Warman's
ANTIQUES AND
COLLECTIBLES
PRICE GUIDE
33RD EDITION

EDITED BY ELLEN T. SCHROY

Volumes in the Encyclopedia of Antiques and Collectibles

Warman's Americana & Collectibles, 8th Edition,
edited by Ellen Tischbein Schroy

Warman's American Pottery & Porcelain,
by Susan and Al Bagdade

Warman's Coins & Currency, 2nd Edition,
by Allen G. Berman and Alex G. Malloy

Warman's Country Antiques & Collectibles, 3rd Edition,
by Dana Gehman Morykan and Harry L. Rinker

Warman's English & Continental Pottery & Porcelain, 3rd Edition,
by Susan and Al Bagdade

Warman's Glass, 3rd Edition,
by Ellen Tischbein Schroy

Warman's Jewelry, 2nd Edition,
by Christie Romero

Warman's Paper,
by Norman E. Martinus and Harry L. Rinker

© 1999 by Krause Publications
Depression Glass Illustrations Copyright © by Jerry O'Brien

Special thanks to the auction houses and individuals who provided the photos for the cover, which are, Clockwise from top right: Doll, Kestner, 20" h, Baby Jean, $1,050; sculpture, Theseus Slaying the Minotaur, by French sculptor Antoine Louis Byre, $12,075; desk, Victorian, walnut, $3,575; Nippon vase, 17" h, hp, scenic, $7,480; and Navajo blanket, 80" x 50", $9,200. The doll photo is courtesy of McMasters Doll Auctions; the other photos are courtesy of Jackson's Auctioneers & Appraisers.

Published by

 **krause publications**

700 E. State Street • Iola, WI 54990-0001
Telephone: 715/445-2214

Please call or write for our free catalog of publications. Our toll-free number to place an order or obtain a free catalog is 800-258-0929 or please use our regular business telephone 715-445-2214 for editioral comment and further information.

ISBN: 0-87341-698-8
Library of Congress Catalog Card No. 82-643543

Printed in the United States of America

BOARD of ADVISORS

INTRODUCTION

Warman's: Serving the trade for more than 50 years

In 1994, *Warman's Antiques and Their Prices* became *Warman's Antiques and Collectibles Price Guide*. The last edition is bigger than ever—physically, that is. Longtime *Warman's* users may find it difficult to imagine that the amount of information in this larger-size book is identical to that found in the earlier smaller-size editions. Yet, it is true. While the page, text, and photograph sizes are larger, the content is the same. You can always expect more, never less, from *Warman's*.

Individuals in the trade refer to this book simply as *Warman's*, a fitting tribute to E. G. Warman and the product he created. *Warman's* has been around for 50 years, 25 years longer than its closest rival. We are proud as peacocks that *Warman's* continues to establish the standards for general antiques and collectibles price guides in 1999, just as it did in 1972 when its first rival appeared on the scene.

Warman's, the antiques and collectibles "bible," covers objects made between 1700 and the present. It always has. Because it reflects market trends, *Warman's* has added more and more 20th-century material to each edition. Remember, 1900 was 99 years ago—the distant past to the new generation of twenty-something and thirty-something collectors.

The general "antiques" market consists of antiques (for the purposes of this book, objects made before 1945), collectibles (objects of the post-World War II era that enjoy an established secondary market), and desirables (contemporary objects that are collected, but speculative in price). Although *Warman's* contains information on all three market segments, its greatest emphasis is on antiques and collectibles.

'Warman's is the Key'

Warman's provides the keys needed by auctioneers, collectors, dealers, and others to understand and deal with the complexities of the antiques and collectibles market. A price list is only one of many keys needed today. *Warman's 33rd Edition* contains many additional keys including: histories, marks, reference books, periodicals, collectors' clubs, museums, reproductions, videotapes, and special auctions. Useful buying and collecting hints also are provided. Used properly, there are few doors these keys will not open.

Warman's is designed to be your first key to the exciting world of antiques and collectibles. As you use the keys this book provides to advance further in your specialized collecting areas, *Warman's* hopes you will remember with fondness where you received your start. When you encounter items outside your area of specialty, remember *Warman's* remains your key to unlocking the information you need, just as it has for more than 49 years.

Organization

Listings: Objects are listed alphabetically by category, beginning with ABC Plates and ending with Zsolnay Pottery. If you have trouble identifying the category to which your object belongs, use the extensive index in the back of the book. It will guide you to the proper category.

We have made the listings descriptive enough so that specific objects can be identified. We also emphasize items that are actively being sold in the marketplace. Some harder-to-find objects are included to demonstrate market spread—useful information worth considering when you have not traded actively in a category recently.

Each year as the market changes, we carefully review our categories—adding, dropping, and combining to provide the most comprehensive coverage possible. *Warman's* quick response to developing trends in the marketplace is one of the prime reasons for its continued leadership in the field.

Krause Publications also publishes other Warman's titles. Each utilizes the *Warman's* format and concentrates on a specific collecting group, e.g., American pottery and porcelain, Americana and collectibles, coins and currency, country, English and continental pottery and porcelain, glass, and jewelry Several are second or subsequent editions. Their expanded coverage compliments the information found in *Warman's Antiques and Collectibles Price Guide*.

History: Collectors and dealers enhance their appreciation of objects by knowing something about their history. We present a capsule history for each category. In many cases, this history contains collecting hints or other useful information.

References: Books are listed in most categories to help you learn more about the objects. Included are author, title, publisher, and date of publication or most recent edition. If a book has been published by a small firm or individual, we have indicated (published by author). To assist in finding these sometimes hard-to-locate authors, we have included the address.

Many of the books included in the lists are hard to find. The antiques and collectibles field is blessed with a dedicated core of book dealers who stock these specialized publications. You will find them at flea markets and antiques shows and through their advertisements in trade publications. Books go out of print quickly, yet many books printed more than 25 years ago remain the standard work in a category. Used book dealers often can locate many of these valuable reference sources. Many dealers publish annual or semi-annual catalogs. Ask to be put on their mailing lists.

Periodicals: The newsletter or bulletin of a collectors' club usually provides the concentrated focus sought by specialty collectors and dealers. However, there are publications, not associated with collectors' clubs, about which collectors and dealers should be aware. These are listed in their appropriate category introductions.

In addition, there are several general interest newspapers and magazines which deserve to be brought to our users' attention. These are:

Antique & The Arts Weekly, Bee Publishing Company, 5 Church Hill Road, Newton, CT 06470; http://www.the-bee.com/aweb

Antique Review, P.O. Box 538, Worthington, OH 43085

Antique Trader Weekly, P.O. Box 1050, Dubuque, IA 52001; http://www.csmonline.com

AntiqueWeek, P.O. Box 90, Knightstown, IN 46148; http://www.antiqueweek.com

Antiques (The Magazine Antiques), 551 Fifth Avenue, New York, NY 10017

Antiques & Collecting 1006 South Michigan Avenue, Chicago, IL 60605

Inside Collector, 225 Main St., Suite 300, Northport, NY 11768

Maine Antique Digest, P.O. Box 358, Waldoboro, ME 04572; http://www.maineantiquedigest.com

MidAtlantic Monthly Antiques Magazine, P.O. Box 908, Henderson, NC 27536

New England Antiques Journal, 4 Church St., Ware, MA 01082

New York-Pennsylvania Collector, Drawer C, Fishers, NY 14453

Space does not permit listing all the national and regional publications in the antiques and collectibles field. The above is a sampling. See David J. Maloney Jr.'s *Maloney's Antiques & Collectibles Resource Directory*, 4th Edition (Antique Trader Books, 1997).

Collectors' Clubs: Collectors' clubs add vitality to the antiques and collectibles field. Their publications and conventions produce knowledge which often cannot be found elsewhere. Many of these clubs are short-lived; others are so strong that they have regional and local chapters.

Museums: The best way to study a specific field is to see as many documented examples as possible. For this reason, we have listed museums where significant collections in that category are on display. Special attention must be directed to the complex of museums which make up the Smithsonian Institution in Washington, D.C.

Reproductions: Reproductions are a major concern to all collectors and dealers. Throughout this edition, boxes will alert you to known reproductions and keys to recognizing them. Most reproductions are unmarked; the newness of their appearance is often the best clue to uncovering them. Specific objects known to be reproduced are marked within the listings with an asterisk (*). The information is designed to serve as a reminder of past reproductions and prevent you from buying them believing them to be period.

We strongly recommend subscribing to *Antique & Collectors Reproduction News*, a monthly newsletter that reports on past and present reproductions, copycats, fantasies, and fakes. Send $32 for twelve issues to: ACRN, Box 12130, Des Moines, IA 50312-9403. This newsletter has been published for several years. Consider buying all available back issues. The information they contain will be of service long into the future.

Special Auctions: In the 33rd Edition, we have chosen to again feature boxes highlighting auction houses. To qualify for placement in one of these boxes, auction houses had to meet several specific requirements. First, they must actively hold auctions solely devoted to that specialty. Second, they must provide a catalog and prices realized. Often the catalogs become an important part of a collection, serving as reference and identification guides. Many of the auction companies featured hold more than one auction annually; some work with a particular collectors' club or society. It is our hope that these boxes will give collectors and those searching for specific objects a better idea of who to contact. *Warman's* is designed to give collectors and dealers a lot of clues to find out what they have, what it is worth, and where to sell it!

These special auction boxes are not intended, however, to diminish the outstanding work done by the generalists, those auctioneers who handle all types of material. The fine auctions like Garth's, Skinner's, and Sloan's, provide us with excellent catalogs all through the year covering many aspects of the antiques and collectibles marketplace. Several categories had too many auction houses to list. For example, most auctioneers sell furniture, clocks, and fine arts. We just couldn't list them all. In addition to these auction house boxes, we hope you will consult the master list of auction houses included in this edition. We are sure that any one of them will be eager to assist in consigning or selling antiques and collectibles.

Index: A great deal of effort has been expended to make our index useful. Always begin by looking for the most specific reference. For example, if you have a piece of china, look first for the maker's name and second for the type. Remember, many objects can be classified in three or more categories. If at first you don't succeed, try, try again.

Black-and-White Photographs: You may encounter a piece you cannot identify well enough to use the index. Consult the photographs and marks. If you own several editions of *Warman's*, you have available a valuable photographic reference to the antiques and collectibles field. Learn to use it.

Price notes

In assigning prices, we assume the object is in very good condition. If otherwise, we note this in our description. It would be ideal to suggest that mint, or unused, examples of all objects exist. The reality is that objects from the past were used, whether they be glass, china, dolls, or toys. Because of this, some normal wear must be expected. In fact, if an object such as a piece of furniture does not show wear, its origins may be more suspect than if it does show wear.

Whenever possible, we have tried to provide a broad listing of prices within a category so you have a "feel" for the market. We emphasize the middle range of prices within a category, while also listing some objects of high and low value to show market spread.

We do not use ranges because they tend to confuse rather than help the collector and dealer. How do you determine if your object is at the high or low end of the range? There is a high degree of flexibility in pricing in the antiques field. If you want to set ranges, add or subtract 10 percent from our prices.

One of the hardest variants with which to deal is the regional fluctuations of prices. Victorian furniture brings widely differing prices in New York, Chicago, New Orleans, or San Francisco. We have tried to strike a balance. Know your region and subject before investing heavily. If the best buys for cameo glass are in Montreal or Toronto, then be prepared to go there if you want to save money or add choice pieces to your collection. Research and patience are key factors to building a collection of merit.

Another factor that affects prices is a sale by a leading dealer or private collector. We temper both dealer and auction house figures.

Price research

Everyone asks, "Where do you get your prices?"
They come from many sources.

First, we rely on auctions. Auction houses and auctioneers do not always command the highest prices. If they did, why do so many dealers buy from them? The key to understanding auction prices is to know when a price is high or low in the range. We think we do this and do it well. The 33rd edition represents a concentrated effort to contact more regional auction houses, both large and small. The cooperation has been outstanding and has resulted in an ever growing pool of auction prices and trends to help us determine the most up-to-date auction prices.

Second, we work closely with dealers. We screen our contacts to make certain they have full knowledge of the market. Dealers make their living from selling antiques; they cannot afford to have a price guide which is not in touch with the market.

More than 50 antiques and collectibles magazines, newspapers, and journals come into our office regularly. They are excellent barometers of what is moving and what is not. We don't hesitate to call an advertiser and ask if his listed merchandise sold.

When the editorial staff is doing field work, we identify ourselves. Our conversations with dealers and collectors around the country have enhanced this book. Teams from *Warman's* are in the field at antiques shows, malls, flea markets, and auctions recording prices and taking photographs.

Collectors work closely with us. They are specialists whose devotion to research and accurate information is inspiring. Generally, they are not dealers. Whenever we have asked them for help, they have responded willingly and admirably.

Board of advisors

Our Board of Advisors is made up of specialists, both dealers and collectors, who feel a commitment to accurate information. You'll find their names listed in the front of the book. Several have authored a major reference work on their subject.

Our esteemed Board of Advisors has increased in number and scope. Participants have all provided detailed information regarding the history and reference section of their particular area of expertise as well as preparing price listings. Many furnished excellent photographs and even shared with us their thoughts on the state of the market.

We are delighted to include those who are valuable members, officers, and founders of collectors' clubs. They are authors of books and articles, and many frequently lecture to groups about their specialties. Most of our advisors have been involved with antiques and collectibles for more than 20 years. Several are retired, and the antiques and collectibles business is a hobby which encompasses most of their free time. Others are a bit younger and either work full time or part time in the antiques and collectibles profession. We asked them about their favorite publications, and most responded with the names of specialized trade papers. Many told us they are regular readers of *AntiqueWeek* and the *Maine Antique Digest*.

One thing they all have in common is their enthusiasm for the antiques and collectibles marketplace. They are eager to share their knowledge with collectors. Many have developed wonderful friendships through their efforts and are enriched by them. If you wish to buy or sell an object in the field of expertise of any of our advisors, drop them a note along with an SASE. If time permits, they will respond.

Buyer's guide, not seller's guide

Warman's is designed to be a buyer's guide, suggesting what you would have to pay to purchase an object on the open market from a dealer or collector. **It is not a seller's guide to prices**. People frequently make this mistake. In doing so, they deceive themselves. If you have an object listed in this book and wish to sell it to a dealer, you should expect to receive approximately 50 percent of the listed value. If the object will not resell quickly, expect to receive even less.

Private collectors may pay more, perhaps 70 to 80 percent of our listed price, if your object is something needed for their collection. If you have an extremely rare object or an object of exceptionally high value, these guidelines do not apply.

Examine your piece as objectively as possible. As an antiques and collectibles appraiser, I spend a great deal of time telling people their treasures are not "rare" at all, but items readily available in the marketplace.

In respect to buying and selling, a simple philosophy is that a good purchase occurs when the buyer and seller are happy with the price. Don't look back. Hindsight has little value in the antiques and collectibles field. Given time, things tend to balance out.

Always improving

Warman's is always trying to improve. Space is freely given to long price descriptions, to help you understand that the piece looks like, perhaps what's special about it. With this edition, we've arranged some old formats, using more **bold** words to help you find what you're looking for. Some categories have been arranged so that if the only thing you know is how high, you can start there. Many times identifying that you've got is the hardest part. Well, the first place to start is how big—grab that ruler and see what you can find that's a comparable size. You are still going to have to make a determination about what the object is made of, be it china, glass, porcelain, wood, or other materials. Use all your senses to discover what you've got. Ask questions about your object, who made it, and why, how was it used, where, and when. As you find answers to these questions, you'll be helping yourself figure out just what the treasure is all about. Now take that information and you'll be able to look it up and discover the value.

Eager to hear from readers

At *Warman's* and Krause Publications, we're always eager to hear what you think about *Warman's* and how we can improve it. Write to either Ellen Schroy, Warman's Editor, P.O. Box 392, Quakertown, PA 18951-0392 or e-mail at schroy@voicenet.com. The fine staff at Krause Publications can be reached at 700 E. State St., Iola, WI 54990. It's our goal to continue in the *Warman's* tradition and make it the best price guide available.

State of the Market

As the calendar pages flip and the decade gets ready to turn, as the millennium comes racing toward us, perhaps it's time to pause and think about what kind of impact this historic date is going to have on the antiques and collectibles marketplace.

Few of our treasures will suffer from the Y2K problem; they were made far in advance of that, possibly even in the century before. How wonderful to think that something made in the 17th, 18th or 19th century may have survived this long. When you think of how many times some of these objects have changed hands, it becomes even more amazing that so many examples have survived in good condition.

Sometimes it's hard to imagine that our treasures were made as objects to be used: a chair to be sat in, a cup and saucer to enjoy our tea. Surely the first owner of our treasures thought they had the latest in style and form, perhaps they were as proud of that fact as we are of our treasures. But, for some reason, they parted company with that owner, and the object entered a new marketplace, the second hand or used market. Again, someone probably purchased the item to be used, perhaps to complete a set, or to set up house keeping. That old fashioned phrase brings to mind the image of a young couple fitting out their first living quarters, perhaps with some hand-me-downs, perhaps with some new pieces, but trying to take an eclectic mix and make it their own statement. As electricity became the rage, old lamp fixtures and cast iron fireplace utensils were relegated to the attic or cast off in other ways. Today, the thought of going too long without electricity is sheer horror to us and we have invented battery-operated gizmos of all types in the event of such a disaster. But, some of us have learned to treasure those pre-electric lamps and find them attractive additions to our collections. Perhaps it was Grandma, who was only too glad to stop fussing with trimming wicks and filling lamps as she carried the old lamps to the attic. Today, we're more likely to find Grandma hooked to the Internet, paying her electric bill online.

When E. G. Warman started publishing the first price guide in America in 1948, he was on the cutting edge. Part of the reason his little pocket guides were so popular is that folks like to take them along as they jumped in their cars and scoured the countryside in search of antiques. The time was perfect to take longer car trips, the automobiles were more comfortable, the roads much improved, and conveniences like gas stations and even McDonald's were luring folks to travel more. Antique shops popped up around the countryside, offering those lamps Grandma had stashed in the attic, along with other items that were no longer necessities, but now were becoming objects for decoration and enjoyment. Today, collectors can hit the antique malls and view the wares of dozens of vendors in one stop, or perhaps visit an antiques show where hundreds of dealers are displaying merchandise. If the desired object hasn't been found through these traditional avenues, today's collector can now jump on-line and visit the World Wide Web and the virtual malls, galleries, shops of thousands of dealers.

Internet impacts collecting

I don't think the full impact of the Internet on the antiques and collectibles marketplace is known as of today. It's true that many of us are becoming savvy in the ways of surfing the net. However, there are also still many collectors and dealers who are not connected. Are they being left behind? I don't think so, or we would be seeing malls and antique shops closing. Could they supplement their business by learning to use the Internet? Probably. Will we always have shows and shops to visit? I sure hope so, for where else can you excite all the senses with an object of generations past?

There is something to be said for the thrill of the hunt, for the excitement of finding that perfect addition to a collection. If you're collecting an object that is easily shipped, like paper ephemera, perhaps searching the Internet will yield the treasure. But, other categories, like stoneware, are suffering because virtual shopping is not realistic. You need to feel the texture of the body, the weight of the piece, to closely examine the decoration. Actually, in the case of a paper collector, the Internet might be yielding a hidden asset. By not having to take paper objects from flea market to shop to show, perhaps the elements will not effect it as much, less hands to soil it. Dealers must learn to adequately describe, measure, and taut their wares and price them attractively. Many are finding this venue to be very appealing and their virtual shops can be open 24 hours a day, all around the world.

As an experiment and a way to test how the Internet is impacting on the antiques and collectibles marketplace, I decided to run a simple survey with assistance of Depression Glass On-Line Shopper, an interactive on-line magazine devoted to Depression-era glassware. The results were a little surprising, and one needs to factor in the idea that this was a devoted group of computer users. By answering a set of ten questions, they told me that 75% are now spending more time shopping on-line than they did a year ago. Where they did not agree was on the question as to whether the urge to shop was as satisfied by jumping on-line or traveling and physically searching for an addition to their collection: 38% said they were satisfied, while 62% said they preferred to go hunting at shops, shows, and flea markets. I asked whether they thought more rare items appeared on-line or at shops and shows, and 60% said they thought rare items appeared on-line. The question that surprised me was one where I asked them if they had $100 to spend, where would they get the most for the money? Fifty percent said on-line, while 50% were ready to grab their coats and go shopping. Some noted that on-line shopping is more convenient, always there for the asking; while others noted that you can't feel an object, check it adequately for damage, sense the color with on-line shopping.

Some felt on-line shopping was just fine to round out a collection, when searching for a specific item. Some indicated that they are tired of seeing the same merchandise at shops and shows and that the Internet offered them "fresh" merchandise. Others were concerned that perhaps the seller had a different quality scale then they expected. Most felt comfortable making on-line purchases of Depression glass, but were not as comfortable in purchasing other types of antiques and collectibles in this manner.

To an auction devotee, perhaps it's the thrill of finding that wonderful treasure and believing no one else in the room knows just what you know and then bidding and securing the object of your passion for a price you feel is right. Today you can attend auctions that are similar to those held in your grandparents' day, right off the front porch, or you can now travel to a warm, clean, auction hall and sit and enjoy the auction. By taking time to preview objects and ask questions of the auctioneer and his staff, you can often learn much about the provenance of the object. Many auctioneers have taken to having long preview hours before the actual auction, allowing potential buyers plenty of time to examine pieces, to decide that they wish to buy. Catalogs sent through the mail act as previews, too, and allow readers to sit in the comfort of their home and consider what to buy. Perhaps the buyers are then motivated to visit the auction gallery and place a bid, either during the auction or by an absentee process. Today it's not unusual to see an auctioneer taking bids from a real person on the floor of the auction, while a member of his staff is relaying the bid price to someone bidding over the telephone, while perhaps another staff member bids in absentia for another bidder. Because of pre-auction faxes, telephone calls in lieu of a physical inspection, collectors and dealers are growing accustomed to bidding in this manner. Their trust in reputable auctioneers is well founded, as many of the auctioneers have developed excellent reputations and rapport with their clients. Today's cell phones also allow a potential bidder to check with another about an object offered for sale, allowing one party to view an object, answer questions, report on condition, etc.

Add to this the ability to bid on-line for all kinds of antiques and collectibles. Last year there were several hundred on-line dealers. Today there are thousands, perhaps even a million or so. Websites, "dot.com" this and "dot.com" that and faster search engines, allow collectors to search the Internet quickly. More and more traditional auction houses are posting catalogs and prices realized on-line. It's probably too soon to fully understand how this is impacting on their business, but it must be worth their trouble as few seem to be vanishing. Krause Publications has launched an on-line auction site for collectors. Collectit.net is geared toward collectors of all types of antiques, collectibles, and memorabilia. Since this venture is still so new, it's too soon to report on its success, but it certainly represents a beginning of a way to expand services to collectors and hobbyists.

So, as 1998 closes, I believe that the antiques marketplace is alive and doing very well. Some segments of it are a bit soft, like stoneware, but others are taking off. From art glass to Depression glass to collectible toys and dolls, objects are changing from one owner to another. A few traditional categories that once mattered to old E. G. Warman, like bootjacks, are becoming almost obsolete. Many of today's collectors might not even know what they are, or care for that matter. However, wave a fishing lure or copy of Lewis Carroll's *Alice in Wonderland* at them, and you'll get a different reaction, one of excitement and record prices. However, to be objective about this, these prices were realized at live auctions, not virtual ones. Perhaps it is still the thought of seeking out that most wonderful lure in a mint original box. Or, perhaps it's the thought that Lewis Carroll himself drew the illustrations in this rare book, believed to be one of six known copies, that pushed its selling price at Christie's to $1.6 million, a lot of money for a little book that was used and read by several different generations.

Record-setting prices

If children's books are not the collectible that sets your heart a flutter, perhaps a few other record setting prices which occurred this past year will.

In August, at James D. Julia's End-of-Summer Sale in Rockport, Maine, participants were taken on a voyage of discovery that included choice pieces from estates gathered through the year. This auction grossed $1.4 million. One of the top sellers was a rare Tiffany Favrile glass and bronze Daffodil table lamp that sold for $60,375. This example is 25" h and in excellent

Geisha Girl, entry door knob, Russell & Erwin, c1884, $1,600. Photo courtesy of Web Wilson Auctions.

condition, showing a warm brown-green patina. Other similar examples of Tiffany lamps were also strong. The second day of the auction brought strong bidding on a tall case clock by I. Simpson of Bardstown, KY. This clock, with a moon dial with a ship and house scene, sold for $39,100, nearly ten times its pre-sale estimate.

Another tall case clock, this one made by Philadelphian David Rittenhouse, sold at Freeman\Fine Arts of Philadelphia for $53,200. This fine example of a Chippendale carved walnut clock, c1770, has a flat top bonnet with swan neck pedestal (replaced) and finials, engraved steel face with calendar dial signed "David Rittenhouse" over shaped pendulum door flanked by quarter fluted columnar sides, the base with shaped panel front terminating on ogival bracket feet (replaced). The provenance of this particular clock notes it was descended from Peter Ozeas (1738-1824) to Capt. John Ramborger (1781-1849) whose first wife was the granddaughter of Peter Ozeas to William Keehmle Ramborger (1837-1919) to the present owner. Perhaps it was the excellent condition of the clock, or its stately looks, or perhaps being made by a rather famous Philadelphian and sold there had a bit to do with this great price. The clock was originally estimated at $8,000 to $12,000.

It wasn't just clocks setting record prices this year. Swann Galleries, Inc. did quite handsomely with some autographs in its February auction. A letter signed in French from Paul Gauguin to his good friend Charles Morice, written shortly after the artist arrived in Tahiti, May 1896, sold for $23,000. The contents of the letter related his boredom, poor health, and financial problems. Another letter signed by John Hancock as President of the Continental Congress, Philadelphia, dated June 1775, brought $11,500. Swann Galleries also did quite well with Audubon's this year, including the sale of a *White Heron* for $16,100. This hand-colored plate was from the double elephant folio Haverll edition of *Birds of America,* printed in London, 1837. A book of poetry by Phillis Wheatley, titled *Poems on Various Subjects,* sold for $19,500. This wide margined first edition was printed in London in 1773.

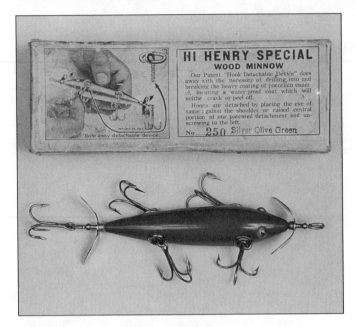

Fishing Lure, Pflueger, #250, silver and green enamel, 5 hook, wooden minnow, orig "Hi Henry Special" box, $4,840. Photo courtesy of Lang's Sporting Collectables, Inc.

Postcards International reports that the top price paid this year for a single postcard in auction was $8,500. This advertising postcard was published in 1898 and featured the popular Waverly Cycles, with artwork done by the famous Art Nouveau artist Alphonse Mucha. This postcard is known as the Mucha Waverly, and was first discovered in postcard collectors in the late 1970s. Only nine copies of this card have surfaced. The one auctioned by Postcards International had been sent from France in 1898 and had a written message relating to the art of Mucha. Perhaps this enhanced the price just a bit.

Another high-priced postcard category are those relating to black history. A real photo of a black execution, c1910, brought the second highest price at auction at $2,500.

If your tastes run to other small items, perhaps you might be more interested in the elegant Arts & Crafts gold and tourmaline necklace sold by Skinner's, Boston, in September. This necklace was designed by Louis Comfort Tiffany, in collaboration with the original owner. The piece centered an oval plaque set with graduated tourmalines surrounded by Montana sapphires and edges with various color natural pearls. The original estimate of $7,000 to $9,000 soon got passed by as bidding soared to $49,450.

Skinner's also did well this year with rare books. Its November auction included a two-volume *Atlas Maior Terrarum Orbis Imperia,* which was compiled by Johann Baptist Homann, c1820. Bidding soared to $64,100 for this rare atlas.

Probably one of the neatest auction success stories for the year belongs to Lang Sporting Collectables, Inc. It reported that an elderly couple from rural Ohio called after they saw an article about the Heddon Dowagiac Minnow that sold for $9,900 (also at a Lang auction). Unfortunately, the catalog for the next sale had gone to the printers, but Langs urged the couple to send the four boxed lures anyway and they would add them to the auction. The couple's Heddon #150 in a wooden box sold for $3,850 and a Heddon #151 sold for $1,430. A Rhodes frog set a new record price at $4,125 and a Shakespeare #64 minnow also broke a record with its winning bid of $1,815. Yes, all parties were gratified, the Langs, the elderly couple, and the new owners of the lures, too! Langs also sold a rare "Hi Henry Special" box with the original Pflueger lure for a record of $4,840. So, before cleaning out the garage or that tackle box, check for original vintage boxes!

AUCTION HOUSES

The following auction houses cooperate with *Warman's* by providing catalogs of their auctions and price lists. This information is used to prepare *Warman's Antiques and Collectibles Price Guide*, volumes in the Warman's Encyclopedia of Antiques and Collectibles. This support is truly appreciated.

Albrecht & Cooper Auction
Services
3884 Saginaw Rd.
Vassar, MI 48768
(517) 823-8835

Sanford Alderfer Auction
Company
501 Fairgrounds Rd.
Hatfield, PA 19440
(215) 393-3000
web site: http://www.alderfer
company.com

Andre Ammelounx
The Stein Auction Company
P.O. Box 136
Palantine, IL 60078
(847) 991-5927

Apple Tree Auction Center
1616 W. Church St.
Newark, OH 43055
(614) 344-4282

The Armans' Collector's Sales
and Services
P.O. Box 4037
Middletown, RI 02842
(401) 849-5012

Arthur Auctioneering
RD 2, P.O. Box 155
Hughesville, PA 17737
(717) 584-3697

Aston Macek Auctions
2825 Country Club Rd.
Endwell, NY 13760-3349
(607) 785-6598

Auction Team Köln
Jane Herz
6731 Ashley Court
Sarasota, FL 34241
(941) 925-0385

Auction Team Köln
Postfach 501168 D 5000
Köln 50, W. Germany

Bailey's Antiques
102 E Main St.
Homer, MI 49245
(517) 568-4014

Noel Barrett Antiques & Auctions,
Ltd.
P.O. Box 1001
Carversville, PA 18913
(610) 297-5109

Robert F. Batchelder
1 W Butler Ave.
Ambler, PA 19002
(610) 643-1430

Bear Pen Antiques
2318 Bear Pen Hollow Road
Lock Haven, PA 17745
(717) 769-6655

Beverly Hills Auctioneers
9454 Wilshire Blvd., Suite 202
Beverly Hills, CA 90212
(310) 278-8115

Bill Bertoia Auctions
1881 Spring Rd.
Vineland, NJ 08360
(609) 692-1881

Biders Antiques Inc.
241 S Union St.
Lawrence, MA 01843
(508) 688-4347

Brown Auction & Real Estate
900 East Kansas
Greensburg, KS 67054
(316) 723-2111

Butterfield, Butterfield & Dunning
755 Church Rd.
Elgin, IL 60123
(847) 741-3483
web site: http://www.butter-
fields.com

Butterfield, Butterfield & Dunning
7601 Sunset Blvd.
Los Angeles, CA 90046
(213) 850-7500
web site: http://www:butter-
fields.com

Butterfield, Butterfield & Dunning
220 San Bruno Ave.
San Francisco, CA 94103
(415) 861-7500
web site: http://www:butter-
fields.com

C. C. Auction Gallery
416 Court
Clay Center, KS 67432
(913) 632-6021

W. E. Channing & Co., Inc.
53 Old Santa Fe Trail
Santa Fe, NM 87501
(505) 988-1078

Chicago Art Galleries
5039 Oakton St.
Skokie, IL 60077
(847) 677-6080

Childers & Smith
1415 Horseshoe Pike
Glenmoore, PA 19343
(610) 269-1036
e-mail: harold@smithau-
tionco.com

Christie's
502 Park Ave.
New York, NY 10022
(212) 546-1000
web site: http://www.sir-
ius.com/~christie/

Christie's East
219 E 67th St.
New York, NY 10021
(212) 606-0400

Cincinnati Art Galleries
635 Main St.
Cincinnati, OH 45202
(513) 381-2128

Mike Clum, Inc.
P.O. Box 2
Rushville, OH 43150
(614) 536-9220

Cohasco Inc.
Postal 821
Yonkers, NY 10702
(914) 476-8500

Collection Liquidators Auction
Service
Suite 407
341 Lafayette St.
New York, NY 10012
(212) 505-2455
website: http://www.rtam.com/
coliq/bid.html
e-mail: coliq@erols.com

Coole Park Books and
Autographs
P.O. Box 199049
Indianapolis, IN 46219
(317) 351-8495
e-mail: cooleprk@indy.net

Samuel J. Cottonne
15 Genesee St.
Mt. Morris, NY 14510
(716) 583-3119

Craftsman Auctions
1485 W. Housatoric
Pittsfield MA 01202
(413) 442-7003
web site: http://www.artsn-
crafts.com

Dargate Auction Galleries
5607 Baum Blvd.
Pittsburgh, PA 15206
(412) 362-3558
web site: http://www.dargate.com

DeWolfe & Wood
P.O. Box 425
Alfred, ME 04002
(207) 490-5572

Marlin G. Denlinger
RR3, Box 3775
Morrisville, VT 05661
(802) 888-2775

Dixie Sporting Collectibles
1206 Rama Rd.
Charlotte, NC 28211
(704) 364-2900
web site: http://www.sportauction

William Doyle Galleries, Inc.
175 E 87th St.
New York, NY 10128
(212) 427-2730
web site: http://www.doylegaller-
ies.com

Dunbar Gallery
76 Haven St.
Milford, MA 01757
(508) 634-8697

Early Auction Co.
123 Main St.
Milford, OH 45150
(513) 831-4833

Fain & Co.
P.O. Box 1330
Grants Pass, OR 97526
(888) 324-6726

Ken Farmer Realty & Auction Co.
105A Harrison St.
Radford, VA 24141
(703) 639-0939
web site: http://kenfarmer.com

Fine Tool Journal
27 Fickett Rd.
Pownal, ME 04069
(207) 688-4962
web site: http://www.wow-
    pages.com/FTJ/

Steve Finer Rare Books
P.O. Box 758
Greenfield, MA 01302
(413) 773-5811

Flomaton Antique Auction
207 Palafox St.
Flomaton, AL 36441
(334) 296-3059

William A. Fox Auctions Inc.
676 Morris Ave.
Springfield, NJ 07081
(201) 467-2366

Freeman\Fine Arts Co. of Phila-
    delphia, Inc.
1808 Chestnut St.
Philadelphia, PA 19103
(215) 563-9275

Garth's Auction, Inc.
2690 Stratford Rd.
P.O. Box 369
Delaware, OH 43015
(740) 362-4771

Greenberg Auctions
7566 Main St.
Skysville, MD 21784
(410) 795-7447

Green Valley Auction Inc.
Route 2, Box 434
Mt. Crawford, VA 22841
(540) 434-4260

Guerney's
136 E 73rd St.
New York, NY 10021
(212) 794-2280

Hake's Americana & Collectibles
P.O. Box 1444
York, PA 17405
(717) 848-1333

Gene Harris Antique Auction
    Center, Inc.
203 South 18th Ave.
P.O. Box 476
Marshalltown, IA 50158
(515) 752-0600

Norman C. Heckler & Company
Bradford Corner Rd.
Woodstock Valley, CT 06282
(203) 974-1634

High Noon
9929 Venice Blvd.
Los Angeles CA 90034
(310) 202-9010

Michael Ivankovich Auction Co.
P.O. Box 2458
Doylestown, PA 18901
(215) 345-6094

Jackson's Auctioneers &
    Appraisers
2229 Lincoln St.
Cedar Falls, IA 50613
(319) 277-2256
e-mail: jacksons @corenet.net

James D. Julia Inc.
Rt. 201 Skowhegan Rd.
P.O. Box 830
Fairfield, ME 04937
(207) 453-7125

J. W. Auction Co.
54 Rochester Hill Rd.
Rochester, NH 03867
(603) 332-0192

Lang's Sporting Collectables, Inc.
31 R Turthle Cove
Raymond, ME 04071
(207) 655-4265

La Rue Auction Service
201 S. Miller St.
Sweet Springs, MO 65351
(816) 335-4538

Leonard's Auction Company
1631 State Rd.
Duncannon, PA 17020
(717) 957-3324

Howard Lowery
3818 W Magnolia Blvd.
Burbank, CA 91505
(818) 972-9080

Joy Luke
The Gallery
300 E Grove St.
Bloomington, IL 61701
(309) 828-5533

Mapes Auctioneers & Appraisers
1729 Vestal Pkwy
Vestal, NY 13850
(607) 754-9193

Martin Auctioneers Inc.
P.O. Box 477
Intercourse, PA 17534
(717) 768-8108

McMasters Doll Auctions
P.O. Box 1755
Cambridge, OH 43725
(614) 432-4419

Metropolitan Book Auction
123 W. 18th St., 4th Floor
New York, NY 10011
(212) 929-7099

William Frost Mobley
P.O. Box 10
Schoharie, NY 12157
(518) 295-7978

William Morford
RD #2
Cazenovia, NY 13035
(315) 662-7625

New England Auction Gallery
P.O. Box 2273
W. Peabody, MA 01960
(508) 535-3140

New Orleans Auction St. Charles
    Auction Gallery, Inc.
1330 St. Charles Avenue
New Orleans, LA 70130
(504) 586-8733

New Hampshire Book Auctions
P.O. Box 460
92 Woodbury Rd.
Weare, NH 03281
(603) 529-7432

Norton Auctioneers of Michigan
    Inc.
50 West Pearl at Monroe
Coldwater MI 49036
(517) 279-9063

Old Barn Auction
10040 St. Rt. 224 West
Findlay, OH 45840
(419) 422-8531
web site: http://www.oldbarn.com

Ohio Cola Traders
4411 Bazetta Rd.
Cortland, OH 44410

Richard Opfer Auctioneering Inc.
1919 Greenspring Dr.
Timonium, MD 21093
(410) 252-5035

Pacific Book Auction Galleries
133 Kerney St., 4th Floor
San Francisco, CA 94108
(415) 989-2665
web site:
    http://www.nbn.com/~pba/

Pettigrew Auction Company
1645 S. Tejon St.
Colorado Springs, CO 80906
(719) 633-7963

Phillips Fine Art Auctions
406 E. 79th St.
New York, NY 10021
(212) 570-4830

Postcards International
2321 Whitney Ave., Suite 102
P.O. Box 5398
Hamden, CT 06518
(203) 248-6621
web site: http://www.csm
    online.com/postcardsint/

Poster Auctions International
601 W. 26th St.
New York, NY 10001
(212) 787-4000

Profitt Auction Company
P.O. Box 796
Columbia, VA 23038
(804) 747-6353

Provenance
P.O. Box 3487
Wallington, NJ 07057
(201) 779-8725

David Rago Auctions, Inc.
333 S. Main St.
Lambertville, NJ 08530
(609) 397-9374

Lloyd Ralston Toys
173 Post Rd.
Fairfield, CT 06432
(203) 255-1233

James J. Reeves
P.O. Box 219
Huntingdon, PA 16652-0219
(814) 643-5497
website:
    www.JamesJReeves.com
e-mail: Reeves5@vicon.net

Mickey Reichel Auctioneer
1440 Ashley Rd.
Boonville MO 65233
(816) 882-5292

Sandy Rosnick Auctions
15 Front St.
Salem MA 01970
(508) 741-1130

Thomas Schmidt
7099 McKean Rd.
Ypsilanti, MI 48197
(313) 485-8606

Seeck Auctions
P.O. Box 377
Mason City, IA 50402
(515) 424-1116
website: www.wil-
    lowtree.com/~seeckauctions

L. H. Selman Ltd.
761 Chestnut St.
Santa Cruz, CA 95060
(408) 427-1177
web site: http://www.selman.com

Sentry Auction
113 School St.
Apollo, PA 15613
(412) 478-1989

Skinner Inc.
Bolton Gallery
357 Main St.
Bolton, MA 01740
(978) 779-6241

Skinner, Inc.
The Heritage on the Garden

63 Park Plaza
Boston MA 02116
(978) 350-5429

C. G. Sloan & Company Inc.
4920 Wyaconda Rd.
North Bethesda, MD 20852
(301) 468-4911
web site: http://www.cgsloan.com

Smith & Jones, Inc., Auctions
12 Clark Lane
Sudbury MA 01776
(508) 443-5517

Smith House Toy Sales
26 Adlington Rd.
Eliot, ME 03903
(207) 439-4614

R. M. Smythe & Co.
26 Broadway
New York, NY 10004-1710
(212) 943-1880
web site:
    http://www.rm-smythe.com

Sotheby's
1334 York Ave.
New York, NY 10021
(212) 606-7000
web site: http://www.
    sothebys.com

Southern Folk Pottery Collectors
    Society
1828 N. Howard Mill Rd.
Robbins, NC 27325
(910) 464-3961

Stanton's Auctioneers
P.O. Box 146
144 South Main St.
Vermontville, MI 49096
(517) 726-0181

Stout Auctions
11 W. Third St.
Williamsport, IN 47993-1119
(765) 764-6901

Michael Strawser
200 N. Main St., P.O. Box 332
Wolcottville, IN 46795
(219) 854-2859

Swann Galleries Inc.
104 E 25th St.
New York, NY 10010
(212) 254-4710

Swartz Auction Services
2404 N. Mattis Ave.
Champaign, IL 61826-7166
(217) 357-0197
web site: http://www/
    SwartzAuction.com

The House In The Woods
S91 W37851 Antique Lane
Eagle, WI 53119
(414) 594-2334

Theriault's
P.O. Box 151
Annapolis, MD 21401
(301) 224-3655

Toy Scouts
137 Casterton Ave.
Akron, OH 44303
(216) 836-0668
e-mail: toyscout@salamander.net

Treadway Gallery, Inc.
2029 Madison Rd.
Cincinnati, OH 45208
(513) 321-6742
web site:
    http://www.a3c2net.com/tread-
    waygallery

Unique Antiques & Auction Gal-
    lery
449 Highway 72 West
Collierville, TN 38017
(901) 854-1141

Venable Estate Auction
423 West Fayette St.
Pittsfield, IL 62363
(217) 285-2560
e-mail: sandiv@msn.com

Victorian Images
P.O. Box 284
Marlton, NJ 08053
(609) 985-7711

Victorian Lady
P.O. Box 424
Waxhaw, NC 28173
(704) 843-4467

Vintage Cover Story
P.O. Box 975
Burlington, NC 27215
(919) 584-6900

Bruce and Vicki Waasdorp
P.O. Box 434
10931 Main St.
Clarence, NY 14031
(716) 759-2361

Web Wilson Antiques
P.O. Box 506
Portsmouth, RI 02871
1-800-508-0022

Winter Associates
21 Cooke St. Box 823
Plainville, CT 06062
(203) 793-0288

Wolf's Auctioneers
1239 W. 6th St.
Cleveland, OH 44113
(614) 362-4711

Woody Auction
Douglass, KS 67039
(316) 746-2694

York Town Auction, Inc.
1625 Haviland Rd.
York, PA 17404
(717) 751-0211
e-mail: yorktownauction@
    cyberia.com

ABBREVIATIONS

The following are standard abbreviations which we have used throughout this edition of *Warman's*.

4to = 8" x 10"
8vo = 5" x 7"
12mo = 3" x 5"
ABP = American Brilliant Period
ADS = Autograph Document Signed
adv = advertising
ah = applied handle
ALS = Autograph Letter Signed
AQS = Autograph Quotation Signed
C = century
c = circa
Cal. = caliber
circ = circular
cov = cover
CS = Card Signed
d = diameter or depth
dec = decorated
dj = dust jacket
DQ = Diamond Quilted
DS = Document Signed
ed = edition
emb = embossed
ext. = exterior
eyep. = eyepiece
Folio = 12" x 16"
ftd = footed
gal = gallon
ground = background
h = height
horiz. = horizontal
hp = hand painted
hs = high standard
illus = illustrated, illustration
imp = impressed
int. = interior
irid = iridescent
IVT = inverted thumbprint
j = jewels
K = karat
l = length

lb = pound
litho = lithograph
ll = lower left
lr = lower right
ls = low standard
LS = Letter Signed
mfg = manufactured
MIB = mint in box
MOP = mother-of-pearl
n/c = no closure
NE = New England
No. = number
r/c = reproduction closure
o/c = original closure
opal = opalescent
orig = original
os = orig stopper
oz = ounce
pat = patent
pcs = pieces
pgs = pages
PUG = printed under the glaze
pr = pair
PS = Photograph Signed
pt = pint
qt = quart
rect = rectangular
sgd = signed
S. N. = Serial Number
sngl = single
SP = silver plated
SS = Sterling silver
sq = square
TLS = Typed Letter Signed
unp = unpaged
vert. = vertical
vol = volume
w = width
yg = yellow gold
# = numbered

ABC PLATES

History: The majority of early ABC plates were manufactured in England and imported into the United States. They achieved their greatest popularity from 1780 to 1860. Since a formal education was uncommon in the early 19th century, the ABC plate was a method of educating the poor for a few pennies.

ABC plates were made of glass, pewter, porcelain, pottery, or tin. Porcelain plates range in diameter from 4-3/8 to slightly over 9-1/2 inches. The rim usually contains the alphabet and/or numbers; the center features animals, great men, maxims, or nursery rhymes.

References: Susan and Al Bagdade, *Warman's English & Continental Pottery & Porcelain*, 3rd Edition, Krause Publications, 1998; Mildred L. and Joseph P. Chalala, *A Collector's Guide to ABC Plates, Mugs and Things*, Pridemark Press, 1980; Irene and Ralph Lindsey, *ABC Plates & Mugs,* Collector Books, 1997; Noel Riley, *Gifts for Good Children*, Richard Dennis Publications, 1991.

Collectors' Club: ABC Plate/Mug Collector's Circle, 67 Stevens Ave., Old Bridge, NJ 08857.

Glass

6" d
- Cane pattern, alphabet on stippled rim, clear 45.00
- Dog's head center 45.00
- Jumbo, emb alphabet border 95.00
- President Garfield, profile bust center, clear, frosted alphabet border. 50.00
- Starburst pattern, alphabet border, scalloped rim, clear, New Martinsville 35.00

7" d, milk glass, plain center, emb alphabet border, beaded rim 50.00
8" d, Stork pattern, clear 85.00

(Porcelain) English, Cruose Rescues Friday, mkd "Tunstall England, Ivory," and registration number, 8-1/8" d, $175.

Porcelain or pottery

5 1/2" d, children, dog, parrot, and verse, multicolored transfer scene, emb alphabet border. 45.00
5-3/4" d, red transfer print, from Month's series, Staffordshire, stained
- January. 125.00
- February, cracked 100.00

6" d
- Fox and Grapes, black transfer, red trim, marked "J Meir & Son, Tunstall, England" 55.00
- Dr Franklin Maxim Proverb, two men in office scene, "If You Would Know The Value Of Money Try To Borrow Some-Creditors Have Better Memories Than Debtors" 145.00

6-1/4" d, Staffordshire
- Brown transfer print, polychrome dec, Crusoe Rescues Friday 175.00
- Green transfer print "Baseball. Running to first base," from American Sports series, minor staining, chips to rim 300.00

6-3/8" d, brown transfer print, Staffordshire
- Children playing, stained, chips 110.00
- Rifle Band, stained chips 115.00

7" d, colored transfer, boy in period attire carrying basket, imp "Meakin" 110.00
7-1/4" d, blue transfer, Robin Crusoe, Staffordshire 175.00
7 1/2" d, cricket game, multicolored transfer center, Staffordshire 135.00

Tin

3" d, girl and boy rolling hoop 110.00
5 1/2" d, Liberty 65.00
6" d, two kittens playing with yarn 50.00
7 1/8" d, Who Killed Cock Robin 115.00
8" d
- Mary Had A Little Lamb 140.00
- Monkey on Barrel, litho dec 65.00

9" d, Hey Diddle Diddle 55.00

ADVERTISING

History: Before the days of mass media, advertisers relied on colorful product labels and advertising giveaways to promote their products. Containers were made to appeal to the buyer through the use of stylish lithographs and bright colors. Many of the illustrations used the product in the advertisement so that even an illiterate buyer could identify a product.

Advertisements were put on almost every household object imaginable and were constant reminders to use the product or visit a certain establishment.

References: *Advertising & Figural Tape Measures*, L-W Book Sales, 1995; Art Anderson, *Casinos and Their Ashtrays,* 1994, printed by author (P.O. Box 4103, Flint, MI 48504); Al Bergevin, *Drugstore Tins and Their Prices*, Wallace-Homestead, 1990; A. Walker Bingham, *Snake-Oil Syndrome*, Christopher Publishing House, 1994; Michael Bruner, *Advertising Clocks*, Schiffer Publishing, 1995; ——, *Encyclopedia of Porcelain Enamel Advertising*, Schiffer Publishing, 1994; ——, *More Porcelain Enamel Advertising*, Schiffer Publishing, 1997; *Collector's Digest Letter Openers: Advertising & Figural*, L-W Book Sales, 1996; Doug Collins, *America's Favorite Food: The Story of Campbell Soup Company*, Harry N

Abrams, 1994; Douglas Congdon-Martin, *America for Sale*, Schiffer Publishing, 1991; ——, *Tobacco Tins*, Schiffer Publishing, 1992; Douglas Congdon-Martin and Robert Biondi, *Country Store Antiques*, Schiffer Publishing, 1991; ——, *Country Store Collectibles*, Schiffer Publishing, 1990; James D. Davis, *Collectible Novelty Phones*, Schiffer, 1998; Fred Dodge, *Antique Tins*, 1995, 1997 value update, Collector Books; ——, *Antique Tins, Book II*, Collector Books, 1998; Warren Dotz, *Advertising Character Collectibles*, Collector Books, 1993, 1997 values updated; ——, *What a Character! 20th Century American Advertising Icons*, Chronicle Books, 1996; James L. Dundas, *Collecting Whistles*, Schiffer Publishing, 1995; Tony Fusco, *Posters Identification and Price Guide*, 2nd ed., Avon Books, 1994.

Ted Hake, *Hake's Guide to Advertising Collectibles*, Wallace-Homestead, 1992; Bill and Pauline Hogan, *Charlton Standard Catalogue of Canadian Country Store Collectables*, Charlton Press, 1996; Bob and Sharon Huxford, *Huxford's Collectible Advertising*, 3rd ed., Collector Books, 1996; Thomas Patrick Jacobsen, *Pat Jacobsen's First International Price Guide to Fruit Crate Labels*, Patco Enterprise (437 Minton Ct, Pleasant Hill, CA 94523), 1994; Ray Klug, *Antique Advertising Encyclopedia*, Vol. 1 (1978, 1993 value update) and Vol. 2 (1985), L-W Promotions; Mary Jane Lamphier, *Zany Characters of the Ad World*, Collector Books, 1995; Patricia McDaniel, *Drugstore Collectibles*, Wallace-Homestead, 1994; Tom Morrison, *More Root Beer Advertising & Collectibles*, Schiffer Publishing, 1997; Gerald S. Petrone, *Tobacco Advertising*, Schiffer Publishing, 1996; Don and Carol Raycraft, *Wallace-Homestead Price Guide to American Country Antiques*, 15th ed., Krause Publications, 1997; Bob Sloan and Steve Guarnaccia, *A Stiff Drink and a Close Shave*, Chronicle Books, 1995; Louis Storino, *Chewing Tobacco Tin Tags*, Schiffer Publishing, 1995; Neil Wood, *Smoking Collectibles*, L-W Book Sales, 1994.

Periodicals: *Creamers*, P.O. Box 11, Lake Villa, IL 60046; *Paper Collectors' Marketplace*, P.O. Box 128, Scandinavia, WI 54917; *Advertising Collectors Express*, P.O. Box 221, Mayview, MO 64071.

Collectors' Clubs: Antique Advertising Society of America, P.O. Box 1121, Morton Grove, IL 60053; Inner Seal Collectors Club, 4585 Saron Drive, Lexington, KY 40515; National Society of Paper and Advertising Collectibles, P.O. Box 500, Mount Joy, PA 17552; Porcelain Advertising Collectors Club, P.O. Box 381, Marshfield Hills, MA 02051; Ephemera Society of America, P.O. Box 95, Cazenovia, NY 13035; Tin Container Collectors Association, P.O. Box 440101, Aurora, CO 80044.

Museums: American Advertising Museum, Portland, OR; Museum of Transportation, Brookline, MA; National Museum of American History, Archives Center, Smithsonian Institution, Washington, DC.

Additional Listings: See *Warman's Americana & Collectibles* for more examples.

Ashtray, Electrolux, Sculptural Promotions, pottery, 1950s 125.00
Bag Holder, 15-1/2" h, wood counter top type, adv "Dixie Nerve & Bone Liniment" on one side and "Dixie Hog and Chicken Cholera" on other side, tapered to accommodate different size bags 1,100.00
Banner, 31" l, 17" w, Hills Bros. Coffee, paper sign, metal strip at top, red background, 1920s 160.00

Cabinet, Diamond Dye, emb tin front with children playing in park, copyright 1906, some wear to tin, 23" x 30" x 9", $650. Photo courtesy of James D. Julia, Inc.

Bill Hook, 6-1/8" h, 2-1/2" d, American Ironing Machine Co., Chicago, celluloid disk with image of Victorian woman using Simplex ironer 180.00

Blotter, 4" w, 9-1/2" l, Honey Fruit Gum, Franklin-Caro Co, Richmond, VA 200.00

Box

Adam's Gum, 3-3/4" w, 6-1/2" l, 1" h, paper litho label with detailed New York City street scene, dated 1880 ..... 475.00

Barnum's Animal Crackers, c1923 .... 220.00

Carter's Inky Racer, cardboard..................... 140.00

Fanny Farmer Candy, c1944, cylinder, depicts Uncle Sam, removable hat 135.00

Hershey's Mint Flavor Chewing Gum, 6 Sticks For 5¢, 6" l, 4-1/4" w, 1-3/8" h, cardboard.................. 700.00

J. J. Joubert Ice Cream, Canada, half gallon, illus of children at the beach 200.00

Kis-Me Gum, 5-3/8" l, 6-5/8" w, 1-3/8" d, glass display insert, alligator finish 350.00

Mickey Mouse Cookies, Nabisco, Mickey on one side, Donald Duck on other, string holder, c1940 .... 185.00

Pages Seeds, 11-1/4" w, 11" d, 7-3/4" h, oak display box, orig early graphic seed packages 220.00

Purity Ice Cream, Canada, half gallon, illus of children at the beach 200.00

President's Fruit Jar Rubbers, cardboard, George Washington illus, orig contents........................... 75.00

Richardson's Kola Pepsin Gum, 5-3/4" w, 4-5/8" d, 1-1/8" h, cardboard litho, image of Sampson knocking down pillars, some creasing and fading 425.00

Calendar

1903, DuPont, 6-1/4" h, 3-1/4" w, cardboard, full pad, scene of father and son hunting, bird dogs in field 675.00

1904, Deering Harvesters, 20-1/4" x 13-3/8" w, full pad, farm kid in wagon, some edge chipping 190.00

1907, Dupont, two hunters and dogs, illus by Edm H. Osthaus, Sept pad only, 29-1/4" h, 15" w 700.00

1908, Batchelder & Lincoln Co., titled "A Good Catch," pretty woman with a fishing rod, 21-1/4" h, 14-3/4" w, orig metal at top and bottom, full calendar pad................ 125.00

1913, 22-1/4" x 15", Ess-Tee-Dee Dandruff Remedy, full pad, advertisement for barbers to carry product, multicolored graphics of couple fence, billboard with pitch in background 1,550.00

1925, Remington, image titled "Let 'er Rain," duck hunter in boat, full pad, 28-1/2" h, 15" w 625.00

1946, Hercules Powder, titled "The Spirit of '46," three men walking in unity representing the three branches of Armed Services, artist sgd "N. C. Wyeth," full calendar pad loose, 30-1/2" h, 15" w 250.00

Candy Pail, tin litho

California Peanut Co., Kiddie Kandies, comical figures carrying candy pieces, 1 lb, 3-3/8" h, 3-3/4" d 525.00

Merry Christmas And A Happy New Year, 3-1/4" h, 3-1/2" d, scene of children sledding and playing under tree... 100.00

Schrafft's, Trideco, nursery rhyme scene, orig mkd lid, 9 oz, 3-3/4" h, 3-7/8" d 1,750.00

Scudder's Confection Butter, Maple Flavor, Palmer Cox Brownie images, 3-1/2" h, 4-1/4" d..................... 325.00

Chair, Piedmont Cigarettes, folding, two sided porcelain sign back 110.00

Cigar Box, Nations Call, 50 count, wood, c1890, graphic of lady Liberty between vignettes of sea and land battles... 160.00

Cigar Cutter, Betsy Ross, cast iron and tin, paper litho cameo of Betsy Ross in shield-shaped holder, c1880 ...... 775.00

Cigar Tin

Apache Trail, 5-1/2" h, 6" w, 4-1/4" d, Liberty Can Co., even all over fading 650.00

Blue Jay, 6-1/4" h, 5-1/2" w, 4-1/4" d 400.00

Miss Detroit Cigars, National Can Co., 12 count, tin, round, litho of woman and flag 2,490.00

Orcico Cigars, 6-1/4" h, 5-1/2" w, 4" d, Orrison Cigar Co., Indian scenes, © 1919 .... 350.00

Popper's Ace Cigars, 5-3/4" h, 5" w, 5" d, vertical box, image of single engine plane on 2 sides and top 90.00

Sunset Trail, 5-1/2" h, 6" w, 4-1/4" d, dark blue ground, even all over fading 350.00

War Eagle Cigars, tin litho, eagle with shield 400.00

Yellow Cab, 5-1/2" h, 2-1/2" d, lid missing 750.00

Clock

Electric Ad Clock Co., Chicago, cathedral shape, drum in lower window rotates to promote advertising, wood front, sheet metal body, c1933, 21-1/2" h, 14" w 100.00

Gruen Watches, octagonal, blue neon perimeter, Williams Jewelry Co. on marquee at bottom, 15" w 500.00

White King Soap, tin litho body, light-up clock face, reverse painted on glass, c1927, 17" x 24" 1,400.00

Coffee Tin, litho tin

Aunt Nellie's, Harrisburg, PA, 1 lb........... 300.00

Blanke's Tin Cup, l lb, inset lid and handle 185.00

Blue Bird Coffee, 9-1/4" h, 5-1/2" d, Stone-Orlean-Wells Co., image on both sides, American Can Co., fade to litho lid, dents 100.00

Blue Bonnet, Springfield, MO, 1 lb 380.00

Bridal Coffee, 5-5/8" h, 4-1/4" d, Thomas Roberts Co., Phila, 1 lb, paper label, portrait of bride in center 550.00

Coffee, 6-3/4" h, 4-1/4" d, l lb, image of William Jennings Bryan as Democratic Presidential candidate, scattering chipping, general overall wear and light rust 600.00

Cupid Coffee, 6-1/2" h, 3-3/4" d, E. B. Miller & Co., Excelsior Mills, Chicago, paper label over tin, 1 lb 210.00

Chair, Piedmont Cigarettes, folding wooden chair, two sided porcelain sign as back, $110. Photo courtesy of James D. Julia, Inc.

Devotion, St. Joseph, MO, 1 lb, early pry lid 120.00

Federal Club Coffee, 5-5/8" h, 4-1/4" d, Euclid Coffee Co., Cleveland, 1 lb, paper label over tin, label shows early cars parked n drive of country club 400.00

Kamo Coffee, 5" h, 4-3/8" d, Paxton & Gallagher, Omaha, NE, paper label over tin, 1 lb size 210.00

King Cole, 1 lb, tall type, pry lid 535.00

Mount Cross Coffee, 10 lb, bail handle, handled inset lid, 14" h, 9" d 245.00

P of H, 6" x 4-5/8" x 3-1/8", early paper label over cardboard, 1 lb, multicolored scene of plantation worker with donkey returning from mountains 275.00

Pride of Arabia, Toronto, 1 lb 110.00

Samson Coffee & Chicory, 5-1/8" h, 4-1/4" d, C. W. Antrim, Richmond, pry lid, 1 lb, red, white, and black 120.00

Splendora Coffee, 5-3/4" h, 4-1/4" d, Granger & Co., Buffalo, NY, 1 lb, image on both sides of woman in Grecian style gown, red top and base bands with white lettering 1,600.00

Tartan Coffee, 5-1/4" h, 3" d, half pound, paper label over tin, Lowry Coffee Co., Philadelphia, red plaid label with kilted Scotsman, wear, some staining 140.00

Wampum Coffee, 9-1/4" h, 5-1/2" d, partially bare breasted Indian maiden, Stone-Orlean-Wells Co., image on both sides, American Can Co., 3 lb, slip lid 650.00

Warrior Coffee, 5-5/8" h, 4-1/4" d, paper label, 1 lb, pry type, Philip Becker, Buffalo, NY, Indian brave graphics . . . 475.00

White Swan, 3 lb, keywind 180.00

Condom Tin, tin litho

Altex, Western Rubber Co., Canada. 325.00

Coffee Tin, Campfire, Blue Ribbon Products, pry lid, 2-1/2 lb, $215. Photo courtesy of Bear Pen Auction.

Artistocrat, Midwest Drug Co., orig contents
   Rect, three-pack 550.00
   Round, trademark Chinese pheasants 810.00

Caravan, 1-5/8" x 2-1/8", camel with rider leading others thru desert 190.00

Dr. Robinson's Rx #333, 1-5/8" x 2-1/8", Wilson-Robinson Co., Boston, blue and white 140.00

Duble Tip, 1-5/8" x 2-3/16", woman seated at water's edge, Department Sales Co., NY 500.00

Golden Eagles, 1-5/8" x 2-1/8", Real Products Co., Philadelphia, PA, green and white box, eagle in center 575.00

Hy-Pure, 1-5/8" x 2-1/8", Hardy Newman, Chicago, red, black, and white 650.00

Silver Bell, Tiger Skin Rubber Co., New York 400.00

Container, Blue Jay Rolled Oats, Pipestone and Marshall, cardboard, graphic of bird 900.00

Counter Display

Baker Chocolate, 22-1/2" h, tin, urn, pedestal base, trademark logo, serving tray top 1,500.00

Beech Nut Gum Rack, 14-1/2" h, 6-1/4" w, 6-1/2" d, emb tin litho, complete with 2 orig insert boxes 1,100.00

Bull Frog Shoe Polish, 4-1/2" x 3-3/4" x 2-1/2", emb tin litho, green, white, and black frog, green and black lettering, tan ground 375.00

Diamond Dye, 30" h, 23" w, 9" d, emb tin front with children playing park with Governess, © 1906, some damage to tin 650.00

Green River Whiskey, full figure, elderly black gentleman with swayback horse, 14" w. 535.00

Harris Flavoring Extracts, 8" h, 8" w, cardboard diecut, two children standing by frame to hold bottle 120.00

Libby's, 13-1/4" w, 17-1/2" h, 6" d, cardboard, nine 2" to 2-5/8" h orig Libby miniature tin litho fruit and vegetable display tins, some damage to hanging shelves 190.00

Light Bulb, 24" h, 15" w, 14" d, tin litho, electric store type display and tester, blue light bulb shape with woman in black dress showing light bulbs 1,900.00

Milliken's Violet Talcum Powder, 5-3/8" h, 6-1/2" d, hinged lid, celluloid, Whitehead & Hoag 300.00

Primley Chewing Gum, 3-3/4" h, 6-1/2" l, diecut, figural bear standing on stick of gum. 210.00

Sanfords Ink, oak and glass, slanting front, 16" h, 12" w, some chipping to decals. 500.00

Squirrel Peanut Butter, 24" h, 7-3/4" w, 7-3/8" d, tin litho, diecut squirrel at top 750.00

Utica Drop Forge Tool Co., 14" x 17", tin and pine, drawers, litho of tools 250.00

Waterman's Ink, 21" h, 14-1/2" w, 17" d, tin litho, fountain pen ink bottles. 775.00

Counter Sign

Carter's Alma Infants Underwear, 14" h, toddler illus . . . 465.00

Fairy Soap, diecut, easel back, 23-1/2" h, girl on bar of Fairy soap 2,035.00

Kis-Me-Gum, 14" h, 12" w, three-dimensional diecut cardboard, beautiful young lady looking out of window at winter scene, 2 side pieces separated 600.00

Touch Down Smoking Tobacco, 6" x 9-1/2", players scrambling for football. 450.00

Wrigley's Spearmint Gum, 14" h, 10-1/2" w, diecut cardboard, little boy holding oversized pack of gum, easel back . . 400.00

Dispenser, Armour's Veribest Root Beer, milk glass barrel, dispenser missing 1,335.00

Door Push

9-3/4" h, 4-1/4" w, Old Reliable Coffee, tin litho, 1920s . 600.00

13-1/4" h, 3-3/4" w, Copenhagen Tobacco, porcelain, orange, white, and blue 475.00

Counter Display, Baker's Chocolate, tin, urn shape, trademark logo, oval tray on top featuring 4 different products, light overall wear, 22-1/2" h, $1,500. Photo courtesy of James D. Julia, Inc.

Figure, 17" h, Le Belle Chocolatiere, porcelain, lavender top, bustle hoop skirt, white apron dec with small pink flowers, light yellow skirt dec with large pink and blue flowers, blue and white shawl, carries tray of two cocoa cups, late 19th C 1,200.00
Firkin, 6-3/4" h, 6" d top, 6-3/4" d base, Heinz's Peach Butter, wooden, bail handle, paper label on front 200.00
Gum Store Display Box, American Chicle Co., 5-3/4" w, 6-5/8" l, 4-7/8" h, tin litho 350.00
Adams California Fruit Chewing Gum Fruiti 325.00
Adams Pepsin Tutti Fruit....................... 450.00
Adams Spearmint Chewing Fruiti, blue and white, some rust spots... 250.00
Yucatan Gum, yellow, red, white, and black.......... 325.00
Humidor, 6-1/2" h, Lucky Strike, glass, orig red, green, and gold paper label 325.00
Jar, glass
Heinz Apple Butter, 7-1/2" h, orig paper label, lid missing 175.00
H. J. Heinz Keystone Brand, 12-1/4" h, 5-1/4" d, orig label, ground glass lid 575.00
Planters Peanuts
    Barrel shape, large etched lid, emb running Mr. Peanut 315.00
    Fishbowl shape, 13-1/2" h, 9-1/2" d, variation label, red lettering "Planters Salted Peanuts," flanked by Mr. Peanut figure on left and "5" on right, lid with peanut finial 525.00

Football, 1930, emb "Planters Salted Peanuts" on front and back, chipped lip 335.00
Walla Walla Pepsin Gum, 4-3/4" w, 13" h, emb Indian Chief and lettering, ground glass lid 325.00
Ledger Marker, tin litho, diecut
Springfield Insurance, 12" l, 3" w, illus of Indian, Wells & Hope Co. litho 135.00
Western Assurance Company, 12-1/2" l, 3" w, trademark crest with unicorn, lion and array of flags, Kellogg & Bulkeley Co. litho 115.00
Lunch Box, tin litho
Blue and Scarlet Plug Cut........................ 440.00
Dixie Kid Tobacco, 3-5/8" l, 7-3/4" l, 5-1/8" h, Nail & Williams Tobacco Co., white child illus 575.00
Pedro Tobacco, 7-3/4" l, 5-1/4" l, 4" d............... 165.00
Marquis, 10-7/8" h, 11-3/4" w, diamond shaped, one side with Diamond Dyes cloth fabric color wheel, other side with black kids on fence, ornate silver borders, both sides behind glass 375.00
Mirror, celluloid covered
Brotherhood Overalls, 2" d, bare breasted lady putting on pair of overalls, discoloration to mirror 125.00
Buster Brown Shoes, 1-3/4" d, titled "The little girl on the other side should wear Buster Brown Shoes," shows head shot of Buster Brown and Tige, some denting to celluloid, discoloration to mirror................................ 150.00
Sanitary Brand Pillows, 3-1/2" d, child in pajamas standing in stack of pillows, Parisian Novelty Co. 275.00
Watertown Daily Times, Mirror of the Day's News, 2" d, Uncle Sam in center............................... 425.00
Paperweight
A. T. A. Nelson Co, naked woman hiding behind leather hide, 2-1/2" w, 4" l, glass......................... 125.00
Carnation Malted Milk, 2-3/4" h, 1-3/4" d, miniature soda fountain metal canister, glossy paper label, chromed metal top, velvet bottom 425.00
Henry Booker & Co. Carriage Manufacturers, 2-1/2" w, 4" l, rect, light scratching to top of glass 100.00
Indian Brand Cream Canned Corn, 4" h, 2-5/8" w, glass, white ground, black lettering and image of Indian Chief, Merrell & Soule, Syracuse, NY 230.00
Lanigan Automobile Sales Co., 3" w, 4-1/2" l, 7/8" h, glass, adv Lanigan Automobiles, white ground, sepia illus of car, scalloped edge 220.00
Lovell Diamond Cycles, 2-1/2" w, 4" l, rect, glass, vintage John P. Lovell Arms Co. bicycle, wear 100.00
New England Mutual Accident Insurance, 2-1/2" w, 4" l, rect, glass, multicolored, vintage railroad on one side, paddle steamboat on other 125.00
Peanut Butter Pail, tin litho
Armour's Veribest, 3-3/4" h, 3-1/2" d, 1 lb........... 100.00
Capitol Peanut Butter, 3-3/8" d, 3-1/2" d, 14 oz size, Andrus Schofield Co, Columbus, OH, scenes of children playing with toys................................... 475.00
Eat More Brand, Erb & Zarlin Co., Shamokin, PA, 4" d, 3-3/4" h, 1 lb, animal figures on back and sides, some scratches and light overall wear 170.00
Hoody's, 3-1/2" h, 3-3/4" d, two young girls seesawing over large peanut, 1 lb.................................. 170.00
Jack and Jill, 3-1/2" h, 3-3/8" d, 13 oz size, Loblaw Grocers, Toronto, light denting...................... 210.00
Jackie Coogan, 3-1/4" h, 3-3/4" d, red ground, 12 oz .. 225.00
Le-Hi Peanut Butter, 3-1/2" h, 3-3/8" d, 1 lb, Lehmann Higginson Grocers, Wichita, Kansas, some light surface rust on lid 825.00
King's, Suffolk, VA, 1 lb........................ 865.00

Monarch, 2" h, 1-3/8" d, "Free Sample," paper label "Teenie Weenie," wrap around label with images of children carrying giant peanuts, never opened 250.00

Pallas, 2-3/4" h, 2-3/4" d, Ridenour-Baker Groc., 7 oz . . 180.00

Peter Pan, 2-3/4" h, 3-1/4" d, E. K. Pond Co., snap top lid, 11 oz 60.00

Roundy's, 3-3/4" h, 3-1/2" d, scene of children playing at beach, 14 oz, mismatched lid. 250.00

School Boy, 3-3/4" h, 3-1/4" d, 1 lb 170.00

School Days, 3-1/4" h, 3-3/4" d, scenes of children at recess, United Fig & Date Co., Continental Can Co., 14 oz . . 325.00

Scowcroft, 3-3/4" h, 3-1/4" d, scenes of children picnicking and at play, 1 lb. 450.00

Squirrel Peanut Butter
3-1/2" h, 3-3/4" w, 1 lb size. 300.00
6-1/2" h, 6-1/4" w, 5 lb size, image of squirrel on both sides 400.00

Sunny Boy, 9-1/2" h, 10" d, Brundage Bros. Co., Toledo, OH, 25 lb. 100.00

Teddie, 3-1/2" h, 3-3/4" d, John W. Levin Co., 1 lb 80.00

Toy Land, 4" h, 3-1-2" d, E. K. Pond Co., 1 lb 150.00

Van Dyks, 3-7/8" h, 3-5/8" d, I lb, Mother Hubbard and children scene 875.00

Plate, Vienna Art, 10" d, adv on back
Anheuser Busch Malt-Nutrine, lady with low cut diaphanous top 95.00

Dr. Pepper, girl holding large vase 675.00

Playing Cards, Planter's Peanut, Mr. Peanut paddling a pretty lady in a peanut canoe, complete deck, linen finish, c1920 . . . . 775.00

Puzzle, Singer, Buffalo, c1890, 50 pcs, orig envelope, 2 buffalo pulling buggy advertising "Singer," framed and matted 365.00

Salesman's Sample
Adams Leaning Wheel Grader, J. D. Adams Co., Indianapolis, IN, name on side, gray colored metal, fiber and wood carrying case, several metal pieces packed inside, 22" l, 8-1/2" w 3,500.00

Boston Stove, cast iron, emb "Little Eva N. S. Kate Boston Stove". 375.00

Sign
Admiration Cigars, 7-1/2" h, 5-3/4" w, tin, easel back, colonial lady admiring herself in mirror 275.00

Allied Mills, 32" h, 24-1/2" d, diecut porcelain, grain bag shape, some chipping, staining 275.00

Anheuser-Busch, 9-1/2" d, reverse painting on glass, vibrant reds and golds, trademark eagle among letter "A" . . . 900.00

Bernard Gloeckler Co. Butcher, Pittsburgh, PA, 20" h, 24" w, cast aluminum, figural wall mounted type, relief model of bull, hack saw, clever, and butcher knife, painted silver . . 700.00

Blu-J Brooms, 9-3/4" h, 4" w, litho diecut cardboard, figural bird perched on handle of upright broom 220.00

Budweiser Beer, 16" d, titled "Say When," couple fonduing with Budweiser Beer, girl on left side, dark ground 700.00

Bull Dog Cut Plug Won't Bite, 10-1/4" x 7-1/4", tin litho, red dog, red and white lettering, minor scattered chipping and wear, antique oak frame 450.00

Calumet Baking Powder, 23-1/2" h, 17-1/2" w, curved tin litho corner display, orig wooden base, red can in center, yellow ground 1,900.00

C. D. Kenny Che-On-Tea, 20" h, 15" w, early litho paper, patriotic child holding oversized box, © 1906 Gothic Litho, matted and framed. 400.00

Danahay's Perfecto Cigars, 19" h, 13" w, oval, tin litho self frame, child and roses in center. 1,100.00

Diamond Wedding Whiskey, 12" d, round, tin litho self frame, saloon girl in center holding shot glass 500.00

Dr. Hartshorn's Bitters Cures Jaundice and Dyspepsia, 18" h, 14-3/4" w, paper, matted and framed 325.00

Fatima Cigarettes, 28" h, 49-1/2" l, diecut cardboard, stand-up window type, yellow canoe with woman with parasol, gentleman seated at other end .5,500.00

Fautless Pepsin Gum Chips, 9-1/2" x 9", emb cardboard, white lettering, dark blue ground 375.00

Fehr's Malt Tonic for Health and Strength, 28-1/2" h, 23" w, rolled self framed tin, oval, semi-clad beauty teasing winged cherubs, H. D. Beach Co. litho, c1910 . . . . 500.00

Foster Hose Supporters, 16-1/2" h, 8-1/2" w, made out of Pulveroid (celluloid-type material), sgd "F. F. Pulver Co.," image of woman wearing corset, framed 550.00

Illinois Springfield Watches, 17-1/2" h, 23-1/2" l, tin, illus of Observatory of Illinois Watch Co., Springfield, orig wood frame with adv 200.00

Imperial Suspenders, 15-1/2" h, 10-1/2" w, cardboard, titled "Are good enough for us," shows police, firemen, and mechanics all wearing Imperial Suspenders, framed 300.00

I. W. Harper Whiskey, 29-1/4" h, 23-1/2" w, vitrolite milk glass, detailed int. scene of hunting cabin, repainted frame 825.00

Jesse Welden 10¢ Cigar, 20" h, 13-3/4" w, emb tin litho, curved corner type, wooden back mount, Donovan Co., St. Albans, VT. 675.00

Kis-Me-Gum, 17-1/4" h, 9-1/4" l, emb diecut cardboard, silhouettes turn of century full figured lady, c1890, notation that same picture without writing is available for postage and 16 gum wrappers 2,500.00

Knox Gelatin, 20" h, 26" w, canvas-type paper, dated 1901, black woman and young girl preparing dessert 1,375.00

Lipton's Tea, paper, dated 1899, American Litho Co., young woman ready to serve tea 1,500.00

Little General Bread, 9-3/4" h, 12-3/8" l, tin litho, 2-sided flange sign, bright yellow background, red lettering, child in colonial dress, blue hat and tricorn hat, white pants, black boots 2,800.00

Sign, Dawson's Diamond Ale, porcelain curved corner type, King of Diamonds playing card advertising "Dawson's Diamond Ale, A Royal Brew," 25" x 17-1/2", $1,900. Photo courtesy of James D. Julia, Inc.

Mellin's Food, 24" h, 13-3/4" w, diecut, baby, pink crepe paper dress. 350.00

Meriden Brewing Co. Nutmeg Beer, 14" h, 20" l, wood, Uncle Sam enjoying beer by fireside, text includes "Bottled at the Brewery for Family and Medicinal Use," Sentenne & Greene litho. 300.00

Moxie, 6" d, diecut tin, beautiful girl drinking Moxie from flared fountain glass 700.00

Munsingwear, 38" h, 25" w, self framed diecut tin, titled "The Munsingwear Twins," girl in long johns looking at herself in mirror, © 1910, some inpainting, some surface rust . 750.00

Nabisco, 17" h, 25" l, diecut, Santa holding products, Merry Christmas in yellow, red suit, long white beard, blue ground 230.00

New England Brewing, 23" h, 33" l, self framed tin, moose overlooking very busy bountiful camping scene, hunters and fisherman, quantities of New England Ales and Lagers throughout, sign on shed in scene shows factory scene and bottles of New England Brewing Beer, Meek Co. litho, previously varnished, fair to good condition 650.00

Old Boone Distillery, 29" h, 21" l, tin litho, Thikxon Milett & Co., Louisville, KY, illus of elderly Daniel Boone sitting outside cabin in wooded setting, framed. 775.00

Old Tucker Rye Whiskey, 9-1/4" h, 13-1/8" l, tin litho self framed, Brown Forman, whiskey jug with funnel, white and brown dog, green ground 325.00

Oshkosh B'Gosh Overalls, 10" h, 30" l, porcelain 625.00

Orange Crush, 18-1/2" x 17-1/2", cardboard, diecut, easel back, pretty girl with two bottles on tray, c1930 . . . . 500.00

Orient Motor Buckboard, 14" h, 21" l, string hung cardboard, image of man and caddie driving to golf course in early car, minor damage and restoration 1,150.00

Philip Morris, 4" h, 25-3/4" l, porcelain, pack of Philip Morris Cigarettes and "Do you inhale? - If so call for Philip Morris Smoking pleasure without smoking penalties," small rim chip 700.00

Prince Albert, 25" h, 19-1/4" w, tin, titled "Chief Joseph, Nez Perce," colorful Indian Chief in full headdress, some inpainting to Prince Albert can, background, framed 1,100.00

Recruit Cigars, 28" h, 22-1/4" w, self framed tin, dashing young recruit in uniform, H. D. Beach Co. litho 3,750.00

Round Oak Stoves, Ranges, Furnaces, 22-1/2" h, 17-1/2" w, curved corner Vitrolite, orig copper flashed frame, colorful image of Doe-Wah-Jack, © 1905 . . . . 7,750.00

Schlitz, 24" d, pre-prohibition, titled "Ah! Isn't Schlitz Always Good?" couple enjoying glass of beer while blacksmith works to repair their automobile, Schlitz advertisement on door, Chas. W. Shonk Co. litho, light overall scratching, orig hanging band on back 800.00

Sherwin-William Paints and Varnishes, 16" h, 22" l, two sided flanged porcelain, trademark paint covering earth . . . 650.00

Soda Mint Pepsin Gum, 17" h, 25-1/2" l, cardboard, detailed graphics, red ground, matted, framed 625.00

Texaco Marine Lubricants, 15" h, 30" w, porcelain, motorboats and gulls 1,650.00

Velvet Tobacco, 22" x 16", tin litho self frame, vibrant colors, few dents and some professional restoration 800.00

Whistle Soda, 9-1/2" h, 27-3/4" l, emb tin litho, "Thirsty? Just Demand the Genuine Whistle," shows hand with bottle, orig sheen, American Art Works 725.00

Wm Wrigley Jr. & Co., 18" h, 13-1/2" w, paper, Teddy Roosevelt leading Rough Riders, 1901 . . . . 2,000.00

Stool, 18" l, 13" w, 10" h, Indian Motorcycle, metal, folding, name in script on canvas top, c1920 . . . . 300.00

Store Bin, tin litho

A. B. Davis Spices, 32" l, 12" d, eight compartments, rolled front, orig covers, swans painted at top 1,250.00

Beech Nut Chewing Tobacco, slant front, red and white package
6" w, 10" l, 8" h, blue ground, white lettering 850.00
8-5/8" w, 9-7/8" l, 8-1/4" h, yellow ground, red lettering 650.00

Game Cut Tobacco, 7-1/2" w, 11-1/2" l, 7-3/4" h, Bagley & Co., Detroit, game birds pictured on front and back 625.00

J. A. Folger & Co., 14-1/4" w, 16" l, 20" h, rolled front, large center ship, smaller ships. 2,225.00

Jamo Coffee, 13" w, 10" d, 16" h, slant front, man with large white beard on horse, reads "The World's Best," W. J. Gould & Co., yellow painted sides and rear 1,200.00

Pastime Tobacco, 12-1/2" l, 9-1/4" w, 4-1/4" h, John Finzer & Bros., top litho faded 125.00

Sure Shot Chewing Tobacco, 6-3/4" h, 15-1/4" l, 10-1/4" d, Indian image on front and back 1,350.00

Sweet Cuba Tobacco, 18" l, 14" w, 12" h, slant front, porcelain knob added. 925.00

Tape Measure, 1-1/2" d, Edison Mazda Lamps, Parrish "Get Together" design, bottom adv Worcester Suburban Electric Co., Uxbridge, MA, celluloid 200.00

Tin

Blue Ribbon Butter, Washington Creamy, Seattle, 3-1/2" x 5-1/8", 2 lb size, tin litho 210.00

Chieftain Brand Typewriter Ribbon, Southwestern Stationery & Bank Supply, 2-5/8" d, 3/4" h, red image of Indian Chief on cover, yellow ground 325.00

Sign, Kis-Me Gum, emb diecut cardboard, full figured lady, c1890, 17-1/4" x 9-1/4", $2,500. Photo courtesy of James D. Julia, Inc.

Clark's Teaberry Pepsin Chewing Gum, 5-1/4" w, 6-3/4" l, 2-3/8" h, hinged, red, yellow, floral dec 550.00

Cyrus Nobel Whiskey, 13" h, 3-1/2" d, artillery shell shape, wooden top, WWI soldier firing cannon on front, adv on back 210.00

Dayton Nuts, Dayton, OH, 8-1/4" h, 7-1/8" d, 5 lb, large bi-wing airplane illus 275.00

Etoile Talc, 5-3/4" h, 2" d, Zuane Perfumers, two nudes, dark blue background. 275.00

Ginna & Co., 4" x 6" x 2", hinged, Christmas theme, graphics on all sides 575.00

Grebb Oysters, Louis Grebb Packers, Baltimore, 7-1/4" h, 6-3/4" d, 1 gallon, blue illus. 150.00

Licorice Forbidden Fruit Gum, Zeno Mfg. Co. 5/8" w, 3-1/4" l, 1" h, slide top, red and black 1,400.00

Majestic Brand Raw Oysters, Atlantic Packing Co, Baltimore, 7-1/4" h, 6-3/4" d, red and yellow 350.00

Minty's Brise Charmante Talcum, tin litho, woman in flower, Canadian, some darkening to gold lid 700.00

Snowdrop Marshmallows, Gottmann & Sons, Chicago, 6" h, 9-3/4" d, 5 lb size, Palmer Cox Brownies roasting marshmallows over campfire 325.00

Standard Brand Carriage & Harness Lubricant, New York Refining Co, 3-3/4" h, 3" d, litho of stork holding pail, yellow ground 160.00

Vivaudo's Astringent Cream, 5/8" x 1", red background, cherub applying cream to scantily clad woman, some wear to base 250.00

Vision Baking Powder, paper label with cherubs eating grapes, tending a fire, c1900. . . . . 300.00

Winchester Talc, hunter and dog 225.00

Zeno Mfg. Co. Pepsin Chewing Gum, 5/8" w, 3-1/4" l, 1" h, slide top 600.00

Tip Tray

Buffalo Brewing Co., 4-1/4" d, semi-clad lady wearing diaphanous top, some minor scratching 350.00

Cortez Cigars, shows Herman Cortez, 6" d, some overall crazing and soiling 275.00

De Laval Cream Separators, 4-1/4" d, titled "The World's Standard," Victorian lady separating cream while little boy in Little Lord Fontaroy outfit goes out to play, © 1905 . . . . . . 270.00

Evinrude Outboard Motor, vivid color scene of lady dressed in red in boat, c1920, 4" d 500.00

Fairy Soap, 4-1/4" d, titled "Have you a little 'Fairy' in your home?" little girl sitting atop oversized cake of Fairy Soap, name on upper rim, Passaic Metal Ware Co. litho, light overall crazing. 150.00

J. Chr. G. Hupfel Brg. Co, 5" d, factory scene, vintage truck and horse-drawn vehicles, Kaufmann & Strauss Co. litho, some chipping to rim 250.00

Kenny's Teas & Coffees, 4-1/4" d, three monkeys, Kaufmann & Strauss Co. litho. 150.00

Lindquist's Crackers, titled "Two Roosevelt Beers had a home out west. In a big ravine near a mountain crest," humorous bears wearing Teddy Roosevelt type items, scalloped rim with additional Roosevelt Bears, © 1906, 5" h, 3-3/4" w 225.00

Log Cabin Inn, titled "I won't sleep upstairs said Teddy G. I want a window. I want to see," showing Teddy-G trying down from upper berth of train, scalloped rim with additional Roosevelt Bears, © 1906, 5" h, 3-3/4" w. 325.00

Manure Spreader, horse drawn manure spreading named "The Success Spreader," 3-1/2" h, 4-3/4" l 275.00

Moxie, titled "I Just Love Moxie Don't You?" young lady drinking from flared soda glass emb "Moxie," 6" d. 275.00

Store Bin, J. & A. Folger & Co., Young Hysont, litho tin, rolled front, shows large ship with small ships nearby, 20" x 14-1/4" x 16", $2,225. Photo courtesy of James D. Julia, Inc.

President Suspenders, 4-1/4" d, Grecian looking lady, glass insert of face 95.00

Red Raven, 4-1/4" d, titled "Great for Headache," little girl looking at Red Raven display, Chas. W. Shonk Co. litho 130.00

Stegmaier Brewing, 4-1/4" d, busy factory scene, horse-drawn vehicles, C. W. Shonk Co. litho 250.00

Wagner Brewing Co., 5" d, Imperial Export Beer bottle, Kaufmann & Strauss Co. litho 200.00

Welsbach Lighting, 4-1/4" d, shows lady reading in wicker chair, child plays in vintage house lit with Welsbach Lighting fixtures 100.00

Tobacco Tin, tin litho

Cardinal Cut Plug, 4-1/2" h, 3" w, vertical pocket type, even fading. 200.00

Century, Lorilard & Co., Somers Bros., 2-1/4" x 3-1/2" x 5/8" h, flat pocket type, dial under lid rotates to show 1880 Presidential and Vice Presidential candidates, Garfield, Arthur, Hancock, and English, black lettering, red ground 650.00

Checkers, Weisart Bros., St. Louis, 4-1/2" h, 3" w, black and red check, slight surface scuffs 400.00

Colonial Cubes, 5" h, 3-1/2" w, 1-1/8" d, pocket type, image of George Washington, American Tobacco, slight surface rusting, loss of luster 650.00

Dixie Queen, American Tobacco Co., 6-1/2" h, 4-3/4" d, small top, canister shape. 175.00

Edgeworth Juniors, 4-3/8" h, 3" w, unopened, intact revenue stamp 120.00

Edgeworth Ready-Rubbed, unopened, orig cellophane . 520.00

Eve, 3-1/2" h, 3-1/2" w, vertical, pocket, Eve only covered by a fig leaf. 100.00

Fast Mail Tobacco, Hasker & Marcuse, 3-3/4" h, 2-1/4" w, 1/2" d, flat pocket type. 275.00

Forest & Stream, two fishermen in canoe. 400.00

Fountain Tobacco, Penn Tobacco Co., 6-1/4" h, 5-1/4" w, slip lid, canister. 225.00

Greek Slave Tobacco, Snead & Carrington Tobacco Co, Lynchburg, VA, 2-1/4" w, 4-1/4" l, 3-1/4" h, black lettering, statue, red ground 300.00

Honey Moon Tobacco, 4-1/2" h, 3" w, 7/8" d, vertical pocket type, couple seated in moon on front, pipe and cigarette on back 900.00

Lucky Curve Plug Cut Tobacco, 4-1/4" w, 6-7/8" l, 4-1/2" h, baseball player, red ground 1,850.00

Maryland Club, 4-1/4" h, 3-1/8" w, 1" d, vertical pocket type, Marburg Bros.. . . . . 550.00

North Pole Tobacco, United States Tobacco Co., 6-1/4" h, 4" w, 5-1/2" d, Hasker & Marcuse litho, two polar bears killing walrus 140.00

Old Rip, 4-3/4" h, 3-1/4" w, 2-1/8" d, Rip Van Winkle in Catskills, black image and lettering, dark red ground, 1890s . . 350.00

Pedro Cut Plug, 6-1/2" h, 5" d, Royal Straight Flush on one side, Jack of Spades on other, small top, canister 250.00

Plaza, 5" h, 4-3/4" d, emb, small top, canister 350.00

Real Thing, 6-1/4" h, 5" d, Laurus & Bros. Co., small top, canister 250.00

Rothenberg's Schloss Mixture, Kansas City, MO, 3" h, 3-1/2" l, 1-1/4" d, vertical pocket type, red ground, white lettering, portrait center 450.00

Squadron Leader, airplane, 1920s, mint. 75.00

Three Feathers, 4" h, 3-1/4" w, vertical pocket type 250.00

Time's Square Smoking Mixture, 4-3/8" x 3-7/8", vertical pocket type, night time view of New York skyline 425.00

Three States, Harry Weissinger Tob. Co., 7" h, 5" w, paper label, small top, canister 375.00

Tuxedo, 6-1/2" l, 4" w, 5" d, oval, small top, canister . . . 100.00

Union World Tobacco, Globe Tobacco Co., 6-1/4" h, 5" d, small top, canister 200.00

Yankee Boy, Scotten, Dillon, Detroit, 4" h, 3-1/2" w, 1-1/8" d, vertical pocket type, blond haired boy playing baseball, red and white stripes 625.00

Whip, octagonal canister. 465.00

Tray, tin litho

American Brewing Co., 18-1/2" h, 15-1/4" w, oval, lady overlooking factory water scene, pointing to pedestal with A. B. C. trademark, two cherubs crowning bottle sitting on pedestal "A. B. C. Sold Around the World," Chas. W. Shonk CO. litho, rim chips, small dent at top. 475.00

Anheuser Busch Brewing, 15" l, 18" w, titled "America's Largest and Favorite Brewery," busy factory complex, early trains, trolleys, and horse drawn vehicles, Standard Advertising Co. litho. 650.00

Arctic Brand Ice Cream, 13-1/2" d, detailed graphic of white polar bear floating on ice chunk 775.00

Columbia Brewing, 9-3/4" d, Lady Liberty holding glass of beer, standing next to American eagle and keg of beer, rim chips 225.00

Crescent Brewing Co., 12" d, factory scene, multiple horse drawn carriages in fore front, Crescent logo with hops background painted in sky 500.00

DeLaval, tin. 550.00

E. Robinson's Sons Pilsener, 12" d, boaters in vintage garb, stopping for brew served by black waiter, Haeusermann litho 225.00

Fan Tan Chewing Gum, 10-1/2" h, 13-1/4" l, colorful scene of Geisha and mountains, very slight rim chipping. 350.00

Golden West Brewing Co., 13" d, factory scene, early trolleys and horse drawn cards, American Art Works litho . . . 300.00

Grand Rapids Brewing Co., 13-1/4" d, factory scene, early automobilia, trolleys, and horse drawn carts, "Silver Foam" Our Special Brew, Kaufmann & Strauss Co. litho 400.00

Hall Co., 13-1/4" h, 10-1/2" w, colorful scene of children being served ice cream by woman, 1920s, unused condition 1,500.00

Los Angeles Brewing Co., 13" l, 16" w, pre-prohibition, factory scene with early automobilia and horse drawn vehicles, some inpainting to sky, rim chips 325.00

Mathie Brewing Co., Red Ribbon Beer, Old Dutch Lager, Polynesian woman stroking her ukulele 200.00

Olympia's Exquisiting Butte Beer, 12" d, titled "Best in the West," Gypsy woman, Chas. W. Shonk Co. litho, © 1907, rim chips and wear. 700.00

Red Ribbon Beer, Mathie Brewing Co., 13" sq, titled "On the Square," happy bear finding full case of Red Ribbon Beer 700.00

Trommer's Evergreen Brewery, 12" l, 17" w, people in old time touring car stopping at tavern, curve corner sign on building in background, some inpainting 375.00

ADVERTISING TRADE CARDS

History: Advertising trade cards are small, thin cardboard cards made to advertise the merits of a product. They usually bear the name and address of a merchant.

With the invention of lithography, colorful trade cards became a popular way to advertise in the late 19th and early 20th centuries. They were made to appeal especially to children. Young and old alike collected and treasured them in albums and scrapbooks. Very few are dated; the prime years for trade card production were 1880 to 1893; cards made between 1810 and 1850 can be found, but rarely. By 1900 trade cards were rapidly losing their popularity, and by 1910 they had all but vanished.

References: Kit Barry, *Advertising Trade Card*, Book 1, published by author, 1981; Dave Cheadle, *Victorian Trade Cards*, Collector Books, 1996; Robert Jay, *Trade Card in Nineteenth-Century America*, University of Missouri Press, 1987; Murray Cards (International) Ltd. (comp.), *Cigarette Card Values*, Murray Cards (International) Ltd., 1994.

Periodicals: *Card Times*, 70 Winified Lane, Aughton, Ormskirk, Lancashire L38 5DL England; *Trade Card Journal*, 109 Main St, Brattleboro, VT 05301.

Collectors' Club: Trade Card Collector's Society, P.O. Box 284, Marlton, NJ 08053

Additional Listings: See *Warman's Americana & Collectibles* for more examples.

Beverages

California Wine, woman, bear, flags, and grapes, 1860s . 25.00

Great Atlantic & Pacific Tea Co, Dinah praises A & P teas and coffees, black landlord and renter's conversation on bottom, adv on back, 1884, 8" x 9" 25.00

Hires Root Beer, An Uninvited Guest 20.00

James Mumm & Co. Reins Chamganes, L. Sanborn & Co., gold trim, Heppenheimer & Mauere 60.00
Royal Garden Teas, September with birthstone 5.00
Wolff's Schnapps, Columbian Exposition adv on back . . . 15.00

Clothing and accessories

Alaska Down Bustles, woman wearing bustle 17.50
AST Co, black tip shoes, school teacher illus, 1880 . . . . . 7.50
Automatic Shoe Heel Co, diecut, black shoe, brown sole. 45.00
Ball's Health Preserving Corsets, multicolored 10.00
Beals. Torrey & Co, Boots and Shoes, Palmer Cox Brownies
. . . . 10.00
Best & Co. Liputian Bazaar, NY, children's wear, gold trim, Wemple & Co. 25.00
Broadhead Dress Goods, litho illus 12.00
Buster Brown Shoes, children and dog, 1909 . . . . 12.00
Cherry, Robt, Germantown, Phila, shoes, woman looking at shoe box 12.00
Draper & Maynard Co Gloves & Mittens, plant vignette on reverse 12.00
Fisk, Clark & Flaggs Gloves, two gentlemen, gold ground
. . . . 10.00
Libby & Spier, clothing, New Year greeting, steel engraving
. . . . 15.00
Marshall & Ball Clothiers, horse, adv on back 5.00
New Globe Patented Shirts, caricature illus, sepia and black
. . . . 18.00
Prevost, M.V., Fine Millinery, diecut, fan shape, comical animals
. . . . 55.00
Reed's, Joseph, Finest Clothing, Philadelphia 12.00
Solar Tip Shoes, wise – foolish man story 155.00
Spun Glass Rusil Finish Dress Linings, litho illus 17.50
Strawbridge & Clothier, man carrying packages 10.00
Taylor & Rogers Clothing, black and green, vignette 25.00

Coffee

Arbuckle Coffee, pictorial US history with maps 5.00
Arbuckle Coffee, Trip Around the World Series, 3" x 5"
    Arabia 5.00
    Bavaria 6.00
    Sweden 6.00
C. D. Kenny
    5" x 6-1/2", store locations ad on front, stain on back
    . . . . 20.00
    5-1/4" x 8-1/4", dry roasted coffee ad on back 24.00
Black Cross Coffee, fortune telling fish, rd and gold, orig envelope 25.00
Lion Coffee, Mrs. President Cleveland 10.00
Standard Java, boy on donkey, double sided 15.00
Victor Coffee, four horses pulling chariot 7.50

Farm machinery and supplies

Advance Thresher Co., Battle Creek, MI, wheat girl, Calvert Litho 15.00
Bickford & Huffman, Macedon, NY, farm tools, 1886 . . . . 25.00
Bucker & Gibbs Plow Co, Canton, OH 20.00
Clinton Plow Co., Clinton, MI, children illus 25.00
Deering Implements, mower on reverse 15.00
Dietericks Harness Oil, horse and elves 35.00
Eureka Mower, farmer on porch 18.00
McCormick, diecut, hand shape 12.00
Princess Plow Co, Canton, OH, The Princess of Wale Plow, full color, four pages, Princess on cov 17.50
Russell & Co, Massillon, OH, threshers, engines, saw mills, litho illus 17.50

Sharples Bros., Philadelphia, cream separator, chromolithograph of girl and bunny 15.00
Star Wind Engines, Flint & Watling Mfg. Co. Kendalville, IN, fold-over, Giles & Co. Litho 20.00

Food

American Breakfast Cereals, 1883 . . . . 15.00
Baltimore Oyster Co, 1884 calendar on reverse 40.00
Bordens Eagle Brand Condensed Milk, child and cat illus . 7.50
Butterine, three girls on log 10.00
Compliments of Clark Bell, The Cash Grocers, adv on reverse
. . . . 15.00
Deep Sea Mess Mackerel, litho illus 7.50
Dixon's Ice Cream, Keamy statue in military park 7.50
Emmerson's Albumenoid Food, 1886 . . . . 5.00
Fleischmann & Co Yeast, litho illus 10.00
Greenfield's Chocolate Sponge, child carrying box, policeman directs traffic, 1915 . . . . 12.00
Hecker's Buckwheat, hold to light type 20.00
Kenton Baking Powder, owl and moon 10.00
Libbey's Extracts of Beef, calendar on reverse 20.00
Mellins Food, litho illus 10.00
Niox de Coco, For Puddings, Pies, Pastries, woman served by blacks 12.00
Quaker Oats, mechanical 40.00
Ridges Food For Infants & Invalids, litho illus 10.00
Shaker Oven Baked Beans, 2" x 3-1/2" 35.00
Syrup of Figs, Fig Syrup Co, CA, folder 12.00
Thurber's Canned Vegetables 7.50
Tip Top Baking Powder, litho dog illus 15.00
Van Houtens Cocoa, litho trains illus 12.00
Walter Baker & Co. cocoa, woman 10.00

Laundry and soaps

Bon-Ton Polish, two girls playing with dolls and dog 5.00
Conqueror Wringer, "Baking Day," women baking, Donaldson Bros 12.00
Empire Wringer, fox wedding 15.00
Fairbanks Gold Dust Twins 50.00
Lifebuoy Soap, woman holding life preserver with boy holding product 24.00
New Process Starch, double view, Chinaman and woman
. . . . 12.00
Niagara Starch, well dressed long haired lady holding product, full color 5.00
Packer's Tar Soap, mother washing baby, full color 4.00
Sapillo, diecut, watermelon shape, black face 20.00
Sweet Home Family Soap, Larkin & Co, Palmer Cox Brownies riding bicycle 15.00
Viola Cream Skin Soap, folder, skin care information . . . 17.50
Williams' Yankee Soap, red, white, and blue flag, beige ground
. . . . 100.00

Medical

Ayer's Hair Vigor 15.00
Browns Bronchial Troches, flag weather warning, Forbes Litho
. . . . 12.00
Burdocks Blood Bitters, lady, Cosack & Co., Buffalo, NY, 5" x 6-1/2" 10.00
Carter's Little Nerve Pills, boy and girl hugging large dog
. . . . 17.50
German Corn Remover, metamorphic 35.00
Horsford's Acid Phosphate, 3-1/2" x 4-1/2" 25.00
Jayne's Expectorant, children begging, 1890 . . . . 7.50
Loose's Red Clover, As a Cure For Cancer, men fighting bear
. . . . 7.50

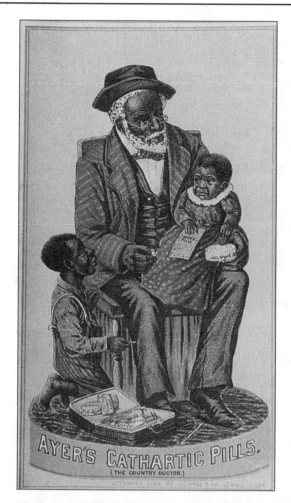

Ayer's Carthatic Pills, Dr. S. C. Ayer & Co., Lowell, MA, The Country Doctor, seated black male with children, multicolored scene, copyright 1883, $25.

Krauter Bitters, elaborate center panel, three folds 5.00
Peckhams Croup Remedy, woman and girl 5.00
Schenk's Pulmonic Syrup, hold to light type, sleeping children and kitten 12.00
Tarrants Seltzer Aperient, metamorphic 20.00

Miscellaneous

Agate Iron Ware, cat in coffee pot. 25.00
Buckingham's Dye for The Whiskers, metamorphic, gentleman with chest length white beard changes to black beard, adv on back 22.00
Campbell's Hair Cutting & Shaving Saloon, black and blue 45.00
Claredon Pianos, little girl holding tennis racket and ball . 35.00
Colaine Headache Powders, puzzle reverse 40.00
Compliments of Seely Manuf Co. Perfumer's, Detroit, MI 10.00
Dutch Boy Paints, mechanical, diecut, blue, white, yellow, and red 25.00
Entertainment and Shaker Sale, 2-1/2" x 3 3/4" 35.00
Finck's "Detroit-Special" Overalls, diecut, 2-3/4" x 5", adv on back 185.00
Gardner, R D, Organs, black illus, light green ground ... 15.00
Hotel & Cafe Butler, Seattle, Halloween card, 1907, Tiny Tads Co, NY, artist sgd 250.00

Hoyt, E W, & Co, perfumed calendar, 1893 .... 10.00
Knaust Bros. & Co, Cincinnati, OH, toy bazaar, Santa illus 17.50
McAuslan & Wahelin Co, Toyland, Holyoke, MA, mechanical, Santa writes on blackboard, black, white, and red, adv on reverse. 40.00
Metropolitan Life, diecut, chromolithograph, three little girls having tea party, boy wearing baker's hat 30.00
Nationals Life and Accident Insurance Co., mechanical, diecut, duck, pull feet, lower bill moves 25.00
Newton's Pepsin Gum, 3-1/2" w x 4-7/8" l, comical image of black kids on front, "Echoes from the Moon" poem on back 70.00
Rochester Lamps, Bridal Chamber, hotel int. view 10.00
Union Web Hammock, US Conant Boston 12.00
Youth's Companion, A National Family Paper, litho illus, 1889, folder 20.00
Weathersbury, Eliza, Froliques, Petite Opera, litho illus .. 10.00
Weaver Organ Factory, multicolored 27.50
Wheellock Piano, litho illus 12.00

Stoves and ranges

Corrugated Stove Pipe Elbow, double picture 18.00
Dixon's Stove Polish, child listening to watch 7.50
Florence Oil Stoves, restaurant kitchen scene 40.00
Glenwood Ranges & Heaters, pretty girl in hat......... 7.50
Gold Coin & Gold Medal Stoves & Ranges, litho illus.... 15.00
Happy Thought Range, diecut, jelly roll shape 7.50

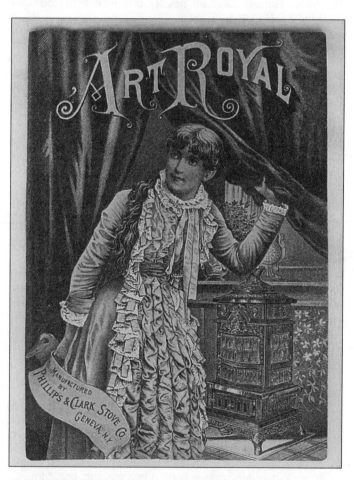

Art Royal Stoves, Philips & Clark Stove Co., Geneva, KY, 1865, multicolored parlor scene, 3-3/4" x 5-1/4", $15.

Jewel Stoves, litho illus 17.50
Monarch Vapor Ranges, diecut, loaf of bread shape 45.00
Rising Sun Stove Polish, folder 20.00

Thread and sewing

Clarks ONT Thread, boy fishing 10.00
De Long Hook and Eye, Eclipses Everything, Columbus show-
    ing Indians eclipse 32.00
Domestic Sewing Machine, father playing with children . . 15.00
Eureka Silk, girl having tea party 10.00
Merrick's Thread, hot air balloon, In Search of the North Pole
    . . . . 10.00
New Home Sewing Machine, dogs chasing man 15.00
Packards Sewing Machine Needles, case photo pasted on card
    . . . . 17.50
Singer Sewing Machine Co., All Nations Series, 5-1/4" x 3-1/8"
    Bosnia 8.00
    Georgia, crease on corner 6.00
    Hungary 6.00
Singer Sewing Machines, women seated at sewing machine,
    children having tea party, 1889, folder 25.00
Standard Sewing Machine, woman playing croquelle . . . 15.00
Wheeler & Wilson, delivery of sewing machine by horse and
    buggy, full color, black and white illus on back with adv, hor-
    izontal 15.00
Williamatic Thread, The People Favorite Hobby 17.50

Tobacco

Blackwells Genuine Durham, novelty, pull-out man in pipe bowl,
    Burrow Giles Litho 25.00
Capadura Cigar, comical jockey illus 10.00
Clinton, Harry, Tobacco Dealer, children holding king cigar, man
    smoking 12.00
Horsehead Tobacco, horse's head, plug in mouth 10.00
Keisey's Cigars, soldiers 7.50
King Bull 3¢ Cigar, risque metamorphic, diecut opening, adv on
    back 35.00
Liggett & Meyers 35.00
Newspaper Plug, "Where is Mother," five puppies 7.50
Old Judge Cigarettes 12.00
Target Plug Tobacco, multicolored 35.00

AGATA GLASS

History: Agata glass was invented in 1887 by Joseph Locke of the New England Glass Company, Cambridge, Massachusetts.

Agata glass was produced by coating a piece of peachblow glass with metallic stain, spattering the surface with alcohol, and firing. The resulting high-gloss, mottled finish looked like oil droplets floating on a watery surface. Shading usually ranged from opaque pink to dark rose, although pieces in a pastel opaque green also exist. A few pieces have been found in a satin finish.

Bowl
    4" d, green opaque body, mottled border with scalloped gold
        tracery 650.00
    5-1/4" d, 2-1/2" h, ten ruffled rim, shaded rose pink, all over
        blue and gold oil spots 550.00
    5-3/8" d, deep rose, crimped rim 700.00
    8" w, 4" h, green opaque body, agata staining, gold trim
        . . . . 1,150.00
Celery Vase, 6-1/2" h, scalloped sq top, opaque pink shading to
    deep rose body, glossy finish 725.00

Tumbler, green opaque, oil dec band, gold line, 3-3/4" h, $615.

Creamer, opaque pink shading to rose body, applied handle
    . . . . 1,200.00
Cruet, 6" h, pale green opaque bulbous body, random oil spot
    dec, applied handle, acid finish, orig faceted dark green stop-
    per 600.00
Finger Bowl, 4-1/2" d, ruffled rim, opaque pink shading to rose
    body, pronounced mottling, deep pink lining 800.00
Juice Tumbler, 3-3/4", opaque pink shading to rose body, mot-
    tling, deep pink lining 825.00
Lemonade Tumbler, 1-5/8" d base, 2-1/2" d top, 5-1/8" h, New
    England peachblow shading, pronounced mottling, gold trac-
    ery 1,250.00
Pitcher, 6-3/8" h, crimped rim, opaque pink shading to rose
    body, pronounced mottling, deep pink lining 1,750.00
Plate, 6-5/8" d, opaque pink shading to rose body, ribbon candy
    fluted rim 875.00
Punch Cup, 3" d, 2-3/4" h, deep color, oily spots with blue high-
    lights, applied handle with mottling 625.00
Salt Shaker, delicate shading of pink to rose 625.00
Spooner, 3-3/4" h, green opaque body, mottled upper band and
    narrow gold band 950.00
Toothpick Holder, 2-1/4" h, flared, green opaque, orig blue oil
    spots, green trim 795.00
Tumbler, 3-3/4" h, 2-1/4", c1887 . . . . 615.00
Vase
    4-1/2" h, quatraform, flared rim, opaque pink shading to deep
        rose body, random oil spot dec 900.00
    5" h, 6" w, round, acid cut peachblow, four way scalloped top,
        good mineral staining 2,900.00
    7-1/4" h, baluster, opaque pink shading to deep rose body,
        random oil spot dec, satin finish 1,650.00
Whiskey Taster, 2-5/8" h, opaque pink shading to rose body,
    acid finish 750.00

AMBERINA GLASS

History: Joseph Locke developed Amberina glass in 1883 for the New England Glass Works. "Amberina," a trade name, describes a transparent glass which shades from deep ruby to amber. It was made by adding powdered gold to the ingredients for an amber-glass batch. A portion of the glass was reheated later to produce the shading effect. Usually it was the bottom which was reheated to form the deep red; however, reverse examples have been found.

Most early Amberina is flint-quality glass, blown or pattern molded. Patterns include Diamond Quilted, Daisy and Button, Venetian Diamond, Diamond and Star, and Thumbprint.

In addition to the New England Glass Works, the Mount Washington Glass Company of New Bedford, Massachusetts, copied the glass in the 1880s and sold it at first under the Amberina trade name and later as "Rose Amber." It is difficult to distinguish pieces from these two New England factories. Boston and Sandwich Glass Works never produced the glass.

Amberina glass also was made in the 1890s by several Midwest factories, among which was Hobbs, Brockunier & Co. Trade names included "Ruby Amber Ware" and "Watermelon." The Midwest glass shaded from cranberry to amber, and the color resulted from the application of a thin flashing of cranberry to the reheated portion. This created a sharp demarcation between the two colors. This less-expensive version was the death knell for the New England variety.

In 1884, Edward D. Libbey was given the use of the trade name "Amberina" by the New England Glass Works. Production took place during 1900, but ceased shortly thereafter. In the 1920s Edward Libbey renewed production at his Toledo, Ohio, plant for a short period. The glass was of high quality.

Marks: Amberina made by Edward Libbey in the 1920s is marked "Libbey" in script on the pontil.

References: Gary Baker et al., *Wheeling Glass 1829-1939*, Oglebay Institute, 1994 (distributed by Antique Publications); Neila and Tom Bredehoft, *Hobbs, Brockunier & Co. Glass*, Collector Books, 1997; Kenneth Wilson, *American Glass 1760-1930*, 2 vols., Hudson Hill Press and The Toledo Museum of Art, 1994.

Reproduction Alert: Reproductions abound.

Additional Listings: Mount Washington.

Basket
  7" h, applied amber wishbone dec, loop handle, attributed to New England Glass Works. 1,300.00
  8" h, 5" w, rose bowl shape, enameled white, blue, and gold floral dec, deep amberina coloration, applied amber-green handle 200.00
  15" h, 10" w, Swirl pattern, gold rose dec, fence design, elaborate gold floral design, applied feet, applied amber rigaree handle 350.00
Berry Set, 9" sq master bowl, ten 4-7/8" sq individual bowls, Daisy and Button pattern, minor edge roughness, small flakes, some color variation, assembled 11 pc set 110.00
Bowl
  7" d, applied vaseline ribbon edge, pinched feet, attributed to New England 225.00
  7-1/2" d, Diamond Quilted pattern, rolled over scalloped edge 195.00
  9" w, square, Daisy and Button pattern 250.00
Butter Dish, cov, 7" d, 5" h, Inverted Thumbprint pattern top, amber knob, amber Daisy and Button type pattern base 300.00
Carafe, 7-1/8" h, Inverted Thumbprint pattern, reversed color, swirled neck 175.00

Celery Vase, 6-1/2" h, Diamond Optic pattern 375.00
Compote, 8-3/4" d, Inverted Thumbprint pattern 350.00
Cordial, 4-1/2" h, trumpet shape 225.00
Cracker Jar, cov, 5" h, 5-1/2" w, Joseph Locke, New England Glass Works, cov missing 550.00
Creamer and Sugar, 4-1/2" h, Diamond Quilted pattern, crimped top, amber reeded handles 650.00
Cruet, 6-3/4" h, 3" d, applied amber handle, orig amber cut faceted stopper, attributed to New England Glass Works 275.00
Dish, leaf shape, ftd, pressed, Gillander 1,200.00
Finger Bowl, fluted, bell tone 355.00
Hair Receiver, 4-1/2" d, 2" h, two pc, deep fuchsia shading to amber, partial Libbey label 1,750.00
Lamp, Lincoln Drape, Aladdin 800.00
Lemonade Tumbler, 5-1/4" h, Swirl pattern, gold dec, applied handle. 250.00
Marmalade, cov, 5-1/4" h, Inverted Thumbprint pattern, white metal cov, Mt. Washington 250.00
Parfait, 6-1/2" h, Swirl pattern, gold leaf and bud dec . . 295.00
Pitcher
  6-3/4" h, 4" w, Inverted Thumbprint pattern, ruffled rim, applied amber loop handle. 195.00
  8-1/4" h, 6" w, ruffled, melon ribbed form, Inverted Thumbprint pattern, applied amber glass loop handle 325.00
Posy Pot, 3" d, applied wishbone feet, berry pontil 300.00
Punch Cup, 2-1/2" h, 3-1/2" w, Diamond Quilted pattern, applied reeded amber handle, good coloration to two-thirds of rounded body, set of 5 . . . . 325.00
Ramekin and Underplate, 4-1/4" d, 2-1/4" h, slightly ribbed 250.00
Rose Bowl, 5-1/2" d, 5-1/2" h, Diamond Quilted pattern, deep color, pinched tricorn rim, applied amber reeded shell feet, attributed to New England Glass Works 550.00
Salt Shaker, elongated Baby Thumbprint pattern, orig top 150.00
Sauce, Daisy and Button pattern 40.00
Spooner, 5" h, Diamond Quilted pattern, pinched scalloped top 150.00
Sugar Bowl, cov, 4-1/4" h, Inverted Thumbprint pattern, New England Glass Works 375.00

Punch Cup, Baby Thumbprint pattern, applied ribbed colorless handle, 2-1/2" h, $190.

Sugar Shaker, 4" h, globular, Inverted Thumbprint pattern, emb floral and butterfly lid 425.00

Syrup Pitcher, 5-5/8" h, Inverted Thumbprint pattern, New England Glass Works, fuchsia to amber with rosy tint, silver plate fitting, slight in the making internal air-trap in glass collar 750.00

Toothpick Holder
  Inverted Thumbprint, pedestal base, NTHCS #82 . . 235.00
  Venetian Diamond, Libbey 200.00

Tumbler, Optic, reverse amberina. 140.00

Vase
  4-5/8" h, 6" d, deep fuchsia color, shape #3013, flowerform, six petal like scallops, sgd "Amberina" above "Libbey" in circle 1,250.00
  5-3/4" h, lily, elongated blossom, brilliant fuchsia shading to Alexandrite blue to amber foot, New England, int. stain 500.00
  7" h, lily, ribbed body, applied amber feet, attributed to New England Glass Works 395.00
  7-1/2" h, 11-1/4" l, fan shape, swirled and ribbed, applied amber rigaree edge and wishbone feet, pastoral landscape scene dec highlighted with gold edge, minor loss to painting 195.00
  8" h, Hobbs, 2 handles 345.00
  12" h, trumpet, ribbed body, attributed to New England Glass Works. 350.00
  23" h, trumpet, ribbed body, knobbed stem, raised circular base, attributed to New England Glass Works . . .1,250.00

Whimsey, 3-1/4" d, 2-3/8" h, hat, Expanded Diamond pattern, ground pontil. 175.00

Whiskey Taster, 2-3/4" h, Baby Diamond Quilted pattern, deep fuchsia to deep amber, minor surface scratches 50.00

AMBERINA GLASS, PLATED

History: The New England Glass Company, Cambridge, Massachusetts, first made Plated Amberina in 1886; Edward Libbey patented the process for the company in 1889.

Plated Amberina was made by taking a gather of chartreuse or cream opalescent glass, dipping it in Amberina, and working the two, often utilizing a mold. The finished product had a deep amber to deep ruby red shading, a fiery opalescent lining, and often vertical ribbing for enhancement. Designs ranged from simple forms to complex pieces with collars, feet, gilding, and etching.

A cased Wheeling glass of similar appearance had an opaque white lining but is not opalescent and does not have a ribbed body.

Bowl, 8" w, border of deep dark mahogany, 12 vertical stripes alternating with 12 vertical opalescent fuchsia stripes, off-white casing. 7,500.00

Celery Vase, vertical ribbing .2,750.00

Cream Pitcher, 2-3/4" h, 3-1/2" w, bulbous, vertical ribbing, raspberry shading two-thirds down to golden amber base, elaborate strap handle, deep oil spots dec 1,950.00

Cruet, 6-3/4" h, faceted amber stopper. 3,200.00

Parfait, vertical ribbing, applied amber handle, c1886 . . . . .1,500.00

Pitcher, 6-1/2" h, vertical ribbing, applied amber handle 4,500.00

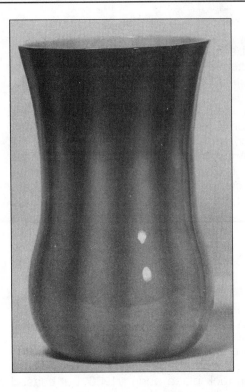

Vase, bulbous base, ribbed motif, $2,400.

Punch Cup, vertical ribs, applied handle. 1,500.00

Salt Shaker, vertical ribs, orig top 1,200.00

Spooner, 4" h, vertical ribbing, ground pontil 2,000.00

Syrup Pitcher, vertical ribbing, orig top, applied amber handle 5,600.00

Tumbler, 3-3/4" h, 2-1/2" d, good color 2,400.00

Vase
  3-1/4" h, bulbous, vertical ribbing, bluish-white lining 2,500.00
  6-1/4" h, flared cylinder, twelve ribs, deep fuchsia shading to amber, cased in opal white, thin walls 4,025.00

AMPHORA

History: The Amphora Porcelain Works was one of several pottery companies located in the Teplitz-Turn region of Bohemia in the late 19th and early 20th centuries. It is best known for art pottery, especially Art Nouveau and Art Deco pieces.

Marks: Several markings were used, including the name and location of the pottery and the Imperial mark, which included a crown. Prior to World War I, Bohemia was part of the Austro-Hungarian Empire, so the word "Austria" may appear as part of the mark. After World War I the word "Czechoslovakia" may be part of the mark.

Additional Listings: Teplitz.

Basket, 8-1/2" h, 9" sq, applied green hops blossoms on basketweave body 500.00

Centerpiece, 17" h, figural, Art Nouveau-style female, wrapped in shell, reaches out to touch tail fin of fish below . . . 850.00

Ewer
  5-1/2" h, molded green grapes, leaves, irid body . . . 100.00
  7-1/2" h, 5" d, relief floral bosses, old, green jewels and spout, 3 handles 320.00

Vase, octagonal, mottled gold, tan stripes, enameled tear drop, red and white ram's head on base, aqua band, mkd "Made in Czecho-slovakia," 10-3/4" h, $225.

Figure

16-1/4" h, peasant woman, basket on back, reaches for another basket at feet, tan clothes, gold highlights, "Austria" and crown mark 550.00

18-1/2" h, peasant woman empties apron of greens into large basket, tan clothes, gold highlights, "Austria" and crown mark 550.00

Vase

6" h, reticulated top with four dragonflies surrounding rim, eight dragonflies below, open handles at side, green, gold, and cream matte glaze, imp marks, minor flake at top 1,200.00

7" h, silhouette portrait, multicolored, gold outlines, imp and stamped mark 850.00

8" h, two handled form, blue butterfly, outlined in gold, gold detailed flowers, imp mark 650.00

10" x 8-1/4" x 5", oval, applied raspberries. 220.00

10" x 9-1/2", applied blackberry cluster on cream basketweave, braided shoulder handles 650.00

13" h, flattened form, irregular top, woman's profile with flowers in long flowing hair, forest scene on reverse, imp and stamped marks 1,700.00

13" h, molded eagles on sides, geometric designs, blue and gold, imp marks 800.00

13" h, two-handled form, textured and quilted body with vertical ribs, divided by applied jewels at top, gunmetal to black glaze with gold highlights at top, designed by Paul Daschel 4,400.00

16-1/2" h, molded floral design at top and bottom, two cut-out handles above drip glaze, red, green and yellow ground, imp and stamped marks 2,500.00

17" h, 14" w, detailed relief dragon/serpent wraps around base, cov in bronze gunmetal glaze with slight irid, green, red, black, brown, and gold body with overall irid, imp mark, minor restoration to dragon, drill hole 5,000.00

17-1/2" h, relief of bold trees, imp marks, filled base chip 1,200.00

Vessel, 9" h, gold bizarre creature figural handle, stylized tree design, applied white enameled flowers with yellow centers, cream and green mottled ground, imp marks 550.00

ANIMAL COLLECTIBLES

History: The representation of animals in fine arts, decorative arts, and on utilitarian products dates back to antiquity. Some religions endowed certain animals with mystical properties. Authors throughout written history used human characteristics when portraying animals.

Glass has been a popular material in making animal-related collectibles. Dishes with an animal-theme cover were fashionable in the early 19th century. In the years between World Wars I and II, glass manufacturers such as Fostoria Glass Company and A. H. Heisey & Company created a number of glass animal figures for the novelty and decorative-accessory markets. In the 1950s and early 1960s, a second glass-animal craze swept America led by companies such as Duncan & Miller and New Martinsville-Viking Glass Company. A third craze struck in the early 1980s when companies such as Boyd Crystal Art Glass, Guernsey Glass, Pisello Art Glass, and Summit Art Glass began offering the same animal figure in a wide variety of collectible glass colors, with some colors in limited production.

The formation of collectors' clubs and marketing crazes, e.g., flamingo, pig, and penguin, during the 1970s increased the popularity of this collecting field.

References: Elaine Butler, *Poodle Collectibles of the 50's & 60's*, L-W Book Sales, 1995; Diana Callow et al., *Charlton Price Guide to Beswick Animals*, The Charlton Press, 1994; Jean Dale, *Charlton Standard Catalogue of Royal Doulton Animals*, 2nd Edition, The Charlton Press, 1998; —, *Charlton Standard Catalogue of Royal Doulton Beswick Storybook Figurines*, The Charlton Press, 1994; Marbena Jean Fyke, *Collectible Cats*, Book I (1993, 1995 value update), Book II (1996), Collector Books; Lee Garmon and Dick Spencer, *Glass Animals of the Depression Era*, Collector Books, 1993; Everett Grist, *Covered Animal Dishes*, Collector Books, 1988, 1993 value update; Frank L. Hahn and Paul Kikeli, *Collector's Guide to Heisey* and *Heisey By Imperial Glass Animals*, Golden Era Publications, 1991; Todd Holmes, *Boyd Glass Workbook*, published by author, 1992; Jan Lindenberger, *501 Collectible Horses*, Schiffer Publishing, 1996; Jessie Walker, *Country Living Collectibles: Rabbits*, Hearst Books, 1996.

Periodicals: *Boyd Crystal Art Glass Newsletter*, P.O. Box 127, 1203 Morton Ave., Cambridge, OH 43725; *Canine Collector's Companion*, P.O. Box 2948, Portland, OR 97208; *Collectively Speaking*, 428 Philadelphia Rd, Joppa, MD 21085 *Collie Courier*, 428 Philadelphia Rd, Joppa, MD 21085; *Hobby Horse News*, 5492 Tallapoosa Rd, Tallahassee, FL 32303; *Jody & Darrell's Glass Collectibles Newsletter*, P.O. Box 180833, Arlington, TX 76096; *Jumbo Jargon*, 1002 West 25th St., Erie, PA 16502; *MOOsletter*, 240 Wahl Ave., Evans City, PA 16033; *TRR Pony Express*, 71 Aloha Circle, Little Rock, AR 72120.

Collectors' Clubs: Boyd Art Glass Collectors Guild, P.O. Box 52, Hatboro, PA 19040; Canine Collectibles Club of America, Suite 314, 736 N. Western Ave., Lake Forest, IL 60045; Cat Collectors, 33161 Wendy Dr, Sterling Heights, MI 48310; Folk Art Society of America, P.O. Box 17041, Richmond, VA 23226; Frog Pond, P.O. Box 193, Beech Grove, IN 46107; National Elephant Collector's Society, 380 Medford St., Somerville, MA 02145; Squirrel Lovers Club, 318 W. Fremont Ave., Elmhurst, IL 60126; Wee Scots, Inc., P.O. Box 1597, Winchester, VA 22604-1597.

Museums: American Kennel Club, New York, NY; American Saddle Horse Museum Society, Lexington, KY; Dog Museum, St Louis, MO; Frog Fantasies Museum, Eureka Springs, AR; International Museum of the Horse, Lexington, KY; Stradling Museum of the Horse, Patagonia, AZ.

Additional Listings: See specific animal collectible categories in *Warman's Americana & Collectibles*.

Advisor: Jocelyn C. Mousley.

Barnyard

Bank, 4-1/2" h, seated pig, cast iron, gold paint 50.00
Bottle Opener, rooster, cast iron, orig polychrome paint
. . . . 95.00
Butter Stamp, 3-3/4" d, wood, goose, half-lb size 165.00
Candy Container, 4-1/2" l, duck, glass, painted 45.00
Cane, 37" l, carved wood, duck's head handle, chased silver neck band, relief carved leaves on shaft, late 19th C
. . . . 800.00
Charger, 16-1/4" d, polychrome dec, various flowering branches, reserves of animals, russet ground, gilt highlights, painted mark "UPW" on base (Union Porcelain Works, Greenpoint, NY,) late 19th C 700.00
Cookie Cutter, 4-1/2" sq, tin, primitive rooster design, spot soldering 65.00
Cookie Jar, figural, cow, cat finial, brown, mkd "W 10 Brush USA," early 1950s 80.00
Creamer, 7" l, 5-1/4" h, cow, flint enamel, old paper label on base "J. Panim's Crockery Store,...107 W. Water St. Elmira N.Y.," 19th C, very minor chip to one horn 230.00
Figure
　Cow, papier-mâché, worn black and white paint, 45"
　　l 190.00
　Donkey, Metzler 50.00
　Pig, 11-1/4" h, 20-1/4" l, carved wood, glass eyes, leather ears, metal tail, paint dec, 20th C 865.00
Hen on Nest, porcelain
　Jackfield, black ground, white enamel polka-dots and gilt trim, 5-3/8" h 200.00
　Staffordshire, polychrome enameling, imp "P&S XII," 11-1/4" l 615.00

Unknown maker, polychrome floral enameling, gilt trim, 7-1/4" h 275.00
Painting, oil on canvas, sheep, lake, mountains, sgd "WT Longmire," British, 19th C, 13-1/2" x 20", modern gilt frame
. . . . 825.00
Pie Bird, figural, chicken, glazed ceramic 50.00
Poster, rooster, chromolithograph, "I Crow for Cleveland and Stevenson," unframed, backed on foam core, some stains and repairs, 44" x 20" 200.00
Salt, 2-1/2" l, three pigs around trough 60.00
Sign
　27-3/4" h, 20-1/2" w, International Stockfood, paper, titled "This hog gained 400 lbs in 100 days," shows before and after picture of pig, pail of product in background, framed
　　. . . . . 325.00
　34" h, 22" w, Monarch Poultry Feeds, figural, crowing rooster, wood 900.00
Tin, 3-1/4" d, 5-3/4" h, Buttermilk and Soda Baking Powder, round paper label, woman and cow illus 40.00
Toy, pull, 10" l, cow, wood, hide covering, leather collar with bell, metal wheels 120.00
Wind Mill Weight, 20-1/2" h, cast iron, figural, full bodied rooster, traces of old white paint, wood base 990.00

Birds

Andirons, pr, 23" h, owls, cast iron, glass eyes 100.00
Box, cov, 18" x 12" x 10-1/2", American Biscuit & Mfg. Co., wood, paper label with parrot illus 85.00
Candlesticks, pr, 14-3/4" h, herons, turtle on base, waterlily candle arm and socket, brass, Oriental 120.00
Clock, bird in cage, nickel plated brass, black onyx base, brass colored globe with revolving hours in center, bird rocks as minutes tick off, mkd "Japan," 10-1/2" h 250.00
Cookie Cutter, 5-3/4" x 3-1/2", dove, flatback, handle . . . 15.00
Doorstop, 10" h, cast iron, full figured penguin, facing sideways, black, white chest, top hat and bow tie, yellow feet and beak, unsgd Hubley 255.00
Figure
　8-1/4" h, 11-1/4" l, blue-jay, wood, relief carved, burl base, early 1900s 450.00
　14" h, peacock, Royal Dux 125.00
　18" h, owl, claw holding shrew, Copeland 545.00
Jardiniere, swallows, McCoy Pottery, 7" h 100.00
Painting, oil on canvas, "For a Crust of Bread," boy trying to save his bread from geese, Continental, 19th C, 36" x 29", framed, minor loss, retouched, craquelure 2,415.00
Paperweight, 7-1/4" h, crystal, eagle perched on rock, wings extended above, base stamped "Sevres Cristal France
　" 250.00
Pin, owl, enameled, David Anderson 70.00
Pip Squeak, duck, worn polychrome, 6" h 200.00
Plate, 9-1/2" d, black transfer pheasants and flowers design, polychrome dec, set of four 90.00
Toy, friction, duck, sheet metal, old polychrome paint, Dayton Toy Co., 8-1/2" h 140.00

Cats

Ashtray, cat playing with ball, Bavaria 40.00
Bookends, Cheshire cats, brass, c1930 . . . . 140.00
Chimney Flue Cover, 9-1/2" d, picture of golden curled girl holding tabby cat 70.00
Doorstop, 7-1/2" h, full bodied sitting cat, old worn repaint
. . . . 165.00
Music Box, litho tin, Felix the Cat, France 80.00
Nodder, 3-1/2" h, 6" l, primitive kitten, carved pine, painted black, head bobs and tail moves, late 19th C 370.00

Painting, 18-1/4" h, 11-3/4" w, oil on board, tiger cat, sgd "G. W. Chadeayne" lower right, American School, 19th C .7,475.00

Sign

11" x 21", Wrigley's Spearmint Gum, trolley card sign, cardboard, black cat shading to gray image, illus by Shepard 325.00

14" d, Burke's Ale, counter top reverse painting on glass, cat in center, mounted on tripod base 350.00

String Holder, chalkware, kitten's head over ball of yarn, white 65.00

Toy, Figaro, litho tin windup 170.00

Dogs

Andirons, pr, Bulldog, cast iron, front view, heads turned opposite directions, c1870 . . . . 225.00

Box, cov, 3-1/2" h, silver, rect box, Field Spaniel on cov, engraved and applied detail, Continental, 19th C 1,610.00

Broadside, 10-1/2" h, 10-3/4" w, litho, dog dressed in blue jacket, red ascot, glass of whiskey before him, tobacco pouch, printed by Liebler Mass Litho, matted and framed 85.00

Calendar, 1937, Du Pont Explosives, two bird dogs, artist sgd "Edm. H. Osthau," 28" h, 15" w, several paint drips on full calendar pad 275.00

Figure

Boxer, Morton 145.00

Cocker, Morton 145.00

Dalmatian, Morton 145.00

Liquor Bottle, Scottie 45.00

Painting

Black Poodle, sgd "Will Rannells," watercolor on paper, matted and framed, 25" x 21" 90.00

On The Alert, inscribed "T. Blinks" lower left, oil on canvas, framed, lined, retouched, craquelure, 14" x 18-3/8" 1,955.00

Sarah Podmore's Dash, titled lower center, unsgd, American School, 19th C, oil on canvas, 21-1/2" h, 29" l, framed, scattered punctures, some repairs, note affixed to stretcher places Sarah and Dash in Boston, c1800 . . . . . .6,900.00

"Star, an English Setter, 1977," sgd "Will Rannells," watercolor on paper matted and framed, 28-1/2" x 25-1/2" . . 200.00

Advertising Sign, Brown's Jumbo Bread, diecut tin, circus elephant wearing banner with name, 12-3/4" x 15", $700. Photo courtesy of James D. Julia, Inc.

Paperweight, 3-1/2" d, colorless dome top, white sulfide of dog, cranberry ground 275.00

Pip Squeak, seated, yellow, white, red, and black, wear, some flaking, bottom portion of bellows missing, 4-5/8" h . . 165.00

Pitcher, Rockingham, hound handle, molded hanging game, 9-5/8" h 275.00

Print, hunting dog, Louis Prang, c1906 . . . . 150.00

Rug, hooked, 30" x 39", pair of Scotties, one brown, one white, wearing red collars, black ground, unused 500.00

Sign

Northland Greyhound Lines, cast iron 550.00

"Old Gold Cigarettes - You can't improve on nature - Not a cough in a carload," Art Deco diecut cardboard, young woman in flowing dress walking two Borzoi dogs, crease from center fold, some light staining, 38" h, 40" w 350.00

Two Friends-2 Cigars 5¢, round, two-sided, same image on both sides, cardboard, string hung, lady in blue dress shaking paw of brown and white St. Bernard, yellow ground, red outer rim with white lettering, 7-1/2" d 575.00

Toy, pull, dog with basket, green, white, and black, wear and rust, 6-1/2" l 260.00

Tray

4-3/4" h, Pug Dog, metal mounted Opalware glass dish, hp, red collared pug, artist sgd "Bauer," mounted on base, partial Handel Ware shield, and number 650.00

13" d, Yuengling's Beer, titled "Beauty and the Beast," lady hugging bulldog, © 1911, American Art Works litho, vivid colors, some overall crazing 1,000.00

Whimsey, 7-7/8" l, 5-3/4", carved wood, dog emerging from shoe, 19th C 225.00

Horses

Bookends, pr, cast iron 50.00

Catalog, D. F. Mangels Co. Carousel Works, Coney Island, NY, 28 pgs, 1938 edition 250.00

Door Knocker, 5-1/2", brass, head 140.00

Figure

Black Beauty, Beswick 150.00

Viennese Porcelain, equestrian, "Pirouette Spanische Reitschule, Hofburg Wien," 9-3/4" h 220.00

Hitching Post, 68" h, cast iron horse head, steel post . . . 95.00

Lunch Box, 7" l, 4-1/2" w, 4-1/4" d, Dan Patch Tobacco, Scotten, Dillin Co., tin litho, brass catch, single handle 125.00

Match Safe, 2" l, brass, figural horseshoe with horse and rider in middle, striker 200.00

Painting, oil on canvas

15-1/2" x 23-1/2", fox hunting scene, two horses with riders jumping over hedge row, three dogs pursing, landscape, sgd "J. F. Herring," gilt gesso frame, restored 1,750.00

30-3/4" x 41-3/4", horses and cowboys, sgd "Pietro Montana 1945," framed 330.00

Paperweight, 2-1/2" w, 4" l, Prince Albert, The World's Champion Harness Gelding, Compliments James Hanley Brewing Co., rect, minor scratching to glass 150.00

Print, lithograph, horses racing, Currier & Ives, matted and framed, 27-1/2" x 35-1/2" 770.00

Sign, 15-1/4" h, 19-1/2" l, Turf Club Gin, reverse painting on glass, jockey riding thoroughbred race horse, framed 500.00

Toy

Hobby Horse, dapple gray, green saddle, heart shaped supports, New England, early 19th C, 24-1/4" h, 51" l.1,400.00

Horse and cart, with driver, white, blue, red, black, gold stenciling on cart, 7" l 660.00

Advertising Sign, Polar Bear Tobacco, litho tin, diecut, 13-1/2" x 9-1/2", $2,400. Photo courtesy of Bear Pen Auction.

Horse and rider, green, brown, blue, yellow, red, and black paint, good color, resoldered horse to base, 9" l . . . 660.00
Horse and rider, rocking-type, old repaint, green, gold, black, and white, 6-3/8" h 475.00
Horse pulling tin Conestoga-style wagon, celluloid driver, wind-up, orig box, Occupied Japan, 9" 225.00
Jockey on horse, orig paint, wood base, 15" l 1,045.00
Walking horse and cart, cast iron, worn polychrome, 9-3/4" l
. . . . 660.00
Watch Fob, horse and horseshoe, gold filled, chain . . . 115.00
Windmill Weight, cast iron, bob tail, Dempster Mfg. Co.. 350.00

Wild Animals

Bank, elephant, Jumbo, cast iron, old gold paint, wear and touch up paint. 90.00
Bell Toy, elephant, cast iron, nickel finish, red wheels, light rust, 7-1/2" l 90.00
Candy Stick Jar, Smokey the Bear 600.00
Chocolate Mold, 6" h, tin, cameo, two parts, hinged 70.00
Cookie Jar, bear with honey 165.00
Egg, 4-1/2" h, 3-1/4" d, two pc, tin litho, Harrison Cady Peter Rabbit figures on front and back 400.00
Figure
　Bear, fish in mouth, carved wood, detailed, 8-1/2" h . . 85.00
　Boar, 14" l, 12" h, carved serpentine, realistically carved, seated on haunches. 550.00
　Chamois, 24-1/2" h, carved wood, polychrome dec, 19th C, mounted on contemporary base, minor cracks, paint loss, craquelure, repair to antler 1,150.00
Mask, 11" h, carved and painted wood, leopard's head, open mouth, snarling teeth, sgd, dated 250.00

Figure, white clay lion, mottled brown coat, cobalt blue name, tail, feet, and nose, sky blue base, imp "Moore Ceramics, Uhrichsville, O," small chips, some glaze flaking on base, 11" l, $5,775. Photo courtesy of Garth's Auctions, Inc.

Match Safe, 2" l, plated metal, figural, fox head, red eyes, opens at base 280.00
Noah's Ark Set, ninety-one pairs of animals, seventeen singles, three people, animals later replacements, 25-1/4" l .2,860.00
Pail, 2-1/2" d, 3-3/4" h, Schepps Cocoanut, monkey in jungle illus. 185.00
Pip Squeak, lion, papier-mâché, yellow and green, flakes, leather bellows loose, 5" l. 165.00
Pitcher, water buffalo, Royal Bayreuth, c1903, 5" h 200.00
Ring, snake, sterling silver, mkd "Mexico". 25.00
Sign
　Brown's Jumbo Bread, diecut litho tin, figural circus elephant wearing banner advertising, 12-3/4" h, 15" w 700.00
　Compliments C. D. Kenny Co., two little girls having tea with mother bunny while baby bunnies nibble on carrots, self-framed tin, oval, some denting to frame, 12" h, 8-1/2" w
. . . . 200.00
Tin
　Buffalo Brand Peanuts, F. M. Hoyt & Co., standing buffalo, 9" h, 8-1/2" d, 10-lb size 150.00
　Mammoth Jumbo Whole Blanched Salted Peanuts, The Kelly Co., elephants, 11" h, 8-1/2" d, 10-lb size 150.00
　Tiger Chewing Tobacco, tiger head illus, 6" x 3-3/4" x 2-1/4"
. . . . 250.00
Toy, pull
　Camel, worn old green and tan paint, some damage, 8-1/2" l
. . . . 315.00
　Jonah and the Whale, on wheels, worn black and blue paint, one wheel glued to axle, 5-3/4" l 525.00

APOTHECARY

History: Early man discovered that by combining herbs and other natural elements into salves, powders, etc., that he was able to create miracles that could be used to attempt a cure for disease and minor aliments. When civilization created villages and towns, one of the first shops that developed was often the apothecary.

Today, examples from early apothecary shops are eagerly sought by collectors. Items collected range from actual fixtures to containers. While a premium may be paid for an object with original contents, collectors are warned to treat those contents with respect as they be contain decomposing chemicals and may be unstable.

Apothecary and pharmaceutical items include those things commonly found in a drugstore and used to store or prepare medications.

References: A. Walker Bingham, *Snake-Oil Syndrome: Patent Medicine Advertising*, Christopher Publishing House, 1994; James M. Edmonson, *American Surgical Instruments, An Illustrated History of Their Manufacture and A Directory of Instrument Makers to 1900*, Norman Publishing, (720 Market St., 3rd Fl., San Francisco, CA 94102), 1997; J Douglas Congdon-Martin, *Drugstore and Soda Fountain Antiques*, Schiffer Publishing, 1991; Patricia McDaniel, *Drugstore Collectibles*, Wallace-Homestead, 1994; J. William Rosenthal, *Spectacles and Other Vision Aids*, Norman Publishing (720 Market St., 3rd Fl., San Francisco, CA 94102), 1996.

Periodical: *Scientific, Medical & Mechanical Antiques*, 11824 Taneytown Pike, Taneytown, MD 21787.

Collectors' Clubs: Maryland Microscopical Society, 8621 Polk St., McLean, VA 22102; Medical Collectors Association, 1685A Eastchester Rd, Bronx, NY 10461.

Museums: Dittrick Museum of Medical History, Cleveland, OH; International Museum of Surgical Science & Hall of Fame, Chicago, IL; National Museum of Health & Medicine, Walter Reed Medical Center, Washington, DC; National Museum of History and Technology, Smithsonian Institution, Washington, DC; Schmidt Apothecary Shop, New England Fire & History Museum, Brewster, MA; Waring Historical Library, Medical University of South Carolina, Charleston, SC.

Advertising Trade Card, 6" x 4-1/2", set of six, Taylor's Sure Cure, Chinese scene and humorous black scene, framed 200.00

Apothecary Chest

14-3/4" h, 15-1/2" w, 7" d, seven nailed drawers, arranged as two columns of 3 small drawers over long base drawer, poplar and walnut, old finish, two brass pulls missing . . . 385.00
19-1/2" h, mahogany, fitted int. of 25 bottles and four small drawers over two long graduated drawers, Victorian, 19th C, some loss to bottles 1,150.00
37" h, 13-1/2" w, 64" l, twelve drawer wood chest, each drawer with decorative cast iron pull with frame for label and keyhole 700.00

Bottle

7-1/2" h, CERA FLAV., early hand blown, cylindrical, applied reverse painted on glass label, tin slip on lid, product inside 115.00
7-1/2" h, P.CAPSICI, early hand blown, cylindrical, applied reverse painted on glass label, tin slip on lid, product inside 75.00
7-1/2" h, P. CINNAM, early hand blown, cylindrical, applied reverse painted on glass label, tin slip on lid, product inside 75.00
8" h, CARUM, early hand blown, cylindrical, applied reverse painted on glass label, tin slip on lid, product inside . . 95.00

8-1/2" h, EX.PLEURISY.-R.RI., hand blown, cylindrical, applied reverse painted on glass label, some light staining to bottle 100.00
8-1/2" h, OL.CHENOPOD, cobalt blue cylindrical, recessed reverse painted on glass label, mkd "Pat'd Sept 23, 1862," ground stopper with flat top 200.00
8-1/2" h, OL.LIMONIS, cobalt blue cylindrical, recessed reverse painted on glass label, mkd "Pat'd Sept 23, 1862," ground stopper with flat top 250.00
8-3/4" h, R.E.GLYCYRR, early hand blown cylindrical, applied figural reverse painted on glass label, ground stopper with flat top, some soiling to label and bottle 50.00
9" h, F. E. SIMURUBA, cylindrical, shaped applied reverse painted on glass label, ground stopper with flat top, light chipping and staining to edge of label 200.00
9-1/2" h, ACID OXALIC, cobalt blue, rect, beveled edges, applied reverse painted on glass label, ground stopper with flat top, minor chipping to label, some color loss around edges 250.00
9-1/2" h, FLE.GAMBIR, brown cylindrical, applied reverse painted on glass label, domed measuring cup top 450.00
9-1/2" h, OI.ANISI, early hand-blown cylindrical, cobalt blue, applied reverse painted on glass label, ground stopper with flat top, label fair condition 150.00
9-1/2" h, SP.AMMON.AROM, cylindrical, notched pattern at shoulder and base, applied reverse painted on glass label, ground stopper with flat top, orig tax stamp on bottom 125.00
10" h, AQ.ANISI, cylindrical, recessed reverse painted on glass label, ground stopper with flat top, some minor paint listing around edges of label 50.00
10" h, IGNATIA AM, brown cylindrical bottle, recessed reverse painted on glass label, ground stopper with flat top, some minor chips to bottle 50.00
10" h, OL.SPERM, cylindrical, applied reverse painted on glass label, ground stopper with flat top, product inside, some chipping around edges of label, crack in neck of bottle . . 225.00
10-1/2" h, SYR.SENEGA, hand blown cylindrical, colorful applied reverse painted on glass label with fancy filigree, ground stopper with flat top 130.00
10-1/2" h, TR.CAPSICI, rect, recessed colorful reverse painted on glass label, ground stopper with ribbed top, product inside 250.00
11" h, AC.AECTIC, hand blown cylindrical, applied gold, white, black, and red, reverse painted label, umbrella shaped stopper 125.00
11" h, LIN.CAMPHOR, cylindrical, recessed reverse painted on glass label, measuring cup top, detachable spout, small stain at bottom of label 350.00
11" h, OL.AMYDG.DULC, cylindrical, applied reverse painted on glass label, ground neck with measuring cup, detachable spout, minor chipping and discoloration around label edge 350.00
12" h, P.PIP.NIB, rect, colorful recessed reverse painted on glass label, ground stopper, ribbed top, product inside 200.00
12" h, PV.GENTIAN, early hand blown cobalt blue cylindrical, colorful applied reverse painted on glass label, ground stopper with flat top, crack in label 400.00
12" h, SENNA, rect, rect, colorful recessed reverse painted on glass label, ground stopper, ribbed top, product inside 300.00
12" h, SULPHER, rect, colorful recessed reverse painted on glass label, ground stopper, ribbed top, product inside 100.00

Bottle, FLE.GAMBIR, cylindrical, brown, bottle, applied r.o.g. label, domed measuring cup top, 9-1/2" h, $450. Photo courtesy of James D. Julia, Inc.

12-1/2" h, MIST.GONNORR, hand blown cobalt blue cylindrical, three-part mold, gold, white, black, white, and red applied reverse painted on glass label, c1880, some minor chipping around edges of label. 500.00

12-1/2" h, OLEUM.MORRUAE, cobalt blue cylindrical, gold applied reverse painted on glass label, crack in label . . 300.00

12-1/2" h, OL.OLIVAE, cylindrical, applied reverse painted on glass label with filigree background, ground top in shape of spout, some minor chipping and light staining around edges of label 275.00

12-1/2" h, TONIC PIL.BLAUD, cylindrical, applied reverse glass painted label with six-pointed star with fancy filigree 300.00

12-1/2" h, TONIC PHOSPHATE, cylindrical, pedestal, orig paper label, faceted tear drop stopper, product inside 600.00

Clock, 31" h, 16" w, Wm. L Gilbert pendulum clock, colorful adv for "Safe-Dependable, Nature's Remedy, Vegetable Laxative". 800.00

Counter

32" h, 72" l, mahogany, four rect columns as legs 300.00

32" h, 144" l, grain painted, paneled wood, two pc 500.00

72" h, 72" l 27" deep, pharmacist's, two pc, grain painted over mahogany, center ruby cut to clear window mkd "Prescriptions Accurately Compounded," cabinets on either side held customers prescriptions, c1900 . . . . .1,300.00

96" h, 72" l 24" deep, pharmacist's, cherry, Victorian Eastlake ornamentation, tall mirrored center section with cobalt blue windows on either side, two wooden mortar and pestles as finials on top, sides with cubicles with marbleized amber stained glass windows, c1880 .2,600.00

Display Case

29" h, counter top type, oak, cash register, upright display case on front, fret work on top, front adv "Shiloh's Remedies," some minor stains 1,200.00

56" h, 21" w, wood, glass sliding door with reverse painted on glass name "Parke Davis & Co. Manufacturing Chemicals" 750.00

Display Rack, 32" h, 22-1/2" w, oak, front angles back to reveal 63 places for labels, multi-compartment and large drawer at base, adv "Playing Cards" on top. 375.00

Display Top, 62" l, 20" h, carved wood, mortar and pestle in center, repainted 250.00

Graduate, 25-1/2" h, oversized, glass, adv "Drugs & Pure Chemicals" on reverse painted banners, some repainting to banner and graduation lines 3,000.00

Jar

9" h, ARSENIC IODIDE, cylindrical Dakota jar, paper label 500.00

9-3/4" h, S.CARUI, hand blown cylindrical, colorful applied reverse painted on glass label, ground stopper with flat top 125.00

10" h, LEECHES, ceramic, crock shape, breathing holes in lid, small knob handles, chip on one handle 5,500.00

10" h, POT.BICHROM, cylindrical, colorful recessed reverse painted on glass label with fancy filigree background, Pat'd March 31, 1891, pattern on base matches ribbed top, multiple chips on bottom of stopper. 150.00

10-1/2" h, MERCURY PROTO.IODIDE, bulbous shape, pedestal base, hexagon umbrella shaped lid. 900.00

10-1/2" h, SANTONIA, gold, white, and red applied reverse painted on glass label, domed lid with faceted tear shaped knob, minor chipping to label edge. 200.00

12" h, QUININE, gold, blue, red and black reverse painted on glass label, mirrored gold domed lid 1,600.00

12-1/2" h, MACIS, cylindrical, colorful recessed reverse painted on glass label with filigree background, Pat'd March 31, 1891, pattern on base matches ribbon on lid, chips to lid . . 135.00

12-1/2" h, TONIC PIL.BLAUD, cylindrical, applied reverse painted on glass label with 6-pointed star, fancy filigree background, adv "Soluble Sugar Coated Tonic Pil.Blaud," pedestal base emb "W. R. Warner & Co. Pat'd Sept 18, 1875," faceted pyramid shaped top, minor color loss and tiny crack around edges of label. 1,200.00

13" h, PENICK'S INITIAL LINE, tall cylindrical, pedestal, swirled patterned lid, cardboard label, product inside 450.00

18" h, ELM BARK SLABS, N.H., early hand blown cylindrical, frosted, paper label, ground stopper with flat top, product inside. 125.00

Light, three-dimensional, mortar, stained glass, multifaceted jewels trim

12" h, hanging, amber red, and green, crack on two panels 250.00

13" h, wall mounted, brass trim, red, green, amber, blue, purple, wood pestle, one jewel missing. 2,000.00

15-1/2" h, hanging, amber, red, and green, small crack in bottom panel 900.00

Mirror, 23-1/2" h, 31" w, center mirror with early paper adv for "Dr. White's Dandelion Alternative The Great Corrector, Blood Purifier, and Tonic," and "Dr. White's Pulmonaria for Coughs, Colds, Croup, Whooping Cough, and Consumption," highly textured wood frame, replaced mirror . . 850.00

Mortar and Pestle

6" h, Beggs' Acme Plasters, nickel plated, emb adv on hinged lid, some denting and wear 475.00

7-3/4" h, brass, cast iron bottom, removable lid mkd "Pat'd Oct 25, '87," shows overall wear. 600.00

Scale, balance, 33" h, all brass, lever mounted on candle stick shaped pedestal. 600.00

Show Globe

13" h, hanging, hand blown, round, brass plated cast iron hanging collar. 350.00

Pharmacists Counter, cherry, Eastlake Victorian ornamentation, tall mirrored enter section with cobalt blue windows on either side, two wooden mortar and pestles mounted on top, sides of cubical have marbleized amber stained glass windows, c1880, 72" w, 24" d, 96" h, $2,600. Photo courtesy of James D. Julia, Inc.

13-1/2" h, hanging, hand blown, round, ornate flanged cast iron bracket, brass plated cast iron collar matches bracket
. . . . 450.00
15" h, hanging, hand blown, emb brass collar, mkd "Mfg. by Dorin Selles, N.Y.C.," some discoloration to globe 575.00
17" h, counter top flared show globe, cast iron pedestal and urn-type collar, fogging to inside of globe, cast iron repainted old. 1,800.00
18-1/2" h, illuminated cluster globe apothecary symbol, wall mounted filigree brass bracket, five globes, each filled with colored liquid, blue, red, yellow, and green, brass collars are figural oak leaves, electric, c1900 . . . . .3,450.00
23" h, hanging, hand blown, very ornate flanged cast iron bracket, repainted collar 450.00
23" h, hanging, hand blown, very ornate flanged cast iron bracket, brass plated cast iron collar. 550.00
24" h, stacking, candy, graduated, pressed block and diamond pattern, chips around base. 1,150.00
24-1/2" h, ornate cast iron pitcher with large hand blown counter top globe. 2,100.00
30" h, stacking, bulbous shaped globes, filled with different colored liquid, chips around base 950.00

36" h, stacking, cut glass pedestal, three graduated sizes, filled with different colored liquid, chips around base 2,850.00
37" h, sitting inside emb flanged bracket, hand blown cut glass glove, large ornate cast iron pitcher 2,800.00

Show Jar

22" h, Hippocratic, reverse painted on glass, figural urn-shape, silhouette of Hippocratic against marbleized background, poor condition, lid mission 350.00
24" h, Dakota, cylindrical, colorless, pedestal, filled with apothecary product, several chips on lid, lid frozen 375.00
27" h, Choice Perfumery, reverse painted on glass, figural urn-shape, brilliant metallic gold design against marbleized background, paint missing from lid, some loss to reverse painting. 1,150.00
39" h, Choice Perfumery, reverse painted on glass, figural urn-shape, lettering in bright metallic gold, marbleized brown background, green and brown marbleized lid with gold trim, blue/green marbleized base, separate dark blue marbleized pedestal, flaking and paint loss to lid, some flaking to gold in body 2,500.00
40" h, Aesculapius, reverse painted on glass, figural urn-shape, cameo of God of Medicine and Healing, marbleized brown background, green and brown marbleized lid, blue/green marbleized base, brown marbleized pedestal with gold trim, some paint loss to lid, some inpainting. 2,400.00
44" h, Fine Chemicals, reverse painted on glass, figural urn-shape, separate black and gold pedestal base, metallic gold banner with "Fine Chemicals" weaves through background of floral displays, paint loss to lid 3,000.00

Trade Sign, figural, zinc, mortar and pestle, some wear and chipping to gold paint, 22-1/2" h, 23" w, $1,000. Photo courtesy of James D. Julia, Inc.

Sign

12" h mortar, 19" h matching hollow pestle, reverse painted on glass with gold mirror like finish, "Pure Drugs" on one wide 5,000.00

17-1/2" h, mortar and pestle, three dimensional, wall mounted wood, paint finish 550.00

22-1/2" h, 33-1/2" w, Herrick's Pills and Plasters, paper, framed, some inpainting 300.00

25" h, mortar and pestle, three-dimensional zinc, could be hung or placed on counter top. 1,000.00

27" h, 12-3/4" w, Hoptonic, paper over linen cloth, titled "Health to the World," trademark cherub with bottle of Hoptonic flying over world, Shober & Carqueville Litho. Co., orig metal rims at top and bottom 400.00

27-1/2" h, 21-1/2" w, Boschee's German Syrup, framed tin, adv "Boschee's German Syrup" and "Green's August Flower," cameo of young girl, framed, overall crazing, chipping, scratching, and soiling 300.00

28" h, mortar and pestle, three-dimensional, American eagle landing on top, could be used as counter top or window display, repainted gold 2,000.00

29" h, 10-1/2" w, Drugs and Soda, trapezoidal, reverse painted on glass, crinkled background, orig copper frame, minor background color change 725.00

29-1/4" h, 11-3/4" w, Prescriptions Carefully Compounded, framed reverse painted on glass, mortar and pestle in center, black background, gold lettering, some loss to lettering 1,000.00

30" h, mortar and pestle, figural, copper, red, blue, amber, and crystal jewels in mortar, red, opalescent, turquoise, and purple smaller jewels in pestle, some jewels missing from back 2,000.00

30" h, 23" w, Wyeth Preparations Here, clear beveled glass sign, shield shape, reverse painting on glass lettering 700.00

33" h, 44-1/2" w, Laxative Bromo Quinine, diecut trifold cardboard, titled "All Nations use Laxative Bromo Quinine," pyramid shaped display of product, images of men from around the world, Uncle Sam on left side, gentleman on right with British flag as vest, some minor damage 300.00

33-1/2" h, 23" w, mortar and pestle, hanging, figural zinc, outdoor type 1,000.00

34" h, 24" w, Dr. J. H. McLean's Liver and Kidney Balm, cardboard, titled "Gives Perfect Health," thankfully looking lady, pictures of products around perimeter, Forbes Co. Litho, © 1898, framed, some discoloration 1,400.00

34" h, 24" w, Morses' Candy, colorful cardboard, shows tin with illus of The Duchess, jar with many varieties of candy, Niagara Litho Co., © 1924, framed 550.00

72" h, McCrea & Williams Druggists, primitive diecut sheet metal, shield shaped tubular border, mortar and pestle. . 600.00

ARCHITECTURAL ELEMENTS

History: Architectural elements, many of which are handcrafted, are those items which have been removed or salvaged from buildings, ships, or gardens. Part of their desirability is due to the fact that it would be extremely costly to duplicate the items today.

Beginning about 1840, decorative building styles began to feature carved wood and stone, stained glass, and ornate ironwork. At the same time, builders and manufacturers also began to use fancy doorknobs, doorplates, hinges, bells, window locks, shutter pulls, and other decorative hardware as finishing touches to elaborate new homes and commercial buildings.

Hardware was primarily produced from bronze, brass, and iron, and doorknobs also were made from clear, colored, and cut glass. Highly ornate hardware began appearing in the late 1860s and remained popular through the early 1900s. Figural pieces that featured animals, birds, and heroic and mythological images were very popular, as were ornate and very graphic designs that complimented the many architectural styles that emerged in the late 19th century.

Fraternal groups, government and educational institutions, and individual businesses all ordered special hardware for their buildings. Catalogs from the era show hundreds of patterns, often with a dozen different pieces available in each design.

The current trends of preservation and recycling of architectural elements has led to the establishment and growth of organized salvage operations that specialize in removal and resale of elements. Special auctions are now held to sell architectural elements from churches, mansions, office buildings, etc. Today's decorators often design an entire room around one architectural element, such as a Victorian marble bar or mural, or use several as key accent pieces.

References: Ronald S. Barlow (comp.), *Victorian Houseware, Hardware and Kitchenware*, Windmill Publishing, 1991; Margarete Baur-Heinhold, *Decorative Ironwork*, Schiffer Publishing, 1996; Len Blumin, *Victorian Decorative Art*, available from ADCA (P.O. Box 126, Eola, IL 60519), n.d.; Michael Breza and Craig R. Olson (eds.), *Identification and Dating of Round Oak Heating Stoves*, Southwestern Michigan College Museum (58900 Cherry Grove Rd, Dowagiac, MI 49047), 1995; Maude Eastwood wrote several books about doorknobs which are available from P.O. Box 126, Eola, IL 60519; Constance M Greiff, *Early Victorian*, Abbeville Press, 1995; Philip G. Knobloch, *A Treasure of Fine Construction Design*, Astragal Press, 1995; Henrie Martinie, *Art Deco Ornamental Ironwork*, Dover Publications, 1996; James Massey and Shirley Maxwell, *Arts & Crafts*, Abbeville Press, 1995; Ted Menten (comp.), *Art Nouveau Decorative Ironwork*, Dover Publications, n.d.; *Ornamental French Hardware Designs*, Dover Publications, 1995; Ernest Rettelbusch, *Handbook of Historic Ornament from Ancient Times to Biedermeier*, Dover Publications, 1996; Edward Shaw, *Modern Architect* (reprint), Dover Publications, 1996; *Turn of the Century Doors, Windows and Decorative Millwork*, Dover Publications, 1995 reprint; Stanley Shuler, *Architectal Details from Old New England Homes*, Schiffer Publishing, 1997; Web Wilson, *Antique Hardware Price Guide*, Krause Publications, 1999; ——, *Great Glass in American Architecture*, E. P. Dutton, New York, 1986.

Periodical: *American Bungalow*, P.O. Box 756, Sierra Madre, CA 91204.

Collectors' Club: Antique Doorknob Collectors of America, Inc., P.O. Box 126, Eola, IL 60519.

Additional Listings: Doorknobs & Builders' Hardware, Stained Glass.

Aquarium, cast iron and glass, attributed to J. W. Fiske & Co., NY, last quarter 19th C
47-3/4" h, 36-3/4" d, shell and foliate dec octagonal tank, rockery form fountain above figural heron-form standard, molded circular base, imperfections 3,335.00
48" h, 28" d, foliate dec octagonal form tank, shaped skirt, center baluster-form fountain, pierced baluster form foliate and scroll dec standard, shaped tripod base, verdigris patination, bowl int. sgd "J. W. Fiske 41...Place N.Y. pat'd Feby...1875" 2,100.00
Apothecary Globe Holder, 10" h, three-dimensional cast iron griffin, originally held globe from mouth 600.00
Bench, 60" l, 19-1/2" d, 20-1/2" h, cast stone, Neoclassical-style, Italian, 20th C 250.00
Birdcage, 20-1/4" w, 15-3/4" d, 19-1/4" h, Victorian Gothic Revival, carved and painted wood and wire, removable carved acanthus leaf base, 19th C. 1,400.00
Boot Scraper, 12" w, 8-1/2" h, cast iron, lyre shape, diamond shaped base. 185.00
Bracket, 19" h, three-dimensional cast iron eagle standing on ledge, chains suspended from beak, originally served as flange for apothecary globe, detailed casting, eagle repainted gold. 1,750.00
Calendar and Sun Dial, 45" l, 9" w, carved wood chip dec board with hanging holes on each end, three copper plates, bottom one forming sundial with engraved numbers, sun and "Umbrar Sumus," middle copper plate with center revolving disk with Roman numerals 1 to 12, diamond shaped plate has twelve-month rays with sun dec, top plate is shield design "Anno MDCXVII" with engraved knights helmet and swords 250.00
Chimney Top, 14-1/2" h, sewerpipe, pagoda shape, attributed to Ohio, chips 330.00
Ceiling Medallion, 31" d, plaster, acanthus leaf dec . . . 150.00
Curtain Tiebacks, 3-1/8" l, transfer dec of neoclassical maiden against memorial, "Sacred to Friendship," pressed brass frames, hp enamel highlights, English, minor dents and enamel loss 450.00

Garden Ornament, Greyhound, cast iron, old finish, traces of old paint, rust, price for pair, $8,250. Photo courtesy of Garth's Auctions, Inc.

Door, entrance, spider web paneled transom, five beveled glass panes on each side, carved moldings 900.00
Down Spout, 25-1/2" l, 23" h, tin, applied cast stars and spread eagle, America, dated 1830, imperfections 460.00
Eagle, attributed to John Hales Bellamy
25-1/4" l, 4-1/2" h, carved pine, orig polychrome, minor losses, minor repair to beak, two minor nail holes 1,725.00
27" l, 10" h, carved pine, polychrome dec, holding American flag, repainted, repairs to one wing 575.00
30-1/2" w, carved pine, old red, white, blue, and gold paint, several applied stars missing, glued split in one flag 5,225.00
Finial, 61-1/2" h, molded copper, fine verdigris, America, 19th C, contemporary wood base, repair, minor dents, purportedly removed from Hunter College, New York City 3,220.00
Fountain
10" h, 47" w, 47-1/4" d, floor type, Moghul style, Rajasthan, c1850, inlaid marble, shallow, fluted, circular basin centered by lotus flowerhead jet, edged in scalloped molding, within rect deeply molded frame with black marble stringing, spandrels inlaid with polychrome floral arabesques . . .7,500.00
28" h, 22-1/2" l, cast metal, trumpeting merman, unsgd, verdigris patination, from Rockport, MA, estate 3,500.00
36" h, patinated bronze, young female standing in careful post on base surrounded by frogs 1,700.00
46-1/2" h, patinated bronze, large fanciful modeled fish, upright position on swirling dome of waves 1,500.00
62" h, 41-1/2" h, cast-bronze, Renaissance style, scrolled cartouche form back plate with dramatic lion head, semi-circular reservoir of lobed campana form, rect base cast with lotus leaves 4,250.00
Garden Ornament
15" l, frog, glazed ceramic, green and brown high glaze, mkd "Brush" 500.00
43" h, 47-1/2" l, cast zinc, polychromed stag, J. W. Fiske, late 19th C, imperfections 4,150.00
Garden Seat, 18-3/4" h, barrel form, polychrome dec symbol medallions, geometric designs, porcelain, Chinese, late 19th/early 20th C, pr 575.00
Garden Settee, cast iron
33" h, 43" l, 15" d, back and legs with grapevine design, pierced seat, several coats of weathered paint, America, late 19th C 230.00
36" h, 46" l, 17" d, three panel pierced back joined to scrolled arms, rect seat, Gothic valance on legs, joined by stretchers, painted black, John McLean maker, New York, repairs 900.00
Garden Urn
13-1/2" h, 16" d, cast iron, two handles, foliate relief, painted black, set of four. 1,495.00
19-1/4" h, 18" d, bronze, Neoclassical style, complex everted baluster form, mounted with sphinxes, lion-mask handles, female masks, and portrait medallions, pr 850.00
22" h, 18" d, cast iron, campana-form, painted beige, American, late 19th C, pr 700.00
30-1/2" h, 20-1/2" d, cast iron, campana form, shaped foliate rim, ribbed body, eagle's head handles, sq base, 19th C, corrosion 700.00
31" h, cast iron, campana form, painted, pr 700.00
36" h, 33-1/2" d, bronze, lobed baluster form, fruiting swags, lion-mask handles mounted with contemplative cupids, 18th C, pr 3,000.00
Gate, 24" w, 59-1/2" h, picket fence, paneled section in base, various sized spires, orig cast iron hardware and latch, Southern, weathered 170.00

Hitching Post, 37" h, cast iron, black child, cap, outstretched arm with ring in hand, plinth base, old polychrome repaint 250.00

Jamb Hooks, 2-3/4" h, brass, urn top, England or America, early 19th C 525.00

Keystone, granite, carved fruit dec 225.00

Mantle, 6-1/4" w, 58-3/4" l, 52-3/4" h, Federal, pine, old black repaint, applied moldings, reeded and fluted detail . . . 1,100.00

Newell Post Finial, 10" h, pine, realistically carved as eagle and squirrel, South German, 19th C, pr 525.00

Pedestal

36-1/2" h, 9-1/2" sq, alabaster, revolving top, octagonal base, reeded and spiral column ending in cut corner sq top 1,400.00

39" h, rotating 17" sq top, mahogany, round cylinder column, sq base, labeled "Paine Furniture," orig finish 1,250.00

39-1/2" h, gray veined marble, sq top, circular support, sq base, Italian, 20th C 175.00

40-3/4" h, onyx, revolving top, fissures and repaired break 440.00

41" h, alabaster, circular top, spiral-carved support, octagonal stepped base, Italian, early 20th C 750.00

43" h, green marble, fluted standard, octagonal foot, Continental, 20th C, chips 350.00

43" h, onyx and gilt metal, sq top, band of gilt-metal foliage, columnar standard and stepped base, Continental, late 19th/early 20th C 920.00

48" h, hardwood, ebonized finish, paw feet, acanthus scrolls and satyr heads, Empire Revival 1,100.00

Shelf Bracket, marble, white, finely carved, Renaissance style, 19th C 175.00

Shield with Eagle, 15-3/8" h, 10-1/4" w, carved wood, polychrome dec, America, 19th C, eagle possibly repainted 1,380.00

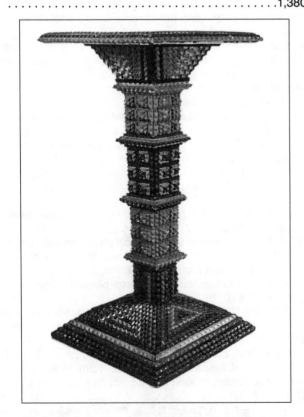

Pedestal, Tramp Art, polychrome paint dec, 12" w, 12" d, 24" h, $1,800. Photo courtesy of Clifford Wallach.

Shutters, pr, 17-1/2" w, 74-1/2" h, movable louvers, cut-out moon and star on top panel, old worn blue plaint, age cracks 480.00

Sign, 44-1/4" h, 66" w, painted and dec, two-sided, Thompson Hotel, Vernon Stiles 1831, gilt letters flanking scene of men in a carriage drawn by two white horses pulling in front of early 19th C dwelling, black ground, other side similarly painted, but shows weathering, orig iron hangers 17,250.00

Sink, pedestal, oval bowl, fluted column standard 150.00

Sun Dial, 17-1/2" d, bronze, dark brown patination, male golfer, both hands gripping club extended in front, titled "Slow Back-Time Right," C. E. Codman, stamped "Gorham" 4,600.00

Tombstone, 9" x 11", gray sandstone fragment, top shaped and carved to form heart, date 1704 and initials BG, small box and arrow 600.00

Wall Bracket, 23-1/2" h, wrought iron, figural rooster, Hunt Diederich artist, includes photograph of orig sketch . 5,750.00

Window, 33-1/2" d, painted wood, circular, eight divided lights, America, 19th C 435.00

ART DECO

History: The Art Deco period was named after an exhibition, "l'Exposition Internationale des Arts Déecorative et Industriels Modernes," held in Paris in 1927. Its beginnings succeed those of the Art Nouveau period, but the two overlap in time as well as in style.

Art Deco designs are angular with simple lines. This was the period of skyscrapers, movie idols, and the Cubist works of Picasso and Legras. Art Deco motifs were used for every conceivable object being produced in the 1920s and 1930s (ceramics, furniture, glass, and metals) not only in Europe but in America as well.

References: Victor Arwas, *Glass: Art Nouveau to Art Deco*, Rizzoli, 1977; Lillian Baker, *Art Nouveau & Art Deco Jewelry*, Collector Books, 1981, 1994 value update; Bryan Catley, *Art Deco and Other Figures*, Antique Collectors' Club, n.d.; Jean L. Druesedow (ed.), *Authentic Art Deco Interiors and Furniture in Full Color,* Dover Pub., 1997; Alfred W. Edward, *Art Deco Sculpture and Metalware*, Schiffer Publishing, 1996; Tony Fusco, *Art Deco Identification and Price Guide*, Avon Books, 1993; Mary Gaston, *Collector's Guide to Art Deco*, 2nd ed., Collector Books, 1997; Steven Heller and Louise Fili, *Italian Art Deco: Graphic Design between the Wars*, Chronicle Books, 1993; ——, *Streamline: American Art Deco Graphic Design*, Chronicle Books, 1995; Francis Joseph, *Collecting Carlton Ware*, Francis Joseph Publications, 1994; Henrie Martinie, *Art Deco Ornamental Ironwork*, Dover Publications, 1996; Theodore Menten, *Art Deco Style*, Dover Publications, n.d.; Paul Ockner and Leslie Piña, *Art Deco Aluminum: Kensington,* Schiffer Publishing, 1997; Francis Salmon, *Collecting Susie Cooper*, Francis Joseph Books, 1995; Tina Skinner, *Art Deco Era Textile Designs,* Schiffer Publishing, 1998; Wolf Uecker, *Art Nouveau and Art Deco Lamps and Candlesticks*, Abbeville Press, 1986; Howard and Pat Watson, *Collecting Art Deco Ceramics*, Kevin Francis, 1993.

Periodical: *Echoes Report*, P.O. Box 2321, Mashpee, MA 02649.

Collectors' Clubs: Canadian Art Deco Society, #302-884 Bute St., Vancouver, British Columbia V6E 1YA Canada; Carlton Ware International, P.O. Box 161, Sevenoaks, Kent TN15 6GA England; Chase Collectors Society, 2149 W Jibsail Loop, Mesa, AZ 85202; International Coalition of Art Deco Societies, One Murdock Terrace, Brighton, MA 02135; Miami Design Preservation League, P.O. Box Bin L, Miami Beach, FL 33119; Twentieth Century Society, 70 Cowcross St., London EC1M 6DR England.

Museums: Art Institute of Chicago, Chicago, IL; Copper-Hewitt Museum, National Museum of Design, Smithsonian Institution, New York, NY; Corning Museum of Glass, Corning, NY; Jones Museum of Glass and Ceramics, Sebago, ME; Virginia Museum of Fine Arts, Richmond, VA.

Additional Listings: Furniture; Jewelry. Also check glass, pottery, and metal categories.

Architect's Table, American, 1935, white lacquer, painted black metal, and oak 4,500.00
Belt Buckle, silver, openwork geometric design, cabochon amethyst accents, Theodore Fahrner hallmark 700.00
Bookends, pr, dancing flappers, colorful, cold painted bronze 150.00
Box, cov
   4" l, bronze, cover with child and two geese, light patina, attributed to Alice M. Wright, initialed "AMW" 200.00
   5-3/8" h, alabaster box, gilded filigree frame, supported by three kneeling women, one head glued, mkd "Made in Germany" 165.00
   7-1/2" l, 1" d, 4" w, hammered brass, enamel top, green, red, and brown geometric design 110.00
Chandelier, 26" l, 15" d, six radiating chrome ribs with gilded accents, base of six angular peach frosted glass shield shaped wing forms, trumpet form ceiling cap with stepped cone and ball at base, shades sgd in cameo "Maynadier," French, c1930 . . . . .3,000.00
Cigarette Case, 4-1/4" h, enameled and silver gilt, rect, black ground, two red bands, white metal geometric inlay, gilt int., inscribed, French 250.00
Clock, 23-1/2" l, 3-1/2" d, 9" h, mantel, alabaster and onyx base, round centerpiece, clock face bordered by two metal peacock figures with brass patina 130.00
Compact, Cigarette Box, and Lighter, white metal, reeded geometric finish, center pave-set with rose-cut diamonds, bordered in 18K yellow gold, sgd "Van Cleef and Arpels," orig leather pouches 900.00
Decanter, 13-5/8" h, 4-1/4" d, amethyst, three sided, enameled gold, brown, and red Art Deco designs, three sided spear point stopper. 110.00
Dish, 9-5/8" h, silver, octagonal, raised dec border, monogram, French, 32 troy oz, pr 700.00
Figure
   12-1/4" h, nude dancer, bronze, cast from model by D Charol, sgd 300.00
   29-1/2" l, muscular male moving marble block with pole, marble and black onyx base, sgd "Bezin" 1,350.00
Furniture
  Chair
    Armchair, fireside type, embroidered cornucopia with flowers, rose colored velvet upholstery, 36" h, price for pr 1,495.00

    Side, carved walnut, arched back, reeded fans, bowed seat rail, reeded tapering cylindrical legs, c1925, French, price for pr 750.00
  Corner Cabinet, France, c1925, mahogany, rect top with rounded corner, single small glazed gilt-bronze door, mirrored compartment, above three short drawers each set with rect shagreen escutcheon, flanked by quarter round door opening to mirrored and glass shelved int., molded feet with gilt-bronze sabots, 34-1/2" w, 16" d, 35-1/2" h 2,650.00
  Dresser, aluminum, porthole handles, orig salmon vinyl trim, c1930, pr, 43" w, 19" d, 34" h 1,500.00
  Kitchen Cabinet, two matching side cabinets, hardwood veneer, worn orig finish, white striping, ivory plastic hardware, enameled pullout shelf, int. bread box and breadboard, labeled "Sellers," center unit 40" w, 22-1/4" d, 69" h, side unit 18" w, 11-1/2" d, 68-3/4" h 400.00
  Suite, silvered bronze, 32" w, 19" d, 78" h domed top vitrine, conforming etched frosted glass panel, single door opening to shelves, mirrored back; 35" w, 14" d, 16" h coffee table, inset black glass top, scroll feet; 35" w, 14" d, 85" h, domed mirrored console, divided into beveled sections, floral and scroll work 3/4 frame, half round table, black glass top, 2 scroll supports; framed mirror; 22" w, 12" d, 46" h black plinth, rect top, sq standard continuing to stair step base 24,150.00
Lamp
  Ceiling, 14-1/2" d, frosted colorless bowl, molded with angular Art Deco stylized foliate elements in high relief, "Muller Freres Luneville" molded in design, three black metal flower finials covering suspension hooks, chains, ceiling arrangement, two chains missing 450.00
  Chandelier, 14" d shade, 39" drop, deeply frosted light bowl, colorless glass molded with stylized foliate designs, gilt metal fittings, six matching glass shades, brass stems extending to elaborate ceiling cap 1,400.00
  Desk, 15" h, angular adjustable gilt metal drop socket base, fitted with frosted blue art glass shade, green, orange, and white dec swirls 300.00

Coffee Maker/Hotplate, Sunbeam, Chicago Flexible Shaft Co., nickel plated, black line dec, black bakelite handles, tab feet, c1930, $90.

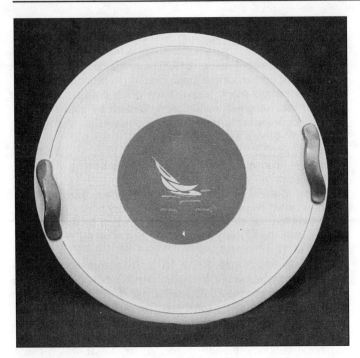

Plate, blue handles, blue center, white sailboat, mkd "Sailboat, Japan," 11-3/4" d, $30.

Table
  15-1/2" h, sculptural figure of woman dancer poised atop alabaster drum platform base housing electrical fittings, base mkd "Italy"........................... 450.00
  24-1/2" h, 16" d reverse painted glass shade, Art Deco foliate design in black, frosted clear and orange accented motif on mottled lavender ground, columnar lamp base fitted with copper colored three-socket mounts, Rookwood Pottery, c1920 ....1,275.00
Torchère, 7-1/2" d, 24" h, silver matte metal base overlapping staircase sequences, eight frosted trapezoidal glass panels in shade, one cracked panel, base flaws........ 100.00
Jug, pottery, 5 3/4" h, multicolored leaf dec, gray ground, green trim, mkd "Charlotte Rhead"................... 390.00
Necklace, 14" l, colorless glass ovals with stylized bird and leaf design, center pendant drop, designed in Rene Lalique manner, frame imp "Made in France" 225.00
Perfume Bottle, yellow, black triangles, deep rose, gold lines blue base, clear neck.......................... 95.00
Pitcher, 8-5/8" h, porcelain, stylized figural cat, yellow and white, base inscribed "Theodore Haviland Limoges/France Copyright Depose," and "E. M. San Doz sc"........... 750.00
Postcard
  Christmas Gifts, set of six, women giving, carrying, and receiving Christmas gifts, snow scenes, Italian, sgd "Bompard," 6 pcs 250.00
  Pierrot Couple, man and woman in pierrot costumes dancing at party, Italian, sgd "Chiostri" 40.00
  Portrait of a Woman, sultry post, Italian, sgd "Bompard," Series 472-3..................................... 40.00
  The Butterflies, French woman, butterfly with real feather wings, sgd "Xavier Sager," Series #104 .... 30.00
  The Fetishes of Fashion, set of seven, French women in flimsy fashions, French, sgd "Koister," Series 71, 7 pcs
  .... 200.00
  Woman and Cupid, cupid riding on shoulder of woman holding love letter, Italian, sgd "Colombo" 40.00

Woman in Provincial Dress, Spanish woman, red rose between her teeth, sgd "Usabel" 40.00
Women in Gossamer, six card set, each different post, Italian, sgd "Guerzoni," used, 1913, Belgium, 6 pcs 200.00
Sculpture, 14" w, 5" d, 14" h, stylized woman and fawn, alabaster, mkd "Made in Italy"......................... 230.00
Smoking Set, 12-3/4" l tray, cigar and cigarette humidors, four ashtrays, brass, worn smoked and bright finish, black striped detail, mkd "Bradley & Hubbard" 225.00
Table Service, 18 pc "Cut Star and Punty" pattern, engraved moon and star motif, designed by Bolas Mankowski, c1934, six 8" plates, six stemmed water goblets, six champagnes, base inscribed "S" or "Steuben" 675.00
Tea Caddy, 3-3/4" h, Danish silver, ovoid, waisted tapering neck, Georg Jensen, c1925 .... 450.00
Toothbrush Holder, sitting dog, ceramic 90.00
Vanity Set, 5 pc, light blue enamel and silver mounts, hairbrush, clothes brush, shoehorn, nail file, and nail buffer, French
.... 175.00
Vanity Bag, mesh, goldtone, attached top with Art Deco design
.... 135.00
Vase
  7-5/8" h, bulbous colorless body, overlaid in opaque white, deeply cameo etched or sandblasted as three repeating design elements, stylized monogram on base "SN/NS"
  .... 175.00
  8" h, colorless oval body, cased with champagne colored layer with mica specks, amethyst int., surface deeply etched or sandblasted with deep curvilinear designs, frosted in recessed, base inscribed "Muller Fres Luneville" ...1,450.00
  9-1/2" h, opalescent glass, ribbed form, emb P. D'Avesn mark.. 190.00
  17" h, flared oval, internally dec with blue, yellow, and white swirls, colorless surround, aubergine pedestal foot inscribed "Degue" 500.00
Wristwatch, lady's, dress
  Platinum and diamond, Abra Watch Co., Swiss, 17 jewels, rect dial, Arabic numerals, diamond bezel flanked by two old European-cut diamonds, engraved link bracelet, some blue stones missing 2,070.00
  Platinum and diamond, small rect dial marked "Gubelin," eight adjustments, 18 jewels, movement no. 39566, flanked by baguette and fancy bullet-shaped diamonds, French-cut synthetic ruby line bracelet 2,650.00
Whitetone dial, black Arabic numerals, geometric design sapphire and diamond bezel, black cord band, accompanied by orig Gubelin proof of authentic, discoloration to dial . 750.00

ART NOUVEAU

History: Art Nouveau is the French term for the "new art" which had its beginning in the early 1890s and continued for the next 40 years. The flowing and sensuous female forms used in this period were popular in Europe and America. Among the most recognized artists of this period were Gallé, Lalique, and Tiffany.

The Art Nouveau style can be identified by flowing, sensuous lines, florals, insects, and the feminine form. These designs were incorporated into almost everything produced during the period, from art glass to furniture, silver, and personal objects. Later wares demonstrate some of the characteristics of the evolving Art Deco style.

References: Victor Arwas, *Glass: Art Nouveau to Art Deco*, Rizzoli, 1977; Lillian Baker, *Art Nouveau & Art Deco*

Jewelry, Collector Books, 1981, 1994 value update; Constance M Greiff, *Art Nouveau*, Abbeville Press, 1995; Ted Menten (comp.), *Art Nouveau Decorative Ironwork*, Dover Publications, n.d.; Bengt Nystrom, *Rorstrand Porcelain*, Abbeville Press, 1995; Albert Christian Revi, *American Art Nouveau Glass*, reprint, Schiffer Publishing, 1981; Wolf Uecker, *Art Nouveau and Art Deco Lamps and Candlesticks*, Abbeville Press, 1986; Roberta Waddell, *Art Nouveau Style*, Dover Publications, n.d.; Kenneth Wilson, *American Glass 1760-1930*, 2 vols., Hudson Hill Press and The Toledo Museum of Art, 1994.

Museum: Virginia Museum of Fine Arts, Richmond, VA.

Additional Listings: Furniture; Jewelry. Also check glass, pottery, and metal categories.

Andirons, pr, gilt brass, scroll dec, bust of woman 750.00
Basket, 14" h, 8-1/2" w, engraved colorless glass, wild rose pattern cut up to edge, applied crystal loop handle. 150.00
Blotter Corners, 14kt yellow gold, elaborate pierced and engraved floral and scroll motifs, 26.80 dwt 300.00
Bowl, 11-1/2" d, sterling silver, elaborate raised floral dec, pierced border, Mauser, 21 troy oz 800.00
Bust, 9-1/2" h, bronze, style of Emmanuel Villanis, brown patina
. . . . 300.00
Candlesticks, pr
   5-3/4" h, silver, Georg Jensen 4,600.00

Clock, Louis Majorelle, rosewood and ironwork, bronze patina, 8" h, $1,750.

12" h, bronze, bobeche suspended on baluster tripod standard, leaf form legs 750.00
Carpet, 18' 7" x 14', wool, beige field strewn with olive and tan scrolling designs, sgd "Victor Horta," c1900. . . . . .19,550.00
Chamberstick, Kayserzinn pewter, floral dec 85.00
Clock
   18" h, ivory and bronze, porcelain dial in drum case, works mkd "Paris" monogrammed, sides with Hippopotamus teeth, scrolling bronze vines 1,150.00
   23-3/4" h, bronze, figural, dark brown patina, inscribed "Marcel Debut 98," Siot foundry stamp, dated 1898 . . .3,500.00
Coal Hod, 15" l, 10-3/4" w, 13-1/2" h, nickel plated, lift lid and back hinged plate, reticulated floral dec, metal handle, slot for shovel, int. liner, sgd and numbered 160.00
Dish, bronze, figural, maiden seated on edge of waterlily blossom, sgd "Cahuzac" 325.00
Dish, cov, 6-1/2" d, pewter, double handle, Art Nouveau dec, raised design, ftd, #4037 . . . . 300.00
Dresser Set
   Silverplated, 10-1/2" l hand mirror, hair brush, and comb, chased repousse, maiden in backless gown, long flowing tresses, wave scrolls and flowers border, Britannia Artistic Silver Co, Chicago, c1905, 3 pcs. 195.00
   Sterling silver, elaborate floral repousse, putti bearing fruit baskets, 9" l handled brush, 7-1/2" comb, 7" l hand brush, 11" hand mirror, 4-1/4" d powder jar, Gorham 900.00
Ewer, bronze, high looped handle, molded with foliage, light gilt patina, sgd "P. Loiseau-Rousseau," French. 150.00
Figure, 8-3/4" h, ivory, young nude woman, poised on right foot, drapery, ebony base, inscribed "R Middegaels," c1925
. . . . .2,950.00
Frame, 11-1/2" h, sterling silver, arched crest, chased pendant husks, clusters of fruit, velvet cov back with easel support back, marked "Walker & Hall, Birmingham," 1911 . .1,125.00
Furniture
   Bedroom Suite, 74" w x 56" h double bed headboard and footboard inlaid with trumpet creeper, floral carved crest rails, carved whiplash borders, marble top dresser with carved mirror, pr of night tables, price for 5 pc set
   . . . . .7,900.00
   Chair, arm, Karpen Bros., mahogany, reed and tendril carved frame, undulating crest rail, high relief carving of female heads and poppy blossoms, poppy carved scrolled armrests, conforming seat rail, cabriole legs, upholstered, c1900 . . . . .1,250.00
   Music Cabinet, Emile Galle, France, c1900, walnut and marquetry, two doors above two drawers, overall iris design, incised signature, 23" w, 16" d, 51" h 2,200.00
   Suite, carved walnut, two-seat settee, padded back with pierced crest rail carved with flowering passion-fruit vines, downswept arms similarly carved, serpentine front, overstuffed seat, conforming rails continuing into splayed legs, frame molded, matching arm and side chairs 2,500.00
Glove Box, silverplated, 15-1/2" l, 6" w, 6-1/2" h, rect, hinged domed lid, chased sides, repeating band of dragonflies
. . . . 450.00
Inkwell, 8-1/4" l, bronze, figural, female scribe holding quill and globe, shaped tray 635.00
Jardiniere, 18" h, terra cotta, rect, figural, nypmh in flowing gown holding blossom, standing against vine cov wall, sgd "J Causse," orig liner 595.00
Jewelry
   Pin, dragonfly, colored enamel large wings, fiery opal small lower wings, large diamond and nine smaller diamonds

Mug, majolica, yellow, brown, and green, German, 3-3/4" h, 3-3/4" d, $115.

body, head with two faceted ruby eyes and one diamond, 18K. 6,000.00

Watch, lapel-type, Smith Patterson Co., 14k yellow gold, goldtone dial with black Roman numerals, initialed case, suspended from chased and engraved griffin brooch, hallmark for Bippart, Griscom & Osborn 435.00

Lamp
15" h, 9-1/2" d cameo glass shade, bronzed metal base, elephant and tree supporting mottled green, white, and brown leaves and vines dec shade, attributed to Mueller, minor base flaws, flakes to shade 950.00
26" h, bronzed floral trim and fittings, red enameled metal base, electrified, replaced milk glass globe with painted rose, wear to base, some damage. 200.00

Lorgnette, 14k gold, repousse iris dec 1,265.00

Match Safe, 2-3/8" h, brass, one side with relief woman, reverse "The Louisiana Purchase Monument" 230.00

Mug, 3" h, sterling silver, monogrammed and dated 1905, numbered "7565" on base, Marcus & Co., NY 300.00

Perfume Lamp, 9-1/4" h, opal white vase, Art Nouveau style replication heat cap, single socket fittings 815.00

Pillbox Pendant, 18k gold, hinged lidded box design, repousse foliate motif, 11.20 dwt 635.00

Postcard
Iris, Japanese woman, illus of the Mascagni opera, sgd "Hohenstein," published in Italy 75.00
Mountain and Field, travelers by field at foot of snow capped mountain, monogrammed, Japonism. 40.00
Nurse Maid, nurse accompanies woman on her walk, from 'Types of St. Petersburg" series by M. Dhoujinsky, Russia, Series, published by Society of St. Eugenea of the Red Cross 40.00
Procession, wagons pulled by ox, onlookers, monogrammed, published by Mikumo Wood-Block Print Co, Kyoto, Japan 40.00
Snow Rabbit, white rabbit running through brush, monogrammed, Japonism 40.00
Springtime, woman with tree blossoms, swallows and morning bell, published by Stengel & Co., Germany, sgd "L. Gauvey," Russia back 75.00

Woman in Nature, bust of woman with light purple flowers in her hair, classic Art Nouveau nature patterns in greens and browns, used, America, 1902 . . . . 60.00
Woman wearing emerald jewelry, German 45.00

Powder Box, cov, 4" d, sterling silver lid, repousse design of maiden and roses, cut glass base 250.00

Tea Set, porcelain, 10-1/2" h teapot, creamer, sugar, four cups and saucers, painted pink and green thistle leaves, acorns, and dragonflies, white ground, printed "J & C Kopenhagen" mark 300.00

Torchère, 84" h, Louis XVI, gilt bronze, marble, five light candelabra, c1880, electrified, price for 4 pc set 28,750.00

Tray, 11-1/4" l, bronze, shaped oval, nude long haired woman and mermaid, two bodies form sides of rippled pool, medium green patination, c1900 . . . . 900.00

Urn, 12-1/4" h, silver, two handles, chased floral and leaf dec, serpentine rim and base, monogram, Gorham, c1873, 40 troy oz 2,300.00

Vase
7-3/4" h, 4" d, bronze, emb pansies, Baubien, imp mark 325.00
15" h, lady circling treelike vase, covered with leaves, Ernest Wahlis 995.00

ART POTTERY (GENERAL)

History: America's interest in art pottery can be traced to the Centennial Exposition in Philadelphia, Pennsylvania, in 1877, where Europe's finest producers of decorative art displayed an impressive selection of their wares. Our young artists rose to the challenge immediately, and by 1900, native artisans were winning gold medals for decorative ceramics here and abroad.

The Art Pottery "Movement" in America lasted from about 1880 until the first World War. During this time, more than 200 companies, in most states, produced decorative ceramics ranging from borderline production ware to intricately decorated, labor intensive artware establishing America as a decorative art powerhouse.

Below is a listing of the work by various factories and studios, with pricing, from a number of these companies. The location of these outlets are included to give the reader a sense of how nationally-based the industry was.

References: Susan and Al Bagdade, *Warman's Americana Pottery and Porcelain*, Wallace-Homestead, 1994; Carol and Jim Carlton, *Colorado Pottery*, Collector Books, 1994; Paul Evans, *Art Pottery of the United States*, 2nd ed., Feingold & Lewis Publishing, 1987; Lucile Henzke, *Art Pottery of America*, revised ed., Schiffer Publishing, 1996; Ralph and Terry Kovel, *Kovels' American Art Pottery*, Crown Publishers, 1993; Richard and Hilary Myers, *William Morris Tiles*, Richard Dennis (distributed by Antique Collectors' Club), 1996; David Rago, *American Art Pottery*, Knickerbocker Press, 1997; Jim Riebel, *Sanfords Guide to Nicodemus*, Adelmore Press, 1998.

Periodicals: *Style 1900*, 17 S. Main St., Lambertville, NJ 08530.

Collectors' Clubs: American Art Pottery Society, P.O. Box 1226, Westport, MA 02790; Pottery Lovers Reunion, 4969 Hudson Dr., Stow, OH 44224.

Videotapes: Ralph and Terry Kovel, *Collecting with the Kovels: American Art Pottery*, 2 tapes, Antiques, Inc., 1995.

Museums: Cincinnati Art Museum, Cincinnati, OH; Everson Museum of Art of Syracuse and Onondaga County, Syracuse, NY; Los Angeles County Museum of Art, Los Angeles, CA; Metropolitan Museum of Art, New York, NY; Newcomb College Art Gallery, New Orleans, LA; Zanesville Art Center, Zanesville, OH.

Additional Listings: See Clewell; Clifton; Cowan; Dedham; Fulper; Grueby; Jugtown; Marblehead; Moorcroft; Newcomb; North Dakota School of Mines; Ohr; Paul Revere; Peters and Reed; Rookwood; Roseville; Van Briggle; Weller; Zanesville.

Notes: Condition, design, size, execution, and glaze quality are the key considerations when buying art pottery. This category includes only companies not found elsewhere in this book.

Advisor: David Rago.

Arequipa Pottery, Fairfax, CA
Cabinet Vase, 5" h, 3" d, squeezebag dec, stylized blue and yellow leaves, green ground, blue mark 3,500.00
Vase
6" h, 4" d, hand modeled, stylized flowers, blue matte glaze, imp mark 925.00
7" h, 6" d, bulbous, blue feathered glaze, three color squeezebag design, green, yellow, and brown. 7,500.00
Crook, Russel, Massachusetts, New England
Vessel
8" h, 4" d, ovoid, stoneware, gray mouse in tall trees, black ground, minor glaze flecks to rim, unmarked. 1,700.00
9" h, 9" d, stoneware, herd of moose in clay color, black ground, firing lines through body, chips to rim, incised palette mark 1,100.00
Denaura, Denver, vase, 8-1/2" h, 5" d, ovoid, small opening, incised with tulips, cover in smooth green glaze, ink mark and "Denaura/Denver/1903/160". 2,400.00
FHR Pottery, Los Angeles
Bowl, 3" x 4", low, closed, pink flambé glaze 850.00
Vase, 6" h, 3" d, crystalline, silvery crystals on flowing brown ground, imp mark 1,200.00
Merrimac Pottery, Newburyport, MA
Cabinet Vase, 4" h, 3-1/2" d, feathered matte green and gunmetal glaze, mark partially obscured by glaze 400.00

Merrimac Pottery, vase, left, reticulations at base, modeled stylized flowers, leathery matte green glaze, incised "AN," 9" h, $4,510; center, vase, applied leaves, brownish-green dead-matte glaze, unmarked, 6" h, $1,430; right, vessel, tooled and applied leaves, leathery green and black semi-matte glaze, touch-ups to leaf edges, mark obscured by glaze, 10" h, $2,420. Photo courtesy of David Rago Auctions, Inc.

Pitcher, 6-3/4" h, 6-1/2" h, rich matte green glaze, restoration to chip at rim, stamped 350.00
Vase
Slope-shouldered, stylized seaweed, flowing green matte glaze, minor rim repair 3,300.00
Squat bulbous, two handles, green matte glaze, unmarked 300.00
Overbeck Pottery
Cabinet Vase, 3" x 1-1/2", carved panels of pine cones and needles, brown, yellow, and green, cracked 1,100.00
Vase
5" x 3", three panel carved floral design, brown and beige 4,500.00
15" h, incised dec of wisteria vine and blossoms, two kiln marks, c1931 . . . . .13,000.00
Pewabic Pottery, Detroit, MI
Bowl, 5" d, 2" h, ext. covered in shimmering burgundy glaze, int. with richly lustered gold glaze, stamped. 450.00
Vase
7" h, 5" d, bulbous, flaring rim, rich metallic lustered blue and gray glaze, circular imp mark 865.00
8" h, metallic glaze, blue, green, gunmetal luster, imp mark 550.00
8-1/4" h, 5-1/4" d, tapering shoulder, lustered gold, green, and burgundy glaze, mark partially obscured by glaze 1,300.00
9-1/4" h, 7-1/4" d, bulbous, lustered cobalt blue glaze, slight bruise to side, in making, circular stamp 1,000.00
9-3/4" h, 5-3/4" d, classically shaped, flaring rim, blue-green crystalline glaze, imp mark, paper label. 2,000.00
Roblin Pottery, San Francisco, CA
Miniature Vase, 3" h, 2" d, bulbous, beaded rim, buff clay, imp mark 350.00
Plate, 7" d, hammered surface, incised frogs and lily pads, sgd "I. Irelan" and "Roblin," short hairline 990.00
Shearwater, vase, 5-1/2" h, molded design of fish, birds, pelican and horse with rider, light blue glaze, imp mark. 450.00

Teco, Terra Cotta, IL
Vase
    5-1/2" h, four buttress form, gray matte glaze, mkd, chips
    . . . . 450.00
    6" h, 4-3/4" d, bulbous, flaring rim, satin matte green glaze,
    imp "Teco" twice. 450.00
    10-1/4" h, 5-1/2" d, buttressed, satin matte green glaze, imp
    "Teco" three times 3,500.00
    11" h, blades of grass, reticulated handles, porous matte
    green finish 9,500.00
    11" h, 5-3/4" d, ikebana, emb tulips and tall intertwining
    leaves, smooth matte green glaze, minor restoration to one
    leaf tip, imp "TECO". 6,000.00
    13" h, 10" w, #119, circular form, four buttress handles, satin
    green finish, imp "Teco 119," repair to rim chips, repair to
    glaze nicks. 5,000.00
University City Pottery, St. Louis, MO
Trivet, pate-sur-pate, pink maple leaves, cream ground, dec by
    Taxile Doat. 3,000.00
Vase
    7" h, 4" d, crystalline, gold snowflake crystals on cream
    ground, imp mark. 1,800.00
    9" h, faceted double gourd, flowing gold snowflake crystals,
    cream ground. 12,100.00
Valentien Pottery, San Diego, CA
Bud Vase, 8" x 3", thin, molded design, curdled light green matte
    glaze, imp mark 1,700.00
Vase, 7" h, 3" d, painted stylized Greek key design, matte paint-
    ing technique, imp mark. 4,000.00
Walley Pottery, West Sterling, MA
Candlestick, 10" h, 4-1/4" h, bulbous top, flared base, striated
    brown-yellow high glaze, smooth green ground, looped han-
    dle, imp "WJW.". 350.00
Mug, 5" h, 4" d, molded head of devil with garnet eyes, imp mark
    . . . . .1,000.00
Tile, 7-1/2" d, circular form, large relief turtle design, thick crack-
    le matte green glaze, imp "WJW" 460.00
Vase
    4-1/2" h, 3-1/2" d, elongated neck, mottled, dripping green
    high glaze, imp mark 345.00
    5-1/2" h, 5-3/4" d, high gloss glaze, brown speckles with yel-
    lowish brown striation on olive green ground, imp "WSH"
    mark for "Worcester State Hospital, minor glaze nick and
    scratches 575.00
    7" h, 7 d, oviform, overlapping leaves in high relief, deep
    matte green glaze, slivery black edges, imp "WJW," glaze
    imperfections, minor glaze nick 1,725.00
    13-1/2" h, 5-1/4" d, tapering cylindrical form, four rising han-
    dles mounted with rolled rim enclosing int. rim with scal-
    loped edges, thick sliding green high glaze rippling towards
    base on brown ground, imp "WJW". 6,325.00
Walrath Pottery, Rochester, NY
Chamberstick, 5" h 250.00
Mug, 4-1/2" w, 3-1/4" h, reddish-brown foliate design, brown
    ground, imp mark, price for pr 435.00
Vase, 7-3/4" h, 3-3/4" d, stylized blue leaf forms, light matte blue
    ground, tight hairline. 1,380.00
Wheatley Pottery Co., Cincinnati, OH
Lamp Base, 11-1/2" h, 9-1/2" d, buttressed, curdled matte green
    glaze, glaze scrape small nicks to feet. 2,600.00
Vase
    10" h, 5" d, handle, emb leaves, matte green finish, imp mark
    . . . . .1,500.00
    12-3/4" h, ovoid, white and green flowers, mottled blue and
    light blue high glaze, inscribed "J. T. Wheatley, Cincinnati,
    1879" 865.00

    14" h, 6" d, two handles, buttresses, green matte, small chip
    repair 3,700.00
Vessel, 11" h, 10" d, matte green glaze, overlaid with silver
    leaves, branches, and simulated net, minor losses
    . . . . .2,500.00

ARTS and CRAFTS MOVEMENT

History: The Arts and Crafts Movement in American decorative arts took place between 1895 and 1920. Leading
proponents of the movement were Elbert Hubbard and
his Roycrofters, the brothers Stickley, Frank Lloyd Wright,
Charles and Henry Greene, George Niedecken, and Lu-
cia and Arthur Mathews.

The movement was marked by individualistic design
(although the movement was national in scope) and
re-emphasis on handcraftsmanship and appearance. A
reform of industrial Society was part of the long-range
goal. Most pieces of furniture favored a rectilinear approach and were made of oak.

The Arts and Crafts Movement embraced all aspects of
the decorative arts, including metalwork, ceramics, embroidery, woodblock printing, and the crafting of jewelry.

References: Steven Adams, *Arts & Crafts Movement*,
Chartwell Books, 1987; *Arts and Crafts Furniture: The
Complete Brooks Catalog of 1912*, Dover Publications,
1996; Michael E. Clark and Jill Thomas-Clark (eds.), *J. M.
Young Arts and Crafts Furniture*, Dover Publications,
1994; Paul Evans, *Art Pottery of the United States*, 2nd
ed., Feingold & Lewis Publishing, 1987; *Furniture of the
Arts & Crafts Period With Prices*, L-W Book Sales, 1992,
1995 value update; Bruce Johnson, *Official Identification
and Price Guide to Arts and Crafts*, 2nd ed., House of
Collectibles, 1992; ——, *Pegged Joint*, Knock on Wood
Publications, 1995; Elyse Zorn Karlin, *Jewelry and Metalwork in the Arts and Crafts Tradition*, Schiffer Publishing,
1993; *Limbert Arts and Crafts Furniture: The Complete
1903 Catalog*, Dover Publications, n.d.; Thomas K. Maher, *The Jarvie Shop: The Candlesticks and Metalwork of
Robert R. Jarvie,* Turn of the Century Editions, 1997;
James Massey and Shirley Maxwell, *Arts & Crafts*, Abbeville Press, 1995; ——, *Arts & Crafts Design in America:
A State-By-State Guide,* Chronicle Books, 1998; Kevin
McConnell, *More Roycroft Art Metal*, Schiffer Publishing,
1995; Richard and Hilary Myers, *William Morris Tiles*, Richard Dennis (distributed by Antique Collectors' Club),
1996; David Rago, *American Art Pottery,* Knickerbocker
Press, 1997; Roycrofters, *Roycroft Furniture Catalog,
1906,* Dover Publications, 1994; Paul Royka, *Mission Furniture ,from the American Arts & Crafts Movement,*
Schiffer Publishing, 1997; Joanna Wissinger, *Arts and
Crafts: Metalwork and Silver* and *Pottery and Ceramics*,
Chronicle Books, 1994.

Periodicals: *American Bungalow*, P.O. Box 756, Sierra
Madre, CA 91204; *Style 1900,* 333 N. Main St, Lambertville, NJ 08530. *American Bungalow* focuses on the
contemporary owner of Period homes and the refurbish-
ing of same. *Style 1900* has a more historically oriented
approach to the turn of the century artisans.

Collectors' Clubs: Foundation for the Study of the Arts & Crafts Movement, Roycroft Campus, 31 S Grove St., East Aurora, NY 14052; Roycrofters-At-Large Society, P.O. Box 417, East Aurora, NY 14052; William Morris Society of Canada, 1942 Delaney Dr., Mississaugua, Ontario, L5J 3L1, Canada. Students of the Arts and Crafts Movement are encouraged to participate in the two major conferences now available. The Grove Park Inn Conference is held annually in Ashville, NC, in February, by Bruce Johnson.

Museums: Cooper Hewitt Museum, Manhattan, NY; Elbert Hubbard Library-Museum, East Aurora, NY; Los Angeles County Museum of Art, Los Angeles, CA; Metropolitan Museum of Art, Manhattan, NY; Museum of Modern Art, New York, NY; Richmond Museum of Art, Richmond, VA.

Advisor: David Rago.

Additional Listings: Roycroft; Stickleys; art pottery categories.

SPECIAL AUCTIONS

Craftsman Auctions
1485 West Housatonic
Pittsfield, MA 01201
(413) 448-8922

David Rago Auctions, Inc.
333 North Main St.
Lambertville, NJ 08530
(609) 397-9374

Treadway Gallery, Inc.
2029 Madison Rd.
Cincinnati, OH 45208
(513) 321-6742

Andirons, pr, 56" h, 19" w, 28" d, wrought iron, wrapped with protruding animal faces, attributed to Samuel Yetlin, c1920 . . . . .2,300.00
Bowl, 5-3/4" d, 2-3/4" h, copper and silver, chased and repousse waves highlighted with silver beads of spray and silver rim, rich patina, early imp Arthur J Stone mark, c1901-12 . . . . .6,325.00
Box
    4" sq, 2-1/2" h, copper, small brass mushrooms and decorative stone, rich dark patina, price for pr 750.00
    4-1/2" w, 3-1/4" d, 1-3/4" h, hand-hammered, enameled black lined sailing ship, yellow ground 260.00
Creamer, 3-1/4" h, silver, oviform, rolled rim, mkd with Arthur Stone logo and initial "G" for Herman Glendenning, c1920, approx. 6 troy oz. 290.00
Fish Tureen, 12" d, 12-1/2" h, hand hammered pewter, applied fish handles, orig ladle, imp Old Newbury marks 460.00
Furniture
  Bookcase
    33-3/4" l, 14" d, 50-1/2" h, J. M. Young, single glazed door with twelve mullions, refinished 2,250.00
    48" w, Gustav Stickley, two door, through tenons and keys, orig finish, red clamp mark 8,500.00

48" w, L. & J. G. Stickley, two door, through tenons and keys, chamfered back, orig finish 13,200.00
Cabinet, 39" w, 13" d, 76-1/2" h, attributed to England, c1910, oak, two leaded glass doors, copper hinges and pulls over open shelf, orig finish, breaks to glass, minor wear 920.00
Chair, dining, price for 8 pc set
    17-1/2" w, 16-1/2" d, 37-1/2" h, one arm chair, seven side chairs, refinished 865.00
    18-1/2" w, 18-1/2" h, 36-1/2" h, three vertical slats, orig black leather and tacks seat 1,150.00
China Cabinet, 48", Lifetime, two doors, orig dark finish 3,250.00
Hall Mirror, 48-3/4" w, 28-1/4" h, Lifetime, similar to #512, two color glass, orig finish and pulls, inverted "V" crest rail 750.00
Morris Chair
    Gustav Stickle, early bow-arm, orig dark finish, early clamp mark 18,700.00
    L. & J. G. Stickley, rocking, open sides, orig finish 3,850.00
    J. M. Young, slatted sides, orig finish, mkd with paper label 4,400.00
Settle
    72" l, 30" d, 36" h, even arms with slats all around, orig dark brown finish, mkd "J. M. Young and Company" 2,500.00

Chair, Limbert, three vertical back slats, fabric covered drop in spring seat, orig finish, branded mark, 37-1/2" h, $250. Photo courtesy of David Rago Auctions, Inc.

74" l, 29" d, 34-1/2" h, Conant Furniture Co, fifteen vertical back slats, sloping side rails, five vertical side slats, orig finish, new leather upholstery 2,300.00

74" l, 30" d, 36" h, Limbert, oak, eight vertical back slats, three vertical side slats, orig medium brown finish, some wear, missing cushions 2,990.00

Sewing Rocker, 17" w, 15-1/4" d, 32-1/4" h, three vertical slats, orig finish 460.00

Stand, 42-1/2" h, 20-1/2" w, 12-1/2" d, Limbert, horizontal support stretchers under top and bottom shelves on four sides gently arched on underside, support stretchers mortised through the vertical posts, 3 middle shelves held with round pegs, burned in mark, number 303, orig condition 1,025.00

Table

Dining

48" d, Limbert, split pedestal, three leaves, orig finish, wear top, unmarked 2,750.00

54" d, 30" h, quarter-sawn oak, mortise and tenon stretcher base, orig finish, veneer chips 920.00

Lamp

30" d, Limbert, flaring legs, cut-out cross stretchers with squares, orig finish, some wear to top 4,500.00

30" h, 30" w, round top and round lower shelf, supported by 4 legs, orig medium-dark brown finish, Paine Furniture Co 60.00

Library, 48" w, 28" d, 30" h, two drawers, flat medial stretcher, worn orig dark brown finish, Stickley Brother/Quaint label 750.00

Limbert

36-1/2" d, 26-1/4" h, round, stretcher base, through tenons, cut down, orig finish 575.00

45" l, 30" d, 29" h, #146, oak, square cut outs and arched apron, branded mark, orig finish, some color added 2,990.00

Lamp

Chandelier, wood and slag glass, center drop with four small drops, orig finish. 1,200.00

Floor, 72" h, 24-1/2" sq shade, three bookshelves with oval cut-outs, red, green, yellow, and white leaded glass shade over orig oil burner lamp, orig dark finish, paper label, "Shop of the Crafters, #153" 4,600.00

Hanging, 32" h, 9" w, brass patina cattail overlay, yellow and green slag glass. 1,150.00

Table

18" h, 18" d, Dirk Van Erp, copper and mica, paneled shade, orig dark patina, 3 lights, mica panel, imp mark 15,000.00

21" h, 16" sq shade, painted gold metal frame, geometric panels over purple, blue, and yellow slag glass, Prairie School, Bradley and Hubbard 1,380.00

24" h, 11" w, four green and white glass panels in shade and base, oak frame 415.00

Jewelry, brooch, attributed to S G Panis, silver, foliate pattern mounted with two sapphires, three diamonds, marked "S.G.P., STERLING," 2-1/4" l 800.00

Loving Cup, 6-1/2" w, 6-1/4" h, silver, two applied angular handles, bulbous form, chased with wave and spray dec, monogrammed, minor scratched, marked with Stone logo and initial "T" for Herbert Taylor, underside engraved as Red Cross presentation, 12 troy oz 635.00

Match Striker, 7" h, 5" w, inlaid wall hanging, glass butterflies on copper mount, imp "Burdick" 4,500.00

Plaque, 11" h, 14" w, patinated repousse copper, semi-precious stones, executed by Maria Longworth Nichols Storer, Cincin-

nati, OH, 1909, rect, eight crabs and starfish in midst of irid pagination and raking, sgd "MLS/1915," wood frame
4,025.00

Porringer, 6-1/4" d, 1-3/4" h, silver, finely pierced and chased handle, engraved "Mary Louise Lawser-Christmas 1909 - from Auntie Mary," mkd with Arthur Stone logo, initial "B" for William Blair, 6 troy oz 460.00

Print

Color linoleumcut on paper, Moonlight on Cape Cod, Tod Lindenmuth, sgd "Tod Lindenmuth" in pencil lower right, titled in pencil lower left, identified on label on mat, image size 9-1/4" x 7", matted 1,265.00

Color woodblock on paper, William Rice, lone pine off the Carmel, CA, coat, 6" x 4" .1,200.00

Color woodcut on paper, Gearhart, Frances Hammel, sgd "Frances H. Gearhart" in pencil lower right, initialed in block lower left, identified on label on mat

7-3/4" x 4-1/2", Coastal Scene, matted 2,100.00

8" x 4-1/2", Point Lobos, matted 1,380.00

Salt, 3-1/4" w, 1-1/4" h, silver, oblong, flared base, set of six, four marked with Arthur Stone logo, and initial "T" for Herbert Taylor, other two with stone logo and initial "C", 18 troy oz 460.00

Serving Piece, silver, 8-1/2" l, hammered finish, pierced and engraved dec, monogram, imp "F. Porter, Sterling," c1925, 2 troy oz. 210.00

Smoking Stand, 9-1/4" sq, 25" h, copper top, new pyramid tacks, push button lock, caned sides and door, quarter-sawn oak, unmarked 1,100.00

Tray, 9" w, 12" l, silver, openwork handles, mid with Arthur Stone logo, initial "C," minor scratches, 15 troy oz 865.00

Vase

Derby, 7" h, 11" d, silver plate, bulbous, hand hammered surface, rim dec with four riveted mounts 320.00

Heinz Art Metal Shop, bronze

8" h, 3-1/2" d, applied silver tree design, imp logo, patent Aug 27, 12, D, orig patina, some denting 175.00

8" h, 5" d, silver foliate design, good patina, imp mark 290.00

8-1/2" h, bulbous top tapering to base, silver foliate design, cleaned 400.00

AUSTRIAN WARE

History: More than 100 potteries were located in the Austro-Hungarian Empire in the late 19th and early 20th centuries. Although Carlsbad was the center of the industry, the factories spread as far as the modern-day Czech Republic.

Many of the factories were either owned or supported by Americans; hence, their wares were produced mainly for export to the United States.

Marks: Many wares do not have a factory mark but only the word "Austrian" in response to the 1891 law specifying that the country of origin had to be marked on imported products.

Additional Listings: Amphora; Carlsbad; Royal Dux; Royal Vienna.

Bowl, 9" d, 4" h, hammered brass, four arched supports, Arts & Crafts style, unsigned, orig patina 300.00

Cabinet Plate, 9-1/2" d, enamel and gilt dec, one titled "Verlobung," other titled "Orthello Relates his Adventures," artist sgd "Kroiller," late 19th/early 20th C, pr 460.00

Chocolate Set, chocolate pot, cov sugar, six cups and saucers, tray, transfer dec of Georgian scene, beehive mark, 15 pc set 500.00

Clock, 14-1/2" h, mantel, carved wood and gesso gilt-wood case, acanthus leaves, shell spandrel, surmounted by four acorn finials, two handled urn with flame finial, one piece silvered dial, 2 gongs with "Grand Sonniere," c1810 ... 460.00

Compote, 7-1/2" d, 5-1/4" h, colorless and amber glass bowl, faceted pedestal, six repeating intricate black and gold enameled designs, attributed to Karl Massanetz 1,850.00

Creamer, 7-1/8" h, blue glaze, floral dec panel......... 45.00

Dish, 8" w, woman with long flowing hair, clutching applied flower among large waterlilies, imp and stamped marks, minor edge roughness 190.00

Dresser Set, pin tray, two boxes, dresser tray, multicolored, 4 pc set... 110.00

Ewer
11-3/4" h, 6" d, rococo gold scroll handle, HP pink and yellow wild roses outlined in gold 125.00
16" h, bulbous top and base, 2-1/2" d waist, jagged yellow and gold swirls on cobalt body, fancy gold mouth and lip 180.00

Fish Set, 25" l, eight 8-1/2" d plates, porcelain, 9 pc set 375.00

Inkwell, 5" sq, art glass, waffle shape, metal lid 360.00

Match Holder, 7" h, little girl, holding flower, standing by open tree stump match holder vase, beige, ecru, gold, and green, gilt highlights, Alexandra Workshop of Ernst Wahlis, Turn-Wien, crown mark, incised #4733, c1900 ..... 860.00

Pitcher, 13-1/2" h, applied gold lizard handle, flowers, cream ground, sgd "Stellmacher No. 228" 195.00

Plaque, 12" d, majolica-type, raised, dec gnomes, blue, brown, and tan, mkd "Made in Austria 540," pr 125.00

Pokal, 23" h, bronze, enameled green glass insert with florals and crests, ornate bronze pierced and molded frame with lion's heads, bronze lid, knight in armor finial 690.00

Portrait Plate, 11-1/2" d, sgd "Kaufman," beehive mark 275.00

Potpourri Urn, 13-1/2" h, red ground, painted scene of Venus and Bellona, gilt scrolls, 19th C 490.00

Salt, hp, open pink roses, green leaves, gold feet, 4 pc set 75.00

Tray, 15" d, pierced handles, beaded rim, ornate gold, green, and purple grape clusters, sgd "Koch" 90.00

Vase
5-1/2" h, tooled ruffled rim, colorless body, gold oil-spots, applied aubergine threads and trailings, polished pontil, attributed to Pallme Konig 225.00
8" h, baluster form, deep emerald green, four applied trailing scallop shell prunts, polished pontil 550.00
8-3/4" h, tapered pastel green glass cylinder, acid-etched surface, subtle integrated floral dec, overall irid.... 750.00
11" h, green glass body, purple irid, pewter base ... 350.00
12" h, hand painted red poppies, butterfly and foliage, pastel shaded ground, gold trim 100.00
13" h, opaque red cased bulbed body, quatraform rim, pulled and swirled black-green irid dec, polished pontil attributed to Pallme Konig 325.00
13-1/2" h, scene dec, titled "After the Day's Work," man on horseback in field with horses, cottage in background 275.00
20" h, pierced and applied lilies, brown hi-glaze, blue and green irid, white and lavender blossoms protruding from vase, illegible imp mark, some minor flakes, pr 750.00

AUTOGRAPHS

History: Autographs appear on a wide variety of formats—letters, documents, photographs, books, cards, etc. Most collectors focus on a particular person, country, or category, e.g., signers of the Declaration of Independence.

References: Mark Allen Baker, *All-Sport Autographs*, Krause Publications, 1995; ——, *Collector's Guide to Celebrity Autographs*, Krause Publications, 1996; George S. Lowry, *Autographs: Identification and Price Guide*, Avon Books, 1994; J. B. Muns, *Musical Autographs*, 2nd Supplement, published by author, 1994; Susan and Steve Raab, *Movie Star Autographs of the Golden Era*, published by authors, 1994; Kenneth W. Rendell, *Forging History: The Detection of Fake Letters & Documents*, University of Oklahoma Press, 1994; ——, *History Comes to Life*, University of Oklahoma Press, 1996; George Sanders, Helen Sanders and Ralph Roberts, *Sanders Price Guide to Sports Autographs*, 1994 ed., Scott Publishing, 1993; ——, *1994 Sanders Price Guide to Autographs*, Number 3, Alexander Books, 1994.

Periodicals: *Autograph Collector*, 510-A S Corona Mall, Corona, CA 91720; *Autograph Review*, 305 Carlton Rd, Syracuse, NY 13207; *Autograph Times*, 2303 N 44th St., No. 225, Phoenix, AZ 85008; *Autographs & Memorabilia*, P.O. Box 224, Coffeyville, KS 67337; *The Collector*, P.O. Box 255, Hunter, NY 12442.

Collectors' Clubs: Manuscript Society, 350 N. Niagara Street, Burbank, CA 95105; Universal Autograph Collectors Club, P.O. Box 6181, Washington, DC 20044.

Additional Listings: See *Warman's Americana & Collectibles* for more examples.

Shaving Mug, fraternal, Knights of Pythias, multicolored dec, gold name and trim, mkd "Austria," $180.

SPECIAL AUCTION

Swann Galleries, Inc.
104 E. 25th St.
New York, NY 10010
(212) 254-4710

Notes: The condition and content of letters and documents bear significantly on value. Collectors should know their source since forgeries abound and copy machines compound the problem. Further, some signatures of recent presidents and movie stars were done by machine rather than by the persons themselves. A good dealer or advanced collector can help spot the differences.

Abbreviations: The following are used to describe autograph materials and their sizes.

Materials:

ADS	Autograph Document Signed
ALS	Autograph Letter Signed
AQS	Autograph Quotation Signed
CS	Card Signed
DS	Document Signed
FDC	First Day Cover
LS	Letter Signed
PS	Photograph Signed
TLS	Typed Letter Signed

Sizes (approximate):

Folio	12 x 16 inches
4to	8 x 10 inches
8vo	7 x 7 inches
12mo	3 x 5 inches

Colonial America

Hart, John, sgd Colonial Paper currency, three-shilling note of the Colony of New Jersey, issued March 25, 1776, also sgd by Jonathan Deare and John Stevens, Jr., printed in red and black 550.00

Henry, Patrick, partially printed DS, 1 page small 4to, May 9, 1785, as Governor of Virginia, military commission, paper seal, ornate borders, double matted with engraving of Henry, housed in maple and black wood frame 4,200.00

Hopkins, Stephen, DS, 1 page 8vo, Newport, Rhode Island, Jan. 14, 1756, ordering State Treasurer Thomas Richardson to pay Daniel Jenckes 5,000 pounds "for the pay for six northern companies raised by the Colony of Rhode Island to go against Crown Point..." 950.00

Slavery Emancipation, manuscript document sgd, 1 page 4to, Henrico Co., Virginia, Dec. 6, 1803, deep of emancipation, by John Ellis for his "...Negroe Woman Nanny...about the age of 43 years...," sgd by three witnesses including Peyton Randolph. 775.00

Williams, William, ADS, 1 page small oblong 8vo, Lebanon, Connecticut, Oct. 3, 1780, certifying Flavel Clark as Soldier in Continental Army 600.00

Wilson, James, ALS, 1 page 4to, Aug. 14, 1793 to Pres. of the Bank of Pa on financial matters 2,400.00

Foreign

Bormann, Martin, Nazi officer, partly printed DS, in German, 4 pgs, large 4to, Berlin, Jan. 31, 1943, huge signature in red crayon on final page, architect's copy of contract for work on Party Chancellery building in Berlin 1,200.00

Freud, Sigmund, ALS in German, 1923, 3" x 5" postcard 5,500.00

Napoleon I, Emperor of France, LS, 1 page 4to, Paris, March 19, 1811, to Count Nicholas-Francois Mollien, Minister of Public Treasure," request for funds. 1,195.00

Princess Diana and Prince Charles, sgd and inscribed Christmas Card, c1967 . . . . 2,150.00

General

Barton, Clara, ALS, 3 pages 8vo, Oxford, (Massachusetts), Aug. 27, 1910 to "My dear Secretary" 375.00

Blanc, Mel, CS, sgd, inscribed color card of Blanc and cartoon characters, May 1978. . . . . 60.00

Einstein, Albert, TLS, 1 page 4to, Princeton, May 6, 1939, to Albrecht Buschke, declining invitation to speak. 1,875.00

Flagg, James Montgomery, sgd bust pose taken from book about him 275.00

Johnson, Eastman, ALS, June 8, 1895, New York City, concerning identify of sitters for painting "Two Men," 2-1/4" pages, 12mo 320.00

Kalakua, King of Hawaii, partly printed DS, sgd "Kalakau R., in Hawaiian, Molokai land grant, countersigned by Minister of Interior, March 7, 1878, Honolulu, green seal, 2 pages, folio, signatures and land plan on integral leaf, professionally encapsulated 300.00

Lindbergh, Charles, sgd copy of first edition of his book *The Wartime Journals of Charles A. Lindbergh,* New York, 1970, boldly signed in black ink on title page 875.00

Wells, Henry and William G. Fargo, stock certificate sgd, 1 page oblong folio, New York, Jan. 9, 1865, for two shares, vignette of harbor and transportation scene, center small round vignette of dog's head surmounted by eagle, surrounded by stars and words "Safety & Dispatch," elaborate vertical cartouche with patriotic symbols 800.00

Literature

Aks, Frank, DS, 6" x 8" paperback edition of *Titanic/Destination Disaster,* inscribed "To the Parrish's from Frank Aks/Titanic Baby" 6/10/88. . . . . 350.00

Bromfield, Louis, page of orig manuscript of short story, sgd at later date 150.00

Carroll, Lewis, ALS, 1 page oblong 8vo, Nov. 26, 1886, as curator of the Common Room at Christ Church, Oxford, re bequests. 1,350.00

Dickens, Charles, ALS, to son Henry Fielding Dickens, 1-1/2 pages, two small 8vo personal stationery, Oct. 7, 1867, Gads Hall, Higham by Rochester. 1,495.00

Hemingway, Ernest, PS, 8" x 10", black and white of Hemingway and John Grath, as war correspondents near Siegfriend Line 2,300.00

Bryant, William Cullen, ALS, 1 page 8vo, Oct. 21, 1856, to fellow poet John Greenleaf Whittier, sending check as price 850.00

Kipling, Rudyard, TLS, 8" x 10" personal stationery, Sussex, England, 1920. . . . . 650.00

Tolstoy, Leo, Russian author, ALS, 1 page small 4to, in English, Nov. 16, 1894, concerning his views on church. . . . 2,500.00

Twain, Mark, 8vo page of orig manuscript of book *The Gilded Age,* written in conjunction with Charles Dudley Warner, published 1873. . . . . 1,800.00

Military

Custer, George Armstrong, DS, envelope addressed to his wife, c1866 . . . . .1,925.00

Grant, US, manuscript, sgd presidential pardon, May 3, 1870, sgd "U. S. Grant" 1,500.00

Jackson, Andrew, manuscript document, sgd as Major General, 1 page folio March 25, 1813, issuing 500 rations for regiment of Tennessee Volunteers, raised in response to Indian massacre. 2,250.00

Lee, Stephen D., Confederate General, manuscript document sgd as Major Genera, 1 page small folio, light blue stationery, April 25, 1864, loyalty oath of British citizen Stephen Monaghan Underill, Acting Aide-de-Camp to Lee, to the Confederacy and state of Alabama 1,800.00

Patton, George S. Jr., censoring letter "Censored/G. S. Patton Jr./Lt. Gen." on 3-1/8" x 2-1/8" sheet from corner of envelope, cut from envelope sent by Patton to his wife January 1944, writing dark. 850.00

Welles, Gideon, Civil War Secretary of Navy, SL, 3 pages 4 to, Sept. 19, 1862 to Henry Flanders, Prize Commissioner, Philadelphia, concerning capture of Confederate ship. . . 850.00

Music

Caruso, Enrico, large sgd drawing, in ink, back of 4to sheet of Hotel Knickerbocker stationery, bold profile caricature of older man, sgd "Enrico Caruso 1913" 950.00

Handy, W. C., TLS, 1 full page 4to, Handy Bros. Music Co. letterhead, NY, March 2, 1950, to Robert W. Bruce, Reno, Nevada 275.00

Honegger, Arthur, Swiss composer, autographed musical quotation, 1 page 12 mo, 1952, two double bars, words "Gloria in Excelcis," on music paper 575.00

Kodalyh, Zoltan, Hungarian composer, autographed musical quotation, 1 page oblong 8vo on music paper, six bars of opera 1,150.00

Menotti, Gian Carlo, printed program for Curtis Institute of Music, Philadelphia, Dec. 13, 1981, bold signature on cover
. . . . 185.00

Prokofieff, Serge, Russian composer, autographed musical quotation, 1 page, 6-1/4" c 5-1/8", two bars of music identified by him as being from his *Piano Concerto Number 2,* sgd in full, dated 1929 . . . . .3,200.00

Puccini, Giacomo, Italian composer, ALS, in Italian, 4 full pages 8vo, slightly risqué content, possibly to girlfriend . . .1,175.00

Sousa, John Philip, American composer and bandmaster, TLS, Sousa and His Band letterhead, small vignette portrait of Sousa in his uniform, 1 page 4to, Willow Grove, PA, Sept. 13, 1924, to Mrs. Ralph Willis, wife of a friend, thanking her for gift. 275.00

Presidents

Adams, John, DS, 1 page small folio on vellum, June 3, 1797, land grant to trustees of creditors of Robert Ballard, awarded land for 3 years of military service 3,900.00

Coolidge, Calvin, PS, framed, by Harris & Hewing, sgd "Calvin Coolidge" 150.00

Davis, Jefferson, Confederate President, ALS, 4 pages 8vo, Memphis, Tennessee, Dec. 8, 1869, to his sister Margaret Howell, at Liverpool, England, regarding new employment position 1,900.00

Fillmore, Millard, DS, envelope, sgd "M. Filmore" in upper right corner of franked mailing envelope, addressed in his hand to Issac Newton, Philadelphia, verso with remains of red wax seal, pieces of kraft mounting paper 200.00

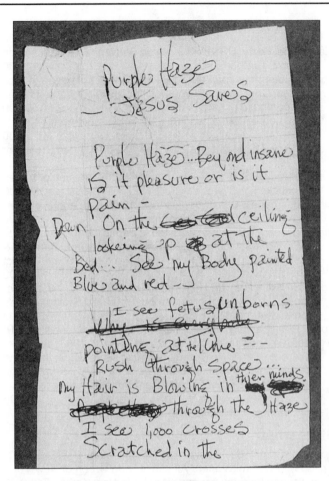

Document Signed, Jimi Hendrix, handwritten lyrics, "Purple Haze," $18,000.

Harrison, William Henry, ALS, 2 pages, small 4to, Headquarters, Piqua, Sept. 25, 1812, to General James Taylor, concerning man's accounts 2,300.00

Lincoln, Abraham, ALS, 1 page 4to, Springfield, IL, Nov. 1, 1958, to Kersey H. Fell. 11,000.00

Madison, Dolley P., first lady, ALS, 1 page small 4to, Montpellier, Virginia, March 22, 1836 to Miss Maury, writes of former President's fragile health .2,500.00

Madison, James, 4to Free Franked address lead, addressed to The Revd. W.B. Sprague/West Springfield/Massachusetts, franked upper right, manuscript postal marking 775.00

Nixon, Richard M., PS, Vice President, August 1957, 4to black and white, bust-length photo, long inscription to Samuel K. McConnell, Republican congressman from PA, accompanied by typed letter on Vice Presidential stationery, auto pen sgd "Dick" 650.00

Roosevelt, Eleanor, PS, matted and framed photo with typed letter, dated April 29, 1940, White House stationery, sgd by Eleanor, 14" x 19". 250.00

Roosevelt, Theodore, TLS, 1 page 4to, Civil Service Commission letterhead, Washington, DC, Dec. 8, 1891, to publisher S. S. McClure, submitted articles to be published, retaining rights, etc. 1,200.00

Taft, William, PS, portrait in holder, sgd "Sincerely your, The White House, July 9, 1913, William H. Taft" 300.00

Show Business

Barrymore, John, sgd self caricature, small 8vo piece of lined paper, pen and ink profile sketch 675.00

Berlin, Irving, TLS, June 13, 1949, regarding recent Philadelphia concert performance 275.00

Blackstone, Harry, DS, 9" x 12" Magic Souvenir Program, sgd on front cov, 1945 . . . . 140.00

Bogart, Humphrey and Lauren Bacall, TLS, 1 full page 4to, Los Angeles, CA, Oct. 3, 1952, agreeing to give right of first refusal for purchase of land 1,500.00

DiCaprio, Leonardo, PS, sgd 8" x 10" color photo from Titanic 125.00

Disney, Roy, DS, loan papers for The Absent-Minded Professor 295.00

Garland Judy, DS, 1 page 4to, Aug. 14, 1957, receipt for traveler's checks 550.00

Ringling, Charles, 8" x 3" bank check, 1912, sgd, engraved portrait vignette of 5 Ringling brothers 400.00

Ringling, John, DS, partially printed, 2 pages legal folio, Jan. 25, 1915, "Artist's Contract and Release" between Barnum & Bailey circus and the 4 Melillo sisters, acrobatic contortion act 475.00

Rogers, Will, sgd and inscribed photo, 8" x 10" sepia, semi-gloss, undated, close-up bust portrait, photographer's imprint lower right. 650.00

Rose, Billy, partially printed DS, sgd once in full, initialed 10 times, 6 pages small folio, New York, Feb. 6, 1963, an agreement between Billy Rose's diamond Horseshoe, Inc. and Theatre Guild Productions for The Jack Benny Show, to be booked at the Ziegfeld Theatre for nine performances 385.00

Stewart, James, canceled check, Dec. 18, 1970 . . . . 75.00

Statesmen

Houston, Sam, ALS, 1 page 8vo, Washington, D.C. , July 27, 1859, to Commissioners Alexander and Green of New York, explaining he does not expect to be in New York . . 2,350.00

Jay, John, ALS, 1 page 8vo, Bedford, June 24, 1822 to son, Peter Augustus, discussing personal matters. 2,000.00

Rockfeller, John D., TLS, 1 page 8vo, Pocantico Hills, NY, letterhead, Jan. 12, 1912, to Charles H. Brown, Jr., of Yonkers, NY, orig envelope 1,400.00

Salinger, J. D., TLS, July 18, 1976, response to request for photo 1,375.00

Seward, William H., ALS, 3 pages 4to, Albany, June 25, 1814, to The Honorable Seth C. Hawley, mkd "Private," regarding efforts to get proper schools for immigrants in New York City 775.00

Supreme Court, c1962-67, sgd by Chief Justice Earl Warren and Associate Justices Hugo Black, William J. Brennan, Tom Clark, William O. Douglas, Arthur Goldberg, John Marshal Harlan, Potter Stewart, and Byron R. White, inscribed to the Chief Justice of Ireland "with best wishes of…," matted and framed, 21-1/4" w, 17-1/4" h. 850.00

Webster, Daniel, letter sgd as Secretary of State, 1 page 4to, Washington, Nov. 25, 1850 to Governor of New Hampshire, regarding resolution of Congress. 250.00

Webster, Noah, ALS, 1 page oblong 8vo, New Haven, Sept. 28, 1842, to Mr. Shuburn, regarding pamphlets. 875.00

AUTOMOBILES

History: Automobiles are generally classified into two categories: prewar, those manufactured before World War II; and those manufactured after the conflict. The Antique Automobile Club of America, the world's oldest and largest automobile historical Society, considers motor vehicles, including cars, buses, motorcycles, and trucks, manufactured prior to 1930 "antique." The Contemporary Historical Vehicle Society, however, accepts automobiles that are at least twenty-five years old. There are also speculate clubs dedicated to specific marquees, like the Wills/Kaiser/AMC Jeep Club, and the Edsel Owners Club.

Some states, such as Pennsylvania, have devised a dual registration system for older cars—antique and classic. Models from the 1960s and 1970s, especially convertibles and limited-production models, fall into the "classic" designation if they are not used as daily transportation. Many states have also allowed collectible vehicles to sport "year of issue" license plates, thus allowing a owner of a 1964 1/2 Mustang to register a 1964 license plate from their home state.

References: Robert Ackerson, Standard Catalog of 4x4s, 1945-1993, Krause Publications, 1993; Dennis A. Adler, Corvettes, Krause Publications, 1996; Quentin Craft, Classic Old Car Value Guide, 23rd ed., published by author, 1989; John Chevedden & Ron Kowalke, Standard Catalog of Oldsmobile, 1897-1997, Krause Publications, 1997; James M. Flammang, Standard Catalog of American Cars, 1976-1986, 2nd ed., Krause Publications, 1989; ——, Standard Catalog of Imported Cars, 1946-1990, Krause Publications, 1992; ——, Volkswagen Beetles, Buses and Beyond, Krause Publications, 1996; Patrick R. Foster, American Motors, The Last Independent, Krause Publications, 1993; The Metropolitan Story, Krause Publications, 1996; John Gunnell, American Work Trucks, Krause Publications, 1994; ——, Marques of America, Krause Publications, 1994; —— (ed.), 100 Years of American Cars, Krause Publications, 1993; ——, Standard Catalog of American Light Duty Trucks, 1896-1986, 2nd ed., Krause Publications, 1993; ——, Standard Catalog of Chevrolet Trucks, Pickups & Other Light Duty Trucks, 1918-1995, Krause Publications, 1995; Beverly Kimes and Henry Austin Clark, Jr., Standard Catalog of American Cars, 1805–1942, 3rd ed., Krause Publications, 1996; Ron Kowalke, Old Car Wrecks, Krause Publications, 1997; ——, Standard Guide to American Cars, 1946-1975, 3rd ed., Krause Publications, 1997; ——, Standard Guide to American Muscle Cars, 1949-1995, 2nd ed., Krause Publications, 1996; Jim Lenzke and Ken Buttolph, Standard Guide to Cars & Prices, 10th ed., Krause Publications, 1997; Albert Mroz, The Illustrated Encyclopedia of American Trucks & Commercial Vehicles, Krause Publications, 1996; Robert Murfin (ed.), Miller's Collectors Cars Price Guide, Reed International Books (distributed by Antique Collectors' Club), 1996; Gerald Perschbacher, Wheels in Motion, Krause Publications, 1996; Edwin J. Sanow, Chevrolet Police Cars, Krause Publications, 1997; Donald F. Wood and Wayne Sorensen, Big City Fire Trucks, 1951-1997,, Krause Publications, Volume I, 1996, Volume II, 1997. Krause Publications' Standard Catalog series includes special marque volumes, including Standard Catalog of Cadillac, 1903-1990; Standard Catalog of Chrysler, 1925-1990; Standard Catalog of Pontiac, 1926-1995; Standard Catalog of Ford, 1903-1990; Standard Catalog of Chevrolet, 1912-1990; Standard Catalog of American Motors, 1902-1987; Standard Catalog of Oldsmobile, 1897-1997; Standard Catalog of Buick, 1903-1990.

Periodicals: *Automobile Quarterly*, 15040 Kutztown Rd, P.O. Box 348, Kutztown, PA 19530; *Cars & Parts*, P.O. Box 482, Sydney, OH 45365; *Classic Car Source*, http://www.classicar.com; *Hemmings Motor News*, P.O. Box 256, Bennington, VT 05201; *Old Cars Price Guide*, 700 E State St., Iola, WI 54990; *Old Cars Weekly, News & Markeplace*, 700 E State St., Iola, WI 54990.

Collectors' Clubs: Antique Automobile Club of America, 501 West Governor Rd, P.O. Box 417, Hershey, PA 17033, http://www.aaca.org; Classic Car Club of America, 1645 Des Plaines River Rd, Suite 7, Des Plaines, IL 60018; Contemporary Historical Vehicle Association, P.O. Box 98, Tecumseh, KS 66542; Horseless Carriage Club of America, 128 S. Cypress St., Orange, CA 92866, http://www.horseless.com; Milestone Car Society, P.O. Box 24612, Indianapolis, IN 46224; Veteran Motor Car Club of America, P.O. Box 360788, Strongsville, OH 44136; Willys/Kaiser/AMC Jeep Club, 1511 19th Ave. W, Bradenton, FL 34205.

Advisors: Jim and Nancy Schaut.

Notes: The prices below are for cars in running condition, with a high proportion of original parts and somewhere between 60% and 80% restoration. *Prices can vary by as much as 30% in either direction.* Prices of unrestored automobiles, or those not running, or missing original parts can be 50% to 75% below prices listed.

Many older cars, especially if restored, are now worth more than $15,000. Their limited availability makes them difficult to price. Auctions, more than any other source, are the true determinant of value at this level.

Prices of high-powered 1964 to 1972 "muscle cars" will continue to escalate, while the value of pre-war cars will remain steady for all but unique custom-built roadsters and limousines. There is renewed interest in the original Volkswagen Beetle since the introduction of the updated nineties version. Look for prices of these economical little cars to climb as well.

Alfa Romeo
1938, Spyder, red and black 225,000.00
1961, Spyder Veloce, small taillights, orig int., rebuilt engine 15,000.00
1964, Giulia Sprint Speciale, red and black leather, one owner 36,000.00

AMC
1965, Rambler Ambassador 990, new int. and paint 2,875.00
1987, Renault GTA, convertible, 5 speed, needs top 1,650.00

Aston Martin
1978, V8 couple, gray and black int., 5 speed 28,500.00
1984, Lagonda, dark blue, tan int. 49,500.00
Auburn, 1936, 852 all weather phaeton, tan, brown trim, orange striping and wheels, dark brown leather, tan top and boot 115,000.00

Austin
1962, A60 Cambridge Wagon 3,800.00
1967, Mini 850 Countryman Van Deluxe, beige and red 3,000.00

BMW
1959 Isetta, ground-up restoration, blue and gray .10,500.00
1973, 2002TH, gold brown Recaro int., ground-up restoration 10,000.00
1977, 320I, orig paperwork, manuals 3,950.00

Buick
1924, Model 51A Brougham, 4 door sedan, restored 12,000.00
1937, Special Model 46C, rumble seat convertible coupe, old highline restoration.............17,500.00
1940, 585 Coupe, green.....................14,500.00
1941, coupe, convertible, all orig, one owner.....14,500.00
1946, Straight Eight, all orig 11,900.00
1951, Deluxe, four door, all orig 9,500.00
1954, Century, convertible, automatic, burnt orange and white...18,500.00
1961, LeSabre, 4 door, bubbletop sedan, white, second owner...19,500.00
1966, Riveria, turquoise, new motor............3,200.00

Cadillac
1930, V16 4335, convertible, four tones of red, sweep cowl panel 295,000.00
1934, 35D, biplane bumpers, needs restoration ...7,900.00
1939, Imperial sedan, jump seats, restored gray int., black lacquer paint 20,000.00
1942, 75 Series, limousine, needs restoration 3,900.00
1948, Fleetwood Series 75, bar behind seat, new chrome and paint 20,995.00
1949, sedan, 4 door, orig int., silver gray 7,000.00
1953, deVille, green, needs restoration 3,900.00
1955, Eldorado, convertible, black, red int., sabre wheels 25,000.00
1959, 4 door hardtop, light blue, orig owner......15,500.00
1978, Eldorado Barritz, white, leather seats......10,000.00

Chevrolet
1918, touring, low mileage 15,000.00
1931, coupe, 5 window, olive and medium brown, pale yellow pinstriping, brown mohair int..............8,500.00
1933, coupe, 3 window, rumble seat, runs, needs work 8,500.00
1939, Master Deluxe, sedan, 2 door, Granville gray 9,500.00
1958, Corvette, 327, 2 tops, needs paint 20,000.00
1959, El Camino, 350 V8 ....3,950.00
1966, Corvette, 327, Nassau blue, teak, all orig ..27,000.00
1968, Nova, sedan, 2 door, 6 cylinder 3,000.00

Ford Model A, Phaeton, 1930, $27,880. Photo courtesy of Auction Team Breker.

Chrysl*er
  1929, Roadster, convertible, 6 cylinder, green and black
  . . . . .19,500.00
  1930, coupe, rumble seat, blue and black wood spoke wheels
  . . . . .8,900.00
  1949, Town & Country convertible, woody, brown, tan top
  . . . . .40,000.00
  1956, New Yorker, St Regis, 2 door, hardtop, red, white, and
  black, wire wheels 7,500.00
Daimler, 1979, DS420 limousine, claret and black, fawn leather
  . . . . .12,500.00
Datsun, 1965, SPL-310 Fairlady, convertible, red, older amateur
  restoration 3,200.00
DeSoto, 1959, Sportsman, 2 door hardtop, heather blue and
  white, restored 11,950.00
Dodge
  1929, sedan, 4 door 5,000.00
  1934, fire truck 7,995.00
  1973, Charger, 340 Magnum, yellow, side stripes, orig tires,
  black bucket seats 13,500.00
Ferrari, 1956, 250 GT Boano, low roof coupe, dark bronze metallic, tan leather 75,000.00
Ford
  1926, Model T, roadster, folding "fat man" steering wheel
  . . . . .5,750.00
  1936, coupe, 3 window, orig int. 18,000.00
  1946, business coupe 12,995.00
  1953, pick-up, F-100 . . . . .5,500.00
  1956, Sunliner, convertible, blue and white, new top and int.
  . . . . .10,000.00
  1964, XL, convertible, red, red int., white top 5,900.00
  1965, Mustang, hard top, ivy, gold vinyl top, rebuilt engine
  and transmission 7,500.00
Jacguar, 1954, XK 120, roadster, red and black 29,500.00
Lamborghini, 1970, Espada, silver, black leather, full mechanical restoration. 28,500.00
Mercedes, 3000D-6 cylinder, 1981, blue, red leather upholstery,
  19,831 miles. 23,650.00
MG
  1957, MGA, roadster, mineral blue, gray int., ground-up restoration. 12,000.00
  1967, MBG roaster, red, black leather, wire wheels
  . . . . .4,500.00
Oldsmobile
  1949, 88, fastback, rust, needs restoration 3,000.00
  1956, 98 Starfire, convertible, white, green leather
  . . . . .19,500.00
  1968, Supreme, 2 door, hardtop 2,500.00
Packard, 1937, Twelve, coupe roadster 195,000.00
Pontiac
  1941, Streamliner Torpedo, 2 door, new int., repainted
  . . . . .8,400.00
  1955, Starchief Custom, 2 door, new turquoise and cream
  paint, new int. 9,300.00
  1962, Grand Prix, new paint and top 13,500.00
  1967, Firebird, black. 5,900.00
  1980, Trans Am, Indy pace car 4,300.00
Plymouth
  1941, Special Deluxe, 2 door. 2,500.00
  1946, wagon, woody, needs restoration. 5,000.00
  1963, Belvedere, hardtop. 1,800.00
Porsche, 1958, Speedster, black and red, restored . .49,500.00
Rolls-Royce, 1951, Silver Dawn, burgundy and silver
  . . . . .28,500.00
Saab, 1968, Sonett 4,000.00
Studebaker, 1962, GT Hawk, 3 speed, bucket seats . .2,000.00

Toyota, 1977, Land Cruiser FJ40, 2 door, factory yellow, removable hardtop 10,500.00
Triumph, 1967, Mk III, two tops, needs paint 2,750.00
VW
  1959, Rometsch Coupe, restored, Okrasa motor .35,000.00
  1966, convertible, custom int., restored 4,500.00
  1971, Super Beetle, convertible, yellow, needs work
  . . . . .2,995.00
Willys, 1949, Jeepster, convertible, yellow, black top and int.
  . . . . .6,900.00

AUTOMOBILIA

History: Automobilia is a wide-ranging category. It includes just about anything that represents a vehicle, from
cookie jars to toys. Car parts are not usually considered
automobilia, although there are a few exceptions, like the
Lalique radiator ornaments. Most sought after are automobile advertising, especially signs and deal promotional models. The number of items related to the automobile
are endless. Even collectors who do not own an antique
car are interested in automobile, bus, truck, and motorcycle advertising memorabilia. Many people collect only
items from a certain marquee, like Hupmobiles or Mus-
tangs, while others may collect all advertising, like match-
books or color brochures showing the new models for a
certain year. Most material changes hands at automobile
swap meets, and specialty auctions held throughout the
year. Notably "hot" items on the market are service station and trucking company hat badges.

References: Mark Anderton and Sherry Mullen, *Gas Station Collectibles*, Wallace-Homestead/Krause, 1994;
Mark Allen Baker, *Auto Racing Memorabilia and Price
Guide*, Krause Publications, 1996; Leila Dunbar, *Automobilia*, Schiffer Publishing, 1998; Scott Benjamin and
Wayne Henderson, *Gas Pump Globes*, Motorbooks International, 1993; Mike Bruner, *Gasoline Treasures*, Schiffer
Publishing, 1996; Bob and Chuck Crisler, *License Plates
of the United States*, Interstate Directory Publishing Co.
(420 Jericho Tpk., Jericho, NY 11753), 1997; Leila Dun-
bar, *Motorcycle Collectibles*, Schiffer Publishing, 1996;
John A. Gunnell, *Car Memorabilia Price Guide*, Krause
Publications, 1995; James K. Fox, *License Plates of the
United States, A Pictorial History 1903 to the Present*, In-
terstate Directory Publishing Co., 1996; Todd Helms and
Chip Flohe, *A Collection of Vintage Gas Station Photo-
graphs*, Schiffer Publishing, 1997; Ron Kowalke and Ken
Buttolph, *Car Memorabilia Price Guide*, 2nd ed., Krause
Publications, 1997; Rick Pease, *A Tour With Texaco*,
Schiffer Publishing, 1997; ——, *Service Station Collecti-
bles*, Schiffer Publishing, 1996; Jim and Nancy Schaut,
American Automobilia, Wallace-Homestead, 1994; Don
Stewart, *Antique Classic Marque Car Keys*, 2nd ed., Key
Collectors International, 1993.

Periodicals: *Hemmings Motor News*, P.O. Box 256, Bennington, VT 05201; *Mobilia*, P.O. Box 575, Middlebury, VT
05753; *Petroleum Collectibles Monthly*, 411 Forest St.,
LaGrange, OH 44050; PL8S, P.O. Box 222, East Texas,
PA 18046; *WOCCO*, 36100 Chardon Rd., Willoughby, OH
44094.

Collectors' Clubs: Automobile Objects D'Art Club, 252 N. 7th St., Allentown, PA 18102; Classic Gauge & Oiler Hounds, Rte 1, Box 9, Farview, SD 57027; Hubcap Collectors Club, P.O. Box 54, Buckley, MI 49620; International Petroliana Collectors Society, P.O. Box 937, Powell, OH 43065; Spark Plug Collectors of America, 14018 NE 85th St., Elk River, MN 55330.

Advisors: Jim and Nancy Schaut.

Badge
   Sinclair Grease, celluloid 300.00
   Trailways Bus Lines, hat, enamel. 225.00
Display Case, 13" h, 13" w, Esso, sixteen unopened bottles
   . . . . 120.00
Grill Badge, Sports Car Club of America, wire wheel logo, black
   and red cloisonné. 50.00
Oil Bottle, 14-3/4" h, 4" d, Skelly Tagolene, label under glass
   . . . . 125.00
Oil Can, quart size
   Ben Hur Motor Oil, 5-1/2" h, 3-7/8" d, full, unopened, bright
     red ground, black and white lettering 325.00
   Bisonoil, 5-1/2" h, 4" d, Bison Motor Co., Buffalo, NY, tin litho,
     crimped seam, red and black buffalo image 425.00
   Tiopet Oil, 5-1/2" h, 4" d, Tiona Petroleum, Phila, tin litho, sol-
     dered seam, Indian chief on front 700.00
Original Art, 15" h, 19" l, painting of Jenkintown Buick Service
   Station, Clyde S. Adams, artist, 1926, pencil and watercolor,
   matted and framed 125.00
Pen Holder, General Motors Trucks, Yellow Cabs, and Coach-
   es, Pontiac, MI, factory scene, porcelain blue, white, and gold
   inserts, bronze, 5" d, pen missing 80.00
Pennant, 11" h, 32" l, Fisk Tires, felt, painted image of Fisk Tires
   Kid 250.00
Service Pin
   Buick, 25 years, screwback, 10K gold 50.00
   Lincoln-Mercury, 10K gold filled, hatpin type back with clasp
   . . . . 25.00
   Shell Oil, 15 year tiebar, 10K gold, dated 1944 . . . . . . 75.00
Sign
   Esso Girl, Bonne Route, 15" h, 5-3/8" w, French diecut tin
   . . . . 300.00

Clock, Ford trademark, octagon, neon, 18" x 18", $650. Photo courtesy of James D. Julia, Inc.

Power-Lube Motor Oil, 20" h, 28" l, two-sided porcelain,
   prowling tiger 1,400.00
Rex Spark Plugs, 9-1/8" h, 6-1/4" w, tin litho over cardboard,
   beveled corners, dark background, red and white logo and
   spark plug 450.00
Tire Patch Repair Kit, Blenord/Cornell Tires (Pep Boys), tin, orig
   contents 25.00

BACCARAT GLASS

History: The Sainte-Anne glassworks at Baccarat in Voges, France, was founded in 1764 and produced utilitarian soda glass. In 1816, Aime-Gabriel d'Artiques purchased the glassworks, and a Royal Warrant was issued in 1817 for the opening of Verrerie de Vonâoche éa Baccarat. The firm concentrated on lead-crystal glass products. In 1824, a limited company was created.

From 1823 to 1857, Baccarat and Saint-Louis glassworks had a commercial agreement and used the same outlets. No merger occurred. Baccarat began the production of paperweights in 1846. In the late 19th century, the firm achieved an international reputation for cut glass table services, chandeliers, display vases, centerpieces, and sculptures. Products eventually included all forms of glassware. The firm still is active today.

Reference: Jean-Louis Curtis, *Baccarat*, Harry N. Abrams, 1992; Paul Jokelson and Dena Tarshis, *Baccarat Paperweights and Related Glass*, Paperweight Press, 1990 (distributed by Charles E. Tuttle Co.).

Additional Listings: Paperweights.

Ashtray, 4-1/2" d, Pinwheel, sgd 85.00
Atomizer, 5" h, 3-1/2" l, oval, etched crystal body, metal chrome
   top, sgd. 90.00
Biscuit Jar, cov, 6" h, crystal, etched ground, cranberry flowers,
   leaves, and vines, marked inside lid. 600.00
Bookends, pr, 12" h, crystal, serpentine tube on molded rocky
   form base, etched "Baccarat, France" 150.00
Bowl, 5-1/2" d, cameo, colorless etched leaf ground, carved
   chartreuse floral dec. 100.00
Brandy Snifter, crystal, gilded foliate cartouche, monogrammed
   "N," set of 12. . . . . 275.00
Calling Card Holder, 5-1/2" h, opaline, fan shape, pedestal base,
   relief butterflies, trees, and flowers, sgd. 195.00
Candlesticks, pr, 9" h, Swirled. 225.00
Celery Tray, 9-1/2" l, 3-1/2" w, Rose Tiente 45.00
Champagne Bucket, 9-1/4" h, tapering cylinder, rect stop fluted
   molded sides, stamped "Baccarat, France" 400.00
Cologne Bottle, 5-1/2" h, Rose Tiente, Diamond Point Swirl, orig
   stopper 125.00
Creamer, 4-1/2" h, lacy, colorless, minor chips 90.00
Decanter, 8-1/2" h, crystal, cut, orig stopper, mkd "Baccarat
   France". 110.00
Dish, 8-3/4" l, oval, lacy, colorless, minor chips 80.00
Dresser Jar, cov, 2-1/2" h, 4-1/2" w, cranberry cut to green base,
   finely textured bark-like ground, finely cut tiny flowers and
   leaves, irregular border bands, gold checkerboard type pat-
   tern, mkd in pontil, monogrammed lid marked "Sterling"
   . . . . 2,350.00

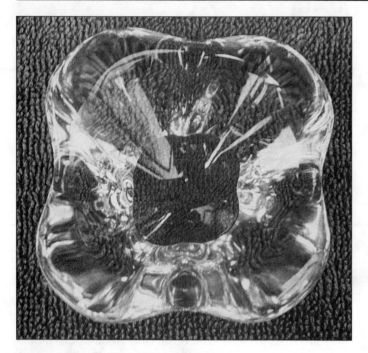

Salt, colorless, 2-1/2" w, $30.

Fairy Lamp, 3-7/8" h, shaded white to clear 275.00
Goblet, Perfection pattern 40.00
Heart, crystal, orig box 80.00
Jar, cov
   6" h, 3-3/4" d, sapphire blue, Swirl, mkd 95.00
   7" d, cameo cut, gilt metal mounts, imp "Baccarat" . . 350.00
Jewelry Box, cov, 4" d, 2-3/4" h, hinged lid, Button and Bow pattern, sapphire blue, brass fittings 145.00
Mustard Jar, cov, 3" d, 5" h, Rose Tiente, Swirl 85.00
Perfume Bottle, black, Art Deco style, D'Orsay. 225.00
Rose Bowl, 3" d, cranberry, lace enamel dec 155.00
Sugar Bowl, cov, 7-1/4" h, lacy, colorless, rim chips. . . . 95.00
Sweetmeat Jar, cov, cranberry colored strawberries, blossoms, and leaves, cut back to clear ground of ferns, silver plated cover and handle, sgd 350.00
Toasting Goblet, 7" h, #340103, pr 150.00
Tumbler, 3-1/2" h, Rose Tiente 5.00
Tumble-Up, carafe and tumbler, Rose Tiente, Swirl pattern
  . . . . 350.00
Vase
   9-1/4" h, ovoid, crystal, large thumbprint design, acid stamped mark 200.00
   10-1/4" h, inverted bell form, five etched urns with tall scrolling branches, printed factory mark, 20th C 800.00

BANKS, MECHANICAL

History: Banks which display some form of action while accepting a coin are considered mechanical banks. Mechanical banks date back to ancient Greece and Rome, but the majority of collectors are interested in those made between 1867 and 1928 in Germany, England, and the United States. Recently, there has been an upsurge of interest in later types, some of which date into the 1970s.

Initial research suggested that approximately 250 to 300 different or variant designs of banks were made in the early period. Today that number has been revised to 2,000-3,000 types and varieties. The field remains ripe for discovery and research.

More than 80% of all cast-iron mechanical banks produced between 1869 and 1928 were made by J. E. Stevens Co., Cromwell, Connecticut. Tin banks are usually of German origin.

References: *Collectors Encyclopedia of Toys and Banks*, L-W Book Sales, 1986, 1993 value update; Al Davidson, Penny Lane, *A History of Antique Mechanical Toy Banks*, Long's Americana, 1987; Don Duer, *A Penny Saved: Still and Mechanical Banks*, Schiffer Publishing, 1993; Bill Norman, *The Bank Book: The Encyclopedia of Mechanical Bank Collecting*, Collectors' Showcase, 1984.

Collectors' Club: Mechanical Bank Collectors of America, P.O. Box 128, Allegan, MI 49010.

REPRODUCTION ALERT

Reproductions, fakes, and forgeries exist for many banks. Forgeries of some mechanical banks were made as early as 1937, so age alone is not a guarantee of authenticity. In the following price listing, two asterisks indicate banks for which serious forgeries exist, and one asterisk indicates banks for which casual reproductions have been made.

Notes: While rarity is a factor in value, appeal of design, action, quality of manufacture, country of origin, and history of collector interest also are important. Radical price fluctuations may occur when there is an imbalance in these factors. Rare banks may sell for a few hundred dollars while one of more common design with greater appeal will sell in the thousands.

The values in the list below accurately represent the selling prices of mechanical banks in the specialized collectors' market. As some banks are hard to find, and the market is quite volatile both up and down in price structure, consultation of a competent specialist in mechanical banks, with up to the moment information, is advised prior to selling any mechanical bank.

The prices listed are for original old mechanical banks with no repairs, in sound operating condition, and with a majority of the original paint intact.

Advisor: James S. Maxwell Jr.

Note: Prices quoted are for 100% original examples, with no repairs, no repaint, and have at least 90% bright original paint. An asterisk indicates casual reproductions. A † denotes examples where casual reproductions and serious fakes exist.

†Acrobat 1,500.00
†Afghanistan 675.00
African Bank, black bust, back emb "African Bank" 750.00
American Bank, sewing machine 600.00
*Artillery 1,800.00
Atlas, iron, steel, wood, paper. 750.00
Automatic Chocolate Vending, tin 750.00
Automatic Coin Savings, predicts future, tin 250.00
Automatic Fortune Bank, tin 4,500.00
Automatic Savings Bank, tin, soldier 300.00

Automatic Savings Bank, tin, sailor................ 200.00
Automatic Surprise Money Box, wood 6,500.00
†Baby Elephant X-O'clock, lead and wood........ .2,000.00
*Bad Accident 3,700.00
Bambovila, black bust, back emb "Bambula" 3,000.00
Bank Teller, man behind 3-sided fancy grillwork..... .5,500.00
Bank of Education and Economy, must have orig paper reel
.... .2,800.00
Barking Dog, wood 500.00
Bear, tin............................... 375.00
†Bear and Tree Stump 3,500.00
†Bear, slot in chest 400.00
†Bill E. Grin........................... 500.00
†Billy Goat Bank 350.00
Bird In Cage, tin 250.00
†Bird on Roof 1,245.00
†Bismark Bank .... .15,000.00
Bonzo, tin 350.00
Book-Keepers Magic Bank, tin......... .22,000.00
Bow-ery Bank, iron, paper, wood 2,500.00
Bowing Man in Cupola 3,200.00
†Bowling Alley......................... .4,500.00
†Boy Robbing Birds Nest 1,750.00
*Boy Scout Camp 2,500.00
†Boy and bull dog 8,500.00
†Boy on trapeze 6,000.00
†Boys stealing watermelons 1,350.00
Bread Winners 2,700.00
British Clown, tin...................... 12,000
†Bucking Mule........................ .4,500.00
*Bull Dog, place coin on nose 3,700.00
†Bull and Bear....................... .75,000.00
Bull Dog Savings, clockwork........... .1,000.00
†Bull Dog, standing................... .1,500.00
Bureau, wood, Serrill patent 4,500.00
Bureau, Lewando's, wood............. .18,000.00
Bureau, wood, John R. Jennings Patent........ .5,500.00
Burnett Postman, tin man with tray 3,500.00
†Butting Buffalo....................... 850.00
†Butting Goat 2,700.00
†Butting Ram 375.00
*Cabin, black man flips 1,400.00
Caller Vending, tin.................... .3,500.00
†Calamity 4,500.00
†Called Out.......................... .2,800.00
Calumet, tin and cardboard, with Calumet kid 200.00
Calumet, tin and cardboard, with sailor........... .14,000.00
Calumet, tin and cardboard, with soldier.......... .18,000.00
†Camera............................. .1,100.00
*Cat and Mouse 1,200.00
†Cat and Mouse, giant cat standing on top........ .30,000.00
Chandlers 2,000.00
Chandlers with clock.................. 350.00
*Chief Big Moon 1,800.00
Child's Bank, wood 850.00
Monkey, pot metal, nods head 750.00
Monkey, chimpanzee in ornate circular blgd, iron..... .1,050.00
Chinaman in Boat, lead................ .3,500.00
Chinaman with queue, tin 400.00
Chocolate Menier, tin 1,750.00
†Chrysler Pig........................ 400.00
Cigarette Vending, tin 700.00
Cigarette Vending, lead............... .2,000.00
Circus, clown on card in circular ring 2,000.00
†Circus, ticket collector.............. 350.00
Clever Dick, tin 200.00

Clown Bust, iron 5,050.00
Clown, Chein, tin..................... 65.00
†Clown on Bar, tin and iron........... .2,800.00
*Clown on Globe...................... .5,500.00
Clown and Dog, tin 250.00
Clown with arched top, tin............ 250.00
Clown with black face, tin 2,000.00
Clown with white face, tin 125.00
Clown with white face, round, tin...... .3,700.00
Cockatoo Pelican, tin 200.00
Coin Registering, many variants 25.00-1,000.00
Columbian Magic Savings, iron........ 200.00
Columbian magic Savings, wood and Paper ...... .15,000.00
Confectionery 2,200.00
Coolie Bust, lead.................... 400.00
Cowboy with tray, tin................ 350.00
†Creedmoor 1,275.00
Crescent Cash Register 4,200.00
Cross Legged Minstrel, tin 350.00
Crowing Rooster, circular base, tin...... .6,500.00
Cupid at Piano, pot metal, musical 750.00
†Cupola............................ .1,050.00
Dapper Dan, tin.................... .2,500.00
*Darktown Battery.................. .3,500.00
Darky Bust, tin, tiny size 200.00
†Darky Fisherman, lead 8,500.00
†Darky Watermelon, man kicks football at watermelon
.... .7,500.00
†Dentist........................... .3,700.00
Dinah, iron........................ 500.00
Dinah, aluminum................... 250.00
Ding Dong Bell, tin, windup........ .3,500.00
Dog on turntable 950.00
†Dog with tray..................... 650.00
Domed vending, tin................ .4,000.00
Driver's Service Vending, tin........ .2,800.00
Droste Chocolate 1,500.00
*Eagle and Eaglettes.............. .1,200.00
Electric Safe, steel 2,200.00
*Elephant and Three Clowns 1,850.00
*Elephant, locked howdah.......... 450.00
Elephant, made in Canada 6,500.00
Elephant, man pops out, wood, cloth, iron 550.00
†Elephant, no stars............... .3,700.00
*Elephant, pull tail................ .1,050.00
Elephant, three stars.............. .1,200.00
*Elephant, trunk swings, large....... 350.00
*Elephant, trunk swings, small 250.00
Elephant, trunk swings, raised coin slot 1,500.00
†Elephant with tusks, on wheels....... 500.00
Empire Cinema, tin 700.00
English Bulldog, tin 450.00
Feed the Goose, pot metal 800.00
5 cents Adding 250.00
Flip the Frog, tin 375.00
Football, English football.......... .1,800.00
Fortune Savings, tin, horse race...... .1,050.00
Fortune Teller, Savings, safe,...... .2,200.00
†Fowler........................... .2,200.00
†Freedman's Bank, wood, lead, brass, tin, paper, etc.
.... .75,000.00
Frog on arched track, tin.......... .1,200.00
Frog on rock 1,400.00
*Frog on round base 950.00
†Frogs, two frogs 1,200.00
Fun Producing Savings, tin........ .2,200.00
*Gem, dog with blgd 2,800.00

German Sportsman, lead and iron 1,500.00
German Vending, tin. 1,500.00
†Germania Exchange, iron, lead, tin. 2,000.00
†Giant in Tower. 1,200.00
†Giant, standing by rock 2,700.00
Girl Feeding Geese, tin, paper, lead. 22,000.00
†Girl Skipping Rope 16,000.00
†Girl in Victorian chair. 2,000.00
Give Me A Penny, wood 8,000.00
Grenadier 1,875.00
Guessing, man's figure, lead, steel, iron. 8,800.00
Guessing, woman's figure, iron. 2,200.00
Guessing, woman's figure, lead 1,400.00
Gwenda Money Box, tin 3,500.00
Hall's Excelsior, iron, wood. 750.00
Hall's Liliput, no tray 400.00
Hall's Liliput, with tray 250.00
†Harlequin. 7,500.00
Harold Lloyd, tin 450.00
Hartwig and Vogel, vending, tin 1,500.00
Hen and Chick. 1,650.00
Highwayman, tin 650.00
Hillman Coin Target 1,500.00
*Hindu, bust. 750.00
†Hold the Fort, 2 varieties, each. 1,050.00
Home, tin building 950.00
*Home, iron. 400.00
Hoop-La 5,500.00
*Horse Race, 2 varieties, each 2,000.00
†Humpty Dumpty, bust of clown with name on back, iron
. . . . .2,800.00
Humpty Dumpty, aluminum, English. 350.00
Huntley and Palmers, tin, vending 1,400.00
*I Always Did 'spise a Mule, black man on bench. 1,050.00
*I Always Did 'spise a Mule, black man on mule. 1,550.00
Ideal Bureau, tin 3,700.00
*Indian and Bear 1,250.00
†Indian Chief, black man bust with Indian feathered headdress,
aluminum 750.00
Indiana Paddlewheel Boat .1,050.00
†Initiating Bank, first degree 1,000.00
Initiating Bank, second degree 1,200.00
*Jolly Nigger, American. 650.00
*Jolly Nigger, English 350.00
Jolly Nigger, lettering in Greek 375.00
Jolly Nigger, lettering in Arabic 1,500.00
*Jolly Nigger, raises hat, lead 1,500.00
*Jolly Nigger, raises hat, iron 2,200.00
*Jolly Nigger, stationary ears 250.00
*Jolly Nigger, stationary eyes 450.00
"Jolly Nigger, with fez, aluminum 750.00
Japanese Ball Tosser, tin, wood, paper 1,875.00
John R. Jennings Trick Drawer Money Box, wood . . .15,000.00
Joe Socko Novelty Bank, tin 250.00
John Bull's Money Box 2,000.00
Jolly Joe Clown, tin 3,200.00
Jolly Sambo Bank 2,800.00
*Jonah and The Whale Bank, large rectangular base
. . . . .2,000.00
†Jonah and The Whale Bank, stands on 2 ornate legs with rect-
angular coin box at center 8,500.00
†Jumbo, elephant on wheels 500.00
Kick Inn Bank, wood 2,200.00
Kiltie 650.00
Lawrence Steinberg's Bureau Bank, wood. 12,000.00
†Leap Frog 2,200.00

Frog, round lattice base, $950.

Lehmann Berlin Tower, tin 350.00
Lehmann,. London Tower, tin 400.00
†Light of Asia 450.00
†Lighthouse Bank 500.00
Lion, tin 575.00
Lion Hunter 1,650.00
†Lion and Two Monkeys 1,850.00
*Little High Hat 1,500.00
Little Jocko, tin 650.00
*Little Joe Bank 950.00
Little Moe Bank 350.00
Lucky wheel Money Box, tin 3,500.00
*Magic Bank, iron house 650.00
Magic Bank, tin 300.00
Magic, safe, tin 450.00
†Magician 1,800.00
†Mama Katzenjammer 2,650.00
†Mammy and Child 2,000.00
*Mason 2,800.00
Memorial Money Box 400.00
*Merry-Go-Round, mechanical, coin activates 2,800.00
†Merry-Go-Round, semi-mechanical, spin by hand 750.00
Mickey Mouse, tin 2,350.00
Mikado Bank 7,500.00
†Milking Cow. 3,600.00
Minstrel, tin 2,800.00
Model Railroad Drink Dispenser, tin 15,000.00
Model Savings Bank, tin, cash register. 4,200.00
*Monkey and Coconut. 1,600.00
Monkey and Parrot, tin 1,400.00
†Monkey Bank 1,450.00
Monkey Face, tin with arched top 3,200.00
†Monkey, slot in stomach 350.00
Monkey, tin, tips hat 450.00
Monkey with Tray, tin 875.00
Mosque 450.00
Motor Bank, coin activates trolley 2,000.00
Mule Entering Barn 1,875.00
Music Bank, tin 375.00
Musical Church, wood. 575.00

Musical Savings Bank, Regina 2,800.00
Musical Savings, tin 325.00
Musical Savings, velvet covered easel 450.00
Musical Savings, velvet covered frame. 500.00
Musical Savings, wood house. 950.00
National Bank 950.00
National, Your Savings, cash register. 2,800.00
Nestle's Automatic Chocolate, cardboard, vending . . .2,800.00
*New Bank, lever at center 400.00
*New Bank, lever at left. 300.00
†New Creedmoor Bank. 320.00
Nodding Clown, pewter and Brass 675.00
Nodding Dog, painted tin. 375.00
†North Pole Bank 1,875.00
*Novelty Bank 1,450.00
Octagonal Fort Bank. 1,600.00
Old Mother Hubbard, tin 750.00
*Organ Bank, boy and girl. 950.00
*Organ Bank, cat and dog. 750.00
*Organ Bank, medium, only monkey figure. 450.00
*Organ Bank, tiny, only monkey figure 350.00
Organ Grinder and Dancing Bear. 1,275.00
Owl, slot in book 275.00
Owl, slot in head 325.00
*Owl, turns head 400.00
*Paddy and the Pig 1,850.00
Panorama Bank 1,675.00
Pascal Chocolate Cigarettes, vending, tin 1,800.00
Patronize the Blind Man 1,200.00
Pay Phone Bank, iron. 2,800.00
Pay Phone Bank, tin. 450.00
†Peg-Leg Beggar 675.00
*Pelican, Arab head pops out 575.00
*Pelican, Mammy head pops out 525.00
*Pelican, man thumbs nose 500.00

Organ Bank, cat and dog, Ksyer & Rex Co., $750.

*Pelican, rabbit pops out 450.00
†Perfection Registering, girl and dog at blackboard . . .1,850.00
Piano, musical. 450.00
*Picture Gallery 2,650.00
Pig in High Chair 450.00
Pinball Vending, tin 1,600.00
Pistol Bank, iron 575.00
Pistol Bank, iron, Uncle Sam figure pops out 2,200.00
Pistol Bank, litho, tin 3,700.00
Pistol Bank, sheet steel. .1,200.00
Policeman, tin 500.00
Popeye Knockout, tin 1,650.00
Post Office Savings, steel. 1,700.00
†Preacher in the Pulpit 9,500.00
†Presto, iron building 950.00
Presto, mouse on roof, wood and paper. 950.00
*Presto, penny changes optically to quarter 1,275.00
*Professor Pug Frog 4,200.00
Pump and Bucket 4,700.00
*Punch and Judy, iron. 2,450.00
Punch and Judy, iron front, tin back 750.00
Punch and Judy, litho tin, circa 1910 . . . . 475.00
Punch and Judy, litho tin, circa 1930 . . . . 275.00
†Queen Victoria. bust, brass. 2,800.00
†Queen Victoria, bust, iron. 4,200.00
Rabbit in Cabbage 350.00
†Rabbit Standing, large. 675.00
†Rabbit Standing, small 375.00
Reclining Chinaman with cards. 2,100.00
Record Money Box, tin scales. 5,500.00
†Red Riding Hood, iron. 3,300.00
Red Riding Hood, tin, vending 1,500.00
†Rival Bank. 2,650.00
Robot Bank, aluminum 650.00
Robot Bank, iron 1,050.00
Roller-Skating Bank 2,850.00
Rooster 1,600.00
Royal Trick Elephant, tin. .5,500.00
Safe Deposit Bank, tin, elephant. 1,650.00
Safety Locomotive, semi. .1,850.00
Sailor Face, tin, pointed top 3,200.00
Sailor Money Box, wood 450.00
Saluting Sailor, tin. 850.00
Sam Segal's Aim to Save, brass and wood 1,300.00
Sam Segal's Aim to Save, iron 1,800.00
*Santa Claus. 1,650.00
Savo, circular, tin. 650.00
Savo, rectangular, tin 575.00
†Schley Bottling Up Cevera 975.00
Schokolade Automat, tin, vending. 1,450.00
School Teacher, tin and wood, American 1,200.00
School Teacher, tin, German 675.00
Scotchman, tin 1,875.00
Seek Him Frisk 3,200.00
Sentry Bank, tin. 375.00
Sentry Bugler, tin. 275.00
†Shoot That Hat Bank. 2,700.00
†Shoot the Chute Bank. 2,300.00
Signal Cabin, tin 1,875.00
†Smith X-ray Bank 1,275.00
Snake and Frog in Pond, tin 12,000.00
*Snap-It Bank 1,400.00
Snow White, tin and lead 875.00
*Speaking Dog 1,875.00
Spring Jawed Alligator, pot metal 250.00
Spring Jawed Bonzo, pot metal 250.00

Stump Speaker, Shepard Hardware Co., Buffalo, NY, $2,800.

Spring Jawed Bulldog, pot metal	225.00
Spring Jawed Cat, pot metal	275.00
Spring Jawed Chinaman, pot metal	1,400.00
Spring Jawed Donkey, pot metal	225.00
Spring Jawed Felix the Cat, pot metal	3,700.00
Spring Jawed Mickey Mouse, pot metal	12,500.00
Spring Jawed Monkey, pot metal	225.00
Spring Jawed Parrot, pot metal	250.00
Spring Jawed Penguin, pot metal	275.00
Springing Cat	4,200.00
†Squirrel and Tree Stump	675.00
Starkies Aeroplane, aluminum, cardboard	12,000.00
Starkies Aeroplane, aluminum, steel	16,000.00
Stollwerk Bros., vending, tin	1,050.00
Stollwerk Bros., 2 penny, vending, tin	1,400.00
Stollwerk Bros., Progressive Sampler, tin	375.00
Stollwerk Bros., Victoria, spar-automat, tin	950.00
Stollwerk Bros., large vending, tin	1,600.00
*Stump Speaker Bank	2,800.00
Sweet Thrift, tin, vending	575.00
Symphonium Musical Savings, wood	2,400.00
†Tabby	375.00
*Tammany Bank	375.00
Tank and Cannon, aluminum	2,000.00
Tank and Cannon, iron	2,800.00
†Target Bank	875.00
†Target In Vestibule	950.00
*Teddy and The Bear	1,650.00
Ten Cent Adding Bank	3,800.00
Thrifty Animal Bank, tin	850.00
Thrift Scotchman, wood, paper	4,500.00
Thrifty Tom's Jigger, tin	2,500.00
Tid-Bits Money Box, tin	350.00
Tiger, tin	450.00
Time Is Money	1,050.00
Time Lock Savings	575.00
Time Registering Bank	750.00

*Toad on Stump	750.00
Toilet Bank, tin	650.00
Tommy Bank	950.00
Treasure Chest Music Bank	250.00
*Trick Dog, 6 part base	2,300.00
*Trick Dog, solid base	850.00
*Trick Pony Bank	1,200.00
Trick Savings, wood, end drawer	950.00
Trick Savings, wood, side drawer	950.00
Tropical Chocolate Vending, tin	3,000.00
Try your Weight, tin, semi	950.00
Try Your Weight, tin, mechanical	2,600.00
†Turtle Bank	3,200.00
Twentieth Century Savings Bank	500.00
Two Ducks Bank, lead	9,000.00
U.S. Bank, Building	850.00
†U.S. and Spain	1,200.00
†Uncle Remus Bank	1,275.00
†Uncle Sam Bank, standing figure with satchel	1,875.00
†Uncle Sam, bust	400.00
†Uncle Tom, no lapels, with star	425.00
†Uncle Tom, lapels, with star	400.00
†Uncle Tom, no star	350.00
United States Bank, safe	550.00
Viennese soldier	1,050.00
Volunteer bank	950.00
Watch Bank, blank face, tin	200.00
Watch Bank, dime disappears, tin	275.00
Watch Bank, stamped face, tin	140.00
Watchdog Safe	650.00
Weeden's Plantation, tin, wood	850.00
Weight Lifter, tin	650.00
Whale Bank, pot metal	850.00
*William Tell, iron	2,175.00
William Tell, crossbow, Australian, sheet steel, aluminum	3,200.00
Wimbledon Bank	1,500.00
Winner Savings Bank, tin	1,050.00
Wireless Bank, tin, wood, iron	875.00
Woodpecker Bank, tin	875.00
World's Banker, tin	750.00
*World's Fair Bank	1,200.00
Zentral Sparkasse, steel	1,350.00
Zig Zag Bank, iron, tin, papier-mâché	4,200.00
*Zoo	1,500.00

BANKS, STILL

History: Banks with no mechanical action are known as still banks. The first still banks were made of wood or pottery or from gourds. Redware and stoneware banks, made by America's early potters, are prized possessions of today's collectors.

Still banks reached a golden age with the arrival of the cast-iron bank. Leading manufacturing companies include Arcade Mfg. Co., J. Chein & Co., Hubley, J. & E. Stevens, and A. C. Williams. The banks often were ornately painted to enhance their appeal. During the cast-iron era, banks and other businesses used the still bank as a form of advertising.

The tin lithograph bank, again frequently a tool for advertising, reach its zenith during the years 1930 to 1955. The tin bank was an important premium, whether a Pabst Blue Ribbon beer can bank or a Gerber's Orange Juice bank. Most tin advertising banks resembled the packaging of the product.

Almost every substance has been used to make a still bank—die-cast white metal, aluminum, brass, plastic, glass, etc. Many of the early glass candy containers also converted to a bank after the candy was eaten. Thousands of varieties of still banks were made, and hundreds of new varieties appear on the market each year.

References: Savi Arbola and Marco Onesti, *Piggy Banks*, Chronicle Books, 1992; *Collector's Encyclopedia of Toys and Banks*, L-W Book Sales, 1986, 1993 value update; Don Duer, *Penny Banks Around the World*, Schiffer Publishing, 1997; Earnest Ida and Jane Pitman, *Dictionary of Still Banks*, Long's Americana, 1980; Andy and Susan Moore, *Penny Bank Book, Collecting Still Banks*, Schiffer Publishing, 1984, 1997 value update; Tom and Loretta Stoddard, *Ceramic Coin Banks*, Collector Books, 1997.

Periodical: *Glass Bank Collector*, P.O. Box 155, Poland, NY 13431.

Collectors' Club: Still Bank Collectors Club of America, 4175 Millersville Rd., Indianapolis, IN 46205.

Museum: Margaret Woodbury Strong Museum, Rochester, NY.

Cast Iron

Andy Gump, leaning against box of money, money bag finial, metal insert, 5" x 6" 350.00
Beehive, gold paint, 2-1/2" h 150.00
Black Boy, two faces, polychrome repaint, 4" h 65.00
Boy Scout Camper, J & E Stevens Co., c1915, 9-7/8" l base
. . . . .1,150.00
Building
    Bank, cupola, polychrome dec, 5-1/2" h 145.00
    House, two story, green and silver dec, 4-1/8" h 120.00
    Palace, 7-3/4" h, Ives, 1885, traces of accent gilding
    . . . . 980.00
    State Bank, Kenton, c1900, 8" l 260.00
    Villa, Kyser & Rex, c1894, 5-5/8" h 920.00
Buster Brown and Tige, A. C. Williams, gilt with red accents, 5-1/4" h, c1910 . . . . 115.00
Cat with Ball, 5-5/8" d, dark gray and black cat playing with gold ball, A. C. Williams, c1905 . . . . 345.00
Donkey, traces of gold paint, 4-1/2" h 60.00
Elephant, howdah, very work red paint over gold, 3-1/2" h
. . . . 60.00
Ford Delivery, 1932, Ertl, MIB 95.00
Gas Stove, black paint, traces of gold trim, 5-1/2" h 135.00
Globe, red and gold, 5-1/2" h 90.00
Goose, gold paint, 5" h 150.00
Horse, prancing, 4-3/4" l 55.00
Lion, orig gold paint, red mouth, A. C. Williams, 1920s, 6-1/4" h
. . . . 50.00
Mammy, black face, worn polychrome dec, 6" h 160.00
Merry Go Round, worn and faded polychrome, 4-5/8" h
. . . . 150.00
Mulligan, polychrome, 5-3/4" h 145.00
Mutt and Jeff, gold paint, 5-1/4" h 170.00
Owl, "Be Wise Save Money," worn gold paint, 5" h 95.00
Pig
    Seated, gold paint, 4-1/2" l 55.00
    Standing, worn green paint over gold, replaced screw, 7" l
    . . . . 50.00

Rabbit, gold paint, 5-1/4" h 100.00
Rooster, worn red and gold paint, 4-7/8" h 70.00
Safe
    Daisy, tin sides and back, nickel plated, 3-1/2" h 35.00
    Ideal Security, 5-1/2" h 45.00
Sailor, worn polychrome dec, 5-1/4" h 145.00
Sewing Machine, Singer trademark 300.00
Soldier, tan and gold paint, 6" h 90.00
Tank, worn gold paint, 4-3/8" l 100.00
Turkey, brown japanning and red paint, 3-1/2" h 145.00
Zeppelin, *Graf*, 6-3/4" l 170.00

Ceramic/Pottery

Advertising, figural acorn, "Acorn Stoves will save half your fuel money," green glaze, 3" h 70.00
Cat's Head, white clay, green glaze, 3" h 115.00
Cylindrical, emb hen and chicks, redware, 12" h 500.00
Dog's Head, molded fur and retriever-type features, green glaze on dark brown clay, 3-1/2" h. 265.00
Dutch Girl, worn polychrome, 4-3/4" h, chips 60.00
Elf's Head, white clay, brown glaze, 3-5/8" h 60.00
Jug, wide ovoid body, tapering from button finial, Albany brown slip glaze, 6-3/8" h 200.00
Lion, Hubert, Lefton. 45.00
Pear, naturalistic yellow-green glaze, pink blush, 3-7/8" h
. . . . 120.00
Piggy, American Bisque, large 65.00
Uncle Sam, blue and white, 4-1/2" h 20.00

Chalk

Dove, 11" h, worn green, red, and yellow ochre paint. . . 250.00
Pig, 7-1/8" l, old white repaint, pink ears 90.00

Tin, Commonwealth Bank, Registering and Savings, patented 1905 and 1915, Shank Works, American Can Co., Maywood, IL, green and yellow, 4" x 5-1/2" x 5-1/4", $60.

Glass

Bank of Independence Hall, clear, tin base, 7-1/4" h, chips
. . . . 65.00
Clock, mantle type, painted, tin closure, 3-3/4" h 40.00
Devil, worn red paint, 4-1/2" h 165.00
Dog, sitting on drum, 4-1/8" h 85.00
Donkey, polychrome dec, 7" h 140.00
Duck, round, polychrome dec, 4" h 190.00
Elephant, gold and red, replaced tin wheels, 4" h, minor wear
. . . . 190.00
Log Cabin, milk glass, paper insert, worn gold, 3-7/8" h. . 40.00
Pig, painted gold, 4-1/4" l 30.00
Radio, clear, emb details. 35.00
Skookum, clear, mkd "S. Sears, 1916," 3-1/2" h 35.00

Papier-mâché

Advertising, James Taffy, tin top, 7" h 20.00
Charlie McCarthy, "Feed Me...," worn polychrome 45.00
Kewpie, worn polychrome, trap missing, 5" h 40.00
Scottie, pink and white, 5-3/4" h 35.00

Tin

Advertising, Red Circle Coffee, yellow, black letters, red circle,
3-7/8" h. 35.00
Andy Gump, 4-3/8" h, 3" w, 7/8" d, litho images of Gump cartoon
characters on front and back 140.00
Barrel, Happy Days, J. Chein & Co. 45.00
Mailbox, emb "Save for Savings Bonds," red, white, and blue, 9"
h. 60.00

Wood

Fidelity Trust, black and gold, decoupage scenes on sides and
top, drawer, 8-1/2" h. 120.00
First National Bank, worn decoupage, 5-3/4" h. 90.00
Fort, oak, pull-out coin slot, 6-1/8" h, worn 25.00
Tramp Art, secret access to coins, 4" w, 4" d, 6" h 335.00

BARBER BOTTLES

History: Barber bottles, colorful glass bottles found on shelves and counters in barber shops, held the liquids barbers used daily. A specific liquid was kept in a specific bottle, which the barber knew by color, design, or lettering. The bulk liquids were kept in utilitarian containers under the counter or in a storage room.

Barber bottles are found in many types of glass—art glass with various decorations, pattern glass, and commercially prepared and labeled bottles.

References: *Barbershop Collectibles*, L-W Book Sales, 1996; Keith E. Estep, *Shaving Mug & Barber Bottle Book*, Schiffer Publishing, 1995; Richard Holiner, *Collecting Barber Bottles*, Collector Books, 1986; Ralph & Terry Kovel, *Kovels' Bottles Price List*, 10th ed., Crown Publishers, 1996; John Odell, *Digger Odell's Official Antique Bottle and Glass Collector Magazine Price Guide Series*, Vol. 1, published by author (1910 Shawhan Rd,. Morrow, OH 45152), 1995.

Note: Prices are for bottles without original stoppers unless otherwise noted.

Amethyst, enameled flowers. 135.00
Art Glass, cylindrical, bulbous body, long bulbous neck, amethyst and light yellow amber mottled design, all over pink irid, ground mouth, smooth base, 7-1/4" h 325.00

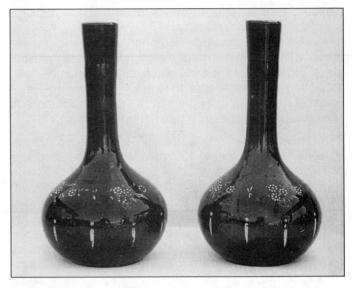

Amethyst, white, orange, and gold raised enamel daisy and dot pattern, 7-1/2" h, pr, $300.

Blue, horizontal brown band design, applied white enamel floral pattern, sheared lip, exposed pontil, 8" h 115.00
Canary, Hobnail pattern, three pouring rings, round lip, smooth base, 7-1/4" h 85.00
Clambroth, emb "Water" in red letters across front, porcelain stopper, 8" h 50.00
Cobalt Blue, bell shape, raised white and orange enameled flowers, sheared lip, exposed pontil, 8-1/2" h 125.00
Colorless, ribbed, dec band around center, gold trim, raised enamel dot pattern, pontil, 6-1/2" h 75.00
Crackle, cranberry, swirl 220.00
Cranberry, rings of hobnails on neck, 6-3/4" h 175.00
Cut Glass, hobstar base, pewter top, 5" h. 90.00
Electric Blue, cylindrical corset waisted form, long neck, opalescent wandering vine dec, tooled mouth, smooth base, 7-1/2" h. 210.00
Emerald Green, cylindrical modified corset waisted form, long neck, lighter green enamel and floral gilt dec, tooled mouth, pontil scar, 7-1/2" h, ... 275.00
Milk Glass, Bay Rum, hand painted pink and white flowers, green leaves, pastel ground, rolled lip, pontil, 9" h. . . 150.00
Opalescent
   Hobbs Hobnail, cranberry. 225.00
   Seaweed, cranberry, teepee shape 495.00
Satin, Hobnail, dark green. 250.00
Spatter, cranberry ground, opalescent white mottling, sq, long neck, tooled mouth, smooth base, 8-1/2" h 160.00

BAROMETERS

History: A barometer is an instrument which measures atmospheric pressure, which, in turn, aids weather forecasting. Low pressure indicates the coming of rain, snow, or storm; high pressure signifies fair weather.

Most barometers use an evacuated and graduated glass tube which contains a column of mercury. These are classified by the shape of the case. An aneroid barometer has no liquid and works by a needle connected to the top of a metal box in which a partial vacuum is maintained. The movement of the top moves the needle.

2-3/4" d, pocket, brass, pocket watch shaped case, mkd "Made in England," worn orig cardboard case with paper label "Henry J. Green, Brooklyn, NY, 1899" 275.00

5-1/2" h, Aneroid, Holosteric, brass, ring hanging mount, mkd "France, USLH Establishment" from New London Lighthouse 295.00

6" h, desk, Gustave Keller, gilt bronze, barometer, thermometer, and clock, c1900 . . . . .1,200.00

15-3/8" l, 5" w, 2-1/4" d, cistern, Currier & Simpson, pat'd Jan. 31, 1860, glass front mahogany case, silver wash barometer and thermometer scales, old instruction sheet 920.00

35-1/4" h, A. S. and J. A., West Rochester, NY, c1840, walnut, rippled molded cornice above glazed panel, framing engraved silvered dial showing temperature and barometric pressure, ripple molded box mirrored base, maker's label on back 635.00

35-3/4" h, 3-1/2" w, 1-5/8" d, stick, Charles Wilder, Peterborough, NH, mahogany, patent date June 5, 1860, cockbeaded case with applied rosette and oval aperture with printed label 1,725.00

37" h, stick, William IV, rosewood, waited case, ivory scale with brass border, sgd "S. A. Callie, Newcastle," c1835 . . . . .1,750.00

37-1/2" h, 4-3/8" w, stick, Charles Wilder, Petterborough, NH, wood case, silver wash and black wax scales, mercury barometer reads 27.00 to 31.00, thermometer 6º to 124º, case needs repair 635.00

38" h, banjo, James Kirby, St. Neotes, early 19th C, walnut, swan's neck cresting above thermometer and barometer, engraved silvered dials, shaped case 425.00

38" h, wheel, S. Crocker, Kingston, mahogany, thermometer and hydrometer 500.00

38-1/2" h, banjo, Pastorelli, Bowling St., Westminster, mahogany, inlaid case, thermometer, silvered dial, sgd, Victorian 650.00

39" h, wheel, late George III, Holbn, London, inlaid mahogany, inlaid shell dec 850.00

40" h, W. Fraiser, Cleveland, Ohio, c1860, walnut, shaped and molded edge, white printed dial with thermometer to the left, continuing to vase and ring split baluster ending in applied turned boss at base 575.00

40-1/2" h, stick, oak case, "Pinkam and Smith," molded case with white painted rect dial above throat thermometer, beveled glass, base with raised panel, molded bracket, England, 19th C. 1,200.00

42-1/2" h, wheel, late Georgian, F. Amadio & Son, London, satinwood, rosewood crossbanding, shrinkage 2,070.00

44" h, split baluster, George III, D. Luvate, Preston, faded mahogany, hygrometer, thermometer, convex mirror, barometer, and level, late 18th C 750.00

50-1/2" h, banjo, V. Zanetti, Manchester, mahogany, 12" d silvered scale, mercury thermometer, hygrometer, spirit level, inscribed name 2,600.00

BASKETS

History: Baskets were invented when man first required containers to gather, store, and transport goods. Today's collectors, influenced by the country look, focus on baskets made of splint, rye straw, or willow. Emphasis is placed on handmade examples. Nails or staples, wide splints which are thin and evenly cut, or a wire bail handle denote factory construction which can date back to the mid-19th century. Decorated painted or woven baskets rarely are handmade, unless they are American Indian in origin.

Baskets are collected by (a) type—berry, egg, or field, (b) region—Nantucket or Shaker, and (c) composition—splint, rye, or willow.

Reference: Don and Carol Raycraft, *Collector's Guide to Country Baskets*, Collector Books, 1985, 1994 value update.

Museums: Heard Museum, Phoenix, AZ; Old Salem, Inc., Winston-Salem, NC.

REPRODUCTION ALERT

Modern reproductions abound, made by diverse groups ranging from craft revivalists to foreign manufacturers.

Note: Limit purchases to baskets in very good condition; damaged ones are a poor investment even at a low price.

3-1/4" h, 10" l, 5" w, key, leather, tapering oval form, decorative tooling and stitching, imp mark "J. H. Laymeyer, Petersburg, VA" on bottom, 19th C, hand reinforced with glue . .1,400.00

4" l, 3-3/4" h, miniature, melon, sgd and dated in ink on handle "Louise 1908," very minor cracks and breaks 265.00

4-1/2" h, 7-3/4" h, splint, pitcher-form, banded rim and base, ash handle, America, 19th C. 900.00

5-3/8" d, 5-1/4" h, Nantucket, Mitchell Ray, 20th C, partial paper label on base, very minor cracks 750.00

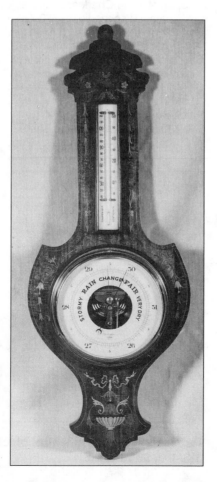

Banjo, Short & Mason, London, #2468, mahogany, inlaid dec, Fahrenheit and centigrade scales, 33-1/2" l, 12-1/2" w, $1,400.

Rye Straw, storage type, 18-1/2" d, $195.

5-3/4" w, 7" l, 3-3/8" h, woven splint, bentwood handle . 200.00

8" l, rect, Eastern Woodland Indian, painted swab dec, fading, breaks. 100.00

8-3/8" d, 4-3/8" h, Nantucket, early 20th C, remnants of paper label. 1,265.00

10-1/4" l, 16" h, picnic, twenty-two ribs, woven natural and colored splint, bentwood handle, double hinged cov . . . 225.00

10-1/2" d, 18" h, weaver's, woven splint, orange and blue watercolor designs, divided in., rounded corners 250.00

11" l, 10" d, 7" h, gathering, plus bentwood handle, woven splint, finely woven 240.00

13" d, 13-1/4" h, splint, circular, banded rim and base, shaped wooden fixed handle, painted blue, America, 19th C 1,380.00

13" l, 14" d, 7-1/2" h, plus handle, market, woven splint, buttocks, red stripe, bentwood handle mkd "Rev. Clerke," minor damage 290.00

13-1/2" d, 9" h, Nantucket, turned and incised wood base, late 19th C. 975.00

13-3/4" d, 9-7/8" h, Nantucket, early 19th C, imperfections 1,265.00

14" d, gathering, splint, painted red and green dec, imperfection 750.00

14" x 17", 8" h plus handle, woven splint, buttocks, tightly woven, wide plaited medial band, wide bentwood handle, pencil inscription on handle "Mrs. W. A. Brown...," found near Lexington, VA 1,450.00

15" d, bread, rye straw, PA, early 20th C, coil work, open handles. 90.00

16-1/4" d, 15-1/4" h, burden, twined weave, worn dyed design, Apache, c1900, wear and missing stitches, native leather repair 250.00

17-3/4" d, 6-1/2" h, cheese, splint, circular, six shaped wooden fixed handles, America, 19th C 850.00

18" d, cotton picking, woven splint, worn blue paint, leather shoulder strap. 400.00

20" d, 9-3/4" h, round, rye straw, bentwood rim handles, wear and rim damage 650.00

Arts & Crafts, bulbous, split-reed, two angular handles, openwork on sides, orig condition 275.00

21-3/4" l, 12" d, 9-1/4" h plus handle, market, woven splint and stick, rect, wooden bottom, damaged rim. 70.00

22" h, field, oak splint, oval, plaited weaving pattern, carved hickory handle. 250.00

BATTERSEA ENAMELS

History: Battersea enamel is a generic term for English enamel-on-copper objects of the 18th century.

In 1753, Stephen Theodore Janssen established a factory to produce "Trinkets and Curiosities Enamelled on Copper" at York House, Battersea, London. Here the new invention of transfer printing developed to a high degree of excellence, and the resulting trifles delighted fashionable Georgian society.

Recent research has shown that enamels actually were being produced in London and the Midlands several years before York House was established. However, most enamel trinkets still are referred to as "Battersea Enamels," even though they were probably made in other workshops in London, Birmingham, Bilston, Wednesbury, or Liverpool.

All manner of charming items were made, including snuff and patch boxes bearing mottos and memory gems. (By adding a mirror inside the lid, a snuff box became a patch box). Many figural whimsies, called "toys," were created to amuse a gay and fashionable world. Many other elaborate articles, e.g., candlesticks, salts, tea caddies, and bonbonnières, were made for the tables of the newly rich middle classes.

Reference: Susan Benjamin, *English Enamel Boxes*, Merrimack Publishers Circle, 1978.

Bonbonnier

Otter's head, natural colors, floral slip on lid, c1770, Bilston 2,650.00

Spaniel, King Charles, oval, black and white, yellow ground, pastoral scene lid, c1770, Bilston 3,200.00

Box, 2" x 1-1/2" d, yellow, bird on nest, inside top fitted with mirror, minor cracking 300.00

Candlestick, 10-1/2" h, white ground, landscape vignettes within pink ground, gilt scroll borders, c1770, Bilston. 4,200.00

Cloak Hooks, 2" l, oval, rose festooned anchors, white ground, c1775, South Staffordshire. 650.00

Patch Box

1-1/2" l, oval, "Always the Same," love birds on white lid, pink base, c1780, Bilston 750.00

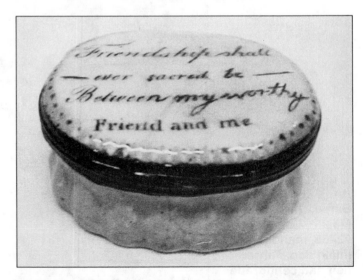

Patch Box, blue and white, black lettering, oval, 1-3/4" l, $300.

2-1/4" l, oval, red checked gingham, green raised ivy, c1770, Bilston 700.00
Scent Bottle Holder, 1/2" x 1-1/4" x 2-1/4", allover pink floral with trellis, leafy green, c1775, Bilston. 400.00
Snuff Box, 2-1/2" l, white, lovers in pastoral setting, ruin background, c1780, Bilston 825.00

BAVARIAN CHINA

History: Bavaria, Germany, was an important porcelain production center, similar to the Staffordshire district in England. The phrase "Bavarian China" refers to the products of companies operating in Bavaria, among which were Hutschenreuther, Thomas, and Zeh, Scherzer & Co. (Z. S. & Co.). Very little of the production from this area was imported into the United States prior to 1870.

Bowl, 10" d, 2-1/4" h, deeply scalloped and scrolled rim, brushed gold trim, large pink roses and buds, green leaves, castle mark and "RC Monbijou" 35.00
Celery Tray, hp, multicolored parrots, white ground 40.00
Chocolate Set, roses and floral bouquets, gold trim, cov chocolate pot, six cups and saucers, price for 13 pc set . . . 225.00
Coffee Set, 9-1/4" h cov coffeepot, creamer, cov sugar, scrolled and melon ribbed blank, multicolored floral dec, gold rim and trim, crown mark with "Bavaria, Creidlitz, Germany," price for 5 pc set. 125.00
Compote, 8-1/4" d, openwork edge, fruit dec 35.00
Demitasse Set, porcelain, white ground, polychrome birds transfer dec, gilt trim, teapot, creamer, sugar, five cups, six saucers, Schwarzenhammer, 20th C, price for 16 pc set
. . . . 45.00
Dish, 7-3/4" x 11-1/4", fluted and scalloped rim, two sections, center scrolled handle, medallions of Venus, Mars, Neptune, blue ground, gold tracery and trim, crown mark with "Royal Bavarian, Germany" 75.00
Dresser Set, hand mirror and brush, hp portrait of lady, long flowing hair entwined with gold streamers and flowers, ornate handles, mkd "R.C. Bavaria," price for 2 pc set 155.00
Fish Set, fish in underwater setting, different scene of each of ten plates and serving platter, mkd "Mignon, Bavaria," price for 11 pc set 1,800.00
Marmalade Jar, cov, matching underplate, two handles, hp pink roses, cream ground, black and gold trim 115.00

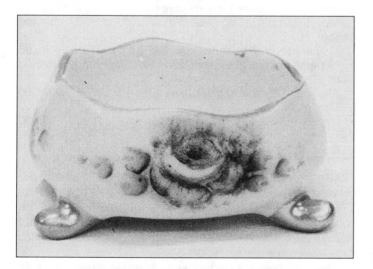

Salt, white int. and ext., two pink roses, green leaves, gold scalloped rim and feet, 2" x 3/4", $24.

Oyster Plate, 9" w, crescent shape, shaded blue ground, five shell shaped depressions, one round shell 115.00
Plaque, 12" d, hp, deer, gold border 85.00
Plate
   7-3/4" d, Arbutus pattern, pink and green draped flowers border, gold trim 12.00
   8-1/2" d, cat and roses 35.00
   10-3/4" d, white center, wide gold encrusted rim band, delicate floral design, mkd "Bavaria," price for 12 pc set
   . . . . 430.00
   11" d, encrusted gold surface with fairies, minor wear and scratches, sgd "Bavaria, Germany" 50.00
Portrait Plate, 10-1/2" d, Edwardian woman, crown mark and "Bayreuth" 100.00
Table Set, hp roses and gold trim, artist sgd, mkd "J & C," creamer, cov sugar, salt and pepper shakers, toothpick holder, price for 5 pc set 150.00
Toothpick Holder, pink flowers, green leaves, shaded ground, gold rim, mkd "Versailles/R C Bavaria" 45.00
Vase, 11-1/2" h, gold luster, floral dec, sgd "Sisters of Notre Dame" 95.00

BELLEEK

History: Belleek, a thin, ivory-colored, almost-iridescent porcelain, was first made in 1857 in county Fermanagh, Ireland. Production continued until World War I, was discontinued for a period of time, and then resumed. The Shamrock pattern is most familiar, but many patterns were made, including Limpet, Tridacna, and Grasses.

There is an Irish saying: If a newly married couple receives a gift of Belleek, their marriage will be blessed with lasting happiness.

Several American firms made a Belleek-type porcelain. The first was Ott and Brewer Co. of Trenton, New Jersey, in 1884, followed by Willets. Other firms producing this ware included The Ceramic Art Co. (1889), American Art China Works (1892), Columbian Art Co. (1893), and Lenox, Inc. (1904).

Marks: The European Belleek company used specific marks during given time periods, which makes it relatively easy to date a piece of Irish Belleek. Variations in mark color are important, as well as the symbols and words.

First mark	Black	Harp, Hound, and Castle	1863-1890
Second mark	Black	Harp, Hound, and Castle and the words "Co. Fermanagh, Ireland"	1891-1826
Third mark	Black	"Deanta in Eirinn" added	1926-1946
Fourth mark	Green	same as third mark except for color	1946-1955
Fifth mark	Green	"R" inside a circle added	1955-1965
Sixth mark	Green	"Co. Fermanagh" omitted	1965- March 1980
Seventh mark	Gold	"Deanta in Eirinn" omitted	April 1980- December 1992
Eighth mark	Blue	Blue version of the second mark with "R" inside a circle added	January 1993- present

References: Susan and Al Bagdade, *Warman's English & Continental Pottery & Porcelain*, 3rd Edition, Krause Publications, 1998; Richard K. Degenhardt, *Belleek*, 2nd ed., Wallace-Homestead, 1993; Mary Frank Gaston, *Collector's Encyclopedia of Knowles, Taylor & Knowles China*, Collector Books, 1996; Timothy J. Kearns, *Knowles, Taylor & Knowles*, Schiffer Publishing, 1994; Marion Langham, *Belleek Irish Porcelain*, Quiller Press, 1993.

Collectors' Club: The Belleek Collectors' Society, 144 W Britannia St., Taunton, MA 02780.

Museum: Museum of Ceramics at East Liverpool, East Liverpool, OH.

Additional Listings: Lenox.

American

Bowl
   5-1/4" d, pearl luster and green, gold trim, three small feet, Willets 50.00
   8-3/4" d, shallow, ruffled sides, roses dec, artist sgd, Willets. 300.00
Chalice, 12" h, hp, monk smoking cigar, Willets 690.00
Charger, 10-1/2" d, hp, gold and bronze enamel floral center, scalloped rim, Willets 190.00
Creamer, 4" h, pale pink ground, gold paste flowers, lavender palette mark, Ceramic Art Co. 90.00
Cup and Saucer
   Bouquet pattern, Coxon 140.00
   Gold paste floral dec, wishbone handle, Ott & Brewer 150.00
Demitasse Set, cov coffeepot, creamer, cov sugar, four ftd cups and saucers, hp, Harvard University tiger and crest, white ground, gold trim, c1899. . . . . 1,200.00
Egg Stand, ftd flat plate pierced with six holes, figural dolphin center handle, applied gold floral dec, sponged gold dec, Ott & Brewer. 125.00
Goblet, 6" h, Princeton University, Willets. 75.00
Hatpin Holder, gold scrolling, green enameled dots on top and base, gold trim 245.00
Lemonade Pitcher, 7" h, 8" d, scalloped top, gold trim, gold scroll handle, yellow, orange, green, and white water lilies dec, Willets 275.00

Bowl, Shell pattern, 3rd black mark, $65.

Mug, 6" h, dragon handle, Willets 275.00
Mustache Cup, gold leaves, butterflies 100.00
Stein, 7-1/4" h, hp, monk drinking from bottle, other bottles tucked in his apron, green palette mark 165.00
Tray, 5" l, lotus leaf shape, hp currents and violets, sgd Willets, pr 160.00
Vase, 6" h, narrow neck tapers to bulbous body, lemon, tan, and light green Art Nouveau florals and swirling ribbons, artist sgd, palette mark 375.00

Irish

Basket, Forget Me Not, #524, 2nd black mark 200.00
Belleek Pot, #538, 2nd black mark 300.00
Biscuit Jar, 8" h, Diamond Pattern, Victoria Tea Ware, 1st black mark 1,200.00
Bust, 10" h, Sorrow, 2nd black mark 2,850.00
Butter, cov, cottage, figural, 6th mark 160.00
Compote, 9-3/4" d, 4-3/4" h, openwork edge, Green pattern, aqua trim, 2nd black mark 675.00
Cornucopia, 7" h, figural cherub holding cornucopia base, 1st black mark 1,800.00
Creamer
   3" h, Irish pattern, ftd, yellow irid int. and handle, 3rd black mark. 65.00
   3" h, Lotus pattern, pink handle and trim, 2nd black mark 70.00
   3-1/2" h, Lily pattern, green handle and trim, 2nd black mark 70.00
Creamer and Sugar
   Ivy pattern, 3rd black mark. 125.00
   Ribbon pattern, 1st green mark 80.00
   Shamrock pattern, 3rd black mark 150.00
Cup and Saucer
   Grass pattern, 1st black mark 265.00
   Harp Shamrock pattern, 3rd black mark. 120.00
   Shell pattern cob luster, 3rd black mark. 85.00
Dish, coral and shell, 6th mark 35.00
Heart Basket
   4" x 4-1/2", #464, 3rd black mark 250.00
   5" x 5", #464, 3rd black mark 350.00
Mustache Cup, Tridacna pattern, first black mark. 125.00
Plate
   8" d, Shell pattern, cob luster, 3rd black mark 85.00
   10-1/2" d, Basketweave pattern, 1st green mark 40.00
Spill Vase, Flower, #509, black mark 150.00
Sugar, cov, Shamrock Basketweave pattern, 2nd black mark 140.00
Teapot, cov
   Limpet pattern, 3rd black mark. 285.00
   Neptune pattern, green trim, 2nd black mark 325.00
Vase
   Aberdeen, #500, 2nd black mark 325.00
   Owl, 8", 6th mark 60.00
   Vintage, 7" x 3-1/2", 6th mark. 70.00

BELLS

History: Bells have been used for centuries for many different purposes. They have been traced as far back as 2697 B.C., though at that time they did not have any true tone. One of the oldest bells is the "crotal," a tiny sphere with small holes, a ball, and a stone or metal interior. This type now appears as sleigh bells.

   True bell making began when bronze, a mixture of tin and copper, was invented. Bells are now made out of many types of materials—almost as many materials as there are uses for them.

Bells of the late 19th century show a high degree of workmanship and artistic style. Glass bells from this period are examples of the glassblower's talent and the glass manufacturer's product.

Collectors' Clubs: American Bell Association, Alter Rd., Box 386, Natrona Heights, PA 15065; American Bell Association International, Inc., 7210 Bellbrook Dr., San Antonio, TX 78227.

Museum: Bell Haven, Tarentum, PA.

Altar, 2-1/2" h, brass, emb angels and Latin script 90.00
Cigar Counter, brass, cast iron base, marked "Russel & Erwin Mfg Co., New Britain, CT, USA, Pat'd Aug. 1, 96, Rd No. 269895" 275.00
Church
    20" d, steeple, molded signature "Made by Meneely Bell Co. at Troy, N.Y., 1911," orig mounting bracket, wooden base 325.00
    27" h, triple, graduated stand, domed cross finial 95.00
Commemorative, 6" h, metal, R.A.F. Victory, 1939-45, R. A. F. Benevolent Fund, emb head of Stalin, Churchill, and Franklin Roosevelt 120.00
Desk
    Side tap, bronze, white marble base, c1875 . . . . 45.00
    Twister type, double chime, c1850 . . . . 75.00
Elephant, 4" h, bronze, Khmer, 14th C 175.00
Fire, 11-1/2" l, hand, metal, iron spring loaded clapper, turned wood handle 225.00
Hand
    Brass, figural
    Napoleon, raised Battle of Waterloo scene 75.00
    Victorian Lady, plumed hat 70.00
    Bronze, figural, windmill, turning blades, emb stonework 90.00

Brass, black metal holding bracket, 9" h x 11" d bell, $400. Photo courtesy of James D. Julia, Inc.

French Faience type, figural, lady 125.00
Glass, 5" h, Bohemian, pink ext. overlay, cream int., amber glass handle, rigaree, and clapper, applied pink and cream flower, green glass leaves 195.00
Pot Metal, police helmet shape, Queen Elizabeth II coronation. 38.00
Pottery, 5-1/4" h, Southern Belle, Ceramic Arts Studio 75.00
Silver, 4-5/8" h, sterling, cupid blowing horn, figural handle, frosted finish, foliate strapwork border, Gorham Mfg Co., c1870. . . . . 725.00
Liberty Bell, 19-1/2" h, brass, black metal holding bracket 400.00
School
    Desk type 25.00
    Hand held, brass, No. 7, wood handle 45.00
Sleigh
    28 brass graduated bells from 1-1/8" to 3-3/4" d, 105" l leather strap. 300.00
    34 bells, leather strap 75.00
    42 bells, straight throats, leather strap 70.00
Souvenir, 5-3/4" h, glass, 1893 World's Far, clear, circular logo surrounded by acid etched florals and banners, int. shoulder emb "1893 WORLD'S COLUMBIAN XPOSITION (sic)", frosted finish twisted handle with star at top, metal clapper, attributed to Libbey Glass. 285.00
Trolley Car, brass 150.00

BENNINGTON and BENNINGTON-TYPE POTTERY

J. NORTON
BENNINGTON
VT.

History: In 1845, Christopher Webber Fenton joined Julius Norton, his brother-in-law, in the manufacturing of stoneware pottery in Bennington, Vermont. Fenton sought to expand the company's products and glazes; Norton wanted to concentrate solely on stoneware. In 1847, Fenton broke away and established his own factory.

Fenton introduced to America the famous Rockingham glaze, developed in England and named after the Marquis of Rockingham. In 1849, he patented a flint enamel glaze, "Fenton's Enamel," which added flecks, spots, or streaks of color (usually blues, greens, yellows, and oranges) to the brown Rockingham glaze. Forms included candlesticks, coachman bottles, cow creamers, poodles, sugar bowls, and toby pitchers.

Fenton produced the little-known scroddled ware, commonly called lava or agate ware. Scroddled ware is composed of differently colored clays which are mixed with cream-colored clay, molded, turned on a potter's wheel, coated with feldspar and flint, and fired. It was not produced in quantity as there was little demand for it.

Fenton also introduced Parian ware to America. Parian was developed in England in 1842 and known as "Statuary ware." Parian is a translucent porcelain which has no glaze and resembles marble. Bennington made the blue and white variety in the form of vases, cologne bottles, and trinkets.

The hound-handled pitcher is probably the best-known Bennington piece. Hound-handled pitchers were made by about 30 different potteries in over 55 variations. Rockingham glaze was used by over 150 potteries in 11 states, mainly in the Midwest, between 1830 and 1900.

Marks: Five different marks were used, with many variations. Only about 20% of the pieces carried any mark; some forms were almost always marked, others never. Marks include:

1849 mark (4 variations) for flint enamel and Rockingham

E. Fenton's Works, 1845-1847, on Parian and occasionally on scroddled ware

U. S. Pottery Co., ribbon mark, 1852-1858, on Parian and blue and white porcelain

U. S. Pottery Co., lozenge mark, 1852-1858, on Parian

U. S. Pottery, oval mark, 1853-1858, mainly on scroddled ware.

References: Richard Carter Barret, *How to Identify Bennington Pottery*, Stephen Greene Press, 1964; William C. Ketchum, Jr., *American Pottery and Porcelain*, Avon Books, 1994.

Museums: Bennington Museum, Bennington, VT; East Liverpool Museum of Ceramics, East Liverpool, OH.

Additional Listings: Stoneware.

Bennington Pottery

Book Flask, flint enamel, minor edge wear
5-5/8" h, *Departed Spirits*. 500.00
5-3/4" h, *Life of Kossuth*, "J" mark, 1849-58, Barret, plate 411
. . . . 490.00
6" h, *Battle of Bennington*, one corner chipped 400.00
Bottle, 9-3/8" h, figural, coachman, brown and tan Rockingham glaze, c1850. . . . . 225.00
Bowl, 11-7/8" d, flint enamel, imp 1849 mark 145.00

Serving Plate, sq, rounded corners, ribbed design, scroll center, 8-3/4" w, $350.

Snuff Jar, toby holding mug, dark brown glaze, 1850 mark, $425.

Bust, 5" h, parian, girl with bird on shoulder 75.00
Candlestick
6-5/8" h, flint enamel glaze, Barret Plate 198. . . . . . . 465.00
6-7/8" h, flint enamel glaze, Barret Plate 198. . . . . . . 715.00
7-3/4" h, Rockingham glaze, Barret Plate 197 . . . . . . 360.00
8" h, Rockingham glaze with black flecks, Barret Plate 198
. . . . 470.00
8-3/8" h, mottled olive glaze, Barret Plate 196, lip has old professional repair. 360.00
Coffeepot, 12-3/4" h, flint enamel, paneled sides, helmet shaped cov, pale cream underglaze, flowing tan, deep blue, and orange glaze, Barret Plate 136, professional restoration to tip of spout and edges. 1,980.00
Crock
7-1/4" h, stoneware, two handles, cobalt blue dec of house flanked by fencing, tree, label "J. & E. Norton, Bennington," 1850-61, minor chips, hairlines 2,760.00
10-1/4" h, stoneware, two handles, two gallon, label "J. & E. Norton, Bennington," cobalt blue foliate devices, chips, cracks, staining, drilled base 200.00
Curtain Tiebacks, 4-1/2" h, 4-1/2" d, flint enamel, pale cream underglaze, flowing medium brown to dark brown, semi-flowing green, Barret, plate 200, price for pr 440.00
Cuspidor, 9" d, paneled, Rockingham glaze, imp "1849" mark
. . . . 110.00
Ewer, 7" h, parian, raised grapevine dec 195.00
Name Plate
7-3/8" l, Rockingham glaze, one white letter "F," scrolling type shape, Barret Plate 203 . . . . 250.00
8-1/4" l, Rockingham glaze, rect shape, Barret Plate 203, chip on one end 250.00

Pie Plate, 8-1/4" d, imp 1849 mark 175.00
Pitcher
  8-1/8" h, flint enamel, Alternate Rib pattern, 1849 mark, Barret, plate 24 . . . . 375.00
  10" h, flint enamel, lobed alternate rib form, 1849 mark on base, hairline, base chip, glaze wear. 325.00
  12-1/2" h, flint enamel, tapering panel design, 1849 mark 425.00
Relish Dish, 10" l, Rockingham glaze 350.00
Teapot, cov, flint enamel glaze, Alternate Rib pattern, pierced pouring spout, period cov. 420.00
Toby Bottle, 10-1/2" h, Rockingham glaze, 1847, imp mark on base, Barret, plate 419. 460.00
Toothbrush Holder, cov, flint enamel, Alternate Rib pattern 500.00
Vase, 10" h, tulip shape, black olive flint enamel, Barret Plate 213, pinpoint flakes 910.00
Wash Bowl and Pitcher, 4-1/2" h, 13-1/2" d bowl, 12-1/2" h pitcher, flint enamel, Alternate Rib pattern, scrolled handle, emb scrolls on bowl, pale cream underglaze with yellow and brown bowl, additional blue on pitcher, imp "United States Pottery Company\Bennington, VT" on bowl, Barret Plate 169, minor glaze rubs on bowl .4,200.00

Bennington-type

Candlesticks, pr, 9-1/4" h, Rockingham glaze, circular kiln separations. 725.00
Frame, 8" x 7", oval, Rockingham glaze 325.00
Marbles, assorted sizes
  Blue glazed, 86 pcs. 220.00
  Brown glazed, 88 pcs 200.00
Mixing Bowl, 9-1/2" d, 4-1/2" h, Rockingham glaze, small chip on foot rim 110.00
Pitcher, 9-1/4" h, hound handle, emb hunt scenes, base hairlines, wear and chip on table ring. 330.00
Plate, 9 sq, emb design, Rockingham glaze. 290.00
Soap Dish, round, Rockingham glaze. 85.00
Vase, 4" h, Majolica 285.00

BISCUIT JARS

History: The biscuit or cracker jar was the forerunner of the cookie jar. Biscuit jars were made of various materials by leading glassworks and potteries of the late 19th and early 20th centuries.

Note: All items listed have silver-plated mountings unless otherwise noted.

Bristol Glass, satin finish, opaque beige ground, pink roses, gold leaves, gray foliage, SP top, rim, and handle, 6-1/2" h, 5-1/4" d. 195.00
Carlton Ware, multicolored floral dec, cobalt blue trim, SP handle, Staffordshire, 9-1/2" h 120.00
Crown Milano, barrel shape, pale yellow ground shades to cream white, deep pink apple blossoms, green leaves, gray-green branches, SP Pairpoint lid and collar, "P" in diamond logo emb in floral motif, 6" h, 5-1/2" d 685.00
Mt. Washington, clear ground, tapering body, molded in scrolls, gold highlights, gold single petaled blossoms each framed by elaborate gold feather scrolls, small side cartouches of clear glass framed by fancy gold scrolls, lid sgd "MM 4425," collar, flame finial, and bail with worn gilt finish, 8-1/2" h . .1,500.00
Opalescent Glass, watermelon striping, dark green ground, vertical white stripes opalescent stripes, SP lid and handle, 6-3/4" h, 4" d. 375.00

Crown Milano, coral, yellow ground, gold enameled flowers, leaves, gold beading, ruffled rim, top mkd "MW," numbered, 8" h, 8" d, $1,400.

Pairpoint, white ground, enameled gold poppy, SP collar and handle. 395.00
Royal Bonn, sq, floral design, SP top and handle, 7" h 140.00
Wavecrest, shaded yellow to opal, morning glories dec, pewter lid and bail, 9-1/2" h, 5-1/2" d, ... 230.00
Wedgwood
  Britannia Ware, cylindrical, white on blue, classical figure and tree dec, swing handle, ball feet, late 19th or early 20th C, 7-1/2" h. 220.00
  Jasperware, light green jasper dipped body, applied yellow trellis, white floral dec, SP rim, handle, and cov, imp mark, 5-1/2" d. 900.00

BISQUE

History: Bisque or biscuit china is the name given to wares that have been fired once and have not been glazed.

Bisque figurines and busts, which were popular during the Victorian era, were used on fireplace mantels, dining room buffets, and end tables. Manufacturing was centered in the United States and Europe. By the mid-20th century, Japan was the principal source of bisque items, especially character-related items.

References: Susan and Al Bagdade, *Warman's English & Continental Pottery .& Porcelain*, 3rd Edition, Krause Publications, 1998; Elyse Karlin, *Children Figurines of Bisque and Chinawares*, Schiffer Publishing, 1990; Sharon Weintraub, *Naughties, Nudies and Bathing Beauties*, Hobby House Press, 1993.

Bank, 3" h, fox head, wearing eyeglasses 375.00
Bottle, 4" h, figural, sailor boy, cork stopper, paper label, "Verbena" 65.00

Bust
    11" h, 6-1/2" d, young man, blond hair, blue eyes, gray hat,
        colored flowers, tan vest with pink and blue, allover dainty
        pink florals on shirt, blue base, imp "M. B." 325.00
    16" h, young boy, after Houdon, cobalt blue base, French
        . . . . 175.00
Cake Figures, bride and groom, traditional clothing, c1947,
    mounted on white base, floral garland overhead 150.00
Candleholder, 8" h, double, figural, girl leaning against bridge in
    woods, Germany, late 19th C 50.00
Cigar Holder, 4-1/4" h, tree stump, bird chasing insect, Germa-
    ny, 19th C 45.00
Doll
    4-3/4" h, Betty Boop-style, blond bobbed molded hair, large
        painted blue eyes to one side, one piece body and head,
        arms need re-stringing, Japan 45.00
    6-1/2" h, moveable arms, original clothes, mkd "Nippon,"
        damage to clothes 95.00
Figure
    3" h, Nun, white habit, gold rosary painted waist and trailing
        down left front, holding book open, singing, mkd "La Bom-
        boniera Sicilia Catania Corso Sicilia 3," blue and gold foil
        label 30.00
    3-1/2" h, bird, gray, crown on head 15.00
    7-1/2" h, elegantly dressed couple, French, late 19th C, price
        for pr 230.00
    12-1/4" h, 3-3/4" d, French style blond couple, girl carrying
        tambourine, boy with horn, fancy pink hats and baskets,
        raised gold dot dec, German, price for pair 325.00
    13" h, The Engagement, price for pair 400.00
    18" h, 18th C French maiden, green anchor mark, stamped
        "Exposition 1878 Medaille Do'or, Paris" 145.00
    18-1/2" h, Medieval courting couple, stamped "M.F. #122"
        . . . . 290.00

Half Doll, 5" h, 3" d, gray hair, band in hair, both hands and arms
    away from body, nude bust, marked "5275 Germany"
    . . . . 130.00
Lamp Base, 9-3/4" h, figural, candlestick type, shepherdess and
    shepherd, pr 40.00
Match Holder, 8" h, figural, hunter with pipe, dog with bird in
    mouth, marked "Made in Germany," c1900 . . . . 105.00
Nodder, 4-3/4" h, poodle and bulldog, oval base 165.00
Piano Baby, 7-1/4" h, boy and girl, Heubach 75.00
Planter, figural, fox with boots, jacket, pipe and musket, Germa-
    ny 110.00
Plaque
    11" h, 14" w, shepherdess with sheep on one, shepherd with
        pipe on other, pr 450.00
    19" h, 16" w, multicolored foliate still life, molded in high relief,
        set of four plaques mounted in giltwood shadowbox frame,
        early 20th C 1,265.00
Snow Baby, 1" h, sitting, arms outstretched, marked "Germany"
    . . . . 50.00
Toothbrush Holder, Three Little Pigs, Walt Disney Productions,
    mkd "Made in Japan," c1930 . . . . 125.00
Toothpick Holder, 4-1/2" h, figural, dwarf, blue pants, green hat
    . . . . 30.00
Vase, 6-1/4" h, 3-1/2" d, figural, Indian Chief head, feather head-
    dress, braids, blue crown and "NP" mark, c1900 . . . . 155.00

BITTERS BOTTLES

History: Bitters, a "remedy" made from natural herbs and other mixtures with an alcohol base, often was viewed as the universal cure-all. The names given to various bitter mixtures were imaginative, though the bitters seldom cured what their makers claimed.

The manufacturers of bitters needed a way to sell and advertise their products. They designed bottles in many shapes, sizes, and colors to attract the buyer. Many forms of advertising, including trade cards, billboards, signs, almanacs, and novelties, proclaimed the virtues of a specific bitter.

During the Civil War a tax was levied on alcoholic beverages. Since bitters were identified as medicines, they were exempt from this tax. The alcoholic content was never mentioned. In 1907, when the Pure Foods Regulations went into effect, "an honest statement of content on every label" put most of the manufacturers out of business.

References: Ralph and Terry Kovel, *Kovels' Bottles Price List*, 10th ed., Crown Publishers, 1996; John Odell, *Digger Odell's Official Antique Bottle and Glass Collector Magazine Price Guide Series*, Vol. 2, published by author (1910 Shawhan Rd, Morrow, OH 45152), 1995; Carlyn Ring, *For Bitters Only*, published by author 203 Kensington Rd., Hampton Falls, NH 03844), 1980; J. H. Thompson, *Bitters Bottles*, Century House, 1947; Richard Watson, *Bitters Bottles*, Thomas Nelson and Sons, 1965.

Periodicals: *Antique Bottle and Glass Collector*, P.O. Box 187, East Greenville, PA 18041; *Bitters Report*, P.O. Box 1253, Bunnell, FL 32110.

Figure, black minstrels, one playing French horn, other with tambourine, blue and white clothes, white hats, 8-3/4" h, $585.

Atwood's Jaundice Bitters, American, c1850, twelve sided,
    aqua, applied sq collar lip, open pontil base, 6-3/8" h 295.00
Begg Dandelion Bitters, Chicago, IL, sq, amber 150.00

Ben Franklin, America, 1840-60, tapered barrel form, light blue green, applied collared mouth with ring, pontil scar, 10" h 3,280.00

Brown's Celebrated Indian Herb Bitters/Patented Feb. 11, 1868, figural Indian maiden, emb, golden amber, ground lip, smooth base, 12-1/4" h 350.00

Cannon's Dyspeptic Bitters, America, 1860-90, sq, beveled corners, emb with cannon balls and ramrods, three full panels with emb cannon barrels, golden amber, applied sloping collared mouth, smooth base, 10" h, 3/4" bruise and repair to top of mouth, some int. residue 3,250.00

Cherry Cordial Bitters, America, 1870-90, sq, beveled corners and indented panels, light yellow amber, tooled sloping collared mouth with ring, smooth base, 8-7/8" h roughness to do manufacturer's tool 140.00

Dingens Napoleon Cocktail Bitters, Dingens Brothers Buffalo, NY, olive amber, iron pontil, applied sloping lip, 10" h 5,390.00

Drake's Plantation Bitters, puce, Arabesque design, tapered lip, smooth base, 9-3/4" h 295.00

Dr. A. S. Hopkins Union Stomach Bitters, F. S. Amodon, Sole Prop., Hartford, Conn, USA, sq amber bottle, orig neck seal 98% orig graphic front label, 95% rear label, orig contents, 9-1/2" h. 240.00

Dr. Bell's Blood Purifying Bitters The Great English Remedy, America, 1860-90, rect, indented panels, bright golden yellow, applied sq collared mouth, smooth base, 9-1/2" h 140.00

Dr. C. D. Warner, honey amber, tooled lip, smooth base, emb "Dr. C. D. Warner, Reading, Mich\German Hop Bitters\Warner 1880\Warner\1880," 9-7/8" h 375.00

Doyles 1872, amber, raised fruit design, 9-3/4" h, $115.

Dr. J Hostetter's Stomach Bitters, American, c1870, olive green, applied tapered lip, smooth base, 8-1/2" h 150.00

Dr. John Bull's Compound Cedron Bitters, Louisville, KY, c1870, sq, olive green, applied tapered lip, smooth base, 9-3/4" h 1,000.00

Dr. Petzold's Genuine German Bitters Incpt 1862, medium amber, colorful graphic front label, oval, 10-1/2" h 950.00

Dr. Stephen Jewetts' Celebrated Health Restoring Bitters, American, c1840, rect, beveled corners, honey amber, sq collar lip, iron pontil base, orig label, 7-1/8" h 1,500.00

Dr. Walkinshaw's Curative Bitters, Batavia, NY, sq amber bottle, 90% orig label, orig contents, 10" h 315.00

East India Root Bitters, Geo P Clapp, sq, tapered, golden amber, applied tapered lip, smooth base, emb, 9-1/2" h, c1870 . . . . 450.00

E. E. Hall's Bitters, amber, broken blister on base, 9" h 75.00

Electric Brand Bitters, HE Bucklen & Co., Chicago, IL, sq, amber 50.00

Greeley's Bourbon Bitters, America, 1860-80, barrel shape, applied sq collared mouth, smooth base
   Apricot puce, 9-1/8" h, shallow 3/8" burst bubble on top barrel ring. 180.00
   Copper puce, 9-1/4" h, shallow 1/4" flake on side of flanged mouth 120.00
   Root beer brown with puce overtones, 9-1/8" h, pinhead sized bruise on top corner of mouth 230.00

Hall's Bitters, America, 1860-80, barrel form, light yellow amber, applied sq collared mouth, smooth base, 9-1/8" h . . . 230.00

Hasterlik's Celebrated Stomach Biters, sq amber, 98% front label with eagle, shield, and flags, 9-1/4" h 55.00

I. Newton's Jaundice Butters, Norwich VT, 1940-60, rect, wide beveled corners, deep aquamarine, tooled flared mouth, pontil scar, 6-7/8" h 700.00

John Moffit, Phoenix Bitters, NY, olive amber, eight sided, round collar pontil, 6-3/8" h. 2,500.00

John Root's Bitters/1834/Buffalo, N.Y., rect, beveled corners, recessed panels, cabin type roof, bluish green, applied sloping collared mouth with ring, smooth base, 10" h, 3" crack in one shoulder 190.00

Johnson's Calisaya Bitters, Burlington VT, 1870-90, sq, beveled corners, indented panels
   Golden yellow, 10" h. 120.00
   Yellow amber, applied sloping collared mouth with ring, smooth base, 10" h, two shallow partial burst bubbles on shoulder 210.00

McKeevers' Army Bitters, stylized drum with cannon balls on top, golden amber, applied tapered lip, smooth base, 10-3/4" h, c1875 . . . . .1,800.00

National Bitters patent 1867, figural, ear of corn, amber 250.00

Old Homestead Wild Cherry Bitters, America, 1860-90, tall house form, yellow amber, applied sloping collared mouth, smooth base, 9-1/2" h, crudely applied lip has air under some of natural folds, sand grain above door 150.00

Old Sachem Bitters and Wigwam Tonic, America, 1840-60, barrel form, applied sq collared mouth, pontil scar
   Deep plum amethyst, 9" h, minor ext. scratches 550.00
   Golden amber, 9-1/4" h 600.00
   Olive yellow, 9-1/4" h 1,700.00

Pond's Bitters, Unexcelled Laxative, sq, amber, paper label 30.00

Simons Centennial Bitters, figural, bust of George Washington, golden amber, applied ring lip, smooth base, 10" h, c1876 . . . . .1,500.00

Sir Robert, Edgar's English Life Bitters-G E Graves Proprietor Rutland, Vt. USA, American, 1860-80, sq, beveled corners,

yellow amber, applied sloping collared mouth, smooth base, 8-1/2" h, 1/4" shallow burst bubble 170.00
Star Kidney and Liver Bitters, sq, amber, 8-7/8" 50.00
S T Drake's Plantation Bitters, amber, six logs, 9-3/4" h
. . . . 115.00
Suffolk Bitters, Philbrook & Tucker, Boston, figural, pig, yellow-ish amber, ground lip, emb, 10" l, c1870 . . . . 225.00
Tonola Bitter, J T Higby, Milford, CT, sq, amber. 165.00
Traveller's Bitters, America, 1834-70, man standing with cane, oval, amber, 10-1/2" h 265.00
Walker's Cocktail Bitters, round, lady's leg neck, amber 650.00
Ware Patented 1866\The Fish Bitters, clear, tooled lip, smooth base, emb, 11-1/2" h 475.00
Warner's Safe Tonic Bitters, America, 1870-90, oval, golden yellow, tooled double collared mouth, smooth base, 7-3/8" h, some minor ext. high point wear 650.00
Zingan Bitters, amber, applied mouth, smooth base, 11-7/8" h
. . . . 150.00

BLACK MEMORABILIA

History: The term "Black memorabilia" refers to a broad range of collectibles that often overlap other collecting fields, e.g., toys and postcards. It also encompasses African artifacts, items created by slaves or related to the slavery era, modern Black cultural contributions to literature, art, etc., and material associated with the Civil Rights Movement and the Black experience throughout history.

The earliest known examples of Black memorabilia include primitive African designs and tribal artifacts. Black Americana dates back to the arrival of African natives upon American shores.

The advent of the 1900s saw an incredible amount and variety of material depicting Blacks, most often in a derogatory and dehumanizing manner that clearly reflected the stereotypical attitude held toward the Black race during this period. The popularity of Black portrayals in this unflattering fashion flourished as the century wore on.

As the growth of the Civil Rights Movement escalated and aroused public awareness to the Black plight, attitudes changed. Public outrage and pressure during the early 1950s eventually put a halt to these offensive stereotypes.

Black representations are still being produced in many forms, but no longer in the demoralizing designs of the past. These modern objects, while not as historically significant as earlier examples, will become the Black memorabilia of tomorrow.

References: Patiki Gibbs, *Black Collectibles Sold in America*, Collector Books, 1987, 1996 value update; Kenneth Goings, *Mammy and Uncle Mose*, Indiana University Press, 1994; Dee Hockenberry, *Enchanting Friends: Collectible Poohs, Raggedies, Golliwoggs & Roosevelt Bears*, Schiffer Publishing, 1995; Kyle Husfloen (ed.), *Black Americana Price Guide*, Antique Trader Books, 1997; Jan Lindenberger, *More Black Memorabilia*, Schiffer Publishing, 1995; J. L. Mashburn, *Black Americana: A Century of History Preserved on Postcards*, Colonial House, 1996; Myla Perkins, *Black Dolls 1820-1991* (1993, 1995 value update), *Book II* (1995), Collector Books; Dawn Reno, *Encyclopedia of Black Collectibles*, Wallace-Homestead/Krause, 1996; J. P. Thompson, *Collecting Black Memorabilia*, L-W Book Sales, 1996; Jean Williams Turner, *Collectible Aunt Jemima*, Schiffer Publishing, 1994.

Periodical: *Blackin*, 559 22nd Ave., Rock Island, IL 61201.

Collectors' Club: Black Memorabilia Collector's Association, 2482 Devoe Ter, Bronx, NY 10468.

Museums: Great Plains Black Museum, Omaha, NE 68110; Museum of African American History, Detroit, MI.

REPRODUCTION ALERT

Reproductions are becoming an increasing problem, from advertising signs (Bull Durham tobacco) to mechanical banks (Jolly Nigger). If the object looks new to you, chances are that it is new.

Ashtray, boy with alligator, fishing pole 50.00
Autograph, George Washington Carver, letter signed, 4 pages 4to, Tuskegee Institute letterhead, orig envelope addressed by Carver, Aug. 4, 1931, to Ralph Douberly of Columbus, GA, young poet friend 585.00
Bill Hook, 7-1/2" h, 3" w, Deluth Flour adv, cardboard, flour sacks, black baker holding loaf, minor wear, some damage to hanging hole. 325.00
Book, *Uncle Tom's Cabin,* Harriet Beecher Stowe 20.00
Cabinet, 20" h, 12-1/8" w, 8-1/8" d, Mammys' Favorite Extract, wood and glass display case, orig wood shelves, orig label with black woman on box of Mammys' Favorite Extract"
. . . . 2,600.00
Carnival Mask, 14" h, figural, carved and painted wood, black man with hair wig, America, 19th C, minor losses, scattered paint loss 750.00
Coffee Tin, 6" h, 4-7/8" w, 3" d, Mity Good Coffee, cardboard litho, tin top and bottom, H & K brand, l lb, black waiter serving coffee, light wear to label 180.00
Coin Operated Jazz Band, "The Five Pence Band," men playing piano, drum, horn, and bass, 5¢, 66" h, 44" w, 22" deep, minor chip to one band member 2,000.00
Cookie Jar
  Chef, National Silver. 250.00
  Mammy, blue, Mosaic Tile 425.00
  Mammy, yellow, Mosaic Tile 375.00
  Mammy, National Silver 200.00
Dart Board, 14" h, 10-1/2" w, tin over cardboard, stereotype black boy as bull's eye 225.00
Doll
  Beloved Melindy, Georgene, 18" h. 800.00
  Uncle Mose, cloth, uncut 225.00
Egg Timer, Chef 75.00
Humidor, cov, 7-1/2" h, Black Arab, purple striped turban
. . . . 225.00
Inkwell, Johnny Griffin. 350.00
Letter, written by young boy to aunt in 1850, mentioning runaway slave. 325.00
Match Holder, black Nubian 250.00
Match Safe
  Figural, 5" h, ceramic baby doll 100.00
  Wall, De Handy Man, little boy holding pouch for matches, "Don't scratch your matches on de wall, scratch 'em on my overalls" 250.00

Advertising Sign, Oxydol Laundry Powder, double sided cardboard, 8-3/4" x 9-1/2", $210. Photo courtesy of Bear Pen Auction.

Original Art, framed

16-1/2" h, 18" w, shows product from start as raw cotton ending up as finished box of Johnson Bandages, Mammy says "Yas-Suh Johnson Bandages are only 25¢" 400.00

22" h, 14" w, stereotype black boy in colorful clothing holding emb bottle of Rochette orange soda, heavily soiled 400.00

35" h, 9-1/2" w, four pc set, pin and ink sketches by Edwin Kemble, raccoon angry at black boy in coon skin cap, final scene raccoon wearing black boys' clothes, cartoon appeared in February 1913 *Cosmopolitan* Magazine 300.00

Pancake Flour Sack, Aunt Jemima 225.00
Paper Holder, Johnny Griffin 100.00
Pillow Cover, framed

21-1/2" sq, humorous wedding scene, elegantly dressed couple, friends and family tossing old shoes 225.00

22" h, black scene of three city boys playing craps with shoe shine money 250.00

Pipe Rack, Johnny Griffin 350.00
Postcard

Aunt Shug, "Who makes the pralines at Afton Village, Famous Ante Bellum House, St. Francisville, Louisiana," cook with pralines, black and white 30.00

Cranberry Scooper, Ocean Spray Cranberry Sauce and Cranberry Cocktail adv, smiling youth in field with scoop, Curt Teich, linen 95.00

Happy New Year, black caricature, published in England 35.00

Hedspath, American Champion on his bicycle, L'Albatros, tires Le Persan, French, black rider. 60.00

Negro Baptism, near Norfolk, VA, crowds of blacks gathered in boats and on shore, used, 1924, Norfolk 30.00

Poor family, real photo of large family posed in front of shack home, "Greetings from the Sand Hills of North Carolina," photo by E. D. Putnam & Son, Atrim, NH 45.00

Poster, paper, framed

22-1/2" h, 19-1/2" w, titled "5 cent limit," black poker game, humorous dialogue between Uncle Remus and Bruer

Gumson, advertising Red Crow Cigars, artist sgd "Van," some restoration 1,100.00

23-1/2" h, 29-1/2" w, Lime Kiln Club Cigars, comical scene of black town meeting, © 1882, some overall scratching 750.00

65-1/2" h, 46-1/2" w, paper, Bougie Oleo Huile Auto'D, black face with huge red lips, artist sgd "Raoul Vion" ... 600.00

79" h, 40-1/2" w, black banjo player, big red lips, oversized polka dot bow-tie, forty people in band and orchestra, multiple folds and overall creasing 400.00

88" h, 39-1/2" w, three sheet, paper, Uncle Tom's Cabin, unusual black face with enlarged facial features, "Jes Yo come along an 'laff at Uncle Tom's Cabin," artist sgd "Robt Kemp" 1,000.00

Print, 15-1/2" h, 19-1/2" w, log cabin scene of black family, father plays banjo, son struts, © 1898, framed, some staining in background. 150.00

Quilt, pieced cotton gauze, Sawtooth/Target pattern, red, blue, green, and white spiral design, trimmed in white border with white and red stripes, hand pieced, machine finished 1,600.00

Salt and Pepper Shakers, pr, black boys with blue jackets and caps 40.00

Sign

5" h, 28" l, emb tin, Gold Dust Twins holding package of washing powder, titled "Let The Gold Dust Twins Do Your Work," Chas W. Shonk Co. litho 550.00

11-1/2" h, 7" w, diecut cardboard, scene of elderly black rural doctor helping constipated black child with his satchel of Ayers remedies, framed 175.00

13-1/2" h, 19-1/2" w, curled corner tin sign, titled "The temptation of St. Anthony," black father uncorking bottle of Paul Jones Whiskey while Aunt Jemima looking mother holds watermelon, Meek Co. litho, some minor fading to sky and roof of house 1,000.00

14" h, 7-1/2" w, diecut cardboard, easel back, one of Gold Dust Twins, creased, some damage 225.00

16" h, 6-1/2" w, two sided diecut cardboard, black man holding sign "Shut the Door," wearing hat advertising German Syrup and August Flower with cures Coughs, Consumption, Dyspepsia & Liver Ailments, framed 175.00

21-3/4" h, 31-1/2" w, paper, Great Atlantic & Pacific Tea Co., titled "Ten Minutes for Refreshments," very busy coffee house scene, customers frantically finishing refreshments before they board train, black waiters serving coffee from great copper urns, framed 1,250.00

23-3/4" d, Green River Whiskey, tin litho charger, trademark black man and mule on front 700.00

39" h, 22" w, three piece diecut cardboard, Sealy All Cotton Beds, little black boy and girl carrying cotton representing twin beds, while father carries large basket of cotton representing Sealy full size cotton mattress, children are 39" h x 22" w, father 73" h, 29" w, some wear 1,000.00

47" l, 11-3/4" w, wood, folk type hand painted store sign, Olewine's General Store, Hazleton, PA, black man in chair smoking pipe 1,000.00

48" h, 12" w, set of five roadside signs, designed to be placed a mile apart, each different, one mile sign with Will Rogers type minstrel in black face, two mile marker with alligator bait scene, three mile marker with little boy being rammed by goat, four mile sign with little boy showing bagged possum, five mile marker with Aunt Jemima type woman, each read "Short's Cash and Carry, Use Your Sense And Save Your Dollars, Sutherland, Iowa," produced by Ithaca Sign Works 1,700.00

51" h, three-dimensional plaster, life size black boy wearing straw hat, straddling wooden crate while holding sign reading "Giletts Lye Eats Dirt," wooden crate lettered "Mammy Beverage" 3,500.00

Soap Pad Holder, 5" h, young Mammy 125.00

Statue, 12" h, three-dimensional, chalk, black boys watching cock fight through split rail fence, ©1898, some paint chips 500.00

String Holder

Chef, chalkware, flowers 345.00

Mammy 185.00

Mammy, ceramic, flowers 270.00

Mammy, ceramic, plaid dress 175.00

Mammy, chalkware, flowers 350.00

Mammy, red neck ribbon 260.00

Mammy, scissors in apron 350.00

Tin

2-1/2" w, 2-1/2" l, 3/4" h, Old Hickory Brand Typewriter Ribbon, southern plantation scene, black man resting under tree, other blacks picking cotton in field 550.00

6-3/4" h, 5-1/2" d, Niggerhair Tobacco, pail, yellow ground, B. Leidersdorf Co., black woman with rings 450.00

9-1/2" h, 8-1/2" d, Pickaninny Brand Peanuts, orig litho lid, F. M. Hoyt & Co., 10 lb size 200.00

Tip Tray, 4-1/4" d, Cottolene, black woman and child picking cotton, titled "Best for Shortening, Best for Frying," some overall crazing 75.00

Tobacco Card, set of six

Sweet Lavender Tobacco, 9-1/4" x 10" cardboard card, comical story told scene by scene, titled "A Sure Thing on a Possum," hunting to last scene titled "Fo' De Lawd It's A Skunk," set of six cards matted and framed as 35" h x 25-1/2" 950.00

Toy, hand painted tin

Seated black figure holding musical drum in hand, feet attached to spoke wheels and pulley for drum, tube on back used as handle to pull toy, 8" l 660.00

Seated black figure in rocking chair, cloth suit, clockwork mechanism activates rocking motion, 6-1/2" h, 7" w 1,210.00

Tray, 12" d, Green River Whiskey, titled "She was bred in old Kentucky," black man holding nag with oversized jug of

Green River Whiskey hanging from saddle, "The Whiskey without a headache," Chas. W. Shonk & Co. litho . . . 200.00

Vending Machine, 76" h, Smilin Sam The Voo Doo Man, black face changes expression after quarter inserted, dispenses cardboard lucky charm pocket piece 1,500.00

BLOWN THREE MOLD

History: The Jamestown colony in Virginia introduced glassmaking into America. The artisans used a "free-blown" method.

Blowing molten glass into molds was not introduced into America until the early 1800s. Blown three-mold glass used a predesigned mold that consisted of two, three, or more hinged parts. The glassmaker placed a quantity of molten glass on the tip of a rod or tube, inserted it into the mold, blew air into the tube, waited until the glass cooled, and removed the finished product. The three-part mold is the most common and lends its name to this entire category.

The impressed decorations on blown-mold glass usually are reversed, i.e., what is raised or convex on the outside will be concave on the inside. This is useful in identifying the blown form.

By 1850, American-made glassware was relatively common. Increased demand led to large factories and the creation of a technology which eliminated the smaller companies.

Reference: George S. and Helen McKearin, *American Glass*, reprint, Crown Publishers, 1941, 1948.

Collectors' Club: Early American Pattern Glass Society, P.O. Box 266, Colesburg, IA 52035; National Early American Glass Club, P.O. Box 8489, Silver Spring, MD 20907.

Museum: Sandwich Glass Museum, Sandwich, MA.

Basket, 4-1/2" h, 4" d, colorless, rayed base, solid applied handle, pontil scar 300.00

Bird Cage Fountain, 5-1/4" h, colorless, ground mouth, pontil scar, McKearin GI-12 . . . . 50.00

Bowl, colorless

5" d, rounded sides, outward folded rim, rayed base, pontil scar 200.00

6" d, 1-3/4" h, outward folded rim, straight slanting sides, sixteen diamond base, pontil 140.00

6-3/8" d, 5-3/4" h, folded rim, sixteen diamond base, ftd, pontil, tilts to one side, McKearin GII-18 . . . . .4,800.00

Carafe, 9-1/4" h, dark yellow amber, rayed base, deep pontil scar 2,400.00

Creamer, 3" h, colorless, applied handle, rigaree on end of handle ground, some residue under rigaree, McKearin GII-18 . . . . 200.00

Cruet, 5-3/8" h, colorless, plain base, formed pouring lip, pontil, McKearin GII-28 . . . . 150.00

Cup Plate, 3-7/8" d, folded rim, rayed base, pontil scar, three McKearin labels, ex-collection George McKearin and TMR Culbertson, McKearin GII-1 . . . . 600.00

Decanter

6-3/4" h, colorless, orig stopper, minor stains, McKearin GI-15 . . . . 225.00

9-3/4" h, colorless, sunburst and diamond pattern, orig stopper 300.00

13-3/4" h, colorless, paneled neck, band of geometric motifs above hobnail body, quilted stopper 350.00

Figure, chalk, three black boys watching cock fight through split rail fence, copyright 1898, 12", $500. Photo courtesy of James D. Julia, Inc.

Toilet Water Bottle, amethyst, orig stopper, McKearin GI-7, type 5, 6-5/8" h, $275.

Dish, colorless
    5" d, outward rolled rim, pontil scar, McKearin GIII-21 130.00
    6-3/8" d, folded rim, rayed base, iron pontil 90.00
Flip Glass, colorless, 6" h, McKearin GII-18 . . . . 125.00
Hat
    2-1/8" h, colorless, fifteen diamond base, pontil, folded rim
    . . . . 275.00
    2-1/4" h, colorless, swirled rayed base, pontil, folded rim
    . . . . 125.00
Inkwell
    1-7/8" h, 2-3/4" d, amber, drum shape, faint ringed base, pontil scar 125.00
    2" h, 2-5/8" d, olive green, McKearin GII-18 . . . . 125.00
Lamp
    4" h, 3" d, peg, colorless, heavy applied solid pegs, period tin matching double burners, short factory ground neck, McKearin GII-18, pr 1,450.00
    6-1/2" h, colorless, double paw pressed base, orig brass collar, mkd "BTM font/Mt. Vernon Works," McKearin GI-30
    . . . . 800.00
Mustard, 5" h, colorless, clear sheared ball finial, flanged, folded lip, pontil, orig matching cov 125.00
Pan, 1-1/2" h, 5" d, colorless, McKearin GI-6 . . . . 185.00
Pitcher, colorless
    8-1/2" h, tool mark at lower part of applied handle . . . 250.00
    10-3/4" h, McKearin GV-17 . . . . 420.00
Plate, 5-3/8" d, colorless, folded rim, plain base, pontil
    . . . . 150.00
Salt, 2-3/8" h, colorless, pinpoint lip flakes, McKearin GII-21
    . . . . 165.00
Salt Shaker, colorless
    4-5/8" h, pontil base, orig metal cap 75.00
    5" h, sheared lip, orig metal cap and pontil 75.00

Sugar, 2-1/2" h, 5" d, brilliant sapphire blue, rolled flanged lip, solid applied base with pontil attributed to Boston & Sandwich, c1820, McKearin GI-29 . . . . 3,250.00
Toddy Plate, 4-1/4" d, colorless, folded rim, rayed base, pontil
    . . . . 265.00
Toilet Water Bottle, 6-3/4" h, violet, flared lip, smooth base, period tam-o-shanter stopper 650.00
Tumbler, colorless
    3-1/4" h, McKearin GII-18 . . . . 200.00
    5-1/2" h, McKearin GII-18 . . . . 210.00
    5-5/8" h, McKearin GII-18 . . . . 300.00
    5-3/4" h, McKearin GII-18 . . . . 275.00
Whiskey Taster, colorless, 1-5/8" h, ringed base, pontil
    . . . . 200.00

BOEHM PORCELAINS

History: Edward Marshall Boehm was born on Aug. 21, 1913. Boehm's childhood was spent at the McConogh School, a rural Baltimore County, Maryland, school. He studied animal husbandry at the University of Maryland, serving as manager of Longacre Farms on the Eastern Shore of Maryland upon graduation. After serving in the air force during World War II, Boehm moved to Great Neck, Long Island, and worked as an assistant veterinarian.

In 1949, Boehm opened a pottery studio in Trenton, New Jersey. His initial hard-paste porcelain sculptures consisted of Herefords, Percherons, and dogs. The first five to six years were a struggle, with several partnerships beginning and ending during the period. In the early 1950s, Boehm's art porcelain sculptures began appearing in major department stores. When Eisenhower presented a Boehm sculpture to Queen Elizabeth and Prince Philip during their visit to the United States in 1957, Boehm's career accelerated.

Boehm contributed the ideas for the images and the techniques used to produce the sculptures. Thousands of prototype sculptures were made, with more than 400 put into production. The actual work was done by skilled artisans. Boehm died on Jan. 29, 1969.

In the early 1970s, a second production site, called Boehm Studios, was opened in Malvern, England. The tradition begun by Boehm continues today.

Many collectors specialize in Boehm porcelain birds or flowers. Like all of Boehm's sculptures, pieces in these series are highly detailed, signed, and numbered.

Reference: Reese Palley, *Porcelain Art of Edward Marshall Boehm*, Harrison House, 1988.

Collectors' Club: Boehm Porcelain Society, P.O. Box 5051, Trenton, NJ 08638.

Birds

Baby Blue Jay, No. 436, 4-1/2" h 170.00
Baby Robin, No. 437D, 3-1/2" h 170.00
Carolina Wren, mushrooms, Malvern Studio, England
    . . . . 625.00
Catbird, two hyacinths base 1,320.00
Chick, No. 412, yellow glaze, 3-1/2" h 200.00
Jenny wren, No. 201, Malvern Studio, England, 4" x 6"
    . . . . 350.00

Junco, No. 400-12, pyracantha base, 10-1/2" x 11-1/2"
. . . . 875.00
Little Owl, No. 1002, Malvern Studio, England, 6" x 9"
. . . . 600.00
Orchard Oriole, No. 400-11, tulip, 14" h. 570.00
Ruffled Grouse, No. 456, 12" h 1,350.00
The Great Egret, #40221, limited edition #798/1029
. . . . .2,200.00
Warblers. 1,320.00

Other

Daisies, #3002 . . . . 800.00
Magnolia Grandiflora, #300-12. . . . . .1,600.00
Panda Cub, No. 400-47, reclining on bamboo, 6-1/2" x 8"
. . . . 425.00
Polo Player, a 1964 replica of a piece commissioned in 1957
by President Eisenhower for Queen Elizabeth . .1,210.00
Rose on log, 6" l, yellow flower, English. 175.00

BOHEMIAN GLASS

History: The once independent country of Bohemia, now
a part of the Czech Republic, produced a variety of fine
glassware: etched, cut, overlay, and colored. Their glassware, which first appeared in America in the early 1820s,
continues to be exported to the U.S. today.

Bohemia is known for its "flashed" glass that was produced in the familiar ruby color, as well as in amber,
green, blue, and black. Common patterns include Deer
and Castle, Deer and Pine Tree, and Vintage.

Most of the Bohemian glass encountered in today's
market is from 1875 to 1900. Bohemian-type glass also
was made in England, Switzerland, and Germany.

References: Sylvia Petrova and Jean-Luc Olivie (eds.),
Bohemian Glass, Abrams, 1990; Robert and Deborah
Truitt, *Collectible Bohemian Glass*, R & D Glass, 1995.

Reproduction Alert.

Beaker
4-1/2" h, blue and white overlay, arched panels with gilt ivy
and stylized foliage on oval white overlay, flaring base,
mid 19th C 225.00
5-1/4"h, white on amethyst overlay, quatrefoil and circular cut
windows, painted trailing roses 250.00
Bottle, 16" h
Bulbous, slim neck, painted floral and gilt design, long, slender stopper 115.00
Cylindrical, gilt dec green body and stopper 90.00
Cake Stand, 9-1/2" h, 14-1/2" d, white overlay, painted springs
of foliage, gilding, late 19th C, wear. 800.00
Canister, cov, 9" h, ruby overlay, landscape scene, cut with foliage 150.00
Center Bowl, 9" d, 11-1/2" h, ribbed and ruffled green irid glass
bowl, elaborate metal base with three cherubs playing flutes
. . . . 520.00
Cruet, amber cut to clear, carved floral arrangement intaglio,
three oval panels with ruby flashing, carved floral swags, five
cut to clear neck panels with gold scrollwork, sixteen dec cut
panels on amber cut to clear stopper, gold edges, base sgd
"4," stopper base sgd "4" 750.00
Decanter
15-1/2" h, ruby cut to clear, geese dec, cut stopper
. . . . 140.00
15-3/4" h, ruby cut to clear, floral dec, orig stopper
. . . . 120.00

Goblet, 6-3/8" h, enameled, ruby flashed ground, paneled octagonal body, floral and scrolled foliate design, gilt wear, pr
. . . . 690.00
Jar, cov, 5-1/4" d, frosted colorless base and top, cased to
off-white, layered on enameled orange and black, etched
leaves and bellflowers, cameo mark at side. 575.00
Perfume Bottle, 4-1/8" h, black glass, cut design, silver gilt fittings and rhinestones, clear stopper, paper label "Aristo,
Genuine Bohemian Glass" 200.00
Service Plate, 10-3/4" d, porcelain, burgundy ground border, gilt
scrolls and foliage, 20th C, set of 15 . . . . 865.00
Tumbler, 4-1/4" h, clear, leaded glass, pontil scar, enameled
German inscription, florals, heart, two hands shaking, dated
1727 . . . . 550.00
Vase
5" h, mold blown oval green body, looped drapery, irid surface, mounted with copper-colored pressed metal grapevine motif collar 250.00
10" h, ruby overlay, cut with foliage, early 20th C . . . 100.00
13-1/2" h, green, gilt stars and band dec, enameled portrait
ovals, pr. 700.00
14" h, cranberry, painted portrait of gypsy girl, gilded floral
surround 290.00
23" h, pigeon blood red oval body, purple irid surface,
opal-gray random threading, mounted in elaborate
bronzed metal ftd platform base, tubular frames, handle
protrusions, price for pr 3,910.00
Wine Ewer, 10-1/4" h, amber flashed, cut and etched grape
vines and clusters dec 400.00

**Decanter, Vintage pat-
tern, ruby, 14" h, $125.**

Wine Glass, 7-3/4" h, ruby overlay, raised blue, amethyst, and ruby panels, faceted body, gilt scrolled ground, late 19th/early 20th C, wear, chips, price for 12 pc set 1,850.00

BOOKS, CIVIL WAR

History: Books pertaining to America's Civil War are becoming increasingly popular with collectors. Some prefer to seek out period books and discover what the author was trying to portray. Other collectors prefer to specialize on books relating to specific battles or geographic areas. No matter what your interest, there are many Civil War related books to choose from.

Some of these books have interesting engravings and detailed illustrations, maps, etc. Like other period books, look for examples with good bindings, well preserved covers, etc. Avoid any that have signs of insect damage or mold.

References: Allen and Patricia Ahearn, *Book Collecting: A Comprehensive Guide*, G. P. Putnam's Sons, 1995; *American Book Prices Current*, Bankcroft Parkman, published annually; Geoffrey Ashall Glaister, *Encyclopedia of the Book*, 2nd ed., available from Spoon River Press, 1996; John R. Gretton, *Baedeker's Guidebooks: A Checklist of English-Language Editions 1861-1939*, available from Spoon River Press, 1994; Sharon and Bob Huxford, *Huxford's Old Book Value Guide*, 9th ed., Collector Books, 1997; Charlie Lovett, *Everybody's Guide to Book Collecting*, available from Spoon River Press), 1993; Ian C. Ellis, *Book Finds*, available from Spoon River Press, 1996; Norma Levarie, *Art & History of Books*, available from Spoon River Press, 1995; Catherine Porter, *Collecting Books*, available from Spoon River Press, 1995; Caroline Seebohm, Estelle Ellis, and Christopher Simon Sykes, *At Home with Books: How Book Lovers Live with and Care for Their Libraries*, available from Spoon River Press, 1996; Henry Toledano, *The Modern Library Price Guide 1917–1995*, available from Spoon River Press, 1995; John Wade, *Tomart's Price Guide to 20th Century Books*, Tomart Publications, 1994; Nancy Wright, *Books: Identification and Price Guide*, Avon Books, 1993; Edward N. Zempel and Linda A. Verkler (eds.), *Book Prices: Used and Rare 1996*, Spoon River Press, 1996; ——, *First Editions: A Guide to Identification*, 3rd ed., Spoon River Press, (2319C W Rohmann, Peoria, IL 61604) 1995.

Periodicals: *A B Bookman's Weekly*, P.O. Box AB, Clifton, NJ 07015; *Biblio*, 845 Willamette St., Eugene, OR 87401; *Bookseller*, P.O. Box 8183, Ann Arbor, MI 48107; *Book Source Monthly*, 2007 Syossett Dr., P.O. Box 567, Cazenovia, NY 13035; *Firsts*, P.O. Box 65166, Tucson, AZ 85728-5166; *Rare Book Bulletin*, P.O. Box 201, Peoria, IL 61650.

Additional Listings: Warman's Americana & Collectibles.

Notes: The prices listed below serve as a model for civil war-history publications. Compare similar items to this listing—prices are approximately the same nationwide for the identical type of material. More recent publications, i.e., within the last 25 years, rarely are valued above their initial selling price.

Remember, condition is perhaps the greatest factor in correctly pricing a book. Local and regional books will bring slightly higher prices in the areas about which they are written.

Bates, William C., ed., *The Stars and Stripes in Rebeldom: A Series of Papers Written By Federal Prisoners (Private) in Richmond, Tuscaloosa, New Orleans, and Salisbury, N. C.*, 1862, two volumes, orig cloth. 40.00

Baxter, J. H., *Statistics, Medical and Anthropological...Derived From...The Examinations For Military Service in the Armies of the United States During the Late War of the Rebellion of Over a Million...Men,* 1987, two thick volumes, orig cloth, 568 pgs and 767 pgs, sgd letter from author laid -in, fold-out maps and charts. 295.00

Boker, George H., *Poems of the War,* Ticknor and Fields, 1864, orig cloth, 202 pgs 25.00

Carter, William H., *Life of Lieutenant General Chaffee*, Chicago, c1917, cloth 90.00

Chesnut, Mary, *Mary Chesnut's Civil War*, edited by C. Vann Woodward, New Haven: 1981, first edition, dj with two closed tears 50.00

Dean, Henry Clay, *Crimes of the Civil War, and Curse of the Funding System*, Innes & Co., 1868, 512 pgs, original cloth, first edition, front hinge weak 120.00

Dodge, W.C., *Memorial To the Hon. Secretary of War, or How to Strengthen Our Army and Crush the Rebellion With a Saving of Life and Treasure,* McGill & Witherow, 1864, 12 pgs, some discoloration to front wrap 40.00

Douglas, Henry, *I Rode With Stonewall, Being Chiefly the War Experiences of the Youngest Member of Jackson's Staff,* UNC Press, 1943, worn dj, plates, 401 pgs, 8th printing 30.00

Dyer, Frederick H., *A Compedium of The Army of The Rebellion Complied...From Official Records of the Federal and Confederate Armies...of the Battles...(and) a Concise History of Each And Every Regiment, Battery, Battalion...Mustered...For Service in the Union Army...,"* Dyer Publishing Co., 1908, 1,796 pgs, orig half leather and cloth, 1st edition, leather spine lightly chipped. 195.00

Foote, Shelby, *The Civil War, A Narrative,* Random House, 1958-1974, three volumes, dj. 115.00

Gould, John Mead, *Joseph K. F. Mansfield, ... A Narrative of Events Connected With His Mortal Wounding At Antietam, September 17, 1862,* Stephen Berry, printer, 1895. 32 pgs,

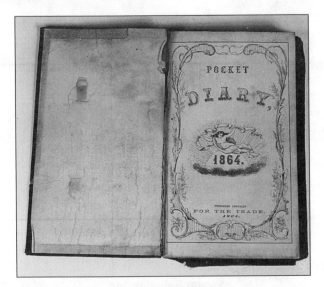

Diary, Lt. George Hill, 7th Michigan Cavalry, 1864, $2,475. Photo courtesy of Jackson's Auctioneers & Appraisers.

portrait, printed tan wrappers; minor tear at foot of front wrapper 45.00

Haskell, Frank Aretas, *The Battle of Gettysburg,* Wisconsin History Commission, reprint No. 1, 1908, portrait, ex.lib. 75.00

Henderson, G. F. R., *The Civil War: A Soldier's View,* Chicago, 1958, cloth, dj, laid-in folding mak 15.00

Henry, Robert S., *The Story of the Confederacy,* Garden City, 1931, cloth, worn dj 10.00

Henry, Robert Selph, *The First With the Most Forest,* Indianapolis, 1944, cloth, plates, 558 pgs, 1st edition 25.00

Hill, W.B. et al., *Address of the Unconditional Union State Committee to the People of Maryland, September 16th, 1863,* Sherwood & Co., 1863, 20 pgs 30.00

Hosmer, James, *The Color-Guard: Being a Corpora's Notes of Military Service in the Nineteenth Army Corps,* Walker, Wise, and Company, 1864, 244 pgs, rebound in black cloth 35.00

Johnson, Robert U. and Buel, Clarence C., eds., *Battles and Leaders of the Civil War, The Century War Book, People's Pictorial Edition,* Century Co., 1894, oblong folio, twenty parts, staples in pictorial wrappers 25.00

King, W. C. and W. P. Derby, *Campfire Sketches And Battlefield Echoes of 61-5,* Springfield, MA, 1888, pictorial cloth 20.00

Liddell, B. H., *Sherman: Soldier, Realist, American,* New York, 1929, cloth 15.00

McClellan, George B., *Report on the Organization And Campaigns of the Army of the Potomac, to Which is Added An Account of the Campaign in Western Virginia,* New York, 1864, cloth, lacks front flyleaf, four maps 65.00

Mills, Lewis Este. *General Pope's Virginia Campaign of 1862.* Read before the Cincinnati Literary Club, Feb. 5, 1870, Tribune Book and Job Office, Detroit, 1870, 32 pgs, printed paper wrapper 80.00

Morgan, Mrs. Irby (Julia), *How It Was: Four Years Among the Rebels,* Nashville, 1892, 12mo, orig dec cloth, 204 pgs, portraits, first edition 250.00

Nichols, George Ward, *The Story of the Great March. From the Diary of a Staff Officer, with a map and illustrations,* NY, 1865, 394 pgs, folding map with color line representing Sherman's route through Georgia and the Carolinas, first edition 100.00

Poore, Ben. Perley, *Life and Public Serves of Ambrose E. Burnside, Soldier-Citizen-Statesman,* Providence, 1882, decorated cloth 50.00

Riley, Harvey, *The Mule, A Treatise on the Breeding, Training and Uses to which He May Be Put,* Philadelphia, Claxton, Remsen & Haffelfinger, 1869. 107 pp. 14 full page illustrations, orig cloth boards, gilt Sherman mule on upper cover, dull boards with wear at extremities, owner's rubber stamp 125.00

Robotham, Tom, *The Civil War Album,* New York, 1992, 304 pgs 30.00

Ross, Ishbel, *Rebel Rose, Life of Rose O'Neal Geenhow, Confederate Spy,* Harper, 1954, paper wraps, uncorrected proof prior to publication with pencil notes throughout by reviewer. 30.00

Steele, Henry, *The Blue and the Gray, The Story of the Civil War As Told By Participants,* 1950, two volumes, orig cloth 30.00

Taylor, Richard, *Destruction and Reconstruction: Personal Experiences of the Late War,* Appleton, 1879, first edition 200.00

Wheeler, A. O., *Eye-Witness; Or, Life Scenes in the Old North State, Depicting the Trials and Sufferings of the Unionists During The Rebellion,* Boston, 1866, 2nd edition, cloth 125.00

Williams, George, *Bullet and Shell, War As the Soldier Saw It...Illustrated, From Sketches Among the Actual Scenes By Edward Forbes,* NY, c1882, pictorial cloth 20.00

Williams, William, G., *Days of Darkness: The Gettysburg Civilians,* Shippensburg, PA, 1986, dj, 254 pages 20.00

Adjutant General of Indiana Report on the Civil War, multi-volume set, professionally rebound 575.00

A Review of the Minority Report, on the Navy Yard Question, With An Appendix, Containing Letters From Maj. General John A. Dix, Starr and Farnham, 1864. 36 pgs, folded map 70.00

Have We the Best Possible Ambulance System? Walker, Wise, and Company, 1864, 18 pgs 40.00

Key To Bachelder's Isometrical Drawing of the Gettysburg Battlefield With a Brief Description of the Battle, C.A. Alvord, 1868. 12 pgs, faded blue wraps 45.00

Kindton, Whitehall And Goldsboro (North Carolina) Expedition, December, 1862, W.W. Howe, 1890 . . . . 90.00

Laws Relating to the Direct and Excise Taxes, Passed During the Thirty-Seventh Congress, Government Printing Office, 1862. 117 pgs, sewn 50.00

Opinions of Loyalists Concerning the Great Questions of the Times;... On Occasion of the Inauguration of the Royal National League, in Mass Meeting on Union Square, New York, on the 11th of April, 1863, The Anniversary of the Attack On Fort Sumter, C.S. Westcott & Co., 1863, 144 pgs 35.00

The Boot on the Other Leg: Or, Loyalty Above Party, "Printed for Gratuitous Distribution," Philadelphia, 1863, 16 pgs . .30.00.

The Conduct of the War. Report of the Congressional Committee on the Operations of the Army of the Potomac. Causes of Its Inaction and Ill Success. Its Several Campaigns. Why M'clellan Was Removed. The Battle Of Fredericksburg. Removal of Burnside, Tribune Association, New York, 1863., 30 Pgs 65.00

The American Soldier and Sailor in War. A Pictorial History of...the War Between the States...And Our Country's War With Spain..., Edward J. Stanley, folio, orig cloth, 568 pgs, cover rubbed 30.00

The Shaping of a Battle: Gettysburg, Montgomery, 1st ed., 1959 . . . . 20.00

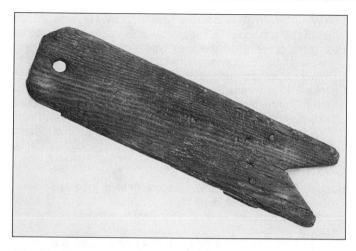

Wood, pine, one piece, primitive, 17" l, $20.

BOOTJACKS

History: Bootjacks are metal or wooden devices that facilitate the removal of boots. Bootjacks are used by placing the heel of the boot in the U-shaped opening, putting the other foot on the back of the bootjack, and pulling the boot off the front foot.

Advertising, Mussleman's Plug Tobacco, cast iron 125.00
Bronze, 9-/2" l, Naughty Nellie 175.00
Cast Iron
    9-/4" l, beetle, worn black paint 40.00
    10-/2" l, cricket, labeled "Boot Jack, the Tri State Foundry Co.
      Cincinnati, Ohio," worn black paint 40.00
    13" l, open heart and circle, scalloped sides 220.00
    19" l, two pheasants, brushes 225.00
Wood
    11" l, folding 40.00
    17" l, pine, primitive, hole for hanging 40.00
    22" l, walnut, hearts and diamonds openwork 50.00

BOTTLES, GENERAL

History: Cosmetic bottles held special creams, oils, and cosmetics designed to enhance the beauty of the user. Some also claimed, especially on their colorful labels, to cure or provide relief from common ailments.

A number of household items, e.g., cleaning fluids and polishes, required glass storage containers. Many are collected for their fine lithographed labels.

Mineral water bottles contained water from a natural spring. Spring water was favored by health-conscious people between the 1850s and 1900s.

Nursing bottles, used to feed the young and sickly, were a great help to the housewife because of their graduated measure markings, replaceable nipples, and the ease with which they could be cleaned, sterilized, and reused.

References: Ralph & Terry Kovel, *Kovels' Bottles Price List,* 10th ed., Crown Publishers, 1996; Peck and Audie Markota, *Western Blob Top Soda and Mineral Bottles,* 2nd ed., published by authors, 1994; John Odell, *Digger Odell's Official Antique Bottle and Glass Collector Maga-* *zine Price Guide Series,* Vols. 1 through 8, published by author (1910 Shawhan Rd, Morrow, OH 45152), 1995; Diane Ostrander, *Guide to American Nursing Bottles,* 1984, revised ed. by American Collectors of Infant Feeders, 1992; Michael Polak, *Bottles,* Avon Books, 1994; Dick Roller (comp.), *Indiana Glass Factories Notes,* Acorn Press, 1994; Carlo and Dorothy Sellari, *The Standard Old Bottle Price Guide,* 1989, 1997 value update, Collector Books.

Periodicals: *Antique Bottle and Glass Collector,* P.O. Box 187, East Greenville, PA 18041; *Canadian Bottle and Stoneware Collector,* 179D Woodridge Crescent, Nepean, Ontario K2B 7T2 Canada.

Collectors' Clubs: American Collectors of Infant Feeders, 5161 W 59th St., Indianapolis, IN 46254; Federation of Historical Bottle Collectors, Inc.; 1485 Buck Hill Drive, Southampton, PA 18966; Midwest Antique Fruit Jar & Bottle Club, P.O. Box 38, Flat Rock, IN 47234; New England Antique Bottle Club, 120 Commonwealth Rd, Lynn, MA 01904; San Bernardino County Historical Bottle and Collectible Club, P.O. Box 6759, San Bernardino, CA 92412.

Museums: Hawaii Bottle Museum, Honolulu, HI; National Bottle Museum, Ballston Spa, NY; Old Bottle Museum, Salem, NJ.

Additional Listings: Barber Bottles; Bitter Bottles; Figural Bottles; Food Bottles; Ink Bottles; Medicine Bottles; Poison Bottles; Sarsaparilla Bottles; Snuff Bottles. Also see the bottle categories in *Warman's Americana & Collectibles* for more examples.

SPECIAL AUCTION

Norman C. Heckler & Company
Bradford Corner Rd.
Woodstock Valley, CT 02682

Baby and Nursing

Acme, clear, lay-down, emb 65.00
Baby's Delight 45.00
Bunny, Hazel Atlas 15.50
Cala Nurser, oval, clear, emb, ring on neck, 7-1/8" h 8.00
Cat, Anchor Hocking 25.00
Cats and Kittens, enamel dec with oz measurements . . . 21.50
Comfy, bottle with orig nipple 15.00
Dominion Glass Co., Canada, 8 oz, narrow mouth, orig filled with
    Vanilla Extract from Pure Standard Products, orig label, nursery rhyme, "I had a little hobby horse," imp image of little boy
    riding rocking horse, 1940s 15.00
Empire Nursing Bottle, bent neck, 6-1/2" h 50.00
Evenflo, 4 oz, black plastic ring, flat cap, rubber nipple orig cardboard sleeve, paper adv flyer, date 1956 on sleeve. . . 12.00
Fire King, sapphire blue
    8 oz. 60.00
Binky's Nip Cap. 210.00
Steri-Seal Nipple Cover, colorless, emb on cover. 25.00
Griptight, banana shape, hole at both ends, colorless, emb
    name 25.00

Hailwoods Graduated Feeding Bottle, aqua, applied top, flattened bladder shape, 2" neck, markings up to 8 oz on back, front emb with name, 7" h 75.00
Happy Baby 10.00
Hygeia, adv on panels 15.00
Hygienic Feeder, emb, open on both ends 30.00
Manx Feeding Bottle, bulbous, clear, tooled sq collar, emb "Patent July 4, 1876," 3" h 200.00
Marguerite Feeding Bottle, inside screw, daisy on top . . . 35.00
Mother's Comfort, clear, turtle type 25.00
Nonpareil Nurser, aqua, 5-1/2" h 20.00
Nursery Rhyme, enameled Jack and Jill 15.00
Ovale Nurser, Non-Rolling, Whitall Tatum & Co., 6 oz, applied lip, narrow mouth 10.00
Pottstown, PA, dairy giveaway, set of five bottles, each enameled with nursery rhyme, one with bank top, other with plastic closure, nipple, yellow and blue congratulations box, never used 25.00
Pyrex
 4 oz, narrow mouth, orig cardboard sleeve 12.00
 8 oz, air vent feature, six-sided, narrow top, pink and blue graphics, orig box 20.00
Sure Feed Ltd. Carfidd, flat turtle shape, long neck, colorless, emb on top 40.00
Sweet Babee Nurser, colorless, emb "Easy Clean, Pat'd May 3, 1910" 15.00
Teddy's Pet, Peaceful Nights, colorless, emb, turtle shape, 4 oz 70.00
The Hygienic Feeder, banana shape, hole at both ends, colorless, emb name 25.00
Tuffy Kap, nipple cov, colorless, emb "Tuffy KAP U.S.A." around cap, "B" in circle on flat top 10.00

Beverage

Drink Howel's Original Orange-Julep, 12" h, cylindrical, colorless, white, gold, red, and yellow orange label under glass, sheared mouth, metal cap, smooth base, America, 1880-90. . . . . 125.00
Grapette, 1946 . . . . 10.00
J. M. Roseberry & Co., Alexandria, VA, eagle wreath and shield, soda water, attributed to Baltimore Glass Works, Baltimore, MD, 1845-60, squat cylindrical form, yellowish green, applied sloping collared mouth, iron pontil mark, half pint, overall ext. wear, 3/8" flat chip 800.00

Left: amber blown globular bottle, 24 swirled ribs, Zanesville, stain, 7-1/2" h, $385; center: golden amber blown chestnut, 24 vertical ribs, Zanesville, wear and scratches, 5-1/4" h, $275; right: amber blown globular bottle, 24 swirled ribs, Zanesville, stain and wear, 7-1/2" h, $220. Photo courtesy of Garth's Auctions, Inc.

Port Wine, brown glass, backbar type, emb, oval reverse painted label, 12" h 155.00
Port Wine, green glass, backbar type, colorful applied reverse painted label, cork stopper, metal top chained to bottle, 13" h, minor chipping on edges of label 125.00
Steinke & Kornahrens/Soda Water/Return This Bottle/Charleston SC, America, 1845-60, octagonal, cobalt blue, applied sloping collared mouth, iron pontil mark, oversize half pint, 7-3/4" h, professionally cleaned to orig luster, some remaining scratches 650.00

Cosmetic

Boswell & Warner's Colorific, rect, cobalt blue, indented panels, tooled sq lip, c1880, 5-1/2" h 85.00
Edwards Harlene Astol Hair Colour Restorer, three sunken panels, cobalt blue, 7" h 55.00
Ferd. Muhlens Inc., New York No. 4711 Bath Salts, orig label 20.00
Harrisons Hair Colour Restorer, Amber, Reading, sunken panel, emb on front, 6" h 18.00
Hind's Honey and Almond Cream, 5-1/2" h 7.50
Hyacinthia Toilet hair Dressing, rect, aqua, crude applied lip, open pontil, 6" h 25.00
Lavender Salts, cylinder, recessed reverse painted label, raised bottom with same pattern as ribbed stop, ground stopper, 6-3/4" h 100.00
Mrs. S. A. Allens World's Hair Restorer, amber, rect, three sunken panels, emb name and "London" on base, 7" h . . . 30.00
Oriental Lotion The Persian Secret Beautifier, blue, emb, paper label, lady admiring her image in mirror, back emb "Elysian Mfg. Co. Chemists & Perfumers," unopened, 7" h 95.00
Prichard & Constance, London & New York, Tonic Bath Crystals, orig label 20.00
 The Mexican Hair Renewer, rounded shoulder, rect emb on edges, cobalt blue, 7" h 35.00

Household

Ammonia, Parson's, aqua, 1882 . . . . 20.00
Blueing, Jennings, aqua, blob top, 7" h 8.00
Cleaning, Lysol, amber, Lysol Boots All British around shoulder, jug, 6-1/2" h 20.00
Furniture Polish
 Alma Polish, aqua, name emb on shoulder, mkd "M & Go" on base, 5" h 8.00
Gordon's Chafola Furniture Polish, emb, open pontil . . . 150.00
Osborn's Liquid Polish, cylindrical, yellow olive, inward rolled mouth, tubular pontil scar, American, 1840-60, 3-5/8" h 475.00
Oil, Standard Oil Co., colorless, orig label, 6" h 7.50

Mineral or spring water

Artesian Water, round, golden chocolate amber, twelve panled base, iron pontil, 1850-60, pint 450.00
B. R. Lippincott & Co., Stockton Superior, Mineral Water, Union Glass Works, 1852-58, cobalt blue, applied top, iron pontil, 7-3/8" h 450.00
Buffalo Mineral Water Springs Natures, Materia Medica Trade Mark, yellow, lady sitting on stool, 10-1/2" h 125.00
Chase & Co. Mineral Water, San Francisco, CA, green, applied top, iron pontil, 7-3/8" h 60.00
Clarke & Co., New York, America, 1840-60, cylindrical, olive amber, applied sloping collared mouth with ring pontil scar, quart 170.00
D. A. Knowlton, Saratoga, NY, America, 1960-80, high shouldered cylinder, olive green, applied sloping collared mouth with ring, smooth base, quart 100.00

G. W. Weston & Co., Saratoga, NY, America, 1840-60, cylindrical, yellow olive, applied sloping collared mouth with ring, pontil scar, pint, 1" vertical body crack on reverse . . . 375.00

Lancaster Glass Works, round, sapphire blue, applied blob top, iron pontil, 1850-60, 7" h 120.00

Lynch & Clarke, New York, America, 1840-60, cylindrical, yellowish olive, applied sloping collared mouth with ring, pontil scar, pint 275.00

Lynde & Putnam, Mineral Waters, San Francisco Cala, Union Glass Works, Philada, teal blue, applied top, iron pontil, 7-1/2" h 100.00

M. T. Crawford/Springfield-Superior Mineral Water, Union Glass Works, Philadelphia, PA, 1845-60, squat cylindrical form, mug base, cobalt blue, heavy applied collared mouth, iron pontil mark, half pint, some int. stain, 1/2" bruise on top of mouth 160.00

Oak Orchard Acid Springs, H. W. Bostwick, Broadway, NY, golden olive green, whittled three part mold, bottom emb "Glass from F. Hitchins Factory Lockport, NY," applied sloping lip with small flakes, 9" h 200.00

Round Lake Mineral Water, red amber, 9-1/4" h 750.00

Rutherford's Premium Mineral Water, ground pontil, dark olive, 7-1/2" h 60.00

San Francisco Glass Works, tapered neck, blob top, sea green, 6-7/8" h 15.00

Saratoga Highrock Spring (fancy rock) Saratoga, NY, America, 1860-80, cylindrical, bright medium green, applied sloping collared mouth with ring, smooth base, pint, 1/2" shallow chip on mouth 850.00

Saratoga Seltzer Water, cylindrical, teal blue-green, applied ring lip, c1890, 7-1/2" h 85.00

Veronica Mineral Water, amber, sq 10.00

Utility

3-5/8" h, freeblown, flattened chestnut form, short neck, bright green, sheared mouth, pontil scar, American, 1800-30 . . . . 300.00

7-7/8" h, freeblown, rect, chamfered corners, dark olive amber, applied sloping collared mouth with ring, pontil scar, America, 1800-30, ext. wear 275.00

9-1/4" h, freeblown, globular, golden amber, heavy applied mouth, pontil scar, attributed to Midwest America, 1800-30, some int. stain 230.00

BRASS

History: Brass is a durable, malleable, and ductile metal alloy consisting mainly of copper and zinc. The height of its popularity for utilitarian and decorative art items occurred in the 18th and 19th centuries.

References: Mary Frank Gaston, *Antique Brass & Copper*, Collector Books, 1992, 1994 value update; Rupert Gentle and Rachael Feild, *Domestic Metalwork 1640-1820*, Revised, Antique Collectors' Club, 1994; Henry J. Kaufmann, *Early American Copper, Tin & Brass*, Astragal Press, 1995.

REPRODUCTION ALERT

Many modern reproductions are being made of earlier brass forms, especially such items as buckets, fireplace equipment, and kettles.

Additional Listings: Bells; Candlesticks; Fireplace Equipment; Scientific Instruments.

Andirons, pr, 15" h, early 225.00

Bed Warmer
40" l, floral engraved lid, turned wooden handle with old finish 420.00
42" l, engraved lid, turned wooden handle, age crack in handle 275.00
43" l, brass and copper, engraved lid, turned wooden handle, old repairs 220.00
43-3/4" l, foliage engraved lid, turned wood handle, minor imperfections 200.00

Bird Cage, sq, ornate, brass and copper, 19th C 300.00

Bookends, pr, 7-3/4" h, George Washington, red, white, and gold paint, 1932 . . . . 75.00

Box
3-3/8" d, hexagonal, gilded, inset ivory with miniature painting of man and woman, sgd 110.00
11" l, repousse dec, rampant lions, Victorian-style . . . 100.00

Candleholder, 12" w, 6" h, Arts & Crafts, three candles, imp "Hand Wrought L. C. Shellabarger" 600.00

Candlestick
Set, graduated set, baluster shaft, pr 14-1/2" h Ace of Diamonds, pr 12-1/4" h King of Diamonds, pr 11-3/4" Queen of Diamonds, pr 11-3/4" h, Diamond Prince, pr 10-3/4" h, Diamond Princess, English 1,350.00
Single, 9" h, Queen Anne, Continental, first half 18th C, very minor dents 290.00

Candy Thermometer, 12" l 80.00

Carriage Lamp
9-1/2" h, marked "Neverout Insulated Kerosene Safety, Rose Mfg. Co., Philadelphia, USA," price for pr 250.00
23-1/2" h, ball finials, two etched glass side panels, ball ends, price for pr 160.00

Clock Jack, 15" h, mkd "No. 7 Warranted," John Linwood, heart shaped key 300.00

Coal Bucket, 13" h, bail handle, foliate design, repousse 175.00

Fireplace Fender, 42" l, three-bar design above pierced skirt, molded base 275.00

Fireplace Set, 16-1/2" h belted ball top andirons, matching tongs, and shovel, America, late 19th C, repairs to dogs 425.00

Heater, 8-1/4" d, 7-1/2" h, octagonal, pierced, four turned feet, bail handle, four lines inscribed on top in Dutch 300.00

Icon, Russian, cast
4 x 5-1/2" open, triptcyh, St. Nicholas center panel, wings display Annunciation and Feast Days, 18th C 165.00
7 x 15-1/2" open, folding, Church Feasts, each leaf divided into quadrants with different feast, back panel displaying cross and outer walls of Jersualem 440.00

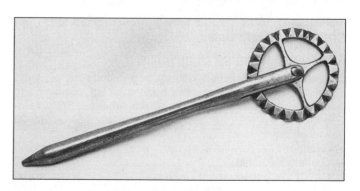

Pie Crimper, 5-1/2" l, $20.

Inkwell, 8-1/4" w, 3" h, Arts and Crafts design, hammered finish, strip work hinges, dark patina, ceramic insert 200.00

Kettle, 13" d, spun, iron bale handle, orig label "American Brass Kettle" 85.00

Lamp
10-1/2" h, gimbal, saucer base 140.00
20" h, cranberry flash receptacle and shade, trefoil shaped stem and base, faceted prisms, marked "J & I Cox, New York," c1880, electrified 550.00
25" h, Baroque Revival, oil, molded high relief figures and foliage, scrolled base, converted, price for pr 1,610.00
28" support tube, hanging, gas light, two burners, etched crystal shades, black and copper stripes 165.00

Noodle Maker Roller, 8-1/2" w, marked "F Crafts, Rochester, NY" 60.00

Pail, 9-1/2" h, 6" h, spun, iron bale handle, marked "Haydens Patent" 75.00

Sauce Pan, 5-3/4" to 8-1/2", wrought iron handles, price for assembled set of 5 . . . . 330.00

Skimmer, 18-1/4" l, star flower shape holes, wrought iron handle 60.00

Steelyard, 18-1/4" l, mkd "Wm. B Preston, Boston" 95.00

Sundial Compass, sunburst on lid, 1940s 275.00

Taper Jack, with wick, English, early 19th C 380.00

Tea Kettle, 8" h, gooseneck spout, turned wooden handle 60.00

Telescope, five sections, orig lens cap 165.00

Tool, leg calipers 60.00

Trivet
7-1/4" x 12-1/4" x 5-1/2" h, reticulated, lion and unicorn, English 195.00
10-5/8" l, punch engraved date 1826, replaced feet . . 60.00

Wall Sconces, pr, 13-1/2" h, 8" w, hand wrought, double light, hammered on front "A.N.N.O. 1698" and "A.N.N.O. 1693" 475.00

Wick Trimmer, 9-1/2" l, orig tray 90.00

BREAD PLATES

History: Beginning in the mid-1880s, special trays or platters were made for serving bread and rolls. Designated "bread plates" by collectors, these small trays or platters can be found in porcelain, glass (especially pattern glass), and metals.

Bread plates often were part of a china or glass set. However, many glass companies made special plates which honored national heroes, commemorated historical or special events, offered a moral maxim, or supported a religious attitude. The subject matter appears either horizontally or vertically. Most of these plates are oval and ten inches in length.

Reference: Anna Maude Stuart, *Bread Plates and Platters*, published by author, 1965.

Additional Listings: Pattern Glass.

Cut Glass, 13" x 6", allover hobstar in diamonds cutting, large satin flower with multi-diamond buttons in center cover inside of base, self handles, cut sawtooth rim, American Brilliant Period 165.00

Historical Glass
Beecher 65.00
Garfield Memorial 45.00
Liberty and Freedom 65.00
Three Presidents, frosted 75.00

Train, locomotive and cars, colorless, $90.

US Grant 50.00

Majolica
Etruscan, emb fern leaves and wheat sheaves 265.00
Pond Lily pattern 200.00

Pattern Glass
Basketweave, amber 40.00
Beaded Loop 30.00
Crying Baby, frog on plate, 13" d 99.00
Deer and Pine Tree 45.00
Finecut and Panel, amber 48.00
Garden of Eden, 9-1/4" x 12-1/2" 40.00
Minerva 60.00
Rock of Ages, clear, milk glass center 125.00
Royal Lady, vaseline 130.00
Scroll with Flowers 30.00
Three Graces 50.00
Wheat 30.00

Silver
12" l, reticulated sides, wheat design, monogrammed, marked "Tiffany & Co., Sterling," 15 troy oz, minor dents 440.00
14" l, basketweave tray partially covered by tromp d'eoil causally folded napkin with linen look, fringed hem, Pavel Ovchinnikov, Moscow, 1874 . . . . 5,520.00

BRIDE'S BASKETS

History: A ruffled-edge glass bowl in a metal holder was a popular wedding gift between 1880 and 1910, hence the name "bride's basket." These bowls can be found in most glass types of the period. The metal holder was generally silver plated with a bail handle, thus enhancing the basket image.

Over the years, bowls and bases became separated and married pieces resulted. If the base has been lost, the bowl should be sold separately.

Reference: John Mebane, *Collecting Bride's Baskets and Other Glass Fancies*, Wallace-Homestead, 1976.

Reproduction Alert: The glass bowls have been reproduced.

Note: Items listed below have a silver-plated holder unless otherwise noted.

8" d, blue cased glass shading to white bowl, enameled dec, Victorian 100.00

8" d, cased, red to white, small elegant SP frame 250.00

8" d, 10-1/2" h, Loetz-type glass, irid blue, and purple, recessed indentations, ruffled, ground pontil, ftd metal stand . . 345.00

8" d, 10-1/2" h, sq crimped edge bowl, white cased to rose-red, cameo cut winged griffins, floral bouquets and swags, fitted SP metal frame with leaf and berry embellished handle, Mt. Washington Glass Co. bowl, frame mkd "Pairpoint". . 825.00

8-1/2" d, 14-1/2" h, heavenly blue satin glass shading to pale white, diamond quilted design, pie crust crimped edge, orig fancy silver plated holder, Mt. Washington. 400.00

9" d, Peachblow, shiny finish bowl, applied amber rim, SP Wilcox holder. 215.00

9" d, 12" h, Mt. Washington, Rose Amber, Coin Spot pattern, deep color, fancy silver plated Pairpoint stand. 875.00

9-1/4" d, blue opalescent, crimped rim, reticulated SP holder mkd "Wallingford, Biggins & Rodgers Co.". 225.00

9-1/2" d, MOP satin, Diamond Quilted pattern, deep blue shading to pale blue int., blue shading to white ext., applied frosted crimped edge, Mt. Washington. 600.00

9-1/2" d, pigeon blood, enamel floral dec, SP holder . . . 225.00

9-3/4" d, 11" h, off-white ext., shaded rose int., crystal ruffled edge, Rogers & Bros. SP basket with two small hands, chains, fruit design on holder 300.00

10" d, 2-1/2" h, deep rose shading to pink satin bowl, ruffled, enameled floral dec 225.00

10-1/2" h, colorless frosted bowl, overlaid in pink crystal, etched acorn and oak leaf dec, gilt metal frame with basket handles, Victorian 250.00

10-1/2" d, 10-3/4" h, MOP satin, Diamond Quilted pattern, deep pink shading to pale pink to off-white, Mt. Washington rectangular form bowl, applied frosted edge, orig fancy silver plated Victorian "Manhattan Silver Company," holder has been resilvered 400.00

10-1/2" d, 12-1/2" h, oval satin bow, blue int., white ext., pleated rim, applied frosted ribbon edge, ornate ftd Forbes frame 250.00

11" d, cased, pink ext., peachblow int., gold stylized flowers, ornate SP holder with aquatic marine life motif, mkd "Pairpoint Mfg. Co.". 825.00

11" d, 10-1/2" h, white and vaseline bowl, all over floral enamel dec, fancy silver plated frame, sgd "Meriden," minor handle restoration 300.00

Cased white ext., shaded pink int., gold floral dec, clear ruffled rim, stand mkd "Superior Silver Co. Quad Plate 1000," $125.

11-1/2" h, sapphire blue bowl, applied ruffled rim, gold tracery and courting scene dec, ornate ftd Meriden stand . . . 325.00

11-1/2" d, 12" h, dark red satin glass shaded to cream, ruffled and crimped rim, SP stand. 275.00

11-1/2" d, 13-1/2" h, ruffled white shading to pink to raspberry bowl, cased in white, plum dec, gold ranches, hanging ferns, gold dotted florals, ornate double handled silver frame, figural flowers on handle and base 400.00

13" l, 12-1/2" h, oval satin bowl, shaded raspberry ext., brilliant turquoise int., tightly ruffed pleated and fold-in edge, rect shape, white and gold enameled floral leaf and berry dec on ornate ftd rope handled silver plated orig frame. 650.00

13-1/2" h, robin's egg blue shaded to white, scalloped rim, applied frosted ribbon, frosted Optic Petal pattern, SP base with engraved griffins, butterflies, and bees on sides, full figural swan inside, figural lilies and berries on handle, mkd "Reed & Barton" 300.00

BRISTOL GLASS

History: Bristol glass is a designation given to a semi-opaque glass, usually decorated with enamel and cased with another color.

Initially, the term referred only to glass made in Bristol, England, in the 17th and 18th centuries. By the Victorian era, firms on the Continent and in America were copying the glass and its forms.

Biscuit Jar, cov, 5" d, 7-1/2" h, apple green body, enameled green and yellow flowers and plants, SP rim, cov, handle, and base, figural strawberry finial 195.00

Bowl, colorless, cinched, ruffled, crimped, hp 65.00

Box, cov

   1-5/8" l, 1" h, turquoise body, gold dec. 110.00

   5-3/4" l, 3-5/8" h, egg shape, white body, pink, cream, blue, and yellow flowers 225.00

Compote, fluted, white body, hand painted cat scene, metal base 95.00

Condiment Set, cov mustard pot, pepper shaker with orig lid, open salt, milk white, pink and blue flowers and green leaves dec, 4-1/4" x 5-3/4" SP holder 175.00

Creamer and Sugar, cov, white body, multicolored floral dec 65.00

Cruet, 6-3/4" h, enameled floral dec 50.00

Decanter

   8-3/8" h, gray, encrusted floral engraving, butterflies, gilt trim, vase-like stopper 60.00

   9-1/4" h, 3-1/2" d, apple green body, reeded gold trimmed green handles, matching stopper 120.00

Egg Cup, white body, gold bands 25.00

Ewer, 4-1/2" h, 2-3/4" d, turquoise, enameled pink flowers, white and green leaves, yellow scrolls, gold trim, applied turquoise handles, pr 190.00

Garniture Set, 19-1/2" h cov jar, 14-1/2" vases, pink, dec with courtship scenes, black and gold highlights, green vines, small chip to vase rim. 300.00

Goblet, 10-3/4" h, pedestal base, opaque blue ground, polychrome enamel floral dec, gilt trim 95.00

Lamp

   13-1/4" h, blue body, enameled white egret, multicolored flowers and foliage, brass oil fittings, black base 300.00

   31" h, black ground, white enameled scene of woman on tree branch 180.00

Mantle Vase, 11" h, painted transfer scene of boy with poodle, large hand painted florals, 19th C, pr 150.00

Miniature Lamp, 10" h, 4-3/4" d, white shaded to soft blue, dainty enameled orange flowers, green leaves, sq ruffled shade, base with matching flowers, brown flying bird, applied opalescent shell feet, orig burner and chimney 885.00

Patch Box, 1" h, 1-1/4" d, hinged, soft pink ground, enameled brown and white bird 100.00

Perfume Bottle, 3-7/8" h, hourglass shape, opaque blue, silver mounted cap. 175.00

Pitcher, 8-1/4" h, light green body, enameled bird and flowers, applied clear handle 95.00

Plate, 14-1/2" d, white body, hand painted, lavender and ochre French lilacs, green leaves. 80.00

Ring Box, cov, 1-3/4" h, 1-3/4" d, turquoise body, gold flowers and leaves 50.00

Salt, 2-3/4" d, light gray body, enameled herons and foliage, SP rim and handle 48.00

Sweetmeat Jar, 4-1/2" d, 5-1/2" h, floral garlands and butterflies dec, SP top and bail handle 125.00

Tumbler, 6-3/4" h, 2-3/4" d, turquoise body, gold and white rope garlands, gold foot 72.00

Vase

    4" h, caramel acid finish, hand painted scenic and floral dec, remnants of French retailer's label 50.00

    8" h, 2-3/4" w, Fireglow, beige ground, white flowers, green and gold leaves, worn gold accents, matched pr 100.00

Vase, opaque blue, hand painted white florals, green leaves, scalloped rim, $70.

8-1/2" h, light pink shading to dark pink, hp enameled design 65.00

8-1/2" h, white body, enameled floral and leaf dec, ruffled top, ram's head handles 75.00

9" h, white body, portrait of young boy and girl, facing pr 165.00

9-3/8" h, white body, hand painted, flowers, gold trim, raised enameling, pr. 150.00

10" h, blue body, cut-out base, enameled floral dec, pr 120.00

13" h, 6" d, shaded pastel yellow ground, red and purple poppies and white daisies, tapered cylinder 100.00

BRITISH ROYALTY COMMEMORATIVES

History: British commemorative china, souvenirs to commemorate coronations and other royal events, dates from the 1600s, with the early pieces being rather crude in design and form. With the development of transfer printing, c1780, the images on the wares more closely resembled the monarchs.

Few commemorative pieces predating Queen Victoria's reign are found today at popular prices. Items associated with Queen Elizabeth II and her children, e.g., the wedding of HRH Prince Andrew and Miss Sarah Ferguson and the subsequent birth of their daughter HRH Princess Beatrice, are very common.

Some British Royalty commemoratives are easily recognized by their portraits of past or present monarchs. Some may be in silhouette profile. Royal symbols include crowns, dragons, royal coats of arms, national flowers, swords, scepters, dates, messages, and monograms.

References: Susan and Al Bagdade, *Warman's English & Continental Pottery & Porcelain*, 3rd Edition, Krause Publications, 1998; Douglas H. Flynn and Alan H. Bolton, *British Royalty Commemoratives*, Schiffer Publishing, 1994; Lincoln Hallinan, *British Commemoratives*, Antique Collectors' Club, 1993; Eric Knowles, *Miller's Royal Memorabilia*, Reed Consumer Books, 1994.

Collectors' Club: Commemorative Collector's Society, The Gardens, Gainsborough Rd, Winthrope, New Newark, Nottingham NG24 2NR England.

Periodical: *The Commemorative Collector Newsletter*, Douglas H. Flynn, P.O. Box 294, Lititz, PA 17543-0294.

Additional Listings: See *Warman's Americana & Collectibles* for more examples.

Autograph

    Christmas Card, Elizabeth II, 1954, photo showing Queen, Prince Philip flanking 6-year-old Prince Charles and 4-year-old Princess Anne, sgd in lower blank margin by Queen, "Elizabeth R" and Prince "Phillip," 1 page, oblong 8vo, emb royal crown on cover 250.00

    Document Signed, Charles II, Dec. 20, 1680, London, instructing Sir Robert Howard to pay sum, 1 page 4to, soiled 690.00

    Manuscript Document, Charles II, countersigned by Samuel Pepys, Sept. 29, 1674, London, reassigning naval cook, 1 page, small folio, matted with reproductions of early Charles II and Pepys portraits 980.00

Mug, Edward VIII Coronation, decal dec, dated May, 1937, Minton, $40.

Note Signed, Edward VIII, sgd "Edward" in pencil, both sides of 3-1/2" x 4-1/2" printed Marlborough House card, dated London July 3, 1904, note regarding forgotten prayer book 850.00

Typed Letter Signed, Duke of Windsor, sgd "Edward," September 1940, to John Royal, Vice President of NBC 220.00

Beaker, 3-1/2" h
Elizabeth II, 1953 Coronation, Poole 35.00
George V\Mary, 1911 Coronation, Bishop and Stonier 75.00

Bell, metal, police helmet shape, Queen Elizabeth II 38.00
Bottle, Coca-Cola, Royal Wedding, 7/29/81, illus of Diana 60.00

Bowl
Edward VIII, 1937 Coronation, Grindly, 6-1/4" d 45.00
Elizabeth II, crown shaped, marked "Queen Elizabeth II, 2 June 1953" to commemorate coronation, 8" d, 4" h 50.00
Victoria, In Memoriam, 1901, pressed glass, 9-1/2" d 120.00

Box, Elizabeth II, 1977 Jubilee, raised flowers, Crown Staffordshire, 1-7/8" d 20.00
Bust, Victoria, parian, circular plinth base, inscribed "To Commemorate the 60th Year of Her Reign 1837-1897" . . 750.00
Cake Plate, Victoria, 1907 Jubilee, sepia portraits, residences, Man of War, 10-3/4" d 140.00
Coronation Chair, 4-5/8" h, sterling silver, gold overlay, Stone of Scone under seat, chair supported by four lions, commemorative plaque, fitted case, Birmingham, 1953, 11 troy oz 750.00
Cup and Saucer, Edward VII\Alexandria, 1888 Silver Wedding Anniversary, coat of arms, oversized 175.00
Folio, Edward VIII Collection, 9" x 11" cover, 8-1/2" x 10-3/4" commemorative tribute folder, orig envelope, following 1936 abdication 30.00
Glass, George IV Coronation, 3-3/4" h, red finish design, one with portrait and inscription "H. M. King George IV Coronation May 12, 1937," second with different portrait view, royalty symbols, inscription "May 1937 Coronation," pr 60.00

Jug, George VI\Elizabeth 1937 Coronation, musical, sepia portraits, Princess Elizabeth\Margaret on reverse, Shelley 275.00
Lithophane, crown, and cypher, 2-3/4" h
Alexandra, 1902, cup 200.00
George V, 1911, mug 175.00
Mary, 1911, cup 275.00
Loving Cup, Elizabeth II, 1972 Silver Wedding Anniversary, Paragon, 3" h 150.00
Match Safe
1-5/8" h, brass, relief of King Edward VII on front, "Long Live the King" on back, c1902 . . . . 85.00
2-1/8" h, Vulcanite, encased picture of King Edward VI 160.00
Mug
Charles, 1969 Investiture as Prince of Wales, gold dragon, feathers, black ground, Portmerion Pottery, 4" h . . . 45.00
Duke and Duchess of Windsor, In Memoriam, black and white portraits, Dorincourt, 3-3/8" h 60.00
Edward VIII, Coronation 50.00
Victoria, 1887 Jubilee, color beaded crown and ribbon, William Whiteley, 3-1/4" h 95.00
Paperweight, Victoria\Albert, black and white portraits, color, glitter, 2-7/8" d 45.00
Photograph, formal wedding photograph by Soper, Duke and Duchess of Windsor, sgd "Edward Duke of Windsor" and "Wallis Duchess of Windsor," dated in Duke's hand, June 3, 1937, 11-1/2" x 9-1/2", mounted, photographer's signature on mount, period standing frame 3,910.00
Pinback Button
Edward VII and Alexandria, multicolored portraits, gold trim, c1902 . . . . 60.00
Edward VIII
1920, Prince of Wales, black and white military portrait, blue rim, white letters 35.00
1937, Coronation, multicolored portrait, white trim 30.00
George V, blue portrait, military uniform, light blue rim inscribed "Unley-April 21, 1917," Gallipoli Day 20.00
George VI, Elizabeth I, red, white, and blue portrait, 1939 Canadian visit 20.00
Queen Victoria, Diamond Jubilee, 1897, two sided cello disk, color images of her as young queen in 1837 and reigning in 1897, reverse inset black and white commemorative text, made by Whitehead & Hoag 75.00
Pin Tray, George VI, 1937 Coronation, sepia portrait, Royal Crown Derby, 3" sq 40.00
Pitcher, William\Adelaide Coronation, white china, portraits and decorative floral accents, in lavender and violet tones, "King William IV & Queen Adelaide, Crowned Sept. 6, 1831," tribute inscriptions, chips to pitcher spout, some wear, 8" h 90.00
Plate
Edward VII\Alexandra, 1902 Coronation, color portraits, scalloped edge, 9-1/2" d 60.00
Elizabeth II, 60th Birthday, large color portrait, Coalport 75.00
George\Mary, white china, full color royalty symbols, sepia-tone oval portraits, "Crowned June 22, 1911," inscribed "Long May They Reign," artwork of St. George slaying dragon, 6" d 65.00
Princess Margaret, birth, parakeets, flowers, Paragon, 6" d 75.00
Victoria, 150th Anniversary of Coronation, gold portrait, 10-1/2" d 140.00
Ribbon, Queen Victoria Reign Anniversary, 2" x 6-1/2", blue silk, inked in black, profile portrait, inscription "H.R.H. Queen Victoria 1837/1887 Jubilee Anniversary June 21" 90.00

Shaving Mug, Edward VIII, 1937 Coronation, sepia portrait
. . . . 75.00
Stickpin, Queen Victoria, Jubilee 1887, diecut thin brass holding
sepia paper inset photo 60.00
Teapot
Edward VII\Alexandra, 1902 Coronation, color portraits,
4-3/4" h 75.00
George V\Mary, 1911 Coronation, color portraits with Prince
of Wales, bone china. 250.00
Tea Set, Elizabeth II, 1953 Coronation, teapot, creamer, and
sugar, relief portraits, Jasperware, white on royal blue,
Wedgwood. Price for set 350.00
Tin, color portrait
Edward VII\Alexandra, 1902 Coronation, Ridgway Ltd. Tea
. . . . 120.00
Elizabeth II, 1953 Coronation, hinged lid, Rowntree . . 25.00

BRONZE

History: Bronze is an alloy of copper, tin, and traces of
other metals. It has been used since Biblical times not
only for art objects, but also for utilitarian wares. After a
slump in the Middle Ages, the use of bronze was revived
in the 17th century and continued to be popular until the
early 20th century.

References: Harold Berman, *Bronzes: Sculptors &
Founders 1800-1930*, Vols. 1-4 and Index, distributed by
Schiffer Publishing, 1996; *Catalog of the Society des
Beaux Arts, Paris*, Schiffer Publishing, 1995 reprint; *1886
Catalog of the French Bronze Foundry of F. Barbedienne
of Paris*, Schiffer Publishing, 1995 reprint; Pierre Kjell-
berg, *Bronzes of the Nineteenth Century*, Schiffer Pub-
lishing, 1994; Lynne and Fritz Weber, *Jacobsen's
Thirteenth Painting and Bronze Price Guide*, January
1992 to January 1994, Weber Publications, 1994.

Notes: Do not confuse a "bronzed" object with a true
bronze. A bronzed item usually is made of white metal
and then coated with a reddish-brown material to give it
a bronze appearance. A magnet will stick to it but not to
anything made of true bronze. A signed bronze com-
mands a higher market price than an unsigned one.
There also are "signed" reproductions on the market. It is
very important to know the history of the mold and the
background of the foundry.

Andirons, pr, 13-3/4" h, Diego Giacometti style, stamped "Made
in France". 1,850.00
Bookends, pr
6-1/4" h, kneeling youth, partially clothed, marked "J Konti,
1911". 440.00
7" h, seated classical philosopher with scroll and hand, by
Thullman, retailed by B Altman & Co., German. . . 575.00
7-3/4" h, cranes, marked "Oscar B Bach". 440.00
Brush Holder, 9-1/2" h, cylindrical, high relief sculpted dragon,
sgd with three characters and kakihan within rect cartouche,
Japanese, Meiji period 400.00
Buddha, 29" h, finely molded figure, seated on stylized lotus
base on top of floral dec cushion, heavy gold lacquer, inlaid
eyes, Bangkok period, 19th C 1,035.00
Bust
10" h, jester, sgd "Dee Frank," sq slate base 120.00
14-1/2" h, man, sgd "F Peleschka," early 20th C, Continental
. . . . 210.00

Sculpture, Wood-Music, deep olive green patina, inscribed "Beatrice Fenton," c1920, 29" h, $3,475. Photo courtesy of Freeman\Fine Arts of Philadelphia, Inc.

Door pulls, store-type, dated July 22, 1879, price for pr, $220. Photo courtesy of Web Wilson Auctions.

Candelabra, 13" h, five seahorses, standing upright on tails, holding candle holders on heads, orig patina, sgd "E. T. Hurley," dated 1914 . . . . .1,200.00

Candlesticks, pr
8" h, Baroque Revival, molded in high relief, C-scrolls and foliage. 175.00
10-1/2" h, open design candle holder, three ftd base with curled feet, green patina, mated pair. 450.00

Cannon, 6-3/4" h, 15" l, signal type, steel, mkd "Chas. A. Briggs," 19th C. 920.00

Cash Register, 21" h, labeled "Lincoln Hotel," National Cash Register 625.00

Compote, 15-1/4" x 12-1/4" oval, cylindrical cut crystal bowl, four columns, circular bronze base, claw feet, Empire style, Austrian 1,200.00

Desk Garniture, champleve dec, calendar, two inkwells, hand blotter, and wax seal 140.00

Doorknocker, 12" h, figural, scrolled tail and head of Savonarola, brown patina, Continental. 600.00

Dresser Tray, 14" l, twin handled tray, scrolling Baroque border, polychrome champleve enamel dec, French 500.00

Fountain Figure, 20-1/2" x 15" Faun figure, 21-1/4" x 19-1/2" rusticated marble plinth, 18th C, restoration 1,100.00

Figure
5" x 6", bulldog chewing slipper, sgd, French. 800.00
5" l, 9" h, unicorn, brown patina, sgd "Edris Eckhardt" 650.00
12-1/2" l, seated Neoclassical female, French, 19th C 980.00

Figural Group
15" w, 7" d, 7-1/2" h, three different breeds of dogs cornering prey under a rock, by Pierre Jules Mene, sgd "P. J. Mene" 1,300.00
16" w, 16-1/2" h, jockey atop horse, holding reins, oval base, by Pierre Jules Mene, sgd "P. J. Mene" 5,230.00
33" h, man and woman dancing hand in hand, detailed costumes and hat, man with sword and scabbard, dark brown patina, sgd in base, "A. Guadez". 2,000.00

Incense Burner, 23" h, 20" d, elephant feet and handles, low relief of exotic birds among foliage, cov dec with pierced floral design, elephant finial, gold highlights, Chinese . . .1,325.00

Inkwell, 7-1/2" l, sparrow on branch, painted, c1910 . . . 350.00

Lamp, 22-1/2" h, braised dragons on base, brass font, opaque white shade with gold painted dragons, electrified, 19th C 350.00

Plaque
4" x 4", circular, two golden brown, two light brown, two Adagio, Allegro, and Profile Portrait of Lady, each sgd "St. Schwart," set of four 450.00
8-1/4" x 11", Allegory of Summer, high relief, verso with foundry mark "Metallic Compress Casting, Boston, MA," brown patina, velvet lined frame 435.00

Spoon Mold, 8-3/4" l, two part mold for large pewter spoon, rat tail bowl, decorative round finial. 450.00

Standish, 14-1/2" l, bird-form finial, foliate form covered wells, leaf shaped tray, gilt, French, c1900 . . . . 230.00

Vase, 14-1/4" h, 12" d, ftd, low relief dragon among waves, multi patinated, brown finish, Japanese 490.00

BUFFALO POTTERY

History: Buffalo Pottery Co., Buffalo, New York, was chartered in 1901. The first kiln

was fired in October 1903. Larkin Soap Company established Buffalo Pottery to produce premiums for its extensive mail-order business. Wares also were sold to the public by better department and jewelry stores. Elbert Hubbard and Frank Lloyd Wright, who designed the Larkin Administration Building in Buffalo in 1904, were two prominent names associated with the Larkin Company.

Early Buffalo Pottery production consisted mainly of semi-vitreous china dinner sets. Buffalo was the first pottery in the United States to produce successfully the Blue Willow pattern. Buffalo also made a line of hand-decorated, multicolored willow ware, called Gaudy Willow. Other early items include a series of game, fowl, and fish sets, pitchers, jugs, and a line of commemorative, historical, and advertising plates and mugs.

From 1908 to 1909 and again from 1921 to 1923, Buffalo Pottery produced the line for which it is most famous—Deldare Ware. The earliest of this olive green, semi-vitreous china displays hand-decorated scenes from English artist Cecil Aldin's *Fallowfield Hunt*. Hunt scenes were done only from 1908 to 1909. English village scenes also were characteristic of the ware and were used during both periods. Most pieces are artist signed.

In 1911 Buffalo Pottery produced Emerald Deldare, which used scenes from Goldsmith's *The Three Tours of Dr. Syntax* and an Art Nouveau-type border. Completely decorated Art Nouveau pieces also were made.

Abino, which was introduced in 1912, had a Deldare body and displayed scenes of sailboats, windmills, or the sea. Rust was the main color used, and all pieces were signed by the artist and numbered.

In 1915, the manufacturing process was modernized, giving the company the ability to produce vitrified china. Consequently, hotel and institutional ware became the main production items, with hand-decorated ware de-emphasized. The Buffalo firm became a leader in producing and designing the most-famous railroad, hotel, and restaurant patterns. These wares, especially railroad items, are eagerly sought by collectors.

In the early 1920s, fine china was made for home use. Bluebird is one of the patterns from this era. In 1950 Buffalo made their first Christmas plate. These were given away to customers and employees primarily from 1950 to 1960. However, it is known that Hample Equipment Co. ordered some as late as 1962. The Christmas plates are very scarce in today's resale market.

The Buffalo China Company made "Buffalo Pottery" and "Buffalo China"—the difference being that one is semi-vitreous ware and the other vitrified. In 1956 the company was reorganized, and Buffalo China became the corporate name. Today Buffalo China is owned by Oneida Silver Company. The Larkin family no longer is involved.

Marks: Blue Willow pattern is marked "First Old Willow Ware Mfg. in America."

Reference: Seymour and Violet Altman, *Book of Buffalo Pottery*, reprinted by Schiffer Publishing, 1987.

Blue Willow
Butter Pat 14.00

Cup and Saucer 35.00
Plate, 9" d 20.00
Platter, 13" x 11", dated 1909 . . . . 100.00
Vegetable Bowl 50.00

Commercial

Bowl, 6" d, made for Roycroft Inn, East Aurora, NY 75.00
Calendar Plate, 8" d, 1911, red open touring car 45.00
Cup and Saucer, George Washington 275.00
Plate
    Automobile Club of Buffalo 25.00
    Hotel Astor, Art Nouveau 25.00

Deldare

Ashtray/matchbox 675.00
Bowl, 8" d, Ye Village Tavern, 1908 . . . . 300.00
Calling Card Tray
    Fallowfield Hunt, 1908 . . . . 250.00
    Ye Lion Inn, sgd by artist M Gerhardt 300.00
Candlestick, shield shape 700.00
Chop Plate, 14" d 600.00
Fruit Bowl 500.00
Hair Receiver 425.00
Humidor 800.00
Mug
    3-1/2" h 300.00
    4-1/2" h 350.00
    Ye Lion Inn 310.00
Pitcher
    6" h 425.00
    7" h 475.00
    8" h 625.00
    9" h 650.00
Plate
    6-1/4" d 85.00
    7-1/4" d 95.00
    8-1/4" d 140.00
    9-3/8" d 140.00

(Adv) Saucer, green and white, The Wanamaker Store, Philadelphia, Largest in the World, 1861-Jubilee Year-1911, on back with Buffalo Pottery mark and 1911, 4-3/8" d, $65.

10" d, Village Gossips, 1909 . . . . 125.00
13-3/4" d, An Evening at Ye Lion Inn 625.00
Tankard 950.00
Teapot, cov, large 350.00
Tea Tile 300.00
Tea Tray 550.00
Vase, 7" h 400.00

Emerald Deldare

Charger, 12-1/2" d, Dr. Syntax Sketching the Lake, polychrome dec of man on horseback, emerald border, green ink stamp mark 850.00
Cup and Saucer, Dr. Syntax at Liverpool 500.00
Fern Dish, 8" d, butterflies and flowers 850.00
Plate, 8-1/4" d, Art Nouveau dec 400.00
Vase, 8" h, kingfisher, dragonflies, iris, and waterlilies 1,200.00

Historical and Commemorative

Mug, 3-1/2" h, Beechland Farms 100.00
Pitcher
    5-1/8" h, Geranium pattern, strong blues, transfer type logo 275.00
    6-1/2" h, Landing of Roger Williams, scenes include view of Betsy Williams' cottage, logo and dated 1906 and 1907 on base 400.00
    6-3/4" h, The Whirl of the Town - Fox Hunt, unique logo, obscured date, c1906 . . . . 500.00
Plate
    7-1/2" d, Niagara Falls 65.00
    10" d, Capitol Building, Washington, DC, canton green, eagle and banner mark, c1905 . . . . 55.00
    10-1/4" d, Independence Hall, Philadelphia, PA, green transfer 70.00

Miscellaneous

Butter Pat, Gaudy Willow 35.00
Child's Feeding Dish, Mary Had A Little Lamb 65.00
Dinner Service, Maple Leaf, price for 100 pc set 400.00
Dresser Tray, 10-1/2" x 13-3/4", Abino Ware, rect, band of sheep on village street, blue highlights, 1913 . . . . 1,750.00
Hair Receiver, Abino Ware, sailing ship, blue highlights, 1913, sgd "WE Simpson" 650.00
Plate
    9-1/4" d
        American Herring Gull 65.00
        Ducky Goose 65.00
        Wild Ducks 65.00
    10-1/2" d, Gaudy Willow 150.00
Platter
    11" x 14", Buffalo Hunt, adapted from Frederick Remington's painting "Her Calf," deep blue-green transfer dec, logo and date 1907 . . . . 250.00
    Deer 110.00

BURMESE GLASS

History: Burmese glass is a translucent art glass originated by Frederick Shirley and manufactured by the Mt. Washington Glass Co., New Bedford, Massachusetts, from 1885 to c1891.

Burmese glass colors shade from a soft lemon to a salmon pink. Uranium was used to attain the yellow color, and gold was added to the batch so that on reheating, one end turned pink. Upon reheating again, the edges would revert to the yellow coloring. The blending of the colors was so gradual that it is difficult to determine where one color ends and the other begins.

Although some of the glass has a glossy surface, most pieces were acid finished. The majority of the items were free blown, but some were blown molded in a ribbed, hobnail, or diamond-quilted design.

American-made Burmese is quite thin and, therefore, is fragile, and brittle. English Burmese was made by Thos. Webb & Sons. Out of deference to Queen Victoria, they called their wares "Queen's Burmese Ware."

Collectors Club: Mount Washington Art Glass Society, P.O. Box 24094, Fort Worth, TX 76124.-1094

REPRODUCTION ALERT

Reproductions abound in almost every form. Since uranium can no longer be used, some of the reproductions are easy to spot. In the 1950s, Gundersen produced many pieces in imitation of Burmese.

Abbreviations:
  MW Mount Washington
  Wb Webb
  a.f. acid finish
  s.f. shiny finish

Advisors: Clarence and Betty Maier.

Bon Bon Bowl, 2" h, 5-1/4" l, 4-1/2" w, optic-ribbed sides, turned-in edges, s.f., MW 385.00
Creamer, 2-5/8" h, enameled vintage dec, ruffled rim . . 275.00
Cruet, 6-1/2" h, melon ribbed, orig mushroom stopper
  Bluish to yellow shading, s.f., MW 1,100.00
  Decorated, MW 2,950.00
Fairy Lamp
  3-1/2" h, Cricklite base, lemon-yellow connecting wafer, pink bowl, piecrust edge, Wb 750.00
  3-3/4" h, pyramid, Burmese shade, clear base, Wb. . 250.00
  5-1/2" h, 5-3/4" w, cup holder sgd "Clarke's Cricklite Trademark," flaring crimped skirt, bowl-shaped base, Wb
  . . . . 950.00
Gaslight Shades, pr, 3-1/4" h, 5" d, 2-3/8" fitter, fluted edge, MW, price for pr 750.00
Jack In The Pulpit, 7-1/2" h, ruffled rim, MW 275.00
Lamp, fluid, 20" h, 10" d shade, fine pink to yellow body, hp and enameled Egyptian pyramids and palm tree oasis scene, orig Burmese glass chimney, gilt metal mounts, MW, not electrified 10,350.00
Mustard Pot, 4-1/2" h, barrel shape, vertical ribs, bail, metal collar, hinged lid, s.f., MW. 375.00
Rose Bowl
  3" h, hexagonal mouth, polychrome enameled flowers
  . . . . 385.00
  3-1/4" h, prunus blossoms dec, yellow ground, square top, Wb. 350.00
Salt Shaker, 4-1/4" h, cylindrical, ribbed body, s.f., MW
  . . . . 200.00
Toothpick Holder, 2-3/4" h
  Elongated diamond quilted design, s.f., MW 285.00
  Prunus blossoms dec, bulbous shape, Wb 750.00
Tumbler
  Paneled salmon shading to creamy yellow, MW 285.00
  Peaches and cream coloring, s.f., MW. 375.00

Vase
  5" h, flower-shaped bowl, butter-cream to lemon-yellow blush, s.f., Wb 750.00
  7" h, trumpet shape, MW 335.00
  8" h, double-gourd shape, turquoise forget-me-nots and peach-colored roses, MW 1,250.00
  8-1/2" h, Pairpoint quadruple-plate holder in shape of Oriental man, MW 385.00
  11" h, Queen's Design dec, MW 2,950.00
  11" h, 6" d, white daisies, lemon-yellow ground, No. 146, MW
  . . . . .1,750.00
  12" h, ibis in flight, pyramids, palm tree, and sand dunes, rosy-pink blush, drilled 3/8" hole in base, MW. . .2,750.00
  14-1/2" h, folded crimped rim of pastel pink shaded to yellow, trumpet form body, flat disk foot, MW 1,150.00
  23-1/2" h, trumpet shape, c1890, MW 1,250.00

BUSTS

History: The portrait bust has its origins in pagan and Christian traditions. Greek and Roman heroes dominate the earliest examples. Later, images of Christian saints were used. Busts of the "ordinary man" first appeared during the Renaissance.

During the 18th and 19th centuries, nobility, poets, and other notable persons were the most frequent subjects, especially on those busts designed for use in a home library. Because of the large number of these library busts, excellent examples can be found at reasonable prices, depending on artist, subject, and material.

Reference: Lynne and Fritz Weber, *Jacobsen's Thirteenth Painting and Bronze Price Guide*, January 1992 to January 1994, Weber Publications, 1994.

Additional Listings: Ivory; Parian Ware; Soapstone; Wedgwood.

4-1/4" h, girl, porcelain, flowers in hair, Vienna 300.00
6" h, woman, carved mahogany, America, 19th C, contemporary stand, minor losses 750.00
8-1/2" h, Reverend John Wesley, creamware, gray hair, pink tinted flesh, black and white clerical robes, black self socle base, inscribed "The Revd John Wesley M. Died Mar 2, 1891, Aged 88, Enoch Wood Sculp. Burslem," Staffordshire, c1791, chips to base 400.00
9-1/2" h
  Athena, bronze, wearing helmet, defined facial features, fish-scale yoke with relief Medusa head, 19th C 200.00
  Joseph de Carayon La Tour, bronze, sgd "h. Chapu" (Henri Michel Antoine Chapu,) inscribed "E. Coni & Co. fondeur,"
  . . . . 275.00
9-3/4" h, 7" l, base, young woman, green marble base, sgd "E. Battiglia, "Italian, some chips 350.00
10-1/2" h, John Wesley, porcelain, pink luster, enamel dec, Staffordshire, England, c1825 . . . . .1,035.00
11-1/4" h, Charles Dickens, parian, raised circular base, attributed to Robinson & Leadbeater, late 19th C 290.00
11-3/4" h, Alexandra, parian, pedestal base, imp "Crystal Palace Art Union, F M Miller Sculpt, Pub'd Feb 11, 1863, Copeland"
  . . . . 225.00
12" h, 7-1/4" l, Busto di Donna Vecchia," bronze, reddish and greenish brown patina, sgd "Gemito" (Vincenzo Gemito), inscribed "V-VIII' and indecipherable foundry seal 325.00
13-1/2" h, 7-3/4" d, Diana, marble, socle base, Italian, 19th C
  . . . . 575.00

Left: marble, woman shrouded I diaphanous veil, three-quarters length portrait, sgd "O. Andreoni Roma," 19th C, 30-1/2" h, $6,440; right: young girl with dove and floral garland dec, three-quarters length portrait, sgd "C. Lapini Firenze 1891," 23-1/2" h, $3,150. Photo courtesy of Freeman\Fine Arts of Philadelphia, Inc.

1" h, girl with large ruffled hat, looking down on bird perched on shoulder, lace dressed, carved flowers, alabaster, mounted on small alabaster circular pedestal atop wood platform, 1" chip to hat. 350.00

16" h, maiden, parian, garland of flowers in hair, black pedestal base 195.00

17" h, Victorian lady, bonnet and blouse, alabaster, some roughness to bonnet 125.00

17-3/4" h, maiden, bronze, parcel gilt, gilt and dark brown patina, socle base, inscribed "G" 1,950.00

19" h, maiden, marble, drape extending over one shoulder, one breast exposed, flowing hair, flower and fruit garland in hair extending to shoulder, after Carpeaux, 19th C, price for pr 2,600.00

21" h, 14" d, Napoleon, marble, incised "A. Cipriani," Italian, 19th C, losses. 490.00

21-1/4" h, Caesar Augustus, marble, Continental, c1900 . . . . 1,950.00

22" h, 16" d, Sara Bernhardt, marble, platform base, incised "Pineschi G" 1,265.00

23-1/4" h, Benjamin Franklin, bronze, after Jean-Antoine Houdon, French, 19th C, green patina 750.00

24" h
   Caesar Augustus, carrara marble and gilded bronze, seal "Pinedo Bronzes Paris" 6,325.00
   Maiden, terra cotta, sgd "A Carrier-Belleuse," French, c1850 . . . . 6,000.00

25" h, Venice, three-quarters length, sq base, marble 1,150.00

25-1/2" h
   Greek Slave, after Hiram Powers, c1850-70, nude, bead and leaf tip molded edge on circular sole, carved carrara marble, Italian 8,050.00

Venus, clamshell and pearl headdress, shell covered bust, carved carrara marble, Italian 5,750.00

26" h
   Young lady, pierced and carved lace hat with flowers, 5" h turned pedestal, alabaster 1,550.00
   Young maiden, intricate coiffure, sq base, alabaster, Continental 1,955.00

29" h, marble, lady, 18th C costume, 42-1/4" h mottled marble column 1,600.00

31-1/2" h
   Lincoln, bronze, George Edwin Bissell, copyright 1904, cast by Gorham Foundries, Inc. 4,840.00
   Young man, plaster, socle base, 41-3/4" h fluted Ionic plaster column 175.00

42-1/2" h, classical youth, white marble, variegated marble pedestal base, edge chips on base 1,650.00

BUTTER PRINTS

History: There are two types of butter prints: butter molds and butter stamps. Butter molds are generally of three-piece construction—the design, the screw-in handle, and the case. Molds both shape and stamp the butter at the same time. Butter stamps are generally of one-piece construction but can be of two-piece construction if the handle is from a separate piece of wood. Stamps decorate the top of butter after it is molded.

The earliest prints are one piece and were hand carved, often heavily and deeply. Later prints were factory made with the design forced into the wood by a metal die.

Some of the most common designs are sheaves of wheat, leaves, flowers, and pineapples. Animal designs and Germanic tulips are difficult to find. Prints with designs on both sides are rare, as are those in unusual shapes, such as half-rounded or lollipop.

Reference: Paul E. Kindig, *Butter Prints and Molds*, Schiffer Publishing, 1986.

REPRODUCTION ALERT

Reproductions of butter prints were made as early as the 1940s.

Mold

Cherries, carved wood, oblong, almond shaped indented mold carved with stylized cluster of cherries, leafy twig, serrated border, two part, dark finish, 10-1/2" l 90.00

Cornflower, hand carved maple, round, c1830, 4-3/4" x 9" 125.00

Cow pattern, hinged wood frame 360.00

Grapes pattern, porcelain, individual size 85.00

Heart, anchor, and cross, carved wood, dished form, fluted sides, old brown patina, 4-5/8" d, 2" h 90.00

Klappmodel, Maltese cross, five sections, woman drawing water from pump house with pine tree, flowers, tree in bloom, radiating tulips in center pc, 6-1/2" d 420.00

Swan, carved wood, cased, old finish, 5" d 190.00

Print

Acorn with two leaves, deeply carved maple, round, knob handle, c1820, 3-1/4" d 250.00

Print, eagle, 3-3/4" d, 3" h, $195.

Berries and leaves, round, cross-hatched design above cluster of long pointed serrated leaves, three round berries, serrated rim, one piece turned handle, old patina, 4-1/2" d 80.00
Bird and flowers, rect, chip carved border, old patina and dark stains, inserted turned handle, 1-3/4" x 2-1/2" x 4-3/4" 250.00
Cow, tree, poplar, round, one piece turned handle, dark patina, 4-1/2" d 195.00
Double
  Carved intaglio star and leaves with chip carved fluted border, floral pattern on reverse, lathe turned from single piece of wood, c1840, 5" d, small age crack 220.00
  Chip carved, falling leaves pattern, small leaf print on handle 75.00
  Eagle and rose, pedestal form, highly chip carved, whittle marks 600.00
  Palm held, deep gouge and chip carved rosette designs, concentric border 220.00
  Pestle shape, chip carved radiating leaf patterns, notched border 200.00
Eagle, scrubbed poplar, round, one piece turned handle, 4-1/4" d, minor age cracks 385.00
Elliptical, lightly carved two way design, primitive form ... 55.00
Floral over leaf, lollipop handle, deeply carved from one pc of wood, PA, c1830, age crack in handle 210.00
Flower on one side, pinwheel on other, scrubbed poplar, lollipop, handle marked "Grandma's Butter Printer," 7-3/4" l . 360.00
Fox, running, carved, scrubbed finish, one piece turned handle, 3-1/2" d 675.00
Geometric starflower scrubbed poplar, lollipop, 9" l 250.00
Intaglio floral design, round, fluted border, c1840, 4-1/2" d 80.00
Leaf, round, carved wood, sprig of three large serrated leaves in center, thin chip-carved border, turned handle, 3-3/4" d 75.00
Maple Hill Dairy, relief carved 65.00
Pennsylvania Crown Tulip, chip carved 85.00
Pineapple, semi-circular, pine, 3-3/8" x 7", worn patina, replaced turned inserted handle 110.00
Rosette, chip and gouge carved, chip carved fluted border, round, c1850, 3-1/2" d 55.00

Rosette, six pointed design alternating crosshatch and striated designs, chip and gouge carved, round, c1850, 3-1/2" d 95.00
Starflower, concave circle, carved wood, old patina, 3-3/4" d 80.00
Striated Tulip, deeply gouge carved, border of chip and gouge carved radiating triangles, round, PA, 1830, 4" d 270.00
Swan, carved wood, round, carved border, 4-1/8" d 365.00
The Union, hearts and stars, butternut, scrubbed finish, 3-1/8" x 5", added tin hanger 360.00
Tulip, stylized, pine, old patina, 3" h, 4-7/8", added tin hanger 250.00

CALENDAR PLATES

History: Calendar plates were first made in England in the late 1880s. They became popular in the United States after 1900, the peak years being 1909 to 1915. The majority of the advertising plates were made of porcelain or pottery and the design included a calendar, the name of a store or business, and either a scene, portrait, animal, or flowers. Some also were made of glass or tin.

Periodical: *The Calendar*, 710 N. Lake Shore Dr., Barrington, IL 60010.

Additional Listings: See *Warman's Americana & Collectibles* for more examples.

1907, 9-1/4" d, Santa Claus center, River Falls, Wisconsin, advertising 85.00
1908, 8" d, holly sprays, Russell Clothing House adv.... 20.00
1908, 9-1/4" d, four cat faces, "Merry Christmas, B. L. Schermerhorn, Lowville, New York" 65.00
1909, 8-1/2" d, flower girl, souvenir Abrams, WI........ 40.00
1909, 9" d, John Kemper Harness Maker, Butler, PA, Mediterranean woman in center, marked "Vorrey" 30.00
1909, 9-1/2" d, Gibson girl type portrait, calendar months, fruit, and floral border, WI adv 35.00

1909, Compliments T. J. Augustine, Gen. Merchandise, Addison, PA, green transfer, Gibson Girl type portrait center, gold trim, $65.

1910, 6-7/8" d, compliments of Geo H Farguhasson, Cooperstown, NY, marked "Semi Porcelain" 35.00
1910, 7" d, violets with ribbon banner, emb gold scalloped edge, JL McCue adv 30.00
1910, 10" d, woman in garden center, calendar months border 30.00
1911, 8-1/2" d, gray fence with three rabbits and two birds, JW Morey adv. 30.00
1912, 7-1/2" d, owl on open book, calendars on pages, August, Illinois, advertising 45.00
1912, 8-1/4" d, Indian husking corn 40.00
1912, 8-1/2" d, flowers and cherubs center 35.00
1912, 8-1/2" d, hot air balloon. 75.00
1913, 8" d, calendar months center, rose garland and holly border 30.00
1913, 8-1/4" d, sweet peas, pink and lavender ground. . . 50.00
1914, 9-1/4" d, Washington's Tomb, Milford, DE, artist sgd "A Smith". 40.00
1914, 9-1/2" d, sandpiper center, sgd "R. K. Beck". 50.00
1916, 8-1/4" d, American flag, eagle with shield. 35.00
1919, 8-1/4" d, American flag, John J Rutgers Co., Holland, MI adv 40.00
1919, 8" d, Walnut Grove, MN 50.00
1921, Tabor & Pukwana, SD. 60.00
1922, game birds and hunting dog 45.00
1928, 8-1/2" d, deer looking at road sign "To Old Orchard Beach, Maine" 60.00

CALLING CARD CASES and RECEIVERS

History: Calling cards, usually carried in specially designed cases, played an important social role in the United States from the Civil War until the end of World War I. When making formal visits, callers left their card in a receiver (card dish) in the front hall. Strict rules of etiquette developed. For example, the lady in a family was expected to make calls of congratulations and condolence and visits to the ill.

The cards themselves were small, embossed or engraved with the caller's name and often decorated with a floral design. Many handmade examples, especially in Spencerian script, can be found. The cards themselves are considered collectible and range in price from a few cents to several dollars.

Note: Don't confuse a calling card case with a match safe.

Calling Card Case
Gold
  Elaborately chased and engraved, fan design within floral motifs, textured background, monogrammed curved lid, European hallmarks, 50.1 dwt 1,100.00
  Tiffany & Co., 18K yellow gold, rect design, textured black leather and yellow gold frame, sgd "Tiffany & Co." . 320.00
  Ivory, 4-1/4" x 3" 50.00
Mother-of-pearl and tortoiseshell, Continental, 4" l. 225.00
Silver, English, Victorian, maker's mark, Birmingham, Rect, bright-cut engraved foliate surface dec, hinged flip-top lid, central lever device to push cards out of case, on chain with ring, monogram, 1898, 3-1/4" l, 2 troy oz 300.00
  Rect, hinged flip-top lid, chain, monogram, 3-7/8" l, c1900, 2 troy oz 150.00
  Slim rect shape, hinged lid, engine-turned surface dec, engraved foliate frame border, central medallion with mono-

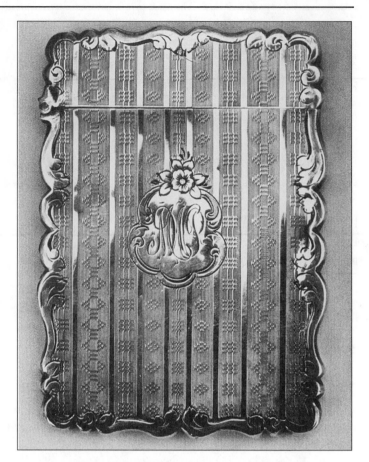

Calling Card Case, sterling silver, four English hallmarks, 3-1/2" x 2-1/2", $115.

gram, illegible maker's mark, 1872, 3-7/8" l, 2 troy oz 250.00
Tortoiseshell
  Inset silver shield, engraved crest, mother-of-pearl inlay, 4-1/8" x 3-1/8" 200.00
  Regency, 4" x 3" 165.00

Calling Card Receiver
Arab and woven basket, 9-3/4" h, bronze, 19th C 420.00
Butler, 33-1/4" h, cast iron, African-American, holding tray 225.00
Flower shape, 6-1/2" d, green five-petaled blossom in center of amber plate, overall gold irid, base inscribed "L. C. T. N9511" for Tiffany Studios 575.00
Frog shape, 7-1/2" l, hammered surface, Tiffany & Co., 1875-91, 5 troy oz 1,100.00
Shell shape, 18kt yellow gold wash over sterling silver, sgd "Tiffany & Co." 260.00
Shell shape, engraved mermaid, ftd, SP, Rogers 100.00
Stand, 5-1/8" h, sterling, easel back, projecting rect card holder, molded scroll border, top pointed arch, America, 20th C, 2 troy oz. 100.00

CAMBRIDGE GLASS

History: Cambridge Glass Company, Cambridge, Ohio, was incorporated in 1901. Initially, the company made clear tableware, later expanding into colored, etched, and engraved glass. More than 40 different hues were produced in blown and pressed glass.

The plant closed in 1954. Some of the molds were later sold to the Imperial Glass Company, Bellaire, Ohio.

Marks: Five different marks were employed during the production years, but not every piece was marked.

References: Gene Florence, *Elegant Glassware of the Depression Era*, Revised 6th ed., Collector Books, 1995; National Cambridge Collectors, Inc., *Cambridge Glass Co., Cambridge, Ohio* (reprint of 1930 catalog and supplements through 1934), Collector Books, 1976, 1996 value update; ——, *Cambridge Glass Co., Cambridge, Ohio, 1949 through 1953* (catalog reprint), Collector Books, 1976, 1996 value update; ——, *Colors in Cambridge Glass*, Collector Books, 1984, 1993 value update; Naomi L. Over, *Ruby Glass of the 20th Century*, Antique Publications, 1990, 1993-94 value update; Bill and Phyllis Smith, *Cambridge Glass 1927-1929* (1986) and *Identification Guide to Cambridge Glass 1927-1929* (updated prices 1996), published by authors (4003 Old Columbus Rd., Springfield, OH 45502).

Periodical: *The Daze*, P.O. Box 57, Otisville, MI 48463.

Collectors' Club: National Cambridge Collectors, Inc., P.O. Box 416, Cambridge, OH 43725.

Museums: Cambridge Glass Museum, Cambridge, OH; Museum of the National Cambridge Collectors, Inc., Cambridge, OH.

Ashtray
    Caprice, Blue Alpine. 30.00
    Portia, sq 45.00
Bon Bon
    Apple Blossom, #3400/1180, blue, 5-1/4" d 60.00
    Rose Point, #205 . . . . 200.00
    Bouillon, Decagon, light blue 20.00
Bowl
    Caprice, blue, 11" d, 4 ftd, crimped 115.00
    Rose Point, 9-1/2" d 80.00
    Tally Ho, red, 12-1/8", flat rim. 75.00
    Windsor Blue, 10" d, seashell, 3-toed 250.00
Brandy, Nudes, mocha 175.00
Bridge Hound, emerald green 65.00
Bud Vase, Rose Point, 6" h. 95.00
Butter, cov, #3400/52
    Apple Blossom, pink 500.00
    Wildflower 200.00
Cake Plate
    Rose Point, #3500/110, ftd, 13" d 145.00
    Wildflower, 13" d 145.00
Candleholder, Cherub, #1191, ebony 2,950.00
Candlesticks, pr
    Apple Blossom, #3400/646, pink 110.00
    Decagon, #627, black, 4" h 55.00
    Wildflower, #646, 1-lite 75.00
Candy Box, cov, Cascade, yellow 60.00
Candy Dish, cov
    Cleo, #103, 3-part 115.00
    Rose Point, Crown Tuscan, gold edge, 3-part 165.00
    Wildflower, 3-part 150.00
Celery/Relish
    Apple Blossom, #3500/152, 4-part 65.00
    Diane, 5-part 60.00
    Rose Point, 3-part, 9" l 70.00
    Wildflower, #397 . . . . 60.00

Champagne
    Decagon, light blue. 25.00
    Wildflower, #3121. . . . . 35.00
Cheese and Cracker Set, Wildflower 110.00
Cheese Comport, Wildflower 50.00
Cheese Dish, cov, Cordeilia, #980, 5" d 85.00
Cigarette Box, cov
    Nudes, Carmen 600.00
    Rose Point, 3-1/2" w, 1-1/2" l 500.00
Cigarette Holder
    Caprice, blue, 2-1/4" h. 75.00
    Diane, gold encrusted, ashtray foot 300.00
Claret
    Nudes, Carmen 175.00
    Tally Ho, red, 4-1/2 oz 45.00
    Wildflower, #3121, 4-1/2 oz 42.00
Cocktail
    Caprice, blue, #3. . . . . 65.00
    Chantilly, #3775 . . . . 25.00
    Gloria, #3122, pink. 165.00
    Hunt's Scene, #3077 . . . . 60.00
    Nudes, pistachio. 200.00
    Rose Point, #3121 . . . . 32.50
    Tally Ho, forest green, 3 oz 18.00
Cocktail Shaker, Chantilly, 32 oz 135.00
Compote
    Apple Blossom, yellow, 7" h. 85.00
    Nudes, Carmen, cupped 300.00
    Rose Point, 5-1/2" 125.00
Cordial
Chantilly, 1 oz 80.00
    Portia 125.00
    Rose Point 75.00
    Tally Ho, red, thick 65.00
    Wildflower, #3121, 1 oz 60.00
Cracker Plate, Apple Blossom, #3400/6, yellow 50.00
Creamer and Sugar, Elaine. 45.00
Cruet
    Caprice, Blue Alpine. 175.00
    Nautilus, amethyst 60.00
Cup and Saucer
    Portia 45.00
    Rose Point 55.00
Decanter
    Portia, #3400/113. . . . . 300.00
    Rose Chintz, amber 400.00

Console Bowl, Heliotrope, 10" w, $90.

Finger Bowl, Heatherbloom, #3111, optic 60.00
Flower Frog, Draped Lady, 8-1/2" h, light blue 450.00
Flower Holder, Crown Tuscan. 175.00
Goblet, water
    Chantilly, #3775 . . . . 25.00
    Elaine 60.00
    Nudes, Carmen 275.00
    Portia 35.00
    Rose Point, #3121 . . . . 32.50
    Tally Ho, red, 10 oz, thick 35.00
Honey Dish, cov, Rubina, 8" h 175.00
Ice Bucket
    Cleo, light blue 225.00
    Decagon, pink 90.00
Iced Tea Tumbler
    Chantilly, #3625 . . . . 30.00
    Gloria, #3122, pink 165.00
    Roselie, blue. 65.00
    Wildflower, #3121, 12 oz 32.50
Ivy Ball
    Nudes, Carmen 500.00
    Rose Point 585.00
Lemon Plate, Caprice, blue, 6" d, handle 40.00
Jelly, Caprice, blue, 7" d, crimped. 65.00
Jug
    Elaine, 80 oz. 400.00
    Nautilus, 84 oz, amethyst. 175.00
    Rose Point, ball, 80 oz 260.00
Juice Tumbler
    Elaine, ftd 35.00
    Rose Point, #3121, ftd 35.00
Marmalade, cov
    Diane 185.00
    Portia, ftd 75.00
    Wildflower. 175.00
Martini Pitcher, Portia, orig plunger, 60 oz 1,500.00
Mayonnaise
    Diane, SS base 85.00
    Rose Point 55.00
    Wildflower, pink, liner 165.00
Mustard, cov, Two Town, amber. 50.00
Nappy, Rose Point, 6" d 85.00
Oyster Cocktail, Portia 40.00
Parfait
    Hunt's Scene 85.00
    Portia 95.00
Pickle Dish
    Rose Point, 9" l. 65.00
    Wildflower, 9-1/2" l 48.00
Plate
    Cleo, blue, 8-1/4" d 30.00
    Portia, 6" d 15.00
    Tally Ho, red, 8" d 20.00
Platter, Apple Blossom, #3400/1186, 12-1/2" l 175.00
Punch Bowl Set, Tally Ho, red, ftd bowl, 8 mugs 800.00
Punch Mug, Tally Ho, red 35.00
Relish
    Candlelight, 3-part, 12" l 55.00
    Elaine, 3-part 85.00
Rose Point, 3-part, center handle, 7-1/2" d 165.00
Salad Bowl, Caprice, #80, pink, cupped, 13" d 500.00
Salad Dressing
    Caprice, blue, twin, handle. 500.00
    Decagon, #1263, amber. 110.00
Salt and Pepper Shakers, pr, Decagon, cobalt blue 125.00
Sherbet
    Diane, low. 24.00

    Rose Point, #3121, tall 22.00
    Wildflower, #3121, 6 oz, tall 20.00
Sherry
    Diane, 2 oz 75.00
    Trumpet, amethyst, 2-1/2 oz 30.00
Sugar Bowl, cov, Decagon, light blue 20.00
Sugar Pail, Cleo, bail handle, green 350.00
Sugar Shaker, Decagon, pink 165.00
Syrup, cov, Decagon, pink 125.00
Swan
    Type I, ebony, 3" h 110.00
    Type II, crystal, 8-1/2" h 95.00
    Type II, pink, 3". 45.00
    Type IIIB, Mandarin gold, 3". 75.00
Sweet Pea Vase, Wildflower, green, 3-3/4" h 300.00
Tankard Pitcher, Portia 500.00
Tray for creamer and sugar, Decagon, black 45.00
Tumbler, water
    Apple Blossom, yellow, 12 oz, ftd. 40.00
    Heatherbloom, #3111, optic, 12 oz, ftd 55.00
    Marjorie, #7606, 10 oz 35.00
    Nautilus, amethyst, 4-3/4" h, 12 oz. 25.00
    Rosalie, #119, amber. 45.00
    Rose Point, #3121, 12 oz, ftd. 35.00
Vase
    Caprice, blue, 3-1/2" h 200.00
    Cleo, #1023, pink, 9-1/2" h. 450.00
    Portia, Crown Tuscan, gold inlay, 6" h, 6" d 185.00
    Rose Point, Crown Tuscan, gold edge, 6-1/2" h 165.00
    Two Tone, forest green, 12" h 75.00
Wine
    Chantilly, #3775 . . . . 32.50
    Decagon, amethyst 30.00
    Nude, amber. 325.00
    Portia 50.00

CAMBRIDGE POTTERY

History: The Cambridge Art Pottery was incorporated in Ohio in 1900. Between 1901 and 1909 the firm produced the usual line of jardinieres, tankards, and vases with underglaze slip decorations and glazes similar to that of other Ohio potteries. Line names included Terrhea, Oakwood, and Otoe.

In 1904 the company introduced Guernsey kitchenware. It was so well received that it became the plant's primary product. In 1909 the company's name was changed to Guernsey Earthenware Company.

Marks: All wares were marked, although a variety of different backstamps were used, and both printed and impressed marks can be found. Many pieces are marked with the pattern name and/or the CAP monogram inside an acorn. Sometimes the monogram alone was used.

Bowl, 6-1/2" d, 3" h, Acorn, green glossy glaze, mkd 60.00
Candlestick, 4" h, Terrhea, standard brown glaze 80.00
Ewer, 7-1/2" h, Oakwood, cream, yellow, and green blended glaze, numbered. 90.00
Pitcher, 6" h, 3 ftd, handle, dark brown ground, honeysuckle dec, sgd "DL," marked "Cambridge," and "CAP" 300.00
Tile, 6" w, floral, high relief majolica type 40.00
Vase
    8" h, brown high glaze, wild rose dec, artist sgd, restored top
        . . . . 200.00

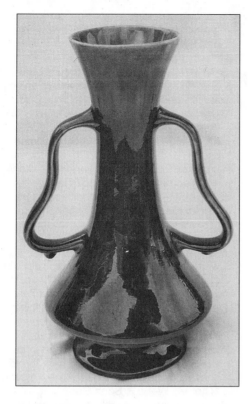

Cambridge Vase, Oakwood, high glaze, mold 235, applied shaped handles, yellow, green, and brown, 8" h, $300.

15-1/2" h, brown glaze, donkey dec, imp mark, glaze flaws, restoration to top 750.00

CAMEO GLASS

History: Cameo glass is a form of cased glass. A shell of glass was prepared; then one or more layers of glass of a different color(s) was faced to the first. A design was then cut through the outer layer(s) leaving the inner layer(s) exposed.

This type of art glass originated in Alexandria, Egypt between 100 and 200 A.D. The oldest and most famous example of cameo glass is the Barberini or Portland vase which was found near Rome in 1582. It contained the ashes of Emperor Alexander Serverus, who was assassinated in 235 A.D.

Emile Gallé is probably one of the best-known cameo glass artists. He established a factory at Nancy, France, in 1884. Although much of the glass bears his signature, he was primarily the designer. Assistants did the actual work on many pieces, even signing Gallé's name. Other makers of French cameo glass include D'Argental, Daum Nancy, LeGras, and Delatte.

English cameo pieces do not have as many layers of glass (colors) and cuttings as do French pieces. The outer layer is usually white, and cuttings are very fine and delicate. Most pieces are not signed. The best-known makers are Thomas Webb & Sons and Stevens and Williams.

Marks: A star before the name Gallé on a piece by that company indicates that it was made after Gallé's death in 1904.

References: Victor Arwas, *Glass Art Nouveau to Art Deco*, Rizzoli International Publications, 1977; Alastair Dun-can and George DeBartha, *Glass by Gallé*, Harry N. Abrams, 1984; Ray and Lee Grover, *English Cameo Glass*, Crown Publishers, 1980; Albert C. Revi, *Nineteenth Century Glass*, reprint, Schiffer Publishing, 1981; John A. Shuman, III, *Collector's Encyclopedia of American Art Glass*, Collector Books, 1988, 1994 value update.

American

Durand, vase, 6" h, cut floral rose color ext., white int., sgd "V. Durand" 385.00
Gillander American Glass Co., attributed to
  Lamp Shade, 4-1/2" h, 3-7/8" fitter ring, crimped rim, flared cased body, Pink, three birds among blossoms, minor rim chips. 250.00
  Vase, 4" h, overlaid in white, cameo etched morning glory blossoms, buds, and leafy vines, shaded blue cased to white oval body 825.00
Mount Washington
  Bowl, 10" d, sq crimped rim, white overlay, cameo carved ribbons and flowers, rose ground. 475.00
  Lamp, 21" h, 10" d shade, brilliant deep yellow over white, base figural woman with basket of flowers, matching floral design on shade, fancy brass base and font, orig chimney 8,500.00

English

Carder, Frederick, attributed to, vase, 8" h, baluster, olive green body, thickly layered in white, deeply carved blossoms on convoluted leafy stems. 4,350.00
Stevens and Williams
  Bowl, 6-1/4" d, 4" h, ftd, cased yellow ground, carved seaweed, applied glass prunt 250.00
  Decanter, 15-1/2" h, citron yellow and colorless ground, sapphire blue overlay, wheel cut and engraved cactus rose blossoms on spiked leaf-forms, matching teardrop stopper 1,265.00

(English) Vase, white fuchsia on royal blue ground, attributed to Stevens & Williams, 3-3/4" h, $990. Photo courtesy of Garth's Auctions, Inc.

Vase

4-1/4" h, 3-1/4" w, pale blue ground, dainty carved leaves, single large butterfly, band of white beaded cutting at throat, base fully sgd "Stevens & Williams Art Glass, Stourbridge" 1,250.00

4-1/2" h, broad bright blue oval, overlaid in opaque white glass, cameo etched and cut clusters of cherries on leafy boughs, circular mark on base "Stevens & Williams Art Glass Stourbridge". 1,265.00

Unknown Maker

Vase

5" h, frosted red body, white cameo blossoms and leafy stems, reverse with two butterflies. 750.00

7-3/4" h, yellow ivory oval body, overlaid in glossy amber brown, etched with Persian influenced scrolling foliate reserves 900.00

Webb, Thomas, & Sons

Perfume Bottle

2-1/2" h, sphere, opalescent translucent body, white overlay, cameo etched with repeating blossom and vine tracery, mounted with mkd "sterling" silver rim and hinged wreath dec cap, orig glass stopper 1,035.00

3-1/8" h, sphere, ruby red, cameo cut shell and seaweed motif, fitted with hallmarked silver rim, hinged dome cov 2,100.00

4" l, teardrop, green oval, white snowdrop blossoms and buds dec, hallmarked silver rim, hinged cover with glass int. 1,400.00

4-1/4" l, flattened oval teardrop, turquoise blue, overlaid in white, cameo etched and carved fantasy scene, downcast boy carrying bundle of kindling sticks on back among thorny branches, silver rim and hinged foliate chased cap 13,800.00

5" h, cased oval, red ground, white cameo overlay, etched blossom motif, three applied thorny camphor glass feet, hallmarked silver rim fitted with silver clad glass stopper, silver over-cover 1,850.00

11" l, figural, carp, red glass overlaid in white, cameo carved intricate scales and details, mounted with hallmarked two-part hinged rim and "tail" cover which enclosed orig glass stopper, underside inscribed "Rd. 15711," orig satin fitted box mkd "A. M. Raper/London," and 1961 authentication letter, dating registry number to 1884 . . . . . .25,300.00

Plaque, 7-3/4" h, 4-3/4" w, attributed to George Woodall, yellow amber overlaid in white, cameo etched lilac blossoms, bordered and scalloped at edge, mounted to foil lined metal frame for hanging. 4,900.00

Rose Bowl

2-1/4" h, 2-1/2" d, etched blackberry dec in white, dark plum ground 920.00

6" h, translucent ruby red, white overlay carved and etched with brambles and thorny rosa rugosa bushes, butterfly and caterpillar at reverse, base stamped for retailer "Theodore B. Starr, New York" 2,875.00

Scent

2" h, sphere, frosted colorless cased to opal, overlaid with white over red, cameo etched trumpet blossoms and leafy vine, hallmarked silver threaded rim and screw cap 1,380.00

2-1/4" l, sphere, red body, detailed white floral spray, screw rim, chased cap with elaborate foliate design, cross threaded. 1,100.00

3" h, cylinder, deep amber ground, white carved flowers and leaves, borders above and below, hallmarked hinged rim and silver cap (dented) .1,495.00

Vase

3" h, 3-1/4" d, squat bulbous, raisin brown ground, white blossoming leafy vines, borders above and below, Webb medallion on base 690.00

3-1/2" h, oval red body, white fuchsia blossoms, linear borders 1,265.00

4" h, design attributed to George Woodall, oval body, deep cobalt blue, overlaid in pastel cornflower blue, cameo carved six Japanesque floral medallions, latticework foliate and geometric ground, polished top rim. 6,900.00

5" h, bottle-form, simulated ivory, turquoise blue oak leaf cluster dec, three gold enhanced acorns, base stamped "Thomas Webb & Sons Gem Cameo" circular mark 1,25.00

5-1/4" h, flared Northwood blue oval body, deeply overlaid in white, cameo etched and carved with sculptural blossoming plants obverse and reverse with insects in flight at sides 3,650.00

5-3/4" h, bulbous lily, chartreuse yellow cased body, overlaid in white over deep red, cameo etched orchid lilies, butterfly at reverse, linear borders. 2,500.00

7" h, bright yellow oval body, lined in creamy ivory, overlaid with white over crimson red, cameo etched five-petal blossoming plant on front, leafy branch on reverse, base mkd "Thomas Webb & Sons Gem Cameo" 5,000.00

7-1/2" h, complex oval body, transparent ice blue overlaid at top quarter in stippled ruby red with white layer below, etched and carved as pond lilies and leaf pods, clear blue water background, base borders center ""Webb" medallion, possible restoration to center base 20,700.00

7-3/4" h, Peking tricolor, bright olive green overlaid on ivory, lined in raspberry pink, etched and carved blossoms and foliate devices in Asian manner, elaborate borders interspersed, framed mark on base "Thos. Webb & Sons" 6,900.00

8" h, flared trumpet form, bright blue overlaid in white, oak leaves dec, elaborate lower border 1,725.00

8-1/2" h, flared cone, bright yellow-green cased to opal, overlaid in white over deep blue, cameo etched and carved blackberry branches, bumblebee below 3,450.00

9" h, double gourd George Woodall design, ivory, carved alternating bird and floral reserves in six panels, enhanced by gold outlines and borders, dotted background executed in Jules Barbe technique, provenance: purchased from George Woodall's estate .9,775.00

10" h, flared baluster, yellow-green body overlaid in white over ruby red, cameo etched and carved chrysanthemums and bumblebee and butterfly at reverse, linear borders, small surface scratch at center 1,200.00

10-1/2" h, elongated oval baluster, brilliant red overlaid in white, cameo etched intricate blossoming leafy stems, butterfly at reverse, int. base stain 1,850.00

French

D'Argental

Box, cov, 3-1/2" d, 3-1/4" h, cylindrical, amber layered in burgundy-red, cameo etched Art Deco style blossoms in overlapping designs, flower mkd "D'Argental" 600.00

Vase

8" h, brown berries, leaves, and vines, lime green ground, cameo sgd. 900.00

8" h, oval body, fiery golden amber, overlaid in bright and burgundy-red, cameo etched expansive riverside scene with

mountains, tall trees in foreground, sgd "D'Argental" in motif
. . . . .1,150.00
12" h, bottle form, fiery golden amber, overlaid in red-amber and maroon, etched landscape and riverside scenes, framed in scrolling arches, etched "D'Argental (cross)" 950.00
13" h, detailed purple wisteria, frosted and purple ground, cameo sgd. 1,200.00

Daum Nancy
  Lamp
    14" h, matching base and shade, purple-aubergine at top shaded to mottled green at lower edge, overlaid in white and green, cameo etched as broad leafy trees, crowns on shade, trunks o base, period bronze lamp fittings, inscribed "Daum Nancy (cross)" under base and on shade rim 5,175.00
    19" h, matching base and ball shade, green and black glass layered over turquoise blue, cameo etched riverside scene with tall trees and grass on foreground shore, island views beyond, sgd "Daum Nancy (cross)" on both, black metal fittings with sockets above and below
    . . . . .12,650.00
  Salt Dish, 2" h, 3" l, angular oval, ftd, one fiery golden amber, other emerald green cased to clear, etched gilded maiden hair fern motif, four applied glass ball feet, each inscribed in gold "Daum (cross) Nancy," price for pr. 1,400.00
  Vase
    3-1/2" h, bleeding hearts in red, blue centers, green leaves, brown stems, green, purple, and white mottled ground, carved floral design at bottom, enamel highlights, cameo sgd .1,300.00
    3-1/2" h, mistletoe, gold and white enameling, frosted light blue ground, enamel signature 475.00
    4-1/2" h, boats at sea, brown and black enamel, mustard/yellow ground, sgd. 1,300.00
    5" h, purple violets, green leaves, green, purple, and white mottled ground, carved stylized design at bottom, enamel highlights, cameo sgd 2,100.00
    5-1/2" h, flared oval, mottled white and purple, etched naturally colored blossoming fuchsias, sgd "Daum (cross) Nancy" at side 2,000.00
    5-5/8" h, oval body, raised rim, mottled blue ground, etched landscape, painted naturalistic vitrified colors, sgd "Daum Nancy (cross)" on lower scene. . . .2,775.00
    8-1/2" h, detailed flowers, shades of brown, yellow frosted and modeled ground, cameo sgd 1,600.00
    14" h, flared mottled gold and red-amber oval body, acid-etched forest scene, enhanced by vitrified autumn colors on falling leaves, sgd "Daum Nancy (cross)" in middle 4,600.00
DeVez, vase, 3-3/4" h, frosted colorless oval, overlaid in pink, cameo etched five-petaled blossoms, cameo sgd "deVez" at side, top edge smoothed 300.00
Galle
  Atomizer, 7" h, deeply cut blue trees, blue mountain range, green lake, frosted and yellow sky, cameo sgd. . . . 800.00
  Bowl, 5-3/4" d, 1-1/2" d, colorless and yellow overlaid in aubergine, cameo etched in organic leaf forms, sgd "Galle" at rim 350.00
  Lamp, 14" h, cameo shade and base, 9" d shade carved with blue eagles, frosted and blue ground, base with deep blue evergreens, light blue mountains, green lake, both cameo sgd, shade cracked 1,200.00
  Perfume Bottle
    5-1/4" h, oval body, frosted yellow overlaid in green-brown, etched spring flowers, sgd "Galle" at side,

fitted with gilt metal atomizer top, some parts missing
. . . . 520.00
    5-3/8" h, conical, cased yellow overlaid in brown, cameo etched leafy stems and blossoms, sgd "Galle" at reverse, top sheared 550.00
    6-3/4" h, oval body, frosted golden amber, amethyst disk foot, overlaid in lavender and brown, cameo etched blossoms above spiked leaves, sgd "Galle" on reverse
    . . . . 500.00
  Vase
    4-3/4" h, vasiform, frosted colorless cased to fiery amber, layered in brown, cameo etched blossoming leafy stems, cameo sgd "Galle" on lower side. 500.00
    5" h, oval body, frosted green and ambergris, layered in forest green, cameo etched fiddleback and maidenhair fern fronds, sgd "(star) Galle" 950.00
    5-1/4" h, flattened oval body, frosted colorless cased to pink opal, layered in lavender and aubergine, applied conforming handles, cameo etched blossom cluster above leafy plant stem, sgd "Galle" on reverse between falling blossoms. 1,000.00
    5-1/4" h, frosted ovoid, bright fiery golden-amber glass layered in ruby and maroon-red, cameo etched upright butterfly cyclamen blossoms and buds above dense leaves, cameo sgd "Galle" on reverse 2,200.00
    7-1/4" h, flattened oval, frosted aqua-blue layered in blue and aubergine, cameo etched riverside scene, tall trees in foreground, cameo sgd "Galle" on reverse . .1,610.00
    8" h, carved brown and green leaves and stems, frosted shading to yellow ground, cameo sgd. 1,100.00

(French) Vase, Legras, with summer scene, 8" h, $1,485. Photo courtesy Jackson's Auctions.

9-3/4" h, 5-3/4" w, elongated elliptical body, frosted color-less and fiery golden amber, layered in chartreuse and dark green, cameo etched as fiddlehead, maiden hair fern fronds, and wild grasses, sgd "Galle" on reverse 2,500.00

10-1/2" h, elongated neck on flattened oval body, pastel pink and colorless, overlaid in green under brown, cam-eo etched and carved riverscape with tall trees along foreground waterfront, sgd "Galle" in river 1,200.00

10-3/4" h, flattened oval, elongated neck, frosted fiery golden amber, layered in amethyst aubergine, cameo etched broad blossom on leafy branches, cameo sgd "Galle" on reverse 1,000.00

12" h, flattened form, intricate cameo carved red limbs, leaves, and berries, frosted red and yellow ground, cam-eo sgd 1,500.00

13-1/4" h, baluster form, frosted colorless, turquoise body lower int., overlaid in bright pink and olive green, cameo etched pendant bleeding heart blossoms attached to leafy vines, falling tree on reverse, cameo sgd "(star) Galle" for Emile Galle 1,650.00

14-1/2" h, oval body, frosted fiery golden amber and color-less, layered in lavender, amber, and aubergine, cameo etched decumbent blossoms, buds, and leafy branches, cameo sgd "Galle" on reverse, minor int. stain 1,725.00

15-3/4" h, tapered oval body, frosted colorless body, cased with opaque white, pink, overlaid in olive green on lavender, cameo etched wisteria cluster pendant from velvet finish green rim, falling blossom on reverse, sgd "Galle" on reverse, int. stain and scratches. 2,500.00

17" h, baluster form, frosted colorless body, layered in bright cornflower blue, green, and black, etched and wheel cut naturalistic cineraria blossoms and buds, leafy stems rising from black earth base, cameo sgd "Galle" on reverse 7,250.00

Legras, vase, 7" h, red and pink pheasant in trees, frosted glass ground 800.00

Muller Fres, vase, 9" h, flared elongated oval, cased white over-laid in orange, green, and black, cameo etched lakeside scene with tall trees on shore, islands beyond, cameo sgd "Muller," some restoration 900.00

Richard, chandelier, 14-1/2" d, brown pinecones and butterfly, mottled yellow, brown, and green ground, cameo sgd, orig hardware 3,250.00

Schneider LeVerre, vase

11-1/2" h, mottled orange on yellow oval, three stylized etched horseshoe crabs alternating with repeating de-sign elements, candy cane signature at lower edge 1,200.00

19-1/2" h, tall tapered pale orange oval, layered in aub-ergine-brown, etched pendant seed clusters and spiked leaves, embedded candy cane signature 950.00

CAMERAS

History: Photography became a viable enterprise in the 1840s, but few early cameras have survived. Cameras made before the 1880s are seldom available on the mar-ket, and when found, their prices are prohibitive for most collectors.

George Eastman's introduction of the Kodak camera in 1888, the first commercially marketed roll film camera, put photography in the hands of the public.

Most collectors start with a general interest that be-comes more defined. After collecting a broad range of

Kodak cameras, a collector may decide to specialize in Retina models. Camera collectors tend to prefer unusual and scarce cameras to the most common models, which were mass-produced by the millions.

Because a surplus exists for many common cameras, such as most Kodak box and folding models, collectors are wise to acquire only examples in excellent condition. Shutters should function properly. Minimal wear is gener-ally acceptable. Avoid cameras that have missing parts, damaged bellows, and major cosmetic problems.

References: Brian Coe and Paul Gates, *The Snapshot Photograph,* Ash and Grant Ltd., 1977; John F. Maloney, *Vintage Cameras and Images,* Books Americana, 1981; James and Joan McKeown, *McKeown's Price Guide to Antique & Classic Cameras, 1997-1998*, Centennial Pho-to Service, 1996; Beaumont Newhall, *The History of Pho-tography,* The Museum of Modern Art, 1982.

Periodicals: *Camera Shopper,* P.O. Box 1086, New Can-nan, CT 06840; *Classic Camera,* P.O. Box 1270, New York, NY 10157-2078; *Shutterbug,* 5211 S. Washington Ave., Titusville, FL 32780.

Collectors' Clubs: American Photographic Historical Society, Inc., 1150 Avenue of the Americas, New York, NY 10036; American Society of Camera Collectors, 4918 Alcove Ave., North Hollywood, CA 91607; International Kodak Historical Society, P.O. Box 21, Flourtown, PA 19301; Leica Historical Society of America, 7611 Dor-noch Lane, Dallas, TX 75248; National Stereoscopic As-sociation, P.O. Box 14801, Columbus, OH 43214; Nikon Historical Society, P.O. Box 3213, Munster, IN 46321; Photographic Historical Society, P.O. Box 39563, Roch-ester, NY 14604; The Movie Machine Society, 50 Old Country Rd., Hudson, MA 01749; Zeiss Historical Soci-ety, 300 Waxwing Drive, Cranbury, NJ 08512.

Museums: Cameras & Images International, Boston, MA; Fleetwood Museum, North Plainfield, NJ; George Eastman Museum, Rochester, NY; International Cinema Museum, Chicago, IL; Smithsonian Institution, Washing-ton, DC.

Additional Listings: See *Warman's Americana & Col-lectibles* for more examples.

Advisor: Tom Hoepf.

Adams & Westlake, Adlake Special box camera, c1897, with 12 aluminum plate holders, 4" x 5" images 100.00

Ansco Vest-Pocket No. 2, strut-type folding camera, c1917, Modico f7.5 Anastigmat lens or Ansco Anastigmat f6.3 lens in extraspeed Bionic shutter, hinged lens cover........ 35.00

Blair Camera Co., Blair Hawk-Eye Junior box camera, c1897, 3-1/2" x 3-1/2" pictures from glass plates...........75.00

Beier (Germany), Rifax folding camera, range finger model, c1939, split-image focusing, Trinar f2.9 Anastigmat lens, Compur rapid shutter, 120 roll film...............100.00

Burke & James, Ingento Junior No. 3A, folding camera, c1915, Ilex shutter, for 3-1/4" x 5-1/2" photos 20.00

Eastman Kodak

2C Autographic Kodak Jr., folding camera, c1916-27, ball bearing shutter with Kodak Anastigmat f7.7 lens, for 2-7/8" x 4-7/8" postcard size image 20.00

Film Premo No. 1, film pack folding camera, c1915, Meniscus Achromatic lens, ball bearing shutter, for 3-1/4" x 5-1/2" postcard size image 40.00

Kodak 35, 35mm camera, c1937, with f3.5, 4.5 or 5.6 lens, flip-up viewfinder atop camera body, no rangefinder 20.00

Retina II, 35mm camera, c1938, f2 or f2.8 Retina-Xenon lens, Compur-rapid shutter, coupled rangefinder 100.00

Speed Graphic, focal plane shutter camera, c1917, black bellows, black oxidized metal, black ebonized woodwork, folding viewfinder with cross hairs, leather handle on top, four sizes, 3-1/4" x 4-1/4", 3-1/4" x 5-1/2", 4" x 5", 5" x 7" 150.00

Vest Pocket Autographic Kodak, folding camera, c1915, Kodak Anastigmat f7.7 lens, for 1-5/8" x 2-1/2" photos 45.00

Folmer Graflex Corp., National Graflex reflex camera, c1938, ground glass focusing, f3.5 Bausch & Lomb Tessar lens, focal plan shutter with speeds to 1/500 . . . . 125.00

Houghton (London), Ensignette, c1914, strut-type folding camera, brass body, 3/4" x 1-7/8" x 3-7/8", f11 Meniscus lens, 1-1/2" x 2-1/4" pictures on roll film 75.00

R. F. Hunter (London), Purma Special, c1940, miniature camera, modern design made of Bakelite and metal, 1-1/4" x 1-1/4" image on 127 roll film, f6.3-3 Beck lens, fixed focus 50.00

Kozy Camera Co., Pocket Kozy Camera, 1898, folding camera with bellows that open like a book, 3-1/2" x 3-1/2" pictures on cartridge (roll) film, size when closed: 4-1/2" x 5-3/4" x 1-5/8" thick, waist-level viewfinder 1,500.00

Mutschler, Robertson & Co. Ray No. 2, 5-x-7 folding plate camera, c1895, Rapid Rectilinear lens, Unicum shutter, leather-covered exterior, mahogany interior, red bellows, brass fittings 100.00

Monroe Camera Co., Tourist Pocket Camera, 1898, folding strut-type plate camera, 3-1/4" x 4-1/4" pictures, pocket size: 1-1/2" x 4-1/4" x 5-1/4" when closed, leather bellows, leather covered aluminum 300.00

Rochester Camera Co.

Cycle Poco 4-x-5 and 5-x-7 folding plate cameras, c1897, leather covered wood body, polished wood interior, red bellows 150.00

Empire State View Camera, c1895, folding field camera, polished wood, brass fittings, 5" x 7" 110.00

Seneca Camera Co., View Camera, 5-x-7, Uno shutter, folding bed, black bellows, black interior, black leather exterior 80.00

Voiglander Bess 66, "Baby Bessa," 1930s folding camera, folding frame viewfinder, f3.5 Voitgar lens, Compur shutter, 120 roll film 50.00

Western Camera Mfg Co., Magazine Cyclone box camera, c1898, three sizes: No. 1 for 2-1/2" by 2-1/2" pictures; No. 2 for 3-1/4" x 4-1/4"; No. 3 for 4" x 5", "takes 12 pictures in 12 seconds," price for each size 75.00

Yale Camera No. 2, small cardboard box camera, c1900, takes 3-1/2" x 3-1/2" dry plates 100.00

Ziess, Tenax II, c1938, 35mm camera, coupled built-in rangefinder, interchangeable 40mm Tessar f2.8 or Sonnar f2 lens, compur rapid shutter 300.00

CANDLESTICKS

History: The domestic use of candlesticks is traced to the 14th century. The earliest was a picket type, named for the sharp point used to hold the candle. The socket type was established by the mid-1660s.

From 1700 to the present, candlestick design mirrored furniture design. By the late 17th century, a baluster stem was introduced, replacing the earlier Doric or clustered column stem. After 1730 candlesticks reflected rococo ornateness. Neoclassic styles followed in the 1760s. Each new era produced a new style of candlesticks; however, some styles became universal and remained in production for centuries. Therefore, when attempting to date a candlestick, it is important to try to determine the techniques used to manufacture the piece.

References: Margaret and Douglas Archer, *Collector's Encyclopedia of Glass Candlesticks*, Collector Books, 1983; Veronika Baur, *Metal Candlesticks*, Schiffer Publishing, 1996; Kenneth Wilson, *American Glass 1760-1930*, 2 vols., Hudson Hills Press and The Toledo Museum of Art, 1994.

Note: Prices listed below are for pairs.

Brass

6-7/8" h, Queen Anne, scalloped base, baluster stems, dents, ... 615.00

7" h, Neoclassical, worn orig gilding, 19th C 180.00

7-9/16" h, trumpet base, sausage turnings, English, second half 17th C 13,800.00

7-7/8" h, Queen Anne, petal base, conforming shaped bobeches, England, c1740, minor cracks, repair to one base 1,050.00

8" h, Queen Anne, sq base with invected corners, well detailed stem, scalloped lip 1,045.00

8-1/8" h, Queen Anne, scalloped lip and foot 330.00

8-3/8" h, Queen Anne, petal base, push-up, England, mid 18th C, minor dents, loss to one push-up 920.00

8-3/8" h, Queen Anne, sq base with invected corners, push ups missing, well executed repairs, not seamed . . . 615.00

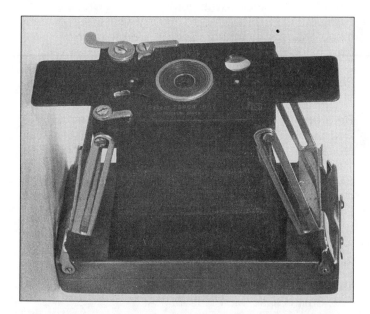

Houghton Ensignette, c1914, strut-type folding camera, early brass body, $75. Photo courtesy of Tom Hoepf.

Glass, blue opalescent socket, dolphin standard, petticoat base, 6-1/2" h, $95.

10-3/4" h, machine turned classical and floral dec, 19th C, one slightly crooked 420.00

12-1/4" h, overall cast rococo design and flowerheads, mkd "Fraget, Warzawie," Polish, late, 19th C 320.00

12-3/8" h, Dutch, domed base, baluster stem, mid-drip pan 3,520.00

26-1/2" h, long turned shaft supported by tall multi-tiered dome, shaped drip pan, tall turned and long socketed candle holder, 17th C. 1,450.00

Bronze

10-1/4" h, cylindrical rope twist standard, acanthus cast flaring nozzle, acanthus, anthemion, and flowerhead cast stepped circular base, late 18th C 1,800.00

17-1/2" h, blown glass inserts, orig patina, one orig bobeche imp "Tiffany Studios, New York" 2,600.00

Copper, hammered, 8" h, Princess style, Karl Kipp, minor cleaning to patina 500.00

Faience, 18" h, blue and white, figural rampant lion, minor edge chips, pr 500.00

Gilt Bronze, 19-3/4" h, elongated slit candlecup, green glass blown throughout, screwed into turned shaft, swirled organic pad foot 575.00

Gilt Metal, 11-1/8" h, 5-1/2" w, rows of flat leaves from top to bottom, diagonal banding on stem, base dec with flat leaves and acanthus, c1800-10, French Empire 2,530.00

Glass

3" h, mottled blue shading to lavender, Monart 80.00

7-1/4" h, translucent powder blue, hexagonal, attributed to New England Glass Co. 850.00

9-5/8" h, flint, colorless, pewter socket liner, Pittsburgh, mid 19th C 90.00

Iron, 6-5/8" h, hogscraper, pushup and hanging lip, mkd "Shaw" 275.00

Pewter, 9-3/4" h, unmarked, married pr 255.00

Pottery, 6-1/2" h, handled form, green matte glaze, imp Teco mark, cov with wax, glued crack to bottom edge 110.00

Silver

3-1/2" d, traveling type, circular dished form, detachable candle socket, loop handle, monogram, Black, Starr & Frost, NY, late 19th C. 400.00

4-1/2" d, traveling type, circular form, shaped edges, bright-cut dec, Hebrew text, unmarked, late 19th/early 20th C 1,100.00

9-1/4" h, repousse, spiral column form, domed bell shaped foot, heavily foliate dec, mkd "A.B.," Continental, late 18th/early 19th C 2,650.00

Silver Plated, 14" h, overall cast foliate and winged griffin's heads, paw feet, mkd "WMF," German, late 19th C, minor damage to one 350.00

Tin, 11-1/2" h, double wedding ring, hogscraper type base 625.00

Wrought Iron, 19-5/8" h, primitive, spring loaded splint holder, tripod base. 470.00

CANDY CONTAINERS

History: In 1876, Croft, Wilbur and Co. filled small glass Liberty Bells with candy and sold them at the Centennial Exposition in Philadelphia. From that date until the 1960s, glass candy containers remained popular. They reflect historical changes, particularly in transportation.

Jeannette, Pennsylvania, a center for the packaging of candy in containers, was home for J. C. Crosetti, J. H. Millstein, T. H. Stough, and Victory Glass. Other early manufacturers included: George Borgfeldt, New York, New York; Cambridge Glass, Cambridge, Ohio; Eagle Glass, Wheeling, West Virginia; L. E. Smith, Mt. Pleasant, Pennsylvania; and West Brothers, Grapeville, Pennsylvania.

References: *Candy Containers*, L-W Book Sales, 1996; Douglas M. Dezso, J. Lion Poirier & Rose D. Poirier, *Collector's Guide to Candy Containers*, Collector Books, 1997; George Eikelberner and Serge Agadjanian, *Complete American Glass Candy Containers Handbook*, revised and published by Adele L. Bowden, 1986; Jennie Long, *Album of Candy Containers*, published by author, Vol. I (1978), Vol. II (1983).

Collectors' Club: Candy Container Collectors of America, P.O. Box 352, Chelmsford, MA 01824-0352.

Museums: Cambridge Glass Museum, Cambridge, OH; L. E. Smith Glass, Mt. Pleasant, PA.

Additional Listings: See *Warman's Americana & Collectibles* for more examples.

Notes: Candy containers with original paint, candy, and closures command a high premium, but beware of reproduced parts and repainting. The closure is a critical part of each container; if it is missing, the value of the container drops considerably.

Small figural perfumes and other miniatures often are sold as candy containers.

Abbreviations:

o/c = orig closure

n/c= no closure

r/c = reproduction closure

E&A refers to George Eikelberner and Serge Agadjanian, *Complete American Glass Candy Containers Handbook*

Long refers to Jennie Long, *Album of Candy Containers*

Airplane

Musical Toy, o/c, E&A 3, Long 331 . . . . 66.00

P-38 Lightning, orig candy, o/c, E&A 12, Long 326 . . 310.00

Spirit of Goodwill, o/c, 50% orig paint, orig propeller, E&A 8b
. . . . 125.00

Spirit of St. Louis, clear, all orig tin, E&A 9, Long 321
. . . . 425.00

Amos and Andy, 70% orig paint, o/c, E&A 21, Long 77
. . . . 580.00

Automobile

Coupe with Long Hood, U.S.A., green glass, roughness on roof, r/c, E&A 51b, Long 359 . . . . 80.00

Electric Coupe, pat Feb 18, 1913, chip on roof corner, n/c, E&A 49, Long 354 . . . . 45.00

Hearse #2, r/c, E&A 40, Long 361 . . . . 100.00

Limousine, rear trunk and tire, 95% orig blue paint, tiny nick on truck, o/c, E&A 38, Long 367 . . . . 200.00

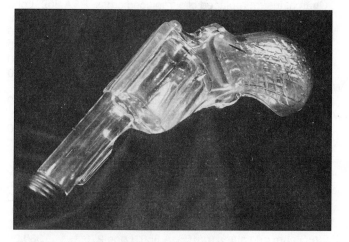

Revolver, orig screw cap, 8" l, $45.

Streamlined, orig paint, o/c, E&A 34, Long 372 . . . . . . 42.00

V.G. Co. Sedan, 70% orig yellow paint, small chips on running board, replaced wheels and closure, E&A 57b, Long 370 . . . . 72.00

West Bros. Co. Limousine, orig wheels, chip under closure, o/c, E&A 43, Long 350 . . . . 95.00

Barney Google and Ball, repainted, o/c, E&A 72, Long 79
. . . . 200.00

Battleship, 3 stacks, orig tin base 40.00

Bell, Liberty Bell with Hanger, E&A 85, Long 229 . . . . . 110.00

Big Show Candy Box, four giraffes 16.50

Black Cat

2-1/2" h, composition, US zone, set of 3 . . . . 60.00

5" h, composition 25.00

6" x 9", emb, scrap pictures 45.00

Boat, Submarine F6, E&A 101, Long 337 . . . . 440.00

Buddy Bank, o/c, Long 449 . . . . 245.00

Bus, Jitney, orig wheels, small chip under front grill, o/c, E&A 114b, Long 340 . . . . 290.00

Candlestick, with handles, "Souvenir of South Fork, PA," o/c, E&A 119b, Long 203 . . . . 245.00

Cannon, two wheel mount #1, all orig, o/c, E&A 123, Long 137
. . . . 210.00

Carpet Sweeper, "Baby Sweeper," all orig, o/c, E&A 132, Long 242 . . . . 385.00

Charlie Chaplin, Borgfeldt, 80% orig paint, o/c, E&A 137, Long 83 . . . . 175.00

Chicken on Sagging Basket, traces of paint, tiny corner chip under closure, o/c, E&A 148a, Long 8 . . . . 50.00

Clock

Mantel, orig dial, mkd on reverse "Contents 3 oz. Av.," o/c, E&A 104a, Long 116 . . . . 235.00

Octagon, 80% orig paint, orig dial, tiny crack front corner, o/c, E&A 163, Long 117 . . . . 275.00

"Souvenir of Platte, S. D.," milk white, o/c, E&A 162, Long 114
. . . . 235.00

Dirigible, *Los Angeles,* 95% orig paint, o/c, E&A 176a, Long 322
. . . . 195.00

Duck on Plain Top Basket, 80% orig paint, o/c, E&A 197, Long 30 . . . . 110.00

Easter, composition

6-1/2" h, boy, round body shape 40.00

6-1/2" h, duck, egg body shape 45.00

6-1/2" h, chick, egg body shape 45.00

6-1/2" h, girl, round body shape 40.00

Elephant with Howdah, camphor glass, chipped foot, n/c, Long 32 . . . . 35.00

Fire Engine

Fire Dept. No. 99, o/c, E&A 214, Long 384 . . . . 50.00

Ladder Truck, chip on left running board, orig wheels, o/c, E&A 216, Long 384 . . . . 165.00

Gas Pump, Gas 23c today, 70% orig paint, replaced hose, o/c, E&A 240a, Long 316 . . . . 320.00

Girl, with two geese, n/c, E&A 241 . . . . 22.00

Halloween, candy box, 5" x 7" 10.00

Hen on Nest, 6" 50.00

Horn, trumpet, two bears, worn, age cracks, o/c, E&A 313, Long 280 . . . . 100.00

House, "All Glass," 95% paint, o/c, E&A 324b, Long 75 . 205.00

Independence Hall, minor edge nick, o/c, E&A 342, Long 74
. . . . 275.00

Jack O Lantern, 95% orig paint, blue glass, orig bail and rim, E&A 349a, Long 159 . . . . 330.00

Kewpie by Barrel, 90% orig paint, o/c, E&A 359, Long 91
. . . . 110.00

Kiddie Kar, 75% orig paint, small chip under closure, o/c, E&A 360, Long 253 . . . . 125.00

Lamp
  Inside Ribbed Base, "Souvenir Boston, Mass," o/c, E&A 367, Long 208 . . . . 125.00
  Kerosene, o/c, E&A 371, Long 21255.00
  Lantern, "Beveled Panel Square," o/c, E&A 396, Long 175 . . . . 72.00
Locomotive
  American Flyer Type #23, blue glass, r/c, E&A 480, Long 417 . . . . 110.00
  "Jeant. Glass C. #888," orig wheels, small chip on wheel flange, o/c, E&A 485a, Long 395 . . . . 165.00
  "Mapother's 1892," o/c, E&A 494a, Long 404 . . . . 80.00
  Mail Box, 80% gray paint, o/c, E&A 521, Long 254 . . . . 190.00
  Midget Washer, E&A 526 . . . . 50.00
  Milk Bottle Carrier, four bottles, Long 451 . . . . 25.00
  Mule Pulling Two Wheeled Barrel, with driver, o/c, E&A 539a, Long 38 . . . . 70.00
  Opera Glass, Swirl Ribs, o/c, E&A 559, Long 260 . . . . . 125.00
Phonograph
  Inkwell Type, orig horn, orig record faded, o/c, E&A 575a, Long 287 . . . . 290.00
  With Glass Horn, 80% orig paint, o/c, E&A 576, Long 286 . . . . 300.00
Piano, upright, 95% orig paint, o/c, E&A 577, Long 289 . . . . 275.00
Pipe, glass, blue 160.00
Powder Horn with Hanger, E&A 588h 18.00
Pumpkin Man, papier-mâché, 5-1/2" h, wire neck 25.00
Puss & Boots, Long, 468 . . . . 140.00
Rabbit
  Glass, crouching, 80% orig paint, o/c, E&A 615, Long 41 . . . . 155.00
  Glass, feet together, sq nose, o/c, E&A 614 . . . . 85.00
  Glass, in egg shell, 80% orig paint, o/c, E&A 608b, Long 48 . . . . 125.00
  Glass, laid back ears, 95% orig paint, o/c, E&A 616a, Long 40 . . . . 100.00
  Glass, legs apart, 95% orig paint, o/c, E&A 611b, Long 50 . . . . 110.00
  Glass, Peter Rabbit, all orig, o/c, E&A 618a, Long 55 . . . . 30.00
  Papier-mâché 600.00
Racer
  "6," #4 on grill, o/c, E&A 641b, Long 430 . . . . 90.00
  "12," 90% orig paint, o/c, E&A 642, Long 432 . . . . . . 350.00
Radio, "Tune In," 90% orig paint, o/c, E&A 643a, Long 290 . . . . 100.00
Rocking Horse, small chip under front, o/c, E&A 651, Long 58 . . . . 155.00
Safe, clear, o/c, E&A 661b, Long 268 . . . . 90.00
Santa Claus, glass
  By square chimney, 80% orig paint, o/c, E&A 672a, Long 99 . . . . 430.00
  Double cuff, 95% orig paint, o/c, E&A 671, Long 101 . . . . 355.00
  Leaving chimney, 60% orig paint, o/c, E&A 673a, Long 102 . . . . 100.00
  Paneled Coat, o/c, E&A 670, Long 98 . . . . 175.00
  Plastic head, all orig, o/c, E&A 674, Long 103 . . . . . . 35.00
  Skookum by tree stump, 75% orig paint, o/c, E&A 681, Long 106 . . . . 220.00
Snowman, composition or papier-mâché
  4-1/2" h, round body 15.00
  5" h, round body, glass eyes, marked "Germany" 40.00
  5-1/2" h, top hat, glass eyes 30.00
  6-1/4" h, glass eyes 24.00

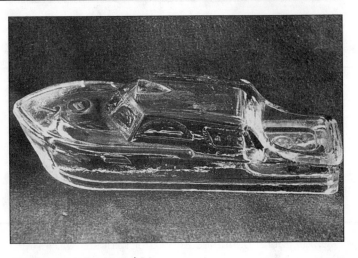

Yacht, no closure, $20.

  6-1/2" h, umbrella 40.00
  7-1/4" h, top hat, tree, carrot nose 30.00
  9" h, stick, musical hat 40.00
Spark Plug, 60% orig paint, rough under closure, r/c, E&A 699 . . . . 115.00
Stop and Go, all orig tin, o/c, E&A 706, Long 317 . . . . . 360.00
Suitcase, milk glass, bear decal, orig handle, o/c, E&A 707, Long 216 . . . . 220.00
Swan Boat, rabbit and chick, 95% orig paint, r/c, E&A 713, Long 60 . . . . 825.00
Tank, World War I, o/c, E&A 721, Long 434 . . . . 160.00
Telephone
  Millstein's ToT, all orig, o/c, E&A 744, Long 306 . . . . . 50.00
  Tall V.G. Co., all orig, o/c, E&A 746, Long 299 . . . . . 160.00
Toonerville Depot Line, traces of paint, large chip on rear, o/c, E&A 767, Long 111 . . . . 90.00
Top, "Spinning Top," all orig, winder, o/c, E&A 775, Long 271 . . . . 100.00
Trunk, round top, milk glass, 90% orig paint, o/c, E&A 789a, Long 219 . . . . 125.00
Turkey, papier-mâché
  3" h, Tom 24.00
  4-1/4" h, Hen 28.00
  4-1/2" h, Tom 40.00
  5-1/2" h, Hen 40.00
  5-1/2" h, Tom 50.00
Village
  Bank, insert, E&A 804, Long, 76b 190.00
  Church, insert, replaced clip, replaced cross, E&A 809, Long 76c 100.00
  City Garage, insert, E&A 811, Long 76g 100.00
  Confectionery, insert, E&A 812, Long 76q 100.00
  Drug Store, insert, E&A 810, Long 76d 110.00
  Engine No. 23, insert, E&A 815, Long 76e 140.00
Wagon, "U. S. Express," all tin replaced, E&A 821b, Long 440 . . . . 110.00
Well, "Ye Old Oaken Bucket," 50% paint, replaced handle, o/c, E&A 831a, Long 137 . . . . 27.50
Windmill
  Dutch Wind Mill, orig blades, n/c, E&A 243, Long 448 . . . . 50.00
  Five Windows, ruby flashed, replaced blades, o/c, E&A 844a, Long 446 . . . . 220.00
  Teddy Wind Mill, replaced tin super structure, tiny corner bottom chip, o/c, E&A 860, Long 276 . . . . 90.00
World Globe, orig stand, o/c, E&A 860, Long 276 . . . . . 330.00

CANES

History: Canes and walking sticks were important accessories in a gentleman's wardrobe in the 18th and 19th centuries. They often served both a decorative and utilitarian function. Glass canes and walking sticks were glassmakers' whimsies, ornamental rather than practical.

References: Linda L. Beeman, *Cane Collector's Directory*, published by author, 1993; Joyce E. Blake, *Glasshouse Whimsies*, published by author, 1984; Catherine Dike, *Cane Curiosa*, Cane Curiosa Press (250 Dielman Rd., Ladue, MO 63124), 1983; ——, *Canes in the United States*, Cane Curiosa Press (250 Dielman Rd., Ladue, MO 63124), 1994; ——, *La Cane Object díArt;* Cane Curiosa Press (250 Dielman Rd., Ladue, MO 63124), 1988; Ulrich Klever, *Walkingsticks*, Schiffer Publishing, 1996; George H. Meyer, *American Folk Art Canes,* Sandringham Press, 1992, Francis H. Monek, *Canes through the Ages*, Schiffer Publishing, 1995; Jeffrey B. Snyder, *Canes from the Seventeenth to the Twentieth Century*, Schiffer Publishing, 1993.

Periodical: *Cane Collector's Chronicle*, 99 Ludlum Crescent, Lower Hutt Welling, New Zealand.

Collectors' Club: International Cane Collectors, 24 Magnolia Ave., Manchester-by-the-Sea, MA 01944; The Cane Collector's Chronicle, 99 Ludlum Crescent, Lower Hutt, Weelington, New Zealand.

Museums: Essex Institute, Salem, MA; Remington Gun Museum, Ilion, NY; Valley Forge Historical Society, Valley Forge, PA.

Notes: Carved wood and ivory canes are frequently considered folk art and collectors pay higher prices for them.

Cane

32" l, zebrawood, carved handle 90.00
33-3/4" l, panbone, rope carved shaft, crosshatched and flute caved handle, 19th C 1,200.00
34" l, ebony shaft, gold dog's head handle, patterned neck, c1901 . . . . 900.00
34-1/4" l, maple, pistol handle, shaft with high relief carving of cow, chicken, home, two dogs' heads, two plants, mother with child. 260.00
35" l
  Pine, carved and painted, handle carved in form of recumbent striped cat tugging at a plaque, relief carved American eagle, crossed cannon, flag and stars and "GAR," with two hearts, tapering shaft relief carved with another striped cat figure, late 19th C. 2,000.00
  Rounded ivory knob above tapering whalebone shaft, 19th C 200.00
  Wood, handle carved with stylized bearded man head, tasseled cord carved on shaft, attributed to Bally Carver, southeastern PA, 19th C, split at top 750.00
36" l
  Bamboo, sterling silver knob set with small clock, enameled face, mkd "Brevete," silver mkd "Sterling" 250.00
  Glass, colorless cased over 1" w opalescent ribbon, red stripe down one edge, blue stripe down other, shepherd's crook handle, fancy knurl. 275.00
37" l, carved wood, figural, knob in form of antelope's head, glass eyes, polychrome highlights, 19th C, minor cracks
. . . . 250.00

44" l, ivory handle over arching horn shaft, ivory top, minor cracks, 19th C 200.00
52" l, glass, pale green, ribbed tapered twist last 18", twist in handle, ... 295.00

Walking Stick

30-3/4" l, carved wood, eagle head knob, swelled tapering shaft, relief dec of two swimmers, lion, dog, and ballerina, inscribed "George Hynes Waterbury Conn. Cut from Camp Bradley Aug. 17th, 1894". 500.00
32-1/2" l, carved hardwood, two snakes grabbing both ends of small quadruped, roothead handle with some burl, very worn black and yellow paint 480.00
32-1/2" l, curly maple, octagonal, good old finish 125.00
33" l, tin, cast white metal knob with McKinley bust, 1896
. . . . 200.00
33-1/4" l, sapling, dog head handle, two tone relief carved figure, leaf, alligator, and giraffe 110.00
34-1/4" l, carved softwood, snake with fist handle, branded inscription "A. M. Gregg, Dec. 3, 1891, Waulpgy Pike, Ohio," old brown crusty finish, some edge damage 175.00
35" l, gold plated knob with cased scrolling design, inscribed "J. H. Hynes Waterbury Ct.," tapering ebonized wood shaft, minor cracks, late 19th C 400.00
35" l, mahogany, open grip handle, relief carved arms and hands, old alligatored varnish, dovetail joining handle and shaft with damage, old repair 85.00

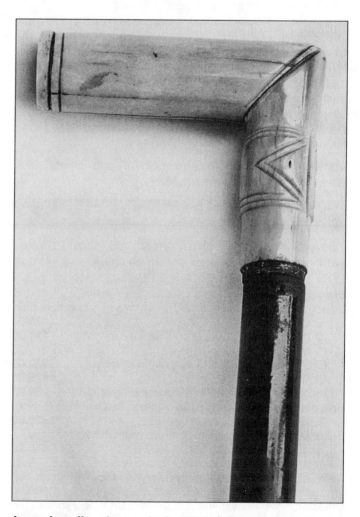

Ivory handle, ebony shaft, 35" l, $90.

35-1/4" l, carved roothead, two snakes, old black and brown paint, brass top. 110.00

36" l, bamboo, natural bark on handle 30.00

36" l, carved softwood, snake with fist handle, carved name "J. F. Williams," old varnish. 165.00

36" l, hardwood, cast white metal man's head handle, carved bamboo-like shaft. 165.00

36-1/2" h, wood, painted black, gold accents, horse's hoof terminal to handle, late 19th/early 20th C, minor paint loss 250.00

37" l, Indian head, lizard, bird, snake, and dated "1926," two tone brown and red finish. 550.00

37-1/2" h, primitive, tattoo type, pony, gazelle, fish, crane, lizard, and snake, knob handle. 325.00

38" l, primitive, root type 85.00

39-1/8" l, polyhedron knob, die-stamped shaft "From W. R. Taylor to Henry Ford Sept 1916," carved whimsey ending in spiral carved shaft, two serpents with bead eyes, old repaired crack, losses to bead eyes. 250.00

CANTON CHINA

History: Canton china is a type of Oriental porcelain made in the Canton region of China from the late 18th century to the present. It was produced largely for export. Canton china has a hand-decorated light- to dark-blue underglaze on white ground. Design motifs include houses, mountains, trees, boats, and bridges. A design similar to willow pattern is the most common.

Borders on early Canton feature a rain and cloud motif (a thick band of diagonal lines with a scalloped bottom). Later pieces usually have a straight-line border.

Early, c1790-1840, plates are very heavy and often have an unfinished bottom, while serving pieces have an overall "orange peel" bottom. Early covered pieces, such as tureens, vegetable dishes, and sugars, have strawberry finials and twisted handles. Later ones have round finials and a straight, single handle.

Marks: The markings "Made in China" and "China" indicate wares which date after 1891.

REPRODUCTION ALERT
Several museum gift shops and private manufacturers are issuing reproductions of Canton china.

Bowl

9-1/4" d, 4-3/4" h, cut-corner, minor area of restoration, hairline 435.00

10-1/2" d, shallow, deeply scalloped rim, rim chip . . . 110.00

10-1/2" d, 3" h, scallop edge 375.00

10-3/4" d, scalloped, low, very minor rim chip 920.00

12" d, 2" h, round 425.00

13-3/4" x 10-3/4" x 2-1/4" h, cut corner, rect 250.00

Box, dome top, sq, cloud and rain border, first half 19th C, pr 6,270.00

Butter Dish, domed lid, pierced insert, mismatched, repaired 440.00

Cann, 5-1/8" h. 175.00

Cider Jug, 11-1/2" h, cracks, staple repair to lid, 19th C 1,500.00

Creamer, 4-1/4" h, helmet shape, 7-1/4" x 5-1/4" leaf shaped underdish 500.00

Platter, blue and white, small rim chip, 18-3/4" l, $1,430. Photo courtesy of Garth's Auctions, Inc.

Dinner Plate, 10" d, set of 14, very minor chips, hairlines 1,150.00

Dish

7-3/8" l, leaf shape, small chips 95.00

10-1/2" l, almond shape, small chips 110.00

Fruit Basket and Undertray, 9" l, two handles, reticulated 300.00

Ginger Jar, 7" h, 7" d, hardwood turned and carved cover 150.00

Pitcher, 4-1/4" h. 220.00

Planter, 13" w, 10" h, hexagonal, ftd trays, 20th C, pr . . 300.00

Plate

7" d, set of nine, minor rim chips 200.00

8-1/2" d, set of six, minor rim chips 175.00

9-1/2" d, rim chips, short hairlines 50.00

Platter

11-1/4" l, rect 315.00

12-1/2" x 15-1/2", octagonal, deep blue and white. . . 450.00

12-3/4" l, octagonal, pearlware. 375.00

13-3/4" l, deep, very minor chips 375.00

15-7/8" l, very minor rim chips, rim roughness 260.00

16" l, chips on front of rim. 55.00

17-1/4" l, deep, pierced insert. 1,035.00

17-1/2" l 550.00

17-3/4" l, 15" w, cut corner 475.00

18" l, well and tree 700.00

18-1/2" l, well and tree 750.00

Sauce Tureen, cov, undertray

6-3/4" h, 3-3/4" h, mismatched. 600.00

7" l, 8" d undertray, cut corner rect, conforming lid with finial, boars head handles 500.00

7-1/8" l, very minor chips 500.00

Soup Tureen, 10" l, 6" h 875.00

Sugar Bowl, cov

5" h, intertwined strap handles. 150.00

5-7/8" h, ear handles, mismatched lid 275.00

Syllabub, set of eight. 900.00

Tea Caddy, cov, 6" h, pr 275.00

Teacup, cov, 3-3/4" h, intertwined strap handles, similar finial on lid 100.00

Teacup and Saucer, minor chips and hairlines, set of ten 250.00

Teapot, cov
  6-1/4" h. 500.00
  6-1/2" h, barrel-form, foo dog handle, mismatched lid, chips 690.00
  6-1/2" h, twined handle, mismatched lid. 420.00
Tray
  8-3/4" x 9", chip on table ring 220.00
  10" l, oval 165.00
Tureen, cov, 12-3/4" l, boar's head handles, minor chips 935.00
Umbrella Holder, 24-1/2" h, 8-1/2" d, side dec with deer, trees, and landscape 600.00
Vegetable, cov
  9" l, mismatched lid 200.00
  9" l, pine cone finial 275.00
  9-1/2" l, pine cone finial 200.00
  10" l, pine cone finial, orange peel glaze 330.00
  10-1/4" l, mismatched lid 400.00
  13-1/2" l, 8-3/4" d, 9" h, blue and white, cut corner form, boars head handles, raised base, large finial on lid. 850.00
Warming Dish
  10-1/2" d, octagonal, handle and spout 250.00
  14-1/4" l, 10" w, oval. 750.00
  15-7/8" l 400.00

CAPO-DI-MONTE

History: In 1743, King Charles of Naples established a soft-paste porcelain factory near Naples. The firm made figurines and dinnerware. In 1760, many of the workmen and most of the molds were moved to Buen Retiro, near Madrid, Spain. A new factory, which also made hard-paste porcelains, opened in Naples in 1771. In 1834, the Doccia factory in Florence purchased the molds and continued production with them in Italy.

Capo-di-Monte was copied heavily by other factories in Hungary, Germany, France, and Italy.

Museums: Metropolitan Museum of Art, New York, NY; Museo of Capodimonte, Naples, Italy; Woodmere Art Museum, Philadelphia, PA.

REPRODUCTION ALERT

Many of the pieces in today's market are of recent vintage. Do not be fooled by the crown over the "N" mark; it also was copied.

Bowl, 14" d, relief molded leopard scene, c1860 . . . . . . 190.00
Box, cov
  6" x 4" x 3-1/2", c1940, minor flakes. 145.00
  8" l, hinged, molded classical Roman bacchanalian scene 500.00
Chocolate Cup and Saucer, relief molded figures, cupid finial cov, c1870 . . . . 165.00
Coffeepot, cov, 6" h relief molded nude figures and trees near lake, pear finial, c1890 . . . . 225.00
Compote, 13" d, shell shape, relief molded cherubs and classical figures, scroll base 125.00
Demitasse Cup and Saucer, maiden, dog, tree, and mountain scene, pastels, branch handle 90.00
Figure, 11" h, dancing woman, 18th C dress 200.00

Figure, boy and dog, sgd "G. Armanis," 9" h, $160.

Jewelry Box, 3-1/4" h, Roman and biblical motif on lid . . 165.00
Pitcher, 8" h, relief molded satyrs and cherubs, polychrome enameling, gilt trim 90.00
Plate, multicolored, raised classical figure border, crown N mark 200.00
Tankard, cov, 13" h, relief molded classical scenes, elephant head handle, relief molded cherubs on rim cov, cupid finial, blue underglaze crown N mark. 500.00
Tea Set, teapot, creamer, cup and saucer, relief carved classical scenes, gold overglaze crown N mark 425.00
Tile, paneled, relief molded nude maidens and Roman bath scene 190.00

Vase, bulbous, narrow cobalt blue neck, gold handle, floral dec, chrysanthemums, rose, blue, and gold dec, mkd "Austria, Victoria, Carlsbad," 8-3/8" h, $80.

Tureen, cov, undertray, 13" l, ovoid body, relief molded with ca-
vorting figures, int. dec with floral springs, cover surmounted
by drunken cherub finial, matching undertray, losses
. . . . 750.00
Urn, 12" h, relief molded classical scenes, blue overglaze crown
N mark, pr. 850.00
Urn, cov, 15" h, baluster shape, domed cov, relief molded sides
with cupids and grapevines, relief molded florals on cover,
molded Bacchus heads at base of handles, pr 600.00

CARLSBAD CHINA

History: Because of changing European boundaries
during the last 100 years, German-speaking Carlsbad
has found itself located first in the Austro-Hungarian Empire, then in Germany, and currently in the Czech Republic. Carlsbad was one of the leading pottery
manufacturing centers in Bohemia.

Wares from the numerous Carlsbad potteries are
lumped together under the term "Carlsbad China." Most
pieces on the market are post-1891, although several
potteries date to the early 19th century.

Biscuit Jar, cov, 5-1/2" d, 6-3/8" h, multicolored florals, gold trim,
mkd "Victoria-Carlsbad" 70.00
Bowl, 12" w, sq, pale peach shading to pale blue, center transfer
of five classical maidens, gold foliage, mkd "Victoria-Carls-
bad" 75.00
Cake Plate, 12" d, violets, pierced gold handles, mkd "Victoria,
Carlsbad, Austria". 45.00
Chocolate Pot, 10" h, multicolored daisies, gold trim, white
ground 110.00
Dessert Set, 9-1/2" d master bowl, twelve 5-1/2" d bowls, scalloped and fluted, four winter scenes, apple blossom boughs,
cream ground, ... 200.00
Ewer, 10" h, divided rim forms two spouts, large dolphin handles
with gold scales, raised gold florals on cream, mkd "Victoria,
Carlsbad" 125.00
Miniature Lamp, 8-1/2" h, porcelain base, Bristol glass shade,
orange, blue, and lavender flowers, scrolling gold trim, nutmeg burner, mkd "Victoria, Carlsbad, Austria" 450.00
Mug, 4" h, decal portrait of monk, violin, mkd "Victoria-Carlsbad"
. . . . 80.00
Pitcher, 11" h, cobalt blue bands, gold trim, pink ground
. . . . 100.00
Portrait Plate, cherubs, rich dark green and cream background,
ruffled edges, sgd "Kaufman" 145.00
Relish, pierced handles, multicolored flowers, pink border,
cream ground 40.00
Teapot, cov, relief scrolls, hp flowers, mkd "Carlsbad, Austria
1892" 70.00
Vase
10-1/2" h, 4-1/2" w, reticulated handles, pedestal, peacock on
balcony, aqua, rose, green, and brown, sgd "Carlsbad Aus-
tria". 265.00
13-3/8" h, 6-1/2" d, hp flowers and holly, colorful shaded
ground, raised enameling, gold tracery, pr 320.00

CARNIVAL GLASS

History: Carnival glass, an American invention, is colored pressed glass with a fired-on iridescent finish. It was
first manufactured about 1905 and was immensely popular both in America and abroad. More than 1,000 differ-

ent patterns have been identified. Production of old
carnival glass patterns ended in 1930.

Most of the popular patterns of carnival glass were
produced by five companies—Dugan, Fenton, Imperial,
Millersburg, and Northwood.

Marks: Northwood patterns frequently are found with the
"N" trademark. Dugan used a diamond trademark on
several patterns.

References: Gary E. Baker et al., *Wheeling Glass*, Ogle-
bay Institute, 1994 (distributed by Antique Publications);
Elaine and Fred Blair, *Carnival Hunter's Companion: A
Guide to Pattern Recognition*, published by authors (P.O.
Box 116335, Carrolton, TX 75011), 1995; Carl O. Burns,
Collector's Guide to Northwood Carnival Glass, L-W Book
Sales, 1994; Dave Doty, *A Field Guide to Carnival Glass*,
Antique Trader Publications, 1998; Bill Edwards, *Stan-
dard Encyclopedia of Carnival Glass*, 5th ed., Collector
Books, 1996; Marion T. Hartung, *First Book of Carnival
Glass to Tenth Book* of Carnival Glass (series of 10
books), published by author, 1968 to 1982; William Hea-
cock, James Measell and Berry Wiggins, *Dugan/Dia-
mond*, Antique Publications, 1993; ——, *Harry Northwood,
The Wheeling Years, 1901-1925*, Antique Publications,
1991; Marie McGee, *Millersburg Glass*, Antique Publications, 1995; Tom and Sharon Mordini, *Carnival Glass
Auction Price for Auctions Conducted in 1995*, published
by authors (36 N. Mernitz, Freeport, IL 61032), 1996;
Glen and Steven Thistlewood, *Carnival Glass, The Magic
& The Mystery,* Schiffer Publishing, 1998.

Collectors' Clubs: American Carnival Glass Association, 9621 Springwater Lane, Miamisburg, OH 45342; Canadian Carnival Glass Association, 107 Montcalm Dr.,
Kitchener, Ontario N2B 2R4 Canada; Collectible Carnival
Glass Association, 3103 Brentwood Circle, Grand Island,
NE 68801; Heart of America Carnival Glass Association,
4305 W 78th St., Prairie Village, KS 66208; International

Carnival Glass Association, P.O. Box 306, Mentone, IN 46539; Lincoln-Land Carnival Glass Club, N951, Hwy 27, Conrath, WI 54731; National Duncan Glass Society, P.O. Box 965, Washington, PA 15301; New England Carnival Glass Club, 27 Wells Rd., Broad Brooks, CT 06016; Tampa Bay Carnival Glass Club, 101st Ave. N., Pinellas Park, FL 34666; WWW.CGA at http://www.woodsland.com/woodland.carnivalglass

Museums: National Duncan Glass Society, Washington, PA; Fenton Art Glass Co., Williamstown, WV.

Notes: Color is the most important factor in pricing carnival glass. The color of a piece is determined by holding it to the light and looking through it.

Acorn, Fenton, ice cream bowl, red 750.00
African Shield, English maker, vase, wire flower arranger, marigold. 145.00
Amaryllis, Northwood
    Compote, marigold. 155.00
    Compote, tri-corner, purple, whimsy shape 175.00
Apple Blossom Twigs, Dugan, bowl, low, ruffled, peach opal
. . . . 150.00
Arched Flute, unknown maker, toothpick, ice green 300.00
Asters, unknown maker, plate, 5" d, marigold. 125.00
Banded Diamonds, Australian maker, tumbler, marigold
. . . . 175.00
Band of Roses, unknown maker
    Cordial Set, decanter, six cordials, undertray, marigold
    . . . . 575.00
    Tumbler, marigold 185.00
Barley & Hops, unknown maker
    Beer Pitcher, marigold, painted 160.00
    Tumbler, marigold, painted. 50.00
Beaded Cable, Northwood, rose bowl, aqua opal. 425.00
Beaded Spears, unknown maker
    Pitcher, marigold 425.00
    Tumbler, marigold 145.00
    Tumbler, teal 30.00
Beaded Swirl, English maker, miniature lamp, marigold. 115.00
Big Basketweave, Dugan, vase, 10-3/4" h, white 165.00
Blackberry, Northwood, basket, open edge, round, red
. . . . 400.00
Blossomtime, Northwood, compote, marigold. 375.00
Boggy Bayou, Fenton, vase, 5" h, lime green opal 950.00
Bull's Eye & Loops, Millersburg, vase, amethyst 350.00
Butterfly, Fenton, ornament, miniature, marigold 1,000.00
Butterfly & Berry, Fenton
    Creamer, blue. 75.00
    Hatpin Holder, blue. 2,100.00
Buzz Saw, Cambridge, cruet, small, green. 350.00
Cane Panels, unknown maker, tumble-up, marigold . . . 175.00
Cherry Circles, Fenton
    Bon Bon, green 350.00
    Bowl, 6" d, ruffled, marigold 40.00
Classic Arts, Czechoslovakian maker, powder box, marigold
. . . . 280.00
Coin Spot, Dugan, compote, celeste blue. 550.00
Colonial Flute, Imperial, toothpick, two handles, marigold, old
    mark 235.00
Colonial Lady, Imperial, vase
    Marigold. 700.00
    Purple. 850.00
Color Burst, unknown maker, perfume, marigold 105.00
Concord, Fenton, bowl, dark marigold 375.00

Corinth, Dugan, jack in the pulpit vase, blue opalescent
. . . . 300.00
Corn, Imperial
    Bottle, helios. 165.00
    Bottle, smoke 350.00
    Vase, green 600.00
    Vase, ice green 375.00
    Vase, white, lavender tint 300.00
Cosmos & Cane, US Glass
    Rose Bowl, volcano shape, honey amber 475.00
    Tumbler, white 335.00
Country Kitchen, Millersburg, spooner, marigold 175.00
Curved Star, unknown maker, child's dish, marigold . . . 175.00
Cut Cosmos, Millersburg, tumbler, marigold. 135.00
Daisy Cup, unknown maker, bell, marigold. 215.00
Daisy Squares, unknown maker
    Goblet, crimped, flared out edge, green. 200.00
    Rose Bowl, crimped edge, two sides turned up, marigold
    . . . . 275.00
Daisy Web, Dugan, hat, Beaded Panels back, two sides up,
    marigold 200.00
Dandelion, Northwood, tumbler, ice blue 175.00
Diamond Fountain, Higbee, cruet, marigold 325.00
Diamond Point, Northwood, vase, amethyst. 90.00
Dimples and Brilliants, maker unknown, hatpin, purple
. . . . 115.00
Dragon & Lotus, Fenton
    Bowl, 3 in 1, amethyst 125.00
    Bowl, 3 in 1, peach opal 275.00
    Ice Cream Bowl, amber opalescent 2,800.00
    Ice Cream Bowl, red. 4,500.00
    Plate, marigold 900.00
Drapery, Northwood
    Vase, ice green 225.00

Acorn Burrs, tumbler, marigold, $48.

Rose Bowl, aqua opal 400.00
Drapery Variant, Northwood, vase, 8" h, marigold 125.00
Elephant, unknown maker, paperweight, miniature, marigold
. . . . 700.00
Embroidered Mums, Northwood, bowl, sapphire blue .1,200.00
Farmyard, Dugan, bowl, 8 ruffle, purple 3,250.00
Feathers, Northwood, vase, 7-1/2" h, green shaded to marigold
. . . . 80.00
Field Thistle, US Glass plate, 6" d, scalloped edge, marigold
. . . . 275.00
Fishscale and Beads, Dugan, plate, 7-1/2" d, amethyst
. . . . 500.00
Five Hearts, Dugan, compote, marigold 275.00
Fleur de Lis, Czechoslovakian maker, plate, 6" d, marigold
. . . . 185.00
Floral and Grape, Fenton
    Tumbler, blue 35.00
    Water Pitcher, blue 400.00
Floral Spray, unknown maker
    Pitcher, clear, very good iridescence 375.00
    Tumbler, clear, very good iridescence 30.00
Flowers & Frames, Dugan, bowl, ftd, purple 450.00
Formal, Dugan, hatpin holder, marigold 700.00
Four Flowers Variant, chop plate, purple, roughness on bottom
. . . . 700.00
Four Pillars, Northwood and Dugan, vase, 9" h, green . . . 85.00
Fruit & Flowers, Northwood
    Bon Bon, ftd, electric blue 185.00
    Bowl, 10" d, dark marigold 125.00
Garden Mums, Northwood, plate, 6" d, amethyst 300.00
Garden Path Variant, chop plate, purple 4,500.00
Garland, Fenton, rose bowl, blue 165.00
Good Luck, Northwood, bowl
    Aqua opalescent, small nick 950.00
    Purple 425.00
    Ribbed back, amethyst 700.00
Grape & Cable, Northwood
    Bon Bon, stippled, green 200.00
    Candle Lamp, green 950.00
    Hatpin Holder, purple 375.00
    Miniature Lamp, purple 200.00
    Plate, purple 200.00
    Powder Jar, purple 200.00
    Punch Bowl and Base, medium, purple 800.00
Hanging Cherries, Millersburg, ice cream bowl, amethyst
. . . . 300.00
Hattie, Imperial, rose bowl, marigold 650.00
Hearts and Flowers, Northwood
    Bowl, aqua opal tips 1,500.00
    Bowl, ice green 650.00
    Bowl, PCE, lime green, 2 heat checks in base 250.00
    Compote, blue, ribbed back 450.00
    Compote, ice blue 700.00
    Compote, marigold 250.00
    Compote, purple 600.00
    Plate, ice green 1,700.00
Hearts and Trees, unknown maker, bowl, ftd, marigold
. . . . 275.00
Heavy Vine, unknown maker, miniature rose bowl, marigold
. . . . 130.00
Herringbone, unknown maker, demitasse cup and saucer,
    marigold 200.00
Hobnail, Millersburg, rose bowl, amethyst 425.00
Hobnail Swirl, Millersburg
    Cuspidor, green 1,700.00
    Cuspidor, purple 600.00

Hobstar & Fruit, Westmoreland
    Card Tray, marigold over milk glass 775.00
    Sauce, 5" d, aqua opal 225.00
Hobstar & Shield, unknown maker, tumbler, marigold . . 265.00
Holly, Fenton
    Bowl, blue satin 125.00
    Plate, electric blue 255.00
Horse Medallion, unknown maker, rose bowl
    Marigold, heat check 155.00
    Red 5,500.00
Imperial Grape, Imperial
    Fruit Bowl, 10-1/4" d, smoke 200.00
    Goblet, amethyst, blue highlights 225.00
    Water Pitcher, marigold 135.00
Inverted Fan and Feather, Dugan, fruit bowl, ftd, marigold
. . . . 85.00
Inverted Feather, Cambridge, cordial, marigold 500.00
Jacobean Ranger, Czechoslovakian or English maker, perfume,
    marigold 215.00
Jockey Club, Northwood, bowl, 6" d, amethyst 1,500.00
Kittens, unknown maker
    Bowl, 2 sides up, 2 kittens, marigold 215.00
    Bowl, 4 sides up, marigold 155.00
    Bowl, six ruffles, marigold 200.00
    Cereal Bowl, marigold 200.00
    Toothpick Holder, marigold 150.00
Leaf & Beads, Northwood, Dugan, rose bowl, aqua opal
. . . . 400.00
Lion, Fenton, paperweight, miniature, marigold 800.00
Little Barrel, Imperial
    Green 185.00
    Marigold 95.00
    Smoke 185.00
Little Stars, Millersburg, bowl, 3 in 1 edge, dark marigold
. . . . 375.00
Loganberry, Imperial, vase
    Amber 400.00
    Green 575.00
Lotus & Grape, Fenton, rose bowl, marigold 400.00

Good Luck, bowl, ribbed back, ruffled, sapphire, $1,600. Photo courtesy of Mickey Reichel Auction Company.

Grape and Cable, centerpiece bowl, white, $1,100. Photo courtesy of Mickey Reichel Auction Company.

Lucille, unknown maker
    Tumbler, blue 245.00
    Water Pitcher, blue 500.00
Many Stars, Millersburg, ice cream bowl, green, 6 point star, radium finish 850.00
Memphis, Northwood, fruit set, bowl and six matching cups, ice blue 4,100.00
Mirrored Lotus, Fenton, rose bowl, marigold 175.00
Moonprint, English maker
    Cordial Set, decanter, six cordials, matching under tray, marigold 450.00
    Vase, 8" h, marigold 425.00
Morning Glory, Imperial, vase, 3-3/4" h, purple 215.00
Omnibus, U. S. Glass, tumbler, blue 275.00

Open Edge, unknown maker, basket, red, two sides up
    . . . . 350.00
Orange Tree, Fenton
    Loving Cup, blue 325.00
    Loving Cup, green 350.00
    Mug, sapphire blue, small size 105.00
    Plate, blue 600.00
    Shaving Mug, blue 75.00
Orange Tree Orchard, Fenton, tumbler, white 55.00
Paneled Dandelion, Fenton, tankard, blue 550.00
Peach, Northwood, berry set, white, gold trim 325.00
Peacock & Urn, Fenton
    Bowl, amethyst 270.00
    Compote, blue 180.00
Peacock & Urn, Northwood, ice cream bowl, dark marigold
    . . . . 500.00
Peacock at Fountain, Northwood, pitcher, electric blue
    . . . . 800.00
Peacock at Urn, Millersburg, shotgun bowl, green 650.00
Peacock at Urn Variant, Millersburg, sauce, amethyst, three rows of beads 145.00
Peacocks, Northwood
    Bowl, aqua 475.00
    Bowl, green 1,050.00
    Bowl, ice green 1,275.00
    Plate, amethyst 775.00
Peacock Tail, Fenton, bowl, 3 in 1 edge, green 255.00
Perfection, Millersburg, tumbler, amethyst 275.00
Persian Garden, Dugan, bowl, 10" d, ten ruffles, amethyst
    . . . . 650.00
Persian Medallion, Fenton
    Compote, large, green 400.00
    Compote, small, white 215.00

Greek Key, plate, basketweave ext., green, $825. Photo courtesy of Mickey Reichel Auction Company.

Heavy Iris, tumbler, marigold, $35.

Fruit Bowl, Grape & Cable ext., marigold 200.00
Plate, 6" d, black amethyst 275.00
Petal & Fan, Dugan
    Bowl, peach opal 95.00
    Bowl, purple 550.00
    Rose Bowl, tightly crimped, purple 235.00
Pine Cone, Fenton, plate, 7-1/2" d, amber 325.00
Plum & Cherry, Northwood, tumbler, marigold 50.00
Plume Panel & Bows, unknown maker, tumbler, marigold
     . . . . 285.00
Poinsettia & Lattice, unknown maker, bowl
    Ice blue 3,200.00
    Marigold, dark 500.00
Pony, Dugan
    Bowl, ice green 1,500.00
    Bowl, ten ruffles, purple 350.00
Poppy, Millersburg, compote, green 450.00
Poppy Show, Northwood, bowl, marigold 500.00
Princeton, unknown maker, vase, 10" h, dark marigold
     . . . . 800.00
Pulled Loops, Dugan, vase
    Celeste blue 900.00
    Green 175.00
Raspberry, Northwood, water pitcher, marigold 175.00
Regal Cane, unknown maker, clock, marigold 800.00
Ripple, Imperial, vase, 11" h, purple 120.00
Rising Sun, US Glass
    Juice Tumbler, marigold 75.00
    Tumbler, blue 300.00
    Tumbler, marigold 135.00
    Rococo, Imperial, vase
    Dark marigold 155.00
    Smoke 175.00
Rosalind, Millersburg, bowl, 10" d, amethyst 220.00
Rosalind Variant, compote, green 600.00
Rose Show Variant, bowl, blue 675.00
Rosettes & Beads, unknown maker, plate, amethyst, 7" d
     . . . . 100.00
    Sailboats, Fenton, plate, 6" d, blue 900.00
    Scroll Embossed, Imperial
    Compote, small, purple 315.00
    Plate, amber 350.00
    Plate, purple 425.00
Singing Birds, Northwood, water set, 7 pcs

Green 800.00
Marigold 800.00
Six Petals, Dugan
    Bowl, 3 in 1 edge, purple 135.00
    Bowl, 7" d, peach opalescent 70.00
Skaters, unknown maker, bowl, dark marigold 225.00
Ski Star, Dugan, banana boat, peach opal 105.00
Star & File, Imperial, compote, marigold 50.00
Star of David, Northwood, bowl, purple 325.00
Stippled Estate Variant, Dugan, vase, ice green 25.00
Stork Rushes, Dugan, basket, handles, marigold 145.00
Strawberry, Millersburg and Northwood, plate, basketweave
    back, green 255.00
Strawberry & Cable, Northwood, creamer, marigold 65.00
Sunken Daisy, English maker, rose bowl, blue 475.00
Swallow, unknown maker, tankard, tall, enameled, irid, clear
     . . . . 375.00
Ten Mums, Fenton, bowl, 3 in 1 edge, amethyst 220.00
The States, US Glass, butter dish, marigold 375.00
Thin Rib, Fenton, vase, 7-1/2" h, blue 155.00
Three Fruits, Northwood, plate, purple 175.00
Tree Trunk, Northwood, vase
    10" h, electric blue 175.00
    10" h, purple 145.00
    10" h, white 125.00
    11" h, ice green 400.00
Trout & Fly, Millersburg, bowl, 8-1/2" d, scalloped, marigold
     . . . . 500.00
Tulip & Cane, Imperial, cordial, marigold 200.00
Vintage, Fenton, Millersburg, Northwood
    Bowl, 6-3/4" d, ruffled, cherry red 2,200.00
    Epergne, large, green 300.00
    Epergne, small, amethyst, some roughness on base
     . . . . 155.00
Weeping Cherry, Dugan, bowl, crimped edge, marigold . . 95.00
Western Thistle, unknown maker
    Tumbler, blue 215.00
    Vase, marigold 500.00
Wild Rose, Northwood, rose bowl, marigold 250.00
Wishbone, Northwood, plate, ftd, marigold 800.00
Wooden Shoe, unknown maker, miniature, marigold . . . 100.00
X-Ray, US Glass, cruet, marigold, enameled flowers . . . 225.00
Zig-Zag, Millersburg
    Bowl, tri-corner, green 800.00
    Bowl, tri-corner, crimped edge, amethyst, radium . . . 350.00
    Ice Cream Bowl, amethyst, radium 600.00

CAROUSEL FIGURES

History: By the late 17th century, carousels were found in most capital cities of Europe. In 1867 Gustav Dentzel carved America's first carousel. Other leading American firms include Charles I. D. Looff, Allan Herschell, Charles Parker, and William F. Mangels.

References: Charlotte Dinger, *Art of the Carousel*, Carousel Art, 1983; Tobin Fraley, *The Carousel Animal*, Tobin Fraley Studios, 1983; Frederick Fried, *Pictorial History of the Carrousel*, Vestal Press, 1964; William Manns, Peggy Shank, and Marianne Stevens, *Painted Ponies*, Zon International Publishing, 1986.

Periodicals: *Carousel Collecting & Crafting*, 3755 Avocado Blvd., Suite 164, La Mesa, CA 91941; *Carousel News & Trader*, Suite 206, 87 Park Avenue West, Mansfield, OH 44902; *Carousel Shopper*, Zon International Publishing, P.O. Box 6459, Santa Fe, NM 87502.

Orange Tree, mug, purple, $35.

Collectors' Clubs: American Carousel Society, 3845 Telegraph Rd., Elkton, MD 21921; National Amusement Park Historical Association, P.O. Box 83, Mount Prospect, IL 60056; National Carousel Association, P.O. Box 4333, Evansville, IN 47724.

Museums: Carousel Museum of America, San Francisco, CA; Heritage Plantation of Sandwich, Sandwich, MA; Herschell Carrousel Factory Museum, North Tonawanda, NY; International Museum of Carousel Art, Portland, OR; Merry-Go-Round Museum, Sandusky, OH; New England Carousel Museum, Inc., Bristol, CT.

Notes: Since carousel figures were repainted annually, original paint is not a critical factor to collectors. "Park paint" indicates layers of accumulated paint; "stripped" means paint has been removed to show carving; "restored" involves stripping and repainting in the original colors.

Bull, Heyn, Germany, c1904, old red park paint, brass horns
. . . . .2,000.00
Camel, Charles Dare, c1890, restored by Tina Veder .5,750.00
Cat, Dentzel, fish in mouth, c1915, professionally restored
. . . . .26,000.00
Chariot Seat, Looff, 1884, complete, early park paint
. . . . .4,000.00
Deer
    Dentzel, leaping, early paint, real antlers 10,500.00
    E. J. Morris, stander converted to jumper by C. W. Parker in 1925, early paint 12,00.00
Frog, Herschell-Spillman, North Tonawanda, NY, c1914, leaping, green painted body, yellow waistcoat, orange shorts, 42" l
. . . . .20,000.00
Giraffe, E. Joy Morris, Philadelphia, old park paint . . .15,000.00
Horse
    Anderson, English, named "Nina" on neck. 2,000.00
    Carmel, Charles, stander, later heavily jeweled by Borelli
. . . . .25,000.00
    Dentzel, Gustave
        Listener, ears cocked, dapple gray, c1905, restored by Layton Studios, New Castle, PA 13,500.00

        Prancer, restored by Layton Studios, New Castle, PA
. . . . .12,000.00
        Prancer, second row, restored by Layton Studios, New Castle, PA 12,000.00
        Second row jumper, old paint 8,000.00
    Herschell, Allan, second row jumper, c1920, Navajo symbols in glass jewels on blanket, restored 2,600.00
    Illions & Sons, M. D., jumper, flame mane, restored
. . . . .30,000.00
    Looff, Charles I. D.
        Inside row prancer, good condition 4,250.00
        Outside row stander, restored, starburst mirrors and tassels 8,500.00
        Outside row stander, three legs replaced 11,500.00
        Second row prancer, c1900. . . . . .4,000.00
    Parker, C. W., Abiliene, KA, c1905, carved mane, saddle, American flag, glass eyes, old polychrome repaint, 56" h, added bass and brass post, replaced tail and stirrups, old sheet metal repairs over seams and breaks in legs
. . . . .1,760.00
    Spillman
        Jumper, restored 3,500.00
        Stander, animal pelt. .4,600.00
    Stein & Goldstein, jumper. 2,850.00
    Unidentified Maker, second row stander, stripped, restored woodwork. 9,000.00
Ostrich, Savages of King's Lynn, England, c1875, running, carved leathers and saddle, hinged neck, 56" h, 58" l, refinished. 3,500.00
Running Board (cornice), 10' l, 2' h, orig paint, portrait of Sir Harcourt, elaborate dec, English 1,600.00
Tiger, Gustav Dentzel, Daniel Muller, c1895, walking, raised head, carved saddle, restored 24,000.00

CASTLEFORD

History: Castleford is a soft-paste porcelain made in Yorkshire, England, in the 1800s for the American trade. The wares have a warm, white ground, scalloped rims (resembling castle tops), and are trimmed in deep blue. Occasionally pieces are decorated further with a coat of arms, eagles, or Lady Liberty.

Bowl, 5" d, scalloped, white ground, blue bands. 190.00
Creamer, 3-1/2" h, three brown oval medallions, one with white applied eagle and shield, second with Lady Liberty, third with cherubs and eagle on cloud 315.00
Sugar, cov, round, mythological scenes, vertical panels, twisted rope band near top, scalloped edge with oval medallions, blue enamel lines, double lid, floral knob 220.00
Tea set, 6-1/2" h teapot, molded white salt glaze, blue enameled trim, 3 pcs, all with some damage 225.00

CASTOR SETS

History: A castor set consists of matched condiment bottles held within a frame or holder. The bottles are for condiments such as salt, pepper, oil, vinegar, and mustard. The most commonly found castor sets consist of three, four, or five glass bottles in a silver-plated frame.

    Although castor sets were made as early as the 1700s, most of the sets encountered today date from 1870 to 1915, the period when they enjoyed their greatest popularity.

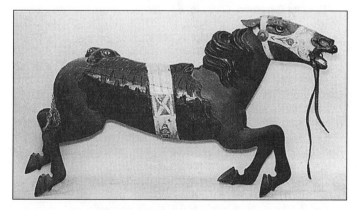

Horse, attributed to Dentzel, carved wood, harness, animal skin, repainted brown, black, and yellow, wear, replaced rope tail, 60" l, $2,750. Photo courtesy of Garth's Auctions, Inc.

6 bottle, silver plated holder, $190.

2 Bottle, silver mounted cut glass bottles, engraved crest on hinged bottles, pierced and forked handles, open frame with applied shellwork cartouche, engraved crest, four scroll supports, rococo shell terminals, George II period, Samuel Wood, London, 1750, 10-1/4" h 2,500.00

3 Bottle, Bristol glass, enameled flowers, SP holder. . . . 125.00

3 Bottle, green glass shaded to clear bottles, cut panels, ornate SP frame, 3-1/2" x 4" x 5" h 190.00

3 Bottle, Mt. Washington glass, opaque white bottles, hp floral dec on salt and pepper, hummingbird dec on mustard, pastels, round hammered SP frame, mkd "Pairpoint 724" 200.00

4 Bottle, blown three mold glass, cruet with solid ball stopper, mustard with ribbed cov, two shakers with orig metal caps, sq tin frame painted red, McKearin GI-7 . . . . 420.00

4 Bottle, cobalt blue glass bottles, SP tops, fitted in oval galleried SP frame, four columns supporting pierced cupola, Germany, c1795, 14-1/2" h. 4,200.00

4 Bottle, Fenton, opaque turquoise glass bottles, matching holder 120.00

4 Bottle, opalescent glass bottles, horizontal ribbing, vertical enameled band with multicolored flowers, ornate SP ftd and handled frame, mkd "Simpson, Hall, Miller & Co." . . . 275.00

4 Bottle, Daisy and Button pattern, blue patterned glass bottles, matching blue glass holder with metal center handle 180.00

5 Bottle, Daisy and Button pattern, clear patterned glass bottles, ornate SP frame with bell at top, resilvered 500.00

5 Bottle, Heavy Paneled Finecut pattern, SP holder. . . . 190.00

5 Bottle, ivory, mahogany case, SP tops 190.00

5 Bottle, vaseline glass, fern engraving, orig tops and stoppers, handled frame sgd "Meriden". 290.00

5 Bottle, willow ware china, blue dec, white ground, matching ceramic holder 180.00

6 Bottle, amberina glass, metal holder, mkd "Aurora 487" 2,400.00

6 Bottle, cut glass, SP oval Sheffield holder, baluster stem, loop handle, 9-3/4" h 395.00

7 Bottle, cut glass, SS collars and caps, George II silver galleried canoe-shaped tray, scroll feet, mkd "Peter, Ann & William Bateman, London," 1801, 8-1/2" h 1,400.00

CATALOGS

History: The first American mail-order catalog was issued by Benjamin Franklin in 1744. This popular advertising tool helped to spread inventions, innovations, fashions, and necessities of life to rural America. Catalogs were profusely illustrated and are studied today to date an object, identify its manufacturer, study its distribution, and determine its historical importance.

References: Ron Barlow and Ray Reynolds, *Insider's Guide to Old Books, Magazines, Newspapers, Trade Catalogs*, Windmill Publishing (2147 Windmill View Rd., Cajon, CA 92020), 1995; Lawrence B. Romaine, *Guide to American Trade Catalogs 1744-1900*, Dover Publications, n.d.

Museums: Grand Rapids Public Museum, Grand Rapids, MI; National Museum of Health and Medicine, Walter Reed Medical Center, Washington, DC.

Additional Listings: See *Warman's Americana & Collectibles* for more examples.

Advisor: Kenneth Schneringer.

Alfred Box & Co., Philadelphia, PA, c1880, 32 pgs, 3-3/4" x 5-3/4", machinery 35.00

American Lace Paper Co., Milwaukee, WI, 1927, 18 pgs, 4-1/4" x 10", fall catalog 42.00

Baxendale & Co., Ltd., Manchester, Great Britain, c1938, 16 pgs, 5-1/2" x 8-3/4", bell fireplaces. 35.00

Bellas Hess & Co., New York, NY, 1913, 64 pgs, 6-1/4" x 8-3/4", Special Bargains, Cat. No. 61, Women's Clothes and Shoes 25.00

Berger Bros. Co., Philadelphia, 1932, 182 pages, 4" x 5-3/4", General Cat. No. 10-B, Tinners & Roofers Supplies . . 35.00

Bigelow-Hartford Carpet, New York, NY, 1922, 6-1/2" x 8-1/2", Hartford-Saxony rubs 35.00

Breck's of Boston, Boston, MA, 1954, 56 pgs, 8" x 10", Christmas gifts 26.00

Brooks Mfg. Co., Saginaw, MI, 1909, 22 pgs, 6-1/2" x 10-1/4", orig mailing envelope, boats and patterns 55.00

Buffalo Spring & Gear Co., Buffalo, NY, 1902, 63 pgs, 6" x 9", carriages and wagons, roughed and damped 78.00

Burgess Battery Co., Chicago, IL, 1930, 4 pgs, 8-1/2" x 10", Dealers Price List No. 3008 . . . . 20.00

Butler Brothers, New York, NY, "Our Drummer"
  1924, 442 pgs, 9-3/8" x 13-1/2", April, clothing, shoes, etc. 85.00
  1928, 626 pgs, 9-1/2" x 13-1/2", October, dolls, toys, Halloween dec, Christmas dec, etc. 110.00

Carlin Comforts, Inc., New York, NY, 1926, 24 pgs, 7-1/4" x 9", 7 pgs of color, "Vogue" Relates Our Bedtime Story . . . 44.00

Chicago House Wrecking Co., Chicago, IL, 1902, 227, 6" x 9-1/4", Cat. No. 127, building supplies 42.00

Colman Levin Co., Boston, MA, 1924, 34 pgs, 9" x 12", general floor covering 30.00

Copenhaver, Laura, Marion, VA, 1957, 32 pages, 4-1/4" x 6-1/2", Rosemont Colonial Reproductions, halftones. . 20.00

Crandall-Bennett-Porter, Montoursville, PA, 1907, 35 pgs, 6" x 9", golden oak extension tables 46.00

Crescent Washing Machine Co., New Rochelle, NY, 1922, 12 pgs, 6" x 9", washing machines 24.00

Deere & Co., Moline, IL, 1957, 279 pgs, 6" x 9", 28th edition 42.00

Des Moines Iron Co., Des Moines, IA, 1930, 16 pgs, 6" x 8-1/2", hardware 20.00

Detroit Mantel & Tile Co., Detroit, MI, c1950, 40 pages, 6-1/4" x 9", fireplace equipment 24.00

Enterprise Mfg. Co., Philadelphia, PA, 96 pgs, 1906, 5" x 6-3/4", The Enterprising Housekeeper. 38.00

Eastman Kodak Co., Rochester, NY, 1917, 188 pgs, 7" x 9-3/4", professional apparatus 55.00

Graham Bros., Detroit, MI, 1926, 40 pgs, 8-1/2" x 11", school buses 85.00

Grand Rapids Fibre Cord, Grand Rapids, MI, 1927, 161 pgs, 6" x 9", laid-in Art Fibre Wave Booklet 36.00

Granite State Evaporator, Marlow, NH, 1897, 32 pgs, 5-3/4" x 8-1/4", sugar making supplies 58.00

Henderson-Ames Co., Kalamazoo, MI, 1914, 96 pgs, 6" x 9", uniforms, supplement and measure sheet laid-in. . . . 150.00

Higgins & Seiter, New York, NY, c1908, 245 pgs, 5-3/4" x 8-1/2", Cat. No. 13, fine china and cut glass, 9 colored sheets 95.00

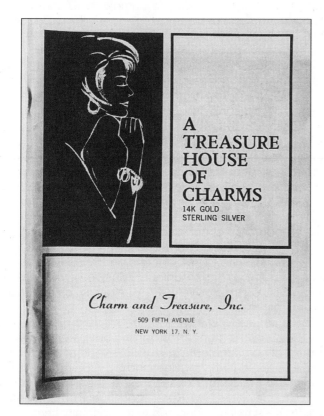

A Treasure House of Charms, Charm and Treasure, Inc., NY, jewelry, 138 pgs, black and white photos, 1950s, $20.

Hudson Mfg. Co., Minneapolis, MN, 1918, 16 pgs, 6" x 9-1/2", shelf wraps, Booklet No. 127, Profitable Seasonable Specialties 18.00

International Harvester, Chicago, IL, 1939, 63 pgs, 6-1/2" x 9-1/2", Models D-2 and D-15 trucks 28.00

Keystone Varnish Co., Brooklyn, NY, 1922, 36 pgs, 9" x 12", Keystona Flat Finish. 50.00

Kimball Bros., Council Bluffs, IA, 1900, 48 pgs, 6" x 9", elevators 45.00

Lippincott & Co., Philadelphia, PA, 1904, 41 pgs, 2-7/8" x 6-1/8", wholesale groceries 12.00

Mason & Lawrence, Elgin, IL, 12 pgs, 4" x 9-1/4", "When Better Silos Are Built, We Will Build Them" 10.00

Maxwell Motor Co., Detroit, MI, 1916, 114 pgs, 6" x 9", hard cover 45.00

Miller & Co., Chicago, IL, c1925, 24 pgs, 7-1/4" x 10-3/4", fur coats. 20.00

Montgomery Ward, Albany, NY, 1941, 1,174 pgs, 9-1/4" x 13-1/2", Fall & Winter Clothing 35.00

Nestle's Food Co., New York, NY, 1914, 72 pgs, 4-3/4" x 5-3/4", "Cupid's Advice, Give The Babies Nestle's Food" 16.00

Northampton Emery Wheel, Leeds, MA, 1901, 40 pgs, 6" x 9-1/4", machinery 45.00

Novelty Knitting Co., Albany, NY, 1905, 50 pgs, 5" x 6-1/2", invalid clothing. 24.00

Nutting, Wallace, Ashland, MA, 1921, 40 pgs, 9-1/4" x 12-1/2", "The Great American Idea," colonial reproduction furniture 80.00

Otis Bed Mfg. Co., Buffalo, NY, 1922, 30 pgs, 5-1/4" x 7", "A Journey with Masters of Fine Bedding" 26.00

Penn Metal Co., PA, 1922, 34 pgs, 3-1/2" x 6", sheet metal 30.00

Piedmont Red Cedar Crest, Statesville, NC, 1914, 64 pgs, 6" x 9-1/4" 35.00

Real Silk Hosiery Mills, Indianapolis, IN,1925, 6 pgs, 3-1/2" x 6", real silk costume color harmony charts, 144 color patches 20.00

Reo Motor Co., Lansing, MI, 1933, 16 pgs, 8-1/2" x 11", The Reo-Royale Eight 52.00

Sears Roebuck & Co.
Boston, MA, 1935, 54 pgs, 8-1/2" x 11", older form laid-in, specialty type, refrigerators, sewing machines, bedding, furniture, kitchen cabinets 16.00
Chicago, IL, 1933, 30 pgs, 5-1/2" x 8-1/2", Tips to Trappers by Johnny Muskrat & His Trapper Friends. 45.00
Chicago, IL, 1968, 1,596 pgs, 8-1/4" x 11", Spring & Summer 33.00

Spiegel, Chicago, IL, 1968, 584 pgs, 9-1/8" x 13-1/4", Spring & Summer 24.00

Standard Engine Co., Minneapolis, MN, c1930, 68 pgs, 6" x 9" 32.00

Stern Brothers, New York, NY, 1912, 128 pgs, 7-3/4" x 10", Spring & Summer Catalog No. 122 . . . . 38.00

Suttle Equipment Co., Lawrenceville, IL 1933, 79 pgs, 7-1/4" x 9-1/2", Cat. No. 28, Spring & Summer, telephones . . . 55.00

Taylor Fireworks Co., Kansas City, MO, 1961, 8 pgs, 8-1/2" x 11", spring fireworks. 35.00

Tucker Furniture & Carpet., Clinton, IA, c1936, 12 pgs, 3-1/4" x 5-1/8", sepia 11-3/4" x 9-3/4" folded-in shade 30.00

United Cigar Stores, New York, NY, 1929, 50 pgs, 5-1/4" x 8", United Cigar Stores of America Premiums. 15.00

Whip-O-Will Furniture, Scranton, PA, c1925, 52 pgs, 9" x 12" 75.00

White Van Glahnt & Co., New York, NY, c1930, 6 pgs, 3-1/8" x 5-1/2", Alabastine, The Sanitary Wall Covering 22.00

Wood, Bishop & Co., Bangor, ME, 1876, 24 pgs, 4" x 6-1/4", Clarion Portable Cooking Stove 50.00

World's Star Knitting Co., Bay City, MI, 1919, 64 pgs, 6" x 9", hosiery and Klen Knit underwear 42.00
Wrinch & Sons, Ipswich, GA, 1910, 52 pgs, 6-1/4" x 10", outdoor furniture 62.00

CELADON

History: The term "celadon," meaning a pale grayish green color, is derived from the theatrical character Celadon, who wore costumes of varying shades of grayish green, in Honore d'Urfe's 17th-century pastoral romance, *L'Astree*. French Jesuits living in China used the name to refer to a specific type of Chinese porcelain.

Celadon divides into two types. Northern celadon, made during the Sung Dynasty up to the 1120s, has a gray to brownish body, relief decoration, and monochromatic olive green glaze. Southern (Lung-ch'uan) celadon, made during the Sung Dynasty and much later, is paint-decorated with floral and other scenic designs and is found in forms which would appeal to the European and American export market. Many of the southern pieces date from 1825 to 1885. A blue square with Chinese or pseudo-Chinese characters appears on pieces after 1850. Later pieces also have a larger and sparser decorative patterning.

Reproduction Alert.

Bottle, Korean, 12th C, Koryo Dynasty 500.00
Bowl
    6-1/2" d, 3" h, Ching Par ware, blue-green glaze, carved combed lotus scroll dec, Southern Sung Period, 1127-1279 . . . . 230.00
    7-3/4" d, foliate form, shallow draft, pale green-blue, Ying Ching, Sung period, 960-1270 . . . . 175.00
Cup, 6" d, tan colored glass, Korean Koryo, 13th C 150.00
Dish, 10-1/2 d, incised peony blossom, crackled deep green glaze, everted rim, Ming Dynasty 300.00
Ewer, 3-5/8" h, ovoid form, ribbed, plain shoulder, loop handle, upright spout, blue-green glaze, burnt orange foot rim, Southern Sung Dynasty 950.00
Jar, 5" h, globular form, pale green glaze, Yongzheng mark, 1723-35 . . . . .5,000.00

Nut Dish, Mandarian dec, $400.

Urn, cov, 6" h, low relief carved Indian lotus motif, exotic bloom carved handles, surmounted by lotus form knot cover, Moghul style 2,950.00
Vase
    8" h, mallet shape, carved dragon roundels, underglaze blue double-circle mark, 19th C, pr 320.00
    13" h, inlaid floral dec, Korean, mounted as lamp . . . 350.00
Water Dropper, bird shape, Korean, Koryo Dynasty, 12th/13th C 785.00

CELLULOID ITEMS

History: In 1869, Albany, New York, printer John W. Hyatt developed and patented the world's first commercially successful semi-synthetic thermoplastic. Made from camphor and pyroxylin, a type of cellulose nitrate,. Hyatt and his brother Isaiah named the material "Celluloid," a contraction of the words cellulose and colloid.

By the mid-1870s, the Hyatts' were successfully making pyroxylin plastic in imitation of expensive luxury materials at the Celluloid Manufacturing Company of Newark, NJ. In the early days of its commercial development, celluloid was used for only a few utilitarian applications. However, by the 1880s fabricating companies were busy molding the plastic into a variety of fancy articles, fashion accessories, and novelty items.

As the industry grew, several other factories went into business making pyroxylin plastic identical to Hyatt's Celluloid, but licensed under different trade names: Pyralin (manufactured by Arlington Co., Arlington, New Jersey), Fiberloid (Fiberloid Corp., Indian Orchard, Massachusetts), and Viscoloid (Viscoloid Co., Leominster, Massachusetts). Even though these companies branded their products with proper trade names, today the word "celluloid" is used generically and encompasses all forms of this early plastic.

The ease with which celluloid can be manipulated and the abundance of available man-made material helped the industry to grow tremendously. However, pyroxylin plastic did have one major drawback, because of the cellulose nitrate used in its production, it was dangerously flammable. Nevertheless, because celluloid products imitated expensive luxury items, the plastic copies became increasingly popular with the working and middle classes.

Used as a replacement for ivory, amber, and tortoiseshell in hundreds of different utilitarian and novelty applications, it wasn't until the development of the motion picture industry that celluloid gained it's own special purpose. In addition to camera film, it was also used by animation artists who drew cartoons on transparent sheets cels. By fulfilling these unique roles, celluloid was no longer viewed exclusively as a imitation for expensive natural materials.

By 1930, and the advent of the modern plastics age, the use of celluloid began to decline dramatically. Development of nonflammable safety film eventually ended the use of celluloid in the movies, and by 1950 production in the United States had ceased altogether. However, Japan, France, Italy and Korea continue to manufacture celluloid in small amounts today for specialty items such as musical-instrument inlay and ping-pong balls, designer fountain pens and jewelry.

Beware of celluloid items that show signs of deterioration: oily residue, cracking, discoloration, and crystallization. Take care when cleaning celluloid items. It is best o use mild soap and water, avoiding alcohol or acetone based cleaners. Never expose celluloid to excessive heat or flame and avoid extreme sunlight.

Marks: Viscoloid Co. manufactured a large variety of small hollow animals that ranged in size from 2 to 8 inches. Most of these toys are embossed with one of three trademarks: "Made in USA," an intertwined "VCO," or an eagle with a shield.

Advisor: Julie P. Robinson.

Advertising and souvenir keepsakes

Badge, 2-7/8" Fraternal Badge, Chaplin-Ladies Auxiliary, FOE. Thick printed celluloid layered over amber tone, Whitehead & Hoag Co., Newark, NJ 20.00

Booklet
  4-1/4" x 2-1/2" leather-bound notepad with celluloid covers, children with bird and advertisement "Presented By Germania Savings Bank, Pittsburgh, PA," 1906 calendar on reverse 30.00
  5-5/8" x 3-1/4" leather-bound folding note booklet, "Valentine & Company, Coach & Railway Varnishes and Colors," on front and 1896 calendar on back; printed on shiny ivory-grained sheet celluloid by Thomas Jay Gleason Co. NY 35.00

Bookmark
  1-1/2" diecut heart with grape motif and picture of Christ, Brooklyn Tabernacle 18.00
  4-1/2" diecut with rose motif on grained celluloid advertising Bair & Lane of Greensburg, PA; The Meek Company, Coshocton, Ohio 22.00
  4-3/4" diecut ivory-grained celluloid with butterfly motif in red, yellow, dark blue, and green and 1st Psalm; Westminster Press 20.00

Card, 4-3/4" x 3", engraved "Baldwin & Gleason," ivory-grained sheet celluloid with pastoral scene and "A Joyous Season" 12.00

Christmas Card, 4" x 3" folding paper card, embossed celluloid front showing a cruise ship scene with poinsettias, "Greetings" 12.00

Clothing Brush
  3" d circular brush, black and white photograph of Gettysburg Memorial, Gettysburg, PA 35.00
  3-1/2" d, advertising, celluloid laminated printed paper showing Parisian Novelty Company of Chicago, USA - "Supplies for making Fiberloid Novelties and Advertising Specialties" 125.00

Comb with case, 4-1/2" x 7/8" ivory-grained comb in case with blue and black graphics "New England Made Cigars" . 40.00

Compact, Souvenir
  1-1/4" x 2" metal powder compact, celluloid top featuring scenic view of Cypress Gardens 12.00
  1-3/4" octagonal metal compact, inset pearlized celluloid lid in light amber tone, pink and blue floral motif; reverse shield shaped medallion of Harrisburg, PA 15.00

Fan, 4" h when closed, mottled turquoise and cream celluloid Brise fan with light blue ribbon, Washington Monument and "Washington, D.C." in gold tone paint 15.00

Ink Blotter, advertising
  2-1/2" x 6" rect booklet of blotter, decorative celluloid cover, shepherds overseeing sheep; A Merry Christmas; Keller

Mfg. Co. of Allentown, PA, Christmas 1921, printed by Whitehead and Hoag Co.. . . . . 25.00
  4-1/8" x 2 7/8" ivory grained celluloid, front and back covers with blotters inside, engraved scene of Black Diamond File Works, Philadelphia, PA and 1890 calendar, Baldwin & Gleason Co.. . . . . 45.00

Letter Opener
  5" l, ivory grained, sickle shaped with "Zylonite Novelties, John A. Lowell & Co. 147 Franklin St. Boston," also features and engraved floral design. 90.00
  6-3/4" multi-purpose bookmark/opener connected by string; round medallion of Indian profile while the pointed letter knife says SOUVENIR of QUEBEC 15.00

Match Safe, 2-1/2" x 1-1/2"
  Advertising, ivory grained safety match holder with blue and black graphics "New England Made Cigars, Carry This Blue Union Label On The Box & Before Purchasing A Cigar Be Sure & See that This Blue Label is on The Box" 65.00
  Souvenir, celluloid photo decorations in green tones, scenic views of Atlantic City, NJ 20.00

Pencil Clip
  5/8" d, celluloid disc, red, white, and green graphics, "7 UP" soda adv 20.00
  3/4" celluloid disc, red, white, and blue graphics showing a Star - "Star Brand Shoes Are Better" 18.00

Pinback Button
  5/8" d, J. Fred Talbott for Congress, no date-unknown politician, original box and back paper, made by the Hyatt Mfg. Co. Baltimore, MD 15.00
  3/4" d Rally Day pin, shows open Bible with verse and church 5.00
  1-1/2" d Patrons of Husbandry motif, sheaf of wheat and plow 15.00
  1-1/2" x 1/2" oval, turquoise blue with black trim and lettering "Johnstown" c1920. . . . . 10.00
  Pinback Button Set, 1-1/4" d, Bird Series, Cardinal, Blue Jay, Robin, Goldfinch, Whitehead & Hoag Co., Newark, NJ 8.00

Pin Holder, 1-3/4" d, celluloid disc, metal framework, "F Krupps Steel Works, Thomas Prosser & Son, NY" front shows advertising, back shows small child, engraved ivory grained celluloid 40.00

Pocket Mirror
  1-3/4" d "Take Duffy's Pure Malt Whiskey When You Are Not Looking Well-Makes The Weak Strong," printed image of old man working with lab equipment, JB Carroll, Chicago 70.00
  2-1/4" d, keepsake mirror, photograph of girl on a preprinted celluloid backing, "February Birthstone, Amethyst & Birthflower, Carnation," winter scene, pink and red carnations, purple gemstone 25.00
  2-3/4" x 1-3/4", oval, pink rose motif, "Use Mennen's Flesh Tint Talcum Powder," or violet motif with "Mennen's Violet Talcum Toilet Powder," information on the curl "Duplicate mirror 5cents postage, Gerhard Mennen Company, Newark, NJ, each 55.00

Postcard, 5 1/2" x 3 12", "Best Wishes" embossed celluloid with applied fabric butterfly and pansies, c1908 . . . . 8.00

Shoe Horn, 5-1/2" l, two-tone amber and cream pearlescent, "HR Holden & Co. Inc.-Shoe Store Supplies, 184 Summer St. Boston," c1925 . . . . 18.00

Tape measure, advertising
  1-1/2" d, Fab Detergent, mfg by JB Carroll Co. of Chicago 20.00
  1-1/4" d, pull-out tape, colorful picture of pretty girl with flowers, adv for "The First National Bank of Boswell, The Same Old Bank in its New Home," printed by P.N. Co. (Parisian

Novelty Co. of Chicago), Patent 7-10-17, embossed in side
. . . . 65.00
Template, 3-7/16" x 1-13/16", typewriter correction template, "Remtico Typewriter Supplies" Remington Typewriter Co., printed by Whitehead & Hoag of Newark, NJ. 20.00

Decorative albums and boxes

Album music box in base, 8" x 11" multi-colored floral printed, celluloid with center motif of a child holding bouquet of lilacs and wearing a large bonnet, orig music box. 180.00
Autograph Album
    4" x 5-1/2", printed pastoral scene, celluloid front and back
    . . . . 65.00
    6" x 4-1/2" embossed cream colored celluloid, "Album" in script, maroon velvet back and binding 50.00
Collar Box, 7-1/2" x 7-1/2" x 6", octagonal, completely covered with multicolored celluloid, embossed gilt trimming on top and bottom, satin lining with mirror in lid 85.00
Decorative Dresser Tray, 7-1/2" x 5" oval, imitation tortoiseshell framework with Normandy lace and glass bottom, c1925
. . . . 30.00
Dresser Set, 3-1/2" d x 8" x 6-1/4" box, embossed white celluloid with floral motif, satin lined, fitted with brush, mirror, salve box, file and nail cleaner, mkd "Celluloid". 135.00
Glove Box, 12-1/2" x 4", pink satin lining, embossed "Gloves" in script, cream-colored celluloid with pink highlights. . . . 50.00
Hankie Box, 3-1/2" h, 7" sq, variegated sweet pea motif with centered snow scene on lid, trimmed with embossed celluloid
. . . . 65.00
Jewelry Box, 3" h x 5-1/2" w, piano shape, imitation amber celluloid with gold embossed trim and black and gold flowers, velvet lined 55.00

Collar Box, bottom drawer, heavy printed paper sides with pansy and forget-me-not dec, celluloid top with apple blossom and ivy design, gilt emb edging, pink fabric lining, mirror in lid, drawer in base, 6" sq, 7" h, $40. Photo courtesy of Julie Robinson.

Manicure Set, 7-3/4" x 6", leaf and bright floral design on violet background, oval medallion picture top, puffed satin lining with manicure implements 110.00
Photograph Album, 8" x 11", celluloid covered album, picture of a pretty girl in center, lily of the valley and violet floral background 115.00
Trinket Box, 5" oval, 2" deep, amber box with butterfly, grass and milkweed silk decorative lid under clear celluloid. 35.00

Fashion accessories

Backcomb, 3-1/2" x 3 1/2" imitation tortoise backcomb with molded Art Nouveau naturalistic design of swags and leaves on a stippled background, 18 slightly curved teeth . . . 45.00
Bangle Bracelet, ivory colored, embedded with 4 rows of aqua and clear rhinestones. 55.00
Bar Pin
    2-1/2" l, ivory grained ovide shape, orange brown swirled pearlescent laminate and hand-painted floral motif in center
    . . . . 15.00
Belt, 22" l, 3/4" x 1-1/2" rect mottled green celluloid slabs; applied silvertone filigree dec, labs linked together by chain
. . . . 35.00
Bracelet
    3" d, molded imitation coral, imitation ivory or imitation jade celluloid bangle with all over floral designs, "Made in Japan" blue ink stamp inside 28.00
    3" d, link bracelet, 4 oblong two-tone cream and ivory links, attached with round cream links of smaller size 45.00
    3" l, translucent amber, applied blue flowers in center, clasp
    . . . . 20.00
Brooch
    1-1/4" x 1-1/2" rect, filigree edging and molded floral center, faded hand painted flowers, "Made in Japan" on safety clasp. 20.00
    1-1/2" x 1", lavender pearlessence, black and white silhouette of swan, pink rhinestone trim, c1926 . . . . 25.00
Comb with case for purse, 3-1/4" x 1" pearlized amber and gray rhinestone studded case for 3" cream colored hair comb
. . . . 15.00
Compact, 1-1/2" d x 1-1/2" tall celluloid powder box, ornate wreath and fleur-de-lis motif, with pink and white cameo lid
. . . . 45.00
Compact/Powder Container, 2-1/4" d powder box, mottled orange, mottled pink or mottled brown. Lid is powder puff . .50
Cuff Links, pr
    Jem Snap Links, separable, round green or purple celluloid disc set in metal frame, orig paper display. 40.00
    Toggle back, realistic molded celluloid lion heads, c1896
    . . . . 115.00
Dress Clips, pr, molded floral motif, semi-translucent cream celluloid, marked "Japan" 35.00
Eyeglasses, Harold Lloyd type with black frames. 15.00
Fan
    Brise-style with diecut and embossed imitation ivory, silk ribbon and violet motif, linked celluloid chain. 45.00
    Cockade-style, celluloid handles in cream, link clasp on bottom to hold handles together when fan is opened, fan made of pleated linen which opens to reveal a full circle. . . 50.00
    Hand-held mechanical device with plunger mechanism, 3 blades, variegated brown pearlessence, patented 1922
    . . . . 65.00
Hair Pin Container, 2-1/2" holder with lid; ivory with bird motif; dark gray lid 40.00
Hair ornament
    7/8" double-prong imitation tortoise ornament with triple row of topaz rhinestones and three-prong imitation tortoise

comb with Art Deco styling and topaz colored rhinestones 50.00

6-1/2" double-prong hair ornament in imitation tortoiseshell, carved out lattice work and leaf spray design 30.00

Hat Pin

Imitation ivory, 4" long elephant head with tusks and black glass eyes 100.00

Imitation tortoise, hollow tusk shape, 12" l 18.00

Question mark shape, pearlized gray and cream swirled, hollow celluloid, 12" l 40.00

Hat Ornament

3-1/2" h, Art-Deco ornament with pearlized red and pearlized cream half circles, rhinestone trimming 40.00

4" black leaf with white painted lines and dots, studded with rhinestones 20.00

4-1/2" h, calla lily, amber celluloid with applied gold paint, studded with yellow rhinestones 30.00

Necklace

Art Nouveau filigree pendant, cream celluloid with oval cameo, profile of a beautiful woman, 2" l, suspended from 20" cream celluloid beaded necklace 100.00

Imitation coral pendant on chain, molded floral design, "Made in Japan" on back. 12.00

Necklace Pendant, 1-1/2" x 1-1/4" filigree pendant with rose and leaf center, molded in cream-colored celluloid and handpainted with shades of green and pink, faded, made in Japan 20.00

Ornamental comb

5-1/2" x 4" molded Cream backcomb with intertwined flowers and vines forming a heart motif, symbolic of the Edwardian Era 45.00

6" tall ivory comb, 3 prongs with hand-etched and decorated rose motif 55.00

6-1/4" teal blue comb decorated with swirled pearlessence and matching blue rhinestones, Art Deco 80.00

Ornamental Sidecombs, pair of 4-1/2" imitation amber side ornaments shaped like long hair pins, painted with delicate floral motif 35.00

Purse Frame

5 1/2" crescent-shaped purse frame with black berry and bird motif, ivory with painted bluebirds, leaves and fruit, push button clasp and link chain. 125.00

6 1/4" Egyptian motif purse frame, ivory with applied orange and gold paint 175.00

Purse

4" d round clam shell-type purse, imitation tortoiseshell and ivory; leather strap with celluloid findings and finger ring, applied celluloid leaf decoration. 85.00

4-1/2" x 4-1/2" basketweave purse with link celluloid chain, mottled grain ivory and green 190.00

6" long linked chain bag with satin lining, lid is solid celluloid, 4" x 3" oval shaped with painted flowers, 4" wide at top and goes to a point at the bottom. 140.00

Figural dolls and toys

Aviator, 5-1/2", VCO/USA, peach with grayish purple highlights 75.00

Baby Rattle

4", pink and green variegated ball, white teething ring 35.00

4-1/4", yellow parrot on red ring, bright red and green highlights, "VCO/USA" trademark near foot 40.00

4-1/2", white clown playing lute with pink and brown highlights. Intertwined "VCO/USA" trademark on back. . . 50.00

6-1/2", ivory grained dumbbell rattle with remnants of blue paint in a floral design 30.00

6-1/2", pink shield shape with hand-painted flowers and "BABY" cream celluloid-covered wooden handle with amber ring 27.00

Bathing Beauty, figural toy, 4", double figural showing two little girls with umbrella in pink and green bathing suit, Floral trademark, Made in Japan 65.00

Battleship, 5-1/2", gray w/gold anchor; Made in USA 35.00

Cowboy, 6-1/4", holding gun, strung arms, standing on bright green base. House in Circle with Japan. 35.00

Dolls

3-1/4", black baby doll with strung arms and legs, unidentified Lantern trademark, Made in Japan 50.00

3-1/2", Peach blow molded doll with strung arms, matching hat and dress in red and teal, no trademark 20.00

3-3/4", toddler in pink snowsuit, yellow and red trim; F in Diamond, Made in JAPAN. 20.00

4" tall, Kewpie-type figure with green painted trousers and yellow shoes, only one leg is movable. Unidentified SS in Diamond trademark. No wings. 35.00

5-3/4", Dutch girl with green, pink, yellow and black details; Butterfly trademark- Made in JAPAN. 35.00

6", girl and boy dressed in ethnic costumes, Turtle in Diamond trademark/Rheinische Gummiund Celluloid Fabrik Co. of Germany. Pr 125.00

8-1/2" tall, side-glancing googly-eyed doll with blue and white printed dress and kerchief trimmed in ric-rac. Trademarked

Powder Shaker, side glancing carnival-type doll, opening in back for talcum, ribbon and fabric clothing, 12" h, $75. Photo courtesy of Julie Robinson.

with unidentified lantern trademark and Made in Japan
. . . . 50.00
10", Carnival Kewpie w/glitter and feathers, top hat and cane, Royal Japan, fleur-de-lis trademark 40.00
12" tall, googly-eyed powder shaker doll has movable arms and satin bloomers. Trademarked with the Star in Circle, Japan 70.00
Flower, novelty w/smiling face attached to spring on base, original sticker on bottom: 10 cents 8.00
Food, 2-1/4", oval platter with turkey, ham or fish, VCO
. . . . 110.00
Football player, 4-1/2" h, red and black uniform, pin back button and ribbon attached with a rubber band to the neck . . 40.00
Roly Poly
   3-1/2", gray man with spectacles; black and white highlights on pink base; Embossed: Palitoy, Made in England
   . . . . 60.00
   4-1/2", baby face w/green and white base and orange bow tie; sticker on bottom: Made in China. 35.00
Steamer
   4", double stacks, dark pink and black, Japan 24.00
   5", gray and red steamer w/flag; intertwined PH 45.00
Whistle
   3-1/4" l, 2-1/4" h, Nightingale, yellow celluloid with green and red highlights; VCO/USA 20.00
   4-1/2" l, 1-1/2" and 3-1/4" ends; black and cream graduated pipe whistle, "Baby Grand". 24.00
   9-1/2" x 3/4" recorder, in transparent teal celluloid, molded mouthpiece and 6 holes for playing . . . .

Holiday items

Christmas
   Angels
      Set of three 1-1/2" tall figures, each holding a different item; a cross, star and lantern. Japan with Mt. Fuji trademark; the set 20.00
   Ornament
      Horn, 6-1/2", red, pink and yellow 75.00
      Roly Poly-type house with opening in back for a small bulb, shows Santa approaching door. Red and intertwined VCO/USA trademark 90.00
      Santa, 3-3/4" figure with horn and sack, hole in back for Christmas light bulb; trademarked S in Circle, Japan
      . . . . 50.00
   Reindeer
      3-1/2" white, with gold glitter, red eyes and mouth and molded ears and antlers; USA . 12.004-3/4" white, with red eyes and mouth, ears and antlers are applied separately; Japan 18.00
   Santa
      4-1/4", waving while holding lantern, Japanese . . . 42.00
      5", figure with basket of flower, nice detail in fur-trimmed suit, VCO/USA trademark . . 50.007-1/2" tall, holding gift box in arm, cream celluloid with red painted detailing, marked with oval Made in USA 80.00
   Toy
      3-5/8" x 2", Santa driving house-shaped automobile, white with applied red, yellow and green painted highlights, VCO/USA trademark 105.00
      4" x 2-1/8", figural reindeer pulling sleigh with Santa Claus, white with red and gold paint. VCO/USA trademark
      . . . . 90.00
      5-3/8" x 2" Santa, riding on a train laden with holiday decorations and gifts including a doll, puppy and rocking

horse. Greatly detailed cream celluloid with red and green highlights; VCO/USA on Santa 135.00
Easter
   3" x 3-1/2" bunny, in top hat and tails in teal shoe; Crossed circle, Japan. 80.00
   3-1/4" rabbit, driving egg-shell car, yellow with green wheels-rattle; intertwined VCO/USA, 10 cents on bottom
   . . . . 105.00
   3-1/2" cream bunny, pulling egg with chick, red details; intertwined VCO/USA 85.00
   3-3/4" swan boat, with rabbit and chick in egg shell; intertwined VCO/USA 100.003-3/4" x 4-3/8" white bird, with red wings in blue shoe; intertwined VCO.USA. 70.00
   7-3/4" cream rabbit figure, with pink and blue highlights, holding bird; no trademark 70.00
Halloween
   Favor, 4", orange horn with black witch and trimming; intertwined VCO/USA 100.00
   Figural toy
      3-1/2", black cat pushing a witch in a pumpkin carriage; intertwined VCO/USA 160.00
      3-3/4" standing black cat with orange bow, on grass, rattle; intertwined VCO/USA 125.00
   Roly poly
      3-1/4", black cat on orange pumpkin, intertwined VCO/USA 130.00
      4", yellow owl with orange and black highlights; intertwined VCO/USA. 120.00
Independence Day
   5-1/4" Uncle Sam figural in white celluloid with painted red, white and blue patriotic clothing. 100.00
St. Patrick's Day
   Figural toy, Paddy riding the Pig, 4-3/4" h; pig has movable legs; little boy with dunce cap riding on the back; JAPAN
   . . . . 170.00

Novelty items

Basket of Flowers, 1-1/4" d, Made in Germany. 150.00
Letter opener
   10-1/4" solid molded opener in grained ivory with intricate rose handle 70.00
   7-1/2" souvenir of Montreal with applied molded Indian, marked French Ivory, Made in Canada 15.00
   7-5/8" hollow blade with solid handle showing three horse heads 80.00
   8" blade topped with intricately detailed full figure lady holding a flask-solid celluloid 85.00
Pincushion
   2" tall, rabbit with pin cushion baskets, marked Germany
   . . . . 135.00
   2-1/4" tall, straight pin holder with brown hen on base
   . . . . 65.00+
Tape measure
   1-1/8" sq., dice, ivory with black dots 225.00
   1-1/2", strawberry 225.00
   1-3/4", chariot with Horses & Rider, imitation bronze
   . . . . 235.00
   2" tall, swashbuckler, ivory with brown & tan highlights
   . . . . 260.00
   2-1/4", pear with ladybug pull 215.00
   2-1/2", Billiken, in cream celluloid with applied brown highlights. Trademarked JAPAN on tape 190.00
   3-1/4", mirror, red & white polka dot, shell shaped back
   . . . . 260.00

Toys

Animal Set, 6 circus animals, garish bright colors, Made in Occupied Japan, Elephant, Gorilla, Giraffe, Tiger, Lion and Hippo, set. 60.00

Alligator
3", green with white tail tip, VCO/USA 10.00
5-3/4", tan with brown highlights, VCO/USA trademark
. . . . 18.00

Bear
2-1/4" l, white polar bear, made in USA 7.00
4" l, peach bear with purple highlights, poor details, Japan
. . . . 15.00
5" w, cream bear with pink and gray highlights, VCO/USA
. . . . 18.00

Bison, 3-1/4" l, dk. brown with Eagle and Shield trademark
. . . . 18.00

Boar, 3-1/4", brown, Paul Haneaus of Germany/PH trademark
. . . . 65.00+

Camel
2-1/4" l, cream camel with light brown highlights, Made in USA trademark 15.00
3-1/2" x 2-1/2" peach celluloid with pink and black highlights, crossed circle and Made in Japan 15.00

Cat
3" l x 2-1/4" h, cream or peach celluloid with black spots, pink bows, ears and mouth; Floral trademark - JAPAN and Made in Occupied Japan; for each one 30.00
5-1/4" cream cat with pink and black highlights, molded collar and bell. Made in USA trademark, rare 60.00

Chick, 7/8" yellow, black eyes and beak, no trademark . . . 5.00

Chicken
2-3/4" hen with metal feet, Double Diamond with Made in Japan 15.00
3" standing hen in grass, cream with gray, yellow feet, VCO/USA trademark 25.00

Cow
4-1/2" cream and orange, intertwined VCO/USA 20.00
5-1/2" purple and cream cow with red rhinestone eyes, crossed circle, Made in Japan 30.00
7-1/2" cream with orange and black highlights, hand-painted facial features, marked with Eagle 55.00

Dog
Airedale, 3" w, 2-1/2" tall, white with pink and dark purple highlights and hand-painted collar, plaster filled, nice detailing; trademark - Made in Japan 18.00
Bulldog, 4-3/4" l and 2-1/2" h, with a spiked neck collar. Translucent green color with rhinestone eyes; intertwined VCO/USA. 30.00
Hound, 5" with long tail, peach celluloid with gray highlights, crossed circle Japan 20.00
Scotty, 3-1/4" l, plaster filled cream colored celluloid, no detailing, marked JAPAN. 15.00
St. Bernard, 3-1/4", tan with black highlights; intertwined VCO/USA. 20.00

Donkey
3/4" l x 4", cream-colored celluloid with orange/pink highlighting, fleur-de-lies-Royal Japan 30.00
2-1/4", dark gray, Made in USA 15.00
4" l x 3-3/4" h, molded harnesses, saddles and blankets; grayish brown with red and orange highlights; intertwined VCO/USA. 40.00

Duck
2-1/4", standing duck or chicken, cream colored celluloid with hand-painted eyes and bills; original paper label and Made in Japan 12.00

3-1/2", yellow with green highlights, VCO/USA and Circle
. . . . 12.00
4", yellow celluloid with applied green and orange, PH (Paul Hunaeus) with 25 cents on bottom 20.00
4", glossy surface with red and green, VCO/USA 15.00

Elephant
2-3/8" x 1-1/2", white with gray highlights, VCO/USA . . 8.00
3", white and gray with purple ears, Made in Occupied Japan
. . . . 20.00
3-1/2" x 2", peach with gray highlights, poor detailing; no trademark. 5.00
6 3/4" x 4-3/4", gray with tusks; Made in USA 40.00

Fish
2-7/8", yellow with brown highlights, molded scales, intertwined VCO/Circle 10.00
3-1/2", medium reddish pink, molded scales and fins, nicely detailed, Japan. 12.00
4-1/2", whimsical whale with curled tail, smooth molded details in cream celluloid highlighted with green, red and yellow. Uncommon 50.00
4-1/2", yellow and red with molded scales, Made in USA
. . . . 14.00
6", red rattle fish with sharp fin and molded scales, gold eyes, Intertwined YM trademark and Japan 22.00
6-3/4", white and red, smooth shiny surface, molded fin, VCO/USA. 18.00

Frog
1-1/4", green or yellow frogs, stripe on back; Intertwined VCO/USA. 12.00
2-3/8", green painted, molded from white or yellow Celluloid, spotted backs; Made in USA inside circle or VCO in Circle over USA 14.00
2-3/4", white with painted green and black striped back, Made in Japan 12.00

Giraffe, yellow with brown spots, excellent molding by Petticolin of France/Eagle head trademark 80.00

Goat
2-1/8", white with hand-painted facial features, no trademark, poor detail 15.00
3-1/2", white with gray, billy goat with beard and horns, VCO/USA. 22.00
3", white goat with curled horns, flower with N in Circle and Japan. 18.00

Hippopotamus, 3-3/4", pink with closed mouth, Crossed Circle and Japan. 15.00

Horse
2-1/4" x 2", cream with brown highlights, Made in USA . 7.00
4", yellow with orange highlights, painted reigns and saddle, rattles, Made in USA 20.00
5-1/4", pink with black highlights, crossed circle, Japan
. . . . 15.00
9-1/4" x 7-3/4", cream with grayish brown highlights, Made in USA 50.00
7", cream with purple and pink highlights, Made in USA
. . . . 22.00

Leopard, 4-1/2", white with orange highlights and black spots, Made in Occupied Japan 20.00

Lion
3", orange with black highlights, Made in USA. 12.00
3-3/4", tan with brown highlights, TS, Made in Japan
. . . . 15.00
4", rattles; tan with brown and black, "VCO/USA" trademark on belly. 20.00

Lobster
1-3/4", bright red, detailed shell, no trademark. 40.00
3-1/4", shiny red lobster, smooth surface, intertwined VCO/USA. 65.00

Parakeet, 6-3/8" l, cream colored with yellow and black highlighting. Marked Germany 40.00

Parrot, 4", white with bright pink, green and yellow highlights, fine detailing; CT-Made in JAPAN 18.00

Pig
    1-1/8", cream pig with pink highlights, VCO 20.00
    4-1/2", pink with painted eyes, Made in USA 28.00

Ram
    2-1/2", cream colored, poor detailing, Japan 7.00
    4-1/2", cream with gray highlights, Made in USA 18.00

Rhino
    4", white with gray, smiling with double horn, Made in Occupied Japan 18.00
    5", gray, fine detail, PH trademark, Paul Haneaus 45.00

Seal, 4-1/2", gray balancing red ball, VCO/USA 55.00

Sparrows
    3-1/4", balancing sparrow, yellow or teal, tail weighted, oval Made in USA trademark near talon 12.00
    4-1/2", yellow with red highlighting, Made in Japan . . . 15.00

Squirrel, 2-7/8", brown celluloid, holding a nut, Made in USA 30.00

Stork, 6-3/4", standing, white with pink legs, Flower mark and Japan 18.00

Swan
    3-3/8", multicolored purple, pink, yellow, Crossed Circle 15.00
    4", cream swan with gray, pink and orange highlights, VCO/USA 18.00

Turtle
    1-3/8", two tone, brown top, yellow bottom, USA on foot 13.00
    3", cream with brown highlights, VCO/USA with Circle 18.00
    4", cream with brownish gray highlights, CC in Diamond and Made in Japan 20.00

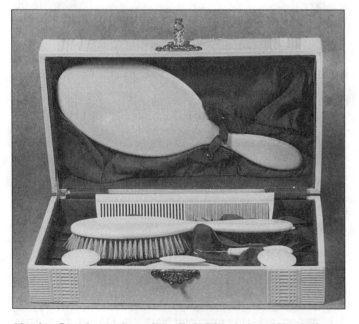

Vanity Set, boxed, emb celluloid cov box, bachelor button dec trim on lid, lined with red satin, mirror, brush, comb, nail buffer, button hook, and two salve jars, mirror mkd "Celluloid," $135. Photo courtesy of Julie Robinson.

Utilitarian and household items

Alarm Clock, 4", 3" h, gray pearlescent with amber accents, Greek Revival style 25.00

Bookends, pr., 4-1/4" h, 3-1/4" w, 2-1/4" d, plaster weighted, mottled pink celluloid embossed with an ornamental gold Neo-classic drape, c1930 . . . . 30.00

Candle holders, 5-1/4" h, sq-shaped holders, sq-weighted base and top 50.00

Clock
    3-1/2" w, 4-1/2" h, ivory grained rect mantle clock 25.00
    5-1/2" x 6-1/2", Classical design with columns, pink pearlessence celluloid, round clock face, c1930 . . . . 50.00

Cutlery, solid imitation ivory-grained handle utensils, 8 forks and 8 knives in original box, Standard Mfg. Co. 30.00

Crumb Tray Set, two dust pan-shaped trays, ivory-colored celluloid, one large and one small, scalloped and curved rim 12.00

Frame
    5-1/2" x 4", semi-oval, ftd scalloped base, peach celluloid, oval metal decoration in black and gold floral design, oval 3"x 5" opening 20.00
    6" x 8", plain oval, imitation ivory grained celluloid with glass, easel back 28.00

Napkin ring
    1" wide, translucent amber with sterling monogram . . . 20.00
    1-1/2" wide, lacy embossed ivory celluloid 8.00

Vase, 7" h, yellow, bulbous bottom, narrow opening with fluted top, painted pink and blue floral motif on bottom, no trademark 25.00

Watch Holder, 6-1/2" l, pearlescent blue green and amber banjo clock-style watch holder with Wilcox trademark on back; designed to hang on wall and hold pocket watch, late 1920s 22.00

Vanity items

Dresser Set
    Arch Amerith, Beverly pattern, ivory with amber edging, scalloped beveled edge; mirror, comb, rect clothing brush, imitation ivory tray with amber trimming, matching powder jar and hair receiver, perfume bottle with celluloid holder, ivory pin cushion base with scalloped amber trim, mkd "Arch Amereth, Beverly" 125.00
    Cleopatra pattern, Fiberloid Company, translucent amber, gold and black decorative trimming, 3-pc. coiffure set (comb, brush and mirror), 3-pc. powder box, hair receiver and tray; perfume bottle, clock and frame, manicure set (file, scissors, cuticle knife, buffer) and salve jars, button hook and clothing brush, 17 pcs, c1924 . . . . 225.00
    Plain, Pyralin, imitation grained ivory: brush and comb, button hook, clothing brush, dresser tray, hair receiver, hand mirror, manicure implements, buffer and salve box, powder box, vase and frame 115.00

Hair Receiver/Powder Box Set
    Ivory grained 3-1/2" d, dark blue monogrammed initials, Pyralin 35.00
    Pale amber containers with pearlescent mottled lids in gray, no trademark 18.00

Hat Pin Holder, 5" h, weighted base
    Circular, cream celluloid, cranberry colored velvet cushion, center post with round circular disc on top 85.00
    Triangular, pale green celluloid, painted flower 20.00

Manicure Set, rolled up leather pouch with fitted manicure tools, salve jars and scissors, green velvet lining, unmarked ivory grained implements 30.00

Straight Razor
    Marbleized cream celluloid, handle with beaded trim, Germany 20.00
    Plain black handle, Duplex 6.00
Vanity Set, black with green pearlescent surface, dresser tray with oval glass center, comb, brush, mirror, glass powder jar, matching celluloid lid, c1930 . . . . 40.00

CHALKWARE

History: William Hutchinson, an Englishman, invented chalkware in 1848. It was a substance used by sculptors to imitate marble and also was used to harden plaster of paris, creating confusion between the two products.

Chalkware pieces, which often copied many of the popular Staffordshire items made between 1820 and 1870, was cheap, gaily decorated, and sold by vendors. The Pennsylvania German folk art pieces are from this period.

Carnivals, circuses, fairs, and amusement parks gave away chalkware prizes during the late 19th and the 20th centuries. These pieces often were poorly made and gaudy.

Additional Listings: See Carnival Chalkware in *Warman's Americana & Collectibles*.

Notes: Don't confuse the chalkware carnival giveaways with the earlier pieces.

Bank, 10-1/2" h, seated cat, black and red ribbon collar and pipe, PA, 19th C 225.00
Bust, 11-1/2" h, woman, pedestal base, titled "Micaela," numbered on back. 145.00
Figure
    7-1/2" h, dog, worn orig red and black paint 200.00
    10" h, rabbit, black and yellow details 200.00
    18-1/2" h, seated girl, reading, head down, holding book on lap, 19th C, minor paint wear 525.00
Mantel Ornament
    5-5/8" h, dog, full figured, oval base 225.00
    5-5/8" h, pr of lovebirds, plinth base 250.00
    7-1/4" h, dog, facing left, stepped rect base 275.00
Match Holder, 6" h, figural, man with long nose and beard, Northwestern Insurance Co., c1890 . . . . 115.00
Plaque, 9" h, horse head, orig polychrome paint 115.00
Urn, 9" h, shades of brown and green, Arts and Crafts style floral motif at neck, two handles formed by kneeling male figures 175.00
Watch Hutch, 14" h, figural, compote of fruit, polychrome dec, 19th C. 350.00

CHARACTER and PERSONALITY ITEMS

History: In many cases, toys and other products using the images of fictional comic, movie, and radio characters occur simultaneously with the origin of the character. The first Dick Tracy toy was manufactured within less than a year after the strip first appeared.

The golden age of character material is the TV era of the mid-1950s through the late 1960s. Some radio premium collectors might argue this point. Today, television and movie producers often have their product licensing arranged well in advance of the initial release.

Do not overlook the characters created by advertising agencies, e.g., Tony the Tiger. They represent a major collecting subcategory.

References: Pauline Bartel, *Everything Elvis*, Taylor Publishing, 1995; Bill Blackbeard (ed.), *R. F. Outcault's The Yellow Kid*, Kitchen Sink Press, 1995; Bill Bruegman, *Cartoon Friends of the Baby Boom Era*, Cap'n Penny Productions, 1993; ——, *Superhero Collectibles*, Toy Scouts, 1996; *Cartoon & Character Toys of the 50s, 60s, & 70s*, L-W Book Sales, 1995; Rudy D'Angelo, *Cowboy Hero Cap Pistols*, Antique Trader Books, 1997; James D. Davis, *Collectible Novelty Phones*, Schiffer, 1998; Warren Dotz, *Advertising Character Collectibles*, Collector Books, 1993; ——, *What a Character! 20th Century American Advertising Icons*, Chronicle Books, 1996; David R. Greenland, *Bonanza, A Viewer's Guide to the TV Legend*, R & G Publications (P.O. Box 605, Hillside, IL 60162); Ted Hake, *Hake's Guide to Cowboy Character Collectibles*, Wallace-Homestead, 1994; ——, *Hake's Price Guide to Character Toys*, Gemstone Publishing, 1998; Jim Harmon, *Radio & TV Premiums*, Krause Publications, 1997. Jack Koch, *Howdy Doody*, Collector Books, 1996; Mary Jane Lamphier, *Zany Characters of the Ad World*, Collector Books, 1995; Cynthia Boris Liljeblad, *TV Toys and the Shows That Inspired Them*, Krause Publications, 1996; David Longest, *Character Toys and Collectibles* (1984, 1992 value update), 2nd Series (1987, 1990 value update), Collector Books; Rex Miller, *The Investor's Guide To Vintage Collectibles*, Krause Publications, 1998; Richard O'Brien, Collecting Toys, 7th ed., Books Americana, 1993; Susan and Steve Raab, *Movie Star Autographs of the Golden Era*, published by authors, 1994; Jon D. Swartz and Robert C. Reinehr, *Handbook of Old-Time Radio*, Scarecrow Press, 1993; Jon R. Warren, *Collecting Hollywood: The Movie Poster Price Guide*, 3rd ed., American Collectors Exchange, 1994; David and Micki Young, *Campbell's Soup Collectibles from A to Z*, Krause Publications, 1998.

Periodicals: *Autograph Times*, 2303 N 44th St, #225, Phoenix, AZ 85008; *Baby Boomer*, P.O. Box 1050, Dubuque, IA 52004; *Big Reel*, P.O. Box 1050, Dubuque, IA 52004; *Button Pusher*, P.O. Box 4, Coopersburg, PA 18036; *Celebrity Collector*, PO Box 1115, Boston, MA 02117; *Classic Images*, P.O. Box 809, Muscatine, IA 52761; *Collecting Hollywood*, American Collectors Exchange, 2401 Broad St., Chattanooga, TN 37408; *Cowboy Collector Newsletter*, P.O. Box 7486, Long Beach, CA 90807; *Frostbite Falls Far-Flung Flier*, P.O. Box 39, Macedonia, OH 44056; *Hollywood & Vine*, Box 717, Madison, NC 27025; *Hollywood Collectibles*, 4099 McEwen Dr., Suite 350, Dallas, TX 75224; *Movie Advertising Collector*, P.O. Box 28587, Philadelphia, PA 19149; *Movie Collector's World*, 17230 13 Mile Rd., Roseville, MI 48066; *Television History Magazine*, 700 E Macoupin St., Staunton, IL 62088; *TV Collector Magazine*, P.O. Box 1088, Easton, MA 02334.

Collectors' Clubs: All About Marilyn, P.O. Box 291176, Hollywood, CA 90029; Beatles Fan Club, 397 Edgewood Ave., New Haven, CT 06511; Betty Boop Fan Club, P.O.

Box 42, Moorhead, MN 56561; C.A.L./N-X-211 Collectors Society, 2820 Echo Way, Sacramento, CA 95821; Camel Joe & Friends, 2205 Hess Dr., Cresthill, IL 60435; Charlie Tuna Collectors Club, 7812 NW Hampton Rd., Kansas City, MO 64152; Dagwood-Blondie Fan Club, 541 El Paso, Jacksonville, TX 75766; Dick Tracy Fan Club, P.O. Box 632, Manitou Springs, CO 80829; Dionne Quint Collectors, P.O. Box 2527, Woburn, MA 01888; Howdy Doody Memorabilia Collectors Club, 8 Hunt Ct., Flemington, NJ 08822; Official Popeye Fan Club, 1001 State St., Chester, IL 62233; R. F. Outcault Society, 103 Doubloon Dr., Slidell, LA 70461; Three Stooges Fan Club, P.O. Box 747, Gwynedd Valley, PA 19437.

Videotapes: *Dionne Quintuplet Dolls: 1934-1939*, Sirocco Productions, 1992; *Shirley Temple Dolls & Memorabilia*, Sirocco Productions, 1994.

Additional Listings: See *Warman's Americana & Collectibles* for expanded listings in Cartoon Characters, Cowboy Collectibles, Movie Personalities and Memorabilia, Shirley Temple, Space Adventurers, and TV Personalities and Memorabilia.

SPECIAL AUCTIONS

Hake's Americana & Collectibles
P.O. Box 1444
York, PA 17405
(717) 848-1333

Toy Scouts
137 Casterton Ave.
Akron, OH 44303
(216) 836-0668

Character

Boop, Betty
Animation Art, 8-1/2" x 11", Betty in top hat, ink on paper, Max Fleischer Studios, c1930, unframed 950.00
Perfume Bottle, 3-1/2" h, glass, figural, painted facial features, dark red plastic cap, c1930 . . . . 50.00
Pin, 1" h, enamel on silvered brass, Betty playing violin, 1930s 200.00
Pinback Button, 7/8" d, "Betty Boop A Paramount Star Created By Fleischer Studios," black and white, 1930s, backpaper from Phila. Badge Co. 100.00
String Holder, wooden, wall mounted, souvenir type decal
. . . . 50.00
Bounce, Billie, W. W. Denslow character, pinback button, 1-1/4" d
"Billie Bounce in the Sunday Sentinel," multicolored, Billy with white bear holding blue umbrella, man holding lunch pail, orig backpaper 300.00
"Compliments of Billie Bounce," red ground, blue uniform, 1904 T C McClure copyright 250.00
Brown, Buster
Child's Book, *My Resolutions,* R. F. Outcault, black and white illus, Frederick A Stokes Co., 1906, 6" x 5" 35.00
Christmas Tree Light Bulb Cover, 5" h, celluloid, Buster Brown hiding Tige 125.00
Doll, 25" h Buster Brown, 16-1/2" h Tige, composition head and hands, stuffed Tige with composition head. . .1,150.00

Advertising Sign, Buster Brown, illus Buster and Tige, plastic, 7-1/4" x 6-1/2", $35.

Mechanical Display, 50" h, 53-1/2" w, three-dimensional, Buster Brown and Tige swimming at "Old Swimming Hole" with Tom Sawyer, Huckleberry Finn, and Becky Thatcher, some fading 1,550.00
Sign
  14" h, 14-1/2" l, Buster Brown Shoes, Buster Brown and Tige in center 60.00
  19-3/4" h, 27-3/4" l, Buster Brown Bread, emb tin, shows Buster Brown and Tige and sheaf of wheat, some paint splatters, trimmed at top 350.00
  89" h, 42" w, wood, "Hand-Up Matches, First In Safety," Buster Brown standing on stool, arm up stretched unable to reach "Hand-up noiseless licenses matches," National Match, Joliet, Ill, large lettering "Spohn & Thaner Sole Agents," green ground, ivy and red stripe border, two board construction. 1,100.00
Statue, 29" h, composition, Buster wearing sailor's hat, red jacket, red checked shorts, Tige sitting beside him, base reads "Buster Brown," with picture of Buster Brown and Tige playing tug-of-war, Buster redressed 225.00
Brownies, Palmer Cox
Stud, 1-3/8" h, white porcelain oval, hp dancing Brownie, wearing tam, brown, c1890 . . . . 70.00
Tray, 10-1/2" w, 13-1/4" h, Benham's Ice Cream, H. D. Beach Co. Coshocoton, OH, litho tin 175.00
Campbell Kids
Doll, squeeze, Chef, painted hollow rubber, early 1950s
. . . . 170.00
Feeding Dish, Buffalo Pottery. 50.00
Spoon, 6" l, SP, boy on handle, c1920. . . . . 15.00
Elsie, Borden's
Apron, cloth 85.00
Book, *Funbook Cut Out Toys and Games*, 7" x 10", 1940s, mint, unused 70.00
Buttons, 3" x 4-1/4" store card, full color Elsie image as cut-out after buttons removed, 3/4" diecut white plastic Elsie in daisy ring border, copyright 1949. . . . . 25.00

Christmas Card, 4-3/4" x 6-1/2", glossy stiff paper, color pop-up center of Elsie and family, printed greeting, Borden copyright, 1940s. 40.00

Clapper, tin. 160.00

Coffee Mug. 125.00

Flashlight, tractor trailer 150.00

Ice Cream Container, 1940s, pink, illus of Elsie and slogan "If It's Borden's, It's Got To Be Good," 4" h 10.00

Lamp Base, 4" x 4" x 7", glazed ceramic, 3" h metal bulb socket, Elsie reading book to baby Beauregard in diaper 185.00

Push Puppet, 2-1/2" x 2-1/2" x 5-1/2" h, jointed wood, Mesgo Products Co., late 1940s, brown and pink figure, white muzzle, green base, played-with condition. 80.00

Felix the Cat

Clicker, 1 1/2" h, black Felix, dark reddish brown ground, angry expression, 1930s 50.00

Pinback Button

1" d, black and white, portrait center, "Member Katz Kitten Klub," 1930s 125.00

1-1/8" d, litho, red and black center reads "31 Comics in Color Sunday Detroit Times," Felix, Skippy, Papa Katzenjammer, Jiggs, Barney Google, the Toonerville Trolley Skipper, and two female characters peeking around of center, yellow ground. 1930s 40.00

Valentine, mechanical, German, framed. 65.00

Google, Barney, pinback button

1" d, "Detroit Times Barney Google," black, white, red, and fleshtone, serial number on front, plus backpaper describing prizes 50.00

1-1/8" d, "Sunday Herald and Examiner 30 Comics," litho, dark blue on white, bright orange ground, 1930s. . . . 20.00

Gump, Andy

Bank, 4-3/8" h, cast iron, worn polychrome, newspaper missing 600.00

Pinback Button, 1-1/4" d, "Andy Gump for President," black, white, and red portrait, pale blue rim with "My Platform Eat Papendick's Dinner Belle Bread," c1932 . . . . 50.00

Sheet Music, 9-1/4" x 12-1/4", full color images on front cov, 1923 copyright 35.00

Hooligan, Happy, pinback button, 1-1/4" d, ""Is Everybody Happy?" full Happy figure, cream ground, light red type, c1910 . . . . 20.00

Howdy Doody

Bank, 4" x 7", china, red and blue striped shirt, blue neckerchief, rubber trap, 1950s 450.00

Mask, 8" x 9", molded rubber, orig red, white, and blue tag with characters, Bob Smith copyright, c1948-51 . . . . 85.00

Plaque, Howdy, Clarabelle, Mr. Bluster, multicolored 100.00

Prize, Doodle Booklet, 1954. . . . . 10.00

Shake-Up Mug, directions 75.00

Watch, silvered metal case, plastic crystal over Howdy dial, diecut eyes slowly move clockwise, plaid fabric band, Bob Smith copyright, 1948-51 . . . . 195.00

Jiggs and Maggie

Ashtray, 38" h, carved and painted flat wood silhouette, metal tray, c1930. . . . . 150.00

Pin, 1-1/4" h, enamel dec, blue and white Jiggs with cigar, Maggie in purple dress, yellow waist sash. 100.00

Pinback Button, 1" d, Detroit Times Contest, black, white, and red, lucky number 25.00

Puzzles, set of 4, 1932. . . . . 45.00

Katzenjammer Kids, pinback button, 1-1/8" d, "Sunday Herald and Examiner 30 Comics," dark blue on white, bright orange ground, Papa Katzenjammer smoking cigar, 1930s. . . 25.00

Killowatt, Reddy

Mechanical Pencil, 5" l, hard plastic and chrome, pocket clip, c1950 . . . . 20.00

Plate, 9" d, Syracuse China, 1940s 125.00

Krazy Kat

Pin, 1-1/4" h, brass, black enamel, white enamel bow, yellow rhinestone eyes, c1920 . . . . 80.00

Pinback Button

1" d, black on white, Ignatz, 1970s 15.00

1-3/8" d, dark green, black image and printing, Los Angeles Evening Herald & Express, serial number. . . . 25.00

Lil Abner

Charm, 1" h, figural plastic, white Shmoo, late 1940s . 45.00

Comic Strip Orig Artwork, Al Capp, daily strip, 4-9-43, Moonbeam McSwine 450.00

Keychain Puzzle, 2" h, white Shmoo, green and dark red, late 1940s. 60.00

Pinback Button

15/16" d, dark blue and white, Abner running with arms in fighting position, "Get in the Scrap! McKeesport," facsimile of All Capp 65.00

1-5/8" d, Knoxville Shmoo Booster - Be a Shmoo, black and white, c1940. . . . . 100.00

Tab, litho tin, 2 1/4" h, Sealtest Ice Cream Shmoo Club, black and white Shmoo, orange ground, c1949 . . . . 25.00

Little Orphan Annie

Clicker, Secret Guard. 70.00

Coin Collection Folder, complete with coins, orig mailer 75.00

Dog Whistle, 3-1/4" l, brass tube extends to 5-1/4", flat diecut image of Sandy, 1940 Ovaltine premium. 80.00

Magic Transfers, complete. 60.00

Manual, orig mailer, 1941. . . . . 125.00

Mug, 3" h, plastic, Ovaltine premium 30.00

Nodder, 4" h, bisque, Germany 90.00

Pinback Button, Voters. 525.00

Ring, magnifying. 800.00

Shadowettes, contest, orig mailer, fold-out, instructions, unfinished. 185.00

Watch, brass, compass and sundial combination, Egyptian hieroglyphics on back, Ovaltine, 1938 . . . . 70.00

MAD

Model Kit, Alfred E Neuman, plastic pieces, orig instruction sheet, uncut sign sheet, orig box, 1965 E C Publications copyright 225.00

Pinback Button

1-1/2" d, full color, Easter rabbit holding basket ready to descend down chimney on snow covered roof, subscription premium, copyright 1987 . . . . 20.00

2-1/2" d, Alfred E. Neuman for President, full color portrait, bright red and blue background 70.00

Mr. Peanut, Planters

Coloring Book, 8" x 11", Planters Nut & Chocolate Co. publication, c1920, 32 pages, only one page colored 50.00

Top, 2-1/2" h wooden spinner, red, yellow and blue decal on large end with Mr. Peanut, c1930s 80.00

Tray, 5-3/4" d, 4-1/2" h, brass finish, base mkd "Planters Peanuts/1906-1956," Mr. Peanut inscription on hatband 40.00

Mullins, Moon, pinback button

13/16" d, Kellogg's Pep, white background 15.00

1-3/8" d, dark green, black image and printing, Los Angeles Evening Herald & Express, serial number 25.00

Mutt & Jeff

Blotter, 4" x 9", black, white, and red, "The Musical Comedy Sensation of the Age," unused. 30.00

Movie Poster, 28" x 41", "A Tropical Eggspedition," 1920s
. . . . 425.00

Pinback Button, 1-1/4" d

Join The Evening Telegraph Mutt & Jeff Club, black on cream, c1920 . . . . 75.00

Meet Us At Forest Park, striking blue and white illus, bright yellow background, Parisian Novelty, early 1930s
. . . . 90.00

Peanuts Gang

Commemorative Medal, 1-1/2" d, Snoopy Moon Landing, silver, Snoopy in space suit and helmet, inscribed "All Systems Are Go!," reverse with Snoopy in space helmet seating on top of doghouse and slogan "First Landing On The Moon/Commemorative 1969," facsimile Schulz signature, 1969 copyright on back 30.00

Pin, 1-5/8" h, Charlie Brown, heavy brass, enameled orange shirt, black shoes. 75.00

Pinback Button

1-3/4" d, "Happy Birthday America, 1776-1976," red, white, blue, and yellow, Woodstock and Snoopy with birthday cake, Simon Simple Originals, various UFS copyrights on curl 20.00

2-1/4" d, "U of M Homecoming," white, maroon, and bright yellow, Charlie Brown in Indian headdress in a pot over campfire as Snoopy and other Peanuts characters look on, curl reads "Peanuts © United Features Syndicate, Inc. Appear Daily in Minneapolis Star and Sunday Tribune". 40.00

Pillsbury Doughboy

Bank, 7" h, 2-1/2" d base, figural, ceramic, c1985 . . . . 20.00

Cookie Jar, 5" x 5-1/5" x 10-1/2", heavy ceramic, 1970s
. . . . 70.00

Popeye

Bank, dime register, 1929 . . . . 90.00

Big Little Book, *Popeye,* Saalfield, 1934, Elzie Cristler Segar
. . . . 35.00

Cereal Bowl, 1935 . . . . 60.00

Egg Cup, china, figural. 120.00

Fountain Pen, 1930 . . . . 25.00

Pinback Button

1-3/8" d, dark green, black image and printing, Los Angeles Evening Herald & Express, serial number. . . . 25.00

1-1/4 d", "I Yam Strong For King Comics," blue and white Popeye, c1936 . . . . 70.00

1-1/4" d, "Popeye for President," multicolored, 1980 KFS copyright 10.00

1-5/8" d, "Onward Popeye," white figure, blue outline, light blue ground, c1960 . . . . 15.00

Skippy, pinback button, 1" d, Detroit Times contest button, black, white, and red. 20.00

Smokey Bear

Key Ring and Fob, 3 1/4" h, bright brass luster, darker brass fob, c1970 . . . . 15.00

Pinback Button

1" d, red and yellow litho, "Keep California Green and Golden/Smokey's Reading Club," c1960 . . . . . . 25.00

2-1/8" d, Smokey's Timbertennial, bright red and white, 1964 International Falls, MN, event, pr of small bears stand by Smokey's legs and slogan 85.00

Ring, plastic, raised brown image, yellow plastic, c1970
. . . . 15.00

Tab, litho tin, 2-1/4" d, I'm Helping Smokey Prevent Forest Fires, brown lettering, bright yellow ground, unbent, 1980s
. . . . 5.00

Token, 1-1/4" d, aluminum, illus of Smokey saying "Please! Only You Can Prevent Forest Fires," reverse with pledge to protect fires, US Dept. of Agriculture-Forest Service and Your State Forester 10.00

Tarzan

Advertising Poster, 5" x 18", "Delicious Ice Cream in Tarzan Cups," full-color illus, 1930s. 115.00

Better Little Book, *The Son of Tarzan*, Whitman, Edgar Rice Burroughs, 1939 copyright. 60.00

Tracy, Dick

Big Little Book, *The Super Detective*, Whitman Better Little Book, 1939, Chester Gould artist and author, 432 pages, hardcover. 30.00

Camera, orig box 175.00

Children's Book, Dick Tracy Meets the Night Crawler, orig dust jacket 25.00

Comic Strip Orig Artwork

Fletcher, Rick, Sunday page, 12-9-79 . . . . 200.00

Gould, Chester, daily strip, 8-1-47 . . . . 600.00

Pinback Button, Dick Tracy Secret Service Patrol, 1940s
. . . . 35.00

Toy, tin, ramp walker, Nurse Nora figure pushing Bonnie Braid in carriage, orig box 175.00

Uneeda Kid, Nabisco

Doll, 16" h, composition, orig yellow slicker and hat, holding package, orig box. 2,000.00

Store Scoop, china, decal on inside and ext. 250.00

Yellow Kid

Doll, 8" h, composition head, wooden jointed body, all orig, yellow cloth outfit, some damage to left hand 425.00

Gum Tin, 7/8" w, 3" l, 3/8" h, Pulver's Kola Pepsin 5¢ Gum, litho tin, Yellow Kid Gum machines on back, substantial wear on base. 525.00

Pin Cushion, 4" h, 3" w, 1-1/5" d, figural, pot metal, carrying red pin cushion at side. 350.00

Sheet Music, 11-1/2" h, 8-1/4" w, *Hogan's Alley Songster*, ©1897 Press Publishing Co. 925.00

Personality

Allen, Jimmie

Album, Skelly Oil Club, complete 40.00

Member Certificate, 8" x 11", parchment paper, green border, red seal, "Full Fledged Pilot Member," Richfield Oil issue, c1934. . . . . 50.00

Whistle, secret signal 20.00

Autry, Gene

Badge, 1-1/4", "Gene Autry Official Club Badge," black and white, bright orange top rim, c1940 . . . . 50.00

Child's Book, *Gene Autry Makes A New Friend,* Elizabeth Beecher, illus by Richard Case, Whitman Tell n Tale, 1952
. . . . 8.00

Pinback Button, 1-1/4" d

"Gene Autry," black and white image, dark red shirt accents, face, kerchief, and hat band, bright yellow ground . . 15.00

"Gene Autry/Durst Bros Dairy," Gene holding six gun in black over yellow printing, black and yellow rim 125.00

Watch, orig band 140.00

Bergen, Edgar and Charlie McCarthy

Bank, 7-1/2" h, white metal, polychrome dec. 85.00

Pinback Button

3/4" d, black and white "Charlie McCarthy," late 1930s
. . . . 60.00

1" d, black and white, "An Effanbee Play-Product," late 1930s 150.00
Radio Show Ticket, 1-1/2" x 3-1/2", tan and black, from "Edgar Bergen With Charlie McCarthy," March, 1951 show, Columbia Broadcasting System, Coca-Cola sponsor
. . . . 25.00
Sheet Music, *Love Walked In,* 1938 Goldwyn Follies musical
. . . . 85.00

Cassidy, Hopalong
Button, 1/2" d, silvered brass, black lettered name . . . 15.00
Charm, 1" h, silvered plastic, inset glossy real photo, c1960
. . . . 15.00
Compass Ring, black metal hat missing 40.00
Employee Button, 4" d, "Hoppy's Favorite Bond Bread," black and white photo, red and black ground, used by delivery men and/or store clerks 50.00
Pinback Button, 2-1/4" d, "Hopalong Cassidy's Saving Rodeo (Bar 20) Foreman," black and gold, pale cream rim
. . . . 200.00
Tab, 2" h, litho tin, "Burry's Hopalong Cassidy Cookies," multicolored, Sheriff, unbent 45.00
Tie Slide, 2-1/2" w, Long-Horn Steer, white metal, bright silver luster, inset red rhinestone eyes 40.00

Chaplin, Charlie
Figure, 2-1/2" d, lead 95.00
Pencil Box, tin, sgd "H. Clive". 75.00
Pinback Button, 7/8" d, "Charlie Chaplin in Modern Times," blue, bright yellow round, string holding celluloid charm of Charlie with cane, red outfit, black derby, 1936. . . . . 50.00
Premium, figure, 13" h, "Dancing Charlie Illusion," jointed, orig package and instructions 145.00

Crabbe, Buster
Pinback Button
1-1/4" d, black and white photo, bright orange ground, c1950 . . . . 35.00
1-5/8" d, litho, black and white photo, red ground, white rim "Member Buster Crabbe Western Club," c1950
. . . . 80.00
Program, Aqua Parade, 1948. . . . . 20.00

Dionne Quintuplets
Bowl, five girls illus 170.00
Broadside, 14-3/4" h, 32" l, five girls promoting Quaker Oats, multicolored 100.00
Cake Plate, serving knife 300.00
Candy Box, Baby Ruth. 190.00
Magazine Adv, 31-1/2" x 14-1/2" h, color, 1935, girls and house adv 125.00
Mug, one girl illus 75.00

Durante, Jimmy, puppet, hand, Umbraigo, sidekick, composition face, mustache and hat, 1945 . . . . 120.00
Fields, W C, pinback button, 2-1/4" d, black and white, litho, "W. C.," slogan "Be Safe-We Care," Upjohn, 1970s 12.00
Gish, Lillian, pinback button, 13/16" d, black and white photo, Egyptian Oasis Cigarettes, c1920 . . . . 20.00

Laurel & Hardy
Figure, Knickerbocker, bend-em's, rubber faces, clothed soft bodies, price for set 75.00
Mask, 9" h, paper, printed caricature face, marked "Laurel & Hardy's Laughing 20s," c1966, price for pr 40.00
Planter, 7-1/2" h, porcelain, standing together, planter in back, 1940s 145.00

Lone Ranger
Badge, "The Lone Ranger-A Republic Picture," 1-1/4" horseshoe-shaped, brass, luster worn, Lone Ranger riding Silver
. . . . 35.00

Charm, 1" d, dark red plastic frame, inset full color cardboard photo of Tonto, 1950s 12.00
Comic Strip Orig Artwork, Charles Flanders, four consecutive daily strips, 1-20 to 1-23-63 . . . . 100.00
Deputy Kit, orig mailer, 1980 . . . . 12.00
Frontier Town, four sections, unpunched, blue backs, orig mailers 850.00
Game Token, 1" d, aluminum disk, portraits of Lone Ranger and Tonto, c1950 . . . . 15.00
Good Luck Token, 1-1/2" h, aluminum casing, 1948 penny, good luck symbols, "Keep Me And Never Go Broke," reverse reads "Pioneer/Belts/Braces/Wallets/Superman-Lone Ranger For Boys" 100.00
Ring, Six Gun 75.00
Silver Bullet, 1-1/4" l, removable end cap holds compass, 1940s, scattered tarnish. 25.00

Marx Brothers, program, 8-1/2" x 11", Curtain Time Variety Show, 16 pgs, 1945, black, white, and maroon cov . . . 70.00

Mix, Tom
Bird Call, orig mailer, directions 100.00
Belt Buckle, 1-1/2" x 1-3/4", solid brass, facsimile signature stamped vertically on left side, 1930s 200.00
Bracelet, leather. 45.00
Branding Iron 45.00
Fountain Pen 75.00
Magnetic Compass Gun with Whistle, orig mailer . . . 160.00

Postcard, Sarah Bernhardt, M. Mucha, $600. Photo courtesy of Postcards International.

Pinback Button
   7/8" d, dark brown and light tan litho, Tom surrounded by lasso as border, issued by Canvas Products Co., 1935 . . . . 75.00
   1-3/4" d, Tom Mix Circus, black and white photo, black ground, 1930s 120.00
   Ring, cat's eye, orig mailer, directions 275.00
Monroe, Marilyn
   Bridge Set, two decks of cards. 32.00
   Calendar, 1954, unused. 20.00
   Candy Dish. 8.00
   Snow Dome 15.00
   Statue, 4" h, porcelain, pink dress 15.00
Pervis, Melvin
   Premium Photo. 65.00
   Ring, scarab 600.00
Presley, Elvis
   Christmas Ornament 12.00
   Coloring Book. 5.00
   Locket, 5/8" h, heart shape, name in black, c1956 . . . 40.00
   Miniature TV Film Viewer, 1" l black plastic television set, loop on one edge to serve as key fob, front with white plastic screen, reverse with viewing hole, six black and white photos to be viewed, also shows Pat Boone, Ava Gardner, Deborah Kerr, Sandra Dee, and Connie Francis, late 1950s, mkd "H0 597 Made in Hong Kong" 85.00
   Newspaper, death headline 12.00
   Pinback Button, 7/8" d
      Any Way You Want Me, 1956, black and white photo, gold rim 20.00
      Love Me Tender, red, white, and blue litho 15.00
Rogers, Roy
   Bowl 85.00
   Charm, 1" h, blue plastic frame, black and white glossy paper photo, seated sideways, face turned front 35.00
   Paint Set, Post, orig box. 80.00
   Pinback Button, 13/16" d, Post's Grape-Nut Flakes, Canadian, 1953 copyright
      Buttermilk. 65.00
      Dale Evans 65.00
      Roy Rogers, yellow ground 70.00
   Poster, Ranch Set 125.00
   Ring, sterling, image of Roy on rearing Trigger, crossed branding irons on each side. 200.00
Sky King
   Dectecto Microscope, orig box, complete 350.00
   Magni-Glo Writing Ring 45.00
   Mystery Picture Ring, 1948 Peter Pan premium, adjustable brass base, propeller and wing design, top with glow-in-dark white plastic square with dark gray plastic circular inset on top, image visible. 900.00
   Photo, 4" x 5" 12.00
   Radar Ring. 80.00
   Stamping King, 1-1/4" x 1-3/4" white tin box with red designs, rubber stamp with name and address, felt ink pad on lid, 1953. . . . . 80.00
Temple, Shirley
   Children's Book, *Birthday Book,* 6th birthday, unused 65.00
   Paper Dolls, ten outfit, cut, orig box 35.00
   Pin, 7/8" disk, real black and white photo, thin silvered rim, silvered metal English-style safety pin 100.00
   Pinback Button
      15/16", Kline's Shirley Temple Beret Club, blue on white, 1930s 200.00

   1-1/4" d, browntone photo, light pink rim, Ideal Dolls, 1930s 75.00
Wayne, John
   Charm, 7/8" h, white plastic frame holds inset black and white photo, wearing cowboy outfit, early 1950s. 15.00
   Dixie Cup Lid, 2-3/4" d, bluetone photo 5.00
   Pinback Button
      1-1/4" d, black and white portraits of Wayne and Ronald Reagan, c1968 . . . . 30.00
      2-1/4" d, black and white photo, red, white, and blue flag ground 15.00
Wynn, Ed, figure, 10" h, cardboard, bright paper label, Fire Chief outfit, movable arms, legs, and leg, c1930. . . . . 65.00

CHELSEA

History: Chelsea is a fine English porcelain which was designed to compete with Meissen. The factory began operating in the Chelsea area of London, England, in the 1740s. Chelsea products are divided into four periods: Early (1740s), 1750s, 1760s, and Derby (1770-1783). In 1924, a large number of the molds and models of figurines were found at the Spode-Copeland Works, and many items were brought back into circulation.

References: John C. Austin, *Chelsea Porcelain at Williamsburg,* Colonial Williamsburg Foundation, 1977; Susan and Al Bagdade, *Warman's English & Continental Pottery & Porcelain,* 3rd Edition, Krause Publications, 1998; John Bedford, *Chelsea & Derby China,* Walker & Co., 1967.

Museums: Colonial Williamsburg Foundation, Williamsburg, VA; Fine Arts Museums, San Francisco, CA; Fitzwilliam Museum, Cambridge, England; Gardiner Museum of Ceramic Arts, Toronto, Canada; Henry E. Huntington Library & Art Gallery, San Marino, CA; Museum of Fine Arts, Boston, MA; Seattle Art Museum, Seattle, WA; Victoria & Albert Museum, London, England; Wadsworth Atheneum, Hartford, CT; Walters Art Gallery, Baltimore, MD.

Marks: Different marks were used during the different Chelsea periods:

Early	incised triangle and raised anchor
1750s	red raised anchor
1760s	gold anchor

Basket, 12-1/8" l oval, deep reticulated sides, upright end loop handles, rose, blue, iron-red, yellow, green, gray, and brown floral bouquet, scattered sprigs and two insects, ext. molded with open wickerwork, brown edge scalloped rim, puce-bound stem end handles, yellow and brown mottled branches, iron-red blossoms, green leaves, c1775, slight glaze chips, handle chipped 700.00
Dessert Plate, 8-1/2" d, c1755, red anchor mark 3,450.00
Dish
   8-1/8" d, puce, iron-red, and yellow painted tulip and flowers bouquet, scattered flowers, brown edged shaped rim, c1755, red anchor mark. 255.00
   9-7/8" l, leaf shape, two overlapping cos lettuce leaves, puce veins, edged in bright green, c1755, red anchor mark 1,500.00

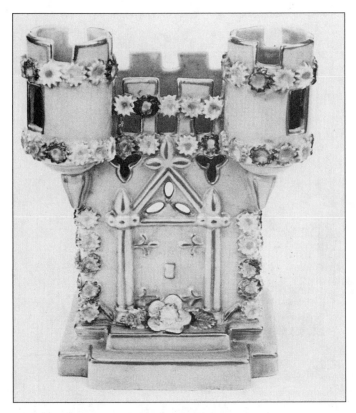

Pastille Burner, purple ground, red, pink, blue, yellow pastel flowers, gold trim, gold anchor mark, 5-1/2" h, 4-1/8" w, $265.

Figure
  6" h, drummer, light green jacket, puce pantaloons, black drumsticks in hands, drum at side, flower encrusted circular base, imp "R" mark, restored 925.00
  7-1/16" h, young sportsman, black hat, turquoise jacket, gold, black, and iron-red waistcoat, pale yellow pants, tan topped black boots, holding bird in right hand, another between feet, brown riffle to left, recumbent brown spotted white hound to right, tree stump with iron-red berries and green leaves, scroll molded mound base trimmed in turquoise and gold, c1765, gold anchor mark, chips 1,250.00
Flower Holder, 9-1/2" h, figural, seated fisherman, green hat, light mauve coat, iron-red breeches, open pierced basket between knees, 1758 . . . . 520.00
Pipe Tamper, 3-5/8" h, modeled bust, brown hair, ruffle, tapered pedestal, orange, yellow, and blue lines, blue flower on base, c1780 . . . . .2,250.00
Plate
  8-1/2" d, silver shape, painted exotic birds, green and brown foliage, three molded rose-pink and gilt shells on border, painted leaf on reverse, gold anchor mark, repaired
  . . . . .1,850.00
  9-5/16" d, scalloped border, rose, iron-red, yellow, blue, purple, brown, green and gray, small floral sprigs, brown edged rim, c1755, red anchor mark 650.00
Tea Bowl and Saucer, octagonal, multicolored painted bouquets and insects, scattered floral sprays, c1760 . . . . 310.00

CHILDREN'S BOOKS

History: Because there is a bit of the child in all of us, collectors always have been attracted to children's books. In the 19th century, books were popular gifts for children, with many of the children's classics written and published during this time. These books were treasured and often kept throughout a lifetime.

Developments in printing made it possible to include more attractive black and white illustrations and color plates. The work of artists and illustrators has added value beyond the text itself.

References: E. Lee Baumgarten, *Price Guide for Children's & Illustrated Books for the Years 1880-1960 Sorted by Artist* and *Sorted by Author*, published by author, 1996; David & Virginia Brown, *Whitman Juvenile Books*, Collector Books, 1996; Richard E. Dickerson, *Brownie Bibliography*, 2nd ed., Golden Pippin Press, 1995; Virginia Haviland, *Children's Literature, a Guide to Reference Sources* (1966), first supplement (1972), second supplement (1977), third supplement (1982), Library of Congress; Alan Horne, *Dictionary of 20th Century British Book Illustrators*, available from Spoon River Press, 1994; Simon Houfe, *Dictionary of 19th Century British Book Illustrators*, revised ed., available from Spoon River Press, 1996; Diane McClure Jones and Rosemary Jones, *Collector's Guide to Children's Books, 1850 to 1950*, Collector Books, 1997; Jack Matthews, *Toys Go to War*, Pictorial Histories Publishing, 1994; Edward S. Postal, *Price Guide & Bibliography to Children's & Illustrated Books*, M & P Press (available from Spoon River Press, 2319C W. Rohmann, Peoria, IL 61604), 1995; *Price Guide to Big Little Books & Better Little, Jumbo Tiny Tales, A Fast Action Story, etc.*, L-W Book Sales, 1995; Steve Santi, *Collecting Little Golden Books*, 3rd ed., Krause Publications, 1998.

Periodicals: *Book Source Monthly*, 2007 Syossett Dr., P.O. Box 567, Cazenovia, NY 13035; *Martha's KidLit Newsletter*, P.O. Box 1488, Ames, IA 50010; *Mystery & Adventure Series Review*, P.O. Box 3488, Tucson, AZ 85722; *Yellowback Library*, P.O. Box 36172, Des Moines, IA 50315.

Collectors' Clubs: Horatio Alger Society, 4907 Allison Dr., Lansing, MI 48910; Society of Phanton Friends, 4100 Cornelia Way, North Highlands, CA 95660.

Libraries: American Antiquarian Society, Worcester, MA; Free Library of Philadelphia, Philadelphia, PA; Library of Congress, Washington, DC; Lucile Clark Memorial Children's Library, Central Michigan University, Mount Pleasant, MI; Pierpont Morgan Library, New York, NY; Toronto Public Library, Toronto, Ontario, Canada.

Additional Listings: See *Warman's Americana & Collectibles* for more examples and an extensive listing of collectors' clubs.

Abbreviations:

dj	dust jacket
n.d.	no date
pgs	pages
teg	top edges gilt
unp	unpaged
wraps	paper covers

Adventures of Paddy Beaver, The, Thornton Burgess, Toronto, McClelland & Stewart, 1943, 1st ed, drawings, dj 20.00

Adventures of Ray Coon, Nancy Bryd Turner, 1934, Barnes & Bridgman, 1923 . . . . 15.00

Alice's Adventures in Wonderland, 42 illus by Tenniel, McMillan, 1914, blue cover, gold Alice, gold edges on pages . . . 25.00

Alice in Wonderland with Cut Out Pictures, cover by Julia Green, 1917 . . . . 148.00

Alphabet Book, Whitman, 1935, linen finish, soft cov, 10" x 13"
. . . . 10.00

American Boys Book of Birds & Brownies of the Woods, Woodcraft Series, Lippincott, 1931, 242 pgs, dj 18.00

Black Beauty, Edgar Lee version, illus by H. L. Miller, Saalfield, 1905 . . . . 20.00

Book of Penny Toys, The, illus by Mabel Dearmer, 1899
. . . . 375.00

Boys and Girls of Book Lane, Nora Smith, 1923, 11 stories, Jessie Wilcox Smith plates. 300.00

Camel with the Wrinkled Knees, Johnny Gruelle, Volland
. . . . 75.00

Charlotte's Web, E. B. White, Harper, 1952, 1st edition, Garth Williams illus, child's name on flyleaf 110.00

Chatterbox for 1928, J. Erksine Clarke, Boston, 1928 . . . 40.00

Children's Classics Illustrated, 5 book series 60.00

Child's Garden of Verses, A, Robert Louis Stevenson, illus by Jesse Wilcox Smith 35.00

Comical Doings, Ernest Nister, dressed animals, Lewis Wain illus. 175.00

Daddy Long Legs, J Webster, Thrushwood Books, 1940
. . . . 10.00

Danny Decoy, John Held, A. S. Barnes, 1942, author sgd
. . . . 20.00

Doings of Little Bear, Frances Margaret Fox, color and black and white illus by Warner Carr, Rand McNally & Co., 1932
. . . . 10.00

Dr. Rabbit & Grumpy Bear, Thomas Clark Hinkle, illus by M. Winter, Rand McNally, 1934. . . . . 15.00

Edith and the Bear Lend A Hand, Dare Wright, dust jacket
. . . . 45.00

Flower Children, Elizabeth Gordon, M. T. Ross illus, 1910, Volland, 78th ed. 70.00

Friendly Fairies, Johnny Gruelle, 1919, Volland, 27th ed
. . . . 60.00

Girl in the Woods, The, Grace L Hill, Lipcott, 1st ed, 1942
. . . . 10.00

Golden Arrow, Bill and Bernard Martin, Tell-Well Press, 1950, 1st ed, sgd by Bill Martin 25.00

Grimm's Fairy Tales, Anderson, matched set in slip box, 1945, bright blue pictorial covers, 373 and 343 pgs, lavish color
. . . . 45.00

Honey Bunch Her First Tour of Toy Town, Helen L. Thorndyke, 1951, 180 pgs. 8.00

Hunting for the Hidden Gold, Hardy Boys, F. W. Dixon, 1928, gray cover. 10.00

Jolly Jump-Ups, The, R. L. Stevenson, McLoughlin, 1941, pop-up, loose hinge 25.00

Kantner's Illustrated Book of Objects, 1895, 2,000 engravings, explanations in English and German 95.00

Kids Cooking - A Very Slightly Messy Manual, Klutz Press, 1987, 78 pgs, spiral bound. 10.00

King Arthur and His Knights, Chicago, 1924, colored plates
. . . . 15.00

Little Brown Bear, The, Johnny Gruelle, P. F. Volland Co., 1920, 34th edition. 35.00

Little Brown Koko Has Fun, 2nd edition, 1945, dust jacket
. . . . 95.00

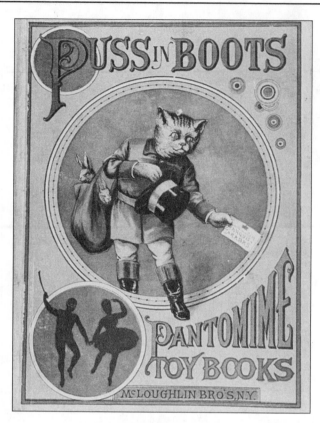

***Puss n' Boots Pantomine Toy Books,
McLoughlin Bros., NY, 7-1/2" x 10-1/8", $60.***

Little Engine That Could, The, Lois Lenski, retold Watty Pipe, 1930 . . . . 25.00

Little Garden People, Marion Bryson, illus by Ann Pearsal Sharp, Akron, Saalfield, 1938, 8" x 10" 45.00

Little Golden Book of Nursery Songs, arranged by Leah Gale, Corinne Malvern illus, Simon & Schuster, 1942. . . . . . 90.00

Little Slam Bang, Helen Vanderveer, illus by F. C. Ransom, Volland, 1928, 1st ed. 30.00

Lone Ranger at the Haunted Gulch, Fran Striker 20.00

Lost Princess, The, A Fairy Tale, Maple Lucie Attwell, Fred Warne pub, six tip-in color pictures, 1st edition 45.00

Lost Wagon Train, The, Zane Grey, 1936, binding loose . . 5.00

Mistress Mary The Secret Garden, Frances H. Burnette, Ottenheimer, retold by Andrea Leach, pop-ups 8.00

Modern Explorers, Thomas Frost, McLoughlin Bros., Arctic explorers on cov. 55.00

Mrs. Piggle Wiggle, Betty MacDonald, black and white Hillary Knight illus, J. B. Lippincott Co., 1957, dj. 20.00

Nancy Drew Cookbook Clues to Good Cooking, Keene, NY, 1974, 159 pgs. 15.00

Peter Puzzlemaker, John Martin Puzzle Book, George Carlson compiler, Platt & Munk Co., 1929. . . . . 20.00

Popeye and the Pirates, animated, Julian Wehs, 1943 . 125.00

Puppy Stories, Evien Beaudry, illus by Diana Thorne, Akron, Saalfield, Pub, 1934, pictorial cov 20.00

Puss N Boots, NY 20.00

Raggedy Ann Stories, Johnny Gruelle, Volland 75.00

Return of Tarzan, The, Edgar Burroughs, 1967, Western Pub
. . . . 10.00

Seven Ages of Childhood, Jessie Wilcox Smith, 1st ed
. . . . 175.00

Strawberry Girl, Lois Lenski, author and illus, Lippincott, 1945, 8" x 6-1/2", Sunbonnet girl on cover. 25.00

Sunbonnet Babies Book, The, E O Grover, 1902, orig jacket
....55.00
Sunny Bunny, Nina Wilcox Patnum, Johnny Gruelle illus, P. F. Volland Co., 1918, 5th edition 50.00
Tale of Mr. Toad, The, Beatrice Potter, 1939, dust jacket
....50.00
Tale of Peter Rabbit, The, Beatrice Potter, Fern Bisel Peat illus, Harter, 1931, soft cover, 9" x 13" 45.00
Tarzan and the Jewels of Opar, Edgar Burroughs, 1918 . 10.00
Tasha Tudor's Bedtime Book, Tasha Tudor, 1977 ......45.00
Teddy Bears in Hot Water, The, 1907................75.00
Ten Seconds to Play, Chip Hilton, Clair Bee, black and white illus, 1960s..................................10.00
Three Bears, The, linen, 1933....................552.00
Through the Looking Glass, Tenniel illus, McMillan, 1914
....25.00
Thundering Herd, The, Zane Grey, Harper's, 1925, 1st ed
....24.00
Tom Swift & His Sky Racer, Victor Appleton, 1911, 207 pgs, ads in back 10.00
Twins in the West, The, D. Whitehall, Barse & Hopkins, 1920, 1st ed, bright cov 10.00
Uncle Wiggly & Jackie & Pettie Bow Wow, Howard Garis, Louis Wisa color illus A. L. Burt Co...................18.00
Uncle Wiggly's Happy Days, 1947, color illus by Rache. . 45.00
Winnie The Pooh, Dutton, Shepard illus, 1945.........15.00
Wizard of Oz Series, illus by John R. Neill
   Dorothy and the Wizard of Oz, L. Frank Baum, Chicago, 1908
....125.00
   Kabumpo in Oz, Ruth Plumly Thompson, Chicago, 1922
....125.00
   Ozma of Oz, L. Frank Baum, Chicago, 1907 ....180.00
   Rinkitink In Oz, L. Frank Baum, Chicago, 1916 ......70.00
   The Cowardly Lion of Oz, Ruth Plumly Thompson, Chicago, 1923.......................................65.00
   The Emerald City of Oz, L. Frank Baum, Chicago, 1910
....75.00
   The Magic of Oz, L. Frank Baum, Chicago, 1919 ....95.00
   The Road to Oz, L. Frank Baum, Chicago, 1909....115.00
   The Scarecrow of Oz, L. Frank Baum, Chicago, 1915
....70.00
   The Tin Woodsman of Oz, L. Frank Baum, Chicago, 1918
....90.00
   The Wishing Horse of Oz, Ruth Plumly Thompson, Chicago, 1935..200.00
   Tic-Tok of Oz, L. Frank Baum, Chicago, 1914.......95.00

CHILDREN'S FEEDING DISHES

History: Unlike toy dishes meant for play, children's feeding dishes are the items actually used in the feeding of a child. Their colorful designs of animals, nursery rhymes, and children's activities are meant to appeal to the child and make mealtimes fun. Many plates have a unit to hold hot water, thus keeping the food warm.

Although glass and porcelain examples from the late 19th and early 20th centuries are most popular, collectors are beginning to seek some of the plastic examples from the 1920s to 1940s, especially those with Disney designs on them.

References: Maureen Batkin, *Gifts for Good Children, Part II, 1890-1990,* Antique Collectors' Club, 1996; Doris Lechler, *Children's Glass Dishes, China and Furniture,* Vol. I (1983), Vol. II (1986, 1993 value update), Collector

Baby's Plate, chick dec, yellow ground, Roseville, 7-1/2" d, $70.

Books; Noel Riley, *Gifts for Good Children: The History of Children's China, Part I, 1790-1890,* Richard Dennis Publications, 1991; Margaret and Kenn Whitmyer, *Collector's Encyclopedia of Children's Dishes: An Illustrated Value Guide,* Collector Books, 1993.

Bowl, 7-1/2" d, two Dutch children 85.00
Cereal Bowl, seven nursery rhyme scenes and captions
....60.00
Cereal Set, cereal bowl, mug, and 6" d plate, Nursery Rhyme, Jack and Jill, marked "Royal Bayreuth" 145.00
Cup Plate, 3-1/2" d, children at play, rust-brown transfer, imp "Woods" 75.00
Dish, 6-1/2" d, 1-1/2" h, Peter Rabbit and Farmer, Beatrix Potter, Wedgwood 40.00
Feeding Dish
   Animals, divided, Walker China 20.00
   Birds perched on branch, dressed in clothes, children's toys on border, red "Made in Czechoslovakia" mark, 5-1/2" d
....65.00
   Duck in Hat, Blue Ridge Pottery.................55.00
   Girl feeding teddy, 8" d 65.00
   Jigsaw, Blue Ridge Pottery 90.00
   Peter Rabbit and Mr. McGregor, multicolored, Wedgwood, 6-3/8" d.......................................45.00
   Scottie and girl, 7" d.........................65.00
Mug
   ABC, African animals 70.00
   Ann, black transfer, geometric rim, applied leaf tip handle, pearlware, 2-3/8" h..........................15.00
   A Present For James, man and woman in landscape, fences, trees, and house, purple transfer, blue lined rim and outer border, c1820..38.00
   For My Dear Girl, black transfer, pink luster trim, 2-1/4" h
....225.00
   Little Bo Peep, glass, 3-1/2" h 65.00
   Raggedy Ann, © 1940 Johnny Gruelle, crazing......68.00
   Remember Me, gold lettering, pink luster trim 50.00

The Sisters, barrel shape, blue and white transfer, c1860
. . . . 140.00
Uniformed boy in automobile 38.00
Plate
5-1/2" d, Punch and Judy, red transfer, Allerton, early 20th C
. . . . 85.00
6" d, sleeping girls and angels, polychrome transfer . . 70.00
6-1/8" d, My Pretty Bird, girl with bird on wrist, black transfer, emb floral border 125.00
6-1/2" d, Dr. Franklin Maxim, "It Is Hard For An Empty Bag to Stand Free," pawn shop scene, black line border . . . 95.00
8" d, Little Tommy Tucker, Royal Doulton 65.00
Teapot, cov, Duck in Hat, Blue Ridge Pottery 125.00

CHILDREN'S NURSERY ITEMS

History: The nursery is a place where children live in a miniature world. Things come in two sizes. Child scale designates items actually used for the care, housing, and feeding of the child. Toy or doll scale denotes items used by the child in play and for creating a fantasy environment which copies that of an adult or his own.

Cheap labor and building costs during the Victorian era encouraged the popularity of the nursery. Most collectors focus on items from the years 1880 to 1930.

References: Marguerite Fawdry, *International Survey of Rocking Horse Manufacture*, New Cavendish Books, 1992; Marcia Hersey, *Collecting Baby Rattles and Teethers: Identification and Value Guide*, Krause Publications, 1998; Doris Lechler, *Children's Glass Dishes, China and Furniture*, Vol. I (1983), Vol. II (1986, 1993 value update), Collector Books; Patricia Mullins, *Rocking Horse: A History of Moving Toy Horses*, New Cavendish Books, 1992; Lorraine May Punchard, *Playtime Kitchen Items and Table Accessories*, published by author, 1993; Herbert F. Schiffer and Peter B. Schiffer, *Miniature Antique Furniture: Doll House and Children's Furniture from the United States & Europe*, Schiffer Publishing, 1995; Tony Stevenson and Eva Marsden, *Rocking Horses: The Collector's Guide to Selecting, Restoring, and Enjoying New and Vintage Rocking Horses*, Courage Books, 1993.

Museum: The Victorian Perambulator Museum of Jefferson, Jefferson, OH.

Additional Listings: Children's Books; Children's Feeding Dishes; Children's Toy Dishes; Dolls; Games; Miniatures; Toys.

Baby Vehicle, 39" l, 21" h with handle, painted wood, blue seat and base with red striping, rubber rimmed spoked rear wheels, small cast iron front wheel, mohair covered horse mounted on front of base, some paint wear and fabric loss
. . . . 690.00
Bean Bag Toss Game Board, 15" w, 30" h, rect board, sq openings, dec in greens, orange, pink, and yellow, stenciled "Bessie," hinged support on back, minor surface abrasion, areas of repaint 575.00
Bowl and Spoon, sterling silver, Wm. B. Kerr & Co., early 20th C, acid-etched design of children riding different animals from seven countries, minor dents, Gorham monogrammed spoon, 5 troy oz 200.00
Christening Outfit, gown, slip, and cap, white cotton, c1920
. . . . 85.00

Noah's Ark, 3 people, 91 prs of animals, 17 single animals, animals of varying ages, paint wear to ark, some edge damage, 25-1/4" l, $2,860. Photo courtesy of Garth's Auctions, Inc.

Cup, Bowl, and Plate, sterling silver, International Silver Co., early 20th C, acid-etched animals, fitted case, 7 troy oz
. . . . 400.00
Dog Sled, 29" l bed, wood, worn orig varnish, red paint with silver stenciled leaf, dumpster bed 200.00
Doll Carriage, 36" l, 33" h, wood and steel frame, wood wheels, orig varnish, dark brown paint, yellow striping, leatherized cloth top, worn fringe, int. cushion and wallpaper trim
. . . . 385.00
Doll Cradle, 10-1/4" l, walnut, old finish. 200.00
Flatware Set, sterling silver, fork, knife, and spoon
Bright-cut shell and flower dec, monogram, Bingham, Walk & Mayhew, c1883, fitted case, 4 troy oz 135.00
Engraved leaf dec, rope carved MOP handles, Victorian, George Unite maker, Birmingham, 1881, inscription, fitted case 175.00
Leaf and fern engraved design, HW LD makers, Sheffield, England, 1911, fitted case, 2 troy oz 90.00
Low relief scroll dec, monogram, fitted case, Gorham, c1871, 2 troy oz 115.00
Gliding Horse, 33" l, 31-1/2" h, painted dapple gray, leather and leatherette, harness and saddle, leather ears, steel and celluloid eyes, horsehair tail, dark red base with white striping, early 20th C, some paint lose, wear to mane 750.00
High Chair, 21-1/2" h, Windsor, New England, 1820-30, arrow-back, shaped and incised seat, foot rest, turned played legs, early red paint, 21-1/2" h seat, 36" h 2,875.00
Perambulator, 55" l, 24" w, 41" h, convertible leatherette top, faille tufted and upholstered seat, wooden spoke wheels with iron rims, yellow paint on body with dark blue and orange striping, cream wheels with similar color accents, America, 1860 . . . . 460.00
Portrait
7-3/4" h, 6" w, watercolor and pencil on paper, portrait of Joan Elizabeth Cook, aged 5, four months, 1835, full-length profile, wearing white dress, holding bouquet of flowers, calligraphic identification info beneath portrait, by Joseph H. Davis, descended through family 46,000.00
25" h, 20" w, oil and graphic on canvas, portrait of Francis E. West as a Child, holding toy lamp, period frame, craquelure, descended through family 68,500.00
Rattle
3-3/4" l, Palmer Cox Brownie head with bells, sterling and mother-of-pearl, late 19th C 150.00
5-1/2" l, Santa, celluloid, colorful 75.00

Rocker, 30-1/4" h, youth size, oak, turned and pressed detail, flat arms over spindles, old finish 200.00
Rocking Horse, 36" l, 35" h, 32-1/2" l, 12" d platform, 46" l wooden rockers, brown and white fur, glass eyes, horsehair mane and tail, red leatherette saddle, felt blanket, mid 20th C
. . . . 920.00
Sailboat Model, 49" h, wood and wire, old paint, some damage
. . . . 385.00
Sled, wooden
33-1/2" l, steep tipped runners, worn orig varnish, braces, red paint, stenciled and free hand floral design in silver and polychrome, underside stenciled "W. E. Ambrose, Nashua, N.H." 330.00
36" l, steep tipped runners, worn orig varnish, yellow striping, red paint, black stenciled lion, bird, and spider web
. . . . 250.00
48" l, double wooden runners, painted reserve of cardinal in marsh setting, other foliate devices, paint wear, minor repair, craquelure 875.00
Wagon
22" l, 8" h, painted wood, "The Flyer," rect red body, mustard wheels, black lettering on sides, paint wear, repairs
. . . . 175.00
34" l, wood and steel, wood spoke wheels, old worn red repaint, hand brake 330.00
Wheelbarrow, 33" l, 14-1/2" h, red and green painted wood, gilt and black dec, painted landscapes on sides, America, 19th C, paint wear, missing one iron brace 525.00

CHILDREN'S TOY DISHES

History: Dishes made for children often served a dual purpose—playthings and a means of learning social graces. Dish sets came in two sizes. The first was for actual use by the child when entertaining friends. The second, a smaller size than the first, was for use with dolls.

Children's dish sets often were made as a sideline to a major manufacturing line, either as a complement to the family service or as a way to use up the last of the day's batch of materials. The artwork of famous illustrators, such as Palmer Cox, Kate Greenaway, and Rose O'Neill, can be found on porcelain children's sets.

References: Doris Lechler, *Children's Glass Dishes, China and Furniture,* Vol. I (1983), Vol. II (1986, 1993 value

Tea Set, celluloid, cream colored, 4" d plates, 2" d cups, 15 pc set, $75. Photo courtesy of Julie Robinson.

update), Collector Books; Lorraine May Punchard, *Playtime Kitchen Items and Table Accessories,* published by author, 1993; ——, *Playtime Pottery & Porcelain from Europe and Asia,* Schiffer Publishing, 1996; ——, *Playtime Pottery and Porcelain from the United Kingdom and the United States,* Schiffer Publishing, 1996; Margaret and Kenn Whitmyer, *Collector's Encyclopedia of Children's Dishes,* Collector Books, 1993.

Collectors' Club: Toy Dish Collectors, P.O. Box 159, Bethlehem, CT 06751.

Akro Agate
Teapot, cov, Chiquita, green opaque 18.00
Tea Set, Interior Panel, green cups and saucers, green creamer, pink sugar, pink teapot, white lid, small size
. . . . 290.00
Tumbler, Stacked Disk and Panel, transparent green, 2" h
. . . . 12.00
Water Set, Stippled Band, green, pitcher, six tumblers
. . . . 110.00
China
Creamer and Sugar, cov, Willow Ware, blue and white
. . . . 30.00
Cup and Saucer, green luster, saucer with scene of girl and Golliwog 48.00
Dinner Set, fruit dec, 16 pcs, c1910 . . . . 125.00
Tea Set
7 pcs, transfer scene of Santa Claus in balloon, dropping gifts to children, pink trim, 5-5/8" h teapot, six cups and saucers, some damage, replaced teapot lid 200.00
11 pcs, blue willow transfer, teapot, creamer, sugar, four 3-3/8" d plates, three cups and saucers, 6-1/4" l platter, most mkd "Made in Occupied Japan," small chips . . 50.00
Cut Glass, vase, 5-3/4" h, trumpet shape, cut allover in hobstars, fans, sawtooth cut rim, American Brilliant Period 110.00
Milk Glass
Basket, cov, emb "Peepers" 185.00
Candleholders, pr, Swirl pattern
Green 60.00
White 35.00
Pattern Glass
Butter Dish, cov, Pennsylvania, dark green, gold trim
. . . . 110.00
Cake Stand, Thistle, 6-1/2" d, 3-1/2" h 75.00
Creamer
Amazon 20.00
Liberty Bell 90.00
Cup, Dahlia, apple green 85.00
Cup and Saucer, Wee Branches 90.00
Dish, Sandwich, lacy, oval, minor damage 60.00
Mug, Wee Branches 30.00
Pitcher, Hobb's Hobnail, cranberry 275.00
Punch Set, Thumbelina, 7 pc set 50.00
Spooner, Sultan, chocolate glass 375.00
Sugar, cov, Rooster, dog finial 250.00
Table Set
Doyle's 500, amber 325.00
Stippled Vine and Beads 350.00
Twin Snowshoes 250.00
Tin
Mug, 2 1/2" h, Little Bo Peep 20.00
Tea Set, dogs and cats, red, blue, and white, marked "Germany," price for 9 pc set 95.00

CHINESE CERAMICS

History: The Chinese pottery tradition has existed for thousands of years. By the 16th century, Chinese ceramic wares were being exported to India, Persia, and Egypt. During the Ming dynasty (1368-1643), earthenwares became more highly developed. The Ch'ien Lung period (1736-1795) of the Ch'ing dynasty marked the golden age of interchange with the West.

Trade between China and the West began in the 16th century when the Portuguese established Macao. The Dutch entered the trade early in the 17th century. With the establishment of the English East India Company, all of Europe sought Chinese-made pottery and porcelain. Styles, shapes, and colors were developed to suit Western tastes, a tradition which continued until the late 19th century.

Fine Oriental ceramics continued to be made into the 20th century, and modern artists enjoy equal fame with older counterparts.

Reference: Gloria and Robert Mascarelli, *Warman's Oriental Antiques*, Wallace-Homestead, 1992; Nancy N. Schiffer, *Imari, Satsuma, and Other Japanese Export Ceramics,* Schiffer Publishing, 1997.

Periodical: *Orientalia Journal*, P.O. Box 94, Little Neck, NY 11363.

Collectors' Club: China Student's Club, 59 Standish Rd., Wellesley, MA 02181.

Museums: Art Institute of Chicago, Chicago, IL; Asian Art Museum of San Francisco, San Francisco, CA; George Walter Vincent Smith Art Museum, Springfield, MA; Morikami Museum & Japanese Gardens, Delray Beach, FL; Pacific Asia Museum, Pasadena, CA.

Additional Listings: Canton; Fitzhugh; Imari; Kutani; Nanking; Rose Medallion; Satsuma.

Candlesticks, pr, Qianlong period 3,300.00
Hat Stand, 11" h, hexagonal, floral piercings, landscape design, blue and white, 19th C 200.00
Figure
    7-1/2" h, pygmy, Tang dynasty. 125.00
    8" h, horse, Tang dynasty 500.00
    9-1/4" h, dancers, Tang dynasty, set of five 650.00
    11" h, horse and rider, Tang dynasty 550.00
    16" h, camel, Tang dynasty 700.00
    20" h, Guanyin, Blanc-de-Chine. 175.00
    21" h, court lady, Tang dynasty 700.00
    23" h, guardian, Tang dynasty 550.00
Fruit Bowl, 7-1/2" d, flowers in baskets, floral sprays, 18th/19th C
. . . . 200.00
Garden Seat, 18-1/4" h, blue and white, chrysanthemum and bird design, China, 19th C, minute glaze chips to top
. . . . .1,250.00
Inkwell, 5-1/4" h, blue glaze, elephant form, hinged neck and brass collar, late 19th C 520.00
Jar, cov, 10" h, Wucai, figural dec, Qing dynasty 375.00
Lamp Base, vase
    12" h, blue and white, flattened ovoid body, painted riverscape dec, electrified, pr 400.00
    12" h, blue and white, pagoda dec, high relief molded deer form handles, pr. 200.00

Mug, mauve, pink, green floral dec, white ground, 1750-1800, $285.

    12" h, Imperial yellow and blue, floral dec, yellow ground, molded fruit form handles, electrified, pr 275.00
    14" h, monochrome turquoise, electrified, pr 250.00
    15" h, orange fu dog dec on white ground, Foo dog handles. 125.00
Low Dish, 7-1/2" d, painted scholar in garden, price for pr
. . . . 150.00
Mantel Garniture, rouge-de-fer dec, 5 pc 3,575.00
Plate, 14" d, central gilt flower, heavily potted, brown tones, imp seal, boxed with extensive inscription, Tamba Ware, 19th/early 20th C 550.00
Platter
    15" l, Thousand Butterfly dec, mid-19th C 400.00
    18-3/4" l, Garden pattern, crest of Clerke or Clarke, motto, in memory of the Victory of King Henry VIII at Battle of Spurs, 1513, drain, c1845-63 . . . . .2,100.00
Punch Bowl
    9" d, elaborate floral and landscape reserves, restored
. . . . 650.00
    9-1/4" d, figural and bird reserves 400.00
Teapot
    6" h, drum form, braided handle, strawberry finial lid, floral sprays, black enamel gilding, late 18th C 450.00
    7-1/2" h, sq form, raised panels, bamboo spout and handle, allover polychrome dec with figures and landscape reserves, restoration to handle, spout, and lid 1,100.00
Topiary, 10" h, aubergine and yellow glazed fruit 150.00
Tureen, 11" l, seated rooster form. 200.00
Warming Dish, 9-3/4" d, Hundred Butterfly, sepia, gilt highlights, 19th C, hairline 350.00
Water Jar, 19" h, stylized dec, pottery. 300.00
Water Pot, 5" l, figural, two boys carrying boat, blue and white, Chia Ching mark, 19th C 375.00

Chinese Export

Bough Pot, 8" h, applied shapes of squirrels among grapes and Famille Rose painted panels, made for the European market, pr 13,800.00

Bowl
   7-3/4" d, cobalt blue border, sepia dec, band border of stars and foliate sprays, center Arabic reserve, gilt highlights
. . . . 225.00
   13-1/2" d, 5" h, blue and white, scalloped edge, inside dec with seven robed men among bamboo trees, center dec with two storks among plants, similar dec on ext. . . 600.00
Brush Pot, 4" h, ivory ground, pierced relief carving of people and pavilions in garden, cash/coin design ground, 19th C
. . . . 200.00
Charger, 13-3/4" d, Armorial, floral spray border, center armorial, gilt highlights, 18th C, gilt and enamel wear, rim chips, glaze wear 750.00
Garden Seat, pr. 17,250.00
Garniture Vases, pr. 7,765.00
Jardiniere, stag form, copper red and cobalt blue. 8,625.00
Mug
   4-3/4" h, 4" w, Mandarian, three vignettes of people in colorful outfits, colorful flowers, blue and white images 590.00
   5-1/4" h, 4" d, colorful bands to top rim, round scenic vignette in black at center of side, interlaced strapped handle
. . . . 400.00
Ornament, 15-1/2" h, stag's head, pr 85,000.00
Plate, 9-1/2" d, Nanking-style border, center polychrome dec reserve of figures in landscape 300.00
Platter, 14-1/2" l, armorial, blue scroll border, 18th C . .2,300.00
Salt Cellar, 3-1/8" l, polychrome and sepia dec, reserves of court figures, birds, and village views, gilt highlights, 18th C
. . . . 460.00
Sauceboat, from DeWitt Clinton NY governor service .1,320.00
Serving Dish, scalloped edge, blue and white, pr 5,750.00
Tea Canister, 4-1/9" h, 4-1/2" d top, blue and white, reserves of figures in landscape, 19th C, hairlines 375.00
Tureen, cov, 14-3/4" l, 7-3/4" h, orange crane and floral dec, orange Foo dog handles and finial, c1775, losses . .4,320.00
Urn, pistol handles, pr 20,700.00
Vase, fish-shape, mounted in ormolu base, French crown "C" tax stamp, 1745-49 . . . . .25,200.00
Vegetable Tureen, cov 4,140.00
Wash Basin, 16" d, 5" h, butterfly, bird, and foliate border, center diapered field, reserves of precious objects, restoration, gilt and enamel wear 250.00
Water Dropper, 9-1/2" h, iron-red and cobalt blue Imari palette foliate designs 115.00

CHINTZ CHINA

History: Chintz china has been produced since the 17th century. The brightly colored exotic patterns produced on fabric imported from India to England during this century was then recreated on ceramics. Early chintz patterns were hand painted and featured large flowers, fantastical birds and widely spaced patterns. The advent of transfer printing resulted in the development of chintz dishes, which could be produced cheaply enough to sell to the masses. By the 1830s, a number of Staffordshire potteries were producing chintzware for everyday use. These early patterns have not yet attracted the interest of most chintz collectors.

Collectors typically want the patterns dating from roughly 1920 until the 1950s. In 1920, A.G. Richardson "Crown Ducal" produced a range of all-over-transfer chintz patterns which were very popular in North America, particularly the East Coast. Patterns such as Florida,

Festival, and Blue Chintz were originally introduced as tea sets and then expanded to full dinner services. Florida is the most popular of the Crown Ducal patterns in North America but Peony has become increasingly popular in the past year or two.

What most collectors consider the first modern chintz was designed by Leonard Grimwade in 1928 and named Marguerite. This pattern was very successful for many years but has never been highly regarded by collectors. Every year at the British Industries Fair, factories vied with each other to introduce new patterns which would catch the buyers' eye. From the late 1920s until the mid-1950s, Royal Winton produced more than 80 chintz patterns. In some cases, the background color was varied and the name changed: Hazel, Spring and Welbeck is the same pattern in different colorways. After the second world war, Royal Winton created more than fifteen new patterns, many of which were more modern looking with large flowers and rich dark burgundy, blue or black backgrounds patterns such as May Festival, Spring Glory and Peony. These patterns have not been very popular with collectors, although other 1950s patterns, such as Florence and Stratford, have become almost as popular as Julia and Welbeck in the past year.

The 1930s were hard times in the Potteries and factories struggled to survive. They copied any successful patterns from any other factories. James Kent Ltd. produced chintzes such as DuBarry, Apple Blossom and Rosalynde. These patterns were sold widely in North America and complete dinner sets still occasionally turn up. The most popular pattern for collectors is the white Hydrangea although Apple Blossom seems to be more and more sought after. Elijah Cotton "Lord Nelson" was another factory which produced large amounts of chintz. Cotton had always been known for the hundreds of utilitarian jugs they produced and they continued to be great producers of institutional ware. The workers at Elijah Cotton were never as skilled as the Grimwades' workers and usually the handles and the spouts of teapots and coffeepots were left undecorated. The shapes are chunky and the pottery thicker than the other factories. Collectors, however, love the Nelson Ware jugs and stacking teapots especially in Black Beauty and Green Tulip.

Although a number of factories produced bone china after World War II, only Shelley Pottery seems to be highly desired by today's collector.

By the late 1950s, young brides didn't want the dishes of their mothers and grandmothers but preferred the clean lines of modern Scandinavian furniture and dishes. Chintz gradually died out by the early 1960s and it was not until the 1990s that collectors began to search for the dishes their mothers had scorned.

References: Eileen Busby, *Royal Winton Porcelain*, The Glass Press Inc., 1998; Linda Eberle and Susan Scott, *Charlton Standard Catalogue of Chintz*, Charlton Press *2nd Edition*, 1997, *3rd Edition*; 1999; Heller/Feljoy, *Chintz by Design*, Chintz International, 1997; Muriel Miller, *Collecting Royal Winton Chintz,* Francis Joseph Publications, 1996, Jo Anne Welch, *Chintz Ceramics*, 2nd Edition, Schiffer Publishing 1998.

Collectors' Clubs: Royal Winton International Collectors' Club, Dancer's End, Northall, Bedfordshire, England LU6 2EU; Royal Winton Collectors' Club, 2 Kareela Road, Baulkham Hills, Australia 2153.

REPRODUCTION ALERT

In the last couple of years, with the rising prices of chintz, both Royal Winton and James Kent have started to reproduce some of their more popular patterns. Royal Winton is reproducing Welbeck, Florence, Summertime and Julia while James Kent has so far reproduced Du Barry and Hydrangea. The Old Chintz Company has bought the Lord Nelson backstamp and there are plans to reproduce some of the Elijah Cotton patterns as well. The new Royal Winton backstamp has a black circle around the original deco backstamp; the new James Kent backstamp includes 100-year anniversary. Contact the factories for current production lists to avoid confusing old and new chintz.

Advisor: Susan Scott.

Elijah Cotton "Lord Nelson"

Cake Plate, tab handles, Black Beauty pattern 250.00
Cup and Saucer
    Rosetime pattern 150.00
    Royal Brocade pattern 75.00
Plate, 8-1/2" sq, Pansy pattern 175.00
Stacking Teapot, totally patterned, Heather pattern . . . 1,695.00
Teapot, cov, six cup, Briar Rose pattern 850.00

Grimwades Royal Winton

Breakfast Set, Royalty pattern 1,800.00
Butter Dish, rect, Ascot shape, Summertime pattern . . . 295.00
Cake Stand, 3 tier, metal handle, Summertime pattern . 425.00
Coffeepot, Perth shape, Fireglow white pattern 1,150.00
Cream and Sugar, Balmoral pattern 225.00
Cream and Sugar, on tray, May Festival pattern 195.00
Cup and Saucer, Bedale pattern 95.00
Hot Water Pot, Countess shape, Welbeck pattern 995.00
Jug, Albans shape 4-1/2", Cotswold pattern 475.00
Plate, 10" sq, Sweet Pea pattern 225.00

Royal Winton, "Julia," salt and pepper on a tray, $395. Photo courtesy Susan Scott.

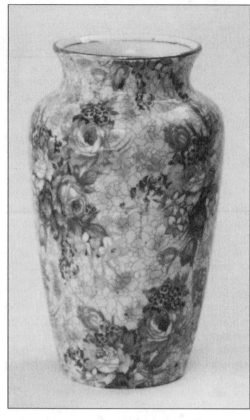

Royal Winton bud vase, "Welbeck," 5", $295. Photo courtesy Susan Scott.

Salt and Pepper, on tray, Chelsea pattern 345.00
Stacking Teapot, Balmoral pattern 1,850.00
Teapot, cov
    Four cup, Albans shape, Eleanor pattern 1,100.00
    One cup, Countess shape, Majestic pattern 795.00
Toast Rack, five bar, Julia pattern 750.00
Vase, Gem shape, Hazel pattern 395.00
Wall Pocket, Nita shape, Evesham pattern 950.00

James Kent Ltd.

Breakfast Set, Apple Blossom pattern 1,200.00
Cream and Sugar, Rosalynde pattern 195.00
Egg Cup Set, four egg cups on tray, Marigold pattern . . 395.00
Mint Sauce, liner, Du Barry pattern 375.00
Nut Dish, 3" sq, Florita pattern 95.00
Plate, 7" round, Rosalynde pattern 135.00
Toast rack, five bar, large, Du Barry pattern 550.00

Midwinter Ltd.

Biscuit Barrel, chrome lid, Brama pattern 350.00
Chop Plate, 11" d, Lorna Doone pattern 225.00

A.G. Richardson "Crown Ducal"

Bowl, 9-1/2" octagonal, Florida pattern 495.00
Breakfast Set, Peony pattern 3,000.00
Cup and Saucer, Pansy pattern 195.00
Plate, 8" d, Ivory Chintz pattern 95.00
Teapot, cov, four cup, Priscilla pattern 495.00

Shelley Potteries Ltd.

Bonbon Dish, tab handles, 4-3/4", Maytime pattern 65.00
Cup and Saucer, Primrose pattern 115.00
Plate, 6" d, Rock Garden pattern 95.00
Teapot, cov, three cup, Melody pattern 875.00

CHRISTMAS ITEMS

History: The celebration of Christmas dates back to Roman times. Several customs associated with modern Christmas celebrations are traced back to early pagan rituals.

Father Christmas, believed to have evolved in Europe in the 7th century, was a combination of the pagan god Thor, who judged and punished the good and bad, and St. Nicholas, the generous Bishop of Myra. Kris Kringle originated in Germany and was brought to America by the Germans and Swiss who settled in Pennsylvania in the late 18th century.

In 1822, Clement C. Moore wrote "A Visit from St. Nicholas" and developed the character of Santa Claus into the one we know today. Thomas Nast did a series of drawings for Harper's Weekly from 1863 until 1886 and further solidified the character and appearance of Santa Claus.

References: Robert Brenner, *Christmas Past*, 3rd ed., Schiffer Publishing, 1996; ——, *Christmas through the Decades*, Schiffer Publishing, 1993; Barbara Fahs Charles and J. R. Taylor, *Dream of Santa,* Gramercy Books, 1992; Beth Dees, *Santa's Guide to Contemporary Christmas Collectibles,* Krause Publications, 1997; Jill Gallina, *Christmas Pins Past and Present*, Collector Books, 1996; George Johnson, *Christmas Ornaments, Lights & Decorations* (1987, 1998 value update), Vol. II (1996), Vol. III (1996), Collector Books; Chris Kirk, *Joy of Christmas Collecting*, L-W Book Sales, 1994; James S. Morrison, *Vintage View of Christmas Past*, Shuman Heritage Press, 1995; Mary Morrison, *Snow Babies, Santas and Elves: Collecting Christmas Bisque Figures*, Schiffer Publishing, 1993; Margaret Schiffer, *Christmas Ornaments: A Festive Study*, Schiffer Publisher, 1984, 1995 value update; Clara Johnson Scroggins, *Silver Christmas Ornaments,* Krause Publications, 1997; Lissa and Dick Smith, *Christmas Collectibles*, Chartwell Books, 1993; Margaret and Kenn Whitmyer, *Christmas Collectibles*, 2nd ed., 1994, 1996 value update, Collector Books.

Collectors' Club: Golden Glow of Christmas Past, 6401 Winsdale St., Golden Valley, MN 55427.

Additional Listings: See *Warman's Americana & Collectibles* for more examples.

Advisors: Lissa Bryan-Smith and Richard M. Smith.

Bank, 4-1/8" h, Santa Claus, Shephard Hardware Co., patent 10/15/1889, some chipping to paint 4,320.00
Book
  Santa Claus Comes to America, written and illus by Caroline Singer and Cyrus Leroy Baldridge, Alfred A. Knopf, New York, 1942 . . . . 30.00
  The Night Before Christmas, advertising give-away for Bush and Bull Co. Dept. Store, Williamsport, PA, 12-3/4" h
. . . . 25.00
  The Night Before Christmas, Clement C. Moore, 8 double page paintings by Grandma Moses, Random House, 1976
. . . . 12.00

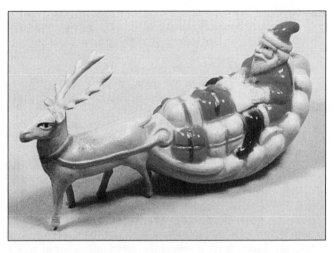

Santa, shell shaped sleigh, reindeer, red and black trim, celluloid, Viscoloid Company, 3-1/2" l, $80. Photo courtesy of Julie Robinson.

The Romance of a Christmas Card, Kate Douglas Wiggin, Hough-Mifflin, 1916, 1st edition, fancy gold trim cover with Christmas card scene 15.00
Watching for Santa Claus, Hurst Co., New York, 1212, 9-1/2" h. 15.00
Booklet, *Christmas Carol by Charles Dickens,* L. L. Stearn's and Sons, 100 pgs, 5" h 7.00
Bubble Light Candoliere, off-white plastic candleholder, holds five candles with bubble lights 35.00
Candy Box, cardboard
  4-1/2" l, 3" h, Christmas Greetings, three carolers, USA
. . . . 5.00
  8" h, Merry Christmas, four sided cornucopia, sleigh, and reindeer over village rooftops, string bail, USA 35.00
Candy Container
  5" h, glass, red Santa climbing into chimney, metal screw-on base, Victory Co., Jeannette, PA. 80.00
  7" h, Santa, fur beard, wire neck 30.00
  7-1/2" h, papier-mâché, Santa, fur beard, red cloth coat
. . . . 70.00
  10" h, Santa, fur beard, toy bag, tree 35.00
  12" h, Santa, fur beard, wire neck, tree 40.00
Clicker, Santa, red, black, white, and blue portrait, black lettering "Washington Park National Bank," 1920s 125.00
Coin Holder, stocking shape, 1st National Bank of Milton, Milton, PA, 6" h 5.00
Feather Tree, 48" h, green goose feather wrapped branches, metal candleholders, round wooden base painted white with green trim, mkd "Germany" 400.00
Figure
  Father Christmas, 8" h, papier-mâché, hollow molded, plaster covered, white coat, black boots, sprinkled with mica
. . . . 300.00
  Nativity, 7" h, composition, mkd "Germany" 15.00
  Reindeer, 1" h, pot metal, mkd "Germany" 18.00
  Santa Claus, cloth, handmade, embroidered facial features, cotton batting stuffing, 1940s. 30.00
  Santa Claus, cotton batting, 3" h, rd, attached to cardboard house, mkd "Japan" 48.00
  Santa Claus, pressed cardboard, 10" h, red felt hat and jacket, black boots 90.00

Greeting Card
  Christmas Greetings, booklet style, emb diecut cover, color litho pictures on pint. pages, Art Lithographic Publishing Co. 20.00
  Merry Christmas, Whitman, dime coin slots, 1950s 5.00
  Sincere Good Wishes, purple pansy with green leaves, greeting inside, Raphael Tuck & Sons, 1892 . . . . 8.00
House, cardboard
  2" x 2", covered with mica and/or glitter, wire loop on top, mkd "Czechoslovakia" 8.00
  4" x 5", cardboard base and fence, sponge trees, mkd "USA" 12.00
  7" x 8", street scene, four houses and a church, covered with mica, mkd "Germany" 30.00
House, log, 3" x 4", wood roof covered with mica, red wooden chimney, mkd "Germany" 15.00
Lantern, 8" h, four sided, peaked top, wire bail, metal candleholder in base, black cardboard colored tissue paper scenes, 1940s 30.00
Ornament
  Angel, 4" h, wax over composition, human hair wig, spun glass wings, cloth dress, Germany 60.00
  Ball, 2" d, glass, silvered, any color 3.00
  Bulldog, 3" h, Dresden, three-dimensional, mkd "Germany" 250.00
  Camel, 4" h, cotton batting, Germany 165.00
  Drummer Boy, 3" h, wax, hollow, metal ring hanger, USA 5.00
  Father Christmas, 10" h, chromolitho, blue robe, riding donkey, tinsel trim 30.00
  Mandolin, 5" h, glass, unsilvered, wrapped in lametta and tinsel 45.00
  Pear, 3" h, cotton batting, mica highlights, paper leaf, wire hanger, Japan 15.00
  Santa Claus in Chimney, 4" h, glass, multicolored, Germany 75.00
  Tree Top, 11" h, three spheres staked with small clear glass balls, silvered, lametta and tinsel trim, attached to blown glass hooks 95.00
Pin, celluloid on straight pin, "Gifts for Everybody," cut-out Santa figure, C. K. Whitner & Co., Reading, PA, 1-1/2" h . . . 15.00
Pinback Button
  Christmas Village, multicolored Santa portrait, white ground, red lettering, Decatur, IL, c1940 . . . . 40.00
  McAllister's, multicolored image of Santa eyeing Christmas stocks, two tiny lighted candles, black lettering "Meet Me At McAllister's," early 1900s 125.00
  The Santa Claus Club, multicolored, early 1900s . . . 575.00
  Wanamaker's Santa, multicolored, gold lettering "You Will Find Me At Wanamaker's," early 1900s 75.00
Post Card, Germany, May Your Christmas Be Merry and Gay, photo card, sepia tones, Father Christmas with fur cap peeking between two large wooden doors 20.00
Nativity Set, eight hand carved pieces, hand painted, orig box mkd ""Made by the Peasants of the Tyrolean Alps" . . 30.00
Putz
  Brush Tree, 6" h, green, mica covered branches, wooden base 10.00
  Chick, 1" h, composition, metal feet, Germany 10.00
  Christmas Tree Fence, cast iron, silver, ornate gold trim, fifteen 10" segments with posts, Germany 600.00
  Cow, 3/4" h, brown and white, penny wooden type, Nuremberg 10.00
  Dog, 1-1/2" h, standing, composition, wooden legs, Germany 20.00
  Elves, 1" h, various poses, set of six, penny wooden type, Nuremberg, mkd "Germany" 65.00

Giraffe, 5-1/2" h, composition, wooden legs and horns, cloth ears and tail, yellow with brown spots, Germany 55.00
Horse, 5" h, rubber, brown 10.00
Turkey, 2" h, celluloid, metal legs, blue 10.00
Rug, 27" x 42", hand hooked, half moon-shape, Santa Claus in sleigh, basket of toys on roof top, chimney and moon, light blue border with mistletoe, hooked by Florentine Heath, Searsport, ME 275.00
Santa, 7-7/8" h, electrified, papier-mâché head, hands, and feet, fur beard, red flannel outfit, calico bag, feather tree, wired candles and lantern, early 20th C 635.00

CIGAR CUTTERS

History: Counter and pocket cigar cutters were used at the end of the 19th and the beginning of the 20th centuries. They were a popular form of advertising. Pocket-type cigar cutters often were a fine piece of jewelry that attached to a watch chain.

Reference: Jerry Terranova and Douglas Congdon-Martin, *Antique Cigar Cutters and Lighters*, Schiffer Publishing, 1996; ——, *Great Cigar Stuff for Collectors,* Schiffer Publishing, 1997.

3" h, front emb "Smoke Country Gentleman 5 cent. American Thoroughbred 10 cents, Bennett, Sloan & Co., N.Y.," manuf by Brunhoff Mfg. Co. 150.00
3-1/4" h, nickel plated cast iron
  Front emb "R. G. Sullivan's 7-20-4-10 cent cigar," manuf by Brunhoff Mfg. Co., Pat'd May 19, 1891, orig condition, light surface rust and wear 210.00
  Top emb "Smoke Dona Marina Mexican Cigars - Highest Grade Imported," clockwork mechanism, manuf by Erie Specialty Co., Pat'd 1889, professionally restored 325.00
3-1/2" h, cast iron
  Emb fancy filigree on front and base, front lever operates cutter, spring missing 200.00
  Nickel plated, top emb "Automatic Cigar Tip Cutter, Pat'd in U.S. and European Countries," clockwork mechanism, mounted on wood base 415.00
  Nickel plated, top emb "Hermann cent cigar, Stoddard, Gilbert & Co.," image of elf, clockwork mechanism, missing base plate, restored 450.00
  Top emb "We Sell the J. U. Divilbiss Co.'s Celebrated Fine Cigars, Try Them," clockwork mechanism, c1889 . . 450.00
3-3/4" h
  Cast iron, base, reverse painting on glass adv "Mi Favorita Cigars," cameo of lady, clockwork mechanism, manuf by Brunhoff Mfg. Co., some loss to reverse painting . . 400.00
  Nickel plated cast iron, adv "Flor De Melba The Cigar Superior," highly dec patter on base, some paint loss to revere glass on sign, worn nickel plating 500.00
4-3/4" h, marquee emb "Waitt & Bond's Blackstone, Leads the World," professionally restored with copper tiger striping 300.00
5" h, reverse painting on glass sign on front reads "B-Y's and buy Y-B's," cutter operates mechanically when customer pulls down lever in front, manuf by Brunhoff Mfg. Co. 450.00
5-1/2" h, cast iron machine emb "Havana High Grade Cigars," paper picture showing open box of cigars, one wooden match dispensed with cigar cut with lever action 850.00
6" h, front emb with shield adv "Kenteria Hanna Cigars Kent's Extra 5 cents, Mac's Best, I. S. Kent - McCathy Co., Jackson-

ville, IL," cast iron top and front, Pat'd Aug 7, 1906, missing base plate 500.00

7" h, cast iron body, emb with embellishments on all four sides of body, shield with stars and stripes on top, Yankee, Pat'd July 13, 1909, also dispensed one lit match at a time, top of shield copper flashed 700.00

7-1/2" h

Metal marquee, figural cast iron cigar center, engraved "The New York Specials, Havana Cigars, Bondy & Lederer, N.Y. Makers," manuf by Brunhoff Mfg. Co. 750.00

Table top, detailed frame with painting of cows, farm house, stream, and wild life, frame titled "H. A. Schneck Allentown Cigars of Quality Maker," minor rusting 1,300.00

8" h, cast iron

Figural marquee emb "Above the Average" atop the world, perimeter and cigar copper plated, rest painted, manuf by Brunhoff Mfg. Co. 1,200.00

Figural, portly man singing from hymnal, man mouth is cutter, operated by moving left arm, cast iron base, pot metal figure, orig paint, wear 600.00

8-1/2" h, 7" w, donkey, cast iron, cigar cutter and trade stimulator, overall wear to paint, 1890s 1,250.00

8-3/4" h, nickel plated cast iron, shape of customer's cigar determined whether left round hole or right oval hole was used, two bulbous handles mechanically operate cutter, marquee emb "Declarencia Havana Cigars" with trademark, ornate base also ashtray, manuf by Brunhoff Mfg. Co. 900.00

9" h, figural cast iron, marquee emb "Havana Cigars of Excellent Quality" around paper picture of H. W. Longfellow, emb base also ashtray, manuf by Brunhoff Mfg. Co. 750.00

10" h, figural, giraffe shape, brass, holder for matches and butting tray on base, raise giraffe's neck up to cut cigar, wear on neck 225.00

11" h, figural, parrot shape, brass wings, raise head up to cut cigar 350.00

19-1/2" h, combination cigar cutter and cigar lighter, mail box shape with lamp post and fence post, lever on side of cast iron chest opens cigar cutter, cast lighter, finials atop fence posts become wicks, could be lit from lantern at top of lamp post. 375.00

CIGAR STORE FIGURES

History: Cigar store figures were familiar sights in front of cigar stores and tobacco shops starting about 1840. Figural themes included Sir Walter Raleigh, sailors, Punch figures, and ladies, with Indians being the most popular.

Most figures were carved in wood, although some also were made in metal and papier-mâché for a short time. Most carvings were life size or slightly smaller and were brightly painted. A coating of tar acted as a preservative against the weather. Of the few surviving figures, only a small number have their original bases. Most replacements were necessary because of years of wear and usage by dogs.

Use of figures declined when local ordinances were passed requiring shopkeepers to move the figures inside at night. This soon became too much trouble, and other forms of advertising developed.

References: Edwin O. Christensen, *Early American Wood Carvings*, Dover Publications, out of print; A.W. Pendergast and W. Porter Ware, *Cigar Store Figures*, The Lightner Publishing Corp., out of print.

Declarencia, nickel plated cast iron, counter top, emb name and trademark, manuf by Brunhoff Mfg. Co., 8-3/4" h, $900. Photo courtesy of James D. Julia, Inc.

Indian Princess, mkd "Kaspar," carved headdress, beads, fluted details on sleeves and hem, old repairs, weathered surface, modern plinth base, 72-1/2" h, $25,850. Photo courtesy of Garth's Auctions, Inc.

Counter-top, painted black, except feathers, possible repaint
. . . . .5,500.00
Indian, standing
   65" h, full costume, holding hands out, sq base with four iron
      wheels, repainted. 2,600.00
   69" h, full headdress with 11 feathers, painted red, green, and
      cream, base reads "Cigars 5 Cents" 450.00
   70" h, polychrome paint over gesso over carved wood, full fig-
      ured Indian with ""Illinois" stamped on back, one cigar bro-
      ken. 2,240.00
   77-1/2" h, brightly painted, full dress 29,900.00
Princess, carved and painted, muted polychrome dec
. . . . .29,900.00
Punch Figure, carved and painted pine, inscribed "Cigars" on
   front and "Tobacco" on sides, America, 1850-75
. . . . .107,000.00
Squaw, 57-1/2" h, carved and painted, holding tobacco leaf in
   left hand 15,000.00

CINNABAR

History: Cinnabar, a ware made of numerous layers of a heavy mercuric sulfide, often is referred to as vermilion because of the red hue of most pieces. It was carved into boxes, buttons, snuff bottles, and vases. The best examples were made in China.

Bowl, cov, 13" d, shallow 715.00
Box, cov, 9-3/4" sq, carved cinnabar lacquer, Chinese, 18th C,
   pr 20,700.00
Cabinet, 10-1/2" w, 22" d, 5" h, upper case of staggered shelves,
   two short drawers, pair of cupboard doors, gilt landscapes,
   20th C. 475.00
Cup, 4-1/2" d, dragon handles, c1900 . . . . 225.00
Dish, 10-3/4" d, deeply carved, leafy melon vines, black lacquer
   base 900.00
Incense Burner, pagoda type, Taoist mask design, c1900
. . . . .1,300.00
Jar, 4" h, flowering plants, carved floral scrolls, diaper ground,
   domed cov, gilt metal rim and finial, price for pr. 150.00
Plate, 12 3/4" d, double dragon design. 375.00
Snuff Bottle, cylindrical, carved figures in landscape, chrysanthemum borders and top, metal mounted base with gold
   four-character Ch'ien Lung mark on black ground . . . 250.00
Stand, 14-1/2" l, 30" h, sq top, lacquered mountain scenes,
   brass pan, Chinese, c1900. . . . . 240.00
Tray, 15" l, bird and flower scene, reddish brown 625.00
Vase, 10-1/2" h, ovoid, long cylindrical neck, carved lotus flowers and leaves, high foot rim with scrolling floral band, price
   for pr. 295.00

CLEWELL POTTERY

History: Charles Walter Clewell was first a metal worker and secondarily a potter. In the early 1900s, he opened a small shop in Canton, Ohio, to produce metal overlay pottery.

Metal on pottery was not a new idea, but Clewell was perhaps the first to completely mask the ceramic body with copper, brass or "silvered" or "bronzed" metals. One result was a product whose patina added to the character of the piece over time.

Since Clewell operated on a small scale with little outside assistance, only a limited quantity of his artwork exists. He retired at the age of 79 in 1955, choosing not to reveal his technique to anyone else.

Box, cov, floral carvings, red, ground, black int., 2" x 3-3/4" x 5-5/8", $90.

Marks: Most of the wares are marked with a simple incised "Clewell" along with a code number. Because Clewell used pottery blanks from other firms, the names "Owens" or "Weller" are sometimes found.

References: Paul Evans, *Art Pottery of the United States*, 2nd ed., Feingold & Lewis Publishing Corp., 1987; Ralph and Terry Kovel, *Kovels' American Art Pottery*, Crown Publishers, 1993.

Museum: John Besser Museum, Alpena, MI.

Ashtray, 3-1/4" d, copper, circular imp mark "Clewell, Canton,
   OH," 1922. . . . . 190.00
Bowl, 4-1/2" d, riveted overlay finish, sgd, circular imp seal
   "Clewell Coppers". 215.00
Jardiniere, copper-clad pottery
   6-1/2" d, 5-1/4" h, verdigris and bronze patina, incised
      "Clewell 418-2-9" 950.00

Vase, copper-clad, squat base, verdigris patina, incised "Clewell 5-2-6," 10-1/4" h, 4-1/2" d, $1,700. Photo courtesy of David Rago Auctions, Inc.

12" d, 9" h, uneven patina, incised mark 450.00
Vase, copper-clad pottery
  5" h, 4-1/4" d, spherical, fine verdigris and bronze patina, incised "Clewell 300-25" 1,100.00
  6" h, 3" d, ovoid, fine verdigris patina, incised "Clewell 331-6" 475.00
  7-1/2" h, 3-1/2" d, classic shape, fine verdigris and bronze patina, incised "Clewell 351-24" 1,900.00
  8-1/2" h, 7" d, classic shape, fine brown to verdigris patina, incised "Lcewell/463-26" 1,800.00
  8-3/4" h, 7" d, classic shape, fine verdigris patina, incised "Clewell 323-6" 1,100.00
  10" h, 3-1/2" d, faceted, verdigris and bronze patina, incised "Clewell 439-2-6" 2,4000.00
  10" h, 5" d, flat shoulder, fine verdigris patina, unmarked 1,000.00
  10-1/4" h, 4-1/2" d, squatty base, fine verdigris patina, incised "Clewell 5-2-6" 1,700.00
  11" h, bulbous shoulder, orig orange, green and blue patina, incised "Clewell 272-2-6" 1,300.00
  11-1/2" h, orig patina, incised mark 375.00
  11-1/2" h, orig patina, orange, green, and blue drip effect, sgd "Clewell 302-2-6" 1,300.00
  12" h, exceptional orig patina 4,750.00
  19" h, orig patina, orange, green, and blue, sgd "Clewell 430-2-6" 6,000.00

CLARICE CLIFF

History: Clarice Cliff, born on Jan. 20, 1899, in Tunstall, Staffordshire, England, was one of the major pottery designers of the 20th century. At the age of thirteen, she left school and went to Lingard, Webster & Company where she learned freehand painting. In 1916 Cliff was employed at A. J. Wilkinson's Royal Staffordshire Pottery, Burslem. She supplemented her in-house training by attending a local school of art in the evening.

In 1927, her employer sent her to study sculpture for a few months at the Royal College of Art in London. Upon returning, she was placed in charge of a small team of female painters at the Newport Pottery, taken over by Wilkinson in 1920. Cliff designed a series of decorative motifs, which were marketed as "Bizarre Ware" at the 1928 British Industries Fair.

Throughout the 1930s, Cliff added new shapes and designs to the line. Her inspiration came from art magazines, books on gardening, and plants and flowers. Cliff and her Bizarre Girls gave painting demonstrations in the stores of leading English retailers. The popularity of the line increased.

World War II halted production. When the war ended, the hand painting of china was not resumed. In 1964, Midwinter bought the Wilkinson and Newport firms.

The original names for some patterns have not survived. It is safe to rely on the handwritten or transfer-printed name on the base. The Newport pattern books in the Wilkinson's archives at the Hanley Library also are helpful.

Since 1999 marks the centenary of Clarice Cliff's birth, there are several major exhibitions of her work planned. Christie's South Kensington, in London, is holding three Clarice Cliff auctions this year. They now include a section on the Wedgwood Reproductions from 1992 and later.

Marks: In the summer of 1985, Midwinters produced a series of limited-edition reproductions to honor Clarice Cliff. They are clearly marked "1985" and contain a special amalgamated backstamp.

References: Susan and Al Bagdade, *Warman's English & Continental Pottery & Porcelain*, 3rd Edition, Krause Publications, 1998; Richard Green and Des Jones, *Rich Designs of Clarice Cliff*, published by authors, 1995 (available from Carole A. Berk, Ltd, 8020 Norfolk Ave., Bethesda, MD 20814); Leonard R. Griffin, *The Fantastic Flowers of Clarice Cliff,* Pavilion Books, 1998; Leonard R. Griffin and Susan Pear Meisel, *Clarice Cliff*, Harry N. Abrams, 1994; Howard and Pat Watson, *Clarice Cliff Price Guide*, Francis-Joseph Books, 1995.

Collectors' Club: Clarice Cliff Collector's Club, Fantasque House, Tennis Drive, The Park, Nottingham, NG7 1AE, England.

Advisor: Susan Scott.

REPRODUCTION ALERT

In 1986, fake *Lotus* vases appeared in London and quickly spread worldwide. Very poor painting and patchy, uneven toffee-colored honey glaze are the clues to spotting them. Collectors also must be alert to marked pieces on which patterns were added to originally plain ground.

Notes: Bizarre and Fantasque are not patterns. Rather, they indicate the time frame of production—Bizarre being used from 1928 to 1937 and Fantasque from 1929 to 1934.

Cup and Saucer
  Bizarre, conical shape, Orange Autumn, printed factory marks 425.00
  Fantasque Bizarre, Pastel Melon, printed factory marks 550.00

Lotus jug, Fantasque Bizarre, "Melon," 12" h, $2,875. Photo courtesy Christie's, South Kensington.

Conical sugar, Fantasque Bizarre, 5-1/2", $3,500. Photo courtesy Christie's South Kensington.

Honey Pot
  3-3/4" h, Bizarre, Orange Roof Cottage, printed factory marks
    . . . . .1,565.00
  4" h, Beehive, Crocus, printed factory marks 585.00
Lotus Jug
  11-1/2" h, Fantasque Bizarre, twin handles, Autumn between
    orange bands 3,125.00
  12" h, Bizarre, single-handle, Viscaria, printed factory marks
    . . . . .1,475.00
Plate, Fantasque Bizarre
  7" d, Red Gardenia inside orange and yellow bands, printed
    factory marks 625.00
  9" d, House & Bridge inside orange, yellow, and black bands,
    printed factory marks 1,465.00
  10" d, Windbells inside green, yellow, and orange bands,
    printed factory marks 1,270.00
Preserve, 4-1/4" h, Bon Jour shape, Rhodanthe, printed factory
    marks 395.00
Sugar Shifter
  5" h, Bizarre, Bon Jour shape, Blue Firs, printed factory
    marks 3,125.00
  5" h, Bizarre, Lynton shape, Newlyn, printed factory marks
    . . . . 785.00
  5" h, Bon Jour Shape, Coral First, printed factory marks
    . . . . .1,750.00
  5-1/2" h, Bizarre, Conical, Mountain, printed factory marks
    . . . . .3,715.00
Vase
  2" h, miniature, ovoid, Sliced Fruit, between yellow and or-
    ange bands, printed factory marks. 585.00
  6" h, Original Bizarre, shape 186, band of triangles in red,
    blue, and yellow between red and blue bands, printed fac-
    tory marks 780.00
  8" h, Bizarre, shape 358, Appliqué Avignon between orange
    and black bands, printed and painted marks 3,500.00
  8" h, Fantasque Bizarre, shape 360, Floreat between yellow
    and orange bands, printed factory marks 1,175.00
Zodiac Sign, 6-3/4" d, star shape, modeled in low relief, "Pisces"
    . . . . 875.00

Wedgwood Reproductions

Bowl, 7" d, conical, Tennis, orig box with certificate 89/250
    . . . . 875.00

Figure, Age of Jazz, double dancer, orig box with certificate
    26/150 . . . . 700.00
Sugar Shifter, conical, May Avenue, orig box with certificate
    444/500 . . . . 400.00
Vase, 12" h, Meiping, Solitude, orig box with certificate 142/250
    . . . . 875.00

CLIFTON POTTERY

History: The Clifton Art Pottery, Newark, New Jersey, was established by William A. Long, once associated with Lonhuda Pottery, and Fred Tschirner, a chemist.

Production consisted of two major lines: Crystal Patina, which resembled true porcelain with a subdued crystal-like glaze, and Indian Ware or Western Influence, an adaptation of the American Indians' unglazed and decorated pottery with a high-glazed black interior. Other lines included Robin's-Egg Blue and Tirrube. Robin's-Egg Blue is a variation of the crystal patina line but in blue-green instead of straw-colored hues and with a less-prominent crushed-crystal effect in the glaze. Tirrube, which is often artist signed, features brightly colored, slip-decorated flowers on a terra-cotta ground.

Marks: Marks are incised or impressed. Early pieces may be dated and impressed with a shape number. Indian wares are identified by tribes.

References: Paul Evans, *Art Pottery of the United States*, 2nd ed., Feingold & Lewis Publishing Corp., 1987; Ralph and Terry Kovel, *Kovels' American Art Pottery*, Crown Publishers, 1993.

Biscuit Jar, cov, 7" h, 4-1/4" d, gray-brown ground, enameled
    running ostrich and stork, florals, bail handle 300.00

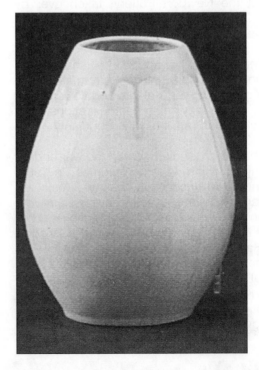

Vase, Crystal Patina, ovoid, ochre glaze dripping over golden micro-crystalline ground, incised mark and "1906," 8-1/2" h, 6" w, $350. Photo courtesy of David Rago Auctions, Inc.

Cruet, 5-3/4" h, hp swallows, blue ground, orig stopper . . 45.00

Decanter, 11-1/2" h, rose shading to deep rose, purple flowers, gilt butterfly on neck, applied handle, marbleized rose and white stopper 150.00

Jardiniere, 8-1/2" h, 11" d, Four Mile Ruin, Arizona, incised and painted motif, buff and black on brown ground, imp mark and incised inscription, hairline to rim 400.00

Sweetmeat Jar, 4" h, hp ducks and cranes, robin's egg blue ground, cow finial 375.00

Teapot, 6" h, brown and black geometric design 200.00

Vase, 8-1/2" h, 5" d, bottle shape, Crystal Patina, incised "Clifton" and dates 1906 and 1907, pr 450.00

CLOCKS

History: The sundial was the first man-made device for measuring time. Its basic disadvantage is well expressed by the saying: "Do like the sundial, count only the sunny days."

Needing greater dependability, man developed the water clock, oil clock, and the sand clock, respectively. All these clocks worked on the same principle—time was measured by the amount of material passing from one container to another.

The wheel clock was the next major step. These clocks can be traced back to the 13th century. Many improvements on the basic wheel clock were made and continue to be made. In 1934 the quartz crystal movement was introduced.

The recently invented atomic clock, which measures time by radiation frequency, only varies one second in a thousand years.

References: Robert W. D. Ball, *American Shelf and Wall Clocks*, Schiffer Publishing, 1992; Philip Collins, *Pastime*, Chronicle Books, 1993; Brian Loomes, *Painted Dial Clocks*, Antique Collector's Club, 1994; Tran Duy Ly, *Seth Thomas Clocks & Movements*, Arlington Book Co., 1996; Derek Roberts, *Carriage and Other Traveling Clocks*, Schiffer Publishing, 1993; Robert and Harriet Swedberg, *Price Guide to Antique Clocks*, Krause Publications, 1998; John Ware Willard, *Simon Willard and His Clocks*, Dover Publications, n.d.

Periodicals: *Clocks*, 4314 W 238th St., Torrance, CA 90505.

Collectors' Club: National Association of Watch and Clock Collectors, Inc., 514 Poplar St, Columbia, PA 17512.

Museums: American Clock & Watch Museum, Bristol, CT; Greensboro Clock Museum, Greensboro, NC; National Association of Watch and Clock Collectors Museum, Columbia, PA; National Museum of American History, Washington, DC; Old Clock Museum, Pharr, TX; The Time Museum, Rockford, IL; Willard House & Clock Museum, Grafton, MA.

Notes: Identifying the proper model name for a clock is critical in establishing price. Condition of the works also is a critical factor. Examine the works to see how many original parts remain. If repairs are needed, try to include this in your estimate of purchase price. Few clocks are purchased purely for decorative value.

Advertising

Calumet Baking Powder, Time to Buy Best By Test, Regulator, Sessions, oak case, 38-1/2" h 400.00

Chevrolet, trademark from PA dealership, neon, 19" d 550.00

Chew Friendship Cut Plug, face of man with moving mouth, chewing Friendship Tobacco, patent March 2, 1886, 4" h 900.00

Ever-Ready Safety Razors, tin litho, man shaving in center of face, some scattered rust and scuffs, 17-3/4" h, 12-1/2" 1,550.00

Ford, octagonal, center trademark, neon, 18" d 650.00

Hire's Root Beer, "Drink Hires Root Beer with Root Bark Herbs," light-up, 15" d 250.00

Philadelphia Light and Electric, image of Reddy Kilowatt, Westclox alarm, 5" d 350.00

Wolf's Head Motor Oil, rect, shows oil can and round clock, outlined in pink neon, 19" h, 30" l 1,500.00

Alarm

Attleboro, 36 hour, nickel plated case, owl dec, 9" h . . 75.00

Bradley, brass, double bells, Germany 40.00

Champion, 30 hour, American movement, metal frame, ornamental feet, 9" h 75.00

New Haven, c1900, 30 hour, SP case, perfume bottle shape, beveled glass mirror, removable cut glass scent bottle, beaded handle 185.00

Thomas, Seth 1919, one day time and alarm movement, second bit, metal case, 10 1/4" h 50.00

Animated, The Bartender, Roosevelt 145.00

Automation, George III, 3rd quarter 18th C, bracket, gilt bronze mounted mahogany, quarter striking, made by Thomas Gardner, triple fusee, striking nest of eight bells, elaborately engraved backplate, dial with dials for strike/silent and chime/not chime and date aperture, arch with automation of blacksmith's shop, domed case fitted with figural and foliate mounts, ogee bracket feet, 20" h, 14-1/2" w, 9" d 18,700.00

Advertising, Ever-Ready Razor, emb tin, jovial man shaving, 8 day clock, 17-1/2" x 12-1/2", $1,800. Photo courtesy of James D. Julia, Inc.

Blinking Eye, figural, owl, unknown maker, c1920, nickel plated white metal front, green eyes, 30 hour level movement, hardwood case, paper dial, nickel plated bezel, beveled glass, 6-1/2" h 375.00

Boat, Seth Thomas, Thomaston, CT, 1880, nickel plated brass case, painted dial, seconds indicator, 8 day double wind movement with lever escapement, 6-1/4" d 100.00

Bracket

George III, signed

John Ferry, London, c1770, ebonized and brass mounted, chiming and quarter striking, inverted bell top, pierced spandrels and dial in each for jig/minuet, engraved backplate and nest of eight bells, 20" h, 13-1/2" w 5,465.00

Steph. Rimbault, London, gilt metal mounts, ebonized, etched backplate, date aperture, phases of moon, strike/silent and pendulum adjustment, nest of four bells, 19" h, restorations 4,890.00

Regency, Bennett & Co., Norwich, c1810, brass inlaid and gilt bronze mounted mahogany, dial and backplate sgd, oak leaf spandrels, case inlaid with scrolls, gadrooned bun feet, 17" h, chips 4,325.00

Regency, London, c1800, mahogany, painted dial, double fusee movement, hour strike with repeat lever, painted face and openwork brass panels, 14" h, minor losses 1,380.00

Tiffany & Co., bronze, stepped rect shaped top, four acorn finials, cast foliate frieze, four capitals with reeded columns, shaped and foliate cast base, beveled glass door and panels, circular face dial with Roman numerals, mkd "Famiel Marti Medaille…Paris 1900, Tiffany & Co."13" h 600.00

Calendar, parlor, Ithaca Clock Co., Ithaca, NY, c1875, walnut case with fine carved dec, black and silver hour dial, glass silver calendar dial, cut glass pendulum bob, maker's label, 10-1/4" w, 5-1/4" d, 20-1/2" h 1,800.00

Carriage

French, oval, brass, four beveled glass panels, fine cut flowers in border to sides, top oval glass panels initialed "M.E.H.," dial painted with woman and cupid, decorative D-shaped handle on top, 5-1/2" h 1,150.00

New Haven Clock Co., gilded brass case, beveled glass, gold repaint to case, orig pendulum and key, 11-1/2" h 315.00

Garniture, 3 pc

Louis XV/XVI, c1895, porcelain, ormolu and gilt metal mounted, painted figures and portraits, foliate and masks mounts, pr of conforming candlesticks, 16-1/2" h 1,035.00

Louis XVI Style, marble and ormolu, works stamped "L. P. Japy & Cie," dial sgd "R. Moyson," 16 1/2" h, pr of three light candelabra 750.00

Gaslight, American, 1900, cast brass bezel and feet, 30 hour lever movement, milk glass shade, 5 3/4" d 175.00

Gravity

American, c1925, brass case, powered by weight of clock movement descending along two posts, lifting movement back winds the clock for another 24 hours, marked "Patented 8/2/21," 10-1/4" h 200.00

French, c1940, retailed by Shreve, Crump & Low, Boston, powered by the fall of the movement along brass rails, reminding accomplished by lifting the movement back to the top of rails, mahogany case, turned columns and brass finials, 30 hour movement, porcelain dial, polished stone drum case, 17" h. 800.00

Kitchen, New Haven Clock Co., c1930, white painted case, 8 day time movement, 1-3/4" h 65.00

Mantel

Brown, J. C., Bristol, CT, mid 19th C, carved rosewood, ripple molded gilt dec rect case, glazed circular molded bezel opening, white painted dial showing balance wheel of lever movement, inscribed "J. C. Brown Bristol Co. U.S.," 8-1/4" h, 6" w, 2-1/2" d 2,990.00

Eastlake, mahogany, Welch Mfg. Co., Forestville, CT, paper dial with Roman numerals, flower-painted glazed door, pierced crest, plinth base, 22-3/4" h 120.00

Empire Revival, late 19th C, bronze and black patinated metal, winged horse finial, touch-form stiles, case with mount of Apollo driving chariot, paw feet, 20" h 1,610.00

English, Regency, early 19th C, gilt bronze and white marble, retailed by Morice Cornhill, London, glass case, no pendulum, crack to case, 7-5/8" h 1,725.00

Figural, woman playing violin, cherub holding music, round clock dial with enamel flowers, red marble base, short ormolu feet, 20" w, 6-1/2" d, 16-1/2" h 500.00

French, Classical style, c1825, ebonized ormolu mounted, circular brass dial framed by scrolled bezel, housed in case of four columns on stepped base, pendulum emb with American eagle and shield motif, 9-3/8" w, 5-1/2" d, 17-1/4" h. 850.00

French, cloisonné, bronze, green onyx, and glass, c1900, mercury filled pendulum and foliate enamel borders, 11" h 500.00

French, Martin Baskett & Cie., Paris, late 19th C, fruitwood inlaid, sliding beveled glass panel, enamel face, chips around winding holes, minor damage 980.00

French, Louis XVI-style, 19th C, gilt-spelter, circular dial with Roman numerals, drum case, base with lady in 18th C costume, 10-1/2" h. 325.00

French, Sevres-style, gilt metal and porcelain, bird-form finial, foliate molded metal mounts, enamel dial painted with cherub, pink ground, 20" h. 460.00

French, S. Marti Medaille d'or Paris 1900, gilt bronze, porcelain face mounted in drum case, top with large bank of gilt bronze clouds with angel blowing trumpet, putto holding scroll inscribed "Raphael, Poussin, Montesquieu, Michelange" above dial, 22-1/4" h. 1,265.00

New Haven Clock Co., French Empire style, cast iron and cast metal, bronze finish, brass works, porcelain dial mkd "New Haven Clock Co.," wear, damage, chips to beveled glass, 15-1/2" h, 20" l. 500.00

Royal Bonn-Style, Germany, late 19th/early 20th C, porcelain, enamel and gilt dec, dark blue ground, scrolled floral relief, molded front hoof feet, 15-1/2" h 1,035.00

Night Light, Standard Novelty Co., NY, nickel plated case, 30 hour lever Ansonia movement, revolving milk glass dome, 6" h. 225.00

Paperweight, E. N. Welch, Bristol, CT, 1860, Briggs Rotary Patent, rotary escapement mounted on turned wood base, cast feet, orig glass dome, nickel plated pendulum ball, 8" h 300.00

Pillar and Scroll, shelf, Eli Terry

Mahogany and curly maple refinished case with mahogany veneer, wooden works, painted wooden face and weights, pendulum, and key, paper label "Eli Terry, Plymouth Hollow, Connecticut," orig reverse glass painting very worn and flaking, replaced brass finials, repairs to case, 31-1/4" h 2,000.00

Mahogany, Federal, c1822, miniature, swan's neck cresting above glazed door with eglomise tablet showing classical building, white painted gilt dec wooden dial, thirty-hour wooden weight driven movement, case with freestanding turned columns, cutout feet, old refinish, 22-1/2" h, 13-1/2" w, 4" d 7,475.00

Regulator, jeweler's, standing, carved mahogany case, large door fitted with dome top beveled edge glass pane, large enameled brass ring supporting large brass pendulum, 66" h, 27-1/2" w, 10" d 2,000.00

Shelf

Ansonia, Victorian, walnut case, old finish, brass works mkd "The King Clock by Ansonia," orig glass with gold enameling, missing 3 medallions, loose finial, 23-1/2" h . . . 250.00

Atkins and Downs

Eight day triple, reverse painted glass with buildings, pendulum window and split columns, middle section with mirror and full columns, top section with dec dial, split columns, top crest with spread eagle, most of orig label remains, 38" h, 17" w, 6" d 450.00

Reverse painted portrait of Henry Clay, stenciled top crest, half columns, orig paper label, 32" h, 16-1/4" w, 4-1/2" d 800.00

Botsford's Improved Patent Timepiece, Coe & Co. 52 Dey St., New York, papier-mâché, scrolled front, gilt, polychrome embellishments, mother of pearl floral designs, circular enamel dial inscribed "Saml. S. Spencer," lever spring-driven movement, mounted on dec oval base, brass ball feet, glass dome, 11" h 1,265.00

Shelf, walnut case, worn finish, traces of gilding, incised carved detail, brass works, blue and white enameled face mkd "Tiffany & Comp. New York," pendulum and key, 20" h, $935. Photo courtesy of Garth's Auctions, Inc.

Classical, Norris North, Torrington, CT, c1825, mahogany, flat cornice above glazed door, eglomise tablet of young woman flanked by engaged black paint stenciled columns, polychrome and gilt white painted dial, thirty-hour wooden weight driven movement, 23-3/4" h, 13-1/2" w, 5-1/4" d 4,900.00

Empire, mahogany veneer, ebonized and stencil gilded pilasters and crest, wooden works with weights, key, and pendulum, very worn paper label "William Orion & Co.," door with mirror in base, replaced reverse painted glass in middle section, finials missing, some veneer damage and repair 350.00

Federal, New England, early 19th C, mahogany and mahogany veneer, shaped fretwork joining three plinths and brass urn finials, flat cornice, glazed veneer door, white painted wood dial with red painted drapery, lower projecting base with crossbanded frame and flame mahogany panel pierced for viewing pendulum, slightly flaring French feet, 39" h, 13-3/4" w, 5-1/2" d, imperfections, replaced old movement 1,500.00

Tiffany & Company, walnut case, worn finish, traces of gilding in incised carved detail, brass works, blue and white enameled face, mkd "Tiffany & Comp. New York," orig pendulum and key, 20" h 935.00

Willard, Aaron, Boston, c1825, Federal

Mahogany and mahogany veneer, mahogany case with pierced fretwork centering fluted plinth and brass ball finial, flat half-round molded cornice, glazed door with half-round molding framing eglomise tablet with shield spandrels, inscribed "Aaron Willard Jr. Boston," iron concave white and gilt dial, brass eight-day weight driven striking movement, lower mahogany hinged door, rounded base, ball feet, refinished and restored, 36-1/4" h, 13" w, 6" d 2,990.00

Mahogany, molded plinth above glazed door, eglomise tablet of lyre spandrels and foliate designs, oval inscribed "Aaron Willard Boston," wooden framed white painted concave iron dial, eight-day weight-drive brass movement, lower section with mirror, framed by rounded moldings, ball feet, refinished, imperfections, 31" h 7,500.00

Ship, Chelsea, 1920, 8 day time brass movement, second bit, 5 1/4" d 200.00

Skeleton, metal figure of man and dog on wood base, glass dome missing, 19" h 900.00

Tall Case

American

Colonial Revival, carved mahogany, beveled glass panel door, gilt brass and silvered dial, Westminster & Whittington chimes, retailed by Bigelow, Kennard & Co., Boston, late 19th/early 20th C, 95" h 4,890.00

Connecticut, c1820, grain painted pine, scrolled fretwork joining three plinths, brass ball finials, arched cornice molding, flared tombstone door, polychrome wooden dial, thirty-hour wooden movement, molded tombstone waist door, base with cutout bracket feet, old red-ochre graining, minor imperfections, 88" h 2,200.00

Country, poplar, old refinishing, dovetailed bonnet with free standing columns, broken arch pediment, turned finials, overlapping door and cove molding between sections, chamfered corners, paneled base, turned feet, wag on wall works with brass gears in wooden plates, painted metal face, replaced feet, case separated at waist and made into 2 sections, replaced finials, minor repairs, weights and pendulum, 82" h 1,500.00

Kentucky, I. Simpson, Bardstown, mahogany, moon dial with scenes of ship and house, four corners of dial dec with sea shells, brass works, back of brass plate etched "...by J. C. Russell 1815 Bardstown, KY," mahogany case, plain mahogany veneer, spiral turned corner columns to base, four beehive turned ball feet, hood with four delicate turned corner posts, broken swan neck pediment with rosette carvings, two finials present, 96-1/2" h 34,000.00

Maine, William & Phineas Quimby, Belfast, 1820, mahogany, bonnet with pierced fret, arched top glazed door, white painted enamel dial inscribed "W & P Quimby, Belfast 1920," shell dec on corners, globes and moon phased dial, ship and American flag and other scenes, waisted case with reeded quarter columns, fitted brass caps, panel door and panel in base, cut-out shaped skirt, eagle brass finial, refinished, some restoration, 95" h 6,500.00

New England, early 19th C, attributed to Boston area, mahogany, brass and silvered dial with upper strike indicating dial, sgd "Sam'l Mulliken," bottom ring dial silvered on engraved brass plate, dec corner pieces, brass works, mahogany case with brass dec reeded corner columns, beginning and ending with brass pieces, door fitted with glass, brass weights and pendulums, bottom section with rippled molding, stepped ogee ftd base, hood with dec fretwork, matching brass and wood columns, brass ball and spire finial 6,500.00

New England, early 19th C, painted pine, hood with molded swan's neck cresting, outlined in stringing above three inlaid stars, glazed tombstone door, white polychrome dec wooden dial showing grove of trees in arch, Arabic numerals, thirty-hour wooden movement, flanked by turned and reeded columns, waist with shaped door and canted corners, inlaid stringing and "1776," base with inlaid eagle and shield, bordered by stringing, old dark brown paint, contrasting inlay, seat board stamped "J. B.". 12,650.00

New Hampshire, c1810, birch, hood with pierced fret joining three reeded plinths, brass ball finials, arched cornice molding, glazed tombstone door, painted iron dial with bird in arch, floral spandrels, second and calendar indicators, flanked by reeded freestanding columns, waist with thumb-molded door flanked by reeded quarter columns on base, ogee bracket feet, orig finish, minor imperfections, 90-1/4" h 12,075.00

Plymouth, CT, S. Hoadley, c1820, painted pine, hood with flat cornice above tombstone panel, framing wooden dial lettered "S. Hoadley Plymouth," thirty-hour wooden movement, rect waist door on cut-out base, old cream paint, door missing, dial retouched, 84" h 2,185.00

English

Figured mahogany veneer with inlay, scalloped crest, rope carved columns with brass Corinthian capitals, cove molding between sections, bracket feet, brass works, painted metal face with phases of moon dial, ship, and calendar movement, weights and pendulum, second hand missing, replaced eagle finials, center finial missing, replaced feet, 82-3/4" h 3,250.00

George III, mahogany, J. McKibain, Lisburn, c1800, arched bonnet, brass dial with lunar aperture and subsidiary dial, waisted case, plinth base. 1,610.00

George III, mahogany, inscribed "Martin Crosby," c1775, engraved face with brass chapter ring, date aperture, subsidiary seconds dial and cherub spandrels, rolling moon in arch, hood with broken pediment, gilt-glass

frieze and free-standing columns, shaped trunk door flanked by reeded quarter columns, outset molded base with paneled front, canted corners, and ogee bracket feet, 95" h 6,250.00

Gothic Revival, mahogany, old finish, brass works, phase of moon dial, cast and engraved detail, labeled "Elliott, London," tubular Westminster and Whittington chimes, weights, key, and pendulum (with mercury removed), 97" h 7,700.00

Philadelphia, PA, David Rittenhouse, c1770, Chippendale, carved walnut, flat top, bonnet with replaced swan neck pedestal and finials, engraved steel face with calendar dial sgd "David Rittenhouse," shaped pendulum door flanked by quarter fluted columnar sides, base with shaped panel front, replaced ogival bracket feet, 22" w, 12" d, 99-1/2" h, $53,200. Photo courtesy of Freeman\Fine Arts of Philadelphia, Inc.

Wall, Howard E. Davis, Boston, $2,500.

Straus Farringdon, dial dec with fox hunting scene at top, dec floral corners, brass works, oak case with mahogany veneer dec banding, dec diamond shaped inlaid bird on branch in door, split column front with matching split columns on hood, scroll top, ogee bracket base, glass cracked in door, minor chips to veneer, 86" h
. . . . .2,200.00

Federal, New England or New York, early 19th C, mahogany and tiger maple inlaid, shaped crest inlaid with central urn, vines, and leafage, banded of inlay above glazed door with stringing, flanked by inlaid columns, brass bases and capitals, oval inlays flank inlaid swags with tassels above inlaid waist door, flanked by engaged tiger maple quarter columns, center inlaid shell reserve on banded circle, shaped skirt, flaring French feet, old refinish, brass eight-day movement, repainted moon dial, two old brass belted finials, pendulum and key, imperfections. 26,450.00

French, Meslin, red and black grain painted case, gold painted leaf-flower dec, large round porcelain dial sgd "Meslin A La Haye-du-Puits," surmounted by flower dec gold gilt frame, shaped hood with flat top, Bombay-style waist with pendulum window, sq box base with molding, case also sgd "Meslin A La Haye-du-Puits," 81-1/2" h
. . . . .1,850.00

Wall
Banjo

28-1/2" h, E. Howard & Co., Boston, #5, rosewood grained, circular molded bezel enclosing white painted metal dial inscribed "Howard & Co., Boston," eight-day weight-driven movement above half round moldings

framing throat and pendulum box eglomise black and maroon tablets, very minor imperfections 2,450.00

28-3/4" h, Federal, mahogany and mahogany veneer, molded circular bezel enclosing painted metal dial, eight-day weight driven movement, throat and pendulum box tablets of a sea battle framed by mahogany veneer and flanked by scroll brackets, restored 875.00

30" h, Federal, mahogany and gilt gesso, Massachusetts, c1820, circular molded brass bezel, convex glass, white painted iron dial, brass weight driven-movement above throat and pendulum box, eglomise tablets inscribed "Patent" and shows classical building, framed by spiral gilt gesso moldings, flanked by pierced brass brackets
. . . . .1,850.00

32-1/2" h, Federal, mahogany and gilt gesso, Massachusetts, c1820, circular molded brass bezel, convex glass, white painted iron dial, brass weight driven-movement above throat and pendulum box, scene of sea battle "*Constitution* and *Guerriere*" framed by silk rope moldings, flanked by pierced brass brackets, restored
. . . . .1,500.00

33-1/2" h, mahogany, facade with gold repaint, brass trim and finial, brass works with weight, pendulum, and key bottom door with remains of old reverse painting, waist panel with replaced mirror glass 500.00

34" h, Federal, Boston, c1815, mahogany case, gilt finial, molded brass bezel, white painted iron dial, eight-day brass weight driven movement with T-bridge escapement above throat and pendulum mirror tablets, framed by mahogany cross-banding flanked by brass side pieces, old finish 8,625.00

37" h, Federal, eastern MA, c1820, mahogany case, molded brass bezel, white painted dial and eight-day weight driven movement, eglomise tablets showing harbor scene, framed by reeded mahogany moldings, flanked by brass side pieces, later gilded bracket, restored
. . . . .1,035.00

39" h, Federal, MA, c1820, mahogany and gilt gesso, presentation, molded brass bezel and convex glass, white painted dial, eight-day weight drive movement, eglomise tablets showing eagle and shield and sea battle, framed by gilt spiral moldings, flanked by brass side pieces, gilded bracket, restored 920.00

41" h, Federal, MA, c1820, mahogany and gilt gesso, mahogany case, brass bezel, convex glass, white painted dial, eight-day weight drive movement, throat and landscape pendulum tablets framed by gilt spiral moldings, flanked by brass side pieces, giltwood bracket, restored
. . . . .1,840.00

43" h, Federal, attributed to Boston, c1820, mahogany, gilt gesso eagle above circular molded brass bezel, convex glass, painted metal dial, brass eight-day weight-drive movement, eglomise throat and pendulum box tablets showing mill on a stream, framed by gilt gesso spiral moldings flanked by brass pierced brackets, restored
. . . . 750.00

44" h, Federal, bottom glass sgd "S. Willard's Patent," presentation style, drop pendent, gilt dec beaded wood, eglomise throat and bottom panel in gold, brown, and white, brass side arms, large spread eagle brass finial, some paint loss, restoration 1,500.00

European, 24" h, ebonized convoluted oval frame with inner facade with nacre inlay around brass ring, repainted metal face, brass works, pendulum and key, repairs. 225.00

French, Ferdinand Berthoud, white enamel dial with black second and hour numbers, sgd "Fd. Berthoud A PARIS," round brass housing with applied ormolu cornucopias of flowers on sides, intertwined with bow at bottom, works sgd "L. Moinet A PARIS," key and pendulum present, weights missing, 13" h, 11" 1,500.00

French Normandy, embossed brass facade and pendulum, brass works in sheet steel case, enameled face with "Andre Spéth à la Charité" and flowers, hairlines and yellowed repair to face, weights and key, replacement wrought iron shelf, 56" l 950.00

CLOISONNÉ

History: Cloisonné is the art of enameling on metal. The design is drawn on the metal body, then wires, which follow the design, are glued or soldered on. The cells thus created are packed with enamel and fired; this step is repeated several times until the level of enamel is higher than the wires. A buffing and polishing process brings the level of enamels flush to the surface of the wires.

This art form has been practiced in various countries since 1300 B.C. and in the Orient since the early 15th century. Most cloisonné found today is from the late Victorian era, 1870-1900, and was made in China or Japan.

Reference: Lawrence A. Cohen and Dorothy C. Ferster, *Japanese Cloisonné*, Charles E. Tuttle Co., 1990.

Collectors' Club: Cloisonne Collectors Club, P.O. Box 96, Rockport, MA 01966.

Museum: George Walter Vincent Smith Art Museum, Springfield, MA.

Box, cov, silver wire, chrysanthemums, pale mustard ground, Meiji period 300.00
Candelabra, moon flask shape, ormolu mounts, sgd "F. Barbedienne, France," c1870, pr .8,250.00
Censer, cov
  Archaism dec, ornate finial, 18th C 34,100.00
  Chinese, Qianlong period, 13" d 48,875.00
  Namikawa Sosuke style, tripod, wireless 6,100.00
Charger, 12" d, floral dec, light blue ground, Meiji period, Japanese 200.00
Figure, 10" h, parrot, green and yellow, perched position, carved wood 4" d x 1-1/2" h base, 19th C, pr. 500.00
Jar, 4-3/4" h, globular, cranes, red ground, Japanese, 19th C 125.00
Tray, Namikawa Sosuke, (1847-1910), Japanese
  10-1/2" w, kidney shape, sgd on front and back . .14,850.00
  10-1/2" w, lobed form, single bird on branch, sgd on front and back, badly cracked 3,025.00
  10-1/2" w, lobed form, two birds on branches, sgd on front and back 27,500.00
  11-5/8" w, 9-1/4" h, heart shaped, ocher ground around edges shades to lighter ocher and light gray, white dove with brown feet, orange beak, and black eyes, second larger black and gray dove in front, sgd on front with red Japanese seal and gray characters, "Namikawa Sosuke," reverse chocolate brown, two tone brown floral design with gilt wire, Sosuke seal in center, brass mounts, very minor restoration on one side, c1880. . . . . .5,800.00
Vase
  8" h, dark blue enamel with fan-shape medallions of tsikijippo enclosed flowers, one sgd with character inside butterfly, Meiji period. 635.00

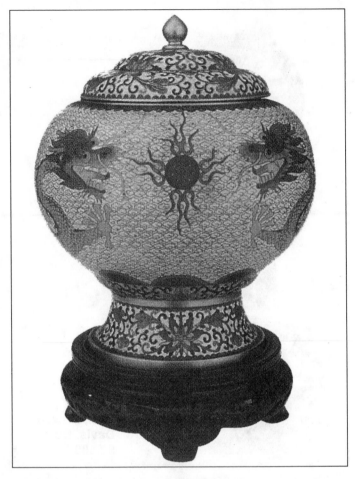

Jar, dragons and intricate colorful floral dec, white ground, wooden stand, Chinese, 8-1/4" w, price for pr, one shown, $770. Photo courtesy of Garth's Auctions, Inc.

9-1/2" h, hexagonal, silver wire, iris design, midnight blue ground, Japanese 690.00
10" h, tall, thin shaped, six panels to tapered center, flaring lip and base, black ground, decorative panels of birds, dragons, and flower bands 200.00
10-7/8" w, 7-1/2" w, flared neck, jade green ground, silver mounts at top and bottom, stylized leaf and Greek key design top border, stylized leaf designs around center, Greek Key design at base, apple green counter enamel, silver wire, Art Deco Style, c1920, Ando Jubei mark on base in silver wire 4,500.00
30-1/4" h, hexagonal, damage to corners, three replaced rings. 7,975.00
Tulip shape, seven butterflies dec. 4,100.00

CLOTHING and CLOTHING ACCESSORIES

History: While museums and a few private individuals have collected clothing for decades, it is only recently that collecting clothing has achieved a widespread popularity. Clothing reflects the social attitudes of a historical period.

Christening and wedding gowns abound and, hence, are not in large demand. Among the hardest items to find are men's clothing from the 19th and early 20th centuries.

The most sought after clothing is by designers, such as Fortuny, Poirret, and Vionnet.

References: Maryanne Dolan, *Vintage Clothing*, 3rd ed., Books Americana, 1995; Roseanne Ettinger, *'50s Popular Fashions for Men, Women, Boys & Girls*, Schiffer Publishing, 1995; Roselyn Gerson, *Vintage & Contemporary Purse Accessories*, Collector Books, 1997; ——, *Vintage Ladies Compacts*, Collector Books, 1996; ——,*Vintage Vanity Bags and Purses*, Collector Books, 1994, 1997 value update; Michael Jay Goldberg, *The Ties That Blind*, Schiffer Publishing, 1997; Carol Belanger Grafton, *Fashions of the Thirties*, Dover Publications, 1993; Kristina Harris, *Victorian & Edwardian Fashions for Women*, Schiffer Publishing, 1995; ——, *Vintage Fashions for Women*, Schiffer Publishing, 1996; Richard Holiner, *Antique Purses*, Collector Books, 1996 value update; Susan Langley, *Vintage Hats & Bonnets, 1770-1970*, Collector Books, 1997; Ellie Laubner, *Fashions of the Roaring '20s*, Schiffer Publishing, 1996; Jan Lindenberger, *Clothing & Accessories from the '40s, '50s, & '60s*, Schiffer Publishing, 1996; Phillip Livoni (ed.), *Russell's Standard Fashions: 1915-1919*, Dover Publications, 1996; Sally C. Luscomb, *The Collector's Encyclopedia of Buttons*, Schiffer Publishing, 1997; Maureen Reilly, *Hot Shoes, 100 Years*, Schiffer Publishing, 1998; Desire Smith, *Hats*, Schiffer Publishing, 1996; ——, *Vintage Styles: 1920-1960*, Schiffer Publishing, 1997; Pamela Smith, *Vintage Fashion & Fabrics*, Alliance Publishers, 1995; Jeffrey B. Snyder, *Stetson Hats & The John B. Stetson Company 1865-1970*, Schiffer Publishing, 1997; Diane Snyder-Haug, *Antique & Vintage Clothing*, Collector Books, 1996; Geoffrey Warren, *Fashion & Accessories, 1840-1980*, Schiffer Publishing, 1997; Debra Wisniewski, *Antique and Collectible Buttons*, Collector Books, 1997.

Periodicals: *Glass Slipper*, 653 S. Orange Ave., Sarasota, FL 34236; *Lady's Gallery*, P.O. Box 1761, Independence, MO 64055; *Lill's Vintage Clothing Newsletter*, 19 Jamestown Dr., Cincinnati, OH 45241; *Vintage Clothing Newsletter*, P.O. Box 88892, Seattle, WA 98138; *Vintage Connection*, 904 N. 65th St., Springfield, OR 97478; *Vintage Gazette*, 194 Amity St., Amherst, MA 01002.

Collectors' Clubs: The Costume Society of America, P.O. Box 73, Earleville, MD 21919; Vintage Fashion and Costume Jewelry Club, P.O. Box 265, Glen Oaks, NY 11004.

Museums: Bata Shoe Museum, Toronto, Canada; Fashion Institute of Technology, New York, NY; Los Angeles County Museum (Costume and Textile Dept.), Los Angeles, CA; Metropolitan Museum of Art, New York, NY; Museum of Costume, Bath, England; Philadelphia Museum of Art, Philadelphia, PA; Smithsonian Institution (Inaugural Gown Collection), Washington, DC; Wadsworth Athenaeum, Hartford, CT; Whiting and Davis Handbag Museum, Attleboro Falls, MA.

Additional Listings: See *Warman's Americana & Collectibles* for more examples.

Note: Condition, size, age, and completeness are critical factors in purchasing clothing. Collectors divide into two groups: those collecting for aesthetic and historic value and those desiring to wear the garment. Prices are higher on the West Coast; major auction houses focus on designer clothes and high-fashion items.

Apron, cotton, green and white check, hand sewn 40.00
Belt, Judith Lieber
    Bow, brushed and polished goldtone bow, wide adjustable lizard belt 175.00
    Frogs, buckle designed with two goldtone frogs, Austrian crystals and colored stones accent, adjustable lizard belt, sgd 520.00
Bonnet, spoon type, minor wear, 1860s 60.00
Booties, baby's, wool, cream, red braid trim, c1850 . . . . . 85.00
Blouse
    Rayon, long sleeve, red and yellow 10.00
    Silk chiffon, beaded front, 1915 . . . . 30.00
Camisole, cotton, white, 1 pc, lace, Victorian 60.00
Coat, fur, natural Russian sable, orig bill of sale from Nieman-Marcus, size 6-8, monogrammed, made for Ann Landers and accompanied by sgd photo of her 6,325.00
Collar
    Leopard, 3-1/4" w, 1930s 85.00
    Satin, 2" w, beaded, braided 16.00
Dress, day
    Chiffon, print, medium 35.00
    Linen, white, satin stitched embroidery, three-quarter sleeves, Edwardian style 75.00
    Silk, black, flapper style drop waist, belt, MOP buckle, ecru neck inset, c1920 . . . . 75.00
Evening Dress
    Chiffon, black, bloused bodice, floating lace panels to waist, black velvet cummerbund, sheer long sleeves with lace cuff, pleated skirt with two lace tiers, Worth, Paris, c1913
    . . . . 750.00
    French cloth, gold, poiret-esque roses and spots, ten pleated panels, weighted waistline, covered leather belt, wine lining, Mylneux, c1928 . . . . .1,200.00
    Lace, mauve overdress, mauve silk underskirt, V neck, keyhole back, sleeveless matching jacket trimmed in burgundy velvet 85.00
    Net, 2 pc, black, satin appliqués, c1890 . . . . 125.00
    Satin, apricot, rhinestone straps, c1930 . . . . 90.00
    Silk, brown, gold, and beige stripes, bodice lined with homespun check, America, c1820, discoloration and fiber loss
    . . . . 120.00

Apron, white cotton, embroidered florals, $45.

Gloves, pr, over the elbow type, black suede, applied beaded abstract rhinestone design, red beads, silver threading detail 200.00

Handkerchief

13" x 15", silk, printed red, yellow, and green dec, worn 130.00

24" x 17", red, white, and blue, Washington commemorative, c1876, framed, faded. 460.00

34" x 32-3/4" , printed silk, center with steam coach crash, stylized floral border, English, 19th C 225.00

Hat

Cloche, felt flowers, 1920s. 55.00

Derby, black felt 25.00

Plush, Edwardian, plumes, coral flowers 245.00

Straw, white, navy under brim, white flower, Frank Olive 22.50

Jacket, silk, blue stamped gold floral dec, cord trimmed neckline ending with single bead, Venetian bead hemline, Fortuny label, early 1900s 1,200.00

Morning Coat, pink, velvet and wool, moiré taffeta collar and inner bodice front, pale pink cutout overlay of fruits and flowers, embroidered raised centers, flared skirt, taffeta lining, France, 1890-1900. . . . . 1,200.00

Necktie

Books, rows of multicolored books, dark background. . . . 40.00

General Motors Corps, men's club logo 10.00

Santa Claus, multicolored Santa figures, dark blue ground 20.00

Nightgown

Cotton, white, crocheted bodice. 45.00

Satin, pink, lace trim, medium 40.00

Silk, pink, Saks 5th Avenue label, large 34.00

Nightshirt, man's cotton, white, long. 48.00

Opera Cape, velvet, sea green, bold stenciled 19th C design, raised collar, nine applied panels with crimped green chiffon edge, six green glass beads, blue chiffon lining with gold stenciled palmettos, French, 1910-20 . . . . 995.00

Pajamas

Satin, peach, medium. 35.00

Silk, pink, ribbon rosettes, crochet trim, c1920. . . . . . 100.00

Parasol, child's, silk and lace, bond handle, 1860s. . . . 165.00

Petticoat

Cotton, brown, hand quilted 140.00

Flannel, small. 25.00

Sateen, black 40.00

Viole, white, tucks, wide crocheted ruffle, Victorian . . . 48.00

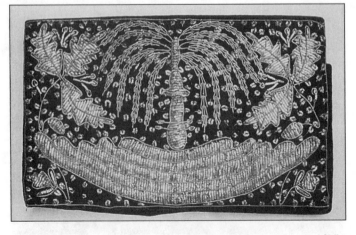

Handbag, black velvet, silver embroidery, 8" x 5-1/2" h, $65.

Purse

Alligator 50.00

Beaded

Art Deco style, green carnival beads, silvertone frame, 5" x 7" 75.00

French, multicolored frame, cloisonné enamel work 250.00

Clutch

French, silver, rhinestone closure 50.00

Judith Lieber, designed as nesting bird, all-over Austrian crystal dec, change purse, comb, and small mirror, sgd 815.00

Evening, jet, Judith Lieber, sq, all-over faceted jet, gold-tone zipper link chain, change purse, comb, and mirror, orig cloth pouch, all sgd. 550.00

Evening, mesh, 14K gold, clasp with five red stones, trace link chain, spring ring, 18.2 dwt. 320.00

Evening, silver, chain

4-1/2" h, 3" h, serpentine form, acid-etched scroll foliate detail, monogram, Wm. B. Kerr & Co., c1900, 3 troy oz 490.00

5-1/4" l, 3" h, bright-cut scroll foliate border, central medallion, monogram, La Secla, Fried & Co., 1909, 5 troy oz 230.00

6-3/4" l, 5-1/8" h, acid-etched scroll foliate design, monogram, American, c1900, 10 troy oz 750.00

4-1/4" l, 2-3/4" h, envelope style, bright-cut floral design flap, W.H.H. maker, Birmingham, England, 1913, 3 troy oz 250.00

Whiting Davis, gold and MOP frame 60.00

Fur, Gucci, navy fur, sq, bamboo handle, leather shoulder strap 635.00

Mesh, 14kt gold, herringbone design, flap highlighted by plaque of fancy-cut sapphires surrounded by diamonds, small matching change purse, fancy link chain handle attached to 14kt yellow gold band, band sgd "S.C.& L." for Shreve Crump and Low, 161.30 dwt 2,300.00

Shoulder Bag

Emilio Pucci, rect, pink, purple, cream, and orange floral design, blue background, flat bow at closure, goldtone curb link straps, sgd, slight staining 150.00

Judith Lieber, pave set with Austrian colorless crystals and black jet beads, silvertone zipper link chain shoulder strap, matching change purse, small mirror, and comb, sgd "Judith Lieber" 1,150.00

Gucci, suede, navy blue, brown double "G" logo, gold closure. 460.00

Suede, clutch, green, accordion bottom, flap closure, accented with marcasite, onyx, and black onyx bar, Cartier, mkd "Made in France". 320.00

Suede and Leather, Gucci, navy suede front, leather buckle design, leather back, goldtone barrel, leather strap 175.00

Purse and Belt, Chanel, rect clutch, quilted black leather, goldtone linked C-logo clasp, detachable black leather belt with interwoven chair of goldtone curb links, sgd "Chanel, Paris" 435.00

Purse, shoes, and scarf, Gucci, royal blue suede bag with gold "G" accent, royal blue suede loafers with twisted gold buckle, blue silk scarf with floral motif. 460.00

Robe

Cotton, breakfast, green print, medium, 1893 . . . . 60.00

Flannel, plaid, man's, c1920. . . . . 40.00

Silk, gold thread embroidered scrolling vine design, royal blue ground, Middle East, 19th C. 375.00

Velvet, green, sq cut, gilt printed, Belini stylized foliate motif, Fortuny label 2,400.00

Sari, gold thread embroidered magenta silk, Indian. . . 50.00
Scarf
 Bottega Veneta, chiffon and charmeuse, navy background, pink pearl and yellow chain motif, sgd, 68" l, 30" w
. . . . 115.00
 Chanel, silk, cream background, jewelry motif, sgd . . . 90.00
 Emilio Pucci, silk
  Bright pink background, abstract green, purple, maroon, and cream design, sgd 250.00
  Yellow border, brightly colored abstract design, sgd, minor stains. 230.00
 Erto, silk, royal blue, turquoise, and red background, paisley design, purple center, sgd, 54" sq 200.00
 Hermes, silk twill
  Antique gold and white perfume bottles, black ground
. . . . 150.00
  "Faux D'Artifice," celebrating 150 years of Hermes, Paris, costumed figure on horse, red and white sq on yellow, blue, red, and white background. 200.00
  Floral print, pale purple, white, and blue flowers, green leaf motif, royal blue background. 200.00
  "Giverny," stylized garden scene, lavender, yellow, pink, and green on fuchsia background. 320.00
  "Mozart," blues, brown, reds, and yellows 400.00
  "Napoleon," light blues, yellows, browns, and cream, minor stains. 200.00
  "Poste et Cavaleerie," gold coat of arms, tassel motif, pale blue and white background. 150.00
  "Rialto," stylized Venetian scene, red, blue, and white on blue background 200.00
  "The Pony Express," black, navy, brown, tan, red, and green. 400.00
  Women wearing antique costumes, pastoral scene, pink background, blue floral border 200.00
 Yves St. Laurent, chiffon and charmeuse, leopard print, black and brown spots, gold background, 84" l, 45" w
. . . . 230.00
Shawl, 128" l, 64" w, paisley, jacquard weave, Victorian, third quarter 19th C 750.00
Shirt, man's, homespun, c1890. . . . . 70.00
Skirt
 Felt, circular, brown, appliquéd poodle, flowers, and beads, c1950. . . . . 30.00
 Muslin, white, full length, deep tucks, ruffled flounce, hand embroidered. 50.00
Slip
 Cotton, white, rows of tucks and lace inserts, crocheted top and flowers. 40.00
 Wool, baby's. 20.00
Suit
 Silk gauze, yellow, jacket with swallow tail overlap to collar, similar shaped hem, two applied brown and ivory buttons, V-shaped stitching on waist and sleeves, curved skirt pockets, 1916-18. . . . . 200.00
 Tweed, gray, double breasted jacket with six buttons, below knee skirt, France, c1963. . . . . 170.00
Stockings, nylon, orig package 35.00
Sweater
 Child's, puppies motif, red, tan, and white, c1950 . . . . 25.00
 Lady's, white rabbit fur trim, beading 50.00
Swimsuit, Spandex, shiny black, back buttons, flared skirt, c1930. . . . . 45.00
Tea Gown, silk, forest green, sleeveless, pleated, matching belt, stenciled floral motif, Venetian beads on sides, Fortuny Die label 1,100.00
Teddy
 Batiste, c1920. . . . . 15.00

Crepe, peach 30.00
Silk, peach, hairpin lace yoke. 40.00
Veil, ecru net and lace, full length, 1918 . . . . 120.00
Waistcoat, gentleman's, satin weave silk, embroidered with silk and metallic threads, spangles, late 18th C, some fiber loss, minor discoloration 650.00
Wedding Gown, satin, wax flowers, beaded hat, Victorian
. . . . 250.00

COALPORT

History: In the mid-1750s, Ambrose Gallimore established a pottery at Caughley in the Severn Gorge, Shropshire, England. Several other potteries, including Jackfield, developed in the area.

About 1795, John Rose and Edward Blakeway built a pottery at Coalport, a new town founded along the right-of-way of the Shropshire Canal. Other potteries located adjacent to the canal were those of Walter Bradley and Anstice, Horton, and Rose. In 1799, Rose and Blakeway bought the Royal Salopian China Manufactory at Caughley. In 1814, this operation was moved to Coalport.

A bankruptcy in 1803 led to refinancing and a new name—John Rose and Company. In 1814, Anstice, Horton, and Rose was acquired. The South Wales potteries at Swansea and Nantgarw were added. The expanded firm made fine-quality, highly decorated ware. The plant enjoyed a renaissance from 1888 to 1900.

World War I, decline in trade, and shift of the pottery industry away from the Severn Gorge brought hard times to Coalport. In 1926, the firm, now owned by Cauldon Potteries, moved from Coalport to Shelton. Later owners included Crescent Potteries, Brain & Co., Ltd., and finally, in 1967, Wedgwood.

References: Susan and Al Bagdade, *Warman's English & Continental Pottery & Porcelain*, 3rd Edition, Krause Publications, 1998; Michael Messenger, *Coalport 1795-1926*, Antique Collectors' Club, 1995; Tom Power, *The Charlton Standard Catalogue of Coalport Figures*, Charlton Press, 1997.

Museums: Cincinnati Museum of Art, Cincinnati, OH; Coalport China works Museum, Ironbridge Gorge Museum Trust, Shropshire, England; Victoria & Albert Museum, London, England.

Additional Listings: Indian Tree Pattern.

Box, cov, 3" l, egg form, gilt dec, applied turquoise, red, and blue enamel jewels, c1900. . . . . 1,725.00
Cup and Saucer, 4-3/4" d saucer, gilt dec, turquoise enamel jewels, c1900, married. 260.00
Dessert Service, partial, assembled, Rock and Tree pattern, Imari palette, gilt edges, c1805-10, price for 19 pc set
. . . . 3,575.00
Dinner Service, partial, gilt blue, 25 pcs 440.00
Ink Stand, 6-1/2" l, crescent shape, yellow foliate scroll border, gilt edged orange band, gold diamond devices border, gilt foliate dec on top, four pen holes, three larger apertures, two ink pots, pounce pot, c1805 . . . . 500.00

Plate, Cigar pattern, blue slashes on back, c1810-20, 8-1/2" d, $195.

Luncheon Plate, 9" d, apple green ground, border dec in gilt, black and white enamels, retailed by Tiffany * Co., 20th C, set of sixteen 500.00
Plate, floral dec, pr 750.00
Platter, 10-3/4" l, Tobacco Leaf pattern, Chinese Export style, underglaze blue, turquoise, chartreuse, iron-red, yellow, green, salmon, rose, puce, and gold, scalloped rim with underglaze blue band, four underglaze blue flowering branches on underside, c1805, pr 2,500.00
Ramekin, scalloped floral, mkd "Coalport, England" 40.00
Teapot, 6" h, cobalt blue underglaze, red floral enamel, gilt trim, wear, repaired finial 360.00
Vase
   4-1/2" d, cobalt blue center, raised gilt foliate dec, oval portrait medallion titled "Omphale," c1900 . . . . .1,035.00
   8 3/4" d, gilt dec, turquoise enameled jewels, raised gold foliate designs, shield shaped panels, swan handle, c1900
   . . . . 635.00

COCA-COLA ITEMS

History: The originator of Coca-Cola was John Pemberton, a pharmacist from Atlanta, Georgia. In 1886, Dr. Pemberton introduced a patent medicine to relieve headaches, stomach disorders, and other minor maladies. Unfortunately, his failing health and meager finances forced him to sell his interest.

In 1888, Asa G. Candler became the sole owner of Coca-Cola. Candler improved the formula, increased the advertising budget, and widened the distribution. A "patient" was accidentally given a dose of the syrup mixed with carbonated water instead of still water. The result was a tastier, more refreshing drink.

As sales increased in the 1890s, Candler recognized that the product was more suitable for the soft-drink market and began advertising it as such. From these beginnings a myriad of advertising items have been issued to invite all to "Drink Coca-Cola."

References: Gael de Courtivron, *Collectible Coca-Cola Toy Trucks*, Collector Books, 1995; Steve Ebner, *Vintage Coca-Cola Machines*, Vol. II, published by author (available from FunTronics, Inc., P.O. Box 448, Middletown, MD 21769; Shelly Goldstein, *Goldstein's Coca-Cola Collectibles*, Collector Books, 1991, 1996 value update; Deborah Goldstein Hill, *Price Guide to Vintage Coca-Cola Collections: 1896-1965,* Krause Publications, 1999; *Coca-Cola Trays*, William McClintock, Schiffer Publishing, 1996; Allan Petretti, *Petretti's Coca-Cola Collectibles Price Guide*, 10th ed., Antique Trader Books, 1997; Randy Schaeffer and Bill Bateman, *Coca-Cola*, Running Books, 1995; B. J. Summers, *B. J. Summers' Guide to Coca-Cola*, Collector Books, 1996; Jeff Walters, *Complete Guide to Collectible Picnic Coolers & Ice Chests*, Memory Lane Publishing, 1994; Al Wilson, *Collectors Guide to Coca-Cola Items*, Vol. I (revised: 1987, 1993 value update), Vol. II (1987, 1993 value update), L-W Book Sales; Al and Helen Wilson, *Wilson's Coca-Cola Guide*, Schiffer Publishing, 1997.

Collectors' Club: Cavanagh's Coca-Cola Christmas Collector's Society, 1000 Holcomb Woods Parkway, Suite 440B, Roswell, GA 30076; Coca-Cola Collectors Club, 400 Monemar Ave., Baltimore, MD 21228-5213; Coca-Cola Collectors Club International, P.O. Box 49166, Atlanta, GA 30359-1166.

Museums: Coca-Cola Memorabilia Museum of Elizabethtown, Inc., Elizabethtown, KY; World of Coca-Cola Pavilion, Atlanta, GA.

Additional Listings: See *Warman's Americana & Collectibles* for more examples.

Notes: Dates of interest: "Coke" was first used in advertising in 1941. The distinctively shaped bottle was registered as a trademark on April 12, 1960.

Ashtray, 4" x 5", aluminum, rect, "Coke adds life to everything nice," 1970s 18.00
Ashtray and Matches set, c1980, logo, "Springtime in Atlanta," unused 20.00
Banner, 13 x 41", "Have a Coke Compliments of this Store," 1950s 30.00
Bingo Game, MIB 45.00
Blotter, 1955, children at party scene 5.00
Bottle Carrier, sic holder, cardboard, 1930s 40.00
Bottle Opener, eagle head, 1912-20 . . . . 100.00
Broadside, 24" h, 18-1/2" w, Baseball Greats series, Stan Musial, action shot and brief write-up 50.00
Button, 3/4" d, uniform type, c1910 . . . . 45.00
Calculator, rect, Unisonic, says "Enjoy Coca-Cola," 1960s, orig case 10.00
Calendar Top, 8-1/8" h, 6-1/8" w, 1903, image of Victorian woman holding early Coke fountain glass, glossy cardboard
. . . . 825.00
Chalkboard, tin, 1958 . . . . 95.00
Clock, electric, wall, "Drink Coca-Cola," 18" d litho metal, plastic cover, Telechron, General Electric, early 1950s 250.00
Coke Dispenser, child's, plastic, 10" h, one glass 45.00
Cooler
   32" h, 20" d, 38" w, lead lined wood, c1934 . . . . . .1,750.00

34" h, bottle cap opener and catcher on side, professionally restored 500.00

Crossing Guard Sign, tin, double sided, diecut of policeman on one side, logo and bottle on other, two bases, c1950 . . . . .1,870.00

Cuff Links, pr, 1/2" d silvered brass with red and white paper insert under celluloid, two paper adv on threaded center spindle, red ground, orig card, c1921 . . . . 50.00

Display Case, watches, 1950 . . . . 145.00

Door Push, plastic, bottle shape, c1950 . . . . 145.00

Game, Game of Health, 8-1/2 x 17-1/4" folded cardboard game board, 1934 Canadian copyright, youthful health activities from rising to bedtime, full color bottled Coke and Canadian maple leaf symbol 125.00

Glass, bell shape, 1929-40 . . . . 5.00

Glass, 4" h, 2-1/2" d, etched, fountain type, set of four. . 160.00

Magazine, *Pause for Living,* 1960s. 4.00

Menu Board, tin, 1939. . . . . 75.00

Needle Case, 2" x 3" stiff paper, full color art front and back, copyright 1924, adv text on inner panels, orig small package of needles. 75.00

Pencil Clip, cello disk mounted on bright silver luster tin clip, red ground, 1940-50
 Drink Coca-Cola, yellow lettering. 22.00
 Drink Coca-Cola In Bottles, white lettering. 20.00

Pencil Sharpener, metal, bottle shape, orig full box with twelve unused sharpeners, c1920. 350.00

Advertising Sign, cardboard, lady wearing ice skates, seated on log, 1941, 50" x 30", some water warping and staining on right side, $250. Photo courtesy of James D. Julia, Inc.

Pinback Button, Hi Fi Club, yellow and green lettering, brown Coke bottle, red 45 rpm record, 1950s. 25.00

Pocket Knife, two stainless blades, marked "Remington," c1930 . . . . 100.00

Pocket Mirror, 2-1/2" h, 1-3/4" w, celluloid, Duster Girl, mfg. by Cruver Mfg. Co., 1911 . . . . .6,750.00

Pocket Watch, "Time for Cold Bottle of Coca-Cola," 1920s 750.00

Premium, tie, 15" l red cord bolo tie, emb brass 1" slide clasp, frontal portrait of Kit Carson by Coca-Cola bottle, two small brass balls on ends, sponsorship premium for TV series "The Adventures of Kit Carson," c1951 . . . . 85.00

Salesman's Sample, cooler, Glasscock, 1929, four miniature cases of bottles, 13-1/4" h 19,550.00

Script, Coke Time TV Broadcast, 8-1/2" x 11" mimeographed paper 16 page typewritten script, Wed., July 22, 1953, starring Eddie Fisher, host Don Ameche, DeMarco Sisters as special guests. 35.00

Shooting gallery, 50" h, Coca-Cola on side panels, marquee, backfield, and gun barrel 1,100.00

Sign
 11" h, 9" w, wood, metal trim, two glasses of Coca-Cola, Kay Displays, Inc., c1930, part of three pc display set 450.00
 11-3/4" h, 28" l, porcelain, "Drink Coca Cola Fountain Service," bright yellow, red, green, and white 950.00
 27-3/4" h, 19-1/2" l, tin, "Take Home a Carton," six-pack carrier with metal handle, c1951 . . . . 750.00
 34" h, 62" w, cardboard, "Hospitality," young man with red bow-tie sitting on sofa with two attractive young ladies, orig gold-colored wood molded frame. 800.00
 48" h, round porcelain, minor scratch. 950.00
 50" h, 30" w, cardboard, lady wearing ice skates, sitting on log, enjoying bottle of Coca Cola, 1941, some warping and staining. 250.00
 57" h, 36" w, cardboard, lady in full length gown holding glass of Coca Cola waiting for her partner, artist sgd, 1936, orig frame 375.00
 62" h, 30-1/2" d, standing, round porcelain sign, orig base emb "Drink Coca Cola," considerable porcelain loss and wear 225.00

Tip Tray, 6" l, 4-1/4" w, titled "Relieves Fatigue," lady enjoying beverage in flared glass, Chas. W. Shonk Co. litho, some age spotting. 250.00

Tray
 1914, 15-1/4" h, 12-1/4" w, Betty, wearing bonnet, Passaic Metal Ware Co. litho, color loss, chips, poor condition 200.00
 1931, Norman Rockwell design, boy in straw hat sitting on ground with puppy 665.00
 1934, 10-1/2" h, 13-1/4" w, Maureen O'Sullivan and John Weissmuller both enjoying bottles of Coca Cola, American Art Works Inc. litho, some rubbing and chipping . . . 725.00
 1935, Madge Evans 415.00
 1937, 13-1/4" h, 10-/2" w, rect, lady in full length gown holding glass, Canadian version, titled in French "Baviez Cocae Cola". 125.00

Umbrella, 1920s 750.00

Vending Machine, 36" h, 24" w, V-23, "Coca-Cola 10 Cents, Drink Coca-Cola In Bottles," revolving white top, orig working condition. 1,895.00

Vienna Art Plate, 10" tin litho, issued by Western Coca-Cola Bottling Co., orig ornate gold leaf frame, 16" sq ornate shadow box frame, 1905 . . . . 925.00

Window Display
 Bathing Beauty, water skiing, trifold, 1922 . . . . . . .6,000.00

Circus, big top with several smaller tents, circus wagons, animals, bands, concession stands, 17 individual pcs, c1929 .... .3,200.00

COFFEE MILLS

History: Coffee mills or grinders are utilitarian objects designed to grind fresh coffee beans. Before the advent of stay-fresh packaging, coffee mills were a necessity.

The first home-size coffee grinders were introduced about 1890. The large commercial grinders designed for use in stores, restaurants, and hotels often bear an earlier patent date.

Reference: Joseph Edward MacMillan, *MacMillan Index of Antique Coffee Mills*, Cherokee Publishing (657 Old Mountain Rd., Marietta, GA 30064), 1995; Michael L. White and Derek S. White, *Early American Coffee Mills*, published by authors (P.O. Box 483, Fraser, CO 80442).

Collectors' Club: Association of Coffee Mill Enthusiasts, 5941 Wilkerson Rd., Rex, GA 30273.

Commercial

Elgin, #40, double-wheel, missing finial and handle 550.00
Enterprise
   #3, double wheel, orig red paint and stenciling, 1875 .... 990.00
   #5, double wheel, worn orig paint 600.00
Landers, Frary & Clark, No. 10, double wheel, cast iron, orig condition 950.00
Simmons Koffee Krusher, double wheel, orig dark blue paint, gilt stenciling, mkd "KK 13" on front of drawer 1,350.00

Crescent #705, Crescent Mfg Co., Louisville, KY, $75.

Star Mill, 28" h, cast iron, red and gold repaint over pitted iron, damaged brass hopper, replaced coffee container, crank and gear case with welded repair, mkd "Star Mill, Philadelphia" 500.00

Domestic

Arcade No. 25, wall type, cast iron, clear glass base, metal lid 70.00
Imperial No. 705, long cast iron crank handle, domed cast-iron top, molded scrolls above dovetailed case, small drawers, remnants of label above drawer, 6" h, 11" h 60.00
Parker No. 50, wall type, tin and iron, orig mounting board 90.00
Pine, fingered joints, one drawer, iron pull, iron top cup and handle, wooden knob, c1880, 5-3/4" sq, 6" h 90.00
Poplar, round pewter cup on top, iron turn handle, wooden knob grip, dovetailed sq wooden base, single drawer, old soft finish, 9-1/4" h 140.00
Walnut, Louis XIV, 18th C, mkd "Martin Laisnez," small old repair 4,850.00

COIN-OPERATED ITEMS

History: Coin-operated items include amusement games, pinball machines, jukeboxes, slot machines, vending machines, cash registers, and other items operated by coins.

The first jukebox was developed about 1934 and played 78-RPM records. Jukeboxes were important to teenagers before the advent of portable radios and television.

The first pinball machine was introduced in 1931 by Gottlieb. Pinball machines continued to be popular until the advent of solid-state games in 1977 and advanced electronic video games after that.

The first three-reel slot machine, the Liberty Bell, was invented in 1905 by Charles Fey in San Francisco. In 1910, Mills Novelty Company copyrighted the classic fruit symbols. Improvements and advancements have led to the sophisticated machines of today.

Vending machines for candy, gum, and peanuts were popular from 1910 until 1940 and can be found in a wide range of sizes and shapes.

References: Michael Adams, Jurgen Lukas, and Thomas Maschke, *Jukeboxes*, Schiffer Publishing, 1995; Michael F. Baute, *Always Jukin' Official Guide to Collectible Jukeboxes*, published by author (221 Yesler Way, Seattle, WA 98104), 1996; Richard M. Bueschel, *Collector's Guide to Vintage Coin Machines*, Schiffer Publishing, 1995; ——, *Guide to Vintage Trade Stimulators & Counter Games*, Schiffer Publishing, 1997; ——, *Lemons, Cherries and Bell-Fruit-Gum*, Royal Bell Books, 1995; ——, *Pinball 1*, Hoflin Publishing, 1988; ——, *Slots 1*, Hoflin Publishing, 1989; Richard Bueschel and Steve Gronowski, *Arcade 1*, Hoflin Publishing, 1993; Herbert Eiden and Jurgen Lukas, *Pinball Machines*, Schiffer Publishing, 1992, values updated 1997; Bill Enes, *Silent Salesmen Too, The Encyclopedia of Collectible Vending Machines*, published by author (8520 Lewis Dr., Lenexa, KS 66227), 1995; Eric Hatchell and Dick Bueschel, *Coin-Ops on Location*, published by authors, 1993; Bill Kurtz, *Arcade Treasures*, Schiffer Publishing, 1994.

Periodicals: *Always Jukin'*, 221 Yesler Way, Seattle, WA 98104; *Antique Amusements Slot Machines & Jukebox Gazette*, 909 26th St NW, Washington, DC 20037; *Around the Vending Wheel*, 5417 Castana Ave., Lakewood, CA 90712; *Coin Drop International*, 5815 W 52nd Ave., Denver, CO 80212; *Coin Machine Trader*, 569 Kansas SE, P.O. Box 602, Huron, SD 57350; *Coin-Op Classics*, 17844 Toiyabe St., Fountain Valley, CA 92708; *Coin Slot*, 4401 Zephyr St., Wheat Ridge, CO 80033; *Gameroom Magazine*, 1014 Mt. Tabor Rd., New Albany, IN 47150; *Jukebox Collector*, 2545 SE 60th St., Des Moines, IA 50317; *Loose Change*, 1515 S Commerce St., Las Vegas, NV 89102; *Pin Game Journal*, 31937 Olde Franklin Dr., Farmington, MI, 48334; *Scopitone Newsletter*, 810 Courtland Dr., Ballwin, MO 63021.

Collectors' Club: Bubble-Gum Charm Collectors, 24 Seafoam St., Staten Island, NY 10306

Museum: Liberty Belle Saloon and Slot Machine Collection, Reno, NV.

Additional Listings: See *Warman's Americana & Collectibles* for separate categories for Jukeboxes, Pinball Machines, Slot Machines, and Vending Machines.

Advisor: Bob Levy.

Notes: Because of the heavy usage these coin-operated items received, many are restored or, at the very least, have been repainted by either the operator or manufacturer. Using reproduced mechanisms to restore pieces is acceptable in many cases, especially when the restored piece will then perform as originally intended.

Arcade

Fortune Teller, Grandma, Genco, c1940	1,800.00
Grip Strength Test, Gottlieb, c1940	200.00

Slot Machines, left: Jennings 10¢ Standard Chief, chrome plated case, red trim, brass Indian head on front, lock restored, $1,210; center: O. D. Jennings & Co., Little Duke, 1¢, oak cast, cast deco detail, silver, orange, black, red, and yellow enamel, working condition, $1,650; right: Wattling Manuf. Rol-A-Top, twin jackpot, yellow and black enameled finish, cast cornucopia, eagle, and coins, working condition, $2,420. Photo courtesy of Garth's Auctions, Inc.

Merchandiser Digger, exhibit, c1930	2,200.00
Rifle, Williams, c1968	300.00
Shuffle Alley, United, c1953	300.00

Gum Machine

Atlas

Bantam, c1947, tray type, 11"	100.00
Deluxe, c146, bulk vendor, 16"	100.00
Master, c1954, penny/nickel, 16"	40.00
Midget, c1950, 14-sided, 11"	125.00
Columbus, Model "A," c1915, round globe, 15-1/2"	200.00
Intl Mutoscope, Old Mill, c1930, floor model	2,000.00
Manikin Vendor, Baker Boy, c1927, automated, 16"	2,500.00
Mansfield, Automatic Clerk, beveled glass, flips package of gum, c1902, 16"	600.00
Norris Mfg., Master Special, c1923, 4-sided porcelain, 16"	225.00

Jukebox

AMI, Model D-40, c1951	1,300.00
Rockola, Model 1455, c1957	3,000.00
Seeburg	
Model 147, c1947	2,500.00
Model HF-100R, c1954	3,500.00
Wurlitzer	
Model 1100, c1948	6,000.00
Model 1800, c1955	3,500.00

Slot Machine

Caille

Dough Boy, c1935, three reel, inferior, 5¢	700.00
Upright Centaur, 1907, single wheel, magnificent, 5¢	14,000.00
Jennings	
Dutch Boy, c1930, three reel, nice wood cabinet, 25¢	1,200.00
Silver Moon Chief, c1840, three reel, jackpot, club machine, 10¢	1,100.00
Mills	
Black Cherry, c1946, three reel, first after World War II, 5¢	1,000.00
Poinsettia, c1929, three reel, fancy design, 5¢	1,200.00
War Eagle, c1931, three reel, 10¢	1,500.00
Pace	
Bantam, c1928, three reel, three-quarter size, 1¢	1,000.00
Comet Vendor, c1933, three reel, vends mints, 5¢	1,400.00
Watling	
Bird of Paradise, c1937, three reel, very desirable, 10¢	3,500.00
Blue Seal, c1928, three reel, jackpot, plain, 5¢	800.00
Treasury, c1936, three reel, twin jackpot, beautiful gold coins, 5¢	3,500.00

Soda Machine

Coke

Cavalier C51, 1950s, 64-1/2" h, 24-3/4" w, 20-1/4" d	300 to 800.00
Vendo V-44, 1956-59, 57-1/2" h, 16" w, 15-1/2"d	1,200 to 1,800.00
Vendolator 88, late 1950s, 58" h, 26-1/4" w, 18" d	800 to 1,500.00
Pepsi	
Ideal 49B, mid 1950s, 62-1/4" h, 24" w, 22-3/4" d	200 to 600.00
Ideal 55B, 1940-50, 42" h, 37" w, 19-1/2" w	200 to 700.00

Vending Machine

Cigaret Special, Rowe Mfg., c1935, 36" 700.00
Fresh Gum, 6-column tabs, c1940, 18-1/2" 75.00
Hershey's Bar, Shipman Mfg., c1937, 16" 125.00
Model D Match Vendor, Specialty Mfg., c1920, 14-1/2"
. . . . 250.00
National Postage, Northwestern, c1940, 13" 75.00
Novelty Card, exhibit, c1930, 12" 150.00
Pocket Combs, Advance Machine, c1950, 10" 50.00
Pulver Short Case, c1930, 21" 600.00
Reed's Aspirin, Kayem Prod., c1940, 13-1/2" 175.00
Sabelle No. 5 Perfume, H. L. Blake, c1950, 20" 75.00
Van-Lite, 1¢ lighter fluid, Van Lansing, c1933, 19" 600.00

COMIC BOOKS

History: Shortly after comics first appeared in newspapers of the 1890s, they were reprinted in book format and often used as promotional giveaways by manufacturers, movie theaters, and candy and stationery stores. The first modern-format comic was issued in 1933.

The magic date in comic collecting is June 1938 when DC issued Action Comics No. 1, marking the first appearance of Superman. Thus began the golden age of comics, which lasted until the mid-1950s and witnessed the birth of the major comic book publishers, titles, and characters.

In 1954, Fredric Wertham authored *Seduction of the Innocent*, a book which pointed a guilt-laden finger at the comic industry for corrupting youth, causing juvenile delinquency, and undermining American values. Many publishers were forced out of business while others established a "comics code" to assure parents that their comics were compliant with morality and decency standards upheld by the code authority.

The silver age of comics, mid-1950s through the end of the 1960s, witnessed the revival of many of the characters from the golden age in new comic formats. The era began with Showcase No. 4 in October 1956, which marked the origin and first appearance of the Silver-Age Flash.

While comics survived into the 1970s, it was a low point for the genre; but in the early 1980s a revival occurred. In 1983 comic book publishers, other than Marvel and DC, issued more titles than had existed in total during the previous 40 years. The mid- and late 1980s were a boom time, a trend which appears to be continuing into the 1990s.

References: *Comic Buyer's Guide Annual*, Krause Publications, issued annually; Alex G. Malloy, *Comics Values Annual 1998*, Antique Trader Books, 1997; Duncan McAlpine (comp.), *Comic Values Annual*, 1996 ed., Antique Trader Books, 1995; Robert M. Overstreet, *Overstreet Comic Book Price Guide*, 27th ed., Avon Books, 1997; Don and Maggie Thompson (eds.), *Comic Book Superstars*, Krause Publications, 1993; —— (eds.), *Marvel Comics Checklist & Price Guide*, Krause Publications, 1993; Maggie Thompson and Brent Frankenhoff, *Comic Book Checklist & Price Guide*, 4th ed., Krause Publications, 1997; Maggie Thompson and John Jackson Miller, *Comic Buyer's Guide 1997 Annual*, 6th ed., Krause Publi-

cations, 1996; Stuart W. Wells and Alex G. Malloy, *Comics Collectibles and Their Values*, Wallace-Homestead, 1996.

Periodicals: *Archie Fan Magazine*, 185 Ashland St., Holliston, MA 01746; *Comic Book Market Place*, P.O. Box 180900, Coronado, CO 92178; *Comics Buyer's Guide*, 700 E State St., Iola, WI 54990; *Comics Interview*, 234 Fifth Ave., New York, NY 10001; *Comics Source*, 2401 Broad St., Chattanooga, TN 37408; *Duckburg Times*, 3010 Wilshire Blvd. #362, Los Angeles, CA 90010; *Hogan's Alley*, P.O. Box 47684, Atlanta, GA 30362; *Overstreet Comic Book Marketplace*, 1996 Greenspring Dr., Suite 405, Timonium, MD 21093; *Western Comics Journal*, 1703 N Aster Place, Broken Arrow, OK 74012; *Wizard: The Guide To Comics*, 151 Wells Ave., Congers, NY 10920.

Collectors' Clubs: American Comics Exchange, 351-T Baldwin Rd., Hempstead, NY 11550; Fawcett Collectors of America & Magazine Enterprise, too!, 301 E Buena Vista Ave., North Augusta, SC 29841.

Videotape: *Overstreet World of Comic Books*, Overstreet Productions and Tom Barker Video, 1994.

Museums: International Museum of Cartoon Art, 300 SE 5th Ave., #5150, Boca Raton, FL 33432; Museum of Cartoon Art, Rye, NY.

REPRODUCTION ALERT

Publishers frequently reprint popular stories, even complete books, so the buyer must pay strict attention to the title, not just the portion printed in oversized letters on the front cover. If there is any doubt, look inside at the fine print on the bottom of the inside cover or first page. The correct title will be printed there in capital letters. Also pay attention to the dimensions of the comic book. Reprints often differ in size from the original.

Note: The comics listed below are in near-mint condition, meaning they have a flat, clean, shiny cover that has no wear other than tiny corner creases; no subscription creases, writing, yellowing at margins, or tape repairs; staples are straight and rust free; pages are supple and like new; generally just-off-the-shelf quality.

Action Comics, D. C.
23, April 1940 . . . . 1,975.00
#228 . . . . 95.00
#252 . . . . 400.00
#254 . . . . 160.00
Adventure, D. C.
#258 . . . . 40.00
#268 . . . . 35.00
#273 . . . . 40.00
#369 . . . . 5.00
Adventures of Dean Martin & Jerry Lewis, D. C., #37 . . . . 16.00
All-American Men of War, D. C., #23 . . . . 45.00
Amazing Spider-Man, Marvel
#6 . . . . 160.00
#12 . . . . 100.00
28, Sept. 1965 . . . . 650.00
#37 . . . . 18.00

Aquaman, D. C.
  #6 . . . . 35.00
  #50 . . . . 12.00
Atom and Hawkman, D. C., #40 . . . . 25.00
Avengers, Marvel
  #2 . . . . 90.00
  #4 . . . . 200.00
Banana Splits, Gold Key, #1 . . . . 45.00
Batman, D. C.
  #71 . . . . 75.00
  #100 . . . . 240.00
  #131 . . . . 50.00
  #213 . . . . 30.00
Blackhawk, D. C., 1st D.C. issue, #108 . . . . 120.00
Bonanza, Gold Key, #35 . . . . 44.00
Brave and the Bold, D. C., #7 . . . . 40.00
Captain America Comics, Marvel
  # 6, Sept. 1941 . . . . 1,275.00
  #100 . . . . 105.00
  #108 . . . . 30.00
Conan, Marvel
  #1 . . . . 105.00
  #8 . . . . 15.00
Daredevil, #4 . . . . 65.00
Dark Mansion of Forbidden Love, D. C., #1 . . . . 32.00
Dark Shadows, Gold Key
  #2 . . . . 85.00
  #5 . . . . 60.00
  #12 . . . . 40.00
Detective Comics, D. C.
  # 54, Aug.1941 . . . . 450.00
  # 87, June 1944 . . . . 625.00
Fantastic Four, Marvel
  # 5, July 1962 . . . . 875.00
  # 10, Dec. 1962 . . . . 875.00
  # 12, March 1963 . . . . 850.00
  #57 . . . . 55.00
  #99 . . . . 25.00
Flash Comics, D. C.
  # 12, Dec. 1940 . . . . 700.00
  # 15, March 1941 . . . . 700.00
  # 26, Feb. 1942 . . . . 975.00
Green Hornet, Gold Key
  #1 . . . . 135.00
  #3 . . . . 110.00
Green Lantern, D. C.
  #1 . . . . 2,500.00
  #22 . . . . 165.00
  #80 . . . . 35.00
Hot Wheels, D. C., #1 . . . . 65.00
House of Mystery, D. C., #1 . . . . 400.00
House of Secrets, D. C., #2 . . . . 100.00
Incredible Hulk, Marvel
  # 3, Sept. 1962 . . . . 375.00
  # 4, Nov. 1962 . . . . 450.00
  #107 . . . . 40.00
Iron Man, Marvel
  #2 . . . . 80.00
  #3 . . . . 55.00
Justice League of America, D. C. #31 . . . . 30.00
Laurel & Hardy, D. C., #1 . . . . 45.00
Legion of Super Heroes, #3 . . . . 12.00
Mars Patrol, Gold Key, #9 . . . . 20.00
Marvel Super Heroes, Marvel, #1 . . . . 60.00
Marvel Mystery Comics, # 5, March 1940 . . . . 1,200.00
Munsters, Gold Key, #15 . . . . 30.00
Mystery in Space, D. C., #4 . . . . 200.00

My Greatest Adventure, D. C., #23 . . . . 55.00
Night Nurse Marvel, #1 . . . . 55.00
Our Army At War, D. C., #185 . . . . 10.00
Rawhide, Gold Key, #1160 . . . . 100.00
Rifleman, Gold Key, #2 . . . . 30.00
Rocky and his Friends, Gold Key, #1 . . . . 65.00
Scooby Doo, Gold Key, #8 . . . . 28.00
Silver Surfer, Marvel, #2 . . . . 110.00
Star Spangled War Stories, D. C., #141 . . . . 25.00
Star Trek, Gold Key
  #4 . . . . 70.00
  #5 . . . . 105.00
  #38 . . . . 21.00
Strange Adventures, D. C., #8 . . . . 75.00
Strange Tales, Marvel
  #69 . . . . 22.00
  #78 . . . . 200.00
Sub-Mariner Comics
  # 2, Summer 1941 . . . . 3,400.00
  # 3, Fall 1941 . . . . 1,100.00
Tales of Suspense, Marvel, #24 . . . . 36.00
Tales to Astonish, Marvel, #10 . . . . 140.00
Teen Titans, D. C., #20 . . . . 36.00
Thor, Marvel, #142 . . . . 30.00
Witching Hour, D. C., #3 . . . . 28.00
World's Finest, D. C.
  #99 . . . . 120.00
  #119 . . . . 100.00
Wyatt Earp, Gold Key, #7 . . . . 20.00
X-Men, Marvel
  #2 . . . . 630.00
  #12 . . . . 75.00
  #32 . . . . 70.00
Young Romance, D. C., #197 . . . . 120.00

COMPACTS

History: In the first quarter of the 20th century, attitudes regarding cosmetics changed drastically. The use of make-up during the day was no longer looked upon with disdain. As women became "liberated," and as more and more of them entered the business world, the use of cosmetics became a routine and necessary part of a woman's grooming. Portable containers for cosmetics became a necessity.

Compacts were made in myriad shapes, styles, combinations and motifs, all reflecting the mood of the times. Every conceivable natural or man-made material was used in the manufacture of compacts. Commemorative, premium, souvenir, patriotic, figural, Art Deco, and enamel compacts are a few examples of the types of compacts that were made in the United States and abroad. Compacts combined with other forms, such as cigarette cases, music boxes, watches, hatpins, canes, and lighters, also were very popular.

Compacts were made and used until the late 1950s when women opted for the "Au Naturel" look. The term "vintage" is used to describe the compacts from the first half of the 20th century as distinguished from contemporary examples.

References: Juliette Edwards, *Compacts*, published by author, 1994; Roselyn Gerson, *Ladies Compacts*, Wallace-Homestead, 1996; ——, *Vintage and Contemporary Purse Accessories, Solid Perfumes, Lipsticks, & Mirrors,*

Collector Books, 1997; ——, *Vintage Ladies Compacts*, Collector Books, 1996; ——, *Vintage Vanity Bags and Purses: An Identification and Value Guide*, 1994, 1997 value update, Collector Books; Frances Johnson, *Compacts, Powder and Paint*, Schiffer Publishing, 1996; Laura M. Mueller, *Collector's Encyclopedia of Compacts, Carryalls & Face Powder Boxes* (1994, 1996 value update), Vol. II (1997), Collector Books.

Collectors' Club: Compact Collectors Club, P.O. Box 40, Lynbrook, NY 11563.

Additional Listings: See *Warman's Americana & Collectibles* for more examples.

Advisor: Roselyn Gerson.

Coty, #405, envelope box 65.00
Daniel, black leather, portrait of lady encased in plastic dome, Paris 90.00
Djer Kiss, with fairy 95.00
Evans, goldtone, heart shape, black twisted carrying cord, lipstick concealed in black tassel suspended from bottom
. . . . 250.00
Fifth Avenue, vanity case "Cosmetist," aquamarine enamel, powder, rouge, lipstick, cleansing cream, and mascara, England. 175.00
Fiato, goldtone, jeweled horse and carriage mounted on lid, blue velvet protective case, sleeve for jeweled lipstick 90.00
Foster & Bailey, vanity case, blue cloisonné suspended from enameled perfume container, powder and rouge compartments, lipstick attached at base, tassel and black enameled finger carrying ring 950.00
Gray, Dorothy, engine turned goldtone, hat shape, ribbon and fruit dec. 80.00
Halston, SP, name on puff, used 150.00

Souvenir, 1937 Great Lakes Expo, Cleveland Centennial, metal, back and silver, raised sailboats, powder and rouge compartments, 2-1/2" d, $85.

Italian, hand mirror shape, SS, stylized floral engraving, lipstick concealed in handle, coral cabochon thumb piece . . 325.00
Kigu, compact and cigarette case, silvered and goldtone, tandem lipstick and carrying chain, England. 80.00
Lampi, light blue enamel, five colorful three dimensional scenes from Alice in Wonderland enclosed in plastic domes on lid 180.00
Norida, emb lady, silver tone. 75.00
Rex Fifth Avenue, vanity-pochette, navy blue, gold polka dots, taffeta drawstring, mirror on outside base 90.00
R. G. & Co., vanity case, SS, yellow cloisonné enamel, finger chain, painted flowers on lid, chain, perfume tube suspended from enameled and silver finger ring chain 290.00
Tiffany & Co.
   14K yellow gold, mirrored compartment, engraved case, engine turned design, sgd "Tiffany & Co.," minor dents
   . . . . 320.00
   Sterling silver and 14K yellow gold, Art Deco, reeded silver sunburst, ruby and gold accents, brushed gold int
   . . . . 345.00
Unknown Maker, compact
   Castanets shape, ebony wood, metal Paris insignia centered on lid, orange tasseled carrying cord. 220.00
   Flamingo motif 90.00
   Telephone dial shape, red, white, and blue, slogan "I Like Ike" imprinted on lid, red map of USA on lid center 225.00
   Yellow gold, 14k, reeded and engraved design, Greek key border, monogrammed, hallmarked, and numbered, scratches to int. 175.00
Unknown Maker, compact and matching cigarette case, SS and 14K gold, reeded silver case with applied gold bow plaque, red stone accents, sgd "WAB" 490.00
Unknown Maker, powder tier, silvertone triple tier vanity case, swivel compartments for powder, rouge, and lipstick. 195.00
Unknown Maker, vanity bag, SS mesh, hallmarked, octagonal, goldtone int. and finger ring carrying chain 500.00
Unknown Maker, vanity case, antique goldtone, two sided filigree, red stones set in lids, powder and rouge compartments, lipstick concealed in tassel, carrying chain. 245.00
Volupte, 2-7/8" sq, gold metal, top black, beaded bold edge, gold center medallion with shell-like raised edge, inlaid on gold leaves and rhinestone flowers, flannel case, orig Franklin Simon box 75.00
Whiting & Davis Co., vanity bag, purple, black, and silver mesh, purple enameled vanity case on outside corner of frame, lined int., powder sifter, metal mirror, and rouge compartment on lid, carrying chain 500.00

CONSOLIDATED GLASS COMPANY

History: The Consolidated Lamp and Glass Company was formed as a result of the 1893 merger of the Wallace and McAfee Company, glass and lamp jobbers of Pittsburgh, and the Fostoria Shade & Lamp Company of Fostoria, Ohio. When the Fostoria, Ohio, plant burned down in 1895, Corapolis, Pennsylvania, donated a seven-acre tract of land near the center of town for a new factory. In 1911, the company was the largest lamp, globe, and shade works in the United States, employing more than 400 workers.

In 1925, Reuben Haley, owner of an independent design firm, convinced John Lewis, president of Consolidated, to enter the giftware field utilizing a series of designs inspired by the 1925 Paris Exposition (l'Exposition Internationale des Arts Décorative et Industriels Modernes) and the work of René Lalique. Initially, the glass was marketed by Howard Selden through his showroom at 225 Fifth Avenue in New York City. The first two lines were Catalonian and Martele.

Additional patterns were added in the late 1920s: Florentine (January 1927), Chintz (January 1927), Ruba Rombic (January 1928), and Line 700 (January 1929). On April 2, 1932, Consolidated closed it doors. Kenneth Harley moved about 40 molds to Phoenix. In March 1936, Consolidated reopened under new management, and the "Harley" molds were returned. During this period the famous Dancing Nymph line, based on an eight-inch salad plate in the 1926 Martele series, was introduced.

In August 1962, Consolidated was sold to Dietz Brothers. A major fire damaged the plant during a 1963 labor dispute and in 1964 the company permanently closed its doors.

References: Ann Gilbert McDonald, *Evolution of the Night Lamp*, Wallace-Homestead, 1979; Jack D. Wilson, *Phoenix & Consolidated Art Glass, 1926-1980*, Antique Publications, 1989.

Collectors' Club: Phoenix and Consolidated Glass Collectors, P.O. Box 81974, Chicago, IL 60681.

Ashtray, Santa Maria, green wash 200.00
Berry Bowl, master, Criss-Cross, cranberry opalescent, 8" d
. . . . 175.00
Bon Bon, Ruba Rhombic, 6" d, smoky topaz 125.00
Bowl
    5-1/2" d, Coronation, Martelé, flared, blue 75.00
    8" d, Dancing Nymph, dark blue wash 365.00
Box, cov, 7" l, 5" w, Martelé line, Fruit and Leaf pattern, scalloped edge 85.00
Butter Dish, cov, Cosmos, pink band 200.00
Candlesticks, pr
    Hummingbird, Martelé line, oval body, jade green, 6-3/4" h
    . . . . 245.00
    Ruba Rhombic, smoky topaz 215.00
Cocktail, Dancing Nymph, French Crystal 90.00
Cologne Bottle, orig stopper, 4-1/2" h, Cosmos 120.00
Cookie Jar, 6-1/2" h, Regent Line, #3758, Florette, rose pink over white opal casing 370.00
Cruet, orig stopper, Florette, pink satin 225.00
Cup and Saucer, Dancing Nymph, ruby flashed 265.00
Goblet, Dancing Nymph, French Crystal 90.00
Humidor, Florette, pink satin 225.00
Jar, cov, Con-Cora, #3758-9, pine cone dec, irid 165.00
Jug, Spanish Knobs, 5-1/2" h, handle, pink 125.00
Lamp
    Cockatoo, 13" h, figural, orange and blue, black beak, brown stump, black base 450.00
    Elk, 13" h, chocolate brown, blue clock mounted between horns, black bass base, shallow annealing mark . .1,000.00
    Flower Basket, 8" h, bouquet of roses and poppies, yellows, pinks, green leaves, brown basketweave, black glass base
    . . . . 300.00
Mayonnaise Comport, Martelé Iris, green wash 55.00
Miniature Lamp, Cosmos, 7" h, fish net ground 350.00
Night Light, Santa Maria, block base 450.00
Old Fashioned Tumbler, 3-7/8" h, Catalonian, yellow 20.00
Pitcher, water, Florette, pink satin 200.00
Plate
    7" d, Catalonian, green 25.00

Pitcher, Cosmos pattern, pale pink band, blue, pink, and yellow flowers, 9" h, $245.

    8-1/4" d, Bird of Paradise, amber wash 40.00
    8-1/4" d, Dancing Nymph, French Crystal 85.00
    8-1/2" d, Five Fruits, green 40.00
    10-1/4" d, Catalonian, yellow 40.00
    12" d, Five Fruits, white 65.00
    12" d, Martelé, Orchid, pink, birds and flowers 115.00
Platter, Dancing Nymph, Palace, dark blue wash 1,000.00
Puff Box, cov
    Hummingbirds, milk glass 75.00
    Lovebirds, blue 95.00
Salt and Pepper Shakers, pr
    Cone, pink 75.00
    Cosmos 185.00
    Guttate, green 85.00
Sauce Dish, Criss-Cross, cranberry opalescent 55.00
Sherbet, ftd
    Catalonian, green 20.00
    Dancing Nymph, French Crystal 80.00
Snack Set, Martelé Fruits, pink 45.00
Spooner, Criss-Cross, cranberry opalescent 75.00
Sugar Bowl, cov
    Catalonian, green 30.00
    Guttate, cased pink 120.00
Sugar Shaker, orig top
    Cone, green 95.00
    Guttate, cased pink, pewter top 200.00
Sundae, Martelé Russet Yellow Fruits 35.00
Syrup
    Cone, squatty, pink 295.00
    Cosmos, SP top 275.00
Toilet Bottle, Ruba Rhombic, cased jade green 650.00
Toothpick Holder
    Florette, cased pink 75.00

Guttate, cranberry 185.00
Tumbler
    Catalonian, ftd, green, 5-1/4" h 30.00
    Cosmos 85.00
    Dancing Nymph, frosted pink, 6" h. 175.00
    Guttate, pink satin 60.00
    Katydid, clambroth 165.00
    Martelé Russet Yellow Fruits, ftd, 5-3/4" h. 5.00
    Ruba Rhombic, jade, 5-1/2" h 325.00
    Umbrella Vase, Blackberry. 550.00
Vase
    Catalonian, #1183, three tiers, honey, 6" h 165.00
    Con-Cora, milk glass, hp flowers, 12" h, 8-1/2" d 95.00
    Dancing Nymph, crimped, ruby stain, reverse French Crystal highlights, 5" h 135.00
    Dancing Nymph, crimped, rust stain, reverse highlights, 5" h
    . . . . 140.00
    Florentine, collared, flat, green, 12" h 275.00
    Freesia, white ceramic wash, fan. 225.00
    Hummingbird, #2588, turquoise on satin custard, 5-1/2" h
    . . . . 90.00
    Katydid, blue wash, fan shaped top, 8-1/2" h. 300.00
    Lovebirds, custard yellow ground, pale green birds, coral colored flowers, 11-1/4" h, 10" w 600.00
    Poppy, green cased 550.00
    Purple leaf and berry design, opalescent, 9-3/4" h . . 225.00
    Regent Line, #3758, cased blue stretch over white opal, pinched, 6" h 175.00
    Ruba Rhombic, French Silver, 9-1/2" h 4,000.00

CONTINENTAL CHINA and PORCELAIN (GENERAL)

History: By 1700, porcelain factories existed in large numbers throughout Europe. In the mid-18th century, the German factories at Meissen and Nymphenburg were dominant. As the century ended, French potteries assumed the leadership role. The 1740s to the 1840s were the golden age of Continental china and porcelains.

Americans living in the last half of the 19th century eagerly sought the masterpieces of the European porcelain factories. In the early 20th century, this style of china and porcelain was considered "blue chip" by antiques collectors.

References: Susan and Al Bagdade, *Warman's English & Continental Pottery & Porcelain*, 3rd Edition, Krause Publications, 1998; Rachael Feild, *Macdonald Guide to Buying Antique Pottery & Porcelain*, Wallace-Homestead, 1987; Geoffrey Godden, *Godden's Guide to European Porcelain*, Random House, 1993.

Additional Listings: French—Haviland, Limoges, Old Paris, Sarreguemines, and Sevres; German—Austrian Ware, Bavarian China, Carlsbad China, Dresden/Meissen, Rosenthal, Royal Bayreuth, Royal Bonn, Royal Rudolstadt, Royal Vienna, Schlegelmilch, and Villeroy and Boch; Italian—Capo-di-Monte.

French

Chantilly
    Dish, 9-3/4" l, quatrefoil, Kakiemon palette, chrysanthemum, chocolate rim, c1740 . . . . 200.00

Plate, 9-1/2" d, blue and white, carnations, basketwork border, blue hunting horn mark, c1845, price for 12 pc set
. . . . 750.00
Faience
    Bowl, ftd, two scrolling vine handles, bowl with fleur-de-lis, dragonfly, and grotesque dec 325.00
    Milk Pitcher, floral spray dec, sgd "L. M. & Son, Creil & Montereau," pr 180.00
    Tile Plaque, 30" h, 72" w, rect panel of 78 tiles, youths encouraging anger of dog, 19th C 1,500.00
Galle Faience
    Compote, 9" d, scalloping rim, waisted cylindrical base, dark blue and yellow, blossom sprays, central unicorn and centaur, sgd "E Galle Nancy," price for pr 990.00
    Figure, 13-1/4" h, seated brown tabby cat, green glass eyes, sgd "Galle Nancy," minor restoration 500.00
Longwy
    Box, cov, 7-1/2" d, circular, polychrome parrot on lid
. . . . 225.00
    Plaque, 8 x 6-1/2" oval, crane in marsh, cobalt blue field
. . . . 80.00
Paris
    Box, cov, circular, Napoleonic dec within circular cartouche, royal blue ground 500.00
    Figure, 19-3/4" h, flamingo and crane, scroll dec base, pr
. . . . .2,200.00
    Fruit Basket, 14-1/4" l, 6" h, openwork, oval body, gilt dec scrolled foliage dec, pierced galleries surrounded by central blue enamel monogrammed medallions, 19th C, hairlines
. . . . 230.00
    Supper Service, each pc painted with foliate sprays and mustard yellow borders, ftd basket, six bowls, ten cups and saucers, seven plates, three platters, sauceboat and tray, three open serving bowls, one covered serving bowl, second quarter 19th C, some restoration and wear 1,265.00
    Vase, 14-1/2" h, goat head and fruiting grapevine handles, blue enamel ground, figural and floral cartouches, restoration, pr 575.00
Samson
    Jar, 14" h, Famille Rose, Phoenix, floral, and dragon dec, mounted as lamp 500.00
    Salts, cov, figural, 7-1/2" h, male and female figures supporting oval two handled baskets on their laps, enamel dec, late 19th C, pr. 350.00
St. Cloud, cup and saucer, 2 3/4" d, white, plum tree branches, mid 18th C, price for pr. .1,700.00
Unknown Maker, centerpiece, 12" l, oval porcelain dish, Commedia del Arte figures in landscape on gilt and sky blue ground, four scrolling legs terminating in oval base, ormolu mounts 1,200.00

German

Ansbach, coffeepot, 8" h, pear shape, dome cov with fruit finial, scrolling handle, short spout, molded female mask and feathers, loose bouquets and scattered flowers dec, c1765, blue coat of arms and "A" mark, restored finial 1,200.00
Berlin
    Plaque, 8-1/2" l, oval, peasant boy with recorder, imp marks, early 20th C 980.00
    Presentation Vase, 31" h, Munchner form, blue ground, gilt foliate and paneled borders, polychrome enamel dec with half portrait to one side, flanked by ascending promotions in rank to one side and victories in Napolenic War to the other, panels of Prussian soldiers below each handle reverse inscribed in gilt "Dem Koniglichen General Lietenant, Com-

mandeur der Sten Division, Ersten Commandauten von Erfurt, hern Hans Friederich August von Vols, ihrem wahrahaft Vaterlichen und hoctiverehrten Fuhrer bei seinem funfzigjahrigen Dienst Jubilaum, van der Officerem der Division," mid 19th C, restoration to handles and base socles. 41,400.00

Furtstenburg, charger, 15-1/4" d, blue floral dec, 18th C
. . . . 800.00

Herend
    Dinnerware Service, green band and floral spray dec, 11 soup plates, 12 dinner plates, 9 salad plates, 5 bread plates, sauce boat with two handles, low fruit bowl, oval 14" platter
. . . . .1,100.00
    Fruit Bowl, 10-1/2" l oval, open work, hp center, pink, gold, and blue dec 250.00

Hoechst, figure, 5-1/2" w, 5-1/2" h, two children dancing, painted factory marks, mid-19th C 375.00

Nymphenburg
    Cup and Saucer, 3-3/4" d, bell shaped bowl, Maximillian Joseph Platz, burnished gilt int. and scroll handle, c1835
. . . . .1,900.00
    Figure, 3-1/4" h, sparrow, realistic color enamels . . . 125.00
    Tea Set, black border, magenta rim, magenta floral sprays, spherical teapot, creamer, 12 teacups and saucers, cake plates, circular tray, damage to teapot. 550.00

(French) Urns, enameled ovoid body, 18th C scene gallant, blue trumpet necks with gilt scrollwork, slender feet flaring to conforming sq chamfered corner plinth base, Rococo style applied handles, pr, 21" h, $4,500. Photo courtesy of Freeman\Fine Arts of Philadelphia, Inc.

Sitzendorf
    Candelabrum, five-light, scrolled arms and putti form standard, courting couple, base with plethora of foliage, late 19th C, restorations, chips 460.00
    Compote, 10" h, maiden with bird and cage in bocage surrounded with lamp, late 19th C, minor chips 300.00
    Potpourri Urn, 11" h, cupid handles, high relief modeling with flowering vines, late 19th C, minor chips 200.00

Thieme, Carl, Saxonian Porcelain Factory
    Candlesticks, pr, 6-1/2" h, enamel dec scrolled panels of cherubs between gilt lattice and enameled floral designs
. . . . 150.00
    Teapot, cov, 6" h, globular form, applied flowers and leaves, figural landscape, floral panels, mark for Carl Thieme Saxonian Porcelain Factory, chips. 400.00

Thuringia Factory, compote, 4-1/4" h, figural, pierced dish with floral and fruit dec, supported by three cherubs, Thuringia mark, late 19th C 175.00

Unknown Maker
    Fruit Bowl, ftd, 15" h, openwork basket, cupid standard, foliate molded base, chips, repairs 350.00

Woflsohn, Helene, urn, cov, 13" h, magenta ground, painted reserves of battle scenes on both sides, attributed, Dresden, late 19th C, pr. 1,725.00

Volkstedt, figure, 13-3/4" h, 27" l, white glazed, eight figures clad in 18th C dress, surrounding piano, rococo framed oval base, underglazed printed mark, restorations, hairline . . .1,495.00

Italian

Deruta, jar, 7 1/4" h, majolica, scrollwork, grotesques and leaf forms, inscribed "Ghoma di Lava" 500.00

Doccia
    Cup and Saucer, flaring cylindrical cup, C-scroll handle, purple highlights, c1755, price for pr. 145.00
    Dish, 9 5/8" w, shell shape, central bouquet of purple flowers surrounded by floral sprays, continuous twisting branches of leaves and nuts border, five point purple star mark, c1780
. . . . 165.00

Istoriato, charger, 16" d, majolica, underglaze blue, yellow, and red luster enamels dec, central scene of Roman legions rallying around their standards, wide scrolling grotesque border
. . . . 200.00

Savona, compote, 14" d, blue and white dec, floral border, pierced, blue lighthouse mark 1,200.00

COOKIE JARS

History: Cookie jars, colorful and often whimsical, are now an established collecting category. Some large collections have now begun to come to the antiques and collectibles marketplace. Prices seem to be steady and increasing. However, collectors are becoming more discerning when selecting cookie jars and seek the finest examples.

Cookie jars often were redesigned to reflect newer tastes. Hence, the same jar may be found in several different variations.

Marks: Many cookie jar shapes were manufactured by more than one company and, as a result, can be found with different marks. This often happened because of mergers or separations, e.g., Brush-McCoy which became Nelson McCoy. Molds also were traded and sold among companies.

References: Mary Jane Giacomini, *American Bisque*, Schiffer Publishing, 1994; *1995 Cookie Jar Express Pricing Guide to Cookie Jars*, Paradise Publications, 1995; Fred and Joyce Roerig, *Collector's Encyclopedia of Cookie Jars*, Book I (1991, 1993 value update), Book II (1994), Book III (1997), Collector Books; Mark and Ellen Supnick, *Wonderful World of Cookie Jars*, L-W Book Sales, 1995; Ermagene Westfall, *Illustrated Value Guide to Cookie Jars*, Book I (1983, 1995 value update), Book II (1993, 1995 value update), Collector Books.

Periodicals: *Cookie Jar Collectors Express*, P.O. Box 221, Mayview, MO 64071; *Cookie Jarrin'*, RR 2, Box 504, Walterboro, SC 29488.

Collectors' Club: The Cookie Jar Collector's Club, 595 Cross River Rd., Katonah, NY 10536.

Museum: The Cookie Jar Museum, Lemont, IL.

Abingdon
Humpty Dumpty	295.00
Jack in Box	450.00
Jack O'Lantern	350.00
Old Lady, #471	235.00
Train, turquoise	200.00

American Bisque
Baby Elephant	175.00
Casper the Friendly Ghost	450.00
Cow Jumping Over The Moon, flasher	975.00
Donkey pulling cart	75.00
Humpty Dumpty	455.00

Robinson Ransbottom, Hi Diddle Diddle, $310. Photo courtesy of House in the Woods Auction Gallery.

Mohawk Indian	2,200.00
Paddle Boat	275.00
Saddle, "Mustn't Forget" blackboard	300.00
Seal, igloo	350.00

Appleman, Glenn, Rolls Royce 850.00

Brayton Laguna
Matilda	900.00
Plaid Dog	360.00

Brechner, Dan
Mickey Mouse School Bus	750.00
Mickey's 60th Anniversary, giant cake, 1988	425.00

Brush
Covered Wagon	500.00
Davy Crockett	225.00
Dog, basket	350.00
Hillbilly Frog	4,200.00
Little Red Riding Hood	795.00

California Originals
Koala on Stump	275.00
Pinocchio	950.00
Tigger	200.00

Cavanaugh, Henry, Good Humor Truck 225.00

Disney
Bambi on Tree Stump, small chip	1,000.00
Donald Duck, on pumpkin	400.00
Dumbo with Timothy	175.00
Mickey in car	450.00

Doranne of California
Brown Shoe	40.00
Cow Jumped Over the Moon, green	200.00
Dragon	275.00

Enesco
Betsy Ross	75.00
Sugar Town General Store	65.00

Fitz and Floyd
Busy Bunnies Tree	150.00
English Garden Wheelbarrow	165.00
Hydrangea Bears	170.00
Rolls Royce	175.00
Santa, in airplane	200.00
Sock Hoppers	300.00

Goode, George, Tazmanian Devil in Whirlwind 200.00

Lefton
Bluebird	165.00
Miss Priss	85.00
Old Lady	110.00
Pixie Baby	125.00
Scottish Mist	200.00
Young Lady	95.00

McCoy
Cat on Coal Bucket	200.00
Christmas Tree	725.00
Clyde Dog	200.00
Football Boy	295.00
Train, yellow	150.00

Metlox
Frosty the Penguin	100.00
Koala Bear	100.00
Little Red Riding Hood	1,275.00
Pinocchio Head	235.00
Pretty Anne	205.00
Rabbit on Cabbage	110.00
Scottie Dog, black	75.00
Squirrel on Pine Cone	75.00
Walrus	235.00
Watermelon	365.00

Mosaic Tile, Mammy, yellow 500.00
Napco
    Bo Peep 175.00
    Cinderella 175.00
    Little Red Riding Hood 175.00
Regal
    Chef 475.00
    Diaper-Pin Pig 450.00
    Fifi Poodle 525.00
    Goldilocks 225.00
    Hobby Horse 275.00
    Three Bears 325.00
Roehrig, Smokey Bear, 50th Anniversary 275.00
Roman Ceramics
    C3PO, orig box 550.00
    Mickey Mouse on Drum 350.00
Sigma, Circus Lady 200.00
Star Jars, Wizard of Oz, complete set, Dorothy and Toto, Cowardly Lion, Scarecrow, Tin Man, Wicked Witch, Glenda, Winged Monkey, Munchkin Mayor, Wizard of Oz, Professor Marvel, Emerald City, Ruby Slippers 1,900.00
Starnes
    Barn Happy Face 300.00
    Bear Blocks 150.00
Twin Winton
    Ark 150.00
    Bambi 180.00
    Dutch Girl 115.00
    Gunfighter Rabbit 250.00
    Jack In Box 500.00
    Santa, black 625.00
    Smokey the Bear 90.00
Warner Bros.
    Roadrunner and Acme TNT 400.00
    Superman 110.00
    Tweety on Flour Sack 100.00

COPELAND and SPODE

History: In 1749, Josiah Spode was apprenticed to Thomas Whieldon and in 1754 worked for William Banks in Stoke-on-Trent. In the early 1760s, Spode started his own pottery, making cream-colored earthenware and blue-printed whiteware. In 1770, he returned to Banks' factory as master, purchasing it in 1776.

Spode pioneered the use of steam-powered pottery-making machinery and mastered the art of transfer printing from copper plates. Spode opened a London shop in 1778 and sent William Copeland there about 1784. A number of larger London locations followed. At the turn of the century, Spode introduced bone china. In 1805, Josiah Spode II and William Copeland entered into a partnership for the London business. A series of partnerships between Josiah Spode II, Josiah Spode III, and William Taylor Copeland resulted.

In 1833, Copeland acquired Spode's London operations and seven years later the Stoke plants. William Taylor Copeland managed the business until his death in 1868. The firm remained in the hands of Copeland heirs. In 1923, the plant was electrified; other modernization followed.

In 1976, Spode merged with Worcester Royal Porcelain to become Royal Worcester Spode, Ltd.

References: Susan and Al Bagdade, *Warman's English & Continental Pottery & Porcelain*, 3rd Edition, Krause Publications, 1998; Robert Copeland, *Spode & Copeland Marks*, Cassell Academic, 1993; ——, *Spode's Willow Pattern & Other Designs After the Chinese*, Blanford Press, 1990; D. Drakard & P. Holdway, *Spode Printed Wares*, Longmans, 1983; L. Whiter, *Spode: A History of the Family, Factory, and Wares, 1733-1833*, Random Century, 1989; Sydney B. Williams, *Antique Blue & White Spode*, David & Charles, 1988.

Museums: Cincinnati Art Museum, Cincinnati, OH; City of Stoke-On-Trent Museum, Hanley, England; Jones Museum of Glass & Ceramics, Sebago, ME; Spode Museum, Stoke-on-Trent, UK; Victoria & Albert Museum, London, England.

Bowl
    8-1/2" d, Imari type, blue, green, and range, scalloped edge, pedestal base, c1850 . . . . 85.00
    9-3/4" sq, cut corner, Imari-style dec, c1825, Spode mark, minor gilding and over glaze enamel wear 650.00
Bust, 8-1/4" h, Sir Walter Scott, parian, mounted to raised circular base, imp Copeland mark, c1875 . . . . 230.00
Centerpiece, 12" h, majolica, shell molded bowl surmounted by putto supporting small shell molded bowl on head, molded coral base, imp mark, c1875, rim chip repair 990.00
Charger, 13-1/2" d, Imari style, red and blue enamels, gilt trim, floral border with scroll pattern and Chinese motif, imp "Spode New Stone China," c1810 . . . . 550.00
Compote, 10" h, figural, reticulated dish, putti form standard, late 19th C, pr, one with damage to rim 1,265.00
Creamer and Sugar, 3-1/4" h, Blue Willow, marked "Copeland's China England" 200.00
Demitasse Cup and Saucer, 4-1/2" d, gilt trim enamel floral design, pink ground, c1900, set of six 700.00
Dinner Service, elegant gold and multicolored floral design, large, c1805-15 . . . . 5,500.00
Figure
    12" h, Lady of the Lake, nude figure, loosely draped cloth, seated on back, molded fish and reeds below, parian, imp marks "Marshall Fect SC, Copeland," mid 19th C . . 400.00
    19 1/8" h, Young Shrimper, holding shell, dragging net, parian, c1880, imp Copeland marks, chips 550.00
Flower Pot, 5" h, ftd base, gilted sea serpent head handles and trim, hp floral panels, striped bodies, painted Spode mark, gilt rim wear, price for pr 2,185.00
Luncheon Service, pattern 1721, Kakiemon style, enameled and gilt dec, twenty-one 8-1/2" d plates, four shrimp dishes, four 9-1/2" oval vegetable dishes, 10-1/4" d oval vegetable dish, three 9" d round vegetable dishes, two 7" cov oval sauce tureens with underplates, 14" l oval compote, Spode, early 19th C, price for 40 pc set 2,875.00
Oyster Plate, hp, insects and flowers 50.00
Pitcher, jasper, blue, 19th C 150.00
Plate, Imari palette, ironstone, c1833, Copeland and Garrett mark, pr 175.00
Platter, 21" l 15-1/2" w, Imari-style, well and tree, c1840, mkd "Copeland & Garrett" 450.00
Punch Bowl, 12-1/2" d, multicolored, Chinese garden scene, gold trim, c1810 . . . . 750.00
Salt and Pepper Shakers, pr, Red Tower pattern 20.00

Basket, white exterior, shaded pink to white int., gold floral and leaf trim, basketweave, intertwined pink handle, gold trim, c1851-85, 11-1/4" l, 8-1/2" h, $250.

Service Plate, 10-1/4" d, wide blue ground rim bounded by emb gilt bands, 20th C, set of twelve 690.00

Tea and Dessert Service, semi-porcelain, Black Bird pattern, red on white, teapot, cov sugar, creamer, cov warm milk jug, eight dessert plates, seven cups and saucers, sq serving plate, minor damage, price for 31 pc set 75.00

Tureen, cov, Imari palette, ironstone, c1833, Copeland and Garrett mark 690.00

Wall Brackets, parian, from Mississippi antebellum mansion, mkd "Copeland," pr. 3,740.00

COPPER

History: Copper objects, such as kettles, teakettles, warming pans, and measures, played an important part in the 19th-century household. Outdoors, the apple-butter kettle and still were the two principal copper items. Copper culinary objects were lined with a thin protective coating of tin to prevent poisoning. They were relined as needed.

References: Mary Frank Gaston, *Antique Brass & Copper*, Collector Books, 1992, 1994 value update; Henry J. Kauffman, *Early American Copper, Tin, and Brass: Handcrafted Metalware from Colonial Times*, Astragal Press, 1995.

Reproduction Alert: Many modern reproductions exist.

Additional Listings: Arts and Crafts Movement; Roycroft.

Notes: Collectors place great emphasis on signed pieces, especially those by American craftsmen. Since copper objects were made abroad as well, it is hard to identify unsigned examples.

Apple Butter Kettle, applied iron handle, cramped seam joining, large 75.00

Bed Warmer, 45" l, engraved floral and bird, turned wood handle
. . . . 375.00

Bookends, pr, 5-1/2" h, hammered, Dirk van Erp, imp mark, cleaned patina 300.00

Bowl

8-1/2" d, 3-1/2" h, hand hammered, curving rim, light patina, imp Kalo Shops mark. 195.00

15-1/2" d, 4" h, symbol shape, rolled edge, light patina, imp Marie Zimmerman mark, No. 95 . . . . .1,495.00

Box, 7" l, 2-1/2" h, hammered, cedar lined, Dirk van Erp, imp mark, lightly cleaned patina 550.00

Candleholder, four holders, sgd "W L Fletcher" 40.00

Chafing Dish, 11" h, dish supported by three realistically modeled rabbits, wooden base, marked "Black, Starr & Forest"
. . . . 450.00

Coal Hod, 17" h, brass handles, 19th C 165.00

Coffeepot, 11" h, wrought, tapering, lift lid with small turned copper finial, curved spout, side apple wood handle, attached to stylized copper heart mounting 350.00

Coffee Urn, 14-/2" h, brass fittings, label inside lid "Parkinson's Manufactury, London" 225.00

Dipper, 80" l, orig pole with wrought iron fittings 650.00

Fish Cooker, 10" w, 7" h, punched tin insert, hinged top, handles
. . . . 40.00

Hotwater Bottle, 17-1/2" l, oval, pewter fittings, screw cap with ring, old patina 140.00

Kettle, 18" d, 16-1/2" h, wrought iron rim, bale handle, old patina
. . . . 165.00

Lamp, 9" h, 5-3/4" w, compressed sq, circular foot rim, beaded mid molding, patinated, applied silver seaweed, fish, seashells, and crab dec, orig wick holder now fitted for electricity, marked "Gorham," 1884 . . . . .3,850.00

Measure

5" d, 3-7/8" h, cylindrical, brass rim, labeled "Fairbanks & Co., US Standard New York". 300.00

6-1/4" h, haystack, Continental, 19th C 75.00

Pitcher, 9-1/4" h, tankard shape, marked "D Bentley & Sons, N 3rd St., Phila" 75.00

Preserving Pot, 28" d, loop wrought iron handle, 19th C 450.00

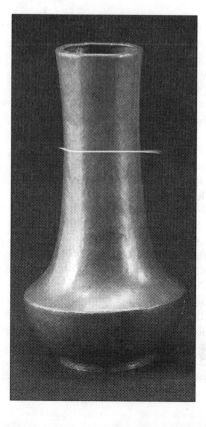

Vase, Jauchen's Old Copper Shop, hammered, bottle shape, orig medium patina, die-stamped mark, 10-1/2" h, 5" d, $1,100. Photo courtesy of David Rago Auctions, Inc.

Sauce Pan, 8" d, dovetailed, wrought copper handle 75.00
Tea Kettle
   5" h, dovetailed, polished, swivel handle, replaced lid
      . . . . 200.00
   6" h, dovetailed, polished, swivel handle, dents, pinpoint
      holes in bottom. 200.00
   6-1/2" h, dovetailed, stamped "D. M. D." 160.00
   7-1/4" h, dovetailed, goose neck spout 165.00
   8" d, circular, brass knob finial, flat serving handle, marked "P
      Apple, Philadelphia," 18th/19th C 575.00
   8-1/2" d, circular, brass knob finial, flat serving handle,
      marked "C Tryon". 550.00
Trade Sign, 16" w, 14" h, coppersmith's, candle with candleholder shape, Arts and Crafts era, American 275.00
Vase, 9" h, 9" w, hammered, bulbous form, rolled rim, Arts &
   Crafts style, attributed to San Francisco School, orig patina
      . . . . 800.00
Vessel, 11" d, 7-1/2" h, hammered copper, warty design, rich red
   patina, applied handle, Arts & Crafts style, attributed to San
   Francisco School 750.00

CORALENE

History: Coralene refers to glass or china objects which
have the design painted on the surface of the piece along
with tiny colorless glass beads which were applied with a
fixative. The piece was placed in a muffle to fix the enamel and set the beads.

Several American and English companies made glass
coralene in the 1880s. Seaweed or coral were the most
common design. Other motifs were Wheat Sheaf and
Fleur-de-Lis. Most of the base glass was satin finished.

China and pottery coralene, made from the late 1890s
until after World War II, is referred to as Japanese coralene. The beading is opaque and inserted into the soft
clay. Hence, it is only one-half to three-quarters visible.

REPRODUCTION ALERT

Reproductions are on the market, some using an old
glass base. The beaded decoration on new coralene
has been glued and can be scraped off.

China

Box, cov, 1-1/2" x 2" x 3", copper matte ground, pink, lavender,
   and green thistle, mkd "Kinran Pat. 16132 Japan". . . 140.00
Sugar Shaker, white ground, orange coralene seaweed dec,
   orig top 180.00
Vase, 8" h, bulbous, scalloped and fluted rim, shaded lavender
   to light blue ground, multicolored snapdragons 250.00

Glass

Bowl, 5-1/2" d, peachblow, ruffled, yellow coralene seaweed dec
   . . . . 190.00
Pickle Castor, 7" h, rubena inverted thumbprint insert, coralene
   butterflies, floral wreath, bird finial cov, cucumbers and
   leaves on vine, ring handle, low silverplated frame, marked
   "Derby Silver Co. #147" 825.00
Pitcher
   5-1/4" h, cased white ground, bright pink lining, gold seaweed
      coralene, applied amber reeded handle 225.00
   6-1/4" h, shaded yellow ground, white lining, coralene sea-
      weed dec 350.00

**Vase, seaweed coralene, rainbow ground, attrib-
uted to Mt. Washington, 5-3/4" h, $375.**

   6-1/2" h, pink and white satin stripes, yellow branch coralene,
      rose int., bulbous shape, tricorner mouth, amber applied
      handle, polished pontil 500.00
Sweetmeat, blue ground, flowers and leaves, SP holder
   . . . . 400.00
Toothpick Holder, 2-1/2" h, glossy peachblow, sq raised rim, bul-
   bous body, opaque lining, yellow seaweed coralene dec
   . . . . 275.00
Vase
   4-1/2" h, Snowflake pattern, golden amber blending to pastel
      pink, cased in ivory 425.00
   4-1/2" h, 3-3/8" d, Diamond Quilted pattern, shaded pink, yel-
      low beaded coralene starts in centers of diamonds, white
      enameled beading around top edge 500.00
   5" h, 4" w, double handles, ruffled rim, orange, pattern mark
      on base, Oriental 80.00
   .5-3/8" h, golden yellow snowflake MOP satin ground, white
      lining, yellow wheat coralene dec 520.00
   5-1/2" h, 4-5/8" d, fan shaped top, opaque pink satin ground
      blends to frosted base, all over dec of yellow three leaf
      sprays with coralene beads 235.00
   6" h, white cased to yellow, yellow coralene beading, ruffled
      rim 250.00
   7" h, ruffled pink top shading to white mother of pearl, cor-
      alene flowers and butterfly 90.00
   7-1/2" h, blue ground, bulbous, yellow coralene seaweed dec
      . . . . 265.00
   7-1/2" h, peachblow satin, deep rose shading to pale pink,
      yellow coralene seaweed dec, gold trim top, white casing,
      polished pontil, c1870, mkd "PATENT" 850.00
   7-3/4" h, 4-3/4" d, pink and green striped satin ground,
      off-white lining, heavy yellow beaded coralene 475.00

8" h, crimped wave mouth, yellow seaweed pattern, shaded pink ground 200.00

8" h, 5" d, alternating pink, white, and green striped satin ground, shades to white base, yellow coralene beading 520.00

8-1/2" h, green shaded ground, green beading, gold tracery 350.00

CORKSCREWS

History: The corkscrew is composed of three parts: handle, shaft, and worm or screw. The earliest known reference to "a Steele Worme used for drawing corks out of bottles" is 1681. Samuel Henshall, an Englishman, was granted the first patent in 1795.

Elaborate mechanisms were invented and patented from the early 1800s onward, especially in England. However, three basic types emerged: T handle (the most basic, simple form), lever, and mechanism. Variations on these three types run into the hundreds. Miniature corkscrews, employed for drawing corks from perfume and medicine bottles between 1750 and 1920, are among those most eagerly sought by collectors.

Corkscrew styles tend to reflect the preferences of specific nationalities. The English favored the helix worm and often coppertoned their steel products. By the mid-18th century, English and Irish silversmiths were making handles noted for their clean lines and practicality. Most English silver handles were hallmarked.

The Germans preferred the center worm and nickel plate. The Italians used chrome plate or massive solid brass. In the early 1800s, the Dutch and French developed elaborately artistic silver handles.

Americans did not begin to manufacture quality corkscrews until the late 19th century. They favored the center worm and specialized in silver-mounted tusks and carved staghorn for handles.

Reference: Fred O'Leary, *Corkscrews*, Schiffer Publishing, 1996.

Collectors' Clubs: Canadian Corkscrew Collectors Club, 670 Meadow Wood Rd., Mississaugua, Ontario, L5J 2S6 Canada; Just For Openers, 3712 Sunningdale Way, Durham, NC 27707.

Bone Handle
   Mechanism type, English rack and pinion corkscrew, polished, brush and hanging ring, four plain post open barrel, narrow rack, long wire helix, side handle, sgd "Verinder" 410.00
   T-handle, Henshall, incised button, helical worm, c1820 . . . . 125.00
Brass Case, mechanism type, secondary wood swivel jointed handle, brush, applied Royal supporters, marked "Thomson Patent New Plus Ultra" 300.00
Brass, rack and pinion type, double, steel shaft, center worm, cap lifter in handle, Italian, 1920. . . . . 40.00
Bronzed Steel, lever, Heeley A1, double lever patent, helical worm. 65.00
Cast Iron, clamp on mechanism type, lacy openwork, emb "Phoenix," patented 1887 . . . . 200.00
Celluloid, novelty type, figural mermaid, bends at waist, marked "Geschutz" 275.00
Chrome, lever, zig-zag design, French, 10-1/2" l extended 65.00
Ebony Handle, mechanism type, steel frame, foliate scrolling raised arm, steel ciphered worm, marked "Champion, Made in USA" 110.00
Ivory Handle, miniature, crescent shape, chromed turned steel shaft wire helix, c1790-1820. . . . . 75.00
Palmette Handle, miniature, carved handle with MOP, helical worm. 30.00
Silver, novelty type, gaucho and horse, oblong platform handle, Archimedian screw. 775.00
Staghorn Handle, T-handle, ornate SS cap 100.00
Wood Handle, duck bill cap, simple Archimedian screw, German 85.00

COWAN POTTERY

History: R. Guy Cowan founded the Cowan Pottery in 1913 in Cleveland, Ohio. The establishment remained in almost continuous operation until 1931, when financial difficulties forced closure.

Early production was redware pottery. Later a porcelain-like finish was perfected with special emphasis placed on glazes, with lustreware being one of the most common types. Commercial wares marked "Lakeware" were produced from 1927 to 1931.

Marks: Early marks include an incised "Cowan Pottery" on the redware (1913-1917), an impressed "Cowan," and an impressed "Lakewood." The imprinted stylized semicircle, with or without the initials "R. G.," came later.

References: Mark Bassett and Victorian Naumann, *Cowan Pottery and the Cleveland School,* Schiffer Publishing, 1997; Leslie Piña, *Pottery, Modern Wares 1920-1960,* Schiffer Publishing, 1994; Tim and Jamie Saloff, *Collec-*

Dutch Silver, Baroque pattern, Amsterdam mark, late 18th C, pipe tamper base, $775.

tor's Encyclopedia of Cowan Pottery: Identification and Values, Collector Books, 1994.

Museums: Cowan Pottery Museum, Rocky River Public Library, Rocky River, OH; Everson Museum of Art, Syracuse, NY.

Bookends, pr, Push and Pull Elephants 1,400.00
Bowl
    8" d, irid blue luster glaze, minor roughness on base . 50.00
    12" d, irid blue luster glaze, ink mark 70.00
Candlesticks, pr, 5-1/2" h, 10-1/2" l, swirling molded floral design, ivory with yellow tint, imp mark 170.00
Cigarette Holder, ashtray, figural duck, yellow 85.00
Console Set, Art Deco styled bowl with radial lines, Nubian design, April Green glaze, matching pr of candleholders
    . . . . 400.00
Decanter, Standing Queen from Alice in Wonderland, Oriental Red, by artist Waylande DeSantis Gregory 675.00
Figure
    Bird on Wave, by Alexander Blazys, 12" h, melon green, broken and repaired 775.00
    Horse, 9" l, by Ralph Howard Cowan, Egyptian blue glaze
    . . . . .1,500.00
    Nautch Dancer, by Waylande Gregory ,17-3/4" h
    . . . . .10,450.00
    Russian Accordion Player (#34), artist Alexander Blazys
    . . . . .1,000.00
    Russian Balalaika Player (#44), by Alexander Blazys
    . . . . .1,800.00
Flower Frog, 6-1/2" h, Pavlova flower figure (#698), designed by R. Guy Cowan and Walter Sinz 270.00
Lamp, 19" h, molded squirrel and birds, brown and ivory, imp mark, orig fittings, later fabric shade 350.00

Flower Figure, swan, Special Ivory glaze, imp circular mark and "Cowan," 1930, 12" h, 6" d, $1,300. Photo courtesy of David Rago Auctions, Inc.

Lamp Base
    16-1/2" h, Art Deco birds, wing-like handles, Guava glaze
    . . . . 800.00
    19" h, molded leaves, gray and ivory semi-gloss glaze, orig fittings. 100.00
Vase
    5" h, shouldered form, pink and maroon high glaze, imp mark
    . . . . 70.00
    7" h, molded design, nude woman, long flowing hair, red hi-glaze, imp mark, minor line to lip 1,000.00

CRANBERRY GLASS

History: Cranberry glass is transparent and named for its color, achieved by adding powdered gold to a molten batch of amber glass and reheating at a low temperature to develop the cranberry or ruby color. The glass color first appeared in the last half of the 17th century but was not made in American glass factories until the last half of the 19th century.

    Cranberry glass was blown, mold blown, or pressed. Examples often are decorated with gold or enamel. Less-expensive cranberry glass, made by substituting copper for gold, can be identified by its bluish purple tint.

Reference: William Heacock and William Gamble, *Encyclopedia of Victorian Colored Pattern Glass: Book 9, Cranberry Opalescent from A to Z*, Antique Publications, 1987.

REPRODUCTION ALERT

Reproductions abound. These pieces are heavier, off-color, and lack the quality of older examples.

Additional Listings: See specific categories, such as Bride's Baskets; Cruets; Jack-in-the-Pulpit Vases; etc.

Barber Bottle, sterling silver tip 350.00
Basket
    7" h. 5" w, petticoat shape, ruffled edge, colorless loop handle, Victorian 250.00
    7-1/2" h, 6-3/4" w, boat-shaped basket, dark cranberry, all over gold dec, white florals, wide gold band, brass ftd vase with flower form handle 200.00
    8" h, 5" w, deep color, ruffled edge, applied colorless handle, Victorian. 90.00
    8-1/2" h, 5" w, rose bowl form, Diamond Quilted pattern, ruffled edge, applied wishbone feet, V-shaped loop handle
    . . . . 150.00
    9" h, 5" w, deep cranberry int., amber casing on ext., white and gold aventurine flecks, applied amber feet, amber U-shaped handle 90.00
    9" h, 5" w, very deep cranberry int., slight ribbed int., applied colorless wishbone rigaree around top, twelve applied feet, applied colorless twisted loop handle, Victorian, flake on one foot, ... 100.00
Biscuit Barrel, frosted, bear finial top 450.00
Bottle, 9-3/4" h, 3-1/2" d, dainty white enameled flowers around middle, white enameled dots dec, colorless teardrop stopper
    . . . . 175.00
Bowl, 5-1/2" d, 6-1/2" d underplate, swirl pattern 65.00
Bride's Bowl, 9" sq, 3-1/2" h, finely executed enameled apple blossom dec, fancy ornate SP orig holder mkd "Middletown Silver Co.," Mt. Washington 950.00
Candlesticks, pr, 10-5/8" h, heavily encrusted gold and polychrome dec. 190.00

Decanters, English, colorless handles and stoppers, left: 8-1/2" h, $80; right: 9-1/2" h, $95.

Celery Vase, 10" h, Thumbprint pattern, enameled flowers and birds, ornate handles, ftd mount, orig silverplated Jas. Tufts Co. frame 550.00
Claret Jug, 10-3/4" h, 4-5/8" h, French emb pewter hinged top, foot, and handle 320.00
Cologne Bottle, 8-5/8" h, 2-3/8" d, gold scrolls, small gold flowers, matching sq cranberry bubble stopper 185.00
Creamer, 5" h, 2-3/4" d, Optic pattern, fluted top, applied colorless handle 95.00
Cruet, orig stopper
    6-1/2" h, 2-3/4" d, applied colorless wafer foot, applied colorless twisted rope handle with flower prunt at base, colorless ribbed bubble stopper 135.00
    10-1/2" h, 3-7/8" d, acid cut herringbone double band around middle, applied colorless foot, applied colorless handle, colorless cut faceted stopper 190.00
Decanter
    10" h, cut to colorless, flattened colorless oval, obverse medallion engraved "Mollies Pony 1869" centering scene with horse, cut star on reverse, conforming teardrop stopper, some internal bubbles 990.00
    10-1/2" h, 3-1/4" d, cut to colorless, matching mushroom bubble stopper 250.00
    11-1/2" h, 3-7/8" d, bulbous base, pinched-in sides, lacy gold enamel dec, dark red flowers, gold enameled centers, applied colorless handle, colorless cut faceted stopper 250.00
Epergne, 19" h, 11" d, 5 pc, large ruffled bowl, tall center lily, three jack-in-the-pulpit vases 1,150.00
Jack In The Pulpit Vase, 9" h, 5" w, deep cranberry, white opal edge, applied crystal base, Hobbs 325.00
Lamp, oil
    Hobnail cranberry glass font, opaque white shade . . . 75.00
    Opaque white cut to cranberry font, replaced metal base 275.00
Lantern, masthead type, cranberry glass lens, heavy Reverse Coin Dot design, orig brass maker's label mkd "Shubert & Cottingham Philadelphia," removable fuel container patented by Hugh Sangster in 1851, 1854, and 1867 . . . . . . 4,600.00
Mantel Luster, Victorian, electrified 190.00

Mug, 4" h, 2-3/4" d, Baby Inverted Thumbprint pattern, applied colorless handle and pedestal foot 65.00
Music Box, 12-1/4" h, 5-1/4" d decanter, emb ribs with etched leaves and stars, orig colorless cut bubble stopper, not working. 310.00
Night Light, 6-1/4" h, 3-1/4" d, cranberry shade with white sanded scallops, grapes, and leaves, openwork brass top rim, gold-washed ormolu ftd frame 275.00
Perfume Bottle, 2-1/4" d, round, filigree, gilt collar 695.00
Pickle Castor, enamel dec, American silver holder and tongs 1,250.00
Pitcher
    Coin Spot, shading to white base, rippled top, applied reeded colorless glass handle, 7-1/2" h, hairline crack 65.00
    Crackle, bulbous. 245.00
    Cut Glass, cranberry cut to clear, 9" h 225.00
    Venetian pattern, large 120.00
Rose Bowl
    3-3/4" h, 3-3/4" d, worn gold rim, six-crimp top 90.00
    4" h, optic ribs, scalloped turned in rim, colorless ruffled applied pedestal base 125.00
Salt, master, crystal rigaree around middle. 150.00
Smoke Bell, 6-1/2" d, swirled, ruffled edge 600.00
Spooner, Paneled Sprig pattern 125.00
Sugar Shaker, Inverted Thumbprint pattern, nine panels 150.00
Tumbler, enameled flowers, set of 3 . . . . 70.00
Vase, 8" h
    Painted portrait of young girl, gilded floral surround, Bohemian. 175.00
    Vertical bands below diamond points, deep cut to colorless 315.00
    Vertical bands of ribbed thumbprints cut to colorless, ground pontil 110.00
Water Set, Swirl pitcher, ruffled rim, six tumblers 250.00
Wine Decanter, 12" h, opaque white cased over cranberry, enameled flowers and gilt scrollwork dec, pr 500.00

CROWN MILANO

History: Crown Milano is an American art glass produced by the Mt. Washington Glass Works, New Bedford, Massachusetts. The original patent was issued in 1886 to Frederick Shirley and Albert Steffin.

Normally, it is an opaque-white satin glass finished with light-beige or ivory-colored ground embellished with fancy florals, decorations, and elaborate and thick raised gold.

Collectors Club: Mount Washington Art Glass Society, P.O. Box 24094, Fort Worth, TX 76124-1094

Marks: Marked pieces have a purple enamel entwined "CM" with a crown on the base. Sometimes paper labels were used. Since both Mount Washington and Pairpoint supplied mountings, the silver-plated mounts often have "MW" impressed or a Pairpoint mark.

Advisors: Clarence and Betty Maier.

Biscuit Jar, 7-1/2" d, 9" h, colorful painting of couple in Colonial garb covers entire front, reverse side is a small white reserve, outlined in raised gold, gold line-drawn florals, cream colored body, base sgd "3912/80," lid sgd "M.W. 4419/c". . . . 975.00
Muffineer, 3" h, 4" d, melon-ribbed shape, chalk-white body, sprays of violet colored Johnny-Jump-Up blossoms, silvery bright metal collar and lid, embossed with butterfly, dragonfly, and blossoms 585.00

Sweetmeat Jar, Holly dec, diamond quilted body, swirls of taupe, gold, emerald leaves, red bead berries, metal top with flowers, 4" h, $650.

Salt Shaker, 4" h, ribbed, dainty blue and white daisy blossoms, Burmese-colored background 185.00

Vase

6" h, 5-3/4" d, cream-colored body, 24 swirling molded-in ribs, white peony blossoms 1,250.00

6" h, 6" d, springtime blossoms, glorious pastel hues, opposite side of flowering white dogwood, four raised gold circular embellishment, large circle with cherub riding mythical sea creature, one with a sun face surrounded by stylized dolphins, two smaller circles with geometric designs, Crown Milano logo and "583" 1,950.00

9-1/4" h, opaque white body, cup-shaped top, exquisite floral dec, two applied handles, orig paper label 1,750.00

9-1/2" h, bulbed satin white body, flared elongated neck split at rim in four decorative points, delicate pink blossoms, gold leaves and overall tracery, base mkd "(Crown) CM" in purple 950.00

12-1/4" h, satin finish, white bulbous body, graceful elongated neck, beaded gold and bronze shaded rose blossoms, buds, and thorny branches, purple crown CM mark over 565 on base 950.00

CRUETS

History: Cruets are small glass bottles used on the table and holding condiments such as oil, vinegar, and wine. The pinnacle of cruet use occurred during the Victorian era when a myriad of glass manufacturers made cruets in a wide assortment of patterns, colors, and sizes. All cruets had stoppers; most had handles.

References: Elaine Ezell and George Newhouse, *Cruets, Cruets, Cruets*, Vol. I, Antique Publications, 1991; William Heacock, *Encyclopedia of Victorian Colored Pattern*

Glass: Book 6, Oil Cruets from A to Z, Antique Publications, 1981.

Additional Listings: Pattern Glass and specific glass categories such as Amberina, Cranberry, and Satin.

Amber

Blown, ftd ovoid body, short neck, tricorn rim, blue daisies and gold leaves, applied handle, amber ball stopper, 8" h 125.00

Pressed, Log and Star pattern, orig stopper 70.00

Amberina, plated, 6-3/4" h, amber handle, orig stopper, New England Glass Co., c1886 . . . . 6,000.00

Blue Opaque, Challinor's Tree of Life pattern, orig stopper 120.00

Chinese Porcelain, Kangxi period cruet set and stand, decorated in Imari palette 12,100.00

Chocolate, Geneva pattern, Greentown Glass 1,200.00

Cobalt Blue, Medallion Sprig pattern, orig cobalt blue to clear stopper 180.00

Cranberry, bulbous base, Hobbs, orig stopper 110.00

Green, pressed

Beaded Ovals in Sand pattern, orig stopper 190.00

Beaumont's Flora pattern, gold trim, orig stopper . . . 250.00

Lavender, blown, ftd spherical body, slender cylindrical neck, gold flowers and bows, applied colorless handle and foot, colorless facet cut stopper, 7-1/4" h 225.00

Milk Glass, Beaded Swag pattern, gold trim, orig stopper 190.00

Nippon China, floral and gold dec 375.00

Opalescent

Hobb's Hobnail pattern, cranberry, orig stopper 315.00

Reverse Swirl pattern, cranberry, chrysanthemum mold base 360.00

Opalescent Hobnail, cranberry ground shading to white neck, tricorn lip, applied colorless handle, orig hobnail stopper, Fenton, $90.

Peachblow, Wheeling, petticoat type, amber handle, cut amber stopper 1,300.00
Satin, Diamond Quilted, MOP, pink, thorn handle and stopper, 5" h 590.00
Spatter, red and white, tricorn top, colorless handle, 4-1/2" h 170.00

CUP PLATES

History: Many early cups were handleless and came with deep saucers. The hot liquid was poured into the saucer and sipped from it. This necessitated another plate for the cup, hence the "cup plate."

The first cup plates made of pottery were of the Staffordshire variety. From the mid-1830s to 1840s, glass cup plates were favored. The Boston and Sandwich Glass Company was one of the main manufacturers of the lacy glass type.

References: Ruth Webb Lee and James H. Rose, *American Glass Cup Plates*, published by author, 1948, Charles E. Tuttle Co. reprint, 1985; Kenneth Wilson, *American Glass 1760-1930*, 2 Vols., Hudson Hills Press and The Toledo Museum of Art, 1994.

Collectors' Club: Pairpoint Cup Plate Collectors of America, P.O. Box 52D, East Weymouth, MA 02189.

Notes: It is extremely difficult to find glass cup plates in outstanding (mint) condition. Collectors expect some signs of use, such as slight rim roughness, minor chipping (best if under the rim), and, in rarer patterns, portions of scallops missing.

The numbers used are from the Lee-Rose book in which all plates are illustrated.

Prices are based on plates in average condition.

Glass

LR 13, deep blue, A-type mold, plain rim, New England. . 65.00
LR 28, colorless, 17 even scallops, New England or Sandwich origin. 35.00
LR 36, opal opaque, 17 even scallops 475.00
LR 46, lavender, 15 even scallops 125.00
LR 70, plain rope, Midwest origin 125.00
LR 82, acorn and leaves, silver opaque blue, fiery opalescent 575.00
LR 95, opal opaque, 10 sided, rope top and bottom. . . . 175.00
LR 109, George Washington, 6" d, small chips 150.00
LR 135, 24 bull's eyes, Midwest origin 75.00
LR 163, light green, 34 scallops, Midwest origin. 65.00
LR 179, lavender, 10 scallops, rope top and bottom, Philadelphia origin. 135.00
LR 197-E 65.00
LR 200, 96 sawtooth scallops, Midwest orig. 40.00
LR 216-C 35.00
LR 257. . . . . 35.00
LR 271. . . . . 30.00
LR 272, 43 scallops. 65.00
LR 323, opalescent 75.00
LR 332-B 30.00
LR 343-B 45.00
LR 399. . . . . 119.00
LR 412, 10 sided, Sandwich origin 100.00
LR 439-C 40.00
LR 440-B 35.00
LR 455, 48 even scallops, Sandwich origin 275.00

LR 456. . . . . 40.00
LR 458-A 15.00
LR 465-F 15.00
LR 477. . . . . 15.00
LR 479. . . . . 25.00
LR 500. . . . . 65.00
LR 522, amber, flint. 375.00
LR 547. . . . . 20.00
LR 561-A, octagonal, clear, gray striations, Washington, tilted head, Midwest origin 4,000.00
LR 565-A 30.00
LR 575. . . . . 65.00

Glass, historical

LR 576, medium blue, Sandwich origin. 95.00
LR 580, colorless, Victoria & Albert, 5-1/8" d, lacy 100.00
LR 605-A, octagonal, ship. 95.00
LR 619. . . . . 185.00
LR 653, eagle, laurel wreath 165.00
LR 658, emerald green, Boston & Sandwich origin, two tiny scallops missing 4,250.00
LR 670. . . . . 65.00
LR 676, 60 even scallops, Curling's Ft Pitt Glass Works . 75.00
LR 677-A 40.00
LR 836, Geo. Peabody, Heart & Crown, 4 3/4" d 85.00
LR 888. . . . . 30.00

Porcelain or Pottery

Davenport, pink luster, imp mark, 3-7/8" d 35.00
Pearlware, free-brushed
    Eagle dec 660.00
Green scalloped edge, polychrome flowers, 4-1/2" d . .1,485.00
Octagonal, brown band, 4" d .1,130.00
Ridgway
    Blind Boy pattern, scene of boy and mother seated on bench, floral border, medium blue transfer, c1830, 4-1/4" d 80.00
    India Temple pattern, blue, emb white border, 3-7/8" d 50.00

(Porcelain) Staffordshire, Battery, NY, dark blue transfer, 3-5/8" d, $270.

Spatter Ware, 5-1/8" d, blue morning glory center 3,245.00
Staffordshire
  American Eagle with Shield pattern, paneled sides, medium
    blue and white, 3-3/4" d 385.00
  Asian landscape scene, imp "Opaque Granite China, W. R. &
    Co.," light blue and white, 4" d, light stain 20.00
  Basket of Flowers, imp "Adams," dark blue transfer, 4" d
    . . . . 155.00
  Ben Franklin, boy with kite, blue and white, 3-1/2" d
    . . . . 110.00
  Bosphorous pattern, marked "T Mayer," c1840, light blue and
    white, 4" d 45.00
  Boy with hoop, blue and white, 3-1/2" d 90.00
  Center fruit cluster with bird, flowers, and scroll border,
    c1830, dark blue transfer, 4-1/4" d 125.00
  Cottage in woods scene, spearhead and trefoil border,
    marked "Clews," 3-5/8" d 125.00
  Landing of Lafayette, blue transfer 275.00
  William Penn's Treaty, Thomas Goodwin, 1830-40, brown
    and white, 3-3/4" d 100.00
  Woodlands Near Philadelphia, Joseph Stubbs and Stubbs &
    Kent, 1790-1831, blue and white, 3-3/4" d 265.00

CUSTARD GLASS

History: Custard glass was developed in England in the early 1880s. Harry Northwood made the first American custard glass at his Indiana, Pennsylvania, factory in 1898.

From 1898 until 1915, many manufacturers produced custard glass patterns, e.g., Dugan Glass, Fenton, A. H. Heisey Glass Co., Jefferson Glass, Northwood, Tarentum Glass, and U.S. Glass. Cambridge and McKee continued the production of custard glass into the Depression.

The ivory or creamy yellow custard color is achieved by adding uranium salts to the molten hot glass. The chemical content makes the glass glow when held under a black light. The more uranium, the more luminous the color. Northwood's custard glass has the smallest amount of uranium, creating an ivory color; Heisey used more, creating a deep yellow color.

Custard glass was made in patterned tableware pieces. It also was made as souvenir items and novelty pieces. Souvenir pieces include a place name or hand-painted decorations, e.g., flowers. Patterns of custard glass often were highlighted in gold, enameled colors, and stains.

REPRODUCTION ALERT

L. G. Wright Glass Co. has reproduced pieces in the Argonaut Shell and Grape and Cable patterns. It also introduced new patterns, such as Floral and Grape and Vintage Band. Mosser reproduced toothpicks in Argonaut Shell, Chrysanthemum Sprig, and Inverted Fan & Feather.

References: Gary E. Baker et al., *Wheeling Glass 1829-1939*, Oglebay Institute, 1994, distributed by Antique Publications; William Heacock, *Encyclopedia of Victorian Colored Pattern Glass, Book IV: Custard Glass from A to Z*, Peacock Publications, 1980; William Heacock, James Measell and Berry Wiggins, *Harry Northwood: The Early Years 1881-1900*, Antique Publications, 1990.

Additional Listings: Pattern Glass.

Banana Boat
  Grape and Gothic Arches, Northwood, 6" h, 12" l . . . 200.00
  Grape and Thumbprint, Northwood 375.00
Berry Bowl, master
  Argonaut Shell, Northwood, 10-1/2" l 150.00
  Beaded Circle, Northwood 185.00
  Cherry and Scale, Fenton 120.00
  Intaglio, ftd 125.00
  Ring Band, Heisey 125.00
  Victoria, Tarentum 175.00
Bowl, Delaware, US Glass 65.00
Butter Dish, cov
  Argonaut Shell, Northwood 250.00
  Beaded Circle, Northwood 275.00
  Cherry and Scale, Fenton 240.00
  Chrysanthemum Sprig, Northwood, blue 750.00
  Fan, Dugan. 225.00
  Geneva, Northwood, red and green dec 165.00
  Intaglio, Northwood 225.00
  Inverted Fan and Feather, Northwood 250.00
  Jefferson Optic, Jefferson 200.00
  Maple Leaf, Northwood 200.00
  Wild Bouquet, Northwood. 275.00
  Winged Scroll, Heisey, dec 185.00
Celery
  Ivorina Verde, Heisey. 250.00
  Victoria, Tarentum, gold trim 190.00
Cigarette Box, Ivorina Verde, Heisey 250.00
Cologne Bottle, orig stopper
  Ivorina Verde, Heisey. 250.00
  Northwood Grape, Northwood, nutmeg stain. 425.00
Compote, Intaglio, Northwood, 9" d 385.00
Condiment Set
  Chrysanthemum Sprig, Northwood, 4 pcs 2,000.00
  Ring Band, Heisey, 5 pcs. 800.00
Cracker Jar, cov, Grape and Cable, Northwood, two handles
  . . . . 700.00
Creamer
  Argonaut Shell, Northwood 150.00
  Beaded Circle, Northwood, 4-1/2" h, slight gold loss
    . . . . 350.00
  Cherry and Scale, Fenton 145.00
  Delaware, US Glass, rose dec 85.00
  Diamond with Peg, Jefferson 90.00
  Fan, Dugan. 100.00
  Fluted Scrolls, Heisey. 85.00
  Intaglio, Northwood 115.00
  Inverted Fan and Feather, Northwood 150.00
  Jackson, Northwood. 100.00
  Jefferson Optic, Jefferson 95.00
  Louis XV, Northwood 85.00
  Maple Leaf, Northwood 125.00
  Northwood Grape, Northwood, nutmeg stain. 115.00
  Ribbed Drape, Jefferson 120.00
  Ring and Beads, Heisey. 50.00
  Vermont, US Glass Co. 100.00
  Victoria, Tarentum 125.00
  Wild Bouquet, Northwood. 145.00
  Winged Scroll, Heisey, dec 110.00

Cruet
  Argonaut Shell, Northwood, gold trim............ 885.00
  Beaded Circle, Northwood, 6-1/2" h, slight gold loss
    ....1,250.00
  Georgia Gem, Tarentum, green, orig stopper 300.00
  Louis XV, Northwood, clear faceted stopper 185.00
  Maple Leaf, Northwood 950.00
  Ribbed Drape, Jefferson 400.00
  Ring Band, Heisey 400.00
  Wild Bouquet, Northwood....................... 525.00
Custard Cup
  Empress, Riverside, green, gold trim............. 45.00
  Winged Scroll, Heisey 65.00
Goblet
  Beaded Swag, Heisey 75.00
  Grape and Cable, Northwood.................... 70.00
  Humidor, Winged Scroll, Heisey................. 225.00
Jelly Compote
  Argonaut Shell, Northwood 110.00
  Beaded Circle, Northwood...................... 365.00
  Chrysanthemum Sprig, Northwood 200.00
  Geneva, Northwood........................... 100.00
  Intaglio, Northwood, gold trim................. 150.00
  Maple Leaf, Northwood 375.00
  Ribbed Drape, Jefferson 190.00
  Ring Band, Heisey 200.00
Lamp, Heart with Thumbprint, Tarentum, kerosene 400.00
Mug
  Diamond with Peg, Jefferson.................... 60.00
  Punty Band, Heisey 70.00
  Ring Band, Heisey 60.00
  Nappy, Winged Scroll, Heisey 65.00
Pickle Dish
  Beaded Swag, Heisey 265.00
  Vermont, US Glass............................. 60.00
  Pin Dish, Delaware, US Glass, dec 80.00
Pitcher
  Cherry and Scale, Fenton 350.00
  Chrysanthemum Sprig, Northwood 375.00
  Intaglio, Northwood, blue and gold dec 235.00
  Inverted Fan and Feather, Northwood 400.00
  Maple Leaf, Northwood 385.00

Ring Band, Heisey, floral dec.................... 450.00
Vermont, US Glass............................. 250.00
Winged Scroll, Heisey, dec 270.00
Plate
  Grape & Cable, Northwood, nutmeg stain 60.00
  Prayer Rug, Imperial, 7-1/2" d 35.00
  Three Fruits, Northwood, 7-1/2" d 30.00
Punch Bowl, matching base, Grape and Cable, Northwood
  ....900.00
Punch Cup
  Grape and Cable, Northwood.................... 50.00
  Inverted Fan and Feather, Northwood 200.00
  Ring Band, Heisey 60.00
Salt and Pepper Shakers, pr
  Argonaut Shell, Northwood 350.00
  Beaded Circle, Northwood...................... 275.00
  Carnelian, Northwood......................... 450.00
  Fluted Scrolls with Flower Band, Northwood 150.00
  Geneva, Northwood........................... 185.00
  Georgia Gem, Tarentum, orig top 100.00
  Heart, Northwood............................ 175.00
  Intaglio, Northwood.......................... 175.00
  Louis XV, Northwood.......................... 350.00
  Maple Leaf, Northwood 475.00
  Trailing Vine, Couderspot Glass............... 165.00
Sauce/Berry Bowl, individual size
  Argonaut Shell, Northwood, dec................. 90.00
  Beaded Circle, Northwood...................... 65.00
  Chrysanthemum Sprig, Northwood 85.00
  Delaware, US Glass, rose stain 65.00
  Fan, Dugan.................................. 70.00
  Geneva, Northwood, oval...................... 45.00
  Georgia Gem, Tarentum 40.00
  Inverted Fan and Feather, Northwood 55.00
  Louis XV, Northwood, gold trim 45.00
  Maple Leaf, Northwood 80.00
  Pecock and Urn, Northwood 45.00
  Ribbed Drape, Jefferson 45.00
  Victoria, Tarentum 50.00
  Wild Bouquet, Northwood...................... 50.00
Spooner
  Beaded Circle, Northwood, 4-1/4" h, slight gold loss
    .... 350.00
  Chrysanthemum Sprig, Northwood 125.00
  Everglades, Northwood 145.00
  Fan, Dugan.................................. 85.00
  Intaglio, Northwood 95.00
  Louis XV, Northwood 75.00
  Ribbed Drape, Jefferson 65.00
  Trailing Vine, Couderspot Glass, blue 70.00
  Victoria, Tarentum 65.00
  Wild Bouquet, Northwood...................... 70.00
  Winged Scroll, Heisey 100.00
Sugar, cov
  Argonaut Shell, Northwood 150.00
  Beaded Circle, Northwood, 6-3/4" h, slight gold loss
    .... 485.00
  Cherry and Scale, Fenton 145.00
  Chrysanthemum Sprig, Northwood, blue, gold dec .. 395.00
  Delaware, US Glass, rose dec 85.00
  Diamond with Peg, Jefferson 110.00
  Everglades, Northwood 125.00
  Fan, Dugan.................................. 100.00
  Fluted Scrolls, Heisey......................... 85.00
  Jackson, Northwood.......................... 100.00
  Northwood Grape, Northwood, nutmeg stain....... 115.00

Creamer, Argonaut Shell, 4-3/4" h, $150.

Ribbed Drape, Jefferson 120.00
Ring and Beads, Heisey 50.00
Vermont, US Glass Co. 100.00
Winged Scroll, Heisey 175.00
Syrup, orig top
Geneva, Northwood 250.00
Ring Band, Heisey 315.00
Table Set, cov butter, creamer, cov sugar, spooner
Carnelian 850.00
Geneva, Northwood 550.00
Georgia Gem, Tarentum, gold trim 300.00
Louis XV, Northwood, gold trim 500.00
Ring Band, Heisey 550.00
Toothpick Holder
Argonaut Shell, Northwood, dec. 465.00
Chrysanthemum Sprig, Northwood, blue, gold trim . . 315.00
Diamond with Peg, Jefferson 85.00
Ivorina Verde, Heisey 85.00
Maple Leaf, Northwood 475.00
Ribbed Drape, Jefferson 150.00
Vermont, US Glass, green dec. 145.00
Tumbler
Argonaut Shell, Northwood 90.00
Delaware, US Glass, green dec. 65.00
Fan, Dugan. 60.00
Fluted Scrolls, Heisey. 45.00
Grape and Cable, Northwood, nutmeg stain 50.00
Grape and Gothic Arches, Northwood, , 6" h. 65.00
Prayer Rug, Imperial 80.00
Punty Band, Heisey, souvenir 40.00
Ribbed Drape, Jefferson, floral dec 100.00
Winged Scroll, Heisey 70.00
Vase
Grape Arbor, Northwood, nutmeg stain 85.00
Prayer Rug, Imperial 65.00
Victorian, baluster, crown-style top, gold dec, intertwining foliage around center, 15" h, 4-1/2" h, matched pr
. . . . .2,500.00
Whiskey, Diamond with Peg, Jefferson souvenir 45.00
Wine
Beaded Swag, Heisey 70.00
Diamond with Peg, Jefferson 50.00
Punty Band, Heisey 50.00
Tiny Thumbprint 50.00

CUT GLASS, AMERICAN

History: Glass is cut by grinding decorations into the glass by means of abrasive-carrying metal or stone wheels. A very ancient craft, it was revived in 1600 by Bohemians and spread through Europe to Great Britain and America.

American cut glass came of age at the Centennial Exposition in 1876 and the World Columbian Exposition in 1893. The American public recognized American cut glass to be exceptional in quality and workmanship. America's most significant output of this high-quality glass occurred from 1880 to 1917, a period now known as the Brilliant Period.

Marks: Around 1890, some companies began adding an acid-etched "signature" to their glass. This signature may be the actual company name, its logo, or a chosen symbol. Today, signed pieces command a premium over unsigned pieces since the signature clearly establishes the

origin. However, signatures should be carefully verified for authenticity since objects with forged signatures have been in existence for some time. One way to check is to run a finger tip or fingernail lightly over the signature area. As a general rule, a genuine signature cannot be felt; a forged signature has a raised surface.

Many companies never used the acid-etched signature on their glass and may or may not have affixed paper labels to the items originally. Dorflinger Glass and the Meriden Glass Co. made cut glass of the highest quality, yet never used an acid-etched signature. Furthermore, cut glass made before the 1890s was not signed. Many of these wood-polished items, cut on blown blanks, were of excellent quality and often won awards at exhibitions.

References: Bill and Louis Boggess, *Identifying American Brilliant Cut Glass*, 3rd ed., Schiffer Publishing, 1996; ——, *Reflections on American Brilliant Cut Glass*, Schiffer Publishing, 1995; Jo Evers, *Evers' Standard Cut Glass Value Guide*, Collector Books, 1975, 1995 value update; Bob Page and Dale Fredericksen, *A Collection of American Crystal*, Page-Fredericksen Publishing, 1995; ——, *Seneca Glass Company 1891-1983*, Page-Fredericksen Publishing, 1995; J. Michael Pearson, *Encyclopedia of American Cut & Engraved Glass*, Vols. I to III, published by author, 1975; Albert C. Revi, *American Cut & Engraved Glass*, Schiffer Publishing, 1965; Martha Louise Swan, *American Cut and Engraved Glass*, Krause Publications, 1998 value update; Kenneth Wilson, *American Glass 1760-1930*, 2 vols., Hudson Hills Press and The Toledo Museum of Art, 1994.

Collectors' Club: American Cut Glass Association, P.O. Box 482, Ramona, CA 92065.

Museums: Corning Museum of Glass, Corning, NY; High Museum of Art, Atlanta, GA; Huntington Galleries, Huntington, WV; Lightner Museum, St. Augustine, FL; Toledo Museum of Art, Toledo, OH.

Note: ABP - American Brilliant Period

Atomizer, 4" h, 2-1/2" sq, Harvard pattern, gold washed atomizer, ABP. 145.00
Banana Boat, elaborate cutting, ABP 8,000.00
Basket
4-5/8" d, floral cutting, sterling openwork rim and reeded swing handle, Watson Co., early 20th C 260.00
6" h, 6" d, step cut base with large hobstar, band of four hobstars with diamond point, fan and cane cutting, triple notched handle, ABP 950.00
6" h, 7" d, four cut hobstars, strawberry, diamond, and fan cutting, triple notched square cut handle, brilliant blank, ABP 350.00
6" h, 8" d, low form, eight-sided, all over brilliant cut design of hobstars and numerous brilliant cuttings, applied twisted rope handle, ABP. 225.00
8" h, 7" d, Cactus pattern, Pairpoint 275.00
8" h, 8-1/2" d, Angelica pattern, applied loop crystal rope handle, deep cut pattern, sgd "Fyre" 550.00
9" h, 10-1/2" d, low flaring basket, bands of twelve hobstars around side with fan cutting and panels of cross hatching, cut with huge hobstar in base, flat arched handle with

Punch Bowl, on stand, American Brilliant Period, $600.

notched edges and leaf cutting in center, clearly sgd "Hoare" on int. 3,500.00

10-1/2" h, 10-3/4" d, brilliant and heavy glass blank, four hobstars with fan and strawberry point cutting, double notched handle, ABP. 425.00

12-1/2" h, 8" d, all over scrolls and leaf design, quadruple notched handle resembles snake with tongue coming out, sgd "Hawkes Gravic" 900.00

13" h, 9" d, notched cut step pedestal, open flaring shaped basket, band of hobstars, brilliant cutting, applied crystal rope twisted handle, large hobstar cut base, ABP 1,850.00

16" h, 10" d, ruffled shaped form, dahlia-like flower cut with leaves, elaborate swirls, cut and notched applied loop handle, base sgd "Hawkes Gravic Glass" 1,800.00

17" h, 11-1/2" d, numerous cut hobstars, step cutting, heavy serrated edge, large star cut base, triple notched handle, ABP 2,900.00

18" h, 12" d, alternating hobstars and pinwheels, double notched handle, extremely heavy and brilliant blank, ABP 1,200.00

21" h, floral cutting, narrow base, narrow handle, ABP 3,100.00

21" h, Harvard pattern base, etched flowers, cut leaf and vine dec, scalloped rim, thumbprints on handle, ABP . . . 350.00

Bell, 6-3/4" h, sharply cut strawberry diamond and fans, pattern also cut on stem end knob 550.00

Bowl

7-3/4" d, 3-1/2" h, China Aster pattern, highly cut pattern, sgd "Hawkes Gravic" 450.00

8" d, clusters of hobstars and cross hatched diamonds, ABP 90.00

8" d, hobstar border, fern leaves in center, sgd "Hoare," ABP 500.00

8" d, sunbursts and feathered arches, ABP 90.00

8" d, 2" h, eight lobes, hobstars and triangular panels cut on base, cross hatching and small star cutting 90.00

8" d, 3-1/2" h, slanted sides cut in pattern of eight hobstars, hobstar base, vertical panels of notches, ABP 50.00

8" d, 3-3/4" h, large hobstar with band of 8 hobstars, ABP, large chip on rim 110.00

8-1/2" d, deep cut, medallions, large pointed ovals, arches, and base, ABP. 110.00

9" d, six large deep cut hobstars and Gothic arches, ABP, minor flakes 250.00

9" d, 4-1/4" deep, Russian pattern, ABP 275.00

10" d, deep cut buttons, stars, and fans, ABP 220.00

10" d, Lotus pattern, Eggingston 275.00

12" d, 4-1/2" h, rolled down edge, cut and engraved flowers, leaves, and center thistle, notched serrated edge . . 275.00

Box, cov, 6-1/2" d, 4-1/4" h, Bishop's hat shape, large center hobstar, cross hatching and fans on lid, silver plated fittings 850.00

Bread Tray, 13-3/4" x 6-1/4", hobstars and cane, rim flake 250.00

Butter Dish, cov, Hobstar, ABP. 250.00

Butter Pat, Cypress, Laurel. 35.00

Candlesticks, pr

8" h, hobstars, hobnail, and diamonds, hollow teardrop stems, rayed bases 975.00

9-1/2" h, hobstars, teardrop stem, hobstar base 250.00

Canoe, 11-1/4" l, Harvard pattern sides, hobstar base, ABP 185.00

Celery Tray, 11" l, nailhead filled diamonds and sunbursts, ABP 90.00

Champagne

Double teardrop stems, strawberry diamonds and fans, set of six. 360.00

Flared bowls, delicate stems, hobstar chain, set of nine 450.00

Monarch pattern, saucer style, set of 12 . . . . .1,200.00

Rayed Button Russian pattern, Russian bases, tumbler type, set of six, ABP 500.00

Champagne Pitcher, 12-1/2" h, Cane pattern, other cuttings, sterling silver rim, ABP 400.00

Chandelier, 12" d, flared curved rim with diamond cutting, light bowl with floral wheel cut design, suspended from three gilt-metal linked rods, central tripartite lighting device, drop adjustable, ABP 650.00

Cheese and Cracker Tray, 10" l, handle, heavy blank, florals alternating with hobstar ellipses 140.00

Cider Pitcher, hobstars, zippers, fine diamonds, honeycomb cut handle, 7" h, ABP. 175.00

Cigar Humidor, 9" h, cylindrical jar, strawberry diamond and fine cut, conforming glass cover with elaborate star cutting on knob, rayed star-cut base, ABP 500.00

Cologne Bottle

6" h, Hob and Lace pattern, green cased to clear, pattern cut stopper, Dorflinger 625.00

6-1/4" h, sq, red cut to clear, Octagon Diamond pattern, horizontal stepped shoulder, matching starred stopper, ABP, chips at inner stopper edge 575.00

7-1/2" h, 2-3/4" d, Parisian pattern, sq shape, Dorflinger, ABP, pr. 700.00

8" h, St. James pattern, sgd "Hoare" 200.00

Compote

6" d bowl, Carnation pattern, sgd "Hawkes Gravic" . . 465.00

7" d, intaglio floral sprays, heavy sterling silver base, monogrammed "K," sgd "Hawkes" 135.00

7-1/2" h, hobstar with file cuts, deep miters, tear drop stem, rayed base 210.00

8" d, Alhambra design, notched edges on rim and foot, attributed to Hawkes, ABP, minor chips. 1,380.00

8" d, 8" h, pinwheel strawberry diamond pattern, air twist stem, rayed base 140.00

10" d, 13" h, teardrop step, 36 point hobstar base, ABP 1,800.00

Console Set, 12" d ftd bowl with wide flat rim, p 9-1/8" h baluster form candlesticks, cross-hatched diamond and flute cutting, ABP 750.00

Cordial, engraved, faceted stem, sgd "Hawkes" 75.00

Cracker Jar, cov, 7" d, floral cut, silver plate and bail handle, Pairpoint 275.00

Creamer and Sugar

6" d, 4" h, large center hobstar with triangular panels of cross hatching, handles with large notches and end in three leaf clover at base, unsigned brilliant heavy blank 350.00

8-1/2" d, hobstars and sunburst, plantation size, ABP 385.00

Cruet, orig stopper, 6" h, Chrysanthemum pattern, tri-pour spout, cut handle and stopper, sgd "Hawkes," ABP. . 350.00

Decanter, orig stopper

11-1/2" h, stars, arches, fans, cut neck, star cut mushroom stopper 95.00

12-3/4" h, hobstar and fan pattern, large notched handle, sgd "Hoare," firing check at handle. 75.00

13" h, paneled neck above sunburst, fine diamond and pineapple cuttings, ABP, minor flake at bottom of stopper 100.00

Fern Dish, 3-3/4" h, 8" w, round, silver-plate rim, C. F. Monroe, minor roughness to cut pattern, normal wear on base, no liner 200.00

Flower Basket, 9-1/2" x 5" x 13", flowers with hobstar centers, cut leaves, honeycomb pattern stand base, cut scalloped rim, thumbprint cut handle, ABP 275.00

Flower Center

5" h, 6" d, hobstars, flashed fans, hobstar chain and base, ABP 325.00

7-1/2" h, paneled zipper and pointed stem above bulbous bowl, star cut sunburst arches and medallions 200.00

7-3/4" h, 12" d, etched and wheel cut motif, honeycomb flared neck, some wear 500.00

8" d, large hobstar base, step cut neck, ABP 325.00

Goblet

Clear Button Russian pattern, facet cut teardrop stem, ABP 140.00

Rayed Button Russian, 6" h, teardrop stems, sgd "Hawkes," set of nine 1,200.00

Strawberry diamond and fans, double teardrop stems, wood polished, set of twelve 800.00

Ice Bucket, 6" d, Jewel pattern, hobstar bases, two handles, 8-1/2" d underplate, Clark, ABP 550.00

Ice Cream Tray, 10-1/2" x 17-3/4", hobstar with chain base 1,395.00

Jug, 7" h, spherical body, offset stoppered spout, applied notched handle, Sinclaire, ABP 520.00

Knife Rest, 4-1/2" l, ABP 145.00

Lamp, ABP

13" h, 6-1/2" d mushroom shade with engraved and clear cut large flowers and leaves, vining tendrils, notch cup stepped base with matching pattern cut on bottom 350.00

13-1/2" h, domed shade with strawberry diamond and horizontal ribbed cutting, Hawkes-Sinclaire manner, silvered metal two-socket electrical fittings 690.00

14" h, teardrop shade with engraved tulip blossoms, star-cut closed top, columnar shaft with sq silver plated platform base, dec with cherubs in vineyard scene, attributed to Pairpoint 550.00

23-3/4" h, 10" d shade, large expanding cut star in heavy brilliant period pattern of band of daisy-like flowers and leaves, matching conforming base, inverted trumpet form, with matching band of flowers, notched prism band, band of strawberry, diamond, and fan circling base, orig prisms 2,000.00

Mustard Pot, cov, 3-1/2" h, panel and notched prism, underplate, sgd "Maple City Glass" 225.00

Nappy, 9" d, deep cut arches, pointed sunbursts and medallions, two handles, ABP 135.00

Orange Bowl, 9-3/4" x 6-3/4" x 3-3/4" h, hobstars and strawberry diamond, ABP 200.00

Perfume Bottle

5-1/2" h, 3" d, six-sided, alternating panels of Harvard pattern and engraved florals, rayed base, matching faceted stopper, ABP 175.00

6-1/2" h, bulbous, all over cutting, orig stopper, ABP 220.00

Pitcher

5" d, ball shape, flattened diamond pattern, Hawkes . 125.00

14" h, star, can, fine cut, and fan motifs, tankard shape, notched handle, ABP, price for matched pair 1,100.00

Plate, 7" d, Thos. Singleton for Mt. Washington 110.00

Powder Box, cov, 5-1/2" d, buzz saw base and large buzz saw lid 125.00

Punch Bowl

10-1/2" d, 12" h, hobstar and fan, 2 pcs 1,600.00

12-1/4" d, 6" h sgd "Libbey," ABP 1,100.00

14-1/2" d, 7-1/2" h, scalloped bowl, star, fan, and fine cut elements, sgd "Hawkes," some rim chipping, silver ladle stamped "Pairpoint Mfg. Co." with cut glass knob, ABP 1,380.00

Punch Bowl Ladle, Hobstar and Pineapple, silver fittings, Meriden Silver Co., c1890 . . . . 500.00

Punch Cup

Hobstars, pedestal, handle 85.00

Monarch pattern, set of ten 320.00

Relish, 13" l, leaf shape, Clear Button Russian pattern, ABP 375.00

Rose Bowl, 6" d, zipper rim, Pattern #682, Dorflinger. . . 385.00

Salad Bowl and Underplate, 10" d, 6" h bowl, 11-1/2" d underplate, Spilane (Trefoil & Rosette) pattern, cross-cut vesicas, notched prism, hobstars and fans, sgd "Libbey" . . .2,200.00

Salt, Sawtooth, ftd, individual size 30.00

Salt Shaker, notched prism columns 30.00

Spooner, cut stars, ferns, cross hatching, cut handles and sawtooth rim, ABP 150.00

Tankard Pitcher

10-1/4" h, Harvard cut sides, pinwheel top, mini hobnails, thumbprint notched handle, ABP 200.00

12" h, diamond band and leaf design, large applied notched handle, ABP 200.00

17-1/4" h, 7" w base, three rows of hobstars, diamond point cutting, fancy silver rim, applied loop cut handle, ABP 700.00

Tray

4-1/2" w, 1-3/4" h, cutting of diamond notches, star cut base, floral emb silver plated rim, C. F. Monroe 75.00

10" l, deep cut hobstar medallions and cross hatched arches, ABP 225.00

12" l, 8" w, Cane pattern, ABP 400.00

Tumble-Up, handled pitcher and matching tumbler, geometric and floral 450.00

Tumbler

Bristol Rose pattern, Mt. Washington 75.00

Clear Button Russian pattern 95.00

Harvard, rayed base 45.00

Hobstars. 40.00
Hobstars, strawberry diamonds, fans, hobstar cluster and
    base, set of six. 360.00
Russian Button pattern, set of nine 350.00
Vase
    5" h, 2" w, Kalana, lily dec, Dorflinger 150.00
    8" h, trumpet set, hobstar and diamond arches, ABP
    . . . . 90.00
    9" h, deep cut zippered ribs with panels of sunburst and fine
        cut, ABP, minor flake 150.00
    9-1/2 h, deep cut arched stars, windows, and zippered ribs,
        ABP 100.00
    10" h, arches, pointed triangles and buzz stars, ABP 100.00
    10" h, ovoid shape bowl, cut with buzz saw, button and daisy,
        deep arches, zipper cut paneled stem, faceted paperweight
        and fine cut foot, ABP 275.00
    10" h, trumpet, zipper and thumbprint cut, star cut paper-
        weight base 100.00
    10-1/4" h, engraved dragon, clear ground, deep amber flash-
        ing, applied sterling rim, both glass and silver rim sgd
        "Hawkes" 250.00
    11" h, bulbous top, fluted rim, tapering cylindrical stem, wide
        base, bulbous top cut with double row of thumbprints and di-
        amond patterns and cross hatching, step cutting under-
        neath, stem cut with hobstars, cross hatching, and flat
        flutes, heavy brilliant blank, clearly sgd "Hawkes" . . 550.00
    11" h, sunburst and finecut pattern, zippered panel stem, star
        cut base 175.00
    12" h, 5-1/2" w, triangular, three large and three small hob-
        stars, double notched pedestal and flaring base, ABP
        . . . . 150.00
    12-1/2" h, 6-1/2" d, floral and diamond point engraving, sgd
        "Hawkes" 250.00
    14" h, bowling pin shape, three 24 point hobstars on sides
        surrounded by notched prisms, strawberry diamond, hob-
        stars, star, and checkered diamond fields 700.00
    14" h, corset shape, Harvard pattern, deep floral engraving
        . . . . 925.00
    14" h, trumpet shape, 8" w at top, Venetian pattern, Hawkes,
        ABP 750.00
    16" h, hobstar and cross hatch panels, 24 point base star
        . . . . 950.00
    16" h, intaglio-cut trumpet-form pedestal-base, bellflower
        dec, floral borders top and bottom, ABP 550.00
    16" h rounded shoulders and large panels with fern decora-
        tion, intaglio dec, ABP 450.00
    24" h, baluster, hobstar fan and stippled design, ABP
        . . . . .5,720.00
    24" h, tapered and flared, elaborate basketweave design,
        ABP 4,620.00
Water Carafe, 7-1/2" h, sunburst variant. 300.00
Water Pitcher, 11" h, Harvard pattern, rayed base, double punty
    handle, sgd "Hawkes," ABP 400.00
Wine, 4-3/4" h, amethyst cut to clear, deep cut grapes and
    leaves, champagne type bowl, knob stems, cut ovals on
    base, 4-3/4" h, set of 10 . . . . 350.00

CUT VELVET

History: Several glass manufacturers made cut velvet during the late Victorian era, c1870-1900. An outer layer of pastel color was applied over a white casing. The piece then was molded or cut in a high-relief ribbed or diamond shape, exposing portions of the casing. The finish had a satin velvety feel, hence the name "cut velvet."

Vase, cut velvet, 9-1/2" h, Diamond Quilted, ruffled and crimped top, twisted reeding on neck, spherical pedestal base, 9-1/2" h, $280.

Basket, 11-1/2" h, 9" w, brilliant yellow ext., Diamond Quilted pattern, bright pink shaded int., tightly crimped and ruffled edge, applied crystal loop handle. 300.00
Biscuit Jar, cov, pink, SP mountings and lid 275.00

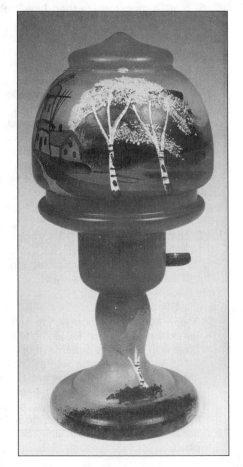

Lamp, Czechoslovakian, white birch trees, landscape background, 9" h, $250. Photo courtesy of Jackson's Auctioneers & Appraisers.

Celery Vase, 6-1/2" h, deep blue over white, Diamond Quilted design, box pleated top 725.00

Creamer, 5-1/4" h, raised ribbed pattern, butterscotch body, white lining 200.00

Finger Bowl, 4-1/2" d, Diamond Quilted pattern, blue . . . 185.00

Rose Bowl, 3-1/4" d, 3-3/4" h, egg shape, raised Diamond Quilted pattern, rose body, white lining, six crimp top 195.00

Vase

6-1/2" d, stick type, raised Diamond Quilted pattern, rose body, white lining 250.00

7-1/2" h, 3-1/2" w, bulbous shape, ruffled top, Herringbone pattern, deep Alice Blue, white lining, c1880 . . . . . . 450.00

9" h, cylindrical, raised Diamond Quilted pattern, blue body, ruffled rim 250.00

9" h, slight flare to end of elongated neck, robin's egg blue, diamond quilt body, daisy blossom like design at base 385.00

9" h, 6" tall cylinder over short bulbous base, deeply ruffled 9" w top, deep orange Diamond Quilted pattern 675.00

10" h, ruffled and crimped top, purple cased to opal white body, Diamond Quilted pattern, Victorian 575.00

11-1/2" h, 6" w, glossy satin, Herringbone pattern, deep blue shading to pale blue, bright opaque white lining, applied crystal edge 250.00

13-1/2" h, 6" w, double gourd, long pumpkin stem neck, pale gold Diamond Quilted body 650.00

CZECHOSLOVAKIAN ITEMS

History: Objects marked "Made in Czechoslovakia" were produced after 1918 when the country claimed its independence from the Austro-Hungarian Empire. The people became more cosmopolitan and liberated and expanded the scope of their lives. Their porcelains, pottery, and glassware reflect many influences.

Marks: A specific manufacturer's mark may include a date, which precedes 1918, but this only indicates the factory existed during the years of the Bohemian or Austro-Hungarian Empire.

References: Dale and Diane Barta and Helen M. Rose, *Czechoslovakian Glass & Collectibles* (1992, 1995 values), Book II (1997) Collector Books; *Bohemian Glass*, n.d., distributed by Antique Publications; Ruth A. Forsythe, *Made in Czechoslovakia*, Antique Publications, 1993; Jacquelyne Y. Jones-North, *Czechoslovakian Perfume Bottles and Boudoir Accessories*, Antique Publications, 1990; Leslie Piña, *Pottery, Modern Wares 1920–1960*, Schiffer Publishing, 1994.

Periodical: *New Glass Review*, Bardounova 2140 149 00 Praha 4, Prague, Czech Republic.

Collectors' Club: Czechoslovakian Collectors Guild International, P.O. Box 901395, Kansas City, MO 64190.

Museum: Friends of the Glass Museum of Novy Bor, Kensington, MD.

Box, cov, 4" h, rect, ruby red faceted glass body, brass mounts, marked "Made in Czechoslovakia," C1920 . . . . 275.00

Candy Dish, multicolored spatter, black feet 45.00

Compote, 7-1/2" d, 5-3/4" h, art glass, bright orange cased to colorless glass, pulled black stripes, wafer, and rim rap, attributed to Michael Powolny 415.00

Console Set, porcelain, Art Deco style, turquoise raised drapery with knotted corners, 10" x 6" x 2-1/2" bowl, pr candlesticks 85.00

Creamer, gold luster ex., black handles and trim, marked "Czechoslovakia" 15.00

Figure, 3-1/2" h, girl with basket 25.00

Gravy Boat, 10-1/8" l, 5-1/4" h, silver, attached trays, Colonial Revival style, triple ribbed rim detail, hallmarked, 800 fine, 41 troy oz, price for pr 635.00

Jardiniere, 4-1/2" h, cameo, white cased to colorless, maroon and pink layers, acid etched grape vines and clusters, partial oval mark on base "Czecho Slovakia" 260.00

Lamp

Basket, 10-1/2" h, colorful faceted fruit and flower form beads form lampshade, basket frame, electrical base imp "Made in Czechoslovakia" 525.00

Desk, two figural Scottie dogs, multicolored spatter geometric glass globe 265.00

Luncheon Set, flowing irid, magenta, orange, brown, and lavender on MOP, teapot and lid, creamer, sugar, cov butter, handled cake plate, twelve 7-1/2" d plates, 5-3/4" bowl, eight cups and saucers, sgd 280.00

Lemonade Set, 10" h pitcher, two matching tumblers, sapphire blue, green, and aubergine ground, sapphire blue threaded shoulder, blue ribbed handles, sgd, c1930 . . . . 250.00

Perfume Bottle, black base, etched lady design, orig clear stopper 95.00

Pin Tray, 3-3/8" l, yellow-green glass, intaglio of nude woman, frosted int., cut edges 100.00

Pitcher, 8-1/2" h, goat's head 375.00

Plate, sq, green border, floral dec 37.50

Scent Bottle, amber, 1" h, paneled cut glass, sterling silver hinged emb lid 195.00

Vase

5"h , white pearlescent vase hugged by angel, holly, berries, and star 25.00

10" h, black, Art Deco form 50.00

10-1/2" h, applied handles, paper label, additional orig NY store label 225.00

DAIRY ITEMS

History: The history of collecting dairy-related items is as varied as there are items. Advertising pieces can go back to mid 1800s. Post cards, trade cards, and pinback buttons were used as advertising, as well as more household utilitarian items, such as match holders and pot holders. The cream separator, milk cans, various testing equipment and cow bells followed as more advertising items were developed. In more recent years, these items are used as promotion or give-aways by the numerous dairy companies.

There were hundreds of small dairies and creameries scattered throughout the United States during the late 19th to mid 20th centuries. Many gave away a variety of materials to promote their products.

Eventually, regional cooperatives expanded the marketing regions, and many smaller dairies closed. Companies such as Borden distributed products on a national level. Borden created the advertising character of "Elsie, the Borden Cow" to help sell its products. Additional consolidation of firms occurred, encouraged in part by state milk marketing boards and federal subsidies.

One area of Dairy Collecting that is popular is the collecting of milk bottle caps. Prices for these range from 25 cents to $2 for the hundreds of dairies commonly found throughout the United States. Milk bottle caps issued for special events or by special organizations can range from $1 to $2.50 or higher. Bottle caps with war-time slogans are also in the $2.50 range.

Many collectors specialize, for instance, in cream separators, milk cans, farm equipment, or creamers used in the diners across America. Individually, or in combination, there will be competition with other collectors of similar items. As with almost any type of collecting, dairy collectibles can be enhanced by so-called "go withs." Dairy items, such as post cards, trade cards, cream separators, and other advertising items can enrich a milk bottle collection. Dairy collecting continues to gain in popularity.

Reference: Paul Dettloff, *Cream Separator Guide,* D. V. M., published by author, 1993; C. H. Wendel, *Encyclopedia of American Farm Implements & Antiques,* Krause Publications, 1997.

Collectors' Clubs: Cream Separator and Dairy Collectors, Rt. 3, P.O. Box 488, Arcadia, WI, 54612; National Association of Milk Bottle Collectors, 4 Ox Bow Rd, Westport, CT 06880; National Association of Soda Jerks, P.O. Box 115, Omaha, NE, 68101.

Periodicals: Creamers, P.O. Box 11, Lake Villa, IL 60046; Cream Separator and Dairy Collectors Newsletter, Route 3, P.O. Box 488, Arcadia, WI 54612; Fiz Biz, P.O. Box 115, Omaha, NE, 68101. The Milk Route, 4 Ox Bow Rd., Westport, CT 06880.

Museums: Museum Village, Monroe, NY; New York State Historical Association Farmers Museum, Cooperstown, NY.

Advisors: Tony Knipp and Tom Gallagher.

Also see: Milk Bottles.

Cartoon Book, 3-1/4" x 4", *Borden's, Compliments of Elsie,* 16 pgs, 14 color cartoons and captions, black, white, and yellow illus on back with six Borden products, mid 1940s.... 45.00

Charm, "Horlick's All-American," football, metal, copper luster finish, 1930s.................................. 15.00

Cookbook, Cloverland Dairy, Good Food Is Good Living, 48 pgs, c1940 .... 5.00

Game, Elsie's Ice Cream Cone Top Game, 6-3/4" d top, 5-1/2" h cardboard canister, copyright Borden Co., 1958, Wilkening Mfg. Co., unopened 60.00

Jar, 9-1/4" h, 4-1/4" d, Horlick's Malted Milk, Hot or Cold, blue enameled lettering, ground lid stopper, emb back ... 525.00

Milk Bottle, 8-1/2" h, 4" d, clear glass, quart, red applied art of WWII Infantry soldiers in action, text "Back Their Attack/Buy More War Bonds/Drink Milk For Health," same design on both sides, glass inscription in neck "Use Sealtest Dairy Products" 125.00

Pinback Button
  Ayrshire Milk, maroon ion white, youngster in Scottish tam and kilt, 1938 copyright, Ayrshire Breeders' Assn. . . 30.00
  Champion Dairy Cow of the World, May Rilma, Record 1073.41 lb. Butter Fan, sepia photo cow in center, mellowed white ground, green lettering, 1930s 35.00

Creamery Package Company, multicolored, center wooden barrel carton, red and white lettering, c1900 .... 20.00

I Drink Milk Only, blue and white, milk bottle center image with "Power" man flexing his muscle, 1930s 20.00

Ohio Dairy, multicolored, infant, slogan "If You Would Have Your baby Look Like This/Get Your Milk Supply From The Ohio Dairy Co." 75.00

Pellisier Club, black, white and red, cow, identified as "Pansco Hazel," c1930.......................... 25.00

Pitcher, 4" x 4" x 5-1/2", glazed china, figural, Borden's Elmer, brown blending to white muzzle, pink nose, yellow simulated nose ring, black eyes, black bow tie, whit collar, c1940 .... 40.00

Sign
  6" h, 19" l, porcelain, Alta Crest Farm Milk, Beaver Falls, PA, "No Milk Can Be Too Good For Your Baby, Alta Crest Farms Certified Milk - Ask Your Doctor - He Knows" white lettering, dark blue ground.................... 275.00
  15" w, 14" h, Carnation Fresh Milk, red top, white bottom, green border, milk bottle center 450.00

Stickpin, celluloid, metal stick pin
  National Cream Separator, thin diecut, red, white, blue, and black flag, National Dairy Machine Co., ad text on back 75.00
  Omega Cream Separator, multicolored, reverse brass insert inscription "Omega Separator Co./Lansing, Mich. U.S.A." 90.00

Sharples Cream Separator, multicolored, oval, reverse brass inscription "The Sharples Separator, West Chester, Pa" 70.00

Stickpin/Clicker, Empire Cream Separator, black and white product, blue rim, white lettering "I Chirp For The Empire Because It Makes The Most Dollars For Me," tin cricket clicker 80.00

Tin, 5-3/8" h, 3" sq, Coors Malted Milk, blue and white, illus of cow standing in front of billboard, farmer and horses cutting field in background 450.00

Advertising Display, Alka Seltzer Barn Dance, three dimensional, 9-1/2" x 9", $50. Photo courtesy of Bear Pen Auctions.

Tip Tray, 4-1/4" d, DeLaval Cream Separator, shows cream separator, Savage Mfg. Co. litho, wear to rim 100.00

Toy, tin, milk delivery wagon, hand painted white, blue roof and chassis, gold striping, enclosed cap with opening door, open bed body with partitions for orig eight tin milk cans, metal wheels, Germany 1,980.00

Toy, wood, horse-drawn wagon
    Abbott's, "Abbottmaid Ice Cream" on banner on top of wagon, "Abbott's 'A' Milk" on side of wagon with image of cow, stuffed horse, 12-3/4" h, 23" l, 6-1/4" d 2,100.00
    H. P. Hood & Sons, Schoenhut, early 20th C, multicolored 3,105.00

Tray
    12" d, Jersey-Creme, titled "The Perfect Drink," beautiful girl, dressed in green, Chas. W. Shonk Co. litho 225.00
    13" h, 10-5/8" w, Dairy Made Ice Cream, litho tin, child seated in center 425.00

DAVENPORT

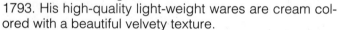

History: John Davenport opened a pottery in Longport, Staffordshire, England, in 1793. His high-quality light-weight wares are cream colored with a beautiful velvety texture.

The firm's output included soft-paste (Old Blue) products, luster-trimmed pieces, and pink luster wares with black transfer. Pieces of Gaudy Dutch and Spatterware also have been found with the Davenport mark. Later Davenport became a leading maker of ironstone and early flow blue. His famous Cyprus pattern in mulberry became very popular. His heirs continued the business until the factory closed in 1886.

Reference: T. A. Lockett and Geoffrey A. Godden, *China, Earthenware & Glass, 1794-1884,* Random Century, 1990.

Museums: British Museum, London, England; Cincinnati Art Museum, Cincinnati, OH; Hanley Museum, Stoke-on-Trent, England; Liverpool Museum, Liverpool, England; Victoria & Albert Museum, London, England.

Biscuit Jar, 6-1/2" h, Imari style dec, SP cover and bail, c1870 . . . . 160.00

Compote, 10-1/4" d, romantic landscape scene, gilt border, apple green ground, two handles 120.00

Cup and Saucer
    Clifford pattern 115.00
    Hawthorn pattern, blue transfers, handleless. 95.00

Dessert Service, 20 pc set, multicolored floral sprays, scroll surrounds, gilt stylized foliage on green border, puce printed mark, c1850 . . . . .1,250.00

Dish, 9-1/2" l, molded cobalt and gilt handle, Oriental style gilt dec outlined in blue, yellow, green, and red exotic birds, orange-red chrysanthemums, pink and magenta flowerheads on scrolling branches, blue "Davenport Stone China" anchor mark, c1820 . . . . 295.00

Ewer, 9" h, multicolored floral dec, c1830. . . . . 200.00

Gravy Boat, blue and white flowers. 90.00

Jug, 5-7/8" h, "The Litchfield Jug," black outlined white Greek warriors, orange ground, white handle, title on bottom, c1850 . . . . 395.00

Plate
    7-1/2" w, hexagonal, emb floral border, green transfer of child and at 90.00

Tureen, cov, undertray, underglaze blue, polychrome Gaudy Welsh type enamel, and gilt dec, transfer mark "Davenport China," yellowed professional repair to tray, lid is damaged and unstable, repairs to handles, 15-1/2" l, $1,265. Photo courtesy of Garth's Auctions, Inc.

8-3/4" d, earthenware, medium blue transfer, English landscape, ruined abbey, imp "Davenport" 60.00

10" d, Muleteer pattern, man riding mule, C-scroll and flower border, blue transfer. 100.00

10-1/2" d, Indian Festoon pattern, red, green, and yellow bower and flowers in center, green floral transfer border 125.00

Platter, 18-3/4" l, rect, cut corners, blue transfer, large house with Chinese junk in front in center, willow trees on shore, floral border 675.00

Sauce Tureen, cov, underplate, 8-1/4" l, Japan pattern, iron-red, cobalt, and gilt, gilt curved horizontal handles, pr . .1,450.00

Soup Tureen, 15" l, 9-1/2" h, Java pattern, flowers, bird, and fruit, blue and white 395.00

Tray, 11" w, 9" l, cloverleaf design, c1850 . . . . 150.00

DECOYS

History: During the past several years, carved wooden decoys, used to lure ducks and geese to the hunter, have become widely recognized as an indigenous American folk art form. Many decoys are from the years 1880 to 1930 when commercial gunners commonly hunted using rigs of several hundred decoys. Many fine carvers also worked through the 1930s and 1940s. Fish decoys were also carved by individuals and commercial decoy makers.

Because decoys were both hand made and machine made, and many examples exist, firm pricing is difficult to establish. The skill of the carver, rarity, type of bird, and age all effect the value.

References: Joel Barber, *Wild Fowl Decoys,* Dover Publications, n.d.; Russell J. Goldberger and Alan G. Haid, *Mason Decoys – A Complete Pictorial Guide,* Decoy Magazine, 1993; Bob and Sharon Huxford, *Collector's Guide to Decoys,* Vol. II, Collector Books, 1992; Linda and Gene Kangas, *Collector's Guide to Decoys,* Wallace-Homestead, 1992; Carl F. Luckey, *Collecting Antique Bird Decoys and Duck Calls: An Identification & Value Guide*, 2nd ed., Books Americana, 1992; Donald J. Peterson, *Folk Art Fish Decoys*, Schiffer Publishing, 1996.

Periodicals: *Decoy Magazine*, P.O. Box 787, Lewes, DE, 19558; *North America Decoys*, P.O. Box 246, Spanish Fork, UT 84660; *Sporting Collector's Monthly*, RW Publishing, P.O. Box 305, Camden, DE 19934; *Wildfowl Art*, Ward Foundation, 909 South Schumaker Dr., Salisbury, MD 21801; *Wildfowl Carving & Collecting*, 500 Vaughn St., Harrisburg, PA 17110.

Collectors' Clubs: Midwest Collectors Association, 1100 Bayview Dr., Fox River Grove, IL 60021; Minnesota Decoy Collectors Association, P.O. Box 130084, St. Paul, MN 55113; Ohio Decoy Collectors & Carvers Association, P.O. Box 499, Richfield, OH 44286.

Museums: Havre de Grace Decoy Museum, Havre de Grace, MD; Museum at Stony Brook, Stony Brook, NY; Noyes Museum of Art, Oceanville, NJ; Peabody Museum of Salem, Salem, MA; Refuge Waterfowl Museum, Chincoteague, VA; Shelburne Museum, Inc., Shelburne, VT; Ward Museum of Wildfowl Art, Salisbury, MD.

Reproduction Alert.

Notes: A decoy's value is based on several factors: (1) fame of the carver, (2) quality of the carving, (3) species of wild fowl—the most desirable are herons, swans, mergansers, and shorebirds—and (4) condition of the original paint.

The inexperienced collector should be aware of several facts. The age of a decoy, per se, is usually of no importance in determining value. However, age does have some influence when it comes to a rare or important example. Since very few decoys were ever signed, it is quite difficult to attribute most decoys to known carvers. Anyone who has not examined a known carver's work will be hard pressed to determine if the paint on one of his decoys is indeed original. Repainting severely decreases a decoy's value. In addition, there are many fakes and reproductions on the market and even experienced collectors are occasionally fooled. Decoys represent a subject where dealing with a reputable dealer or auction house is important, especially those who offer a guarantee as to authenticity.

Decoys listed below are of average wear unless otherwise noted.

Black-Bellied Plover
    Cobb, Nathan, Cobb Island, VA, c1895 . . . . .18,700.00
    Dilley, some damage 990.00
    Holmes, Lothrop, Kingston, MA 11,550.00

Black Duck
    Canvas covered, George Boyd, Seabrook, NH 1,650.00
    Hollow carved, Dan Lake Leads, Pleasantville, NJ
    . . . . .2,200.00
    Ward Brothers, Crisfield, MD, 1936 . . . . .3,190.00
Blue-Breasted Plover, unknown maker, Long Island, carved wings, split tail, old paint. 400.00
Bluebill
    Drake, G. W. Stevens Factory, Weedsport, NY, orig paint, replacement eyes, branded "G W Stevens" 1,500.00
    Hen, Hayes Decoy Factory, orig paint, age split 175.00
Blue Goose, Ben Schmidt, early 11,550.00
Brant
    Cobb, Nathan, VA, hollow carved, slightly turned head, cocked down, "V" detail, c1860 . . . . .5,750.00
    Parker, Lloyd, hollow carved, old repaint 900.00
    Shourds, Harry V., Tuckertown, NJ, hollow, branded
    . . . . 385.00
Bufflehead
    Drake, J. L. Saltonstall 100.00
    Hen, Harry V. Shourds, Tuckertown, NJ, c1890, hollow carved 18,700.00
Canada Goose
    Reeves, Phineas, Point, Ontario, c1870, hollow carved
    . . . . .10,120.00
    Schmidt, Marvin, Peru, IL, early 1900s, 19" l, 13" h, neck reattached 100.00
    Unknown maker, Long Beach Island, NJ, area, working decoy, 24" l, 11" h, probably overpainted 300.00
    Unknown maker, working decoy, weights attached to base and leather attaching ring, body painted bray, white and black, 25-1/2" l, 10" h, neck reattached, old repaint. 200.00
    Watson, Dave "Umbrella," Chincoteague, VA, hollow carved, c1920 . . . . .11,000.00
    Wheeler, Shang, Stratford, CT, c1935 . . . . .18,700.00
    Wheeler, Shang, Stratford, CT, hollow-carved, sleeping, c1910 . . . . .27,500.00
Cape Cod Shore Bird, 10" l, 5" h, underneath sgd "J. Mulak L. Cayman Chatham, 84," head reattached, some paint loss
    . . . . 100.00
Common Yellow Throat, 4" x 6", round wood pedestal. . 275.00
Curlew
    Boyd, George, Seabrook, NH. 4,840.00
    Bowman, William, Long Island, NY, 1870-90, hunched up in cold weather. 90,500.00
    Bowman, William, Long Island, NY, 1870-90, standing
    . . . . .57,500.00
    Crowell, A. Elmer, East Harwich, MA. 6,380.00

Bluebill Drake, Rozell Bliss, Stratford, CT, c1910, $290.

Gelston, Thomas, Quogue, Long Island, New York, long billed, head repair, replaced bill, 1890 . . . . .11,550.00

Unknown maker, MA, c1890, running, sickle-billed, 21-1/2" l 335,500.00

Unknown maker, Brigatine, NJ, c1800, long-billed 18,000.00

Unknown maker, VA, c1880. . . . . .20,900.00

Verity, Obediah, Seaford, NY, c1870, oversized 30,800.00

Wheeler, Shang, unique. 7,150.00

Dowticher, William Bowman, Long Island, NY, 1870-90 . . . . .13,475.00

Eider Drake, wide-bodied, oversized 4,070.00

Eider Hen, Gus Wilson, South Portland, mussel in bill 5,500.00

Goldeneye, Maurice Eaton, Deer Island, ME
Drake 2,530.00
Hen. 2,090.00

Golden Plover, A. Elmer Crowell, East Harwich, MA . .7,260.00

Gull, Bill Cranmer, hollow carved, orig paint, weathered 450.00

Hutchins Goose, preening, unknown maker 9,900.00

Ice Fishing
9" l, cream colored body, dark lateral line, fine gold sand glued to the back above the line, gold tin tail and fins, pressed painted eyes, and multi-loop line tie, Leroy Howell 365.00

9" l, tan, black markings on back, red gill and mouth lines, metal fins, a wooden tail, and large tack eyes, wear on belly and fins, gently curved Cadillac style by Leonard Zelinski 50.00

12" l, cedar, red nailed bead eyes, heavy copper fins, wood tail, burned or carved gill lines, possibly stripped and re-painted 25.00

Labrador Duck, Northeast, 19th C 5,500.00

Loons, miniature, George Boyd, Seabrook, NH, made for display at 1939 New York World's Fair
Drake 2,970.00
Hen. 1,210.00

Mallard, Nathan Rowley Horner, West Creek, NJ, hollow carved, pr 71,500.00

Merganser Drake
Huey, George. 4,180.00
Unknown maker, Maine 990.00

Merganser Hen, Mason Factory Premier-grade 7,150.00

Oldsquaw, canvas covered, Clinton Keith, Kingston, MA 770.00

Pied Bill Grebe, Jim Polite, carved minnow in mouth, sgd and dated 1974 . . . . 375.00

Pintail
Drake, John Blair, Philadelphia, c1895, hollow carved 19,800.00
Hen, Charles Perdew, Henry, IL, c1930. . . . . .6,600.00
Red-breasted Merganser
Gelston, Thomas, Long Island, NY 8,250.00
Shourds, Harry V., Tuckerton, NJ, hollow carved, c1890 . . . . .13,200.00
Smith, Ben, Martha's Vineyard, MA, c1900, hollow carved, restored to orig paint 3,300.00
Unknown, horseshoe weights, Maine, pr 2,970.00
Wilson, Gus, South Portland, ME. 55,000.00

Rig Plover, Morton 7,700.00

Ruddy Turnstone, William Bowman, Lawrence, NY . .57,750.00

Shovelier Hen, Bob Schaber. 300.00

Snowy Egret, branded "H. Conklin" on bottom 500.00

Surf Scoter, with mussel, Gus Wilson, Portland, ME 28,600.00

Swan, 25" l, 18-1/2" h, horseshoe weight, over painted, some paint flaking 825.00

Teal, green-winged, Ward Brothers, Crisfield, MD, 1936, pr 38,500.00

Tern, life size, A. Elmer Crowell, East Harwich, MA . . .5,280.00

Wigeon
Crowell, A. Elmer, East Harwich, MA 33,000.00
Lincoln, Joe, Accord, MA, restored bill top 12,650.00
Woodcock, A. Elmer Crowell, East Harwich, MA . .13,200.00

Wood Duck
Crowell, A. Elmer, East Harwich, MA, three-quarter size, flying 11,500.00
Lincoln, Joe, Accord, MA 165,000.00

Yellowlegs, feeding, Fred Nichols, Lynn, MA 25,850.00

DEDHAM POTTERY

History: Alexander W. Robertson established a pottery in Chelsea, Massachusetts, about 1866. After his brother, Hugh Cornwall Robertson, joined him in 1868 the firm was called A. W. & H. C. Robertson. Their father, James Robertson, joined his sons in 1872, and the name Chelsea Keramic Art Works Robertson and Sons was used.

Their initial products were simple flower and bean pots, but the firm quickly expanded their output to include a wide variety of artistic pottery. They produced a very fine redware body used in classical forms, some with black backgrounds imitating ancient Greek and Apulian works. They experimented with underglaze slip decoration on vases. The Chelsea Keramic Art Works Pottery also produced high-glazed vases, pitchers, and plaques with a buff clay body with either sculpted or molded applied decoration.

James Robertson died in 1880 and Alexander moved to California in 1884 leaving Hugh C. Robertson alone in Chelsea where his tireless experiments eventually yielded a stunning imitation of the prized Chinese Ming-era blood-red glaze. Hugh's vases with that glaze were marked with an impressed "CKAW." Creating these red-glazed vases was very expensive, and even though they received great critical acclaim, the company declared bankruptcy in 1889.

Recapitalized by a circle of Boston art patrons in 1891, Hugh started the Chelsea Pottery U.S., which produced gray crackle-glazed dinnerware with cobalt blue decorations, the rabbit pattern being the most popular.

The business moved to new facilities in Dedham, Massachusetts, and began production in 1896 under the name Dedham Pottery. Hugh's son and grandson operated the business until it closed in 1943, by which time between 50 and 80 patterns had been produced, some very briefly.

Marks: The following marks help determine the approximate age of items:

"Chelsea Keramic Art Works Robertson and Sons," impressed, 1874-1880

"CKAW," impressed, 1875-1889

"CPUS," impressed in a cloverleaf, 1891-1895

Foreshortened rabbit only, impressed, 1894-1896

Conventional rabbit with "Dedham Pottery" in square blue stamped mark along with one impressed foreshortened rabbit, 1896-1928

Blue rabbit stamped mark with "registered" beneath along with two impressed foreshortened rabbit marks, 1929-1943

References: Lloyd E. Hawes, *Dedham Pottery and the Earlier Robertson's Chelsea Potteries*, Dedham Historical Society, 1968; Paul Evans, *Art Pottery of the United States*, Feingold & Lewis, 1974; Ralph and Terry Kovel, *Kovels' American Art Pottery*, Crown Publishers, 1993.

Collectors' Club: Dedham Pottery Collectors Society, 248 Highland St., Dedham, MA 02026.

Museum: Dedham Historical Society, Dedham, MA.

REPRODUCTION ALERT

Two companies make Dedham-like reproductions primarily utilizing the rabbit pattern, but always mark their work very differently from the original.

Advisor: James D. Kaufman.

Bowl, 8-1/2" sq
    Rabbit pattern, reg. stamp 600.00
    Rabbit pattern, reg. stamp, hairline crack. 275.00
    Swan pattern, reg. stamp 725.00
Candlesticks, pr
    Elephant pattern, reg. blue stamp 525.00
    Rabbit pattern, reg. blue stamp 325.00
Creamer and Sugar, type #1, 3-1/4" h, Duck pattern, blue stamp
    . . . . 650.00
Demitasse Cup and Saucer, Rabbit pattern, blue stamp
    . . . . 320.00

Bread and Butter Plate, Horse Chestnut pattern, 6-1/8" d, $115.

Knife Rest, Rabbit form, blue reg. stamp 575.00
Paperweight, Rabbit form, blue reg. stamp. 495.00
Pickle Dish, 10-1/2" l, Elephant pattern, blue reg. stamp 750.00
Pitcher
    5" h, Rabbit pattern, blue stamp. 325.00
    5-1/8" h, Chickens pattern, blue stamp 2,300.00
    7" h, Turkey pattern, blue stamp 585.00
    9" h, Rabbit pattern, blue stamp. 700.00
    Style of 1850, blue reg. stamp 975.00
Plate
    6" d
        Clover pattern, reg. stamp 625.00
        Dolphin pattern, blue reg. stamp, chip. 225.00
        Iris pattern, blue stamp, Maude Davenport's "O" rebus
        . . . . 280.00
        Rabbit pattern, blue stamp 145.00
        8" d, Iris pattern, reg. stamp 230.00
    8-1/2" d
    Chicken pattern, reg. blue stamp 1,450.00
    Crab central design, blue stamp. 550.00
    Duck pattern, blue stamp, Maude Davenport's "O" rebus
    . . . . 375.00
    Elephant pattern, blue reg. stamp 650.00
    French Mushroom pattern, blue stamp 1,100.00
    Lobster central design, blue stamp 575.00
    Magnolia pattern, blue stamp. 165.00
    Rabbit pattern, blue stamp 170.00
    Rabbit pattern, blue stamp, Maude Davenport's "O" rebus
    . . . . 235.00
    Snow Tree pattern, blue stamp 210.00
    Upside down dolphin, CPUS 900.00
    10" d
        Clover pattern, blue stamp 825.00
        Dolphin pattern, blue reg. stamp. 875.00
        Elephant pattern, blue reg. stamp. 900.00
        Elephant pattern, blue reg. stamp, three small rim nicks
        . . . . 450.00
        Pine Apple pattern, CPUS 775.00
        Turkey pattern, blue stamp, Maude Davenport's "O" rebus 475.00
        Turtle pattern, reg. blue stamp 1,125.00
Platter, 14" x 8", oval, steak platter, Rabbit pattern, blue reg. stamp 825.00
Sherbet, two handles, Rabbit pattern, blue stamp 350.00
Tea Cup and Saucer
    Azalea pattern, reg. stamp 130.00
    Butterfly pattern, blue stamp 345.00
    Duck pattern, reg. stamp 190.00
    Iris pattern, reg. stamp 155.00
    Rabbit pattern, reg. stamp 155.00
    Turtle pattern, reg. stamp. 680.00
    Water Lily pattern, reg. stamp 130.00
Teapot, 6-1/8" h, Rabbit pattern, blue stamp 875.00

DELFTWARE

History: Delftware is pottery with a soft, red-clay body and tin-enamel glaze. The white, dense, opaque color came from adding tin ash to lead glaze. The first examples had blue designs on a white ground. Polychrome examples followed.

The name originally applied to pottery made in the region around Delft, Holland, beginning in the 16th century and ending in the late 18th century. The tin used came from the Cornish mines in England. By the 17th and 18th centuries, English potters in London, Bristol, and Liverpool were copying the glaze and designs. Some designs unique to English potters also developed.

In Germany and France, the ware is known as Faience, and in Italy as Majolica.

Bowl
11-5/8" d, shallow, polychrome flowers and squirrel, English, edge chips 935.00
13" d, 6" h, polychrome floral dec with butterfly, wear, rim hairline, and small chips. 1,705.00
Bust, 11-3/4" h, Napoleon, ceramic, artist sgd "S.B.," dated 1809 . . . . 500.00
Charger
12-3/4" d, polychrome floral dec, chips and hairline. . 275.00
13-1/2" d, blue and white, central scene of flowers and trees, cross-banded border, Liverpool, 18th C, some roughness to rim edge 550.00
13-1/2" d, blue and white, central scene of house and tall tree, stylized birds, Liverpool, 18th C, small glaze edge chips 350.00
13-3/4" d, polychrome floral dec, Holland, late 18th/early 19th C 550.00
15-1/2" d, blue and white, Rembrandt portrait, mkd "Delft," imp "Joost Thooft & Labduchere". 200.00
Dish, 10-5/8" d, blue and white floral dec, Dutch, 18th C 150.00
Flask, 7" h, flattened round base, narrow short neck, round foot, blue, white, and black floral dec, windmill landscape scene of man and harp, loops for rope, sgd "AK," Holland, minor edge chips. 300.00
Ginger Jar, blue and white, birds, flowers, and human figures, 18th C, set of three. 3,960.00
Inkstand, 9-3/4" l, cov central pot, raised pen stand, blue and white landscape, floral, and insect dec, Dutch, late 18th C, glaze wear, rim chips 460.00
Jar, 8-1/4" h, chicken-shape, polychrome, pink and green dec, sgd, chips. 400.00
Plate
8-3/4" d, flowers and bird, polychrome dec, English, small chips. 385.00
8-7/8" d, polychrome, profiles of regal couple, mkd "FSW-PVOR," chips and glued rim repair 770.00
9 1/2" d, blue tin glaze, landscape and border dec, 18th C, price for pr 350.00
10 1/2" d, blue tin glaze, garden dec, 18th C 260.00
Posset Pot, cov, 10" h, polychrome floral and floral dec, Dutch, c1770, glaze loss to spout rim, restorations. 1,495.00
Pot, cov, 4" h, two handles, blue and white dec bird and floral designs, English, mid 18th C, rim chip to cov, glaze loss 550.00
Soup Plate, 8-3/4" d, blue and white floral dec, Dutch, 18th C 150.00
Tile, 5-3/4 x 12-1/4", painted blue and white, cows on coast, framed, late 19th/early 20th C 280.00
Tobacco Jar, 10" h, blue and white dec, pipe smoking Indian seated by large cov jar, titled "St Domingo," Dutch sailing

Charger, blue and white wind mill scene, 12-3/4" d, $225.

ships in distance, brass cov, Dutch, late 18th/early 19th C, glaze wear to rim, old repair to body 575.00
Trivet, 8-1/2" l, triangular form, black outlined blue and white leaves dec, circular frieze of figures in landscape, Dutch, early 19th C, slight glaze loss to rim 100.00
Vase
3-1/8" h, shaped flaring rim, ribbed baluster form body, figural and foliage devices, 18th C, minor chips, hairline . . 350.00
8-1/4" h, blue and white floral dec, oval scene of youth in landscape with windmills, chips, hairline, repair . . . 275.00
8-1/2" h, tin glazed blue and white earthenware, bishop praying in landscape dec, dated 1742, repairs, Continental 40.00

DEPRESSION GLASS

History: Depression glass was made from 1920 to 1940. It was an inexpensive machine-made glass and was produced by several companies in various patterns and colors. The number of forms made in different patterns also varied.

Depression glass was sold through variety stores, given away as premiums, or packaged with certain products. Movie houses gave it away from 1935 until well into the 1940s.

Like pattern glass, knowing the proper name of a pattern is the key to collecting. Collectors should be prepared to do research.

References: Gene Florence, *Collectible Glassware from the 40's, 50's, 60's*, 4th ed., Collector Books, 1997; ——, *Collector's Encyclopedia of Depression Glass*, 13th ed., Collector Books, 1997; ——, *Elegant Glassware of the Depression Era*, 7th ed., Collector Books, 1997; ——, *Pocket Guide to Depression Glass & More*, 1920-1960s, 11th ed., Collector Books, 1998; ——, *Stemware Identification Featuring Cordials with Values*, 1920s-1960s, Collector

Books, 1997; ——, *Very Rare Glassware of the Depression Era*, 1st Series (1988, 1991 value update), 2nd Series (1991), 3rd Series (1993), 4th Series (1996), 5th Series (1996), Collector Books; Ralph and Terry Kovel, *Kovels' Depression Glass & American Dinnerware Price List*, 5th ed., Crown, 1995; Carl F. Luckey and Mary Burris, *Identification & Value Guide to Depression Era Glassware*, 3rd ed., Books Americana, 1994; Ellen T. Schroy, *Warman's Depression Glass*, Krause Publications, 1997; Kent G. Washburn, Price Survey, 4th ed., published by author, 1994; Hazel Marie Weatherman, *Colored Glassware of the Depression Era*, Book 2, published by author 1974, available in reprint; ——, *1984 Supplement & Price Trends for Colored Glassware of the Depression Era*, Book 1, published by author, 1984.

Periodical: *The Daze*, P.O. Box 57, Otisville, MI 48463.

Collectors' Clubs: Canadian Depression Glass Club, 1026 Forestwood Drive, Mississauga, Ontario L5C 1G8, Canada; National Depression Glass Association, Inc., P.O. Box 8264, Wichita, KS 67209; 20-30-40 Society, Inc., P.O. Box 856, LaGrange, IL 60525.

Videotape: *Living Glass:* Popular Patterns of the Depression Era, 2 Vols., Ro Cliff Communications, 1993.

REPRODUCTION ALERT

The following is a partial listing of Depression Glass patterns that have been reproduced. When available, the name of the reproduction manufacturer, shapes, and colors are given.

Adam (produced in the Far East and distributed through AA Importing of St. Louis) butter dish, pink.

Avocado (Indiana Glass Company) pitcher and tumbler, in amethyst, blue, green, pink, frosted pink, red, and yellow.

Cherry Blossom (large number of manufacturers and importers) numerous forms including two-handled tray, cup and saucer, and children's set, in blue, cobalt blue, Delphite, green, iridized colors, pink, and red.

Madrid (Indiana Glass Company) goblet, grill plate, shakers, vase, and more, in crystal (clear), blue, pink, and teal.

Mayfair, cookie jars, juice pitchers, shakers, shot glasses, and more, in amethyst, blue, cobalt blue, green, pink, and red.

Miss America, covered butter dish, pitcher, shakers, and tumbler, in cobalt blue, crystal (clear), green, ice blue, pink, and red amberina.

Sharon (privately produced) covered butter in blue, cobalt blue, green (light and dark), opalescent blue, red, and umber (burnt).

AMERICAN PIONEER

Manufactured by Liberty Works, Egg Harbor, NJ, from 1931 to 1934. Made in amber, crystal, green, and pink.

	Amber	Crystal	Green	Pink
Bowl, 5" d, handle	44.00	22.00	24.00	22.00
Bowl, 8-3/4" d, cov	—	85.00	125.00	85.00
Bowl, 9" d, handle	—	24.00	30.00	24.00
Bowl, 9-1/4" d, cov	—	95.00	130.00	95.00
Bowl, 10" d	—	50.00	70.00	50.00
Candlesticks, pr, 6-1/2" h	—	75.00	95.00	75.00
Candy Jar, cov, 1 pound	—	100.00	115.00	110.00
Candy Jar, cov, 1-1/2 pound	—	70.00	125.00	95.00
Cheese and Cracker Set, indented plate and compote	—	50.00	65.00	55.00
Coaster, 3-1/2" d	—	18.00	32.00	30.00
Cocktail, 3 oz, 3-13/16" h	45.00	—	—	—
Cocktail, 3-1/2 oz, 3 -15/16" h	45.00	—	—	—
Console Bowl, 10-3/4" d	—	50.00	75.00	60.00
Creamer, 2-3/4" h	—	18.00	20.00	25.00
Creamer, 3-1/2" h	60.00	30.00	32.00	30.00
Cup	24.00	10.00	12.00	12.00
Dresser Set, 2 cologne bottles, powder jar, 7-1/2" tray	—	300.00	345.00	365.00
Goblet, 8 oz, 6" h, water	—	40.00	45.00	40.00

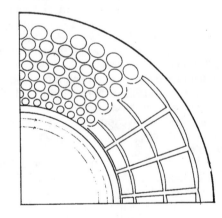

	Amber	Crystal	Green	Pink
Ice Bucket, 6" h	—	50.00	80.00	65.00
Juice Tumbler, 5 oz	—	32.00	37.50	35.00
Lamp, 1-3/4", metal pole, 9-1/2"	—	—	65.00	—
Lamp, 5-1/2" round, ball shape	—	—	—	70.00
Lamp, 8-1/2" h	—	90.00	115.00	110.00
Mayonnaise, 4-1/4"	—	60.00	90.00	60.00
Pilsner, 5-3/4" h, 11 oz	—	100.00	110.00	100.00
Pitcher, cov, 5" h	265.00	150.00	225.00	165.00
Pitcher, cov, 7" h	300.00	175.00	250.00	195.00
Plate, 6" d	—	12.50	17.50	12.50
Plate, 6" d, handle	25.00	12.50	17.50	12.50
Plate, 8" d	28.00	10.00	13.00	14.00
Plate, 11-1/2" d, handle	40.00	20.00	24.00	20.00
Rose Bowl, 4-1/4" d, ftd	—	40.00	50.00	45.00
Saucer, 6" sq	11.00	4.00	5.00	5.50
Sherbet, 3-1/2" h	—	18.00	22.00	20.00
Sherbet, 4-3/4" h	—	32.50	40.00	30.00
Sugar, 2-3/4" h	—	20.00	27.50	25.00
Sugar, 3-1/2" h	50.00	20.00	27.50	25.00
Tumbler, 8 oz, 4" h	—	32.00	55.00	35.00
Tumbler, 12 oz, 5" h	—	40.00	55.00	40.00
Vase, 7" h, 4 styles	—	85.00	110.00	90.00
Vase, 9" h, round	—	—	235.00	—
Whiskey, 2 oz, 2-1/4" h	—	48.00	—	48.00

AUNT POLLY

Manufactured by U.S. Glass Company, Pittsburgh, PA, in the late 1920s. Made in blue, green, and iridescent. Reproduction cups and saucers.

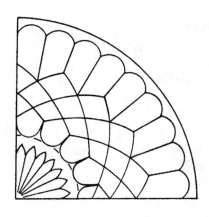

	Blue	Green	Iridescent
Berry Bowl, 4-3/4" d, individual	18.00	8.50	8.50
Berry Bowl, 7-1/8" d, master	45.00	22.00	22.00
Bowl, 4-3/4" d, 2" h	—	15.00	15.00
Bowl, 5-1/2" d, one handle	22.00	15.00	15.00
Bowl, 8-3/8" l, oval	100.00	42.00	42.00
Butter Dish, cov	215.00	200.00	200.00
Candy Jar, cov, 2 handles	39.00	27.50	27.50
Candy Jar, ftd, 2 handles	—	26.00	26.00
Creamer	48.00	32.00	32.00
Pickle, 7-1/4" l, oval, handle	42.00	17.50	17.50
Pitcher, 48 oz, 8" h	175.00	—	—
Plate, 6" d, sherbet	12.00	6.00	6.00
Plate, 8" d, luncheon	20.00	—	—
Salt and Pepper Shakers, pr	220.00	—	—
Sherbet	15.00	12.00	12.00
Sugar	48.00	32.00	32.00
Tumbler, 8 oz, 3-5/8" h	30.00	—	—
Vase, 6-1/2" h, ftd	48.00	30.00	30.00

BEADED BLOCK

Manufactured by Imperial Glass Company, Bellaire, OH, from 1927 to the 1930s. Made in amber, crystal, green, ice blue, iridescent, milk white (1950s), opalescent, pink, red, and vaseline. Some pieces are still being made in pink and are embossed with the "IG" trademark.

	Amber	Crystal	Green	Ice Blue	Irid.	Opal	Pink	Vaseline
Bowl, 4-1/2" d, lily	8.00	6.00	10.00	18.00	15.00	18.00	15.00	18.00
Bowl, 4-1/2" d, 2 handles	10.00	8.00	10.00	18.00	16.00	18.00	10.00	20.00
Bowl, 5-1/2" sq	8.50	6.00	8.50	9.00	7.50	9.00	8.50	9.00
Bowl, 5 -/2 d, 1 handle	8.50	6.00	8.50	9.00	7.50	9.00	18.00	9.00
Bowl, 6" deep	12.00	10.00	12.00	12.50	10.00	12.50	15.00	12.00
Bowl, 6-1/4" d	9.00	7.00	9.00	9.50	9.00	9.50	8.00	9.00
Bowl, 6-1/2" d, 2 handles	9.00	7.00	9.00	9.50	9.00	9.50	8.00	9.00
Bowl, 6-3/4" d	12.00	10.00	12.00	11.00	12.00	12.00	11.00	10.00
Bowl, 7-1/4" d, flared	12.00	10.00	12.00	11.00	12.00	12.00	11.00	10.00
Bowl, 7-1/2" d, fluted	22.00	20.00	22.00	21.00	18.00	22.00	21.00	22.00
Bowl, 7-1/2" plain	20.00	18.00	20.00	18.50	18.50	20.00	18.00	20.00
Candy Dish, cov, pear shaped	—	—	275.00	—	—	—	—	600.00
Celery, 8-1/4" d	15.00	12.00	15.00	16.00	15.00	15.00	14.00	15.00
Creamer, ftd	20.00	16.00	20.00	18.50	18.50	20.00	18.00	20.00
Jelly, 4-1/2" h, stemmed	10.00	8.00	10.00	10.00	9.00	8.50	9.00	10.00
Jelly, 4-1/2" h, stemmed, flared lid	12.00	10.00	12.00	11.00	12.00	12.00	11.00	10.00
Pitcher, 1 pt, 5-1/4" h	85.00	95.00	100.00	95.00	90.00	85.00	175.00	85.00
Plate, 7-3/4" sq	7.50	5.00	7.50	7.50	7.00	7.00	6.00	7.50
Plate, 8-3/4"	20.00	16.00	20.00	20.00	17.50	17.50	16.00	17.50
Sugar, ftd	20.00	16.00	20.00	20.00	17.50	17.50	16.00	17.50
Syrup	—	—	—	—	—	—	—	150.00
Vase, 6" h, ftd	15.00	12.00	18.00	20.00	15.00	15.00	14.00	20.00

CHERRYBERRY

Manufactured by U. S. Glass Company, Pittsburgh, PA, early 1930s. Made in crystal, green, iridescent, and pink.

	Crystal	Green	Iridescent	Pink
Berry Bowl, 4" d	6.50	8.75	6.50	8.75
Berry Bowl, 7-1/2" d, deep	17.50	20.00	17.50	20.00
Bowl. 6-1/4" d, 2" deep	40.00	55.00	40.00	55.00
Butter Dish, cov	150.00	170.00	150.00	170.00
Comport, 5-3/4"	17.50	25.00	17.50	25.00
Creamer, large, 4-5/8"	40.00	45.00	40.00	45.00
Creamer, small	15.00	20.00	15.00	20.00
Olive Dish, 5" l, one handle	10.00	15.00	10.00	15.00
Pickle Dish, 8-1/4" l, oval	10.00	15.00	10.00	15.00
Pitcher, 7-3/4" h	165.00	175.00	165.00	175.00
Plate, 6" d, sherbet	6.50	11.00	6.50	11.00
Plate, 7-1/2" d, salad	8.50	15.00	9.00	15.00
Salad Bowl, 6-1/2" d, deep	17.50	22.00	17.50	22.00
Sherbet	9.00	10.00	9.50	12.00
Sugar, large, cov	45.00	75.00	45.00	75.00
Sugar, small, open	15.00	20.00	15.00	20.00
Tumbler, 9 oz, 3-5/8" h	20.00	35.00	20.00	35.00

CHRISTMAS CANDY, No. 624.

Manufactured by Indiana Glass Company, Dunkirk, IN, 1950s. Made in crystal and Terrace Green (teal).

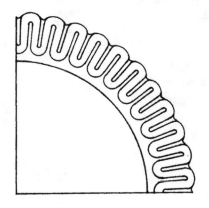

	Crystal	Terrace Green
Bowl, 5-3/4" d	5.00	—
Creamer	12.00	27.50
Cup	8.00	35.00
Mayonnaise, ladle, liner	24.00	—
Plate, 6" d, bread and butter	4.00	16.00
Plate, 8-1/4" d, luncheon	8.00	28.00
Plate, 9-5/8"d, dinner	12.00	36.00
Sandwich Plate, 11-1/4" d	24.00	65.00
Saucer	5.00	15.00
Soup Bowl, 7-3/8" d	11.00	75.00
Sugar	12.00	35.00
Tidbit, 2 tier	20.00	—
Vegetable Bowl, 9-1/2" d	—	235.00

COLONIAL FLUTED, Rope

Manufactured by Federal Glass Company, Columbus, OH, from 1928 to 1933. Made in crystal and green.

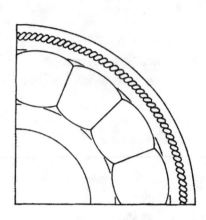

	Crystal	Green
Berry Bowl, 4" d	10.00	11.00
Berry Bowl, 7-1/2" d	16.00	18.00
Cereal Bowl, 6" d	12.00	14.00
Creamer, ftd	12.00	14.00
Cup	5.00	7.50
Plate, 6" d, sherbet	2.50	4.00
Plate, 8" d, luncheon	5.00	10.00
Salad Bowl, 6-1/2" d, 2-1/2" deep	18.00	20.00
Saucer	2.50	4.00
Sherbet	6.00	8.50
Sugar, cov	21.00	25.00
Sugar, open	4.00	5.00

COLUMBIA

Manufactured by Federal Glass Company, Columbus,. OH, from 1938 to 1942. Made in crystal and pink. Several flashed (stained) colors are found and some decaled pieces are known.

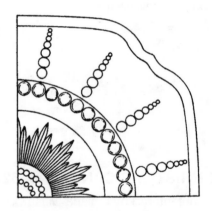

	Crystal	Flashed	Pink
Bowl, 10-1/2" d, ruffled edge	24.00	20.00	—
Butter Dish, cov	20.00	18.00	—
Cereal Bowl, 5" d	17.00	—	—
Chop Plate, 11" d	17.00	12.00	—
Crescent Shaped Salad	27.00	—	—
Cup	8.00	9.00	24.00
Cup and Saucer	11.00	11.50	34.00
Plate, 6" d, bread & butter	5.00	—	14.00
Plate, 9-1/2" d, luncheon	15.00	—	32.00
Salad Bowl, 8-1/2" d	20.00	—	—
Saucer	3.00	2.50	10.00
Soup Bowl, 8" d, low	22.00	—	—
Tumbler, 4 oz.	30.00	—	—
Tumbler, 9 oz.	42.50	—	—

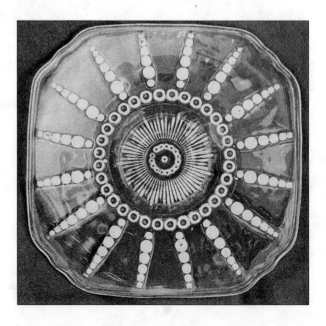

Columbia, saucer, crystal, $3.

DAISY, No. 620

Manufactured by Indiana Glass Company, Dunkirk, IN, from late 1930s to 1980s. Made in amber (1940s), crystal (1933-40), dark green (1960s-80s), fired-on red (late 1930s), and milk glass (1960s-80s).

Daisy, amber creamer, $8.50; amber sugar, $8.50.

	Amber or Fired-On Red	Crystal	Dark Green or Milk White
Berry Bowl, 4-1/2" d	9.00	5.00	5.00
Berry Bowl, 7-3/8" d deep	15.00	7.50	7.50
Berry Bowl, 9-3/8" d, deep	30.00	12.00	12.00
Cake Plate, 11-1/2" d	14.50	12.00	12.00
Cereal Bowl, 6" d	25.00	10.00	10.00
Cream Soup Bowl, 4-1/2" d	13.50	7.50	7.50
Creamer, ftd	8.50	6.00	6.00
Cup	5.00	4.50	6.00
Plate, 6" d, sherbet	3.00	2.50	2.50
Plate, 7-3/8" d, salad	7.00	3.00	3.00
Plate, 8-3/8" d, luncheon	7.75	5.00	5.00
Plate, 9-3/8" d, dinner	9.00	7.50	7.50
Plate, 10-3/8" d, grill	15.00	8.00	8.00
Plate, 10-3/8" d, grill, indent for soup	15.00	8.00	8.00
Platter, 10-3/4" d	14.00	11.00	11.00
Relish Dish, 8-3/8" d, 3 part	22.00	12.00	12.00
Sandwich Plate, 11-1/2" d	14.50	12.00	12.00
Saucer	2.00	1.50	2.00
Sherbet, ftd	9.00	5.00	5.00
Sugar, ftd	8.50	6.00	6.00
Tumbler, 9 oz, ftd	16.00	10.00	10.00
Tumbler, 12 oz, ftd	40.00	15.00	15.00
Vegetable Bowl, 10" l, oval	15.00	10.00	10.00

FLORENTINE NO. 2, Poppy No. 2

Manufactured by Hazel Atlas Glass Company, Clarksburg, WV, and Zanesville, OH, from 1932 to 1935. Made in amber, cobalt blue, crystal, green, ice blue, pink, and yellow. Reproductions: † 7-1/2" h cone-shaped pitcher and 4" h ftd tumbler. Reproductions found in cobalt blue, crystal, deep green, and pink.

	Crystal	Green	Pink	Yellow
Ashtray, 3-1/2" d	18.00	18.00	—	25.00
Ashtray, 5-1/2" d	20.00	25.00	—	35.00
Berry Bowl, 4-1/2" d	12.00	15.00	17.50	22.50
Berry Bowl, 8" d	24.00	26.00	30.00	35.00
Bowl, 5-1/2" d	32.00	35.00	—	42.00
Bowl, 7-1/2" d, shallow	—	—	—	85.00
Bowl, 9" d, flat	27.50	27.50	—	—
Butter Dish, cov	100.00	115.00		155.00
Candlesticks, pr, 2-3/4" h	45.00	48.00	—	60.00
Candy Dish, cov	100.00	95.00	95.00	150.00
Cereal Bowl, 6" d	26.00	26.00		38.00
Coaster, 3-1/4" d	—	—	—	22.50
Coaster, 3-3/4" d	18.00	18.00	—	25.00
Coaster, 5-1/2" d	20.00	25.00	—	35.00
Cocktail, 3-1/4" h, ftd	—	—	—	12.00
Comport, 3-1/2" d, ruffled	25.00	25.00	25.00	—
Condiment Tray, round	—	—	—	65.00
Cream Soup, 4-3/4" d, 2 handles	14.00	16.00	18.00	20.00
Creamer	8.00	11.00	—	12.00
Cup	7.50	7.50	—	10.00
Custard Cup	60.00	60.00	—	85.00
Gravy Boat	—	—	—	49.00
Gravy Boat Underplate, 11-1/2" l	—	—	—	115.00
Iced Tea Tumbler, 12 oz, 5" h	35.00	35.00	—	45.00
Juice Tumbler, 5 oz, 3-1/8" h, flat	12.00	12.00	12.00	22.00
Juice Tumbler, 5 oz, 3-1/8" h, ftd	13.00	15.00	—	21.00
Parfait, 6" h	30.00	32.00	—	60.00
Pitcher, 24 oz, cone, ftd, 6-1/4" h	—	—	—	35.00
Pitcher, 28 oz, cone ftd, 7-1/2" h †	31.50	35.00	—	42.00
Pitcher, 48 oz, 7-1/2" h	60.00	70.00	120.00	32.00
Pitcher, 76 oz, 8-1/4" h	90.00	95.00	225.00	400.00
Plate, 6" d, sherbet	4.00	4.00	—	6.50
Plate, 6-1/2" d, indent	16.00	17.50	—	30.00
Plate, 8-1/2" d, salad	8.50	9.00	9.00	10.00
Plate, 10" d, dinner	14.00	16.00	—	19.00
Plate, 10-1/4" d, grill	15.00	15.00	—	12.00
Plate, 10-1/4" d, grill, cream soup ring	35.00	35.00	—	—
Platter, 11" oval	15.00	16.00	18.00	24.00
Relish, 10" d, divided, 3 part	20.00	22.50	24.00	30.00
Relish, 10" d, plain	20.00	20.00	24.00	30.00
Salt and Pepper Shakers, pr	45.00	45.00	—	55.00

	Crystal	Green	Pink	Yellow
Saucer	5.00	4.00	—	3.50
Sherbet, ftd	10.00	10.00	—	12.00
Sugar, cov	8.50	9.00	—	38.00
Tumbler, 5 oz, 3-1/4" h, ftd	15.00	15.00	15.00	—
Tumbler, 5 oz, 4" h, ftd †	13.00	13.00	17.50	16.50
Tumbler, 5 oz, 3-5/16" h, blown	18.00	18.00	—	—
Tumbler, 6 oz, 3-9/16" h, blown	16.00	18.00	—	—
Tumbler, 9 oz, 4" h	12.00	18.00	16.00	22.50
Tumbler, 9 oz, 4-1/2" h, ftd	25.00	25.00	—	38.00
Tumbler, 10 oz, 4-11/16, blown	19.00	19.00	—	—
Tumbler, 12 oz, 5" h, blown	20.00	20.00	—	20.00
Vase, 6" h	30.00	32.00	—	60.00
Vegetable Bowl, cov, 9" l, oval	55.00	60.00	—	65.00

HEX OPTIC, Honeycomb

Manufactured by Jeannette Glass Company, Jeannette, PA, from 1928 to 1932. Made in green and green. Ultramarine tumblers have been found. Iridescent tumblers and pitchers were made about 1960 and it is assumed that they were made by Jeannette.

	Green	Pink
Berry Bowl, 4-1/4" d, ruffled	5.50	6.00
Berry Bowl, 7-1/2" d	8.00	8.00
Bucket Reamer	60.00	50.00
Butter Dish, cov, rect, 1 lb size	75.00	72.00
Creamer, two style handles	6.00	7.00
Cup, two style handles	5.00	5.00
Ice Bucket, metal handle	20.00	20.00
Mixing Bowl, 7-1/4" d	14.00	14.00
Mixing Bowl, 8-1/4" d	16.00	16.00
Mixing Bowl, 9" d	18.00	18.00
Mixing Bowl, 10" d	20.00	20.00
Pitcher, 32 oz, 5" h	24.00	24.00
Pitcher, 48 oz, 9" h, ftd	48.00	50.00
Pitcher, 96 oz, 8" h	235.00	245.00
Plate, 6" d, sherbet	3.00	3.00
Plate, 8" d, luncheon	6.00	6.00
Platter, 11" d, round	14.00	16.00
Refrigerator Dish, 4 x 4"	10.00	10.00
Refrigerator Stack Set, 4 pc	60.00	60.00
Salt and Pepper Shakers, pr	30.00	30.00
Saucer	4.00	4.00

	Green	Pink
Sherbet, 5 oz, ftd	5.00	5.00
Sugar, two styles of handles	6.00	6.00
Sugar Shaker	175.00	175.00
Tumbler, 12 oz, 5" h	8.00	8.00
Tumbler, 5-3/4" h, ftd	10.00	10.00
Tumbler, 7" h, ftd	12.00	12.00
Tumbler, 7 oz, 4-3/4" h, ftd	8.00	8.00
Tumbler, 9 oz, 3-3/4" h	5.00	5.00
Whiskey, 1 oz, 2" h	8.50	8.50

INDIANA CUSTARD, Flower and Leaf Band

Manufactured by Indiana Glass Company, Dunkirk, IN, 1930s; 1950s. Made in custard color, known as French Ivory. White was made in the 1950s.

	French Ivory	White
Berry Bowl, 5-1/2" d	14.00	5.50
Berry Bowl, 9" d, 1-3/4" deep	32.00	—
Butter Dish, cov	68.00	—
Cereal Bowl, 6-1/2" d	4.00	—
Creamer	17.50	—
Cup	38.00	17.00
Plate, 5-3/4" d, bread and butter	7.00	—
Plate, 7-1/2" d, salad	16.00	—
Plate, 8-7/8" d, luncheon	16.00	—
Plate, 9-3/4" d, dinner	28.00	—
Platter, 11-1/2" l, oval	30.00	—
Saucer	12.00	5.00
Sherbet	90.00	—
Soup Bowl, 7-1/2" d, flat	32.00	—
Sugar, cov	30.00	—

LORAIN, Basket, No. 615.

Manufactured by Indiana Glass Company, Dunkirk, IN, from 1929 to 1939. Made in crystal, green, and yellow.

	Crystal	Green	Yellow
Berry Bowl, 8" d	80.00	85.00	155.00
Cereal Bowl, 6" d	35.00	35.00	59.00
Creamer, ftd	15.00	15.00	27.00
Cup and Saucer	15.00	15.00	20.00
Plate, 5-1/2" d, sherbet	6.50	7.50	12.50
Plate, 7-3/4" d, salad	10.00	10.00	15.00
Plate, 8-3/4" d, luncheon	15.00	15.00	25.00
Plate, 10-1/4" d, dinner	30.00	35.00	60.00
Platter, 11-1/2" l	25.00	25.00	40.00
Relish, 8" d, 4 part	17.50	17.50	35.00
Salad Bowl, 7-3/4" d	36.00	36.00	75.00
Saucer	5.00	5.00	7.00
Sherbet, ftd	17.50	20.00	35.00
Snack Tray, crystal trim	22.00	25.00	—
Sugar, ftd	15.00	18.00	24.00
Tumbler, 9 oz, 4-3/4" h, ftd	17.50	20.00	36.50
Vegetable Bowl, 9-3/4" l, oval	36.00	40.00	47.00

MADRID

Manufactured by Federal Glass Company, Lancaster, OH, from 1932 to 1939. Made in amber, blue, crystal, green, iridescent, and pink. Reproductions: † Reproductions include candlesticks, cups, saucers, and vegetable bowl. Reproductions are found in amber, blue, crystal, and pink.. Federal Glass Company reissued this pattern under the name "Recollection." Some of these pieces were dated 1976. When Federal went bankrupt, the molds were sold to Indiana Glass who removed the date and began production of crystal, then pink. Several pieces were made recently that were not part of the original production and include a footed cake stand, goblet, two section grill plate, preserves stand, squatty salt and pepper shakers, 11 oz tumbler, and vase.

Iridized pieces are limited to a console set, consisting of a low bowl and pair of candlesticks, valued at $35.00.

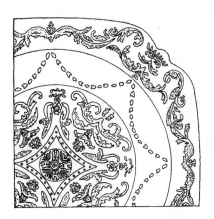

Madrid, pitcher, 60oz, sq, amber, 8" h, $44.

	Amber	Blue	Crystal	Green	Pink
Ashtray, 6" sq	265.00	—	250.00	160.00	—
Berry Bowl, small	5.00	—	5.00	—	—
Berry Bowl, 9-3/8" d	22.00	—	22.00	—	20.00
Bowl, 7" d	12.00	—	6.00	15.50	—
Butter Dish, cov	70.00	—	64.00	90.00	—
Cake Plate, 11-1/4" d	24.00	—	20.00	—	28.00
Candlesticks, 2-1/4" h, pr †	18.50	—	14.50	—	28.00
Coaster, 5" d	40.00	—	40.00	35.00	—
Console Bowl, 11" d	20.00	—	18.00	—	36.00
Cookie Jar	48.00	—	40.00	—	34.00
Creamer	12.00	18.00	7.00	10.00	—
Cream Soup, 4 3/4" d	15.00	—	15.00	—	—
Cup †	6.50	18.00	4.50	10.00	7.50
Gelatin Mold, 2-1/2" h	13.50	—	13.50	—	—
Gravy Boat and Platter	500.00	—	500.00	—	—
Iced Tea Tumbler, round	18.00	—	18.00	20.00	—
Jam Dish, 7" d	21.00	33.00	10.00	25.00	—
Juice Pitcher	50.00	—	45.00	—	—
Juice Tumbler, 5 oz, 3 7/8 h, ftd	16.50	40.00	35.00	30.00	—
Pitcher, jug-type	60.00	—	24.00	190.00	—
Pitcher, 60 oz, 8" h, sq	44.00	150.00	150.00	135.00	36.00
Pitcher, 80 oz, 8-1/2" h, ice lip	55.00	—	50.00	200.00	—
Plate, 6" d, sherbet	5.50	12.00	4.00	4.50	4.00
Plate, 7-1/2" d, salad	12.00	17.00	12.00	9.00	9.00
Plate, 8-7/8" d, luncheon	8.50	18.50	5.50	10.00	8.00
Plate, 10-1/2" d, dinner	42.50	60.00	21.00	40.00	—

	Amber	Blue	Crystal	Green	Pink
Plate, 10-1/2" d, grill	12.00	—	10.00	18.50	—
Platter, 11-1/2" oval	16.00	24.00	15.00	16.00	15.00
Relish Dish, 10-1/2" d	14.50	—	7.00	16.00	20.00
Salad Bowl, 8" d	17.00	—	9.50	15.50	—
Salad Bowl, 9-1/2" d	32.00	—	30.00	—	—
Salt and Pepper Shakers, 3-1/2" h	125.00	135.00	95.00	68.00	—
Sauce Bowl, 5" d	9.00	—	7.50	8.50	11.00
Saucer †	5.00	8.00	4.00	5.00	5.00
Sherbet, cone	7.00	18.00	6.50	9.50	—
Sherbet, ftd	7.50	15.00	6.00	11.00	—
Soup Bowl, 8" d	15.00	20.00	6.00	15.50	—
Sugar, cov	46.00	175.00	32.50	48.00	—
Sugar, open	7.00	15.00	6.00	9.00	—
Tumbler, 9 oz, 4-1/2" h	17.50	38.00	15.0	23.50	24.00
Tumbler, 12 oz, 5-1/4" h, ftd	33.50	—	30.00	40.00	—
12 oz, 5-1/4" h	23.00	—	14.00	33.50	—
12 oz, 5-1/2" h, flat	22.50	32.00	20.00	40.00	—
Vegetable Bowl, 10" l, oval †	18.00	33.00	18.00	22.00	27.00

MANHATTAN, Horizontal Ribbed.

Manufactured by Anchor Hocking Glass Company, from 1938 to 1943. Made in crystal, green, iridized, pink, and ruby. Anchor Hocking introduced a similar pattern, Park Avenue, in 1987. Anchor Hocking was very careful to preserve the Manhattan pattern. Collectors should pay careful attention to measurements if they are uncertain of the pattern.

Ruby pieces are limited to relish tray inserts, currently valued at $6 each. Green and iridized production was limited to ftd tumblers, currently valued at $17.50.

	Crystal	Pink
Ashtray, 4" d, round	11.00	8.00
Ashtray, 4-1/2" w, sq	25.00	—
Berry Bowl, 5-3/8" d, handles	18.00	22.00
Berry Bowl, 7-1/2" d	15.00	—
Bowl, 4-1/2" d	9.00	—
Bowl, 8" d, closed handles	28.00	25.00
Bowl, 8" d, metal handle	25.00	—
Bowl, 9-1/2" d, handle	—	45.00
Candlesticks, pr, 4-1/2" h	25.00	—
Candy Dish, 3 legs	—	15.00
Candy Dish, cov	40.00	—
Cereal Bowl, 5-1/4" d, no handles	30.00	—
Coaster, 3-1/2"	19.50	—
Cocktail	15.00	—
Comport, 5-3/4" h	32.00	32.00
Cookie Jar, cov	35.00	30.00
Creamer, oval	9.00	17.50

	Crystal	Pink
Cup	20.00	160.00
Fruit Bowl, 9-1/2" d, 2 open handles	40.00	35.00
Juice Pitcher, 24 oz	35.00	—
Pitcher, 80 oz, tilted	55.00	85.00
Plate, 6" d, sherbet	7.00	50.00

	Crystal	Pink
Plate, 8-1/2" d, salad	18.00	—
Plate, 10-1/4" d, dinner	24.00	120.00
Relish Tray Insert	2.50	6.00
Relish Tray, 14" d, inserts	22.00	50.00
Relish Tray, 14" d, 4 part	65.00	—
Salad Bowl, 9" d	20.00	—
Salt and Pepper Shakers, pr, 2" h, sq	50.00	48.00
Sandwich Plate, 14" d	22.00	—
Sauce Bowl, 4-1/2" d, handles	10.00	—
Saucer	7.00	50.00
Sherbet	13.50	15.00
Sugar, oval	12.00	17.50
Tumbler, 10 oz, 5-1/4" h, ftd	16.00	25.00
Vase, 8" h	17.50	—
Wine, 3-1/2" h	12.50	—

Manhattan, sherbet plate, 6" d, crystal, $7.50.

OLD CAFE

Manufactured by Hocking Glass Company, Lancaster, OH, from 1936 to 1940. Made in crystal, pink, and royal ruby.

	Crystal	Pink	Royal Ruby
Berry Bowl, 3-3/4" d	3.50	4.00	6.00
Bowl, 5" d	5.00	5.00	—
Bowl, 9" d, closed handles	10.00	10.00	15.00
Candy Dish, 8" d, low	7.00	11.00	15.00
Candy Jar, 5-1/2" d, crystal w/ruby cover	—	—	15.00
Cereal Bowl, 5-1/2" d	8.00	8.00	12.00
Cup	6.00	6.00	10.00
Juice Tumbler, 3" h	10.00	10.00	12.00
Lamp	24.00	24.00	35.00
Olive Dish, 6" l, oblong	6.00	7.50	—
Pitcher, 36 oz, 6" h	72.00	75.00	—
Pitcher, 80 oz	90.00	90.00	—
Plate, 6" d, sherbet	4.00	4.00	—
Plate, 10" d, dinner	35.00	35.00	—
Saucer	4.00	4.00	—
Sherbet, low, ftd	7.00	7.00	12.00
Tumbler, 4" h	12.00	12.00	18.00
Vase, 7-1/4" h	15.00	17.50	22.00

PATRICIAN, Spoke

Manufactured by Federal Glass Company, Columbus, OH, from 1933 to 1937. Made in amber (also called Golden Glo), crystal, green, and pink.

	Amber	Crystal	Green	Pink
Berry Bowl, 5" d	12.00	9.50	12.00	17.00
Berry Bowl, 8-1/2" d	47.00	9.00	37.50	35.00
Butter Dish, cov	95.00	100.00	215.00	225.00
Cereal Bowl, 6" d	29.00	27.50	27.50	25.00
Cookie Jar, cov	85.00	80.00	525.00	—
Cream Soup, 4-3/4" d	26.00	24.00	22.50	20.00
Creamer, ftd	12.00	9.00	12.00	12.00
Cup	10.00	8.00	10.00	10.00
Jam Dish	30.00	25.00	35.00	30.00
Pitcher, 75 oz, 8" h, molded handle	120.00	125.00	125.00	115.00
Pitcher, 75 oz, 8-1/4" h, applied handle	150.00	140.00	150.00	145.00
Plate, 6" d, sherbet	10.00	8.50	10.00	10.00
Plate, 7-1/2" d, salad	17.50	15.00	12.50	15.00
Plate, 9" d, luncheon	13.00	12.00	11.00	12.00
Plate, 10-1/2" d, grill	15.00	13.50	20.00	20.00
Plate, 10-1/2 d, dinner	8.00	12.75	32.00	36.00
Platter, 11-1/2" l, oval	32.50	30.00	30.00	28.00
Salt and Pepper Shakers, pr	55.00	45.00	65.00	85.00
Saucer	10.00	9.25	9.00	9.50
Sherbet	13.00	10.00	14.00	16.00
Sugar	12.00	9.00	12.00	12.00
Tumbler, 5 oz, 4" h	30.00	28.50	30.00	32.00
Tumbler, 8 oz, 5-1/4" h, ftd	47.00	42.00	50.00	—
Tumbler, 9 oz, 4-1/4" h	33.50	28.50	25.00	28.00
Tumbler, 12 oz	42.00	—	—	—
Tumbler, 14 oz, 5-1/2" h	42.00	38.00	40.00	46.00
Vegetable Bowl, 10" l, oval	28.00	30.00	38.50	30.00

QUEEN MARY, Prismatic Line, Vertical Ribbed

Manufactured by Hocking Glass Company, Lancaster, OH, from 1936 to 1948. Made in crystal, pink, and royal ruby.

	Crystal	Pink	Royal Ruby
Ashtray, 2 x 3-3/4" l, oval	4.00	5.50	5.00
Ashtray, 3-1/2" d, round	4.00	—	—
Berry Bowl, 4-1/2" d	3.00	5.00	—
Berry Bowl, 5" d	4.00	10.00	—
Berry Bowl, 8-3/4" d	10.00	17.50	—
Bowl, 4" d, one handle	4.00	12.50	—
Bowl, 5-1/2" d, two handles	6.00	13.00	—
Bowl, 7" d	7.50	35.00	—
Butter Dish, cov	38.00	125.00	—

	Crystal	Pink	Royal Ruby
Candlesticks, pr, two lite, 4-1/2" h	24.00	—	70.00
Candy Dish, cov	30.00	38.00	—
Celery Tray, 5 x 10"	10.00	24.00	—
Cereal Bowl, 6" d	8.00	24.00	—
Cigarette Jar, 2 x 3" oval	6.00	7.50	—
Coaster, 3-1/2" d	4.00	5.00	—
Coaster/Ashtray, 4-1/4" sq	4.00	6.00	—
Comport, 5-3/4"	9.00	14.00	—
Creamer, ftd	6.00	40.00	—
Creamer, oval	6.00	12.00	—
Cup, large	5.00	7.00	—
Cup, small	8.50	10.00	—
Juice Tumbler, 5 oz, 3-1/2" h	4.50	10.00	—
Pickle Dish, 5 x 10"	10.00	24.00	—
Plate, 6" d, sherbet	4.00	5.00	—
Plate, 6-1/2" d, bread and butter	6.00	—	—
Plate, 8-1/4" d, salad	6.00	—	—
Plate, 9-1/2" d, dinner	15.00	60.00	—
Preserve, cov	30.00	125.00	—
Relish, clover-shape	15.00	17.50	—
Relish, 12" d, 3 part	10.00	15.00	—
Relish, 14" d, 4 part	15.00	17.50	—
Salt and Pepper Shakers, pr	20.00	—	—
Sandwich Plate, 12" d	16.00	15.00	—
Saucer	2.00	5.00	—
Serving Tray, 14" d	15.00	9.00	—
Sherbet, ftd	6.50	9.00	—
Sugar, ftd	—	40.00	—
Sugar, oval	6.00	12.00	—
Tumbler, 9 oz, 4" h	6.00	12.00	—
Tumbler, 10 oz, 5" h, ftd	28.50	66.00	—

Queen Mary, tumbler, 10 oz, pink, 5" h, $66.

RADIANCE

Manufactured by New Martinsville Glass Company, New Martinsville, WV, from 1936 to 1939. Made in amber, cobalt blue, crystal, emerald green, ice blue, pink, and red.

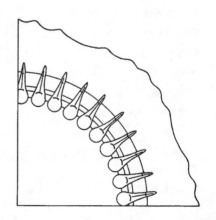

	Amber	Cobalt Blue	Crystal	Emerald Green	Ice Blue	Pink	Red
Bonbon, 6" d	16.00	—	8.00	—	32.00	—	32.00
Bonbon, 6" d, cov	48.00	—	24.00	—	95.00	—	95.00
Bonbon, 6" d, ftd	18.00	—	9.00	—	35.00	—	35.00
Bowl, 6" d, ruffled	—	—	—	—	35.00	—	—
Bowl, 6-1/2" d, ftd, metal holder	—	—	—	—	—	—	32.00
Bowl, 10" d, crimped	28.00	—	14.00	—	48.00	—	48.00
Bowl, 10" d, flared	22.00	—	11.00	—	48.00	—	48.00
Bowl, 12" d, crimped	30.00	—	15.00	—	50.00	—	50.00
Bowl, 12" d, flared	28.00	—	14.00	—	50.00	—	50.00
Butter Dish, cov	210.00	—	100.00	—	460.00	—	460.00
Butter Dish, chrome lid	40.00	—	20.00	—	—	—	—
Cake Salver	—	—	—	—	175.00	—	175.00
Candlesticks, pr, 2 lite	75.00	—	37.50	—	120.00	—	120.00
Candlesticks, pr, 6" h, ruffled	85.00	—	40.00	—	175.00	—	175.00
Candlesticks, pr, 8" h	60.00	—	30.00	—	110.00	—	110.00
Candy Dish, cov, 3 part	—	125.00	—	—	125.00	—	125.00
Celery Tray, 10" l	18.00	—	9.00	—	32.00	—	32.00
Cheese and Cracker Set, 11" d plate	32.00	—	15.00	—	55.00	—	55.00
Comport, 5" h	18.00	—	9.00	—	30.00	—	30.00
Comport, 6" h	24.00	—	12.00	—	35.00	—	35.00
Condiment Set., 4 pc, tray	160.00	—	85.00	—	295.00	—	295.00
Cordial, 1 oz	30.00	—	15.00	—	45.00	—	45.00
Creamer	14.00	—	7.00	—	30.00	32.00	32.00
Cruet, individual	40.00	—	20.00	—	26.00	—	27.50
Cup, ftd	15.00	18.00	8.00	—	18.00	20.00	20.00
Decanter, stopper, handle	90.00	195.00	45.00	—	175.00	—	175.00
Lamp, 12" h	60.00	—	30.00	—	115.00	—	115.00
Mayonnaise, 3 pc set	37.50	—	19.00	—	85.00	—	85.00
Nut Bowl, 5" d, 2 handles	12.00	—	6.50	—	20.00	—	24.00
Pickle, 7"d	16.00	—	8.00	—	25.00	—	27.50
Pitcher, 64 oz	150.00	350.00	75.00	—	225.00	—	235.00
Pitcher, silver overlay	—	—	—	—	—	—	125.00
Plate, 8" d, luncheon	10.00	—	5.00	—	12.00	—	12.00
Punch Bowl, 9" d	110.00	—	65.00	135.00	185.00	—	185.00
Punch Bowl Liner, 14" d	48.00	—	24.00	35.00	85.00	—	85.00
Punch Cup	8.00	—	5.00	—	15.00	—	15.00
Punch Ladle	100.00	—	45.00	—	120.00	—	120.00
Relish, 7"d, 2 part	18.00	—	9.00	—	32.00	—	32.00
Relish, 8" d, 3 part	28.00	—	14.00	—	35.00	—	35.00
Salt and Pepper Shakers, pr	50.00	—	25.00	—	90.00	95.00	95.00
Saucer	6.00	7.50	3.50	—	7.50	8.00	8.00
Sugar	16.00	—	8.00	—	30.00	32.00	32.00
Tray, oval	25.00	—	15.00	—	32.00	32.00	32.00
Tumbler, 9" oz	20.00	35.00	10.00	—	30.00	—	35.00

	Amber	Cobalt Blue	Crystal	Emerald Green	Ice Blue	Pink	Red
Vase, 10" h, crimped	48.00	75.00	24.00	—	60.00	—	70.00
Vase, 10" h, flared	48.00	75.00	24.00	—	60.00	—	70.00
Vase, 12" h, crimped	60.00	50.00	30.00	—	55.00	—	85.00
Vase, 12" h, flared	60.00	—	30.00	—	55.00	—	85.00

SANDWICH

Manufactured by Indiana Glass Company, Dunkirk, IN, 1920s to 1980s. Made in crystal, late 1920s to 1990s; amber, late 1920s to 1980s; milk white, mid 1950s; teal blue, 1950s- 1960s; red, 1933, and early 1970s; smokey blue, 1976-1977.

	Amber	Crystal	Teal Blue	Red
Ashtray, club	2.00	3.00	—	—
Ashtray, diamond	2.00	3.00	—	—
Ashtray, heart	2.00	3.00	1.00	—
Ashtray, set	8.00	12.00	—	—
Ashtray, spade	2.00	3.00	—	—
Basket, 10" h	35.00	35.00	—	—
Berry Bowl, 4-1/4" d	3.00	4.00	—	—
Bowl, 6" w, hexagonal	4.50	4.00	15.00	—
Bowl, 8-1/2" d	10.00	11.00	—	—
Butter Dish, cov	25.00	25.00	150.00	—
Candlesticks, pr, 3-1/2" h	18.00	18.00	—	—
Candlesticks, pr, 7" h	25.00	25.00	—	—
Celery Tray, 10-1/2" l	17.50	14.00	—	—
Cereal Bowl, 6" d	12.00	6.50	—	—
Cocktail, 3 oz, ftd	7.50	7.50	—	—
Console Bowl, 9" d	17.50	17.50	—	—
Console Bowl, 11-1/2" d	20.00	20.00	—	—
Creamer	6.00	6.00	—	48.00
Creamer and Sugar, tray	18.00	18.00	35.00	—
Cruet, 6-1/2 oz, stopper	—	—	145.00	—
Cup	4.00	4.00	8.50	30.00
Decanter, stopper	25.00	25.00	—	90.00
Fairy Lamp	15.00	—	—	—
Goblet, 9 oz	10.00	13.00	—	45.00
Iced Tea Tumbler, 12 oz, ftd	10.00	10.00	—	—
Mayonnaise, ftd	14.00	14.00	—	—
Pitcher, 68 oz	24.00	24.00	—	175.00
Plate, 6" d, sherbet	3.50	3.50	7.50	—
Plate, 7" d, bread and butter	4.00	4.00	—	—
Plate, 8" d, oval, indent	—	4.00	6.50	15.00
Plate, 8-3/8" d, luncheon	7.50	8.00	—	20.00
Plate, 10-1/2" d, dinner	9.00	8.50	—	—
Puff Box	18.00	18.00	—	—
Salt and Pepper Shakers, pr	18.00	18.00	—	—
Sandwich Plate, 13" d	14.50	14.50	25.00	35.00

	Amber	Crystal	Teal Blue	Red
Sandwich Server, center handle	20.00	20.00	—	50.00
Saucer	2.50	1.50	7.00	7.50
Sherbet, 3-1/4" h	6.00	5.00	12.00	—
Sugar, cov, large	20.00	20.00	—	48.00
Tumbler, 8 oz, ftd, water	10.00	10.00	—	—
Wine, 3" h, 4 oz	10.00	11.00	—	15.00

TEA ROOM

Manufactured by Indiana Glass Company, Dunkirk, IN, from 1926 to 1931. Made in amber, crystal, green, and pink.

	Amber	Crystal	Green	Pink
Banana Split Bowl, 7-1/2" l	—	75.00	100.00	145.00
Candlesticks, pr,	—	—	48.00	85.00
Celery Bowl, 8-1/2"d	—	—	35.00	27.50
Creamer, 3-1/4" h	—	—	30.00	28.00
Creamer, 4-1/2" h, ftd	80.00	—	20.00	18.00
Creamer and Sugar on Tray	—	—	180.00	75.00
Cup	—	—	65.00	60.00
Finger Bowl	—	79.00	50.00	40.00
Goblet, 9 oz.	—	—	75.00	65.00
Ice Bucket	—	—	85.00	80.00
Lamp, electric	—	140.00	175.00	145.00
Mustard, cov	—	—	160.00	140.00
Parfait	—	—	72.00	65.00
Pitcher, 64 oz	425.00	400.00	150.00	135.00
Plate, 6-1/2" d, sherbet	—	—	35.00	32.00
Plate, 8-1/4" d, luncheon	—	—	37.50	35.00
Plates, 10-1/2" d, two handles	—	—	50.00	45.00
Relish, divided	—	—	30.00	25.00
Salad Bowl, 8-3/4" d, deep	—	—	150.00	135.00
Salt and Pepper Shakers, pr, ftd	—	—	60.00	55.00
Saucer	—	—	30.00	25.00
Sherbet	—	—	35.00	30.00
Sugar, 3" h, cov	—	—	115.00	100.00
Sugar, 4-1/2" h, ftd	80.00	—	20.00	18.00
Sugar, cov, flat	—	—	200.00	170.00
Sundae, ftd, ruffled	—	—	85.00	70.00
Tumbler, 6 oz., ftd	—	—	35.00	32.00
Tumbler, 8 oz, 5-1/4" h, ftd	75.00	—	35.00	32.00
Tumbler, 11 oz., ftd	—	—	45.00	40.00
Tumbler, 12 oz., ftd	—	—	60.00	55.00
Vase, 6-1/2" h, ruffled edge	—	—	145.00	125.00
Vase, 9-1/2" h, ruffled	—	50.00	110.00	100.00
Vase, 9-1/2"h, straight	—	175.00	95.00	225.00
Vase, 11" h, ruffled edge	—	—	350.00	395.00
Vase, 11" h, straight	—	—	200.00	395.00
Vegetable Bowl, 9-1/2" l, oval	—	—	75.00	65.00

DISNEYANA

History: Walt Disney and the creations of the famous Disney Studios hold a place of fondness and enchantment in the hearts of people throughout the world. The 1928 release of "Steamboat Willie," featuring Mickey Mouse, heralded an entertainment empire.

Walt and his brother, Roy, were shrewd businessmen. From the beginning, they licensed the reproduction of Disney characters on products ranging from wristwatches to clothing.

In 1984, Donald Duck celebrated his 50th birthday, and collectors took a renewed interest in material related to him.

References: Ted Hake, *Hake's Guide to Character Toys*, Gemstone Publishing (1966 Greenspring, Ste. 405, Timonium, MD 21093), 1998; Robert Heide and John Gilman, Disneyana, Hyperion, 1994; Maxine A. Pinsky, *Marx Toys: Robots, Space, Comic, Disney & TV Characters*, Schiffer Publishing, 1996; Carol J. Smith, *Identification & Price Guide to Winnie the Pooh Collectibles*, Hobby House Press, 1994; Tom Tumbusch, *Tomart's Illustrated Disneyana Catalog and Price Guide*, Vols. 1, 2, 3, and 4, Tomart Publications, 1985; ——, *Tomart's Illustrated Disneyana Catalog and Price Guide, Condensed Edition*, Wallace-Homestead, 1989.

Periodicals: *Mouse Rap Monthly*, P.O. Box 1064, Ojai, CA 93024; *Tomart's Disneyana Digest*, 3300 Encrete Lane, Dayton, OH 45439; *Tomart's Disneyana Update*, 3300 Encrete Lane, Dayton, OH 45439.

Collectors' Clubs: Imagination Guild, P.O. Box 907, Boulder Creek, CA 95006; Mouse Club East, P.O. Box 3195, Wakefield, MA 01880; National Fantasy Fan Club for Disneyana Collectors and Enthusiasts, P.O. Box 19212, Irvine, CA 92713.

Archives/Museum: Walt Disney Archives, Burbank, CA 91521.

Additional Listings: See *Warman's Americana & Collectibles* for more examples.

Advisor: Theodore L. Hake.

SPECIAL AUCTION

Hake's Americana & Collectibles
P.O. Box 1444, Dept. 344
York, PA 17405
(717) 848-1333

Bambi
Figure, 3-1/4" h, Flower, the Skunk, glazed ceramic, flower, black and white, deep pink accents, label missing, 1940s 65.00
Push Puppet, 2-3/4" h, 1940s, yellow base, gold foil sticker, Kohner Brothers #3990 copyright Walt Disney Productions, c1960, label slightly faded 24.00
Tiny Golden Book, 2-1/8" x 31/8", full color, 20 pgs, *Bambi*, Simon & Schuster, copyright 1950, art by Campbell Grant 10.00

Davy Crockett, children's book, *Davy Crockett Big Golden Book,* Simon & Schuster, 1955 copyright, 8-1/2" x 11", color hardcover, 48 pgs, color illus on every page 20.00

Disneyland
Guide Book
6 x 8-3/4", *Disneyland,* full color softcover, 20 pages, stiff glossy covers, artwork rather than real photos, text dealing with each attraction, copyright 1955 . . . . 95.00
10-1/2" x 10-1/2", *Walt Disney's Disneyland,* glossy full color softcover, 32 pages of photos and illus of park attractions, copyright 1965, one page fold-out for new Haunted Mansion 45.00
Miniature Cup and Saucer and Plate, 2-3/4" d x 1-3/4" h cup, image of Tinker Bell on inside, Cinderella's castle on outside, matching 4-1/2" d plate with color art of Disneyland castle, "Disneyland Copyright Walt Disney Productions" stamp, c1950 . . . . 65.00
Pennant, 8-1/2" x 26-1/2", orange felt, large name in white and design of Tinker Bell and castle in red, white, and blue, pair of purple streamers, first year 28.00
Postcard Folder, 4" x 6", color, unfolds to 54" l, 26 different photo scenes, plus introduction from Walt Disney, c1960 . . . . 35.00
Salt and Pepper Shakers, pr, 2-1/2" h, glazed china, figural bells, white, gold accents, colorful image of Disneyland castle, other with flying Tinker Bell, "Disneyland" stamped in gold on front, Japan sticker on underside, c1950, plastic stopper. 30.00

Disney Studios, stock certificate, 8" x 12-1/4", Walt Disney Productions Common Stock, unissued, purple, black and white logo, bank note imprint, smiling image of Walt at top in simulated TV screen, Mickey on his shoulder, Fantasyland castle background, masthead showing various Disney characters smiling at Walt and Mickey, "Void" stamped on blue ink three times at bottom where offer's facsimile signatures are printed, including "Michael Esner," two punch holes at bottom as issued, c1980. . . . . 30.00

Donald Duck
Big Little Book, *Donald Duck in Volcano Valley,* Whiteman #1457, copyright 1949 . . . . 24.00
Figure, 3-1/4" h, bisque, Donald with hands on hips, head titled upward smiling, 1930s 75.00
Fork and Spoon, 5-3/4" l, figural, Donald wearing sailor suit, left hand raised, Bonny, Japan, copyright Walt Disney Productions, c1980 . . . . 19.00
Ink Blotter, 3-3/4" x 6", Sunoco Oil, color illus of Donald driving car out of garage and into snow, 1942, printed "Buy War Bonds" logo on bottom, station imprint 60.00
Pencil, 7-1/2" l, unused, red and blue design on white, text "Harvest Donald Duck Bread/Ungles Baking Company," illus of bread loaf with Donald images on wrapper . . . 35.00
Salt and Pepper Shakers, pr, glazed ceramic, 3-1/4" h smiling and waving Donald, dark green shirt, brown cap, pink tie, orange beak and feet, pink flower in right hand, 3" h Daisy dressed like mother hen, green sweater, purple scarf, red apron, pink hat with "Souvenir of Endicott, N.Y." decal on front brim, unlicensed, made in Japan, late 1940s . . 55.00
Sheet Music, 9" x 12", *Der Fuehrer's Face,* four pages of words and music by Oliver Wallace, from film *Donald Duck in Nutzi Land,* copyright 1942, Donald hitting Hitler in eye with tomato while reverse has victory garden symbol design with Disney characters. 60.00
Straws, 4-1/2" x 12-1/4", Donald Duck Sunshine Straws, unused, orange stiff paper, color image of Donald on one side, holding straw to beak with bottom of straw going into cellophane-covered diecut window, reverse with colorful images

of Donald, Mickey, Pluto, and Mickey with Donald, Herz Mfg. Crop, New York City, 1950s 18.00

Fantasia

Original Art, 10" x 12" sheet of animation paper, concept drawing, 6" x 7-3/4" outlined area at center with 4-1/2" x 7-3/4" lead and orange pencil drawing of baby Pegasus sitting on large tree branch, minor pinpoint holes, scattered traces of soiling 325.00

Souvenir Album, 9-1/2" x 12-1/2", *Walt Disney Presents Fantasia*, softcover, orig 1940 movie release, Western Printing Co., color plates, black and white photos of Disney and other contributors to film 45.00

Mickey Mouse

Big Little Book, *Mickey Mouse in the World of Tomorrow*, Whitman #1444, copyright 1948 . . . . 48.00

Bubble Gum Wrapper, 5" x 7", waxed paper, color illus of Mickey, Minnie, Pluto, Horace, and Clarabell, 1930s Gum Inc. 145.00

Candy Box, 5-3/4" x 9" x 2-3/4", Mickey Mouse Sugar Babies, cardboard, countertop box, originally contained 24 five-cent packages of candy, tan and red lid, design of Mickey holding birthday cake with test "Free Mickey Mouse Surprise Birthday Party Comic Strip And Card Game Offer On Each Bag," same design on four sides 35.00

Cereal Box, 11" x 12", Post Toasties Mickey Mouse Cut-Outs, back panel, attached right, left, and bottom flaps, copyright 1934 . . . . 48.00

Figure

1-3/4" h, bisque, smiling full figure, hand on right hip, light green shorts, brown shoes, 70% orig paint 25.00

3-1/2" h, Mickey dressed as hunter, holding book, sitting on log, log with silver oil sticker reading "Walt Disney

Cookie Jar, Mickey Mouse in Toy Sack, "Merry Christmas" on front, $150. Photo courtesy of House in the Woods Auction Gallery.

Character W.D.P. FFM Copyright," incised "78," and Goebel full bee mark, 1950s 225.00

5" h, glazed ceramic, smiling full figure, yellow shirt, red bow tie, blue pants, green shoes, dark green base, stickers missing 38.00

Fork and Spoon, 5-1/2" l spoon with 2" full figure of smiling Mickey wearing T-shirt and shorts, 5-1/2" l fork with 2" smiling seated image of Pluto, Bonny, Japan, copyright Walt Disney Productions, c1980 . . . . 18.00

Ice Cream Lid, 2-3/4" d, Mickey Mouse Southern Dairies Ice Cream, stiff paper, black and orange design of Mickey holding ice cream cup which features his image, 1930s, blank reverse 20.00

Ink Blotter, 3-1/2" x 6", Sunoco Oil, color illus of Mickey as artillery man giving victory symbol, standing behind artillery gun with Sunoco oil bottle as it's body, bottom printed label "Keep 'Em Flying! Buy Defense Bonds," 1942 . . . . . . 75.00

Premium Folder, 5-3/4" x 8", "The Happy Homemakers Weekly," April 17-22, 1938 issue, four pages, color front and back covers, black and white inside 70.00

Sheet Music, *The Wedding Party of Mickey Mouse*, 9" x 12", copyright 1931, black, white, and red cover, Mickey and Minnie at head of laughing animals wedding party, bright red background 125.00

Spoon, 5-1/2" l, 1-1/2" h smiling full figure relief image of Mickey on handle, c1934, offered by Post Toasties as cereal premium 28.00

Toy, 2-3/8" x 6-1/2" x 3-1/2" h, Sun Rubber fire truck, bright red soft rubber, hard rubber white wheels, Mickey wearing fireman's helmet, smiling as driver while Donald stands on rear of truck holding his hat, most of paint on Mickey's head worn off, no paint on Donald, rest 80% complete, early 1950s 55.00

Watch, 4" x 4-1/2" x 5-3/4" h, boxed, U.S. Time, c1958, white box with illus on rd on all sides of Mickey, Minnie and nephews, lifts off to reveal yellow cardboard box bottom/display, 5" h colorful hard plastic figure and watch with 1" d silvered metal case, dial features Mickey image and his hands point at numerals, orig red leather straps, running, orig warranty card 325.00

Mickey Mouse Club

Certificate, 8-1/2" x 11", tan parchment-like paper, black text, black and white image of Mickey in center, red accents, simulated full color seal with him at lower left, smiling black art images of Mouseketeers around margins, copyright Walt Disney productions, c1970s 28.00

Letterhead, 8-1/2" x 11", "Walt Disney's Mickey Mouse Club," unused white paper sheet, light red design of Mickey as band leader, c1950 . . . . 2.00

Magazine, Walt Disney's Mickey Mouse Club Magazine, 8-1/4" x 11-1/2", 42 pages, Western Printing

Vol. 2, #1, Dec, 1956, Christmas theme cover 75.00

Vol. 3, #3, 1958, Zorro cover 30.00

Pencil Case, 4-3/4" x 10" x 2" deep, stiff cardboard, red paper cov, snap closure, full color paper label on lid with clubhouse, Mickey, Pluto, Donald, and nephews, copyright Walt Disney Productions, mid 1950s 40.00

Poster, 19-3/4" x 44", full color, "Walt Disney's Mickey Mouse Club," Welch's, full color Mickey holding club sign as cartoon Indians and fox holding Welch's products, ride around on roller coaster, copyright Walt Disney Productions ABC-TV, mid-1950s, rolled 95.00

Minnie Mouse

Animation Cel, 10" x 12-1/2" acetate sheet, 3-1/4" x 6-3/4" cel image of Minnie in pink and cranberry outfit, "24" of numbered sequence, 1970s 125.00

Figure, 3-3/4" h, wood and wire, Fun-E-Flex, 70% of orig decal on chest, orig tail, professionally replaced ears, light paint wear 75.00

Plate, 5" d, glazed white ceramic, red trim, Minnie as falling down Jill, mkd "J. & G. Meakin, England," 1930s . . . 50.00

Pinocchio

Bank, 7-3/4" h, hard vinyl, smiling image of Pinocchio in black chair, looking up, yellow shirt, hat, and shoes, blue shorts, red tie, copyright Walt Disney Prod. Play Pay Plastics Inc., c1970, no coin trap 28.00

Figure

3" h, bisque, blue, red, and yellow outfit, brown shoes, c1940 . . . . 40.00

4-1/2" h, composition wood, Jiminy Cricket, blue coat and hat, red tie and hat band holding red umbrella, name incised on base, copyright Walt Disney Prod. Multi Products, Chicago, c1940 . . . . 95.00

5" h, composition wood, smiling full Pinocchio figure, nicely painted brown wood design, red shorts, blue tie, yellow hat, red feather, name on base, copyright Walt Disney Prod., Multi Products Chicago, c1940 . . . . 95.00

Sheet Music, 9" x 12", *When You Wish Upon A Star,* 6 pages of words and music, copyright 1940 Irving Berlin Inc., front cover with black, white, and orange image of smiling Pinocchio and Jiminy Cricket 24.00

Song Folio, 9" x 12", *Pinocchio Song Hit Folio,* 16 pgs of words and music, copyright 1950, Australian issue by Allan & Co. Pty. Ltd., front cover with black, white, and red illus 28.00

Spoon, 5-3/8" l, relief of Pinocchio with name and donkey with his name on handle, Duchess Silver Plate, c1939, lightly tarnished around edges of bowl 28.00

Pluto

Figure, 3-1/4" h, bisque, smiling seated Pluto looking at green crab, yellow base, Disney Gift-Ware stamped on base, gold foil UCGC Taiwan sticker, c1970 . . . . 35.00

Soaky, 8-1/2" h, one-piece, empty, deep orange, black and red accents, 1960s. 15.00

Toy, push bottom, 2-1/2" x 3" x 2-1/2" h, hard plastic, Pluto's doghouse, white, orange, roof, Kohner Brothers, 1970s 22.00

Snow White

Bread Label Picture, 11" x 11-1/2" full color, Snow White cottage with background of forest setting, wood grain design margins, white silhouettes for application of cut-out bread characters, red, white, and blue design on reverse with directions from sponsor Skylark Bread, Safeway Stores, 1950s. 85.00

Glass, 4-3/4" h, Walt Disney All Star Parade, wrap-around design of Snow White and the Seven Dwarfs, dark blue, title at top in light blue. 45.00

Paper Dolls, 10" x 12-3/4", *Snow White and the Seven Dwarfs Paperdolls' Book,* Whitman, copyright 1972, full color covers, two stiff paper pages with punch-outs, price sticker on front cover. 38.00

Valentine, 3" x 5-3/4", mechanical, diecut, stiff paper, smiling image of Snow White sweeping, tab on one side which lifts up to smiling squirrel from under broom holding valentine heart, caption "You Are The Fairest in The Land, If You'll Be My Mine-Twil Be Just Grand," copyright 1938 W.D. Ent., ink inscription on back. 35.00

Three Little Pigs

Glass, 4-7/8" h, 2nd Little Pig, blue accent, smiling and dancing Fiddler Pig next to his name, copyright WD, c1936 . . . . 35.00

Spoon, 4-1/4" l, 2-1/2" l handle, image of three pigs, titled on reverse "Wm. Rogers & Son" imprint, bit tarnished, c1933 . . . . 35.00

Tiny Golden Book, 2-1/8" x 31/8", full color, 20 pgs, *Three Little Pigs, Bambi, Bongo,* Simon & Schuster, copyright 1950, art by Campbell Grant 10.00

Toothbrush Holder, 4" l x 4" h, 1-1/4" deep, bisque, Practical Pig with bricks in center between Fiddler and Fifer Pigs, 95% complete paint, Made in Japan, copyright Walt Disney incised on reverse 95.00

Zorro

Action Figure, 6" x 9", blister card, 3-3/4" poseable figure, accessories

Captain Ramon, Gabriel #32714, copyright 1981 . . 30.00

Sergeant Gonzalez, Gabriel #32716, copyright 1981 . . . . 30.00

Zorro, Gabriel #32710, copyright 1981 . . . . 75.00

Children's Book, *Zorro,* Whitman, copyright 1958, 5-1/2" x 7-3/4", hardcover, full-color wraparound cover 15.00

DOLLHOUSES

History: Dollhouses date from the 18th century to modern times. Early dollhouses often were handmade, sometimes with only one room. The most common type was made for a young girl to fill with replicas of furniture scaled especially to fit into a dollhouse. Specially sized dolls also were made for dollhouses. All types of accessories in all types of styles were available, and dollhouses could portray any historical period.

References: Evelyn Ackerman, *Genius of Moritz Gottschalk,* Gold House Publishing, 1994; Mary Brett, *Tomart's Price Guide to Tin Litho Doll Houses and Plastic Doll House Furnishings,* Tomart Publications, 1997; Caroline Clifton-Mogg, *Dollhouse Sourcebook,* Abbeville Press, 1993; Nora Earnshaw, *Collecting Dolls' Houses and Miniatures,* Pincushion Press, 1993; Flora Bill Jacobs, *Dolls' Houses in America: Historic Preservation in Miniature,* Charles Scribner's Sons, 1974; Margaret Towner, *Dollhouse Furniture,* Courage Books, 1993; Dian Zillner, *American Dollhouses and Furniture from the 20th Century,* Schiffer Publishing, 1995.

Periodicals: *Doll Castle News,* P.O. Box 247, Washington, NJ 07882; *International Dolls' House News,* P.O. Box 79, Southampton S09 7EZ England; *Miniature Collector,* 30595 Eight Mill, Livonia, MI 48152; *Miniatures Showcase,* P.O. Box 1612, Waukesha, WI 53187; *Nutshell News,* 21027 Crossroads Circle, P.O. Box 1612, Waukesha, WI 53187.

Collectors' Clubs: Dollhouse & Miniature Collectors, 9451 Lee Hwy #515, Fairfax, VA 22302; National Association of Miniature Enthusiasts, P.O. Box 69, Carmel, IN 46032; National Organization of Miniaturists and Dollers, 1300 Schroder, Normal, IL 61761.

Museums: Art Institute of Chicago, Chicago, IL; Margaret Woodbury Strong Museum, Rochester, NY; Museums at Stony Brook, Stony Brook, NY; Toy and Miniature Museum of Kansas City, Kansas City, MO; Washington Dolls' House and Toy Museum, Washington, DC.

10" x 13" x 13", Bliss, Wild Rose Cottage, litho paper on wood, potted geraniums and Little Red Riding Hood at the door on front facade 1,600.00

15" h, Stirn & Lynn, wood "Combination Dollhouse," patent 1911, litho paper illus on cover, stenciled wood building sections, crayon dec 175.00

15-5/8" h, 19" w, 9-1/2" d, stable, litho paper on wood, late 19th C, some parts missing 115.00

18-1/2" h, 12-5/8" w, 1-1/2" d, McLoughlin Bros., Dolly's Playhouse, litho paper on board, folding two room house, folded printed paper furniture, orig worn box 375.00

23" h, 26"l, 22-3/4" d, Victorian, cottage, yellow with red trim, green shingled roof, two rooms down, one room up, early 20th C, miscellaneous furniture and accessories. . . . 500.00

28" h, 23" w, 23" d, eight rooms, attic, gray blocks, Schoenhut, c1917 . . . . .1,400.00

28" h, 36-3/4" l, 27-1/4" d, Japanese, scale model, copper accents, light soft wood, one room, sliding glass and cloth solji screen door, 20th C 500.00

34" h, painted, front stucco facade, five rooms, 2-1/2 story, steeple roof, two chimneys, bay window, papered int., Christian Hacker, Nuremberg, Germany, FAO Schwartz label . 750.00

36" h, 25" w, Victorian, mansard roof, belvedere, mustard yellow, brown trim, gray roofs, red accents, two rooms down, two rooms up, attic, staircases, cast iron fence, cast iron lions on wooden plinths, wooden outhouse, 49" sq lawn, late 19th C, some restoration needed. 2,875.00

40" h, 33" l, 20" d, four room, blue and green painted ext., chamfered wood trim, paneled hinged doors, pierced windows, scroll-out lintels, int. with parquetry floors, hinged doorways with two windows, attic rooms, late 19th C. 1,100.00

DOLLS

History: Dolls have been children's play toys for centuries. Dolls also have served other functions. From the 14th through 18th centuries, doll making was centered in Europe, mainly in Germany and France. The French dolls produced in this era were representations of adults and were dressed in the latest couturier designs. They were not children's toys.

During the mid-19th century, child and baby dolls, made in wax, cloth, bisque, and porcelain, were introduced. Facial features were hand painted; wigs were made of mohair and human hair; and the dolls were dressed in the current fashions for babies or children.

Doll making in the United States began to flourish in the 1900s with companies such as Effanbee, Madame Alexander, and Ideal.

Marks: Marks of the various manufacturers are found on the back of the head or neck or on the doll's back. These marks are very important in identifying a doll and its date of manufacture.

References: Johana Gast Anderton, *More Twentieth Century Dolls from Bisque to Vinyl*, Vols. A–H, I–Z, revised eds., Wallace-Homestead, 1974; J. Michael Augustyniak, *Thirty Years of Mattel Fashion Dolls, 1967 Through 1997: Identification and Value Guide*, Collector Books, 1998; Kim Avery, *The World of Raggedy Ann Collectibles,* Collector Books, 1997; John Axe, *Encyclopedia of Celebrity Dolls*, Hobby House Press, 1983; Carol Corson, *Schoenhut Dolls*, Hobby House Press, 1993; Carla Marie Cross, *Modern Doll Rarities,* Antique Trader Books, 1997; Linda Crowsey, *Madame Alexander Collector's Dolls Price Guide,* Collector Books, 1998; Maryanne Dolan, *The World of Dolls, A Collector's Identification and Value Guide,* Krause Publications, 1998; Jan Foulke, *Doll Classics,* Hobby House Press, 1997; ——, *Insider's Guide to China Doll Collecting*, Hobby House Press, 1995;——, *Insider's Guide to Doll Buying and Selling*, Hobby House Press, 1995; ——, *Insider's Guide to Germany "Dolly" Collecting*, Hobby House Press, 1995; ——, *32nd Blue Book Dolls and Values*, Hobby House Press, 1997; Cynthia Gaskill, *Legendary Dolls of Madame Alexander*, Theriault's, 1995; Patricia Hall, *Johnny Gruelle: Creator of Raggedy Ann and Andy*, Pelican Publishing (1101 Monroe St., Gretna, LA 70053), 1993; Dawn Herlocher, *200 Years of Dolls*, Antique Trader Books, 1996; R. Lane Herron, *Warman's Dolls,* Krause Publications, 1998; Judith Izen and Carol Sover, *Collector's Guide to Vogue Dolls*, Collector Books, 1997; Polly Judd, *African and Asian Costumed Dolls*, Hobby House Press, 1995: ——, *Cloth Dolls*, Hobby House Press, 1990; Polly and Pam Judd, *Composition Dolls*, Vol. I (1991), Vol. II (1994), Hobby House Press; ——, *European Costume Dolls*, Hobby House Press, 1994; ——, *Glamour Dolls of the 1950s & 1960s*, revised ed., Hobby House Press, 1993; ——, *Hard Plastic Dolls*, 3rd ed. (1993), Book II (1994), Hobby House Press; Michele Karl, *Composition & Wood Dolls and Toys: A Collector's Reference Guide,* Antique Trader Books, 1998; A. Glenn Mandeville, *Alexander Dolls*, 2nd ed., Hobby House Press, 1995; ——, *Ginny*, 2nd ed., Hobby House Press, 1994; Marcie Melilo, *The Ultimate Barbie Doll Book*, Krause Publications, 1997; Patsy Moyer, *Doll Values, Antique to Modern*, Collector Books, 1997; --, *Modern Collectible Dolls*, Collector Books, 1997; Myra Yellin Outwater, *Advertising Dolls,* Schiffer Publishing, 1997; Edward R. Pardella, *Shirley Temple Dolls and Fashion*, Schiffer Publishing, 1992; Sabine Reinelt, *Magic of Character Dolls*, Hobby House Press, 1993.

Lydia Richter, *China, Parian, and Bisque German Dolls*, Hobby House Press, 1993; Lydia and Joachim F. Richter, *Bru Dolls*, Hobby House Press, 1989; Lydia Richter and Karin Schmelcher, *Heubach Character Dolls and Figurines*, Hobby House Press, 1992; Joyce Rinehart, *Wonderful Raggedy Anns,* Schiffer Publishing, 1997; Jane Sarasohn-Kahn, *Contemporary Barbie,* Antique Trader Books, 1997; Patricia R. Smith, *Antique Collector's Dolls*, Vol. I (1975, 1991 value update), Vol. II (1976, 1991 Value update), Collector Books; ——, *Effanbee Dolls,* Collector Books, 1998 values update; ——, *Madame Alexander Collector's Dolls Price Guide #20*, Collector Books, 1995; ——, *Madame Alexander Dolls 1965-1990*, 1991, 1997 values update, Collector Books; ——, *Modern Collector's Dolls*, Series I through VIII (1973-1996 value updates), Collector Books; ——, *Patricia Smith's Doll Values Antique to Modern*, Eleventh Series, Collector Books, 1995; ——, *Shirley Temple Dolls and Collectibles*, Vol. I (1977, 1992 value update), Vol. II (1979, 1992 value update), Collector Books; Evelyn Robson Stahlendorf, *Charlton Standard Catalogue of Canadian Dolls*, 3rd ed., Charlton Press, 1995; Carl P. Stirn, *Turn-of-the-Century Dolls, Toys and Games* (1893 catalog reprint), Dover Publications, 1990; Margaret Whitton, *Jumeau Doll*, Dover Publications, 1981.

Periodicals: *Antique Doll World*, 225 Main St., Suite 300, Northport, NY 11768; *Cloth Doll Magazine*, P.O. Box 2167 Lake Oswego, OR 97035; *Costume Quarterly for Doll Collectors*, 118-01 Sutter Ave., Jamaica, NY 11420; *Doll Castle News*, P.O. Box 247, Washington, NJ 07882; *Doll Collector's Price Guide*, 306 East Parr Rd., Berne, IN 46711; *Doll Life*, 243 Newton-Sparta Rd., Newton, NJ 07860; *Doll Reader*, 6405 Flank Dr., Harrisburg, PA 17112; *Doll Times*, 218 W Woodin Blvd., Dallas, TX 75224; *Doll World*, 306 East Parr Rd., Berne, IN 46711; *Dollmasters*, P.O. Box 151, Annapolis, MD 21404; *Dolls—The Collector's Magazine*, 170 Fifth Ave., 12th Floor, New York, NY 10010; *National Doll & Teddy Bear Collector*, P.O. Box 4032, Portland, OR 97208.

Collectors' Clubs: Doll Collector International, P.O. Box 2761, Oshkosh, WI 54903; Madame Alexander Doll Fan Club, P.O. Box 330, Mundeline, IL 60060; United Federation of Doll Clubs, P.O. Box 14146, Parkville, MO 64152.

Videotapes: *Doll Makers: Women Entrepreneurs 1865-1945*, Sirocco Productions, 1995; *Dolls of the Golden Age: 1880-1915*, Sirocco Productions, 1993; *Extraordinary World of Doll Collecting*, Cinebar Productions, 1994.

Museums: Aunt Len's Doll House, Inc., New York, NY; Children's Museum, Detroit, MI; Doll Castle Doll Museum, Washington, NJ; Doll Museum, Newport, RI; Toy and Miniature Museum of Kansas City, Kansas City, MO; Gay Nineties Button & Doll Museum, Eureka Springs, AR; Margaret Woodbury Strong Museum, Rochester, NY; Mary Merritt Doll Museum, Douglassville, PA; Mary Miller Doll Museum, Brunswick, GA; Prairie Museum of Art & History, Colby, KS; Washington Dolls' House & Toy Museum, Washington, DC; Yesteryears Museum, Sandwich, MA.

Additional Listings: See *Warman's Americana & Collectibles* for more examples.

SPECIAL AUCTIONS

McMasters Doll Auctions
P.O. Box 1755
Cambridge, OH 43725
(614) 432-4419

Skinner Inc.
Bolton Gallery
357 Main St.
Bolton, MA 01740
(508) 779-6241

Alt, Beck & Gottschalck, 25" h, bisque head, blond mohair wig, brown glass sleep eyes, open mouth, pierced ears, fully jointed composition body, imp "1362," some paint wear, damage to knee joint 320.00

Bahr & Proschild, 12-1/2" h, 224 Belton, bisque socket head, flat area and three holes on top, set blue threaded eyes, feathered brows, painted upper and lower lashes, closed mouth, accented lips, accent line and white space between lips, pierced ears, orig mohair wig, jointed wood and composition body with straight wrists, old pale blue print dress, eyelet trim, underclothing, socks, and shoes, marked "224,5" on back of head, slight damage to body finish, neck socket loose 1,500.00

Bergmann, C. M.
16" h, character, bisque head, brown glass sleep eyes, open mouth, bent limb composition body, imp "Spezial," needs restringing 375.00
24" h, bisque socket head, set blue eyes, real and painted lashes, feathered brows, open mouth, four upper teeth, synthetic wig, jointed wood and composition body, antique blue and white dress, underclothing, new socks, and shoes, marked "C. M. Bergmann, Simon & Halbig, S & H, 3" on back of head, tiny flake on lower right lid, broken eyes set with plaster showing, unmatched legs, foot repaired 250.00
30" h, bisque socket head, brown sleep eyes, real lashes, molded and feathered brows, painted lower lashes, open mouth, accepted lips, four upper teeth, pierced ears, human hair wig, jointed wood and composition body, antique low-waisted dress, antique underclothing, stockings, high button shoes, marked "C. M. Bergmann, Simon & Halbig, 13-1/2" on back of head, light rub on cheek, finish worn on front of torso. 400.00

Borgfelt, 24" h, bisque head, orig blond mohair wig, blue glass sleep eyes, open mouth, fully jointed composition body, imp "GB" mark, some paint wear 230.00

German, mkd "51," 19-1/2" h, $1,500. Photo courtesy of McMasters Auctions.

Bru, Casimir

17" h, pressed bisque head, brown paperweight eyes, outlined open/closed mouth, cork pate, pierced ears, wood jointed body, key wound mechanical music box, marked "Bte S.G.D.G." 6,600.00

23" h, bisque swivel head, shoulder plate, brown paperweight eyes, highlighted lids, outlined open/closed mouth, cork pate, pierced ears, kid body, bisque lower arms, repainted wood lower legs, circle dot mark "Bru Jne 19" 1,320.00

Bye-Lo

5" h, bisque swivel head, tiny brown sleep eyes, softly blushed brows, painted upper and lower lashes, closed mouth, all bisque body, jointed at shoulders and hips, orig crocheted diaper with belly band, white baby dress, crocheted sweater, marked "12" on front of neck, "6-12, Copr. by Grace S. Putnam, Germany" on back, "20-32" on top of right leg 275.00

18" h, bisque flange head, blue sleep eyes, softly blushed brows, painted upper and lower lashes, closed mouth, lightly molded and painted hair, cloth body with frog legs, celluloid hands, antique white lace trimmed christening dress, underclothing, baby booties, embroidered bib, bonnet, marked "Copr. by Grace S. Putnam, Made in Germany" on back of head, turtle mark on celluloid hands, very fine flake at upper left eye rim, light rub to cheek 525.00

Cameo, 11" h, composition, jointed at shoulders, black Kewpie, catalog #1347, Noma Toys Limited, Owen Sound, Ontario, Canada, orig box 375.00

Chase Type, 18-1/2" h, oil painted stockinette head, stiff neck, painted brown eyes, single stroke brows, painted hair, applied ears, cloth body with sateen covering, oil painted stock-

Kestner, Baby Jean, 20", $1,050. Photo courtesy McMasters Auctions.

inette lower arms and legs, jointed at shoulders, hips and knees, pink tint on stitched fingers and toes, plain white baby dress, underclothing, old blue cotton socks, light wear, slight flaking, left ankle repaired, unmarked 550.00

China Head

21" h, china shoulder head, light pink tint, painted brown eyes with red accent line, single stroke brows, closed smiling mouth with white space between lips, molded and painted black hair with center part, cloth body, leather arms, individually stitched fingers, orig red print dress, black velvet ribbon trim, underclothing, socks, old hand made leather shoes, unmarked, well repaired hairline on left side of shoulder, dark spot of kiln debris on left shoulder, fragile dress 350.00

24" h, boy, china shoulder plate, painted blue eyes, red accent line, single stroke brows, closed mouth, molded and painted curly hair, cloth body, leather lower arms, redressed in black and white checked two piece suit, underclothing, black socks, marked "880 11" on back of shoulder plate 275.00

Cloth

Advertising, 14" h, Hamilton Brown Shoe Co., Twinkie, composition character head, molded hair and features, sleeping and flirty steep eyes, cream flannel body and limbs, celluloid hands, red and yellow jester vest, cuffs, and boots 225.00

Columbia, 22" h, painted blond hair, brown eyes, painted hands, stitched fingers, some paint wear and loss, period cotton outfit, 1890s. 2,185.00

Printed, 15-1/2" h, Harry, full round arms and legs, printed union suit, socks, and shoes, printed separate white shirt, blue jacket, and trousers 175.00

Volland, 15" h, Raggedy Ann, c1918 . . . . 850.00

Effanbee

13-1/2" h, Suzanne, brown sleep eyes, light hair, orig red and white dress, straw hat, bracelet tags, orig suitcase with four outfits 265.00

18" h, cloth body, composition hands, lower legs, and flange head, brown glass sleep eyes, real lashes, closed mouth, molded and painted hair, painted facial features, orig clothes 120.00

26" h, Patsy Ruth 3,600.00

French Fashion, 16" h, bisque socket head, bisque shoulder plate, set cobalt blue eyes, multi-stroke brows, painted upper and lower lashes, closed mouth, accented lips, pierced ears, orig mohair wig, kid body with gussets at hips, individually stitched fingers, dark brown velvet suit with long train and bustle, lace trim, flowers on blue hat, hand made shoes, marked "B 3 S"" on bottom of rear shoulder plate, minor repairs 1,600.00

Gaulthier, Francois, 26" h, bisque swivel shoulder head, Ethel, cork pate, orig mohair wig, stationary blue paperweight eyes, open/closed mouth, pierced ears, cloth shoulder and legs, kid upper arms, fragments of celluloid hands, mkd "F 9 G," right shoulder mkd "FG," c1870, imperfection to neck, front of shoulder plate damaged. .4,320.00

Greiner, 28" h, papier-mâché shoulder head, painted blue eyes, single strike brows, painted upper lashes, closed mouth, molded and painted hair with twelve vertical curls, cloth body, leather lower arms, orig black and gold plaid dress, underclothing replaced socks and shoes, white apron, marked "Greiner's Improved Patent Heads, Pat. March 30, '58" on label on back shoulder plate, very light touch-up on face, light crazing on face, left ankle mended, water stains on orig body, lower kind arms discolored, orig silk dress deteriorating badly in places 450.00

Handwerck, Heinrich

26" h, bisque socket head, blue sleep eyes, real lashes, molded and feathered brows, open mouth, four upper teeth, pierced ears, antique human hair wig, jointed wood and composition body, antique white eyelet dress, underclothing, socks, and shoes, marked "Germany, Heinrich Handwerck, Simon & Halbig" on back of head, "W" on front of head at crown, worn body finish, repairs at knees and neck socket, finger missing 425.00

30" h, bisque head, replaced human hair wig, brown glass sleep eyes, open mouth, pierced ears, fully jointed composition body, imp "Handwerck Simon & Halbig" mark 635.00

Heubach, E., 12" h, #417, googlie, toddler body 1,695.00

Heubach, Gebrüder, bisque-head character, brown mohair wig with ear braids, weighted blue eyes, jointed wood and composition body, original underwear and chemise, c1912 . . . . .1,955.00

Holz-Masse, 40" h, character, papier-mâché, mkd on shoulder plate 1,300.00

Horsman

13" h, character, Snowball, designed by Bernard Lipfert, from Gene Carr's comic strip, molded composition head and hands, orig costume, 1916, fabric fading and wear, paint cracks. 225.00

19" h, character, Ella Cinders, from Bill Conselman and Charlie Plumb comic strip, molded composition head, arms, and legs, orig outfit, 1925, paint cracked, some fading to fabric 300.00

Ideal

14" h, Miss Curity, hard plastic head, blue sleep eyes, real lashes, feathered brows, closed mouth, orig saran wig, five piece hard plastic body, orig tagged nurse's uniform with cape and hat, underclothing, socks, and shoes, marked "Ideal Doll, Made in USA" on back of head, "Ideal Dolls, P-90" on back, "Miss Curity" on hat. "The First Lady of First Aid, Miss Curity, The Famous Nurse Doll" on dress tag, unplayed with condition, orig play nurse kit, orig box 650.00

21" h, Shirley Temple, composition, orig blond mohair wig, sleep eyes, open mouth, body jointed at shoulders and hips, orig dark blue cotton twill version of Captain January sailor suit, orig rayon tag and orig pin, ruffled pink party dress, mid 1930s, pupils crazed 1,265.00

Jumeau

14" h, bisque socket head, blue paperweight eyes, open/closed mouth, pierced ears, straight wrist jointed composition body, body stamped "Jumeau," orig lambskin pelt (fur missing), c1880 . . . . .3,450.00

16" h, bisque socket head, closed mouth, dark brown paperweight eyes, pale creamy bisque, fully mkd orig body, orig shoes 4,495.00

19" h, bisque socket head, blond mohair wig, blue paperweight eyes, and maroon printed satin/velvet dress, with matching hat, brown Jumeau shoes, and a white dress, c1900 . . . . .9,775.00

20" h, bisque socket head, bulbous pale blue paperweight eyes, heavy feathered brows, long painted upper and lower lashes, closed mouth with accented lips, pierced ears, mohair replaced wig, jointed wood and composition body with jointed wrists, redressed, marked "Depose, Tete Jumeau, 9" stamped in red, incised "D" and "9," red and black artist marks on back of head, partial oval label on lower back 3,300.00

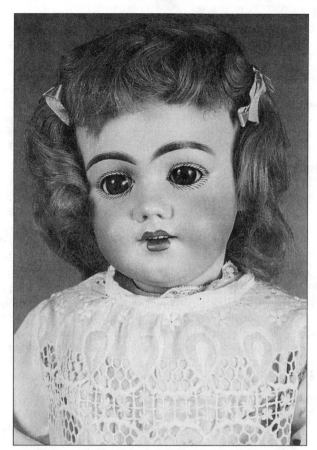

Simon & Halbig, #1009, 27" h, $1,500. Photo courtesy of McMasters Auctions.

Kammer & Reinhardt

10" h, character, bisque head, painted hair, molded features, painted eyes, open/closed mouth, jointed bent limb composition body, imp "K star R 100". 345.00

19" h, character, bisque head, orig blond mohair wig, light blue sleep eyes, open mouth, bent limb composition body, imp "K star R Simon & Halbig 126," 1920s, damage and repainting to body 320.00

23" h, character, bisque, c1910, eyes 14,300.00

24" h, character, Gretchen, bisque head, replaced strawberry blond human hair wig, brown glass eyes, closed mouth, fully jointed composition body, imp "114," c1909, paint wear, body and knee joint damage 11,500.00

Marie, character, bisque head, slight wear. 1,150.00

Kestner

7" h, bisque head, blond mohair wig, blue glass sleep eyes, open mouth, composition body jointed at shoulders, hips, and knees, imp "143" 500.00

11" h, character, orig brown mohair wig, brown glass sleep eyes, open mouth, bent limb composition body, imp "247" 825.00

16" h, character, bisque head, orig blond mohair wig, brown glass sleep eyes, open/closed mouth with teeth, fully jointed composition body, imp "183," some paint loss, needs restringing 3,735.00

26" h, bisque head, blue glass sleep eyes, open mouth, fully jointed composition body, imp "171," replaced synthetic wig, one finger damaged, paint wear 460.00

28" h, bisque head, orig strawberry blond mohair wig, brown glass sleep eyes, open mouth, fully jointed composition body, imp "164" 825.00

29" h, bisque shoulder head, replaced wig, brown glass sleep eyes, open mouth, fully jointed composition arms, imp "154" mark. 500.00

Kley & Hahn, 11" h, character baby, orig blond mohair wig, blue sleep eyes, open mouth with two molded teeth, molded roof and tongue insert in open mouth, bent limp composition body, imp "K & H 176" 320.00

Kruse, Kathe

12" h, boy, blue overalls 4,888.00

16"h, molded muslin painted head, painted short brown hair, brush stroked curls, painted blue-gray eyes, closed pouty mouth, cloth body jointed at shoulders and hips, red and white cotton dress, marked "Kathe Kruse" and numbers on sole of foot 1,750.00

Lenci

28" h, Harlequin, pressed and painted felt head, cream, tan, orange, and yellow costume, 1930s, slight moth damage, face somewhat soiled 865.00

36" h, Czechoslovakian Bride, pressed and painted felt face, blond mohair wig, felt outfit, kidskin books, some moth damage. 750.00

Limoges, 14" h, friction, playing drum 1,045.00

Madame Alexander

10" h, Cissette Queen, plastic, jointed body, blue sleep eyes, closed mouth, synthetic wig, orig Queen clothing, crown, and red banner. 320.00

14" h, Wendy Bride, hard plastic, orig dress tag 100.00

16" h, baby, cloth body, composition flange head, composition arms and legs, hazel sleep eyes, open mouth, two-upper teeth, felt tongue, molded painted hears, orig clothing, coat, and bonnet, c1936 . . . . 375.00

Marseille, Armand

27" h, bisque head, light brown human hair wig, brown glass sleep eyes, open mouth, fully jointed composition body, imp "AM390" mark, some paint wear and chipping 375.00

Boy, #1394, pale bisque, orig mohair hair, brown paper-weight eyes, fully jointed straight wrist composition body 995.00

Mascotte, 23" h, fine quality bisque head, bulging blue paper-weight glass stationary eyes, pierced ears, closed mouth, long brown curls, real French hair wig, French composition jointed body, straight wrists, marked "M," blue satin dress with lace, matching blue hat with ostrich plume 2,900.00

Morimura, 19-1/2" h, bisque shoulder head, orig strawberry blond wig, blue glass sleep eyes, open mouth, oil cloth body and legs, bisque hands, imp mark, several pcs of clothing, early 1920s. 200.00

Papier-mâché

7-3/4" h, shoulder head, molded head with elaborate hairdo, kid body wooden arms and legs, period outfit, c1845 . . . . 575.00

8-3/8" h, man, molded head with short curly hairdo, kid body, wooden arms and legs, felt period frock coat and trousers, c1845. . . . . 460.00

26" h, French, shoulder head, stationary pupil-less brown glass eyes, open mouth, four bamboo teeth, painted hair, kid body and limbs, c1850, some damage and paint loss, arm repairs. 460.00

Poured Wax, 20" h, French, child, well detailed facial features, blue-gray spiral eyes, all orig, wax arms and legs . .1,995.00

Sasha Morgenthaler

21" h, boy, gray tweed suit 10,500.00

21" h, girl, lamb's-wool coat and tam. 14,500.00

Schmidt, Bruno, 16" h, 2072 Toddler 2,550.00

Schmidt, Franz, 19" h, character, bisque head, orig light brown mohair wig, blue glass sleep eyes, open mouth, pierced nostrils, bent limb composition body, imp "F S & Co. 1271/50" 490.00

Schoenau Hoffmesiter, 19" h, 170 toddler, painted bisque socket head, blue sleep eyes, real lashes, feathered brows, open mouth, two upper teeth, replaced synthetic wig, five piece composition toddler body, black corduroy jumper, new socks, and shoes, marked "S PB [in star] H, 170 3-1/2" on back of head, light wear, crazed replaced arms, torso finish cracked and damaged, legs repainted 215.00

Simon & Halbig

17" h, character, orig blond mohair wig, brown glass sleep/flirty eyes, bent limp composition body, imp "133" mark, restored, repainted. 460.00

23" h, bisque head, replaced wig, blue glass sleep eyes, open mouth, pierced ears, jointed composition body, imp "S & H 1078," slight paint scuffing 435.00

Societe Francaise de Bebes et Jouets

16" h, bisque head, fixed eyes, open mouth with upper teeth, brown hair, composition ball jointed body, dress and black shoes 180.00

19" h, 236 toddler, bisque socket head, set dark brown eyes, feathered brows, painted lashes, open/closed mouth, two upper teeth, human hair wig, jointed wood and composition toddler body, brown knit romper, socks, and shoes, marked "S.F.B.J. 236, Paris, -10-" on back of head, "S.F.B.J., 7" imp on body, repaired hairline on back of head, minor firing line in left ear, body finish yellowed, flaking on hands 500.00

21" h, character, boy, fine quality bisque head, open/closed mouth, two upper molded teeth, blue glass open/close eyes, dark blond orig hair, orig chunky French toddler composition jointed body, jointed wrists, white shirt, black and white striped shorts, red and white striped cap, new shoes, marked "S.F.B.J. 247 Paris". 2,750.00

Steiner, Jules Nicholas, 24" h, bisque head, blue paperweight eyes, pierced ears, closed mouth, brown wig, composition jointed body, marked "Steiner/Paris/Fre A.17" 4,675.00

Unis France, 13-1/2" h, bisque socket head, blue sleep eyes, real lashes, feathered brows, open mouth, four upper teeth, jointed composition body with jointed wrists, orig labeled regional costume, underclothing, socks, and shoes, orig paper label on skirt, paper wrist tag "fabrication Jumeau Paris, Made in France," marked "Unis France, 71 301 149" on back of head, "Made in France" circular stamp, facial coloring pale 475.00

Walker, Izannah, 17" h, painted brown hair and eyes, closed mouth, dark brown orig clothes, kid boots, 1860s, paint wear and fiber loss, arms repaired 2,415.00

Walkure, 23-3/4"h, bisque head, replaced wig, brown glass sleep eyes, open mouth, pierced ears, fully jointed composition body, imp mark 350.00

DOORKNOBS and other BUILDER'S HARDWARE

History: Man's home has always been his castle, whether grand and ornate, or simple and homey. The use of decorative doorknobs, back plates, doorbells, knockers, and mail slots helped decorate and distinguish one's door. Creating a grand entrance was as important to our ancestors as it is today.

Before the advent of the mechanical bell or electrical buzzer and chime, a doorknocker was considered an essential door ornament to announce the arrival of visitors. Metal was used to cast or forge the various forms; many cast-iron examples were painted. Collectors like to find doorknockers with English registry marks.

Collectors of doorknobs and other types of builders' hardware are growing as we learn to treasure the decorative elements of our past. Often old house lovers seek out these elements to refurbish their homes, adding to the demand.

References: Ronald S. Barlow (comp.), *Victorian Houseware, Hardware and Kitchenware*, Windmill Publishing, 1991; Margarete Baur-Heinhold, *Decorative Ironwork*, Schiffer Publishing, 1996; Len Blumin, *Victorian Decorative Art*, available from ADCA (P.O. Box 126, Eola, IL 60519), n.d.; Maude Eastwood wrote several books about doorknobs which are available from P.O. Box 126, Eola, IL 60519; Constance M Greiff, *Early Victorian*, Abbeville Press, 1995; Philip G. Knobloch, *A Treasure of Fine Construction Design*, Astragal Press, 1995; Henrie Martinie, *Art Deco Ornamental Ironwork*, Dover Publications, 1996; James Massey and Shirley Maxwell, *Arts & Crafts*, Abbeville Press, 1995; Ted Menten (comp.), *Art Nouveau Decorative Ironwork*, Dover Publications, n.d.; *Ornamental French Hardware Designs*, Dover Publications, 1995; Ernest Rettelbusch, *Handbook of Historic Ornament from Ancient Times to Biedermeier*, Dover Publications, 1996; Alan Robertson, *Architectural Antiques*, Chronicle Books, 1987; Edward Shaw, *Modern Architect* (reprint), Dover Publications, 1996; *Turn of the Century Doors, Windows and Decorative Millwork*, Dover Publications, 1995 reprint; Web Wilson, *Antique Hardware Price Guide*, Krause Publications, 1999; ——, *Great Glass in American Architecture*, E. P. Dutton, New York, 1986.

Periodical: *American Bungalow*, P.O. Box 756, Sierra Madre, CA 91204.

Collectors' Club: Antique Doorknob Collectors of America, Inc., P.O. Box 126, Eola, IL 60519.

Additional Listings: Architectural Elements, Stained Glass.

Advisor: Web Wilson.

SPECIAL AUCTION

**Web Wilson Antique Hardware Auction
PO Box 506
Portsmouth, RI 02871
(800) 508-0022**

Doorbell
  Cast Iron, Aesthetic design 65.00
  Nickel plated, lever action, fancy, dated 1870 . . . . . . 160.00
Doorbell Pull and Backplate, nickel-plated, Neo-Grec style
  . . . . 140.00
Doorbell Pull, glass and cast iron, 1860s 20.00
Doorbell Push Button Plate, La Grande pattern by Reading
  . . . . 75.00
Doorknob
  Geisha Girl, Russell & Erwin, c1774 . . . . .1,600.00
  Gothic design, c1900, entry size 50.00
  Hexagonal, fancy, c1875, entry size 170.00
  Millefiori, knurled brass shank, c1850, small 475.00
  New York City Public School, oval 35.00
  Nickel-plated, Art Deco circle design 165.00
  Walnut, fancy pressed design 40.00
  Wedgwood, blue and white medallion, cast with classical ladies, entry size 375.00
Doorknob and Plate
  Hummingbird, figural backplate, entry size, R & E . . . 500.00

Doorbell Pull and Backplate, Neo-Grec style, nickel-plated, $140. Photo courtesy of Web Wilson Auctions.

Door Pull, Egyptian Pharaoh face, cast iron, 20th C, $100. Photo courtesy of Web Wilson Auctions.

Knights of Pythias. 65.00
Statler Hotel, New York City, cast iron 375.00
Doorknob and Rosette, gutta percha, fancy design, dated 1860
. . . . 40.00

Doorknocker
Masonic, lion head, with peephole 300.00
Sailing ship 65.00
Doorplate, large, single keyhole, Bamboo pattern by Branford
. . . . 160.00

Door Pull
Bronze, store type, dated July 22, 1879, pr 220.00
Cast Iron, Egyptian Pharaoh face, 20th C 100.00
Hinges, pr, bronze, Aesthetic design, 4" 110.00
Keyhole Doorplate, single, Windsor pattern 35.00
Keyhole Escutcheon, large, swing cover, Ekado pattern
. . . . 95.00

Knob
Clear acrylic, pink roses inside, set of three 45.00
Oval, painted, French. 65.00
Mail Slot, bronze, orig spring 75.00

Passage Knob
Aesthetic design. 90.00
Argillo Glass, red and black swirl pattern 55.00
Masonic Crest 55.00
Newark Public Schools. 60.00
Odd Fellows logo 140.00
Pressed Glass, amber 55.00

Passage Knob and Backplate
Broken Leaf pattern 170.00
Bronze, triangle backplate, R & E, c1870. . . . . 550.00
Gothic. 180.00
Rice pattern, Yale. 45.00
Rim Lock, entry size, keeper and key, early 19th C 325.00
Sash Lifts, cast iron, fancy, set of eight. 70.00
Shutter Latches, bronze, Veroccio pattern, four sets 55.00
Thumb Latch, entry, Arts & Crafts style, bronze 200.00

DOORSTOPS

History: Doorstops became popular in the late 19th century. They are either flat or three-dimensional and were made out of a variety of different materials, such as cast iron, bronze, or wood. Hubley, a leading toy manufacturer, made many examples.

All prices listed are for excellent original paint unless otherwise noted. Original paint and condition greatly influence the price of a doorstop. To get top money, the piece must be close to mint original paint. Chipping of paint, paint loss, and wear reduce the value. Repainting severely reduces value and eliminates a good deal of the piece's market value, thereby reducing it's value. A broken piece has little value to none.

References: Jeanne Bertoia, *Doorstops*, Collector Books, 1985, 1996 value update; Douglas Congdon-Martin, *Figurative Cast Iron*, Schiffer Publishing, 1994.

Collectors' Club: Doorstop Collectors of America, 2413 Madison Ave., Vineland, NJ 08630.

Videotape: *Off the Ground & Off the Wall*, Gary Roma, Iron Frog Productions.

Advisor: Craig Dinner.

Notes: Pieces described below contain at least 80% or more of the original paint and are in very good condition. Repainting drastically reduces price and desirability. Poor original paint is preferred over repaint.

All listings are cast-iron and flat-back castings unless otherwise noted.

Doorstops marked with an asterisk are currently being reproduced.

Ann Hathaway's Cottage, 7-1/2" x 6-1/8", three dimensional, marked "AM Greenblatt copyright 1927 #114" 1,050.00
Aunt Jemima, 13-1/4" x 6-1/2", Littco Products 450.00
Basket of Flowers, 6-1/2" h, 4" w, yellow, red, and blue flowers, green vase, white pedestal base, 75% paint 60.00
Bear with Honey, 15" x 6-1/2", full figured 2,250.00
Black Man on Cotton Bale, 6-7/8 x 6-7/8", full figured pot metal figure on cast iron bale 2,000.00
Bloodhound, 15-1/4 x 4-3/8", Spencer, wedge bottom . . 250.00
Bobby Blake, 9-1/2 x 5-1/4", Hubley, Grace Drayton design
. . . . 330.00
Boston Terrier, 8-1/2" w, 10 1/2" h, black and white, significant paint loss to body 150.00
Butler, 11-1/4 x 5-7/8", Bradley & Hubbard. 650.00
Cape Cod, 5-3/4 x 8-3/4", Eastern Specialty Mfg. Co., repainted
. . . . 360.00
Cape Cod Cottage, 5-1/2 x 7-3/4", Hubley, marked "444"
. . . . 420.00
Cat, 11" w, 6" h, reclining, white, green eyes, Hubley
Original paint 150.00
Repainted. 75.00
Cat Scratch Fever, 8-3/4 x 4-1/4", Judd Co., sgd "A Diouhy" on front and marked "cJo 1271" on back. 1,000.00
Charleston Dancers, 8-7/8 x 5-3/8", Hubley, Fish design, Art Deco style
75% paint 800.00
90% paint 2,000.00
100% original paint. 3,000.00
Cherubs, 10" x 6", partial overpaint. 275.00
Cocker Spaniel, 6-3/4 x 11", full figured, Hubley. 375.00
Colonial Lady, pink dress, red flower dots, white collar and cuffs, pink and black bonnet, red flowers, green leaves, orig paint
. . . . 125.00
Colonial Lawyer, 9-5/8 x 5-1/4", orange jacket, Waverly Studios, marked "W5 Mark," orig paint 350.00
Cornucopia of Fruit, 7-1/2 x 7", vibrant colors 300.00
Cottage, 5-3/4 x 7-1/2", National Foundry. 220.00
Crossed Out, 7-1/4 x 5-5/8", orig paint 750.00
Daisy Bowl, 7-1/2 x 5-1/8", Hubley, marked "452" 200.00
Doberman Pinscher, 8 x 8-1/2", full figured, Hubley 690.00

Dolly Dimple, 7-3/4 x 3-3/4", Full figured, Hubley, Grace Drayton design
    85% paint 250.00
    100% original paint 500.00
Drum Major, 13-1/2" x 6-1/2", full figured 190.00
Duck, 5" x 3-3/4", Hubley, wedge back 360.00
Dutch Boy
    7-1/2" x 6", Judd Co., marked "1275" 750.00
    11" x 3-1/2", full figured 400.00
Farm House, 6" x 8", Bradley & Hubbard, orig rubber knobs
    . . . . .1,000.00
Flapper, 8-7/8" x 4-1/2", slight wedge 550.00
Flower Basket, 11" x 10-3/4", detailed assorted spring flowers, intricate basket base
    95% orig paint 650.00
    100% original paint 1,265.00
Flowered Doorway, 7-5/8" x 7 12" 350.00
Footmen, Hubley, Fish design, Art Deco style
    9-1/8" x 6", orig paint 1,000.00
    12-1/8" x 8-1/4", orig paint 1,250.00
French Basket, 11" x 6-3/4", country style basket of flowers, Hubley, marked "69" 225.00
Fruit Basket, 11-1/2" x 10", cherries on base, basketweave basket. 650.00
Geese, 8" x 8", Hubley, Fred Everett design. 385.00
Geisha, 10-1/4" x 3-1/2", full figured, Hubley 450.00
Giraffe, 12-1/2" x 9", full figured, Hubley, 99% orig paint
    . . . . .4,070.00
Goldenrods, 7-1/8" x 5-1/2", Hubley, marked "268" 360.00
Golfer, 8-3/8" x 7", putting, Hubley, marked "34" 375.00

Drum Major, full figured, 13-1/2" h, $190.

Grandpa Rabbit, 8-5/8" x 4-7/8", red jacket 1,250.00
House, 8-1/8" x 4-1/2", Judd Co., marked "cJo 1288". . . 325.00
House with Woman, 5-3/4" x 8-1/2", pink house, Eastern Specialty Mfg. Co., No. 50 . . . . 550.00
Huckleberry Finn, Littco Products 585.00
Iris, 10-5/8" x 6-3/4", Hubley, marked "469" 325.00
Jonquils, 7" x 6", bright colors, Hubley, marked "534" . . 275.00
Mammy, 8-1/2" x 4-1/2", blue dress, full figured, Hubley
    . . . . 275.00
Man with Flowers, 9" x 5-3/4", vibrant paint 375.00
Marigolds, 7-1/2" x 8", pastels, Hubley, marked "315 Made in USA". 215.00
Mary Quite Contrary, 11-3/8" x 9-5/8", Littco Products
    90% original paint. 500.00
    100% original paint. 850.00
Minuet Girl, 8-1/2" x 5", Judd Co., marked "1278" 210.00
Modernistic Flower, 10" x 9-3/4", blue flowers, yellow and orange centers, green leaves, black base with dot dec. 500.00
Narcissus, 7-1/4" x 6-3/4", Hubley, marked "266". 325.00
Old Fashioned Lady, 7-3/4" x 4", blue dress, Hubley, marked "Hubley 296". 500.00
Oriental Man, 9" x 7-1/4", full figured 225.00
Owl, 15-1/2" x 5", Bradley & Hubbard
    Mint original paint. 1,250.00
    Wear, paint loss 400.00
Parrot, 12-1/2" x 7-1/2", Albany Foundry 220.00
Penguin, 9-1/2" x 5-1/4", sgd "No. 1, c1930, Taylor Cook," near mint condition 2,500.00
Persian Cat, 8-1/2" x 6-1/2", full figured, Hubley. 175.00
Peter Rabbit, 9-1/2" x 4-3/4", Hubley, Grace Drayton design
    . . . . 330.00
Pheasant, 9-1/4" x 14", full figured 475.00
Pirate with Sack, 11-7/8" x 9-5/8", vibrant colors 650.00
Popeye, 9" x 4-1/2", full figured, Hubley, marked "c1929 King Features Syn Made in USA"
    80% original paint. 600.00
    90% original paint. 1,200.00
    95% original paint. 1,750.00
    99% original paint. 2,310.00
Poppies and Cornflowers, 7-1/4" x 6-1/2", Hubley, marked "265"
    . . . . 360.00
Primrose, -3/8" x 6-1/4", yellow flowers, Hubley, marked "488"
    . . . . 195.00
Rabbit Eating Cabbage, 8-1/8" x 4-7/8" 375.00
Reading Girls, 5" x 8-5/8", two girls with sun bonnets, seated back to back, heads bent down to read books on laps
    . . . . 750.00
Red Riding Hood, 9-/2" x 5", Hubley, Grace Drayton design
    . . . . 650.00
Rooster, 13" x 8-1/2". 660.00
Rose Basket, 11" x 8", Hubley, marked "121". 225.00
Sailor, 11-3/8" x 5", Art Deco style 650.00
Senorita, 11-1/4" x 7", holding basket of flowers in one hand at side. 375.00
Southern Belle, 6-1/2" h, pink and green dress, crisscross dec, holding bouquet 150.00
Spanish Girl, 9-7/8" x 5-1/2", green and orange dress . . 275.00
Stork, 5-1/2" x 3-1/2", Hubley, wedge back. 350.00
Street Singers, 6-1/4" x 7-1/2", Hubley, marked "445" . . 650.00
Sunbonnet Sue, 9" x 5-1/2", orange hat, blue dress 450.00
Tiger Lilies, 10-1/2" x 6", Hubley, marked "472" 250.00
Toko, 5-1/2" x 6-1/4", full figured, Hubley 275.00
Tropical Woman, 12" x 6-1/4" h, basket of fruit on head
    . . . . 325.00
Twin Cats, 7" x 5-1/4", Hubley, Grace Drayton design . . 275.00

Vase of Flowers, 11-3/4" x 6", Bradley & Hubbard
  Original rubber knobs and paint 360.00
  Worn paint 175.00
Whistling Boy, 10" x 5-1/2", full figured, pot metal black boy on
  cast iron base, rubber back knobs, marked "98" 600.00
Whistling Jim, 14-1/2" x 5-1/2", striped shirt, pants rolled up to
  knees, orig rubber knobs .2,800.00
Windmill
  6-3/4" x 6 7/8", National Foundry 220.00
  9-7/8" x 11 1/2", marked "AM Greenblatt Studios Boston
    copyright 1926"
      Mint 695.00
      Poor paint 250.00
Wineman, 9-1/2" x 7", full figured 1,045.00
Wire-haired Terrier, orig black and white paint, minor paint chips
  . . . . 120.00
Woman, 11-1/2" x 9", large hooped skirt 450.00
Zinnias, 9-3/4" x - 1/2", Hubley,
  marked "316"200.00

DRESDEN/ MEISSEN

History: Augustus II, Elector of Saxony and King of Poland, founded the Royal Saxon Porcelain Manufactory in the Albrechtsburg, Meissen, in 1710. Johann Frederick Boettger, an alchemist, and Tschirnhaus, a nobleman, experimented with kaolin from the Dresden area to produce porcelain. By 1720, the factory produced a whiter hard-paste porcelain than that from the Far East. The factory experienced its golden age from the 1730s to the 1750s under the leadership of Samuel Stolzel, kiln master, and Johann Gregor Herold, enameler.

The Meissen factory was destroyed and looted by forces of Frederick the Great during the Seven Years' War (1756-1763). It was reopened, but never achieved its former greatness.

In the 19th century, the factory reissued some of its earlier forms. These later wares are called "Dresden" to differentiate them from the earlier examples. Further, there were several other porcelain factories in the Dresden region and their products also are grouped under the "Dresden" designation.

Marks: Many marks were used by the Meissen factory. The first was a pseudo-Oriental mark in a square. The famous crossed swords mark was adopted in 1724. A small dot between the hilts was used from 1763 to 1774, and a star between the hilts from 1774 to 1814. Two modern marks are swords with a hammer and sickle and swords with a crown.

References: Susan and Al Bagdade, *Warman's English & Continental Pottery & Porcelain*, 3rd Edition, Krause Publications, 1998; Robert E. Röntgen, *The Book of Meissen*, revised ed., Schiffer Publishing, 1996.

Museums: Art Institute of Chicago, Chicago, IL; Cincinnati Art Museum, Cincinnati, OH; Dresden Museum of Art & History, Dresden, Germany; Gardiner Museum of Ceramic Art, Toronto, Canada; Meissen Porcelain Museum, Meissen, Germany; Metropolitan Museum of Art, New York, NY; National Museum of American History, Smithsonian Institution, Washington, DC, Robertson Center for the Arts and Sciences, Binghamton, NY; Schlossmuseum, Berlin, Germany; Stadtmuseum, Cologne, Germany; Wadsoworth Atheneum, Hartford, CT; Woodmere Art Museum, Philadelphia, PA; Zwinger Museum, Dresden, Germany.

Dresden

Centerpiece, 15" h, Art Deco-style female, gilt hair and shoes, peach bathing suit, lilac wrap, standing on octagonal base, round center bowl with molded floral gilt rim, ivory and gilt ground 1,200.00
Charger, 18" d, soldiers receiving provisions, flower garland border, black enamel pseudo AR cipher, 19th C 650.00
Compote, 18" h, three detailed figurines playing around tall stem, multicolored flowers, white ground, round pedestal base, c1870 . . . . .1,500.00
Figure, 4 1/2" h, peasant couple, seated on rocks, chickens and flowers 280.00
Fruit Dish, circular, low front, scalloped, open wide sides, floral panels, floral center, price for pr 300.00
Plaque, 2-1/2" x 3-1/4" and 3-1/2" x 4-1/2" d, oval, female portrait, mounted in giltwood frame, c1900, pr 375.00
Punch Bowl, cover, stand, 11-3/4" d, 15-1/4" d stand, sliced lemon finial, enamel dec, titled figures depicting the "Punch Society," c1750 . . . . .27,600.00
Relish Dish, 7-1/2" l, 4-part, handled, hp flowers 125.00
Shrimp Server, circular, floral dec, openwork border . . . 125.00
Urn, cov, 17-1/4" h, baluster, scroll handles, reticulated neck and cov, floral and landscape cartouches, white ground, floral spray dec 750.00
Vase, cov, 20-1/2" h, 9" w, white ground, two Victorian multicolored romantic scenes, multicolored floral dec on each side of detailed white and gold handles, neck and base with gilt and white pebble border, gold border with magenta and orange roses, green leaves, detailed elongated oval gilt design at base, gilt short pedestal with floral dec, Dresden mark on bottom with crown on top, number 11018, c1883 . . . . .1,600.00

Figure, shepherd and shepherdess, multicolored, interlocking mark, 8" h, $250.

Wall Sconce, 33" h, shaped mirror plate and frame, elaborately modeled with putti and foliate, three-light standard, 20th C, cracks, minor losses 635.00

Meissen

Box, cov, 6" d, central floral cartouche, cobalt blue ground, gilt highlights 750.00

Candelabra, 15" h, five-light, modeled with elaborate foliate, standards depicting four seasons, late 19th C, pr, minor chips and losses 4,325.00

Clock, mantel, 22-1/2" h, elaborate foliate molded case mounted with four seasons, gilt metal face, plateau form stand also mounted with foliage, late 19th C, minor chips 6,900.00

Cream Jug, cov, 5-1/2" h, scenes of miners at work, 19th C 650.00

Cup and Saucer, 5-1/4" d, scenes of miners at work, 19th C 700.00

Deep Dish, 15-1/4" d, scalloped border, slip dec, raised foliate and scrolled cartouches, enameled floral sprays, early 19th C 1,265.00

Desk Set, 7-1/2" x 11-1/4" shaped rect tray, 9" l oval pen tray, 3" h sander, 3-1/4" h cov ink pot, underglaze blue bird and floral ground, overglazed iron red enamel and gilding, late 19th C 650.00

Figure

    5" h, 4-1/2" l, seated couple facing each other, late 19th C, minor losses 375.00

    5-1/4" h, seated woman at table with flowers on lap, basket of flowers, fluted base, minor loss 550.00

    5-3/4" h, lady with birdcage, enamel and gilt dec, model E4 . . . . 635.00

    6" h, boy playing flute, dressed in 18th C costume . . 425.00

    7-1/4" h, three cherubs surrounding easel as another cherub paints, late 19th/early 20th C 2,530.00

    8" h, cherub, enamel dec, gilt trim, late 19th/early 20th C 1,150.00

    8-1/4" h, beggar cherub, figure standing with crutches, enamel dec, gilt trim, late 19th/early 20th C 875.00

    8-1/4" h, embracing male and female, sheep and got at their feet, model A29, late 19th/early 20th C, losses 920.00

    8-1/4" h, female cherub, enamel dec, gilt trim, late 19th/early 20th C 1,035.00

    8-1/2" h, Bacchanalian scene, drunken male, supported by standing male, seated on mule, woman feeding mule grapes while child plays with his tail 3,000.00

    8-1/2" l, three birds on sunflowers 1,800.00

    8-3/4" h, The Good Mother, mother seated in armchair, surrounded by three children, model E69, late 19th/early 20th C, losses 2,415.00

Plate

    8-5/8" d, raised gilt foliate dec, set of six 550.00

    9" d, monochrome white, molded foliate and cattail dec, gilt rim 75.00

    9-3/4" h, Apple Picker, group, enamel dec, gilt trim, model 2229, losses. 865.00

Serving Tray, 10" x 13-3/8" oval, molded laurel leaves and grape border, gilt framed central cartouche, enamel dec figural landscape scene, late 18th C/early 19th 1,840.00

Soup Plate, 9-5/8" d, scrolled gilt vine borders, enameled landscape and floral dec, early 19th C, pr. 230.00

Standish, 14" w, 9-1/2" d, 10" h, figural sander and inkwell, center Chinoiserie figural group with small well, scrolled base, late 19th C, minor restorations. 4,025.00

Tea Service, partial

    Cobalt blue ground, cartouche of colorful flowers, gold dec, cov teapot, creamer, cov sugar, tray, eleven cups, twelve saucers, twelve 7" d plates 1,100.00

    Enamel floral dec, 4-1/4" h teapot, two tea bowls and saucers, 4" h cream jug, 6-3/4" d waste bowl, 19th C . . 690.00

    Miners dec, scrolled gilt trim, central enamel dec of miners at work, 3-1/2" cov teapot, 5" h cov tea canister, six cups and saucers, 18th C 13,800.00

DUNCAN and MILLER

History: George Duncan, Harry B. and James B., his sons, and Augustus Heisey, his son-in-law, formed George Duncan & Sons in Pittsburgh, Pennsylvania, in 1865. The factory was located just two blocks from the Monongahela River, providing easy and inexpensive access by barge for materials needed to produce glass. The men, from Pittsburgh's south side, were descendants of generations of skilled glassmakers.

The plant burned to the ground in 1892. James E. Duncan Sr., selected a site for a new factory in Washington, Pennsylvania, where operations began on Feb. 9, 1893. The plant prospered, producing fine glassware and table services for many years.

John E. Miller, one of the stockholders, was responsible for designing many fine patterns, the most famous being Three Face. The firm incorporated and used the name The Duncan and Miller Glass Company until the plant closed in 1955. The company's slogan was "The Loveliest Glassware in America." The U.S. Glass Co. purchased the molds, equipment, and machinery in 1956.

References: Gene Florence, *Elegant Glassware of the Depression Era*, 6th ed., Collector Books, 1995; Naomi L. Over, *Ruby Glass of the 20th Century*, Antique Publications, 1990, 1993-94 value update.

Collectors' Club: National Duncan Glass Society, P.O. Box 965, Washington, PA 15301.

Additional Listings: Pattern Glass.

Ashtray, clear

    Canterbury 18.50

    Duck, 6" 40.00

    Tulip 30.00

Bowl

    Caribbean, 5" d, blue 20.00

    Sandwich, 5" d 10.00

    Butter, cov, Tear Drop, clear, silverplated lid 30.00

    Cake Plate, King Arthur, clear, 9-1/2" d, skirted. 55.00

    Candlesticks, pr, Canterbury, clear, etched 30.00

    Candy Box, cov, Canterbury, pink opalescent 55.00

    Celery and Relish Tray, First Love, #30, 12" l 90.00

    Cheese Compote, Tear Drop, clear 20.00

    Cigarette Holder, Spiral Flutes, green, cutting 70.00

    Cocktail, Canterbury, clear, 4-1/4" h, 3-1/2" oz 10.00

    Cologne, stopper, Hobnail Opalescent Blue, 9 oz . . . 120.00

Comport

    First Love, 5-1/2" 50.00

    Terrace, amber, 7" 45.00

Cordial, Indian Tree, 1 oz 65.00

Cornucopia Vase, Three Feathers, #117, pink opalescent, 8" h, ftd 140.00

Creamer and Sugar, First Love, stacking 95.00

Cruet, Caribbean. 70.00
Cup and Saucer
    Caribbean, blue 70.00
    Sandwich 13.00
    Terrace. 20.00
Decanter, Laguna, #154/49, 32 oz, Biscayne Green . . . 130.00
Deviled Egg Plate, Sandwich, clear 50.00
Flower Basket, Teardrop, loop handle, 12" h 175.00
Fruit Bowl, Sandwich, flared, 12" d 70.00
Gardenia Bowl, Canterbury, clear. 35.00
Goblet
    Hobnail Opalescent Blue, 9 oz. 40.00
    Sandwich, 9 oz. 18.00
Hat, Hobnail Opalescent Blue, 6" h. 200.00
Iced Tea Tumbler, clear
    Canterbury, 7" h. 15.00
    Indian Tree, ftd, 6" h. 22.00
Jelly Compote, Caribbean, clear. 30.00
Lemon Tray, Puritan, green, clear handle. 25.00
Mayonnaise, Language of Flowers, clear, price for 3 pc set
. . . . 37.50
Nappy
    Indian Tree, clear, triangular, handle 20.00
    Murano, clear, ruffled, 6" d. 20.00
Nut Bowl, Sandwich, 3-1/2" d 10.00
Olive Dish, Tear Drop, clear, divided, 6" l 15.00
Pickle/Olive, Indian tree, 8-1/2" l 40.00
Plate
    Canterbury, 8" d, lily of the valley cutting 15.00
    Caribbean, dinner, blue 125.00
    Sandwich, 16" d 90.00
Puff Box, cov, Hobnail Opalescent Blue, 4" 100.00
Relish, Sandwich, 3-part, 10-1/2" d, rect. 42.00
Salt and Pepper Shakers, pr
    Caribbean, blue, salt cloudy. 70.00
    Sandwich, 2-1/2" h, metal lids 18.00

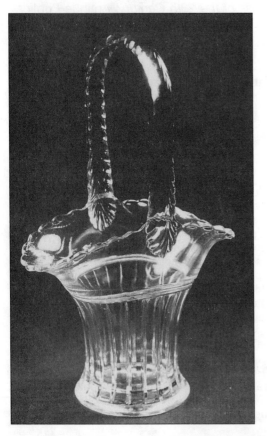

Basket, colorless, ribbed bands, $85.

Serving Plate, Sandwich, clear, 13" d 40.00
Sherbet
    Sandwich 10.00
    Tear Drop, clear, tall. 10.00
Sugar, clear
    Canterbury 10.00
    First Love 15.00
    Language of Flowers 18.00
Swan, ruby, clear neck
    10" 60.00
    12" 95.00
Torte Plate, Sandwich, 12" d 50.00
Tumbler, Sandwich, 9 oz, ftd. 15.00
Vase
    Caribbean, blue, flared, 7-1/2" h. 60.00
    Sandwich, 10" h, ftd, #41 . . . . 90.00
Wine, Indian Tree, 3 oz. 35.00

DURAND

History: Victor Durand (1870-1931), born in Baccarat, France, apprenticed at the Baccarat glassworks where several generations of his family had worked. In 1884 Victor came to America to join his father at Whitall-Tatum & Co. in New Jersey. In 1897 father and son leased the Vineland Glass Manufacturing Company in Vineland, New Jersey. Products included inexpensive bottles, jars, and glass for scientific and medical purposes. By 1920, four separate companies existed.

When Quezal Art Glass and Decorating Company failed, Victor Durand recruited Martin Bach, Jr., Emil J. Larsen, William Wiedebine, and other Quezal men and opened an art-glass shop at Vineland in December 1924. Quezal-style iridescent pieces were made. New innovations included cameo and intaglio designs, geometric Art Deco shapes, Venetian Lace, and Oriental-style pieces. In 1928, crackled glass, called Moorish Crackle and Egyptian Crackle, was made.

Durand died in 1931. The Vineland Flint Glass Works was merged with Kimble Glass Company a year later, and the art glass line was discontinued.

Marks: Many Durand glass pieces are not marked. Some have a sticker with the words "Durand Art Glass," others have the name "Durand" scratched on the pontil or "Durand" inside a large V. Etched numbers may be part of the marking.

Bowl, 8" d, 6-1/2" h, orange cased to opal, overall irid green leaf and vine dec, sgd in V 1,500.00
Candlesticks, pr, 9-1/2" h, baluster, amber, pulled blue feather tips, flanged rim with etched wheat and leaves 300.00
Chandelier, baluster-form central blue glass shaft, conforming irid threading mounted on six-light ceiling lamp, adjustable drop 350.00
Compote, 8" d, white feather dec, blue ground, pale green stem and foot 750.00
Lamp, 14" h, shade with gold and green hearts and vines, irid opal ground, applied heavy gold threading, yellow int., bronze tree-form standard 2,250.00
Vase
    6" h, flared, tapered body, white heart and vine dec, blue ground, sgd 1,200.00
    7-1/2" h, ovoid, everted lip, amber, mottled amber int., inscribed "Durand/1968-6" 295.00

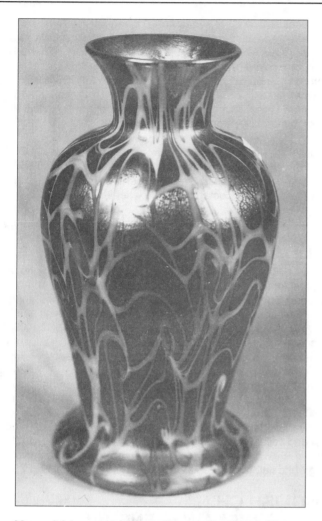

Vase, iridescent blue, white pulled dec, 7" h, $345.

10" h, King Tut, broad shouldered cased oval body, strong green pulled and coiled dec, lustrous irid gold surface, gold int. over opal, base inscribed "Durand 1964-10" . .2,450.00
15-1/2" h, Genie, bulbous cobalt ribbed body, elongated slender neck, lustrous blue-silver irid, mirror bright near base 2,415.00

EARLY AMERICAN GLASS

History: The term "Early American glass" covers glass made in America from the colonial period through the mid-19th century. As such, it includes the early pressed glass and lacy glass made between 1827 and 1840.

Major glass-producing centers prior to 1850 were Massachusetts (New England Glass Company and the Boston and Sandwich Glass Company), South Jersey, Pennsylvania (Stiegel's Manheim factory and many Pittsburgh-area firms), and Ohio (several different companies in Kent, Mantua, and Zanesville).

Early American glass was popular with collectors from 1920 to 1950. It has now regained some of its earlier prominence. Leading auction sources for early American glass include Garth's, Heckler & Company, James D. Julia, and Skinner, Inc.

References: William E. Covill, *Ink Bottles and Inkwells*, William S. Sullwold Publishing, out of print; George and Helen McKearin, American Glass, Crown, 1975; ——, *Two Hundred Years of American Blown Glass*, Doubleday and Company, 1950; Helen McKearin and Kenneth Wilson, *American Bottles and Flasks*, Crown, 1978; Dick Roller (comp.), *Indiana Glass Factories Notes*, Acorn Press, 1994; Jane S. Spillman, *American and European Pressed Glass*, Corning Museum of Glass, 1981; Kenneth Wilson, *American Glass 1760-1930*, 2 Vols., Hudson Hills Press and The Toledo Museum of Art, 1994; ——, *New England Glass and Glassmaking*, Crowell, 1972.

Periodicals: *Antique Bottle & Glass Collector*, P.O. Box 187, East Greenville, PA 18041; *Glass Collector's Digest*, Antique Publications, P.O. Box 553, Marietta, OH 45750.

Collectors' Clubs: Early American Glass Traders, RD 5, Box 638, Milford, DE 19963; Early American Pattern Glass Society, P.O. Box 266, Colesburg, IA 52035; Glass Research Society of New Jersey, Wheaton Village, Glasstown Rd., Millville, NJ 08332; National Early American Glass Club, P.O. Box 8489, Silver Spring, MD 20907.

Museums: Bennington Museum, Bennington, VT; Chrysler Museum, Norfolk, VA; Corning Museum of Glass, Corning, NY; Glass Museum, Dunkirk, IN; Glass Museum Foundation, Redlands, CA; New Bedford Glass Museum, New Bedford, MA; Sandwich Glass Museum, Sandwich, MA; Toledo Museum of Art, Toledo, OH; Wheaton Historical Village Association Museum of Glass, Millville, NJ.

Additional Listings: Blown Three Mold; Cup Plates; Flasks; Sandwich Glass; Stiegel-Type Glass.

Blown

Bottle
8-3/4" h, club shape, aqua, twenty-four ribs broken swirl, Zanesville, OH, wear 150.00
9-1/2" h, globular, aqua, twenty-four swirled ribs, Zanesville, OH, residue, large ext. broken blister and stone . . . 325.00
Bowl
5-5/8" d, 3-3/4" h, colorless, applied sapphire blue rim, late 125.00
8-1/4" d, 2-7/8" h, light green, folded rim, ftd, Eastern 550.00
Candlestick
7" h, opaque medium blue, hexagonal, wafer, minor edge damage and damage to base of socket 185.00
7-3/8" h, canary, petal detail, mated pair, some damage on both 120.00
7-1/2" d, canary, hexagonal, flaring base, wafer, broken blister inside socket 150.00
7-5/8" h, canary, hexagonal, wafer, small chips 150.00
8-1/8" h, colorless, blown hollow socket, baluster stem, pressed base, firing checks in base, pr 400.00
9-1/4" h, canary, opalescent socket, hexagonal socket and stem, round base, pewter insert missing, Pittsburgh, chips and crack in socket 135.00
9-1/8" h, colorless, hollow socket with two knob stem, stepped pressed base, pewter insert, chips on base 150.00
9-3/8" h, grass-green, hexagonal, Pittsburgh, chips, check in socket 75.00

9-1/2" h, opaque medium blue, hexagonal, Pittsburgh, sanded finish, pewter socket missing, edge wear and chips
. . . . 100.00

9-5/8" h, opaque medium blue, hexagonal, Pittsburgh, pewter socket missing, small edge chips. 250.00

Canister, 9-1/2" h, colorless, two applied sapphire rings, matching ring on lid, colorless finial 995.00

Compote

4-5/8" h, 5-5/8" d, blue bowl cased in clambroth-colored glass, deep cobalt blue base, applied foot, baluster stem, worn int. 550.00

6-7/8" h, 8" d, colorless with slight amber tint, cut ovals, strawberry diamonds and fans on bowl, applied foot with star, Pittsburgh, wear, pinpoints and scratches 200.00

7-1/4" h, 9-1/2" d, colorless, flared bowl with folded rim, engraved vining floral design on bowl, knob step, applied foot, wear, New England Glass Co. 250.00

11-1/4" d, green 550.00

Decanter, stopper, 8-1/4" h, colorless, cut strawberry diamonds and fans, three applied rings and flared lip, mismatched stopper, Pittsburgh 150.00

Hurricane Shade, 11-3/4" h, 10-1/8" d, brown 75.00

Lamp

7-1/8" h, colorless, font with cut roundels and fans, brass collar, wafer stem, sq base, Pittsburgh, chips on base
. . . . .300.00

9-7/8" h, amethyst, hexagonal three printie font, octagonal stem, sq base, brass collar, chips on base 550.00

10-3/8" h, colorless, hollow stem, puce font with drapery swags. 865.00

Mug

4" h, yellow green, applied ear handle, Diamond smocked design, wear and small chips, rigaree on end of handle chipped 185.00

5-3/8" h, opalescent, enamel dec floral sprays, reserve of gentleman smoking, very minor enamel wear 550.00

Pan, 5-3/4" d, aqua, folded rim 115.00

Pitcher, colorless

5-3/4" h, squatty, cut swags and fans in bowl, applied foot and handle, cut rayed foot, grinding at base of handle and on spout, attributed to Pittsburgh 175.00

5-7/8" h, fifteen slightly swirled ribs, applied handle, Midwestern, broken int. blisters, rim roughness 125.00

Sugar Bowl, cov

3-1/4" h, witch ball cover, applied handles, aqua, South Jersey 3,500.00

3-3/8" h, colorless, gallery rim, applied foot, bruise on foot and chips on finial 115.00

Vase

8-3/4" h, folded over lip with cut flutes, bowl with cut panels and daisy diamonds, knob stem, applied foot with rays, Pittsburgh, wear, pinpoints, and slight stain. 175.00

8-3/4" h, hexagonal, ellipse and circle bowl, ruffled rim, amethyst, base chips, pr. 825.00

12-1/4" h, cobalt blue, applied foot and stem, wafer, applied rim, ruffled lip 4,730.00

Lacy

Bowl

6" d, rope rim, eight spoke center, minor chips 250.00

7-3/8" d, 1-5/8" h, Nectarine, chips. 100.00

9-3/4" d, Thistle and Beehive, octagonal, shallow, edge chips
. . . . 50.00

Candlesticks, pr, 6" h, reeded and ribbed socket attached with wafer, reeded stem, sq stepped base, chips, checks in socket
. . . . 450.00

Compote, cov, 9-1/2" h, 8-1/4" d, Sawtooth, flint, chips . 150.00

Compote, open, 8" h, 8-1/2" d, Diamond Point, flint, wear and small flakes. 145.00

Miniature Lamp, 4" h, lacy cup plate base, blown spherical font, knob stem, chips on base. 385.00

Plate

5-3/8" d, side wheeler, Pittsburgh, round 220.00

7" d, eagle, chips 160.00

Relish, 7-1/2" l, Peacock Eye, Midwestern, chips 65.00

Tea Plate, 6-1/2" d, octagonal, side wheeler, Pittsburgh
. . . . 800.00

Toddy Plate, 7-1/8" d, Peacock Eye, chips, set of six. . . 200.00

Pillar Mold

Bowl, 4-3/8" h, emerald green, cut design at top of each rib, applied foot, ground pontil, attributed to Pittsburgh . . .1,100.00

Cologne Bottle, 5-5/8" h, cobalt blue, eight ribs, two applied rings, flared lip, mushroom stopper, stopper base chipped
. . . . 400.00

Decanter

9-3/4" h, cobalt blue, applied handle and collar, pewter jigger cap 7,920.00

10-1/2" h, apple green, eight ribs swirled to the right, double ringed lip, polished pontil, pewter stopper, 1840-50, price for pr, one with minor stain. 700.00

Pillar molded, decanter, 9-3/4" h, cobalt blue, applied handle and collar, pewter jigger cap 7,920.00

Pitcher, 5-5/8" h, colorless, applied handle, Pittsburgh, bottom ground flat, minor wear. 275.00

ENGLISH CHINA and PORCELAIN (GENERAL)

History: By the 19th century, more than 1,000 china and porcelain manufacturers were scattered throughout England, with the majority of the factories located in the Staffordshire district.

By the 19th century, English china and porcelain had achieved a worldwide reputation for excellence. American stores imported large quantities for their customers. The special-production English pieces of the 18th and early 19th centuries held a position of great importance among early American antiques collectors.

References: Susan and Al Bagdade, *Warman's English & Continental Pottery & Porcelain*, 3rd Edition, Krause Publications, 1998; John A. Bartlett, *British Ceramic Art: 1870-1940*, Schiffer Publishing, 1993; David Battie and Michael Turner, *19th and 20th Century British Porcelain Price Guide*, Antique Collectors' Club, 1994; Peter Bradshaw, *English Eighteenth Century Porcelain Figures, 1745-1795*, Antiques Collectors' Club, 1980; John and Margaret Cushion, *Collector's History of British Porcelain*, Antique Collectors' Club, 1992; Rachael Feild, *Macdonald Guide to Buying Antique Pottery & Porcelain*, Wallace-Homestead, 1987; Mary J. Finegan, *Johnson Brothers Dinnerware: Pattern Directory & Price Guide*, Marfine Antiques, 1993; Geoffrey A. Godden, *Godden's Guide to Mason's China and the Ironstone Wares*, Antique Collectors' Club, out of print; ——, *Godden's Guide* *to English Porcelain*, Wallace-Homestead, 1992; Pat Halfpenny, *English Earthenware Figures 1740-1840*, Antique Collectors' Club, 1992; R. K. Henrywood, *Relief Molded Jugs, 1820-1900*, Antique Collectors' Club; Kathy Hughes, *Collector's Guide to Nineteenth-Century Jugs* (Routledge Kegan Paul, 1985), Vol. II (Taylor Publishing, 1991); Llewellyn Jewitt, *Ceramic Art of Great Britain*, Sterling Publishing, 1985 (reprint of 1883 classic); Griselda Lewis, *Collector's History of English Pottery*, Antique Collectors' Club, 1987.

Additional Listings: Castleford; Chelsea; Coalport; Copeland and Spode; Liverpool; Royal Crown Derby; Royal Doulton; Royal Worcester; Staffordshire, Historical; Staffordshire, Romantic; Wedgwood; Whieldon.

Bow

Coffee Cup and Saucer, Golfer and Caddy pattern, blue, c1758 . . . . 475.00

Dish, 10-5/8" l, rect, cur corners, oval reserve f Chinese water scene, border with four fan reserves of Oriental landscapes, four round reserves of flowers, powder blue, c1765 . . . . 690.00

Figure, 3-1/2" h, goldfinch, iron-red patches on black head, puce back, black tail, black and yellow wings, seated on flowered branch, 1760, repairs, pr 1,950.00

Salt, 7-5/8" w, white, molded scallop shell, shell covered coral base, c1755, chips and cracks 920.00

Bristol

Charger, 12" d, man standing with boy, balcony overhead, oval panels of leaves border, criss-cross and dots between, blue and white, c1720-60, pr 2,100.00

Dish, 9" d, Cracked Ice pattern, blue and manganese 1,350.00

Mug, 7-1/8" h, polychrome stylized peacock, large stylized flowerheads and insects, scroll design on rim, dot handle, mid 18th C, repairs 400.00

Plate, 9" d, light blue ground, blue center scene of Oriental village, fisherman on dock and boat, bianco soopra bianco border band of white flowerheads, fruit, and leaves, hairline and chips 200.00

Caughley

Dessert Plate, 8" d, four floral sprigs painted in center cavetto, floral garlands dec, blue edged scalloped rim, blue "S" mark 185.00

Mug, 4-3/4" h, blue printed dec, late 18th century, crescent mark, rim restoration 175.00

Pitcher, 7-1/2" h, leaf molded body, blue printed bouquets of garden flowers, mask spout, scroll handle with thumb rest, c1785 . . . . 460.00

Derby

Cream Jug, 2-3/8" h, painted Chinoiserie scene, pagoda flanked by rockwork and pines, int. with boulder and grasses, brown lined rim, c1760 . . . . 2,465.00

Dish, 9-7/8" x 7-1/4", diamond shape, green scattered floral bouquets and sprigs, gilt lined and dentil rim, gilt anchor and "D" mark, Chelsea-Derby, c1775 . . . . 425.00

Figure, 6-1/8" h, standing shepherd, flower in hand, pink hat, light yellow coat, striped waistcoat, iron-red breeches, gilt accents, leaning on flower encrusted stump, hound at side, mound base, c1765, chips and repairs 300.00

New Hall, teapot, Pattern 422, bulbous body, helmet top, oval finial, red and blue florals, gold trim, $360.

Plate, 8-7/8" d multicolored center, exotic birds in landscape, stiff gilt leaves border, pale blue ground, gilt stylized flower heads on rim bands, c1820, iron-red crown mark, crossed batons and "D" mark, gilder's mark attributed to John Moscrop 360.00

Potpourri, cov, 8-3/4" h, deep pink enamel and gilt dec pot supported by three goat's mask columns, hood feet, coiled snake, red baton mark, early 19th C, rim cov nicks, snake restored, one horn repaired, gilt wear 650.00

Vase, 16" h, Persian bottle form, two pierced handles, gilt floral dec, pale yellow ground, red beaded dec. 2,500.00

English Soft Paste yellow-glazed, mug, silver luster trim, 2" h, 1-7/8" d, $245.

Flight, Barr, & Barr, Worcester

Coffee Can and Saucer, painted yellow and black, moonlight classical ruins scene, gilt scroll panel, dark blue ground, incised mark, c1807, pr..........................4,450.00

Crocus Pot, 9" w, 4" h, D-form, molded pilasters and panels, arcaded base, pale salmon ground, gilt stylized anthemion and foliage, painted still-life panel of shells and coral, conforming top pierced panel, early 19th C................8,000.00

Plate, 8" d, Exotic Birds by G. Davis, c1807-13, wear to gilding 350.00

Ralph Wood

Bust, 9-1/4" h, Handel, brown wig, green lined puce drapery, blue coat, waisted socle, imp mark, c1790, repainted 990.00

Figure, 5-1/4" h, Admiral Rodney, uniform with open coat, green enamel with manganese dots, emblems of war at feet, molded tree stump with name, sheathed sword, c1780, restored 950.00

Spill Vase, 10-3/8" h, seated shepherd and shepherdess with sheep, gnarled tree with three openings, rocky mound base, late 18th C, restored.......................1,000.00

Worcester

Coffeepot, 7-1/2" h, 6-1/2" handle to spout, Rock & Strata Island pattern, Dr. Wall, c1770, very minor chips and wear to floral finial 950.00

Creamer, 3-1/2" h, pear shape, blue Oriental dec, 18th C 250.00

Dish, 3-3/4" h, sheep shape, blue and white, Two Peony Rock Bird pattern, scrolls, underglaze blue workman's mark, c1755 .... 575.00

Plate, 8" d, blue Chinoiserie landscape and fisherman, blue oyster border, c1765 .... 400.00

Sauceboat, 7-1/2" l, floral molded body, blue painted floral sprays, c1765................................. 320.00

ENGLISH SOFT PASTE

History: Between 1820 and 1860, a large number of potteries in England's Staffordshire district produced decorative wares with a soft earthenware (creamware) base and a plain white or yellow glazed ground.

Design or "stick" spatterware was created by a cut sponge (stamp), hand painting, or transfers. Blue was the predominant color. The earliest patterns were carefully arranged geometrics, which generally covered the entire piece. Later pieces had a decorative border with a central motif, usually a tulip. In the 1850s, Elsmore and Foster developed the Holly Leaf pattern.

King's Rose features a large, cabbage-type rose in red, pale red, or pink. The pink rose often is called "Queen's Rose." Secondary colors are pastels—yellow, pink, and, occasionally, green. The borders vary: a solid band, vined, lined, or sectional. The King's Rose exists in an oyster motif.

Strawberry China ware comes in three types: strawberries and strawberry leaves (often called strawberry luster), green featherlike leaves with pink flowers (often called cut-strawberry, primrose, or old strawberry), and relief decoration. The first two types are characterized by rust-red moldings. Most pieces have a cream ground.

Davenport was only one of the many potteries which made this ware.

Yellow-glazed earthenware (canary luster) has a canary yellow ground, a transfer design, which is usually in black, and occasional luster decoration. The earliest pieces date from the 1780s and have a fine creamware base. A few hand-painted pieces are known. Not every piece has luster decoration.

Because the base material is soft paste, the ware is subject to cracking and chipping. Enamel colors and other types of decoration do not hold well. It is not unusual to see a piece with the decoration worn off.

Marks: Marked pieces are uncommon.

Additional Listings: Adams Rose; Gaudy Dutch; Salopian Ware; Staffordshire Items.

Adams Rose

Bowl, 9" d, early, rare size, mint condition 500.00
Creamer, 5 3/4" h, early 325.00
Cup and Saucer, handleless
    Early.. 215.00
    Late, rose dec on saucer, blue spatter........... 115.00
Pitcher, 7" h............................... 550.00
Plate
    6-7/8" d, two purple luster bands on border 65.00
    7-1/2" d, single rose, rust and green florals, raised basketweave order, two purple luster bands on border 125.00
    8-1/2" d, red, blue, green, and black flowers, imp "Adams," wear, minor pinpoints, stains, price for pr 250.00
    9" d, red, green, and black design 75.00
    10-1/2" d, red, green, and black design 150.00
Platter, 17-5/8" d, early, emb scalloped rim 450.00
Soup Plate, 10-1/4" d 175.00
Sugar Bowl, cov, early 345.00
Teapot, cov, late 265.00
Vegetable Dish, cov, 12 5/8" d, early 500.00

Creamware

Pitcher, 8" h, polychrome dec, floral swags, sheath of wheat, various farm implements, dated 1793, hairlines, glaze wear, minor base chip 1,725.00

Plaque, 5-7/8" h, 5-1/2" l, oval, transfer dec, "Fayette The Nation's Guest," portrait reserve of Lafayette, hairlines, second quarter 19th C 300.00

Plate, 10" d, Last Rites scene, dec for Dutch Market ... 250.00

Stirrup Cub, 4-7/8" h, figural cow, late 18th C, restored, hairlines 345.00

Design Spatterware

Bowl, 9-1/2" d, serrated rim, blue, white, and black trim . 300.00
Cup and Saucer, floral, blue, green, ochre, and red 150.00
Mug, 6" h, rosettes, blue, green bands 100.00
Plate, 9-3/4" d, red concentric center circles, narrow red line border, stars circled in blue 140.00

Earthenware

Mantel ornaments, 9-3/4" and 10-1/4" h, classical maidens with cornucopias, polychrome dec, Neale-type, imp arrow mark, chips, hairlines, glaze wear 635.00

King's Rose, plate, pink floral dec, 8-3/16" d, $200.

King's Rose

Creamer, helmet shape, brick red rose 260.00
Cup and Saucer, solid border 190.00
Plate, 7-1/2" d, vine border 150.00
Platter, 11" l, pierced edge, hairline crack. 825.00
Soup Plate, 9" d 190.00
Sugar, cov, pink rose 200.00

Pearlware

Bowl, 14-3/4" d, transfer dec, polychrome dec, various foliate
    devices, 19th C, hairline, very minor base chip 250.00
Cup and Saucer, handleless
    Bird dec 1,240.00
    Floral pattern, yellow and green. 550.00
    Gaudy blue, green, yellow and yellow-ochre floral dec, imp
    "Wood & Sons," stains and wear 275.00
Cup Plate, free-brushed, eagle dec 660.00
Pitcher
    Black transfer "Country Lad and Lass" with "Sailor's Farewell"
    and vase, polychrome enamel and pink luster, wear
    . . . . 550.00
    Chinoiserie, 6" h, 6-3/4" w handle to lip, vibrant polychrome
    dec 575.00
    Three color, 8-1/4" h. 990.00
Plate
    7-1/2" d, blue feather-edge, Peafowl dec. 600.00
    7-1/2" d, green shell edge, hexagonal, Peafowl dec 1,210.00
    7-1/2" d, green shell scalloped-edge, pineapple and urn dec-
    oration 1,100.00
    7-1/2" d, green shell edge, five color floral dec 1,705.00
    8-1/4" d, scalloped edge, five color floral, brown band, run-
    ning vine border 935.00
    10" d, blue shell edge, bold floral design 2,860.00
Toddy Plate, 4-1/2" d, chicken transfer. 550.00
Wash Bowl and Pitcher, blue, yellow, and tan flowers .1,595.00

Strawberry China

Bowl, 6-1/4" d, pink luster, red and green enamel, wide straw-
    berry border, c1820 . . . . 200.00

Creamer, 6-1/4" h 225.00
Cup and Saucer, handleless. 150.00
Plate, 8-1/4" d, Cut Strawberry 225.00
Sugar, cov, raised strawberries, strawberry finial 225.00

Yellow Glaze

Child's Mug
    Come Up Donkey, transfer dec, 2" h, second quarter 19th C,
    minor rim chips, hairlines 375.00
    Polychrome and luster dec. 825.00
Child's Teapot, 3-1/2" h, floral dec, spout repaired, hairline crack
    . . . . 635.00
Cup and Saucer, handleless, brown transfer, couple at tea
    . . . . 300.00
Jug, 5-1/4" h, black transfer print, silver-luster dec, inscribed
    "Accept this trifle from a friend whose love for thee shall never
    end," and "George Lawton, 1809" under spout 700.00
Cup and Saucer, handleless
    Luster print of mother and children. 360.00
    Transfer print of fishing scene 495.00
Mug, 2-1/2" h, yellow ground, pink luster dec 330.00
Pitcher, bulbous, floral dec 600.00
Plate
    6-1/2" d, floral pattern, yellow border 247.50
    7-1/2" d, floral dec, scalloped edge 440.00
    8-1/4" d, deep, emb fruit and floral border 2,750.00
    8-1/4" d, floral pattern. 415.00
Tea Bowl, 4-3/8" d, repair on base 412.50
Teapot
    6" h, 8" w handle to spout, black transfer, lady with urn in me-
    dallion, florals, Staffordshire, minor chips to spout foot rim
    . . . . 800.00
    7" h, 8-1/2" w handle to spout, black transfer scenic view,
    Staffordshire. 1,000.00

FAIRINGS, MATCH-STRIKERS, and TRINKET BOXES

History: Fairings are small, charming china objects which were purchased or given away as prizes at English fairs in the 19th century. Although fairings are generally identified with England, they actually were manufactured in Germany by Conte and Boehme of Possneck.

Fairings depict an amusing scene, either of courtship and marriage, politics, war, children, or animals behaving as children. More than 400 varieties have been identified. Most fairings include a caption. Early examples, 1860-1870, were of better quality than later ones. After 1890, the colors became more garish, and gilding was introduced.

The manufacturers of fairings also made match safes and trinket boxes. Some of these were also captioned. The figures on the lids were identical to those on fairings. The market for the match safes and trinket boxes was the same as that for the fairings.

Reference: Janice and Richard Vogel, *Victorian Trinket Boxes*, published by authors (4720 S.E. Ft. King St., Ocala, FL 34470), 1996.

Fairings

Baby's First Step, three children, hand in hand 200.00

Fairing, Paddling His Own Canoe, white and green, gold trim, 2-3/4" x 2" x 4-1/8", $145.

Bisque, painted, gold trim, detailed molding, marked "Conte & Boehme" 195.00
For Heaven's Sake Marie, Give Us Rest, woman standing over man in bed, pale blue blanket, white ground, gold trim, German mark 220.00
Home Rule, couple by bed 270.00
O Do Leave Me A Drop, two cats at bowl 250.00
Twelve Months After Marriage 200.00

Match-Strikers

Crown and scepter, oval, applied flowers on border 275.00
Drum and drumsticks, red, white, and blue, gilt accents
. . . . 250.00
Tea Party, three ladies around tea table 300.00

Trinket Boxes

Boy gathering apples, 3-3/4" l 60.00
Cameo, musical instruments on lid, 3-3/4" d 115.00
Chest of Drawers, bombe front, pocket watch on top . . . 195.00
Girl putting on stockings, white ground, blue dec, imp marks, 3-1/2 x 4 x 2" 150.00
Passenger Pigeon, blue beak, package around neck, brown and yellow wings, white base, blue band, gilt trim. 200.00
Piano, 2-3/8" 95.00
Sailor, anchor on cover, 4-7/8" l 90.00

FAIRY LAMPS

History: Fairy lamps, which originated in England in the 1840s, are candle-burning night lamps. They were used in nurseries, hallways, and dim corners of the home.

Two leading candle manufacturers, the Price Candle Company and the Samuel Clarke Company, promoted fairy lamps as a means to sell candles. Both contracted with glass, porcelain, and metal manufacturers to produce the needed shades and cups. For example, Clarke used Worcester Royal Porcelain Company, Stuart & Sons, and Red House Glass Works in England, plus firms in France and Germany.

Fittings were produced in a wide variety of styles. Shades ranged from pressed to cut glass, from Burmese to Nailsea. Cups are found in glass, porcelain, brass, nickel, and silver plate.

American firms selling fairy lamps included Diamond Candle Company of Brooklyn, Blue Cross Safety Candle Co., and Hobbs-Brockunier of Wheeling, West Virginia.

Two-piece (cup and shade) and three-piece (cup with matching shade and saucer) fairy lamps can be found. Married pieces are common.

Marks: Clarke's trademark was a small fairy with a wand surrounded by the words "Clarke Fairy Pyramid, Trade Mark."

References: Bob and Pat Ruf Pullin, *Fairy Lamps*, Schiffer Publishing, 1996; John F. Solverson (comp.), *Those Fascinating Little Lamps: Miniature Lamps Value Guide*, Antique Publications, 1988.

Periodical: *Light Revival*, 35 West Elm Ave., Quincy, MA 02170.

Collectors' Club: Night Light Club, 38619 Wakefield Ct., Northville, MI 48167.

Reproduction Alert: Reproductions abound.

Ribbed Drape shade, vaseline shade, green Clarke base, $195.

Amber, 4" h, Diamond Point pattern, matching, clear marked Clarke insert 265.00

Blue, 3-5/8" h, 2-7/8" d, Diamond Quilted pattern, MOP satin glass shade, white lining, clear marked Clarke insert
. . . . 180.00

Burmese, 6 1/2"h, 8" d, dome shade dec with red flowers, yellow centers, tapestry flower bowl base with cream ground, pink flowers, aqua and gold trim, base marked "Clarke" . . 995.00

Cranberry, 3-1/2" h, 2-7/8" d, Diamond Quilted pattern, clear marked Clarke insert 120.00

Figural
3-1/2" h, monkey, natural coloring, amber eyes 375.00
4-1/2" h, 3-3/4" d, owl's head, frosted green, red enameled eyes, clear marked Clarke base 300.00

Goofus Glass, 7" h, rose dec, flash fired green and red dec, three smoke holes in top, wood base 45.00

Nailsea, Verre Moiré
5" h, 5-1/2" d, white loopings, frosted cranberry body, dome shaped shade, bowl shaped base with ruffled edge, clear marked Clarke insert 450.00
6-1/2" h, 5-3/4" d, white loopings, red satin body, dome shaped shade, bowl shaped base with six pinched-in pleats, clear insert marked "S Clarke/Patent/Trade Mark/Fairy" 865.00

Opalescent, 3-3/4 x 2-7/8", blue emb rib, pyramid, clear marked Clarke base 95.00

Overshot, 4-1/2" h, frosted white dec, yellow ground, white porcelain base mkd "Clarke Patent" 300.00

Peachblow, 5-1/4"h , clear glass candle cup, Mt. Washington
. . . . 250.00

Satin Glass
5" h, Diamond Quilted shade, clear marked Clarke's Cricklite base 120.00
6 3/4" h, cranberry, opaque white loopings, clear marked Clarke base 700.00

Spatter Glass, 3-1/2" h, 2-7/8" h, yellow and white spatter shade, clear marked Clarke base 150.00

Teal Blue and White Swirl, 4-7/8" h, overlay, emb swirl pattern shade, white lining, clear marked Clarke base 250.00

FAMILLE ROSE

History: Famille Rose is Chinese export enameled porcelain on which the pink color predominates. It was made primarily in the 18th and 19th centuries. Other porcelains in the same group are Famille Jaune (yellow), Famille Noire (black), and Famille Verte (green).

Decorations include courtyard and home scenes, birds, and insects. Secondary colors are yellow, green, blue, aubergine, and black.

Rose Canton, Rose Mandarin, and Rose Medallion are mid- to late 19th-century Chinese export wares which are similar to Famille Rose.

Famille Jaune

Bowl, 10-1/4" d, 4-1/4" h, alternating reserves of birds among trees and carp pounds, center reserve of stag with monkey, foliage, fish, and butterfly borders, 19th C, minor gilt and enamel wear, minor glaze chips 635.00

Standish, 7-1/2" l, French silver maquet, chased with birds, fish, and scrolling foliate, one cover and one glass liner missing, Chinese Export, late 19th C 920.00

Famille Rose

Basin, 17" d, multicolored scene of pheasants perched on pierced rockwork, peonies and chrysanthemums, cavetto border with suspended pomegranates alternating with ruyi heads, stylized hibiscus blossom, gilt highlights, four iron-red peony sprigs on underside 10,350.00

Bird, figural
12-1/2" h, parrot, posed on weathered rock base, blues, greens, purples, and yellow, black highlights, late 19th C, pr
. . . . 575.00
15-1/4" h, phoenix atop flower covered rocks, brilliant enamels, late 19th C, pr 690.00

Bowl
8" d, iron-red five-clawed dragon, cloud scattered ground, iron-red six-character Ch'ien Lung mark, 19th C . . . 200.00
13-1/4" d, 19th C, very minor rim chips, minor gilt wear
. . . . 980.00

Charger, 15-3/4" d, courtesans panels, red enamel ground, scrolling lotus and dragons, 20th C 190.00

Garden Seat, 19" h, barrel shape, squirrel and grape design, Chinese, 19th C 865.00

Ginger Jar, cov
9" h, floral and butterfly dec, mounted as lamps 220.00
11-1/2" h, 8-1/2" d, pink, blue, green, and yellow flowers, 18th C, pr 600.00

Jar, 10" h
Cabbage leaf, 19th C, mounted as lamp, pr 375.00
Floral dec, rose ground, 19th C, mounted as lamp . . 150.00

Punch Bowl
13" d, hongs at Canton 70,700.00
16" d, underglaze blue and white enamels, Chinese domestic scenes 8,625.00

Tankard, 6" h, cylindrical, rose, iron-red, turquoise, green, and blue, trailing branch of flowering peonies, iron-red scalloped band, ribbed base, brown rim with gilt blossoms and leaves, S-scroll handle, iron-red heart shaped terminal, c1745
. . . . 750.00

Vase
5-1/2" h, cha dou shape, mirror image painting of children playing with rooster between gourd and peony plants, goldfish pond, Kuang Hsu mark and period, 1875-1908, repairs to one, pr 230.00
10" h, painted port scene with flags, mounted as lamp, electrified, pr 150.00
24-3/4" h, Rouleau, shaped panels of birds, flowers, and scenes from the Peking Opera, gold ground decorated with pink flowers and green tendrils, Jiaquing Period (1796-1820) 1,380.00

Vase, cov, floral sprays, rooster dec, 19th C 980.00

Wine Ewer, 10" h, phoenix on rock with flowers, leafy tree forms handle, late 19th C 250.00

Famille Verte

Vase
7-1/2" h, oviform, four women, top with green cracked ice ground and flowers, mouth with grisaille bamboo, K'ang His period, 1662-1722 . . . . 1,555.00
13" h, bird and floral dec, mounted as lamps, pr 175.00
17-1/2" d, mallet form, shaped reserves of landscapes, floral groups, birds among foliage and antiques, famille verte enamels, powder blue ground, mounted as lamps, pr
. . . . 750.00

FENTON GLASS

History: The Fenton Art Glass Company began as a cutting shop in Martins Ferry, Ohio, in 1905. In 1906, Frank L. Fenton started to build a plant in Williamstown, West Virginia, and produced the first piece of glass there in 1907. Early production included carnival, chocolate, custard, and pressed glass, plus mold-blown opalescent glass. In the 1920s, stretch glass, Fenton dolphins, jade green, ruby, and art glass were added.

In the 1930s, boudoir lamps, Dancing Ladies, and slag glass in various colors were produced. The 1940s saw crests of different colors being added to each piece by hand. Hobnail, opalescent, and two-color overlay pieces were popular items. Handles were added to different shapes, making the baskets they created as popular then as they are today.

Through the years Fenton has beautified their glass by decorating it with hand painting, acid etching, and copper-wheel cutting

Marks: Several different paper labels have been used. In 1970, an oval raised trademark also was adopted.

References: William Heacock, *Fenton Glass: The First Twenty-Five Years* (1978), *The Second Twenty-Five Years* (1980), *The Third Twenty-Five Years* (1989), available from Antique Publications; Alan Linn, *Fenton Story of Glass Making*, Antique Publications, 1996; James Measell (ed.), *Fenton Glass: The 1980s Decade*, Antique Publications, 1996; Naomi L. Over, *Ruby Glass of the 20th Century*, Antique Publications, 1990, 1993-94 value update; Ferill J. Rice (ed.), *Caught in the Butterfly Net*, Fenton Art Glass Collectors of America, Inc., 1991; Margaret and Kenn Whitmyer, *Fenton Art Glass 1907-1939*, Collector Books, 1996.

Periodical: *Butterfly Net*, 302 Pheasant Run, Kaukauna, WI 54130.

Collectors' Clubs: Fenton Art Glass Collectors of America, Inc., P.O. Box 384, Williamstown, WV 26187; National Fenton Glass Society, P.O. Box 4008, Marietta, OH 45750; Pacific Northwest Fenton Association, 8225 Kilchis River Rd., Tillamook, OR 97141.

Videotape: *Making Fenton Glass, 1992*, Fenton Art Glass Co. Museum, 1992.

Museum: Fenton Art Glass Co., Williamstown, WV.

Advisor: Ferill J. Rice.

Additional Listings: Carnival Glass.

Ashtray
#848 Jade Green, three feet	30.00
#5173 Bird, Old Virginia Line	35.00
#9176 Swirl, Colonial Green	9.00

Basket
#1615 Diamond Optic, Ruby, no handle	60.00
#2632 8 Blue Ridge, 80th Anniversary	75.00
#3837 7 Hobnail, Blue Pastel	45.00
#7437 Violets in the Snow	70.00
Hobnail, Black Rose, sgd "Frank Fenton" (QVC)	75.00
Lion, Rosalene (QVC)	50.00

Bell
Bicentennial, Patriot Red	32.50
Bluebirds, custard	40.00
Lily of the Valley, Blue Opalescent	28.00
Milk, Ruby Crest	30.00
Sable Arch, Cameo Opalescent	30.00

Bon Bon
5" Daisy & Button, Blue Opalescent	12.50
5" Dolphin, Jade	15.00
5-1/2" Emerald Crest, double crimped	2.00
#1502 Round Bridge, Ruby Diamond Optic	20.00

Bowl
#7222 Low Dessert, Emerald Crest	17.50
#7320 Soup, Emerald Crest	12.50
Rose, Hobnail, Green Opalescent	45.00
10" d, Hobnail, Plum Opalescent, ftd	150.00
11" d, Hobnail, Green Opalescent	35.00

Bucket, #1615, Bridge, Ruby Diamond Optic 30.00

Candlestick
#951 Cornucopia, Silver Crest	50.00
#1523 Crystal Crest	62.50
#1623 Dolphin, Ruby	22.50

Candy Jar or Puff Box
#7580 Dolphin handled, with cover, Velva Rosa	55.00
#8288 Medallion, Pink Blossom on Custard Satin	37.50
#8480 Waterlily	20.00
#9185 Panelled Daisy, Orange Carnival	20.00

Comport
#1533 5-1/2" Dolphin, Ruby	70.00
#3627 Hobnail, Milk Glass	16.50
#3885 Hobnail, Milk Glass, covered (scarce)	33.50
#8422 Waterlily, Rosalene, ftd	50.00
#9222 Rose, Jonquil Yellow (rare)	115.00

Creamer and Sugar
#1639 Ruby 2, crystal foot	55.00
#1903 Daisy & Button, Milk Glass	30.00
#3906 Hobnail, Milk Glass	20.50
#5604 Block & Star, Turquoise	50.00

Creatures (animals and birds)
#5106 Frog, Chocolate Roses	42.00
#5147 Mallard, Berries & Blossom	45.00
#5161 Swan, Blue Satin	47.50

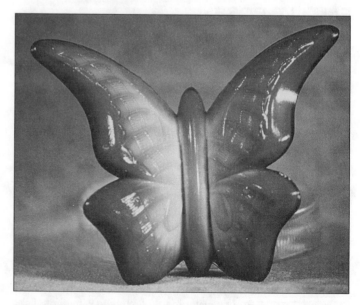

Butterfly, #5170, chocolate, FAGCA, $55. Photo courtesy of Ferill Rice.

#5170 Butterfly, Colonial Orange, cut off 45.00
#5177 Alley Cat, Burmese 85.00
#5193 Fish Paperweight, Rosalene 25.00
#5197 Happiness Bird, Bluebirds on Custard 35.00
Cat Slipper, Hobnail Topaz Opalescent 35.00
Fairy Light
    #2604 Blue Ridge, 3 pc, 80th Anniversary 90.00
    #3608 Hobnail, Colonial Orange 22.50
    #3608 Hobnail, Milk Glass 15.00
    #7501 Pink Dogwood on Burmese, 3 pc 220.00
    #8406 Heart, Rosalene 65.00
Hobnail, Blue Bells on Milk Glass 40.00
Holly on Ruby, 2 pc 35.00
Log Cabin on Custard 40.00
Goblet
    #3845 Hobnail, Milk Glass 12.00
    #4445 Thumbprint, Colonial Blue 16.00
    #4445 Thumbprint, Colonial Green 9.00
Lamp
    #1700 Hurricane, Emerald Green Snow Crest, 2 pc . 165.00
    Black Rose, black base 170.00
    Courting Lamp, Blue Overlay, electric 120.00
Miniature
    #37 Jug, Blue Opalescent 50.00
    #7436 Basket, Black Crest 125.00
Oil Bottle, with stopper, Emerald Crest 85.00
Plate
    #1502 7-1/2" d, salad, Ruby with Diamond Optic 8.00
    #1639 7-1/2" d, salad Ruby with cutting 35.00
    8" Leaf, Rosalene 38.00
Salt and Pepper Shakers, pr
    #4306 Lambs Tongue, Turquoise 47.50
    Hobnail, French Opalescent, ftd 57.50
    Relish, Emerald Crest, two heart shaped dishes in metal
        stand 60.00
Toothpick, Paneled Daisy, Lime Sherbet 22.50
Vase
    #1356 Bubble Optic, Apple Green, 7-1/2" h 45.00
    #1356 Bubble Optic, Coral, 7-1/2" h 75.00
    #1924 Crystal Crest, 4" h 30.00
    #9153 Jaquelyn, Pink Opaline, 5-1/2" h 35.00
    5" h, Custard Hanging Heart 95.00
    6" h, Emerald Crest, double crimped 25.00
    8" h, Spiral Optic, Stiegel Blue 55.00
    8" h, Stiegel Blue, square top 20.00

Happiness Birds, #5197, ruby, hand painted by Louis Piper, $85 each. Photo courtesy of Ferill Rice.

FIESTA

History: The Homer Laughlin China Company introduced Fiesta dinnerware in January 1936 at the Pottery and Glass Show in Pittsburgh, Pennsylvania. Frederick Rhead designed the pattern; Arthur Kraft and Bill Bensford molded it. Dr. A. V. Bleininger and H. W. Thiemecke developed the glazes.

The original five colors were red, dark blue, light green (with a trace of blue), brilliant yellow, and ivory. A vigorous marketing campaign took place between 1939 and 1943. In mid-1937 turquoise was added. Red was removed in 1943 because some of the chemicals used to produce it were essential to the war effort; it did not reappear until 1959. In 1951, light green, dark blue, and ivory were retired and forest green, rose, chartreuse, and gray were added to the line. Other color changes took place in the late 1950s, including the addition of a medium green.

Fiesta ware was redesigned in 1969 and discontinued about 1972. In 1986 Fiesta was reintroduced by Homer Laughlin China Company. The new china body shrinks more than the old semi-vitreous and ironstone pieces, thus making the new pieces slightly smaller than the earlier pieces. The modern colors are also different in tone or hue, e.g., the cobalt blue is darker than the old blue. Other modern colors are black, white, apricot, and rose.

References: Susan and Al Bagdade, *Warman's American Pottery and Porcelain*, Wallace-Homestead, 1994; Sharon and Bob Huxford, *Collector's Encyclopedia of Fiesta*, Revised 7th ed., Collector Books, 1996; Jeffrey B. Snyder, *Fiesta, Homer Laughlin China Company's Colorful Dinnerware*, Schiffer Publishing, 1997.

Collectors' Clubs: Fiesta Club of America, P.O. Box 15383, Loves Park, IL 61132-5383; Fiesta Collectors Club, 19238 Dorchester Circle, Strongsville, OH 44136; Fiesta Collector's Quarterly, P.O. Box 471, Valley City, OH 44280.

Reproduction Alert.

Additional Listings: See *Warman's Americana & Collectibles* for more examples.

After Dinner Coffeepot, cov
    Green 475.00
    Red 725.00
After Dinner Cup and Saucer
    Chartreuse 625.00
    Cobalt Blue 95.00
    Green 85.00
    Ivory 125.00
    Red 125.00
    Rose 750.00
    Turquoise 115.00
    Yellow 95.00
Ashtray, medium green 260.00
Bud Vase
    Green 85.00

Fruit Bowl, cobalt blue, 11-5/8" d, 2-3/4" h, $485.

Red.	130.00
Turquoise	125.00
Calendar Plate, 1955, 10" d, green.	45.00
Cake Plate, green	1,950.00
Candlesticks, pr, bulb	
Cobalt Blue.	125.00
Ivory	125.00
Turquoise	110.00
Candlesticks, pr, tripod	
Cobalt Blue.	950.00
Ivory	950.00
Yellow.	750.00
Carafe	
Green	300.00
Ivory	650.00
Red.	475.00
Turquoise	380.00
Casserole, cov	
Dark Green.	425.00
Gray	375.00
Turquoise	135.00
Yellow.	130.00
Chop Plate, 13" d, gray	95.00
Coffeepot	
Chartreuse	575.00
Cobalt Blue.	350.00
Dark Green.	750.00
Gray	750.00
Rose	850.00
Turquoise	250.00
Creamer, individual	
Red.	385.00
Yellow.	75.00
Creamer, stick handle	
Cobalt Blue.	65.00
Red.	85.00
Turquoise	115.00
Cream Soup	
Chartreuse	95.00
Dark Green.	95.00
Red.	75.00

Rose.	95.00
Deep Plate	
Gray	50.00
Medium Green	135.00
Dessert Bowl, 6" d, Chartreuse.	50.00
Eggcup	
Cobalt Blue.	90.00
Dark Green.	180.00
Gray	175.00
Light Green.	80.00
Red.	100.00
Yellow.	80.00
Fruit Bowl, 11-3/4" d, yellow	350.00
Juice Pitcher, red	750.00
Juice Tumbler, 4-1/4" h	
Cobalt Blue.	45.00
Ivory	45.00
Red.	55.00
Rose.	60.00
Turquoise	125.00
Marmalade, yellow	360.00
Mixing Bowl	
#1, cobalt blue	375.00
#1, green	230.00
#1, ivory	390.00
#1, red	275.00
#1, yellow	325.00
#2, cobalt blue	200.00
#2, yellow	150.00
#3, green, double marks.	225.00
#4, green	200.00
#4, ivory	225.00
#4, turquoise.	220.00
#4, yellow	145.00
#5, cobalt blue	325.00
#5, ivory	275.00
#7, ivory	590.00
Mixing Bowl Lid	
#1, green	1,150.00
#1, red	1,600.00
#2, ivory	1,550.00
#2, yellow	1,375.00
#3, ivory	1,950.00
Mug	
Chartreuse	90.00
Cobalt Blue.	85.00
Gray	95.00
Ivory, marked	125.00
Medium Green	150.00
Rose	95.00
Turquoise	55.00
Mustard, cov	
Cobalt Blue.	325.00
Green	250.00
Turquoise	265.00
Yellow.	350.00
Onion Soup, cov	
Green	850.00
Ivory	950.00
Pitcher, disk, rose	275.00
Pitcher, ice lip, turquoise	200.00
Pitcher, jug, cobalt blue.	120.00
Plate	
6" d, medium green	35.00
10" d, chartreuse	50.00
10" d, cobalt blue	55.00

10" d, ivory 40.00
10" d, red 50.00
12" d, compartment, cobalt blue. 75.00
Platter, medium green. 175.00
Relish
   Red, center and side segments 425.00
Salad Bowl, ftd, yellow 470.00
Salt and Pepper Shakers, pr
   Medium Green 270.00
   Turquoise 135.00
Sauce Boat, medium green. 225.00
Sugar, cov
   Medium Green 265.00
   Turquoise 55.00
Sweets Compote
   Turquoise 125.00
   Yellow. 95.00
Syrup
   Ivory 600.00
   Red. 600.00
   Turquoise, mkd "Dripcut" 760.00
Tea Cup
   Medium Green 165.00
   Red. 100.00
Teapot, large
   Cobalt Blue. 335.00
   Green 225.00
   Turquoise 280.00
Teapot, medium
   Ivory 245.00
   Rose. 350.00
   Turquoise 150.00
Utility Tray, figure 8, turquoise 400.00
Vase, 8"h
   Cobalt Blue, light streaks on one side, in the making
   . . . . 700.00
   Ivory 850.00
   Light Green. 750.00
   Red. 750.00
Vase, 12" h
   Cobalt Blue. 1,500.00
   Ivory 1,500.00
Water Tumbler, turquoise 85.00

FIGURAL BOTTLES

History: Porcelain figural bottles, which have an average height of three to eight and were made either in a glazed or bisque finish, achieved popularity in the late 1800s and remained popular into the 1930s. The majority of figural bottles were made in Germany, with Austria and Japan accounting for the balance.

Empty figural bottles were shipped to the United States and filled upon arrival. They were then given away to customers by brothels, dance halls, hotels, liquor stores, and taverns. Some were lettered with the names and addresses of the establishment, others had paper labels. Many were used for holidays, e.g., Christmas and New Year.

Figural bottles also were made in glass and other materials. The glass bottles held perfumes, food, or beverages.

References: Ralph & Terry Kovel, *Kovels' Bottles Price List*, 10th ed., Crown Publishers, 1996; Kenneth Wilson,

American Glass 1760-1930, 2 Vols., Hudson Hills Press and The Toledo Museum of Art, 1994.

Periodical: *Antique Bottle and Glass Collector*, P.O. Box 187, East Greenville, PA 18041.

Collectors' Clubs: Federation of Historical Bottle Clubs, 88 Sweetbriar Branch, Longwood, FL 32750; New England Antique Bottle Club, 120 Commonwealth Rd., Lynn, MA 01904.

Museums: National Bottle Museum, Ballston Spa, NY; National Bottle Museum, Barnsley, S Yorkshire, England; Old Bottle Museum, Salem, NJ.

Barrel Form, 4-7/8" h, yellow olive green, fancy rigaree trailing around body, two sleigh runner feet serve as base, each emb with repeating sunburst motif, tooled mouth, pontil scar, Europe, 18th C 450.00
Bear, 10-5/8" h, dense yellow amber, sheared mouth, applied face, Russia, 1860-80, flat chip on back 400.00
Big Stick, Teddy Roosevelt's, 7-1/2" h, golden amber, sheared mouth, smooth base, flat flake at mouth 170.00
Boy crying against brick wall, "I'm So Discouraged" 100.00
Fish, 11-1/2" h, "Doctor Fisch's Bitters," golden amber, applied small round collared mouth, smooth base, America, 1860-80, some ext. highpoint wear, burst bubble on base 160.00
Garfield, James, President, 8" h, colorless glass bust set in turned wood base, ground mouth, smooth base, America, 1880-1900 . . . . 80.00
Huntsman with snooty dog, comical expression, Goebel crown mark, 10" h 275.00
Indian Maiden, 12-1/4" h, "Brown's Celebrated Indian Herb Bitters," yellow amber, inward rolled mouth, smooth base, America, 1860-80 . . . . 600.00
Man, Toasting Your Health, flask shape, bisque front, tree bark back, 4-1/2" x 4" 40.00
One of the Boys, man in tux, tall stool, Schafer & Vater
. . . . 165.00
Pig, pottery, Kirkpatrick Brothers, Anna, Illinois; incised "From the World's Fair/ With a little good Old Rye in [arrow] 1893/Cut Rates/To All Points East," 7-1/4" l 1,760.00
Pig, Suffolk Bitters, America, 1860-90, shaded yellow amber, applied double collared mouth, smooth base, 10-1/8" l, minor ext. high point wear 750.00
Pineapple, 8-3/4" h, "W & Co./N.Y.," America, 1845-60, brilliant yellow green with strong olive tone, applied double collard mouth, iron pontil mark, 8" meandering crack through body
. . . . 425.00
Shoe, dark amethyst, ground mouth, smooth base 125.00

Fish, Bennington type pottery, brown glaze, 9" l, $495.

Washington, George, 10" h, "Simon's Centennial Bitters," aquamarine, applied double collared mouth, smooth base, America, 1860-80 . . . . 650.00

FINDLAY ONYX GLASS

History: Findlay onyx glass, produced by Dalzell, Gilmore & Leighton Company, Findlay, Ohio, was patented for the firm in 1889 by George W. Leighton. Due to high production costs resulting from a complex manufacturing process, the glass was made only for a short time.

Layers of glass were plated to a bulb of opalescent glass through repeated dippings into a glass pot. Each layer was cooled and reheated to develop opalescent qualities. A pattern mold then was used to produce raised decorations of flowers and leaves. A second mold gave the glass bulb its full shape and form.

A platinum luster paint, producing pieces identified as silver or platinum onyx, was applied to the raised decorations. The color was fixed in a muffle kiln. Other colors such as cinnamon, cranberry, cream, raspberry, and rose were achieved by using an outer glass plating which reacted strongly to reheating. For example, a purple or orchid color came from the addition of manganese and cobalt to the glass mixture.

References: Neila and Tom Bredenhoft, *Findlay Toothpick Holders*, Cherry Hill Publications, 1995; James Measell and Don E. Smith, *Findlay Glass: The Glass Tableware Manufacturers, 1886-1902*, Antique Publications, 1986.

Collectors' Club: Collectors of Findlay Glass, P.O. Box 256, Findlay, OH 45839.

Bowl
    7" d, 2-3/4" h, silver onyx 320.00
    7-1/2" d, cream onyx 390.00
    7-1/2" d, raspberry onyx 425.00
Butter Dish, cov, 5-1/2" d, silver onyx 850.00
Celery, cream onyx, gold florals 400.00

Tumbler, platinum floral dec, 3-5/8" h, $375.

Creamer, 4-1/2" h, raspberry onyx, platinum colored dec, opalescent glass handle 550.00
Mustard, cov, 3" h, hinged metal cov, orig spoon mkd "sterling"
    Cream onyx 400.00
    Raspberry onyx 600.00
Pitcher, 8" h, cream onyx, amber florals and handle, minor bubbles in inner liner 700.00
Salt and Pepper Shakers, pr, 3" h, platinum onyx 550.00
Spooner, 4-1/2" h, platinum blossoms, rough edge 265.00
Sugar Bowl, cov, 5-1/2" h
    Cream onyx 475.00
    Raspberry onyx 650.00
Sugar Shaker, 6" h, silver onyx 400.00
Toothpick Holder, 2-1/2" h, cinnamon onyx 425.00
Tumbler, raspberry onyx, Floradine pattern 785.00

FINE ARTS

Notes: There is no way a listing of less than one hundred paintings can accurately represent the breadth and depth of the examples sold during the last year. To attempt to make such a list would be ludicrous.

In any calendar year, tens, if not hundreds of thousands of paintings are sold. Prices range from a few dollars to millions. Since each painting is essentially a unique creation, it is difficult to compare prices.

Since an essential purpose of *Warman's Antiques And Collectibles Price Guide* is to assist its users in finding information about a category, this Fine Arts introduction has been written primarily to identify the reference books that you will need to find out more about a painting in your possession.

Artist Dictionaries: Emmanuel Benezit, *Dictionnaire Critique et Documentaire des Peintres, Sculpteurs, Dessinateurs et Graveurs*, 10 volumes, 3rd ed., Grund, 1976; John Castagno, *Old Masters: Signatures and Monograms*, Scarecrow Press, 1996; Ian Chilvers, *Concise Oxford Dictionary of Arts & Artists*, 2nd ed., Oxford University Press, 1996; Peter Hastings Falk, *Dictionary of Signatures & Monograms of American Artists*, Sound View Press, 1988; Mantle Fielding, *Dictionary of American Painters, Sculptors and Engravers*, Apollo Books, 1983; J. Johnson and A. Greutzner, *Dictionary of British Artists, 1880-1940: An Antique Collector's Club Research Project Listing 41,000 Artists*, Antique Collector's Club, 1976; Les Krantz, American Artists, Facts on File, 1985.

Introductory Information: Alan Bamberger, *Buy Art Smart*, Wallace-Homestead Book Company, 1990; ——, *How to Buy Fine Art You Can Afford*, Wallace-Homestead, 1994.

Price Guide References, Basic: *Art at Auction in America*, 1994 ed., Krexpress, 1994; William T. Currier (comp.), *Currier's Price Guide to American Artists 1645-1945 at Auction*, 6th ed., Currier Publications, 1994; —— (comp.), *Currier's Price Guide to European Artists 1545-1945 at Auction*, 4th ed., Currier Publications, 1994; Susan Theran, *Fine Art: Identification and Price Guide*, 3rd ed., Avon Books, 1996.

Price Guide References, Advanced: R. J. Davenport, *Davenport's Art Reference & Price Guide: 1996-97*, 8th ed., Davenport Publishing, 1996; Peter Hastings Falk (ed.), *Art Price Index International '96*, Sound View Press

Stone Fruit, oil on canvas by Marvin Cone (1891-1964, Iowa), $57,750. Photo courtesy of Jackson's Auctioneers & Appraisers.

(859 Boston Post Rd., Madison, CT 06443), 1995; Richard Hislop (ed.), *Annual Art Sales Index*, 28th ed., Art Sales Index Ltd., 1996; Enrique Mayer, *International Auction Record*, Paris, Editions Enrique Mayer, since 1967; Judith and Martin Miller (comps. & eds.), *Miller's Picture Price Guide*, Millers Publications, 1994; Susan Theran (ed.), *Leonard's Price Index of Art Auctions*, Auction Index, since 1980.

Museum Directories: *American Art Directory*, R. R. Bowker, 1995; American Association of Museums, *Official Museum Directory: United States and Canada*, R. R. Bowker, updated periodically.

Collectors' Club: American Art Collectors, 610 N Delaware Ave., Roswell, NM 88201.

FIREARM ACCESSORIES

History: Muzzle-loading weapons of the 18th and early 19th centuries varied in caliber and required the owner to carry a variety of equipment, including a powder horn or flask, patches, flints or percussion caps, bullets, and bullet molds. In addition, military personnel were responsible for bayonets, slings, and miscellaneous cleaning equipment and spare parts.

During the French and Indian War, soldiers began to personalize their powder horns with intricate engraving, in addition to the usual name or initial used for identification. Sometimes professional hornsmiths were employed to customize these objects, which have been elevated to a form of folk art by some collectors.

In the mid-19th century, cartridge weapons replaced their black-powder ancestors. Collectors seek anything associated with early ammunition—from the cartridges themselves to advertising material. Handling old ammunition can be extremely dangerous because of decomposition of compounds. Seek advice from an experienced collector before becoming involved in this area.

References: Ralf Coykendall Jr., *Coykendall's Complete Guide to Sporting Collectibles*, Wallace-Homestead, 1996; John Delph, *Firearms and Tackle Memorabilia*, Schiffer Publishing, 1991; Jim Dresslar, *Folk Art of Early America—The Engraved Powder Horn*, Dresslar Publishing (P.O. Box 635, Bargersville, IN 46106), 1996; John Ogle, *Colt Memorabilia Price Guide*, Krause Publications, 1998.

Periodical: Military Trader, P.O. Box 1050, Dubuque, IA 52004.

Museums: Fort Ticonderoga Museum, Ticonderoga, NY; Huntington Museum of Art, Huntington, WV.

REPRODUCTION ALERT

There are a large number of reproduction and fake powder horns. Be very cautious!

Notes: Military-related firearm accessories generally are worth more than their civilian counterparts.

Additional Listings: Militaria.

Advertising Display, 14" h, 11" w, litho cardboard, easel back, Remington UMC Firearms and Ammunition, illus of Remington bear cubs, strong color. 500.00
Award Fob, 1-3/4" d, 2-sided, celluloid, 1899 shooting tournament
    DuPont Powder 600.00
    Hazard Powder. 575.00
Belt, 36" l, 2" w, thirty nickel metal clips for holding shot shells, canvas shoulder straps, nickel plated buckle with Savage Arms logo cast into it, nickel plated hook 350.00
Book
    Custom Guns, Richard Simmons, illus, 1949. . . . . 30.00
    Western Ammunition Handbook, 1938, 72 pgs 35.00
Bullet Mold, 9", brass, casting six round buttons with central raised letter "I" for infantry, one 25 mm, one 18 mm, and four 14.5 mm d, American, 18th C. 750.00

Advertising Sign, Marlin Firearms, framed paper sign, two determined hunters in pursuit of prey, copyright 1907, artist sgd "Philip R. Goodwin," 24-1/4" x 13-3/4", $1,800. Photo courtesy of James D. Julia, Inc.

Calendar

26-3/4" h, 13-3/4" w, Harrington & Richardson Arms Co., 1908, hunter taking bead on caribou, oilcloth, orig metal rim top and bottom, calendar pad missing 800.00

27" h, 13-3/4" w, Peters Cartridges, 1910, titled "The First Lesson STEADY," mother pointer teaching pups, © 1908, artist sgd "A. Muss Arnolt," oilcloth, framed 1,100.00

29-1/2" h, 14-1/2" w, Winchester, 1915, eagle attacking mountain goats, Forbes Litho Mfg. Co., artist sgd "Lynn Bogue Hunt," paper, framed, calendar pad missing
. . . . .1,500.00

Cartridge Board, 30-1/4 x 32-1/4", US Cartridge Co., plaster casting of early board, displaying line of self contained ammunition, bullets, and primers, rifle, handgun, and shot shell ammunition, laminated oak frame, refinished c1960, provenance includes display at 1892 Chicago Expo and 1904 St. Louis World's Fair. 1,800.00

Cartridge Box

3-7/8" x 2" x 1", Hall & Hubbard, cal. 22, green and black label "100 No. 1/2 2-100/PISTOL CARTRIDGES," molted cream and black paper, empty, half green side label missing
. . . . 350.00

4" x 2-1/8" x 1-1/4", Union Metallic Cartridge Co., cream and black label "FIFTY .32 CALIBRE/No. 2/PISTOL CARTRIDGES," engraving of Smith & Wesson 1st Model 3rd Issue, checkered covering, orange and black side labels, unopened 250.00

Catalog

Colt Industries, Inc., Hartford, CT, 1976, 24 pgs, 8-1/4" x 11"
. . . . 40.00

Colt's Patent Fire Arms, Hartford, CT, 1920s, 40 pgs, 3-1/4" x 5-1/4". 40.00

Winchester-Western, New Haven, CT, 1976, 5-3/4" x 7-1/2", Bicentennial edition 40.00

Display Cabinet, 56" l, 7-1/4" d, 33-1/2" h, oak, glass front lift door, three drawers across bottom, rests for two Thompson carbines, back lined with red cloth, USMC logo in center, key locks at each end 500.00

Holster, Colt Single Action Holster, tooled dec along borders on both sides, brown leather 125.00

Powder Flask

7-3/4" h, copper, pear shape, emb on both sides with group of hounds fighting with bear in woods, script initials below, brass top 100.00

8-1/4" h, brass, body emb "Rifle Horn" within a curved panel surrounded with a toothed design, orig lacquer finish, orig faded green carrying cord 170.00

Powder Horn

9" l, engraved ship, hearts, house, trees, two inscriptions "Jeremiah Donohue, Age 21, M. 11, 1871," and "Patrick Donohue born 1866," another date of 1885, crack in end, may be cut down, very worn old plug. 150.00

10-1/2" l, engraved map of fort and roads leading to it, stag hunt scene, plug engraved "JR," very minor loss to plug
. . . . .2,760.00

11-1/4" l, engraved stags, foliate, and geometric devices, name "Samuel Evens," late 18th/early 19th C, minor cracks
. . . . 650.00

Powder Keg, 9-1/4" h, 6-1/4" d, wood, black painted number 56, 3-1/4" h black and white "Oriental Powder Mills" label, 2" "Eastern Sporting FFG Gun Powder," other end with 5" "Oriental Powder Mills Boston FF Western Sporting Powder G" purple and gold label, orig wooden screw plug with slight chips. 500.00

Sign, framed paper

24-1/4" h, 13-3/4" w, Marlin Firearms, two determined hunters in canoe in hot pursuit of pray, © 1907, artist sgd Philip B. Goodwin 1,800.00

24-1/4" h, 15" w, Marlin Rifles and Shotguns, hunting scene with hunter, two shot ducks, © 1908 . . . . .1,600.00

26-1/2" h, 16" w, Ithaca Guns, wild turkey in winter scene, © 1908, artist sgd Louis Agassiz Fuertes 1,800.00

29" h, 15-1/4" w, Winchester, hunter standing tall with his Winchester as ferocious wolves attack, © 1906 . .3,300.00

29" h, 18-3/4" w, Remington Shotgun, oil cloth, flock of ducks landing among decoys at dawn, both Remington Repeating Shotgun and Remington Auto Loading Shotgun pictured, © 1908. . . . . .2,250.00

29-1/4" h, 15" w, UMC Shot Shells, flying covey of quails, © 1908, textured paper 1,100.00

Target Ball, 2-3/4" d, molded amber glass, overall net pattern, bottom with raised sunburst pattern, middle 1/2" band emb "Bogardus Glass Ball Ptd April 10, 1877," chips at neck
. . . . 200.00

FIREARMS

History: The 15th-century Matchlock Arquebus was the forerunner of the modern firearm. The Germans refined the wheelock firing mechanism during the 16th and 17th centuries. English settlers arrived in America with the smoothbore musket; German settlers had rifled arms. Both used the new flintlock firing mechanism.

A major advance was achieved when Whitney introduced interchangeable parts into the manufacturing of rifles. Continued refinements in firearms continued in the 19th century. The percussion ignition system was developed by the 1840s. Minie, a French military officer, produced a viable projectile. By the end of the 19th century cartridge weapons dominated the field.

References: Robert W. D. Ball, *Mauser Military Rifles of the World*, Krause Publications, 1996; ——, *Remington Firearms*, Krause Publications; ——, *Springfield Armory Shoulder Weapons, 1795–1968*, Antique Trader Books, 1997; Ralf Coykendall, Jr., *Coykendall's Complete Guide to Sporting Collectibles*, Wallace-Homestead, 1996; Norman Flayderman, *Flayderman's Guide to Antique American Firearms And Their Values*, 7th ed., Krause Publications, 1998; *Gun Trader's Guide*, 15th ed., Stoeger Publishing, 1992; Herbert G. Houze, *Colt Rifles and Muskets from 1847–1870*, Krause Publications, 1996; ——, *History of Winchester Repeating Arms Company*, Krause Publications, 1994; John Ogle, *Colt Memorabilia Price Guide,* Krause Publications, 1998; Russell and Steve Quertermous, *Modern Guns Identification & Values*, 11th ed., Collector Books, 1997; Ned Schwing, *Browning Superposed*, Krause Publications, 1996; Ned Schwing and Herbert Houze, *Standard Catalog of Firearms*, 7th ed., Krause Publications, 1997; Jim Supica and Richard Nahas, *Standard Catalog of Smith & Wesson*, Krause Publications, 1996; John Taffin, *Big Bore Sixguns*, Krause Publications, 1997; ——, *Modern Custom Guns*, Krause Publications, 1997; Ken Warner (ed.), *Gun Digest 1998,* 52nd ed., Krause Publications, 1997; Frederick Wilkinson, Handguns, New Burlington Books, 1993; A. B. Zhuk, *Illustrated Encyclopedia of Handguns*, Greenhill Books, 1995.

Periodicals: *Gun List*, 700 E State St., Iola, WI 54990; *Gun Report*, P.O. Box 38, Aledo, IL 61231; *Historic Weapons & Relics*, 2650 Palmyra Rd., Palmyra, TN 37142; *Man at Arms*, P.O. Box 460, Lincoln, RI 02865; *Military Trader*, P.O. Box 1050, Dubuque, IA 52004; *Sporting Gun*, P.O. Box 301369, Escondido, CA 92030; *Wildcat Collectors Journal*, 15158 NE 6 Ave., Miami, FL 33162.

Collectors' Clubs: American Society of Military History, Los Angeles Patriotic Hall, 1816 S Figuerora, Los Angeles, CA 90015; Winchester Arms Collectors Association, Inc., P.O. Box 6754, Great Falls, MT 59406.

Museums: Battlefield Military Museum, Gettysburg, PA; National Firearms Museum, Washington, DC; Remington Gun Museum, Ilion, NY; Springfield Armory National Historic Site, Springfield, MA; Winchester Mystery House, Historic Firearms Museum, San Jose, CA.

Notes: Two factors control the pricing of firearms—condition and rarity. Variations in these factors can cause a wide range in the value of antique firearms. For instance, a Colt 1849 pocket-model revolver with a 5-inch barrel can be priced from $100 to $700, depending on whether all the component parts are original, whether some are missing, how much of the original finish (bluing) remains on the barrel and frame, how much silver plating remains on the brass trigger guard and back strap, and the condition and finish of the walnut grips.

Be careful to note a weapon's negative qualities. A Colt Peterson belt revolver in fair condition will command a much higher price than the Colt pocket model in very fine condition. Know the production run of a firearm before buying it.

SPECIAL AUCTION

James D. Julia, Inc.
P.O. Box 830
Fairfield, ME 04937
(207) 453-7125

Cane Gun

Days Pat., percussion, 28" round barrel, brown finish, walnut grip with age cracks, chip on toe, 34-1/2" l 525.00

Derringer

Colt

No. 1, Cal. 41, standard engraved frame, nickel barrel, plain steel frame, 80% nickel on barrel, bare steel frame, 30% case color on hammer 800.00

No. 2, Cal. 41, checkered wood drips, standard engraved frame 500.00

No. 3, Cal. 41, Thieur, last type, nickel plated frame and barrel, walnut grips 375.00

Henry, medium size, Cal. 47, 4" barrel, overall 8-1/4", mkd "Deringer Philadela" on lock and barrel, German silver mounted with ramrods, all mounts engraved, shield shaped thumb pieces inscribed "WBJ," pair. 1,750.00

Colt Model 1851 Navy, engraved to corporal in 15th Kansas Cavalry, $2,750. Photo courtesy of Jackson's Auctioneers & Appraisers.

Marston, William, .32 Cal., three barrel, 4" barrels, bold signature and brass frame, rosewood grips, spots of pitting, 7" l overall 550.00

Mossberg Brownie, Cal. 22, 4 shot, 2-1/2" tip down barrel, serrated wood grip panels, missing ejector pin, fair bores, cracked left grip 95.00

Philadelphia

Early, Cal. 45, 3" barrel stamped "Deringer/Philadel'a," two gold bands at breech and single "P" proof, 6-3/4" overall, scroll engraved lock sgd "Deringer/Philadel'a," well grained walnut stock, engraved silver barrel key plates, side plate, small inlay below nipple bolster, trigger guard and shield shaped wrist escutcheon, lightly engraved German silver butt cup with plain iron cover, ramrod and horn forend cap missing, modern replacement nipple 800.00

Vest Pocket, Cal. 42 Perc, 2-1/2" octagon round barrel with markings on lock and breech, single "P" proof, normal German silver fittings, lightly engraved with checkered butt and grip 950.00

Sharp's Four Barrel, Model 2, Cal. 30, rimfire, medium size, nickel plated brass frame, 2 pc checkered ivory grips, no orig finish, pin does not revolve 350.00

Musket

Confederate, Richmond Armory, Cal. 58, 40" round barrel, three bands, walnut stock, lockplate mkd "CS/Richmond, VA," dated 1863, 1855 type rear sight, iron mounted with brass butt plate 2,000.00

Flagg, B., 1842 Pattern, percussion, Cal. 69, usual 1842 pattern, 42" barrel, usual proofs, lock plate markings with eagle obliterated over "US" with maker's name and address over "1849" behind hammer, three barrel bands, trumpet ramer, rocket bayonet mkd "GL" on flat without scabbard 700.00

Springfield Cadet, Cal. 57 Perc., 1851 dated lock and tang, made for Virginia Military Institute, slim 40" barrel, three bands, iron mounted on walnut stock, bottom bayonet lug, trumpet ramrod, middle band and 2 pc trigger guard fitted with sling swivels, lock and small eagle over "US" ahead of hammer, "Springfield 1851" behind hammer, tan also dated 1851, breech mkd with small "VP" proof and eagle head, left flat with crisp tiny cartouche, orig cadet socket 14-1/4" l bayonet 4,150.00

US Model 1855 Harpers Ferry, Cal. 58, 40" round barrel, three barrel bands, iron mounted, brass nose cap, walnut stock, lockplate dated "1857," long range rear sight, no patch box, dark brown uncleaned patina on all metal parts, medium to heavy pitting hear breech 2,000.00

Winchester Low Wall Winder, Cal. 22 short, regular musket configuration, 28" barrel, ramp front sight, no barrel sight, receiver with Lyman side mount sight, full length wood forestock, military style butt stock, marked "US" and flaming bomb on top tang, 93-94% barrel blue turning plum, scattered surface rust, thinning near muzzle, some heavier pitting at muzzle, stock with pinned wrist, normal handling and use marks, strong bore 330.00

Pepperbox

Allen & Thurber, Worcester
Dragoon, Cal. 36, 6" barrel group, ribbed, long curved grip, trigger guard made without second finger spur, engraved frame, engraved nipple shield, 1845 date on hammer, no finish, overall dark gray/black with scattered light pitting and discolorations, one nipple missing, trigger guard needs re-securing, orig grips. 300.00
6-shot, Cal. 31, 4-3/4" barrel group, Norwich style engraved frame, engraved nipple shield, silver spangled grips, cased in orig mahogany Allen case, cylindrical plunger flask mkd "J. Camm" on top, orig accessories 1,050.00

Robbins & Lawrence, Cal. 31, 5-shot, mkd Leonard's patent 1848, ring trigger, concealed hammer, 2-pc rosewood grips, engraved frame and barrels, traces of factory finish, light pitting in small areas 550.00

Spies, A. W., Cal. 31, 3-3/4" barrel, engraved frame, narrow ribs on barrel, 1837 patent barrel, mkd "Allen" ring trigger, shield-less, light gray to black engraved frame, engraving on left side, 75% on right side, hammer markings clear, no finish on barrels, light speckling and dings, grips and spangles intact, right grip with 17 notches cut in it, no finish on grips, mechanically fine. 350.00

Stocking & Co., Worcester, Cal. 31, 4" barrel group with ribs, engraved frame, second finger spur on trigger guard, rounded spangled walnut rips, worn overall, no finish remaining, light to medium pitting on nipple shield, mottled medium gray barrels, bright steel frame, clear hammer and barrel markings 450.00

Percussion rifle

Half stock, curly maple, refinished, gold curl, brass butt plate, nickel silver inlays, and patchbox, restoration with replacements, 50-1/2" l 400.00

Half stock, walnut stock, beaver tail cheek piece, engraved German silver cap box with squirrel and eagle, 30" octagonal barrel with silver bands, hook breech with bright finish, 48" l 1,550.00

Half stock, walnut stock, 36" barrel, brass hardware, Golcher lock, stock has been varnished, minor age cracks, 53-1/2" l 350.00

Pistol, flintlock

Danish, Revolutionary War Period, Calvary, 10-3/4" barrel, Danish proof at breech, brass blade sight, relief carved walnut stock, heavy cast brass furniture, ramrod assembly with swivel and iron swivel mounted to butt cap, large convex banana shaped flintlock. 1,550.00

European, walnut stock, brass hardware, horn nose cap, 8-1/4" octagonal to round barrel, dark surface with pitting, lock bolts stripped, 13-1/2" l 330.00

US Model 1819, contract by Simeon North, dated 1821, Cal. 54, 10" round barrel with swivel ramrod, iron furniture, walnut stock, markings clear, cleaned, minor pitting, orig flintlock 1,200.00

US Model 1836, contract by Robert Johnson, dated 1838 on lock plate, Cal. 54, 8-1/2" round barrel, iron mounted, walnut stock, dark gray uncleaned patina, minor pitting, double

stamped on lock plate, visible inspector's cartouche on stock, orig flintlock 1,050.00

US Model 1837, contract by Asa Waters, dated 1837, Cal. 54, 8-1/2" round barrel, iron furniture, walnut stuck, light peppery pitting near breech, clear inspector's cartouches . . .1,500.00

Pistol, percussion

Allen & Thurber Grafton Tubehammer, Cal. 38, 2-5/8" round/octagon barrel, engraved frame, sharp drop grip with spangles, mkd "cast sleeve/warrented" on one barrel flat, "pocket rifle" on next flat, "Allen & Thurber" on next flat, "Grafton, Mass," on next flat, and "P. M.E.A. 183" on another, mkd "Allens Patent" on side plate, no finish, cleaned bright overall, light pitting and metal deterioration lightly scattered 1,400.00

Allen & Wheelock
Double Barrel, 2-shot, Cal. 34, 3-1/8" barrel, two hammer single trigger system, 40% faded blue on barrels, traces of blue on frame, right grip replaced 300.00

Single Shot, medium frame, orig Allen combination mold/wrench, Cal. 36, 3" round/octagon barrel mkd "Allen & Wheelock" on top flat, standard engraved frame, walnut grips, one handle is octagonal barrel wrench, no finish, steel gray metal with mottled brown, 75% varnish grips. . 200.00

Stocking & Co., Worcester, MA, single shot, Cal. 34, 4-1/8" round/octagon barrel, engraved frame, single action hammer with spur, walnut grips, excellent barrel and hammer markings, gray barrel with some light dark pitting at muzzle, cleaned gray frame, overall speckled pitting, orig grips, 40% varnish 200.00

Pistol, semi-auto

Astra Cub, Cal. 22 short, tiny pocket model, full coverage factory arabesque engraving pattern, silver plated, artificial pearl grips, spare mag and orig owner's manual 150.00

High Standard Model, HD Military, Cal. 22 LR, blued finish, 6-3/4" barrel, adjustable sights, full checkered walnut grips, Lt. Col., insignia stuck on left grip 225.00

Revolver

Allen & Wheelock
Belt Model, lip fire, converted to rimfire, Cal. 32, 5-7/8" barrel, no blue remaining except on striker level which is 50%, rest gray steel, with metal surfaces fairly good, 80% varnish on grips, mechanically fine 400.00

.25 lip fire, Cal., 25, 3" barrel, no markings, blue finish overall, nicely figured walnut grips, 80% orig bright blue barrel, 25% on cylinder, balance flaked brown, 15-20% on frame, balance flaked, grips with 80% varnish, mechanically fine 300.00

32 side hammer, Cal. 32, 4" barrel, brass frame, traces of silver, replaced cylinder pin, bare stele barrel, weak cylinder scene, no finished on cylinder, 85% orig varnish on grips, mechanically fine 300.00

Colt
Army Special, Cal. 38, regular configuration, 6" barrel, blued finish, black Colt composition grips, orig hinged lid maroon box and instruction sheet 300.00

Detective Special, Cal. 28 Spel., nickel finish, 2" bbl with reproduction stag grips, Tyler grip adapter 200.00

Model 1851 Navy, Cal. 36, six shot, 7-1/2" barrel, brass back strap and trigger guard, "US" marked on left side of frame, cleaned with areas of light pitting, 20% seam remains on cylinder, worn grips 1,250.00

Model 1851 Navy, Cal. 36, Perc., 4-screw, scarce shoulder stock model, extended screws each side of receiver, iron trigger guard, back strap with small swivel installed just to front of trigger guard, 1 pc wood grips 1,200.00

Model 1860 Army, Cal. 44, Perc, 8" round barrel, three screw frame, brass trigger guard, 1 pc walnut grips, no orig finish, dark gray patina overall, 50% cylinder scene, mechanically sound 1,600.00

Police Positive Flattop Target, Cal. 22, small frame, 6" barrel, adjustable front and rear sights, checkered medallion wood grips, checkered trigger and back strap, 94-96% strong blue, thin and turning at muzzle, grip frame and sharp edges, moderate wear to sound grips, bright bore 350.00

Ethan Allen & Co.

Lip Fire, Cal. 32, 5" barrel, full silver plate finish, 75% silver finish, 90% clear markings, 40% varnish on grips, inoperable cylinder stop 475.00

Side Hammer, Cal. 32, last variety, 3-7/8" octagon barrel mkd on top flat, no cylinder engraving, iron frame, walnut grips, traces of blue in protected areas, balance turned mottled gray/brown, orig grips, 75% varnish, hammer with 50% case colors, mechanically fine 200.00

Moore, Belt Model, Cal. 32, RF, blued finish, engraved brass silver plated frame, trigger guard with back strap, 1 pc varnished walnut grips complete with ejector rod, traces of finish on barrel, 40-50% thinning blue on cylinder, 75-80% silver plate on brass, most varnish finish on wood, excellent bore 600.00

Rogers & Spencer

Army, Cal. 44, 7-1/2" barrel, military inspected, excellent grips with triangular repair to toe of right grip, excellent cartouche, 25% bright blue, balance thin blue/gray to brown, mechanically excellent, apparently unfired 1,200.00

Percussion, Cal. 44, all matching serial numbers, 7-1/2" octagonal barrel, 2 pc walnut grips, sharp US Inspector's marks, 40% bright factory blue remains. 1,200.00

US Military, Cal. 44, Perc, 7-1/2" barrel, military inspected, dings and small areas of pitting, 50% blue overall, no finish on cylinder, grips not original, mechanically fine . . . 800.00

Ruger Bearcat, single action, Cal. 22, standard configuration, blued finish, brass coated trigger guard, 2 pc varnished wood grips, orig box and papers 300.00

Smith & Wesson

M28-2 Highway Patrolman DA, Cal.357 Mag., blued finish, 4" barrel, adjustable sights and checkered medallion walnut grips, strong orig finish. 175.00

No 1-1/2 Spur Trigger, Cal. 32, nickel finished, 3" ribbed barrel, half moon sight, black composition logo grips, orig green cloth cov hinged lid box 400.00

Star Number 38, Prescott Pistol Co., Hatfield, MA, Cal. 38, 2-7/8" octagon barrel, marked only with star and "No. 38" on top strap, wood grips color of walnut but with tight dark grain, nickel finish, case colored hammer, orig black label picture box, 60% nickel on barrel, 85% on brass frame, 40% cylinder, 70% case colors on hammer, excellent grips, 95% varnish, one ding, mechanically fine 625.00

Rifle

Ballard Single Shot, Sporting, Cal. 22, 22-1/2" octagonal barrel, iron frame, ring style lever, walnut stocks with iron butt plate, 90% factory blue barrel, orig varnish on stock, excellent bore 1,700.00

Jenks Mule Ear Navy, Cal. 54 Perc., 30" round barrel, three brass bands, bayonet lug at bottom of muzzle, lock with Ames and Jenks marks, mkd on breech with usual marks, dated 1844, full length wood stock 2,500.00

Kimber Model 82 Bolt Action, Cal. 22 LR, early model, 22" tapered round barrel, straight grain checkered 1 pc stock, 13-5/8" over a flat checkered steel butt plate, grooved receiver and 5-shot mag. 475.00

Marine Corps 1903 Sniper, Cal. 30-06, Regulation 1903, scope blocks mounted to barrel and rear sight, barrel markings "SA/5-21," mounted with Lyman 48 receiver sight with bright bolt and rails, straight grip stock cartouche "WJS," with "T" in cutoff recess, Unertl 8X scope mkd "USMC-Sniper," military mounts, white paint on target knobs, clean smooth wood, 97-98% gray/black parkerizing thin over front barrel area, muzzle recrowned during period of use, brilliant bore, excellent optics 2,600.00

Remington

Flintlock, barreled full stock, Bedford County, KY, type, Cal. 50, 39" octagon barrel mkd on top flat "Remington," stepped lock plate with teardrop at back, lightly engraved with name "Spencer/Stafford/Warranted," recent reconversion using nice period hammer and older parts, full length curly maple stock secured with three oval head wedges, brass furniture including three ramrod guides, nose cap, trigger guard, butt plate, pierced plain patchbox, release on toe tiny beavertail push, full iron sideplate secured with three wood screws, two lockplate screws 1,500.00

Military, Rolling Block, Cal. 58 center fire, 39" round barrel with M1864 type rear sight, three iron bands on walnut stock, unmarked except for Remington name and patent data on tang, manuf utilizing altered Civil War musket stock, bayonet standard cal. 58 triangular socket, mkd "US," light to medium overall pitting, heavy patches on frame and butt plate, missing ramrod, stock heavily worn, worm damage on end 450.00

Model 1867 Navy Cadet, rolling block, 32-1/2" round barrel, .50/45 center fire cadet cal., right side of frame mkd "P/F.C.W.," left side frame mkd with anchor stamp, Remington patent info on tang, butt plate stamped "U.S." with rack No. 158, right side of butt stock stamped "B/103," single leaf Springfield musket type rear site, knurled slotted ramrod, two barrel bands with retaining springs on black walnut stock, lightly cleaned, light gray patina, clean sharp bore, hammer and block blued .2,100.00

Model 1903A3 Military, Cal. 30-06, regular 03A3 configuration, barrel marking "RA/9-43" and various cartouches, old military sling, pristine condition, new, unfired, very minor handling and storage, some roughness, couple of bruises to handguard and forend top 400.00

Model 1917 Military, Cal. 30-06, barrel mkd "R/9-18," regular 1917 configuration, bright blued metal, British proofed Remington bayonet with green leather scabbard and leather sling 400.00

Springfield

Air Force M-1 Garand Match, Cal. 30-06, National Match configuration, "NM" marked sights, op-roc, barrel and gas cylinder, glass bedded stock, barrel dated "4-63," Air Force paperwork 950.00

M-1 Garand, Cal. 30-06, usual configuration, barrel dated "6-43," early battled sight, small wheeled "EM c F" cartouche, "114" at left toe, 90-99% dark green parkerizing, thin gas tube, dark oiled wood, bright shiny bore 750.00

M-1 Gas Trap Garand, Cal. 30-06, early configuration, all numbered parts including wood, replacement gas trap, barrel, cylinder, sight, plug, ferrule, follower rod and springs, early stock without butt trap and checkered steel butt plate inspected "SPG," 96-98% orig gray/green parkerizing, restored finish to wood, pins through wrist 1,750.00

Winchester Model 677, single shot, Cal. 22, normal Model 67 with smooth stock, never fitted with signs, mounted with target scope blocks on barrel, British proofed with British military broad arrow marking, nickeled bolt, no serial no., 98-99% orig barrel blue, solid wood showing light handling and use marks, filled knot bottom of forearm, bright shiny bore 775.00

Shotgun

Browning, pre-war GR-1, Over-Under, Cal. 20 ga., long tang, round knob model with 26-1/2" barrels, imp cyl/mod, narrow vent rib, checkered round forearm and round knob grip, 14" over a Pachmayr pad, single trigger and ejectors . . . 600.00

Daly, Charles, Over-Under, Cal. 28 ga., early Browning infringement model, 26" barrels, choked Skeet/Skeet, checkered rounded forearm and round knob painted grip stock 15" over black composition butt plate, single selective trigger and ejectors, 97-99% orig blue on barrels, sound clean wood with 2 bruises to forearm checkering, few light handling and use marks 650.00

Winchester Model 1887, lever action, Cal. 10 ga., regular configuration, 32" steel barrel, wood forestock panels, semi-pistol grip stock, refinished wood, replaced tang screw, butt plate missing 325.00

FIREHOUSE COLLECTIBLES

History: The volunteer fire company has played a vital role in the protection and social growth of many towns and rural areas. Paid professional firemen usually are found only in large metropolitan areas. Each fire company prided itself on equipment and uniforms. Conventions and parades gave the fire companies a chance to show off their equipment. These events produced a wealth of firehouse-related memorabilia.

References: Andrew G. Gurka, *Hot Stuff! Firefighting Collectibles*, L-W Book Sales, 1994; James Piatti, *Firehouse Memorabilia: Identification and Price Guide*, Avon Books, 1994; Donald F. Wood and Wayne Sorensen, *American Volunteer Fire Trucks*, Krause Publications, 199_; --. *Big City Fire Trucks, 1900-1950*, Krause Publications, 1996 (Volume I), 1997 (Volume II).

Periodical: *Fire Apparatus Journal*, P.O. Box 141295, Staten Island, NY 10314.

Collectors' Clubs: Antique Fire Apparatus Club of America, 5420 S Kedvale Ave., Chicago, IL 60632; Fire Collectors Club, P.O. Box 992, Milwaukee, WI 53201; Fire Mark Circle of the Americas, 2859 Marlin Dr., Chamblee, GA 30341; Great Lakes International Antique Fire Apparatus Association, 4457 285th St., Toledo, OH 43611; International Fire Buff Associationiates, Inc., 7509 Chesapeake Ave., Baltimore, MD 21219; International Fire Photographers Association, P.O. Box 8337, Rolling Meadows, IL 60008; Society for the Preservation & Appreciation of Motor Fire Apparatus in America, P.O. Box 2005, Syracuse, NY 13320.

Museums: American Museum of Fire Fighting, Corton Falls, NY; Fire Museum of Maryland, Lutherville, MD; Hall of Flame, Scottsdale, AZ; Insurance Company of North America (INA) Museum, Philadelphia, PA; New England Fire & History Museum, Brewster, MA; New York City Fire Museum, New York, NY; Oklahoma State Fireman's Association Museum, Oklahoma City, OK; San Francisco Fire Dept. Memorial Museum, San Francisco, CA.

Additional Listings: See *Warman's Americana & Collectibles* for more examples.

Alarm Box
    Gamewell Excelsior, cast iron, code wheel and number plate telegraph door, orig weathered paint 300.00
    Utica Fire Alarm and Telegraph, telegraph door 500.00
Alarm Gong
    Star Electric, Binghamton, NY, fancy case with star on top, 12" 1,800.00
    US Fire and Police Telegraph, maple ""Moses Crane" case, fig leaf finial, 8" 1,250.00
Badge
    Eureka Fire Co., bronze luster, metal link, "Compliments of Eureka Fire House Co., N.Y.," pendent rimmed in coiled hose design, center eagle, "Eureka/Paragon/Red Cross," early 1900s 40.00
    Union Hose Co., bright silver luster brass, also inscribed "Annville, PA," fire symbols of primitive pumper, hook and ladder, c1930s 25.00
Bell, American La France, 700 series type base, eagle finial, orig, 12" 550.00
Belt, leather
    32" l, brass trim "Old Town," one side painted white, buckle stamped "Dirigo No. 1," some paint flaking 150.00
    48" l, brown leather, applied brass "2nd Assistant," large "2" by buckle, wear 100.00
Catalog, Daly & Bryan, Boston, MA, 1886, 26 pgs, 4-1/2" x 6-1/4", "Illustrated Catalog & Price List of Firemen's Equipment," 19 illustrations 135.00
Charm, Cracker Jack, fire pumper, dark silver flashing over white metal, 1930s 30.00
Extinguisher, foam type, 2-1/2 gal
    Ahrens Fox 215.00
    Mack, nickel and glass 175.00
Fire Bucket, 12-3/4" h, leather, painted "Benj. Pitman 1830" on scrolling banner design, painted in black and yellow, green ground, break and losses t handle, paint loss 460.00
Fire Wagon Lantern, 23-1/4" h, nickel plated, mkd "DeVoursney Bros. makers 389 Broome St. New York," acid etched and engraved blue, red, and clear glass panels showing fire fighting equipment, geometric and foliate device, and "Prospect 4," removable oil font 1,725.00
Hat, 13" x 11-3/4" x 6", leather, top hat style, black paint, gold writing on front "Good Will 1802," back with "G.W.," top with "T.M.S.," number "15734" on brim, piece missing from brim 2,750.00
Helmet, 13" l, leather, worn black paint, gilded eagle, shield missing, battered 150.00
Horn
    17" h, brass, painted red int., inscribed "From Mrs. PH Bowman to GP Mason" 500.00
    17" h, brass, plain 450.00
    18" h, silverplated, inscribed "Presented to EB Ackerman of Lafayette Co. No. 1" 700.00
    23" h, silverplated, repousse flowers, unsigned 700.00
Hose Nozzle, 19-1/2" l, "Chief" model, two man type, Elkhart Brass Mfg. Co., professionally restored 150.00
Lapel Stud, York Fire Co., blue and white celluloid, bull head image, "Vigilient S & C F. E. Co. No. 1," metal lapel stud, late 1890s/early 1900s 25.00

Pinback Button

Martin Fire Engine, blue and white, adv "Martin Carriage Works," York, PA, c1920 . . . . 25.00

Pioneer Hose Co. Fire Engine, black and white real photo, American-LaFrance engine, Robesonia, Pennsylvania, Oct 25, 1924 . . . . 50.00

York County Building, sepia real photo of "Royal Fire Co. No. 6," 1900s 30.00

Poster, 22" x 27", Fire! Fire! Fire!, "Chicago Lost But J. Dearman of Knoxville, Penna. Continues to Roll Up, Bundle Up, and Box Up As Many Goods As Ever!" red and black, some replacement to border, Oct 15th, 1871 . . . . 225.00

Print, lithograph with hand-coloring, "The American Fireman, Rushing to the Conflict," Currier and Ives, Louis Maurer lithographer, 1858, identified in inscriptions in matrix, 22-1/2" x 17-1/4" sheet size, framed 700.00

Ribbon, convention, brass scroll, 1922, San Francisco Fire Chiefs, hanging blue glove fire lantern 195.00

Shot Glass, 2-3/4" h, silver plated, fire bucket shape, Gorham Co., white badge with ladder, and fire hydrant, blue lettering "Little Giant Engine Company 1871, Chicago Fire Department" 150.00

Siren, hand crank, sterling silver, orig mounting bracket 450.00

Stereocard, The Summer St. Fire, Boston, Mass, Nov. 9 & 10, 1872, shows rubble of burned out buildings, people . . 25.00

Toy, cast iron

Fire Patrol Wagon, 16" l, red and yellow wagon, driver missing leg, seat missing, horse, poor paint, some rust 275.00

Fire Patrol Wagon, 17" x 7", three horses, bell on chassis, orig fireman and driver, blue paint, red trim, some paint loss to figures 750.00

Fire Pumper, 11-1/2" l, 4-1/2" h, two horses, yellow metal spoked wheels, overall paint loss 75.00

Fire Truck, 6-1/2" l, driver, worn red paint, replaced wheels, Kenton 100.00

Fire Wagon, 15" l, red paint, yellow wheels, orig figures and horses, two ladders, Dent 150.00

Ladder Wagon, 21" l, red and yellow painted wagon, ladders missing, non-matching nickel plated figure at rear, painted three horse team 100.00

Ladder Wagon, 30" l, horse-drawn, red and white painted wagon, one complete and one broken ladder, two repainted figures, horse painted black and white, Hubley 100.00

Toy, tin, ladder truck, four tin firemen, hard rubber wheels, Gunthermann, 14" x 5" 200.00

Watch Fob, double sided cello, York County Convention, Red Lion, Pennsylvania, Sept. 4, 1916, red lettered inscription, black and white firehouse, red, white, and blue US flat at top, back with tinted color image of woman in showgirl outfit, dark brown background 35.00

FIREPLACE EQUIPMENT

History: In the colonial home, the fireplace was the gathering point for heat, meals, and social interaction. It maintained its dominant position until the introduction of central heating in the mid-19th century.

Because of the continued popularity of the fireplace, accessories still are manufactured, usually in an early-American motif.

References: Rupert Gentle and Rachael Feild, *Domestic Metalwork 1640-1820*, Revised, Antique Collectors' Club, 1994; George C. Neumann, *Early American Antique Country Furnishings*, L-W Book Sales, 1984, 1993 reprint.

REPRODUCTION ALERT

Modern blacksmiths are reproducing many old iron implements.

Additional Listings: Brass; Ironware.

Andirons, pr

13-1/8" h, brass, figural dolphins, minor loss to one dog 2,520.00

15" h, brass, lemon top, iron knife blade, penny feet, America, late 19th C 550.00

17" h, brass, belted ball top, John Hunneman, Boston, c1800, mkd "Hunneman," minor cracks 1,380.00

18-1/2" h, brass, double lemon top 500.00

19-1/2" h, brass, belted ball top, America, c1800, repair to one dog 920.00

20-1/2" h, cast iron, figural Hessian soldiers 250.00

22" h, steel and brass, knife blade, brass urn-form finials, penny feet 450.00

23" h, brass and wrought iron, flame and chamfered ball-top, knife bade, American, third quarter 18th C, corrosion, very minor loss to penny feet .2,185.00

23-1/2" h, Chippendale, double urn top, acorn finial, matching log stops, replaced dogs 750.00

25-1/2" h, brass, double lemon top, attributed to New York, early 19th C 1,500.00

28" h, Neoclassical, urn finials, early 19th C, small casting hole in one 990.00

Bellows

17-1/2" l, turtle back, orig mustard paint, green leaves, red applies, green highlights, crack to front wood, leather brittle 100.00

18" l, paint dec, new leather strap to handle 85.00

22" l, 8" w, center carved with two-masted ship, handle with anchor and chain, leather deteriorated 100.00

Chenet, 40" l, Louis XVI-style, gilt and patinated bronze, mounted with two bacchanalian putti, fender and base molded with foliate, late 19th C 3,150.00

Chimney Cover, 12" h, oval, marked "Compliments of C. D. Denny Co., Kaufmann & Strauss Co., N. Y. 1058," metal cover with picture of two little girls having tea party in lush spring garden, large bunny seated at table, eight smaller bunnies on ground, doll lying under table. gold border 210.00

Clock Jack, 19" h, brass, cast iron rotating wheel for roasting small game, replaced key, working 715.00

Coal Box, 12" w, 12" d, 13" h, copper, emb laurel wreath dec 150.00

Coal Grate, 32" w, 17" d, 38-1/2" h, bell metal, rect basket, cast iron back plate, dancing maidens ornament, pierced front skirt, surmounted by urns, straight tapered legs, spade feet, George III, late 18th C 315.00

Crane, 41" h, 39" w, wrought iron, attached kettle tilter, scrolled detail, pitted and rust damage 615.00

Fender

36-1/2" w, 12" d, 13-3/4" h, steel and brass, brass ball feet and finials, wire grill 550.00

37-1/4" w, 24-1/4" h, brass and wire, English, early 19th C 1,200.00

43" l, 13" d, 11-1/2" h, brass, reticulated grill, paw feet 275.00

44" l, 16" d, 3" h, hammered copper, repousse stylized floral motif, Arts & Crafts style, cleaned orig patina 450.00

48" l, brass, rope twist rails 175.00

Andirons, pr, bronze, top surmounted by full length putti, tripod plinth, ram's head and satyr supports, base with inverted griffin supports, center allegorical figure flanked by putti, mid 19th C, 36" h, $4,375. Photo courtesy of Freeman\Fine Arts of Philadelphia, Inc.

51-1/4" l, pierced brass, English, 19th C, minor dents and losses. 250.00

52-3/4" l, pierced brass and sheet metal, applied ribbed banding, center engraved grape leaf and foliate design, English, 19th C. 375.00

57" w, 19" d, 12" h, serpentine, steel and wire, brass top rail, some battering and damage 1,210.00

Fire Back, 21-3/4" w, 27" h, cast iron, curved crest with cherubs and garlands, heat damage, crack in base 125.00

Fire Board, 22-3/4 x 36-1/4", painted, geometric blue, yellow, green, sienna, black, and white pattern, American, 19th C 2,000.00

Fireplace Set, gilt bronze, pr andirons, matching set of tools, ornate winged sphinx heads, Egyptian Revival. 2,760.00

Fireplace Tool Set

25" l, shovel and tongs, matching brass handles 220.00

29-1/4" h, five mismatched tools, steel and brass, stone base, two tongs, shovel, poker, and stand 110.00

31" l, pair of tongs, matching shovel, brass and iron, paneled steeple top, attributed to New York, early 19th C . . 575.00

Firescreen

26-1/4" w, 13" d, 40-3/4" h, Classical, mid Atlantic states, 1815-25, tiger maple and mahogany veneer, rolled crest about silk textile panel flanked by veneered columns, brass capitals and bases, arched feet. 1,610.00

48" h, rosewood and needlework, Renaissance Revival, c1875 . . . . 575.00

Hearth Fork, 15-1/4" l, wrought steel, engraved geometric design, late 18th C 115.00

Mantle Set, china clock and garniture urns, ormolu turned and gilt dec, ivory ground, white reserves with polychrome scenes, enameled face, brass works mkd "Tiffany & Co. New York," no key or pendulum, minor damage, 12" h . .1,210.00

60-1/2" h, classical, mahogany, brass inlay, veneered surface, turned finial, turned and reeded column, ormolu trim,

adjustable oval screen with painting of urn on silk, trefoil base, carved paw feet, some damage to veneer . . . 770.00

Steelyard, 37" l, brass inlay, brass weight. 330.00

Surround, white marble, carved

Baroque Style, rect mantel over stepped leaf carved arched opening, flanked on either side by male and female leaf-carved terminals, central putti supporting cartouche 6,325.00

Rococo Style, serpentine mantel, central carved cartouche issuing carved foliage and C-scrolls continuing to side supports, slip with urn, floral and rope carving 3,163.00

Tinder Lighter, 7" l, flint lock, wooden pistol grip, engraved and cast detail 500.00

Trammel, wrought iron, sawtooth, simple tooling, "B.S. 1781," adjusts from 36" 165.00

FISCHER CHINA

FISCHER J. BUDAPEST.

History: In 1893, Moritz Fischer founded his factory in Herend, Hungary, a center of porcelain production since the 1790s.

Confusion exists about Fischer china because of its resemblance to Meissen, Sevres, and Oriental export wares. It often was bought and sold as the product of these firms.

Fischer's Herend is hard-paste ware with luminosity and exquisite decoration. Pieces are designated by pattern names, the best known being Chantilly Fruit, Rothschild Bird, Chinese Bouquet, Victoria Butterfly, and Parsley.

Fischer also made figural birds and animal groups, Magyar figures (individually and in groups), and Herend eagles poised for flight.

Museum: Victoria & Albert Museum, London, England.

Marks: Forged marks of other potteries are found on Herend pieces. The initials "MF," often joined together, is the mark of Moritz Fischer's pottery.

Ewer, 15-3/4" h, multicolored florals with gold trim, long spout and handle 375.00

Figures, bisque, pair, 18th C garb, mkd "M. F." 250.00

Jug, 10-3/4" h, Oriental style multicolored florals, butterflies, and fans, gold outlines 200.00

Planter, 19" w, painted green and brown flowerheads, cream ground, green and brown reticulated raised diamonds around base, blue "J. Fischer, Budapest" mark 1,650.00

Plaque, 11-1/2" h, 8-1/4" l, seated lady, wearing 18th C costume, low-cut bodice, rose in one hand, table with open book and glove by side, two figures in distance in formal garden setting, script title "Mondespan C Netscher, Dresden Museum," imp "CF" for Christian Fischer, c1860-80, framed. 8,500.00

Plate, 9-1/2" d, reticulated, gold, rose, and turquoise medallions, marked "Budapest, Hungary" price for pr 350.00

Puzzle Jug, 13" h, brown transfer of three gentlemen, polychrome and gilt accents, marked "Fischer, Budapest" 175.00

Vase, 13" h, moon flask shape, two loop handles, Iznik design, red flowerheads and green vines, cream ground, gold brocade ground on sides, base, and handles, mkd "Fischer, J., Budapest," c1882 . . . . 850.00

FITZHUGH

History: Fitzhugh, one of the most-recognized Chinese Export porcelain patterns, was named for the Fitzhugh family for whom the first dinner service was made. The peak years of production were 1780 to 1850.

Fitzhugh features an oval center medallion or monogram surrounded by four groups of flowers or emblems. The border is similar to that on Nanking china. Occasional border variations are found. Butterfly and honeycomb are among the rarest.

REPRODUCTION ALERT

Spode Porcelain Company, England, and Vista Alegre, Portugal, currently are producing copies of the Fitzhugh pattern. Oriental copies also are available.

Notes: Color is a key factor in pricing. Blue is the most common color; rarer colors are ranked in the following ascending order: orange, green, sepia, mulberry, yellow, black, and gold. Combinations of colors are scarce.

Bowl, 10-1/2" d, scalloped edge, blue and white 2,20.00
Cider Jug, cov, 11 1/2" h, underglaze blue, 19th C. . . .2,500.00
Hot Water Dish, 10 5/8" d, underglaze blue, center pine cone and beast medallion, four clusters of flowers and precious objects in trellis diaper border, spearhead and dumbbell border, blue spouts, c1840 . . . . 450.00
Plate, 9" d, green, 19th C, chips, gilt wear, price for nine pc set 1,150.00
Platter, oval, brown, monogrammed, pr 3,335.00
Punch Bowl, 11" d, white underglaze blue, Fitzhugh border, famille rose floral sprays and shield shaped cartouche, monogram, scalloped rim, restoration 500.00
Salt, 4" l, oval, underglaze blue, center pine cone and beast medallion, four clusters of flowers and precious objects spearhead and dumbbell border, ruffled rim, Mared pattern border, feathered edge, fluted sides, c1820, price for pr . . .1,450.00
Serving Dish, ogee-shaped, crest of the Manigault family of Charleston, SC. 7,765.00
Tureen, 14" l, underglaze blue dec, braided handles, restored pineapple knop finial. 1,400.00
Vegetable Dish, 9-1/2" w, 8-1/4" h, 2" h, blue and white 110.00

FLASKS

History: A flask, which usually has a narrow neck, is a container for liquids. Early American glass companies frequently formed them in molds which left a relief design on the front and/or back. Historical flasks with a portrait, building, scene, or name are the most desirable.

A chestnut is hand-blown, small, and has a flattened bulbous body. The pitkin has a blown globular body with a spiral rib overlay on vertical ribs. Teardrop flasks are generally fiddle-shaped and have a scroll or geometric design.

References: Gary Baker et al., *Wheeling Glass 1829-1939*, Oglebay Institute, 1994, distributed by Antique Publications; Ralph and Terry Kovel, *Kovels' Bottles Price List*, 10th ed., Crown Publishers, 1996; George L.

and Helen McKearin, *American Glass*, Crown Publishers, 1941 and 1948; John Odell, *Digger Odell's Official Antique Bottle and Glass Collector Magazine Price Guide Series*, Vol. 3, published by author (1910 Shawhan Rd, Morrow, OH 45152), 1995; Michael Polak, Bottles, Avon Books, 1994; Kenneth Wilson, *American Glass 1760-1930*, 2 vols., Hudson Hills Press and The Toledo Museum of Art, 1994.

Periodical: *Antique Bottle & Glass Collector*, P.O. Box 187, East Greenville, PA 18041.

Collectors' Clubs: Federation of Historical Bottle Clubs, 88 Sweetbriar Branch, Longwood, FL 32750; The National Early American Glass Club, P.O. Box 8489, Silver Spring, MD 20907.

Notes: Dimensions can differ for the same flask because of variations in the molding process. Color is important in determining value—aqua and amber are the most common colors; scarcer colors demand more money. Bottles with "sickness," an opalescent scaling which eliminates clarity, are worth much less.

SPECIAL AUCTION

Norman C. Heckler & Company
Bradford Corner Rd.
Woodstock Valley, CT 06282

Ceramic, Bennington-type, book shape, glazed, chips

5" h, Comin thro the Rye. 175.00
5-3/4" h, History of Holland 175.00
7" h, History of Burbon County, blue glaze 225.00

Chestnut

5-1/8" h, citron, half pint, fifteen vertical ribs, attributed to OH maker 675.00
6" h, cobalt blue, eighteen swirled ribs 715.00
10" h, Germany, 1650-1700, freeblown, olive yellow, sheared mouth, applied decorated string rim, smooth base . . 325.00

Historical

Baltimore Monument-Sloop, Baltimore Glass Works, Baltimore, MD, 1840-60, light yellow with olive tone, sheared mouth, pontil scar, half pint, some ext. high point wear and scratches 2,100.00
Clasped Hands-Cannon, Pittsburgh district, Pittsburgh, PA 1860-80
   Aquamarine, applied collared mouth with ring, smooth base, pint, McKearin GXII-41, some minor int. haze 70.00
   Golden yellow, applied collared mouth with ring, smooth base, pint, McKearin GXII-41, some minor ex. Scratches below cannon, 1/8" chip on top of mouth 300.00
Eagle, pint, blown
   Deep olive green, double eagle and "Pittsburgh, PA" in oval, broken blister on lip, some other surface chips, small star at stone 125.00
   Green, McKearin GII-64, minor rim chip. 750.00

Eagle-Cornucopia, attributed to Keene Marlboro Street Glassworks, Keene, NH, 1830-50
Bright aquamarine with bluish bone, sheared mouth, pontil scar, pint, McKearin GII-74 . . . . 140.00
Emerald green, sheared mouth, pontil scar, pint, McKearin GII-74, pinhead sized flake on top of mouth, two 3/8" potstone cracks 210.00
Pale aquamarine, sheared mouth, pontil scar, pint, McKearin GII-72, some minor int. stain near base 130.00
Yellowish olive amber, sheared mouth, pontil scar, pint, McKearin GII-72 . . . . 150.00
Eagle-Westford Glass Co., Westford Glass Co., Westford, CT, 1860-73, bright medium reddish amber, malformed applied double collared mouth, smooth base, half pint, McKearin GII-65 . . . . 120.00
Horse and Cart-Eagle, Coventry Glass Works, Coventry, CT, 1830-48, bright light yellow amber with olive tone, sheared mouth, pontil scar, pint, McKearin GV-9 . . . . 170.00
Lowell/Railroad-Eagle, Coventry Glass Works, Coventry, CT, 1830-48, yellow amber with olive tone, sheared mouth, pontil scar, half pint, McKearin GV-10, some minor ext. highlight wear, lettered emb weak 170.00
Masonic-Eagle, Keene Marlboro Street Glassworks, Keene, NH, 1815-30, deep bluish aquamarine, shared mouth, pontil scar, pint, McKearin GIV-27 . . . . 275.00
Masonic-Eagle, New England, possibly CT glasshouse, 1815-30, brilliant aquamarine, inward rolled mouth, pontil scar, pint, McKearin GIV-16 . . . . .3,000.00
Masonic-Eagle, White Glass Works, Zanesville, OH, 1820-30
Light blue green, sheared mouth, pontil scar, pint, McKearin GIV-32 . . . . 325.00
Light yellow amber, sheared mouth, pontil scar, pint, McKearin GIV-32, shallow bubble burst on left column of Masonic emblem 500.00
Masonic-NEG Eagle, attributed to New England Glass Bottle Co., Cambridge, MA, 1820-30, deep greenish aquamarine, sheared mouth, ground pontil, half pint, McKearin GIV-26 . . . . .1,200.00
Seeing Eye Masonic, attributed to Stoddard glasshouse, Stoddard, NH, 1846-60, olive amber, sheared mouth, pontil scar, pint, McKearin GIV-43, moderate ext. highpoint wear 150.00
Success to the Railroad, Coventry Glass Works, Coventry, CT, 1830-48, brilliant light yellowish olive, sheared mouth, pontil scar, pint, McKearin GV-8, pinhead sized flake on side of mouth 325.00
Success to the Railroad, Lancaster Glass Works, Lancaster, NY, 1849-60, aquamarine, sheared mouth, tubular pontil scar, pint, McKearin GV-1a, 3/8" brush on inside of mouth, other minor mouth roughness 200.00
Success to the Railroad, Mount Vernon Glass Works, Vernon, NY, 1830-44, forest green, sheared mouth, pontil scar, pint, McKearin GV-5, pinhead sized flake on medial rib . . 375.00

Pictorial

Baltimore/Glass Works and anchor-Resurgam Eagle, Baltimore Glass Works, Baltimore, MD, 1860-70, variegated yellow amber, applied collared mouth, smooth base, pint, McKearin GXIII-54, two 1/4" shallow flakes at side of base 475.00
Cornucopia-Large Medallion, Midwest America, 1820-40, very pale blue green, sheared mouth, pontil scar, half pint, McKearin GIII-1 . . . . .3,000.00
Cornucopia-Urn, attributed to Coventry Glass Works, Coventry, CT, 1830-48, bright green, sheared mouth, pontil scar, pint, McKearin GIII-4, small flake appears to have been ground 230.00

Cornucopia-Urn, attributed to New England, 1830-50, yellow olive, sheared mouth, pontil scar, half pint, McKearin GIII-2, small chip 130.00
Isabella/Glass Works and anchor-Factory, Isabella Glass Works, Brooklyn, NJ, 1850-60, aquamarine, sheared mouth, pontil scar, qt, McKearin GXIII-55, 3/4" open bubble burst to right of factory 210.00
Sailor-Banjo Player, Maryland Glass Works, Baltimore, MD, 1840-60, aquamarine, inward rolled mouth, pontil scar, half pint, McKearin GXIII-8 . . . . 180.00
Sheaf of Wheat-Star, attributed to Bulltown Glass Works, Bulltown, NJ, 1858-60, bright medium green, applied double collared mouth, pontil scar, pint, McKearin GIII-39 . . . . . 750.00
Sheaf of Wheat-Westford Glass Co., Westford Glass Works, Westford, CT, 1860-73
Golden amber, reddish tone, applied double collared mouth, smooth base, pint, McKearin GXIII-35 . . . . 120.00
Reddish amber, applied double collared mouth, smooth base, pint, McKearin GXIII-35 . . . . 140.00
Yellow olive, applied double collared mouth, smooth base, pint, McKearin GXIII-36 . . . . 120.00
Yellow olive, applied double collared mouth, smooth base, pint, McKearin GXIII-37 . . . . 120.00
Summer-Winter, attributed to Baltimore Glass works, Baltimore, MD, 1860-70, citron with olive tone, applied double collared mouth, smooth base, pint, McKearin GX-15 . . . . 900.00

Pitkin Type

Midwest, 1800-30, 5-1/4" h, light green, sixteen ribs broken swirl, Midwestern, worn ext. 450.00
New England, 1783-1830, sheared mouth, pontil scar
5" h, 36 ribs swirled to the right, yellow olive 400.00
5-1/4" h, 36 swirled ribs, olive green, half post neck
. . . . 255.00
6-3/4" h, olive green, 36 ribs, broken swirl 220.00

Pocket

6-3/4" l, colorless, fiery opalescent ribs 225.00
7-5/8" l, opaque white, blue spatter 195.00

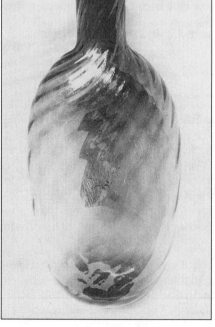

Pitkin, medium green, 14 right swirls, pontil mark, $195.

Portrait

Lafayette, Thomas Stebbins, Coventry, CT, 19th C, olive amber, pint, reverse with DeWitt Clinton, McKearin GI-80, 8-1/2" h
. . . . 575.00

Lafayette-Masonic, Coventry Glass Works, Coventry, CT, 1824-45, yellowish-olive, sheared mouth, pontil scar, half pint, McKearin Gi-84, some minor exterior highpoint wear
. . . . 1,700.00

Rough and Ready Taylor-Eagle, Midwest, 1830-40, aquamarine, sheared mouth, pontil scar, pint, McKearin GI-77
. . . . 1,200.00

Washington-Albany Glass Works/NY, Albany Glass Works, Albany, NY, 1847-50, greenish-aquamarine, sheared mouth, pontil scar, half pint, McKearin GI-30 . . . . .2,200.00

Washington-Eagle, Kensington Glass Works, Philadelphia, PA, 1820-38, bright aquamarine, sheared mouth, pontil scar, pint, McKearin GI-14 . . . . 375.00

Washington-Jackson, Coventry, CT, Glass Works, olive amber, half pint, reverse with portrait of Jackson, McKearin GI-34, 5-1/2" h. 250.00

Washington-Taylor, Dyottville Glass Works, Philadelphia, PA 1840-60
Bright bluish-green, applied double collared mouth, pontil scar, quart, McKearin GI-42. . . . . 400.00
Brilliant olive yellow, sheared mouth, pontil scar, pint, McKearin GI-38. . . . . 900.00

Scroll

America, 1845-60
Brilliant golden amber, applied collared mouth, iron pontil mark, pint, McKearin GIX-10 . . . . 425.00
Medium lime green, sheared mouth, iron pontil mark, McKearin GIX-11, 1/4" flat flake on top of mouth 325.00
Miniature, America, 1845-60, cobalt blue, inward rolled mouth, pontil scar, 2-5/8" h, approx. 1 oz, McKearin GIX-40, extremely rare, deep color 5,000.00

Sunburst

Baltimore Glass Works, Baltimore, MD, 1820-30, attributed to, sheared and tooled mouth, pontil scar
Colorless, light gray hue, pint, McKearin GVIII-26, some light overall int. haze 375.00
Olive green, half pint, McKearin GVIII-27. . . . . .3,000.00
Coventry Glass Works, Coventry, CT, 1814-30
Brilliant light olive yellow, sheared mouth, pontil scar, pint, McKearin GVIII-3 . . . . 450.00
Variegated brilliant yellowish amber with olive tone, sheared mouth, pontil scar, half pint, McKearin GVIII-18 . . . 850.00
Keene Marlboro Street Glassworks, Keene, NY, 1815-30
Brilliant yellow amber with olive tone, sheared mouth, pontil scar, half pint, McKearin GVIII-8, 3/4" faint fissure in one of rays 200.00
New England, 1820-30, attributed to, blue green, inward rolled mouth, pontil scar, half pint, McKearin GVIII-29 . . . . . 190.00

FLOW BLUE

History: Flow blue, or flown blue, is the name applied to china of cobalt and white china whose color, when fired in a kiln, produced a flowing or blurred effect. The blue varies from dark royal cobalt to a navy or steel blue. The flow may be very slight to a heavy blur where the pattern cannot be easily recognized. The blue color does not permeate through the body of the china. The amount of flow on the back of a piece is determined by the position of the piece in the sagger during firing.

Flow blue was first produced around 1830 in the Staffordshire area of England and credit is generally given to Josiah Wedgwood. He worked in the Staffordshire area of England. Many other potters followed, including Alcock, Davenport, Grindley, Johnson Brothers, Meakin, and New Wharf. Early flow blue, 1830s to 1870s, was usually of the ironstone. Variety. The later patterns, 1880s to 1900s, and modern patterns, after 1910, usually were made of the more delicate semi-porcelain. Approximately 90% of the flow blue was made in England, with the remainder made in Germany, Holland, France, Belgium, Wales and Scotland. A few patterns were also made in the United States by Mercer, Warwick, and the Wheeling Pottery companies.

References: Susan and Al Bagdade, *Warman's English & Continental Pottery & Porcelain*, 3rd Edition, Krause Publications, 1998; Mary F. Gaston, *Collector's Encyclopedia of Flow Blue China*, Collector Books, 1983, 1993 value update; ——, Collector's Encyclopedia of Flow Blue China, 2nd Series, Collector Books, 1994; Ellen R. Hill, *Mulberry Ironstone: Flow Blue's Best Kept Little Secret*, published by author, 1993; Norma Jean Hoener, *Flow Blue China, Additional Patterns and New Information*, Flow Blue International Collectors' Club, Inc. (P.O. Box 1526, Dickensen, TX 77539), 1996; Jeffrey Snyder, *Fascinating Flow Blue,* Schiffer Publishing, 1997; ——, *Flow Blue, A Collector's Guide to Pattern, History, and Values,* Schiffer, 1992; ——, *Historic Flow Blue*, Schiffer Publishing, 1994; Petra Williams, *Flow Blue China: An Aid to Identification*, revised ed. (1981), *Flow Blue China II* (1981), *Flow Blue China and Mulberry Ware: Similarity and Value Guide*, revised ed. (1993), Fountain House East (P.O. Box 99298, Jeffersontown, KY 40269).

Collectors' Club: Flow Blue International Collectors' Club, Inc., P.O. Box 1526, Dickenson, TX 77539.

Museum: The Margaret Woodbury Strong Museum, Rochester, New York.

Advisor: Ellen G. King.

Alaska, Grindley, butter dish, cov. 450.00
Amoy, Davenport
Creamer, 4" h, restoration. 350.00
Plate, 9-1/4" d 100.00
Platter, 20" l. 1,150.00
Punch Cup 600.00
Teapot, cov 875.00
Vegetable Tureen, cov 650.00
Anemone, Minton, drainer, 12-1/4" l. 500.00

Arabesque, Mayer
Creamer, restoration to lip 450.00
Sauce Tureen, cov 300.00
Teapot, cov 500.00
Argyle, Grindley
Plate
      6-3/4" d 50.00
      7-3/4" d 60.00
Platter, 15-1/4" l, restoration to edge 175.00
Soup Bowl, 9" d 80.00
Teapot, cov, lid restored 400.00
Vegetable Tureen, cov 350.00
Athens, Meigh, posset cup, price for set of four 250.00
Basket Japan, Minton, sauce tureen, polychrome, lid, tureen,
    undertray 300.00
Beaufort, Grindley
Honey Jar, cov 150.00
Punch Bowl 200.00
Beauties of China, Mellor, Venables, vegetable tureen 935.00
Blue Onion, Meissen, pie wheel 125.00
Brushstroke, various makers
Creamer, Tulip pattern 275.00
Teapot, cov, Grapeshot pattern 650.00
Burleigh, Burgess and Leigh
Gravy Boat 85.00
Plate, 10-1/2" d 90.00
Platter, 11-1/2" l 155.00
Sauce Tureen, lid, tureen, tray, ladle 375.00
Candia, Cauldon, syrup, pewter lid 275.00
Carlton, Alcock, platter, 19" l 450.00
Cashmere, Ridgway and Morley
Plate, 7" d 185.00

Cashmere, wash pitcher, green polychrome dec, gilt highlights $1,000. Photo courtesy of Ellen King.

Platter, 18" l, restoration 900.00
Punch Cup 1,100.00
Soup Plate, 10-1/2" d 325.00
Wash Pitcher, polychrome 1,000.00
Cavendish, Keeling
Biscuit Jar, cov, reeded handle 550.00
Vase, 11" h 165.00
Chapoo, Wedgwood
Coffeepot, cov, lid restored .1,100.00
Sauce Tureen, cov 700.00
Wash Basin 950.00
Chusan, Morley, low tazza, 10-1/2" d 325.00
Claremont, Johnson Bros., gravy boat, undertray 110.00
Clayton, Johnson Bros., open vegetable bowl 80.00
Cleopatra, Meakin, pitcher, 6-1/2" h 250.00
Coburg, Edwards
Plate, 10-1/2" d 125.00
Teapot, cov, spout restoration 500.00
Delft, Minton, plate, 10-1/4" d 50.00
Delft, Warwick, biscuit jar, cov 275.00
Denmark, Minton, platter, 12" l 120.00
Dorothy, Johnson Bros., vegetable tureen, cov 225.00
Duchess, Grindley, demitasse cup and saucer 50.00
Egerton, Doulton, sauce tureen, cov, tureen, tray, ladle
    . . . . 275.00
Fairy Villas, Adams
Plate, 10" d 85.00
Vegetable Bowl, round, open 125.00
Vegetable Tureen, cov 325.00
Ferrara, Wedgwood, toothpick holder 150.00
Floral and Vase, Ashworth, footed compote, polychrome
    . . . . 275.00
Florida, Ford and Son, platter, 19" l 350.00
Florida, Grindley, gravy boat, base restoration 75.00
Formosa, Mayer
Plate, 10-1/2" d 125.00
Platter, 15-1/2" l 385.00
Gainsborough, Ridgway, jardiniere, crazing, small hairline
    . . . . 400.00
Gem, Hammersley
Plate, 8-1/2" d 75.00
Tea Cup and Saucer 65.00
Gironde, Grindley
Butter Dish, cov, base, insert 350.00
Butter Pat 45.00
Girton, Grindley, soup tureen, cov, tureen 175.00
Grace, Grindley, gravy boat 185.00
Gothic, Furnivals
Platter, 13-1/2" l 150.00
Razor Box, cov 525.00
Sauce Tureen, cov 250.00
Hamilton, Keeling, jardiniere 275.00
Hofburg, The, Grindley
Gravy Boat 125.00
Pitcher, 8" h 200.00
Platter, 18" l 175.00
Holland, Johnson Bros., salt dip 165.00
Holland, The, Alcock
Plate, 10" d 120.00
Tea Cup and Saucer 85.00
Honc, maker unknown, soup plate, 10" d 125.00
Hong Kong, Meigh, plate, 10-1/2" d 115.00
Hopberry Sprig Variant, Meigh, plate, 10" d 145.00
Humphreys Clock, Ridgway
Creamer, 4" h 225.00
Plate, 10" d 65.00

Sauce Tureen, cov, tureen, tray, ladle 400.00
Tea Cup and Saucer. 95.00
Indian, Pratt
Soup Bowl, 9" d. 90.00
Vegetable Bowl, open, oval. 100.00
Indian Empress, Brown-Westhead, vegetable tureen, cov
. . . . 300.00
Indian Jar, Furnivals, creamer 200.00
Indian Jar, Wedgwood, platter, 18" l 255.00
Iris, Adderly, urn with lid, 20" h 900.00
Iris, Wood & Son
Biscuit Jar, cov 350.00
Condiment Set, 3 pcs, silverplated holder. 425.00
Japan, Minton, sauce tureen, cov, polychrome 355.00
Kelvin, Meakin
Soup Tureen, cov, restoration. 150.00
Vegetable Tureen, cov 250.00
Kin Shan, Challinor, sugar, cov 375.00
Kyber, Adams
Creamer 125.00
Dessert Bowl, 5" d. 45.00
Plate, 5-3/4" d. 30.00
Platter, 14-1/2" l 350.00
La Belle, Wheeling Pottery Co.
Charger, round, 13" d 295.00
Chocolate Pot, cov, rim restored. 550.00
Creamer 350.00
Dresser Tray 250.00
Gravy Boat, two handles, spout hairline 450.00
Platter, 13-1/2" l 115.00
Punch Cup 700.00
Soup Tureen, cov, tureen, undertray 2,000.00
La Francaise, French China Co., fish platter 250.00
Lancaster, New Wharf, butter pat 35.00
Lonsdale, Ridgways
Demitasse Cup and Saucer 65.00
Gravy Boat, undertray. 150.00
Lorne, Grindley
Platter
      14-1/2" l 150.00
      16-1/2" l 175.00
Soup Bowl, 9" d. 85.00

Hopberry Sprig Variant, plate, 10" d, $145. Photo courtesy of Ellen King.

Lugano, Ridgways, gravy boat. 95.00
Madras, Alcock
Fruit Compote, reticulated. 650.00
Pedestal Bowl 155.00
Madras, Doulton, open vegetable, 9-5/8" l 125.00
Manilla, Podmore, Walker
Plate, 7-3/4" d 85.00
Platter, 10-1/2" l. 250.00
Relish Dish 225.00
Tea Cup and Saucer, handleless 165.00
Vegetable Tureen, cov 650.00
Melbourne, Grindley
Compote 700.00
Creamer 250.00
Soup Ladle 650.00
Melrose, Doulton, sauce ladle, 8" l. 150.00
Mikado, Wilkinson, soup tureen, cov, tureen, undertray
. . . . 675.00
Montrose, Wedgwood, sauce tureen, cov, tureen, tray, ladle
. . . . 400.00
Moyune, Ridgways, polychrome
Platter, 19-1/2" l. 650.00
Soup Tureen, cov, tureen, ladle 675.00
Mt. Vernon, Adams, plate, 10" d 85.00
Nakin, Pratt, shaving mug 175.00
Ning Po, Ralph Hall, honey dish. 100.00
Non Pariel, Burgess & Leigh
Chop Plate 225.00
Platter
      15-1/2" l 400.00
      18" l 450.00
Tea Cup and Saucer. 90.00
Vegetable Tureen, cov, restoration. 275.00
Normandy, Johnson Bros.
Platter, 14" l. 400.00
Vegetable Bowl, open, tab handles, 8" l 175.00
Oakley, Meakin, butter, cov, no insert 150.00
Oregon, Mayer
Butter Dish, cov. 750.00
Waste Bowl. 250.00
Oriental, Ridgways
Demitasse Cup and Saucer 100.00
Sugar Bowl, cov 155.00
Teapot, cov 875.00
Vegetable Tureen, cov 475.00
Olympia, Grindley, toothbrush holder. 90.00
Oxford, Johnson Bros.
Butter Pat 40.00
Mustard Pot, cov. 475.00
Pagoda, Ridgways, sugar bowl, cov. 275.00
Paisley, Mercer, punch cup 80.00
Pansy, Warwick
Chocolate Cup and Saucer. 400.00
Pitcher, 7-1/2" h. 200.00
Pekin, Dimmock, vegetable tureen, cov 175.00
Provence, Doulton, charger, round, 13" d 100.00
Quails, Cauldon, pitcher, 8" h. 250.00
Queen, T. Rathbone
Plate, 9" d 70.00
Soup Tureen, cov, tureen, ladle 250.00
Rhine, Dimmock, soup bowl, 10" d. 55.00
Rose and Lily, Davenport, gravy boat, undertray 95.00
Scinde, Alcock
Cup Plate 120.00
Plate, 10-1/2" d 150.00
Sauce Tureen, cov, tureen, tray, ladle 4,250.00

Undertray, handles, reticulated 500.00
Shanghai, Grindley
Plate
    7" d 80.00
    10" d 95.00
Vegetable Tureen, cov, 10-1/2" l 500.00
Shapoo, Hughes, plate, 8-1/2" d 85.00
Shell, Challinor
Creamer 450.00
Plate, 9-1/2" d 80.00
Sobraon, unknown maker
Plate, 9-1/2" d 115.00
Platter, 22" l, well and tree, hairline 600.00
Syria, Grindley, waste jar, cov, restoration 950.00
Temple, Podmore, Walker
Creamer 375.00
Plate, 9" d 135.00
Soup Bowl, 10" d 100.00
Vegetable Tureen, cov, octagonal 650.00
Togo, Colonial Pottery, creamer and sugar, cov 225.00
Touraine, Alcock
Chop Plate 215.00
Creamer, spout restoration 175.00
Dessert Bowl, oval, individual 150.00
Platter
    12-1/2" l 125.00
    15" l 200.00
Vegetable Bowl, open, oval 110.00
Waste Bowl 250.00
Touraine, Stanley, sugar bowl, cov 400.00
Trent, Ford & Sons, vegetable tureen, cov 200.00
Trilby, Grindley, wash bowl and pitcher set 950.00
Vermont, Burgess & Leigh, sauce tureen, cov, tureen, tray, la-
dle 350.00
Verona, Wood & Son
Creamer 225.00
Sugar Bowl, cov 275.00
Victor, Rathbone, jardiniere 450.00
Waldorf, New Wharf Pottery, plate, 10" d 95.00
Watteau, New Wharf Pottery
Compote, undertray, both reticulated 800.00
Plate, 7-1/2" d 45.00
Vegetable Bowl, open, oval 100.00
Whampoa, Mellor, Venables, relish dish 135.00
Willow, Doulton, teapot, cov 225.00
Wreath Japan, Minton
Plate, 10-1/2" d 90.00
Platter, 11" l, reticulated 150.00

FOLK ART

History: Exactly what constitutes folk art is a question still being vigorously debated among collectors, dealers, museum curators, and scholars. Some want to confine folk art to non-academic, handmade objects. Others are willing to include manufactured material. In truth, the term is used to cover objects ranging from crude drawings by obviously untalented children to academically trained artists' paintings of "common" people and scenery.

References: Edwin O. Christensen, *Early American Wood Carvings*, Dover Publications, n.d.; Country Living Magazine, *Living with Folk Art*, Hearst Books, 1994; Catherine Dike, *Canes in the United States*, Cane Curiosa Press, 1995; Jim Dresslar, *Folk Art of Early America—The Engraved Powder Horn*, Dresslar Publishing (P.O. Box 635, Bargersville, IN 46106), 1996; Wendy Lavitt, *Animals in American Folk Art,* Knopf, 1990; Jean Lipman, *American Folk Art in Wood, Metal, and Stone*, Dover Publications, n.d. George H. Meyer, *American Folk Art Canes*, Sandringham Press, Museum of American Folk Art, and University of Washington Press, 1992; Donald J. Petersen, *Folk Art Fish Decoys*, Schiffer Publishing, 1996; Beatrix Rumford and Carolyn Weekly, *Treasures in American Folk Art from the Abby Aldrich Rockefeller Folk Art Center,* Little Brown, 1989.

Periodical: *Folk Art Illustrated*, P.O. Box 906, Marietta, OH 45750.

Museums: Abby Aldrich Rockefeller Folk Art Center, Williamsburg, VA; Daughters of the American Revolution Museum, Washington, DC; Landis Valley Farm Museum, Lancaster, PA; Museum of American Folk Art, New York, NY; Museum of Early Southern Decorative Arts, Winston-Salem, NC; Museum of International Folk Art, Sante Fe, NM.

SPECIAL AUCTIONS

Aston Macek Auction Company
2825 Country Club Rd.
Endwell, NY 13760
(607) 785-6598

Garth's Auction Inc.
2690 Stratford Rd.
P.O. Box 369
Delaware, OH 43015

Calligraphy, 19-1/2" h, 15" w, pen and ink drawing of General George Washington atop rearing horse, saddle blanket and uniform colored red, blue, and black, wearing hat, holds telescope, flowing blue cape, surrounded by circle wreath, "Executed with the pen of Samuel G. Hayes," framed and matted 1,500.00
Doll, America, late 19th C
    22" h, black cotton, embroidered features, plaid cotton dress 175.00
    22" h, cotton, pen and inked features, brown calico dress, blue and white striped bonnet 850.00
Drawing, 21" h, 30-3/4" h, black and white charcoal drawing on sandpaper, pleasure and cargo boats and mountains, very worn, tears, paper backed on masonite, framed 110.00
Figure
    Carved wood, life size, standing position, 69" h Jim Bowie, one hand with leather outfit and carved belt with knife in sheath, fringed moccasins, arms down at side, right hand holding wide brimmed hat, 70" h Davy Crockett, one hand holding long rifle, other resting on coonskin hat, leather-type carved outfit with fringe on arms and labels, leather shoes and leggings, each carved from 4' high cut corner block of wood, found in San Francisco area, price for pair 12,500.00
    Sheet metal, man, wearing hat, coat with tails, articulated, 13-1/4" h, America, 19th C, minor dents and corrosion 550.00
Painting, 9-5/8" h, 8-1/8" w, watercolor on paper, pen and ink verse, "A jay bird set on a hicory (sic) limb...," green and yel-

low bird on branch, buildings in background, fold line an tears, top edge glued to backing, framed 385.00

Portrait, 13-1/2" x 11-1/2", watercolor, George Washington on his horse above the inscription "General Georg Washington," attributed to Center County, PA, artist Henry Young, paper has darkened with age 7,150.00

Sculpture

Carved wood whimsy in bottle, 23-3/4" h, James McCowan Davis, PA, late 19th C, seated man in blue suit and hat as finial, red, white, and blue shaft ends in green, blue, black, and white painted structure with gilt cannon, boy with blue hat, Dalmatian, and hanging blocks, minor loss to polychrome paint, very minor chips to bottle rim, sold with photo of carver holding piece and Davis family records

. . . . .4,500.00

Sandstone Indian head, by Ohio folk sculptor Popeye Reed, sgd "E. Reed". 150.00

Schnerenschnitte (paper cutting), attributed to Seymour Lindsay, Lexington, OH, 1848-1927

7" h, 7" w, white paper, blue ground, tree with seven birds, glue stains, 10-3/8" x 10-3/8" modern frame 440.00

7-1/4" h, 7-1/2" w, coated black paper, yellow ground, large tree, rabbit, twenty-three birds, and four squirrels, modern 8-5/8" h x 8-7/8" w frame 1,375.00

8-1/2" h, 11" w, white paper, coated blue paper ground, two women with plants and birdcage, tree, thirteen birds, two squirrels, and butterfly, damage and glue stains, 11-1/2" x 14-1/2" oak frame 825.00

11-3/4" h, 13" w, white paper, black ground, tree, deer family, two squirrels, bird, three birds in nest, 15-1/4" h x 17-1/4" w walnut frame labeled "Ralph & Seymour Lindsay Ex Marie Baker" 1,100.00

12" h, 10" w, white lined paper, black ground, large tree, man, twenty-two birds and nests, pencil inscription "Nov. 1878, this figure was cut by a boy of 10 years of age at Lexington, O. without mark or pattern," stains, 15" h x 13" w frame

. . . . 550.00

Theorem

8" h, 10-1/2" w, watercolor on velvet, basket of fruit, period frame, unsigned. 1,725.00

9-3/4" h, 7-7/8" w, watercolor on velvet, compote of fruit, unsigned, American school, 19th C, ripple molded frame

. . . . 990.00

10-1/16" h, 8-1/16" w, watercolor on paper, red tulips, purple five petal flower, green leaves, stains, molded frame with gilded liner 250.00

10-1/2" h, 8-1/2" w, watercolor on velvet, basket of flowers, framed, toning, foxing, minor staining 500.00

11-1/8" h, 13-1/8" w, watercolor on paper, pinprick highlights, fruit compote, framed, toning, minor foxing 850.00

13-3/4" h, 16-1/2" w, painting on velvet, basket of strawberries, fruit, and bird, initialed "D.Y.E." (David Ellinger), grained frame. 1,705.00

21" h, 19" w, painting on velvet, crowing rooster, William Rank, sponged dec frame 580.00

21" h, 23" w, painting on velvet, ship with American flag, sgd "Bill Rank," sponged dec frame 220.00

21-3/4" h, 27-3/4" w, painting on velvet, basket of fruit, unsigned Ellinger, matted, old gilt frame 1,870.00

22" h, 26-1/4" w, watercolor on paper, well executed flowers in many colors, brown background uneven in color, glued to underside of mat, bird's eye veneer frame. 660.00

22" h, 27-3/4" w, painting on velvet, basket of fruit with bee, sgd "D. Y. Ellinger," fabric loose in frame, matted, old gilt frame 880.00

Watercolor, two bird sitting on tulip branch potted in heart, David Y. Ellinger, sgd "D. Y. Ellinger" on left corner, 11-1/2" h, 9-1/2" w, $880. Photo courtesy of Alderfer Auction Company, Inc.

25-1/4" h, 31-1/4" w, watercolor on paper, bowl and compote of stylized flowers and fruit, poor condition, tears and old repairs, faint signature. 385.00

28-3/4" h, 33-3/4" w, painting on velvet, cornucopia with fruit and bird, sgd "Wm Rank," pine frame 580.00

28-3/4" h, 36-3/4" w, painting on velvet, landscape with stone end barn and house, horse and buggy, sgd "Bill Rank," sponge dec frame 450.00

Toy, America, late 19th C

19" h, Jumping Jack, carved wood, polychrome dec

. . . . 115.00

41-1/2" w, 16" d, 38-1/2" h, jig dancers, carved wood and wrought iron, articulate figures with period clothing, remnants of hair wigs, imperfections 825.00

FOOD BOTTLES

History: Food bottles were made in many sizes, shapes, and colors. Manufacturers tried to make an attractive bottle that would ship well and allow the purchaser to see the product, thus giving assurance that the product was as good and as well-made as home preserves.

References: Ralph & Terry Kovel, *Kovels' Bottle Price List*, 10th ed., Crown Publishers, 1996; John Odell, *Digger Odell's Official Antique Bottle and Glass Collector Magazine Price Guide Series*, Vol. 6, published by author (1910 Shawhan Rd., Morrow, OH 45152), 1995.

Periodical: *Antique Bottle and Glass Collector*, P.O. Box 187, East Greenville, PA 18041.

Collectors' Club: Federation of Historical Bottle Collectors, Inc., 88 Sweetbriar Branch, Longwood, Fl 32750.

Baking Powder, Eddy's, tin top 12.00
Banana Flavoring, Herberlings, paper label, 8" h 10.00
Candy, Prices Patent Candie Company, England, 1840-60, rect wedge form, cobalt blue, applied sloping collared mouth with ring, pontil scar, 7" h 350.00
Catsup
    Curtis Brothers, colorless, blue label 12.00
    Quickshank, paper label 5.00
Extract
    Baker's Flavoring Extracts, 4-3/4" h, aqua, sq ring lip
    . . . . 15.00
    L. C. Extract, label, orig box 180.00
Honey, Land of Lakes, honeycomb, metal cap 8.00
Horseradish, Heinz Nobel & Co., emb, two anchors, horse head on lid, 1873, 5" h 275.00
Lemonade, G. Foster Clark & Co., Eiffel Tower, 2-3/4" h
    . . . . 10.00
Lemon Extract, Louis & Company 10.00
Lime Juice, 13" h, tapered cylinder, blob top, overall emb lime foliage, emb "L. Rose & Co." 35.00
Malted Milk, Horlick's Malted Milk, Racine, half pint 20.00
Olive, Chef, 5" h 5.00
Pepper Sauce, 8" h, S & P Pat. Appl. For, teal blue, smooth base, tooled lip 50.00
Pickle, cathedral, America, 1845-80, sq, beveled corners,
    10-5/8" h, 4 fancy cathedral arch designs, medium green, tooled rolled mouth, smooth base 650.00
    11-1/2" h, 3 fancy cathedral designs, greenish-aqua, tooled rolled mouth, smooth base 150.00
    11-3/4" h, 4 different fancy cathedral arch designs, protruding irregular panels, aquamarine, tooled sq mouth, iron pontil mark 170.00
Snuff, freeblown, rect, wide beveled corners, olive green, sheared mouth, pontil scar, attributed to New England, 1800-30, 4-1/2" h 130.00
Valentine's Vanilla, rect, recessed reverse painted label, Pat'd Apr 2, 1889, ground stopper with flat top, 10" h, light crazing and staining to label 100.00
Vinegar, jug shape, Whitehouse, 10" h 20.00

FOOD MOLDS

History: Food molds were used both commercially and in the home. Generally, pewter ice cream molds and candy molds were used commercially; pottery and copper molds were used in homes. Today, both types are collected largely for decorative purposes.

The majority of pewter ice cream molds are individual serving molds. One quart of ice cream would make eight to ten pieces. Scarcer, but still available, are banquet molds which used two to four pints of ice cream. European-made pewter molds are available.

Marks: Pewter ice cream molds were made primarily by two American companies: Eppelsheimer & Co. (molds marked "E & Co., N.Y.") and Schall & Co. (marked "S & Co."). Both companies used a numbering system for their molds. The Krauss Co. bought out Schall & Co., removed the "S & Co." from some, but not all, of the molds, and added more designs (pieces marked "K" or "Krauss"). "CC" is a French mold mark.

Manufacturers of chocolate molds are more difficult to determine. Unlike the pewter ice cream molds, makers' marks were not always used or were covered by frames. Eppelsheimer & Co. of New York marked many of their molds, either with their name or with a design resembling a child's toy top and the words "Trade Mark" and "NY." Many chocolate molds were imported from Germany and Holland and were marked with the country of origin and, in some cases, the mold-maker's name.

Reference: Judene Divone, *Chocolate Moulds*, Oakton Hills Publications, 1987.

Museum: Wilbur's American Candy Museum, Lititz, PA.

Additional Listings: Butter Prints.

Cake
    Rabbit, cast iron, Griswold 225.00
    Swirl, copper, domed half round shape, bold design, 6-5/8" d
    . . . . 90.00
    Turk's Turban, redware, reddish glaze, brown flecks, white slip and dark brown dec at top, 10-1/4" d, minor chips
    . . . . 125.00
Chocolate
    Alligators, Anton Reiche, 1885, price for four pc set . 125.00
    Bulldog, tin, 5" h 90.00
    Camel, tin, two-part, 6" h 80.00
    Cat, bird and rabbit, three cavities, relief carved wood, 3-3/8" x 11-3/4", frame type 125.00
    Clown, 9" h, numbered 15262, two pc type 75.00
    Dog with hat, tin, 6-1/2" h 120.00
    Duck, clamp and hinge, Germany 70.00
    Hen on nest, tin, removable handled base, orig long clipped top, sgd "K & M," 7" h, 7" w 300.00
    Rabbit and chicken, six rows, 11" x 17", tray type . . . 100.00
    Rooster, 12" x 10", single cavity, tray type 75.00
    Snowman, wearing hat, two pc type 50.00
Ice Cream, pewter
    Black boy killing turkey, L & Co., 4" h 95.00
    Boy swinging golf club, 1900s 145.00
    Child, 5" h 45.00
    Cucumber, E & Co., #228, 4-1/2" w, 2" h 42.00
    Drum, 2-1/2" h 40.00
    Eagle with shield, 5" h 200.00
    Halloween Witch, 511/2" h 175.00
    Horse, 3" h 65.00
    Girl, golfer, 1900s 150.00

Cake Mold, Lamb, No. 866, #2 size, $80.

Orange, 2-1/2" d
    D & Co., #120 . . . . 32.00
    E & Co., #807 . . . . 35.00
Pear, E & Co., 4" w, 2-1/2" h 35.00
Pears, three joined pears, L & Co., 3 5/8" l 45.00
Plum, D & Co., #121, 2-1/2" d 32.00
Tomato, E & Co., #239 2-1/2" d 35.00
Washington, George and Martha, 5-1/2" h, price for pr
    . . . . 250.00
Pastry, two-sided, horse on one side, two chickens on other, cast iron, late 19th/early 20th C, 6-1/2" 300.00
Pudding
    Basket of flowers, china, 7" x 7" x 3", Germany 45.00
    Ear of Corn, copper, rect, rounded corners, deep ruffled sides, design stamped in top, tin-washed, 4" x 6" . . 165.00
    Lion, ironstone 95.00
    Melon, tin, two mark, marked "Kraemer" 48.00
Pear, tin, oval, deep ruffled sides, design stamped in top, framed by raised rim band, 3-1/2" x 5-1/2" 90.00
Pomegranate, tin, oval sides, inset top with stamped design of large and small fruit, scrolling leaves, 7-1/4" l 80.00

FOSTORIA GLASS

History: Fostoria Glass Co. began operations at Fostoria, Ohio, in 1887, and moved to Moundsville, West Virginia, its present location, in 1891. By 1925, Fostoria had five furnaces and a variety of special shops. In 1924, a line of colored tableware was introduced. Fostoria was purchased by Lancaster Colony in 1983 and continues to operate under the Fostoria name.

Reference: Gene Florence, *Elegant Glassware of the Depression Era*, Revised 5th ed., Collector Books, 1993; Ann Kerr, *Fostoria: An Identification and Value Guide of Pressed, Blown, & Hand Molded Shapes* (1994, 1997 values), *Etched, Carved & Cut Designs* (1996, 1997 values) Collector Books; Milbra Long and Emily Seate, *Fostoria Stemware*, Collector Books, 1995; Leslie Piña, *Fostoria Designer George Sakier*, Schiffer Publishing, 1996; ——, *Fostoria*, Schiffer Publishing, 1995; JoAnn Schleismann, *Price Guide to Fostoria*, 3rd ed., Park Avenue Publications, n.d.

Periodical: The Daze, P.O. Box 57, Otisville, MI 48463.

Collectors' Clubs: Fostoria Glass Collectors, Inc., P.O. Box 1625, Orange, CA 92856; Fostoria Glass Society of America, P.O. Box 826, Moundsville, WV 26041.

Museums: Fostoria Glass Museum, Moundsville, WV; Huntington Galleries, Huntington, WV.

After Dinner Cup and Saucer
    Beverly, green 30.00
    June, blue. 160.00
    Versailles, yellow 48.00
Almond Dish, Colony, ftd. 15.00
Ashtray
    Fairfax, yellow, 4" d 12.00
    Manor, yellow, sq 40.00
Baker
    June, oval. 180.00
    Trojan, yellow 100.00
Bon Bon
    Baroque, blue, 3 toes 40.00
    Lafayette, burgundy, 5" d, handle 40.00

Meadow Rose, 7" d, 3 legs. 35.00
Bouillon, liner
    Beverly, green 22.00
    June 40.00
Bowl
    America, 8" d, 5-1/8" h, ftd 250.00
    Baroque, blue, 11" d, rolled edge. 95.00
    Chintz, 10-1/2" d, 4 toes. 70.00
    Navarre, 12" d, flared 62.50
Brandy Inhaler, Navarre 115.00
Butter Dish, cov
    America, round. 125.00
    Colony, 1/4 lb 60.00
Cake Plate
    Chintz, 2 handles, 10" d 40.00
Cake Stand
    American, 10"
        Round 100.00
        Square. 125.00
    Bouquet, ftd 135.00
Candlesticks, pr
    American, #282, 3" h, round, ftd. 40.00
    Baroque, blue, 4" d 35.00
    Camelia, duo 130.00
    June, blue, 3 ftd 110.00
    June, yellow, 3" h 75.00
    Lido, 5-1/2" h 90.00
    Meadow Rose, #2496, double 70.00
    Morning Glory cutting, 2 lite 70.00
    Versailles, pink, mushroom shape 135.00
Candy Dish, cov
    American, 3 part. 90.00
    Lido, crystal, 3 part. 85.00
Celery
    Baroque, blue. 85.00
    June, blue. 130.00
Centerpiece Bowl
    American, 11" d 175.00
    Seascape, blue, ftd. 140.00
Cereal Bowl
    Beverly, green 30.00
    Vernon, orchid 55.00
Champagne
    Beacon 15.00
    Florentine, yellow 18.00
    June, blue. 50.00
    Meadow Rose, saucer 22.00
    Navarre, saucer 24.00
    Rambler, hollow stem. 30.00
    Romance, saucer 15.00
Cheese and Cracker
    Chintz 145.00
    Navarre. 150.00
    Vernon, orchid 90.00
Chop Plate, June, pink, 13" d 230.00
Claret
    Navarre, 4-1/2 oz 45.00
    Wilma, pink. 40.00
Cocktail
    American Lady 12.00
    Buttercup 18.00
    Colony 12.00
    Fairfax, #5299, yellow 18.00
    Hermitage, yellow, cone 10.00
    Meadow Rose, #6016, 3-1/2 oz, 5-1/4" h. 25.00
    Versailles, yellow, 3-1/2 oz. 25.00

Compote, cov, Colony, low 45.00
Compote, open
   Baroque, blue, 5-1/2" d, 6-1/2" h 140.00
   Beverly, amber, 8" d, ftd. 85.00
   Navarre, #2496. . . . . 45.00
   Romance, 8" d, Sonata 130.00
   Trojan, yellow, 4-1/2" d. 40.00
Console Bowl, June, blue, scroll 200.00
Cordial, Corsage 50.00
Creamer
   Meadow Rose, 3-3/4" h 18.00
   Navarre. 20.00
   Willowmere. 18.00
Cream Soup, June, blue 100.00
Cup and Saucer
   Baroque, blue. 40.00
   Century. 18.00
   Fairfax, yellow 10.00
   Lafayette, wisteria 28.00
   Meadow Rose 22.50
   Navarre. 24.00
   Romance 24.00
   Versailles, yellow 22.00
Decanter
   American, Rye 180.00
   Hermitage, azure 260.00
Dessert Bowl, two handles
   Century. 45.00
   Lido. 65.00
Finger Bowl, liner
   Beverly, green 25.00
   June, yellow 60.00
Floating Garden, American, 10" d. 60.00
Fruit Bowl
   Buttercup, 13" d 75.00
   Colony, 10" d 35.00
Goblet, water
   American Lady, amethyst. 35.00
   Arcady 28.00
   Baroque, blue. 30.00
   Capri, cinnamon 20.00
   Chintz, 7-5/8" h. 30.00
   Colony, 9 oz 20.00
   Florentine, yellow 25.00
   June, blue. 80.00
   Meadow Rose, #6016, 10 oz, 7-5/8" h 30.00
   Navarre. 30.00
   Neo Classic, amethyst 35.00
   Wilma, pink. 30.00
Grapefruit, liner, June, crystal 125.00
Gravy, liner
   June, pink. 500.00
   Versailles, green. 260.00
Ice Bucket
   Arcady 125.00
   Baroque, blue. 190.00
   June, yellow 140.00
   Navarre, Baroque style. 160.00
   Versailles, blue. 210.00
Iced Tea Tumbler, ftd
   Baroque, blue, 6" h. 90.00
   Chintz, 13 oz 30.00
   Holly 18.00
   June, pink. 70.00
   June, yellow 45.00
   Meadow Rose, #6016, 13 oz, 5-7/8" h 35.00

Goblet, Colonial Mirror, c1930, $45.

   Navarre, pink 55.00
   Neo Classic, amethyst 25.00
   Trojan, yellow, 12 oz 36.00
Jelly, cov
   Baroque, blue. 200.00
   Garland. 100.00
Jewelry Box, America, 5-1/2" x 2-5/8" 500.00
Jug, ftd
   Arcady 490.00
   Beverly, amber 400.00
   Hermitage, yellow. 130.00
Juice Tumbler
   Chintz, 5 oz, ftd 26.00
   Fairfax, #2375, 5 oz, ftd, yellow 11.00
   Plymouth 12.00
Mayonnaise, 3 piece, (bowl, liner, spoon)
   Buttercup 90.00
   Chintz 100.00
   Lido. 230.00
   Meadow Rose 90.00
   Morning Glory cutting 75.00
Mint Tray
   Baroque, blue, tab handle 28.00
   Seascape, blue, 7" l 45.00
Nappy
   Baroque, blue, 5" w, handle, ftd 55.00
   Lido, tricorn. 30.00
Nut Cup
   Baroque, blue, 3 toes 40.00
   Chintz, 3 toes 50.00
   Fairfax, yellow 25.00
Oil Bottle, stopper
   Baroque, yellow 225.00
   June, crystal, ftd 400.00
Old Fashioned Tumbler, Baroque, blue 95.00
Oyster Cocktail
   Colony 12.50
   Meadow Rose 25.00
   Rambler 20.00
Pansy Bowl, Seascape, 4" d, blue 25.00
Parfait
   June 70.00

Vernon, orchid 55.00
Versailles, pink 90.00

Pickle Dish
   Baroque, blue 55.00
   Romance 40.00

Pin Box, cov, Jenny Lind, 5" d, milk glass 70.00

Pitcher
   Century, pint 70.00
   Colony, 48 oz, ftd, ice lip 215.00
   Vernon, orchid 500.00
   Versailles, green, #5000 . . . . 760.00

Plate
   Baroque, blue, 8" d 20.00
   Baroque, 8" d, crystal 10.00
   Beacon, 7-1/2" d 9.00
   Chintz, 7-1/2" d 14.00
   June, 8-1/4" d, pink 22.00
   Lafayette, 8-3/8" d, wisteria 25.00
   Meadow Rose, 7-1/2" d 14.00
   Navarre, 7-1/4" d 16.50

Platter
   America, 12" l 60.00
   June, 12" l 75.00

Pomade Box, cov, American 200.00

Punch Bowl Set, Coin, crystal, punch bowl, base, twelve cups
. . . . 625.00

Relish
   Baroque, blue, 2 part, 6-1/2" l 55.00
   Buttercup, 3 part 60.00
   Chintz, 2 part 30.00
   June, 2 part, pink 70.00
   Meadow Rose, 3 part 45.00
   Navarre, 3 part 48.00
   Rambler, 5 part, gold trim 70.00
   Versailles, yellow, #2375, 2 part 35.00

Salad Bowl, Morning Glory cutting, 12" d 55.00

Salad Dressing Bottle
   Buttercup, #2063 . . . . 460.00
   June, crystal 290.00
   Navarre 490.00

Salad Plate, Romance, crescent shape 100.00

Salt and Pepper Shakers, pr
   American, glass tops 50.00
   Baroque, blue, individual size 340.00
   Baroque, crystal 45.00
   June, yellow 185.00
   Navarre, glass tops, #2375, ftd 160.00
   Versailles, pink 190.00

Sauce Boat
   Chintz, #2496, oval 75.00
   June, yellow 115.00
   Sauce Boat, liner
   Baroque, blue 150.00
   Lafayette, red 125.00

Sauce Dish
   Baroque, blue, divided 75.00
   Lafayette, #2440, pink 65.00
   Navarre, #2496 . . . . 125.00
   Shirley, 6-1/2" x 5-1/4" 95.00

Server, center handle
   Brocade, Oakwood, blue 200.00
   Buttercup 50.00
   Chintz 80.00
   June, pink, 11" d 75.00
   Morning Glory cutting 50.00
   Vernon, orchid 90.00
   Willowmere, #2560 . . . . 48.00

Sherbet
   Baroque, yellow, 3-3/4" h, 5 oz 17.00
   Chintz, low 18.00
   Colony 9.00
   Fairfax, #2375, yellow, 4-1/4" 10.00
   June, yellow 26.00
   Meadow Rose, low 20.00
   Plymouth 14.00

Sherry, Neo Classic, amethyst 40.00

Snack Tray, Colony, 10-1/2" d 45.00

Sugar Bowl, cov
   June, pink 38.00
   Meadow Rose, 3-3/4" h 18.00
   Navarre 22.00
   Willowmere 18.00

Sugar Cuber, America, orig tongs 325.00

Sugar Pail, Trojan, yellow 240.00

Sweet Meat
   Beacon 25.00
   June, pink 60.00
   Versailles, yellow 15.00

Tidbit
   Baroque, blue, 3 toe 45.00
   Chintz, 3 ftd, 8-1/4" d 24.00

Torte Plate
   American, 13-1/2" l, oval 70.00
   Chintz, 14" d, used 70.00
   Lido, 13" d 70.00

Tumbler, water
   American Lady, 10 oz 12.00
   Baroque, blue, 12 oz, ftd 40.00
   Beacon, 9 oz, ftd 12.00
   Chintz, 10 oz, ftd 22.00
   Colony, 12 oz, ftd 35.00
   Jamestown, amber, 9 oz 7.00
   Jamestown, amber, 12 oz 7.00
   June, pink 48.00
   Lido, crystal, 12 oz, ftd 22.00
   Meadow Rose, 13 oz, ftd 35.00
   Navarre, 13 oz, ftd 32.50
   Romance, 12 oz, ftd 25.00
   Willowmere, #6024, 12 oz, ftd 28.00

Vase
   American, 9-1/2" h, flared, swung 400.00
   Arcady, #2470, 10" h, ftd 260.00
   Baroque, yellow, 7" h 95.00
   Brocade, #4105, pink, palm leaf, 8" h 220.00
   Colony, bud, yellow, 6-1/2" h 50.00
   Morning Glory cutting, #2577, 14" h 400.00

Vegetable Bowl, Century, oval 45.00

Wedding Bowl, cov, America, milk glass 90.00

Whipped Cream Bowl
   Fairfax, yellow 15.00
   Versailles, yellow 15.00

Whipped Cream Pail
   June, pink 300.00
   Versailles, blue 240.00

Whiskey
   June, yellow, ftd 90.00
   Manor, ftd 25.00

Wine
   Colony 28.00
   Meadow Rose 37.50
   Navarre 40.00
   Romance 40.00

FRAKTUR

History: Fraktur, the calligraphy associated with the Pennsylvania Germans, is named for the elaborate first letter found in many of the hand-drawn examples. Throughout its history, printed, partially printed/partially hand-drawn, and fully hand-drawn works existed side by side. Frakturs often were made by schoolteachers or ministers living in rural areas of Pennsylvania, Maryland, and Virginia. Many artists are unknown.

Fraktur exists in several forms—geburts and taufschein (birth and baptismal certificates), vorschrift (writing examples, often with alphabet), haus sagen (house blessings), bookplates and bookmarks, rewards of merit, illuminated religious texts, valentines, and drawings. Although collected for decoration, the key element in fraktur is the text.

References: Donald A. Shelley, *Fraktur-Writings or Illuminated Manuscripts of the Pennsylvania Germans*, Pennsylvania German Society, 1961; Frederick S. Weiser and Howell J. Heaney (comps.), *Pennsylvania German Fraktur of the Free Library of Philadelphia*, 2 Vols., Pennsylvania German Society, 1976.

Museums: Franklin & Marshall College, Lancaster, PA; The Free Library of Philadelphia, Philadelphia, PA.

SPECIAL AUCTION

Sanford Alderfer Auction Company
501 Fairgrounds Rd.
Hatfield, PA 19440
(610) 368-5477

Notes: Fraktur prices rise and fall along with the American folk-art market. The key marketplaces are Pennsylvania and the Middle Atlantic states.

Almanac Holder, dated 1800. . . . . .2,090.00
Birth Certificate, Geburts und Taufschein
  1775 birth of John Eichelberger, by Hanover Township artist, fair condition. 3,850.00
  1790, by Johannes Ernst Spangenberg, Bucks County, PA, 7 1/2" x 13",. 6,325.00
  1794, Brunswick Township, Berks County, PA, birds, hearts, and tree of life design. 5,225.00
  1798, hand-drawn and colored, by the artist identified as "Busy Artist" (active c. 1787-98, Dauphin Co., PA), certificate of Elisabetha Beili, born Oct. 30, 1798, Annville Township, Dauphin Co., Pennsylvania, daughter of Johan Adam Biele and wife Lisabet, is in orange, green, yellow, brown, and black with some foxing and soiling. It was matted in a modern walnut frame, 18" x 21-1/8". 13,000.00
  1800, watercolor on paper fraktur by so-called Wild Turkey Artist, three hearts on the top edge centered by two yellow birds, green and yellow foliate scrolls throughout, double tulip and two blue stars at the bottom with stylized urns on either side, translation of the inscription reads: "In the year of Christ, Anno, on the 16th of July, David was born to the light of this world. The father is Adam Rosenbaum, and the mother, Susanna, was born Spraker, and the baptismal witnesses are Christopher Spraker and his wife," David Rosenbaum was baptized on Sept. 13, 1800, at Zion Luth-

eran Church, located at Cripple Creek, 12-1/2" x 16"
. . . . .19,040.00
  1808, printed, hand blocked red, yellow, blue, and green, Ohio birth, "Printed by John Herman, Lancaster, Ohio," 14" h, 15" w, damage, stains, crease in paper. 660.00
  1810, printed and handcolored, birth in York County, PA, printed by "D. P. Lange, Hanover, Pennsylvania, 1826," eagles, angels, and birds, red, green, and yellow, 12" h, 15" w, rebacked on adv litho, old gilt 13-1/4" h, 13-7/8" w frame
. . . . 330.00
  1811 birth of twin brothers, Abraham and Jacob Lang, printed, hand dec, polychrome flowers and birds, pr . .5,775.00
  1815, with yellow birds, blue-green peacock, and woman in a green dress, by Francis Portzline 12,650.00
  Printed and hand-decorated fraktur for Elisabeth Stambach of Codorus Twp., York County, printed in Hanover, Pennsylvania, by Stark and Lange, period paint-grained frame, foxed 475.00

Bookplate
  6-1/2" x 4", attributed to Andreas Kolb (1749-1811) of Berks, Bucks, Chester, Lehigh, Montgomery, and Northampton counties, dated 1797, translates as "This New Testament belongs to Elizabeth Schei-mer...25th day March...1797..."
. . . . .5,980.00
  6-1/2" x 4", signed by George Gerhart (1791-1846) of Lehigh or Washington County, dated Feb. 12, 1837, illustrated in Pastor Frederick Weiser's *The Gift Is Small, the Love Is Great* 27,600.00
  17" x 21", double, fraktur artist Christian Strenge of Lancaster County, PA, for Christian Steman 18,000.00

Copybook, Vorschriften
  Christian Frederick Helener, 6-1/2" x 8-1/8". 1,495.00
  Wilhelm Munch, 5" x 8-1/8" 6,900.00

Drawing
  6-1/2" x 7 7/8", by Maria Schultz, Schwenkfelder, decorated with tulips and other flowers in green, red, blue, and brown, loss to lower edge 4,180.00
  9-1/2" x 7-1/8", red, green, and black interlaced calligraphic figure-eight with four angel heads in corners, attributed to the Gottschall family, 19th C 3,750.00
  9-3/4" x 7-7/8", printed and hand-colored fraktur by artist David Bixler, Fivepointville, Brecknock Township, Lancaster County, PA, translation by Pastor Frederick Weiser of the texts: in the heart, "Restrain yourself and do not curse in my house or go right out the door! Otherwise God will punish both you and me alike from heaven," and across the bottom, "Hearken! Flowers in the meadows! Hearken! Birdies in the air! I will trust my Jesus in love who calls me. I am his and he is mine...eternal shall my love befoxed," small damp-stain at bottom, orig period molded softwood frame, painted black over earlier red, backboard has "A. B. Bixler" written in pencil 25,000.00
  12-1/2" x 15-1/2", watercolor on paper, sgd "Carl Munch, Heidelberg Township, Dauphin Co., 1799," decorated with a basket of flowers and a vase of tulips flanking an interior scene of a woman spinning, and featured a Windsor and a ladder-back chair and a six-plate stove, paper has darkened over the years 22,000.00
  12-1/2" x 18-1/2", crown and birds, David Ellinger, PA
. . . . .1,650.00
  13-3/4" x 14", basket of strawberries, David Ellinger, PA
. . . . .1,925.00
  13-3/4" x 16-3/4", attributed to Daniel Peterman, inscribed "The Birds of Paradise in all their Joys" across the top and "A walk in the garden by two sisters" and "A Christmas gift

Daniel Peterman, Manheim Township, York County, PA, wove paper, watermark, colored dec, bird, distelfink, and floral motifs, two women, 15-3/4" x 12-1/2", $1,750.

for Miss Mary Ann Rickert. Presented by M. Palmer, December the 23rd, 1838" 13,800.00
14" x 17", crowns and peacocks, David Ellinger, PA 1,650.00
14-1/2" x 10-1/2", parrot, David Ellinger, PA 1,265.00
15-1/2" x 11-1/2", urn of tulips, David Ellinger, PA. .1,155.00
16" x 13", urn of flowers, David Ellinger, PA 1,155.00
16" x 13-1/2", George Washington on horseback, David Ellinger, PA 2,200.00
16-5/16" x 13-2/16" hand-drawn by Mary Toms, a celibate member of the Snow Hill Society, words "American Eagle" in yellow and green above a large calligraphic eagle 4,500.00
Family Record, 15-1/4" h, 11-1/4" w, pen, ink, and watercolor on paper, gilt highlights, Mayberry Family, Windham, Maine area, framed, some scattered staining, minor tears, old repairs 500.00
Marriage Certificate, watercolor, Col. Edward Anderson of Windham, Maine, born 1753 and married in 1774, water-stained 2,750.00
Portrait, pen, ink, and watercolor, wove paper, full length portrait of woman in yellow dress, holding purse and bouquet of flowers, inscribed "Miss Susannah Kern her Picture AD 1831," red, yellow, pink, green, and black, Centre County, PA, artist, 10-5/8"h, 7-1/2" w, orig walnut frame, 11-3/4" h, 9-5/8" w 21,010.00
Religious Text, pen, ink, and watercolor on paper
14" x 12" religious text fraktur by Heinrich Engelhard, dated 1830, text in Pennsylvania German. 2,420.00
17" h, 13-3/4" w, text in English, excerpt from Exodus, Chapter 20, architectural frame work with columns, picket fence, gable roof and steeples with plumes of flowers, red, green, yellow, and black, paper has darkened and very fragile, 1889 presentation inscription on old gilt frame backing 2,860.00
Wall Chart, 23-3/4" x 17-3/4", Ephrata Cloister, German text reads: "The lambkin's not alone, the dove-let has a mate, And I no playmate have, nor shepherd who will wait. How long now must my heart in passionate longing burn, Till my dear precious Friend myself his own will term? I know within my heart my love will ne're grow cold, Yet premature this power is wont to waxen old. I ever shall embrace the wisdom of my heart, Which raises me in it, and remedies my smart. But still it's not enough, to comprehend all this. I want the most beloved, our heavenly mate to kiss; And since 'twill surely be; he'll take me at the last. So will I choose him now and ever forth hold fast." Lacks color, worn condition 10,000.00
Writing Book (Schreibbuch), Catherine Rohr, New Britain Township, PA, 1784-1824, and her husband, John Frick of Hatfield Township, Montgomery County, legal-size softcover manuscript, for years 1784-1788, 1798-1800, and 1823-24, 45 pages written mostly in German script with several full pages of fraktur 4,400.00

FRANKART

History: Arthur Von Frankenberg, artist and sculptor, founded Frankart, Inc., in New York City in the mid-1920s. Frankart, Inc., mass produced practical "art objects" in the Art Deco style into the 1930s. Pieces include aquariums, ashtrays, bookends, flower vases, and lamps. Although Von Frankenberg used live female models as his subjects, his figures are characterized by their form and style rather than specific features. Nudes are the most collectible; caricatures of animals and human figures were also produced, no doubt, to increase sales.

Pieces were cast in white metal in one of the following finishes: cream—a pale iridescent white; bronzoid—oxidized copper, silver, or gold; french—medium brown with green in the crevices; gunmetal—iridescent gray; jap—very dark brown, almost black, with green in the crevices; pearl green—pale iridescent green; and verde—dull light green. Cream and bronzoid were used primarily in the 1930s.

Marks: With few exceptions, pieces were marked "Frankart, Inc.," with a patent number or "pat. appl. for."

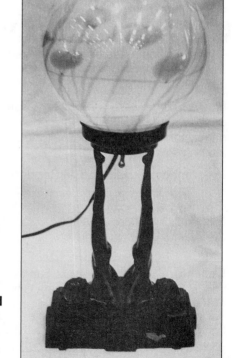

Lamp, No. L220X, two inverted figures balance 8" ball of glass with gold irid dec, green leaves, mkd "Patented Design No. D77202," 1928, 17" h, $900.

Note: All pieces listed have totally original parts and are in very good condition unless otherwise indicated.

Ashtray, stylized pigeon, puffed out chest, holding 3" removable glass insert ashtray between wings 170.00
Bookends, pr, 7" h, female heads, long necks 220.00
Centerpiece Bowl, 15" d dish, 8-1/2" h nude flower frog 275.00
Incense Burner, 5" h, female head on burner base, leaning back to blow smoke through mouth 195.00
Lamp
    9" h, two kneeling nudes, embracing 8" d crackle glass globe 495.00
    23" h, two female figures wearing pajamas and wide brimmed hats, strolling across base, silk shade 400.00
Match Holder, 8" h, burrow, pack on back 165.00
Smoker's Set, 7" h, nude, seated and leaning back, geometric base, arms resting on removable glass cigarette box, 3" d removable glass ashtray at feet. 300.00
Wall Plaque, 6"h, seated nude, floral framework 275.00

FRANKOMA POTTERY

History: John N. Frank founded a ceramic art department at Oklahoma University in Norman and taught there for several years. In 1933, he established his own business and began making Oklahoma's first commercial pottery. Frankoma moved from Norman to Sapulpa, Oklahoma, in 1938.

A fire completely destroyed the new plant later the same year, but rebuilding began almost immediately. The company remained in Sapulpa and continued to grow. Frankoma is the only American pottery to have pieces on permanent exhibit at the International Ceramic Museum of Italy.

In September 1983, a disastrous fire struck once again, destroying 97% of Frankoma's facilities. The rebuilt Frankoma Pottery reopened on July 2, 1984. Production has been limited to 1983 production molds. All other molds were lost in the fire.

Prior to 1954, all Frankoma pottery was made with a honey-tan-colored clay from Ada, Oklahoma. Since 1954, Frankoma has used a brick-red clay from Sapulpa. During the early 1970s the clay became lighter and is now pink in color.

Marks: There were a number of early marks. One most eagerly sought is the leopard pacing on the "Frankoma" name. Since the 1938 fire, all pieces have carried only the name.

References: Susan and Al Bagdade, *Warman's American Pottery and Porcelain*, Wallace-Homestead, 1994; Phyllis and Tom Bess, *Frankoma and Other Oklahoma Potteries*, Schiffer Publishing, 1995; Donna Frank, *Clay in the Master's Hands*, 2nd ed., Cock-A-Hoop Publishing, 1995.

Collectors' Club: Frankoma Family Collectors Association, P.O. Box 32571, Oklahoma City, OK 73123-0771.

Ashtray, Can-Tex, green/brown glaze. 18.00
Bank, elephant 18.00
Bicentennial Plates, series 125.00

Bookends, pr, ocelot, walking, logo. 275.00
Bowl
    Lazybones, blue 7.00
    Wagon Wheel, prairie green. 7.50
Candleholders, Prickly Pear, Prairie Green, Ada clay, mold #306 . . . . 150.00
Canteen, small, Ada clay, mold #59 . . . . 40.00
Center Bowl, Prickly Pear, Prairie Green, Ada clay, mold #206 . . . . 45.00
Christmas Plate, 1968-75, set. 125.00
Cigarette Set, interlocking cov 3 3/4" l cigarette keeper and 3 3/4" l ashtray, forms state of Oklahoma shape, green/brown glaze, Ada clay. 50.00
Creamer, 4" h, Wagon Wheel, brown/gold/butterscotch glaze, Ada clay, imp mark. 15.00
Cup and Saucer
    Mayan, Aztec white 10.00
    Westwind, yellow 12.00
Figure
    Boots, 3 3/4" h, connected by leather thong, pink clay. 15.00
Gardener Girl and Boy
    Blue 210.00
    Desert Gold 230.00
Jug, 7"h, 4" w, Golda's Corn, reddish brown glaze, incised "Frankoma 810 1951". 35.00
Mug
    Donkey
        1969, 1st edition 25.00
        1975. . . . . 35.00
    Elephant
        1968, 1st edition 75.00
        1972. . . . . 35.00
Mayan Aztec, 5" h, turquoise drip glaze, Ada clay, incised "82M" and "Frankoma" 15.00
Uncle Sam, red, white, or blue 15.00
Pitcher, 2-1/2" h, Thunderbird, green/brown glaze, red clay, incised "555" 15.00
Plate
    Conestoga, 8 1/4" d, 1971, gray-blue glaze, relief "Conestoga Wagon 1725-1850" and "1971 John Frank Oklahoma Association For Retarded Children, Oklahoma Jaycees 1971 State Seal," red Sapulpa clay, ink stamped #559 . . 125.00
    Easter, 1972. . . . . 25.00
    Flight to Egypt 35.00
    Fifty Year Commemorative. 25.00
    7" d, Wagon Wheel, prairie green 6.50
    10" d
        Mayan, Aztec white 10.00
        Wagon Wheel, prairie green 7.50

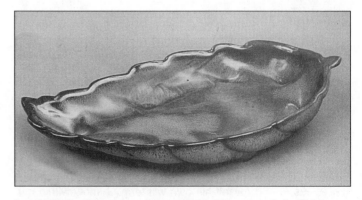

Leaf Dish, Gracetone, green and brown, ftd, #226, 12-1/4" l, 6-1/8" w, 1-7/8" h, $45.

Salt and Pepper Shakers, pr, 3-1/4" h, oil derrick shape, ivory glaze, Ada clay, stamped "Frankoma" on bottom..... 20.00
Vase, mold #28, Ada clay........................ 30.00
Wall Mask
    Indian, 3 3/4" l,. mahogany glaze, Ada clay........ 35.00
    Tragedy and Comedy, white, price for pr.......... 95.00
Wall Pocket, Acorn, green, early clay, #190.......... 45.00

FRATERNAL ORGANIZATIONS

History: Benevolent and secret societies played an important part in America from the late 18th to the mid-20th centuries. Initially, the societies were organized to aid members and their families in times of distress. They evolved from this purpose into important social clubs by the late 19th century.

In the 1950s, with the arrival of the civil rights movement, an attack occurred on the secretiveness and often discriminatory practices of these societies. Membership in fraternal organizations, with the exception of the Masonic group, dropped significantly. Many local chapters closed and sold their lodge halls. This resulted in the appearance of many fraternal items in the antiques market.

Museums: Iowa Masonic Library & Museum, Cedar Rapids, IA; Knights of Columbus Headquarters Museum, New Haven, CT; Masonic Grand Lodge Library & Museum of Texas, Waco, TX; Museum of Our National Heritage, Lexington, MA; Odd Fellows Historical Society, Caldwell, ID.

Additional Listings: See *Warman's Americana & Collectibles* for more examples.

Benevolent & Protective Order of the Elks (BPOE)
Badge, metal
    1913, Rochester.............................. 30.00
    1940, Houston.............................. 25.00
Bowl, 1910, Detroit, Fenton, amethyst carnival glass... 650.00
Calling Card Case, 1-1/2" x 2", sterling silver, inscribed and dated 1913........................... 100.00
Cap, Keokuk, IA, purple and white.................. 5.00
Mug, purple, elk's head and clock, silver handle and trim
    .... 40.00
Pipe Holder, ceramic, white, gold trim, "Elks Lodge, South Bend, Ind."....................... 22.00
Pitcher, 12" h, china, purple shaded elk's head and clock emblems, white ground, marked "National Art China, Trenton, NJ"................................ 115.00
Program, souvenir, 1940........................... 10.00
Shaving Mug, gold on white, elk emblem............. 50.00
Fraternal Order of Eagles
Match Safe, 2-3/4" h, plated metal, metal inserts, encased wording, "Compliments of H. Fetter, Toledo, Ohio," very worn
    .... 15.00
Stein Set, tankard, six matching steins............1,250.00
Improved Order of Redmen, match safe, 2-3/4" h, plated metal, metal inserts, "The Improved Order of Redmen," name tag inserted on back.......................... 150.00
Independent Order of Foresters, match box cover, 2-1/2" w, 1-5/8 d, brass, hinged top, relief with home, Toronto, Canada
    .... 50.00
Independent Order of Odd Fellows, IOOF
Bow, 48" l....................................... 85.00
Certificate, 16" h, 19" w, Grand Lodge of Ontario....... 50.00

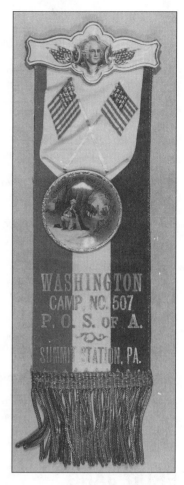

Patriotic Order Sons of America, top pin printed celluloid, center portrait of George Washington, gold trim, center medallion with image of Washington kneeling in prayer, made by Whitehead & Hoag, 7" l, $125. Photo courtesy of Julie Robinson.

Cookie Board, 5" x 6-3/4", oval, cast iron, center insignia, initials "F.L.T." within links..................... 150.00
Degree Chart, 31-1/2" h, 25-1/2" w, framed, stains.... 100.00
Match Safe, 2-3/4" h, plated metal, metal inserts...... 130.00
Quiver with Arrows, 5-1/2" h, silver plated pendant with scroll, quill pens, and heart in hand................... 85.00
Receipt, 2-1/2" x 4", 1955....................... 15.00
Secretary, 31-1/4" w, 24-1/2" d, 81-1/2" h, two pc, oak, molded cornice with Odd Fellows insignia on crest, top door with single pane of glass, two drawers, slant top writing surface, one drawer base, fluted and turned legs, old worn finish. 700.00
Staff of Life, 62-1/2" l, serpent, worn polychrome....... 90.00
Knights of Pythias
Goblet, green, 1900............................. 50.00
Match Safe, 2-3/4" h, plated metal, inserts with Knights of Pythias emblems and Friendship, Charity and Benevolence wording, some wear............................. 90.00
Rug, hooked, 36" l, 24" w, oval with knight and crossed arms, red/brown border, late 19th or early 20th C, needs rebinding
    .... 250.00
Tankard and Mug Set, 11-1/2" h tankard, six 5" h mugs, multicolored decal transfers, mkd "Roseville," minor flaws... 350.00
Masonic
Apron, 13-1/2" l, 15" w, silver bullion embroidery and fringe, scrolling foliate, crossed swords, crossed keys, skull and crossbones, open book with crossed quills, Masonic compass and sq, all-seeing eyes, velvet ground, painted highlights, 19th C, some loss and fading.............. 100.00
Book, Arthur E. Waite, *A New Encyclopedia of Free Masonry*, Combined Edition, Weathervane Books, NY, 16 full page plates, 900 pgs................................ 15.00

Bowl, 10 1/8" d, Sunderland pink luster, polychromed enameled black transfers, farmers arm verse "God Speed the Plow," sailors farewell with verse, Masonic emblems on ext., pink luster trim and berries on int. vinework border, central figural landscape with hp titled "Thomas & Susanna Gray," printed "Dixon, Austin & Co. Sunderland" mark, English, c1825, rim wear 635.00

Letter Opener, miniature trowel, Franklin Lodge, wooden handle 25.00

Loving Cup, St. Paul, MN, 1907, Pittsburgh PA 65.00

Match Safe, 2-3/4" h, plated metal, metal inserts with Masonic emblem on both sides 90.00

Photograph, 10-1/2" x 8-1/2", President McKinley in full Masonic outfit, sgd "Courtney, Canton, Ohio," matted and framed 110.00

Plate, 8-1/4"" d, Toledo, 1906, polychrome center scene, fraternal symbols around scalloped rim, inscribed "64th Annual Conclave of Toledo Commandery, 1906," marked "Knowles, Taylor & Knowles" 40.00

Saucer, 6" d, Pittsburgh, Syria, Los Angeles, May 1908 . 30.00

Tumbler, "Landmark Lodge No. 127, Baltimore, 1866-1916," milk glass 45.00

Shriner

Dinner Set, Rajah, 52 pcs, various makers. 150.00

Goblet, ruby stained, St. Paul, 1908 . . . . 60.00

Hat, fez, felt. 25.00

Plate, 10-1/2" d, comic beat-up Shriner center, camel border, desert and palms 65.00

Shot Glass, cranberry, gold sheaf of wheat pattern, Shrine symbol, marked "Syria Temple Pittsburgh 1908, Brown, Motheral, Moore, Robinson". 175.00

Wine Glass, sgd "Buffalo 1899," clear, gold dec. 115.00

FRUIT JARS

History: Fruit jars are canning jars used to preserve food. Thomas W. Dyott, one of Philadelphia's earliest and most innovative glassmakers, was promoting his glass canning jars in 1829. John Landis Mason patented his screw-type canning jar on Nov. 30, 1858. This date refers to the patent date, not the age of the jar. There are thousands of different jars and a variety of colors, types of closures, sizes, and embossings.

References: Douglas M. Leybourne, Jr., *Red Book No. 7*, published by author (P.O. Box 5417, N. Muskegon, MI 49445), 1993; Jerry McCann, *Fruit Jar Annual*, published by author (5003 W. Berwyn Ave., Chicago, IL 60630), 1995; Dick Roller (comp.), *Indiana Glass Factories Notes*, Acorn Press, 1994; Bill Schroeder, *1000 Fruit Jars: Priced and Illustrated*, 5th ed., Collector Books, 1987, 1996 value update.

Periodical: *Fruit Jar Newsletter*, 364 Gregory Ave., West Orange, NJ 07052.

Collectors' Clubs: Ball Collectors Club, 22203 Doncaster, Riverview, MI 48192; Federation of Historical Bottle Collectors, Inc., 88 Sweetbriar Branch, Longwood, FL 32750; Midwest Antique Fruit Jar & Bottle Club, P.O. Box 38, Flat Rock, IN 47234.

Additional Listings: See *Warman's Americana & Collectibles* for more examples.

Advance, Pat Apld For, aquamarine, qt, ground lip 80.00

All Right, aquamarine, qt, cylindrical, ground mouth, metal cap, wire clamp, smooth base, wispy amber streaks in neck, 1868-1880, old closure, crudely made jar, Leybourne #61 . . . . 225.00

American Fruit Jar, light green, qt, handmade, glass lid, wire bail 100.00

Anchor Hocking, clear, qt, machine made, glass lid, wire bail, anchor emb on side H superimposed on anchor 5.00

Ball

Aqua, qt, handmade, glass lid, ground top, emb script "The Ball, Pat. Apl'd For" 40.00

Blue, Sure Seal, smooth lip, lightning beaded neck seal 5.00

Belle, Pat. Dec 14th, 1968, aquamarine, qt, three raised feet, ground lip, lid, metal neck band, wire bail 775.00

Blue Ribbon, clear, qt, glass lid, wire clip 8.00

Cadiz, aqua, ground lip 450.00

Clark Fruit Jar Co., blue, qt, handmade, glass lid emb "Clark Fruit Jar Cleveland" 50.00

Conserve, clear, qt, handmade, glass lid, wire bail. 9.00

Dexter, aqua, ground lip, glass insert and screw band, patd Aug. 8th, 1865 . . . . 35.00

Doolittle, aqua, qt, handmade, glass lid, emb "Doolittle The Self Sealer" 65.00

Eagle, aquamarine, qt, applied mouth, lid, cast iron yoke 125.00

Economy, amber, pt, metal lid, spring clip 5.00

Forster Jar, clear, smooth lip, glass insert and screw band 10.00

Good House Keepers, clear, 2 qt, machine made, zinc lid . 2.50

Hamilton, clear, qt, handmade, glass lid, metal clip 45.00

Improved Gem, L G Co., aqua, ground lip, glass insert, screw band 400.00

Kerr, self sealing trademark, patented Mason, sky blue, pt, smooth lip, 2 pc lid 95.00

Lafayette, aqua, script. 2.50

Mason

Aqua, ground lip, X patent Nov 30th 1858 . . . . 15.00

Green, qt, hand made, zinc lid, emb "S Mason's Patent 1858" 5.00

Millville Atmospheric Fruit Jar, NJ, aqua, cast iron lid fastener, aqua lid marked "Whitall's Patent," chip on lid, 9" h . . . 50.00

Ohio Quality Mason, clear, 2 qt, handmade, zinc lid. 15.00

Drey Mason, sq, emb, zinc lid, half pint, $20.

Pine Deluxe Jar, clear, pt, machine made, glass lid, wire bail
. . . . 5.00

Potter & Bodine/Air Tight/Fruit Jar, aquamarine, cylindrical, barrel form, tooled mouth, pontil scar, 1840-60, two flat mouth chips, some int,. minor stain, 9" h 500.00

Protector, aquamarine, qt, cylindrical, ground mouth, smooth base, 1867-90, no closure, Leybourne #2420 . . . . 45.00

Sure, aqua, qt, handmade, glass lid, spring wire clip . . . 225.00

Tillyer, aquamarine, qt, ground lip, lid, wire clamp 60.00

Trade Mark Lightning, light yellow amber, qt, cylindrical, ground mouth, smooth base, yellow glass lid, wire bail, 1882-1900, Leybourne #1499 . . . . 60.00

Turn Mold, golden amber, cylindrical, applied wax sealer mouth, aquamarine lid, half gallon, 1860-90, Leybourne #3045-3
. . . . 90.00

Western Pride, aquamarine, qt, cylindrical, applied collared mouth, smooth base, 1875-90, no closure, Leybourne #2495
. . . . 120.00

Woodbury Improved WGW, aquamarine, qt, cylindrical, ground mouth, smooth base, 1880-90, Leybourne #3029 . . . . 40.00

Yeoman's Fruit Bottle, aqua, wax cork closure 50.00

FRY GLASS

History: The H. C. Fry Glass Co. of Rochester, Pennsylvania, began operating in 1901 and continued in business until 1933. Their first products were brilliant-period cut glass. They later produced Depression glass tablewares. In 1922, they patented heat-resisting ovenware in an opalescent color. This "Pearl Oven Glass," which was produced in a variety of pieces for oven and table, included casseroles, meat trays, and pie and cake pans.

Fry's beautiful art line, Foval, was produced only in 1926 and 1927. It is pearly opalescent, with jade green or delft blue trim. It is always evenly opalescent, never striped like Fenton's opalescent line.

Marks: Most pieces of the oven glass are marked "Fry" with model numbers and sizes. Foval examples are rarely signed, except for occasional silver-overlay pieces marked "Rockwell."

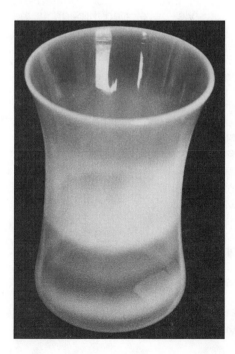

Tumbler, Foval, waisted, 3-7/8" h, $40.

Reference: Fry Glass Society, *Collector's Encyclopedia of Fry Glass*, Collector Books, 1989, 1998 value update.

Collectors' Club: H. C. Fry Glass Society, P.O. Box 41, Beaver, PA 15009.

REPRODUCTION ALERT

In the 1970s, reproductions of Foval were made in abundance in Murano, Italy. These pieces, including items such as candlesticks and toothpicks, have teal blue transparent trim.

Bouillon Cup and Saucer, Foval, pearl white, two cobalt blue handles. 85.00

Bud Vase, 9-1/2" h, Foval, pearl white, Delft blue wafer attachment 125.00

Candleholder, Azure blue 25.00

Casserole, Pearl Oven Ware, etched gold dec lid, metal holder, 1938 . . . . 75.00

Child's Pie Plate, Pearl Oven Ware 50.00

Compote, 6-3/4" d, Foval, alabaster white bowl and foot, jade green stem 120.00

Creamer, 4" h, pinched top, yellow body, three blue-green loops, applied deep blue handle 175.00

Cup and Saucer, Foval, pearl white, Delft blue handles . . 65.00

Goblet
    Rose etch, #7816, 10 oz 24.00
    Royal Blue, 6-1/4" h 35.00

Grill Plate, 10-1/2" d, mkd "Pearl Oven Ware" 35.00

Iced Tea Set, Japanese Maid, deeply etched, ftd pitcher, six handled, ftd tumblers 525.00

Ivy Ball, Emerald Green, crystal swirl connector. 60.00

Lemonade Pitcher, 6" h, Pearl Ware, Delft blue handle . 165.00

Pie Plate, Pearl Oven Ware 35.00

Pitcher, 9-1/4" h, Diamond Optic pattern, chrome green, ground pontil. 85.00

Plate
    7-1/2" d, jade, sterling silver floral overlay 185.00
    9-1/2" d, Foval, pearl white, Delft blue rim 75.00

Soda Tumbler, Wild Rose etch, 5" h, 12 oz, handle, 16 point cut star base. 28.00

Teapot, Foval, pearl white, cobalt blue spout, handle and knob
. . . . 250.00

Toothpick Holder, Foval, pearl white, Delft blue handle . . 85.00

Tumbler, Wild Rose etch, #51, 3-1/2" h, 8 oz, cut fluted base
. . . . 24.00

Vase, 12" h, opalescent body, pink loopings. 215.00

Wine Glass, Wild Rose etch, 5-1/4" h, 3 oz, cut fluted stem
. . . . 28.00

FULPER POTTERY

History: The Fulper Pottery Company of Flemington, New Jersey, made stoneware pottery and utilitarian ware beginning in the early 1800s. It switched to the production of art pottery in 1909 and continued until about 1935.

Its earliest artware was called the Vasekraft line (1910-1915), featuring intense glazine and rectilinear, Germanic forms. Its middle period (1915-1925) included some of the earlier shapes, but it also incorporated Oriental forms.

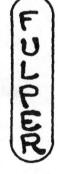

The company's glazing at this time was less consistent but more diverse. Its last period (1925-1935) was characterized by water-down Art Deco forms with relatively week glazing.

Pieces were almost always molded, though careful hand-glazing distinguished this pottery as one of the premier semi-commercial producers. Pieces from all periods are almost always marked.

Marks: A rectangular mark, FULPER, in a rectangle is known as the "ink mark" and dates from 1910-1915. The second mark, as shown, dates from 1915-1925, it was incised or in black ink. The final mark, FULPER, die-stamped, dates from about 1925 to 1935.

References: Susan and Al Bagdade, *Warman's American Pottery and Porcelain*, Wallace-Homestead, 1994; Ralph and Terry Kovel, *Kovels' American Art Pottery*, Crown Publishers, 1993; David Rago, *American Art Pottery*, Knickerbocker Press, 1977; ---, *Fulper Pottery*, Arts & Crafts Quarterly Press, n.d.

Collectors' Club: American Art Pottery Association, P.O. Box 525, Cedar Hill, MO 63016; Stangl/Fulper Collectors Club, P.O. Box 538, Flemington, NJ 08822.

Advisor: David Rago.

Bookends, pr, 8" h, Egyptian, Rameses, green matte, early mark 550.00
Bowl
   12" d, 6" h, Effigy, 3 apes holding flat bowl, blue glossy flambé over blue matte, early mark 600.00

Lamp, flaring base, mushroom shade, green and ivory leaded glass pieces, Cat's Eye flambe glaze, rectangular ink mark, rare, $11,000. Photo courtesy of David Rago Auctions, Inc.

13" d, 5" h, curled edge, Leopard skin Crystalline glaze, early mark 800.00
Cabinet Vase
   5" h, 4" d, cylindrical neck, squat base, ivory flambé over mustard matte glaze, early mark 250.00
   7" h, three curving feet, mustard and white matte flambé, early mark 400.00
Centerpiece Bowl, flaring, flutes and ruffled edge, green flambé, late mark 300.00
Doorstop, Siamese cat, cream and black, early mark. .1,100.00
Lamp, table, 18" h, Japanese, ceramic and leaded glass shade 22,000.00
Vase
   6" h, 8" d, bulbous, 3 handles, white glossy glaze, late mark 125.00
   7" h, 5" d, bulbous, 3 curling handles at rim, blue semi-mate crystalline glaze, late mark. 150.00
   8" h, 5" d, tapering hexagonal, Chinese blue and mahogany flambé glaze, middle mark. 450.00
   10" h, 4" d, reticulated cylindrical, emb mushrooms, ivory and mahogany flambé glaze, early mark 900.00
   11" h, cylindrical, green and black flambé glaze, early mark 550.00
   13" h, bulbous, four handles, blue crystalline glaze, middle period mark 1,870.00
Wall Sconce, 13" h, glossy and matte finishes, electrified, early mark, set of three 3,300.00

FURNITURE

History: Two major currents dominate the American furniture marketplace—furniture made in Great Britain and furniture made in the United States. American buyers continue to show a strong prejudice for objects manufactured in the United States. They will pay a premium for such pieces and accept them above technically superior and more aesthetically appealing English examples.

Until the last half of the 19th century, formal American styles were dictated by English examples and design books. Regional furniture, such as the Hudson River Valley (Dutch) and the Pennsylvania German styles, did develop. A less-formal furniture, often designated as "country" or vernacular style, developed throughout the 19th and early 20th centuries. These country pieces deviated from the accepted formal styles and have a charm that many collectors find irresistible.

America did contribute a number of unique decorative elements to English styles. The American Federal period is a reaction to the English Hepplewhite period. American designers created furniture which influenced, rather than reacted to, world taste in the Gothic Revival style and Arts and Crafts, Art Deco, and Modern International movements.

Furniture styles, approx. dates

William and Mary	1690-1730
Queen Anne	1720-1760
Chippendale	1755-1790
Federal (Hepplewhite)	1790-1815
Sheraton	1790-1810
Empire (Classical)	1805-1830
Victorian	
French Restauration	1830-1850
Gothic Revival	1840-1860

Rococo Revival	1845-1870
Elizabethan	1850-1915
Louis XIV	1850-1914
Naturalistic	1850-1914
Renaissance Revival	1850-1880
Néo-Greek	1855-1885
Eastlake	1870-1890
Art Furniture	1880-1914
Arts and Crafts	1895-1915
Art Nouveau	1896-1914
Art Deco	1920-1945
International Movement	1940-Present

REPRODUCTION ALERT

Beware of the large number of reproductions. During the 25 years following the American Centennial of 1876, there was a great revival in copying furniture styles and manufacturing techniques of earlier eras. These centennial pieces now are more than 100 years old. They confuse many dealers, as well as collectors.

References: *Antique Wicker from the Heywood-Wakefield Catalog*, Schiffer Publishing, 1994; Luke Beckerdite (ed.), *American Furniture*, Chipstone Foundation, 1994; Joseph T. Butler, Field Guide to American Furniture, Facts on File Publications, 1985; Robert Judson Clark et al., *Design in America*, Harry N. Abrams, Detroit Institute of Arts and The Metropolitan Museum of Art, 1983; Wendy Cooper, *Classical Taste in America*, Abbeville Press, 1993; Madeleine Deschamps, *Empire*, Abbeville Press, 1994; Eileen and Richard Dubrow, *Styles of American Furniture, 1860-1960,* Schiffer Publishing, 1997; Nancy Goyne Evans, *American Windsor Chairs*, Hudson Hills Press, 1996; ——, *American Windsor Furniture: Specialized Forms,* Hudson House Press, 1997.

Fine Furniture Reproductions, Schiffer Publishing, 1996; Oscar Fitzgerald, *Four Centuries of American Furniture*, Wallace-Homestead, 1995; Tim Forrest, *Bulfinch Anatomy of Antique Furniture*, Bulfinch Press, 1996; Benno M. Forman, *American Seating Furniture*, Winterthur Museum, W. W. Norton & Company, 1988; Don Fredgant, *American Manufactured Furniture*, revised and updated ed., Schiffer Publishing, 1996; *Furniture of the Arts & Crafts Period*, L-W Book Sales, 1992, 1995 value update; Phillipe Garner, *Twentieth-Century Furniture*, Van Nostrand Reinhold, 1980; Cara Greenberg, *Mid-Century Modern*, Harmony Books, 1995; George Hepplewhite, *Cabinet-Maker and Upholsterer's Guide* (reprint), Dover Publications, 1969; Heywood Brothers and Wakefield Company, Katherine S. Howe, et al., *Herter Brothers*, Harry N. Abrams, 1994; Conover Hill, *Antique Oak Furniture,* 1997 value update, Collector Books; Bruce Johnson, *The Pegged Joint*, Knock on Wood Publications, 1995.

Myrna Kaye, F*ake, Fraud, or Genuine*, New York Graphic Society Book, 1987; William C. Ketchum, Jr., *American Cabinetmakers*, Crown, 1995; Russell Hawes Kettell, *Pine Furniture of Early New England*, Dover Pub-

lications, 1929; Thomas King, *Neo-Classical Furniture Designs* (reprint of 1829 catalog), Dover Publications, n.d.; Ralph Kylloe, *History of the Old Hickory Chair Company and the Indiana Hickory Furniture Movement*, published by author, 1995; ——, Rustic Traditions, Gibbs-Smith, 1993; David P. Lindquist and Caroline C. Warren, *Colonial Revival Furniture with Prices*, Wallace-Homestead, 1993; ——, *English & Continental Furniture with Prices*, Wallace-Homestead, 1994; ——, *Victorian Furniture with Prices*, Wallace-Homestead, 1995; Robert F. McGiffin, *Furniture Care and Conservation*, revised 3rd ed., American Association for State and Local History Press, 1992; Kathryn McNerny, *Victorian Furniture, Our American Heritage,* Book I, 1997 value update, Book II, 1997 value update; Collector Books; Edgar G. Miller, Jr., *American Antique Furniture*, 2 vols., Dover Publications, 1966; *Herman Miller 1939 Catalog, Gilbert Rohde Modern Design,* Schiffer Publishing, 1998; Marie Purnell Musser, *Country Chairs of Central Pennsylvania*, published by author, 1990.

Milo M. Naeve, *Identifying American Furniture*, 2nd ed., American Association for State and Local History, 1989; George C. Neumann, *Early American Antique Country Furnishings*, L-W Book Sales, 1984, 1993 reprint; Jacquelyn Peake, *How to Recognize and Refinish Antiques for Pleasure and Profit*, 3rd ed., Globe Pequot Press (P.O. Box 833, Old Saybrook, CT 06475), 1995; Peter Philip, Gillian Walkling, and John Bly, *Field Guide to Antique Furniture*, Houghton Mifflin, 1992; Leslie Piña, *Fifties Furniture*, Schiffer Publishing, 1996; Rudolf Pressler and Robin Staub, *Biedermeier Furniture*, Schiffer Publishing, 1996; Don and Carol Raycraft, *Wallace-Homestead Price Guide To American Country Antiques, 15th Edition,* Krause Publications, 1997; Ernest Rettelbusch, *Handbook of Historic Ornament from Ancient Times to Biedermeier*, Dover Publications, 1996; Michael Regan (ed.), *American & European Furniture Price Guide*, Antique Trader Books, 1995; Steve and Roger W. Rouland, *Heywood-Wakefield Modern Furniture*, 1995, 1997 value update, Collector Books; Paul Royka, *Mission Furniture from the American Arts & Crafts Movement,* Schiffer Publishing, 1997.

Ibert Sack, *New Fine Points of Furniture*, Crown, 1993; *American Wooden Chairs, 1895-1907,* Schiffer Publishing, 1997; Klaus-Jurgen Sembach, *Modern Furniture Designs, 1950-1980s,* Schiffer Publishing, 1997; Nancy A. Smith, *Old Furniture*, 2nd ed., Dover Publications, 1990; Robert W. and Harriett Swedberg, *Collector's Encyclopedia of American Furniture*, Vol. 1 (1990, 1996 value update), Vol. 2 (1992, 1996 value update), Vol. 3 (1998), Collector Books; ——, *Furniture of the Depression Era*, Collector Books, 1987, 1996 value update; ——, *Swedberg's Price Guide to Antique Oak Furniture*, 1st Series, Collector Books, 1994; Thonet Co., *Thonet Bentwood and Other Furniture* (1904 catalog reprint), Dover Publications, 1980; Eli Wilner, *Antique American Frames*, Avon Books, 1995; Ghenete Zelleke, Eva B. Ottillinger, and Nina Stritzler, *Against the Grain*, The Art Institute of Chicago, 1993.

There are hundreds of specialized books on individual furniture forms and styles. Two of note are: Monroe H. Fabian, *Pennsylvania-German Decorated Chest*, Universe Books, 1978, and Charles Santore, *Windsor Style In America*, Revised, vols. I and II, Dover Publications, n.d.

Videotapes: BBC Enterprises Ltd., *Story of English Furniture*, 2 Vols., Home Vision, 1981; John Bivens, *Authenticating Antique Furniture*, 2 Vols., Pilaster Publications, 1994.

Additional Listings: Arts and Craft Movement; Art Deco; Art Nouveau; Children's Nursery Items; Orientalia; Shaker Items; Stickley.

Notes: Furniture is one of the types of antiques for which regional preferences are a factor in pricing. Victorian furniture is popular in New Orleans and unpopular in New England. Oak is in demand in the Northwest, not as much so in the Middle Atlantic states.

Prices vary considerably on furniture. Shop around. Furniture is plentiful unless you are after a truly rare example. Examine all pieces thoroughly—avoid buying on impulse. Turn items upside down; take them apart. Price is heavily influenced by the amount of repairs and restoration. Make certain you know if any such work has been done to a piece before buying it.

The prices listed below are "average" prices. They are only a guide. High and low prices are given to show market range.

Beds

Aesthetic Movement, American, c1880, ebonized, gilt incised, and marquetry, 76" l, 64-1/2" w, 73" h 3,165.00
Art Nouveau, Louis Marjorelle, France, c1900, carved and inlaid mahogany, arched headboard with whiplash carved and molded corners, footboard with molded panels, both inlaid with various woods, mother-of-pearl, and copper, stylized poppy blossoms and undulating foliage, 85" l, 69" w, 71-3/4" h 15,500.00
Arts and Crafts
American, oak, full size, five vertical slats at headboard and footboard, orig varnish, 78" l, 57" w, 48" h 850.00
Limbert, #651, daybed, angled headrest with spade cut-out, orig finish, recovered cushions, branded, numbered, 74" w, 25" d, 23" h 650.00
Arts and Crafts-Style, quarter-sawn oak, three vertical panels in head and foot board, 42" x 53" h headboard, 34-1/2" h footboard 375.00
Baroque, Italian, simulated marble high scrolling headboard dec in patiglia with vacant cartouches and foliage, carved scrolling feet, painted, green and blue marbleized dec, losses to paint and gilt, pr, 45-3/4" w, 84" h 3,750.00
Biedermeier, figured mahogany veneer, octagonal posts, turned feet and finials, paneled head and footboards, orig rails, some veneer damage, 38" w, 72" l, 45" h, pr. . . 750.00
Chippendale, tall post, curly maple, turned posts, scrolled headboard with poplar panel, orig side rails, old mellow refinishing, minor repairs to posts, 60" w, 72" l, 80" h . . .3,000.00
Classical
Massachusetts, c1825-35, carved mahogany, tall post, scrolled mahogany headboard flanked by reeded, carved, and ring-turned posts, acanthus leaf, beading, gothic arches, and foliage carving, reeded and turned feet, orig rails later fitted for angle irons and bed bolts,

orig surface, central finial missing, 59" w, 81" d, 98" h 6,900.00
Middle Atlantic States, 1835-45, carved mahogany veneer low post, scrolled and paneled headboard, leaf carved finials flanked by posts with pineapple finials, acanthus leaves above spiral carved and ring-turned posts, orig rails, bed bolts, and covers, refinished, imperfections, 58-1/2" w, 78" d, 56-1/2" h 1,100.00
Tall post, four turned, carved, and reeded posts continuing to turned feet on castors, flanked by scrolled recessed panel headboard with rolled veneered crest, shaped footboard, joined by flat tester, rails with added angle irons, old refinish, height loss, 61-1/2" w, 72" d, 77-1/2" h 2,550.00
New England, c1820, painted, turned tall post, turned and tapering headposts flanking shaped headboard, spiral carved footpost joined by rails fitted for roping, accompanying tester, old red paint, restored, 54" w, 79" l, 60-1/2" h 1,400.00
Country, American, rope
Curly maple, turned posts and crest rails, paneled head and footboards with raised walnut panel, old varnish finish, replaced walnut side rails, 51-1/2" w, 72" l, 42" h 750.00
Poplar, old red paint, turned posts with cannonball finials, paneled headboard with scrolled detail and turned finials, footboard posts cut down, extended orig rails, 54-3/4" w, 78" l, 53" h 750.00
Empire, American
Single, fitted as daybed or sofa, mahogany and mahogany figured veneer, turned and acanthus carved posts, upholstered cushion, 31-1/2" x 80" x 43-3/4" h 825.00
Tall Post, curly maple posts, poplar scrolled headboard with old soft finish, turned detail, acorn finials, rails and headboard replaced, 57-1/4" w, 72-1/2" l rails, 89" h. . .1,650.00
Empire Style, cannonball, mahogany, bold detail, replaced headboard with carved eagle, originally rope bed, side rails

Hepplewhite Style, mahogany, satinwood inlay, c1920-30, $300.

changed, other repairs, replaced rails, 78" l, 54" w, 59" h
. . . . .1,200.00

Federal
American, first half 19th C, cherry, tester, three-quarter, rect headboard with concave side edges, footboard lower, baluster-turned posts continuing to turned legs, rails with rope pegs, 81-1/2" l, 53-1/2" w, 78-1/4" h 500.00
New England, c1820, painted red, tall post, vase and ring turned and reeded foot posts joined to turned head posts and shaped pine headboard, arched canopy frame, old red stain, minor imperfections, 48" w, 69" l, 75" h 2,750.00
New England, early 19th C, painted low post, folding, turned headposts planking shaped headboard, joined to footposts by joined rails fitted for roping and folding, old Spanish brown paint, 52-3/4" w, 77-1/2" d, 33-1/2" h 700.00
Salem, MA, c1810-30, carved mahogany, tall post, flat tester frame joining vase and ring reeded and swelled acanthus leaf carved footposts, sq tapering legs, molded spade feet, leaf carved vase and ring reeded and swelled head posts, shaped headboard, old finish, 62" w, 78-1/2" d, 87" h
. . . . .10,925.00

George III, four poster, carved walnut, brass mounted, circular tapered head posts, shaped mahogany headboard, reeded and acanthus-carved footposts, ring-turned feet, casters, 9-1/2" h. 10,000.00

Gothic Revival, American, c1850, carved mahogany, tall headboard with three Gothic arch panels, leaf-carved crest rail, flanked by heavy round ribbed posts topped by ring-turned finials, arched and paneled footboard flanked by lower footposts, heavy bun feet. 4,750.00

Queen Anne, Pennsylvania, early 19th C, low poster, turned and painted pine, head and footposts with flattened ball finials, shaped head and footboards, tapered feet, orig rope rails, orig green paint, 48-1/2" w, 74-3/4" h 3,600.00

Sheraton
Canopy
Carved mahogany, headboard posts simple turned with ring and block turnings, simple headboard, heavily carved footboard posts with spiral turnings and acanthus leaf bell, sq tester with curtains, 58" w, 73-1/2" l, 88" without finials. 3,200.00
Painted, headboard with D-type cut outs on side, footboard with reeded and turned posts, canopy frame, painted red, 52" w, 76" l, 68" h 750.00
Tall post, refinished maple an birch, pine headboard, turned posts with reeded detail on foot posts, rope end

Regency, chaise lounge, rosewood, tufted shaped back, over-scrolled head and end, brass rosettes, three bolsters, three loose cushions, splayed legs, brass paw feet, 83" l, 25" d, $2,400. Photo courtesy of Alderfer Auction Company, Inc.

rails, replaced side rails, curved canopy frame covered in white cotton with floral embroidery, matching bed clothes included, 55" w, 78" l, 66-3/4" h 1,550.00

Victorian
American, refinished walnut, paneled head and footboards with applied scroll and fruit detail, matching crest, orig 73" l side rails, 54" w, 71-1/2" h 450.00
Brass, c1900, straight top rail, curved corners, ring shaped capitals, cast iron side rails, 55" w, 61" h
. . . . .1,200.00
Half Tester, attributed to Prudent Mallard, New Orleans, LA, c1850, carved rosewood, tall arched headboard, shell carved crest, fruit and nuts, scroll carved borders, shaped bordered panels flanked by tall tapering turned headposts supporting upholstered half tester, scroll carved crest, turned finials, paneled sideboards and footboard, turned and carved details, scroll carved corner braces 15,000.00

Benches

Arts & Crafts, oak, rect top with raised edge, pierced and arched apron supported by side slabs, scrolled cut-outs at base, refinished top, orig finish to base, 42" w, 14" d, 18" h
. . . . .1,600.00

Classical, window
Boston, 1835-45, carved mahogany veneer, upholstered seat, veneered rail, leaf-carved cyma curved ends, joined by ring-turned medial stretcher, 48" w, 16-1/4" d, 17-1/2" h
. . . . .2,185.00
New York, 1815-25, mahogany veneer, curving upholstered seat flanked by scrolled ends, scrolled base, old refinish, some veneer cracking and loss, 20th C olive green velvet upholstery, 39-1/2" w, 14" d, 23-5/8" h. 3,500.00
New York, c1820, mahogany and mahogany veneer, upholstered slip seat, veneered rect frame, beaded curule legs joined by vase and ring-turned stretcher, old finish, 24-1/4" w, 15" d, 19" h 1,035.00

Classical Revival, mahogany, carved paw feet and lion's heads, maroon velvet cushion, old finish, 16-1/2" l, 29-1/4" w, 23" h. 600.00

Country
68-1/2" l, Canadian, settle, pine, paneled construction, shaped arms, turned spindles, shaped crest, folds open into bed, old worn finish, traces of paint 600.00
96" l, 18-1/4" w, 13" h, pine, orig red paint, PA, early 19th C
. . . . 750.00
104" l, 13-1/2" w, pine, old worn and weathered green repaint, one board top with rounded front corners, beaded edge apron, cut-out feet mortised through top, age crack in one end of top 325.00

Federal
New England, c1810, window, mahogany, upholstered seat and rolled arms, sq tapering legs, H-form stretchers, refinished, minor repair to one leg, 39-1/2" l, 16" d, 29" h
. . . . 900.00
New York, c1825, window, figured mahogany, each end with rect crotch-figured crest centering removable slip seat, matching seat rail, saber legs, 40-1/2" l. 3,500.00

George III, English, mid-18th C, window, mahogany, rect seat, scrolling arms, later velvet cov, straight legs, blind fret craved, H-form stretcher, pr, 38" l. 4,750.00

Gothic Revival, American, c1820-40, carved mahogany, angled over-upholstered seat, carved seat rails centering quatrefoil, facet lancet-carved legs, molded faceted feet, 65" l, 20" d, 15-1/2" h. 1,750.00

Louis XVI-Style, window
   Carved cherry, overstuffed seat, channeled rails, flanked by molded, overscroll arms carved with be-ribboned foliate sprays, turned, tapered, and leaf-capped legs. 200.00
   Mahogany, out-curved overscroll arms with X-splats, close-nailed, horsehair upholstered seat, sabre legs with castors, frame reeded and carved with paterae, brass plaque reading, "...Colonial Mft Co., Zeeland, Michigan" 550.00
Neoclassical-Style, Italian, 19th C, giltwood, worn leather top, 44-1/2" w, 20" d, 21" h 2,530.00
Wagon Seat, New England, late 18th C, painted, two pairs of arched slats joining three turned stiles, double rush seat flanked by turned arms ending in turned hand-holds, tapering legs, old brown paint over earlier gray, 15" h seat, 30" h 1,200.00
Wicker, painted white, hooped crest rail flanked by rows of dec curlicues, spiral wrapped posts and six spindles, pressed-in oval seat, dec curlicue apron, wrapped cabriole legs, X-form stretcher, 35" w, 31" h 500.00
Windsor
   Country, kneeling, gray over olive green and red paint, reeded edge top, bamboo-turned legs, splayed base, 36-3/4" l, 6-3/4" d, 6" h 350.00
   Mammy, painted black over red, gold stenciling, back crest with stenciled flowers, removable front gate, bench fitted with orig rockers, light brown painted scrolled arms, 48" w, 29-1/4" h 1,000.00
   Pennsylvania-Style, deep seat, white cushion, half spindle back, shaped top crest, curved and scrolled arms, eight legs, box stretchers, medium to light brown finish, 19-1/2" d seat, 34" h 1,200.00

Bentwood

In 1856, Michael Thonet of Vienna perfected the process of bending wood using steam. Shortly afterward, Bentwood furniture became popular. Other manufacturers of Bentwood furniture were Jacob and Joseph Kohn; Philip Strobel and Son; Sheboygan Chair Co.; and Tidoute Chair Co. Bentwood furniture is still being produced today by the Thonet firm and others.

Box
   6-3/4" h, oval, Shaker, Harvard type, finger construction, steel tacks, presentation inscription on inside of lid, old varnish finish, lid has some damage. 175.00
   8" d, 7" h, round, worn orig paint resembles wallpaper, yellow and black foliage scrolls on blue ground, some edge damage to lid 750.00
   12" d, round, old dark finish, swivel handle, minor lid edge damage 200.00
   14-3/4" l, oblong, pine, laced seams, old blue paint, edge damage 250.00
   17-1/4" l, band, pine, orig blue paint, unusual decoupage paper scene of black man, woman, and child, foreign inscription, wear and loose bottom board. 550.00
Chair
   Austrian, Vienna Secession-style, c1910, side, back splat with three circular perforations, three slender spindles, painted black, set of eight 5,500.00
   Thonet, arm, c1935, lacquered, pine frame, upholstered back and seat, 43" h 600.00
Cradle, 41" l, 39" h, ivory fittings 440.00
Hall Tree, Thonet, c1910, bentwood frame, contrasting striped wood inlay, coat hooks with central beveled mirror above one

door, metal drip pan, orig label, 57" w, 13" d, 76" h 2,750.00
Rocker, Thonet, arched twined top rail, cut-velvet fabric fitted back, armrests, and seat, elaborate scrolling frame, curved runners, 53" l 750.00
Stool, Thonet, attributed to Marcel Kammerer, Austria, 1901, beech, sq seat, four legs, U-shaped braces forming spandrels, shaped bronze sabot feet, 14-1/4" sq, 18-1/2" h 1,500.00
Table, Josef Hoffman, c1905, circular top, wooden spheres dec below rim, 21-1/4" h 500.00

Blanket Chests

Chippendale, country, pine, molded rect and hinged top, storage well, front with two simulated drawer fronts over two drawers, molded surrounds, outset molded base with bracket feet, 37-1/2" w, 20" d, 41" h 750.00
Decorated
   Berks County, PA, early 19th C, pine and poplar, lift top, two drawers in base, four bracket feet, old green ground paint striped with red, three tablets, center one with uniform, tulips and vines dec on drawers, later paint, flaking, 43-1/2" w, 18-1/2" d, 38-1/2" h 1,265.00
   Ohio or Pennsylvania, c1840-50, walnut, white pine, poplar, and chestnut secondary woods, punched tulip dec, painted dec and punched green and mustard highlights, six-board construction, dovetailed case, till with lid, single drawer, later turned feet, minor repairs, 39-3/4" w, 19-1/2" d, 25-1/4" h 3,500.00
   Pennsylvania, Perry County, c1825, dower, poplar dovetailed case, orig lime green rag dec, marked "S. Z." on front, two bottom drawers, scalloped dovetailed bracket feet with applied wafers and black paint, reeded between drawers, crab lock, sgd "Sarah Zook Bakner" on back, 48" w, 24" d, 29" h 6,000.00
   Pennsylvania, pine, old worn orig vinegar graining, tombstone panels, half and whole circles and compass stars in red and white, bluish-green ground, dovetailed case, lid edge and base moldings, turned feet, two dovetailed drawers in till, wrought iron strap hinges and bear trap lock with key, old label on back "H. Sowers, Crestline, Oh," 51-1/2" w, 21-1/2" d, 25-1/2" h 2,200.00
Dowry, Mahantango Valley, Pennsylvania, "Samuel Grebiel 1799," orig paint dec, red, blue, mustard, black, and white, two shaped polygons painted in blue grain painting, identical polygons on each side, two in front with banner above with name and date, int. lidded till, black painted dovetailed bracket base, off-set strap hinges, orig lock, 48-1/2" w, 21" d, 23-1/2" h 3,000.00
Grain Painted, New York sate, c1830, molded hinged lift top, lidded till, molded bracket black painted base, orig fanciful ochre and raw umber graining, 48" w, 22" d, 29" h .1,265.00
Jacobean, oak, paneled construction with relief carving, drawer and feet replaced, repairs to lid and molding, old dark finish, 44-1/2" w, 19-1/2" d, 31-3/4" h 825.00
Italian Renaissance-Style, walnut, antique elements, 60-1/2" w, 20" d, 21-3/4" h 4,000.00
Mule, America, pine, thumb-molded top, two overlapping dovetailed drawers, bracket feet, old dark finishing, int. lined with 1875 Boston newspaper, pierced repairs to feet and drawer fronts, 40" w, 18" d, 34-3/4" h. 700.00
Painted
   Massachusetts, western, 18th C, pine, hinged top with molded edge, lidded molded till, single base drawer, molded bracket feet, old green paint over red, old replaced glass pulls, paint wear on top, 45" w, 17" d, 31-5/8" h . .2,650.00

Milford, Connecticut, early 18th C, yellow pine, six board construction, vestiges of painted dec, replaced ball feet, imperfections, 42-1/2" w, 20" d, 26-1/2" h 950.00

New England, c1780, six-board, molded hinged top, dovetail constructed base, bracket feet, orig red paint, minor imperfections, 43-3/4" w, 19" d, 26" h 700.00

New England, late 18th C, molded lift top, two thumb-molded drawers on bracket base, old blue paint, brasses and hinges replaced, 36" w, 19" d, 44" h 1,955.00

New England, late 18th C, pine, hinged molded lid, dovetailed box, applied carved ropetwist beading, applied molded base, orig blue paint, 43-1/2" w, 18" d, 17" h 2,645.00

Pennsylvania, c1780, pine, green and blue paint, one board top with breadboard ends, applied lower molding, dovetailed case, strap hinges, till with molded lid, ogee feet, 45" w, 19" d, 25-1/4" h 1,500.00

Pennsylvania, poplar, old brownish-red finish, dovetailed case, hinged lid, three dovetailed drawers, dovetailed bracket feet, applied moldings, till with lid, tattered printed Haus Segen fraktur on int. of lid, bear trap lock, 50-1/4" w, 23" d, 30" h 2,100.00

Pilgrim Century, attributed to Peter Blin, Wethersfield, CT, 1675-1710, carved, painted, and ebonized oak, rect hinged lid, storage well with till, front carved with two rect inset panels of stylized tulips and leaves, center octagonal panel carved with sunflowers, ebonized splint balusters, mid molding, two long drawers with egg appliqués, stiles continue to form feet, replaced lid, reduced feet, traces of orig red and black pigment, 47-1/2" w, 20-3/4" d, 34-1/4" h 12,000.00

Queen Anne, New England, c1750, marriage chest, pine, hinged rect lift lid, upper half faced with faux drawer fronts, brown paint, 35" 4,000.00

Sheraton, country, pine and poplar, orig red paint, molded edge top, paneled front and ends, sq corner posts, mortised and pinned frame, scalloped apron, turned feet, 44" w, 19-1/2" d, 25-1/2" h 900.00

William and Mary, New England, c1700, oak and yellow pine, joined, drawer base, old finish, minor imperfections, 48-1/2" w, 22" d, 32-3/4" h 4,500.00

Bookcases

Arts & Crafts

Paine Furniture Co., three sliding doors, arched leaded glass panel at top with organic design over single pane of glass, eight adjustable shelves, missing backsplash, orig dark finish, sgd with metal tag, 60" w, 14" d, 59" h 2,200.00

Stickley Brothers, oak, three door form, arched gallery top, leaded stained glass at top above two vertical panes on each door, orig copper hardware, orig finish, unsigned, 59" w, 12" d, 60" h 4,750.00

Stickley, L. & J. G., #645, oak, double door with twelve panes of glass in each, orig copper hardware, keyed tenon construction at sides, orig finish, sgd "The Work of...," 53" w, 12" d, 55" h 7,000.00

Viking, oak, four stacking units, single drawer base, orig copper hardware, orig finish, paper bel, 34" w, 13""d, 60" h 650.00

Biedermeier-Style

Inlaid cherry, outset molded cornice with ebonized bead, front with two recessed glazed doors, four shelves, outset molded base raised on black feet, burr poplar panels, ebonized stringing, 53-1/2" w, 21" d, 72" h 700.00

Mahogany, outset molded top, front with two glazed doors, three shelves, sq section stile feet, 35-3/4" w, 15" d, 52" h 375.00

Chippendale, Maryland or Pennsylvania, 1765-65, mahogany, three sections, upper: dentiled triangular pediment, plinth with contemporary bust of William Shakespeare, plain veneered frieze; center: bookcase with double glazed cupboard doors, astragal mullions, Chinoiserie pattern, molded base; lower: chest with short thumb-molded central drawer flanked by two similar box drawers, two graduated long box drawers, two graduated long drawers, flanked by fluted quarter columns, ogee bracket feet, 44-3/4" d, 25-1/4" d, 106-1/4" h 18,500.00

Chippendale-Style, New England, mahogany, broken arch pedestal over two arched panele3d doors, fitted secretary int. with pigeonholes, six small drawers, lower section with fall front, stepped fitted int., straight front, two small and two wide drawers, brass bail handle, escutcheons, lock plates, straight bracket feet, 42" w, 24" d 93-3/4" h 3,200.00

Classical, New York, 1810-30, mahogany, three-part construction, upper: deeply projecting rect cornice over arched frieze; middle: conforming case fitted with pair of geometric glazed cupboard doors, two int. shelves; lower: rect white marble top above bolection-molded frieze drawer, pair of paneled cupboard doors enclosing shelf, centered by engaged colonettes, foliate-carved and gadrooned bun feet, 47-1/2" w, 24-1/4" d, 92-1/4" h 3,500.00

Eastlake, America, c1880, cherry, rect top, flaring bead trimmed cornice, pair of single-pan glazed cupboard doors, carved oval paterae and scrolls across top, adjustable shelved int., stepped base with line-incised drawers, bail handles, 47-1/2" w, 15-1/4" d, 69-1/4" h 1,200.00

Empire, crotch mahogany veneers, top section: large architectural type cornice, two large glass doors with cathedral top muttons, three adjustable shelves; base: eleven drawers, oval brass knobs, applied base molding, two panes of glass cracked, 66" w, 83" h 5,500.00

Renaissance Revival, walnut, 3 sections, $11,500. Photo courtesy of Jackson's Auctioneers & Appraisers.

Empire-Style, mahogany, two door bookcase top with cathedral type door, base with one top drawer over two doors, three smaller drawers under doors, shelved int., 43-1/2" w, 83-1/2" h 1,700.00

Federal, Philadelphia, 1790-1810, mahogany veneered, four part construction: long rect top with detachable molded cornice; two bookcase sections each with pairs of glazed cupboard doors, twelve rect panes below top row of arched panes, adjustable shelves int.; lower: center butler's fall-front desk drawer, kneehole area flanked by bands of three cockbeaded short drawers, large paneled cupboard doors, molded base, 119" w, 17-1/2" d, 105-3/4" h 27,500.00

George III, late 18th C, mahogany, breakfront, later cornice, damage, losses, 85" w, 21" d, 83-1/2" h 3,750.00

George III-Style

Mahogany, stepped dentiled cornice, four glazed lattice doors, shelves int., lower section with two small over two wide cockbeaded drawers flanked by twin panel doors, ogival bracket feet, 74-3/4" w, 17-1/2" d, 77-1/2" h 2,500.00

Pine, revolving, four circular tiers, simulated books for supports, quadruped base, 26" d, 60" h, pr 6,000.00

Georgian-Style, mahogany, outset molded cornice, front with three glazed doors, each with simulated eighteen-pane tracery, adjustable shelves, molded plinth base, bracket feet, 71-1/4" w, 15" d, 54-1/4" h 600.00

Louis XVI-Style, 19th C, inlaid mahogany, parquetry top, low three-quarter gallery and center oval panel inlaid with fleur-de-lis, open shelf raised on sq-section tapered legs, conforming sabots, 24" w, 8-1/4" d, 27-1/4" h, pr 900.00

Regency, mahogany, projecting molded cornice over two mullion glazed doors, two lower cupboard doors, int. shelves, bracket feet, 56" w, 22" d, 89" h 9,000.00

Revolving, American, second half 19th C, oak, molded rect top, five compartmentalized shelves with slatted ends, quadruped base with castors, stamped "Danners Revolving Book Case...Ohio," 24" w, 24" d, 68-1/4" h 1,100.00

Victorian

Globe-Wernicke, barrister type, stacking, oak, glass fronted drawers, drawer in base, metal bands, orig finish . . 700.00

Macey, barrister type, stacking, oak, leaded glass door, drawer in base, three sections of varying height, needs regluing, 34" w, 11" d 400.00

Boxes

Band, wallpaper covering, oval

6-5/8" l, 2-3/4" h, America, 19th C 550.00

23" l, cardboard, scene of Castle Garden, red, brown, white, and green, blue ground, wear, bottom loose, bottom sgd in ink "Joel Post" 3,300.00

Bible, chestnut, some curl in lid, molded edges, front panel with punched design, initials and date "L. T. 1705," int. with cov till and single drawer, wrought-iron lock, old dark patina, hasp missing, some edge damage, pulls added to drawer, 27" l 650.00

Book, walnut, dovetailed, old varnish on cover and marbleized paper, minor age cracks, edge damage, 12-1/2" l . . . 350.00

Bride, 18-1/2" l, pine, orig blue paint, polychrome flowers and fruit, lid with bowl of flowers, wear, some edge damage, glued split on lid 880.00

Candle

12" l, 4-1/2" w, 4-1/4" h, dovetailed, rect, sliding lid, cherry lid, pine box 300.00

14" l, 20" h, hanging, pine, two compartments, old red repaint, minor wear 625.00

22" l, 10" d, 6-3/8" h, pine, slide top, painted red, America, early 19th C 425.00

Cheese, 6-1/2" h, 12-1/8" d, pine, circular, incised "E. Temple" on lid, painted blue, America, 19th C, cracks, paint wear, minor losses 175.00

Collar, 13" l, 5" h, wallpaper covering, oval, mkd "E. Stone no. 116 1/2 William Street, New York" 575.00

Decorated

Pine, orig dark red paint, red, black, yellow, and green stylized floral dec, two painted panels on front and two on lid with hearts on corners, stenciled back with freehand inscription "J. K. Hoadle, So. Woodstock, Jan. 1816," dovetailed case, molded edge lid, staple hinges, oval brass bale handles, int. baffle removed, some alligatoring and flaking of paint on lid, 20-1/2" w, 10-5/8" d, 10-1/2" h 2,750.00

Poplar, worn orig red paint, black striping, Roman numerals and decals of children, made to look like stack of books, floral wallpaper-lined int., secret compartment in base, keyhole hidden by sliding book, some edge damage, 9-3/4" l 325.00

Walnut and poplar, vinegar grained, worn orig brown graining, wrought iron lock, incomplete hasp, 31" l 295.00

Document

10-5/8" l, 6-1/8" d, 6-1/2" h, mahogany and flame birch veneer inlaid, shield-form escutcheon, Boston, MA, early 19th C 750.00

18" l, 9-1/2" d, 8-1/4" h, paint dec poplar, lidded till, ochre paint on red ground, gilt lettering "G.W.S.," brass bail handle, America, 19th C 1,150.00

Dome Top, 30" w, 15" d, 13" h, painted red, front panel dec with Adam and Eve in garden of Eden, under pillared gate, flowers and birds, flanking gate, pinwheel style flowers scattered throughout, green, red, white, and brown, pine painted with curve at corners, top with central white lined red heart, back and sides sponge dec 950.00

Dough, pine and poplar, rect removable top, tapering well, splayed ring-turned legs, ball feet, Pennsylvania, 19th C, 38" w, 19-3/4" w, 29-1/2" h 500.00

Hatbox, wallpaper covered

10-3/4" h, 16-3/4" l, birds among foliage, architectural view, imperfections 500.00

11" h, 17-3/4" l, scene of stagecoach among hunters, imperfections 150.00

12-1/4" h, 17-3/4" l, 12-1/2" d, Clayton's Ascent, showing hot air balloons in flight, labeled on underside of lid "From J. M. Hulbert's paste board band box manufactory no. 25 Court Street, Boston," imperfections . . . . 980.

Knife

5-1/4" h, 13-1/8" l, ivory inlaid rosewood, attributed to New England, 19th C, very minor cracks, minor inlay loss 1,850.00

8-3/4" h, 15-3/4" l, walnut, dovetailed, high sides, scalloped divider with heart cut out handle 880.00

14-1/2" h, mahogany veneer with inlay, edge veneer damage, int. incomplete, inlaid oval on inside of lid 225.00

14-1/2" h, mahogany veneer with inlay, short feet, banded corner inlay, inlaid star on lid and also inside lid, edge and veneer damage, int. incomplete 425.00

16" h, 9-3/4" w, 14-1/2" d, Federal, flamed grained mahogany, serpentine and block front, reeded front columns, fitted int., orig keys, pr 2,500.00

Letter, oblong honeycomb, wood and metal, 26 octagonal lettered slots 375.00

Pantry, circular, nailed construction, swing handle

7-1/2" d, 3-1/2" h, green, two finger construction, orig paint 250.00

10-7/8" d, 7" h, orig red painted surface, 19th C, chip to top and bottom, paint wear 550.00

12" d, 6-3/4" h, orig green painted surface, 19th C, minor surface abrasion 550.00

Pencil, 10-1/2" l, swivel lid, carved from one piece of pine, old red paint 175.00

Pipe

17-1/8" h, 7-1/2" w, 5-1/4" d, red painted poplar and yellow pine, reverse sgd "Emma E. Robbins," southern New England, early 19th C, minor loss on molded edge . . 1,200.00

19-1/2" h, 8-3/8" w, 5-1/4" d, carved cherry, painted red, metal lined int., old finish, CT River Valley, late 18th/early 19th C 6,000.00

21-1/4" h, 6" w, 4-1/4" d, yellow pine, traces of red paint, old finish, southern New England, early 19th C, very minor losses, crack, minor insect damage to base 2,650.00

21-5/8" h, 8-5/8" w, 5" d, one drawer, old black paint, New England, 18th C, minor losses, cracks 3,450.00

Salt, 11-1/2" w, 7-1/4" d, 9" h, oak, dovetailed, lift lid, crest, divided int., old finish. 120.00

Sewing, 9-1/2" l, 6-3/4" w, 7-3/4" h, bird's eye maple and inlaid walnut, tiered, one drawer, America, mid-19th C, very minor losses to finials. 375.00

Spice, 9-3/8" d, circular, maple, eight spice containers with stenciled names, America, late 19th C 450.00

Spill, 10-1/8" h, 3" w, 2-3/4" d, hanging, walnut and poplar, New England, late 18th/early 19th C, old refinish, front molding replaced. 550.00

Storage, 14-3/8" h, 26-3/4" l, 19-3/4" d, pine, oval, two handles, painted blue, America, 19th C 1,500.00

Tea Bin, 24-1/8" h, 17-1/2" w, 25" d, dec of gentleman toasting lady, dec by Ralph Cahoon, oil on wood, with certificate of authenticity from Cahoon Museum of American Art. . . 2,530.00

Wall

9-3/4" l, 3-3/8" d, 17-3/4" h, pine, inscribed on reverse with three-masted sailing ship under sail, New England, late 18th C, old refinish, minor cracks. 700.00

20-1/2" l, 8" w, 6-3/4" h, red painted pine, shaped back, canted sides, beveled edge base, New England, early 19th C, paint wear, minor cracks 1,850.00

Work, 12" w, 10-1/2" d, 7-1/4" h, European, marquetry inlaid mahogany veneer, pine secondary wood, slant top lid with pincushion covered in old burgundy velvet, paper lined int., till with lid, engraved strap hinges, old finish, repairs . . . 275.00

Cabinets

Bar, Art Deco, walnut, sarcophagus form, two doors, sq top with drop-front cabinet on left, mirrored bar, small drawer on right between two open bays, 48" w, 21" d, 54-1/2" d 600.00

China

Art Moderne, mahogany, double doors, floral-carved relief panels, int. shelves, two drawers below, 45" w, 17" d, 62" h 2,000.00

Arts & Crafts

Limbert, #428, trapezoidal form, two doors, each with four windows at top over one large window, orig copper pulls, sides with two windows over one, refinished, branded, 40" w, 19" d, 63" h. 4,250.00

Secessionist style, gallery top set on pillars around mirror, two glass panel doors over open shelf, inlaid ebony and MOP detail, orig mahogany finish, orig hardware, 42" w, 15" d, 72" h 3,500.00

Biedermeier, highly figured and burl olive wood veneer, ebonized trim, classical-style details, architectural cornice, single glass door, two dovetailed drawers, refinished, 52" w, 32" d, 58" h 1,200.00

Edwardian-Style, curved glass sides, single flat glazed door, illuminated int., mirrored back, 42" w, 16""d, 64" h, pr 1,675.00

International Movement, Gilbert Rhode, manufactured by Herman Miller, glass-sided china cabinet top over two doors with burled fronts, brushed steel pulls, refinished, glass doors and shelves missing, 36" w, 17" d, 58" h 800.00

Victorian, American, c1900, shaped crest with lion's head and carved foliage, curved central door flanked by curved glass to either side, four ball and claw feet, 48" w, 16" d, 72" h 1,500.00

Chinoiserie, two drawers, double doors, two adjustable int. shelves, walnut veneer with inlay and black lacquer, gilded detail, attached base with turned legs, 20th C, 43" w, 15-1/2" d, 63" h. 625.00

Corner Display, Georgian-Style, c1880, mahogany and inlay, swan's crest, pair of glazed mullioned doors, int. shelves, pair of cabinet doors with marquetry, bracket feet 2,415.00

Curio, Louis XV, French, mahogany and mahogany veneer, well detailed ormolu with cherubs, marble top, beveled glass panel in door and plain glass in sides, lighted int., lined with very work silk moiré, 20th C, 28" w, 14" d, 65" h . . . 3,410.00

Display

Biedermeier-style

Inlaid walnut, single door, outset, molded cornice over front, three-lane door with shaped panels, opening to three mirror-backed shelves supporting shaped half-shelves, glazed sides, block feet, inlaid foliate arabesques and stringing, 30" w, 14" d, 60-1/2" h . . 600.00

Poplar and burr-poplar, single door, outset molded cornice, three-pane glazed door flanked by similar stiles and sides, three mirror-backed shelves supporting shaped half shelves, block feet, 41" w, 16" d, 68" h 800.00

Edwardian, c1900, paint dec, satinwood, breakfront top, glazed doors, int. shelves, splayed legs, 42" w, 15" d, 4-1/2" h 900.00

Neoclassical-style, London, late 19th/early 20th C, oak and parcel-gilt, presentation plaque inscribed "Presented by Mr. and Mrs. Sidney H. Cotton (The Knoll 1874-1876)," ivory plaque for F. Sage & Co. (1905), 37" w, 31" d, 78" h 4,900.00

Rococo, South Germany, 18th C, walnut, scrolling heavily molded open pediment, center gilt-bronze cartouche plate, two arched doors of fielded panels, mahogany figures of court ladies, basal-molded and conforming stand, shaped apron, cabriole legs, 46" w, 19-1/2" d, 71-1/2" h 4,750.00

Filing, American, c1910, golden oak, plain vertical stack, five drawers, orig brass nameplates and pulls 650.00

Ledger, American, 19th C, walnut and mixed hardwoods, poplar secondary wood, dovetailed case, single paneled door, int. with divided compartments, later salmon paint, pr, 15-1/2" w, 12" d, 24" h. 600.00

Music, walnut, two dovetailed drawers, two paneled doors, molded and punched designs, four adjustable shelves, old varnish finish, orig castors, 22" w, 16-1/4" d, 37-1/2" h 450.00

Side

Arts & Crafts, oak, single door, orig sq copper pull, notched toe-board, refinished, 22" w, 22" d, 38" h. 700.00

Biedermeier, late 19th C

Fruitwood parquetry, rect top, canted corners, pr of cabinet doors enclosing shelves, bracket feet, 55-1/4" w, 24-3/4" d, 40-1/2" h 1,725.00

Inlaid walnut, single door, outset molded cornice, door with arched, sunken panel, flanked by bowed stiles continuing to molded stile feet, three int. shelves, 39-1/2" w, 19" d, 65-1/4" h 1,500.00

Empire-Style, late 19th/early 20th C, gilt bronze mounted mahogany, rect marble top, conforming case fitted with cabinet door, pull-out shelves, plinth base, 20-3/4" w, 16-1/4" d, 52-1/4" h 750.00

Louis XVI, Provincial, late 18th/early 19th C, oak, paneled door carved with urns, 41" w, 18-1/2" d, 73" h .1,380.00

Renaissance Revival, attributed to New York, c1865-75, ebonized, marquetry, and parcel-gilt, central elevated cupboard flanked by two similar cupboards, 75" w, 15" d, 64" h 4,900.00

Vitrine

Edwardian, c1900, mahogany and boxwood inlay, rect, Gothic-style mullioned glazed doors, sq tapering legs, spade feet, 41-1/2" w, 14-1/4" d, 63-1/4" h 1,200.00

George III-Style, late 19th/early early 20th C, mahogany, rect lift top, chamfered legs, joined by shelf stretcher and fretwork, 21-1/4" l, 15-1/2" d, 31-3/4" h 850.00

Louis XV-Style, late 19th/early 20th C, giltwood, boxed glass on each side, cabriole legs, 19" w, 17" d, 38" h.... 800.00

Louis XVI-Style, c1850, giltwood, outset molded rect top, frieze with beribboned floral garlands, front with glazed door with inset corners, flanked by fluted stiles, opening to two shelves, glazed sides, paneled skirt with swags, turned, tapered, and fluted legs with paterae, 27-1/4" w, 16" d, 61-1/2" h.......................................1,200.00

Candle Shields

Chippendale, Philadelphia, c1770, attributed to Thomas Afleck, carving attributed to Bernard and Jugiez, carved mahogany, turned cylindrical pole, adjustable screen with intricately carved frame, tapering fluted shaft, acanthus carved baluster, swirl gadroon, carved ball, acanthus carved tripod cabriole legs overlaid with trailing husk and vines, carved hairy paw feet, 60" h 68,000.00

George II, English, mid 18th C, carved mahogany, turned standard surmounted by urn shaped finial, spirally fluted multi-knopped shaft, acanthus carved tripod base, claw and ball feet, adjustable rect screen with beaded edge, orange, red, blue, and green needlepoint panel of floral bouquet, reverse inset with painted leather panel of Chinese figures in parquetry floored pavilion in garden, finials added, some damage to fabric, 59-1/2" h 3,750.00

Regency-Style, giltwood, rect panel with molded border, scrolling frame, shells, and ornaments at corners with volutes, 33" w, 48" h 1,500.00

Victorian, English, c1840, fluted stem surmounted by an urn finial, circular plinth base on three scrolled feet, adjustable shield shaped frame carved with scrolling leaves and enclosing floral needlework screen, 24" w, 77" h.......1,400.00

Candlestands

Chippendale

Connecticut River Valley, late 18th C, cherry, old refinish, minor imperfections, 17" w, 16-1/2" d, 25-1/2" h ...16,100.00

New England, late 18th C
Dish-top, cherry, turned pedestal, cabriole legs, pad feet, refinished, 18-1/4" d, 26-3/4" h 2,185.00

Tilt top, refinished walnut, one board dish turned top, turned column, tripod base, snake feet, hinge block and latch are old replacements, pieced repairs on top, minor age cracks, 21-3/4" d, 29" h 935.00

Chippendale, American, mahogany, serpent feet, 18" d, 27-1/2" h, $1,850.

New Hampshire, attributed to Lt. Samuel Dunlap, old refinish, birch, painted red, imperfections, 16-1/2" 2, 16-1/8" d, 26-1/2" h 2,950.00

Pennsylvania, late 18th C, walnut, circular molded top, turned birdcage support, vase and ring-turned post, tripod cabriole leg base, pad feet on platforms, old refinish, 20-1/2" d, 29" h 3,450.00

Country

Cherry and Maple, southeastern New England, late 18th C, circular top, vase and ring turned post and tripod base, three tapering legs, remnants of old dark green paint, imperfections, 12" d, 25" h 1,150.00

Stained cherry, Connecticut, late 18th C, tilt-top, dished top, ring-turned swelled pedestal, cabriole lets, pad feet, old surface, 20-1/4" d, 28-3/4" h 3,220.00

Federal

Massachusetts, c1800, mahogany, octagonal tilt-top, vase and ring-turned post, tripod spider leg base, spade feet, refinished, 21-1/4" w, 15-3/4" d, 29-1/2" h.........1,500.00

New England, c1790, maple, octagonal top, vase and ring-turned post, tripod cabriole leg base, pad feet, old finish, imperfections, 15" w, 15-1/8" d, 27" h 1,610.00

New England, early 19th C, painted, octagonal shaped top, outlined in black, painted checkerboard and four gilt scrolled flourishes dec, pedestal, cabriole legs with similar Victorian dec, 18" w, 17-3/4" d, 29" h.........12,650.00

New Hampshire, c1810-20, maple, carved tilt top, swelled reeded post, chip-carved detail, old red varnish, minor imperfections, 20" x 15-5/8" top, 29-1/2" h 1,000.00

Hepplewhite, American, cherry, one-board octagonal top, turned column with chip carving, tripod base, spider legs, old refinishing, minor damage, old repair, 17-1/4" x 18-1/8" top, 27" h 500.00

Primitive, 40" h, wooden, adjustable candle arm, dark brown patina, early 19th C 715.00

Queen Anne

Attributed to Vermont, 18th C, cherry, circular top, vase and ring turned post, tripod cabriole leg base ending in arris pad feet on platforms, old refinish, 15-1/4" d top, 25-3/4" h 1,150.00

Country, mahogany, piecrust tilt top, center turned pedestal, graceful legs, pad feet, 20" d, 28-1/2" h 275.00

Chairs

Aesthetic Movement, America, c1800

Arm, rosewood, stylized floral carving, open arms, 39" h 115.00

Side, cherry and mahogany, Herter Brothers, from Washburn Commission, crest rail with garland of flowers ending in bow ties, bottom rail pierced carved with flowers, turned ring and block legs, spindles and stretchers, seat covers missing, back leg branded "Washburn," commissioned by Hon. William Drew Washburn for MN Greek Revival house, copy of orig bill, 17-1/4" w, 16" h seat, 37" h 28,000.00

Art Deco

Arm, France, c1925, giltwood, sloping U-form back rail ending in gently swollen reeded arm supports, D-shaped seat upholstered seat cushion, pr 15,750.00

Side, Europe, wooden gondola backs, ivory sabots on front legs, cream striped fabric upholstery, pr, 25" h . . .2,000.00

Art Nouveau, L. Majorelle, France, c1900, arm, carved mahogany, horseshoe-shaped back rail, upholstered back, front of arm supports carved with pine cones and needles, continuing to form molded front legs with similar carving, dark green leather upholstery. 7,000.00

Arts & Crafts

Indiana Hickory, arm, twig construction, orig hickory splint seat, weathered finish, branded signature, 26" w, 17" d, 37" h. 50.00

Limbert

#79, hall chair, unique "bicycle" shape, orig leather back and shaped seat over slab leg with keyed construction, orig finish, branded and numbered, orig leather has been reinforced, 19" w, 20" d, 42" h. 1,100.00

#931, arm, three vertical back slats, recovered drop-in leather cushion, orig finish, branded, 28" w, 24" d, 37" h 800.00

#1825, five #1821, dining, one armchair, two horizontal slats over three vertical slats, orig leather and tacks, orig finish, branded, #1825: 24" w, 18" d, 38" h, #1821 17" w, 17" d, 38" h 2,900.00

#8073, arm, two curved horizontal slats to back, torn orig leather seat and tacks, orig finish, paper label, 23" w, 20" d, 35" h 210.00

Stickley, Charles, arm, four back slats, recovered spring cushion seat, orig finish, remnant of decal, 26" w, 22" d, 41" h. 230.00

Biedermeier, dining, fruitwood and part ebonized, black faux-leather upholstery, restorations, set of four, 36" h 2,500.00

Centennial, Colonial Revival

Chippendale-Style, side, carved mahogany, shaped shell-carved crest rail, pierced vasiform back splat, balloon slip seat, shell-carved apron, cabriole legs, leaf-carved knees, claw and ball feet, pr 850.00

Queen Anne-Style, arm, wing back, hardwood cabriole legs, turned stretcher, upholstery removed, old dark finish, 46" h 900.00

Sheraton-style, dining, mahogany, two arm, eight side, shield back, reeded front legs, corner posts with carving of urns, needlepoint slip seats, 19-1/2" w, 17-1/4" d, 37-1/2" h 3,000.00

Chippendale

Side

Boston or North Shore, c1760-80, carved mahogany, leaf carved lunettes and C-scrolls centered in shaped crests, raked molded terminals above pierced splats and over-upholstered seats, cabriole front legs terminating in scratch carved high pad feet, old refinish, 18" h seat, 37-1/4" h, price for pair 13,800.00

Boston or Salem, MA, 1760-80, carved walnut, raked terminals of crest above pierced splat with C-scrolls, compass slip seat, cabriole legs, high pad feet, old refinish, restoration to stiles, 16-1/2" h seat, 38-1/2" h 2,185.00

Connecticut River Valley, tiger maple, serpentine crest with raked molded terminals above pierced splat, old rush seat, block and vase turned front legs joined by turned stretcher, old refinish, 17-1/4" h seat, 39" h 900.00

Country, maple with some curl, pierced spat and shaped crest with carved ears, sq legs, mortised and pinned stretchers, old mellow refinishing, damage to paper rush seat because of breaks in front seal rail, 39" h . . 110.00

Country, refinished birch, pierced splat and crest with carved ears, replaced paper rush seat, sq legs with molded corners, 15-3/4" seat, 36-1/2" h 450.00

Massachusetts, c1780, carved mahogany, shaped crest rail with carved terminals, pierced splat, raked stiles, trapezoidal slip seat, frontal cabriole lets ending in pad feet on platforms, raked chamfered rear legs, old refinish, 17-1/2" h seat, 37" h. 1,725.00

New London, CT, 1760-95, carved cherry, serpentine crest rails, pierced splats with C-scrolls and beaded edges, molded shoes, flanked by stiles and rounded backs, molded seat frames and straight legs with beaded edges, pierced brackets joined by sq stretchers, old refinish, set of five, 17" h seat, 39" h 10,350.00

New York, 1755-65, carved mahogany, carved crest ending in raked molded terminals above pierced splat with C-scrolls, slip seat, molded seat frame, front carved cabriole legs ending in ball and claw feet, rear raked legs, old surface, imperfections, 18" h seat, 39-1/2" h 2,990.00

Wingback, arm, country, birch base, old dark finish, sq slightly tapered legs with molded corners, H stretcher, reupholstered, glued split on one foot, 47-1/2" h 1,650.00

Chippendale-Style, English, early 20th C, dining, refinished mahogany, one arm and five side chairs, pierced splat, hand carving, slip seat, ball and claw feet, 18" h seat, 38" h, price for set of six 2,400.00

Classical

Dining, New England, c1830, tiger maple, concave crests, horizontal splat, turned raked stiles, caned seat, rein-turned legs, joined by stretchers, old finish, minor imperfections, 33-1/2" h, price for set of eight 2,500.00

Side

Baltimore, painted and dec, scrolled crest above inverted vase-shaped splat, cane seat, dec front legs joined by medial stretcher, stencil dec, orig gilt classical motifs on black ground, 34-1/2" h 750.00

Connecticut, 1830-50, tiger maple, curving shaped crests, curving front rail, Grecian legs, branded "A. G. Case," refinished, seats missing caning, other imperfections, 17-3/4" h seat, 33-1/2" h, set of six 3,200.00

Middle Atlantic States, 1830s, mahogany veneer, curving veneered crests, similar horizontal splats, upholstered seats, Klismos-type legs, old refinish, 17-3/4" h seat, 33-1/2" h, set of seven 1,850.00

New York, 1810-20, carved mahogany veneer, scroll back, beaded edges, horizontal splats carved with leafage and other classical motifs, slip seat, curving legs, old surface, 16-1/2" h, 32" h, set of six 5,200.00

Eastlake, American, c1870, dining, mahogany, one armchair, six side chairs, fan-carved crest rail, reeded stiles and stretchers, block-carved front legs, minor damage, seven pc set, 35" h 850.00

Egyptian Revival, American, c1865, ebonized and parcel-gilt, arm, upholstered scrolling back and seat, matching upholstered arm pads, sphinx head arm supports, claw feet, 39-1/2" h. 8,050.00

Empire-Style, arm, mahogany, rect padded back, padded arms, ormolu-mounted classical busts, bowed padded seat, sq tapering legs with brass caps, white striped upholstery 850.00

Federal

Dining, Rhode Island or Salem, MA, c1795, mahogany carved, set of four side and matching arm chair, shield back with molded crest and stiles above carved kylix with festoons draped from flanking carved rosettes, pierced splat terminating in carved lunette at base above molded rear seat rail, seat with serpentine front rail, sq tapering legs joined by stretchers, over-upholstered seats covered in old black horsehair with scalloped trim, old surface, 16-1/2" h seat, 37-3/4" h 23,000.00

Side

Massachusetts, early 19th C, carved mahogany, shaped crests and stiles above stay rails, beaded edges, seat with serpentine front, sq tapering molded legs, beaded edges, joined by sq stretchers, old surface, over-upholstered needlepoint seats, 17" h seat, 36" h, set of three 1,150.00

Massachusetts or Rhode Island, c1780, mahogany inlaid, shield back, arched molded crest above five molded spindles and inlaid quarter fan, overupholstered seats with serpentine fronts, molded tapering legs joined by stretchers, 17-1/2" h seat, 37" h, pr 5,475.00

New Hampshire, Portsmouth, attributed to Langley Boardman, 1774-1833, mahogany, sq back, reeded on rest rail, stiles, and stay rail, over upholstered serpentine seat, molded sq tapering front legs, sq stretchers and rakes rear legs, refinish, minor imperfections, 18" h seat, 36" h 1,035.00

George III, c1800

Arm, French taste, giltwood, channel molded frame, cartouche panel back, center pad arms, bowed seat, fluted seat rail, stop-fluted turned tapering supports headed by rect floral paterae, figured cut green velvet upholstery. . .2,000.00

Dining, carved mahogany, yoke back, upswept reeded terminals, carved openwork vasiform splat with center pendant tassels over three flowerheads, green leather over upholstered seat, nailhead trim, fluted, molded, and chamfered front supports, H-form stretchers, swept rear supports, six pc set 5,500.00

Library, mahogany and caned, pink upholstered loose cushion, 33-1/2" h 2,070.00

Gothic Revival

Arm, America, walnut, old finish, reupholstered in damask, age cracks, 52-1/2" h 200.00

Side, New York City, 1850s, mahogany veneer, trefoil pierced splats, curved stay rails, veneered seal rails, curving rococo legs, old refinish, 20th C upholstery, 16-1/2" h seat, 33-1/2" h, set of eight 6,900.00

Hepplewhite, American, side, mahogany, shield back, rush seat. 325.00

Hitchcock, Hitchcocksville, CT, 1825-32, side

Painted and dec, crown tops, wide horizontal splats, cane seats, turned gold leaf dec legs, orig graining and gilt dec, red-brown ground, 36" h, price for set of six 1,000.00

Rosewood grained surface, orig gilt dec, urn centering cornucopia splat, old rush seats, ring-turned legs, orig surface, 35-1/2" h, price for set of four. 1,265.00

International Movement

Cherner, Norman, manufactured by Plycraft, arm, molded walnut seat backs, bent wood arms, orig label, set of six, 25" w, 23" d, 32" h 4,250.00

Eames, Charles, manufactured by Herman Miller, #670, lounge chair and ottoman, richly grained rosewood shell, tufted black leather inserts, polished aluminum base, 33" w, 32" d, 33" h chair, 26" w, 22" d, x 16" h ottoman 2,900.00

Evans, Paul, manufactured by Directional, arm, sculptural bronze ext. with abstract design, orig off-white upholstery, c1966, minor losses to ext., 28" w, 29" d, 25" h. . . . 850.00

Ladder Back, American

Arm, maple shaped arms, four graduated arched slats, turned finials, rush seat, turned posts and legs, all wooden casters, old refinishing, 15-3/4" h seat, 45-1/4" h . . 550.00

Side, hardwood, four graduated arched slat, turned finials, old rush seat, turned legs, bulbous front feet and stretcher, refinished, 42" h. 800.00

Louis XVI-Style, 19th C, side, L'Anglaise, painted and lacquered, pierced fan splat within hoop frame, serpentine front, over stuffed dropped-in seat, turned, tapered and flared legs with feathered annulation 250.00

Neoclassical

Arm, Italian, late 18th/early 19th C, walnut, urn and wheat carved splat, downswept arms, raised sq tapering legs, 34-1/4" h. 1,100.00

Side, attributed to workshop of Duncan Phyfe, New York City, 1810-15, carved mahogany and tiger maple veneer, spiral carved crest rail flanked by curving beaded stiles, flanking carved scrolls above horizontal splat with oval tiger maple veneer reserve flanked by carving, beaded seat rail, klismos-type molded legs, 17" h seat, 32-1/4" h, price for set of three. 4,900.00

Plank, northern New England, 1830s, side, arrow-back, yellow ground, stencil dec with dark green and blue leafage and fruit, gold accents, shaped plank seat, splayed bamboo turned legs, paint loss, minor imperfections, 17-3/4" h seat, 35" h, set of five 1,725.00

Queen Anne

Arm

Country, banister back, old black repaint, gold leaf on crest, shaped arms, turned legs, posts, and stretchers, replaced rush seat, mortised joints redoweled, wear and some edge damage, 16" seat, 45" h 500.00

New Hampshire, hardwood with old black repaint, molded and curved back posts with vase splat and carved crest, turned posts support molded and scrolled arms, turned legs, Spanish feet, turned rungs with bulbous front stretcher, old rush seat, some loss of height to feet, 15-3/8" seat, 41" h 4,125.00

New Hampshire, maple and other hardwood, old worn brown finish, molded arms, vase splat, shaped back posts with crest, turned legs, Spanish feet, bulbous front stretcher, old rush seat, 16-1/2" seat, 41-1/2" h 2,475.00

Commode, corner, New England, maple, shaped crest, scrolled arm, shaped splat, molded seat, frontal cabriole leg ending in pad foot, old refinish, minor imperfections, 16-1/2" h, 31" h.....................................2,100.00

Side

Country, maple, molded back posts and crest with vase splat, primitive relief carvings with scrolled detail, turned legs, Spanish feet, turned rungs, old refinishing with traces of red, replaced rush seat, some restorations, 17" w seat, 42" h..............................1,265.00

Country, yoke crest, old worn rush seat, turned legs and posts, bulbous front stretcher, old dark finish, feed ended out, 38-1/4" h..............................575.00

Pennsylania,1740-60 figured maple, molded yoked crest rail over earred vasiform splat flanked by molded serpentine stiles, balloon-shaped slip seat, cabriole legs, stockinged pad feet, 40-1/4" h 9,950.00

Transitional, Newport, RI, 1750-75, walnut, crest and shaped splat, molded compass seat, frontal cabriole legs ending in pad feet, joined to rear chamfered legs by block and baluster shaped stretcher, 20th C needlepoint slip seat, old surface, 17" h, 38-1/2" h.......2,650.00

Rococo Revival, rosewood, laminated curved backs, Stanton Hall pattern carving, attributed to J. & J. Meeks, old needlepoint upholstery, minor age cracks, 43-3/4" h, $3,450. Photo courtesy of Garth's Auctions, Inc.

Regency-Style, late 19th/early 20th C, dining, mahogany and inlay

Two armchairs, four side chairs, back splats with dark and light veneer inlays, carved lyre form supports with rosettes, reeded arms terminating in turned supports, crimson red floral upholstered seat, 36-1/2" h 3,900.00

Two armchairs, six side chairs, curved inlaid crest rail, dec horizontal splats, pale blue silk upholstery, Greek key design, 33-3/4" h 10,350.00

Renaissance Revival, American, c1865, arm

Walnut, attributed to Pottier & Stymus, New York, scrolled arms, upholstered back and seed, spherules on seat rail, 38" h..................................1,100.00

Walnut, burl walnut and marquetry, upholstered, pr, 44-1/2" h 1,850.00

Rococo Revival

Arm, rosewood, attributed to

John H. Belter, Rosalie pattern, laminated, solid back, crest carved with large rose, fruit, and grape clusters, yellow silk upholstery, tufted back, 42-1/2" h ..3,500.00

J. & J. Meeks, Stanton Hall pattern, laminated curved back, tufted gold velvet brocade reupholstery, minor age cracks, 43-3/4" h 3,450.00

Recaimer, John H. Belter, rosewood, finger carved, laminated wood, French style feet, brass casters, tufted red silk front and back upholstery, one faces left, other faces right, 42" w, 34" h, pr....................7.250.00

Side, rosewood, attributed to

John H. Belter, Rosalie without the Grapes pattern, laminated, solid back, crest carved with large rose and fruit, red silk upholstery, casters, pr, 37-1/2" h 2,550.00

J. & J. Meeks, Stanton Hall pattern, laminated curved back, floral brocade reupholstery, minor age cracks, 40-1/2" h 1,870.00

Sheraton, Hitchcock type, two arm chairs, six side chairs, old red and black repaint, yellow striping, stenciled and freehand dec, replaced rush seats, 18" h seat, 33-1/2" h 2,500.00

Victorian

Arm, George Huntzinger, NY, patent March 30, 1869, walnut, pierce carved crest, rect upholstered back panel flanked by turned and curved slats and stiles, low upholstered barrel-back, arm frame carved with classical heads, upholstered seat, pierced and scroll-carved front drop under seat connected to turned rung joining carved and turned front legs, ball feet, front leg stamped 2,100.00

Office, Philadelphia, c1850, carved rosewood, arched flower carved crest rail joining curved and carved stiles framing tufted leather upholstered back, padded closed arms, curved and scroll carved arm supports, upholstered seat above serpentine seat rail, boldly scroll carved drop, short pedestal base, four scrolled legs, caters, 33-1/2" w, 48" h 6,750.00

William and Mary

Chair Table, southeastern New England, early 18th C, oval two-board top, base of two horizontal supports ending in scrolled hand holds joining four block vase and ring turned legs, medial seat and box stretchers, turned feet, orig Spanish brown paint, minor imperfections, 51-1/4" w, 47-1/4" d, 26" h.................................20,700.00

Corner

New England, 18th C, shaped backrest and chamfered crest, scrolled handholds, three vase and ring-turned stiles continuing to turned legs, joined to front leg by turned double stretchers, old dark brown paint, replaced wood seat, 30" h 1,380.00

Southern New England, late 17th C, roundabout, maple, shaped crest above scrolled arms, turned arm supports joining shaped horizontal splats over replaced rush seat, turned stretchers, old refinish, 16" h, 28" h 1,100.00

Great Chair

America or England, turned maple and ash, baluster turned stiles topped by finials joining three shaped slats, rush seat, front posts crowned by large hand-holds, continuing to baluster turned front legs, joined by double turned stretchers, 17" h seat, 43-1/4" h. 6,900.00

Southern New England, late 17th C, painted, balustered turned stiles joining shaped slats, shaped flat arms ending in knob hand holds, turned legs joined by turned double stretchers, rush seat, old red paint, 17" h seat, 43" h 4,100.00

William IV, c1830-40, side, mahogany, caned, rope carved rail, carved tablet back, carved seat with reeded seat rail, sabre legs, pr, 32" h 250.00

Windsor

Bow-Back, Salem, MA, c1796-1805, painted, nine-spindle chair, incised seat rail, shaped seat, splayed legs, old black paint, incised "J. C. Tuttle," considerable paint wear, 17-1/2" h seat, 37" h. 750.00

Brace-Back, New York, c1770-90, arm, black paint, yellow dec, oak scrolled crest rail, hickory back posts and five spindles, maple arms, legs, and stretcher, poplar seat, 26" w, 19-1/2" d, 17-1/4" h seat, 43" h 9,500.00

Comb-Back, New England, early 19th C

Continuous arm, pine and maple, remnants of old resin varnish surface, rockers added, height loss, 15" h seat, 44" h 750.00

Writing arm, painted, shaped crest rail, five spindles, shaped back, writing surface with two drawers beneath, shaped seat with drawer, splayed bamboo turned legs joined by stretchers, old black paint, restoration to drawers, 17" h seat, 42-1/2" h. 4,025.00

Continuous Arm, New England, early 19th C, pine and maple, shaped incised seats, turned splayed legs, refinished, 35" h, price for pr 1,100.00

Fan-Back, New England, early 19th C, painted, curving crests, tapering spindles, shaped seats, splayed lets, repainted dark red, 35-1/2" h, price for set of four . .3,200.00

High Back, Pennsylvania, 1770-80, arm, painted, serpentine crest terminates in carved scrolls above spindles, open arms ending in carved knuckles, shaped incised seat, bulbous turned legs joined by swelled stretchers, old red paint, 18-1/2" h seat, 39-3/4" h 6,325.00

High Chair, child's, rod-back, New England, early 19th C, painted, incised tapering spindles, 21-3/4" h seat, 33-1/2" h 980.00

Hoop-Back, American, early 19th C, side, bamboo-turned spindle back, saddle seat, rakish legs, H-form stretcher, painted green. 700.00

Rod Back, William Dalton, Boston, c1800, side, slightly concave crest rail, seven spindles, bamboo-turned stiles, shaped incised seat, splayed legs joined by stretchers, old dark brown surface, branded "W. Dalton," 17" h, 33" h, set of six. 4,325.00

Sack Back

New England, c1780, maple and ash, bowed crest rail above seven spindles, shaped arms, vase and ring-turned supports, shaped saddle seat, splayed vase and ring-turned legs joined by stretchers, old varnish, repair to crest rail, 16-1/2" h seat, 38" h. 2,185.00

New England, late 18th C, painted, bowed crest rail above seven spindles, shaped arms, vase and ring-turned sup-

ports, shaped saddle seat, splayed vase, ring-turned legs joined by swelled stretchers, old black paint, 17" h seat, 35-1/4" h. 2,300.00

Southern New England, late 18th C, later rosewood graining and yellow outlines, old surface, 17-5/8" h seat, 38" h 1,500.00

Side, New England, 1820-30, painted yellow ground, green and red stenciled leaf and berry dec, green accents, shaped plank seats, splayed bamboo turned legs, some repaint, 17" h seat, 33-1/4" h, set of four. 900.00

Chests of Drawers

Art Deco, Quigley, France, c1925, parchment covered, rect top, three tapering drawers, pyramid mirrored stiles, bracket feet, back branded, 44-1/2" x 35". 2,750.00

Chippendale

Boston, 1750-90, mahogany, block front, thumb-molded shaped top, conforming case, four graduated drawers, molded base, bracket feet, old refinish, replaced brass, rear foot missing, backboard inscribed "G. Russell" (George Russell, 1800-1866, born in Providence, RI, married Sarah Shaw, and died in Manchester, MA,) 33" w, 19-1/4" w, 29-1/4" h. 46,000.00

Chester County, PA, late 18th C, high, cherry, cornice cove molding above single drawer, visually divided into three, over split drawer, four graduated drawers below, flanked by quarter engaged fluted columns with capitals and bases, molded base, four bracket on platforms characteristic of Octorara, (area between Chester and Lancaster counties), imp "T. Stock-ton" on backboard, old surface, casters added, minor imperfections, 38" w, 21-3/8" d, 66-3/4" h 19,550.00

Country, curly maple, four dovetailed drawers, bracket feet, refinished, bottom backboard and feet replaced, brasses replaced, 41-1/4" w, 19-1/2" d, 37-1/2" h 2,450.00

Massachusetts, c1720, wavy birch, overhanging molded top, cockbeaded case, four graduated drawers, bracket feet, replaced brasses, old refinish, 35-1/4" w, 19" d, 32-3/4" h 2,990.00

Massachusetts, c1780, birch, overhanging top with molded edge, serpentine front, conforming cockbeaded case, four graduated drawers, central drop pendant, bracket feet, old brasses, refinished, 40" w, 21-1/2" d, 36-3/4" h . . .3,750.00

New England, c1780, birch, tall, flat molded cornice, case with six thumb-molded graduated drawers, bracket feet, replaced brasses, old refinish, imperfections, 36" w, 18" d, 51" h. 3,150.00

New England, c1800, maple, tall, cornice molding, case with six thumb-molded graduated drawers, bracket base with central drop, old refinish, old replaced brass, 40-1/2" w, 20" d, 55" h. 9,200.00

New England, southeastern, c1770, maple, flat molded cornice, case with two thumb-molded short drawers over five long drawers, tall bracket feet, old brasses, old refinish, 35" w, 17-1/8" d, 62" h 4,900.00

New England, southeastern, late 18th C, maple, molded cornice, case with six thumb-molded drawers, top one visually divided into thirds, central fan carving, bracket base, replaced brasses, refinished, 37" w, 17-1/2" d, 57" h 4,900.00

Rhode Island, late 18th C, carved tiger maple, tall, cornice with dentil molding, case of seven graduated thumb-molded drawers, molded tall bracket base with central drop, top drawer with fan-carving, orig brasses, early surface, 38" w, 18-3/4" d, 63-3/4" h 27,600.00

Classical, northshore MA, c1825, carved mahogany and mahogany veneer, scrolled backboard over three short drawers on projecting case of two half drawers over three long drawers, flanked by recessed panels and pineapple, acanthus leaf and spiral carved columns continuing to turned feet, replaced glass pulls, refinished, imperfections, 42-3/4' w, 22" w, 45" h 1,000.00

Eastlake, curly walnut, burl veneer, carved detail, scrolled crest, four dovetailed drawers, two handkerchief drawers, well detailed molded panel fronts, refinished, 39" w, 17-1/2" d, 46" h 750.00

Empire

American, c1830, ebonized mahogany, gilt stenciled, step back fitted with swing mirror, three small drawers, lower section with single beveled drawer over two deep drawers, circular wood pulls, flanked by half-ebonized columnar sides, ring-turned legs, ball feet, 38-1/2" d, 21-1/2" d, 45" h 1,400.00

Country, miniature, cherry, curly maple drawer fronts, poplar secondary wood, three dovetailed graduated drawers, paneled ends, turned feet, turned walnut pulls, old refinishing, 19-3/4" w, 11-3/8" d, 19-1/2" h 2,100.00

Maine, pine, orig red and black graining, yellow and green striping, old brasses, edge damage, top poorly executed replacement, 41" w, 21-1/4" d, 40-1/2" h. 350.00

Federal

American, early 19th C, cherry, bow front, reeded edge top, four graduated dovetailed drawers with applied edge beading, paneled ends, shaped apron, turned feet, inlaid shield shaped escutcheons, old finish, pieced repairs to drawer edges and bottom drawer, 42-5/8" w, 20" d, 39" h 1,650.00

Country, mahogany and satin wood veneer, biscuit corners, "D" shaped facade, four dovetailed drawers with applied edge beading and inlay, turned and reeded feet and pilasters, ring turned posts, turned wooden pulls, backboards mkd "J. J. Drew, Norwalk, O," repairs, some veneer and edge damage, age cracks in top and side panels, 45-1/2" w, 23-5/8" d, 37-3/4" h 2,000.00

Massachusetts, c1815, mahogany and mahogany veneer, rect bowfront top with ovolo corners and cross-banded inlaid edge, conforming case with four cockbeaded drawers, quarter engaged ring-turned beaded posts continuing to tapering ring-turned reeded legs, arched cross-banded skirt, circular brass pulls, old refinish, 41" w, 21-3/4" d, 39-1/2" h 1,840.00

Massachusetts, c1815-20, mahogany inlaid, rect top with ovolo corners, inlaid edge, case with four cockbeaded drawers bordered with tiger maple cross-banding, flanked by quarter engaged ring-turned reeded posts continuing to vase and ring turned legs and joined by shaped apron with tiger maple banding continuing around legs to sides, replaced old brasses, old refinish, veneer losses, 43" w, 20" d, 41-1/4" h 1,610.00

Massachusetts, c1820, cherry, bird's eye maple, and mahogany veneer, rect top with bowfront, case of four cockbeaded graduated drawers veneered with bird's eye maple panels and bordered by mahogany cross-banding, flanking ring-turned legs joined by scrolled maple and mahogany veneered skirt, sgd "Samuel Stonington," replaced brasses, old refinish, imperfections, 40-1/2" w, 21-1/4" h, 40" h 4,500.00

Massachusetts, c1820, mahogany and mahogany veneer, rect top with bowfront and ovolo corners, conforming case with four cockbeaded graduated drawers flanked by quarter engaged ring-turned reeded posts continuing to turned legs

joined by cut-out skirt, turned wooden pulls, old refinish, sun bleached, other imperfections, 40" w, 18" d, 38-1/2" h 1,650.00

Massachusetts, early 19th C, bird's eye maple, ovolo corners, four drawers, reeded columns, turned feet, orig brasses, old surface, 40" w, 19-1/2" d, 41" h 1,500.00

New England, c1820, maple, rect top with ovolo corners, ring-turned columns ending in turned tapering legs, flanking four reverse graduated drawers, refinished, replaced brasses, 41" w, 18-1/2" d, 41" h 900.00

New England, early 19th C, cherry, bowfront, four cockbeaded graduated drawers, veneer cyma curved skirt, orig brasses, old refinish, surface imperfections, 41-1/2" w, 21-3/8" d, 37" h 2,875.00

New England, early 19th C, cherry inlaid, bowfront, bowed top edged in inlay, case with four cockbeaded drawers, skirt outlined in veneer, flaring platform feet, castors, orig brass pulls, old refinish, 38-3/4" w, 22-1/4" d, 38-1/2" h 3,000.00

New Hampshire, Portsmouth or Greenland, attributed to Joseph Clark, 1810-14, inlaid bowfront, rect overhanging top with bowfront, case with four cockbeaded drawers with mahogany veneer flanked by contrasting inlaid stringing and wavy birch panels, all bordered by mahogany cross-banding, flaring French feet, center rect drop panel of wavy birch

Hepplewhite, PA, walnut, inlay, molded cornice, dovetailed case, 8 dovetailed overlapping drawers, French feet, inlaid escutcheons, orig oval brasses, 42" w, 66-1/2" h, $6,325. Photo courtesy of Garth's Auctions, Inc.

bordered by checkered and contrasting inlaid banding, orig brasses, old refinish, imperfections, 39-1/4" w, 20-3/4" d, 38-3/4" h 5,465.00

George III, Late, early 19th C, mahogany, bowfront, plain top, pair of drawers over three graduated drawers, French feet 1,380.00

Gothic Revival, Cottage Style, MA, late 19th C, pine, pediment and molded scalloped cornice over rect mirror flanked by frame with candle plateaus, shelf under mirror, four drawers, brown and orange comb-graining, black and gold accent striping on olive green, rose and gold floral motif on top, painted round reserve with landscape scene on front, castors, orig brass and paint, 38" w, 18-3/4" d, 76" h 950.00

Hepplewhite

Bowfront, refinished cherry, facade of curly maple and mahogany veneer and inlay, four dovetailed drawers, banding around base, drawer edges, and top, inlaid diamond escutcheons and oval medallion on top drawer with urn, scrolled apron, French feet, turned mahogany pulls, some repairs, damage to veneer, top has been reworked, 43" w, 22" d, 39-1/2" h 3,500.00

Bowfront, refinished cherry, figured cherry veneer drawer fronts and mahogany veneer along top edge, four dovetailed drawers with applied edge beading, French feet, replaced brasses, some damage to feet, 40" w, 22-3/4" d, 38-1/2" h 2,200.00

Country, refinished pine, red stain, solid bird's eye maple drawer fronts with natural finish, four dovetailed drawers, cut out feet and apron, old brass knobs, age cracks in front feet, 37-3/4" w, 35-3/4" h .1,100.00

High, Pennsylvania, walnut, orig wood facade and line inlay, nine dovetailed drawers with applied edge beading, chamfered corners with fluting and molded cornice, ogee feet, old worn finish, replaced brasses with ghost image of oval brasses, 41" w, 60-3/4" h 3,850.00

Miniature, refinished mahogany, pine secondary wood, six dovetailed drawers with applied edge beading and molded edge top, inlaid base around base, French feet, two drawers with inlaid diamond escutcheons, one with wood escutcheon, edge damage, old repairs, one side warped and split along back edge, 23-3/8" w, 10-3/4" d, 21" h 2,550.00

Louis XV-Style, bureau-plat, kingwood, parquetry, and gilt-metal mounts, rect top, leatherette-lined writing surface, cast acanthus edge, frieze with central drawer flanked by shaped drawers, keeled cabriole legs, molding, chutes, and sabots, 33" w, 70" l, 30-1/2" h 2,100.00

Queen Anne, Southeastern New England, c1700, painted oak, cedar, and yellow pine, rect top with applied edge, case of four drawers each with molded fronts, chamfered mitered borders, separated by applied horizontal moldings, sides with two recessed vertical molded panels above single horizontal panel, base with applied molding, four turned ball feet, old red paint, minor imperfections, 37-3/4" w, 20-1/2" w, 35" h 26,450.00

Sheraton

America

Bowfront, mahogany and mahogany veneer, pine secondary wood, four drawers with applied edge beading, molded stiles with reeding, turned feet, old finish, orig oval brasses, wear and minor edge damage, filed age cracks in top, one foot with age crack, 41-3/8" w, 23-1/2" d, 38-1/2" h 1,100.00

Cookie Corner, mahogany, shaped backsplash, three quartered reeded corner columns, shaped apron, turned feet, orig hardware, 42-1/2" w at front, 39-3/4" h 1,50.00

Ohio, c1820-30, walnut, white pine secondary wood, four graduated drawers, scratch bead and inlaid diamond escutcheons, double lined inlay on stiles and on top board, 41-1/2" w, 20" d, 46-1/4" h 1,650.00

Victorian, American

Poplar, mahogany veneer facade, serpentine top drawer, two serpentine stepback drawers, five dovetailed drawers, applied beading, worn finish, 40" w, 19-3/4" d, 47" h . . 330.00

Rosewood, ivory inlaid, rect top, four short and four long drawers, free standing reeded columns, inlaid base, turned feet, restoration on lower left base molding, 41-1/2" w, 20-1/4" d, 45" h 5,775.00

William and Mary

American

Burl veneer, bachelor's, five dovetailed drawers, pull-out shelf, worn finish, veneer damage, replaced base molding, turned feet, and backboards, orig brasses, 30" w, 19" d, 35" h 1,980.00

Oak, molded edge top, five dovetailed drawers, facade with applied moldings, bracket feet, old worn finish, orig engraved brasses, repairs, feet replaced, 36" w, 35-3/4" h 1,350.00

Southern Massachusetts or Rhode Island, tiger maple, graduated drawer construction, two over four drawers, applied moldings to top and bottom, turned turnip feet, old grunge finish, 3 escutcheon plates present, rest of hardware missing, some repair, 36-1/4" w, 18-1/4" d, 48" h 2,950.00

Chests of Drawers, Other

Bachelor, late George III, English, early 19th C, mahogany, rect top with molded edge, slide, four graduated cockbeaded drawers, bracket feet, veneer damage, restoration to feet, 37" l, 33-1/2" h 2,750.00

Campaign, mahogany, pine secondary wood, brass trim, dovetailed case, int. with lift-out tray, one dovetailed drawer, some shrinkage to lid, 30-3/4" w, 18-1/4" d, 19" h 385.00

Chest on Chest

Chippendale, cherry, pine secondary wood, molded cornice, dovetailed cases, nine dovetailed overlapping drawers, scalloped apron, bracket feet, old mellow refinishing, interiors of drawers varnished, old brasses in orig holes, repairs, age cracks, 77-3/4" h 13,200.00

Queen Anne, Connecticut, c1780, carved cherry, molded and scrolled crest with carved urn finials, dentil molding, top section with three thumb-molded short drawers, central short drawer with pinwheel carving, four graduated long drawers, flanking engaged quarter columns; lower section: three graduated drawers, flanked by engaged quarter columns gadrooning below skirt with pinwheel carved pendant, four cabriole legs ending in pad feet, replaced brasses, restored, 37-1/2" w, 18-1/2" d, 48" h 9,200.00

Chest on Frame

Queen Anne, New England, last half 18th C, maple, pine, and cherry, rect molded slightly overhanging top, case with five thumb-molded graduated drawers, frame with skirt and drop pendant, cabriole legs, pad feet on platforms, replaced brasses, refinished, restoration, 36" w, 19" d, 52-1/2" h 1,380.00

Queen Anne style, English, walnut and burl veneer, mahogany secondary wood, case with four dovetailed drawers, brass teardrop pulls, cabriole legs, duck feet, 20th C, 19-1/4" x 33-1/2" base, 38-1/2" h 825.00

Southeastern New England, early 18th C, painted maple, cherry, oak, and pine, top with flat molded cornice, double arch molded case, two short drawers, frame with valanced skirt, four ring turned legs, disc feet, old engraved brasses, old Spanish brown paint, imperfections, 35" w, 19" d, 54-1/2" h 3,500.00

Chest over Drawer, Queen Anne
Massachusetts, mid 18th C, salmon-red painted pin and maple, molded hinged top, double arch molded case, single drawer, applied molding at base, shaped skirt joining four cabriole legs, pad feet on platforms, orig engraved brasses, 35-1/2" w, 16" d, 40-1/2" h 54,625.00
Rhode Island, 1830-40, grain painted pine, molded lift top, single drawer, shaped bracket base with high arched sides, orig red and yellow paint simulating tiger maple, orig turned pulls, old dry surface, 39-3/4" w, 20" d, 36" h 2,100.00

Commode
Biedermeier, north Germany or Scandinavia, c1840, pearwood, stepped rect top, three drawers, shaped apron, 35" w, 20" d, 31" h 2,000.00
Directorie, c1800, fruitwood, rect to, two long drawers, sq tapered legs, restored, 36-1/2" w, 32" h 2,500.00
French Provincial, 19th C, walnut, rect top, canted corners with carved dec, arched paneled door, one with three shelf int., other with six drawers int., fiche hinges, inset panel sides, scalloped apron, short cabriole legs, pr, 33-34" w, 18-3/4" d, 39-1/2" h 1,700.00
Neoclassical, Continental, walnut, rect verde antico marble top with canted corners, three graduated cockbeaded drawers, chamfered stiles, sq tapered legs, cracked marble, missing some molding, 45-1/2' w, 36-1/2" h 750.00

Credenza, attributed to Horner, New York, ebonized, marquetry inlaid, shaped inset marble top, ormolu bronze figural mounts, two drawers over two doors with concave sides, side panels inlay with flowers on green ground, front door panels inlay with baskets of flowers with bow tie ribbon, int. fitted with shelves, 67-1/2" w, 19-1/2' d, 41" h 8,000.00

Highboy
Queen Anne
American, maple, curly facade, molded cornice, top dovetailed case with seven overhanging dovetailed drawers, four overlapping dovetailed drawers in base, scrolled apron, cabriole legs with trifid feet, orig brasses, refinished, pine secondary wood, base reworked, several brasses incomplete, one escutcheon missing, 35" w, 20-7/8" d, 70-1/4" h 7,500.00
American, walnut with figured veneer, herringbone cross banding on drawers, applied moldings, top: molded cornice, dovetailed case, five dovetailed drawers, scrolled apron with turned drops and three dovetailed drawers, cabriole legs, duck feet, old refinishing, replaced brasses, cornice and molding between sections replaced, facade veneer has damage and restoration, apron drops replaced, other repairs, 35-1/2" w, 22" x 39-3/4" cornice, 21-1/2" d, 38-1/2" w base, 64-1/4" h 3,300.00
Massachusetts, c1760, maple, top section with flat molded cornice, case with 2 thumb-molded short drawers, four graduated long drawers; lower case with one long drawer over three short drawers, four cabriole legs, pad feet on platforms, valanced apron, replaced brasses, old refinish, imperfections, 38" w, 21" d, 72" h 9,775.00
New England, 19th C, maple, cornice molding on upper case, five graduated thumb-molded drawers, lower case with similar drawers, shaped skirt, cabriole legs, high pad feet, replaced brasses, old refinish, minor restoration, 38" w, 17" d, 70-7/8" h 12,650.00
North Shore, MA, 18th C, walnut and maple, cove molding, five graduated thumb-molded drawers, lower case

Linen Press, Chippendale, poplar, reeded quarter columns, top dental molding, two arched top drawers, secret compartment, base with three drawers over two drawers, replaced ogee bracket feet, 56" w, 23-1/4" d, 81" h, $4,125. Photo courtesy of Alderfer Auction Company, Inc.

with small drawers centered by fan-carved drawer, shaped skirt, cabriole legs, pad feet, some old brasses, old refinish, restoration, 37" w, 19-3/4" d, 72" h 8,100.00
Salem, MA, c1760-75, carved walnut, cornice molding above three small drawers, central one with fan-carving, four thumb-molded graduated drawers, lower case with one long drawer above three small drawers, central one fan-carved, scrolled skirt, cabriole legs ending in arris pad feet, old brasses, refinished, two replaced moldings, 37" w, 19-3/4" d, 72-1/4" h 16,100.00
William and Mary, southeastern New England, early 18th C, painted pine, top section with flat molded cornice, single arch molded case with two short drawers and three long graduated drawers, base with three short drawers, four turned legs joined by flat shaped stretchers, turned feet, brasses may be orig, painted dark brown, restoration, 33" w, 18" d, 55" h 16,100.00

Linen Press, Federal, New York, c1820, mahogany inlaid, top section with arched molding above inlaid frieze flanked by ball finials, two cupboard doors with applied molding opening to mahogany, cedar, and pine linen drawers, lower case with two cockbeaded short drawers, three graduated long drawers, flaring French feet joined by valanced skirt, old finish, 48" w, 22" d, 87-3/4" h 9,775.00

Liquor, England, late 18th C, oak, two handles, iron mounts, compartmented int. with thirteen etched foliate dec bottles, ten pressed brass and cork stoppers, 17-5/8" w, 12-3/8" d, 11-3/4" h 460.00

Low Boy, Queen Anne, burl walnut, molded edge top, matched veneer rectangles, bordered in two borders with matching veneers, front has two sq drawers flanking central drawer with burl walnut veneer, center with shaped apron, four cabriole legs, pad feet, old brasses, 29-1/2" w, 18-3/4" d, 28" h 3,000.00

Spice, Pennsylvania, 1780-1800, walnut, dovetailed, cove-molded cornice, raised panel hinged door, opens to int. of eleven small drawers, brass pulls, molded base, old surface, 15-1/2" w, 11" d, 18-1/4" h 14,950.00

Wardrobe, Classical, mid Atlantic states, 1840, mahogany veneer, two recessed panel doors, similar sides, int. with veneered drawers, base with platform feet, small int. drawers added, 65" w, 26" d, 79-1/2" h 3,200.00

Cradles

Chippendale-Style, birch, canted sides, scalloped headboard, turned posts and rails, refinished, 37-1/2" l 400.00

Country

New England, 18th C, painted pine, arched hood continuing to shaped and carved dovetailed sides, rockers, old light green paint, old repairs, 40" l 300.00

Pennsylvania, late 18th C, dovetailed, refinished curly maple, cut-out hearts, age cracks and shrinkage . . . ., 41" l550.00

Pennsylvania, 19th C, walnut, scrolled back and sides, shaped rockers, old refinish, repaired crest, 39" l, 18-1/4" d, 21" h 250.00

Eastlake, 1875, walnut, paneled headboard, footboard, and sides, scrolling crest above short turned spindles, platform support, orig finish, dated. 495.00

Rustic, twig construction, rocker base, unsigned, 33" l, 22" d, 22" h 100.00

Victorian, cast iron, painted black, wooden slat bottom, finial missing, 37" l, 21" d, 36" h 200.00

Windsor, New England, c1800-20, bamboo turned spindles, worn finish 850.00

Cupboards

Armoire

Classical, New York, c1835, mahogany, bold projecting molded Roman arch cornice, two paneled doors flanked by tapered veneered columns, ogee bracket feet, 74" w, 31" d, 94" h. 3,200.00

Empire-Style, French, late 19th C, oak, outstepped shaped cornice, ogee frieze, paneled sides, molded outline on doors, divided base drawers, shaped bracket feet, 63" w, 80" h. 2,000.00

Louis XV/XVI-style, transitional, 19th C, kingwood and parquetry, molded marble top with serpentine sides, pair of doors, each with two shaped and quarter-veneered flush panels, serpentine sides, coated stiles with gilt-brass chutes, sq-section cabriole legs joined by shaped skirt, stamped "Dubreuil," 44" w, 18-1/2" d, 59" h. 950.00

Restoration, New York, c1830, mahogany, flat top with cornice molding, two doors, birds' eye maple lined int., concealed drawer below, ribbed blocked feet, 56" w, 19-1/2" d, 90" h. 2,800.00

Victorian, American, c1840, walnut, bold double ogee molded cornice, two arched paneled doors, shelved int., plinth base, ogee bracket feet, 62" w, 24" d, 89" h 1,400.00

Chifforobe, Art Deco, 1935, herringbone design waterfall veneer, arched center mirror, dropped center section, four deep drawers flanked by tall cupboard doors, shaped apron 450.00

Corner

Architectural, American, curly maple, arched cornice with molded details, carved rosettes, turned finials, arched upper paneled cupboard doors over paneled cupboard base doors, ogee feet, old refinishing, finials, upper sections of goosenecks, and feet replaced, 44-1/2" h, 99-1/2" h 10,450.00

Chippendale

Pennsylvania, early 19th C, carved cherry, scrolled molded pediment flanking fluted keystone with flame finial, arched door flanked by reeded columns, three serpentine-shaped painted shelves, recessed panel doors also flanked by reeded columns, single shelf base int., cyma curved skirt, old refinish, hardware changes, minor patching, 41-1/2" w, 17-3/4" d, 95" h 9,200.00

Pennsylvania, late 18th C, poplar, glazed arched doors, int. of one bowed and two serpentine shelves with plate rails, lower case of raised panel doors, serpentine skirt, flaring bracket feet, old surface, imperfections, 51" w, 25-1/2" d, 67" h. 3,700.00

Country, late 18th C, one piece, poplar, distressed two tone orange repaint, molded cornice, two paneled doors, scalloped base, 5-1/4" w, 81" h .1,100.00

Country, 19th C, two piece

Cherry and chestnut, upper: outset, ogee-molded cornice, canted corners, conforming front with nine-pane door opening to two shelves; lower: two doors over two sunken-panel doors, between canted stiles, bracket feet, 48-1/4" w, 24-3/4" d, 83" h 1,400.00

Walnut, upper: outset cavetto cornice, twelve-pane glazed door, three shelves int.; lower: two panel cupboard doors, shaped skirt, bracket feet, 43" w, 19-1/2" d, 81-1/4" h 2,750.00

Hepplewhite

One piece, refinished cherry with inlay banding around base, waist and top, inlaid fan in apron, line inlay with invected corners on doors, cove molded cornice, paneled doors with molded edge stiles and rails, cut-out feet and scrolled apron, replaced feet, repairs, 42-1/4" w, 82-1/2" h 3,300.00

Two piece, cherry, old dark finish, figured wood veneer on door panels, drawers, and cornice, molded cornice, top with double doors, each with eight panes of old glass, arched top lights, three drawer fronts with chamfered edges, center drawer dovetailed, two flanking faux drawers, paneled base doors, orig brass "H" hinges, other hardware replaced, bracket feet are old replacements, top int. covered in old worn yellow-green brocade, minor repairs to cornice, 54" w, 86" h. 3,850.00

Two piece, curly maple, cove molded cornice, dovetailed case, double top doors each with eight panes of old glass, paneled doors in base, French feet, int. with pale yellow repaint, replaced hardware, old refinishing, minor edge damage, 49" w, 83" h 8,500.00

Hanging, corner, English, mahogany, open curved shelves, shaped top edge, old finish, center of three base drawers missing, 22-3/4" w, 39" h 770.00

Jelly, country, refinished poplar, molded edge top with crest, two dovetailed drawers, paneled doors, paneled ends, turned feet, minor edge damage, age cracks, 39-1/2" w, 20-1/2" x 42" top, 53" h 625.00

Kas, Long Island, NY, c1730-80, cherry, pine, and polar, architectural cornice molding, two raised panel thumb-molded doors flanked by reeded pilasters, applied moldings, single drawer, painted detachable disc and stretcher feet, replaced hardware, refinished, restored, 65-1/2" w, 26-1/4" d, 77-1/4" h 4,500.00

Kitchen (Hoosier), American, early 20th C, oak, scalloped cornice over three cupboard doors, two glazed over two larger paneled doors, outset lower section with aluminum-lined work surface, over cupboard door flanked by three graduated drawers, 39-1/2" w, 28" d, 71-3/4" h 650.00

Pewter, two part, top: cornice molding, two six glass pane doors, two shelves, open pie shelf; base: two drawers over raised panel doors, one shelf int., short turned feet, 56" w, 20" d, 87" h 2,250.00

Pie Safe, country

Butternut and poplar, dovetailed case, corner and base moldings, tin paneled doors with star flower and bird dec, old

Chippendale, butler's, mahogany, 3 dovetailed drawers, top drawer fitted as desk with 6 dovetailed drawers, 8 pigeon holes with scalloped brackets, open center compartment, paneled doors, pull out linen shelves, removable molded cornice, replaced bracket feet, replaced brasses, 44-3/8" w, 81-1/4" h, $3,520. Photo courtesy of Garth's Auctions, Inc.

worn green over red paint, orig cast iron latch, porcelain knob, removable batten, insect damage, 48-1/2" w, 72" h 900.00

Poplar, attributed to east Tennessee, worn old red paint, tin panel on each side, two pairs on each door with soldered seams, stylized urns of flowers and oak leaves, turned feet, 53" w, 48" h 1,650.00

Poplar, attributed to Zanesville, OH, area, 12 punched tins with snowflake designs, joined with solderless crimped seams, stripped of orig paint, later red wash 1,980.00

Slant Back, New England, late 18th C, pine

Flat molded cornice above beaded canted front flanking shelves, projecting base with single raised panel door, old refinish, doors missing from top, imperfections, 37-1/2" w, 18" d, 73" h 2,300.00

Flat overhanging cornice, cockbeaded front, three shelves, paneled door with wrought iron "H" and "L" hinges, old refinish, replaced door, 29-1/2" w, 12-3/4" d, 39" h. . . .1,650.00

Spice, northern Europe, last half 18th C, wall-type, painted, flat molded cornice, hinged cupboard door, molded recessed panel opening, compartmentalized int., molded base, old dark green paint bordered by red, int. drawers missing, imperfections, 16" w, 8" d, 17" h 1,500.00

Step Back

Mennonite, one piece, top section with twelve dec frosted panes of glass, two int. shelves, plate rack, bottom with two paneled door with one shelf int., orig finish, pie shelf, simple cut out base and cornice, 42" w, 16-1/2" d, 80" h 2,000.00

New England, 18th C, primitive, two pc, top: three shelves with plate groove; lower: two drawers, two panel doors, traces of orig red paint, 56-1/2" w, 23-1/2" d, 81" h . . .1,700.00

Pennsylvania, two piece, pine and poplar, upper: flat top with dove molded cornice, two paneled doors, shelf int., turned quarter columns, pie shelf; lower: three small dovetailed overlapping drawers, two paneled cupboard doors, turned quarter columns, straight apron, bracket feet, wood knob handles, brownish-red paint traces, repainted black trim, 55" w, 22" d, 84" h 4,500.00

Wall

Country, refinished pine and poplar, top: molded cornice, double doors with "H" hinges, nine panes of glass, high pie shelf, base: three dovetailed drawers, paneled doors (probably from earlier piece), 64-1/2" w, 18" d, 85" h. . .2,550.00

New England, early 19th C, red painted pine, one-pat, double raised panel upper door, three-shelved painted int., similar base door with one shelf int., shaped skirt, orig red paint, int. repaint, hardware changes, minor height and cornice loss, 43-1/2" w, 19-1/4" d, 81" h 1,200.00

New England, southeastern, 18th C, pine, molded cornice, two sliding doors, int. with three shelves, gadrooned molding, four paneled hinged door, flanked by paneled pilasters on molded capitals and bases, old refinish, remnants of blue-green paint, minor imperfections, 37-1/2" w, 19-1/2" d, 78" h. 9,775.00

Ohio, early 19th C, cherry inlaid, flat molded cornice, door with flush cockbeaded panel inlaid with two symmetrically arranged leafy branches, rect escutcheon, int. with three shelves, flanked by ring-turned columns, flat molded base, 19-1/2" w, 7-1/2" d, 27-1/4" h 1,495.00

Pennsylvania, 19th C, pine, two sections, upper: cavetto cornice, two six-pane doors over arched open shelf; lower: outset with three drawers over two sunken-panel doors, shield int., short turned feet, 51" w, 19" d, 81" h 2,500.00

Desks

Aesthetic Movement, Herter Brothers, Washburn Commission, mahogany, fall front, top section: shelf with gallery top supported by turned and blocked posts, back panel with dec gold threaded material; middle section: slant lid, two supporting pull-out arms, central panel of marquetry inlaid with garland of flowers ending in bows, int. with two drawers, five cubbyholes, supported by two turned front legs, two bottom section with shelf and paneled back, missing orig writing surface, raised panel back, needs restoration, commissioned by Hon. William Drew Washburn for MN Greek Revival house, copy of orig bill of sale, 30" w, 20" w, 53-1/2" h 9,000.00

Art Deco, Paul Frankl, Frankl Studios, New York, c1928, known as "Puzzle Desk," Chinese red lacquered body, four silver-leaf drawers with whimsical silver metal pulls, beveled mirrored top, fully restored, 40" w, 24" d, 28" h . . .16,000.00

Arts & Crafts

McHugh, oak, partners, four drawers on each side, Mackmurdo feet, X-design applied to sides, orig dark finish, one knob replaced, 56" w, 37" d, 29" h 1,300.00

Stickley Brothers, #6515, oak, slant front, copper strap hinges, over single drawer, orig oval copper hardware, four tapered posts on shoefoot base, cleaned orig finish, unsigned, 30" w, 15" d, 47" h 1,900.00

Chippendale

Connecticut, late 18th C, mahogany, block front, slant front lid, fitted tiered int. with nine dovetailed drawers, pigeonholes, two pull-out letter drawers with fluted columns, flame carved finials and door with blocking and fan carving, dovetailed case, four dovetailed drawers, conforming apron, bracket feet, replaced brasses, old refinishing, feet replaced, repairs to case, 41-3/4" w, 21-1/2" d, 42-3/4" h
. . . . .3,850.00

Delaware River Valley, c1770, walnut, slant front, int. of central prospect door with recessed thumb-molded tombstone panel opening to valanced two-drawer int. flanked by document drawers with engaged columns and four valanced compartments and four short drawers, case with four thumb-molded graduated drawers, flanked by reeded quarter columns, ogee bracket feet on platforms, orig Chippendale brass pulls and escutcheons, old finish, minor imperfections, provenance: made for Captain John Lambert, Revolutionary War captain for whom Lambertville, NJ, was named. 25,300.00

Massachusetts, c1760-80, maple, slant front, two-stepped int., four balanced compartments, fourteen drawers, case with four thumb-molded graduated drawers, bracket feet, old refinish, minor imperfections, 35" w, 19-3/4" d, 41-1/2" h
. . . . .4,200.00

Massachusetts, 18th C, carved mahogany, reverse serpentine, slant lid, two-stepped int. of valanced compartments and small drawers, case with four graduated scratch beaded serpentine drawers, conforming molded base with central drop, frontal ball and claw feet, shaped bracket rear feed, old refinish, repairs, 42" w, 22" d, 44-1/2" h
. . . . .5,175.00

New England, c1760-80, maple, slant front, int. with tan-carved concave drawer, conforming drawer below flanked by shaped valanced compartments above shaped drawers, two projecting compartments, case with four thumb-molded graduated drawers, bracket feet, replaced pulls, old finish, imperfections, 35-3/4" w, 17" d, 40-3/4" h
. . . . .5,175.00

New England, c1780, maple, slant front, int. of eight valanced compartments, two document drawers, five drawers, case

with four thumb-molded graduated drawers, bracket feet, replaced brasses, refinished, 35" w, 18-1/8" d, 41-1/2" h
. . . . .3,800.00

New England, 18th C, maple, slant front, walnut stepped int. with valanced compartments above small drawers, some with end blocking, central convex end blocked drawers with flanking document drawers with turned columns, case with four thumb-molded graduated drawers, bracket base, replaced brasses, old refinish, repairs, 35-1/4" w, 19-1/2" d, 40" h. 3,450.00

New England, late 18th C, tiger maple, slat front, two-tiered int., valanced compartments, small drawers, carved central drawer flanked by document drawers with turned columns, four graduated drawers, replaced brasses, refinished, restoration, 36" w, 18" d, 39" h 2,550.00

Newport, RI, c1780-1810, mahogany, oxbow, inlaid, slant front, lid opens to int. of six cusped pencil drawers flanking document drawers, inlaid prospect door, opening to two-shelved int., small drawers above reverse serpentine case of cockbeaded graduated drawings beginning with top arched drawer on molded conforming base, ogee bracket feet, old dry surface, orig brasses, imperfections, descended in family from orig owner Captain Daniel Stillwell, 40" w, 23-1/4" d, 42-1/4" h 13,800.00

Rhode Island, 18th C, cherry and maple, slant front, two-tiered int. of small compartments and drawers, thumb-molded case ad four graduated drawers, shaped bracket feet, casters, replaced brasses, old refinish, repairs, 36-3/4" w, 18-1/4" d, 40-1/2" h. 2,675.00

Rhode Island, late 18th C, cherry, slant front, stepped int. of small drawers, central one with shaping, case of beaded graduated drawers, ogee bracket feet, orig brasses, old refinish, restoration, 39" w, 20" d, 43" h 3,800.00

Eastlake, lady's, walnut, two part, top section sits on pegs, top: mirror with two columns supported shelves, fancy carving, pressed dec; base section: double hinged writing surface with dec floral carving, writing surface with two panels of green felt, lifts to reveal compartment desk int. with two drawers, one side fitted with two long drawers, gallery shelf in base, dec applied pieces, shoe foot base, metal asters, 31-1/2" w, 19" d, 57" h 1,150.00

Edwardian, c1900, kneehole, mahogany, rect crossbanded top with central oval medallion, front canted corners, long frieze drawer, two banks of three drawers, center cupboard door, foliate marquetry dec, 37-1/2" w, 31" h 600.00

Empire, butler's, cherry and curly maple, poplar secondary wood, scrolled crest with turned rosettes, pull-out desk drawer with arched pigeon holes and three dovetailed drawers, three dovetailed drawers with applied edge beading, turned and carved pilasters, paneled ends, paw feet, old finish, some edge damage, 44-1/2" w, 23" d, 57-3/4" h . . .1,925.00

Federal

Central Massachusetts, early 19th C, lady's, mahogany inlaid, cove-molded top above three drawers with inlaid floral vines, checkered veneer banding opening to three-section int., end sections each with three drawers above openings flanking two central compartments over fold-out writing surface, cockbeaded bird's eye maple and mahogany veneer drawers flanked by colonettes above spiral carved engraved columns ending in turned feet, replaced brass, old surface, door inscribed "F. A. Butler, Deerfield, March 1864," legs pieced, other repairs, 40-3/4" w, 20-1/2" d, 54" h
. . . . .4,325.00

Massachusetts, c1820, tiger maple and mahogany inlaid, top section with cross-banded cornice board over two tambour doors, int. of nine valanced compartments over fifteen drawers with mahogany cockbeaded surrounds, center prospect door, pen and ink on paper "Commandments 10" within arched glass panel set in mahogany panel framed by tombstone stringing, lower section: fold-out writing surface, two cockbeaded long drawers, straight skirt joining block ring-turned tapering legs, old refinish, replaced pulls, minor restoration, 39-1/4" w, 18-1/2" d, 54" h 17,250.00

New England, early 19th C, mahogany and mahogany veneer inlaid, top section shaped gallery above flat molded cornice, two glazed doors enclosing compartments and drawer, flanking door and small drawer; projecting base with fold-out writing surface, two cockbeaded short drawers, two graduated long drawers, four sq tapering legs, inlaid cross-banding, old refinish, some restoration, inscribed "22 Geo. L. Deblois Sept. 12th 1810," 37-1/8" w, 20" d, 51-1/2" 3,000.00

New York State, early 19th C, mahogany veneer inlaid, slant lid and three graduated drawers outlined in stringing with ovolo corners, int. of veneer and outline stringing on drawers, valanced compartments, prospect door opening to inner compartments and drawers, flanking document drawers, orig brasses, old surface, veneer cracking loss and patching, other surface imperfections, 41-1/2" w, 21-1/2" d, 44" h 2,550.00

Pennsylvania, early 19th C, walnut inlaid, slant front, lid and cockbeaded drawers outlined in stringing, base with band of contrasting veneers, int. of small drawers above valanced compartments, scrolled dividers flanking prospect door which opens to two small drawers, three drawers, old refinish, repairs, 40" w, 20" d, 44-1/2" h 3,550.00

Pennsylvania or New York, c1790, mahogany inlaid, slant front, string inlaid lid opens to multi-compartmented int., center prospect door, case of four graduated drawers, inlaid stringing flanked by inlaid lambrequin corners, inlaid flaring French feet, old replaced brasses, refinished, repairs, 41-1/2" w, 20-1/4" d, 42-3/4" h. 2,770.00

George III, late, English, burl elmwood, slant front with rect crossbanding, fitted int. of pigeonholes and drawers, three graduated crossbanded drawers, serpentine apron, bracket feet, restorations, 30-1/2" w, 38" h. 1,800.00

George III-Style, partner's, third quarter, 19th C, burl elm, rect top, gold tooled green leather writing surface, molded edge, four crossbanded cockbeaded frieze drawers, two banks of three crossbanded cockbeaded and opposing cupboard doors, plinth base, 72" w, 31" h 2,875.00

Hepplewhite

American, cherry, slant front, dovetailed case, four dovetailed drawers with edge beading, fitted int. with eight dovetailed drawers, two letter drawers and center door, scrolled apron, French feet, replaced brasses, old mellow refinishing, old pieced repairs, 41-1/2" w, 19" d, 35" h writing surface, 46" h 3,350.00

Pennsylvania, early 19th C, walnut, rect top, thumb molded edge, string and quarter fan inlaid hinged slant front, fitted int., four line inlaid graduated long drawers, oval brass handles, shaped skirt with banded inlay, French feet, 42" w, 45" h. 3,000.00

Louis XV-Style, mid 20th C, mahogany, gilt bronze mounts, molded rect top, leather-lined writing surface, outset corners, frieze drawer, 70-1/2" d, 33-1/2" d, 30-1/4" h 2,760.00

Louis XVI-Style, late 19th C, mahogany, brass mounts, molded rect top, leather-lined writing surface, outset corners, frieze drawer over kneehole, flanked by three graduated drawers on each side, opposing faux drawers, toupee feet, 59-1/4" w, 25" d, 30-1/4" h. 900.00

Neoclassical, Italian, c1790-1810, walnut and burl walnut, roll-top, four drawers, damages, 43-1/2" w, 24" d, 43" h 4,600.00

Queen Anne

Northern Maine, 19th C, maple, slant front, int. with valanced compartments above small drawers, end drawers separated by scrolled dividers, case of three thumb-molded drawers, molded bracket base with central drop pendant, old darkened surface, 35-1/2" w, 17-1/2" d, 40-1/4" h 5,175.00

Vermont, c1750, tiger maple and cherry, slant front, int. with central fan-carved drawer, two valanced compartments flanked by molded document drawers, four valanced compartments, three drawers, case with four thumb-molded graduated drawers, bracket feet, replaced brasses, old refinish, imperfections, and repairs, 36" w, 18" d, 41-1/2" h 3,220.00

Renaissance Revival, English, partner's, carved oak, rect top with rounded corners, molded edge, front and back each carved with three frieze drawers, one pedestal with three drawers, other with paneled door opening int. with drawers and shelves, canted corners with figural pilasters, conforming molded plinth base, compressed bun feet, profusely carved with fruiting swags, grotesque masks, and heraldic devices, 72" w, 39-1/2" d, 30" h .5,500.00

Sheraton, Maine, birch, slant front, three drawers, dec inlaid skirt, tapering ridge feet, int. with five drawers and five cubbyholes, turned legs, refinished, 37-1/2" w, 19" d, 45" h 1,200.00

Victorian, English, second half 19th C, davenport, carved walnut, three-quarter galleried rect top, tooled green leather slant writing surface, int. drawers, bank of four drawers, turned and carved supports, plinth base, distressed leather, veneer chips, 23" w, 34" h 1,400.00

William and Mary, attributed to CT, early 18th C, tulipwood and oak, fall-front lid with raised panel, int. of four compartments, three drawers, well with sliding closure, double arched molded front, base with long drawer, four turned legs, joined by valanced skirt, shaped flat cross stretchers, turned feet, replaced brasses, old refinish, minor imperfections, 24-3/4" w, 15" d, 42-1/2" h. 17,250.00

William and Mary Style, American, 20th C, oak, seven dovetailed drawers, applied moldings, molded edge top, brass tear drop pulls, old finish, turned legs and stretchers, one pc of molding missing from drawer, 27-3/4" x 59" x 31" h 500.00

Dry Sinks

Curly Maple, rect well, work surface on right with small drawer, two poplar wood cupboard doors, short bracket feet, hardwood edge stripes, minor repairs, refinished, 55" w, 34-1/2" h 2,400.00

Grain Painted, New England, rect well with tin lining, rounded splashboard, two small drawers, two cupboard doors, shelf int., bracket feet, brown and yellow pine graining, 49" w, 38" h 900.00

Pine, three drawers on high back, sink with back-curved sides, paneled doors opening to self, stile feet, c1900, 43" w, 18-1/2" d, 33-1/2" h 900.00

Pine and Poplar, galleried well, one small dovetailed drawer, two paneled doors, cut-out feet, 46" w, 18-1/4" d, 37-3/4" h 600.00

Poplar, painted, rect well above pair of paneled cupboard doors, scroll-cut apron continuing to low bracket feet, cast iron thumb latch replaced, layers of old worn green paint, 39-1/2" w, 16-13/4" d, 33" h 650.00

Hall Trees and Hat Racks

Art Nouveau, France, early 20th C, hall rack, mahogany, flaring mahogany panel, five brass curved coat hooks centered by mirror, umbrella stand below, 47" w, 85" h 1,200.00

Arts & Crafts, attributed to Charles Rohls, early 20th C, oak, tall sq shaft, two tiers of four wooden hooks, each near the top, half buttresses running up from the cross base on all four sides, sq wafer feet, 64" h 1,100.00

Colonial Revival, Baroque-Style, American, 1910, cherry, shell carved crest over cartouche and griffin carved panel back, lift seat, high arms, mask carved base, paw feet, 39-1/2" w, 21-1/2" d, 51" h 700.00

International Movement

Eames, Charles, hat rack, "Hang-It-All," manufactured by Tigrett Enterprises, c1953, white enameled metal frame, multicolored wooden balls, 20" w, 6" d, 16" h 800.00

McArthur, Warren, coat rack, manufactured by Warren McArthur Industries, 1930s, anodized tubular aluminum frame with rubber "doughnut" feet, orig label, 24" d, 67" h 3,250.00

Victorian, American, burl walnut, ball finials above paneled and shaped cornice, rect mirror flanked by turned garment holders, marble top drawer supported by turned legs, shaped base, painted metal plant holders, 29" w, 14" d, 93" h 1,400.00

Windsor, American, pine, bamboo turned, six knob like hooks, orig yellow varnish, black striping, 33-3/4" w 200.00

Mirrors

Aesthetic Movement, America, c1880, over mantel, gilt, central cornice supported by two small columns over frieze dec with scene of snake attaching bird in tree, mirror plate highly dec with leaves, orig label of L. Utler, 47 Royal St., New Orleans, 64" w, 6" d, 84" h 3,600.00

Art Deco, French, c1930, giltwood, frame closed at bottom and sides, carved chevrons, stylized sundials and Chinese scrolls, hung by gilt thread rope, tapered rect beveled mirror plate, 27" w, 37" h 1,500.00

Arts & Crafts

Boston Society of Arts and Crafts, 1910, carved wood, rect, carved and gilded frame, ink mark, initials, orig paper label, 11-1/4" w, 18-1/2" h 700.00

Limbert, oak, frame with geometric inlaid design over rect cane panel shoefoot base, recoated orig frame, orig glass, 20" w, 8" d, 22" h 600.00

Centennial, Queen Anne-style, American, late 19th C, mahogany faced, scalloped, shell pendant, 32" h. 250.00

Cheval, German, ebonized, swivel rect mirror, rounded ends, low sq mount, artist sgd, 70" h 425.00

Chippendale, scroll

Mahogany, England, late 18th C, gilt stenciled star on crest over molded liner, orig finish, 12-1/4" w, 19-3/4" h . 600.00

Mahogany, old finish, molded frame, old replaced ears, some edge damage, replaced mirror, Philadelphia paper label in very poor condition, 16-1/2" w, 30" h 420.00

Mahogany, orig finish, molded frame with gilded liner, composition eagle in crest with old gilding, orig mirror glass with minor wear to silvering, 19-3/4" w, 40-1/2" h 3,575.00

Refinished mahogany, molded frame, repairs, mirror replaced, 11-1/2" w, 19-3/4" h 225.00

Walnut, England, last half 18th C

Scrolled crest, pierced foliate and scroll device, gilt molded liner, remnants of orig label on back, imperfections, 21-1/2" w, 41-1/2" h 1,725.00

Scrolled framed, pierced foliate and scroll device in crest, gilt incised and molded liner, flanked by gilded gesso fillets, restored, imperfections, 24-1/2" w, 46" h 1,265.00

Classical

Dressing, America or England, 1810-20, carved mahogany and mahogany veneer, cylinder top opens to reveal four drawers, centering one door, ivory pulls, above single divided long drawer, restoration, 19" w, 10-5/8" d, 32" h 1,610.00

Girandole, America or England, 1810-20 gilt gesso, crest with eagle flanked by acanthus leaves, convex glass, ebonized molded liner with affixed candle branches, foliate and floral pendant, imperfections, 23" w, 35" h 5,175.00

Overmantel, New England, c1825, carved gilt gesso, rect frame, acanthus leaf and spiral carved split balusters joining corner pieces, floral rosettes, reeded ebonized liner enclosed three-part glass, some regilding, 58-3/4" w, 38" h 2,425.00

Courting, wooden frame, reverse painted glass inserts and crest with bird and flowers, orig mirror glass with worn silvering, penciled inscription on back with "restored 1914," touch-up to reverse painting, brass back corner braces, 10-7/8" w, 16-1/2" h 935.00

Empire

Architectural, two part glass replaced, orig gilding, touch up repair, 20-1/2" w, 40-1/2" h 250.00

Convex, c1820, giltwood, eagle finial, carved, gessoed, and gilded frame, foliage, acorns, and oak laves, replaced mirror, repairs, 32" h 2,400.00

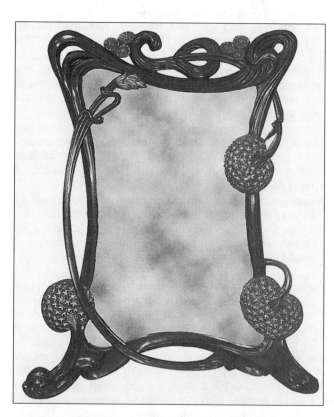

Art Nouveau-Style, mahogany, old finish and gilding, age cracks, 47-1/2" h, 38" w, $715. Photo courtesy of Garth's Auctions, Inc.

Federal

Architectural, old gold repaint, 26" w, 38-3/4" h 360.00

Girandole, America or England, 1810-20, gilt gesso carved, eagle with outstretched wings on rocky plinth, flanking foliate devices, circular frame with acanthus leaves, ebonized reeded liner with flanking candle sconces, foliate and floral drop pendant, regilding, 24" w, 43" h 5,475.00

Overmantel, Boston, MA, c1820, gilt gesso, rect frame, central frieze of shell and grape vines in relief, mirror plate flanked by floral panes and mirrors, framed by spiral moldings, corner blocks with lions' heads, regilded, replaced mirrors, 56" w, 28" h 4,615.00

Shaving mahogany veneer on pine, oval beveled mirror with scrolled posts, four dovetailed drawers, edge and veneer damage, one foot missing, 24-3/4" w, 9-1/4" d, 29-1/4" h 300.00

Wall

Gilt eglomise, attributed to Barnard Cermenati, Newburyport, MA, 1807-19, entablature with gilt spherules above reverse painted white panel with gilt eagle, swagged garland of flowers, 19-1/2" w, 36" h 3,350.00

Gilt and eglomise, Boston or North Shore, MA, early 19th C, molded cornice with gilt spherules overhangs reverse painted tablet with light blue paint, white rect reserve with gilt urn and gilt flowerettes, imperfections and regilding, 22-1/2" w, 38" h 2,100.00

Giltwood, labeled "Parker and Clover Looking Glass and Picture Frame Makers 180 Fulton St. New York," molded cornice with applied spherules above eglomise table of girl in pasture landscape holding dove, mirror flanked by spiral carved pilasters, 13-3/4" w, 29-1/8" h . . .2,875.00

George II Style, English, 19th C, carved gesso and giltwood, C-scroll and shell carved arched crest, serpentine and rect mirror plate, scrolled foliate corner pendants, C-scroll, shell, and acanthus carved shaped apron, 29" w, 65-1/2" h

. . . . .1,800.00

Hepplewhite, shaving, mahogany, inlay, two dovetailed drawers, feet, posts, and mirror are old replacements, 17-3/4" h

. . . . 225.00

Neoclassical, English, c1810-15, giltwood, flat molded cornice above eglomise tablet with center sailing vessel within a black oval, red and silver lattice panel bordered by black and white, mirror below flanked by reeded columns on sq plinths with rosettes, 18-1/8" w, 36" h 1,725.00

Queen Anne, English

Mahogany, top carved round shell with gold highlights, scrolled crest, bottom with small shell carved circle, gold dec gesso liner, replaced beveled glass, 26" l 60.00

Figured walnut veneer on pine, rubbed down finish, molded frame and scrolled crest, replaced glass, minor edge damage and some veneer repairs, 9" w, 15-3/4" h 770.00

Oak, old finish, old glass with some wear to silvering, old replaced backboards, 13" w, 21-1/4" h 330.00

Scroll, mahogany, old finish, molded frame, detailed scrolled crest, minor split in bottom edge of frame, 9" w, 16-1/4" h

. . . . 550.00

Walnut and parcel-gilt, scrolled crest, center pierced gilt gesso Prince of Wales device, gilt incised liner framing two-part beveled mirror, England, c1760, imperfections, 16" w, 40-1/4" h 1,955.00

Walnut, scrolled cornice and pendant, molded liner framing mirror plate, England, 18th C, some imperfections and restoration, 18" w, 38-1/8" h 1,380.00

Regency, carved and giltwood, convex, ebonized horse with dragon tail on shaped cliff mounted with lion's head in scrolled oak leaves, circular frame mounted with gold spher-

ules, center molded ebonized slip and convex plate, carved two headed serpent flat and arrow pendant below, gilded finish, back label "Ciceri & Co. Edinburgh," 25-1/2" w, 38" h
. . . . .8,000.00

Renaissance Revival, American, c1875, carved oak, pier, finely carved with game, putti, centered Ceres, glass shelves on sides, curved molded shaped base, 85" w, 124" h

. . . . .9,200.00

Rococo Revival, c1860-80, pier

Carved, well executed, some repaired breaks and areas of regilding, 36-1/2" w, 94" h 1,200.00

Giltwood and composition, cresting carved with flutist within cartouche, frame elaborately carved in high relief with C-scrolls and foliage, minor restoration, 40" w, 77" h
. . . . .3,450.00

Sheraton, mahogany, spiral turned split columns and bottom rail, inlaid panels of mahogany, rosewood, and cherry, architectural top cornice, split mirror, 24-1/2" w, 47" h 300.00

Victorian, English

Carved gesso and giltwood, scrolled and acanthus carved crest, center grape clusters over shaped mirror plate, deep frame, C-scroll corner brackets, pr, 41" w, 70" h . .1,400.00

Oak, late 19th C, pier, rect, paneled cornice flanked by columns over marble shelf, turned feet, 25" w, 11" d, 96" h
. . . . 600.00

Rockers

Art Nouveau, American, c1900, oak, fumed finish, carved arms, saddle seat, three splats with floral type capitals 400.00

Arts & Crafts

American, oak, four vertical back slats, corbel supports under arms, recovered orig spring cushion, orig finish, 29" w, 34" d, 36" h 200.00

Limbert, #580, oak, T-back design, orig recovered drop-in cushion, recent finish, branded, 24" w, 29" d, 34" h
. . . . 150.00

Plail, oak, slatted barrel back, D-shaped recovered seat, refinished, unsigned, 26" w, 28" d, 31" h 2,500.00

Stickley Brothers, oak, six vertical back slats, recovered orig spring cushion, worn orig finish, branded, 25" w, 27" d, 35" h
. . . . 220.00

Stickley, Charles, five slats under each arm, through-tenon construction, recovered cushions, minor wear to orig finish, remnant of decal, 34" w, 37" d, 41" h 1,400.00

Stickley, L. & J. G., #831, Morris-type, adjustable back, open under arms, orig finish, sgd "The Work of…," back bar replaced, 30" w, 35" d, 38" h 1,500.00

Boston, American, 19th C, maple, spindle back 200.00

Colonial Revival, Windsor-style, Colonial Furniture Co., Grand Rapids, MI, comb back, birch, mahogany finish, turned legs, 21" w, 17" d, 27-1/2" h 200.00

International Movement, Charles Eames, manufactured by Herman Miller, salmon fiberglass zenith shell, rope edge, black wire struts, birch runners, c1950, 25" w, 27" d, 27" h
. . . . .1,400.00

Renaissance Revival, George Huntzinger, NY, 1876, walnut, ring turned armrests and stretchers, cloth wrapped wire seat and back, dated, 21" w, 33" h 400.00

Wicker, painted white, sq back, basket weave pattern over openwork back, rect armrests with wrapped braces, openwork sides, braided edge on basketweave seat and skirt, X-form stretcher, 32" w, 33" h 200.00

Windsor, American, c1850, grain painted, stencil dec, scrolled crest, tail spindle back, shaped seat, bamboo turned legs, box stretcher 450.00

Secretaries

Biedermeier-Style

Inlaid walnut, molded rect top, four drawers, top drawer with fall front, fitted int. with ebonized writing-surface, molded block feet, 50-1/4" w, 23-3/4" d, 35-1/2" h 1,000.00

Walnut and parquetry, cavetto-molded cornice, front with frieze drawer, fall front opening to fitted int. with box-fronted cupboard and similar drawers, base of two door cupboard, flanked by convex stiles, molded plinth base, 42-1/2" w, 21-1/4" d, 67" h 2,300.00

Centennial, inlay mahogany, two part: top with four drawers over six cubbyholes center, line inlay door opening to reveal two cubbyholes and large drawer, sliding tambour doors flanked by inlay panels with simulated columns; lower: fold-over line inlay lid, two drawers with line inlay, diamond inlay on legs, some lifting to veneer, replaced cloth writing-face, 37-1/4" w, 19-3/4" d, 46" h. 800.00

Chippendale

Massachusetts, c1770-90, carved mahogany, scrolled and molded pediment above tympanum with projecting shell and arched raised panel doors flanked by fluted pilasters, candleslides, raised panel slant lid with blocked facade, molded conforming base, bracket feet, int. of upper bookcase divided into nine open compartments above four small drawers, int. of lower case with two fan-carved blocked drawers, similar prospect door, small blocked and plain drawers, scrolled compartment dividers, replaced brasses, old finish, restored, 39" w, 22" d, 93-1/2" h 19,550.00

New England, c1780, cherry, two pc, top section: flat cove molded cornice, two cupboard doors, molded recessed panels, projecting base with slant lid opening to int. of central prospect door flanked by three valanced compartments and drawers; lower section: case of four thumb-molded graduated drawers, bracket feet, replaced brasses, refinished, restored, 39-1/4" w, 20-1/8" d, 86" h 4,500.00

Classical, Boston, 1820-25, secretaire a'abattant, carved mahogany and mahogany veneer, marble top above cove molding, mahogany veneer facade flanked by veneered columns topped by Corinthian capitals, terminating in ebonized ball feet, recessed panel sides, fall front opens to desk int. over two cupboard doors, old refinish, 35" w, 17-1/2" d, 57-1/2" h 16,100.00

Colonial Revival, Colonial Desk Co., Rockford, IL, c1930, mahogany, broken arch pediment, center finial, two glazed mullioned doors, fluted columns, center prospect with acanthus carving flanked by columns, four graduated drawers, brass eagle, carved claw and ball feet, 41" w, 21" d, 87" h 1,000.00

Eastlake, American, burl walnut and mahogany, shaped cornice, pair of glazed cabinet doors, cylinder front, writing-face, two doors in base, shaped apron, 27" w, 22" d, 66" h 1,500.00

Empire-Style, late 19th C, gilt bronze mounted mahogany, rect top, fall front with fitted int., over pr of recessed cupboard doors, flanked by columns, paw feet, 44-1/4" w, 23-1/2" d, 49-1/4" h. 1,955.00

Federal, Boston or North Shore, MA, early 19th, mahogany inlaid, top section: central panel of bird's eye maple with cross-banded mahogany veneer border and stringing joined to the plinths by a curving gallery above flat molded cornice, glazed beaded doors with Gothic arches and bird's eye maple panels and mahogany cross-banding and stringing enclosing shelves, compartments, and drawers; lower: projecting section with fold-out surface inlaid with oval bird's eye maple panel set in mitered rect with cross-banded border and cockbeaded case, two drawers veneered with bird's eye maple panels bordered by mahogany cross-banding and stringing, flanked by inlaid panels continuing to sq double tapered legs, lower edge of case and leg cuffs with lunette inlaid banding, old finish, replaced brasses, imperfections, 41" w, 21-3/4" d, 74-1/2" h 9,775.00

George III, English, early 19th C, japanned, swan neck pediment, rosette carved terminals, two glazed cupboard doors, fitted int. of compartments and small drawers, fall front writing surface with cubbyholes and drawers, four graduated drawers, shaped apron, bracket feet, gilt and polychrome warrior and figural landscape scenes, birds, and flowering trees, green ground, over painting and minor reconstruction, 40-1/4" w, 21-1/2" d, 96-1/2" h 5,000.00

George III/Early Federal, America, third quarter 18th C, mahogany, two sections, upper: shaped architectural pediment with gilt-metal ball and spike finials, cavetto cornice over crossbanded frieze, chequer-banding, front with pair of thirteen-pane astragal doors, two adjustable shelves; base: outset fall-front opening, fitted int., four graduated cockbeaded oxbow-fronted drawers, conforming molded plinth base, molded and spurred bracket feet, 44-1/4" w, 24-1/4" d, 93-1/2" h. 17,000.00

Hepplewhite, two pc, walnut and figured walnut veneer with inlay, pine and poplar secondary wood, top: removable cornice with high goosenecks, keystone and turned finials, double doors with adjustable shelves, stringing inlay with invected corners and inlay on cornice, base: slant front lid, fitted int., with pigeon holes and ten dovetailed drawers, center door, four dovetailed drawers with applied edge beading, bracket feet, old finish, period replaced brasses, pieced repairs, some edge damage, replaced finials, 39-5/8" w, 11" h x 42-1/4" cornice, 21" d x 40-1/2" w base, 90" h 20,900.00

International Movement, Gilbert Rhode, manufactured by Herman Miller, upper bookcase with drop front desk over four doors, carved wooden pulls in burl and paldio veneers, refinished, c1940, 66" w, 15" d, 72" h 2,600.00

Renaissance Revival, American, c1865, walnut, two sections, upper: bookcase section, S-curved pediment with center applied grapes and foliage carving, two arched and molded glazed doors, shelved int., three small drawers with applied grapes and foliage carved pulls; lower: fold-out writing surface, two short drawers over two long drawers with oval molding and applied grapes and foliage carved pulls, matching ornamentation on skirt, 48" w, 21" d, 95" h 5,000.00

Sheraton, late, American, c1925, walnut and oak, projecting molded cornice, pair of glazed doors, fold-out writing surface, long drawer, turned tapering legs, 35" w, 1-1/2" d, 75" h 900.00

Victorian, two pc, walnut, top: crown molding cornice, two glazed doors with burl and walnut buttons; base: burl cylinder roll with two drawer walnut int., pigeon holes, slide-out writing surface, base: three long drawers with burl dec, tear drop pulls, refinished, 40" w, 23" d, 86" h 1,850.00

Settees

Art Deco, attributed to Warren McArthur, c1930, tubular aluminum frame, sheet aluminum seat and back supports, removable vinyl cushions, 68" l .5,750.00

Arts & Crafts

Limbert, #939, oak, eleven back slats, corbels under arm, recovered orig drop-in cushion, branded, refinished, 75" w, 27" d, 40" h 800.00

Stickley, L. & J. G., oak, drop-arm form, twelve vertical slats to back and drop-in orig spring cushion, recovered in brown

leather, refinished, unsigned, 65" w, 25" d, 36" h
. . . . .1,800.00

Baroque Revival, Flemish, scroll, mahogany, old cane in back medallion, cane seat has been upholstered, old dark finish, 66" w, 50" h 750.00

Biedermeier-Style, beechwood, curved open back, three vasiform splats, outcurved arms, caned seat raised on six sq-section sabre legs 650.00

Classical, American, c1850, mahogany, serpentine front, carved crest, transitional rococo design elements, 82" l
. . . . 600.00

Colonial Revival, William and Mary style, American, c1930, loose cushions, turned baluster legs and stretcher, 48" l
. . . . 750.00

Empire-Style, late 19th/early 20th C
Mahogany and parcel-gilt, two seat canapé, curved and padded back, reeded frame continuing into arms with swan-form supports, overstuffed seat, sabre legs . . 400.00
Mahogany, two seat, curved backs, each armrest ending on ram's head, hoof-foot feet 2,100.00

French Restauration, New York City, c1840, rosewood, arched upholstered back, scrolled arms outlined in satinwood terminating in volutes, rect seat frame with similar inlay, bracket feet, 80" l, 27" d, 33-1/2" h 1,200.00

Gothic Revival, American, c1850, carved walnut, shaped crest rail surmounted by center carved finial, stiles with arched recessed panel and similarly carved finials, upholstered back and seat, open arms with padded armrests and scrolled handholds, carved seat rail, ring turned legs, ball feet, 67-1/2" w, 23-1/2" d, 49-3/4" h 800.00

Louis XVI-Style, third quarter 19th C
Gilt bronze mounted ebonized maple, Leon Marcotte, New York City, c1860, 55-1/2" l, 25" d, 41-1/2" h 2,185.00
Giltwood, two-seat canapé, upholstered with Fortuny fabric, flaking, 55" l, 36" h 1,610.00

Renaissance Revival, America, c1875, carved walnut, triple back, each having carved crest and ebonized plaque inlaid with musical instruments, red floral damask upholstery
. . . . .1,200.00

Rococo Revival, rosewood, laminated curved backs, Stanton Hall pattern, attributed to J. & J. Meeks, rose crest in scrolled foliage and vintage, tufted gold velvet brocade reupholstery, age cracks and some edge damage, 65-1/2" l 5,500.00

Victorian
Carved rosewood, c1870, shaped and padded back, two arched end sections joined by dipped section, each with pierced foliate crest, over upholstered serpentine front seat, flanked by scroll arms, conforming rail continue to cabriole legs, frame leaf carved. 850.00
Wrought and cast brass, lion finials on back posts, red and gold brocade seat cushions and upholstered back, 48-1/2" l
. . . . 825.00

Wicker, tightly woven rect back, inverted triangle-dec, tightly woven arms, rect seat with woven diamond herringbone pattern, continuous braided edging from crest to front legs, turned spindle apron, 43" w, 36" h 500.00

Sideboards

Art Nouveau, Louis Majorelle, 1900, oak and mahogany, rect, bowed front, inset marble top, tow long drawers, undulating brass pulls cast with sheaves of wheat, tow cupboard doors with large applied brass sheaves of wheat and undulating leaves, molded apron, four lug feet, 65" w, 39-1/8" h
. . . . .6,000.00

Arts & Crafts, Charles P. Limbert, Grand Rapids, MI, c1910, oak, oblong top, mirrored back above case, three short drawers flanked by paneled cupboard doors over long drawer, cooper pulls and strap hinges, sq legs, chamfered tenons, branded mark, 49-1/2" w, 53-1/2" h 900.00

Centennial, Chippendale-Style, America, late 19th C, mahogany, block front with shell carving, four drawers, front cabinet doors, gadrooned apron, cabriole legs, claw and ball feet, 68" w, 24" d, 40" h 950.00

Classical, mid Atlantic States, 1840-45, carved mahogany and cherry veneer, rect top over mahogany veneered drawer, two recessed panel doors opening to one shelf int., flanked by veneered scrolled supports, veneered base, old refinish, hardware changes, splashboard missing, 40" w, 18-3/4" d, 40-1/8" h 2,550.00

Empire, late, mahogany, three drawers over four drawers, mahogany veneer front on center drawer, two pull-out working surfaces above two smaller drawers, four mahogany turned front posts, four front hairy paw feet, two turned rear feet, glass pulls, 73" w, 24" d, 42" h 750.00

Federal
Boston, c1790, mahogany inlaid, rect top with ovolo corners, conforming case with two central drawers inlaid with ovals within mitered frames flanked by rectangles formed by cross-banding and stringing, arched apron, flanked by drawers and cupboards, tapering legs on castors, replaced brasses, old finish, repairs, loss of height, 68-1/2" w, 27" d, 38" h 1,850.00
Boston, 1810-20, mahogany, maple, and rosewood veneer, two-tiered case, demilune superstructure, maple inlaid panels surrounded by cross-banded rosewood veneer above cockbeaded end drawers, small central drawer flanked by end cupboards, six ring turned tapering legs, case with concentric turnings, reeding, cockbeading, and scenic landscape jointed on underside of arched opening, old surface, replaced pulls, replaced leg, veneer loss, later landscape painting, 74-1/2" l, 24-1/2" d, 44-3/4" h 9,200.00
Massachusetts, c1810, mahogany inlaid, shaped top outlined in inlay, conforming case with central drawer with reserve, flanked by end drawers outlined in Greek key inlays, two central cupboard doors with beaded ovals, flanked by cupboard doors, legs with bellflower inlays on front of the upper and lower sections, replaced brasses, old surface, 71-1/2" w, 26-1/2" d, 42" h 21,850.00
Middle Atlantic States, c1790, attributed to, mahogany and cherry inlaid, overhanging top with canted corners and serpentine front, central cockbeaded door inlaid with cherry panel with quarter fan inlays and mahogany mitered border, cockbeaded wine drawer with three-drawer facade at one end, three cockbeaded graduated drawers on other, ends with cherry veneered panels, four sq inlaid tapering legs ending in molded spade feet, lower edge of case with molding, old finish, minor imperfections, 48-1/2" w, 21-5/8" d, 37" h
. . . . 19,950.00
New England, c1790, mahogany and mahogany veneer, overhanging top with shaped front, conforming case, central pullout surface, bowed cockbeaded drawers, two cupboard doors flanked by concave drawers and cupboard doors, six sq tapering legs, replaced brasses, old refinish, imperfections, 64" w, 20-1/8" d, 37-1/2" h 5,500.00
Virginia, 1790-1810, walnut and yellow pine, molded rect top, cockbeaded case with end drawers, right drawer visually divided into two drawers, left with two working drawers, central cupboard cockbeaded door, four square tapering legs, old brass pulls, old refinish, repairs, inscription on drawer reads "Virginia Hunt Board, early 19th cent. from family of

Admiral Todd, Naval Commander prior to and during the Civil War, Virginia," 56" w, 22" d, 39" h 5,520.00

Federal-Style, 19th C, inlaid mahogany, shaped rect top, inlaid edges, center section with two short cockbeaded drawers over one cockbeaded cupboard door flanked by two cockbeaded cellarette drawers, flanked by reeded half columns, flanked by two short, cockbeaded drawers, over two cockbeaded cupboard doors, flanked by reeded three-quarter columns, reeded cylindrical tapering legs, 73-1/4" w, 24" d, 40" h 4,500.00

George III, late 18th C, mahogany, demilune top, frieze fitted with angled drawers, sq tapering legs, 66" w, 29-1/2" d, 37-1/2" h 2,550.00

Gothic, Kimbel & Cabus, New York, c1875, design no. 377, walnut, galleried top over two cupboard doors over open self over slant front over central drawer over open well flanked by two cupboard doors, galleried base shelf, bracket feet, 39-1/4" w, 17-3/4" d, 73" h 9,775.00

Henri II-Style, carved walnut, upper section with three-carved doors divided by fluted, free-standing columns, surmounted by foliate crest, raised on baluster turned columns, lower section with two molded frieze drawers over carved doors, similar columns, molded base on compressed bun feet, 58-3/4" w, 21-3/4" d, 98" h 1,900.00

English, late 19th C, two piece, ornate dyed ivory marquetry inlay, beveled edge mirrors, broken arch top over turned columns, spindled rails on top with single door, base with drawer over door over shelf on each side, center with domed door, French feet, 72-1/2" w, 23-1/2" d, 84-1/2" h, $8,525. Photo courtesy of Alderfer Auction Company, Inc.

Hepplewhite, mahogany and mahogany veneer with inlay, bowed center section with conforming doors and dovetailed drawer, two flat side doors, sq tapered legs, banding and stringing with bell flowers on legs, corner fans on doors and drawers, reworked, repairs, replaced brasses, 58-1/4" w, 18-1/2" d, 37-3/4" h 2,200.00

Renaissance Revival, America, cherry, curled mahogany drawer fronts, burled arched panel doors. 900.00

Sheraton, country, walnut and curly maple, beaded edge top, four dovetailed drawers, scalloped aprons, turned legs, line inlay around apron and drawer fronts, old varnish finish, replaced glass pulls, wear and edge damage, one heart inlay missing, large water stain on top, 69-1/2" w, 21-1/2" d, 43-1/2" h 5,500.00

Victorian, American, late 19th C, pine, serpentine crest, rect top, four small drawers over two banks of four drawers, center cupboard, 65" w, 19' d, 51-1/2" h 750.00

Sofas

Art Nouveau, Carlo Bugatti, 1900, ebonized wood, rect back, mechanical seat, slightly scrolling rect arms, parchment upholstery, painted swallows and leafy branches, hammered brass trim, four block form feet, 68-3/8" l 1,900.00

Centennial, Chippendale-style, American, late 19th C, mahogany, shaped back, rolled arms, yellow velvet upholstered seat, gadrooned apron, cabriole legs with carved knees, claw and ball feet, 62" l 1,500.00

Chippendale, country, step down back with step down arms, bowed front with large down filled cushions, eight molded carved legs, cup caster feet, reupholstered, 76" w, 32" d, 36" h 3,000.00

Classical

Mid Atlantic States, 1805-20, carved mahogany and bird's eye maple veneer, Grecian style, scrolled and reeded arm and foot, punctuated with brass rosettes, continuing to similar reeded seat rail with inlaid dies, reeded saber legs flanked by brass flowerettes, brass paw feet on castors, old surface, 75" l, 14-1/2" h seat, 35" h 3,680.00

New England, 1820-40, carved mahogany veneer, cylindrical crest ends, leaf carved volutes, upholstered seat and rolled veneer seat rail, leaf carved supports, carved paw feet, 92" w, 16-1/2" h seat, 34-3/4" h 1,650.00

Empire

Mahogany and figured mahogany veneer frame, well detailed carving with sea serpent front legs, turned back legs, lyre arms with relief carved flowers and cornucopia, rope turned crest rail, refinished, reupholstered in floral tapestry on ivory ground, bolster pillows, 107" l 3,850.00

Mahogany veneer with carving, reupholstered in old rose and green floral brocade on beige ground, some damage to frame, 92" l 750.00

Federal

America, carved mahogany, mahogany veer paneled top crest with scrolled sides, front carved with rosette and leaf dec, carved paw feet with front stylized wings, red flower dec upholstery, 96" w, 19-1/2" d, 32" h 1,000.00

New Hampshire, c1815, carved mahogany, upholstered, straight crest continuing to shaped sides with carved arms on vase and ring reeded and swelled posts and cockbeaded panels, bowed seat rail, vase and ring-turned legs with cockbeaded rect inlaid dies, old finish, minor imperfections, 78" w, 24" d, 17" h seat, 34" h back 2,415.00

George III-Style, English, carved oak, double arched upholstered high backrest, scrolled arms, loose cushion seat, acanthus carved legs, claw and ball feet, 58" l 1,200.00

Chippendale-Style, camel back, scrolled arms, sq legs, stretcher base, 74" l, 25" d, $2,290. Photo courtesy of Alderfer Auction Company, Inc.

Louis XV-Style, 19th C, walnut, shaped, foliate carved crest rail, padded back, out-scrolled arms, foliate carved scrolled armrests, conforming molded seat rail, cabriole legs, pad feet, 85" l 800.00

Rococo Revival, John B. Belter, carved rosewood, triple back, carved central rose and fruit on sides, scroll band underneath, carved segmented scroll, tufted back red silk upholstery, brass caster feet, old restoration to central crest, worn seat fabric, 62" w, 42" h 4,500.00

Victorian, late, American, c1890, camel back, reupholstered, turned legs, 60" l 750.00

Stands

Baker, wrought iron, 48" h, 14-1/2" d, 84" h 500.00

Bird Cage, wicker, painted white, tightly woven quarter moon shaped cage holder, wrapped pole standard, tightly woven conical base, 74" h 225.00

Book, Georgian-style, early 20th C, mahogany, revolving, custom, 53-1/4" h 1,850.00

Canterbury, Regency, early 19th C, mahogany, drawer with paper label for "G. Ibison Furniture Broker & Appraiser, Cumberland Place, Near the Elephant & Castle," restoration, 19-1/4" l, 14" d, 22-1/2" h 1,380.00

Cellaret, George III, English, mid 19th C, mahogany, lozenge form, brass bands, twin loop carry handles, racked chamfered tapering legs, 24" w, 17-1/2" d, 27-1/2" h 7,500.00

Chamber, Federal

New England, early 19th C, painted and dec, dec splashboard above wash stand top with round cut-out for basin, medial shelf with drawer below, orig yellow paint with green and gold stenciling and striping, paint wear, imperfections, 18-1/4" h, 1" d, 39-1/4" h 350.00

North Shore, MA, c1815-25, carved mahogany, shaped splashboard, veneered cabinet door flanked by ovolu corners, carved columns of leaves and grapes on punchwork ground, ring turned tapering legs, brass casters, old replaced brasses, old refinish, minor restoration, 21-1/2" w, 16" d, 35-5/8" h 2,300.00

Portsmouth, NH, c1800, mahogany inlaid, shaped splashboard with center quarter round shelf, pierced top with bow front, square string inlaid supports continue to outward flaring legs with patterned inlays, medial shelf, satinwood skirt, small center drawer with patterned inlaid lower edge, shaped stretchers with inlaid paterae, old finish, minor imperfections, 23" w, 16-1/2" d, 41" h 5,750.00

Dumbwaiter, Queen Anne style, walnut, three circular shelves, splayed legs, pad feet, 21" d, 39" h 300.00

Easel

Aesthetic Movement, attributed to Cincinnati furniture maker, cherry, intricate carved sunflowers and oak leaves, orig finish, 23" w, 36" d, 75" h 2,500.00

Louis XVI-style, mahogany and parcel-gilt, picture support hung with berried laurel swags, trestle-end frame carved with acanthus, imbrication, and dolphins, 25" w, 23-1/2" d, 82" h 950.00

Etagere

Napoleon III, c1875, Chinoiserie, walnut and inlay, applied bronze dragon and inset ivory, MOP floral design on slant front lid, towering display areas, single long drawer, base divided with shelves 1,840.00

Regency, late, English, early 19th C, six tiers, corner, columnar supports, basal drawer, brass casters, 18" w, 14" d, 62" h 3,000.00

Victorian, late, English, bamboo and Japanese lacquer, three tiers, corner, scalloped form shelves, raised, colored and gilt Chinoiseries, 16-1/2" w, 45" h 800.00

Fernery, wicker, painted white, tightly woven, rect well, wrapped braced legs, X-form stretcher, 25-1/2" w, 18-1/2" d, 32" h 300.00

Game Board, New England, early 19th C, grain painted checkerboard top, single drawer, sq tapering legs, turned pull, paint imperfections, 17" w, 16" d, 29" h 700.00

Lamp, Federal-style, mahogany, molded rect top, two drawers, sq-section tapered legs, 18-1/4" w, 18" d, 28" h 800.00

Magazine, Arts & Crafts, oak

Lakestand Craftshop, three vertical slots under back, containing give square cut-offs with arched and cut-out side, recent finish, unsigned, 14" w, 10" d, 38" h 1,100.00

Michigan Chair Co., two cabinet doors with cross cut-out design over three open shelves, arched toe board, refinished, 20" w, 12" d, 44" h 700.00

Music, Napoleon III, second half 19th C, ebonized and parcel-gilt, lyre fronted upper section with folio rack divided by spindle galleries, open shelf, lower section with open shelf, turned, tapered, and fluted supports, incised dec of floral arabesques, gilt-metal mounts, 21-3/4' w, 11-1/4" d, 54-1/2" h 600.00

Pedestal, Arts & Crafts, Limbert, #269, oak, sq top, tapered column, sq base, orig finish, branded signature, 12" w, 12" d, 35" h 1,200.00

Plant

Arts & Crafts, Limbert, ebon-oak line, overhanging top, four caned panels on each side, recent finish, branded signature, 14" w, 14" d, 34" h 2,100.00

New England, 19th C, painted, three graduated demilune shelves, vase and ring turned supports joined by sq rails, old green paint, 40" w, 20" d, 39" h 1,650.00

Victorian, wirework, painted, late 19th C, demilune, three-tier, each tier with ornately curled rim, four slender legs heading by scrolled wire design, joined by single stretchers, X-bracing at back, casters, 45" l, 40" h 750.00

Portfolio, William IV, English, c1830, carved rosewood, folding mechanism 3,500.00

Reading, Federal, Albany, NY, early 19th C, mahogany, reading stand above ring-turned tapering post on rect shaped canterbury, turned tapering spindles, castors, 22-1/4" w, 14" d, 47-1/2" h 3,200.00

Sewing

Heywood Brothers, wicker, lift top, painted off-white, wrapped large D-shaped handle, hinged lid, sq basket, shelf below, paper label on bottom "Hayward Brothers & Wakefield Co.," 27" h, 17" w, 14" d 150.00

Sheraton, mahogany and curly maple veneer, biscuit corner top, case with two dovetailed drawers with applied edge beading and chamfered corners, pull-out bag frame, slender turned, reeded, and ring turned legs, brass feet, fitted compartments along one side of top drawer, replaced turned wooden pulls, old finish, 15-1/2" w, 19-3/4" d, 27" h 2,500.00

Side

French style, kidney shaped, inlay, drawer, base shelf with metal label "Watson and Walton, Chicago," damage, drawer locked, no key, 10-1/2" x 19-3/4" x 28-1/2" h. . . . 425.00

Grain Painted, New England, early 19th C, pine, top with shaped corners, single drawer, sq tapered legs, old burnt sienna and ochre fanciful graining, top worn, replaced pull, 18" w, 18-1/2" l, 27" h 1,725.00

Hepplewhite, country, birch with old red, pine secondary wood, one board top with serpentine cut edge, one dovetailed drawer, beaded edge apron, sq tapered legs, 17-1/4" w, 17-1/2" l, 26-3/4" h. 4,180.00

Sheraton

Country, curly maple, one board top (reattached), two dovetailed drawers, turned legs, old mellow refinishing, some plugged holes, replaced brass pulls, 18-3/4" w, 18-3/4" d, 29" h 1,185.00

New York State, tiger maple two drawer, oversized, two curved front drawers, two glass knobs on each, boldly turned tall legs, rounded front sq top, 26-1/2" w, 19-1/4" d, 35-1/2" h 750.00

Tier, Sheraton, English, three tiers, rosewood, single dovetailed drawer, turned finials, posts, and legs, old finish, 15" x 19" x 42" h. 1,450.00

Vitrine, transitional Louis XV/XVI style, kingwood, hinged, glazed, rect top, quilted int. with glazed sides, keeled cabriole legs, gilt-brass beading, chutes and sabots, 29-1/2" w, 20" d, 32" h. 375.00

Wash

Federal

American, mahogany and figured mahogany veneer, bow front with two small drawers, cutout for bowl, cutout sides, single dovetailed drawer in base, turned legs, worn finish, some water damage, replaced top and two small drawers, 20-1/4" w, 17-1/4" d, 30-1/4" h . . 275.00

Rhode Island, c1790, mahogany veneer, top with four shaped corners, canted corners, engaged ring-turned columns ending in reeded legs flanking cockbeaded drawers outlined in cross-banded veneer, top two drawers with sections, replaced brasses, old refinish, imperfections, 20-3/4" w, 15-1/2" d, 28-1/2' h 4,025.00

Hepplewhite, American, polar and pine, painted yellow ground, black blocking and linear dec, shaped gallery, cutouts for bowls and accessories, sq tapering legs, base shelf, emb brass pulls, nailed drawer, 18-1/2" w, 15-1/2" d, 37-1/4" h. 650.00

Work

Hepplewhite, New England, c1810, cherry inlaid, sq top, outline stringing and quarter fan inlays on ovolo corners, line inlaid drawer and skirt, line inlaid sq tapering legs, crossbanded cuffs, brass drawer pull, refinished, 19" w, 19" dc, 27" h. 2,650.00

Renaissance Revival, American, c1860, lift top opening to real satinwood interior fitted with compartments, narrow drawer above semi-circular bag drawer, pair of stylized lyre form ends jointed by arched stretcher surmounted by turned finial 875.00

Sheraton, New England, 1805-15, mahogany, veneered, outset rounded corners, shaped top, pull-out suspended fabric bag below single drawer, ring-turned and reeded round tapering legs ending in ring-turned tapering vasiform feet, old refinish, 16-1/2" w, 18-1/2" d, 28-1/4" h 3,500.00

Steps

Bed, New England, early 19th C, pine and tulipwood, two steps, thumb-molded drawer below bottom one, flanked by shaped sides, demilune base, old color, repaired, 15-1/2" w, 10" d, 17-1/2" h. 575.00

Library

George III, English, late 18th C, mahogany, rect molded hinged top, eight steps, 49-1/2" w, 53-1/2" h 2,500.00

Regency, English, early 19th C, mahogany, three steps, inset green leather treads, scrolling banister, sq balusters, feet with brass casters, 46" w, 27" w, 56" h 2,400.00

Stools

Cricket, Arts & Crafts, Limbert, #205-1/2", rect top covered with new leather, splayed sides, inverted heart cut-out, single stretcher with through-tenon, replaced keys, orig finish, branded, 20" w, 15" d, 18" h. 950.00

Foot

Arts & Crafts, oak

Barber Brothers, oak, nicely replaced leather seat, some color added to orig finish, paper label, 13" w, 13" d, 11" h 110.00

Limbert, cricket, #205-1/2, rect orig leather top and tacks, splayed sides with inverted heart cut-out having single stretcher with through-tenon construction, orig finish, branded and numbered, 20" w, 15" d, 19" h 2,000.00

Orig leather and tacks, slightly arched rails, orig finish, 12" sq, 8" h 90.00

Worn orig drop-in leather cushion with four vertical slats to side, orig finish, 16" w, 14" d, 14" h 260.00

Queen Anne, 18th C, walnut, rect frieze, four cabriole legs each with shell carving on knees, pad feet, slip seat, 22-1/2" w, 17" d, 17" h 1,950.00

Sheraton, curly and bird's eye maple, old finish, cane top, minor damage to top, 7-3/4" w, 13" l, 6-1/2" h 440.00

Victorian, walnut, floral needlework top with brown ground, 14" x 17 3/4" x 14" h. 220.00

Hepplewhite, mahogany with old finish, sq tapered and reeded legs, upholstered top recovered in gold brocade, 17" w, 17" l, 19-1/2" h. 935.00

Joint

Early, oak, old finish, wear and age cracks, 11" w, 16-1/2" l, 17-3/4" h. 990.00

Jacobean, 17th/18th C, oak

17" w, 7-1/2" d, 19" h 490.00

17-1/2" w, 10-1/2" d, 22" h 635.00

Piano

Louis XVI-Style, late 19th C, carved beech, circular, adjustable, close-nailed over stuffed top, petal-carved frieze, leaf-capped turned, tapered, and fluted legs, wavy cross-stretcher 850.00

Renaissance Revival, American, 1870, walnut, sq upholstered seat, acanthus carved baluster supports, four outswept legs, hoof feet 350.00

Seat-type

Country, folk art, attributed to Fredericksburg, PA, late 19th/early 20th C, painted and dec, octagonal seat, chamfered edge, trimmed with border band of carved hearts, tall splayed and chamfered legs also trimmed with carved

hearts and joined by slender rungs, overall polychrome
....1,850.00
George III, late 19th C, mahogany, gold floral satin upholstered rest seat, sq tapering supports, molded H-form
stretchers, pr, 19-1/2" l, 17" h 1,650.00
International Movement
　Eames, Charles, manufactured by Herman Miller,
　　Time-Life, walnut, concave seat, 13" d, 15" h ..1,000.00
　Platner, Warren, manufactured by Knoll, bronze wire
　　base, peach fabric upholstered seat, 17" d, 21" h
　　...325.00
　Windsor, American, 19th C, oblong plant seat raised on
　　three tall, turned and slightly swelled legs joined by
　　T-stretcher, traces of old green paint, 15" w, 24-1/2" h
　　...200.00

Tables

Architect's, George III, English, late 19th C, mahogany, hinged
tooled leather work surface above opposing hinged work surface, turned pedestal on three splayed legs, pad feet, some
reconstruction, 29" w, 19-1/4" d, 29-1/2" h 2,300.00

Breakfast
　Chippendale to Hepplewhite, transitional, walnut, one board
　top, beaded edge apron, sq legs with slight taper, molded
　corner, and inside chamfer, H stretcher, old finish, stains on
　top, 19" w, 29-1/4" l, 28-1/4" h 8,250.00

Classical, New York, 1820-30
　Carved mahogany inlaid, top with brass inlay in outline,
　stamped brass on edge of shaped leaves, one working and
　one faux drawers, flanked by drop pendants, four pillar
　curved platform support, leafage carved legs, carved paw
　feet, castors, replaced pulls, old finish, repairs, losses, 39"
　w, 24" d, 28" h 2,450.00
　Carved mahogany veneer, rect leaves with rounded ends,
　straight veneered skirt with panels and turned pendants,
　one end with working and one with faux drawer, fluted and
　turned four pillar veneer and shaped platform, four carved
　legs ending in carved paw feet and casters, old refinish, mi-
　nor veneer imperfections, 22-1/2" w, 47-1/4" l extended,
　30-1/4" h 2,300.00
　Carved mahogany veneer, shaped drop leaves with reeded
　edge, four spiral-carved supports on veneered shaped plat-
　form, leaf carved legs, carved paw feet, castors, one work-
　ing and one faux drawer, replaced brass pulls, old surface,
　imperfections, 25-1/4" w, 37" d, 28-1/2" h 2,000.00

Federal
　Massachusetts, central, c1810, inlaid cherry, rect hinged top
　with ovolo corners, base with straight skirt, edged with lu-
　nette inlay, flanked by sq tapering legs outlined in stringing,
　topped with icicle inlay, old refinish, 36" w, 17" d, 29" h
　...1,150.00
　New York City, attributed to William Whitehead, 1792-1900,
　mahogany, line inlaid top with hinged leaves and stringing
　banded the edge above oval inlaid frieze, one with working
　and one with false drawer, sq tapering inlaid legs with begin
　with twelve-point paterae and continue with V-shaped and
　looped stringing in conjunction with three-point bellflowers,
　terminate in cuff inlays, old surface, brass appears to be
　orig, some minor stains, some missing cuff inlays, descend-
　ed through family from Captain Francis E. West, Essex, CT,
　32" w, 18-1/4" w, 28-1/4" h 134,500.00
　New York City, c1810, mahogany veneer, rect top, double el-
　liptic hinged leaves, single veneer drawer, reeded legs,
　elongated and turned feet, orig brass pull, old refinish, cas-
　tors missing, height loss, 31-5/8" h, 19-1/2" d, 26-1/4" h
　...1,380.00

Federal, New York City, c1815, carved mahogany veneer,
rect top, shaped leaves, one working and one faux end
drawers, cross-banded mahogany veneer, turned acanthus
leaf carved pedestal, four acanthus leaf carved legs, brass
hairy paw feet, old refinish, repairs, 25" w closed, 38-1/2" l,
30-1/4" h...................................1,725.00

Card
　Empire, mahogany, satinwood and mahogany veneer,
　hinged swing top with rounded corners, turned and carved
　pedestal, four paw feet with acanthus carving, old worn and
　alligatored finish, old wallpaper lined int., 18" x 36" x 29" h
　...1,265.00

Federal
　Athol, MA, 1803-13, mahogany and flame birch veneer,
　stamped "Spooner & Fitts, Athol," elliptic shaped top, inlay
　outlining top edge above conforming frieze, inlaid oval pat-
　erae outlined in patterned inlay, cross-banded mahogany
　veneer outlined skirt, four reeded tapering legs with inlaid
　dies at top outlined in patterned inlaid banding, multiple ring
　turnings above turned feet, old refinish, 36" w, 7-1/2" d,
　29-3/4" h...................................4,950.00
　Boston or Salem, MA, c1790-1910, mahogany, inlaid, figured
　maple and flame birch veneer, sq hinged top, elliptic front,
　serpentine ends above under edge of lower top over tiger
　maple frieze, banded by mahogany veneer, central ve-
　neered panel centering satinwood veneer paterae over sq
　tapering legs, bird's eye maple frontal inlaid panels outlined
　in stringing, cuff inlays about double tapered termination,
　old refinished surface, 36-1/4" w, 17-1/2" d, 29-1/4" h
　...16,100.00
　Coastal Massachusetts or New Hampshire, c1800, mahoga-
　ny inlaid, folding top, half serpentine ends, serpentine front,
　ovolu corners and edge inlaid with cross-banding and
　stringing, conforming skirt with tiger maple panels, string-
　ing, and cross-banding, quarter engaged turned, reeded,
　and swelled legs, old refinish, 35" w, 17-1/2" d, 30-1/2" h
　...3,800.00
　Massachusetts, c1790, mahogany inlaid, rect top with ovolo
　corners, string inlaid edge, conforming base with inlaid
　stringing on five sq inlaid tapering legs, dies with contrasting
　panels bordered in patterned banding, lower edge with dart
　banding, old refinish, 16" w, 18" d, 29-1/2" h.....2,185.00
　Massachusetts, c1815-20, carved mahogany and mahogany
　veneer, shaped folding top, molded edge and ovolo cor-
　ners, conforming shaped skirt with reeded lower edge join-
　ing vase and ring-turned legs, turned tapered feet, old
　refinish, 36" w, 17-3/4" w, 29" h...............1,850.00
　Massachusetts, early 19th C, mahogany inlaid, rect top with
　ovolo corners, skirt divided into panels by stringing, central
　one with oval reserve of tiger maple above legs outlined in
　stringing, inlaid dies and cuff inlays, old refinish, 34" w,
　16-1/4" d, 31-1/8" h.........................3,000.00
　North Shore, MA, early 19th C, mahogany and flame birch
　veneer inlaid, edge of top outlined in banding, veneered
　skirt with central inlaid birch veneer reserve, ring turned and
　reeded legs, 34-3/4" w, 17-1/2" d, 29-3/8" h 4,600.00
　Salem, MA, c1800, carved mahogany and flame birch ve-
　neer, serpentine top with ovolo corners, conforming veneer
　frieze with cockbeaded skirt, flanked by legs with stippled
　background and carving, reeded legs, old refinish, 37" w,
　18" d, 30-1/4" h.............................7,500.00

Hepplewhite
　American, inlaid mahogany, demilune, top edge with band of
　alternating tooth inlay, apron and legs with line inlay, 36" w,
　18" d, 31" h 1,300.00
　Newburyport, sgd "G. Parker," inlaid mahogany, shaped top,
　inlaid edge band, apron inlay with light figured wood rect

with outside rosewood band, dec rect panels to top of legs with line inlay, cuff bands, sgd underneath in chalk, 35-3/4" w, 16-1/4" d, 28-1/2" h 1,750.00

Center

Biedermeier, inlaid walnut, shaped rect top, molded frieze with drawer, canted, sq-section cabriole legs, 25" w, 37" l, 27-3/4" h 1,100.00

Classical

Boston, c1840, carved mahogany veneer, circular top with rounded edge, conforming veneered apron with banded lower edge, carved and turned pedestal, shaped veneered platform above incised ball feet, 40-1/2" d top, 30-3/4" h 1,955.00

Philadelphia, c1827, carved mahogany veneer, rect top with molded edge, cockbeaded frieze with single central working drawer flanked by faux drawers, turned and carved pedestal ending in gadrooning above stepped, curved pedestal, four belted ball feet, old surface, minor imperfections, carving similar to work of Anthony G. Quervelle (1789-1856), Philadelphia, 45-1/4" w, 20" d, 34-3/4" h 2,550.00

George III-style, Irish, late 19th C, mahogany, 36" d, 21-1/2" d, 31-1/2" h 2,875.00

International Movement, Wienerwerkstatte, c1930, mahogany and brass, circular top with crossbanded edge, conforming frieze, sq-section support flanked by four further cylindrical supports, raised on truncated pyramidal base, 25-1/4" d, 30-1/2" h 550.00

Louis XV-Style, 19th C, mahogany inlaid, ormolu mounted walnut, shaped rect top, one short drawer, opposite faux drawer, cabriole legs, cast sabots, 35" w, 22" d, 28" h 600.00

Chair

American, late 18th C, cherry, three board top, hinged seat lid, scalloped edge sides, apron, shoe feet, black paint on underside of top, old refinishing on base, minor repairs, 45-1/2" d top, 28-1/2" h 9,350.00

New England, late 18th C, pine and birch, top tilts above plant seat flanked by sq tapering arm supports which continue to chamfered legs, four sq stretchers, old refinish, 40-1/2" w, 42" d, 28-3/4" h 1,100.00

New England, 19th C, painted pine, rect cleated top, old red painted surface tilts above seat and shaped sides, 36" w, 43" d, 27-1/2" h 3,220.00

Console

Art Nouveau, mahogany, shaped top, modified cabriole legs, curved brackets, hoof feet, 45" w, 19" d, 33" h 825.00

Sheraton-style, hardwood and figured veneer, inlay, old worn finish, English, early 20th C, age cracks, 17-1/4" x 29-1/2" x 31" h. 2,100.00

Dining, extending

Art Deco, Palisanderwood, rect top with bowed ends, conforming frieze, oval pedestal with ebonised molding, spreading foot capped with hammered brass, 43-1/4" w, 90" l extended, 31-3/4" h 300.00

Arts & Crafts

Limbert, #403, cut-corner top over intricate base, slab supports with three spindles in an oval cut-out keyed stretchers connecting to a center leg, one leaf, orig finish, numbered, 50" w, 50" d, 30" h 2,500.00

Limbert, circular top, sq pedestal, four extended feet, two orig leaves, orig finish, veneer chip to apron, 48" d, 30" h 1,900.00

Empire-Style, Continental, 19th C, walnut, quarter-veneered top with crossbanded border, conforming frieze, four canted scroll supports, rect platform stretcher with concave sides, gilt lion-paw feet, octagonal center support, one leaf, 46-1/4" w, 94-3/4" l extended, 31-1/4" h 2,300.00

Federal, New England, c1820-25, cherry and bird's eye maple, two part, two rect ends each with hinged drop-leaf, ring-turned tapering legs ending in ball feet, orig surface, minor surface mars, 82" w, 44-1/2" d, 28-3/4" h . .1,725.00

George III-Style, mahogany, D-shaped top with rounded corners and reeded edge, twin pedestal bases of column raised on tripod base, downswept legs, brass toe caps and castors, 120" l, 44" w, 29-1/4" h 2,100.00

International Movement, Paul Evans, manufactured by Directional, sculptured bronzed metal abstract design base, plate-glass top, c1966, 72" w, 37" d, 29" h 2,300.00

Regency, England, 1815-25, mahogany, rect top, rounded corners, reeded edge, turned pedestals with curving reeded legs ending in brass paw feet, castors, connected by single leaf, old refinish, 36-1/4" w, 74-1/4" d, 29-3/4" h . .1,500.00

Victorian, America, c1875, carved walnut, molded rect top with rounded corners, molded conforming frieze, baluster-turned legs, acanthus scroll feet joined at each end by molded U-stretcher, seven leaves, 53-1/2" w. 140-3/4" l extended, 30-1/4" h 2,500.00

Dressing

Aesthetic Movement, Herter Brothers, molded edge cherry top, chest with orig frame, feet, and top drawer with orig hardware and marquetry inlaid garland of flowers ending in bows, side posts have incised lines, large button feet, fine-grained mahogany panels, later fitted with 3 drawers where orig open space with shelf was, matching rect mirror with beveled edge, originally supported by two arms that attached to top of dressing table (now missing), holes plugged, from commission for furniture by Hon. William Drew Washburn, for his Greek Revival house in Minneapolis, MN, copy of orig bill, 30-3/4" w, 17" d, 29" h . .2,350.00

Federal, New York state, c1825, carved mahogany and mahogany veneer, brass inlaid, cockbeaded rect mirror, scrolled acanthus leaf carved supports with brass emb rosettes above three short drawers, projecting case of two short drawers, one long drawer joining four vase and ring-turned acanthus carved legs, castors, refinished, repaired, 36-1/4" w, 21-1/2" d, 55" h 1,725.00

Painted and Decorated, New Hampshire or Massachusetts, early 19th C, shaped splashboard, table top with single drawer below, ring-turned legs, orig yellow ground, green and gold stencil dec, gold striping, replaced brasses, paint loss and wear, 34-1/4" w, 17-1/2" d, 37" h 1,150.00

Queen Anne

American, walnut, pine secondary wood, two board top with thumb-molded edge, mortised and pinned apron, two dovetailed overlapping drawers, round tapered legs, duck feet, old finish, edge damage to replaced top and drawer fronts, some damage to period brasses, 21-1/2" x 36" x 30-1/2" h 7,700.00

Massachusetts, c1750-60, carved walnut, molded overhanging top with shaped corners, thumb-molded case with long drawer over three small drawers, central one with fan carving, four cabriole legs, pad feet on platforms, concave carved valanced apron with two turned drop pendants, replaced brasses, refinished, repaired rear legs, provenance indicates table descended from Jealous Bates, Cohasset, MA, (1754-1831) American Revolution war soldier, 29-3/4" w, 17-1/2" d, 30" h 24,150.00

Rhode Island, c1760, walnut, overhanging top with molded edge, shaped corners, case with three short thumb-molded drawers, valanced skirt joining four cabriole legs with arris knees, pointed slipper feet, replaced pulls, old finish, repairs, 31" w, 19" d, 29-1/2" h 16,100.00

Transitional, New England, early 19th C, painted and dec, shaped backsplash, gold and green stenciled dec, green and mustard grained surface, single drawer, ring-turned tapering legs, old replaced opalescent drawer pulls, 32-1/4" w, 15" w, 34" h 1,380.00

Drop Leaf

Chippendale

Pennsylvania, late 18th C, walnut, shaped skirt, molded Marlborough legs, old surface, minor imperfections, 15-1/2" w, 46-3/4" l, 29" h 550.00

Rhode Island, c1780, carved mahogany, rect drop leaf top, four sq molded stop fluted legs joined by cut-out apron, repairs, 47-3/4" w, 38-1/4" d, 29" h 2,100.00

Federal

New England, c1810, cherry, sq hinged leaves, straight skirt, sq tapering legs, surface imperfections, 41" w, 14-1/2" d, 28-1/4" h 575.00

New England, c1820, mahogany, rect hinged leaves, ring-turned legs, castors, 47-1/2" w, 25" d, 20" h
. . . . 575.00

Hepplewhite, country, birch and maple with some curl in legs, worn old red scrubbed top, replaced or reset hinges, added extension brackets, 39" w, 18" d, 10-1/4" leaves, 28-1/2" h 550.00

Queen Anne

Country, cherry top, refinished maple base, pine and chestnut secondary wood, two board oval top, cabriole legs, swing leg, duck feet, leaves have been reattached, minor age cracks, 14-3/4" w, 43-1/2" l, 14-1/4" leaves, 27-1/4" h 2,200.00

Country, maple, scrubbed top, old reddish brown finish on base, round tapered legs, duck feet, swing legs, wrought iron butterfly hinges, old seam in each leaf, age cracks in top, 18" w, 47-3/4" l, 16-1/2" l leaves, 28-1/4" h
. . . . .4,125.00

Country, walnut, two board top, two board rounded leaves, six round tapering legs, duck feet, swing legs, old soft refinishing, top braced, frame has minor repairs, leaves have pierced repairs at rule joints and hinges, 50-1/2" l, 17-1/2" d, 29-1/4" h 2,500.00

New England, c1760, cherry, circular overhanging drop leaf, valanced apron, four cabriole legs with arris knees, pad feet on platforms, old finish, 35" d, 27" h
. . . . .42,550.00

Southern New England, 18th C, maple, half rounded hinged leaves, cabriole legs, pad feet, old refinish, 42-3/4" w, 13-1/2 d, 27" h 4,900.00

Folding, International Movement, Bruno Mathsson, manufactured by Carl Mathsson, walnut, refinished, 36" w, 10" d, 29" h
. . . . 850.00

Gallery, English, mahogany, turned column and round top and shelf with galleries, tripod base, old finish, wear and edge damage, some age cracks and repairs, late 19th C, 24" d, 30-3/4" h 330.00

Games

Empire, tilt top, ebonized veneer, inlaid checker board top with brass edging, ivory segments in turned, reeded, and rope carved column, ivory inlay on trefoil foot, 18-1/4" x 18-1/2" x 30" h, some edge damage and repairs. .1,430.00

Hepplewhite, American, 19th C, inlaid cherry, hinged demi-lune to, conforming apron, sq tapering legs. 400.00

Renaissance Revival, A. Cutler & Son, Buffalo, NY, c1874, ebonized and parcel-gilt, drop leaf, orig paper label, wear to baise, 36" w, 13-3/4" d, 28-3/4" h 700.00

William IV, English, c1830, rosewood, rect top, leather cov playing surface, apron with bead edge panel extending to

pair of leaf carved brackets, turned columns, concave plinth base, scroll feet 975.00

Library

Arts & Crafts

Imperial Furniture Co., #981, two drawers, elaborate copper hardware, cleaned orig finish, remnant of decal, 54" w, 30" d, 29" h 1,600.00

Limbert, #132, rect top, single drawer, orig brass pulls flanked by book shelves opening at sides, branded signature, orig red brown finish, 45" w, 28" d, 29" h
. . . . 850.00

Limbert, #999, rect top, two drawers, orig hardware, long corbels on legs, six wide slats on each side, orig finish, paper label, some veneer restoration, 54" w, 30" d, 30" h
. . . . 900.00

George III, c1800, mahogany and inlay, circular drum top, alternating working and faux drawers, inset gilt tooled green leather top, 42" d, 31" h 8,625.00

Renaissance Revival, American, late 19th C, mahogany, oblong top, carved edge, gadroon carved apron, trestle base with caryatid supports at each side joined by flat stretcher shelf, acanthus carved wide scroll feet, 60" l 30" h 3,500.00

Parlor

Victorian, walnut, molded detail, white marble turtle top, carved dog on base shelf, old dark finish, old repairs, top cracked, 23" x 3" x 29" h 770.00

Victorian, Gothic Revival, walnut, rosewood veneer apron, replaced top, 20" x 36" x 29-1/4" h. 500.00

Pedestal

Biedermeier-Style, cherry and burr poplar, circular top with crossbanded edge, conforming apron, hexagonal support rising from triangular platform base with concave sides, three scroll supports, 29-1/2" d, 27-1/2" h 600.00

Second Empire-Style, walnut, marquetry, and parcel-gilt, quarter-veneered circular top, polychrome floral marquetry, gilt-metal gadrooned edge, sq section tapered pedestal with concave sides and canted corners, gilt hairy-paw feet, 33-1/2" d, 28-1/4" h 1,000.00

Pembroke

Chippendale, New England, 1760-80, cherry, serpentine top, drawer, molded chamfered legs, refinished, 33" w, 33" d, 28" h. 875.00

Federal

New England, late 18th C, mahogany, old refinish, restored, 19" w, 30" d, 28" h. 2,185.00

New York, c1790-1800, mahogany inlaid, rect top with hinged leaves, shaped corners bordered by inlaid stringing, four sq tapering legs inlaid with satinwood panels, stringing and cross-banding, straight skirt with working and false drawers, old brasses, old finish, imperfections, 19" w closed, 32" d, 28-1/2" h 2,990.00

Sheraton, New York, mahogany, double drop shaped leaves, single end drawer, well proportioned tapering turned elongated legs fitted with brass ferrules and castors, inlaid mahogany tombstone panels beside drawer, fine reeding to legs, 43" w open, 21" closed, 35-1/2" d, 29" h 6,500.00

Pier, Classical, Boston, 1835-40, mahogany veneer, replaced carrara marble top, straight paneled veneered frieze above scrolled and carved frontal supports with flattened veneered columns flanking pier glass, old refinish, feet missing, some veneer loss, 41" w, 17-3/4" d, 36" h, price for matched pair
. . . . .10,925.00

Poker, Arts & Crafts, sectional apron with small drawers, arched cross- stretchers, added varnish, 36" ,d 30-1/2" h . . . 950.00

Refectory, Jacobean-style, 19th C, carved oak, rect top with molded apron, each trestle end with lobed, cup and cover support, arched acanthus capped feet, joined by molded platform stretcher, 94" l, 29" w, 31-1/2" h 3,250.00

Serving, George III, c1800

Mahogany, slightly bowed top, pair of drawers, sq tapering legs 1,725.00

Satinwood and marquetry, demilune, later fitted with spring action drawers, restoration, 62-1/4" w, 23-1/2" d, 32-3/4" h 19,550.00

Sewing

Federal

Boston, MA, c1805, mahogany veneer, mahogany top with outset corners above two veneered cockbeaded drawers, sliding bag frame, flanked by legs with colonettes above reeding, ending in turned tapering feet, old brass, old finish, 20-3/4" w, 15-3/4" d, 28-1/4" h 1,610.00

New England, mahogany veneer, mahogany top with hinged drop leaves, reeded edge, flanking three veneered drawers, top fitted for writing, bottom with sliding sewing bag frame, ring-turned and spiral carved legs, castors, old refinish, replaced brasses, 18-1/2" w, 18-1/8" d, 29-1/4" h .1,150.00

Sheraton, mahogany, drop leaf, two drawers over one drawer, ring and spiral turned legs, brass cup and caster feet, 20-1/2" closed, 27-3/4" open, 18" d, 28-1/2" h 1,200.00

Silver, George III, c1765, carved mahogany, galleried tray top, low relief carved everted lip, repeating border of C-scrolls and foliage, swirling scroll bordered apron, molded sq cabriole supports with trailing acanthus carving at knees, Spanish feet, alternations to top, repairs, 31-3/4" l 28-3/4" h 2,000.00

Sofa

Hepplewhite, Salem, MA, 1790-1810, mahogany, satinwood inlaid, rect top flanked by D-shaped drop leaves, skirt fitted with two cockbeaded inlaid working and two faux drawers,

Pembroke, Chippendale, American, 18th C, carved mahogany, 38" l, 27-1/2" h, $2,750.

drawers flanked by diamond inlaid dies, stringing on lower skirt edge, two upright rect columns each continuing to two line inlaid tapering down curving legs, brass animal paw casters, ring-turned transverse stretcher, repairs to legs and uprights, 53-3/4" w extended, 27-1/4" d, 28-1/2" h 82,500.00

Neoclassical, Continental, second quarter 19th C, brass and ivory inlaid rosewood, 52-1/2" w extended, 28-1/4" d, 29-1/2" h 3,335.00

Tavern

Hepplewhite, two board breadboard top, large overhang, one drawer base, tapered sq legs, grungy finish, 42-1/2" w, 29-3/4" d, 28" h 750.00

Queen Anne, PA, walnut, removable one board top, mortised and pinned apron, beaded edge, two overlapping drawers, splayed base, rounded tapered legs, duck feet, old finish, orig brasses and pins, age crack in top, 16-3/4" w, 30-3/8" l, 29-3/4" h 27,500.00

Southeastern New England, 18th C, painted cherry and pine, rect top, valanced apron, two small end drawers, four block vase and ring turned splayed legs, sq box stretchers, turned feet, orig red paint, minor imperfections, 24-1/2" w, 16-1/2" d, 25" h 14,950.00

William and Mary, New England, 18th C, maple and pine, rect overhanging top, straight skirt with drawer, joining block base and ring turned legs, feet joined by square stretchers, old refinish, minor imperfections, 33" w, 21" d, 27" h 1,610.00

Tea

Chippendale

Connecticut, attributed to Amzi Chapin, 1780-1800, cherry, round top, reel and baluster turned pedestal, cabriole legs, pad feet, old dark stained surface, imperfections, 36" d, 26-3/4" h 2,650.00

Deerfield, MA, late 18th C, mahogany, serpentine molded tilt-top, turned pedestal, cabriole leg base, pad feet, one damaged foot, 30-1/2" w, 32-1/2" l, 28-1/2" h . .1,100.00

Massachusetts, 18th C, carved mahogany, scrolled piecrust tilt top, pedestal with spiral carving at base, leaf carved cabriole legs, ball and claw feet, old refinish, leg fractures, 29-1/2" d, 27-1/2" h 2,990.00

Nantucket, MA, 1780-1810, mahogany and cherry, serpentine shaped tilt top, ring turned pedestal, cabriole legs, chip carved knees, scratch beaded edges, old refinish, imperfections, 20" w, 20-1/2" d, 29" h . . .2,990.00

Newport, RI, 18th C, carved mahogany, tilt top, chamfered underside, spiral carved pedestal, cabriole legs, small ball and claw feet, top with old refinish, 32-3/4" d, 27-3/4" h 2,760.00

Pennsylvania, c1770, carved mahogany, circular tilt-top, birdcage support, vase and ring-turned post, tripod cabriole leg base, carved claw and ball feet, refinished, imperfections, 29-3/4" d, 28" h 2,100.00

Hepplewhite, tilt top, poplar one board top with cut corners, birch tripod base with spider legs, turned column, old refinishing with painted foliage border designs in shades of gold and black, top replaced, repairs, 15-1/2" w, 23-1/2" l, 28-3/4" h 440.00

Queen Anne, curly maple, molded edge tray top, scrolled apron, cabriole legs, duck feet, refinished, top is old replacement, 20" w, 30-1/2" l, 27-1/4" h 3,025.00

Tray, Edwardian, c1900, satinwood and inlay, two oval tiers, removable wood and glass tray, slightly splayed sq tapering legs joined by stretcher, 36" w, 20-1/4" d, 32" h 1,150.00

Trestle, New England, 18th C, oak and pine, rect top, three chamfered cleats, two shaped legs resting on trestle feet, joined by shaped medial stretcher with mortise and tenon construction, additional shaped center support, old finish, 92-1/2" l, 28" d, 29" h 8,625.00

Tripod, Renaissance Revival, c1865, rosewood, part ebonized, parcel-gilt, and beadwork, 26-3/4" w, 44-3/4" h 1,380.00

Work

Biedermeier-Style, cherry wood and burr popular, rect top, molded frieze with drawer, inverted, pierced, and lyre-form supports joined by pole stretcher, 22-1/2" l, 15-3/4" w, 25-1/4" h 650.00

Classical, New England, c1820-30, tiger maple, rect drop leaf top, two drawers with convex fronts, sq tapering pedestal, stepped sq platform, four turned and belted feet, old finish, 16-1/2" w, 17" d, 30-1/2" h 1,500.00

Federal

New England, c1800, mahogany and mahogany veneer, rect top, two drawers, straight skirt joining four sq taper-ing legs, replaced brass pulls, old finish, 18-3/4" w, 15-1/8" d, 29-1/2" h 980.00

New York, c1815-20, mahogany astragal-end carved and mahogany veneer, rect top flanked by hinged tops above conforming case of two cockbeaded drawers flanked by reeded pilasters and acorn-turned drop pendants and compartments, vase and ring turned pedestal, four acan-thus leaf carved and molded shaped legs, cast brass hairy paw feet, replaced brasses, imperfections, some sun-bleaching, 25-1/4" w, 14" d, 30-1/4" h 2,300.00

Queen Anne

Black walnut and pine, painted, PA, c1760-1800, remov-able blank three-board pine top, supported by cleats and four dowels, two thumb-molded drawers, straight skirt with breaded edge above straight cabriole legs ending in pad feet, orig apple green paint, old replaced wooden pulls, surface imperfections, cracked foot, 48-1/2" w, 32" d, 27" h 2,500.00

Maple and pine, New England, late 18th C, scrubbed top, straight skirt with beaded edge, turned tapering legs ending in turned button feet, old surface, remnants of red on base, 28" w, 28-1/2" l, 27" h 2,530.00

Painted Pine, New England, 18th C, overhanging oval scrubbed top, straight molded skirt, splayed ring-turned legs ending in turned feet, orig red paint on base, 35" w, 26-3/8" l, 26-1/4" h 14,950.00

Pine and maple, two board pine bread board top with good old patina, mortised and pinned apron, turned tapered legs, button feet, maple base with traces of old paint, reddish brown finish, one corner of top has damage, 31-3/4" w, 64-1/2" l, 27-3/4" h 550.00

Walnut, removable three board top, two dovetailed over-lapping drawers, mortised and pinned apron with edge beading, turned legs, weathered duck feet, old refinish-ing, period replaced brasses, pieced repairs to top, age cracks, 32" w, 49-1/2" l, 28" h 2,750.00

Sheraton, mahogany and mahogany veneer, three dove-tailed drawers, turned legs with ring turned detail, orig gild-ed lion head brasses, old finish, top drawer is fitted with tilt-up writing surface, age cracks in sides, some veneer damage to writing tablet, 16" w, 18" l, 27-3/4" h . .1,430.00

William and Mary-Style, walnut, ebonized trim, two board top, one dovetailed drawer, turned stretchers and legs, repairs and old replacements, 22-3/4" w, 34" d, 27-1/4" h. . 935.00

GAME PLATES

History: Game plates, popular between 1870 and 1915, are specially decorated plates used to serve fish and game. Sets originally included a platter, serving plates,

Fish, 10-3/4" x 23-3/4" platter, twelve 9-1/2" d plates, gravy boat and underplate, peach shading to ivory ground, gold trim, fish school dec, unmarked, gravy boat damaged, flakes to some plates, $550. Photo courtesy of Alderfer Auction Company, Inc.

and a sauce or gravy boat. Many sets have been divided. Today, individual plates are often used as wall hangings.

Birds

Plaque, 14-1/2" d, multicolored flaying ducks over march, print-ed under glaze, gold trim, #1044-9030, Mettlach 350.00

Plate

8-3/4" d, hp, brown quail standing in green and tan land-scape, white ground, inner border of yellow flowers and green leaves, raised outer border with gilt leaves, shaped rim, sgd "C. T." and eagle mark 55.00

9-1/2" d, sgd "Max," Limoges Coronet 65.00

9-3/4" d, blue grouse, brown grouse, shielded green field, shaded brown borer, brown lined rim, Bavaria 25.00

10" d, duck, white, gray, and black body, emerald green head, standing in marsh, gadrooned gilt border within tradi-tional border, Royal Copenhagen 990.00

10-1/2" d, Asiatic Pheasants, R Hall. 3.00

12-1/4"" d, birds in flight, hp, gold scalloped edge, marked "Li-moges" 200.00

Platter

13-3/4" x 9-1/2", oval, duck, p, natural setting, gold handles, artist sgd, Limoges blank 225.00

18" l, pheasants, multicolored center scene, marked "R K Beck" 500.00

Set, 20-1/2" l platter with two turkeys, twelve plates with hp de-signs, artist sgd, marked "Limoges, France" 625.00

Deer

Plate, 13-3/4"" h, stag in woods, hp, raised enamel dec 200.00

Platter, 15-1/4" x 12-1/8", antlered deer fighting, multicolored transfer, cobalt blue border, gold stencil trim, gold striped rim 50.00

Set, platter, twelve plates, deer, bear, and game birds, yellow ground, scalloped border, marked "Haviland China," artist sgd "MC Haywood". 3,000.00

Fish

Plaque, 14" d, multicolored hanging fish and lobster, printed un-der glaze, gold trim, Mettlach 375.00

Plate

9" d, bass, artist sgd "Morley," marked "Lenox" 75.00
10-1/2" d, trout, cobalt blue border, marked "M Z Austria"
. . . . 85.00

Platter, 16-1/2" l, bass, water lilies, emb, artist sgd "Max," marked "Limoges" 175.00

Set

21" platter, nine 8-1/2" d plates, sauceboat with undertray, hp reserves of leaping trout, seaweed border, heavy gold accents, Limoges. 990.00
23-1/2" platter, twelve plates, different species on each plate, yellow border, gold trim, marked "Limoges, France" 500.00

Miscellaneous

Plaque, 11-5/8" d, brown moose in woods, dark blue shaded border, gold overlay, pierced for hanging. 45.00

Plate

9" d, elk, natural colors, scalloped edge. 45.00
10" d, wild boar, multicolored, Limoges 160.00

Platter, 18" l, weasel carrying red squirrel in mouth, winter scene, sky blue ground, paneled and beaded border, dentil rim, gilt and ground highlights, numbered, Royal Copenhagen 1,200.00

GAMES

History: Board games have been commercially produced in this country since at least 1822, and card games since the 1780s. However, it was not until the 1840s that large numbers of games were produced that survive to this day. The W. & S. B. Ives Company produced many board and card games in the 1840s and 1950s. Milton Bradley and McLoughlin Brothers became major producers of games starting in the 1860s, followed by Parker Brothers in the 1880s. Other major producers of games in this period were Bliss, Chaffee and Selchow, Selchow and Righter, and Singer.

Today, most games from the 19th century are rare and highly collectible, primarily because of their spectacular lithography. McLoughlin and Bliss command a premium because of the rarity. The quality of materials, and the extraordinary art that was created to grace the covers and boards of their games.

In the 20th century, Milton Bradley, Selchow and Righter and Parker Brothers became the primary manufacturers of boxed games. They have all now been absorbed by toy giant Hasbro Corporation. Other noteworthy producers were All-Fair, Pressman, and Transogram, all of which are no longer in business. Today, the hottest part of the game collecting market is in rare character games from the 1960s. Parker Brothers and All-Fair games from the 1920s to 1940s also have some excellent lithography and are highly collectible.

References: *Board Games of the 50's, 60's & 70's with Prices*, L-W Books, 1994; Mark Cooper, *Baseball Games*, Schiffer Publishing, 1995; Lee Dennis, *Warman's Antique American* Games, 1840-1940, Wallace-Homestead, 1991; *Dexterity Games and Other Hand-Held Puzzles*, L-W Book Sales, 1995; Jack Matthews, *Toys Go to War*, Pictorial Histories Publishing, 1994; Rick Polizzi, *Baby Boomer Games*, Collector Books, 1995; Rick Polizzi and

Fred Schaefer, *Spin Again*, Chronicle Books, 1991; Desi Scarpone, *Board Games*, Schiffer Publishing, 1995; Carl P. Stirn, *Turn-of-the-Century Dolls, Toys and Games* (1893 catalog reprint), Dover Publications, 1990; Bruce Whitehill, *Games: American Boxed Games and Their Makers*, Wallace-Homestead, 1992.

Periodicals: *The Games Annual,* 5575 Arapahoe Rd., Suite D, Boulder, CO 80303; *Toy Shop,* 700 E. State St., Iola, WI 54990; *Toy Trader,* P.O. Box 1050, Dubuque, IA 52004.

Collectors' Clubs: American Game Collectors Association, P.O. Box 44, Dresher, PA, 19025; Gamers Alliance, P.O. Box 197, East Meadow, NY 11554.

Museums: Checkers Hall of Fame, Petal, MS; Essex Institute, Salem, MA; Margaret Woodbury Strong Museum, Rochester, NY; University of Waterloo Museum & Archive of Games, Waterloo, Ontario, Canada; Washington Dolls' House and Toy Museum, Washington, D.C.

Additional Listings: See *Warman's Americana & Collectibles.*

Notes: While people collect games for many reasons, it is strong graphic images that bring the highest prices. Games which are collected because they are fun to play or for nostalgic reasons are still collectible but will not bring high prices. Also, game collectors are not interested in common and "public domain" games such as checkers, tiddley winks, Authors, Anagrams, Jackstraws, Rook, Pit, Flinch, and Peter Coodles. The game market today is characterized by fairly stable prices for ordinary items, increasing discrimination for grades of condition, and continually rising prices for rare material in excellent condition. Whether you are a dealer or a collector, be careful to buy games in good condition. Avoid games with taped or split corners or other box damage. Games made after about 1950 are difficult to sell unless they are complete and in excellent condition. As games get older, there is a forgiveness factor for condition and completeness that increases with age.

These listings are for games that are complete and in excellent condition. Be sure that the game you're looking to price is the same as the one described in the listing. The 19th century makers routinely published the same title on several different versions of the game, varying in size and graphics.

Aero-Chute Target Game, American Toy Works, boxed board game, 19-3/16" x 13-3/16" x 2-5/8", 8 pcs 40.00
American Boys, McLoughlin Bros., early 1900s, boxed board game, 11" x 20", some damage to orig box 200.00
Auto Race Game, Milton Bradley, c1925, boxed board game, 16-7/8" x 8-3/4", 8 pcs 125.00
Bagatelle, early push-type, 1-5/8" x 9-15/16" x 19-1/4", wooden, multicolored litho pasted to face marking points, wooden stick with wooden block to push ball, one wood and one clay ball, instructions pasted on back 135.00
Bicycle Race, McLoughlin Bros., c1890, boxed board game
. . . . 925.00
Big Trail Game, boxed board game, 13-1/2" x 17" x 1-1/2", 1930 Movietone picture with John Wayne and Tyrone Power Sr., 14" x 26" multicolored board, wagon train illus, instruction

booklet, wooden pawns, metal figures, full color illus box, several pawns and four figures missing 75.00

Bradley's Toy Town Post Office, Milton Bradley, c1910, educational, 8-3/4" x 11", 10 pcs 110.00

Buster Brown and Tige, Bliss, target game 575.00

Champion Game of Baseball, Proctor Amusement, c1900, boxed board game, 9" x 12", instructions inside cov, unused score card, litho heavy paper gameboard with baseball diamond, attached spinner, bleachers, and stands, paper markers in orig envelopes 140.00

Charlie Chan, Whitman, 1939, boxed card game, 5" x 6" x 1", 35 playing cards, instruction card, black, white, and red crime fighting scenes, multicolored box 75.00

Cinderella, Milton Bradley, c1900, card game, 6-3/4" x 5-1/2", 33 cards. 20.00

Comic Conversations, Parker Bros., card game, 5" x 6-1/2"
. . . . 45.00

Down the Pike with Mrs. Wiggs at the St. Louis Exposition, Milton Bradley, c1904, card game, 7-1/2" x 5-1/2", instructions on front of reading booklet, small cards 20.00

Excursion to Coney Island, Milton Bradley, c1885, card game, printed cards, reading booklet 35.00

Flap Jacks, Alderman-Fairchild, 1931, skill game, 15-1/2" x 12-1/2", 30 pcs 35.00

Game of Balloon, R Bliss Manuf, 1889, skill game, 31" x 10-1/2", 17 pcs, wooden stand and hoop, all wood dovetailed and hinged box 275.00

Game of Bang, McLoughlin Bros., 1912, boxed board game, 15" x 8", orig spinner, game board on box bottom, playing pcs
. . . . 85.00

Game of Boy Scouts, McLoughlin Bros. 290.00

Game of Louisa, McLoughlin Bros., 1888, platform type board, repairs to orig box. 625.00

Game of Old Mother Hubbard, Milton Bradley, c1890, boxed board game, 15" x 16", 8 pcs 95.00

Game of Parlor Baseball, McLoughlin Bros., 1897, boxed board game, 17" x 19", vivid litho cov of early baseball players, board with playing field, two litho spinners, 18 wooden playing markers. 1,600.00

Game of Poor Jenny, Alderman-Fairchild, c1927, boxed board game, 11-1/2" x 11-1/2", 9 pcs 50.00

Game of Zulu, McLoughlin Bros., target game, 12" x 20", 8 parts
. . . . 110.00

Gypsy Fortune Telling Game, Milton Bradley, 1930, fold out board, fortune telling cards. 150.00

Honey Bee Game, Milton Bradley, c1913, boxed board game, 12-3/4" sq, 26 pcs 60.00

Jack and the Bean Stalk, Parker Bros., 1901, box bottom is playing board, two playing pieces, teetotum, cover edge wear, 15" l, 9-1/2" w, 5/8" h 115.00

Japanese Games of Mon, Blind Pilgrim, and Cash, McLoughlin Bros., 1890, book type 275.00

Klondyke Nugget Game, c1890, boxed board game, 4" x 8" x 1", full color illus of mine, miner holding "Boss Nugget," multicolored game board, mine covers, gold nuggets 85.00

Lee at Havana Game, c1898, boxed board game, 5" x 7" x 1", Spanish-American War, set of 52 cards, instruction sheet, full color paper label on lid 75.00

Magnetic Fish Pond, Parker Bros., c1930, boxed board game
. . . . 75.00

Mansion of Happiness, Henry P. Ives, 1864, hand colored board, 15" x 18", slight damage to box. 250.00

Motor Cycle Game, Milton Bradley, c1905, boxed board game, 9" sq, 5 pcs. 40.00

Naval Engagement, McLoughlin Bros., 1870, folding box board, teetotum, peg, and card, wooden tokens, orig 9-3/16" x 5-5/8" x 1-1/2" box 230.00

Oriental Color Game, McLoughlin Bros., 1875, 7-1/2" x 4-1/2", wooden box, 54 multicolored litho cards, litho double arrowed block spinner, instruction booklet 85.00

Psychology of the Hand, Baker & Bennett Co., card game, 8-3/4" x 12-1/4" x 1-1/2", copyright by Gertrude Ann Lindsay, five cards of hands, instruction booklet 35.00

Raggedy Ann's Magic Pebble Game, Johnny Gruelle Co., Milton Bradley, 1941, 15-1/2" x 8-11/16" x 1-3/4", 18 pcs. . . . 65.00

Round the World with Nellie Bly, c1895, Statue of Liberty on board 125.00

Strange Game of Forbidding Fruit, Parker Bros., c1900, boxed card game, 4" x 5-1/2", forty cards, full color paper label on lid of three men steeling apples, charging farm yard dog
. . . . 75.00

Tally-Ho, Snow, Woodman & Co., c1880, 11-1/4" x 11-1/4", thirty-six white wooden pegs, thirty-six black wooden pegs, lift out board, instruction sheet, multicolored litho board with red star center 60.00

The Two Friends, French, 19th C, litho paper on wood, flat picture blocks, view of people in national costumes, 9-5/8" w, 7-1/2" d, 1-1/8" h 288.00

Tiddle Tennis, Schonlat, 1930s, tiddly wink type, 6" x 12-1/2", 8 playing pcs 45.00

Tug of War, Chafee/Selchow, 1898, boxed board game, 10-1/2" x 19-1/2", repairs to orig box 425.00

When My Ship Comes In, George S. Parker, & Co., c1888, 5-1/2" x 4", boxed card game, 84 cards, instruction sheet
. . . . 30.00

GAUDY DUTCH

History: Gaudy Dutch is an opaque, soft-paste ware made between 1790 and 1825 in England's Staffordshire district.

The wares first were hand decorated in an underglaze blue and fired; then additional decorations were added over the glaze. The over-glaze decoration is extensively worn on many of the antique pieces. Gaudy Dutch found a ready market in the Pennsylvania German community because it was inexpensive and extremely colorful. It had little appeal in England.

Collectors' Club: Gaudy Collector's Society, P.O. Box 274, Gates Mills, OH 44040.

Museums: Henry Ford Museum, Dearborn, MI; Philadelphia Museum of Art, Philadelphia, PA; Reading Art Museum, Reading, PA.

Marks: Marks of various potters, including the impressed marks of Riley and Wood, have been found on some pieces, although most are unmarked.

References: Susan and Al Bagdade, *Warman's English & Continental Pottery & Porcelain*, 3rd Edition, Krause Publications, 1998; Eleanor and Edward Fox, *Gaudy Dutch*, published by author, 1970, out of print; John A. Shuman, III, *Collector's Encyclopedia of Gaudy Dutch & Welsh*, Collector Books, 1990, 1998 value update.

Collectors' Club: Gaudy Collector's Society, P.O. Box 274, Gates Mills, OH 44040.

Advisor: John D. Querry.

Butterfly
Bowl, 11" d 3,900.00
Coffeepot, 11" h 4,500.00
Cup and Saucer, handleless 600.00
Plate, 6-1/2" d 650.00
Plate, 9-1/2" d 1,500.00
Sugar Bowl, cov 900.00
Teapot, 5" h, squat baluster form 1,400.00
Waste Bowl, 1,275.00

Carnation
Bowl, 5-1/2" d 625.00
Bowl, 6-1/4" d 750.00
Creamer, 4-3/4" h 700.00
Pitcher, 6" h 675.00
Plate, 5-1/2" d 575.00
Plate, 8" d 850.00
Teabowl and Saucer 495.00
Teapot, cov 1,275.00
Toddy Plate 525.00
Waste Bowl 375.00

Dahlia
Bowl, 6-1/4" d 675.00
Plate, 8" d 1,100.00
Teabowl and Saucer 700.00

Double Rose
Bowl, 6-1/4" d 400.00
Creamer, 4" h, squatty 1,075.00
Gravy Boat 300.00
Plate, 7" d 675.00
Plate, 10" d 750.00
Soup Plate, 9-3/4" d 1,595.00

Oyster pattern, plate, 8-3/4" d, $425.

Sugar Bowl, cov 775.00
Teapot, cov. 800.00
Toddy Plate, 4-1/2" d 350.00
Waste Bowl, 6-1/2" d, 3" h 550.00

Dove
Creamer 675.00
Cup and Saucer, handleless 990.00
Plate, 10" d 750.00
Waste Bowl 650.00

Flower Basket, plate, 6-1/2" d 195.00

Grape
Bowl, 6-1/2" d, lustered rim 385.00
Plate, 6" d 450.00
Plate, 7-1/2" d 525.00
Sugar Bowl, cov 450.00
Teabowl and Saucer 475.00
Teapot, squatty, minor paint loss 4,070.00
Toddy Plate, 5" d 395.00

Oyster
Bowl, 5-1/2" d 300.00
Coffeepot, cov, 12" h 3,000.00
Plate, 7-1/2" d 525.00
Plate, 8-3/4" d 425.00
Plate, 9-1/2" d 575.00
Soup Plate, 8-1/2" d 550.00
Teabowl and Saucer 400.00
Toddy Plate, 5-1/2" d 425.00

Single Rose
Bowl, 6" d 275.00
Coffeepot, dome lid, repaired 3,025.00
Cup and Saucer 400.00
Plate, 7" d 550.00
Plate, 8-1/4" d 650.00
Quill Holder, cov 2,500.00
Sugar Bowl, cov 700.00
Toddy Plate, 5-1/4" d 250.00

Sunflower
Bowl, 6-1/2" d 950.00
Coffeepot, cov, 9-1/2" h .6,500.00
Creamer 850.00
Cup and Saucer, handleless 850.00
Plate, 5-1/2" d 650.00
Teabowl and Saucer 775.00

Urn
Creamer 450.00
Plate, 8-1/4" d 1,100.00
Sugar Bowl, cov, 6-1/2" h, round, tip and base restored
. . . . 395.00

War Bonnet
Bowl, cov 225.00
Coffeepot, cov 9,500.00
Plate, 7" d 475.00
Plate, 8-1/2" d 775.00
Teapot, cov. 2,400.00
Toddy Plate, 4-1/2" d 525.00

GAUDY IRONSTONE

History: Gaudy Ironstone was made in England around 1850. Ironstone is an opaque, heavy-bodied earthenware which contains large proportions of flint and slag. Gaudy Ironstone is decorated in patterns and colors similar to those of Gaudy Welsh.

Collectors' Club: Gaudy Collector's Society, P.O. Box 274, Gates Mills, OH 44040.

Left: plate, floral with eye, underglaze blue, red and green enamel and luster, imp "E. Walley, Niagara Shape," registry mark, wear and scratches, 8-1/2" d, $120; center: Strawberry platter, underglaze blue with red, pink, and green enamel and luster, wear, stains, some enamel flaking, 13-1/2" l, $770; right: plate, Pinwheel, underglaze blue with red and green enamel and luster, imp "Ironstone," minor wear, 8-3/8" d, $175. Photo courtesy of Garth's Auctions, Inc.

Museums: Henry Ford Museum, Dearborn, MI; Philadelphia Museum of Art, Philadelphia, PA; Reading Art Museum, Reading, PA.

Marks: Most pieces are impressed "Ironstone" and bear a registry mark.

Coffeepot, cov, 10" h, Strawberry pattern 650.00
Cup and Saucer
    Morning Glory pattern, underglaze blue, polychrome enamels 170.00
    Seeing Eye pattern 180.00
Jug, 7-1/2" h, yellow, red, white, and blue tulips on sides, light blue pebble ground, luster trim, rim outlined 350.00
Pitcher, 8-1/2" h, Strawberry pattern. paneled 1,045.00
Plate
    6-1/4" d, Morning Glories and Strawberries pattern, underglaze blue, polychrome enamel and luster trim 80.00
    7-7/8" d, Urn pattern 70.00
    9-1/2" d, Strawberry pattern, wear to red enamels 45.00
Platter
    14-1/4" , red, green, blue, and black floral rim, mkd "Allertons, England" 185.00
    17-1/4" l, underglaze blue, red transfer, imp "Derby," underglaze blue crown mark 200.00
Sugar Bowl, cov, 8-1/2" h, Strawberry pattern 425.00
Toddy Plate, 4-3/4" d, Urn pattern, underglaze blue, polychrome enamel and luster 210.00

GAUDY WELSH

History: Gaudy Welsh is a translucent porcelain that was originally made in the Swansea area of England from 1830 to 1845. Although the designs resemble Gaudy Dutch, the body texture and weight differ. One of the characteristics is the gold luster on top of the glaze.

In 1890, Allerton made a similar ware from heavier opaque porcelain.

Collectors' Club: Gaudy Collector's Society, P.O. Box 274, Gates Mills, OH 44040.

Museums: Royal Institution of South Wales, Swansea Mills; St. Fagen's Welsh Folk Museum, Cardiff, Wales; Welsh National Museum, Cardiff, Wales.

Marks: Allerton pieces usually bear an export mark.

References: Susan and Al Bagdade, *Warman's English & Continental Pottery & Porcelain*, 3rd Edition, Krause Publications, 1998; John A. Shuman, III, *Collector's Encyclopedia of Gaudy Dutch and Welsh*, Collector Books, 1990, 1991 value update, out-of-print; Howard Y. Williams, *Gaudy Welsh China*, Wallace-Homestead, out-of-print.

Collectors' Club: Gaudy Collector's Society, P.O. Box 274, Gates Mills, OH 44040.

Columbine
    Bowl, 10" d, 5-1/2" h, ftd, underglaze blue and polychrome enamel floral dec 400.00
    Plate, 5-1/2" d 65.00
    Tea Set, c1810, 17 pc set 625.00
Daisy and Chain
    Creamer 175.00
    Cup and Saucer 95.00
    Sugar, cov 195.00
    Teapot, cov 225.00
Flower Basket
    Bowl, 10-1/2" d 190.00
    Mug, 4" h 90.00
    Plate 65.00
    Sugar, cov, luster trim 165.00
Grape
    Bowl, 5-1/4"" d 50.00
    Cup and Saucer 75.00
    Mug, 2-1/2" h 65.00
    Plate, 5-1/4"" d 65.00
Oyster
    Bowl, 6" d 80.00
    Creamer, 3" h 100.00
    Cup and Saucer 75.00
    Jug, 5-3/4" h, c1820 . . . . 85.00
    Soup Plate, 10" d, flange rim 85.00
Strawberry
    Creamer 90.00
    Cup and Saucer 75.00
    Mug, 4 1/8" h 125.00
    Plate, 8-1/4"" d 150.00
Tulip
    Bowl, 6-1/4"" d 50.00
    Cake Plate, 10" d, molded handles 120.00
    Creamer, 5-1/4"" h 90.00
    Sugar, cov, 6-3/4"" h 110.00
    Teapot, 7-1/4"" h 175.00
Wagon Wheel
    Cup and Saucer 75.00
    Mug, 2-1/2" h 95.00

Cup and Saucer, peppermint transfer, Shan We See, $75.

Pitcher, 8-1/2" h 195.00
Plate, 8-3/4"" d 85.00
Platter. 125.00

GIRANDOLES and MANTEL LUSTRES

History: A girandole is a very elaborate branched candleholder, often featuring cut glass prisms surrounding the mountings. A mantel lustre is a glass vase with attached cut glass prisms.

Girandoles and mantel lustres usually are found in pairs. It is not uncommon for girandoles to be part of a large garniture set. Girandoles and mantel lustres achieved their greatest popularity in the last half of the 19th century both in the United States and Europe.

Girandoles, pr

10-1/2" h, William IV, ormolu, Napoleon exiled on Elba, staring out to sea, marble bases, c1835 . . . . 600.00
12" h, bronze, 3-light, Roman Centurion form support, prisms, American, c1855 . . . . 200.00
15" h, gilt brass and marble, naturalistically scrolling arms, neoclassical urns, stepped marble bases, pr 230.00
17" h, brass and marble, 3 candle arms, colorless cut prisms, gold repaint. 95.00
18" h, brass relief, 3-light, courting couple, colorless cut prisms, marble base 225.00
21" h, Louis Philippe style, gilt metal, 3-light, gilt metal, faceted glass prisms 500.00
50" h, giltwood, 2-light, three-part mirrored plate, frame with sloping cresting and pendant bellflowers, 20th C, pr, minor losses 865.00

Mantel Lusters

11" h, George III, black amethyst, ten colorless crystal prisms, colorless knop stem 300.00
14" h, ruby glass, enameled forget-me-not dec 500.00
14-1/2" h, pink cased, enamel painted flower swags, gilt scrolls, scalloped bulbous bowl, two rows of colorless faceted prisms 300.00

Ruby Glass, enamel forget-me-not dec, orig prisms, 14" h, $450.

GOLDSCHEIDER

History: Friedrich Goldscheider founded a porcelain and faience factory in Vienna, Austria, in 1885. Upon his death, his widow carried on operations. In 1920, Walter and Marcell, Friedrich's sons gained control. During the Art Deco period, the firm commissioned several artists to create figural statues, among which were Pierrettes and sleek wolfhounds. During the 1930s, the company's products were mostly traditional.

In the early 1940s, the Goldscheiders fled to the United States and re-established operations in Trenton, New Jersey. The Goldscheider Everlast Corporation was listed in Trenton City directories between 1943 and 1950. Goldscheider Ceramics, located at 1441 Heath Avenue, Trenton, New Jersey, was listed in the *1952 Crockery and Glass Journal Directory* but was not listed in 1954.

Reference: Susan and Al Bagdade, *Warman's English & Continental Pottery & Porcelain*, 3rd Edition, Krause Publications, 1998.

Bust, 9" h, Madonna 115.00
Charger, 18-1/2" d, earthenware, riverscape scenes with cottages, one sgd "A. Keller," other sgd "A. Wagner," pr 1,200.00
Figure
  Lady with flower basket, #801 . . . . 50.00
  Lady with hands in muffler, #802 . . . . 50.00
  Marie Antoniette, 6-1/2" h, Peggy Porscher 85.00
  Morning in Paris, authentication letter from Mr. Goldschneider 80.00
  Southern lady, #951779 . . . . 35.00
Lamp Base, 32" h, figural, standing bare breasted female, long lavender gown, holding garland of fruit and grains, column standard, stepped base, printed and imp marks, matching silk beaded shade, minor restoration to base. 2,400.00

Dish, cov, multicolored bird, c1925, mkd "Goldschneider Wein," 11" h, $425.

Plaque, 13-1/2" w, 25-1/8" h, earthenware, rect, molded, maiden in profile, garland of blossoms and berries in hair, large blossom and cluster on left, earth tones, designer sgd "Lamassi," Goldscheider mark, c1900 .1,200.00

Vase, 8-7/8" h, thistle form, stylized leaf and heart motifs, blue and white glazes, black ground with orange banding
. . . . 500.00

Wall Mask, 7-1/4" h, woman's face, dark brown hair, red lips, light beige face 275.00

GONDER POTTERY

History: Lawton Gonder established Gonder Ceramic Arts, Inc., at Zanesville, Ohio, in 1941. He had gained experience while working for other factories in the area. Gonder experimented with glazes, including Chinese crackle, gold crackle, and flambé. Lamp bases were manufactured under the name "Eglee" at a second plant location.

The company ceased operation in 1957.

Marks: Pieces are clearly marked with the word "Gonder" in various forms.

References: Susan and Al Bagdade, *Warman's American Pottery and Porcelain*, Wallace-Homestead, 1994; Ron Hoppes, *Collector's Guide and History of Gonder Pottery*, L-W Book Sales, 1992.

Collectors' Club: Gonder Collectors Club, P.O. Box 4263, North Myrtle Beach, SC 29597.

Basket, 8-1/2" h, pink floral motif 28.00
Bowl, 7-3/4" d, 7" h, blue and brown glossy glaze, swirl, orig flower frog 30.00
Cornucopia, 7" h, turquoise and brown 25.00
Ewer, 12" h, figural swan 40.00
Figure, gazelle 45.00
Panther
    15" l 135.00
    19" l, green 200.00
Planter
    Gazelle 60.00
    Swan 65.00
Teapot, P31 . . . . 25.00

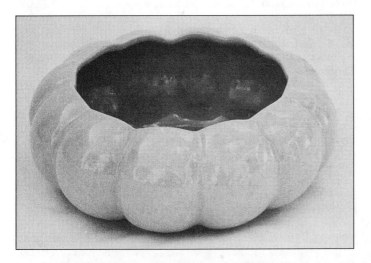

Bowl, melon shape, turquoise ext., pink int., imp "E-12/Gonder/USA," 7" d, $20.

Vase
    E-3, pr. 20.00
    E-4 . . . . 25.00
    E-49 . . . . 20.00
    E-64 . . . . 20.00
    E-94 . . . . 22.50
    J35, yellow, 11" h 60.00
    Pine Cone 95.00
    Swan 35.00

GOOFUS GLASS

History: Goofus glass, also known as Mexican ware, hooligan glass, and pickle glass, is a pressed glass with relief designs that were painted either on the back or front. The designs are usually in red and green with a metallic gold ground. It was popular from 1890 to 1920 and was used as a premium at carnivals.

The cold painted, unfired, decoration did not wear well and easily chipped off. This may be why the name goofus was derived, the manufacturers "goofed" with this technique. The goofus decoration was applied to colorless, transparent green, blue, or amber grounds, as well as opalescent and milk glass grounds. Surfaces were sometimes acid etched (giving a satin ground), crackled, or pressed in a basketweave pattern.

It was produced by several companies: Crescent Glass Company, Wellsburg, West Virginia; Imperial Glass Corporation, Bellaire, Ohio; LaBelle Glass Works, Bridgeport, Ohio; and Northwood Glass Co., Indiana, Pennsylvania, Wheeling, West Virginia, and Bridgeport, Ohio.

Marks: Goofus glass made by Northwood includes one of the following marks: "N," "N" in one circle, "N" in two circles, or one or two circles without the "N."

Periodical: *The Goofus Glass Gazette*, #9, NW 61st St., Gladstone, MO 64118-4002.

Website: Goofus Glass Information Center, http://sundial.sundial.net~gballens.

Ashtray, red rose dec, emb adv 12.00
Basket, 5" h, strawberry dec 50.00
Bon Bon, 4" d, Strawberry pattern, gold, red, and green dec
. . . . 40.00
Bowl
    6-1/2" d, Grape and Lattice pattern, red grapes, gold ground, ruffled rim 45.00
    7" d, Iris pattern, gold and red dec 35.00
    7" d, thistle and scrolling leaves, red dec, gold ground, ruffled rim 35.00
    8-3/4" d, fluted, beaded rim, relief molded, teardrops and red hearts 45.00
    9" d, Roses pattern, red roses, ruffled, relief molded . . 30.00
    10" d, pears and apples dec 35.00
    10-1/2" d, water lilies dec 50.00
    11" d, red cherries, relief molded, ruffled 35.00
Bread Plate, 7" w, 11" l, Last Supper pattern, red and gold, grapes and foliage border 65.00
Candy Dish, 8-1/2" d, figure eight design, serrated rim, dome foot 60.00
Coaster, 3" d, red floral dec, gold ground 12.00
Compote
    4" d, Grape and Cable pattern 35.00

6" d, Strawberry pattern, red and green strawberries and foliage, ruffled 40.00

6-1/2" d, Poppy pattern, red flowers, gold foliage, green ground, sgd "Northwood" 40.00

9-1/2" d, red and green floral and foliage dec, green ground, crimped and fluted rim, pedestal foot, sgd "Northwood" 40.00

Decanter, orig stopper, La Belle Rose 50.00

Dresser Tray, 6" l, Cabbage Rose pattern, red roses dec, gold foliage, clear ground. 35.00

Fairy Lamp, red roses dec, green trim, clear candle cup 45.00

Jar, cov, butterflies, red and gold 35.00

Jewel Box, 4" d, 2" h, basketweave, rose dec 50.00

Mug, Cabbage Rose pattern, gold ground 35.00

Nappy, 6-1/2" d, Cherries pattern, red cherries, gold foliage, clear ground. 35.00

Perfume Bottle, 3-1/2" h, pink tulips dec. 20.00

Pickle Jar, aqua, molded, gold, blue, and red painted floral design. 50.00

Pin Dish, 6-1/2" l, oval, red and black florals. 20.00

Plate

6"d, Rose and Lattice pattern, relief molded 20.00

6" d, Sunflower pattern, red dec center, relief molded . . 20.00

7-3/4" d, Carnations pattern, red carnations, gold ground 20.00

10-1/2" d, grapes dec, gold ground, irid pink edge. . . . 35.00

11" d, Dahlia pattern, red and gold. 40.00

Platter, 18" l, red rose dec, gold ground 65.00

Powder Jar, cov

3" d, puffy, rose dec, red and gold 40.00

4-1/2" d, Cabbage Rose pattern, white cabbage rose, relief molded. 35.00

Salt and Pepper Shakers, pr, Grape and Leaf pattern . . . 45.00

Syrup, relief molded, red roses dec, lattice work ground, orig top 85.00

Oil Lamp, raised floral design, yellow and red flowers, green highlights, gold background, $40.

Toothpick Holder, red rose and foliage dec, gold ground . . 40.00

Tray, 8-1/4" d, 11" d, red chrysanthemum dec, gold ground 45.00

Tumbler, 6" h, red rose dec, gold ground 35.00

Vase

6" h, Cabbage Rose pattern, red dec, gold ground . . . 45.00

6-1/2" h, Grape and Rose pattern, red and gold dec, crackle glass ground 35.00

9" h, Poppies pattern, blue and red dec, gold ground 45.00

10-1/2" h, Peacock pattern. 75.00

12" h, Parrot pattern, red and blue bird, molded foliage 85.00

GOUDA POTTERY

History: Gouda and the surrounding areas of Holland have been principal Dutch pottery centers for centuries. Originally, the potteries produced a simple utilitarian tin-glazed Delft-type earthenware and the famous clay smoker's pipes.

When pipe making declined in the early 1900s, the Gouda potteries turned to art pottery. Influenced by the Art Nouveau and Art Deco movements, artists expressed themselves with free-form and stylized designs in bold colors.

References: Susan and Al Bagdade, *Warman's English & Continental Pottery & Porcelain*, 3rd Edition, Krause Publications, 1998; Phyllis T. Ritvo, *The World of Gouda Pottery,* Font & Center Press, 1998.

Periodical: *Dutch Potter*, 47 London Terrace, New Rochelle, NY 10804.

REPRODUCTION ALERT

With the Art Nouveau and Art Deco revivals of recent years, modern reproductions of Gouda pottery currently are on the market. They are difficult to distinguish from the originals.

Biscuit Jar, cov, 8" h, multicolored 135.00

Bowl

5-1/2" d, 3-1/2" h, Damascus mark 60.00

11-1/2" l, 4-1/2" w, 4-1/4" h, stylized floral black, yellow, orange and teal design 265.00

Candlestick

3" h, 6-1/2" d, circular, handle, matte green, yellow, blue, and cream dec, marked "0139 DAM II Holland," c1885 . 100.00

3-3/4" h, green, rust, cobalt blue, ochre, marked "Candis 1137" and house mark 55.00

Charger, 12" d, multicolored flowers, rope border, black trim 150.00

Compote, 7-5/8", black ground, geometric design, multicolored scroll int. 175.00

Ewer, 9-1/2" h, matte finish, Anjer house mark 125.00

Humidor, cov, light green and tan floral, sgd "Kitty Royal" 185.00

Incense Burner, 8" h, Roba, flowers and geometric designs, green ground 110.00

Jug, 10" h, multicolored dec, black matte ground, orig stopper 195.00

Tobacco Humidor, cov, Verona pattern, 5" h, $200.

Match Holder, striker on bottom, mkd "Regina Holland" . . 45.00
Plate, 10-1/2" d, matte multicolored dec 100.00
Set, 10-1/2" h decanter, 4" h vase, 13" d tray, multicolored floral dec, black and cream ground, all sgd, paper labels. . 450.00
Tobacco Jar, cov, 5" h, Verona pattern. 100.00
Tumbler, 4 3/8" h, 3 5/8" d, multicolored flowers, green leaves, black ground, satin finish, marked "Neri" and house mark
. . . . 65.00
Vase
   9" h, multicolored floral design, green and white ground, sgd "Made in Holland". 160.00
   9" h, multicolored tulip design, green hi-glaze ground, painted marks 375.00
   12-1/2" h, 4-3/4" w, green, peasant woman dec, mkd "7052 RR Holland Gouda" and #1852R, flake on bottom . 350.00

GRANITEWARE

History: Graniteware is the name commonly given to enamel-coated iron or steel kitchenware.

The first graniteware was made in Germany in the 1830s. Graniteware was not produced in the United States until the 1860s. At the start of World War I, when European companies turned to manufacturing war weapons, American producers took over the market.

Gray and white were the most common graniteware colors, although each company made their own special color in shades of blue, green, brown, violet, cream, or red.

Older graniteware is heavier than the new. Pieces with cast-iron handles date between 1870 to 1890; wood handles between 1900 to 1910. Other dating clues are seams, wooden knobs, and tin lids.

References: Helen Greguire, *Collector's Encyclopedia of Granite Ware: Colors Shapes and Values*, Book 1 (1990, 1994 value update), Book 2 (1993, 1998 value update), Collector Books.

Collectors' Club: National Graniteware Society, P.O. Box 10013, Cedar Rapids, IA 52410.

Additional Listings: See *Warman's Americana & Collectibles* for more examples.

Baby Bottle Warmer, gray and white speckled, electric . . 70.00
Bacon Platter, blue and white swirl 115.00
Baking Pan, 11-1/2" l, gray mottled, wire handle 25.00
Basin, 9-1/2" d, blue and white swirl 75.00
Berry Bucket, cov, brown and white swirl, tin lid, bail handle
. . . . 120.00
Bread Dough Riser, cov, gray mottled 100.00
Bread Pan, robin's egg blue, 9" l. 35.00
Butter Churn, blue and white swirl, orig lid 950.00
Cake Pan, 10" x 14", blue and white swirl, molded handles
. . . . 150.00
Candleholder, cobalt blue and white, medium spatter . . . 90.00
Casserole, cov, cobalt blue and white swirl 60.00
Chamber Pot, cov, robin's egg blue and white 145.00
Coffee Boiler, cov, blue and white speckled, large 90.00
Coffeepot, cov, gray mottled, copper bottom 140.00
Colander, ftd, blue and white mottled 80.00
Creamer, multicolored dec 325.00
Dipper, gray mottled 25.00
Double Boiler, cov, yellow and black. 200.00
Frying Pan, brown and white swirl 80.00
Funnel, gray spatter 18.00
Grater, cream and green, flat 100.00
Jelly Kettle, cov, brown and white swirl. 90.00
Kettle, cov, tan, green trim 40.00
Ladle, 12" l, gray mottled. 20.00
Lunch Bucket, cov, light blue and white swirl 100.00
Measure, 4 cup size, gray mottled 140.00
Milk Pan, 11" d, gray mottled 40.00
Milk Pitcher, large blue and white swirls 190.00
Miniature, basin, white, royal blue rim. 40.00
Muffin Pan, 8 cup, brown and white swirl 140.00
Mug, blue and white swirl 90.00
Pail, blue and white mottled, white int., wire bail handle, wood grip 65.00
Pie Pan
   Cobalt Blue. 10.00

Berry Pail, gray and black, 7" d, 4-3/4" h, $40.

Green and white swirl, Emerald Ware, Strong Mfg. Co., Sebring, OH 170.00
White, rose decal 20.00
Plate
8" d, blue-gray speckled 15.00
10" d, gray mottled 20.00
Roaster, cov, tan, green trim, large 180.00
Salt Box, cream and red 125.00
Spittoon, red and white swirl 160.00
Sugar Bowl, tin cover, gray mottled, mkd "L & G Mfg. Co." 325.00
Tea Kettle
Apple green, gooseneck spout 200.00
Blue and white speckle 90.00
Cream and green, gooseneck spout 95.00
Tea Strainer, blue, star perforations 70.00
Wash Basin, green and white mottled 70.00
Wash Board, dark blue insert, mkd "Enamel King" 65.00

GREENAWAY, KATE

History: Kate Greenaway, or "K.G." as she initialed her famous drawings, was born in 1846 in London. Her father was a prominent wood engraver. Kate's natural talent for drawing soon was evident, and she began art classes at the age of 12. In 1868, she had her first public exhibition.

Her talents were used primarily in illustrating. The cards she decorated for Marcus Ward are largely unsigned. China and pottery companies soon had her drawings of children appearing on many of their wares. By the 1880s she was one of the foremost children's book illustrators in England.

Reference: Ina Taylor, *Art of Kate Greenaway: A Nostalgic Portrait of Childhood*, Pelican Publishing, 1991.

Pie Bird, bisque, girl, 5" h, $50.

Collectors' Club: Kate Greenaway Society, P.O. Box 8, Norwood, PA 19074.

Reproduction Alert: Some Greenaway buttons have been reproduced in Europe and sold in the United States.

Bowl, 8-1/2" h, 3-1/4" h, mottled opaque white glass on clear ground, painted and enameled three young children standing in garden, enamel spray of pink daisies on reverse, cut edge, brass-plated stand 300.00
Box, cov, three girls sitting atop log 200.00
Children's Book, *Birthday Book*, Warne, color illus 50.00
Children's Feeding Dish, nursery rhyme dec with children and dog, Haviland 100.00
Children's Play Dishes, tea set, children and dachshund pulling tablecloth, price for 7 pc set 150.00
Figure, 9-1/2" h, children jumping rope, price for pr 600.00
Match Holder, girl helping little girl over log, place for matches and striker 100.00
Nodder, bisque, elderly couple, wearing eyeglasses, cloak, bonnet, and high hat 135.00
Plate, 9" d, children playing, oversized fruit, birds, and flowers 100.00
Print, 6" x 8", Outdoor Tea Party, fifteen girls, sgd 95.00
Sugar Shaker, boy in long coat, white ground 95.00
Thimble Holder, girl holding sterling silver thimble 125.00
Tile, Pipe Thee High, scene with small boy and horn, Wedgwood 85.00
Vase, 4" h, figural girl, holder with orig frosted dec bud vase, sq ornate ftd base, marked "Tufts" 150.00

GREENTOWN GLASS

K. G.

History: The Indiana Tumbler and Goblet Co., Greentown, Indiana, produced its first clear, pressed glass table and bar wares in late 1894. Initial success led to a doubling of the plant size in 1895 and other subsequent expansions, one in 1897 to allow for the manufacture of colored glass. In 1899 the firm joined the combine known as the National Glass Company.

In 1900, just before arriving in Greentown, Jacob Rosenthal developed an opaque brown glass, called "chocolate," which ranged in color from a dark, rich chocolate to a lighter coffee-with-cream hue. Production of chocolate glass saved the financially pressed Indiana Tumbler and Goblet Works. The Cactus and Leaf Bracket patterns were made almost exclusively in chocolate glass. Other popular chocolate patterns include Austrian, Dewey, Shuttle, and Teardrop and Tassel. In 1902 National Glass Company bought Rosenthal's chocolate glass formula so other plants in the combine could use the color.

In 1902, Rosenthal developed the Golden Agate and Rose Agate colors. All work ceased on June 13, 1903, when a fire of suspicious origin destroyed the Indiana Tumbler and Goblet Company Works.

After the fire, other companies, e.g., McKee and Brothers, produced chocolate glass in the same pattern designs used by Greentown. Later reproductions also have been made, with Cactus among the most-heavily copied patterns.

Reference: James Measell, *Greentown Glass*, Grand Rapids Public Museum, 1979, 1992-93 value update, distributed by Antique Publications.

Collectors' Clubs: Collectors of Findlay Glass, P.O. Box 256, Findlay, OH 45839; National Greentown Glass Association, P.O. Box 107, Greentown, IN 46936.

Videotapes: *Centennial Exhibit of Greentown Glass* and *Reproductions of Greentown Glass*, National Greentown Glass Association, P.O. Box 107, Greentown, IN 46936.

Museums: Grand Rapids Public Museum, Ruth Herrick Greentown Glass Collection, Grand Rapids, MI; Greentown Glass Museum, Greentown, IN.

Additional Listings: Holly Amber; Pattern Glass.

Reproduction Alert.

Animal Covered dish
 Bird with Berry, blue 475.00
 Bird with Berry, chocolate, minor repair 650.00
 Cat, hamper base, amber. 465.00
 Hen on Nest, blue. 265.00
 Hen on Nest, chocolate 725.00
 Robin, nest base, opaque white 225.00
Berry Set, Leaf Bracket, chocolate, 7 pcs 275.00
Bowl
 6-1/4" d, No. 11, blue 200.00
 6-1/2" d, Cactus, chocolate 100.00
 10-1/4" d, Geneva, chocolate. 450.00
Butter, cov
 Cactus, chocolate. 300.00
 Daisy, opaque white. 100.00
 Herringbone Buttress, green 250.00
 Leaf Bracket, chocolate 250.00
 Oval Lattice, colorless 75.00
 Shuttle, chocolate. 1,100.00
Compote, Geneva, 4-1/2" d, 3-1/2" h, chocolate. 150.00
Cookie Jar, Cactus, chocolate 300.00
Cordial
 Austrian, canary. 125.00
 Overall Lattice, colorless 45.00
 Shuttle, colorless 45.00
Creamer
 Austrian, colorless 40.00
 Cactus, chocolate. 125.00
 Cord Drapery, colorless 65.00
 Cupid, Nile green 400.00
 Indian Head, opaque white. 450.00
 Indoor Drinking Scene, chocolate, 5-1/2" h 500.00
 Shuttle, colorless, tankard style 65.00
Cruet, orig stopper
 Cactus, chocolate. 325.00
 Chrysanthemum Leaf, chocolate 1,275.00
 Dewey, vaseline. 300.00
 Geneva, chocolate 1,000.00
Dish, Dolphin, chocolate, sawtooth 200.00
Dresser Tray, Wild Rose and Bowknot, chocolate 350.00
Goblet
 Beehive, colorless 65.00
 Diamond Prisms, colorless. 70.00
Jelly Compote
 Cactus, chocolate. 200.00
 Pleat Band, chocolate 130.00
 Lemonade Tumbler, Cactus, chocolate 100.00

Mug
 Elf, green 115.00
 Herringbone Buttress, chocolate 80.00
 Serenade, colorless 75.00
 Troubadour, 6-1/2" h, opaque white, cov 70.00
Nappy, Leaf Bracket, chocolate, triangular 85.00
Pitcher, water
 Cord Drapery, colorless 95.00
 Fleur De Lis, colorless 265.00
 Racing Deer and Doe, colorless. 200.00
 Ruffled Eye, chocolate 550.00
 Squirrel, colorless. 200.00
 Teardrop and Tassel, cobalt blue. 200.00
Punch Cup, Shuttle, colorless. 15.00
Relish, Cord Drapery, amber 110.00
Rose Bowl, Austrian, colorless 45.00
Salt, wheelbarrow shape, Nile green 350.00
Sauce
 Cactus, chocolate, ftd. 65.00
 Leaf Bracket, chocolate 50.00
 Water Lily and Cattails, chocolate 100.00
 Wild Rose and Bowknot, chocolate 95.00
Spooner
 Austrian, colorless 65.00
 Cactus, chocolate. 80.00
 Cupid, colorless 145.00
 Wild Rose and Bowknot, chocolate 150.00
Stein, Serenade, colorless 50.00
Sugar, cov, Cupid, opaque white 115.00
Syrup, Cord Drapery, chocolate 350.00
Tumbler
 Cord Drapery, chocolate 245.00
 Geneva, chocolate 115.00

Syrup, Geneva pattern, chocolate glass, orig tin top, $615.

Icicle, chocolate 150.00
Teardrop and Tassel, blue 65.00
Wildflower, amber. 45.00
Wine, Shuttle, colorless. 20.00

GRUEBY POTTERY

History: William Grueby was active in the ceramic industry for several years before he developed his own method of producing matte-glazed pottery and founded the Grueby Faience Company in Boston, Massachusetts, in 1897.

The art pottery was hand thrown in natural shapes, hand molded, and hand tooled. A variety of colored glazes, singly or in combinations, were produced, but green was the most popular. In 1908, the firm was divided into the Grueby Pottery Company and the Grueby Faience and Tile Co. The Grueby Faience and Tile Company made art tile until 1917, although their pottery production was phased out about 1910.

Minor damage is acceptable to most collectors of Grueby Pottery.

References: Paul Evans, *Art Pottery of the United States*, 2nd ed., Feingold & Lewis Publishing, 1987; Ralph and Terry Kovel, *Kovels' American Art Pottery*, Crown Publishers, 1993; Susan Montgomery, *The Ceramics of William H. Grueby,* Arts and Crafts Quarterly Press, 1993; David Rago, *American Art Pottery,* Knickerbocker Press, 1997.

Advisor: David Rago.

Bowl
7" d, flaring, curving leaves, green matte finish, stamped mark. 3,250.00
8" d, 2" h, flat, green matte ext., glossy dark green int., circle mark. 350.00

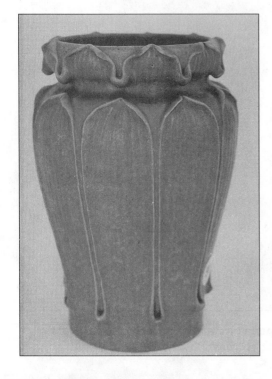

Vase, 12" h, emb upright leaves, one row ends at shoulder, other row extends to opening, $20,000. Photo courtesy of David Rago Auctions, Inc.

Bud Vase, white bellflowers, green stems, stamped mark
. . . . .41,800.00
Cabinet Vase
5" x 4", flowing green matte finish, obscured stamp mark
. . . . 650.00
6" h, two color, white crocus, blue ground, stamped mark
. . . . .19,800.00
Candlestick, 8" h, 3" d, tapering cylindrical, bulbous top, tooled leaves, dark blue glaze, unmarked. 2,000.00
Jardiniere, 6" h, 11" d, flaring vessel, tooled leaves, yellow matte glaze, circle mark 3,000.00
Paperweight, 3" h, 4" l, Scarab beetle, matte blue glaze, circle mark, nicks to bottom edge 600.00
Vase
7" h, 13" d, bulbous, squatty, tooled leaves, three-petal flowers, matte green glaze, circle mark 5,000.00
8:" h, bulbous bottom, corseted neck, tooled leaves and buds, green matte glaze, stamped mark 2,850.00
8" h, cylindrical, vertical ribbing, pumpkin matte finish, stamped mark 2,800.00
8" h, 4" d, cylindrical, green matte glaze, mkd 750.00
8" h, 5" d, bulbous, cylindrical neck, tooled and applied leaves and buds, green matte glaze, circle stamp mark . .1,500.00
9" h, 5" d, five-sided, yellow daffodils and green leaves, green matte ground, circle mark, small chip to rim 6,000.00

HAIR ORNAMENTS

History: Hair ornaments, among the first accessories developed by primitive man, were used to remove tangles and keep hair out of one's face. Remnants of early combs have been found in many archaeological excavations.

As fashion styles evolved through the centuries, hair ornaments kept pace with changes in design and usage. Hair combs and other hair ornaments are made in a wide variety of materials, e.g., precious metals, ivory, tortoiseshell, plastics, and wood.

Combs were first made in America during the Revolution when imports from England were restricted. Early American combs were made of horn and treasured as toiletry articles.

References: Mary Bachman, *Collector's Guide to Hair Combs, Identification and Values,* Collector Books, 1998; Evelyn Haetig, *Antique Combs and Purses*, Gallery Graphics Press, 1983.

Collectors' Club: Antique Comb Collectors Club International, 8712 Pleasant View Road, Bangor, PA 18013; Antique Fancy Comb Collectors Club, 3291 N River Rd., Libertyville, IL 60048; National Antique Comb Collectors Club, 3748 Sunray Dr., Holiday, FL 34691.

Museums: Leominster Historical Society, Field School Museum, Leominster, MA; Miller's Museum of Antique Combs, Homer, AK.

Back Comb
Bakelite, coral and gold-wash filigree, c1890 . . . . 290.00
Imitation goldstone, green stone, Victorian style, c1900
. . . . 150.00
Clip, rhinestone dec, c1930, pr 40.00
Comb
Tortoiseshell, wide plain top. 30.00
Tortoiseshell, set four graduated combs with 14kt yellow gold beaded dec 40.00

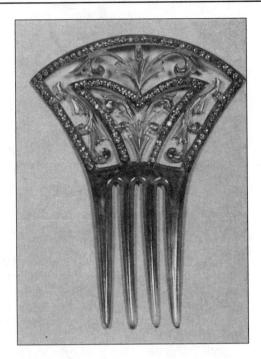

Comb, celluloid to imitate tortoise shell, filigree ornamentation, set with blue rhinestones, 6-1/4" l, $45. Photo courtesy of Julie Robinson.

Hairpin
    Silver, butterfly shape, celadon green jade wings, 7" l, Sung
      Dynasty 200.00
    Staghorn, hand with insect on wrist, 19th C. 80.00
    Tortoiseshell, openwork naturalistic carving. 45.00
Headband, 14K yellow gold, double band, engraved scroll and
    leaf dec, Edwardian, matching gold hairpins 275.00
Ornament, Art Nouveau, tortoiseshell, c1910 . . . . 90.00

HALL CHINA COMPANY

History: Robert Hall founded the Hall China Company in 1903 in East Liverpool, Ohio. He died in 1904 and was succeeded by his son, Robert Taggart Hall. After years of experimentation, Robert T. Hall developed a leadless glaze in 1911, opening the way for production of glazed household products.

The Hall China Company made many types of kitchenware, refrigerator sets, and dinnerware in a wide variety of patterns. Some patterns were made exclusively for a particular retailer, such as Heather Rose for Sears.

One of the most popular patterns was Autumn Leaf, a premium designed by Arden Richards in 1933 for the exclusive use of the Jewel Tea Company. Still a Jewel Tea property, Autumn Leaf has not been listed in catalogs since 1978 but is produced on a replacement basis with the date stamped on the back.

References: Susan and Al Bagdade, *Warman's American Pottery and Porcelain*, Wallace-Homestead, 1994; Harvey Duke, *Hall China: Price Guide Update Two*, ELO Books, 1995; ——, *Official Price Guide to Pottery and Porcelain*, 8th ed., House of Collectibles, 1995; C. L. Miller, *Jewel Tea Grocery Products with Values*, Schiffer Publishing, 1996; ——, *Jewel Tea: Sales and Housewares Collectibles*, Schiffer Publishing, 1995; Jim and Lynn Salko, *Halls Autumn Leaf China and Jewel Tea Collectible*, published by authors (143 Topeg Dr., Severna Park, MD 21146); Margaret and Kenn Whitmyer, *Collector's Ency-*clopedia of Hall China, 2nd ed., Collector Books, 1994, 1997 values update.

Periodicals: *The Daze*, P.O. Box 57, Otisville, MI 48463; *Hall China Encore*, 317 N. Pleasant St., Oberlin, OH 44074.

Collectors' Clubs: Hall Collector's Club, P.O. Box 360488, Cleveland, OH 44136; National Autumn Leaf Collectors Club, Route 16, Box 275, Tulsa, OK 74131.

Additional Listings: See *Warman's Americana & Collectibles* for more examples.

Patterns
Autumn Leaf
    Berry Bowl, small 6.50
    Cream Soup 15.00
    Custard Cup 10.00
    Plate, 8" d 15.00
    Platter, 9" l 20.00
    Teapot, long spout 45.00
    Vegetable, oval. 25.00
Blue Blossom
    Bean Pot, New England type 225.00
    Casserole 95.00
    Cookie Jar, five band 240.00
    Jug, loop handle. 195.00
    Syrup, cov, five band 165.00
Blue Bouquet
    Creamer and Sugar 40.00
    Teapot, Aladdin 135.00
Chinese Red
    Batter Bowl. 125.00
    Bean Pot, New England type 85.00
    Custard. 12.00
    Donut Jar 70.00
    Jug, loop handle. 100.00
    Teapot, Streamline. 125.00
Crocus
    Leftover, cov, set of 3 . . . . 300.00
    Pretzel Jar 195.00

Teapot, Philadelphia, pink, gold trim, Gold Label Line, mid 1940s, 5 cup, $40.

Teapot
    Boston 225.00
    Medallion 65.00
    New York 275.00
Game Birds
    Coffee Pot, electric perk 95.00
    Cookie Jar, cov 250.00
Orange Poppy
    Baker, fluted 25.00
    Bean Pot, New England type 110.00
    Casserole, cov, oval 40.00
    Cup and Saucer 10.00
    Plate, 9" h 12.00
    Spoon 145.00
    Teapot
        Boston 210.00
        Melody 400.00
        Streamline 35.00
Red Poppy
    Milk Jug, Daniel 60.00
    Recipe Box 52.00
    Teapot, New York 90.00
Rose Parade
    Casserole 50.00
    Jug, pert 40.00
    Salt and Pepper Shakers, pr, pert 45.00
Royal Rose
    Ball Jug 95.00
    Mixing Bowl, large 30.00
Wild Poppy
    Bean Pot, New England type 235.00
    Teapot, 4 cup
        Manhattan 220.00
        New York 295.00

Miscellaneous

Coffee Pot
    Duse Drip-O-Later 50.00
    Golden Glow, #2 . . . . 200.00
    Waverly Minuet 65.00
    Tankard, Silhouette 75.00
    Tom and Jerry Set, 12 cups, ivory, gold trim 90.00
Water Server
    Hercules, cobalt blue 125.00
    Montgomery Ward 40.00
    Phoenix 65.00

Teapots

Addison, globe, dripless, gold trim, 6 cup 95.00
Airflow, 6 cup
    Cobalt blue, gold 95.00
    Warm Yellow, gold 95.00
Aladdin, 6 cup
    Blue, oval lid 50.00
    Blue Bouquet 135.00
    Cobalt Blue, gold trim 95.00
Albany, mahogany, gold trim, 6 cup 95.00
Biggin Stock, brown, 2 cup 110.00
Birdcage, maroon, gold, 6 cup 335.00
Boston, white, gold lettering, 2 cup 35.00
Connie, celadon green, 6 cup 50.00
Coverlet, white, gold cover, 6 cup 40.00
Donut, Chinese red, 6 cup 425.00
French
    Maroon, gold trim, 6 cup 45.00
    Seaspray, gold trim, 2 cup 40.00
Illinois, maroon, gold spirals 240.00
Indiana, warm yellow, gold trim, 6 cup 350.00

Manhattan, warm yellow, 6 cup 85.00
McCormick, mahogany, gold trim 85.00
Nautilus, turquoise, gold trim 225.00
Ohio, brown, gold trim 200.00
Parade, Chinese Red, flake 160.00
Rhythm, yellow, gold trim, 6 cup 125.00
Royal Rose, French 100.00
Streamline, Chinese Red 110.00
Sundial
    Canary, gold trim 75.00
    Yellow, gold trim 95.00
T-Ball, black, gold label, 6 cup 195.00
Tip Top, yellow, 6 cup, stand missing 95.00
Windshield Gold Dot, 6 cup 95.00

HAMPSHIRE POTTERY

History: In 1871, James S. Taft founded the Hampshire Pottery Company in Keene, New Hampshire. Production began with redwares and stonewares, followed by majolica in 1879. A semi-porcelain, with the recognizable matte glazes plus the Royal Worcester glaze, was introduced in 1883.

Until World War I the factory made an extensive line of utilitarian and art wares including souvenir items. After the war the firm resumed operations but made only hotel dinnerware and tiles. The company was dissolved in 1923.

References: Susan and Al Bagdade, *Warman's American Pottery and Porcelain*, Wallace-Homestead, 1994; Ralph and Terry Kovel, *Kovels' American Art Pottery*, Crown Publishers, 1993.

Bowl, 10" d, 3" h, emb water lily pads and buds, leathery matte brown-green glaze, emb mark 400.00
Dresser Tray, 8" x 6-1/2", cream, pink florals, gold trim, "Mt. Mansfield" in gold script, sgd "Hampshire Pottery, Keene, NH" 110.00

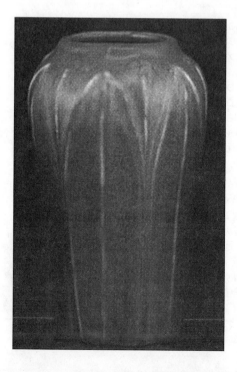

Vase, modeled full length leaves alternating with buds, fine leathery matte teal blue glaze, imp mark, 6-3/4" h, 4" w, $600. Photo courtesy of David Rago Auctions, Inc.

Lamp, 22" h, pottery base with green matte glaze, bulbous form, vertical ribs, imp mark, leaded glass shade with geometric design 1,500.00

Plate, 6-1/2" d, Royal Worcester-style, oyster white, light green rim, gold edge, imprinted with Hampshire majolica mark, age discoloration 50.00

Pitcher, 6" h, majolica, lustrous brown with amber highlights and white int., "Spring Lake" in gold script on bulbous section, unmarked 55.00

Vase
3-1/2" h, closed form, green matte glaze, emb mark
. . . . 280.00

4" h, 6" w, molded leaves on side, blue matte glaze, emb mark. 500.00

5" h, 6" w, closed form, blue and green matte glaze, imp mark
. . . . 375.00

6" h, molded corn design, green matte glaze, imp mark, repair to lip 160.00

6" h, 3-3/4" d, ovoid, raspberry semi-matte curdled glaze, unmarked. 350.00

7" h, green matte glaze, molded leaves and stems with buds, imp mark and "M" in circle 550.00

8" h, molded design at shoulder, incised whiplash design, green matte glaze, black highlights 375.00

Vessel, 5-1/4" h, matte green glaze, incised "Hampshire" and "JST & Co. Keene, NH," stress crack on base, 1/2" hairline at lip 125.00

HAND-PAINTED CHINA

History: Hand painting on china began in the Victorian era and remained popular through the 1920s. It was considered an accomplished art form for women in upper- and upper-middle-class households. It developed first in England, but spread rapidly to the Continent and America.

China factories in Europe, America, and the Orient made the blanks. Belleek, Haviland, Limoges, and Rosenthal were among the European manufacturers. American firms included A. H. Hews Co., Cambridge, Massachusetts; Willetts Mfg. Co., Trenton, New Jersey; and Knowles, Taylor and Knowles, East Liverpool, Ohio. Nippon blanks from Japan were used frequently during the early 20th century.

Marks: Many pieces were signed and dated by the artist.

Reference: Dorothy Kamm, *American Painted Porcelain,* Collector Books, 1997.

Collectors' Club: World Organization of China Painters, 2641 NW 10th St., Oklahoma City, OK 73107.

Museum: World Organization of China Painters, Oklahoma City, OK.

Notes: The quality and design of the blank is a key factor in pricing. Some blanks were very elaborate. Aesthetics is critical. Value is higher for a piece which has unique decorations and pleasing and unusual designs.

Bowl, 9" w, sq, flowers, pink and blue dec 45.00

Brooch, blue forget-me-nots, green leaves, gold border, painted gold back 65.00

Cake Plate, 10-1/2" d, open handles, pastel ground, deep purple blackberries and foliage 60.00

Candlestick, 5-3/4" h, pink roses, shaded yellow and blue ground, gold trim 35.00

Candlesticks, pr, blue ground, gold stripes, white owl, painted by "M. Hooker, 1914," 8-1/4" h, $125.

Celery Tray, 6" w, 11" l, scrolled rim, pastel ground, small rust berry dec, artist sgd, Limoges blank, dated 1899. . . . . 75.00

Cheese Dish, cov, pink floral sprays, green leaves, pale blue shaded to white ground, gold trim, applied handles . . 125.00

Compote, multicolored flowers, romantic landscape, matched pr
. . . . 215.00

Cup, yellow, 1-1/2" figural butterfly on handle. 35.00

Dresser Tray, 11" w, 16" l, center spray of multicolored flowers, gold floral wreath, white ground, pink border, sgd 90.00

Dust Pan, 8" w, mkd "Limoges". 90.00

Hatpin Holder, corset shape, cobalt blue band around center, pastel blue to white background, hp florals with dotted centers, hallmarked sterling rim, English 225.00

Pitcher, 6" h, leaves, gold handle and trim, Limoges blank
. . . . 90.00

Plaque, 12-7/8" x 18-7/8", enameled figures in courtyard, Elizabethan dress, sgd "A. Armand apres M. Gossman," giltwood frame, Limoges-style, 19th C 1,495.00

Plate, 11" d, scalloped gold border, pastel yellow single rose, green foliage, artist sgd, Haviland blank, 1901 . . . . . . 70.00

Punch Bowl, 12" d, 7-1/2" h, pedestal base, hp cherries inside and out, green ground, Serves blank 225.00

Ring Tree, scalloped edge, pink flowers, T. V. Limoges, France, bank 45.00

Toothpick Holder, 2" h, shaded pink to blue, pink flowers, gold trim 35.00

Vase, 8-1/2" h, 6-1/4" d, two handles, two inverted ruffles at mouth, pink and red roses, gold beading swirling to top, unsigned, some wear to gold 125.00

HATPINS and HATPIN HOLDERS

History: When oversized hats were in vogue, around 1850, hatpins became popular. Designers used a variety of materials to decorate the pin ends, including china, crystal, enamel, gem stones, precious metals, and shells. Decorative subjects ranged from commemorative designs to insects.

Hatpin holders, generally placed on a dresser, are porcelain containers which were designed specifically to hold these pins. The holders were produced by major manufacturers, among which were Meissen, Nippon, R. S. Germany, R. S. Prussia, and Wedgwood.

Reference: Lillian Baker, *Hatpins & Hatpin Holders: An Illustrated Value Guide*, Collector Books, 1983, 1997 value update.

Collectors' Clubs: American Hatpin Society, 20 Montecillo Drive, Rolling Hills Estates, CA 90274; International Club for Collectors of Hatpins and Hatpin Holders, 1013 Medhurst Rd., Columbus, OH 43220.

Museum: Los Angeles Art Museum, Costume Dept., Los Angeles, CA.

Hatpin

Art Deco, 1-1/2" d round painted porcelain disc, Eye of Horis motif, bezel mount, brass button type sleeve, c1920 .... 50.00
Art Nouveau style lacy design, escutcheon head, brass filigree, 9" l 90.00
Bear, ruby eyes, sterling silver, English hallmarks 200.00
Bird perched on foliate spray, diamond accents, silver and 18K yellow gold mount. 200.00
Cherub, 3/4" d, sterling silver 75.00
Cloisonné, foil back, mkd in Japanese script 90.00
Elephant, ivory, hand carved. 95.00
Fan shaped head cast in low relief, four muscular mice tormenting furry cat, dark green enamel ground, gold de, imp "Lalique," France, c1900 .... 6,500.00
Four kittens dec, brass, 9" l. 80.00
Jet Glass, 3-1/4" d, cut and faceted, wire frame, japanned shank 200.00
Mosaic, brass button sleeve type metallic mounting, gold wire trim, 8" brass pin, stamped "GS," c1875 .... 80.00

Hatpin holder, Belleek, African violets dec, Willet mark, 5" h, $90.

Owl, figural, brass 50.00
Triangular frame, rhinestones, filigree border, Austria, 12-1/4" l pin. 150.00

Hatpin Holder

Austria, hp violets dec, mkd "Royal Austria" 90.00
Bavarian, floral dec 75.00
Bisque, Art Nouveau style, lavender 190.00
Carnival Glass, Grape and Cable pattern, marigold 170.00
Nippon, shaped, raised beading 65.00
Royal Bayreuth, Goose Girl 375.00
RS Germany, hexagonal, tiny gold feet, roses dec, sgd 90.00
Silver, etched and engraved, holes for sixteen hatpins, 5-1/2" h, unmarked, c1880 .... 135.00
Torquay Pottery, hp rooster dec, "Keep Me on the Dressing Table," ftd, 5" h 120.00

HAVILAND CHINA

History: In 1842, American china importer David Haviland moved to Limoges, France, where he began manufacturing and decorating china specifically for the U.S. market. Haviland is synonymous with fine, white, translucent porcelain, although early hand-painted patterns were generally larger and darker colored on heavier whiteware blanks than were later ones.

David revolutionized French china factories by both manufacturing the whiteware blank and decorating it at the same site. In addition, Haviland and Company pioneered the use of decals in decorating china.

David's sons, Charles Edward and Theodore, split the company in 1892. In 1936, Theodore opened an American division, which still operates today. In 1941, Theodore bought out Charles Edward's heirs and recombined both companies under the original name of H. and Co. The Haviland family sold the firm in 1981.

Charles Field Haviland, cousin of Charles Edward and Theodore, worked for and then, after his marriage in 1857, ran the Casseaux Works until 1882. Items continued to carry his name as decorator until 1941.

Thousands of Haviland patterns were made, but were not consistently named until after 1926. The similarities in many of the patterns make identification difficult. Numbers assigned by Arlene Schleiger and illustrated in her books have become the identification standard.

References: Susan and Al Bagdade, *Warman's American Pottery and Porcelain*, Wallace-Homestead, 1994; Mary Frank Gaston, *Haviland Collectibles & Art Objects*, Collector Books, 1984; Arlene Schleiger, *Two Hundred Patterns of Haviland China*, Books I-V, published by author, 1950-1977; Nora Travis, *Haviland China*, Schiffer Publishing, 1997.

Collectors' Club: Haviland Collectors International Foundation, P.O. Box 802462, Santa Clarita, CA 91380; Matching Services: Charles E. & Carol M. Ulrey, *Matching Services for Haviland China*, P.O. Box 15815, San Diego, CA 92175.

Game Platter, dark green border, gold trim, partridge center, artist sgd, $265.

Bouillon Cup and Saucer, small green flowers and leaves
.... 30.00
Bowl, 5-1/2" d, Greek Key dec, black and yellow 15.00
Cake Plate, open handles, Schleiger #705............. 45.00
Coffee Service, coffeepot, creamer, and sugar, Wedding Anniversary pattern, marked "H & Co." 140.00
Compote, 9" d, 2-3/4" h, blue and pink flowers, gold scalloped edge 65.00
Cup, Autumn Leaves pattern 23.00
Dresser Set, hair receiver, cov powder jar, fitted tray with handle, yellow florals, gilt borders..................... 150.00
Gravy Boat, cov, attached underplate, oval, green and gold geometric dec.................................... 50.00
Oyster Plate, white, gold trim, mkd "Haviland/Limoges" . . 85.00
Plate
    Autumn Leaf pattern, 6" d 15.00
    Baltimore Rose pattern, 8-1/2" d, pink, Ranson blank, marked "Haviland & Co" 25.00
    Silver Anniversary pattern, 8-1/2" d 25.00
    Blank 211, blue flowers, set of 5 .... 55.00
Platter, 11-3/4" l, Arbor pattern 60.00
Ramekin and Saucer, No. 24 pattern, Ranson blank 35.00
Relish, white, scattered pink flowers, scalloped edge.... 30.00
Soup Tureen, cov, Baltimore Rose pattern........... 295.00
Saucer, Ranson pattern 12.00
Vegetable Dish, cov, 9-1/2" w, octagonal, Persia pattern
.... 200.00

HEISEY GLASS

History: The A. H. Heisey Glass Co. began producing glasswares in April 1896, in Newark, Ohio. Heisey, the firm's founder, was not a newcomer to the field, having been associated with the craft since his youth.

Many blown and molded patterns were produced in crystal, colored, milk (opalescent), and Ivorina Verde (custard) glass. Decorative techniques of cutting, etching, and silver deposit were employed. Glass figurines were introduced in 1933 and continued in production until 1957 when the factory closed. All Heisey glass is notable for its clarity.

Marks: Not all pieces have the familiar H-within-a-diamond mark.

References: Neila Bredehoft, *Collector's Encyclopedia of Heisey Glass, 1925-1938*, Collector Books, 1986, 1997 value update; Lyle Conder, *Collector's Guide to Heisey's Glassware for Your Table*, L-W Books, 1984, 1993-94 value update; Gene Florence, *Elegant Glassware of the Depression Era*, Revised 5th ed., Collector Books, 1993.

Collectors' Clubs: Bay State Heisey Collectors Club, 354 Washington St., East Walpole, MA 02032; Heisey Collectors of America, 169 W Church St., Newark, OH, 43055; National Capital Heisey Collectors, P.O. Box 23, Clinton, MD 20735.

Videotape: Heisey Glass Collectors of America, Inc., *Legacy of American Craftsmanship: The National Heisey Glass Museum*, Heisey Collectors of America, Inc., 1994.

Museum: National Heisey Glass Museum, Newark, OH.

REPRODUCTION ALERT
Some Heisey molds were sold to Imperial Glass of Bellaire, Ohio, and certain items were reissued. These pieces may be mistaken for the original Heisey. Some of the reproductions were produced in colors, which were never made by Heisey and have become collectible in their own right. Examples include: the Colt family in Crystal, Caramel Slag, Ultra Blue, and Horizon Blue; the mallard with wings up in Caramel Slag; Whirlpool (Provincial) in crystal and colors; and Waverly, a 7-inch, oval, footed compote in Caramel Slag.

Ashtray, #1435, individual, Orchid etch.............. 35.00
Bar Glass, #2052, 1-1/2 oz, Tally Ho etch 25.00
Bowl, Titania, #1519, 11" d, 3 seahorse feet......... 115.00
Candlesticks, pr
    Plantation, duo 150.00
    Queen Anne, 3" h, 3 ftd 45.00
Candy Dish, cov
    #1506 Whirlpool, ftd 70.00
    #3947, ladle, cut, blue dec, "H" mark 225.00
Celery, #407 Coarse Rib, marigold flashed, metal holder
.... 25.00
Centerpiece Vase, #1405 Ipswich, ftd, candle holder missing
.... 70.00
Champagne
    #3390 Carcassone, 6 oz, cobalt bowl, saucer 80.00
    #4069 Ridgeleigh, 5 oz, Mariemont cutting 85.00
    #4083 Stanhope, 4-1/2 oz, zircon bowl and foot, saucer
.... 50.00
    #5025 Tyrolean, 6 oz, Orchid etch, saucer 35.00
    #5057 Suez, 6 oz, Sultana stem 45.00
    #5072 Rose, 6 oz, Rose etch, saucer 30.00
Claret, #3390 Carcassone, 4 oz, cobalt bowl 85.00
Coaster, Plantation 60.00
Cocktail
    #5025 Tyrolean, 4 oz, Orchid etch 35.00
    #5072 Rose, 4 oz, Rose etch................... 25.00
Cordial, 1 oz
    #5010 Symphone, Minuet etch................. 115.00
    #5022 Graceful, Orchid etch 125.00
    #5072 Rose, Rose etch 105.00

Cruet, faceted stopper
 #305 Punty & Diamond Point, 6 oz, slightly cloudy . . . 50.00
 #1201 Fandango, 6 oz 50.00
Cup, Empress, Sahara 30.00
Cup and Saucer #1509 Queen Ann, Orchid etch 60.00
Dessert, #1637A Town and Country, 5 oz, flared, dawn. . 25.00
French Dressing Bowl, underplate, ladle, #412 Tudor,
 Moongleam green 75.00
Gardenia Bowl, orchid etch 250.00
Goblet
 #4069 Ridgeleigh, 8 oz, cutting, monogram 25.00
 #5025 Tyrolean, 10 oz, tall, Orchid etch 65.00
 #5072 Rose, 9 oz, Rose etch 40.00
Iced Tea Tumbler, Puritan, ftd 30.00
Ice Tub, #393 Narrow Flute, pat'd 30.00
Jello Dish, #1495 Fern, 12" d, zircon 50.00
Mayonnaise, cov, #1509 Queen Ann, Rosalie etch 25.00
Mayonnaise, open, #1401 Empress, Sahara, dolphin feet
 . . . . 60.00
Nappy, #1225 Sawtooth Band, 4" d, scalloped 20.00
Party Plate, #1519 Waverly, unknown floral etch, 13" d . . 20.00
Plate
 Twist, green, 7" d 10.00
 #1183 Revere, Westpoint etch, 8" d 25.00
 #1228 Swirl, Moongleam green, 10" d 45.00
 #1236 Eagle, Moongleam green, 8" d 25.00
 #1401 Empress, Alexandrite, 7" d 150.00
 #1401 Empress, Sahara, 6" sq 15.00
 #1401 Empress, Sahara, 6" round 20.00
 #1509 Orchid Etch, 10-1/2" d 175.00
Punch Bowl, Colonial 135.00
Punch Cup, Greek Key 20.00
Salt, master, #1503 Crystolite, swan 35.00
Sherbet
 #349 Colonial, 4 oz, ftd 20.00
 #349 Colonial, 4-1/2 oz, flared 35.00
 #4085 Kohinoor, 5-1/2 oz, zircon 175.00
 #5025 Tyrolean, 6 oz, low, ftd, Orchid etch 25.00
 #5072 Rose, 6 oz, Rose etch 20.00
Soda Tumbler
 #2041 Oakwood, fisherman etch 55.00
 #3381 Creole, Sahara, 8 oz, ftd 95.00
Torte Plate, Rose Etch, #1519, 14" d 95.00
Tumbler
 Old Sandwich, Sahara, 12 oz, ftd 45.00
 Plantation, 12 oz, ftd, pressed 80.00

Twist, green, ftd, 9oz 50.00
300-1/2 Flamingo, 8 oz 50.00
#1506 Whirlpool, 9 oz, limelight 40.00
#2351 Tally Ho etch, 14 oz 50.00
Vase, #4045 Wide Optic, cobalt blue, ball, 7" h 180.00
Wine, #5025 Tyrolean, 3 oz, Orchid etch 55.00

HOLLY AMBER

History: Holly Amber, originally called Golden Agate, was produced by the Indiana Tumbler and Goblet Works of the National Glass Co., Greentown, Indiana. Jacob Rosenthal created the color in 1902. Holly Amber is a gold-colored glass with a marbleized onyx color on raised parts.

Holly (No. 450), a pattern created by Frank Jackson, was designed specifically for the Golden Agate color. Between January 1903 and June of that year, when the factory was destroyed by fire, more than 35 different forms were made in this pattern.

Reference: James Measell, *Greentown Glass, The Indiana Tumbler & Goblet Co.*, Grand Rapids Public Museum, 1979, 1992-93 value update, distributed by Antique Publications.

Collectors' Club: National Greentown Glass Association, 19596 Glendale Ave., South Bend, IN 46637.

Museums: Grand Rapids Public Museum, Ruth Herrick Greentown Glass Collection, Grand Rapids, MI; Greentown Glass Museum, Greentown, IN.

Additional Listings: Greentown Glass.

Bowl, 7-1/2" l, oval 375.00
Butter, cov 1,875.00
Cake Stand 2,500.00
Compote, 8-1/2" h, 12" d, cov 2,500.00
Creamer, 4-1/2" h 650.00
Cruet, orig stopper 1,850.00
Honey, cov, Holly Amber 850.00
Mug, 4-1/2" h, ring handle 550.00
Nappy 385.00
Parfait 600.00
Salt & Pepper Shakers, pr 500.00

Sherbet, Victorian pattern, ftd, sgd, $20.

Tumbler, 3-7/8" h, $400.

Sauce	250.00
Spooner	475.00
Syrup, 5-3/4" h, SP hinged lid	2,000.00
Toothpick, 2-1/4" h	585.00
Tumbler	400.00

Tumbler, 5" h, engraved hunt scene	70.00

Vinaigrette, curled horn surmounted by pierced screen, silver cap with repousse acorns and oak leaves, faceted foil-backed quartz, trace link chain and ring, minor crack in horn ... 290.00

HORNS

History: For centuries, horns from animals have been used for various items, e.g., drinking cups, spoons, powder horns, and small dishes. Some pieces of horn have designs scratched in them. Around 1880 furniture made from the horns of Texas longhorn steers was popular in Texas and the southwestern United States.

Additional Listings: Firearm Accessories.

Beaker
5-1/8" h, harvest scene dec, sgd "Ion Stead," 19th C, minor losses and cracks to rim ... 250.00
7-1/2" h, silver mounted rims, and crest, Victorian, pr 600.00
Box, cov, 2-3/4" d, brass hinges ... 35.00
Figure, 8-1/2" h, courtesan, standing, carrying branch and basket, Chinese, 18th/19th C ... 345.00
Flask, 8-1/2" h, dark patina, silver mounds, 19th C ... 250.00
Foot Stool, hide covering, horns form legs ... 165.00
Libation Cup, 4" h, carved rhinoceros horn, lotus blossom carving, carved hardwood stand, Chinese, minor damage ... 920.00
Parlor Chair, 39-1/2" h, rect back splat, shaped seat, scrolling horns as crest rail, side supports, apron, and legs, Victorian, third quarter 19th C ... 920.00

Chair, various horns and antlers used in arms and back, wooden seat frame, carved animal legs with hoofs, old dark finish, seat reupholstered in brown moire silk, 36" h, pr, $825. Photo courtesy of Garth's Auctions, Inc.

HULL POTTERY

History: In 1905, Addis E. Hull purchased the Acme Pottery Company, Crooksville, Ohio. In 1917, the A. E. Hull Pottery Company began making art pottery, novelties, stoneware, and kitchenware, later including the famous Little Red Riding Hood line. Most items had a matte finish with shades of pink and blue or brown predominating.

After a disastrous flood and fire in 1950, J. Brandon Hull reopened the factory in 1952 as the Hull Pottery Company. New, more-modern-style pieces, mostly with glossy finish, were produced. The company currently produces wares for florists, e.g. the Regal and Floraline lines.

Marks: Hull pottery molds and patterns are easily identified. Pre-1950 vases are marked "Hull USA" or "Hull Art USA" on the bottom. Many also retain their paper labels. Post-1950 pieces are marked "Hull" in large script or "HULL" in block letters.

Each pattern has a distinctive letter or number, e.g., Wildflower has a "W" and a number; Waterlily, "L" and number; Poppy, numbers in the 600s; Orchid, in the 300s. Early stoneware pieces are marked with an "H."

References: Susan and Al Bagdade, *Warman's American Pottery and Porcelain*, Wallace-Homestead, 1994; Barbara Loveless Gick-Burke, *Collector's Guide to Hull Pottery*, Collector Books, 1993; Joan Hull, *Hull, The Heavenly Pottery*, 6th ed., published by author (1376 Nevada, Huron, SD 57350), 1999; ----, *Hull, The Heavenly Pottery Shirt Pocket Price List,* published by author, 1998; Brenda Roberts, *The Ultimate Encyclopedia of Hull Pottery*, Collector Books, 1995; Mark and Ellen Supnick, *Collecting Hull Pottery's Little Red Riding Hood, Revised Edition,* L-W Books, 1998.

Periodicals: *Hull Pottery Association,* 11023 Tunnel Hill NE, New Lexington, OH 43764; *Hull Pottery Newsletter,* 7768 Meadow Dr., Hillsboro, MO 60350.

Additional Listings: See *Warman's Americana & Collectibles* for more examples.

Advisor: Joan Hull.

Pre-1950 (matte)

Bowknot
B-1 5-1/2" pitcher ... 195.00
B-5 7-1/2" cornucopia ... 250.00
B-10 10-1/2" vase ... 500.00
B-12 10-1/2" basket ... 750.00
Calla Lily (Jack-in-the-Pulpit), 500-32 bowl ... 185.00
Dogwood (Wildrose)
508 10-1/2" window box ... 495.00
513 6-1/2" vase ... 125.00
Little Red Riding Hood
Dresser or Cracker Jar ... 800.00
Salt and pepper shakers, pr, small ... 95.00
Wall pocket planter ... 600.00

Open Rose (Camelia)
116 and 117, console and dove candleholders 600.00
126 8-1/2" hand vase 325.00
136 6-1/4" vase 140.00

Orchid
301 6" vase 145.00
302 8" vase 195.00
304 10" vase 325.00
310 9-1/2" jardiniere 450.00

Poppy
604 8" cornucopia 325.00
607 8-1/2" vase 250.00
610 13" pitcher 1,350.00

Tulip
103-33-6" suspended vase 250.00
105-33-8" vase 225.00
109-33-8" pitcher 235.00

Waterlily
L-2-5-1/2" vase 65.00
L-11-9-1/2" vase 200.00
L-14-10-1/2" vase 350.00

Wildflower
W-6-7-1/2" vase 90.00
W-12-9-1/2" vase 165.00
W-20-15" floor vase 500.00

Wild Flower No. Series
55, 10-1/4" basket 2,000.00
72, 73, and 74 tea set 1,700.00
76 8-1/2" vase 350.00

Woodland (matte)
W-11 5-1/2" flower pot/saucer 175.00
W-12 7-1/2" hanging basket 575.00
W-18 10-1/2" vase 185.00

Post 1950

Blossom Flight
T4 8-1/2" basket 125.00
T7 9-1/2" vase 95.00

Butterfly
B2 6" cornucopia 40.00
B9 9" vase 55.00

Capri
C47 8" round flower bowl 30.00
C50 9" lion head goblet 45.00

Continental
C29 12" vase 95.00
C55 12-1/2" basket 150.00

Little Red Riding Hood, cookie jars, $300 to $1,000 each. Photo courtesy of Joan Hull.

Ebb Tide
E-2 7" twin fish 95.00
E-8 ashtray with mermaid 225.00

Parchment & Pine
S-5 10-1/2" window box 85.00
S-15 8" coffeepot 150.00

Serenade
S13 13-1/2" pitcher 375.00
S17 teapot, creamer, and sugar 265.00

Sunglow
83 iron wall pocket 65.00
85 8-3/4" bird vase 50.00

Tokay/Tuscany
11 10-1/2" moon basket 125.00
12 12" vase 125.00

Tropicana
T51 13" flower dish 550.00
T57 hanging planter 750.00

HUMMEL ITEMS

History: Hummel items are the original creations of Berta Hummel, who was born in 1909 in Massing, Bavaria, Germany. At age 18, she was enrolled in the Academy of Fine Arts in Munich to further her mastery of drawing and the palette. Berta entered the Convent of Siessen and became Sister Maria Innocentia in 1934. In this Franciscan cloister, she continued drawing and painting images of her childhood friends.

In 1935, W. Goebel Co. in Rodental, Germany, began producing Sister Maria Innocentia's sketches as three-dimensional bisque figurines. The Schmid Brothers of Randolph, Massachusetts, introduced the figurines to America and became Goebel's U.S. distributor.

In 1967, Goebel began distributing Hummel items in the U.S. A controversy developed between the two companies, the Hummel family, and the convent. Lawsuits and counter-suits ensued. The German courts finally effected a compromise: the convent held legal rights to all works produced by Sister Maria Innocentia from 1934 until her death in 1946 and licensed Goebel to reproduce these works; Schmid was to deal directly with the Hummel family for permission to reproduce any pre-convent art.

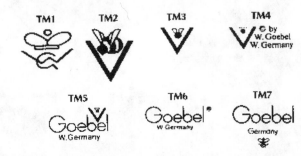

Marks: All authentic Hummel pieces bear both the signature "M. I. Hummel" and a Goebel trademark. Various trademarks were used to identify the year of production:

Crown Mark (trademark 1)	1935 through 1949
Full Bee (trademark 2)	1950-1959
Stylized Bee (trademark 3)	1957-1972
Three Line Mark (trademark 4)	1964-1972

Last Bee Mark (trademark 5)	1972-1979
Missing Bee Mark (trademark 6)	1979-1990
Current Mark or	1991 to the present
New Crown Mark (trademark 7)	

References: Ken Armke, *Hummel: An Illustrated History and Price Guide*, Wallace-Homestead, 1995; Carl F. Luckey, *Luckey's Hummel Figurines and Plates: A Collector's Identification and Value Guide*, 11th ed., Krause Publications, 1997; Robert L. Miller, *No. 1 Price Guide to M. I. Hummel: Figurines, Plates, More...*, 6th ed., ——, *Hummels 1978-1998: 20 Years of "Miller on Hummel" Columns*, Collector News, 1998; Portfolio Press, 1995; Wolfgang Schwalto, *M. I. Hummel Collector's Handbook, Part I: Rarities and Collector Pieces*, Schwalto, GMBH, 1994; Lawrence L. Wonsch, *Hummel Copycats with Values*, Wallace-Homestead, 1987, out-of-print.

Collectors' Clubs: Hummel Collector's Club, Inc., 1261 University Dr., Yardley, PA 19067; M. I. Hummel Club, Goebel Plaza, Rte 31, P.O. Box 11, Pennington, NJ 08534.

Museum: Hummel Museum, New Braunfels, TX.

Additional Listings: See *Warman's Americana & Collectibles* for more examples.

Ashtray
    Boy with bird, #166, trademark 3 . . . . 95.00
    Joyful, #33, trademark 2, 6" x 3-1/2" 165.00
Bell, 1980, third issue, 6-1/4" h, MIB 70.00
Bookends, pr, Farm Boy and Goose Girl, #60/A and B, trademark 1, 4-3/4" h 775.00
Candleholder, Silent Night, #54, trademark 2, 3-1/2" x 4-3/4"
    . . . . 265.00
Candy Box, cov, Happy Pastime, #111/69, trademark 4, 5-1/4" h
    . . . . 125.00

Harmony in Four Parts, #471, trademark 6, $1,155. Photo courtesy of Jackson's Auctioneers & Appraisers.

Figure
    Accordion Boy, #185, trademark e 150.00
    Apple Tree Boy, #142/I, trademark 3, 6" h 290.00
    Apple Tree Girl, #141/I, trademark 3, 6" h 290.00
    Auf Wiedersehn, #153/0, trademark 3 . . . . 175.00
    Bookworm, trademark 3 . . . . 490.00
    Brother, #95, trademark 3 . . . . 150.00
    Chicken Licken, trademark 4 . . . . 240.00
    Coquettes, #179, trademark 2 . . . . 280.00
    Duet, #130, trademark 2 . . . . 275.00
    Hello, #124/0, trademark 3 . . . . 175.00
    Home from Market, #198/2/0, trademark 4 . . . . 100.00
    Just Resting, #112/3/0, trademark 4 . . . . 100.00
    Little Sweeper, #171/0, artist sgd, trademark 6, 4-1/2" h
    . . . . 195.00
    Not for You, #317, trademark 3 . . . . 375.00
    Shepherd, #214F, trademark 4 . . . . 110.00
    Stormy Weather, #71/I, artist sgd, trademark 7, 6" h
    . . . . 495.00
    Trumpet Boy, #97, trademark 5, 4-5/8" h 195.00
    Wayside Harmony, #111/1, trademark 3 . . . . 195.00
Font
    Angel Shrine, #147, trademark 3, 3" x 5" 40.00
    Holy Family, #246, trademark 3, 3-1/8" x 4-1/2" 65.00
Lamp
    Culprits, #44, trademark 1, c1930, orig wiring, 9-1/4" h
    . . . . 475.00
    Happy Days, #235, trademark 2 . . . . 400.00
Nativity Set, #214/A-O, trade mark 3, color, 14 pcs 850.00
Wall Plaque
    Flitting Butterfly, #139, trademark 1, 2-1/2" x 2-1/2"
    . . . . 275.00
    Swaying Lullaby, #165, trademark 1, 4-1/2" x 5-1/4"
    . . . . 700.00

IMARI

History: Imari derives its name from a Japanese port city. Although Imari ware was manufactured in the 17th century, the pieces most commonly encountered are those made between 1770 and 1900.

Early Imari was decorated simply, quite unlike the later heavily decorated brocade pattern commonly associated with Imari. Most of the decorative patterns are an underglaze blue and overglaze "seal wax" red complimented by turquoise and yellow.

The Chinese copied Imari ware. The Japanese examples can be identified by grayer clay, thicker glaze, runny and darker blue, and deep red opaque hues.

The pattern and colors of Imari inspired many English and European potteries, such as Derby and Meissen, to adopt a similar style of decoration for their wares.

Reference: Nancy N. Schiffer, *Imari, Satsuma, and Other Japanese Export Ceramics*, Schiffer Publishing, 1997.

REPRODUCTION ALERT

Reproductions abound, and many manufacturers continue to produce pieces in the traditional style.

Bottle, 10" h, bulbous, tall elongated body, phoenix, medallions, and flowers, 19th C, pr 460.00
Bowl
    7" d, floral dec, Showa period, set of 3 . . . . 250.00

Jardiniere, diamond shape, four small monster mask feet, flowers and floral scrolls dec, underglaze blue, red, and gold enamels, Sansai, Edo period, 18th C, rubbing to enamel, 9-1/2" l, $850. Photo courtesy of Freeman\Fine Arts of Philadelphia, Inc.

8-1/4" d, fish on waves dec 125.00
9" d, shaped reserves enclosing flowers, Edo period 300.00
10" d, 3" h, scalloped edge, multicolored, green, blues, rusts, and ivory, petal-form sides. 350.00
11-3/4" d, peacock in landscape dec 175.00
Charger
  15-1/2" d, landscape dec, Meiji period, pr 550.00
  17-1/2" d, scalloped, central flower filled basket dec, border with bird, butterfly, floral, and brocade dec 475.00
  18-1/4" d, center dec of large green dragon. 500.00
  18-1/2" d, rockery, pavilion, flying peacock on wave and brocade ground dec, Meiji period, Japanese 425.00
Dish, 9-1/2" l, boat shape, wave and bird dec. 120.00
Jar, 5-1/2" h, lion mask handles, underglaze blue borders and rocks, red and gold floral dec, early 19th C, pr. 350.00
Pie Plate, 9-1/2" w, 1-1/2" h, ten sided, Chinese, 19th C 225.00
Plaque, 15" x 11", rect, foliated edges, Kutani color palette, orange, purple, green, and gold, boldly painted with seven gods of luck, gold ground, mid 19th C, pr 3,220.00
Plate
  9" d, floral dec, Showa period, set of 8. . . . . 350.00
  11-3/4" d, decorative cartouches 150.00
Platter, 16-1/2" l, gilt highlights, gilt and enamel wear, knife marks 225.00
Soup Tureen, cov, ladle, 11" h, gilt highlights, gilt and enamel wear 450.00
Tea Bowl and Saucer, 6-3/4" d, scalloped rim 150.00
Tea Cup, Showa period, set of eight. 225.00
Vase, 26-3/4" h, dragon in relief surrounding body, enamel dec with bird and floral designs in medallion shaped panels, Japanese, late 19th C 1,035.00

IMPERIAL GLASS

History: Imperial Glass Co., Bellaire, Ohio, was organized in 1901. Its primary product was pattern (pressed) glass. Soon other lines were added, including carnival glass, Nuart, Nucut, and Near Cut. In 1916, the company introduced Free-Hand, a lustered art glass line, and Imperial Jewels, an iridescent stretch glass that carried the Imperial cross trademark. In the 1930s, the company was reorganized into the Imperial Glass Corporation, and the firm is still producing a great variety of wares.

Imperial recently acquired the molds and equipment of several other glass companies—Central, Cambridge, and Heisey. Many of the retired molds of these companies are once again in use.

Marks: The Imperial reissues are marked to distinguish them from the originals.

References: Margaret and Douglas Archer, *Imperial Glass*, Collector Books, 1978, 1993 value update; Gene Florence, *Elegant Glassware of the Depression Era*, 6th ed., Collector Books, 1994; National Imperial Glass Collectors Society, *Imperial Glass Encyclopedia: Volume I, A–Cane*, Antique Publications, 1995; ——, *Imperial Glass 1966 Catalog*, reprint, 1991 price guide, Antique Publications; Mary M. Wetzel, *Candlewick: The Jewel of Imperial Price Guide II*, Revised 2nd ed., published by author, 1993, 1995 value update.

Collectors' Clubs: National Candlewick Collector's Club, 275 Milledge Terrace, Athens, GA 30606; National Imperial Glass Collectors Society, P.O. Box 534, Bellaire, OH 43906.

Videotapes: National Imperial Glass Collectors Society, *Candlewick: at Home, In Any Home, Vol. I: Imperial Beauty, Vol. II: Virginia and Mary*, RoCliff Communications, 1993; ——, *Glass of Yesteryears: The Renaissance of Slag Glass*, RoCliff Communications, 1994.

Additional Listings: See Carnival Glass; Pattern Glass; and *Warman's Americana & Collectibles* for more examples.

Art Glass

Bowl, 9" d, Jewel Ware, irid amber 90.00
Candlesticks, pr, 9-1/4" h, Free HandWare, orange mirror luster 275.00
Compote, 7-1/2" d, Jewel Ware, irid teal blue 75.00
Creamer, Jewel Ware, amethyst, pearl, and green luster 80.00
Rose Bowl, 6" d, Free Hand Ware, irid orange, white floral cutting 85.00
Vanity Jar, 7-5/8" h, Spun, pink, reeded 95.00
Vase
  6" h, Free Hand Ware, bulbous yellow, orange int. rim 200.00

Rose Bowl, Molly pattern, pink, short foot, four wide toes, eight scalloped top, light ribbed body, 4-1/2" h, 5-1/2" w, $25. Photo courtesy of Johanna Billings.

6-1/2" h, Mosaic, deep cobalt blue body, shaded and swirled with opal, irid orange lining 550.00
6-5/8" h, 4-1/8" d, Free Hand Ware, ovoid tapering body, short neck, flattened flaring rim, oyster white irid body, green hearts and vines dec, deep bronze int. 350.00
8" h, Jewel Ware, flared rim, irid silver, mulberry ground 180.00
8-3/4" h, Free Hand Ware, green heart and vine free hand dec, opaque white body, overall irid luster. 750.00
11-1/4" h, Free Hand Ware, tall slender ovoid body, tapering slightly to flared rim, glossy cobalt blue ext., white hearts and random vine dec, orig irid int. 600.00
11-1/2" h, Free Hand Ware, orange ground, deep blue Drag Loops over white, iridescent surface 875.00

Pressed

Animal, owl, milk glass 50.00
Basket, miniature, basketweave, marigold carnival 275.00
Bowl
    7-1/2" d, Beaded Block, green 45.00
    9" d, Roses pattern, milk glass. 25.00
Bud Vase, Candlewick, fan, floral cutting, 8-1/2" h 90.00
Candy Jar, cov, 1 lb, Cape Cod 100.00
Cigarette Holder, Candlewick, eagle. 95.00
Cocktail, Cape Cod. 12.00
Cologne Bottle, Hobnail, blue milk glass, ruffled stopper, pr 75.00
Creamer and Sugar, Beaded Block, deep blue. 95.00
Goblet, 5-1/2" h, Tradition. 35.00
Parfait, Cape Cod 12.00
Pitcher, Windmill, red slag. 60.00
Plate, Katy, blue opalescent, 8" d 65.00
Salt and Pepper Shakers, pr, Cape Cod, fern green 75.00
Sherbet, Mt. Vernon, ruby. 30.00
Toothpick, Ivory, orig label 24.00
Vase, Beaded Block, deep blue opal 95.00

INDIAN ARTIFACTS, AMERICAN

History: During the historic period, there were approximately 350 Indian tribes grouped into the following regions: Eskimo, Northeast and Woodland, Northwest Coast, Plains, and West and Southwest.

American Indian artifacts are quite popular. Currently, the market is stable following a rapid increase in prices during the 1970s.

References: Susan and Al Bagdade, *Warman's American Pottery and Porcelain*, Wallace-Homestead, 1994; C. J. Brafford and Laine Thom (comps.), *Dancing Colors: Paths of Native American Women*, Chronicle Books, 1992; Harold S. Colton, *Hopi Kachina Dolls*, revised ed., University of New Mexico Press, 1959, 1990 reprint; Gary L. Fogelman, *Identification and Price Guide for Indian Artifacts of the Northeast*, Fogelman Publishing, 1994; Lar Hothem, *Arrowheads & Projectile Points*, Collector Books, 1983, 1997 value update; —, *Indian Artifacts of the Midwest*, Book I (1992, 1996 value update), Book II (1995), Book III (1997), Collector Books; —, *Indian Axes & Related Stone Artifacts,* Collector Books, 1996; Robert M. Overstreet, *Overstreet Indian Arrowheads Identification and Price Guide*, Avon Books, 1997; Lillian Peaster, *Pueblo Pottery Families,* Schiffer Publishing, 1997; Dawn E. Reno, *Native American Collectibles*, Avon Books,

1994; Nancy N. Schiffer, *Indian Dolls,* Schiffer Publishing, 1997; Peter N. Schiffer, *Indian Jewelry on the Market,* Schiffer Publishing, 1996; John Shuman, *Warman's Native American Collectibles,* Krause Publications, 1998; Lawrence N. Tully & Steven N. Tully, *Field Guide to Flint Arrowheads & Knives of North American Indians,* Collector Books, 1997; Sarah Peabody Turnbaugh and William A. Turnbaugh, *Indian Baskets,* Schiffer Publishing, 1997.

Periodicals: *American Indian Art Magazine,* 7314 E Osborn Dr., Scottsdale, AZ 85251; *American Indian Basketry Magazine,* P.O. Box 66124, Portland, OR 97266; *Indian-Artifact Magazine,* RD #1 Box 240, Turbotville, PA 17772; *Indian Trader,* P.O. Box 1421, Gallup, NM 87305; *Whispering Wind Magazine,* 8009 Wales St., New Orleans, LA 70126.

Collectors' Club: Genuine Indian Relic Society, Int., 8117 Preston Road, Dallas, TX 75225-6324; Indian Arts & Crafts Association, Suite B, 122 Laveta NE, Suite B, Albuquerque, NM 87108.

Museums: Amerind Foundation, Inc., Dragoon, AZ; The Heard Museum, Phoenix, AZ; Colorado River Indian Tribes Museum, Parker, AZ; Favell Museum of Western Art & Indian Artifacts, Klamath Falls, OR; Field Museum of Natural History, Chicago, IL; Grand Rapids Public Museum, Grand Rapids, MI; Indian Center Museum, Wichita, KS; Institute of American Indian Arts Museum, Sante Fe, NM; Maryhill Museum of Art, Goldendale, WA; Museum of Classical Antiquities & Primitive Arts, Medford, NJ; Museum of the American Indian, Heye Foundation, New York, NY; US Dept. of the Interior Museum, Washington, DC; Wheelwright Museum of the American Indian, Sante Fe, NM.

Note: American Indian artifacts listed below are prehistoric or historic objects made on the North American continent.

Bag
11-3/4" l, Plateau, beaded asymmetrical flora pattern, mauve ground, backed with yarn adorned corn husk bag fragment, c1910 . . . . 175.00
18" l, Nez Perce, Plateau, cornhusk, dyed husk, repeated diamonds and stepped geometric motifs, blue, orange, pink, and yellow, slight fading. 980.00

22" l, 16" w, Nez Perce, Plateau, cornhusk, dyed husk and yarn geometric motifs, one side in purple and green repeating parallelogram motif, ...1,610.00

Bandoleer, 40" l, Ojibwa, Great Lakes, c1880, beaded cloth, backed in cotton and wool trade cloth, shoulder strap with beaded bilateral geometric and flora design, heart and rhombodial devices, pumpkin, greasy yellow, navy, and bottle green beads, white field, bag sides bound with olive worsted tape with pumpkin, white, and yellow-amber beadwork, central panel of bilateral design of beads similar to strap, loom beaded tabs of repeated heart and rhomboidal devices, red and olive wool yard tassels, c1880. . . . . .3,780.00

Basket

2-1/2" h, 4" d, Pima/Papago, four stylized figures on sides 250.00

3-1/4" h, 14" d, Pima, shallow, geometric pattern dec 225.00

3-1/2" h, 7-1/8" d, Alaskan Eskimo, lidded, diamond design in light and dark fiber, missing stitches, rim splits 200.00

8" h, 10" w, Pima, stepped geometric pattern dec, damage to bottom 100.00

8" h, 10-1/2" w, Pima/Papago, sides dec with geometric pattern. 100.00

11" h, Apache, Southwest, burden-style, twined, two rows of tin cone danglers, inverted cone at base, early 20th C 350.00

13-1/4" d, 26" h, Taconic, oblong cylindrical form, two wooden fixed handles, hinged cov, 19th C, cover detached, minor breaks 250.00

Bird Effigy Jar, 5" h, pottery, Casa Grandes, Southwest, cream, red, and brown slip painted geometric devices, 12th/13th C, loss and cracks. 300.00

Blanket Strip, 58" l, 3-1/2" w, Lakota, beaded buffalo hide, repeated cross-roundel device separated by barred designs, white heart red, apple green, dark blue, and faceted metallic beds, white field, c1880, minor bead loss 2,100.00

Bracelet

1/2" w, Navajo, silver and turquoise, sq stone, stamped design, applied silver beading, c1920 . . . . 400.00

3/4" w, Navajo, silver and turquoise, round and elliptical turquoise stones, stamped and twisted silver, c1930. . 575.00

3-1/2" h, Navajo, silver, 2 pcs of turquoise, berry and leaf silver work, soldered repair on back 140.00

Bottle, basketry, 10-1/2" h, Nootka, Northwest, twined, finely woven, decorative bands, sea birds, and boats, early 20th C 320.00

Bowl, basketry

11" d, Washoe, Southwest, finely coiled, unusually patterned geometric devices, c1800 . . . . .1,955.00

14" d, Pima, Southwest, coiled, abstract rosette pattern with geometric devices 980.00

15" l, Apache, Southwest, oval, shallow, positive/negative stepped devices, four sets of paired dogs, c1920 . . . . .1,150.00

17-3/4" d, Yokuts, CA, finely woven, two rows of hourglass devices, pair of small bear paw like motifs, c1800 . . . . .1,265.00

Bowl, pottery

3" h, Santa Clara Pueblo, Southwest, sgd "Joy Cain" in slip, deeply carved geometric motifs 15.00

3-3/4" h, Hopi, Southwest, sgd "Adelle Nampeyo," highly stylized bear paw motif, some abrasion at lip 345.00

4-3/4" d, Zuni, Southwest, red, cream, and brown slip designs, geometric neck band with deer, heart lines, and floral motif, c1920, minor surface wear. 350.00

5" d, Southwest, black and red geometric devices, cream ground, applied snake at rim, mid 20th C 115.00

5" h, Acoma Pueblo, Southwest, body painted in geometric and foliate motif, labeled in pencil "Acoma $1.00" at shoulder, indented base, chipped, surface discoloration, pitting 230.00

5-1/4" d, Hopi, Southwest, sgd "Nellie Nampeyo" at base, creamy orange ground, brown slip flora design. . . . 150.00

Canteen, pottery, 4-1/2" d, Hopi, Southwest, red and black painted Kachina head design, creamy orange ground. . . . 690.00

Cradle Board

27" l, 9" w, carved wood head with painted eyes, wrapped in green cloth, deerskin wrapping with white bead dec 200.00

33" l, Paiute, Great Basin, wicker frame and damaged sun shade, covered in buckskin hide, applied and loomed beadwork, beaded cotton cloth pillow fastened to wicker structure, double rows of fringed danglers with shells and large multicolored beads, back with elongated fringe, top front with loomed strips and two applied beaded celestial motifs, c1900 . . . . 460.00

44" l, Central Plains, beaded buffalo hide calico lined cradle, edge roll beaded in bottle green and devices to white field, form beaded in stepped geometric devices, crossed, forked linear devices, hourglasses and arrows, pumpkin, light and dark blue, white heart red, greasy yellow, white ground, stained yellow hide ties, side trim of barley corn beads and skeleton key suspensions, profusely tacked wood slats, c1880 . . . . .59,700.00

Cradle Cover, 13-1/2" l, Plains, beaded and quilled, native tanned hide, roll beaded edge, white, apple green, and greasy yellow beads, continuous-lopped lined faded red and cream quillwork on sides, yellow quilled "elk dreamer" motif top, c1880, damage, loss, tears to hide and quillwork, some old repairs. 690.00

Cribbage Board, 20" l, Eskimo, carved ivory, incised and carved animal motifs, seals, whales, caribou, fox, fish, and sea birds, repaired and unrepaired cracks 460.00

Dance Kilt, 30" h, 41" w, Santa Domingo Pueblo, painted single cloth panel, pair of classic facing Avanyo (plumed serpents) in black, tin cone rattles, red band at bottom, aged patina, fold lines, soiling, few missing cones 440.00

Doll

Arapaho, Southern Plains, 12" h, beaded hide, cloth form, white fringed leggings and dress, white, wine, red, powder blue, and green dec, braided horsehair coiffure, beaded facial features, c1890 . . . . .1,265.00

Arapaho, Southern Plains, attributed to, 14" h, beaded hide, cloth torso, hide legs, clothes, and head, yoked dress with beaded white heart, red, white, powder blue, and green beads, face beaded and heavily painted, horsehair coiffure 2,070.00

Iroquois, 13" h, cornhusk, male and female, well clothed in stroud cloth and cotton, edge beaded satin trim, late 19th C, pr 635.00

Mohave, painted clay, late 19th C 920.00

Ute, Plains, beaded hide, cloth form, hide leggings, clothes, and head, yellow paint on leggings and yoke, multicolored beadwork, beaded and modeled facial features, plaited horse hair, late 19th C 865.00

Yuma, maternity, painted clay, cloth, beads, and horsehair, 19th C 2,875.00

Yuma, polychrome figure, face, and torso painted in linear tattoo motif, skirt, sash, hair, and band of organic matter, damage, one leg partially missing, 5-1/2" h 1,035.00

Dough Bowl

11-1/2" d, Acoma Pueblo, Southwest, black and orange stepped geometric devices, cream ground, int. with band of elliptical devices, deeply patinated, c1920, repaired cracks at lip 575.00

19-1/2" d, Santo Domingo Pueblo, Southwest, band of dec geometric devices, drill hole at base, paint loss, major surface abrasion 865.00

Drum

16" d, 3-1/2" d, hand held, painted rawhide head, reinforced wood frame, flat side painted yellow, green dot center, sgd in several different places, two old sinew repairs, green painted edges, rawhide lacing and hand hold 450.00

25" d, Southwest, attributed to Tarahumara, hide covered, painted brick red cross, multi-pointed star, c1940 . . 490.00

Hat

3-1/2" h, 7" d, basketry, Northern California, attributed to Hupa, decorative bands, main one triangles with bracken fern root, minor wear 310.00

6" h, 15" d, basketry, Northwest, Nootka or Tingit, cone shaped outside, inner round attached insert to hold to head, yellow, blue, red, green, and black paint dec, one side is face, other eyes and patterns, rough rim edge . . . 2,600.00

7-1/2" h, Eastern Woodlands Iroquois, four black velvet triangular panels, white, yellow, red, blue, green, and opalescent floral beading, some bead loss, wear, damage to silk lining. 660.00

Jar, basketry

5" h, Tulare, CA, finely woven, polychrome, double rattlesnake bands, some minor loss 1,265.00

9-1/2" d, Tubatulatal, CA, finely coiled, repeated cross devices in four rows at neck and shoulder, followed by two rows of rhomboidal devices with male and female figures, 19th C 3,110.00

Jar, pottery

3" h, Southwest, sgd "Fannie Nampeyo," cream, orange, and brown highly stylized geometric bear paw motif . . . 320.00

3-1/2" h, San Ildefonso Pueblo, Southwest, sgd "Maria" and "Santana" at base, highly polished gunmetal finish, decorative band of repeated geometric devices at neck, minor abrasion to finish 375.00

4-3/8" h, 5" d, Acoma Pueblo, Southwest, white polished slip with umber and red heartline deer, base sgd "Lucy M. Lewis, Acoma Pueblo, Southwest, N.M.," small scratches and flakes. 275.00

5-1/2" h, Acoma Pueblo, Southwest, sgd "Lucy M. Lewis," brown and creamy slip, linear and geometric design, minor surface wear 920.00

6-1/4" h, Santa Clara Pueblo, Southwest, sgd "Tina Garcia" at base, Blackware, highly polished surface 230.00

6-1/2" h, Santa Domingo Pueblo, Southwest, black and cream repeated geometric devices 300.00

12-1/4" h, San Ildefonso Pueblo, Southwest, sgd "Marie," highly polished gunmetal finish, repeated geometrics motifs below lip, anther decorative band below neck with Avanyu water serpent and rain cloud motifs, abrasions and small chips to mouth 1,610.00

Kachina, 10" h, Southwest, Hopi, felt kilt and tunic clad priest figure, articulated arms, 20th C 320.00

Kayak, 27" l, Eskimo, hide covered, wood frame, two person, 19th C. 635.00

Leggings, pr, 33" l, Plains Apache, natural hide, fringed outside edges, bottoms finished with short fringe and scalloped edges, c1880 . . . . 865.00

Mask

11-1/2" h, 7-1/2" w, Northwest Coast, painted and carved wood, white highlights around crescent-shaped eyes, red nose and lips, black ground 2,000.00

8-1/2" h, 14-1/2" l, 8" w, Northwest Coast, wolf, articulated form, wolfs teeth and bone teeth, abalone eyes, copper eyebrows, painted red, blue, and black, movable jaw, early 20th C 2,400.00

Moccasins, pr

7" l, Plains, attributed to Arapaho, youth, white beaded bands with medium blue fields, checkered terraced dark blue, lavender, and pink bands 330.00

10" l, Cheyenne, full spot stitch beading, concentric medallions on fronts surmounted by cross, red, dark blue, and green beads on white ground, some beads missing 615.00

10-1/2" l, Sioux, Plains, fully beaded uppers, geometric motifs, white ground, similarly beaded bifurcated tongues with tin cone danglers, sinew and thread sewn, c1900 . . 865.00

12" l, Plains, adult, buffalo hide, blue, red, green, and white beads 850.00

17" h, Arapaho, Central Plain's, woman's beaded high top, medium blue, white heart, red and translucent dark blue geometric motifs, white ground, jointed to buffalo hide Lakota leggings with brass and metallic faceted beads and other beads on white ground, exposed hide stained yellow, c1890 . . . . 2,990.00

Necklace

12-1/2" l, Pueblo, four-strand disk carved clamshells, polished shell, turquoise, and other stone nuggets, strung on organic cording, c1880. . . . . 320.00

16" l, Navajo, squash blossom, silver, 18 pcs of turquoise, support chain broken, minor dents to blossoms . . . 385.00

Olla

7-1/2" h, Zia Pueblo, Southwest, flared form, black and white, repeated geometric forms with hatching, indented base, c1920 . . . . 1,610.00

7-3/4" d, Acoma Pueblo, Southwest, geometric stepped and elliptical devices, hatching in black and light orange, white ground, base indented, c1920, small puncture 750.00

8-1/2" h, 11" d, Acoma Pueblo, Southwest, black and white geometric pattern of feathers and arrowheads 450.00

9" h, Zia Pueblo, Southwest, upper body painted in cream, black, and red, alternating road runner and avian form, floral motifs, banded arched devices, indented base, c1920, minor slip loss 1,495.00

11" h, 13" w, Acoma Pueblo, Southwest, three red, black, and white parrots, three large flowers and geometric patterns, pieced together from several parts, one 2-1/2" sq missing dec 400.00

Olla, cov, 10-1/2" h, Tesuque Pueblo, Southwest, black stylized cloud and rain motif, geometric motifs, white ground, lid with conforming dec, labeled "3780" inside, indented bottom, c1900, some burn marks 11,500.00

Paddle, 42" l, Northwest Coast, carved cedar, one side carved with eagle motif, other with stylized bear, 19th C 175.00

Pipe Bag, 21" l, western Sioux, Lakota, native tanned hide, roll beaded top with descending three row beaded edgework, lower panel with geometric devices topped with coup feather, teepee, and cross devices, faceted metallic, dark blue, white heart red, apple green, and cobalt blue beads, white ground, lowest panel of aniline-dyed quillwork with fringe, c1880 . . . . 2,415.00

Pitcher

6" h, Southwest, Roosevelt, black slip geometric motifs, white ground, repair to handle, chip at lip 230.00

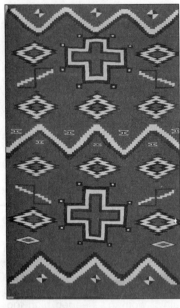

Navajo Germantown blanket, 80" x 50", $9,200. Photo courtesy of Jackson's.

8-1/2" h, Cochiti Pueblo, Southwest, black flora and foliate design, cream ground, handle, light fire spots 145.00

Plate, 5-3/4" d, San Ildefonso Pueblo, Southwest, sgd in slip "Marie-Popovi," polished gunmetal finish, abstract feather design, 20th C 1,380.00

Rug, Navajo
4' 7" x 6' 6", transitional period, Crystal, c1910, diamonds interspersed with comb like elements in dark red, dark brown, and natural, carded gray ground, piano key like edge selvage design with stepped terrace and dark brown design, edge damage, small holes, stains, some bleeding . 605.00

7' 8" x 4' 1", pictorial, center dec with opposing eagles on shields, serrated border, gold, white, and gray . . .1,100.00

Saddle Blanket, 59" x 34", Navajo, double twill weave, red, gray, and brown wool 460.00

Seed Jar, pottery
4" h, San Ildefonso Pueblo, Southwest, sgd "Blue Corn," repeated black and tan feather motif, light umber ground
. . . . 490.00

5-1/2" h, Hopi, Southwest, sgd "Dextra" with ear of corn at base, sq opening, intricate geometric design on shoulder and body 920.00

6-1/4" h, Hopi, Southwest, sgd "Clinton Polacca Nampeyo," red and brown slip, creamy ground, stylized bear paw motif, 20th C 230.00

Shirt
9" l, toddler's, attributed to Blackfeet, Plains, green felt, highly adorned with pearl, blue, and caramel straw beads, straw and cowry danglers at sleeves, thimbles at waist, c1920
. . . . .1,095.00

18" l, youth's, Plains Apache, buckskin with Southern Plains long fringe and ochre paint, poncho cut neck hemmed on both sides with sparsely spaced white beads, center front with thirteen inches of narrow fringe, body and sleeves painted dark ochre, shoulder seams surrounded by fine long fringe, edged in white, navy, and translucent wine red beads, each sleeve with red-ochre stripe with traces of dark horizontal stripes of varying width, outside sleeve edge trimmed with long fringe running about three-quarters of the length, cuff trimmed with single lane of lazy stitch white, wine red, black, and pony trader blue beadwork, c1880
. . . . .6,900.00

Shirt and Leggings, 21" l each, child's, Southern Plains, native tanned hide, trace yellow ochre, shirt fringed at yoke, shoul-

der, sleeves, and bottom, front and back yoke trimmed with narrow bands of white, translucent dark blue and pumpkin beads, front with cross device, cuffs with similar double band of beadwork, thicker hide leggings with outseam joined by leather straps, edged in double banded single row beadwork of white, light blue, and dark blue, fringe at outseams and cuff, c1900 . . . . .2,645.00

Shirt and Pants, man's, Northeast, buckskin, laced front pull-over shirt, machine sewn, scalloped edge yoke and fringe across back and back of sleeves, fancy stitched wide cuffs with red cotton edging, same red cloth lining down front, around collar and top of yoke, sleeves lined with natural cotton cloth; pants with wide waist band, four pockets of white cotton cloth, seven button fly, early trade buttons, watch pocket, outside seam with fine fringe, cuffs with eleven silvery buttons in gusset, all lined with red wool, some wear, and repairs, bullet hole 1,550.00

Slippers, 10" l, Eskimo, seal skin, hand pink felt trim, tag "Louis H. Werner Co.," early 20th C 175.00

Spoon, 16-1/2" l, Northwest Coast, carved horn, pierced and incised goat horn totem handle attached to sheep horn ladle with nail 375.00

Storyteller Bear, 9" h, Cochiti Pueblo, Southwest, sgd "Seferina Ortiz," black, cream, and orange, seated, open mouth, four listening cubs 825.00

Totem Pole, 25-1/2" h, Northwest Coast, tongue and groove, sliding parts, some labeled on back, shaman, frog, raven, and eagle motifs 460.00

Tray, basketry, 12-3/4" d, Pima, Southwest, maze motif, coiled rim and Navajo silver and turquoise button 690.00

Vessel, pottery
4-1/2" h, Hopi, Southwest, sgd "S" with feather (Sylvia Naha Humphrey), globular, painted with stylized turtles and intricate geometric devices 865.00

6-1/2" h, Zuni, Southwest, olla-form, stepped geometric devices, flora and deer motifs, red and brown slip, white ground, corrugated band at lip, three sets of applied coupling frogs, late 19th C 3,105.00

7-3/4" h, Cochiti Pueblo, Southwest, horned owl form, small outlet under each wing, red and brown abstract feather motif on cream ground 1,095.00

8" h, Cochiti Pueblo, Southwest, clay form, surprised feline, black slip, creamy ground, hairline crack at neck . . 865.00

Vest
17" l, Lakota, Central Plain's, man's, fully beaded, native tanned buckskin, abstract teepee and geometric designs, white heart, red, greasy yellow, dark blue, medium blue, and faceted metallic beads, white ground, fringed bottom, late 19th C 1,840.00

18" l, Northern Plains, beaded buckskin and cloth, asymmetrical floral motif, multicolored beads, pearl button closure, lined in brown cotton, printed tan cotton cloth backing, c1920 . . . . 750.00

Vest and Belt, Woodlands, flora beaded and fringed buckskin vest, cotton lining, 40" l commercial leather belt with orange, blue, and white beads in geometric design, c1920 . . 400.00

Wall Pocket, 23-3/4" l, Tlingit, Northwest Coast, edge beaded seal skin, two stroud cloth panels, bilateral beading of avian and flora forms 520.00

INDIAN TREE PATTERN

History: Indian Tree pattern is a popular pattern of porcelain made from the last half of the 19th century until the present. The pattern, consisting of an Oriental crooked

Grill Plate, mkd "Union, made in Czechoslovakia, Mustershutz o. 4589, 9-1/2" d, $30.

tree branch, landscape, exotic flowers, and foliage, is found predominantly in greens, pinks, blues, and oranges on a white ground. Several English potteries, including Burgess and Leigh, Coalport, and Maddock, made wares in the Indian Tree pattern.

Bowl, 7-1/4" d, handles 20.00
Compote, 8" d, ftd, marked "Coalport" 60.00
Egg Cup, marked "Coalport" 15.00
Fruit Bowl, 10" d, ftd, scalloped, marked "Copeland and Spode"
. . . . 135.00
Pitcher, marked "Coalport" 25.00
Plate
    8" d, fluted, marked "Coalport" 15.00
    9-1/2" d, marked "KPM" 17.50
Sauce Boat, matching underplate, marked "Maddock & Sons"
. . . . 135.00
Soup Plate, 9" d, marked "Maddock, England" 25.00
Sugar, cov, marked "Minton" 50.00
Teapot, cov, 2 cup size, mkd "Sadler, England" 75.00

INK BOTTLES

History: Ink was sold in glass or pottery bottles in the early 1700s in England. Retailers mixed their own formula and bottled it. The commercial production of ink did not begin in England until the late 18th century and in America until the early 19th century.

Initially, ink was supplied in often poorly manufactured pint or quart bottles from which smaller bottles could be filled. By the mid-19th century, when writing implements had been improved, emphasis was placed on making an "untippable" bottle. Shapes ranging from umbrellas to turtles were tried. Since ink bottles were usually displayed, shaped or molded bottles were popular.

The advent of the fountain pen relegated the ink bottle to the back drawer. Bottles lost their decorative design and became merely functional items.

References: Ralph & Terry Kovel, *Kovels' Bottles Price List*, 10th ed., Crown Publishers, 1996; John Odell, *Digger Odell's Official Antique Bottle and Glass Collector Magazine Price Guide Series*, vol. 4, published by author (1910 Shawhan Rd, Morrow, OH 45152), 1995.

Periodical: *Antique Bottle and Glass Collector*, P.O. Box 187, East Greenville, PA 18041.

Additional Listings: See *Warman's Americana & Collectibles* for more examples.

Bell
    2-1/2" h, aqua 10.00
    3-1/2" h, "M" emb on body, colorless 35.00
Boat
    Cobalt blue, shear top 28.00
    Moss green, sear top, two pen rests, 2-1/2" h 30.00
Cylindrical
    2" h, cobalt blue, ringed neck 28.00
    4-1/4" h, Waterman's, colorless, paper label with bottle of ink, wooden bullet shaped case, orig paper label. 10.00
    5-1/2" h, ice blue, 2 rings at bottom, 2 at top, 1-1/2" neck with pour lip 30.00
    6" h, Hyde London, cobalt blue, emb, 1-1/2" neck with pour lip
    . . . . 60.00
Figural, America, 1860-90
    2" h, house, domed offset neck for, emb architectural features of front door and 4 windows, colorless, sheared mouth, smooth base, Carter's Ink, some remaining int. ink residue, C #614 . . . . 650.00
    2" h, locomotive, aquamarine, ground mouth, smooth base, C #715 . . . . 800.00
    2-5/8" h, house, 1-1/2 story cottage form, full label on reverse "Bank of Writing Fluid, Manuf by the Senate Ink Co Philadelphia," aquamarine, tooled sq collared mouth, smooth base, small area of label slightly faded, C # 682 . . . 300.00
    3-1/8" h, rect log cabin, colorless, ground mouth, smooth base, 1/8" bruise on int. of mouth, possibly done at manufacture 375.00
Hexagonal, 9-7/8" h, America, 1900-20, "Carter," cathedral panels, colorless with pale yellow cast, machined mouth, smooth base, similar to C #820 . . . . 700.00

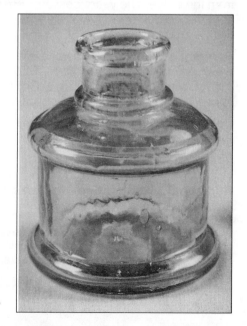

Aqua, applied lip and collar, c1880, 3" h, $12.

Inverted Concial
  2-3/8" h, Stoddard, NH, 1846-60, deep yellow-olive, sheared mouth, pontil scar, pinhead flake on mouth edge, C #15 . . . . 170.00
  2-1/2" h, America, 1840-60, "Woods/Black Ink/Portland," aquamarine, inward rolled mouth, pontil scar, C #12, unearthed with some remaining stain 170.00
Master
  6" h, cobalt blue, round, pour spout, emb "Hyde London" 85.00
  8-1/2" h, aqua, 2" neck, crude applied pour lip, some bubbles 40.00
  10-1/2" h, eighteen sides, cobalt blue 95.00
Octagonal
  Aqua, cut away base to lay on side 20.00
  Harrison's Columbian Ink, light green 60.00
  Light forest green with slight amber swirls, burst top, 3-1/2" h 18.00
Square, Temple London, emb top, one pen rest, aqua. . . 24.00
Teakettle, sapphire blue, long curved spout, orig metal cap, 2" h, C #1257 . . . . 500.00
Tent, light cornflower blue, ribbing from bottom of neck to base, single pen rest 85.00
Triangular, Derby's All British, emb, aqua, sheared lip . . . 30.00
Umbrella, America, 1840-60
  2-1/4" h, New England, 1840-60, octagonal, golden amber, sheared mouth, C #145 . . . . 160.00
  2-3/8" h, octagonal, sapphire blue, inward rolled mouth, pontil, scar, C #141 . . . . 700.00
  2-5/8" h, octagonal, lime green, labeled "Williams/Black/Empire/Ink/New York," tooled mouth, smooth base, label 95% intact, C #173. . . . . 160.00
  2-5/8" h, octagonal, sapphire blue, inward rolled mouth, pontil, scar, C #129 . . . . 950.00

INKWELLS

History: Most of the commonly found inkwells were produced in the United States or Europe between the early 1800s and the 1930s. The most popular materials were glass and pottery because these substances resisted the corrosive effects of ink.

Inkwells were a sign of the office or wealth of an individual. The common man tended to dip his ink directly from the bottle. The years between 1870 and 1920 represent the golden age of inkwells when elaborate designs were produced.

References: Veldon Badders, *Collector's Guide to Inkwells: Identification and Values*, Book I (1995), Book II, 1997, Collector Books; William E. Covill Jr., *Inkbottles and Inkwells*, William S. Sullwold Publishing, out of print.

Collectors' Clubs: St. Louis Inkwell Collectors Society, P.O. Box 29396, St. Louis, MO 63126; The Society of Inkwell Collectors, 5136 Thomas Ave. So., Minneapolis, MN 55410.

Additional Listings: See *Warman's Americana & Collectibles* for more examples.

Brass, 4-1/2" sq inkwell, 9" l, 5" w tray, Clarence Crafters, butterfly design, brass patina, green highlights, imp mark . 110.00
Bronze, 4-3/4" x 4-1/2", elephant with chicken top, Chinese, sgd, c1850 . . . . 400.00
Cast Iron, 5" h, seated rotund man, eating turkey, polychrome dec, late 19th C 350.00

Porcelain, white ground, pink edge, gold floral dec, German, $60.

Copper, 5" h, tooled and riveted, Forest Craft Guild, orig patina, imp mark. 400.00
Faience, French
  5-1/4" x 5-1/4", colorful glaze, hunters dec, small chips 150.00
  13-1/2" l, 7" w, 6-1/2" h, harpsichord shape, front panel opens up showing keyboard and two inkwells, back opens to store pens, scene of people in courtyard on top, back panel with scene of mountains and group of people sitting in a garden, 5 different scenes with groups of people around sides, border of green leaves, magenta accents, thin yellow line outlined by magenta and green, splashes of green and pink with conforming outlines, scenes pained in pink, turquoise, yellow, magenta, green, and earth tones, 6 sq cartouches on top with pink and magenta raised pinwheel design in middle with splashes of green and pink on corners, six legs, with gilt and magenta liner design, 4 decorative brass hinges, 18th C fleur-de-lis mark, minor professional restoration to legs, some gilt restored 6,800.00
Glass
  1-1/2" h, 1-1/2" d, irid gold free-blown cylinder, recessed top, concave polished base 200.00
  3-3/4" h, cut glass, inset sulfide flowers in front panel, attributed to Baccarat. 235.00
  4" d, daisy form cranberry glass body, hinged pewter lid 240.00
Newcomb Pottery, 2" h, circular, flaring base, pink blossoms, blue ground, low relief, matte glaze, imp mark, potter and decorator marks, 1929 . . . . 600.00
Pewter, honeypot with underplate, blown-out bees, Kayserzinn 400.00
Sheffield Silver, 11" w, 9" d, 5 h, Regency, mahogany, one drawer box, set of four silver ball feet, top section in silver over copper, two pen trays, silver topped inkwell, silver topped sander, central ring holder, inlay to drawer, small silver drawer knob 600.00
Silver, round hinged lid, front hinged compartment with gold wash int. for stamps, Birmingham, England, 20th C . 260.00
Staffordshire, 4-5/8" h, salmon and gray enameled, gilt trim, stag and doe dec, pr 275.00

IRONS

History: Ironing devices have been used for many centuries, with the earliest references dating from 1100. Irons from the medieval, Renaissance, and early industrial eras can be found in Europe but are rare. Fine engraved brass irons and hand-wrought irons predominated prior to

1850. After 1850 the iron underwent a series of rapid evolutionary changes.

Between 1850 and 1910, irons were heated in four ways: 1) a hot metal slug was inserted into the body, 2) a burning solid, e.g., coal or charcoal, was placed in the body, 3) a liquid or gas, e.g., alcohol, gasoline, or natural gas, was fed from an external tank and burned in the body, or 4) conduction heat, usually drawing heat from a stove top.

Electric irons are just beginning to find favor among iron collectors.

References: Dave Irons, *Irons by Irons*, published by author (223 Covered Bridge Rd., Northampton, PA 18067), 1994; ——, *More Irons by Irons*, published by author 1996; ——, *Pressing Iron Patents*, published by author, 1994.

Periodical: *Iron Talk*, P.O. Box 68, Waelder, TX 78959.

Collectors' Clubs: Club of the Friends of Ancient Smoothing Irons, P.O. Box 215, Carlsbad, CA 92008; Midwest Sad Iron Collectors Club, 24 Nob Hill Dr., St. Louis, MO 63138.

Museums: Henry Ford Museum, Dearborn, MI; Shelburne Museum, Shelburne, VT; Sturbridge Village, Sturbridge, MA.

Additional Listings: See *Warman's Americana & Collectibles* for more examples.

Advisors: David and Sue Irons.

Charcoal

Acme Carbon Iron, 1910	110.00
All brass, oversize Indian, sole plate extends over 1"	100.00
Chinese, brass pan, carved handle	125.00
European, turned chimney, brass heat shield	150.00
Ne Plus Ultra 1902, double chimney	200.00

Box, lift gate, wood handle, $120.

Electric

Eureka, cordless, shoe is outlet to heat	130.00
K & M Flat Work Ironer, round iron	200.00
Petipoint, Art Deco style	250.00
Proctor Never Lift, stand in base	90.00

Flat

Colebrookdale Crown, all cast	15.00
Dover Sad Iron, 2 piece	40.00
Hood's, soapstone base, 3 sizes	190.00
Le Gaulois #5, thin base, French	85.00
Slant handle, 2 piece	180.00

Fulter

Am. Machine, roller type	80.00
English, fine flutes, coffee mill base	300.00
Johnson's, cross roll, brass plates	285.00
Star, machine fluter, good paint	250.00
"The Best," rocker type	85.00

Goffering

All wrought, tripod base	300.00
Double barrel, on tripod base	400.00
Kenrigg, "S" post, round base	85.00

Iron Heater

Laundry Stove, holds 6 irons, Union	400.00
Pyramid Stove Top, holds 3 irons	150.00
Tray, round, sad iron heater	125.00

Liquid Fuel

Coleman 609A, black	110.00
European, ox tongue, gas jet heated	100.00
Imperial Gas Iron, natural gas	130.00
Peerless, tank under handle	180.00
Skelgas, natural gas	140.00
Tilley, cream color, English	170.00

Mangle Board

Geometric carved decorations, circles, and stars, Danish	300.00

Slug

Bless-Drake, top lifts off	250.00
English, box, lift-up gate	110.00
NR Streeter, top lifts off	180.00
Ox tongue, all brass, rainbow handle	220.00

Small

Asbestos Sad, 3-1/2"	40.00
English, box, all brass, 3-1/4"	150.00
European, charcoal, 5"	150.00
Geneva, 2-1/2"	120.00
Star #12, Stevens, 4"	125.00
Tribump, all cast, 2-3/8"	40.00
Wire handle, 2-3/4"	25.00

Special Purpose

Billiard Table, English	160.00
Egg, hand held, wood handle	75.00
Flower, 2 pc, brass, used to imprint design	110.00
Hat, two groove, wood handle	110.00
Polisher, Cooks, rounded edges	110.00
Sleeve, Ober	70.00

IRONWARE

History: Iron, a metallic element that occurs abundantly in combined forms, has been known for centuries. Items made from iron range from the utilitarian to the decorative. Early hand-forged ironwares are of considerable interest to Americana collectors.

References: *Collectors Guide to Wagner Ware and Other Companies,* L-W Book Sales, 1994; Douglas Congdon-Martin, *Figurative Cast Iron,* Schiffer Publishing, 1994; *Griswold Cast Iron,* L-W Book Sales, 1997; Jon B. Haussler, *Griswold Muffin Pans,* Schiffer Publishing, 1997; Henrie Martinie, *Art Deco Ornamental Ironwork,* Dover Publications, 1996; Kathryn McNerney, *Antique Iron Identification and Values,* Collector Books, 1984, 1998 value update; J. L. Mott Iron Works, *Mott's Illustrated Catalog of Victorian Plumbing Fixtures for Bathrooms and Kitchens* (reprint of 1888 catalog), Dover Publications, 1987; George C. Neumann, *Early American Antique Country Furnishings,* L-W Book Sales, 1984, 1993 reprint; David G. Smith and Charles Wafford, *Book of Griswold & Wagner,* Schiffer Publishing, 1995; Diane Stoneback, *Kitchen Collectibles,* Wallace-Homestead, 1994.

Periodicals: *Cast Iron Cookware News,* 28 Angela Ave., San Anselmo, CA 94960; *Kettles 'n Cookware,* Drawer B, Perrysburg, NY 14129.

REPRODUCTION ALERT

Use the following checklist to determine if a metal object is a period piece or modern reproduction. This checklist applies to all cast-metal items, from mechanical banks to trivets.

Period cast-iron pieces feature well-defined details, carefully fitted pieces, and carefully finished and smooth castings. Reproductions, especially those produced by making a new mold from a period piece, often lack detail in the casting (lines not well defined, surface details blurred) and parts have gaps at the seams and a rough surface. Reproductions from period pieces tend to be slightly smaller in size than the period piece from which they were copied.

Period paint mellows, i.e., softens in tone. Colors look flat. Beware of any cast-iron object whose paint is bright and fresh. Painted period pieces should show wear. Make certain the wear is in places it is supposed to be.

Period cast-iron pieces develop a surface patina that prevents rust. When rust is encountered on a period piece, it generally has a greasy feel and is dark in color. The rust on artificially aged reproductions is flaky and orange.

Collectors' Club: Griswold & Cast Iron Cookware Association, P.O. Drawer B, Perrysburg, NY 14129-0301.

Additional Listings: Banks; Boot Jacks; Doorstops; Fireplace Equipment; Food Molds; Irons; Kitchen Collectibles; Lamps; Tools.

Andirons, pr, wrought iron
15" h, goose neck, triple-split holder, England or America, 18th C 720.00
26" h, 14" w, 23" d, Arts & Crafts style, hammered, curled and twisted stem, three circular brass disks at top, incised floral design, orig patina 750.00
Bill Clip, 2" x 2-3/4", cast, figural Indian Chief, headdress and earrings, facing left, old brass color, hole for hanging 90.00
Bird House, 13' h, 12" x 10" base, cast iron, two story sq house, bow windows and doorway, large back open door, red paint with gold trim, cupola on top, Victorian, one corner of roof gone 1,750.00
Bookends, pr, 6" h, cast, Indian with full headdress, painted dec, late 19th C 125.00
Bottle Opener, cast
3-1/4" l, steel worker, worn polychrome dec. 140.00
5-1/8" l, lion, gold dec 75.00
5-1/2" l, parrot on perch, polychrome dec 65.00
Candleholder, 21-1/2" h, 12" w, wrought iron, double adjustable, table top, center shaft with turned stopping knob, tripod base, penny feet, candleholder adjusts on metal springs, horizontal bar holds two candleholders with drip pans, two decorative hooks on side of metal supports. 2,750.00
Candlestand, 36" h, primitive, wrought iron, pricket, tripod base, pitted with rust 420.00
Candlesticks, pr, 54-1/2" h, tripod base, adjustable sockets with push-ups, wrought iron. .1,430.00
Coffin Stand, 24-1/4" h, 49-3/4" w, 13" d, wrought iron, America, 19th C. 150.00
Cookie Board, 3-1/4" x 5-1/4", cat, rect, bird on leafy branch surrounded by dots, sawtooth oval frame 160.00
Dough Scraper, 4-1/4" w, hand wrought, snake head, bent handle. 150.00
Holder, 2-1/4" h, wrought iron, snake-form, clasping ball joint caliper form clamp, coiled body forms base, America, 19th C 2,530.00
Kettle Shelf, 11-1/4" x 17", cast, reticulated top, straight narrow lets 75.00
Mailbox, cast, Griswold No. 106 . . . . 90.00
Paper Clip, cast, wall-type, figural, collie. 160.00
Pipe Tongs, wrought iron
15-3/4" l, pierced tobacco tamp, 18th C 1,000.00
16-1/2" l, England or America, 18th C, very minor losses 635.00
Plaque, 26-1/2" h, 21-1/2" w, cast iron, medallion of George Washington, contemporary wood frame. 575.00
Roaster
12" l, wrought iron, pierced pan, hinged lid, wooden handle 360.00

Christmas Tree Holder, painted green, holly dec, 4" h, 7" sq base, $60.

27-1/2" h, wrought iron, standing, ball finial above double and single pronged meat holders, sliding circular frame, tripod base, penny feet, England, late 18th C 500.00

Rush Light, 11-1/2" h, candle socket counter weight, twisted detail, turned wooden base with age cracks, wrought iron
. . . . 385.00

Shooting Gallery Figure, 4-1/2" h, cast, rooster, black finish
. . . . 35.00

Stand, 53-3/4" w, 22-1/2" h, wrought iron, English or America, late 18th/early 19th C 490.00

Stove, 51" h, cast iron and enamel, cast neoclassical style dec, painted putti, birds, and foliage, urn form finial, F. Kuppersbusch & Sonne 1,400.00

Trivet, 14-1/2" h, wrought, scrolled and pierced heart dec
. . . . 160.00

Trough, 26" l, 11" w, 4-7/8" h, cast iron, painted blue, corrosion, 19th C 300.00

Umbrella Stand, 29" h, cast, cupid holding snake, Victorian, late 19th C 900.00

Urn, 32" h, cast, classical-style, painted black, two handles, figures on sides, waisted socle on sq plinth base, early 20th C
. . . . 2,070.00

Wall Sconce, wrought iron, America, late 18th/early 19th C, corrosion
   19-1/2" l, cutout pinwheel design 425.00
   26" h, trammel bracket 450.00

Windmill Weight, cast, horse, Dempster, repainted 300.00

IVORY

History: Ivory, a yellowish white organic material, comes from the teeth or tusks of animals and lends itself to carving. Many cultures have used it for centuries to make artistic and utilitarian items.

A cross section of elephant ivory will have a reticulated crisscross pattern. Hippopotamus teeth, walrus tusks, whale teeth, narwhal tusks, and boar tusks also are forms of ivory. Vegetable ivory, bone, stag horn, and plastic are ivory substitutes, which often confuse collectors. For information on how to identify real ivory, see Bernard Rosett's "Is It Genuine Ivory" in Sandra Andacht's *Oriental Antiques & Art: An Identification and Value Guide* (Wallace-Homestead, 1987).

References: Edgard O. Espinoza and Mary-Jacque Mann, *Identification for Ivory and Ivory Substitutes*, 2nd ed., World Wildlife Fund, 1992; Gloria and Robert Mascarelli, *Oriental Antiques*, Wallace-Homestead, out of print.

Periodical: *Netsuke & Ivory Carving Newsletter*, 3203 Adams Way, Ambler, PA 19002.

Collectors' Club: International Ivory Society, 11109 Nicholas Dr., Wheaton, MD 20902.

Note: Dealers and collectors should be familiar with The Endangered Species Act of 1973, amended in 1978, which limits the importation and sale of antique ivory and tortoiseshell items.

Box, 9-1/4" l, reticulated, figural and foliate dec, Continental
. . . . 1,750.00

Bust
   7-1/2" h, General Sherman, Continental 525.00
   10-1/2" h, carved head and headdress, some seams and cracks poorly glued 370.00

Figure, Madonna and Child, Gothic-style, 21" h, $5,170. Photo courtesy of Jackson's Auctioneers & Appraisers.

Chess Set, carved ivory and wood, playing board, fitted box, Japanese 300.00

Chess Set Figures, carved ivory pieces, Chinese Export, early 19th C 4,320.00

Cup, 5-1/2" h, relief carved dec of retriever, Continental
. . . . 500.00

Cylinder, 7" h, pierce carved scenes, pagodas, trees, animals, people, Oriental carved 440.00

Figure
   3-7/8" h, peasant boy, standing on pedestal, wearing torn shirt, floppy hat, holding rifle, Continental 360.00
   4-3/8" h, Madonna and Child, Madonna's crown accented with faux jewels, Continental 440.00
   4-1/2" h, Pu Tai, draped with rosary bead necklace, Chinese, late 19th C 260.00
   6" h, Death, Oriental carved 550.00
   6" h, woman with flower, polychrome dec, Japanese . 150.00
   6-1/4" h, woman with revolving face, holding sac, riding dragon, Japanese 150.00
   6-3/4" l, elephant, Indian carved, glued to wooden base
   . . . . 220.00
   7-1/2" h, musicians, one playing cello, other playing drum, mounted to wood base, Continental 450.00
   8" l, physician's figure, woman, Oriental carved, wooden base 525.00
   8-3/4" h, woman with fan and peach, fine line engraving, reddish-brown highlights, Japanese 260.00
   9" h, Meirin holding fan and flower, Chinese 250.00
   9" h, woman with flowers, bright colored polychrome, Oriental carved, attached wooden base 220.00
   10-1/4" l, woman with flower, colored beads set on costume, Oriental carved, wooden bench, glued head rest and floor
   . . . . 275.00
   11-1/4" h, woman with fan and cage on chains, polychrome detail, Oriental carved, attached wooden base 330.00

14-1/2" h, Mu LAN, woman warrior, sword in hand, bow over her shoulder, dressed in armor, tinted with ink, 19th C, fitted rosewood stand, mounted as lamp, ivory finial 750.00

18-1/4" l, two elephants and two big cats, Indian carved, glued to wooden base 425.00

30" l, dragon, fully articulated, Japanese, Meiji period, minor losses. 2,185.00

Letter Opener, 10-3/4" l, relief carved lion lying on shield, Continental 400.00

Miniature, vase and stand, 2-3/4" h, pomegranate shape, relief carving of gardens, pavilions, and mountains, sgd, base carved with flowers, Japanese 460.00

Necessaries, 4" l, paint dec, fitted, tools, French, 1870
. . . . 230.00

Okimono

Bishamonten and Hoitei, sd "Gyokusan," 19th C . . .1,850.00

Man and boy dancing, sgd, 19th C. 980.00

Pendant and Necklace, 2" l pendant carved with Ho Ho Er Hsien, tow boys with branch of beaches, necklace of cord string with horn and bone beads, Japanese, Meiji period 435.00

Puzzle Ball, 5" d, ext. carved with intertwined dragons surrounding multiple geometrically pierced int. spheres, Chinese, 19th C. 850.00

Ruler, 6" l, folding brass fittings. 40.00

Standish, 7-1/4" l, ivory and tortoiseshell Boullework, Continental, late 19th C, minor losses 690.00

Snuff Bottle, 3" h, flattened round shape, tall neck, foot rim, carved on both sides with masks, brocade carving on sides and neck, polychrome dec, two-character seal from signature to base, Japanese 375.00

Tankard, 9-3/8" h, silver fittings, detailed relief carving, scenes of Dionysian revelry, mermaid handle, cherub finial, age cracks in ivory, silver base loose, old repair to hinge
. . . . .5,300.00

Vase, cov, entirely carved, 19th C

9-1/2" h, people in garden scenes, lion mask handles with jump rings, lids carved with foo dogs, pr 2,300.00

10-3/4" h, women, pavilions, and gardens, elephant mask handles with jump rings, one finial of a woman and child, other with man and small boy, pr 2,530.00

11" h, dozens of musicians, various musical instruments, palace scene, carved Buddhas on lids, lion mask jump ring handles, pr 2,450.00

20" h, Buddist and Taoist figures in landscape setting, iron mask handles with jump rings, lid surmounted by figure of an immortal with demon, small child and peacock, Chinese, mid 19th C, inlaid stand, mounted without drilling to lamp base. 6,050.00

JADE

History: Jade is the generic name for two distinct minerals: nephrite and jadeite. Nephrite, an amphibole mineral from Central Asia that was used in pre-18th-century pieces, has a waxy surface and hues that range from white to an almost-black green. Jadeite, a pyroxene mineral found in Burma and used from 1700 to the present, has a glassy appearance and comes in various shades of white, green, yellow-brown, and violet.

Jade cannot be carved because of its hardness. Shapes are achieved by sawing and grinding with wet abrasives such as quartz, crushed garnets, and carborundum.

Prior to 1800, few items were signed or dated. Stylistic considerations are used to date pieces. The Ch'ien Lung period (1736-1795) is considered the golden age of jade.

Periodical: *Bulletin of the Friends of Jade*, 5004 Ensign St., San Diego, CA 92117.

Museum: Avery Brundage Collection, de Young Museum, San Francisco, CA.

Belt Buckle

Horse form, gray color stone, blue, black, and tan inclusions, reverse with two bosses for suspension, 3/4" x 2-3/4"
. . . . .3,565.00

Three-part type, celadon colored stone, tan veins, relief carved lotus and two foo dog heads, 19th C 230.00

Bottle, Nephrite, even celadon colored, rounded four-side oblong form, flat sq foot, finely carved bamboo and lotuses
. . . . .2,300.00

Boulder, carved, 8" x 6", mountain landscape, three figures, nephrite stone with celadon color, brown, black, and gray markings. 1,495.00

Bracelet

Lavender and tomato red, even tone stone, bright red markings, fitted embroidered box, 3-1/2" d, pr 7,200.00

Uniform pale green stone, brilliant apple green inclusions
. . . . 920.00

Brush Washer, 3-1/8" h, peach on gnarled branch form, slender leaves encompassing sides, gray with dark brown, calcified to opaque buff base, Ming Dynasty 2,400.00

Buddha, 1-3/4" h, apple green stone, Pu Tai seated with rosary around his neck, 19th C 115.00

Chrysanthemum Bowl, carved in form of flower, Mughal-style, 19th C

4" d, highly translucent celadon color stone, white inclusions
. . . . 290.00

4-3/4" d, 1-1/4" h, gray stone, white clouds and mossy inclusions, raised flower shaped foot, Mughal-style, 19th C
. . . . 460.00

Clasp, 3" l, dragon, carved lotus button, 19th C 90.00

Ewer, cov, 9-3/4" h, mottled gray stone, baluster body, six vertical lobes, barbed rim encircled with key fret border, faceted spout and handle carved with clouds and surmounted by chliong, handle with tab, sage figure sleep amidst rocks and pine on conforming cov, Ming Dynasty 3,500.00

Figure

Horse, green stone, brilliant apple green marking, darker inclusions, Chinese, 19th C, 2-1/2" l. 230.00

Kylin, yellow jade with cinnabar, giving red and orange hue, carved openwork motif of birds and exotic animals, Chinese
. . . . .7,770.00

Pair of crabs on lotus pod, tied with silk ribbon, pure white stone, slight greenish blue tone,3" l 325.00

Pendant

2-1/2" l, 2" w, gray stone, bright amber brown skin, carved bats and peaches, 19th C 260.00

3-1/2" l, green spinach stone, form of lock composed of chih lung dragons and phoenix around a central medallion, four character seal, script inscription on reverse, mounted in enameled gilt silver box, 19th C. 1,035.00

Pendant and Necklace, 2" l bright olive green pendant, carved with bird and pair of cucumbers, necklace of cord stung with six 1/2" d jade beads, two 1-1/2" l ornately carved peach pits
. . . . 230.00

Snuff Bottle, natural form pebble, off-white with yellow and brown skin, carved dragon, stem-shaped green Peking glass top 300.00

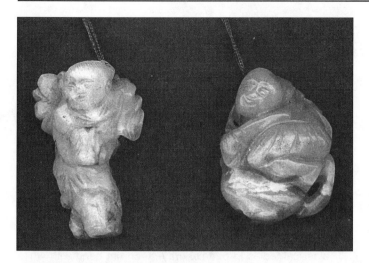

Pendants, type used in burial tombs, each $125.

Tray, 5" x 4", highly translucent stone, rect, carved allover with chrysanthemum petals radiating from central medallion, Mughai-style, 19th C 2,185.00

Water Cup, 5" l, highly translucent celadon tone stone, brown veins, carved blossoming peach branch and fruit, ftd with wood stand 460.00

Wine Ewer, 6" x 3-1/2", burnt opaque green-gray stone with black veining, animal-form handle and spout, body and lid in flowering lotus form 230.00

JAPANESE CERAMICS

History: Like the Chinese, the Japanese spent centuries developing their ceramic arts. Each region established its own forms, designs, and glazes. Individual artists added their unique touches.

Japanese ceramics began to be exported to the West in the mid-19th century. Their beauty quickly made them favorites of the patrician class.

Fine Japanese ceramics continued to be made into the 20th century, and modern artists enjoy equal fame with older counterparts.

References: Christopher Dresser, *Traditional Arts and Crafts of Japan*, Dover Publications, 1994; Gloria and Robert Mascarelli, *Warman's Oriental Antiques*, Wallace-Homestead, 1992; Nancy N. Schiffer, *Imari, Satsuma, and Other Japanese Export Ceramics,* Schiffer Publishing, 1997.

Periodical: *Orientalia Journal*, P.O. Box 94, Little Neck, NY 11363.

Collectors' Club: China Student's Club, 59 Standish Rd., Wellesley, MA 02181.

Museums: Art Institute of Chicago, Chicago, IL; Asian Art Museum of San Francisco, San Francisco, CA; George Walter Vincent Smith Art Museum, Springfield, MA; Morikami Museum & Japanese Gardens, Delray Beach, FL; Pacific Asia Museum, Pasadena, CA.

Bowl, 12-1/2" d, ext. dec with three underglaze opine boughs., int. roughened for grinding 200.00

Charger, 12-1/2" d, blue and white, mountainous riverscape dec, scalloped, Meiji period, pr. 200.00

Jar, cov, Koransha Fukagawa, underglaze blue pair of cranes beneath flowering prunus, blossoming water flora, enameled aubergine, yellow, red, gold, white, and black, lid with shishi knop and underglaze blue and enamel small birds, red marks on base, knob reattached, c1880, 32" h, $1,290. Photo courtesy of Freeman\Fine Arts of Philadelphia, Inc.

Dish, 7" l, oval, scalloped, Kakiemon, Meiji period 250.00

Ewer, 9" h, two panels with foliage and figure dec, one panel with herons on plum branches, band of stylized flower heads on neck, loop handle, underglaze blue and white, Arita, late 19th C 1,650.00

Figure, 6" h, bird, polychrome dec, Showa period 100.00

Planter, 16" d, stenciled cobalt blue designs of landscapes in reserves, floral brocade ground 225.00

Teapot, cov, 6" w, two figures in high relief, underglaze blue and glazed color dec, Sumidagawa 260.00

Vase

7" h, bulbous, widely flaring neck, olive green glaze blushing purple, brown infusions, Meiji period 175.00

7-1/2" h, shoulder with molded floral dec, polychrome dec, Meiji period. 600.00

12" h, figural dec, Sumidagawa 120.00

15-1/2" h, covered, bird on flowering branch dec, mounted as lamp 120.00

12-1/4" h, ovoid body, molded to depict polychrome wagon wheels floating in silt sear, irregular teal border, gilt foliate dec, rim molded with gilt, brown, and black birds, Meiji period. 650.00

JASPERWARE

History: Jasperware is a hard, unglazed porcelain with a colored ground varying from the most common blues and greens to lavender, yellow, red, or black. The white designs, often classical in nature, are applied in relief. Jasperware was first produced at Wedgwood's Etruria Works in 1775. Josiah Wedgwood described it as "a fine terra-cotta of great beauty and delicacy proper for cameos."

In addition to Wedgwood, many other English potters produced jasperware. Two of the leaders were Adams and Copeland and Spode. Several Continental potters, e.g., Heubach, also produced the ware.

References: Susan and Al Bagdade, *Warman's English & Continental Pottery & Porcelain*, 3rd Edition, Krause Publications, 1998; R. K. Henrywood, *Relief-Moulded Jugs*, 1820-1900, Antique Collectors' Club.

Museums: British Museum, London, England; Memorial Hall Museum, Philadelphia, PA; Museum of Fine Arts, Boston, MA; Victoria & Albert Museum, London, England.

REPRODUCTION ALERT

Jasperware still is made today, especially by Wedgwood.

Note: This category includes jasperware pieces which were made by companies other than Wedgwood. Wedgwood jasperware is found in the Wedgwood listing.

Biscuit Jar, cov, 6" d, 6" h, bulbous, dark blue ground, white relief hunting scene, SP cover, rim, and handle, mkd "Adams, England" 150.00
Bookends, pr, 6" h, white figural colonial man with cane, woman with basket, blue ground, Germany 140.00
Bowl, 7" d, white classical figures, dark blue ground . . . 225.00
Box, cov, 5" l, oval, white relief carved cherub and nymph, blue ground, mkd "Schafer & Vater, Germany" 70.00

Cassolette, cov, 11" h, solid blue, white classical dec, pierced, recessed rim, c1785, pr 4,600.00
Cheese dish, cov, 11" d, 11-1/4" h, high domed blue cov, white relief figures of classical ladies in panels, rolled base rim with white relief flower and leaf band, acorn finial, Dudson Bros., England 575.00
Hair Receiver, 3-3/8" d, 3-1/2" h, white relief classical ladies and flowers, cupids on lid, blue ground, mkd "Germany" . . 75.00
Jardiniere, 7-1/2" h, light blue ground, white relief scene of Columbus landing, mkd "Copeland" 225.00
Jug, 4-7/8" h, 4-3/8" d, blue ground, white relief hunting scene, man on horse with dogs and stag, white relief band, Copeland, 19th C 90.00
Pin Dish, green ground, white relief figures of Indian Chief holding bow and arrow, sgd "Heubach" 70.00
Pitcher
  6-7/8" h, 4-1/8" d, cylindrical, dark green ground, white relief classical ladies in panels, gray-green rim band with white relief band, Dudson Bros., England, 19th C 125.00
  7-7/8" h, 5" d, cylindrical, dark blue ground, band of small white relief classical figures around base, band of white relief floral Swags around rim, angled white handle, Copeland, 19th C 140.00
Plaque, pierced for hanging
  Angel holding baby, cupid beside her, sage green ground, white relief figures and floral border, Germany, late 19th C 90.00
  Chief Painted Horse, Indian in full headdress, owl border, white relief figures, green ground 125.00
  Cupid kissing bust of lady, sage green ground, white relief figures and floral border, Germany, 6" d 120.00
  Fisherman in rowboat being embraced by young lady, blue ground, white relief figure and floral border, Germany, 7-7/8" 150.00
Tray, 6" x 5", oval, green ground, Indian on horseback aiming arrow at running buffalo, sgd "Heubach" 135.00
Urn, 8" h, dark blue ground, white classical hunting scene, mkd "Adams, Tunstall, England" 210.00

JEWEL BOXES

History: The evolution of jewelry was paralleled by the development of boxes in which to store it. Jewel-box design followed the fashion trends dictated by furniture styles. Many jewel boxes are lined.

Pitcher, brown ground, football motif, Copeland, mkd "JMSD & S" Rg. 180288, 1895, 5-3/8" h, $250.

German Silver, ftd, pink velvet lining, raised figures of people and animals, 4-3/4" x 3" x 3-1/2", $120.

3-1/2" l, oval, silver, repousse crown and laurel wreath with monogram, engraved sides, lid set with colored glass jewels and two miniature portraits on ivory, mkd "930" and partial European hallmarks 385.00

3-1/2" h, 4-1/4" d, light sapphire blue glass, white and cream enameled flowers on lid and sides, lacy gold leaves and vines on side, hinged 200.00

4-1/2" w, Bella Ware, Helmschmeid Manufacturing Co., Meriden, CT, pale lavender ground, violet bunches within scroll, orig brass hardware, sgd on base 250.00

5-5/8" l, 3-1/4" h, oval, gilded grass, detailed flowers and garlands, pink fabric inserts on lid, portrait on ivory of young woman, sgd "Michel," mkd "France, Ovington, NY" . . 440.00

6" d, silver, rect, green velvet lined int. compartments, engraved rooster on lid, Japanese, 20th C 290.00

6" sq, 15-1/2" h, burl veneer, inlaid fans, watch hutch with lift top jewelry compartment, revolving center section with door and watch holder window, four black painted columns surround revolving box, sq base, round black feet, urn finish 1,000.00

7" l, sterling silver, rect, repousse floral design, maroon velvet lining, Jacob & Jenkins, early 20th C, 18 troy oz . . . 1,100.00

8-1/2" x 8-1/2" x 3-1/2", ivory, rect, two doors including two drawers, two drawers below, stone appliqué and gilding, Oriental, losses to gilding 775.00

11-3/4" l, walnut, old dark alligatored finish, applied rope and bead molding, oval beveled mirror in lid, carved foliage fans, lined with old green felt, some molding missing 85.00

13-1/8" l, ebony and Pietra Dura, shaped octagon, inset with foliate and insect panels, red velvet int., Italian, cracks to case and one panel. 1,725.00

17-1/2" l, 12" d, 12" h, colonial steel mounted ebony and ivory, rect, ext. fitted with openwork mounts, int. fitted with drawers and doors, each fronted with decorative ivory plaques, Portuguese, lines, minor losses 3,335.00

20-1/2" l, 15" w, painted, bronze frame, floral feet, hinged lid panel dec with figural landscape, sides with floral sprays, Rococo Revival, France, 19th C 1,265.00

JEWELRY

History: Jewelry has been a part of every culture. It is a way of displaying wealth, power, or love of beauty. In the current antiques marketplace, it is easiest to find jewelry dating after 1830.

Jewelry items were treasured and handed down as heirlooms from generation to generation. In the United States, antique jewelry is any jewelry at least 100 years old, a definition linked to U.S. Customs law. Pieces that do not meet the antique criteria but are at least 25 years old are called "period" or "heirloom/estate" jewelry.

The names of historical periods are commonly used when describing jewelry. The following list indicates the approximate dates for each era.

Georgian	1714-1830
Victorian	1837-1901
Edwardian	1890-1920
Arts and Crafts	1890-1920
Art Nouveau	1895-1910
Art Deco	1920-1935
Retro Modern	1935-1945
Post-War Modern	1945-1965

References: Lillian Baker, *Art Nouveau & Art Deco Jewelry*, Collector Books, 1981, 1994 value update; ——, *100 Years of Collectible Jewelry, 1850-1950*, Collector Books, 1978, 1997 value update; Howard L. Bell, Jr., *Cuff Jewelry*, published by author (P.O. Box 11695, Raytown, MO 64138), 1994; C. Jeanenne Bell, *Answers to Questions about Old Jewelry*, 4th ed., Books Americana, 1996; ——, *Collector's Encyclopedia of Hairwork Jewelry: Identification and Values,* Collector Books, 1998; David Bennett and Daniela Mascetti, *Understanding Jewellery*, revised ed., Antique Collectors' Club, 1994; France Borel, *Splendor of Ethnic Jewelry*, Harry N. Abrams, 1994; Shirley Bury, *Jewellery 1789-1910*, Vols. I and II, Antique Collectors' Club, 1991; Franco Cologni and Eric Nussbaum, *Platinum By Cartier, Triumphs of the Jewelers' Art,* Harry N. Abrams, 1996; Genevieve Cummins and Neryvalle Taunton, *Chatelaines*, Antique Collector's Club, 1994.

Lydia Darbyshire and Janet Swarbrick (eds). *Jewelry, The Decorative Arts Library,* Chartwell Books, 1996; Ginny Redington Dawes and Corinne Davidov, *Victorian Jewelry*, Abbeville Press, 1991; Ulysses Grant Dietz, Janet Zapata et. al., *The Glitter & the Gold, Fashioning America's Jewelry,* The Newark Museum, 1997; Janet Drucker, *Georg Jensen, A Tradition of Splendid Silver,* Schiffer Publishing, 1997; Alastair Duncan, *Paris Salons 1895-1914,* Jewelry, 2 Vols., Antique Collectors' Club, 1994; Martin Eidelberg, (ed.), *Messengers of Modernism, American Studio Jewelry 1940-1960,* Flammarion, 1996; Lodovica Rizzoli Eleuteri, *Twentieth–Century Jewelry*, Electa, Abbeville, 1994; Joan Evans, *History of Jewellery 1100-1870,* Dover Publications, 1988; Stephen Giles, *Jewelry, Miller's Antiques Checklist,* Reed International Books Ltd., 1997; Geza von Habsburg, *Fabergé in America,* Thomas and Hudson, 1996; S. Sylvia Henzel, *Collectible Costume Jewelry, Third Edition,* Krause Publications, 1997; Susan Jonas and Marilyn Nissenor, *Cuff Links*, Harry N. Abrams, 1991; Arthur Guy Kaplan, *Official Identification and Price Guide to Antique Jewelry*, 6th ed., House of Collectibles, 1990, reprinted 1994; Elyse Zorn Karlin, *Jewelry and Metalwork in the Arts and Crafts Tradition*, Schiffer Publishing, 1993; Jack and Pet Kerins, *Collecting Antique Stickpins*, Collector Books, 1995; George Frederick Kunz, *Curious Lore of Precious Stones,* Dover Publications, 1970; ——, *Rings for the Finger*, Dover Publications, n.d.; George Frederick Kunz and Charles Hugh Stevenson, *Book of the Pearl*, Dover Publications, 1973; David Lancaster, *Art Nouveau Jewelry, Christie's Collectibles,* Bulfinch Press, Little Brown and Co., 1996.

Daniel Mascetti and Amanda Triossi, *Bulgari,* Abbeville Press, 1996; Daniel Mascetti and Amanda Triossi, *The Necklace, From Antiquity to the Present,* Harry N. Abrams, Inc., 1997; Antionette Matlins, *The Pearl Book,* GemStone Press, 1996; Patrick Mauries, *Jewelry by Chanel,* Bulfinch Press, 1993; Anna M. Miller, *Cameos Old and New,* Van Nostrand Reinhold, 1991; ——, *Illustrated Guide to Jewelry Appraising: Antique Period & Modern*, Chapman & Hall, 1990; Penny C. Morrill, *Silver Masters of Mexico,* Schiffer Publishing, 1996; Penny Chittim Morrill and Carol A. Beck, *Mexican Silver: 20th Century Handwrought Jewelry and Metalwork*, Schiffer Publishing, 1994; Gabriel Mourey et al., *Art Nouveau*

Jewellery & Fans, Dover Publications, n.d.; Clare Phillips, *Jewelry, From Antiquity to the Present,* Thames and Hudson, 1996; Michael Poynder, *Price Guide to Jewellery 3000 b.c.-1950 a.d.,* Antique Collectors' Club, 1990 reprint; Penny Proddow and Marion Fasel, *Diamonds, A Century of Spectacular Jewels,* Harry N. Abrams, 1996; Penny Proddow, Debra Healy, and Marion Fasel, *Hollywood Jewels*, Harry L. Abrams, 1992; Dorothy T. Rainwater, *American Jewelry Manufacturers*, Schiffer Publishing, 1988; Christie Romero, *Warman's Jewelry,* 2nd ed., Krause Publications, 1998; Judy Rudoe, *Cartier 1900-1939,* Harry N. Abrams, 1997; Nancy N. Schiffer, *Silver Jewelry Designs*, Schiffer Publishing, 1996; Sheryl Gross Shatz, *What's It Made Of? A Jewelry Materials Identification Guide*, 3rd ed., published by author (10931 Hunting Horn Dr., Santa Ana, CA 92705), 1991; Doris J. Snell, *Antique Jewelry with Prices, Second Edition,* Krause Publications, 1997; Ralph Turner, *Jewelry in Europe and America, New Times, New Thinking,* Thames and Hudson, 1995; Fred Ward, *Opals,* Gem Book Publishers, 1997; Janet Zapata, *Jewelry and Enamels of Louis Comfort Tiffany*, Harry N. Abrams, 1993.

Periodicals: *Auction Market Resource for Gems & Jewelry,* P.O. Box 7683, Rego Park, NY 11374; *Gems & Gemology*, Gemological Institute of America, 5355 Armada Drive, Carlsbad, CA 92008; *Jewelers' Circular Keystone/Heritage,* P.O. Box 2085, Radnor, PA 19080; *The Estate Jeweler,* Estate Jewelers Association of America, 209 Post St., Suite 718, San Francisco, CA 94108; *Professional Jeweler,* Bond Communications, 1500 Walnut St., Suite 1200, Philadelphia, PA 19102.

Collectors' Clubs: American Hatpin Society, 2101 Via Aguila, San Celemnte, CA 92672; American Society of Jewelry Historians, Box 103, 133A North Avenue, New Rochelle, NY 10804; Leaping Frog Antique Jewelry and Collectable Club, 4841 Martin Luther Blvd., Sacramento, CA 95820; National Antique Comb Collectors Club, 3748 Sunray Rd., Holiday, Fl 34691; National Cuff Link Society, P.O. Box 346, Prospect Heights, IL 60070; Society of Antique & Estate Jewelry, Ltd., 570 7th Ave., Suite 1900, New York, NY 10018.

Videotapes: C. Jeanne Bell, *Antique and Collectible Jewelry Video Series*, Vol. I: *Victorian Jewelry, Circa 1837-1901*, Vol. II: *Edwardian, Art Nouveau & Art Deco Jewelry, Circa 1887-1930's*, Antique Images, 1994; Leigh Leshner and Christie Romero, *Hidden Treasures*, Venture Entertainment (P.O. Box 55113, Sherman Oaks, CA 91413), 1992, includes updated printed price guide, 1995.

Notes: The value of a piece of old jewelry is derived from several criteria, including craftsmanship, scarcity, and the current value of precious metals and gemstones. Note that antique and period pieces should be set with stones that were cut in the manner in use at the time the piece was made. Antique jewelry is not comparable to contemporary pieces set with modern-cut stones and should not be appraised with the same standards. Nor should old-mine, old-European, or rose-cut stones be replaced with modern brilliant cuts.

The pieces listed here are antique or period and represent fine jewelry (i.e., made from gemstones and/or precious metals). The list contains no new reproduction pieces. Inexpensive and mass-produced costume jewelry is covered in Warman's Americana & Collectibles.

Bracelet

Art Deco

Flexible, platinum, diamonds

Central old European-cut diamond, approx 1.74 cts, within sq frame of calibré-cut black onyx, flanked by flexible strap, line of grad calibré-cut black onyx outlined with 178 old-European single-cut diamonds, approx 3.50 cts tw, sgd Cartier, 1/2" w x 6-7/8" l 16,100.00

Line of thirty-six old European-cut diamonds and five circ-cut diamonds, approx 4.00 cts tw, central buckle motif set with eleven Fr-cut and calibré-cut blue stones, in engr plat mount, 1/2" w x 7-1/4" 3,990.00

Pierced equal width strap pavé-set throughout with sm circ-cut diamonds, approx 9.50 cts tw, three pierced quatrefoil motifs collet-set with larger circ-cut diamond centers alternating with three pierced opposed V-shaped motifs enclosing carré-set diamonds, 1/2" w x 7" tl
. . . . .15,525.00

Link

Five open rounded rect links joined with arched double bars, set throughout with 228 old European-cut diamonds, approx 7.89 cts tw, sgd "B.S. & F." for Black, Starr & Frost, New York, 5/8" w x 7-1/8" 14,950.00

Three pairs of diamond-set open oval links alternating with narrow pierced rect plaques, pavé-set with three hundred forty-two sm circ-cut diamonds, approx 8.10 cts tw, v-spring and box clasp, fitted case, 1/2" w x 7"
. . . . .12,075.00

Art Nouveau, link, 14k yg, diamonds, rect linked plaques with undulating borders, pierced openwork curv floral/foliate motif, four plaques surmounted by a three-dimensional lizard motif with a row of sixteen old European-cut diamonds down the back, maker's mk for Riker Bros. (R over a scimitar), Newark, NJ, 5/8" w x 6-1/4" 4,887.00

Arts and Crafts, link, silver, enamel, seed pearls, blue stones, four rect plaques, each with a rounded *plique à jour* enameled stylized design of web-like netting in shades of blue, green and red, radiating from a sq-cut lt blue stone at the base, corners set with seed pearls, plaques joined at equal intervals with seven lengths of cable link silver chain, sliding hingepin closure, illegible hmk and maker's mk, probably German or Austrian, approx 1-1/2" w x 7" 2,300.00

Georgian, link, c. 1825, lg cushion-shaped clasp of floral and foliate motif in yg, rose gold, and green gold, with appl bead and wirework edges, centering a circ emerald surrounded by four lg oval amethysts alternating with four sm oval foiled rubies set in cut-down collets, on a band of three rows of circ links set alternately with sm circ emeralds and rubies, clasp 1-3/4" w x 1-3/4", 6-1/2" tl. 6,900.00

Retro Modern

Link, 18k yg, "tank track" style, lg rounded open rect links joined with sm domed links, each channel-set with a central row of calibré-cut rubies, 64 dwt, 8" x 1" 5,750.00

18k yg, central floral scroll clasp, bands of pave-set diamonds bisecting three yg scrolls, sm circ-cut diamonds surrounded by lg prong-set ruby cabs, one central flowerhead of a domed diamond-set cluster encircled by lg prong-set blue sapphires, double tubular link band, foldover box clasp, sgd "Boucheron," Fr hmk (eagle's head) for 18k gold, clasp 2-3/8" w x 1-3/8", 6-1/4" tl 8,050.00

Victorian

Bangle, hinged

9k yg, engraved throughout with allover scrolled foliate design, sgd "Birks," 27.7 dwt, 1-1/4" w x 2-1/2" dia. 321.45

14k yg, allover stippled pattern with central engraved scroll and quatrefoil motif decorated with black enamel tracery (*taille d'épargne*), safety chain, 5/8" w x 2-1/2" dia 431.25

Flexible, yg, wide honeycomb mesh band, lg oval blue enameled front clasp, lg central incised star motif set with sm rc diamonds, surrounded by single star-set rc diamonds, tubular yg frame with scroll and wirework decoration, damage to enamel, clasp 2-1/4" w x 2-7/8", band 1-3/4" w x 6-1/2" tl. 2,530.00

Link, 14k yg, textured and pierced chain links alternating with polished fancy links, clasp a hand with gemstone ring and floral motif cuff, 1/2" w x 7" tl. 1,150.00

Brooch/pin

Art Deco

Bar pin

14k yg, Egyptian Revival falcon wing and serpent motif flanking central round crystal opal (cracked), surmounted by a sm old European-cut diamond, wings enameled in shades of yellow, red and green, European hmks, 2" x 5/8" 977.50

Platinum, pierced rounded oblong plaque, one lg and two sm old European-cut diamonds in a navette-shaped center, flanked by four sm brilliant-cut diamonds, two rows of calibré-cut emeralds (one missing, one replaced), and

Brooch/pin, sterling, C. 1935, round rect plaque, chased and repoussé cornucopia motif, mkd "PEER SMED STERLING HAND CHASED," safety clasp, 2-1/2" w x 2", $750. Janet Zapata collection.

two triangular-cut diamonds forming opposed arrow motifs, and set throughout with sm brilliant-cut diamonds, 2" w x 1/2" 1,955.00

Platinum, stylized bow shape, center set with a row of 18 old European-cut diamonds flanked by rows of channel-set calibré-cut black onyx (one missing), repair, new wg pinstem, 2-1/2" x 3/4" 1,380.00

Black onyx, diamonds, platinum, emeralds, c. 1920, open rounded black onyx oval, two pierced plat foliate motifs set throughout with circ-cut diamonds with sm calibré-cut emerald centers, mounted diagonally opposed across oval, 1-1/2" w x 1" 1,495.00

"Fruit salad" basket motif, pierced platinum mount set throughout with 85 old European-cut diamonds and three baguette diamonds, four carved rubies, two carved emeralds, 1-3/4" x 1-1/4" 7,647.50

Pierced and cutout circ platinum plaque, central stylized fountain motif, set throughout with 216 old European-cut diamonds, two narrow black enamel bands at the base flanked by four sm calibré-cut emeralds, 1-3/8" dia 7,475.00

Pierced circ platinum plaque, latticework motif with open central quatrefoil, old European-cut diamond, approx .75 ct, set in sq bezel in center, and set throughout with 74 old European and single-cut diamonds, approx 7.50 cts tw, sgd "Cartier, Paris," 1-5/8" dia 19,550.00

Art Nouveau

18k yg, circ medallion of a young woman's profile in an elaborate floral and foliate scroll frame, Fr hmk (eagle's head) for 18k gold, 1-1/8" w x 1-3/8" 920.00

Polychrome enameled yg plaque, undulating outline, depicting profile of a woman looking at a flower framed by floral/foliate motifs, set with one sm old European-cut diamond, watch hook on rev, 1-1/4" x 1" 4,312.00

Six-petaled open flowerhead, enameled yg in shades of pink with central old European-cut diamond, hmkd, 1" dia
. . . . .1,437.00

Arts and Crafts

18k yg pierced circ plaque with cutout C-scrolls encircling central circ-cut peridot, triangular segments of green plique à jour enamel around outside edge, sgd "Tiffany & Co.," 1-1/4" dia 8,912.00

Silver, three lg lobed leaves within oval scrolled wire and beaded frame set with four circ-cut citrines, maker's mark for Theodor Fahrner, Germany, 1-7/8" x 1-1/2" 632.50

SS, oval frame with openwork design of appl foliate motif and scrolled wire accented with collet-set zircons, attributed to Edward Oakes, Medalist, Boston Society of Arts & Crafts, 2-1/2" w x 1-3/4". 1,380.00

Edwardian

Bar pin, platinum-topped 18k yg tapered ellipse, open foliate motif set with twenty-five old European-cut diamonds in bead and bezel settings, approx 1.00 cts tw, 3" w x 1/2" 1,083.00

Cusped scallop-edged navette-shaped pierced platinum plaque centering one lg collet-set old European-cut diamond, approx 0.85 ct, surrounded by sm old European-cut diamonds, approx 4.50 cts tw, 2-3/4" w x 1-1/8" . .3,450.00

Retro Modern

14k green and yg, bow motif, central knot set with six single-cut diamonds, .18 ct tw, maker's mk for Eckfeldt & Ackley, Newark, NJ (acorn), 3-1/2" x 1-1/2". 345.00

14k yg, a step-cut cut-corner rect amethyst, 22.9 x 18 mm, within a scrolling spray and ribbon bow motif set with two grad rows of five and four circ-cut amethysts, sgd "Trabert & Hoeffer, Mauboussin-Reflection," provenance: the estate of Lana Turner, 3" x 2-1/8". 11,500.00

Three-dimensional five-petaled flower, leaves and ribbon bow design in polished yg, center and edges set with twenty-nine sm circ-cut and old European-cut diamonds, circ-cut and calibré-cut rubies, 1-1/2" w x 2-1/2" 978.00

Yg, stylized Athena's helmet with lg circ-cut green tourmaline in center, clip and brooch findings, Am, sgd "FLATO" for Paul Flato, 2-1/2" w x 1-1/2". .5,750.00

Victorian

Bar pin

Arrow motif suspending a central foliate swag, forty-five sm rose-cut diamonds throughout, a horizontal row of four sm pearls along shaft, sm pearl at center of swag suspending a pear-shaped pearl drop, 2-3/4" w x 1-1/8" tl 570.00

Butterfly motif, the body a lg pear-shaped diamond and a button pearl, two ruby cab eyes, the wings set throughout with old European-cut diamonds in silver-topped yg, 1-1/2" w x 1-1/4" 5,463.00

Carved coral, cherub amongst flowers and leaves, mounted on yg armature, 1-1/2" x 1" 488.75

Crown motif, points set with five oval turquoise cabochons and four circ-cut diamonds, two rows of seed pearls at the base, yg mount, sgd "B.S. & F." for Black, Star & Frost, New York, 2-5/8" w x 1-5/8" 1,495.00

Floral spray motif, set throughout with 104 rose-cut diamonds, one old mine cut diamond in flower center, in silver-topped yg, 2-7/8" w x 1" 2,090.00

Four-leaf-clover motif centering one lg old mine-cut diamond, each leaf centering a bezel-set oval emerald cab surrounded by old mine-cut diamonds, a lg old mine-cut diamond flanking one side of diamond-set stem, mounted in silver-topped 18k yg, French hmks, (one emerald cracked), 1-1/2" w x 1-3/8" 5,175.00

Multi-rayed starburst motif set throughout with old mine and rose-cut diamonds mounted in silver-topped yg, 1-1/2" dia. 3,450.00

Oval polychrome mosaic depicting Roman ruins in a black onyx ground, mounted in a bead and wirework bezel within a lobed and concave/convex rect 18k yg frame, engr with blue enameled foliate scroll decoration, 1-3/4" w x 1-1/2" 920.00

Cameo

Hardstone, high relief cameo of woman's profile within a plain 18k yg frame, fitted box, 1-1/2" w x 2" . . .2,415.00

Lava, chocolate brown monochrome depicting a mythological embracing couple in high relief with well-detailed drapery and features, plain 18k yg frame, Russian hmks, 1-1/2" w x 2" 2,070.00

Shell

Profile of goddess Diana in beaded yg frame, 1-3/8" x 1" 184.00

Profile of classical woman with crescent man-in-the-moon motif below, good detail, set in 14k yg frame with ropetwist border, undulating ribbon trefoils at compass points, 1-3/4" w x 2" 718.75

Chain

Edwardian, fine curb link platinum chain interspersed at equal intervals with prong-set diamonds in open circ frames, grad in size, approx 10.00 cts tw, 36" tl 8,625.00

Retro Modern, 14k yg snake chain, foldover clasp, 24.2 dwt, 15-1/2" tl. 690.00

Victorian

14k yg, fancy double circular links terminating in a swivel hook, 21.6 dwt, 61" tl 460.00

18k yg, textured domed circ links, 54.2 dwt, 58" tl 3,105.00

Yg, loop-in-loop circ links with beaded textured surface, clasp a matte finish hand wearing a red stone jeweled ring, engr floral cuff, 3/8" w x 57-1/2" tl 7,475.00

Clips, pr

Art Deco, scrolling ribbon cascade motif, forty-seven baguette diamonds, approx 2.00 cts tw, twenty-seven lg circ diamonds, approx 7.00 cts tw, one hundred sixty sm circ-cut diamonds, approx 6.50 cts tw, set in platinum, 1-3/8" w x 1-5/8" 12,075.00

Retro Modern, pr of three-dimensional feathers, one a yg shaft and diamond-set platinum barbs, the other diamond-set platinum shaft with yg barbs, featured in a Paul Flato advertisement in Vogue Magazine, page 33, Oct. 15, 1939, provenance: from the estate of Ginger Rogers, each 1-3/4" w x 2-3/4". 43,700.00

Cuff links, pr

Art Deco, double-sided circ disks, each centering a sapphire cab surmounting a MOP disk within an engr wg-topped yg frame, yg bar connectors, mkd "585 XX". 275.00

Art Nouveau, 14k yg oval disks with chased bulldog design, 5.3 dwt, hmk for Bippart, Griscom & Osborne (torch), Newark, NJ, 1/2" w x 3/4", pr 374.00

Edwardian, platinum-topped yg, double-sided octagonal plaques with engr geometric border centering a bezel-set rect-cut blue sapphire on one side and a single-cut diamond on the other, mkd "PLAT. ON 14k," 1/2" dia 200.00

Post-war Modern, SS, double-sided ovals, the fronts depicting an engr design of Kukla on one, and Ollie on the other (puppets from the popular 1950s children's television show, "Kukla, Fran, and Ollie"), sgd "KALO" for The Kalo Shop, Chicago, IL, 5/8" w x 3/4" 316.00

Retro Modern, 14k yg, each in the shape of a threaded bolt with slotted head and a screw-on nut, attributed to Paul Flato, 5/8" dia, pr 1,150.00

Victorian, circ disks, polychrome mosaic depiction of a swan in a floral bg, blue and white geo border, 18k yg bead and wiretwist decoration, yg mount, 7/8" dia. 748.00

Dress set

Art Deco, pr of double cuff links, three vest studs, four shirt buttons, octagonal MOP top centering a sm circ-cut diamond in

an engr platinum frame on a yg base, cuff links 1/2" dia
....2,300.00
Victorian, 14k yg, dumbbell-type cuff links, each set with a lg and
sm oval gold-in-quartz cab, 5/8" x 1/2", three shirt studs, each
with a circ disk of gold-in-quartz, 1/2" dia........1,265.00

Earrings, pr

Art Deco, fan-shaped black onyx surmount suspending a line of
old European-, rose- and single-cut diamonds, terminating in
a rounded triangular black onyx plaque, platinum mount, 2" tl
x 5/8"...3,162.50
Edwardian, prong-set old European-cut diamond drops, approx
3.79 cts and 4.10 cts, suspended from knife edge bar tops,
each with two sm prong-set old European diamonds, approx
0.50 ct tw, plat mounts, yg fittings, Fr hmks, 1-1/8" tl x 1/2" w
....42,550.00
Georgian, modified *girandole* style, a chain of paired foliate motifs alternating with single old mine-cut diamonds in cut-down
collets terminating in a pear-shaped foliate frame suspending
an old European-cut diamond drop in the open center, and
three articulated drops of similar design to top chain,
eighty-eight old mine-cut and rose-cut diamonds, silver-topped yg mount, European backs, 3-1/8" tl x 5/8" w
....3,450.00

Retro Modern

14k yg, V-shape with cutout center and scrolled top centering
a stepped cylinder, screwbacks, sgd "TIFFANY & CO.," 7/8" x
7/8"...518.00
Three prong-set rect-cut aquamarines surmounting a pierced
diamond-set scroll motif, platinum and yg mount, clipbacks,
1-1/4" tl x 1" w...................................1,840.00

Victorian

Coral, *girandole* style, circ cab surmount, suspending lg center circ cab bordered with three sm circ cabs alternating with
seed pearls, suspending three pear-shaped drops topped
with seed pearls, with yg ropework swags, kidney earwires,
2-3/8" tl x 1" w.....................................747.00
Garnets, cab surmount and drop, each with an incised star
motif set with rose-cut diamonds, surmount suspending
central yg crossed keys motif with appl wirework and bead
decoration with sm circ central garnet cab, later-added
screwbacks, 1-5/8" l x 5/8" w......................1,610.00
Hardstone cameos, navette-shaped drops, each centering a
woman's profile, white on black, within a floral scrollwork yg
frame with beaded border, seed pearl accents, fishhook
earwires, 1/2" w x 1-1/2".............................863.00
Micromosaic, circ yg surmount with bead and wire decoration
surmounting a horizontal bar with appl beads at each end,

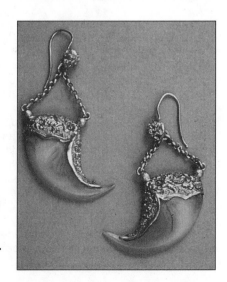

**Tiger's claw ear-
rings, C. 1880,
claw mounted on
floral motif gf
frame suspended
by two chains from
floral motif sur-
mount, shep-
herd's hook
earwires, 3/4" w x
2" tl, pr, $350.
Courtesy of E.
Foxe Harrell Jewel-
ers, Clinton, IA.**

suspending a central inverted balustered conical drop,
flanked by balustered tubular rods suspending a circ disk
centering a polychrome mosaic of a man's profile in one, a
woman's profile in the other, terminating in a round yg bead,
shepherd's hook findings, 2-1/4" tl x 3/4" w.....2,760.00

Hair Comb, Victorian, curved yg bar with appl three-dimensional filigree floral and foliate motif, sm pearl cluster and lg
prong-set pearls (some pearls missing), surmounting a
hinged iron five-toothed comb, 4-3/4" w x 4" tl.....1,150.00

Hatpin, Art Nouveau, wreath of green enameled yg leaves enclosing four freshwater pearls, ym pinstem, 1/2" w x 8" tl
....920.00

Jabot Pin, Art Deco, arrow motif, head with three collet-set old
European-cut diamonds and calibré-cut black onyx forming V
shape through diamonds, feather at opposite terminal
pierced and set with triangular calibré-cut onyx, surmounted
by a collet-set old European-cut diamond, four old European-cut diamonds approx 0.61 ct tw, set throughout with sm
rose-cut diamonds in millegrained platinum on yg, 2" w x 1/2"
....1,150.00

Lavalier, Edwardian, central shield-shaped platinum plaque set
with sm old European-cut diamonds around a lg button pearl,
suspending *négligée* two chains of navette-shaped filigree alternating with collet-set old European-cut diamonds, terminating in lg pear-shaped pearl drops, suspended from a
similar diamond-set chain of navette-shaped filigree, each
set with a sm central old European-cut diamond, alternating
with collet-set old European-cut diamonds, GIA report stating
pearls of natural origin and approx 15, 17, and 18 mm, orig
fitted box mkd "J.F. Hayward, Boston," 3" top to bottom at
center, 17" tl............................18,975.00

Locket

Victorian

Yg, Etruscan-style cartouche shape, a central horizontal row
of four seed pearls within appl bead and scrolled wirework
design, ropetwist border around oval locket compartment,
10.9 dwt, 1-1/4" w x 2-1/4" tl...................632.00
Yg, oval with central appl grape motif pearl cluster surrounded by conforming seed pearl border, opening to reveal two
photo compartments, surmounted by a cutout scroll motif
and pearl-set bail, one hundred five natural pearls total,
1-1/4" w x 2-1/2"...............................747.00

Locket and Chain, Victorian, wide rounded circ chevron-pat-
terned 18k yg links suspending a heart-shaped yg locket with
appl beads, multicolor yg floral motifs encircling a central tur-
quoise-set forget-me-not motif of two intertwined flowers
flanking an oval-cut red stone, opens to reveal a hair design
in a glazed compartment, gem-set beaded barrel clasp, locket 1-1/8" w x 1-3/4" tl, chain 38-1/2" tl...........2,300.00

Lorgnette

Art Nouveau, 14k yg, Beaux-arts style, foliate and scroll decorations on handle continuing to border of cover for lenses,
spring mechanism for releasing folded spectacles, small
dent, 1-1/4" w x 5-1/2" tl...........................748.00
Edwardian, pierced openwork platinum, geometric design, handle set with a central vertical row of sm circ-cut diamonds,
suspended from an oval link platinum chain, spring ring clasp
to chain, 1-1/4" w x 3-1/2".......................1,380.00

Necklace

Art Deco, central shield-shaped platinum plaque of open geometric design with pierced and lobed trefoils set with old
mine-cut and old European-cut diamonds, suspending a grad
fringe of sm circ collet-set diamonds, each row terminating in
an inverted pear-shaped collet-set diamond drop, diamond-set circ bail attached to two diamond-set triangular
open geometric terminals set with old European and sm
circ-cut diamonds, joined to a woven seed pearl band, Fr hmk

(dog's head) for platinum, 1-1/8" w x 3", 16-3/8" tl
....23,000.00

Art Nouveau, festoon, centering an open heart shape with central sm post-set pearl and suspending a lg pink pearl drop, flanked by two smaller open circ motifs each suspending a pearl, attached by triple swagged yg chain, double chain to pearl bead, single chain to closure, 1" w (at center), 16" tl
....1,840.00

Edwardian, dog collar, latticework of platinum chains forming open rectangles, vertically set rows of seed pearls at the intersections, 1-3/8" w x 13-1/2" tl................5,462.00

Georgian, twelve grad flowerhead links with yg bead decoration, each link centering an oval foiled pink topaz surrounded by alternating split pearls and circ turquoise cabs in sawtooth bezels, beaded borders, interlinks of split pearls with appl bead decoration, in a fitted box (two pearls missing), 7/8" w (at center), 15" tl.............................2,875.00

Retro Modern, double strand of flexible 18k yg tubes, reeded alternating with polished segments, dome-shaped front terminals with circ-cut diamond borders suspending an open pear-shaped drop, scalloped edges set with a row of circ-cut diamonds, two intertwined flexible loops of polished yg tubular segments interspersed with diamond-set rings suspended from open center, Fr hmks, sgd "Regner, Paris," 15" tl, center 1" w x 3-1/8" top to bottom....................6,325.00

Victorian

14k yg, snake motif of grad scale-like links terminating in a turquoise-colored enameled snake's head front clasp, head set with seed pearls, suspending an inverted pear-shaped drop surmounted by an enameled fleur-de-lis motif set with seed pearls (some enamel loss), 15" tl.........1,035.00

18k yg, Egyptian Revival, seven grad bezel-set carved hardstone scarabs in wiretwist frames, mounted on two trace link chains accented with appl disks, mkd "C.G." for Carlo Giuliano, 3/4" w (at center), 14-1/2" l...........4,600.00

Cameo, seven graduated oval shell cameos depicting mythological scenes, in engr 14k yg frames with scrolls surmounted by bead finials at top and bottom, alternating with swagged chains suspending inverted pear-shaped and spherical bead drops, joined by pierced scalloped-shaped bars (solder, repair and small breaks to chain), 3" w (at center), 14" tl.................................5,865.00

Fringe of lozenge shapes, sm ones bezel-set with a single lozenge-shaped turquoise cab alternating with larger ones set with a cluster of four lozenge-shaped turquoise cabs within one bezel, suspended by short and long yg rods from tubular reeded yg links alternating with sq turquoise cabs in hollow sq bezels, strung on chain, 1-3/8" x 16" tl
....4,600.00

Scottish agate, a linked series of paired octagonal variegated agate cylinders with floral engr silver caps, shield-shaped padlock clasp set with a cut-to-shape agate plaque surmounted by a pyramidal lozenge-shaped agate, 7/8" w x 18" tl, clasp 7/8" w x 1" 1,150.00

Pendant

Art Nouveau, yg, figure of a woman holding two sm circ-cut prong-set diamonds in her outstretched hands, surrounded by a diaphanous billowing robe with a scale-like pattern of *plique à jour* enamel in shades of lt pink and green, plain yg bail, 1-1/8" w x 1-3/8" tl 4,025.00

Arts and Crafts, SS and enamel, rectilinear with lobed base suspending a pear-shaped drop, hammered texture enameled in shades of blue and green, Birmingham (England) hmks, date letter for 1908, 2-1/2" tl x 1" 345.00

Edwardian, platinum-topped 18k yg, open circle set with 56 calibré-cut rubies framing knife-edge platinum wire forming grid

pattern suspending nine old European-cut diamonds in open centers, diamond-set bail, 1-3/8" tl x 1" dia 1,610.00

Georgian, openwork Maltese cross with lg central old mine-cut diamond surrounded by four open arms each centering a lg old mine-cut diamond surrounded by oval and old mine-cut diamonds bead-set in a frame of silver-topped rose gold, formerly the property of The Trustees of the late 7th Duke of Newcastle, 2-3/8" w x 2-3/4" (with bail) 51,750.00

Victorian

Egyptian Revival, depicting the head of a pharaoh with a ruby and diamond-set headdress, mounted in the center of a circ chalcedony cab within a beaded frame bordered with scrolled wirework and foliate motifs, diamond accents, cusped bail, 1-3/4" w x 2-3/8" 2,530.00

Micromosaic equilateral cross with trefoil terminals, depicting a dove in central disk, scrolled foliate and Christian motifs on arms, shades of blue, red, yellow, pink, and white tesserae, yg mount, attributed to Antonio Civilotti, 2-1/2" tl x 1-3/4"
....4,025.00

Pendant and chain

Art Deco, Egyptian Revival, yg, depicting a pharaoh's head flanked by ibis and surmounted by lotus motifs, set with 17 rose-cut diamonds and four ruby cabs, suspended from 18" chain, 1-3/8" l x 1-3/4" 1,955.00

Art Nouveau, depicting a semi-nude dancing woman, lower torso clad in a diaphanous gown, arms overhead holding a tambourine, gown of pink *plique à jour* enamel bordered with rose-cut diamonds, bg plaque in green *plique à jour* enamel, undulating yg border, heart-shaped terminal set with a ruby, suspending a pearl, suspended from two lengths of knot-like link chain attached at top sides, caught by a sm open cusped and lobed lozenge-shaped plaque with diamond-set paired wings through the center, Fr, 2" w x 2-3/4" 4,600.00

Arts and Crafts

SS, oval dyed blue agate bezel-set in the center of a lobed oval frame with pierced geo design, suspended from a paper clip chain, maker's mk for The Art Silver Shop, Chicago, IL, 18" tl, 1" w x 1-1/2"..................................595.00

SS, oval openwork Celtic knot plaque enameled in violet and blue, suspended from sm circ enameled disk, fine cable link chain, spring ring closure, hmks for Chester (England), date letter for 1909, mkd "CH" for Charles Horner, 1" w x 7/8", chain 15" tl 500.00

Edwardian, platinum-topped yg, ribbon motif of sm bead-set diamonds with central collet-set diamond, suspending a sm collet-set diamond and a lg faceted oval pink topaz in a millegrained collet, trace link chain, pendant 7/8" w x 1-1/2"
....1,840.00

Art Nouveau, yg, three-dimensional butterfly with *plique à jour* enameled wings in shades of dk and lt blue, violet, and green, partially outlined by sm rose-cut diamonds, each wing bezel-set with a blue sapphire cab, central sapphire cab in body, ruby eyes, rows of sm rose-cut diamonds on lower body, engr yg legs and antennae, a total of one hundred thirty-eight rc diamonds, 3-1/8" w x 2-1/8 ....8,050.00

Edwardian, platinum-topped yg, open scrolled stylized fleur-de-lis motif, small pearl at top and bottom, set throughout with thirty-three circ-cut diamonds, approx 1.00 ct tw, sgd "T.B.STARR" for Theodore B. Starr, New York, NY, 1-1/4" w x 1-3/8" 1,495.00

Victorian

18k yg, a bow motif top suspending a heart-shaped locket, allover turquoise-colored enamel, appl diamond-set butterfly motif surmounting bow, diamond-set flower surmounting heart, fitted box (minor enamel repair), 1-1/8" w x 1-1/2" tl
....805.00

Openwork star shape centering lg collet-set and sm prong-set old mine-cut diamonds surrounded by sm old mine-cut diamonds bead-set in platinum, pendant hoop, sgd "Tiffany & Co.," 1-3/4" w x 1-3/4".........23,000.00

Ring

Art Deco, platinum

Blue star sapphire, approx 30.00 cts, flanked by geometric stepped design of forty-two channel-set baguette diamonds, approx 1.00 ct tw, 1" w x 3/4", size 6-1/2
....3,450.00

Central circ-cut diamond, approx 1.75 cts, flanked by two tapered baguette diamonds and two trapeze-cut diamonds, approx 0.60 ct tw, maker's mk for W.J. Harber Co. Inc. (H in a circle), New York, NY, 1931-50, 5/8" w x 1/4"...9,775.00

Green jadeite cab measuring approx 16.22 x 11.20 x 6.76 mm, flanked by stepped geometric design of baguette and sm circ-cut diamonds, 3/4" w x 5/8"...........4,888.00

Lozenge-shaped plaque with central old mine-cut diamond framed by eight sm sugarloaf ruby cabs forming opposed V-shapes surmounted by two old European diamonds top and bottom, surrounded by sixteen single-cut diamonds, approx 2.00 cts tw, two triangular ruby cabs at each side, 1/2" w x 3/4"..............................2,850.00

Art Nouveau, oval-cut aquamarine flanked by green-enameled foliate motifs continuing to shoulders, a spray of collet-set sm rose-cut diamonds at top and bottom, mounted on a narrow yg shank, French hmks, maker's mk "LD," approx 3/4" w x 1"
....2,645.00

Arts and Crafts, 6.5 mm pearl center flanked by circ-cut green tourmalines, hessonite and rhodolite garnets bezel-set in the corners of a cushion-shaped openwork foliate 14k yg mount on a narrow shank, attributed to Everett Oakes, 3/4" x 3/4"
.... 978.00

Edwardian

Old mine-cut diamond, approx 1.50 cts, framed by fifty-two sm old European-cut and single-cut diamonds in bead settings, engr platinum mounting with pierced openwork set with eight sm calibré-cut emeralds in curved rows at shoulders, 3/4" w x 1/2", size 6-1/2 ....2,875.00

Platinum-topped 18k yg, cusped navette shape of nine old mine-cut diamonds, approx 5.75 cts tw, thirty sm rose-cut diamonds on shoulders (one missing), mkd "Tiffany & Co.," 3/4" w x 1" 8,625.00

Georgian, central old mine-cut diamond of approx 1.50 cts flanked by four sm old mine-cut diamonds set in silver-topped yg, two sm circ-cut emeralds and five sm circ-cut green stones set in 18k yg, mounted in cut-down collets on a split tapered shank, 3/8" w (at center), approx size 4
....2,166.00

Retro Modern, lg central emerald-cut prong-set aquamarine, approx 42.50 cts, flanked by domed shoulders of pavé-set sm circ-cut diamonds each bordered by rows of calibré-cut rubies, platinum and yg shank, 1-1/4" w x 1".....6,900.00

Victorian

Lozenge-shaped engr yg plaque set with nine old mine-cut diamonds, approx 1.30 cts tw, plain shank, 1/2" w x 3/4", approx size 5 .... 912.00

Yg band of appl scroll motif *cannetille* and beads centering a row of sm circ turquoise cabs, 1/4" w, size 6-3/4... 978.00

Scarf Pin/Stickpin

Art Deco, disk with central collet-set diamond of approx .65 ct encircled by calibré-cut rubies in a platinum mount, 14k yg pinstem, maker's mk for Allsopp and Allsopp, Newark, NJ, 3/8" dia..1,093.00

Art Nouveau

Egyptian Revival, oval bezel-set moonstone in a 18k yg frame flanked by serpent and lotus motifs, two sm old European-cut diamonds, enamel accents, sgd "T.B. STARR" for Theodore B. Starr, New York, NY, 1/2" w x 2-1/2" tl 431.00

Yg, woman's head in profile, long flowing hair with diamond and seed pearl-set headdress, enameled features, 5/8" w x 7/8", 3" tl 633.00

Edwardian, platinum-topped 14k yg, open circle centering a collet-set circ blue stone surrounded by four rc diamonds and four seed pearls, yg pinstem, maker's mk for Carter, Howe & Co., Newark, NJ, 1/2" dia 124.00

Victorian

Crescent moon and star, central carved moonstone depicting the man in the moon, surrounded by a crescent of pave-set sm old European-cut diamonds in a 14k yg mount, a diamond-set star suspended from top terminal, 1/2" w x 5/8", 2-1/2" tl 1,495.00

Micromosaic disk depicting a scarab beetle in polychrome tesserae, beaded and wiretwist 18k yg frame, Vatican hmk, 5/8" dia, 3" tl....................... 747.50

Suite

Arts and Crafts, necklace, bracelet, and earrings, SS, link necklace centering a lg shield-shaped pierced and engr plaque of cherry and foliate motif, flanked by sm oval plaques of similar design, bracelet of lg circ plaques of similar motif, earrings of three cherries with one leaf, sgd "KALO" (Chicago), necklace, 15" tl, bracelet 1-1/4" w x 7-1/2" l, earrings, 3/4" w x 1", suite
....1,093.00

Georgian, necklace, pendant and brooch/pin, necklace of eleven grad floral and scroll motif *cannetille* links set with a total of sixteen lg oval bezel-set foiled pink topaz with pearl accents, suspended from a triple strand cable link chain to v-spring and box clasp, box decorated with one lg oval pink topaz and appl *cannetille* decoration, cruciform brooch and pendant of similar design, fitted box (missing earrings), necklace 1-1/4" w (at center), 15" tl, pendant 2-1/4" dia, brooch 1-1/2" dia 2,588.00

Retro Modern, double-clip brooch, earrings, ring, pr of clips of opposed scrolling ribbon motif in polished rose gold with prong and bead-set diamond borders, rays of diamonds and calibré-cut rubies, removable pinback mechanism, matching ring and clipback earrings, one hundred twenty circ-cut and old European-cut diamonds total, brooch 3" w x 1-1/4", earrings 1/2" w x 3/4", ring 1" w x 1/2", size 6........4,600.00

Victorian

Brooch/pin and bracelet, brooch a scalloped lozenge shape centering a lg cluster of seed pearls in grape motif flanked by engr green gold grape leaves, surmounted by a yg grape leaf flanked by two sm seed pearl grape clusters, within an open yg textured frame, C-catch, extended pinstem, matching bracelet of nine links, the central link with a lg seed pearl grape cluster surrounded by four lg green gold engr leaves and two sm yg engr leaves, flanked by sm circ links with a sm cluster of seed pearls and a green gold engr leaf, continuing to grad links surmounted by engr leaves, v-spring and box clasp, brooch 2-1/2" w 2", bracelet 1-1/2" w (at center), 7-1/2" tl, fitted case....................2,875.00

Brooch/pin and earrings, brooch a carved coral head of a Bacchante with grapes and leaves suspending three carved coral amphorae decorated with flowers, grapes and leaves, matching pendent earrings, mounted in 18k yg, French hmk, brooch 1-5/8" w x 3-1/4" l, earrings, later-added clip backs, 2-3/4" l x 7/8" w......................2,070.00

Pendant/locket and earrings, pietra dura (Florentine) mosaic, floral motif oval plaque set into bead and wiretwist 14k yg frames and pendant bail, matching earrings with sm oval pietra dura plaque surmounts, larger drops, kidney earwires, pendant 1" w x 2" l, earrings, 1-3/4" tl x 3/4" 510.00

Watch Chain

Victorian

14k yg, elliptical open links with foliate motif centers alternating with sm circ links, 16.7 dwt, 1/2" w x 8-1/2" tl. . . 488.00

Shakudo, silver, yg, double strand of sm circ links with floral motif tops, appl silver and yg details, swivel hook clasp, 1/4" w x 56" tl 2,185.00

Watch Chain and Fob, Victorian, 14k yg, open rounded rect links, terminating at one end with a swivel hook, the other with a T-bar, and suspending a double-sided oval banded agate tablet in a gp brass frame, chain 16" tl 741.00

Watch Fob, Art Nouveau, yg, open shield-shaped intertwined floral and foliate motif suspending an unengr seal, short chain at opposite end terminating in a swivel hook, in a fitted leather, silk, and velvet box stamped "Spaulding & Co., Jewelers and Silversmiths, 36 Avenue de l'Opéra, Paris," 1" w x 5-1/4" tl 2,875.00

JUDAICA

History: Throughout history, Jews have expressed themselves artistically in both the religious and secular spheres. Most Jewish art objects were created as part of the concept of Hiddur Mitzva, i.e., adornment of implements used in performing rituals both in the synagogue and home.

For almost 2,000 years, since the destruction of the Jerusalem Temple in 70 A.D., Jews have lived in many lands. The widely differing environments gave traditional Jewish life and art a multifaceted character. Unlike Greek, Byzantine, or Roman art which have definite territorial and historical boundaries, Jewish art is found throughout Europe, the Middle East, North Africa, and other areas.

Ceremonial objects incorporated not only liturgical appurtenances, but also ethnographic artifacts such as amulets and ritual costumes. The style of each ceremonial object responded to the artistic and cultural milieu in which it was created. Although diverse stylistically, ceremonial objects, whether for Sabbath, holidays, or the life cycle, still possess a unity of purpose.

Reference: Penny Forstner and Lael Bower, *Collecting Religious Artifacts (Christian and Judaic)*, Books Americana, 1996.

Collectors' Club: Judaica Collectors Society, P.O. Box 854, Van Nuys, CA 91408.

Museums: B'nai B'rith Klutznick Museum, Washington, DC; H.U.C., Skirball Museum, Los Angeles, CA; Jewish Museum, New York, NY; Yeshiva University Museum, New York, NY; Judah L. Magnes Museum, Berkeley, CA; Judaic Museum, Rockville, MD; Spertus Museum of Judaica, Chicago, IL; Morton B. Weiss Museum of Judaica, Chicago, IL; National Museum of American Jewish History, Philadelphia, PA; Plotkin Judaica Museum of Greater Phoenix, Phoenix, AZ.

Notes: Judaica has been crafted in all media, though silver is the most collectible.

Almanac, small 8vo, 10 pages, "The Oxford Almanac/The Jewish Kalendar," printed 1692, "explanation of Jewish Kalendar," brown calf gilt, covers scuffed, spine ends worn 6,900.00

Amulet

3-1/4" h, silver, oval shape, applied cast dec to edges, glass inset on front and verso, Italian-style 400.00

3-1/4" h, silvered metal, oval shape, crenelated surround, reverse painted tablet depicting binding of Isaac, verso with amulet against evil eye, Italian-style 635.00

5-3/4" h, enamel dec and parcel-gilt porcelain, rect, painted star, gilt-metal mounts, painted mark on reverse, attributed to Limoges, France, 20th C 800.00

Belt Buckle, Yom Kippur

5" d, silver-gilt and jewel mounted, domed circular form, various inset stones, unmarked, Polish, 18th/19th C . . 875.00

8" l, silver, silver filigree, and gem mounted, double paisley form, repousse silver panels depicting binding of Isaac and Jonah and the whale, unmarked, Italian 6,900.00

Candlesticks, pr, 7-1/2" h, silver and silver filigree, tapering form, dished bobeche, domed circular foot, stylized dec, applied mark, Bezalel, early 20th C, dents 1,850.00

Charity Container

7" h, domed cylindrical form, slop on top, door to side, dec with Jewish subjects, Hebrew text, Damascene, 20th C 800.00

7-1/2" h, brass, cylindrical form, hasp and loop handle, Polish, late 19th/early 20th C 400.00

10-3/4" h, paint dec pine, rect box, hinged lid, slot on top, back with swan's neck cresting, painted with deer holding an oval inscribed "Torah Fund," flanked by columns, plain base, painted yellow and dark green, attributed to Philadelphia, PA, area, late 19th/early 20th C 4,600.00

Charity Collection Dish, 5-1/2" d, silver, circular bowl, applied handle, foliate engraved thumb-piece, engraved Hebrew inscription on rim, fitted with small candle socket, Continental, late 18th C 3,795.00

Children's Game, "The New and Fashionable Game of the Jew," London, J. Wallis, M. Dunnet and J. Wallis Juner, 27 May 1807, uncut broad-sheet game board, hand colored engravings, minor old repairs, matted and framed 2,760.00

Esther Scroll, silver cased, vellum scroll, unmarked

8" h, Salonic, heavy floral repousse, floral-form finial, turned winder, hand lettered ink, 18th/19th C 1,495.00

15-1/4" h, North African, repousse floral dec, crown finial, handwritten ink, vellum scroll, unmarked, late 19th/early 20th C 875.00

Etrog Container, 7-1/2" l, carved walnut, fruit fork, hinged top, realistically carved leafy base, America, late 19th C . . . 920.00

Hanukah Lamp

5" h, bronze, arched and scrolled backplate above row of eight oil fonts, Italian Renaissance, late 16th/early 17th C, replaced servant lamp 1,725.00

8-3/4" h, brass, cartouche-shaped backplate stamped with lions, crowns, and foliage, central etched menorah design, rect base with eight candleholders, cast feet, Polish, 19th C, lacking servant light 1,265.00

9-3/4" h, silver, paneled baluster stem, eight thin arms holding candle sockets, removable snuffer with star of David finial, servant light, domed paneled foot, obscured maker's mark, Birmingham, England, 1929, bent 325.00

10-1/2" h, silver, paneled tapering stem, eight thin arms holding candle sockets, servant light to side, Star of David finial, sq domed foot, maker "A. S.," Birmingham, England, 1963 . . . . 575.00

11-3/4" h, brass, arched backplate pierced with exotic beasts, tree branches, central heart device, over row of eight oil fonts, rect drip-pan, servant light above right, Dutch, 18th C 2,070.00

Kiddush Cup

4-1/4" h, silver, finely chased floral motifs, engraved Hebrew text, illegible maker's mark, Continental, 19th C . . . 920.00

5-1/2" h, silver-gilt, paneled form, cast foliate dec, Hebrew text, molded octagonal foot, German-style, 20th C 9,200.00

Laver, 4-3/4" h, copper, applied loop handle, engraved Hebrew text, Continental, 18th/19th C. 175.00

Magazine, *Der Hammer Worker's Monthly,* New York, 1926, cov illus designed by Gropper, Lozowick, Yiddish text, orig pictorial wrappers, no. 1 to 10 bound into contemporary cloth volume, folio 290.00

Manuscript

Bible, Pentateuch, Hebrew, 1740-42, [The Pentateuch] with the order of the Haftarot that belong to each of the books. According to the rites of Germanic Jews with vocalization and accents," written on vellum, drawings, Simha ben Yona Segal, Scribe, Mannheim, five volumes, orig leather binding, marbleized end papers, fitted leather case 145,500.00

Seder Tefillah M'Kol Hashanah, (The Order of Prayers for the whole year), according to rites of German, Polish, Lithuania, and Russian Jews, Hebrew and Yiddish, Raphael de Gedalia Halevi Luria, Scribe, Vilna, 1827, enameled and jeweled binding, later name plate for Helene Ratner, fitted leather slip-case. 5,630.00

Map, 21-1/2" x 25-1/4", Holy Land, etching, later hand coloring, Generalle Kaart van het Beloofde Land, Jan Berend Elwe, Amsterdam, 1792. . . . . 650.00

Marriage Bowl, 5-1/4" d, silver, silver-gilt, and niello, inscribed with text relating to seven benedictions of marriage, Buchara, Persia, dated 1683, modern fitted box 12,650.00

Marriage Contract (Ketubah), 13" x 18-1/4", illuminated parchment, Livorno, dated 1817, rect, flowers, foliage, and text, framed 865.00

Mezuzah

3-3/4" h, cast bronze, architectural form, lion, inscribed in Hebrew "Shadai" and "Yerushaliem," Bezalel, early 20th C 700.00

4" h, Ottoman silver and stone inset, rect form, hand and "Shadai," rounded scroll case set with gemstones, overall engraved geometric and foliate dec, bosses to sides, indistinctly marked, 19th/20th C 575.00

9-1/2" h, German silver, cylindrical, peaked top and bottom, adjustable bracket, Anton Gutwein, maker, Augsburg, c1800. . . . . .2,415.00

Oil Can, one gallon, Planters Edible Oil Co., Suffolk, VA, shows fried foods along sides, Star of David, Hebrew writing on front and back, red ground, yellow and black lettering, unopened, large dent in back. 400.00

Painting

13-3/4" h, 10-1/8" w, oil on panel, "The Marriage Broker," sgd and inscribed "PR. B. Schatz, Jerusalem" (Boris Schatz,

1866-1932), lower left, monogram and inscribed "Jerusalem" in Hebrew lower right, titled on label on reverse, repousse brass frame, under glass. 25,300.00

24" h, 20" w, oil on canvas, "Portrait of a Rabbi," sgd "Bromberg," lower right, framed. 350.00

Picture Frame, 9" h, silver, clasps depicting Moses and Aaron, small with hallmarks, int. 5" x 7". 345.00

Plaque

7-1/4" h, 5" w, bronze, titled "In The Old City," mounted on patinated bronze frame, M. Murro, early 20th C 350.00

8-1/2" h, 6-1/2" w, hammered brass, titled "At The Kotel," mounted on silvered metal and ebonized wood frame, mkd "Bezalel," M. Murro, early 20th C 230.00

9-3/4" h, scene titled "Blessing of the Rabbi," arched frame, stylized dec, title, easel back, reverse with paper label for Bezalel, numbered A15, Boris Schatz, c1906 . . . .3,450.00

Purim Noisemaker (Gregger), 7" h, wood, maple handle, later applied silver dec depicting Haman and Purim scenes, late 19th C. 500.00

Rose Water Container, 11-1/4" h, silver, flattened inverted heart-shaped form, domed pierced top, oval domed foot, chased with foliage, unmarked, Persian, late 19th/early 20th C. 375.00

Rug, wool, double candelabra device, Bezalel, early 20th C

50-1/2" x 28-1/2", mosque, green, blue, beige, and rust, overall wear. 520.00

55-1/4" x 21", panorama of Jerusalem, blue, rust, and beige, overall wear, borders re-woven 460.00

Seal, 5" h, silver, for Bassevi von Trefeld, created 1622, formed as rampant lion holding shield, crest three stars and two lion/leopards, Austrian, Baroque-style 575.00

Shabat Bottle Opener, bronze, key-form, incised blessing for wine, early 20th C. 920.00

Shabat Knife, 5-1/2" l, metal and mother-of-pearl, inscribed in Hebrew, Czechoslovakian 290.00

Shabat Table Cover, 23-1/2" w, 20-1/2" h, Balkan, gilt-metal thread embroidered silk, purple ground, sequined dec, early 20th C, minor discoloration. 230.00

Shabat Tray, 15-3/4" l, Sheffield silver, oval, repousse dec of braided challah loafs, vintage border, Hebrew text, base mkd "England," 20th C. 345.00

Kiddush Cup, Russia, silver, engraved dec, hallmarked, c1888, 2-1/8" h, $145.

Sheet Music, *The Titanic Disaster,* New York, Hebrew Publishing Co., copyright 1912, blue and white cover art work by J. Keller 260.00

Shofar, 13-1/4" l, ram's head, geometric carving at edge, scalloped end section, Continental, 19th/20th C 200.00

Snuff Box

    2-1/4" h, silver-gilt mounted polychrome dec porcelain, rect, painted with Biblical scenes, French, 19th C, restoration to lid 2,185.00

    2-3/4" h, silver-gilt, later worked lid with binding of Isaac, George III, London, c1778, adapted 575.00

    3" d, silver-mounted enamel, circular, painted with Biblical scenes, base with moth, German, 18th/19th C, some restoration to lid 1,380.00

    3" d, silver-mounted enamel, circular, painted with Biblical scenes, base with floral de, German, 18th/19th C 1,725.00

Spice Container, silver

    2-1/4" h, grand piano form, hinged lid, ivorine keys, hallmarked, 20th C 345.00

    3-1/2" l, round openwork container, tapering stem, filigree cover, Russian, 19th C. 980.00

    4" l, horn form, heavily dec with birds, foliage, and scrollwork, lid engraved with crest of Sir Moses Montefiore, carnelian mount, chain, London, 1871, maker "T.J.". 1,955.00

    4-1/4" h, two compartments, rooster finials, dolphin-form legs, Birmingham, England, 1808, maker "M.L." . . . 750.00

    6" h, fruit-form, curved stem, applied leaves, apple set on leaf-form base, Polish, 19th C 1,035.00

Spice Tower, spire with pendant

    7-1/4" h, silver, 800 fine, hexagonal compartment, floral repousse panels, hinged door, tapering stem, hexagonal domed foot, German, late 19th/early 20th C 635.00

    7-1/4" h, silver and silver filigree, central filigree compartment, emb dec, tapering stem, domed circular foot, attributed to Berlin, early 19th C 520.00

    9" h, silver and silver filigree, sq filigree compartment, hinged door, flags, and bells, baluster stem, domed circular foot, London, 1902, maker "H.A.". 690.00

    10-1/4" h, silver and silver filigree, sq compartment with hinged door and flags, tapering stem, circular domed foot, Continental, late 19th/early 20th C 600.00

Tefflin Case, 1-1/4" h, miniature, silver, engraved dec, late 19th C, pr 1,265.00

Torah Binder, 112" l, painted linen, dated 15th day of Elul, 1870, inscribe to Yehuah ben Eli Gold, printed in bright colors, Hebrew inscriptions and birds, some staining. 750.00

Torah Crown, 19-1/4" h, silver and silver filigree, heavily pierced and cast, foliate dec, surmounted by bird perched on ball, pendant bells, J. Perlman, maker, Warsaw, c1900, some bells replaced 2,300.00

Torah Pointer, silver

    9" l, tapering form, heavily cast with rococo style dec, tapering knopped finial, lower section terminating in cuffed hand, hallmarked, Dutch, 19th C 375.00

    11" h, oval stem cast with leaf-tip and molded dec, finial formed as rampant lion holding shield, lower section terminating in cuffed hand, unmarked, Bohemian, late 19th/early 20th C 800.00

    12" l, tapering cylindrical stem, baluster shaped chased with foliage, ovoid knop finial, lower section terminating with hand, loop, and chain, hallmarked, Polish-style, 20th C 350.00

Torah Shield, 14" h, silver, 950 fine, cartouche form, crown above two winged griffins, lions, and tablets to center, supported by scroll-work, suspension chain, Johann Aiehrer maker, Austro-Hungary, c1880, repairs 750.00

Vase, Bezalel, bronze, early 20th C

    6" h, tapered hexagonal form, stylized designs and Hebrew text on sides, mkd on base 350.00

    11-3/4" h, flattened moon-flask form, circular stylized dec, flaring rim, loop handles, domed foot, applied mark 1,495.00

JUGTOWN POTTERY

History: In 1920, Jacques and Julianna Busbee left their cosmopolitan environs and returned to North Carolina to revive the state's dying pottery-making craft. Jugtown Pottery, a colorful and somewhat off-beat operation, was located in Moore County, miles away from any large city and accessible only "if mud permits."

Ben Owens, a talented young potter, turned the wares. Jacques Busbee did most of the designing and glazing. Julianna handled promotion.

Utilitarian and decorative items were produced. Although many colorful glazes were used, orange predominated. A Chinese blue glaze that ranged from light blue to deep turquoise was a prized glaze reserved for the very finest pieces.

Jacques Busbee died in 1947. Julianna, with the help of Owens, ran the pottery until 1958 when it was closed. After long legal battles, the pottery was reopened in 1960. It now is owned by Country Roads, Inc., a nonprofit organization. The pottery still is operating and using the old mark.

Bowl

    4" h, 7-1/4" d, Chinese Blue glaze, stamped "Jugtown Ware" 500.00

    11-1/2" d, Chinese Blue glaze 250.00

Cabinet Vase

    3" h, Chinese Blue glaze, stamped "Jugtown Ware" . 375.00

    3-3/4" h, Chinese Blue glaze, stamped "Jugtown Ware" 325.00

    4" h, Chinese Blue hi-glaze, imp mark 150.00

Candlesticks, pr, 4 1/2" h, tapered stems, broad cups supporting candleholders, mottled blue and black high glaze, imp mark 110.00

Urn, 7" h, 5-1/4" d, bulbous, predominately red Chinese Blue glaze, stamped "Jugtown Ware". 3,500.00

Vessel

    3-1/2" h, 4-3/4" d, flaring, Chinese Blue glaze, stamped "Jugtown Ware," small rim chip. 250.00

    5-1/2" h, 4" d, pear shaped, red Chinese Blue glaze, stamped "Jugtown Ware" 1,400.00

    5-1/2" h, 4-1/4" d, bulbous, thick, dripping purple and green glossy glaze, stamped "Jugtown Ware". 1,500.00

    5-1/2" h, 6-1/2" d, flaring, incised band on top, red and turquoise Chinese Blue glaze, stamped "Jugtown Ware" 2,500.00

    5-3/4" h, 6-1/2" d, bulbous, Chinese Blue glaze dripping over brown clay bisque body, stamped "Jugtown Ware" 1,300.00

    6-1/4" h, 7" d, bulbous, tapered shoulder, Chinese Blue glaze, stamped "Jugtown Ware" 700.00

    7-1/2" h, 4" d, two applied medallions, predominately red Chinese Blue glaze, stamped "Jugtown Ware," restoration to two rim chips 2,400.00

Vessel, Chinese Blue glaze dripping over bisque brown clay body, stamped mark, 5-3/4" h, 4-1/2" d, $1,300. Photo courtesy of David Rago Auctions, Inc.

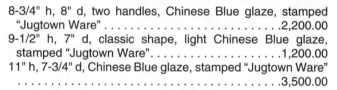

8-3/4" h, 8" d, two handles, Chinese Blue glaze, stamped "Jugtown Ware" 2,200.00
9-1/2" h, 7" d, classic shape, light Chinese Blue glaze, stamped "Jugtown Ware". 1,200.00
11" h, 7-3/4" d, Chinese Blue glaze, stamped "Jugtown Ware" 3,500.00

KAUFFMANN, ANGELICA

History: Marie Angelique Catherine Kauffmann was a Swiss artist who lived from 1741 until 1807. Many artists who hand-decorated porcelain during the 19th century copied her paintings. The majority of the paintings are neoclassical in style.

References: Susan and Al Bagdade, *Warman's English & Continental Pottery & Porcelain*, 3rd Edition, Krause Publications, 1998; Wendy Wassying Roworth (ed.), *Angelica Kauffmann*, Reaktion Books, 1993, distributed by University of Washington Press.

Biscuit Jar, cov, 7" h, 5" d, scenic panel of three ladies and gentleman, pastels, alternating gold and maroon panels, gold grim, SP rim, cov, and handle 165.00
Bowl, 9-1/2" d, two maidens and child 65.00
Condensed Milk Can Holder, cov, matching underplate, classical maiden, green ground, gold tracery 115.00
Dresser Set, green ground, multicolored portraits on each of 3 cov pots, matching tray 150.00
Marmalade jar, cov, Three Graces scene. 90.00
Plate, 8-5/8" d, scalloped edge, gilt and magenta border with gilt foliage and 3 cartouches of multicolored floral sprays, cream ground with gilt leaves, center painting of chariot with cupid, 3 maidens, artist sgd "Angelica Kaufmann" on front, mkd "Imperial Crown China Austria" with crown and wreath mark with "Austria" underneath on back. 550.00
Portrait Plate, 8-1/2" d, emerald green, gold, and cream, fancy edges, ladies in orange and purple gowns, cherub, sgd, mkd "Carlsbad, Austria". 100.00
Tobacco Jar, cov, portrait front, muted dark green, orange and yellow trim, SP rim and lid, pipe finial. 325.00
Vase, 8-3/8" h, medallion of classical maidens, gold filigree and trim, sgd, mkd "Austria" 120.00

Cake Plate, four classical maidens, gold border, $115.

KEW BLAS

History: Amory and Francis Houghton established the Union Glass Company, Somerville, Massachusetts, in 1851. The company went bankrupt in 1860, but was reorganized. Between 1870 and 1885, the Union Glass Company made pressed glass and blanks for cut glass.

Art-glass production began in 1893 under the direction of William S. Blake and Julian de Cordova. Two styles were introduced: a Venetian style, which consisted of graceful shapes in colored glass, often flecked with gold; and an iridescent glass, called Kew Blas, made in plain and decorated forms. The pieces are similar in design and form to Quezel products but lack the subtlety of Tiffany items.

The company ceased production in 1924.

Museum: Sandwich Glass Museum, Sandwich, MA.

Bowl, 5-1/2" d, irid gold ground, shaped rim, shallow round bowl, sgd "Kew Blas" on base 250.00
Compote, 7" h, irid gold ground, pink highlights, ribbed bowl, twisted stem 550.00
Console Set, 10" d compote, 6-3/4" h pr candlesticks, Alexandrite, heat reactive red shaded to blue, chocolate shading, central air trap bubble stem 1,265.00
Cuspidor, 5-3/4" d, 2-1/2" h, amber ground, irid gold dec, squatty, flattened flared rim, sgd "Kew Blas". 285.00
Decanter, 14-1/2" h, gold, ribbed and painted stopper, purple-pink highlights, sgd on base. 1,450.00
Finger Bowl and Underplate, 5" d, 7" d plate, twelve ribbed body, scalloped edge, gold irid, inscribed and numbered . . 425.00
Goblet, 4-3/4" h, irid gold ground, curved stem. 250.00
Pitcher, 5" h, King Tut, white ground, green and gold irid dec, irid blue lining, blue handle, sgd. 2,000.00
Rose Bowl
5-1/2" w, 3-1/2" h, ovoid, soft beige over oyster white, green hooked and swirled feather, brilliant orange/gold int., band of gold going thru design, sgd in pontil 950.00

5-1/2" w, 4" h, ovoid, oyster white ground, interlocking circles, one irid gold, other green, brilliant gold int. 1,200.00
Tumbler, 3-1/2" h, 3" d, brilliant irid gold exterior, purple irid interior, sgd 275.00
Vase
4-1/4" h, 5-1/4" d, deep emerald green, honeycomb pattern, highly irid purple int., sgd 800.00
4-1/4" h, 5-1/4" d, flared amber ribbed trumpet form, pulled emerald green int. dec, base engraved "Kew-Blas"
. . . . 815.00
7" h, cased ambergris oval body, gold irid feathers on opal body, folded irid rim, base inscribed "Kew-Blas" . . . 980.00
8-1/4" h, elongated goblet form, gold irid luster, splotched and spotted technique, base inscribed "Kew Blas" 450.00
10" h, tooled spiked top rim, flared amber cylinder, green pulled feather dec, irid luster, base inscribed "Kew Blas"
. . . . 550.00

KITCHEN COLLECTIBLES

History: The kitchen was the focal point in a family's environment until the 1960s. Many early kitchen utensils were handmade and prized by their owners. Next came a period of utilitarian products made of tin and other metals. When the housewife no longer wished to work in a sterile environment, enamel and plastic products added color, and their unique design served both aesthetic and functional purposes.

The advent of home electricity changed the type and style of kitchen products. Fads affected many items. High technology already has made inroads into the kitchen, and another revolution seems at hand.

References: E. Townsend Artman, *Toasters: 1909-1960*, Schiffer Publishing, 1996; Ronald S. Barlow, *Victorian Houseware*, Windmill Publishing, 1992; *Collector's Digest Price Guide to Griswold Mfg. Co. 1918 Catalog Reprint*, L-W Book Sales, 1996; *Collectors Guide to Wagner Ware and Other Companies*, L-W Book Sales, 1994; Linda Fields, *Four & Twenty Blackbirds: A Pictorial Identification and Value Guide for Pie Birds*, published by author, (158 Bagsby Hill Lane, Dover, TN 37058); Gene Florence, *Kitchen Glassware of the Depression Years*, 5th ed., Collector Books, 1997; Linda Campbell Franklin, *300 Years of Housekeeping Collectibles*, Books Americana, 1992; ——, *300 Hundred Years of Kitchen Collectibles*, Krause Publications, 1997; Ambrogio Fumagalli, *Coffee Makers*, Chronicle Books, 1995; Michael J. Goldberg, *Collectible Plastic Kitchenware and Dinnerware*, Schiffer Publishing, 1995; ——, *Groovy Kitchen Designs for Collectors*, Schiffer Publishing, 1996; Helen Greguire, *Collector's Guide to Toasters & Accessories*, Collector Books, 1997; Susan E. Grindberg, *Collector's Guide to Porcelier China*, Collector Books, 1996; Jon B. Haussler, *Griswold Muffin Pans*, Schiffer Publishing, 1997; *Griswold Cast Iron*, L-W Book Sales, 1997; Frances Johnson, *Kitchen Antiques*, Schiffer Publishing, 1996; Jan Lindenberger, *The 50s & 60s Kitchen*, Schiffer Publishing, 1994; ——, *Fun Kitchen Collectibles*, Schiffer Publishing, 1996.

Kathryn McNerney, *Kitchen Antiques 1790-1940*, Collector Books, 1991, 1997 value update; Gary Miller and K. M. Mitchell, *Price Guide to Collectible Kitchen Appliances*, Wallace-Homestead, 1991; Jim Moffett, *American Corn Huskers*, Off Beat Books (1345 Poplar Ave., Sunny-

vale, CA 94087), 1994; Ellen M. Plante, *Kitchen Collectibles*, Wallace-Homestead, 1991; Don and Carol Raycraft, *Wallace-Homestead Price Guide to American Country Antiques*, 15th ed., Krause Publications, 1997; James Rollband, *American Nutcrackers*, Off Beat Books (1345 Poplar Ave., Sunnyvale, CA 94087), 1996; David G. Smith and Charles Wafford, *Book of Griswold & Wagner*, Schiffer Publishing, 1996; Diane Stoneback, *Kitchen Collectibles*, Wallace-Homestead, 1994; Don Thornton, *Apple Parers,* Off Beat Books, (1345 Poplar Ave., Sunnyvale, CA 94087) 1997; ——, *Beat This: The Eggbeater Chronicles*, Off Beat Books, 1994; *Toasters and Small Kitchen Appliances*, L-W Book Sales, 1995; Jean Williams Turner, *Collectible Aunt Jemima*, Schiffer Publishing, 1994; April M. Tvorak, *Fire-King Fever '96*, published by author, 1995.

Periodicals: *Cast Iron Cookware News*, 28 Angela Ave., San Anselmo, CA 94960; *Kettles 'n' Cookware*, P.O. Box B, Perrysburg, NY 14129; *Kitchen Antiques & Collectible News*, 4645 Laurel Ridge Dr., Harrisburg, PA 17110; *Piebirds Unlimited*, 14 Harmony School Rd., Flemington, NJ 08822.

Collectors' Clubs: Cook Book Collectors Club of America, P.O. Box 56, St. James, MO 65559-0056; Cookie Cutter Collectors Club, 1167 Teal Rd., SW, Dellroy, OH 44620; Glass Knife Collectors Club, 711 Kelly Dr., Lebanon, TN 37087; Griswold & Cast Iron Cookware Association, P.O. Drawer B, Perrysburg, NY 14119-0301; International Society for Apple Parer Enthusiasts, 17 E. High, Mount Vernon, OH 43050; National Cookie Cutters Collectors Club, 2763 310th St., Cannon Falls, MN 55009; National Reamer Collectors Association, 47 Midline Court, Gaithersburg, MD 20878.

Museums: Corning Glass Museum, Corning, NY; Kern County Museum, Bakersfield, CA; Landis Valley Farm Museum, Lancaster, PA.

Additional Listings: Baskets; Brass; Butter Prints; Copper; Fruit Jars; Food Molds; Graniteware; Ironware; Tinware; Woodenware. See *Warman's Americana & Collectibles* for more examples including electrical appliances.

Apple Peeler, cast iron, Hudson Co, Leominster, MA, patent 1882 . . . . 75.00
Bread Stick Pan, cast iron, Griswold #23 . . . . 75.00
Broiler, 6-1/2" d, wrought iron, wavy cross bars 75.00
Butter Churn, 8-3/4" d, 26" h, wood, blue painted, America, late 18th/early 19th C, wear to paint 375.00
Butter Paddle, 10" l, maple, curved handle, some curl, old worn patina, age crack in bowl 55.00
Cake Board, 13" x 17", carved walnut, three lozenge-shaped molds of dog, soldier on horseback, and flower filled base, imp mark "J. Conger, New York," 19th C 825.00
Cookie Board, 3-7/8" x 7", pewter, fifteen segments, well detailed animals, flowers, and buildings, walnut back . . 220.00
Cream and Egg Whip, Whippit, Durometal Products Co, 14" l
. . . . 25.00
Dutch Oven, cov, cast iron, Griswold #8, large trademark
. . . . 100.00
Egg Beater
Dover, 13" l, 4 hole wheel standard, pat. Dec 27-98 . . 65.00

Instant Whip, 11-1/2" l, aluminum, Pat April 20, 1920 . . . . 25.00

Ladd No. 2, 12-1/2", Pat July 7, 1907, Oct 18, 1912, Other Pats Pending 25.00

Taplin Improved Dover Pattern, 10-1/2" l, Pat Feb 9, 1904 . . . . 45.00

Fish Broiler, 18" l, wrought iron, America, late 18th/early 19th C 175.00

Flour Scoop, 14" l, maple, Shaker type, carved, shaped handle, finger grip 170.00

Food Grinder, cast iron, Griswold #4 . . . . 25.00

Grater, 9-5/8" l, tin, pine box with sliding lid and drawer, old brown varnish, wire nail construction 95.00

Griddle, Erie, #12, bailed. 40.00

Ice Chest Refrigerator, 34" w, 20-1/2" d, 30-1/4" h, poplar, old worn refinishing, metal lined int. with double wooden lid, turned feet with castors, paper label "Eddy Refrigerator, Boston..." 250.00

Kettle, cast iron, 5 qt, Wagnerware and Griswold trademarks 80.00

Kraut Cutter, 13" x 41", ash, cherry dovetailed hopper, refinished 80.00

Muffin Pan, cast iron, Griswold #10 . . . . 40.00

Nutmeg Grater, 5-1/4" l, tin, wood handle. 65.00

Pie Bird
    Duck
        Pink 50.00
        Yellow 50.00
        White, gold flowers 275.00

Pie Crimper, 7" l, wood handle, brass crimper 75.00

Potscraper, 3" h, 3-1/2" l, King Midas Flour adv, diecut, black ground, Sunbonnet girl in white, orange lettering and trim 300.00

Refrigerator, 33-3/4" w, 48-1/4" h, refinished pine, lift top for ice, paneled doors, turned feet, metal lining 450.00

Rolling Pin, 15" l, glass, blown, amethyst, worn painted floral dec 135.00

Skewer Holder, six flat skewers, wrought iron, 18th C
    12-3/4" l, imp "RE" mark. 520.00
    16" l 700.00

Skillet, cast iron
    Griswold #0, heat ring, large trademark 65.00
    Griswold #3, smooth bottom, small trademark. 15.00
    Griswold #5, smooth bottom, small trademark. 35.00
    Griswold #7, smooth bottom, small trademark. 15.00
    Griswold #9, hinge, small trademark 35.00

Victor, #8 . . . . 50.00

Wagnerware, #0, Randall Wagnerware paper label. . . 15.00

Wapak, #8, heat ring 100.00

Sugar Nippers, wrought steel and brass, turned wooden handle, molded edge base, 11" l. 175.00

Trivet, wrought iron, heart shape 90.00

Wafer Iron, 28" l, 5-1/2" w, eagle motif, late 18th/early 19th C 550.00

KUTANI

History: Kutani originated in the mid-1600s in the Kaga province of Japan. Kutani comes in a variety of color patterns, one of the most popular being Ao Kutani, a green glaze with colors such as green, yellow, and purple enclosed in a black outline. Export wares made since the 1870s are enameled in a wide variety of colors and styles.

Berry Set, master bowl, six serving bowls, multicolored enamel floral dec, red border, price for 7 pc set 175.00

Bowl, 4-3/4" sq, polychrome, gold flowers, unglazed foot, sgd gold seal form. 320.00

Charger, 14" d, figural landscape, multicolored, gold border 225.00

Chocolate Pot, 8-1/2" h, red, orange, and gold, reserve panels of peonies and birds, people in gardens, Japanese. . 165.00

Ewer, 8-1/4" h, duck on floral base, keyfret band, green, yellow, aubergine, and blue enamel. 195.00

Ginger Jar, cov, 5" h, blue, green, and carmine enamel dec, foo dog finial. 150.00

Low Bowl, 13-1/2" d, yellow, blue, green, and aubergine enamels, central reserve of scholar and attendant in pavilion, wide lappet border 650.00

Sake Cup, 1-7/8" h, floriform rim, short ring foot, enamel and gold dec, painted rim band, gold scrolling flower and trellis dec 125.00

Umbrella Stand, 28" h, multicolored butterflies, flowers, foliage, and medallions 500.00

Vase, 26" h, medallions of birds and flowers, gold brocade dec orange ground, Aka-Kutani, late 19th C, mounted as lamp 300.00

Funnel, wood, 7-1/4" h, 4-3/4" d, $85.

Bowl, three men in red, 7-1/2" d, $170.

LACE and LINENS

History: Lace, lacy linens, embroidery, and hand-decorated textiles are different from any other antique. They are valued both as a handmade substance and as the thing the substance is made into. Thread is manipulated into stitches, stitches are assembled into lace, lace is made into handkerchiefs, edgings, tablecloths, bedspreads. Things eventually go out of style or are damaged or worn, and just as the diamonds and rubies are taken from old jewelry and placed into new settings, fine stitchery of embroidery and lace is saved and reused. Lace from a handkerchief is used to decorate a blouse, fragments of a bridal veil are made into a scarf; shreds of old lace are remounted onto fine net and used again as a veil.

At each stage in the cycle, different people become interested. Some see fragments as bits and pieces of a collage, and seek raw materials for accent pieces. Others use Victorian whites and turn-of-the-century embroidered linens to complement a life style. Collectors value and admire the stitches themselves, and when those stitches are remarkable enough, they will pay hundreds of dollars for fragments a few inches square.

Until the 1940s, lace collecting was a highly respected avocation of the wealthy. The prosperity of the New World was a magnet for insolvent European royalty, who carried suitcases of old Hapsburg, Bourbon, Stuart, and Romanov laces to suites at New York's Waldorf hotel for dealers to select from. Even Napoleon's bed hangings of handmade Alencon lace, designed for Josephine and finished for Marie Louise, found their way here. In 1932, *Fortune* magazine profiled socially prominent collectors and lace dealers. For the entire first half of this century, New York City's Needle and Bobbin Club provided a forum for showing off acquisitions.

Until 1940, upscale department stores offered antique lace and lacy linens. Dealers specializing in antique lace and lacy linens had prominent upscale shops, and offered repair, restoration, remodeling, and cleaning services along with the antique linens. In addition to collecting major pieces—intact jabots from the French Ancient Regime, Napoleonic-era Alencon, huge mid-Victorian lace shawls, Georgian bed hangings appliquéd with 17th-century needle lace—collectors assembled study collections of postcard-size samples of each known style of antique lace.

When styles changed round the 1940s and 1950s and the market for antique lace and linens crashed, some of the best collections did go to museums; others just went into hiding. With renewed interest in a gracious, romantic lifestyle, turn-of-the-century lacy cloths from the linen closets of the barons of the industrial revolution are coming out of hiding. Collectors and wise dealers know that many of the small study-pieces of irreplaceable stitchery—fragments collectors will pay ten to hundreds of dollars for—still emerge in rummage and estate sales.

Very large banquet-sized lace tablecloths, especially those with napkins, continue to be especially popular. Appenzell, a white-on-white embroidered lacework of 19th C Switzerland, has become one of the hottest collector's items. Strong interest continues in patterned silk ribbons, all cotton lace yardage, and other lacy materials for heirloom sewing and fashion.

The market for antique lace definitely is changing. Interest is still rising for elaborate lace for home decorating and entertaining, and interest in fine quality lace collars is increasing. Large lace shawls and veils, especially for bridal wear, continue to be in demand. Internet auctions and chat groups make it possible for a dealer in Wyoming to link up with a collector in Louisiana, and find a home for an interesting piece. Those interested in fine quality lace are realizing they need to start buying at market prices instead of waiting for that lucky find that they alone recognize. Current market prices, although rising, still are usually far below what the pieces would have cost when new, or during the early twentieth century heyday of lace collecting.

As prices rise, buyers more often want an accurate identification: what is it, where was it made, how old is it? What makes it worth the price? Word spreads quickly over the Internet when it is obvious a dealer has mislabeled something, especially labeling something as handmade that is obviously machine. Lace has long been a sideline for most dealers, and they did not bother to learn to identify it. As long as they could turn it over quickly for a small markup, they were satisfied. That is changing. More sophisticated buyers won't put up with that without comment.

The basic techniques are bobbin lace, needle lace, crochet, tatting, knitting, knotting, and needleweaving. Identifying how a piece was made is the easy part, and there is no excuse for a dealer not being able to separate crochet from bobbin lace. Anyone can identify the technique after just a weekend workshop, or by comparing a piece to pictures in a good textbook. The technique, plus the quality of the design, and the condition, provides nearly all the information anyone needs to decide what a piece is worth.

After identifying the technique, many like to apply a name to the style (Duchesse bobbin lace, Point de Gaze needle lace, Irish crochet). This serves as a useful shorthand in talking about lace, but adds nothing to the value of the piece. This is often the confusing part. Unlike most antiques, there is no uniformity in labeling styles of lace. Names changed at different points in time, different names were used for similar products made in different countries, and foreign names often were translated differently. Any dealer should be expected to be able to explain why they chose to use any specific style name.

The Internet offers a unique access to a wide variety of kinds of lace and lacy linens. The small pictures available on the Internet, however, rarely show enough detail to know just what you are buying. Insist on a return policy for any lace purchased sight unseen on the Internet. Even well intentioned dealers may miss details that significantly affect the value of lace. Handmade meshes cannot be positively identified without high powered magnification. Repairs often go unnoticed and unreported. Color and texture make a great deal of difference in determining whether a piece of lace is attractive or not.

Whether purchasing fine quality collector's study samples, or boxes and bags of recyclable fragments for sewing, it is worth taking a close look at all the details. It is not uncommon for good quality study samples that a collector will pay $10 to $100 for in the "rag bags."

Those who learn to recognize the artistry and value of old stitchery will not only enhance their lives with beauty, they may find a windfall.

References: Pat Earnshaw, *Identification of Lace*, Lubrecht and Cramer, 1989; Frances Johnson, *Collecting Antique Linens, Lace, and Needlework*, Wallace-Homestead, 1991; ——, *Collecting More Household Linens,* Schiffer Publishing, 1997; Elizabeth Kurella, *Guide To Lace and Linens,* Antique Trader Books, 1998; ——, *Secrets of Real Lace*, The Lace Merchant (P.O. Box 222, Plainwell, MI 49080), 1994; ——, *Pocket Guide to Valuable Old Lace and Lacy Linens*, The Lace Merchant (P.O. Box 222, Plainwell, MI 49080), 1996; Santina Levy, *Lace, A History,* Victoria and Albert Museum, London, reprinted in 1997; Marsha L. Manchester, *Vintage White Linens A to Z*, Schiffer Publishing, 1997; Elizabeth Scofield and Peggy Zalamea, *Twentieth Century Linens and Lace*, Schiffer Publishing, 1997; Warnick and Nilsson, *Legacy of Lace,* Crown, 1988.

Collectors' Club: International Old Lacers, P.O. Box 554, Flanders, NJ 07836.

Museums: Chicago Art Institute, Chicago, IL; Cooper Hewitt (Smithsonian), New York, NY; Metropolitan Museum of Art, New York, NY; Museum of Early Southern Decorative Arts (MESDA), Winston-Salem, NC; Museum of Fine Arts, Boston, MA; Rockwood Museum, Wilmington, DE; Shelburne, Museum, Shelburne, VT; Smithsonian Institution, Washington, DC.

Advisor: Elizabeth M. Kurella.

Collars

Honiton English bobbin lace, traditional design of roses, thistles, and shamrocks, inch-long robin-like bird hidden in each lapel, 38" l, 9" deep at center back, mid 19th C 385.00

Irish Crochet, round cape-like collar, exceptional design of heavy flowers with lots of raised work, imitates 17th C Gros Point needle lace, 12" deep 325.00

Maltese bobbin lace, round style, honey color silk, geometric design with Maltese crosses, background grid of fat wheatears, c1900, 7" deep 285.00

Needle lace, large stylized flowers with raised outlines, c1900 . . . . 375.00

Tape lace, heavy millinery-style cotton tape in scrolling design, simple looping and needle-woven stitches, deep beige, early 20th C. 175.00

Vieux Flandre Berthe, combination of bobbin lace motifs with needle lace background, deep beige, early 20th C, 5" x 56" 185.00

Collector's Lace

Alencon needle lace lappets (headdress streamers) with stylized floral design, c1730, 28" l, pr 725.00

Brussels bobbin lace flounce fragment in exceptional design of full-blown roses with shaded petals, unusual bobbin lace fillings, 16" deep, 28" l 485.00

Dutch bonnet, late nineteenth century, decorated with about a yard of four-inch deep handmade Beveren bobbin lace 54.00

Gros Point de Venise, design of stylized flowers with heavy raised outlines decorated with picots, background repaired, 2" x 18" 125.00

Point de France needle lace border fragment, with a Berainesque design of small, symmetrical flower vases and stylized flowers, background of hexagonal bars covered with buttonhole stitches and decorated with picots, 3.8" x 25" 125.00

Point de France needle lace engegeant (sleeve ruffle) with a hunting scene design including fox and hounds in exotic floral and foliage background, c1720 . . . . 1,100.00

Point de Gaze needle lace, flounce fragment with design of traditional rose and scroll, 6" x 14" 45.00

Point de Gaze needle lace. tablier (dress front) with design of flower bouquets and scrolls with two heraldic shields each with tree, castles, and fleur-de-lis, 42" l 3,700.00

Doilies

Bobbin lace, design of butterflies typical of 20th C Chinese, 8" d round 5.00

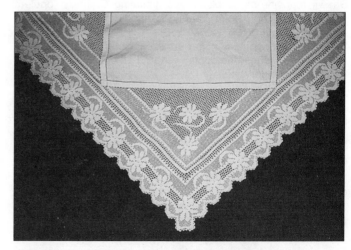

Tea Cloth, white linen center, hemstitched border, surrounded by intricate hand crochet floral and mesh design, white, c1900, 54" sq, $150.

Bobbin lace, meandering scrollwork design, probably early 20th
C, Chinese, 8" d round 5.00
Crochet, unusual dragon-like design, probably eastern Europe-
an, early 20th C, 8" d round 35.00
Needle lace, well-designed rose motif with shaded petals, fine
thread, 20"th C, 9" d round 25.00

Handkerchiefs

French embroidery, drawnwork, and needle lace inserts, large
satin stitch leaves design, 10" sq, fair condition 75.00
Irish Youghal needle edge, 4" w lace in stylized foliate design,
background of bars with picots, 14" sq 425.00
Linen, 12" sq
Edged with 1/4" of tatted rings with picots 8.00
Edged with 2" of scallops of crochet chain stitch and double
crochet 5.00
Point de Gaze needle lace edged with 4" of design of cattails
and flower sprays, c1870 . . . . 375.00

Tablecloths

Combination of bobbin lace and needle lace, scrolling design including dragon-like figures, early 20th C, 68" x 108"
. . . . .1,250.00
Crochet, round design of scallop chain stitch, 38" d, some small
repairs 28.00
Normandy work, a patchwork of machine, crochet, torchon bob-
bin lace, needle lace, filet in good symmetrical design, ecru,
48" x 68" 750.00

Veils and shawls

Brussels bobbin lace flowers and bouquets appliquéd on machine net, c1870, 96" x 28" 1,800.00
Brussels needle and bobbin lace flowers arranged in bouquets
at the corners and in sprays at the border, applied to machine
net, sprigs and spots scattered across the net, 51" x 78"
. . . . .1,530.00
Brussels needlelace flowers appliquéd in scalloped border on
machine net, scattered sprigs, 74" x 69 " 625.00
English Honiton bobbin lace appliqué on machine net, spray of
flowers at each corner, scattered springs and scalloped border, late 19th C, 71" x 69" 238.00
English Honiton bobbin lace appliqué on machine net, stylized
posies at each corner and roses along the border, late 19th
C, 75" x 73" 660.00
Shawl, machine-made black lace, imitating Chantilly, opulent
design of flower bouquets and garlands of flowers and foliage, triangular, 105" l x 54" w 145.00
Veil, rect, large, bouquet of flowers at each corner, formal posies
at border, sprigs and spots scattered across net in fine tambour embroidery, 92" x 74" 325.00

LALIQUE

History: René Lalique (1860-1945) first gained prominence as a jewelry designer. Around 1900, he began ex-
perimenting with molded-glass brooches and pendants,
often embellishing them with semiprecious stones. By
1905, he was devoting himself exclusively to the manufacture of glass articles.

In 1908, Lalique began designing packaging for the
French cosmetic houses. He also produced many ob-
jects, especially vases, bowls, and figurines, in the Art
Nouveau and Art Deco styles. The full scope of Lalique's

genius was seen at the 1925 Paris l'Exposition Internationale des Arts Décorative et Industriels Modernes.

Marks: The mark "R. LALIQUE FRANCE" in block letters
is found on pressed articles, tableware, vases, paperweights, and automobile mascots. The script signature,
with or without "France," is found on hand-blown objects.
Occasionally, a design number is included. The word
"France" in any form indicates a piece made after 1926.

The post-1945 mark is generally "Lalique France" without the "R," but there are exceptions.

References: Hugh D. Guinn (ed.), *Glass of René Lalique
at Auction*, Guindex Publications, 1992.

Collectors' Club: Lalique Collectors Society, 400 Veterans Blvd., Carlstadt, NJ 07072; Lalique Society of America, 400 Veterans Blvd., Carlstadt, NJ 07072.

Videotape: Nicholas M. Dawes, *World of Lalique Glass*,
Award Video and Film Distributors, 1993.

REPRODUCTION ALERT

The Lalique signature has often been forged, the most
common fake includes an "R" with the post-1945 mark.

Animal
Fox, 2-3/4" h, frosted, circular, engraved script sgd "R. Lal-
ique France" 550.00
Rooster, 9" h, numbered, sgd "R. Lalique, France," orig paper
label 2,000.00
Ashtray, 3-1/2" h, Soucis, opal figure of vase with flowers at center, base stamped "R. Lalique France" 460.00
Atomizer, cylindrical, 3-3/4" h, relief molded frieze of six nude
maidens, holding floral garland, waisted gilt metal mount, Le
Provencal fragrance, molded "R Lalique, Made in France"
. . . . 265.00

Perfume Bottle, Flausa, created for Roget & Gallet, 4-3/4" h, $6,325. Photo courtesy of Jackson's Auctioneers & Appraisers.

Auto Mascot, 8-1/4" h, rooster, molded, polished and frosted, ruffled tail feathers, low disk base, etched block mark, numbered on base 750.00

Bookends, pr
6-1/4" h, florals, birds, sgd 500.00
7-1/8" h, three molded putti bearing garlands, frosted, stenciled "Lalique France" 600.00

Bottle, 13" h, double dove, swirl, stopper, never opened, signed, numbered 900.00

Bowl
5-3/8" h, frosted and colorless, overall raised foliate and bird dec 275.00
11-3/8" d, foliate dec, amber patina, V.D.A. 325.00

Box, cov, 3-1/2" d, Emiliane, frosted, molded flowerheads, engraved "R. Lalique France" 250.00

Carafe, 7-1/4" h, clear, indented and molded large blossoms, brown patine in recesses, inscribed "R. Lalique" 450.00

Champagne Glass, 4-1/2" h, Strasbourg, frosted androgynous nude couple on stem, Art Deco pattern exhibited at Paris Exhibition, 1925, Rene Lalique, set of 6 . . . . 920.00

Chandelier, 13-1/2" d domed shade, Charmes, frosted all over leaf pattern, rect components with similar pattern, orig metal fixtures, molded "R. Lalique" 4,000.00

Charger
12" d, Peacock Feather 550.00
14-1/2" d, Martigues, opalescent, deeply molded swimming fish, molded mark "R. Lalique" 2,700.00

Cigarette Lighter, 5" h, highly emb frosted lion's heads, pedestal, sgd in script 90.00

Clock, 8-1/2" l, 6" h, demilune, circular mate finished silvered metal face, stylized dahlia encircled by polished Arabic numerals, arching frosted glass case, relief molded pairs of finches among flowering vines, inscribed in block letters "R. Lalique France," dial inscribed "ATO" and impressed "Made in France," c1930 . . . . .2,750.00

Cordial Set, Wingen, 8" h bulbous bottle, conforming stopper, two 3" h wine glasses, each with fine vertical striping, molded "R. Lalique" 575.00

Candleholder, 3-1/2" h, frosted and colorless, molded flower, block mark 160.00

Coupe, 3-1/2" h, 9-1/2" d, Coquilles, molded overlapping scallop shell design, strong opal blue color at base, inscribed in block letters "R. Lalique France" 500.00

Dresser Box, cov, 4" d, Emiliane, LeLys, floral dec, colorless pressed molded glass, retains some sepia patine . . . 250.00

Jardiniere, 18-1/4" l, 5-1/8" h, Saint Hubert, frosted elliptical bowl, ends spreading to form reticulated ear shaped handle, molded relief of leaping antelope among clear leafy branches, wheel cut block letters "R. Lalique/France," incised script "No. 3461," c1932. . . . . .3,500.00

Light Bowl, 13-1/2" d, partial luster, press molded design, four exotic birds among stylized berries and foliage, sepia patina in recesses, pierced at four panels and base for hanging, panel inscribed "Lalique France" 500.00

Paperweight, Tete D'Aigle, eagle head, clear and frosted, sgd in mold at side "R. Lalique" 1,200.00

Perfume Bottle
3-1/4" h, Le Jade, flattened snuff bottle form, molded jungle bird dec, bright green crystal, matching stopper, mkd "Le Jade/Roger et Gallet Paris/R. Lalique" in mold . . .2,185.00
3-3/4" h, Elgance, for D'Orsay, sq molded bottle, two nude women standing among flowering ranches, molded "D'ORSAY". 2,000.00
4-3/4" h, Bouchon Cassis, vertically ribbed colorless barrel form, integrated tiara stopper molded as currant berries, selectively polished and frosted, base molded, also engraved "R. Lalique" 7,200.00

Place Card Holder, 1-5/8" h, demilune form, clear and frosted, molded baskets of flowers and fruit, engraved "R. Lalique," set of 8 . . . . 850.00

Plaque, 4" h, 3-1/2" w, frosted and clear, floral design, mkd "Lalique," orig velvet lined box. 100.00

Plate
7-7/8" d, crescent-form, colorless, frosted thistle dec, pr
. . . . 125.00
12-1/2" d, molded swirling fish, opalescent, raised signature, few scratches. 400.00

Sign, 1-1/2" h, 5" l, free standing colorless glass wedge, frosted recessed trademark "Lalique Cristallerie France" . . . 150.00

Table Ornament, 8" h, Luxembourg, catalog no. 11619/11620, selectively frosted colorless crystal, molded three full-length cherubs in half circle, semi-circular platform foot, inscribed "Lalique France," price of pr. 900.00

Tray, 10-1/2" d, blue opalescence, all over shell pattern, sgd "R. Lalique". 300.00

Vase
3-1/2" h, Oleron Fish, colorless gray frosted oval, molded petits poissons overlapping and intertwined, rim edge of base inscribed "R. Lalique France No. 1008" 475.00
6" h, Esterel, broad oval, frosted opalescent, overall molded relief leaf design, blue patina, base rim inscribed "R. Lalique France". 1,610.00
6-3/4" h, Gui, spherical, molded with leafing and fruiting mistletoe plants, script sgd "R. Lalique," No. 948 . . . . . 800.00
7" h, Laurier, frosted cylinder, cigar jar-form, berries and spiked leaf design, lower side with molded mark "R. Lalique"
. . . . 350.00
8" h, protruding disks, colorless glass on frosted ground, script signature, minor flaw to lip 210.00
9-1/4" h, Ronces, small raised rim, oval body, swirled thorny bramble branches, molded in high relief, rim inscribed "R. Lalique No. 946," minor int. stain 575.00
9-1/2" h, Marisa, charcoal gray, spherical, spiral design with trout, base script sgd "R. Lalique" 2,600.00

LAMP SHADES

History: Lamp shades were made to diffuse the harsh light produced by early gas lighting fixtures. These early shades were made by popular Art Nouveau manufacturers including Durand, Quezal, Steuben, and Tiffany. Many shades are not marked.

Acid Etched, 8" d, hummingbirds and leaves, clear and frosted, c1870, price for pr 175.00

Burmese, 8 3/4' d, birds, butterflies, and floral dec, gas style fitter ring 275.00

Carnival Glass, marigold, swirled ribs, 10" d. 200.00

Durand, 3 1/2" d, irid gold, candle lamp type 150.00

Fostoria, 5"h, gold, green leaves and vines, white luster ground
. . . . 150.00

Fry, 8" w, 2-1/2" d fitter ring, turret-shape, dark cream ribs, pale translucent panels, unmarked, pr. 550.00

Hobbs Brockunier, 4 1/2" h, 7" d, Coinspot pattern, opalescent and amber optic, c1880 . . . . 65.00

Leaded Dome
12 1/4" d, 4 3/4" h, red, green, and opalescent white chunks of glass shards, some cracks, slightly out of round, European. 460.00
20" d, angular, clusters of red bead grapes among green and amber glass segments, bent glass crown, replacement two-light socket 425.00

Carnival Glass, hand painted forest scenes, pr, $175.

Lotton, 4-1/2" l, lily, gold, pink and platinum irid highlights, made by fit Tiffany lily lamps, sgd and dated 1975, set of three
.... 160.00
Northwood, 8 1/4" d, light pink, etched flowers, frosted, ruffled
.... 150.00
Quezal
    5" h, ivory ground, green pulled feather outlined in gold, gold int., incised signature, small flake on fitter rim 125.00
    6" h, ribbed, flaring, gold irid, incised signature 260.00
Tiffany
    3" h, 5-1/4" d lower opening, Candlelamp, Pine Needle pattern, conical, reticulated etched metal, imp "Tiffany Studios," price for pr 280.00
    5" h, 3" d top opening, opal glass, optic-ribbed, pink damascene striping, rim mkd "L. C. T.," both cracked, price for pr
.... 300.00
    6-3/4" h, 16" d, leaded, Pomegranate pattern, band of yellow fruit, segmented two-tone green ground, imp "Tiffany Studios/New York/1-57-109" 8,750.00

LAMPS and LIGHTING

History: Lighting devices have evolved from simple stone-age oil lamps to the popular electrified models of today. Aimé Argand patented the first oil lamp in 1784. Around 1850, kerosene became a popular lamp-burning fluid, replacing whale oil and other fluids. In 1879, Thomas A. Edison invented the electric light, causing fluid lamps to lose favor and creating a new field for lamp manufacturers. Companies like Tiffany and Handel became skillful at manufacturing electric lamps, and their decorators produced beautiful bases and shades.

References: James Edward Black (ed.), *Electric Lighting of the 20s-30s* (1988, 1993 value update), *Volume 2 with Price Guide* (1990, 1993 value update), L-W Book Sales; J. W. Courter, *Aladdin Collectors Manual & Price Guide #16*, published by author (3935 Kelley Rd., Kevil, KY 42053), 1996; ——, *Aladdan, The Magic Name in Lamps, Revised Edition*, published by author, 1997; Susan E. Grindberg, *Collector's Guide to Porcelier China*, Collector Books, 1996; Arthur H. Hayward, *Colonial and Early American Lighting*, 3rd ed., Dover Publications, 1962; Marjorie Hulsebus, *Miniature Victorian Lamps*, Schiffer Publishing, 1996; Nadja Maril, *American Lighting*, Schiffer Publishing, 1995; Calvin Shepherd, *50s T.V.*

Lamps, Schiffer Publishing, 1998; Richard Miller and John Solverson, *Student Lamps of the Victorian Era*, Antique Publications, 1992, 1992-93 value guide; Bill and Linda Montgomery, *Animated Motion Lamps 1920s to Present*, L-W Book Sales, 1991; Denys Peter Myers, *Gaslighting in America*, Dover Publications, 1990; Henry A. Pohs, *Miner's Flame Light Book*, Hiram Press, 1995; *Quality Electric Lamps*, L-W Book Sales, 1992; Catherine M. V. Thuro, *Oil Lamps*, Wallace-Homestead, 1976, 1992 value update; ——, *Oil Lamps II*, Collector Books, 1983, 1994 value update; Kenneth Wilson, *American Glass 1760-1930*, 2 Vols., Hudson Hills Press and The Toledo Museum of Art, 1994.

Periodical: *Light Revival*, 35 West Elm Ave., Quincy, MA 02170.

REPRODUCTION ALERT

The following is a partial list of reproduction kerosene lamps. Colors in italics indicate a period color:

Button & Swirl, 8" high—*clear, cobalt blue*, ruby
Coolidge Drake (a.k.a. Waterfall), 10" high—*clear, cobalt blue, milk glass*, ruby
Lincoln Drape, short, 8-3/4" high—*amber, clear, green, and other colors*
Lincoln Drape, tall, 9-3/4" high—*amber, clear, cobalt blue, moonstone, ruby*
Shield & Star, 7" high—*clear,* cobalt blue
Sweetheart (a.k.a. Beaded Heart), 10" h—*clear,* milk glass, pink, pink cased font with clear base

General clues that help identify a new lamp include parts that are glued together and hardware that is lacquered solid brass.

Collectors' Clubs: Aladdin Knights of the Mystic Light, 3935 Kelley Rd., Kevil, KY 42053; Coleman Collector Network, 1822 E Fernwood, Wichita, KS 67216; Historical Lighting Society of Canada, P.O. Box 561, Postal Station R, Toronto, Ontario M4G 4EI, Canada; Incandescent Lamp Collectors Association, Museum of Lighting, 717 Washington Place, Baltimore, MD 21201; International Coleman Collectors Club, 2710 Nebraska St., Amarillo, TX 79106; International Colmean Collector's Network, 3404 West 450 North Rochester, IN 46975-8370; Night Light, 38619 Wakefiled Ct., Northville, MI 48167; Rushlight Club, Inc., Suite 196, 1657 The Fairway, Jenkintown, PA 19046.

SPECIAL AUCTIONS

Green Valley Auctions, Inc.
Rte. 2, Box 434
Mt. Crawford, VA 22841
(540) 434-4260

James D. Julia, Inc.
P.O. Box 830
Fairfield, ME 04937
(207) 453-7125

Museums: Kerosene Lamp Museum, Winchester Center, CT; Pairpoint Lamp Museum, River Edge, NJ.

Astral

11" h, socket, marble base, two tone gilding, mkd "Cornelius & Co., Philda," drilled and fitted as electric table lamp, pr 200.00

13" h, molded opalescent stem, brass font labeled "Patented by J. G. Webb, NY, Oct 14, 1851," marble base, font altered and collar replaced 200.00

13-1/2" h, molded cranberry stem, brass font labeled "Patented by J. G. Webb, NY, Oct 14, 1851," marble and brass base, font altered and collar added, rings for prism and globe, top of glass insert chipped 225.00

16" h, gilded stem with resist floral dec, stepped marble base, font labeled "Cornelius & Baker, Philadelphia," mismatched parts, drilled and fitted as electric table lamp 60.00

17" h, brass fluted columnar stem, Corinthian capital, ornate scroll base, marble base, font mkd "Cornelius & Co., Philad," labeled "Patent April 1st 1843," drilled and fitted as table lamp 165.00

21" h, Classical, ormolu and etched glass, mid 19th C. . 690.00

25-1/2" h, ormolu and etched glass, elaborate, electrified 1,150.00

26" h, gilt brass, wheel-cut and acid finished foliate and swag dec shade, Corinthian column standard on C-scroll and foliate dec sq base, Cornelius & Co., Philadelphia, dated April 1, 1843 . . . . .1,035.00

27-1/4" h, banquet, frosted cut to clear shade, late font, brass and marble base. 400.00

Boudoir

Classique, 14" h, 8" d, reverse painted shade with landscape along river bank, sgd and numbered bronzed metal base, orig patina 900.00

Moe Bridges, 18" h, 8" d reverse painted shade, landscape dec, bronzed metal base, orig patina, mkd 900.00

Pairpoint
  13-1/2" h, 8-1/2" d reverse painted shade, Art Deco orange flowers with green centers, ivory ground, green leaves, black stems, nickel plated bronzed metal base, imp mark, shade sgd 950.00
  14-1/2" h, 9-1/2" d obverse painted shade, butterflies, multi-colored trees, and flowers, frosted ground, bronzed metal base, orig patina, mkd 50.00

Ceiling

Pittsburgh Glass Co., 10" d amber glass globe with etched crackle surface, painted blue parrot motif repeated on obverse, 16" d round flush-mount bronzed metal ceiling fixture, four figural wol heads applied to edge surface. 1,150.00

Chandelier

Brass
  20" h, 23" d, six candle arms, made for electric candles, wiring removed, early 20th C 715.00
  21" h, six candle arms, large circular center, 20th C, needs re-wiring 550.00

Gilt-Metal, 20" h, six light, foliate dec, half globe crosshatched tier with press-cut glass, Empire-style, 20th C 1,035.00

Painted maple, brass, and iron, 12-1/2" h, 22-1/2" d, five-light, turned maple shaft with scribe line dec, brass candle holders and cups, wear to red paint, cracks, America, late 19th C 2,185.00

Regency, 41" h, 22-1/2" w, cut glass and gilt bronze, eight-light, orig shades, c1810-20 . . . . .11,500.00

Desk

Emerlite, 50" h, 4-1/2" x 9 x 5" green cased glass shade, tag on inside of shade bracket 275.00

Tiffany Studios, 15" h, 7" d gold Favrile glass shade, bright gold and rose irid, three-arm bronze base, orig patina, shade mkd "L. C. T. Favrile," base mkd "Tiffany Studios, N.Y., #322" 5,000.00

Early American

Grease, hanging, 28-1/4" h, wrought iron, sq pan, one corner partitioned, twisted post, ratchet trammel. 315.00

Loom Light, 23" h, wrought iron, adjustable betty lamp and candle socket on rod with ring top finial, round base with punched brass washer trim, three feet, wire link wick pick . . .1,100.00

Rush Light Holder, 7-1/4" h, wrought iron, three feet, twisted detail. 385.00

Floor

Arts & Crafts style, 63" h, 20" d domed shade, central woven design, ribbed base, wicker, natural finish, relined. . . .1,100.00

Empire Style, 73-1/2" h, carved wood, griffin base, old ebonized finish, gold trim, black and gold velvet brocade fringed shade, wear and damage to shade 450.00

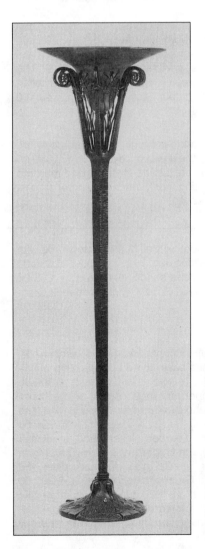

Floor, Torchiere, Art Nouveau, wrought iron, 19" d mottled orange glass inverted bell shaped shade sgd "Daum Nancy," alternating stylized flowers and scrolling projections support shade, tapering hexagonal standard, bronze spreading circular base, c1930, 66" h, $9,000.

Gurschner, Gustave, 40-1/4" h, bronze, amorous couple in embrace, bowl-lie globe shade with colored glass circles in copper foil, bronze top rim, sgd 1,870.00
Handel
  55-1/2" h bronze frame, unsigned 10" d Steuben brown aurene with platinum border shade, base mkd "Handel," worn gilding. 3,300.00
  57" h, 10" d brown chipped ice shade, bronzed metal harp, recent patina, shade and base sgd 2,300.00
  58" h bronze frame, old patina, 10" d, Steuben green shade, platinum irid rim, band of green and white, minor chips on top edge of unmarked shade 3,150.00
  58" h bronze frame, old patina, 10" d gold irid Tiffany-style shade cased white, minor chips to metal ring on shade
  . . . . .3,795.00

Fluid

9-1/8" h, purple cut to clear font, brass collar and fluted stem, marble base 375.00
10" h, white cut to cranberry font and stem insert, brass fittings and collar, black ceramic base. 565.00
10-1/4" h, white cut to cranberry overlay font, brass connector and collar, opaque white base, minor chips to base . 350.00
11-5/8" h, opaque blue font, clambroth base, lightly sanded, Acanthus, chips and bruise on edge of font, replaced brass collar. 395.00
12-1/4" h, clear pressed font with cut panels and engraved floral band, brass collar and stem, stepped marble base with brass trim 125.00
13-1/4" h, blue cut to white to clear font, brass connector and collar, fluted column on opaque white base 935.00
15" h, cobalt blue cut to clear font, brass plated figural stem and font fittings, black stone base, Victorian. 500.00
20-3/4" h, banquet, emerald green cut to clear font, brass collar, ornate gilded brass stem, marble base 400.00

Hall

12" h, polished and lacquered brass frame, red swirled cylindrical insert, no burner, orig chain and pulleys. 350.00
12" h, Duffner & Kimberly, 12" h, leaded glass, closed teardrop form, stylized floral repeating motif, deep red-amber scrolls, single socket mount, large cap. 825.00

Student

20-1/4" h, brass, adjustable font with oil burner, tole shade with orig red paint, stenciled gilded dec. 2,550.00
21-1/4" h, brass, old opaque white shade, electrified . . . 275.00
23-1/2" h, brass, two green cased 6" h x 7" w glass shades, Manhattan Brass Co.. . . . . 350.00

Table

Arts & Crafts Style, 28" h, 20" d, copper and mica conical shade, hammered copper bulbous base, three sockets, orig patina and mica. 1,300.00
Benedict, 32" h, 20" d, copper and mica conical shade, hammered copper tapered and banded base, orig patina and mica 3,250.00
Bigelow Kennard, 23" h, 18" d leaded glass shade, sunflower blossom configuration, green lappet motif above petal-form border, deep gold amber "granite" glass, bronze spider and socket, green matte glaze Grueby pottery base. . . .9,200.00
Duffner & Kimberly, 22-1/2" h, 19-1/2" d leaded glass mosaic shade, gold leading, multicolored domed shade, six repeating red-orange shell forms space by green scrolls and sky

blue glass segments, yellow-amber shield reserves, Duffner gilt bronze four-socket base, bowed tripartite shaft, elaborate paw feet 13,800.00
Erp, Dirk van
  20" h, 17" d, hammered copper and mica four panel shade, supported by four socket trumpet base, recent mica and patina 4,500.00
  22" h, 19" d hammered copper and mice four panel shade, four light base, imp marks, recent patina, replaced mica
  . . . . .8,500.00
Figural, 18" l, 22-1/2" h, cast metal, "Soldat Spartiate," old worn polychrome paint, soldier's outstretched arm holds replaced light socket with yellow glass flower segment shade
. . . . 325.00
Handel
  20-1/2" h, 14" d domed shade, Teroma textured glass reverse painted mountainous scene with leafy trees in foreground, mkd "Handel 7147," copper-colored two-socket base with "Handel" label on felt, some wear to metal patina, needs rewiring 4,025.00
  21-1/2" h, 16" d domed shade, Wild Rose, Teroma textured glass reverse painted, soft pastel pink, blue, yellow, and green, realistic rose blossoms, buds, and leafy stems, lower edge inscribed "Handel 6422," three-socket ribbed base with cast "Handel" mark, some metal patina wear
  . . . . .6,900.00
  22" h, 17" d amber slag glass shade with bent panels framed with metal overlay to depict flowers painted yellow, three-socket bronzed base with Teroma-style texture, molded Handel mark, minor damage to metal overlay .3,335.00
  22-1/2" h, 12-1/2" d obverse painted flared Tam o'Shanter shade, tall leafy and evergreen trees, pale yellow and sunset pink textured ground, rim sgd "Handel 2967," minor nicks, spider ring base with brass and white columnar base
  . . . . .1,150.00
  23-1/2" h, 18" d reverse painted conical shade, textured Teroma ext., inside hp with yellow and yellow-orange daffodils among green spiked leaves, inscribed "Handel 5851," stamped "U.S. patent 879664" at lower edge, oversized bronze three-socket base with organic form, damage to platform base. 10,350.00
  24" h, 20" w x 14" d trapezoidal leaded shade, caramel, green, and red, four socket bronzed base with strong Prairie School elements, orig patina, base sgd. 16,000.00
  24-3/4" h, 16-3/4" d new copper foil shade with pink and green flowers, bronze stick base mkd "Handel". . .1,540.00
  28" h, 24" d octagonal shade, red and green sunset slag glass, decorative cast metal overlay trees dec, simple green enameled dec on glass, bronze base with verdigris finish mkd "Handel," unmarked shade with several damaged panels 2,860.00
Jefferson
  21-1/2" d, 16" d domed glass shade, pebbled surface, hp on int. with riverside scene, including fence and red-roofed buildings, lower edge numbered "2365," mounted on cast metal two-socket ribbed base inscribed "Jefferson" at lower edge. 1,650.00
  21-1/2" d, 16" d domed glass shade, pebbled surface, reverse painted with three repeating border elements of purple iris blossoms, buds, and stylized leaf forms, deep orange-amber ground, two-socket ribbed cast metal baluster base, shade rim and base imp "Jefferson" 920.00
  22" h, 18" d conical reverse painted shade, yellow, green, and brown landscape, scene of trees surrounding body of water, bulbous green textured glass base, worn orig patina, shade sgd, minor chips to base under fittings 1,800.00

23" h, 18" d reverse painted shade, multicolored landscape, bronzed metal base, orig patina 2,200.00

Moe Bridges, 23" h, 17" d, heavy walled domed shade with pebbled surface, reverse painted colorful riverside scene, sheep under tall leafy trees, mkd "Moe Bridges Milwaukee, San Fran," two-socket metal vasiform lamp base, painted copper color with green accents .1,100.00

Pairpoint, 20-1/4" h, 15" d Exeter reverse painted flared shade, two urn and griffin mounts space by floral reserves, two-socket baluster form base, imp "Pairpoint" and numbered, two small rim chips 1,200.00

Pittsburgh, 18-1/2" h, 14" d conical shade, reverse painted with winter scene of evergreens, snowy landscape, orange-purple sky, obverse accented with snow-capped dark trees, single-socket cast metal foliate base 1,100.00

Tiffany

18-1/4" h, 12" d Damascene green and gold shade, cased in white, mkd "favrile," bronze base with verdigris finish, mkd "Tiffany Studios New York," crack in top edge of shade 2,860.00

Unknown American Maker, 18" h, 14" d leaded glass shade, 4-1/4" d top opening, golden-yellow, opal, and amber mosaic glass daffodil blossoms, green spiked leaves and stems, bronzed leading and rounded rim, three-arm spider above brass and bronze converted fluid lamp base 14,950.00

Wilkinson, Brooklyn, NY, 24" h, 20" d leaded glass shade, broad border band of poppy blossoms and pods, amber slag glass brickwork dome, three-socket ribbed bronze base, cushion ftd library-style 4,025.00

LANTERNS

History: A lantern is an enclosed, portable light source, hand carried or attached to a bracket or pole to illuminate an area. Many lanterns have a protected flame and can be used both indoors and outdoors. Light-producing materials used in early lanterns included candles, kerosene, whale oil, and coal oil, and, later, gasoline, natural gas, and batteries.

References: *Collectible Lanterns*, L-W Book Sales, 1997; Anthony Hobson, *Lanterns That Lit Our World*, Hiram Press, reprinted 1996; Neil S. Wood, *Collectible Dietz Lanterns*, L-W Book Sales, 1996.

Collectors' Club: Coleman Collectors Network, 1822 E Fernwood, Wichita, KS 67216.

Barn, 11 1/2" h, wood, pine, worn red finish, hinged door, wire bail handle, age cracks, top board cracked 440.00

Bicycle, 7 3/4" h, Majestic model, nickel plated, clear lens, faceted red and green side lights, c1900 . . . . 175.00

Buggy, 9" h, E T Wright & Co., orig black paint, late 19th C 85.00

Candle, 10" h, tin, candle, pierced and tooled pyramid top, traces of brown japanning, ring handle 110.00

Dashboard, 15" h, spring clips, reflector, orig red paint, sgd brass label, Kemp Mfg. Co., c1900 . . . . 165.00

Inspector's, globe marked "New York Central System" and logo, pressed mark on back "Ideal Inspector Lamp," Dietz, late 19th C. 75.00

Miner, 8" h, wrought iron, chicken finial, wick pick 250.00

Navy, brass, Dietz, marked "US Navy" 75.00

Paul Revere Type, 13" h, punched tin, dented, ring handle 140.00

Table lamp, Tiffany, banded dogwood, mottled blue leaded glass, orig base, sgd, 16" h, $13,200. Photo courtesy of James D. Julia Auctions, Inc.

Pocket, 5 3/4" h, folding, black and gold lithograph f man seated on train, ruby glass panel, c1870 . . . . 200.00

Post, 26" h, tin, orig glass globe, orig brass burner, marked "Dietz Tubular Globe #3," old worn green paint, light rust 220.00

Railroad, 11 1/8" h, NL Piper Railway Supply Co. Ltd., bull's eye front lens, orig red and green side glass, corrugated reflector lined door, Simplex burner 200.00

Rayo, No. 60 CB 90.00

Skater's, 7" h, brass, bail, kerosene burner, clear globe. 145.00

Tin

12 1/2" h, clear blown globe, pierced air vents in diamond design, five and six point stars, removable front, whale oil burner, mismatched parts, wire guard missing, ring handle 215.00

14-3/4" h, pierced tin and blown colorless glass, star and diamond design on tin, base separates for removable font, 19th C 1,955.00

Wall, Prairie School

8" l, 5" sq, zinc and slag glass, alternating bands of cream and yellow glass, orig dark patina on metal, price for pr 400.00

9 1/2" h, 6" sq, four sided brass and leaded glass, yellow, opalescent and frosted glass, orig gas fittings, price for pr 650.00

LEEDS CHINA

History: The Leeds Pottery in Yorkshire, England, began production about 1758. Among its products was creamware that

was competitive with that of Wedgwood. The original factory closed in 1820, but various subsequent owners continued until 1880. They made exceptional cream-colored wares, either plain, salt glazed, or painted with colored enamels, and glazed and unglazed redware.

Marks: Early wares are unmarked. Later pieces are marked "Leeds Pottery," sometimes followed by "Hartley-Green and Co." or the letters "LP."

REPRODUCTION ALERT

Reproductions have the same marks as the antique pieces.

Bough Pot, 9" l, D-shaped, silver resist luster fruiting vine dec within arched panels, pierced cov, c1815 . . . . 750.00
Charger, 15-1/2" d, five color urn, floral spray, blue feathered edge 450.00
Chestnut Bowl, cov, reticulated band, twisted rope handles, c1790 . . . . 775.00
Creamer, 3-3/8" h, brown, yellow dec 145.00
Cup and Saucer, five color, floral and cross hatched dec 125.00
Jug, 4-1/2" h, baluster, transfer print, underglaze blue, iron-red, yellow, green, and brown enameled scene of hunter and two hounds, silver resist border, blue floral garland, c1815 . . . . 295.00
Pitcher, 8-1/2" h, pearlware, ovoid body, painted spout and strap handle, blue hp three-leaf sprig, surrounded by small stylized flowers and leaf sprigs, early 19th C 900.00
Plate
    7" d, spatterware, peafowl and green dec, green border, early 19th C 1,650.00
    8" d, earthenware, molded shell edge, green glazed rim, center dec of stylized American eagle crest, early 19th C 650.00
    9 5/8" d, cream, blue edge, some damage and variation to sizes, price for five pc set. 150.00
Potpourri, cov, 4-5/8" h, basket form, pierced cover, silver resist leaf and berry dec. 275.00
Sauce Tureen, cov, underplate, basketweave, green edges, floral finial, early 19th C, one handle repaired 450.00

Teapot, blue and white leafy dec, imp "L. Wood" in bottom, c1820, 7-1/2" h, 11" w, $425.

Snuff Box, cov, 2 3/4" d, waisted cylinder, iron-red, puce, yellow, and green painted floral sprays, floral wreath, inscribed "When This You See, Remember Me, W. G. 1779," and "A Pinch of This Deserv's A Kiss" 595.00
Tea Caddy, cov, 5-1/4" h, pearlware, deep rect body, short block feet, low domed cov with center loop handle, hp, bouquet of stylized green, dark, brown and yellow ochre flowers, thin band edge trim, chips, minor edge wear 1,200.00

LEFTON CHINA

History: China, porcelain, and ceramic with that now familiar "Lefton" mark has been around since the early 1940s and is highly sought by collectors in the secondary marketplace today. The company was founded by George Zoltan Lefton, a Hungarian immigrant who arrived in the United States in 1939. In the 1930s, he was a sportswear designer and manufacturer, but his hobby of collecting fine china and porcelain led him to a new business venture.

After the bombing of Pearl Harbor in 1941, Mr. Lefton aided a Japanese-American friend by helping him to protect his property from anti-Japanese groups. As a result, Lefton came in contact with and began marketing pieces from a Japanese factory owned by Kowa Toki KK. At this time he embarked on a new career and began shaping a business that sprang from his passion for collecting fine china and porcelains. Though his fund were very limited, his vision was to develop a source from which to obtain fine porcelains by reviving the postwar Japanese ceramic industry, which dated back to antiquity. As a trailblazer, George Zoltan Lefton soon earned the reputation of "The China King."

Figurines and animals, plus many of the whimsical pieces such as the Bluebirds, Dainty Miss, Miss Priss, Angels, Cabbage Cutie, Elf Head, Mr. Toodles, and the Dutch Girl, are popular with collectors. All types of dinnerware and tea-related items are eagerly acquired by collectors. As is true with any antique or collectibles, prices vary, depending on location, condition, and availability.

Marks: Until 1980, wares from the Japanese factory include a "KW."

Reference: Loretta DeLozier, *Collector's Encyclopedia of Lefton China*, Vol. 1 (1995), Vol. 2 (1997), Collector Books; *1998 Lefton Price Guide.*

Collectors' Club: National Society of Lefton Collectors, 1101 Polk St., Bedford, IA 50833.

Advisor: Loretta DeLozier.

Animal
    4" h, camel, Bethlehem Collection, #05381 . . . . 35.00
    5" h, spaniel, #80521 . . . . 50.00
    7" h, cat, luster, stones, #871 . . . . 35.00
Baby Set, bowl and mug, Bluebirds, #435 . . . . 80.00
Bank, 7-3/4", kangaroo with baby, #2778 . . . . 25.00
Beer Mug, 5" h, Paul Bunyan, #609 . . . . 28.00
Bird
    5-1/2" h, bobwhite, #300. . . . . 40.00
    6-3/4" h, bird of paradise. #140 . . . . 85.00
    7" h, seagull. #02715 . . . . 60.00
    7-1/2" h, owl and waxwing. #8018 . . . . 250.00
    12" h, pheasant, closed wings, #210 . . . . 200.00

Box, cov, 5" d, round, Flower Garden, #2152 . . . . 80.00
Butter Dish, Mr. Toodles, #3294 . . . . 95.00
Candleholders, pr, Vineyard line, #3035 . . . . 30.00
Candy Box, 9", Santa in rocker, #7923 . . . . 65.00
Canister Set, 4 pieces
 Americana, #946 . . . . 215.00
 Blue Plum, #4981 . . . . 125.00
Cheese Dish, cov, Honey Bee, #1285 . . . . 55.00
Cigarette Set, 4 pieces, Violets with stones, #4557 . . . . . 65.00
Coffee Pot, cov
 Gingham, #3265 . . . . 80.00
 Green Heritage, #3065 . . . . 165.00
 Magnolia, #2518 . . . . 175.00
 Rose Garden, 8-1/2" h, #6570 . . . . 110.00
Cookie Jar, 10-1/4" h, Honey Bear, #7439 . . . . 85.00
Creamer and Sugar
 Bossie the Cow, #6512 . . . . 35.00
 Dutch Girl, #2698 . . . . 85.00
 Festival, #2615 . . . . 65.00
 Heavenly Rose, #2689 . . . . 65.00
 Magnolia, #2520 . . . . 65.00
Cup and Saucer
 Americana, #963 . . . . 38.00
 Magnolia, #2523 . . . . 35.00
Dish
 6" l, leaf, sponge gold and raised pink roses, #961 . . . 60.00
 7" l, butter, Sweet Violets. #2854 . . . . 28.00
Eggcup, Bluebirds, #286 . . . . 60.00
Egg Tray, 12-1/2" d, Country Squire, #1601 . . . . 35.00
Figure
 8" h, Don Quixote and Sancho Panza, #4721 . . . . . . 120.00
 10-1/2" h, Colonial man and woman, pr, #2256 . . . . 350.00
 11" h, Napoleon on horse, #4908 . . . . 285.00
Jam Jar
 Fruit, teapot-shape, #6973 . . . . 35.00
 Grapes, 5", #4852 . . . . 30.00
 Miss Priss, #1515 . . . . 105.00
Mug, Winter Holly, #6066 . . . . 12.00
Nappy, 8" sq, Roses, #2874 . . . . 35.00

Teapot, #2032, Dresden-type, violets dec, gold trim, 7-1/2" h, $215. Photo courtesy of Loretta DeLozier.

Pin Box, 2-1/4" d, pink, rhinestones, #90254 . . . . 35.00
Planter
 5", bucket, Mardi Gras, #50442 . . . . 45.00
 9", cherub holding urn, antique ivory, #193 . . . . 48.00
Plate
 7-1/2" d, Fruit, latticed, #711 . . . . 35.00
 8" d, Elegant Rose, #2854 . . . . 28.00
 8" d, Moss Rose, #3169 . . . . 20.00
 10-1/2" d, Americana, #963 . . . . 40.00
Religious, 5", Sacred Heart of Jesus, #479 . . . . 32.00
Salt and Pepper Shakers, pr
 Chicks with hats, #4926 . . . . 12.00
 Fruit, jug-shape, #4418 . . . . 12.00
Sleigh, 8" l, Green Holly, #1346 . . . . 50.00
Snack Set
 Elegant Rose, #2124 . . . . 35.00
 Magnolia, #2599 . . . . 25.00
 Rose Heirloom, #1376 . . . . 32.00
 To A Wild Rose, #2580 . . . . 25.00
 White with violets. #20054 . . . . 28.00
Swan, 3-1/2" h, pink, lily of the valley, #194 . . . . 18.00
Teapot, cov
 Fleur De Lis, #1799 . . . . 70.00
 Miss Priss, #1516 . . . . 155.00
 Poinsettia, #4388 . . . . 175.00
 Violets, Dresden-shape, #2439 . . . . 215.00
Tray, 2 tier
 Green Heritage, #1153 . . . . 85.00
 Green Holly, #1364 . . . . 70.00
Vase
 4" h, Italian Romance, beige, #781 . . . . 18.00
 5" h, lyre, white china, #955 . . . . 85.00
 6-1/4" h, fan, milk china, #840 . . . . 85.00
 6-1/2" h, tree trunk with child, #840, pr 180.00
Wall Plaque, 8"
 Fruit, #094 . . . . 20.00
 Fruit, latticed edges, #6350 . . . . 25.00

LENOX CHINA

History: In 1889, Jonathan Cox and Walter Scott Lenox established The Ceramic Art Co. at Trenton, New Jersey. By 1906, Lenox formed his own company, Lenox, Inc. Using potters lured from Belleek, Lenox began making an

Figures, #3058, Colonial Couple, 10" h, pr, $200. Photo courtesy of Loretta DeLozier.

American version of the famous Irish ware. The firm is still in business.

Marks: Older Lenox china has one of two marks: a green wreath or a palette. The palette mark appears on blanks supplied to amateurs who hand painted china as a hobby. The Lenox company currently uses a gold stamped mark.

References: Susan and Al Bagdade, *Warman's American Pottery and Porcelain*, Wallace-Homestead, 1994; Richard E. Morin, *Lenox Collectibles*, Sixty-Ninth Street Zoo, 1993.

Additional Listings: Belleek.

Bon Bon, Shell
   Brushed gold rim, blue mark 100.00
   Small sawtooth edge, green mark 45.00
Bouillon Cup and Saucer, Detroit Yacht Club, palette mark
   . . . . 565.00
Bowl, 2 handles, etched told trim, pre1930 . . . . 45.00
Box, cov, 3-3/4" x 4-3/4", spray of flowers, green wreath mark
   . . . . 50.00
Cake Set, Mimosa pattern, 10-1/2" d low pedestal plate, six 7-1/2" d plates, green wreath mark, 7 pc set 225.00
Compote, 2" h, 5" d, brown rim, white ground, hp black insignia, pre-1930 . . . . 40.00
Creamer and Sugar, Wheat pattern 45.00
Cup and Saucer, Kingsley pattern, X445 . . . . 30.00
Decanter Set, ivory, gold trim, green wreath mark, price for decanter and five shot glasses 125.00
Demitasse Cup and Saucer, made for Tiffany 18.00
Dinner Service, 48 pcs, gilt fruit, floral and basket dec, ivory and mint ground, service for 12 of bread plates, cream soup cups, dessert plates, and dinner plates, retailed by Ovington, New York City 500.00
Mug, cobalt blue, sterling silver overlay bands 75.00
Pitcher, Cottage pattern 75.00
Place Setting, 5 pc, Autumn pattern 100.00
Plate, Kingsley pattern, X445
   Bread and butter 15.00
   Dinner 30.00
   Salad 20.00
Plate, Lenox Rose pattern
   Bread and butter 12.00

Swan, salt, light coral body, green mark, 3" l, 2" h, $30., 7-1/2" h, 11" w, $425.

   Dinner 25.00
   Salad 18.00
Platter
   13" l, Lenox Rose pattern 75.00
   16" l, Kingsley pattern, X445 . . . . 95.00
Salt, palette mark 15.00
Swan
   4-1/2" h, green mark 45.00
   5" h, green mark 32.00
Teapot, 4-1/4" h, individual, salmon color, metal lid and handle, made for Waldorf Astoria, 1931 . . . . 125.00
Toby, William Penn, 7-1/2" h, yellow, green mark 300.00
Vase
   7" l, basket form, round loop center handle, silver bands down center and around rims, c1930 . . . . 120.00
   9-3/4" h, cylindrical, rounded shoulder, short rolled neck, cobalt blue ground, silver overlay, small pierced scrolls
   . . . . 650.00

LIBBEY GLASS

History: Edward Libbey established the Libbey Glass Company in Toledo, Ohio, in 1888 after the New England Glass Works of W. L. Libbey and Son closed in East Cambridge, Massachusetts. The new Libbey company produced quality cut glass which today is considered to belong to the brilliant period.

In 1930, Libbey's interest in art-glass production was renewed, and A. Douglas Nash was employed as a designer in 1931.

The factory continues production today as Libbey Glass Co.

References: Bob Page and Dale Frederickson, *Collection of American Crystal*, Page-Frederickson Publishing, 1995; Kenneth Wilson, *American Glass 1760-1930*, 2 Vols., Hudson Hills Press and The Toledo Museum of Art, 1994.

Additional Listings: Amberina Glass; Cut Glass.

Basket, 18 1/2" h, cut, pressed, and engraved floral and geometric dec, notched rim, star-cut base stamped "Libbey" in circle
   . . . . 520.00
Bon Bon, 7" d, 1 1/2" h, amberina, shape #3029, six pointed 1 1/2" fuchsia rim, shallow pale amber bowl, sgd 595.00
Bowl, 7" d, amberina, ruffled, flared rim, sgd 350.00
Butter, cov, Maize, blue husks, custard ground 475.00
Celery Vase, Maize, colorless, amber irid kernels, blue husks
   . . . . 170.00
Champagne, Silhouette pattern, colorless bowl, figural squirrel stem 165.00
Claret, Silhouette pattern, colorless bowl, opalescent figural bear stem 200.00
Compote
   8" w, 6 1/4" h, rolled edge, flower engraving on bowl, twisted hollow oval stem, sgd 150.00
   10 1/2" d, 4" h, clear crystal bowl with pink Nailsea type loops, flaring top, sgd 595.00
   11" d, white opalescent elephant stem, sgd 975.00
Console Set, green and white pulled feather, sgd 825.00
Cruet, Maize pattern, milk glass, painted yellow leaves, orig stopper 875.00
Goblet, Silhouette pattern, colorless bowl, opalescent figural cat stem 170.00

Hair Receiver, cov, 4 1/2" w, 2" h, two pc, amberina, deep fuchsia shading to amber, partial label 1,750.00
Pitcher, 5 1/2" h, ribbed opal body, combed pink striping, applied
cased glass handle, peppermint pink stripe, colorless foot
stamped "Libbey" in circular mark 345.00
Punch Bowl, 16-1/4" x 14-1/2", cut glass, sgd "Libbey"
. . . . .3,500.00
Rose Bowl, 3-1/2" w, 2-1/2" d, melon-ribbed bowl, beige ground,
two pansies and leaves, white beading, sgd "Libbey"
. . . . 550.00
Salt and Pepper Shakers, pr, Maize, small size 75.00
Serving Dish, 12" x 7-1/2", cut glass, ABP, sgd 500.00
Sherbet, Silhouette pattern, colorless bowl
Opalescent figural rabbit stem 75.00
Opalescent figural squirrel stem. 110.00
Sugar Shaker, Maize, creamy opaque, yellow husks, gold trim,
orig top 245.00
Vase, 14" h, Talisman, optic ribbed flared oval, colorless glass
with spiraled green internal thread, applied colorless foot,
base mkd "Libbey" 250.00

LIMOGES

History: Limoges porcelain has been produced in Limoges, France, for over a century by numerous factories in
addition to the famed Haviland.

Marks: One of the most frequently encountered marks is
"T. & V. Limoges," which is on the wares made by Tress-
man and Vought. Other identifiable Limoges marks are
"A. L." (A. Lanternier), "J. P. L." (J. Pouyat, Limoges), "M.
R." (M. Reddon), "Elite," and "Coronet."

References: Susan and Al Bagdade, *Warman's English
& Continental Pottery & Porcelain*, 3rd Edition, Krause
Publications, 1998; Mary Frank Gaston, *Collector's Encyclopedia of Limoges Porcelain*, 2nd ed., Collector Books,
1992, 1998 value update.

Additional Listings: Haviland China.

Bowl, Charles Ahrensteld, large 75.00
Box, cov, green ground, floral dec, crown mark 225.00
Charger, 16" d, still life fruit, gold rococo rim, sgd "Duval"
. . . . 350.00
Cracker Jar, cov, ivory ground, flowers, green and gold trim, TV
mark 250.00
Cuspidor, hp, cottage and boat in background, 1890s . . 175.00
Ice Cream Tray 125.00
Oyster Plate, indentations for oysters outlined in gold, small pink
flowers dec, mkd "GDA France". 150.00
Plate
8-1/4" d, hp, blackberries, gold border and dec, sgd, c1900
. . . . 125.00
8-1/4" d, hp, cherries, gold border and dec, sgd, c1900
. . . . 125.00
9-1/2" d, hp, Cupid's Sail with Cupid, playing lyre, leading lovers across water, Flora's Triumph with woman crowned by
putto and attendants; Harvest with scene of women lying in
wheat field; Spell with scene of putto eating berries; all with
scrolling gilt borders, sgd "Soustre," retailed by Tiffany Co.,
New York, set of 4 . . . . 400.00
10" d, scenic, hp, boats, day scene, Flambeau China
. . . . 165.00
Pot De Creme, set of eight, matching lids and tray, polychrome
transfer of birds and flowers, gilt trim, mkd "Limoges France"
. . . . 325.00

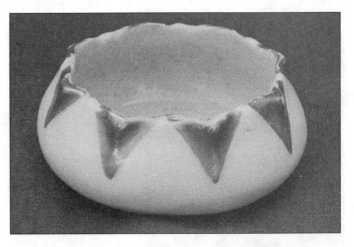

**Salt, individual, white ext., green int., scalloped
edge, gold trim, mkd "D. & C. France," 1-5/8" x
1-3/4", $15.**

Powder Box, cov
Courting couple on lid, dark pink bowl, small Elite mark
. . . . 200.00
Hand painted, sgd by two artists, early 1900s 110.00
Tankard Set, 13-1/2" h tankard with figural female handle, six
mugs, all dec with red poppies and daisies, each sgd "Os-
borne". 2,600.00
Vase
12" h, 9" w, bulbous body, small neck opening with brass rim,
floral arrangement on front and back, raised white daisies
with yellow centers, shaded coral poppies with mauve centers, mauve and blue shaded poppies with dark purple centers, pink shaded with white poppies with yellow and black
centers, yellow daisies with orange centers, light and dark
shaded foliage, flowers on silver-foil backed mottled background of mauve, emerald green, light and deep turquoise,
and pink, copper base, sgd in gold "Faure, Limoges,
France," c1930. . . . . .7,800.00
13-1/2" h, hp scene of Victorian woman smelling pink rose,
overlooking pond, artist sgd "K. Ryboe". 525.00
16-1/4" h, 5" d, cylindrical, gilded peacocks and moths, black
ground, mkd "Limoges France" 350.00

LITHOPHANES

History: Lithophanes are highly translucent porcelain
panels with impressed designs. The designs result from
differences in the thickness of the plaque; thin parts
transmit an abundance of light while thicker parts represent shadows.

Lithophanes were first made by the Royal Berlin Porcelain Works in 1828. Other factories in Germany,
France, and England later produced them. The majority
of lithophanes on the market today were made between
1850 and 1900.

Collectors' Club: Lithophane Collectors Club, 2030
Robinwood Ave., P.O. Box 4557, Toledo, OH 43620.

Museum: Blair Museum of Lithophanes and Carved
Waxes, Toledo, OH.

Candle Shield, 9" h, bronze collar, rococo frame, two country
boys, goat and castle in background 265.00

Plaque, windmill and ship, imp "KPM/36S," c1860, 5-3/8" x 3-7/8", $190.

Cup and Saucer, nude lady, moriage and dragon dec . . . 60.00
Fairy Lamp, lady leaning from tower window, two panels, rural romantic scene 1,400.00
Lamp, 23-1/2" h, double student type, four scenes, brass base, mkd "Germany" 1,950.00
Lamp Shade, 10" d, 5-1/4" h, five panels, childhood scenes, emb brass frame, mkd "PPM" 650.00
Panel
   4-1/2" x 5", PR Sickle, cupid and girl fishing 220.00
   6-1/2" x 8", PPM, elderly lady teaching girl to knit, lead mounted edge 195.00
   8" x 16", KK, General Zachary Taylor, holding telescope in left arm, men fighting battle in background, wreath, eagle, and two flags, leaded frame, ruby flashed 750.00
Stein, half liter, dancing couple 115.00
Tea Set, cov teapot, creamer, cov sugar, six cups and saucers, romantic scenes 175.00
Tea Warmer, 6" x 6", four panels, scenic, pierced top, metal frame, molded ftd base, Germany 195.00

LIVERPOOL CHINA

History: Liverpool is the name given to products made at several potteries in Liverpool, England, between 1750 and 1840. Seth and James Pennington and Richard Chaffers were among the early potters who made tin-enameled earthenware.

By the 1780s, tin-glazed earthenware gave way to cream-colored wares decorated with cobalt blue, enameled colors, and blue or black transfers.

The Liverpool glaze is characterized by bubbles and frequent clouding under the foot rims. By 1800, about 80 potteries were working in the town producing not only creamware, but soft paste, soapstone, and bone porcelain.

References: Susan and Al Bagdade, *Warman's English & Continental Pottery & Porcelain*, 3rd Edition, Krause Publications, 1998; Robert McCauley, *Liverpool Transfer*

Designs on Anglo-American Pottery, Southworth-Anthoensen Press; Bernard M. Watney, *Liverpool Porcelain of the Eighteenth Century*, Antique Collectors' Club, Ltd., 1997.

Museums: City of Liverpool Museum, Liverpool, England; Henry Ford Museum, Dearborn, MI; Potsdam Public Museum, Potsdam, NY.

REPRODUCTION ALERT

Reproduction Liverpool pieces were documented as early as 1942. One example is a black transfer-decorated jug which was made in the 1930s. The jugs vary in height from 8-1/2 to 11 inches. On one side is "The Shipwright's Arms"; on the other, the ship Caroline flying the American flag; and under the spout, a wreath with the words "James Leech."

A transfer of the *Caroline* also was used on a Sunderland bowl about 1936 and reproduction mugs were made bearing the name "James Leech" and an eagle. The reproduction pieces have a crackled glaze and often age cracks have been artificially produced. When compared to genuine pieces, reproductions are thicker and heavier and have weaker transfers, grayish color (not as crisp and black), ecru or gray body color instead of cream, and crazing that does not spiral upward.

Bowl, 10-1/2" d, int. painted with two men standing next to ale cask, border of blue alternating panels of trellis and half flowerheads, ext. painted blue vignettes of Chinese houses and rockery, c1754 . . . . .9,200.00
Charger, 13-3/4" d, black, iron-red, yellow, green and blue Fazackerly floral pattern, scattered flowers on rim 825.00
Cream Jug, 3-1/4" h, spiral fluted base, rocaille scrolls, iron-red, blue, turquoise, green-yellow, and black painted Chinese man beside tree, another holding stick, scalloped rim, C-scroll handle, c1776 . . . . 460.00
Cup and Saucer, handleless, Washington and Lafayette portraits on cup, bust of Washington and "Washington, His Country's Father" on saucer, black transfers, hairlines 330.00
Jug, transfer dec, early 19th C
   6-7/8" h, reverse of three-masted ship under sail, verse "Poor Jack," staining, cracks, transfer and glaze wear . . . 460.00
   8" h, reserve of masons congregating "Vertias Prevalerus," various Masonic and regalia motifs, "Holiness to the Lord, it is found," cracks, staining, minor glaze wear 450.00
   8-1/4" h, reserve of Ship Caroline, Shipwrights Arms, spread eagle with shield, "James Leech," polychrome highlights, minor spout chips, cracks, staple repair 350.00
   9-3/4" h, reserve of portrait of Washington surrounded by Justice, Liberty, and Victory, encircled by fifteen stars, names of fifteen states, reserve of Peace, Plenty, and Independence, "Phillip & Jane Gilkey" under spout, base chip, minor staining, rim roughness 1,725.00
   9-3/4" h, Proscribed Patriots of America, three-masted hip flying American flag, spread eagle with American shield, polychrome highlights, restoration, minor abrasions to transfers 1,725.00
   10-1/8" h, reserve of three-masted ship under sail, flying American flag, Masonic elements, "United for the Benefit of Mankind," spread eagle with shield, polychrome highlights,

Pitcher, American eagle on one side, poem "Oh Liberty thou Goddess" on other, border of 15 states, base chip, 8-1/4" h, $450.

shadows of gilt highlights, chips to spout, minor cracks, staining, transfer wear 1,150.00

10-1/2" h, "Washington in Glory America in Tears," reverse with transfer of Masonic elements, below spout monogram and eagle, "SOS" within Masonic reserve, staining, old repair to handle, minor hairlines 1,380.00

11-3/8" h, three Masonic reserves "United for the Benefit of Mankind," reserve of woman with three children "to judge with candor...," various Masonic elements, "EW" under spout, polychrome and gilt highlights. 1,380.00

Pitcher, transfer dec

5-1/2" h, reserve of naval battle, "Lepervier and Peacock," restoration to spout, cracks, minor rim chips, surface abrasions. 700.00

8-7/8" h, "Washington in Glory America in Tears," reverse dec with "The Macedonian & The United States," spout with spread eagle, minor rim nick and glaze wear, base chip 2,300.00

10-5/8" h, frame of ribbon bearing names of fifteen states, sgd at base "F. Morris Shelton," reverse dec with American three-masted ship under sail, spread eagle, polychrome highlights, cracks, minor chips, and staining 875.00

Plate, creamware

7-3/4" d, Nelson's Monument in Liverpool harbor, black transfer, black lined rim 165.00

10" d, Hope, woman seated under tree, sailing ship in background, bird border, black transfer, polychrome enamel accents, c1800. . . . . 175.00

Puzzle Jug, 7-1/2" h, neck pierced with outlined hearts and ellipses, body inscribed with rhyme, blue Chinese landscape, c1760 . . . . .2,185.00

LOETZ

History: Loetz is a type of iridescent art glass that was made in Austria by J. Loetz Witwe in the late 1890s. Loetz was a contemporary of L. C. Tiffany's, and he had worked in the Tiffany factory before establishing his own operation; therefore, much of the wares are similar in appearance to Tiffany products. The Loetz factory also produced items with fine cameos on cased glass.

Marks: Some pieces are signed "Loetz," "Loetz, Austria," or "Austria."

Reference: Robert and Deborah Truitt, *Collectible Bohemian Glass: 1880-1940*, R & D Glass, 1995.

Basket

10-1/2" h overall, 4-1/2" h x 7" w glass, oyster white glass, mottled medium yellow raindrop patter, four bands of pulled deep ruby brown horizontal stripes, pinched and dimpled, four pulled down edges, fancy ormolu and silver bronzed Art Nouveau holder with Japanese chrysanthemum dec 600.00

16" h, 10" w, mottled oyster white int., deep gold mottled ground, applied tall crystal loop handle with floral prunts 250.00

18-1/4" h, 11-1/2" w, medium green, purple and blue irid 200.00

Bottle, 11-3/4" h, bulbous, extended neck, everted rim, four upturned handles, rose gold irid ground, rainbow irid oil spot dec 19,800.00

Bowl

5-3/4" d, cylindrical, ruffled rim, orange int., green shading to silver ext. 600.00

9" d, 6" h, irid gold, textured crackle finish, polished pontil 250.00

13" l, 7-1/2" h, large shell form, resting on seaweed base, green ground, blue irid 1,700.00

Candlesticks, pr

9-1/2" h, slender baluster form, raised circular foot, gold irid 300.00

15-3/8" h, cobalt blue ground, annulated round tapering stem, stepped cushion foot, bell form nozzle, conical drip pan, rainbow irid oil spot dec 2,400.00

Compote

10" d, 9-1/2" h, brilliant irid green, diamond quilted raised pattern, highly irid surface, fancy Art Nouveau reticulated floral design metal holder 300.00

10-5/8" d, 5-1/4" h, bright orange int., deep black ext., white flaring circular rim, 3 ball feet, c1920 . . . . 310.00

Dish, 8-1/2" d, 2-3/4" h "M" and "L" 200.00

Garniture Set, blood red, multicolored variegated oil-spot motif, matched pr of sq 9-3/4" h vases in metal frames, rect match-

Art glass vase with silver overlay, 5", $1,870. Photo courtesy of Jackson's.

ing 4-1/2" h x 9" l x 4" d planter in ornate brass mounted frame, emb pond lily dec 1,950.00

Jack In The Pulpit Vase

10" h, Persian flask shape, dimpled bulbous body, spotted irid papillon surface dec, polished pontil 635.00

14" h, silver blue gold irid surface, floriform blossom, green body, knotty tree bark texture, polished pontil 425.00

Lamp, 22" h, 15" d glass paperweight-type shade, green and platinum designs, three arm holder supports ring of limbs and leaves, bronzed gilt base, sculpted base with ribbed neck, detailed floral dec at top, shade chip hidden by fitter ring 4,250.00

Salt, 2-3/4" d, 1" h, irid blue ground, blue and gold oil-spot motif 600.00

Town Pump and Trough, 10" h, 9" w, all over random threading, slight irid colors, applied base with pale pink-peach open flower, green leaves 400.00

Vase

4" h, dimpled and waisted base, flaring neck, gold, blue, green, and rose irid 250.00

4-1/2" h, crimped top, six lobes, oil spot dec, maroon ground, pink and platinum irid 250.00

6" h, pale green, two applied blue handles, blue disks, purple and green irid 300.00

6-1/2" h, quilted green body, applied copper collar with protruding glass balls, orig patina 550.00

8" h, pale green and glass, blue threading wrapped around neck, three applied disks at shoulder, purple and green irid 325.00

9" h, bronze mount at top and bottom of flowers and leaves, oil spot body with purple and green irid, orig patina. 750.00

LUSTER WARE

History: Lustering on a piece of pottery creates a metallic, sometimes iridescent, appearance. Josiah Wedgwood experimented with the technique in the 1790s. Between 1805 and 1840, lustered earthenware pieces were created in England by makers such as Adams, Bailey and Batkin, Copeland and Garrett, Wedgwood, and Enoch Wood.

Luster decorations often were used in conjunction with enamels and transfers. Transfers used for luster decoration covered a wide range of public and domestic subjects. They frequently were accompanied by pious or sentimental doggerel as well phrases which reflected on the humors of everyday life.

Copper luster was created by the addition of a copper compound to the glaze. It was very popular in America during the 19th century, and collecting it became a fad from the 1920s to the 1950s. Today it has a limited market.

Pink luster was made by using a gold mixture. Silver luster pieces were first covered completely with a thin coating of a "steel luster" mixture, containing a small quantity of platinum oxide. An additional coating of platinum, worked in water, was then applied before firing.

Sunderland is a coarse type of cream-colored earthenware with a marbled or spotted pink luster decoration which shades from pink to purple. A solution of gold compound applied to the white body developed the many shades of pink.

The development of electroplating in 1840 created a sharp decline in the demands for metal-surfaced earthenware.

Additional Listings: English Soft Paste.

Canary

Child's Mug, 1-3/4" h

"A Present for Charles," pink luster trim, minor wear 625.00

Bird on branch, silver luster trim, handle broken and glued 40.00

Creamer, 3-3/4" h, silver luster resist bands with floral dec, damage and repairs 125.00

Pitcher, 6-1/2" h, enameled red, green, blue and pink flowers, wear and crazing, hairline in spout. 650.00

Copper

Bowl, 5-3/4" d, yellow band with enameled raised flowers 50.00

Compote, 3-1/4" h, pedestal base, flared sides, wide blue band with copper luster house design 55.00

Creamer

3" h, copper luster trim, marbleized, chips on spout. . . 75.00

4-1/8" h, canary band with white reserves, purple transfer of woman and child in classical attire, polychrome enamel, repairs 185.00

Goblet, 3-3/4" h, blue center band with red and brown enameled flowerhead, beaded ring on stem 90.00

Hen on Nest, 10" h, 7" w, Italian 225.00

Mug, copper luster body

3-1/8" h, blue band, white polychrome cherubs and classical figures at play, scroll handle 25.00

3-1/2" h, medium blue center band, multicolored children and goat 60.00

Pitcher

3-1/2" h, blue bands, yellow berries 55.00

Silver luster, bowl, ftd., beaded rim, ribbed sides, copper luster int., 5-1/8" d, 3" h, $85

4-1/4" h, cobalt blue lower band with yellow and brown enameled scene of dog, boy, and trees 85.00

5" h, polychrome badminton scene on canary band, copper luster body, unmkd. 125.00

6-1/2" h, cream center and neck band, pink luster streaks 110.00

Salt, 2" h, pedestal base, yellow band, stylized luster leaves 65.00

Tumbler, 2-3/4" h, blue band, polychrome molded flowers 100.00

Pink

Creamer, 3-7/8" h, light blue ground, alternating molded green acanthus leaves and pink and green floral springs, molded green grapevine border band, pink luster spout, rim, and handle. 120.00

Cup and Saucer, handleless, pearlware, pink luster reserve of trees and picket fence, pink luster stripes and banded rims 20.00

Jug, 4-7/8" h, relief molded running hunting dogs, berried vine border, pink luster accents, Staffordshire, c1825. . . . 450.00

Mug, 4-3/4" h, church pattern, fencing 500.00

Pitcher, 5-1/4" h, Masonic transfers "Protestant Ascendancy, Let Brotherly Love Continue," and statue of William of Orange on horseback, polychrome dec, glaze wear to spout and handle, wear to luster 230.00

Teabowl and Saucer, landscape scene with villa, pink lustered rims, c1825. . . . . 50.00

Silver

Bough Pot, cov, 9" w, demilune shape, pierced cov, urn knob, pearlware, central panels of fruit flanked by molded columns and leaves, stylized floral reserves, ball feet, Staffordshire, c1820, pr 2,100.00

Creamer, 4-3/8" h, helmet shape, overall luster 45.00

Cup and Saucer, hanging red painted flowerheads, green dots, silver luster scrolling leaves and borders 110.00

Jug, 53/8" h, red and yellow owl seated on brown branch, silver resist leaves on body 750.00

Relish Tray, leaf design, Myott 55.00

Teapot, 5-1/4" h, squatty, molded reeded borders, overall luster 140.00

Vase, 7-1/4" h, bulbous, floral dec on wide black band, cream ground, Wedgwood, 1920 . . . . 375.00

Sunderland

Bowl, 11-3/4" d, Odd Fellows transfers and verses, splashed and wavy pink luster designs 1,250.00

Cream Pitcher, 3-1/2" h, paneled body, overall splashed pink luster. 115.00

Jug, 6-1/2" h, Battle of Wasp and Reindeer, "Constitution" on reverse, black transfers, pink luster trim, chips 400.00

Mug

4" h, Mariners Arms, polychrome dec transfer 125.00

4-1/8" h, Sailor's Farewell, poem "The Sailor's Tears," polychrome highlights. 175.00

Plaque, pierced for hanging

7" x 8-1/2", pink and silver luster frame, center with black transfer ship and "May peace and plenty on our nation smile and trade with commerce bless the British Isle" . . . 175.00

8-5/8" l, rect, *Flying Cloud, Boston,* black transfer, pink luster border, copper luster rim 450.00

9-3/8" l, 8-1/4" w, rect, *Victoria and Albert Yacht,* black transfer, green water, pink splashed border, molded brown rim 450.00

Puzzle Jug, 6-1/2" h, pink luster house and landscape scene, lustered rim and nozzles, chips 750.00

Tumbler, 2-1/4" h, wear and flakes 75.00

Watch Stand, 11" h, figural tall case clock, flanked by two classical children, black, yellow, red, and green enamels, splashed pink luster on base, imp "Dixon, Austin" . . 1,100.00

LUTZ-TYPE GLASS

History: Lutz-type glass is an art glass attributed to Nicholas Lutz. He made this type of glass while at the Boston and Sandwich Glass Co. from 1869 until 1888. Since Lutz-type glass was popular, copied by many capable glassmakers, and unsigned, it is nearly impossible to distinguish genuine Lutz products.

Lutz is believed to have made two distinct types of glass: striped and threaded. The striped glass was made by using threaded glass rods in the Venetian manner, and this style is often confused with authentic Venetian glass. Threaded glass was blown and decorated with winding threads of glass.

Barber Bottle, 8" h, colorless ground, multicolored threaded latticino and opaque stripes 250.00

Beverage Set, 70-1/2" h tankard pitcher, four lemonade tumblers, four large tumblers, colorless ground, cranberry threading, engraved pattern of water plants and Grape Blue Heron on pitcher. 650.00

Bowl, 3-1/4" d, 3" h, colorless, white, amethyst, and yellow latticino, goldstone border 75.00

Cake Stand, threaded, colorless, white threads 125.00

Compote, 7" h, colorless ground, lavender, pink, and opalescent swirls, entwined serpent stem 275.00

Dish, 12" w, leaf shape, colorless, white latticino, goldstone and white waves 175.00

Lemonade Tumbler, 5-1/2" d, colorless ground, cranberry threading, engraved dec, applied colorless handle . . 145.00

Marble

1-3/4" d, colorless ground, green, red, white, and blue threaded twists, minor bruises, some roughness. 35.00

2-1/8" d, colorless ground, cranberry and white swirl. . 95.00

2-3/8" d, multicolored, minor roughness and bruises . 110.00

Bowl, latticinio, blue ribbons, goldstone, clear bands, 4-1/4" d, 2" h, $95.

Pitcher, 10" h, colorless ground, pink threading 200.00

Plate, 6-1/4" d, threaded, rose shading to amber body, gold-stone dec, ruffled 125.00

Scent Bottle, 2-1/8" l, blown, colorless, figural sea horse, opaque white spiral ribs, applied blue rigaree 115.00

Syrup Pitcher, blue ground, white stripes, frosted handle
. . . . 175.00

Tea Service, creamer, cov sugar, two cups and saucers, color-less ground, light pink, blue, and white latticino 250.00

Tumbler, colorless ground

3" h, gold and white latticino, threaded, six applied strawber-ries, ftd 115.00

3-1/2" h, white, green, and orange latticino 120.00

Vase, colorless ground

7" h, cylindrical, cranberry threading 125.00

8" h, bulbous, white latticino, applied colorless handle
. . . . 150.00

Whimsy, 6-3/8" h, tiny Frozen Charlotte doll in colorless glass tube, latticino rings dec, bulbous finial, knob stem, colorless foot 375.00

MAASTRICHT WARE

History: Petrus Regout founded the De Sphinx Pottery in 1836 in Maastricht, Holland. The firm specialized in transfer-printed earthenwares. Other factories also were established in the area, many employing English workmen and adopting their techniques. Maastricht china was exported to the United States in competition with English products.

Bowl

6" d, ftd, Honc pattern, green transfer, polychrome accents
. . . . 40.00

7-3/4" d, ftd, Slamat pattern, orange and green oriental scene with young boy, green Petrus Regout sphinx mark . . 45.00

Plate, multicolored Oriental type scene, mkd "Made in Holland/Society Ceramique Potiche," 7-3/4" d, $15.

9" d, ftd, Honc pattern, green transfer, polychrome accents
. . . . 45.00

Charger, 13" d, rose, blue, and green flowers and lines in center, brown and yellow inner circles, border with blue triangles, cream ground, mkd "Maastricht, Made in Holland" . . . 45.00

Cup Plate, 4-1/2" d, Lasso pattern, horse hunting scenes, red transfer, mkd "Petrus Regout & Co. Maastricht, Made in Holland" 20.00

Cup and Saucer

Honc pattern, blue-black oriental design, orange accents
. . . . 20.00

Oriental pattern, overall floral design, red transfers, mkd "Societe Ceramique Maastricht" 12.00

Timor pattern, green, iron-red, blue, and luster dec . . . 38.00

Plate

7" d, Tea Party pattern, brown transfer, rampant lion and "M. Maastricht" marks 25.00

8-1/2" d, Canton pattern, multicolored . . .25.08-3/4" d, Honc pattern, green, orange-red, and orange accents 25.00

9" d, Pajong pattern, oriental scene of man and woman with umbrella, black transfer, orange luster, Petrus Regout sphinx mark 35.00

9-1/8" d, red, blue, and yellow floral border band, sphinx mark
. . . . 20.00

Soup Plate, 9-1/8" d, Willow pattern, blue transfer, mkd . 45.00

Tureen, cov, matching ladle, white 60.00

Waste Bowl, 4" d, Pompeia pattern, flow blue, c1875. . . 55.00

MAJOLICA

History: Majolica, an opaque, tin-glazed pottery, has been produced in many countries for centuries. It was named after the Spanish Island of Majorca, where figuline (a potter's clay) is found. Today, however, the term "majolica" denotes a type of pottery which was made during the last half of the 19th century in Europe and America.

Majolica frequently depicts elements of nature: leaves, flowers, birds, and fish. Designs were painted on the soft clay body using vitreous colors and fired under a clear lead glaze to impart the rich color and brilliance characteristic of majolica.

Victorian decorative art philosophy dictated that the primary function of design was to attract the eye; usefulness was secondary. Majolica was a welcome and colorful change from the familiar blue and white wares, creamwares, and white ironstone of the day.

Marks: Wedgwood, George Jones, Holdcraft, and Minton were a few of the English majolica manufacturers who marked their wares. Most of their pieces can be identified through the English Registry mark and/or the potter-designer's mark. Sarreguemines in France and Villeroy and Boch in Baden, Germany, produced majolica that compared favorably with the finer English majolica. Most Continental pieces had an incised number on the base.

Although 600-plus American potteries produced majolica between 1850 and 1900, only a handful chose to identify their wares. Among these manufacturers were George Morely, Edwin Bennett, the Chesapeake Pottery Company, the New Milford-Wannoppee Pottery Company, and the firm of Griffen, Smith, and Hill. The others hoped their unmarked pieces would be taken for English examples.

References: Susan and Al Bagdade, *Warman's American Pottery and Porcelain*, Wallace-Homestead, 1994; ——, *Warman's English & Continental Pottery & Porcelain*, 3rd ed., Krause Publications, 1998; Victoria Bergesen, *Majolica: British, Continental, and American Wares, 1851-1915*, Barrie & Jenkins, 1989; Leslie Bockol, *Victorian Majolica*, Schiffer Publishing, 1996; Helen Cunningham, *Majolica Figures*, Schiffer Publishing, 1997; Nicholas M. Dawes, *Majolica, Crown*, 1990; Marilyn G. Karmason and Joan B. Stacke, *Majolica, A Complete History and Illustrated Survey*, Abrams, 1989; Mariann Katz-Marks, *Collector's Encyclopedia of Majolica*, Collector Books, 1992, 1996 value update; Marshall P. Katz and Robert Lehr, *Palissy Ware: Nineteenth Century French Ceramics from Avisseau to Renoleau*, Athlone Press, 1996; *Price Guide to Majolica*, L-W Book Sales, 1997; Mike Schneider, *Majolica*, Schiffer Publishing, 1990, 1995 value update; Jeffrey B. Snyder and Leslie J. Bockol, *Majolica: European and American Wares*, Schiffer Publishing, 1994.

Periodical: Majolica Market, 2720 N. 45 Rd., Manton, MI 49663.

Collectors' Club: Majolica International Society, 1275 First Ave., Ste. 103, New York, NY 10021.

REPRODUCTION ALERT

Majolica-style pieces are a favorite of today's interior decorators. Many exact copies of period pieces are being manufactured. In addition, fantasy pieces incorporating late Victorian era design motifs have entered the market and confused many novice collectors.

Modern majolica reproductions differ from period pieces in these ways: (1) modern reproductions tend to be lighter in weight than their Victorian ancestors; (2) the glaze on newer pieces may not be as rich or deeply colored as on period pieces; (3) new pieces usually have a plain white bottom, period pieces almost always have colored or mottled bases; (4) a bisque finish either inside or on the bottom generally means the piece is new; and (5) if the design prevents the piece from being functional—e.g., a lip of a pitcher that does not allow proper pouring—it is a new piece made primarily for decorative purposes.

Some reproductions bear old marks. Period marks found on modern pieces include (a) ""Etruscan Majolica" (the mark of Griffen, Smith and Hill) and (b) a British registry mark.

SPECIAL AUCTION

**Michael G. Strawser
200 N. Main, P.O. Box 332
Wolcottville, IN 46795
(219) 854-2859**

Advisor: Mary D. Harris.

Note: Prices listed below are for pieces with good color and in mint condition. For less-than-perfect pieces, decrease value proportionately according to the degree of damage or restoration.

Bud Vase, German, 6" h, golfer swinging at a ball, blue ground, pink and yellow flowers at top, multicolored golfer, cap on head, unsigned 150.00
Butter Pat
   Etruscan, Pansy, multicolored petals, sgd 135.00
   Fielding, Butterfly, brown trim, multicolored one butterfly, one flower, bamboo shoot, white ground 200.00
   Wedgwood, Sunflower, brown and yellow, white ground, sgd 185.00
Compote
   English, 3" h, 9" w, Bird and Fan, colorful birds and fans alternating on top, white ground, trimmed in turquoise, unsigned 200.00
   Morley, 5" h, 9" d, large mottled leaf on top, mottled base, blue, green, white, and yellow, sgd, Wellsville, OH 200.00
Creamer, Shell and Seaweed, 4" h, dragonfly spout, brown, yellow, and red shells, green waves, brown handle, white ground, unsigned, attributed to James Carr 150.00
Cup and Saucer
   English, Pineapple, green and yellow, unsigned 225.00
   Etruscan, Shell and Seaweed, pink, green, blue, and brown, sgd 250.00
   Humidor, 6-1/2" d, clown head, blue dec on hat, painted nose, green ruffled collar 125.00
Pitcher
   English, 7-3/4" h, Bamboo Paneled, brown ground, bamboo sticks dividing floral and leaf panels, green and cobalt blue floral panels, English registry mark 185.00
   St. Clements, 12" h, figural, duck, blue, green, and brown, sgd "K. G. St. Clement, France" 175.00
   Unsigned, 7-1/2" h, Acorn and Leaf pattern, brown base and handle, middle section with yellow ground, green acorn leaves, brown and yellow acorns, light pink int. 175.00
Plate
   French, 10" d, rabbit, three rabbits hopping in vegetable garden, natural colors, patent date 12/4/1900 . . . . 225.00

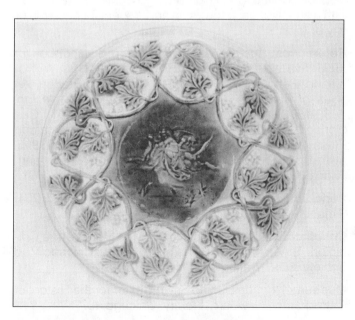

Bowl, low, Classical, white ground, green leaves, pink flowers, green center, Etruscan, 9-1/2" d, $110.

St. Clement, 8-1/4" d, peach, gray-white ground, red and yellow peaches, green leaves, mkd "St. Clement, made in France". 50.00

Wedgwood, 9" d, Chrysanthemum, Argenta series, yellow, purple, and pink flowers, white ground with gray trim, sgd 225.00

Wedgwood, 9" d, Chrysanthemum, Argenta series, yellow, purple, and pink flowers, white ground with turquoise trim, sgd 350.00

Platter

English, Wild Rose and Rope, 13" l handle to handle, cobalt blue center, yellow trim, pink wild roses and green and brown leaves and bark, unsigned 385.00

Etruscan, Geranium, 13" l handle to handle, white ground, pink and yellow geraniums, green leaves, yellow trim, sgd 350.00

Spittoon, English, 8" x 4", Bamboo pattern, brown and green mottled inside, brown and green bamboo on ext., unsigned 250.00

Teapot, Samuel Lear, Water Lily pattern, white ground, yellow lily, green leaves, turquoise trim, flower finial on lid, unsigned 275.00

Vase, unsigned, boy dressed like colorful clown riding boar planter/vase, apples decorate base 150.00

MAPS

History: Maps provide one of the best ways to study the growth of a country or region. From the 16th to the early 20th century, maps were both informative and decorative. Engravers provided ornamental detailing, such as ornate calligraphy and scrolling, especially on bird's-eye views and city maps. Many maps were hand colored to enhance their beauty.

Maps generally were published as plates in books. Many of the maps available today are simply single sheets from cut-apart books.

In the last quarter of the 19th century, representatives from firms in Philadelphia, Chicago, and elsewhere traveled the United States preparing county atlases, often with a sheet for each township and a sheet for each major city or town.

References: *Antique Map Price Record & Handbook for 1996*, available from Spoon River Press (2319C W. Rohmann, Peoria, IL 61604), 1996; Melville C. Branch, *An Atlas of Rare City Maps: Comparative Urban Design, 1830-1842*, Princeton Architectural Press, 1997; Carl Morland and David Bannister, *Antique Maps*, Phaidon Press, 1993; K. A. Sheets, *American Maps 1795-1895*, available from Spoon River Press (2319C W. Rohmann, Peoria, IL 61604), 1995.

Periodical: *Antique Map & Print Quarterly*, P.O. Box 254, Simsbury, CT 06070.

Collectors' Clubs: Association of Map Memorabilia Collectors, 8 Amherst Rd., Pelham, MA 01002; Chicago Map Society, 60 W Walton St., Chicago, IL 60610.

Museum: Hermon Dunlap Smith Center for the History of Cartography, Newberry Library, Chicago, IL.

Notes: Although mass produced, county atlases are eagerly sought by collectors. Individual sheets sell for $25 to $75. The atlases themselves can usually be purchased in the $200 to $400 range. Individual sheets should be viewed solely as decorative and not as investment material.

"Africa," James Wyld, London, 1823, double page, engraved, 520 x 595 mm, wide margins, hand colored in outline, some offsetting, scattered browning, few short marginal tears, second edition 490.00

"America With Those Known Parts In That Unknowne Worlde," John Speed, Bassett and Chiswell, London, 1626, double page, engraved, 395 x 520 mm, English text on verso, vertical fold reinforced with paper tape on verso, very slight browning along fold 3,910.00

"A New And Accurate Map of All The Known World," Emanuel Bowen, London, c1750, double page, engraved, double hemispheric, 310 x 535 mm, side margins trimmed to platemark, few closed tears, paper backing 460.00

"A New and Accurate Map of the North Pole," Emanuel Bowen, London, 1747, double page, engraved, 380 x 430 mm, top margin trimmed to platemark, slight browning along vertical fold 230.00

"A New and Accurate Map of the World," John Speed, Humble, London, c1627, double page, engraved, double hemispheric, 405 x 510 mm, margins trimmed, hand colored in outline, small tears 2,530.00

"A New Map of Ireland," John Cary, London, 1799, double page, engraved, 495 x 555 mm, wide margins, hand colored in outline 230.00

"A New Map of the Terraqueous Globe," Edward Wells, London, 1704, engraved, folding, double hemispheric, 375 x 515 mm 1,265.00

Battle of Long Island, William Faden, London, Oct. 19, 1776, double page, engraved battle plan, supporting letterpress text, 525 x 440 mm, sheet measuring 765 x 550 mm, wide margins, hand colored, browned along horizontal fold 3,680.00

"Charte uber die XIII Vereinigte Satten von Nord-America...," F. L. Gussefeld and Heirs of Homann, 1784, hand colored engraving, 17-1/2" h, 22-5/8" w 1,100.00

"Colton's Kentucky and Tennessee," J. H. Colton, New York, 1863, hand colored, engraved, folding, 350 x 415 mm, folds into orig 16mo cloth case, case damp stained 490.00

"Colton's New Topographical Map of the States of Virginia, West Virginia, Maryland & Delaware," G. W. and C. B. Colton, New York, 1879, hand colored, engraved, folding, 800 x 1130 mm, folds into orig 12 mo cloth case 980.00

Europe, Hartmann Schedel, Nuremberg, 1493, extracted from Latin edition of Nuremberg Chronicle, 395 x 580 mm image size, wide margins, Latin text on verso, vertical fold with expert closures, slight browning 2,990.00

"Hydrographical Basin of the Upper Mississippi River," J. N. Nicollet, Washington, 1843, engraved, two joined sheets, folded, 970 x 800 mm, scattered minor browning 490.00

Jerusalem, Braun & Hogenberg, c1580, hand colored engraving, 14-1/2" h, 19-1/8" w 550.00

"Map of the Cities of Pittsburgh, Allegheny, and the adjoining Boroughs," G. M. Hopkins, Philadelphia, 1872, hand colored litho, folding, 475 x 600 mm, folds into orig 12mo cloth case 550.00

"Map of the City of Milwaukee," Silas Chapman, Milwaukee, 1882, hand-colored litho, folding, 510 x 435 mm, minor separation at several intersection folds, orig 16mo cloth case 375.00

"Map of the Republic of Switzerland," William Faden, London, 1820, double page, engraved, 575 x 830 mm, wide margins, partly hand colored, some browning 115.00

"Map of the United States Projected by Olive Little Marshfield A.D. 1830," pen, ink, and watercolor on paper, 27" h, 38-1/4" w, mounted to canvas, unframed, varnished, minor tears and creases 2,530.00

"Map of the White Mountains," Snow and Bradlee, Boston, 1873, relief map, 220 x 270 mm, orig cloth backed boards, map box binding loose 230.00

Northern hemisphere, John Churchman, published in "Philadelphia: 1790" and dedicated "To George Washington President of the United States of America This Magnetic Atlas or Variation Chart is Humbly Inscribed" 3,450.00

"Plan of the City of New York," William Bridges, New York, 1807, engraved, 310 x 33 mm, trimmed, loss at intersection folds, scattered minor staining, paper backed 635.00

Prussia, Abramah Ortelius, c1580, hand colored engraving, 15-1/8" h, 19-5/8" w 375.00

"The Kindome of China," John Speed, Bassett and Chiswell, London, 1626, double page, engraved, 395 x 115 mm, English text on verso, map hand colored in outline, hand colored side figures, faintly evenly browned 2,530.00

"The Kindome of Persia," John Speed, Humble, London, 1627, double page, engraved, 395 x 510 mm, English text on verso, map hand colored in outline, hand colored side figures 750.00.00

"The Tourist's Map of the State of Ohio, S. Augustus Mitchell," Philadelphia, 1938, hand colored, engraved, folding, 325 x 390 mm, lightly toned overall, folds into orig 16mo road case 400.00

"The Turkish Empire," John Speed, Humble, London, 1626, double page, engraved, 395 x 515 mm, margins trimmed to platemark, English text on verso, hand colored in outline, hand colored vignettes, scattered light soiling 865.00

United States, published in 1849, mkd "New York: J.H. Colton," 23" x 30" 260.00

World, school girl exercise, sgd "Elizabeth Whiton," lower center, watercolor, pen, and ink on paper, framed, 6-1/4" h, 9-1/2" w 500.00

MARBLEHEAD POTTERY

History: This hand-thrown pottery was first made in 1905 as part of a therapeutic program introduced by Dr. J. Hall for the patients confined to a sanitarium located in Marblehead, Massachusetts. In 1916, production was removed from the hospital to another site. The factory continued under the directorship of Arthur E. Baggs until it closed in 1936.

Most pieces found today are glazed with a smooth, porous, even finish in a single color. The most desirable pieces have a conventional design in one or more subordinate colors.

Reference: David Rago, *American Art Pottery,* Knickerbocker Press, 1997.

Bowl
    3-1/4" d, 1-1/2" h, low, matching flower frog, green matte glaze, imp ship mark 365.00
    5" d, 3-1/2" d opening, 3" h, brown matte, yellow int., old 2" base crack 400.00
    5" d, 6" d, blue speckled, imp ship mark 400.00
    6" d, 3" h, red metallic glaze, imp sink mark 350.00
    6-1/2" d, 2-3/4" h, dark blue ext., light blue int. 375.00
    7-1/2" d, 2" h, matte, mustard yellow, cream color int. 450.00
    8-1/2" d, 2-1/4" h, matte, two-tone blue, navy blue ext., light blue int. 450.00
    8-1/2" d, 3-1/4" h, flaring, emb lotus-leaf pattern, dark blue ext. glaze, light blue int., imp ship mark 375.00
Bud Vase, 6" h, 3" d, squatty base, matte gray ground, imp ship mark 125.00
Cabinet Vase, 3-3/4" h, 3-1/2" d, ovoid, pink matte glaze, imp ship mark, hairline to rim 125.00
Candlestick, 6" h, three handle form, green matte glaze, imp mark, slight damage 75.00
Flower Pot, 5" h, 6" w at top, dark blue, imp ship mark. . 400.00
Pitcher, handle
    3-1/2" h, semi-gloss blue glaze, imp ship mark 100.00
    5" h, blue hi-glaze, incised dec of ship at sea, imp ship mark 300.00
Tile, 4" sq, emb white ship at sea, blue sky, imp ship mark, minor edge flakes 210.00
Vase
    3-1/2" h, closed form, blue matte glaze, imp ship mark 260.00
    3-1/2" h, closed form, brown matte glaze, imp ship mark, paper label, burst bubble on side. 180.00
    3-1/2" h, closed form, pink matte glaze, imp ship mark 250.00

Vase, stylized fish, beige and blue, gray ground, imp ship mark, 4-1/2" x 4", $4,500. Photo courtesy of David Rago Auctions, Inc.

3-1/2" h, painted and molded green floral design, rust berries, blue ground 1,300.00

3-1/2" h, cylindrical, gray, blue 325.00

3-1/2" h, 5-1/2" d, tapering closed form, yellow matte glaze, imp ship mark. 600.00

4-1/2" h, flared base, mottled green, brown int. 375.00

4-1/2" h, 4" d, cylindrical, stylized fish, painted in beige and blue, gray ground, imp ship mark. 4,500.00

5" h, lilac, imp ship mark 240.00

5" h, tapered, matte gray, blue matte int., imp ship mark 375.00

5" h, 3" d, ovoid, green, brown, and blue grapevine dec, mustard matte ground, Hannah Tuff, ship mark and "HT," restored rim chip 1,300.00

5" d, 5" h, matte finish, two-tone blue, navy blue ext., light blue int., hairline rack. 250.00

5-1/2" h, 3-1/2" d, stylized blossoming standards blue trees, gray ground, Hannah Tutt, painted mark "HT". . . .1,600.00

6" h, 5" w, pear shaped, smooth matte blue glaze, stamped ship mark 500.00

6" h, cylindrical, four carved and painted dragonflies alternating in blue and grown, at top, green matte ground, imp mark, artist sgd "Hanna Tutt," small flake to base 1,600.00

8" h, 4" d, tapering, mottled green, brown, and blue matte glaze, stamped mark, paper label 1,100.00

Vessel

6-3/4" h, 3" d, squatty, gray and indigo grapevine dec, smooth matte speckled gray ground, Hannah Tuff, imp ship mark and "HT". 1,300.00

8-1/2" h, 4" d, dark brown stylized peacock feathers, dark green matte ground, incised initials for Hannah Tutt, imp ship mark 3,750.00

MARY GREGORY TYPE GLASS

History: The use of enameled decoration on glass, an inexpensive way to imitate cameo glass, developed in Bohemia in the late 19th century. The Boston and Sandwich Glass Co. copied this process in the late 1880s.

Mary Gregory (1856-1908) was employed for two years at the Boston and Sandwich Glass factory when the enameled decorated glass was being manufactured. Some collectors argue that Gregory was inspired to paint her white enamel figures on glass by the work of Kate Greenaway and a desire to imitate pate-sur-pate. However, evidence for these assertions is very weak. Further, it has never been proven that Mary Gregory even decorated glass as part of her job at Sandwich. The result is that "Mary Gregory type" is a better term to describe this glass.

Reference: R. and D. Truitt, *Mary Gregory Glassware*, published by authors, 1992.

Museum: Sandwich Glass Museum, Sandwich, MA.

REPRODUCTION ALERT

Collectors should recognize that most examples of Mary Gregory type glass seen today are either European or modern reproductions.

Box, cov, amethyst ground, white enamel girl in garden setting, 5-1/2" d, $260.

Atomizer, cranberry ground, white enameled little girl, gold washed atomizer mounting 345.00

Barber Bottle, 7-5/8" h, deep amethyst ground, white enameled young girl, landscape setting pr 300.00

Beverage Set, pitcher and six tumblers, colorless ground, white enameled girl, garden setting. 295.00

Box, cov, 5-3/4" d, 4-3/4" h, sapphire blue ground, white enameled young girl holding basket of flowers on lid, multicolored enamel dec on base, fancy wire legs 645.00

Cologne Bottle, sapphire blue, white enameled child . . . 155.00

Cruet, orig stopper, 7-1/2" h, green, white enameled girl and trees 145.00

Decanter, stopper, 12" h, colorless, white enameled woman with basket. 175.00

Dresser Set, pr 10-1/2" h perfume bottles, 7" h cov dresser jar, cobalt blue, white enamel dec of young children and angels, floral sprays, crown tops. 900.00

Dresser Tray, 10-1/2" l, 8" w, oval, emerald green ground, white enameled boy and girl dancing white another girl plays the mandolin. 295.00

Ewer, 10" h, 3-1/8" d, cranberry ground, white enameled girl in garden setting, applied colorless handle 225.00

Jewel Box, 10" l, 4" w, blue ground, white enameled boy and girl pulling cart, girl astride huge bottle, boy carrying goblet, floral garlands, SP edges, base and feet, sgd "Middletown Plate Co" 850.00

Mug

3" h, 2-1/8" d, cranberry ground, white enameled boy, applied colorless handle. 85.00

3-7/8" h, 2-1/4" d, amber ground, applied amber handles, white enameled boy on one, girl on other, pr. 150.00

Paperweight, 4" l, rect, black glass ground, white enameled little boy and girl in garden. 300.00

Perfume Bottle

4-5/8" h, 2" d, cranberry ground, white enameled little girl dec, colorless bubble stopper 165.00

5-3/4" h, 3" d, sapphire blue ground, white enameled boy chasing butterfly, tinted facial features, blue ball stopper 225.00

Pitcher

6-1/2" h, blue ground, white enameled boy with boat. 150.00

6-5/8" h, 4-1/4' d, lime green ground, bulbous, optic effect, round mouth, white enameled boy, applied green handle 145.00

12" h, 6-1/2" w, sapphire blue ground, bulbous, applied amber handle, white enameled young woman holding her hat and staff, standing in scenic spot, minor paint loss on front 150.00

Rose Bowl, cranberry ground, crimped top, white enameled girl holding flower 325.00

Tumble-Up, cranberry ground, white enameled girl on carafe, boy on tumbler 415.00

Tumbler

4-1/4" h, cranberry ground, white enameled girl holding basket of flowers 115.00

4-1/2" h, sapphire blue ground, white enameled boy, ribbed body 85.00

5" h, 2-1/2" d, sapphire blue ground, white enameled girl carrying basket of flowers 90.00

5-1/2" h, cobalt blue ground, white enameled girl picking flowers, narrow gold band at top 115.00

Vase

6-1/4" h, 2-1/4" d, blue ground, white enameled child, matched pr 275.00

6-1/2" h, green ground, white enameled young man . . 90.00

7" h, cobalt blue ground, gilded rim, white enameled flowers and cupids 175.00

8-7/8" h, 4" d, cranberry ground, white enameled young girls carrying watering cans, facing pr 425.00

9" h, 4" d, frosted emerald green ground, white enameled girl holds flowers in her apron and hand 165.00

9-7/8" h, cranberry ground, white enameled boy running with butterfly net, girl with bouquet of flowers, holding apron, colorless pedestal foot, facing pr 475.00

10-1/4" h, 5" w, cranberry ground, large white enameled dec of young girl holding flower, paneled int. 300.00

12" h, emerald green ground, finely white enameled scene of boy picking flowers. 190.00

Scalloped top, applied colorless reeded snail handles 420.00

Wine Bottle, 9" h, 3-1/8" d, cranberry ground, white enameled girl holding floral spray, orig colorless bubble stopper 195.00

MATCH HOLDERS

History: The friction match achieved popularity after 1850. The early matches were packaged and sold in sliding cardboard boxes. To facilitate storage and to eliminate the clumsiness of using the box, match holders were developed.

The first match holders were cast iron or tin, the latter often displaying advertisements. A patent for a wall-hanging match holder was issued in 1849. By 1880, match holders also were being made from glass and china. Match holders began to lose their popularity in the late 1930s with the advent of gas and electric heat and ranges.

Reference: Denis B. Alsford, *Match Holders*, Schiffer Publishing, 1994.

Advertising

Arnold Stern Cookers, 7-1/8" h, 4-1/4" w, cardboard litho, Statue of Liberty image, detailed scene of bridges and boats in background, never used. 400.00

Chef Spices, Berdan & Co., Toledo, OH, tin litho, wall type, wear on front basket, 4-7/8" h, 3-7/8" w, 1-1/4" d . . 375.00

Roycroft, hammered copper, nested ashtray, 3-1/4" h, 3-1/4" d, $90.

Dr. Smith's Columbo Tonic Bitters, Scranton, PA, hanging, cardboard, litho of seated bear, match holder wood barrel between legs, sandpaper paws for striking, 7" h, 5-1/4" w 300.00

Empire steam Laundry, figural frog, cast iron, 4" x 2-1/2" x 2" 225.00

Pointer Stoves and Ranges, figural fly, cast iron, 4" x 3-1/8" x 1-1/2" 225.00

Bisque, 2-1/2" h, figural, dog in house 25.00

Composition Plaster, 8-1/2" h, Palmer Cox Brownie, holding bucket to side for matches, scratching spot on belly, paint worn, small chips 275.00

Glass, 5" l, cornstarch blue, reeded and serrated detail, chip on one corner of base 150.00

Hanging, 2-7/8" h, 2-1/8" w, Cambridge Crest, Goss China 25.00

Jasperware, 2-3/8" h, 2-1/2" w, light green and white classical scene, Wedgwood, England. 30.00

Plated Metal, 3" h, figural, boot, open top, striker on base 10.00

Porcelain

1-3/4" h, ball shape, woman's portrait on front. 15.00

4-1/4" h, 3" base, Cunard Ship Lines 40.00

4-1/2" h, figural, boy with backpack, floral dec, German, chips on top of pack 35.00

4-5/8" h, figural, boy selling matches, green and white, German 20.00

4-5/8" h, figural, girl holding flags, German 60.00

Silicon Ware, 3" h, 2-3/4" w, tan, white, light blue, and dark blue, Doulton, Lambeth, minor chip at base of cover 40.00

MATCH SAFES

History: Pocket match safes are small containers used to safely carry matches in one's pocket. They were first used in the 1850's. Match safes are often figural with a hinged lid and striking surface, but they come in many shapes and were made from numerous materials.

References: Denis Alsford, *Match Holders, 100 Years of Ingenuity*, Schiffer Publishing, 1994; W. Eugene Sanders Jr., and Christine C. Sanders, *Pocket Matchsafes, Reflections of Life & Art, 1840-1920*, Schiffer Publishing, 1997;

Audrey G. Sullivan, *History of Match Safes in the United States*, published by author, 1978.

Collectors' Club: International Match Safe Association, P.O. Box 791, Malaga, NJ 08328-0791; e-mail:IMSAoc@aol.com

Advisor: George Sparacio.

REPRODUCTION ALERT

Reproduction, copycat and fantasy sterling match safes include:

Art Nouveau style nude with veil, rectangular case with C-scroll edges

Boot, figural

Embracing wood nymphs

Jack Daniel's, 1970s fantasy item, nickel plated

Mermaid, with upper torso out of water, combing her hair

Owl, figural

Moon, figural

Devil head, figural

Many of these match safes are only marked "Sterling" or "925." Any match safe so marked requires careful inspection. Period American match safes are marked with the name of the manufacturer and/or a patent date in about half of the instances. Period English safes have the proper hallmarks. Beware of English reproduction match safes bearing the "DAB" marking. Always verify the date mark on English safes.

Note: While not all match safes have a striking surface, this is one test, besides size, to distinguish a match safe from a calling card case.

Advertising

Age & Purity Make Sunny Brook a Perfect Whiskey, copper plated metal, wording on both sides, 2-1/4" x 1" 50.00

Anheuser Busch, embossed with large A and eagle trademark on both sides, nickel plated brass, 2-7/8" x 1-1/2" 125.00

Arm & Hammer trade mark, slip top, thermoplastic, 3" x 1-1/2" 125.00

Compliments United Hatters, Buy No Hat Without This Label, celluloid wrapped, multi-colored graphics, 2-1/2" x 1-1/2" 125.00

Cowboy roping buffalo one side, adv under clear cello on other, insert type, nickel plated brass, 2-3/4" x 1-1/2". . 115.00

Henry Wehr's Buffet, Milwaukee, Choice Whiskies, High Grade Cigars, celluloid wrapped, illus of nude on waves on front, adv on back, 2-3/8" x 1-1/2" 250.00

Hunt & Mitton Engineers and Hydraulic Brass Finishers, Lubricators, Pressure Gauges and Fire Appliances, Birmingham, book shape, plated metal, opens both ends, 1-1/8" x 2" 85.00

Shannon & Co., Phila., Derricks, Railroad Supplies, etc. celluloid wrapped, black graphics, 2-3/4" x 1-1/2" 85.00

United Brewery Workers Against Prohibition, celluloid wrapped, multi-colored graphics, 2-7/8" x 1-1/2" . . . 175.00

Brass and Nickel Plated Brass

Barrel shape, flattened, flower on front, some wear, 2-1/8" l 130.00

Book shape, floral design, double ender, worn plating, 1-5/8" x 2" 55.00

Book shape, one side matches, other side stamps, 1-7/8" x 1-3/8" 60.00

Bullet shape, blue, screw top, French, 3-1/8" h 70.00

Canada and Shield, spring drawer type, worn, 2-5/8" x 1-3/4" 50.00

Cavaliers in relief, stone striker, slide type, 2-3/8" x 1-5/8" 125.00

Drill press on front, mkd "Ludw. Kaufman & Co.," slide type, 2-3/8" x 1-5/8" 50.00

Engraved sides, hinged top, slight denting, 1-7/8 x 7/8" 40.00

Neptune riding waves, pill box style, 2-3/8" x 1-5/8" . . 85.00

Oriental with dragons, sea life and people, 2-1/2" x 1-1/2" 250.00

Outdoor tavern scene on both sides in relief, slide type, 2-3/8" x 1-5/8" 125.00

Stork and baby design, cigar cutter in hinged lid, slightly rough, 2-3/4" x 1-1/2" 25.00

Bristol Silver, flattened barrel shape, relief figures of woman, bird, dog and gun, mkd "Bristol," 2-3/8" x 1-1/2" 250.00

Figural

Baby holding rattle wrapped in swaddling clothes, plated brass, 2-1/4" x 3/4". 245.00

Billiken, ring on side, brass, 1-5/8" x 1" 325.00

Boy's head sticking out of folded shirt, "Tim & Co., Tim Wallerstein & Co.," late 19th C, 2-2/3" x 1-1/8" 275.00

Columbus, some wear, hinge needs repair, plated brass, 2-5/8" x 1-5/8" 180.00

Devil's head, ivory horns, glass eyes, push nose to open, nickel plated brass, 2" x 1-3/8". 425.00

Heart, figural, 1-1/2" x 1-5/8" 50.00

Kidney bean, hinged cover, striker in curve, 2-1/4" x 1" 110.00

Overalls/pants, advertising on top of lid, pewter, 2-7/8" x 1-1/4" 135.00

Pig standing on all fours, vesta hole in nose, brass, 7/8" x 1-7/8" 135.00

Rooster head, glass eyes, squeeze beak to open, nickel plated brass, 2" x 2-1/4" 290.00

Violin, striker on lid, nickel plated brass, 2-5/8" x 1" . . 140.00

Padlock, sterling silver, English, c1882, 1-3/4" h, $285.

Gold, textured body design, inset stone striker, slide type, .585 (14K), Continental, 2-1/4" x 1-5/8" 400.00
Leather and Metal, Hamburg crest on top, 2-5/8" x 1-3/4" 110.00
Pewter
    Deer and scrolls on top, pill box-style, 2" w 50.00
    Hunting dog on cover, pill box-style, 2-1/2" x 1" 100.00
Sterling
    "Butterfly lady" embossed on side, Gorham maker marks, 2-1/2" x 1-1/2" 550.00
    Oval, engraved scrolling design, monogram, Victorian, maker's mark, London, 1893, 2 troy oz 115.00
    Repousse scrolling floral dec, central female figure, American, late 19th C, 1 troy oz, 2-1/2" x 1-1/2" 125.00
Vulcanite
    Advertising, "Chloride" on top, 1-5/8" x 1-1/2" 75.00
    Book shape, flip up cover on both ends, 1-3/4" x 1-1/2" 45.00

McCOY POTTERY

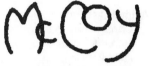

History: The J. W. McCoy Pottery Co. was established in Roseville, Ohio, in September 1899. The early McCoy company produced both stoneware and some art pottery lines, including Rosewood. In October 1911, three potteries merged creating the Brush-McCoy Pottery Co. This firm continued to produce the original McCoy lines and added several new art lines. Much of the early pottery is not marked.

In 1910, Nelson McCoy and his father, J. W. McCoy, founded the Nelson McCoy Sanitary Stoneware Co. In 1925, the McCoy family sold their interest in the Brush-McCoy Pottery Co. and started to expand and improve the Nelson McCoy Co. The new company produced stoneware, earthenware specialties, and artware.

Marks: Most of the pottery marked "McCoy" was made by the Nelson McCoy Co.

REPRODUCTION ALERT

Unfortunately, Nelson McCoy never registered his McCoy trademark, a fact discovered by Roger Jensen of Tennessee. As a result, Jensen began using the McCoy mark on a series of ceramic reproductions made in the early 1990s. While the marks on these recently made pieces copy the original, Jensen made objects which were never produced by the Nelson McCoy Co. The best known example is the Red Riding Hood cookie jar which was originally designed by Hull and also made by Regal China.

The McCoy fakes are a perfect example of how a mark on a piece can be deceptive. A mark alone is not proof that a piece is period or old. Knowing the proper marks and what was and was not made in respect to forms, shapes, and decorative motifs is critical in authenticating a pattern.

References: Susan and Al Bagdade, *Warman's American Pottery and Porcelain*, Wallace-Homestead, 1994; Bob Hanson, Craig Nissen and Margaret Hanson, *McCoy Pottery, Collector's Reference*, Collector Books, 1996; Sharon and Bob Huxford, *Collector's Encyclopedia of Brush-McCoy Pottery*, Collector Books, 1996; ——, *Collectors Encyclopedia of McCoy Pottery*, Collector Books, 1980, 1997 value update; Martha and Steve Sanford, *Sanfords' Guide to Brush-McCoy Pottery*, Book 2, Adelmore Press (230 Harrison Ave., Campbell, CA 95008), 1996; ——, *Sanfords' Guide to McCoy Pottery*, Adelmore Press, 1997.

Periodicals: *NM Express*, 3081 Rock Creek Dr., Broomfield, CO 80020.

Additional Listings: See *Warman's Americana & Collectibles* for more examples.

Bookends, pr, Yellow Dog, #205 . . . . 95.00
Bowl, blue, bird 30.00
Candleholder, bisque, cobalt blue 40.00
Cookie Jar
    Bugs Bunny, cylinder 185.00
    Happy Face 75.00
    Indian 245.00
    Kissing Penguins 50.00
    Teepee, slant lid 350.00
    WC Fields 250.00
Creamer and Sugar
    Elmer and Elsie 90.00
    Sunburst, gold orig paper inventory tags 125.00
Decanter, Pierce Arrow 90.00
Dresser Caddy, buffalo 55.00
Flower Pot, saucer, hobnail and leaf 40.00
Hanging Basket
    Pine Cone Rustic 40.00
    Yellow, chain 35.00
Hanging Strawberry Jar, chain 40.00
Jardiniere
    Blended glaze, 12" h 90.00
    Nasturtiums, standard glaze, 7" w, 5" h 70.00
    Tulips dec, orange and yellow flowers, green leaves, dark to light brown standard glaze, ruffled top, 11" d, 11" h 280.00
    Tulips, standard glaze, mkd, 8" h, minor flaking to feet 210.00
    Yellow, 4" h 35.00
    White, 4" h 35.00
Lamp
    Boot, no shade 100.00
    Cobweb, bedroom type, pink 55.00
    Fireplace, green, #208 . . . . 85.00
    Lamp Base, orange and yellow iris dec, green leaves, dark standard glaze, orig drill hole, 10" h 190.00
    Mug, green 24.00
Pitcher
    Blue Butterfly 235.00
    Hobnail 160.00
Planter
    Auto, Birchwood 35.00
    Duck with egg 30.00
    Duck with umbrella 130.00
    Parrot, white 36.00
    Pelican, yellow 55.00
    Pirate head 110.00
    Shoes, #135-1-2 . . . . 1,500.00
    Stretching Goat 110.00
    Turtle, cold painted 45.00
    Umbrella Carriage, green 177.00

Cookie Jar, Pumpkin Face, $375. Photo courtesy of House in the Woods Auction Gallery.

Umbrella Duck	130.00
Water Lily and Pheasants	95.00
Strawberry Jar	
Bird dec	40.00
Black, 7" h	65.00
Tankard	
Green	60.00
Standard glaze, green and orange leaves, 11-1/2" h, 6" w	210.00
Teapot, Leaf and Berry	
Blue	185.00
Yellow	165.00
Tea Set, Daisy	70.00
Vase and Flower Frog, Onyx	50.00
Vase	
Antiqua, strap handle	155.00
Blossom Time	45.00
Feather, maroon	55.00
Flowers, green, yellow and orange flowers and leaves, dark brown to green ground, standard glaze, imp "232," 5" h, 8" w, base chip	80.00
Pillow, orange and yellow floral dec, orange to brown ground, imp "#400," 5" h, 5" w	120.00
Springwood, large	40.00
Swan, 9" h, turquoise, white matte	50.00
Wall Pocket	
Apple, repaired	45.00
Cornucopia	100.00
Flower and bird, blue flower, pink bird	60.00
Grape	65.00
Mexican	95.00
Window Box, Pine Cone Rustic	35.00

McKEE GLASS

History: The McKee Glass Co. was established in 1843 in Pittsburgh, Pennsylvania. In 1852, it opened a factory to produce pattern glass. In 1888, the factory was relocated to Jeannette, Pennsylvania, and began to produce many types of glass kitchenwares, including several patterns of Depression glass. The factory continued until 1951 when it was sold to the Thatcher Manufacturing Co.

McKee named its colors Chalaine Blue, Custard, Seville Yellow, and Skokie Green. McKee glass may also be found with painted patterns, e.g., dots and ships. A few items were decaled. Many of the canisters and shakers were lettered in black to show the purpose for which they were intended.

References: Gene Florence, *Kitchen Glassware of the Depression Years*, 6th ed., Collector Books, 1995; ——, *Very Rare Glassware of the Depression Years*, 3rd Series, (1993, 1995 value update), 4th Series (1995), Collector Books.

Additional Listings: See *Warman's Americana & Collectibles* for more examples.

Animal Dish, cov	
Canary, nest base, milk glass	145.00
Hen, milk glass, orig eyes	140.00
Rabbit, milk glass	170.00
Squirrel, split rib base, milk glass	150.00
Basket, 15-1/2" h, 11" w, cut and pressed, floral and bird with butterfly	50.00
Bird House, gray body, red roof	165.00
Bottoms Up Tumbler, orig coaster, Seville Yellow	180.00
Bowl, 8" d, Star Rosetted pattern	18.00
Bread Plate	
Queen pattern, canary yellow	40.00
Star Rosetted pattern, "A Good Mother Makes A Happy Home"	65.00
Butter Dish, cov	
Eureka pattern, heavy brilliant flint	75.00
Gothic pattern, colorless, pyramid shaped finial	50.00
Queen pattern, canary yellow, domed lid	85.00
Strigil pattern, colorless	45.00
Cake Stand, Queen pattern, amber	65.00
Candlesticks, pr, 10" h, crucifix form, Christ figure and "INRI" plaque, hexagonal base, colorless	125.00
Candy Dish, cov, 7-3/4" h, orange body, gold trim, gold finial, colorless pedestal base	35.00
Castor Set, 3 bottle, toothpick handle	270.00
Celery Vase, Eugenia pattern, heavy brilliant flint	95.00
Champagne, colorless, heavy brilliant flint	
Eugenia	90.00
Eureka	90.00
Cheese and Cracker Set, Rock Crystal, red	170.00
Clock, Daisy and Button pattern, tambour shape, vaseline	450.00
Compote	
Queen pattern, apple green	85.00
Star Rosetted pattern, colorless, 8-1/2" d	70.00
Cordial, colorless, heavy brilliant flint	
Eugenia pattern	90.00
Eureka pattern	85.00
Creamer	
Comet pattern, colorless	55.00
Gothic pattern, ruby stain	65.00
Masonic pattern, colorless	45.00
Queen pattern, canary yellow	45.00
Strigil pattern, colorless	35.00
Decanter Set, decanter, six whiskey glasses, pink ground, ring dec	125.00

Fruit Bowl, 12" d, Colonial pattern, caramel 140.00
Goblet
    French Ivory 40.00
    Gothic pattern, ruby stain 65.00
    Puritan pattern, pink stem 35.00
Grapefruit Bowl, Rock Crystal, red 45.00
Iced Tea Tumbler, Rock Crystal, red 35.00
Jelly Compote, Gothic pattern, colorless, scalloped rim . . 20.00
Lamp
    Dance de Lumierre, green 750.00
    Eugenia pattern, heavy brilliant flint, whale oil burner
    . . . . 165.00
    Ribbed Tulip pattern, 9-1/2" h, colorless font, milk glass base
    . . . . 125.00
Measuring Cup
    Glassbake, 4 cup, crystal, red lettering 25.00
    Red ships, white ground 28.00
    Seville Yellow, red dots, 2 cup 55.00
Mug, Bottoms Down, Seville Yellow 150.00
Mustard Bottle, Eugenia pattern, heavy brilliant flint 35.00
Pepper Bottle, Eugenia pattern, heavy brilliant flint 30.00
Pickle Dish, oval
    Queen pattern, blue 25.00
    Star Rosetted, colorless 20.00
Pin Tray, hand shape, milk glass 20.00
Pitcher
    Aztec pattern, 5" h, colorless 20.00
    Gothic pattern, colorless 75.00
    Queen pattern, blue 85.00
    Yutec, Eclipse, marked "Prescut" 45.00
Plate
    Holly pattern, 8" d, Skokie Green 12.00
    Serenade pattern, 6-3/8" d, opaque white 60.00
Punch Bowl Set, bowl, 12 mugs, Tom and Jerry, red scroll dec
    . . . . 65.00
Relish
    Hickman, 8" l, green, gold trim 30.00
    Prescut, milk glass 25.00
Salt and Pepper Shakers, pr
    Red Dots, Seville Yellow ground 75.00
    Roman Arches, black 60.00

Sauce
    Gothic pattern, ruby stain 20.00
    Strigil pattern, colorless 8.00
Sandwich Server, 10-1/2" d, Brocade, pink, center handle
    . . . . 50.00
Spooner
    Queen pattern, amber 35.00
    Strigil pattern, colorless 20.00
Sugar Bowl, cov
    Comet pattern, colorless 55.00
    Laurel pattern, Skokie Green 15.00
    Masonic pattern, colorless 45.00
    Queen pattern, canary yellow 45.00
    Strigil pattern, colorless 35.00
Sugar Shaker, Chalaine Blue 125.00
Toothbrush Holder, Skokie Green 20.00
Toothpick Holder, figural, hat shape, vaseline 35.00
Tumbler
    Gladiator pattern, cobalt blue, gold trim 50.00
    Gothic pattern, colorless 35.00
    Queen pattern, blue 45.00
    Ribbed Palm pattern, colorless 70.00
    Sextec, colorless, 4" h, flat 20.00
Vase
    7-1/2" h, Brocade, crystal, two handles, gold trim 50.00
    10" h, Hickman, green, gold trim 65.00
Window Box, 5" x 9", lion, Skokie Green 85.00

MEDICAL ITEMS

History: Modern medicine and medical instruments are well documented. Some instruments are virtually unchanged since their invention; others have changed drastically.

The concept of sterilization phased out decorative handles. Handles on early instruments, which were often carved, were made of materials such as mother-of-pearl, ebony, and ivory. Today's sleek instruments are not as desirable to collectors.

References: A. Walker Bingham, *Snake-Oil Syndrome: Patent Medicine Advertising*, Christopher Publishing House, 1994; James M. Edmonson, *American Surgical Instruments, An Illustrated History of Their Manufacture and A Directory of Instrument Makers to 1900*, Norman Publishing, (720 Market St., 3rd Fl., San Francisco, CA 94102), 1997; James M. Edmonson, intro, *Surgical and Dental Instrument Catalogues from the Civil War Era*, Snowden and Brother (1860) and John Weiss and Son (1863), Norman Publishing in association with National Museum of Health and Medicine, Armed Forces Institute of Pathology, 1997; Douglas Congdon-Martin, *Drugstore and Soda Fountain Antiques*, Schiffer Publishing, 1991; Patricia McDaniel, *Drugstore Collectibles*, Wallace-Homestead, 1994; J. William Rosenthal, *Spectacles and Other Vision Aids*, Norman Publishing (720 Market St., 3rd Fl., San Francisco, CA 94102), 1996.

Periodical: Scientific, Medical & Mechanical Antiques, 11824 Taneytown Pike, Taneytown, MD 21787.

Collectors' Clubs: Maryland Microscopical Society, 8621 Polk St., McLean, VA 22102; Medical Collectors Association, 1685A Eastchester Rd., Bronx, NY 10461.

Museums: Dittrick Museum of Medical History, Cleveland, OH; International Museum of Surgical Science &

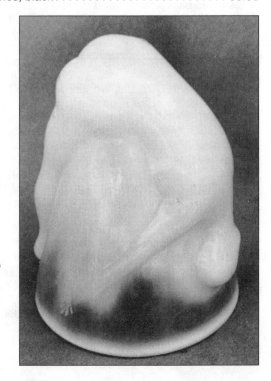

Bottoms Up Tumbler, opalescent, Pat. No. 77726, 3-1/4" h, $325.

Hall of Fame, Chicago, IL; National Museum of Health & Medicine, Walter Reed Medical Center, Washington, DC; National Museum of History and Technology, Smithsonian Institution, Washington, DC; Schmidt Apothecary Shop, New England Fire & History Museum, Brewster, MA; Waring Historical Library, Medical University of South Carolina, Charleston, SC.

Advertisement, 10-1/4" h, 6" w image, Use Dr. H. w. Clouds Invigorating Cordial (Ague tonic), Victorian lady in green dress holding flowers, framed 50.00

Box, 9" h, 6-1/2" w, Drs. Starkey and Panel Compound Oxygen, wood, dovetailed, brass catch, paper labels showing woman taking oxygen from a bottle 100.00

Diecut, 17" h, 11-1/2" w, emb cardboard, center young lady, message about painless dental extracting, matted, framed 800.00

Display Case, 12-1/2" h, 22" l, 27" d, Dr. Johnson's Celebrated Remedies, Collins Ague Cure, Collins Bro.'s Drug Co., Sole Prop's Saint Louis, MO, curved corner German silver case, name etched on inside of glass, back door mirror missing 2,600.00

Dissectable Eye-Ball, composition, colorfully painted, celluloid tag reads "F. E. Becker and Co., Hatton Wall, London" 575.00

Jar, colorless glass, orig stopper

6-1/2" h, "Dr. Pierce's Pleasant Pellets," squatty rect, etched name, three packages of "Pierce's Pleasant Purgative Pellets" 350.00

8-1/2" h, "Squibb's Brown Mixt. Lozenges," rect, recessed reverse painted on glass label, mkd "Pat'd Apr 2, 1889," ground stopper with flat top, minor discoloration to label 200.00

8-3/4" h, "Bromo Bracer Cures Headaches. Sold only by Albert Pick & Co.," rect, painted label, some chips on bottom of lid, minor lip roughness 950.00

10-1/2" h, "Duff's Colic & Diarrhoea Remedy," cylindrical, recessed reverse painted on glass label, ground stopper matches pattern at base, some minor staining 250.00

11" h, "Gono Pills - Man's Friend for Gonorrhea, City Drug, Johnson City, Tenn," cylindrical, etched label, ribbed pressed glass lid 1,000.00

12" h, "Dent's Toothache Gum," tapered jar, etched label, ribbed pressed glass lid 550.00

12" h, "Dr. Simmon's Aspirin Laxative Tablets for Pain," beveled corner, reverse painted on glass label, chip on lid, small crack in glass label 450.00

12" h, "Foley's Kidney Pills," reverse painted on glass label, black printing on orange background, orig contents, some color loss and fogging to label around edges, lid cracked 600.00

16-1/2" h, "Dr. Miles Anti-Pain Pills Cure Headache," beveled corners, reverse painted on glass label, ground lid with swirled design, chip on upper rim, minor discoloration to corners of label 650.00

Letter, from doctor to another doctor, 1835, describes use of leeches, politics, tools 125.00

Poster, 16-1/4" h, 22" l, International Worm Powder, International Stock Food Co., MN, paper litho, multicolored illus with white horse in center .1,100.00

Pill Machine, 7-1/2" w, 15" l base, grooved wood top and base, brass construction, c1870 . . . . 225.00

Shadowbox Frame, containing chromolithograph advertising poster, "President Garfield and Cabinet, Warner's Safe Pills," two old business cards of "B. F. Phillips, druggist and jeweler,

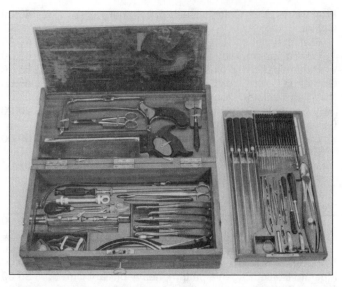

Surgical Set, Baker, 244 Holborn, London, c1850, $13,940. Photo courtesy of Auction Team Breker.

North Jackson, Ohio," walnut frame, 9-1/4" h, 25-1/4" w 275.00

Sign

4-1/2" h, 5-1/2" w, Lavoris, emb tin, easel back, orig envelope, shows white jaw, red lettering, black background, white border 300.00

9-1/4" h, 7" w, D. B. Cough Drops, D. Bacon Co., Harrisburg, PA, diecut, little girl leaning on counter 140.00

12-1/2" h, 41" l, C. F. Hussey Optometrist, zinc, double sided, polychrome and gilt dec, figural eyeglasses, name and title in banner at base, late 19th C, imperfections 2,650.00

17" h, 17" l, Dr. Drake's German Cough Remedy, two sided diecut cardboard, hanging, figural white duck 1,600.00

18" h, 14" w, Dr. Trovillion, Skin Diseases and Skin Cancer, gold letters, black galvanized metal ground, double sided, worn decoration 45.00

19" h, 16" w, Dr. L. Ray Temple, Dentist, gold letters, black sanded background, wood frame 35.00

20-1/2" h, 17-3/4" w, Dr. Sweet's Bone Setter Liniment, detailed graphics, matted and framed 500.00

21-1/4" h, 15-1/4" w, Humphrey's Specifics, framed tin, trademark bare breasted lady with lion, orig ornate frame emb "Humphreys" 4,700.00

22" h, 23-3/4" l, Dr. Bell Wonder Medicine Co., diecut cardboard, horse, some minor damage 190.00

25" h, 18-1/4" w, Dr. Pierce's Golden Medical Discovery, paper litho, two young Indian maidens preparing herbs for "Spring Time for the Blood," crude mortar and pestles, framed 350.00

26-1/2" h, 33" w, Perry Davis Pain Killer, paper litho, early graphics, some professional stain removal, orig frame, new matting 425.00

Tin

3" l, 3" w, 1" h, Dr. Dick's Gail Cure, Pecan Oil Mfg. Co., Davenport, IA, farmer and plow horses in field 275.00

4" h, 2-1/4" w, 1-3/4" d, Skyes Comfort Talcum Powder, two little girls on front, nurse on back 275.00

4-1/2" h, 2-1/4" w, Hemstreet's Antiseptic Foot Powder, unused, black illus on tan ground 600.00

4-1/2" h, 2-1/2" w, Royce's Talcum Powder, Abner Royce Co., Cleveland, tin litho, baby in center 300.00

6" h, 3" w, 1/2" d, Dr. Tepper's Gum Lyke, Industrial Rubber Corp., shows dentures on front 500.00

8" h, 5-1/8" w, F. W. 5¢ Cough Tablets, Geo. Miller & Son, Phila., graphics of woman and ornate script, yellow ground, 1880's 1,700.00

Tip Tray
   3-1/2" d, Luden's Cough Drop, 5¢ package 400.00
   4-1/4" d, titled "The Great eye remedy," cherub placing eye drops in lady's eye, H. D. Beach Co. Litho, minor rim chips 110.00
   5" l, 3-3/4" h, Sheldon Optical, titled "But the play that caused the biggest laugh was Teddy-G on a big giraffe," shows Roosevelt Bear humorously riding giraffe, scalloped rim with multiple Roosevelt Bears, copyright 1906 . . . . 225.00
Tray, Hicks Capudine Liquid, flying cherubs around package 75.00
Veterinary Cabinet, counter type display case
   27-3/4" h, 20" w, 10-1/4" d, Humphrey's Remedies, tin front lists remedies, seven different unopened remedies in cabinet, some damage 400.00
   33" h, 16-1/2" l, 7" d, Pratt Remedies, oak, emb tin front with trademark logo of horse's head, lists products, some damage 700.00
Veterinarian Emergency Medicine Kit, 8" h, 12-1/2" l, 6-1/2" d, Dr. Daniel's, trimmed oak box, paper label inside describing contents, unused 1,200.00

MEDICINE BOTTLES

History: The local apothecary and his book of formulas played a major role in early America. In 1796, the first patent for a medicine was issued by the U.S. Patent Office. At that time, anyone could apply for a medicinal patent; as long as the dosage was not poisonous, the patent was granted.

Patent medicines were advertised in newspapers and magazines and sold through the general store and at "medicine" shows. In 1907, the Pure Food and Drug Act, requiring an accurate description of contents on a medicine container's label, put an end to the patent medicine industry. Not all medicines were patented.

Most medicines were sold in distinctive bottles, often with the name of the medicine and location of manufacture in relief. Many early bottles were made in the glass-manufacturing area of southern New Jersey. Later, companies in western Pennsylvania and Ohio manufactured bottles.

References: Joseph K. Baldwin, *Collector's Guide to Patent and Proprietary Medicine Bottles of the Nineteenth Century*, Thomas Nelson, 1973; Ralph and Terry Kovel, *Kovels' Bottles Price List*, 10th ed., Crown Publishers, 1996; John Odell, *Digger Odell's Official Antique Bottle and Glass Collector Magazine Price Guide Series*, Vol. 5, published by author (1910 Shawhan Rd., Morrow, OH 45152), 1995.

Periodical: Antique Bottle and Glass Collector, P.O. Box 187, East Greenville, PA 18041.

Collectors' Club: Federation of Historical Bottle Collectors, Inc., 88 Sweetbriar Branch, Longwood, FL 32750.

Alexander's Silameau, America, 1840-60, violin form, bulbous neck, sapphire blue, applied sq collared mouth, pontil scar, 6-1/8" h, professionally cleaned, some remaining residue 425.00

Bateman's, hand blown cylinder, applied reverse painted label, some light crazing to label, 10" h, slight in-making imperfections in bottle 70.00
Bennetts Hyssop Cure Stockport, rect, aqua, sunken panel, 5-1/2" h. 30.00
Black Swamp Syrup, colorless, light staining on orig label, orig contents, 7" h 50.00
C. W. Roback, MD, Dr. Roback Swedish Remedy, America, 1840-60, octagonal, bright aquamarine, applied sq collared mouth, pontil scar, 6" h. 160.00
Dr. Davis' Compound Syrup of Wild Cherry and Tar, America, 1840-60, octagonal, indented panels, greenish aquamarine, applied sloping collared mouth, pontil scar, 6-5/8" h, 1/4" chip under mouth 40.00
Dr. Henley's Celery, Beef and Iron, C B & I Extract Co., America, 1884-94, amber, tooled top, smooth base, 9-1/4" h . . 120.00
Dr. J. Webster's Cerevisa Angelica Duplex (coat of arms), America, 1840-60, rect, beveled corners, brilliant medium yellowish green, applied sloping collared mouth with ring, pontil scar, 7-1/8" l, some light int. stain on shoulders. . . .1,300.00
Dr. McMunn's Elixir of Opium, round aqua, orig inside paper wrapper, bottle emb "Opium," 4-1/2" h 140.00
Dr. Phelp's-Arcanum-Genuine, deep olive amber hexagonal form, blown molded, c1830-45, 8-1/4" h, chips to collar and base, mold roughness 3,450.00
Dr. Roback Swedish Remedy, C. W. Roback, MD, America, 1840-60, octagonal, bright aquamarine, applied sq collared mouth, pontil scar, 4-1/2" h. 140.00
Dr. Rookes Rheumatic Lixile, dense cobalt blue, slope shouldered rect, double collar, three sunken panels, 5" h . . 50.00
Elipizone A Safe Cure For Fits & Epilepsy H. C. Root London, aqua, rect, emb front panel, 6-1/2" h 55.00
Granular Citrate of Magnesia, kite with letter inside, ring top, cobalt blue, 8" h 35.00
G. W. House Clemens Indian Tonic, ring top, aqua, 5" h 100.00
Hayman's Balsam of Horehound, ice blue, emb on front panel, 5" h. 20.00
Hicks' Capudine Cure, brown cylinder, recessed reverse painted label with name, and man's head above trademark, ground stopper with flat top, 8-3/4" h, two cracks on label, some edge chips. 325.00
Iceland Balsam For Pulmonary Consumption, Iceland Balsam, America, 1830-50, rect, beveled corners, emb on 3 sides, yellow olive, short applied sloping collared mouth, pontil scar, 6-1/2" h, professionally cleaned, light emb lettering 5,500.00
I. L. St. John's Cough Syrup, America, 1840-60, octagonal, brilliant aquamarine, applied sloping collared mouth, pontil scar, 6-1/4" h. 140.00
Kimball's Anodyne Toothache Drops, Troy, NH, olive green, three pc mold, cylinder, pontil scarred base, 9" h. . . . 425.00
Manchester Wilds Gout & Rheumatic Mixture, aqua, two sunken panels, 6" h. 18.00
O. K. Plantation, triangular, amber, 11" h 200.00
Morrow's Kid-Ne-Oids, paper label showing man bent over with pain, cork closure, 2-3/4" h. 50.00
Phelp's Arcanum Worcester, Mass, olive amber cylinder, blown molded, recess panel, c1830-45, 8-1/2" h, minor mold imperfection to base 1,380.00
Radium Radia, colorless, colorful graphic label wraps around 3 sides, orig contents, 5-1/4" h 210.00
Roshoton & Aspinwall, new York, Compound Chlorine Tooth Wash, golden olive, flared top, pontil, 6" h. 250.00
Rushton Clark & Co., Chemist's New York, aqua, applied top, open pontil, 9-1/2" h. 100.00

Sanderson's Blood Renovator Milton VT, America, 1840-60, oval, aquamarine, applied sq collared mouth, pontil scar, 8-1/8" h, very minor ext. high point wear 650.00

Security Rheumatic Liniment, colorless, colorful graphic label wraps around 3 sides, orig contents, orig box (top missing), 7-1/2" h. 325.00

Shaker Anodyne, NTH, Enfield, NH, aqua, front and rear labels, orig contents, 4" h 250.00

Shaker Digestive Cordial/AJ White New York, aqua, orig front and rear labels, orig contents, 5-1/2" h 110.00

Smith's Anodyne Cough Drops Montpelier, America, 1840-60, rect, beveled corners, aquamarine, applied sloping collared mouth, pontil scar, 5-7/8" l 140.00

Sun Drug Co., Los Angeles, CA, America, 1890-1905, light amber, tooled top, smooth base, winged mortar and pestle motif, 5-3/4" h. 175.00

The Calqueur, Quehen & Smith, pillar with sunken panels on 4 sides, cobalt blue 30.00

Thymo Borine, rect, emb "Thymo Borine" on one side, recessed reverse painted on glass label on other side adv "Thymo Borine The True Antiseptic," ground stopper with flat top, 5-1/2" h. 200.00

True Daff's Elixir, England, 1830-50, rect, beveled edges, yellow green, applied ring lip, bail pontil base, 4-7/8" h 360.00

Use Pritchard's Teething Powders, aqua, rect, emb front panel, 3-1/2" l 12.00

Warner's Safe Cure, London
   Olive green, pint 90.00
   Yellow amber, heavy embossing, half pint 45.00

Warner's "Tinct.Kino," pedestal cylinder, oval applied reverse painted label, pedestal emb "Pat'd Sept 18, 1875, W. R. Warner & Co.," 9" h, crack, some chipping around edge of label. 250.00

White Rose Extract, cylinder, colorful applied reverse painted label, pedestal base emb "W. R. Warner & Co., Pat'd Sept. 18, 1875," 10-1/2" h 600.00

Whitwell's Liquid Improved Opodeloc, cylindrical, colorless, emb, sloping flanged lip, pontil, two part mold, 4-5/8" h 110.00

Winans Bros. (Indian) Indian Cure for the Blood, orig contents 525.00

MERCURY GLASS

History: Mercury glass is a light-bodied, double-walled glass that was "silvered" by applying a solution of silver nitrate to the inside of the object through a hole in its base.

F. Hale Thomas of London patented the method in 1849. In 1855, the New England Glass Co. filed a patent for the same type of process. Other American glassmakers soon followed. The glass reached the height of its popularity in the early 20th century.

Atomizer, colored floral bud shaped glass stopper 50.00

Bottle, 7-1/2" h, 4-1/4"d, bulbous, flashed amber panel cut neck, etched grapes and leaves dec, corked metal stopper, c1840 . . . . 175.00

Bowl, 6" d, enameled white floral dec 45.00

Candlesticks, pr, 6-1/4" h, gold, minor wear 95.00

Carafe, 12" h, 5-1/2" d, mushroom stopper, dated 1909. . 65.00

Compote, 7" h, 6-1/2" d, enameled white floral dec, gold luster int. 65.00

Creamer, 6" h, etched grapevine dec, applied colorless handle 115.00

Vases, floral dec, 10" h, pr, $440. Photo courtesy of Jackson's Auctioneers & Appraisers.

Cup and Saucer, etched floral dec 65.00

Curtain Tieback, 2-5/8" d, pewter fitting, starflower dec . . 65.00

Garniture, 14" h, baluster, raised circular molded foot, everted rim, enameled foliate motif 215.00

Goblet
   6-7/8" h, silver, etched Vintage pattern, gold luster int 65.00
   7-1/2" h, Ivy pattern, engraved grape leaves and grapes 145.00

Mug, 2-7/8" h, silver, applied colorless handle 35.00

Perfume Bottle, emerald green ground, cut and enameled dec, orig stopper 225.00

Pitcher, 12-1/2" h, bulbous, applied colorless handle . . . 185.00

Reflecting Globe, 10" d, silver int., rests on white columnar form satin glass base, 19th C, minor silver loss, base chip, pr 450.00

Salt, 3 x 3", price for pr 100.00

Spooner, 4-1/2" h, silver, etched vintage dec, gold int. . . 120.00

Sweetmeat Dish, cov, 4" d, 7-1/2" h, pedestal base, colorless cov 50.00

Tazza, 5-3/4" d, 2-3/4" h, etched birds and leaves dec. . . 75.00

Toothpick Holder
   3-1/2" h, gold, pedestal base 40.00
   5" h, gold, pedestal base, etched ferns 45.00

Urn, 13" h, baluster, mkd "Harnish & Co. London" 250.00

Vase
   8" h, cut to show emerald glass ground, mkd "Harnish & Co. London Pat." 115.00
   8-7/8" h, silver, minor wear. 145.00
   10-1/2" h, cylindrical, hand painted floral and leaf band around center. 125.00
   12" h, ribbed, emerald green, enameled floral and bird dec 145.00
   13" h, trumpet shape, enameled panel of orange, yellow, green, and blue floral clusters and butterflies 220.00

Walking Stick, 42-1/2" l, red, blue, yellow, and silver swirls, some wear to silvering 200.00
Witch Ball, emerald green, attached base 185.00

METTLACH

History: In 1809, Jean Francis Boch established a pottery at Mettlach in Germany's Moselle Valley. His father had started a pottery at Septfontaines in 1767. Nicholas Villeroy began his pottery career at Wallerfanger in 1789.

In 1841, these three factories merged. They pioneered underglaze printing on earthenware, using transfers from copper plates, and also were among the first companies to use coal-fired kilns. Other factories were developed at Dresden, Wadgassen, and Danischburg. Mettlach decorations include relief and etched designs, prints under the glaze, and cameos.

Marks: The castle and Mercury emblems are the two chief marks although secondary marks are known. The base of each piece also displays a shape mark and usually a decorator's mark.

References: Susan and Al Bagdade, *Warman's English & Continental Pottery & Porcelain*, 3rd Edition, Krause Publications, 1998; Gary Kirsner, *Mettlach Book*, 3rd ed., Glentiques (P.O. Box 8807, Coral Springs, FL 33075), 1994.

Periodical: *Beer Stein Journal*, P.O. Box 8807, Coral Springs, FL 33075.

Collectors' Clubs: Stein Collectors International, 281 Shore Dr., Burr Ridge, IL 60521; Sun Steiners, P.O. Box 11782, Fort Lauderdale, FL 33339.

Additional Listings: Villeroy & Boch.

Pitcher, Hires Root Beer, trademark boy toasting with tall mug that has his image on it, "Join Health and Cheer - Drink Hires Rootbeer," pewter thumb press with ceramic insert picture of oak leaf, 8-1/2" h, $25,000. Photo courtesy of James J. Julia, Inc.

Note: Prices in this listing are for print-under-glaze pieces unless otherwise specified.

Beaker, #3883/553, 1/4 liter, German man leaning on rifle 90.00
Bowl, 9-1/4" d, 4" h, six-sided, Secessionist-style, stylized trees, blue, ochre, and ivory, imp mark 500.00
Cigar Holder, figural, boy with basket on back, wearing pointed hat 250.00
Coaster, #2820, etched, college boy holding stein 200.00
Mug, 5-1/2" h, #1028, half liter, brown tree-trunk ground, relief of may carrying hay while walking with woman, lids and thumb rests missing, set of 8. . . . . 50.00
Pitcher
    8-1/2" h, trademark Hires Root Beer boy toasting with tall mug with same image on it, "Join Health and Cheer - Drink Hires Rootbeer," pewter thumb press lid with ceramic insert with image of oak leaf .25,000.00
    13-1/2" h, quarter liter, brown tree-trunk ground, relief of may carrying hay while walking with woman, inlaid lid, pewter rim, and thumbrest, repainted handle 250.00
Plaque
    #1607, 11" d, etched, ladies representing summer and fall, sgd "Warth, 1893" 550.00
    #2875, 17-1/2" d, cameo, blue-green, white classical woman and man depicting industry 775.00
Plate, #3096, octagonal, Art Deco design, burnt gold, ream, and royal blue 75.00
Pokal, #2058, monkeys among branches, monkey on lid 775.00
Punch Bowl, underplate, 13" d, 11" h, 16-1/2" d underplate, #2806, two handles, two cameo panels, cover missing 350.00
Stein
    #1527, half liter, continuous scene of drunken men and musicians 320.00
    #2025, half liter, inlaid lid, carousing cherubs 250.00
    #2182, quarter liter, PUG printed design of maiden with stem, 6-1/2" h. 200.00
    #2752, half liter, two men drinking in tavern scene, sgd "Schlitt". 200.00
    #2782, Rookwood type, man drinking, shades of green and brown, mkd "Villeroy & Boch," imp number, transfer number 6127, hinged pewter lid, 18-3/4" h 900.00
    #3395, blue, bowling ball and scene, 12" h, 7" w. . . . 350.00
Tumbler, #1191, old man in boat with windmill background, quarter liter, set of six, hairlines 100.00
Vase
    9-1/2" h, detailed red and turquoise floral design, blue ground, imp arks 300.00
    10" h, incised and painted geometric red and green design, cream ground, imp marks 500.00

MILITARIA

History: Wars have occurred throughout recorded history. Until the mid-19th century, soldiers often had to provide for their own needs, including supplying their own weapons. Even in the 20th century a soldier's uniform and some of his gear are viewed as his personal property, even though issued by a military agency.

Conquering armed forces made a habit of acquiring souvenirs from their vanquished foes. They also brought their own uniforms and accessories home as badges of triumph and service.

Saving militaria may be one of the oldest collecting traditions. Militaria collectors tend to have their own special shows and view themselves outside the normal antiques channels. However, they haunt small indoor shows and flea markets in hopes of finding additional materials.

References: Robert W. D. Ball, *Collector's Guide to British Army Campaign Medals*, Antique Trader Books, 1996; Thomas Berndt, *Standard Catalog of U.S. Military Vehicles*, Krause Publications, 1993; Ray A. Bows, *Vietnam Military Lore 1959-1973*, Bows & Sons, 1988; Gary R. Carpenter, *What's It Worth: A Beginner Collector's Guide to U.S. Army Patches of WW II*, published by author, 1994; W. K. Cross, *Charlton Standard Catalogue of First World War Canadian Corps Badges*, Charlton Press, 1995; ——, *Charlton Standard Catalogue of First World War Canadian Infantry Badges*, 2nd ed., Charlton Press, 1995; Robert Fisch, *Field Equipment of the Infantry 1914-1945*, Greenberg Publications, 1989; Gary Howard, *America's Finest: U.S. Airborne Uniforms, Equipment and Insignia of World War Two* (ETO), Greenhill Books, Stackpole Books, 1994.

Jon A. Maguire, *Silver Wings, Pinks & Greens: Uniforms, Wings, & Insignia of USAAF Airmen in World War II*, Schiffer Publishing, 1994; Jon A. Maguire and John P. Conway, *Art of the Flight Jacket*, Schiffer Publishing, 1995; Ron Manion, *American Military Collectibles Price Guide*, Antique Trader Books, 1995; ——, *German Military Collectibles Price Guide*, Antique Trader Publications, 1995; *North South Trader's Civil War Collector's Price Guide*, 5th ed., North South Trader's Civil War, 1991; Harry Rinker Jr., and Robert Heistand, *World War II Collectibles*, Running Press, Courage Books, 1993; *Schuyler, Hartley & Graham Illustrated Catalog of Civil War Military Goods* (reprint of 1864 catalog), Dover Publications, n.d.; Sydney B. Vernon, *Vernon's Collectors' Guide to Orders, Medals, and Decorations*, published by author, 1986; Ron L. Willis and Thomas Carmichael, *United States Navy Wings of Gold*, Schiffer Publishing; 1995; Richard Windrow and Tim Hawkins, *World War II GI, U.S. Army Uniforms*, Motorbooks International, 1993.

Periodicals: *Men at Arms*, 222 W Exchange St., Providence, RI 02903; *Militaria Magazine*, P.O. Box 995, Southbury, CT 06488; *Military Collector Magazine*, P.O. Box 245, Lyon Station, PA 19536; *Military Collector News*, P.O. Box 702073, Tulsa, OK 74170; *Military Images*, RD1 Box 99A, Henryville, PA 18332; *Military Trader*, P.O. Box 1050, Dubuque, IA 52004; *North South Trader's Civil War*, P.O. Box Drawer 631, Orange, VA 22960; *Wildcat Collectors Journal*, 15158 NE 6th Ave., Miami, FL 33162; *WWII Military Journal*, P.O. Box 28906, San Diego, CA 92198.

Collectors' Clubs: American Society of Military Insignia Collectors, 526 Lafayette Ave., Palmerton, PA 18071; Association of American Military Uniform Collectors, P.O. Box 1876, Elyria, OH 44036; Company of Military Historians, North Main Street, Westbrook, CT, 06498; Imperial German Military Collectors Association, 82 Atlantic St., Keyport, NJ 07735; Karabiner Collector's Network, P.O. Box 5773, High Point, NC 27262; Militaria Collectors Society, 137 S Almar Dr., Ft Lauderdale, FL 33334; Orders and Medals Society of America, P.O. Box 484, Glassboro, NJ 08028.

REPRODUCTION ALERT

Pay careful attention to Civil War and Nazi material.

Additional Listings: Firearms; Nazi; Swords. See World War I and World War II in *Warman's Americana & Collectibles* for more examples.

French and Indian War

Enlistment Document, 1 page small oblong 8vo, Hampshire County, Massachusetts, April 6, 1759, for Ebenezer Warner who volunteered "in the present Expedition forming for the invasion of Canada" 675.00

Powder Horn, scrimshaw dec, bottom of horn engraved "Jonathon Barker, Jonathon, His, A. D. 1760, Horn, Dated At Oswago, July 14, Aug, ...Montreal, September, the 8," other names of places, etc., many figural engravings, pie crust pattern base, base held on by wrought iron tacks, five iron tacks missing 4,500.00

Revolutionary War

Autograph

Letter signed

Adams, John, 1 page 4to, The Hague, Oct. 1, 1782, to John Jay in Paris, written while both were in Europe to negotiate peace with Great Britain 16,000.00

Arnold, Benedict, 2 pages folio, London, April 30, 1787, writing for assistance with business affairs, detailing travel plans from London to St. John, Canada, insight into scorn and financial difficulties. 6,800.00

Note signed, back of a three of spades playing card, Aug. 11, 1778, permit to pass through lines issued to army wagon driver 550.00

Broadside, 1 page small folio, Hartford, Nov. 29, 1780, printed by Hudson & Goodwin, recruiting Connecticut regiment of 575 soldiers 1,200.00

Document Signed

Bond, 1-1/3 pages small folio, Cambridge, Massachusetts, Nov 4, 1777, to Seth Sumner to supply provisions to British brought to Boston Market, sgd by Sumner and several witnesses 1,250.00

Commission, 1 page oblong small folio, Boston, July 13, 1780, to David Holbrook as Captain of 4th Regiment of Foot, sgd by James Bowdoin as President of the Mass Provincial Council, intact MA paper seal. 975.00

Oath of Allegiance, partially printed, 6-1/4 x 2-3/4" oblong, printed in Lancaster, PA, "...voluntarily taken and subscribed by the Oath Affirmation of Allegiance and Fidelity, as directed by an Act of General Assembly of Pennsylvania, passed the 13th Day of June, A.D. 1777" 275.00

Pay Voucher, part printed, part manuscript, approx. 6-1/2 x 7-1/2", sgd by "Jed[ediah] Huntington, Major General in the Continental Army," 1789 . . . . 55.00

Powder Horn

14-1/4" l, covered with scrimshawed scenes of shipping and buildings, long thin banner engraved "Prince Hamblen His Horn Made In The Year 1780," year going around at right angle, 2-3/4" wooden base plug well carved in swirled pattern. 1,200.00

15" l, medium green color, plain wood base plug secured with early nails, wire staple strap holder inserted, tip end with octagonal carved raised ridge, side incised rect box with "Eliphas Hunt," light scroll carving, dark patina to wood, few bug bites, small crack at base edge. 400.00

Sword and Scabbard, 26" single edged slightly curved blade, brass hilt with stirrup guard, flat pommel, ribbed horn grip, brown leather scabbard, single brass mount 400.00

Civil War

Autograph, Elziwah W. Langworthy, four letters, written 1862-54, 5th US Artillery Battery E, from Washington, Bristol Station, Chester, PA, and Rochester, NY hospital. . . . 40.00

Baldrick, US Officer, shoulder strap of tarred leather, gilt-cloth facing, brass mounts, tiger head chain and American shield applied, tarred leather brass bound box with spread winged American eagle on outer flap 1,150.00

Belt and Buckle, period belt, oval US buckle plate, attributed to Pvt. Arthur E. Parker, Co. F., killed at Vicksburg, Miss 8/10/1863 . . . . 200.00

Broadside, Alexander H. Stephens, *Who Is Responsible For The War? Who Accountable For Its Horrors And Desolation? Extracts From A Speech...Delivered In The Secession Convention of Georgia...January 1861,* Boston, 1864, 11-1/2" x 9-1/4" 45.00

Cannonball, 6 lb., solid iron shot engraved in script "Gettsburg/1863," floral dec on wood base, breaks to base 350.00

Captains Epaulettes, 4-1/4" x 5-1/8", velvet ground, one pair with pressed brass surround, other with gold braid, provenance:

Mexican Border Patrol Grouping, Sgt. Orie Donley, 2 uniforms, 3 hats, cartridge belt, spats, 2 newspapers, trunk, etc., $2,750. Photo courtesy of Jackson's Auctioneers & Appraisers.

reportedly belonged to MA Volunteers Captain A. J. Clough, 53rd Regiment, price for two pairs 250.00

Cartridge Box, woodburn, metal lined 95.00

Cabinet Card
Admiral Faragut, full dress, sword, Sarony 225.00
Fort Marion, St. Augustine, FL, oversized 45.00

CDV
Admiral Faragut, Fredericks 75.00
Admiral Foote 65.00

Chair, camp, folding, orig carpet seat 90.00

Diary, Timothy B. Robbins, Newburyport, MA, *Pocket Almanac and Memorandum for 1861,* daily entries, member of Company B, 1st Battalion of Rifles, typed transcription of diary is included. 140.00

Forage Cap, enlisted man's, tall, dark blue wool, tarred leather chip strap with two eagle "I" buttons, tarred leather visor with full sweat band and int., dark blue polished cotton lining, brown polished cotton body and crown 2,500.00

Kepi, GAR, dark blue wool, light blue silk lining, partially obscured mark's label, tarred leather visor, leather chip strap, two GAR buttons, late 7th US Cavalry brass insignia added to front, lining loose 225.00

Muster Roll, Union, 28th Regiment of PA Volunteers, Company B, 1-1/2 pgs long oblong folio, Chancellorsville, VA, April 30, 1863, covers Feb. 28 to April 30, lists 14 officers, 2 drummers, wagoner, 51 privates, 3 men discharged, chart form, 10 line record of events, fold wear 450.00

Newspaper, Daily Mirror-Extra, Manchester, NH, June 30, 1862, 12" x 6", special edition with headline "Startling Rumors! Reported Capture of Richmond! The Enemy Routed! A Four Days Fight!" 40.00

Photographs, cartes des visites of three generals, identified in pencil as Kearny, Strong, and A. S. Williams, Brady imprint on verso, unidentified portraits of one general, two sergeants, and two corporals, also two tintypes of unidentified privates, two litho portraits of Generals Hancock and James Shields, published by L. Prang, set of 12 . . . . 450.00

Shako, leather body, int. chin strap and visor, underside painted green, insignia missing, red, white, and blue rosette, mildewed, several creases 300.00

Stereoview
Anthony, Rebel Artillery Soldier's, killed in trenches of Fort Mahone, two dead soldiers, horse 180.00
Taylor, Brady view of Confederate prisoners on way to rear guard 95.00

Surgeon's Kit, partial, 15 different surgical and doctor's tools, saws, scalpels, probes, stethoscope, knives, forceps, some mkd "Gemrig/Phila," some with tortoise shell handles, 16-1/2" x 6" x 4" walnut box, brass fixtures. 600.00

Sword Belt and Plate, Union officer's, folded leather waist belt, both sets of sword hangers attached, model 1851 eagle belt plate 325.00

Tintype
1-7/8 x 2-1/16", head and shoulders of young lad in uniform, plastic case marked "S Peck & Co. A Union Case Improved" 110.00
3-3/8 x 3-3/4", soldier posing with unsheathed sword, Army tents in background, c1861, plastic case marked "S Peck & Co., The Crossed Cannons" 290.00

War Bond, Confederate, $500, issued 1864, $15 coupon, dry mounted and framed 20.00

Spanish American

Canteen and strap, regular canvas covered ovoid shaped metal canteen, cork stopper, mkd on one side "US" and other with penciled name "JM Rudd," scattered blood spots, black strap with brass hooks and hangers mkd "Rock Island Arsenal," with inspector's marks 325.00

World War I

Bayonet, Remington, case, 1917 . . . . 90.00
Buckle, US Balloon Corps, emb hot air balloon 30.00
Flare Pistol, French, marked "Modele 1918" 125.00
Map Case, leather, strap, nine orig tour maps of France
. . . . 45.00
Measure, angle, US Army Engineer's Corps, case, 1916
. . . . 45.00
Postcard
    Army and Navy Forever, patriotic salute to U. S. Soldiers, lyrics to "My Country 'tis of Thee" at top 40.00
    Fatal Wound, Brittannia bull dog wounds German Kaiser's backside, Belgian 50.00
    Well Done 77th, Homecoming, Statue of Liberty, 77th of Buffalo, sgd "Lawrence Wilber" 75.00
Saddle Cloth, 7th Cavalry, yellow trim, blue felt, worn . . 150.00
Sheet Music
    After the War is Over, 1917 . . . . 5.00
    How 'Ya Gonna Keep 'em Down on the Farm After They've Seen Paree?, 1919 . . . . 8.00
    Madelon, I'll Be True to the Whole Regiment, 1919 . . . . 6.00
    Since Katy the Waitress Became An Aviatress, 1919 . . 8.00
Trench Knife, L. F. & C., 1917, stamped knuckle guard, wood handle, 9" blued triangle blade with green leather scabbard, metal tip and throat 225.00
Uniform
    Army, wool blouse, 4th M.G. Battalion discs, machine gun, pin, trousers with ankle laces 225.00
    Captain's, tunic and trousers, collar insignia, captain's bars, 2nd division patch 295.00
    Enlisted Man's, dress blues, tunic and trousers, no pockets
    . . . . 175.00

World War II

Button, Royal Air Force, brass, emb wings and king's crown
. . . . 5.00
Field Glasses, German 100.00
Fighting Knife, 12-1/2" l, 1 pc blade and handle, 7-13/16" exposed spearpoint blade mkd "John Ek KNIFE/HAMDEN CONN," number "ID765" on left ricasso, 3-1/4" back grind, attached finger groove wood scales secured with three metal rivets, 3/4" exposed skull breaker accompanied by orig simple brown leather sheath 310.00
Flyers Goggles, Japanese, gray fur lined cups, yellow lenses, boxed 15.00
Knife, side, Imperial German, leather scabbard, well marked
. . . . 75.00
Medal, St. Christopher, USMC 32.00
Paperweight, bronze, marked "Captured Japanese Material" from Yokosuka Naval Air Station, *USS Webster* 60.00
Plate, General Marshall surrounded by Allied Nations flags
. . . . 30.00
Tunic, flight, German Luftwaffe 200.00
Wings
    Army Corp., sterling
        AVG, American Volunteer Group, Flying Tigers . . 250.00
        WASP, Women Army Service Pilots 265.00
    Gunner's, 1st Model, open G 100.00

MILK BOTTLES

History: Milk bottles were known to have been used in the last quarter of the 19th century. Their popularity was enhanced by the inventions of Dr. Hervey Thatcher, who in 1889, developed the bottle with the cap seat holding a cardboard disk following the successful introduction of the Milk Protector system of milk distribution. This system used the now poplar Milk Protector bottle with the glass top and picture of a man milking a cow. The use of the bottle was wide spread by the mid teens. With the growth of fluid milk industry, competition resulted in numerous patents. The cream top in 1925, the baby faced and cream separators were popular. Bottles continued well into the 1950s, enhanced by the addition of color and inexpensive manufacturing process. Milk bottles died with the advent of the supermarket and the growing use of fiber board and plastic. There has been a reintroduction recently and a growing number of dairies are now back to using glass.

Milk bottles come in many sizes, colors, and shapes. The beginning collector will very likely collect bottles from the area in which he resides. Other areas can be size, such as quarter pints (gills) or the colorfully painted bottles generally termed "pyro." Other collectors will go to the baby tops, war slogans, or the older tin top closures. Yet even another group may be collected by type, including the modern ones currently in use, or by dairy such as Borden or Carnation. Bottles may be found in shops, at flea markets, or dug in country dumps. History tells us that condition is important and will influence value and collectability. Regional values will vary.

References: Jeffrey L. Giarde, *Glass Milk Bottles: Their Makers and Marks,* printed by author, Donald E. Lord, *California Milks,* published by author, John Tutton, *Udder Delightful, Udder Fantastic, and Udderly Beautiful,* published by author (Rt. 4, Box 929, Front Royal, VA 22630).

Collectors' Club: The National Association of Milk Bottles Collectors, 4 Ox Bow Road, Westport, CT 06880.

Museums: Billings Farm Museum, Woodstock, VT, National Bottle Museum, Ballston Spa, NY; Southwest Dairy Museum, Arlington, TX.

Advisors: Tony Knipp and Tom Gallagher.

REPRODUCTION ALERT

Milk bottles are being reproduced. Most, by use of blank bottles, then being processed with color slogans, designs, and fictitious farms. Reproduction Elsie the Borden's popular cow, Hopalong Cassidy, and Disney characters have crept into the market. The process has improved and some are virtually undetectable, except to the serious collector. A low price for a very unusual bottle may be a tip off.

Also see: Dairy Items.

Alta Crest Farm, Spencer, MA, quart, round, green glass, emb cow's head 1,000.00
Brambridge Dairy, Established 1900, bust of Lincoln, trademark, Pomery, O - Toe Washed and Returned, amber, quart, smooth base, tooled lip, c1900-10 . . . . 700.00

Borden's Condensed Milk, quart, Borden Eagle trademark, clear, emb, tin top 100.00

Capital Dairy, North Dartmouth, MA, quart, round, clear, emb capital dome emb on front slug plate 15.00

Cream Top, generic, quart, sq, dish of ice cream, green/orange 15.00

Dairylea, quart, square, red, Miss Dairylea, picture of fruit and vegetables 15.00

Empire State Dairy Co., Brooklyn, half pint, round, emb, state seal in frame. 10.00

Firestone Farms, Columbiana, OH, one half pint, round, clear, emb, Firestone emblem emb in slug plate 25.00

Fort Wayne Dairy Co.'s Buttermilk, amber, half pint, smooth base, tooled lip, c1900-10 . . . . 950.00

Gettysburg Ice and Storage Co., Gettysburg, PA, quart, round, clear, emb name. 12.00

Ideal Dairy, N. Ray Bourbonnais, Ill, This Side Up, Cream Separator Bottle, Inc., quart, emb, smooth base, ABM lip, c1925-35 . . . . 90.00

Metzgers, quart, emb baby face 90.00

Peoria Sanitary Milk Co., Wash and Return, amber, half pint, smooth base, tooled lip, c1900-10 . . . . 225.00

R. F. S., R. F. Stevens Co., 90-92-94 Third Ave., Brooklyn, To Be Washed and Returned, quart, emb "S" on smooth base, ABM lip, tin lid and wire bail, c1910-20 . . . . 90.00

Standard Cream Line, Whiteman's Patent Feb. 18, 1890, quart, emb, tooled lip, orig glass lid and wire bail, 1900. . . . 145.00

Thatcher's Dairy, quart, emb man milking cow, 1884 patent 265.00

University of Connecticut, Storrs, CT, one half pint, round, clear, emb name 8.00

Use Sealtest Dairy Products, Buy War Bonds, Everybody Every Payday 10%, No Better Home Guard, Buy War Bonds & Stamps, red and blue pyroglaze, quart, emb Toledo, Ohio on base, ABM lip, c1941-45 . . . . 280.00

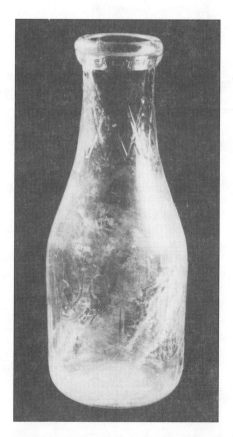

Garners Dairy Co., Uniontown, PA, quart, $20.

Warren Creamery, 323 Warren St. This Bottle To Be Washed and Returned, aqua, pint, emb, tin lid and wire bail, tooled lip, c1900-10 . . . . 120.00

White Springs Farm Dairy, Geneva, quart, orange pyro . . 12.00

Wm Brewer Farm Prop. Dairy, quart, J. B. Brooks, 86 Fulton St., New York, Maker on base 150.00

MILK GLASS

History: Opaque white glass attained its greatest popularity at the end of the 19th century. American glass manufacturers made opaque white tablewares as a substitute for costly European china and glass. Other opaque colors, e.g., blue and green, also were made. Production of milk glass novelties came in with the Edwardian era.

The surge of popularity in milk glass subsided after World War I. However, milk glass continues to be made in the 20th century. Some modern products are reissues and reproductions of earlier forms. This presents a significant problem for collectors, although it is partially obviated by patent dates or company markings on the originals and by the telltale signs of age.

Collectors favor milk glass from the pre-World War I era, especially animal-covered dishes. The most prolific manufacturers of these animal covers were Atterbury, Challinor-Taylor, Flaccus, and McKee.

References: E. McCamley Belknap, *Milk Glass*, Crown Publishers, 1949, out of print; Regis F. and Mary F. Ferson, *Today's Prices for Yesterday's Milk Glass*, published by authors, 1985; ——, *Yesterday's Milk Glass Today*, published by authors, 1981; Everett Grist, *Covered Animal Dishes*, Collector Books, 1988, 1993 value update; Lorraine Kovar, *Westmoreland Glass*, 2 Vols., Antique Publications, 1991; S. T. Millard, *Opaque Glass*, 4th ed., Wallace Homestead, 1975, out of print; Betty and Bill Newbound, *Collector's Encyclopedia of Milk Glass*, Collector Books, 1995.

Collectors' Club: National Milk Glass Collectors Society, 46 Almond Dr., Hershey, PA 17033.

Museum: Houston Antique Museum, Chattanooga, TN.

Notes: There are many so-called "McKee" animal-covered dishes. Caution must be exercised in evaluating pieces because some authentic covers were not signed. Furthermore, many factories have made, and many still are making, split-rib bases with McKee-like animal covers or with different animal covers. The prices below are for authentic McKee pieces with either the cover or base signed.

Numbers in listings prefixed with a letter refer to books listed in the references, wherein the letter identifies the first letter of the author's name.

Animal Dish, cov

Baboon, fleur de lis base, seated baboon, facing to one side, attributed to Flaccus (F114) 600.00

Chick emerging from egg, basketweave base 80.00

Deer, fallen tree base, sgd "E. C. Flaccus Co., Wheeling, WV" (F34) 185.00

Elephant with Rider (F1). 700.00

Hen, large, blue head, white body 45.00

Rabbit, patent date on base, Atterbury (F48) 175.00

Robin with Berry (F217) 75.00
Squirrel, acorn base (F15) 145.00
Bon Bon, scoop shape, Eagle Glass Co., 1899 (F597) . . 45.00
Bowl
　Arch Border pattern, 8" d, alternating wade curved arches
　　and interlocking narrow pointed arches, Challinor, Taylor
　　(B100a) 50.00
　Cut Star pattern, 7-1/4" d, blue, scalloped edge, twelve rated
　　stars (F289) 75.00
Bread Tray, basketweave border, motto "Give Us Our Daily
　Bread" inscribed on rim, Atterbury (F345) 75.00
Butter Dish, cov
　Crossed Fern pattern, 6"d, animal claw grasping ball feet and
　　finial, scalloped edge, Atterbury (F232) 75.00
　Gooseberry pattern, narrow beaded edges, band of fruit on
　　cov and base, berry finial, Sandwich (F248) 120.00
Candlestick, 3-3/8" h, clown, bust rises from wide curved neck
　ruffle (F129) 75.00
Celery Vase, Burred Hobnail pattern 45.00
Charger, Grape 40.00
Child's Mug, Little Bo Peep (M-92) 85.00
Compote
　Blackberry pattern, 9" h, large figural blackberry finial on cov,
　　Hobbs Brockunier (B121) 160.00
　Chick and Eggs, 11" h, pedestal, chick emerging from
　　heaped eggs, finial cov, mounted on curved tripod, central
　　support, rounded lacy edge base, emb Atterbury patent
　　date, Aug 6., 1889 inside cov (F362) 185.00
　Prism pattern, 8" d, 5-1/2" h, wafer connection between Prism
　　bowl and foot 155.00
Creamer
　Blackberry pattern 45.00
　Burred Hobnail pattern 45.00
　Forget Me Not pattern 40.00
　Paneled Wheat pattern, Hobbs Brockunier (F255) . . . 65.00
　Roman Cross pattern (F239) 50.00
Cruet, Tree of Life pattern, blue 80.00
Fish Set, figural fish platter, four serving dishes, Atterbury, emb
　patent date 250.00
Inkwell, horseshoe, circular inkwell in center, pen rests (F449)
　. . . . . 45.00
Lamp, 20-1/4" h, clear and milk glass shade, clear font with cut
　stars, ovals, and strawberry point roundels, brass collar and
　connector, brass kerosene burner, milk glass base . . 275.00
Jar, cov, figural
　Eagle, "Old Abe," leafy base, "E. Pluribus Unum" on encircled
　　banner, gray (F568) 115.00
　Owl, glass eyes 85.00
Match Holder
　Indian Head (B219) 125.00
　Jolly Jester, patent date on rear (F201) 135.00
Miniature Lamp, 9" h, Chrysanthemum pattern, emb swirls and
　pink and yellow flowers, matching shade and base . . 290.00
Perfume Bottle, 7-1/2" h, Lightner's, emb cylindrical bottle, col-
　orful oval recessed reverse painted label, bulbous shaped
　stopper
　Helitrope Perfume, very minor paint loss around label edge
　　. . . . . 275.00
　Lily of the Valley Perfume. 375.00
　Maid of the Mist Perfume 375.00
　West End Perfume, crack in label, some discoloration
　　. . . . . 175.00
Pitcher
　Birds on Branch pattern, trio of small birds on leafy branch,
　　cold painted dec (F519) 110.00
　Dart and Bar pattern, 8" h, blue, rect handle, ftd (B85a)
　　. . . . . 100.00

Miniature Lamp, Daisy and Button Variant pattern, orig fittings and chimney, Smith #419, 7-3/8" h, $150.

Fish pattern, 7-1/4" h, finely detailed, Atterbury (F328)
. . . . 185.00
Plate
　Backward C with Lincoln 50.00
　Contrary Mule. 25.00
　Cupid & Psyche 25.00
　Easter Chicks 38.00
　Easter Verse. 20.00
　Gothic and Chain border, black 35.00
　Pinwheel, black 20.00
　Scroll and Waffle, McKee. 20.00
　Serenade, Greentown 55.00
　Wicket. 20.00
Platter, 13-1/4" l, Retriever, swimming dog pursuing duck
　through cattails, lily pad border (B53). 120.00
Salt Shaker
　Atterbury Dredge, 3-3/8" h, combination octagonal paneled
　　and pepper shapers shaped as small cov stein (F415)
　　. . . . . 95.00
　Diamond Point and Leaf pattern, 2-3/4" h, blue (F489)
　　. . . . . 50.00
Spooner
　Melon with Leaf and Net, Atterbury 40.00
　Paneled Flower, 4-5/8" h, ribbing separates six diamond
　　point panels, stylized floral dec, scalloped edges, Challinor,
　　Taylor (F284) 60.00
Sugar Bowl, cov
　Almond Thumbprint, 7-1/2" h, large scalloped edges (F367)
　　. . . . . 120.00
　Ceres pattern, 7-1/4" h, cameo profiles in beaded circles,
　　leafy sprays, bust finial (B127). 115.00
　Forget Me Not pattern 40.00
　Melon with Leaf and Net pattern, Atterbury 45.00
　Roman Cross pattern (F239) 50.00
　Sunflower pattern (B82b) 65.00
Sugar Shaker
　Netted Oak pattern, 4-1/4" h, oak leaf centered on netted
　　panels, green top band, Northwood (F495) 85.00
　Royal Oak pattern 90.00
Syrup, Pattern #87, Hobbs, orig top 110.00
Tumbler, Louisiana Purchase 55.00

MILLEFIORI

History: Millefiori (thousand flowers) is an ornamental glass composed of bundles of colored glass rods fused together into canes. The canes were pulled to the desired length while still ductile, sliced, arranged in a pattern, and fused together again. The Egyptians developed this technique in the first century B.C. it was revived in the 1880s.

REPRODUCTION ALERT

Millefiori items, such as paperweights, cruets, and toothpicks, are being made by many modern companies.

Basket, 10-1/2" h, 6-1/2" w, random pattern of millefiori canes, white opal ground cased in colorless, butterscotch irid surface, applied pale pink loop handle 200.00
Bowl
    2" d, pink, green, and white canes, applied colorless handles
    . . . . 48.00
    4" d, blue and white canes, applied colorless handles
    . . . . 80.00
Box, cov, 3" d, multicolored. 125.00
Creamer, 4" h, white ground, scattered millefiori, applied handle
    . . . . 250.00
Dish
    4-3/8" d, 1-1/2" h, close concentric millefiori, blue, white, and amethyst canes, signature Whitefriars monk cane, dated "1977". 80.00
    5" d, octagonal, blue and white canes 125.00

Miniature Lamp, cobalt blue, orange and ochre canes, brass trim, electrified, 12" h, $625.

Flask, 4-1/2" x 3" x 1", millefiori separated by blue and white filigrana threads 275.00
Jack In The Pulpit Vase, multicolored canes, matte finish, Italian, c1950 . . . . 65.00
Inkwell, 4-1/2" h, sgd "Paul Ysart". 200.00
Jug, 2-1/4" h, multicolored canes, applied colorless handle
    . . . . 95.00
Miniature Lamp
    8-1/2" h, mushroom cap shade, bulbous base, multicolored canes 375.00
    11" h, mushroom cap shade, matching glass lamp shaft, red, blue, and white, gilt metal "Bryant electrical fittings"
    . . . . 1,200.00
Perfume Bottle, 8-1/2" h, varicolored fitted canes, colorless tapered body, conforming integrated stopper 225.00
Vase
    3-1/2" h, waisted, ruffled top, light blue, cobalt blue, medium blue, and white canes, four applied knob handles . . . 65.00
    4" d, handkerchief, red ground, gold dust ext. 180.00
    5-1/2" h, purple bands, white oval lines and bands, red flowers, yellow centers 175.00
    8" h, ruffled rim, multicolored canes, applied colorless handles 190.00

MINIATURE LAMPS

History: Miniature oil and kerosene lamps, often called "night lamps," are diminutive replicas of larger lamps. Simple and utilitarian in design, miniature lamps found a place in the parlor (as "courting" lamps), hallway, children's rooms, and sickrooms.

Miniature lamps are found in many glass types, from amberina to satin glass. Miniature lamps measure 2-1/2 to 12 inches in height, with the principle parts being the base, collar, burner, chimney, and shade. In 1877, both L. J. Atwood and L. H. Olmsted patented burners for miniature lamps. Their burners made the lamps into a popular household accessory.

References: Marjorie Hulsebus, *Miniature Victorian Lamps*, Schiffer Publishing, 1996; Frank R. and Ruth E. Smith, *Miniature Lamps* (1981), Book II (1982) Schiffer Publishing; John F. Solverson, *Those Fascinating Little Lamps: Miniature Lamps and Their Values*, Antique Publications, 1988, includes prices for Smith numbers.

Collectors' Club: Night Light, 38619 Wakefield Ct., Northville, MI 48167.

REPRODUCTION ALERT

Study a lamp carefully to make certain all parts are original; married pieces are common. Reproductions abound.

Note: The numbers given below refer to the figure numbers found in the Smith books.

#23-I, Time, clear, emb "Time and Light, Pride of America, Grand Vals Perfect Time Indicating Lamp," white beehive chimney, 6-5/8"h. 265.00
#36-I, Little Buttercup, amethyst, applied handle, nutmeg burner, 2-3/4" h 100.00
#109-I, Beaded Heart, green, six toed foot, acorn burner, 5-3/8" h 315.00

China, blue Delft dec, 6-1/8" h, $180.

#112-I, Bull's Eye, emerald green, acorn burner, 4-7/8" h 100.00
#209-I, white milk glass, emb design and flowers, multicolored paint, nutmeg burner, 9-1/2" h 150.00
#228-II, amber, 5-7/8" h 125.00
#276-I, Pineapple in the Basket, white milk glass, fired-on brown paint, ruffled burner, 7-3/8" h 175.00
#288-I, red satin glass, emb designs, P & A Victor burner, 11-1/2" h 300.00
#317-I, white milk glass base and shade, green ground, pink and yellow daisy dec, nutmeg burner, 8-1/2" h 375.00
#385-I, peachblow, 6 7/8" h, chips on shade rim 440.00
#390-I, bright yellow, melon ribbed shade and base, glossy finish, nutmeg burner, 7" h 525.00
#425-I, irid green, emb dec, nutmeg burner, 9-3/4" h . . . 450.00
#458-II, white milk glass, heavily emb daisies and leaves, large white milk glass balls around base 400.00
#467-II, blue opal, applied clear feet, foreign burner, 7-3/4" h 325.00
#513-I, Swirl, blue opal, acorn burner, 4-3/4" h 165.00

MINIATURE PAINTINGS

History: Prior to the advent of the photograph, miniature portraits and silhouettes were the principal way of preserving a person's image. Miniaturists were plentiful, and they often made more than one copy of a drawing. The extras were distributed to family and friends.

Miniaturists worked in watercolors and oil and on surfaces such as paper, vellum, porcelain, and ivory. The miniature paintings were often inserted into jewelry or mounted inside or on the lids of snuff boxes. The artists often supplemented commission work by painting popular figures of the times and copying important works of art.

After careful study miniature paintings have been divided into schools, and numerous artists are now being researched. Many fine examples may be found in today's antiques marketplace.

Reference: Dale T. Johnson, *American Portrait Miniatures in the Manney Collection*, The Metropolitan Museum of Art, 1990.

Museum: Colonial Williamsburg Foundation, Williamsburg, VA; Gibbes Museum of Art, Charleston, SC.

2" h, 1-5/8" w, watercolor on ivory, portraits of young couple, unsgd, American School, 19th C, common frame 1,265.00
2" h, 2-1/2" w, watercolor on ivory, memorial portrait of small child, unsgd, America School, 19th C, in leather case 825.00
2-1/4" d, watercolor on ivory, young lady with lace bonnet and collar, blue and white ribbon, round brass frame, sgd on reverse of paper baking "Verschinden 1839" 200.00
2-1/4" h, watercolor on ivory, gentleman in dark blue coat, Continental School, 19th C, oval locket case with matching tooling, added easel back 115.00
2-3/8" h, 1-7/8" w, watercolor on ivory, gentleman, unsgd, American School, 19th C, pendant frame 650.00
2-3/8" h, 1-7/8" w, watercolor on ivory, heightened with gum arabic, woman in black dress, unsgd, American School, 19th C, framed, split, minor losses, minor pigment loss, surface abrasions 225.00
2-5/8" h, 2-1/8" w, watercolor on paper, gentleman in blue frock coat, unsgd, American School, 19th C, pendant frame, scattered pigment loss, toning 230.00
2-3/4" h, 2-1/4" d, watercolor in ivory, Miss Trumansburg of New York, unsgd, American School, 19th C, identified on label, framed 650.00
2-7/8" h, 2-3/8" w, watercolor on paper, reverse identified "John R. Risle 22 years old," unsgd, American School, 19th C, period frame, toning, minor pigment loss, very minor staining, cut down 435.00
3-1/16" h, 2-3/8" w, watercolor on ivory, lady with gold necklace, unsgd, American School, 19th C, framed, very minor pigment loss, surface grime 200.00
3-1/16" h, 2-5/8" w, watercolor on paper, heightened with gum arabic, Morrill Children of Strafford, VT, unsigned, period gilt gesso frames, pr 8,100.00
3-1/8" h, 2-1/2" w, watercolor in ivory, Franklin Pierce, identified on paper label, unsgd, attributed to Elkanah Tisdale, leather case, ... 450.00
3-1/8" h, 2-1/2" w, watercolor on ivory, Miss Harriet Pierce of Providence, Rhode Island, unsgd, American School, 19th C, unframed, laid down, very minor pigment loss 1,610.00
3-1/4" h, 2-1/2" w, watercolor on ivory, gentleman, unsgd, Anglo/American School, 19th C, framed 500.00
3-1/4" h, 2-5/8" w, watercolor on ivory, uniformed Naval officer, period frame, American School, 19th C 550.00
3-1/4" h, 2-5/8" w, watercolor on paper, gentleman, attributed to Justus Dalee, framed, toning, scattered staining 350.00
3-1/4" h, 2-5/8" w, watercolor on paper, gum arabic highlights, Mr. & Mrs. E. F. Wade, East Avon, NY, 1848, unsigned, identified on reverse of frame, pr in common frame 2,185.00

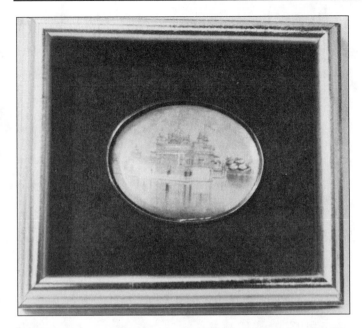

Hand painted on ivory, cene of house by lake, Continental School, 19th C, 2-3/4" x 2-1/4" without frame, $225.

3-1/4" h, 4-3/4" w, watercolor on paper, two children, sgd illegibly and dated lower right "L. K. Kov...1881," American School, framed, minor toning and staining 230.00

3-3/8" h, 2-3/4" w, watercolor on paper, unsgd, American School, identified as "Susan 1834 age 3...years," period frame 350.00

3-3/8" h, 3" w, watercolor on paper, gentleman, blue coat, unsgd, American School, 19th C, inscribed "painted January the 16th 1824," framed, toning, scattered foxing, creases, text, tack hole 425.00

3-1/2" h, oil on porcelain, profile of elegant woman, Renaissance-style costume, Continental School, 19th C, oval, framed 150.00

3-1/2" h, watercolor on celluloid, bust portrait of young lady, American School, c1920-30, mounted in silver frame 100.00

3-1/2" h, 2-1/2" w, watercolor on ivory, gentleman in frock coat, unsgd, American School, 19th C, framed. 350.00

3-1/2" h, 2-7/8" w, watercolor on ivory, regal lady, sgd "Rubens," minor edge wear, narrow brass frame 220.00

3-5/8" h, 2-3/4" w, watercolor on ivory, woman with shawl, unsgd, American School, 19th C, framed. 920.00

3-5/8" h, 3-1/8" w, watercolor on porcelain, gentleman with handlebar mustache, Continental School, 19th C, mounted as brooch, oval frame 110.00

3-3/4" h, 2-5/8" w, watercolor on paper, young couple, reverse sgd "drawn by Peter Louise, Taken June 12th 1824," birth dates of sitters, period common frame, toning, scattered staining, very minor tear and losses. 3,105.00

3-3/4" h, 3" w, oil on ivory, Napoleon and Josephine, Continental School, 19th C, similar brass frames, stains and discoloration 475.00

3-3/4" h, 3" w, watercolor on paper, gentleman in black waistcoat, framed, unsgd, but attributed to Rufus Porter, toning, scattered minor staining, tear, minor loss to lower edge, minor pigment loss. 750.00

3-9/16" h, 2-1/2" w, watercolor on paper, gentleman, unsgd, attributed to Rufus Porter, framed, toning, minor fading 350.00

4" h, 3-1/4" w, watercolor on ivory, American School, 19th C, framed, identified as Frances Pamela Howe, age 3, on paper label 7,475.00

4" h, 3-1/4" w, watercolor on paper, gentleman, attributed to Rufus Porter, framed. .1,265.00

4-1/8" h, 3-3/8" w, watercolor on ivory, young woman with dog, sgd "Pomney," gilded frame, easel back 440.00

4-3/8" h, 3-3/4" w, watercolor and gouache on paper, young lady in white dress, unsgd, American School, 19th, framed in period pressed brass frame 575.00

4-1/2" h, 3-3/8" w, oil on ivory, young woman, classical attire, floral garland, sgd "Piahant," worn dark finish on frame 325.00

4-7/8" h, 4-1/4" w, watercolor and graphite with gum arabic on paper, lady in black dress, unsgd, American School, 19th C, period style grain painted frame, toning, scattered minor staining. 700.00

4-11/16" h, 3-3/4" w, watercolor on ivory, Mrs. A. Mills of Brookline, identified on reverse, ornate gilt gesso frame with brass mat, mkd "WW," laid down, very minor surface abrasions. 500.00

5" h, 3-7/8" w, and 4-5/8" h, 3-7/8" w, watercolor on paper, Captain and Mrs. David Williams, unsgd, identified on reverse as "this likeness was teken at the age of 34, 1827 Cap.n David Williams...St. Paul, Bristol," heightened with gum arabic, period frames, laid down, minor toning, pr 1,725.00

5" h, 4-1/4" d, watercolor on paper, lady holding roses, framed, American School, 19th C 5,650.00

5-1/4" h, 4-1/2" w, watercolor on ivory, woman with white laced bonnet and collar with black dress, minor edge damage, American School, 19th C, black lacquer frame with gilded band and brass trim, wear and edge damage 360.00

5-1/4" h, 4-3/4" w, watercolor on ivory, Napoleon, Josephine, and attendant Marshall, landscape scene, Continental School, late 19th C, gilt metal frame 1,380.00

5-1/2" h, oil on porcelain, bust portrait of 19th C woman, sgd "Rucqver," Continental School, rococo gilt metal frame 200.00

5-3/4" h, 5-1/8" w, watercolor on ivory, gentleman with white hair, dark blue frock coat, Continental School, 19th C, repainted background, black lacquered frame with brass trim 330.00

5-7/8" h, 5-1/4" w, watercolor and graphite heightened with gum arabic on paper, young lady with book, unsgd, American School, 19th C, D. Felt & Co. London watermark, period style grain painted frame, toning, minor staining, fading 6,325.00

6-1/2" h, 5-3/4" w, oil on ivory, French military officer, sgd "Lovaghy," ebonized frame mkd "Made in France" and inscribed "LaFayette" 385.00

6-1/2" h, 6-1/4" w, watercolor and graphite on paper, heightened with gum arabic, young lady holding book, Jane A. Davis, period veneer frame, very minor staining. 2,300.00

7-1/4" h, 5-1/2" w, oil on ivory, French woman, elaborate coiffure, playing keyboard instrument, sgd "Bouillard," stain in one corner, ivory and brass frame 860.00

7-3/8" h, 6-1/4' w, oil on canvas, scene of woman kneeling with book beside young girl in bed, illegible signature in lower right, edge wear 550.00

7-1/2" h, 6-3/4" w, oil on porcelain, classical likeness of Dauphne, laurel wreath, sgd, Continental School, 19th C, Florentine frame 250.00

7-7/8" h, 9-5/8" w, watercolor on ivory, pair, busts, Continental School, 19th C, mounted on green velvet, gilded brass and brown brocade frame 660.00

8" h, 7" w, oil on pressed board, portrait of man with beard, later label on backing "Howard Woodward, painted for bride to be, Clinton, Michigan," edge and surface wear, ornate frame with gold repaint. 400.00

8" h, 7-1/4" w, watercolor on ivory, young Indian woman, richly dressed, adorned with jewels, sgd "Bender" 325.00

9-1/4" h, 7-7/8" w, watercolor on paper, mother and child surrounded by garland of flowers, sgd on reverse "Betsey E. Scott," framed, toning, scattered foxing, minor losses to corners 1,840.00

MINIATURES

History: There are three sizes of miniatures: dollhouse scale (ranging from 1/2 to 1 inch), sample size, and child's size. Since most early material is in museums or is extremely expensive, the most common examples in the marketplace today are from the 20th century.

Many mediums were used for miniatures: silver, copper, tin, wood, glass, and ivory. Even books were printed in miniature. Price ranges are broad, influenced by scarcity and quality of workmanship.

The collecting of miniatures dates back to the 18th century. It remains one of the world's leading hobbies.

References: George M. Beylerian, *Chairmania*, Harry N. Abrams, 1994; Caroline Clifton-Mogg, *Dollhouse Sourcebook*, Abbeville Press, 1993; Nora Earnshaw, *Collecting Dolls' Houses and Miniatures*, Pincushion Press, 1993; Flora Gill Jacobs, *Dolls Houses in America*, Charles Scribner's Sons, 1974; ——, *History of Dolls Houses*, Charles Scribner's Sons; Constance Eileen King, *Dolls and Dolls Houses*, Hamlyn, 1989; Herbert F. Schiffer and Peter B. Schiffer, *Miniature Antique Furniture*, Schiffer Publishing, 1995; Margaret Towner, *Dollhouse Furniture*, Courage Books, Running Press, 1993.

Periodicals: *Doll Castle News*, P.O. Box 247, Washington, NJ 07882; *Miniature Collector*, Scott Publications, 30595 Eight Mile Rd., Livonia, MI 48152; *Nutshell News*, 21027 Crossroads Circle, P.O. Box 1612, Waukesha, WI 53187.

Collectors' Clubs: International Guild Miniature Artisans, P.O. Box 71, Bridgeport, NY 18080; Miniature Industry Association of America Member News, 2270 Jacquelyn Dr., Madison, WI 53711; National Association of Miniature Enthusiasts, 2621 Anaheim, CA 92804-3883.

Museums: Colonial Williamsburg Foundation, Williamsburg, VA; Margaret Woodbury Strong Museum, Rochester, NY; Mildred Mahoney Jubilee Doll House Museum, Fort Erie, Canada; Museums at Stony Brook, Stony Brook, NY; Toy and Miniature Museum of Kansas City, Kansas City, MO; Toy Museum of Atlanta, Atlanta, GA; Washington Dolls' House and Toy Museum, Washington, DC.

Additional Listings: See Dollhouse Furnishings in *Warman's Americana & Collectibles* for more examples.

Child size

Blanket Chest

15-3/8" l, cherry, dovetailed case, dovetailed bracket feet, applied lid edge molding, till with lid, old finish, faint pencil inscription on bottom "Made by Mr. ___," in the year of 1847,

Loudoun Co., Va., "Presented to R. G. Axline by Mrs. Mary Axline" 3,575.00

Cart, wood, America, 19th C, minor losses, very minor paint wear

24" l, 10" h, green painted body, red wheels, black striping 500.00

29-1/2" l, pumpkin dec on dark blue ground, yellow wheels, black highlights, dated "Pat. Jan 12 1869". 500.00

Chair

Hitchcock, Hitchocksville, CT, early 19th C, side, rolled crest above rect splat, rush seat, ring-turned legs, black painted ground, some graining, gold leaf dec, minor surface imperfections, 16" h seat, 21" h 900.00

Windsor, bow-back, painted, remnants of old ochre paint, ew England, 19th C, minor imperfections, 13-1/4" h seat, 29" h 2,760.00

Chest of Drawers

Empire, refinished cherry and curly maple, decorative inlay on facade, two dovetailed top drawers, three graduated long drawers (bottoms and backs removed to create hollow int. compartment) paneled ends, half column pilasters, turned legs, back board missing, 21-1/2" w, 12-1/2"d, 25-1/2" h. 2,310.00

Federal, refinished cherry, top posts with inlaid panels, four dovetailed drawers with applied edge beading, scrolled apron with inlaid heart, turned and rope carved half column pilasters and feet, replaced clear glass pulls, repairs to feet, 24" w, 12-1/4" d, 26" h 3,250.00

Hepplewhite, cherry, inlay, four dovetailed drawers with striped banded inlay on edges, scrolled apron, French feet, old finish, replaced brasses, 15" w, 8-1/4" d, 19-1/4" h 3,960.00

Chest over Drawer, William and Mary, attributed to coastal MA, early 18th C, painted pine, hinged molded top over half-round molded case, applied molded drawer on base, four turned ball feet, top carved "B. Swale," front and sides red painted wash and brown freehand design of concentric rings, demi-lune and meandering lines, drawer painted in salmon, red, and brown, single arch molding painted black, minor imperfections, 28" w, 17-1/8" d, 19" h 9,200.00

Sofa, china, hp pastel floral motif, gold trim, late 19th C, French or German, $80.

Rocker

9-1/2" h seat, 24-3/4" h back, New England, 1860-80, painted and dec, floral painted crest rail over spindles, natural arms, plank seat with rolled rail above rockers, old blue paint, surface imperfections 350.00

23" h, 14" d, 16" d, red stained birch, New England, early 19th C, shaped back and sides, pierced handles, trapezoidal seat, cut-out skirt, seat replaced 425.00

School Desk and Chair, 29" h chair, 26" w x 26-1/2" h desk, wood, adjustable wrought iron base patented June 1896, polychrome scenic, scrolling devices, foliate dec, sgd "Peter Hunt from Cape Cod," surface imperfections 450.00

Storage Chest, painted dec, New England, 19th C, dovetail construction

6-3/4" h, 14" d, 7-1/4" d, lid and base with applied molded edge, dark umber on mustard ground dec, very minor wear, crack in top 1,100.00

7-3/4" h, 14-1/2" 2, 7-3/4" d, lid and base with applied molded rim, black and white, red checked design, minor paint loss, crack in top 1,495.00

Dollhouse size

Andirons, pr, 5-1/4" h, brass, ribbed, English, 19th C . . . 300.00
Basket, metal, moveable handle, 3" x 1-1/2" 50.00
Bathroom Set, Tootsietoy, metal, c1920, 8 pcs 95.00
Bed, maple, honey finish, scalloped head and footboard, 6-1/4" h, c1900 . . . . 110.00
Candlesticks, pr, brass, 1" h, c1900 . . . . 42.00
Chair, carved wood, scrolled back and arms, blue velvet upholstery, 5-1/2" h, pr 60.00
Chest, walnut, Victorian, step back top, hinged doors with Gothic shaped arches, inset mirrors, two drawer base, curved Federal style feet, 11" h 65.00
Christmas Tree, undecorated 20.00
Coffee Grinder, wood base, iron fittings 90.00
Cradle, earthenware, deep yellow glaze, molded interlocking circle design, 4-5/8" l 300.00
Desk, Biedermeier, marble top, stencil dec, black ground, c1860 . . . . 350.00
Dining Room Suite, maple, Art Nouveau style, rect extension table with two leaves, four matching scrolled back chairs, black leather seats and backs 125.00
Dresser Set, hp, china, 15 pcs 35.00
Fireplace, Victorian, filigree metal, orig tools 95.00
Lamp, banquet style, gilt metal, urn shaped emb base, circular blown glass shade 200.00
Living Room Suite, metal, 4 pcs, love seat, recliner chair, two side chairs, pink velvet upholstered, mkd "The Fairy Furniture Set, Always For Cooke's Indestructable Toys," orig wood box 90.00
Mirror, brass, ormolu, turned columns support oval mirror, 1" x 2", 19th C 115.00
Park Bench, metal 10.00
Piano, upright, tin, brown painted ground, gilt trim, scrolled crest, emb back, scrolled swivel candle arms, hinged keyboard cov, 3 legged stool with painted red seat, 3-1/4" x 3-1/2" . . 85.00
Sofa, Regency, black walnut, green velvet upholstery, needlepoint and velvet pillows, 1840 styling, 9-1/2" l 215.00
Table, carved wood, painted scene on top 65.00
Tea Set, cov teapot, creamer, and sugar, English silver, Birmingham hallmarks, 1-1/4" h, 1906 . . . . 160.00
Towel Rack, Victorian, wooden 30.00
Waffle Iron, 7-1/2" l, mkd "Wagner Mfg. Co. Sidney, O" 175.00
Wardrobe, oak, golden finish, 1" scale, c1900 . . . . 100.00

MINTON CHINA

History: In 1793, Thomas Minton joined other men to form a partnership and build a small pottery at Stoke-on-Trent, Staffordshire, England. Production began in 1798 with blue-printed earthenware, mostly in the Willow pattern. In 1798, cream-colored earthenware and bone china were introduced.

A wide range of styles and wares was produced. Minton introduced porcelain figures in 1826, Parian wares in 1846, encaustic tiles in the late 1840s, and Majolica wares in 1850. Many famous designers and artists in the English pottery industry worked for Minton.

In 1883, the modern company was formed and called Mintons Limited. The "s" was dropped in 1968. Minton still produces bone-china tablewares and some ornamental pieces.

Marks: Many early pieces are unmarked or have a Sevres-type marking. The "ermine" mark was used in the early 19th century. Date codes can be found on tableware and majolica. The mark used between 1873 and 1911 was a small globe with a crown on top and the word "Minton."

References: Paul Atterbury and Maureen Batkin, *Dictionary of Minton*, Antique Collectors' Club; Susan and Al Bagdade, *Warman's English & Continental Pottery & Porcelain*, 3rd Edition, Krause Publications, 1998; Joan Jones, *Minton: The First Two Hundred Years of Design and Production*, Swan Hill, 1993.

Museum: Minton Museum, Staffordshire, England; Victoria & Albert Museum, London, England.

Bowl, 12-1/2" d, floral reserves, cobalt blue ground, gold trim, c1810 . . . . 1,450.00
Breakfast Set, plate with attached toast rack, salt and pepper shapers, Dejeuneau, green mark 200.00
Bulb Planter, 10-3/4" l, majolica, emb brown fence, green leaves, turquoise lining, mkd 150.00
Cup and Saucer, hp, bird vignettes and flower blossoms, aqua borders 55.00
Cup Plate, 3-7/8" d, central medium blue transfer floral design, zig-zag rim border, c1830 . . . . 100.00
Demitasse Cup and Saucer, scrolling reserves of flowers, gilt dec, cobalt blue ground, c1900 . . . . 295.00
Floor Vase, 25" h, 12" d, Aesthetic Movement, squat, scalloped base, transfer-printed blue and yellow flowers, ivory ground, stamped "Minton's/Made in England" 500.00
Jardiniere, 22" h, two figural handles, multicolored floral design, navy blue ground, imp mark, minor glaze flaws, chip repair 1,300.00
Marmalade Jar, butterflies, blue ground, c1920 . . . . 50.00
Oyster Plate, emb fish, white ground 60.00
Plate

8-7/8" d, multicolored, tortoise and hare in field near lake, basketweave molded border, loop pierced rim, Bernard Rischgitz 75.00

10-1/4" d, pate-sur-pate, blue border, white classical scenes, sgd "Birks" 160.00

10-1/2" d, cream center, parcel gilt cornucopia, husk, and swag draping, retailed for Tiffany, set of 12 . . . . . . 1,840.00

Wash Bowl, Gaudy English Imari pattern, blue transfer, red and yellow enameling, imp mark, wear, crazing, and some possible hairlines, 15-1/2" d, 5" h, $165. Photo courtesy of Garth's Auctions, Inc.

Portrait Plate, 9-1/8" d, young woman, Victorian dress, multicolored, plique-a-jour border, sgd "A. Bouilemier," pr . .1,800.00
Tile, 6" sq, King Henry 70.00
Tureen, cov, undertray, 14-1/4" w, Oriental garden scene, black transfers with enameled accents, ribbed handles, loop knob, c1882 . . . . 400.00
Vase
    5-1/2" h, bulbous, handled, green, white cameo 95.00
    11-1/2" h, tapered cylindrical shape, flaring rim, Arts and Crafts style green and yellow flowerheads and stems, blue ground 400.00
Wash Bowl and Pitcher, amethyst, ruby red, and yellow floral dec 200.00

MOCHA

History: Mocha decoration usually is·found on utilitarian creamware and stoneware pieces and was produced through a simple chemical action. A color pigment of brown, blue, green, or black was made acidic by an infusion of tobacco or hops. When the acidic colorant was applied in blobs to an alkaline ground, it reacted by spreading in feathery designs resembling sea plants. This type of decoration usually was supplemented with bands of light-colored slip.

Types of decoration vary greatly, from those done in a combination of motifs, such as Cat's Eye and Earthworm, to a plain pink mug decorated with green ribbed bands. Most forms of mocha are hollow, e.g., mugs, jugs, bowls, and shakers.

English potters made the vast majority of the pieces. Collectors group the wares into three chronological periods: 1780-1820, 1820-1840, and 1840-1880.

Marks: Marked pieces are extremely rare.

References: Susan and Al Bagdade, *Warman's English & Continental Pottery & Porcelain*, 3rd Edition, Krause Publications, 1998.

Reproduction Alert.

Bowl
    7-1/2" d, 5-1/2" h, agate glaze, hairline, minor chips . 575.00
    8-1/2" d, blue, white, and dark brown earthworm design, blue band, hairline on base 385.00
Creamer, 2-5/8" h, bulbous, black seaweed, amber center band, brown and white stripes, ribbed leaf handle 220.00
Milk Pitcher, 4-5/8" h, dark gray-blue band, black stripes, emb band, green and black seaweed, leaf hand 440.00
Mug
    3-1/2" h, center cream band with dark brown vertical stripes, dark brown ground, band of brown and cream circlets on rim, applied acanthus leaf handle 325.00
    3-5/8" h, gray band, brown and white stripes, black seaweed dec, leaf handle 165.00
    5" h, dark tan center band, blue, white, and dark brown earthworm design, dark brown and white stripe, leaf handle, hairlines 495.00
    5-1/2" h, earthworm design, impressed geometric border, dark brown, blue, and cream, pumpkin ground, hairlines, glaze wear to rim and handle, minute rim chips. . . . 525.00
    6-1/2" h, two small blue bands flanking wide central gray band, four large stocks of seaweed, applied handle 250.00
Mug Measure, 6" h, white ground, tan, blue, and black stripes and seaweed, leaf handle, mkd "Quart," stains and minor chips, short hairlines. 220.00
Mustard Pot, 4-1/8" h, bulbous, blue, tan, and white earthworm and cat's eye design, blue-gray center band, tan and white stripes, leaf handles, chips 220.00
Pitcher
    6-1/2" h, molded spout, leaf handle, machine tooled band, orange band with earthworm, white, light blue, pale green, and dark brown (black) bands and stripes, wear and chips, hairlines in foot 1,265.00
    7-1/2" h, 9" w, incised green band, two bands of blue, brown, and white cat eyes on black ground, central band of brown, blue, white, and black spot mottled dec on gray ground, ap-

Cream Pitcher, white ground, narrow black bands, blue wide bands, 3-3/4" h, $175.

plied dec handle, molded spout, crack on bottom, discoloration at base, side crack 1,750.00

8" h, earthworm and polka dots, tooled band, white, gray, black, yellow, brown, and green stripes, blue in earthworm, wear and damage, old repairs to handle, spout, and rim
. . . . 880.00

Waste Bowl, 5-5/8" d, white, blue, and dark brown earthworm design, red-orange band, dark brown stripes, emb green rim, hairlines 275.00

MONART GLASS

History: Monart glass is a heavy, simply shaped art glass in which colored enamels are suspended in the glass during the glassmaking process. This technique was originally developed by the Ysart family in Spain in 1923. John Moncrief, a Scottish glassmaker, discovered the glass while vacationing in Spain, recognized the beauty and potential market, and began production in his Perth glassworks in 1924.

The name "Monart" is derived from the surnames Moncrief and Ysart. Two types of Monart were manufactured: a commercial line which incorporated colored enamels and a touch of aventurine in crystal, and the art line in which the suspended enamels formed designs such as feathers or scrolls.

Marks: Monart glass, in most instances, is not marked. The factory used paper labels.

Bowl
7-1/4" d, 1-3/4" h, Cluthra, internally swirled and hooked green, amber, and aubergine, yellow ground, gold dust, orig label "Monart Glass/Moncreiff Scotland/YXI" 225.00

9" d, Aventurine, blue, mottled brown, and goldstone, pebbled texture 150.00

Vase, green pedestal shading to brown to clear to green rim, $65.

Candlestick, two shades of green, goldstone mica, paper label
. . . . 120.00

Vase
5-7/8" h, 5-5/8" d, mottled shades of blue, goldstone flecks, orig paper label 200.00

6-1/2" h, mottled shades of red and blue, white lining
. . . . 225.00

7" h, colorless, interior sapphire blue pulled elements enhanced by golden amber threading, blue rim border
. . . . 250.00

7" h, 7" w, gray, blue, and white swirls on dark red ground, orig paper label 215.00

8-1/2" h, goldstone shading to clear, cylindrical, flaring rim, Scottish Cluthra 225.00

11" h, mottled orange shade to deep orange at flared rim
. . . . 260.00

14" h, bulbous, tapered, extended neck, flared rim, blue shaded to pink, gold highlights, Cluthra 650.00

MONT JOYE GLASS

History: Mont Joye is a type of glass produced by Saint-Hilaire, Touvier, de Varreaux & Company at their glassworks in Pantin, France. Most pieces were lightly acid etched to give them a frosted appearance and were also decorated with enameled florals.

Note: Pieces listed below are frosted unless otherwise noted.

Bowl, 3-3/4" d, frosted ground, enameled floral dec, sgd
. . . . 275.00

Ewer, cov, cameo cutting, crystal, green, and gold, brass spout and handle, removable cover, artist sgd "Cristalle Rie Depantin" 550.00

Jar, cov, 8" h, cylindrical, crystal ground, etched, enameled iris, gilt leaves, crystal knob, gilt factory mark, c1900 . . . . 275.00

Vase
5-1/8" h, spherical, cylindrical neck and foot, frosted ground, etched and gilt oak leaves and acorns, gilt signature
. . . . 215.00

5-3/4" h, green glitter body, gold leaf painted dec, applied opal glass spheres 375.00

6-1/2" h, green frosted ground, cut poppies, crimson enamel and gilt trim 265.00

7-1/2" h, dark green satin ground, enameled pink iris dec
. . . . 400.00

8" h, light turquoise ground, etched iris dec, gold highlights, acid etched frosting, gold band around crimped edge
. . . . 395.00

8-1/2" h, cameo, icy frosted ground, enameled leaves, deep red poppies, sgd 450.00

9" h, frosted ground, enameled purple orchids, green leaves
. . . . 200.00

9-1/2" h, 6" w, ovoid, acid etched, lilies outlined in gold, body slightly ribbed, indented fluted top with gold accents, sgd, c1900 . . . . 600.00

11" h, tomato red ground, lacy gold dec, enameled iris and foliage dec. 250.00

13-3/4" h, flattened ovoid shape, cameo, crystal ground, etched, molded and enameled iris, gilt leaves, c1900
. . . . 350.00

Violet Vase, 6" h, frosted etched surface, colorless glass, naturalistic enameled purple violet blossoms, gold highlights, base mkd "Dimier Geneve" 260.00

MOORCROFT

History: William Moorcroft was first employed as a potter by James Macintyre & Co., Ltd., of Burslem in 1897. He established the Moorcroft pottery in 1913.

The majority of the art pottery wares were hand thrown, resulting in a great variation among similarly styled pieces. Color and marks are keys to determining age.

Walker, William's son, continued the business upon his father's death and made wares in the same style.

References: Paul Atterbury, *Moorcroft: A Guide to Moorcroft Pottery 1897-1993, Rev. Ed.,* Richard Dennis and Hugh Edwards, 1990; Susan and Al Bagdade, *Warman's English & Continental Pottery & Porcelain*, 3rd Edition, Krause Publications, 1998; A. W. Coysh, *British Art Pottery, 1870-1940*, Charles E. Tuttle, 1976; Frances Salmon, *Collecting Moorcroft*, Francis-Joseph Books, 1994.

Collectors' Club: Moorcroft Collectors' Club, Lipert International Inc., 2922 M. Street, NW, Washington, DC 20007.

Museums: Everson Museum of Art, Syracuse, NY; Moorcroft Museum, Stoke-on-Trent, England; Victoria & Albert Museum, London, England.

Marks: The company initially used an impressed mark, "Moorcroft, Burslem"; a signature mark, "W. Moorcroft" followed. Modern pieces are marked simply "Moorcroft" with export pieces also marked "Made in England."

Bowl, 4-1/2" d, pink and yellow flower dec, green leaves, cobalt blue glaze 60.00
Bulb Bowl, 6-1/2" d, white and purple narcissus, dark blue and green ground, "Potter to the Queen" mark 150.00
Compote, 7-1/2" x 5-1/2", Cornflower pattern, mottled green ground, mkd "W. Moorcroft" 500.00
Creamer and Sugar, Pomegranate pattern, celadon ground, sgd in ink "W. Moorcroft". 1,900.00
Floor Vase, 19-1/2" h, 8" d, Eventide pattern, squeezebag dec, green trees, shaded cobalt blue sky, copper liner, imp "MOORCROFT/MADE IN ENGLAND," small base chip
. . . . .7,000.00
Ginger Jar, 7" h, mkd "Walter Moorcroft, 1960" 110.00
Jardiniere, 5-3/4" h, multicolored panels, white ground, gilt trim, sgd "MacIntyre" 600.00
Lamp, 10-1/2" h, fruit and leaves flambe, 1928-34 . . . .1,400.00
Match Holder, 2-3/4" h, pink thistle flowers, mottled green ground, coat of arms, MacIntyre mark, green painted initials, "WM," printed "Redley Hall," c1897 . . . . 350.00
Vase
3-1/2" h, multicolored orchid design, orig label 375.00
6" h, Pomegranate design, hammered pewter top, imp and script marks, pr 1,300.00
6-1/2" h, multicolored floral design, green and blue ground, imp and painted marks. 325.00
7" h, 5" d, bulbous, Orchid pattern, dark flowers, teal green ground, stamped, imp "MOORCROFT/MADE IN ENGLAND/M74". 2,300.00
8-1/2" h, painted red, green, and yellow mushrooms, blue ground, imp and painted marks, Claremont. 2,400.00
10" h, 7" d, Florian Ware, two handles, blue and yellow anemones, white ground, sgd "W. Moorcfott des./Florian Ware" ink stamp 2,900.00

Bowl, Florian Ware, blue tones, 7-5/8" h, 2-1/2" h, $595.

13" h, 7-1/4" d, baluster, Pansy pattern, large pink and purple flowers, cobalt blue ground, , imp "MOORCROFT/MADE IN ENGLAND," ink signature 1,700.00

MORGANTOWN GLASS WORKS

History: The Morgantown Glass Works, Morgantown, West Virginia, was founded in 1899 and began production in 1901. Reorganized in 1903, it operated as the Economy Tumbler Company for 20 years until, in 1923, the word "Tumbler" was dropped from the corporate title. The firm was then known as The Economy Glass Company until reversion to its original name, Morgantown Glass Works, Inc., in 1929, the name it kept until its first closing in 1937. In 1939, the factory was reopened under the aegis of a guild of glassworkers and operated as the Morgantown Glassware Guild from that time until its final closing. Purchased by Fostoria in 1965, the factory operated as a subsidiary of the Moundsville-based parent company until 1971 when Fostoria opted to terminate production of glass at the Morgantown facility. Today, collectors use the generic term, "Morgantown Glass," to include all periods of production from 1901 to 1971.

Morgantown was a 1920s leader in the manufacture of colorful wares for table and ornamental use in American homes. The company pioneered the processes of iridization on glass as well as gold and platinum encrustation of patterns. They enhanced Crystal offerings with contrasting handle and foot of India Black, Spanish Red (ruby), and Ritz Blue (cobalt blue), and other intense and pastel colors for which they are famous. They conceived the use of contrasting shades of fired enamel to add color to their etchings. They were the only American company to use a chromatic silk-screen printing process on glass, their two most famous and collectible designs being Queen Louise and Manchester Pheasant.

The company is also known for ornamental "open stems" produced during the late 1920s. Open stems separate to form an open design midway between the bowl and foot, e.g., an open square, a "Y," or two diamond-shaped designs. Many of these open stems were purchased and decorated by Dorothy C. Thorpe in her California studio, and her signed open stems command high prices from today's collectors. Morgantown also produced figural stems for commercial clients such as

Koscherak Brothers and Marks & Rosenfeld. Chanticleer (rooster) and Mai Tai (Polynesian bis) cocktails are two of the most popular figurals collected today.

Morgantown is best known for the diversity of design in its stemware patterns as well as for their four patented optics: Festoon, Palm, Peacock, and Pineapple. These optics were used to embellish stems, jugs, bowls, liquor sets, guest sets, salvers, ivy and witch balls, vases, and smoking items.

Two well-known lines of Morgantown Glass are recognized by most glass collectors today: #758 Sunrise Medallion and #7643 Golf Ball Stem Line. When Economy introduced #758 in 1928, it was originally identified as "Nymph." By 1931, the Morgantown front office had renamed it Sunrise Medallion. Recent publications erred in labeling it "dancing girl." Upon careful study of the medallion, you can see the figure is poised on one tiptoe, musically saluting the dawn with her horn. The second well-known line, #7643 Golf Ball, was patented in 1928; production commenced immediately and continued until the company closed in 1971. More Golf Ball than any other Morgantown product is found on the market today.

References: Jerry Gallagher, *Handbook of Old Morgantown Glass*, Vol. I, published by author (420 First Ave. NW, Plainview, MN 55964), 1995; ——, *Old Morgantown, Catalogue of Glassware, 1931*, Morgantown Collectors of America Research Society, n.d.; Ellen Schroy, *Warman's Depression Glass*, Krause Publications, 1997; Hazel Marie Weatherman, *Colored Glassware of the Depression Era*, Book 2 published by author, 1974, available in reprint; ——, *1984 Supplement & Price Trends for Colored Glassware of the Depression Era*, Book 1, published by author, 1984.

Periodical: *Morgantown Newscaster*, Morgantown Collectors of America, 420 First Ave., NW, Plainview, MN 55964.

Collectors' Clubs: Old Morgantown Glass Collectors' Guild, P.O. Box 894, Morgantown, WV 26507.

Advisor: Jerry Gallagher.

Bowl
#1 Berkshire, Crystal w/#90 Starlet Cutting, 8" d 58.00
#12-1/2 Woodsfield, Genova Line, 12-1/2" d 545.00
#14 Fairlee, Glacier decoration, 8" d 525.00
#19 Kelsha, Genova Line, 12" d 425.00
#26 Greer, Neubian Line, 10" d 750.00
#35-1/2 Elena, Old Amethyst, applied Crystal rim, 8" d
. . . . 425.00
#67 Fantasia, Bristol Blue, 5-1/2" d 75.00
#101 Heritage, Gypsy Fire, Matte Finish, 8" d 70.00
#103 Elyse, Steel Blue, 7" d 48.00
#1102 Crown, Moss Green, 9" d 45.00
#1933 El Mexicana, console, Seaweed, 10" d 385.00
#1933 El Mexicano Ice Tub, Ice or Seaweed, 6" d . . 210.00
#4355 Janice, Ritz Blue or Spanish Red, 13" d 445.00
#4355 Janice, Crystal, Glacier Decor w/Snow Flowers, 13" d
. . . . 565.00
#7643 Truman, Spanish Red, Crystal trim, rare, 10" d
. . . . .4,500.00

Candleholders, pair
#37 Emperor, Stiegel Green or 14K Topaz, 8" h 625.00

#80 Modern, Moss Green, 7-1/2" h 70.00
#81 Bravo, Peacock Blue, 4-1/2" h528.00
#82 Cosmopolitan, Moss Green, slant, 7" h 75.00
#87 Hamilton, Evergreen, 5" h 75.00
#88 Classic, Nutmeg, 4-3/4" h 55.00
#105 Coronet, Ebony or Cobalt, slant, 8-3/4" h 120.00
#7620 Fontanne, Ebony filament, #781 Fontinelle etch
. . . . .1,000.00
#7643 Golf Ball, Torch Candle, single, Ritz Blue, 6" h
. . . . 280.00
#7662 Majesty, Randall Blue, 4" h 750.00
#7690 Monroe, Ritz Blue, 7" h, rare 1,200.00
#7951 Stafford, Crystal w/#25 gold band, 3-1/8" h . . . 685.00
#9923 Colonial, Pineapple, 2-pc hurricane, 8-1/2" h . 140.00
Candy Jar
#14 Edmond, Danube Line, #4 cover, rare, 8-1/2" h . 625.00
#16 Rachel, Crystal, Pandora Cutting, 6" h 385.00
#108 Bethann, Topreen Line, 5" h 595.00
#200, Mansfield, Burgundy matte, 12" h 195.00
#1212 Michael, Spanish Red, Crystal finial, 5-1/2" h
. . . . .1,000.00
#7643-1 Alexandra, Randall Blue/Crystal Duo-Tone, 5" h
. . . . 825.00
#9952 Palace, Ruby, 6-12" h 60.00
Champagne
#7577 Venus, Ritz Blue, Pillar Optic, 5-1/2 oz 55.00
#7606-1/2 Athena, Ebony filament, #777 Baden etch, 7 oz
. . . . 75.00
#7621 Ringer, Aquamarine, 6 oz 55.00
#7623 Pygon, D.C. Thorpe satin open stem, 6-1/2 oz 165.00
#7640 Art Moderne, Ebony open stem, 5 oz 85.00
#7643 Golf Ball, 5-1/2 oz , Spanish Red 50.00
#7678 Old English, 6-1/2 oz, Ritz Blue. 52.00
#7860 Lawton, Azure, Festoon Optic, 5 oz 50.00
Cocktail
Chanticleer, Pink Champagne bowl, 4 oz 45.00
Mai Tai, Topaz stem, 4 oz. 50.00
Old Crown, 6-1/4" h, 5-1/2 oz 85.00
#7577 Venus, Anna Rose, Palm Optic, 3 oz 38.00
#7577 Venus, Venetian Green, Palm Optic, 3 oz 35.00

Goblet, Yale, Spanish Red bowl, crystal stem and foot, 9-1/2 oz, $145.

#7620 Fontanne, Ebony filament, #781 Fontinelle etch, 3-1/2 oz 135.00

#7643 Golf Ball, 3-1/2 oz, Ritz Blue 42.00

#7643 Golf Ball, 3-1/2 oz, Stiegel Green 42.00

#7654-1/2 Legacy, Spanish Red, 3 oz 45.00

#7654-1/2 Legacy, Manchester Pheasant Silk Screen, 3-1/2 oz 185.00

Compote

#201 Inverness, Meadow Green, Peacock Optic, 4-1/2" d, 7-1/2" h 155.00

#206 Colette, Burgundy, 7-1/2" h 65.00

#7556 Toledo, high with cover, Crystal, Forever Cutting, 4-1/2" d 315.00

#7654 Reverse Twist, Aquamarine, 6-1/2" d, 6-3/4" h 195.00

Cordial

#7565 Astrid, Anna Rose, #734 American Beauty etch, 3/4 oz 155.00

#7577 Venus, Anna Rose, #743 Bramble Rose etch, 1-1/2 oz 165.00

#7643 Golf Ball, 1-1/2 oz, Pastels 55.00

#7643 Golf Ball, 1-1/2 oz, Spanish Red 55.00

#7643 Golf Ball, 1-1/2 oz, Stiegel Green 52.00

#7617 Brilliant, Spanish Red, 1-1/2 oz 135.00

#7654 Lorna, Nantucket etch, 1-1/2 oz 105.00

#7668 Galaxy, Mayfair etch, 1-1/2 oz 87.50

#7673 Lexington, Ritz Blue filament, #790 Fairwin etch, 1-1/2 oz 165.00

Goblet

#300 Festival, Gloria Blue, 8 oz 35.00

#7568 Horizon, #735 Richmond etch, 10 oz 48.00

#7577 Venus, Anna Rose, Palm Optic, 9 oz 55.00

#7577 Venus, Crystal, #743 Bramble Rose etch, 9 oz 80.00

#7604-1/2 Heirloom, 14-K Topaz, #751 Adonis etch, 9 oz 125.00

#7614 Hampton, Golden iris, Virginia etch, 9 oz . . . 65.00

#7617 Brilliant, Spanish Red, 10 oz 95.00

#7624 Paragon, Ebony open stem, 10 oz 200.00

#7630 Ballerina, Aquamarine/Azure, Yukon cutting, 10 oz 120.00

#7637 Courtney, D.C. Thorpe satin open stem, 9 oz. 195.00

#7640 Art Moderne, Ritz Blue, Crystal open stem, 9 oz 155.00

#7643 Golf Ball, 9 oz, Alabaster 150.00

#7643 Golf Ball, 9 oz, Pastels 55.00

#7643 Golf Ball, 9 oz, Ritz Blue 58.00

#7643 Golf Ball, 9 oz, Spanish Red 55.00

#7643 Golf Ball, 9 oz, Stiegel Green 52.00

#7644-1/2 Vernon, Venetian Green, Pineapple Optic, 9 oz 55.00

#7659 Cynthia, #746 Sonoma etch, 10 oz 68.00

#7664 Queen Anne, Manchester Pheasant Silk Screen, 10 oz 275.00

#7678 Old English, 10 oz, Spanish Red 55.00

#7690 Monroe, Golden Iris, Amber, 9 oz 80.00

Guest Set

#23 Trudy, 6-3/8" h

Alabaster 175.00

Baby Blue 85.00

Bristol Blue 125.00

Opaque Yellow carafe, India Black tumbler 195.00

#24 Margaret, 5-7/8" h

Anna Rose, enamel decor 170.00

Azure/Aquamarine, enamel decor 575.00

Jade Green 185.00

Jug

#6 Kaufmann, #510 Doric Star Sand Blast, 54 oz 275.00

#8 Orleans, #131 Brittany Cutting, 54 oz 385.00

#33 Martina, #518 Lily of the Valley Sand Blast dec, 46 oz, 7-piece set 585.00

#36 Bolero, Pomona Two-Tone Line, 54 oz 985.00

#37 Barry, Anna Rose handle and foot, Palm Optic, 48 oz 390.00

#303 Cyrano, #203 needle etch, 54 oz 385.00

#1933 LMX Del Rey, Randall Blue non-opaque, rare, 54 oz 675.00

#1962 Ockner, Crinkle Line, 64 oz, Amethyst 145.00

#1962 Ockner, Crinkle Line, 64 oz, Pink Champagne, frosted 165.00

#7622-1/2 Ringling, 54 oz, Golden Iris 650.00

#7622-1/2 Ringling, 54 oz, Spanish Red 695.00

#20069 Melon, Alabaster, Ritz Blue trim 1,250.00

Plate, #1500

Alexandrite, #776 Nasreen etch, dessert, 7" d 135.00

Anna Rose, #734 American Beauty etch, dessert, 7" d 55.00

Crystal, Hollywood Platinum/Red band decor, torte, 14" d 395.00

Crystal, #810 Sear's Lace Bouquet etch, dessert, 7" d 25.00

Ritz Blue, Vernay decoration, dessert, 7-1/2" d 135.00

Stiegel Green, salad/luncheon, 8-1/2" d 55.00

14-K Topaz, Carlton Madrid, liner, 6" d 35.00

14-K Topaz, #776 Nasreen etch, salad, 7-3/4" d 60.00

Sherbet

#1962 Crinkle, 6 oz, Pink 24.00

#3011 Montego, Gypsy Fired, 6-1/2" oz 38.00

#7620 Fontanne, #781 Fontinelle etch, 6 oz 165.00

#7643 Golf Ball, 5-1/2 oz, Pastels 35.00

#7643 Golf Ball, 5-1/2 oz, Ritz Blue 45.00

#7643 Golf Ball, 5-1/2 oz, Spanish Red 38.00

#7643 Golf Ball, 5-1/2 oz, Stiegel Green 35.00

#7646 Sophisticate, Picardy etch, 5-1/2 oz 48.00

#7654-1/2 Legacy, Manchester Pheasant Silk Screen, 6-1/2 oz 135.00

#7690 Monroe, Old Amethyst, 6 oz 85.00

#7780 The President's House, 6 oz 20.00

Tumbler

#1928 Ivy, Stiegel Green, ice tea, 15 oz 75.00

#1962 Crinkle, India Black, flat juice, 6 oz 85.00

#7622 Bracelet, Ritz Blue, ice tea, 14 oz 85.00

#7664 Queen Anne, Aquamarine/Azure, #758 Elizabeth etch, 11 oz 115.00

#7668 Galaxy, #778 Carlton etch, 9 oz 22.00

#9051 Zenith, Venetian Green, Peacock Optic, bar, 2 oz 45.00

#9074 Belton, Primrose, Vaseline, Pillar Optic, 9 oz . 125.00

Vase

#12 Viola, Rainbow Line, Spiral Optic, 8" d 120.00

#25 Olympic, #734 American Beauty etch, 12" h 650.00

#26 Catherine 10" bud, Azure, #758 Sunrise Medallion etch 250.00

#35-1/2 Electra, Continental Line, Old Amethyst, 10" 1,000.00

#53 Serenade 10" bud, Opaque Yellow 430.00

#53 Serenade 10" bud, Venetian Green, #756 Tinker Bell etch 595.00

#67 Grecian, Ebony, Saracenic Art Line, 6" h 1,200.00

#73 Radio, Ritz Blue, 6" 895.00

#90 Daisy, Crystal, Green and White Wash, 9-1/2" w 450.00

#91 Lalique, Crystal Satin, 8-1/4" h 650.00

#1933 Gaydos, LMX Seaweed, 6-1/2" 785.00
#7621 Ringer, 10" bud, Opaque Yellow 475.00
Wine
   #7565 Astrid, Anna Rose, #734 American Beauty etch, 3 oz
   . . . . 125.00
   #7577 Venus, Anna Rose, #743 Bramble Rose etch, 3-1/2 oz
   . . . . 145.00
   #7643 Golf Ball, 3 oz, Alabaster 145.00
   #7643 Golf Ball, 3 oz, Ritz Blue 65.00
   #7643 Golf Ball, 3 oz, Stiegel Green 55.00
   #7640 Art Moderne, ebony stem, 3 oz 145.00
   #7660-1/2 Empress, Spanish Red, 3 oz. 85.00
   #7668 Galaxy, #810 Sears' Lace Bouquet etch, 2-1/2 oz
   . . . . 48.00
   #7693 Warwick, Stiegel Green, 2-1/2 oz 55.00
   #7721 Panama, Sharon decoration, 3 oz. 225.00
   #8446 Summer Cornucopia, Copen Blue bowl, 3 oz . 325.00

MOSER GLASS

History: Ludwig Moser (1833-1916) founded his polishing and engraving workshop in 1857 in Karlsbad (Karlovy Vary), Czechoslovakia. He employed many famous glass designers, e.g., Johann Hoffmann, Josef Urban, and Rudolf Miller. In 1900, Moser and his sons, Rudolf and Gustav, incorporated Ludwig Moser & Söhne.

Moser art glass included clear pieces with inserted blobs of colored glass, cut colored glass with classical scenes, cameo glass, and intaglio cut items. Many inexpensive enameled pieces also were made.

In 1922, Leo and Richard Moser bought Meyr's Neffe, their biggest Bohemian art glass rival. Moser executed many pieces for the Wiener Werkstätte in the 1920s. The Moser glass factory continues to produce new items.

References: Gary Baldwin and Lee Carno, *Moser—Artistry in Glass*, Antique Publications, 1988; Mural K. Charon and John Mareska, *Ludvik Moser, King of Glass*, published by author, 1984.

Bell, 5-1/2" h, cranberry cut to colorless, gold scrolling, orig clapper 110.00
Bowl, 7-1/4" d, 5-5/8" h, opalescent pink shaded ground, multicolored enameled oak leaves and foliage, applied lustered acorns, sgd in gold on base 1,200.00
Box, cov
   3-3/8" h, circular, deep purple ground, gold enameled fauns and maidens, fitted cov, four ball feet, etched "Made in Czechoslovakia Moser Karlsbad" 1,200.00
   4-1/2" l, red ground, enameled blue and white floral motif, gilt highlights 550.00
   6" d, 3-3/4" h, cranberry ground, white enameled woman carrying cornucopia and grapes, gold enameled vine and berries 650.00
Cabinet Vase, 2" h, 2-1/2" w, bulbous, citron green ground, applied brass rim, three black glass acorns, gold and yellow florals and leaves, three flying insects, sgd "Moser Carlsbad" under base 200.00
Calling Card Holder, cranberry ground, turquoise jewels, gold prunts, four scrolled feet. 375.00
Chalice, cov, 9-1/2" h, amber and colorless ground, faceted, central landscape frieze, gold leaves outlined in white, gold and black dots, white dotted blossoms, neck, base, and orange stopper heavily gold encrusted 425.00

Cologne Bottle, 9-1/2" h, deep cobalt blue ground, enameled floral scene, matching stopper, script engraved "Moser"
. . . . 225.00
Compote
   4" h, 8-1/4" d, hollow base, pale amber ground, electric blue rigaree and four applied dec, int. deck of twelve painted leaves, brown branches, gold leaves, white cherries, matching branch on base. 650.00
   9-1/2" h, quatraform, crystal ground, gilt enameled heavy scrollwork reserves, matching dec on pedestal foot, crystal stem, pr 400.00
Cordial, 1-3/8" h, cranberry bowl, colorless stem, multicolored enameled flowers, bee, and insect dec on base 100.00
Cruet, 13" h, pigeon blood ground, eleven raised acorns, raised enameled tracery branches and dragonfly, trefoil spout, applied handle, orig paper label 1,850.00
Cup and Saucer, amber ground, gold scrolls, multicolored enameled flowers 295.00
Decanter
   10-1/2" h, ovoid, flattened sides, colorless ground. . . 125.00
   11-1/2" h, 4-1/4" d base, cranberry and white opaque overlay, six opaque petal shapes with gold tree and branch design, gilt dec around each petal, top formed by six cut petals edged in gold, gold vertical lines, tulip-shaped stopper with six opaque white petal shapes with conforming dec, c1880
   . . . . 1,375.00
Ewer, 9" h, cov, horn shape, aquamarine ground, all over gold leaves, vines and flowers, pedestal base. 925.00
Fernery, 7" d, deep amethyst ground, inverted thumbprint, enameled florals, script sgd "Moser" 450.00
Goblet, 4-1/2" h, cranberry ground, enameled, gold overlay, wheel cut design, ftd stem with gold overlay on base, 6 pc set
. . . . 500.00
Ice Cream Set, master bowl and four serving bowls, clear shading to gold ground, mermaid relief, gilt highlights. . . . 395.00
Jar, cov, 10-3/4" h, goblet form, amber ground, polished faceted panels, conforming inset cov 315.00
Juice Tumbler, colorless ground, enameled florals, lace-type trim, 83 applied glass jewels 235.00
Lamp, 18" h, 7-1/4" w globe, cranberry opaque ground, multicolored enamel floral dec, gilt scroll dec, finely cut pattern on globe and base, acid etched signature on base, c1920
. . . . 4,800.00
Mug, 4-1/4" h, topaz colored crackle ground, heavy gold handle and base edging, four applied insects with polychrome dec
. . . . 345.00
Nappy, 5" w, 1-3/4" h, pastel green, yellow, blue, and pink, four enameled foxes, applied loop handle, polished disc base
. . . . 500.00
Pansy Vase, 14" h, colorless ground, multicolored dec
. . . . 1,000.00
Perfume Bottle, 6-1/2" h, 4-1/4" d, Malachite ground, molded bottle and stopper, slab polished sides and top 295.00
Pitcher, 11-3/4" h, bright transparent blue ground, heavy gilding, enameled fern fronds, birds, and insects, applied salamander handle. 2,400.00
Plate, 7-3/8" d, amber ground, gold dec 150.00
Pokal, cov, 8" h, cut, faceted, and enameled, amethyst body with cut panels, gold and high relief floral dec, wafer foot with cut stem 700.00
Scent Bottle, 5" h, emerald green ground,, multicolored leaves and berries, ball stopper. 195.00
Sweetmeat Dish, round, cranberry ground, engraved, gold band
. . . . 225.00
Toothpick, cranberry cased with clear, fancy gold band trim, acid etched signature. 150.00

Tray, 12-7/8" l, cranberry, enamel foliate dec, gilt highlights, two handles 1,100.00
Tumbler
3-1/2" h, octagonal, ruby cut to clear ground, gold dec 85.00
4" h, green, red, and blue, elaborately dec with floral, scrolled, beading, and gild, some beads missing, 9 pc set 460.00
Vase
5" h, Lithyalin, six nymphs, mkd "Moser" 315.00
5-1/4" h, 2-5/8" w, light green ground, coralene beaded dec around top, gilt coralene leaf design, white enameled branches, blue dot enameled highlights, center 5-petal flower with 2 sprays of leaves, white enameled opaque scene of tree and mountains, between spray of leaves on front, c1890 . . . . 500.00
6" h, flared vaseline goblet form, faceted, gold medial band of etched Amazon women, sq base inscribed "Moser Czecko/Slovakia Karlsbad" 420.00
7-3/4" h, long neck shading from emerald green shading to clear ground, bulbous base, gold and platinum floral dec, diamond point signature 375.00
8-1/4" h, 6-1/2" w, bulbous base, narrow neck, three applied rolled handles, blue ground, enameled dec of green and pink grasshopper, delicate pastel flowers, and leaves, round pink enameled circle with brown and turquoise beetle and spray of pink and blue flowers with green leaves, gilt dec, vertical stripe, enameled pink and white flowers, gilt and turquoise green leaves 1,200.00
10" h, flared purple cylinder, broad medial band of etched griffins, urns, and swags, enameled in gold, polished pontil 375.00

10" h, trumpet, red Venetian ground, heavy gold filigree surrounding central Greek Goddess Diana wearing clinging dress, one bare breast, standing next to buck, other side with Diana holding bird, standing next to doe 450.00
11" h, stick, cranberry ground, enameled gold florals and scrolls, script engraved "Moser" 150.00
11-1/2" h, alternating blue and yellow bands, ivory enameled florals, script engraved "Moser" 385.00
12" h, triangular baluster, ruby ground, gold enameled children dec 265.00
12-1/8" h, 3-7/8" w, flaring neck, stepped pedestal base, delicate gold all over fern and floral design on neck and body, 2-3/8" border with gold design, acid cutback dots above and below border, pink, white, purple, orange and magenta floral dec of pansies, bell flowers, mums, daisies and clematis, shaded green foliage all around base, orig paper label with design number, c1880 . . . . .2,800.00
12-1/4" h, cobalt blue ground, large enameled florals and gold dec, script engraved "Moser" 220.00
15-1/2" h, clear and frosted ground, deeply etched thistles, inscribed "Moser/Karlsbad" 420.00
Wine
Rainbow glass, funnel shaped cup, Inverted Baby Thumbprint pattern, enameled grapes and leaves dec, applied row of gold knobs around top 365.00
Turquoise shading to clear ground, all over gold leaf dec, heavy applied prunts 425.00

MOUNT WASHINGTON GLASS COMPANY

History: In 1837, Deming Jarves, founder of the Boston and Sandwich Glass Company, established for George D. Jarves, his son, the Mount Washington Glass Company in Boston, Massachusetts. In the following years, the leadership and the name of the company changed several times as George Jarves formed different associations.

In the 1860s, the company was owned and operated by Timothy Howe and William L. Libbey. In 1869, Libbey bought a new factory in New Bedford, Massachusetts. The Mount Washington Glass Company began operating again there under its original name. Henry Libbey became associated with the company early in 1871. He resigned in 1874 during the general depression, and the glassworks was closed. William Libbey had resigned in 1872 when he went to work for the New England Glass Company.

The Mount Washington Glass Company opened again in the fall of 1874 under the presidency of A. H. Seabury and the management of Frederick S. Shirley. In 1894, the glassworks became a part of the Pairpoint Manufacturing Company.

Throughout its history, the Mount Washington Glass Company made different types of glass including pressed, blown, art, lava, Napoli, cameo, cut, Albertine, and Verona.

References: Edward and Sheila Malakoff, *Pairpoint Lamps*, Schiffer Publishing, 1990; John A. Shuman III, *Collector's Encyclopedia of American Art Glass*, Collector Books, 1988, 1994 value update.

Collectors Club: Mount Washington Art Glass Society, P.O. Box 24094, Fort Worth, TX 76124.-1094.

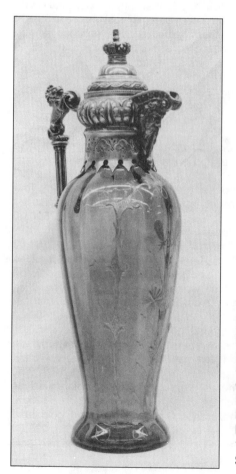

Tankard, cranberry body with gold dec, elaborate silver top, spout as face of old man, standing lion handle, inscribed mark, blue paper label, 14" h, 6-1/4" w, $495.

Museum: The New Bedford Glass Museum, New Bedford, MA.

Additional Listings: Burmese; Crown Milano; Peachblow; Royal Flemish.

Advisor: Louis O. St. Aubin Jr.

Biscuit Jar, 7-1/2" h, 6" d, Opalware, shaded peach to pale yellow ground, purple and yellow pansies, lid mkd "M. W. 4404," base mkd "3926"" 650.00

Bowl
  4-1/2" d, 2-3/4" h, Rose Amber, Swirl pattern, blue swirl bands, bell tone 295.00
  8" d, 4" h, Cameo, blue over white, sq shape, ruffled edge, two winged griffins holding up scroll, spray of flowers 1,475.00

Box, 6-1/2" d, 4-1/2" h, Opalware, mint green ground, deep pink roses, small red cornflowers, gold trim, blown-out floral and ribbon design, #3212/20. . . . . 1,750.00

Collars and Cuffs Box, Opalware, shape of two collars, big bright blue with white polka dots bow in front, orange and pink Oriental poppies on top and bottom, white ground, gold trim, poppy-shaped silver finial with gold trim, bottom sgd "Patent applied for April 10, 1884, #2390/128" 950.00

Cracker Jar, Opalware, bright yellow ground, pink Oriental poppies and green leaves, blown-out floral and leaf design, orig metal hardware, base mkd "3930/230," cover mkd "Pairpoint" 525.00

Dish, 6" l, 4" w, 2-1/2" h, basket form, Burmese, matte finish, applied border of Burmese glass brilliant yellow drippings 1,750.00

Ewer, 9-1/4" h, 5" w, MOP satin, shaded rose to pink, herringbone design, applied frosted thorn handle, tightly ruffled edge, double step base 450.00

Fruit Bowl, 10" d, 6" h, Napoli, solid green ground, outside dec with pale pink and white pond lilies, green and pink leaves and blossoms, int. dec with gold highlight traceries, 7-1/2" h SP base with pond lily design and two applied loop handles, four feet of buds, base sgd "Pairpoint Mfg. Co. B4704" 2,200.00

Humidor, cov
  6-1/2" h, 4-1/2" w, Opalware, shaded yellow background, yellow and pink spider mums, molded gold beaded top, silver-plated finial, base #2382, int. edge flakes 525.00
  7-1/2" h, 5-1/2" w, Delft, all over brilliant blue Delft dec, large central cartouche with windmill and boat, rest covered in snowflakes, cover with windmill and seascape, silver-plated metal rim and ftd base, mkd "Pairpoint #2769," glass stamped "Delft 2769/73" 1,875.00

Jack In The Pulpit Vase
  5-1/2" h, 3-1/2" w, Vasa Murrina, blue, yellow, and brown spatter, white ground, all-over silver flecks, applied crystal edge, swirled body 250.00
  6-1/4" h, 3" w, Burmese, matte finish 425.00

Jewel Box, cov
  4-1/2" d top, base 5-1/4" d, 3-1/4" h, Opalware, portrait of monk drinking glass of red wine, solid shaded green ground on cover and base, elaborate gold washed silver-plated rim and hinge, orig satin lining, artist sgd "Schindler" . . 550.00
  5-1/4" d, 3-1/4" h, Colonial Ware, glass base painted pale pink, four panels of purple and yellow pansies, fancy blown-molded blank with scroll, orig metal cover mkd "M.W.," silver-plated gold-washed and orig cloth cov wooden top 525.00

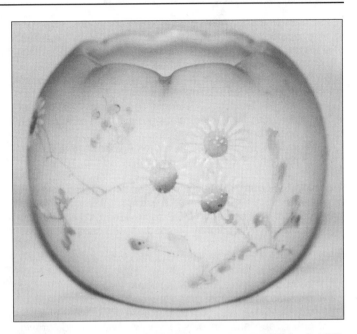

Rose Bowl, Florian Ware, blue tones, 7-5/8" h, 2-1/2" h, $595.

Jug, 6" h, 4" w, MOP satin, Polka Dot, deep peachblow pink, white air traps, DQ, unlined, applied frosted loop handle 475.00

Lamp
  Banquet, 17" h, 4-1/2" d shade, Delft dec, egg shaped shade, bright milk glass with Delft blue houses and trees, orig metal fittings, dec attributed to Frank Guba. 795.00
  Hanging, hall-type, Burmese, Hobnail pattern, orig fixtures 2,500.00

Lamp Shade, 4-1/4" h, 5" w top, 2" d opening, Rose Amber, ruffled, fuchsia shading to deep blue, DQ design. 575.00

Milk Pitcher, 7-1/4" h, 4" w, tankard, Burmese, matte finish, applied loop handle, 1880s 950.00

Mustard Pot, 4-1/2" h, ribbed, bright yellow and pink ground, painted white and magenta wild roses, orig SP hardware 185.00

Nappy, 6" l, 2-1/2" h, MOP satin, white, triangular shaped top, applied frosted handle, all over gold dec, DQ, deeply crimped edge 425.00

Perfume Bottle, 5-1/4" h, 3" w, Opalware, dark green and brown glossy ground, red and yellow nasturtiums, green leaves, sprinkler top 375.00

Pickle Castor Insert, 5-1/2" h, 4-1/2" w, rubena, petticoat shape with int. ribs, orig cov 295.00

Pitcher, 6" h, 3" w, Pearl Satin, DQ, large loop frosted camphor shell handle 325.00

Salt Shaker, fig, white ground, floral dec, orig top. 225.00

Sugar Bowl, 3" h, 4" w, Burmese, petticoat shape, ruffled top, matte finish 425.00

Toothpick Holder, 3" h, 3" d, Burmese, matte finish, naturalistic pine cone and branches dec, 7 pine cones, 1880s . . 675.00

Tumbler, 3-3/4" h
  Burmese, matte finish. 175.00
  MOP satin, DQ, one shaded blue, bright pink daisies, other deep rose with bright blue flowers, pr 550.00

Vase
  5" h, 7" l, 5" w, pouch shape, glossy finish, applied dec, one side with 5-1/2" l feather, reverse with large spray of three Burmese glass leaves, two stems, two open poppies, bright

salmon pink and yellow ground, ext. vertical ribs, scalloped top, one flower chipped 4,250.00
6-1/4" h, 5-1/2" w, MOP satin, bridal white, muslin pattern, melon-ribbed, applied frosted edge, 1880s 425.00
7-3/4" h, 5" w base, MOP satin, bulbous base, ruffled top, applied frosted edge, spring yellow, white lining, Drape pattern, 1880s 500.00
8" h, cylindrical, Ring, black glass ground, gold storks in flight dec, spoke bottom, matched pr 550.00
8-1/4" h, 5" w, MOP satin, DQ, red-orange background, deep gold diamonds, white lining, slightly ruffled top, 1880s 1,250.00
9" h, flaring gourd, bright crystal, green parrot tulips dec, gold leaves. 375.00
9" h, 3-1/2" w at shoulder, MOP satin, deep gold color, Raindrop pattern lining, tightly crimped applied camphor edge 285.00
9-1/4" h, 4-1/4" w, MOP satin, DQ, shaded rose, white lining, ruffled edges, pr. 875.00
10" h, ribbed flaring form, Neapolitan, yellow, purple, rust, and gold spider mums, green leaves, #880 . . . . .1,450.00
11-1/2" h, 6-1/2" w, gourd, Burmese, dec with bamboo shoots, deep salmon pink to yellow, heavy gold, brown, green, tan and rust dec, 1880s 1,875.00
11-7/8" h, bulbous stick, Colonial Ware, glossy white ground, all-over vine and berry dec, two wreath and bow dec at top, sgd, #1010 . . . . 550.00
12-1/2" h, lily, Burmese, matte finish, 1880s 750.00
12-3/4" h, 5-1/2" w, Persian water jug shape, Colonial Ware, loop handle on top, small spout at base of bulbous body, pedestal base, glossy white ground, pale pink and purple lilies, green leaves and stems, overlaid gold dec of leaves, stems, and daisies, scrollwork, sgd, #1022 . . . . . .2,200.00

MULBERRY CHINA

History: Mulberry china was made primarily in the Staffordshire district of England between 1830 and 1860. The ware often has a flowing effect similar to Flow Blue. It is the color of crushed mulberries, a dark purple, sometimes with a gray tinge or bordering almost on black. The potteries that manufactured Flow Blue also made Mulberry china, and, in fact, frequently made some patterns in both types of wares. To date, there are no known reproductions.

References: Susan and Al Bagdade, *Warman's English & Continental Pottery & Porcelain*, 3rd Edition, Krause Publications, 1998; Ellen R. Hill, *Mulberry Ironstone*, published by author, 1993; Petra Williams, *Flow Blue China and Mulberry Ware*, revised ed., Fountain House East, 1993.

Advisor: Ellen G. King.

Astor and Grapeshot, Dimmock, pitcher, 11-3/4" h . . . 105.00
Beauties of China, Mellor, Venables, sauce tureen, cov 200.00
Bryonia, Utzschneider
    Cake Plate, stemmed, 12" d. 450.00
    Dessert Dish, 4-1/2" d 35.00
    Plate, 7" d. 45.00
    Tea Cup and Sauer 55.00
Corean, Podmore, Walker
Creamer 150.00
    Plate, 9-3/4" d. 60.00

    Platter, 13-1/2" l 250.00
    Sauce Tureen, cov, tureen, tray 450.00
Eagle, Podmore Walker, soup tureen, cov, tureen, tray 325.00
Flora, Walker
    Plate, 8" d. 65.00
    Wash Pitcher 300.00
Floral, maker unknown, relish dish, mitten-shaped 75.00
Florentine, Dimmock, wash basin, polychrome 450.00
Jardinere, Utzschneider, plate, 9" d. 55.00
Lady Peel, Morley, cup plate 115.00
Leipsic, Clementson, sauce tureen, cov 250.00
Marble, maker unknown
    Chamber Pot 95.00
    Inhaler 150.00
    Wash Basin and Pitcher, small edge chip 475.00
Moss Rose, Furnivals
    Creamer 85.00
    Plate, 10" d. 70.00
Pelew, Challinor
    Pitcher, 6-1/2" h 250.00
    Sugar Bowl, cov 100.00
    Tea Cup and Saucer, handleless 55.00
    Teapot, cov, handle restored 200.00
Rhone Scenery, Mayer
    Plate, 9" d. 65.00
    Razor Box, cov. 145.00
    Relish 100.00
    Soup Tureen, cov, tureen, tray. 135.00
Seville, Wood & Son
    Gravy Boat, tray. 100.00
    Platter, 14-1/4" l 150.00
    Vegetable Bowl, open, 9" l, oval. 200.00
    Vegetable Tureen, cov. 200.00
Summer Flowers, Alcock, low tazza, polychrome 250.00
Tonquin, Heath
    Sugar Bowl, cov 195.00
    Wash Pitcher 425.00
Vienna, Johnson Bros., soup bowl, 9" d 40.00
Vincennes, Alcock
    Gravy Boat 100.00
    Platter, 13-3/8" l 175.00
    Underplate 80.00
Washington Vase, Podmore, Walker
    Butter Dish, cov, base, orig insert 450.00
    Creamer, 4-1/2" h. 135.00
    Plate, 10" d. 80.00
    Wash Basin and Pitcher. 625.00

Bryonia, Utzschneider, left: dessert dish, $35 each, center: cake plate, $450; right: 7" d plate, $45 each. Photo courtesy of Ellen King.

MUSICAL INSTRUMENTS

History: From the first beat of the prehistoric drum to the very latest in electronic music makers, musical instruments have been popular modes of communication and relaxation.

The most popular antique instruments are violins, flutes, oboes, and other instruments associated with the classical music period of 1650 to 1900. Many of the modern instruments, such as trumpets, guitars, and drums, have value on the "used" rather than antiques market.

The collecting of musical instruments is in its infancy. The field is growing very rapidly. Investors and speculators have played a role since the 1930s, especially in early string instruments.

References: Tony Bacon (ed.), *Classic Guitars of the '50s*, Miller Freeman Books (6600 Silacci Way, Gilroy, CA 95020), 1996; S. P. Fjestad (ed.), *Blue Book of Guitar Values*, 2nd ed., Blue Book Publications, 1994; George Gruhn and Walter Carter, *Acoustic Guitars and Other Fretted Instruments*, GPI Books, 1993; ——, *Electric Guitars and Basses*, Miller Freeman Books, GPI Books, 1994; ——, *Gruhn's Guide to Vintage Guitars*, GPI Books, 1991; Mike Longworth, *C. F. Martin & Co.*, 4 Maples Press, 1994; Paul Trynka (ed.), *Electric Guitar*, Chronicle Books, 1993.

Periodicals: *Concertina & Squeezebox*, P.O. Box 6706, Ithaca, NY 14851; *Jerry's Musical Newsletter*, 4624 W Woodland Rd., Minneapolis, MN 55424; *Piano & Keyboard*, P.O. Box 767, San Anselmo, CA 94979; *Strings*, P.O. Box 767, San Anselmo, CA 94979; *Twentieth Century Guitar*, 135 Oser Ave., Hauppauge, NY 11788; *Vintage Guitar Classics*, P.O. Box 7301, Bismarck, ND 58507.

Collectors' Clubs: American Musical Instrument Society, RD 3, Box 205-B, Franklin, PA 16323; Automatic Musical Instrument Collectors Association, 919 Lantern Glow Trail, Dayton, OH 45431; Fretted Instrument Guild of America, 2344 S. Oakley Ave., Chicago, IL 60608; Musical Box Society International, 887 Orange Ave. E, St. Paul, MN 55106; Reed Organ Society, Inc., P.O. Box 901, Deansboro, NY 13328.

Museums: C. F. Martin Guitar Museum, Nazareth, PA; International Piano Archives at Maryland, Neil Ratliff Music Library, College Park, MD; Miles Musical Museum, Eureka Springs, AR; Museum of the American Piano, New York, NY; Musical Museum, Deansboro, NY; Streitwieser Foundation Trumpet Museum, Pottstown, PA; University of Michigan, Stearns Collection of Musical Instruments, Ann Arbor, MI; Yale University Collection of Musical Instruments, New Haven, CT.

Bassoon, fifteen-keyed, maple, brass mounts and keys, c1900, unstamped, 50-1/4" l 460.00
Bugle, nickel plated, minor dents, wooden case with black paint 100.00
Clarinet, ten-keyed boxwood, key of C, c1860, brass mountings, brass keys with round covers, orig mouthpiece, 21-1/2" l 400.00
Cornet
 "Class A New Creation, Besson & Co. Prototype 198 Euston Road, London England, Agents, Thos. Claxton Ltd., Toron-to," silverplated brass tubing, three piston values, case, mouthpiece 175.00
 "Lyric, The Rudolph Wurlitzer Co. USA," silverplated brass tubing engraved at the bell, three piston values with pearl buttons, stamped "P21766," fitted case, two period mouthpieces, turning crook, and mute 150.00
 "Made By C. G. Conn, Elkhart Ind. & Worcester, Mass," brass and silver tubing, three piston valves, stamped "50246," three period mouthpieces, extra crook, two mutes, and music holder, orig fitted case, c1900 . . . . 750.00
Flute
 Firth Hall and Pond, c1855, eight keys, cocuswood and nickel silver mounts, c1855, stamped "Firth, Hall & Pond, Franklin Sq, New York, 1242," inlaid lip plate, nickel-silver keys with salt spoon cup cover, adjustable stopper, 26-1/4" l, fitted mahogany case 230.00
 Hall, William and Son, one key, boxwood, faintly stamped "William Hall & Son, 239 Broadway, N. York," ivory mounts, one brass key with round cover, 19-7/8" l 300.00
 Haynes, William S., Boehm System, silver, engraved "The Haynes Flute Mfd. By Wm. S. Haynes Co., Boston, Mass, 25428, Reg Trade Mark," silver body and closed hole key work, "C" foot, 26-11/16" l, fitted case, 1956 . . . . . 2,070.00
 Melodeon, rosewood veneer, lyre shaped ends, ivory and ebony keyboard, 4-1/2 octaves, mkd "Carhart & Needham, New York," wear and veneer damage, lyre and bench mismatched, one bellows rod is missing, 32-1/2" w, 16-1/4" d, 28" h. 175.00
 Orguinette, "Mechanical Orguinette Co., New York," small roller organ, walnut case, silver stenciled label and dec, working condition, paper rolls, 12" w, 9-1/4" d, 10" h 500.00
 Piano, Chickering, baby grand, mahogany, old finish, Ampico reproducing mechanism with 210 rolls, ivory and ebony keys, 59" w, 65" l, orig bench. 5,225.00

"Steinway & Sons Patent Grand, New York," worn ebonized finish, gilt label, turned and reeded legs, Eastlake carving, ebony and ivory keyboard, cracked soundboard, 1885, 54" w, 71" l, $1,100. Photo courtesy of Garth's Auctions, Inc.

Piano Forte

Fearn, Robert, sgd "Robert Fearn Jr. Upright Grand and Square Piano Forte Maker," London, c1810, mahogany inlaid, rect case, string inlay, string inlaid frame, sq tapering legs, casters, refinished, 5-1/4" l, 23" w, 31-1/4" h 2,300.00

Firth & Hall, c1935, inscribed on nameboard "Manufactured by Firth & Hall No. 1 Franklin Square, New York," birch case cov in walnut veneer, solid walnut cover, turned and fluted walnut legs, 43 ivory cov naturals, 30 stained accidentals, 68-3/16" l, 27" w, with adjustable piano stool with fluted legs, cast brass ball feet 920.00

Pianola, Aeolian, quartersawn oak, 36" h, 45" w, foot petals, repairs required to bellows, 60 orig rolls 400.00

Piano Roll Cabinet, Adam style, mahogany veneer, painted panels on doors, incomplete applied ornament, English, 40" w, 16" d, 38-1/4" h 330.00

Scottish Pipes, blackwood and ivory mounts, canter stamped "P. Henderson, Glasgow," turned drones with nickel ferrules, leather bag........................520.00

Tenor Recorder, branded "Friedrich Von Huene, Boston, 878," rosewood and ivory mounts, four brass keys, case 1,610.00

Viola

French, c1900, labeled "Made in France, Copie e J. Bte. Vuillaume, A Paris," two piece back with narrow curl, similar ribs, strong narrow curl scroll, fine grain top, red-brown varnish, back length 16-1/8", with case 920.00

German, c1930, labeled "Made Expressly For, William Lewis and Son, Chicago, Illinois, No. 2526-16," two piece back with irregular curl, similar ribs, light narrow curl scroll, fine to medium grain top, golden red varnish, back length 16" l, with case and bow 920.00

Mittenwald, Neuner and Hornsteiner, c1980, labeled "Neuner & Hornsteiner," one piece back with light narrow curl, similar ribs, faint curl scroll, fine grain top, red varnish, back length 15-1/2", with case and silver mounted bow 1,610.00

Violin

American, John Bodor Jr., Churchville, PA, labeled "Joseph Guaranerius Fecit, Cremonae Anno 1773 LHS," two piece back with irregular narrow curl, ribs and scroll similar, fine grain top, brown varnish, 13-15/16" l back, with case 2,875.00

French, Auguste Sebastien Bernardel, Paris, labeled "Bernardel Luthier Eleve De Lupot, Rue Croix Des Petits Champs No. 23, A Paris 1827," one piece back with strong broad curl, similar ribs and scroll, medium grain top, red varnish, back length 14-1/8", with fitted wood violin case labeled "Gustave Bernardel Luthiers Du Conservatoire, 4 Passage Saulnier A Paris"...................19,550.00

Italian, Paul Vettori, Florence, labeled "Paolo Vettori Di Dario, Fece in Firenze 1978," one piece back with strong irregular curl, similar ribs, scroll of narrow cut curl, medium grain top, golden orange varnish, 13-7/8" l back 4,315.00

South German, labeled "Aegidius Berzellini Fecit, Ecole Amatius Cremonen 16??," one piece back with narrow curl, ribs of irregular narrow curl, scroll of narrow curl, fine to medium grain top, golden brown varnish, back length 13-7/8" 2,300.00

Violin Bow

Bazin, Charles Nicolas, in the style of J. B. Vuillaume, silver mounted, round stick faintly stamped "C. Bazin" at butt, ebony frog with pearl eye, silver and ebony adjuster with missing pearl eye, 51 grams 1,150.00

Fréres, Louis Morizot, silver mounted, round stick faintly stamped "L. Morizot" at butt, ebony frog with pearl eye, silver and ebony adjuster with pearl eye, 62 grams 1,840.00

Mohr, Rodney Duane, Chicago, silver mounted, round stick stamped "Rodney D Mohr" at butt, ebony frog with pearl eye, silver and ebony adjuster with parisian eye, 60 grams 700.00

Nürnberger Workshop, silver mounted, round stick stamped "?? Superior" at butt, ebony frog with parisian eye, silver and ebony adjuster, 62 grams 1,265.00

Schuster, Max Kurt, gold and ebony mounted, octagonal stick stamped "M. K. Schuster" at butt, ebony frog with parisian eye, gold and ebony adjuster, 62 grams ...1,035.00

Vuillaume, Jean Baptiste, silver mounted, round stick faintly stamped "J. B. Vuillaume A Paris" at butt, ebony frog with pearl eye, silver and ebony adjuster, 63 grams ...7,765.00

Violincello

Derazey School, Catalogue Number 8688, two piece back with narrow curl, irregular curl ribs, light curl scroll, fine to wide grain top, red varnish, back length 29-9/16" 4,325.00

Farotti, Celeste, Milan, labeled "Farotti Celeste, Da San Germano Di Casale, Fece In Milano Nell Anno 1912," inscribed by maker "Medaglio Oro Milano 1906," "Torino 1911, Farotti Celeste," strongly figured two-piece poplar back, similar ribs, maple scroll of medium curl, fine to medium grain top, red-gold varnish, back length 29-15/16", with case 68,500.00

Panormo School, labeled "Nicholas Amatus Cremonen Hieronymi Fil Ac An Antonii Nepos Fecit 167?," two piece back with irregular curl, faint irregular curl ribs, plain scroll, medium to wide grain top, golden brown varnish, back length 28-7/8", with case 9,200.00

MUSIC BOXES

History: Music boxes, invented in Switzerland around 1825, encompass a broad array of forms, from small boxes to huge circus calliopes.

A cylinder box consists of a comb with teeth which vibrate when striking a pin in the cylinder. The music these boxes produce ranges from light tunes to opera and overtures.

The first disc music box was invented by Paul Lochmann of Leipzig, Germany, in 1886. It used an interchangeable steel disc with pierced holes bent to a point which hit the star-wheel as the disc revolved, and thus produced the tune. Discs were easily stamped out of metal, allowing a single music box to play an endless variety of tunes. Disc boxes reached the height of their popularity from 1890 to 1910 when the phonograph replaced them.

Music boxes also were incorporated in many items, e.g., clocks, sewing and jewelry boxes, steins, plates, toys, perfume bottles, and furniture.

References: Gilbert Bahl, *Music Boxes*, Courage Books, Running Press, 1993; Arthur W. J. G. Ord-Hume, *Musical Box*, Schiffer Publishing, 1995.

Collectors' Clubs: Music Box Society of Great Britain, P.O. Box 299, Waterbeach, Cambridge CB4 4DJ England; Musical Box Society International, 1209 CR 78 West, LaBelle, FL 33935.

Museums: Bellms Cars and Music of Yesterday, Sarasota, FL; Lockwood Matthews Mansion Museum, Norwalk,

CT; Miles Musical Museum, Eureka Springs, AR; The Musical Museum, Deansboro, NY; The Musical Wonder House Museum, Iscasset, ME.

Additional Listings: See *Warman's Americana & Collectibles* for more examples.

Animated, 10" h, 7" w, composition grandmother sitting in chair grinding coffee in coffee mill, moves her lips and eyes as she churns, red printed dress, white apron, white bun hairdo, mounted on wood litho box, side crank handle 1,400.00

Bells in Sight, litho paper label, list of eight tunes, mahogany veneer case, inlay and ebonized trim, 6" cylinder, 17-3/4" l 1,320.00

Bells in Vue, Switzerland, litho paper label, list of ten tunes, mahogany veneer case, ebonized trim and clock in crest, 17-1/2" h, 11-1/2" d, 25-1/2" h 2,860.00

Columbia Grafonola, Deluxe, quarter sawed oak veneer case, lion handles, old finish, combination mechanism plays 78 records as well as Regina type metal disks, includes 28 disks, minor edge damage to case, 52" h 12,650.00

Ideal Sublime Harmonie, Orpheus, labeled "Switzerland," patent dates 1885 and 1890, oak case

Molded detail and applied cast metal ornaments, two 11" d cylinders, needs some adjustments, 30-1/2" l 2,750.00

Relief carving, three 11" cylinders, storage drawer, 20-1/2" l 5,225.00

Imperial Symphonion, 15-3/4" disc, stained mahogany case with cable and leaf tip lower borders, single comb, litho tune sheet, coffered lid, six discs, c1900, 23" w. 3,500.00

Jacots, oak case, cylinder, Swiss, pat'd safety check Sept. 22, 1886, refinished, applied filigree carving on front, 12 tunes, mechanism by Mermod Freres, late 19th C, plays well, 27" x 11" x 8" h case 1,700.00

Kalliope No. 50, 9-1/8" disc, walnut case, bone inlaid lid, nine discs, 11-1/4" w 900.00

Maliginon, cylinder, inlaid rosewood case, eight tunes, 13" cylinder, keywind, orig label inside outlining eight classical tunes, sgd "A. Maliginon," 20-1/4" x 6-1/2" 1,650.00

Nichole Freres, keywind, line inlaid mahogany rect case, musical trophy, 8-1/8" cylinder, 15" w 1,300.00

Olympia II, 11-5/8" disc, oak case with coffered lid, flanged base, molded and pressed repeating leaf tip and palmette dec, 22 discs, 15-1/4" w 1,500.00

Paillard, 13" cylinder, inlaid and rosewood grained case, eight air playing selection, zither attachment, late 19th C, 22-1/2" 1,650.00

Polyphon, Karl Morat, Eisenbach, Braden, walnut, penny operated, crank handles, c1904, 21 tin discs, 24" w, 13" d, 43" h 3,750.00

Regina, 11" inch, single cone box, old litho label on inside of lid, oak case, box restored, 14" x 12" x 9" 1,400.00

Regina Style, works labeled "Scrutz-Marke. Made in Germany," retailer's label "Ilsen & Co. Cincinnati, O.," mahogany case, base drawer holds 20 disks, 21" w, 17-1/4" d, 14" h 3,850.00

Swiss
6" cylinder, inlaid rosewood grained case, litho tune sheet, eight air playing selection, late 19th C, 16-1/4" h 1,200.00
8" cylinder, ebonized case, litho tune sheet, 18" w . . 950.00

Swiss Imperial, 11-1/2" disc, rect inlaid walnut and rosewood crossbanded case, 17 discs, late 19th C, 23-1/2" w 1,450.00

Thornes, 4-1/2" disc, silvered metal, engraved floral scrolling arabesque case, domed and colonnaded hinged upper section, divided drawer in base, 25 discs, 14" 1,750.00

Troubadour, 8-7/8" disc, walnut case, single comb, four saucer bells, eight disks, 10-7/8" w 1,200.00

Ultman, Charles, eight air playing selection, inlaid and rosewood grained case, stamped comb, gilt circular medallion behind cylinder, late 19th C, 21-1/4" w. 1,750.00

Zimbailist, Swiss movement, 42 disks, bright metal silver colored case shaped like bureau, cast machine tooled and engraved dec, 20th C, 12-1/2" l 500.00

NAILSEA-TYPE GLASS

History: Nailsea-type glass is characterized by swirls and loopings, usually white, on a clear or colored ground. One of the first areas where this glass was made was Nailsea, England, 1788-1873, hence the name. Several glass houses, including American factories, made this type of glass.

Basket, 5-1/2" h, 5" w, pink loopings, white satin ground, applied frosted feet, applied frosted handle 385.00

Bottle
6-1/2" h, medium gray-blue ground, white loopings, pewter threading, pontil scar, cap missing, attributed to Germany, mid 18th C 1,750.00
7-5/8" h, rect, beveled edges, medium sapphire blue ground, white loopings, pewter threads, pontil scar, attributed to Germany or Northern Europe, c1750. . . . . 1,250.00
8-1/2" h, gemel, colorless ground, white loopings, sheared lip, pontil scar, 1860-80 . . . . 200.00
8-3/4" h, gemel, cranberry ground, white loopings, applied rigaree 275.00

Bowl, 4-1/4" d, 2-1/4" h, citron ground, narrow white looping, applied rigaree loop dec, rim, ground pontil 200.00

Cologne Bottle, 5-3/8" h, opaque white body, blue and cranberry loopings, colorless stopper with white, pink, and blue loopings, pontil scar, New England, 1840-60 . . . . 485.00

Creamer, 4" h, aqua, white and red spatter, applied handle, surface chips 125.00

Ideal Sublione Harmonie, Orpheus, Switzerland, three 11" cylinders, oak case with relief carving, patent dates of 1885 and 1890, 20-1/2" l, $5,225. Photo courtesy of Garth's Auctions, Inc.

Fairy Lamp, 6" h, blue shade, matching ruffled trifold rim base, colorless glass candle cup insert 750.00

Finger Bowl, 4-1/4" d, ftd, colorless ground, swirled streaks of deep blue ad white, foot drawn from body, applied colorless handles imp with cherub's face 85.00

Flask
6-1/2" h, 5" w, cranberry ground, white and deep pink feathering 150.00
6-3/4" h, colorless ground, white loopings, flattened round body, short sheared lip, small rough pontil, attributed to South Jersey 185.00
7-1/4" h, broad oval form, ruby red ground, white herringbone type loopings, applied double collared mouth, pontil scar 400.00
7-3/4" l, clear cased in white, pink loops 200.00
8-3/4" l, clear cased in white, pink loops 250.00
8-3/4" l, clear cased in white, red and blue loops. . . . 225.00

Mug, 5-1/4" h, 3-5/8" d, colorless ground, white and blue loopings, cylindrical, tapering slightly to rim, applied colorless solid handle, rough pontil 375.00

Pipe, 18" l, white ground, red loopings, bulbous bowl, knopped stem 275.00

Pitcher, 9-1/2" h, cranberry ground, thick white loopings, applied clear handle with five crimps, applied colorless handle with five crimps, applied colorless foot, pontil scar, attributed to South Jersey, c1840-50 . . . . 4,100.00

Powder Horn
11" h, colorless ground, blue and white loopings, tooled lip, pontil scar, ground lip, mid 19th C 125.00
13" l, colorless ground, white loopings and red stripes, stand 250.00

Rolling Pin, 18" l, colorless ground, pink and white loopings 265.00

Salt, open, 3-1/4" d, 1-1/4" h, colorless ground, white loopings, wide gauffered rolled rim, applied cobalt blue rim band, applied solid foot, polished pontil 450.00

Vase
9-3/4" h, medium blue ground, white loopings, hollow knop stem containing 1842 dime, applied foot, pontil scar, stem previously broken off and re-glued, attributed to Pittsburgh or South Jersey, 1840-50. . . . . 625.00
9-7/8" h, bulbous, flaring neck, ftd, colorless ground, spiraling white bands, applied colorless swagging, applied colorless baluster stem, thick round base, attributed to New England, 19th C 3,200.00

Witch Ball, 5-1/4" d, colorless ground, opaque white casing, red loopings, attributed to Pittsburgh 275.00

NANKING

History: Nanking is a type of Chinese porcelain made in Canton, China, from the early 1800s into the 20th century. It was made for export to America and England.

Four elements help distinguish Nanking from Canton, two similar types of ware. Nanking has a spear-and-post border, as opposed to the scalloped-line style of Canton. Second, in the water's edge or Willow pattern, Canton usually has no figures; Nanking includes a standing figure with open umbrella on the bridge. In addition, the blues tend to be darker on the Nanking ware. Finally, Nanking wares often are embellished with gold, Canton is not.

Green and orange variations of Nanking survive, although they are scarce.

REPRODUCTION ALERT

Copies of Nanking ware currently are being produced in China. They are of inferior quality and are decorated in a lighter rather than in the darker blues.

Bowl
10" d, 5" h, cut corner, blue and white, minute rim chips 980.00
15" l, oval, flat octagonal rim, blue and white, c1800 . 750.00

Fairy Lamp, rose with white loopings, frosted, S. Clarke clear glass base, 4-3/4" h, 4" d base, $325.

Platter, 11-1/2" x 14-1/2", $345.

Chocolate Pot, 9" h, pear shape, blue and white, Buddhistic lion finial 775.00

Cider Jug, 7-3/4" h, blue and white, spearhead and lattice borders, coastal village scene, double entwined handle, molded flowers and leaves terminal, early 19th C, base rim chip 400.00

Mug, 6-1/8" h, blue and white water's edge scene 350.00

Platter, 17-3/8 x 20", oval, blue and white, coastal village scene, spearhead and lattice borders, minor glaze wear, early 19th C. 875.00

Sauce Tureen, cov, underplates, 8" l, blue and white, twin braided handles, floral knops, 19th C, base chips, price for pr 1,250.00

Serving Dish, cov, 11" l, two handles, blue and white, staple repair to lid. 200.00

Sugar Bowl, cov, 6-1/2" h, cylindrical, blue and white, gilt highlights, strawberry knop finial 325.00

Tea Caddy, 5" h, blue and white, gilt trim 750.00

Teapot, 5-1/2" h, lobed form, reeded strap handle, blue and white, gilt highlights, China, late 18th/early 19th C, minor chips, gilt wear 525.00

Warming Dish, 11-1/2" l, blue and white, 19th C 180.00

NAPKIN RINGS, FIGURAL

History: Gracious home dining during the Victorian era required a personal napkin ring for each household member. Figural napkin rings were first patented in 1869. During the remainder of the 19th century, most plating companies, including Cromwell, Eureka, Meriden, and Reed and Barton, manufactured figural rings, many copying and only slightly varying the designs of other companies.

Reference: Lillian Gottschalk and Sandra Whitson, *Figural Napkin Rings*, Collector Books, 1996.

Reproduction Alert: Quality reproductions do exist.

Additional Listings: See *Warman's Americana & Collectibles* for a listing of non-figural napkin rings.

Notes: Values are determined by the subject matter of the ring, the quality of the workmanship, and the condition.

Bird, perched on top of ring, long tail, elaborately scrolled base, Apollo Silver Plate Co. 185.00

Boy and Dog, SP, mkd Meriden, #199 . . . . 245.00

Butterfly and fan 175.00

Cap, beneath ring, horns and swords at side 335.00

Cats, two cats peeking around ring, rect base 450.00

Cherub, pulling cart, movable wheels 225.00

Chick and Eggshell, SP, mkd "Derby". 100.00

Dog and Bird, SP, Aurora, #27 . . . . 185.00

Fox, sitting, oval ring on back, rect base. 250.00

Greenaway, Kate, boy feeding begging dog 450.00

Horse pulling ring on wheels 450.00

Lily and lily pad 175.00

Monkey, standing, oval base, Derby Silver Co. 295.00

Naked boy pushing ring, ornate base, Middletown Plate Co. 395.00

Squirrel, SP. 360.00

Turtle Doves, spread wings support ring, Middletown Plate 195.00

NASH GLASS

History: Nash glass is a type of art glass attributed to Arthur John Nash and his sons, Leslie H. and A. Douglas. Arthur John Nash, originally employed by Webb in Stourbridge, England, came to America and was employed in 1889 by Tiffany Furnaces at its Corona, Long Island, plant.

While managing the plant for Tiffany, Nash designed and produced iridescent glass. In 1928, A. Douglas Nash purchased the facilities of Tiffany Furnaces. The A. Douglas Nash Corporation remained in operation until 1931.

Bowl

5-1/4" d, inverted rim, leaf design, sgd 200.00

8" d, aventurine Chintz, gold irid striping, base inscribed "Nash" 200.00

8" d, rose petal Chintz, magenta stripes, base inscribed "Nash" 200.00

15-1/2" d, Chintz amber, blue, and green opalescent, turned down rim 325.00

Candlestick, 5" h, Chintz blood red and silver dec 550.00

Champagne, 5" h, pale irid amber, shallow cup splitting to three stems continuing to domed circular base 750.00

Chick and egg, engraved "Best Wishes," Derby Silver, Birmingham, CT, 3-1/2" w, 2-1/4" h, $100.

Dish, irid gold, blue-green, etched grape leaves and vines, mkd "Nash 569 C-1," 5-3/8" d, 1/2" h, $315.

Cologne Bottle, 6" h, cylindrical, Chintz paperweight stopper 275.00

Compote, 6" d, 2" h, fold over rim, Chintz, green-blue bowl, colorless pedestal foot, sgd 225.00

Creamer, 4-1/4" h, pale orchid and green design, applied colorless handle 325.00

Dish, cov, 5" d, 2-1/2" h, internally molded leaf design, amber ground, lustrous gold irid, conforming cover, rim chips 260.00

Finger Bowl, 4-3/4" d, matching underplate, opalescent rays, cranberry rim, sgd 225.00

Goblet, 6-1/2" h, Chintz 185.00

Perfume Bottle, 7-1/2" h, bulbous bottle shape over blown-in-mold apron, irid gold, conforming stopper with 7" l wand, sgd "Nash 523" 975.00

Plate

4-1/2" d, irid amber, scalloped edge, sgd and numbered 325.00

6-1/2" d, Spiral pattern, orchid and clear spirals, sgd 200.00

Salt, open, 4" d, 1-1/4" h, irid gold, ruffled rim, sgd and numbered 350.00

Vase

4-3/4" h, blue-gold irid, pedestal base, inscribed "Nash 644" 350.00

5-1/4" h, Chintz, flared rim, oval colorless body, internally dec with orange stripes alternating with yellow-amber pulled threading 195.00

6-1/4" h, 3-1/2" d, trumpet shade, Chintz, sgd and numbered 375.00

7-1/2" h, beaker, Chintz, blood red, sgd "Nash RD 1025" 475.00

7-3/4" h, baluster, brilliant irid pumpkin, lemon-yellow int. 3,500.00

8-1/2" h, Chintz, green, brown, and gold flecks 325.00

9" h, Chintz, blood red and ray, ball shaped clear stem 475.00

9-1/2" h, green and gold irid body, colorless irid circular base 325.00

Wine, 6" h, Chintz, pink and green 175.00

NAUTICAL ITEMS

History: The seas have fascinated man since time began. The artifacts of sailors have been collected and treasured for years. Because of their environment, merchant and naval items, whether factory or handmade, must be of quality construction and long lasting. Many of these items are aesthetically appealing as well.

References: Jon Baddeley, *Nautical Antiques & Collectables*, Sotheby's Publications, 1993; Robert W. D. Ball, *Nautical Antiques*, Schiffer Publishing, 1994.

Periodicals: *Nautical Brass*, P.O. Box 3966, North Ft. Myers, FL 33918; *Nautical Collector*, P.O. Box 949, New London, CT 06320.

Collectors' Club: Nautical Research Guild, 62 Marlboro St., Newburyport, MA 01950.

Museums: Kittery Historical & Naval Museum, Kittery, ME; Lyons Maritime Museum, St. Augustine, FL; Mariners' Museum, Newport News, VA; Maritime Museum of Monterey, Monterey, CA; Museum of Science and Industry, Chicago, IL; Mystic Seaport Museum, Mystic, CT; Peabody Museum of Salem, Salem, MA; Philadelphia Maritime Museum, Philadelphia, PA; San Francisco Maritime National Historical Park, San Francisco, CA; U.S. Naval Academy Museum, Naval Academy, MD.

Backstaff, wood, inlaid label "Made by William Hart in Portsmouth, NE/for 1767," 18th C 8,000.00

Bell, brass, 14" d, inscribed *SS Pacific Prince* 500.00

Binnacle, 56" h, brass, mahogany base, complete 750.00

Book

Cram, W Bartlett, *Picture History of New England Passenger Vessels,* 8" x 10", dj, 414 pgs, 1980, 1st ed. 75.00

Spears, John, *Captain Nathaniel Brown Palmer, An Old-Time Sailor of the Sea,* 3" x 5", orig cloth, plates, 252 pgs, NY, 1922. . . . . 20.00

Captain's Box, 16-1/2" w, 9-3/4" d, 7" h, paint dec, bird's eye maple, stamped "J. E. French," lid dec with floral reserve and anchors, "Capt J. E. French, New Bedford, Mass," sides dec with reserve of mountain scenery, compartmentalized int. with removable tray, 19th C 1,500.00

Chronometer, 7-1/2" h, 4-3/4" d timepiece, two-day type, rosewood gimbal case, MOP plaque, flush brass carrying handles, Victor Kulberg, London, retailed by W. Bond and Son, Boston 5,465.00

Clock, 11" h, nickel-plated, wall, outside bell 400.00

Communicating Tower, 39" h, ship's engine room, brass, lamp housing on side, labeled "A. Robinson & Co. Liverpool & Glasgow," lamp missing 1,100.00

Foghorn, bellows operated, 1910 . . . . 175.00

Octant, 15-3/4" l, Spencer, Browning & Rust, London, 1787-1842, ebony, brass, and ivory, painted wood case 575.00

Painting

12" h, 20" l, oil on board, portrait of American ship *Gatherer,* indistinctly inscribed lower right, vessel identified on bow, framed, abraded area lower right, craquelure, attributed to Antonio Jacobsen 2,100.00

12-1/2" h, 22-1/2" l, watercolor, graphic and gouache on paper/board, portrait of Bark *Dora* under full said, sgd "H. Bode" lower right, identification on info affixed to reverse, framed 875.00

14" h, 22" l, oil on board, portrait of four-masted schooner *Clara Davis* on high seas, sgd and dated "Antonio Jacobsen, 1908" lower right, vessel identified on bow and stern, identified on inscription on reverse, unframed . . . 10,350.00

15-3/4" h, 28" l, oil on board, portrait of Steam Screw *El Siglo* on high seas, sgd and inscribed "Antonio Jacobsen. 1920 31 Paradise Ave. West Hoboken, NJ" lower right, vessel identified on bow, framed. 4,350.00

20" h, 30" w, oil on canvas, scene of shipwreck and life saving efforts on shore, two master steamer adrift on rocks, lighthouse and crowd assembled on rocky shore sending signal flare, initials H. G. (attributed to Hans Frederick Gude), unframed, cleaned, some restoration, restretched . . . 600.00

22" h, 36" l, oil on canvas, portrait of American Schooner *Shepherd King,* under full sail, bluffs, lighthouse in distance, sgd "S. F. M. Badger" lower left, sgd and inscribed with artist's address on reverse, vessel identified on bow and banner, framed, puncture, some canvas loss, surface grime, craquelure 7,475.00

22" h, 36" l, oil on canvas, portrait of *U.S.S. Constitution,* sgd and dated "Antonio Jacobsen 1916" lower right, vessel identified on stern, framed, lined, scattered retouch, craquelure 17,250.00

24" h, 35" l, oil on canvas, portrait of American Schooner *Sky Lark,* sgd and dated "Stubbs 1879" (William Pierce Stubbs),

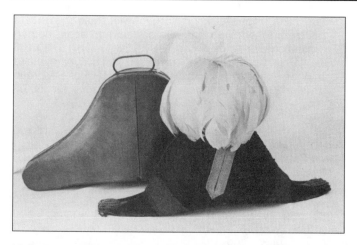

Hat, French officer's, black felt, silver thread and fabric, white feather plume, orig travel case, c1812, 17" l, 11" h, $300.

sgd lower left, vessel identified on banner and near stern, period frame 12,650.00

Rug, 58" d, round, hooked, designed by Joan Moshimer, hooked by Forestine Heath, Searsport, ME, Door Mills teacher, 1879, all wool, two women on shore with telescope looking out to sea at American sailing vessel, mermaid on shore looking through seashell-type telescope, sgd "FMH" 1,500.00

Porthole, 15"d, brass, storm cov 120.00

Print, color woodcut on paper, framed
7-1/2 x 8", Lemos, Pedro J, Driftwood, Oakland Shipyard, sgd in pencil lower right, titled in pencil lower left 635.00
15-1/4 x 12-1/2", Lindenmuth, Tod, The Riding Light, sgd in pencil lower right, titled in pencil lower left 865.00

Quadrant, ebony, ivory inlays 550.00

Sailor's Valentine, 9" h, 9-1/6" w, octagonal segmented case, various exotic shells, center reads "To One I Love" on left, heart center and initials on right panel, minor losses to case, 19th C 2,185.00

Sea Chest, 37 l, orig green and brown paint and ropework beckets, 19th C 600.00

Sextant
13" l, ebony, brass and ivory trim, mkd "J. Good, High St. Hull," damage to ivory 450.00
17" l, mahogany, engraved brass radial arm, ivory nameplate engraved "H Duren, New York," Gregory & Wright, London, 18th C 1,200.00

Ship's Block, 13 1/2" l, wood, one lignium vitae, one metal pulley 125.00

Ship's Log
Bark *Petrea,* 65 pages folio, entries from March 17 to Dec. 15, 1858, voyages from Le Havre to Portsmouth, New York, and Melbourne, details activities while in port, at sea, hourly speeds, courses, winds, weather, including near disaster, towing to Portsmouth, repairs, trying to save mud-covered cargo, mate with small pox 585.00
Merchantman *Hanover,* 155 pages, manuscript journal for two Atlantic crossings, kept by Captain James Drummond, sailing from New Orleans to Le Havre and Cadiz in 1839 and 1841 . . . . 815.00

Ship Model, shadowbox
14-1/2" h, 29-1/2" l, three-masted ship under full sail, painted background, glass missing 635.00
16-1/2" h, 24-3/8" l, three-masted ship *Augusta* under full sail, painted and decoupage background, 19th C, minor imperfections 575.00

23-1/2" h, 32-1/2" w, 12" d walnut case, four masted Barque ship, *Great Republic,* 20th C, minor imperfections . . 950.00
36-1/2" h, 56" w, 15-1/2" d, three-masted ship *Fair Wind* in full sail, painted hull fitted with lifeboats and anchors, linen sails, flying American flag, back panel painted with coastal scene showing water and waves, boat flying American flag and back painted lighthouse has top with holes fitted with light in back, sgd "Perk, 1925 (Charles Perkins,) constructed by Capt. Forest Fillmore Cole," late 1920s 1,900.00

Speaking Trumpet, 17-1/2" l, nickel plated, applied spread eagle, inscribed "E. D. Hurlbut & Co. to Capt. Francis West," 19th C 1,400.00

Sternboard, 54" w, carved mahogany, gilded eagle, P Libbey, Maine, sgd on back 1,500.00

Telescope
4-3/4" h, brass, Swan, Hunter & Wingham Richardson Ltd., Neptune Works, dated 1840 . . . . 750.00
20-1/4" h, canvas cov brass, from ship *Edwina,* Capt. Francis West 1,200.00

Trailboard, 58-1/2" l, gilded, foliate scroll carving, black ground, 19th C 450.00

Whip, 52" l, wood and braided leather, die stamped "Owned by Capt. Nickerson Yarmouth, N.S. cat o'nine tail whip used in slave days on the old windjammer in the old sailing days 1864," losses to leather 460.00

NAZI ITEMS

History: The National Societyialist German Workers Party (NSDAP) was created on Feb. 24, 1920, by Anton Drexler and Adolf Hitler. Its 25-point nationalistic program was designed to revive the depressed German economy and revitalize the government.

In 1923, after the failed Beer Hall Putsch, Hitler was sentenced to a five-year term in Landsberg Prison. He spent only a year in prison, during which time he wrote the first volume of Mein Kampf.

In the late 1920s and early 1930s, the NSDAP developed from a regional party into a major national party. In the spring of 1933, Hitler became the Reich's chancellor. Shortly after the death of President von Hindenberg in 1934, Hitler combined the offices of president and chancellor into a single position, giving him full control over the German government as well as NSDAP. From that point until May 1945, the National Societyialist German Worker's Party dominated all aspects of German life.

In the mid-1930s, Hitler initiated a widespread plan—ranging from re-arming to territorial acquisition—designed to unite the German-speaking peoples of Europe into a single nation. Germany's invasion of Poland in 1939 triggered the hostilities that led to the Second World War. The war in Europe ended on VE Day, May 7, 1945.

Reference: Ron Manion, *German Military Collectibles Price Guide*, Antique Trader Publications, 1995.

Periodicals: *Der Gauleiter*, P.O. Box 721288, Houston, TX 77272; *Military Collector Magazine*, P.O. Box 245, Lyon Station, PA 19536; *Military Collectors News*, P.O. Box 702073, Tulsa, OK 74170; *Military History*, 602 S. King St., Suite 300, Leesburg, VA 22075; *Military Trader*, P.O. Box 1050, Dubuque, IA 52004.

Note: The objects that appear below are associated with the NSDAP as a political party. See the Militaria listing for objects associated with the German military prior to and during World War II.

Arm Band
Concentration Cap Prisoner, colored triangle on white cotton
Black, Political 55.00
Blue, Gypsy 65.00
Green, Criminal 55.00
Pink, Homosexual 90.00
Red, Communist 55.00
Yellow, half Jewish 65.00
Purple, Jehovah Witness 75.00
Jewish, yellow star of David 42.00
Waffen SS 29.00

Autograph
Bormann, Martin, private secretary to Adolf Hitler, letter sgd as Deputy to the Fuhrer and Chief of Staff, in German, 1 page, 8" x 10", on National Socialist German Labor Party letterhead, Obersalzberg, Aug. 26, 1937, telling storm trooper that he has been exceeding his jurisdiction and asking him to confirm activity 850.00
Goering, Hermann, typed letter sgd as Reichsminister for Air Travel and Commander in Chief of the Luftwaffe, in German, 1 page, 8" x 10", on official letterhead with emb eagle and swastika at upper left, Berlin, July 9, 1938, letter regarding sums for support of housing or studios for artists, sgd in magenta ink 1,275.00

Bayonet, dress, 9-7/8" chrome blade, single unstopped fuller, nickeled handguard and eagle head pommel, dark stag grip lanes, mkd on left ricasso "Alcoso," right mkd "Albert Kuhl/Munster-Essen," black metal scabbard 95.00
Belt Buckle, enlisted man's 20.00
Book, *The Nazi Movement in the United States 1924-1941*, Sander A. Diamond, Cornell Univ. Press, 1974, 5" x 7", 330 pgs 20.00
Broadside, "The National Socialist Germany Greets Their National Socialist Austria and the New National Socialist Regime in Honor of Unerasuable Fellowship - Hiel Hitler" 42.00
Cap Badge, Labor Corps, aluminum, mkd "Ges. Gesch" 35.00
Cigarette Case, SS, German silver, inscribed to "Das Reich Div, SS," name and rank 750.00

Dagger
Army, 10" blade, later type by Carl Ju. Krebs, aluminum spread winged Nazi eagle and pommel cap, yellow handle material, pebble finish aluminum scabbard 325.00
Army, officer's, 10" blade, later type by Siegfried, aluminum spread winged Nazi eagle and pommel cal, yellow handle material, pebble finish aluminum scabbard, pommel cap fitted with anodized gray-brown color 245.00
Luftwaffe, 10" blade, standard late issue, eagle and swastika hand guard, dark orange synthetic handle with twisted silver wire dec, standard pommel cap with gold enameled swasti-

kas, mkd "original/eickhorn/soligen" with squirrel, standard pebble finished scabbard with oakleaf and acorn dec on bottom quarter 300.00
SA, standard configuration, brown grip and scabbard, blade b WLH Kober & Co., crossguard mkd "TH" for SA group Thurigen 250.00

Dog Tag
Lufwaffe 120.00
SS 150.00

Medal
Iron Cross, 2nd Class, ribbon, 1939 . . . . 30.00
Mayday Tinny 35.00
National Socialist Medal, ribbons 25.00
War Merit Cross, swords, ribbon 35.00
Parade Flag, 10" x 9", National Socialist 20.00
Pin, lady's, swastika, flower, red glass center 15.00
Plate, 9" d, green and white porcelain, green Luftwaffe eagle, Unit #O-H-2 . . . . 20.00
Pocket Knife, brass, small, thin 2 blade, mkd "Soligen/Germany" on ricasso, repoussed brass handles depicting Adolph Hitler in full Nazi uniform on one side, Nazi eagle on wreath with swastika, acorns, and oak leaves and "Deutschland Erwacht" 70.00
Podium Banner, 40" x 30", National Socialist Party 35.00
Postage Stamps, sheet of 100, Hitler portrait, WWII era . 35.00
Print, 8" x 11", Luftwaffe crew, preparing bomber for strike, marked "Berlin, 1940" 20.00
Shirt, SA, brown, arm band and chest ribbon 700.00
Stickpin, Nazi Industrial Cogwheel 30.00
Sword, 29-1/2" l single edged blade, quill back, unmarked, heavily etched scene on both sides showing battleships and biplanes, oak leaf clusters, cast brass hilt with folding clam shell guard lions head pommel, red and green rhinestone eyes, ivory grip with twisted wire wrap, leather scabbard with brass mounts 1,400.00

NETSUKES

History: The traditional Japanese kimono has no pockets. Daily necessities, such as money and tobacco supplies, were carried in leather pouches, or inros, which hung from a cord with a netsuke toggle. The word netsuke comes from "ne"—to root—and "tsuke"—to fasten.

Netsukes originated in the 14th century and initially were favored by the middle class. By the mid-18th century, all levels of Japanese society used them. Some of the most famous artists, e.g., Shuzan and Yamada Hojitsu, worked in the netsuke form.

Netsukes average from 1 to 2 inches in length and are made from wood, ivory, bone, ceramics, metal, horn, nutshells, etc. The subject matter is broad based, but always portrayed in a lighthearted, humorous manner. A netsuke must have smooth edges and balance in order to hang correctly on the sash.

Reference: Raymond Bushell, *Introduction to Netsuke*, Charles E. Tuttle Co., 1971; George Lazarnick, *The Signature Book of Netsuke, Inro and Ojime Artists in Photographs,* first edition 1976, 2 volume second edition 1981.

Periodical: *Netsuke & Ivory Carving Newsletter*, 3203 Adams Way, Ambler, PA 19002.

Collectors' Clubs: International Netsuke Society, P.O. Box 471686, San Francisco, CA 94147; Netsuke Kenkyukai Society, P.O. Box 31595, Oakland, CA 94604.

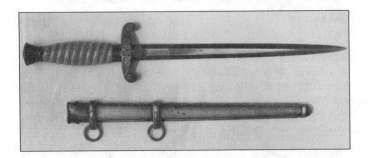

Officer's dress dagger, 15" l, $245.

Notes: Value depends on artist, region, material, and skill of craftsmanship. Western collectors favor katabori, pieces which represent an identifiable object.

Cinnabar, wrestler, sgd within cartouche 400.00
Ivory, 19th C
  Ashinaga and octopus, inlaid eyes, 2-3/4" l, 19th C
  . . . . 920.00
  Blind leading the blind, sgd, 19th C 635.00
  Daikoku and Ebisu sharing bottle of sake, sgd "Tamayuki," 19th C 175.00
  Daruma, scowling, robed, holding hoso (fly wisk), leaning on elbow rest, sgd "Jokuzan," 19th C, chip to foot 345.00
  Dragon head, bell, deeply colored patina, 18th C . . . 230.00
  Dragon rising from clouds, inlaid eyes, stained, 1-1/2" h
  . . . . 525.00
  Five deities in boat, sgd with three characters, 19th C
  . . . . 475.00
  Hoitei dancing, sgd with inlaid cinnabar seal, 19th C
  . . . . 700.00
  Hoitei, bag of wealth over his shoulder, sgd "Jogyoku," late 19th C 300.00
  Manjo Dancer, lacquer and gilt details, noted carver Hideyuki
  . . . . 575.00
  Manju-type, carved octopus and various plants, attached to tobacco pouch 400.00
  Man with basket, sgd "Ryutei," 18th/19th C 400.00
  Man with three boys, sgd "Masatomo," 19th C. 380.00
  Monkey, inlaid eyes, sgd "Gyokusai," 19th C 400.00
  Noh mask, 19th C. 175.00
  Oni, carrying pole balancing bell and lantern, sgd "Unsei" or "Kumaharu," 19th C 850.00
  Ox, reclining, color details, sgd "Yasuchika" 350.00
  Shinto priests struggling to move huge conch shell, 19th C
  . . . . 460.00
  Three men in a sake cup, fine detail, sgd "Chokyu," seven characters and seal, 19th C. 1,265.00
  Tradesmen and other subjects. 345.00
  Traveler with large backpack, holding basket of flowers, accosted by miniature badgers dressed as humans, 19th C
  . . . . 700.00
  Two children playing with Hoitei's bag, 18th C. 550.00
  Two men, one picking pine branches, other falling after being startled by snake in tree, sgd "Seimei," 19th C 800.00
  Two quail and pair of millet pots, finely detailed feathers, stained natural color, inlaid eyes, sgd "Okatomo"
  . . . . 1,000.00
  Woman, bare chest, awakened from sleep, yawning, stretching, colored, sgd, 2-1/4" h 920.00
  Woman, holding ball of flowers, sgd with seal, 19th C
  . . . . 288.00
Ivory and Wood, Bukkan Zenshi, sleeping on tiger, accompanied by two daruma figures, two different types of wood and ivory, sgd with Kakiban reading Sorin, one hand missing
. . . . 1,380.00
Staghorn, 19th C
  Lotus pod with seeds of inlaid horn, frog perched on side
  . . . . 320.00
  Sashi carved as ling chih mushroom 175.00

Carved ivory, 19th C, $115.

Wood, carved
  Bell, eggplant shape, cov with negoro lacquer, sgd "Hidemasa" 320.00
  Daruma, hardwood, 4-1/2" h, repair to bottom of robe
  . . . . 230.00
  Farmer, hoeing, accompanied by dog, boxwood, 19th C, cartouche missing. 290.00
  Group of nuts, Japanese 75.00
  Group of shells, Japanese 85.00
  Hoitei with his bag, inlaid eyes, by noted carved Chuichi, Taisho period. 750.00
  Toad, 1-1/2" l, Japanese 150.00

NEWCOMB POTTERY

History: The Sophie Newcomb Memorial College, an adjunct of Tulane University in New Orleans, LA, was originated as a school to train local women in the decorative arts. While metal working, painting, and embroidery were among the classes taught, the production of fine, hand-crafted art pottery remains their most popular and collectible pursuit.

Pottery was made by the Newcomb women for nearly 50 years, with earlier work being the rarest and the most valuable. This is characterized by shiny finishes and broad, flat-painted and modeled designs. More common, though still quite valuable, are their matte glaze pieces, often depicting bayou scenes and native flora. All bear the impressed NC mark.

References: Ralph and Terry Kovel, *Kovels' American Art Pottery*, Crown Publishers, 1993; Jessie Poesch, *Newcomb Pottery: An Enterprise for Southern Women*, Schiffer Publishing, 1984; David Rago, *American Art Pottery,* Knickerbocker Press, 1997.

Collectors' Club: American Art Pottery Association, P.O. Box 1226, Westport, MA 02790.

Museum: Newcomb College, Tulane University, New Orleans, LA.

Advisor: David Rago.

Bowl
　4" d, 5" h, Matte Ware, closed form, stylized yellow flowers, blue ground, border design 1,200.00
　6-1/2" d, 3" h, incised and painted green, blue, and ivory high-glaze floral design, deeply carved, incised marks, "C. Payne, J.M.". 2,500.00
　7" d, squatty, three-sided rim, green and blue hi-glaze, with flower frog, imp marks 600.00
　8" d, 3-1/2" h, shoulder dec with yellow, red, and green flowers, matte blue body, imp "NC, HF, 64, 259" 1,100.00
　9-1/2" d, carved and painted pink florals, yellow centers, green leaves, blue matte glaze, imp marks, A. F. Simpson, J.M., tight line. 900.00
Cabinet Vase, 4" h, 4" h, Matte Ware, blue and white molded flowers, blue ground. 900.00
Candleholder, 5" h, 5" d, Matte Ware, transitional, green flowers, blue ground, lightly molded, markings underneath
　. . . . . .1,700.00
Cream Pitcher, 4" x 3", green trefoils, blue leaves, light blue ground 1,500.00
Cup and Saucer, 3" h cup, 5-1/2" d saucer, incised and painted flowers, blue hi-glaze, light blue ground, imp marks, C. Luria 1,900.00
Inkwell, 4" x 4", stylized yellow flowers and green leaves, cream ground, orig lid and inkpot 1,500.00
Match Holder, 4" h, 3" d, Matte Ware, yellow flowers, blue ground 800.00
Pitcher
　5-1/2" h, 4" d, deep gray-green metallic dripping glaze, brown ground, imp "CN, GM" 260.00
　8" h, painted hi-glaze, green berries and leaves, ivory and blue ground, imp mark, R. Kennon, J.M.. . . . . .6,500.00
Plaque, 8" x 6", scenic, carved bayou scene, matte blue finish, Henrietta Bailey 7,700.00
Vase
　4-1/2" h, 2" d, crisply molded high relief flowers, mate blue ground, imp "NC RQ3 IS, JH" 1,380.00
　6" h, early high glazed, yellow jonquils, cream ground, Desiree Roman artist 7,150.00
　6" h, 6" d, Matte Ware, bulbous, squatty, carved bayou scene in blues, yellow moon 2,500.00

Left, vase: carved matte, by F. Simpson, 1929, $7,700; right: vase, M. Ross, 1904, $8,500. Photo courtesy of David Rago Auctions, Inc.

　6" h, 6-3/4" d, slab built, crackle high glaze, base marked with monogram for Leoni Nicholson, minor hairline 260.00
　7" h, 4" d, stylized flowers, blue and white, shiny finish
　. . . . . .2,000.00
　7" h, 6" d, Matte Ware, bulbous, allover design of carved flowers in blue and green, blue ground 2,200.00
　8" h, early high glazed tall corseted vase, white flowers, blue ground, Marie LeBlanc. .5,500.00
　8" h, 6" w, bulbous, white and yellow jonquil, dark green leaves, dark blue and white ground, early 26,400.00
　10" h, 7" d, Matte Ware, carved iris blossoms in blue and white, blue ground 3,500.00
　11" h, 5" d, bulbous, modeled yellow fleur-de-lis, green leaves, cream ground .20,000.00

NILOAK POTTERY, MISSION WARE

History: Niloak Pottery was made near Benton, Arkansas. Charles Dean Hyten experimented with native clay, trying to preserve its natural colors. By 1911, he perfected Mission Ware, a marbleized pottery in which the cream and brown colors predominate. The company name is the word "kaolin" spelled backwards.

After a devastating fire, the pottery was rebuilt and named Eagle Pottery. This factory included enough space to add a novelty pottery line in 1929. Mr. Hyten left the pottery in 1941, and in 1946 operations ceased.

Marks: The early pieces were marked "Niloak." Eagle Pottery products usually were marked "Hywood-Niloak" until 1934, when the "Hywood" was dropped from the mark.

References: Susan and Al Bagdade, *Warman's American Pottery and Porcelain*, Wallace-Homestead, 1994; David Edwin Gifford, *Collector's Encyclopedia of Niloak*, Collector Books, 1993.

Collectors' Club: Arkansas Pottery Collectors Society, P.O. Box 7617, Little Rock, AR 72217.

Additional Listings: See *Warman's Americana & Collectibles* for more examples, especially the novelty pieces.

Ashtray, 3-1/2" w, Mission Ware. 80.00
Bowl
　4" d, Mission Ware. 100.00
　5" d, Mission Ware 80.00
　10" d, w, Mission Ware, imp mark 325.00
Box, cov, 5" d, Mission Ware, lid chip 190.00
Bud Vase, 6" h, Mission Ware, imp mark 180.00
Candlestick, 3-1/2" h, Mission Ware 160.00
Chamber Pot, infant's, 5-1/2" w, Mission Ware. 550.00
Cigarette Jar, cov, Mission Ware 350.00
Drinking Cup, Mission Ware, set of six, various colors, minor flakes 600.00
Flower Pot, 10" h, 9" w underplate, drainage hole, Mission Ware
　. . . . . 950.00
Humidor, cov, 6-1/2" h, tan, cream, and light beige Mission Ware, bell-bottom shape, rare mark. 1,300.00
Jardiniere, 8" h, 8-1/2" w, Mission Ware, four incised rings at top, paper label 600.00

Vase, Mission Ware, yellow, blue, and brown swirl, imp mark, 5-1/4" h, $95.

Jardiniere Pedestal, 7" h, Mission Ware, bruise to bottom
.... 325.00
Jug, 6" h, Mission Ware 325.00
Match Holder, 5" w, ashtray base, Mission Ware, paper label
.... 400.00
Mug, Mission Ware
    4" h, dark brown, dark cream, set of six, patent pending mark
.... 900.00
    5" h... 230.00
Necklace, 18" l 750.00
Pitcher, 10-1/2" h, Mission Ware, handle, early patent pending
    mark and imp mark........................... 950.00
Punch Bowl, 13" d, 9" h, glazed int., Mission Ware . . .2,400.00
Rose Jar, 8" h, Mission Ware 850.00
Shot Glass, 2-1/2" h, Mission Ware, set of six, one chip
.... 425.00
Stem Holders, Mission Ware, set of three, 4-1/2" w, minor flakes
.... 110.00
Tankard Pitcher, 10" h, brown, tan, cream, and turquoise Mis-
    sion Ware, chip repair and line.................. 290.00
Tile, 4" sq, Mission Ware, unmarked, minor flakes..... 110.00
Tobacco Jar, 5-1/2" w, 5-1/2" h, Mission Ware........ 700.00
Toothpick Holder, 2" h, Mission Ware, cylindrical, imp mark
.... 110.00
Tray, Mission Ware
    10-1/2" d, cream, beige, tan, red, and turquoise 400.00
    13" d, cream, tan, red, turquoise 950.00
Tumble-Up, 8-1/2" h, Mission Ware, imp mark........ 475.00
Umbrella Stand, Mission Ware
    20" h, firing crack in base....................2,100.00
    21" h, crack to base 1,500.00
Vase, Mission Ware
    3" h, cream, brown, blue, and red, closed cylinder form, imp
      mark.. 140.00
    3-1/2" h... 60.00
    4" h... 100.00
    4" h, 5" w 100.00
    4-1/2" h, swelled ovoid, lip, imp mark............ 130.00
    6" h, tapering ovoid with slightly flared base, slightly turned in
      shoulder, imp mark........................... 100.00
    6-1/2" h, waisted form, bulbous base............ 150.00

    8" h, baluster, wide flat top rim, imp mark 130.00
    8-1/2" h, hourglass form...................... 170.00
    10" h, waisted form, blue, red, brown, and cream swirls, imp
      mark.. 250.00
    11-1/2" h, cylindrical 375.00
    13-1/2" h, long neck over swelled base 475.00
    14" h.. 800.00
    16" h, baluster, wide flat top rim, imp mark 1,700.00
    18" h, baluster, wide flat top rim, orig paper label . .3,000.00
Violet Vase, 3-1/2" h, Mission Ware 375.00
Wall Pocket, 5-1/2" l, Mission Ware 375.00
Water Bottle, cov, 8" h, Mission Ware, top may not be orig, minor
    chip... 250.00

NIPPON CHINA, 1891-1921

History: Nippon, Japanese hand-painted porcelain, was made for export between 1891 and 1921. In 1891, when the McKinley tariff act proclaimed that all items of foreign manufacture be stamped with their country of origin, Japan chose to use "Nippon." In 1921, the United States decided the word "Nippon" no longer was acceptable and required all Japanese wares to be marked "Japan," ending the Nippon era.

Marks: There are more than 220 recorded Nippon backstamps or marks; the three most popular are the wreath, maple leaf, and rising sun. Wares with variations of all three marks are being reproduced today. A knowledgeable collector can easily spot the reproductions by the mark variances.

The majority of the marks are found in three different colors: green, blue, or magenta. Colors indicate the quality of the porcelain used: green for first-grade porcelain, blue for second-grade, and magenta for third-grade. Marks were applied by two methods: decal stickers under glaze and imprinting directly on the porcelain.

REPRODUCTION ALERT

Distinguishing Old Marks from New:
A common old mark consisted of a central wreath open at the top with the letter M in the center. "Hand Painted" flowed around the top of the wreath; "NIPPO Box N" around the bottom. The modern fake mark reverses the wreath (it is open at the bottom) and places an hourglass form not an "M" in its middle.
An old leaf mark, approximately one-quarter inch wide, has "Hand" with "Painted" below to the left of the stem and "NIPPO Box N" beneath. The newer mark has the identical lettering but the size is now one-half, rather than one-quarter, inch.
An old mark consisted of "Hand Painted" arched above a solid rising sun logo with "NIPPO Box N" in a straight line beneath. The modern fake mark has the same lettering pattern but the central logo looks like a mound with a jagged line enclosing a blank space above it.

References: Joan Van Patten, *Collector's Encyclopedia of Nippon Porcelain*, 1st Series (1979, 1997 value update), 2nd Series (1982, 1997 value update), 3rd Series

(1986, 1996 value update), 4th Series, (1997), Collector Books; 5th Series (1998); Kathy Wojciechowski, *Wonderful World of Nippon Porcelain*, Schiffer Publishing, 1992.

Collectors' Clubs: ARK-LA-TEX Nippon Club, 6800 Arapaho Rd, #1057, Dallas, TX 75248; Dixieland Nippon Club, P.O. Box 1712, Centerville, VA 22020; International Nippon Collectors Club, 1417 Steele St., Fort Myers, FL 33901; Lakes & Plains Nippon Collectors Society, P.O. Box 230, Peotone, IL 60468-0230; Long Island Nippon Collectors Club, 145 Andover Place, W Hempstead, NY 11552; MD-PA Collectors' Club, 1016 Erwin Dr., Joppa, MD 21085; New England Nippon Collectors Club, 64 Burt Rd., Springfield, MA 01118; Sunshine State Nippon Collectors' Club, P.O. Box 425, Frostproof, FL 33843; Upstate New York Nippon Collectors' Club, 122 Laurel Ave., Herkimer, NY 13350.

Additional Listings: See *Warman's Americana & Collectibles.*

SPECIAL AUCTION

Jackson's Auctioneers & Appraisers
2229 Lincoln St.
Cedar Falls, IA 50613
(319) 277-2256
e-mail:jacksons@corenet.net

Biscuit Jar, 4-1/2" h, painted maroon and gold, blue maple leaf mark 70.00
Bowl
    7" d, ftd, raised nut design, green "M" in wreath mark . 85.00
    7-1/4" d, 4" h, tan and beige, hp chestnuts int., ext. with leaves and gold beaded dec, three legs, blue maple leaf mark 100.00
    10" d, light green faded ground, yellow, red, and pink hp roses, gold dec rim, two small closed handles, blue maple leaf mark 100.00
Cake Plate, 11" d, floral design, gold trim, green "M" in wreath mark 40.00
Candlestick, 11" h, 5" base, hp gold highlights, light green ground pedestal base, green maple leaf mark 115.00
Celery Tray, 10-1/4" l, scalloped edge, green "M" in wreath mark 75.00
Cheese Dish, cov, 7-3/4" l, slanted, floral design, gold trim, blue Komaro mark 70.00
Chocolate Set, 9-1/2" h chocolate pot, four cups and saucers, orange and tan floral dec, white ground, gold highlights, green "M" in wreath mark 100.00
Compote, 5-1/4" h, floral dec, green "M" in wreath mark . 30.00
Dish, 9" w, two section, handle, butterfly design, blue rising sun mark 50.00
Dresser Set, hair receiver, trinket box, powder box, Van Patten Book I, plate 65 . . . . 375.00
Dresser Tray, 18" l, 6-1/4" w, delicate hp pink floral design, gold trim, closed handles, green "M" in wreath mark, minor gold wear 50.00
Egg Caddy, 4" h, 6" d, holds four eggs, handle over stopper, hp landscape scene, green "M" in wreath mark 75.00
Hatpin Holder, shaped, raised beading 65.00
Humidor, cov
    Bulldog 200.00
    Hand painted cottage landscape, trees, fence, green "M" in wreath mark 275.00

Lemonade Set, 6-1/2" h pitcher, four matching tumblers, grape design, gold trim, 5 pc, China JE-OH mark 125.00
Milk Pitcher, cov, 7" h, lavender ground, Egyptian style boats, island with trees and buildings, brow handle, geometric devices, blue maple leaf mark 185.00
Muffineer, 5" h, handle, two oval panels of hp flowers, gold dec, blue maple leaf mark 70.00
Nut Dish, 9" d, nut in nest design, double handles, green "M" in wreath mark 55.00
Pitcher
    6" h, lavender ground, hp scene of Mediterranean sailboats, island with trees and buildings, geometric beading around rim, applied hp brown handle, bulbous ribbed body
    . . . . 145.00
    6-1/2" h, 5" w, Moorage dec, tan ground, handle dec, green, and white beading, blue maple leaf mark 50.00
Plaque
    Elk, blown-out 800.00
    Horses, 10-3/4" d, molded in relief, five tan and brown horses, fence and trees in back ground, green M in wreath mark
    . . . . 550.00
    Indian Warrior, 10-1/2" d, molded in relief, full feather bonnet, hunter clad in buffalo cap, green "M" in wreath mark
    . . . . 750.00
    Moose, blown-out 450.00
    Waiting by Shore,10" d, Dutch mother and two children looking over bay, dec rim, blue "M" in wreath mark 100.00
Plate
    9" d, Flying Phoenix, dark blue 45.00
    9-1/2" d, hp landscape of water, trees, and mountain in background, 1" w gold border with green and pink hp jewels, blue maple leaf mark 70.00
Platter, 15" l, Flying Phoenix, dark blue 110.00
Portrait Vase, 5" h, 4" w, hp, portrait of young lady on one side, hp floral scene on reverse, two open handles, ruffled top, unmarked 325.00
Salt and Pepper Shakers, pr, HoHo birds 45.00
Serving Tray, 11-3/4" l, swan dec, gold trim, blue "M" in wreath mark 110.00
Tankard, 10" h, 6" d, flared base, raised gold enameled dec, central hp floral medallion, green maple leaf mark, some wear to gold 225.00

Sugar Bowl, cov, hp scene, $40.

Tea Set, 6" h cov teapot, creamer, sugar, six cups and saucers, hp swans in pond, mill in background, gold highlighted beading, green M in wreath mark, wear to gold 150.00

Tiered Plate, 9" d, floral border, gold trim, magenta "M" in wreath mark 30.00

Vase

5-1/4" h, bulbous, two handles, black, pink, red, and yellow roses, Royal Kinran mark. 125.00

6" h, four handles, scenic design, green "M" in wreath mark, pr 165.00

6-1/2" h, hp, grapes on vines, gold dec, bulbous, green maple leaf mark 70.00

7-1/2" h, 7" w, Madame Recamier portrait, handle, cobalt blue ground, three bright floral inserts, beaded, bulbous, pedestal 415.00

8-1/2" h, double handles, Lilac pattern, gold trim, blue maple leaf mark 150.00

8-1/2" h, double handles, scenic design, gold trim, green "M" in wreath mark, pr 265.00

8-1/2" h, 4-3/4" w, four sided, hp scenes of water views with trees, gold beading around each panel, green M in wreath mark. 150.00

8-3/4" h, double elephant trunk handles, florals, gold trim, green "M" mark, pr 300.00

9-1/2" h, 4-1/2" d, iris dec, two small handles, 2" heavy gold band around top, blue maple leaf mark 325.00

10" h, black pottery, Gouda type design, green wreath mark 200.00

12-1/2" h, double handles, blue floral dec, gold trim, green "M" in wreath mark. 100.00

13" h, two handles, hp flowers, gold painted griffins, black, red, and green, gold highlights, ruffled top, white and pink flowers, blue "M" in wreath mark 250.00

13-1/2" h, two handles, small roses hp in portrait style, gold dec, two large ovals, green maple leaf mark, some minor gold wear, pr 450.00

14" h, 6" d, hp white and red roses and leaves on one side, gold beaded highlights at rim and base, blue maple leaf mark, some wear to gold at rim 200.00

Vegetable Bowl, 10-1/4" d, two handles, scalloped edge, acorn design, green "M" in wreath mark. 90.00

Wall Plaque, 10" d, portrait 435.00

Wine Jug, monk portrait, Moriage stopper 750.00

NODDERS

History: Nodders are figurines with heads and/or arms attached to the body with wires to enable movement. They are made in a variety of materials—bisque, celluloid, papier-mâché, porcelain, or wood.

Most nodders date from the late 19th century, with Germany being the principal source of supply. Among the American-made nodders, those of Disney and cartoon characters are most eagerly sought.

Reference: Hilma R. Irtz, *Figural Nodders*, Collector Books, 1996.

Black Boy, 24" h, papier-mâché, clockwork, felt and cotton outfit, c1900 . . . . .1,265.00

Black Woman, seated, holding removable watermelon, gray hair, head nods, salt shaker type 75.00

Bull Dog Terrier, articulated head, papier-mâché, minor losses to paint 375.00

Cat, 5" h, composition, black. 65.00

Donkey, 3" h, celluloid. 45.00

Donkey, semi-translucent, pink-purple celluloid, dark gray highlights, yellow blanket, mkd "Made in Occupied Japan", $45. Photo courtesy of Julie Robinson.

Duck, 15-1/2" h, clockwork, yellow dyed rabbit fur, glass eyes, papier-mâché feet, articulated bill, French, early 20th C 690.00

Hobo, 3-1/2" h, 2-1/4" w, green coat, bottle in pocket, tan pants and hat, sitting in chair, holding stick 225.00

Little Orphan Annie, bisque, mkd "Germany" 125.00

Monkey, 6-1/2" h, celluloid 70.00

Mother Goose, papier-mâché, old woman in red cape riding on back of white goose 3,960.00

Oriental Lady, 6-3/4" h, bisque, seated, holding fan behind nodding head, Continental 200.00

Rabbit, 7" h, papier-mâché, glass eyes. 75.00

Turkey, 3-3/4" h, papier-mâché, male and female, orig black paint, polychrome trim, pewter feet 120.00

NORITAKE CHINA

History: Morimura Brothers founded Noritake China in 1904 in Nagoya, Japan. They made high-quality chinaware for export to the United States and also produced a line of china blanks for hand painting. In 1910, the company perfected a technique for the production of high-quality dinnerware and introduced streamlined production.

During the 1920s, the Larkin Company of Buffalo, New York, was a prime distributor of Noritake China. Larkin offered Azalea, Briarcliff, Linden, Modjeska, Savory, Sheridan, and Tree in the Meadow patterns as part of their premium line.

The factory was heavily damaged during World War II, and production was reduced. Between 1946 and 1948 the company sold their china under the "Rose China" mark, since the quality of production did not match the earlier Noritake China. Expansion in 1948 brought about the resumption of quality production and the use of the Noritake name once again.

Marks: There are close to 100 different marks for Noritake, the careful study of which can determine the date of production. Most pieces are marked "Noritake" with a wreath, "M," "N," or "Nippon." The use of the letter N was registered in 1953.

References: Aimee Neff Alden, *Collector's Encyclopedia of Early Noritake,* Collector Books, 1995; Joan Van Patten, *Collector's Encyclopedia of Noritake,* 1st Series (1984, 1997 value update), 2nd Series, (1994), Collector Books; David Spain, *Noritake Collectibles A to Z, A Pictorial Record and Guide to Values,* Schiffer Publishing, 1997.

Collectors' Club: Noritake Collectors' Society, 145 Andover Place, West Hempstead, NY 115532-1603.

Additional Listings: See *Warman's Americana & Collectibles* for Azalea pattern prices.

Ashtray, 4-3/4' w, tree trunk, relief molded raccoon, green M in wreath mark 200.00
Bowl, 7" sq, 3 ftd, turned-in sides, autumn leaves, molded filbert nuts 80.00
Bread Plate, 12" l, ear of corn dec 50.00
Butter Dish, cov, Tree in the Meadow pattern, orig insert 65.00
Butter Tub, Azalea pattern 45.00
Cake plate, Baroda pattern 25.00
Candlesticks, pr, 3-1/2" h, 4-1/2" d, tan luster, blue roses, black handle and trim, three ftd base. 75.00
Card Holder, Art Deco style, double handles, pedestal base, blue and orange luster, gentleman in checkered cape 225.00
Celery Tray, 12" l, Azalea pattern 45.00
Chocolate Pot, cov, Tree in the Meadow pattern 200.00
Compote, blue, gold, and white, fruit dec, 2 pcs 175.00
Condiment Set, figural, lady, pr salt and pepper shakers, and mustard pot, price for set 85.00
Cookie Plate, 10-1/2" d, orange luster, vibrant sunflowers, handles. 125.00

Cracker Jar, cov, Tree in the Meadow pattern, melon ribbed 135.00
Creamer and Sugar, cov, Tree in the Meadow pattern . . . 70.00
Cup and Saucer, Chelsea pattern 30.00
Dessert Set, Art Deco lady in cup, large geometric tray, blue luster 125.00
Dresser Set, orange luster, figural bird final on ftd powder box, matching tray 250.00
Jam Dish, gray luster, figural locust, multicolored emb fruits 65.00
Lemon Dish, 5-1/2" d, Tree in the Meadow pattern. 35.00
Napkin Ring, gentleman 50.00
Nut Bowl Set, 6" d bowl, open chestnut form, holds six 2" d nut dishes, painted nuts and leaves, earthtones, green mark 150.00
Plate, 8-1/2" d, Tree in the Meadow pattern 20.00
Potpourri Jar, 6" h , blue and white, pierced cov with red and yellow rosebud finial 85.00
Salt and Pepper Shakers, pr, Art Deco style. 75.00
Sandwich Server, 8" d, pearlized center, fruit dec, bird finial 175.00
Teapot, cov, Tree in the Meadow pattern 100.00
Vase
    7" h, pink, flowers 42.00
    10" h, moriage dragon, two handles, green mark. . . . 175.00
    13" h, two handles, Tree in Meadow scene, green "M" in wreath mark 125.00
Vegetable Dish, cov, 8-1/2" w, 5" h, floral design, heavy gold trim, mkd "Noritake China, 'M' in wreath, Made in Occupied Japan" (Mark #91), very slight wear to gold 125.00
Wall Pocket, orange luster, figural bird peering over top 180.00

NORTH DAKOTA SCHOOL of MINES

History: The North Dakota School of Mines was established in 1890. Earle J. Babcock, a chemistry instructor, was impressed with the high purity level of North Dakota potter's clay. In 1898, Babcock received funds to develop his finds. He tried to interest commercial potteries in the North Dakota clay but had limited success.

In 1910, Babcock persuaded the school to establish a Ceramics Department. Margaret Cable, who studied under Charles Binns and Frederick H. Rhead, was appointed head. She remained until her retirement in 1949.

Decorative emphasis was placed on native themes, e.g., flowers and animals. Art Nouveau, Art Deco, and fairly plain pieces were made.

Marks: The pottery is marked with a cobalt blue underglaze circle of the words "University of North Dakota/Grand Forks, N.D./Made at School of Mines/N.D. Clay." Some early pieces are marked only "U.N.D." or "U.N.D./Grand Forks, N.D." Most pieces are numbered (they can be dated from University records) and signed by both the instructor and student. Cable-signed pieces are the most desirable.

References: Susan and Al Bagdade, *Warman's American Pottery and Porcelain,* Wallace-Homestead, 1994; Darlene Hurst Dommel, *Collector's Encyclopedia of the Dakota Potteries,* Collector Books, 1996; Ralph and Terry Kovel, *Kovels' American Art Pottery,* Crown Publishers, 1993.

Plate, Azalea pattern, 7-1/2" h, $12.

Vase, The Plowsman, carved field plowing scene, matte brown glaze, dec by F. Huckfield, ink stamp, carved title and artist, 5" x 6-1/2", $1,700. Photo courtesy of David Rago Auctions, Inc.

Collectors' Club: North Dakota Pottery Collectors Society, P.O. Box 14, Beach, ND 58621.

Bowl, 6-1/2" d, 3-1/2" h, squatty, Red River Ox Cart, emb panels of ox carts, brown and green matte glaze, Margaret Cable, ink stamp, incised title, and artist 1,400.00

Cabinet Vase, 3" h, 3-1/2" d, spherical, Prairie Rose, carved dec, green matte glaze, F. Huckfield, 1951, ink stamp mark, incised title, and "Huck/51" 450.00

Charger, 9-3/4" d, dark brown flowers, burnt sienna ground, Margaret Cable, 1932, ink stamp, "M. Cable #844/1932" 900.00

Humidor, 6" h, 6-1/4" d, brown and green berries, matte mustard ground, painted by Margaret Cable, 1917, ink stamp/MKC 1917/SM/#40 . . . . .4,750.00

Jardiniere, 7" h, 4-3/4" d, brown emb band of cowboys, green matte ground, Julia Mattson, ink stamp, incised "Mattson" 2,900.00

Trivet
 4-3/4" d, Bentonite, carved stylized black eagle, brick red ground, Julia Mattson, 1958, ink stamp mark and "JM58" 250.00
 5" d, green and ochre fish, light ground, carved by Julia Mattson, imp stamp/JM58. . . . . 250.00

Vase . .3" h, 3-1/2" d, Bentonite, squatty, evergreens and deer, tribal style, brown and yellow, red ground, Julia Mattson, ink stamp "JH" 750.00
 4" h, 4-1/2" d, squatty, blue and green Viking ships, light blue ground, Julia Mattson, ink stamp "JH" 700.00
 4-1/4" h, 3-1/2" d, bulbous, carved haystacks, green matte ground, F. Huckfield, ink stamp mark, incised "H 164" 550.00
 5" h, 3" d, cowboys in chaps, standing arm in arm, matte brown and green glaze, Julia Mattson, ink stamp "JM" 1,300.00
 5" h, 6-1/2" d, The Plowman, carved field-plowing scenes, mate brown glaze, dec by F. Huckfield, ink stamp, carved title, and artist 1,700.00
 7-1/4" h, 5" d, daffodils, light green semi-matte glaze, Margaret Cable, ink stamp "M. Cable" 2,600.00

7-1/2" h, 3-1/4" d, stylized red and blue flowers, green stems, blue ground, carved by Reinert, 1938, ink stamp/Reinert 1938, some firing glaze flakes 1,800.00

8-1/2" h, deeply molded floral dec on shoulder, red clay body, pale cream and lightly tinted blue matte glaze, stamp mark, incised Cable and Prairie Rose 550.00

8-1/2" h, 5-1/4" d, carved prairie roses, glossy pink glaze, Julia Mattson, ink stamp "JM" 600.00

11" h, 6" d, classic shape, Trees/Thorne, incised trees, matte green glaze, F. Huckfield, ink stamp, carved title, and artist 4,500.00

Vessel
 3-1/4" h, 3-3/4" d, squatty, incised turkeys, matte green glaze, Julia Mattson, ink stamp mark, incised "JM 170" . . . 500.00
 6-1/4" h, 7-1/2" d, spherical, blue and turquoise carved stylized mushrooms, white ground, ink stamp mark, incised "June?maths(?)/May 1949" 1,500.00

NUTTING, WALLACE

History: Wallace Nutting (1861-1941) was America's most famous photographer of the early 20th century. A retired minister, Nutting took more than 50,000 pictures, keeping 10,000 of his best and destroying the rest. His popular and best-selling scenes included "Exterior Scenes" (apple blossoms, country lanes, orchards, calm streams, and rural American country sides), "Interior Scenes" (usually featuring a colonial woman working near a hearth), and "Foreign Scenes" (typically thatch-roofed cottages). Those pictures which were least popular in his day have become the rarest and most-highly collectible today and are classified as "Miscellaneous Unusual Scenes." This category encompasses such things as animals, architecturals, children, florals, men, seascapes, and snow scenes.

Nutting sold literally millions of his hand-colored platinotype pictures between 1900 and his death in 1941. Starting first in Southbury, Connecticut, and later moving his business to Framingham, Massachusetts, the peak of Wallace Nutting's picture production was 1915 to 1925. During this period, Nutting employed nearly 200 people, including colorists, darkroom staff, salesmen, and assorted office personnel. Wallace Nutting pictures proved to be a huge commercial success and hardly an American household was without one by 1925.

While attempting to seek out the finest and best early American furniture as props for his colonial Interior Scenes, Nutting became an expert in American antiques. He published nearly twenty books in his lifetime, including his ten-volume *State Beautiful* series and various other books on furniture, photography, clocks, and his autobiography. He also contributed many photographs which were published in magazines and books other than his own.

Nutting also became widely known for his reproduction furniture. His furniture shop produced literally hundreds of different furniture forms: clocks, stools, chairs, settles, settees, tables, stands, desks, mirrors, beds, chests of drawers, cabinet pieces, and treenware.

The overall synergy of the Wallace Nutting name, pictures, books, and furniture, has made anything "Wallace Nutting" quite collectible.

Marks: Wallace Nutting furniture is clearly marked with his distinctive paper label (which was glued directly onto the piece) or with a block or script signature brand (which was literally branded into his furniture).

Note: "Process Prints" are 1930s machine-produced reprints of twelve of Nutting's most popular pictures. These have minimal value and can be detected by using a magnifying glass.

References: Michael Ivankovich, *Alphabetical & Numerical Index to Wallace Nutting Pictures*, Diamond Press, 1988; ——, *Collector's Guide to Wallace Nutting Pictures*, Collector Books, 1997; ——, *Guide to Wallace Nutting Furniture*, Diamond Press, 1990; ——, *Wallace Nutting Expansible Catalog* (reprint of 1915 catalog), Diamond Press, 1987; Wallace Nutting, *Wallace Nutting: A Great American Idea* (reprint of 1922 catalog), Diamond Press, 1992; ——, *Wallace Nutting General Catalog* (reprint of 1930 catalog), Schiffer Publishing, 1977; ——, *Wallace Nutting's Windsors* (reprint of 1918 catalog), Diamond Press, 1992.

Collectors' Club: Wallace Nutting Collectors Club, P.O. Box 2458, Doylestown, PA 18901.

Museum: Wadsworth Athenaeum, Hartford, CT.

Advisor: Michael Ivankovich.

SPECIAL AUCTION

Michael Ivankovich Auction Co.
P.O. Box 2458
Doylestown, PA 18901
(215) 345-6094

Books

American Windsors	85.00
England Beautiful, 1st ed.	125.00
Furniture of the Pilgrim Century, 1st ed.	140.00
Furniture Treasury, Vol. I	125.00
Furniture Treasury, Vol. II	140.00
Furniture Treasury, Vol. III	105.00
Ireland Beautiful, 1st ed.	45.00
Pathways of the Puritans	85.00
Social Life in Old New England	72.00

State Beautiful Series

Connecticut Beautiful, 1st ed.	72.00
Maine Beautiful, 1st ed.	45.00
Massachusetts Beautiful, 2nd ed.	35.00
New Hampshire Beautiful, 1st ed.	72.00
New York Beautiful, 1st ed.	85.00
Pennsylvania Beautiful, 1st ed.	45.00
Vermont Beautiful, 2nd ed.	40.00
Virginia Beautiful, 1st ed.	60.00
The Cruise of the 800	95.00

Furniture

Chair

Arm, mahogany, chip	1,265.00
Bedroom, mahogany	440.00
Side, Windsor	600.00
Slipper	715.00

Costumer/Coat Rack	415.00
Desk, child's	770.00
Stool, 4 legged, maple, rushed	235.00
Trestle Table	60.00

Miscellaneous

Calendar, 1939, 6" x 10"	75.00

Catalog

Christmas Picture, 1912	135.00
Furniture, 1937	95.00
Christmas Card, 4" x 5"	155.00
Easter Card, 5" x 9"	200.00
Plate, treenware	245.00

Pictures

A Berkshire Cross Road, 14" x 17"	160.00
A Call for More, 10" x 13"	330.00
A Cluster of Zinnias, 13" x 16"	330.00
A Fair Orchard Way, 11' x 14"	105.00
A Gettysburg Crossing, 14" x 17"	200.00
A Keene Road, 13" x 17"	165.00
All the Comforts of Home, 13" x 15"	210.00
A Perkiomen October, 9" x 11"	250.00
Among the Ferns, 14" x 17"	165.00
An Elaborate Dinner, 14" x 17"	200.00
Better than Mowing, 16" x 20"	490.00
Between the Spruces, 10" x 14"	200.00
Birch Hilltop, 15" x 22"	100.00
By the Fireside, 9" x 13"	100.00
California Hilltops, 11" x 14"	165.00
Dog-On-It, 7" x 11"	1,265.00
Elm Drapery, 15" x 22"	385.00
Fleur-de-lis and Spirea, 13" x 16"	685.00
Flume Falls, 12" x 15"	310.00
Four O'Clock, 14" x 17	855.00
Gloucester Cloister, 16" x 20"	1,100.00
Grandmother's Hollyhocks, 9" x 11"	400.00
Helping Mother, 14" x 17"	410.00
Hesitation, 10" x 16"	220.00
Home Charm, 15" x 22"	315.00
Honeymoon Cottage, 11" x 17	125.00
Into the West, 10" x 16"	45.00
Mountain Born, 10" x 12"	165.00
On The Heights, 10" x 16"	100.00
Parting at the Gate, 10" x 14"	550.00
Pennsylvania Arches, 14" x 17"	300.00
Priscilla's Cottage, 14" x 17"	360.00
Russet and Gold, 16" x 20"	315.00
Shadowy Orchard Curves, 11" x 14"	85.00
Stepping Stones to Bolton Abbey, 11" x 14"	330.00

Picture, On the Slope, #312, Rhode Island, 11" x 17", $245.

The Footbridge by the Ford, 16" x 20" 440.00
The Guardian Mother, 11" x 17" 2,970.00
The Manchester Battenkill, 16" x 20" 245.00
The River Farm, 10" x 12" 180.00
Toward Slumberland, 13" x 17" 770.00
Trumpets, 8" x 10" 580.00
Two Lilies, 9" x 11" 440.00
Village Spires, 10" x 12" 125.00
Watching for Papa, 13" x 16" 420.00
Wilton Waters, 13" x 16" 155.00
Winding an Old Tall clock, 14" x 17" 165.00

Silhouettes

George and Martha Washington, 3" x 4" 90.00
Girl at Vanity Desk, 4" x 4" 79,99
Girl by Garden Urn, 4" x 4" 75.00
Girl by Spider Web, 5" x 4" 50.00
Scenes 40.00

WALLACE NUTTING-LIKE PHOTOGRAPHERS

History: Although Wallace Nutting was widely recognized as the country's leading producer of hand-colored photographs during the early 20th century, he was by no means the only photographer selling this style of picture. Throughout the country, literally hundreds of regional photographers were selling hand-colored photographs from their home regions or travels. The subject matter of these photographers was comparable to Nutting's, including Interior, Exterior, Foreign, And Miscellaneous Unusual scenes.

Several photographers operated large businesses, and, although not as large or well-known as Wallace Nutting, they sold a substantial volume of pictures which can still be readily found today. The vast majority of their work was photographed in their home regions and sold primarily to local residents or visiting tourists. It should come as little surprise that three of the major Wallace Nutting-like photographers—David Davidson, Fred Thompson, and the Sawyer Art Co.—each had ties to Wallace Nutting.

Hundreds of other smaller local and regional photographers attempted to market hand-colored pictures comparable to Wallace Nutting's during the period of 1900 to the 1930s. Although quite attractive, most were not as appealing to the general public as Wallace Nutting pictures. However, as the price of Wallace Nutting pictures has escalated, the work of these lesser-known Wallace Nutting-like photographers have become increasingly collectible.

A partial listing of some of these minor Wallace Nutting-like photographers includes: Babcock; J. C. Bicknell; Blair; Ralph Blood (Portland, Maine); Bragg; Brehmer; Brooks; Burrowes; Busch; Carlock; Pedro Cacciola; Croft; Currier; Depue Brothers; Derek; Dowly; Eddy; May Farini (hand-colored colonial lithographs); George Forest; Gandara; Gardner (Nantucket, Bermuda, Florida); Gibson; Gideon; Gunn; Bessie Pease Gutmann (hand-colored colonial lithographs); Edward Guy; Harris; C. Hazen; Knoffe; Haynes (Yellowstone Park); Margaret Hennesey; Hodges; Homer; Krabel; Kattleman; La Bushe; Lake; Lamson (Portland, Maine); M. Lightstrum;

Machering; Rossiler Mackinae; Merrill; Meyers; William Moehring; Moran; Murrey; Lyman Nelson; J. Robinson Neville (New England); Patterson; Own Perry; Phelps; Phinney; Reynolds; F. Robbins; Royce; Frederick Scheetz (Philadelphia, Pennsylvania); Shelton, Standley (Colorado); Stott; Summers; Esther Svenson; Florence Thompson; Thomas Thompson; M. A. Trott; Sanford Tull; Underhill; Villar; Ward; Wilmot; Edith Wilson; and Wright.

References: Carol Begley Gray, *History of the Sawyer Pictures*, published by author, 1995 (available from Wallace Nutting Collector's Club, P.O. Box 2458, Doylestown, PA 18901); Michael Ivankovich, *Guide to Wallace-Nutting Like Photographers of the Early 20th Century*, Diamond Press, 1991.

Collectors' Club: Wallace Nutting Collector's Club, P.O. Box 2458, Doylestown, PA 18901.

Advisor: Michael Ivankovich.

Notes: The key determinants of value include the collectibility of the particular photographer, subject matter, condition, and size. Exterior Scenes are the most common.

Keep in mind that only the rarest pictures, in the best condition, will bring top prices. Discoloration and/or damage to the picture or matting can reduce value significantly.

David Davidson

Second to Nutting in overall production, Davidson worked primarily in the Rhode and Southern Massachusetts area. While a student at Brown University around 1900, Davidson learned the art of hand-colored photography from Wallace Nutting, who happened to be the Minister at Davidson's church. After Nutting moved to Southbury in 1905, Davidson graduated from Brown and started a successful photography business in Providence, Rhode Island, which he operated until his death in 1967.

A Puritan Lady 70.00
A Real D.A.R. 150.00
Berkshire Sunset 80.00
Christmas Day 160.00
Driving Home The Cows 120.00
Heart's Desire 30.00
Her House in Order 75.00
Neighbors 170.00
Old Ironsides 170.00
On A News Hunt 120.00
Plymouth Elm 20.00
Rosemary Club 40.00
Snowbound Brook 55.00
The Brook's Mirro 95.00
The Lamb's May Feast 130.00
The Seine Reel 190.00
The Silent Wave 35.00
Vanity 70.00

Sawyer

A father and son team, Charles H. Sawyer and Harold B. Sawyer, operated the very successful Sawyer Art Company from 1903 until the 1970s. Beginning in Maine, the Sawyer Art Company moved to Concord, New Hampshire, in 1920 to be closer to their primary market—New Hampshire's White Mountains. Charles H. Sawyer briefly worked for Nutting from 1902 to 1903 while living in southern Maine. Sawyer's production volume ranks third behind Wallace Nutting and David Davidson.

A February Morning	210.00
A New England Sugar Birth	300.00
At the Bend of the Road	35.00
Crystal Lake	65.00
Echo Lake, Franconia Notch	50.00
Indian Summer	35.00
Lake Morey	30.00
Lake Willoughby	50.00
Mt. Washington in October	55.00
Newfound Lake	73.00
Old Man of the Mountains	35.00
Original Dennison Plant	100.00
Silver Birches, Lake George	50.00
The Meadow Stream	80.00

Fred Thompson

Frederick H. Thompson and Frederick M. Thompson, another father and son team, operated the Thompson Art Company (TACO) from 1908 to 1923, working primarily in the Portland, Maine, area. We know that Thompson and Nutting had collaborated because Thompson widely marketed an interior scene he had taken in Nutting's Southbury home. The production volume of the Thompson Art Company ranks fourth behind Nutting, Davidson, and Sawyer.

Apple Tree Road	45.00
Blossom Dale	75.00
Brook in Winter	190.00
Calm of Fall	50.00
Fernbank	35.00
Fireside Fancy Work	140.00
High and Dry	45.00
Knitting for the Boys	160.00
Lombardy Poplar	100.00
Nature's Carpet	50.00
Neath the Blossoms	95.00
Peace River	30.00
Six Master	100.00
Sunset on the Suwanee	45.00
The Gossips	80.00
White Head	90.00

Minor Wallace Nutting-Like Photographers

Generally speaking, prices for works by minor Wallace Nutting-like photographers would break down as follows: smaller pictures (5" x 7" to 10" x 12"), $10–$75; medium pictures (11" x 14" to 14" x 17"), $50–$200; larger pictures (larger than 14" x 17"), $75–$200+.

Baker, Florian A., Rushing Waters	50.00
Farini, In Her Boudoir	30.00
Gibson, Mountain Road	20.00
Haynes, Untitled Waterfalls	20.00
Higgins, Charles A., A Colonial Stairway	65.00
Payne, George S., Weekly Letter	25.00

OCCUPIED JAPAN

History: The Japanese economy was devastated when World War II ended. To secure necessary hard currency, the Japanese pottery industry produced thousands of figurines and other knickknacks for export. The variety of products is endless—ashtrays, dinnerware, lamps, planters, souvenir items, toys, vases, etc. Initially, the figurines attracted the largest number of collectors; today many collectors focus on other types of pieces.

Marks: From the beginning of the American occupation of Japan until April 28, 1952, objects made in that country were marked "Japan," "Made in Japan," "Occupied Japan," or "Made in Occupied Japan." Only pieces marked with the last two designations are of major interest to Occupied Japan collectors. The first two marks also were used during other time periods.

References: Gene Florence, *Price Guide to Collector's Encyclopedia of Occupied Japan*, Collector Books, 1997 (updated prices for 5-book series *Collector's Encyclopedia of Occupied Japan*); David C. Gould and Donna Crevar-Donaldson, *Occupied Japan Toys with Prices*, L-W Book Sales, 1993; Anthony Marsella, *Toys from Occupied Japan*, Schiffer Publishing, 1995; Lynette Parmer, *Collecting Occupied Japan*, Schiffer Publishing, 1996; Carole Bess White, *Collector's Guide to Made in Japan Ceramics*, Book I (1996), Book II (1997), Collector Books.

Collectors' Club: The Occupied Japan Club, 29 Freeborn St., Newport, RI 02840.

Additional Listings: See *Warman's Americana & Collectibles* for more examples.

Ashtray, Niagara falls, hp, mkd "Occupied Japan" 20.00
Bank, 2" h, 3-1/4" l, piggy, "I'm A Little Piggy," blue ink mark "Made in Occupied Japan" 15.00
Biscuit Barrel, hp, raised gold dec, Japanese characters painted on bottom and "Made in Occupied Japan" 175.00
Box, cov, figural
    1-1/2" h, 1-3/4" w, chest of drawers, mkd "Made In Occupied Japan" 18.00
    1-1/2" h, 1-1/2" l, piano, mkd "Made in Occupied Japan" 18.00
Child's Toy Plate, 2-3/4" d, hp floral pattern in center, mkd "PICO, Made in Occupied Japan" 8.00
Condiment Set, figural hen and rooster salt and pepper shakers, orig lids and spoon, mkd "Made in Occupied Japan" 125.00
Crib Toy, 3" h, composition, Mickey Mouse, mkd "Occupied Japan," c1945-52, tip of nose broken off 125.00
Cup and Saucer, flower design, scalloped saucer, mkd "SGK China" 25.00
Demitasse Cup and Saucer, 1-3/4" h x 2-1/2" d cup, 3-7/8" d saucer, mkd "Made In Occupied Japan" 25.00
Figure
    2" h, Snow Birds, male in blue tie and black hat, female with brown scar, green hat, black mark 7.50
    2-7/8" h, Colonial man, mkd "Made in Occupied Japan" 12.00
    3-1/4" h, baseball player, red mark "Made in Occupied Japan" 12.50
    3-1/4" h, boy in pink checked shirt, blue pants, white overcoat, girl with pink checked skirt, red "Hand Painted Made in Occupied Japan" mark, pr 24.00

3-1/2" d, boy with baseball bat, one eye on ball, other closed, black mark 22.00

3-3/4" h, show girl, ethnic caricature, dark brown skin tone, red lips, side glance eyes, real fur tutu, green bandeaux, gold shoes, pink bow in black curly hair. 65.00

4" h, cat and kittens in basket 30.00

4" h, Hummel type, golfer boy, golf clubs. 25.00

4" h, Oriental figure with basket, brown jacket, yellow sleeves, green paints, black mark 12.00

4" h, Victorian lady, black ink mark "Made in Occupied Japan" 12.50

4-1/4" h, Hummel type, boy sitting on bench, violin, red stamp mark, minor paint loss 20.00

4-1/4" h, 4" l, elf riding snail, green mark "Made in Occupied Japan" 35.00

4-1/2" h, boy playing drum, red mark "Made in Occupied Japan" 18.00

5" h, Colonial couple, both mkd in red "Made in Occupied Japan" 35.00

5-1/2" h, accordion player, red "Made in Occupied Japan" mark. 18.00

5-3/4" h, man, brown coat, blue vest, burnt orange pants, black mark 15.00

7-3/4" h, lady with lute, white flowered dress, pink bodice, blue hat, black mark. 30.00

8" h, 3-1/2" w, man holding flower, bright colors 40.00

Jar, 3" h, hp, gold detailing around mixed flower transfer, red "Hand Painted Made in Occupied Japan" mark 10.00

Pin, 2" x 1-1/2", dog, celluloid 32.00

Planter

3" h, dog, strolling outside basketweave planter, blue and tan, mkd "Occupied Japan" 18.00

5-1/4" h, 5-1/2" w, 5" d, bisque, girl with planter, red ink mark "Paulux Made in Occupied Japan" 52.00

Salt and Pepper Shakers, pr

2-3/4" h, Art Deco birds, black mark. 18.00

3-1/4" h, Indians in Canoe, mkd "Made in Occupied Japan" 30.00

3-1/2" h, 3-1/2" w, pelicans, nesting, stand, bisque, green mark on stand "Urango China, Occupied Japan," red mark "Japan" on pelicans 35.00

3-3/4" h, little Indian boy and girl, mkd "Made in Occupied Japan" 45.00

Scarf, 31-1/2" x 34", blue, brown, pink floral design on white, gray border, partial orig tag reads: Pure Silk, a 'Top Hit' Fashion (rest of tag is missing) 35.00

Tea Set, teapot, 6 cups and saucers, 6 plates, cov sugar bowl, luster, paint dec 95.00

Toothpick Holder, 2-1/2" h, cornucopia, stenciled flowers, hp details, red "Made in Occupied Japan" mark 5.00

Toby Jug, 2-1/4" h, old woman, black bonnet, blue polka-dot dress, black mark 18.00

Toothbrush Holder, 4-1/4" h, Scotties playing cards, base mkd "Made in Occupied Japan"" 150.00

Vase

5" vase, white painting, blue rose on front, mkd "Made in Occupied Japan" 35.00

7-1/2" h, Dragonware, green ink mark "Made in Occupied Japan Hand painted" with wreath and ferns mark 60.00

8-1/2" h, Souvenir of Toronto, worn decal dec, bird mark, molded "Made in Occupied Japan" 15.00

Wall Plaque, 4-1/2" x 7-1/2", Colonial gentleman, mkd "Occupied Japan, Chase" 30.00

OHR POTTERY

G.E.OHR, BILOXI.

History: Ohr pottery was produced by George E. Ohr in Biloxi, Mississippi. There is a discrepancy as to when he actually established his pottery; some say 1878, but Ohr's autobiography indicates 1883. In 1884, Ohr exhibited 600 pieces of his work, suggesting that he had been a potter for some time.

Ohr's techniques included twisting, crushing, folding, denting, and crinkling thin-walled clay into odd, grotesque, and, sometimes, graceful forms. His later pieces were often left unglazed.

In 1906, Ohr closed the pottery and stored over 6,000 pieces as a legacy to his family. He had hoped it would be purchased by the U.S. government, which never happened. The entire collection remained in storage until it was rediscovered in 1972.

Today Ohr is recognized as one of the leaders in the American art pottery movement. Some greedy individuals have taken the later unglazed pieces and covered them with poor-quality glazes in hopes of making them more valuable. These pieces do not have stilt marks on the bottom.

Marks: Much of Ohr's early work was signed with an impressed stamp including his name and location in block letters. His later work was often marked with the flowing script designation "G. E. Ohr."

Figure, man, blue turban, olive green jacket, rust pants, mkd, 8-1/4" h, $30.

References: Susan and Al Bagdade, *Warman's American Pottery and Porcelain*, Wallace-Homestead, 1994; Garth Clark, Robert Ellison Jr., and Eugene Hecht, *Mad Potter of Biloxi: The Art & Life of George Ohr*, Abbeville Press, 1989; Ralph and Terry Kovel, *Kovels' American Art Pottery*, Crown Publishers, 1993; David Rago, *American Art Pottery,* Knickerbocker Press, 1997.

Bowl
  2" h, 5" d, free form, ext. covered in gunmetal, green, and ochre glaze, glossy raspberry int., imp "G. E. OHR/BILOXI" 4,250.00
  2-1/4" h, 4" d, folded rim, dimpled body, ext. cov with speckled brown-black glaze, black int., imp "G. E. OHR/Biloxi, Miss" 1,200.00
  2-1/4" h, 4-1/4" d, free-form, collapsed rim, ext. cov in glossy dripping green and purple glaze, int. with mottled ochre, imp "G. E. OHR/Biloxi, Miss," small restored base chip 1,100.00
  4" h, 6" d, in-body twist, folded rim, glossy dark green and raspberry glazed ext., gunmetal green int., incised "OHR/1903," restoration to nicks and bruise at base 3,500.00
Bottle, 4" h, 3-3/4" d, squatty base, gunmetal, raspberry, and green frothy glaze, script signature 2,500.00
Chamberstick, 6" h, 4" d, sq dimpled base, ribbon handle, frothy raspberry and green matte glaze, script signature, stilt-pull to base 2,600.00
Pitcher, 3-3/4" h, 3-1/4" w, asymmetrical, deeply folded and pinched rim, gunmetal black glaze, imp "G. E. OHR/Biloxi, Miss" 1,600.00
Puzzle Jug, 8" h, 6-3/4" d, incised wheat-sheaf and landscape dec, glossy brown and green glaze, script sgd "Biloxi/Miss/1899," and stamped mark 1,400.00
Vase
  3-1/2" h, 2-1/2" d, corseted, pinched rim, in-body twist, dimpled base, dark brown ext., ochre int., imp "Geo. E. OHR/Biloxi, Miss," two minute rim flecks 1,100.00
  4-1/2" h, 4-1/2" d, bulbous, deeply twisted top, cov in glossy dripping dark blue glaze, imp "E. G. OHR/Biloxi, Miss" 2,000.00
  5" h, bisque, folded in middle, flared bottom, unglazed, script signature 1,660.00
  5" h, two handles, bulbous base cov in gunmetal to brown glaze, imp mark 1,800.00

Creamer, slightly pinched spout, angular handle, $9,350. Photo courtesy of David Rago Auctions, Inc.

Vessel, free-form
  3" h, 4" d, closed-in, folded rim, sponged blue, green, and black dec, buff clay body, clear glossy glaze, "G. E. OHR/Biloxi, Miss," chip and small circular crack to rim 2,300.00
  3" h, 6" d, covered in mottled gunmetal and ochre glaze, imp "E. G. OHR/BILOXI".......................3,500.00
  3-1/4" h, 3-3/4" d, one side pinched and one side dimpled, dark brown and red bisque scroddled clay, tightly folded rim, incised "Biloxi" 550.00
  3-1/2" h, 4-1/4" d, squatty, straight neck, green-speckled matte purple glaze, script signature, restoration to small rim chip, kiln kiss 800.00
  3-3/4" h, 3-3/4" d, tapering, tightly folded rim, granular dark brown lustered glaze, incised "Biloxi"............700.00
  3-3/4" h, 4-1/2" d, asymmetrical, folded and twisted rim, mottled green glaze, "G. E. OHR/Biloxi, Miss," minute glaze nicks to rim.....................................2,300.00
  3-3/4" h, 4-1/2" d, deep in-body twist, folded rim, ext. cov in glossy deep purple glaze, imp "E. G. OHR/BILOXI" 4,750.00
  4" h, 5-1/2" d, bisque, scroddled clay, incised script signature, small edge chip 4,250.00
  4-1/2" h, 4-3/4" d, folded label rim, sheer, mottled glossy green glaze, "G. E. OHR/Biloxi, Miss" 3,000.00
  4-3/4" h, 3-1/2" d, corset shape, bisque, brown and red scroddled clay, folded rim, notched base, imp "G. E. OHR/Biloxi," two small rim chips..........................750.00
  5" h, 5-1/2" d, red clay, folded and collapsed in three lobes, incised script signature 1,800.00

OLD IVORY CHINA

OLD IVORY
84

History: Old Ivory derives its name from the background color of the china. It was made in Silesia, Germany, during the second half of the 19th century.

Marks: Marked pieces usually have a pattern number (pattern names are not common), a crown, and the word "Silesia."

References: Susan and Al Bagdade, *Warman's English & Continental Pottery & Porcelain*, 3rd Edition, Krause Publications, 1998; Alma Hillman, David Goldschmidt & Adam Szynkiewica, *Collector's Encyclopedia of Old Ivory China, The Mystery Explored,* Collector Books, 1997.

Periodical: *Old Ivory Newsletter*, P.O. Box 1004, Wilsonville, OR 97070.

Collectors' Club: Old Ivory Porcelain Society, Route 3, Box 188, Spring Valley, MN 55975.

Berry Set, master bowl and four serving bowls, 5 pc set
  #11 ....145.00
  #84 ....200.00
Biscuit Jar, cov, #15 ....350.00
Biscuit Barrel, 8-1/2" h, Yellow Rose..................500.00
Bowl, 9-1/2" d, Yellow Rose 225.00
Cake Plate
  #16, Clarion 160.00
  #XI, mkd "Germany Clarion: XI," 13" d, some wear to gold int. border..150.00
Celery Bowl, #84, 11 x 5-1/2" 150.00
Chocolate Pot, 11, pedestal 410.00

Plate, floral dec, mkd "VIII," 9" d, $50.

Creamer
#16, Clarion	165.00
#32	48.00

Cup, Yellow Rose 45.00

Cup and Saucer
Clarion, #16	75.00
Yellow Rose	75.00

Demitasse Pot, cov, #16 . . . . 395.00

Dessert Plate, sgd "Old Ivory, Germany," Hillman, p 200, top
   right, 6 pc set 75.00

Dinner Plate, 8-1/2" d, Yellow Rose, set of 6 . . . . 400.00

Ladle Holder, #84 . . . . 95.00

Luncheon Plate
71/2" d, Yellow Rose	75.00
8-1/2" d, U30, Alice blank	22.00

Luncheon Set, No. 84, assembled 47 pc set, six small bowls,
   creamer, twelve cups, six small plates, six luncheon plates,
   14 saucers, sugar, 12" rect tray, some mkd "Silesia No. 84"
   . . . . .1,000.00

Mustard Pot, cov, #16 . . . . 100.00

Oyster Bowl, #11 . . . . 175.00

Salad Plate, Clarion 75.00

Salt and Pepper Shakers, #84, ftd 55.00

Serving Bowl, #84 . . . . 100.00

Sugar, cov, #75 . . . . 50.00

Tea Plate, pink and white daisies, gold trim, mkd "Old Ivory, Germany," set of 6 . . . . 90.00

Teapot, cov, #15 . . . . 395.00

Toothpick Holder
#16	195.00
#84	285.00

OLD PARIS CHINA

History: Old Paris china is fine-quality porcelain made by various French factories located in and around Paris during the 18th and 19th centuries. Some pieces were marked, but most were not. In addition to its fine quality, this type of ware is characterized by beautiful decorations and gilding. Favored colors are dark maroon, deep cobalt blue, and a dark green.

Urns, pr Italianate Village, handles with masks and foliage, deep rose ground, gold trim, 9-1/2" h, $700.

Additional Listings: Continental China and Porcelain (General).

Basket, reticulated, gold and white dec, c1825 . . . . . .1,400.00

Cake Stand, Honore style, green border, c1845 . . . . . . 200.00

Figure, 18-3/4" h, Napoleon, standing, one arm tucked behind
   his back, other tucked into shirt, full military dress, gilt dec,
   low sq base, inscribed "Roussel-Bardell," late 19th C
   . . . . 650.00

Mantel Vase, bell-like flowered handles, blue ground, paneled
   enamel portraits of lovers, gilt trim, minor flower damage,
   price for pr 325.00

Plate, 9-1/4" d, flower basket center, gilt line and borders, ochre
   ground, c1830, price for pr 250.00

Tea Set, partial, enamel dec central medallions of portraits and
   musical instruments surrounded by gilt shields and spearhead border, 5-3/4" h cov teapot, creamer, compote, twelve
   coffee cans and saucers, 19th C, gilt wear, minor damage,
   price for 15 pc set 2,875.00

Urn, cov, 14-1/2" h, painted hunting scenes, molded acanthus
   and palmette scrolled double handles, gilt border, sq plinth
   base, price for pr 1,200.00

OLD SLEEPY EYE

History: Sleepy Eye, a Sioux Indian chief who reportedly had a droopy eye, gave his name to Sleepy Eye, Minnesota, and one of its leading flour mills. In the early 1900s, Old Sleepy Eye Flour offered four Flemish-gray heavy stoneware premiums decorated in cobalt blue: a straight-sided butter crock, curved salt bowl, stein, and vase. The premiums were made by Weir Pottery Company, later to become Monmouth Pottery Company, and finally to emerge as the present-day Western Stoneware Company of Monmouth, Illinois.

Additional pottery and stoneware pieces also were issued. Forms included five sizes of pitchers (4, 5-1/2, 6-1/2, 8, and 9 inches), mugs, steins, sugar bowls, and tea tiles (hot plates). Most were cobalt blue on white, but other glaze hues, such as browns, golds, and greens, were used.

Old Sleepy Eye also issued many other items, including bakers' caps, lithographed barrel covers, beanies, fans, multicolored pillow tops, postcards, and trade cards. Regular production of Old Sleepy Eye stoneware ended in 1937.

In 1952, Western Stoneware Company made 22- and 40-ounce steins in chestnut brown glaze with a redesigned Indian's head. From 1961 to 1972, gift editions were made for the board of directors and others within the company. Beginning in 1973, Western Stoneware Company issued an annual limited edition stein for collectors.

Marks: The gift editions made in the 1960s and 1970s were dated and signed with a maple leaf mark. The annual limited edition steins are marked and dated.

REPRODUCTION ALERT

Blue-and-white pitchers, crazed, weighted, and often with a stamp or the word "Ironstone" are the most common reproductions. The stein and salt bowl also have been made. Many reproductions come from Taiwan. A line of fantasy items, new items which never existed as Old Sleepy Eye originals, includes an advertising pocket mirror with miniature flour-barrel label, small glass plates, fruit jars, toothpick holders, glass and pottery miniature pitchers, and salt and pepper shakers. One mill item has been made: a sack marked as though it were old but of a size that could not possibly hold the amount of flour indicated.

References: Susan and Al Bagdade, *Warman's American Pottery and Porcelain*, Wallace-Homestead, 1994; Elinor Meugnoit, *Old Sleepy Eye*, published by author, 1979.

Collectors' Club: Old Sleepy Eye Collectors Club of America, P.O. Box 12, Monmouth, IL 61462.

Mug, Indian head on handle, Indian and village scenes, 7-1/2" h, $350.

Mill items

Advertising Sign, 24" h, 20" w, self framed tin, trademark picture of Chief Old Sleepy Eye, multiple Indian scenes on border, surface rust and staining on frame 2,300.00
Cookbook, Sleepy Eye Milling Co., loaf of bread shape, portrait of chief 145.00
Demitasse Spoon, roses in bowl. 145.00
Letter Opener, bronze, Indian head handle, marked "Sleep Eye Milling Co., Sleep Eye, MN" 750.00
Pinback Button, Old Sleepy Eye For Me, bust portrait of chief 165.00
Spoon, Unity SP 110.00

Pottery and stoneware

Mug, cobalt blue on white, Indian head on handle, 1906-37 . . . . 350.00
Pitcher, 6" h. 285.00
Stein, 7-3/4" h, Flemish blue, gray stoneware ground, Weir Pottery Co., 1903. . . . . 525.00
Tile, cobalt blue and white. 950.00
Vase, 9" h, gray and cobalt blue, cattails 475.00

ONION MEISSEN

History: The blue onion or bulb pattern is of Chinese origin and depicts peaches and pomegranates, not onions. It was first made in the 18th century by Meissen, hence the name Onion Meissen.

Factories in Europe, Japan, and elsewhere copied the pattern. Many still have the pattern in production, including the Meissen factory in Germany.

Marks: Many pieces are marked with a company's logo; after 1891, the country of origin is indicated on imported pieces.

Reference: Robert E. Röntgen, *Book of Meissen*, revised ed., Schiffer Publishing, 1996.

Note: Prices given are for pieces produced between 1870 and 1930. Early Meissen examples bring a high premium.

Bowl, 8-1/2" d, reticulated, blue crossed swords mark, 19th C 395.00
Box, cov, 4-1/2" d, round, rose finial 75.00
Cake Stand, 13-1/2" d, 4-1/2" h 215.00
Candlesticks, pr, 7" h 80.00
Canister, marked "Prunes" 200.00
Centerpiece, 19" h, three-tier, reticulated 300.00
Creamer and Sugar, gold edge, c1900. . . . . 175.00
Demitasse Cup and Saucer, blue, gilt dec, underglaze crossed swords mark, price for 8 pc set 295.00
Fruit Compote, 9" h, circular, openwork bowl, five oval floral medallions 375.00
Fruit Knives, price for 6 pc set. 75.00
Funnel, small. 55.00
Hot Plate, handles. 125.00
Ladle, wooden handle. 115.00
Mold, melon, handle 45.00
Pie Crimper, wood handle. 35.00
Plate
    8-1/2" d. 35.00
    10" d 75.00

Platter, Meissen mark, imp "11.27.00/128," 12-1/2" w x 25" l, $525.

Platter, oval
   12" l 95.00
   13-1/2" l 120.00
   18" l, oval, mkd "Meissen" in oval, pr 275.00
Pot de Creme 65.00
Salt and Pepper Shakers, pr. 50.00
Serving Dish, 9-1/4" w, 11" l, handle with floral design . . 200.00
Tea Set, teapot, creamer, sugar, four cups and saucers, tray
   . . . . 400.00
Tea Strainer, wood handle 25.00
Tray, 17" l, cartouche shape, blue and white design, gilt edge
   . . . . 425.00
Vase, 6-1/2" d, bud 60.00
Vegetable Dish, cov, 10" w, sq 145.00

OPALESCENT GLASS

History: Opalescent glass, a clear or colored glass with milky white decorations, looks fiery or opalescent when held to light. This effect was achieved by applying bone ash chemicals to designated areas while a piece was still hot and then refiring it at extremely high temperatures.

There are three basic categories of opalescent glass: (1) blown (or mold blown) patterns, e.g., Daisy & Fern and Spanish Lace; (2) novelties, pressed glass patterns made in limited quantity and often in unusual shapes such as corn or a trough; and (3) traditional pattern (pressed) glass forms.

Opalescent glass was produced in England in the 1870s. Northwood began the American production in 1897 at its Indiana, Pennsylvania, plant. Jefferson, National Glass, Hobbs, and Fenton soon followed.

References: Gary Baker et al., *Wheeling Glass 1829-1939*, Oglebay Institute, 1994, distributed by Antique Publications; Bill Banks, *Complete Price Guide for Opalescent Glass*, 2nd ed., published by author, 1996; Bill Edwards, *Standard Encyclopedia of Opalescent Glass*, Collector Books, 1997; William Heacock, *Encyclopedia of Victorian Colored Pattern Glass*, Book II, 2nd ed., Antique Publications, 1977; William Heacock and William Gamble, *Encyclopedia of Victorian Colored Pattern Glass*, Book 9, Antique Publications, 1987; William Heacock, James Measell, and Berry Wiggins, *Dugan/Diamond*, Antique Publications, 1993; ——, *Harry Northwood* (1990), Book 2 (1991) Antique Publications.

Blown

Barber Bottle, Swirl, ketchup bottle shape, cranberry . . . 425.00
Basket, Daisy and Fern, vaseline, looped handle 190.00
Bowl
   Ruffles and Rings, green 40.00
   Seaweed, white, 9" d 80.00
Butter Dish, cov, Spanish Lace, blue 265.00
Celery Vase
   Chrysanthemum Swirl, blue 140.00
   Hobbs Hobnail, blue. 90.00
   Seaweed, cranberry 225.00
   Spanish Lace, vaseline 135.00
   Stripe, white 90.00
   Windows, cranberry, ruffled rim 115.00
Cheese Dish, Hobb's Swirl, cranberry 350.00
Compote, Ribbed Spiral, blue 70.00
Creamer, Windows Swirl, cranberry 500.00
Cruet, orig stopper
   Hobb's Hobnail, blue 225.00
   Spanish Lace, canary yellow 185.00
   Stripe, blue, applied blue handle 185.00
   Windows, Swirled, cranberry 350.00
Finger Bowl
   Hobb's Optic Diamond, cranberry 70.00
   Spanish Lace, blue. 50.00
Lamp, oil, Snowflake, cranberry 735.00
Miniature Lamp, Reverse Swirl, vaseline 95.00
Pitcher
   Bubble Lattice, cranberry 950.00
   Coinspot, cranberry, #127 . . . . 300.00
   Coinspot, cranberry, #261, corner ruffle. 545.00
   Coinspot, cranberry, 3 tier 1,375.00
   Fern, blue, square 445.00
   Honeycomb & Clover, green 325.00
   Poinsettia, blue, rare shape 425.00
   Raised Swirl, cranberry, #79 . . . . 685.00
   Seaweed, blue, square. 515.00
   Swag with Brackets, green. 200.00
   Thumbprint, 10" h, ruffled, colorless, white dots and rim, applied colorless handle 250.00
   Windows, blue, square. 485.00
   Windows, cranberry, #111, square. 485.00
Salt Shaker, orig top
   Coin Spot, cranberry 200.00
   Reverse Swirl, blue 65.00
Spooner
   Bubble Lattice, cranberry 145.00
   Ribbed Spiral, blue. 110.00
Sugar, cov
   Bubble Lattice, cranberry 195.00
   Spanish Lace, blue. 175.00
Sugar Shaker
   Argus Swirl, cranberry 300.00
   Bubble Lattice, cranberry 500.00
   Daisy and Fern, Parian Swirl, cranberry. 350.00
Seaweed, cranberry 685.00
Syrup
   Coin Spot, 9 panel, blue. 200.00
   Leaf Umbrella, cranberry, heat check 395.00
   Polka Dot, blue
      Bulbous 245.00
      Tall. 315.00
   Reverse Swirl, cranberry 800.00
Tankard, Coin Spot, 3 tier, cranberry 1,375.00
Toothpick Holder, Ribbed Lattice, blue 165.00

Tumbler

    Reverse Swirl, cranberry 105.00

    Seaweed, cranberry 150.00

    Spanish Lace, green 65.00

    Windows, cranberry 125.00

Vase, Stripe, vaseline 65.00

Novelties

Basket

    4" h, 5" w, cranberry, white opalescent stripes and clear rib-
bing interspersed with silver mica, ruffled edge, applied
clear twisted center loop handle 150.00

    7-1/2" h, 5" w, rose bowl form, cranberry, deep white opales-
cent extends half way down, applied clear rigaree top, applied crystal five-footed base, small loop applied crystal
handle 200.00

Bowl

    Cashews, blue, crimped 60.00

    Greek Key and Ribs, green 75.00

    Jolly Bear, white 85.00

    Leaf and Beads, green, twig feet 60.00

    Many Loops, blue, crimped, fluted 65.00

Compote

    Dolphin, vaseline 95.00

    Squirrel and Acorn, green, ruffled 175.00

Dish, Lined Lattice, green 85.00

Hanging Vase, 8-1/2" h, green opalescent vase with thorns,
clear crystal vine as holder for vase, pressed green daisy-like
flower on holder, Victorian 115.00

Hat, Opal Swirl, white 35.00

Mug, Singing Birds, blue 145.00

Plate, Wishbone and Drape, green 35.00

Rose Bowl. Cashews, white 85.00

Vase, Lorna, blue 60.00

Pressed

Banana Boat, Jewel and Fan, green 115.00

Berry Bowl, master

    Alaska, blue 195.00

    Beatty Rib, white 50.00

**Rose Bowl, Opalescent Swirl, Fenton, green, 5-1/2"
h, 4-1/2" d, $90.**

Everglades, vaseline, gold trim 200.00

    Tokyo, green 55.00

Berry Set, Wreath & Shell, blue, 7 pc 475.00

Bowl

    Beaded Stars, low base, green 45.00

    Beatty Rib, blue, rect 65.00

    Jewel and Fan, blue 35.00

    Peacock and Fence, blue 300.00

Butter Dish, cov

    Argonaut Shell, white 245.00

    Wreath & Shell, blue 255.00

Calling Card Receiver, Inverted Feather, vaseline 225.00

Celery

    Beatty Swirl, blue 90.00

    Wreath & Shell, vaseline 225.00

Compote

    Intaglio, vaseline 70.00

    Tokyo, blue 60.00

Cracker Jar, cov, Wreath & Shell, blue 600.00

Creamer

    Alaska, blue 85.00

    Beaded Shell, green 165.00

    Paneled Holly, white 70.00

    Scroll with Acanthus, green 65.00

    Swag with Brackets, green 90.00

    Wild Bouquet, blue 125.00

    Wreath and Shell, vaseline, dec 135.00

Cruet

    Alaska, vaseline, enameled dec 275.00

    Christmas Pearls, white 260.00

    Jackson, blue 185.00

    Scroll with Acanthus, blue 200.00

Jelly Compote

    Diamond Spearhead, vaseline 85.00

    Everglades, blue, gold trim 85.00

    Iris with Meander, vaseline 95.00

    Wild Bouquet, blue 160.00

Match Holder, Beatty Rib, white 35.00

Mug

    Diamond Spearhead, cobalt blue 85.00

    Stork and Rushes, blue 90.00

Pitcher

    Beatty Swirl, canary yellow 195.00

    Fluted Scrolls, vaseline 300.00

    Intaglio, blue 215.00

    Jeweled Heart, blue 250.00

    Swag with Brackets, vaseline 225.00

    Wild Bouquet, blue 300.00

Plate

    Palm Beach, blue, 10" d, set of 6 . . . . 895.00

    Tokyo, ftd, green 70.00

    Water Lily and Cattail, amethyst 85.00

Rose Bowl

    Beaded Drape, blue 60.00

    Fancy Fantails, cranberry, four clear applied feet . . . 650.00

    Fluted Scrolls, blue 125.00

    Water Lily and Cattails, amethyst 110.00

Salt and Pepper Shakers, pr, Everglades, vaseline 400.00

Salt, open, individual

    Beatty Rib, white 50.00

    Wreath & Shell, vaseline 120.00

Sauce

    Argonaut Shell, blue 40.00

    Circled Scrolls, blue 50.00

    Iris with Meander, yellow 25.00

    Water Lily and Cattails, white 35.00

    Wild Bouquet, blue 40.00

Spooner

    Argonaut Shell, French Opal 170.00
    Beatty Rib, white 45.00
    Flora, blue 110.00
    Iris with Meander, canary yellow 95.00
    Palm Beach, vaseline. 95.00
    Tokyo, blue. 85.00
    Wreath and Shell, vaseline. 120.00

Sugar, cov

    Alaska, vaseline 155.00
    Circled Scroll, green. 85.00
    Diamond Spearhead, vaseline 235.00
    Fluted Scrolls, blue. 130.00
    Intaglio, blue. 75.00
    Swag with Brackets, blue 95.00
    Tokyo, blue, gold trim. 115.00

Syrup, Flora, white, gold trim 275.00

Table Set, Wreath & Shell, vaseline 700.00

Toothpick Holder

    Diamond Spearhead, vaseline. 80.00
    Flora, white, gold trim. 150.00
    Gonterman Swirl, amber top 150.00
    Iris with Meander, blue. 115.00
    Wreath & Shell, vaseline 245.00

Tumbler

    Alaska, vaseline. 85.00
    Beatty Rib, white 35.00
    Beatty Swirl, white 45.00
    Everglades, vaseline 50.00
    Fluted Scrolls, vaseline 75.00
    Intaglio, white. 45.00
    Paneled Holly, blue 100.00
    S-Repeat, blue. 45.00
    Wreath and Shell, ftd, blue. 375.00

Vase

    Fluted Scrolls and Vine, blue 70.00
    Inverted Fan and Feather, blue 85.00
    Water Lily and Cattail, amethyst. 75.00

OPALINE GLASS

History: Opaline glass was a popular mid- to late 19th-century European glass. The glass has a certain amount of translucency and often is found decorated with enamel designs and trimmed in gold.

Basket

    5" h, ruffled, applied colorless handle 60.00
    6-1/2" h, 6" d, clambroth color, applied pink snake loop around handle, gold rim. 100.00

Bottle, 7" h, white, squatty bulbous body, trumpet neck, gilt scrolling vine dec, orig stopper, Continental, pr 225.00

Box, cov, 4-1/4" l, 3-1/4" h, rect, blue, roundel studded brass strapwork, French, early 20th C 460.00

Bowl, 6-1/2" d, shallow, blue, gold painted trim, some wear to gold, set of six 100.00

Candlestick, 7-1/4" h, white opaque clambroth body, rib molded 150.00

Cheese dish, cov, white opaque body, gold enamel dec 185.00

Child's Mug, 2-1/4" h, paneled scenes of Dutch children, pr 65.00

Clock, 6" d, white opaque body, hanging type, circular frame, hand painted, Welch Company, Forestville, CT, clockworks, orig brass chain 275.00

Cologne Bottle

    6" h, jade green opaque body, orig stopper 95.00
    8-3/4" h, jade green opaque body, gold ring dec, orig stopper 90.00

Creamer, shaded yellow to white opaque body, pink roses and blue forget me nots, SP rim and handle 125.00

Cup Plate, Lee-Rose 258, white opaque body, minute rim roughage 75.00

Fairy Lamp, 17" h, French blue, four large faceted purple and dark blue jewels, filigree brass mountings 285.00

Jack In the Pulpit Vase, 5-1/2" h, robin's egg blue opaque body, applied amber feet 95.00

Match Holder, 1-3/8" h, blue opaque body, gold flowers and leaves 40.00

Perfume Bottle

    2-3/4" h, blue opaque body, gold flowers and leaves, matching stopper 60.00
    4" h, blue opaque body, gold, white, and yellow dec, matching stopper 75.00

Pitcher

    4-1/4" h, pink opaque body, applied white handle 75.00
    12" h, pink, applied ruby paste stones, beaded enamel swag, applied handle, French, 19th C 110.00

Posy Holder, 8" h, blue opaque body, figural hand holding small vase, ruffled rim 85.00

Salt and Pepper Shakers, pr, 4" h, pansy dec, damage to both covers, worn dec, pr. 45.00

Sugar, cov, shaded yellow to white opaque body, pink roses and blue forget me nots, SP cover, rim, and handle 150.00

Toothpick Holder, lavender opaque body, small ball feet . 85.00

Tumbler, white opaque body, enameled pink rose 25.00

Tumble-Up, carafe, tumbler, and underplate, pale green opaque body, gold beading, black and white jeweled dec, three pcs 325.00

Urn, 13" h, blue opaque body, enameled blue flowers, gilt trim, flared rim, pr. 350.00

Mug, Opaline glass, white opaque ground, cobalt blue trim, French, 4" h, $95.

Vase

5" h, blue, platinum stars dec, Czechoslovakian 55.00

5-1/2" h, cased light blue opaline, blue applied ribbon handles, mkd "Czecho-slovakia" 50.00

8" h, swirled and mottled colors over opaline, applied clear pinched handles, Czechoslovakian 35.00

16-1/4" h, oviform, circular cushioned foot, parcel gilt, enameled, turquoise blue opaque body, gilt rimmed molded border and handles, oval panels with artists' portraits, one with Raphel, other Van Dyke, brown, claret, white, and flesh tones, gilt borders with scrolling foliate edges, French, 19th C, pr 2,500.00

Violet Bowl, 3-1/2" d, 3" h, peachblow pink ground, blue and white enameled flowers, gray leaves and vines, base sgd, Mt. Washington 275.00

Whiskey Taster, white opaque clambroth colored body

Lacy, Sandwich, Lee, plate 150-5, minute rim nicks . . 45.00

Ten Panel, handle, small chip on bottom 85.00

ORIENTALIA

History: Orientalia is a term applied to objects made in the Orient, an area which encompasses the Far East, Asia, China, and Japan. The diversity of cultures produced a variety of objects and styles.

References: Sandra Andacht, *Collector's Guide to Oriental Decorative Arts,* Antique Trader Books, 1997; Christopher Dresser, *Traditional Arts and Crafts of Japan*, Dover Publications, 1994; R. L. Hobson and A L. Hetherington, *Art of the Chinese Potter*, Dover Publications, 1983; Duncan Macintosh, *Chinese Blue and White Porcelain*, Antique Collectors Club, 1994; Gloria and Robert Mascarelli, *Warman's Oriental Antiques*, Wallace-Homestead, 1992; Nancy N. Schiffer, *Imari, Satsuma, and Other Japanese Export Ceramics,* Schiffer Publishing, 1997; Jana Volf, *Treasures of the Chinese Glass Work Shops,* Asiantiques, 1997.

Periodical: *Orientalia Journal*, P.O. Box 94, Little Neck, NY 11363.

Collectors' Club: China Student's Club, 59 Standish Rd., Wellesley, MA 02181.

Museums: Art Institute of Chicago, Chicago, IL; Asian Art Museum of San Francisco, San Francisco, CA; George Walter Vincent Smith Art Museum, Springfield, MA; Morikami Museum & Japanese Gardens, Delray Beach, FL; Pacific Asia Museum, Pasadena, CA.

Additional Listings: Canton; Celadon; Cloisonné; Fitzhugh; Nanking; Netsukes; Rose Medallion; Japanese Prints; and other related categories.

SPECIAL AUCTION

Skinner Inc.
Bolton Gallery
357 Main St.
Bolton, MA 01740
(508) 779-6241

Bowl, 7" d, enameled, finely drawn water palace, extensive seal character poem on reverse, two red seals, Ch'ia Ching, 1796-1821, iron-red mark on base, boxed 1,725.00

Box, cov

2-3/4" x 1-3/4" x 1-1/4", mixed metal, top inlaid with pair of cranes by stream, assorted flowers, side panels with Li Po fishing, magnolias, dandelions, and puffer fish, inlay of gold, silver, and copper, Japanese, Meiji period, 19th C 400.00

3-3/4" sq, inlaid iron, with deer, crane, and lotus designs, Korean, 19th C 1,045.00

5-1/2" x 4", rosewood, covered in silver inlaid, bamboo design in copper, Japanese. 300.00

Lacquer, karma kuri-buri method, covered in layers of black lacquer and then red lacquer, creating surface of true red, Japanese,17th/18th C, orig presentation box 1,840.00

Brush Pot, porcelain, reticulated, Korean, 18th or 19th C 620.00

Buddha, 9-1/2" h, bronze, standing on lotus throne, hands clasped in prayer at chest, long loose fitting robes, incised scrolling floral design, traces of gilt, red and green pigment, Ming dynasty 875.00

Censer, 24-1/2" h, bronze, rising from oval base, finely detailed dragoon, large bulbous body with birds, handles with zoomorphic heads, vented lid, foo dog finial, Chinese, Ching Dynasty, dark brown patina 575.00

Ceremonial Bowl, 2-3/4" to 6-1/2" d, nested set of nine, lacquer, gilt and silver dec, Japanese 850.00

Charger, 15-3/8" d, porcelain, underglaze blue dec, Vietnamese, 15th/16th C. 7,475.00

Chopsticks Set, 10" l, ivory and jade, Qing dynasty, Chinese 150.00

Drapes, embroidered silk, cream, white, and beige wisteria, chrysanthemums, and roses, ecru ground, matching valance, Chinese, mid 19th C. 150.00

Dresser Set, silver, dragon dec, two mirrors, comb, rect brush, two oval brushes, shoe horn, and box 700.00

Figure

1-3/4" h, carved turquoise, fu dog, Chinese 90.00

2-3/4" l, carved lapis lazuli, cat, Chinese, attached to wood stand 65.00

6" h, bronze, Buddha and attendants. 150.00

7-1/2" h, carved spinach jade, woman warriors on horseback, Chinese 475.00

8" h, enameled and gilt silver, elephant, blanketed back mounted with turquoise and other semi-precious stones, Chinese 550.00

15" l, bronze, lion, reared head, bared teeth, sgd, Japanese 450.00

15" h, bronze, man seated on duck, Japanese 1,750.00

16-1/2" h, bronze, fish, Japanese. 375.00

Furniture

Altar Table, Chinese, 19th C, cypress, rect top, molded and upturned ends, splayed rect legs with scroll brackets and pierced foliate panels, 73-3/4" l, 15-1/2" w, 37-1/2" h 950.00

Armoire, Chinese, red painted, rect top over two paneled cupboard doors flanked by stiles, shaped and molded apron, molded sq-section legs, 32-1/2" w, 20" d, 73-1/4" h 900.00

Bench, Chinese, 18th C, huali wood, rect, flush-paneled seat, molded rails continuing into similar legs joined by stepped box stretcher, pr. 700.00

Bench, Chinese, 19thC, carved elm wood, molded rect seat, splayed cylindrical legs with carved brackets 200.00

Bookshelf, Chinese, pine, outset molded cornice, four open shelves over two molded drawers with recessed panels, molded plinth base, 42-1/2" w, 14-1/2" d, 71" h. . . . 225.00

Cabinet, Chinese, side, painted, rect top over two paneled cupboard doors, shaped and molded apron, molded

square-section legs, 23" w, 14-1/2" d, 32-3/4" h, pr
.... 450.00
Cabinet, Chinese, 19th C, side, red-lacquer, molded cornice over front with two doors, large circular escutcheon, opening to three shelves and two drawers, deep skirt, bracket feet, 41-1/4" w, 23" d, 68-1/2" h............... 900.00
Center Table, Chinese Export, rosewood and brass, circular tray-top, suspended from dragon-head finials, four bowed legs joined by fretted cross-stretcher, applied Chinese characters, 31" d, 30-1/4" h 275.00
Chair, Chinese, stained elm, horseshoe-back, arm, curved crest continuing into arms on three stile supports, molded out-curved splat over paneled seat, molded seat rail, raised on molded square-section legs joined by stretchers
.... 200.00
Chair, Chinese, stained elm, yoke-back, side, yoke-form crest, curved splat, rattan seat over molded seat rail with pierced corners, molded sq section legs joined by stretchers, pr. 500.00
Chair, Chinese, 19th C, willowwood, yoke-back, arm, downswept, curved back with bent splat, woven-cane seat with shaped rails, splayed, sq-section legs, box stretcher
.... 250.00
Chest, Chinese, 19th C, red lacquer, hinged lid opens to storage well, sides applied with bale handles, floral scrollwork dec, later stand, 21" w, 24" l, 12-1/2" h 300.00
Chest, Korean, 19th C, finely grained burled veneer on each panel and drawer front, rounded fronts on frame to simulate bamboo, large brasses on plates, 66" h 1,100.00
Gaming Table, Chinese, stained elm, rect top, molded edges, shaped, molded, and pierced apron, cylindrical legs, 38" w, 38-1/2" l, 33-1/4" h...................... 250.00
Mirror, Chinese Export, pierced and carved teak, framed with 4" carved outside border carved with warriors in battle scenes, corners with stylized butterflies, inside 1-1/2" frame, inlaid with ivory birds and carved symbols, orig wavy glass, 26" w, 29" h 1,000.00
Side Table, Chinese, 19th C, bamboo, rect top, paling frieze, legs joined by slatted platform stretcher, 36" l, 18" w, 34" h
.... 400.00
Stand, nesting, Chinese, Chinoiserie dec, shaped tops supported by pierced side elements, four gold dec paw feet, sides supported by curved stretcher, three largest size tops dec with matching scenic scrolls with palace scene flanked by women with cane pole next to bamboo trees, smallest stand dec with oval scene of people and house, set of four, 11-3/4" w x 10-12" d x 25-1/2" h to 21" w, 14" d, 27-3/4" h
.... 1,250.00
Stool, Chinese, 19th C, elm wood, trapezoidal, flush-paneled top with molded frieze, cylindrical legs joined by shaped box stretcher, 22-1/2" w, 10-1/2" d, 29-1/4" h......... 250.00
Hand Scroll
Chinese, Night Banquet, color on paper, sgd "Tang Yin," comments by "Jiang Ting Xi" and "Yun Shou Ping," 19th C
.... 3,450.00
Korean, two birds among prunus branches, tears 50.00
Hot Water Kettle, sculptured in high relief, rustic scene, sgd copper cover, Japanese, late 19th C 460.00
Incense Burner, Archaic-style, bronze, Kuei form, deep chestnut brown, inlaid with silver cloud motifs, scrolling, and Tao Tieh masks, sgd in silver wire Shih Sou, 18th/19th C 260.00
Inkstand, 8-3/4 x 6-1/2", rect, incised dragons, fitted box with character inscriptions on lid 230.00
Inro, four compartment, cricket cage surrounded by vines, maki-e and kin-kan gai, Nashiji int., 19th C, some rubbing
.... 635.00

Inro, Ojime, and Netsuke
Burlwood, single compartment, dec with pine tree, pewter trunk brass cones, MOP buds, gold lacquer leaves, carved wooden ojime, natural form netsuke, 19th C 900.00
Cinnabar lacquer, three compartment, carved brocade pattern, Mahiji int., mixed metal cylindrical ojime with squares of different colors, ivory puppy netsuke with inlaid eyes
.... 550.00
Ivory, four compartment, carved dragons on wood grain textured ground, mixed metals in form of man reading from scroll ojime, ivory netsuke of sennin, sgd "Goraku," 19th C
.... 1,265.00
Lacquer, four compartment, black, dec in maki-e of two shades of gold with children playing with flowers, Nahiji int., small boy bone oijime, Fukujoroki riding stag attended by child ivory netsuke, sgd.................... 1,610.00
Lacquer, four compartment, front with man in boat with MOP and gilt lacquer birds, back with landscape of prunus trees and birds, Nashiji int., coral ojime and sgd wood netsuke carved as man riding toad, sgd, Japanese, Meiji period ...1,200.00
Lacquer, single compartment with gold lacquer maki-e of carriage on one side, and Fukujuroku's staff on other, Nashiji int., carved cinnabar ojimie, ivory netsuke of boy with drum trying on smiling mask, sgd "Ikusan," 19th C 550.00
Wood, single compartment inro carved in form of skull, bone ojimie, cowry shell netsuke, 19th C 345.00
Jar
Porcelain, underglaze red dec, precisely faceted octagonal form, each panel simply arched above and below, conforming foot, Korean, Yi Dynasty (1392-1910), attributed to middle period................................ 4,620.00

Drum, bronze, inverted bell form, central twelve pointed star on top surrounded by concentric bands of flowers, diamonds, and birds dec, four sets of three frogs proceed around perimeter, two pairs of strap handles, six graduated elephants march down one side, brown patina with emerald green patina, Han Dynasty, 27" d, 18-1/2" h, $7,280. Photo courtesy of Freeman\Fine Arts of Philadelphia, Inc.

Stoneware, globular, iron-red dragon dec over white glazed stoneware body, Korean, broken and glued together
. . . . .11,000.00
Koro, 16" h, bronze, bulbous, twin beast head handles, two reserves of bids among foliage, tripod legs, pierced lid surmounted by mythical beast, cast seal on base, Japanese
. . . . 250.00

Medicine Chest
31-1/8" h, multiple drawers with Chinese characters over two doors carved with relief dec of women in landscape scene
. . . . 300.00
54-1/2" h, 92 drawers, two cupboards, Korean 1,870.00

Planter, 8" x 8" x 6-3/4", sq shape, formal lotus scrolls, Tou Tsi, mid 19th C, attributed to Tao Kuang period, 1821-50
. . . . 690.00

Rice Barrel, 17" h, black lacquered, octagonal, landscapes painted on sides, Chinese, 19th C, pr 400.00

Robe, silk, embroidered floral sprays and clouds, multicolored figures and floral trim, medium blue, Chinese 200.00

Saucer Dish, 6-1/2" d, blue and white, central five-clawed dragon and pearl int., two dragons flanking pearls on ext., Tao Kung mark and period, 1821-50. . . . . .1,150.00

Screen, folding, Korean, 17th C 2,200.00

Scroll Painting
40-5/8" x 26-1/4", ink and color on silk, "Sakyamuni and Moonlight Buddha, Sunshine Buddha and Daoist Immortals," Chinese, 18th C 375.00
54-3/4" x 31-1/2", ink and color on paper, "Double Ancestor Portrait," Qing Dynasty, Chinese, 19th C. 225.00
69" x 28-5/8", ink and color on paper, "Guanyin with Foo Lion and Goddess Protector," Qing Dynasty, Chinese . . 250.00
69-1/4" x 28-3/4", ink and color on paper, "Guanyin with Elephant and Attendant," inscribed "Young Family who hired someone to draw Puchine Buddha to Bless their Family," Qing Dynasty, Chinese 350.00

Sculpture, 11" h, elephant locked in combat with two tigers, sgd, carved wood base, Japanese, Meiji period 500.00

Shrine
14" h, lacquer and gilt wood, int. with seated Bodhisattva on lotus, Japanese 300.00
17-1/2" h, carved and lacquered, twin doors, birds, foliage, and offering on int., text on diaper ground, int. with well painted trompe l'oeil landscape screen, gilt ext. trim, Chinese, minor chips. 325.00

Storage Jar, 23-1/2" h, stoneware, ovoid, broad shoulders, tapering to base, white glaze, Korean, 18th C . . 1,020,000.00

Sword, Samuri, Japanese. 700.00

Tsuba, 3" d, iron, gilt copper inlays, Mychin style, 16th C
. . . . 400.00

Vanity Box, 13" l, mother-of-pearl inlaid black lacquer, bird on flowering branch and foliate dec, Chinese 225.00

Vase, cov, 15-1/2" h, carved malachite, dragon and man in boat, Chinese, mounted as lamp. 900.00

Vase
6-3/4" h, bronze form, slightly flaring mouth and foot, tubular handles, bow string marks, pale green glaze with blue tint, broad crackle with finer crackle within, burnt-reddish brown foot, Kuan Yao, 12/13th C, southern Sung dynasty, Lung Chuan kilns 13,800.00
20" h, kuan, deep purple-blue coloring, white ground, painting of Shao Lao surrounded by Taoist immortals, scrolling at neck, band of jewel motifs at shoulder, waves and rocks at base, unglazed base, Ming Dynasty, Chia Ching period, 1522-66, slight hairline to rim. 9,775.00
23" h, 1" d, wide body, well proportioned neck, two cylindrical bamboo-shaped lugs and bowstring marks, deep crushed

strawberry color with controlled purple to upper registers, fitted carved stand, Sang de Bouef, Chinese, 19th C
. . . . .2,300.00
Vessel, 17" h, bronze, body dec with figural relief, S-form handle, attached spout form dish with bird and leaf motif, reticulated foot, Asian 200.00

ORIENTAL RUGS

History: Oriental rugs or carpets date back to 3,000 b.c.; but it was in the 16th century that they became prevalent. The rugs originated in the regions of Central Asia, Iran (Persia), Caucasus, and Anatolia. Early rugs can be classified into basic categories: Iranian, Caucasian, Turkoman, Turkish, and Chinese. Later India, Pakistan, and Iraq produced rugs in the Oriental style.

The pattern name is derived from the tribe which produced the rug, e.g., Iran is the source for Hamadan, Herez, Sarouk, and Tabriz.

References: J. R. Azizollahoff, *The Illustrated Buyer's Guide to Oriental Carpets,* Schiffer, 1998; George O'Bannon, *Oriental Rugs,* Running Press, Courage Books, 1995; Walter A. Hawley, *Oriental Rugs, Antique and Modern,* Dover Publications, 1970; Charles W. Jacobsen, *Check Points on How to Buy Oriental Rugs,* Charles E. Tuttle Co., 1981; Friedrich Sarre and Hermann Trenkwald, *Oriental Carpet Designs in Full Color,* Dover Publications, 1980.

Periodicals: *HALI,* P.O. Box 4312, Philadelphia, PA 19118; *Oriental Rug Review,* P.O. Box 709, Meredith, NH 03253; *Rug News,* 34 West 37th St., New York, NY 10018.

REPRODUCTION ALERT

Beware! There are repainted rugs on the market.

Notes: When evaluating an Oriental rug, age, design, color, weave, knots per square inch, and condition determine the final value. Silk rugs and prayer rugs bring higher prices than other types.

SPECIAL AUCTION

Skinner Inc.
Bolton Gallery
357 Main St.
Bolton, MA 01740
(508) 779-6241

Afshar, South Persia, late 19th C
Bagface, large hexagonal medallion inset with two palmettes and spot motifs, midnight blue, ivory, gold, light brown, and light blue-green, red field, midnight blue floral meander border, 3' x 1' 6", slight even wear to center, guard stripes partially missing from both ends 1,840.00
Rug, two hooked diamond medallions inset on two superimposed stepped cartouches, midnight blue, red, ivory, gold, aubergine, and blue-green, royal blue field, ivory blossoming vine border, 6' 4" x 4' 8" 1,840.00
Agra, Northwest India, late 19th C, overall Herati variant design, midnight blue, navy blue, sky blue, rose, ivory, apricot, brown,

aubergine, and light blue-green, abrashed rust field, midnight blue cypress vase and floral spray border, 19' 4" x 11' 2"
.............................13,800.00

Anatolian Kelim, second half 19th C, wide horizontal bands of eli-belinde motifs, red, rose, blue, apricot, dark brown, aubergine, and light blue-green alternate with narrow ivory meander bands, 12' 9" x 5' 4", wear, small holes, repairs
..................................1,150.00

Baluch, Northeast Persia, late 19th C
Rug, column of four hooked medallions surrounded by small rosettes, navy blue, ivory, and aubergine, abrashed red field, midnight blue curled leaf border, 6' 8" x 3' 10", slight even wear 865.00
Tent Pole Cover, column of hooked diamonds, aubergine, dark red, and dark blue-green, heavily abrashed camel-dark brown field, zig-zag border, 5' 8" x 10", good pile, slight moth damage 750.00
Trapping, column of seven hourglass motifs, aubergine, ivory, brown, and silk highlights, midnight blue field, sq motif border, 1' 8" x 1", elaborate tassels 460.00

Bidjar, Northwest Persia, late 19th/early 20th C, serrated hexagonal medallion, large scale Herati design, light slate blue, rose, red-brown, gold, light blue and dark blue-green, red field, ivory rosette and leaf border, 4' 9" x 3' 7" 3,220.00

Eagle Karabagh, South Caucasus, last quarter 19th C, two large sunburst medallions, navy blue, ivory, gold, camel, and blue-green, red field, ivory "crab" border, 6' 9" x 4'
..................................3,105.00

Ersari, West Turkestan, second half 19th C, two columns of six midnight blue, apricot, and blue-green main carpet guls, rust-red field, ashik gul-in-diamond border, rust plainweave elems, 10' 4" x 7' 8" 4,600.00

Fachralo Kazak, Southwest Caucasus, last quarter 19th C, hooked diamond medallion and four hooked cruciform motifs, navy blue, ivory, cream, light-brown, and blue-green, red field, two reciprocal trefoil borders, 5' 6" x 4' 2" 4,485.00

Sarouk, rust red border, midnight blue spandrels, ivory ground, 4'3" x 6'10", $3,575. Photo courtesy of Garth's Auctions, Inc.

Fereghan-Sarouk, West Persia
Early 20th C, large flowerhead medallion, pendants, and blossoming vines, red, ivory, came, rose, sky blue, and blue-green, on might blue field, red spandrels, midnight blue rosette border, 6' 2" x 4' 2" 2,875.00
Late 19th C, serrated diamond medallion, delicate flowering vines, midnight blue, ice blue, royal blue, rose, tan, and light blue-green, terra cotta red field, ivory spandrels, midnight blue palmette and vine border, 13' x 8' 4", even wear, small creases 13,800.00

Heriz, Northwest Persia, second quarter 20th C
Overall design with large curved, serrated leaves and blossoming vines, midnight blue, sky blue, ice blue, ivory, gold, rose, and blue-green, terra cotta red field, midnight blue "turtle" border, 11' 3" x 8' 2" 8,625.00
Overall design with staggered flowerheads and paired palmettes, royal blue, sky blue, rose, light red, tan-told, ivory, and blue-green, abrashed rust-red field, midnight blue "turtle" border, 10' 6" x 8' 4" 5,750.00

Isphahan, Central Persia, second quarter 20th C, overall dense floral sprays and leafy vines, dark red, rose, sky blue, ivory, gold, aubergine, brown, tan, light blue-green, and dark blue-green, midnight blue field, similar border, 7' 6" x 4' 9"
..................................3,740.00

Karachoph Kazak, Southwest Caucasus, third quarter 19th C, octagonal medallion and four star-filled squares, navy blue, ivory, and blue-green, red field, dark brown hooked shield motif border, 7' 5" x 5' 8", crease repairs, small areas of repiling.......................................1,265.00

Karadja, runner, Northwest Persia, second quarter 20th C, column with seven gabled square and hooked hexagonal medallions, royal blue, rose, gold, camel, ivory, aubergine, and blue-green, terra-cotta red field, camel floral meander border, 14' 6" x 3', reduced in length, slight stair wear 2,415.00

Kashan, West Central Persia, early 20th C, overall Herati design variant, paired serrated leaves, red, rose, sky blue, camel, ivory, and light blue-green, navy blue field, red palmette and flowering vine border, 12' x 8' 10".............6,900.00

Kerman, Southeast Persia, last quarter 19th C
Rug, nine circular medallions, circular groups of twelve radiating boteh, midnight blue, gold, rose, tan, ivory, and blue-green, cochineal field, ivory "turtle" variant border, 17' 6" x 11' 10", small areas of wear, stain, small end gouge
....20,700.00
Saddle Cover, central palmette surrounded by blossoming vines, cochineal, rose, sky blue, came, ivory, and blue-green, midnight blue field, narrow cochineal rosette and vine border, 3' 6" x 3' 6", small areas of wear, small repair.. 920.00

Kuba, Northwest Causacus, last quarter 19th C, column of plant motifs surrounded by small stars, rosettes, and other geometric motifs, midnight and royal blue, rust, gold, ivory, and light blue on terra-cotta red field, black "pinwheel" motif border, slight wear to center, small repair, 4' 6" x 3' 3"
..................................1,725.00

Kurd, Northwest Persia, late 19th C, two columns, octagons, and palmette motifs, red, navy blue, gold, ivory, aubergine, and dark blue-green, midnight blue field, red meander border, 5' 6", 4' 6", areas of wear, small hole and repair, creases
.... 690.00

Lori Pambak Kazak, Southwest Caucasus, last quarter 19th C, stepped medallion flanked by octagonal medallions, navy blue and sky blue, ivory, gold, aubergine, and blue-green, red field, sky blue wine glass border, 7' x 5' 2", even wear to center, small repairs.........................3,200.00

Luri, Southwest Persia, early 20th C, diamond medallion and six octagons, red, navy blue, gold, coral, light and dark blue-green, midnight blue field, ivory geometric border, bag-face, 2' 4" x 1' 10", small area of minor wear 350.00

Mahal, West Persia, early 20th C
Overall floral groups, blossoming vines and large serrated leaves, royal blue, ice blue, red, rose, gold, ivory, and blue-green, midnight blue field, red flowering vine border, 14'2" x 10' 6", areas of minor wear 11,500.00
Overall palmettes, dense blossoming vines, red, sky blue, green-gold, rose, tan, ivory, aubergine, and blue-green, midnight blue field, red border, 15' 8" x 9' 4", reduced in length 5,750.00

Malayer Sarouk, West Persia, early 20th C, overall Herati design, red, rose, royal blue, gold, dark rust-red, and blue-green, navy blue field, ivory spandrels, red palmette and vine border, 5' x 3' 7" 2,185.00

Mudjar, Central Anatolia, mid 19th C, prayer, small royal blue, ivory, and dark brown geometric motifs, red field, blue-green spandrels, wide gold rosette and blossoming shrub border, 4' 2" x 4", areas of moth damage, 4" hole, guard stripes missing from both ends 690.00

Qashqai Kelim, Southwest Persia, late 19th/early 20th C, two large stepped diamond medallion flanked by triangles in navy and royal blue, tan, gold, cottonwhite, and dark blue-green, red field, multicolored reciprocal trefoil border, 9'8" x 5'3", small hole 6,325.00

Sarouk, West Persia, late 19th/early 20th C
Large oval medallion, matching spandrels and blossoming vines, serrated leaves, midnight blue, navy blue, rosy red, ivory, gold, tan, and blue-green, terra-cotta red field, midnight blue palmette and vine border, 18' 10" x 12' 6" 24,150.00
Lobed circular medallion, delicate flowering vines, ivory, black, slate blue, gold, rose, and blue-green, rust field, black flowerhead border, 4' 10" x 3' 4" 2,645.00

Senneh Northwest Persia, late 19th C
Kelim, hexagonal medallion and matching spandrels inset with Herati design, midnight blue, navy blue, red, rose, gold, and dark blue-green, red field, gold floral meander border, 6' 10" x 4' 2", small stain, small repairs 2,530.00
Saddle Cover, overall Herati design, red, rose, sky blue, ivory, gold, and blue-green, midnight blue field, gold floral meander border, 3' 2" x 3' 2" .2,185.00

Shirvan East Caucacus, last quarter 19th C
Kelium, wide horizontal bands, large hexagons, navy blue, sky blue, light red, brown, gold, and blue-green alternate with narrow bands of stepped polygons, ivory field, 9' 10" x 5' 5" 805.00
Rug, four large Lesghi stars, red, ivory, gold, and pale blue-green, abrashed navy-slate blue field, ivory askik gul border, 7' x 3' 10" 1,610.00

Soumak, Northeast Caucasus, late 19th C
Four large indented diamond medallions surrounded by lobed diamonds and palmettes, navy blue, sky blue, rose, gold, and blue-green, rust field, black meander border, 9' 10" x 9', rewoven areas 9,200.00
Three indented diamond medallions, eight octagons, small floral motifs, navy and ice blue, rosy red, gold, rose, ivory, and blue-green, red field, aubergine-brown octagon and cruciform motif border, rewoven areas, 9' 4" x 7' 4" 4,888.00

Sultanabad Sampler, West Persia, late 19th C, large flower-heads, small rosettes, curved, serrated leaves, navy blue, sky blue, red, rose, camel, gold, and blue-green, ivory field, narrow gold boteh border, 3' 6" x 1' 7", small area of wear, slight moth damage 1,035.00

Tabriz, Northwest Persia, late 19th C, large rosette medallion and matching spandrels, midnight blue, light slate blue, red-gold, pale blue-green, light gold field, red palmette and leafy vine border, 5'6" x 4'2", slight moth damage 2,875.00

Tekee, West Turkestan, second half 19th C
Chuval, twelve chuval guls, midnight blue, ivory, apricot, and dark blue-green, rust-red field, gotshak border, flowering plant elm of similar coloration, 3' 10" x 3', edges reduced, tear, small holes 2,300.00
Mat, four columns of ten aina guls, midnight blue, apricot, rust, ivory, blue-green, and magenta silk highlights, serrated leaf border and elems of similar coloration, 2' 87" x 2' 2", small areas of wear, slight moth damage 400.00

Ushak, West Anatolia, last quarter 19th C
Overall design with palmettes, rosettes, and wide curved leaves, red, sky blue, and apricot, olive-tan field, wide red "turtle" border, 13' 2" x 9' 9" 7,475.00

Veramin, North Persia, early 20th C
Three columns of hooked quatrefoil medallions surrounded by rosettes and octagons, red, rose, navy blue, camel, light green, and dark green, tan field, red "Kufic" border, 8' 9" x 6' 6" 1,955.00
Bagface, diamond lattice with hooked diamonds, dark red, royal blue, apricot, ivory, and blue-green, ivory star border, 2' x 1' 5", small repair 575.00

Torba, partial Herati design, red, sky blue, rust, apricot, ivory, and blue-green, midnight blue field, ivory floral meander border, 3' 5" x 1' 9", slight wear to center, minor end fraying 490.00

Yomud West Turkestan, late 19th C
Chuval, nine chuval guls, midnight blue and royal blue, red, ivory, and gold, rust field, red stepped polygon border, plant motif elem, 4' x 2' 6", slight even wear, small area of moth damage 800.00
Ensi, quarter aubergine field, red, midnight blue, and blue-green plant motifs, red syrga border, navy blue diamond motif elem, 5' 7" x 4' 3", areas of wear 1,840.00

OVERSHOT GLASS

History: Overshot glass was developed in the mid-1800s. To produce overshot glass, a gather of molten glass was rolled over the marver upon which had been placed crushed glass. The piece then was blown into the desired shape. The finished product appeared to be frosted or iced.

Early pieces were made mainly in clear glass. As the demand for colored glass increased, color was added to the base piece and occasionally to the crushed glass.

Pieces of overshot generally are attributed to the Boston and Sandwich Glass Co. although many other companies also made it as it grew in popularity.

Museum: Sandwich Glass Museum, Sandwich, MA.

Basket
7" h, 9" w, pink opalescent ruffled body, 3 rows of hobnails, twisted vaseline handle 190.00
10" h, 7-1/2" d, rect, shaded cranberry to crystal, applied crystal ruffled edge, applied thorn overshot handle 225.00

Biscuit Jar, cov, 7" h, 5" d, colorless melon ribbed body, applied cranberry overshot, coiled snake handle 250.00

Pitcher, amber, applied dark amber handle, Boston & Sandwich, 6-3/4" h, $325.

Bride's Bowl, 8-5/8" d, 6-5/8" h, shaded clear to blue ground, lobed, crimped edge, dec brass holder 215.00
Compote
    6-3/4" h, 8-3/8" d, cranberry shaded to clear bowl, applied clear scalloped and ruffled edge, fancy brass dome ftd pedestal base. 125.00
    9" h, 8-7/8" d, colorless ground, applied gold dec, cranberry serpent around stem 125.00
Custard Cup, pink ground, applied clear ground, Sandwich
    . . . . 60.00
Decanter, colorless ground, ice bladder, orig stopper. . . 750.00
Ewer, 13-1/2" h, trefoil top, colorless ground, twisted rope handle, Sandwich. 275.00
Finger Bowl, pink ground, fluted and swirled 115.00
Goblet, flint, cut cotton twist stem, American 300.00
Ice Cream Tray, 13" l, colorless, gold trim, Portland. 40.00
Lamp Shade, 7-7/8" d, 2-7/8" d fitter ring, sapphire blue shaded to clear ground, ruffled 125.00
Marmalade Jar, cov, matching underplate, green ground, gold snake entwined on cov, attributed to Boston and Sandwich Glass Co. 315.00
Mug, 3" h, colorless ground, applied colorless handle . . . 35.00
Pitcher
    6" d, cranberry ground, bulbous, applied colorless reeded handle 125.00
    8" d, bulbous, colorless ground, heavy enamel dec of white roses, blue forget me nots and green leaves, applied colorless handle. 150.00
    10-1/2" h, colorless, rope twist handle, ice bladder . . . 90.00
Punch Cup, pink ground, applied colorless handle, attributed to Boston and Sandwich Glass Co. set of 8 . . . . 300.00
Rose Bowl, 3-3/4" d, rubena ground, applied flowers and pale green leaves. 165.00
Tazza, 5-3/4" h, 7-3/4" d, colorless ground, flint glass . . 195.00
Vase
    7-1/2" h, bulbous base, slender neck, colorless ground, gold overshot, silver floral dec. 125.00
    8-1/2" h, opalescent pink ground, fluted, applied colorless handle 135.00

OWENS POTTERY

History: J. B. Owens began making pottery in 1885 near Roseville, Ohio. In 1891, he built a plant in Zanesville and in 1897 began producing art pottery. After 1907, most of the firm's production centered on tiles.

Owens Pottery, employing many of the same artists and designs as its two cross-town rivals, Roseville and Weller, can appear very similar to that of its competitors, e.g., Utopian (brown glaze), Lotus (light glaze), Aqua Verde (green glaze).

There were a few techniques used exclusively at Owens. These included Red Flame ware (slip decoration under a high red glaze) and Mission (over-glaze, slip decorations in mineral colors) depicting Spanish Missions. Other specialties included Opalesce (semi-gloss designs in lustered gold and orange) and Coralene (small beads affixed to the surface of the decorated vases).

References: Susan and Al Bagdade, *Warman's American Pottery and Porcelain*, Wallace-Homestead, 1994; Paul Evans, *Art Pottery of the United States*, 2nd ed., Feingold & Lewis Publishing, 1987; Frank Hahn, *Collector's Guide to Owens Pottery*, Golden Era Publications (available from Green Gate Books, P.O. Box 934, Lima, OH 45802), 1996; Ralph and Terry Kovel, *Kovels' American Art Pottery*, Crown Publishers, 1993; Kristy and Rick McKibben and Jeanette and Martin Stofft, *Owens Pottery Unearthed*, published by authors (45 12th St., Tell City, IN 47586), 1996.

Bud Vase
    6-1/4" h, 2-1/2" w, standard glaze, yellow roses, mkd "#804," initials for Harry Robinson 150.00
    9" h, molded body under metallic glaze, hairline to body
    . . . . 160.00
Ewer, 10" h, brown high glaze, cherry design 200.00

Vase, Utopia, 3 handles, brown glaze, grape leaf dec, artist sgd "J. B. Owens, Utopia," 7" h, $215.

Jug, 8" w, 4-1/2" w, standard glaze, ear of corn dec, mkd and sgd "Tot Steele"................................ 230.00
Lamp Base
   10" h, brown glaze, yellow daffodil dec, green leaves and stems, orig lamp hole in base 190.00
   10" h, 4-1/2" w, standard glaze, tulips and leaves, ftd form, mkd 90.00
Mug, 7-1/2" h, standard glaze, cherries, mkd "#830," sgd "Henry R. Robinson," hairlines to int.................. 110.00
Pitcher, 8-1/2" h, dark brown to green, orange and brown flowers, green leaves, mkd "JBO" intertwined, artist sgd "HK," crack in handle.............................. 110.00
Tankard
   7" h, brown high glaze, Indian design, incised signature, restored.. 325.00
   12" h, brown glaze, artist sgd, imp mark 210.00
Vase
   3-3/4" h, Utopia, dark brown, lighter brown, orange, and yellow floral dec, imp mark "#110," small base flake .. 100.00
   4" h, Lotus, bee flying above green blades of grass, ivory to blue ground, imp mark, artist initials 400.00
   4" h, Utopian, floral........................... 135.00
   4" h, 4" w, yellow chick surrounded by thinly painted grass, four feet, artist sgd.................... 300.00
   5-3/4" h, brown flowers, mkd 100.00
   5-3/4" h, 3-3/4" w, brown clover, standard glaze, mkd "#232" 100.00
   6" h, Lotus, #1177, tiny repair 200.00
   7" h, fluted, Ida Steel, floral 625.00
   7-1/2" h, high glaze, orange, white, and green grapes, vines, and leaves, pink to green ground, imp "Owens #1260" 300.00
   8" h, Aqua Verdi, green matte, textured surface, incised geometrics, four handles around neck, unmarked..... 550.00
   8" h, 8-1/2" w, ftd pillow, dark to light brown with yellow ground, Indian portrait, cream and red vest, blue in hair, imp mark, repaired top 1,100.00
   8-1/2" h, standard glaze, yellow berry dec, green leaves, imp mark................................... 100.00
   10" h, orange and yellow tulips, green leaves, brown ground, imp mark 250.00
   10" h, 5" w, standard glaze, mkd "Owens #010" 210.00
   11"h, Utopia, rose with green leaves, brown stems, orange and brown ground, mkd, artist sgd............ 260.00
   11-1/2" h, 5" w, Utopian, standard glaze, mkd "Owens Utopian #1031," sgd "Sarah Timberlake" 375.00
   12" h, molded flowers and heads, green matte glaze, hairline 160.00
   12-1/2" h, pink poppy, green stems and leaves, pink, ivory, and light blue ground, artist initialed, imp mark 600.00
   12-1/2" h, 8" w, standard glaze, yellow flowers and petals, mkd "#8," minor roughness on bottom.......... 190.00
   13" h, matte, Utopian 425.00
   13-1/2" h, green, yellow, and brown leaves, swirling mahogany, yellow, and dark brown ground, artist initials "A. H.," incised bottom, sunburst "J. B. Owens"".......... 650.00
   16-1/2" h, Lotus, rose, pink, purple, and yellow iris, green leaves, ivory, gray, and peach ground, artist sgd, imp mark 1,400.00

PAIRPOINT

History: The Pairpoint Manufacturing Co. was organized in 1880 as a silver-plating firm in New Bedford, Massachusetts. The company merged with Mount Washington Glass Co. in 1894 and became the Pairpoint Corporation.

The new company produced specialty glass items often accented with metal frames.

Pairpoint Corp. was sold in 1938 and Robert Gunderson became manager. He operated it as the Gunderson Glass Works until his death in 1952. From 1952 until the plant closed in 1956, operations were maintained under the name Gunderson-Pairpoint. Robert Bryden reopened the glass manufacturing business in 1970, moving it back to the New Bedford area.

References: Edward and Sheila Malakoff, *Pairpoint Lamps*, Schiffer Publishing, 1990; John A. Shumann III, *Collector's Encyclopedia of American Art Glass*, Collector Books, 1988, 1994 value update.

Collectors' Clubs: Mount Washington Art Glass Society, P.O. Box 24094, Fort Worth, TX 76124.-1094; Pairpoint Cup Plate Collectors, P.O. Box 890052, East Weymouth, MA 02189.

Museum: Pairpoint Museum, Sagamore, MA.

Butter Dish, 5" d, silvered metal, chased ext., glass insert with cow's head, knife rest, period butter knife, monogrammed 250.00
Candle Shade, 9" d, flared colorless chimney shade, chipped ice surface, scenic dec, mounted on gilt metal inserts for sconces or candlesticks, stamped "patented July 19, 1901, The Pairpoint Corp." inside, pr....................... 575.00
Chalice, 12" h, sapphire blue and white pulled loop, controlled bubble colorless stem, disk foot, Bryden Art 230.00
Chocolate Pot, 10" h, porcelain, butter yellow ground, delicate lilac blossoms, gold embellishments, molded in swirls on body, handle, and finial, marked "Pairpoint-Limoges 2500 114" 485.00
Cologne Bottle, 7" h, green, clear foot, faceted paperweight stopper 200.00
Compote, 10-1/2" x 11", cranberry reverse painted, peaches and gold highlights, SP handled pedestal base, sgd 1,200.00
Console Bowl, 12" d, 6-3/4" h, applied green, bubble ball connector, engraved Vintage pattern................. 175.00
Cornucopia Vase, colorless, bubble filled paperweight bases, pr 150.00

Salt Shaker, white opaque body, yellow and pink flowers, green leaves, wreath, 12 panels, 3-1/4" h, 2-3/4" d, $55.

Creamer, opal glass, Delft blue windmill and landscape, five sailing ships on reverse, painted blue blown-out scrolls encircle base, SP handle, rim, and spout 350.00

Ice Pail, 6" d, 7-1/2"h, clear, engraved Vintage pattern, nickel silver rim and drain plate 195.00

Lamp

13-3/4" h, 8" d shade, boudoir, blown out closed top sq glass shade, rose red blossoms, four butterflies, reverse painted, white ground, marked "The Pairpoint Corp.," gilt metal base, fully sgd 5,750.00

21" h, 16" d domed Copley shade, hp on interior, broad landscape scene, silver-plated two-socket base, chipped rim 1,100.00

22" h, 18" d flared Berkeley glass reverse painted shade, New Bedford harbor scene, tall masted ships in foreground, men in small boat rowing toward town, church spires and village on distant shore, marked "The Pairpoint Corp.," SP triple dolphin base stamped "Pairpoint" 4,715.00

Mantel Lamp, 14" h, 10-1/2" d, two-arm candelabra-form, elaborate silver-plated metal fittings joined by controlled bubble ball stems and finals, imp "Pairpoint" marks under candlecups, silver worn, old wiring, pr 700.00

Mantel Vase, cov, 17" h, Rosaria, Gunderson period goblet-form, red, colorless twisted ball, stem, and foot, flame finials, pr. 650.00

Miniature Lamp, 16-3/8" h, 9" d San Remo barrel shape reverse painted puffy shade, blown out butterflies, asters, and roses against green accented white ground, gold ext. accents, millefiori green patina metal base. 6,900.00

Pickle Castor Frame, silver plate, orig lid 135.00

Smoking Stand, three opal glass bowls mounted in shield-shaped maple wood stand, brass trim and feet, brass cigar holder, Delft dec of windmills, houses, people, and sailing ships. 650.00

Vase

6" h, Tavern Glass, thousands of bubble inclusions, sailing galleon on wavy sea dec, c1900-38. . . . . 300.00

10" h, 3" d, cone shape, opal, floral sprigs, sgd 225.00

PAPER EPHEMERA

History: Maurice Rickards, author of *Collecting Paper Ephemera*, suggests that ephemera are the "minor transient documents of everyday life," material destined for the wastebasket but never quite making it. This definition is more fitting than traditional dictionary definitions that emphasize time, e.g., "lasting a very short time." A driver's license, which is used for a year or longer, is as much a piece of ephemera as is a ticket to a sporting event or music concert. The transient nature of the object is the key.

Collecting ephemera has a long and distinguished history. Among the English pioneers were John Seldon (1584-1654), Samuel Pepys (1633-1703), and John Bagford (1650-1716). Large American collections can be found at historical societies and libraries across the country, and museums, e.g., Wadsworth Athenaeum, Hartford, CT, and the Museum of the City of New York.

When used by collectors, "ephemera" usually means paper objects, e.g., billheads and letterheads, bookplates, documents, labels, stocks and bonds, tickets, and valentines. However, more and more ephemera collectors are recognizing the transient nature of some three-dimensional material, e.g., advertising tins and pinback buttons. Today's specialized paper shows include

dealers selling other types of ephemera in both two- and three-dimensional form.

References: Warren R. Anderson, *Owning Western History*, Mountain Press Publishing, 1993; Patricia Fenn and Alfred P. Malpa, *Rewards of Merit*, Ephemera Society, 1994; Norman E. Martinus and Harry L. Rinker, *Warman's Paper*, Wallace-Homestead, 1994; Robert Reed, *Paper Collectibles*, Wallace-Homestead/Krause, 1995; Kenneth W. Rendell, *Forging History*, University of Oklahoma Press, 1994; Gene Utz, *Collecting Paper*, Books Americana, 1993.

Periodical: *Biblio*, 845 Willamette St., Eugene, OR 87401; *Paper Collectors' Marketplace*, P.O. Box 128, Scandinavia, WI 54977.

Collectors' Clubs: Ephemera Society, 12 Fitzroy Sq, London W1P 5HQ England; Ephemera Society of America, Inc., P.O. Box 95, Cazenovia, NY 13035; The Ephemera Society of Canada, 36 Macauley Dr., Thornhill, Ontario L3T 5S5 Canada; National Association of Paper & Advertising Collectors, P.O. Box 500, Mount Joy, PA 17552.

SPECIAL AUCTIONS

Postcards International
P.O. Box 185398
Hamden CT 06518
(203) 248-6621

R. M. Smythe & Co.
26 Broadway
New York, NY 10004-1701

Swann Galleries, Inc.
104 E 25th St.
New York, NY 10010
(212) 254-4710

Additional Listings: See Advertising Trade Cards; Catalogs; Comic Books; Photographs; Sports Cards. Also see Calendars, Catalogs, Magazines, Newspapers, Photographs, Postcards, and Sheet Music in *Warman's Americana & Collectibles*.

Billheads and invoices

Reference: Leslie Cabarga, *Letterheads*, Chronicle Books, 1992.

Alliance First National Bank, Alliance, OH, Capital & Surplus $600,000 . . . . 5.00

Amey, George, Coal & Lumber, blue lines, quarter page . . 3.50

Antietam Paper Company, Hagerstown, Md. Manufacturers and Distributors of Paper, quarter page 3.50

Bank of Northumberland, Incorporated of Heathsville, Virginia, fold line. 5.00

Burlington Coffin Company, Burlington, NC "The House of Quality". 5.00

Ewald Hildebrand & Co., half page 3.50

First and Tri State National Bank and Trust Company, Fort Wayne, Indiana. Capital and Surplus $3,375,000, illus at bottom corner 5.00

Ford., E. G., Philadelphia, PA, 1899, 2 pgs, 4-3/4" x 8-1/2", for repairs to sweeper, illus of New Columbia Clothes Wringer and Bissell Sweeper, set of 2 . . . . 6.00

Freed Brothers Shoes, Richlandtown, PA, black and white 5.00

Greensboro Bank & Trust Company, Greensboro, NC. Capital & Surplus, $1,500,000 . . . . 5.00

Greensboro Life Insurance Company, Greensboro, NC . . . 5.00

Haddon Motors, Inc., Camden, NJ, "great cars, fine service, a square deal," quarter page 3.50

Hotel Utica, Utica, New York, Mohawk Valley Hotel Company, Inc. NY, 1939 World's Fair logo on bottom. "An easy drive to New York World's Fair" 6.50

Hydro, The Most Beautiful Tire in America. Insured for one year against all road hazards, quarter page 3.50

Miller Brothers Co., Wilmington, DE, Furniture & Floor Coverings, "The Happy Home is the well furnished home" 5.00

Mitchell & Lewis Co., Ltd., Racine, WI, c1900, 1 pg, 8-1/2" x 11", letterhead with 3-1/4" x 6" illus of green farm wagon with red wheels, text of letter pertains to selling wagons to agents 30.00

Norge Electric Refrigeration, Columbus, OH, illus of woman opening refrigerator 10.00

Richardson Dry Goods Co., St. Joseph, Mo. Dry Goods, Notions, Furnishing Goods, quarter page size 3.50

Standard Watch Co., Syracuse, NY, c1905, 1 pg, 8" x 10", blue ink, Jewelry Dept. sales letter regarding patent show case for jewelry, two black and white illus 20.00

The Bridgeport Machine Company, Witchita, Kansas. Oil Well Drilling and Fishing Tools, quarter page. 3.50

The First and Farmers National Bank and Trust Company, Montrose, Pa. Surplus & Profits Over $200,000, quarter page 3.50

The Mallory Hat Co., Danbury, Conn. Fur, felt & straw hats, since 1823 . . . . 5.00

The Savings Bank of Utica, Utica, NY, Established 1839, center fold 5.00

The Sussex & Merchants National Bank of Newton, NJ Capital $400,000, some damage 3.50

The Van Wert Overall Mfg. Co., Van Wert, OH, Excelsor Work Clothes 5.00

Booklets

Amberg File & Index Co., New York, NY, 1899, 9-1/4" x 12-1/4", Amberg's Imperial Cabinets, 9 illus, folded 30.00

Caldwell & Peterson Mfg., Wheeling, WV, c1893, 4 pgs, 8 x 11-1/4", sheet metal roofing for sale by jobbing hardware houses and agents, 5 illus of workings laying sheet steel roofing. 22.00

Church, Stephen B., Semour, CT, 1910, 4 pgs, 8-1/" x 11", Engineering & Contracting for Suburban Water works, wells, etc. 26.00

Colgate, nursery rhymes, 5-1/4" x 3-1/4"
Little Miss Muffet Sat On A Tuffet. 45.00
One Foot Up The Other Foot Down 45.00
Peter Peter Pumpkin Eater. 45.00
Ring Around The Roses. 45.00

Kent, Woodman & Co., Boston, MA, c1894, 5 pgs, 5-1/4" x 8-1/4", 4 illus of telephones and parts 32.00

Michigan Buggy Co., Kalamazoo, MI, c1904, 4 pgs, 6" x 9", 4 illus, 3 folds 22.00

Old Dutch Cleanser, Chicago, IL, 1933, 32 pgs, 6" x 9", orig World's Fair picture envelope, "Cleanliness Through The Ages," cuts of various means of people throughout the world keeping themselves clean 22.00

Quick Meal Gasoline Stoves, Buster Brown, illus to make shadow images, 3" x 5" 135.00

The Favorite Mfg. Co., Chicago, IL, c1894, 4 pgs, 9-1/4" x 12-1/4", 1 pink, 1 green sheet, 6 illus of sewing machine and features 20.00

Brochures and flyers

American Knitting Machine Co., Boston, MA, 1870, 6 pgs, 5" x 8", one stamped envelope, one advertising return envelope, two single sheet flyers, one 4 pg brochure, picture of Family Knitting Machine. 25.00

Bigelow & Dowse, Boston, MA, 1 pg, 8-1/2" x 10-3/4", Excelsior Weather Strip 12.00

Buck Trolley Clothes Dry, Worchester, MA, c1890, 1 pg, 6" x 9-1/2", illus, "Don't fail to see this Dryer" 20.00

Buffalo Spring & Gear Co., Buffalo, NY, c1885, 1 pg, 8-1/2" x 11", folded, directions for hanging up Thomas Coil Springs for new buggies, product illus 13.00

Clawson Machine Co., Flagtown, NJ, c1929, 1 pc, 10" x 12-3/4", illus of vending machines 24.00

Cox, J. B. Manuf, Chicago, IL, c1890, 1 pg, 8" x 10-3/4", "The Vesuvius Flambeau," flaming torch, red and blue ink, announcing torch that throws flames 20 to 30 feet, two illus 22.00

Department of Public Park, U.S., pre 1900, 1 pg, 6" x 10", illus of new boulevard lap posts. 15.00

Dorr's Son, J. O., New York, NY, c1892, 1 pg, 5-1/2" x 8-1/4", red and black ink, price list for electric light oil, export, and western oils 13.00

Empire Electric Supply Co., Chicago, IL, c1923, 1 pg, 6" x 7", improved "Harter Ringer" for telephone exchanges 10.00

Hubbard, J. A., Plainfield, NJ, c1889, 1 pg, 8" x 10", announcing "Standard's Clothes Washer Patented June 8, 1868," illus of washer 12.00

Lilley, C. M., & Co., Columbus, OH, c1908, 3 pgs, 8" x 11", price list of Patriarch Militant Supplies, brochures of uniforms 15.00

Mahoney Chair Co., Gardner, MA, c1938, 2 pgs, 8-1/2" x 11", mail-out type, folded, orig stamp, folding chairs 10.00

Palmer & Harden, Louisville, KY
1920, 2 pgs, 20-1/4" x 30-1/2", Special Offering No. 7, bed lounges and bed couches, 15 models, tear at center fold 21.00
1921, 2 pcs, 22" x 32", Special Offering No. 8, parlor furniture, lounges, couches, mattresses, 60 items illus, chips on edges, fold tears 23.00

Rathbun, Geo. W., N. Providence, RI, c1890, 1 pg, 9" x 12-1/4", "Necessity" saw sharpening machine. 24.00

Richmond Casket Co., Richmond, IN, 1911, 2 pgs, 11-1/4" x 24", 14 models illus 26.00

Rogers, George W., Chesterfield, MA, 1 pg, 5-3/4" x 9-1/4", illus of Newman Best & Cheapest Wire Truss Fence 15.00

Spear, James, & Co., Philadelphia, PA, c1880, 1 pg, 8-1/2" x 11-1/4", description of Caloric and Spear's heat regulating or heat distributing anti-rust cooking stove, list of fixtures, prices 22.00

The IHC of America, Inc., Chicago, IL, 1917, 2 pgs, 18" x 19-1/2", folded as issued, 2 colored illus, hay and grain harvesting machines, parts 23.00

Calendars

Collectors' Club: Calendar Collector Society, American Resources, 18222 Flower Hill Way #299, Gaithersburg, MD 20879.

1908, DuPont, portrait of Geneva, winner of National Field Trial Championship, Bird Dog of the Year, 1903, artist Edm O. Os-

thaus, orig metal rim at top and bottom, 30-1/2" h, 20" w, framed 1,100.00
1916, post card photo, 5-1/2 x 10 ....18.00
1925, E Huckerby Tailor, Belle Vernon PA, Lincoln 20.00
1928, American Book Co., school calendar 13.50
1932, Historical Art Calendar, George Washington 30.00
1938, Mt. Airy Milling, Gold Medal Flour..............25.00
1941, American Book Co., school calendar, churches ...15.00
1944, Stem Brothers, Skyesville, AMOCO 18.50
1950, Welch Florists, Reistertown, MD, 12 flower pictures
....12.00
1952, Classic Masters, Bach, Beethoven, et., 4-1/2" x 8"
....8.00
1952, Real No Squeek Fong. All kinds of Naval and Army Shoes, High Grade Gentlemen, Boots and Shoes, Made to Order and Best Repairing, etc. H.K. Branch, 34 Pilkem St., Kowloon, H.K...................................18.00
1955, Farmer's Supply, 24 pgs, colorful, orig envelope ...8.00

Cigar labels

References: Edwin Barnes and Wayne Dunn, *Cigar-Label Art Visual Encyclopedia with Index and Price Guide*, published by authors (P.O. Box 3, Lake Forest, CA 92630), 1995.

Collectors' Clubs: Cigar Label Collectors International, P.O. Box 66, Sharon Center, OH 44274; International Seal, Label & Cigar Band Society, 8915 E Bellevue St, Tucson, AZ 85715; Society of Antique Label Collectors, P.O. Box 24811, Tampa, FL 33623.

Aficionado. Faber, Coe & Gregg, Inc..................8.00
Apter's Don-Remo......................................6.50
Commoner, A Man of the People 7.00
Conning, Geo..8.00
den de Bances y Lopez, Tampa 6.00
Dolly Madison 5.00
Golden Veil, Chas. L. Boak, Harrisburg, Pa...........10.00
Ideolo 8.00
Kohler's Hand Made. Big Value 9.00
La Estampa...3.50
La Favorita de Tampa.................................3.50
La Flor de Garcia y Vega, Fine Cigars Since 1882......10.00
La Granda, Quality Cigar 3.50
La Saolo, Mild Blend 10.00
Marshall Field, Don't Bite - Just Lite 10.00
Miss Primrose 8.00
Natividad. El Primo Cigar Company, San Francisco, CA ..8.00
Our Kitties, black and white cat, white ground 10.00
Quaker Cigar..10.00
Reina Bella 10.00
Senator Dixon 7.00
Sonny Boy, Quality Cigar 3.50
Souvenir National Convention, 1948, Phila. Pa.........7.50

Cook booklets

References: Bob Allen, *Guide to Collecting Cookbooks and Advertising Cookbooks*, Collector Books, 1990, 1995 value update; Mary Barilie, *Cookbooks Worth Collecting*, Wallace-Homestead, 1994; Linda Dickinson, *Price Guide to Cookbooks and Recipe Leaflets*, Collector Books, 1990, 1995 value update.

Collectors' Club: Cook Book Collectors Club of America, Inc., P.O. Box 56, St. James, MO 66559-0056; Cook-

book Collectors' Exchange, P.O. Box 3269, San Jose, CA 95152.

Arm & Hammer, New Fashioned Old Fashion Recipes, 18 pgs, 1949 ....9.00
Armour Ham, 60 Ways To Serve ham, 28 pgs, 1930s ...15.00
Baker's Choice, Choice Recipes, 64 pgs, 1926 ....15.00
Betty Crocker, Your Share, 48 pgs, 1943 ....5.00
Bond Bread, Bond Bread Cook Book, 72 pgs, 1935.....15.00
Borden-Eagle, New Magic In The Kitchen, 68 pgs, c1930
....12.00
Crisco, Recipes For Good Eating, 64 pgs, 1944........10.00
Del Monte, Del Monte Peaches, 11 Food Experts. 1927
....15.00
Diamond Walnuts Menu Magic in Nutshell, 32 pgs, 1940
....9.00
Dole Pineapple, Kingdom That Grew Out of Little Boy's Garden, 1930 ....14.00
Duryea's Cornstarch, Recipes & Cooking Suggestions, 48 pgs, 1907 ....10.00
Foss Extract, Sixteen Dainty Desserts, 32 pgs, c1920 ....7.50
General Foods, Recipes For Today, 40 pgs, 1943......10.00
Gold Medal Party Cakes, 24 pgs, 1931 ....8.00
Heinz, 57 Ways To Use Heinz Condensed Soups, 38 pgs, 1944
....6.00
Hellmann's, Salad Ideas, 16 pgs, 1929................16.00
Hershey Cocoa, Story of Chocolate and Cocoa, 24 pgs, 1934
....10.00
McCormack Cookbook; 5" x 7-7/8", 32 pgs 34.00
Sealtest, Food Advisor For November, 16 pgs, 1936.....7.50
Spry, Aunt Jenny's Favorite Recipes, 48 pgs, 1943......8.00
Standard Brands, The Bread Basket, 40 pgs, 1942......7.50
Sucaryl, Calorie Saving Recipes, 32 pgs, 1951 ....5.00
Swans Down, How to Bake by Ration Book, 24 pgs, 1943
....10.00
Watkins Products, Watkins Salad Book, spiral, 252 pgs, 1946
....18.00
Worchester Salt Cook Book, 32 pgs, 1931 ....12.50

Miscellaneous

Checks
　　Commercial Bank of St. Augustine 3.50
　　State Emergency Relief Board, Harrisburg, PA 3.50
　　The State Bank of Belmont 3.50
Cut-out, baptismal gift for god child, inscribed in ink, watercolor and pinpick highlights, Europe, 19th C, minor imperfections, 12-1/2" d...375.00
Document, Monmouth Mutual Fire Insurance Company, policy, partly printed, 1846, filled out by hand 75.00
Fan, McCormick Bee Brand Spices, 7" sq, wood handle, creased, bright colors.............................100.00
Ink Blotter
　　Gulf Fuel Oil, 5-3/4" x 2-3/4"......................28.00
　　Kelly Heavy Duty Cord, 6-1/4" x 3-3/8", slight rubbing to corners 35.00
　　Kelly Springfield Tires, ink blotter; 10" x 3-7/8" 65.00
Instruction Sheet, C. Gautschi & Co., Philadelphia, PA c1897, 2 pgs, 8" x 11-1/4", for Swiss made music boxes 23.00
Menu, The Grist Mill Gazette, New York, NY, 1884, 4 pgs, 11-1/2" x 16-1/2", Vol. XVII, no. 22, heavy stock paper, Jimmy Denicola's Grist Mill Bill of Fare, plus history of mill ...28.00
Premium List, E. H. Pardee, New Haven, CT, c1888, 4 pgs, 10-3/4" x 16-1/4", folded, jewelry, silverware, novelties, 69 illus. 26.00

Price List

Jesse Lazear & Co. Props., Baltimore, MD, 1874, 4 pgs, 8" x 10", Baltimore City Roasted Coffee & Spice Mills, 1 illus of Lockwood's portable coffee roaster, folds 24.00

The John Danner Mfg. Co., Canton, OH, c1889, 4 pgs, 9" x 12", revolving goods cases, 4 large illus of revolving print shelf, Eureka Goods Rack, novelty goods, and star goods 28.00

Wallpaper Book, Sears, Roebuck & Co., Chicago, IL, 62 pgs, 8-3/4" x 12-3/4", 1931 Style Book, "Certified Fadeproof Wall Paper & Colored Pages of Pressed Wall Hangings, Wall Hangings, Panel Binders, Art Cloth, etc." actual wall paper samples 42.00

Postcards

Here is a small sampling of the millions of postcards available to collectors. Examples have been selected to show the wide range of images available. While these illustrate some of the rarer cards, remember postcards range from a few cents to hundreds of dollars.

References: Janet Banneck, *Antique Postcards of Rose O'Neill*, Greater Chicago Publications, 1992; J. L. Mashburn, *Artist-Signed Postcard Price Guide*, Colonial House, 1993; ——, *Black Americana: A Century of History Preserved on Postcards*, Colonial House, 1996; ——, *Fantasy Postcards with Price Guide*, Colonial House, 1996; ——, *Postcard Price Guide*, 3rd ed., Colonial House, 1997; ——, *Super Rare Postcards of Harrison Fisher with Price Guide*, Colonial House, 1992; Frederic and Mary Megson, *American Exposition Postcards*, The Postcard Lovers, 1992; Ron Menchine, *Picture Postcard History of Baseball*, Almar Press, 1992; Susan Brown Nicholson, *Encyclopedia of Antique Postcards*, Wallace-Homestead, 1994; Cynthia Rubin and Morgan Williams, *Larger than Life: The American Tall-Tall Postcard 1905-1915*, Abbeville Press, 1990; Nouhad A. Saleh, *Guide to Artist's Signatures and Monograms*

on Postcards, Minerva Press, 1993; Robert Ward, *Investment Guide to North American Real Photo Postcards*, Antique Paper Guide, 1991; Jane Wood, *Collector's Guide to Post Cards*, L-W Book Sales, 1984, 1995 value update.

Periodicals: *Barr's Post Card News*, 70 S. 6th St., Lansing, IA 52151; *Gloria's Corner*, P.O. Box 507, Denison, TX 75021; *Postcard Collector*, P.O. Box 1050, Dubuque, IA 52004.

Collectors' Clubs: *Barr's Post Card News* and *Postcard Collector* publish lists of more than 50 regional clubs in the United States and Canada; Deltiologists of America, P.O. Box 8, Norwood, PA 19074; Granite State Postcard Collectors Club, P.O. Box 79, West Franklin, NH 03235; International Postcard Association Inc., P.O. Box 66, 1217 F S K Hwy, Keymar, MD 21757; Monumental Postcard Club, 3013 St. Paul St., Baltimore, MD 21218; Postcard History Society, P.O. Box 1765, Manassas, VA 22110.

Bud Piper's Twin Filling Station, Beer and Gasoline, Champaign, IL, real photo, adv with multi-views 60.00

Carnival float, woman rides tiger, fish in his mouth, real photo, float parked on French street 30.00

Chief Blackhorn, "Souvenir of the American Indian Villages, Real Sioux Indians," Brussels Exposition, 1935, black and white 40.00

Christmas hold to light, child chases a turkey, diecut . . . 150.00

Donald Duck with Toothache, "It has the air of truth that sugar causes pain in the teeth," Donald, nephews, and Pluto, French 50.00

4th of July, "Be proud that you were born in the U.S.A.," boy lights big firecracker, girl with flag and dog watches . . 40.00

German Red Cross, Christmas angel, red hat and robe, brings lighted tree, "Thanks to our brave troops!" official postcard of the Local Fundraising Committee of the Nürmburg Red Cross, Germany, Christmas, 1915 . . . . 50.00

Girl Scouts, "Choose the right path, and stick to it until the end - Baden Powell," Belgian, sgd "Wandy," published by Catholic Scouts of Belgium 40.00

Grand Army of the Republic, real photo, studio portrait of aged Civil War veteran, in uniform with medals, notation on back "James Henry Barrett, 70 years old, 1915" 45.00

Halloween Night, child lifts top of jack-o-lantern, Freixas design, published by Winsch, 1914, embossed 125.00

National Apple Show, Nov 14 to 19, 1910, Spokane, Wash., pretty red apple on front 65.00

"New Departure Coaster Brakes gives absolute control of wheel anywhere," bears chasing Scots scientist on bicycle, from series of eight published by New Departure Manuf Co., Bristol, CT 85.00

Telegraph Boy, real photo, from London Life series, Rotary Photo 40.00

World War I, "War knows no justice," drawing of church in ruins, German, used, 1915 German Infantry Fieldpost 45.00

The Encampment, boy scouts setting up their tent, French, sgd "Job," adv on back for Belle Jardiniere department store, Paris 65.00

Zuni, photo view of adobe village, E. S. Curtis, 1904, brown and white 85.00

PAPERWEIGHTS

History: Although paperweights had their origin in ancient Egypt, it was in the mid-19th century that this art

Postcard, Mid-Pacific Carnival, Hawaii, 1910, $600. Photo courtesy of Postcards International.

form reached its zenith. The finest paperweights were produced between 1834 and 1855 in France by the Clichy, Baccarat, and Saint Louis factories. Other weights made in England, Italy, and Bohemia during this period rarely match the quality of the French weights.

In the early 1850s, the New England Glass Co. in Cambridge, Massachusetts, and the Boston and Sandwich Glass Co. in Sandwich, Massachusetts, became the first American factories to make paperweights.

Popularity peaked during the classic period (1845-1855) and faded toward the end of the 19th century. Paperweight production was rediscovered nearly a century later in the mid-1900s. Contemporary weights still are made by Baccarat, Saint Louis, Perthshire, and many studio craftsmen in the U.S. and Europe.

References: *Annual Bulletin of the Paperweight Collectors Association, Inc.*, available from association (P.O. Box 1263, Beltsville, MD 20704), 1996; Monika Flemming and Peter Pommerencke, *Paperweights of the World*, Schiffer Publishing, 1994; Robert G. Hall, *Old English Paperweights*, Schiffer Publishing, 1998; John D. Hawley, *Glass Menagerie*, Paperweight Press, 1995; Sibylle Jargstorf, *Paperweights*, Schiffer Publishing, 1991; Paul Jokelson and Dena Tarshis, *Baccarat Paperweights and Related Glass*, Paperweight Press, 1990; Edith Mannoni, *Classic French Paperweights*, Paperweight Press, 1984; Bonnie Pruitt, *St. Clair Glass Collectors Guide*, published by author, 1992; Pat Reilly, *Paperweights*, Running Press, Courage Books, 1994; Lawrence H. Selman, *All About Paperweights*, Paperweight Press, 1992; ——, *Art of the Paperweight*, Paperweight Press, 1988; ——, *Art of the Paperweight, Perthshire*, Paperweight Press, 1983; ——, *Art of the Paperweight, Saint Louis*, Paperweight Press, 1981 (all of the Paperweight Press books are distributed by Charles E. Tuttle Co., 1996).

Collectors' Clubs: Caithness Collectors Club, 141 Lanza Ave., Building 12, Garfield, NJ 07026; International Paperweight Society, 761 Chestnut St., Santa Cruz, CA 95060; Paperweight Collectors Association Inc., P.O. Box 1059, Easthampton, MA 01027; Paperweight Collectors Association of Chicago, 535 Delkir Ct., Naperville, IL 60565; Paperweight Collectors Association of Texas, 1631 Aguarena Springs Dr., #408, San Marcos, TX 78666.

Museums: Bergstrom-Mahler Museum, Neenah, WI; Corning Museum of Glass, Corning, NY; Degenhart Paperweight & Glass Museum, Inc., Cambridge, OH; Museum of American Glass at Wheaton Village, Millville, NJ.

Additional Listings: See Warman's Americana & Collectibles for examples of advertising paperweights.

Antique

Baccarat
    Concentric, arrowhead and star canes, three Gridel animal silhouettes, 3-1/8" d 1,400.00
    Floral, two red and yellow star centered striped blossoms, one purple, one white, millefiore cane garland surround, 2-1/2" d 1,650.00

Millefiore, close pack intricate canes with "B1846," some scratches and side blemish 1,725.00
    Strawberry, central green branch with seven leaves, three strawberries, star-cut base, minor chips to base, 3" d 4,600.00
    Yellow Wheatflower, two rows of six black-spotted petals, centered by two rows of white stars, red and white whorl, green stalk, surrounded by seven green leaves, star-cut base, 2-1/2" d 3,750.00
Clichy
    Patterned Millefiori, red ground, central pink, white, and green cane surrounded by five looped garlands of blue and white canes, each divided by white and green florals, 3" d 1,200.00
    Scatter, colorful six-pointed millefiori scatter, center pink rose, white rose aside, bubble afloat, 3" d 900.00
    Swirl, rose, green, and white pinwheel swirl, pink center and turquoise center, shall drill hole center base, 3" d 1,100.00
New England
    Floral, pink blossom, dew-drop bubbles spaced at petals, blue and white jasper ground, attributed to Sandwich, 3" d 450.00
    Fruit, five red and yellow pears, four cherries, leaves, white lattice conical ground, 2-1/2" d 325.00
    Poinsettia, ten-petal red blossom, blue and white center cane, white lattice bed, elaborate millefiore cane garland surround, faceted edging, 2-3/4" d 425.00
St. Louis
    Faceted floral, upright bouquet, fourteen-point inside cane, recessed diamond-cut base, 3-1/8" d 2,000.00
    Fruit, white latticino basket enclosing cluster of two green pears, striped apple, four cherries, green serrated leaves, 3-1/4" d 1,850.00
Sandwich
    Cherries, two shaded red cherries pendent from green branch, four serrated leaves, 2-15/16" d 700.00
    Poinsettia, flower composed of two rows of six overlapping red pointed petals, red, green, and white Clichy rose cane stamen, curved stem, four variegated leaves, one leaf off to side, 3-7/16" d 800.00

Paul Ysart, dahlia, purple flower, circle of red and white canes, cobalt blue carpet, orig paper label, sgd "PY," $375.

Modern

Ayotte, Rick
    Bird, compound weight, black-capped tan bird on blossoming branches, yellow cased to white ground, inscribed "Ayotte 1/1 '85," 3-1/2" d 575.00
    Flower, fruit, seed pod, white, red, and purple cycle, green leafy stem, "Ayotte Ed. 50 '92," 3-3/4" d 550.00

Baccarat
    Concentric ring, multicolored millefiore garlands, central cane of arrowheads, 2-1/2" d 250.00
    Dahlia, pink and white fleur-de-lis center cane, twelve-petal white blossom, side bud, blue transparent ground, "B1970" cane, 3-3/8" d. 150.00

Banford, Bob
    Cornflower, blue flower, yellow center, pink and white twisted torsade, "B" cane at stem, 3" d 550.00
    Flower bouquet, five red stemmed blossoms, "B" cane below, diamond cut recessed base, 3-1/4" d 475.00
    Iris and rose, purple, blue, and pink irises, center pink roe, recessed diamond-cut base, "B" cane at stem, 3" d . . 250.00

Banford, Bobbie, aquarium, three exotic green fish among sea plants and shells, "B" cane on and, 3-3/8" d 350.00

Clichy, panel pattern, pink, white, and rose red clusters around central red on white cane, green cushion, fold at edge, 2-1/2" d. 475.00

Italian, attributed to Arte Vetraria Muranese, hollow glass dome, stretched millefiore canes, filigrana and latticino slices above aventurine green layer, 7-1/2" d, 4-1/2" h. 200.00

Kaziun, Charles
    Millefiori, cluster of canes, one with gold "K," pink torsade, clear pedestal base, 1-1/2" h. 500.00
    Yellow rose, upright flower, four green leaves, center "K" and seven hearts, star-cut base, 2-1/4" d. 575.00

Rosenfeld, Ken, bouquet
    Red, lavender, and two white blossoms, four buds on leafy stems, transparent blue ground, "R" cane and "Ken Rosenfeld '93 12/25" at side, 3-1/4" d 500.00
    Spray of exotic lavender bellflowers, dark centered yellow flowers on leafy stems, "R" cane, sgd "Ken Rosenfeld '94" at side, 3-3/8" d 500.00

Salazar, David, compound floral, lavender six-petal poinsettia star blossom, three-leaf stem over green and red wreath, white ground, inscribed "David Salazar/111405/Lundberg Studios 1991," 3-1/4" d. 225.00

St. Louis, Honeycomb, carpet of numerous hollow sienna canes, central red, white, and blue composite cane, sgd and dated "SL 1988" 1,200.00

Stankard, Paul J., Ants and Indian Pipes, white blossoms, tan buds, complex root system, two nude root spirits and banners "seeds/scent/moist/fertile," three realistic ants interspersed, inscribed "Paul J. Stankard V30 '97," 3" d 1,955.00

Taristano, Debbie, floral
    Brilliant red-orange dahlia, yellow and blue smaller blossoms, spotted bug on green leaf, "DT" cane under flower, 3-1/4" d 1,100.00
    Colorless, complex centered six-petal pink blossom and bud, "DT" cane on reverse, 2-1/2" d 300.00
    Yellow centered five-petal blossom and bud, shaded blue scrambled cane ground, flat-top, fancy fluted rim, obscured "DT" cane, 3-1/2" d 475.00

Trabucco, Victor
    Magnum snake, green and yellow bellied black snake, silvered rocky sanded ground, inscribed "Trabucco 1997" at lower edge, 3-3/4" d. 700.00
    Pear branch, yellow centered white blossom and buds, two red and yellow fruits, inscribed "Trabucco 1995"" at lower edge, 3-1/4" d 650.00

PAPIER-MÂCHÉ

History: Papier-mâché is a mixture of wood pulp, glue, resin, and fine sand which is subjected to great pressure and then dried. The finished product is tough, durable, and heat resistant. Various finishing treatments are used, such as enameling, japanning, lacquering, mother-of-pearl inlaying, and painting.

During the Victorian era, papier-mâché articles such as boxes, trays, and tables were in high fashion. Banks, candy containers, masks, toys, and other children's articles were also made of papier-mâché.

Box, cov, floral dec and parcel-gilt, fitted int., Victorian, England, c1860 . . . . 500.00
Bread Tray, 14-1/4" l, cartouche shape, blood red, floral spray and butterfly dec, cavetto and shaped border, gilt edge, black under surface, England, c1820 . . . . 500.00
Figure, 23-1/4" h, comic male figure, brightly colored polychrome paint, spot welded high wheel bicycle, 20th C 1,750.00
Folio Cover, 16-1/2" l, MOP inlaid, painted, depicting Pliny Doves, foliate borders, Victorian, mid 19th C, losses. 200.00
Lap Desk, 14" w, 11" d, 4-1/2" h, painted and gilt stenciled, MOP inlaid, lid painted with still life of fruit, bombe sides resting on flattened feet, foliate gilt stenciling throughout ext. and int., minor losses to stenciling, Victorian mid 19th C. 865.00
Match Safe, pill box-style
    2-1/2" w, copper foil finish, name "Robert Schneider" . 80.00
    2-1/2" w, large cathedral on cover 95.00
    2-5/8", gilt design, name inside cover. 45.00
Music Stand, MOP and parcel gilt dec, labeled "Chinnocks Patent Screen," Victorian, 2nd half 19th C 700.00
Pip-Squeak, 6-1/2" h, rooster, spring legs, wood bellow base, orig polychrome paint. 75.00
Snuff Box, Dr. Syntax, The Shooting Pony, round, yellow and brown transfer 145.00
Stand
    28" h, 17" d, shaped papier-mâché circular top with central wreath of flowers on greens, cut-out fleur-de-lis dec edge,

Cup, gold ground, black base, red band at top, floral dec, mkd "Made in USSR," 2-1/2" h, $30.

tilts above turned pine standard, shaped legs, painted mustard ground, red and black classical embellishments, attributed to Litchfield Mfg. Co., Litchfield, CT, mid 19th C 2,645.00

29" h, 20" d, checkerboard top with inlaid mother-of-pearl, ripple edge with red painted dec, tilt-top turned wooden center post with papier-mâché base supported by three wooden feet, roughness to edges, crack to base, brass latch missing 150.00

Table, tripod, tilt-top, MOP and parcel gilt dec, Jennins & Bettridge, Victorian, c1850 . . . . 350.00

Tea Caddy, 5-3/4" h, 7 2/3" w, MOP inlay, English 200.00

Tray, floral dec and parcel-gilt, shaped, Victorian, England, c1860 . . . . 350.00

Wig Stand, 13" h, figural, woman's head, white, tan, and brown paint, gesso, age cracks, wear. 625.00

PARIAN WARE

History: Parian ware is a creamy white, translucent porcelain that resembles marble. It originated in England in 1842 and was first called "statuary porcelain." Minton and Copeland have been credited with its development; Wedgwood also made it. In America, parian ware objects were manufactured by Christopher Fenton in Bennington, Vermont.

At first parian ware was used only for figures and figural groups. By the 1850s, it became so popular that a vast range of items was manufactured.

References: Paul Atterbury, ed., *The Parian Phenomenon*, Shepton Beauchamp, 1989; Susan and Al Bagdade, *Warman's English & Continental Pottery & Porcelain*, 3rd Edition, Krause Publications, 1998; G. A. Godden, *Victorian Porcelain*, Herbert Jenkins, 1961; Kathy Hughes, *Collector's Guide to Nineteenth-Century Jugs* (1985, Routledge & Kegan Paul), Vol. II (1991, Taylor Publishing).

Museum: Victoria & Albert Museum, London, England.

Bust
16-1/2" h, young Bacchante maiden, after Owen Hale, dated 1881, imp Copeland marks 1,035.00
17-1/2" d, John Milton, folding verse inscribed scroll, English, c1880 . . . . 300.00
Compote, 10-1/4" h, low relief grapes and vines, English 275.00

Doll, 15" h, child, untinted bisque shoulder head, painted blue eyes with red accent lines, single strike brows, closed mouth, molded and painted blond hair with blue ribbon, kid body, bisque lower arms, new blue low-waisted dress, lace trim, underclothing, socks, and shoes, unmarked, faint rub on back of hair, replaced arms, kid repairs on both legs 525.00

Ewer, raised scrollwork, glazed green and pink roping, Copeland, c1853, one handle damaged, price for pr 415.00

Figure
13-1/2" h, nude Diana, wrist shackles, cylindrical plinth 300.00
14-1/4" h, nude female seated on panther, rect base, imp "Minton," 1857 year mark. 700.00
15-1/4" h, The Lion in Love, simply draped female pulling thorn from lion's paw, glazed base, imp "Minton," cipher mark. 1,500.00
16-3/4" h, classic beauty drawing water from well, cream ground, gold and antique green highlights, raised pink triangle seal mark with acorn logo "P.P.M," stamped "1257" 520.00
19-1/8" h, The Young Shrimper, holding shell, dragging net, imp Copeland marks, c1880 . . . . 550.00

Pitcher, 9" h, blue and white ear of corn dec, Bennington, crow's foot in base. 120.00

Posy Holder, 9-1/2" h, boy holding wheat sheaf, unmarked, attributed to Bennington 175.00

PATE-DE-VERRE

History: The term "pate-de-verre" can be translated simply as "glass paste." It is manufactured by grinding lead glass into a powder or crystal form, making it into a paste by adding a 2% or 3% solution of sodium silicate, molding, firing, and carving. The Egyptians discovered the process as early as 1500 b.c.

In the late 19th century, the process was rediscovered by a group of French glassmakers. Almaric Walter, Henri Cros, Georges Despret, and the Daum brothers were leading manufacturers.

Contemporary sculptors are creating a second renaissance, led by the technical research of Jacques Daum.

Ashtray, 6-1/4" l, 3-1/2" w, center medallion with Egyptian head, molded in reds and purples, small flower buds around edge, raised lattice work on bottom 1,650.00

Atomizer, 5-3/4" h, red berries, green leaves, molded signature "H. Berge". 1,200.00

Pitcher, twig handle, raised foliage, grapes, Copeland, 4-1/2" h, $80.

Bowl, pedestal, purple grape relief inside and out, sgd "Gargy-Rousseau," 4" d, 1-5/8" h, $900.

Bowl

4-3/4" h, oviform, turquoise blue ground, molded green band of stylized flowers, molded "A. Walter Nancy" 1,600.00

9-3/4" d, 4" h, octagonal coupe, solid foot, dec by swags of stylized leafy purple and black branches, mottled colorless near transparent background, ext. molded "G. Argy Rousseau" 6,500.00

Dish, large, butterfly, script sgd "Daum Nancy, France" . 200.00

Inkwell, double, 6-1/2" l, 3" h, black and brown beetle, brilliant orange and yellow glass, central beetle motif, orig conforming covers, sgd "Walter" 4,500.00

Jewelry

Earrings, pr, 2-3/4" l, teardrop for, molded violet and rose shaded tulip blossom, suspended from rose colored swirl molded circle 2,200.00

Pendant, 2-1/8" x 2-1/4", pierced glass, butterfly, blue, green, red-orange wings, colorless and gray ground, inscribed "GAR" in design (G. Argy-Rousseau) 2,415.00

Paperweight, 3-1/2" l, 1" h, swan, brown, green opalescent ground, sgd "A. Walter," some wear 150.00

Plaque, 6-1/2" d, 7-1/4" h, amber ground, two stalking black striped orange tigers emerging from stylized panels ribbed as tall grasses, molded "G. Argy-Rousseau," No. 28.11, designed as lighting plate on electrolier stand 5,750.00

Sculpture

8" h, Faune, man/goat, gray-green glass, inscribed "66/250" on base, mkd "Daum/J. P. Demarchi" on neck and plinth, 1980s 690.00

10-3/4" h, seated cat, gray-green glass, inscribed "53/250" on base, mkd in mold, c1980 . . . . 690.00

Tray, 7" l, 5" w, angular mottled orange-yellow oval, full bodied black and brown center scarab, imp "A. Walter/Nancy" 2,750.00

Vase

5-1/8" h, striated aubergine purple and colorless cone shaped body, integrated disk foot molded with four repeating spiked devices, imp "Decorchemont" in horseshoe stamp, numbered C199 on base 3,600.00

5-1/4" h, 4-7/8" l, golden amber and brown ground, central conical bud vase in oval plinth base, molded and stylized birds of prey at each side, mkd "G. Argy-Rousseau" 4,025.00

9" h, molded goblet form, yellow amber ground, shaded green to orange at base, highly detailed and realistic green-black lizard wrapped around stem, imp "A. Walter" and "H. Berge SC," orig thin rim area 6,325.00

Veilleuse, night light, 6-1/2" h, domed form, deep aqua blue glass, molded trailing vines, yellow flower, mounted on circular wrought-iron stand, removable domed cap molded "A. Walter Nancy". 6,000.00

Vide Pouche, irregular shaped dish

6-1/4" l, welled crescent shape, mottled tangerine shading to pale lemon, molded along with side with two spotted langoustines, one teal, the other burgundy, molded "A. Walter Nancy" and "Berge S.C." 4,000.00

6-3/4" l, 3-3/4" h, shallow oval, mottled orange and black, surmounted by green spotted black lizard molded in full relief, molded "A. Walter Nancy Berge" 4,500.00

PATE-SUR-PATE

History: Pate-sur-pate, paste-on-paste, is a 19th-century porcelain-decorating method featuring relief designs achieved by painting layers of thin pottery paste one on top of the other.

About 1880, Marc Solon and other Sevres artists, inspired by a Chinese celadon vase in the Ceramic Museum at Sevres, experimented with this process. Solon emigrated to England at the outbreak of the Franco-Prussian War and worked at Minton, where he perfected pate-sur-pate.

References: Paul Atterbury and Maureen Batkin, *Dictionary of Minton,* Antique Collectors Club, Ltd., 1996; Susan and Al Bagdade, *Warman's English & Continental Pottery & Porcelain*, 3rd Edition, Krause Publications, 1998; Bernard Bumpers, *Pate-Sur-Pate,* Barrie & Jenkins, 1992; G. .A. Godden, *Victorian Porcelains,* Herbert Jenkins, 1961.

Museums: National Collection of Fine Arts, Smithsonian Institution, Washington, DC; Victoria & Albert Museum, London, England.

Book Stand, 16" l, walnut veneer, pate-sur-pate end panels with cupids playing badminton, Bettemann's patent, sold by Shreve Crump and Low 500.00

Box, cov, 7-3/4" d, circular, white relief of figure on chariot, blue ground, cobalt blue rim band, gilt trim lines, illegible printed marks, Continental, late 19th/early 20th C 175.00

Centerpiece, 11" l, cartouches with putti, ivory and gilt reserves, brown ground, imp and printed Minton factory m arks, dec by H Holls, c1872 . . . . .1,500.00

Lamp Base

11-1/2" h vase, dark brown ground, white classical relief of female with cherub, gilt trim, Lawrence Birks, England, late 19th C 1,495.00

15-3/4" h vase, dark brown ground, white classical relief, sgd "F Peyrat," France, c1875 . . . . .1,100.00

Plaque

6" d, circular, Helios and his horses, white figures, celadon ground, inscribed monogram and "Limoges" 120.00

10-3/4" d, oval, blue ground, white dec of child reaching for bunch of grapes, dec and sgd "Taxile Doat, France, 1874" 1,495.00

19-1/4" d, brown and green Art Nouveau style, floral dec ground, five blue ground rect-form pate-sur-pate panels with classical genre scenes, sgd "Taxile Doat, 1901," marked "Sevres" 29,900.00

Portrait Vase, 9-1/2" h, Art Nouveau style, central mauve ground, portrait on teal blue ground, cherub in relief, gilt banded borders and foliate relief, France, late 19th C 460.00

Tray, 5 x 3", elegant lady, cobalt blue ground, Limoges Barbatine 75.00

Plaque, sowing scene, dark green ground, 4-3/8" h, 7-1/2" l, $325.

Vase, 13" h, porcelain, gilt banded and foliate borders, central relief of birds within landscape, France, 19th C, pr . . 920.00

PATTERN GLASS

History: Pattern glass is clear or colored glass pressed into one of hundreds of patterns. Deming Jarves of the Boston and Sandwich Glass Co. invented one of the first successful pressing machines in 1828. By the 1860s, glass-pressing machinery had been improved, and mass production of good-quality matched tableware sets began. The idea of a matched glassware table service (including goblets, tumblers, creamers, sugars, compotes, cruets, etc.) quickly caught on in America. Many pattern glass table services had numerous accessory pieces such as banana stands, molasses cans, and water bottles.

Early pattern glass (flint) was made with a lead formula, giving many items a ringing sound when tapped. Lead became too valuable to be used in glass manufacturing during the Civil War; and in 1864 Hobbs, Brockunier & Co., West Virginia, developed a soda lime (non-flint) formula. Pattern glass also was produced in transparent colors, milk glass, opalescent glass, slag glass, and custard glass.

The hundreds of companies that produced pattern glass experienced periods of development, expansions, personnel problems, material and supply demands, fires, and mergers. In 1899 the National Glass Co. was formed as a combine of 19 glass companies in Pennsylvania, Ohio, Indiana, West Virginia, and Maryland. U.S. Glass, another consortium, was founded in 1891. These combines resulted from attempts to save small companies by pooling talents, resources, and patterns. Because of this pooling, the same pattern often can be attributed to several companies.

Sometimes various companies produced the same patterns at different times and used different names to reflect current fashion trends. U.S. Glass created the States series by using state names for various patterns, several of which were new issues while others were former patterns renamed.

References: Gary Baker et al., *Wheeling Glass 1829-1939*, Oglebay Institute, 1994, distributed by Antique Publications; George and Linda Breeze, *Mysteries of the Moon & Star*, published by authors, 1995; William Heacock, *Encyclopedia of Victorian Colored Pattern Glass: Book 1: Toothpick Holders from A to Z*, 2nd ed. (1976, 1992 value update) *Book 5: U. S. Glass from A to Z* (1980), *Book 7: Ruby Stained Glass from A To Z* (1986), *Book 8: More Ruby Stained Glass* (1987), Antique Publications; ——, *Old Pattern Glass*, Antique Publications, 1981; ——, *1000 Toothpick Holders*, Antique Publications, 1977; ——, *Rare and Unlisted Toothpick Holders*, Antique Publications, 1984; Kyle Husfloen, *Collector's Guide to American Pressed Glass*, Wallace-Homestead, 1992; Bill Jenks and Jerry Luna, *Early American Pattern Glass— 1850 to 1910*, Wallace-Homestead, 1990; Bill Jenks, Jerry Luna, and Darryl Reilly, *Identifying Pattern Glass Reproductions*, Wallace-Homestead, 1993; William J. Jenks and Darryl Reilly, *American Price Guide to Unitt's Canadian & American Goblets Volumes I & II*, Author! Author! Books (P.O. Box 1964, Kingston, PA 18704), 1996.

Minnie Watson Kamm, *Pattern Glass Pitchers*, Books 1 through 8, published by author, 1970, 4th printing; Ruth Webb Lee, *Early American Pressed Glass*, 36th ed., Lee Publications, 1966; ——, *Victorian Glass*, 13th ed., Lee Publications, 1944; Bessie M. Lindsey, *American Historical Glass*, Charles E. Tuttle, 1967; Robert Irwin Lucas, *Tarentum Pattern Glass*, privately printed, 1981; Mollie H. McCain, *Collector's Encyclopedia of Pattern Glass*, Collector Books, 1982, 1994 value update; George P. and Helen McKearin, *American Glass*, Crown Publishers, 1941; James Measell, *Greentown Glass*, Grand Rapids Public Museum Association, 1979, 1992-93 value update, distributed by Antique Publications; Alice Hulett Metz, *Early American Pattern Glass*, published by author, 1958; ——, *Much More Early American Pattern Glass*, published by author, 1965; S. T. Millard, *Goblets I* (1938), *Goblets II* (1940), privately printed, reprinted Wallace-Homestead, 1975; John B. Mordock and Walter L. Adams, *Pattern Glass* Mugs, Antique Publications, 1995.

Arthur G. Peterson, *Glass Salt Shakers*, Wallace-Homestead, 1970; Ellen T. Schroy, *Warman's Pattern Glass*, Wallace-Homestead, 1993; Jane Shadel Spillman, *American and European Pressed Glass in the Corning Museum of Glass*, Corning Museum of Glass, 1981; ——, *Knopf Collectors Guides to American Antiques, Glass*, Vol. 1 (1982), Vol. 2 (1983), Alfred A. Knopf; Doris and Peter Unitt, *American and Canadian Goblets*, Clock House, 1970, reprinted by The Love of Glass Publishing (Box 629, Arthur, Ontario, Canada NOG 1AO), 1996; ——, *Treasury of Canadian Glass*, 2nd ed., Clock House, 1969; Peter Unitt and Anne Worrall, *Canadian Handbook, Pressed Glass Tableware*, Clock House Productions, 1983; Kenneth Wilson, *American Glass 1760-1930*, 2 Vols., Hudson Hills Press and The Toledo Museum of Art, 1994.

SPECIAL AUCTIONS

Bailey's Antiques
102 E. Main St.
Homer, MI 49245
(517) 568-4014

Mike Clum
P.O. Box 2
Rushville, OH 43150
(614) 536-9220

Green Valley Auctions, Inc.
Rt. 2, Box 434
Mt. Crawford, VA 22841
(540) 434-4260

REPRODUCTION ALERT

Pattern glass has been widely reproduced.

Museums: Corning Museum of Glass, Corning, NY; Jones Museum of Glass and Ceramics, Sebago, ME; National Museum of Man, Ottawa, Ontario, Canada; Sandwich Glass Museum, Sandwich, MA; Schminck Memorial Museum, Lakeview, OR.

Additional Listings: Bread Plates; Children's Toy Dishes; Cruets; Custard Glass; Milk Glass; Sugar Shakers; Toothpicks; and specific companies.

Advisors: John and Alice Ahlfeld.

Periodical: *Glass Collector's Digest*, The Glass Press, P.O. Box 553, Marietta, OH 45750.

Collectors' Clubs: Early American Pattern Glass Society, P.O. Box 266, Colesburg, IA 52035; The National Early American Glass Club, P.O. Box 8489, Silver Spring, MD 20907.

Notes: Research in pattern glass is continuing. As always, we try to use correct pattern names, histories, and forms. Reflecting the most current thinking, the listing by pattern places colored, opalescent, and clear items together, avoiding duplication.

Items in the listing marked with an * are those for which reproductions are known to exist. Care should be exercised when purchasing such pieces.

Abbreviations:

ah	applied handle
GUTDODB	Give Us This Day Our Daily Bread
hs	high standard
ind	individual
ls	low standard
os	original stopper

ACTRESS

Made by Adams & Company, Pittsburgh, PA, c1880. All clear 20% less. Imperial Glass Co. has reproduced some items, including an amethyst pickle dish, in clear and color.

Clear and Frosted

Bowl
- 6," ftd 45.00
- 7," ftd 50.00
- 8," Miss Neilson 85.00
- 9-1/2," ftd 85.00

Bread Plate
- 7" x 12," HMS Pinafore 90.00
- 9" x 13," Miss Neilson 72.00

Butter, cov 90.00
Cake Stand, 10" 145.00
Candlesticks, pr 250.00
Celery Vase
- Actress Head 130.00
- HMS Pinafore, pedestal 145.00

Cheese Dish, cov, The Lone Fisherman on cov, Two Dromios on base 250.00

Compote
- Cov, hs, 6" d 250.00
- Cov, hs, 12" d 300.00
- Open, hs, 10" d 90.00
- Open, hs, 12" d 120.00
- Open, ls, 5" d 45.00

Clear and Frosted

Creamer 75.00
Dresser Tray 60.00
Goblet, Kate Claxton (two portraits) 85.00
Marmalade Jar, cov 125.00
Mug, HMS Pinafore 50.00
*Pickle Dish, Love's Request is Pickles 45.00
Pickle Relish, different actresses
- 4-1/2" x 7" 35.00
- 5" x 8" 35.00
- 5-1/2" x 9" 35.00

Pitcher
- Milk, 6-1/2," HMS Pinafore 295.00
- Water, 9," Romeo & Juliet 250.00

Salt, master 70.00
Salt Shaker, orig pewter top 42.50
Sauce
- Flat 15.00
- Footed 20.00

Spooner 60.00
Sugar, cov 100.00

ALMOND THUMBPRINT (Pointed Thumbprint, Finger Print)

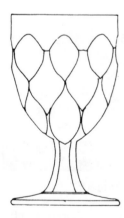

An early flint glass pattern with variants in flint and non-flint. Pattern has been attributed to Bryce, Bakewell, and U.S. Glass Co. Sometimes found in milk glass.

	Flint	Non-Flint		Flint	Non-Flint
Bowl, 4-1/2" d, ftd	—	20.00	Decanter	70.00	—
Butter, cov	80.00	40.00	Eggcup	45.00	25.00
Celery Vase	50.00	25.00	Goblet	45.00	12.00
Champagne	60.00	35.00	Punch Bowl	—	75.00
Compote			Salt		
Cov, hs, 4-3/4," jelly	70.00	40.00	Flat, large	25.00	15.00
Cov, hs, 10"	110.00	45.00	Ftd, cov	45.00	25.00
Cov, ls, 4-3/4"	75.00	30.00	Ftd, open	25.00	10.00
Cov, ls, 7"	70.00	25.00	Spooner	20.00	15.00
Open, hs, 10-1/2"	70.00	—	Sugar, cov	65.00	40.00
Cordial	40.00	30.00	Sweetmeat Jar, cov	75.00	50.00
Creamer	60.00	40.00	Tumbler	60.00	20.00
Cruet, ftd, os	55.00	—	Wine	28.00	12.00

APOLLO (Canadian Horseshoe, Shield Band)

Non-flint first made by Adams & Co., Pittsburgh, PA, c1890, and later by U.S. Glass Co. Frosted increases price 20%. Also found in ruby stained and engraved. Lamp found also in blue and yellow, valued at $250.00

	Clear		Clear		Clear
Bowl		Celery Vase	35.00	Plate, 9-1/2," sq	25.00
4"	10.00	Compote		Salt	20.00
5"	10.00	Cov, hs	65.00	Salt Shaker	25.00
6"	12.00	Open, hs	35.00	Sauce	
7"	15.00	Open, ls, 7"	25.00	Flat	10.00
8"	20.00	Creamer	35.00	Ftd, 5"	12.00
Butter, cov	40.00	Cruet	60.00	Spooner	30.00
Cake Stand		Eggcup	30.00	Sugar, cov	45.00
8"	35.00	Goblet	35.00	Syrup	110.00
9"	40.00	Lamp, 10"	125.00	Tray, water	45.00
10"	50.00	Pickle Dish	15.00	Tumbler	30.00
Celery Tray, rect	20.00	Pitcher, water	65.00	Wine	35.00

ARCHED GRAPE

Non-flint made by Boston and Sandwich Glass Co., Sandwich, MA, c1880.

	Non-flint		Non-flint		Non-flint
Butter, cov	45.00	Creamer	40.00	Spooner	30.00
Celery vase	35.00	Goblet	25.00	Sugar, cov	45.00
Champagne	35.00	Pitcher, water, ah	60.00	Wine	25.00
Compote, cov, hs	50.00	Sauce, flat	8.00		

ARGUS

Flint thumbprint-type pattern made by Bakewell, Pears and Co., Pittsburgh, PA, in the early 1860s. Copiously reproduced, some by Fostoria Glass Co. with raised "H.F.M." trademark for henry Ford Museum, Dearborn, MI. Reproduction colors include clear, red, green and cobalt blue.

	Clear		Clear		Clear
Ale Glass	75.00	*Creamer, ah	115.00	Salt, master, open	30.00
Bitters Bottle	60.00	Decanter, qt	95.00	*Spooner	45.00
Bowl, 5-1/2"	30.00	Eggcup	30.00	*Sugar, cov	65.00
*Butter, cov	85.00	*Goblet	60.00	*Tumbler, bar	65.00
Celery vase	90.00	Lamp, ftd	100.00	Whiskey, ah	75.00
Champagne	65.00	Mug, ah	65.00	Wine	35.00
Compote, open 8," scalloped	50.00	Pitcher, water, ah	400.00		

ASHBURTON

A popular pattern produced by Boston and Sandwich Glass Co. and by McKee & Bros. Glass Co. from the 1850s to the late 1870s with many variations. Originally made in flint by New England Glass Co. and others and later in non-flint. Prices are for flint. Non-flint values 65% less. Also reported are an amber-handled whiskey mug, flint canary celery vase ($750), and a scarce emerald green wineglass ($200). Some items known in fiery opalescent.

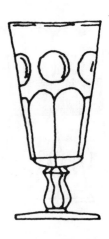

	Clear		Clear		Clear
Ale Glass, 5"	90.00	*Creamer, ah	210.00	Plate, 6-5/8"	75.00
Bar Bottle		Decanter, qt, cut		Sauce	10.00
Pint	55.00	and pressed, os	250.00	*Sugar, cov	90.00
Quart	75.00	Eggcup		Toddy Jar, cov	375.00
Bitters Bottle	55.00	Double	80.00	*Tumbler	
*Bowl, 6-1/2"	75.00	Single	30.00	Bar	75.00
Carafe	175.00	Flip Glass, handled	140.00	Water	75.00
Celery vase, scalloped top	100.00	*Goblet	50.00	Whiskey	60.00
Champagne, cut	85.00	Honey Dish	15.00	Water Bottle, tumble up	95.00
*Claret, 5-1/4"	50.00	*Jug, qt	90.00	Whiskey, ah	125.00
*Compote, open, ls, 7-1/2"	65.00	Lamp	75.00	*Wine	
		*Lemonade Glass	55.00	Cut	65.00
Cordial, 4-1/4" h	70.00	Mug, 7"	100.00	Pressed	40.00
		*Pitcher, water	450.00		

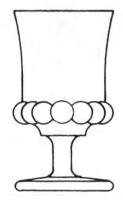

ATLAS (Bullet, Cannon Ball, Crystal Ball)

Non-flint, occasionally ruby stained and etched, made by Adams & Co.; U.S. Glass Co. in 1891; and Bryce Bros., Mt. Pleasant, PA, in 1889.

	Clear	Ruby Stained		Clear	Ruby Stained
Bowl, 9"	20.00	—	Molasses Can	65.00	—
Butter, cov, regular	45.00	75.00	Pitcher, water	65.00	—
Cake Stand			Salt		
8"	35.00	—	Master	20.00	—
9"	40.00	95.00	Individual	15.00	—
Celery Vase	28.00	—	Salt & Pepper, pr	20.00	—
Champagne, 5-1/2" h	25.00	55.00	Sauce		
Compote			Flat	10.00	—
Cov, hs, 8"	65.00	—	Footed	15.00	25.00
Cov, hs, 5," jelly	50.00	80.00	Spooner	30.00	45.00
Open, ls, 7"	40.00	—	Sugar, cov	40.00	65.00
Cordial	35.00	—	Syrup	65.00	—
Creamer			Toothpick	20.00	50.00
Table, ah	30.00	55.00	Tray, water	75.00	—
Tankard	25.00	—	Tumbler	28.00	—
Goblet	35.00	65.00	Whiskey	20.00	45.00
Marmalade Jar	45.00	—	Wine	25.00	—

AUSTRIAN (Finecut Medallion)

Made by Indiana Tumbler and Goblet Co., Greentown, IN, 1897. Experimental pieces were made in cobalt blue, Nile green, and opaque colors. Some pieces were made in Chocolate glass.

	Amber	Canary	Clear	Emerald Green
Bowl				
8," round	—	150.00	50.00	—
8-1/4," rect	—	150.00	50.00	—
Butter, cov	185.00	300.00	90.00	—
Children's table set	—	550.00	325.00	—
Compote, open, ls	—	150.00	75.00	—
Cordial	145.00	150.00	50.00	150.00
Creamer	120.00	125.00	40.00	120.00
Goblet	—	150.00	40.00	—
Mug, child's	—	—	45.00	—
Nappy, cov	—	135.00	55.00	—
Pitcher, water	—	350.00	100.00	—
Plate, 10"	—	—	40.00	—
Punch Cup	150.00	150.00	18.00	125.00
Rose Bowl	—	150.00	50.00	—
Sauce, 4-5/8" d	—	50.00	20.00	—
Spooner	—	100.00	40.00	—
Sugar, cov	—	175.00	45.00	—
Tumbler	175.00	85.00	25.00	—
Wine	175.00	150.00	30.00	150.00

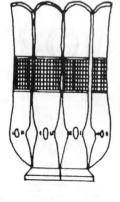

BANDED PORTLAND (Virginia #1, Maiden's Blush)

States pattern, originally named Virginia, by Portland Glass Co., Portland, ME. Painted and fired green, yellow, blue, and possibly pink; ruby stained, and rose-flashed (which Lee notes is Maiden's Blush, referring to the color rather than the pattern, as Metz lists it). Double-flashed refers to color above and below the band, single-flashed refers to color above or below the band only.

	Clear	Color-Flashed	Maiden's Blush Pink
Bowl			
4" d, open	10.00	—	20.00
6" d, cov	40.00	—	55.00
7-1/2" d, shallow	30.00	—	55.00
8"d, cov	50.00	—	75.00
Butter, cov	50.00	195.00	85.00

	Clear	Color-Flashed	Maiden's Blush Pink
Cake Stand	55.00	—	90.00
Candlesticks, pr.	80.00	—	125.00
Carafe	80.00	—	90.00
Celery Tray	25.00	—	40.00
Celery Vase	35.00	—	45.00
Cologne Bottle	50.00	125.00	85.00
Compote			
Cov, hs, 7"	75.00	—	125.00
Cov, hs, 8"	85.00	—	150.00
Cov, jelly, 6"	40.00	95.00	90.00
Creamer			
Individual, oval	25.00	55.00	40.00
Regular, 6 oz.	35.00	85.00	50.00
Cruet, os	60.00	175.00	300.00
Decanter, handled	50.00	—	100.00
Dresser Tray	50.00	—	65.00
Goblet	40.00	75.00	95.00
Lamp			
Flat	45.00	—	—
Tall	50.00	—	—
Nappy, sq	15.00	55.00	65.00
Olive	18.00	25.00	35.00
Pin Tray	16.00	—	25.00
Pitcher, tankard	75.00	115.00	240.00
Pomade Jar, cov	35.00	75.00	95.00
Punch Bowl, hs	110.00	—	300.00
Punch Cup	20.00	—	30.00
Relish			
6-1/2"	25.00	35.00	25.00
8-1/4"	20.00	40.00	45.00
Ring Holder	75.00	—	125.00
Salt & Pepper, pr.	45.00	95.00	75.00
Sardine Box	55.00	—	90.00
Sauce, round, flat, 4 or 4-1/2"	10.00	—	25.00
Spooner	28.00	—	45.00
Sugar, cov	48.00	95.00	75.00
Sugar Shaker, orig top	45.00	—	85.00
Syrup	50.00	—	135.00
Toothpick	40.00	55.00	45.00
Tumbler	25.00	45.00	45.00
Vase			
6"	20.00	—	50.00
9"	35.00	—	65.00
Wine	35.00	—	85.00

BASKETWEAVE

Non-flint, c1880. Some covered pieces have a stippled cat's-head finial.

	Amber or Canary	Apple Green	Blue	Clear	Vaseline
Bowl	20.00	—	25.00	15.00	—
Bread Plate, 11"	35.00	—	35.00	10.00	—
Butter, cov	35.00	60.00	40.00	30.00	40.00
Compote, cov, 7"	—	—	—	40.00	—
Cordial	25.00	40.00	28.00	20.00	30.00
Creamer	30.00	50.00	35.00	28.00	36.00
Cup and Saucer	35.00	60.00	35.00	30.00	38.00
Dish, oval	12.00	20.00	15.00	10.00	16.00
Eggcup	20.00	30.00	25.00	15.00	25.00
*Goblet	28.00	50.00	35.00	20.00	35.00
Mug	25.00	40.00	25.00	15.00	30.00
Pickle	20.00	30.00	20.00	15.00	25.00
Pitcher					
Milk	95.00	95.00	95.00	95.00	95.00
*Water	75.00	75.00	75.00	45.00	80.00

	Amber or Canary	Apple Green	Blue	Clear	Vaseline
Plate, 11," handled............	25.00	35.00	25.00	20.00	30.00
Sauce......................	10.00	10.00	12.00	8.00	12.00
Spooner....................	30.00	36.00	30.00	20.00	30.00
Sugar, cov	35.00	60.00	35.00	30.00	40.00
Syrup	50.00	75.00	50.00	45.00	55.00
*Tray, water, scenic center	45.00	50.00	60.00	35.00	55.00
Tumbler, ftd	18.00	30.00	20.00	15.00	20.00
Waste Bowl	20.00	35.00	25.00	18.00	25.00
Wine......................	30.00	50.00	30.00	20.00	30.00

BEADED GRAPE (Beaded Grape and Vine, California, Grape and Vine)

Non-flint made by U.S. Glass Co., Pittsburgh, PA, c1890. Also attributed to Burlington Glass Works, Hamilton, Ontario, and Sydenham Glass Co., Wallaceburg, Ontario, Canada, c1910. Made in clear and emerald green, sometimes with gilt trim. Reproduced in clear, milk glass, and several colors by many, including Westmoreland Glass Co.

	Clear	Emerald Green		Clear	Emerald Green
Bowl			*Goblet..............	35.00	50.00
5-1/2," sq.........	17.50	20.00	Olive, handle	20.00	35.00
7-1/2," sq.........	25.00	35.00	Pickle...............	20.00	30.00
8," round	28.00	35.00	Pitcher		
Bread Plate	25.00	45.00	Milk..............	75.00	90.00
Butter, cov	65.00	85.00	Water	85.00	120.00
Cake Stand, 9".......	65.00	85.00	*Plate, 8-1/4," sq	28.00	40.00
Celery Tray	30.00	45.00	Salt & Pepper	45.00	65.00
Celery Vase	40.00	60.00	Sauce, 4"...........	15.00	20.00
*Compote			Spooner.............	35.00	45.00
Cov, hs, 7"........	75.00	85.00	Sugar, cov	45.00	55.00
Cov, hs, 9"........	100.00	110.00	Toothpick...........	40.00	65.00
Open, hs, 5," sq	55.00	75.00	*Tumbler	25.00	40.00
Open, hs, 8"	55.00	70.00	Vase, 6" h	25.00	40.00
Creamer............	40.00	50.00	*Wine..............	35.00	65.00
Cruet, os	65.00	125.00			

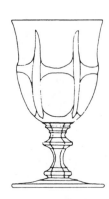

BIGLER

Flint made by Boston and Sandwich Glass Co., Sandwich, MA, and by other early factories. A scarce pattern in which goblets are most common and vary in height, shape and flare. Rare in color. The goblet has been reproduced as a commemorative item for Biglerville, PA.

	Clear		Clear		Clear
Ale Glass	65.00	Cordial	65.00	Lamp, whale oil,	
Bar Bottle, qt	95.00	Creamer.............	75.00	monument base	155.00
Bowl, 10" d..........	40.00	Cup Plate	30.00	Mug, ah..............	60.00
Butter, cov	125.00	Eggcup, double	50.00	Plate, 6" d	30.00
Celery Vase	100.00	*Goblet		Salt, master...........	20.00
Champagne	95.00	Regular	48.00	Tumbler, water	65.00
Compote, open, 7" d ...	40.00	Short Stem........	50.00	Whiskey, handled	100.00
				Wine	65.00

BIRD and STRAWBERRY (Bluebird, Flying Bird and Strawberry, Strawberry and Bird)

Non-flint, c1914. Made by Indiana Glass Co., Dunkirk, IN. Pieces occasionally highlighted by blue birds, pink strawberries, and green leaves, plus the addition of gliding.

	Clear	Colors		Clear	Colors
Bowl			Compote		
5"................	25.00	45.00	*Cov, hs	125.00	200.00
9-1/2," ftd.........	50.00	85.00	Open, ls, ruffled	65.00	125.00
10-1/2"..........	55.00	95.00	Jelly, cov, hs	150.00	225.00
Butter, cov	100.00	175.00	Creamer.............	55.00	135.00
Cake Stand	65.00	125.00	Cup	25.00	35.00
*Celery Vase	45.00	85.00	Goblet	600.00	1,000.00

	Clear	Colors		Clear	Colors
Nappy	40.00	65.00	Relish	20.00	45.00
Pitcher, water	235.00	350.00	Spooner	50.00	120.00
Plate, 12"	125.00	175.00	Sugar, cov	65.00	125.00
Punch Cup	25.00	35.00	Tumbler	45.00	75.00
			Wine	65.00	100.00

BLEEDING HEART

Non-flint originally made by King Son & Co., Pittsburgh, PA, c1875, and by U.S. Glass Co. c1898. Also found in milk glass. Goblets are found in six variations. Note: A goblet with a tin lid, containing a condiment (mustard, jelly, or baking powder) was made. It is of inferior quality compared to the original goblet.

	Clear		Clear		Clear
Bowl		Cov, ls, 7-1/2"	60.00	Pitcher, water, ah	150.00
7-1/4," oval	30.00	Cov, ls, 8"	75.00	Plate	75.00
8"	35.00	Open, ls, 8-1/2"	30.00	Platter, oval	65.00
9-1/4," oval, cov	65.00	Creamer		Relish, oval,	
Butter, cov	75.00	Applied Handle	60.00	5-1/2" x 3-5/8"	35.00
Cake Stand		Molded Handle	30.00	Salt, master, ftd	60.00
9"	75.00	Dish, cov, 7"	55.00	Salt, oval, flat	20.00
10"	90.00	Eggcup	45.00	Sauce, flat	15.00
11"	100.00	Egg Rack, 3 eggs	350.00	Spooner	25.00
Compote		Goblet, knob stem	35.00	Sugar, cov	60.00
Cov, hs, 8"	75.00	Honey Dish	15.00	Tumbler, ftd	80.00
Cov, hs, 9"	95.00	Mug, 3-1/4"	40.00	Wine	150.00
Cov, ls, 7"	60.00	Pickle, 8-3/4" l, 5" w	30.00		

BLOCK and FAN (Red Block and Fan, Romeo)

Non-flint made by Richard and Hartley Glass Co., Tarentum, PA, in the late 1880s. Continued by U.S. Glass Co. after 1891.

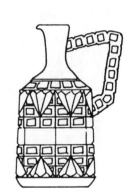

	Clear	Ruby Stained		Clear	Ruby Stained
Biscuit Jar, cov	65.00	150.00	Orange Bowl	50.00	—
Bowl, 4," flat	15.00	—	Pickle Dish	20.00	—
Butter, cov	50.00	85.00	Pitcher		
Cake Stand			Milk	35.00	—
9"	35.00	—	Water	48.00	125.00
10"	42.00	—	Plate		
Carafe	50.00	95.00	6"	15.00	—
Celery Tray	30.00	—	10"	18.00	—
Celery Vase	35.00	75.00	Relish, rect	25.00	—
Compote, open, hs, 8"	40.00	165.00	Rose Bowl	25.00	—
Condiment Set, salt, pepper			Salt & Pepper	30.00	—
and cruet on tray	75.00	—	Sauce		
Creamer			Flat, 5"	8.00	—
Individual	—	35.00	Ftd, 3-3/4"	12.00	25.00
Large	30.00	100.00	Spooner	25.00	—
Regular	25.00	45.00	Sugar, cov	50.00	—
Small	35.00	75.00	Sugar Shaker	40.00	—
Cruet, os	35.00	—	Syrup	75.00	95.00
Dish, large, rect	25.00	—	Tray, ice cream, rect	75.00	—
Finger Bowl	55.00	—	Tumbler	30.00	40.00
Goblet	48.00	120.00	Waste Bowl	30.00	—
Ice Tub	45.00	50.00	Wine	45.00	80.00

BOW TIE (American Bow Tie)

Non-flint made by Thompson Glass Co., Uniontown, PA, c1889.

	Clear		Clear		Clear
Bowl		Cake Stand, large, 9" d	60.00	ls, 8"	55.00
8"	35.00	Compote, open		Creamer	45.00
10-1/4" d, 5" h	65.00	hs, 5-1/2"	60.00	Goblet	60.00
Butter, cov	65.00	hs, 9-1/4"	65.00	Honey, cov	55.00
Butter Pat	25.00	ls, 6-1/2"	45.00	Marmalade Jar	75.00

	Clear
Orange Bowl, ftd, hs, 10"	110.00
Pitcher	
Milk	85.00
Water	75.00
Punch Bowl	100.00

	Clear
Relish, rect	25.00
Salt	
Individual	20.00
Master	45.00
Salt Shaker	40.00
Sauce, flat	15.00

	Clear
Spooner	35.00
Sugar	
Cov.	55.00
Open	40.00
Tumbler	45.00

BRIDAL ROSETTE (Checkerboard)

Made by Westmoreland Glass Co. in the early 1900s. Add 150% for ruby-stained values. Reproduced since the 1950s in milk glass and, in recent years, with pink satin. The Cambridge Ribbon pattern, usually marked "Nearcut," is similar.

	Clear
Bowl, 9," shallow	20.00
Butter, cov	40.00
Celery Tray	20.00
Celery vase	30.00
Compote, open, ls, 8"	25.00
Creamer	25.00
Cruet, os	40.00
Cup	8.00
Goblet	28.00

	Clear
Honey Dish, cov, sq, pedestal	45.00
Pitcher	
Milk	40.00
Water	35.00
Plate	
7"	15.00
10"	20.00
Punch Cup	5.00

	Clear
Salt & Pepper	40.00
Sauce, flat	5.00
Spooner	20.00
Sugar, cov.	35.00
Tumbler	
Iced tea	25.00
Water	20.00
Wine	15.00

BUCKLE (Early Buckle)

Flint and non-flint pattern. The original maker is unknown. Shards have been found at the sites of the following glasshouses: Boston and Sandwich Glass Co., Sandwich, MA; Union Glass Co., Somerville, MA; and Burlington Glass Works, Hamilton, Ontario, Canada. Gillinder and Sons, Philadelphia, PA made the non-flint production, in the late 1870s.

	Flint	Non-Flint
Bowl		
8"	60.00	50.00
10"	65.00	50.00
Butter, cov	65.00	60.00
Cake Stand, 9-3/4"	—	30.00
Champagne	60.00	—
Compote		
Cov, hs, 6" d	95.00	40.00
Open, hs, 8-1/2"	40.00	35.00
Open, ls	40.00	35.00
Creamer, ah	120.00	40.00

	Flint	Non-Flint
Eggcup	35.00	25.00
Goblet	40.00	25.00
Pickle	40.00	15.00
Pitcher, water, ah	600.00	85.00
Salt		
flat, oval	30.00	15.00
footed	20.00	18.00
Sauce, flat	10.00	8.00
Spooner	35.00	27.50
Sugar, cov	75.00	55.00
Tumbler	55.00	30.00
Wine	75.00	35.00

BULL'S EYE

Flint made by the New England Glass Co. in the 1850s. Also found in colors and milk glass, which are worth more than double the price of clear.

	Clear
Bitters Bottle	80.00
Butter, cov	150.00
Carafe	45.00
Castor Bottle	35.00
Celery Vase	85.00
Champagne	95.00
Cologne Bottle	85.00
Cordial	75.00
Creamer, ah	125.00
Cruet, os	125.00

	Clear
Decanter, qt, bar lip	120.00
Eggcup	
Cov	165.00
Open	48.00
*Goblet	65.00
Lamp	100.00
Mug, 3-1/2," ah	110.00
Pitcher, water	285.00
Relish, oval	25.00
Salt	
Individual	40.00

	Clear
Master, ftd	100.00
Spill holder	85.00
Spooner	40.00
Sugar, cov	125.00
Sweetmeat, cov	125.00
Tumbler	85.00
Water Bottle, tumble up	125.00
Whiskey	70.00
Wine	50.00

BULL'S EYE and DAISY

Made by U.S. Glass Co. in 1909. Also made with amethyst, blue, green, and pink stain in eyes.

	Clear	Emerald Green	Ruby Stained
Bowl	15.00	20.00	30.00
Butter, cov	25.00	45.00	90.00
Celery Vase	20.00	25.00	40.00
Creamer	25.00	25.00	50.00
Decanter	—	110.00	—
Goblet	25.00	25.00	50.00
Pitcher, water	35.00	40.00	95.00
Salt Shaker	20.00	20.00	35.00
Sauce	7.50	10.00	20.00
Spooner	20.00	25.00	40.00
Sugar	22.00	30.00	45.00
Tumbler	15.00	20.00	35.00
Wine	20.00	25.00	40.00

BULL'S EYE WITH DIAMOND POINT (Owl, Union)

Flint made by New England Glass Co. c1869.

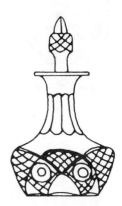

	Clear		Clear		Clear
Butter, cov	250.00	Goblet	135.00	Spooner	125.00
Celery Vase	150.00	Honey Dish, flat	25.00	Sugar, cov	175.00
Champagne	145.00	Lamp, finger, ah	165.00	Syrup	175.00
Cologne Bottle, os	90.00	Pitcher, water,		Tumbler	145.00
Creamer	200.00	10-1/4," tankard	650.00	Tumble-Up	165.00
Cruet, os	225.00	Salt, master, cov	100.00	Whiskey	150.00
Decanter, qt, os	200.00	Sauce	20.00	Wine	135.00
Eggcup	90.00	Spill	75.00		

CABBAGE ROSE

Non-flint made by Central Glass Co., Wheeling, WV, c1870. Reproduced in clear and colors by Mosser Glass Co., Cambridge, OH, during the early 1960s.

	Clear		Clear		Clear
Basket, handled, 12"	125.00	Champagne	50.00	Pitcher	
Bitters Bottle, 6-1/2" h	125.00	Compote		Milk	150.00
Bowl, oval		Cov, hs, 8-1/2"	120.00	Water	125.00
7-1/2"	30.00	Cov, ls, 6"	95.00	Relish, 8-1/2" l, 5" w,	
9-1/2"	40.00	Cov, ls, 7-1/2"	100.00	rose-filled horn of	
Bowl, round		Open, hs, 7-1/2"	75.00	plenty center	35.00
6"	25.00	Open, hs, 9-1/2"	100.00	Salt, master, ftd	25.00
7-1/2," cov	65.00	Creamer, 5-1/2," ah	55.00	*Sauce, 4"	10.00
Butter, cov	60.00	Eggcup	45.00	Spooner	25.00
Cake Stand		*Goblet	40.00	Sugar, cov	55.00
11"	40.00	Mug	60.00	Tumbler	40.00
12-1/2"	50.00	Pickle Dish	35.00	Wine	40.00
Celery Vase	48.00				

CABLE

Flint, c1860. Made by Boston and Sandwich Glass Co. to commemorate the laying of the Atlantic Cable. Also found with amber-stained panels and in opaque colors and other colors (rare).

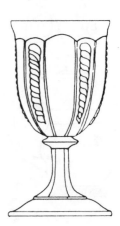

	Clear		Clear		Clear
Bowl		Decanter, qt,		Plate, 6"	75.00
8," ftd	45.00	ground stopper	295.00	Salt, individual, flat	35.00
9"	70.00	Eggcup		Salt, master	
Butter, cov	100.00	Cov	225.00	Cov	95.00
Cake Stand, 9"	100.00	Open	60.00	Ftd	45.00
Celery Vase	70.00	*Goblet	70.00	Sauce, flat	15.00
Champagne	250.00	Honey Dish	15.00	Spooner	40.00
Compote, open		Lamp, 8-3/4"		Sugar, cov	120.00
hs, 5-1/2"	65.00	Glass Base	135.00	Syrup	225.00
ls, 7"	50.00	Marble Base	100.00	Tumbler, ftd	200.00
ls, 9"	35.00	Miniature Lamp	500.00	Wine	175.00
ls, 11"	75.00	Pitcher, water, rare	650.00		
Creamer	225.00				

CANADIAN

Non-flint possibly made by Burlington Glass Works, Hamilton, Ontario, Canada, c1870.

	Clear
Bowl, 7" d, 4-1/2" h, ftd	65.00
Bread Plate, 10"	45.00
Butter, cov	85.00
Cake Stand, 9-1/4"	85.00
Celery Vase	65.00
Compote	
Cov, hs, 6"	90.00
Cov, hs, 7"	100.00

	Clear
Cov, hs, 8"	110.00
Cov, ls, 6"	50.00
Cov, ls, 8"	75.00
Open, ls, 7"	35.00
Creamer	65.00
Goblet	45.00
Mug, small	45.00
Pitcher	
Milk	90.00

	Clear
Water	125.00
Plate, 6," handles	30.00
Sauce	
Flat	15.00
Footed	20.00
Spooner	45.00
Sugar, cov	90.00
Wine	45.00

CANE (Cane, Insert, Hobnailed Diamond and Star)

Non-flint made by Gillinder and Sons Glass Co., Philadelphia, PA, and by McKee Bros. Glass Co., c1885. Goblets and toddy plates with inverted "buttons" are known.

	Amber	Apple Green	Blue	Clear	Vaseline
Butter, cov	45.00	60.00	75.00	40.00	60.00
Celery Vase	38.00	40.00	50.00	32.50	40.00
Compote, open, ls, 5-3/4"	28.00	30.00	35.00	25.00	35.00
Cordial	—	—	—	25.00	—
Creamer	35.00	40.00	50.00	25.00	30.00
Finger Bowl	20.00	30.00	35.00	15.00	30.00
Goblet	25.00	40.00	35.00	20.00	40.00
Honey Dish	—	—	—	15.00	—
Match Holder, kettle	20.00	—	35.00	30.00	35.00
Pickle	25.00	20.00	25.00	15.00	20.00
Pitcher					
Milk	60.00	55.00	65.00	40.00	55.00
Water	80.00	85.00	80.00	48.00	85.00
Plate, toddy, 4-1/2"	20.00	25.00	30.00	16.50	20.00
Relish	25.00	26.00	25.00	15.00	20.00
Salt & Pepper	60.00	50.00	80.00	30.00	70.00
Sauce, flat	—	10.00	—	7.00	—
Slipper	30.00	—	25.00	15.00	30.00
Spooner	42.00	35.00	30.00	20.00	30.00
Sugar, cov	45.00	45.00	45.00	25.00	45.00
Tray, water	35.00	40.00	50.00	30.00	45.00
Tumbler	24.00	30.00	35.00	20.00	25.00
Waste Bowl, 7-1/2"	32.50	30.00	35.00	20.00	30.00
Wine	35.00	40.00	35.00	20.00	35.00

COMET

Flint, possibly made by Boston and Sandwich Glass Co. in the early 1850s.

	Clear
Butter, cov	200.00
Compote, open, ls	140.00
Creamer	175.00

	Clear
Goblet	135.00
Mug	135.00
Pitcher, water	750.00
Spooner	95.00

	Clear
Sugar, cov	175.00
Tumbler	110.00
Whiskey, w/handle	250.00

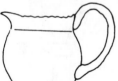

CONNECTICUT

Non-flint, one of the States patterns made by U.S. Glass Co. c1900. Found in plain and engraved. Two varieties of ruby-stained toothpicks ($90.00) have been identified.

	Clear
Biscuit jar	25.00
Bowl	
4"	10.00
8"	15.00
Butter, cov	35.00
Cake Stand	40.00
Celery Tray	20.00
Celery Vase	25.00

	Clear
Compote	
Cov, hs	40.00
Open, hs, 7"	25.00
Creamer	28.00
Dish, 8," oblong	20.00
Lamp, enamel dec	85.00
Lemonade, handled	20.00
Pitcher, water	40.00

	Clear
Relish	15.00
Salt & Pepper	35.00
Spooner	25.00
Sugar, cov	35.00
Sugar Shaker	35.00
Toothpick	50.00
Tumbler, water	20.00
Wine	35.00

CRYSTAL WEDDING (Collins, Crystal Anniversary)

Non-flint made by Adams Glass Co., Pittsburgh, PA, c1890 and by U.S. Glass Co. in 1891. Also found in frosted, amber stained, and cobalt blue (rare). Heavily reproduced in clear, ruby stained, and milk with enamel.

	Clear	Ruby Stained
Banana Stand	95.00	—
Bowl		
4-1/2," individual berry	15.00	—
7," sq, cov	75.00	85.00
8," sq, berry	50.00	85.00
8," sq, cov	60.00	95.00
Butter, cov	75.00	125.00
Cake Plate, sq	45.00	85.00
Cake Stand, 10"	65.00	—
Celery Vase	45.00	75.00
Compote		
*Cov, hs, 7" x 13"	100.00	110.00
Open, ls, 5," sq	50.00	55.00
Creamer	50.00	75.00
Cruet	125.00	200.00
*Goblet	55.00	85.00
Nappy, handle	25.00	—
Pickle	25.00	40.00
Pitcher		
Milk, round	110.00	125.00
Milk, sq	125.00	200.00
Water, round	110.00	210.00
Water, sq	165.00	225.00
Plate, 10"	25.00	40.00
Relish	20.00	40.00
Salt		
Individual	25.00	40.00
Master	35.00	65.00
Salt Shaker	65.00	75.00
Sauce	15.00	20.00
Spooner	30.00	60.00
Sugar, cov	70.00	85.00
Syrup	150.00	200.00
Tumbler	35.00	45.00
Vase		
Footed, twisted	25.00	—
Swung	25.00	—
Wine	45.00	70.00

DAISY and BUTTON

Non-flint made in the 1880s by several companies in many different forms. In continuous production since inception. Original manufacturers include: Bryce Brothers, Doyle & Co., Hobbs, Brockunier & Co., George Duncan & Sons, Boston & Sandwich Glass Co., Beatty & Sons, and U.S. Glass Co. Reproductions have existed since the early 1930s in original and new colors. Several companies, including L.G. Wright, Imperial Glass Co., Fenton Art Glass Co., and Degenhart Glass Co., too, have made reproductions. Also found in amberina, amber stain, and ruby stained.

	Amber	Apple Green	Blue	Clear	Vaseline
Bowl, triangular	40.00	45.00	45.00	25.00	65.00
Bread Plate, 13"	35.00	60.00	35.00	20.00	40.00
*Butter, cov					
Round	70.00	90.00	70.00	65.00	95.00
Square	110.00	115.00	110.00	100.00	120.00
Butter Pat	30.00	40.00	35.00	25.00	35.00
*Canoe					
4"	12.00	24.00	15.00	10.00	24.00
8-1/2"	30.00	35.00	30.00	25.00	35.00
12"	60.00	35.00	28.00	20.00	40.00
14"	30.00	40.00	35.00	25.00	40.00
*Castor Set					
4 bottle, glass standard	90.00	85.00	95.00	65.00	75.00
5 bottle, metal standard	100.00	100.00	110.00	100.00	95.00
Celery Vase	48.00	55.00	40.00	30.00	55.00
*Compote					
Cov, hs, 6"	35.00	50.00	45.00	25.00	50.00
Open, hs, 8"	75.00	65.00	60.00	40.00	65.00
*Creamer	35.00	40.00	40.00	18.00	35.00
*Cruet, os	100.00	80.00	75.00	45.00	80.00
Eggcup	20.00	30.00	25.00	15.00	30.00
Finger Bowl	30.00	50.00	35.00	30.00	42.00
*Goblet	40.00	50.00	40.00	25.00	40.00
*Hat, 2-1/2"	30.00	35.00	40.00	20.00	40.00
Ice Cream Tray, 14" x 9" x 2"	75.00	50.00	55.00	35.00	55.00
Ice Tub	—	35.00	—	—	75.00
Inkwell	40.00	50.00	45.00	30.00	45.00

	Amber	Apple Green	Blue	Clear	Vaseline
Parfait	25.00	35.00	30.00	20.00	35.00
Pickle Castor	125.00	90.00	150.00	75.00	150.00
*Pitcher, water					
Bulbous, reed handle	125.00	95.00	90.00	75.00	90.00
Tankard	62.00	65.00	62.00	60.00	65.00
*Plate					
5," leaf shape	20.00	24.00	12.00	12.00	25.00
6," round	10.00	22.00	15.00	6.50	24.00
7," square	25.00	35.00	25.00	15.00	35.00
Punch Bowl, stand	90.00	100.00	95.00	85.00	100.00
*Salt & Pepper	30.00	40.00	30.00	20.00	35.00
*Sauce, 4"	18.00	25.00	18.00	15.00	25.00
*Slipper					
5"	45.00	48.00	50.00	45.00	50.00
11-1/2"	40.00	50.00	30.00	35.00	50.00
*Spooner	40.00	40.00	45.00	35.00	45.00
*Sugar, cov	45.00	50.00	45.00	35.00	50.00
Syrup	45.00	50.00	45.00	30.00	45.00
*Toothpick					
Round	40.00	55.00	25.00	40.00	45.00
Urn	25.00	30.00	25.00	15.00	30.00
*Tray	65.00	65.00	60.00	35.00	60.00
Tumbler	18.00	30.00	35.00	15.00	25.00
Vase, wall pocket	125.00	—	—	—	—
*Wine	15.00	25.00	20.00	10.00	45.00

DAKOTA (Baby Thumbprint, Thumbprint Band)

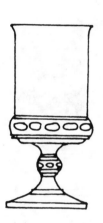

Non-flint made by Ripley and Co., Pittsburgh, PA, in the late 1880s and early 1890s. Later re-issued by U.S. Glass Co. as one of the States patterns. Prices listed are for etched fern and berry pattern; also found with fern and no berry, and oak-leaf etching, and scarcer grape etching. Other etchings known include fish, swan, peacock, bird and insect, bird and flowers, ivy and berry, stag, spider and insect in web, buzzard on dead tree and crane catching fish. Sometimes ruby stained with or without souvenir markings; ftd. Sauce known in cobalt blue. There is a four-piece table set available in a "hotel" variant. Prices are about 20 percent higher than for the regular type.

	Clear Etched	Clear Plain	Ruby Stained
Basket, 10" x 2"	205.00	175.00	300.00
Bottle, 5-1/2"	85.00	65.00	—
Bowl, berry	45.00	35.00	—
Butter, cov	65.00	40.00	125.00
Cake Cover, 8" d	300.00	200.00	—
Cake Stand, 10-1/2"	95.00	75.00	—
Celery Tray	40.00	25.00	—
Celery Vase	40.00	30.00	—
Compote			
Cov, hs, 5"	60.00	50.00	—
Cov, hs, 7"	70.00	55.00	—
Cov, hs, 10"	125.00	100.00	—
Open, ls, 6"	45.00	35.00	—
Open, ls, 8"	50.00	40.00	—
Open, ls, 10"	75.00	65.00	—
Condiment Tray	—	75.00	—
Creamer	55.00	30.00	—
Cruet	125.00	100.00	175.00
Goblet	35.00	25.00	75.00
Pitcher			
Milk	145.00	80.00	200.00
Water	125.00	75.00	190.00
Plate, 10"	85.00	75.00	—
Salt Shaker	65.00	50.00	125.00
Sauce			
Flat, 4" d	20.00	15.00	30.00
Footed, 5" d	25.00	15.00	35.00

	Clear Etched	Clear Plain	Ruby Stained
Spooner.	30.00	25.00	65.00
Sugar, cov.	65.00	55.00	85.00
Tankard.	125.00	95.00	205.00
Tray			
Water, 13" d	100.00	75.00	—
Wine, 10" to 12"	125.00	90.00	—
Tumbler.	35.00	30.00	55.00
Waste Bowl.	65.00	50.00	75.00
Wine	30.00	20.00	55.00

DIAMOND POINT (Diamond Point with Ribs, Pineapple, Sawtooth, Stepped Diamond Point)

Flint originally made by Boston and Sandwich Glass Co. c1850 and by the New England Glass Co., East Cambridge, MA, c1860. Many other companies manufactured this pattern throughout the 19th century. Rare in color.

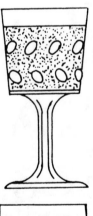

	Flint	Non-Flint		Flint	Non-Flint
Ale Glass, 6-1/4" h	85.00	—	Eggcup		
Bowl			Cov.	75.00	50.00
7," cov	60.00	20.00	Open	40.00	20.00
8," cov	60.00	20.00	Goblet	45.00	35.00
8," open	45.00	15.00	Honey Dish	15.00	—
Butter, cov	95.00	50.00	Lemonade	55.00	—
Cake Stand, 14"	185.00	—	Mustard, cov	25.00	—
Candlesticks, pr.	165.00	—	Pitcher		
Castor Bottle	25.00	15.00	Pint	200.00	—
Celery Vase.	75.00	30.00	Quart	300.00	—
Champagne.	85.00	35.00	Plate		
Claret.	90.00	—	6"	30.00	—
Compote			8"	50.00	—
Cov, hs, 8"	185.00	60.00	Salt, master, cov	75.00	—
Open, hs, 10-1/2", flared	100.00	—	Sauce, flat.	15.00	—
			Spill Holder	45.00	—
Open, hs, 11", scalloped rim	110.00	—	Spooner	45.00	30.00
			Sugar, cov.	95.00	55.00
Open, ls, 7-1/2"	50.00	40.00	Syrup	170.00	—
Cordial.	165.00	—	Tumbler, bar	65.00	30.00
Creamer, ah	115.00	—	Whiskey, ah	85.00	—
Decanter, qt, os.	200.00	—	Wine	75.00	30.00

EGG IN SAND (Bean, Stippled Oval)

Non-flint, c1885. Has been reported in colors, including blue and amber, but rare.

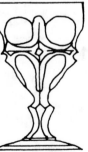

	Clear		Clear		Clear
Bread Plate, octagonal	25.00	Goblet	30.00	Spooner, flat rim	30.00
Butter, cov.	40.00	Pitcher, water.	45.00	Sugar, cov	35.00
Compote, cov, jelly	45.00	Relish.	15.00	Tray, water.	40.00
Creamer	30.00	Salt & Pepper	65.00	Tumbler	30.00
Dish, swan center	40.00	Sauce	10.00	Wine.	35.00

EXCELSIOR

Flint attributed to several firms, including Boston and Sandwich Glass Co., Sandwich, MA; McKee Bros., Pittsburgh, PA; and Ihmsen & Co., Pittsburgh, PA, 1850s-60s. Quality and design vary. Prices are for high-quality flint. Very rare in color.

	Clear		Clear		Clear
Ale Glass.	50.00	Champagne.	60.00	Decanter	
Bar Bottle	85.00	Claret.	45.00	Pint	85.00
Bitters Bottle	95.00	Compote		Quart	85.00
Bowl, 10," open	125.00	Cov, ls	125.00	Eggcup	
Butter, cov.	100.00	Open, hs	85.00	Double.	45.00
Candlestick, 9-1/2" h	125.00	Cordial.	40.00	Single	40.00
Celery Vase, scalloped top	85.00	Creamer.	85.00	Goblet	50.00

	Clear		Clear		Clear
Lamp, hand	95.00	Salt, master	30.00	Syrup	125.00
Mug	30.00	Spillholder	75.00	Tumbler, bar	50.00
Pickle Jar, cov	45.00	Spooner	60.00	Whiskey, Maltese Cross	65.00
Pitcher, water	400.00	Sugar, cov	110.00	Wine	45.00

EYEWINKER (Cannon Ball, Crystal Ball, Winking Eye)

Non-flint made in Findlay, Ohio, in 1889. Reportedly made by Dalzell, Gilmore and Leighton Glass Co., which was organized in 1883 in West Virginia and moved to Findlay in 1888. Made only in clear glass; reproduced in color by several companies, including L. G. Wright Co. A goblet and toothpick were not originally made in this pattern.

	Clear		Clear		Clear
Banana Stand, hs	135.00	Open, 4-1/2," jelly	45.00	9," sq, upturned	
Bowl		Creamer	65.00	sides	65.00
6-1/2"	25.00	Cruet	65.00	10," upturned sides	85.00
9," cov	75.00	*Honey Dish	40.00	Salt Shaker	35.00
*Butter, cov	70.00	Lamp, kerosene	125.00	Sauce	15.00
Cake Stand, 8"	55.00	Nappy, folded sides,		Spooner	35.00
Celery Vase	45.00	7-1/4"	30.00	*Sugar, cov	55.00
*Compote		*Pitcher, water	95.00	Syrup, pewter top	125.00
Cov, hs, 6-1/2"	85.00	Plate		*Tumbler	45.00
Cov, hs, 9-1/2"	150.00	7"	30.00		
Open, 7-1/4," fluted	65.00				

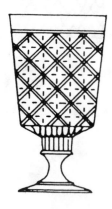

FINECUT (Flower in Square)

Non-flint made by Bryce Bros., Pittsburgh, PA, c1885, and by U.S. Glass Co. in 1891.

	Amber	Blue	Clear	Vaseline
Bowl, 8-1/4"	15.00	20.00	10.00	15.00
Bread Plate	50.00	60.00	25.00	50.00
Butter, cov	55.00	75.00	45.00	60.00
Cake Stand	—	—	35.00	—
Celery Tray	—	45.00	25.00	40.00
Celery Vase, SP holder	—	—	—	115.00
Creamer	60.00	40.00	35.00	75.00
Goblet	45.00	55.00	22.00	42.00
Pitcher, water	100.00	100.00	60.00	115.00
Plate				
7"	25.00	40.00	15.00	20.00
10"	30.00	50.00	21.00	45.00
Relish	15.00	25.00	10.00	20.00
Sauce, flat	14.00	15.00	10.00	14.00
Spooner	30.00	45.00	18.00	40.00
Sugar, cov	45.00	55.00	35.00	45.00
Tray, water	50.00	55.00	25.00	50.00
Tumbler	—	—	18.00	28.00
Wine	—	—	24.00	30.00

FLAMINGO HABITAT

Non-flint, maker unknown, c1870, etched pattern.

	Clear		Clear		Clear
Bowl, 10," oval	40.00	Compote		Goblet	45.00
Butter, cov	65.00	Cov, 4-1/2"	75.00	Sauce, ftd	15.00
Celery Vase	45.00	Cov, 6-1/2"	95.00	Spooner	25.00
Champagne	45.00	Open, 5," jelly	35.00	Sugar, cov	50.00
Cheese Dish, blown	110.00	Open, 6"	40.00	Tumbler	30.00
		Creamer	40.00	Wine	45.00

FLORIDA (Emerald Green Herringbone, Paneled Herringbone)

Non-flint made by U.S. Glass Co., in the 1890s. One of the States patterns. Goblet reproduced in green, amber, and other colors.

	Clear	Emerald Green		Clear	Emerald Green
Berry Set	75.00	110.00	Nappy	15.00	25.00
Bowl, 7-3/4"	10.00	15.00	Pitcher, water	50.00	75.00
Butter, cov	50.00	85.00	Plate		
Cake Stand			7-1/2"	12.00	18.00
Large	60.00	75.00	9-1/4"	15.00	25.00
Small	30.00	40.00	Relish		
Celery Vase	30.00	35.00	6," sq	10.00	15.00
Compote, open, hs,			8-1/2," sq	15.00	20.00
6-1/2", sq	—	40.00	Salt Shaker	25.00	50.00
Creamer	30.00	45.00	Sauce	5.00	7.50
Cruet, os	40.00	110.00	Spooner	20.00	35.00
*Goblet, 5-3/4" h	25.00	40.00	Sugar, cov	35.00	50.00
Mustard Pot, attached			Syrup	60.00	175.00
under plate, cov	25.00	45.00	Tumbler	20.00	35.00
			Wine	25.00	50.00

GARFIELD DRAPE (Canadian Drape)

Non-flint issued in 1881 by Adams & Co., Pittsburgh, PA, after the assassination of President Garfield.

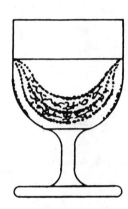

	Clear		Clear		Clear
Bread Plate		Compote		Water, ah	75.00
Memorial, portrait		Cov, hs, 8"	100.00	Water, strap handle	100.00
of Garfield	65.00	Cov, ls, 6"	85.00	Relish, oval	20.00
"We Mourn Our		Open, hs, 8-1/2"	40.00	Sauce	
Nation's Loss,"		Creamer	40.00	Flat	8.50
portrait	75.00	Goblet	40.00	Footed	12.00
Butter, cov	70.00	Honey Dish	15.00	Spooner	35.00
Cake Stand, 9-1/2"	70.00	Pitcher		Sugar, cov	60.00
Celery Vase	55.00	Milk	70.00	Tumbler	35.00

GEORGIA (Peacock Feather)

Non-flint made by Richards and Hartley Glass Co., Tarentum, PA, and reissued by U.S. Glass Co. in 1902 as part of the States series. Rare in blue. (Chamber lamp, pedestal base, $275.00). No goblet known in pattern.

	Clear		Clear		Clear
Bonbon, ftd	25.00	Cov, hs, 8"	50.00	Hand, oil, 7"	80.00
Bowl, 8"	30.00	Open, hs, 5"	20.00	Mug	25.00
Butter, cov	45.00	Open, hs, 6"	25.00	Nappy	25.00
Cake Stand, 10"	50.00	Open, hs, 7"	30.00	Pitcher, water	70.00
Castor Set, 2 bottles	60.00	Open, hs, 8"	35.00	Plate, 5-1/4"	15.00
Celery Tray, 11-3/4"	35.00	Condiment Set, tray,		Relish	15.00
Children's Cake Stand	35.00	oil cruet,		Salt Shaker	40.00
Creamer	35.00	salt & pepper	75.00	Sauce	10.00
Compote		Creamer	35.00	Spooner	35.00
Cov, hs, 5"	35.00	Cruet, os	55.00	Sugar, cov	45.00
Cov, hs, 6"	40.00	Decanter	70.00	Syrup, metal lid	65.00
Cov, hs, 7"	45.00	Lamp		Tumbler	35.00
		Chamber, pedestal	85.00		

HONEYCOMB

A popular pattern made in flint and non-flint glass by numerous firms, c1850-1900, resulting in many pattern variations. Found with copper-wheel engraving. Rare in color.

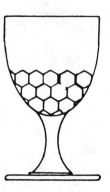

	Flint	Non-Flint		Flint	Non-Flint
Ale Glass	50.00	25.00	Champagne	50.00	25.00
Barber Bottle	45.00	25.00	Claret	35.00	35.00
Bowl, cov, 7-1/4" pat'd			Compote, cov, hs		
1869, acorn finial	100.00	45.00	6-1/2" x 18-1/2" h	60.00	40.00
Butter, cov	75.00	45.00	9-1/4" x 11-1/2" h	110.00	65.00
Cake Stand	55.00	35.00	Compote, open, hs		
Castor Bottle	25.00	18.00	7" x 7" h	60.00	40.00
Celery Vase	45.00	20.00	7-1/2," scalloped	40.00	25.00

	Flint	Non-Flint
8" x 6-1/4" h.	65.00	40.00
Compote, open, ls		
6" d, Saucer Bowl	35.00	25.00
7-1/2," scalloped	40.00	25.00
Cordial, 3-1/2"	35.00	25.00
Creamer, ah	35.00	20.00
Decanter		
Pint, os	85.00	45.00
Quart, os	85.00	65.00
Eggcup	20.00	15.00
Finger Bowl	45.00	—
Goblet	25.00	15.00
Honey Dish, cov	15.00	25.00
Lamp		
All Glass	—	85.00
Marble base	—	90.00
Lemonade	40.00	20.00
Mug, half pint	25.00	15.00
Pitcher, water, ah	165.00	60.00

	Flint	Non-Flint
Plate, 6"	—	12.50
Pomade Jar, cov	50.00	20.00
Relish	30.00	20.00
Salt, master, cov, ftd	35.00	30.00
Salt Shaker, orig top	—	35.00
Sauce	12.00	7.50
Spillholder	35.00	20.00
Spooner	65.00	35.00
Sugar		
Frosted rosebud finial	—	50.00
Regular	75.00	45.00
Tumbler		
Bar	35.00	—
Flat	40.00	12.50
Footed	45.00	15.00
Vase		
7-1/2"	45.00	—
10-1/2"	75.00	—
Whiskey, handled	125.00	—
Wine	35.00	15.00

HORSESHOE (Good Luck, Prayer Rug)

Non-flint made by Adams & Co., Pittsburgh, PA, and others in late 1880s.

	Clear
Bowl, cov, oval	
7"	150.00
8"	195.00
Bread Plate, 14" x10"	
Double horseshoe handles	65.00
Single horseshoe handles	40.00
Butter, cov	95.00
Cake Plate	40.00
Cake Stand	
9"	70.00
10"	90.00
Celery Vase, knob stem	40.00
Cheese, cov, woman churning	275.00

	Clear
Compote	
Cov, hs, 7," horseshoe finial	95.00
Cov, hs, 8" x 12-1/4"	125.00
Cov, hs, 11"	135.00
Creamer, 6-1/2"	55.00
Doughnut Stand	75.00
Finger Bowl	80.00
Goblet	
Knob Stem	40.00
Plain Stem	38.00
Marmalade Jar, cov	110.00
Pitcher	
Milk	125.00
Water	100.00
Plate	
7"	45.00
10"	55.00

	Clear
Relish	
5" x 7"	20.00
8," wheelbarrow, pewter wheels	75.00
Salt	
Individual, horseshoe shape	20.00
Master, horseshoe shape	100.00
Master, wheelbarrow, pewter wheels	75.00
Sauce	
Flat	10.00
Footed	15.00
Spooner	35.00
Sugar, cov	65.00
Vegetable Dish, oblong	35.00
Waste Bowl	45.00
Water Tray	125.00
Wine	150.00

ILLINOIS (Clarissa, Star of the East)

Non-flint. One of the States patterns made by U.S. Glass Co. c1897. Most forms are square. A few items are known in ruby stained, including a salt ($50.00) and a lidless straw holder with the stain on the inside ($95.00).

	Clear	Emerald Green
Basket, ah, 11-1/2"	100.00	—
Bowl		
5," round	20.00	—
6," sq	25.00	—
8," round	25.00	—
9," sq	35.00	—
*Butter, cov	60.00	—
Candlesticks, pr	95.00	—
Celery Tray, 11"	40.00	—
Cheese, cov	75.00	—
Compote, open		
hs, 5"	40.00	—
hs, 9"	60.00	—

	Clear	Emerald Green
Creamer		
Individual	30.00	—
Table	40.00	—
Cruet	65.00	—
Finger Bowl	25.00	—
Marmalade Jar	135.00	—
Olive	18.00	—
Pitcher, milk		
Round, SP rim	175.00	—
Square	65.00	—
Pitcher, water, square	65.00	—
Plate, 7," sq	25.00	—
Relish		

	Clear	Emerald Green
7-1/2" x 4"	10.00	40.00
8-1/2" x 3"	18.00	—
Salt		
Individual	15.00	—
Master	25.00	—
Salt & Pepper, pr.	40.00	—
Sauce	15.00	—
Spooner	35.00	—
Straw Holder, cov	275.00	400.00
Sugar		
Individual	30.00	—

	Clear	Emerald Green
Table, cov	55.00	—
Sugar Shaker	65.00	—
Syrup, pewter top	95.00	—
Tankard, SP rim	80.00	135.00
Toothpick		
Adv emb in base	45.00	—
Plain	30.00	—
Tray, 12" x 8,"		
turned up sides	50.00	—
Tumbler	30.00	40.00
Vase, 6," sq.	35.00	45.00
Vase, 9-1/2"	—	125.00

JACOB'S LADDER (Maltese)

Non-flint made by Bryce Bros., Pittsburgh, PA, in 1876 and by U.S. Glass Co. in 1891. A few pieces found in amber, yellow, blue, pale blue, and pale green. Bowls in variant of pattern found in flint, sometimes in metal holders.

	Clear
Bowl	
6" x 8-3/4"	15.00
6-3/4" x 9-3/4"	20.00
7-1/2" x 10-3/4"	20.00
9," berry, ornate, SP holder, ftd (variant)	125.00
Butter, cov	75.00
Cake Stand	
8" or 9"	50.00
11" or 12"	60.00
Castor Bottle	18.00
Castor Set, 4 bottles	100.00
Celery Vase	45.00
Cologne Bottle, Maltese-cross stopper, ftd	85.00

	Clear
Compote	
Cov, hs, 6"	80.00
Cov, hs, 7-1/2"	100.00
Cov, hs, 9-1/2"	135.00
Open, hs, 7-1/2"	35.00
Open, hs, 8-1/2," scalloped	30.00
Open, hs, 9-1/2," scalloped	38.00
Open, hs, 10"	40.00
Creamer	35.00
Cruet, os, ftd	85.00
Goblet	65.00
Honey Dish, 3-1/2"	10.00
Marmalade Jar	75.00

	Clear
Mug	100.00
Pitcher, water, ah	175.00
Plate, 6-1/4"	20.00
Relish, 9-1/2" x 5-1/2"	15.00
Salt, master, ftd	20.00
Sauce	
Flat, 4" or 5"	8.00
Footed, 4"	12.00
Spooner	35.00
Sugar, cov	80.00
Syrup	
Knight's Head finial	125.00
Plain top	100.00
Tumbler, bar	100.00
Wine	30.00

JERSEY SWIRL (Swirl)

Non-flint made by Windsor Glass Co., Pittsburgh, PA, c1887. Heavily reproduced in color by L. G. Wright Co. The clear goblet is also reproduced.

	Amber	Blue	Canary	Clear
Bowl, 9-1/4"	55.00	55.00	45.00	35.00
Butter, cov	55.00	55.00	50.00	40.00
Cake Stand, 9"	75.00	70.00	45.00	30.00
*Celery Case	42.00	42.00	35.00	30.00
*Compote, hs, 8"	50.00	50.00	45.00	35.00
Creamer	45.00	45.00	40.00	30.00
Cruet, os	—	—	—	25.00
*Goblet				
Buttermilk	40.00	40.00	35.00	30.00
Water	40.00	40.00	35.00	30.00
Marmalade Jar	—	—	—	50.00
Pickle Castor, SP frame and lid	—	—	—	125.00
Pitcher, water	50.00	50.00	45.00	35.00
Plate, round				
6"	25.00	25.00	20.00	15.00
8"	30.00	30.00	25.00	20.00
10"	38.00	38.00	35.00	30.00
*Salt, ind	20.00	20.00	18.00	15.00
Salt Shaker	30.00	30.00	25.00	20.00
Sauce, 4-1/2," flat	20.00	20.00	15.00	10.00
Spooner	30.00	30.00	25.00	20.00
Sugar, cov	40.00	40.00	35.00	30.00
Tumbler	30.00	30.00	25.00	20.00
*Wine	50.00	50.00	40.00	15.00

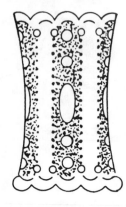

KANSAS (Jewel with Dewdrop)

Non-flint originally produced by Co-Operative Glass Co., Beaver Falls, PA. Later produced as part of the States pattern series by U.S. Glass Co. in 1901 and Jenkins Glass Co. c1915-25. Also known with jewels stained in pink or gold. Mugs (smaller and of inferior quality) have been reproduced in clear, vaseline, amber and blue).

	Clear		Clear		Clear
Banana Stand	90.00	Compote		Water	100.00
Bowl		Cov, hs, 6"	60.00	Relish, 8-1/2," oval	20.00
7," oval	35.00	Cov, hs, 8"	85.00	Salt Shaker	50.00
8"	40.00	Cov, ls, 5"	60.00	Sauce, flat, 4"	12.00
Bread Plate, ODB	45.00	Open, hs, 6"	30.00	Sugar, cov	65.00
Butter, cov	65.00	Open, hs, 8"	45.00	Syrup	125.00
Cake Plate	45.00	Creamer	40.00	Toothpick	65.00
Cake Stand		*Goblet	55.00	Tumbler	45.00
7-5/8"	50.00	*Mug		Whiskey	25.00
10"	85.00	Regular	45.00	Wine	50.00
Celery Vase	80.00	Tall	25.00		
Champagne	100.00	*Pitcher			
		Milk	80.00		

KENTUCKY

Non-flint made by U.S. Glass Co. c1897 as part of the States pattern series. The goblet is found in ruby stained ($50). A footed, square sauce ($30) is known in cobalt blue with gold. A toothpick holder is also known in ruby stained ($150).

	Clear	Emerald Green		Clear	Emerald Green
Bowl, 8" d	20.00	—	Plate, 7," sq	15.00	—
Butter, cov	50.00	—	Punch Cup	10.00	15.00
Cake Stand, 9-1/2"	40.00	—	Salt Shaker, orig top	10.00	—
Creamer	25.00	—	Sauce, ftd, sq	10.00	15.00
Cruet, os	45.00	—	Spooner	35.00	—
Cup	10.00	20.00	Sugar, cov	30.00	—
Goblet	30.00	50.00	Toothpick, sq	35.00	85.00
Nappy	10.00	15.00	Tumbler	20.00	30.00
Olive, handle	25.00	—	Wine	28.00	38.00
Pitcher, water	55.00	—			

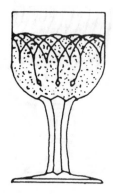

LOOP and DART

Clear and stippled flint and non-flint of the late 1860s and early 1870s. Made by Boston and Sandwich Glass Co., Sandwich, MA, and Richards and Hartley, Tarentum, PA. Flint adds 25%.

	Clear		Clear		Clear
Bowl, 9," oval	30.00	Cruet, os	95.00	Sauce	5.00
Butter, cov	45.00	Eggcup	25.00	Spooner	25.00
Cake Stand, 10"	40.00	Goblet	25.00	Sugar, cov	50.00
Celery Vase	35.00	Lamp, oil	85.00	Tumbler	
Compote		Pitcher, water	75.00	Footed	30.00
Cov, hs, 8"	85.00	Plate, 6"	35.00	Water	25.00
Cov, ls, 8"	65.00	Relish	20.00	Wine	35.00
Creamer	35.00	Salt, master	50.00		

LOUISIANA (Sharp Oval and Diamond, Granby)

Made by Bryce Bros., Pittsburgh, PA, in the 1870s. Reissued by U.S. Glass Co. c1898 as one of the States patterns. Available with gold and also comes frosted.

	Clear		Clear		Clear
Bowl, 9," berry	20.00	Open, hs, 5," jelly	40.00	Pitcher, water	65.00
Butter, cov	75.00	Creamer	30.00	Relish	15.00
Cake Stand	65.00	Goblet	30.00	Spooner	30.00
Celery Vase	30.00	Match Holder	35.00	Sugar, cov	45.00
Compote		Mug, handled, gold top	25.00	Tumbler	25.00
Cov, hs, 8"	75.00	Nappy, 4," cov	30.00	Wine	35.00

MAINE (Paneled Stippled Flower, Stippled Primrose)

Non-flint made by U.S. Glass Co., Pittsburgh, PA, c1899. Researchers dispute if goblet was made originally. Sometimes found with enamel trim or overall turquoise stain.

	Clear	Emerald Green		Clear	Emerald Green
Bowl, 8"	30.00	40.00	Mug	35.00	—
Bread Plate, oval			Pitcher		
10" x 7-1/4"	30.00	—	Milk	65.00	85.00
Butter, cov	48.00	—	Water	50.00	125.00
Cake Stand	40.00	60.00	Relish	15.00	—
Compote			Salt Shaker, single	30.00	—
Cov, jelly	50.00	75.00	Sauce	15.00	—
Open, hs, 7"	20.00	45.00	Sugar, cov	45.00	75.00
Open, ls, 8"	38.00	55.00	Syrup	75.00	225.00
Open, ls, 9"	30.00	65.00	Toothpick	125.00	—
Creamer	30.00	—	Tumbler	30.00	45.00
Cruet, os	80.00	—	Wine	50.00	75.00

MARYLAND (Inverted Loop and Fan, Loop and Diamond)

Made originally by Bryce Bros., Pittsburgh, PA. Continued by U.S. Glass Co. as one of its States patterns.

	Clear with Gold	Ruby Stained		Clear with Gold	Ruby Stained
Banana Dish	35.00	105.00	Olive, handled	15.00	—
Bowl, berry	15.00	35.00	Pitcher		
Bread Plate	25.00	—	Milk	42.50	135.00
Butter, cov	65.00	95.00	Water	50.00	100.00
Cake Stand, 8"	40.00	—	Plate, 7," round	25.00	—
Celery Tray	20.00	35.00	Relish, oval	15.00	55.00
Celery Vase	30.00	65.00	Salt Shaker, single	30.00	—
Compote			Sauce, flat	10.00	15.00
Cov, hs	65.00	100.00	Spooner	30.00	55.00
Open, jelly	25.00	45.00	Sugar, cov	45.00	60.00
Creamer	25.00	55.00	Toothpick	125.00	175.00
Goblet	30.00	60.00	Tumbler	25.00	50.00
			Wine	40.00	75.00

MASCOTTE (Dominion, Etched Fern and Waffle, Minor Block)

Non-flint made by Ripley and Co., Pittsburgh, PA, in the 1880s. Reissued by U.S. Glass Co. in 1891. The butter dish shown on Plate 77 of Ruth Webb Lee's *Victorian Glass* is said to go with this pattern. It has a horseshoe finial and was named for the famous "Maude S," "Queen of the Turf" trotting horse during the 1880s. Apothecary jar and pyramid jars made by Tiffin Glass Co. in the 1950s.

	Clear	Etched		Clear	Etched
Bowl			Creamer	30.00	45.00
Cov, 5"	—	35.00	Goblet	40.00	45.00
Cov, 7"	—	45.00	Pitcher, water	55.00	65.00
Open 9"	35.00	40.00	Plate, turned in sides	40.00	45.00
Butter Pat	15.00	20.00	Pyramid Jar, 7" d, one fits		
Butter, cov			into other and forms tall		
"Maude S"	100.00	110.00	jar-type container with		
Regular	50.00	65.00	lid, three sizes with		
Cake Basket, handle	80.00	95.00	flat separators	50.00	55.00
Cake Stand	35.00	50.00	Salt Dip	25.00	—
Celery Vase	35.00	40.00	Salt Shaker, single	25.00	25.00
Cheese, cov	70.00	80.00	Sauce		
Compote			Flat	8.00	15.00
Cov, hs, 5"	35.00	40.00	Footed	12.00	15.00
Cov, hs, 7"	45.00	55.00	Spooner	30.00	35.00
Cov, hs, 8"	60.00	75.00	Sugar, cov	40.00	45.00
Cov, hs, 9"	65.00	90.00	Tray, water	40.00	55.00
Open, hs, 6"	20.00	25.00	Tumbler	20.00	35.00
Open, hs, 8"	30.00	35.00	Wine	25.00	30.00
Open, ls, 8"	30.00	45.00			

MICHIGAN (Loop and Pillar)

Non-flint made by U.S. Glass Co. c1902 as one of the States pattern series. The 10-1/4" bowl ($42) and punch cup ($12) are found with yellow or blue stain. Also found with painted carnations. Other colors include "Sunrise," gold and ruby stained.

	Clear	Rose Stained		Clear	Rose Stained
Bowl			Olive, two handles 10.00		25.00
7-1/2". 15.00		30.00	Pickle. 12.00		20.00
9". 35.00		60.00	Pitcher		
10-1/4". 35.00		62.00	8". 50.00		—
Butter, cov			12," tankard. 70.00		150.00
Large. 60.00		125.00	Plate, 5-1/2" d 15.00		—
Small 65.00		—	Punch Bowl, 8" 50.00		—
Celery Vase 40.00		85.00	Punch Cup. 8.00		—
Compote			Relish. 20.00		35.00
Jelly, 4-1/2" 45.00		75.00	Salt Shaker, single,		
Open, hs, 9-1/4" 65.00		85.00	3 types 20.00		30.00
Creamer			Sauce 12.00		22.00
Ind, 6 oz., tankard . . . 20.00		65.00	Sherbet cup, handles. . . .15.00		20.00
Table. 30.00		70.00	Spooner. 50.00		75.00
Cruet, os 60.00		225.00	Sugar, cov 50.00		85.00
Crushed Fruit Bowl 75.00		—	Syrup 95.00		175.00
Custard Cup. 15.00		—	*Toothpick 45.00		100.00
Finger Bowl 15.00		—	Tumbler 30.00		40.00
Goblet 45.00		65.00	Vase		
Honey Dish 10.00		—	Bud 35.00		40.00
Lemonade Mug 24.00		40.00	Ftd, large. 45.00		—
Nappy, Gainsborough			Wine 35.00		50.00
handle 35.00		—			

MINNESOTA

Non-flint made by U.S. Glass Co. in the late 1890s as one of the States patterns.

	Clear	Ruby Stained		Clear	Ruby Stained
Banana Stand 65.00		—	Match Safe 25.00		—
Basket 65.00		—	Mug 25.00		—
Biscuit Jar, cov. 55.00		150.00	Olive 15.00		25.00
Bonbon, 5" 15.00		—	Pitcher, tankard 85.00		200.00
Butter, cov 50.00			Plate		
Carafe 35.00		—	5," turned up edges. . .25.00		—
Celery Tray, 13". 25.00		—	7-3/8" d 15.00		—
Compote			Pomade Jar, cov 35.00		—
Open, hs, 10," flared . 60.00		—	Relish. 20.00		—
Open, ls, 9," sq 55.00		—	Salt Shaker 25.00		—
Creamer			Sauce, boat shape. 10.00		25.00
Individual. 20.00		—	Spooner. 25.00		—
Table. 30.00		—	Sugar, cov 35.00		—
Cruet 35.00		—	Syrup 65.00		—
Cup 18.00		—	Toothpick, 3 handles 30.00		150.00
Goblet 35.00		75.00	Tray, 8" l 15.00		—
Hair Receiver. 30.00		—	Tumbler 20.00		—
Juice Glass 20.00		—	Wine 40.00		—

NEVADA

Non-flint made by U.S. Glass Co., Pittsburgh, PA, c1902 as a States pattern. Pieces are sometimes partly frosted and have enamel decoration. Add 20% for frosted.

	Clear		Clear		Clear
Biscuit Jar 45.00		Celery Vase 25.00		Open, hs, 8" 35.00	
Bowl		Compote		Creamer 30.00	
6" d, cov 35.00		Cov, hs, 6" 40.00		Cruet. 35.00	
7" d, open 20.00		Cov, hs, 7" 45.00		Cup, custard 12.00	
8" d, cov 45.00		Cov, hs, 8" 55.00		Finger Bowl. 25.00	
Butter, cov 70.00		Open, hs, 6" 20.00		Jug 35.00	
Cake Stand, 10". 35.00		Open, hs, 7". 30.00		Pickle, oval 10.00	

	Clear		Clear		Clear
Pitcher		**Salt**		Spooner	35.00
Milk, tankard	45.00	Individual	15.00	Sugar, cov	35.00
Water, bulbous	50.00	Master	20.00	Syrup, tin top	45.00
Water, tankard	45.00	Salt Shaker, table	15.00	Toothpick	35.00
		Sauce, 4" d	10.00	Tumbler	15.00

NEW JERSEY (Loops and Drops)

Non-flint made by U.S. Glass Co., Pittsburgh, PA, c1900-08 in States pattern series. Prices are for items with perfect gold. An emerald green 11" vase is known (value $75).

	Clear with Gold	Ruby Stained		Clear with Gold	Ruby Stained
Bowl			Molasses Can	90.00	—
8," flared	25.00	55.00	Olive	15.00	—
9," saucer	32.50	70.00	Pickle, rect	15.00	—
10," oval	30.00	85.00	**Pitcher**		
Bread Plate	30.00	—	Milk, ah	75.00	185.00
Butter, cov			Water		
Flat	75.00	100.00	Applied Handle	80.00	210.00
Footed	125.00	—	Pressured Handle . . .	50.00	185.00
Cake Stand, 8"	65.00	—	Plate, 8" d	30.00	50.00
Carafe	60.00	—	**Salt & Pepper, pr**		
Celery Tray, rect	25.00	45.00	Hotel	50.00	120.00
Compote			Small	35.00	60.00
Cov, hs, 5," jelly	45.00	65.00	Sauce	10.00	35.00
Cov, hs, 8"	65.00	95.00	Spooner	27.00	80.00
Open, hs, 6-3/4"	35.00	70.00	Sugar, cov	60.00	80.00
Open, hs, 8"	60.00	80.00	Sweetmeat, 8"	70.00	110.00
Open, hs, 10-1/2,"			Syrup	90.00	—
shallow	65.00	—	Toothpick	55.00	225.00
Creamer	35.00	65.00	Tumbler	30.00	60.00
Cruet	50.00	—	Water Bottle	55.00	110.00
Fruit bowl	40.00	70.00	Wine	45.00	65.00

ONE HUNDRED ONE (Beaded 101)

Non-flint made by Bellaire Goblet Co., Findlay, Ohio, in the late 1880s.

	Clear		Clear		Clear
Bread Plate, 101 border		Cov, ls	60.00	8"	30.00
Farm implement		Creamer	45.00	Relish	15.00
center, 11"	75.00	*Goblet	50.00	**Sauce**	
Butter, cov	40.00	Lamp, hand, oil, 10"	80.00	Flat	10.00
Cake Stand, 9"	65.00	Pickle	20.00	Footed	15.00
Celery Vase	50.00	Pitcher, water, ah	125.00	Spooner	25.00
Compote		**Plate**		Sugar, cov	45.00
Cov, hs, 7"	60.00	6"	20.00	Wine	60.00

PALMETTE (Hearts and Spades, Spades)

Non-flint, unknown maker, late 1870s. Shards have been found at Burlington Glass Works, Hamilton, Ontario, Canada. Syrup known in milk glass.

	Clear		Clear		Clear
Bottle, vinegar	80.00	**Compote**		Salt, master, ftd	22.00
Bowl, scalloped rim		Cov, hs, 8-1/2"	75.00	Salt Shaker	55.00
8"	25.00	Cov, hs, 9-3/4"	85.00	Sauce, flat, 6"	10.00
9"	20.00	Open, ls, 7"	30.00	**Shaker, saloon,**	
Butter Dish, cov	60.00	Creamer, ah	65.00	oversize	80.00
Cake Plate,		Cup Plate	55.00	Spooner	35.00
tab handles	35.00	Eggcup	40.00	Sugar, cov	55.00
Cake Stand		Goblet	35.00	Syrup, ah	125.00
(two sizes)	100.00	Lamp, various sizes	95.00	**Tumbler**	
Castor Set, 5 bottles,		Pickle, scoop shape	20.00	Bar	75.00
sp holder	125.00	**Pitcher, bulbous, ah**		Water, ftd	40.00
Celery Vase	55.00	Milk	135.00	Wine	110.00
Champagne	75.00	Water	125.00		
		Relish (3 sauces)	18.00		

PENNSYLVANIA (Balder)

Non-flint issued by U.S. Glass Co. in 1898. Also known in ruby stained. A ruffled jelly compote is documented in orange carnival.

	Clear with Gold	Emerald Green
Biscuit Jar, cov	75.00	125.00
Bowl		
4"	20.00	—
8," berry	25.00	35.00
8," sq	20.00	40.00
Butter, cov	60.00	85.00
Carafe	45.00	—
Celery Tray	30.00	—
Celery Vase	45.00	—
Champagne	25.00	—
Cheese Dish, cov	65.00	—
Compote, hs, jelly	50.00	—
Creamer	25.00	50.00
Cruet, os	45.00	—
Decanter, os	100.00	—
Goblet	24.00	—
Juice Tumbler	10.00	20.00
Molasses Can	75.00	—
Pitcher, water	60.00	—
Punch Bowl	175.00	—
Punch Cup	10.00	—
Salt Shaker	10.00	—
Sauce	7.50	—
*Spooner	24.00	35.00
Sugar, cov	40.00	55.00
Syrup	50.00	—
Tankard	110.00	—
Toothpick	35.00	90.00
Tumbler	28.00	40.00
Whiskey	20.00	35.00
Wine	15.00	40.00

PICKET (London, Picket Fence)

Non-flint made by the King, Son and Co., Pittsburgh, PA, c1890. Toothpick holders are known in apple green, vaseline, and purple slag.

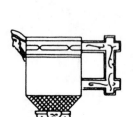

	Clear
Bowl, 9-1/2," sq	30.00
Bread Plate	70.00
Butter, cov	65.00
Celery Vase	40.00
Compote	
Cov, hs, 8"	135.00
Cov, ls, 8"	125.00
Open, hs, 7," sq	35.00
Open, hs, 10," sq	70.00
Open, ls, 7"	50.00
Creamer	50.00
Goblet	50.00
Pitcher, water	95.00

	Clear
Salt	
Individual	10.00
Master	35.00
Sauce	
Flat	15.00
Footed	20.00
Spooner	30.00
Sugar, cov	50.00
Toothpick	35.00
Tray, water	65.00
Waste Bowl	40.00
Wine	85.00

QUEEN ANNE (Bearded Man)

Non-flint made by LaBelle Glass Co., Bridgeport, Ohio, c1879. Finials are Maltese cross. At least 28 pieces are documented. A table set and water pitcher are known in amber.

	Clear
Bowl, cov	
8," oval	45.00
9," oval	55.00
Bread Plate	50.00
Butter, cov	65.00
Celery Vase	35.00

	Clear
Compote, cov, ls, 9"	85.00
Creamer	45.00
Eggcup	45.00
Pitcher	
Milk	75.00
Water	85.00

	Clear
Salt Shaker	40.00
Sauce	15.00
Spooner	40.00
Sugar, cov	55.00
Syrup	100.00

RED BLOCK (Late Block)

Non-flint with red stain made by Doyle and Co., Pittsburgh, PA. Later made by five companies, plus U.S. Glass Co. in 1892. Prices for clear 50% less.

	Ruby Stained
Banana Boat	75.00
Bowl, 8"	75.00
Butter, cov	110.00
Celery Vase, 6-1/2"	85.00
Cheese Dish, cov	125.00
Creamer	
Individual	45.00
Table	70.00

	Ruby Stained
Decanter, 12," os, variant	175.00
*Goblet	35.00
Mug	50.00
Mustard, cov	55.00
Pitcher, water, 8" h	175.00
Relish Tray	25.00
Rose Bowl	75.00

	Ruby Stained
Salt Dip, individual	50.00
Salt Shaker	75.00
Sauce, flat, 4-1/2"	20.00
Spooner	45.00
Sugar, cov	90.00
Tumbler	40.00
*Wine	40.00

SKILTON (Early Oregon)

Made by Richards and Hartley of Tarentum, PA, in 1888 and by U.S. Glass Co. after 1891. This is not one of the U.S. Glass States pattern series and should not be confused with Beaded Loop, which is Oregon #1, named by U.S. Glass Co. It is better as Skilton (named by Millard) to avoid confusion with Beaded Loop.

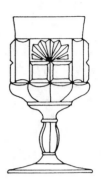

	Clear	Ruby Stained		Clear	Ruby Stained
Bowl			Goblet	35.00	50.00
5," round	15.00	—	Olive, handled	20.00	—
7," rect	20.00	—	Pickle	15.00	—
9," rect	30.00	—	Pitcher		
Butter, cov	45.00	110.00	Milk	45.00	125.00
Cake Stand	35.00	—	Water	50.00	125.00
Celery Vase	35.00	95.00	Salt & Pepper, pr	45.00	—
Compote			Sauce, ftd	12.00	20.00
Cov, hs, 8"	45.00	—	Spooner, flat	25.00	55.00
Open, ls, 8"	30.00	75.00	Sugar, cov	35.00	85.00
Creamer	30.00	55.00	Tray, water	45.00	—
Dish, oblong, sq	25.00	—	Tumbler	25.00	40.00
			Wine	35.00	50.00

SPIREA BAND (Earl, Nailhead Variant, Spirea, Squared Dot)

Non-flint made by Bryce, Higbee and Co., Pittsburgh, PA, c1885.

	Amber	Blue	Clear	Vaseline
Bowl, 8"	25.00	40.00	20.00	30.00
Butter, cov	50.00	55.00	35.00	45.00
Cake Stand, 11"	45.00	55.00	40.00	45.00
Celery Vase	40.00	50.00	25.00	40.00
Compote, cov, hs, 7"	44.00	65.00	40.00	44.00
Cordial	38.00	42.00	20.00	38.00
Creamer	32.50	44.00	35.00	35.00
Goblet	30.00	35.00	25.00	35.00
Pitcher, water	65.00	80.00	35.00	60.00
Platter, 10-1/2"	32.00	42.00	20.00	32.00
Relish	30.00	35.00	18.00	30.00
Sauce				
Flat	10.00	12.00	5.00	10.00
Ftd	15.00	15.00	8.00	15.00
Spooner	30.00	35.00	20.00	35.00
Sugar, open	32.00	40.00	25.00	32.00
Tumbler	24.00	35.00	20.00	30.00
Wine	30.00	35.00	20.00	30.00

TENNESSEE (Jewel and Crescent, Jeweled Rosette)

Non-flint made by King, Son & Co., Pittsburgh, PA, and continued by U.S. Glass Co. in 1899 as part of the States series.

	Clear	Colored Jewels		Clear	Colored Jewels
Bowl			Open, ls, 7"	35.00	—
Cov, 7"	40.00	—	Creamer	30.00	—
Open, 8"	35.00	40.00	Cruet	65.00	—
Bread Plate	40.00	75.00	Goblet	40.00	—
Butter, cov	55.00	—	Mug	40.00	—
Cake Stand			Pitcher		
8"	35.00	—	Milk	55.00	—
9-1/2"	38.00	—	Water	65.00	—
10-1/2"	45.00	—	Relish	20.00	—
Celery Vase	35.00	—	Salt Shaker	30.00	—
Compote			Spooner	35.00	—
Cov, hs, 5"	40.00	55.00	Sugar, cov	45.00	—
Cov, hs, 7"	50.00	—	Syrup	90.00	—
Open, hs, 6"	30.00	—	Toothpick	75.00	85.00
Open, hs, 8"	40.00	—	Tumbler	35.00	—
Open, hs, 10"	65.00	—	Wine	65.00	85.00

TEXAS (Loop with Stippled Panels)

Non-flint made by U.S. Glass Co., Pittsburgh, PA, c1900, in the States pattern series. Occasionally pieces are found in ruby stained (wine, $175). Reproduced in solid colors, including cobalt blue, by Crystal Art Glass Co. and Boyd Glass Co., Cambridge, Ohio.

	Clear with Gold	Rose Stained		Clear with Gold	Rose Stained
Bowl			Pickle, 8-1/2"	25.00	50.00
7"	20.00	40.00	Pitcher, water.	125.00	400.00
9," scalloped	35.00	50.00	Plate, 9"	35.00	60.00
Butter, cov	75.00	125.00	Salt Shaker	25.00	—
Cake Stand, 9-1/2"	65.00	125.00	Sauce		
Celery Tray	30.00	50.00	Flat	10.00	20.00
Celery Vase	40.00	85.00	Footed.	20.00	25.00
Compote			Spooner.	35.00	80.00
Cov, hs, 6"	60.00	125.00	Sugar		
Cov, hs, 7"	70.00	150.00	*Individual, cov	45.00	—
Cov, hs, 8"	75.00	175.00	Table, cov	75.00	125.00
Open, hs, 5"	45.00	75.00	Syrup	75.00	175.00
Creamer			Toothpick.	25.00	95.00
*Individual	20.00	45.00	Tumbler	40.00	100.00
Table.	45.00	85.00	Vase		
Cruet, os	75.00	165.00	6-1/2"	25.00	—
Goblet	95.00	110.00	9".	35.00	—
Horseradish, cov	50.00	—	*Wine.	75.00	140.00

THREE-FACE

Non-flint made by George A. Duncan & Son, Pittsburgh, PA, c1878. Designed by John E. Miller, a designer with Duncan, who later became a member of the firm. It has been heavily reproduced by L. G. Wright Glass Co. and other companies as early as the 1930s. Imperial Glass Co. was commissioned by the Metropolitan Museum of Art, New York, to reproduce a series of Three-Face items, each marked with the "M.M.A." monogram.

	Clear		Clear		Clear
Biscuit Jar, cov.	300.00	*Claret	110.00	*Lamp. Oil	150.00
*Butter, cov	165.00	*Compote		Marmalade Jar	275.00
*Cake Stand		Cov, hs, 8"	175.00	Pitcher, water	325.00
9"	175.00	Cov, hs, 9"	190.00	*Salt Dip	35.00
12-1/2".	225.00	Cov, hs, 10"	225.00	*Salt & Pepper	75.00
Celery Vase		Cov, ls, 6"	160.00	*Sauce, ftd	25.00
Plain	110.00	Open, hs, 9".	165.00	*Spooner.	80.00
Scalloped	110.00	Open, ls, 6"	95.00	*Sugar, cov	125.00
*Champagne		*Creamer	135.00	*Wine	150.00
Hollow stem.	250.00	*Goblet	85.00		
Saucer type.	150.00				

TRUNCATED CUBE (Thompson's #77)

Non-flint made by Thompson Glass Co., Uniontown, PA, c1894. Also found with copper-wheel engraving.

	Clear	Ruby Stained		Clear	Ruby Stained
Bowl, 8"	—	40.00	Water, 1/2 gal	60.00	115.00
Butter, cov	50.00	90.00	Salt Shaker, single	15.00	30.00
Celery Vase	40.00	55.00	Sauce, 4"	30.00	50.00
Creamer			Spooner	30.00	50.00
Individual	20.00	30.00	Sugar, cov		
Regular	35.00	65.00	Individual	20.00	35.00
Cruet, os, ph	35.00	90.00	Regular	30.00	65.00
Decanter, os, 12" h	60.00	150.00	Syrup	40.00	100.00
Goblet	30.00	50.00	Toothpick	30.00	45.00
Pitcher, ah			Tray, water	20.00	40.00
Milk, 1 qt	50.00	100.00	Tumbler	22.50	35.00
			Wine	25.00	40.00

U.S. COIN

Non-flint frosted, clear, and gilded pattern made by U.S. Glass Co., Pittsburgh, PA, in 1892 for three or four months. The U.S. Treasury stopped production because real coins, dated as early as 1878, were used in the molds. The 1892 coin date is the most common. Lamps with coins on font and stem would be 50% more. Heavily reproduced for the gift-shop trade.

	Clear	Frosted		Clear	Frosted
Ale Glass	250.00	350.00	Cruet, os	375.00	500.00
*Bowl			Epergne	—	1,000.00
6"	170.00	220.00	Goblet	300.00	450.00
9"	215.00	325.00	Goblet, dimes	200.00	295.00
*Bread Plate	175.00	325.00	Lamp		
Butter, cov,			Round font	275.00	450.00
dollars and halves	250.00	450.00	Square font	300.00	—
Cake Stand, 10"	225.00	400.00	Mug, handled	200.00	300.00
Celery Tray	200.00	—	Pickle	200.00	—
Celery Vase, quarters	135.00	350.00	Pitcher		
Champagne	—	400.00	Milk	500.00	800.00
*Compote			Water	400.00	800.00
Cov, hs, 7"	300.00	500.00	Sauce, ftd, 4,"		
Cov, hs, 8,"			quarters	100.00	185.00
quarters and dimes	—	550.00	*Spooner, quarters	225.00	325.00
Open, hs, 7,"			*Sugar, cov	225.00	450.00
quarters and dimes	200.00	300.00	Syrup, dated pewter lid	—	650.00
Open, hs, 7,"			*Toothpick	180.00	275.00
quarters and halves	225.00	350.00	Tray, water, 10," round	450.00	550.00
Open, 8-3/8" d,			*Tumbler	135.00	235.00
6-1/2" h	—	240.00	Waste Bowl	225.00	250.00
*Creamer	350.00	600.00	Wine	225.00	375.00

U.S. SHERATON (Greek Key)

Made by U.S. Glass Co., Pittsburgh, PA, in 1912. This pattern was made only in clear, but can be found trimmed with gold or platinum or with a green stain. Some pieces are marked with the intertwined U.S. Glass trademark.

	Clear		Clear		Clear
Bowl		Berry, bulbous, sq ft	15.00	Pin Tray	12.00
6," ftd, sq	15.00	Large	18.00	Pitcher, water, 1/2 gal	30.00
8," flat	12.00	Cruet, os	25.00	Squat, medium	30.00
Bureau Tray	30.00	Finger Bowl,		Tankard	35.00
Butter, cov	35.00	under plate	24.00	Plate, sq	
Celery Tray	30.00	Goblet	18.00	4-1/2"	8.00
Compote		Iced Tea	20.00	9"	12.00
Open, 4," jelly	12.00	Lamp, miniature	50.00	Pomade Jar	14.00
Open, 6"	14.00	Marmalade Jar	35.00	Puff Box	14.00
Creamer		Mug	15.00	Punch Bowl, cov, 14"	90.00
After dinner,		Mustard Jar, cov	30.00	Ring Tree	25.00
tall, sq ft	12.00	Pickle	10.00		

	Clear			Clear			Clear
Salt Shaker		Spooner			Regular		20.00
Squat	12.00	Handled	25.00		Sundae Dish		10.00
Tall	15.00	Tray	12.00		Syrup, glass lid		35.00
Salt, individual	17.00	Sugar, cov			Toothpick		35.00
Sardine Box	35.00	Individual	15.00		Tumbler		15.00

VERMONT (Honeycomb with Flower Rim, Inverted Thumbprint with Daisy Band)

Non-flint made by U.S. Glass Co., Pittsburgh, PA, 1899-1903. Also made in custard (usually decorated), chocolate, caramel, novelty slag, milk glass, and blue. Crystal Art Glass Co., Mosser Glass Co., and Degenhart Glass (which marks its colored line) have reproduced toothpick holders.

	Clear with Gold	Green with Gold		Clear with Gold	Green with Gold
Basket, handle	30.00	45.00	Goblet	40.00	50.00
Bowl, berry	25.00	45.00	Pickle	20.00	30.00
Butter, cov	40.00	75.00	Pitcher, water	50.00	125.00
Card Tray	20.00	35.00	Salt Shaker	20.00	35.00
Celery Tray	30.00	35.00	Sauce	15.00	20.00
Compote, hs			Spooner	25.00	75.00
Cov	55.00	125.00	Sugar, cov	35.00	80.00
Open	35.00	65.00	*Toothpick	30.00	50.00
Creamer, 4-1/4"	30.00	55.00	Tumbler	20.00	40.00
			Vase	20.00	45.00

VIKING (Bearded Head, Bearded Prophet, Hobb's Centennial, Old Man of the Mountain)

Non-flint made by Hobbs, Brockunier, & Co., Wheeling, WV, in 1876 as its Centennial pattern. No tumbler or goblet originally made. Very rare in milk glass.

	Clear		Clear		Clear
Apothecary Jar, cov	60.00	Cov, ls, 8," oval	95.00	Pitcher, water	125.00
Bowl		Open, hs	60.00		
Cov, 8," oval	55.00	Creamer, 2 types	50.00	Relish	20.00
Cov, 9," oval	65.00	Cup, ftd	35.00	Salt, master	40.00
Bread Plate	70.00	Eggcup	40.00		
Butter, cov	75.00	Marmalade Jar	85.00	Sauce	15.00
Celery Vase	45.00	Mug, ah	50.00	Spooner	35.00
Compote		Pickle	20.00		
Cov, hs, 9"	165.00			Sugar, cov	65.00

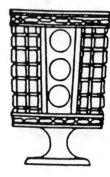

WAFFLE and THUMBPRINT (Bull's Eye and Waffle, Palace, Triple Bull's Eye)

Flint made by the New England Glass Co., East Cambridge, MA, c1868 and by Curling, Robertson & Co., Pittsburgh, PA, c1856. Shards have been found at the Boston and Sandwich Glass Co., Sandwich, MA.

	Clear		Clear		Clear
Bottle, ftd	135.00	Decanter, os		Salt, master	45.00
Bowl, 5" x 7"	30.00	Pint	165.00	Spooner	45.00
Butter, cov	95.00	Quart	195.00	Sugar, cov	125.00
Celery Vase	105.00	Eggcup	45.00	Sweetmeat, cov, hs, 6"	150.00
Champagne	90.00	Goblet, knob stem	65.00	Tumbler	
Claret	110.00	Lamp		Flip Glass	125.00
Compote, cov, hs	150.00	9-1/2"	115.00	Water, ftd	75.00
Cordial	100.00	11," whale oil	175.00	Whiskey	75.00
Creamer	125.00	Pitcher, water	500.00		

WHEAT and BARLEY (Duquesne, Hops and Barley, Oats and Barley)

Non-flint made by Bryce Bros., Pittsburgh, PA, c1880. Later made by U.S. Glass Co., Pittsburgh, PA, after 1891.

	Amber	Blue	Clear	Vaseline
Bowl, 8," cov	35.00	40.00	25.00	55.00
Butter, cov	45.00	60.00	35.00	80.00
Cake Stand				
8"	30.00	45.00	20.00	60.00
10"	40.00	50.00	30.00	70.00
Compote				
Cov, hs, 7"	45.00	55.00	40.00	75.00
Cov, hs, 8"	50.00	55.00	45.00	75.00
Open, hs, jelly	32.50	40.00	30.00	55.00
*Creamer	30.00	40.00	28.00	55.00
*Goblet	40.00	55.00	25.00	75.00
Mug	30.00	40.00	20.00	55.00
Pitcher				
Milk	70.00	85.00	40.00	110.00
Water	85.00	95.00	45.00	125.00
Plate				
7"	20.00	30.00	15.00	40.00
9," closed handles	25.00	35.00	20.00	45.00
Relish	20.00	30.00	15.00	40.00
Salt Shaker	25.00	30.00	20.00	40.00
Sauce				
Flat, handled	15.00	15.00	10.00	20.00
Footed	15.00	15.00	10.00	20.00
Spooner	30.00	40.00	24.00	55.00
Sugar, cov	40.00	50.00	35.00	65.00
Syrup	175.00	195.00	85.00	—
Tumbler	35.00	40.00	20.00	55.00

WILLOW OAK (Acorn, Acorn and Oak Leaf, Bryce's Wreath, Stippled Daisy, Thistle and Sunflower)

Non-flint made by Bryce Bros., Pittsburgh, PA, c1885 and by U.S. Glass Company in 1891.

	Amber	Blue	Canary	Clear
Bowl, 8"	45.00	40.00	50.00	20.00
Butter, cov	65.00	65.00	80.00	40.00
Cake Stand, 8-1/2"	55.00	65.00	70.00	45.00
Celery Vase	45.00	60.00	75.00	35.00
Compote				
Cov, hs, 7-1/2"	50.00	65.00	80.00	40.00
Open, 7"	30.00	40.00	48.00	25.00
Creamer	45.00	50.00	60.00	40.00
Goblet	40.00	50.00	60.00	30.00
Mug	35.00	45.00	54.00	30.00
Pitcher				
Milk	50.00	60.00	70.00	45.00
Water	55.00	60.00	75.00	50.00
Plate				
7"	35.00	45.00	50.00	25.00
9"	35.00	35.00	40.00	25.00
Salt Shaker	25.00	40.00	55.00	20.00
Sauce				
Flat, handled, sq	15.00	20.00	24.00	10.00
Footed, 4"	20.00	25.00	30.00	15.00
Spooner	35.00	40.00	48.00	30.00
Sugar, cov	68.50	70.00	75.00	40.00
Tray, water, 10-1/2"	35.00	50.00	60.00	30.00
Tumbler	35.00	40.00	45.00	30.00
Waste Bowl	35.00	40.00	40.00	30.00

WISCONSIN (Beaded Dewdrop)

Non-flint made by U.S. Glass Co. in Gas City, IN, in 1903. One of the States patterns. Toothpick reproduced in colors.

	Clear
Banana Stand	75.00
Bowl	
6". oval, handled, cov	40.00
7", rounded	42.00
Butter, flat flange	75.00
*Cake Stand	
8-1/2"	60.00
9-1/2"	70.00
Celery Tray	40.00
Celery Vase	60.00
Compote	
Cov, hs, 5"	60.00
Cov, hs, 6"	65.00
Cov, hs, 7"	75.00
Cov, hs, 8"	90.00

	Clear
Open, hs, 6"	35.00
Open, hs, 8"	50.00
Open, hs, 10"	75.00
Condiment Set, salt & pepper, mustard, horseradish, tray	110.00
*Creamer	60.00
Cruet, os	80.00
Cup and Saucer	50.00
*Goblet	75.00
Marmalade Jar, straight sides, glass lid	125.00
Mug	35.00

	Clear
Pitcher	
Milk	75.00
Water	85.00
Plate, 6-3/4"	25.00
Punch Cup	12.00
Relish	25.00
Salt Shaker	30.00
Spooner	30.00
Sugar, cov	60.00
Sugar Shaker	90.00
Sweetmeat, 5", ftd, cov	40.00
Syrup	110.00
*Toothpick, kettle	55.00
Tumbler	45.00
Wine	75.00

X-RAY

Non-flint made by Riverside Glass Works, Wellsburgh, WV, 1896-98. Prices are for pieces with gold trim.

	Clear	Emerald Green
Bowl, berry, 8," beaded rim	25.00	45.00
Bread Plate	30.00	50.00
Butter, cov	40.00	75.00
Celery Vase	—	50.00
Compote		
Cov, hs	40.00	65.00
Jelly	—	40.00
Creamer		
Individual	20.00	50.00
Regular	35.00	65.00
Cruet Set, 4-leaf clover tray	125.00	350.00

	Clear	Emerald Green
Goblet	20.00	35.00
Pitcher, water	40.00	75.00
Salt Shaker	10.00	15.00
Sauce, flat, 4-1/2" d	8.00	10.00
Spooner	25.00	40.00
Sugar		
Individual, open	20.00	45.00
Regular, cov	35.00	65.00
Tumbler shape	—	75.00
Syrup	—	265.00
Toothpick	25.00	50.00
Tumbler	15.00	25.00

YALE (Crow-foot, Turkey Track)

Non-flint made by McKee & Bros. Co., Jeannette, PA, patented in 1887.

	Clear
Bowl, berry, 10-1/2"	20.00
Butter, cov	45.00
Cake Stand	55.00
Celery Vase	40.00
Compote	
Cov, hs	50.00

	Clear
Open, scalloped rim	25.00
Creamer	60.00
Goblet	45.00
Pitcher, water	65.00
Relish, oval	10.00
Salt Shaker	30.00

	Clear
Sauce, flat	10.00
Spooner	45.00
Sugar, cov	35.00
Syrup	65.00
Tumbler	25.00

ZIPPER (Cobb)

Non-flint made by Richards & Hartley, Tarentum, PA, c1888.

	Clear
Bowl, 7" d	15.00
Butter, cov	45.00
Celery Vase	25.00
Cheese, cov	55.00
Compote, cov, ls, 8" d	40.00
Creamer	35.00

	Clear
Cruet, os	45.00
Goblet	20.00
Marmalade Jar, cov	45.00
Pitcher, water, 1/2 gal.	40.00
Relish, 10" l	15.00
Salt Dip	5.00

	Clear
Sauce	
Flat	7.50
Footed	12.00
Spooner	30.00
Sugar, cov	45.00
Tumbler	20.00

PAUL REVERE POTTERY

S.E.G.

History: Paul Revere Pottery, Boston, Massachusetts, was an outgrowth of a club known as The Saturday Evening Girls. The S.E.G. was composed of young female immigrants who met on Saturday nights to read and participate in craft projects, such as ceramics.

Regular pottery production began in 1908, and the name "Paul Revere" was adopted because the pottery was located near the Old North Church. In 1915, the firm moved to Brighton, Massachusetts. Known as the "Bowl Shop," the pottery grew steadily. In spite of popular acceptance and technical advancements, the pottery required continual subsidies. It finally closed in January 1942.

Items produced range from plain and decorated vases to tablewares to illustrated tiles. Many decorated wares were incised and glazed either in an Art Nouveau matte finish or an occasional high glaze.

Marks: In addition to an impressed mark, paper "Bowl Shop" labels were used prior to 1915. Pieces also can be found with a date and "P.R.P." or "S.E.G." painted on the base.

References: Susan and Al Bagdade, *Warman's American Pottery and Porcelain*, Wallace-Homestead, 1994; Paul Evans, *Art Pottery of the United States*, 2nd ed., Feingold & Lewis Publishing, 1987; Ralph and Terry Kovel, *Kovels' American Art Pottery*, Crown Publishers, 1993; David Rago, *American Art Pottery*, Knickerbocker Press, 1977.

Collectors' Club: American Art Pottery Association, P.O. Box 1226, Westport, MA 02790.

Bowl, cuerda seca decoration
    5-1/2" d, 2-1/2" h, white rabbits, yellow ground, repair to rim chip, mkd "265-3-11/I.G./S.E.G., 1911" 700.00
    5-1/2" d, 2-1/2" h, landscape dec, brown trees, outlined in black, yellow ground, white sky, repaired chips. . . . 450.00

Tea Caddy, cuerda seca dec, indigo irises, brown and green ground, ink mark, small chips to lid, short tight line on jar, 4" h, 3-1/2" d, $1,200. Photo courtesy of David Rago Auctions, Inc.

Breakfast Set, cuerda seca dec, white running rabbits, blue ground, inscribed to "Bruce Learned," sgd and dated "12-18" in ink, 1918, hairline and chip repair to bowl, chip repair to plate 1,300.00
Cereal Bowl, 6" d, 1-3/4" d, cuerda seca dec, yellow and white hen and chicks, inscribed "To Eliza," sgd and dated "241-4-09, F. L.," 1909, two short tight hairlines, slight surface wear 750.00
Plate, cuerda sec decoration
    5-1/2" d, pine cone dec, green, black, and brown, light cream ground, sgd, dated 5-22, artist sgd 170.00
    6-1/2" d, chicken and chicks, cream and yellow ground, sgd and initialed "EG," dated 9-13 . . . . 350.00
    6-1/2" d, whimsical chick, outlined in black, cream and yellow ground, artist sgd and dated 650.00
    7-1/2" d, green and brown trees, dark blue ground, ink sgd "7-14 S.E.G./A.M." 1914, tight hairline and minor touch-up to rim 350.00
    8-1/2" d, ivory trotting pigs, yellow, ochre, and ivory ground, inscribed "HOS" for Helen Osborn Storrow, as a Christmas gift from her workers, sgd and dated "241-4-09" and "F. I.". 2,700.00
Tankard Set, 7-1/2" h, 9-1/2" d tankard, six mugs, blue-green matte glaze, imp Paul Revere mark 650.00
Tea Caddy, cov, 4" h, 3-1/2" d, cuerda seca dec, indigo irises, brown and green ground, ink sgd "S. E. G. 11-14," small chips to lid, tight line on jar 1,200.00
Tile, 5" d, brown and green geometric, blue ground, black outline, sgd, framed in oak Arts & Crafts frame. 250.00
Tray, 7" l, incised and painted tree, two tones of green, blue, and black, sgd, cracked and glued 280.00
Vase
    4-1/2" h, blue semi-gloss glaze, imp Paul Revere mark 120.00
    8-3/4" h, 7-1/4" d, swirling, robin's egg blue semi-matte glaze, ink mark "P.R.P./11-20,"" c1920 . . . . 400.00

PEACHBLOW

History: Peachblow, an art glass which derives its name from a fine Chinese glazed porcelain, resembles a peach or crushed strawberries in color. Three American glass manufacturers and two English firms produced peachblow glass in the late 1880s. A fourth American company resumed the process in the 1950s. The glass from each firm has its own identifying characteristics.

Hobbs, Brockunier & Co., Wheeling peachblow: Opalescent glass, plated or cased with a transparent amber glass; shading from yellow at the base to a deep red at top; glossy or satin finish.

Mt. Washington "Peach Blow": A homogeneous glass, shading from a pale gray-blue to a soft rose color; some pieces enhanced with glass appliqués, enameling, and gilding.

New England Glass Works, New England peachblow (advertised as Wild Rose, but called Peach Blow at the plant): Translucent, shading from rose to white; acid or glossy finish; some pieces enameled and gilded.

Thomas Webb & Sons and Stevens and Williams (English firms): Peachblow-style cased art glass, shading from yellow to red; some pieces with cameo-type relief designs.

Gunderson Glass Co.: Produced peachblow-type art glass to order during the 1950s; shades from an opaque faint tint of pink, which is almost white, to a deep rose.

Marks: Pieces made in England are marked "Peach Blow" or "Peach Bloom."

References: Gary E. Baker et al., *Wheeling Glass 1829-1939*, Oglebay Institute, 1994, distributed by Antique Publications; Neila and Tom Bredehoft, *Hobbs, Brockunier & Co. Glass*, Collector Books, 1997; James Measell, *New Martinsville Glass*, Antique Publications, 1994; John A. Shuman III, *Collector's Encyclopedia of American Glass*, Collector Books, 1988, 1994 value update; Kenneth Wilson, *American Glass 1760-1930*, 2 Vols., Hudson Hills Press and The Toledo Museum of Art, 1994.

Gunderson

Cornucopia Vase, acid finish, deep rose shading to white, ruffled top, curled tip 525.00
Creamer and Sugar, 3-1/2" h, 5-3/4" w, acid finish, deep pink, vertical stripes, applied reeded handles 485.00
Cruet, 8" h, 3-1/2" d, matte finish, ribbed shell handle, matching stopper 875.00
Decanter, 10" h, bulbous, ftd, pouring lip, deep raspberry shaded to pale pink to white, orig peachblow stopper, reeded shell applied peachblow handle 775.00
Goblet, acid finish, deep raspberry, applied peachblow foot 275.00
Jug, 4-1/2" h, 4" w, bulbous, applied loop handle, acid finish 450.00
Toothpick Holder 150.00
Tumbler, 3-3/4" h, matte finish 275.00
Vase, 9" h, 3-1/4" w at base, Tappan, acid finish 425.00
Wine Glass, 5" h, glossy finish 175.00

Mt. Washington

Creamer, 5-1/4" h, ribbon edge, applied handle, orig paper label "Patented/Peach/Mt. W G Co/Blow/Dec 15 '85" 2,950.00
Cruet, 5-1/2" h, cylindrical ribbed body, blackberry vine dec, orig white faceted molded stopper with blue-gray tint, two small foot flakes on base 1,000.00
Jack In The Pulpit, 9" h, bright pink shading to blue,, matte finish, c1880 . . . . .4,250.00
Sugar, cov, orig paper label .2,950.00

New England

Bowl, 5-1/2" d, ruffled rim 375.00
Bride's Bowl, 10" d, shiny finish 285.00
Celery, shiny finish, scalloped 685.00
Creamer, 3" h, bulbous, ribbed, deep raspberry to white, white violets, leaves, and buds dec, gold trimmed handle and rim 650.00
Hat Stand, ground pontil 140.00
Lamp, 16" h, base with ribbed font, floral enameling, matching lift out font, brass collar and burner 275.00
Pitcher, 6-1/4" h, crimped top, applied handle 1,300.00
Punch Cup, acid finish, deep rose shading to white, applied white handle 425.00
Salt and Pepper Shakers, pr, orig sterling tops 1,100.00
Spooner, sq top, acid finish 825.00
Tumbler, 3-3/4" h, satin finish, deep raspberry red extending two-thirds down to pure white base 475.00
Vase
5-1/2" h, shiny finish, deep color 485.00
6" h, Wild Rose tricorn dec 1,150.00
7" h, trumpet, tricorn, deep raspberry pink shading to white base 550.00

Rose Bowl, gold Jules Barbe enameled floral dec, on front, gold enamel butterfly on back, eight soft crimps, lined with gold enamel, creamy white lining, polished pontil, 3" h, 3" w, $550. Photo courtesy of Johanna Billings.

10-1/2" h, 5" d, bulbous, tapering neck and cup top, deep color, orig glossy finish 1,250.00

Webb

Bowl, 3-3/4" d, folded and pinched rim, stamped on bottom "Queen's Burmese Ware Patented Thos Webb & Sons" 425.00
Scent Bottle, 2-3/4" d, acid finish, enameled blue, white, and yellow forget-me-nots, green leaves, creamy white lining, hallmarked SS screw-on dome top 695.00
Vase
8-1/2" h, butterfly hovering near tree, gold flowers and buds, deep pink shading to white, creamy lining 795.00
11-1/4" h, 6-1/2" w, deep cherry red shading to pink-peach, creamy white lining, gold trim, James Barbe dec pine needles, boughs, trailing prunus blossoms, buds, and branches, two butterflies in flight 750.00

Wheeling

Cruet, petticoat type, amber handle, cut amber stopper 1,300.00
Finger Bowl, 4-3/4" d, yellow shading to deep red, opaque white int. 400.00
Lemonade Tumbler, 5-1/2" h, acid finish, elongated, Hobbs Brockunier 365.00
Milk Pitcher, 7-1/2" h, glossy finish, Hobbs Brockunier, c1890 . . . . .1,000.00
Pitcher
8" h, bulbous, quatrefoil top, glossy, deep coloration, white casing, applied amber handle 400.00
11" h, acid finish, tankard, red to amber shading, opal glass int., applied amber reeded handle, Hobbs Brockunier 2,415.00
Punch Cup
2-1/4" h, satin finish, chalk white lining, clear amber glass curled handle 575.00
2-1/2" h, Hobbs, Brockunier 535.00
Salt Shaker, large, satin 650.00

Tumbler, shiny finish 485.00
Vase
    2-1/2" h, bulbous, short collared rim, glossy, deep coloration
    . . . . 300.00
    8" h, cased, white int., glossy finish, yellow to amber to red,
    unmarked, minute flake at top 500.00
    9-1/4" h, shiny finish, creamy yellow ball shaped lower half,
    dark mahogany slender 5" h neck, Hobbs, Brockunier
    . . . . 885.00
    10" h, stick, glossy, c1890 . . . . .1,100.00

PEKING GLASS

History: Peking glass is a type of cameo glass of Chinese origin. Its production began in the 1700s and continued well into the 19th century. The background color of Peking glass may be a delicate shade of yellow, green, or white. One style of white background is so transparent that it often is referred to as the "snowflake" ground. The overlay colors include a rich garnet red, deep blue, and emerald green.

Bottle, 3-1/2" h, amber colored, interior painting of kingfishers and lotus plants, sgd "Kuan Yu Tien," c1900 . . . . 690.00
Bowl
    5-7/8" d, 2-5/8" h, rounded sides, raised foot, ext. with floral branches in relief, opaque pink, 19th C, minor hairline
    . . . . 250.00
    6-1/2" h, deep rounded sides, gently flared rim, low foot, ruby, early 19th C 520.00
    9" d, foliate form, fitted carved stand, mkd "China," early 20th C 100.00
Cup, 3" d, deep red, bell form, late 19th C 215.00
Jar, cov, 5-3/4" h, urn shape, cobalt blue, geometric pattern
    . . . . 600.00
Snuff Bottle, 2-1/2" h
    Flattened oviform shape, four-color overlay, red, green, yellow, and blue, carved pumpkin plant, 19th C 350.00
    Flattened round form, tapering neck, red overlay on snowflake ground, finely carved boy in boat holding lotus, lion mask handles to side, bright apple green stopper, 19th C
    . . . . 290.00

Pink overlaid white glass, finely carved with Shao Lao on his crane, double gourd, staff, peaches, bats, and four-character seal inscription, reverse with Lan Tsai Ho scattering her basket of flowers, crescent moon, bird, sides with rui jump rings and seal, jade cabochon in silver top, Suchou School, 19th C 450.00
Vase
    3-1/2" h, carved pomegranate and leaves, 19th C, some chips. 2,530.00
    5" h, deep amethyst, double gourd form, covered with vines and smaller gourds, Chi'en Lung mark 700.00
    6" h, ruby overlay carved as to snowflake ground, allover pattern of chih lung and clouds, four character Chi'en Lung mark. 635.00
    9-1/4" h, yellow overlay on white, allover pattern of chih lung and clouds, four character Chi'en Lung mark, pr . . . 300.00
    12" h, carved yellow on white, fish dec. 375.00

PELOTON

History: Wilhelm Kralik of Bohemia patented Peloton art glass in 1880. Later it was also patented in America and England.

Peloton glass is found with both transparent and opaque grounds, although opaque is more common. Opaque colored glass filaments (strings) are applied by dipping or rolling the hot glass. Generally, the filaments (threads) are pink, blue, yellow, and white (rainbow colors) or a single color. Items also may have a satin finish and enamel decorations.

Bowl, 6-1/2" d, 6" h, white ground, all over brown and yellow filaments, ribbed surface, three applied colorless thorn feet, eight point star top 325.00
Fairy Lamp, white ground, pastel filaments, undulating ruffled saucer base, colorless Clarke insert 365.00
Pitcher, 4-3/4" h, green filaments on colorless body 75.00
Plate, 7-3/4" d, colorless ground, blue filaments, enameled floral dec 125.00
Rose Bowl
    4" d, 4" h, bowl form, four pulled edges, sq shape, applied crystal edge and six shell feet, glossy finish blue shaded body, yellow, pink, white, red, and blue filaments . . 400.00

Vase, blue and white, honeycomb cut overlay, 9-1/2" h, $395.

Vase, bulbous, cranberry red filaments, 7" h, $270.

5-1/2" w, 6" h, star shaped top with eight points, white lining, ribbed and swirled body, shades of brown filaments, applied crystal feet 325.00
Toothpick Holder, 3" h, colorless ground, white filaments145.00
Tumbler, 3-3/4" h, colorless ground, yellow, pink, red, light blue, and white filaments. 125.00
Vase

4" h, 4-3/4" d, bulbous shape, folded over tricorn shape top, white ribbed cased body, pink, yellow, blue, and white applied filaments 290.00

6" h, 4-1/2" d, shaded lavender to off-white opaque ground, cased in crystal, all over pink, white, yellow, blue, and red filaments, corset type shape, vertical ribs, tightly crimped top 450.00

6" h, 5" w, ribbed, bright pink ground, yellow, blue, white, red, pink, and purple filaments, white lining, two applied ribbed handles 450.00

PERFUME, COLOGNE, and SCENT BOTTLES

History: The second half of the 19th century was the golden age for decorative bottles made to hold scents. These bottles were made in a variety of shapes and sizes.

An atomizer is a perfume bottle with a spray mechanism. Cologne bottles usually are larger and have stoppers which also may be used as applicators. A perfume bottle has a stopper that often is elongated and designed to be an applicator.

Scent bottles are small bottles used to hold a scent or smelling salts. A vinaigrette is an ornamental box or bottle that has a perforated top and is used to hold aromatic vinegar or smelling salts. Fashionable women of the late 18th and 19th centuries carried them in purses or slipped them into gloves in case of a sudden fainting spell.

Perfume display bottles are frequently oversized bottles, sometimes found with bases. Many are found with advertising and claims exclaiming the virtue or source of the scent. As many small drugstores are being closed, several of these large attractive display bottles are appearing in the marketplace and commanding high prices.

References: Joanne Dubbs Ball and Dorothy Hehl Torem, *Commercial Fragrance Bottles*, Schiffer Publishing, 1993; ——, *Fragrance Bottle Masterpieces*, Schiffer Publishing, 1996; Carla Bordignon, *Perfume Bottles*, Chronicle Books, 1995; Glinda Bowman, *Miniature Perfume Bottles*, Schiffer Publishing, 1994; ——, *More Miniature Perfume Bottles*, Schiffer Publishing, 1996; Jacquelyne Jones-North, *Commercial Perfume Bottles*, revised and updated ed., Schiffer Publishing, 1996; Christie Mayer Lefkowith, *Art of Perfume*, Thames and Hudson, 1994; Monsen and Baer, *Beauty of Perfume*, published by authors (Box 529, Vienna, VA 22183), 1996; ——, *Legacies of Perfume*, published by authors, 1997; ——, *Memories of Perfume*, published by authors, 1998; John Odell, *Digger Odell's Official Antique Bottle and Glass Collector Magazine Price Guide Series*, vol. 6, published by author (1910 Shawhan Rd., Morrow, OH 45152), 1995; Jeri Lyn Ringblum, *Collector's Handbook of Miniature Perfume Bottles*, Schiffer Publishing, 1996.

Periodical: *Perfume & Scent Bottle Quarterly*, P.O. Box 187, Galena, OH 43021.

Collectors' Clubs: International Perfume Bottle Association, P.O. Box 529, Vienna, VA 22183-0529; Mini-Scents, 7 Saint John's Rd., West Hollywood, CA 90069; Parfum Plus Collections, 1590 Louis-Carrier Ste. 502, Montreal Quebec H4N 2Z1 Canada.

Atomizers

Baccarat, 5" h, 3-1/2" l, oval, etched crystal body, metal chrome top, marked 115.00
Opalescent, 5-1/2" h cranberry striped, orig fittings 125.00
Steuben, 4" h, Aurene. 230.00

Colognes

Baccarat, 6-1/8" h, cut and pressed body, mkd "Baccarat France," chips on stopper. 30.00
Blown Three-Mold, 6" h, purple, tooled flared lip, pontil, ribbed 650.00
Bohemian Glass, 3" x 6-3/4", Vintage pattern, ruby and clear, orig steeple stopper 150.00
Cut, 7-3/4" h, turquoise blue cut to white cut to clear, matching swirled teardrop stopper. 375.00
Opalescent, 4-5/8" h, eight tooled panels, c1860 . . . . . . 150.00
Pairpoint, 7" h, clear, elaborate floral engraving, orig open red rose in paperweight stopper, Charles Kaziun signature cane 750.00
Sandwich, 9" h, opaque white, elaborate dec, satin finish, price for pr 225.00

Perfumes

Black Glass, 6-3/8" h, gilt filigree, glass stones and jade glass medallion, clear stopper, applicator broken 250.00
Cameo, 3-1/2" h, red trailing flowers, SS top, English 750.00
Commercial

Belter's New Mown Hay Perfume, 9-1/2" h, cylindrical bottle, oval applied reverse painted label with vintage lady, light staining and streaking to int. 150.00

Jockey Club Perfume, 7-1/4" h, milk glass, rect, colorful recessed reverse painted label, stopper with flat top, Pat'd April 2, 1889. . . . . 175.00

Lightner's White Rose Perfume, 7" h, emb cylindrical bottle, colorful oval recessed reverse painted label, ground stopper with flat top, product inside 200.00

Orange Flower Perfume, 7-1/4" h, milk glass, rect, colorful recessed reverse painted label, stopper with flat top, Pat'd April 2, 1889, two chips on bottle. 225.00

Palmer's Bouquet Perfume, 9" h, emb cylindrical bottle, recessed reverse painted label, ground stopper with bulbous top, chip on stopper 325.00

Palmer's Jockey Club Perfume, 9" h, emb, black, gold, white, and red reverse painted label, bulbous stopper. . . . 275.00

Victorian King Edward, 9-1/2" h, cylindrical bottle, recessed colorful reverse painted label, ground stopper, ribbed top

Crab Apple Perfume 325.00

Jasmine Perfume. 325.00

Rose Perfume 325.00

Cranberry

2-1/4" h, round, cranberry, filigree, gilt collar 695.00

2-1/4" x 5-3/4", sanded gold enameled leaves, white enameled flowers, clear ball stopper, gold trim. 135.00

Cut Glass, 6" h, cut glass, SS collar, cut stopper 180.00

Display Bottle, Shalimar, figural, multifaceted top, body, and base, amber body, blue ground stopper, clear foot, 18" h, $750. Photo courtesy of James D. Julia, Inc.

Czechoslovakian
  4-1/2" h, clear and frosted, butterfly stopper, chip on stopper, incomplete applicator, mkd "Made in Czechoslovakia" 200.00
  5-3/4" h, amethyst cut and pressed body, clear stopper, Aristo paper label, mkd "Made in Czechoslovakia" 250.00
  5-3/4" h, pale blue cut and pressed body, gilded filigree, blue glass stones and faux pearls, mkd "Made in Czechoslovakia" 825.00
  8-1/2" h, waisted, amber, eight panel cut, orig conforming stopper. 150.00
Golliwogg, 2-5/8" h, figural, orig paper label 185.00
Moser, 4-1/2" l, lay down type, cranberry, white overlay, gold holly leaves and thistles 250.00
Opaline, 8" h, green, bell shaped base, tulip rim, enameled gold florals and dec, orig gold enameled stopper, polished pontil, c1870 . . . . 195.00
Staffordshire, 2-3/4" h, pillow shape, hp, garlands, gold dec, corner tassels, price for pr. 250.00

Perfume Display

Richard Hudnut Violet Sec, Toilet Water, 23" h, oversized emb bottle, paper label on front, back, and neck, crown-shaped top, paper labels in fair condition 800.00
Rieger's Perfumes, 9" h, wooden lazy Susan base holds eight beveled bottles, each with emb ground stoppers and holding a variety of Rieger's Perfumes, minor paper loss to one paper label 1,500.00
Shalimar, 18" h, figural bottle, multifaceted top, body, and base, amber body, clear glass base, blue ground stopper . 750.00

Scents

Blown Three Mold, cobalt blue, sunburst pattern 95.00
Northwood, 1-3/4" h, pull-up design, eight horizontal bands, alternating stripes of rust, chartreuse, and white, SS cap
. . . . 390.00
Opalescent, 3-1/4" l, horizontal and vertical ribs. 85.00
Paris, 9-3/4" h, porcelain, figural, couple, slight restoration to lady, cracked to base of both 190.00
Rock Crystal, 2-1/4" h, slightly bulbous swirled base, paneled neck with gold mouth chased leafage at neck, domed cov with translucent enameled royal blue over gillouche ground,

moonstone thumbpiece, marked with initials of Workmaster "Henrik Wigstrom," 72 standard, incised signature of Fabergé in Cyrillic, St Petersburg, c1910 . . . . .4,888.00
Satin
  3-3/4" h, white, mother of pearl, Peacock Eye design, monogrammed silver plated lid, orig glass stopper. 435.00
  4" d, white, mother of pearl, 24 white vertical stripes, collar stamped "CS, FS, Std, SILr," name engraved on sterling cap, several minor dents in flip top 400.00
Steuben, 5-1/4" h, Aurene-type, lightly striated green, gold irid heart and vine dec, polished base, ribbed leaf-flame stopper with dauber, attributed to Carder Steuben 635.00

Vinaigrettes

Cranberry, 2-1/2 x 1", rect, cut, enameled pink roses, green leaves, gold dec hinged lid, stopper, finger chain . . . 195.00
Cut Glass, oval design, 14kt rose gold lid with cabochon red stone, pierced floral design filter. 920.00
German Silver, 1" h, stein shape, enameled, marked "Gruss a Munchen" 500.00
Silver-gilt
  1" x 3/4", chased top, grill pierced and gilt, oval, English hallmarks on inside of cover "IT," attributed to Joseph Taylor, Birmingham 150.00
  1" x 1-1/2", chased top, grill pierced and gilt, rect, bottom engraved "Anna," English hallmarks on inside of cover "IT," attributed to Joseph Taylor, Birmingham 150.00
  1-1/4" h, George III, Thomas Willmore maker, Birmingham, 1814, engraved scroll foliate dec, .5 troy oz 350.00
  1-1/2" x 3/4", chased top, grill pierced and gilt, rect, English hallmarks inside of cover "S&S" 100.00

PETERS and REED POTTERY

History: J. D. Peters and Adam Reed founded their pottery company in South Zanesville, Ohio, in 1900. Common flowerpots, jardinieres, and cooking wares comprised the majority of their early output. Occasionally art pottery was attempted, but it was not until 1912 that their Moss Aztec line was introduced and widely accepted. Other art wares include Chromal, Landsun, Montene, Pereco, and Persian.

Peters retired in 1921 and Reed changed the name of the firm to Zane Pottery Company.

Marks: Marked pieces of Peters and Reed Pottery are unknown.

Bowl
  7" d, Moss Aztec, green and brown 120.00
  11-1/2" d, horizontal stripes inside and out 160.00
Jug, 7-1/2" h, swirled form, brown glaze, portrait of Cavalier in yellow 50.00
Mug, 5-3/4" h, high glaze, floral sprigs. 45.00
Nursing Feeder, grape and leaf garland dec around spout, glossy brown glaze. 45.00
Planter, 10-1/2" l, marbleized 75.00
Pitcher, 4" h, brown glaze, yellow floral dec, unmarked, price for pr 70.00
Sand Jar, 21" h, molded design, maiden in forest with horse and rider, castle in trees, green wash over red clay, minor flaws
. . . . 700.00
Vase
  6-1/2" h, blue, green, and brown dec, imp mark. 165.00

Vase, pine cones and needles, terra cotta with green wash, 9-3/4" h, $70.

10" h, hexagonal, marbleized blue and gold, unmarked
. . . . 125.00
10" h, Moss Aztec, emb florals, green and red matte
. . . . 350.00
Wall Pocket
Floral, glossy 135.00
Grapes and vines, molded design, bisque finish, brown and green, incised mark, 8" h 100.00

PEWTER

History: Pewter is a metal alloy consisting mostly of tin with small amounts of lead, copper, antimony, and bismuth added to make the shaping of products easier and to increase the hardness of the material. The metal can be cast, formed around a mold, spun, easily cut, and soldered to form a wide variety of utilitarian articles.

Pewter was known to the ancient Chinese, Egyptians, and Romans. England was the primary source of pewter for the American colonies for nearly 150 years until the American Revolution ended the embargo on raw tin, allowing the small American pewter industry to flourish until the Civil War.

References: Marilyn E. Dragowick (ed.), *Metalwares Price Guide*, Antique Trader Books, 1995; Donald M. Herr, *Pewter in Pennsylvania German Churches*, Vol. XXIX, The Pennsylvania German Society, 1995; Henry J. Kauffman, *American Pewterer*, Astragal Press, 1994.

Collectors' Club: Pewter Collectors Club of America, 504 W Lafayette St., West Chester, PA 19380.

Museum: The Currier Gallery of Art, Manchester, NH.

Note: The listings concentrate on the American and English pewter forms most often encountered by the collector.

Basin
7-3/4" d, Samuel Hamlin, pitted, faint touchmark 125.00
7-3/4" d, Spencer Stafford, Albany, NY, c1820 . . . . . 325.00

8" d, Thomas Danforth Boardman, faint eagle touch
. . . . 225.00
9-1/8" d, Samuel Ellis, London, 18th C. 200.00
Beaker, 3" h, J B Woodbury, Beverly, MA and Philadelphia, PA, 1830-38, handle, good mark 400.00
Bowl
11-1/2" d, shallow, eagle touch with "TD" and "T. Danforth, Philadelphia," 330.00
13-1/4" d, shallow, partial touch for Samuel Danforth, Hartford, CT 440.00
Candlesticks, pr
6" h, Rufus Dunham, Westbrook, ME, c1840, straight line touch, pr 900.00
9-1/2" h, Plumey & Felton, Philadelphia, early 19th C, flaring around stems, circular base 110.00
9-3/4" h, attributed to Horman, Cincinnati, unmarked
. . . . 225.00
9-3/4" h, unmarked American, married pair, one with slight battering, other with foot repair 200.00
10" h, William Calder, Providence, RI, 1817-56, minor pitting on base 325.00
Charger
12-1/4" d, English, crowned rose touchmark, rim stamped with initials, some wear 275.00
13-3/8" d, Thomas Badger, Boston, MA, eagle touch, 13-3/8" d 650.00
13-1/2" d, Nathaniel Austin, Charleston, MA, 13-1/2" d
. . . . 500.00
14-3/4" d, Charles White Leigh, London, England
. . . . 325.00
15" d, English, crowned rose touchmarks and "London," wear and battering 350.00
16-1/2" d, Richard King, London, England 375.00
Compote, 8-5/8" d, 6" h, unmarked 420.00
Coffeepot
10" h, H. B. Ward & Co, Guilford or Wallingford, CT, c1840, lighthouse form, minor pitting and dents 250.00
10-1/2" h, Ashbill Griswold, Meriden, CT, pyriform. . . 250.00
11" h, Roswell Gleason, Dorchester, MA, 19th C, straight line touch mark 250.00
11-1/2" h, Boardman & Hart, Hartford, CT, 1830-50, double belly form 230.00
Communion Bowl, 10-1/2" d, 5-3/4" h, ftd, Hiram Yale & Co., Yalesville, CT, c1824-35 . . . . 600.00

Left: lamp, mkd "Yale & Curtis, NY," whale oil burner, 8-1/4" h, $220; center: tall pot, mkd "G. Richardson" (Boston), 10-1/2" h, shaped wood handle, $335; right: lamp, unmarked American, repair on base, fluid burner with brass tubes, pewter snuffer caps and chain, 7-3/4" h, $250. Photo courtesy of Garth's Auctions, Inc.

Communion Flagon, 10-1/2" h, Eben Smith, Beverly, MA, 1814-56, lighthouse shape, heart motifs dec 450.00

Communion Plate, 13-1/8" d, Thomas Boardman, Hartford, CT, c1805-60, eagle touch mark. 600.00

Creamer, 4-1/2" h, Philadelphia, attributed to William Will
. . . . .6,900.00

Deep Dish, Samuel Hamlin, Hartford, CT, late 18th C . . 600.00

Flagon, 12" h, Smith & Fletman, Albany 350.00

Food Dome, 16-1/2" l, marked "James Dixon & Sons, Sheffield," traces of silver plating, one nut holding handle missing
. . . . 125.00

Funnel, American, unmarked, ring handle, 6-3/8" l 125.00

Ladle
13-1/4" l, Josiah Danforth, Middletown, CT 600.00
13-1/2" l, John Yates, Birmingham, England, c1835, minor pitting on bowl int., ... 90.00

Lamp
6" h, Freeman Porter, Westbrook, MA, brass and tin, whale oil burner, ring handle, ... 425.00
6-1/2" h, unmarked, cast ear handle, fluid burner, snuffer caps on chains, minor battering, wear 140.00
7" h, Henry Hopper, New York, NY, 1842-47, orig whale oil burner, straight line touch, pr 850.00
7-3/4" h, Roswell Gleason, Dorchester, MA, c1830, acorn camphene font 285.00
8-1/2" h, Ostrander & Noyes, New York, NY, 1845-50, camphene, resoldered handle, saucer base 400.00

Measure, English, 1750-1800, Channel Island Jersey type, one half pint 375.00

Mug
Eddon, William, London, c1750, pint, tulip shape . . . 175.00
Whitmore, Jacob, Middletown, CT, c1758-90, quart, fair mark
. . . . .1,750.00

Pitcher
5-1/2" h, unmarked, American, pigeon breasted, reverse C-handle, removable lid 325.00
6-1/2" h, Rufus Dunham, Westbrook, ME, c1845, cider type, two quart size 350.00
12" h, Homan & Co, Cincinnati, hinged lid, resoldered finial
. . . . 150.00

Plate
7-3/4" d, Thomas Danforth III, eagle touch and "T. Danford, Phila," wear, pitting, small rim split. 200.00
8" d, partial eagle touch, attributed to Parks Boyd, Phila, worn and battered. 220.00
8" d, partial rampant lion touch, attributed to Thomas Danford, II, Middletown, CT, worn and battered. 200.00
8-1/4" d, English, Townsend & Compton touch, wear and scratches with small splits in metal, pr 175.00
9" d, Thomas Danforth touch 160.00
9-3/16" d, John Skinner, Boston, 1760-90, imp "EF" on rim, minor pitting and scratches 350.00
11-1/4" d, Blakeslee Barns, eagle touch with "Barnes, Phila" in rect, wear, scratches, and edge damage 300.00

Porringer
5" d, unmarked, attributed to David Mellville, Newport, RI, c1780-90, flowered handle initialed "FGW" 200.00
5-1/4" d, cast flowered handle, Calder, Provid. (William Calder, Providene, RI), eagle touch, minor dents
. . . . 660.00
5-1/2" d, Samuel Green, Boston, MA, cast crown handle
. . . . 550.00
5-1/2" d, Samuel Hamlin, Providence, RI, c1790, flowered handle, minor int. pitting, good touch mark 500.00

Salt, Boyd, Parks, Philadelphia, PA, 1795-1819, beaded rim and base, ftd 950.00

Sugar Bowl
Boardman & Hart, NY, c1835, orig lid, little minor denting, 8" h
. . . . 375.00
Unmarked, attributed to Boyd Parks, Philadelphia, PA, c1795-1819, beaded lid, rim and foot 7,500.00

Tall Pot, cov
10-3/4" h, "F. Porter, Westbrook No. 1" touch, Freeman Porter, Westbrook, Maine, finial wafer missing 325.00
10-3/4" h, "T. S. Derby" touch, J#126, Thomas S. Derby, Middletown, CT, corroded surface and soldered repairs
. . . . 220.00
11-3/8" h, unmarked American, dents and repairs, bottom replaced, very worn wooden finial. 95.00

Tankard Pitcher, 7-5/8" h, Boardman & Co., eagle touch, damage to bottom edge, battered spout 660.00

Teapot, cov
7-7/8" h, Sellew & Co. Cincinnati, eagle touch, repairs
. . . . 225.00
8" h, H. Yale & Co. Wallingford, touch inside, dents and some repairs 200.00
8" h, Roswell Gleason, painted metal handle, turned wood finial, rect touch mark to base 250.00
11" h, George Richardson, bear shaped, domed lid with finial, black painted metal handle, rect touch mark 350.00
Henry Joseph, London (1736-1771), wood handle and finial. 4,180.00

PHOENIX GLASS

History: Phoenix Glass Company, Beaver, Pennsylvania, was established in 1880. Known primarily for commercial glassware, the firm also produced a molded, sculptured, cameo-type line from the 1930s until the 1950s.

References: Jack D. Wilson, *Phoenix & Consolidated Art Glass*, Antique Publications, 1989.

Collectors' Club: Phoenix & Consolidated Glass Collectors Club, P.O. Box 159, Burlington, VT 05402-0159.

Lamp, white ground, red berries, green leaves, brown stems, bronze plated base, 22" h, $145.

Ashtray, Praying Mantis, white ground, relief molded insect, triangular 65.00
Basket, 4-1/2" h, pink ground, relief molded dogwood dec 65.00
Bowl, Bittersweet, relief molded, white ground, 9-1/2" d, 5-1/2" h 165.00
Candlesticks, pr
   3-1/4" h, blue ground, bubbles and swirls 65.00
   4" h, blue ground, frosted 50.00
Canoe, 8" l, white ground, sculptured green lemons and foliage
   . . . . 95.00
Centerpiece Bowl, 14" d, opaque white ground, sculptured diving nudes, three colors 250.00
Charger, 14" d, blue ground, relief molded white daffodils
   . . . . 100.00
Cigarette Box, Phlox, white milk glass, Wedgwood blue 125.00
Compote, 8-1/2" d, butterscotch ground, relief molded dragonflies and water lilies dec 85.00
Dish, cov, 8-1/2" l, oval, amber ground, sculptured lotus blossoms and dragonflies 100.00
Ginger Jar, cov, frosted ground, bird finial 80.00
Lamp
   Boudoir, Wild Rose, brown highlights, milk glass ground
   . . . . 150.00
   Table, 23" h, 16" d reverse painted shade, landscape with windmill, cottage, and barn, pale pink, yellow, and blue ground, green and brown landscape, minor edge flake
   . . . . 650.00
Planter, 8-1/2" l, 3-1/4" h, white ground, relief molded green lion
   . . . . 95.00
Plate, 8-1/2" d, frosted and clear ground, relief molded cherries
   . . . . 60.00
Powder Box, cov, 7-1/4" d, pale lavender ground, sculptured white violets 115.00
Rose Bowl, rose pink ground, relief molded starflowers and white bands 150.00
Tumbler, Lace Dew Drop, blue and white, set of 4 . . . . . . 75.00
Vase
   6" h, Cameo, #345, sculptured, blue highlights 130.00
   7" h, Fern, #261, sculptured crystal, very light blue frosted design 130.00
   8-3/4" h, grasshoppers and reeds dec, clear and frosted
   . . . . 125.00
   9" h, 9" w, Cockatoos, aqua, bulbous, cream ground, beige branches, lavender berries 325.00
   9-1/4" h, 8" w, Gold Fish, pale green, peach colored fish
   . . . . 425.00
   9-1/2" h, Bittersweet, gold over milk glass, worn gold 125.00
   9-1/2" h, Peony, yellow, green, custard 160.00
   9-1/2" h, 9" w, Daisies, white milk glass, pale blue/gray painted ground, all over daisies 500.00
   10" h, Wild Geese, #357, pearlized white birds, light green ground 195.00
   10-1/2" h, Foxglove, rose, green, white 125.00
   10-1/2" h, Wild Rose, medium green, milk glass ground, partial label 150.00

PHONOGRAPHS

History: Early phonographs were commonly called "talking machines." Thomas A. Edison invented the first successful phonograph in 1877; other manufacturers followed with their variations.

References: Timothy C. Fabrizio and George F. Paul, *The Talking Machine: An Illustrated Compendium, 1877-1929*, Schiffer Publishing, 1997; Neil Maker,

Hand-Cranked Phonographs, Promar Publishing, 1993; Arnold Schwartzman, *Phono-Graphics*, Chronicle Books, 1993.

Periodicals: *Horn Speaker*, P.O. Box 1193, Mabank, TX 75147; *New Amberola Graphic*, 37 Caledonia St., St. Johnsbury, VT 05819.

Collectors' Clubs: Buckeye Radio & Phonograph Club, 4572 Mark Trail, Copley, OH 44321; California Antique Phonograph Society, P.O. Box 67, Duarte, CA 91010; Hudson Valley Antique Radio & Phonograph Society, P.O. Box 207, Campbell Hall, NY 10916; Michigan Antique Phonograph Society, Inc., 2609 Devonshire, Lansing, MI 48910; Vintage Radio & Phonograph Society, Inc., P.O. Box 165345, Irving, TX 75016.

Museums: Edison National Historic Site, West Orange, NJ; Johnson's Memorial, Dover, DE; Seven Acres Antique Village & Museum, Union, IL.

Advisor: Lewis S. Walters.
Columbia
   BQ cylinder player 1,200.00
   HG cylinder player 2,400.00
Decca, Junior, portable, leather case and handle. 150.00
Edison
   Amberola 30. . . . . 350.00
   Army-Navy, World War I era 1,200.00
   Excelsior, coin op 2,500.00
   Fireside, orig horn 900.00
   Gem, maroon, 2/4 minute reproducer 1,700.00
   Opera, moving mandrel and fixed reproducer . . .2,500.00
   S-19 Diamond Disc, floor model, oak case 400.00
   Standard, Model A, oak case, metal horn 550.00
   Truimph, cygnet horn, mahogany case 2,500.00
Graphone
   12.0 oak case, columns on corners, nickel plated platform, metal horn, stenciled cast iron parts 725.00
   12.5 oak case, metal horn, cylinder, retailer's mark . . 450.00
Home Grand, oak case, nickel plated works #6, spring motor
   . . . . .1,300.00

Pathé Le Gaulois, orig glass horn, 1900-1903, $5,230. Photo courtesy of Auction Team Breker.

Harvard, trumpet style horn 300.00
Kalamazoo, Duplex, reproducer, orig horns with decals, patent
    date 1904 . . . . .3,300.00
Odeon Talking Machine Co., table model, crank wind, brass
    horn, straight tone arm 500.00
Silvertone (Sears), two reproducers 500.00
Sonora
    Gothic Deluxe, walnut case, triple spring, gold plated parts,
      automatic stop and storage 400.00
    Luzerne, Renaissance-style case with storage 200.00
Talk-O-Phone, Brooke, table model, oak case, rope decora-
    tions, steel horn 200.00
Victor
    Credenza, crank 1,100.00
    Monarch, table model, corner columns, brass bell, horn
    . . . . .1,500.00
    School House 2,500.00
    Victor I, mahogany case, corner columns, bell horn 1,500.00
    Victor II, oak case, black bell horn 1,200.00
    Victor III, papier-mâché horn 1,400.00
    Victor V, oak case, corner columns, no horn 1,400.00

PHOTOGRAPHS

History: A vintage print is a positive image developed from the original negative by the photographer or under the photographer's supervision at the time the negative is made. A non-vintage print is a print made from an original negative at a later date. It is quite common for a photographer to make prints from the same negative over several decades. Changes between the original and subsequent prints usually can be identified. Limited edition prints must be clearly labeled.

References: Helmut Gernsheim, *Concise History of Photography*, 3rd ed., Dover Publications, 1986; —, *Creative Photography*, Dover Publications, 1991; Susan Theran (ed.), *Leonard's Annual Price Index of Posters & Photographs*, Auction Index (30 Valentine Park, Newton, MA 02165), 1995.

Periodicals: *CameraShopper*, 313 N Quaker Lane, P.O. Box 37029, W Hartford, CT 06137; *History of Photography*, 1900 Frost Rd., Suite 101, Tullytown, PA 19007; *Photograph Collector*, Photographic Arts Center, 163 Amsterdam Ave. #201, New York, NY 10023.

Collectors' Clubs: American Photographic Historical Society, Inc., 1150 Avenue of the Americas, New York, NY 10036; Association of International Photography Art Dealers, 1609 Connecticut Ave. NW #200, Washington, DC 20009; Daguerrean Society, 625 Liberty Ave., Ste. 1790, Pittsburgh, PA 15222; National Stereoscopic Association, P.O. Box 14801, Columbus, OH 43214; Photographic Historical Society, Inc., P.O. Box 39563, Rochester, NY 14604; Photographic Historical Society of Canada, P.O. Box 54620, Toronto, Ontario M5M 4N5 Canada; Photographic Historical Society of New England, P.O. .Box 189, Boston, MA 02165; Western Photographic Collectors Association Inc., P.O. Box 4294, Whittier, CA 90607.

Museums: Center for Creative Photography, Tucson, AZ; International Center of Photography, New York, NY; International Museum of Photography at George East-

man House, Rochester, NY; International Photographic Historical Association, San Francisco, CA; National Portrait Gallery, Washington, DC.

Additional Listings: See *Warman's Americana & Collectibles* for more examples.

Album
    Alaska and the Northwest, 1903,documenting American's travels, views of totems and Indians, Skaguay, White Pass, and Sitka views, Russian trading post and cemetery, views from Washington, Oregon, California, and Minnesota, North Dakota, and Arkansas, silver prints, 4" x 3" prints, mounted one to 3 per page, many captioned by hand, in ink, on mount, printed wrappers, pr 625.00
    Caribbean, ninety 3-1/2" x 4-1/2" silver print photographs of Cuba, Puerto Rico and St. Thomas, street and market scenes, genre portraits, architectural views, mounted on Kodak Photographs album pages, photographer's caption below, gilt leathered cloth, soiled, disbound, pages loose, 1891 . . . . 950.00
    Class, Massachusetts Agricultural College, fifty-eight faculty and student portraits, campus life, each identified, photographer's imprint on mount recto, gilt letters and edges, buckled, worn, 1876 . . . . 650.00
Albumen Print
    Arkansas River, train in distance, W. H. Jackson, Canton City, CO photographer, 14" x 10-1/2", period frame, 1870s 700.00
    Buffalo Bill, young man with curly long hair, long mustache and goatee, black suit and bow tie, sgd at top in pencil, 8-1/2" x 6-1/2" 800.00
    Lincoln, Abraham, bust portrait by Alexander Hesler, printed by George B. Ayres from Hesler's orig negative, penciled notations on verso, oval, 8" x 6", 1860, printed 1890s 625.00
Cabinet Card
    Buffalo Bill, decorative jacket, hat, looking sideways, printed "Stacy, Brooklyn," titled "W. F. Cody, Col. "Buffalo Bill," pen sgd on right side in blue ink "Buffalo Bill," 6-1/2" x 4-1/2" 650.00
    Chief Geronimo, front emb "Overstreet Studio, Chickasha, I. T., back inscribed "Geronimo, Chief of Apache Indians now prisoner of war at Fort Sill," 5-3/4" x 4" 1,840.00
    Civil War Infantryman, camp scene background, color tint 75.00
    Comanche Quannah Parker, traditional chief garb, c1890, 5-1/2" x 4" 1,150.00
    Imperial, formal portrait of three Yuma warriors, front labeled "Yuma Indians, Arizona., E. A. Bonine phot. Lamonda Park, Los Angeles, Cal," c1890, 7-1/4" x 4-1/2" 690.00
    Imperial, portrait of elaborately dressed Apache warrior, applying war paint to face, stamped on back "A. F. Randall, photographer, Wilcox, A. T.," c1880, 8-1/2" x 4-1/4" 1,035.00
    Kiowa woman, fully beaded and tacked cradle board, emb "Russell, Anadarko O. T.," 6-1/2" x 4-1/4" 550.00
    Nude Woman in Bondage, long haired, full figured . . 200.00

Owens, John G., Armless Guitar Player, with wife at side
. . . . 125.00
Portrait of three children in native dress, back labeled "Laguna Pueblo children from New Mexico," pen and printed "J. N. Choate, photographer for Indian training school, Carlisle Barracks PA," 6-1/2" x 4-1/4". 260.00
Portrait of tightly cradled Indian infant, back labeled "Parker, photographer...San Diego, Cal...," and "804 Moqui Indian baby,..." on front, 8-1/2" x 5-1/4" 150.00
Portrait of young woman, labeled "Dakotah" or "Sioux Indians, C. A. Zimmerman, photographer, St. Paul, Minn," 1870s, 6-1/2" x 4-1/4" 350.00
CDV
Convicted Murder in Chains, identified as Charles Eighmy on back 80.00
Portrait of eastern Plains native man holding pipe with bow to side, 4" x 2-3/8", framed. 490.00
Tatooed Man 150.00
CDV Case, 4" x 2-3/4", relief dragon in clouds on one side, intaglio dragon on other, sgd on intaglio sgd, mounted with silk brocade, Japanese 200.00
Daguerreotype
Capt. Richard T. Goodwin, Indian Army, by Richard Beard, sixth-plate, Beard frame, handwritten notations on reverse, 1840s 220.00
Dog and man, seated on ornate couch, quarter-plate, contemporary seal and half case, 1850s 1,200.00
Greek Revival house, quarter-plate, leather case, 1850s
. . . . 675.00
Policeman, hand tinted, six-plate ambrotype, leather case, 1850s 310.00
Portrait of young girl, basket of roses, 3-5/8" h, 3-1/8" w case, America, mid 19th C 865.00
Timber Mill, Strongsville, OH, sixth-plate, contemporary seal and leather case, 1840s. 2,650.00
Photograph
6-1/2" x 4-1/2", unsigned, portrait of Tlingit man holding carved staff, wearing beaded tunic depicting double headed "Russian Eagle," octopus bag with abstract and flora beading, c1890 . . . . 260.00
7" x 5", President Millard Fillmore, salt print, oval, orig mount
. . . . 715.00

7-1/2" x 5-1/2", portrait of John Brown and Dr. Doy, oval, salt print, ink highlights, Doy's handwritten inscription on mount verso 550.00
7-3/8" x 9-3/8", Nautilus Shell, gelatin silver print, studio stamp on verso "Negative by Edward Weston, print by Cole Weston," sgd in pencil on verso "Cole Weston shell, 1927-15". 1,035.00
7-3/8" x 9-1/2", Row of Houses, Lower Manhattan, 1936, sgd "Berenice Abbott..." in pencil on reverse, artist's stamp on the reverse, gelatin silver print, matted 865.00
7-3/4" x 7-1/2", front emb "Herum Devil's Lake N. D.," formal portrait of four Chippewa man and woman, late 19th/early 20th C 690.00
9" x 6-3/4", unsigned, train stop near Acoma Pueblo, native women peddling pottery jars to train passengers, 1902
. . . . 435.00
13-1/2" x 10-1/2", *Hindenberg* disaster, silver print by Murray Becker, handwritten notations on verso, 1937. . . . . 900.00
Tintype, formal portrait of boy, oval period frame, large hexagonal period frame, memorial wreath of pine cones, pods, and dried flowers, 1850s. 490.00
Tobacco Card, Scanty Dressed Woman Smoking Hashish Pipe
. . . . 150.00

PICKARD CHINA

History: The Pickard China Company was founded by Wilder Pickard in Chicago, Illinois, in 1897. Originally the company imported European china blanks, principally from the Havilands at Limoges, which were then hand painted. The firm presently is located in Antioch, Illinois.

References: Susan and Al Bagdade, *Warman's American Pottery and Porcelain*, Wallace-Homestead, 1994; Alan B. Reed, *Collector's Encyclopedia of Pickard China with Additional Sections on Other Chicago China Studios*, Collector Books, 1996.

Collectors' Club: Pickard Collectors Club, 300 E. Grove St., Bloomington, IL 61701.

SPECIAL AUCTION

Joy Luke Auctions
300 E. Grove St.
Bloomington, IL 61701
(309) 828-5533

Berry Set, apples, blossoms, and leaves, 9-1/2" d bowl sgd "Leon," c1903-05 . . . . 1,050.00
Bowl
5-1/2" d, raspberries and etched gold, sgd "Coufall," 1903-1905 mark. 120.00
5-3/4" d, Regency Water Lilies pattern, sgd "H.E.M.," 1898-1903 mark. 250.00
7-1/4" w, scenic panel wit house, roses and floral border, two handles, 1922-1925 mark 140.00
8-1/4" sq, Peaches Linear pattern, sgd "Beutlich," 1905-1910 mark. 150.00
8-3/4" w, poppies dec, handle, sgd "Fox," 1903-1905 mark
. . . . 325.00

Clearing Winter Storm by Ansel Adams (1902-1984), 15" x 19", $11,787. Photo courtesy of Jackson's Auctioneers & Appraisers.

Chalice, Plain Hops and Matte Green, artist sgd "Hessler," 1905-10 mark, 11-1/4" h, $1,300. Photo courtesy of Joy Luke Auctioneers & Appraisers.

Tankard, monk peeling a turnip, artist sgd "P. Gasper," 1905-10 mark, 13-3/4" h, $2,900. Photo courtesy of Joy Luke Auctioneers & Appraisers.

10-1/4" w, Walled Garden, two handles, sgd "Alex," 1912-1918 mark. 175.00

11" d, Yosemite, sgd "Marker," Nippon blank. 350.00

Cake Plate, 10-3/4" d, two handles, scenic, trees and lake, sgd "Marker," 1912-1918 mark 225.00

Celery Tray, 12" l, 23K gold, sgd 75.00

Chalice, 11-1/4" h, hp, Plain Hops pattern, matte green, artist sgd "Hessler" 1,300.00

Chocolate Pot, cov, grapes and leaves o black and red ground, artist sgd "E. Gibson," c1903-05. . . . . .1,050.00

Cider Pitcher, 8" h, Arabian pattern, 1903-05 mark . . .1,600.00

Creamer and Sugar, hand painted
Apple blossoms, gold dec, fancy blank 110.00
Florals, gold trim, sgd by Curtis Marker 200.00

Cup and Saucer
Aura Argenta Linear pattern, sgd "Vobor," 1918-1919 mark 75.00
Chinese Seasons pattern, sgd "Challinor," 1938-present mark. 30.00
Roses dec, sgd "Blaha," 1903-1905 mark on cup, 1898-1903 mark on saucer 225.00

Jug, 8" h, Alexander strawberries, sgd "Beitler" 1,000.00

Lemonade Pitcher, 5-1/2" h
Daisy Multiflora pattern, 1905-1910 mark 275.00
Encrusted Linear pattern, hexagonal, 1912-1918 mark 450.00

Milk Pitcher, 4" h, Aura Argenta Linear pattern, sgd "O.P.," 1905-1910 mark. 325.00

Mug, elk. 1,500.00

Mustard Pot, cov, Hessler Violets dec, sgd "R.H.," 1903-1905 mark 250.00

Plate
7-1/2" d, hp, cherries, gold web, artist sgd "Beitler" . . . 70.00
8-1/2" d, Easter Lily Swirl pattern, sgd "Schoner," 1903-1905 mark. 250.00
8-3/4" d, White Poppy and Daisy pattern, sgd "Gasper," 1912-1918 mark. 175.00

Punch Bowl, 13" d, 6" h, hp, red currants and leaves, maroon to yellow ground, sgd "Kokral," 1905-10 mark 3,600.00

Salt and Pepper Shakers, pr
Aura Argenta Linear, artist sgd "H". 95.00

Rose and Daisy pattern, etched on gold ground, 2-1/2" h 25.00

Tankard, hp
5" h, 3" d, white pond lily dec, gold trim, artist sgd "Firchs," early sq mark 225.00
14-1/4" h, grapes and leaves, sgd "Coufall," 1905-10 mark 2,250.00
14-1/4" h, monk peeling turnip, artist sgd "GP. Gasper" 2,900.00
14-1/4" h, oranges, blossoms, and leaves, artist sgd "N. R. Gifford," chip restoration to base 1,750.00
15" h, Metallic Grapes dec, sgd "Hessler" 1,100.00

Tray, 15-3/4" l, two handled, scenic Italian Garden pattern, sgd "Gasper," 1912-1918 mark. 350.00

Vase, hp
6-1/4" h, violets, gold trim and rim 95.00
7-1/4" h, scenic, highland cattle, sgd "Kubash," 1904-05 mark 3,500.00
8" h, scenic, walled garden design, ...1,800.00
8-1/2" h, daffodils, artist sgd "Motzfeldt," 1898-1903 . . . . .1,250.00
9-1/2" h, 3-1/4" d, 3 large dark orange poppies, gold, rust, brown, hp, sgd "Gasper" 370.00
10-1/2" h, pink and lavender orchids, sgd "Fuchs," 1905-10 . . . . .1,150.00
14" h, peacock, gold and black, sgd "E. Challinor," dated 1925-30 . . . . .1,700.00
15-1/2" h, pink, yellow, and white chrysanthemums, ornate gilded handles, artist sgd "F. Walters" 2,200.00

PICKLE CASTORS

History: A pickle castor is a table accessory used to serve pickles. It generally consists of a silver-plated frame fitted with a glass insert, matching silver-plated lid, and matching tongs. Pickle castors were very popular during the Victorian era. Inserts are found in pattern glass and colored art glass.

Pattern Glass, Daisy and Button pattern, amber, silver plated Tufts frame, orig tongs, $220.

Biscuit Jar, ribbed body, silver plated fittings, 8-1/2" h, $250.

Cranberry
  Bowl type insert, enameled flowers, gold stems and leaves, ornate frame, 10" h, 8" w 875.00
  Vase type insert, enameled dec, SP lid and orig fork. 495.00
  Crown Milano, Mt. Washington, bowl type insert, pastel pansies, gold tracery, white DQ ground, Pairpoint frame, lid marked "MW 520" 1,495.00
Double
  Clear inserts, vertical panels, band of engraved leaves and vines, Wm Rogers frame 825.00
  Clear inserts, vertical panels, unmarked resilvered frame 750.00
  Florentine insert, frosted blue, enameled dec 550.00
Mt. Washington
  Satin, pink and frosted swirled opalescent stripes, polished pontil, SP frame, small chip under cov 350.00
  Seashell and Seaweed pattern insert, cased, pink to salmon, delicate enameled flowers, leaves, scrolls, Aurora frame, 9-1/2" h 1,150.00
  Opalescent, Daisy and Fern, cranberry 450.00
Pattern
  Daisy and Button, clear, Barbour Bros. #117 resilvered frame 250.00
  Thumbprint, cranberry insert, ornate SP holder 395.00
Pressed Glass, colorless insert
  Castle shaped insert, Warwick Castle, plated white metal stand, 10-1/4" h, 6" d, price for pr 1,250.00
  Engraved flowers on each of six panels, F B Rogers #435 frame, resilvered, 9" h 350.00
Satin
  Blue, cased, egg shape, enameled dec, ornate holder, pickle shaped tongs hook. 700.00
  Rainbow, white to pink insert, Simpson, Hall, Miller frame, 12" h. 1,395.00
  Vaseline, Hobstar (Imperial) pattern insert, Pairpoint frame 750.00

PIGEON BLOOD GLASS

History: Pigeon blood refers to the deep orange-red-colored glassware produced around the turn of the century. Do not confuse it with the many other red glasswares of that period. Pigeon blood has a very definite orange glow.

Berry Bowl, Open Heart	225.00
Biscuit Jar, cov	
Florette	295.00
Little Shrimp	325.00
Butter Dish, cov	
Coreopsis	275.00
Torquay, clear base	195.00
Carafe	
Coreopsis	295.00
Open Heart	295.00
Creamer	
Beaded Drape	150.00
Coreopsis	125.00
Torquay	110.00
Pickle Castor	
Beaded Drape	595.00
Open Heart	375.00
Pitcher, Coreopsis, metal top	400.00
Salt Shaker, Periwinkle Variant	110.00
Syrup, Beaded Drape	595.00
Vase, 10-1/2" h, enameled flowers	195.00

PINK SLAG

History: True pink slag is found only in the molded Inverted Fan and Feather pattern. Quality pieces shade from pink at the top to white at the bottom.

REPRODUCTION ALERT

Recently, pieces of pink slag made from molds of the now-defunct Cambridge Glass Company have been found in the Inverted Strawberry and Inverted Thistle patterns. This is not considered true pink slag and brings only a fraction of the price of the Inverted Fan and Feather pieces.

Tumbler, Inverted Fan and Feather pattern, 4" h, $450.

Bowl

9" d, ftd	600.00
10" d	750.00
Butter Dish, cov, 7-5/8" d, 7" h cov, 2-1/4" h base with 4 molded feet, fiery opalescent coloring	1,485.00
Creamer	465.00
Cruet, 6-1/2" h, orig stopper	1,300.00
Jelly Compote, 5" h, 4-1/2" d, scalloped top	375.00
Marmalade Jar, cov	875.00
Pitcher, water	775.00
Punch Cup, 2-1/2" h, ftd	275.00
Salt Shaker	300.00
Sauce Dish, 4-1/4" d, 2-1/2" h, ball feet	225.00
Spooner	350.00
Sugar Bowl, cov	550.00
Toothpick Holder	825.00
Tumbler, 4-1/2" h	475.00

PIPES

History: Pipe making can be traced as far back as 1575. Pipes were made of almost all types of natural and man-made materials, including amber, base metals, clay, cloisonné, glass, horn, ivory, jade, meerschaum, parian, porcelain, pottery, precious metals, precious stones, semiprecious stones, and assorted woods. Some of these materials retain smoke and some do not. Chronologically, the four most popular materials and their generally accepted introduction dates are: clay, c1575; wood, c1700; porcelain, c1710; and meerschaum, c1725.

Pipe styles reflect nationalities all around the world, wherever tobacco smoking is custom or habit. Pipes represent a broad range of themes and messages, e.g., figurals, important personages, commemoration of historical events, mythological characters, erotic and pornographic subjects, the bucolic, the bizarre, the grotesque, and the graceful.

Pipe collecting began in the mid-1880s; William Bragge, F.S.A., Birmingham, England, was an early collector. Although firmly established through the efforts of freelance writers, auction houses, and museums (but not the tobacco industry), the collecting of antique pipes is an amorphous, maligned, and misunderstood hobby. It is amorphous because there are no defined collecting bounds; maligned because it is perceived as an extension of pipe smoking, and now misunderstood because smoking has become socially unacceptable (even though many pipe collectors are avid non-smokers).

References: R. Fresco-Corbu, *European Pipes*, Lutterworth Press, 1982; Benjamin Rapaport, *Complete Guide to Collecting Antique Pipes*, Schiffer Publishing, 1979.

Periodical: *Complete Smoker Magazine*, P.O. Box 7036, Evanston, IL 60204.

Collectors' Clubs: International Association of Pipe Smokers' Clubs, 47758 Hickory, Apt. 22305, Wixom, MI 48393; New York Pipe Club, P.O. Box 265, Gracie Station, New York, NY 10028; North Texas Pipe Club, 1624 East Cherry St., Sherman, TX 75090; Pipe Collectors Club of America, P.O. Box5179, Woodbridge, VA 22194; Sherlock Holmes Pipe Club Ltd. USA, P.O. Box 221, Westborough, MA 01581; Society for Clay Pipe Research, P.O. Box 817, Bel Air, MD 21014; Southern California Pipe & Cigar Smokers' Association, 1532 South Bundy Dr., Apt. D, Los Angeles, CA 90025.

Museums: Museum of Tobacco Art and History, Nashville, TN; National Tobacco-Textile Museum, Danville, VA; Pipe Smoker's Hall of Fame, Galveston, IN; U.S. Tobacco Museum, Greenwich, CT.

Briar, 11" l, carved bearded man bowl, horn stem	175.00
Clay, 4-1/4" l, blue and white bowl, brown stem, Ohio	165.00
French, Williams Jenning Bryan, Gambier, 2-3/4" l, 2-1/4" h	70.00
Fraternal, c1927, carved, SS bands	125.00
Florida, carved folk art type, c1900	
Black boy being swallowed by alligator, polychrome dec	950.00
Black boy in coat, detailed alligator on back attached to seat of boy's pants, red, green, and black polychrome dec	1,150.00
Snake and alligator	175.00
Meerschaum, carved	
6-1/4" l, girl with spinning wheel, cheroot holder, cracked amber stem, fitted case	550.00

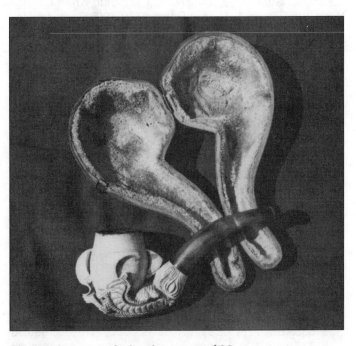

Meerschaum, orig leather case, $90.

6 -7/8" l, tavern scene, maid serving hunter, cheroot holder, amber stem, fitted case 450.00
8" l, 6", laughing bearded soldier, map of France engraved on helmet and tunic, silver fitted case with turquoise .2,650.00
10-1/2" l, hunting, maidens with wolves chase stag around rose, amber stem, fitted case. 1,400.00
Porcelain, 3-1/2" h, Turkish gentleman bowl, bust head, jeweled and beaded turban, underglaze enamels, metal stem mount, hinged bowl cov, German, 19th C 1,500.00
Wood
Civil War, folk art type, highly carved and detailed, emb "Union Forever" 1,300.00
Hand holding bowl 85.00

POCKET KNIVES

History: Alcas, Case, Colonial, Ka-Bar, Queen, and Schrade are the best of the modern pocket-knife manufacturers, with top positions enjoyed by Case and Ka-Bar. Knives by Remington and Winchester, firms no longer in production, are eagerly sought.

References: Jacob N. Jarrett, *Price Guide to Pocket Knives*, L-W Books, 1993, 1995 value update; Bernard Levine, *Levine's Guide to Knives and Their Values*, Krause Publications, 1997; ——, *Pocket Knives*, Apple Press, 1993; Jack Lewis and Roger Combs, *The Gun Digest Book of Knives,* 5th ed., Krause Publications, 1997; Jim Sargent, *Sargent's American Premium Guide to Pocket Knives & Razors*, 4th ed., Books Americana, 1995; Ron Stewart and Roy Ritchie, *Standard Knife Collector's Guide*, 3rd ed., Collector Books, 1993, 1995 value update; J. Bruce Voyles, *International Blade Collectors Association's Price Guide to Antique Knives*, Krause Publications, 1995.

Periodicals: *The Blade*, 700 E. State St., Iola, WI 54990; *Knife World*, P.O. Box 3395, Knoxville, TN 37927.

Collectors' Clubs: American Blade Collectors, P.O. Box 22007, Chattanooga, TN 37422; Canadian Knife Collectors Club, Route 1, Milton, Ontario L9T 2X5 Canada; National Knife Collectors Association, P.O. Box 21070, Chattanooga, TN 37421.

Museum: National Knife Collectors Museum, Chattanooga, TN.

Additional Listings: See *Warman's Americana & Collectibles* for more examples.

Notes: Form is a critical collecting element. The most desirable forms are folding hunters (one or two blades), trappers, peanuts, Barlows, elephant toes, canoes, Texas toothpicks, Coke bottles, gun stocks, and Daddy Barlows. The decorative aspect also heavily influences prices.

Case
265 . . . . 200.00
928R Tested, cracked ice. 350.00
2137, sod buster. 25.00
4200, melon taster, serrated blade. 165.00
5111 1/2 L, SSP Cheetah, 4" 700.00
5165SAB 660.00
5172, 1965-70, XX series. 150.00

Case, Nantaucket Sleigh Ride, scrimshaw handle, $160.

254, 1965-70, XX series. 90.00
5375, stag. 75.00
5391 Tested, red stag 2,000.00
5452 . . . . 300.00
6143, 1965-70, XX series. 45.00
6261 . . . . 125.00
52131, canoe 200.00
61093 Tested, green bone 550.00
Ka-Bar, Union Cutlery Co., Olean, NY
2217, rigger 75.00
6191, knife, fork, spoon 625.00
6260, KF. 100.00
21107, Grizzly 2,000.00
61161, composition handle 125.00
62191, dog's head trapper, bone 1,450.00
Keen Kutter, Simons Hardware, St. Louis, MO
K1771 3/4", Daddy Barlow 150.00
K1898 3/4", toothpick 100.00
K8464 1/4", Kattie. 65.00
New York Knife
20, office, celluloid 170.00
142, hawkbill, wood 150.00
223, sowbelly, bone 470.00
251, rooster comb, celluloid 300.00
2077, peanut, pearl 270.00
2515, cigar, wood. 750.00
Remington
R181, teardrop jack, wood 255.00
R273, Texas Jack. 200.00
R303, one blade trapper, bone. 400.00
R315, two blade trapper, celluloid 435.00
R718, hawkbill, wood 220.00
R945-M, toothpick, celluloid 520.00
R982, peanut, rubber 320.00
R1253, bullet lockback hunter, bone 2,610.00
R1303, bullet trapper, bone 2,320.00
R1535, florist 85.00
Winchester
1613, speying, wood 115.00
1701, Barlow 125.00
1920, hunter 1,000.00
2070, doctor's. 95.00
2078, serpentine pen, celluloid. 75.00
2363, congress, pearl 225.00
2380, doctor's, pearl. 515.00
2879, jumbo sleeveboard 515.00
3022, whittler 250.00
Wostenholm
3B, Art Nouveau, bronze 100.00
5010A, plumber's, wood 75.00
B181X, stock, imitation ivory 100.00
B133, premium stock, bone 180.00

POISON BOTTLES

History: The design of poison bottles was meant to serve as a warning in order to prevent accidental intake or misuse of their poisonous contents. Their unique details were especially helpful in the dark. Poison bottles generally were made of colored glass, embossed with "Poison" or a skull and crossbones, and sometimes were coffin-shaped.

John H. B. Howell of Newton, New Jersey, designed the first safety closure in 1866. The idea did not become popular until the 1930s when bottle designs became simpler and the user had to read the label to identify the contents.

References: Ralph and Terry Kovel, *Kovels' Bottles Price List*, 10th ed., Crown Publishers, 1996; Carlo and Dorothy Sellari, *Standard Old Bottle Price Guide*, Collector Books, 1989.

Periodical: *Antique Bottle and Glass Collector*, P.O. Box 187, East Greenville, PA 18041.

Collectors' Club: Federation of Historical Bottle Collectors, Inc., 88 Sweetbriar Branch, Longwood, FL 32750.

Ammonia around shoulder, three sets of ribbing, Poisonous then ribbing and Not To Be Taken, 6-1/2" h, cylinder 4.00
Bottled By Jeyes, 7" l, dark straw-amber, oval, ribbing down front with name 12.00
Bowker's Pyrox Poison, colorless 30.00
British Household Ammonia, Poisonous Not To Be Taken, 6-1/2" h, aqua, name around neck, panel with emb lettering 20.00
Burdalls Manufacturing Chemists Sheffield Not To Be Taken Internally, 6" l oval, aqua, row of ribbing each side of lettering 22.00
Clark's Ammonia, aqua, offset neck, 8" h 55.00

Not To Be Taken, dark amber, $15.

Coffin, 3" h, irregular hexagonal, emerald green, glass stopper, ribbed 30.00
Figural, skull, America, 1880-1900, cobalt blue, tooled mouth, smooth base. 2-7/8" h, small hole in nose area 475.00
Foultsons Crescent, 5" h, cobalt blue, sunken ribbed front panel, Not To Be Taken and ribbing on side 65.00
Hobnail, 3-1/2" h, cobalt blue 40.00
Ikey Einstein Poison, rect, ring top, colorless, 3-3/4" h . . . 25.00
Killgerm Disinfectant, oval, aqua, front panel with "Poisonous Not To Be Taken" 6-1/2" l 25.00
Kill Pest Non Poisonous Disinfectant, 5" h, aqua, hexagonal, emb lettering on three panels 20.00
Imperial Fluid Co. Poison, 1 gallon, colorless 95.00
J Wilson Bonsetter, light cobalt blue, rect 65.00
Lysol, 3-1/4" h, cylindrical, amber, emb "Not To Be Taken" 12.00
McDonalds Steam System, 5-1/2" h, aqua, Poisonous across shoulder 20.00
Not To Be Taken, cobalt blue, hexagon, 3" h 10.00
Not To Be Taken Gordon Grand Lysol, 5" h, amber jug shape, emb around neck, cross hatching on 2 sides 32.00
Poison, hexagonal, cobalt blue, 3" h 16.00
Poisonous Not To Be Taken
   3-1/2" h, cobalt blue, cylinder, Poison on back base, ribbing down front 48.00
   6-1/2" h oval, aqua, emb on front panel with ribbing . . 22.00
   7" h, hexagon, aqua, formed lip, Poison on one panel, emb down front 35.00
   11-1/2" h, whiskey shaped, green, long neck 50.00
Sano Bolic Disinfectant, 6" h, aqua, cylinder, sheared top 20.00
Sulpholine, 4" h, rect, colorless 10.00
Thretipene Disinfectant, 9" h, amber, emb Poison around cylinder shaped shoulder, central ribbing of 9 panels, tapers to base, professionally cleaned 225.00
Tinct Gelsem Poison and Hydrag Subchlor Poison, 5-1/2" h, green ribbed cylinder, orig label in rect panel, pr 150.00
Towle's Chlorodyne, 4-1/2" h, colorless 40.00
Trioloids Poison, triangular, blue, c1900, 3-5/16" h 25.00
Vapo Cresolene Co., 4" h, sq, bumps on 2 panels, cobalt blue 48.00

POLITICAL ITEMS

History: Since 1800, the American presidency has been a contest between two or more candidates. Initially, souvenirs were issued to celebrate victories. Items issued during a campaign to show support for a candidate were actively being distributed in the William Henry Harrison election of 1840.

There is a wide variety of campaign items—buttons, bandannas, tokens, pins, etc. The only limiting factor has been the promoter's imagination. The advent of television campaigning has reduced the quantity of individual items, and modern campaigns do not seem to have the variety of materials that were issued earlier.

References: Herbert Collins, *Threads of History*, Smithsonian Institution Press, 1979; Theodore L. Hake, *Encyclopedia of Political Buttons, United States, 1896-1972* (1985), *Book II, 1920-1976* (1977), *Book III, 1789-1916* (1978), revised prices for all three books (1998) Americana & Collectibles Press, (P.O. Box 1444, York, PA 17405); —, *Hake's Guide to Presidential Campaign Collectibles*, Wallace-Homestead, 1992; Edward Krohn (ed.), *National Political Convention Tickets and Other Convention Ephemera*, David G. Phillips Publishing (P.O. Box 611388,

N. Miami, FL 33161), 1996; Keith Melder, *Hail to the Candidate*, Smithsonian Institution Press, 1992; James W. Milgram, *Presidential Campaign Illustrated Envelopes and Letter Paper 1840-1872*, David G. Phillips Publishing (P.O. Box 611388, N. Miami, FL 33161), 1996; Edmund B. Sullivan, *American Political Badges and Medalets, 1789-1892*, Quarterman Publications, 1981; ——, *Collecting Political Americana*, Christopher Publishing House, 1991; Mark Warda, *100 Years of Political Campaign Collectibles*, Sphinx Publishing (P.O. Box 25, Clearwater, FL 34617), 1996; ——, *Political Campaign Stamps,* Krause Publications, 1998.

Periodicals: *Political Bandwagon*, P.O. Box 348, Leola, PA 17540; *Political Collector*, P.O. Box 5171, York, PA 17405.

Collectors' Clubs: American Political Items Collectors, P.O. Box 340339, San Antonio, TX 78234; Ford Political Items Collectors, 18222 Flower Hill Way #299, Gaithersburg, MD 20879; NIXCO, Nixon Collectors Organization, 975 Maunawili Cr., Kailua, HI 96734; Third Party & Hopefuls, 503 Kings Canyon Blvd., Galesburg, IL 61401.

Museums: National Museum of American History, Smithsonian Institution, Washington, DC; Western Reserve Historical Society, Cleveland, OH.

REPRODUCTION ALERT

Campaign Buttons:
The reproduction of campaign buttons is rampant. Many originated as promotional sets from companies such as American Oil, Art Fair/Art Forum, Crackerbarrel, Liberty Mint, Kimberly Clark, and United States Boraxo. Most reproductions began life properly marked on the curl, i.e., the turned-under surface edge.
Look for evidence of disturbance on the curl where someone might try to scratch out the modern mark. Most of the backs of these buttons were bare or had a paper label. Beware of any button with a painted back. Finally, pinback buttons were first made in 1896, and nearly all made between 1896 and 1916 were celluloid covered. Any lithographed tin button from the election of 1916 or earlier is very likely a reproduction or fantasy item.

Additional Listings: See *Warman's Americana & Collectibles* for more examples.

Advisor: Theodore L. Hake.

SPECIAL AUCTION

Hake's Americana & Collectibles
P.O. Box 1444, Dept. 344
York, PA 17405
(717) 848-1333

Bust, 5-1/2" h, black vinyl, John F. Kennedy, inscription on front, name, birth and death dates 1917-1963, c1963. . . . . . 40.00
Button
   7/8" d, Theodore Roosevelt, multicolored portrait, Spanish-American war uniform, gold background 125.00

1-1/4" d, red, white, and blue rim, black and white photo, 1" x 3" red, white, and blue fabric ribbon, attached to pinback is 3" d yellow fabric sunflower, white plastic elephant, "Landon For President" 50.00
2-1/2" red, and white, black and white illus of Truman with button sewn on his lip, red inscription reads "I'm For Stevenson," text underneath Truman illus reads "How We'd Like Harry," c1952 . . . . 25.00
3-1/2", black type on white outside rim, large black and white center photo of Franklin D. Roosevelt, c1938-40. . . . 40.00
3-1/2" d, red, white, and blue, pinktone coloring over portrait, "Jacqueline Kennedy" 120.00
4" d, Willkie, black and white litho 40.00
6" d, red, white, and blue, large bluetone center photo, Re-Elect Nixon, yellow cardboard easel back 15.00
9" d, red, white and blue, large black and white photo of Carter at center, cardboard easel back 15.00
Button with Ribbon
   1-3/4" d, red, white and blue, black and white photo button, Franklin D. Roosevelt, attached to 2" x 5" linen-like white fabric ribbon, gold inscription on ribbon "Inauguration President Franklin D. Roosevelt/Washington, D. C./Jan. 20, 1937"80.001-3/4" d, black and white button, attached 2" x 6" red fabric ribbon, 1-1/2" long gold colored plastic donkey on chain, John F. Kennedy Presidential Visit, c1961-63
   . . . . 45.00
3" d, "U.S. For Ike," red, white, and blue with black and white photo at center, cardboard back, 2" x 9" red, white, and blue fabric ribbon with slogan "The People Want Ike" 90.00
Campaign Medalet
   1-1/2", white metal, Lincoln portrait on front "For President Abraham Lincoln Of Illinois," reverse eagle with wings standing on section of globe depicted with the United States shield on his chest, holding arrows and olive branch in his talons, scroll in beak inscribed "E. Plurbius Unum" . 175.00
1-9/16" white metal, Henry Clay "Native American" 1844, full figure of man holding large American flag, torn and tattered, observe slogan "Our Flag Trampled Upon" referring to Philadelphia riots, reverse with eagle flying with long ribbon in beak "Natives/Beware of Foreign Influence/1844". . 225.00
Christmas Card
   4" x 5-3/4", Franklin D. Roosevelt, 1945, white card stock, 2" x 2-3/4" black and white illus of "The White House North Front," inscription in gold, emb mistletoe leaf and two ac-

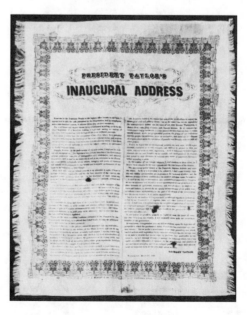

Broadside, silk, President Taylor's Inaugural Address, March 4, 1849, printed by J. Murphy & Co., Baltimore, MD, light green border, frayed edges on sides, 14" w, 17-1/4" l, $375.

companying red emb berries, "With Christmas Greetings And Our Best Wishes For A Happier Nineteen Forty-Five The President And Mrs. Roosevelt". 300.00

4-1/2" x 6-1/2", John F. Kennedy, glossy full color photograph of Creche in East Room, The White House, inside message with gold emb presidential seal above and facsimile signature at bottom of John F. Kennedy and Jacqueline, inscription "With Our Wishes For A Blessed Christmas And A Happy New Year," made by Hallmark, cards arrived at the White House the same day as assassination, never used, few examples saved by assistant to President Kennedy 400.00

Clothing Button, 5/8" d, ferrotype, Grant, thin brass rim, angled ridges surrounding clear ferrotype portrait 200.00

Coloring Book, 8-1/2" x 11", full color caricature cover of Watergate figures leading a parade of people with US, flags, carrying crayons as if they were rifles, "Join the Fun-Color The Facts!," sealed in plastic bag 10.00

Earrings, 5/8" h, rhinestone, slight blue tint, silver metal mountings, orig 2-1/4" x 2-3/4" stiff card, IKE, 1956. . . . . 25.00

Ferrotype, 15/16", Lincoln and Hamlin, Lincoln side with full name and date 1860 with bright and clear ferrotype portrait, Hamlin portrait on reverse 400.00

Flag, 8" x 11", Hoover, red, white, and blue, attached to 19" h, 1/4" wooden dowel painted black, gold painted top, c1928 . . . . 75.00

Inauguration Button

6" d, red, white, and blue, large black and white photo of John F. Kennedy and LBK, Presidential seal in gold and white between two photos, easel back 65.00

6" d, red, white, and blue, with black and white photo of Lyndon B. Johnson and Hubert H. Humphrey, bluetone image of John F. Kennedy at center on dark blue background, gold presidential seal at bottom just above the words "The Great Society," easel back. 40.00

Inauguration Medal

3" d, Franklin D. Roosevelt, second, bronze, Medallic Art, raised image of Franklin D. Roosevelt on one side, "John Nance Garner" on other, dated Jan. 20, 1937 . . . . . 225.00

3" d, Truman, brass, two-sided, unofficial medal, issue of US Mint, front raised image of Truman and inscription "President Of The United States/Harry S. Truman," reverse with raised image of White House, presidential seal above, inscription "Inaugurated April 12 1945/January 20 1949" 35.00

Inauguration Pennant, 4-1/2" x 12" l, red and yellow felt, white image of Franklin D. Roosevelt, Capitol dome, and inscription "I Was At The 1st Third Term Inauguration January 20, 1941" 80.00

Japanese Lantern, 8-1/2" d, Grant & Wilson, names in fuchsia on beige, surrounded by fuchsia circle with star designs, accented by 3 blue circles top and bottom, 1872. . . . . . 250.00

Jugate

1-1/4" d, Grant, hard rubber, black disk, very detailed raised jugate portraits of Grant and Colfax in center, reverse with names and tiny star design 75.00

1-3/4" d, Bryan/Stevenson, black and white photos against bright red, white, and blue shield, bright silver background 80.00

Parker/Davis, black and white photos, gold rim, accented by red, white, and blue stripe 30.00

Lapel Stud, McKinley, gold nugget, emb brass, shaped like nugget, raised letters "Gold Basis," 1896. . . . . 30.00

License Emblem

4" x 4-1/2", Willkie, heavy steel, red and blue, tan ground, orig heavy paper envelope with illus on front 100.00

5" x 10", Win with Truman and Barkley, red, white, and blue metal, 1948 . . . . 150.00

Menu

6-1/4" x 8-1/2", Hoover 1932 trip, "Breakfast Menu" folder, heavy cardboard cover, inscribed "Trip Of The President To Detroit, Michigan and Return October 21st to October 23rd 1932/Pennsylvania Railroad," red fabric spine sash, emb gold-colored eagle at top of cover 150.00

7" x 10", Franklin D. Roosevelt, from return trip from Portland to Washington, D.C., red, white, blue, and gold flag design at top of cover, titled "The President Of The Untied States of America and Party/In Route Via The Chicago & Northwestern Railway/August 8-9, 1934" 125.00

7" x 10", Hoover 1932 trip, "Breakfast Menu" folder, 4 pgs, "The President of the United States of America and Party/Washington, D.C. To Palo Alto, California, Nov. 6, 1932," Union Pacific logo, full color scene of Yosemite Falls/Yosemite National Park on front, text about park on back, stiff paper 165.00

Photo, McClelland, military uniform, c1864, 3/4" x 1" brass frame held by pair of slots with folded brass tabs on the reverse to a 2-1/4" x 4" beige card with ornate frame design in light green 250.00

Pin

Cleveland, figural, diecut aluminum, silver luster, four-leaf clover, raised lettering "Our Four Leaf Clover/Grover" 60.00

Harrison, figural, diecut aluminum, silver luster, five petal pansy, raised lettering "Protection/Reciprocity/Our Nation's Pride/Harrison" reverse with orig pin 60.00

Postcard, Teddy Roosevelt, pen and ink drawing printed postcard, artist "Alla," captioned "Shooting From A Blind," elephant on left with initials "G.O.P." on forehead, large container on back inscribed "Prosperity in Michigan," Theodore Roosevelt crouches behind donkey labeled "Democracy," blank reverse, c1904 . . . . 30.00

Poster, 11" x 16", Win With Ike!, black, white, and light brown, stiff cardboard, large 9-1/2" x 10-1/4" black and white photo of Eisenhower. 40.00

Puzzle, 5-1/2" sq box, "Hoover Wins/Prove It!," wood block puzzle, pieces labeled with Republican Party platform planks from 1929, instructions glued into second box, orig lid 60.00

Rebus, 1-1/4" d, button, Theodore Roosevelt, full color image of Theodore Roosevelt against background accented by pale blue shading to cream, full color red rose with green leaves, blue ribbon with the lettering "Velt," backpaper with union bug and patent dates for Whitehead & Hoag 150.00

Ribbon, fabric

2" x 5", blue and white, "Bull Moose/Watcher," Teddy Roosevelt, coattails type, 1912, 1-1/4" sq at top with blue illus of Bull Moose figure on fabric, reads "Vote Under This Emblem," names Roosevelt, Johnson, Strauss, and Davenport. 125.00

2-1/2" x 10", red, silver type "I'm For Roosevelt in '44" 50.00

Ribbon, silk

2" x 6-1/2", black on light gray silk, McKinley Calendar, memorial, 1902. . . . . 45.00

2-1/4" x 5-3/4", black and white, Republican Candidate for President, Col. J. C. Fremont, The Champion of Liberty, scattered and light small areas of spotting. 350.00

2-1/2" x 4", Harrison & Morton, 1888, red, white, and blue, fringe on sides 50.00

Silk, woven, 1-3/8" x 3-1/2", black and white image of Eisenhower at top, white silhouette of state of New York on yellow background, inscription "We Like Ike!," made in Austria, c1956 . . . . 50.00

Souvenir Card Deck, John F. Kennedy, Air Force One, two sealed decks of playing cards enclosed in gold cardboard box

with blue flocking slip case lid, cards have black, white, and gold design, presidential seal, plane, and world background
. . . . 450.00
Souvenir Key, 3-3/4" l, brass, March 4, 1909 inauguration of Wm. H. Taft, reads "Key Of The White House," full luster
. . . . 50.00

Stereo Card
    3" x 7", Hayes & Wheeler, jugate sepia toned, c1877, photo inset surrounded by white lace and fern design. 35.00
    3" x 7", Mrs. President Hayes, sepia toned, c1877, photo inset surrounded by white lace and fern design 20.00
    3-1/2" x 7", Rough Riders on Parade, stiff cardboard, black and white photos, pinkish colored sky on left, bluish colored sky on right, c1898. . . . . 25.00

Stickpin
    7/8", Bryan, black on ream, vertical, real photo 40.00
    1-1/8" h, Cleveland, spread-winged eagle perched atop brass shield frame which holds inset sepia cardboard photo
. . . . 150.00
    2-1/2" h, Harrison, flat tin 1" x 1-3/4" American flag at top, stenciled blue field, every other stripe is stenciled in red, alternating stripes and star design unpainted, silver luster, blue lettering "American Tin/Protection/Reciprocity" 100.00
    2-1/2" h, Wm. H. Taft, brass, facsimile diecut signature at top, full luster, 1908. . . . . 25.00
    2-3/4" h, Grants Tomb Dedication, 1898, white metal diecut, image of Grant with shield below, full bright brass plating
. . . . 45.00
    Mechanical, red, white, and blue tin shield dated "1888," sides of shield held and then pulled down to reveal sepia paper on tin diecut head of Cleveland, brass stickpin mounted to reverse 250.00

Ticket Stub
    1-3/4" x 5", Truman Inauguration, light orange card stock, black printing, humorous, reverse reads "Compliments of Lafayette Smoke Shop" 20.00
    2" x 4-1/2", Roosevelt-Garner Inaugural Parade, missing stub, orange stock, black type, for address on Pennsylvania Ave. second floor window seat 15.00
    2-1/2" x 4-1/2", Truman and Barkley, red, white, blue, and gold, with black and white photo insets on front, seating information on reverse 25.00
Tintype, 1/2" x 7/8", Abraham Lincoln, orig mount, photo surrounded by black lines and stars, caption reads "Patent'd Oct. 13, 1863, S. Wing 290 Washington Sq, Boston," white background has faint traces of soiling 600.00

Watch Fob
    1-1/4" d, Wm. H. Taft, black and white button with photo image attached to 5-1/2" l black leather strap, c1908 . . 60.00
    2-1/8" d, McKinley, two-sided, celluloid, black and white image of McKinley on white background, red, white, and blue flag design at left, other side with red, white, blue, green, and yellow design of Uncle Sam dancing with woman clad in red, white, and blue dress, wearing blue hose, advertising "Trans-Mississippi Exposition" 150.00

POMONA GLASS

History: Pomona glass, produced only by the New England Glass Works and named for the Roman goddess of fruit and trees, was patented in 1885 by Joseph Locke. It is a delicate lead, blown art glass which has a pale, soft beige ground and a top one-inch band of honey amber.

There are two distinct types of backgrounds. First ground, made only from late 1884 to June 1886, was produced by making fine cuttings through a wax coating fol-

Pitcher, Cornflower, first grind, light amber collar, 4-1/2" h, $490.

lowed by an acid bath. Second ground was made by rolling the piece in acid-resisting particles and acid etching. Second ground was made in Cambridge until 1888 and until the early 1900s in Toledo, where Libbey moved the firm after purchasing New England Glass works. Both methods produced a soft frosted appearance, but fine curlicue lines are more visible on first-ground pieces. Some pieces have designs which were etched and then stained with a color. The most familiar design is blue cornflowers.

Do not confuse Pomona with Midwestern Pomona, a pressed glass with a frosted body and amber band.

References: Joseph and Jane Locke, Locke Art Glass, Dover Publications, 1987; Kenneth Wilson, American Glass 1760-1930, 2 Vols., Hudson Hills Press and The Toledo Museum of Art, 1994.

Bowl
    5" d, Rivulet pattern, second ground, fluted, blue stain . 95.00
    5-1/4" d, Cornflower pattern, second ground, fluted. . . 45.00
Celery Vase, 6-1/2" h, 4" d, Inverted Thumbprint pattern, scalloped amber rim 125.00
Champagne Glass, 5" h, 2nd grind, amber staining 245.00
Cream Pitcher, 3-1/4" h, first ground, amber stain, three dainty applied feet, applied handle with heat check 245.00
Finger Bowl, 2-1/2" d, first ground, gold stain 75.00
Lemonade Tumbler, Leaf pattern, first ground, ring handle
. . . . 85.00
Nappy, 5-1/4" d, Cornflower pattern, first ground, blue stain, applied handle 125.00
Pitcher, 7-1/2" d, honeycomb pattern frosted body, quatraform rim, twisted rope applied necklace and handle, hp polychrome floral dec, polished pontil. 700.00
Punch Cup
    Cornflower, 1st grind, blue staining 145.00
    Cornflower, 2nd grind. 110.00

Inverted Thumbprint, first ground, amber staining, minor wear
. . . . 45.00
Spooner, 5" h, Inverted Thumbprint pattern, second ground, red stemmed blueberry dec, crimped base 140.00
Toothpick Holder, applied rigaree rim 1,000.00
Tumbler, 3-3/4" h, 2-5/8" d, Cornflower pattern, second ground, DQ, honey amber stained top and leaves, blue stained flowers 150.00
Vase, 5-1/4" h, Cornflower pattern, first ground body, ruffled amber rim, gold and blue floral belt at waist, applied wishbone feet 375.00

PORTRAIT WARE

History: Plates, vases, and other articles with portraits on them were popular in the second half of the 19th century. Although male subjects, such as Napoleon or Louis XVI, were used, the ware usually depicts a beautiful, and often unidentified, woman.

A large number of English and Continental china manufacturers made portrait ware. Because most was hand painted, an artist's signature often is found.

Box, cov, 5" w, 3" h, shield shaped dec with elegant portrait of woman, white enamel trim, orig lining, sgd "Nakara" . 900.00
Cup and Saucer, 2-1/2" h, cup with Marie Antoinette portrait in gilt medallion, cobalt blue ground, polychrome pastoral scene on saucer, Sevres, 18th C 300.00
Dresser Tray, 12" l, two portrait medallions, four floral medallions, gold designs, white ground, marked "Nippon" . 250.00
Ewer, 7-1/4" h, 6-1/2" d, Celeste blue ground, five damsels by a brook, maroon, purple, green, and blue gowns, gold Rococo handle, scalloped opening and pedestal, Royal Saxe Germany 300.00
Jewel Box, 10-1/2" x 5", blown-out florals, ribbons on cov, center multicolored portrait of seated woman, 18th C attire, beige ground, gold highlights, marked "Mt. Washington". . . 950.00
Plaque
  4-1/4" x 6-1/4", rect, wrigglework to gilt ground, enameled female portrait, French, late 19th C 550.00
  10-1/4" x 15-3/4", Samson and Dahlia, artist sgd "H Stadler," imp KPM scepter mark, further marked in blue with shield mark, "FD Vienna Austria" 9,200.00

Left: plate, classically robed maiden in five lobed gilt cartouche, gilt flowers on burgundy field, sgd "Wagner," Royal Vienna, late 19th C, 9-9/16" d, $1,050; right: portrait of Daphne, sgd "Wagner," Royal Vienna, early 20th C, 8" d, $800; Photo courtesy of Freeman\Fine Arts of Philadelphia, Inc.

14" x 11" d, Raub der Lubinerinnen, 1436, antique green and gold border with floral dec, artist sgd "F Dorfl," blue shield mark "Vienna, F & D Austria," titled on reverse . . .6,100.00
Plate
  8" d, bust length portrait of Anmuth, Vienna style, gilt scroll, diaper, and foliate pattern border, sgd "Wagner," framed 850.00
  9-1/2" d, George Washington, deep blue, wide garland border, Royal Doulton, c1910 . . . . 125.00
  9-3/4" d, bust length portrait of Ariadne, Vienna style, wide gilt foliage border, metallic red ground, lobed rim, sgd "Wagner" 1,225.00
  10-1/2" d, Rape of Sabine Woman, wide cobalt blue border, gilt floral filigree and trellis pattern, artist sgd "C Landutrut," blue Royal Vienna beehive mark 865.00
  13" d, lobed circular plate,-3/4 length portrait of woman, mountainous landscape, thick gold band border surrounded by russet border, sgd "M Wantzel," Limoges 110.00
  17" d, woman, jade green border, gold trim, marked "Victoria, Austria". 225.00
Vase, 10" h, blond woman, daisies in hair, multicolored flowers, gold scroll handles 260.00

POSTERS

History: Posters were a critical and extremely effective method of mass communication, especially in the period before 1920. Enormous quantities were produced, helped in part by the propaganda role posters played in World War I.

Print runs of two million were not unknown. Posters were not meant to be saved; they usually were destroyed once they had served their purpose. The paradox of high production and low survival is one of the fascinating aspects of poster history.

The posters of the late 19th and early 20th centuries represent the pinnacle of American lithography. The advertising posters of firms such as Strobridge or Courier are true classics. Philadelphia was one center for the poster industry.

Europeans pioneered posters with high artistic and aesthetic content, and poster art still plays a key role in Europe. Many major artists of the 20th century designed posters.

References: George Theofiles, American Posters of World War I, Dafram House Publishers; Susan Theran (ed.), Leonard's Annual Price Index of Posters & Photographs, Auction Index (30 Valentine Park, Newton, MA 02165), 1995; Jon R. Warren, Collecting Hollywood, 3rd ed., American Collector's Exchange, 1994; Bruce Lanier Wright, Yesterday's Tomorrow, Taylor Publishing, 1993.

Periodicals: Biblio, 845 Willamette St., Eugene, OR 87401; Collecting Hollywood, American Collectors Exchange, 2401 Broad St., Chattanooga, TN 37408; Movie Poster Update, American Collectors Exchange, 2401 Broad St., Chattanooga, TN 37408; Plakat Journal, Oskar-Winter Str. 3 D30160 Hannover, Germany.

Museum: Museé de la Publicité, 107 Rue de Rivoli, Paris, France.

Additional Listings: See Warman's Americana & Collectibles for more examples.

Advisor: George Theofiles.

Advertising

Corsets Le Furet, Roger Pérot, Art deco lingerie poster, adv "The Woman's Dream," showing stylized silhouette of woman in Merry Widow-type corset, bright orange and yellow background, 1933, 39" x 55" 500.00

Do It Electrically, Comfort, Convenience, Efficiency in the Home…Save Fuel, Food, Time, Money -By Wire," image of angel holding electric motor, period electrical appliances, full color, blue background, expert restoration to edges,c1915, 27" x 35" 600.00

Ediswan Electric Home Iron, full color, showing 1930s electric iron, c1935, 11" x 18" 60.00

Ferry's Seeds, full color image of pretty young lass amid towering hollyhocks, light fold lines, restoration to edges, thin tears, 1925, 21" x 28" 325.00

Granite Iron Ware, paper, woman carrying milking pail, cow, "For Kitchen and Table Use," 12-1/2" x 28" 75.00

House of Kuppenheimer, J. C. Leyendecker, "Clothes for Men," bold placard showing dandy in white tie and tails, 1919, 14" x 22" 425.00

Lady Esther Face Cream, printed on board, beautiful young woman in oval vignette, "A Skin Food-An Astringent," c1920, 23" x 36" 325.00

Lucite Hosiery, Coles Phillips, full color car, woman pointing horizon at sea next to handsome naval vet in wheelchair, c1918, 21" x 11", damp stain upper right, some border bites . 90.00

Kix Cereal, Lone Ranger 6-shooter ring, General Mills premium, "Only 15 cents plus Kix box top," c1948. 17" x 22" . . 225.00

Miles Shoes, anonymous, "The Best Thing On Foot," yellow and black, detailed locomotive, c1900, 17" x 11", some light residue to small sections of surface, small tack holes . . . 100.00

Popcorn Starch, packages and little girl, color litho, c1900, 10" x 13" 200.00

Richfield Gasoline, race driver in car, c1930, 39" x 53" 1,100.00

Royal Portable Typewriter, dark green detailed manual portable typewriter against leafed red and green ground, c1940, 24" x 36" 285.00

Shamrock Tobacco, canvas, seated man holding knife and tobacco, "Plug Smoking -10 cents a Cut," c1900, 17" x 23" 190.00

Waterman's Ideal Fountain Pen, paper, Uncle Sam at Treaty of Portsmouth, early 1900s, 41-1/2" x 19-1/2" 950.00

Circus, shows, and acts

Barnum and Bailey Circus, Strobridge Litho, Co., "Jockey Races," 1908, 19" x 28" 900.00

Carson & Barnes Circus, anonymous, clowns of all types, full color offset with removable date sheet, white margin wear, 1950s, 42" x 36" 75.00

Clyde Beatty-Cole Bros. Combined Circus, The World's Largest Circus, "Clyde Beatty in Person," Roland butler, lion tamer, multicolored, 19" x 26" 90.00

Cole Brothers Circus - Miss Allen with Her Five Gaied Palomino, anonymous, brilliant 1930s-type litho of Miss Allen and her horse, removable date sheet at bottom, 1945, 21" x 35" 165.00

Downey Bros. Big 3 Ring Circus, "Leaps-Revival of that Astounding and Sensational exhibition," group of elephants, camels, and horses in line, aerial artist leaping overhead, audience background, c1925, 41" x 27" 125.00

Hoxie Bros. Old Time Circus Land, One Mile West of Walt Disney World, multicolored view of circus grounds and big top, 20" x 27" 65.00

Larry Breener's Fantasies of 1929, vaudeville and dance revue, Donaldson Litho, 14" x 22" .80.00Ringling Bros. and Barnum & Bailey Circus, Alfred Court, Master Trainer, G. H., litho image of leopard draped over shoulders of trainer, bears and lions in background, full color, removable data sheet somewhat worn, c1943, 28" x 21", some tape stains and tears to upper edge 125.00

Ringling Bros. Barnum & Bailey Liberty Bandwagon, color litho, ornate wagon with Merle Evans portrait, 1943, 30" x 19" 225.00

Tim McCoy's Wild West, circle of riders around red circle, on canvas, 1938, 54" x 41" 900.00

Magic

Buddha and Heartstone, Polish magician performing tricks, English and Polish text, c1914, 14" x 26" 100.00

Carter the Great-A Baffling Chinese Mystery- The Elongated Maiden, Otis Litho, "A pretty Chinese girl tied to a torture rack without seeming discomfort..," life-sized Chinese nobleman looking down on vignettes of complicated rack, stretched maiden, banshees, imps, devils, in color, c1920, 41" x 81" 650.00

Friedlander Stock Magic, Adolph Friedlander #6966, smiling devil holds card-like vignettes of magic acts in one hand, wand in other, yellow ground, c1919, 14" x 19" 150.00

Kar-Mi Swallows a Loaded gun Barrel, National, "Shoots a cracker from a man's head," Kar-Mi with gun in mouth blasts away at blindfolded assistant, crowd of turbaned Indians, 1914, 42" x 28" 350.00

Movie

African Queen, French release of classic Bogart and Hepburn film, color portraits of both above steamy jungle setting, c1960, 22" x 31" 150.00

Al Capone, Allied Artists, Rod Steiger, full color, 1959, 27" x 41" 100.00

Alias Boston Blackie, Columbia Pictures, Chester Morris, full color, 1942, 27" x 41" 100.00

Amazing Transparent Man, Miller Consolidated, D Kennedy, Marguerite Chapman, sci-fi silhouette against blue, 1959, 27" x 41" 125.00

Anthony Adverse, Warner Bros., Frederick March, Olivia de Havilland, embracing among panorama of runaway coaches and dancing girls, 1936, 27" x 41" 300.00

Atlantic City, Republic, Constance Moore, Jerry Colonna in drag, by James Montgomery Flagg, 1941, 14" x 36" . 200.00

Blondie in the Dough, Columbia Pictures, Penny Singleton, Chick Young's Blondie cartoon film, full color, 1947, 27" x 41" 95.00

Bad Boy, James Dunn and Louise Fazenda,, Fox, 1934, 27" x 41" 150.00

Buck Privates, Relart re-release, Bud Abbott, Lou Costello, the Andrews Sisters, full-color montage, 1953, 27" x 41" . 95.00

Cheaters At Play, Thomas Meighan and Charlotte Greenwood, Fox, 1931, 27" x 41" 275.00

Double Danger, Preston Foster and Whitney Bourne, RKO, 1938, 27" x 41" 110.00

Dr. No, United Artist, Sean Connery, Ursula Andress, 1962, 27" x 41" 325.00

13 Rue Madeleine, Fox, James Cagney, Annabella, Cagney coming from behind looming door, printed in US for So American market. 1947, 27" x 41" 225.00

Farmer's Daughter, RKO, Loretta Young, Joseph Cotton, Ethel Barrymore, Cotton kneeling to pick up blond Young in maid's outfit, 1947, 27" x 41" 125.00

Fear Strikes Out, Paramount, Anthony Perkins, Karl Malden, full color, 1957, 27" x 41" 150.00

Fly, Vincent Price, Fox, "The Monster Created by Atoms Gone Wild!," red, black, yellow, and puce, 1958, 27" x 41" . 325.00

Goodbye Mr. Chips, Robert Donat and Greer Garson, MGM, 1939, 27" x 41" 450.00

I'll Be Seeing You, Ginger Rogers, Joseph Cotton, and Shirley Temple, United Artists 1945, 27" x 41" 150.00

Letter of Introduction, Universal, Charlie McCarthy, Edgar Bergen, Andrea Leeds, full-color dummy. 1938, 27" x 41" 300.00

Love Takes Flight, Bruce Cabot and Beatrice Roberts, Grand National, 1937, 22" x 28" 135.00

Mule Train, Columbia Pictures, Gene Autry, Champion, full-color portraits, 1950, 27" x 41" 150.00

New York, New York, United Artists, Robert Diniro, Liza Minnelli, 1977 . . . . 35.00

One-Eyed Jacks, Paramount, Marlon Brando, Karl Malden, full color, 1959, 27" x 41" 85.00

Pursuit Of The Graf Spee, John Gregson and Anthony Quayle, Rank, c1955, 22" x 28" 150.00

Roll Along Cowboy, Guaranteed Pictures, Smith Ballew, Zane Gray Story, full color, c1940, 27" x 41" 75.00

Smoldering Fires, Pauline Frederick and Laura La Plante, Universal, 1925, 14" x 22" 125.00

South of Caliente, Republic, Roy Rogers, Dale Evans, full color, insert, 1951, 14" x 36", minor tape stain at left edge . 175.00

Streets of Laredo, Paramount, William Holden, Macdonald Carey, full color, 1949, 27" x 41" 125.00

Political and patriotic

America Lets Us Worship As We Wish - Attend The Church Of Your Choice, for American Legion sponsored "Americanism Appreciation Month," full color image of praying Uncle Sam, family at dinner table behind him, c1945, 20" x 26" . . 225.00

Bridge of Peace, Venette Willard Shearer, anti-war poster from American Friends Service Committee, National Council to Prevent War, in color, children of all nations play beneath text of song of peace, c1936, 16" x 22". 125.00

Confidence, large color portrait of Roosevelt over yacht at sea, "Election Day was our salvation/Franklin Roosevelt is the man/Our ship will reach her destination/Under his command...Bring this depression to an end...," c1933, 18" x 25" 250.00

Taft, William H. - James s. Sherman, anonymous, presidential election poster, monochromatic photo images of both, 1908, 28" x 21" 110.00

United Nations Day, blue and white U.N. banner waves over airbrushed stylized brown and yellow globe, minor edge crumple, 1947, 22" x 23" 250.00

Willkie for President, anonymous, "The New America Needs," detailed photo image, orange and white background, 1940, 37" x 48", some repairs at edges 165.00

Theater

Black Dwarf, Beck & Pauli Litho, Milwaukee, detailed stag set with 9 strutting players, cat-like character, a knight, ladies, etc., folio fold, expert restoration to upper cream border, c1870, 28" x 21" 325.00

Bringing Up Father, McManus, "Jiggs, Maggie, Dinty Moore-George McManus's cartoon comedy with music," early newspaper cartoon characters against New York skyline, c1915, 41" x 81" 425.00

Colette Andris, Sierre Thiriot, Art Deco image of Parisian dancer, stylized nude portrait, blue-greens, black, and white, c1930, 30" x 46", minor crumpling 525.00

Gregory Et Sa Panthere, Harfort, semi-nude muscle guy and beautiful female in skin-tight leopard outfit, tussle behind background of palms, yellows, golds, greens, blue, and white, c1938, 20" x 25" 275.00

Les Amours D'Eve, Paul Colin, c1947, 16" x 24", silhouette of blond Eve, serpent, and apple, multicolored, blue background, surrounded by attractions for cabaret, including costumes by Erté and Les Mayfair Lovelies Girls 90.00

No No Nanette, Tony Gibbons, Theatre Mogador, Paris, European production of American musical, c1925, 15" x 22" 375.00

Transportation

Air France - North Africa, Villemot, stylized imagery of mosques and minarets, lavenders, yellow, and blues against sky blue background, plane and Pegasus logo, c1950, 24" x 39" 225.00

Cie De Navigation Transatlantique, Vittorio Grassi, Italian placard, string hanger at top, color image of huge hull of liner plying toward viewer, motif of gulls at borders, c1930, 10" x 17", light scratches at lower blue border, some corner bumps 95.00

Cosulich Line Trieste, Dondou, steamer plies foaming waves, spied on by American Indian chieftain in foreground, c1930, 26" x 35" 475.00

French Line - Ile De France Returns, Mimouca Nebel, impressionist view of New York Harbor, full color, c1950, 20" x 27", light dampstain left edge 150.00

Grace Line - Caribbean South America Cruises, David, stylized natives, sea, and sun, 1959, 28" x 41" 225.00

Royal Mail Atlantis, Padden, tourists in Royal mail motor launch approaching harbor village, mountains in background, c1923, 25" x 38" 675.00

Lets Go! US Marines, by J. A. Thomason, 1942, 29" x 41", $275. Photo courtesy of George Theofiles.

SS France, Bob Peak, launching of French ocean liner, champagne and confection in front of huge, night-lit bow of ship, 1961, 30" x 46"..................................450.00

SS Michelangelo and *SS Raffaello*, Astor, detailed cutaway of Italian ocean liners, designed for use in travel office, printed on plasticized stock, metal frame, 1964, 54" x 22"...300.00

Travel

Arizona - Fly TWA, Austin Briggs, full color western lass in 1950s style, c1955, 25" x 40"...........................300.00

Boston - New Haven Railroad, Nason, full color, stylized montage of Historic Boston by day and night, faint folio folds, c1938, 28" x 42"..............................275.00

Britain in Winter, Terence Cuneo, color rendering of horseman, hunters, and tourists outside rustic inn, 1948, 19" x 29"...125.00

Come to Ulster, Norman Wilkinson, sailboats and fishermen in front of lighthouse, full color, c1935, 50" x 40"......450.00

Fly to Britain by Clipper, Mark von Arenburg, 1948, full color image of coronation carriage and footmen, Buckingham guard at right, 28" x 42"............................300.00

Mexico, C. Uruelá, idealized Mexican children in typical 1930s primitive style, c1938, 18" x 27".................250.00

Nassau - Jet BOAC, Hayes, beautiful Bahamian dancer, sharp detail and color, c1953, 27" x 41".................275.00

Paradise Valley - Mount Ranier National Park, anonymous, Chicago, Milwaukee, St. Paul and Pacific Railroad, painted image of hotel in foreground, snow covered peak in background, c1927, 28" x 22"...................325.00

Paris, Paul Colin, doves floating above stylized Eiffel tower and Arc de Triumph, 1946, 24" x 39"..............600.00

Pistany Spa, Hempel, grand spa imagery, male bathers taking the waters in front of ornate gate, golfers and tourists behind, full color, c1935, 24" x 20"...................375.00

San Remo - Gold - All Sports, L. Polo, Italian Riviera resort, smiling blond lass holds armful of flowers, resort landscape background, c1935, 24" x 38"...................375.00

Travel Flashes - New Fast Bus Service East, Union Pacific Stages, "Direct, Through - 3 Nights Only to Chicago," bright yellow design against black, bus shown at bottom, schedule from Los Angeles to Salt Lake, Cheyenne, Denver, Omaha, Chicago," silk-screen and offset, c1936, 12" x 18".....200.00

Visit Spain, Morell, stylized image of signôrita, c1948, 25" x 39"...250.00

World War I

Beat Back The Hun, F. Srothmann, large Hun lurks on horizon, bloody bayonet, burning city, c1918, 20" x 29", wear to margins, thin tears, edge bites...................200.00

Buy Buy Buy, anonymous, red, white, and blue typographic image for Victory Liberty Loan, c1918, 14" x 21".......75.00

Clear the Way!, Howard Chandler Christy, Columbia points the way for Naval gun crew, c1918, 20" x 30".........250.00

Follow The Flag - Enlist in the Navy, James Daugherty, sailor plants flag on shore, 1917, 27" x 41"............450.00

Foods From Corn - Corn Products Are Plentiful - Use Them, Lloyd Harrison, corn cakes, pies, soups, fillings, etc., tins of corn products all against corn yellow and blue ground, 20" x 30", c1918...................................225.00

For Every Fighter A Woman Worker, Adolph Treidler, woman worker holds detailed biplane and projectile aloft, 30" x 40", expert corner restoration, faint center folio folds....275.00

Treat 'Em Rough - Jon The Tanks, A. Hutaf, window card, electric blue-black cat leaping over tanks in fiery battle, white border, c1917, 14" x 22"......................900.00

You Wireless Fans - Help The Navy Get A Hun Submarine - A Thousand Radio Men Wanted, C. B. Falls, wireless operator reaching up to grab lightening bolt, starry night background, blue, green, red, and white, 1918, 27" x 44".......550.00

Which? Soldier Or Mechanic, L.H., "Enlist in the 57th Engineers (Inlaid Waterways) and Be Both... Camp Laurel, Maryland," 1918, 18" x 23"..............................200.00

World War II

A National Emergency Is Upon Us - Arise Americans, anonymous, for Naval reserve, big flag atop red, white, and blue letters, June 1941, 29" x 42"......................150.00

Army Air Forces Want You! WACS Keep 'Em Flying, anonymous, "Go to your U. S. Army recruiting station now," WAC inspects propeller and motor while AAF pilot walks towards her, c1943, 19" x 27".........................125.00

Be A Marine...Free A Marine To Fight, D. Dickson, "The Marshalls - First pre-war Japanese territory to be conquered in WWII..." charging Marines on beach of jungle stoll, 1945, 29" x 40"......................................225.00

Ideas Will Help Beat The Promise, anonymous, worker peers into robot-like brain in curious, futuristic design, bright color, black ground, c1943, 18" x 22"..................125.00

Keep 'Em Flying - Air Crews Are Vital, Ivan Dimitri, bomber pilots study maps under panoramic flyover of B-17s, full color, very light folio folds, 1942, 25" x 36"..................150.00

Pass The Ammunition - OK Soldier That's Our Job!, Frederick Stanley, brilliantly light image of soldier rushing to line of artillery with ammo, 1943, 28" x 40"...............275.00

Remember Dec. 7th!...We Here Highly Resolve That These Dead Shall Not Have Died In Vain..., Allen Saalburg, powerful image of tattered American flag flying at half mast among smoky Pearl Harbor background, 1942, 22" x 28"...175.00

POT LIDS

History: Pot lids are the lids from pots or small containers which originally held ointments, pomades, or soap. Although some collectors want both the pot and its lid, lids alone are more often collected. The lids frequently are decorated with multicolored underglaze transfers of rural and domestic scenes, portraits, florals, and landmarks.

The majority of the containers with lids were made between 1845 and 1920 by F. & R. Pratt, Fenton, Staffordshire, England. In 1920, F. & R. Pratt merged with Cauldon Ltd. Several lids were reissued by the firm using the original copper engraving plates. They were used for decoration and never served as actual lids. Reissues by Kirkhams Pottery, England, generally have two holes for hanging. Cauldon, Coalport, and Wedgwood were other firms making reissues.

Marks: Kirkhams Pottery reissues are often marked as such.

References: Susan and Al Bagdade, *Warman's English & Continental Pottery & Porcelain*, 3rd Edition, Krause Publications, 1998; A. Ball, *Price Guide to Pot-Lids and Other Underglaze Multicolor Prints on Ware*, 2nd ed., Antique Collectors' Club, 1991 value update.

Note: Sizes given are for actual pot lids; size of any framing not included.

Alexandra Toothpaste, Dr. Ziemer's Matchless for Beautifying and Preserving The Teeth & Gums, London, portrait of Queen Alexandra, facing left, black and gray on white, outer gold band, 3-1/2" d 250.00

Areca Nut Tooth Paste

Army and Navy Co-Operative Society Limited, two military men shaking hands and holding flags, black on white, 3-1/16" d, rust stains 90.00

Barclay and Sons, Farmingdon St., London/A Fleet Marriage Party From a Print Of The time, gold border, black on white, 3-1/2" d 2,400.00

Cleansing Preserving and Beautifying The Teeth/Lewis And Burrows Ltd., London, roses, black on white, 2-3/4" d . 95.00

For Cleansing and Whitening The Teeth and Gums/Timothy White Company Chemists, Portsmouth, geometric center, black on brown, 2-13/16" d 100.00

Cherry Tooth Paste, Patronized by the Queen/For Beautifying and Preserving The Teeth, Prepared by John Gosnell 7 Co, London, young head profile of Queen Victoria facing left, shades of blue, and black on white, gold band, 3-3/16" d 125.00

Cold Cream, R Lemmon, Chemist, The Pharmacy Hythe, geometric border, gray on white, 2-1/2" d 110.00

Higgin's Cherry Tooth Paste/For Cleansing Beautifying and Preserving The Teeth & Gums/Trademark R Higgins, Chemist 235 Strand Next Temple Bar, London, street scene, black on white, 2-3/4" d 185.00

Napoleon Price & Cos., Cherry Toothpaste For Beautying & Preserving The Teeth & Gums, 27 Bond St., London, bust of Queen Victoria and Prince Albert, shades of yellow, black, white ground, 3-3/16" d 900.00

Otto of Rose Cold Cream, SF Goss Chemist, 460 Oxford St., red rose center, green leaves, black letters, white ground, 2-5/8" d 115.00

Rimmels Cherry Tooth Paste, bunch of cherries, deep yellow and pink cherries, green leaves, yellow-orange black band, white ground, 3" d 950.00

Saponaceous Shaving Compound, Prepared by X Bazin, Perfumer, Philadelphia, geometric stars border, black and white, 4-3/8" d 250.00

The Sportsman, multicolored, 4-1/8" d, $90.

Victoria Carbolic Toothpaste/For Preserving and Beautifying The Teeth/Perfumes The Breath, Strengthens The Gums/A. B., warrior with shield lying against lion, black on white, sq, rounded corners, 2-1/2" l 250.00

Worsley Wholesale Perfumer, Philadelphia, Capitol at Washington, linear border, view of Old Capitol Building, violet on white, 3-1/2" d 475.00

PRATT WARE   PRATT

PRATT FENTON

History: The earliest Pratt earthenware was made in the late 18th century by William Pratt, Lane Delph, Staffordshire, England. From 1810 to 1818, Felix and Robert Pratt, William's sons, ran their own firm, F. & R. Pratt, in Fenton in the Staffordshire district. Potters in Yorkshire, Liverpool, Sunderland, Tyneside, and Scotland copied the products.

The wares consisted of relief-molded jugs, commercial pots and tablewares with transfer decoration, commemorative pieces, and figures and figural groups of both people and animals.

Marks: Much of the early ware is unmarked. The mid-19th century wares bear several different marks in conjunction with the name Pratt, including "& Co."

References: Susan and Al Bagdade, *Warman's English & Continental Pottery & Porcelain*, 3rd Edition, Krause Publications, 1998; John and Griselda Lewis, *Pratt Ware 1780-1840*, Antique Collectors' Club, 1984.

Museums: City Museum & Art Gallery, Stoke-On-Trent, England; Fitzwilliam Museum, Cambridge, England; Potsdam Public Museum, Potsdam, NY; Royal Pavilion Art Gallery & Museum, Brighton, England; Royal Scottish Museum, Edinburgh, Scotland; Victoria & Albert Museum, London, England; William Rockhill Nelson Gallery of Art, Kansas City, MO.

Additional Listings: Pot Lids.

Bank, 5" h, house shape, coin slot in roof, open chimney, two figures, faces in windows, professional repair 650.00

Creamer, 4-3/4" h, children at play, heart shaped cartouche, underglaze blue, green, and brown 250.00

Finger Vase, 7" h, four colors, leaves and flowers, minor wear, slight hairline, pr 990.00

Model, 4-1/2" l, baby in cradle, underglaze yellow and blue enamels, early 19th C, nick to bonnet 350.00

Money Box, 5" h, modeled as house, two children peering from windows, flanked by man and woman, blue, ochre, brown, and green, base and chimney restored, c1820 . . . . . 650.00

Pipe, c1800

5" h, sailor form, stem formed as large fish swallowing male figure supporting a mask-head bowl, restored at mouthpiece and bowl stem 890.00

8-1/2" l, 4-1/8" h, monkey form, bowl molded as bird's head, stem and bowl restored 650.00

9-1/4" l, coiled snake, bowl extending from snake's mouth, stains, hairline, and repair 400.00

13-1/2" l, coil, underglaze enamels, molded figural bowl, staining 920.00

Pitcher

7-1/4" h, pearlware, molded dec of children in heart shaped devices, titled "Mischievous Sport" a and "Sportive Inno-

Pitcher, molded form, green, yellow, orange, and brown enamel dec, 5-7/8" h, $165.

cence," yellow, green, tan, blue, and brown, chips on handle and spout 535.00
7-1/2" h, relief busts and floral dec, six colors, minor glaze wear and stains 470.00
Pomade Jar, cov
3-3/4" d, Philadelphia World's Fair, minor roughness to under edges of lid 200.00
4" d, Walmer Castle, roughness to edge of lower lid . 185.00
Relish Bottle, 7-3/4" h, triangular shape, enameled transfers, one with "The Fishbarrow," other with "The Poultry Woman," mid-19th C, minor gilt rim wear, pr 500.00
Sauce Boat, 5" h, 7" w, orange-ochre fox's head as body and spout, white with sponged brown wings swan forming handle, yellow-green acanthus leaves on white wide body base, c1790, body reglazed 850.00
Sugar, cov, 5-34" h, almond shaped relief medallion of woman and child, figural swan finial, stains, minor wear and chips
. . . . 415.00
Tea Bowl and Saucer, 5-1/4" d, peafowl perched on leafy branch, blue, yellow, green, and ochre 300.00
Tea Caddy, 5-1/4" h, applied and glazed floral dec, early 19th C
. . . . 275.00
Toby Jug, 9-1/2" h, seated Mr Toby, holding jug, wearing tricorn hat, jacket, vest, knee breeches, manganese, soft green, brown ochre, yellow, and orange-ochre, 18th C, pipe bowl by chair missing, small flake on one hand 1,540.00
Watch Stand, 10" h, tall case clock flanked by two children wearing yellow crowns, applied sq base with mound beneath their feet, blue, orange-ochre, yellow, brown, and green, small shallow chip on base 500.00

PRINTS

History: Prints serve many purposes. They can be a reproduction of an artist's paintings, drawings, or designs, but often are an original art form. Finally, prints can be developed for mass appeal rather than primarily for aesthetic fulfillment. Much of the production of Currier & Ives fits this latter category. Currier & Ives concentrated on genre, urban, patriotic, and nostalgic scenes.

References: William P. Carl, *Currier's Price Guide to American and European Prints at Auction*, 3rd ed., Curri-

er Publications, 1994; Clifford P. Catania, *Boudoir Art*, Schiffer Publishing, 1994; Karen Choppa and Paul Humphrey, *Maud Humphrey*, Schiffer Publishing, 1993; Max Allen Collins and Drake Elvgren, *Elvgren: His Life & Art*, Collectors Press, 1998; Erwin Flacks, *Maxfield Parrish Identification & Price Guide*, 3rd ed., Collectors Press, 1998; Patricia L. Gibson, *R. Atkinson Fox & William M. Thompson Identification & Price Guide*, Collectors Press, 1994; Michael J. Goldberg, *Maxfield Parrish Vignettes*, Collectors Press, 1998; Martin Gordon (ed.), *Gordon's 1995 Print Price Annual*, Gordon and Lawrence Art Reference, 1995; William R. Holland, Clifford P. Catania, and Nathan D. Isen, *Louis Icart*, Schiffer Publishing, 1994; William R. Holland and Douglas L. Congdon-Martin, *Collectible Maxfield Parrish*, Schiffer Publishing, 1993; Robert Kipp, *Currier's Price Guide to Currier & Ives Prints*, 3rd ed., Currier Publications, 1994; Stephanie Lane, *Maxfield Parrish*, L-W Book Sales, 1993; Coy Ludwig, *Maxfield Parrish*, Schiffer Publishing, 1973, 1993 reprint with value guide; *Maxfield Parrish*, Collectors Press, 1995; Rita C. Mortenson, *R. Atkinson Fox, His Life and Work*, Vol. 1 (1991, 1994 value update), Vol. 2 (1992), L-W Book Sales; Norman I. Platnick, *Coles Phillps*, published by author (50 Brentwood Rd., Bay Shore, NY 11706); Kent Steine and Frederick B. Taraba, *J. C. Leyendecker Collection*, Collectors Press, 1996; Susan Theran, *Prints, Posters & Photographs*, Avon Books, 1993; Susan Theran and Katheryn Acerbo (eds.), *Leonard's Annual Price Index of Prints, Posters & Photographs*, Auction Index, published annually.

Periodicals: *Illustrator Collector's News*, P.O. Box 1958, Sequim, WA 98382; *Journal of the Print World*, 1008 Winona Rd., Meredith, NH 03253; *Print Collector's Newsletter*, 119 East 79th St., New York, NY 10021.

REPRODUCTION ALERT

The reproduction of Maxfield Parrish prints is a continuing process. New reproductions look new, i.e., their surfaces are shiny and the paper crisp and often pure white. The color on older prints develops a mellowing patina. The paper often develops a light brown to dark brown tone, especially if it is acid based or was placed against wooden boards in the back of a frame.

Size is one of the keys to spotting later reproductions. Learn the correct size for the earliest forms. Be alert to earlier examples that have been trimmed to fit into a frame. Check the dimensions before buying any print.

Carefully examine the edges within the print. Any fuzziness indicates a later copy. Also look at the print through a magnifying glass. If the colors separate into dots, this indicates a later version.

Apply the same principles described above for authenticating all prints, especially those attributed to Currier & Ives. Remember, many prints were copied soon after their period introduction. As a result, reproductions can have many of the same aging characteristics as period prints.

Collectors' Clubs: American Antique Graphics Society, 5185 Windfall Rd., Medina, OH 44256; American Historical Print Collectors Society, P.O. Box 201, Fairfield, CT 06430; Gutmann Collector Club, P.O. Box 4743, Lancaster, PA 17604; Prang-Mark Society, P.O. Box 306, Watkins Glen, NY 14891.

Museums: American Museum of Natural History, New York, NY; Audubon Wildlife Sanctuary, Audubon, PA; John James Audubon State Park and Museum, Henderson, KY; Museum of the City of New York, NY; National Portrait Gallery, Washington, DC.

Additional Listings: See Wallace Nutting.

Note: Prints are beginning to attract a wide following. This is partially because prices have not matched the rapid rise in oil paintings and other forms of art.

SPECIAL AUCTIONS

Phillips Fine Art Auctions
406 E. 79th St.
New York, NY 10021
(212) 570-4830

Skinner Inc.
Bolton Gallery
357 Main St.
Bolton, MA 01740

Swann Galleries, Inc.
104 E. 25th St.
New York, NY 10010

Allen, James E, Plowing, lithograph on paper with GCM watermark, sgd "James E. Allen" in pencil lower right, stamped "Collectors of American Art, Inc., New York, N. Y." on reverse, 8-1/4" x 12", unmatted, unframed 435.00

Audobon, John James, etching, engraving, aquatint and hand-colored, wove paper with J Whatman watermark, Blue Gray Flycatcher, 1830, Havell edition, full typographical inscription, 19-3/8" x 12-1/4", good condition, taped edge tears, mount staining, scattered foxing and tape residue, creasing 450.00

Arms, John Taylor

French Lace, sgd and dated "John Taylor Arms 1949" in pencil lower right, inscribed "II" in pencil lower left, etching on paper with watermark "...934 Unbleached Arnold," second sate, edition of 306, plate size 8" x 4-5/8", matted. . 260.00

Memento Vivere, Notre Dame, Evreux, sgd and dated "John Taylor Arms 1947" in pencil lower right, inscribed "II" in pencil lower left, etching on laid paper, second state, edition of 198, plate size 13-1/2" x 7", unmatted, deckled edge on two sides. 550.00

Bacon, Peggy B., The Sights of the Town, sgd "Peggy Bacon" in pencil lower right, titled in pencil lower left, lithograph on paper, watermark "Basingwerk Pap...," image size 8-3/8" x 10-3/8", matted, deckled lower edge 320.00

Baumann, Gustave

Bright Angel Trail, 1919, sgd "Gustave Baumann" in pencil, hand to heart chop lower right, numbered "18 125" in pencil lower right, titled in pencil lower left, identified in artist's orig label affixed to reverse, color woodcut on cream paper, image size 9-3/4" x 11-1/8", framed, laid down, glue reside, 1-1/2" tear to upper margin, annotations to lower margin 8,050.00

Indiana Red Gum, 1909-16, sgd "Gustave Baumann" in pencil, hand to heart chop lower right, numbered "48 125" in pencil lower right, titled in pencil lower left, color wood block on cream wove paper, hand-in-heart watermark, edition of 125, image size 9-3/8" x 11-1/4", framed. 5,465.00

Sycamore Salt Creek, 1916, sgd "Gustave Baumann" in pencil, hand-in-heart chop lower right, numbered "no. 37 of 120" in pencil lower center, titled in pencil lower left, color woodcut on oatmeal paper, image size 9-1/2" x 11-1/4", framed 3,740.00

Benson, Frank Weston

Ducks in the Rain, 1918, sgd "Frank w. Benson" in pencil lower left, stamped "Childs Boston" on reverse, etching on paid paper with partial watermarks, published state, edition of 100 plus proofs, plate size 7-7/8" x 6", framed, deckled edges, annotations to margins and reverse. 1,265.00

Log Driver, 1924, sgd "Frank w. Benson" in pencil lower left, drypoint on laid paper with watermark, "FJ Head & Co.," published state, edition of 150, plate size 9-3/4" x 11-7/8", deckled lower edge, pale mat burn, annotations to lower margin 1,150.00

Wild Goose Drinking, 1915, sgd "Frank W. Benson" in pencil lower left, numbered "1/50" in pencil lower right, label from Holman's Print Shop, Boston, on reverse, etching on Shogun paper with watermark, plate size 7-7/8" x 5-7/8", framed, deckled edges, annotations to lower margin, staining 750.00

Benton, Thomas Hart

Instruction, 1940, sgd "Benton" in pencil lower right, within matrix lower left, lithograph on paper, edition of 250, published by Associated American Artists, image size 10-1/2" x 12-3/8", framed 1,725.00

Nebraska Evening, 1941, sgd "Benton" in pencil and within matrix lower right, lithograph on paper, edition of 250, published by Associated American Artists, image size 10" x 13", matted, deckled edges to 3 sides, pale fox marks. .2,300.00

Berry, Carroll Thayer, Petunia, color woodcut on paper, sgd "Carroll Thayer Berry" in pencil lower right, titled in pencil lower left, 8-5/8" x 6-1/2" d, framed 230.00

Birch, William Russell, High Street from the Country Marketplace, Philadelphia-Procession of the Death of George Washington, engraving, 8-1/4" x 11" 250.00

Calder, Alexander, Circus, sgd "Calder" in pencil lower right, numbered "84/125" in pencil lower left, color lithograph on paper, sight size 25-1/2" x 37-3/8", framed 690.00

Chagall, Marc, Solomon, sgd in pencil, color lithograph, numbered 34/75, 1956, cream wove paper, full sheet printed to edges, 14" x 10-1/4". 1,500.00

Currier & Ives, handcolored litho

A Stopping Place on the Road, The Horse Shed, sgd "T. Worth" in the stone lower left (lithographer), identified in inscriptions in matrix, 21-3/8" h, 31-1/4" l, framed . . . 920.00

Harvesting, 11" h, 15" w, molded frame with gilded liner, stains and minor damage, C#2750 . . . . 220.00

Strawberries, 10" h, 14" w, black beveled frame, margins trimmed, stains, and tear in left margin, C#5838 . . . 250.00

The Haunts of the Wild Swan, 12-3/8" h, 16-1/4" w, foxing and minor edge damage, full margins, new curly maple frame, C#2757 . . . . 300.00

Currier, Nathaniel

Naval Hero's of the United States, C#4397, hand-colored lithograph, minor stains, framed, 14-1/4" h, 18-1/4" w 330.00

Thomas W. Dore, Elected Governor of Rhode Island, hand-colored lithograph, period frame, 13-3/4" x 9-1/2" 150.00

Curry, John Steuart, Elephants, 1936, sgd "John Steuart Corry" in pencil lower right, titled and dated in pencil lower left, initialed within the matrix lower right, identified on the AAA label affixed to reverse, lithograph on BFK Rives paper with watermark, edition of 250, published by Associated American Artists, image size 9" x 12-5/8" 750.00

Darley, F.O.C. and A. H. Ritchie, On The March To The Sea, hand colored, sgd in pencil by both artist and engraver, artist's proof before title, General Sherman mounted watching his troops burn, pillage, and destroy rail tracks, telegraph poles, etc., freed slaves coming in, American flag held high, bridge in distance being destroyed, 42" x 27" plus frame, publisher's description and copy of invoice for hand coloring included 1,300.00

Dehn, Adolf Arthur, Golden Gate, sgd "Adolf Dehn" in pencil lower right, identified on AAA label on reverse, lithograph on paper, published by Associated American Artists, image size 9-1/4" x 13-5/8" 260.00

Dürer, Albrecht, Saint Christopher, 1521, engraving on paper, later impression, monogrammed and dated 1521 within plate, 4-5/8" x 2-7/8", framed 1,265.00

Endicott & Company, handcolored litho, New Bedford Fifty Years Ago, 1858, after William Allen Wall, identified within matrix, diagram of figures and view affixed to reverse, 19-1/2" x 26-1/4", period frame, staining, tears 460.00

Gardiner, Eliza Draper

In The Big Bank, sgd and numbered "Eliza D. Gardner 8/5…" in pencil lower left, titled in pencil lower center, inscribed "no. 8" in pencil lower right, color woodcut on Japan paper, image size 11-7/8" x 10" 350.00

Wading, Low Tide, sgd "Eliza D. Gardiner 2" in pencil lower right, color woodcut on tissue, image size 9" x 7", framed 375.00

Gaugengigl, Ignaz Marcel, Buggy Driving, sgd "I. M. Gaugengigl" in pencil lower right and in plate lower left, etching on paper, image size 8" x 7-3/8", framed 635.00

Hassam, Frederick Childe

The Church Tower, Portsmouth, 1921, monogrammed and inscribed "…imp" in pencil lower right, monogrammed and dated within the plate lower left, identified on label from H. V. Allison & Co., New York, on reverse, etching on thin laid paper, pate size 8-3/8" x 6" 1,610.00

Union Square, 1896, monogrammed and inscribed "…imp" in pencil lower right, monogrammed, dated, and inscribed "New York…" within plate center right, identified on label from William MacBeth, New York, on reverse, etching on wove paper, plate size 4-1/4" x 5-3/4", framed . . .8,525.00

Icart, colored etching on paper, lady at flower vender, Arc de Triomphe in background, sgd "Louis Icart," glued between mat and backboard with emb windmill mark partially covered, matted and framed, 26-1/2" h, 21" w 1,155.00

Kasimir, Luigi, New York - Fog and Mist, 1936, sgd "Luigi Kasimir" in pencil lower right, numbered "20/100" in pencil lower left, dated within the plate, color etching on paper, plate size 12-1/2" x 14-3/4", framed 575.00

Kellogg

Battle of Champion Hills, MS, Mat 16, 1863, lithograph 125.00

Rural Sweets, lithograph 95.00

Kent, Rockwell, Diver, 1931, wood engraving on paper with Japan watermark, edition of 150, sgd "Rockwell Kent," 7-7/8" x 5-3/8", matted, unframed 980.00

Kloss, Gene, Summer Evening in New Mexico, 1941, sgd "Gene Kloss" in pencil lower right, titled in pencil lower left, aquatint and drypoint on paper, edition of 75, plate size 8-7/8" x 12", matted 1,840.00

Grant Wood, Seed Time & Harvest, sgd, 1937, $225.

Lane and Scott, View of New Bedford. From the Fort Near Fairhaven, 1845, identified within the matrix, lithograph on paper, 19-3/8" h x 27-1/4" w, unframed 1,265.00

Marsh, Reginald, Loco - Going Through Jersey City, etching on heavy paper, from the Whitney Museum edition of 100, 1969, Whitney Museum drystamp lower right, annotated in lower margin, unmatted, unframed, 1930, 4-7/8" x 9-7/8" . . 250.00

Mucha, Alphonse, color lithograph on silk, 33-1/2" h, 8-1/2" w, framed, c1896

Lady in long green outer garment, holding bird, three birds sit on snow covered branch .3,750.00

Lady with long brown hair, sitting on rock, feet in stream, red flowers in hair 3,750.00

Lady with long flowing hair, five birds on harp 3,500.00

Maiden picking berries in forest 3,750.00

Parish, Maxfield, Daybreak, marked "The House of Art, N.Y.," 13" x 20-1/2", framed 200.00

Patterson, Margaret Jordan, color woodcut on paper

In The High Hills, sgd "Margaret Patterson" in pencil lower right, indistinctly inscribed in pencil lower left, 11" x 8-3/4", framed 1,380.00

Morning Glories, edition of 100, sgd "Margaret J. Patterson" in pencil lower right and lower center, titled in pencil lower right, numbered "#4/100," 10" x 7-1/4", framed . . .1,380.00

Thayer & Co, Boston, Lithographers, View of the Grand Mass Washingtonian Convention on Boston Common,, on the 30th of May, 1844, lithograph, handcolored on paper, full typographical inscription below image, 8-1/2" x 13-1/2" image, period burl frame, minor staining and fading 225.00

Thornton, Dr. Robert, The Scared Egyptian Bean, 1804, from *The Temple of Flora,* identified within the plate, color aquatint on paper, sheet size 20" x 14", framed 690.00

Wengenroth, Stow, Along the Canal, 1949, sgd "Stow Wengenroth" in pencil lower right, lithograph on paper, edition of approx. 50, image size 7-7/8" x 13-3/9", orig folder, text from Society of American Etchers, Gravers, Lithographers, and Woodcutters, Inc. 350.00

Whistler, James Abbott McNeill

Annie Seated, unsigned, inscribed "Annie" in the plate lower center, etching on thin laid paper, second state, plate size 5-1/8" x 3-3/4", matted 865.00

Billingsgate, c1859, sgd and dated "Whistler 1859" in the plate lower center, etching on J. Whatman laid paper with partial watermark, eighth state, plate size 6" x 8-7/8" 980.00

Drouet, sgd and dated in the plate lower right, titled in the plate lower center, etching on paper, second state, plate size 9" x 5-7/8" 1,035.00

The Winged Hat, butterfly monogram within the matrix, Birnie Philip stamp on reverse, lithograph on paper with watermark "R. Munn & Co. 1824," 1890, edition of approx. 25, matted, unobtrusive soiling, annotations lower left, image size 7" x 6-3/4" 1,265.00

Wood, Grant, March, 1941, sgd "Grant Wood" in pencil lower right, lithograph on wove paper, edition of 250, published by Associated American Artists, image size 8-7/8" x 11-7/8", unmatted 2,300.00

Woodward, Ellsworth, The Oaks in Audubon Park, moss-laden trees in park across from Newcomb College, 5" x 4", orig frame and matting 300.00

Wyllie, William Lionel, Thames View, sgd "W. L. Wyllie" in pencil lower left, etching on paper, plate size 6-1/4" x 14-3/4", framed, pale fox marks, mat staining 520.00

Zorn, Anders, Sappo, 1917, sgd "Zorn" in pencil lower right, monogrammed and dated in the plate lower left, etching on paper, plate size 8-1/8" x 7-1/8", framed 460.00

PRINTS, JAPANESE

History: Buying Japanese woodblock prints requires attention to detail and abundant knowledge of the subject. The quality of the impression (good, moderate, or weak), the color, and condition are critical. Various states and strikes of the same print cause prices to fluctuate. Knowing the proper publisher and censor's seals is helpful in identifying an original print.

Most prints were copied and issued in popular versions. These represent the vast majority of the prints found in the marketplace today. These popular versions should be viewed solely as decorative since they have little monetary value.

A novice buyer should seek expert advice before buying. Talk with a specialized dealer, museum curator, or auction division head.

The following terms are used to describe sizes: chuban, 7-1/2 x 10 inches; hosoban, 6 x 12 inches; and oban, 10 x 15 inches. Tat-e is a vertical print; yoko-e a horizontal one.

Collectors' Club: Ukiyo-E Society of America, Inc., FDR Station, P.O. Box 665, New York, NY 10150.

Museum: Honolulu Academy of Fine Arts, Honolulu, HI.

Note: The listings below include the large amount of detail necessary to determine value. Condition and impression are good unless indicated otherwise.

Chickanobu, half length portrait of beautiful woman, very good impression, color, and condition, 1896. . . . . 115.00

Eisen, courtesan composing poetry, landscape inset printed in blue, good impression and color, framed 230.00

Gekko, eight framed prints from Gekko's Miscellaneous Drawings series, good impression, some fading and toning 300.00

Harunobu, chuban of woman standing in doorway, young man kneeling on verandah, very good impression, faded, toned 400.00

Hasui, Zojoji in the Snow, framed, good impression and color 690.00

Hawagawa Mitsunobu, album sheet, samizuri-e, two women entertain man with shadow puppets and music, c1730, good impression, soil 490.00

Hirosada, chuban of actor, mid 19th C, good impression and color 290.00

Hiroshige
Cherry Trees Along The Tama River Embankment from 100 Famous Views of Edo, framed, fair impressions, faded 215.00

Eijiri, from Hoeido Tokaido, good impression, soiled, framed 250.00

Ishibe from the Hoeido Tokaido, framed, fair impression, faded 200.00

Night View of Sanya Canal from "One Hundred Famous Views of Edo," 1857, moderate impression, good color, backed, centerfold, torn 115.00

Night view of lake with fishermen in small boats, from series "Sixty-odd views of the Provinces," very good impression, faded, backed 320.00

Nihonbshi from "One Hundred Views of Edo," 1856, good impression, faded 375.00

Okabe from "Reisho Tokaido," oban yoko-e, c1850, very good impression and condition, slightly faded 435.00

Scene overlooking river, Fuji in background, from "Thirty-six Views of Fuji," 1858, good impression and color, full margins 290.00

Hiroshige II
Horsemen from series of 100 Famous Views, framed, good impression, faded, c1860. . . . . 260.00

Townspeople from "Thirty-six Views of Fuji," 1860, very good impression and color, album backing. 290.00

Hiroshige III, watery landscape from series of One Hundred famous Views, good impression, faded, c1860 . . . . 200.00

Hiroshi Yoshida
Ajmer Gate, Jaipur, sgd in pencil in margin, Jizuri seal, good impression and color, 14-3/4" x 9-3/4" image size 400.00

Figures on a road, watercolor on paper, sgd lower right, "H Yoshida, 1903," 19-3/8" x 26" 3,740.00

Small Town in Chugoku, pencil sgd in margin, good color and impression 400.00

Hokusai, Sinsho Suwa-Ko, Lake Suma in Shiano Province, from Fugaku sanjurokkei series, "Thirty--six view of Mt. Fuji," sgd Zen Hokusai Iitsui hitsu, publisher's seal Eljudo, 10" x 15" 4,250.00

Kunisada, Utgawa, 1786-1868, 13-1/2" x 9-1/2", $125.

Ishikawa, fisherman's village, watercolor on paper, sgd "T. Ishikawa" bottom left, toned, tear to edge, 19-1/8" x 13-1/8" 2,645.00
Junichiro Sekino, II ne etat, pencil sgd lower right 53, 52/100 . . . . 690.00
Kogyo, set of four framed vertical prints of Noh drama subjects, very good impressions, color, and condition 350.00
Koitsu, good impression and color, framed
    Boats on lake, 20th C. 320.00
    Forest scene. 200.00
    Night scene 115.00
Koryusai, chuban of two woman in an interior, c1770, good impression, some fading and soil. 1,495.00
Kunichika, portrait of Nakamura Shika, moon in distance, very good impression, good color, some soil to margins, 1860s 200.00
Kunimasu, hanshi-bon, actor, c1850, good impression and color 320.00
Kunisada
    Fan print of Genji on shore with two women, fair impression, worn. 60.00
    Figures in front of stations modeled after Hiroshige, from Tokaido series, c1835, framed, good impression and condition 320.00
    Portrait of woman in front of mirror in an interior, c1835, good impression and color, centerfold 316.00
Kuniyoshi, Tuankuk print showing four drunken badgers dancing and singing, illus text passes, sgd "Ichiyusai Kuniyoski-giga," and one Nanushi and anonymous publisher's seal, fair impression and color, slightly faded 10" x 15" 200.00
Okiie Hashimoto, girl with flowers, pencil sgd in lower margin, dated 1952, artist's seal within image, printed character to right margin, 15-1/2" x 21-1/2" 805.00
Sadanubo, chuban yoko-e of snowy landscape, mid 19th C, good impression and color, stain to left third 145.00
Shigemitsu, triptych of warriors on hill overlooking lake, Fuji in distance, framed, very good impression and color. . . 350.00
Tamachika, from chuban series of famous view, framed, good impression and color 175.00
Tokyo, chuban print from series of views, two men on temple ground, framed. 175.00
Toyohiro, tiger, black and gray printed tones, very good impression, some soil 575.00
Toyokuni, portrait of Bando Mitsugoro, good impression, some wear 80.00
Toyokuni II, woman and child, framed 140.00
Toyokuni III
    Actor Print, mounted as scroll, good impression and color, c1860. . . . . 115.00
    Ishikwa Goeman in combat, inset of temple by student of Kunisada, from "Sixty-odd Provinces," c1845 . . . . . 145.00
    Pentaptych of actors by river, 1858, very good impression, some fading, mat line, stains to edges. 435.00
Utamaro, woman on tortoise with fan, toned, faded 175.00
Yasuharu, Meiji period
    Koban size winter landscape, framed 200.00
    Small landscape of walk along river, framed 115.00
    Small winter landscape, framed. 175.00
    Winter landscape with temple, koban size, framed . . 175.00
Yoshitora, scene from Chushinguara, framed, faded, worn 115.00
Youkyo, chuban landscape, framed 175.00

PURPLE SLAG (MARBLE GLASS)

History: Challinor, Taylor & Co., Tarantum, Pennsylvania, c1870s-1880s, was the largest producer of purple slag in

Fluted Rib pattern, Challinor, celery vase, 8-1/4" h, 4-1/4" d, $95.

the United States. Since the quality of pieces varies considerably, there is no doubt other American firms made it as well.

Purple slag also was made in England. English pieces are marked with British Registry marks.

Other slag colors, such as blue, green, and orange, were used, but examples are rare.

Videotape: National Imperial Glass Collectors Society, *Glass of Yesteryears*, The Renaissance of Slag Glass by Imperial, RoCliff Communications, 1994.

Additional Listings: Greentown Glass (chocolate slag); Pink Slag.

REPRODUCTION ALERT

Purple slag has been heavily reproduced over the years and still is reproduced at present.

Animal Dish, cov, duck, Atterbury, ridged base with diamond motif 85.00
Bowl, 8" d, Dart Bar. 50.00
Butter Dish, cov, cow finial 145.00
Cake Stand, plain 125.00
Celery Vase, Jeweled Star, Challinor-Taylor, 1880s. . . . 125.00
Compote, Beaded Hearts 95.00
Match Holder, dolphin head 75.00
Mug, Bird In Nest, cat on base 105.00
Plate, 10" d, lattice edge 75.00
Rose Bowl, ribbed, Northwood 90.00
Sauce Dish, Majestic Crown, Challinor-Taylor, 4" d 25.00
Sherbet, Majestic Crown, Challinor-Taylor, 4" d 35.00
Sugar, cov, Fluted. 195.00
Toothpick, Scroll with Acanthus 150.00
Vase, 10" h, wispy purple swirls, cloudy and clear body. 115.00

PUZZLES

History: The jigsaw puzzle originated in the mid-18th century in Europe. John Spilsbury, a London map maker, was selling dissected-map jigsaw puzzles by the early

1760s. The first jigsaw puzzles in America were English and European imports aimed primarily at children.

Prior to the Civil War, several manufacturers, e.g., Samuel L. Hill, W. and S. B. Ives, and McLoughlin Brothers, included puzzles in their lines. However, it was the post–Civil War period that saw the jigsaw puzzle gain a strong foothold among the children of America.

In the late 1890s puzzles designed specifically for adults first appeared. Both forms—adult and child—have existed side by side ever since. Adult puzzlers were responsible for two 20th-century puzzle crazes: 1908-1909 and 1932-1933.

Prior to the mid-1920s, the vast majority of jigsaw puzzles were cut out of wood for the adult market and composition material for the children's market. In the 1920s, the die-cut, cardboard jigsaw puzzle evolved and was the dominant medium in the 1930s.

Interest in jigsaw puzzles has cycled between peaks and valleys several times since 1933. Mini-revivals occurred during World War II and in the mid-1960s when Springbok entered the American market.

References: *Dexterity Games and Other Hand-Held Puzzles*, L-W Book Sales, 1995; Jack Matthews, *Toys Go to War*, Pictorial Histories Publishing, 1994; Chris McCann, *Master Pieces, The Art History of Jigsaw Puzzles,* The Collectors Press, 1998; Jerry Slocum and Jack Botermans, *Book of Ingenious & Diabolical Puzzles*, Time Books, 1994.

Collectors' Clubs: American Game Collectors Association., P.O. Box 44, Dresher, PA 19025.

Advisor: Bob Armstrong.

Note: Prices listed here are for puzzles which are complete or restored, and in good condition. Most puzzles found in attics do not meet these standards. If evaluating an old puzzle, a discount of 50% should be calculated for moderate damage (1-2 missing pieces, 3-4 broken knobs,) with greater discounts for major damage or missing original box.

Cardboard, pre-1950

Brundage/Modern Scenic, Summer Days, artist Edward Dufner, 1930s, 19-1/2" x 12-3/4", 350 pcs, diecut, crkd line, round edge, orig box. 10.00

Chilcote/Jig Time, Ye Olde Village, 1933, 15-1/2" x 11-1/2", 300 pcs, diecut, square knob stripcut, orig box. 10.00

Consolidated Paper Box/Perfect, Red Fishermen, Indians, artist W. E. Roy, 1930s, 13-1/2" x 10", 250 pcs, diecut, round knob stripcut, interlocking, orig box. 10.00

Einson-Freeman/Every Week, The Challenge, Indian youth stalking bear, artist R. Aufelt, 1933, 14-1/2" x 10-1/2", 160 pcs, diecut, square knob, orig box 10.00

Milton Bradley, The Indian Bear Hunt, 1930s, 26-1/4" x 18-1/2", 465 pcs, diecut, round knob stripcut, interlocking, orig box, gory scene 12.00

Regent Specialties/De Luxe, Nature's Glories, flowers, 1930s, 20" x 16", 400 pcs, diecut, square knob, partly interlocking, orig box. 8.00

Tuco/Art Picture Puzzle, Boy and Rabbit, 1930s, 11" x 15-1/4", 187 pcs, diecut, crkd line stripcut, orig box 8.00

Viking/Picture Puzzle Weekly, The Covered Bridge, 1933, 13-3/4" x 10", 212 pcs, diecut, push-fit, orig box, 7 figures 8.00

Whitman/Guild, The First Step, 1950s, 18" x 14", 304 pcs, diecut, round knob stripcut, interlocking, orig box, No. 4425 . . . . 5.00

Cardboard, post-1950

American Pub/National Challenge, Simple Marbleous, 1980s, 24" x 18", 550 pcs, diecut, round knob stripcut, interlocking, orig box. 5.00

Eaton, Scheaffer, Beyond the Rainbow, 1983, 24" x 18", diecut, round knob, interlocking, orig box 5.00

Hallmark Cards/Springbok, Sensational Sushi, artist Jane McClelland, 1970-80, 20" x 20", 500 pcs, diecut, round knob, interlocking, orig box 5.00

Milton Bradley/Betty Crocker, Chocolate Chip Cookies, 1991, 24" x 18", diecut, round knob stripcut, interlocking, orig box 5.00

Tuco/Scenic, On The Banks of the Scheldt, 1950s, 22" x 14-3/4", 400 pcs, diecut, round knob stripcut, interlocking, orig box 10.00

Children's

Milton Bradley/Little Folks, Sectional Birds, artist Barbar Edgett, 1920-40, cardboard, 6-3/4" x 9", 8 pcs, diecut, round knob stripcut, interlocking 10.00

Western Publishing, Surprise Attach, Masters of Universe, 1983, cardboard, 14" x 18", 100 pcs, diecut, round knob stripcut, interlocking, orig box. 2.00

Parker Brothers, Pastime Puzzles, plywood

Autumnal Beauty, 1931-05, 9" x 9", 139 pcs (1 replaced), curl knob, color line cutting, interlocking, orig box, 12 figures, sawed by #17 . . . . 45.00

Entrance to a Mosque, 1928, 14-3/4" x 22-3/4", 518 pcs (1 replaced) curved knob, color line cutting, knob, orig box, 58 figures, sawed by #16 & 6 . . . . 180.00

Holdup in the Rockies, artist C. M. Russell, 1920s, 13-3/4" x 9-1/4", 205 pcs, curve knob, color line cutting, interlocking, orig box, 24 figures. 75.00

In The Hills of Devon, 1930s, 16-1/4" x 21-3/4", 501 pcs, round knob, color line cutting, interlocking, orig box, 60 figures, sawed by #753 . . . . 180.00

The Charm of Sweet Contentment, 1929-11, 9-1/4" x 7", 109 pcs (1 replaced), ft knob, jagged, color line cutting, partly interlocking, orig box, 13 figures, sawed by #209 . . . . 35.00

Venetian Morning, 1940/50, 13-3/4" x 17-1/4", 364 pcs, round knob, color line cutting, interlocking, orig box, 41 figures, sawed by #757 . . . . 115.00

Washington Monument, artist M. Glover, 1940-50, 7-3/4" x 5-3/4", 68 pcs, bulb knob, interlocking, orig box, 7 figures 25.00

Straus, Joseph K., plywood

Awaiting Spring's Wispful Breeze, windmills, 1930s, 19-3/4" x 15-3/4", 500 pcs, round knob, interlocking, orig box . . 55.00

Etching, old European town, 1930s, 15-3/4" x 19-3/4", 500 pcs, round knob stripcut, interlocking, orig box 35.00

Old Trusty, ranger showing fawn to dogs, artist H. Hintermeister, 1930-40, 20" x 16", 500 pcs (2 replaced), round knob stripcut, interlocking, replaced box. 70.00

Peonies, artist W. P., 1940s, 12" x 16", 300 pcs, round knob stripcut, interlocking, orig box. 35.00

Poppies and Larkspur, artist M. Streckenbach, 1930s, 20" x 16", 500 pcs (2 replaced), ft knob, interlocking, orig box. . . 50.00

Untitled, mountain lake scene, 11-3/4" x 16", 300 pcs (1 replaced), round knob stripcut, interlocking, orig box . . . 20.00

Wood and/or handcut, pre-1930

Madmar, attributed to, The Scout, Indian in full headdress on horse, 1910s, press board, 7-3/4" x 9-3/4", 48 pcs, ckrd line stripcut, partly interlocking, replaced box. 22.00

Milton Bradley Picture Puzzles, Rotterdam, artist Marian, Dutch harbor scene, 1909, solid wood, 6" x 7-1/4", 80 pcs, crkd line stripcut, orig box. 22.00

Parker Brothers, Wild West, horses, western ambush theme, 1910-20, plywood, 11-1/2" x 7-1/2", crkd line sem-stripcut, orig box. 30.00

Unknown Maker

A Breathless Moment, bears, camping action scene, Philip R. Goodwin, artist, 1910-20, plywood, 21" x 16", 582 pcs, big earlets, partly interlocking, replaced box 135.00

An Interesting Passage, cardinal and assistant studying bible, 1909, solid wood, 3-1/2" x 4-3/4", 33 pcs (1 replaced), push-fit, replaced box. 10.00

A Rocky Cliff, western scenery, 1910s, plywood, 9" x 11-1/2", 112 pcs, crkd line, partly interlocking, replaced box . 22.00

Brant Black, flocks of Canadian geese by water, 1910-20, plywood, 10" x 11", 201 pcs (2 pcs replaced), large earlet, round knob, sem-l, orig box 45.00

Castle on the Lake, scenery, 1910-20, plywood, 8" x 6", 99 pcs, push-fit, color line cutting, replaced box, separate 8 lc interlocking wood frame. 30.00

Too late, 18th C courtship scene, mkd "No. 8" in corner, 1909, plywood, 24-3/4" x 17-1/4", 180 pcs, jagged push-fit, replaced box, white border, large pcs 50.00

Whose Meat, bears, artist Philip R. Goodwin, 1914, plywood, 14-1/2" x 10-3/4", 202 pcs (1 replaced), earlets, color line cutting, interlocking, unusual edge cuts, replaced box
. . . . 40.00

Wood and/or handcut, 1930-40s

Bel'Espoir, A Mantle White as Lilly Leaves, winter scene, 1930s, plywood, 10" x 8", 268 pcs, square knob, sem color line cutting, interlocking, orig box. 50.00

Fuller Novelty Co., Fishermans Cove, 1930s, plywood, 14-1/2" x 10-3/4", 250 pcs (1 replaced), random, color line cutting, interlocking, orig box, 7 figures 45.00

Hayes, J. M./J.M.H., Dessert, 1940s, plywood, 20" x 16", 601 pcs (4 replaced), 1-by-1 round knob, interlocking, orig box, still life. 110.00

Hayter/Victory Artistic

Hastings, seaside scene with bathers and fishermen, 1940/50, plywood, 19-1/2" x 20", 700 pcs, round knob, var stripcut, interlocking, orig box, 36 figures. 120.00

Mountain Lake, 1950-60, plywood, 39-1/4"n x 29-1/2", 2,000 pcs, round knob, 1 way stripcut, interlocking, orig box, 120 figures 400.00

Jig Saw Puzzle, At Bailey's Bay, Bermuda, mansion and people, biking scene, artist V. Carlton, 1940-50, plywood, 15-1/2" x 11", 345 pcs, 1-by-1 round knob, interlocking, orig box 50.00

Madmar/Interlox, Springtime Is Blossom Time, Washington Monument, cherry blossoms, 1930s, plywood, 15-3/4" x 19-3/4", 500 pcs (1 replaced), scroll, interlocking, orig box
. . . . 90.00

Merritt, R. H./Delta, 1930s

Lake Louise, artist R. Atkinson Fox, 1930s, plywood, 14-1/2" x 10-1/4", 325 pcs (1 replaced), long/angular, interlocking, orig box 90.00

Winter Moonlight, artist Thompson, 1930s, plywood, 16" x 12", 394 pcs (1 replaced), long/angular, interlocking, orig box. 85.00

Nowell, Bessie, Mignon, women scene, 1930s, press board, 19-3/4" x 14-3/4", 345 pcs, long/rd, color line cutting, partly interlocking, orig box, trick edges, cutter's name and address
. . . . 70.00

Par Puzzles, Off Center, Roman ruins scene, 1930s, plywood, 15-1/4" x 24-1/2", 800 pcs (1 replaced), earlets, jagged, sem color line cutting, orig box, 16 figures, Par Time 4 hrs, 55 min.
. . . . 650.00

Schwartz, FAO/Special Cut, Bearing the Brunt, bears, camping, 1950s, plywood, 23-1/2" x 17-3/4", 750 pcs (2 replaced), random, interlocking, orig box, 17 figures 110.00

Unknown Maker

Lassie with Eyes of Blue, Irish lass, artist W. H. Margetson, 1930s, press board, 9-1/4" x 13", 216 pcs, push-fit, color line cutting, edge-interlocking, orig box 30.00

Opening Tomb of Father C.R.C., 1930s, plywood, 8-3/4" x 13-1/4", 168 pcs, square knob, sem color line cutting, interlocking, orig box, 4 figures. 35.00

Untitled, beached fishing boats, artist Donald Greig, 1930s, plywood, 19-1/4" x 14-1/2", 500 pcs (2 replaced), 1-by-1 round knob, interlocking, replaced box 70.00

Venice, 1930s, plywood, 28" x 20-1/2", 1,116 pcs (5 replaced), 1-by-1 round knob, interlocking, orig box, rich colors 250.00

Wood and/or handcut, post 1950

Atlantic/Kingsbridge, untitled, children in cart pulled by donkey, 1940s, plywood, 15-1/4" x 11-1/2", 364 pcs (1 replaced), round knob stripcut, interlocking. 40.00

Hayter/Victory Popular, Gay Harbour, Cornwall, artist Donald Greir, 1950/60, plywood, 15-1/2" x 11-3/4", round knob stripcut, interlocking, orig box. 38.00

Russell, Charles, Auburn, Mass, Nahuel Haupi National Park, Argentine, 1940/50, plywood, 14" x 10-3/4", 455 pcs, rd, square knob, color line cutting, interlocking, orig box, 42 figures, photo 110.00

Spear/Hayter/Victory Gold, Pembroke Castle, 1970s, plywood, 19-3/4" x 13-3/4", 500 pcs (1 replaced), round knob stripcut, interlocking, orig box, 28 figures. 75.00

Unknown Maker, untitled, women in countryside, artist Picasso, 1950/60, plywood, 11-3/4" x 14", 412 pcs, random, interlocking, replaced box, 35 figures 85.00

QUEZAL

Quezal

History: The Quezal Art Glass Decorating Company, named for the quetzal—a bird with brilliantly colored feathers—was organized in 1901 in Brooklyn, New York, by Martin Bach and Thomas Johnson, two disgruntled Tiffany workers. They soon hired Percy Britton and William Wiedebine, two more Tiffany employees.

The first products, which are unmarked, were exact Tiffany imitations. Quezal pieces differ from Tiffany pieces in that they are more defined and the decorations are more visible and brighter. No new techniques were developed by Quezal.

Johnson left in 1905. T. Conrad Vahlsing, Bach's son-in-law, joined the firm in 1918 but left with Paul Frank in 1920 to form Lustre Art Glass Company, which copied Quezal pieces. Martin Bach died in 1924 and by 1925 Quezal had ceased operations.

Marks: The "Quezal" trademark was first used in 1902 and was placed on the base of vases and bowls and on the rims of shades. The acid-etched or engraved letters vary in size and may be found in amber, black, or gold. A printed label which includes an illustration of a quetzal was used briefly in 1907.

Bowl, 9-1/2" d, gold calcite ground, stretch rim, pedestal foot, sgd "Quezal" 800.00

Candlesticks, pr, 6-1/2" h, white opal ground, orange-green King Tut irid dec, flared bobeches rim, ringed hollow baluster, sgd 950.00

Compote, 4-5/8" h, pale pastel blue ground, pedestal foot, sgd and numbered 525.00

Creamer, 2-1/2" h, irid gold ground, applied lip and handle 550.00

Cruet, white opal ground, green pulled feather design, yellow stopper, applied handle 2,500.00

Desk Lamp, 13" h, 16" l, figural, bronze lion reclining on faceted weighted pedestal foot, offset curved lamp shaft fitted with gold, white, and green pulled feather dec glass shade inscribed "Quezal" 1,100.00

Flask, 8-1/2" h, brilliant irid rainbow ground, finely chased silver overlay carnations, inscribed "Quezal," Alvin Corp. mark stamped on silver 1,200.00

Floor Lamp, 58" h, 10" d, bell shaped shade with green and gold damascene dec, adjustable base, shade sgd, base has been polished 2,100.00

Jack in the Pulpit Vase
 8-3/4" h, squatty bulbous base, tapering to tall slender neck, ending in widely flaring and ruffled rim, int. with gold irid, ext. with tightly drawn mint green and gold striated pulled feather designs, continuing down to base, sgd "Quezal P663" 2,950.00
 9" h, broad mouth, tapering stem, bulbous foot, brilliant orange and salmon irid, inscribed "Quezal" 750.00
 11-3/4" h, squatty bulbous base, tall slender stick neck, widely flared and ruffled rim, int. with deep amber irid, ext. with

pearly opalescent, wintergreen striated feathering edged in amber irid, continues down neck and base, additional amber irid feathering on base, ext. rim with amber irid chain dec, sgd 4,000.00

Lamp Base, 12" h, elaborate pulled and hooked gold feather on green glass, cream ground, pulled gold feather at top, gold int.. . . . . 750.00

Lamp Shade, 5-1/4" h, 2-1/4" fitter ring, pulled feather, gold to white opalescent with green feather edge, gold irid int., sgd inside top fitter rim 350.00

Salt, 2-1/2" d, irid gold, pr 325.00

Table Lamp, 18-1/2" h, cast metal lamp base, Art Nouveau woman and quatraform swirling platform base, gold irid squared glass shade inscribed "Quezal" at rim, pr 2,550.00

Vase
 4" h, compressed bulbous base, wide shoulder, narrow flaring neck, dec with bands of silvery amber, green and blue lappets, rich emerald green irid ground at base, pearly white neck, sgd "Quezal 901" 1,650.00
 5" h, four-edged top, gold irid, inscribed mark 550.00
 5" h, pedestal form, ruffled top, lined with irid gold, green pulled feather with gold border, white ground, inscribed mark, #838. . . . . .1,000.00
 5-1/2" h, long flaring body, flared top, gold body, rose and blue irid highlights, inscribed mark. 375.00
 6-1/2" h, baluster, slightly flared foot, blue, orange, and gold irid pulled and hooked swirling dec, sgd 1,000.00
 7" h, trumpet form, lobed body, amber irid neck, lower section dec with striated amber irid lappets edged in green, reserved against opalescent ground, inscribed "Quezal A982," c1925 . . . . .1,500.00
 8" h, flared oval cased body, int. and ext. golden orange luster, base inscribed "Quezal". 495.00
 9-1/2" h, bottle form, opal white dec, reverse pulled gold irid feathers above symmetrical spider web criss-cross designs, sgd "Quezal C269". .1,500.00
 9-5/8" h, ovoid body, tapering to slender waisted stick neck, lower section dec with amber irid lappets and silvery blue irid striated feathering reserved against caramel irid ground, fine int. ribbing, creamy white neck and shoulder, sgd "Quezal A465," c1920 . . . . .3,500.00
 10-3/4" h, pyriform body, squatty foot, rich opalescent sides dec with brilliant amber irid striated feather devices below amber irid lappets, edged in lime green, sgd "Quezal 937," c1920 . . . . .2,200.00
 12-1/2" h, wide ovoid body, low flared neck, ext. with creamy irid ground, trailing gold vines interspersed with green flowers, large pulled feather design around bottom, sgd 3,500.00

QUILTS

History: Quilts have been passed down as family heirlooms for many generations. Each one is unique. The same pattern may have hundreds of variations in both color and design.

The advent of the sewing machine increased, not decreased, the number of quilts which were made. Quilts are still being sewn today.

References: Cuesta Benberry, *Always There: The African-American Presence in American Quilts*, Kentucky Quilt Project, 1992; Kathryn Berenson, *Quilts of Provence*, Thames and Hudson, 1996; Mary Clare Clark, *Collectible Quilts*, Running Press, Courage Books, 1994; Anne Gilbert, *Instant Expert: Collecting Quilts*, Alliance

Chandelier, five ruffled shades in pulled feather design, sgd, $2,100. Photo courtesy of James D. Julia.

Publishing, 1996; Liz Greenbacker and Kathleen Barach, *Quilts*, Avon Books, 1992; Carter Houck, *Quilt Encyclopedia Illustrated*, Harry N. Abrams and Museum of American Folk Art, 1991; Donald B. Kraybill, Patricia T. Herr, Jonathon Holstein, *A Quiet Spirit: Amish Quilts from the Collection of Cindy Tietze & Stuart Hodosh,* UCLA Fowler Museum of Cultural History (405 Hilgard Ave., Los Angeles, CA 90024); Jeanette Lasansky et. al., *On the Cutting Edge*, Oral Traditions Project, 1994; Patsy and Myron Orlofsky, *Quilts in America*, Abbeville Press, 1992; Nancy and Donald Roan, *Lest I Shall be Forgotten*, Goschenhoppen Historians, Inc. (P.O. Box 476, Green Lane, PA 18054), 1993; Robert Shaw, *The Art Quilt,* Hugh Lauter Levin Associates, Inc., 1997; Shelly Zegart, *American Quilt Collections/Antique Quilt Masterpieces,* Nihon Vogue Ltd., 1996.

Periodicals: *Quilt Journal*, 635 W. Main St., Louisville, KY 40202; *Quilters Newsletter*, P.O. Box 4101, Golden, CO 80401; *Vintage Quilt Newsletter*, 1305 Morphy St., Great Bend, KS 67530.

Collectors' Clubs: American Quilt Study Group, 660 Mission St., Ste. 400, San Francisco, CA 94105; American Quilter's Society, P.O. Box 3290, Paducah, KY 42001; National Quilting Assoc., Inc., P.O. Box 393, Ellicott City, MD 21043.

Museums: Colonial Williamsburg Foundation, Colonial Williamsburg, VA; Doll & Quilts Barn, Rocky Ridge, MD; Museum of the American Quilter's Society, Paducah, KY; National Museum of American History, Washington, DC; New England Quilt Museum, Lowell, MA.

Notes: The key considerations for price are age, condition, aesthetic appeal, and design. Prices are now level, although the very finest examples continue to bring record prices.

Appliqué

Carolina Lily, appliqué and pieced, goldenrod and green calico, white ground, cut-out corners, small stamped ink maker's label on back, 72" x 79". 375.00

Double Fleur-de-Lis, cotton, printed navy blue and white patches, white ground, double sawtooth border, feather wreath and diamond quilting, MI, c1860-70, 78" x 80". 2,250.00

Floral Medallions, four medallions of four stylized stemmed flowers in X-form design, red, green, orange, and beige patches, white ground, diamond quilting, colors slightly faded, 69" x 86" 750.00

Flowering Vines, appliqué and pieced, bands of flowering vines and birds alternating with bands of flying geese within stripes, cotton, red, yellow, and taupe, 19th C, imperfections, 76" x 78" 500.00

Missouri Rose variant, stylized potted flowers, meandering vine border, yellow, green, and red patches, white ground, conforming heart, tea cup and flowerhead quilting, Catherine Jane McPeak Stults, 1858, minor discoloration and fiber loss, 91" x 72" 900.00

Nasturtiums, red and green, white ground, scalloped border, America, early 20th C, staining, 90" x 76" 200.00

Oak Leaf Variant, red, green, and yellow calicos, white ground, crib size, 36" x 28-3/4", America, 19th C 575.00

Poinsettia and Christmas cactus, red and green, white ground, dated "March 14, 1934," 68-1/2" x 62" 250.00

Potted Tulips, border of birds among foliage, green and red calicos, white ground, minor staining, scattered fiber wear, 92-1/2" x 94-1/2". 980.00

Rose and Bud, pink calico, green, and red, white ground, America, mid 19th C, 90" x 73", top only 460.00

Rose Medallion, nine medallions, pink, medium green, and pale pink, white ground, vining border, well quilted, light staining, 84" x 85". 220.00

Rose of Sharon and heart design, scrolling foliate border, green calico and red cotton, white ground, toning, minor fading, America, second half 19th C, 84" x 82-1/2" 900.00

Rose Wreath, similar borders, cut corners, red and teal green, America, mid 19th C, 84" x 82", fading, very minor staining 250.00

Star of Bethlehem, various appliquéd potted flowering plants, plain and printed cottons, white ground, 85" x 88", staining, fading, scattered fiber wear 750.00

Stylized floral medallions, teal blue, red, and burnt orange, minor stains, 86" x 90" 690.00

Stylized floral medallions, vining border, two shades of green, red, and orange, stains, 78""x 81" 715.00

Sunburst and Eagle, green, terra-cotta, and red, white ground, America, mid 19th C, 88" x 90", fading, staining, minor areas of fiber wear 250.00

Sunburst and Rose of Sharon with Birds, variant, red, green, and terra-cotta, white ground, America, mid 19th C, very minor staining to reverse 2,415.00

Crazy, knotted crazy quilt center, multicolored solids, quilted border of faded blue and maroon crepe, Kalona, Iowa, origin, very worn, holes, and stains. 110.00

Pieced

Barn Rising, log cabin variant, calicos and other materials, America, late 19th C, fading, minor fiber wear, 69-1/2" x 68" 375.00

Bow Tie, multicolored colored prints, white ground, stains, one corner with minor damage, 70" x 80" 220.00

Nine floral medallions with birds, matching vining border, puffed berries with embroidered stems, red and green, well quilted, minor stains and fading, frayed edge binding, 86" x 86", $1,320. Photo courtesy of Garth's Auctions, Inc.

Crown of Thorns, blue and black calico on white, alternating squares of olive green calico, overall wear, some repair and stains, 74" x 88" 220.00

Fence 'Round Field, green and goldenrod, brown center, Holmes County, Ohio, minor stains and overall wear, 81" x 82" 325.00

Flower Garden, printed cotton patches, red floral roller printed border, cut-out corners, mid 19th C, 81" x 90-1/4" . . . 400.00

Flying Geese, red and white, reversed with pieced bars backing, 75" x 82" 650.00

Irish Chain Variant, red patches, white ground, red, white, purple, and green occupational embroidery, dated 1885, Stamford, NY, 96" x 79" 1,610.00

LeMoyne Star, calicoes, red and green ground, America, late 19th C, very minor staining, 80" x 66-1/2" 375.00

Log Cabin, concentric diamond design, multicolored prints, solids, and white, red border, machine sewn, hand quilted, minor stains, 83" x 88" 330.00

Lone Star, red, medium blue, goldenrod, and white, small black stains and age stains, machine sewn binding, 80" x 82" 385.00

Mosaic, pinwheel stars, blue, black, green, and yellow, lavender ground, fish scale quilted border, machine sewn binding, Cochranton, PA, origin, overall wear, some stains, 67" x 80" 250.00

Navajo Rug design, green, blue, red, and orchid cotton, white ground, fading, minor staining, America, late 19th/early 20th C, 77" x 69" 300.00

Nine Patch, with cocheco crazy quilt printed border worked in with calicos, green ground, America, 19th C, 81-1/2" x 77" 375.00

Pinetree, blue, green, black, brown, and lavender, machine sewn binding, made by Mrs. Mose Miller, Middlefield, OH, very worn, faded 350.00

Pinwheel and Sunburst, diamond latticework, pinwheel within starburst within quatrefoil in diamonds, pieced triangle border, solid and printed cotton fabrics, green, squash brown, and cream, conforming parallel line quilting, mid 19th C, some discoloration, 92" x 98" 900.00

Postage Stamp Squares, brightly colored prints alternating with white, red binding, corner embroidered "Allie," wear and some loose seams, 66" x 78" 450.00

Star of Bethlehem Variant, red, blue, green, and white printed cotton, paisley printed border, America, late 19th C, 76" x 79-/2" 850.00

Sunshine and Shadow Log Cabin, diagonal bands of red, blue gray and pink contrasted with white, wear and stains, 65" x 73" 220.00

Tumbling Blocks, multicolored silk, satin, and velvet patches, 62" x 82" 500.00

Twelve Stars, four each in blue, pale apricot, and turquoise white ground, blue edge tripe, Reno County, KS, well quilted, 73" x 84" 500.00

QUIMPER

History: Quimper faience, dating back to the 17th century, is named for Quimper, a French town where numerous potteries were located. Several mergers resulted in the evolution of two major houses—the Jules Henriot and Hubaudière-Bousquet factories.

The peasant design first appeared in the 1860s, and many variations exist. Florals and geometrics, equally popular, also were produced in large quantities. During the 1920s the Hubaudière-Bousquet factory introduced the Odetta line which utilized a stone body and Art Deco decorations.

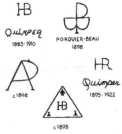

The two major houses merged in 1968, the products retaining the individual characteristics and marks of the originals. The concern suffered from labor problems in the 1980s and was purchased by an American group.

Marks: The "HR" and "HR Quimper" marks are found on Henriot pieces prior to 1922. The "Henriot Quimper" mark was used after 1922. The "HB" mark covers a long time span. Numbers or dots and dashes were added for inventory purposes and are found on later pieces. Most marks are in blue or black. Pieces ordered by department stores, such as Macy's and Carson Pirie Scott, carry the store mark along with the factory mark, making them less desirable to collectors. A comprehensive list of marks is found in Bondhus book.

References: Susan and Al Bagdade, *Warman's English & Continental Pottery & Porcelain*, 3rd Ed., Krause, 1998; Sandra V. Bondhus, *Quimper Pottery: A French Folk Art Faience,* printed by author, 1981, Revised Edition, 1995; Millicent Mali, *French Faience*, United Printing, 1986; Millicent Mali, *Quimper Faience,* Airon, Inc., 1979; Adela Meadows, *Quimper Pottery, A Guide to Origins, Styles, and Values,* Schiffer Publishing, 1998; Ann Marie O'Neill, *Quimper Pottery, 2nd Edition,* Schiffer Publishing, 1998; Marjatta Taburet, *La Faience de Quimper*, Editions Sous le Vent, 1979, (French text).

Museums: Musee des Faiences de Quimper, Quimper, France; Musee Departemental Breton, Quimper, France; Victoria and Albert Museum, French Ceramic Dept., London, England.

Advisors: Susan and Al Bagdade.

Additional Terms:

A la touche border decor - single brush stroke to create floral

Breton Broderie decor - stylized blue and gold pattern inspired by a popular embroidery pattern often used on Breton costumes, dates from the Art Deco era.

Croisille, criss-cross pattern

Decor Riche border - acanthus leaves in two colors

Fleur de lys - the symbol of France

Ivoire Corbeille pattern - red dots circled in sponged blue with red touches forming half a floral blossom, all over a tan ground

Quintal - five fingered vase.

Bank, 8" l, standing figural pig, red, blue, and black standing peasant figure on side, red, blue, and green single stroke flowers, pink pig face, hooves, and curled tail, "HB Quimper" mark 695.00

Bell, 3-1/2" h, figural bagpipe, male peasant on front, floral spray and four blue dot design on reverse, figural blue bow, brown horns on handle, "HenRiot Quimper France" mark . . 150.00

Biberon, 4-1/2" h, red, yellow, and green flowers on sides, blue bands on pedestal base, blue dashes on handle and spout, "HB" under handle, "*Quimper*" on base, 19th C 375.00

Bookends, pr, 7-1/4" h, 6-3/4" l, seated figural male peasant in blue shirt, black jacket, yellow ribboned black hat, gray trousers, blowing horn, seated female in black dress, white coif, yellow apron, holding white goose in lap, cream bases, "HB Quimper" on bases. 995.00

Bowl, 10" d, green stylized bird in center with heart, dark red, yellow, and brown stylized flowers, light yellow to brown shaded ground, green rim, pierced for hanging, "P Fouillen Quimper" mark 185.00

Box, 3-1/4" h, seated female peasant holding egg basket on reverse, red and blue criss-cross panels on ends and cov, four red dot flowers, orange dashes at corners, blue sponged rims, blue swan finial, "HenRiot Quimper" mark. 225.00

Cake Stand, 8" sq, 4-1/2" h, ftd, pink and yellow morning glories on green vine, purple clover and insect, rolled corners, blue and yellow geometric border, green acanthus leaves on under border, wavy scrolled rim, Porquier-Beau 1,700.00

Cheese Dish, cov, 8-1/4" d, 3-1/4" h, cov with male peasant holding pipe, blue pantaloons, orange shirt, black hat, yellow centered blue dot and a la touche flowers, figural serpent handle, octagonal base, blue and orange striped rim, "HenRiot Quimper" mark 475.00

Cider Jug, 6-1/2" h, Breton Broderie design, female peasant bust with white coif and collar, tan ground, dark blue trim, orange a la touche strokes, "HB Quimper" mark 260.00

Compote, 5-1/2" h, 9" d, frontal view of female peasant with basket over arm, flanked by red, blue, and green foliage, bands of red, blue, and green foliage and scattered four blue dot designs on int. and ext. border, blue outlined int. wavy rim and base, "HR Quimper" mark 490.00

Cup and Saucer, heart shape, male peasant with floral sprays on cup, floral garland, sprays and four blue dot designs on saucer, three small feet, "HR Quimper" mark. 150.00

Dish, 9-1/4" d, dancing peasant couple in center, pink bell-shaped scattered ajonc flowers at sides, large yellow flower at top, blue-green piecrust border, figural pink and green butterflies at edges, 3 small green feet, "HR Quimper" mark. 825.00

Egg Cup, 2" h, figural
  Baby chick, yellow body, blue wings, attached underplate with scattered florals, blue outlined lobed rim, "HR Quimper" mark. 165.00
  Swan, blue spotted yellow breast, wings, and feathers, band of floral sprays and blue dots on border, orange outlined rim, "HR Quimper" mark. 160.00

Figure
  3-1/4" h, male peasant in black suit with blue trim, walking arm in arm with female peasant in black dress with blue trim, white collar and coif, J. Sevellec, "HenRiot Quimper France" mark 275.00
  4" h, standing male peasant, orange-lined cobalt jacket, black hat, white pantaloons, leaning on staff, sq green base, orange outlined "LOIK" on front, "HenRiot Quimper" mark 250.00

Fish Platter
  20-1/2" l, 11" w, multicolored center scene of Breton wedding scene, cottage and forest in background, blue acanthus border on light blue ground, crest of Brittany on top, orange outlined shaped rim, "HR Quimper 130" mark. . . . 1,700.00
  24" l, 10" w, seated female peasant with distaff, male peasant playing bagpipe, trees and fencing in background, scattered red and green florals on border, shaped rim, "HR Quimper" mark. 1,250.00

Inkwell, 6" d, figural peasant hat, seated male peasant on cov, yellow criss-cross band around crown, yellow-centered blue dot florals, blue outlined rim, orig insert, "HenRiot Quimper France" mark 375.00

Jardiniere, 8" l, 6-1/2" h, figural swan, green head, yellow beak resting on neck, reserve of seated female peasant holding distaff or male peasant playing bagpipe on breast, blue sponged spotted body, blue outlined wing feathers, "HenRiot Quimper" marks, pr 1,250.00

Liqueur Bottle, 11-1/2" and 12" h, stoneware, charcoal jacket, tan vest, blue trousers, black coif, cream blouse, dark brown dress, blue apron, "Dolfi" on base, "HR Quimper" marks, pr 225.00

Oil and Vinegar Cruet, 7" h, overall black ermine tails, yellow and black fleur-de-lys, blue dash spouts and overhead handle, "HB" mark. 475.00

Picture Frame, 8" l, 6-1/2" w, rect, male peasant at one end, female at other, band of yellow-centered blue floral garlands, green leaves, and red single stroke flowerheads on border, "AP" mark. 1,700.00

Pitcher, 6" h, white coif, green blouse, dark and light blue shawl, "HenRiot Quimper" mark 125.00

Plate
  8-1/4" d, frontal view of peasant man leaning on walking stick, vertical single stroke green and red florals, border band of red, blue, and green florals and leaves, blue lined shaped rim, "HR Quimper" mark. 400.00
  8-3/4" d, black sun face in center with red and yellow rays, yellow-centered blue dot flowers between rays, border of blue swags and green single stroke dashes, yellow outlined shaped rim. 525.00
  9-1/4" d, Convolvuius flowers and leaves, blue-winged insect, yellow outlined indented rim, Porquier Beau, c1875-80 . . . . 880.00
  9-1/2' d, male peasants playing bagpipe or horn, barrel in background, orange outlined blue acanthus border, crest of Brittany at top, shaped indented rim, "HR" mark . . . 595.00
  9-5/8" h, maroon jacket, dark blue trousers, orange shawl, dark blue dress, green apron, orange and blue inner stripes, blue, maroon, and green stylized seagulls, snails, and lines and stripes, "Pecheur Quimper" mark 225.00

Box, seated female peasant holding egg basket on reverse, red and blue criss-cross panels on ends and cov, four red dot flowers, orange dashes at corners, blue sponged rims, blue swan finial, "HenRiot Quimper" mark, 3-1/4" h, $225. Photo courtesy of Susan and Al Bagdade.

Platter

    15" l, 10" w, oval, frontal view of peasant woman holding basket of eggs, flanked by red, blue, and green vertical florals, border band of green and red foliage and yellow centered blue dot florals, blue outlined indented rim, unmarked 535.00

    20" l, yellow cornucopia, red, yellow, and blue chrysanthemums, multicolored flying insects and birds, scattered multicolored florals, indented shaped rim 1,050.00

Quintel, 3-3/4" h, seated peasant woman holding egg basket in orange quatrefoil reserved on band of red and blue criss-cross, orange and blue striped openings and stylized orange, yellow, and blue dogwood blossom, "HenRiot Quimper France" mark 230.00

Serving Dish, 11-1/2" d, 4" h, three overlapping scallop shells, frontal view of male peasant, female peasant, or basket of flowers in colors, blue outlined rim, figural swan handle, "HR Quimper" mark 420.00

Snuff Bottle, 3" d, blue clock face on front, male peasant with pipe and florals on reverse, blue sponged border, "HR Quimper" mark 425.00

Teapot, 11" h, donut shape, male peasant smoking pipe, female leaning on walking stick on front, floral wreath on reverse, scattered red, green, and blue florals and leaves, four blue dots, hairlines 500.00

Trivet

    8-1/2" sq, male fisherman in brown jacket with arm around peasant woman in orange shawl and green apron, sailboats in background, blue squares on border with yellow stylized shells and green seagulls, "Pecheur Quimper" mark . 325.00

    9-3/4" d, figural six-sided star, frontal view of female peasant with basket on head in center, red and blue criss-cross panels on border, stylized chrysanthemums at star points, "HenRiot Quimper" mark 325.00

Tureen, cov, 7" d, 7-1/2" h, band of red, blue, and green flowers and foliage, wide yellow borders with blue stripe, blue knob and scroll handles, "HB Quimper" mark 475.00

Vase

    6-1/2" h, ovoid shape, flared rim, male peasant blowing horn or female peasant holding flower, red, green, yellow, and blue vertical foliage, scattered four blue dot design, band of blue half circles and dots on neck, orange, and blue striped rim, "HenRiot Quimper" marks, pr 350.00

    8" h, figural fleur-de-lys, female peasant on front, floral spray on reverse, red, blue, and green criss-cross ground, orange outlined crest of Brittany on base, "HR Quimper" mark on front 475.00

    8" h, swollen cylinder shape, spread base, female peasant in meadow and blue clouds on body, orange and blue striped rim, orange outlined dark blue on light blue decor riche border on base, "HB Quimper" mark 250.00

    8-1/2" h, stoneware, tapered cylinder shape with shoulder and vertical rim, black, brown, and cream half circles, black and cream horizontal lines, brown ground, "HB Quimper Odetta" mark 675.00

    12-1/2" h, stoneware, ball shape, short neck, flared rim, black glaze with orange circles, lines and wavy lines, "HB Quimper Odetta" mark, c1920 . . . . .1,150.00

Wall Pocket

    4-1/2" h, 4-1/2" w, figural envelope, male peasant, red and green florals in sections, dark blue outlined folds, "HR Quimper" mark 350.00

    8" h, figural bagpipe shape, standing male peasant playing bagpipe on front, molded brown pipes and yellow ribbon at top, "HR Quimper" mark 300.00

    10-1/2" h, overlapped cone shape, standing male peasant blowing horn on front, red, blue, and green vertical florals, blue outlined orange-yellow borders, 19th C 180.00

RADIOS

History: The radio was invented more than 100 years ago. Marconi was the first to assemble and employ the transmission and reception instruments that permitted the sending of electric messages without the use of direct connections. Between 1905 and the end of World War I, many technical advances affected the "wireless," including the invention of the vacuum tube by DeForest. Technology continued its progress, and radios filled the entertainment needs of the average family in the 1920s.

    Changes in design, style, and technology brought the radio from the black boxes of the 1920s to the stylish furniture pieces and console models of the 1930s and 1940s, to midget models of the 1950s, and finally to the high-tech radios of the 1980s.

References: Marty and Sue Bunis, *Collector's Guide to Antique Radios*, 4th ed., Collector Books, 1996; ——, *Collector's Guide to Transistor Radios*, Collector Books, 1994; Marty Bunis and Robert Breed, *Collector's Guide to Novelty Radios*, Collector Books, 1995; Philip Collins, *Radio Redux*, Chronicle Books, 1992; Harold Cones, and John Bryant, *Zenith Radio: The Early Years, 1919-1935*, Schiffer Publishing, 1997; Chuck Dachis, *Radios by Hallicrafters*, Schiffer Publishing, 1996; Alan Douglas, *Radio Manufacturers of the 1920s*, Vol. 1 (1988), Vol. 2 (1989), Vol. 3 (1991), Vestal Press; Roger Handy, Maureen Erbe, and Aileen Farnan Antonier, *Made in Japan*, Chronicle Books, 1993; David and Betty Johnson, *Guide to Old Radios, Pointers, Pictures and Prices*, 2nd ed., Wallace Homestead/Krause, 1995; David R. and Robert A. Lane, *Transistor Radios*, Wallace-Homestead, 1994; Harry Poster, *Poster's Radio & Television Price Guide*, 2nd ed., Wallace-Homestead, 1994; Ron Ramirez, *Philco Radio*, Schiffer Publishing, 1993; B. Eric Rhoads, *Blast from the Past*, available from author (800-226-7857), 1996; Mark Stein, *Machine Age to Jet Age, Radiomania's Guide to Tabletop Radios—1933-1959*, published by author (2109 Carterdale Rd., Baltimore, MD 21209); Eric Wrobbel, *Toy Crystal Radios,* published by author, 1997 (20802 Exhibit Court, Woodland Hills, CA).

Periodicals: *Antique Radio Classified*, P.O. Box 2, Carlisle, MA, 01741; *Horn Speaker*, P.O. Box 1193, Mabank, TX 75147; *Radio Age*, 636 Cambridge Road, Augusta, GA 30909; *Transistor Network*, RR1, Box 36, Bradford, NH 03221.

Collectors' Clubs: Antique Radio Club of America, 81 Steeplechase Rd., Devon, PA 19333; Antique Wireless Assoc., 59 Main St., Bloomfield, NY 14469; New England Antique Radio Club, RR1, Box 36, Bradford, NH 03221; Vintage Radio & Phonograph Society, Inc., P.O. Box 165345, Irving, TX 75016.

Museums: Antique Radio Museum, St. Louis, MO; Antique Wireless Museum, Bloomfield, NY; Caperton's Radio Museum, Louisville, KY; Muchow's Historical Radio Museum, Elgin, IL; Museum of Broadcast Communication, Chicago, IL; Museum of Wonderful Miracles, Minneapolis, MN; New England Wireless and Steam Museum, Inc., East Greenwich, RI; Voice of the Twenties, Orient, NY.

Additional Listings: See *Warman's Americana & Collectibles* for more examples.

Advisor: Lewis S. Walters.

Note: Prices of Catalin radios are dropping by about 10 to 15%. Collectors and dealers feel prices for these radios have reached their high side and are falling into a more realistic range.

Admiral
  Portable
    #33-35-37 . . . . 30.00
    #218, leatherette 40.00
    #909, All World 85.00
    Y-2127, Imperial 8, c1959 . . . . 45.00
Air King, tombstone, Art Deco 3,000.00
Arvin
  Hopalong Cassidy, lariatenna 525.00
  Table
    #444 . . . . 100.00
    #522A 65.00
  Tombstone, #617 Rhythm Maid 215.00
Atwater Kent
  Breadboard
    Model 9A 550.00
    Model 10, orig tags 1,200.00
    Model 10C 930.00
  Cathedral, 80, c1931 . . . . 380.00
  Table
    #55, Keil 225.00
    #318, dome 115.00
  Tombstone, #854 . . . . 155.00
Bulova, clock radio
  #100 . . . . 40.00
  #120 . . . . 40.00
Columbia, table, oak 125.00
Crosley
  Bandbox, #600, 1927 . . . . 80.00
  Battery Operated, #4-28 . . . . 130.00
  Dashboard 120.00
  Gemchest, #609 . . . . 425.00
  Litfella, 1N, cathedral 175.00
  Pup, with orig box 575.00
  Sheraton, cathedral 290.00
  Showbox, #706 . . . . 100.00
  Super Buddy Boy 125.00
Dumont, RA346, table, scroll work, 1938 . . . . 110.00
Emerson
  AU-190, Catalin tombstone 1,500.00

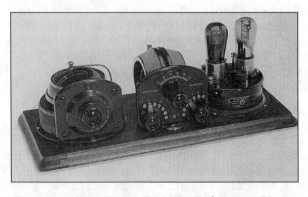

Atwater Kent Type TA, 1924, $1,465. Photo courtesy of Auction Team Breker.

BT-245 . . . . .1,200.00
#409, Mickey 1,400.00
#411, Mickey 1,400.00
#570, Memento 110.00
#640, portable 30.00
#888, Vanguard 60.00
Fada
  #43 . . . . 240.00
  #60W 75.00
  #115, bullet shape 850.00
  #136 . . . . .1,000.00
  #252 . . . . 575.00
  #625, rounded end, slide rule dial 700.00
Federal
  #58DX 500.00
  #100 . . . . 425.00
General Electric
  #81, c1934 . . . . 200.00
  #400 . . . . 30.00
  #410 . . . . 30.00
  #411 . . . . 30.00
  #414 . . . . 30.00
  #515, clock radio 25.00
  #517, clock radio 25.00
  K-126 . . . . 150.00
  Tombstone 250.00
Grebe
  CR-12 . . . . 600.00
  MU-1 . . . . 200.00
Halicrafters
  TW-200 . . . . 125.00
  TW-600 . . . . 100.00
Majestic
  #92 . . . . 125.00
  #381 . . . . 225.00
  Charlie McCarthy 1,000.00
Metrodyne, Super 7, 1925 . . . . 265.00
Motorola
  #68X11Q, Art Deco 75.00
  Jet Plane 55.00
  Jewel Box 80.00
  M logo 25.00
  Pixie 45.00
  Ranger, portable 40.00
  Ranger #700 . . . . 45.00
  Table, plastic 35.00
Olympic, radio with phonograph 40.00
  Paragon
  DA-2, table 475.00
  RD-5, table 600.00
Philco
  #17-20-38, cathedral 250.00
  #37-62, table, 2 tone 75.00
  #37-84, cathedral, 1937 . . . . 65.00
  #40-180, console, wood 130.00
  #46-132, table 20.00
  #49-501, Boomerang 475.00
  #49-506, Transitone 35.00
  #52-544, Transitone 40.00
  #551, 1928 . . . . 145.00
  T07, 126 transistor 65.00
  T1000, clock radio 80.00
Radiobar, decanter and glasses 1,500.00
Radio Corporation of America, RCA
  LaSiesta 300.00
Radiola
  #18, speaker 115.00

#20 . . . . 165.00
#24 . . . . 170.00
#28, console. 200.00
#33 . . . . 40.00
#6X7, table, plastic. 25.00
8BT-7LE, portable 35.00
40X56, World's Fair 1,000.00
Silvertone, Sears
#1, table 75.00
#1582, cathedral, wood 225.00
#1955, tombstone. 135.00
#9205, plastic transistor 40.00
Sony, transistor
TFM-151, 1960. 50.00
TR-63, 1958 . . . . 145.00
Sparton
#506, Blue Bird, Art Deco. 3,300.00
#5218 . . . . 95.00
Stewart-Warner, table, slant 175.00
Stromberg Carlson, #636A, console 125.00
Westinghouse, Model WR-602 . . . . 50.00
Zenith
Royal
#500, transistor, owl eye 75.00
#500D, transistor 55.00
#750L, transistor, leather case 40.00
Trans-Oceanic 175.00
#6D2615, table, boomerang dial 95.00
Zephyr, multiband 95.00

RAILROAD ITEMS

History: Railroad collectors have existed for decades. The merger of the rail systems and the end of passenger service made many objects available to private collectors. The Pennsylvania Railroad sold its archives at public sale.

References: Susan and Al Bagdade, *Warman's American Pottery and Porcelain*, Wallace-Homestead, 1994; Stanley L. Baker, *Railroad Collectibles*, 4th ed., Collector Books, 1990, 1993 value update; Richard C. Barrett, *Illustrated Encyclopedia of Railroad Lighting*, Vol. 1, Railroad Research Publications, 1994; David Dreimiller, *Dressel Railway Lamp & Signal Company*, Hiram Press, 1995; Joseph F. Farrell, Jr., *Illustrated Guide to Peter Gray Railroad Hardware*, Hiram Press, 1994; Anthony Hobson, *Lanterns That Lit Our World*, Hiram Press, reprinted 1996; Richard Luckin, *Dining on Rails*, RK Publishing, 1994; Don Stewart, *Railroad Switch Keys & Padlocks*, 2nd ed., Key Collectors International, 1993.

Periodicals: *Key, Lock and Lantern*, 3 Berkeley Heights Park, Bloomfield, NJ 07003; *Main Line Journal*, PO Box 121, Streamwood, IL 60107.

Collectors' Clubs: Chesapeake & Ohio Historical Society, Inc., P.O. Box 79, Clifton Forge, VA 24422; Illinois Central Railroad Historical Society, 14818 Clifton Park, Midlothian, IL 60445; Railroad Enthusiasts, 102 Dean Rd., Brookline, MA 02146; Railroadiana Collectors Assoc., 795 Aspen Drive, Buffalo Grove, IL 60089; Railway and Locomotive Historical Society, P.O. Box 1418, Westford, MA 01886; Twentieth Century Railroad Club, 329 West 18th St., Ste. 902, Chicago, IL 60616.

Museums: Baltimore and Ohio Railroad, Baltimore, MD; California State Railroad Museum, Sacramento, CA; Frisco Railroad Museum, Van Buren, AR; Museum of Transportation, Brookline, MA; National Railroad Museum, Green Bay, WI; New York Museum of Transportation, West Henrietta, NY; Old Depot Railroad Museum, Dassel, MN.

Additional Listings: See *Warman's Americana & Collectibles* for more examples.

Notes: Railroad enthusiasts have organized into regional and local clubs. Join one if you're interested in this collectible field; your local hobby store can probably point you to the right person. The best pieces pass between collectors and rarely enter the general market.

Ashtray, 3-1/2" d, Cotton Belt Route, copper, logo on bottom
. . . . 25.00
Baggage and Brass Check
1-1/4" d, key tag, GN Ry. 12.00
1 1/2" x 2", SOU PAC RR, 794, strap. 45.00
Bell, 25" h, 15-1/2" h at yoke, nickel plated, mounted on modern mahogany base 2,145.00
Book, *Colorado,* Chicago, Milwaukee & St. Paul Railway, c1910, illustrated travel guide . . . . .28.00.
Button, Erie, large silver dome, Scovill Mfg. Co., Waterbury, CT
. . . . 7.50
Calendar, 27-1/2" h, 18-1/4" w, 1951, New York Central, shows locomotive #4734, complete pad 55.00
Catalog, Pennsylvania Steel Co., Steelton, PA, 1906, 96 pages, 4-1/4" x 6-3/4", hardcover, black, gold emb, spirals, street railway curves, formulas, tables, illus 45.00
Check, Atlantic City & Shore Railroad Co. 10.00
China
Atchinson, Topeka & Sante Fe, gravy boat, Syracuse China, no backstamp. 165.00
Atlantic Coast Line, butter pat, 3-1/2" d, Flora of the South, Buffalo China backstamp 100.00
B & O (Baltimore & Ohio)
Creamer, 4-1/2" h 75.00
Plate, dinner 75.00
Platter 175.00
C & O (Chesapeake & Ohio), plate, 4-3/4" sq, Silhouette, Martha and George Washington dancing with hands up, Syracuse China, no backstamp 250.00
Delaware & Hudson, Canterbury, platter, 10-1/4" x 7", Syracuse China, no backstamp. 120.00
Florida East Coast, Carolina, bowl, 5-3/4" d, Buffalo China backstamp 75.00
Mimbreno, platter, 9-1/4" l, oval, dear motif 175.00
New York Central, Albany, compote, 7-1/4" d, Shenango China backstamp. 275.00
Norfolk & Western, plate, 6-1/4" d, Syracuse China, no backstamp 80.00
UP (Union Pacific), plate, 8-1/4" d, circus theme, monkey, clown, bareback rider. 125.00
Wabash Banner, cup and saucer, logo, Syracuse China, no backstamp 250.00
Glassware
Canadian Pacific, wine, 4" h, etched script logo on side, ornate facets 40.00
Lehigh Valley, highball, 4-1/2" h, maroon and white train, map of northeastern US marking route 75.00
Sante Fe, cordial, 4-1/2" h, applied Sante Fe white script logo
. . . . 60.00

Union Pacific, goblet, 5-1/2" h, etched name inside shield
. . . . 20.00
Hat
    Missouri Pacific, two silver bands, silver "Missouri Pacific
    Lines" buttons on each side, red cap badge with buzz saw
    logo, "Missouri Pacific Lines" and "Trainman" 165.00
    Penn Central, red logo and cap badge with "Station Master"
    . . . . 75.00
Hat Rack, overhead type, coach, wood and brass, six brass dou-
    ble sided hooks 200.00
Head Rest, Pennsylvania, 15" x 16" tan linen-type fabric, brown
    PRR logo and electric train. 15.00
Lamp, caboose interior side, C & O, c1920, price for pr . 350.00
Lantern
    Great Northern Railway, Adams & Westlake, double horizon-
    tal guard, twist-off pot and burner, 5-3/8" h clear globe,
    patent date Nov. 30, '97. 175.00
    Penn RR, Dressel, short clear globe 100.00
    Southern Railway, red globe 150.00
Lock, brass
    Boston & Maine Railroad, switch type, marked "B&M RR LS
    S," made by "Sherburne & Co/Boston, Mass" 150.00
    B & O, orig key 45.00
    Illinois Central Railroad, six lever round style, "ICRR" cast
    over front side 200.00
Map, Atlantic Coast Line, c1950s 150.00
Oil Can, Locomotive Oil 100.00
Paperweight, New York Grand Central Station, 2-1/2" w, 4" l,
    rect, view of station, adv 5 limited trains, Barnes & Abrams
    Co., light scratching to top glass 150.00
Playing Cards
    Louisville & Nashville, engine, six scenes 50.00
    Norfolk & Western, N & W in circle, blue and black . . . 50.00
    Union Pacific, river scene, two horses and riders in fore-
    ground, c1910, 52 cards, joker, extra card, booklet. . 65.00
Ruler, Soo Line, 12" l, tin, map and logo, red letters, white
    ground 10.00
Sign
    Chicago, Rock-Island & Pacific Railway, intricate moth-
    er-of-pearl inlay on reverse painted glass, 137 engine and
    tender, United States express car, five passenger cars, pro-
    moting railroad between Chicago and California, switchman
    in forefront, view is 3 miles east of LaSalle, ornate frame,
    32-1/2" h, 43-1/2" l, minor loss to black background and
    gold border. 275.00
    Railway Express Agency, set of three matched porcelain
    signs, tan and red letters, green ground, each 4" h, length
    varies from 26" to 30-1/4" 425.00
    Railway Express Agency, tin over cardboard, men unloading
    early railroad car while truck comes for pickup, H. D. Beach
    Co. litho, 13-1/2" h, 19-1/2" d, some minor scratching
    . . . . 500.00
Silver Flatware, top marked
    Lackawanna, fruit knife, Cromwell pattern, International Sil-
    ver 25.00
    NPR (North Penn Railroad), iced tea spoon, Winthrop pat-
    tern, Gorham 35.00
    PRR (Pennsylvania Railroad), teaspoon, Kings pattern, Inter-
    national Silver 30.00
    Reading, fork, Kings pattern, International Silver. 30.00
    Soo Line, fork, Windsor pattern, Reed & Barton 35.00
Silver Hollowware
    Chesapeake & Ohio, sugar tongs, 5-1/4" l, Waverly pattern,
    Albert Pick, top marked, no backstamp 165.00
    Pennsylvania, creamer, hinged lid, raised PRR keystone logo
    on side, Gorham, backstamp with name of railroad
    . . . . 175.00

**Conduc-
tor's Hat,
Milwaukee
RR, Carl-
son & Co.,
Chicago,
IL, $45.**

Southern Pacific, teapot, 12 oz, Reed & Barton, backstamp
    reads "S.P. Lines" 145.00
Western Pacific, cheese scoop, 8-1/4" l, Belmont pattern,
    Reed & Barton, top mark reads "W P Ry" 125.00
Stamp Set, Atlantic Coast Line, Jacksonville, FL, freight office,
    wooden drawer, seventy city stamps, c1950 . . . . . . 150.00
Step Stool, SP Co, marked "Morton". 325.00
Stock Certificate
    New York Central, vignette of engine 3404 pulling passenger
    train 20.00
    Western Maryland Railway, Mercury standing in front of die-
    sel locomotive 6.00
    Western Pacific Railroad, male and female flanking stream-
    lined train 8.00
Time Table, Union Pacific, 1945 . . . . 12.00
Watch Fob, brass, Oklahoma International Petroleum Expo,
    train, oil wells, plane 45.00

RAZORS

History: Razors date back several thousand years. Early
man used sharpened stones; the Egyptians, Greeks, and
Romans had metal razors.

Razors made prior to 1800 generally were crudely
stamped "Warranted" or "Cast Steel," with the maker's
mark on the tang. Until 1870 razors were handmade and
almost all razors for the American market were manufactured in Sheffield, England. Most blades were wedge
shaped; many were etched with slogans or scenes. Handles were made of natural materials: horn, tortoiseshell,
bone, ivory, stag, silver, or pearl.

After 1870, razors were machine made with hollow
ground blades and synthetic handle materials. Razors of
this period usually were manufactured in Germany (Solingen) or in American cutlery factories. Hundreds of
molded-celluloid handle patterns were produced.

Cutlery firms produced boxed sets of two, four, and
seven razors. Complete and undamaged sets are very
desirable. The most-popular ones are the seven-day sets
in which each razor is etched with a day of the week.

References: Ronald S. Barlow, *Vanishing American Barber Shop*, Windmill Publishing, 1993; *Safety Razors: A
Price Guide*, L-W Book Sales, 1995; Jim Sargent, *Sargent's American Premium Guide to Pocket Knives & Razors*, 3rd ed., Books Americana, 1992.

Periodical: *Blade Magazine*, P.O. Box 22007, Chattanooga, TN 37422.

Additional Listings: See *Warman's Americana & Collectibles* for more examples.

Notes: The fancier the handle or more intricately etched the blade, the higher the price. Rarest handle materials are pearl, stag, sterling silver, pressed horn, and carved ivory. Rarest blades are those with scenes etched across the entire front. Value is increased by the presence of certain manufacturers' names, e.g., H. Boker, Case, M. Price, Joseph Rogers, Simmons Hardware, Will & Finck, Winchester, and George Wostenholm.

Boker & Co., H., etched blade with American Lines *S. S. St. Louis* ship scene, black celluloid handle 130.00
Challenge Cutlery Co., Bridgeport, CT, blade etched "Rince," black peacock pattern 70.00
Country Club, #76, black handle, orig box 25.00
Kinfolks Straight Razor, good condition 45.00
Lecourtre, Jacques, Swiss, frameback, wafer blade, tang stamped "M. M. & Co.," engraved plated steel blade, "William Ernest Barnes Dec. 30th 1869" 45.00
Morley & Sons, W. H., German, silver overlay hunting scene 55.00
Novelty Cutlery Co., Canton, OH, rounded point blade, handle with cow, horse, train, and owner's name and address, front dated "1921," German silver ends 85.00
Saffa, John S., St. Louis, scene of two gold covered camels, scroll on blade with "Silver Sheet," ivory colored handle 40.00
Sears Craftsman, celluloid handle, orig box 45.00
Three Admirals, one medallion with Admiral Dewey, inscribed "Dewey-Manilla," other with Admiral Sampson, inscribed "Sampson-Santiogo," third with Admiral Schley, inscribed "Schley-Santiogo," gold dec. 175.00
Turniss Cutler & Stacey Sheffield, unusual shaped point blade, tang stamped "For Use," two pressed intertwined snakes on mottled horn handle 650.00
Union razor Cutlery Co., Union City, GA, banded tobacco pattern handle 50.00
Wade & Butcher, hollow ground blade, engraved and ornate escutcheon plate, two inlaid engraved star shaped metal dec, mottled horn handle, blade etched "The Celebrated Hollow Ground Razor," c1850 . . . . 90.00
Westfield Mfg. Co., hollow ground blade, checkered raised shield, ivory handle. 60.00
Wostenholm & Sons, George, Celebrated I'XL Razor Washington Works, wedge blade, etched spread American eagle and "The Congress Razor," notched point, black horn handle, five sided pewter end cap ends, c1930. . . . . 120.00
Yankee Cutlery, celluloid handle, nude woman, orig box . 75.00

F. J. Elwell, Rockdale, NY, 1900, images of political figures, $250.

RECORDS

History: With the advent of the more sophisticated recording materials, such as 33 1/3 RPM long playing records, 8-track tapes, cassettes, and compact discs, earlier phonograph records became collectors' items. Most have little value. The higher-priced items are rare (limited-production) recordings. Condition is critical.

References: Mark Allen Baker, *Goldmine Price Guide to Rock 'n' Roll Memorabilia,* Krause Publications, 1997; Les Docks, *American Premium Record Guide, 1900-1965,* 5th Edition, Krause Publications, 1997; Goldmine Magazine, *Goldmine's 1997 Annual,* Krause Publications, 1996; Ron Lofman, *Goldmine's Celebrity Vocals,* Krause Publications, 1994; William M. Miller, *How to Buy & Sell Used Record Albums,* Loran Publishing, 1994; Tim Neely, *Goldmine Christmas Record Price Guide,* Krause Publications, 1997; *Goldmine's Price Guide to Alternative Records,* Krause Publications, 1996; ——, *Goldmine's Price Guide to 45 RPM Records,* Krause Publications, 1996; Tom Neely and Dave Thompson, *Goldmine British Invasion Record Price Guide,* Krause Publications, 1997; Jerry Osborne (comp.) *Rockin' Records, 1998 Ed.,* Antique Trader Books, 1997; Neal Umphred, *Goldmine's Price Guide to Collectible Jazz Albums,* 1949-1969, 2nd ed., Krause Publications, 1994; ——, *Goldmine's Price Guide to Collectible Record Albums,* 5th ed., Krause Publications, 1996; ——, *Goldmine's Rock 'n' Roll 45 RPM Record Price Guide,* 3rd ed., Krause Publications, 1994.

Periodicals: *Cadence,* Cadence Building, Redwood, NY 13679; *DISCoveries Magazine,* P.O. Box 309, Fraser, MI 48026; *Goldmine,* 700 E. State St., Iola, WI 54990; *Jazz Beat Magazine,* 1206 Decatur St., New Orleans, LA 70116; *Joslin's Jazz Journal,* P.O. Box 213, Parsons, KS 67357; *New Amberola Graphic,* 37 Caledonia St., St. Johnsbury, VT 05819; *Record Collectors Monthly,* P.O. Box 75, Mendham, NJ 07945; *Record Finder,* P.O. Box 1047, Glen Allen, VA 23060.

Collectors' Clubs: Association for Recorded Sound Collections, P.O. Box 453, Annapolis, MD 21404; International Association of Jazz Record Collectors, P.O. Box 75155, Tampa, FL 33605.

Additional Listings: See *Warman's Americana & Collectibles* for more examples.

Note: Most records, especially popular recordings, have a value of less than $3 per disc. The records listed here are for Picture Sleeves, 45 rpm records, which feature a photo of the artist or group.

Atomic Rooster, Save Me/Close Your Eyes, Spain 15.00
Beach Boys
    Good Vibrations/Let's Go Away For Awhile, Germany
    . . . . 20.00
    I Can Hear The Music/All I Want, France. 20.00
Beatles
    John/Cold Turkey, US 60.00
    Love Me Do, 1" bottom seam split 50.00
Bee Gees, Stayin' Alive/If I Can't Have You, Belgium . . . 10.00
David Bowie, Alabama song/Space Oddity, Germany . . . 20.00
Cheap Trick, Dancing the Night Away, promo, Spain 15.00

Petula Clark, Anyone Who Had A Heart, France 20.00
Dave Clark Five, Tabathia Twitchet, Mexico. 45.00
Dead or Alive, Stranger/Some of That, United Kingdom. . 35.00
Doobie Brothers, Eyes of Silver, Germany 8.00
ELO, Strange Magic/Down Home Town, Germany 12.00
Nina Hagen, Spirit in the Sky/My Way, promo, Spain. . . . 25.00
Hollies, Stop, Stop, Stop, Spain 45.00
Jefferson Airplane, Mexico, 3 promo stamps, Brazil. 40.00
Lennie Kravitz, Stand By My Woman/Flowers, France. . . . 8.00
Barry Manilow, Let's Hang On, promo, Spain. 20.00
Meatloaf, Dead Ringer for Love, promo, Spain. 15.00
Monkees, Daydream Believe, promo, Japan 60.00
Willie Nelson, Help Me Make It, Spain 10.00
Donny Osmond, When I Fall In Love, Spain. 15.00
Rolling Stones, Emotional Rescue, France. 20.00
Slade, Bangin Man/She Did It To Me, Germany. 15.00
Bruce Springsteen, Tenth Avenue/Freeze Out, Germany 75.00
Cat Stevens, Two Fine People/A Bad Penny, France 8.00
Supremes, Baby Love, France 75.00
Tears for Fears, Pale Shelter, Spain. 10.00
Ike & Tina Turner, Baby, Get It On, Spain 15.00
Who, My Generation, Czech. 20.00
Yardbirds, Still I'm Sad/Evil Hearted You, Sweden. 60.00

REDWARE

History: The availability of clay, the same used to make bricks and roof tiles, accounted for the great production of red earthenware pottery in the American colonies. Redware pieces are mainly utilitarian—bowls, crocks, jugs, etc.

Lead-glazed redware retained its reddish color, but a variety of colored glazes were obtained by the addition of metals to the basic glaze. Streaks and mottled splotches in redware items resulted from impurities in the clay and/or uneven firing temperatures.

Slipware is the term used to describe redwares decorated by the application of slip, a semi-liquid paste made of clay. Slipwares were made in England, Germany, and elsewhere in Europe for decades before becoming popular in the Pennsylvania German region and other areas in colonial America.

References: Susan and Al Bagdade, *Warman's American Pottery and Porcelain*, Wallace-Homestead, 1994; William C. Ketchum, Jr., *American Pottery and Porcelain*, Avon Books, 1994.

Bank, 6-1/2" h, 5-3/4" d, beehive shape, peg finial clear lead
    glaze, slight greenish int. 225.00
Basin, 18" d, tin glaze 75.00
Basket, 3-1/4" h, 6" d, hanging type, red and white, yellow slip,
    green and brown glaze, notched rim, pot and saucer, three
    pierced holes, restored. 1,300.00
Bottle, 11-3/4" h, donut shape, amber glaze, brown flecks
    . . . . 140.00
Bowl
    11-3/4" d, brown and green striped glaze, cream ground,
        Continental, 19th C, minor chips, glaze wear 635.00
    12-1/2" d, shallow, very worn int., yellow slip bird on branch
        and edge design, green and brown glaze, chips . . . 250.00
    13-1/2" d, 2-1/2" h, shallow, coggle edge, three line yellow
        slip dec, worn, center badly chipped 400.00
Charger, coggle edge
    11 3/8" d, four line slip dec. 1,200.00

    13-3/4" d, yellow slip combware dec 1,350.00
Chestnut Dish, 13-1/2" d, oval, slip dec, rim chips 425.00
Colander, 9-3/4" x 7", clear glaze, brown flecks, orange-ground
    ground, rim handles, three applied feet 350.00
Creamer, 4" h, incised band, four vertical lines of black irid glaze
    . . . . 125.00
Crock, 9" h, clear glaze, brown splotches, applied handles
    . . . . 190.00
Cuspidor, 3 7/8" h, 7-1/2" d, red and white slip, green and brown
    sponged glaze under clear lead glaze, foot chips and wear
    . . . . 100.00
Custard Cup, 2 3/8" h, incised "TS Stahl, Sept. 1, 1940" . 60.00
Desk Set, 5-1/2" l, 6-1/2" h, molded edges, hollow int., dog with
    urn, black brushed design, clear glaze. 525.00
Dish
    7 5/8" d, dark glaze, yellow slip spots, rim flake. . . . 275.00
    8" d, yellow slip dec, wear and chips 200.00
    12-1/8" d, shallow, script slip dec, chips, glaze wear . 225.00
Figure
    7-3/4" l, 7-1/4" h, poodle, in style of Staffordshire spaniel,
        brown glaze, reverse inscribed "H. McD," 19th C, minor los-
        es, cracks, kiln imperfections 200.00
    8-3/4" l, lion, rect base, mottled tan and cream colored un-
        glazed surface, incised label "12-6-'31, WADS, O., L.E." . .
        385.00
    9-1/2" h, seated dog, tooled coat, open front legs, solid cast-
        ing, chips around base, worn black stain 420.00
Flask, 8" h, brown splotches, clear glaze, orange ground, New
    England 275.00
Flower Pot
    5" h, 6 1/8" d, red and white slip, brown sponge dec, clear
        lead glaze ext., attached undertray imp "John Bell/Waynes-
        boro". 200.00
    7 5/8" h, 8 1/8" d, white slip, applied brown slip and dabbed
        green glaze swag design dec, double roulette rim attached
        ruffled undertray, imp "Solomon Bell" 450.00
Foot Warmer, 6-3/4" h, 13-1/2" l, ram-form, glazed, 19th C, very
    minor chips. 520.00
Jar, ovoid
    6" h
        Brown sponging, ribbed strap handle, chips 135.00
        Light amber, brown splotches, ribbed strap handle, minor
            chips 300.00
        Well defined brown and amber glaze, minor flakes 220.00
    6-1/2" h, dark ground, brown splotches, minor chips
        . . . . 275.00
    9-1/2" h, dark green amber glaze, incised initials "SB" on
        side, ripped strap handle, wear, chips 315.00
    9-3/4" h, two handles, glazed, 19th C, chips, glaze wear
        . . . . 375.00
    12" h, applied shoulder handles, reddish amber glaze, chips
        on lip and lid. 110.00

**Bowl, 8" d,
3-1/2" h,
$90.**

Jug, America, 19th C

8" h, minor hairlines, minor chips to base 2,645.00
9-5/8" h, glazed, very minor chips and cracks 400.00
9-3/4" h, gonic glaze, minor chips 775.00

Lamp, 23" h overall, 9" h jar drilled and mounted as lamp base, incised lines, applied ribbed shoulder handles and clear glaze, tan color, dark brown splotches, wear and chips, wooden base, old burlap shade 265.00

Loaf Pan, 13" l, rect, coggle edge, three line yellow slip dec, worn, old chips and scratches 425.00

Meat Roaster, 12" l, scoop shape, applied finger crimped rim, strap handle, end spout, greenish amber glaze 220.00

Milk Pan, 10" d, "1813" in yellow slip between double lines, wavy line border, black back 125.00

Mug, 4 3/8" h, 4-1/4" d, brown sponging, clear lead glaze, top and bottom thumbnail grooves, imp "John Bell" 550.00

Pie Plate, coggle edge

9-3/4" d, three line yellow slip dec 220.00
10" d, three line yellow slip dec, very worn, chips and scratches 100.00
12-1/4" d, yellow slip dec, wear and old chips 315.00

Pitcher

5" h, pinched spout, white slip, mottled brown glaze
. . . . 95.00
7-1/2" h, red and white overall slip, brown spattered dec, clear lead glaze, bold handle 325.00

Plate

8-1/2" d, zigzag and parallel line yellow slip dec, reddish brown glaze, chips 225.00
10-1/4" d, yellow slip dec, parallel zigzag lines and commas, reddish brown glaze, rim chip and roughage 325.00
11-1/4" d, glazed face, unglazed back, applied yellow slip dec reads "Lafayette," yellow slip squiggles above and below name, coggle edge, professional restoration to 6" l rim hairline 2,750.00

Pot, cov

6" h, 5-1/2" w with handle, four bands of yellow slip, bulbous body, applied handle, attributed to CT 400.00
6" h, 7-1/2" w with handle, splotched dec, four vertical swipes, pouring spout, small finial on matching lid, applied handle with thumb print, two chips on lid 450.00

Shaving Mug, 5-3/4" h, brown-green mottled glaze, strap handle
. . . . 290.00

Stirrup Cup, 4-1/2" h, hound form, glazed, English, late 18th C
. . . . 300.00

Turk's Head Mold, 9" d, amber and green, dark brown ext. sponging, swirled flutes, scalloped rim 175.00

Vase, 3 5/8" h, sgraffito, birds and flowers, tricolor, bulbous base, marked "DDR, June 5, 1828, PA" 1,750.00

RED WING POTTERY

History: The Red Wing pottery category includes several potteries from Red Wing, Minnesota. In 1868 David Hallem started Red Wing Stoneware Co., the first pottery with stoneware as its primary product. The Minnesota Stoneware Co. started in 1883. The North Star Stoneware Co. was in business from 1892 to 1896.

The Red Wing Stoneware Co. and the Minnesota Stoneware Co. merged in 1892. The new company, the Red Wing Union Stoneware Co., made stoneware until 1920 when it introduced a pottery line which it continued until the 1940s. In 1936, the name was changed to Red Wing Potteries, Inc. During the 1930s, this firm introduced several popular patterns of hand-painted dinnerware which were distributed through department stores, mail-order catalogs, and gift-stamp centers. Dinnerware production declined in the 1950s and was replaced with hotel and restaurant china in the early 1960s. The plant closed in 1967.

Marks: Red Wing Stoneware Co. was the first firm to mark pieces with a red wing stamped under the glaze. The North Star Stoneware Co. used a raised star and the words "Red Wing" as its mark.

References: Susan and Al Bagdade, *Warman's American Pottery and Porcelain*, Wallace-Homestead, 1994; Dan and Gail DePasquale and Larry Peterson, *Red Wing Collectibles*, Collector Books, 1985, 1997 value update; —, *Red Wing Stoneware*, Collector Books, 1983, 1997 value update; B. L. Dollen, *Red Wing Art Pottery*, Collector Books, 1997; Ray Reiss, *Red Wing Art Pottery Including Pottery Made for Rum Rill*, published by author (2144 N. Leavitt, Chicago, IL 60647), 1996.

Collectors' Clubs: Red Wing Collectors Society, Inc., P.O. Box 184, Galesburg, IL 61402; RumRill Society, P.O. Box 2161, Hudson, OH 44236.

Additional Listings: See *Warman's Americana & Collectibles* for more examples.

Ashtray, Minnesota Twins 1965 World Series, red 88.00
Bank, Hamm's Beer, figural bear, chips and cracks 110.00
Bookends, pr, polar bears, jet black glaze, Rumrill 525.00
Bud Vase, 8-1/2" h, cactus, pale blue-green 345.00
Candleholders, pr, 1-1/2" h, fluted, green 35.00
Child's Feeding Dish, figural, clown, orange-pink glaze, Hankscraft 35.00
Console Bowl, 13" l, mottled green, trumpet flowers dec
. . . . 290.00

Vase, tapered cylinder, straight neck, relief floral design, red matte glaze, stamped "Red Wing/Union/Stoneware/Co./Red Wing/Minn," 8-1/4" h, $75.

Cooler, stoneware, two gallon, litho with boy at well.... 500.00
Cookie Jar, cov
   Dancing Peasants, white stoneware 45.00
   Katrina, tan and brown...................... 80.00
Crock, 10 gallon, ball handles, hairline crack 35.00
Figure, elephant
   Nokomis finish, mottled matte surface of brown, tan, teal,
    bronze, and rust.......................... 800.00
   Pale Yellow, 4" h, #236A 430.00
Lamp Base, Nokomis finish, mottled matte surface of brown,
   teal, bronze, and rust 715.00
Pitcher and Bowl, 7-3/8" h pitcher, 11-3/8" d bowl, early . 95.00
Planter
   Duck, #439............................... 385.00
   Giraffe, Murphy, repairs, tight hairline 330.00
   Muses reclining, bronze finish, Deluxe line, small chip 55.00
   Seal, #941 .... 90.00
   Swan, #440, mustard yellow, Rumrill 60.00
Plaque, Minnesota Centennial, maroon, 1958 .... 100.00
Souvenir Jug, 1992 Red Wing Collectors Society....... 55.00
Urn
   #252, 11" h, pale yellow glaze, blue circle stamp mark
   .... 290.00
   #852, large 80.00
Vase
   4" h, green, elongated tulip shape 95.00
   7" h, Nokomis finish, mottled matte surface of brown, tan,
    teal, bronze, and rust..................... 300.00
   7" h, #175, yellow........................... 75.00
   8" h, #1103 .... 25.00
   8" h, #1357 .... 25.00
   8" h, Tropicana series, Bird of Paradise, mkd "B-2000," de-
    signed by Belle Kogan, 1950................. 65.00
   10" h, 6-1/4" d, light drab green, mkd "Redwing USA
    M-1461," factory flaw..................... 65.00
   11" h, Art Deco............................ 100.00
   15" h, #157, green and white, drilled for lamp base.. 235.00
Two handles, trumpeting elephants, pale yellow 135.00

RELIGIOUS ITEMS

History: Objects used in worship or as expression of man's belief in a superhuman power are collected by many people for many reasons.

This category includes icons since they are religious mementos, usually paintings with a brass encasement. Collecting icons dates from the earliest period of Christianity. Most antique icons in today's market were made in the late 19th century.

Reference: Penny Forstner and Lael Bower, *Collecting Religious Artifacts (Christian and Judaic)*, Books Americana, 1995.

Collectors' Club: Foundation International for Restorers of Religious Medals, P.O. Box 2652, Worcester, MA 01608.

Museum: American Bible Society, New York, NY.

REPRODUCTION ALERT

Icons are frequently reproduced.

Additional Listings: Russian Items.

Alms Box, 10-3/4" w, 16" h, oak, old brown grained repaint, Gothic style, English, wear and one incomplete scalloped bracket 145.00
Altar Cabinet, 18" w, 14" d, 23" h, giltwood, carved columns, masks, foliage, and architectural niches, Italian Renaissance, attributed to Sansovino, late 15th/early 16th C, losses, restorations. 3,105.00
Autograph
   Autographed letter signed, Peter Boehler, Nov. 27, 1763, Bethlehem, (Pennsylvania) to inner conference of the Moravian Brotherhood, in German, relating Bishop's trip to Philadelphia and the hostile attitude there against missionaries and treatment of Indian delegation, mentions well known colonial figures, such as Franklin, Logan, Daniel, 3-1/2 closely written pages, with translation 1,495.00
   Deed of Conveyance, partially printed, granting Brigham Young 99 square feet of land in Salt Lake City for $1.55, sgd by Daniel H. Wells, Mayor, January 10, 1873, 1 page, folio, affixed gold seats of Salt Lake City, notary James Pack 375.00
   Document Signed, Pope Pius IV, sgd "El Cardinal di Medici," Nov. 23 1555, appointment to Church in Cassano, action approved by Duke of Florence and King of England, 1 full page, tall 4to 920.00
Buddha
   5-1/2" h, gilt bronze, seated on double lotus throne, fired gilded with applied cold gold paste to face, blue pigment to hair and unisha, offering plate cover with double vajra, Tibetan, 17th/18th C 1,035.00
   16-1/2" h, bronze, seated, hands in teaching position, seated on pierced double lotus throne, detachable halo at back, Nepal, late 19th/early 20th C 300.00
Bust, 11-1/2" h, Our lady of Lourdes, carved alabaster, amethyst veining, oval plinth, reverse sgd "Causse" for Julian Causse 865.00
Chalice
   9-1/4" h, gold-washed copper, Ecclesiastical, bell-shaped bowl embellished with cut card work featuring bull rushes, grapes, and wheat, emb baluster stem, domed foot emb and inset with images of Mary 460.00
   9-1/4" h, sterling silver and gold-washed base metal, Ecclesiastical, silver bowl with gold-washed lip and int., stem with central gothic-style knop, plain hexafoil foot with emb cross 140.00
   9-1/2" h, silver, Ecclesiastical, slightly flared bowl engraved to one side with stylized sunburst and "IHS," knopped stem with central applied foliate band, spreading repousse foot with foliate edge, gold washed int., former gold wash to ext. removed, 20 troy oz 1,150.00
   9-7/8" h, silver, Ecclesiastical, slightly flared bowl with gold-washed int., stem with egg-shaped knob flanked by compressed knops, gold-washed ribbing, spreading foot with ribbed band and engraved flat leaves and flowers, French, first quarter 19th C, 14 troy oz 460.00
   9-7/8" h, silver-gilt, bell-shaped bowl embellished with gothic-style cut card work, stem with central hexafoil knob, hexafoil base, stamped gothic-style detailing, three painted porcelain plaques depicting religious vignettes, maker's mark Chevron Freres, French, late 19th C 1,495.00
   10" h, silver, Ecclesiastical, plain bell-shaped bowl, int. gold-washed, stem with central egg-shaped knop between flared knobs with bands of guillouche, domed foot stamped with cartouches of grapes, bull ruses, and wheat between roundels depicting biblical images, French, marker's mark H. Puchs, late 19th/early 20th C, 9 troy oz 475.00

Chasuble, velvet, crimson, orphrey embroidered colored silks, metal thread, roundels of Madonna and Child, four Saints within strapwork, Spanish, 16th C 2,750.00

Crucifix, 8-1/4" l, carved ivory, mounted on 21-1/4" l wooden cross, engraved ivory plaque, stepped plinth, southern Germany, 18th C 2,070.00

Ecclesiastical Scepter, 29-1/2" l, carved ivory, hexagonal faceted knob mounted with figural plaques, stem carved with fruiting leafy foliage, Continental, losses 4,025.00

Figure

8-1/2" h, carved ivory, crucifix, finely carved, sculpted hair and lion cloth, Italian, 18th C, mounted in 15-1/2" x 10-1/2" giltwood frame 2,070.00

30" h, painted wood, Madonna & Child, c1700, Baroque, South German, benign expression, hair falling in long tresses over her shoulders, wearing long gown, heavy mantle falling into deep folds, infant Christ delivers blessing and supports gilt orb, both with gilt-metal crowns, ornate plinth base with acanthus leaves and winged cherubs, some worming and cracks, most of polychrome intact, overall patina and craquelure, flat back. 5,100.00

33-1/2" h, St. Peter, high relief carving, tiara on head, stylized hair connecting to stylized hobnail-type beard, left hand holds key, right holds gospels, cape deeply carved folds, painted wood, Continental, 19th C, later paint, flat back 920.00

42-1/2" h, Lindenwood, Ecco Homo, finely carved, high relief, curly cascading hair, fine facial and anatomical features, circle of "Der Rasso-Meister," South German, 16th C, hallowed back, some losses, worming, cracks, and restored nose 4,035.00

64" h, female saint, finely carved, delicately sculpted hair, elaborately draped brocade mantle and tunic, orig "estafado" paint-work, Italian, early 18th C, minor restoration, some worming, orig gilt plinth 650.00

Icon, Christ Enthroned, Russian, 17th C, 35" x 45", $14,950. Photo courtesy of Jackson's Auctioneers & Appraisers.

Incense Burner

9-1/2" h, bronze, archaic-style tripod, Tao Tich masks and frieze of mythical animal on cloud background, animal form handles, dark chocolate brown patina, sgd, Chinese, 18th/19th C 250.00

9-1/2" h, 10" w, bronze, tripod shaped with handles, tall highly elongated feet and understated handles, surface finely inlaid with gold and silver emblems, mons, thunder meander ground, Japanese, 19th C 1,500.00

Icon, Greek, 11-1/2" x 8", Hodigitra Mother of God, 19th C, angels crown Mary as Christ delivers blessing, custom fitted shadow box kit, mother of pearl inlays and double headed eagle at top. 1,555.00

Icon, Russian

10-1/2" x 12-1/4", The Lord Almighty, 19th C, finely executed, Vsederzhitel, Christ delivers blessing with right hand, left hand holds open Gospels to Matthew, entire image overlaid with finely fashioned gilt-metal repousse riza, attached halo, embellished with faux gemstones, executed in 16th C style 1,450.00

10-1/2" x 12-1/2", Christ Immanuel, 17th C, finely detailed on ochre ground, ivory highlights, overlaid with applied gilt-metal halo embellished with faux gemstones and gilt metal open riza 3,335.00

10-1/2" x 12-1/2", The Dormination of the Mother of God, 17th C, Christ stands behind recumbent Mary, receives her soul in the form of an infant, Apostles stand around her, fanatical Jewish priest tires to bush the bier over, hand cut off by sword-welding angel, borders and background with traces of orig gilding, double kovcheg, some early restoration 2,300.00

12" x 10-1/4", St. Paraskeva Paitnista, 18th C, finely executed painting done on gold leaf ground, two angels place a crown upon her head, right hand delivers blessing, left hand supports scroll which begins "I believe in One God the Father, The Almighty Maker of Heaven and Earth…," borders with Guardian Angel left and St. Paul the Confessor Archbishop of Constantinope on right, image overlaid with well crafted gilt repousse metal riza 1,840.00

Monstrance, 19-1/4" h, gilt-brass, Gothic-style, spires with central glass holder for host, small angel-form handle, stem with flattened knob, hexagonal foot, fitted case 690.00

Painting

16-1/2" x 10-1/2", gouache and watercolor on paper, Portrait of a Cleric, sgd "Spy" in pencil lower left, identified on presentation plaque, titled and identified on label on reverse, painted by Sir Leslie Ward, framed 300.00

37-1/2 x 27-1/2", oil on canvas, "St. Jerome Reading Before A Crucifix," unsigned, Italian School, 17th C, lined, retouched, flaking and losses, craquelure. 2,100.00

41" x 68", Congregation Watching the Baptism at the River, Henry Sanderson, oil on canvas, framed, background retouched 8,625.00

Panel, 20" h, 14-1/2" w, carved walnut, Madonna and Child, traces of polychrome dec, Italian, 17th C 1,150.00

Pendant

18k gold, ivory carved Madonna, diamond accented hallow, pink plique-a-jour background, turquoise and seed pearl frame, pearl and diamond accents. 980.00

18k gold, Maltese cross, c1900, designed as pin/pendant, reeded and beaded accents, sgd "T. B. Starr". 550.00

Plaque, 9-1/4" x 7-1/2", Christ with crown of thorns, imp KPM marks, framed 1,265.00

Prei-dieu (kneeling bench), 23-1/4" w, 20-1/2" d, 34-1/2" h, walnut, Italian Renaissance, restorations 1,610.00

Reliquary, 20-1/2" h, Gothic Revival, silver and gilt metal, upper section in two parts, spires and figures within niches, int. lined with amber glass, faceted and shaped stem on arched foot, 19th C. 5,175.00

Reliquary Cross, 9-1/2" x 6-1/2" panel, 2-1/2" x 2-1/4" cross, Russian, 18th C, silver, hollow construction, front engraved with crucifixion, end of each cross bar with hand made silver screws to fasten the lid, final screws pierced for suspension, 2 pc wood cross inside, 6 to 8 relics on front suspended in resin or wax, mounted in wood panel with receptacle for cross, later silvered metal riza with opening for cross to show through, reverse inscribed with names of Saint's relics contained within cross, and other indistinguishable names 1,265.00

Santos, 11-3/4" h, carved and painted wood, robed figured, stepped base, Continental, 19th/20th C 425.00

Stele, 19-1/2" w, 31-3/4" h, carved gray limestone, Buddhist Trinity, Northern Wei style, central standing robed Buddha, two standing bodhisattvas on either side, lotus plinths being held up by animal heads, low relief carved floral motifs on flat ground, reverse with rows of Buddhas, inscriptions, wood stand, repairs 1,100.00

REVERSE PAINTING on GLASS

History: The earliest examples of reverse painting on glass were produced in 13th-century Italy. By the 17th century the technique had spread to central and eastern Europe. It spread Westward as the center of the glassmaking industry moved to Germany in the late 17th century.

The Alsace and Black Forest regions developed a unique portraiture style. The half and three-quarter portraits often were titled below the portrait. Women tend to have generic names while most males are likenesses of famous men.

The English used a mezzotint, rather than free-style, method to create their reverse paintings. Landscapes and allegorical figures were popular. The Chinese began working in the medium in the 17th century, eventually favoring marine and patriotic scenes.

Most American reverse painting was done by folk artists and is unsigned. Portraits, patriotic and mourning scenes, floral compositions, landscapes, and buildings are the favorite subjects. Known American artists include Benjamin Greenleaf, A. Cranfield, and Rowley Jacobs.

In the late 19th century commercially produced reverse paintings, often decorated with mother-of-pearl, became popular. Themes included the Statue of Liberty, the capitol in Washington, D.C., and various world's fairs and expositions.

Reference: Shirley Mace, *Encyclopedia of Silhouette Collectibles on Glass*, Shadow Enterprises, 1992.

Portraits

Emilie, balloon sleeve dress, large collar, 9-1/2" x 12" . . 500.00

Josephina, red, green, white dress, red hair ribbon, green background, 11-1/2"h, 9-1/4" w, wear and white margin retouched, orig frame 220.00

Mallanderin, woman with flowers in her hair, replaced frame, 9-1/2" x 11-1/2". 140.00

Sylvia, woman in red dress, blue ground, orig frame, 7-3/4" x 10-1/2" 120.00

Washington, George, oval portrait, white border, sky blue background, mahogany veneer frame, 12-1/4" h, 10-1/4" w, paint flaking. 220.00

Sign, Drugs and Soda, trapezoidal, crinkle background, orig copper frame, 29" x 10-1/2", $725. Photo courtesy of James D. Julia, Inc.

Oriental women, colorful costumes, 19-3/4" h, 13-5/8" w, price for facing pr 150.00

Scenes

Adoration of the Magi, later carved giltwood frame, Italian, 27" x 18-1/2" 425.00

Blarney Castle, forest scene, castle on right, touches of mica and abalone, 20" x 27". 150.00

Landscape, pink, gray, white, green, and brown, Chinese Export School, 10" x 8" 175.00

Man and woman in landscape, Chinese Export School, late 18th or early 19th C, 15-1/4" x 11-1/2". 2,750.00

Rock of Ages, gold, white, red, blue, and green, black ground, tinsel highlights, orig oak frame, 20-3/4" h, 17-3/4" w 115.00

Summer-Winter, winter landscape with woman in velvet coat, summer landscape with young woman in straw bonnet carrying sickle, sprays of wheat, Chinese Export School, 19th C, 10" x 14-1/2", price for facing pr. 900.00

Titanic, sinking with life rafts in water, 15-1/2" h, 19-1/2" w, silver dec frame, some paint loss 75.00

RIDGWAY

History: Throughout the 19th century, the Ridgway family, through a series of partnerships, held a position of importance in the ceramics industry in Shelton and Hanley, Staffordshire, England. The connection began with Job and George, two brothers, and Job's two sons, John and William. In 1830 John and William dissolved their partnership; John retained the Cauldon Place factory and William the Bell Works. By 1862 the porcelain division of Cauldon was carried on by Coalport China Ltd. William and his heirs continued at the Bell Works and the Church (Hanley) and Bedford (Shelton) works until the end of the 19th century.

Cheese Dish, cov, light brown, floral transfer, 8-1/2" x 10", $65.

Marks: Many early pieces are unmarked. Later marks include the initials of the many different partnerships.

References: Susan and Al Bagdade, *Warman's English & Continental Pottery & Porcelain*, 3rd Edition, Krause Publications, 1998; G. A. Godden, *Ridgway Porcelains*, Antique Collectors' Club, 1985.

Museums: Cincinnati Art Museum, Cincinnati, OH; Potsdam Public Museum, Potsdam, NY.

Additional Listings: Staffordshire, Historical; Staffordshire, Romantic.

Beverage Set, 12-3/8" x 6-1/2" tankard, pitcher, six 4-1/4" x 5" mugs, Coaching Days, caramel ground, black scene, silver luster top bands and handles, price for 7 pc set. 400.00
Bowl
   6" d, Shakespeare 30.00
   8-1/2" w to handles, Coaching Days 35.00
Cheese Dish, cov, light brown floral transfer. 75.00
Child's Teapot and Creamer, Dickensware, Humphrey's Clock, blue and white, c1891-1903 . . . . 165.00
Coffeepot, cov, 7-1/2" h, Coaching Days, silver luster . . . 95.00
Cup Plate, Marmora 45.00
Mug
   4" h, Shakespeare 35.00
   4-3/4" h, Coaching Days, silver luster 30.00
Pitcher, 10-1/2" h, earthenware, blue glaze, molded and enameled foliate dec, pewter lid, base sgd "William Ridgway & Co., Hanley, October 1, 1835," minor chip to handle. 115.00
Plate, 9" d, Coaching Days 25.00
Tankard Pitcher, 12" h, Coaching Days, In A Snowdrift . 300.00
Tea Caddy, cov, 4" x 5-3/4" h, Coaching Days, scenes on all sides 175.00
Tile, 6" d, round, Coaching Days 115.00
Tray, 8-1/4" d, Bank of Savannah, handles 185.00
Vase, 4-7/8" h, egg shape, Coaching Days, caramel ground, black scenes, silver luster top band and handle. 75.00
Vegetable Bowl, cov, 12" w, 6-1/4" h, flow blue, oval, A Deak pattern 210.00

RING TREES

History: A ring tree is a small, generally saucer-shaped object made of glass, porcelain, metal, or wood with a center post in the shape of a hand, branches, or cylinder.

Sterling Silver, saucer base, repousse, three wire ring holders, mkd "RW & S," 3" d base, 2" h, $145.

It is a convenient object for holding finger rings.

Baccarat, 3" h, Swirl pattern, vaseline. 55.00
Bronze, 5" h, figural, parrot 48.00
Fenton, 4-1/2" h, yellow, figural owl 15.00
Hand Painted China, center hand, saucer base, rose dec, maple leaf mark and "Hand Painted" 55.00
Jasperware, 3-1/4" h, deep blue ground, white relief classical bust medallions 50.00
Limoges, hp pink flowers, scalloped edge, mkd "T & V" . . 45.00
Nippon, purple violets dec, gold band, shallow base, maple leaf mark 65.00
Silver, Sheffield, maker's mark, chased base, fluted rim, Victorian, c1900, 2 troy oz 115.00

ROCKINGHAM and ROCKINGHAM BROWN-GLAZED WARES

History: Rockingham ware can be divided into two categories. The first consists of the fine china and porcelain pieces made between 1826 and 1842 by the Rockingham Company of Swinton, Yorkshire, England, and its predecessor firms: Swinton, Bingley, Don, Leeds, and Brameld. The Bramelds developed the cadogan, a lidless teapot. Between 1826 and 1842, a quality soft-paste product with a warm, silky feel was developed by the Bramelds. Elaborate specialty pieces were made. By 1830, the company employed 600 workers and listed 400 designs for dessert sets and 1,000 designs for tea and coffee services in their catalog. Unable to meet its payroll, the company closed in 1842.

The second category of Rockingham ware includes pieces produced in the famous Rockingham brown glaze that became an intense and vivid purple-brown when fired. It had a dark, tortoiseshell appearance. The glaze was copied by many English and American potteries. American manufacturers which used Rockingham glaze include D. & J. Henderson of Jersey City, New Jersey; United States Pottery in Bennington, Vermont; potteries in East Liverpool, Ohio; and several potteries in Indiana and Illinois.

References: Susan and Al Bagdade, *Warman's American Pottery and Porcelain*, Wallace-Homestead, 1994; Susan and Al Bagdade, *Warman's English & Continental Pottery & Porcelain*, 3rd Edition, Krause Publications, 1998; Mary Brewer, *Collector's Guide to Rockingham*, Collector Books, 1996.

Museum: Bennington Museum, Bennington, VT.

Additional Listings: Bennington and Bennington-Type Pottery.

Bowl, 14" d, 6-1/2" h, emb ext. 75.00
Cup and Saucer, enamel painted tulip and poppy dec, white ground, barbed rim, 1826-30 . . . . 550.00
Figure
    6-5/8" h, 9-1/2" l, lion, rect base, good detail and glaze, price for pr. 525.00
    12-5/8" h, 16" l, bull, flint enamel glaze, 19th C, minor losses, restoration 300.00
    18-1/2" h, 36-1/2" w, bulldog, overall brown glaze, finely modeled, glass eyes, late 19th C, restoration to tail . . .2,180.00
Flask, 7-1/4" h, molded hunting dogs, hairline in bottom 330.00
Food Mold, 8-1/2" d, Turk's head, brown glaze, green flint enamel. 85.00
Goblet, 5-3/8" h. 525.00
Inkwell, 4-3/4" l, lion 185.00
Mixing Bowl, 16-1/2" d, 6-5/8" h, 1849 mark. 2,500.00
Pitcher
    7-1/4" h, detailed emb scenes of camel and elephant, imp mark "R Bew, Bliston" 75.00
    7-3/4" h, Paneled Grapevine pattern, brown glaze .1,100.00
Plate, 9-1/4" d, Woodnook, Wentworth Park, Yorkshire, man holding game bird, river and wooded scene, scrolling vine and scattered insects band, 1926-32 . . . . 520.00
Scent Bottle, 6" h, onion shape, applied garden flowers, gilt line rims, 1831-40 . . . . 450.00
Teapot, 8-1/4" h, emb design, portrait of lady 75.00
Tobacco Jar, 8" h, molded oval floral medallions, dark brown glaze, small rim chip. 80.00

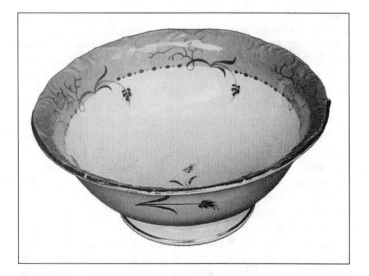

Bowl, mocha and gold dec, 7-3/8" d, 3-1/4" h, $70.

Toby Snuff Jar, 4-1/8" h, flint enamel glaze, 19th C, minor glaze wear to rim 375.00
Wall Pocket, toby shape, brown glaze 375.00

ROCK 'N' ROLL

History: Rock music can be traced back to early rhythm and blues. It progressed until it reached its golden age in the 1950s and 1960s. Most of the memorabilia issued during that period focused on individual singers and groups. The largest quantity of collectible material is connected to Elvis Presley and The Beatles.

In the 1980s two areas—clothing and guitars—associated with key Rock 'n' Roll personalities received special collector attention. Sotheby's and Christie's East regularly feature Rock 'n' Roll memorabilia as part of their collectibles sales. At the moment, the market is highly speculative and driven by nostalgia.

It is important to identify memorabilia issued during the lifetime of an artist or performing group as opposed to material issued after they died or disbanded. Objects of the latter type are identified as "fantasy" items and will never achieve the same degree of collectibility as period counterparts.

References: Jeff Augsburger, Marty Eck, and Rich Rann, *Beatles Memorabilia Price Guide*, 2nd ed., Wallace-Homestead, 1993; Karen and John Lesniewski, *Kiss Collectibles*, Avon Books, 1993; Stephen Maycock, *Miller's Rock & Pop Memorabilia*, Millers Publications, 1994; Greg Moore, *Price Guide to Rock & Roll Collectibles*, published by author, 1993; Michael Stern, Barbara Crawford, and Hollis Lamon, *The Beatles*, Collector Books, 1994; Neal Umphred, *Goldmine's Price Guide to Collectible Record Albums*, 4th ed., Krause Publications, 1994; ——, *Goldmine's Rock 'n' Roll 45 RPM Record Price Guide*, 3rd ed., Krause Publications, 1994.

Periodicals: Beatlefan, P.O. Box 33515, Decatur, GA 30033; *Good Day Sunshine*, 397 Edgewood Ave., New Haven, CT 06511; *Instant Karma*, P.O. Box 256, Sault Ste. Marie, MI 49783.

Collectors' Clubs: Beatles Connection, P.O. Box 1066, Pinellas Park, FL 34665; Beatles Fan Club of Great Britain, Superstore Productions, 123 Marina St., Leonards on Sea, East Sussex, England TN 38 OBN; Elvis Forever TCB Fan Club, P.O. Box 1066, Pinellas Park, FL 34665; Graceland News Fan Club, P.O. Box 452, Rutherford, NJ 07070; Working Class Hero Club, 3311 Niagara St., Pittsburgh, PA 15213.

Additional Listings: See The Beatles, Elvis Presley, and Rock 'n' Roll in *Warman's Americana & Collectibles*.

Anklet, Elvis Presley, dog tag, orig pink photo card, 1956 50.00
Autograph
    Paula Abdul, Head Over Heels Display, matted LP and signature card 50.00
    Elton John, matted *Billboard Magazine* advertisement
    . . . . 30.00
    Monkees, Monkees Greatest Hits LP cover, sgd by Mickey, Davy, Peter 85.00
    Rod Stewart, Blondes Have More Fun, picture disc
    . . . . 75.00
    U-2, matted 12" x 16" display, live Bono photo 65.00
    Zappa, Frank, Mother's of Invention One Size Fits All, LP
    . . . . 325.00
Backstage Pass, cloth
    Aerosmith, Pump, stage hand, 1989 . . . . 10.00
    Billy Idyl, photo pass, large. 15.00
    Black Sabbath, 1974 Civic Arena. 75.00
    Fleetwood Mac, Behind The Mask, dressing room . . . 25.00
    Gloria Estefan, Into the Light 15.00
    Kiss, Kiss Alive, 1983. . . . . 20.00
    Madonna, Like A Virgin, 1985 . . . . 25.00
Backstage Pass, laminated
    Metallica, Snakepit. 15.00
    Pink Floyd, film crew, 1986 . . . . 25.00
Banner, Beatles, printed nylon, four Beatles in black, large blue print heading "The Beatles," Memphis, 1966 . . . . . . 1,150.00
Bubble Gum Cards, Elvis Presley/Bubbles, Inc., set of 66 color cards, plastic protectors, 1956 . . . . 1,000.00
Concert Clothing
    James Brown, stage vest, black leather, gold round buttons, lined in white felt, front left wide cut white leather initials "JB," white leather letters "Mr. D" on other side
    . . . . 1,840.00
    Madonna, stage shorts, low waisted, high-cut purple shorts, ribbed stretch knit, legs lined in black satin, completely decorated with purple sequins, 1992 Girlie Tour 1,725.00
Concert Pin, Elvis Presley, 1978, 25" silver chain 35.00

Drawing, Psychedelic, Jimi Hendrix, 1969, $6,875.

Concert Poster
    Bill Graham Series, marked "Six Days of Sound - Dec 26-New York's Eve 1967," design by Bonnie MacLean, includes The Doors, Chuck Berry, Big Brother & the Holding Co, Winterland 125.00
    Grateful Dead, Skull in Sand, 1981 European Fall tour, design by Stanley Mouse, 22-1/2" x 27" 85.00
    Hells Angels Party, featuring Big Brother, God, Main Squeeze & Janis Joplin, May 21, 1970, design by Don Moses, toned, minor damage 345.00
    Led Zeppelin, July 23-24, 1977, Oakland Stadium, design by Randy Tuten & William Bostedt 175.00
    The Supremes, Trude Heller and G. Keys present - The Supremes - Lincoln Center, Philharmonic Hall, Friday, Oct 15, 1965, design by Eula, 25" x 38" 500.00
Concert Program
    Aerosmith, Nine Lives Tour 10.00
    Jim Hendrix, New York Pop Festival, 1970 . . . . 700.00
Crew Shirt
    Grateful Dead, white, "Grateful Dead - Crew 1994," drawing of cargo plane over pocket area 30.00
    Metallica, black, "Staff 85/86," drawing of wild Father Time and metal babies 30.00
Display, Beatles, Wings, Back to the Egg, promotion, 3-D 25.00
Fun Kit, Beatles, orig 1964 oversized magazine, featuring Hard Day's Night. 30.00
Guitar Pick, custom
    Guns N Roses, Slash 25.00
    Ozzy Osbourne, Zac Wilk. 25.00
    Rolling Stones, Richards/Blamehound. 30.00
    ZZ Top, Dusty Hill. 25.00
Jacket, Rolling Stones, Varsity Tour, red wool body, black leather sleeve, chenille Stones logo on back, breast, and sleeves
    . . . . 225.00
Lobby Card
    Elvis Presley, Blue Hawaii, 1961, 11" x 14", full color
    . . . . 40.00
    Led Zeppelin, John Paul Jones playing bass. 12.00
Lyrics
    Alice Cooper, handwritten for song "Trash," composed in studio, 1989, three verses in black ink, corrections in blue ball point pen, two additional verses in blue ball point pen, written on yellow legal size paper 300.00
    Paul McCartney, handwritten for song "When I'm 64," 1967 Sgt. Pepper album, lyrics and revisions 40,250.00
Magazine, *Sixteen*, 1966, Beatles cover and article 15.00
Make Up Kit, Kiss, sealed in package, showing group in make-up 10.00
Medallion, Beatles, Sgt. Peppers, US promo 30th anniversary
    . . . . 50.00
Mousepad, Kiss, showing group in make-up 10.00
Newspaper, *Memphis Press*, Aug.17, 1977, announcing death of Elvis Presley. 35.00
Patch
    Bon Jovi 10.00
    David Lee Roth, Charlotte, 1986 . . . . 15.00
Pen, Elvis Presley, Tickle Me Feather, mkd "Elvis Presley In Tickle Me It's Your Summer/Block Buster For Release June 30th Allied artists," 1965 . . . . 50.00
Perfume Bottle, Elvis Presley, Teddy Bear, 1965 photo of Elvis on label, gold top, orig contents 100.00
Pinback Button
    7/8" d, Elvis Presley, Hound Dog, 1956 . . . . 40.00
    1" d, Fabian Fan Club, blue on white, litho, late 1950s
    . . . . 15.00

3-1/2" d, Monkeys, black and white photo, red and white logo, 1966 . . . . 25.00

4" d, Jackson Five, black and white photo, bright red ground, copyright 1971, Motown Record Corp. 40.00

Poster

Alice Cooper, black and white, heavy stock, Alice in full make-up, Daisy in his mouth, Warner Bros. 175.00

Guns N Roses, Appetite for Destruction, 1987 . . . . 8.00

Pink Floyd, Roger Waters, Pros & Cons, 36" x 35" . . . 25.00

Promo Tape, Doors, Live At The Hollywood Bowl, advance VHS tape, sealed in MAC Video box 15.00

Road Sign, Led Zeppelin, Walking into Clarkesdale, green and white, 12" x 16". 35.00

Sweatshirt, Rolling Stones, white, "Rockware by Brockum," four different Stones logos. 40.00

Ticket Stub, Bob Dylan, Tom Petty, Greek Theater, Berkeley, CA, 6/13/86 . . . . 12.00

Tour Book

Michael Jackson, *History World*, oversized 12.00

Elton John, *The Big Picture* 10.00

Rolling Stones, *Voodoo Lounge World Tour*, Japanese edition. 12.00

T-shirt

Aerosmith, Get A Grip, XXL 15.00

Guns N Roses, tie dye 25.00

Rolling Stones, Babylonian Tongue, tan 20.00

Van Halen, Right Now 15.00

ROCKWELL, NORMAN

History: Norman Rockwell (Feb. 3, 1894-November 1978) was a famous American artist and illustrator. During the time he painted, from age 18 until his death, he created over 2,000 works.

His first professional efforts were illustrations for a children's book; his next projects were done for *Boy's Life*, the Boy Scout magazine. His most famous works are those that appeared as cover illustrations on the *Saturday Evening Post.*

Norman Rockwell painted everyday people in everyday situations, mixing a little humor with sentiment. His paintings and illustrations are treasured because of this sensitive approach. Rockwell painted people he knew and places with which he was familiar. New England landscapes are found in many of his illustrations.

References: Denis C. Jackson, *Norman Rockwell Identification and Value Guide to: Magazines, Posters, Calendars, Books*, 2nd ed., published by author, 1985; Karal Ann Marling, *Norman Rockwell*, Harry N. Abrams, 1997; Mary Moline, *Norman Rockwell Collectibles*, 6th ed., Green Valley World, 1988.

Collectors' Club: Rockwell Society of America, 597 Saw Mill River Rd., Ardsley, NY 10502.

REPRODUCTION ALERT

Because of the popularity of his works, the images have been reproduced on many objects. These new collectibles, which should not be confused with original artwork and illustrations, provide a wide range of collectibles and prices.

Museums: Museum of Norman Rockwell Art, Reedsburg, WI; Norman Rockwell Museum, Northbrook, IL; Norman Rockwell Museum, Philadelphia, PA; Norman Rockwell Museum, Stockbridge, MA.

Additional Listings: See *Warman's Americana & Collectibles* for more examples.

Historic

Blotter, Fisk Tires, 1924 . . . . 25.00

Book, *Huckleberry Finn*, 1940 edition, no dust jacket. . . . 20.00

Calendar, 1951, Four Seasons 38.00

Orig artwork, advertising, illus for Piso's Cough Remedy, full color 187,000.00

Oil on Canvas

The Choirboy, 29" x 26-1/2" 717,500.00

The Lure of the Sea, 27" x 24", for cover of Oct. 20, 1934, *Saturday Evening Post*, boy perched atop weathervane 396,000.00

Tired Salesgirl on Christmas Eve, 30-1/2" x 28-1/4" 607,500.00

Sheet Music, "*I'm Sorry I Made You Cry*" 7.50

Tray

Coca-Cola, Tom Sawyer, 1931 . . . . 290.00

Who's Having More Fruit? Green Giants Niblets Corn, 1940 . . . . 70.00

Modern

Bell

Butter Girl, Royal Devon, 1976. . . . . 42.00

Tavern Sign Painter, Gorham Fine China, 1976 . . . . . 60.00

Bowl, 8-1/2" d, Yankee Doodle, Gorham Fine China, 1975 . . . . 160.00

Coin, Four Seasons, Hamilton Mint, 4 pc set 110.00

Figure

Caught in the Act, Danbury Mint, 1980 . . . . 60.00

First Prom, Rockwell Museum, 1980 . . . . 85.00

His First Smoke, Goebel Hummelwerk 400.00

Ignot, sterling silver

At The Barber, Franklin Mint, 1973, 10 pc set 375.00

Four Freedoms, Hamilton Mint, 1974, 8 pc set 260.00

Plate

Bedtime, Mother's Day Series, Rockwell Society of America, 1978. . . . . 50.00

Magazine Cover, *Saturday Evening Post*, September 1958, Checkup, 11" x 14", $40.

Flying High, Gorham Fine China, 1982 . . . . 60.00
Toymaker, Rockwell Society, 1977 . . . . 190.00
Print
    Children At The Window, Circle Fine Arts, title edition, sgd
      and numbered 1,750.00
    Football Hero, Ettinger Ltd., sgd and numbered, 1978
       . . . . .2,200.00
Thimble, Tiny Tim, Gorham, 1980. . . . . 25.00

ROGERS & SIMILAR STATUARY

History: John Rogers, born in America in 1829, studied sculpture in Europe and produced his first plaster-of-paris statue, "The Checker Players," in 1859. It was followed by "The Slave Auction" in 1860.

His works were popular parlor pieces in the Victorian era. He produced at least 80 different statues, and the total number of groups made from the originals is estimated to be more than 100,000.

Casper Hennecke, one of Rogers' contemporaries, operated C. Hennecke & Company from 1881 until 1896 in Milwaukee, Wisconsin. His statuary often is confused with Rogers's work since both are very similar.

References: Paul and Meta Bieier, *John Rogers' Groups of Statuary*, published by author, 1971; Betty C. Haverly, *Hennecke's Florentine Statuary*, published by author, 1972; David H. Wallace, *John Rogers*, Wesleyan University, 1976.

Periodical: *Rogers Group*, 4932 Prince George Ave., Beltsville, MD 20705.

Museums: John Rogers Studio & Museum of the New Canaan Historical Society, New Canaan CT; Lightner Museum, Saint Augustine, FL.

Notes: It is difficult to find a statue in undamaged condition and with original paint. Use the following conver-

Checkers at the Farm, c1875, 20" h, $475.

sions: 10% off for minor flaking; 10%, chips; 10 to 20%, piece or pieces broken and reglued; 20%, flaking; 50%, repainting.

Rogers

Campfire 650.00
Challenging Union Vote 1,100.00
Charity Patient, 1866. . . . . 665.00
Courtship Sleepy Hollow 750.00
Elder's Daughter 950.00
Favored Scholar, 1873 . . . . 425.00
Faust and Marguerite 800.00
Fighting Bob 1,800.00
First Ride. 1,800.00
Ha, I Like Not That 500.00
One More Shoot 500.00
Pews 600.00
Phrenology 750.00
Politics. 1,300.00
Private Theatricals 700.00
Referee 900.00
You Are A Spirit. 750.00
We Boys 800.00
Why Don't You Speak. 600.00
Wrestlers. 1,600.00

Rogers Type

Croquet Player 200.00
Evening Devotion 300.00
Family Cares. 120.00
First Love 200.00
Lost & Found. 150.00
Red Riding Hood. 350.00
Welcome, alabaster 300.00

ROOKWOOD POTTERY

History: Mrs. Marie Longworth Nicholas Storer, Cincinnati, Ohio, founded Rookwood Pottery in 1880. The name of this outstanding American art pottery came from her family estate, "Rookwood," named for the rooks (crows) which inhabited the wooded grounds.

Though the Rookwood pottery filed for bankruptcy in 1941, it was soon reorganized under new management. Efforts at maintaining the pottery proved futile, and it was sold in 1956 and again in 1959. The pottery was moved to Starkville, Mississippi, in conjunction with the Hersche-de Clock Co. It finally ceased operating in 1967.

Rookwood wares changed with the times. The variety is endless, in part because of the creativity of the many talented artists responsible for great variations in glazes and designs.

Marks: There are five elements to the Rookwood marking system—the clay or body mark, the size mark, the decorator mark, the date mark, and the factory mark. The best way to date Rookwood art pottery is from factory marks.

From 1880 to 1882, the factory mark was the name "Rookwood" incised or painted on the base. Between 1881 and 1886, the firm name, address, and year appeared in an oval frame. Beginning in 1886, the impressed "RP" monogram appeared and a flame mark was added for each year until 1900. After 1900, a Roman numeral, indicating the last two digits of the year of production, was added at the bottom of the "RP" flame mark. This last mark is the one most often seen on Rookwood pieces in the antiques marketplace.

References: Susan and Al Bagdade, *Warman's American Pottery and Porcelain*, Wallace-Homestead, 1994; Anita J. Ellis, *Rookwood Pottery*, Rizzoli International and Cincinnati Art Museum, 1992; Ralph and Terry Kovel, *Kovels' American Art Pottery*, Crown Publishers, 1993; Herbert Peck, *Book of Rookwood Pottery*, Crown Publishers, 1968; ——, *Second Book of Rookwood Pottery*, published by author, 1985; David Rago, *American Art Pottery,* Knickerbocker Press, 1997.

Videotape: Anita Ellis, *The Collectors Series: Rookwood Pottery*, distributed by Award Video and Film Distributors, Inc., 1994.

Collectors' Club: American Art Pottery Association, P.O. Box 1226, Westport, MA 02790.

SPECIAL AUCTIONS

Cincinnati Art Galleries
635 Main St.
Cincinnati, OH 45202
(513) 381-2128

David Rago Auctions, Inc.
333 North Main St.
Lambertville, NJ 08530
(609) 397-9374

Treadway Gallery, Inc.
2029 Madison Rd.
Cincinnati, OH 45208
(513) 321-6742

Ashtray, #7183 . . . . 25.00
Bookends, 5-1/2" h, molded trees, mottled brown matte glaze, 1929, imp mark #6020, also imp "W. P. McDonald"
. . . . 500.00
Bowl
  3-3/8" h, three repeating lily of the valley sprays, vellum glaze, E. T. Hurley, 1919 . . . . .1,400.00
  9-1/4" d, light orange, clover dec, cameo glaze, 1869
. . . . 385.00
  13-1/8" d, blue roses, repeating patterns dec, blue tinted high glaze, Sara Sax, 1926 . . . . 850.00
Bust, 9-3/4" h, young boy, matte glaze, 1913 . . . . 750.00
Candy Box, 2-5/8" h, fruit blossom dec, three handles, standard glaze, Amelia Sprague, 1893 . . . . 300.00
Cane Handle, 3-3/8" l, dragonfly dec, iris glaze, c1905 . 375.00
Charger, 12-5/8" d, young Indian boy, standard gales, titled on back "Moki Rabbit Hunter," Grace Young, 1898 . . .6,000.00
Chocolate Pot, 9-3/8" h, baluster, jonquils dec, standard glaze, Elizabeth Lincoln, 1904 . . . . 600.00
Creamer, 2-1/4" h, pansy dec, standard glaze, Olga Reed, 1891
. . . . 190.00
Cup and Saucer, daisy dec, cameo glaze, Ed Abel, 1891
. . . . 325.00
Ewer, 11-5/8" h, poppy flower dec, petal rim, standard glaze, Kataro Shirayamadani, 1891 . . . . .2,650.00

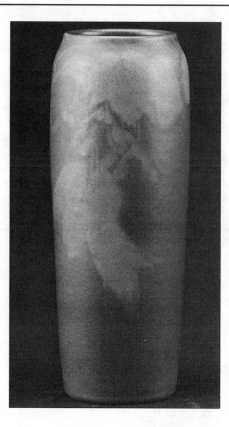

Vase, matte, cylindrical, maple leaves and pods dec, burgundy ground, Olga Geneva Reed, 1907, flame mark, 10-1/2" h, 4" d, $5,500. Photo courtesy of David Rago Auctions, Inc.

Figure, elephant, 4" h, #6488, 1934, white matte, flat flake on ear
. . . . 180.00
Jar, cov, 6" d, #1349, incised geometric design, red and green matte glaze, 1908, minor flake to inner rim 375.00
Jardiniere, 10-1/2" h, grape and leaf dec, standard glaze, Albert Valentien, 1888 . . . . .1,400.00
Match Holder, 1-3/4" h, forget-me-not dec, matches and cigarettes dec, standard glaze, Carl Schmidt, 1898 . . . . . 385.00
Pitcher, 8-3/4" h, 6-1/4" d, cameo, dec in Limoges style, white narcissus, salmon pink ground, A. M. Valentien, 1890, flame mark/343/W/A.M.V. 400.00
Tea Set, porcelain, Shipware, teapot, creamer, sugar, trivet, cups, saucers, and luncheon plates for six, flame mark
. . . . .1,100.00
Tile
  4" sq, pink flower in brown vase, cream ground, Arts & Crafts oak frame 325.00
  6" h, cuenca dec, pink Glasgow rose, green leaves, Arts & Crafts frame, imp "Rookwood Faience/1281Y" . . .1,300.00
Urn, 12-3/4" h, 9-1/2" d, mustard microcrystalline glaze, 1910, flame mark/X/339B 1,300.00
Vase
  3" h, #1186, four-sided top, incised geometric design, green and blue matte glaze, 1904 . . . . 400.00
  4" h, #942F, incised geometric design, green matte glaze, imp mark, 1904 . . . . 425.00
  5" h, 4-1/2" h, vellum, blue, green, pink, and purple stylized flowers and leaves, medium blue ground, Margaret Helen McDonald, 1923, flame mark/XXIII/1343/HMH 600.00
  6-1/2" h, #80C, incised and painted geometric design, light green, red highlights on navy blue ground, matte glaze, deeply carved, artist sgd, 1906 . . . . .1,100.00
  7" h, #1358, incised geometric design, green and blue matte glaze, 1910, minute flake to top 170.00
  7" h, 3-1/4", scenic vellum, purple and apricot landscape of birch trees by lake, Elizabeth McDermott, 1917, flame mark/XVII/30F/EFM 1,400.00

7" h, 6" d, porcelain, brown and cobalt blue geometric pattern, ivory ground, W. Rehn, 1930, flame mark/XXX/1780/WR 1,200.00

7" h, 7" d, jewel porcelain, spherical, gray and white birds and magnolia blossoms, amber ground, Jens Jensen, 1946, flame mark/XLVI/6204/artist's cipher 1,800.00

7-3/4" h, vellum, white roses, ivory and gray ground, M. H. McDonald, 1914, flame mark/XIV/1861/V/M.H.MD 750.00

7-3/4" h, marine scenic vellum, painted sailboats, aqua water and sky, uncrazed, Carl Schmidt, 1923, flame mark/XXI-II/CS/901D 3000.00

7-3/4" h, 3" d, marine scenic vellum, sailboats on water, E. T. Hurley, 1943, uncrazed, flamemark/XLIII/932E/E.T.H. 2,400.00

8" h, #1374, four ftd form, curling fern fronds, rose and green matte glaze, designed by Shirayamadani, 1903 . . . 450.00

8" h, 4-1/2" d, jewel porcelain, bottle shape, brown and red, figures of Adam and Eve, with flowers, fish and fowl, cobalt blue butterfat glaze, Jens Jensen, 1933, flame mark/XXXI-II/5/artist's cipher 2,600.00

8" h, 6" d, jewel porcelain, brown and blue covered figures of Eve, flowers, fish, and fowl, sheer ivory butterfat glaze, Jens Jensen, 1945, flame mark/XLV/8005/64/artist's cipher 1,900.00

8-1/4" h, 3-3/4" d, ovoid, iris glaze, yellow, purple, and blue gooseberry leaves and fruit, shaded gray ground, Ed Diers, 1902, flame mark/II/732/ED 1,200.00

8-1/4" h, 4" d, scenic vellum, silhouetted seagulls in flight against pink sky, over gray waves, E. T. Hurley, 1905, flame mark/V/845d/V/E. T. Hurley 1,300.00

8-1/2" h, #1297, molded poppies dec, two-tone blue matte glaze, 1912 . . . . 550.00

8-1/2" h, 3-1/2" d, carved matte, tooled indigo irises and green leaves, red and green ground, Rose Fescheimer, 1906, flame mark/VI/932D/P.F. 5,500.00

8-3/4" h, 3-3/4" h, marine scenic vellum, sailboats at dust, purple and green sky, Fred Rothenbusch, 1910, flame mark/X/1660D/V/FR, two hairlines. 650.00

8-3/4" h, 4-1/2" d, marine scenic vellum, sailboats at dust, blue and green sky, Ed Diers, 1909, flame mark/IX/1659/D/V/ED. 450.00

8-3/4" h, 5" d, Iris, painted yellow water lilies, dark gray ground, Constance Baker, 1902, flame mark/II/CAP/935c 2,100.00

9-1/2" h, 4" d, wax matte, red flowers, green leaves, shaded orange ground, Eliz. Lincoln, 1923, flame mark/XXI-II/614D/LNL 1,400.00

10-1/4" h, 4" d, marine scenic vellum, baluster, small sailboats against dusk sky, Carl Schmidt, 1920, imp flame marl/XX/937/V/CS 3,750.00

10-1/2" h, geometric design at shoulder, pink and green matte glaze, #2033D, 1912 . . . . 400.00

10-1/2" h, 4" d, painted matte, cylindrical, maple leaves and pods, burgundy ground, Olga Geneva Reed, 1907, well-fired, flame mark/VII/951G/O/G/R 5,500.00

10-1/2" h, 5-1/4" d, wax matte, painted brown and red poppy pods and blossoms, red butterfat ground, Eliz. Lincoln, 1922, flame mark/XXII/614D/LNL". 2,400.00

10-3/4" h, 5-1/4" d, wax matte, purple flowers, green foliage, turquoise butterfat ground, Eliz. Lincoln, 1928, flame mark/XXVIII/614D/LNL" .1,700.00

12" h, molded double leaf form, multi-tone brown matte glaze, #2492, 1921. . . . . .1,700.00

ROSE BOWLS

History: A rose bowl is a decorative open bowls with a crimped, pinched, or petal top which turns in at the top, but does not then turn up or back out again. Rose bowls held fragrant rose petals or potpourri which served as an air freshener in the late Victorian period. Practically every glass manufacturer made rose bowls in virtually every glass type, pattern, and style, including fine art glass.

Collectors' Club: Rose Bowl Collectors, P.O. Box 244, Danielsville, PA 18038-0244.

REPRODUCTION ALERT

Rose bowls have been widely reproduced. Be especially careful of Italian copies of satin, Mother of Pearl satin, peachblow, and Burmese, and recent Czechoslovakian ones with applied flowers.

Additional Listings: See specific glass categories.

Advisor: Johanna S. Billings.

Glass

Carnival, Hobnail pattern, Millersburg, radium purple, collar foot 360.00

Depression, Molly pattern, Imperial, pink, short foot with four wide toes, 8 scalloped top, light ribs in body, 4-1/2" h, 5-1/2" w. 25.00

Fenton, amethyst with collar foot, unfired white painting of wild horses and trees going all the way around, sgd "handpainted by Marilyn Wagner," Fenton stamp, 3-1/4" h, 4-1/4" w 150.00

Latticino, vertical stripes of white zanfirico, transparent red, transparent yellow, and crystal with twisted strands of blue highlighted with mica, rough pontil, c1973, 2-7/8" h, 3" w 165.00

Mt. Washington, light heavenly blue satin top, fading to creamy white bottom, enameled gold daisies with red centers and painted foliate, 9 soft crimps, gold highlights, shiny white int., polished pontil, sgd "620," 2-5/8" h, 3-1/4" w 395.00

Mother-of-Pearl, heavenly blue, Swag pattern, white lining, 8 subtle crimps, rough pontil, 3-1/2" h, 4-1/2" w 150.00

Stevens & Williams, Jewell glass, Zipper pattern, light sapphire blue, six box pleats, polished pontil, Rd. #55693, 4" h, 5" w, $125. Photo courtesy of Johanna Billings.

Opalescent

   Amethyst opalescent vertical stripes, gold enameled scroll work on front, gold enameled bon on back, 12 crimps, gold enamel highlights, polished pontil, 4-1/4" h, 6-1/4" w 225.00

   Daisy and Plume pattern ext., Blackberry pattern int., aqua 960.00

   Intaglio Glass Co., heavy, crystal with vertical white stripes, swirling yellow stripes, hint of pink at bottom, 3 crimps, 1" opening, 4" h, 4" w 35.00

   Peachblow, Thomas Webb & Sons, gold Jules Barbe enameled floral dec on front, gold enamel butterfly on back, 8 soft crimps with gold enamel, creamy white int., polished pontil, 3" h, 3" w 550.00

   Satin, heavenly blue to white, 8 crimps, round pontil, 3-1/3" h, 4" w 65.00

   Threaded, Zipper pattern, Stevens & Williams Jewell Glass, light sapphire blue, 6 box pleats, polished pontil, "Rd 55693," 4" h, 5" w 125.00

Porcelain

Czechoslovakian, old textured stucco-type design, smooth gold "V's" and vertical gold stripes within the "V's", creamy int. with irid finish reflecting pink, blue, and yellow, 8 crimps, bottom mkd with green crown and "TK Czechoslovakia," sgd "H Ludeman '23 to Mother" 85.00

ROSE CANTON, ROSE MANDARIN, and ROSE MEDALLION

History: The pink rose color has given its name to three related groups of Chinese export porcelain: Rose Mandarin, Rose Medallion, and Rose Canton, and Rose Medallion.

Rose Mandarin, which was produced from the late 18th century to approximately 1840, derives its name from the Mandarin figure(s) found in garden scenes with women and children. The women often have gold decorations in their hair. Polychrome enamels and birds separate the scenes.

Rose Medallion, which originated in the early 19th century and was made through the early 20th century, has alternating panels of figures and birds and flowers. The elements are four in number, separated evenly around the center medallion. Peonies and foliage fill voids.

Rose Canton, which was introduced somewhat later than Rose Mandarin and was produced through the first half of the 19th century, is similar to Rose Medallion except the figural panels are replaced by flowers. People are present only if the medallion partitions are absent. Some patterns have been named, e.g., Butterfly and Cabbage and Rooster. Rose Canton actually is a catchall term for any pink enamel ware not fitting into the first two groups.

REPRODUCTION ALERT

Rose Medallion is still made although the quality does not match the earlier examples.

Rose Canton

Bowl, 14-3/4" d, 6" h, mandarin scenes, edge repair . . . 825.00
Creamer, 4" h, gilt dec, double twisted handle 215.00
Dish, 10-1/2" l, shell shape, gold dec, c1850 . . . . 450.00
Plate, 8-1/2" d, Thousand Butterfly border, gilt highlights, 19th C 110.00
Platter, 18-7/8" l, well and tree, mkd on base, late 19th C, very minor rim chips 550.00
Punch Bowl
   21" d, very minor gilt and enamel wear 3,450.00
   13-3/8" d, 5-3/8" h, minor gilt and enamel wear 900.00
Vase, 12-1/2" h, mandarin scenes, drilled and mounted as lamp, chip on base ring 390.00

Rose Celadon

Vase, 16-1/2" h, baluster form, relief blue underglaze, dec of scholars, foo dog handles, gilt highlights, minor gilt and enamel wear, China, 19th C. 700.00

Rose Mandarin

Cache Pot, 8-1/2" h, reserves of court figure, squirrel and grape border, 19th C, restoration, lid missing, minor chips . 700.00
Hot Water Dish, 9-1/4" d, gilt highlights. 545.00
Platter
   14-3/4" l, gilt and enamel wear, minute rim chips, knife marks 635.00
   14-3/4" l, 12" w, some wear 700.00
   15-3/4" l, gilt and enamel wear, minor chips. 1,100.00
   17-1/2" l, well and tree, restoration, gilt and enamel wear 1,150.00
Vase
   9-7/8" h, bottle form, applied kylins and foo dogs, minor gilt and enamel wear 375.00
   12-3/8" h, 7-3/4" d, Ku-form, raised acanthus leaf ribbing, gilt archaic dragon design, blue ground, first half 19th C, pr 3,350.00
   13-5/8" h, Ku-form, chips and cracks, pr 1,035.00
   15-1/4" h, 10" d, Ku-form, very minor rim chip, gilt and enamel wear, 19th C. 575.00
Vase, cov, 10-3/4" h, very minor chips, gilt and enamel wear, pr 3,220.00

Rose Mandarin, platter with insert, armorial crests, fish, monogram, and "Avise La Fin," 17-3/8" l, $3,250. Photo courtesy of Garth's Auctions, Inc.

Rose Medallion

Bowl
    9-3/4" w, 8-1/2" d, 2-3/4" h, shaped 200.00
    10-5/8" d, 4" h, scalloped, minor gilt and enamel wear, minute rim chips. 575.00
Box, cov, small 665.00
Brush Box, 7" l, 3-1/2" w, 2-3/4" h, rect, divided base
    . . . . 475.00
Brush Pot
    4-3/4" h, 3" d, cylinder 450.00
    5-3/4" h, 5" w, cylinder 500.00
Bun Tray, 13-1/2" x 7" x 1-3/4" h, rect. 800.00
Candlestick
    9-3/4" h, minor chips, enamel wear 300.00
    10-1/4" h, minor gilt and enamel wear, pr 1,000.00
Center Bowl, 10-3/8" d, 6-1/2" h, paneled, scalloped rim, ftd, two very minor rim chips, minor gilt and enamel wear
    . . . . 2,875.00
Chamber Pot, 9-5/8" d, minute rim chips 635.00
Charger, 18" d, scenes of people 200.00
Compote, 7-5/8" d, 3-5/8" h, reticulated, pr. 700.00
Creamer
    3-1/4" h, 7" w, repaired. 60.00
    4-1/2" h, curved spout 225.00
Fruit Basket, 9-3/8" h, 9-7/8" l undertray, reticulated basket, very minor chips, minor gilt and enamel wear 950.00
Jar, cov
    3-1/2" h, 3" d, repairs to cover 50.00
    12-1/2" h, sgd on base, 20th C. 50.00
Plate
    8-1/2" d, dinner, minor gilt and enamel wear, set of six
    . . . . 200.00
    9-1/2" d, dinner, scalloped edge, set of four. 250.00
Platter
    13-1/2" l, 11" w 300.00
    14-1/2" l, 11-3/4" w. 250.00
    15-1/2" x 11-1/2" w. 350.00
    16" l, 13' w 300.00
    16-1/2" l, 13-1/4" w, cabbage leaf center 625.00
    18" l, 14-1/2" w, oval. 350.00
    18-3/4" l, well and tree, panels of red flowers and butterflies
    . . . . 800.00
Punch Bowl
    13-1/4" d, 5-1/4" h, gilt and enamel wear 950.00
    14-5/8" d, gilt and enamel wear, hairline 1,100.00
    14-7/8" d, 6" h, gilt and enamel wear, minute rim chips
    . . . . 750.00
    15-1/2" d, 6-1/2" h 1,050.00
    15-3/4" d, 6-1/2" h 1,050.00
Rice Bowl and Spoon, 4-3/4" d x 2-1/4" h bowl, 5" spoon. 45.00
Sauce Tureen, 8-1/8" l, mismatched undertray, gilt and enamel wear 575.00
Serving Bowl, 9-1/2" d, 4-7/8" h, shaped, very minor chips to base 1,100.00
Serving Dish, cov, 7-1/8" d, reversible pierced lid, two handles, circular, minute chip to one handle, minor gilt and enamel wear 650.00
Soap Dish, 6" w, 4-1/2" d, 3" h, three part 275.00
Soup Plate, 9-1/8" d, minor gilt and enamel wear, set of four
    . . . . 200.00
Tazza, 14-1/8" d, 3-1/2" h, minor gilt and enamel wear . 800.00
Teapot, cov, 4-1/2" h, strap handle. 250.00
Tea Set, 5" h cov teapot, creamer, cov sugar. 225.00
Umbrella Holder, 24" h, 9-1/2" w, twelve panels of people in int., setting birds and butterflies with flowers, reeded type molded side. 1,650.00

Vase
    9-1/4" h, baluster, applied kylins and foo dogs, minor gilt and enamel wear, pr. 650.00
    17-1/2" h, converted to lamps, gilt metal mounts, electrified, pr. 1,500.00
    24" h, applied kylins and foo dogs, hardwood stands, minor gilt and enamel wear, pr. 2,300.00
Wash Basin, 16-1/8" d, 4-7/8" h, minor gilt and enamel wear, hardwood stand 1,265.00
Wash Basin and Pitcher
    15-7/8" d basin, 13-1/4" h pitcher, mismatched, restoration, minor gilt and enamel wear 1,100.00
    16" d basin, 14-3/4" h pitcher, heavy enamel wear to basin
    . . . . 650.00
Water Bottle, cov
    14-1/2" h, hairline, minute chip to lid, minor gilt and enamel wear 435.00
    15" h, minor chips to lid, minor gilt and enamel wear, hardwood stand. 890.00

ROSENTHAL

History: Rosenthal Porcelain Manufactory began operating at Selb, Bavaria, in 1880. Specialties were tablewares and figurines. The firm is still in operation.

Reference: Dieter Struss, *Rosenthal,* Schiffer Publishing, 1997.

Bowl, 10-3/4" d, pink, strawberries and leaves, scalloped gold trim, scroll handle, red glazed underside, artist sgd
    . . . . 85.00
Cake Plate, 10" d, multicolored roses, cobalt blue and gold border 55.00
Coffee Cup and Saucer, white porcelain cup, .800 silver holder and saucer, Art Nouveau dec, initials, price for 6 pc set
    . . . . 750.00
Creamer and Sugar, gold trim, sgd "Donatello" 45.00
Cup and Saucer, Maria pattern, heavy silver overlay 65.00
Dessert Set, Maria pattern, teapot, creamer, cov sugar, six cups, saucers, and dessert plates, 1908-48, price for 23 pc set
    . . . . 350.00
Dinner Service, Regina pattern, gold trim, price for 101 pc set
    . . . . 1,000.00
Dresser Set, lavender flowers, gold trim, price for 3 pc set 75.00
Figure
    Bird on branch, artist sgd, 6" h. 155.00
    Harem Dancer, 10" h, artist sgd 600.00
    Springer Spaniel, basket, 1932, 71 /2" h 200.00
    Rabbit, dark brown, 3" h. 165.00
Fruit Set, 10" d bowl, six 8" d plates, blue, green, yellow, and pink, pink roses, gold dec, price for 7 pc set 395.00
Luncheon Service, partial, cobalt blue ground rims, and gilt borders, twelve: 6-1/4" d plates, 7-3/4" d plates, 10-1/8" d plates, 5-1/4" d sauce dishes, 8-1/4" d soup bowls, saucers, eleven teacups, 12-3/4" l oval platter, 14-3/4" oval platter, oval 9-3/4" l serving dish, cov vegetable bowl 2,300.00
Nappy, brown nuts and flowers on gold ground, ruffled rim
    . . . . 50.00
Nut Set, master bowl, six 3-1/2" d serving bowls, Pompadour pattern, cream ground, ornate gold scrolled rim, price for 7 pc set. 65.00
Place Card Holder, small multicolored floral dec 15.00

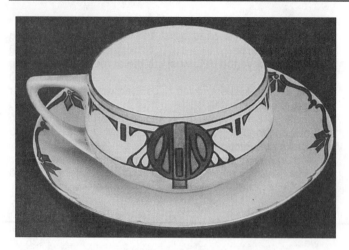

Cup and Saucer, Donatello pattern, light and dark green, gold trim, $20.

Plaque, 10" x 12", snow covered mountain, lake in foreground, orig frame 700.00
Plate, 8" d, pastel daisies, price for 6 pc set 95.00
Sculpture, 16" h, 9-1/2" d base, white, two tropical fish swimming among rising seaweed, wood base, artist sgd "F. Heidenreich," small in-making fracture on seaweed leaf 200.00
Tea Cup and Saucer, Donatello pattern, price for 12 piece set
. . . . 50.00
Vase
   7" h, crackle, rust foliage, artist sgd "Stockmayer," 1946
. . . . 125.00
   17-1/2" h, Studio Line, bisque ext., glazed int., cylindrical, flaring neck, molded bands of figures supporting ribs of flowers, designed by Bjorn Winblad 275.00

ROSEVILLE POTTERY

Roseville
U.S.A.

History: In the late 1880s, a group of investors purchased the J. B. Owens Pottery in Roseville, Ohio, and made utilitarian stoneware items. In 1892, the firm was incorporated and joined by George F. Young who became general manager. Four generations of Youngs controlled Roseville until the early 1950s.

A series of acquisitions began: Midland Pottery of Roseville in 1898, Clark Stoneware Plant in Zanesville (formerly used by Peters and Reed), and Muskingum Stoneware (Mosaic Tile Company) in Zanesville. In 1898 the offices also moved from Roseville to Zanesville.

In 1900, Roseville introduced Rozane, an art pottery. Rozane became a trade name to cover a large series of lines. The art lines were made in limited amounts after 1919.

The success of Roseville depended on its commercial lines, first developed by John J. Herald and Frederick Rhead in the first decades of the 1900s. In 1918, Frank Ferrell became art director and developed more than 80 lines of pottery. The economic depression of the 1930s brought more lines, including Pine Cone.

In the 1940s, a series of high-gloss glazes were tried in an attempt to revive certain lines. In 1952, Raymor dinnerware was produced. None of these changes brought economic success and in November 1954 Roseville was bought by the Mosaic Tile Company.

References: Susan and Al Bagdade, *Warman's American Pottery and Porcelain*, Wallace-Homestead, 1994; Virginia Hillway Buxton, *Roseville Pottery for Love or Money*, updated ed., Tymbre Hill Publishing Co. (P.O. Box 615, Jonesborough, TN 37659), 1996; John W. Humphries, *Price Guide to Roseville Pottery by the Numbers*, published by author, 1993; Sharon and Bob Huxford, *Collectors Encyclopedia of Roseville Pottery*, 1st Series (1976, 1997 value update), 2nd Series (1980, 1997 value update), Collector Books; ——, *The Roseville Pottery Price Guide,* Collector Books, 1997; Ralph and Terry Kovel, *Kovels' American Art Pottery*, Crown Publishers, 1993; Randall B. Monsen, *Collectors' Compendium of Roseville Pottery*, Monsen and Baer (Box 529, Vienna, VA 22183), 1995, ——, *Collectors' Compendium of Roseville Pottery, Volume II,* Monsen and Baer, 1997; David Rago, *American Art Pottery,* Knickerbocker Press, 1997.

Collectors' Clubs: American Art Pottery Assoc., P.O. Box 1226, Westport, MA 02790; Roseville's of the Past Pottery Club, P.O. Box 656, Clarcona, FL 32710.

Additional Listings: See *Warman's Americana & Collectibles* for more examples.

Ashtray
   Silhouette, red, 799 . . . . 130.00
   Wincraft, blue, 240-7 . . . . 135.00
Basket
   Apple Blossom, 309-8 . . . . 250.00
   Blackberry, 7" w, minor flake to top 650.00
   Bushberry, blue, 8" h, 370-8 . . . . 210.00
   Bushberry, blue, 8-1/2" h, 369-6.5 . . . . 175.00
   Monticello, arched handle, incised mark, 6-1/2" h . . . 550.00
   Pine Cone, 11" 700.00
Bookends, pr
   Freesia, delft blue, relief mark 250.00
   Magnolia, blue 250.00
   Water Lily, pink and green, mkd, 5" w, 5" h 180.00
   Zephyr Lily, brown to green, 5-1/2" 210.00
   Zephyr Lily, orange and yellow, #16, 5" h 190.00
Bowl
   Baneda, low form, two handles, 11" l 475.00
   Donatello, 10" d 110.00
   Luffa, two handles, horizontal wavy lines, large green leaves, small white flowers, 7" d 200.00
   Monticello, low, two handles, black and white geometric design, rust, camel, and tan ground, green border, 13" w, 3" h
. . . . 375.00
   Pine Cone, blue 321-9 . . . . 600.00
   Pine Cone, brown, 425-8 . . . . 200.00
   Topeo, two-tone red hi-glaze, paper label, 9" d, minor flakes
. . . . 100.00
   Water Lily, 663, pink. 45.00
   Windsor, maroon, orig black paper label 575.00
   Zephyr Lily, rust, green int., #810. . . . . 125.00
Candleholders, pr
   Carnelian II, aqua and lilac, 1059-2-1/2" 150.00
   Ixia, 3-1/4" h, low, pink, imp mark. 220.00
   Moss, 1107-4-1/2", blue 415.00
   Tuscany, 3-1/2" h 65.00
Candlesticks, pr
   Ming Tree 80.00
   Pine Cone, green, 1099-4-1/2". 200.00
Celery Dish, Raymor, brown, #177 . . . . 65.00

Child's Feeding Dish
   Baby Bunting, rolled edge 150.00
   Chick dec, stamp mark, 8" d 110.00
Child's Mug, Chicks. 130.00
Compote, Silhouette, white, 722 . . . . 110.00
Conch, Peony, pink, 436 . . . . 150.00
Console Bowl
   Bushberry, green, 385-10 . . . . 155.00
   Columbine, pink, 405-12" 165.00
   Gardenia, green, 632 . . . . 70.00
   Pine Cone, blue, 263-14", rect, two handles, rolled edge
   . . . . 1,870.00
   Pine Cone, green, 322-12" 350.00
   Poppy, 10" d, pink 175.00
   White Rose, 393-12 . . . . 225.00
   Console Set, Apple Blossom, blue 275.00
Cookie Jar, cov
   Freesia, brown, 4-8 . . . . 425.00
   Magnolia, blue, 2-8 . . . . 475.00
   Magnolia, orange to green, white and pink flowers, mkd, 8" h
   . . . . 300.00
   Water Lily, brown 440.00
Cornucopia, Silhouette, 8" 85.00
Creamer, Juvenile Ware, chicks 135.00
Egg Cup, Juvenile Ware, chicks 280.00
Ewer
   Clematis, blue, 18-15" 365.00
   Columbine, 7" h, blue, 18-7 . . . . 195.00
   Freesia, blue, 21-15 . . . . 350.00
   Iris, pink, 926-10" 300.00
   Ming Tree, 10" h, white 150.00
   Peony, green, 7-6" 125.00
   Pine Cone, brown, 909-10 . . . . 450.00
   Snowberry, pink, 1TK-6 . . . . 125.00
   Snowberry, pink, 1TI-10 . . . . 225.00
   Zephyr Lily, green and brown, 24-15 . . . . 300.00
Floor Vase
   Bittersweet, #888-16 . . . . 900.00
   Iris, 929-15 . . . . 650.00
   Flower Bowl, low, Florentine, 8" 85.00
Flower Pot
   Clematis, blue, saucer base 140.00
   Thornapple, pink, unmarked, 5" h 250.00
Hanging Basket
   Bittersweet, green, orange berries, 5" h 210.00
   Clematis, blue 250.00
   Pine Cone, blue 550.00
   Pine Cone, brown, unmarked 385.00

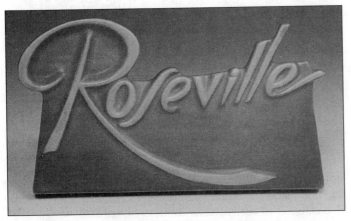

Dealer's Sign, pink, 7-1/2" h, $1,925. Photo courtesy of Jackson's Auctioneers & Appraisers.

Vista, molded landscape design, flower underneath, 7" w
   . . . . 210.00
   Wisteria, brown, rim chip 660.00
Humidor, Dutch 275.00
Jar, Carnelian, blue, brown, and speckled gold underglaze,
   7-3/4" x 5-1/2", minor chip repair 50.00
Jardiniere
   Bleeding Heart, blue, 651-3 . . . . 100.00
   Bushberry, blue, 657-3 . . . . 120.00
   Cosmos, blue, 649-3 . . . . 100.00
   Freesia, brown, 669-8" 385.00
   Futura, two handles, multicolored leaf design, orange to
      green ground, 14" d 400.00
   Futura, two handles, stepped base, shoulder flake . . 415.00
   Old Ivory, 6"d 50.00
   Persian, stylized orange colored fruit, green leaves, white
      matte ground, 7" d 400.00
   Pine Cone, blue, raised mark 660.00
   Pine Cone, green, raised mark 60.00
   Primrose, blue, 634-6" 225.00
Jardiniere and Pedestal
   Apple Blossom, pink, raised mark, small chip 715.00
   Vintage, dark brown ground, yellow and orange design,
      13-1/2" d jardiniere, 30-1/2" h, minute flakes 1,100.00
Lamp Base, Vista, landscape dec, 15" h, drill hole in side
   . . . . 350.00
Mug
   Cornelian, ornate handle, elaborate relief designs, 4" h
   . . . . 50.00
   Della Robbia, incised and painted Dutch girls, blue, white,
      and brown, cut-back ground of dark green bordered by olive
      green, artist initials "F. B.", 4-1/2" h 750.00
   Juvenile Ware, chick, large 145.00
Pedestal, Clematis, 8" h 250.00
Pitcher
   Boy with horn 400.00
   Bushberry, blue, green branch handle, mkd #1325, 9" h
   . . . . 375.00
   Holland, 12" h 480.00
Planter
   Artwood, 10", yellow, 1056-10 . . . . 125.00
   Cosmos, blue, 381-9" 250.00
   Rhead design, squeezebag dec of yellow and black water lil-
      ies, pale green ground, orig liner, 5" h, minor flakes
   . . . . 250.00
Planter Bookends, Pine Cone, green 575.00
Rose Bowl, Foxglove, 6" h, pink 210.00
Sand Jar, Florentine, ivory ground, rust panels and green de-
   sign, 21" h, minor chips 260.00
Strawberry Jar, Earlam, green, blue, and peach matte glaze, 8"
   h, glaze imperfection to side 325.00
Sugar, Magnolia, blue 95.00
Teapot
   Apple Blossom, blue 300.00
   Zephyr Lily, green, emb mark 340.00
Tea Set, teapot, creamer and sugar
   Magnolia, brown 425.00
   Persian, ivory matte glaze, tapering handles and tops
   . . . . 550.00
   Wincraft, green, 7" h teapot, creamer and sugar each 3" h
   . . . . 130.00
   Zephyr Lily, green 475.00
Tobacco Jar, cov, ivory ground, two American colonists enjoying
   long stemmed pipes, 6" x 5", restored finial 220.00
Umbrella Holder, 20" h, 10" d, cylindrical, raised floral design,
   matte green glaze, unsigned 600.00

Urn

- Bittersweet, green, 842-7 . . . . 150.00
- Panel, brown 125.00
- Pine Cone, blue, 623-3 . . . . 250.00
- White Rose, blue, 388-7 . . . . 170.00

Vase

- Apple Blossom, 15" h, pink 360.00
- Apple Blossom, 382-7, pink 155.00
- Baneda, 7-1/2" h, green 475.00
- Blackberry, 6" h 585.00
- Carnelian I, green, 9" h 300.00
- Carnelian II, 7" h. 325.00
- Cherry Blossom, blue, ball shape. 535.00
- Chloron, green suspended matte glass, three legs, 12-1/4" h 900.00
- Clemana, two handles, 6-1/2" h 200.00
- Clematis, 12" h, green, 112-12. . . . . 350.00
- Dahlrose, 10" h, brown, orig black paper label. 295.00
- Della Robbia, cut-back and incised floral design, shades of blue, aqua, olive green, brown, and yellow, 10-1/2" h, restoration to top and bottom. 8,000.00
- Della Robbia, flaring waisted form, incised and cut-back olive green tulips, cut-back aqua background, Rozane wafer, artist sgd. 1,300.00
- Donatello, 5" h 60.00
- Egypto, green suspended matte glaze, six arched linked to each other, 5-3/4" x 5-1/4". 600.00
- Foxglove, pink and green, 54-15 . . . . 900.00
- Fuchsia, brown, 255-B 215.00
- Futura, #380-6 . . . . 485.00
- Imperial I, 71-8 . . . . 165.00
- Iris, blue, 9" h, 924-9 . . . . 255.00
- Iris, tan, 923-8 . . . . 170.00
- Jonquil, 523-3. . . . . 240.00
- Luffa, brown, 683-6 . . . . 325.00
- Magnolia, blue, 86-4. . . . . 100.00
- Magnolia, brown, 184-6 . . . . 125.00
- Morning Glory, white, 7" 525.00
- Mostique, 8" h, incised geometric design, two open handles 1,300.00
- Mostique, 10" h, arrowhead 200.00
- Mostique, 21" h, stylized white floral design, red center, peach ground, dark and light green incised dec . . . 950.00
- Panel Gate, brown 185.00
- Peony, corn green, 171-8. 180.00
- Pine Cone, blue, 705-9 . . . . 400.00
- Pine Cone, blue, ftd, 425F-5 . . . . 575.00
- Pine Cone, blue, 10" h, handles at top, 848-10 . . . . . 825.00
- Pine Cone, blue, 12" h, orig foil label, 712-12 . . . . . . 800.00
- Pine Cone, brown, triple bud type, 113-8" 275.00
- Pine Cone, brown, 704-7 . . . . 350.00
- Pine Cone, green, 10" h, 749-10 410.00 . . . . 585.00
- Pine Cone, green, 12" h. 395.00
- Rozane, pillow, yellow roses, RPCO mark, 20" h, J. Handel signature, rim repair. .1,500.00
- Rozane Mongol, three handles, red hi-glaze, wafer mark, 6-1/4" h 550.00
- Rozane, portrait, broad shoulders, painted portrait of Rembrant, executed and sgd by Arthur Williams, imp mark, 14-1/2" h, minute flake under base 2,000.00
- Rozane Royal, floral dec, hi-glaze, imp mark, artist sgd "M. Timberlake," 11" h 160.00
- Rozane, two handles, ruffled top, painting of hunting dog with pheasant in mouth, unmarked, 11" w, 9" h, well repaired lip chips. 1,300.00
- Russco, blue, 108-7 . . . . 145.00

- Savona, 6" 150.00
- Silhouette, #710-10 . . . . 325.00
- Silhouette, Nude, #74206 . . . . 600.00
- Sunflower, 5" h, two long open handles 400.00
- Sunflower, 6" h, 7-1/2" w, broad shouldered form . . . 750.00
- Sunflower, 6" w, two open handles 650.00
- Sunflower, 7" h. 650.00
- Thornapple, brown, 813-7 . . . . 140.00
- Thornapple, pink, 824-15" 525.00
- Vista, 6-1/2" h, 7-1/2" w, molded landscape design 300.00
- Vista, 8-1/2" h, 10" w, molded landscape design, minor bruise to lip 210.00
- White Rose, blue, 985-8. . . . . 235.00
- Wincraft, green, 282-8 . . . . 175.00
- Wincraft, tan, 241-6 . . . . 150.00
- Wisteria, 6" h, tan 375.00
- Wisteria, brown, 631-6 . . . . 630.00
- Zephyr Lily, 12" h, blue. 250.00

Wall Pocket

- Blackberry, remnant of foil label. 1,450.00
- Carnelian I 250.00
- Cherry Blossom, unmarked, 6" x 9" 1,450.00
- Dahlrose, 9" h. 170.00
- Dogwood, 8-1/2" l, unusual form, minor flakes. 275.00
- Dogwood, 9-1/2" l, stamp mark 325.00
- Egypto, fan shape, unmarked, 8" x 12", glaze nicks 1,045.00
- Futura, geometric design, 8" l, minor chip 250.00
- Ming Tree, green, raised mark 360.00
- Morning Glory, white, bruised. 880.00
- Pine Cone, double, brown, imp mark 500.00
- Snowberry, pink, 8" w. 375.00
- Sunflower, flower pot shape. 1,760.00
- Wisteria, blue, 7" x 9" .1,210.00

Window Box

- Tourist, 13" x 7" x 7", three tight hairlines inside corners 1,760.00
- Vista, 11-1/2" l, orig liner, molded landscape dec, minute flake to top 1,200.00

ROYAL BAYREUTH

History: In 1794, the Royal Bayreuth factory was founded in Tettau, Bavaria. Royal Bayreuth introduced their figural patterns in 1885. Designs of animals, people, fruits, and vegetables decorated a wide array of tablewares and inexpensive souvenir items.

Tapestry wares, in rose and other patterns, were made in the late 19th century. The surface of the piece feels and looks like woven cloth. Tapestry ware was made by covering the porcelain with a piece of fabric tightly stretched over the surface, decorating the fabric, glazing the piece, and firing.

Royal Bayreuth still manufactures dinnerware. It has not maintained production of earlier wares, particularly the figural items. Since thorough records are unavailable, it is difficult to verify the chronology of production.

Marks: The Royal Bayreuth crest used to mark the wares varied in design and color.

References: Susan and Al Bagdade, *Warman's English & Continental Pottery & Porcelain*, 3rd Edition, Krause Publications, 1998; Mary J. McCaslin, *Royal Bayreuth*, Antique Publications, 1994.

Collectors' Club: Royal Bayreuth Collectors Club, 926 Essex Circle, Kalamazoo, MI 49008; Royal Bayreuth International Collectors' Society, P.O. Box 325, Orrville, OH 44667-0325.

Devil & Cards
    Candy Dish 195.00
    Creamer 250.00
    Cup and Saucer 175.00
    Dresser Tray 250.00
    Milk Pitcher 500.00
    Salt, master 175.00
Grape Cluster
    Cracker Jar, cov, white pearl, blue mark 675.00
    Creamer and Sugar
        Purple 395.00
        White pearl, blue mark 475.00
    Salt and Pepper Shakers, pr, purple 165.00
    Wall Pocket 500.00
Lobster, red
    Ashtray 60.00
    Bowl, 8" d, blue mark 375.00
    Creamer 75.00
    Radish Bowl, 5" d, blue mark 275.00
Miscellaneous Patterns
    Bowl, Dutch children, 6" d 65.00
    Candlestick, Basset, marked 600.00
    Cigarette Holder, Oak Leaf, pearl, marked 275.00
    Coffeepot, 8" h, 7" w, Brittany girl with draft horse, scene of trees and meadow, blue mark, lid not orig 450.00
    Creamer
        Alligator, white, unmarked 550.00
        Apple 250.00
        Bull, red, marked 150.00
        Butterfly, open wings, brown, orange, gray, and green, 3-1/2" h, blue mark 325.00

Creamer, Sun Bonnet Babies, laundry day, blue mark, 3-3/8" h, $180.

Chick, unmarked 225.00
Coachman 385.00
Cow, red 300.00
Crow 300.00
Dachshund, unmarked 145.00
Eagle, marked 450.00
Fish Head
    Blue mark 250.00
    Unmarked 95.00
Frog
    Green, blue mark 300.00
    Red, blue mark 195.00
Monkey, green, marked 575.00
Mountain Goat, marked 450.00
Oak Leaf, green luster, Depoinert 125.00
Orange, marked 175.00
Parakeet, red, unmarked 275.00
Pelican 275.00
Pig, gray, blue mark 495.00
Poodle, gray, blue mark 275.00
Robin 280.00
Rococo style, tropical bird scene, blue mark 125.00
Rural landscape, figure and turkeys, 4-1/4" h, blue mark 115.00
Seal, blue mark 400.00
Shell, purple, seahorse handle 225.00
St. Bernard, unmarked 350.00
Creamer and Sugar, figural, oyster and pearl 475.00
Cup and Saucer, Shell, ftd, blue mark 165.00
Dresser Box, cov, 3 x 4-1/2", 3 gold feet, peacock dec 250.00
Ferner, ftd, ornate, Hunter with Dog, in Tree, gold trim, blue mark 450.00
Hair Receiver, Mountain Goat scene, ruffled, blue mark 156.00
Humidor, cov
    Coachman, blue mark 795.00
    Gorilla, black, blue mark 1,075.00
Lamp, 9" h, porcelain base, seated semi-nude Fairy, brass fittings, figural dolphin feet 400.00
Letter Rack, cows, unmarked 465.00
Match Holder
    Arab on horseback, another horse beside him 175.00
    Elk, brown 250.00
Milk Pitcher, snail 300.00
Pitcher
    3-1/4" h, Highland Goats 165.00
    4" h, Little Jack Horner 165.00
Plate, Strawberry, 8" d 165.00
Playing Card Box, ship scene 150.00
Salt and Pepper Shakers, pr, radish, figural 350.00
    Shoe, high laced style, orange 200.00
    String Holder, rooster, marked 500.00
Sugar, cov
    Orange, figural, blue mark 375.00
    Pansy, purple, tiny rim flake 225.00
    Sugar, open, double rooster, unmarked 425.00
    Teapot, cov, figural, pansy, purple, blue mark 625.00
    Tea Trivet, Sand Babies, sgd 95.00
    Toothpick, ovoid, side handle, Dutch boy and goose, mkd 200.00
    Vase, 4" h, scenic, boy sitting between two donkeys, blue mark 95.00
    Water Pitcher, Pelican 1,400.00
Poppy
    Cake Plate, white pearl, open handles 225.00

Creamer, red 145.00
Match Holder, standing, red 550.00
Sugar, cov 225.00
Red Clown
   Ashtray, blue mark 345.00
   Candlestick, 6 1/2 x 4-1/2" 525.00
   Creamer, blue mark 450.00
   Match Holder, hanging, blue mark 425.00
   Mug, unmarked 435.00
Red Devil
   Ashtray, blue mark 165.00
   Creamer, blue mark 550.00
Snowbabies
   Cereal Set, sledding 175.00
   Plate, 6" d, babies playing 85.00
   Salt Shaker 120.00
   Trivet, Snowbabies, blue mark 110.00
Sunbonnet Babies
   Bell, sewing, unmarked 400.00
   Candlestick, babies ironing 300.00
   Creamer and Sugar, open, price for pr. 475.00
   Cup and Saucer, babies sewing 155.00
   Hatpin Holder 250.00
   Plate, 9" d, washing clothes 245.00
Tomato
   Biscuit Jar, cov 200.00
   Bowl, 5-1/2" d, green leaf 35.00
   Creamer and Sugar 75.00
   Cup and Saucer 115.00
   Mustard Jar, lettuce leaf underplate, blue mark 100.00
   Salad Bowl, large 395.00
   Tea Set, 4-1/2" h cov teapot, 3" h creamer, 5-1/2" d plate with
     open handle, 3-1/2" h sugar, 3" h x 4" d cov waste bowl
   . . . . 250.00
   Water Pitcher, marked 315.00

Tapestry

Bell, pink roses 545.00
Box, cov, round, dome lid, three color roses, shape #1187
. . . . 400.00
Candleholder, three color roses, shape #1251 . . . . 860.00
Chocolate Set, chocolate pot, four matching cup and saucers,
   three color roses, blue mark, price for 10 pc set . . .2,800.00
Creamer
   2-1/2" h, red roses 250.00
   3-1/2" h, The Bathers, shape #1038 . . . . 285.00
   3-3/4" h, lady's portrait 350.00
   4" h, pinched spout, Hounds and Stag 350.00
Cup and Saucer, three color roses 400.00
Dish, Colonial Couple, maple leaf shape 225.00
Dresser Tray
   Japanese chrysanthemum dec, leaf shape 225.00
   Roses, large, blue mark 350.00
Hair Receiver, roses 325.00
Match Holder, hanging
   Roses 365.00
   Sheep, shape #1059 . . . . 485.00
Mug, 3-3/8" h, roses, gold handle, blue mark 325.00
Plate, 7-1/2" d, three color roses, shape #1263 . . . . . 190.00
Powder Dish, cov, 5-1/2" x 3-1/2", colonial couple dancing
. . . . 495.00
Relish, 8" l, Chrysanthemum, handles 375.00
Shoe, pink roses, orig lace trim, blue mark 400.00
Sugar, cov, pink roses, shape #1310 . . . . 220.00
Sugar, matching underplate 450.00

Teapot, three color roses 650.00
Vase
   4-1/2" h, Christmas Cactus 325.00
   7-1/2" h, Pheasant Tapestry, gold handles, blue mark
   . . . . 425.00

ROYAL BONN

History: In 1836, Franz Anton Mehlem founded a Rhineland factory that produced earthenware and porcelain, including household, decorative, technical, and sanitary items.

The firm reproduced Hochst figures between 1887 and 1903. These figures, in both porcelain and earthenware, were made from the original molds from the defunct Prince-Electoral Mayence Manufactory in Hochst. The factory was purchased by Villeroy and Boch in 1921 and closed in 1931.

Marks: In 1890, the word "Royal" was added to the mark. All items made after 1890 include the "Royal Bonn" mark.

Biscuit Jar, 6-5/8" h, 5-1/4" d, floral dec, beige and cream color ground, rose, purple, and yellow flowers, green leaves, emb scrolls 210.00
Bowl, 9-1/2" d, cream, floral dec, metal rim, c1760 . . . . . 195.00
Celery Tray, floral dec 85.00
Cheese Dish, cov, pink, floral design 125.00
Cup and Saucer, blue and white, wild roses dec 45.00
Ewer
   6-1/2" h, gold handle, floral tapestry, scene with brick fence
   . . . . 150.00
   10-3/8" h, large red and pink flowers, raised gold, fancy handle 75.00
Mug, 4" h, blackberries and flowers, shaded green ground
. . . . 65.00
Spittoon, two cartouches with Oriental scenes 150.00
Teapot, 4-1/2" x 9-1/2", cream, red, black, and blue florals, gold trim, marked "1755" 125.00

Cake Plate, dark blue floral transfer, 10-1/4" w, $45.

Urn, 15-1/2" h, two handles, floral still life, gilded mask-form handles, paw feet, shaped base, c1900 . . . . 320.00
Vase
　5-1/2" h, Victorian boy and girl sledding, shaded fuchsia ground 150.00
　7" h, globular, Boucher scenes, blue transfers, 1850 . . . . 125.00
　8-1/4" h, portrait type, artist sgd 795.00
　9-1/2" h, floral and gilt dec, blues and greens 100.00
　11" h, Woman with Shawl, green ground, gold overlay base and neck, 4 handles, artist sgd 875.00
　11-1/2" h, gourd shape, hp, numbered, orchids dec, gold border, c1900 . . . . 155.00
　13" h, baluster form, gilt loop handles, bulbous shaped neck, floral cartouche, green, royal blue, and gilt ground, pr 550.00
　20" h, 5" d, raised gold flowers, link handles, hp giant multicolored floral sprays, ftd 250.00

ROYAL COPENHAGEN

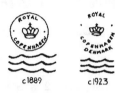

History: Franz Mueller established a porcelain factory at Copenhagen in 1775. When bankruptcy threatened in 1779, the Danish king acquired ownership, appointing Mueller manager and selecting the name "Royal Copenhagen." The crown sold its interest in 1867; the company remains privately owned today.

Blue Fluted, Royal Copenhagen's most famous pattern, was created in 1780. It is of Chinese origin and comes in three styles: smooth edge, closed lace edge, and perforated lace edge (full lace). Many other factories copied it.

Flora Danica, named for a famous botanical work, was introduced in 1789 and remained exclusive to Royal Copenhagen. It is identified by its freehand illustrations of plants and its hand-cut edges and perforations.

Reference: Robert J. Heritage, *Royal Copenhagen Porcelain: Animals and Figurines,* Schiffer Publishing, 1997.

Marks: Royal Copenhagen porcelain is marked with three wavy lines (which signify ancient waterways) and a crown (added in 1889). Stoneware does not have the crown mark.

Additional Listings: Limited Edition Collector Plates.

Bowl, 4-1/2" d, orange blossoms, green leaves 115.00
Box, cov, egg shape, seagulls on cov 195.00
Chocolate Cup and Saucer, Flora Danica, raised paneled border, enamel dec botanical design, titled on reverse, 20th C, set of 12 . . . . 4,325.00
Crocus Pot, 8-1/2" l, armorial dec, white and gilt ground, red highlights, lion form mounts, 19th C 400.00
Cup and Saucer, Blue Fluted Full Lace 100.00
Cup, covered, stand, 3-1/4" h, Floral Danica, triangular, raised paneled border, enameled dec botanical design, titled on reverse 865.00
Dessert Service, blue floral imbricated border, coffeepot, creamer, cov sugar, cake tray, fruit bowl, 12 cake plates, cups, and saucers 450.00

Vase, dogwood spray, butterflies, mkd "1584-271," 4-1/2" h, $170.

Dinner Service
　Blue fluted half lace pattern, service for 8, cups and saucers, dinner plates, bread and butter plates, teapot, sq vegetable, meat platter, serving bowl, nappy, tri-part dish, butter pats, creamer, sugar, and waste bowl, price for 43 pc set 1,600.00
　Blue foliate sprays, molded basketweave borders, dinner, luncheon, bread and butter, salad plates, tea, coffee, and demitasse cups and saucers, tea set, soup bowls, 19 additional pieces, price for 175 pc set 2,645.00
Figure
　Boy, sitting on rocks, whittling stick, sgd on back of rocks, #905, 7-1/2" h 275.00
　Goose Girl, #528 . . . . 210.00
　Mouse, sugar cubes 65.00
　Nude on Rock, #4027 . . . . 150.00
　Pan, sitting on column, holding flute, rabbit at base, 8-1/2" h 375.00
　Pekinese, tan and white, begging on haunches, #1776 . . . . 150.00
　Satyr, holding snake, sitting, #1712, 3" x 5" 225.00
　Siamese Cat, #3281, seated, 7-3/4" h 195.00
　Witch and soldier, #1112, 8" h 500.00
Fruit Compote, Floridian pattern, "Potentilla Nivea L." inscribed underneath bowl 550.00
Jardiniere, 13" h, anemones dec, 1890s 275.00
Monteith, 13-1/8" l, painted with botanical specimens, printed inscriptions, modern, hairline 980.00
Plate
　Blue Fluted Full Lace
　　Bread and butter 40.00
　　Dinner 85.00
　　Salad 60.00
　Flora Danica, raised paneled border, enamel dec botanical design, titled on reverse, 20th C
　　5-3/4" d, set of 12 . . . . 2,875.00
　　7-3/4" d, set of 12 . . . . 3,680.00
　　9" d, set of 12 . . . . 5,575.00
　　10" d, set of 12 . . . . 7,590.00
Platter, 17-1/4" l, oval, Flora Danica pattern, marked and numbered 450.00
Serving Dish, 14-1/4" d, raised paneled border and enamel dec botanical design, titled on reverse 1,610.00

Tea Set, Fluted Lace pattern, blue and white, price for 5 pc set
. . . . 295.00
Tray, 6-1/2" d, round, rose, fish swimming 150.00
Vase
    7" h, mermaid on rocks, gazing into harbor 95.00
    7-3/4" h, floral and dragonfly dec, c1890 . . . . 150.00
    11-3/8" h, swollen cylindrical shape, green, blue, white, and brown wildflowers, hilly landscape in background, blue shaded ground, #2549/1148 . . . . 300.00

ROYAL CROWN DERBY

History: Derby Crown Porcelain Co., established in 1875 in Derby, England, had no connection with earlier Derby factories which operated in the late 18th and early 19th centuries. In 1890, the company was appointed "Manufacturers of Porcelain to Her Majesty" (Queen Victoria) and since that date has been known as "Royal Crown Derby."

Most of these porcelains, both tableware and figural, were hand decorated. A variety of printing processes were used for additional adornment. Today, Royal Crown Derby is a part of Royal Doulton Tableware, Ltd.

References: Susan and Al Bagdade, *Warman's English & Continental Pottery & Porcelain*, 3rd Edition, Krause Publications, 1998; John Twitchett, *Dictionary of Derby Porcelain 1748-1848*, Antique Collectors' Club; John Twitchett and Betty Bailey, *Royal Crown Derby*, Antique Collectors' Club, 1988.

Museums: Cincinnati Art Museum, Cincinnati, OH; Gardiner Museum of Ceramic Art, Toronto, Canada; Royal Crown Derby Museum, Osmaston Road, Derby; Derby Museums & Art Gallery, The Strand, Derby; Victoria & Albert Museum, London, England.

Mug, satyr's face, multicolored, mkd, $65.

Marks: Derby porcelains from 1878 to 1890 carry only the standard crown printed mark. After 1891, the mark includes the "Royal Crown Derby" wording. In the 20th century, "Made in England" and "English Bone China" were added to the mark.

Bowl, Chinoiserie dec, four small feet 145.00
Creamer and Sugar, cov, Dublin shape, Imari pattern . . 300.00
Cup and Saucer 60.00
Demitasse Cup and Saucer 50.00
Dessert Service, eleven 9-1/4" d plates, three 9-1/2" ftd plates, each painted with varying foliate sprays, last quarter 19th C
. . . . 2,415.00
Ewer, 7-1/2" h, raised gold dec on reticulated cobalt blue neck and handle, enameled flowers on gold ground 675.00
Figure, 10-1/4" h, young man, foot on lap of woman, polychrome and gilt, edge chips on foliage 300.00
Jug, Imari palette, pink ground, gold trim, c1885, pr 750.00
Plate, 8-1/4" d, Japan pattern, No. 2451, price for 8 pc set
. . . . 115.00
Tea Cup and Saucer, 2-1/4" h cup, Japan pattern, price for 14 pc set 115.00
Urn, cov, 5" h, yellow ground, leaves and butterflies, molded mask handles, 1887 . . . . 425.00
Vase, cov, 12" h, 8" w, bulbous, raised fruit and leaf dec around handles on body, irregular gilt edge at top resembles waves, raised fruit and gilt bows around neck, delicate gilt flowers on green ground, line drawings of leaves and flowers with some raised leaves on body, raised gilt wavy design around base, round green cov with raised gilt flowers, orange mark 3718786, incised 786D/D, made for J. E. Caldwell and Co., Philadelphia, c1891 . . . . 3,800.00
Vase
    8" h, 6" w, bulbous, Imari pattern, cobalt border at top with gilt dec, 1-1/4" band of cobalt blue with geometric designs in white and orange, gilt panels and cobalt blue panel with white flower with orange lines alternating, center cartouche in cobalt blue with gilt swirls and white flowers with orange accents, cobalt blue base with gilt leaf design, mkd "Royal Crown Derby, England" in orange, incised numbers, c1911
. . . . 875.00
    12" h, teal ground, raised gilt trim, scroll framed floral dec, c1896 . . . . 290.00

ROYAL DOULTON

ROYAL
DOULTON
FLAMBE

History: Doulton pottery began in 1815 under the direction of John Doulton at the Doulton & Watts pottery in Lambeth, England. Early output was limited to salt-glazed industrial stoneware. After John Watts retired in 1854, the firm became Doulton and Company, and production was expanded to include hand-decorated stoneware such as figurines, vases, dinnerware, and flasks.

In 1878, John's son, Sir Henry Doulton, purchased Pinder Bourne & Co. in Burslem. The companies became Doulton & Co., Ltd. in 1882. Decorated porcelain was added to Doulton's earthenware production in 1884.

Most Doulton figurines were produced at the Burslem plants where they were made continuously from 1890 until 1978. After a short interruption, a new line of Doulton figurines was introduced in 1979.

Dickens ware, in earthenware and porcelain, was introduced in 1908. The pieces were decorated with characters from Dickens's novels. Most of the line was withdrawn in the 1940s, except for plates which continued to be made until 1974.

Character jugs, a 20th-century revival of early Toby models, were designed by Charles J. Noke for Doulton in the 1930s. Character jugs are limited to bust portraits while Royal Doulton toby jugs are full figured. The character jugs come in four sizes and feature fictional characters from Dickens, Shakespeare and other English and American novelists, as well as historical heroes. Marks on both character and toby jugs must be carefully identified to determine dates and values.

Doulton's Rouge Flambé (Veined Sung) is a high-glazed, strong-colored ware noted primarily for the fine modeling and exquisite colorings, especially in the animal items. The process used to produce the vibrant colors is a Doulton secret.

Production of stoneware at Lambeth ceased in 1956; production of porcelain continues today at Burslem.

Marks: Beginning in 1872 the "Royal Doulton" mark was used on all types of wares produced by the company.

Beginning in 1913, an "HN" number was assigned to each new Doulton figurine design. The "HN" numbers, which referred originally to Harry Nixon, a Doulton artist, were chronological until 1940, after which blocks of numbers were assigned to each modeler. From 1928 until 1954, a small number was placed to the right of the crown mark; this number added to 1927 gives the year of manufacture.

References: Susan and Al Bagdade, *Warman's English & Continental Pottery & Porcelain*, 3rd Edition, Krause Publications, 1998; Diana and John Callow and Marilyn and Peter Sweet, *Charlton Price Guide to Beswick Animals*, 2nd ed., Charlton Press, 1995; Jean Dale, *Charlton Standard Catalogue of Royal Doulton Animals*, 2nd ed., Charlton Press, 1998; ——, *Charlton Standard Catalogue of Royal Doulton Beswick Jugs*, 4th ed., Charlton Press, 1997; ——, *Charlton Standard Catalogue of Royal Doulton Beswick Storybook Figurines*, Charlton Press, 1994; ——, *Charlton Standard Catalogue of Royal Doulton Figurines*, 4th ed., Charlton Press, 1994; ——, *Charlton Standard Catalogue of Royal Doulton Jugs*, Charlton Press, 1991; Doug Pinchin, *Doulton Figure Collectors Handbook*, 4th ed., Francis-Joseph Books, 1996.

Periodicals: *Collecting Doulton*, BBR Publishing, 2 Strattford Ave., Elsecar, Nr Barnsley, S. Yorkshire, S74 8AA, England; *Doulton Divvy*, P.O. Box 2434, Joliet, IL 60434.

Collectors' Clubs: Heartland Doulton Collectors, P.O. Box 2434, Joliet, IL 60434; Mid-America Doulton Collectors, P.O. Box 483, McHenry, IL 60050; Royal Doulton International Collectors Club, 700 Cottontail Lane, Somerset, NJ 08873; Royal Doulton International Collectors Club, 850 Progress Ave., Scarborough Ontario M1H 3C4 Canada.

Animal
  Bull Dog 245.00
  Cat, HN2580. . . . . 50.00
  Cocker Spaniel with pheasant, HN1137. . . . . 475.00
  Duck, flambé, #7, 3-1/2" h 150.00
  Llama, HM2665, restored. 300.00
  Peacock, HN2576 . . . . 325.00
  Pheasant, HN2577. . . . . 325.00
Biscuit Jar, cov, 6" x 7-3/4", ribbed cream ground, band of turquoise with birds and animals, SP top, rim, and handle, marked "Doulton, Burslem Pottery" 225.00
Bowl, 8-7/8" x 4-1/4", blue, brown geometric borders, grazing cows and horses, sgd "Hannah Barlow, 1885". 675.00
Dinnerware
  Creamer, Glamis Thistle. 30.00
  Cup and Saucer
    Glamis Thistle 30.00
    Glen Auldyn. 30.00
    Plate, bread and butter, Glen Auldyn 12.00
    Plate, dinner, Glen Auldyn. 25.00
    Plate, salad, Glen Auldyn 20.00
    Sugar, open, Glamis Thistle 30.00
Ewer, 9" h, Babes in Wood Series, girl with cape in woods
  . . . . 1,250.00
Figure
  Adirenne, HN2152 . . . . 160.00
  Ascot, HN2356 . . . . 175.00
  Autumn, HN2087 . . . . 450.00
  Balloon Man 200.00
  Bess, HN2002 . . . . 350.00
  Blithe Morning, HN2021 . . . . 245.00
  Blue Beard, HN2105 . . . . 650.00
  Bonnie Lassie, HN1626 . . . . 550.00
  Bridesmaid, M12 . . . . 425.00
  Camelia, HN2222 . . . . 225.00
  Carolyn, HN2112 . . . . 350.00
  Carrie, HN2800 . . . . 225.00
  Celeste, HN2237 . . . . 240.00
  Christmas Time, HN2110. . . . . 425.00
  Cookie, HN2218. . . . . 150.00
  Coralie, HN2307. . . . . 140.00
  Daffy-Down Dilly, HN1712 . . . . 425.00
  Darling, HN1319. . . . . 190.00
  Day Dreams, HN1731 . . . . 300.00
  Emma, HN2834 . . . . 225.00
  Faith, HN3082 . . . . 175.00
  First Dance, HN2803 . . . . 215.00
  Fleur, HN2368 . . . . 200.00
  Gail, HN2937 . . . . 325.00
  Goody Two Shoes, M81. . . . . 1,275.00
  June, HN2027, restored. 575.00
  Kathy, HN2346. . . . . 160.00
  Laura, HN2960. . . . . 175.00
  Laurianne, HN2719 . . . . 175.00
  Lilac Time, HN2137 . . . . 385.00
  Marguerite, HN1928 . . . . 475.00
  Maureen, HN1770 . . . . 325.00
  Maureen, M85 . . . . 1,400.00
  Merely a Minor, HN2531, gray, 12" h, orig sticker . . . 750.00
  Midsummer Noon, HN2033 . . . . 625.00
  Pauline, HN2441 . . . . 200.00
  Penelope, HN1901. . . . . 360.00
  Primroses, HN1617 . . . . 1,100.00
  Roseanna, HN1926 . . . . 425.00
  Silks & Ribbons, HN2017 . . . . 250.00
  Solitude, HN2810. . . . . 250.00
  Sonia, HN1692 . . . . 1,600.00
  Spring Flowers, HN1807 . . . . 350.00
  Spring Morning, HN1922 . . . . 275.00
  Suitor, HN2132. . . . . 385.00

Child's Plate, Out for a Walk, multicolored, 7" d, $65.

Susan, HN2952	185.00
Symphony, HN2287	250.00
The Cobbler, HN1706	350.00
The Rocking Horse, HN2072, restored	1,850.00
Top of the Hill, HN1849	190.00
Vanity, HN2475	120.00
Victorian Lady, M1	400.00
Wizard, HN2877	400.00

Jug, large

Auld Mack, "A"	85.00
Bacchus	90.00
Catherine Parr	135.00
Collector	60.00
Jane Seymour	115.00
Leprechaun	125.00
Ringmaster	175.00
Romeo	100.00
Scaramouche, 2nd version	125.00
Sir Thomas Moore	160.00
Trapper	100.00

Jug, miniature

Bacchus	50.00
Eli	55.00
Falconer	50.00
Falstaff	50.00
Gone Away	55.00
Henry VIII	75.00
John Peel "A"	80.00
Lawyer	50.00
Lobsterman	45.00
Long John Silver	50.00
Merlin	50.00
N. A. Indian	55.00
Tam O Shanter	75.00

Jug, small

Arman	86.00
Bacchus	55.00
Earl Mountbaten of Burma	100.00
Lumberjack	60.00
Neptune	50.00
N. A. Indian	55.00
Pearly King	65.00
Pearly Queen	65.00
Poacher, flow rim	50.00
Rip Van Winkle	55.00
Sailor	65.00
Sleuth	55.00

Smuggler	60.00
Soldier	65.00
Tam O Shanter	65.00
Trapper	55.00
Viscount Montgomery of Alamein	100.00

Mustard Pot, 3-1/2" h, handle, brown and tan stoneware, relief dogs and figurals, Lambeth, lid damaged 175.00

Plate

6-1/2" d, Poor Jo	100.00
7-5/8" d, Juliet	175.00
10" d, George and Martha Washington, flow blue style dec, pr	325.00

Service Plate, 10-1/2" d, apple green borders, gilded scrolls, printed marks, price for 12 pc set 1,100.00

Spittoon

European landscape, blue and white, sgd "Geneva"	275.00
Landscape scene, brown and green luster	160.00
Poppies, inner border with grapes and leaves	110.00

Teapot, two pansy reserves and pale flowers dec, gilt handle, marked "Doulton Burslem," late 19th or early 20th C . 190.00

Toby, large

Auld Mac, "A"	115.00
Lumberjack	150.00
Neptune	125.00

Toothpick Holder

Doulton Burslem, flowers, gold trim	90.00
Gamp	510.00

Umbrella Stand, 24" h, 9" w, cylinder, tapering top, blue birds and flowers, ivory ground, imp and printed mark 500.00

Vase

6-1/2" x 9", double handle, Margueterie pattern, blue/gray ground, gold leaf	475.00
9" h, Welsh Ladies	295.00

ROYAL DUX

History: Royal Dux porcelain was made in Dux, Bohemia (now the Czech Republic), by E. Eichler at the Duxer Porzellan-Manufaktur, established in 1860. Many items were exported to the United States. By the turn of the century Royal Dux figurines, vases, and accessories, especially those featuring Art Nouveau designs, were captivating consumers.

Marks: A raised triangle with an acorn and the letter "E" plus "Dux, Bohemia" was used as a mark between 1900 and 1914.

Bust, 18-1/2" h, woman adorned with flowers, Czechoslovakia, c1915 .... 460.00

Calling Card Receiver, 4", figural, frog standing on large open shell, beige, matte finish, pink triangle mark 125.00

Candlestick, 13" h, figural, boy wearing knickers 175.00

Centerpiece, 11" x 4-1/4" x 7-3/4", pr of kneeling nudes, central flared base, creamy white, cobalt blue, and gold trim 450.00

Compote, 20 5/8" h, three dancing female figures, emb bowl and base, sgd 750.00

Figure

Acrobat Elephant, 4-1/4" h, 3-3/4" w, pastel blue, white, and beige, gold "Royal Dux" triangular sticker, oval gold "Made in Czech Republic" sticker, base with "R" within circle and #970 .... 60.00

Figure, dog, pink triangle mark, 11-3/4" l, $90.

Bulldog, raised pink triangle "Royal Dux Bohemia," blue stamped circle "Czech Republic," #6, #652, #536 . . 120.00
Elephant, 10" x 13", trunk up 170.00
Fox, 4" x 8", glossy glaze, post-war mark 180.00
Grecian Woman, 8-1/2" h, classic Greek-style clothing, pre-war "E" mark 335.00
Hunting Dogs, 7-1/2" h, 11-1/4" l, hp, natural colors and pose 255.00
Lady, sedan chair, 2 courtiers, hound, 14" x 8-1/2" x 15-1/2" 800.00
Male, 12" h, bird in right hand, hp 110.00
Male, 12-1/2" h, 4-1/2" w, playing flute, imp #198 . . . 135.00
Peasant Couple, 12" h, matte glaze, pre-war marking, male damaged and repaired. 395.00
Polar Bear, 10" h, 13" l, detailed expression, back stamp numbered 3/8/4.66.16 with "R" and pink triangle with Royal Dux Bohemia D, circle with triangle inside mkd "Hand Painted, Made in Czech Republic". 250.00
Retriever, duck in jaws, 14" l, matte finish 400.00
Sled Dog Team, 9" x 8", three tethered dogs, pre-war "E" mark. 1,295.00
Stork, 8" h, orig sticker, mkd "353" and "82". 65.00
Woman, 9" h, bright colors, high gloss, "Made in Czechoslovakia," pink triangular mark 285.00
Pin Tray, figural, Art Nouveau maiden on wave 325.00
Serving Dish, 8-1/2" h, open shell-shape, maiden and lovebirds dec 230.00
Tobacco Jar, 8" h, figural, man's head, wearing nightcap, smoking pipe. 200.00
Vase
6-1/2" h, 3-3/4" l, Art Deco, orig gold sticker, back stamp "Royal Dux Bohemia, Hand Painted, Made In Czech Republic," raised, pink triangle. #11295, 3, 6 numbers under glaze, designed by V. Serak 70.00
11" h, Grecian, pre-war "E" mark 595.00
16" h, 5-1/2" d, Grecian maid with drapery on front, heavily gold embellished, creamy white, rust colored vines, leaves, and flower on back, 1arge raised pink triangle mark "Royal Dux Bohemia" with an "E" in center, c1900-18, some glaze wear, wear to gold edging, minor repair to hand . . . 700.00

ROYAL FLEMISH

History: Royal Flemish was produced by the Mount Washington Glass Co., New Bedford, Massachusetts.

The process was patented by Albert Steffin in 1894.

Royal Flemish is a frosted transparent glass with heavy raised gold enamel lines. These lines form sections—often colored in russet tones—giving the appearance of stained glass windows with elaborate floral or coin medallions.

Collectors' Club: Mount Washington Art Glass Society, 60 President Ave., Providence, RI 02906.

Advisors: Clarence and Betty Maier.

Biscuit Jar, cov, 8" h, ovoid, large Roman coins on stained panels, divided by heavy gold lines, ornate SP cov, rim, and bail handle, orig paper label "Mt. W. G. Co. Royal Flemish" 1,750.00
Box, cov, 5-1/2" d, 3-3/4" h, swirled border, gold outlined swirls, gold tracery blossoms, enameled blossom with jeweled center on lid 1,500.00
Ewer, 10-1/2" h, 9" w, 5" d, circular semi-transparent panel on front with youth thrusting spear into chest of winged creature, reverse panel shows mythical fish created with tail changed into stylized florals, raised gold dec, outlines, and scrolls, rust, purple, and gold curlicues, twisted rope handle with brushed gold encircles neck, hp minute gold florals on neck, burnished gold stripes on rim spout and panels. . . .4,950.00
Jar, 8" h, classical Roman coin medallion dec, simulated stained glass panels, SP rim, bail, and cov, paper label "Mt. W. G. Co. Royal Flemish" 1,650.00
Vase
4-1/2" h, 5-1/2" d, raised rim, applied angular handles, bulbous transparent colorless body, overall gold and silvered metallic coin medallions, raised gold enamel outlines and accents, partial label 2,650.00
6" h, double bulbed, frosted, colorful pansies, allover gold enameling 1,210.00
7-1/2" h, 7-1/2" d, squatty, smaller squatty form as collar, 14 pastel pansies, clear frosted ground, 4 rayed suns, painted foliage-like gold tracery .1,400.00

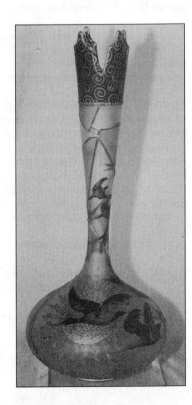

Vase, Guba duck dec, attributed to Frank Guba, raised gold sun, lead mallard, ten other ducks encircle perimeter, irregular panels of pastel tan and frosted clear, mauve, and gold embellishments on upper 3" of crown-like top, 15-3/4" h, $7,200.

13" h, classic handled oval body, gilt enameled panels and medallions, center star-studded scene of cameo with ethnic-costumed rider, body guard with scimitar, Mid-Eastern scrolls and devices on reverse. 13,800.00

ROYAL RUDOLSTADT

History: Johann Fredrich von Schwarzburg-Rudolstadt was the patron of a faience factory located in Rudolstadt, Thuringen, Germany, from 1720 to c1790.

In 1854 Ernst Bohne established a factory in Rudolstadt.

The "Royal Rudolstadt" designation originated with wares which Lewis Straus and Sons (later Nathan Straus and Sons) of New York imported from the New York and Rudolstadt Pottery between 1887 and 1918. The factory manufactured several of the Rose O'Neill (Kewpie) items.

Marks: The first mark of the original pottery was a hayfork; later, crossed two-prong hayforks were used in imitation of the Meissen mark.

"EB" was the mark used by Ernst Bohne.

A crown over a diamond enclosing the initials "RW" is the mark used by the New York and Rudolstadt Pottery.

Bowl
  7-1/4" d, white roses, green leaves, yellow centers, light green to white shaded int., 3 gold feet, crown and "B" mark 70.00
  9-1/8" d, paneled, hummingbird with blue wings, yellow tail, green branch chrysanthemums and peonies on int., black outlined blue luster border, yellow luster int. rim 20.00
Cake Plate
  10-1/4" d, hp, white flowers 75.00
  12" w, large roses, open handles. 195.00
Celery Dish, 13" l, handles, hp, yellow roses, gold trim, artist sgd 90.00
Creamer and Sugar, cov, purple pansies, cream ground, gold trim 85.00
Dresser Set, tray, hatpin holder, hair receiver, hp camellias, green leaves, pastels, gold trim, imp mark "Royal Rudolstadt Coronet B Prussia". 250.00
Ewer, 13-1/4" h, cream and light pink shell body, pebbled ground, brown worm type handle. 195.00
Figure, 3" h, seated Chinese figures, blue and white garb, late 19th C, pr 120.00
Hair Receiver, hp, pastel florals 50.00
Pitcher, 15-1/2" h, jeweled, inlaid gold leaves. 315.00
Plate, 8-1/2" d, chickens and roosters 75.00
Sweetmeat Jar, cov, 5-1/2"x 8", pink florals, green and rust leaves, cream ground, SP holder, marked "Middletown" 150.00
Urn, 25-1/2" h, floral dec, imp mark 595.00
Vase
  5-1/2"h, two children in Victorian winter clothes, stone wall, oval rocky base, polychromed, Ernest Bohne Sons Rudolstadt. 70.00
  9-1/4" h, florals, gold and scroll handles, emb lip. . . . 150.00
  11" h, center medium blue band, painted purple flowerheads, raised enameled centers, molded gilt outlined shoulder and foot, two scroll handles, matte beige ground, c1910 . . . . 250.00

ROYAL VIENNA

History: Production of hard-paste porcelain in Vienna began in 1720 with Claude Innocentius du Paquier, a runaway employee from the Meissen factory. In 1744, Empress Maria Theresa brought the factory under royal patronage; subsequently the ware became known as Royal Vienna. The firm went through many administrative changes until it closed in 1864. The quality of its workmanship always was maintained.

1749-1864

Marks: Several other Austrian and German firms copied the Royal Vienna products, including the use of the "Beehive" mark. Many of the pieces on today's market are from these firms.

Bone Dish, center gilt dot cartouche, multicolored period courting couple, wide gold border, gold flowerheads and gold drops, pale green ground, blue shield mark, set of 4 . . . . 100.00
Charger, 20-1/2" d, titled "Columbus Triumphant Return," landing party, Indians, bountiful scene 1,500.00
Compote, 9-1/2" d, two handles, portrait dec, cobalt blue ground, gold trim 165.00
Cup and Saucer, 3-1/2" d cup, 5-1/2" d saucer, green and gold dec, center scene of colorful rooster in landscape, saucer with similar gold and greed dec, center reads "quand ce coq chantera mon anmite finira" Bindenschild mark 250.00
Ferner, 7-3/4" w, 4" h, portrait of lady on side, portrait of different lady on other side, burgundy, green, gold, beaded, ftd, scalloped edges, sgd, mkd "Royal Vienna, Austria" 425.00
Figure, 8-5/8" h, man playing mandolin and other man playing hurdy-gurdy, one with pink jacket and striped trousers, other with yellow coat and purple trousers, blue shield mark, pr 300.00

Pedestal, two figural bands, one with angel and man comforting a swooning maiden, other with satyr and maiden frolicking with cherub, tooled gold foliage scrollwork bands, deep blue ground, sq plinth base, ormolu mounts, new marble top, minor chips, mid 19th C, 39" h, $10,360. Photo courtesy of Freeman\Fine Arts of Philadelphia, Inc.

Plate

6" d, multicolored scene of seated Cupid and Dido, dark red and gold border 395.00

9-1/2" d, two girls feeding birds in garden setting, multicolored intricate raised border, beehive mark 400.00

Portrait Plate, 15" d, cobalt blue border, gilt lily stylized flowers, center with emerald green ground, pr of facing portraits of young woman, one with orchid shawl on her hair with flowers and stars, red and blue design, other with long blond hair, elaborate hair dec and rose shawl, underglaze beehive mark on back of each, c1890, pr 3,200.00

Portrait Vase, 8-1/2" h, 4" d, bottle shape, cobalt blue, gold beading and flowers, beautiful woman portrait 235.00

Stein, 6" h, seated monk with stein, cobalt blue ground, gold trim, artist sgd "Wagner" 900.00

Urn, 8" h, maidens dancing, small cherub, beehive mark 175.00

Vase, 21-3/4" h, shield shape, painted scene of Bacchus and Ariadne on Island of Naxos on front, Juno and Aolous on reverse, gilt scrolling foliage cartouches, named below, cobalt blue ground, tilt curving scrolling handles ending in leaf terminals, suspended berry wreaths, sq base with canted corners, sgd "Richter Pinx," blue shield marks 4,375.00

ROYAL WORCESTER

History: In 1751, the Worcester Porcelain Company, led by Dr. John Wall and William Davis, acquired the Bristol pottery of Benjamin Lund and moved it to Worcester. The first wares were painted blue under the glaze; soon thereafter decorating was accomplished by painting on the glaze in enamel colors. Among the most-famous 18th-century decorators were James Giles and Jefferys Hamet O'Neale. Transfer-print decoration was developed by the 1760s.

A series of partnerships took place after Davis' death in 1783: Flight (1783-1793); Flight & Barr (1793-1807); Barr, Flight & Barr (1807-1813); and Flight, Barr & Barr (1813-1840). In 1840, the factory was moved to Chamberlain & Co. in Diglis. Decorative wares were discontinued. In 1852, W. H. Kerr and R. W. Binns formed a new company and revived the production of ornamental wares.

In 1862, the firm became the Royal Worcester Porcelain Co. Among the key modelers of the late 19th century were James Hadley, his three sons, and George Owen, an expert with pierced clay pieces. Royal Worcester absorbed the Grainger factory in 1889 and the James Hadley factory in 1905. Modern designers include Dorothy Doughty and Doris Lindner.

References: Susan and Al Bagdade, *Warman's English & Continental Pottery & Porcelain*, 3rd Edition, Krause Publications, 1998; Anthony Cast and John Edwards, *Charlton Price Guide to Royal Worcester Figurines*, Charlton Press, 1997; G. A. Godden, *Victorian Porcelain*, Herbert Jenkins, 1961; Stanley W. Fisher, *Worcester Porcelain*, Ward Lock & Co., Ltd., 1968; David, John, and Henry Sandon, *Sandon Guide to Royal Worcester Figures*, Alderman Press, 1987; Henry Sandon, *Flight & Barr Worcester*, Antique Collectors' Club, 1992; Henry Sandon and John Sandon, *Dictionary of Worcester Porcelain*, vol. II, Antique Collectors' Club, 1995; ——, *Grainger's Worcester Porcelain*, Barrie & Jenkins, 1990; John Sandon, *The Dictionary of Worcester Porcelain*, vol. I, Antique Collectors' Club, 1993.

Museum: Charles William Dyson Perrins Museum, Worcester, England; Roberson Center for the Arts and Sciences, Binghamton, NY.

Biscuit Jar, cov, 7" h, vertical ribbing, cobalt blue bamboo leaves and stems 355.00

Bowl, cov

4-1/4" h, ivory ground, polychrome floral dec and gilt 250.00

6-1/2" h, melon ribbed, ivory ground, polychrome floral dec and gilt 265.00

Cache Pot, 8" d, 7" h, circular, lug handles, Kakiemon style dec, Chamberlain, price for pr .5,995.00

Cheese Dish, 9-3/4" h, modeled bamboo body, brown and gilt dec, dec relief bamboo leaves, printed factory mark and "Richard Briggs Boston," c1879, slight rim nick, minor wear

. . . . 635.00

Claret Jug, 8" h, gilt banded and raised prunus dec, enamel dec flowers and butterfly, printed mark, c1884, gilt rim wear, price for pr 320.00

Cup and Saucer, Blue Arundel 95.00

Dessert Plate, 8-1/2" d, fruit dec, artist "T. Lockyer," factory marks, 1923 date code 345.00

Ewer

6" h, flowers and leaves dec, maroon mark, #1160

. . . . 175.00

9 1 /2" h, enamel dec butterflies among raised and gilt tall grass, printed mark, c1884 . . . . 550.00

Fern Pot, 7" h, figural, boy standing by wood simulated pot, printed mark, c1887, brim of hat restored, gilt wear 345.00

Figure

Eastern water carriers, male and female figures holding vessels, shape 1206, printed and imp marks, c1888, 8" h, one with restored neck, one with rim chip, price for pr

. . . . 575.00

Elizabeth, enamel dec, imp and printed marks, c1807, 6-1/4" h, gilt wear 435.00

Girl and boy dressed in 19th C garb, each holding a basket, enamel and gilt dec, imp and printed marks, c1882, 8-1/2" h, basket restored, price for pr 635.00

June, barefoot boy, playing harmonica, dog at side. . 125.00

Flower Pot, 9-1/4" h, frog and lotus flower, imp and printed marks, c1883, gilt wear, one base restored, price for pr

. . . . 520.00

Ice Cream Set, enamel dec stylized floral and leaf designs, gilt trim, twelve sq shaped 6-1/4" w plates, 14-3/8" l rect tray, printed marks, c1883, glaze scratches, one plate restored, minor damage, price for 13 pc set 115.00

Ice Jug, 9-3/4" h, leaf molded necks, melon shape, enamel and gilt floral sprays, printed marks, c1889, price for pr . . 690.00

Jardiniere

6-3/4" h, leaf molded and basketweave body, scrolled handles, enamel and gilt dec, printed mark, c1897 . . . . 345.00

8-1/4" h, enamel and gilt dec floral sprays with foliate borders, printed mark, c1891, gilt wear 460.00

Lamp, 11" d, 5-1/2" h, 27" to top of harp, inverted funnel shape, floral, gilt, scrolled handles 165.00

Plate

8-3/8"" d, shell shape, gilt rim, enameled floral dec, c1889, four with restored rim chips, three with rim chips, price for 15 pc set 345.00

Plate, cattle dec, sgd "o," 10" d, $1,540. Photo courtesy of Jackson's Auctioneers & Appraisers.

9" d, fruit dec, gilt border on cobalt blue ground, sgd "Albert Shuck," pattern no. W8346, printed marks, c1928, price for 18 pc set 8,100.00
Potpourri Vase, cov, 14-1/2" h, wicker basketweave molded bodies, raised enamel and gilt dec water lilies, pierced borders, printed mark, c1883, finials restored, price for pr
. . . . 920.00
Salad Bowl
6-3/4" w, square-form, leaf molded, scalloped edge, pierced gallery, enamel and gilt dec floral sprays with butterflies, printed mark, c1884 . . . . 230.00
9" d, lobed body, gilt accented polychrome floral dec, printed mark, c1890, int. gilt wear 290.00
9-1/4" d, molded foliate body, enamel floral sprays, gilt trim, printed marks, c1892 . . . . 345.00
Tray, 14-1/2" d, Royal Lily pattern, gilt trim, printed and imp mark, c1878 . . . . 190.00
Urn, 12-1/2" h, painted reserve of two ravens, moonlit landscape, gild trim, c1875-80, lines, chips 175.00
Vase
3-1/2" h, sq, white and gold frog and trim 325.00
4-3/4" h, Japanese style, ivory, ranch form handles, reticulated border above modeled landscape, gilt trim, printed mark, c1886, rim chip restored, price for pr 490.00
5-1/2" h, 6" d, sack shape, applied rope, gold trim, c1886
. . . . 185.00
5-5/8" h, elephant, gilt trimmed body, printed mark, late 19th C 750.00
7-1/4" h, floral relief, enamel and gilt dec, printed mark, c1887
. . . . 635.00
9" h, ivory ground, polychrome floral dec, gilt trim . . . 175.00
9-3/4" h, pink and yellow roses, artist sgd "Jarman"
. . . . 695.00
14-3/4" h, cov, yellow ground, polychrome floral dec, gilt trim, printed mark, c1893, finial repair, gilt wear 690.00
16-3/4" h, gilt and enamel dec, bird perched on branch, moonlit sky, pierced handles and rim, retailed by Bigelow, Kennard & Co., Boston 920.00

ROYCROFT

History: Elbert Hubbard founded the Roycrofters in East Aurora, New York, at the turn of the century. Considered a genius in his day, he was an author, lecturer, manufacturer, salesman, and philosopher.

Hubbard established a campus which included a printing plant where he published The Philistine, *The Fra*, and *The Roycrofter*. His most-famous book was *A Message to Garcia*, published in 1899. His "community" also included a furniture manufacturing plant, a metal shop, and a leather shop.

References: Kevin McConnell, *Roycroft Art Metal*, 2nd ed., Schiffer Publishing, 1994; The Roycrofters, *Roycroft Furniture Catalog, 1906*, Dover, 1994; Paul Royka, *Mission Furniture ,from the American Arts & Crafts Movement,* Schiffer Publishing, 1997; Marie Via and Marjorie B. Searl, *Head, Heart and Hand*, University of Rochester Press (34 Administration Bldg, University of Rochester, Rochester, NY 14627), 1994.

Collectors' Clubs: Foundation for the Study of Arts & Crafts Movement, Roycroft Campus, 31 S. Grove St., East Aurora, NY 14052; Roycrofters-at-Large Assoc., P.O. Box 417, East Aurora, NY 14052.

Museum: Elbert Hubbard Library-Museum, East Aurora, NY.

Additional Listings: Arts and Crafts Movement; Copper.

SPECIAL AUCTIONS

Cincinnati Art Galleries
635 Main St.
Cincinnati, OH 45202
(513) 381-2128

David Rago Auctions, Inc.
333 North Main St.
Lambertville, NJ 08530
(609) 397-9374

Treadway Gallery, Inc.
2029 Madison Rd.
Cincinnati, OH 45208
(513) 321-6742

Ashtray, 8" d, hammered copper, cleaned patina 90.00
Bell, 3" h, hammered copper, orig patina, imp mark 300.00
Bench, 71" w, 17 d, 32" h, from Roycroft Inn, East Aurora, NY, c1912, one of two designed for peristyle, two horizontal back slats, seat with five slats, lower stretcher, keyed tenon construction, orig finish, orb mark, initialed with East Aurora Fish & Game Club Roycroft Inn inventory number 1,600.00
Book
Abe Lincoln and Nancy Hanks, unusual binding, 5-1/2" w, 8-1/2" h 50.00
Little Journeys, volumes one through fourteen, set
. . . . 100.00
The Book of Business, leather bound 100.00
The Dog of Flanders, leather bound 120.00
The Ebert Hubbard Scrapbook, leather bound 100.00

The Notebook of Ebert Hubbard, leather bound 115.00
The Philosophy of Ebert Hubbard, leather bound . . . 110.00
Bookends, pr
    4-1/4" h, 5" w, hammered copper, rectangular, emb with medallion of four-leaf clover against verdigris patinated sq, orig dark patina, orb and cross mark 400.00
    5" h, hammered copper, riveted straps with rings, orig patina 450.00
    5" h, hammered copper, three-legged form, platform base, orig patina, imp mark 280.00
    5" h, 5-1/2" w, hammered copper, poppy dec, orig patina, orb and cross mark 950.00
    5-1/2" w, 5-1/2" h, leather, tooled design, imp marks, minor scuffs 800.00
    6" h, 3-1/2" w, hammered copper, open hemispheres, covered in brass wash, orb and cross mark with ROYCROFT 325.00
Booklet, *The Roycroft Inn,* Aurora, NY 110.00
Book Stand, *Little Journeys,* rect top, two shelves with vertical slats, double keyed tenons, shoefoot, orig finish, metal orb tab, 26"w, 14" d, 26" h 600.00
Bowl
    6" w, 3" h, hammered copper, closed form, orig patina, imp mark 475.00
    10" d, 4" h, hammered copper, three feet, imp mark, worn orig patina 550.00
Box, 7" w, 2" h, hammered copper, stylized floral design on front, orig patina, imp mark 1,500.00
Calendar, 7-1/2" w x 3" h, hammered copper, lightly cleaned patina 100.00
Calling Card Tray, 6-1/4" l, hammered copper, blue patina, emb stylized flowers 100.00
Candleholders, pr, 20-1/2" l, hammered copper, eight candle holders, arranged on hammered length with curled ends, brass wash, orb and cross mark 1,400.00

Candlestand, 10-1/2" w, hammered copper, holds three handles, orig patina, imp mark 210.00
Candlesticks, pr
    9-1/2" h, hammered copper, orig patina 600.00
    9-3/4" h, hammered copper, cylindrical shafts, orig dark patina, orb and cross mark 750.00
Chair
    Arm, sq posts, paddle arms, orig tacked-on Japan leather seat cushion, orig finish, wear t seat, carved "Roycroft," 29-1/2" w, 25" d, 38" h 2,500.00
    Dining, 17" w, 16-1/2" d, 43-1/2" h, highback, newly upholstered seats, Mackmurdo feet, refinished, carved orb and cross mark, set of six 5,000.00
    Morris Chair, 37" w, 40" d, 44" h, four vertical slats under paddle arms, orig velvet covered loose back and seat cushions, orig ebonized finish, color added to arms, replaced back root bar, carved "Roycroft" 8,000.00
    Side, 17" w, 17" d, 36" h, bird's eye maple, two horizontal back slats, Mackmurdo feet, refinished, orb mark under seat rail 1,300.00
Chamberstick, 5-1/2" h, hammered copper and spun brass, orig patina, imp mark 110.00
Child's Chest of Drawers, 26" w, 11" d, 34" h, oak, three drawers, mirror, designed for Elbert Hubbard's granddaughter, carved orb and cross mark, letter of provenance 13,000.00
Console Set, 9" d bowl, brass-washed hammered copper, two handled bowl, pr of candlesticks, orig patina, orb and cross mark 550.00
Desk, #059, single drawer above kneehole opening, flanked by two drawers, orig copper hardware, orig finish, orb mark, 54" w, 30" d, 29" h 5,500.00
Doughboy Hat, 3" d, copper, brass wash, orb and cross mark 375.00
Dressing Table, 39" w, 18" d, 58" h, bird's eye maple, single drawer, orig copper pulls, swivel mirror, Mackmurdo feet, refinished 5,500.00
Foot Stool, 17" w, 12" d, 15" h, mahogany, drop-in cushion, refinished, orb mark 425.00
Goodie Box, 26" w, 9" h, mahogany and hammered latch, trim, and handles, orb signature, slightly worn orig finish, minor split to top 700.00
Inkwell
    2-1/2" h, hammered copper, orig patina 220.00
    3-1/2" h, 15" l, hammered copper pen tray, pair of glass inkwells on each end, orig patina, orb and cross mark 600.00
Lamp, table
    16-1/2" h, 14-1/2" d leaded glass shade, opaque light green and purple glass segments, hammered base, designed by Karl Kipp, Secessionist style, orig dark patina, orb and cross mark 9,000.00
    23" h, 12" h textured acid-etched surface, Steuben Pomona green vasiform lamp shaft mounted to hammered copper platform base, orig finial, cap imp with Roycroft orb, sockets and central shaft replaced 1,100.00
Letter Opener, 10" l, hammered copper, saber shape, orig patina, orb and cross mark 80.00
Plate, 10" d, hammered copper, emb trefoils against verdigris panels, some pitting to patina, orb and cross mark . . 300.00
Poker Chip Holder, 6-1/2" h, 4-1/2" d, hammered copper, orig patina, imp mark 375.00
Sideboard, 60" l, 25" d, 55" h, oak, mirrored back, three small drawers between leaded glass cabinet doors over long linen drawer, orig finish, craved orb and cross mark, crack to one glass pane 28,600.00

Sideboard, mirrored back, two leaded glass cabinet doors flanking 3 drawers over linen drawer, orig hardware, mint orig finish, carved orb and cross mark, $28,600. Photo courtesy of David Rago Auctions, Inc.

Table
#073, circular top, wide apron, cross stretcher base, orig finish, orb signature, 35" d, 30" h 3,000.00
#079, library, rect top, single stretcher, mousehole cut-out and double keyed tenons, orig finish, orb signature, 60" w, 33" d, 30" h 5,500.00
Tabouret, 11-1/4" sq, 18-3/4" h, flaring legs, sq overhanging top, orig ebonized finish, carved "Roycroft" on apron . . .2,600.00
Tray
5-1/2" d, hammered copper, circular, imp geometric pattern, old cleaned patina, orb and cross mark, craftsman's mark, attributed to Walter Jennings 550.00
17" w, 15" d, hammered copper, octagonal, two handles, cleaned patina, orb mark 350.00
Vase, hammered copper
4-1/2" h, tapering ovoid, orig patina, imp mark. 400.00
4-3/4" h, 2-1/4" d, covered in brass wash, stylized quatrefoils, verdigris band, orb and cross mark, minor wear to patina
. . . . 400.00
7" h, 2-1/2" d, cylindrical, etched stylized quatrefoils, orig dark patina, orb and cross mark 3,700.00
10-1/2" h, shaft, riveted base, spotted orig patina . .1,800.00
12" h, 6" d, American Beauty, new patina, orb and cross mark
. . . . .1,600.00
18-1/2" h, American Beauty, orig patina, imp mark
. . . . .5,000.00
21" h, American Beauty, orig patina, imp mark 3,000.00
Wastebasket, 14" sq, slatted, orig ebonized finish, carved orb and crown mark 2,100.00

RUBENA GLASS

History: Rubena crystal is a transparent blown glass which shades from clear to red. It also is found as the background for frosted and overshot glass. It was made in the late 1800s by several glass companies, including Northwood and Hobbs, Brockunier & Co. of Wheeling, West Virginia.

Rubena was used for several patterns of pattern glass including Royal Ivy and Royal Oak.

Basket, 3-1/2"x 5-1/2", threaded dec, clear applied twisted handle. 125.00
Carafe, Aurora. 150.00
Celery Vase, Inverted Thumbprint, ruffled rim 85.00

Pitcher, enameled apple blossom motif, 7-1/2" h, $495.

Compote, 8-1/4" d, Honeycomb, low standard 75.00
Creamer, Medallion Sprig, clear applied handle 165.00
Cruet, Royal Ivy, orig stopper 465.00
Finger Bowl, matching underplate. 85.00
Lamp Shade, 3-7/8" h, applied ribbed petals, opalescent rim, chips at base, one petal glued 50.00
Peg Lamp, 15-1/4" h, 5-1/8" d, fluted top, frosted rubena center shades to cranberry, flowers and scrolls patterning, frosted rubena font with flowers dec, brass candlestick base
. . . . 325.00
Pickle Castor, Royal Oak, frosted insert, orig tongs 395.00
Rose Bowl, 6" d, Hobnail. 230.00
Sugar Bowl, cov, Royal Oak, frosted 155.00
Sugar Shaker, Royal Oak 325.00
Table Set, Royal Oak, frosted. 425.00
Vase, 6" h, bud, enameled floral dec, diamond band 75.00
Water Set, acid etched storks, Hobbs, price for 7 pc set
. . . . 700.00

RUBENA VERDE GLASS

History: Rubena Verde, a transparent glass that shades from red in the upper section to yellow-green in the lower, was made by Hobbs, Brockunier & Co., Wheeling, West Virginia, in the late 1880s. It often is found in the Inverted Thumbprint (IVT) pattern, called "Polka Dot" by Hobbs.

Bowl, 9-1/2" d, IVT, ruffled 175.00
Butter Dish, cov, Daisy and Button 250.00
Celery Vase, 6-1/4" h, IVT. 225.00
Cruet, IVT, orig stopper. 225.00
Creamer and Sugar Bowl, cov, Hobnail, bulbous, applied handle
. . . . 550.00
Finger Bowl, IVT 95.00
Jack In The Pulpit Vase, 8" h 250.00
Pickle Castor, Hobb's Hobnail, SP frame, cov, and tongs
. . . . 500.00
Salt and Pepper Shakers, pr, IVT 210.00
Tumbler, IVT 125.00
Vase, 9-1/4" h, paneled body, enameled daises dec 85.00
Water Pitcher, Hobb's Hobnail 395.00

RUSSIAN ITEMS

History: During the late 19th and early 20th centuries, craftsmen skilled in lacquer, silver, and enamel wares worked in Russia. During the Czarist era (1880-1917), Fabergé, known for his exquisite enamel pieces, led a group of master craftsmen who were located primarily in Moscow. Fabergé also had an establishment in St. Petersburg and enjoyed the patronage of the Russian Imperial family and royalty and nobility throughout Europe.

В РАТЬЕВЪ
Baterin's factory
1812-1820

КорНИЛОВЫХЪ
Korniloff's factory
c1835

Almost all enameling was done on silver. Pieces are signed by the artist and the government assayer.

The Russian Revolution in 1917 brought an abrupt end to the century of Russian craftsmanship. The modern Soviet government has exported some inferior enamel and lacquer work, usually lacking in artistic merit. Modern pieces are not collectible.

References: Vladimir Guliayev, *Fine Art of Russian Lacquered Miniatures*, Chronicle Books, 1993; P. Hare, *The*

Art & Artists of Russia, Methuen & Co., 1965; L. Nikiforova, compiler, *Russian Porcelain in the Hermitage Collection,* Aurora Art Publications, 1973; Marvin Ross, *Russian Porcelains,* University of Oklahoma Press, 1968; A. Kenneth Snowman, *Fabergé,* Harry N. Abrams, 1993; Ian Wardropper, et. al., *Soviet Porcelain,* The Art Institute of Chicago, 1992.

Museums: Cleveland Museum of Art, Cleveland, OH; Forbes Magazine Collection, New York, NY; Hermitage, Leningrade, Russia; Hillwood, The Marjorie Merriweather Post Collection, Washington, DC; Russian Museum, Leningrad, Russia; Virginia Museum of Fine Arts, Lillian Thomas Pratt Collection, Richmond, VA; Walters Art Gallery, Baltimore, MD.

SPECIAL AUCTION

Jackson's Auctioneers & Appraisers
2229 Lincoln St.
Cedar Falls, IA 50613
(319) 277-2256
email: jacksons@corenet.net

Bronze

Angel, 3-1/4" x 1-3/4", cast bronze, 16th C 400.00
Encolpion Cross, 3-3/4" x 2-1/4", cast bronze, 16th C
. . . . 750.00
Sculpture, 6-1/4" h, 7" l, Resting Peasant, detailed, pensive expression, inscribed "Possen" Worffel found mark, dark brown patina 1,850.00

Enamel

Bowl, each handle realistically chased bear's head, set with jeweled eyes, sides with multicolored enamel floral dec, moss green base, silver-gilt, base hallmarked "Moscow," 1899-1907, Cyrillic makers mark "F. R." for Fyodor Rückert
. . . . .9,500.00
Box, cov, low, silver, round
   2" d, hinged lid, five colors of enamel, indistinguishable makers mark, Moscow, c1900 . . . . 400.00
   2-1/2" d, hinged lid, five colors of enamel, St. Petersburg, Cyrillic makers mark "D. O." 575.00
Cigarette Box, 4" x 3", foliage, birds, and butterflies, gold washed stippled ground, gold washed int. with Russian inscription, dated 1899, 5 troy oz 1,265.00
Coronation Cup, 4" h, enameled, gilt and transfer dec, Imperial double headed eagle and Cypher of Tsar Nicholas II above date 1896 . . . . .1,840.00
Kovsh, 3" h, 8-1/2" l, 5" w, blue, red, white, and gold flowers, gold wash to silver areas, int. bowl with enamel circle, base hallmarked "T K" with "84", touch mark under handle . .3,300.00
Match Box Cover, enamel on gold gilt silver, 2-3/8" x 1-1/8" x 1-3/16", I. S. Lebdkin, Moscow Assayers mark
   Illegible maker's mark, mkd with .875 and star and letter "M," 84 standard mark, assayer's initials, some enamel missing
. . . . 300.00
   Maker's mark for V. Agafonov, mkd with 84 silver standard
. . . . 375.00
Miniature Cup, 2-1/8" h, enameled gold, reticulated and ftd, champleve stylized floral dec, painted with military and musical motifs in oval reserves, minor losses 2,300.00

(Enamel) Bowl, silver-gilt and enamel, by Imperial Russian silver maker Fyodor Ruckert, 8", $9,500. Photo courtesy of Jackson's Auctioneers & Appraisers.

Napkin Ring, silver, bright enamels, c1908, hallmarked "84," Cyrillic makers mark "D. O.," set of 12 . . . . .1,840.00
Sugar Container, 5-1/2" h, water bucket form, gilt metal, multicolored enamel dec, 19th C 200.00
Sugar Scoop
   4-1/4" l, five colors of enamel, silver-gilt, twisted handle, hallmarked "Moscow," makers mark of Gustav Klingert
. . . . 690.00
   5-1/2" l, silver-gilt and plique-a-jour enamel, scratched inventory no. 520.00

Icon

5-3/4" x 4-3/4", St. George, 19th C, cast bronze, enamel St. George at center slaying dragon, Deisis on top margin, borders with selected saints 550.00
7" x 7-3/4", The Unburnt Thornbush Mother of God, c1900, finely painted, gold leaf ground, faux enamel borders 520.00
7" x 8-3/4", St. Nicholas, c1900, detailed image, gold leaf background, faux enamel borders 575.00
9" x 10-3/4", The Kursk Sign Mother of God, c1842, Old Testament figures such as King David, King Solomon, Moses, Daniel, Elijak and others all surrounding central image, overlaid with fine silver repousse and chased riza, attached halo and porcelain title plaques, riza hallmarked "84" and dated 1842 with Cyrillic makers' mark "P. N." for Pavel Nikitin
. . . . .3,220.00
10-1/2" x 12", The Lord Almighty, c1900, Christ delivers blessing with right hand, while left hand holds open Gospels to John 13:34, overlaid with very fine silver engraved riza and champleve enamel Gospel text and title plaque, attached halo with 8 colors of cloisonné enamel, hallmarked "84, Moscow," Cyrillic makers mark "D. G." (Dimitriy Gorbonov) . . .3,165.00
10-1/2" x 12-1/4", John The Forerunner As Angel Of The Wilderness, c1900, 16th C revivalist style, John depicted with wings, holds salver with his decapitated head, scroll in hand with text from John 1:29, Holy Napkin at top 1,500.00
10-1/2" x 12-1/4", The Image Not Made By Hands, 19th C, so-called first icon, Christ's face seen as was miraculously transferred onto cloth or napkin, finely executed, gold leaf ground, entire image overlaid with finely crafted silver-gilt, repousse, and chases riza, attached halo, hallmarked "84 Moscow," dated 1864, Cyrillic makers mark "I. G." 3,165.00

10-1/2" x 12-1/4", The Sign Mother of God, 18th C, overlaid with cloth riza heavily embellished with profusion of faux gemstones, beads, and mother of pearl, later silvered metal riza with attached halo covers entire panel 1,495.00

10-1/2" x 12-1/2", The Removal from The Cross, 18th C, top with Joseph of Arimathea and Nicodemus removing Christ's body from cross, Mary present with other women, below Christ, clad in loin cloth, is placed on shroud and laid on stone of anointing, fragmented inscription reads "The Removal from the Cross of the Lord God and Savior of Us Jesus Christ," scattered restorations. 990.00

10-3/4" x 12-1/2", Kazan Mother of God, 18th C, double raised border (kovcheg), silver-gilt riza starts a flat piece of silver, gemstone dec riza, hallmarked Moscow and dated 1781, Cyrillic stamp "Ya. F." (Ya. Frolov) 6,440.00

10-3/4" x 12-1/2", St. Seraphim of Sarov, c1903, finely executed with each hair individually painted, entire image overlaid with silver-gilt repousse and chased riza, applied multicolored enamel corner plaques, multicolored enamel halo, hallmarked "84, Moscow," Cyrillic makers mark "S. E." (Semion Yegornov), title at bottom identifies subject as "The Holy Starets Seraphim" 4,890.00

11" x 12-3/4", Svyenskaya-Percherskaya Mother of God, 18th C, shows Mother of God seated with Christ in her lap, Saints Antoniy and Feodosiy stand beside her holding scrolls, overlaid with later very fine silver repousse and chased riza, attached halo, embellished with river pearls, riza hallmarked "84" city mark of Kirov, Cyrillic makers' mark "L. G." 3,450.00

11" x 13-1/2", St. Demetrius & St. George, 19t C, two warrior saints, Demetrius dressed as warrior and rides charger, below he strikes lance into King of Infidels, who is crowned and seated on fallen horse, angel descends from heaven with crown of victory for saint, above him in church Slavonic inscription "Svatuiy Mouchenik Dimitriy Solunski" (the Holy Martyr Demetriy of Thessalonika), right side with St. George as mounted soldier who strikes with lance at dragon beneath his horse, young princess Elisaba looking on at right, Christ delivers message from above, overlaid with heavy silver-gilt metal repousse riza 3,740.00

11" x 14", The Dormition, c1890, Abramstervo School, Christ at center in mandrola receives soul of his mother in form of an infant, 12 Apostles gather around her, reverse inscribed in Cyrillic script "Abramtsrvo August 15, 1890," borders overlaid with silver engraved riza, hallmarked "84, Moscow," makers mark of Imperial silver smith Ivan Gubkin 1,725.00

11-1/4" x 14", The Tikhvin Mother of God, 19th C, well painted, image overlaid with finely crafted silver-gilt repousse riza, attached silver-gilt halo, halo with city mark of Nizhniy Novgorod, stamped "84" and dated 1825, traditional style plaiting, fine gold highlights on garments of Christ and Mary 2,025.00

11-1/2" x 13", Smolensk Mother of God, 17th C, double kovcheg panel, attributed to Yaroslavi-Kostroma region, overlaid with fine detailed gilt-metal riza, halo dec with angles and seraphim 4,890.00

12" x 14-1/4", Joy To All Who Suffer, 19th C, crowned Mother of God stands at center, infant Christ on her left arm, scepter in right hand, suffering humans gathered on both sides, angels among them, open scrolls with petition of the people, inscription below her is kotakion "O All-Hymed Mother," additional row of stains added, God delivers blessing from above, entire image overlaid with elaborate gilt metal repousse and chased riza 1,995.00

12-1/4" x 10-1/2", The Kazan Mother of God, c1893, 20 individual pieces of gold plated silver decorated with 7 colors of enamel and faux gemstones, finely crafted silver-gilt riza cover, from workshop of Nicholay Vasilevich Alexeyev, Moscow 6,440.00

13-1/2" x 11-1/4", The Resurrection, c1800, Christ standing on fallen gates of Hades, reaches down to grasp hand of Adam, Eve kneels at right, other old Testament Prophets and Patriarchs seen in background preparing to walk forth from bondage, overlaid with fine silvered metal repousse riza 1,495.00

13-3/4" x 11-3/4", scenes from life of Christ, 19th C, losses 320.00

Porcelain

Tea set, hand dec, teapot, coffeepot, and cream pitcher, attributed to Gardner Factory, minor war to gilding, hairline in creamer 300.00

Silver

Baptismal Cross
    2" l, scrolls dec, inscription with applied beads, replaced chain, 18th C 175.00
    2-1/4" x 1-3/4", 18th C 490.00
Beaker, 3-1/2" h, 3" w, gilt and niello, hallmarked "B. C. 1865 BC," Moscow assayers' mark for Viktor Savinkov, attributed to Vasiliy Semenov. 375.00
Cigarette Case
    3-1/2" l, niello and silver, indistinguishable makers mark, c1900 . . . . 350.00
    4-1/4" l, lid with 2 swans, makers mark of Aleksandr Ivanovich Peskarev, Moscow, c1908 . . . . 435.00
    4-1/2" l, lid with peasant plowing, cabochon thumbpiece, markers mark of Ivan Krutykov, Moscow 460.00
Cup and Saucer, finely engraved country cottage scene, makers mark of Peter Baskakov, Moscow, c1890 . . . . 400.00
Goblet, 6 5/8" h, Art Nouveau style, gilt int., maker's marks "NC," Moscow hallmarks, c1890 . . . . 125.00
Priestal Cross, 4-1/4" x 2-1/4", corpus in relief, reverse inscribed with Cypher of Nicholas II, hallmarked "84, Moscow" and dated 1896, Cyrillic makers initials "V. Z.," suspension loop mission. 260.00
Purse, evening type, 2 3/4 x 2 1/4", Russian, hinged lid engraved in Cyrillic "In Remembrance," chain, hallmarked "84, Moscow," Nikolai Alexsev maker 145.00
2 3/4" x 2 1/4", Russian, hinged lid engraved in Cyrillic "In Remembrance," chain, hallmarked "84, Moscow," Nikolai Alexsev maker 145.00
Snuff Box, 3-1/4" l, niello, hinged lid with Peter the Great, side with Russian cottages, back with scene of St. Petersburg, hallmarked "84 Moscow," dated 1932, makers mark of Fedor Maximov. 350.00
Spoon, 5-1/2" l, niello, hallmarks "H.A.," and "A. K.," set of three 125.00
Vodka Cup, 2-1/2" h, bright cut floral dec, fleur-de-lis rim band, mkd "CK," set of six 300.00

Wood

Samovar, brass and wood
    13" h 390.00
    14" h 300.00
Viola, two piece plain back, ribs and scroll similar, medium to wide grain, red-brown varnish, 16-11/16" l back, with case, Cyrillic label, 1988 . . . . 690.00

SABINO GLASS

History: Sabino glass, named for its creator Ernest Marius Sabino, originated in France in the 1920s and is an art glass which was produced in a wide range of decorative styles: frosted, clear, opalescent, and colored. Both blown and pressed moldings were used. Hand-sculpted wooden molds that were cast in iron were used and are still in use at the present time.

In 1960, the company introduced fiery opalescent Art Deco-style pieces, including a line of one- to eight-inch high figurines. Gold was added to a batch of glass to obtain the fiery glow. These are the Sabino pieces most commonly found today.

Marks: Sabino is marked with the name in the mold, as an etched signature, or both.

Ashtray
Butterfly	85.00
Swallow, large	50.00
Thistle	45.00
Berry Bowl	50.00
Bird	75.00
Box, Petalia	95.00
Butterfly, 2-3/4" l	45.00
Elephant	75.00
Hen, 3-5/8" h	40.00
Poodle	30.00
Scent Bottle, Pineapple, 5" h	175.00
Shell	60.00
Snail, 3"	75.00
Sparrow, small	50.00
Squirrel	85.00
Statue, nude woman, long flowing hair, 6-1/2" h	150.00

Vase

6" h, flared trumpet shape, molded squares alternately raised and frosted, golden amber, int. raised mark "Sabino France" 275.00

11" h, 7" w, six lobes, Art Deco geometrics, royal blue, satin finish, polished highlights, sgd 600.00

SALOPIAN WARE   C S SALOPIAN

History: Salopian ware was made at Caughley Pot Works, Salop, Shropshire, England, in the 18th century by Thomas Turner. At one time the product was classified "Polychrome Transfer" because of the method of decoration, but the ware is better known by the more popular name "Salopian." Much of the output was sold through Turner's Salopian warehouse in London.

Marks: Pieces are impressed or painted under the glaze with an "S" or the word "Salopian."

Bowl

9-1/4" d, 4" h, pearlware, blue and white Oriental dec, "S" mark, wear and slightly yellowed rim repair 165.00

11" d, Bird on Branch pattern, blue and white 415.00

Can, 5-3/4" h, transfer dec, foliate devices and reserves of archers, 19th C, hairlines, minor transfer wear 90.00

Creamer and Sugar, man and woman having tea in garden, black and white transfer 450.00

Cup and Saucer, handleless, girl with sheep, small rim chip 385.00

Cup Plate, 4-1/2" d, Deer pattern, polychrome dec 450.00

Mug, 4" h, Bird on Branch pattern 250.00

Pitcher, figures in garden, polychrome dec 220.00

Plate

7-1/2" d, Oriental design 360.00

7-3/4" d, polychromed Creil scene of man, woman, and child, hut and church in background, black transfer with applied yellow, blue, red, and blue-green highlights 45.00

8-1/4" d, harvest scene, polychrome dec 300.00

8-1/2" d, Double Deer, green, yellow, black, and white 225.00

8-3/4" d, octagonal, Oriental scene, blue and white . . 195.00

Saucer, pearlware, deep

Birds, 5-1/2" d 100.00

Birds and animal views, set of three 225.00

Country cottage views, set of four 275.00

Floral dec, restored 50.00

People views, set of three 250.00

Teapot, 4" x 8-1/4", boy carrying lamb, blue and white 495.00

Turkey, molded mark, 2" l, 2-1/4" h, $45.

Teapot, blue transfer of boy carrying lamb, c1790, 8-1/4" l, 4" h, $495.

SALT and PEPPER SHAKERS

History: Collecting salt and pepper shakers, whether late 19th-century glass forms or the contemporary figural and souvenir types, is becoming more and more popular. The supply and variety is practically unlimited; the price for most sets is within the budget of cost-conscious collectors. In addition, their size offers an opportunity to display a large collection in a relatively small space.

Specialty collections can be by type, form, or maker. Great glass artisans, such as Joseph Locke and Nicholas Kopp, designed salt and pepper shakers in the normal course of their work.

References: Gideon Bosker and Lena Lencer, *Salt and Pepper Shakers*, Avon Books, 1994; Larry Carey and Sylvia Tompkins, *1002 Salt and Pepper Shakers*, Schiffer Publishing, 1995; ——, *Salt and Pepper*, Schiffer Publishing, 1994; Melva Davern, *Collector's Encyclopedia of Salt & Pepper Shakers*, 1st Series (1985, 1991 value update), 2nd Series (1990, 1995 value update), Collector Books; Helene Guarnaccia, *Salt & Pepper Shakers*, Vol. I (1985, 1996 value update), Vol. II (1989, 1993 value update), Vol. III (1991, 1995 value update), Vol. IV (1993, 1997 value update), Collector Books; Mildred and Ralph Lechner, *World of Salt Shakers*, 2nd ed., Collector Books, 1992, 1996 value update; Arthur G. Peterson, *Glass Salt Shakers*, Wallace-Homestead, 1970, out of print; Mike Schneider, *Complete Salt and Pepper Shaker Book*, Schiffer Publishing, 1993; Irene Thornburg, *Collecting Salt and Pepper Shakers,* Schiffer, 1998.

Collectors' Clubs: Antique and Art Glass Salt Shaker Collectors Society, 2832 Rapidan Trail, Maitland, FL 32751; Novelty Salt & Pepper Shakers Club, P.O. Box 3617, Lantana, FL 33465.

Museum: Judith Basin Museum, Stanford, MT.

Additional Listings: See *Warman's Americana & Collectibles* for more examples.

Notes: The colored sets, in both transparent and opaque glass, command the highest prices; crystal and white sets the lowest. Although some shakers, e.g., the tomato or fig, have a special patented top and need it to retain their value, it generally is not detrimental to replace the top of a shaker.

The figural and souvenir types are often looked down upon by collectors. Sentiment and whimsy are prime collecting motivations. The large variety and current low prices indicate a potential for long-term price growth.

Generally, older shakers are priced by the piece; figural and souvenir types by the set. Pricing methods are indicated in the listings. All shakers included below are assumed to have original tops unless otherwise noted. Reference numbers are from Arthur Goodwin Peterson's *Glass Salt Shakers*. Peterson made a beginning; there are hundreds, perhaps thousands, of patterns still to be cataloged.

.Prices below are for individual shakers unless otherwise noted.

Art Glass (priced individually)

Cased
    Bulging Petal, pink, pr 45.00
    Flower Band pink 30.00
    Palm Leaf, pink 48.00
    Pineapple, pink 55.00
Mount Washington
    Egg, flat end 85.00
    Tomato, 5 lobe 85.00
Peachblow, Wheeling, orig top 325.00
Pigeon Blood, Periwinkle variant 110.00
Rubena, enamel dec, pewter top 195.00
Spatter, vaseline and cranberry spatter, Leaf Mold, orig top
    . . . . 85.00

China (priced by set)

Bartender, 3 condiment barrels on base 50.00
Black Bears, Rosemead 60.00
Bendel Bugs, green 60.00
Chickens, 3, egg cup base 40.00
Dutch Children and Dutch Shoe 40.00
Old McDonald, boy and girl, Regal China 75.00

Figural and sets (priced by set)

Billiken, white, opaque and crystal, gilt, Buddha shape, inscription on base "The God of things as they ought to be," patent 1908, tin top 75.00
Dogs, cast metal, 3' h, green paint, amber glass eyes, pr 85.00
Metal Frame, tapered panels, pr, marked "C. F. Monroe" 205.00

Opalescent (priced individually)

Argonaut Shell, blue 60.00
Beatty Rib, white, no top 25.00
Fluted Scrolls, canary, orig top 65.00
Reverse Swirl, white, orig top 45.00
Windows Swirl, cranberry 110.00

Opaque (priced individually)

Bird, blue, handle 95.00
Bulging Petal, green, pr 45.00
Ear of Corn, jade green opaque 55.00

Opaque white ground, yellow and orange flowers, green leaves, St. Paul in gold letters, egg shape, orig tops, 2" h, pr, $215.

Forget Me Not, rose opaque, Challinor 110.00
Guttate, green 30.00
Inverted Fan and Feather, pink slag 795.00
Melonette, blue, pr 45.00
Rib & Swirl, blue 45.00
Square Scroll, pink 25.00

Pattern Glass (priced individually)

Acorn, pink, orig top 45.00
Banded Portland, maiden's blush 35.00
Feather 20.00
Fish
    Blue 65.00
    Pink and white 95.00
Klondike, amberette, pr 225.00
Nestor, amethyst, dec 55.00
Nevada 30.00
Red Block 60.00
Thousand Eye, vaseline 40.00
Wheat and Barley, blue 35.00
Whirligig, orig tin top 35.00

SALT-GLAZED WARES

History: Salt-glazed wares have a distinctive pitted surface texture made by throwing salt into the hot kiln during the final firing process. The salt vapors produce sodium oxide and hydrochloric acid, which react on the glaze.

Many Staffordshire potters produced large quantities of this type of ware during the 18th and 19th centuries. A relatively small amount was produced in the United States. Salt-glazed wares still are made today.

References: Susan and Al Bagdade, *Warman's English & Continental Pottery & Porcelain*, 3rd Edition, Krause Publications, 1998; Arnold R. Mountford, *The Illustrated Guide to Staffordshire Salt-Glazed Stoneware*, Barrie & Jenkins, 1971; Louis T. Stanley, *Collecting Staffordshire Pottery*, Doubleday & Co., 1963.

Syrup, celadon hue, classical dec, pewter lid, 7" h, $150.

Museums: American Antiquarian Society, Worcester, MA; City Museum, Stoke-On-Trent, England; British Museum, London, England, Colonial Williamsburg Foundation, Williamsburg, VA; Fitzwilliam Museum, Cambridge, England; Museum of Art, Rhode Island School of Design, Providence, RI; Victoria & Albert Museum, London, England; William Rockhill Nelson Gallery of Art, Kansas City, MO.

Bowl, Oriental translation, green frog-skin glaze, 1930s. 165.00
Cracker Jar, ovoid, two loop handles, orange peel effect on lid
    and shoulder, Ben Owen 1,210.00
Noggins, set of eight, green frog-skin glaze 165.00
Plate, 9-5/8" d, enamel dec 4,315.00
Pitcher, green frog-skin glaze, 1930s 80.00
Sauce Boat, ftd, Staffordshire, cobalt blue highlights . . . 550.00
Storage Jar, two handles, sgd "E. S. Craven," c1850 . .1,265.00
Storage Jug
    Ballard sgd "W. W. Ballard," one handle 600.00
    Hayes, James Madison, one handle, fly ash melting area
    . . . . .1,045.00
    Kirkpatrick, Cornwall, 18-1/2" h, 1886 Union County Fair, imp dozens of names and crosshatching highlighted in cobalt blue, greenish ash glaze on shoulders running in trails from neck to midway down one side, sgd "Cornwall Kirkpatrick," date and place of birth, Anna, IL, 9" fire burn on one side
    . . . . .17,000.00
    Moffitt, sgd "M. R. Moffitt," one wide handle, fly ash melting area, late 1800s 1,210.00
Teapot, cov, enamel dec 980.00
Vase, green frog-skin glaze, four handles, Oriental translation, 1920s 825.00

SALTS, OPEN

History: When salt was first mined, the supply was limited and expensive. The necessity for a receptacle in which to serve the salt resulted in the first open salt, a crude, hand-carved, wooden trencher.

As time passed, salt receptacles were refined in style and materials. In the 1500s, both master and individual salts existed. By the 1700s, firms such as Meissen, Waterford, and Wedgwood were making glass, china, and porcelain salts. Leading glass manufacturers in the 1800s included Libbey, Mount Washington, New England, Smith Bros., Vallerysthal, Wave Crest, and Webb. Many outstanding silversmiths in England, France, and Germany also produced this form.

Open salts were the only means of serving salt until the appearance of the shaker in the late 1800s. The ease of procuring salt from a shaker greatly reduced the use of and need for the open salts.

References: William Heacock and Patricia Johnson, *5,000 Open Salts*, Richardson Printing Corporation, 1982, 1986 value update; Allan B. and Helen B. Smith have authored and published ten books on open salts beginning with *One Thousand Individual Open Salts Illustrated* (1972) and ending with *1,334 Open Salts Illustrated: The Tenth Book* (1984). Daniel Snyder did the master salt sections in volumes 8 and 9. In 1987, Mimi Rudnick compiled a revised price list for the ten Smith Books; Kenneth Wilson, *American Glass 1760-1930*, 2 Vols., Hudson Hills Press and The Toledo Museum of Art, 1994.

Periodical: *Salty Comments*, 401 Nottingham Rd., Newark, DE 19711.

Collectors' Clubs: New England Society of Open Salt Collectors, P.O. Box 177, Sudbury, MA 01776; Open Salt Collectors of the Atlantic Region, 56 Northview Dr., Lancaster, PA 17601.

Note: The numbers in parenthesis refer to plate numbers in the Smiths' books.

Condiment sets with open salts

Porcelain, light pink with gold trim, leaf shaped holder, mkd "Made in Bavaria" (388) 130.00
Silver Plated, 3 pcs, emb pattern around bowls, Oriental (481)
. . . . 65.00

Individuals

Agate, carved hardstone, orange, slight pedestal. 120.00
Basket, metal frame, cobalt blue liner, pierced ribbon handles, mkd "E. P. N. S." (413) 40.00
Belleek, ruffled rim, hp roses, gold trim, Lenox palette mark
. . . . 60.00
Cameo Glass, Webb, red ground, white lacy dec around bowl, sgd, matching spoon 650.00
Copper, heavy, pedestal base, deep maroon enamel (414)
. . . . 35.00
Cut Glass
    Round, alternating zippered and starred panels (361)
    . . . . 30.00
        Triangular, Star and Diamond, sgd "Hawkes" (466). . . 35.00
Dresden Saxony, lily dec on one side (434) 55.00
Heisey, octagonal paneled bowl, sloping octagonal base, H in diamond mark (475) 40.00
Meissen, double salts, floral dec int. and ext., crossed swords and crown mark (460) 85.00
Opaline, blue, boat shape, white garland and scroll enamel dec
. . . . 90.00
Peking Glass, orange-red cut back to white 170.00
Pewter, floral shape, mkd "A E Channal" 35.00
Steuben, Aurene, calcite, gold, pedestal base 290.00
Vallerystahl, turquoise milk glass, double, sgd "Vallerystahl, Made in France" (460) 50.00

Figurals

Cupid driving reindeer pulling sleigh, SS, mkd "Made in Germany" (352). 420.00
Donkey, painted, pulling colorful painted cart (458) 35.00
Flower, 2" w, 3-1/4" l, 3" h, petal top, green swirl glass insert, SP leaf border 135.00
Lafayette Boat, deep cobalt blue, emb "Lafayet [sic] Sandwich, B & S Glass Co.," c1830, several chips 750.00

Masters

Belleek, shell shape (314). 45.00
Cranberry Glass
    2-3/4" d, 1-3/4" h, applied colorless and vaseline shell trim, SP standard. 140.00
    3" d, 2-1/4" h, fluted top, colorless wafer foot. 80.00
Cut Glass, Diamond pattern on top of bowl, ribbed base (404)
. . . . 50.00
Glass, lacy
    Neal, EE2, colorless, 3" l, chips 125.00
    Neal JY2b, medium green, 3" l, chips 200.00
    Neal, LE1, colorless, 3-1/4" l 150.00

Master, lacy glass, green, chips, $200

Neal LE3, deep blue, one foot glued, 3-1/8" l 220.00
Neal Og 7, New England Glass Co, colorless, chip on inside of base 85.00
Neal OP4, green, 3-5/8" l 400.00
Neal SL1a, amber, 31/8" l, corner crack. 150.00
Leeds China, boat shape, pedestal base (313) 70.00
Mercury Glass, 2-3/4" d, 2-1/4" h, vintage etching, pedestal base, gold int. 90.00
Minton, ftd, #57957 (314) 50.00
Pewter, pedestal base, cobalt blue liner (349) 80.00
Pressed Glass
    Eyewinker, pedestal base (346) 85.00
    Hamilton, pedestal base (344) 45.00
    Hobnail pattern, round (407) 35.00
    Palmette pattern (471) 60.00
    Paneled Diamond, pedestal base (331) 50.00
    Square Pillared pattern (341) 30.00
    Vintage pattern (340) 40.00
Silver, 2" h, repousse and chased body, urn form, handles, French hallmarks, late 18th C 115.00

SAMPLERS

History: Samplers served many purposes. For a young child, they were a practice exercise and permanent reminder of stitches and patterns. For a young woman, they were a means to demonstrate skills in a "gentle" art and a way to record family genealogy. For the mature woman they were a useful occupation and method of creating gifts or remembrances, e.g., mourning pieces.

Schools for young ladies of the early 19th century prided themselves on the needlework skills they taught. The Westtown School in Chester County, Pennsylvania, and the Young Ladies Seminary in Bethlehem, Pennsylvania, were two institutions. These schools changed their teaching as styles changed. Berlin work was introduced by the mid-19th century.

Examples of samplers date back to the 1700s. The earliest ones were long and narrow, usually done only with the alphabet and numerals. Later examples were square. At the end of the 19th century, the shape tended to be rectangular.

The same motifs were used throughout the country. The name of the person who stitched the piece is a key factor in determining the region.

References: Ethel Stanwood Bolton and Eva Johnston Coe, *American Samplers*, Dover, 1987; Glee Krueger,

Gallery of American Samplers, Bonanza Books, 1984; Betty Ring, *American Needlework Treasures*, E. P. Dutton, 1987; Anne Sebba, *Samplers*, Thames and Hudson, 1979.

Museums: Cooper-Hewitt Museum, National Museum of Design, New York, NY; Smithsonian Institution, Washington, DC.

Note: Samplers are assumed to be on linen unless otherwise indicated.

1741, "Margaret MacLeroy her work aged 10 year 1741," attributed to Philadelphia, upper panel of alphabets and vases of flowers, various foliate and animal motifs, lower panel of pious verse, scenic panel of Adam and Eve, birds in trees, other animals, figural, and foliate devices, geometric floral border, 17-3/8" x 9-5/8", framed, toning, minor fading
. . . . .8,100.00

1769, "Mary Harvey October 11, 1769," geometric floral border, 7-1/2" x 7", framed, toning, minor fading 575.00

1776, "Rebeckah RSS Tainton 1776," various alphabets and numbers, toning, fading minor losses and holes, 12" x 8-3/4", framed 450.00

1786, Mary Greenleaf born in July the 16 1786, Newbury or Newburyport area, MA, upper panel of alphabets and pious verse above lower panel with vase of flowering vines flanked by parrots and various fruit, foliate, and animal motifs, geometric floral border, 21-1/8" h, 16-1/4" w, unframed, toning, fading, minor staining 10,925.00

1791, "By VROE...Anno 1791," Netherlands, central design of yellow building with blue roof surrounded by various fruit, foliate, animal, and human motifs, foliate border, unframed, fading, toning, together with letter from Betty Ring attesting to origin. 1,150.00

1794, "Lucy Deweys sampler wrought in the eleventh year of her age 1794," upper panel with flowering vine with box, lower panel with potted flowering plant flanked by foliate devices,

1839, Catherine Dickerman, aged 12 years, under the instructions of Miss Beda Dickerman, three sets of alphabets, numeral band, flower, and tree, four different borders, framed, $650.

flowering fine border, unfinished, unframed, 15-1/2" h, 17" w
. . . . .2,100.00

1796, "Havervill Auguft 29 Betsey Gage Plummer Born AD 1782 this wrought in the 14 year of her age...," MA, upper panel of alphabets and pious verse above lower panel of scrolling grape vines, birds, and other foliate devices, checkered basket, flowering vine border, 19-3/8" h, 15-3/4" w, framed, toning, fading, tack holes, very minor staining 10,925.00

180..., "Francis Smith Aged 10 A.D. 180...," upper panel of alphabets and pious verse, lower panel of various animals and flowering trees, plants, geometric floral border, 16-1/4" h, 14-1/8" w, framed, toning, fading, very minor losses . 575.00

1809, family register, Beverly, MA, area, "Amaziah Phillips born Jan 15 1785 Lucy Bates born Aug 14 1789 Married Sept 10 1809," upper panel with genealogical info, lower panel with pious verse, cottage flanked by fencing, trees, and potted plants, foliate border, vibrant colors, unframed, minor toning, very minor staining, 25" x 17". 4,600.00

1814
"Jane Porter her work July 28 1814 Aged 13 year," upper panel of alphabet and pious verses above lower panel of shepherd and his flock, flanked by Adam and Eve and the Crucifixion and various foliate and animal devices, geometric floral borer, staining, toning, minor fading, 16-3/8" x 15-3/8", framed 575.00

"Martha James Aged 11 1814," upper panel of pious verse, lower panel of architectural, animal and floral motifs, geometric floral border, 16" x 12-3/4", framed, losses, fading, minor toning 520.00

182..., "Martha A. Grahams Work Done in her 11th year 182...," upper panel of alphabets and pious verse, lower panel of flowering plants and animals, geometric floral border, unfinished, 18-5/8" h, 16-1/4" w, framed, minor losses, fading
. . . . 850.00

1820, "Paulina F. Freeman, Aged 9 Years August 31, 1820," upper panel of alphabets and pious verse, lower panel of swags of ribbon-tied flowers, geometric floral borer, 16-5/8" h, 17-1/8" w, toning, fading. 1,495.00

1824, "Elizabeth Downess work Aged 12 1824," upper panel of alphabets and pious verse, lower panel of figural foliate and animal motifs, Greek key border, 12-3/4" h, 12-3/4" w, framed, minor repairs, toning 700.00

1828, family register, "Lucy Banta Aged Eighteen years Oct 26th 1828," upper panel of genealogical info flanked by panels of flowering plants, floral and scrolling vine and fan border, 16" h, 14-1/2" w, toned, scattered staining, laid down . . . 950.00

1823, family register, "Dorcas B. Gragin New Ipswich Sept 11th 1823," (New Hampshire), upper panel of alphabets and foliate devices, lower panel of genealogical record surrounded by flowering vine border, geometric floral border, unfinished, toning, faded, scattered minor staining, framed, reverse inscribed "Sampler purchased at the 'Lawrence Girls' auction Spring '62, Ashby, Mass...the Gragins were ancestors of the three Lawrence spinsters..." 500.00

1825, "Jane Oliver 1825 aged 13 years" England, upper panel of pious verse surrounded by foliate and butterfly, lower panel of bird and foliate devices, floral border, 19-1/8" h, 12-7/8" w, framed, toning, fading, minor staining 550.00

1828, "Wrought by Fanny M. Eager 1828," upper panel of genealogical info and alphabets, lower panel with pious verse flanked by flowering plants, basket of fruit, geometric floral border, 16-1/2 h, 17' w, framed, toning, fading. 575.00

1830, "Maria W. Baldwin, Shrewsbury 1830," alphabet rows, 9" x 13", framed, toning, fading, minor losses 400.00

1833
"Ann Shaw Aged 12 Years 1833," silk on linen, alphabets, flowering border, horse, flowers, chairs, verse and name,

brown, green, black, and white, 13-1/4" h, 13-5/8" w, framed, stains 525.00

"Johana McCarthy Middlepice finished this 8 day of March 1833," central design of basket of flowers, birds, and other foliate devices, foliate border, 26-5/8" h, 27-5/8" w, toning, minor repairs, scattered fiber wear 1,850.00

"Juliaette Ballad Sampler Carmel Aged 11 years 1833," upper panel of alphabets and pious verse, lower panel with various architectural, bird, fruit, and foliate motifs, geometric floral border, 18" x 18", framed, toning, scattered staining, minor fading 1,840.00

1836, "Worked in the Town of Cordon by Catherine Farquar, March the 31st, 1836," silk on loosely woven homespun linen, blue, white, brown, and faded green alphabets, attributed to Indiana, minor stains, modern frame, 25" h, 20-14" w 550.00

1837

"Emma Nunns Aged July 18, 1837," alphabet variations, 7-7/8" h, 12-1/2" w, framed 400.00

"Margaret Craigs Sampler done in the 10th year of her age 1837," upper panel with basket of fruit flanked by various human, foliate, animal, and angelic motifs, middle panel with basket of flowers flanked by pious verse, lower panel with neoclassical memorial flanked by human, animal, and foliate motifs, foliate border, edges glued down, toning, minor staining, 22" x 20-1/2" l, framed 1,200.00

1854, "Elizabeth Wheel Finished this work 1854," upper panel of alphabet and pious verse, lower panel of animal, foliate, and architectural motifs, geometric floral border, 20-1/4" h, 15-3/8" w, framed, toning, minor staining, minor holes, insect damage 460.00

Unknown Date

"Easter Ellen Rudd," upper panel of various foliate and animal devices, lower panel with two story house, picket fence, surrounded by various foliage devices, geometric floral border, 18" x 16-1/2", toning, minor staining from tacks, unframed 950.00

"Elizabeth Saunders Aged 10," upper panel of alphabets, lower panel with architectural views, foliate, and animal motifs, geometric floral border, 15-1/4" X 17-1/2", framed, toning, scattered staining, fading 1,725.00

"Harriet French A37 at Miss Hammonds School Boston," upper panel of alphabets and pious verse, lower panel of geometric devices and flowering plants, geometric floral border, 11-7/8" h, 11-3/8" w, framed, toning, scattered staining 1,150.00

"Mary Jowett Work," attributed to PA, c1830, upper panel of fruit and foliate devices, pious verse, Adam and Eve above lower panel of two-story brick house flanked by trees, various animals, 25" h, 24" w, framed, toning, minor losses, scattered staining 2,645.00

"Sarah Justin," 19th C, upper panel with vase of flowers flanked by birds among foliage, middle panel Chinoiserie reserve, lower panel of foliate device flanked by two landscape reserves, 16-1/4" x 17-1/2", tacked down, heavy toning, framed 300.00

SANDWICH GLASS

History: In 1818, Deming Jarves was listed in the Boston Directory as a glass factor. That same year, he was appointed general manager of the newly formed New England Glass Company. In 1824, Jarves toured the glassmaking factories in Pittsburgh, left New England Glass Company, and founded a glass factory in Sandwich.

Originally called the Sandwich Manufacturing Company, it was incorporated in April 1826 as the Boston & Sandwich Glass Company. From 1826 to 1858, Jarves served as general manager. The Boston & Sandwich Glass Company produced a wide variety of wares in differing levels of quality. The factory used the free-blown, blown three mold, and pressed glass manufacturing techniques. Both clear and colored glass were used.

Competition in the American glass industry in the mid-1850s resulted in lower-quality products. Jarves left the Boston & Sandwich company in 1858, founded the Cape Cod Glass Company, and tried to duplicate the high quality of the earlier glass. Meanwhile, at the Boston & Sandwich Glass Company emphasis was placed on mass production. The development of a lime glass (non-flint) led to lower costs for pressed glass. Some free-blown and blown-and-molded pieces, mostly in color, were made. Most of this Victorian-era glass was enameled, painted, or acid etched.

By the 1880s, the Boston & Sandwich Glass Company was operating at a loss. Labor difficulties finally resulted in the closing of the factory on Jan. 1, 1888.

References: Raymond E. Barlow and Joan E. Kaiser, *Glass Industry in Sandwich*, Vol. 1 (1993), Vol. 2 (1989), Vol. 3 (1987), and Vol. 4 (1983), distributed by Schiffer Publishing; ——, *Price Guide for the Glass Industry in Sandwich Vols. 1-4*, Schiffer Publishing, 1993; Ruth Webb Lee, *Sandwich Glass Handbook*, Charles E. Tuttle, 1966; ——, *Sandwich Glass*, Charles E. Tuttle, 1966; George S. and Helen McKearin, *American Glass*, Random House, 1979; Ellen T. Schroy, *Warman's Glass*, 3rd ed., Wallace-Homestead, 1995; Catherine M. V. Thuro, *Oil Lamps II*, Collector Books, 1994 value update; Kenneth Wilson, *American Glass 1760-1930*, 2 Vols., Hudson Hills Press and The Toledo Museum of Art, 1994.

Museum: Sandwich Glass Museum, Sandwich, MA.

Additional Listings: Blown Three Mold; Cup Plates.

Bell, opal, pink ground, autumn leaves dec 165.00
Bowl
    6-1/2" d, Peacock Eye, lacy, slightly clambroth, RWL pate 115. . . . . 175.00
    7-1/4" d, Oak Leaf, lacy, colorless 45.00
    7-1/2" d, Tulip and Acanthus, lacy, colorless 45.00
Candlestick, 9" h, columnar, opaque, powdery purple-blue, rough sandy finish 450.00
Celery Vase, 7" h, 4" w, Hobnail, peachblow, satin finish, pale creamy white shading to rose pink, 11 rows of pointed hobnails 475.00
Compote
    6-1/8" d, 7 1 /2" h, cov, Lincoln Drape, colorless 250.00
    7-1/4" d, Plume, lacy, colorless 175.00
Dish, ftd, 10-5/8" l, 6" h, Princess Feather, medallion and basket of flowers, canary, leaf foot, 1840-45, base of foot ground, base chips, small rim chips, annealing mark 20,700.00
Egg Cup, Horn of Plenty, flint, price for pr. 95.00
Goblet, colorless
    Bull's Eye and Fleur-De-Lis 95.00
    Comet. 90.00
Lamp, Astral, 33" h, wheel cut and acid etched shade with Gothic arches, overlay cut red to white standard, gilt and poly-

Toilet Bottle, colorless, c1820, 5-1/4" h, $70.

chrome foliate and scroll devices, scrolling gilt brass base, electrified, one prism missing, gilt wear, very minor chips to shade, provenance indicates lamp was owned by Deming Jarvis, then George McKearin who sold it to Ruth Webb Lee 3,450.00

Lamp, whale oil
   8-1/2" h, opaque starch blue, shading to bright sapphire blue, small star and punty font attached to wafer to hexagonal stem and base, orig brass collar, c1840 . . . . . . .3,300.00
   9" h, cut faceted glass, missing burners, price for pr 300.00
   9-3/4" h, peacock green, pressed, short loop patterned fonts attached by wafer to octagonal bulbous stem, sq base, orig pewter collar and double burners, c1830, price for matched pr 8,250.00
   10" h
      Blackberry pattern, colorless font, white base. . . . 145.00
      Loop pattern, cobalt blue, some chips. 200.00
Miniature, tureen, cov, 3" l, cobalt blue, lacy. 415.00
Pitcher, 6-3/4" h, 7-1/2" w, 3-1/4" w across top, bulbous, sq top, peachblow, applied frosted handle, ten rows of hobnails 550.00
Relish Dish, 6-1/4" l, Sandwich Star, colorless 65.00
Salt
   Boat, blue opaque 1,450.00
   Crown, 2-1/8" h, 3-1/8" l, fiery opalescent, c1830-50, chips 260.00
   Gothic Arch and Heart, master, 3-7/8" l, fiery blue opalescent 300.00
   Hexagonal, ftd, peacock blue. 250.00
   Shell, pedestal base, lacy, colorless 125.00
Sauce Dish, lacy
   Peacock Eye, 4-1/4" d, sapphire blue, rim chips 175.00
   Sword and Cross, 4-1/2" d, sapphire blue, rim chips 185.00
Spill Holder, Sandwich Star, opaque white. 300.00
Spoon Holder, Loop, colorless 125.00
Sugar, cov, Acanthus Leaf and Shield, lacy, colorless . . 350.00
Vase
   9-1/2" h, Bull's Eye and Diamond Point, colorless . . . 175.00
   9-7/8" h, Tulip, pressed, dark amethyst, octagonal base, Barlow3021b, minute base chips, rim roughness 1,035.00
   10" h, Tulip, pressed, light amethyst, octagonal base, Barlow 3021b, minute rim chips, pr 1,850.00

Whiskey Taster
   Flute, canary. 175.00
   Lacy, colorless 195.00

SARREGUEMINES CHINA

SARREGUEMINES

History: Sarreguemines ware is a faience porcelain, i.e., tin-glazed earthenware. The factory which made it was established in Lorraine, France, in 1770, under the supervision of Utzschneider and Fabry. The factory was regarded as one of the three most prominent manufacturers of French faience. Most of the wares found today were made in the 19th century.

Marks: Later wares are impressed "Sarreguemines" and "Germany" as a result of changes in international boundaries.

Animal Covered Dish, 5-1/4" l, hen and chicks, polychrome dec 175.00
Asparagus, 9" l, majolica, naturalistic colors. 90.00
Box, cov, heart shape, floral dec, ormolu mount, c1760 . . . . 150.00
Character Jug, 7-1/2" h, Scotsman, red hair, blue and red hat 95.00
Creamer, 5" h, ducks and frogs, flower border 75.00
Ewer, 10" h, tan, gold butterflies and flowers 85.00
Luncheon Set, majolica, cov strawberry dish, sq basket, 6 different fruit plates. 650.00
Oyster Plate, price for 4 pc set 200.00
Plate
   7-3/4" d, NY World's Fair, 1939 . . . . 45.00
   8-1/2" d, majolica, strawberries and floral trim, aqua ground 85.00
Tea Service, florals, ornate shapes, c1840, price for 14 pc set 625.00
Tobacco Jar, cov, relief masks, brown, yellow trim. 95.00

Lamp, crystalline glaze, tan, imp mark, 21-1/2" h, $190.

Toby Pitcher, 8-1/4" h, toothy grin, polychrome dec, marked "Sarreguemines, Made in Germany," stains and crazing
.... 45.00

Vase
8-1/2" h, majolica, gargoyles and lizards 150.00
17" h, incised lilies, intricate design of leaves and stems in yellow, brown ground, imp marks, minor flakes at top
.... 250.00

SARSAPARILLA BOTTLES

History: Sarsaparilla refers to the fragrant roots of a number of tropical American, spiny, woody vines of the lily family. An extract was obtained from these dried roots and used for medicinal purposes. The first containers, which date from the 1840s, were stoneware; glass bottles were used later.

Carbonated water often was added to sarsaparilla to make a soft drink or to make consuming it more pleasurable. For this reason, sarsaparilla and soda became synonymous even though they originally were two different concoctions.

References: Ralph and Terry Kovel, *Kovels' Bottles Price List*, 10th ed., Crown Publishers, 1996; Carlo and Dot Sellari, *Standard Old Bottle Price Guide*, Collector Books, 1989.

Periodical: *Antique Bottle and Glass Collector*, P.O. Box 187, East Greenville, PA 18041.

Additional Listings: See *Warman's Americana & Collectibles* for a list of soda bottles.

Brown's Sarsaparilla, aqua 12.00
Dalton's Sarsaparilla and Nerve Tonic, blue label 40.00
Dr. Beldings Wild Cherry Sarsaparilla, Dr. Belding Medicine Co., Minneapolis, MN, aqua, complete label, orig contents, orig fancy box (top missing), 9-1/4" h 180.00
Dr. Guysott's Compound Extract of Yellow Dock and Sarsaparilla, peacock green, sloping lip, iron pontil, 9" h 1,350.00
Dr. Townsend's Sarsaparilla, olive green, pontil 85.00
Lancaster Glassworks, barrel, golden amber 125.00
Sand's Genuine, rect, aqua 95.00
Sawyers Eclipse, aqua 35.00
Wetherell's, aqua 45.00

SATIN GLASS

History: Satin glass, produced in the late 19th century, is an opaque art glass with a velvety matte (satin) finish achieved through treatment with hydrofluoric acid. A large majority of the pieces were cased or had a white lining.

While working at the Phoenix Glass Company, Beaver, Pennsylvania, Joseph Webb perfected mother-of-pearl (MOP) satin glass in 1885. Similar to plain satin glass in respect to casing, MOP satin glass has a distinctive surface finish and an integral or indented design, the most well known being diamond quilted (DQ).

The most common colors are yellow, rose, or blue. Rainbow coloring is considered choice.

Additional Listings: Cruets; Fairy Lamps; Miniature Lamps; Rose Bowls.

REPRODUCTION ALERT

Satin glass, in both the plain and mother-of-pearl varieties, has been widely reproduced.

Bowl, 10-1/4" d, 4-5/8" h, pink and white loops, ruffled rim, gold and yellow encrusted floral dec 470.00
Bride's Bowl, 9-1/2" d, MOP, blue, moiré pattern, SP holder with strawberries and leaves applied to handle, marked "Simpson, Hall, Miller Co.". 375.00
Candlesticks, pr, 8-3/4" h, yellow, brown roses, dark painted rims and bases 170.00
Dresser Jar, cov, 3-1/2" h, yellow, gold flowers, red leaves
.... 185.00

Ewer
8-1/2" h, pink herringbone, mother of pearl, frilly spout, applied fancy thorn handle 385.00
11-3/4" h, 4-1/2" d, shaded heavenly blue, melon sections, white lining, applied frosted handles, peach color flowers and lacy foliage dec, price for pr 485.00
Jam Dish, 6-3/4" h, 5" d, shaded pink, white lining, frosted shell trim applied around top, dark color berries, leaves, and bird dec, SP holder 175.00
Lamp, 19-3/4" h, peg, pale pink shading to deep pink, ribbed base, matching ribbed shades with ruffled rims, orig brass burners, brass base, price for pr 990.00
Miniature Lamp, 9-3/4" h, 3-1/2" d, soft green and blue, enameled purple and white flowers, gold leaves, pedestal
.... 285.00
Mug, 3-1/2" h, pink and gold looping, white ground, applied frosted reeded handle 175.00
Mustard, cov, 4-1/8" h, melon ribs, yellow shaded to pale pink, SP fittings, sterling spoon with enameled bowl 170.00
Nappy, 6" l, triangular shaped top, applied frosted handle, MOP, white, all over gold dec, deeply crimped edge 425.00
Perfume Bottle, 5-1/2" l, teardrop shape, lay down type, mother of pearl shaded blue, DQ, Webb 575.00
Pickle Castor, Heart Arches pattern insert, white, enameled rose color apple blossoms and green leaves, silverplated frame
.... 395.00
Pitcher, 5-1/2" h, scalloped top, gold shaded to white, applied frosted handle, sgd "Webb" 265.00
Plate, 7" d, shaded rose to lighter pink, Drape MOP, marked "Patent" in glossy letters on base 200.00
Rose Bowl
4-1/2" d, bright yellow shading to white, enameled berries, leaves, and stems 150.00
5-1/2" d, 5" h, bright green shading to pale green, enameled blue, pale yellow, and gold floral dec 300.00
Salad Set, 8" d x4-1/2" d bowl, shaded gold ribbon MOP bowl, silver plated top rim, matching silver plated salad fork and spoon, gold ribbon MOP glass handles 900.00
Sweetmeat jar, 6 h, 5" d, shaded blue, DQ, MOP, white lining, white enameled flowers, brown leaves, SP top 565.00
Tumbler
3-1/4" h, pink herringbone, MOP 55.00
3-1/2" h, vertical rainbow bands of vivid pink, blue, and yellow, DQ, MOP, floral dec, applied enamel branch of 3 white and pink singled petal blossoms, partially opened buds, four leaves, stylized stems, gold highlights and rim 885.00
Vase
5-1/2" h, rainbow bands of yellow, blue, white, and mahogany, encrusted gold band at ruffled rim 360.00

Lamp Shade, Tartan pattern, octagonal, pinched base, rippled edge, 8-1/2" d, 4" d fitter ring, $685.

6-1/2" h, 3-3/4" d, shaded heavenly blue, swirl, ruffled, MOP, melon sections, ormolu bases, price for pr 435.00

6-3/4" h, Federzeichnung, pearl satin, brown, undulating air trap dec, marked, Rd 76057 . . . . 1,350.00

6-3/4" h, 3-1/2" d, shaded blue herringbone, MOP, white lining, lavender dot flowers, thin gold leaves 235.00

7-1/4" h, 4" w at shoulder, Rainbow MOP, pink, yellow, blue, and white, DQ pattern, flaring top, broad shouldered, tapered body, glossy white int., sgd "Patent" 1,250.00

8-1/2" h, 7" w, bulbous, MOP, Muslin pattern, Alice Blue, all-over color, Mt. Washington 425.00

9-3/4" h, 5" d, shaded heavenly blue, herringbone, MOP, rect closely ruffled top, white lining, frosted applied thorny handles, three applied frosted feet, price for pr 775.00

10-1/2" h, 5-1/2" w, Heavenly blue shading to pale blue, creamy white lining, English. 265.00

SATSUMA

History: Satsuma, named for a war lord who brought skilled Korean potters to Japan in the early 1600s, is a handcrafted Japanese faience (tin-glazed) pottery. It is finely crackled, has a cream, yellow-cream, or gray-cream color, and is decorated with raised enamels in floral, geometric, and figural motifs.

Figural satsuma was made specifically for export in the 19th century. Later satsuma, referred to as satsuma-style ware, is a Japanese porcelain also hand decorated in raised enamels. From 1912 to the present, satsuma-style ware has been mass-produced. Much of the ware on today's market is of this later period.

Reference: Nancy N. Schiffer, *Imari, Satsuma, and Other Japanese Export Ceramics,* Schiffer Publishing, 1997.

Belt, 36" l, twelve 1-1/2" Satsuma buttons, figures, butterflies, dragons, flowers, two 1-3/4" buttons of dragons at ends
. . . . 300.00

Biscuit Jar, cov, 6-1/2"x 6", orange, bamboo type handles, diaper border. 125.00

Box, 4" d, round, tripartite feet, two panels painted as hanging scrolls, one with plants and flowers, the other with people in

garden, remaining surface cov in gold dec on cobalt blue ground, sgd "Kinkozan," orig label 1,265.00

Bowl

7-1/4" d, int. with textile and teapot-shaped reserves enclosing people and flowers, brocade ground, ext. of milliefleur with lucky objects, sgd, 19th C 1,725.00

11-3/4" d, shallow. 300.00

Brush Pot, water plants dec, Kinkozan 125.00

Button, round

Black border, large gold dots, two detailed multicolored flowers in center, green leaves, heavy gold beading, some glaze crackling 22.00

Black ground, Oriental woman's face, gold border, large gold dots 38.00

Cobalt blue ground, blue rim, small gold dots, complex multicolored floral center 28.00

Charger, 12-7/8" d, red and black flowers and birds, white ground, gold trim 125.00

Creamer and Sugar, cov, floral pattern. 350.00

Cup and Saucer, flowers and butterflies, c1900 . . . . 50.00

Dish, 9-7/8" h, Kannon, arhats and dragon, int. dec, scalloped, gilt ground, c1900. . . . . 275.00

Incense Burner, 4" h, ovoid, three arrow form molded flower-head reserves, cream glaze, tripod feet, reticulated cov, Meiji period 175.00

Jar, cov, 5" h, prunus branch with bird, diaper border neck band and handles 250.00

Koro, 17-1/2" h, earthenware covered, blue field, birds and flowers dec, green foo dog handles to lid and sides, three green foo dog feet, 18th/19th C 425.00

Miniature

Box, 1-1/4" h, drum-shape, cov dec with court scene of eight people, body with landscape of flowering cherry blossoms, sgd "Yabu Meizan" in gold, gold ground 1,725.00

Vases, pr, mountain, river, foliage, and peasant scene, orig velvet lined case, Meji period (1867-1912), 4-3/4" h, $700

Teapot, 3-3/4" h, diamond shaped, four reserves of figures in garden settings, blue ground with gold flowers, cracked ice pattern, sgd "Kinkozan" in gold on back cartouche, orig paper label 690.00

Wine Pot, 3-1/2" h, top and spout dec with brocade fans, body with two medallions with leisure scenes, bottom with gold inscription on back ground "Ryozan made this" 1,610.00

Plate, 9" d, mother and children in garden, flowers and butterflies border, Japanese 300.00

Tea Bowl, 5" d, 33/4" d, high sides, int. dec with hexagons, dragonflies, and butterflies surrounding central medallion of children flying kite, brocade borders, ext. with four medallions of court scenes, brocade ground, landscape around base, two-character Fuzan mark, Meiji period 1,955.00

Tea Caddy, cov, 5-1/2" d, blooming prunus tree, bird, brocade ground, handles 195.00

Tea Set, teapot, creamer, cov sugar, two cups and saucers, pottery, fitted box, Japanese 600.00

Tile, 3-3/4" x 5-1/2", women and children crossing bridge to crowded country inn, polychrome and gilt dec 325.00

Urn, 14" h, Geisha girl scene, bird handle, Awata Satsuma, c1920, price for pr 275.00

Vase

4-1/2" h, baluster, high shoulder, two medallions of girls, birds, and flowers, deep cobalt blue ground, borders sprinkled with gold cherry blossoms, sgd "Kinkozan," Meiji period 920.00

9-1/2" h, long neck, divided round base, three legs, two reserves, one with warriors, other with women and children, cobalt blue ground, bordered with brocade patterns, gold scattered flowers and leaves 1,610.00

10" h, 5-1/4" w, enameled brocade design, one panel with people, large tree, houses, mountains, and lake, other panel with large naturalistic pink, yellow, orchid, and blue mums, pink geraniums, cherry blossoms, 2 brown and beige birds, shaded green leaves, borders of bamboo, flowers, and fan shapes with crests and geometric shapes, rubbed off gilt signature 3,800.00

12-1/2" h, moriage dec, flowers and butterflies, gilt highlights, sgd with kanji characters, late 19th/early 20th C, pr 175.00

15" h, cobalt blue, hp feathers, outlined raised gold, beads, c1915 . . . . 125.00

17-1/2" h, fan-shaped medallions of study room set of tea and poetry competition, ornate banquet scene, brocade green ground, sgd and sealed "Kinkozan," 19th C 2,875.00

SCALES

History: Prior to 1900, the simple balance scale was commonly used for measuring weights. Since then scales have become more sophisticated in design and more accurate. There are a wide variety of styles and types, including beam, platform, postal, and pharmaceutical.

Collectors' Club: International Society of Antique Scale Collectors, 300 W. Adams St., Suite 821, Chicago, IL 60606.

Apothecary, 9" h, 19-1/2" l, 6" d, oak base, window in side to show balance, marble top, matching brass weighing bowls 250.00

Balance, 33-3/4" h, cast iron and brass, Birmingham label, English 275.00

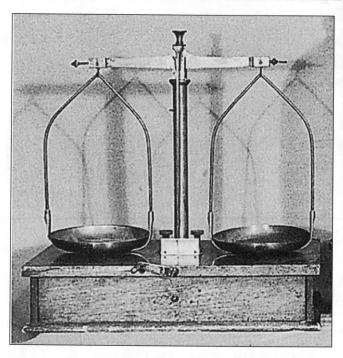

Balance, H. Kohlbusch, NY, brass column, brackets and pans, wood base with drawer, old Kohlbusch label in drawer, 20-1/2" x 20-1/4" x 10-1/2", $165. Photo courtesy of Garth's Auctions, Inc.

Candy

Anderson Computing Scale Co, 2 lb 300.00

Enterprise Manufacturing Co, Phila, PA, tin scoop, brass slide 145.00

National, decal, restored 350.00

Computing, 31" h, 19" w, 18" d, painted, top plate reads "The Computing Scale Co./Dayton, Ohio, U.S.A." 400.00

Country Store, 14" h, cast iron, large hopper, some orig paint and stenciling 150.00

Egg, 8-1/2" x 6-1/2" x 3", aluminum weight indicator, brass head screw, red weighing arm 50.00

Feed, red and white checked top, blue and cream bottom, metal pan, "Purina Feed Saver and Cow Culler" adv 80.00

Home, 8" h, cast iron, porcelain dial printed backwards, when side is angled down it exposes mirror to read scale, 0 to 270 lbs 300.00

Pharmacy, oak case, beveled glass and marble top, 1800s 300.00

Postal, Hanson Bros. Scale Co., c1925 . . . . 45.00

SCHLEGELMILCH PORCELAINS

GERMANY
c 1910-1956

Poland China
R.S.
Made in (German) Poland
c 1945-1956

R S
TILLOWITZ
Silesia
c1920-1930s

History: Erdmann Schlegelmilch founded his porcelain factory in Suhl in the Thuringia region in 1861. Reinhold, his brother, established a porcelain factory at Tillowitz in Upper Silesia in 1869. In the 1860s Prussia controlled Thuringia and Upper Silesia, both rich in the natural ingredients needed for porcelain.

By the late 19th century, an active export business was conducted with the United States and Canada due to a large supply of porcelain at reasonable costs achieved through industrialization and cheap labor.

The Suhl factory ceased production in 1920, unable to recover from the effects of World War I. The Tillowitz plant, located in an area of changing international boundaries, finally came under Polish socialist government control in 1956.

Marks: Both brothers marked their pieces with the "RSP" mark, a designation honoring Rudolph Schlegelmilch, their father. More than 30 mark variations have been discovered.

REPRODUCTION ALERT

Dorothy Hammond in her 1979 book *Confusing Collectibles* illustrated an R. S. Prussia decal which was available from a china-decorating supply company for $14 a sheet. This was the first of several fake R. S. Prussia reproduction marks that have caused confusion among collectors. Acquaint yourself with some of the subtle distinctions between fake and authentic marks as described in the following.

The period mark consists of a wreath that is open at the top. A five-pointed star sits in the opening. An "R" and an "S" flank a wreath twig in the center. The word "Prussia" is located beneath. In the period mark, the leg of the letter "P" extends down past the letter "r." In the reproduction mark, it does not. In the period mark, the letter "i" is dotted. It is dotted in some fake marks but not in others.

The "R" and the "S" in the period mark are in a serif face and are uniform in width. One fake mark uses a lettering style that utilizes a thin/thick letter body. The period mark has a period after the word "Prussia." Some fake marks fail to include it. Several fake marks do not include the word "Prussia" at all.

The period mark has a fine center line within each leaf of the wreath. Several fake marks do not.

References: Susan and Al Bagdade, *Warman's English & Continental Pottery & Porcelain*, 3rd Edition, Krause Publications, 1998; R. H. Capers, *Capers' Notes on the Marks of Prussia*, Alphabet Printing (667 E. 6th St., El Paso, IL 61738), 1996; Mary Frank Gaston, *Collector's Encyclopedia of R. S. Prussia and Other R. S. and E. S. Porcelain*, 1st Series (1982, 1993 value update), 2nd Series (1986, 1994 value update), 3rd Series (1994), 4th Series (1997), Collector Books; Leland and Carol Marple, *R. S. Prussia: The Early Years,* Schiffer Publishing, 1997.

Collectors' Club: International Association of R. S. Prussia Collectors Inc., 212 Wooded Falls Rd, Louisville, KY 40243.

E. S. Germany

Bowl, 14" l, oval, large re roses, orange shaded rose sprays, gold tracery, scalloped, mkd "E. S. Germany Prov. Saxe" 125.00

Candy Dish, 7-1/4" d, lobed body, white camellias, green leaves, gold sponged rim and handle, red "E. S. Germany Prov. Saxe" mark 20.00

Chocolate Pot, Napoleon portrait, mkd "E. S. Prov Saxe" 375.00

Demitasse Cup, Napoleon and Recamier, portrait, mkd "E. S. Prov Saxe" 135.00

Dish, basket type, ruffled edge, Josephine and Hortense portraits, mkd "E. S. Prov Saxe" 175.00

Portrait Plate, 10-1/2" d, Madame DuBarry in center, luster burgundy border, four cartouches of women 400.00

Urn, 6-3/4" h, 3 feet, two Victorian women with cupid, gold beading, cobalt blue ground 195.00

Vase, 9-1/2" h, Lady with Swallows, turquoise and gold beading, white ground 475.00

R. S. Germany

Basket

Peafowls and Asian pheasants 150.00

Scallop & Fan, 5 x 3" 225.00

Bun Tray, 13" d, Medieval house scene, lake with sailboat, mountains 600.00

Cake Plate, 10" w, cottage scene, woods, maiden, and two yoked oxen 235.00

Celery Tray, 10-1/2" l, 5" w, pink flowers, green ground . . 65.00

Creamer and Sugar, Art Deco dec 135.00

Cup and Saucer, Art Deco, blue silhouette of dancing girl and scarf, beige luster ground, blue, black, and white bands 90.00

Dish, 13" l, oval, open handles, pink and yellow roses 45.00

R. S. Germany, cake plate, green ground, white flowers, gold leaves, gilded edge, mkd, 9-3/4" w handle to handle, $60.

Hatpin Holder, 4-1/2" h, large white rose at top, long green stem, shaded brown to green ground, green mark 150.00
Demitasse Cup and Saucer, muted greens and gold, blown roses. 75.00
Mug, head shape, mkd 80.00
Pitcher, 5" h, hidden images 265.00
Plate, 11-1/4" d, lilacs on white, green, and pink shaded ground, green and gold trim, gold rim 110.00
Shaving Mug, Poppy pattern, with soap holder, scalloped base 100.00
Smoke Set, blue borders, match holder and pipe 295.00
Toothpick Holder, white daisies, blue ground, gold handles and top, slight wear to gold 95.00
Tray, 15-1/4" l, white and green poppies, handles 250.00

R. S. Poland

Bowl, 10-1/2" d, Heart mold, poppies, satin finish. 245.00
Candlestick, 6' h, violets, lily of the valley dec, shiny finish 125.00
Hair Receiver, violets, lily of the valley dec. 100.00
Hatpin Holder, 6" h, garland of red roses and green leaves, pale green band below with gold geometrics, pale green pierced top 125.00
Powder Jar, violets, lily of the valley dec. 100.00
Server, 11" d, 8" h, center handle, lavender and orange roses 515.00
Vase
    7-1/4" h, large white roses, yellow centers, green foliage, shaded brown to cream ground 85.00
    8-3/4" h, cream ground, pink and white roses, gold band around top, garlands of gold roses and leaves 195.00

R. S. Prussia

Bell, 3-1/2" h, small purple flowers, white ground, ruffled edge, green twig and leaf handle, unmarked 285.00
Biscuit Jar, cov, Lily mold, double portrait, lady holding chickens and lady with dog, unmarked 950.00
Bowl
    4-1/4" d, ftd, pink and yellow peonies, green leaves, gold trim 425.00

10-1/2" d, carnation mold, lavender and peach colored ground, pink roses, satin finish, mkd 600.00
10-1/2" d, iris mold, large pink poppies and daisies, green ground, red mark 300.00
10-1/2" d, mold 207, green and white, flowers, red mark 230.00
Cake Plate
    10" d, Iris mold, lavender ground, poppies, satin finish, mkd 500.00
    10" d, Ripple 275.00
    10-3/4" d, Art Nouveau forget-me-not mold, beige flowers, pink luster rim, multicolored floral spray, unmarked. 200.00
Chocolate Pot, multicolored flowers, satin finish, ornate handle, large molded base 300.00
Coffee Pot, stipple mold, pastels, raised gold dec, satin finish 850.00
Creamer and Sugar, 5-1/4" h, red roses, green leaves, gilt trim 220.00
Ferner, 6-3/4" d, 3-1/2" h, water lilies, pastels, pie-crust rim, liner, tri-foot, red mark 275.00
Fruit Bowl, 9" d, ftd, pink rose dec. 180.00
Hair Receiver, green ground, white lilies. 250.00
Hatpin Holder, Calla Lily 150.00
Jar, cov, light blue ground, three color roses 425.00
Plate, luster, roses dec, scalloped festoon rim 95.00
Shaving Mug, Old Star mark 175.00
Tankard
    9-3/4" h, Ribbon and Jewel, bronze, soft green, purple and yellow flowers. 365.00
    13-1/4" h, Stipple mold, large roses 625.00

R. S. Suhl

Bowl, 10" d, sheepherder scene, cottage, red mark 500.00
Compote, 4-1/2" d, ftd, creamy roses, gold stencil design, green mark 225.00
Hatpin Holder, 5" h, hp pink roses, satin shaded blue to yellow ground, wreath mark 85.00
Pitcher, 5-1/2" h, white ground, red roses, unmarked 115.00
Spittoon, pale green, pink roses 275.00
Vase, 9-1/2" h, Gibson Girl portrait, red mark 850.00

R. S. Tillowitz

Bowl, 10 x 6-1/4", oval, hp, pheasant hen and cock, blue mark 295.00

R. S. Prussia, bowl, pink rose, green trim, 11" d, $345.

R. S. Suhl, dish, light green ext., green ground, white, pink, and yellow classical maidens, 8" l, 4-5/8" w, $490.

Cheese and Cracker Dish, 8-1/2" d, 2-1/2" h, blue mark, "Germany" in green 65.00
Chocolate Pot, Art Nouveau dec, glossy finish 55.00
Dish, 8-1/2" l, oval, handle, gold trim 38.00
Marmalade, cov, underplate, floral dec. 85.00
Plate, 7" d, stylized butterfly border, gold rim and handles, blue mark 65.00
Relish, basket handle, bird of paradise 350.00
Tray, five sided, roses dec 45.00

SCHNEIDER GLASS

History: Brothers Ernest and Charles Schneider founded a glassworks at Epiney-sur-Seine, France, in 1913. Charles, the artistic designer, previously had worked for Daum and Gallé. Robert, son of Charles, assumed art direction in 1948. Schneider moved to Loris in 1962.

Although Schneider made tablewares, stained glass, and lighting fixtures, its best-known product is art glass which exhibits simplicity of design and often has bubbles and streaking in larger pieces. Other styles include cameo-cut and hydrofluoric-acid-etched designs.

Marks: Schneider glass was signed with a variety of script and block signatures, "Le Verre Francais," or "Charder."

Bowl, 15" d, 4" h, mottled purple, pink, and white, black foot, unmarked 275.00
Center Bowl, 10" d, 4-1/2" h, shaped orange bowl, layered with tortoiseshell brown, etched as five scarab beetles alternating geometric elements, lower edge inscribed "LeVerre Francais France/Ovington New York" 700.00
Compote
   3-1/2" h, 15-1/4" d, broad triangular platter, bright red-orange, short purple striped knob and disk foot, inscribed "Schneider" 350.00
   5-1/4" h, 14-1/2" d, broad shallow mottled burgundy red platter, six-point tooled rim, raised on black aubergine striped stem and disk foot, inscribed "Schneider" 500.00
   7-1/2" h, 6-1/4" d, rolled rim, burnt sienna shaded to pale blue colored dish, slender purple stem and disk foot, inscribed "Schneider France" 1,000.00
Vase
   9" h, amber, green, and white mottled glass, encased in geometric wrought iron holder 1,800.00

Dish, orange shading to dark blue, amethyst with white ribbing base, etched signature, 13-1/2" d, 5-1/2" h, $295.

15-1/2" h, mottled white body, color layered with swirled orange and brown-green glass, etched stylized blossoms around bulbed shoulder, lappet swag panels below, sgd "Charder" in cameo, and "LeVerre Francais"" on edge 1,100.00

SCHOENHUT TOYS

History: Albert Schoenhut, son of a toy maker, was born in Germany in 1849. In 1866, he ventured to America where he worked as a toy-piano repairman for Wanamaker's in Philadelphia, Pennsylvania. Finding the glass sounding bars inadequate, he perfected a toy piano with metal sounding bars. His piano was an instant success, and the A. Schoenhut Company had its beginning.

From that point on, toys seemed to flow out of the factory. Each of his six sons entered the business, and it prospered until 1934, when misfortune forced the company into bankruptcy. In 1935, Otto and George Schoenhut contracted to produce the Pinn Family Dolls.

The Schoenhut Manufacturing Company was formed by two other Schoenhuts. Both companies operated under a partnership agreement that eventually led to O. Schoenhut, Inc., which continues today.

Some dates of interest:
1872—toy piano invented
1903—Humpty Dumpty Circus patented
1911–1924—wooden doll production
1928–1934—composition dolls made

References: E. Ackerman and F. Keller, *Under the Big Top with Schoenhut's Humpty Dumpty Circus*, published by author (P.O. Box 217, Culver City, CA 90230), 1997; Carol Corson, *Schoenhut Dolls*, Hobby House Press, 1993; Richard O'Brien, *Collecting Toys*, 7th ed., Books Americana, 1995.

Collectors' Clubs: Schoenhut Collectors Club, 1003 W. Huron St., Ann Arbor, MI 48103; Schoenhut Toy Collectors, 1916 Cleveland St., Evanston, IL 60202.

Animal, jointed wood construction
   Alligator, painted green, red mouth, white teeth, leather feet, 13" l 500.00
   Brown Bear, hand painted shades of brown, leather ears, 7-1/2" l on hind legs 275.00
   Buffalo, glass eyes, hand painted dark brown, leather horns, rope tail, 8" l 200.00
   Bulldog, painted white, black spot over eye, leather collar and tail, 5" l 410.00
   Camel, painted brown, black hoofs, rope tail, double hump back, 7-1/2" l 250.00
   Cat, olive brown, black stripes, white underbelly, leather tail, 4-1/4" h. 770.00
   Cow, glass eyes, hand painted brown, leather collar, rope tail, horns, and ears, 8-1/2" l 265.00
   Donkey, glass eyes, painted brown, gray nose, fabric mane, price for pr 90.00
   Elephant, glass eyes, hand painted dark gray, rope tail and tusks, large leather ears, orig box 635.00
   Giraffe, painted. 320.00
   Goat, glass eyes, hand painted black and white, leather ears, horns, beard and tail, 8" l 220.00
   Goose, glass eyes, painted white, orange beak and feet, 7" l 360.00
   Gorilla, painted brown, leather ears, 11" arm span . . 3,410.00

Hippo, painted eyes, dark brown, leather tail and ears, wooden carved front teeth, 10" l 185.00

Horse, glass eyes, painted brown, leather ears and saddle, 8" h, missing stirrups, price for pr. 110.00

Hyena, Teddy Roosevelt safari animal, hand painted gray with stripes, leather ears, rope tail, 6" l 1,430.00

Kangaroo, painted shades of brown, white underbelly, leather ears, stands on rear legs and tail, 10-1/2" l 440.00

Leopard, painted yellow with brown spots, rope tail, 7-1/4" l
.... 360.00

Pig, glass eyes, painted light brown, leather ears, 8" l
.... 55.00

Polar Bear, painted white, short rope tail, leather ears, 8" l
.... 660.00

Poodle, glass eyes, painted white, rope tail, 7" l 55.00

Rabbit, painted brown, leather ears and tail, 5-1/4" l
.... 715.00

Rhino, painted eyes, hand painted olive brown with black spots, rope tail, leather ears, 9" l, one ear missing
.... 110.00

Seal, painted dark brow, leather flipper hands, 9" l .. 290.00

Show Horse, glass eyes, ring tail, leather ears, wooden platform mounted on back, 10" l, price for pr. 360.00

. Tiger, hand painted orange, brown spots, rope tail, 7-1/2" l, some paint flaking 230.00

Wolf, painted shades of brown, red mouth, long carved wooden tail, leather ears 1,980.00

Zebra, painted light brown with dark stripes, leather ears, rope tail, 7-3/4" l 330.00

Balancing Bar, painted wood and metal 550.00

Cage Wagon, 12" x 12", wood, red, gray bars, blue wheels, top mkd "Schoenhut's Humpty Dumpty Circus," contains lion with full mane, rear door opens 990.00

Camera, Spirit of America, wood, painted black, movie camera clicks when turned, 10" h, orig box. 935.00

Circus Animal in Cage, wood animal, wire cage

7-1/2" h, brown bear, leather ears, hand painted, shades of brown.. 220.00

8" l, lion, rope tail, carved head, body painted light to medium brown.. 415.00

11" h, giraffe, leather ears, wood short horns, rope tail, natural colors 770.00

Circus Pedestals, painted wood and litho paper, price for 5 pc set. 470.00

Figure, jointed wood construction

Barney Google and Spark Plug, wood hat, fabric suit, yellow blanket with name on Spark Plug 550.00

Black Dude, hand painted face, leather ears, long purple coat, yellow vest, checkered pants, white top hat, 8-1/2" h
.... 315.00

Circus Acrobat, bisque head, hand painted, fabric suit, blue and yellow felt suit, red shorts 300.00

Farmer, straw hat, bucket and rake, 7" h 110.00

Felix the Cat, black and white, large leather ears ... 470.00

Hobo, hand painted face, leather ears, felt jacket and hat, fabric pants and scarf around neck 140.00

Maggie and Jiggs, cloth and fabric suits, animated appearance, Maggie holding rolling pin 525.00

Mary and Her Lamb, cloth outfit, straw hat, white lamb, school desk, feeding trough 1,430.00

Ringmaster, hand painted face, red tails, vest, and pants, orig top hat and whip. 250.00

Golf Game, indoor, 36" l long wooden handles with golfers, tee area, putting green, sand trap, water well, balls. 1,320.00

School Desk, painted wood, for Mary and her lamb set
.... 190.00

Doll, boy, pouty expression, wood, spring jointed body, mkd "75," $495.

Weights, painted wood, lift weights, 50 lb barbells, 100 lb barbells, price for 4 pc set 990.00

SCIENTIFIC INSTRUMENTS

History: Chemists, doctors, geologists, navigators, and surveyors used precision instruments as tools of their trade. Such objects were well designed and beautifully crafted. They are primarily made of brass; fancy hardwood cases also are common.

The 1990s have seen a keen interest in scientific instruments, both in the auction market and at antique shows. The number of collectors of this mechanical wonders is increasing as more and more interesting examples are being offered.

References: Florian Cajori, *History of the Logarithmic Slide Rule and Allied Instruments*, Astragal Press, 1994; Gloria Clifton, *Directory of British Scientific Instrument Makers 1550-1851*, P. Wilson Publishers, 1994; William H. Skerritt, *Catalog of the Charles E. Smart Collection: Antique Surveying Instruments*, published by author, (12 Locust Ave., Troy, NY 12180), 1996; Gerard L. E. Turner, *Scientific Instruments 1500-1900: An Introduction*, University of California Press, 1998.

Periodicals: Rittenhouse, P.O. Box 151, Hastings-on-Hudson, NY 10706; Scientific, Medical & Mechanical Antiques, P.O. Box 412, Taneytown, MD 21787.

Collectors' Clubs: International Calculator Collectors Club, 14561 Livingston St., Tustin, CA 92680; Maryland Microscopical Society, 8261 Polk St., McLean VA, 22102; The Oughtred Society, 2160 Middlefield Rd., Palo Alto, CA 94301; Zeiss Historical Society, P.O. Box 631, Clifton, NJ 07012.

Museum: National Museum of American History, Smithsonian Institution, Washington, DC.

Adder, 6-3/4" l, 4-7/8" w, brass, mahogany backer, brass wall fasteners, mkd "C. H. Webb N.Y. 'The Adder' PATd March 10, 1868, B1108" 520.00

Anemometer, 6 register, 8 blade, 2-5/8" d fan derives 2-1/4" d silvered dial with six registers from 1 to 9,999,999 cubic feet, brass construction, mounting bracket, softwood case, c1875 350.00

Artificial Horizon, unsigned, mercury reservoir with two glass covers, 6-1/4" l, 3-7/8" w, 3-7/8" h, mercury filled container locks into dovetailed mahogany case, c1900 . . . . . . 490.00

Batson Sketching Case, 10-1/2" l, 7" w overall, 4-1/2" x 6-1/8" plotting surface, 5" d graduated plotting scale, 2" l rotating trough compass, 2 paper rollers, varnished hardwood and lacquered brass, sgd "W. & L. E. Gurley, Troy, NY," patent Sept. 28, 1897 . . . . 750.00

Chronometer

Hamilton Watch Co., Lancaster, PA, model 36, 21 jewel, 5 position, motor barrel, double roller, 56 hour, 5" mahogany cube, double lid, gimballed deck case, nickel silver finish, 2-3/4" d bezel, c1918. . . . . .1,495.00

Waltham Watch Co., 8 days, 4-7/8" cube mahogany double lid desk case, weighted brass case in brass gimbals, second hand, winding register, 15 jewels, c1913 . . . . 635.00

Circumferentor, 5-1/4" h, 9" outside diameter, brass, 4-1/8" compass in center, attached to rotating sight vane/vernier

Binocular microscope, C. Collins, London, c1875, $1,325. Photo courtesy of Auction Team Breker.

arm, inset vial, silvered dial, outer ring engraved with 8 point star, 2 outer fixed sight vanes, Dollond London, c1825 . . . . .1,955.00

Drawing Instruments, cased, 6" l ivory and brass sector, 6" l ivory scale, 6" ebony and brass parallel rule, 1-3/4" brass protractor, six brass and iron drafting tools with ram's head screws, 6" l x 3" w black shagreen cov wood case, unsgd, c1800 . . . . 400.00

Fowler's Calculator, Fowler & Co. Manchester, England, 6978, two 11/16" d x 1-1/2" thick with circular logarithmic scales on both faces, two stems for rotating faces and cursor, nickel plated, sq velvet lined case, c1920 . . . . 375.00

Globe, 8" d, 9-1/2" h, Ginn & Heath, revolving cast iron base, adjustable brass daylight/twilight boundry rings and brass moon, c1877, minor defects in Arctic Circle area 3,220.00

Lords Patent Pocket Calculator, 2-1/2" d pocket watch style, three stems move inner dial and its cursor, center ring and minute hand type cursor, three circular logarithmic scales engraved on silvered dial, c1920 . . . . 920.00

Microscope, Binocular, T. W. Watson, 4 Pall Mall, London, No. 287, 18-1/2" h, mounted on case board, 12-1/4" l binocular tubes, single focus for both tubes, fine focus on eyep. End, rect mechanical stage on 4-3/8" d rotating stage with degree scale to 1/2º, gimballed mirror yoke, lacquered brass, "H. B. Gelb," 1879. . . . . 750.00

Microscope, Cary Type

Paul Roescler, New Haven, CT., 7-3/4" h, rack and pinion focus of 2-1/8" d glass stage, horiz. and vert. adjustable eye. Arm, single mirror, lacquered brass, 4-1/2" w x 6-1/2" l x 2-7/8" h mahogany case, c1875 . . . . 920.00

Unsigned, 7" h, rack and pinion focus of 2" d glass stage, vert. and horiz. adjustable lens holder, 3 lenses, single mirror, dissecting knife and tweezers, lacquered brass, mahogany case, c1875 . . . . 750.00

Microscope, Compound Monocular

Bausch & Lomb Optical Co., Rochester, NY
 #1761, Family, 13-3/4" h, 9-5/8" l, 1-1/8" d tube with single objt., rack and pinion focus, rect table, 4 hole diaphragm, single mirror, 1 eyep., 2 obj., japanned and lacquered brass, case, c1882 . . . . .1,100.00
 #11737, 12" h, 8-1/2" l, 1-1/8" d tube with 1 object., fine focus on arm, rect stage, 5 hole diaphragm, double mirror on rotating arm, extra eyep., orig case, japanned and lacquered brass, sgd "Wm. H. Armstrong & Co., Indianapolis, Ind," c1893 . . . . 635.00
 #13668, 13-1/4" h, 9" l, 1-1/2" d single nosepiece tube, 3-1/2" d stage, condenser and double mirror revolve on arms centered on stage, against graduated vertical circular silvered dial, 4 obj. and 3 eyep., lacquered brass, orig case, mkd "Pat. Oct. 13, 1885," c1894 . . . . .1,840.00
Boston Optical Co., Boston, 17-1/4" h, 12" l, 1-3/16" d tube with double nosepiece and calibrated draw tube, fine focus on tube, 4-1/4" d rotatable stage table, condenser with double mirror on rotating arm, lacquered brass, case, c1870 . . . . .5,175.00
Boston Optical Works Tolles, SN 140, 14-1/4" h, 9-1/4" l, 1-1/8" d tube with single obj., fine focus at bottom of tube, mechanical stage, 4 hole diaphragm with tube, double mirror, 3 eyep., 2 obj., slides, case, c1870 . . . . 1,380.00
Spencer, Buffalo, folding, 10-1/4" h, 6-1/4" l x 1-1/2" d tube, triple nosepiece, micrometer drum fine focus on arm, calibrated draw tube, rect. stage, condenser, double mirror, japanned and lacquered brass, heavy metal case, c1900 . . . . . 750.00

Tolles, Boston, 272, 15-1/2" h, 10-1/2" l, 1-1/4" d tube, single nosepiece, fine focus on front of tube, 4-1/2" d stage, 2 sub-stage condensers, double mirror, detachable parabolic mirror, extra 8" l, 1-1/" d, draw tube, detachable stand condenser lens with "bug" holder, prism eyep., 2 objt., 2 eyep., lacquered brass, orig case, c1875 . . . . .2,070.00

Zentmayer, J., Philadelphia, 726," hospital style stand, 15" h, 10-3/4" l, 1-1/2" d, single obj. with fine focus on tube, rect table, slide holder, 4 hole tube diaphragm, double mirror, 4 eyep., 2 obj., lacquered brass, case, condenser stand, c1879 . . . . 980.00

Microscope Compendium, Wilson, 3-1/4" l x 1-1/8" d, screw barrel, brass construction with socket for ivory handle (missing), spring loaded under specimen plate, 11/16" d eyep., detachable simple microscope with six numbered lenses, four with lens caps, four hole brass slide holder, mahogany case, unsigned, c1925 . . . . 575.00

Miner's Dial, hanging, 8-1/4" l, 5-1/2" h, 4" d gimballed 3" compass, silvered dial and outer ring, lacquered bright brass, Otto Fennel Cassel, c1900 . . . . 635.00

Nystrom's Calculator, "Patented March 4, 1851, Made by W. J. Young, Philada," No. 754, 9-1/2" d, 5-1/4" l, "A" and "B" arms, "C" dial with 1" long arrow pointer, brass construction, silver plate scale face, engraved lines, numerals, and letters, c1855 . . . . .10,350.00

Octant

Bassnet, Liverpool, 12-3/4" l, 10-1/2" w, ebony arms, circle, and "T" cross brace, brass accessories, ivory scale, vernier, and nameplate, 3 sun glasses, scratch pad and pencil missing 520.00

F. W. Lincoln Jr. & Co., Boston, 13" x 11-1/2" case, ebony and ivory, brass fittings, ivory scale to 105 degrees, paper label on case. 700.00

Simon Robinson, 16" l, 13" w, 14" rad. ivory circle, ivory vernier with 1' least count, ivory nameplate and scratch pad, adjustable mirrors, brass arm and fittings, ebony arms and braces, 3 smoked glass, pie shaped case, labeled "Richard Patten, NY," c1820 . . . . 750.00

Palmer's Computing Scale/Fuller's Time Telegraph, two 8-1/2" d scale wheels with finger grommets, on 10-7/8" sq outer scale board, computing scale logarithmic, Time Telegraph Scale is liner, gold, brown, black, and pastel green, mkd "Aaron Palmer/John F. Fuller," engraving by Geo. G. Smith, c1846 . . . . .1,035.00

Railroad Compass

Pocket, 7-1/4" l, 6" w, 10" h, 4-1/2" l hinged sight vanes, 4 screw leveling adaptor, 3-1/2" d silvered compass card and ring with declination vernier, 1" single vernier horiz circle, bronzed brass finish, orig case with paper label, made by W. & L. E. Gurley, Troy, NY, c1880. . . . . .2,185.00

Vernier, 15-7/8" l, 71/2" w, 3-7/8" h, without sight vanes, crossed vials, outside 30º, 1' declination vernier, outside 7" d, 1', 2 vernier horizontal scale, needle floats over 5-1/2" d silvered dial engraved with 8 point star, edge engraved out ring, darkened brass, dovetailed mahogany case, sgd "James Meneely made Janry. 1838," Meneeley & Oothout, West Troy, NY, Warranted No. 674 .2,300.00

Sperry Pocket Calculator, Keuffel & Esser Co., NY, Pat. Dec. 26, 11, 777, 2-1/8" d pocket watch style, dual faces, 2 knob stem rotates the dials with logarithmic scale and minute hand style cursors, German silver finish 920.00

Telescope

39" l closed, 52" l extended, brass, French, engraved "Telegraphe No. 22…Bardou Rue St. Martin No. 171…A Paris," brass ends, wood center, wood split 350.00

95" h extended, 59" l telescope, pedestal mounted, counter weighted equatorial mount, mahogany telescope case with 10 eyep., 5 colored lenses, lens caps, sgd "J. H. Steward Ltd. , 406 Strand, London," c1910, including both handwritten and typed copies of approx. 250 pgs *Southern Stars for Small Telescopes…*, by G. V. Hudson, F.R.S.N.Z., 1925 . . . . .4,600.00

SCRIMSHAW

History: Norman Flayderman defined scrimshaw as "the art of carving or otherwise fashioning useful or decorative articles as practiced primarily by whalemen, sailors, or others associated with nautical pursuits." Many collectors expand this to include the work of Eskimos and French POWs from the War of 1812.

References: Stuard M. Frank, *Dictionary of Scrimshaw Artists*, Mystic Seaport Museum, 1991; Nina Hellman and Norman Brouwer, *Mariner's Fancy*, South Street Seaport Museum, Balsam Press, and the University of Washington Press, 1992; Martha Lawrence, *Scrimshaw*, Schiffer Publishing, 1993.

Museums: Cold Spring Whaling Harbor Museum, Cold Spring Harbor, NY; Kendall Whaling Museum, Sharon, MA; Mystic Seaport Museum, Mystic, CT; National Maritime Museum, San Francisco, CA; New Bedford Whaling Museum, New Bedford, MA; Old Dartmouth Historical Society, New Bedford, MA; Pacific Whaling Museum, Waimanalo, HI; Sag Harbor Whaling & Historical Museum, Sag Harbor, NY; San Francisco Maritime National Historical Park, San Francisco, CA; South Street Seaport Museum, New York, NY; Whaling Museum, Nantucket, MA.

REPRODUCTION ALERT

The biggest problem in the field is fakes, although there are some clues to spotting them. A very hot needle will penetrate the common plastics used in reproductions but not the authentic material. Ivory will not generate static electricity when rubbed, plastic will. Patina is not a good indicator; it has been faked by applying tea or tobacco juice, burying in raw rabbit hide, and in other ingenious ways. Usually the depth of cutting in an old design will not be consistent since the ship rocked and tools dulled; however, skilled forgers have even copied this characteristic.

Bracelet, five oval scrimshaw plaques, three depicting nautical scenes, all sgd "Howard Weyahok," joined by 14kt yellow gold trace link chain 60.00

Buggy Whip, 82" l, whale ivory and whalebone sections, baleen rings, two rope carvings, mid 19th C 2,000.00

Busk

11-1/4" l, whale bone, engraved compass, stars, tree, flags, hot air balloon 500.00

11-1/2" h, whalebone, whale, lighthouse, and American eagle, 19th C 550.00

12-1/2" h, whalebone, heralding angel, harp, and two story house, 19th C, repaired crack 230.00

13-1/4" h, baleen, panels of floral and geometric design, 19th C, minor chipping to one side 200.00

13-1/2" h, baleen, panels of palm trees, three story building, ship, 19th C, age cracks and worming. 230.00

14-1/4" h, panels of woman, plants, and heart, 19th C, in two pcs 225.00

Butter Mold, 5-1/8" h, circular, wood, carved rosette, whale ivory handle, early to mid 19th C 275.00

Cane

31-17/8" h, wood and whalebone, whale ivory and baleen rings, 19th C. 295.00

37-1/2" l, wood, whale ivory tip and knob, partially wound baleen and ropework, diamond shape wood inlays, 19th C 275.00

Chest, 20-3/4" x 9-1/2" x 9", walnut or mahogany and pine, hinged top, three inlaid abstract whalebone figures on front panel and initials "G. W. T." 550.00

Cribbage Board, 18-1/2" d, walrus tusk, 7 walruses 300.00

Ostrich Egg, engraved sailor, sweetheart, eagle, flag, stars, and ship, orig ropework hanger. 275.00

Sewing Box

6-3/4" l, engraved baleen, stuffed brocade pin cushion lid, 19th C, small losses. 1,100.00

8" sq, island wood, geometric wood inlays, inlaid whale ivory and abalone shell compass rose, diamonds and spandrel dec, mid 19th C 650.00

Snuff Box, 3 x 1-1/2" l; shaped oval, top diamond inscribed "R. N.," (Royal Navy) and anchor, other side inscribed "Capt. N. C. Norten," dates of service, 1831, 1841, on ends, fluting, highlighted with lampblack 450.00

Watch Fob, whale ivory, book form, engraved colored Masonic symbols, mid 19th C. 395.00

Whale's Tooth, dec

5" l, reserves of church, three-masted ship under sail, minor cracks, 19th C 700.00

5-1/4" h, vases of flowers, 19th C, price for pr 690.00

5-3/4" h, shielded American eagle, American flag flanked by cannons above whale boat disaster on one side, other side

with three-masted ship flying American flag and whale boat, 19th C, small chip to tip 8,625.00

6" h, gentleman writing at desk, 19th C, crack 450.00

6-1/4" h, woman in formal dress, late 19th C, cracks 375.00

6-1/2" h, polychrome dec of "The Mother of Washington Receiving Marquis LaFayette," early 20th C, accompanying note reads "Uncle Benjamin Ball made on one of his sailing trips in the 1850s" 700.00

7-1/4" h, each side with three-masted ship under sail, 19th C, age cracks, price for pr 4,900.00

7-1/2" h, British ship under full sail on one side, screw steamer on other side, 19th C 1,265.00

9-1/4" l, reserve of whaling scene, flanked by whaling implements, rope border, early 20th C 2,760.00

SEVRES

History: The principal patron of the French porcelain industry in early 18th-century France was Jeanne Antoinette Poisson, Marquise de Pompadour. She supported the Vincennes factory of Gilles and Robert Dubois and their successors in their attempt to make soft-paste porcelain in the 1740s. In 1753 she moved the porcelain operations to Sevres, near her home, Chateau de Bellevue.

The Sevres soft-paste formula used sand from Fontainebleau, salt, saltpeter, soda of alicante, powdered alabaster, clay, and soap. Many famous colors were developed, including a cobalt blue. The wonderful scenic designs on the ware were painted by such famous decorators as Watteau, La Tour, and Boucher. In the 18th century Sevres porcelain was the world's foremost diplomatic gift.

In 1769, kaolin was discovered in France, and a hard-paste formula was developed. The baroque gave way to rococo, a style favored by Jeanne du Barry, Louis XV's next mistress. Louis XVI took little interest in Sevres, and many factories began to turn out counterfeits. In 1876, the factory was moved to St. Cloud and was eventually nationalized.

References: Susan and Al Bagdade, *Warman's English & Continental Pottery & Porcelain*, 3rd Edition, Krause Publications, 1998; Carl Christian Dauterman, *Sevres Porcelain, Makers and Marks of the Eighteenth Century,* Metropolitan Museum of Art, 1986; Linda Humphries, *Sevres Porcelain from the Sevres Museum 1740 to the Present,* Hund Humphries, 1997; George Savage, *Seventeenth & Eighteenth Century French Porcelain,* Hamlyn Publishing Co., Ltd., 1969.

Museums: Art Institute of Chicago, Chicago, IL; British Museum, London, England; Frick Collection, New York, NY; Gardiner Museum of Ceramic Art Museum, Toronto, Canada; J. Paul Getty Museum, Los Angeles, CA; Metropolitan Museum of Art, New York, NY; Musee de Louvre, Paris, France, Musee National e Ceramique, Sevres,

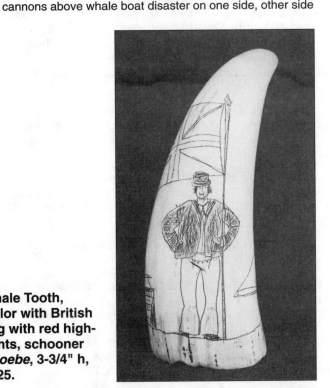

Whale Tooth, sailor with British flag with red highlights, schooner *Phoebe*, 3-3/4" h, $225.

France; Victoria & Albert Museum, London, England; Wadsworth Atheneum, Hartford, CT.

Marks: Louis XV allowed the firm to use the "double L" in its marks.

Reproduction Alert.

Bowl

    8-3/4" d, 3-1/4" h, exotic bird and swags of flowers, early blue mark 500.00

    11-1/4" d, 4-1/4" h, inside of bowl dec with large spray of flowers, outside medium blue, one large panel of colorful flowers, another with cherub flanking Louis Philip seal, crown over intertwined L & P surrounded by wreath mark 400.00

Box, cov, 8" d, octagonal, amorous couple on cov, foliage on int., sgd "George Rocher," early 20th C 550.00

Cache Pot, 5-1/2" h, figural cartouche of putto, sky blue ground, silver overlay floral and swag dec 800.00

Center Bowl, 12-3/4" d, painted reserves of courting couple, landscape, cobalt blue ground, gilt metal mounts, sgd "Guy," c1900 . . . . 400.00

Compote, 10-5/8" d, center portrait medallion of Louis XVI, gilt scroll and floral border, pink ground, two gilt lined flat handles 275.00

Cup and Saucer, gilt and floral panels, apple green ground 75.00

Dresser Box, cov, 5-3/4" l, oval, portrait medallion of lady on cov, floral side dec, gold bronze mounts 350.00

Inkwell

    9" l, floral swag dec, sky blue and gilt ground, attached to quatrefoil dish 550.00

    10-1/2" l, gondola-form, green painted hull, gilt rim and prow 250.00

Magnifying Glass, 14-1/2" l, porcelain handle with figural cartouches, gilt and cobalt blue ground 700.00

Lamp Base, 24-1/4" h, made from urns, green, gold trim, oval reserves of romantic couples, pr 375.00

Cup and Saucer, bird in landscape, trellis and florals in cartouche on wide border, 18th C, $250

Patch Box, 6" l, cobalt blue ground, painted Napoleonic scene, sides painted with landscape panels, gilt scrolls, sgd "Henet," late 19th C 980.00

Plate

    8" d, embracing couple, garden setting, yellow dec, scalloped gold dec rim, artist sgd, marked "Chateau St Cloud" 95.00

    11" d, two putti, monogram, celeste blue borders, factory marks, sgd "Bruny," Louis-Philippe, 1846 . . . . 225.00

Portrait Plate, 9-1/2" d, green and gilt borders encircling portraits of Napoleon and Josephine, pr 600.00

Urn, 18th C courting couples within cartouche, cobalt ground, ormolu mounts, electrified, pr 500.00

Vase, 5" h, ovoid, figural and landscape cartouches, cobalt blue and gilt ground 250.00

SEWING ITEMS

History: As recently as 50 years ago, a wide variety of sewing items were found in almost every home in America. Women of every economic and social status were skilled in sewing and dressmaking.

Iron or brass sewing birds, one of the interesting convenience items, which developed, were used to hold cloth (in the bird's beak) while sewing. They could be attached to a table or shelf with a screw-type fixture. Later models included a pincushion.

References: *Advertising & Figural Tape Measures*, L-W Book Sales, 1995; Elizabeth Arbittier et al., *Collecting Figural Tape Measures*, Schiffer Publishing, 1995; Carter Bays, *Encyclopedia of Early American Sewing Machines*, published by author, 1993; Frieda Marion, *China Half-Figures Called Pincushion Dolls*, published by author, 1974, 1994 reprint; Averil Mathias, *Antique and Collectible Thimbles and Accessories*, Collector Books, 1986, 1995 value update; Wayne Muller, *Darn It!*, L-W Book Sales, 1995; James W. Slaten, *Antique American Sewing Machines*, Singer Dealer Museum (3400 Park Blvd., Oakland, CA 94610), 1992; Glenda Thomas, *Toy and Miniature Sewing Machines* (1995), Book II (1997), Collector Books; Helen Lester Thompson, *Sewing Tools & Trinkets*, Collector Books, 1996; Gertrude Whiting, *Old-Time Tools & Toys of Needlework*, Dover Publications, 1970.

Collectors' Clubs: International Sewing Machine Collectors Society, 1000 E. Charleston Blvd., Las Vegas, NV 89104; Toy Stitchers, 623 Santa Florita Ave., Millbrae, CA 94030.

Museums: Fabric Hall, Historic Deerfield, Deerfield, MA; Museum of American History, Smithsonian Institution, Washington, DC; Sewing Machine Museum, Oakland, CA; Shelburne Museum, Shelburne, VT.

Additional Listings: See Thimbles and *Warman's Americana & Collectibles* for more examples.

Basket, cov, round, birch bark and quill, two bears, damaged 25.00

Bodkin, sterling silver, engraved, floral dec, hallmarked 35.00

Caddy, 8-1/4" w, 5-5/8" d, 8-1/4" h, grain painted, shaped pierced carved galleried top, sixteen spool holders, one drawer, shaped base, America, 19th C 250.00

Spool Dispenser, counter top, Merrick's, curved glass sides, $1,980. Photo courtesy of Jackson's Auctioneers & Appraisers.

Catalog
  Hawkeye Pearl Button Co., Muscatine, IA, c1930, 19 pgs, 7" x 8-1/2".................................... 38.00
  King Sewing Machine Co, Buffalo, NY, 1909, 56 pages, 6" x 9", King sewing machines, cabinets, features...... 25.00
Chatelaine
  Leather, three straps connect to scissors and case, thimble holder and pencil, English, c1900.............. 215.00
  Sterling Silver, ring top, chains connect to note pad, thimble and thimble case, buttonhook, English.......... 575.00
Crochet Hooks, whale bone, carved, price for 3 pc set
  .... 245.00
Darning Ball, Nailsea, blown glass, blue, white pulled loops
  .... 115.00
Display Case, counter top, 31" h, 16" w, 16-1/2" d, E. C. Simmons Keen Kutter, oak, front glass etched with trademark logo and name, "Shears and Scissors" etched at bottom, orig rotating pole and hangers inside, plaque at bottom reads "Simmons Hardware Co.," some replaced molding .. 750.00
Instruction Book, Barbour Brothers, Co., New York, NY, 1883, 5-1/2" x 7-3/4", *Imperial Macrame Lace Book,* illus and instructions 35.00
Knitting Needles, 12-3/4" to 15" l, three pairs, ivory, exotic wood, baleen and whalebone, minor cracks, some insect damage
  ....1,650.00
Needle Cabinet, Standard Sewing Machine, dark brown, black and gilt lettering, one long compartmentalized drawer, six small drawers.................................1,050.00
Needle Case, ivory, book shape, fabric pages........ 125.00
Pin Cushion
  Black Girl, print fabric......................... 40.00
  Chicken, 4" h, spool base....................... 45.00
  Punch, 3-1/8" l, ivory, turnings on top 40.00
Quilt Frame, 36" h, two 111" l rails, two 100-1/2" l rails, curly maple, old soft brown patina, four turned legs and posts, all wooden clamps 660.00
Salesman Sample Book, Ely & Walker, St. Louis, MO, 9 pgs, 89-1/2" x 14", E & W Fast Color American Beauty Batiste Doubled & Rolled Material for dressed and Blouses, 48 sample swatches.................................. 30.00

Sewing Bird, 4-1/2" h, iron, brass heart shaped thumb screw
  .... 125.00
Sewing Box, 8-3/4" w, 6-1/4" d, 9" h, inlaid mahogany and ivory, three-tier, pin cushion finial rests on lift top, int. spool storage area, two drawers, slide-out mirror, ball feet, 19th C
  .... 750.00
Sewing Table
  26-1/2" l, 17-1/4' d, 29-1/2" h, Classical, mahogany veneer and grained drop-leaf, stencil label "J. & J. W. Meeks Makers No. 4 Vesey St., New York" on inside of sectioned drawer, sewing bag fitting, pierced, shaped medial shield flanked by faux bois scrolled supports, serpentine legs with castors, old refinish, c1840 ....1,150.00
  34" l, 22" d, 27" h, curly maple, molded edge top made from six narrow boards, turned edge, folding, early 20th C
  .... 330.00
Spool Cabinet, counter top
  7-1/2" h, 22" w, 15-1/2" deep, two drawers, Clark's O. N. T. Spool Cotton 150.00
  18" h, 18" w, 14" d, five drawers, Heminway & Sons, divided drawers, some damage to wood case........... 350.00
  22" h, 18" d, cylindrical, wood and glass, columns rotate by turning spindle at top, "Merrick's Six Cord Soft Finish Cotton" stenciled in gold on glass in two locations, top plaque reads "Pat'd July 20, 1897," some glass missing on one curved panel 850.00
Swift, 21-1/4" h, cup-form finial, scribe line dec barrel form clamp, whale ivory, wood, and steel, 19th C 350.00
Tape Measure, figural
  Baseball player, celluloid 225.00
  Black man, celluloid 125.00
  Cat, in boot, metal 400.00
  Cello, metal 285.00
  Chick, hatching from egg, celluloid............. 200.00
  Dancing Girl, porcelain, sashed dress 185.00
  Dog and puppy on cushion, celluloid 110.00
  Drum, metal 300.00
  Dutch Boy, porcelain 145.00
  Eiffel Tower, metal 375.00
  Fruit Basket, celluloid........................ 120.00
  Girl, with muff, celluloid 100.00
  Golfer, celluloid............................. 425.00
  Groom, porcelain 225.00
  Indian, boy, wearing headdress, celluloid 110.00
  Man, with monocle, celluloid 375.00
  Turtle, metal 85.00
Thread Caddy, 8-1/2" d, 8-3/4" h, treen, walnut, old varnish finish, turned detail, spire finial, pin cushion inside lid, age crack
  .... 260.00

SHAKER

History: The Shakers, so named because of a dance they used in worship, are one of the oldest communal organizations in the United States. This religious group was founded by Mother Ann Lee, who emigrated from England and established the first Shaker community near Albany, New York, in 1784. The Shakers reached their peak in 1850, when there were 6,000 members.

Shakers lived celibate and self-sufficient lives. Their philosophy stressed cleanliness, order, simplicity, and economy. Highly inventive and motivated, the Shakers created many utilitarian household forms and objects. Their furniture reflected a striving for quality and purity in design.

In the early 19th century, the Shakers produced many items for commercial purposes. Chairmaking and the packaged herb and seed business thrived. In every endeavor and enterprise, the members followed Mother Ann's advice: "Put your hands to work and give your heart to God."

References: Michael Horsham, *Art of the Shakers*, Apple Press, 1989; John T. Kirk, *The Shaker World: Art, Life, Belief,* Harry N. Abrams, 1997; Charles R. Muller and Timothy D. Rieman, *The Shaker Chair*, Canal Press, 1984; June Sprigg and Jim Johnson, *Shaker Woodenware*, Berkshire House, 1991; June Sprigg and David Larkin, *Shaker Life*, Work, and Art, Stewart, Tabori & Chang, 1987; Timothy D. Rieman and Jean M. Burks, *Complete Book of Shaker Furniture*, Harry N. Abrams, 1993.

Periodical: *Shaker Messenger*, P.O. Box 1645 Holland, MI 49422.

Museums: Hancock Shaker Village, Pittsfield, MA; Shaker Historical Museum, Shaker Heights, OH; Shaker Museum and Library, Old Chatham, NY; Shaker Village of Pleasant Hill, Harrodsburg, KY 40330.

Advertisement, newspaper
"Canterbury Shakers' World Renowned Sarsaparilla...," The Canaan Reporter, Sept. 17, 1880, front page adv with engraving of Shaker brother 15.00
"The Tall Shakers' Concert," The Age, ME, June 18, 1846, re traveling apostate performers 20.00
Basket, 19-1/4" h, 14-3/4" h, splint, four handle, 19th C, minor losses 1,495.00
Blanket Chest, 48-1/2" w, 23-3/4" d, 29-1/2" h, pine, orig red paint, applied edge molding top, dovetailed case, dovetailed bracket feet, stenciled label on back "H. B. Bear," attributed to Ohio Community, some wear and edge damage
. . . . 770.00
Bonnet, 7-1/4" h, striped iridescent silk, attributed to Enfield, NH, 19th C, splits, minor tears. 435.00
Book
Allen, Catherine, *Biographical Sketch of Daniel Fraser of the Shaker Community of Mt. Lebanon, Columbia County, NY,* Weed, Parsons & Co., Albany, 1890, 38 pgs 75.00
Anderson*, Martha Jane and others, Social Gathering Dialogue, between Six Sisters of the North Family of Shakers, Mt. Lebanon, Columbia County, N. Y.,* Albany, 1873, 18 pgs, 8vo, orig letterpress wrappers, sewn 70.00
Anderson, Martha Jane, *Social Life and Vegetarianism,* Mt. Lebanon, Guilding Star Printing House, Chicago, 1893, 27 pgs, small stains on cov. 80.00
Chandler, Lloyd, *A Visit to the Shakers of East Canterbury, NH,* printed by the Shakers, 1894, 11 pgs 65.00
Green, Calvin and Seth Wells, *A Brief Exposition of the Established Principles and Regulations of the United Society of Believers called Shakers*, New York, 1879, 32 pgs, 8vo, orig letterpress wrappers 70.00
Green, Calvin and Seth Wells compilers, *A Summary View of the Millenial Church, or United Society of Believers, (Commonly called Shakers),* Albany, 1823, 12mo, orig tree sheep, presentation inscription from Sister Mildred Bonher, dated 1960, on front free endpaper 100.00
Mace, Aurelia Gay, *The Aletheia: Spirit of Truth...by Aureilia,* Farmington, ME, 1899, plates, 8vo publisher's cloth, inscribed "Caroline Helfrich, West Pittsfield, Mass. From Sabbathday Lake Friends," front flyleaf missing 140.00

Mace, Fayette, *Familiar Dialogues on Shakerism,* Portland, ME, 1838, 12mo, orig letterpress wrappers, darkened, owner's signature on front cover 140.00
Wells, Seth Young, compiler, *Millennial Praises,* Hancock, 1813, 12mo, orig tree sheep, contemporary label . . 150.00
Box, cov
2" d, 1-1/4" h, round, top and cover with opposing single finger 50.00
5" w, 3-1/4" d, 2-1/2" h, oval, traces of green paint, one finger base, one finger top, small chip on cover 80.00
6" w, 4-1/2" d, 21/4" h, oval, brown stain, base with two fingers, one finger on top. 150.00
7" w, 5" d, 2-1/2" h, oval, reddish-orange stain, base with four fingers, copper tacks, one finger on top. 850.00
8" d, round, light brown finish, single finger construction, slight reduction to top of base 155.00
9-1/2" d, round, old dark bluish green paint, wire bale, wooden handle, attributed to Enfield, CT, minor edge damage, bottom slightly loose 525.00
11-1/2" l, 4-1/4" h, oval, three finger construction, 19th C, staining, minor cracks and losses 260.00
Broadside, *The Shaker Museum, Founded 1931, Sabbathday Lake, Poland Spring, Maine, c*1970 . . . . 10.00
Bucket, 10-7/8" w, 11-1/2" d, 6-7/8" h, butternut, rect box-form, canted sides, iron bale handle attached with hammered copper pins, 19th C 1,150.00
Candlestand, 13-1/4" d, 22-3/4" h, cherry, attributed to Mt. Lebanon, NY, first half 19th C, refinished. 5,750.00
Carrier, three finger construction
11" l, 6-1/2" h, painted yellow, attributed to Canterbury, NH, even wear, cracks 2,990.00
11-1/4" l, 7-1/4" h, painted yellow, fixed int. handle, Mt. Lebanon, NY, 19th C, minor break lower edge 8,625.00
Catalog
Catalog of Fancy Goods Made At Shaker Village, Alfred, York County, Maine, Fannie Casey, Trustee and General Manager, 1908, 10 pgs. 135.00

Butter Churn, old red paint, strap hinges, $380.

Catalogue of Shaker Herbs and Herbal Teas, Sabbathday, The Shaker Press, 1974, 4 pgs 20.00

Chair, side, ladderback

33-1/2" h, old dark finish, Mt. Lebanon, NY label on bottom slat, "3" imp on top slat, replaced woven blue and gray tape seat 470.00

35-1/8" h, 17" h seat, red stain, two arched slats, splint seat jointed by double stretchers, tilters, early 19th C, minor imperfections 1,840.00

39-1/4" h, 16" h seat, old red paint, three slat back, old splint seat, good turned finials, worn patina, seat missing some splint. 250.00

Clock, tall case, poplar, old red paint, base molding, overlapping door, simple bonnet, wag-on-the-wall works, painted wooden face, brass gears, wooden plates, old inscription "Repaired by Smith Mar 11, 1910 Tiffin O, Written by A.L. Norris," other unreadable notations, 78" h 5,100.00

Dipper, 7-1/4" round, 8-1/2" handle, wood, turned handle, copper tacks, good old staining, 8" horizontal crack to side 250.00

Dust Pan, 16-1/2" l, turned maple handle, 19th C. 360.00

Essay

Blinn, Henry, *What Shall I Do To Be A Shaker?* East Canterbury, 1885, printed on both sides of single sheet 125.00

Hollister, Alzono, *Joyful Tiding,* Mt. Lebanon, 1886, 4 pgs 165.00

Embroidery Hoop, 6-1/4" d, walnut and cherry, table clamp, hand made 145.00

Foot Stool, 11-1/2" x 11-3/4", worn orig dark finish, Mt. Lebanon, NY, label, edge wear, minor corner damage 325.00

Grain Sack, 37-1/2" l, 18-1/2" w, Enfield, NH, woven, stenciled, staining, patches 115.00

Hymnal, *Shaker Hymnal By The Canterbury Shakers,* East Canterbury, NH, Stanhope Press, Gilson Co., Boston, 1908, 273 pgs, pencil inscription, stamped "North Family, Mt. Lebanon, NY" 65.00

Label, canned goods, Butter Beans ad Fresh Tomatoes, Anna Case Trustee South Family Shakers, West Albany, Mt. Lebanon, NY, chromolithographic labels, matted and framed, 15" h, 20" w 315.00

Letter

Canterbury, NH, March 24, 1798, concerning death of a sister, 12" x 7", splits, minor losses, toning, staining 225.00

New Lebanon, NY, July 15, 1849, from Sister Hannah Treadway to her biological sister Nancy Lucks, 6 pgs . . . 525.00

Magazine, The Shaker Herbalist, No. 1, Spring, 1975 . . . 15.00

Peg Board, 38-3/4" l, pine and cherry, old patina, one peg missing. 50.00

Photograph, albumen portrait, cabinet card form, three elderly Shaker sisters doing needlework, cozy indoor setting, orig unmarked mount, reverse filled with two manuscript religious poems, sgd by Nellie J. Watts 175.00

Rocker

35-3/4" h, armless, Mt. Lebanon, NY, late 19th C, production-type, several layers of later upholstery over old tape seat and back. 250.00

41" h, maple, three graduated slat-back, turned post terminating in simple finial, replaced splint seat, refinished 950.00

45" h, 15-1/2" h seat, arms, Enfield, curly maple, four graduated back slats, curved arms, front turned arm supports with mushroom caps 3,750.00

Sander, 3 to 3-1/2" h, wooden, 19th C, staining, price for 3 pc set 230.00

Seed Box, 14-3/4" l, unfinished pine, black and white paper label "Shakers' Garden Seeds, Raised at New Lebanon, NY," broken leather hinges 1,100.00

Sewing Desk, 25" d, 28" h work surface, 40" h overall, top with central paneled door, flanked by three lip molded drawers on either side, top drawers with keyhole escutcheons, mushroom-shaped walnut pulls on lower drawers, lower portion with three large similar drawers in front, side with paneled door above full length lip molded drawers, delicate turned legs, chestnut work surface, refinished soft wood, small chip on one small drawer 10,000.00

Sieve, 6-7/8" l, 3-5/8" h, stained wood, 19th C, minor imperfections 115.00

Spit Box, 10" d, yellow painted, Mt. Lebanon, NY, 19th C, crack, even paint wear 1,955.00

Stove Set, 17-1/2" l shove, 22" l tongs, wrought iron, attributed to Canterbury, NH 495.00

Swift, 15" h, worn orig yellow varnish, minor crack in table clamp, attributed to Hancock, MA 220.00

Table, work

26" x 72", 12-1/4" leaf, 29-1/2" h, walnut, poplar secondary wood, one drop leaf supported by 2 swing legs, dovetailed drawer in each end, turned tapering legs, old refinishing, attributed to Otterbein Shaker, Lebanon, OH, age crack, repairs, replaced hinges 2,100.00

37-1/2" x 48-3/4", 27-1/4" h, Hepplewhite, old red and pine two board top with rounded corners, old scrubbed finish, hardwood base, sq tapered legs, mortised and pinned apron, attributed to Enfield, NH 935.00

Tailor's Counter, six dovetailed lip molded drawers, top with large swing-over work surface, orig iron supports on side, short simple turned legs, each of drawer fronts fitted with walnut mushroom shaped pulls, old mellow patina, 72" w, 40" deep when open, 38" h. 21,000.00

Teapot, 8-1/2" h, tin, side spout 165.00

Wood Box, 37-1/2" w, 21" d, 31" h, pine, old mellow finish, bin top with hinged lid with breadboard ends, one dovetailed overlapping drawer, sq corner posts, chamfered feet, red stain int., wear from kindling, purchased from Shakers in Canterbury, NH, in 1940s, old pierced repair to one end of drawer front 880.00

SHAVING MUGS

History: Shaving mugs, which hold the soap, brush, and hot water used to prepare a beard for shaving, come in a variety of materials including tin, silver, glass, and pottery. One style, which has separate compartments for water and soap, is the scuttle, so called because of its coal-scuttle shape.

Personalized shaving mugs were made exclusively for use in barber shops in the United Sates. They began being produced shortly after the Civil War and continued to be made into the 1930s.

Unlike shaving mugs that were used at home, these mugs were personalized with the owner's name, usually in gilt. The mug was kept in a rack at the barber shop, and it was used only when the owner came in for a shave. This was done for hygienic purposes, to keep from spreading a type of eczema known as barber's itch.

The mugs were usually made on European porcelain blanks, that often contained the mark of "Germany,"

"France," or "Austria" on the bottom. In later years, a few were made on American-made semi-vitreous blanks. The artwork on mugs was done by decorators who worked for major barber supply houses. Occasionally the mark of the barber supply house is also stamped on the bottom of the mug.

After a short time, the mugs became more decorative, including hand-painted floral decorations, as well as birds, butterflies, and a wide variety of nature scenes, etc. These are classified today as "decorative" mugs.

Another category, "fraternal mugs," soon developed. These included the emblem of an organization the owner belonged to, along with his name emblazoned in gold above or below the illustration.

"Occupational mugs" were also very popular. These are mugs, which contained a painting of something that illustrated the owner's occupation, such as a butcher, a bartender, or a plumber. The illustration might be a man working at his job, or perhaps the tools of his trade, or a product, which he made or sold.

Of all these mugs, occupationals are the most prized. Their worth is determined by several factors: rarity (some occupations are rarer than others), size of mug, and size of illustration (the bigger the better), quality of artwork, and condition. Although rare mugs with cracks or chips can still be valuable if the damage does not affect the artwork on the mug. Generally speaking, a mug showing a man at work at his job is usually valued higher than that same occupation illustrated with only the tools or finished product.

The invention of the safety razor by King C. Gillette, issued to three and one-half million servicemen during World War I, brought about changes in personal grooming—men began to shave on their own rather than visiting the barber shop to be shaved. As a result, the need for personalized shaving mugs declined.

References: Susan and Al Bagdade, *Warman's English & Continental Pottery & Porcelain*, 3rd Edition, Krause Publications, 1998; Ronald S. Barlow, *Vanishing American Barber Shop*, Windmill Publishing, 1993; Keith E. Estep, *Shaving Mug & Barber Bottle Book*, Schiffer Publishing, 1995.

Collectors' Club: National Shaving Mug Collectors Association, 320 S. Glenwood St., Allentown, PA 18104.

Advisor: Bill Boyd.

Note: Prices shown are for typical mugs which have no damage and show only moderate wear on the gilt name and decoration.

Decorative

Bunch of violets	50.00
Butterfly hovering over water lily	75.00
Humorous, frog fishing	275.00
Windmill scene	150.00

Fraternal

Foresters of America, emblem over flags	125.00
Knight Templar, man standing in uniform	400.00
Knights of Pyhtias, shield of organization	100.00
Loyal Order of Buffaloes, buffalo head with flowers	450.00
Odd Fellows, chain emblem with eye	100.00
32nd Degree Mason, emblem over name	175.00
Woodman of the World, ax, stump, and bird	175.00

Occupational

Automobile, old touring car	850.00
Bartender, man serving two customers at bar	400.00
Baseball Game, player sliding into home plate, shows entire field	1,000.00
Brick Mason, man laying a brick wall on side of house	650.00
Butcher Tools, saw, sharpener, and cleaver	175.00
Cabinet Maker, man working at wood-working bench	500.00
Cowboy, man roping a steer	800.00
Dentist, man working on a patient in dental chair	700.00
Glass Blower, man blowing glass bottle	750.00
Hat Maker, man's hat in center of floral decorations	400.00
Horse-Drawn Ice Wagon	550.00
House Painter, man painting house on scaffold	550.00
Painter, can of paint and brush	250.00
Railroad Locomotive	250.00

SHAWNEE POTTERY

History: The Shawnee Pottery Co. was founded in 1937 in Zanesville, Ohio. The company acquired a 650,000-square-foot plant that had previously housed the American Encaustic Tiling Company. Shawnee produced as many as 100,000 pieces of pottery a day until 1961, when the plant closed.

Shawnee limited its production to kitchenware, decorative art pottery, and dinnerware. Distribution was primarily through jobbers and chain stores.

Marks: Shawnee can be marked "Shawnee," "Shawnee U.S.A.," "USA #——," "Kenwood," or with character names, e.g., "Pat. Smiley" and "Pat. Winnie."

(Occupational) Bartender, gold trim, $270.

References: Susan and Al Bagdade, *Warman's American Pottery and Porcelain*, Wallace-Homestead, 1994; Pam Curran, *Shawnee Pottery*, Schiffer Publishing, 1995; Jim and Bev Mangus, *Shawnee Pottery*, Collector Books, 1994, 1996 value update; Mark Supnick, *Collecting Shawnee Pottery*, L-W Book Sales, 1997; Duane and Janice Vanderbilt, *Collector's Guide to Shawnee Pottery*, Collector Books, 1992, 1996 value update.

Collectors' Club: Shawnee Pottery Collectors Club, P.O. Box 713, New Smyrna Beach, FL 32170.

Ashtray, Indian Arrowhead 580.00
Bank, Howdy Doody 395.00
Bowl, cov, Lobsterware, #907 . . . . 45.00
Candlesticks, pr, 6-1/2" h, hand dec gold trim 25.00
Casserole, cov, Lobster, Kenwood
   Large, 2 quart, with stand. 95.00
   Medium, 16 oz 68.00
   Small, 10 oz 45.00
Cookie Jar, cov
   Jill the Dutch Girl 80.00
   Muggsy. 650.00
   Puss 'n Boots 225.00
   Sailor Boy. 325.00
   Smiley, gold paint, orig decals 550.00
   Smiley/Winnie, butterscotch bank 1,350.00
Creamer
   Elephant. 40.00
   King Corn, No. 70. . . . . 25.00
   Lobster, Kenwood, 13 oz 100.00
   Puss N Boots, green and yellow 85.00
Cup and Saucer, King Corn, cup marked "90," and saucer marked "91" 45.00
Figure
   Raccoon. 65.00
   Squirrel. 80.00
Hors d'oeuvre Holder, Lobster, Kenwood 265.00
Lamp, emb flowers 45.00
Mixing bowl, King Corn
   5" d 37.00
   6-1/4" d 45.00
Pie Bird 45.00
Pitcher
   Ball style, blue 20.00
   Chanticleer, figural rooster. 125.00
   Embossed, green 20.00
   Little Bo Peep, blue hat, pink coat 100.00
   Little Bo Peep, blue, gold trim 650.00
   Smiley Pig, pink flower. 150.00
Planter
   Buddha, #524. . . . . 25.00
   Dog and jug 24.00
   Fawn, gold trim. 20.00
   Girl at gate 22.00
   Ram, #515 . . . . 25.00
   Water Trough, #716 . . . . 20.00
Plate, King Corn, 8" d 40.00
Range Shakers, pr, Smiley, red bib 5.00
Relish Tray, King Corn, marked "Shawnee 79". 35.00
Salt and Pepper Shakers, pr
   Dutch Boy and Girl. 35.00
   Lobster, Kenwood
      Claw shape 95.00
      Full bodied. 165.00
   Smiley Pig 125.00

Sugar Bowl, cov, Corn pattern, 5-1/4" h, $35.

Sugar, cov
   King Corn 42.00
   Lobster, Kenwood 65.00
Teapot, cov, King Corn 95.00
Vase
   #805, green 25.00
   #827, green 25.00
Wall Pocket
   Birdhouse. 40.00
   Grandfather Clock, #1261 . . . . 45.00

SILHOUETTES

History: Silhouettes (shades) are shadow profiles produced by hollow cutting, mechanical tracing, or painting. They were popular in the 18th and 19th centuries.

The name came from Etienne de Silhouette, a French Minister of Finance, who cut "shades" as a pastime. In America, the Peale family was well known for the silhouettes they made.

Silhouette portraiture lost popularity with the introduction of the daguerreotype prior to the Civil War. In the 1920s and 1930s a brief revival occurred when tourists to Atlantic City and Paris had their profiles cut as souvenirs.

Marks: An impressed stamp marked "PEALE" or "Peale Museum" identifies pieces made by the Peale family.

References: Shirley Mace, *Encyclopedia of Silhouette Collectibles on Glass*, Shadow Enterprises, 1992.

Museums: Essex Institute, Salem, MA; National Portrait Gallery, Washington, DC.

Children

4-3/4" d, girl, hollow cut, turned frame, stains 115.00
4-3/4" l, 3-5/8" w, boy, hollow cut, black cloth backing, discolored and stained paper, old black molded frame 220.00
5" h, 3-7/8 w, boy, hollow cut, black velvet backing, ink inscription "take When A Child, George A. Cushing," printed "Certificate of Merit" on back of frame from Boston school, "Master G. A. Cushing," old frame, wrinkles, taped tears 90.00
10-1/2" h, 9-1/2" w, boy, painted, flaked white coating, mahogany veneer frame, gilded liner 60.00

Groups

7-1/8" h, 9-1/8" l, eight hollow-cut silhouettes, cut-work background, men and woman, framed together in common period frame, attributed to PA 575.00

Woman, hollow cut, minor stains, gilt frame, 5-3/4" h, 4-7/8 w, $85. Photo courtesy of Garth's Auctions, Inc.

18-3/4" x 15-1/2", pen and ink, two men and women, seated on chairs, pencil room int., sgd "Aug Edoart, fecit 1840," bird's eye maple frame 650.00

Men

4-3/4" h, 3-1/2" d, young man, gilt highlights, back labeled "J. I. Magin Artist," black oval frame 115.00

5-1/8" h, 4" w, young man, hollow cut, black cloth backing, modern frame, stains 140.00

5-7/8" h, 4-3/3" w, young man, gilt detail, back scribed "A college friend of G. H. Nurse's 1858," matted and framed 90.00

7-1/2" h, 5-1/2" w, Henry Clay, faded black cloth backing, minor stains, tear at edge, later mat and frame 95.00

8" h, 6-1/4" w, full length profile of stocky man, top hat, old inscription on back of frame "Silhouette of Doctor Johnson," cut from heavy black colored paper, gray paper background, framed 275.00

8-1/4" x 6-3/4", slave, praying pose, rosewood frame, 19th C
. . . . 575.00

11-3/4" h, 5-1/4" w, full length portrait, Lt. Edward M. Yard, U.S. Navy Boston 1st March 1842 on *John Adams* Sloop of War, unsgd, attributed to August Edouart, framed 750.00

Pairs

3-1/2" h, 2-3/4" w, man and woman, penciled highlights in hair and bonnet, man identified on back as Cornelius Wheeler, oval brass and wood frames, pr 200.00

4-1/2" h, 3-1/4" w, pair, Captain Braddock and Martha Bourne Nye of Sandwich, marked on reverse "Gallery of Cuttings cut by Master Hankes with Common Scissors," one with bronze highlights, named on reverse, framed, toning, staining, fold creases 475.00

4-1/2" x 5-3/4", girl and boy, cut, titled "Agnes and Lindsey, sgd "Auguste Edouart, 1831" 450.00

5-1/2" h, 4-1/2" h, woman and child, hollow cut, black cloth backing, worn eglomise glass, price for pr 275.00

6-5/8" h, 5-5/8" w, man and woman, hollow cut, black cloth backing, old mahogany veneer frames with black finish, minor stains, pr 220.00

7-5/8" h, 10-7/8" w, facing pair of men in top hats, sgd in pencil on backing paper "Mary D. Smith" cherry frame, minor stains
. . . . 345.00

8-1/2" h, 7-1/4" w, man and woman, hollow cut, matching emb brass frames with cardboard backs, stains, and damage, pr
. . . . 200.00

Women

3-1/2" h, 2-3/4" w, woman, penciled hair, illegible identification on back, oval brass and wood frame 100.00

4" x 4-7/8", pen and ink, woman wearing lacy collar, orig black reeded frame 295.00

4-3/8" h, 3-1/2" w, young lady, hollow cut, painted highlights, American School, 19th C, toning, minor staining 175.00

5-3/8" h, 5-1/8" w, old woman in bonnet, ink silhouette, old guilt frame, stains 70.00

5-3/4" h, 4-7/8" w, young woman, hollow cut, gilt frame, minor stains 85.00

5-7/8" x 6-5/8", hollow cut, young woman, paper with emb mark "Museum," (Peale Museum), black cloth backing, minor stains and creases, mahogany veneer frame 225.00

6-1/4" h, 4-1/2" w, hollow cut, black cloth ground, molded pine frame 100.00

SILVER

History: The natural beauty of silver lends itself to the designs of artists and craftsmen. It has been mined and worked into an endless variety of useful and decorative items. Pure silver is too soft to be fashioned into strong, durable, and serviceable utensils. Therefore, a way was found to give silver the required degree of hardness by adding alloys of copper and nickel.

Silversmithing in America goes back to the early 17th century in Boston and New York and the early 18th century in Philadelphia. Boston artisans were influenced by the English styles, New Yorkers by the Dutch.

References: Louise Belden, *Marks of American Silversmiths in the Ineson-Bissell Collection*, University of Virginia Press, 1980; Frederick Bradbury, *Bradbury's Book of Hallmarks*, J. W. Northend, 1987; Bonita Campbell and Nan Curtis (curators), *Depression Silver*, California State University, 1995; Maryanne Dolan, *1830's-1900's American Sterling Silver Flatware*, Books Americana, 1993; Janet Drucker, *Georg Jensen: A Tradition of Splendid Silver,* Schiffer Publishing, 1997; Stephen G. C. Ensko, *American Silversmiths and Their Marks*, Dover Publications, 1983; Rachael Feild, *Macdonald Guide to Buying Antique Silver and Sheffield Plate*, Macdonald & Co., 1988; *Fine Victorian Gold- and Silverplate, Exquisite Designs from the 1882 Catalog of the Meriden-Brittania Co.,* Schiffer Publishing, 1997; Nancy Gluck, *Grosvenor Pattern of Silverplate*, Silver Season, 1996; Tere Hagan, *Silverplated Flatware*, 4th ed., Collector Books, 1990, 1998 value update; Kenneth Crisp Jones (ed.), *Silversmiths of Birmingham and Their Marks*, N.A.G. Press, 1981, distributed by Antique Collectors Club; Henry J. Kaufman, *Co-*

Ionial Silversmith, Astragal Press, 1995; Ralph and Terry Kovel, *Kovels' American Silver Marks*, Crown Publishers, 1989.

Joel Langford, *Silver*, Chartwell Books, 1991; Everett L. Maffett, *Silver Banquet* II, Silver Press, 1990; Penny C. Morrill, *Silver Masters of Mexico*, Schiffer Publishing, 1996; Penny Chittim Morrill and Carole A. Berk, *Mexican Silver 20th Century Handwrought Jewelry & Metalwork*, Schiffer Publishing, 1994; Richard Osterberg, *Silver Hollowware for Dining Elegance*, Schiffer Publishing, 1996; ——, *Sterling Silver Flatware for Dining Elegance*, Schiffer Publishing, 1994; Benton Rabinovitch, *Antique Silver Servers for the Dining Table*, Joslin Hall Publishing, 1991; Dorothy T. Rainwater, *Encyclopedia of American Silver Manufacturers*, 3rd ed., Schiffer Publishing, 1986; Dorothy T. and H. Ivan Rainwater, *American Silverplate*, Schiffer Publishing, 1988; *Sterling Silver, Silverplate, and Souvenir Spoons*, revised ed., L-W Book Sales, 1987, 1994 value update; Charles Truman (ed.), *Sotheby's Concise Encyclopedia of Silver*, Antique Collectors' Club, 1996; Charles Venable, *Silver in America 1840-1940*, Harry Abrams, 1994; Joanna Wissinger, *Arts and Crafts Metalwork and Silver*, Chronicle Books, 1994; Seymour B. Wyler, *Book of Old Silver*, Crown Publishers, 1937 (available in reprint).

Periodicals: *Silver Magazine*, P.O. Box 9690, Rancho Santa Fe, CA 92067; *Silver News*, 1112 16th St. NW, Ste. 240, Washington, DC 20036; *Silver Update*, P.O. Box 960, Funkstown, MD 21734.

Collectors' Club: New York Silver Society, 242 E. 7th St., #5, New York, NY 10009.

Museums: Bayou Bend Collection, Houston, TX; Boston Museum of Fine Arts, Boston, MA; Colonial Williamsburg Foundation, Williamsburg, VA; Currier Gallery of Art, Manchester, NH; Yale University Art Gallery, New Haven, CT; Wadsworth Antheneum, Hartford, CT.

Additional Listings: See Silver Flatware in *Warman's Americana & Collectibles* for more examples.

American, 1790-1840

Mostly Coin

Coin silver is slightly less pure than sterling silver. Coin silver has 900 parts silver to 100 parts alloy. Sterling silver has 925 parts silver. American silversmiths followed the coin standards. Coin silver is also called Pure Coin, Dollar, Standard, or Premium.

Beaker, 3-1/8" h, Asa Blanchard, Lexington, KY, 1818-38, barrel form, reeded banding, monogrammed, mkd on base, minor dents, 5 troy oz............................5,475.00
Bowl
3-1/8" h, 5 13/16" d, Lincoln and Foss, Boston, 1848-57, applied beaded rim, chased floral garland design, ftd, mkd on base, 8 troy oz............................350.00
5-1/2" h, 7" d, Francis Bassett, flaring rim, bulging band to shoulder, pedestal with tin rim on base with incised lines, faint "HB" monogram on side, block hallmarked "Bassett" in base.......................................650.00
Butter Dish, cov, 6-1/8" d, 6" h, Lincoln & Foss, Boston, 1848-57, shaped dome top, floral final and chased foliate banding above base, wide flange, applied circular molded base with

pierced inset, mkd "Lincoln & Foss Pure Silver Coin Boston," monogrammed, 14 troy oz....................350.00
Cann, 5-1/8" h, William Swan, Boston, 1757-74, bulbous form, molded rim, applied molded circular foot, cast hollow scroll handle, molded body drop at upper joining, mkd on base, initialed "CTL," dents, 11 troy oz................1,850.00
Chalice, 8" h, 4-1/4" w, mkd "S. Hoyt & Co.," repousse grape clusters, leaves, and vines, chased engraving of three-masted steamship flying American flag in wave sea, reverse with presentation "To Thomas C. Dudley Purcer of Steamship 'City of Richmond' from his friends, the officers and crew in token of their admiration of him as a gentleman and officer Wm. Parrish, 1st offer W. T. Freligh, 1st engr O. Chiciester, 2nd Ino Barrett 2, Geo Tamlyn Stewd, N.Y. March 1st 1852"
....700.00
Coffeepot, 12-3/8" h, Ball, Black & Co., NY, c1850, rosebud finial, domed molded lid, baluster form body, paneled lower portion, applied Greek key banding, engraved Rococo C-scrolls, shells, and other foliate devices, naturalistic handle with rose motif, circular molded base with similar Greek key banding, monogrammed, mkd on base, very minor dents, 33 troy oz
....950.00
Creamer
4-7/8" h, Joseph Lownes, Philadelphia, 1859-1820, neoclassical form, applied reeded banding, strap handle, monogrammed, mkd twice on base, 5 troy oz.........460.00
6" h, Thomas Fletcher, Philadelphia, 1813-15, baluster form, applied foliate banding, mkd on base, 10 troy oz
....350.00
6-1/4" h, America, mid 19th C, baluster form, foliate chasing, applied geometric banding, molded circular base, mkd "Pure Silver Coin," and "T & W," 4 troy oz.......325.00
6-1/2" h, baluster form, applied foliate and geometric banding and handle, molded circular base, monogrammed, possibly resoldered at shoulder, 8 troy oz...............260.00
9-1/4" h, Ball, Black & Co., NY, c1850, rosebud finial, domed molded lid, baluster form body, paneled lower portion, applied Greek key banding, elaborately engraved Rococo C-scrolls, shells, and foliate devices, naturalistic handle with rose motif, circular molded base with similar Greek key banding, monogrammed, mkd on base, minor dents, 15 troy oz..500.00
Creamer and Sugar, 8-3/4" h cov sugar with 2 handles, lobed baluster form, applied thistle and shell banding, reeded strap handles, William Thomson, NY, 1810-45, 28 troy oz.550.00
Cream Jug, 5-1/2" h Joseph Lownes, Philadelphia, 1785-1822, baluster form, applied diagonal ribbed banding, circular molded base, monogrammed, solder repairs to base, minor dents, 6 troy oz..200.00
Crumber, 13-1/8" l, Geradus Boyce, NY, 1820-57, engraved with reserve of castle, scrolling foliage devices, minor dents
....175.00
Ladle, 13-3/4" l, Joseph Richardson, Jr. and Nathaniel Richardson, Philadelphia, 1785-91, molded handle, V-slashed, double molded bowl, mkd three time on handle, monogrammed and dated "1782," 7 troy oz....................875.00
Mug
3-1/2" h, Nicholas N. Weaver, Utica, New York, c1791-1853, applied loop handle, line dec, rolled edge type rim . 250.00
4-3/8" h, Geradus Boyce, NY, 1820-57, flaring paneled shape, foliate and C-scroll engraving, monogrammed,
....200.00
Napkin Ring, 2-1/8" d, unidentified American maker, bas relief foliate design, inscribed "Charles Codman"........200.00

Powder Box, 2-7/8" h, 4" d, low round form, butterfly finial, domed cov, engraved monogram, Gorham, some dents, 6 troy oz. 230.00

Spoon

Serving, 12" l, George Alexander and Peter Riker, New York, 1797-1800, bright cut dec, monogrammed, mkd twice, 3 troy oz. 825.00

Teaspoon, 5-3/4" l, Pelletreau, Bennett & Cook, NY, 1825-28, basket of flowers, outlined shell on bowl, monogrammed, 3 troy oz, price for set of six 275.00

Sugar Bowl

6" d, Jones, Ball & Co., Boston, 1952-54, 4-1/2" h, navette-form, applied beaded rim, chased C-scroll and foliate design, ftd, handle, monogrammed, mkd on base, 7 troy oz. 450.00

7" h, Thomas Fletcher and Sidney Gardner, Boston, 1808-25, acorn finial, domed lid, baluster form body, applied foliate and star banding, sq molded base, monogrammed, mkd twice on base, minor dents, 22 troy oz 350.00

7-3/4" h, Jonathon Stodder and Benjamin Frobisher, Boston, 1816-25, two handles, strawberry finial, molded circular lid, baluster form bowl, acanthus leaf chasing, applied scroll and foliage banding, circular molded base, applied gadrooning, monogrammed, mkd on base, minor dents, 23 troy oz. 425.00

Teapot, cov

10" h, Henry Ball, Erastus Tompkins, and William Black, NY, 1839-1851, basket of fruit finial, domed lid, baluster form, applied grape and foliate banding, scroll handle, oval molded base, engraved, mkd on base, 32 troy oz. 700.00

10-1/2" h, Baldwin Gardiner, Phila and New York, 1814-46, basket of flower finial, domed lid with foliate chasing, baluster form body, applied foliate banding, ornately chased foliate and cornucopia handle, spout with similar chasing, open hands motif, circular molded base, 43 troy oz 990.00

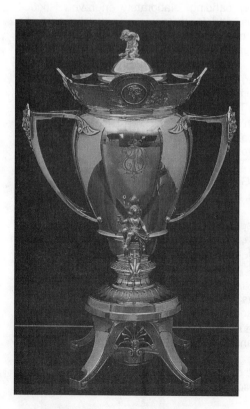

(American) Hot Water Urn, Gorham, cupid finial, putti handle, twin square "C" handles with satyr masks, four raised bust medallions on rim, four flaring feet, orig burner, 18-1/4" h, 105 troy oz., $7,850.

Tea Set

Adams, William, New York, c1830, 9-3/4" h teapot, two handled cov sugar, creamer, floral final over domed lid, paneled baluster body, applied foliate banding, molded circular base, monogrammed, mkd on base, very minor dents, 63 troy oz 1,750.00

Gale, William and Son, New York, teapot on stand, coffeepot, creamer, sugar, teapot, and waste bowl, repousse dec of grape clusters and vine, monogrammed teapot on stand mkd "Tiffany Co. New York sterling," matching silverplated tray. 6,250.00

Monell, John I. And Charles M. Williams, New York, c1825, 10-3/8" h teapot, creamer, two-handled cov sugar, basket of flowers finials, chased scrolling leaf lid over bulbous lobed body, stepped circular base, applied foliate banding, paneled spout, mkd on base, 74 troy oz 2,185.00

Rice, J. T., Albany, New York, 1813-53, 9-5/8" h teapot, creamer, two-handled cov sugar, basket of flower finial, domed lid with foliate chasing, lobed baluster form, applied rose and other foliate banding, strap handle with applied foliate sprays, spout with applied acanthus leaves, grape and leaf motifs on legs ending in paws, ball feet, mkd on base, minor dents and losses, 98 troy oz 2,550.00

Water Jug, 10-7/8" h, America, second quarter 19th C, baluster form, applied foliate banding, molded circular foot, scrolling handle, inscribed "Presented to Esek Saunders. A token of esteem Jany 1st 1833," 30 troy oz, very minor dents 890.00

Water Pitcher

9-1/4" h, Fletcher & Gardinier, Philadelphia, 1811-25, baluster form, applied foliate banding, scrolling handle with eagle's head, molded circular base, mkd on base, minor dents on base, 32 troy oz 1,500.00

10-1/4" h, James Ward, Hartford, CT, 1768-1856, lobed baluster, applied foliate banding, scrolling handle, molded circular base, inscribed "The Boston Light Infantry to their respected past Commander Henry Codman Esquire 1820," mkd "Ward" twice on base, 36 troy oz 1,200.00

Wine Ewer, 10-7/8" h, Lows, Ball & Co., Boston, 1841-47, baluster form, engraved C-scroll and foliate design, monogrammed on base, "S. C. Jan 1, 1845," base mkd, minor dents, 16 troy oz. 575.00

American, 1840-1920

Mostly Sterling

There are two possible sources for the origin o the word sterling. The first is that it is a corruption of the name Easterling. Easterlings were German silversmiths who came to England in the Middle Ages. The second is that it is named for the sterling (little star) used to mark much of the early English silver.

Sterling is 92.5 percent per silver. Copper comprises most of the remaining alloy. American manufacturers began to switch to the sterling standard about the time of the Civil War.

Asparagus Tongs

Bailey & Co., mid/late 19th C, bright-cut engraved leafy floral dec on handle, pierced grips, 6 troy oz 375.00

Mulford, Wendell & Co., mid/late 19th C, teardrop-shaped pierced dec, 6 troy oz. 375.00

Basket

Towle, early 20th C, 13" d, open pierced flower shape, reeded rim, base, and handle, two balls finial, monogram, 26 troy oz 800.00

Reed & Barton, 1946, 13" d, sterling, leaf motif double bowls, central entwined vine handle, 14 troy oz 250.00

Watson Co., c1926, engraved neoclassical dec, garlands and leaves, openwork border under rim, low ftd base, monogram on handle, 28 troy oz 650.00

Bowl

Barbour Silver Co., late 19th C, oblong shape, chased floral motifs and borders, monogram, 23 troy oz 700.00

Gorham, 1906, sterling, open oblong shape, reeded serpentine rim, monogram, 22 troy oz 175.00

S. Kirk & Son, 1868-98, 9" d, sterling, round, repousse floral dec, applied scroll rim, 16 troy oz 635.00

Wood & Hughes, 1871-99, 4-7/8" d, asymmetrical fluted cup-form, textured basketweave surface dec, four cast turtle feet, central monogram, 6 troy oz 865.00

Candelabra, three-light

9-1/8" h, Redlich, 20th C, spreading circulars base, removable bobeches, weighted, pr 435.00

11-1/2" h, Gorham, 20th C, sterling, central tapering column, S-curve reeded arms, weighted 350.00

Candlesticks, pr

6-1/8" h, Gorham, retailed by Foster & Co., 20th C, pointed oval spreading base with fluted detail, paneled stems, fluting under receded nozzle, weighted 400.00

8-1/4" h, Gorham, retailed by Bigelow, Kennard & Co., 1905, Corinthian columns, removable bobeches, weighted
. . . . 750.00

10" h, International, Royal Danish pattern, elongated teardrop body, decorative motif under nozzle and above base, monogram, weighted 520.00

10-1/4" h, Gorham, 1907, Corinthian column style, removable bobeches, sq pedestal base with beaded detail, weighted
. . . . 980.00

Celery Vase, 10-3/8" h, cast stag head handles, Greek key border, mid 19th C. 980.00

Center Dish, 11-3/4" d, Redlich & Co., retailed by A. Stowell & Co., c1914, chased floral border, openwork sides, four cast neoclassical floral motifs, four floral dec raised feet, monogram, 22 troy oz 750.00

Centerpiece

6-15/16" h, 16-3/8" l, Gorham, 1860s, navette-form, engraved inscription and date 1,380.00

9" d, Durgin, late 19th/early 20th C, central circular mirror with four scroll arm candle holders, openwork leaf dec, engraved leaf and bow design on candle nozzles, four ball feet
. . . . .1,265.00

Chamber Stick

4" h, Howard, late 19th C, sterling, repousse floral design, matte background, sq pan, scroll foliate border on pan and nozzle, four claw and ball feet, removable bobeche, 18 troy oz 800.00

6-5/8" h, Gorham, c1900, silver-gilt, oval pan with repousse leaf motifs at end, handle with slot for match, central monogram, Gorham, 2 troy oz 175.00

Cigar Cutter, 2-1/8" h, Herbst & Wassall, early 20th C, matchbox body, four ball feet, cutter on top, side shell-form bowl ashtray, pr, 3 troy oz 400.00

Coffeepot, 8-1/2" h, Whiting, lighthouse-form, fluted spout, 24 troy oz. 275.00

Compote, 4-1/2" h, Durgin, early 20th C, shell-form bow, twisting serpent tail stem, spreading circular base, weighted . 350.00

Creamer, 7-3/4" h, John Burger, New York City, repair urn shape, classical detail, engraved shield and flowers, monogrammed, mkd "Burger" at handle 250.00

Demitasse Coffee Service, Depasse Mfg. Co., New York, 7-1/2" h coffeepot, creamer, open sugar, tapering rect form, cut corners, angular wooden handle and finial, 18 troy oz . . 200.00

Desk Clock, 4-3/4" h, Reed & Barton, early 20th C, tambour, acid-etched scroll foliate dec, ... 435.00

Dessert Plate, 6-3/8" d, Kirk, 1925-32, repousse floral border, central monogram, 32 troy oz, set of eight 650.00

Dish

9-1/4" d, Bigelow Kennard & Co., circular, pierced border with trellis, scrolling foliage, and flowers, field chased with scrolling foliage and flowers, monogrammed, 16 oz 225.00

10-1/4" d, Whiting, 20th C, circular spreading base, openwork floral design, shaped rim, 16 troy oz 230.00

Goblet, 6-3/4" h, Tiffany & Co., 1865-75, applied fretwork band on rim, fretwork border around base, 7 troy oz 400.00

Fish Server, 11-5/8" l, Albert Coles, engraved floral border on blade, central engraved fish, engraved scroll foliate design on handle, monogram, 3 troy oz 175.00

Flask, 5-1/2" h, Gorham, early 20th C, sterling, cigar case shape, hidden twist-off corner spout, 6 troy oz. 325.00

Julep Cup, 4" h, mkd "E. & D Kinsey," Cincinnati, OH . . 425.00

Kettle and Tray, Dominick & Haff, retailed by Shreve, Crump & Low, early 20th C, sterling, round kettle with fluted detail, scroll design joints, sq tray with band of fluting under reeded rim, 48 troy oz. 650.00

Kettle on Stand, 14-1/2" h, Gorham, Plymouth pattern, shaped oval, cut corners, oval molded foot and base, four ball feet, scrolling supports, angular wooden over handle, burner unmarked, 42 troy oz. 800.00

Lady's Flask, 4-1/4" l, Dominick & Haff, c1900, oval shape, repousse floral design on matte ground, 2 troy oz 375.00

Martini Shaker, 5-1/2" h, Reed & Barton, 20th C, individual size, 5 troy oz 115.00

Mug

3-5/8" h, Gorham, 1870, barrel shape, reeded borders and handle, monogram, 5 troy oz. 200.00

4-1/4" h, Colin V. G. Forbes, reeded rim and base borders, scroll handle, monogram, 12 troy oz 800.00

Nutmeg Grater

2-1/8" h, shell form, engraved "Winslow," minor loss and corrosion to grater. 325.00

4-3/8" h, Jacobi & Jenkins, c1900, cov compartment, exposed grating surface, monogram, 2 troy oz 865.00

Patch Box, late 18th C, engraved basketweave design, gold wash int., repaired, 2 troy oz 115.00

Peacock Dish, Gorham, 20th C, cast body, chased tail feathers, pr, 16 troy oz 2,300.00

Pepper Grinder, 3-1/2" h, Gorham, 1898, cylindrical, chased floral dec, monogram 115.00

Pickle Server, 9-3/4" h, three-prong gold wash fork, beaded disk detail, monogram on back, fitted leather case, 1 troy oz
. . . . 150.00

Pitcher, 10-1/8" h, Gorham, early 20th C, paneled baluster, spreading circular base, reeded rim, angular handle, minor dents, 25 troy oz. 500.00

Pitcher and Tray, 7-1/2" h pitcher, 14-7/8" l tray, Theodore B. Starr, 1900-24, sterling, Queen Anne revival style, paneled baluster form, pitcher with reeded detail, two handled tray with reeded border, engraved eagle over crown on both, 40 troy oz. 850.00

Porringer, 4-5/8" d, Gorham, retailed by Spaulding & Co, low relief band under rim, nursery rhymes, pierced scroll design handle, monogram, 7 troy oz 350.00

Powder Jar, 4" h, Black, Starr & Frost, 20th C, chased floral border on top, monogram, cut glass base. 175.00

Presentation Bowl, 9-7/8" d, 3-3/4" h, Gorham, 1880, sterling and mixed metal, four raised feet, hammered surface, applied birds and plants, two applied medallions, owl and bird in trees, inscription on base, 46 troy oz 4,600.00

Presentation Pitcher, 8" h, Gorham, 1880, sterling and mixed metal, hammered surface, applied leaf and fruit motifs, four lower panels with chased figures of mythological women, branch-form handle, inscription on base, 36 troy oz .10,350.00

Punch Bowl, 11-3/4" d, 8-7/8" h, Dominick & Haff, retailed by Smith Patterson & Co., early 20th C, reticulated rim, ladle, twelve cups, monogram, 95 troy oz 2,650.00

Ramekin, 3-1/2" d, Hamilton & Diesinger, circular, pierced, trellis, scrolls, and flowers, handles with pierced terminals, monogram, French porcelain liners, set of twelve, 31 oz, 4 dwt 850.00

Salt and Pepper Shakers, pr, 4-1/4" h, Whiting, late 19th/early 20th C, pear form, hammered surface, applied gold washed birds and flowers, 4 troy oz 435.00

Salver, 10-1/4" d, John B. Jones, Boston, 1816-37, applied shaped foliate rim and feet, monogrammed, minor surface abrasions, 22 troy oz 635.00

Sauce Boat, 5-7/16" l, Gorham, 1886, relief heads on upright handles, engraved name and monogram, price for pr, 19 troy oz 800.00

Sauce Tureen, cov, Towle, late 19th/early 20th C, baluster-form, two applied lion's head ring handles, 11 troy oz. 300.00

Smoker's Set, lower relief scroll foliate design, cigarette case, matchsafe, pocketknife, cigar cutter, fitted case, c1900, 4 troy oz 375.00

Spoon
7-1/2" l, Jacob Hurd, Boston, 1702-58, spatulate end mid-rib handle, double molded drop, monogrammed, mkd, minor dents, wear to bowl 350.00

7-3/4" l, Benjamin Burt, Boston, 1729-1805, spatulate end mid-rib handle, long drop with shell, monogrammed, mkd 375.00

Sugar Bowl, cov, 8-1/2" h, 2 handles, bud finial, domed lid, baluster form, applied rose banding, ram's head mounts on sq molded base, keystone touchmark with "DH," minor dents, 21 troy oz. 350.00

Tazza, 9-7/8" d, Dominick & Haff, 20th C, retailed by Shreve, Crump & Low, openwork design, putti in scroll foliate background, cut-form base, three scroll feet with openwork dec, 22 troy oz 920.00

Tea and Coffee Set
Aldelphia, 20th C, 9-7/8" h coffeepot, teapot, creamer, cov sugar, waste bowl, melon baluster-form, repousse floral and scroll motif, 66 troy oz 1,380.00

Ball, Black & Co., c1868, Greco-Roman Revival, sterling, coffeepot, teapot, cov creamer, cov two-handled sugar, waste bowl, helmet-form finial with beading above scroll engraved lid, 10-1/2" h coffeepot with elaborately engraved body centering reserve of locomotive, reverse with identical center reserve with "1868," beaded handles surmounted by neoclassical heads, anthemion leaves, circular molded base, 9-3/4" h teapot inscribed "Presented to Addison Day Esq. By the Employees of the Rome, Watertown & Ogdensburg Railroad Co., Dec. 1st, 1868," minor loss to one teapot ivory spacer, 98 troy oz 3,450.00

Durgin, retailed by Grogan Company, late 19th C, 9-3/4" h coffeepot, kettle on stand, teapot, creamer, cov sugar, waste bowl, paneled baluster-form, ftd base, ivory finials, monogram, 148 troy oz 3,450.00

Gorham, 1912-51, sterling, coffeepot, teapot, creamer, cov sugar, waste bowl, baluster form, spreading circular base,

reeded borders, baluster finials, monogram, 67 troy oz 875.00

Redlich & Co., retailed for Shreve, Crump and Low, late 19th C, sterling, tea and coffee pots, kettle on stand, creamer, cov sugar, waste bowl with strainer, and tray, baluster-form, chased floral design, 302 troy oz 9,200.00

Rogers, 20th C, 12" h coffeepot, teapot, creamer, open sugar, waste bowl, baluster-form, gadrooned detail, stylized acorn finials, 58 troy oz 900.00

Tea Set, Goodnow & Jenks, retailed by J. E. Caldwell & Co., c1900, 6-1/2" h teapot with wooden handle, creamer, cov sugar, oblong oval form, floral relief rims and handles, four ball feet, hinge on teapot not secured 635.00

Teaspoon, 6" l, James Easton II, Nantucket, c1830, monogrammed, mkd, set of 5, 2 troy oz 230.00

Vase
6-7/8" h, Gorham, 1873, cylindrical, hammered surface, engraved dec band diagonally across height, lower circular foot, band of birds, ivy, and flowers, 5 troy oz 500.00

30" h, Whiting, retailed by C. D. Peacock, 1913, tall trumpet, chased and engraved borders, alternating vertical fluted bands, central applied rosettes, applied neoclassical style motifs of garlands and fruit under rim, 111 troy oz.5,475.00

Wine Coaster, 4-3/4" d, Gorham, 1897, ftd, openwork sides, monogram, 4 troy oz 230.00

Arts & Crafts

Silver of the Arts & Crafts movement encompasses several styles and features well-made craftsmanship. The movement encouraged crafts people to express themselves in whatever medium they were using, thus creating some exciting silver items for today's collector to enjoy. As craftsman, they often chose to hammer and adorn pieces with unique trims and borders, as well as free-flowing forms. Most pieces have impressed marks. Because the Arts & Crafts movement was international, guilds were located in the United States, Great Britain, Germany, and Austria, creating many forms.

Bowl
7" d, Peterson, hammered sterling, five-lobed form, imp mark 210.00

8-1/2" d, 2-1/2" h, F. W. Lawrence, hammered, ftd, fluted body, two scrolled handles, stamped mark, pr 450.00

Candlesticks, pr, 12" h, Kalo, hammered, initials on base, imp mark 2,900.00

Cocktail Shaker, 8" h, LeBolt, hammered, detailed rim, imp mark 700.00

Compote
5-1/2" d, Gorham, hand-hammered, imp mark. 150.00

6" d, Kalo, hand-hammered, five-lobed bowl 550.00

Creamer and Sugar, 4" h, Kalo, hammered, imp mark 750.00

Demitasse Cup, John O. Bellis, hammered, scalloped rim, imp mark, set of six 125.00

Pitcher, 10-1/2" h, 8" d, Kalo, hand hammered, emb sections, monogrammed "B", stamped "Sterling/Handwrought/The Kalo Shop/Chicago/USA/5 Pints" 2,600.00

Serving Spoon, 9-1/2", Kalo, hammered 275.00

Shaker, 7" h, Woolley, hammered, pierced holes in top, finely tooled center floral design, mkd 450.00

Tea Caddy Spoon, 2-1/2" h, 1-1/2" w, Handicraft Guide, hand hammered, c1895, cut-out handle, die-stamped 150.00

Tea Set, LeBolt, hammered, 7-1/2" h teapot, 3-1/2" h creamer, 3-1/2" h sugar, 13" d tray, imp marks 1,000.00
Tray
  9-1/2" d, Kalo, hand-hammered, five-lobed rim, imp mark 500.00
  10-1/2" l, 5" w, hammered, handled, glass bottom, imp mark 325.00
  11" d, LeBolt, hammered, detailed edge dec, imp mark 160.00

Continental

Generally, Continental silver does not have a strong following in the United States, but Danish pieces by Georg Jensen are early sought. As the antiques marketplace continued to expand globally, Continental silver has become more popular.

Austrian
  Bowl, 5-1/8" d, repousse floral design, two medallions of pastoral scenes with cow and horse, spreading circular base, 4 troy oz 175.00
  Box, cov, 9" h, mid 19th C, bombe form, engraved design, mark's mark "WH," 9 troy oz 425.00
  Candlesticks, pr, 12" h, 19th C, Rococo Revival style, floral repousse baluster form standard, molded socle, cast scrolls and wave work feet, 26 troy oz 750.00
  Chalice, 7-7/8" h, c1910, raised repeating geometric and medallion pattern, trumpet base with raised repeating pyramid pattern, imp "WMFM," wear to finish 250.00
Chinese Export, kettle on stand, 14-5/8" h, kettle with chased landscape scenes and figures, floral and plant panels, extensive inscriptions, bamboo finial, handle, and stand, c1900, 44 troy oz 865.00
Denmark
  Cigarette Lighter, 3-1/2" h, lamp-form, leaf dec foot, bud finial, Georg Jensen, 1925-30, 5 troy oz 1,380.00
  Coffeepot, 11-1/8" h, pear-shape, fluted band on bottom of pot and on lid, ball in fluted cup finial, lightly hammered surface, part-wood scroll handle, applied ball and scroll dec, Georg Jensen, 29 troy oz .2,185.00
  Condiment, 5-1/4" h, Andress Holm, Copenhagen, 1795, hinged lid, cobalt blue glass liner 295.00
Dutch
  Basket, 11-1/2" h, pierced border, engraved leaf pattern under rim, 19th C, 28 troy oz 850.00
  Snuff Box, 1-7/8" l, Amsterdam, c1740, cartouche form, molded rim, cov engraved with cipher, hinged lid .1,200.00
  Tankard, 6" h, cup form body, repousse vignettes with artistic cherubs, flattened cov with leaf form thumb piece, claw and ball feet, 17 oz 1,400.00
  Teapot, 6-1/8" h, Gerrit Honing maker, pear-shape, repousse scroll and tassel dec, baluster finial, eagle head spout, cast lion on scroll handle, early 18th C, 12 troy oz 1,265.00
French
  Chocolate Pot, 8-1/4" h, baluster, turned wooden side handle, three pad feet, hinged swing finial, Paris, 1781, 18 troy oz 2,000.00
  Creamer, 5-1/2" h, hinged lid, Rococo detail, monogrammed, indistinct mark 140.00
  Egg Cup Set, 19th C, engraved egg-form container, two pedestal bases, 950 fine, 3 troy oz 300.00
  Sauceboat and undertray, J. C. Camier, Paris, 1809-19, oval, attached undertray, flying handle, foliage and applied figural mask, 23 ox 2,500.00

Tumbler, 4" h, spreading circular base, gadrooned border, Paris, 18th C, some dents, 3 troy oz 300.00
German
  Decanter, 15-1/2" h, glass body, shaped oval, lower body mounted with scrolling foliage, flowers, putti, and trellis, etched foliate glass, long neck, upper neck mounted with similar dec, glass stopper with putti finial 1,700.00
  Figure, knights, .800 silver, gilt dec, ivory faces and details, 20th C, pr 1,850.00
  Reindeer and Sleigh, 9-1/2" l, attachable harness, gold wash int. sleigh, 800 fine, late 18th/early 19th C, 11 troy oz 750.00
  Salt, 3-1/2" l, four paw feet, openwork body, chased floral garlands, ribbons, and mythological heads, cobalt blue glass liners, 18th/19th C, price for pr 200.00
  Sugar Bowl, 4-5/8" d, repousse openwork basket, elaborate floral, fruit, and scroll design, floral openwork swing handle, spreading circular foot, leaf and floral borders, gold wash removable int. bowl, late 19th C 260.00
  Tea and Coffee Service, tea and coffee pots, kettle on stand, creamer, cov sugar, ribbed melon baluster-form, mythological sea figures, 800 fine, late 19th C, 334 troy oz 6,900.00
  Teapot, 8" h, baluster, repousse with scrolling foliage centering putti and birds in landscape, scrolling handle, spout issuing from foliage centered vacant cartouche, hinged cover with similar dec, floral finial, four feet, 17 oz, 2 dwt 275.00
Swedish, urn, 14-1/2" h, ribbed melon baluster-form, two scroll handles, openwork scroll and arcade dec body, ruby glass liner, raised sq base, four repousse scroll foliate feet, c1900, 60 troy oz 1,725.00

English

From the 17th century to the mid-19th century, English silversmiths set the styles which American silversmiths copied. The work from the period exhibits the highest degree of craftsmanship. English silver is actively collected in the American antiques marketplace.

Apple Corer, 5-7/8" l, Victorian, H & T makers, Birmingham, 1870, turned handle, 2 troy oz 460.00
Asparagus Tongs, Victorian, Messrs. Eady makers, London, 1861, beaded borders with openwork, scroll design, 7 troy oz 750.00
Berry Spoon, George IV, Glasgow, 1820, engraved floral handles, chased pear and grape gold wash bowls, monogrammed, price for pr, 5 troy oz 175.00
Candlestick
  10-1/4" h, Georgian, Dublin, late 18th/early 19th C, chased and engraved scroll foliate dec, removable bobeches with engraved heraldic device, set of four, 96 troy oz 4,025.00
  13-1/4" h, George III, IWFK makers, London, 1767, fluted Corinthian columns, sq stepped base with bands of ovolos, removable nozzles with canted corners, beaded rim, one engraved with heraldic symbol, base with wood mounts, price for pr 1,495.00
Caddy Spoon, George III, George Baskerville maker, London, 1798, engraved dec, .5 troy oz 175.00
Cann, London hallmarks for 1770-71, 3-7/8" h, very minor dents 575.00
Caster
  6-1/2" h, London, 1837, baluster, pierced cover, molded foot, 7 oz, 2 dwt 200.00

9" h, Thomas Bradbury & Sons, London, 1895-96, octagonal, waisted reeded band and foot, pierced cover
.... 350.00

Cheese Scoop with Pusher, 8-1/2" l, George III, JT maker, Birmingham, 1803, Stilton, carved palmette-shaped ivory handle. 375.00

Cigar Case
Edwardian, WA maker, Birmingham, 1907, 5-5/8" l, cushion-shape, rect form, 6 troy oz 260.00
Victorian, GHJ maker, London, 1886, gold wash int., holds four cigars, engraved, 5 troy oz 350.00

Coffeepot
6-1/4" h, George III, TK & RS makers, London, 1804-05, cylindrical, wooden handle and finial, gadroon border on lid, engraved crest under spout and on lid. 700.00
11-3/4" h, George III, maker's mark illegible, London, 1774, baluster-form, spreading circular base, beaded and fluted dec, garland swags under rim, scroll rattan handle, later dec, repairs to back under handle, 22 troy oz 750.00

Condiment Set, J. C. Ltd. maker, Birmingham, 1922, mustard pot and salt with cobalt blue glass liners, pepper aster, two condiment spoons, fitted case, 4 troy oz 190.00

Creamer and Sugar, Edward VIII, Birmingham, 1901, oval, bright cut floral dec, angular handles, 7 oz, 8 dwt ... 600.00

Cruet Stand
7-3/8" h, George I, Paul Lamerie maker, marks of Britannia and lion's head erased, London, c1726, double bottle holder, reeded rims, scroll handle, four scroll and ball feet, each compartment with front ring for bottle tops, two cut glass bottles, 22 troy oz.........................4,600.00
8" h, George III, maker's mark, London, 1770, round wood base, openwork band on three paw feet, gadroon and reeded rims, central handle, five-part bottle divider, engraved thistle on front of band 260.00

Cup
3-1/4" h, London hallmarks for 1838-39, tooled lines, dents and small repaired split at handle 125.00
12-3/4" h, cov, Georgian, crowned "W" maker's mark, Dublin, 18th C, urn-form, two scroll handles, spreading circular base, chased scroll foliate dec, shepherd and shepherdess on back, central cartouche with coat of arms, chased dec on front with pastoral scene with woman and basket of flowers, scene of two boat men, chased floral border on base, 65 troy oz 3,750.00

Egg Stand, 7-5/8" h, George III, illegible maker's mark, possibly William Elliot, London, 1817, raised rect shape, double scroll lifting handle, four paw feet, rosette and scroll detail, gadroon borders on frame, six round cup holders, six egg cups with gadroon rim and silver-gilt int., six spoon slots on frame, six George IV egg spoons, four 1823 with maker's mark, other two 1820, attributed to R. Peppin maker, all King's pattern, silver-gilt bowls, same engraved heraldic symbol, repairs to frame base, 34 troy oz 1,265.00

Entree Dish, George III, Richard Cooke maker, London, 1804-05, cushion-shape, deep body, cov, removable liner, cast lion's head handles and scroll finial, gadroon rims, engraved coat of arms on cover and body, paw feet, 168 troy oz
....4,325.00

Epergne, George III, Matthew Boulton maker, Birmingham, 1804, four detachable branches, band around rim with vine motifs, cast lion's masks on each of four supports, bottom incurving quatrefoil plinth, gadroon rim, cast fluted finial, four paw feet, large 11-1/8" d central cut glass dish and four smaller dishes, 98 troy oz........................8,925.00

Fish Knife, Victorian, Hy. Wilkinson & Co. makers, Sheffield, 1880, engine-turned surface dec on handle, beaded border, bright-cut engraved blade, 4 troy oz............. 150.00

(English) Candlesticks, William Café, London hallmarks for 1758-59, each engraved on underside of base "The Gift of Eliz. Sauvaire to her grandson Thos. De Jersey 1759," 8-1/4" h, pr, $5,950. Photo courtesy of Garth's Auctions, Inc.

Fish Server, Regency, John Emes maker, London, 1800, heraldic device surrounded by open wrigglework, 7 troy oz
.... 575.00

Fish Set, Victorian, FE maker, Birmingham, 1876, service for five, ivory handles, floral engraved blades, fitted case
.... 200.00

Fish Slicer
12-7/8" l, William IV, Mary Chawner maker, 1835, King's pattern, engraved stag, openwork foliate blade, 7 troy oz
.... 290.00
13-7/8" l, Victorian, Atkin Brothers maker, Sheffield, 1891, bright-cut engraved floral and scroll dec, carved ivory handle 350.00

Fruit Basket, 10-1/4" d, William IV, Robinson, Edkins and Astor makers, Birmingham, c1831, round, raised central foot, fluted dec overlay, reeded openwork entwined body with vine and grape design draped rim, swing handle, scroll foliate dec and central flower, 22 troy oz 1,200.00

Fruit Spoon, Regency, G. T. maker, London, 1814, repousse fruit dec gold washed bowls, engraved floral handle, price for pr, 4 troy oz 7,475.00

Glove Stretcher, 8-5/8" l, Victorian, D & S maker, Birmingham, 1888, mosaic pattern handle, 2 troy oz 175.00

Goblet, 6-1/4" h, George III, Henry Chawner and John Emes makers, London, 1796, lower body repousse with leaves, circular molded foot, engraved armorials, pr, 22 oz 8 dwt
....1,200.00

Gravy Boat, George III, London, R. Peaston maker, 1774-75, gadroon border, flying scroll handle, engraved stag, three shell feet, minor dents on one, 26 troy oz 2,185.00

Hot Milk Jug, 5-3/4" h, George IV, London, 1938, tapering cylindrical, domed lid, reeded rim and foot, wood handle, engraved crest, 11 oz, 7 dwt 350.00

Hot Water Urn, 21" h, George IV, Daniel Holy & Co., Sheffield, 1925, beehive form, waisted foliate band centering two crested cartouches on shaped sq base, four paw supports issuing from foliage, four paw feet, reeded and foliate handles, dome cover, scrolling foliate finial, with liner, 165 oz 11,000.00

Inkstand, 13-1/4" l, Victorian, Birmingham, Robinson, Edkins and Astor makers, 1840, rect, shell and scroll border, four scrolling shell feet, two pen dips, crystal bodied inkwell and pounce pot, central sealing wafer pot, 31 troy oz. . . . 980.00

Inkwell, traveling, 2" h, Edwardian, illegible maker's mark, London, 1902, cylindrical, twist-off lid, inner glass ink chamber, ext. engraved checkerboard dec, ... 260.00

Ladle

7-1/8" l, George III, Hester Bateman maker, London, 1780, 1 troy oz 350.00

13" l, George III, Hester Bateman maker, London, 1780, long stem handle, shaped oval bow, mkd on back, monogrammed, 4 troy oz 575.00

13-1/2" l, George III, Hester Bateman maker, London, c1780, 4 troy oz. 575.00

14-1/8" l, 3-7/8" d, George II, Elias Cachart maker, London, 1746, rat tail handle, engraved coat of arms, 6 troy oz 300.00

Marrow Scoop

George II, TR maker, London, 1758, 2 troy oz 250.00

George III, Thomas Chawner maker, London, 1775, 8-3/8" l, 1 troy oz. 175.00

Muffineer, 7-7/8" h, George V, R. C. maker, 1931, retailed by Tiffany & Co., tall bulbous shape, spreading circular base, pierced scroll foliate design on cov, bell finial, monogram, 10 troy oz. 265.00

Napkin Ring

George V, Birmingham, 1920, round, engine-turned surface dec, central monogram, pair in fitted case, 2 troy oz 125.00

Victorian, JR maker, London, 1861, floral repousse design, set of six in fitted case, individually numbered, 6 troy oz 800.00

Nutmeg Grater, George III, Matthew Linwood maker, Birmingham, 1809-10

Cushion-shape, lined surface dec, 1 troy oz 760.00

Rect hinged box, 1 troy oz 760.00

Pepper Caster, 6-1/8" h, George II, attributed to Samuel Wood maker, London, 1737, tall bulbous shape, pierced dec on cov, minor dents, 5 troy oz. 300.00

Punch Ladle, 13-1/2" l, George III, Paul Callard maker, fluted bowl, engraved heraldic device on handle, 4 troy oz . 400.00

Salt, London hallmarks for 1772-73, three hoof feet, 2-1/2" d, small dents 275.00

Salver

10-1/2" d, George II, Paul Lamerie maker, London, 1745, engraved scroll foliate detail, central cartouche, engraved rampant lion, four scroll feet, segmented outer fluted border, 26 troy oz 16,100.00

12" d, George III, John Carter maker, London, 1775, gadroon border, central engraved coat of arms, three ball and claw feet, 30 troy oz. 1,265.00

13" d, George III, John Carter maker, London, 1771, gadroon border, engraved coat of arms with heart-shaped shield, floral dec, four feet, 32 troy oz. 2,070.00

Sauce Boat, George III, maker's mark erased, London, 1811, oval, scalloped rim, scroll handle, three pad feet issuing from shells 400.00

Sauce Tureen, cov

George III, William Burwash and Richard Sibley makers, London, 1807, round, spreading circular base, two applied lion head reeded side handles, gadrooned borders on base rim and lid, leaf-clad reeded loop finial, sides, and cover engraved with heraldic device, 72 troy oz, price for pr 4,485.00

Regency, Robert Hennell maker, London, 1818-19, two reeded handles, beaded borders, pedestal foot, 46 troy oz 3,450.00

Shaker, 5-3/4" h, George III, Hester Bateman, London, 1786-87, bulbous center, slightly domed elongated shaker section, criss-crossed lines and holes, top twisted finial, hallmarked on side 325.00

Sifting Spoon, George III, Samuel Pemberton maker, Birmingham, 1805, bright-cut engraved floral handle, engraved rim, sides of bowl with filigree work bottom, monogram, .5 troy oz 320.00

Snuffbox, 3-1/8" l

George III, T. Phipps and E. Robinson makers, London, 1808, rounded rect, hinged central lid, engine-turned surface dec, central oval surrounded by fretwork band, gold wash int., 2 troy oz. 230.00

George IV, Ledsam, Vale, and Wheeler makers, Birmingham, 1829, rect, hinged lid, engine-turned surface dec, scroll relief borders, central engraving of anchor and motto, gold wash int., 2 troy ox 326.00

Spoon, 7-1/2" l, early, partially illegible London marks, trifid end, rat-tail handle, engraved crest and monogram, 1-1/2 troy oz 250.00

Straining Spoon, 12" l, George III, William Eley, William Fearn, and William Chawner makers, London, 1911, plain Fiddle pattern, engraved heraldic animal, vertical straining device in center of bowl, 5 troy oz 230.00

Stuffing Spoon, 12" l, George III, Thomas Ollivant maker, London, 1795, 3 troy oz 175.00

Sugar Sifter, Birmingham, c1900, shell-form, 1 troy oz 260.00

Tablespoon, George III, Richard Crossley maker, London, 1787, engraved figure of rampant horse on handle, set of eight, 18 troy oz. 750.00

Teapot, George III

5"h, Robert Hannell maker, London, 1782-83, oval, fluted sides and spout, engraved dec borders, heraldic symbol on lid, ivory handle and finial. 750.00

10-3/4" l, Peter, Anne, and William Bateman makers, London, 180-2, compressed cylindrical form, gadrooned rim, circular foot, wood finial and loop handle, 212 oz 950.00

Tea Set

Regency, J. McKay maker, Edinburgh, 1819-20, teapot, creamer, open sugar, oblong oval form, four ball feet, gadroon rims, engraved floral and leaf dec, gold washed int. in creamer and sugar, curving leaf-shape handles, repair and split to lid, spout damage, 40 troy oz 750.00

Victorian, GR maker, London, 1850, 9-1/2" h teapot, creamer, open sugar with gold wash int., rounded baluster form, spreading circular base, scroll handles, engraved plain scroll dec, central monogram, molded scroll border, ornate bell finial, 47 troy oz. 750.00

Victorian, Walter and George Sissons, makers, London, 1876, 12-1/2" h coffeepot, teapot, creamer, two handled open sugar, plain baluster shape, beaded rims, circular foot, leaf-capped loop handle with applied beads, bombe hinged cover, baluster finial, monogrammed, 69 oz 1,200.00

Tea Urn

19-3/4" h, George III, London, 1764, chased floral and scroll dec, gadroon rims, four raised ball and claw feet, some dents, missing finial on lever, 83 troy oz 2,070.00

20-1/2" h, George III, Charles Wright maker, London, 1775, center with beaded details, ivory handle, monogrammed, 78 troy oz. 2,415.00

Tray, 20-3/8" d, William IV, London, Paul Storr maker, 1831, cast scroll and floral border, engraved scroll foliate dec, central coat of arms, three foliate feet, 110 troy oz 6,900.00

Wine Coaster, 5-3/4" d, George IV, Matthew Boulton maker, Birmingham, 1824, repousse scroll foliate design, curved petal shaped rim 500.00

English, Sheffield

Sheffield Silver, or Old Sheffield Plate, has a fusion method of silver-plating that was sued from the mid-18th century until the mid 1880s when the process of electroplating silver was introduced.

Sheffield plating was discovered in 1743 when Thomas Boulsover of Sheffield, England, accidentally fused silver and copper. The process consisted of sandwiching a heavy sheet of copper between two thin sheets of silver. The result was a plated sheet of silver, which could be pressed or rolled to a desired thickness. All Sheffield articles are worked from these plated sheets.

Most of the silver-plated items found today marked "Sheffield" are not early Sheffield plate. They are later wares made in Sheffield, England.

Argyle, 6-3/8" h, c1830, cylindrical, beaded rim, raffia wrapped handle, sell terminal, faceted ovoid knob 295.00

Cake Basket, 14-7/8" l, c1820, rect, flower dec gadroon rim, sides chased scrolls and berried foliage, interlaced ribbon-work handle, satyr mask terminals, four paw feet 750.00

Compote, 4-1/2" d, Martin Hall & Co., Ltd. Makers, made for Tiffany & Co., 1911, ftd, pierced fretwork band under rim, price for pr, 13 troy oz 460.00

Entree Dish, 12-3/4" l, applied rim of shells and scrolling foliage, foliate handles, four paw feet, liner 750.00

Fish Slicer, 13" l, ivory handle, maker's mark, 1906 .... 175.00

Ice Tongs, 5-3/4" l, Victorian, maker's mark, bird claw grips, central monogram, 2 troy oz 115.00

Serving Tray
18-1/4" d, oval, central engraved crest of arms, reeded border and handles, four feet 275.00
21" d, Henry Wilkinson maker, c1800, gadroon border, two engraved dogs on rim 300.00

Tea Set, Regency style, 19th C, 6" h, teapot, reamer, and sugar, mkd "TM" 300.00

Wine Cooler, 10-3/4" h, c1810, campana form, applied grapevine dec at shoulder, waist and rims, foliate handles, molded circular foot, liner and collar, monogrammed 2,500.00

Silver, Plated

Englishmen G. R. Elkington and H. Elkington are given credit for being the first to use the electrolytic method of plating silver in 1838.

Argyle, 6-1/2" h, late Georgian, late 19th C, compressed urn form, cut engraved tapered body, raked spout, stepped oval cov with ball finial, wood loop handles, oval reeded scole 500.00

Biscuit Box, 6-1/2" h, oval, lift lid, ftd tray base 200.00

Bowl, Elkington & Co., Birmingham, c1850, shaped oval form, stag head handles, scrolled feet, three pc set 800.00

Candelabra, pr, 23-3/8" h, Elkington & Co., 1950, lobed and fluted baluster stems, serpentine branches, campana shaped detachable scones 2,400.00

Candlesticks, pr, Arts & Crafts style, Marshall Field, brass base, emb and etched floral design 375.00

Collar Button Box, 2-1/4" d, emb sides, figural collar button o lid with engraving "Here's Your Collar Button," marked "Homan Silver Co.," four SS buttons inside 65.00

Compote, 6-1/4" h, figural, dolphin-form, shell form bowl, one with English maker's marks, wear, price for pr. 700.00

Condensed Milk Can Holder, Rogers & Bros., cylindrical body, emb band at top and bottom, simple "C" handle, hole in lid for ladle 75.00

Entree Dish, Elkington & Co., Birmingham, c1850, shaped oval, stag head handles, scrolled feet, orig liner, nested seven pc set 1,200.00

Knife Rest, two squatting children on each end 40.00

Liquor Bottle Tag, "Bourbon," on chain 25.00

Monteith, 12" d, Ellis Barker, early 20th C, round fluted body, spreading circular base, scroll rim, two medallions surrounded by scroll detail, two applied lion's head ring handles, detachable rim to convert to punch bowl 2,990.00

Muffin Basket, 13" l, oval, pierced ribbed sides, twin scrolled handles 95.00

Napkin Ring, child's, narrow, engraved cupid being drawn on chariot by butterflies 25.00

Syrup Pitcher, emb filigree, Wilcox 32.00

Tea and Coffee Service, Reed & Barton, 12-1/4" h coffeepot, teapot, creamer, two handled open sugar, baluster-form, lobed at intervals, chased, scroll and foliate cartouche, loop handle, four scroll feet, flower, and bud finial 200.00

Tray
21-1/4" l, oblong, pierced gallery rim, engraved scroll foliate dec, two side handles, four ball feet, c1900 .... 175.00
30" l, shaped rect, repousse with flowers and leaves border, monogrammed cartouche flanked by flowers and foliage, two scrolling foliate handles, Pairpoint 475.00

Vegetable Dish, cov, 14" l, shaped oval, applied scroll dec, scrolling handles, Sheffield, price for pr 150.00

Wine Cooler, 11-1/4" l, oblong, gadrooned rims, two leaf-form side handles, two removable bottle compartments, Portugal, 20th C 325.00

SILVER DEPOSIT GLASS

History: Silver deposit glass was popular at the turn of the century. A simple electrical process was used to deposit a thin coating of silver on glass products. After the

Vase, green body, Art Nouveau silver dec, c1920, 16" h, $90.

glass and a piece of silver were placed in a solution, an electric current was introduced which caused the silver to decompose, pass through the solution, and remain on those parts of the glass on which a pattern had been outlined.

Bowl, 5-1/2" d, vines and leaves dec, scalloped edge . . . 45.00
Compote, 7" d, floral dec. 85.00
Creamer and Sugar, cov, floral dec 90.00
Decanter, 9" h, emerald green, hollow stopper. 75.00
Serving Plate, 12-1/2" d, dark amethyst, floral dec. 75.00
Toothpick Holder, 2" h, amber ground 50.00
Tumbler, 4-5/8" h, flared top 25.00
Vase, 10" h, baluster, black ground, twin handles, parrot on branch dec 50.00

SILVER OVERLAY

History: Silver overlay is silver applied directly to a finished glass or porcelain object. The overlay is cut and decorated, usually by engraving, prior to being molded around the object.

Glass usually is of high quality and is either crystal or colored. Lenox used silver overlay on some porcelain pieces. Most designs are from the Art Nouveau and Art Deco periods.

Reference: Lillian F. Potter, *Re-Introduction to Silver Overlay on Glass and Ceramics*, published by author, 1992.

Bookends, pr, 4-1/2" h, bronze, sterling silver ships dec, orig patina, imp "Silver Crest" 100.00
Bottle
6" h, spherical form, colorless glass body, chased silver floral and scroll design, orig stopper, monogrammed, price for pr 325.00

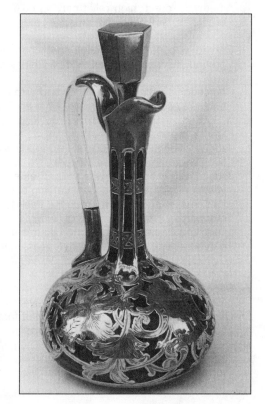

Decanter, cranberry glass, floral and stem motif, hexagonal stopper, 10-1/2" h, $675.

8" h, pinch style, colorless glass body, men, birds, dragons, silver marked "YTK" 50.00
10-1/4" h, colorless glass body, floral overlay, heavy floral center medallion, monogrammed, matching stopper 800.00
Claret Jug, 13" h, baluster form, colorless glass body, base cut with calyx, faceted neck with applied silver mount, hinged shell lid with spout, applied chased handle reaching down to silver mounted base, circular dome foot, repousse and chased floral and foliate design, unclear hallmark 1,100.00
Cruet
7" h, green glass body, cornstalk pattern overlay, orig stopper 1,100.00
8-1/4" h, bulbous form, colorless glass body, base cut with calyx, chased silver floral and foliate design, applied handle, orig stopper, stamped "Black, Star & Frost, 4000" 200.00
Decanter
7-3/4" h, square form, chamfered corners, colorless glass body, chased silver floral and foliate design, base with cut calyx, faceted stopper 440.00
10-1/2" h, bulbous form, shaped base, colorless glass body, chased floral and foliate pattern, rim with tri-spout, applied handle, pinched stopper, monogrammed, unclear stamp mark. 770.00
11-1/2" h, baluster form, colorless glass body, faceted neck, chased grape and foliate design, orig stopper, monogrammed, stamped "Thaihfimer & Frank" 715.00
Ewer, Weller pottery base, floral dec 750.00
Perfume Bottle, 4-1/4" l, tapered black glass body, ball-form knob, silver foil dec, Continental. 150.00
Tea Set, 7-1/2" h cov teapot, creamer, sugar, Art Nouveau silver overlay on brown pottery, graceful form. 550.00
Tray, 6" d, bronze body, sterling Arts & Crafts style dec, imp "Heintz," pr 120.00
Vase
4-1/4" h, flared bulbous amber body, applied scrolling silver imp "I./Sterling". 450.00
12" h, baluster bronze body, Arts & Crafts stylized floral design, orig patina, imp "Heintz," minor flaws 300.00
12" h, cylindrical bronze body, applied Arts & Crafts style dec, sgd "Silver Crest" 600.00

SMITH BROS. GLASS

History: After establishing a decorating department at the Mount Washington Glass Works in 1871, Alfred and Harry Smith struck out on their own in 1875. Their New Bedford, Massachusetts, firm soon became known worldwide for its fine opalescent decorated wares, similar in style to those of Mount Washington.

Marks: Smith Bros. glass often is marked on the base with a red shield enclosing a rampant lion and the word "Trademark.""

References: Kenneth Wilson, *American Glass 1760-1930*, 2 Vols., Hudson Hills Press and The Toledo Museum of Art, 1994.

REPRODUCTION ALERT

Beware of examples marked "Smith Bros."

Bowl, 3" d, melon ribbed body, blue scrolls, dainty yellow flowers, red rampant lion mark 240.00

Box, cov, 5-1/2" d, hinged lid, melon ribbed, opaque white ground, hp pansies. 385.00

Cracker Jar, cov
    6-1/2" h, 6-1/2" d, melon ribbed, peach ground, hp pansies, gold outlines, SP cov, sgd 400.00
    7" h, barrel shape, creamy white, shaded yellow daisies and green foliage, rampant lion mark, SP rim, cover, and bail handle, cov mkd "S. B." 415.00

Creamer and Sugar, blue pansy dec, SP mountings and cov, rampant lion mark. 320.00

Dresser Jar, cov, 5-1/2" d, melon ribbed, multicolored pansy dec 300.00

Ferner, 10" d, melon ribbed, glossy white, violets and leaves, orig metal insert, sgd 675.00

Jar, cov, 4" d, melon ribbed, ivory, polychrome floral dec, gilt trim, rampant lion mark. 170.00

Mustard Jar, 3-1/4" h, heron dec, SP top 85.00

Perfume Bottle, 5" h, enameled floral dec, emb flower cap, sgd 350.00

Plate, 6-1/4" d, scene of Christopher Columbus' ship, Santa Maria 325.00

Rose Bowl, 4-1/2" h, creamy white ground, shaded yellow daisies, green foliage, enameled white beaded rim 225.00

Salt, open, dec, price for pr. 185.00

Sugar Shaker, tapered cylinder, owl dec 350.00

Syrup Pitcher, 6" d, 6" h, bulbous melon ribbed creamy body, dainty flowers, orig SP rim, cover, and handle. 875.00

Sweetmeat jar, cov, 5-1/2" h, 5-1/2" d, squatty, melon ribbed, opaque white ground, hp tiny blue flowers, silver plate cov, rim, and bail handle, sgd 650.00

Toothpick Holder
    2-1/4" h, swag of blossoms, opaque white ribbed barrel shaped body, blue rim dots 265.00
    2-1/2" h, Little Lobe, single petal rose blossoms, pale blue body, raised blue rim dots 245.00

Biscuit Jar, cream ground, pink and green floral dec, silver plated lid and bail handle, 8-1/2" h, $270.

Vase
    6" h, tall conical body, molded double rings near to and base, tapering in at bottom, front with two large overlapping circles, one with scene of two red birds on blossom laden limb, other with land landscape, framed by blossoming branches 400.00
    7-1/4" h, 8" w, double pilgrim style, two flattened round vases, joined at side and short cylindrical neck, creamy white ground, lavender wisteria blossoms, gold outlines, gold beading at top 1,220.00

SNUFF BOTTLES

History: Tobacco usage spread from America to Europe to China during the 17th century. Europeans and Chinese preferred to grind the dried leaves into a powder and sniff it into their nostrils. The elegant Europeans carried their snuff in boxes and took a pinch with their fingertips. The Chinese upper class, because of their lengthy fingernails, found this inconvenient and devised a bottle with a fitted stopper and attached spoon. These utilitarian objects soon became objets d'art.

Snuff bottles were fashioned from precious and semi-precious stones, glass, porcelain and pottery, wood, metals, and ivory. Glass and transparent-stone bottles often were enhanced further with delicate hand paintings, some done on the interior of the bottle.

Collectors' Club: International Chinese Snuff Bottle Society, 2601 No. Charles St., Baltimore, MD 21218.

Bottle

1-1/2" h, jade, translucent pale green, high relief carving of birds in flowering trees 475.00

1-3/4" h, opal, vasiform, relief carving of Kuan Yin and lotus, lion mask handles 290.00

2" h
    Amethyst, round, high relief carving of plum blossoms and branches, well hollowed, amethyst stopper, 19th C 400.00
    Carved coconut shell, relief seal characters on textured ground, inscription on both sides, Chinese, 19th C 700.00
    Chalcedony, cylindrical form, carved with goldfish and bamboo, gray colored stone with orange and tan inclusions 175.00
    Fluorite, green, Chinese 65.00
    Jadeite, even toned celadon stone, spade shape, carved with two fisherman, gilt brass stopper 500.00
    Jadeite, off-white stone with veils of emerald green, natural veins of color used to accent carving of dragonflies, butterflies, rocks, and flowers, rounded flask form, Peking glass stopper 1,380.00
    Lapis Lazuli, deep blue stone, double-gourd form, matrix carved as tiger and gourd with leaves, matching stopper 550.00

2-1/4" h
    Boulder Opal, pearl gray with flashes of color, double gourd form, high relief carved carp and waves 350.00
    Glass, interior painted, oblong flattened form, dec with bird, flowering prunus, vase of flowers, and incense burner 250.00
    Jade, pale green stone, yellow markings, flattened rounded form, brighter green clouds, twenty-character inscription, reverse with children playing 350.00

Cloisonné, floral motif on one side, forest scene with deer on other, wood base, 3-3/8" h, $270.

2-1/2" h

Carnelian, well marked orange hue stone with darker veining, allover carving of flowers and vines, matching carved stopper, fitted stand, 19th C 250.00

Cloisonné, high shouldered flattened form, indented sides, design of hundred antiques on turquoise ground, heavily gilded borders, matching stopper, Ch'ien Lung mark, early 20th C 115.00

Glass, clear, interior painting of mule borne procession through mountain passes, tiger's eye top, sgd "Hsiech Tsao Fu," five character inscription, two seals 175.00

Glass, interior painting with two scholars and serving boy on one side, reverse with extensive inscription, int. heavily stained with snuff 290.00

Ivory, small boy with large bitter melon with leaves, matching stopper 115.00

Jade, even green color, spade shaped, sq foot rim, well hollowed, carved flowering trees and rocks framed within Greek key fret borders, sides carved with floral scrolls 115.00

Jadeite, flattened spade shape, celadon colored, carved tied brocade panel around center, apple green jadeite stopper 490.00

Metal body, butterfly shape, Lac burgaute, kingfisher, butterfly and flowers on one side, two figures in landscape on other, Ch'ien Lung mark on base 460.00

Peking glass, cranberry colored overlay, snowflake ground, covered with scrolling chih lung dragons 175.00

Peking glass, flattened round form, foot rim, coral colored glass carved with carp and crashing waves, reverse with flowering plant and butterfly, dyed ivory top 175.00

Rhodochrosite, deep pink stone with white markings in concentric circles, flattened oblong, relief carved pines and ornamental rocks. 575.00

Rose quartz, slightly flattened flask form, even pastel pink stone, relief carved birds in flowering branches, matching stopper 250.00

Shadow Agate, flattened oblong form, even dove gray colored stone infused with black and brown markings resembling plants and rocks, finely hollowed, turquoise stopper, 19th C 550.00

Sharkskin, graduated oblong form, darkened accents, agate top, 19th C 300.00

2-3/4" h

Amber, Chinese 95.00

Cylindrical, blue and white dec, numerous painted birds on fruit covered branches, deep cobalt blue ground, lapis lazuli stopper 115.00

Peking glass, pear form, high foot, tortoiseshell colored overlay on bubble diffused yellow ground, finely carved wreathes of chih lung dragons enclosing Shou characters, tied fillets and rui for sides, 19th C 450.00

Rose quartz, flattened spade shape, pale pink color, carved birds, trees, and flowering plants, matching cover 400.00

Silver, Mongol-style dec, two archaic dragons confronting each other on both sides, further dec with coral cabochons, turquoise mounted in cloisons, coral set top, 19th C 115.00

Tourmaline, elongated heart shape, pink rubelite material with apricot shadings, carved pine tree and three seals 350.00

2-3/4" x 2-1/2", shadow agate, rounded flattened flash form, well hollowed, delicately carved pair of birds, and tree, agate stopper 1,265.00

2-7/8" h, porcelain, black ground, white figural reserves, Chinese 90.00

3" h

Agate, Chinese 100.00

Glass, blue cut to white, horses, Chinese 325.00

Glass, blue overlay of figures and trees, Chinese . . . 100.00

Glass, four color overlay, white ground, carved pink, yellow, and blue flowers, green stems and leaves. 175.00

Lapis Lazuli, flattened flask form, deep blue stone, veins of gold and white, carved single relief woman with fan and flowing dress, matching high domed stopper 460.00

Pewter and cinnabar, five musicians on one side, reverse with two sages, one on water buffalo, other on mule, two character Ch'ien Lung mark, 20th C 350.00

Porcelain, mei ping shape, celadon ground, enameled in famille rose colors, tourmaline-colored Peking glass stopper 150.00

Porcelain, polychrome, relief carving of Buddhist divinities, jade top, Ch'ien Lung mark, 19th C, chip at mouth . 150.00

Rock crystal, hexagonal, well hollowed, remaining skin of stone carved with flowering plum and pine branches, bud, monkey, bee, and deer, Chinese, 19th C 400.00

3-1/4" h

Amethyst, Chinese 125.00

Glass and interior painted, cylindrical, carved black glass over clear ground, body painted with dragon descending from dark clouds, sgd. 175.00

3-1/2" h

Amber Peking glass surrounded with gilt framed repousse dec, filigree set with garnets, turquoise, and glass, Mongol-style 300.00

Horn, carved all over with dragons and clouds, tortoiseshell coloring, 20th C 115.00

Porcelain, coral glazed, Chinese 100.00

Pottery, unglazed turquoise, form of winged carp ridden by dragon, coral colored glass stopper as celestial pearl 115.00

4" h, ivory, small boy and large Chinese cabbage 115.00

Box

Burlwood, 3-3/8" d, circular, tortoiseshell banding centers eglomise reserve of Benjamin Franklin, tortoiseshell lining, Continental, 18th C, imperfections 575.00
Silver, sterling
  English, George III, London, 1802, rect, applied floral band on front of lid, 2 troy oz 260.00
  English, Victorian, Yapp & Woodward makers, Birmingham, 1853, engine-turned surface, edges with scroll dec, 3 troy oz 326.00
  European, hazelnut form, late 19th C, .5 troy oz 260.00

SOAPSTONE

History: The mineral steatite, known as soapstone because of its greasy feel, has been used for carving figural groups and designs by the Chinese and others. Utilitarian pieces also were made. Soapstone pieces were very popular during the Victorian era.

Reference: *Soapstone*, L-W Book Sales, 1995.

Bookends, pr, elephants, c1890 . . . . 65.00
Box, 3 x 5", inlaid pearl dec, artist sgd 45.00
Figure
  5" h, pomegranate 25.00
  7" h, two boys riding water buffalo, mottled brown and cream color stone, 19th C. 230.00
  16 1/2" h, Shoulao, holding dragon headed staff and peach, Chinese 225.00
Incense Burner, 8" h, black, 19th C 350.00
Inkwell, geometric carving on sides 150.00
Match Holder, elaborate carving. 70.00
Paperweight, three carved monkeys. 75.00
Sculpture
  7" h, four chilongs and two toads carved in relief, ovoid form stone, chestnut and light green colored stone, 19th C 460.00
  28" h, angel, Raymond Coins. 4,950.00

Vase, tan and brown, carved rodent, 2-1/2" h, $85.

Toothpick Holder, carved monkey. 70.00
Urn, 7-1/4" d, 10-1/4" h, carved figures, buildings, florals, and trees, elephant head handles, wood stand. 175.00

SOUVENIR and COMMEMORATIVE CHINA and GLASS

History: Souvenir, commemorative, and historical china and glass includes those items produced to celebrate special events, places, and people.

China plates made by Rowland and Marcellus and Wedgwood are particularly favored by collectors. Rowland and Marcellus, Staffordshire, England, made a series of blue-and-white historic plates with a wide rolled edge. Scenes from the Philadelphia Centennial in 1876 through the 1939 New York World's Fair are depicted. In 1910, Wedgwood collaborated with Jones, McDuffee and Stratton to produce a series of historic dessert-sized plates showing scenes of places throughout the United States.

Many localities issued plates, mugs, glasses, etc., for anniversary celebrations or to honor a local historical event. These items seem to have greater value when sold in the region in which they originated.

Commemorative glass includes several patterns of pressed glass, which celebrate people or events. Historical glass includes campaign and memorial items.

References: Arene Burgess, *Collector's Guide to Souvenir Plates*, Schiffer Publishing, 1996; Monica Lynn Clements and Patricia Rosser Clements, *Popular Souvenir Plates,* Schiffer Publications, 1998; Bessie M. Lindsey, *American Historical Glass*, Charles E. Tuttle Company, 1967; Lawrence W. Williams, *Collector's Guide To Souvenir China,* Collector Books, 1997.

Periodicals: *Antique Souvenir Collectors News*, Box 562, Great Barrington, MA 01230; *Souvenir Building Collector*, 25 Falls Rd., Roxbury, CT 06783.

Collectors' Club: Statue of Liberty Collectors' Club, 26601 Bernwood Rd., Cleveland, OH 44122.

Additional Listings: Cup Plates; Pressed Glass; Political Items; Staffordshire, Historical. Also see *Warman's Americana & Collectibles* for more examples.

China

Cup, DAR, Greenwood China. 5.00
Demitasse Cup and Saucer, Scammeli, Harry Stevens . . 35.00
Dresser Tray, hp, Mt. Vernon, portraits of George and Martha, delicate floral borders. 110.00
Mug, University of Pennsylvania, c1905, football player 250.00
Pitcher, Delmonicos 85.00
Plate
  DAR, Greenwood China. 10.00
  Denver, Rowland & Marsellus 125.00
  Dickens, Charles, 10" d, rolled edge, Rowland & Marsellus 40.00
  Maritime Provinces, Royal Doulton 24.00
  Niagara, Royal Doulton 24.00
  Rochester, 8" d. 45.00

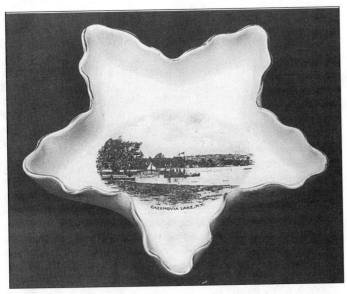

Ashtray, Cazenoia Lake, NY, white ground, multicolored decal transfer center, stamped "Hampshire, Keene, New Hampshire" on back, 5" w, $35.

Roosevelt, Theodore, blue, rolled rim, Rowland & Marsellus 65.00
Texian Campaigne, light blue transfer, Anthony Shaw, restored 300.00
Yale College, 9-1/2" d, light blue transfer, Charles Meigh, chip on foot rim 100.00
Platter, Elkwood, 12" l 25.00
Stein, Cedar Rapids, IA, 2-3/4"" h 75.00

Glass

Badge, paperweight type, cannonball dec, Oldest House, St. Augustine, FL 45.00
Bowl, Detroit, 1910, Elks, Fenton, amethyst carnival glass 650.00
Bust
    4-3/4" h, frosted, Abraham Lincoln, raised name on front of base, "Centennial Exhibition" and "Gillander & Sons Inc." on back, chip on corner of base 425.00
    5-1/4" h, frosted, Columbus, raised "World's Fair" and "1893" on back, minor chips 275.00
    6" h, frosted, Benjamin Harrison 250.00
    6" h, milk glass
        Ulysses S Grant, raised name on front of base, "Gillander & Sons Inc." on back, small chips on bottom and rear edge of base 525.00
        George Washington, raised name on front of base, "Centennial Exhibition" and "Gillander & Sons Inc." on back 450.00
    6-1/2" h, frosted glass, James A Garfield, raised name on front of base 300.00
Butter Dish, cov, 6-1/2" x 5-3/4", Lancaster Fair, 1916, Button Arches pattern, ruby stained 175.00
Candlestick, 8" h, gold script "Souvenir of World's Fair" 35.00
Creamer, Liberty Bell, child size 90.00
Cup, Akron Ohio, custard, Heisey mark, 2-1/2" h 25.00
Goblet, Knights of Pythias, 1900, green 50.00
Mug, Pacific Grove, Button Arches pattern, ruby stained 25.00
Paperweight, Plymouth Rock 65.00

Pitcher, Ocean City, NJ, 1912, King's Crown pattern, ruby stained 95.00
Plate
    Niagara Falls, transfer dec 50.00
    Spectors Dept. Store, marigold carnival glass 1,100.00
Platter, Newark 1952 Sesq, Twist pattern, Heisey 145.00
Statue
    Boy with dog, frosted, 1876 Expo 215.00
    Woman, standing, holding child, 14-1/2" h, raised mark of Gillander, division of United States Glass Co, 1891-1900, on back of base 850.00
Toothpick Holder, Omaha Expo, 1899, Colorado pattern 35.00
Tumbler, Scranton, PA, Mother, Button Arches pattern, ruby stained 50.00
Tray, Old State House, 12" d, blue 225.00
Water Set, 7" h pitcher, three 3-3/4" h tumblers, pink shading to clear, hp dec of Whittier Birthplace, Haverhill, MA . . . 150.00

SOUVENIR and COMMEMORATIVE SPOONS

History: Souvenir and commemorative spoons have been issued for hundreds of years. Early American silversmiths engraved presentation spoons to honor historical personages or mark key events.

In 1881, Myron Kinsley patented a Niagara Falls spoon, and in 1884, Michael Gibney patented a new flatware design. M. W. Galt, Washington, D.C., issued commemorative spoons for George and Martha Washington in 1889. From these beginnings a collecting craze for souvenir and commemorative spoons developed in the late 19th and early 20th centuries.

References: Wayne Bednersch, *Collectible Souvenir Spoons: Identification and Values,* Collector Books, 1998; George B. James, *Souvenir Spoons (1891),* reprinted with 1996 price guide by Bill Boyd (7408 Englewood Lane, Raytown, MO 64133), 1996; Dorothy T. Rainwater and Donna H. Fegler, *American Spoons,* Schiffer Publishing, 1990; —, *Spoons from around the World,* Schiffer Publishing, 1992; *Sterling Silver, Silverplate, and Souvenir Spoons with Prices,* revised ed., L-W Book Sales, 1987, 1994 value update.

Collectors' Clubs: American Spoon Collectors, 7408 Englewood Lane, Raytown, MO 64133; Northeastern Spoon Collectors Guild, 52 Hillcrest Ave., Morristown, NJ 07960; The Scoop Club, 84 Oak Ave., Shelton, CT 06484.

Additional Listings: See *Warman's Americana & Collectibles* for more examples.

Atlantic City, sterling silver, skyline on handle, ocean scenes on back, push cart in bowl, 6" l, $75.

Boston Tea Party 60.00
Cincinnati, OH. 35.00
Colombian Expo, sterling, engraved bowl with Brownies climb-
    ing all over ferris wheel, 1893. . . . . 60.00
Cornell University, seal on handle. 32.00
Easter, SP, ornate handle, demitasse. 25.00
Elk's Temple, Erie, PA, on bowl, SS 40.00
Gate to Union Stockyards, Chicago, IL, on bowl. 45.00
Indianapolis 500, 1913, SS, race cars, balloons, and biplane
    . . . . 120.00
Kaiser Wilhelm II, SP, bust handle, crest, flag, Army and Navy
    figures, mkd "Deutschland," plain bowl 70.00
Kentucky, state seal 35.00
Mackinac Island, MI, Indian Chief, demitasse. 35.00
Montana, cowboy handle 50.00
Mt. Tom Railroad, Holyoke, MA 55.00
Niagara Falls, Indian head handle 45.00
New York City, city hall, engraved bowl, Bridal Rose figural han-
    dle. 30.00
Observatory Peak, Ogden, Utah, in bowl, SS 45.00
San Francisco-Eureka, Golden gate Bridge, bear figural handle,
    SS. 65.00
Santa, SP, ornate handle, demitasse 70.00
Sir Walter Raleigh, figural handle 60.00
Vassar College, Poughkeepsie, NY, scene in bowl 40.00
Wisconsin Dells, figural fish handle. 40.00

SPANGLED GLASS

History: Spangled glass is a blown or blown-molded variegated art glass, similar to spatter glass, with the addition of flakes of mica or metallic aventurine. Many pieces
are cased with a white or clear layer of glass. Spangled
glass was developed in the late 19th century and still is
being manufactured.

Originally, spangled glass was attributed only to the
Vasa Murrhina Art Glass Company of Hartford, Connecticut, which distributed the glass for Dr. Flower of the
Cape Cod Glassworks, Sandwich, Massachusetts. However, research has shown that many companies in Europe, England, and the United States made spangled
glass, and attributing a piece to a specific source is very
difficult.

Vase, egg shape, 8 crimp top, shaded yellow to white base, gold mica flecks, 4" h, 3-1/2" w, $65.

Basket
    5" d, pink, mica flecks, white lining, applied clear twisted thorn
        handle 150.00
    5-1/2" d, pink, crimped handle, clear reeded twisted thorn
        handle 185.00
    7-1/2" d, light green, ribbon candy rim, clear brier form handle
        . . . . 140.00
Bowl
    3-3/4" d, 3-7/8" h, cranberry, three clear scroll feet, embossed
        heads, clear stars with berry centers applied around bowl,
        large mica flakes 165.00
    5-3/4" d, 4-1/2" h, olive green blue stripes, clear applied riga-
        ree around top, clear dripping appliqué, mica flakes in bowl,
        clear berry prunt, applied clear feet 240.00
    8-1/2" d, 3" h, shaded pink overlay, clear ruffled edge, melon
        rib, white lining 175.00
Bride's Basket, 10" h, pink shaded to white, silver flakes, ruffled
    edge, shiny finish 85.00
Candlesticks, pr, 8" h, green and maroon, gold mica flakes,
    white lining 115.00
Condiment Set, 2" x 5-1/2" x 6" h, cov pepper pot, cov mustard
    pot, cruet with orig stopper, cranberry and green spatter,
    mica flecks, SP covers, orig SP holder 275.00
Ewer
    6-7/8" h, 2-3/4" d, blue overlay, white lining, mica flakes, ap-
        plied clear handle, price for pr 135.00
    8-3/8" h, 3-1/2" d, apricot, white lining, mica flakes, applied
        thorn handle 145.00
Fairy Lamp, 3-5/8" h, 2-7/9" d, embossed swirl pyramid cranber-
    ry shade with mica flakes, embedded green threading on
    clear marked "Clarke" base 155.00
Jack in the Pulpit Vase, 5-3/4'"h, white ext., pink int., clear edg-
    ing, mica flakes, ruffled rim. 150.00
Pitcher, 8" h, 5-1/2" w, bulbous, six wide rib blowouts, silver mi-
    ca, rose ground, hp flowers and leaves, white lining, gold trim,
    patented 1883, applied clear handle, Hobbs Brockunier
    . . . . 500.00
Rose Bowl, 3-1/4" d, eight crimp top, shaded blue ext., white int.,
    mica flecks 115.00
Tumble-Up, 7-1/2" h decanter, matching tumbler, cobalt blue,
    mica flecks, white enamel and gilt dec 220.00
Vase
    8-1/2" h, flattened oval, applied cranberry rigaree, copper
        aventurine flecks, scroll handles, c1880 . . . . 320.00
    9-1/2" h, 6" d, squatty bulbous base, tapering to slender cy-
        lindrical body, flaring rolled and crimped rim, pink, cased in
        clear, white lining, silver mica flecks, clear shell trim down
        each side 165.00

SPATTER GLASS

History: Spatter glass is a variegated blown or
blown-molded art glass. It originally was called
"End-of-Day" glass, based on the assumption that it was
made from batches of glass leftover at the end of the day.
However, spatter glass was found to be a standard production item for many glass factories.

Spatter glass was developed at the end of the 19th
century and is still being produced in the United States
and Europe.

References: William Heacock, James Measell and Berry
Wiggins, *Harry Northwood*, Antique Publications, 1990.

Basket
5" w, 7-1/2" h, triangular, bright pink and yellow spatter, white ground, colorless twisted thorn handle 225.00
6" l, 7-1/2" h, brown and jade green spatter, white ground, large thorn handle, ruffled star shaped edge 275.00
6-1/4" l, 5" w, 6-1/2" h, maroon, brown, yellow, blue, red, and green spatter, white int., colorless thorn loop handle, tightly crimped edge with two rows of hobnails, rectangular body
. . . . 250.00
6-1/2" l, 6" w, 6" h, pink and bright yellow spatter, white int., colorless thorn handle, eight point star shaped body
. . . . 250.00
Bowl, 8-1/4" d, 5-1/4" h, crimped rim, peach and white spatter, ornate ftd ormolu base 245.00
Candlestick, 7-1/2" h, flared socket, twisted hourglass stem, domed ribbed base, yellow, red, and white spatter . . . 50.00
Creamer, 4-1/2" h, 2-3/4" d, blue and light blue opaque, embossed swirl, applied blue reeded handle 95.00
Cruet, 8-3/4" h, 3-1/2" d, blue ground, white spatter, clear applied handle, clear heart-shaped stopper 135.00
Darning Egg, red, yellow, and green, clear applied handle
. . . . 125.00
Dish, cov, 4-1/4" d, 5-3/4" h, pink and green spatter, white lining, clear applied leaves on sides, clear applied feet, cover with applied clear finial. 80.00
Jack in the Pulpit Vase, 7-1/4" h, green, peach, yellow, and white spatter, green DQ body 75.00
Jar, cov, 3-3/4" x 6-1/2", maroon, white, yellow, and green, white cased int., clear applied feet and finial 85.00
Pitcher, amber and white, square top, IVT 185.00
Rolling Pin, 16" l, clear ground, red and blue spatter . . . 200.00

Miniature Lamp, Beaded Swirl pattern, brown and green spatter, 8-7/8" h, $275.

Rose Bowl, 3-1/2" d, octagonal crimped top, rose spatter, white cased int. 115.00
Salt, 3-3/4" x 3 x 1-1/2", maroon, yellow, and white spatter, white lining, clear applied shell trim 50.00
Spittoon, amber, wide rim 40.00
Sugar Shaker, cranberry, ring neck 145.00
Tumbler, 3-3/4" h, IVT, pink and cream spatter 48.00
Vase, 8" h, baluster, ringed neck, flared mouth, red, yellow, and green spatter, brown lining 90.00

SPATTERWARE

History: Spatterware generally was made of common earthenware, although occasionally creamware was used. The earliest English examples were made about 1780. The peak period of production was from 1810 to 1840. Firms known to have made spatterware are Adams, Barlow, and Harvey and Cotton.

The amount of spatter decoration varies from piece to piece. Some objects simply have decorated borders. These often were decorated with a brush, requiring several hundred touches per square inch to achieve the spatter effect. Other pieces have the entire surface covered with spatter.

Marks: Marked pieces are rare.

References: Susan and Al Bagdade, *Warman's English & Continental Pottery & Porcelain*, 3rd Edition, Krause Publications, 1998; Kevin McConnell, *Spongeware and Spatterware*, Schiffer Publishing, 1990.

Museum: Henry Ford Museum, Dearborn, MI.

Notes: Collectors today focus on the patterns—Cannon, Castle, Fort, Peafowl, Rainbow, Rose, Thistle, Schoolhouse, etc. The decoration on flatware is in the center of the piece; on hollow ware it occurs on both sides.

Aesthetics and the color of spatter are key to determining value. Blue and red are the most common colors; green, purple, and brown are in a middle group; black and yellow are scarce.

Like any soft paste, spatterware is easily broken or chipped. Prices in this listing are for pieces in very good to mint condition, unless otherwise noted.

Bowl, 11-1/8" d, stamped foliage border, center reserve of hp drapery swags and foliage devices, English, 19th C, hairline, very minor enamel loss, staining 200.00
Bowl and Pitcher, 12-5/8" d, 10-3/4" h, red and green four part flower, edge chip on bowl. 1,375.00
Child's Cup and Saucer, handleless, four-color 5,720.00
Child's Tea Set, teapot, two handleless cups and saucers, cream jug, green and blue spatter, repairs to all pieces
. . . . 1,100.00

Plate, Tulip pattern, yellow rim, wear, knife marks, 8-1/2" d, $265.

Creamer
   Cluster of Buds, blue spatter, 4" h 770.00
   Double-sided red, yellow, blue, green, and black rooster, purple spatter, repaired spout 1,870.00
   Rose, red and green spatter, bulbous creamer, 4" h, repaired spout 330.00
Cream Pitcher, 3-3/4" h, black and brown spatter 525.00
Cup and Saucer, handleless
   Acorn, red spatter, hairline crack on the cup 660.00
   Peafowl, green spatter 745.00
   Rose dec, red and purple spatter 1,210.00
   Thistle, yellow spatter 3,190.00
   Three-color rainbow spatter, impressed "Adams" . . . 495.00
Cup Plate, 5 1/8" d, blue morning glory in center, yellow spatter
. . . . .3,245.00
Pepper Pot, 5-1/8" h, dome top, purple and blue rainbow spatter
. . . . .5,500.00
Pitcher
   7-3/4" h, Tulip, paneled, yellow spatter 2,200.00
   10-1/2" h, Rainbow, red, green, yellow, black, and blue spatter 14,850.00
   10-3/4" h, Cluster of Buds pattern, blue spatter, red buds, green leaves, bulbous .5,390.00
Plate
   5" d, Double Acorn, blue spatter 2,860.00
   8-1/4" d, Schoolhouse, blue schoolhouse, red spatter
. . . . 2,090.00.
   8-1/2" d, Peafowl, ironstone 880.00
   9-1/4" d, Schoolhouse, paneled, blue spatter 3,740.00
   9-1/2" d, Triple Acorn, flake on edge 1,870.00
   9-5/8" d, Fort and Castle, blue spatter 330.00
   9-3/4" d, Cockscomb, paneled, yellow spatter 5,775.00
   9-3/4" d, Dahlia, purple. 385.00
Soup Plate, 10" d, Peafowl, blue spatter. 60.00
Sugar Bowl, cov
   Double-Loop, four-color rainbow spatter, 4" h 3,520.00
   Hollyberry covered sugar bowl, blue spatter, small chip to the rim 522.50
   Peafowl, red spatter, blue, yellow, green, and black Peafowl, 6" h, dark stains, mismatched lid, repaired hole in base
. . . . 550.00

Teapot, cov
   Cluster of Buds pattern teapot, blue spatter. 1,210.00
   Windmill, purple spatter, 5-3/4" h 2,750.00
Toddy, 5-3/4"" d, red design spatter border, blue stripe, purple, green, yellow ochre, and black viola, pinpoint flakes . 180.00
Tray, 11-1/4" l, maroon, very worn and stained 200.00

SPONGEWARE

History: Spongeware is a specific type of decoration, not a type of pottery or glaze.

Spongeware decoration is found on many kinds of pottery bodies—ironstone, redware, stoneware, yellowware, etc. It was made in both England and the United States. Pieces were marked after 1815, and production extended into the 1880s.

Decoration is varied. On some pieces the sponging is minimal with the white underglaze dominant. Other pieces appear to be solidly sponged on both sides. Pieces made between 1840 and 1860 have circular or horizontally streaked sponging.

Blue and white are the most common colors, but browns, greens, ochres, and a greenish blue also were used. The greenish blue results from blue sponging with a pale yellow overglaze. A red overglaze produces a black or navy color. Blue and red were used on English creamware and American earthenware of the 1880s. Other spongeware colors include gray, grayish green, red, dark green on stark white, dark green on mellow yellow, and purple.

References: Susan and Al Bagdade, *Warman's American Pottery and Porcelain*, Wallace-Homestead, 1994; ——, *Warman's English & Continental Pottery & Porcelain*, 3rd Edition, Krause Publications, 1998; William C. Ketchum, Jr., *American Pottery and Porcelain*, Avon Books, 1994; Kevin McConnell, *Spongeware and Spatterware*, Schiffer Publishing, 1990.

Coffeepot, blue and white, c1830, unmarked, $295.

Bowl
    8-1/2" d, 4" h, blue and white, ears for wire bale handle, wear
      and pinpoint flakes 75.00
    9" d, 3-1/2" h, blue and white, molded ribs, chips no foot and
      several open firing blisters 85.00
Butter Crock, 6" d, blue and white, emb label 85.00
Cooler, blue and white
    9-1/2" h, cov, marked "2" and "Ice Water," bung hole, no spig-
      ot, hairlines, chips to lid 110.00
    10" h, black enameled "15," brown Albany slip int., brass
      spigot, surface flake 110.00
    14-3/4" h, marked "5," bung hole, no spigot, chip on one han-
      dle 165.00
    18" h, marked "8," nickel plated spigot, minor chips on inside
      flange of lid. 350.00
Crock, cov, 9-1/2" d, 6-1/2" h, blue and white, chips 75.00
Dish, 6" d, blue and white, molded rim 45.00
Mug, 4-1/8" h, blue and white 40.00
Mustard Pot, cov, 2-1/4" h, blue and white, damaged lid . 55.00
Pitcher, blue and white
    6-1/2" h, bulbous base, labeled "UHL Pottery Co" . . . 770.00
    7-1/2" h
      Barrel shake, small rim flakes 220.00
      Bulbous 200.00
    8-3/8" h, rim chip, minor base flakes 220.00
    8-5/8" h, barrel shapes, stripes, hairlines 315.00
    8-3/4"" h, large pattern, chip on table ring 470.00
    8-7/8" h
      Bulbous base, cylindrical neck, chips 220.00
      Tankard, molded rose, minor open surface blisters
      . . . . 360.00
    9" h, tankard shape, small rim flake 330.00
    9-1/8" h, tankard, hairline, minor flakes 330.00
    9-1/2" h, bulbous base 715.00
Plate
    7-1/2" d, blue and white, molded rim 85.00
    9-1/4" d, blue and white, molded rim 115.00
    10" d, blue and white, molded rim handles 125.00
    10-1/4" d, blue and white, molded rim 120.00
Platter, 15" l, blue and white 325.00
Salt Crock, cov
    5-3/4"" d, blue and white, molded basketweave and vintage,
      hairline 80.00
    6-3/8" h, blue, yellowware ground, lid missing 65.00
Soap Dish, 3-1/2" x 4-3/4"", blue and white 65.00
Sugar, cov, 7-1/2" h, blue and white, attributed to Buford Bros.,
    East Liverpool, OH, professional repair to lid 165.00
Teapot, 6-1/2" h, bluish green and white, small chips
    . . . . 385.00
Toothbrush Holder, 5-1/4" h, blue and white. 45.00
Tray, 9-1/2" l, leaf shape, blue and white 115.00
Umbrella Stand, blue and red sponge dec 715.00
Wash Bowl
    14-1/2" d, 12" h, blue and white, blue stripes, color and width
      of stripes varies 330.00
    14-3/4" d, 4-1/4" h, blue and white 150.00
Water Filter, 22-1/2"h , blue and white, nickel plated spigot, two
    sections and lid, slight color variation 635.00

SPORTS CARDS

History: Baseball cards were first printed in the late 19th century. By 1900, the most common cards, known as "T" cards, were those made by tobacco companies such as American Tobacco Co. The majority of the tobacco-relat-

ed cards were produced between 1909 and 1915. During the 1920s American Caramel, National Caramel, and York Caramel candy companies issued cards identified in lists as "E" cards.

During the 1930s, Goudey Gum Co. of Boston (from 1933 to 1941) and Gum Inc. (in 1939) were prime producers of baseball cards. Following World War II, Bowman Gum of Philadelphia (B.G.H.L.I.), the successor to Gum, Inc., lead the way. Topps, Inc. (T.C.G.) of Brooklyn, New York, followed. Topps bought Bowman in 1956 and enjoyed almost a monopoly in card production until 1981.

In 1981, Topps was challenged by Fleer of Philadelphia and Donruss of Memphis. All three companies annually produce sets numbering 600 cards or more.

Football cards have been printed since the 1890s. However, it was not until 1933 that the first bubble gum football card appeared in the Goudey Sport Kings set. In 1935 National Chickle of Cambridge, Massachusetts, produced the first full set of gum cards devoted exclusively to football.

Both Leaf Gum of Chicago and Bowman Gum of Philadelphia produced sets of football cards in 1948. Leaf discontinued production after their 1949 issue; Bowman continued until 1955.

Topps Chewing Gum entered the market in 1950 with its college-stars set. Topps became a fixture in the football card market with its 1955 All-American set. From 1956 thorough 1963 Topps printed card sets of National Football League players, combining them with the American Football League players in 1961.

Topps produced sets with only American Football League players from 1964 to 1967. The Philadelphia Gum Company made National Football League card sets during this period. Beginning in 1968 and continuing to the present, Topps has produced sets of National Football League cards, the name adopted after the merger of the two leagues.

References: *All Sports Alphabetical Price Guide*, Krause Publications, 1995; Mark Allen Baker, *All-Sport Autograph Guide*, Krause Publications, 1995; Tol Broome, *From Ruth to Ryan*, Krause Publications, 1994; *Charlton Standard Catalogue of Canadian Baseball & Football Cards*, 4th ed., The Charlton Press, 1995; *Charlton Standard Catalogue of Hockey Cards*, 7th ed., Charlton Press, 1995; Gene Florence, *Florence's Standard Baseball Card Price Guide*, 6th ed., Collector Books, 1995.

Jeff Kurowski and Tony Prudom, *Sports Collectors Digest Pre-War Baseball Card Price Guide*, Krause Publications, 1993; Mark Larson, *Complete Guide to Baseball Memorabilia*, 3rd ed., Krause Publications, 1996; --, *Complete Guide to Football, Basketball & Hockey Memorabilia*, Krause Publications, 1995; --, *Sports Collectors Digest Minor League Baseball Card Price Guide*, Krause Publications, 1993; Mark Larson (ed.), *Sports Card Explosion*, Krause Publications, 1993; Bob Lemke and Sally Grace, *Sportscard Counterfeit Detector*, 3rd ed., Krause Publications, 1994; Michael McKeever, *Collecting Sports Cards*, Alliance Publishing, 1996; Alan Rosen, *True Mint*, Krause Publications, 1994; *Sports Collectors Digest, Baseball Card Price Guide*, 11th ed., Krause Publications, 1997; ——, *Premium Insert Sports Cards*, Krause Publications, 1995; ——, *Standard Catalog of Baseball Cards*, 7th ed., Krause Publications, 1997; --, *1998 Standard Catalog of Basketball Cards*, Krause Publications, 1997; --, *1998 Standard Catalog of Football Cards*, Krause Publications, 1997; ——, *Standard Catalog of Football, Basketball, & Hockey Cards*, 2nd ed., Krause Publications, 1996.

Periodicals: *Allan Kaye's Sports Cards News & Price Guides*, 10300 Watson Rd., St. Louis, MO 63127; *Baseball Update*, Suite 284, 220 Sunrise Hwy, Rockville Centre, NY 11570; *Beckett Baseball Card Monthly*, 15850 Dallas Pkwy, Dallas, TX 75248; *Beckett Football Card Magazine*, 15850 Dallas Pkwy, Dallas, TX 75248; *Canadian Sportscard Collector*, P.O. Box 1299, Lewiston, NY 14092; *The Old Judge*, P.O. Box 137, Centerbeach, NY 11720; *Sport Card Economizer*, RFD 1 Box 350, Winthrop, ME 04364; *Sports Cards Magazine & Price Guide*, 700 E. State St., Iola, WI 54490; *Sports Card Trader*, P.O. Box 443, Mt. Morris, IL 61054; *Sports Collectors Digest*, 700 E. State St., Iola, WI 54990; *Tuff Stuff*, P.O. Box 1637, Glen Allen, VA 23060; *Your Season Ticket*, 106 Liberty Rd., Woodsboro, MD 21798.

Sports Cards Language:

As in a dictionary, new terms and abbreviations are added to various antiques and collectibles categories. Here are some commonly used Sports Cards terms.

ACC—American Card Catalog, edited by Jefferson Burdick, Nostalgia Press, 1960. Lists alphabetical and numerical designations as it identifies card sets. They have devised a set of sub-abbreviations, such as F for food inserts. The one, tow, or three-digit number which follows the letter prefix identifies the company and the series.

AS—All Star Card. A special card for players of the all star teams of the National League, American League, or Major League.

AU—Card with autograph.

Blank Back—refers to a card with no printing at all on the back.

Borders—white space, although sometimes colored, which surrounds the picture, used in establishing grading.

Brick—a wrapped group of cards, often of only one year.

Centering—the player should be centered on the card with even borders; an important grading factor.

Chipping—wearing away of a dark-colored border.

Combination Card—shows two or more players but not an entire team.

Common Card—ordinary player, lowest-valued card in a set.

CO—abbreviation for coach.

COR—corrected card.

CY—Cy Young award.

Ding—slight damage to the edge or corner of a card.

DP—double-quantity print run.

DR—draft choice.

ERR—error card. Card with a known mistake, misspell-

ing, etc. When a variation card has been issued, the value of an error card goes down.

First Card—first card of a player in a national set, not necessarily a rookie card.

Foil—foil embossed stamp on card.

F/S—father and son on card.

Gloss—the amount of shine on a card, again a value determination.

Grade—condition that helps determine value.

Key Card—most important cards in a set.

Reverse Negative—common error in which picture negative is flipped so the picture comes out backward.

ROY—Rookie of the Year.

SP—single or short print, printed in lesser amounts than rest of series.

Team Card—card showing entire team.

Wrapper—paper wrapper surrounding wax packs.

YL—yellow letters, Topps, 1958.

Baseball

Bowman
1948

8, Ruzzoto, PSA Grade 9, MT	2,500.00
17, Slaughter, PSA Grade 7, NM	110.00
18, Spahn, PSA Grade 7, NM	300.00

1949

46, Roberts, PSA Grade 7, NM	200.00
84, Campanella, PSA Grade 8, NM-MT	1,250.00
224, Paige, PSA Grade 7, NM	950.00

1950

94, Boudreau, PSA Grade 8, NM-MT	150.00
112, Hodges, PSA Grade 8, NM-MT	275.00
148, Wynn, PSA Grade 7, NM	75.00
215, Lopat, PSA Grade 8, NM-MT	175.00
217, Stengel, PSA Grade 7, NM	125.00

1951

3, Roberts, PSA Grade 7, NM	85.00
58, Slaughter, PSA Grade 8, NM-MT	125.00
254, Exeter, PSA Grade 7, NM	65.00
305, Mayes, PSA Grade 7, NM	3,000.00

1952

1 Berra, PSA Grade 7, NM	595.00
21, Fox, PSA Grade 7, NM	80.00
196, Musical, PSA Grade 7, NM	550.00
218, Mays, PSA Grade 7, NM	1,095.00

1953, color

61, Keil, PSA Grade 8, NM-MT	250.00
73, Pierce, PSA Grade 8, NM-MT	250.00
1954, 66, Williams, PSA Grade 7, NM	3,500.00

1955

23, Kaline, PSA Grade 8, NM-MT	225.00
179, Aaron, PSA Grade 7, NM	225.00

Cracker Jack
1911

81, Delehanty, PSA Grade 7, NM	225.00
122, Bush, PSA Grade 7, NM	225.00
128, Evans, PSA Grade 7, NM	225.00
131, Baumgardner, PSA Grade 6, EX-MT	125.00
140, Murphy, PSA Grade 7, NM	225.00

1915

4, Doyle, PSA Grade 7, NM	225.00
9, Hoffman, PSA Grade 6, EX-MT	125.00
21, Zimmerman, PSA Grade 7, NM	225.00

45, Luderus, PSA Grade 5, EX 70.00
124, Moore, PSA Grade 7, NM 225.00
Diamond Stars, 1934-36
41, Hendrick, PSA Grade 7, NM 75.00
43, Lyons, PSA Grade 7, NM. 175.00
44 Hornsby, PSA Grade 7, NM 500.00
Fleer
1961
14, Cobb, EX-MT 22.00
31, Gehrig, MT 55.00
154, Young, NM 24.00
1963
5, Mays, EX-MT 90.00
29, Persal, EX 6.00
42, Koufax, NM. 140.00
Goudey
1933
6, Dykes, PSA Grade 7, NM. 200.00
14, Johnson, PSA Grade 7, NM. 225.00
59, Miller, PSA 7, NM. 175.00
139, Cantwell, PSA Grade 8, MN-MT 350.00
182, High, PSA Grade 7, NM 125.00
1934
18, Manush, PSA Grade 7, NM 300.00
22, Vaghan, PSA Grade 8, NM-MT 700.00
61, Gehring, PSA Grade 4, VG-EX 1,500.00
75, Werber, PSA Grade 6, EX-MT. 150.00
90, Coyler, PSA Grade 6, EX-MT. 275.00
Mayo Cut Plug, 1895, Anson, PSA Grade 4, VG-EX
. . . . .2,250.00
Sporting Life, 1911
Baker, PSA Grade 8, MN-MT. 800.00
Delehanty, PSA Grade 6, EX-MT. 50.00
Demmitt, PSA Grade 8, NM-MT. 300.00
Tinker, PSA Grade 7, NM. 350.00
Topps
1951, blue back
3, Ashburn, PSA Grade 8, NM-MT. 395.00
6, Schoendenst, PSA Grade 9, MT 395.00
37, Doerr, PSA Grade 8, NM-MT. 175.00
50, Mize, PSA Grade 8, NM-MT. 225.00
1952, 261, Mayes, PSA Grade 5, EX 395.00

1953
27, Campanella, PSA Grade 9, MT 495.00
258, Gillam, PSA Grade 7, NM 295.00
1954
32, Snider, PSA Grade 8, NM-MT 695.00
54, Banks, PSA Grade 7, NM. 895.00
102, Hodges, PSA Grade 7, NM-MT 275.00
1955
123, Koufax, PSA Grade 7, NM 795.00
155 Matthews, PSA 8, NM-MT. 295.00

Football
Bowman
1948
7, Van Buren, PSA Grade 7, NM 150.00
250, McAfee, PSA Grade 8, NM-MT 250.00
1950
6, Griza, PSA Grade 7, NM 175,99
37, Layne, PSA Grade 7, NM. 150.00
45, Graham, PSA Grade 8, NM 1,295.00
53, Huffman, PSA Grade 7, NM. 35.00
108, Lilywhite, PSA Grade 8, NM-MT 85.00
137, Kavanaugh, PSA Grade 8, MN-MT 85.00
Leaf, 1948, 36 Dudley, PSA Grade 7, NM 125.00

SPORTS COLLECTIBLES

History: People have been saving sports-related equipment since the inception of sports. Some was passed down from generation to generation for reuse; the rest was stored in dark spaces in closets, attics, and basements.

In the 1980s, two key trends brought collectors' attention to sports collectibles. First, decorators began using old sports items, especially in restaurant decor. Second, card collectors began to discover the thrill of owning the "real" thing. By the beginning of the 1990s, all sport categories were collectible, with baseball items paramount and golf and football running close behind.

References: Mark Allen Baker, *Sports Collectors Digest Complete Guide to Boxing Collectibles*, Krause Publications, 1995; Don Bevans and Ron Menchine, *Baseball Team Collectibles*, Wallace-Homestead, 1994; David Bushing, *Guide to Spalding Bats 1908-1938*, published by author; ——, *Sports Equipment Price Guide*, Krause Publications, 1995; Dave Bushing and Joe Phillips, *1996 Vintage Baseball Glove Pocket Price Guide*, No. 4, published by authors (217 Homewood, Libertyville, IL 60048), 1996; ——, *Vintage Baseball Bat 1994 Pocket Price Guide*, published by authors, 1994; Bruce Chadwick and David M. Spindel authored a series of books on major-league teams published by Abbeville Press between 1992 and 1995; Duncan Chilcott, *Miller's Societycer Memorabilia*, Miller's Publications, 1994; Douglas Congdon-Martin and John Kashmanian, *Baseball Treasures*, Schiffer Publishing, 1993; Ralf Coykendall, Jr., *Coykendall's Complete Guide to Sporting Collectibles*, Wallace-Homestead, 1996; Sarah Fabian-Baddiel, *Miller's Golf Memorabilia*, Millers Publications, 1994; Chuck Furjanic, *Antique Golf Collectibles, A Price and Reference Guide*, Krause Publications, 1997; John F. Hotchkiss, *500 Years of Golf Balls*, Antique Trader Books, 1997; Mark K. Larson, *Complete*

Topps #311, Mickey Mantle, rookie card, regular back, 1952, $16,000.

Guide to Baseball Memorabilia, 3rd ed., Krause Publications, 1996; Mark Larson, Rick Hines and David Platta (eds.), *Mickey Mantle Memorabilia*, Krause Publications, 1993; Carl Luckey, *Old Fishing Lures and Tackle*, 4th ed., Books Americana, 1996; Roderick A. Malloy, *Malloy's Sports Collectibles Value Guide*, Attic Books Ltd., Wallace-Homestead, 1993; Michael McKeever, *Collecting Sports Memorabilia*, Alliance Publishing (P.O. Box 080377, Brooklyn, NY 11208), 1966; Dudley Murphy and Rick Edmisten, *Fishing Lure Collectibles*, 1995, 1997 value update, Collector Books; *1996 Vintage Baseball Glove Catalog Source Book*, The Glove Collector (14057 Rolling Hills Lane, Dallas, TX 75240), 1996; John M. and Morton W. Olman, *Golf Antiques & Other Treasures of the Game*, Market Street Press, 1993; George Richey, *Made in Michigan Fishing Lures*, published by author (Rte. 1, Box 280, Honor, MI 49640), 1995; George Sanders, Helen Sanders, and Ralph Roberts, *Sanders Price Guide to Sports Autographs*, 1994 ed., Scott Publishing, 1993; Harold E. Smith, *Collector's Guide to Creek Chub Lures & Collectibles*, Collector Books, 1996; Mark Wilson (ed.), *Golf Club Identification and Price Guide III*, Ralph Maltby Enterprises, 1993.

Periodicals: *Baseball Hobby News*, 4540 Kearney Villa Rd., San Diego, CA 92123; *Beckett Focus on Future Stars*, 15850 Dallas Pkwy, Dallas, TX 75248; *Boxing Collectors Newsletter*, 59 Boston St., Revere, MA 02151; *Button Pusher*, P.O. Box 4, Coopersburg, PA 18036; *Diamond Angle*, P.O. Box 409, Kaunakakai, HI 97648; *Diamond Duds*, P.O. Box 10153, Silver Spring, MD 20904; *Fantasy Baseball*, 700 E. State St., Iola, WI 54990; *Golfiana Magazine*, P.O. Box 688, Edwardsville, IL 62025; *Old Tyme Baseball News*, P.O. Box 833, Petoskey, MI 49770; *Sports Collectors Digest*, 700 E. State St., Iola, WI 54990; *Tuff Stuff*, P.O. Box 1637, Glen Allen, VA 23060; *US Golf Classics & Heritage Hickories*, 5407 Pennock Point Rd., Jupiter, FL 33458.

Collectors' Clubs: The (Baseball) Glove Collector, 14507 Rolling Hills Lane, Dallas, TX, 75240; Boxiana & Pugilistica Collectors International, P.O. Box 83135, Portland, OR 97203; Golf Club Collectors Association, 640 E. Liberty St., Girard, OH 44420; Golf Collectors Society, P.O. Box 20546, Dayton, OH 45420; Logo Golf Ball Collector's Association, 4552 Barclay Fairway, Lake Worth, FL 33467; Society for American Baseball Research, P.O. Box 93183, Cleveland, OH 44101.

SPECIAL AUCTIONS

Dixie Sporting Collectibles
1206 Rama Rd.
Charlotte, NC 28211
(704) 364-2900

Lang's
30 Hamlin Rd.
Falmouth, ME 04105
(207) 797-2311

Museums: Aiken Thoroughbred Racing Hall of Fame & Museum, Aiken, SC; International Boxing Hall of Fame, Canastota, NY; Kentucky Derby Museum, Louisville, KY; Metropolitan Museum of Art, The Jefferson Burdich Collection, New York, NY; Naismith Memorial Basketball Hall of Fame, Springfield, MA; National Baseball Hall of Fame & Museum, Inc., Cooperstown, NY; National Bowling Hall of Fame & Museum, St. Louis, MO; New England Sports Museum, Boston, MA; PGA/World Golf Hall of Fame, Pinehurst, NC; University of New Haven National Art Museum of Sport, W Haven, CT.

Baseball

Ball, autographed
  Aaron, Hank 40.00
  DiMaggio, Joe, 1955 . . . . 300.00
  Mickey Mantle and Ted Williams 250.00
  Pete Rose. 90.00
Bank, 3" x 6" x 7", Cleveland Baseball Club, china, figural, Cleveland Baseball Club copyright, Gibbs-Sonner & Co., mid 1950s 225.00
Bat, autographed
  Yogi Berra 180.00
  Kirby Puckett 180.00
  Frank Thomas 140.00
Box, 6-7/8" w, 9-1/4" l, 2-3/8" h, New York Champions Chocolates, paper label, wooden box, inside with illus of uniformed baseball players 650.00
Candy Bar Wrapper, 7-7/8" w, 7" l, wax paper, Bit Hit 10¢ Babe Ruth, Universal Candy Co., Oconto, WI 160.00
Coaster, 4-1/4" d, cardboard, Ballentine Ale & Beer adv, black and white portrait illus of Bob Linger and Virgil Davis, late 1930s 45.00
Jersey, autographed
  Eddie Murray 325.00
  Pete Rose. 250.00
  Lawrence Taylor. 195.00
Medallion, 1-1/2" d, Babe Ruth Shrine, Ruth at bat on one side, Baltimore birthplace on other 60.00
Pennant
  Baltimore Orioles League Championship, 29-1/2" l, black, 1969. . . . . 30.00
  New York Mets, 29-1/2" l, blue, white, and orange inscription and design, late 1960s. 20.00
  San Francisco Giants, 29" l, black, white inscription, 1960s 22.00
Press Pin, New York Yankees, 1938 World Series, two crossed bats, raised baseball, red, white, and blue border mkd "World Series Yankee Stadium". 850.00
Sign, 13-1/2" h, 10-1/2" w, diecut cardboard, Ken-Wel Glove, shows baseball players using Lou Gehrig Model, picture of glove in background, some minor creasing around edges 210.00
Yearbook, Yankees, 1951. . . . . 120.00

Boxing

Autograph, black and white photo signed
  8" x 10", Brett Hart 20.00
  8" x 10", Hollywood Hogan. 25.00
  16" x20", Muhammad Ali, staring at speed back with Howard Cossell's face on it, sgd in blue 75.00
Game, Championship Fight, Frankie Goodman copyright and design, US National & Intercollegiate Champion, 1940-50 . . . . 48.00
Playing Cards, James J. Jeffries Championship, boxer photo on each card, complete deck, 1909 copyright. 120.00

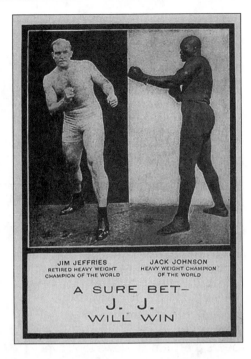

Postcard, Jim Jeffries vs. Jack Johnson, Heavyweights, $200. Photo courtesy of Postcards International.

Program, 1964 Ali vs. Liston, Boston, MA, sgd "Muhammad Ali" 150.00

Fishing

Fish, 31-1/2" l, wood, paint dec, America, early 20th C, minor paint wear and losses........................1,495.00
Folk Art, 25" h, 40-1/4" l, wood carving, titled "Two Fish and a Frog," sgd "L. A. Plummer, 1904" in lower right, polychrome dec, minor cracks.........................17,250.00
Painting, oil on canvas
    13" x 9-1/2", Landscape with Fisherman, monogrammed "RHW" (Richard W. Hubbard) lower right, identified on Cleveland Museum of Art label on reverse, framed, re-touched 660.00
    20" h, 32" l, Salmon and Fishing Rod on a Rock Ledge Beside a Stream, Walter R. Brackett, sgd and dated "W. M. Brackett 1881" on lower right, fish and wave motif carved wood frame 17,250.00
Reel, B. F. Meek & Sons, #33 Bluegrass 200.00
Rod
    F. E. Thomas, three piece fly rod, extra tip, metal case, mkd "Special, Bangor, Maine," 8-1/2' 275.00
    Hardy's of England Salmon Deluxe Rod, extra tip, aluminum case, 9'.. 175.00
    H. L. Leonard, fly, Leonard Tournament, extra tip, metal case, 9' 300.00

Reel, brass P. A. Altmaire, Harrisburg, PA, Pat. Nov. 9, 1869, $2,145. Photo courtesy of Lang's Sporting Collectables, Inc.

L. L. Bean, Bean's Atlantic Salmon Rod, extra tip and case, extra cork handle, 9-1/2'. 95.00

Football

Ashtray, 7-1/2" d, Baltimore Colts Championship, china, white, blue cartoon illus, dated Dec. 29, 1958, orig box..... 75.00
Glass, 5-1/4" h, Ohio State University Football, Champions Western Conference, Appreciation Banquet, Nov. 25, 1968 .... 18.00
Nodder, 6-1/2" h, LA Rams, composition, c1961 .... 55.00
Pennant
    Chicago Bears, 28" l, black, dark orange lettering and design 42.00
    San Diego Chargers, 29-1/2" l, felt, yellow-gold and white lettering and helmet design, blue ground, American Football League insignia, late 1960s.................... 18.00
Program, Chicago Tribune All-Star Charity Football, College All-Americans and Chicago Bears, Soldiers' Field, Chicago, c1935 .... 30.00

Golf

Bowl, Old Foley-Wileman 225.00
Decanter, silver overlay, dark amethyst glass body, figure of golfer 300.00
Doorstop, 8" h, cast iron, figural, wear to old polychrome 770.00
Miniature Cup and Saucer, Old Foley-Wileman 225.00
Mug, white stoneware, hp golfer, Scotland, c1950 ..... 140.00
Plate, small, Old Foley-Wileman.................... 85.00
Tray, 12" d, golfer and caddy on golf course, plane flying overhead pulling banner adv "Famous Beverwyck Beers and Ales," Electro-Chemical Engraving Co. litho, © 1934 .... 225.00

STAFFORDSHIRE, HISTORICAL

W.ADAMS&SONS   ADAMS

History: The Staffordshire district of England is the center of the English pottery industry. There were 80 different potteries operating there in 1786, with the number increasing to 179 by 1802. The district includes Burslem, Cobridge, Etruria, Fenton, Foley, Hanley, Lane, Lane End, Longport, Shelton, Stoke, and Tunstall. Among the many famous potters were Adams, Davenport, Spode, Stevenson, Wedgwood, and Wood.

References: David and Linda Arman, *Historical Staffordshire* (1974), 1st Supplement (1977), published by authors, out of print; Susan and Al Bagdade, *Warman's English & Continental Pottery & Porcelain*, 3rd Edition, Krause Publications, 1998; A. W. Coysh and R. K. Henrywood, *Dictionary of Blue and White Printed Pottery* (1982), Vol. II (1989), Antique Collectors' Club; Mary J. Finegan, *Johnson Brothers Dinnerware*, published by author, 1993; N. Hudson Moore, *The Old China Book*, Charles E. Tuttle, Co., second printing, 1980; Jeffrey B. Snyder, *Historical Staffordshire American Patriots and Views*, Schiffer Publishing, 1995.

Museums: American Antiquarian Society, Worcester, MA; Cincinnati Art Museum, Cincinnati, OH; City Museum & Art Gallery, Stoke-on-Trent, England; Colonial Williamsburg Foundation, Williamsburg, VA; Elverson Museum of Art, Syracuse, NY; Henry Ford Museum, Dearborn, MI;

Hershey Museum, Hershey, PA; Metropolitan Museum of Art, New York, NY; The National Museum of History & Technology, Washington, DC; The Henry Francis DuPont Winterthur Museum, Winterthur, DE; William Rockhill Nelson Gallery of Art, Kansas City, MO; Yale University Gallery of Fine Arts, New Haven, CT.

Notes: The view is the most critical element when establishing the value of historical Staffordshire; American collectors pay much less for non-American views. Dark blue pieces are favored; light views continue to remain under-priced. Among the forms, soup tureens have shown the largest price increases.

Prices listed below are for mint examples. Reduce prices by 20% for a hidden chip, a faint hairline, or an invisible professional repair; by 35% for knife marks through the glaze and a visible professional repair; by 50% for worn glaze and major repairs.

The numbers in parentheses refer to items in the Armans' books, which constitute the most detailed list of American historical views and their forms.

SPECIAL AUCTION

The Armans Collector's Sales and Services
P.O. Box 4037
Middletown, RI 02842
(401) 849-5012

Adams

The Adams family has been associated with ceramics since the mid-17th century. In 1802, William Adams of Stoke-on-Trent produced American views. In 1819, a fourth William Adams, son of William of Stoke, became a partner with his father and was later joined by his three brothers. The firm became William Adams & Sons. The father died in 1829 and William, the eldest son, became manager. The company operated four potteries at Stoke and one at Tunstall. American views were produced at Tunstall in black, light blue, sepia, pink, and green in the 1830-40 period. William Adams died in 1865. All operations were moved to Tunstall. The firm continues today under the name of Wm. Adams & Sons, Ltd.

(Adams) Plate, Mitchell & Freemans China & Glass Warehouse, Chatham Street, Boston, dark blue transfer, c1804-10, mkd, 10" d, $465.

Cup Plate, 4" d, Fair Mount, Hudson River Series, pink transfer (459) 90.00
Plate
7-3/4" d, St. Paul's School, London, dark blue transfer, imp "Adams" 175.00
9" d, Mitchell & Freeman's China & Glass Warehouse, Chatham Street, Boston, dark blue transfer, imp "Adams," wear, chip on back of rim, scratches 385.00
Platter
15-1/2" l, Fountain Scenery, blue transfer, wear and scratches, imp "Adams" 200.00
17" l, Jedburgh Abbey, Roxburghshire, dark blue transfer, imp "Adams," wear and deep knife scratches 360.00
Soup Plate, 10-1/2" d, US Views, Catskill Mountain House, light blue transfer (445) 85.00
Vegetable Bowl, open, 8-1/4" l, Hanover Terrace, Regents Park, dark blue transfer, imp "Adams" 385.00
Waste Bowl, Log Cabin, medallions of Gen. Harrison on border, brown transfer (458) 265.00

Clews

From sketchy historical accounts, that are available, it appears that James Clews took over the closed plant of A. Stevenson in 1819. His brother Ralph entered the business later. The firm continued until about 1836 when James Clews came to America to enter the pottery business at Troy, Indiana. The venture was a failure because of the lack of skilled workmen and the proper type of clay. He returned to England but did not re-enter the pottery business.

Cup and Saucer, Landing of LaFayette, dark blue transfer 300.00
Cup Plate, 4-5/8" d, winter view of Pittsfield, MA, dark blue transfer, imp "Clews,"" chips and hairlines 200.00
Pepper Pot, Landing of Lafayette, dome top, dark blue transfer 1,155.00
Pitcher, 7-7/8" h, Landing of Gen. LaFayette," dark blue transfer, imp "Clews," wear and glaze flakes 1,100.00
Plate
8" d, America and Independence, States series, scene with two story building with curved drive, dark blue transfer, imp "Clews," small rim bruise 330.00
8-3/4" d, Peace, Plenty, dark blue transfer, imp "Clews," minor wear and scratches, small glaze flake near eagle 220.00
9" d, Landing of Gen. LaFayette, dark blue transfer, imp "Clews" 330.00
9" d, Peace and Plenty, basket of flowers and scroll border, dark blue transfer, imp "Clews" 220.00
10-1/8" d, Landing of Gen. LaFayette, dark blue transfer, imp "Clews" 455.00
10-1/4" d, Landing of Lafayette, dark blue transfer, imp "Clews" 385.00
10-1/2" d, Winter View of Pittsfield Elm, dark blue transfer 300.00
Platter
14-3/4" l, America and Independence, dark blue transfer, scene of mansion with small boat and flag, imp "Clews," minor wear and scratches 1,210.00
16-1/2" l, 13-1/4" w, Sandusky, dark blue transfer, misnamed "Detroit," Cities series, minor staining on back ...4,500.00

(Clews) Plate, States series, medallion with Washington, dark blue transfer, 8-3/4" d, $115.

17" l, Peace & Plenty, dark blue transfer, imp "Clews," wear, small edge flakes and deep scratches 715.00
17" l, 13" w, Landing of LaFayette, dark blue transfer, stained, deteriorating repair to chip on front 1,050.00
17-1/2" l, Picturesque View, Little Falls at Luzerne, Hudson River, black transfer, imp "Clews," wear, knife scratches, small flakes 450.00
18-1/2" l, 15-1/2" w, Winter View of Pittsfield Mass, dark blue transfer, scalloped edge, minor staining on back
. . . . .3,000.00
Sauce Boat Tray, 9-3/4" l, Landing of Gen. LaFayette, dark blue transfer, imp "Clews" 965.00
Sauce Tureen, 6" h, 7-3/4" w handle to handle, Hudson River, Fort Montgomery, light blue transfer, Picturesque Views series 350.00
Saucer, English scene with church and fisherman, dark blue transfer, imp "Clews," wear 75.00
Toddy Plate
5-1/2" d, Landing of Gen. LaFayette, dark blue transfer, imp "Clews" 425.00
5-5/8" d, America and Independence, States series, scene of three story building with wings, dark blue transfer, imp "Clews," hairline 110.00

Goodwin, Thomas, 1830-40

Plate, 9-1/4" d
Schuykill Water Works, 9 1/4" d plate, American Views series, brown transfer 160.00
William Penn's Treaty American Views series, dark blue transfer. 85.00
Platter, Crystal Palace, mauve transfer, deteriorating repair to 2" chip, staining 50.00
Soup Plate, 10 1/2" d, William Penn's Treaty American Views series , green transfer 90.00
Vegetable, open, 8" l, oval, William Penn's Treaty American Views series, red transfer. 250.00

Hall, Ralph, Tunstall, 1800-29

Bowl, 9-3/4" d, Select Views, Biddulph Castle Staffordshire, medium blue transfer, glaze wear, minor chips 300.00

Compote, Rode Hall, Cheshire, 3-1/2" x 12" w, ftd, Foliage border series, dark blue transfer, underglaze title, shell and scroll emb handles, four tiny peg feet, light center, dark border, three stilt marks on face, two shallow rim chips 350.00
Plate, 7-1/2" d, Sheltered Peasants, dark blue transfer, wear and scratches, pr. 400.00
Waste Bowl, 6 1/4" d, dark blue transfer, imp "Nest, R. Hall"
. . . . 200.00

Heath, Joseph & Co.

Pitcher, 6-1/4" h, Residence of the Late Richard Jordan, New Jersey, black transfer, crack to handle 250.00

J. & J. Jackson   J&J. JACKSON

Job and John Jackson began operations at the Churchyard Works, Burslem, about 1830. The works formerly were owned by the Wedgwood family. The firm produced transfer scenes in a variety of colors, such as black, light blue, pink, sepia, green, maroon, and mulberry. More than 40 different American views of Connecticut, Massachusetts, Pennsylvania, New York, and Ohio were issued. The firm is believed to have closed about 1844.

Plate
6-1/4" d, Girard's Bank, Philadelphia, one green, one black, two mulberry, 4 pcs 350.00
8-1/4" d, Library, Philadelphia, Beauties of America series, floral border, blue transfer 200.00
8-1/2" d, Dumb Asylum, blue transfer. 160.00
9" d, The Race Bridge, Philadelphia, black transfer
. . . . 100.00
10" d, Water Works, Philadelphia, oak leaf and acorn border, blue transfer. 600.00
10-1/4" d, The President's House, Washington, Jackson's Warranted, red transfer 315.00
Platter, 9-3/4", Upper Ferry Bridge, Philadelphia, red transfer
. . . . 500.00

Thomas Mayer

In 1829, Thomas Mayer and his brothers, John and Joshua, purchased Stubbs's Dale Hall Works of Burslem. They continued to produce a superior grade of ceramics.

Cup Plate, 4" d, Arms of South Carolina, Arms of States series, dark blue transfer, unmarked 700.00
Plate, 8-1/2" d, Arms of Rhode Island, Arms of the American States series, dark blue transfer, minor staining 600.00
Soup Plate, 10" d, Arms of New York, Arms of States series, dark blue transfer, wear, shallow rim flakes, pinpoints on table ring 635.00
Sugar Bowl, Lafayette at Washington's Tomb, cov, dark blue transfer (511) 750.00
Vegetable Dish, 11-3/4" l, Arms of Georgia, Arms of States series, dark blue transfer (500) 3,000.00

J. & W. Ridgway and William Ridgway & Co.

John and William Ridgway, sons of Job Ridgway and nephews of George Ridgway who owned Bell Bank Works and Cauldon Place Works, produced the popular

Beauties of America series at the Cauldon plant. The partnership between the two brothers was dissolved in 1830. John remained at Cauldon. William managed the Bell Bank Works until 1854. Two additional series were produced based upon the etchings of Bartlett's American Scenery. The first series had various borders including narrow lace. The second series is known as Catskill Moss. Beauties of America is in dark blue. The other series are found in light transfer colors of blue, pink, brown, black, and green.

J.W.R.

Stone China

W. RIDGWAY

Bowl, urn shaped, 10" d, Oriental, medium blue transfer, gilt trim, mkd "Ridgways" 275.00
Cup Plate, Exchange Building, Baltimore, Beauties of America series, dark blue transfer (254) 450.00
Gravy Tureen Ladle, 6" l, Portions of a View, College series, dark blue, transfer, repairs to handle 325.00
Gravy Tureen, cov, 6-1/4" h, 8-1/4" w, Trinity Hall, Cambridge, College series, dark blue transfer, underglaze mark, emb handles, floral finial. 600.00
Plate
    7-1/8" d, Insane Hospital, Boston, Beauties of America series, medium to dark blue transfer 350.00
    8-1/2" d, City Hall, New York, Beauties of America series, dark blue transfer, mkd "J. & W. Ridgway," Hanley, 1814-30
    . . . . 200.00
    9" d, Fairmount Gardens, Catskill Moss series, 1844
    . . . . 90.00
    9-1/2" d, Meredith, Catskill Moss series (307) 65.00
    9-3/4" d, City Hall, New York, Beauties of America series, medium to dark blue transfer, imp mark, tiny factory flaws around rim 300.00
Platter
    16" l, Almshouse, New York, Beauties of America series, dark blue transfer (255) 625.00

18-1/2" l, Pennsylvania Hospital, Philadelphia, Beauties of America series, dark blue transfer, octagonal 1,400.00
20-3/4" l, 15-1/2" w, Capitol Washington, Beauties of America series, medium to dark blue, staining, 12" crack, wear to face 200.00
Soup Plate
    8-1/4" d, Straughton's Church, Philadelphia, Beauties of America series, dark blue transfer, pr 350.00
    10" d, Kosciusko's Tomb, Catskill Moss series(305)
    . . . . 75.00
    10" d, Octagon Church, Boston, Beauties of America series, dark blue transfer (A-271) 275.00

Rogers, John & Son, Longport, England

ROGERS

John Rogers and his brother George established a pottery near Longport in 1782. After George's death in 1815, John's son Spencer became a partner, and the firm operated under the name of John Rogers & Sons. John died in 1916. His son continued the use of the name until he dissolved the pottery in 1842.

Cup and Saucer, Boston Harbor, dark blue transfer (441)
. . . . 650.00
Plate, 10" d, Boston State House, dark blue transfer (442)
. . . . 150.00
Platter, 14" l, Boston State House, dark blue transfer (442)
. . . . 495.00
Set, Boston State House, c1815-42, blue and white, 29 dinner plates, 19 luncheon plates, 11 soup plates, 4 bread and butter plates, 10 platters, pierced insert, soup tureen with undertray and ladle, 4 sauce tureens, 3 undertrays, 4 cov serving dishes, sq center bowl, all mkd "Rogers," some with staple and other repairs, minor cracks, chips, staining, price for set
. . . . 16,500.00
Sugar Bowl, Boston Harbor, dark blue transfer (441)
. . . . 675.00

Stevenson

As early as the 17th century, the name Stevenson has been associated with the pottery industry. Andrew Stevenson of Cobridge introduced American scenes with the flower and scroll border. Ralph Stevenson, also of Co-

(Ridgway) Platter, Sydney Sussex College, Cambridge, light blue transfer, lattice edge, 9-1/2" x 11-3/4", $450.

(Stevenson) Left: soup plate, View of Governor's Island, dark blue transfer, imp mark, minor wear and small flakes, 10-3/8" d, $2,475; right: plate, New York from Brooklyn Heights, dark blue transfer, imp mark, minor wear, chip on table ring, 10-1/4" d, $1,485. Photo courtesy of Garth's Auctions, Inc.

bridge, used a vine and leaf border on his dark blue historical views and a lace border on his series in light transfers. The initials R. S. & W. indicate Ralph Stevenson and Williams are associated with the acorn and leaf border. It has been reported that Williams was Ralph's New York agent and the wares were produced by Ralph alone.

Cup and Saucer, New Orleans, Lace border series (387) 150.00

Plate

    5-1/2" d, Baltimore Exchange, Acorn and Oak Leaves border series, dark blue transfer (348) 775.00

    6-1/4" d, Columbia College, New York, Acorn and Oak Leaves border series, dark blue transfer, minor staining and rubbing to edge 600.00

    7" d, City Hall, New York, Floral and Scroll border series, dark blue transfer (397) 1,200.00

    8-3/8" d, Harvard College, Acorn and Oak Leaves series, dark blue transfer 295.00

    10" d, Harvard College, Acorn and Oak Leaves border series, medium to dark blue transfer, hairline on front 300.00

    10" d, Park Theater, New York, Acorn and Oak Leaves border series, dark blue transfer (357) 195.00

    10-1/4" d, New York from Brooklyn Heights, Floral and Scroll border series, dark blue transfer 995.00

Platter, 18-3/4" l, New York from Weehawk, dark blue transfer, imp "Stevenson," wear, knife scratches, hairline . . .1,210.00

Soup Plate, 10" d

    Capitol, Washington, Vine border series (370) 425.00

    Erie Canal at Buffalo, Lace border series (386) 195.00

Tureen, cov, 9-1/4" sq, 5-1/2" h, Pennsylvania Hospital, int. with flowers and Charleston Exchange, Vine border series, leaf molded rim corners, leaf molded base corners with carved feet, base incorrectly painted New York Battery, imp "Stevenson," clover leaf Ralph Stevenson mark, blue and white 7,000.00

Stubbs

In 1790, Joseph Burslem Stubbs established a pottery works at Burslem, England. He operated it until 1829 when he retired and sold the pottery to the Mayer brothers. He probably produced his American views about 1825. Many of his scenes were from Boston, New York, New Jersey, and Philadelphia.

Pitcher, 6-1/2" h, 7-1/4" w, Boston State House/City Hall, New York, dark blue transfer, small lip chip 800.00

Plate

    6-5/8" d, City Hall New York, Spread Eagle border series, medium blue transfer, ... 300.00

    8-3/4" d, Upper Ferry Bridge Over the River Schuykill, Spread Eagle border series, dark blue transfer 160.00

    8-7/8" d, Nahant Hotel, Near Boston, Spread Eagle border series, medium to dark blue transfer, restored 300.00

    10-1/4" d, Fairmount Near Philadelphia, Spread Eagle border series, medium to dark blue transfer, ... 200.00

Platter

    10-5/8" l, Woodlands Near Philadelphia, dark blue transfer 650.00

    14-1/2" l, 12" w, Boston State House, Spread Eagle border series, dark blue transfer, professional restoration . 900.00

    16-1/2" l, 13-1/2" w, Menden Hall Ferry, Spread Eagle border series, dark blue transfer, stained, couple of small pits on front and back, wear to face. 1,100.00

    18-1/2" l, Upper Ferry Bridge Over the River Schuykill, Spread Eagle border series, dark blue transfer . . .1,350.00

    20-1/2" l, Fairmount Near Philadelphia, Spread Eagle border series, dark blue transfer .1,750.00

Sauce Tureen, underplate, oval, Upper Ferry Bridge Over the River Schuykill, Spread Eagle border series, brown transfer 275.00

Soup Plate, 9-7/8" d, Fairmount Near Philadelphia, dark blue transfer, imp "Stubbs" on base, hairlines, very minor base chips, glaze wear, set of three 500.00

Soup Tureen, cov, 9-1/4" h, 14" w, Birds and Fruit, dark blue transfer, large shell emb scroll handles, four paw feet, floral finial, replaced finial, restoration to lid 1,300.00

Vegetable Dish, open, 9-1/8" l, oval, Upper Ferry Bridge Over the River Schuykill, Spread Eagle border series, brown transfer. 575.00

Unknown Maker

Caster, 4-5/8" h, Landing of Gen. Lafayette At New York 1824, medium blue transfer 300.00

Creamer

    6" h, scene of horse drawn sleigh, dark blue transfer, filled in rim flake 440.00

    Lafayette at Franklin's Tomb, dark blue transfer 400.00

Cup Plate

    3-7/8" d, scene of three men, dark blue transfer 110.00

    4" d, Hyena, dark blue transfer, stains, some glaze wear 175.00

Pepper Shaker, 4-5/8" h, floral, English scene of church and fisherman, dark blue transfer, chips on domed top 385.00

Pitcher

    6-1/8" h, scroll and foliate devices, spread eagle, "E. Pluribus Unum,"" blue and white transfer, spout chip, hairlines 750.00

    6-1/4" h, City Hall New York and Insane Asylum, New York, flower and foliage border, dark blue transfer, rim and spout edge wear, circular hairline in base 660.00

    6-3/8" h, Boston State House, spread eagle mark in base, dark blue transfer, restoration to spout, chip, hairlines to base 750.00

    6-1/2" h, The Landing of the Fathers at Plymouth, dark blue transfer, minor chips, star crack, glaze wear 350.00

Plate

    7" d, New York Battery, dark blue transfer, wear, stains, and scratches 110.00

    7-5/8" d, View of Trenton Falls, dark blue transfer, wear and scratches 95.00

    8-1/2" d, American Villa, dark blue transfer, fruit, and flower border, stained, dings, wear and scratches 150.00

    8-1/2" d, Boston State House, medium blue transfer, wear and scratches. 110.00

    9-3/4" d, Boston State House, medium blue transfer, wear and scratches. 125.00

10" d, Arms of New York, dark blue transfer, chip on table rim 500.00

10" d, Baltimore Exchange, dark blue transfer, fruit and flower series, minor staining and rubbing to rim 500.00

10" d, The Dam & Waterworks, Philadelphia, stern wheeler, dark blue transfer, stains and minor wear 445.00

10-1/4" d, Fair Mount Near Philadelphia, medium blue transfer, wear and scratches 150.00

Platter

18-3/4" l, Christianburg Danish Settlement on the Gold Coast, Africa, dark blue transfer, wear, small glaze flakes, and hairline 1,265.00

19" x 15-3/4", Hanibal Crossing the Alps, light to medium blue, minor staining 250.00

20-1/4" l, lakeside scene of fisherman hanging nets out to dry on tree, blue transfer, attributed to Robert Hamilton Stoke, 1811-26, very minor rim chips, glaze wear, knife marks 575.00

Sauce Boat, 7-3/4" l, Hoboken, New Jersey, dark blue transfer, stains, hairline, foot chip. 220.00

Sauce Tureen, 3 pc, 8" x 5-3/4" x 6-1/2" h, Boston Mails, Gentleman's Cabin, brown transfer, tureen with attached undertray, lid, and ladle, base restored 450.00

Saucer, 5-7/8" d, 1-1/8" deep, Railroad, dark blue transfer, floral border, stained, cracks. 400.00

Soup Plate, 9-7/8" d, Harvard College, dark blue transfer, wear and scratches. 165.00

Sugar Bowl, cov

5-7/8" h, Landing of Gen. Lafayette, dark blue transfer, baluster-form, ring handles, mismatched lid. 550.00

6" h, 6-3/4" w handle to handle, Mount Vernon, The Seat of the Late General Washington, dark blue transfer, floral border, floral molded handles, minor chip to lid 800.00

Teapot, 8-1/2" h, 12-1/2" w handle to spout, young girl with basket of flowers, floral border, dark blue transfer, stained, spider crack to side, minor chips on spout, lid damaged, finial replaced. 400.00

Vegetable Bowl, cov, 9-1/2" h, 9-1/2" l, "A Ship of the Lines in the Downs," mismatched lid with unidentified verse, dark blue transfer, both have repaired hairlines (139) 715.00

Waste Bowl, 7" d, 3-5/8" h, Boston Harbor, dark blue transfer, wear and hairline 825.00

Wood

Enoch Wood, sometimes referred to as the father of English pottery, began operating a pottery at Fountain Place, Burslem, in 1783. A cousin, Ralph Wood, was associated with him. In 1790, James Caldwell became a partner and the firm was

known as Wood and Caldwell. In 1819, Wood and his sons took full control. Enoch died in 1840. His sons continued under the name of Enoch Wood & Sons. The American views were first made in the mid-1820s and continued through the 1840s. It is reported that the pottery produced more signed historical views than any other Staffordshire firm. Many of the views attributed to unknown makers probably came from the Woods. Marks vary, although always include the name Wood. The establishment was sold to Messrs. Pinder, Bourne & Hope in 1846.

Coffeepot, dome lid, 12" h, Commodore MacDonnough's Victory, dark blue transfer 3,410.00

Cream Pitcher, 3-1/2" h, Commodore MacDonnough's Victory barrel shape, Floral border series, dark blue transfer (154) 1,850.00

Cup and Saucer, handleless, Lafayette at Franklin Tomb, dark blue transfer, imp "Wood & Sons," cup has chips and hairlines 200.00

Cup Plate

3-5/8" d, English brick bridge, dark blue transfer, imp "Wood" 150.00

3-5/8" d, cottage in the woods, dark blue transfer, imp "Wood," under glaze "A" on back. 165.00

3-3/4" d, Cadmus, dark blue transfer, imp "Wood," chip on table ring 330.00

3-3/4" d, Castle Garden Battery New York, dark blue transfer, imp ""Wood," minor wear and stains 385.00

Gravy Boat, 7" w, 2-3/4" d, 4-1/4" h, Pass in the Catskill Mountain, dark blue transfer, Shell border series, crack in handle, very minor staining 400.00

Plate

7-1/2" d, Pass in the Catskill Mountains, dark blue transfer, imp "Wood & Son" 330.00

7-1/2" d, The Landing of the Fathers at Plymouth, Dec. 22, 1620, medium blue transfer, imp "Wood," wear and scratches, small flake 50.00

7-1/2" d, Trenton Falls, dark blue transfer, shell border series 350.00

8-3/8" d, Fall of Montmorenci, Near Quebec, dark blue transfer, imp "Wood," wear and scratches 175.00

9-1/4" d, Gilpin's Mills, dark blue transfer, shell border series 450.00

9-1/4" d, Transylvania University Lexington, dark blue transfer, imp "Wood" 250.00

9-1/4" d, View de Chateau Ermenonville, dark blue transfer, imp "Wood" 300.00

9-1/2" d, B & O Railroad, inclined view, dark blue transfer, shell border series, imp "Wood & Sons," minor staining and hairline crack 550.00

(Wood) Plate, Erie Canal Aqueduct Bridge at Rochester, dark blue transfer, 7-5/8" d, $145.

9-7/8" d, Albany, dark blue transfer, shell border series
....1,800.00
9-7/8" d, London Views Hanover Lodge Regent's Park, Enoch Wood & Sons, knife marks 200.00
10" d, Naval Battle, *Constitution* and the *Guerriere*, shell border, minor staining 1,200.00
10-1/8" d, The Landing of the Fathers at Plymouth, Dec. 22, 1620, medium blue transfer, transfer mark "Enoch Wood," wear and small edge chips 50.00
10-1/4" d, American Independence, Landing of the Fathers at Plymouth, medium blue transfer, very minor staining and wear to front................................300.00
10-1/4" d, Commodore MacDonnough, dark blue transfer, shell order series 375.00
10-1/4" d, Table Rock Niagara, dark blue transfer, imp "Wood"..300.00
10-1/2" d, Fisherman, red transfer, imp "Wood," pinpoint rim flakes.......................................220.00
Platter
12-1/2" d, Highlands, Hudson River, steam boat, dark blue transfer.....................................1,650.00
16-1/2" l, 13" w, Lake George, NY, Shell border series, dark blue transfer, imp "Wood," 2" crack to rim 1,900.00
18-3/4" l, 14-1/2" w, Castle Garden, Battery, NY, Shell border series, dark blue transfer, three minor stain spots on back
....2,600.00
Saucer, MacDonnough's Victory, dark blue transfer, imp "Wood"
....150.00
Sauce Tureen and Tray, Boston State House, medium blue transfer, tureen unmarked, tray imp "Wood," stains and chip on table ring of tray.........................715.00
Soup Plate, 9-3/8" d, Catskill Mountains, Pine Orchard House, dark blue transfer, minor wear, light scratches......525.00
Sugar Bowl, cov, 6-3/4" h, 6-1/2" w handle to handle, Commodore MacDonnough's Victory, dark blue transfer, teapot lid, repair to bottom rim, cracks in base.............500.00
Teapot, 8" h, 11" w handle to spout, Franklin's Tomb, dark blue transfer of Lafayette at Franklin's Tomb, imp "Enoch Wood & Sons," cracks, replaced rim chip 500.00

STAFFORDSHIRE ITEMS

History: A wide variety of ornamental pottery items originated in England's Staffordshire district, beginning in the 17th century and still continuing today. The height of production took place from 1820 to 1890.

These naive pieces are considered folk art by many collectors. Most items were not made carefully; some even were made and decorated by children.

The types of objects are varied, e.g., animals, cottages, and figurines (chimney ornaments).

References: Susan and Al Bagdade, *Warman's English & Continental Pottery & Porcelain*, 3rd Edition, Krause Publications, 1998; Pat Halfpenny, *English Earthenware Figures*, Antique Collectors' Club, 1992; Adele Kenny, *Staffordshire Spaniels*, Schiffer Publishing, 1997; Arnold R. Mountford, *The Illustrated Guide to Staffordshire Salt-Glazed Stoneware*, Barrie & Jenkins, 1971; Clive Mason Pope, *A-Z of Staffordshire Dogs*, Antique Collectors' Club, Ltd., 1996; P. D. Gordon Pugh, *Staffordshire Portrait Figures of the Victorian Era*, Antique Collectors' Club, 1987; Dennis G. Rice, *English Porcelain Animals of the 19th Century*, Antique Collectors' Club, 1989. Louis T.

Stanley, *Collecting Staffordshire Pottery*, Doubleday & Co., 1963.

Museums: American Antiquarian Society, Worcester, MA; Brighton Museum, England; British Museum, London, England; City Museum and Art Gallery, Stoke-on-Trent, England; The Detroit Museum of Arts, Detroit, MI; Fitzwilliam Museum, Cambridge, England; Victoria & Albert Museum, London, England.

REPRODUCTION ALERT

Early Staffordshire figurines and hollowware forms were molded. Later examples were made using a slip-casting process. Slip casting leaves telltale signs that are easy to spot. Look in the interior. Hand molding created a smooth interior surface. Slip casting produces indentations that conform to the exterior design. Holes occur where handles meet the body of slip-cast pieces. There is not hole in a hand-molded piece.

A checkpoint on figurines is the firing or vent hole, which is a necessary feature on these forms. Early figurines had small holes; modern reproductions feature large holes often the size of a dime or quarter. Vent holes are found on the sides or hidden among the decoration in early Staffordshire figurines; most modern reproductions have them in the base.

These same tips can be used to spot modern reproductions of Flow Blue, Majolica, Old Sleepy Eye, Stoneware, Willow, and other ceramic pieces.

Note: The key to price is age and condition. As a general rule, the older the piece, the higher the price.

ABC Plate, 7" d, dancing figures in center, raised alphabet border, discolored 85.00
Animal Dish, cov, 8" l, hen, black and white, light brown basketweave base...............................285.00
Bank, 5" h, cottage, white snow on roof, two chimneys, black outline, c1885...............................225.00

Figure, lamb and young, beige, brown, black, green, orange, and blue, c1800, 4" x 2-1/2" x 4-3/4", $450.

Box, 3-5/8" l, primrose ground, emb, painted sprays of flowers, gilt metal mounts 275.00

Chimney Ornament, 6" h, two girls at dog house, one on roof, other petting dog at door 165.00

Creamer, 6" h, girl with flower basket, floral border, dark blue transfer, chips and cracks 150.00

Figure

3-1/4" h, stag and doe, polychrome, molded "X" on bottom, minor chips. 220.00

3-3/8" h, seated dog, red, white, yellow, and black, chips on base and damage on back. 110.00

3-5/8" h, goat, flat back, polychrome 220.00

3-7/8" h, facing cats, black and yellow, white ground, later, damage to one of pr. 360.00

4" h, horse, flat back, polychrome dec 330.00

4" h, rooster, red, yellow, and green-yellow, white ground, chip on neck, minor flaking, early. 250.00

4-1/4" h, seated cat, sponged black and yellow, white ground, wear and chips. 275.00

4-1/2" h, seated cat, sponged black and brown, white ground, glazed over crack at seam. 275.00

5-1/8" h, Dalmatian, white, polychrome and gilt, blue base 275.00

5-1/8" h, lute player, restoration to lute 115.00

5-1/4" h, white poodle, two pups, polychrome and gilt, blue base. 300.00

6-1/2" h, girl with oversized dog, red, white, blue, pink, and black, crazing. 1,595.00

7" h, seated dog, black and white, polychrome dec, wear, chips on base and nose. 330.00

7-1/8" h hunter, restoration to gun 175.00

7-7/8" h, courting couple, restoration, pr 1,725.00

7-7/8" h, Scottish couple, very minor chip and loss 230.00

9-1/2" h, earthenware, child with cornucopia, overglaze enamel dec, cornucopia rim chips restored, some retouched painting, early 19th C 225.00

11" h, whippets, pr, each with rabbit in mouth, beige and red, minor chips. 750.00

Mug, 3-7/8" h, molded scenes, white, int. yellow frog with black spots, red eyes, rim chips. 250.00

Pastille Burner, 4-3/8" h, house, yellow sides, gray windows, roofed ochre door, olive green roof, two yellow chimneys with brown edging, green grassy mount base, c1790 . . . . 695.00

Platter, 14-5/8" d, scrolling foliate border, reserves of manor houses, center reserve of game birds, blue and white transfer, second quarter 19th C 635.00

Spill Vase, 12" h, cow with calf, brightly colored 275.00

Stirrup Cup, 5-3/8" h, ironstone, fox head, shaded iron-red and ochre mask, gray and black muzzle and eyes, green collar edged in black and white, gilt center square, c1810 . . . . 595.00

Sugar Bowl, cov, 5-1/2" h, genre scene of figures in foreground of manor house, ring handles, blue and white transfer, 19th C, minor chips, glaze wear. 100.00

Teapot, 5-1/2" h, yellow transfer dec, reserves of three musicians, restoration to finial, minor chips. 450.00

STAFFORDSHIRE, ROMANTIC

History: In the 1830s, two factors transformed the blue-and-white printed wares of the Staffordshire potters into what is now called "Romantic Staffordshire." Technical innovations expanded the range of transfer-printed colors to light blue, pink, purple, black, green, and brown. There was also a shift from historical to imaginary scenes with less printed detail and more white space, adding to the pastel effect.

Shapes from the 1830s are predominately rococo with rounded forms, scrolled handles, and floral finials. Over time, patterns and shapes became simpler and the earthenware bodies coarser. The late 1840s and 1850s saw angular gothic shapes and pieces with the weight and texture of ironstone.

The most dramatic post-1870 change was the impact of the craze for all things Japanese. Staffordshire designs adopted zigzag border elements and motifs such as bamboo, fans, and cranes. Brown printing dominated this style, sometimes with polychrome enamel highlights.

Marks: Wares are often marked with pattern or potter's names, but marking was inconsistent and many authentic, unmarked examples exist. The addition of "England" as a country of origin mark in 1891 helps to distinguish 20th-century wares made in the romantic style.

References: Susan and Al Bagdade, *Warman's English & Continental Pottery & Porcelain*, 3rd Edition, Krause Publications, 1998; Jeffrey B. Snyder, *Romantic Staffordshire Ceramics*, Schiffer Publishing, 1997; Petra Williams, *Staffordshire: Romantic Transfer Patterns* (1978), *Staffordshire II* (1986), *Staffordshire III* (1996), Fountain House East (P.O. Box 99298, Jeffersontown, KY 40269).

Museums: City Museum & Art Gallery, Stoke-on-Trent, England; Henry Ford Museum, Dearborn, MI.

Arabesque, gray-blue, Edwards & Son

Creamer 60.00

Gravy Boat 50.00

Relish, small, oblong 35.00

Vegetable Dish, open. 45.00

Waste Bowl 40.00

Balantyre, J Alcock

Bowl, 8" d 45.00

Cup Plate 55.00

Creamer 50.00

Plate, 10-1/2" d. 35.00

Teapot 195.00

Caledonia, William Adams, c1800-65

Bowl 45.00

Creamer 55.00

Cup and Saucer 45.00

Plate, 8-1/2" d, pink 75.00

Soup Plate, red transfer, 10-3/4" d, imp "Adams," stains, bruise on table ring 150.00

Sugar, cov 85.00

Canna, platter, red transfer, 18" l, edge wear, minor stains 385.00

Canova, T. Mayer

Platter, 17-1/2" x 14-1/2", black transfer, minor staining 300.00

Tureen, Underplate, brown transfer, 13-1/2" x 9" x 9-1/2" h tureen, 15" x 10-3/4" underplate, staining, chips, crack to underplate, lid missing 100.00

Vegetable, cov, red transfer, 12-1/2" l, Mayer, stains, chips 225.00

Etruscan Vase, blue and brown, Thomas, John, Joseph Mayer, c1843-55

Bowl, 7" d 45.00

Plate, 10-1/2" d. 55.00

Soup Bowl, Allegheny Scenery, Bell, pink, 10-3/8" d, $35.

Platter, 16" x 11-1/2" 145.00
Relish, 5" l 45.00
Soup Plate, wide flange 65.00
Fairy Queen, pitcher, 9-1/2" h, purple transfer, edge wear, small flake on foot 275.00
Garden Scenery, pink, Mayer
 Bowl, 4" d 35.00
 Cup and Saucer 65.00
 Cup Plate 45.00
 Plate 55.00
 Sauce Dish 35.00
 Soup Plate 75.00
 Teapot 175.00
 Vegetable Bowl, open 85.00
Ivanhoe, Podmore Walker & Co., 1834-1859
 Bowl 40.00
 Creamer 60.00
 Plate 45.00
 Sugar, cov 80.00
Oriental, Ridgway, c1830-34
 Creamer 75.00
 Cup and Saucer, handleless 75.00
 Cup Plate 60.00
 Plate 85.00
 Tureen, cov, octagonal 225.00
Park Scenery, G. Philips, platter, 18" x 15", brown and white, staining 255.00
Priory, Edward Challinor and Co., c1853-1862
 Bowl 45.00
 Creamer 65.00
 Cup and Saucer, handleless 45.00
 Plate 55.00
 Platter 95.00
 Soup Plate 85.00
 Toddy Plate, 5" d, light blue 45.00
Royal Cottage, sauce tureen, underplate, 8-3/4" l, light blue transfer, plain white ladle 250.00
Undina, black and blue, J Clementson, registered Jan .7, 1852
 Plate 45.00
 Relish, oval, shell shaped 65.00
 Wash Bowl and Pitcher 295.00

STAINED and/or LEADED GLASS PANELS

History: American architects in the second half of the 19th century and the early 20th century used stained- and leaded-glass panels as a chief decorative element. Skilled glass craftsmen assembled the designs, the best known being Louis C. Tiffany.

The panels are held together with soft lead cames or copper wraps. When purchasing a panel, protect your investment by checking the lead and making any necessary repairs.

Reference: Web Wilson, *Great Glass in American Architecture,* E. P. Dutton, New York, 1986.

Periodicals: *Glass Art Magazine,* P.O. Box 260377, Highlands Ranch, CO 80126; *Glass Patterns Quarterly,* P.O. Box 131, Westport, NY 40077; *Professional Stained Glass,* P.O. Box 69, Brewster, NY 10509; *Stained Glass,* 6 SW. 2nd St., #7, Lees Summit, MO 64063.

Collectors' Club: Stained Glass Association of America, P.O. Box 22462, Kansas City, MO 64113.

Museum: Corning Museum of Glass, Corning, NY.

10-1/2" x 23", sign, "Exit-11," red and amber, leaded 185.00
18" h, 36" w, framed, leaded, Art Nouveau lily pads in pond motif, some bowing in glass, few pieces cracked 850.00
21" w, 30" h, Prairie School, leaded, floral design, two frosted white glass lilies, orig frame 1,000.00
29-3/4" l, 69-1/2" w, horizontal, glass jewels and red flowing ribbon against blue and gold background, bordered in gold jewel ripple edge, orig frame, some minor cracks 2,800.00
30" h, 45" w, framed, leaded glass, vase of red petaled flowers, brown and gold background, some slight bowing to stained glass, reinforced frame, some minor cracks in glass 450.00
31-1/2" x 18-1/2", stained pattern of curtains pulled back revealing owl on tree branch, moon and stars, showing books and glowing candle, curtain glass raised to further illustrate a further pulled back curtain, tied with tieback 3,450.00

Stained and leaded window, red petaled flowers, brown and gold background, opalescent jewel centers, slight bowing to stained glass, several cracks in glass, 30" x 45", $450. Photo courtesy of James D. Julia, Inc.

32" w, 70" h, door panel, leaded and stained, Arts & Crafts multicolored florals, fold and white striated background minor flaws 4,000.00

33" h, 16" w, framed leaded glass

Summer, semi-clad woman picking dogwood flowers from tree, birds on top and bottom, floral perimeter design, yellows, reds, light green forest background, multiple small cracks 600.00

Winter, woman wrapped in winter cape, snow scene, birds on top and bottom, floral perimeter design, yellows, reds, light green field background, multiple small cracks, small piece of clear glass missing in upper right corner 400.00

38-1/2" w, 37" h, stained and leaded, Arts & Crafts style water lilies, white and yellow flowers, green glaze background, orig frame, pr 6,000.00

40" h, 25" w, stained, multicolored panels, stenciled boar's head and stenciled horse's head, three large clear panels, several round amber jewels on side 375.00

44-1/2" h, 30" w, stained, scenic view at twilight with trees, path leading across meadow to forest, framed, two glass panels cracked 1,600.00

STANGL POTTERY BIRDS

History: Stangl ceramic birds were produced from 1940 until the Stangl factory closed in 1978. The birds were produced at Stangl's Trenton plant and either decorated there or shipped to their Flemington, New Jersey, outlet for hand painting.

During World War II, the demand for these birds, and other types of Stangl pottery as well, was so great that 40 to 60 decorators could not keep up with the demand. Orders were contracted out to be decorated by individuals in their own homes. These orders then were returned for firing and finishing. Colors used to decorate these birds varied according to the artist.

Marks: As many as ten different trademarks were used. Almost every bird is numbered; many are artist signed. However, the signatures are used only for dating purposes and add very little to the value of the birds.

References: Susan and Al Bagdade, *Warman's American Pottery and Porcelain*, Wallace-Homestead, 1994; Harvey Duke, *Stangl Pottery*, Wallace-Homestead, 1992; Robert C. Runge, Jr., *The Collector's Encyclopedia of Stangl Dinnerware*, 1998; Mike Schneider, *Stangl and Pennsbury Birds*, Schiffer Publishing, 1994.

Collectors' Club: Stangl/Fulper Collectors Club, P.O. Box 538, Flemington, NJ 08822.

Additional Listings: See *Warman's Americana & Collectibles* for more examples.

Advisor: Bob Perzel.

Note: Several birds were reissued between 1972 and 1977. These reissues are dated on the bottom and are worth approximately the same as older birds if well decorated.

3250, Gazing Duck, Antique Gold 60.00
3250, Preening Duck 125.00
3273, Rooster, 5-3/4" h 650.00
3274, Penguin 500.00
3275, Turkey 475.00

3276, Bluebird 80.00
3285, Rooster, 4-1/2" h, early blue green base 100.00
3286, Hen, 4-1/2" h, late lime green base 50.00
3285, 3286, Rooster and Hen shakers, late, pr 100.00
3400, Lovebird, old, wavy base 120.00
3400, Lovebird, revised leaf base 60.00
3402, Pair of Orioles, revised 125.00
3402, Pair of Orioles, old 250.00
3404, Pair of Lovebirds, old 400.00
3404, Pair of Lovebirds, revised 125.00
3405, Pair of Cockatoos, revised, open base 175.00
3406, Pair of Kingfishers, blue 150.00
3407, Owl 350.00
3431, Duck, standing 500.00
3433, Rooster, 16" h 2,000.00
3443, Flying Duck, teal 350.00
3444, Cardinal, pink, glossy 100.00
3445, Rooster, yellow 220.00
3446, Hen, gray 225.00
3449, Paraquet 200.00
3450, Passenger Pigeon 1,300.00
3451, William Ptarmigan 2,500.00
3453, Mountain Bluebird 1,100.00
3454, Key West Quail Dove, single wing up 350.00
3454, Key West Quail Dove, both wings up 750.00
3455, Shoveler Duck 2,300.00
3457, Walking Pheasant 1,800.00
3458, Quail 1,200.00
3459, Falcon/Fish Hawk/Osprey 3,000.00
3490, Pair of Redstarts 225.00
3492, Cock Pheasant 225.00
3518, Pair of White Headed Pigeons 650.00
3580, Cockatoo, medium 165.00
3580, Cockatoo, medium, white 350.00
3581, Group of Chickadees 195.00
3581, Group of Chickadees, black and white 250.00
3582, Pair of Green Parakeets 200.00
3582, Pair of Blue Parakeets 275.00
3584, Cockatoo, large 300.00
3590, Chat 165.00
3591, Brewers Blackbird 150.00
3595, Bobolink 150.00
3596, Gray Cardinal 85.00
3599, Pair of Hummingbirds 300.00
3625, Bird of Paradise, large, 13-1/2" h 2,220.00
3627, Rivoli Hummingbird, with pink flower 150.00
3634, Allen Hummingbird 75.00
3635, Group of Goldfinches 200.00
3715, Blue Jay with peanut 650.00
3717, Pair of Blue Jays 3,500.00
3746, Canary, rose flower 225.00
3749, Scarlet Tanager 350.00
3750, Pair of Western Tanagers 425.00
3751, Red Headed Woodpecker, pink glossy 225.00
3752, Pair of Red Headed Woodpeckers, red matte . . . 350.00
3754, Single White Winged Crossbill 2,500.00
3754, Pair of White Winged Crossbills, pink glossy 350.00
3755, Audubon Warbler 200.00
3756, Pair of Audubon Warblers 500.00
3757, Scissor-tailed Flycatcher 650.00
3758, Magpie Jay 1,250.00
3810, Blackpoll Warbler 165.00
3812, Chestnut Sided Warbler 150.00
3813, Evening Grosbeak 150.00
3814, Blackthroated Green Warbler 165.00
3815, Western Bluebird 400.00
3848, Golden Crowned Kinglet 100.00

3850, Yellow Warbler 150.00
3852, Cliff Swallow 125.00
3853, Group of Golden Crowned Kingfishers 600.00
3868, Summer Tanager 600.00
3921, Yellow-headed Verdin .1,250.00

STEIFF

History: Margarete Steiff, GmbH, established in Germany in 1880, is known for very fine-quality stuffed animals and dolls, as well as other beautifully made collectible toys. It is still in business, and its products are highly respected.

The company's first products were wool-felt elephants made by Margaret Steiff. In a few years, the animal line was expanded to include a donkey, horse, pig, and camel.

By 1903, the company also was producing a jointed mohair teddy bear, whose production dramatically increased to more than 970,000 units in 1907. Margarete's nephews took over the company at this point.

Newly designed animals were added: Molly and Bully, the dogs, and Fluffy, the cat. Pull toys and kites also were produced, as well as larger animals, on which children could ride or play.

Marks: The bear's-head label became the symbol for the firm in about 1907, and the famous "Button in the Ear" round, metal trademark was added.

References: Peter Consalvi, Sr., *2nd Collector Steiff Values*, Hobby House Press, 1996; Margaret and Gerry Grey, *Teddy Bears*, Running Press, Courage Books, 1994; Margaret Fox Mandel, *Teddy Bears and Steiff Animals*, 1st Series (1984, 1997 value update), 2nd Series (1987, 1996 value update), Collector Books; ——, *Teddy Bears, Annalee Animals & Steiff Animals*, 3rd Series, Collector Books, 1990, 1996 value update; Dee Hockenberry, *Big Bear Book*, Schiffer Publishing, 1996; Linda Mullins, *Teddy Bear & Friends Price Guide*, 4th ed., Hobby House Press, 1993.

Collectors' Clubs: Steiff Club USA, 31 E. 28th St., 9th Floor, New York, NY 10016; Steiff Collectors Club, P.O. Box 798, Holland, OH 43528.

Additional Listings: Teddy Bears. See also Stuffed Toys in *Warman's Americana & Collectibles* for more examples.

Notes: Become familiar with genuine Steiff products before purchasing an antique stuffed animal. Plush in old Steiff animals was mohair; trimmings usually were felt or velvet. Unscrupulous individuals have attached the familiar Steiff metal button to animals that are not Steiff.

Cat, 7" h, plush cotton, green glass eyes, orig red rayon bow, c1930 . . . . 100.00
Circus Bear, 8-3/8" h, roly-poly, brown mohair, black steel eyes, shoe button nose, excelsior stuffing, wooden stick and metal chair, weighted wood base, c1897, base repair 1,265.00
Dog
   Dachshund, 18" l, black and brown wool, fully jointed, black shoe button eyes, embroidered nose, mouth and claws, c1930, some fiber loss and repairs 350.00

Fox Terrier, 11" l, rayon fur, mohair face and muzzle, glass eyes, black embroidered nose, mouth, and claws, leatherette collar, paper tag, 1930s, spotty fur loss and yellowing 175.00
Elephant, 17-1/2" l, black button eyes, pull cord sound box, four wood wheels, c1920 . . . . 295.00
Fish, 11" l, mohair, open felt mouth, large eyes 85.00
Fox, 10-1/4" l, 5-1/2", mohair, fully jointed, glass eyes, embroidered nose, mouth, and claws, excelsior stuffing, c1913, ear button missing, slight moth damage 435.00
Lamb, 4-5/8" l, pile wool, felt face, ears, and legs, black bead eyes, pink embroidered nose and mouth, c1913 . . . . 575.00
Teddy Bear
   3" h, buff mohair, fully jointed, black bead eyes, black embroidered nose and mouth, ear button, no pads, c1905 . . . . 690.00
   3" h, white mohair, fully jointed, black bead eyes, rust embroidered nose and mouth, ear button, no pads, c1905
   3-3/4" h, yellow mohair, fully jointed, black embroidered nose and mouth, c1905 . . . . 420.00
   5-1/2" h, light golden mohair, fully jointed, black steel eyes, black embroidered nose and mouth, no pads, excelsior stuffing, c1905, minor fur loss 1,035.00
   5-1/2" h, yellow mohair, fully jointed, glass eyes, black embroidered nose and mouth, no pads, c190u, overall traces of fur, no button 435.00
   9-1/2" h, blond mohair, fully jointed, black steel eyes, brown embroidered nose, mouth, and claws, felt pads, excelsior stuffing, c1905, button missing, spotty moth damage, needs stuffing 550.00
   9-1/2" h, light apricot mohair, fully jointed, black steel eyes, brown embroidered nose, mouth, and claws, felt pads, excelsior stuffing, c1905, button missing 865.00
   12-1/2" h, golden mohair, fully jointed, black steel eyes, brown embroidered nose, mouth, and claws, felt pads, excelsior stuffing, c1909, ear button, spotty fur loss . . . .——.1,380.00
   12-1/2" h, light apricot mohair, fully jointed, black steel eyes, brown embroidered nose, mouth, and claws, felt pads, excelsior stuffing, c1905, fur loss on back and muzzle, needs restuffing, moth damage on pads 460.00
   13" h, light yellow mohair, fully jointed, black steel eyes, black embroidered nose, mouth, and claws, replaced felt pads, c1905, spotty fur loss, new nose stitching 1,495.00

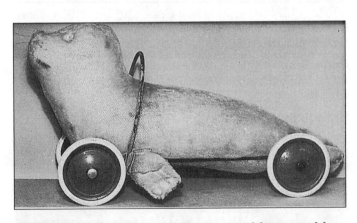

Seal, riding, button on tail flipper, steel frame, rubber tread wheels, worn ivory colored mohair and salmon colored embroidered nose and mouth, nylon filament whiskers, eyes missing, straw stuffing, 28" l, $200. Photo courtesy of Garth's Auctions, Inc.

15" h, light golden mohair, fully jointed, black steel eyes, black embroidered nose, mouth, and claws, tan felt pads, excelsior stuffing, c1905, button missing 3,220.00

15-1/2" h, golden apricot mohair, fully jointed, black steel eyes, brown embroidered nose, mouth, and black claws, felt pads, excelsior stuffing, blank ear button, c1905, cotton jacket, spotty fur loss, pad damage 1,610.00

16" h, golden mohair, fully jointed, black steel eyes, brown embroidered nose, mouth, and claws, felt pads, excelsior stuffing, c1905, button missing 7,475.00

16" h, light apricot mohair, fully jointed, black steel eyes, dark brown embroidered nose, mouth, and claws, felt pads, excelsior stuffing, c1905 .4,325.00

19" h, long curly golden mohair, fully jointed, black steel eyes, black embroidered nose, mouth, and claws, excelsior stuffing, c1905, replaced pad, fiber unstable on muzzle, button missing. 1,850.00

20" h, cinnamon mohair, fully jointed, center seam, black steel eyes, black embroidered nose, mouth, and claws, tan felt pads, c1905, some fur loss on muzzle. 12,650.00

24" h, ginger mohair, fully jointed, center seam, black steel eyes, brown embroidered nose, mouth, and claws, excelsior stuffing, c1905, button missing, fiber loss on muzzle 4,600.00

Tiger, mohair, fully jointed, c1950 . . . . .175.00

STEINS

History: Steins, mugs especially made to hold beer or ale, range in size from the smaller 3/10 and 1/4 liter to the larger 1, 1-1/2, 2, 3, 4, and 5 liters, and in rare cases to 8 liters. (A liter is 1.05 liquid quarts.)

1892–1921

Master steins or pouring steins hold 3 to 5 liters and are called krugs. Most steins are fitted with a metal hinged lid with thumb lift. The earthenware character-type steins usually are German in origin.

References: Susan and Al Bagdade, *Warman's English & Continental Pottery & Porcelain*, 3rd Edition, Krause Publications, 1998; Gary Kirsner, *German Military Steins*, 2nd ed., Glentiques (P.O. Box 8807, Coral Springs, FL 33075), 1996; ——, *Mettlach Book*, 3rd ed., 1994; Gary Kirsner and Jim Gruhl, *The Stein Book, A 400 Year History*, Glentiques, 1990.

Periodicals: *Regimental Quarterly*, P.O. Box 793, Frederick, MD 21705; *The Beer Stein Journal*, P.O. Box 8807, Coral Springs, FL 33075.

Collectors' Clubs: Stein Collectors International, P.O. Box 5005, Laurel, MD 20726-5005; Sun Steiners, P.O. Box 11782, Fort Lauderdale, FL 33339.

Museum: Milwaukee Art Center, Milwaukee, WI.

Anheuser Busch, Ceramarte, color
 Half Liter
  City series, Stuttgart 350.00
  Grant's Farm, "A" and eagle on top 115.00
 Liter, Pilique 990.00

Brewery, stoneware
 Half liter, transfer and enamel dec, Joh. Humbser Furth Bayern, in remembrance of July 31, 1912, matching relief pewter lid with brewery logo .345.00
 Liter, engraved, Augustiner Brau, Munchen, matching relief pewter lid with brewery logo, lid slightly dented 375.00

Capo-di-Monte, 8-1/4" h, painted pottery, lion finial, body with continuous hunt scene, late 19th C 345.00

Character, half liter
 Porcelain
  Indian, E Bohne & Sohne, inlaid lid, chips on feathers 340.00
  Munich child on barrel, Schierholz, porcelain lid, 5" h 395.00
  Skull, E Bohne & Sohne, inlaid lid 465.00
  Von Motlke, tan, brown, Schierholz. 1,250.00
 Pottery, black man in white striped jacket, glazed finish No. 138, inlaid lid 445.00

Glass, blown, third liter, beige, enameled cavalier, matching glass inlaid lid. 215.00

Hauber and Reuther, half liter, pottery, etched, No. 417, Lohengrin's arrival, relief pewter lid of lady in gown with shield, shallow chip on base. 310.00

Marzi & Remy, pottery, half liter, No. 1635, hunting scene, etched scene, inlaid lid, c1900 . . . . .250.00

Mettlach
 No. 1526, half liter, PUG, John C White successor to White & Krafts, Maltsters, Buffalo, NY, woman on one wide with factory scene on other, pewter lid. 575.00
 No. 1526-1108, half liter, PUG, H Schlitt, festive scene with Bock in center, relief pewter lid of barmaid and target, int. stained 220.00
 No. 2028, liter, etched, Gasthaus scene, inlaid lid, large dwarf thumblift 615.00
 No. 2091, half liter, H Schlitt, St. Florian extinguishing fire, orig pewter lid. 640.00
 No. 2778, half liter, etched, H Slitt, carnival scene, inlaid lid 1,375.00
 No. 2833 B, half liter, etched, man sitting under tree, inlaid lid 400.00
 No. 2957, half liter, etched, bowling scene, inlaid lid 450.00
 No. 3135, half liter, etched, American eagle and flags, inlaid lid of American shield. 1,155.00

Military, half liter, stoneware, transfer and enamel dec, 8 Bavarian Infantry, Munchen, center scene, pewter lid with relief initials on top, large lion thumblift. 350.00

Musterschutz , 7" h, porcelain, pig form, German. 475.00

Occupation, half liter, porcelain, transfer and enamel dec
 Coach Driver, named to Diermeier, large scene of horses pulling coach, pewter lid, pewter tear and repair, base chip repaired 565.00
 Farming, named to Josef Fusseder, central scene, pewter lid 480.00
 Jockey, relief pewter lid of horse jumping stone wall with jockey, scratches on handle, base and pewter strap 440.00
 Pottery, liter, transfer and enameled, Remembering the First Year of the Pension Fund for the Munich Streetcar Drivers Oct 19, 1892, elaborate scene of horse drawn streetcar, pewter lid 425.00

High glaze, panoramic view of city of Munich, city seal, highly glazed lion on cover, 19" h, $600.

Regimental, half liter
9-1/2" h
 Porcelain, 1 Chevauleger, Nurnberg 1904-07, named to Chevauleger Fischer, two side scenes, roster, lion thumblift, prism inlaid lid with scene of Chevauleger painted on underside, strap repoured, base chip repaired 580.00
 Stoneware, 15 Infantry, Neuburg 1912-14, in remembrance of military bakery in Munchen 1913/14, named to Hans Leikauf, four side scenes including two at bakery, roster, lion thumblift, screw off lid to reveal prism, screw-off lid missing 810.00
10-1/2" h, porcelain, 171 Infantry, Ludwigsburg, named to Musketier, name removed, pewter lid 200.00
11" h, porcelain, 22 Infantry, Zweibrucken 1902-04, named to Res. Conrad, two side scenes, roster, lion thumblift 465.00
12" h, porcelain
 11 Field Artillery, Cassel 1909-11, named to Res. Grube, four side sides, roster, eagle thumblift 525.00
 23 Infantry, Saargemund 1909-11, named to Res. Schwarz, two side scenes, roster, lion thumblift with stanhope, wear on roster 415.00
12-1/4" h, pottery, 118 Infantry, Worms 1909-11, named to Res. Wolf, four side scenes, roster, lion thumblift, wear on roster 320.00
Schutzen, half liter, stoneware, transfer and enamel dec, center scene of target with crossed weapons, male and female with weapon and target on either side, pewter lid 415.00
Stoneware, liter, transfer and enameled dec
 Leib Rgt. Vereinigun Muncheon 1907, presentation on lid to military serviceman stained in Munchen 580.00

People walking to have steins filled, pewter lid with relief design around edge 375.00
Ringer, Franz
 American Soc. of Mechanical Engineers, Munchen, July 7, 1913, relief pewter lid with logo 465.00
 100 Anniv. Oktoberfest, Muncheon, 1810-1910, relief pewter lid of Munchen 1,510.00
 13 German Turnfes Munchen, 1923, pewter lid, old pewter tear repaired 580.00

STEUBEN GLASS

History: Frederick Carder, an Englishman, and Thomas G. Hawkes of Corning, New York, established the Steuben Glass Works in 1904. In 1918, the Corning Glass Company purchased the Steuben company. Carder remained with the firm and designed many of the pieces bearing the Steuben mark. Probably the most widely recognized wares are Aurene, Verre De Soie, and Rosaline, but many other types were produced.

The firm is still operating, producing glass of exceptional quality.

References: Paul Gardner, *Glass of Frederick Carder*, Crown Publishers, 1971; Paul Perrot, Paul Gardner, and James S. Plaut, *Steuben*, Praeger Publishers, 1974; Kenneth Wilson, *American Glass 1760-1930*, 2 vols., Hudson Hills Press and The Toledo Museum of Art, 1994.

Museums: Corning Museum of Glass, Corning, NY; Rockwell Museum, Corning, NY.

Aurene

Bowl, 8" d, 4" h, gold, closed form, sgd "Aurene #2687" 400.00
Centerbowl, 3-1/4" h, 12" d, catalog no. 2879, planter-form, inward curved rim, red-gold irid surface and int., polished base, inscribed "Aurene 2879," wear scratches on base 450.00
Jar, cov, 3-1/2" h, 5" w, blue ground, silver, blue, and purple irid, sgd "Aurene #1616" 750.00
Perfume Bottle, 7-1/2" h, gold, orig stopper, sgd "Aurene #1414," small flake to lip 600.00
Potpourri Jar, cov, 5-3/4" h, catalog no. 2812, bright gold irid, oval body, conforming cov with three drilled fragrance holes, applied finial 650.00
Stemware, 7" h, deep gold, blue irid, flaring bowl, twisted stem, sgd "Aurene" and numbered, six pc set 2,300.00

Bowl, Aurene, gold irid, pedestal foot, mkd "Aurene/2952," 11" d, 4-3/4" h, $315.

Tumbler, 4-1/2" h, gold, brilliant irid, sgd "Steuben #2361" 120.00

Vase

5" h, flaring neck, blue, sgd 650.00

5" h, flared ten-rib oval body, blue-purple irid luster, mirror bright near base, inscribed "Steuben" 1,100.00

5-1/2" h, catalog no. 913, ten-ribbed flared body, blue, base inscribed "Steuben" 600.00

8-1/4" h, catalog no. 346, gold on calcite, six scallop rim, trumpet form, irid white calcite ext., gold int. 575.00

8-1/4" h, catalog no. 6241, gold, angular six-sided rim, flared irid oval, disk foot, base inscribed "Steuben Aurene 6241" 700.00

8-1/2" h, gold, green loops from top of double gourd form, dimpled bottom, gold, purple, and green irid highlights, sgd "Aurene #2038, F. Carder" 1,300.00

12" h, 11" w, gold, yellow, rose, and platinum irid highlights, incised signature 1,500.00

Calcite

Bowl

6" d, 2-5/8" h, wide flared rim, gold aurene int., unmarked 220.00

13-3/4" d, 3-1/2" h, gold aurene int., unmarked 250.00

Parfait, gold, matching underplate 165.00

Sherbet, gold, matching underplate 155.00

Salt, 2-5/8" d 85.00

Crystal

Animal

Eagle, catalog no. 1172, David Dowler design 2,315.00

Fox, catalog no. 8260, Lloyd Atkins design, seated with tail wrapped, inscribed "Steuben" on base, c1971 . . . 1,265.00

Gazelle, catalog no. 7399, leaping Art Deco figures, molded rect plinth, stylized curvilinear Frederick Carder and Sidney Waugh design, base inscribed "Steuben," price for pr 1,150.00

Geese, catalog no. 8519, 5-1/4" h gander, 4" h preening goose, Lloyd Atkins design, price for pr 350.00

Horse, catalog no. 7727, Sidney Waugh design, stylized Clydesdale, base inscribed "Steuben," 1930s 1,035.00

Koala, catalog no. 8268, Lloyd Atkins design, base inscribed "Steuben," 1976 . . . . 1,100.00

Owl, catalog no. 8064, Donald Polland design, frosted eyes, base inscribed "Steuben," smoothed base edge 300.00

Squirrel, catalog no. 8291, George Thompson design, upright, tail extended, inscribed "Steuben" 900.00

Creamer and Sugar, catalog no. 7907/7906, John Dreves design, each inscribed "Steuben," price for pr 575.00

Paperweight/Doorstop, catalog no. 7257, solid, controlled bubbles and silvered cushion, center bright pink Cintra five-petaled lily blossoms, fleur-de-lis stamp on base, 4" h, 4-1/2" d 300.00

Vase, 12-1/2" h, masterwork, exhibition piece designed by Sidney Waugh to commemorate Paul Revere's ride, three vignettes, base inscribed "Steuben" 3,450.00

Wine, 4-1/2" h, catalog no. 8011, spiral stem with air twist, base inscribed "Steuben," price for 12 pc set 950.00

Grotesque

Bowl

10" d, #7535, ivorene 350.00

12" d, #7535, ivory 260.00

Vase, 11" h

Amethyst top shading to clear, #7090, c1920 . . . . . 525.00

Ivory 300.00

Ivorene

Candleholders, pr, 3-1/2" h, 4" l, catalog no. 7564, Grotesque, irid white, oval ribbed and folded bobeche cups, base inscribed "Steuben," one ruffle rough 435.00

Centerbowl, 7" h, 12" l, 7-1/2" w, catalog no. 7449, Grotesque, four-rib oval, lustrous opaque white, manipulated undulating rim, base evened, minor chips 350.00

Jade

Bowl, 12" d, #3200 . . . . 150.00

Compote, 6" d, 3-1/2" h, green bowl, alabaster stem and base 125.00

Iced Tea Glass, 6" h, translucent white handle 140.00

Vase

7" h, catalog no. 6078, green jade cased to alabaster sphere, acid etched Matzu pattern, Ming trees and stylized clouds 700.00

7" h, 8" d, catalog no. 6078, green jade cased to alabaster sphere, acid etched Asian design of stylized bonsai trees and cloud formations, fleur-de-lis mark, polished base 1,035.00

Wine, 7-1/4" h, alabaster twist stem 110.00

Miscellaneous

Candelabrum, 19" h, Cyprian, catalog no. 7392 variant, aquamarine tinted verre de soie, Celeste blue accent rims, three-arm candle holder, central pink, green, and blue dec floral finial, brass connector, orig conforming verre de soie candlecups, one finial flower petal chipped 1,850.00

Lemonade Mug, 6" h, Matsu Noke catalog no. 3329, optic ribbed colorless goblet form, Pomona green cintra rim, handle, and three fan-shaped dec 230.00

Perfume Bottle, opal, light blue stopper, #5203 . . . . 700.00

Salt, 2-1/8" d, clear, blue threading 85.00

Torchere, 68" h, 9" shade, Oriental Poppy, internally striped pink-opal flared shade, pale green receding under flared rim, inserted into elaborate floor lamp with ram's heads, tassels, and beading above twisted metal shaft 2,875.00

Vase

5" h, Millefiore, catalog no. 573, style J, baluster, gold aurene, internally decorated with green hearts and vines interspersed with clusters of white blossoms, fine platinum-gold irid 2,760.00

10" h, amethyst, flared oval, pattern molded in swirled design, small sand grain dot 350.00

12" h, Black Matzu, catalog no. 6391, flared rim, mirror black oval body, three full-length acid etched Ming trees, stylized cloud formations, triangular foil label 1,100.00

Pomona Green

Candlestick, 10-1/4" h, catalog no. 3374, colorless, Pomona green cintra rim wraps, disk and four berry prunts, base stamped "Steuben" 350.00

Compote, 7" h, twisted hollow stem, applied glass prunts, price for pr 350.00

Console Bowl, 11" d, #3261 . . . . 50.00

Window Box, 9" rect, #6199, amber crackle glass, lion head medallions 175.00

Rosaline

Boullion Cup and Saucer, alabaster handles 150.00
Compote, 8" d, alabaster stem and foot 295.00
Cup and Saucer, alabaster handle 150.00
Goblet, 6" h, flaring rim 135.00
Sherbet, matching underplate 175.00
Vase, 6" h, trumpet, alabaster pedestal foot 195.00

Verre De Soie

Vase
   5" h, ruffled top 200.00
   10" h, clear, overall rainbow irid 210.00

STEVENGRAPHS

History: Thomas Stevens of Coventry, England, first manufactured woven silk designs in 1854. His first bookmark was produced in 1862, followed by the first Stevengraphs, perhaps in 1874, but definitely by 1879 when they were shown at the York Exhibition. The first portrait Stevengraphs (of Disraeli and Gladstone) were produced in 1886, and the first postcards incorporating the woven silk panels in 1904. Stevens offered many other items with silk panels, including valentines, fans, pincushions, and needle cases.

Stevengraphs are miniature silk pictures, matted in cardboard, and usually having a trade announcement or label affixed to the reverse. Other companies, notably W. H. Grant of Coventry, copied Stevens' technique. Their efforts should not be confused with Stevengraphs.

Collectors in the U.S. favor the Stevengraphs with American-related views, such as "Signing of the Declaration of Independence," "Columbus Leaving Spain," and "Landing of Columbus." Sports-related Stevengraphs such as "The First Innings" (baseball), and "The First Set" (tennis) are also popular, as well as portraits of Buffalo Bill, President and Mrs. Cleveland, George Washington, and President Harrison.

Postcards with very fancy embossing around the aperture in the mount almost always have Stevens' name printed on them. The two most popular embossed postcard series in the U.S. are "Ships" and "Hands across the Sea." The latter set incorporates two crossed flags and two hands shaking. Seventeen flag combinations have been found, but only seven are common. These series generally are not printed with Stevens' name. Stevens also produced silks that were used in cards made by the Alpha Publishing Co.

Stevens' bookmarks are longer than they are wide, have mitered corners at the bottom, and are finished with a tassel. Many times his silks were used as the top or bottom half of regular bookmarks.

Marks: Thomas Stevens' name appears on the mat of the early Stevengraphs, directly under the silk panel. Many of the later portraits and the larger silks (produced initially for calendars) have no identification on the front of the mat other than the ""woven in pure silk" and have no label on the back.

Bookmarks originally had Stevens' name woven into the foldover at the top of the silk, but soon the identification was woven into the fold-under mitered corners. Al-most every Stevens' bookmark has such identification, except the ones woven at the World's Columbian Exposition in Chicago, 1892 to 1893.

References: Geoffrey A. Godden, *Stevengraphs and Other Victorian Silk Pictures*, Associationiated University Presses, 1971; Chris Radley, *Woven Silk Postcard*, privately printed, 1978; Austin Sprake, *Price Guide to Stevengraphs*, Antique Collectors' Club, 1972.

Collectors' Club: Stevengraph Collectors' Association, 2829 Arbutus Rd., #2103, Victoria, British Columbia, V8N 5X5, Canada.

Museums: Herbert Art Gallery and Museum, Coventry, England; Paterson Museum, Paterson, NJ.

Note: Prices are for pieces in mint or close-to-mint condition.

Bookmarks

Centennial, USA 1776-1876, General George Washington, The Father of Our Country, The First in Peace, The First in War, The First in the Hearts of Our Countrymen!, few small stains 125.00
General George Washington, The Father of Our Country, The First in Peace, The First in War, The First in the Hearts of Our Countrymen!, water damage to 1" upper piece 70.00
I Wish You A Happy New Year, small stain at bottom . . . 50.00
I Wish You A Merry Christmas and A Happy New Year 65.00
Jesus Behold the Man, He was despised and rejected of men; a man or sorrows, and acquainted with grief 75.00
To My Favorite, I had a little pony his name was dapple gray. I lent him to a lady to ride a mile away. she whipped him and she slashed him, she led him through the mires. I would not lend my pony for all that lady's hire 65.00
To One I Love, Love me little, love me long is the burden of my song, Love that is too hot and strong, burneth soon to waste, Still I would not have thee cold, not too backward or too bold; Love that lasteth till this old fadeth not in haste 65.00

Stevengraph

Are you ready? 175.00
Betsy Making the first Untied States Flag, Anderson Bros., Paterson, NJ, 5" x 8-1/2" 50.00
Buffalo Bill, Nate Salsbury, Indian Chief, orig mat and frame, 8" x7" 500.00
Coventry, 7-1/4" x 13", framed 100.00
Death of Nelson 250.00
Declaration of Independence 375.00
Dick Turpin's last ride on his Bonnie Black Bess 175.00

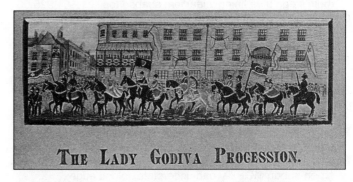

Lady Godiva's Procession #2, orig mat, $145.

For Life or Death, fire engine rushing to burning house, orig mat
    and frame.................................... 350.00
Full Cry.. 175.00
God Speed the Plow............................ 175.00
H. M. Stanley, famous explorer................... 300.00
Jeyhanne d'Arc, F. Lematte, 12-1/2" x 6-1/2" w........ 50.00
Kenilworth Castle, 7-1/4" x 13" framed............. 100.00
Landing of Columbus........................... 350.00
President Cleveland............................. 365.00
The Good Old Days............................. 175.00
The Water Jump................................ 195.00
Untitled, crew boats............................ 175.00
Untitled, life saving boat........................ 175.00

STEVENS and WILLIAMS

History: In 1824, Joseph Silvers and Joseph Stevens leased the Moor Lane Glass House at Briar Lea Hill (Brierley Hill), England, from the Honey-Borne family. In 1847, William Stevens and Samuel Cox Williams took over, giving the firm its present name. In 1870, the company moved to its Stourbridge plant. In the 1880s, the firm employed such renowned glass artisans as Frederick C. Carder, John Northwood, other Northwood family members, James Hill, and Joshua Hodgetts.

Stevens and Williams made cameo glass. Hodgetts developed a more commercial version using thinner-walled blanks, acid etching, and the engraving wheel. Hodgetts, an amateur botanist, was noted for his brilliant floral designs.

Other glass products and designs manufactured by Stevens and Williams include intaglio ware, Peach Bloom (a form of peachblow), moss agate, threaded ware, "jewell" ware, tapestry ware, and Silveria. Stevens and Williams made glass pieces covering the full range of late Victorian fashion.

After World War I, the firm concentrated on refining the production of lead crystal and achieving new glass colors. In 1932, Keith Murray came to Stevens and Williams as a designer. His work stressed the pure nature of the glass form. Murray stayed with Stevens and Williams until World War II and later followed a career in architecture.

Additional Listings: Cameo Glass.

Basket, 5" d, 9" h, creamy opaque, applied green and amber ruffled leaves, applied amber feet and handle, rose pink lining
    .... 365.00
Bowl, 7-3/4" d, 3-3/4" h, shaded gold to aqua, swirl MOP, ruffled, robin's egg blue lining, clear leaf shaped top....... 925.00
Cruet, 7-3/4" h, 3-3/4" d, Arboresque, light blue, opaque white overlay in craquelle-like effect, applied blue handle, orig blue bubble stopper................................ 145.00
Perfume Bottle, 6-1/2" h, 3-3/4" w, deep gold, brown/red, turquoise blue lining, orig cut frosted stopper......... 895.00
Pitcher, 10-1/2" h, applied amber feet and rim, green handle forms green leaves and yellow flower, cranberry overlay, blue int.. 650.00
Plate, 5-3/4" d, ruffled shell shape, swirl satin MOP, pink to green, cream underside....................... 195.00
Rose Bowl, 2-3/4" h, 5" d underplate, light blue ribbon MOP, light green ribbon MOP lily pad underplate, folded edges
    .... 400.00

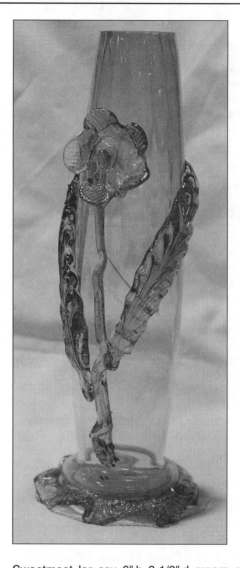

Vase, colorless shading to light green, applied rose flowers, green leaves, and base fringe, 10-3/4" h, $220

Sweetmeat Jar, cov, 6" h, 3-1/2" d, cream, opaque, three applied amber and green leaves, pink lining, SP rim, lid and handle
    .... 495.00
Tumbler, 3-1/4" d, 3-3/4" h, amber, applied amber pear and apple, green leaves, amber branch................. 225.00
Vase
    3-7/8" h, 1-1/2" d, sq, pink overlay, white lining, intaglio cut ferns and flowers, pink opalescent scroll feet..... 175.00
    4-1/4" h, 2-1/8" d, ruffled top, rose pink overlay, white lining, intaglio cut flowers, leaves, and dots, opalescent wafer foot
    .... 235.00
    5-1/8" h, 2-3/4" h, narrow neck, ruffled top, rose pink overlay, white lining, intaglio cut ferns and flowers, clear wafer foot
    .... 250.00
    6" h, 7-3/4" w at flared mouth, twisted form, Silveria, silver foil between clear glass layers, crimson, ruby-red, and rosy-pink top portion highlights, sky-blue and turquoise blue enameled colors on lower portion, streaks and gold blotches throughout, clear green glass entwining vertical ext. lines, sgd "S & W" on pontil mark..............3,950.00
    7-1/4" h, Pompeiian Swirl, MOP, powder blue body, pink air traps, two ext. flakes....................... 545.00
    9" h, 5-1/2" d, deep rose shading to pink, applied cherries, flowers, and vines, rose, amber, yellow, and white
    .... 485.00
    11" h, 6-1/2" w, bulbous bottom, stick neck, amber to bright red, Pompeiian Swirl........................ 950.00

STICKLEYS

History: There were five Stickley brothers: Albert, Gustav, Leopold, George, and John George. Gustav often is credited with creating the Mission style, a variant of the Arts and Crafts style. Gustav headed Craftsman Furniture, a New York firm, much of whose actual production took place near Syracuse. A characteristic of Gustav's furniture is exposed tenon ends. Gustav published The Craftsman, a magazine espousing his antipathy to machines.

Originally Leopold and Gustav worked together. In 1902, Leopold and John George formed the L. and J. G. Stickley Furniture Company. This firm made Mission-style furniture and cherry and maple early-American style pieces.

George and Albert organized the Stickley Brothers Company, located in Grand Rapids, Michigan.

References: Donald A. Davidoff and Robert L. Zarrow, *Early L. & J. G. Stickley Furniture*, Dover Publications, 1992; *Furniture of the Arts & Crafts Period*, L-W Book Sales, 1992, 1995 value update; Thomas K. Maher, *The Kaufmann Collection: The Early Furniture of Gustav Stickley*, Treadway Gallery (2029 Madison Rd., Cincinnati, OH 45208), 1996; Paul Royka, *Mission Furniture, from the American Arts & Crafts Movement*, Schiffer Publishing, 1997.

Periodical: *Style 1900*, 333 Main St., Lambertville, NJ 08530.

Collectors' Club: Foundation for the Study of Arts & Crafts Movement, Roycroft Campus, 31 S. Grove St., East Aurora, NY 14052.

Museum: Craftsman Farms Foundation, Inc., Morris Plains, NJ.

Note: *Gustav* denotes Gustav Stickley and Craftsman Furniture; *L & J G* denotes L. and J. G. Stickley Furniture Company; *Stickley Bros.* denotes Stickley Brothers Company

Stickley Bros. Andirons, pr, 14" w, 19" w, #102, Gustav, wrought iron, curled strap, orig patina 3,750.00
Bed, Gustav, five wide vertical slats under inverted "V" top rail, tapered posts, orig finish, branded signature, 59" w, 48" d, 78" l 8,000.00
Bookcase
    #647, L. & J. G., three doors with twelve panes of glass each, orig hammered copper hardware, V-board back, keyed tenons and slab sides, fine orig finish, Handcraft decal, 73" w, 12" d, 55" h 16,000.00
    #717, Gustav, two doors with eight panes of glass each, orig iron hardware, branded, paper label, recent finish, 48" w, 13" d, 56" h 4,750.00
    #718, Gustav, two doors with eight panes of glass each, orig iron hardware, keyed tenon construction, cleaned orig finish, unsigned, 47" w, 13" d, 56" h 6,000.00
Book Trough, similar to #74, Gustav, ash, V-shaped top rack over lower shelf, slab sides, hand cut-outs, keyed thru-tenon construction, orig green finish, 30" w, 10" d, 31" h. . . 700.00
Candlestick, 12" h, Stickley Brothers, hammered copper, applied and curled handle, orig patina, imp #178. . . . . . 650.00

Cellarette, #86, Gustav, copper lined, pull-out shelf over single drawer, paneled door, orig iron hardware, int. divided compartment, orig finish, red decal, 22" w, 16" d, 40" h 4,000.00
Chair
    Arm, #388, L. & J. G., leather back and seat, orig leather and tacks, orig finish, sgd "The Work of...," 20" w, 17" d, 34" h 6,000.00
    Arm, #810, L. & J. G., five back slats, peaked rail, orig drop-in cushion recovered in black leather, recent finish, sgd "The Work of...," 26" w, 20" d, 39" h 400.00
    Arm, Gustav, inlaid, American white oak, pewter, copper, and exotic woods inlay, designed by Harvey Ellis, c1903 . . . . .46,000.00
    Arm, Gustav, V-back, recent finish and seat covering 400.00
    Billiard, L. & J. G., five vertical backslats, drop-in spring seat covered in new dark brown leather, foot rest, orig finish, stain to one ark, "The Work of..." label, 26" w, 21" d, 62" h 2,000.00
    Dining, #348, Gustav, heavy ladder-back type, three horizontal back slats, rush seat, orig finish, faint signature, 18" w, 18" d, 37" h, set of four .3,000.00
    Dining, #349, one arm, five side, heavy ladderback, three horizontal back slats, seats missing, stripped, unmarked, arm 27" 2, 22" d, 38" h, side 18" w, 17" d, 38" h 3,250.00
    Morris,#400, L. & J. G., fixed-back, five slats under bent arm, recovered leather cushion, cleaned orig finish, sgd "The Work of ...," 33" w, 32" d, 40" h 2,700.00
    Morris, #471, L. & J. G., adjustable back, six slats under wide arm, refinished, unsigned, replaced back bar, recovered orig seat cushion, 32" w, 35" d, 43" h 2,000.00
    Morris, #322, Gustav, five wide slats under arm, thru-tenon construction, refinished, replaced leather cushions, branded, 31" w, 38" d, 40" h .6,500.00
    Morris, #2341, Gustav, adjustable back, legs with inferior corbels flanking two wide slats under each arm, orig sling seat, recent finish, unsigned, 30" w, 34" d, 39" h 3,250.00
    Morris, L. & J. G., rocking type, adjustable back, recovered orig cushions, recoated orig finish, unsigned, 30" w, 36" d, 40" h. 950.00
    Office, L. & J. G., swivel, upholstered back and seat, notched arms, thru-tenon construction, refinished, unsigned, recovered in tan leather, 27" w, 21" d, 36" h. 750.00
    Side, #304, Gustav, four rung ladder-back, recovered orig drop-in spring cushion seat, arched lower slat, orig finish, branded signature, 18" w, 18" d, 36" h, set of three 1,500.00
    Side, #305, Gustav, H-back, wide vertical back slat with cut-outs, recovered orig drop-in seat, branded, recoated orig finish, set of four, 17" w, 15" d, 40" h 2,500.00
    Side, #306, Gustav, three horizontal back slats, recovered seats, orig finish, branded signature, pr, 17" w, 17" d, 36" h 950.00
    Side, #384, L. & J. G., very heavy construction, orig tacked leather back and seat, orig finish, sgd "The Work of...," 20" w, 17" d, 34". 4,250.00
Chamberstick, 6" h, Stickley Bros., hammered copper, orig patina, imp mark, #227. . . . . 400.00
Chandelier, #670, Gustav, four wrought iron and amber glass lanterns, six sq cut-outs at top, suspended from iron cross bar, orig chain and canapes to orig wood cross beam, orig patina and finish, replaced amber glass, 24" w, 24" d, 37" h 32,000.00

Chest of Drawers

#913, Gustav, Harvey Ellis, nine drawers, overhanging rect top, six small drawers over three long graduated drawers, bowed sides, orig wooden knobs, lightly cleaned orig finish, red decal, slight veneer split, 36" w, 20" d, 51" h 7,000.00

L. & J. G., two small drawers over three long drawers, V-backsplash, chamfered sides, large faceted wooden pulls, orig dark finish, 36" w, 20" d, 43" h 13,000.00

Chiffonier, #111, L. & J. G., two door, four small drawers over four wide drawers, paneled doors, orig finish, branded "The Work of...," 40" w, 19" d, 48" h 16,000.00

China Cabinet

#729, L. & J. G., two doors, each with sixteen leaded panes of glass, two cabinet doors, orig hammered copper hardware and straps, eight panes on each side, lightly cleaned orig finish, some glass replaced, branded "The Work of...," numbered, 43" w, 16" d, 66" h 18,000.00

#814, Gustav, two doors, each with eight panes of glass, orig brass hardware, straight tow board with thru-tenon construction, eight panes to sides, lightly cleaned orig finish, branded and paper label, minor distress to top, 42" w, 15" d, 64" h 8,000.00

Stickley Bros., two doors, each with eight panes of glass, four panes on sides, orig copper hardware, plate rail at back, three adjustable shelves, orig finish, illegible number, 42" w, 17" d, 64" h 3,250.00

Costumer (hall tree), Stickley Bros.

#198, single tapered post, four wooden coat supports, orig finish, Quaint decal, 18" d, 65" h 210.00

Double, orig iron hooks, tapered posts, cut-out shoe foot base, drip pan missing, recent finish, unsigned, 14" w, 20" d, 72" h 550.00

Desk

#430, Gustav, writing, orig oil cloth top and tacks, center drawer flanked by two side drawers, orig faceted pulls, chamfered back and sides with vertical keyed tenon supports, orig finish, unsigned, 36" w, 24" d, 29" h 2,300.00

#501, L. & J. G., rect top over single center drawer, two drawers on each side, orig copper hardware, thru-tenon construction, paneled sides and back, orig finish, branded, 48" 2, 30" d, 30" h 1,900.00

#550, Gustav, slant front over three drawers and two cabinet doors, orig copper strap hardware, flush tenons at sides, orig finish, early red decal, c1902, 33" w, 14" d, 48" h 11,000.00

#720, Gustav, pigeonhole organizer over two drawers, orig iron hardware, recent finish, sgd paper label, 38" w, 23" d, 37" h 1,250.00

Foot Stool

#300, Gustav, recovered seat, arched seat rail with orig tacks over four legs, thru-tenon horizontal supports, orig green finish, unsigned, 20" w, 16" d, 15" h 1,200.00

#394, L & J. G., recovered seat, arched stretcher, orig finish, unsigned, 19" w, 15" d, 16" h 500.00

Monk, Gustav, orig leatherette seat, orig tacks, four flared feet, orig finish, sgd with red decal, 12" w, 12" d, 5" h 800.00

Hall Bench, #180, Gustav, heavy thru-tenon construction, vertical keyed tenon lower stretcher, recovered leather seat, refinished, unsigned, 43" w, 22" d, 34" h 1,500.00

Lamp, Gustav

Newel Post, hammered iron, three sq cut-outs at top, replaced hammered amber glass, sgd, 8" w, 8" d, 21" h 3,750.00

Table, #295, hammered copper, slag glass shade, base with two applied handles, orig patina, imp mark, minor cracks and glass loss to shade, 15" w, 18" h 2,800.00

Table, #611, wooden base, four flaring spindles connected to cross stretcher, circular base, orig woven shade rests on hammered copper frame, orig finish, unsigned, restoration to metal work, 13" d, 21" h 21,000.00

Magazine Stand

#45, L. & J. G., four open shelves with arched supports, arched toe-board, paneled back, recent finish, unsigned, 21" w, 12" d, 45" h 1,800.00

#4602, Stickley Bros., five shelves, notched gallery with two wide slats at sides and back, minor stains to orig finish, remnant of paper label, 16" w, 12" d, 51" h 700.00

Music Cabinet, #70, Gustav, single panel door, orig iron hardware, thru-tenon construction, two orig int. shelves, orig light finish, paper label, 20" w, 16" d, 48" h 4,500.00

Rocker

#61, Gustav, wicker, arched back over woven design, natural finish, 21" w, 31" d, 35" h 600.00

#319, Gustav, four vertical back slats, notched top rail, refinished, unsigned, 30" w, 30" d, 39" h 325.00

#323, Gustav, five slats under each arm, cleaned orig finish, replaced cushions, one rocker replaced, branded, 29" w, 33" d, 40" h 1,700.00

Stickley Bros., highback, arm, four vertical back slats, orig leatherette loose cushion, orig finish, unsigned, two slats replaced, 27" w, 32" d, 40" h 300.00

Stickley Bros., six vertical back slats, recovered orig spring cushion, worn orig finish, branded signature, 25" w, 27" d, 35" h 220.00

Thorden, Gustav, two wide horizontal back slats, recovered black leather seat, refinished, 22" w, 28" d, 32" h . . 425.00

Rug, 68" w, 38" l, drugget style, blue on oatmeal ground, Gustav, some wear 350.00

Sconce, #830, Gustav, hammered iron lantern, six sq cut-outs at top over hammered amber glass, supported by L-shaped brackets, orig patina, replaced glass, 6" w, 11" d, 12" h 4,200.00

Server

#816, Gustav, rect top, two drawers, orig iron hardware, branded, refinished, 42" w, 19' d, 38" h 3,250.00

Stickley Bros., rect top, backsplash, rect top, lower shelf, unsigned, recoated orig finish, 36" w, 20" d, 36" h 800.00

Settle

#205, Gustav, five back slats, single wide slat under each arm, thru-tenon construction, orig recovered spring cushion, unsigned, 56" w, 22" d, 30" h 2,900.00

#208, Gustav, even arm form, three wide slats under each arm, eight back slats, thru-tenon construction, recovered cushions, orig finish, faint red decal, 75" w, 32" d, 29" h 8,000.00

#285, L. & J. G., davenport bed, even arms, two slats under each arm, seven back slats, arched front rail pulls out to make 3/4 bed, orig finish, sgd "The Work of...," 70" w, 27" d, 34" h 4,000.00

Sewing Cabinet, #630, Gustav, dropleaf, two drawers, orig copper ring pulls, cleaned orig finish, unsigned, some restoration to top, 18" w, 18" d, 28" h .1,100.00

Sideboard

#631, L. & J. G., from Onodaga Shops, wide over hanging top with cabinet doors, orig copper strap hardware flanking four half drawers over one long drawer, orig early copper pulls, orig dark finish, unsigned, 45" h 5,000.00

#745, L. & J. G., two cabinet doors with orig copper strap hinges flanking four half drawers over one long drawer, orig copper hardware, replaced plate rail, stains to top, cleaned orig finish on base, unsigned, 54" w, 24" d, 48" h 1,900.00

#814-1/2, Gustav, two cabinet doors flanking three drawers, over one long drawer, plate rail, orig copper hardware, recent finish, red decal, height slightly reduced, 54" w, 22" d, 48" h. 2,900.00

Stock Certificate, 11" x 7-1/2", Gustav, matted and framed 170.00

Table

Center, #541, L. & J. G., circular top, circular shelf on cross stretchers, orig finish, some stains, Handcraft decal, 30" d, 29" h. 1,800.00

Center, #2608, Stickley Bros., circular top, lower shelf supported by thru-tenon stretchers, Mackmurdo feet, orig finish, numbered, 32" d, 30" h 1,300.00

Center, #2570, Stickley Bros., prairie design, full length corbels, four sq legs, shoefoot base, orig finish to base, top refinished, branded and Quaint decal, 40" w, 26" d, 30" h 2,100.00

Center, Gustav, hexagonal form, recovered leather top over six legs, notched and thru-tenon stretcher, recent finish, unsigned, 48" w, 48" d, 29" h. 3,750.00

Dining, #632, Gustav, circular top, five tapering legs, four orig leaves, orig finish, paper label, 48" d, 30" h. 4,750.00

Dining, #656, Gustav, circular top, tapered base, four extended feet, six orig leaves in orig case, cleaned orig finish, unsigned, center leg replaced, some rings to top, 54" d, 30" h 5,000.00

Dining, L. & J. G., circular top, cluster of five tapering legs, shoefoot base, three orig leaves, unsigned, refinished, 45" d, 29" h. 3,500.00

Directors, #631, Gustav, rect top, splayed legs, exposed pegs, shoefoot base, refinished, unsigned, 94" w, 46" d, 30" h. 16,000.00

Library, #615, Gustav, rect top, two drawers with oval copper pulls above corbel legs, thru-tenon construction, orig finish, red decal, some distress to top, two replaced corbels, 48" w, 30" d, 30" h 1,600.00

Library, #617, Gustav, rect top, two drawers, orig copper pulls, orig red/brown finish, some color added to stretcher, branded, 54" w, 32" d, 30" h 3,500.00

Library, #619, Gustav, three drawers, orig iron hardware, refinished, paper label, veneer loss to legs, surface scratches, 66" w, 36" d, 30" h 2,100.00

Library, #652, Gustav, rect top, single drawer, orig iron hardware, unsigned, recent finish, drawer bottom replaced, 36" w, 24" d, 29" h 750.00

Side, #440, Gustav, circular top, flared cross-stretcher base, cleaned orig finish, unsigned, 30" d, 29" h. 2,000.00

Side, #573, L. & J. G., circular top over lower shelf supported by arched cross-stretcher, refinished, splits in top, unsigned, 18" d, 29" h 600.00

Spindle, #655, Gustav, rect top, 13 spindles to each side, new finish, unsigned, 36" w, 24" d, 29" h. 3,750.00

Sutherland, #2676, Stickley Bros., narrow drop leaf, opens to six-sided top, gateleg support, cut-out slab sides, shoefoot base, orig finished, numbered, 39" w (closed), 9" d, 29" h 900.00

Tilt-Top, #2577, Stickley Bros., circular top, flaring base, caned insets on ftd platform, refinished, numbered, 30" d, 29" h. 1,500.00

Trestle, Gustav, rect top, thick lower shelf, keyed tenon construction, shoe-foot base, recoated orig finish, branded, 48" w, 29" d, 30" h 1,800.00

Trestle, #595, L. & J. G., rect top, lower stretcher with keyed tenon construction, shoefoot base, unsigned, refinished, some distress, 48" w, 30" d, 29" h 900.00

Trestle, #599, L. & J. G., rect top, keyhole slab sides, vertical stretcher, keyed-tenons, refinished, sgd "The Work of...," 54" w, 32" d, 29" h 2,500.00

Tabouret

#558, L. & J. G., octagonal top over arched cross stretchers and thru-post legs, top recent finish, base orig, branded, 18" w, 18" d, 20" h 1,100.00

#602, Gustav, circular top over arched cross stretchers, orig dark finish, red decal, 16" d, 18" h 1,000.00

#603, Gustav, circular top over arched cross stretchers, thru-tenon construction, cleaned orig finish, sgd with faint box mark, minor splits, 19" d, 20" h 1,300.00

Tray, 23" l, 11" w, oval, hammered copper, riveted handles, new dark patina, "Als Ik Kan" stamp 700.00

Umbrella Stand

#100, Gustav, flaring slatted form, riveted to int. iron hoops, cleaned orig finish, unsigned, drip-pan missing, 12" d, 24" h 1,600.00

#382, Gustav, hammered copper, repousse design, riveted handles, new dark patina, 13" d, 24" h 1,300.00

Urn, 18" h, 10" d, L & J. G., hammered copper, riveted sinewy handles, orig patina, imp LJGS shield and F15 . . . .4,000.00

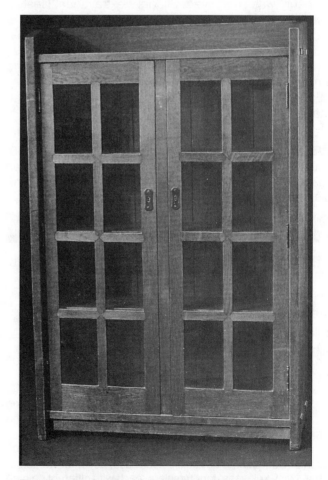

Bookcase, Gustav Stickley, double doors, mitered mullions, eight panes on each door, gallery top, mortised sides, mint orig ebonized finish, closed box decal, 56" x 36" x 12-1/2", $14,000. Photo courtesy of David Rago Auctions, Inc.

Vase

10" h, Stickley Bros., hammered copper, applied handles at shoulder, rolled rim, three emb designs, recent patina, imp #20 . . . . 850.00

17-1/2" h, L. & J. G. hammered copper, vertical lobes at base, cleaned patina, imp mark, drilled at base, dent to one side 2,000.00

Wall Shelf, 25" l, 6-1/4" d, 13-3/4" h, Stickley Bros., hanging, sectional, heart-shaped cut-out top, light overcoat on orig finish, Quaint metal tag 1,400.00

Wastebasket

L. & J. G., flaring sides, cut-out handles, scalloped rim, orig medium finish, 13" sq, 16" h 1,300.00

Stickley Bros., five slats on each side, refinished, numbered, 14" w, 14" d, 16" h 425.00

STIEGEL-TYPE GLASS

History: Baron Henry Stiegel founded America's first flint-glass factory at Manheim, Pennsylvania, in the 1760s. Although clear glass was the most common color made, amethyst, blue (cobalt), and fiery opalescent pieces also are found. Products included bottles, creamers, flasks, flips, perfumes, salts, tumblers, and whiskeys. Prosperity was short-lived; Stiegel's extravagant lifestyle forced the factory to close.

It is very difficult to identify a Stiegel-made item. As a result, the term "Stiegel-type" is used to identify glass made during the time period of Stiegel's firm and in the same shapes and colors as used by that company.

Enamel-decorated ware also is attributed to Stiegel. True Stiegel pieces are rare; an overwhelming majority is of European origin.

References: Frederick W. Hunter, *Stiegel Glass*, 1950, available in Dover reprint; Kenneth Wilson, *American Glass 1760-1930*, 2 Vols., Hudson Hills Press and The Toledo Museum of Art, 1994.

REPRODUCTION ALERT

Beware of modern reproductions, especially in enamel wares.

Enameled

Bottle

4-1/2" h, rect, colorless, enameled girl and flowers 265.00

5" h

Oval, colorless, enameled deer, flowers, and verse, pewter top, dated 1770 . . . . 625.00

Rect, colorless, enameled boy 250.00

6-1/4" h, octagonal, colorless, enameled reserve of bird on each side, pewter top, 18th C 925.00

Decanter Set, painted heraldic unicorn dec, decanter with stopper, twelve glasses, four tumblers, each with different painted heraldic dec, Bavarian 1,500.00

Flip, 3-7/8" h, clear, blown, enameled flower and running deer 175.00

Mug, 3-3/4" h, enameled "Forget Me Not," in blue diamond medallion, forget me nots and other flowers, "C" handle, ribbed base 150.00

Tumbler, 3-1/2" h, 3-1/2" w, colorless, enameled connected hearts, clasped hands, German writing, dated 1708, open pontil, wear marks 600.00

Etched

Flip

5-1/2" h, colorless, etched and ribbed blown 160.00

6" h, colorless, flaring shape, floral and leaf etch 170.00

Mug, 6-1/2" h, colorless, floral and leaf etch, applied flat "C" handle 375.00

Nursing Bottle, 3-1/8" h, blown half-post type, clear, pontil, bow and leaf dec 195.00

Tumbler, 3-5/8" h, colorless, etched and ribbed blown, early 19th C 130.00

Other

Baptismal Bowl, 4-1/4" h, blue, diamond mold, ftd, base repaired 70.00

Bowl, 3 x 2-1/8", blown mold, Expanded DQ, deep cobalt blue, applied foot 1,200.00

Creamer

3-5/8" h, blue, diamond mold, loop handle, circular ftd base, 18th C 450.00

4" h, blue, diamond marble, applied loop handle, circular foot, 18th C 350.00

Cup, 3" h, colorless, inverted pear shape, diamond mold, circular base 350.00

Flask, 5" h, 4" w, amethyst, Daisy and Hexagon pattern, globular, short cylindrical neck and plain lip, two lateral rows of hexagons start at central bottom part and continue up, second horizontal band curves up the neck, terminates at top of shoulder, open pontil, McKearin 435 . . . . .6,500.00

Finger Bowl, 4" d, deep amethyst, diamond mold, 18th/19th C, price for 4 pc set 700.00

Salt, blown mold, Expanded DQ, cobalt blue, ftd 750.00

Scent Bottle, 2-3/4" l, swirled, deep cobalt blue 195.00

Sugar Bowl

3-1/4" h, blue, circular, rimmed base, 18th C 500.00

4-1/2" x 2-3/4", blue, diamond mold, ftd, 18th C 625.00

STONEWARE

History: Made from dense kaolin and commonly salt-glazed, stonewares were hand-thrown and high-fired to produce a simple, bold, vitreous pottery. Stoneware crocks, jugs, and jars were made to store products and fill other utilitarian needs. These intended purposes dictated shape and design—solid, thick-walled forms with heavy rims, necks, and handles and with little or no embellishment. Any decorations were simple: brushed cobalt oxide, incised, slip trailed, stamped, or tooled.

Stoneware has been made for centuries. Early American settlers imported stoneware items at first. As English and European potters refined their earthenware, colonists began to produce their own wares. Two major North American traditions emerged based only on location or type of clay. North Jersey and parts of New York comprise the first area; the second was eastern Pennsylvania spreading westward and into Maryland, Virginia, and West Virginia. These two distinct geographical boundaries, style of decoration, and shape are discernible factors in classifying and dating early stoneware.

By the late 18th century stoneware was manufactured in all sections of the country. This vigorous industry flourished during the 19th century until glass fruit jars appeared and the use of refrigeration became widespread. By 1910, commercial production of salt-glazed stoneware came to an end.

References: Susan and Al Bagdade, *Warman's American Pottery and Porcelain*, Wallace-Homestead, 1994; Georgeanna H. Greer, *American Stoneware*, revised ed., Schiffer Publishing, 1996; William C. Ketchum, Jr., *American Pottery and Porcelain*, 1994; Jim Martin and Bette Cooper, *Monmouth-Western Stoneware*, published by authors, 1983, 1993 value update; Don and Carol Raycraft, *Collector's Guide to Country Stoneware & Pottery*, 1st Series (1985, 1995 value update), 2nd Series (1990, 1996 value update), Collector Books; ——, *Stoneware*, Wallace-Homestead, 1995, -----, *Wallace-Homestead Price Guide to American Country Antiques,* 15th ed., Krause Publications, 1997; Terry G. Taylor and Terry and Kay Lowrance, *Collector's Encyclopedia of Salt Glaze Stoneware*, Collector Books, 1996.

Collectors' Clubs: American Stoneware Association, 208 Crescent Ct., Mars, PA 16066; Federation of Historical Bottle Collectors, Inc., 1485 Buck Hill Drive, Southampton, PA 18966.

Museum: Museum of Ceramics at East Liverpool, East Liverpool, OH.

Apple Butter Crock, 1 gallon, D Ack, Mooresburg, PA, salt-glazed, free hand cobalt blue floral design, rim chip 330.00

Batter Jug, cobalt blue quill work long tailed bird, imp "4," replaced bail handle, tin lids missing, surface flakes, bottom chips, 9" h 550.00

Batter Pail, 1-1/2" gallon
  Cowden & Wilcox, Harrisburg, PA, salt-glazed, free hand cobalt blue dec, professional repairs to ears 925.00
  Sipe, Nicholas & Co., Williamsport, PA, salt-glazed, free hand cobalt blue all around flower design, rim chips 1,100.00

Bowl, 11" d, 4" h, molded shells and foliage scrolls highlighted in cobalt blue, gray ground, molded lip, chips and two short rim hairlines 85.00

Butter Crock, cov, applied side handles, brushed cobalt blue dec, small rim flake, 11-1/2" d 495.00

Butter Churn
  Four gallon, applied shoulder handles, cobalt blue stenciled eagle with "E. Pluribus Unum, 4," hairlines and chips, 15-1/2" h 220.00
  Four gallon, two handles, W. H. Farrar & Co., Geddes, NY, 1841-71, cobalt blue foliate device, cracks, minor chips, kiln imperfections, 16-1/4" h 350.00
  Five gallon, two handles, cobalt blue foliate dec, Worcester, MA, 19th C, minor chips and hairlines, 18-1/4" h
   . . . . 550.00

Canning Jar, WRF Weimer & Bro., Snydertown, PA, 2 quart, wax seal, simple cobalt blue design 550.00

Churn
  Burger, J., Rochester, NY, ovoid, applied shoulder handles, imp label
   Cobalt blue quill work foliate design, minor lime deposits, 22-1/2" h 550.00

Cobalt blue quill work flower and "8," minor lime deposits, 22-3/4" h. 990.00
Unsigned, ovoid, applied shoulder handles, cobalt blue brushed tulip and "6," int. lime deposits and hairline, 18" h
   . . . . 225.00

Cooler, two handles, ftd, cobalt blue grape and foliate dec, dated 1849, staple repairs, minor chips, 18-1/2" h 950.00

Crock
  Bosworth, Seymour, Hartford, CT, cobalt blue traveler viewing directional sign, "11 miles to Hartford," chips, prefiring dent 700.00
  Burger, John, Rochester, applied handles, imp label, cobalt blue quill work flower, chips and hairlines, 9"h. 385.00
  Farrar & Co., W. H., Geedes, NY, 1841-72, five gallon, cobalt blue foliate dec, minor chips, 17-1/2" h 435.00
  Mead, 4 gallon, ovoid, imp mark "I. M. Mead & Co., Portago Co., Ohio," cobalt blue highlights 200.00
  Norton, E. & L. P., Bennington, VT, 1-1/2, cobalt blue floral dec, imp label, applied handles, 8" h 150.00
  Norton & Co., E., Bennington, VT, 3, cobalt blue floral dec, imp label, applied handles, minor chips and lime deposits, 10-1/4" h. 150.00
  New York Stoneware Co., Fort Edward, NY 2," cobalt blue floral dec, imp label, 2 gallon 175.00
  Union Stoneware, two gallon 55.00
  Unsigned
   Five gallon, applied shoulder handles, cobalt blue brushed floral dec, and "5," glaze wear and pitting, 13-1/4" h
    . . . . 110.00
   Four gallon, cobalt blue blooming flower on one side, wave design on other, two handles, 14-1/2" h
    . . . . 200.00

Jar
  A Leet, PA, 3 gallon, merchant stamp, bold floral design
   . . . . 525.00
  Bennett & Choliar, Homer, ovoid, applied shoulder handle, imp label, cobalt blue brushed star, 9" h 420.00
  L. Eberhardt. Toronto, Ont., ovoid, applied shoulder handle, imp label, cobalt blue brushed flower and "2," hairlines and flakes at rim, 13" h 360.00
  Jas Hamilton & Co, Manufacturers, Greensboro, PA, salt-glazed, stenciled mark 125.00
  J Swank & Co, Johnstown, PA, semi-ovoid, simple dec, some blue missing. 385.00
  Whites Utica 2, imp label, cobalt blue quill work bird on flowering branch, applied shoulder handles, 12" h. 550.00
  Brewer, S. T., Havana, 2, cobalt blue floral design, applied handle, hairlines in bottom, small chips on base, 13-1/2" h
   . . . . 250.00
  Lyman & Clark, Gardiner, ME, 1837-41, four gallon, brown dec foliate device, cracks, chips, 15-1/4" h. 1,265.00
  Norton & Co., F. B. Worcester, Mass, 2, cobalt blue brushed leaf design, strap handle, imp label, chip on lip 220.00
  Stedman & Seymour, New Haven or Hartford, CT, c1830, attributed to, double, two ovoid vessels joined in middle with reeded strap handle, dec with cobalt blue pecking chickens below stylized trees, 10-5/8" h .17,250.00
  Unsigned
   Charlestown, MA, imp spread eagle atop cannon, and "Charlestown," 19th C, chips, kiln burn 575.00
   Gray salt glaze, brown highlights, cobalt blue brushed tree-like design, ovoid, ribbed strap handle, fitted with lamp socket, 15" h. 250.00
   New York, c1810-16, ovoid, salt glaze, dec with cobalt blue figure of girl bent over peering between her legs,

Churn, applied handles, cobalt blue brushed floral dec and "6," hairline and small chips, 18-1/4" h, $360. Photo courtesy of Garth's Auctions, Inc.

two horseshoe shaped marks on backside, 17" h
....10,350.00
Welding, W. E., cobalt blue brushed floral design, imp label, strap handle, hairline and minor lip flakes, 13-1/2" h
.... 110.00
White & Son, N. A., Utica, NY, 3, dark cobalt blue quill work flower, strap handle, imp label, hairlines, repair at handle and chips on lip, 15-1/2" h........... 330.00
Milk Bowl
 A Sipe & Son, Williamsport, PA, salt-glazed, free hand cobalt blue floral design, blue at handles, some chips.... 365.00
 Unknown Maker, brushed cobalt blue commas at lip, 9" d, edge chips................................ 115.00
Pitcher
 Cowden & Wilcox, Harrisburg, PA, 1 gallon, salt-glazed, cobalt blue floral design, blue at handles, rim chip
.... 770.00
Preserving Jar, 10" h, cobalt blue stenciled and freehand label "Hamilton & Co. Greensboro, Pa"............... 185.00

STONEWARE, BLUE and WHITE

History: Blue-and-white stoneware refers to molded, blue salt-glazed, domestic, utilitarian earthenware produced in the late 19th and early 20th centuries. Earlier stoneware was usually hand thrown and either undecorated, hand decorated in Spencerian script with flowers and other motifs, or stenciled. The stoneware of the blue-and-white period is molded and designs are impressed, embossed, stenciled, or printed.

Although known as blue-and-white, the base color is generally grayish in tone. The blue cobalt glaze may coat the entire piece, appear as a series of bands, or accent the decorative elements.

All types of household products were available in blue-and-white stoneware. Bowls, crocks, jars, pitchers, mugs, and salts are just a few examples. The ware reached its greatest popularity between 1870 and 1890.

The advent of glass jars, tin containers, and chilled transportation hastened its demise. The last blue-and-white stoneware was manufactured in the 1920s.

References: M. H. Alexander, *Stoneware in the Blue and White*, revised ed., published by author, 1993; Kathyrn McNerney, *Blue & White Stoneware*, Collector Books, 1981, 1996 value update.

Collectors' Club: Blue & White Pottery Club, 224 12th St. NW, Cedar Rapids, IA 52405.

REPRODUCTION ALERT

Many pieces of blue-and-white stoneware found in antiques shops and flea markets are unmarked reproductions from Rushville Pottery, Rushville, Ohio.

Bean Pot, cov, 7-1/2" h, high relief of two children and "Boston Baked Beans".............................330.00
Bowl, bluebirds..................................165.00
Bread/Cake Crock, cov, 12-1/4" d, 8" h, blue bands top and bottom, minor chips on edge of lid................1,100.00
Butter Crock, cov
 7" d, 4" h, molded cherries and lid, wire bale and wooden handle......................................250.00
 7-1/4" d, 4-1/2" h, molded cows and lids, wire bale and wooden handle, minor chips on inner flange.........500.00
Canister, cov, scroll motif
 Cereal.....................................350.00
 Coffee.....................................275.00
 Salt.......................................100.00
Coffeepot, cov
 9-3/4"h, spiral stripes, acorn finial, tin bottom......685.00
 10-1/2" d, spiral stripes, ball finial, tin bottom......1,320.00
Cup, blue flowers and hummingbirds, white ground....225.00
Jar, cov, 7-1/2" d, stippled surface, flowers, holes for wire bale handle, old professional repair to lid..............165.00
Mixing Bowl, Wedding Ring, price for nested set of three
....125.00

Pedestal, tree trunk form, applied branches, leaves, birds, some repair to decoration, firing cracks, 19-1/2" h, $1,075. Photo courtesy of Garth's Auctions, Inc.

Mug, 4-1/8" h, Flying Bird, molded birds, price for set of six, hairlines in three, one with chipped lip 565.00
Pitcher
    7" h, molded cattails 200.00
    7-1/2" h, tree bark and flowers 165.00
    7-5/8" h, molded roadway lined with trees, rim chips
    . . . . 200.00
    7-7/8" h, molded swallows flying, small edge flakes
    . . . . 525.00
    8" h, molded
        Cattle in oval, small chips and int. crazing 200.00
        Cherries, professional repairs 80.00
        Eagles and shields in ovals, minor crazing 385.00
        Leaping deer in one oval and swan in other 550.00
        Leaping stags in oval, surface flakes on spout . . . 375.00
        Swans in ovals, short hairline in spout and minor surface chips 275.00
    8-1/4" h, molded, Indian heads in circles, small chips
    . . . . 415.00
    8-3/4" h, molded brick arches and pillars 440.00
    9" h, molded, roses, small edge flakes 440.00
    9-1/4" h, molded, Vintage, star mark on bottom, small edge flakes 180.00
    9-1/2" h, Colonial garbed gentleman drinking, woman, child with mug, large barrel 225.00
Salt Cellar
    Butterflies design 95.00
    Peacock design 85.00
    Poppies design, cobalt blue flowers 155.00
Soap Dish
    4-1/2" d, lion head, small edge chips 50.00
    5" d
        Floral motif 85.00
        Roses 72.00
Spittoon, Basketweave, rose 85.00
Sugar Crock, 9-1/4" d, 4-1/2" h, stripes, crow's foot in bottom
. . . . 200.00
Teapot, cov, 6-1/2" h, spiral stripes, acorn finial, wire bale and wood handle 725.00
Wash Bowl and Pitcher, Primrose motif, overall swag
. . . . 550.00

STRING HOLDERS

History: The string holder developed as a useful tool to assist the merchant or manufacturer who needed tangle-free string or twine to tie packages. The early holders were made of cast iron, some patents dating to the 1860s.

REPRODUCTION ALERT

As a result of the growing collector interest in string holders, some unscrupulous individuals are hollowing out the backs of 1950s figural-head wall plaques, drilling a hole through the mouth, and passing them off as string holders. A chef, Chinese man, Chinese woman, Indian, masked man, masked woman, and Siamese face are altered forms already found on the market. Figural wall lamps from the 1950s and '60s also are being altered. When the lamp hardware is removed, the base can be easily altered. Two forms that have been discovered are a pineapple face and an apple face, both lamp-base conversions.

When the string holder moved into the household, lighter and more attractive forms developed, many made of chalkware. The string holder remained a key kitchen element until the early 1950s.

Reference: Sharon Ray Jacobs, *Collector's Guide to Stringholders*, L-W Book Sales, 1996.

Advertising
    Cornell White Lead, 13-3/4" w, 19-3/4" h, double sided diecut tin, Dutch Boy painting in opened window 1,000.00
    Heinz, 17" l, hanging, double sided diecut pickle suspended from marquee labeled "57 Varieties" on one side, "Pure Foods" on reverse, spool of thread mounted on top of pickle
    . . . . 5,940.00
    Lipton's Tea, 13-1/3" w, 19-1/2" h, hanging, double sided diecut litho tin 1,665.00
Apple, chalkware
    Bird chasing worm 110.00
    Stem to left 20.00
    Stem to right 40.00
Art Nouveau Lady 90.00
Bear Cub, bee on tummy 230.00
Bird, scissors forms beak, Royal Copley 50.00
Black Cat
    Full figure, red ball, chip on ear 150.00
    Head, red bow 90.00
Bride, groom, one bridesmaid 170.00
Bride and two bridesmaids 120.00
Bridesmaid 85.00
Cat
    Ceramic, pearlized white, string out extended paw . . 150.00
    Chalkware, pink collar 150.00
Clown, comical expression 230.00
Dog, head, sad expression 160.00
Dutch Girl
    Ceramic, flowered hat 95.00
    Chalkware, red hat 45.00
Flapper Girl, head, black, orange, and green hair 170.00

Plaster, man in top hat, 8-3/4" h, $25.

Fox, wearing glasses 160.00
Lemon, chalkware 130.00
Mammy
    Polka dot scarf 400.00
    Red scarf, gray face 425.00
Owl, dark brown 60.00
Pear, chalkware 45.00
Pineapple, smiling, chalkware 150.00
Pumpkin, winking 180.00
Scotty Dog, ceramic 220.00
Strawberry, chalkware
    Face 50.00
    With blossom 65.00
Tomato, wearing hat, chalkware 140.00

SUGAR SHAKERS

History: Sugar shakers, sugar castors, or muffineers all served the same purpose: to "sugar" muffins, scones, or toast. They are larger than salt and pepper shakers, were produced in a variety of materials, and were in vogue in the late Victorian era.

Reference: William Heacock, *Encyclopedia of Victorian Colored Pattern Glass*, Book III, Antique Publications, 1976, 1991-92 value update.

China

Meissen, 6-1/2" h, baluster, hp, multicolored floral spray, ozier band, pierced cov edge in puce, c1750, chip on final
. . . . 450.00
R. S. Prussia, 4-3/4" h, luster finish, rose dec, scalloped base, red mark 250.00
Wedgwood, jasper, blue, white relief classical figures . . . 55.00

Glass

Amerina, 4" h, globular, Inverted Thumbprint pattern, emb floral and butterfly lid 425.00

Milk Glass, Waffle pattern, metal top, bottom emb "Pat'd Appl. For," 7" h, $45.

Bristol, 6-1/4" h, tall tapering cylinder, pink, blue flowers and green leaves dec 75.00
Burmese, 4-1/2" h, 4" w, painted shaded salmon colored ground, enameled blue and white small flowers done in the manner of Timothy Canty, unfired, orig cover 400.00
Camphor, 3-1/2" h, tinted yellow ground, pressed leaf dec, silver plated top 55.00
Cranberry, Optic pattern, orig top 225.00
Crown Milano, melon shape, ribbed, dec, Mt. Washington two-pc top 395.00
Custard, Paneled Teardrop 110.00
Cut Glass, Russian pattern alternating with clear panels, orig SS top 375.00
Hobbs, Venetian Diamond pattern, cranberry 125.00
Imperial, ice blue 35.00
Milk glass, Netted Oak pattern, 4-1/4" h, oak leaf centered on netted panels, green top band, Northwood (F495) 85.00
Mt. Washington, Albertine, egg shape, orig top 295.00
Opalescent
    Beatty Rib, blue 250.00
    Bubble Lattice, blue, bulbous ring neck, orig top 225.00
    Coin Spot, blue, ring neck 135.00
    Daisy and Fern, Parian Swirl mold, cranberry 385.00
    Leaf Umbrella, orig top, Northwood 295.00
    Spanish Lace, cranberry, orig top 150.00
Opaque
    Acorn, pink, heavy floral enamel 225.00
    Parian Swirl, green, dec 110.00
Pattern Glass
    Banded Portland, maiden's blush, orig tip 125.00
    Block and Fan, clear 40.00
    Broken Column, ruby stained 200.00
    Connecticut, clear 35.00
    Galloway, rose stained 100.00
    Illinois, clear 65.00
    Kokomo, ruby stained 75.00
    Pineapple and Fan 40.00
    Royal Oak, frosted crystal, orig top 294.00
    Wisconsin, clear 90.00
Ruby Stained, Duncan Late Block, orig top 294.00
Smith Bros., Ribbed Pillar, dec 375.00
Wave Crest, 3" h, 3-1/4" d, Helmschmeid Swirls, pale lime-yellow ground, pastel pink rococo swags, raised gold borders, tendrils of gray blossoms rising from base of each of eight swirls, metal lid with emb florals and rococo swags . . 585.00

SURVEYORS' INSTRUMENTS

History: From the very beginning of civilized cultures, people have wanted to have a way to clearly delineate what lands they owned. Surveying instruments and equipment of all kinds were developed to help in this important task. The ancients learned to use the sun and other astronomical bodies as their guides. Early statesmen like Washington and Jefferson used brass and ebony instruments as they surveyed the young America. A surveyor must know how to measure lines and angles of a piece of land, using the principles of geometry and trigonometry.

To accomplish this often complicated mathematics, instruments of all types were invented and often patented. Accuracy is important, so many are made with precision components. A surveyor's level is an instrument, which consists of a revolving telescope mounted on a tripod and it is fitted with cross hairs and a spirit level. It is designed to allow surveyors to find points of identical elevation. A transit is used to measure horizontal angles and consists of a telescope mounted at right angles to a horizontal east-west axis. English mathematician, Leonard Digges invented an instrument called a "theodolite" which is used to measure vertical and horizontal angles. From a simple compass to high tech transits, today's collectors are finding these devices interesting. Fine examples of early instruments are coming into the antiques and collectibles marketplace as modern day surveyors now use sophisticated lasers and computers.

References: Florian Cajori, *History of the Logarithmic Slide Rule and Allied Instruments*, Astragal Press, 1994; Gloria Clifton, *Directory of British Scientific Instrument Makers 1550-1851*, P. Wilson Publishers, 1994; William H. Skerritt, *Catalog of the Charles E. Smart Collection: Antique Surveying Instruments*, published by author, (12 Locust Ave., Troy, NY 12180), 1996; Gerard L. E. Turner, *Scientific Instruments 1500-1900: An Introduction*, University of California Press, 1998.

Periodicals: Rittenhouse, P.O. Box 151, Hastings-on-Hudson, NY 10706; Scientific, Medical & Mechanical Antiques, P.O. Box 412, Taneytown, MD 21787.

Collectors' Clubs: International Calculator Collectors Club, 14561 Livingston St., Tustin, CA 92680; The Oughtred Society, 2160 Middlefield Rd., Palo Alto, CA 94301; Zeiss Historical Society, P.O. Box 631, Clifton, NJ 07012.

Museum: National Museum of American History, Smithsonian Institution, Washington, D.C.

SPECIAL AUCTIONS

Auction Team Köln
P.O. Box 50 11 19, D-50981 Koeln
Bonner St., 528-530, D-50968 Koeln
Köln Germany
0221/38 70 49

Skinner, Inc.
357 Main St.
Bolton MA 01740
(508) 779-6241

Alidade

Coast survey type, 11-1/4" h, 5" l strider level, 21" l, 3-3/4" w blade, 16-1/2" l telescope, vert. arc with control level, crossed vials and trough compass on blade, green leather finish, orig case, "Buff & Buff, Boston, 3588," c1905 . . . . .1,100.00

High Post Plane Table, Keuffel & Esser Co., NY 73903, model 5093A, 7-1/2" h, 10" telescope, 3" x 18" l blade, one beveled edge, strider level, 2" rad. Beaman Stradia Arc, trough compass and bull's eye vial on blade, japanned and "leather"" black finish on bras, orig case, c1940 . . . . 460.00

Astronomical Transit, 20" h, 8-1/2" w, 15-3/4" telescope with right angle prism eyep., removable strider, 7" d double frame, 2 vernier, vertical circle with indexing vial and circle control, 6" d, 2 vernier, 15", silver horizontal scale, plate vial with ivory scale, tribrach leveling base, bright brass finish, pine case, "Blunt, New York," c1860 . . . . .7,475.00

Compass/Theodite, 13-1/4" h, 7" w, tribrach leveling base, 9-1/4" l telescope with 4" l telescope vial, 3-1/2" rad , 1' vernier vert. arc., plate vials, 4-1/2" compass with silvered dial and outer ring, 5" rad , 2 vernier, 1' horiz. scale, 4-1/4" l hinged sight vanes, bronzed and lacquered brass, leather clad mahogany case, "Troughton & Simm's London," c1850. . . . . .1,035.00

Compass/Wye Level, 14" h, 5-3/8" w, 17-1/2" l telescope, 8" l ebony encased telescope vial, 4" l, needle over 32 point star mariner's card, 1º ivory ring, 4 ivory leveling screws, "G. L. Whitehouse, Farmington, N.H.," c1840 . . . . .5,520.00

Flat Plate Transit, Edmund Draper, Philadelphia, #259, 13-1/2" h, 7-3/4" w, 10" telescope, 5" d vert. circle, 4-1/2" compass, 6" d single vernier, silver horiz. scale, 2 plate vials, 4 screw leveling, darkened brass finish, pine case, c1850 . .1,725.00

Military Level, 7" h, 6" w, 9-1/4" telescope with high precision vial viewed by prism, quick leveling bull's eye vial, micrometer controlled precise adjustment, battery powered lighting, brass construction, beige enamel finish, orig case with 15 accessories,"10X C. L. Berger & Sons, Boston, Mass, ML1407," c1950 . . . . 375.00

Nonius Compass, 6"

15-1/8" l, 6-7/8" w, 7-1/8" h, 5-1/4" l detachable sight vanes, top designed to hold 7/8" d telescope, plate vials, silvered dial and edge engraved outer ring, unique 5' vernier moves the sough sight vane by means of a worm gear, mahogany case, "J. Hanks, Troy, NY," c1825. . . . . .1,725.00

15-7/8" l, 6-7/8" w, 9-1/2" h, 7-1/4" l detachable sight vanes, 4-3/4" rad , 20º 1' outside vernier, plaint vials, finely engraved and silvered dial and outer ring, staff adapter, lacquered brass, "Phelps & Gurley, Troy, NY," c1850 . . . . .2,530.00

Reconnaissance Transit

Buff & Buff Mfg. Co., Boston, 12007. 10-1/2" h, 5-1/4" w, 8 3/4" l telescope with rt. Angle solar eyep., 3-1/2" vial, 4" d vert. circle, crossed vials, 3" compass 4-1/2" d, 2 vernier, 1', silver horiz. scale, 4 screw leveling., black leather finished brass, mahogany box, c1918 . . . . 920.00

Keuffel & Esser Co., New York, 37037, 10" h, 7-3/4" l telescope, 3-1/2" d vert. circle, 3-1/2" compass, 5" d horiz. circle, telescope and plate vials, 4 screw leveling, orig box with plummet and accessories, c1918 . . . . 800.00

Saegmuller Solar Attachment, Fauth & Co., Washington, DC, Saegmuller's pat May 2, 81, 6-1/2" l, 4" h, brass and aluminum construction, level vial, sun lens, horiz. motion, c1885 . 920.00

Solar Transit, 17" h, Burt Solar Attachment, hour circle, 6.45" engineer's transit, 11" telescope, 3" rad vert. arc., 5" compass, telescope and plate vials, 4 screw leveling, brass construction, rubbed bronze finish, detailed mahogany case, label, brass plummet, accessories, "W. & L. E. Gurley, Troy, NY," c1890 . . . . .3,335.00

Surveying/Astronomical Theodite, 15-1/2" h, 10-1/2" l telescope, 5-1/2" d, 2 vernier vertical circle, 6", 2 vernier 20" horiz. circle, telescope and plate vials, microscope vernier readers, detachable alcohol lamp, detachable 4 screws leveling base, trough compass on telescope, orig. dovetailed mahogany box with accessories, Heller & Brightly label, mahogany ext., leg tripod, "Stanley, Great Turnstile, Holborn, London, 7535," c1890 . . . . .2,185.00

Surveyors' Compass

Chandler, A., Concord, N.H.

13-1/8" l, 5-3/8" w, 7-7/8" h, detachable sight vanes, crossed vials, silvered dial and outer ring, darkened brass, case with key and brass plummet, c1840 . . . . .2,185.00

14" l, 6" w, 8" h, detachable brass sight vanes, mahogany encased compass with 4-3/4" needle, 32 point star, Mass Bay Colony Indian, fleur-de-lis, on paper card engraved by Callender, brass outer ring, old leather and brass tack enclosed box with 2 pole Gunters chain and brass plummet, c1850 . . . . .2,645.00

Davenport, W., Phila., 15-3/4" l, 7" w, 9" h, 6-5/8" l detachable brass sight vanes, single 3" lone E-W level vial with sliding cover, silvered dial and outer ring, 6" l brass adapter and brass cover, worn fitted dovetailed mahogany case with brass fittings, Knox & Shain label, c1820 . . . . 920.00

Draper, Edmund, Philada. Warranted, 4-7/8" l, 3-1/2" w, 2-1/4" h, 1-9/16" l detachable sight vanes and brass cover, brass construction, silvered dial, raised azimuth ring, 4-1/2" x 4-1/2" x 1-5/8" dovetailed fitted mahogany case, c1835. . .1,500.00

Dupee, John, Boston, 14" l, walnut, engraved compass rose "Made & Sold by John Dupee ye North Side Swingbridge Boston New Eng.," protective cover, mid 18th C . . .1,955.00

Surveyors' Instrument, 1-3/4" h, 10-1/4" w, 4-7/8" d, wood and brass, sgd "Made by C. Elliott in New-London 1766," stand missing 3,750.00

Surveyors' and Engineers' Transit

Buff & Burger, Boston, #2149, 11" telescope wit vial, vert. arc., 6-1/4", 30" horiz. circle with inlaid silver scales, plate vials, 4 screw leveling, green leather finish, orig dovetailed mahogany box with labels, c1890 . . . . 920.00

Heller & Brightly Makers Philadelphia 4601, 13-3/4" h, 8-3/8" w, 10-1/2" l telescope, 6-1/4" l, vial 4-1/2" d vert. circle, cross sights, crossed vials, 5" compass with black dial and silver ring, 6-1/4" d, 2 vernier, 1', silver horiz. scale, detachable 4 screw leveling base, sgd by "E. H. Phelps," bronzed brass, orig case and accessories, c1872 . . . . .1,495.00

Pike, B. & Sons, 166 Broadway (N.Y.), 10-1/2" h, 8-3/8" w, 9-1/4" l telescope with vertical circle, 5" compass, 6-1/2" d horiz. scale (single vernier), telescope vial, plate vials, lacquered brass, orig mahogany case with Gurley label, dated 11/11/1873 . . . . 980.00

Theodolite

Stackpole & Brother, New York, 147, city, 8-3/4" h, 6-3/4" w, 14" l telescope with 6" l vial, telescope reversible in yokes, crossed vials, 3-1/4" compass, 6" d, 2 vernier, 20" beveled, silver horiz. scale, 4 screw leveling, sgd "Moody 1886," and "P. Leustn/France Richeau," darkened brass, tripod, c1865 . . . . .1,150.00

Stackpole & Brother, New York, 1559, miniature, 8-1/2" h, 4-1/8" w, 7-1/8" l telescope with vial, 3-1/4" d, 1' vert. circle, 2" compass, 3-1/2" d, 2 vernier, 1' vert. circle, 2" compass, 3-1/2" d 2 vernier, 1' silver horiz. scale, tribrach leveling base, black and brass finish, orig box, extension leg tripod, c1870 . . . . .1,495.00

Theodolite/Level, one minute type, Wm Wurdemann, Washington, DC, 10" l telescope, 5-1/2" h, labeled "Gr. No. 5," 4" d, 1' vernier, silver metal horiz. scale, bull's eye level vial, telescope motion screw, 3 screw leveling base, telescope reversible in its yokes, c1860 . . . . 635.00

Theodolite with Compass, Wm Wurdemann, Washington, DC, No. 155, 10-1/2" reversible telescope, 12-3/4" h, 6" d silver metal horiz. scale, 2 microscope read verniers, 4" compass,

Top left: Bausch, Lomb and Saegmuller level, brass and enameled brass, some wear, rings for tube have engine turnings, mahogany case, 8-3/8" x 21", $330; top right: W. & L. E. Gurley level, orig carrying case and tripod, 6-3/8" x 11-1/4", $300; middle row: left, Wm. Ainsworth & Sons, Denver, CO level, enameled brass, some wear, dovetailed mahogany case with leather strap, $300; middle right: unidentified maker, level, tripod, and carrying case, with wear, 6-3/4" x 11-1/4", $275; bottom row: left: (scientific instrument) J. Dubosco & P. Pelin, Paris, colorimeter, brass, steel base, label "Arthur Thomas, Phila," minor surface rust, 15-1/2", $385; center: Sikes Hydrometer, inlaid mahogany case with label "Re-adjusted by W. R. Loftus Ltd. London," plate missing from ext. lid, 2" x 8" x 4", $110; left: small microscope, mahogany case, 3" x 8-3/4" x 3-1/2", $140. Photo courtesy of Garth's Auctions, Inc.

single plate vial, telescope vial, 3 screw leveling base and truss frame, c1865 . . . . .1,725.00

Vernier Compass

Gurley, W. & L. E., Troy, NY, 13-1/4" h, 11" telescope, 6" compass with outside declination vernier, crossed plate vials, detachable 4 screw leveling base, leveling adapter, sunshade, orig mahogany box with label, bronzed finish brass, c1865 . . . . .2,300.00

Helffricht. Wm, Maker Philadelphia, 14-7/8" l, 6-1/2" w, 9-5/8" h, 7-1/4" l detachable sight vanes, crossed level vials, 16 count outkeeper, 25º 5' vernier, silvered dial and outer ring, brass cover, 6" l, adapter, dovetailed mahogany box with 20 1/2" x 3-1/2" Helffricht label, sgd "C. S. Woolman," c1850 . . . . .1,150.00

Young, Wm. J, Maker 3694 Philadelphia, 13-3/4" l, 6-1/8" w, 9-1/4" h, detachable sight vanes, bull's eye vial (empty), outkeeper, non-reflecting dial and silver ring, 25º 5' vernier, brass cover and 6-1/8" l adapter, darkened brass, case and Jacob staff 1,725.00

Wye Level

Kuebler & Seelhorst Makers Philada, 597, Oct 1, 1867 patent, eyep. attachment, 8-1/4" h, 4" w, 16-1/4" l, 1-3/8" d reversible telescope with 6-3/4" l vial, 4 screw leveling base, horiz. motion clamp and screw, c1870 . . . . 490.00

Young & Sons, Philadelphia 8219, 7-1/2" h, 5-1/4" w, 17-1/2" telescope with 6-1/4" l vial, unique patent pending bayonet-type tripod mount leveling head arrangement, lacquered bright brass, mahogany case, c1907 . . . . .1,265.00

SWORDS

History: The first swords used in America came from Europe. The chief cities for sword manufacturing were Solingen in Germany, Klingenthal in France, and Hounslow and Shotley Bridge in England. Among the American importers of these foreign blades was Horstmann, whose name is found on many military weapons.

New England and Philadelphia were the early centers for American sword manufacturing. By the Franco-Prussian War, the Ames Manufacturing Company of Chicopee, Massachusetts, was exporting American swords to Europe.

Sword collectors concentrate on a variety of styles: commissioned vs. non-commissioned officers' swords, presentation swords, naval weapons, and swords from a specific military branch, such as cavalry or infantry. The type of sword helped identify a person's military rank and, depending on how he had it customized, his personality as well.

Following the invention of repeating firearms in the mid-19th century, the sword lost its functional importance as a combat weapon and became a military dress accessory.

References: *Swords and Hilt Weapons*, Barnes & Noble Books, 1993; Gerald Welond, *Collector's Guide to Swords, Daggers & Cutlasses*, Chartwell Books, 1991.

Museum: Fort Ticonderoga Museum, Ticonderoga, NY.

American, eagle head, militia officer

30" l, single edged blade, etched with cast floral cross guard, shield shaped langets with American eagle, carved ivory grip, eagle head pommel and chain guard, brass scabbard with engraved dec 450.00

30-1/2" l, single edged curved blade, 1-1/4" w with stirrup guard, eagle head pommel and ribbed ivory grip, blued blade, gilt dec, leather scabbard with brass mounts, once

Officer's, Model 1837, eagle hilt, 29" blade, $750.

silver plated, traces of old blue and dec on blade 775.00

French Dragoon Cavalry Officer, 38" l single edged curved blade by Glingenthal, dated 1823, right face of blade engraved "Donne Par Le Roi," cast brass fore branch dec guard with laurel leaf dec on pommel, underside of guard stamped "Manceaus A Paris," leather grip with twisted brass wire, iron scabbard with two carrying rings, bright blade 950.00

Katana, Japanese, 27-1/2" l blade, suri-age nakago, two mekugi-ana, two characters showing on nakago, but very faint, bohi on both sides of blade that run back behind the habakimoto, hobi painted with red lacquer on both sides, blade attributed to Bizen, late Koto/early Shinto period, sword mountings of gold foil habaki, pierced heart design, some wear to sides, iron with gold trim fuchi kashira, gold trim mon in center on one side, tsuka wrapped in black ito maki, menuki of gold, silver with shukudo floral design incorporating shishi dog motif, tsuba is 3" old iron sukashi with cherry blossoms, birds, and mon design, fine patina, saya mounted with iron and gold trim tachi style fittings which match fuchi 2,400.00

Naval Cutlass, 1861 Pattern handle with large basket, brass handguard, riveted to single knuckle bow, 26" l slightly curved iron bade with wide unstopped fuller, completely unmarked on ricasso or spine, pommel cap mkd "13," quillion mkd "11M/644". 300.00

Presentation, Pattern of 1860 Staff Officer's sword, 31" narrow double edge blade etched on both sides or 13-1/2" with pattern of s rolls, eagle, and trophy of arms, obverse ricasso stamped "Ridabock & Co/New York" within oval plus "Made in France" within curved banner, reserve with maker's mark "FBD" combined with vase and torch, all within an oval, very detailed brass hilt with lion head quillion, openwork guard with raised eagle clutching olive branches and arrows, pearl grips would with twisted brass wire, folding langet handsomely engraved "Presented to/Genl. Stillman F. Kneeland/By a few of his friends/Jan. 1st 1897," German silver scabbard with very elaborate cast gilded brass mounts, accompanied by papers relating to Kneeland's military service 2,000.00

Springfield Armory Light Infantry, late ceremonial type, 30" x 7/8" blade, etched both sides with usual pattern, four branch handguard and finger groove wood grip, all nickel plated, orig scabbard, langet and quillion bent, one branch of knuckle guard missing. 150.00

US Civil War Non-Regulation Staff and Field Officer, 32-1/2" l single edged straight blade with etched panels having US and spread-winged eagle ricasso mkd "Clauberg" and "Schuler Hartlery & Graham, New York," iron half basket guard with eagle over US, fish skin wrapped grip with twisted brass wire, iron scabbard, uncleaned blade, medium gray patina, lightly pitted hilt and scabbard 600.00

US Model 1833, Foot Artillery, 19" l double edge wide blade mkd "N. P. Ames/Springfield" and dated 1835, cast brass hilt with fish scale grip eagle on pommel, black leather scabbard with brass mounts, leather belt and frog with two pc US belt plate 950.00

US Model 1840

Light Artillery, 32-1/2" curved single edged blade, manuf by Ames, dated 1863, cast brass D-guard leather and twisted wire wrap grip, iron scabbard with two carrying rings and throat 600.00

Non Commissioned Officer, 32" single edged straight blade, cast brass hilt, clam shell guard, leather scabbard with brass mounts, manuf by Ames, dated 1864. . . . . 500.00

US Model 1850

Foot Officer, 31" l single edged black etched with no makers mark, etching of US eagle, military and floral motifs and "US," cast brass floral half-basket guard, fish skin and twisted wire wrapped grip, brass mounted leather scabbard, top mount stamped "Ames Mfg. Co., Chicaopee, Ma" 800.00

Foot Officer, 31-1/4" l single edged blade with bold etching, military and floral motifs, US and spread-winged eagle, cast brass half basket hilt with leather wrap grip and twisted wire, leather scabbard with brass mounts, manuf. By C. Roby & Co., W Chelmsfort, MA. 1,050.00

Foot Officer, 32" l single edged blade with etched panel having "US" on one side, spread winged eagle opposite, cast brass half-basket hilt with regulation floral motif, fish skin wrapped grip with regulation floral motif, steel scabbard with brass mounts, mkd "Schuyler, Hartley & Graham, New York" 700.00

Staff and Field, 31-1/2" l single edged blade etched with US American eagle, military and floral motifs, unsigned blade, large cast brass floral half-basket guide with US fish skin and twisted wire grip, solid brass scabbard gold plated with line engraved mounts, blade retains most of its frosty etched appearance, hilt has been cleaned, scabbard fine with untouched patina, no dents .2,500.00

Staff and Field, officer's, 31" l single edge etched blade, made by "C. Roby & Co., W. Chemsford, Ma," etching of US eagle, military and floral motifs, and "US," cast brass floral half-basket guard, fish skin and twisted wire wrapped grip, brass mounted leather scabbard .1,100.00

Staff and Field, officer's 33-1/2" l single edged straight blade etched in floral cast brass, half-basket guard with US, fish skin and twisted wire wrapped grip, steel scabbard with dec brass mounts, severely cleaned blade, almost all etching removed, good grip, floral engraving on scabbard 750.00

Staff and Field, officer's, 33-1/2" l single edged straight blade etched in two panels, spread winged eagle and US, mkd "Emerson & Silver/Trenton" on ricasso, floral cast brass half-basket guard with US, fish kin and twisted wire wrapped grip, steel scabbard with dec brass mounts 1,900.00

Staff and Field, presentation grade, 31-3/4" l imported German blade by W. Clauberg of Soligen, standing knight logo, one side floral engravings with "US" in center panel, other side with floral engraving with eagle and "E. Pluribus Unum," some dark spots, overall good condition, etching crisp, hilt gilted brass with some areas of gilt remaining, "US" with floral work to guard, quillion in form of eagle's head, brass drip with wire wrap comprised of small chain link, metal 2 ring scabbard with fancy throat, brass drag and hanger mounts 2,000.00

US Model 1860

General, Staff and Field, 30" double edged straight bade, etched panels covering 75% of length, dec in gold, spread-edged winged eagle, US on one side, presentation "Brig. Gen'l Hunter C. White" on other side, Soligen-made blade etched "The M. C. Lilley & Co., Columbus, Ohio," double clam shell pierced cross guard in high relief, sterling silver American eagle applied to one side, pierced guard on reverse having oak leaf clusters with US in raised oval panel, heavily encrusted two branch D-guard with vines, roses, acanthus leaf, and other dec, standing urn-shaped pommel with relief cast suit of armor on cross swords, two pc mother-of-pearl grips with fancy triple laid brass wire wrap, gilt cloth blackened gold sword knot attached, bright nickel plated steel scabbard with heavy gilt and pierced floral mounts 5,000.00

Light Cavalry, 35" l, single edge curved blade, manuf by Ames, mkd "US" and inspected "G. G. S" on ricasso, dark uncleaned blade, c1860 . . . . 725.00

Light Cavalry, 35" l, single edge curved blade, marked "D. J. Millard/Clayville, NY," US inspected, date 1862, three branch cast brass guard with leather and wire wrapped grip, iron scabbard with two carrying rings 700.00

Light Cavalry, 35" l, single edge curved blade, marked "Mansfield & Lamb…," US inspected, date 1853, three branch cast brass guard with leather and wire wrapped grip, iron scabbard with two carrying rings 500.00

US Model 1862 Pattern, Cavalry, saber, belt, and buckle, standard configuration, 34-3/4" blade, single wide fuller, mkd on right ricasso "R&C" left mkd "IRON/PROOF," 3 branch brass handguard with twisted wire wrapped handle, iron scabbard, black suede textured sword belt and hangars, rect brass spread-winged eagle buckle with applied silver laurel leaves, inside of belt and hangers are light buff colored, with mark "W. Kinney/Newark, N.J." 1,000.00

US Non-Regulation, Staff & Field Officer, 32-1/4" single edged etched blade, iron basket hilt with spread-winged eagle and US cut-out, fish skin and twisted wire wrapped grip, steel scabbard, manuf by "W. Clauberg, Soligen," style known as "Peterson #75" 1,200.00

TEA CADDIES

History: Tea once was a precious commodity and was stored in special boxes or caddies. These containers were made to accommodate different teas and included a special cup for blending.

Around 1700, silver caddies appeared in England. Other materials, such as Sheffield plate, tin, wood, china, and pottery, also were used. Some tea caddies are very ornate.

4-1/2" x 5" x 3-1/2", burl wood inlaid, oval inlaid top with band inlay along sides, handled int. cov, ivory inlay escutcheon, late 18th C. 850.00

5" h, sterling silver, sterling, applied grapevine design, monogram, Frank W Smith Silver Co., Inc., retailed by A Stowell & Co., 19th/20th C, 6 troy oz 230.00

6-1/4" l, black lacquer, gilding, nacre inlay, painted lily of the valley dec, some edge damage 380.00

6-1/4" l, bronze, gold and silver gilding, four sides and lid with relief bull fighting scenes 450.00

7" h, 14" w, 7" d, mahogany, George III, silver mountings, handle marked "London, 1810," int. with two lidded containers, cut glass mixing bowl 230.00

7-1/2" l, fruitwood inlaid mahogany, inlaid shells and leaves, George III, cracking 435.00

7-1/2" h, 13-1/4" l, 6-3/4" d, parquetry, George III, sarcophagus shape, inlaid specimen woods, fitted int., two wells, cut glass mixing bowl, disc feet .1,725.00

7-5/8" l, 4-1/4" d, 5" h, oval, inlaid satinwood veneer, int. with mahogany divider and lids, turned ivory knobs, England or America, early 19th C, losses to leaded paper. 1,265.00

8" w, 4-1/2" w, 5" h, Regency, brass ball feet, two ivory finial cov compartments. 250.00

9" l, dome top

Burl Veneer, dec gilded brass strapping, int. has two compartments with lids with burl veneer, knobs with brass escutcheons initialed "B" and "G," loose strapping
. . . . 275.00

Walnut, openwork foliate mounts, brass mounted, int. with spring loaded domed receptacles, Victorian, 19th C
. . . . 700.00

Whieldon, Cauliflower pattern, beige and green, oval base, 4" h, $725.

11-3/4" l, 6-3/4" d, 8" h, Chippendale, mahogany, dovetailed case and molded edge lid, bracket feet, old finish, orig brass bale handle, mismatched escutcheon, int. dividers missing, repairs 1,650.00
12" l, mahogany veneer, edge inlay, inlaid escutcheon, brass ball feet, int. baffle, lids missing, replaced mixing bowl, English, some veneer damage. 220.00
12-1/2" l, brass mounted walnut, open foliate mounts, fitted int., Victorian, mid 19th C, one foot missing 375.00
14" w, 6-1/2" d, rosewood, Regency, sarcophagus, pearl inlay medallion on top, escutcheon plate, large lion mask end handles on bun feet, two box inserts 350.00
17" x 7-1/2" x 7-1/2", porcelain, sq, round cover, Cabbage and Butterfly, early 20th C. 320.00

TEA LEAF IRONSTONE CHINA

History: Tea Leaf ironstone flowed into America from England in great quantities from 1860 to 1910 and graced the tables of working-class America. It traveled to California and Texas in wagons and down the Mississippi River by boat to Kentucky and Missouri. It was too plain for the rich homes; its simplicity and durability appealed to wives forced to watch pennies. Tea Leaf found its way into the kitchen of Lincoln's Springfield home; sailors ate from it aboard the *Star of India*, now moored in San Diego and still displaying Tea Leaf.

Contrary to popular belief, Tea Leaf was not manufactured exclusively by English potters in Staffordshire. Although there were more than 35 English potters producing Tea Leaf, at least 26 American potters helped satisfy the demand.

Anthony Shaw (1850-1900) is credited with introducing Tea Leaf. The most prolific Tea Leaf makers were Anthony Shaw and Alfred Meakin (1875-present). Johnson Bros. (1883-present), Henry Burgess (1864-1892), Enoch Wedgwood, and Arthur J. Wilkinson (1897-present), all of whom shipped much of their ware to America.

Although most of the English Tea Leaf is copper luster, Powell and Bishop (1868-1878) and their successors,

Bishop and Stonier (1891-1936), worked primarily in gold luster. Beautiful examples of gold luster were also made by H. Burgess; Mellor, Taylor & Co. (1880-1904) used it on children's tea sets. Other English potters also were known to use gold luster, including W. & E. Corn, Thomas Elsmore, and Thomas Hughes, companies which have been recently identified as makers of this type of ware.

J. & E. Mayer, Beaver Falls, Pennsylvania, founded by English potters who immigrated to America, produced a large amount of copper luster Tea Leaf. The majority of the American potters decorated with gold luster that had no brown underglaze beneath the copper luster.

East Liverpool, Ohio, potters such as Cartwright Bros. (1864-1924), East End Pottery (1894-1909) and Knowles, Taylor & Knowles (1870-1934) decorated only in gold luster. This also is true of Trenton, New Jersey, potters, such as Glasgow Pottery, American Crockery Co., and Fell & Thropp Co. Since no underglazing was used with the gold, much of it has been washed away.

By the 1900s, Tea Leaf's popularity had waned. The sturdy ironstone did not disappear; it was stored in barns and relegated to attics and basements. While the manufacture of Tea Leaf did experience a brief resurgence from the late 1950s through the 1970s, copper lustre Tea Leaf didn't recapture the hearts of the American consumer as it had a generation before.

Tea Leaf collectors recognize a number of "variant" decorative motifs as belonging to the Tea Leaf family: Teaberry, Morning Glory, Coral, Cinquefoil, Rose, Pre-Tea Leaf, Tobacco Leaf, Pepper Leaf, Pinwheel, Pomegranate, and Thistle & Berry, as well as white ironstone decorated with copper lustre bands and floral and geometric motifs. Once considered the stepchildren of Tea leaf, these variants are now prized by collectors and generally bring strong prices.

Today's collectors eagerly seek out Tea Leaf and all of its variant motifs, and copper-lustre decorated white ironstone has once again become prized for its durability, beauty, simplicity, craft, and style.

References: Annise Doring Heaivilin, *Grandma's Tea Leaf Ironstone*, Wallace-Homestead, 1981, 1996 reprint distributed by L-W Book Sales; Jean Wetherbee, *White Ironstone, A Collector's Guide*, Tea Leaf Club International (324 Powderhorn Dr., Houghton Lake, MI 48629), 1996.

Collectors' Club: Tea Leaf Club International, 324 Powderhorn Dr., Houghton Lake, MI 48629.

Museums: Lincoln Home, Springfield, IL; Ox Barn Museum, Aurora, OR; Sherman Davidson House, Newark OH.

Advisor: Dale Abrams.

Notes: Tea Leaf values have increased steadily for the last decade, but there are some general rules of thumb for the knowledgeable collector. English Tea Leaf is still more collectible than American, except for rare pieces. The earlier the Tea Leaf production (1850s-1860s), the harder it is to find pieces and, therefore, the more expensive they are. Children's pieces are highly collectible, especially those with copper lustre decorative motifs.

Hard-to-find Tea Leaf pieces include mustache cups, eggcups, covered syrup pitchers, ladles, oversized serving pieces, and pieces with significant embossing. Common pieces (plates, platters) of later production (1880-1900) need to be in excellent condition or should be priced accordingly as they are not that difficult to find.

Apple Bowl, Shaw, low, ftd, fluted	475.00
Baker	
Meakin, 3-3/4" x 5-1/2" x 1-1/2" deep	27.00
Wilkinson, 6-1/2" x 9-1/2" x 1-1/2" deep	45.00
Bone Dish, Meakin	
Crescent shape	55.00
Scalloped edge	65.00
Brush Vase	
Burgess, 2 piece	325.00
Meakin, Chelsea	350.00
Mellor-Talyor, Hearts	450.00
Shaw, plain, round, drain hole	300.00
Butter Dish, 3 pc, top, liner, base	
Meakin, Bamboo	200.00
Wedgwood, simple square	185.00
Butter Pat, Meakin	
Round, Chelsea	25.00
Square	16.00
Cake Plate	
Edwards, Peerless (Feather), square, handles	195.00
Meakin, Bamboo, 8-3/4" d, handles	115.00
Shaw, Cable	180.00
Shaw, Senate shape	150.00
Chamber Pot	
Mellor-Taylor, Hearts	350.00
Shaw, Cable	325.00
Children's Dishes	
Cup and Saucer, handleless, Shaw, Lily of the Valley	425.00
Mug, Shaw	395.00
Tea Set, Mellor-Taylor, slant sided, gold luster, 6 cups and saucers, six plates, teapot, creamer, sugar, waste bowl	1,450.00
Coffeepot, cov	
Meakin, Bamboo	215.00
Meakin, Chelsea	365.00
Meakin, Fishhook	185.00
Shaw, Cable	350.00
Shaw, Chinese shape	425.00
Shaw, Lily of the Valley	525.00
Compote	
Burgess, plain, round	350.00
Red Cliff, (American, 1960s) simple square	150.00
Shaw, square	375.00
Creamer	
Davenport, Fig Cousin	425.00
Meakin, Bamboo	225.00
Meakin, Fishhook	195.00
Shaw, Cable	325.00
Shaw, Lily of the Valley	435.00
Cup and Saucer	
Adams, Empress shape, 1950s	35.00
Meakin	65.00
Shaw, Chinese shape, handleless	125.00
Shaw, Lily of the Valley, handle	125.00
Cup Plate, Meakin, 3-1/2" d	55.00
Egg Cup	
Meakin, Boston Egg Cup, 4" d, 1-3/4" h	395.00
Unmarked, 3-1/2" h	350.00

Platter, Alfred Meakin, England, Royal Ironstone China, oval, scalloped edges, single center Tea Leaf, 12-1/2" l, $55.

Gravy Boat	
Adams, Empress, attached stand, 1950s	150.00
Mayer, American	90.00
Meakin, Bamboo	85.00
Mellor-Taylor, lion's head	100.00
Wilkinson, Daisy 'n Chain	300.00
Mug	
Meakin, Scroll	210.00
Shaw, Chinese shape	125.00
Shaw, Lily of the Valley	425.00
Mush Bowl, Meakin	85.00
Nappy	
Meakin, Chelsea, round	22.00
Meakin, Fishhook, 4-1/4" sq	18.00
Wedgwood, 4-1/4" sq, scalloped edge	20.00
Pitcher/Jug	
Meakin, Chelsea	425.00
Meakin, Fishhook	325.00
Shaw, Cable shape, 7" h	325.00
Shaw, Chinese shape, 7-1/2" h	550.00
Plate	
Furnival, plain, round, 8-1/4" d	12.00
Johnson Bros., Acanthus, 9" d	25.00
Meakin, plain, round, 6-3/4" d	10.00
Shaw, plain, round, 10" d	25.00
Wedgwood, plain, round, 9-1/4"	18.00
Platter	
Meakin, Chelsea, 10" x 14", oval	65.00
Meakin, plain, 9" x 13", rect	35.00
Shaw, Lily of the Valley, 13" l	150.00
Posset Cup, unmarked, plain, round	350.00
Punch Bowl, Shaw, Cable, base and lid	800.00
Relish Dish	
Shaw, Chinese shape	295.00
Wedgwood, square ridged	55.00
Sauce Tureen	
Furnival, Little Cable, 4 pc, including ladle	425.00
Meakin, Bamboo, 4 pc, including label	495.00
Red Cliff, America, 1960s, 4 pc, including ladle	195.00
Serving Bowl, open	
Grindley, round, scalloped edge	150.00
Meakin, square, scalloped edge, 6" sq	55.00
Soap Dish, cov, cover, base, orig liner	
Grindley, Bamboo, rect disk	225.00

Mellor-Taylor, lion's head	250.00
Shaw, Cable, oval	325.00

Soup Bowl

Meakin, plain, round, 8-3/4" d	25.00
Shaw, plain, round, 10" d	50.00

Soup Tureen, 4 pc, cover, base, underplate, ladle

Meakin, Bamboo	1,550.00
Shaw, Cable	1,900.00

Sugar Bowl

Furnival, Victory shape	250.00
Meakin, Bamboo	110.00
Meakin, Fishhook	95.00
Shaw, Cable shape	175.00
Vanity Box, Shaw, Lily of the Valley	635.00

Vegetable Dish, covered

Meakin, Bamboo	165.00
Shaw, Basketweave	325.00
Shaw, Cable	245.00
Shaw, Hexagon	235.00

Wash Bowl and Pitcher Set

Furnival, Cable	495.00
Meakin, Fishhook	425.00
Shaw, Cable	550.00

Waste Bowl

Meakin, plain, round	95.00
Shaw, Niagara Fan	120.00

TEDDY BEARS

History: Originally thought of as "Teddy's Bears," in reference to President Theodore Roosevelt, these stuffed toys are believed to have originated in Germany. The first ones to be made in the United States were produced about 1902.

Most of the earliest teddy bears had humps on their backs, elongated muzzles, and jointed limbs. The fabric used was generally mohair; the eyes were either glass with pin backs or black shoe buttons. The stuffing was usually excelsior. Kapok (for softer bears) and wood-wool (for firmer bears) also were used as stuffing materials.

Quality older bears often have elongated limbs, sometimes with curved arms, oversized feet, and felt paws. Noses and mouths are black and embroidered onto the fabric.

The earliest teddy bears are believed to have been made by the original Ideal Toy Corporation in America and by a German company, Margarete Steiff, GmbH. Bears made in the early 1900s by other companies can be difficult to identify because they were all similar in appearance and most identifying tags or labels were lost during childhood play.

References: Pauline Cockrill, *Teddy Bear Encyclopedia*, Dorling Kindersley, 1993; Margaret and Gerry Grey, *Teddy Bears*, Courage Books, 1994; Pam Hebbs, *Collecting Teddy Bears*, Pincushion Press, 1992; Dee Hockenberry, *Bear Memorabilia*, Hobby House Press, 1992; —, *Big Bear Book*, Schiffer Publishing, 1996; Margaret Fox Mandel, *Teddy Bears and Steiff Animals*, 1st Series (1984, 1997 value update), 2nd Series (1987, 1996 value update), Collector Books; —, *Teddy Bears, Annalee Animals & Steiff Animals*, 3rd Series, Collector Books, 1990, 1996 value update; Linda Mullins, *Teddy Bear & Friends Price Guide*, 4th ed., Hobby House Press, 1993; —,

Raikes Bear & Doll Story, Hobby House, 1991; —, *Teddy Bears Past & Present*, Vol. II, Hobby House Press, 1992; —, *Tribute to Teddy Bear Artists*, Series 2, Hobby House Press, 1996; Jesse Murray, *Teddy Bear Figurines Price Guide*, Hobby House, 1996; Sue Pearson and Dottie Ayers, *Teddy Bears: A Complete Guide to History, Collecting, and Care*, McMillan, 1995; Cynthia Powell, *Collector's Guide to Miniature Teddy Bears*, Collector Books, 1994; Carol J. Smith, *Identification & Price Guide to Winnie the Pooh Collectibles*, Hobby House Press, 1994.

Periodicals: *Antiques & Collectables*, P.O. Box Drawer 1565, El Cajon, CA 92022; *National Doll & Teddy Bear Collector*, P.O. Box 4032, Portland, OR 97208; *Teddy Bear and Friends*, 6405 Flank Dr., Harrisburg, PA 17112; *Teddy Bear Review*, 170 Fifth Ave., New York, NY 10010.

Collectors' Clubs: Good Bears of the World, P.O. Box 13097, Toledo, OH 43613; My Favorite Bear: Collectors Club for Classic Winnie the Pooh, 468 W Alpine #10, Upland, CA 91786.

Museum: Teddy Bear Museum of Naples, Naples, FL.

Additional Listings: See Steiff.

Notes: Teddy bears are rapidly increasing as collectibles and their prices are rising proportionately. As in other fields, desirability should depend upon appeal, quality, uniqueness, and condition. One modern bear already has been firmly accepted as a valuable collectible among its antique counterparts: the Steiff teddy put out in 1980 for the company's 100th anniversary. This is a reproduction of that company's first teddy and has a special box, signed certificate, and numbered ear tag; 11,000 of these were sold worldwide.

Bing, 15" h, white mohair, fully jointed, black shoe button eyes, rust embroidered nose, mouth, and claws, white felt pads, 1910 .... 1,265.00

Bruin, 28" h, golden mohair, fully jointed, glass eyes, tan felt pads, excelsior stuffing, pink silk and mohair jacket, worn, detached partial cloth label, c1907 .... 6,325.00

Clemens, 17" h, long gold mohair, fully jointed, glass eyes, brown embroidered nose and mouth, excelsior stuffing, c1940, spotty fur loss 290.00

Herman, 19" h, golden mohair, no side seams, fully jointed, shoe button eyes, fabric nose, embroidered mouth, excelsior stuffing, replaced pads 175.00

Ideal

10-1/2" h, golden mohair, fully jointed, black shoe button eyes, black embroidered nose, mouth, and claws, beige pads, excelsior stuffing, c1919, remnants of red felt tongue, minor fur loss 425.00

12" h, white mohair, fully jointed, black shoe button eyes, tan embroidered nose, mouth, and claws, felt pads, well loved 575.00

19" h, golden mohair, fully jointed, black steel eyes, tan felt pads, black embroidered nose, mouth, and claws, c1905, fur flattened on back 5,750.00

20" h, golden mohair, fully jointed, glass eyes, fabric nose, embroidered mouth and claws, felt pads, excelsior stuffing, early 1920s 350.00

Mohair, brown, 20" h, $1,025, Hertel, Schwab & Co. #152 baby doll, 12" h, $400. Photo courtesy of McMasters Auctions.

Schuco
    4-3/4" h, Yes/No, yellow mohair, fully jointed, black steel eyes and eye glasses, early 20th C, minor fur loss 435.00
    5" h, dancing, gold mohair, black steel eyes, embroidered nose and mouth, arm jointed at shoulders, red felt beret and trousers, black metal feet, key, 1930, 5" h 290.00

Steiff
    9-1/2" h, blond mohair, fully jointed, felt pads, black steel eyes, dark brown embroidered nose, mouth, and claws, excelsior stuffing, blank ear button, c1905, well loved
    . . . . 500.00
    22" h, golden mohair, few signs of moth damage, c1905
    . . . . .10,065.00

Unknown Maker
    3-3/8" h, cast iron, sitting, brown asphaltum finish fair
    . . . . 150.00
    5-3/4" h, 7-1/2" l, light brown velveteen, glass eyes, wooden platform base, metal wheels, early 20th C, some pile loss
    . . . . 225.00
    12" h, polar, off-white mohair, glass eyes, composition nose and open mouth with teeth, Distler key, French clockwork
    . . . . 980.00
    13" h, yellow mohair, fully jointed, shoe button eyes, tan embroidered nose and claws, excelsior stuffing, well loved
    . . . . 290.00
    19" h, yellow mohair, fully jointed, glass eyes, embroidered nose and mouth, excelsior stuffing, pads replaced, some arm damage, fur loss 1,150.00

Related
    Candy Container, 21" h, yellow plush fur, glass eyes, black embroidered nose and mouth, unjointed, head lifts off to reveal container, blue polka dot overalls, 1920s 460.00
    Sand Pail, 5-5/8" h, litho tin, teddy bear band 345.00
    Teething Ring, 3-7/8" d, sterling, teddy holding bells, mother-of-pearl mouthpiece, early 20th C 375.00

TEPLITZ CHINA

History: Around 1900, there were 26 ceramic manufacturers located in Teplitz, a town in the Bohemian province of what was then known as Czechoslovakia. Other potteries were located in the nearby town of Turn. Wares from these factories were molded, cast, and hand decorated. Most are in the Art Nouveau and Art Deco styles.

Marks: The majority of pieces do not carry a specific manufacturer's mark; they are simply marked "Teplitz," "Turn-Teplitz," or "Turn."

Bowl, 5-1/2" d, girl pulling rooster's tail, marked "Stellmacher"
. . . . 75.00
Candlestick, 5-1/4", figural, woman wearing flowing gown
. . . . 150.00
Compote, 6" d, Art Nouveau woman, high relief florals, marked "Amphora-Teplitz". 400.00
Ewer
    10" h, Art Nouveau, scrolled and gold beaded handle, reticulated ruffled collar, goldfish lip spout, raised gold outlined flowers 425.00
    11-1/2" h, flower dec, ornate handle, marked "Turn Teplitz Bohemia" 225.00
Figure, 18-1/2" h, young woman, elaborate dress 450.00
Loving Cup, 15" h, 9-3/4" w, reticulated outer wall, turquoise, amber, opal, and cobalt blue jewels, gold scalloped rim, foot, and twisted branch handles 350.00
Pitcher, 9-1/2" h, green and pink, lily pad dec, c1895
. . . . 225.00
Vase
    7" h, enameled caped gentleman, mkd "Teplitz Stellmacher"
    . . . . 100.00

Figure, Arab warrior and horse, mkd "Amphora Teplitz," base, imp mark, 10" h, 9-3/4" l oval, $400.

8-1/2" h, molded intricate design, gold highlights, cram ground, blown-out stylized design at top, pink centers, designed by Paul Daschel, stamp mark. 700.00

13" h, 5-1/4" d, Art Nouveau-style, woman's head with flowing hair and blossoms, stems form two asymmetrical handles, ochre and green, ink stamped mark 450.00

14" h, 6" d, corseted, bulbous top, Secessionist-style dec, emb stylized white roses and gilded leaves, blue-gray ground 600.00

15" h, winged gold and ivory creature at neck, reticulated top with applied flowers, bulbous ribbed bottom with painted flowers outlined in gold, stamped mark, minor chips and repairs 290.00

TEXTILES

History: Textiles is the generic term for cloth or fabric items, especially anything woven or knitted. Antique textiles that have survived are usually those that were considered the "best" by their original owners, since these were the objects that were used and stored carefully by the housewife.

Textiles are collected for many reasons—to study fabrics, to understand the elegance of a historical period, for decorative purposes, or to use as was originally intended. The renewed interest in antique clothing has sparked a revived interest in period textiles of all forms.

References: Dilys E. Blum, *The Fine Art of Textiles: The Collection of the Philadelphia Museum of Art*, Philadelphia Museum of Art, 1997; Gideon Bosker, Michele Mancini, John Gramstad, *Fabulous Fabrics of the 50s, and Other Terrific Textiles of the 20s, 30s, and 40s*, Chronicle Books, 1992; M. Dupont-Auberville, *Full-Color Historic Textile Designs*, Dover Publications, 1996; Frances Johnson, *Collecting Household Linens*, Schiffer Publishing, 1997; Sheila Paine, *Embroidered Textiles: Traditional Patterns from Five Continents, With a Worldwide Guide To Identification*, Thames & Hudson, 1997; Pamela Smith, *Vintage Fashion and Fabrics*, Alliance Publishing, 1995; Jessie A. Turbayne, *Hooked Rug Treasury*, Schiffer Publishing, 1997; ——, *Hookers' Art: Evolving Designs in Hooked Rugs*, Schiffer Publishing, 1993; Sigrid Wortmann Weltge, *Women's Work*, Chronicle Press, 1993.

Periodicals: International Old Lacers Bulletin, P.O. Box 481223, Denver, CO 80248; Lace Collector, P.O. Box 222, Plainwell, MI 49080; Textile Museum Newsletter, The Textile Museum, 2320 S. St. NW, Washington, DC 20008.

Collectors' Clubs: Costume Society of America, 55 Edgewater Dr., P.O. Box 73, Earleville, MD 21919; Stumpwork Society, P.O. Box 122, Bogota, NJ 07603.

Museums: Cooper-Hewitt Museum, New York, NY; Currier Gallery of Art, Manchester, NH; Ipswich Historical Society, Ipswich, MA; Lace Museum, Mountain View, CA; Museum of American Textile History, North Andover, MA; Museum of Art, Rhode Island School of Design, Providence, RI; Philadelphia College of Textiles & Science, Philadelphia, PA; Textile Museum, Washington, DC; Valentine Museum, Richmond, VA.

Additional Listings: See Clothing; Lace and Linens; Quilts; Samplers.

Blanket
79" x 82", overshot plaid wool, scarlet, navy, and green 375.00
81-1/2" x 70", twill woven wool, initialed and dated "M. M. March the 10 1840," green, rust, sage, and yellow yarns 850.00
96" x 80", twill woven wool, initialed and dated "R.S. 1886," navy and cream yarns 375.00
97" x 75", twill woven wool, initialed "MDC," navy and cream yarns 375.00
Call Bell Pull, floral needlework, soft colors, gold silk ground, gilded brass fittings, very worn, 79" l 200.00
Coverlet, embroidered, 98" x 104", initialed and dated "E. H. 1804," scrolled green, salmon, yellow, navy, and purple flowering vines, linen ground, toning, scattered staining, minor fiber wear 6,900.00
Coverlet, jacquard, two piece
75" x 82", double weave, navy blue and natural white, "Rough and Ready" and "1847" in corners, commemorates Zachary Taylor, attributed to Samuel Graham, unsewn, stains and wear, incomplete fringe 4,950.00
76" x 85", star medallions, vintage border with trees and birds, corners labeled "Samuel Slaybaugh, Bucyrus, Crawford County, Ohio, 1849," red, green, blue, and natural white, minor damage 550.00
81" x 79", blue and white, floral border on three sides, floral medallion pattern, double weave, dated on opposite ends "1849," small hole, some staining, some fringe missing 250.00
82" x 74", mustard and tomato red, double grape and leaf border, three sides with fringe of mustard and red stripes, double weave, top border of small alternating owl and mouse design. 325.00
83" x 74", nine star variant, navy and red, cream ground 990.00
83" x 83", double flower pattern with eagle and foliate border, corner reads "Caroline I. Mott 1835. French Weaver Waterville," NY, fiber wear, minor repairs 1,100.00
86" x 73", blue, green, and red, two sided fringe mostly gone, double weave, both sides, same end corners sgd "J. Keagy Globe Factory Morrisons Cove, Bedford County, Penn'a," other side corners sgd "J. Keagy Globe J. Keagy" 300.00
86" x 74", double heart and potted plant, eagle border, indistinctly sgd corner block, "wove in 1840". 375.00
86" x 78", double rose, eagle and shield border, navy and white, corner block sgd and dated "J. Impson 1844 Cortland County," minor staining, scattered fiber wear 375.00
89" x 71", red and white, double rose and pedals, leaf border, fringe on one end, double weave. 300.00
89" x 72", red and blue, single star border, three sided fringe with tulips and snowflake design, double weave, sgd opposite corners "John Redick, Troy Township, Richland County, Ohio 1853" 950.00
89" x 82", red and blue, large center medallion of star inside sun design, four corners with large spread winged eagle, cornucopia borders, double weave, sgd on opposite ends "Made by Wm Ney, Myerstown, Lebanon County, PA" 750.00
Coverlet, overshot, 93" x 69", sunrise variant design, red and white, minor fiber wear 200.00
Coverlet, trapunto, 81-1/2" x 83", whitework, scrolling feather border centers reserve of basket of fruit and flowers, surrounded by foliate banding, fruit, birds, and corner fans, sgd "Mary E. Tuutenberg 1873," scattered minor staining and toning. 750.00

Crewel Work Picture, 21-2/3" h, 25-1/8" w, black urn filled with brightly colored flowers and birds, surrounded by various flowers, yellow ground, framed. 200.00

Embroidery, 19-3/4" h, 22-3/4" w, spread eagle clutching arrows and laurel atop American shield and flags, banner reads "E. Pluribus Unum," silver bullion highlights, China, 19th C, very minor staining, framed 920.00

Memorial, silk needlework

15-1/4" h, 15" w, "By Elizabeth Shute 11 years old," early 19th C, ink highlights, eglomise mat, framed 1,150.00

16-1/2" h, 13-1/2" w, oval reserve embroidery of woman kneeling in prayer among neoclassical urns and columns, brass sequin border, flowering vine outer border, watercolor highlights, early 19th C, toning, minor fiber wear, minor sequin loss. 275.00

17-5/8" h, 21" w, New England, early 19th C, young girl at three neoclassical urn-form memorials, tacked down, foxing, minor fading, note on back attributes embroidery to Elmina Clarinda Walker Greene, born 1805, died 1836 . . . . .5,175.00

Memorial Band, 49" l, loom beaded, multicolored geometric designs, "James Watson," wear and repair, stitched to cloth covered mounting board, Victorian. 25.00

Needlework Picture

13" h, 16" w, spread winged eagle over six draped American flags with banner "Pluribus Unum," shield, and anchor in center, black ground, lemon gold frame. 400.00

16-1/2" h, 20-1/2" w, silk, commemorating USS Franklin, eagle above life ring, picture of sailor and gunboat behind, four flags, colorful vine below, deep burgundy ground, frame with dec flowers with burgundy velvet liner and lemon gold liner, water stain on mat. 500.00

20" h, 24-1/2" l, early 19th C, "The Parting of Hector and Romache," military uniformed Hector, two women and child on portico of building in distance, worked with gold, brown, and greenish silk and watered color on silk ground, eglomise mat, period frame, accompanying note reads "Made my Mary Allen age 15, c1790," minor imperfections . . . 750.00

Panel, 32" w, 45" l, homespun, blue and white, blue edge embroidery, white crocheted lace edging, minor stains . 110.00

Reticule, 9-5/8" x 9-1/2", cotton, drawstring, New Hampshire, dated 1817, pen and ink inscription "Sacred to the memory of Nathan Bean obt. Octob. 28, 1817 ae 34 years," landscape reserve of neoclassical urn, willow tree, vine border, reverse with poetic verse, floral spray sgd "Olive Bean," grapevine border, early repairs, toning, scattered staining 500.00

Rug

19" x 32", hooked, pictorial, dog sled underway, label on reverse, Grenfell, early 20th C, splits 950.00

21-5/8" x 30", hooked, figural, house with shed and trees, amethyst, green, brown, red, gray, and pink, America, early 20th C, minor repair and fading 250.00

24-1/2" x 43", hooked, figural, central diamond form reserve with seated cat, perched bird spandrels, gold, terra-cotta, taupe, red, and light gray, on black and gray field, mounted, America, late 19th C/early 20th C, minor hole, fading 1,265.00

27-1/4" x 39", hooked, pictorial, two people with dog sled, label on reverse, Grenfell, early 20th C, minor fading, staining 2,200.00

31-1/2" x 52", hooked, heart border enclosing field of foliate devices and hearts, name "Hattie" in center, red, sage, taupe, brown, ream, and pink on black field, America, late 19th C/early 20th C, minor losses, repairs. 1,150.00

Coverlet, jacquard, two piece, double weave, four rose medallions and stars, floral border, corners labeled "Wove at Newark, Ohio, by G. Stich 1846," blue/black and white, some wear and small holes, 74" x 86", price for pr, $1,100. Photo courtesy of Garth's Auctions, Inc.

49" x 48", yard and cloth, hooked, scrolling vine border, center reserve of stylized potted plant, sage, olive, ecru, red, and gray, homespun ground, backed, New England, first half 19th C, scattered repairs, fading 2,070.00

61" x 61", hooked, striated and scrolling leaf border, center field of repeating geometric and leaf design, red, brown, celery, sage, and burnt umber, backed, America, late 19th/early 20th C, areas of wear 2,550.00

Table Runner, 82" l, 14" w, stumpwork and cut velvet, each end with crowned armorial, red cut velvet foliate design, Continental, 18th C 290.00

Tapestry

78" x 82", Verdure, scene wit dog and guinea hen with chicks, brittle, losses, Flemish, early 18th C 5,175.00

9' x 8' 8", crowd of hunters and dogs about stag, foliate and fruited borders, multicolored, Flemish, late 17th/early 18th C, restorations 13,800.00

Towel, 56" l, 16-1/2" w, woven linen, initialed and dated "BC 1828," red embroidery, cream ground, attributed to PA 100.00

50-3/4" x 30-3/4", wool, thirteen panel design, various pieced, embroidered, and appliquéd foliate motifs, red, green, purple, blue, sage, taupe, and white, black field, New England, first half 19th C, minor losses, scattered minor fiber wear 2,650.00

80" x 41", braided, rect, shaped edge, diamond, heart, and circle designs, pale blue, teal, pink, and black, America, 20th C, minor wear. 460.00

105" x 70", hooked, floral, repeating foliate design, red, salmon, blue, green, sage, and camel, on taupe ground, 20th C 1,150.00

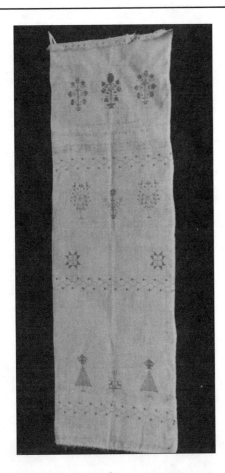

Show Towel, faded red embroidery, 16-1/2" w, 50-1/2" l, $225.

Runner, 2' h, 17' 6" l, hooked, penny design, striped borders, pink, green, blue, yellow, purple, gray, maroon, orange, gold, and taupe, on beige field, America, early 20th C . . .1,850.00

Woven Carpet, 24-1/2" w, 164" l, red, blue, green, and gold, un-used 525.00

THREADED GLASS

History: Threaded glass is glass decorated with applied threads of glass. Before the English invention of a glass-threading machine in 1876, threads were applied by hand. After this invention, threaded glass was produced in quantity by practically every major glass factory.

Threaded glass was revived by the art glass manufacturers such as Durand and Steuben, and it is still made today.

Basket, 3-1/2" d, rubena, clear applied twisted handle . . 135.00

Bowl, 8" d, 3-3/4" h, triangular shape, Tartan, blue, white, and pale pink plaid, clockwise swirl on ext., reversed swirls on int., attributed to Wordsley Flint Glass Works, Stourbridge, small chip off one applied foot 485.00

Cheese Dish, cov, 7-1/2" d, light blue opal threading on upper half of bell shaped dome, faceted knob 125.00

Cocktail Set, 9-1/2" h colorless decanter, applied mirror black threads, stopper and jug monogrammed "H.W.N.," six matching handled cups, Steuben fleur-de-lis mark on jug base, Steuben catalog no. 7056 . . . . 450.00

Epergne, 9-1/2" d, 15" h, four orange to clear threaded vases, petal scalloped tops, clear branches, orange threaded base 675.00

Finger Bowl, 5" d, yellow-green, scalloped rim, price for set of eight 200.00

Vase, green threading, colorless body, 5" h, $65.

Perfume, 5-1/2" h, blown, machine applied threads 250.00

Pitcher, blue rim, applied handle 65.00

Rose Bowl, 2-1/4" d, , clear glass ovals, sgd "Rd 81951," English

Cranberry 275.00

Olive Green 275.00

Salt, 2-3/4" x 1-1/2", opaque white threads, cranberry ground, clear applied petal feet 75.00

Tumbler, 4-1/4", aqua threads, clear ground. 200.00

Vase, 7-1/4" h, tapered, pinched top, irid satin finish, applied threading 110.00

TIFFANY

History: Louis Comfort Tiffany (1849-1934) established a glass house in 1878 primarily to make stained glass windows. In 1890, in order to utilize surplus materials at the plant, Tiffany began to design and produce "small glass" such as iridescent glass lamp shades, vases, stemware, and tableware in the Art Nouveau manner. Commercial production began in 1896.

Tiffany developed a unique type of colored iridescent glass called Favrile, which differs from other art glass in that it was a composition of colored glass worked together while hot. The essential characteristic is that the ornamentation is found within the glass; Favrile was never further decorated. Different effects were achieved by varying the amount and position of colors.

Louis Tiffany and the artists in his studio also are well known for their fine work in other areas—bronzes, pottery, jewelry, silver and enamels.

Marks: Most Tiffany wares are signed with the name "L. C. Tiffany" or the initials "L.C.T." Some pieces also are marked "Favrile" along with a number. A variety of other marks can be found, e.g., "Tiffany Studios" and "Louis C. Tiffany Furnaces."

References: Victor Arwas, *Glass, Art Nouveau and Art Deco*, Rizzoli International Publications, 1977; Alastair Duncan, *Louis Comfort Tiffany*, Harry N. Abrams, 1992; Robert Koch, *Louis C. Tiffany, Rebel in Glass*, Crown Publishers, 1966; David Rago, *American Art Pottery*, Knickerbocker Press, 1997; John A. Shuman III, *Collector's Encyclopedia of American Art Glass*, Collector Books, 1988, 1994 value update.

Museums: Chrysler Museum, Norfolk, VA; Corning Glass Museum, Corning, NY; University of Connecticut, The William Benton Museum of Art, Storrs, CT.

REPRODUCTION ALERT

A large number of brass belt buckles and badges bearing Tiffany markings were imported into the United States and sold at flea markets and auctions in the late 1960s. The most common marking is "Tiffany Studios, New York." Now, more than 25 years later, many of these items are resurfacing and deceiving collectors and dealers.

A partial list of belt buckles includes the Wells Fargo guard dog, Wells Fargo & Company mining stage, Coca-Cola Bottling, Southern Comfort Whiskey, Currier and Ives express train, and U.S. Mail. Beware of examples that have been enhanced through color enameling.

An Indian police shield is among the fake Tiffany badges. The badge features an intertwined "U" and "S" at the top and a bow and arrow motif separating "INDIAN" and "POLICE."

Bronze

Bowl, 9" d, gold doré finish, etched border, sgd "Tiffany Studios New York, #1707". 250.00
Canapé Tray, 12" d, etched gold doré on cleaned gilt bronze, dec border, imp "Tiffany Studios New York 1746" . . . 325.00
Candlesticks, pr, 19" h, etched fore surface, urn-form candlecups on tripod holders, long shaft, swirled organic pad foot, inscribed "Tiffany Studios New York 1213," orig conforming bobeche insets. 2,550.00
Clock, 4-1/8" h, 4-1/4" w, Zodiac pattern, dark doré patina, offset frame, keywind movement, gold dial mkd "Tiffany & Co. New York," base imp "Tiffany Studios 1076" 1,400.00
Desk Set
  Dark doré finish, Russian pattern, blue patina, blotter ends 2021, blotter rocker 2024, complete calendar 2026, inkstand 2022, letter holder 2025, note pad 2027, pen tray 2023, all 7 pcs imp "Tiffany Studios New York" 4,025.00
  Doré finish, Byzantine pattern, orange-red glass jewel inserts, beaded accents and medallions, complete calendar 944, paper rack no. 1006, stamp box, each pc imp "Tiffany Studios New York," minor damage to stamp box
  . . . . .2,760.00
  Doré finish, Pine Needle pattern, etched gold metal, amber slag glass inserts, beaded utility box 809, blotter ends 999, blotter rocker 995, calendar frame 930, inkwell 844, letter holder 1008, letter knife 969, match holder 958, note pad 1022, paper holder 1019, pen tray 1004, stamp box 801, all 12 pcs imp 2,530.00
  Verdigris finish, spider web filigree, green slag glass inserts, 3-1/4" h hexagonal box (hinge broken); 5-1/8" h pin holder

(with crack in glass); 3-3/4" d ink well paperweight (insert missing); 2-1/4" h urn shaped match holder; four blotter corners, all mkd "Tiffany Studios New York". 1,870.00
Inkstand, 3" h, 5-1/4" w, 4-1/4" d, Nautical, dark green patina, shell cov, dolphin corners, imp "Tiffany Studios New York 1842" 1,400.00
Letter Holder, 4-1/2" h, single-tier, Venetian pattern, lower border of ermine, mature doré bronze patina, imp "Tiffany Studios New York 1634" 575.00
Note Pad, molded design, heavy bronze, dark patina, green coloration, base imp "Tiffany Studios New York 1120"
. . . . 750.00
Picture Frame, desk type
  6-1/4" h, 7-1/2" w, etched bronze, blossom pattern, dark patina, beaded edges, green slag, easel back, notched back plate, imp "Tiffany Studios New York" 920.00
  9" h, 7" w, doré, Abalone pattern, shaped vertical frame, some green patina, shell inserts, easel back, imp "Tiffany Studios New York 1178" 1,500.00
Tile, 6-1/2" tile, 7-1/4" sq bronze frame with four extended paw feet, gold and green tessera segments arranged in sq geometric design, center "C," some minor chips on glass segments 1,200.00
Vase, 14" h, elongated frosted favrile glass cylinder, gold pulled leaf dec, base mkd "L. C. T.," inserted into dark and gold doré bronze holder, stamped "Tiffany Studios New York 711," lower edge of cylinder ground to fit holder. 1,500.00

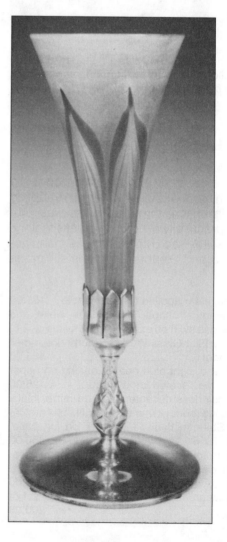

"Pulled Feather" trumpet vase with bronze stand, 12", $2,310. Photo courtesy of Jackson's.

Glass

Basket, 7" h, 7" d, pastel yellow Favrile bowl, opal laurel leaf design, fitted into doré bronze "Tiffany Furnaces" handled holder #516, bowl inscribed "LCT Favrile 1925" 875.00

Bowl and Flower Frog, gold Favrile, green leaves and vines, brilliant gold and pink irid highlights, removable flower frog, both pcs sgd "L. C. Tiffany Favrile #3838" 850.00

Compote
4-1/2" h, 7-1/4" d, conical irid amber dish, swirled pattern, octagonal crimped rim, pedestal foot, inscribed "LCT N2117" 750.00
5-1/2" d, gold Favrile body, blue and white edge, clear body, ftd, sgd "L. C. T. Favrile #1871" 400.00

Cordial, 4-1/2" h, irid gold, base inscribed "L.C.T.," some color variation in set of five 950.00

Goblet, 6-1/2" h, flared optic ribbed bowl, gold glossy ext., irid int., base inscribed "L.C.T. Favrile" 350.00

Paperweight, 1-1/2" l, scarab, deep blue and purple irid 150.00

Salt, 1-1/4" d, irid gold, four-ftd serving pots, each inscribed "LCT" and numbered, two small foot chips, price for matched set of four 900.00

Vase
3" h, dimpled form, gold Favrile, sgd "LCT #N8009" 300.00
3-1/8" h, double bulbed amber body, eighteen-rib design, base inscribed "L.C.T. 4601B" 775.00
3-1/2" h, Favrile body, green pulled feather, gold, brown, pink, and purple irid, sgd "LCT #9078B" 700.00
3-1/2" h, ribbed body, flaring top, uneven rim, gold Favrile, platinum irid, sgd "LCT Favrile #1807D" 450.00
3-7/8" h, eight-ribbed oval, amber body, raised scalloped rim, overall golden luster, base inscribed "LCT 1725A," paper label 775.00
4-1/4" h, flared rim, broad shouldered oval, ten-ribbed cobalt blue favrile glass, overall lusterous irid, base inscribed "L. C. Tiffany Favrile 18" 1,265.00
4-1/2" h, ribbed body, flaring top, uneven rim, gold Favrile, irid, sgd "LCT Favrile #6556Q" 450.00

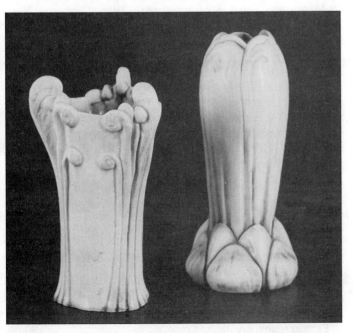

Pottery, vases, left: $13,200; right: $1,650. Photo courtesy of David Rago Auctions, Inc.

5" h, double bulbed gourd-form amber body, green leaves and amber vines, darker gold blossoms, base inscribed "L. C. Tiffany Favrile 8246B" .1,900.00
5-1/4" h, bulbous oval, dark green favrile covered by swirling pulled and coiled irid dec, irregular cypriot surface, base inscribed "L. C. T. K378" 2,550.00
9" h, ribbed neck, bulbous bottom, gold Favrile, blue/purple irid, sgd "LC Tiffany Favrile #1834" 800.00
12" h, elongated eighteen-rib oval, amber body, strong gold luster, two engraved butterflies in flight near upper rim, base inscribed "L. C. Tiffany Inc. Favrile 1547-5694N" 1,750.00
16-1/2" h, floriform, gold favrile insert, bronze base mkd "Tiffany Studios New York 1686" and monogram 1,320.00
20" h, tapering form, gold Favrile, blue/purple irid pulled feather at bottom, sgd "L. C. Tiffany Favrile #3570L" 2,600.00

Wax Seal, 1-3/4" h, gold Favrile, three scarabs 210.00

Lamp

Bridge, 58" h, 12" d shade with amber mottled dichroic glass with green acorns, adjustable harp, slender standard raised on five-leg spade form base, shade sgd "Tiffany Studios, New York, #1410," base sgd twice "Tiffany Studios New York #423" 18,500.00

Chandelier, 20" d, conical hanging shade, favrile glass segments leaded as pastel pink, rose, and opalescent white pond lily blossoms, green pads, blue rippled glass as water, rim imp "Tiffany Studios New York 149-17," some early restoration, fitted onto non-Tiffany light fixture and hanging support 75,100.00

Desk
Adams style, octagonal shade with amber and white slag glass inserts mkd "Tiffany Studio New York 1412," gold Doré stick base mkd "Tiffany Studios, New York 539," one glass panel cracked 5,500.00
18" h, dark patina on spun bronze dome shade, silver color reflective int., two-socket base, reticulated finial cap, flared fluted shaft, conforming base, imp "Tiffany Studios New York 617" 2,000.00

Table
21-1/2" h, twelve-light, orig dark patina on bronze curved drop stems, tiered platform base of lily pads, ribbed gold favrile shades with scalloped rims, base imp "Tiffany Studios New York," some variation in color of shades 23,000.00
25" h base, 20" d Pond Lily shade, pattern of green and white striated lily pads, mottled glass, clear glass tinged with green background, lower border of faceted emerald green glass, bronze base with cylindrical standard cast with overlapping leaf tips at top, shallow incised loops around middle, cushion-form circular base cast with two rows small alternating bosses, bands of loops with raised centers at outer edge, four petal-form feet, cap swirling reticulated shallow cap with small finial, shade sgd "Tiffany Studio, New York," base imp "Tiffany Studios New York #359," some fractures, deep brown/green patina 39,000.00
25" h, 29-1/2" d shade, Narcissus shade, golden yellow mottled daffodils, deep yellow/green mottled foliate, yellow/green stems, grayish pinpoints outlined in deep rich blue/purple background, bronze base inverted trumpet-form, cast with radiating leaves, finial cap with reticulated swirl top and single large finial, shade sgd "Tiffany Studio New York #1919," base sgd "Tiffany Studio, New York #368" 52,500.00

30" h, 22" d geometric green variegated shade, graduated brick shaped segments, bronze twisted vine base with "er-digris finish, shade mkd "Tiffany Studios New York 1501," base mkd "Tiffany Studios New York 443," some minor cracks in glass 31,900.00

Dogwood, white, lavender, and green petals, blue background, fracture, striated, rippled, and mottled glass segments, two bands of rippled greenish opalescent glass, bronze pumpkin-type base, rich brown/green patina, fuel canister, fire-arm shade supports, wired for electricity, micro tag on shade "Tiffany Studio, New York," fuel canister sgd "Tiffany Studio, New York, #21218" 39,000.00

Silver and silver plate

Asparagus Tongs, 10" l, sterling, leaf pattern handle, teardrop shape openwork grips, 5 troy oz 350.00

Bowl

9" d, open cone-shape, three curved leaf feet, 26 troy oz 920.00

9" d, rim dec with clover leaves, flowers, and reeded scroll detail, monogram, 1891-1902, 11 troy oz 435.00

Butter Dish, cov, 6-5/8" d, sterling, round, low foot, scrolled design rim, lid with engraved scroll and floral detail, applied putti flanking two medallions, c1875, 17 troy oz. 800.00

Candelabra, pr, sterling

16" h, 12" w, two arm, center candleholder, monogrammed, mkd "Tiffany & Co. Makers Sterling Silver, 925-1000" 2,200.00

19" h, convertible, repousse floral dec, weighted, late 19th C 8,625.00

Center Bowl, 14-7/8" l, sterling, oval shape, scroll foliate relief band under rim, leafy shell handles, four raised paw feet, 1873-91, 54 troy oz 4,600.00

Cigar Box, 6-1/4" x 3-3/4" x 2-5/8", silver plated, blue dec, hinged metal box, monogrammed "CH" on cov, int. engraved "1852 D.S. 1922," base inscribed "Louis C. Tiffany Furnaces Inc./350," worn silver 900.00

Cocktail Forks, hammered forks, gold wash tines, set of six 200.00

Cocktail Shaker, 9-3/8" h, sterling, Hawkes crystal base, cylindrical, sterling cover and pouring spout, 20th C 230.00

Creamer and Sugar, sterling, 2-1/2" h, rounded rect shape, low foot, leaf design handles, beaded border around body, chased scattered flowers, c1873, 7 troy oz 400.00

Dresser Set, ten piece, 1891-1902, repousse scroll foliate design, hairbrush, three clothes brushes, hand mirror, shoe horn, comb, buttonhook, nail file, buffer handle, monogrammed, some wear. 575.00

Fruit Bowl, 8-7/8" d, round, ftd base, openwork band below reeded rim, handle, 1907-38, 16 troy oz 250.00

Ladle, 11" l, sterling, Audubon pattern, fluted edge, rect form bowl, 1871, 7 troy oz 1,265.00

Nutmeg Grater, 2-3/4" h, cylindrical-form, hinged drop grating surface cov, engine-turned surface dec, c1855, 2 troy oz 920.00

Pepper Casters, pr, 5-5/8" h, Chrysanthemum pattern, 1907, 9 troy oz. 1,150.00

Salt, pr, Chrysanthemum pattern, 1907, 5 troy oz 875.00

Sandwich Tongs, 8-1/4" l, sterling, engraved handle, openwork grips, 5 troy oz 400.00

Sauce Ladle, beaded handle, cast head of mythological figure on back of gold wash bowl, fitted case, 2 troy oz. . . . 175.00

Spoon, shell-shape, gold wash bowl, floral relief pattern handle, 2 troy oz 375.00

Tazza, 9-1/4" d, sterling, round, low ftd base, acid-etched floral and fine border, 16 troy oz 300.00

Tea Service

4-3/8" h teapot, creamer, cov sugar, chased floral design, eagle finial, monogrammed, mkd "Tiffany, Young & Ellis," 27 troy oz 1,150.00

13-1/4" h kettle on stand, teapot, open sugar and pitcher, four lion law feet on kettle, Greek revival style with bands of fretwork, wooden handles and finials on kettle and teapot, 1854-70, 96 troy oz 4,025.00

Toothbrush Protector, 2" h, hinged domed lid, pierced dec, c1902, 1 troy oz 260.00

Tray, 26" l, 18" w, sterling, open handles, monogrammed and dated 1898 . . . . .3,750.00

Trophy, 9-3/4" h, sterling, urn form, two handles, spreading circular base, engraved inscriptions, c1923, 48 troy oz 800.00

Vase, 6-1/2" h, 3-7/8" d, sterling, spreading circular base, beaded detail, tapering fluted form, c1902-07, 4 troy oz 350.00

Waste Bowl, 5-3/16" d, 2-13/16" h, sterling, applied rim border, monogram, c1866, 8 troy oz 200.00

Whistle, sterling, silver mouthpiece, bulbous naturalistic motif center, mother-of-pearl handle, c1900, sgd "Tiffany & Co." 450.00

TIFFIN GLASS

History: A. J. Beatty & Sons built a glass manufacturing plant in Tiffin, Ohio, in 1888. On Jan. 1, 1892, the firm joined the U. S. Glass Co. and was known as factory R. Fine-quality Depression-era items were made at this high-production factory.

From 1923 to 1936, Tiffin produced a line of black glassware called Black Satin. The company discontinued operation in 1980.

Marks: Beginning in 1916, wares were marked with a paper label.

References: Fred Bickenheuser, *Tiffin Glassmasters,* Book I (1979), Book II (1981), Book III (1985), Glassmasters Publications; Bob Page and Dale Fredericksen, *Tiffin Is Forever,* Page-Fredericksen, 1994; Jerry Gallagher and Leslie Piña, *Tiffin Glass,* Schiffer Publishing, 1996; Kelly O'Kane, *Tiffin Glassmasters, The Modern Years,* published by author, 1998 (P.O. Box 16303, St. Paul, MN 55116-0303); Ed Goshe, Ruth Hemminger, and Leslie Piña, *Depression Era Stems & Tableware: Tiffin,* Schiffer Publishing, 1998.

Collectors' Club: Tiffin Glass Collectors Club, P.O. Box 554, Tiffin, OH 44883.

Ashtray, Twilight, 5" d, cloverleaf 45.00

Basket, Twilight, 9" h, 5-1/2" w 300.00

Bowl

Swedish Modern, Copen blue and crystal, 5-1/4" h, ftd 65.00

Twilight, 9-1/4" w, ftd, sq 200.00

Bud Vase

Cherokee Rose, 6" h 25.00

Etched roses, crystal and smoke 190.00

Fuchsia, #14185, 10-1/2" h 40.00

June Night, 8" h 30.00

Vase, black ground, red coralene flowers, 6-1/2" h, $80.

Candlesticks, pr
  #319, 8" h, red satin 175.00
  Cherokee Rose, #5902, 2-lite. 160.00
  Killarney, #6364, green 100.00
Candy Dish, cov, Deerwood, #15320, black, gold encrusted dec,
  6" d 750.00
Centerpiece, 13", #8153
  Fontaine, green, light use. 95.00
  La Fleure, yellow 125.00
Champagne
  Athens Diana 25.00
  Cherokee Rose, #17403 . . . . 16.00
  Empire, optic, pink 20.00
  Fuchsia, #15803. . . . . 12.00
  June Night, #17403 . . . . 30.00
  Killarney, #15074, green 25.00
  Majestic Twilight, #17507 . . . . 35.00
  Persian Peasant, #17358 . . . . 25.00
  Twilight, #17524 . . . . 35.00
Claret
  Cherokee Rose, #17399, 4 oz 55.00
  Persian Peasant, #17358. . . . . 50.00
Cocktail
  Athens Diana 18.00
  Cherokee Rose, #17399 . . . . 16.00
  Classic 35.00
  Flanders, pink. 45.00
  Fuchsia, #15083. . . . . 20.00
  June Night, #17358 . . . . 20.00
  Majestic Twilight, #17507 . . . . 40.00
  Persian Peasant, #17358. . . . . 20.00
Comport, open
  Cherokee Rose, blown, beaded, tall 150.00
  Deerwood, #15320, black, gold encrusted dec, 7" h, ftd
  . . . . 350.00
  Juno, yellow, 6-1/2" h. 65.00
Console Bowl, Flanders, 8" w, 4-1/4" h, blown, pink. . . . 800.00
Console Set, #8088, 7" d bowl, #320 10" h candlesticks, black
  . . . . 250.00

Cordial
  Cameo etching, #17594 . . . . 70.00
  Celestial, #17707, ebony 30.00
  Celestial, #17707, turquoise. 30.00
  Cherokee Rose, #17399 . . . . 55.00
  Classic, #185 . . . . 70.00
  Coventry, #17623. . . . . 30.00
  Fantasy, #17687. . . . . 40.00
  Flanders, crystal 55.00
  June Night, #17358 . . . . 45.00
  Majal, #17594. . . . . 30.00
  Persian Pheasant, #17392 . . . . 65.00
Creamer and Sugar, Cherokee Rose, beaded 60.00
Cup and Saucer
  Athens Diana 25.00
  Rosalind, yellow, blown 40.00
  Dahlia Vase, Flanders, pink, 8" h 800.00
  Decanter, #3700, globe stopper, carved dec
  Jonquil, sgd "Franz Grosz" 300.00
  Roses 260.00
Dessert Plate, Luciana, green, 8" d. 30.00
Flower Basket, Copen, blue and crystal, 13" h 165.00
Goblet, luncheon, June Night, #17358, low 35.00
Goblet, water
  Chalet. 50.00
  Cherokee Rose, #17403 . . . . 35.00
  Classic, #185 . . . . 35.00
  Fuchsia, #15083, 7-1/2" h 22.00
  June Night, #17358 . . . . 35.00
  Killarney, #15074, green 35.00
  Rosalind, yellow 30.00
  Twilight, #17492 . . . . 45.00
Grapefruit, Flanders, yellow, crystal insert 250.00
Iced Tea Tumbler
  Cherokee Rose, #17403 . . . . 35.00
  Flanders, pink, 12 oz 75.00
  Flying Nun, crystal, green base 60.00
  June Night, #17358 . . . . 35.00
  Killarney, #15074, green 30.00
  King's Crown, ruby flashed, 12 oz 14.00
Jug, #128
  Athens Diana 260.00
  Rosalind, yellow 350.00
Juice Tumbler, King's Crown, ruby flashed, 4 oz, ftd 12.00
Martini Jug, Twlight, 11-1/2" h 450.00
Nut Dish, June Night 45.00
Oyster Cocktail, Athens Diana 18.00
Parfait
  Classic, #185 . . . . 70.00
  Flanders, pink, handle 150.00
Pitcher, Cherokee Rose, ftd 700.00
Plate
  Classic, 10-1/2" d, dinner 125.00
  Fuchsia, #8814, 7-7/8" 12.50
  June Night, crystal, 6" d 17.50
  Juno, yellow, 9-1/2" d, dinner 40.00
  La Fleure, yellow, 7-1/4" d 15.00
  Rosalind, yellow, 8" d 12.00
  Rosalind, yellow, dinner 50.00
Server, center handle, Deerwood, #15320, black, gold encrust-
  ed dec, 10-1/2" d 250.00
Sherbet, Cherokee Rose, #17399, low 25.00
Sherry, June Night, #17403 . . . . 30.00
Sugar, cov, Fuchsia, #5902, bead handle. 24.00
Torte Plate, King's Crown, ruby flashed, 14" d 70.00

Tumbler
　Classic, 8 oz, flat 44.00
　Fuchsia, 12 oz, ftd 22.00
　June Night, #17403, 10-1/2 oz, ftd 20.00
Vase
　Canterbury, roses dec, 10" h 190.00
　Cherokee Rose, 10-1/2" h 40.00
　Empress, #6551, red and crystal, 12" h 190.00
　Fuchsia, 11" h, trophy shape, handles 230.00
　Wedding Bowl, cov, King's Crown, ruby flashed, 7-1/2" d
　. . . . . 90.00
Whiskey
　Classic, #185, ftd, 2 oz 75.00
　Flanders, yellow, 2-3/4" h 175.00
Wine, Chalet 55.00

TILES

History: The use of decorated tiles peaked during the latter part of the 19th century. More than 100 companies in England alone were producing tiles by 1880. By 1890, companies had opened in Belgium, France, Australia, Germany, and the United States.

Tiles were not used only as fireplace adornments. Many were installed into furniture, such as washstands, hall stands, and folding screens. Since tiles were easily cleaned and, hence, hygienic, they were installed on the floors and walls of entry halls, hospitals, butcher shops, or any place where sanitation was a concern. Many public buildings and subways also employed tiles to add interest and beauty.

References: Susan and Al Bagdade, *Warman's American Pottery and Porcelain*, Wallace-Homestead, 1994; –—, *Warman's English & Continental Pottery & Porcelain*, 3rd Edition, Krause Publications, 1998; Ralph and Terry Kovel, *Kovels' American Art Pottery*, Crown Publishers, 1993; Hans van Lemmen, *Decorative Tiles Throughout the Centuries*, Moyer Bell, 1997; ——, *Delftware Tiles*, Overlook Press, 1997; ——, *Fired Early 1000 Years of tiles In Europe*, Antique Collectors' Club, Ltd., 1991; Ralph Moore and Dinah Tanner, *Porcelain & Pottery Tea Tiles*, Antique Publications, 1994; Richard and Hilary Myers, *William Morris Tiles*, Richard Dennis (distributed by Antique Collectors' Club), 1996; David Rago, *American Art Pottery*, Knickerbocker Press, 1997; Ronald L. Rindge et al., *Ceramic Art of the Malibu Potteries*, Malibu Lagoon Museum, 1994.

Periodical: *Flash Point*, P.O. Box 1850, Healdsburg, CA 95448.

Collectors' Clubs: Tiles & Architectural Ceramics Society, Reabrook Lodge, 8 Sutton Rd., Shrewsbury, Shopshire SY2 6DD, UK.

Museums: Boymans-van Beunigen Museum, Rotterdam, Holland; City Museum, Stoke-on-Trent, England; Iron Bridge Gorge Museum, Teford, England Lambert Van Meerten Museum, Delft, Holland; Mercer Museum &

Tile Works, Doylestown, PA; Victoria & Albert Museum London, England.

Notes: Condition is an important factor in determining price. A cracked, badly scuffed and scratched, or heavily chipped tile has very little value. Slight chipping around the outer edges of a tile is, at times, considered acceptable by collectors, especially if these chips can be covered by a frame.

It is not uncommon for the highly glazed surface of some tiles to have become crazed. Crazing is not considered detrimental as long as it does not detract from the overall appearance of the tile.

American Encaustic Tile Co., Zanesville, OH
　3" sq, portrait of President Wm. McKinley, blue glazed intaglio, 1896, biography pasted on back 145.00
　4" sq, Oriental junque, pagoda in background 45.00
　6" sq, cherub and dog, small repair 35.00
　18" x 6", hunting dogs, high relief, sponged pale aqua and honey brown glossy glaze 250.00
Arts & Crafts
　5" x 13", pink flamingo, multicolored ground, Arts & Crafts oak frame 375.00
　5-1/2" sq, yellow flowers, green leaves, cut-back brown ground, Arts & Crafts oak frame 200.00
　6" w, 12" h, two tiles, squeezebag dec, stylized light green flower, aqua ground, Arts & Crafts oak frame 600.00
Batchelder, 4" sq
　Hunter and dog in woods, bas relief, reddish brown clay, high gloss light blue rubbed into background 90.00
　Landscape of trees, water, and bridge, deeply imp, red clay, light chalky blue brushed into recessed areas 95.00
Beaver Falls, 6" sq, standing squirrel, incised and outlined in black, squirrel and border medium blue, Kelly green ground, marked 65.00
California Art, 5-1/2" sq, scenic, relief, natural colors 20.00

Grueby Pottery, cuenca dec, bright yellow and green, 6" sq, $1,980. Photo courtesy of David Rago Auctions, Inc.

Claycraft, CA, 35" x 23-1/2", 24 tile frieze, articulated scene of dirt road winding towards stone bridge, grove of fir and maple trees, Cottswald type cottage, molded wooden frame 2,250.00

DeMorgan, William, 6" sq, hedgehog, ruby luster glaze 400.00

Dutch, 9-1/2" x 7-1/2", painted blue and white, man and woman in cart, sgd "O Evrelman," framed, 19th/20th C 110.00

Grueby

    4-1/2" sq, landscape, trees, stream and mountain, green, blue, yellow, and brown, marked "Architectural" ...600.00

    8" sq, mocha brown galleon, billowing white sails, choppy powder blue sea, medium blue sky, black wood frame, sgd "EH," partial black stamp 850.00

Low, J. & J. G., Chelsea, MA

    4" sq, bearded man, laurel wreath, green gloss.....165.00

    6" x 5", cupid on flying bird, olive gloss, 1883 ......175.00

    7" x 7-1/2", flowers, brown shaded to amber 50.00

Marblehead, 6" x 6", scenic, house and trees, deep blue and green, imp ship mark, minor nicks 1,265.00

Minton China Works, 6" sq, transfer printed

    Adam and Eve driven out of Eden, blue cream ground 45.00

    Farmyard scene, sheep, brown on white, sgd "W. Wise," 1879.................................80.00

    Hancock House, brown on white 35.00

    Romeo and Juliet, sepia.......................35.00

Moravian Pottery & Tile Works, Doylestown, PA

    4" sq, Aladdin Lamp...........................70.00

    7-1/4" x 4", Knight in armor on horseback, ochre and blue 85.00

Mosaic Tile Co., Zanesville, OH

    4" sq, German Shepherd dec...................120.00

    6" sq, Little Bo Peep, blue, tan, and cream, Walter Crane 100.00

    6" sq, ship at sea, yellow sail, blue water, imp mark 250.00

Pardee, 4" sq, houses and trees, matte glaze, brown and green, 1910 ....225.00

Pewabic Pottery, Detroit, MI

    2-3/4" sq, bird of paradise, gray-taupe bird, cranberry red ground, high luster finish 65.00

    3" sq, Detroit Skyline, round, emb, brown on blue 75.00

Richards, H, 6" sq, Art Nouveau flower, tube lined, red and green, cream ground 75.00

Robertson, 8" sq, scenic, cloisonné dec, brown road winding through green hills, fortress 1,300.00

Rookwood Faience, 6" sq, geometric, matte ochre glaze, wood box frame, no visible mark 100.00

Solon, 5-1/2" sq, ship at sea, blue against camel ground, Arts & Crafts oak frame..........................500.00

Tiffany, 4" sq, blue-black glass, molded fire-breathing dragon in circular reserve, overall luster irid. 375.00

Trenton Tile Co., Trenton, NJ

    4-1/4" sq, portrait of woman, brown glaze 65.00

    6" sq, flower, tan glossy glaze 25.00

US Encaustic Tile Co.

    6" sq, birds, framed 75.00

    18" x 6", Dawn, woman, emb green glaze 175.00

Wedgwood

    6" sq, Moth from Midsummer's Night Dream, blue transfer, white ground 120.00

    8" sq, hunting dog and bird, brown transfer, white ground 115.00

TINWARE

History: Beginning in the 1700s, many utilitarian household objects were made of tin. Because it is nontoxic, rust resistant, and fairly durable, tin can be used for storing food; and because it was cheap, tinware and tin-plated wares were in the price range of most people. It often was plated to iron to provide strength.

An early center of tinware manufacture in the United States was Berlin, Connecticut, but almost every small town and hamlet had its own tinsmith, tinner, or whitesmith. Tinsmiths used patterns to cut out the pieces, hammered and shaped them, and soldered the parts. If a piece were to be used with heat, a copper bottom was added because of the low melting point of tin. The industrial revolution brought about machine-made, mass-produced tinware pieces. The handmade era had ended by the late 19th century.

References: Dover Stamping Co., *1869 Illustrated Catalog*, Astragal Press, 1994 reprint; Marilyn E. Dragowick (ed.), *Metalwares Price Guide*, Antique Trader Books, 1995; John Player, *Origins and Craft of Antique Tin & Tole*, Norwood Publishing, 1995 (available from Christie & Christie Association, P.O. Box 392, Cookstown, Ontario, Canada LOL 1LO).

Museum: Cooper-Hewitt Museum, New York, NY.

Additional Listings: See Advertising; Kitchen Collectibles; Lanterns; Lamps and Lighting; and Tinware, Decorated.

Note: This category is a catchall for tin objects, which do not fit into other categories in this book.

Battle Axe, 21" x 12", whimsey 150.00

Candle Sconces, pr

    11-1/4" h, 7-1/4" w, octagonal domed panels, crimped edges, pendant candleholders also with crimped edges, old yellow painted surface 2,100.00

    12" h, 6" w, 3-1/2" w, double, shaped crimped top section, rect back, crimped tray with two candleholders, old ivory painted surface 1,035.00

    13-1/2" h, 3" w, chimneyed demi-lune top, elongated body, single candle bobeche, minor corrosion, vestiges of black paint..........................635.00

Candle Tray, 9-1/4" x 19" x 12-3/4", rect, formed strap handle, holds 24 candles 650.00

Canteen, 5 5/8" h, punched star and circle dec 95.00

Centerpiece, 14-1/2" d, whimsey, tiered, traces of green paint 175.00

Churn, 21-1/2" h, wooden dasher 200.00

Coffee Grinder, hanging, Parker..................45.00

Cookie Cutter

    8-1/2" h, man with pipe, hat, and frock coat with tails, punched circle around hole, light rust 525.00

    9" h, woman with hat and long dress 525.00

Figure, 29" h, 24-1/2" l, rooster, silver gilt, carved wood rockery base, Continental 1,025.00

Food Grater, 14-1/4" l, punched, wood frame, mortised and turned handle 95.00

Footwarmer, 7-3/4" x 9", punched circle design with hearts, mortised hardwood frame, turned corner posts, old red stain 140.00

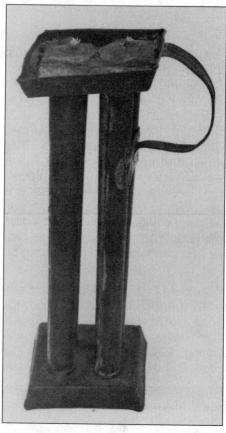

Candle Mold, four candles, handle, 10" h, 3-3/4" w, $70.

Lamp, 6-3/4" h, oil, saucer base, traces of gold and silver paint, Kinnear Patent 150.00
Mistletoe Ball, 6-1/4" d, hinged 450.00
Oyster Ladle 45.00
Quilt Pattern, 5-1/2" l, horse, pitted and rusted 20.00
Spice Canisters and Carrier, 8-1/2" x 8-1/2" x 5-3/4", crimp dec 275.00
Tinder Box, 4-1/4" d, America, late 18th/early 19th C . . . 100.00

TINWARE, DECORATED

History: The art of decorating sheet iron, tin, and tin-coated sheet iron dates back to the mid-18th century. The Welsh called the practice pontypool; the French, tôle peinte. In America, the center for tin-decorated ware in the late 1700s was Berlin, Connecticut.

Several styles of decorating techniques were used: painting, japanning, and stenciling. Designs were done by both professionals and itinerants. English and Oriental motifs strongly influenced both form and design.

A special type of decoration was the punch work on unpainted tin practiced by the Pennsylvania tinsmiths. Forms included coffeepots, spice boxes, and grease lamps.

Reference: Marilyn E. Dragowick (ed), *Metalwares Price Guide*, Antique Trader Books, 1995.

Basket, 10-1/2" x 9", crimp and curl dec 825.00
Box, dome top, orig dark brown japanning
    4-1/4" l, white band, floral dec, red and yellow stripes, wear 115.00
    6-3/4" l, white band, floral dec, red, green, and yellow stripes, wear, one hinge loose 115.00

7" l, white band, yellow, red, green, and black floral dec, hasp end broken 125.00
Canister, 27-1/2" h, country store type, worn old black paint, red striping and gilt letters 275.00
Coal Hod, 23-3/4" h, old black paint, worn gilt and floral transfers, rack in back for tools, marked "GD Manf. Co." . . 225.00
Coffeepot, 10-3/4" h, worn orig dark brown japanning, red, yellow, white, and dark green floral dec, some old touch up repair 715.00
Deed Box, 9-1/4" l, dome top, orig yellow paint, stenciled bowl of fruit and foliage on front, green stripe on lid, wear, front panel dec crazed 500.00
Foot Warmer, 9" l, punched circles, hearts, and diamonds, mortised wood frame, turned posts, worn red finish, int. pan 225.00
Lamp, 20-1/2" h, adjustable candle socket and shade, old paint, red and gold dec, brass post and finial 615.00
Lantern, 16" h, old yellow japanning, hinged door, added candle socket, reflector slot 115.00
Nutmeg Grater, 6" l, brown japanning, hand crank 175.00
Patch Box, 1-1/2" l, 1" w, 1/2" h, curved rect shape, 3/4 hinged top, colorful flower dec 75.00
Tea Caddy, rect bombe shape, floral dec, black ground, ornate bronze bail, scroll feet, three compartment int., 19th C 425.00
Teapot, 8-1/4" h, worn orig red paint, yellow, white, and dark green floral dec, resoldered handle 330.00
Tray
    19-1/2" l, oval, two handles, painted, gilt banding and foliate devices, dark red field, England, 19th C, minor paint loss 435.00
    28-1/2" d, painted with brown and green flowers, red ground, England, first half 19th C, restorations 1,955.00
    29-3/4" l, 21-3/8" w, painted, gold, bronze, and red anthemion leaves, fruit, foliate devices, and pinwheels, black ground, America, 19th C, minor areas of repaint, scattered paint loss 435.00

Milk Can, black ground, orig red and gold stenciled flowers and border, 8-1/2" h, $200.

30" x 21-1/2", painted allegory of time, openwork gallery, late Georgian, attributed to Pontypool, late 18th/early 19th C, minor restoration, wear 1,725.00

TOBACCO CUTTERS

History: Before pre-packaging, tobacco was delivered to merchants in bulk form. Tobacco cutters were used to cut the tobacco into desired sizes.

Ax Shape, cast iron, wood handle and base, 18" l, 7-1/2" h
. . . . 225.00
Dexter, wood base, metal slide and cutter, measures plug
. . . . 100.00
Enterprise Manufacturing Co., Philadelphia, OA, cast iron, emb "E. W. Venables Tobaccos" adv, patented April 15, 1875, 16-1/2" l, 7" h 150.00
European, wrought iron, fancy marking on blade and hinge, wood base with dark patina, dated "1773," some insect damage to base, 35" l 250.00
John Finzer & Brothers, Louisville, KY, cast iron, emb adv, 17" l, 7" h. 140.00
P. J. Song Co., spear head, cast iron, red, black lettering, 16-1/2" l 170.00
R. J. Reynolds Co., black japanned finish. 125.00

TOBACCO JARS

History: A tobacco jar is a container for storing tobacco. Tobacco humidors were made of various materials and in many shapes, including figurals. The earliest jars date to the early 17th century; however, most examples seen in the antiques market today were made in the late 19th or early 20th centuries.

Reference: Joseph Horowitz, *Figural Humidors, Mostly Victorian,* published by author, 1997 (FTJ Publications, 3011 Fallstaff Rd., Baltimore, MD 21209).

Collectors' Club: Society of Tobacco Jar Collectors, 3011 Fallstaff Rd., Baltimore, MD 21209.

Alpine Man, 5" h, bisque, white, green and brown trim. . 150.00
Blackamoor, 7-1/2" h, majolica 250.00
Boy, 5" h, majolica, earflap hat, realistic coloring 175.00

Student, blue cap, yellow band, light green bow tie, high glaze, mkd "6597/71," 4-7/8" h, $90.

Cat, 6" h, majolica, wearing yellow straw hat, mkd "Made in Austria," raised "J. S." in shield, numerals on base 450.00
Cigar Man, 8-3/4" h, terra cotta, mkd "J. M. 3625, Made in Bohemia, Czech" 350.00
Cylinder, 7-1/2" h, pewter, claw and ball feet 95.00
Dog, 5" h, majolica, boxer's head 450.00
Englishman, 7" h, majolica, night hat, mkd "567" and "48" incised in bottom. 250.00
Indian, 5-1/2" h, porcelain, polychrome dec, set-on lid, E Bohne & Sohne 235.00
Man's Head, 6-3/4" h, majolica, high gloss, Japan 150.00
Monk, majolica
  6-3/4" h, high gloss, c1950. . . . . 100.00
  6-3/4" h, realistic coloring, incised "2585" over "27" . . 225.00
  8" h, realistic coloring 350.00
Owl, 7" h, pottery, high glaze, cobalt blue, yellow, and brown
. . . . 350.00
Skull, bisque, sitting on book, wearing golfing cap 150.00

TOBY JUGS

History: Toby jugs are drinking vessels that usually depict a full-figured, robust, genial drinking man. They originated in England in the late 18th century. The term "Toby" probably is related to the character Uncle Toby from Tristram Shandy by Laurence Sterne.

References: Susan and Al Bagdade, *Warman's English & Continental Pottery & Porcelain*, 3rd Edition, Krause Publications, 1998; Vic Schuler, *Collecting British Toby Jugs,* 2nd ed., Kevin Francis Publishing Ltd., 1987.

Museums: American Toby Jug Museum, Evanston, IL; City Museum & Art Gallery, Stoke-on-Trent, England; Victoria & Albert Museum, London, England.

Additional Listings: Royal Doulton.

REPRODUCTION ALERT

During the last 100 years or more, tobies have been copiously reproduced by many potteries in the United States and England.

6-1/8" h, Benjamin Franklin, seated figure, pipe, wine goblet, mottled brown Rockingham glaze, Bennington, 1849-58
. . . . 550.00
7-1/4"h, Huntsman, Royal Doulton, c1910 . . . . 350.00
8-1/4" h, Prattware-type, underglaze palette, restorations to hat brim, handle, and one foot, late 18th C 375.00
9-1/8" h, Mr. Toby, seated, holding jug, tricorner hat, jacket, vest, knee breeches, manganese, soft green, brown ochre, yellow, and orange-ochre, Prattware, 18th C, pipe bowl missing, slight damage 1,540.00
9-1/8" h, seated man, blue and yellow mottled coat, yellow pants, brown hair, hat, and shoes, holding jug on left knee, pipe between legs, Leeds type, c1800 . . . . 850.00
9-1/2" h
  Derbyshire, standing man, yellow-tan glaze, dark brown splashes, mid 19th C 125.00
  Staffordshire, seated man, blue coat, yellow breeches, foaming jug on left knee, late 18th C 900.00
  Wood, Ralph, seated man, green waistcoat, gray jacket, dark hat, one hand raised to mouth 950.00
10-1/2" h
  Napoleon, graniteware, standing, yellow waistcoat, blue vest, marked "Made in Trenton, NJ" 400.00

Pratt type, brown hat, olive green jacket, rust breeches, 6" h, $2,400.

Sailor, seated, tricorn hat, holding jug in one hand, pipe in other, Staffordshire, 19th C, repairs. 345.00
10-3/4" h, Napoleon, ironstone, multicolored enamel, marked "Napoleon Jug-patent applied for Alfred E Evans, Philadelphia, PA". 400.00
11" h
Chained kneeling black woman, eyes turned upward, applied green coat, gold outlines, royal blue and dark red stripes alternating with gold patterned stripes, gold belt, white shirt, gold edged collar with gold dots, royal blue and gold bow at neck, yellow hat with blue, dark red, and yellow stripes, black painted hair, crabstock handle, slight loss to paint
. . . . .6,000.00
Coachman, wearing tassels, Rockingham glaze, Bennington, 1849 mark 450.00
11-1/2" h, Hearty Goodfellow, full figure man, tricorn hat, coat, waistcoat, knee breeches, carrying pitcher and ale glass, rockwork base, manganese, green, pale blue, tan, brown-ochre, olive green, Staffordshire, attributed to Ralph Wood, 18th C, professional restoration 3,575.00

TOOLS

History: Before the advent of the assembly line and mass production, practically everything required for living was handmade at home or by a local tradesman or craftsman. The cooper, the blacksmith, the cabinet maker, and the carpenter all had their special tools.

Early examples of these hand tools are collected for their workmanship, ingenuity, place of manufacture, or design. Modern-day craftsman often search out and use old hand tools in order to authentically recreate the manufacture of an object.

References: Ronald S. Barlow, *Antique Tool Collector's Guide to Value*, Windmill Publishing (2147 Windmill View Rd., El Cajon, CA 92020), 3rd ed., 1991; Kenneth L. Cope, *American Machinist's Tools*, Astragal Press, 1993; Martin J. Donnelly, *Catalogue of Antique Tools*, published by author (31 Rumsey St., Bath, NY 14810), 1997; Garrett Hack, *The Handplane Book*, Taunton Press, 1997; Jerry & Elaine Heuring, *Keen Kutter Collectibles*, Collector Books, 1996; Herbert P. Kean and Emil S. Pollak, *Price Guide to Antique Tools*, Astragal Press, 1992; ——, *Collecting Antique Tools*, Astragal Press, 1990; Kathryn McNerney, *Antique Tools, Our American Heritage*, Collector Books, 1979, 1997 value update; Emil and Martyl Pollak, *Guide to American Wooden Planes and Their Makers*, 3rd ed., The Astragal Press, 1994; ——, *Prices Realized on Rare Imprinted American Wood Planes, 1979-1992*, Astragal Press, 1993; John Walter, *Antique & Collectible Stanley Tools, Guide to Identity & Value*, 2nd ed.., The Tool Merchant, 1996; C. H. Wendel, *Encyclopedia of American Farm Implements & Antiques*, Krause Publications, 1997; John M. Whelan, *The Wooden Plane*, Astragal Press, 1993; Jack Wood, *Town-Country Old Tools*, 6th ed., L-W Book Sales, 1997.

Periodicals: *Fine Tool Journal*, P.O. Box 4001, Pittsford, VT 05763; *Plumb Line*, 10023 St. Clair's Retreat, Fort Wayne, IN 46825; *Stanley Tool Collector News*, 208 Front St., P.O. Box 227, Marietta, OH 45750; *Tool Ads*, P.O. Box 33, Hamilton, MT 59840.

Collectors' Clubs: Blow Torch Collectors Club, 3328 258th Ave. SE, Issaquah, WA 98027-9173; Collectors of Rare & Familiar Tools Society, 38 Colony Ct., Murray Hill, NJ 07974; Early American Industries Association, P.O. Box 2128, Empire State Plaza Station, Albany, NY 12220; Early American Industries-West, 8476 West Way Dr., La Jolla, CA 92038; Mid-West Tool Collectors Association, 104 Engle Court Franklin, TN 37069-6101; Missouri Valley Wrench Club, 613 N. Long St., Shelbyville, IL 62565; New England Tool Collectors Association, 303 Fisher Rd., Fitchburg, MA 01420; Ohio Tool Collectors Association, P.O. Box 261, London, OH 43140; Pacific Northwest Tool Collectors, 2132 NE. 81st St., Seattle, WA 98115; Potomac Antique Tools & Industries Association, 6802 Newbitt Pl, McLean, VA 22101; Rocky Mountain Tool Collectors, 2024 Owens Ct., Denver, CO 80227; Society of Workers in Early Arts & Trades, 606 Lake Lena Blvd., Auburndale, FL 33823; Southwest Tool Collectors Association, 7032 Oak Bluff Dr., Dallas, TX 75240; Three Rivers Tool Collectors, 39 S Rolling Hills, Irwin, PA 15642; Tool Group of Canada, 7 Tottenham Rd., Ontario MC3 2J3 Canada.

Museums: American Precision Museum Association, Windsor, VT; Mercer Museum, Doylestown, PA; Shelburne Museum, Shelburne, VT; World of Tools Museum, Waverly, TN.

Awl, 5-1/4" l, stag horn, old worn patina 100.00
Beader, Stanley No. 66, full set of replacement blades, fences, 70% plating. 100.00
Bit Gauge, Stanley No. 49, orig box, early SR & L label. . 22.50
Brace and Bit, wood, inlaid pewter 500.00
Buck Saw, 8-1/2" l, miniature, dated "1859" 150.00
Butt Gauge, Stanley No. 95G, yellow box with reinforced corners 22.50
Calipers, Goodell Pratt, No. 505, outside spring, 8", faded red box 25.00
Carving Tools, Miller Falls, No. 1, set of 6, rosewood handles, orig oak box with inside paper label 110.00
Clapboard Maker, Stanley 88, adjustable, orig box, early SR & L label 40.00
Dowel Jig, Stanley No. 59, 6 drill guides, orig box 40.00
Dowel Machine, Stanley No. 77, 3/8" cutter, blue finish, orig instructions and cardboard box. 395.00
Drill, Miller Falls type, 90% orig red detail painting, 96% japanning. 110.00
Grooving Router, Preston, adjustable, three cutters, three fences, 80% japanning 85.00
Gouge, Ibbotson Peace & Co., graduated set of 9, cast steel 225.00
Hammer
  Adz head, Cheney No. 777 . . . . 65.00
  Snowball, wrapped handle, fancy brass clip 35.00
Hatchet, 10-3/4" l, hand forged, old hickory handle, mkd "AH" 250.00
Level
  Goodell Pratt, 18", cast iron, double plumb, one dry vial 15.00
  Stratton Brothers No. 10, brass, bound 12", rosewood, 1908 Barber quarter dollar inlaid in side 195.00
Molding Plane, 11" l, adjustable gate, rosewood and boxwood, ivory and brass trim, stamped "Casey & Co. Auburn, N.Y.," wedge replaced 425.00
Parallel Ruler, Carrington's Patent, manufactured by William Hill, Wallingford, CT, wood, paper label 65.00
Pipe tongs, 17-1/4" l, wrought steel, incised dec and "Fort W. M. Henry Capt. B. Williams 1756" 9,200.00
Plane
  Bedrock, 604, bench, type 9, orange frog, Sweet Hart blade, 93% japanning 145.00
  Spiers Ayr, rosewood filled, 2 1/8" inch iron, polished 325.00

Stanley
  No. 47, dado, type 5, 60% japanning 395.00
  No. 50, combination, 15 cutters, B casting, 70% plating 110.00
  No. 97, chisel, 60% japanning 395.00
  No. 278, rabbet, 85% japanning, wrong fence 125.00
Ratchet Brace
  Consolidated Tool Works, Inc., No. 808, knob controlled, hardwood handles, 85% plating. 45.00
  Keystone, W A Ives Mfg Co., Wallingford, CT, lever controlled, hardwood handles 65.00
Sash Router, Preston 40.00
Saw, Disston, right angle 30.00
Saw Set, Stanley 42, orig box. 15.00
Screwdriver, 18-1/2" l, Cowles Hardware Co., Warranted Superior, sold by T.H.E. Co., cabinet maker's type 48.00
Sharpening Stone, 13-3/4" l, mounted on block, carved designs and "James N. Rosser, 1826" 385.00
Socket Set, PS & W Co., set of 12 in orig wood box, 9 apple wood handles, 3 with replaced handles 325.00
Wrench, W & C Wynn & Co., Patent, combination wrench, pliers, buggy wrench, hammer, and screwdriver 75.00

TOOTHPICK HOLDERS

History: Toothpick holders, indispensable table accessories of the Victorian era, are small containers made specifically to hold toothpicks.

They were made in a wide range of materials: china (bisque and porcelain), glass (art, blown, cut, opalescent, pattern, etc.), and metals, especially silver plate. Makers include both American and European firms.

By applying a decal or transfer, a toothpick holder became a souvenir item; by changing the decal or transfer, the same blank could become a memento for any number of locations.

References: William Heacock, *Encyclopedia of Victorian Colored Pattern Glass*, Book I, 2nd ed., Antique Publications, 1976, 1992 value update; ——, *1,000 Toothpick Holders*, Antique Publications, 1977; ——, *Rare & Unlisted Toothpick Holders*, Antique Publications, 1984; National Toothpick Holders Collectors Society, *Toothpick Holders*, Antique Publications, 1992.

Collectors' Club: National Toothpick Holder Collectors, P.O. Box 246, Sawyer, MI 49221.

Additional Listings: See *Warman's Americana & Collectibles* for more examples.

China, three handles, silver deposit design, sgd "R. S. Tillowitz" 65.00
Elfinware, basket. 24.00
Opaque Glass
  Beggar's Hand, white, green base 45.00
  One-O-One, pink 80.00
  Palm Leaf, green 45.00
  Porcelain, figural, nude girl in shell, mkd "Glen Falls, NY" 45.00
Pattern Glass
  Block, hat shape, vaseline 55.00
  Box in Box 30.00
  Cat on a Pillow, amber 60.00
  Frances Ware, 2-1/2" h, 1-1/2" d, bright golden yellow rim, frosted hobnail base, small base chip 150.00

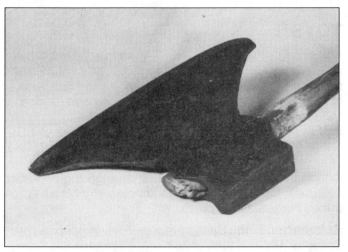

Broad Ax, hand forged, early 1900s, 12-1/4" w blade, $85.

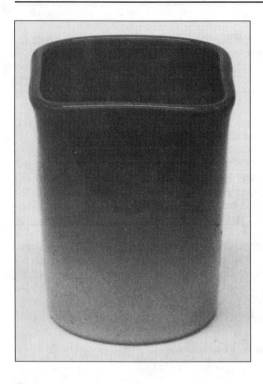

Peachblow, New England, 2-1/4" h, $425.

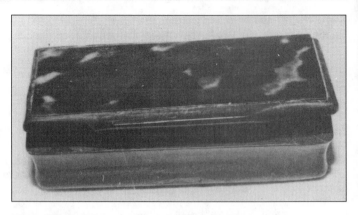

Box, hinged lid, 1-1/2" x 3-1/2", $145.

Pretty Maid	85.00
Rabbit, amber	45.00

Royal Bayreuth
Coal Shuttle, Dutch Boy and goose, unmkd.	200.00
Ovoid, side handle, Dutch boy and goose, mkd.	200.00

Ruby Stained
Daisy and Button, red buttons and rim	65.00
Scroll with Cane band	65.00
Sunk Honeycomb	45.00

Silver Plate, figural
Bird sitting next to eggshell half, wishbone, shell engraved "Best Wishes," Derby No. 2309	60.00
Bird sitting next to goblet, engraved "Take Your Pick"	100.00
Boots, pair on base, Aurora	125.00
Miniature pickle castor, engraved insert	80.00
Rat crouching next to pouch, Derby	85.00

TORTOISESHELL ITEMS

History: For many years amber and mottled tortoiseshell has been used in the manufacture of small items such as boxes, combs, dresser sets, and trinkets.

Note: Anyone dealing in the sale of tortoiseshell objects should be familiar with the Endangered Species Act and Amendment in its entirety. As of November 1978, antique tortoiseshell objects can be legally imported and sold with some restrictions.

Bowl, 7-3/4" d, one turned up side, applied amber feet	115.00
Box, cov, round, small round watercolor of gentleman on top, early 19th C	300.00
Cabinet Door, 28-1/2" h, 18" w, repousse silver scene of descent from cross, reverse with incised giltwood designs, Continental, 19th C, losses	3,850.00
Dance Program Holder, 5-3/4" x3-1/8", rect, Continental silver, tortoise shell, and enamel, floral and shell engraved silver frame, one side with oval-3/4" portrait of damsel, Victorian, mid half 19th C	350.00

Hair Ornament, Art Nouveau
Back Comb, gilt grass, turquoise glass accents	135.00
Side, applied metallic dec, simulated gemstones	75.00
Hairpin, carved poppy blossom, heavy shell	135.00
Inkstand, 8" x16", three cut glass bottles, brass inlay, shaped handles	400.00
Letter Opener, sterling silver, stylized spear design, sterling shaft, tortoiseshell blade, hallmark for William Spratling, Taxco, Mexico	690.00
Match Box Cover, applied red coral trim	65.00
Match Safe, 2-3/8" l, silver trim, felt lined, octagonal, push button opening	200.00
Necessaire, 10" l, tortoiseshell and ivory, rect, fitted int. with sewing implements, ball feet, Victorian, mid 19th C	865.00
Patch Box, 3-1/4" d, brass inlaid, scrolled foliate and bird design, Continental, 19th C, minor breaks	150.00
Snuff Box, 1-3/8" d, ivory medallion with miniature watercolor painting of gentleman in blue coat, Anglo/American School, 18th C	375.00

Tea Caddy
5" w, 5-1/2" h, George III, silver mounts, ivory inlay, late 18th C	1,375.00
6" x 8" x 5-1/2", William IV, oblong top, bread front outline, twin canisters, conforming case resting on molded base, second quarter 19th C	900.00
7-3/4" l, blonde, two cov interior compartments, Regency, 19th C, losses	865.00

TOYS

History: The first cast iron toys began to appear in America shortly after the Civil War. Leading 19th-century manufacturers include Hubley, Dent, Kenton, and Schoenhut. In the first decades of the 20th century, Arcade, Buddy L, Marx, and Tootsie Toy joined these earlier firms. Wooden toys were made by George Brown and other manufacturers who did not sign or label their work.

Nuremberg, Germany, was the European center for the toy industry from the late 18th through the mid-20th centuries. Companies such as Lehman and Marklin produced high-quality toys.

References: Linda Baker, *Modern Toys, American Toys*, Collector Books, 1985, 1993 value update; Bill Bruegman, *Toys of the Sixties*, Cap'n Penny Productions, 1991; Dana Cain, *Collecting Monsters of Film and TV*, Krause

Publications, 1997; Jurgen and Marianne Cieslik, *Lehmann Toys*, New Cavendish Books, 1982; *Collector's Digest Price Guide to Pull Toys*, L-W Book Sales, 1996; Don Cranmer, *Collectors Encyclopedia, Toys—Banks*, L-W Books, 1986, 1993 value update; Charles F. Donovan, Jr., *Renwal, World's Finest Toys*, published by author (11877 US Hwy 431, Ohatchee, AL 36271), 1994; Elmer Duellman, *Elmer's Price Guide to Toys*, vol. 2, L-W Book Sales, 1996; James L. Dundas, *Gap Guns with Values*, Schiffer Publishing, 1996; Edward Force, *Lledo Toys*, Schiffer Publishing, 1996; Tom Frey, *Toy Bop: Kid Classics of the 50's & 60's*, Fuzzy Dice Productions, 1994.

Christine Gentry and Sally Gibson-Downs, *Motorcycle Toys*, Collector Books, 1994; David C. Gould and Donna Crevar-Donaldson, *Occupied Japan Toys with Prices*, L-W Book Sales, 1993; Ted Hake, *Hake's Price Guide To Character Toys,* Gemstone Publishing, 1998; Morton Hirschberg, *Steam Toys*, Schiffer Publishing, 1996; Andrew Gurka, *Pedal Car Restoration and Price Guide,* Krause Publications, 1996; Dee Hockenberry, *Big Bear Book*, Schiffer Publishing, 1996; Don Hultzman, *Collecting Battery Toys*, Books Americana, 1994; Ken Hutchison & Greg Johnson, *Golden Age of Automotive Toys, 1925-1941*, Collector Books, 1996; Charles M. Jacobs, *Kenton Cast Iron Toys*, Schiffer Publishing, 1996;Alan Jaffe, *J. Chein and Co., A Collector's Guide to an American Toymaker,* Schiffer Publishing, 1997; Dana Johnson, *Matchbox Toys 1947-1996*, 2nd ed., Collector Books, 1996; Michele Karl, *Composition & Wood Dolls and Toys: A Collector's Reference Guide*, Antique Trader Books, 1998; Dale Kelley, *Die Cast Price Guide, Post-War: 1946-Present,* Antique Trader Books, 1997; Lisa Kerr, *American Tin-Litho Toys*, Collectors Press, 1995; Constance King, *Metal Toys & Automata*, Chartwell Books, 1989; Sharon Korbeck, *Toys & Prices, 1998*, 5th ed., Krause Publications, 1997.

Cynthia Boris Liljeblad, *TV Toys and the Shows that Inspired Them*, Krause Publications, 1996; Jerrell Little, *Collector's Digest Price Guide to Cowboy Cap Guns and Guitars*, L-W Book Sales, 1996; David Longest, *Antique & Collectible Toys 1870-1950*, Collector Books, 1994; ——, *Character Toys and Collectibles* (1984, 1992 value update), 2nd Series (1987), Collector Books; ——, *Toys*, Collector Books, 1990, 1994 value update; Charlie Mack, *Encyclopedia of Matchbox Toys*, 1947-1996, Schiffer Publishing, 1997; Bill Manzke, *The Encyclopedia of Corgi Toys*, Schiffer Publishing, 1997; Brian Moran, *Battery Toys*, Schiffer Publishing, 1984; Richard O'Brien, *Collecting Toys*, 8th ed., Krause Publications, 1997; ——, *Collecting Toy Cars & Trucks*, 2nd ed., Krause Publications, 1997; ——, *Collecting American Made Toy Soldiers*, Krause Publications, 1997; ——, *Collecting Foreign-Made Toy Soldiers*, Krause Publications, 1997; Bob Parker, *Hot Wheels*, revised ed., Schiffer Publishing, 1996; ——, *Marx Toys*, Schiffer Publishing, 1996.

John Ramsay, *British Diecast Model Toys*, 6th ed., available from Tim Arthurs (Ralston Gallery, 109 Gover Ave., Norwalk, CT 06850), 1996; David E. Richter, *Collector's Guide to Tootsietoys*, 2nd ed., Collector Books, 1996; Vincent Santelmo, *The Complete Encyclopedia to*

G. I. Joe, 2nd ed., Krause Publications, 1997; Martyn L. Schorr, *Guide to Mechanical Toy Collecting*, Performance Media, 1979; *Schroeder's Collectible Toys*, 3rd ed., Collector Books, 1996; Carole and Richard Smith, *Pails by Comparison*, published by author (P.O. Box 2068, Huntington, NY 11743), 1996; Craig Strange, *Collector's Guide to Tinker Toys*, Collector Books, 1996; Carl P. Stirn, *Turn-of-the-Century Dolls, Toys and Games* (1893 catalog reprint), Dover Publications, 1990; Jack Tempest, *Post-War Tin Toys*, Wallace-Homestead, 1991; Carol Turpen, *Baby Boomer Toys and Collectibles*, Schiffer Publishing, 1993; Gerhard G. Walter, *Metal Toys from Nuremberg*, Schiffer Publishing, 1992.

Periodicals: *Antique Toy World*, P.O. Box 34509, Chicago, IL 60634; *Canadian Toy Mania*, P.O. Box 489, Rocanville, Saskatchewan SOA 3LO Canada; *Die Cast & Tin Toy Report*, 559 North Park Ave., Easton, CT 06612; *Model & Toy Collector Magazine*, 137 Casterton Ave., Akron, OH 44303; *Plane News*, P.O. Box 845, Greenwich, CT 06836; *Robot World & Price Guide*, P.O. Box 184, Lenox Hill Station, New York, NY 10021; *Toy Cannon News*, P.O. Box 2052-N, Norcross, GA 30071; *Toy Collector & Price Guide*, 700 E. State St., Iola, WI 54990; *Toy Collector Marketplace*, 1550 Territorial Rd., Benton Harbor, MI 49022; *Toy Gun Collectors of America Newsletter*, 312 Starling Way, Anaheim, CA 92807; *Toy Shop*, 700 East State St., Iola, WI 54990; *Toy Trader*, P.O. Box 1050, Dubuque, IA 52004; Toybox Magazine, 8393 E. Holly Rd., Holly, MI 48442; *U.S. Toy Collector Magazine*, P.O. Box 4244, Missoula, MT 59806; *Yo-Yo Times*, P.O. Box 1519, Herndon, VA 22070.

Collectors' Clubs: American Game Collectors Association, P.O. Box 44, Dresher, PA 19025; Antique Engine, Tractor & Toy Club, Inc., 5731 Paradise Rd., Slatington, PA 18080; Antique Toy Collectors of America, 13th Floor, Two Wall St., New York, NY 10005; Capitol Miniature Auto Collectors Club, 10207 Greenacres Dr., Silver Spring, MD 20903; Diecast Exchange Club, P.O. Box 1066, Pineallas Park, FL 34665; Ertl Collectors Club, Highways 136 & 120, Dyersville, IA 52040; Farm Toy Collectors Club, P.O. Box 38, Boxholm, IA 50040; Majorette Diecast Toy Collectors Association, 13447 NW Albany Ave., Bend, OR 97701; Miniature Piano Enthusiast Club, 633 Pennsylvania Ave., Hagerstown, MD 21740; San Francisco Bay Brooklin Club, P.O. .Box 61018, Palo Alto, CA 94306; Schoenhut Collectors Club, 45 Louis Ave., West Seneca, NY 14224; Southern California Toy Collectors Club, Ste. 300, 1760 Termino, Long Beach, CA 90804.

Museums: American Museum of Automobile Miniatures, Andover, MA; Eugene Field House & Toy Museum, St Louis, MO; Evanston Historical Society, Evanston, IL 60201; Forbes Magazine Collection, New York, NY; Hobby City Doll & Toy Museum, Anaheim, CA; Margaret Woodbury Strong Museum, Rochester, NY; Matchbox & Lesney Toy Museum, Durham, CT; Matchbox Road Museum, Newfield, NJ; Museum of the City of New York, New York, NY; Smithsonian Institution, Washington, DC; Spinning Top Exploratory Museum, Burlington, WI; Toy & Miniature Museum of Kansas City, Kansas City, MO; Toy

Museum of Atlanta, Atlanta, GA; Washington Dolls' House & Toy Museum, Washington, DC; Western Reserve Historical Society, Cleveland, OH.

Additional Listings: Characters; Disneyana; Dolls; Schoenhut. Also see *Warman's Americana & Collectibles* for more examples.

Notes: Every toy is collectible; the key is condition. Good working order is important when considering mechanical toys. Examples in this listing are considered to be at least in good condition, if not better, unless otherwise specified.

Alexander, USA, race car, cast aluminum, front drive gas powered racer, hard rubber tires, 1940s upright spring car styling, orig tires, 20" l, no motor, hood replaced, grill missing 2,100.00
Arcade, USA
  Bus, cast iron, double decker, green, gold trim, nickel plated radiator and wheels, balloon tires, attached driver, three detachable passengers, 1950s 750.00

Bus, cast iron, fair orig white paint, orig wheels with dual tires at rear, nickel driver, 12" l 250.00
Coupe, 6-3/4" l, Chevy Superior, cast iron, black, gold trim, nickel plated driver and tires, 1928 . . . . 550.00
Gasoline Truck, 13" l, Lubrite, orig Mack truck paper labels on cab, red, nickel plated driver and tires, gilt lettering and accents 2,300.00
International Harvester Dump Truck, cast iron, red, nickel plated crank mechanism for lifting rear dump, yellow wheels, 10-1/2" l, fair orig paint, one wheel replaced 350.00
Lindy Airplane, cast iron, painted gray, emb wings read "Lindy," nickeled propeller motors, painted black, aluminum blades, 13-1/2" wingspan, replaced tires 1,870.00
McCormick-Deering Farm Machine, cast iron, orig gray and red paint, Arcade decal, white wheels, 10" l, rust on nickel plated parts 250.00
Model T Sedan, orig black paint, nickel plated driver, 6-1/2" l 195.00
Austin, pedal car, 61" l, J40, low-slung contours, surface rust on left front fender 1,610.00
Bergmann, Althof, USA, boy bell ringer, hand painted, boy mounted on small spoked wheels, wire in hand appears to pull large bell supported on ornate heart-shaped spoke wheels, American cloth flag mounted to center of wires, c1880, 8-1/2" l 1,760.00
Bing, Gebruder, Germany
  Luchs Gunboat, hand painted tin, painted gray, red trim, side guns, two deck mounted cannons, completely railed deck, crows nest, three stacks and funnels, observation deck, lifeboats, clockwork mechanism, 23-1/2" l 3,300.00
  Ocean Liner, hand painted tin, red and blue hull, deck cabin level with windows on each side, upper lever deck contains eight lifeboats on supports, three funnels, three masts, stacks, railed observation decks, two stationary lifeboats and chained anchors, clockwork mechanism, 31" l, some over paint 7,975.00
  Union Ferry Boat, hand painted tin, red hull, brown open deck, white deck housing, railings on side, window cutouts on both sides, stack on roof, clockwork mechanism, 12" l 1,100.00
  Warship, hand painted tin, gray, red striped hull, upper deck with three stacks, five funnels, four lifeboats, cabin, railed observation level, two masts, one with crow's nest, side mounted cannon turrets, chained anchors, two deck mounted guns, clockwork mechanism concealed in body, 27" l 4,950.00
Bing Toy Works, Germany
  Amphibian Airplane, hand painted tin, overhead engines, clockwork housing in fuselage, painted silver and brown, 16" wingspan, some silver over paint. 800.00

Arcade, Greyhound Bus, Century of Progress, Chicago, 1933, cast iron, painted white and white, orig label, rubber tires, 11-1/2" l, $425.

Convertible Touring Car, litho tin, clockwork, yellow, brown trim, simulated top down model, striped seats, seated driver, full running boards, 11-1/2" l 1,980.00

De Dion Runabout, hand painted tin, white, gold trim, red upholstered emb finish, two open seats, front head lamp and curved running boards, 8" l 2,310.00

Limousine, litho tin, clockwork, red body, black roof, full running boards, seated driver, spare mounted on side, gold finished grill, spoke wheels, partial orig box, 10-1/2" l 2,100.00

Pigmyphone, litho tin wind-up, tin container, illus of Little Red Riding Hood, Wolf, Seven Dwarfs, two black banjo players, Little Wonder record plays "The Alcoholic Blues," extra box of needles, 6" x 6" x 3-1/2", some overall soiling 50.00

Taxi limousine. beveled-glass windows, carriage lights, bright red, orange, and green paint with black trim; 14-1/4" l 21,850.00

Tug Boat, hand painted tin, red and black hull, upper deck painted yellow, pilot's house, mast with rigging, stack on cabin, two support beams, clockwork mechanism, 9-1/2" l 1,350.00

Bliss, USA

Buffalo Floor Train, 45" long, litho paper on wood, alphabet blocks cargo and connecting rod missing, c1900 . . . . .7,190.00

Horse Drawn Chariot, wood, paper lithography, drawn by wheeled horse, ornate details, stamped cardboard seat, "C" shaped chariot with curtained back window graphics, covered roof, 15-1/2" h, 23" l 1,540.00

Brown, George, USA, paddle wheeler, tin, hand painted, stenciled, light blue boat, red top deck roof, cast iron spoke wheels, two stacks, stenciled "Monitor" on sides, American tin flag on bowl, ball pole on stem, clockwork 5,280.00

Bub, Karl, Germany, Man Riding Horse Cart, hand painted tin, clockwork, portly man seated in open cart, spoke wheels, pulled by solo horse, 11-3/4" l 420.00

Buddy L, USA

Allied Van Lines, pressed steel, painted orange and black duo-tone, International cab, semi trailer body, adv on sides, rubber tires, metal disc wheels, 28-3/4" l, missing pull rod, fair condition 440.00

Army Truck

Pressed steel, painted olive green, enclosed cab, canopy cov body, mkd "Army" on sides, orig box, 17" l . . 385.00

Wood, painted olive green, yellow dummy lights, canvas top on cargo bed, orig box, 12-1/2" l 420.00

Buddy L, steam shovel, pressed steel, $285

Army Truck and Trailer, pressed steel, painted army green, tractor with open bed body pulling smaller body, wires for canvas canopy, rubber tires, 31" l 135.00

Baggage Truck, pressed steel, painted white and green, enclosed cab, open bed body, automatic tail gate, rubber tires, metal wheels, 1950s, 25" l, missing tail gate and seat 100.00

Circus On Wheels, sheet metal cab, cage sided van body, each compartment with animal, ornately dec, painted red, orig decals, orig box, 25-1/2" l 1,210.00

City Dray, pressed steel, enclosed cab painted green, yellow open stake body, rubber tires with emb spokes, electric headlights, 1934, 18-1/2" l 360.00

Dump Truck, pressed steel, enclosed cab painted black, red dump body, rubber tires, emb spoke wheels, electric lights, 20-1/2" l 440.00

Fire Truck, extension ladder, red, black, white, and silver pressed steel, late 1940s, 32" l, 8" h 350.00

Greyhound Bus, pressed steel, blue and white paint, decaled logo and name, battery operated tail light, wind-up, rolling action opens door, rings bell, 16-1/2" l 275.00

Ice Truck, pressed steel, 1920s International model truck, duo tone green and yellow, open bed body with canvas ice cover, rear platform, rubber tires, emb spoke wheels, 21-1/2" l, cab repainted 500.00

Ladder Truck, International model cab, hood, mounted brass bell, painted red and yellow duo tone, attached trailer with ladders mounted on supports, full running boards, rubber tires, disc wheels, orig decals, 1940s, 29-1/2" l 200.00

Moving Van, No. 204, black cab, red body, 1926, 25" l, decals missing 575.00

Parcel Delivery Truck, pressed steel, brown and beige paint, large slant black body, rear doors, decals on sides, solid rubber wheels, 24" l, pull bar and one headlight missing 990.00

Passenger Bus, pressed steel, light green, 22 chair seats, two benches, spare tires on sides, 29" l, shellacked 3,300.00

Railway Express, pressed steel, 1938 International cab, painted yellow and green duo-tone, van body with removable top, opening rear doors, large side decals adv "Wrigley's Spearmint Chewing Gum," rubber tires, emb spoke wheels, 24" l 715.00

Robotoy, pressed steel, red tractor, green dump body, black chassis, electrical, moves forwards and backwards to automatically dump cargo, orig transformer and box, 21-5/8" l 2,310.00

Shell Oil Truck, pressed steel, International model cab, orange and red duo-tone, decals on tank body "Shell Fuel Oils," rubber wheels, red centers, 20-3/4" l, dent to grill 360.00

Station Wagon, all wood, maroon front, hood fenders, side panels, and roof with simulated wood graining, opening front and rear doors, side decals "Buddy 'L' Station Wagon," orig box, 19" l 1,100.00

Wrecking Truck, pressed steel, painted white, enclosed cab, open bed body, electric lights, crane on rear platform, rubber tires, emb spoke wheels, c1934, 20-1/2" l, fair condition 200.00

Carrette, Germany

Gun Boat, hand painted tin, brown, red hull stripe, railed deck, pilot's house, two stacks, two guns and mast, 16" l, mast loose 660.00

Limousine, hand painted tin, clockwork, maroon, orange trim, two head lamps, two side lanterns, glass windows, opening doors, detailed molded seats, full running boards, rubber tires, 12-1/4" l, professionally restored 2,750.00

Limousine, litho tin, clockwork, deep green, brown and yellow trim, black full running boards, nickel plated head lamps, side lanterns, opening side doors, glass windows, seated hand painted chauffeur, rubber tires, spoke wheels, roof rack, 16" l, replaced lights 7,150.00

River Boat, hand painted tin, red and cream hull, yellow corrugated deck simulating wood flooring, cabin deck with curtained corners, stairs lead to upper deck, railed bow and stern, twin screw activated by clockwork mechanism, 17" l, stairs railway missing 660.00

Chad Valley, England, touring sedan, litho tin, clockwork, green, window graphics of driver and passengers, luggage rack on rear, nickeled grill, 9" l 660.00

Citroen, France

Aviation Fuel Truck, pressed steel, clockwork, painted red, enclosed cab with opening driver's door, tanker body with filler cap and brass drain valve, electric headlights, rear decal "AVIA," 18" l 1,320.00

Coupe, pressed steel, clockwork, painted maroon, black roof and trunk, chromed grill, molded seats, 11-1/2" l, replaced tires, clockwork and lights missing. 495.00

Delivery Truck, litho tin, friction, green, black highlights, covered body, exposed tail end, curved fenders, 9" l . . 825.00

Fire Engine, painted tin, clockwork, red, open bench seats, removable hose reel, ladders mount on rear body, disc wheels, rubber tires, orig box, 19" l 2,860.00

Flat Bed Truck, litho tin, friction, enclosed green cab, nickeled front grill, black flat bed body, removable stake side rear, pulley bar, body hooks, 12-1/4" l 1,045.00

Race Car, pressed steel, clockwork, blue, molded seated figure with hand painted composition head, rubber tires, decal "Petite Rosalie," 12-1/4" l 440.00

Sedan, litho tin, clockwork, bright orange and red, molded black seats, full running boards, dummy headlights, opening driver's door, 11-1/2" l, repainted lights 1,210.00

Stake Truck, litho tin, flywheel on rear axle, enclosed cab painted red, yellow highlights, blue stake side body, curved venders, 9" l 990.00

Converse/Packer Mason, USA, open touring car, orig driver, paint on wood and tin fair, cast wheels, 9" l 250.00

Cor Cor Mfg., USA

Army Truck, sheet metal, painted brown, enclosed cab, low side body, cloth canopy cover reads "Army" on sides, orig box, 17" l 385.00

Bus, pressed steel, painted blue, int. seating, front dummy lights, sides emb "Cor-Cor Toys - Washington, Indiana," 24" l 525.00

C. R., France, bus, litho tin, clockwork, modeled after "De Dion" autobus, extensively detailed, top marquees read "Trocadera-Gare de L'est," seated driver, 11" l 1,980.00

Dent, USA, fire wagon, cast iron, red paint, yellow wheels, orig figures and horses, two ladders, 15" l 150.00

Distler, Germany, limousine, litho tin, clockwork, deep blue, aqua blue trim, full running boards, opening repair box on each side, two brass plated headlights, folding rear rack, c1920, 12" l 1,320.00

Erbl, Hans, Germany

Comic Convertible Car, litho tin, clockwork allows car to rollover onto it's roll bar, extensive graphics of faces in spirited patterns, seated tin clown driver, 10" l, fair condition
. . . . 550.00

Delivery Truck, litho tin, clockwork, blue and red body, black roof, overhead luggage rack, full running boards, spoked

metal wheels, seated driver in doorless open cab, 8" l, fair condition. 660.00

Delivery Truck, litho tin, clockwork, red and black body, black roof, open rear door, open side door, seated driver, sides read "Strawbridge & Clothier," spoke wheels, 7-1/2" l, paint cracked 1,320.00

Fischer, Heinrich, & Co., Germany, penny toy

Fire Engine, pumper truck 145.00

Roadster, open, sloping hood 2,650.00

Fleischmann, Germany

Cargo Ship, hand painted tin, red and black, upper deck features railed cat walks from pilot's house to cabins and observation deck, three funnels, railed sides, multi leveled cabins, clockwork mechanism, 19-1/2" l, missing masts
. . . . 725.00

Ocean Liner, *Bremen* type, hand painted tin, white, blue hull stripe, brown deck, upper deck cabin features windows and port holes, two masts, pilot house crews nest, two stacks and two life boats, clockwork mechanism, 12-3/4" l, small dent on one side 990.00

Ocean Liner, hand painted and litho tin, white, blue hull stripe, upper deck cabin with diecut windows, port holes, lifeboats, pilot's house, two masts, railed bow and stern, clockwork mechanism, 19-1/2" l, one replaced mast 1,210.00

F. V., France, touring car, hand painted tin, yellow, maroon and gold striping, open bench seat painted blue, full curved fenders, nickeled lanterns, front headlamp, rubber tires with spoke wheels, clockwork mechanism, 10-1/2" l 3,100.00

Gunthermann, Germany

Bugle Player, hand painted tin, soldier with bugle in hand, circular base, plans" Soldier to Arms Call" when clockwork activated, 7-7/8" h 990.00

Convertible Touring Car, litho tin, clockwork, blue, gray trim, brown seats, front head lamps, full running boards, simulated top down model, seated driver behind glass windshield, 9-3/4" l 1,100.00

Monkey and Darkey Ministrels, hand painted tin, clarinet playing minstrel, seated monkey violinist, mounted on base, music stand, clockwork mechanism activates movement and rhythmic notes, 7-1/2" h x 6" w 1,320.00

Open Touring Car, litho tin, clockwork, blue, white, silver trim, unit "V" shaped hood, tow front lanterns, curved running boards, tin driver, two tin seated lady passengers, 10" l, repainted figures, new headlights 4,620.00

Saloon, litho tin, red, yellow trim, opening doors, glass windows, seated hand painted tin driver, curved running boards, fifth wheel on rear used with clockwork mechanism, 9-1/2" l 4,675.00

Vis-A-Vis, hand painted and litho tin, clockwork, open seat, railed arm rest and backrest, lamps on front, modeled after Peugeot motor car, rubber tires, spoked wheels, 10-1/4" l, new lamps, figure, two new tires 1,650.00

Vis-A-Vis, litho tin, clockwork, open seat car, seated driver, railed seat with backrest, rubber tires, spoked wheels, 6-1/2" l, replaced figure, mud guards, and lamps
. . . . .1,540.00

Hess Toy Company, Germany, racer, litho tin, open drivers seating for two, hood opens to expose intricate clockwork mechanism, rear tailgate opens, spoked metal wheels, 8-3/4" l, some litho wear 1,045.00

Hot Wheels, USA

Barbie Camaro

1st version 75.00

2nd version 65.00

Hills 1970 Plymouth Barracuda 28.00

J C Whitney
  Fat Fendered '40 . . . . 40.00
  Scorchin' Scooter 30.00
LAPD Series
  Police B Wagon 40.00
  Police Cruiser 40.00
  Lexmark Passion 45.00
  Randy's Stuff, pink VW Bug 75.00
  Yamahauler 20.00

HTMH, Russia, dump truck, litho tin, enclosed green cab, simulated wood stake side body, chassis and disk wheels painted brown, tin emblems on opening doors, bright tin hood trim lights, front grill, 2-1/4" l 150.00

Hubley, USA
  Auto Racer, 9-1/2" d, cast iron, nickel plated, red lift hood, black painted driver, nickel motor, Hustler rubber tires, c1928 . . . . 1,380.00
  Fire Patrol Wagon, 13" l, cast iron and steel, single black horse, red wagon, yellow wheels, driver and three fireman, steel wagon bed and seat, wear 1,380.00
  Grasshopper, cast iron, painted green, articulated back legs 660.00
  Jansen Surfer, cast iron, pull toy, young man in bathing suit mounted on surfboard, cast waves around sides, rubber tires 770.00
  Ladder Wagon, cast iron, horse drawn, fair condition red and white paint on wagon, two repainted figures, detached wheel, 30" l 100.00
  Lindy Airplane, cast iron, painted blue, gold lettering emb on wings, nickeled propeller, 5-5/8" wingspan 825.00
  Mack Dump Truck, cast iron, orig green and red paint, 7" l 325.00
  Monkey Riding Tricycle, cast iron, full figure monkey, three spoked wheels, rubber tires, legs articulate a bicycle moves, 7" l 3,080.00
  Motorcycle with Side Car, 8-3/4" l, cast iron, two removable policeman, balloon tires, 1932 . . . . 1,265.00
  Popeye Patrol Motorcycle, 8-3/4" l, cast iron, rubber tires, orig paint, 1938 . . . . 2,300.00
  Racer, 10-3/4" l, cast iron, aluminum with red accents and driver, rubber wheels, chrome wheel moving pistons, 1938 . . . . 2,130.00
  Santa and Sleigh, cast iron, repainted blue sleigh, orig Santa, white paint on reindeer, intact antlers, 14" l 650.00
  Static Speedboat, cast iron, painted yellow, red trim, seated driver, brown jacket, re cap, holds Johnson throttle in hand, clicker on back axle, nickeled disk wheels with rubber tires, 10" l 4,400.00

Ives, USA
  Coal Cart, cast iron, drawn by donkey, painted red, yellow spoke wheels, emb "Coal" on sides, figure stands in cart, 13" l 385.00
  Fire Patrol Wagon, 19-3/8" l, single running horse, brown with black tack, red wagon and wheels, six fireman, driver with cap and visor, c1890 . . . . 1,850.00
  Fire Pumper, cast iron, painted black, gold trim on stack, open driver's seat, bulb with eagle ornament, large boiler, seated driver, standing firemen on rear platform, red spoke wheels, drawn by two horses attached to frame by center spoke wheel, 24" l 4,750.00
  Gun Ship, hand painted tin, gray, bow and stern guns, pilot's house, two stacks, funnels, two lifeboats and clockwork mechanism, 13" l 200.00

JEP, France
  Airplane, litho tin, single propeller, red, silver front fuselage, extensive graphics, seated pilot, wings mkd "F-255," spoke wheels, clockwork mechanism, 19" wingspan 1,760.00
  Delage Racer, pressed steel, painted blue, open drivers seat, molded seat painted brown, slant front nickeled grill, stenciled #6 on boat tail, clockwork mechanism, composition figure, 17" l 1,550.00
  Fire Apparatus Truck, litho tin, clockwork, red, yellow simulated wood, open bench seats, two tin seated firemen, extension ladder, swivel base, hose reels mounted to running boards, nickeled front grill, 13" l 1,100.00
  Hispano Suiza, auto, yellow, red running boards, nickeled steps, maroon molded seat int., nickeled lights, grill, side horn, windshield bracket, radiator mascot, well detailed, intricate clockwork mechanism with differential axles, disc wheels, rubber tires, 19-1/2" l, professionally restored 2,970.00
  Racer, pressed steel, painted white, open seat with composition figure, molded seats painted brown, muffler runs along side, rubber tires, clockwork mechanism, 18" l, repainted 550.00
  Rolls Royce, pressed steel, green, red trim, simulated top down, molded seats, separate passengers windshield, seated composition figure, electric lights, clockwork mechanism activated from front, full running boards, 19" l, professionally restored 3,850.00
  Rolls Royce Open Phaeton, pressed steel, white and red, fully curved running boards, step runner, separate winged passenger windshield, upholstered look seating, two electric headlights, disc wheels, rubber tires, clockwork, 1928, 19-1/2" l 2,200.00
  Ruban Bleu Speedboat, sheet metal, painted red and ream, sealed figure at wheel behind windshield, rudder lever on deck, clockwork mechanism, sides stenciled with name, 13-1/2" l 440.00
  Touring Car, tin, painted shades of brown, electric headlights, spare tires, full running boards, maroon painted seats, individual passenger's windshield, classic bonnet styled grill, clockwork mechanism activated propeller shaft rear axle with differential, orig book from Rapport General Paris show where car was exhibited, c1925, 17-1/2" l, mint condition 39,600.00

Joustra, France, airplane, Air France, litho tin
  Blue, silver, and white, commercial airplane, four propellers, three fin tail wings, rubber tires, friction powered, orig box, 19-1/2" l 550.00
  Red and yellow, extensive graphics, electric light, six propellers, three fin tail wing, clockwork mechanism, orig box, 23" l 1,045.00

J. P., France, city bus, litho tin, clockwork, green and white, destinations on sides, six spoke wheels, 10-1/2" l 550.00

Kenton, USA
  Farm Wagon, cast iron, green painted wagon, rear yellow wheels, 14" l, fair paint 150.00
  Fire Pumper, cast iron, painted yellow, open seat wagon with large boiler, side cranks, driver's lanterns, two figures, red spoke wheels, three horses in flight attached to frame with two center mounted spoke wheels, 27" l 2,970.00
  Log Carrier, double team, black driver, early 1900s, 15-1/4" l, chains broken 460.00
  Overland Circus, animal cage, yellow vehicle, gold trim, cream and gold wheels, brown bear, 1927, 9" l 1,380.00

Patrol Car, dark blue, gilt lettering and accents, nickel plated and red wheels, driver and three policemen, c1927, 9-1/8" l, paint worn on figures. 1,100.00

Touring Car, cast iron, 1920s, 9-1/4" l, driver and passenger missing. 490.00

Keystone, USA

Bus, pressed steel, gray, cream hinged roof, wooden handles on top of roof for steering, simulated headlights and tail lights, rear railing decal on grill "Packard," side decals "Coast-to-Coast Keystone Bus," large door decals lists 15 cities, greyhound decal on side, 31" l, fair condition 1,430.00

Dump Truck, pressed steel, black open bench seat cab and chassis, red dump body, hand lever for tilting body, disc wheels, rubber tires, 26" l, over painted. 300.00

Ride 'Em Plane, pressed steel, fighter plane, child's seat and handle bars on fuselage, propeller revolves, painted gray, red wings, rubber tires, disc wheels on front, 27" wingspan, fair condition 275.00

Kiddies, USA, Oh-Boy moving van, pressed steel, black cab, red van body, #210 Moving Van decals, disc wheels simulated duals on rear, fender tab broken, fair condition. . . 825.00

Kilgore, USA, Sea Gull airplane, cast iron, painted orange, blue wings, wing mounted nickeled propeller, nickeled disc wheels, 8-1/4" wingspan .1,100.00

Kingsbury Toys, USA

Chrysler Airflow, pressed steel, painted brown, chromed grill, clockwork and battery box 2,640.00

Golden Arrow Racer, Major Segrave as driver, working mechanism, gold paint, 95% orig Kingsbury decal, orig paper tag, 20" l. 1,200.00

KW, Germany, carousel, litho tin wind-up, Victorian dressed women swing around 9" carousel, working 300.00

Latil, France, delivery truck, litho in, van body, green and black, white roof, extensive adv, opening front and rear doors, electric headlights, clockwork mechanism, 16-1/2" l, one replaced door 1,650.00

Lehmann, Germany

Africa, Ostrich Mail, litho tin, string wind drive, 6" l. . . 880.00

Alabama Coon Jigger, litho tin, clockwork, dancer on platform, orig box. 825.00

Also Automobile, litho tin, clockwork, yellow and red, open cab, 3-3/4" l 935.00

Autin, litho and hand painted tin, clockwork, boy in pedal car, 4-1/4" l 615.00

Autohutte, litho tin

One car, Stiller, yellow and black sedan, clockwork mechanism parked in cottage style garage with silhouette of children at play on back, ornate graphics, 6"l 2,860.00

Two car, red scalloped roof, large opening front doors stores sedan EPL No. 760 and the Galop, both included, orig box 6-1/4" x 7" w, missing box lid. 2,320.00

Baker and Sweep, litho and hand painted tin, clockwork, baker with spoon in hand, chimney sweep in charcoal, 5-1/2" l 4,400.00

Balky Mule, litho and hand painted tin, clockwork, comical clown, cart, and donkey, fabric suit, orig box, 8" l . . 550.00

Buster Brown, litho and hand painted tin, friction, seated in open auto, 4" l 1,650.00

Coco, string pull toy, man climbing palm tree, paper leaves, 14-1/2" h 1,045.00

Convertible, litho tin

Berolina, navy blue, red trim and int., tan cloth top, 6-3/4" l 1,380.00

Left, Buck's Junior cast iron stove, $1,150; Stitchwells child's sewing machine, $550; Kenton Novelty cast iron stove, $550. Photo courtesy of Jackson's Auctioneers & Appraisers.

Chromed grill, bumpers, and spare, orig box, 4" l 360.00

Crawling Beetle, litho tin, clockwork, light green wings, wings move, crawls, 4" x 4-1/2" l 440.00

Crocodile, litho tin, clockwork, animated, simulated real life colors, walks and jaw moves, 9-1/2" l 500.00

Dancing Sailor, Columbia on hat, 1903, 7-1/2" h, repairs to box 690.00

Dump Truck, litho tin, red cab, green stationary dump body, chromed grill, rubber tires, orig box, 4-1/4" l 250.00

Express, litho and hand painted tin, clockwork, porter wearing blue jack, pulling trunk carrier, 6" l 660.00

Flying Bird, hand painted tin, paste board bird suspended by two strings, wings, orig box, 10" wingspan, missing box lid 660.00

Galop, litho tin, clockwork, cowboy rider pulled by zebra, c1954, orig box, 7-1/4" l 990.00

Going to the Fair, litho and hand painted tin, flywheel, woman seated in promenade chair, 5" h, 6-1/2" l 3,190.00

Gustav the Miller, litho tin, string pull, figure climbs long shaft to mill, orig box, 18" h. 440.00

Hansom Cab, litho and hand painted tin, clockwork, 5-1/2" l 1,980.00

Kadi, litho and hand painted tin, clockwork, two Chinese figures with tea chest, 7" l 2,310.00

Kamerun, litho tin, string wind drive, ostrich drawn cart, black boy seated on open bench seat, 6" l 1,100.00

Lehmann Family, litho tin, flywheel action, walking figures, 6-1/2" h. 4,400.00

Lolo Automobile, litho tin, friction, open cab, 3-3/4" l . 385.00

Mandarin, litho and hand painted tin, clockwork, Chinese in sedan chair, pulled by two servants, 7" l 2,750.00

Mars Motorcycle, litho and hand painted tin, clockwork, motorcycle, 3" x 4-3/4" l 660.00

Masuyama, litho and hand painted tin, clockwork, rickshaw, floral design on umbrella, 6-3/4" l 3,190.00

May Beetle, litho tin, clockwork, brown wings, 8" l . . . 660.00

Mensa Delivery Van, litho tin, clockwork, 5-1/4" l . . .2,530.00

Mikado Family, Japanese litho and hand painted tin, clockwork, rickshaw with seated woman holding baby, pulled by China man, 7" l. 1,430.00

Mixtum, litho and hand painted tin, clockwork
   Black driver, 4-1/4" l 1,760.00
   White driver, 4-1/4" l 2,420.00
Motor Car, litho tin, steering by front wheels, 5" l, replaced
   key handle 925.00
Naughty Boy, litho and hand painted tin, clockwork, car, driv-
   er, and boy, 5" l 1,430.00
Na-Nu, litho tin, clockwork, white driver, zebra drawn cart,
   7-1/4" l 1,100.00
Nina, Cat and Mouse, litho tin, large black and white cat chas-
   es mouse 1,650.00
Nu-Nu, litho and hand painted tin, clockwork, Chinese with
   tea chest, 5" l 1,210.00
Oho, litho tin, clockwork, open cab automobile, 3-3/4" l
   . . . . 550.00
Paak-Pak, litho tin, clockwork, duck cart and ducklings, 7" l
   . . . . 715.00
Paddy and the Pig, litho and hand painted tin, clockwork, fig-
   ure riding large scaled pig, 5" l 1,100.00
Performing Sea Lion, litho tin, clockwork, orig box, 8" l
   . . . . 600.00
Racer, litho tin, red, sleep body, disc wheels, 4" l . . . 275.00
Rad-Cycle Mars, 4-5/8" l 575.00
Rad Cycle Pulling Anxious Bride, litho and hand painted tin,
   clockwork, woman wearing large brim hat, 8-1/2" l, replaced
   key handle 3,080.00
Shell Filling Station, litho tin, two pumps, orig box, 5-1/2" w,
   4" d. 990.00
Suzi Turtle, litho tin, clockwork, boxer turtle, walking motion,
   orig box, 5" l 715.00
Swing Doll, litho tin, clockwork, seated china doll, cloth dress,
   7-1/4" h 2,970.00
Tap-Tap, litho and hand painted tin, clockwork, walking gar-
   dener, wheelbarrow and shove, 1920s, 7" l 1,045.00
Tut-Tut, litho and hand painted tin, clockwork, automobile
   and driver, 6-1/2" l 1,100.00
Tyras Walking Dog, litho tin, clockwork, 6" l 715.00
Uhu, litho and hand painted tin, clockwork, amphibian auto,
   simulated lights on sides of high windshield, propeller blad-
   ed wheels for water travel, 9" l 1,320.00
Zig-Zag, litho and hand painted tin, clockwork, rocking car,
   4-1/4" h 3,080.00
Zikra-Dare Devil, litho tin, clockwork, cart with driver pulled by
   kicking zebra, orig box, 7-1/4" l 1,650.00
Zikra-Dare Devil Na-Nu, litho tin, clockwork, black man seated in cart pulled by zebra, 7-1/4" l, two replaced legs
   . . . . 500.00
Zulu, litho tin, clockwork, ostrich mail, 7" l 660.00

Liberty Playthings, cruise boat, litho tin, clockwork, large red
   and white wooden wheels, blue wooden hull, bench seats,
   drier, 25" l 440.00
Linemar, Bubble Blowing Popeye, battery operated, 12-1/2" h,
   not working 900.00
Mamod, England, steam roller, chrome and painted, orig box,
   10" l 80.00
Marklin, Germany
   Construction Set, boxed, Chassis Set No. 1101, clockwork
      motor and light, all complete, orig instructions, 13" x 18"
      . . . . .2,250.00
   Military Armored Car, litho tin, painted camouflage colors, re-
      volving roof top gun turret, protruding guns, each window
      has slant lid shell protectors, nickeled bumpers, simulated
      riveting throughout, 14-1/2" l 2,475.00
   Rheinland Battleship, hand painted tin, olive green hull, deck
      painted in simulated wood flooring, railing throughout, four
      guns on each side, six deck cannons, with turrets, observa-
      tion deck, two masts, chained anchors, lifeboats supported
      on rods, two deck cranes, extensive details, stenciled
      "Rheinland," clockwork mechanism, 26-1/2" l 6,600.00
Martin, France
   Farmer with Sickle, hand painted tin face, lead feet and
      hands, farmer wears cloth suit, hold long handled sickle,
      simulates cutting motion when clockwork activated, 7-1/2" l,
      new jacket 1,045.00
   Mystery Ball, litho tin, ball with standing figure, travels down
      spiral band ball opens and then climbs to top for another de-
      scent, 12" h 925.00
   Violinist, hand painted tin face, lead hands and feet, cloth
      suit, top hat, clockwork mechanism activates violin playing,
      7-5/8" h. 615.00
Marx, Louis, Co., USA
   Coca-Cola Truck, pressed steel, yellow, stake sided body,
      orig decals, chromed grill and hood trim, black metal
      wheels, 20" l. 250.00
   Filling Station, litho tin, auto lift, restaurant, gas pumps, oil
      cart, tin truck, electric lights, orig box, 13-1/2" x 10" x 4"
      . . . . .1,000.00
   Fire Truck, sheet metal, painted red, yellow seat for child to
      ride, side mounted ladders, large roof top steering wheel,
      bell mounted to hood support, litho graphics on sides, orig
      box, 31" l 770.00
   Joe Penner Wanna Buy A Duck, litho tin wind-up, c1930,
      8-1/4" h. 230.00
   Mack City Coal Co. Truck, litho steel wind-up, silver with navy
      trim and lettering, black and green wheels, mkd "550 City
      Coal Co. Coal Coke," lever dump action, 13" l. 460.00
   Magic Garage, litho tin wind-up, convertible rolls forward and
      automatically opens garage door, orig box, 10" l. . . 225.00
   Merry Makers band, litho tin wind-up, 1930, minor wear, orig
      box, 9-1/8" h, 9-1/2" l 1,150.00
   Old Jalopy, litho tin wind-up, colorful graphics, 1940s, 7"
      . . . . 210.00
   Pathe News Automobile, mounted movie camera attached to
      roof, 9-1/2" x 9" x 4", some scratching, orig lettering on
      doors, orig paper decal .2,500.00
   Sandy, walking, carrying valise, litho tin, 1930s, 5" l
      . . . . 320.00
   Service Station, Roadside Rest, litho tin, lunch stand, gas
      pumps, free air, auto lift, Mobil motor oil cart, two gas light
      bulbs, 1920s, 5" h, 13-5/8" w, 10" d 635.00
   Warship, litho tin, extensive graphics, sparks from tail gun
      when clockwork activated, orig box, 14-1/2" l 265.00
Meier, Germany, penny toy
   Horse-drawn cab 330.00

Marx, litho tin wind-up, car, $95.

Horse-drawn landau 250.00
Omnibus, Grand Hotel, without horse 440.00
Roadster, open, "948" 750.00
Stake-back truck. 275.00
Touring car with chauffeur and passenger 750.00

Metal Craft, USA

Coca Cola Truck, painted metal, rubber tires, electric head-lights, stenciled, fixed adv logo on top, holds 10 bottles, 11" l 1,015.00

Goodrich Tires Service Truck, painted sheet metal, open bed with tires and winch, adv along side rail, 12" l, minor wear 275.00

Heinz 57 Truck, painted sheet metal, rubber tires, electric lights, 12" l, grill missing headlamp brackets 440.00

Meadow Gold Medal Butter Truck, painted sheet metal, rubber tires, electric lights, 13" l 1,650.00

Samarkand Ice Cream Truck, painted sheet metal, rubber tires, adv on van body, 10-3/4" l 3,250.00

Shell Motor Oil Truck, painted sheet metal, rubber tires, 8 orig cans, 12" l 825.00

Standard Stake Truck, painted shell metal, rubber tires, white stake body, red company name on side, 12" l 1,870.00

St. Louis Truck, painted sheet metal, disc wheels, company name on van body, 11-1/2" l 360.00

Sunshine Biscuit Truck, painted sheet metal, rubber tires, adv on van body, 12" l 1,210.00

Nain Blev, France, Bignan, luxury car, deep blue, wooden boat tail fin, full running boards, rubber tires, spoke wheels, open int. seating done in leather, electric lights mounted to hood, nickeled front grill with radiator cap, elaborate spring leaf suspension, clockwork mechanism, 18" l, professionally restored 2,750.00

Orkin Craft, motor boat, tin, clockwork, painted maroon, white and red hull, cabin deck, fully appointed, deck level open seat, trimmed windows, pilot's doors, funnels, railway, 31" l, chip off rear deck 3,025.00

Orobor, Germany

Cargo Plane, litho tin, three propellers, wood grain simulated cargo, intricate double clockwork mechanism allows propellers to spin while other activates wheel motion, 14-1/4" l 1,540.00

Packard Coupe, litho tin, clockwork, red, black top, rumble seat opens, full running boards, disc wheels, spare attached to trunk, "Packard" written across radiator, missing one great 2,860.00

Pratt and Letchworth, USA, Hanson cab, cast iron, light brown horse with white blanket, gold bridle, yellow and black cab, yellow wheels, driver missing, c1880 . . . . 685.00

Rossignol, C., France

Fire Engine, litho tin, clockwork, red, seated tin firemen on open bench seats, tin driver, silver extension ladder on swivel base, hose reels mounted on full running boards, headlights, spare wheels, 14-1/2" l 880.00

Turbine Car, live steam powered, hand painted, shades of blue, simulated wicker sides in green, gold trim, hand painted multicolored tin lady passenger, seated tin driver, steam powered turbine mechanism, 7" l 22,000.00

Steelcraft, USA, pedal airplane, US Navy Patrol, silver, red and blue trim, spring belt driver propeller, mid 20th C, 48" l 2,990.00

Steiff, Germany, Stratosplan Airplane, wire frame covered with fine paper, rubber tip, molded bears head, wings contain logo and emblems, orig box, 8" wingspan 330.008

Strauss, USA, Yell-O-Taxi, 8-1/2" l, one wheel repaired 410.00

Structo, USA

Loom, pressed steel, free standing, working model, 12-1/2" l 210.00

Transport Truck, pressed steel, painted red and gray, enclosed cab, semi trailer body, additional flat bed trailer, rubber tires, chromed hubs, side decal reads "Hi-Way Transport," 25" l 320.00

Sturditoy, USA, US mail truck, 25-1/2" l, 11" h, green, black, and red pressed steel, paint scratched on edges, 1920s 2,300.00

Tipp Co., Tipp & Co., Tipco, Germany

Army Truck and Cannon, litho tin wind-up, opening door, composition soldiers, well articulated cannon with working lever auction, elevation device, camouflaged, 16" l 100.00

Bomber Airplane, litho, clockwork mechanism drops lead cap bombs from wings underside while in motion, tan, red and blue graphics, 14-1/2" wingspan, replaced bombs 1,650.00

Club Sedan, litho tin, clockwork, bright orange and gray, two opening doors, elaborate int., seated driver, rear trunk lid opens, electric lights, full running boards, 1933, 17" l 1,540.00

Fuhrerwagon, litho tin, clockwork, Mercedes Benz, black, six different lights, two horns, side mounted muffler pipes, spares mounted on full running boards, convertible model, molded seats, 9" l 825.00

Limousine, litho tin, clockwork, green, luxury model, molded seats, tin dashboard with graphics, seated tin chauffeur, opening passenger doors, chromed front grill with hood ornament, 1920s, 15-1/2" l 4,125.00

Luxury Sedan, litho tin clockwork, maroon and brown, full running boards, opening doors, seated tin driver, luggage compartment, electric headlights, 19-1/2" l 2,100.00

Tonka, USA

Ace Hardware Semi Truck, red, decals, 1955 . . . . . . 425.00
Army Troop Carrier, 1964. . . . . 150.00
Bulldozer, orange, rubber treads, 1960 . . . . 75.00
Car Hauler, yellow, 1961 . . . . 250.00
Carnation Milk Van, white, decals, 1955 . . . . 200.00
Deluxe Fisherman, boat and trailer, 1960 . . . . 225.00
Dump Truck, 1949-53. . . . . 135.00
Fire Dept. Rescue Van, 1950s 150.00
Fire Truck, hydraulic aerial ladder, 1957 . . . . 200.00
Gasoline Tanker, red, 1957 . . . . 400.00
Green Giant Transport Truck, white, green lettering, 1953 . . . . 200.00
Hi-Way Mobil Clam, orange, 1961 . . . . 225.00
Hi-Way Sign Set, 1959. . . . . 250.00
Livestock Van, red, 1952 . . . . 150.00
Log Hauler, red cab, orig logs, 1953 . . . . 150.00
Pickup Truck, 1955. . . . . 195.00
Road Grader, orange, 1953 . . . . 75.00
Star-Kist Tuna Box Van, red cab, blue body, 1950-53 . . . . 180.00
Steam Shovel, red, 1949 . . . . 130.00
Tonka Air Express, black, decals, 1959 . . . . 300.00
Wrecker Truck, blue, 1949-53 . . . . 175.00

Tootsietoy, USA

Chrysler Convertible, '50, red, replaced windshield . . 150.00
Ford Station Wagon, '52, gray and blue, 4-1/4" l 45.00
GMC Box Truck, '39, green, 4-1/2" l, repainted 40.00
Jumbo Sedan, '47, #1018, green 35.00
Mercedes, '56, #995, red 195.00

Turner Toys, USA, touring coupe, pressed steel, red body, beige roof, green sun visor, brass striping and simulated

Unique Art, Li'l Abner Band, litho tin wind-up, $550.

headlights, friction mechanism activated by rear wheel, disc wheels, rubber tires, 25-1/2" l, restored 550.00

Unidentified Maker

Acrobat on Rings, hand painted tin, French acrobat performing on chained rings, mounted on base, 13-1/2" h 1,980.00

Bomber Plane, litho tin, lead cap bombs under wings which drop when clockwork is activated 715.00

Clown Riding Pig, hand painted tin, clockwork, clown in cloth suit, spoked wheel cart, pulled by pig, 8-3/4" l 660.00

Clown Weight Lifter, litho tin wind-up, red and blue duck print suit, bends forward and lifts "100" pound weight in his teeth, Germany, early 1900s, 7-1/2" h 1,100.00

Comical Car, litho tin, clockwork initiates clown's wild behavior, open seat, colorful clown in driver's seat, two clowns, one with umbrella in hand, sitting face to face in rear bench seats, comical graphics on all sides, disc wheels, Germany, 7" l 2,750.00

Dog, hand painted tin, clockwork, hunting dog carrying tin rabbit in mouth, two spoked wheels for movement, 6-3/4" l 495.00

Fisherman, litho tin, man with fishing pole spins rapidly in circle, Germany, 1920s, 5-1/2" h 320.00

Gun Ship, hand painted tin, gray, red hull stripe, railed deck, two lifeboats, two stacks, two funnels, two small guns mounted to iron bases, clockwork mechanism, 11-1/2" l, professionally restored. 250.00

Horse-Drawn Coach, detailed tin, hand painted, green, black trim, gold striping, two opening doors, back to back interior bench seats down in hand stitched silk lining, coach body accented with dual folding leather top, nickeled arms, open bench driver's seat with railed bracket, two front lanterns, high splash guard, spoke wheels drawn by gray painted tin horse, gold metal dec, mounted on tin wheeled base, hand painted composition figures of driver, coachman, gentleman, and two lady passengers, Germany, attributed to Lutz, professionally restored. .1,980.00

Limousine, litho tin, clockwork, gray, brown trim, full running boards, opening side doors, open chauffeur's compartment, seated driver, spoked wheels, Germany, 8-3/4" l, roof missing paint 990.00

Monkey Riding Handcar, hand painted tin, clockwork, bell hop uniform, steering platform wagon with spoke wheels, 5-1/2" l 465.00

Ostrich, Rudy, from Barney Google comic strip, litho tin wind-up, Germany, 1924, 8-1/2" h 575.00

Performing Clowns and Dog, hand painted tin, clockwork, two small clowns balancing on standing clown as he counter balance performers holding onto dog's paws, circular wheel platform, 11" h .1,760.00

Street Musician, hand painted tin, clockwork, musician wearing jacket and hat, head sways back and forth, arms and horn follow, 8" h 1,045.00

Unique, USA

Cycling Boy, litho tin wind-up, bell ringing peddling boy on tricycle, working, 9-1/2", some corrosion on bell. 150.00

G. I. Joe and His Jouncing Jeep, litho tin wind-up, 1940s, working, 8" 175.00

Jazzbo Jim, litho tin wind-up, 1920s, 9" h 230.00

Lil' Abner Dogpatch band, litho tin, 1946, 8-1/4" h 550.00

Rodeo Joe, litho tin wind-up, metal cowboy, novelty drive tractor, 7" l 175.00

Williams, A. C., USA

Ford Wrecker, '29, cast iron, dark blue 375.00

Fuel Truck, cast iron. 225.00

Sedan

Desoto Airflow, blue, white rubber tires, red hubs, 1937, 6-7/8" l 635.00

Pierce Arrow, 1933, cast iron, take apart type. . . . 275.00

Truck, 6-3/4" l, stake body, red body, green chassis, balloon tires, nickel plated radiator, late 1920s 635.00

Wyandotte, USA, sedan, La Selle, pressed steel, painted red, white rubber tires, 15" l 715.00

TRAINS, TOY

History: Railroading has always been an important part of childhood, largely because of the romance associated with the railroad and the prominence of toy trains.

The first toy trains were cast iron and tin; wind-up motors added movement. The golden age of toy trains was 1920 to 1955, when electric-powered units and high-quality rolling stock were available and names such as Ives, American Flyer, and Lionel were household words. The advent of plastic in the late 1950s resulted in considerably lower quality.

Toy trains are designated by a model scale or gauge. The most popular are HO, N, O and standard. Narrow gauge was a response to the modern capacity to miniaturize. Its popularity has decreased in the last few years.

References: Paul V. Ambrose, *Greenberg's Guide to Lionel Trains, 1945-1969*, Vol. III, Greenberg Publishing, 1990; Paul V. Ambrose and Joseph P. Algozzini, *Greenberg's Guide to Lionel Trains 1945-1969*, Vol. IV, Uncatalogued Sets (1992), Vol. V, Rare and Unusual (1993), Greenberg Publishing; Susan and Al Bagdade, *Collector's Guide to American Toy Trains*, Wallace-Homestead, 1990; John O. Bradshaw, *Greenberg's Guide to Kusan Trains*, Greenberg Publishing, 1987; Pierce Carlson, *Collecting Toy Trains*, Pincushion Press, 1993; W. G. Claytor, Jr., P. Doyle, and C. McKenney, *Greenberg's Guide to Early American Toy Trains*, Greenberg Publishing, 1993; Joe Deger, *Greenberg's Guide to American Flyer S Gauge*, Vol. I, 4th ed. (1991), Vol. II (1991), Vol. III (1992), Greenberg Publishing; Cindy Lee Floyd (comp.), *Greenberg's Marx Train Catalogues*, Greenberg Publishing,

1993; John Glaab, *Brown Book of Brass Locomotives*, 3rd ed., Chilton, 1993.

Bruce Greenberg, *Greenberg's Guide to Ives Trains*, Vol. I (1991), Vol. II (1992), Greenberg Publishing; —— (Christian F. Rohlfing, ed.), *Greenberg's Guide to Lionel Trains: 1901-1942*, Vol. 1 (1988), Vol. 2 (1988), Greenberg Publishing; ——, *Greenberg's Guide To Lionel Trains: 1945-1969*, Vol. 1, 8th ed. (1992), Vol. 2, 2nd ed. (1993), Greenberg Publishing; *Greenberg's Lionel Catalogues*, Vol. V, Greenberg Publishing, 1992; *Greenberg's Marx Train Catalogues*, Greenberg Publishing, 1992; George Horan, *Greenberg's Guide to Lionel HO*, Vol. II, Greenberg Publishing, 1993; George Horan and Vincent Rosa, *Greenberg's Guide to Lionel HO*, Vol. I, 2nd ed., Greenberg Publishing, 1993; John Hubbard, *Story of Williams Electric Trains*, Greenberg Publishing, 1987; Steven H. Kimball, *Greenberg's Guide to American Flyer Prewar O Gauge*, Greenberg Publishing, 1987; Roland La Voie, *Greenberg's Guide to Lionel Trains, 1970-1991*, Vol. I (1991), Vol. II (1992), Greenberg Publishing.

Lionel Book Committee, *Lionel Trains: Standard of the World, 1900-1943*, Train Collectors Association, 1989; Dallas J. Mallerich III, *Greenberg's American Toy Trains: From 1900 with Current Values*, Greenberg Publishing, 1990; ——, *Greenberg's Guide to Athearn Trains*, Greenberg Publishing, 1987; Eric J. Matzke, *Greenberg's Guide to Marx Trains*, Vol. 1 (1989), Vol. II (1990), Greenberg Publishing; Robert P. Monaghan, *Greenberg's Guide to Marklin OO/HO*, Greenberg Publishing, 1989; Richard O'Brien, *Collecting Toy Trains*, No. 3, Books Americana, 1991; John R. Ottley, *Greenberg's Guide to LGB Trains*, Greenberg Publishing, 1989; Alan R. Schuweiler, *Greenberg's Guide to American Flyer*, Wide Gauge, Greenberg Publishing, 1989; John D. Spanagel, *Greenberg's Guide to Varney Trains*, Greenberg Publishing, 1991; Robert C. Whitacre, *Greenberg's Guide to Marx Trains Sets*, Vol. III, Greenberg Publishing, 1992.

Periodicals: *Classic Toy Trains*, 21027 Crossroads Cr., P.O. Box 1612, Waukesha, WI 53187; *Lionel Collector Series Marketmaker*, Trainmaster, P.O. Box 1499, Gainesville, FL 32602.

Collectors' Clubs: American Flyer Collectors Club, P.O. Box 13269, Pittsburgh, PA 15234; Lionel Collectors Club of America, P.O. Box 479, LaSalle, IL 61301; Lionel Operating Train Society, 18 Eland Ct., Fairfield, OH 45014; Marklin Club-North America, P.O. Box 51559, New Berlin, WI 53151; Marklin Digital Special Interest Group, P.O. Box 51319, New Berlin, WI 53151; The National Model Railroad Association, 4121 Cromwell Road, Chattanooga, TN 37421; The Toy Train Operating Society, Inc., Suite 308, 25 West Walnut St., Pasadena, CA 91103; Train Collector's Association, P.O. Box 248, Strasburg, PA 17579.

Museum: Toy Train Museum of the Train Collectors Association, Strasburg, PA.

Additional Listings: See *Warman's Americana & Collectibles* for more examples.

Notes: Condition of trains is critical when establishing price. Items in fair condition and below (scratched,

chipped, dented, rusted or warped) generally have little value to a collector. Accurate restoration is accepted and may enhance the price by one or two grades. Prices listed below are for trains in very good to mint condition unless otherwise noted.

SPECIAL AUCTIONS

Greenberg Auctions
7566 Main St.
Sykesville, MD 21784
(410) 795-7447

J. W. Auction Co.
54 Rochester Hill Rd.
Rochester, NH 03867
(603) 332-0192

Lloyd Ralston Toys
173 Post Rd.
Fairfield, CT 06432
(203) 255-1233

Stout Auctions
11 W. Third St.
Williamsport, IN 47993-1119
(765) 764-6901

American Flyer

Car
  Baggage, #1202, eight wheel, litho, blue 90.00
  Observation, #9912, aluminum, black lettering, 10-1/8" l
  . . . . 60.00
Locomotive
  Silver Bullet, #356, streamlined, chrome, yellow and blue decals, 1953. . . . . 145.00
  Steeple Cab, #1218, black, 1920-21 . . . . 165.00
Set
  O gauge, cast iron wind-up engine, litho tin tender, #1106 Union Pacific coach, curved track, damaged box . . 500.00
  Standard gauge, Minnie-Ha-Ha, #964-T, locomotive with built-in tender, two coaches, observation car, 1935
  . . . . 200.00

Ives

Car
  Baggage, #550, litho, four wheels, emerald green, black roof, 1913-30, 6-1/2" l. 50.00
  Parlor, #72, NY and Chicago, litho steel, brown sides, 1914-20, 12" l. 375.00
Locomotive, steam, #1122, diecast boiler, black boiler and tender, brass trim, 1929-30 . . . . 320.00
Set, boxed, #14 passenger set, O gauge, windup black cast iron engine, litho tin #11 black tender, #62 red Limited Vestibule Express parlor car, #60, red Limited Vestibule Express Baggage/Mail car, some wear to orig box 4,025.00

Lionel

Accessory
  Bridge Section, bright green, standard, set of four sections, 13-3/4" l 200.00
  City Station, #114, green roof, cream building, green and cream trim, 8-1/2" h, 19-1/2" w, 9-1/8" d 1,150.00
  Freight Station Platform, maroon roof, green stations, orange platform, 18" l 375.00

Manual Switch, #210, bright green, 15-1/2" l, some rust on track 20.00

Mountain, papier-mâché, houses and trees, 36-1/2" l 550.00

Platform and Garden, #129, flowers and lawn, 13" l 575.00

Train Station, #116, red and cream tin, 9" h, 19" l, repainted 460.00

Car

Flatcar, #3830, blue car, gray submarine, 1960-63 . . . 90.00

Hand Car, Mickey and Minnie, #100, composition figures, red vehicle, 1930s, key missing 460.00

Stock, #802, green, Union Stock Line, 1915-28 . . . . . 45.00

Locomotive

Electric, #250, terra cotta body, maroon frame, 1934 . . . . 250.00

Steam, #1681E, red, red frame, 1934-35 . . . . 120.00

Switcher, #625, Lehigh Valley, GE 44 ton, blue, yellow lettering, 1969 . . . . 150.00

Set

Freight, #385E gun metal steam engine, #5 tender, #515 cream tank car, #516 red gondola, #513 orange and green cattle car, #514 cream refrigerator, #511 flatbed with lumber, #65 whistle controller, 1933-39 . . . . 700.00

Freight, #392E black steam engine, #384T black tender, #214 cream and orange box, #212 maroon gondola with eight wooden barrels, #219 green and red crane, #217 red and green caboose, 1932-39 . . . . 1,150.00

Passenger, #8E electric engine, two #337 Pullman cars, #338 observation car, red, standard gauge, repainted 30.00

Passenger, #10 peacock electric engine, #339 peacock Pullman, #341 Observation, #332 Railway Mail, 1926-30, paint slightly dull 435.00

Marklin

Locomotive and Tender, steam, O gauge, wind-up, black and red, green, and gold trim, 8-3/4" l engine, early 20th C 4,315.00

Set, accessories, #V13021 olive green wind-up electric engine, two #1181 olive green Pullman cars, #17611 olive green gondola, brown freight/caboose, #17931 cream freight, brown

flat car, olive green and red hopper, #1037 turntable, derrick and car roof #1046 tunnel, covered station, Kibri concession stand, two boxes of track 1,955.00

TRAMP ART

History: Tramp art was an internationally practiced craft, brought to the United States by European immigrants. Its span of popularity was between the late 1860s to the 1940s.

Made with simple tools usually a pocketknife, and from scrap woods—non-reusable cigar box wood and crate wood, this folk art form can be seen in small boxes to large pieces of furniture. Usually identifiable by the composition of thin layered pieces of wood with chip-carved edges assembled in built-up pyramids, circles, hearts, stars, etc. At times, pieces included velvet, porcelain buttons, brass tacks, glass knobs, shards of china, etc., that the craftsmen used to embellish his work. The pieces were predominantly stained or painted.

Collected as folk art, most of the work was attributed to anonymous makers. A premium is placed on the more whimsical artistic forms, pieces in original painted surfaces, or pieces verified to be from an identified maker.

Reference: Clifford A. Wallach and Michael Cornish, *Tramp Art, One Notch At A Time,* Wallach-Irons Publishing, (277 W. 10th St., New York, NY 10014) 1998.

Advisor: Clifford Wallach

Armoire, 49" w, 15" d, 76" h, scratch built, dec with stars and tulips, 3 shelves 12,500.00

Bank

4" w, 3-1/2" d, 8-1/2" h, mechanical, puzzlework 500.00

4" w, 4" d, 4-1/2" h, square shape, brass tacks, secret access 400.00

Cabinet, 21" w, 15" d, 31" h, wall mounted, painted, layered pyramids on doors 4,800.00

Chest of Drawers, 30" w, 19" d, 42" h, cigar box construction, four pull-out drawers, glass knobs 5,250.00

Church, 6" w, 16" d, 16" h, model, painted white, glass windows, door 550.00

Lionel, O gauge, No. 233, #262 engine, #803 hopper car, #902 gondola car, #806 cattle car, #807 caboose, pre-war, $125.

Clock, table, curlique outline, light and dark woods, 13" h x 15" w, x 4" d, $475. Photo courtesy of Clifford Wallach.

Clock
12" w, 9" d, 29" h, church-shape, bell tower......1,050.00
14" w, 7" d, 23" h, mantel, wide base, tapered top...325.00
14" w, 13" d, 81" h, grandfather, rounded top, large layered hearts and stars on front 6,200.00
15" w, 4" d, 13" h, table, curlicue outline, light and dark woods 475.00
16" w, 8" d, 27" h, house shape, dated 1899 ...... 950.00

Comb Case, 11" w, 5" d, 23" h, rosettes dec, mirror over slot for comb. 475.00

Crucifix, 9" w, 4" d, 16" h, wooden pedestal base, carved figure on cross 200.00

Desk Accessory Box, 18" w, 6" d, 7" h, dec with sea shells, initialed "K. H." 750.00

Doll Furniture
Chair, 7" w, 4" d, 10" h, Crown of Thorns style, woven seat, int. rattle............................. 375.00
Chest of Drawers, 12" w, 7" d, 21", heavily layered, porcelain pulls 650.00
Document Box, 12" w, 6" d, 7" h, on legs, doves carved on top, sgd by Civil War soldier 675.00
Dresser, 9" w, 4" d, 15" h, mirror on top, drawers, pedestal base 275.00

Frame
4" w, 6" h, table top style, easel stand 110.00
7" w, 7" h, table top style, star design, pr......... 495.00
7" w, 10" h, square shape, 3 layers, cigar box wood 95.00
10" w, 14" h, table top style, five openings, sits on base of double notch carving 275.00
10" w, 16" h, table top style, horseshoe shape with hearts, easel stand................................. 400.00
12" w, 14" h, cross corner style, 3 layers, pyramid design 115.00
14" w, 14" h, star shape, round center, surrounded by layered points, painted gold 375.00
16" w, 20" h, block corner, velvet panels 165.00
22" w, 14" h, double oval openings 350.00
24" w, 29" h, frame in frame style, hearts in corners 1,600.00
27" w, 36" h, tulip carved corners, stars, rosettes, and diamonds 2,800.00

Jewelry Box
10" w, 5" d, 6" h, lift top lid, painted, mirror int., top heart dec 375.00
11" w, 6" d, 9" h, pedestal base, heavily layered, painted gold, mirror under lid............................ 395.00
14" w, 7" d, 12" h, double pedestal stand, velvet lined, initials "J. S.".................................. 425.00
15" w, 12" d, 11" h, hinged top, brass lion pulls, dated, clasp for lock 245.00

Lamp
15" w, 15" d, 23" h, table, star shape, light and dark woods 550.00
15" w, 15" d, 70" h, floor, 3 tier base supports slender stem, carved feet...............................1,50.00

Match Safe, 7" w, 4" d, 9" h, open holder for matches, sandpaper for striking. 115.00

Medicine Cabinet, 18" w, 8" d, 25" h, mirrored door, shelved int., heavy crate wood construction, painted white 650.00

Mirror Frame
12" w, 16" h, heart shape, painted red, with mirror 475.00
26" w, 53" h, ornate horn shapes extending off top, 25 layers, with mirror 2,400.00
28" w, 37" h, heavily layered, trees on sides 2,200.00

Night Stand, 22" w, 14" d, 34" h, dark stain, built-up layers around edges, large star on door 725.00

Sewing Box, octagonal, carved and painted vines and leaves, 12" h, 13" w, 13" d, $850. Photo courtesy of Clifford Wallach.

Pedestal Stand
12" w, 12" d, 24" h, polychrome paint. 1,800.00
12" w, 12" d, 31" h, light and dark stain, ball feet 1,200.00

Sewing Box
9" w, 6" d, 8" h, polychrome finish, velvet inserts in sides 475.00
13" w, 13" d, 12" h, octagonal, carved and painted vines and leaves. 850.00

Vanity, 39" w, 17" d, 59" h, mirror on top, three drawers, light stain, sgd 1,800.00

Wall Pocket
12" w, 5" d, 16" h, paint dec, hearts and diamonds, pr 825.00
14" w, 5" d, 32" h, mirror over drawer, rounded top, light and dark woods................................1,100.00

TRUNKS

History: Trunks are portable containers that clasp shut and are used for the storage or transportation of personal possessions. Normally "trunk" means the ribbed flat- or domed-top models of the second half of the 19th century.

References: Martin and Maryann Labuda, *Price & Identification Guide to Antique Trunks*, published by authors, 1980; Jacquelyn Peake, *How to Recognize and Refinish Antiques for Pleasure and Profit*, 3rd ed., Globe Pequot Press (P.O. Box 833, Old Saybrook, CT 06475), 1995.

Notes: Unrestored trunks sell for between $50 and $150. Refinished and relined, the price rises to $200 to $400, with decorators being a principal market.

Early trunks frequently were painted, stenciled, grained, or covered with wallpaper. These are collected for their folk-art qualities and, as such, demand high prices.

Dome
12" l, worn dec black oil cloth and leather trim, brass tacks, lined with 1844 newspaper, hasp missing 45.00
12-1/4" w, 30" l, black and red grain paint, plain int., early 19th C 325.00

Flat Top, wood rim, brass banding on ends, 16-1/4" x 29-1/4" x 15-1/2", $120.

18" w, 16" d, 12" h, leather, alligator texture, strapwork 200.00

23-1/4" x 30-3/4" x 19-1/2", tooled leather covering, int. with two lift-out trays, very bright chromolithograph decorations, some wear to oil cloth, edge wear, handles missing 225.00

24-1/4" l, pine, orig graining in imitation mahogany, line inlay, dovetailed, age cracks in lid, some wear and edge damage, wrought iron lock 200.00

25-3/4" w, 12-3/4" d, 13-1/4" h, grain and fancifully painted, various foliate devices in sienna paint, ochre ground, Vermont, 19th C, cracks, minor paint wear, surface abrasions 3,000.00

46" l, immigrant's, pine, old red paint, ornate dec wrought iron strapping, tooled detail, int. with cov till, shelf along hinge rail, three dovetailed drawers, some edge damage, age cracks. 160.00

47-1/2" l, immigrant's, white oak, old red repaint, dovetailed, orig iron hardware, age cracks and repair in bottom 145.00

Flat Top

7" sq, leather cov, label "George W Tukey Portland, ME" 80.00

11-3/4" h, 18-1/2" l, grain painted, red and brown raised molded plinth base, inscribed in red "1856, PWS". 175.00

27-1/2" l, pine, dec, bowed side and lid, worn light blue repaint int., orig brown graining, orig wrought iron lock and hasp. 200.00

Hide Covered, 12" l, leather and brass tack trim, orig wallpaper int., loose handle 65.00

Leather Bound, 26" l, worn black leather, brass tack trim, flattened seat on lid, engraved brass plaque "J. D. Warner Canandaiqua". 110.00

Louis Vuitton, 43-1/2" w, 21-1/2" d, 13" h, late 19th/early 20th C, surface wear. 575.00

Oriental

31-1/4" w, 13" h, pigskin covering, hinged rect top, conforming case, metal carrying handles, Chinese 150.00

15" l, leather covered wood, worn painted scenes with figures, brass hardware. 275.00

Painted, 30-1/4" w, 22" d, 18-1/2" h, pine, molded hinged rect top, polychrome case, molded rect base, bracket feet 150.00

Traveler's, poplar, dovetailed, dark red mahogany stain, fitted int. with doors and drawers, some repair, int. door rehinged, 24 x 13-1/4" x 34-3/4". 200.00

Tucker China

History: William Ellis Tucker (1800-1832) was the son of a Philadelphia schoolmaster who had a small shop on Market Street, where he sold imported French china. William helped in the shop and became interested in the manufacture of china.

In 1820, kaolin, a white clay which is the prime ingredient for translucence in porcelain, was discovered on a farm in Chester County, Pennsylvania, and William earnestly began producing his own products with the plentiful supply of kaolin close at hand. The business prospered but not without many trials and financial difficulties. He had many partners, a fact reflected in the various marks found on Tucker china including "William Ellis Tucker," "Tucker and Hulme," and "Joseph Hemphill," as well as workmen's incised initials which are sometimes found.

The business operated between 1825 and 1838, when Thomas Tucker, William's brother, was forced by business conditions to close the firm. There are very few pieces available for collectors today, and almost all known pieces are in collections or museums. But you can never tell!

Museum: Pennsylvania Historical Museum, Harrisburg, PA.

Coffee Cup and Saucer, large size, floral spray, green band dec, gilt edges and handle, from set made for Atherton family of Chester County, PA, monogrammed "A" 1,500.00

Creamer and Sugar, black transfer dec, landscape with house, c1830, sugar bowl repaired, pr. 400.00

Fruit Dish, 11" l, oval, serpentine, gilt border, c1830. . .1,150.00

Perfume Vial, 1-1/2" h, heart shape, basket of flowers and floral bouquet dec, gilt trim 450.00

Pin Box, cov, circular, floral dec, gilt trim, wear. 50.00

Pitcher

9-1/4" h, polychrome dec, foliate reserves, gilt highlights, cracks, gilt wear. 200.00

Large, polychrome river scenes with sailboats, scrolling, gilt highlights 16,240.00

Large, floral dec, chip to spout. 815.00

Small, gold fern dec, gilt highlights, squared handle . 700.00

Plate, luncheon, landscape, monogram 95.00

Urn, 11-3/4" h, classical shape, square plinth, Blanc de Chine glaze, twin scroll handles, c1830, slight damage to one, pr 4,750.00

Pitcher, sepia landscape dec on both sides, 9-5/8" h, $1,500.

VAL ST.-LAMBERT

History: Val St.-Lambert, a 12th-century Cistercian abbey, was located during different historical periods in France, Netherlands, and Belgium (1930 to present). In 1822, Francois Kemlin and Auguste Lelievre, along with a group of financiers, bought the abbey and opened a glassworks. In 1846 Val St.-Lambert merged with the Socété Anonyme des Manufactures de Glaces, Verres à Vitre, Cristaux et Gobeletaries. The company bought many other glassworks.

Val St.-Lambert developed a reputation for technological progress in the glass industry. In 1879, Val St.-Lambert became an independent company employing 4,000 workers. The firm concentrated on the export market, making table glass, cut, engraved, etched, and molded pieces, and chandeliers. Some pieces were finished in other countries, e.g., silver mounts were added in the United States.

Val St.-Lambert executed many special commissions for the artists of the Art Nouveau and Art Deco periods. The tradition continues. The company also made cameo-etched vases, covered boxes, and bowls. The firm celebrated its 150th anniversary in 1975.

Box, cov, 3-3/4" h, 4" d, Basketweave pattern, ring shaped finial, opaque blue, fiery opalescent, emb "Val St. Lambert, Belgique" 90.00
Cologne Bottle, 5-1/4" h, transparent green cylinder, overlaid in ruby red, double etched blossoms, swags, and gold accents, fitted with threaded rim, screw top, hallmarks at rim and within, wear to cover 375.00

Atomizer, cut glass, green, bulb missing, mkd "Val St. Lambert for Saks," 6" h, $165.

Decanter, 12-1/2" h, cranberry cut to clear, sgd, orig stopper, orig paper label 175.00
Goblet, 5 3/8" h, clear, blown mold, applied foot and stem 45.00
Plate, Van Dyck 75.00
Powder Jar, 4-1/2" d, transparent green glass, overlaid in ruby red, double etched dec blossoms, swags, and gold accents, orig beaded silver cover, mkd "Sterling 530" 650.00
Sherbet, acid cut back, blue cut to clear, scenes of children playing with animals in gold 225.00
Toothbrush Holder, clear, amber stain, sgd 65.00
Vase
    10" h, cameo, ovoid body, tall slender cylindrical neck, frosted clear overlaid in lavender, cut sprays of wildflowers and leafage, sgd in intaglio "Val St. Lambert - Made in Belgium," c1900 . . . . .1,400.00
    14"h, pink with multicolored design at top and sides, orig label 600.00

VALENTINES

History: Early cards were handmade, often containing both handwritten verses and hand-drawn pictures. Many cards also were hand colored and contained cutwork.

Mass production of machine-made cards featuring chromolithography began after 1840. In 1847, Esther Howland of Worcester, Massachusetts, established a company to make valentines which were hand decorated with paper lace and other materials imported from England. They had a small "H" stamped in red in the top left corner. Howland's company eventually became the New England Valentine Company (N.E.V. Co.).

The company George C. Whitney and his brother founded after the Civil War dominated the market from the 1870s through the first decades of the 20th century. They bought out several competitors, one of which was the New England Valentine Company.

Lace paper was invented in 1834. The golden age of lacy cards took place between 1835 and 1860.

Embossed paper was used in England after 1800. Embossed lithographs and woodcuts developed between 1825 and 1840, and early examples were hand colored.

There was a big revival in the 1920s by large companies, like R. Tuck in England, who did lots of beautiful cards for its 75th Diamond Jubilee; 1925 saw changes in card production, especially for children with paper toys of all sorts, all very collectible now. Little girls were in short dresses, boys in short pants, which helps date that era of valentines. There were an endless variety of toy types of paper items, many companies created similar items and many stayed in production until World War II paper shortages stopped production both here and abroad.

References: Dan & Pauline Campanelli, *Romantic Valentines*, L-W Book Sales, 1996; Roberta B. Etter, *Tokens of Love*, Abbeville Press, 1990; Katherine Kreider, *Valentines with Values*, Schiffer Publishing, 1996.

Collectors' Club: National Valentine Collectors Association, P.O. Box 1404, Santa Ana, CA 92702.

Advisor: Evalene Pulati.

Animated, large
    Felix, half tone, German 22.00
    Jumping Jack, Tuck, 1900 . . . . 65.00

German, diecut stand-up, 6-3/4" x 3-3/4", $20.

Bank True Love note, England, 1865 . . . . 75.00
Bank of Love note, Nister, 1914 . . . . 35.00
Charm String
    Brundage, 3 pcs 45.00
    Four hearts, ribbon 45.00
Comic
    Sheet, 8" x 10", Park, London 20.00
    Sheet, 9" x 14", McLoughlin Co., USA, 1915 . . . . 15.00
    Woodcut, Strong, USA, 1845 . . . . 25.00
Diecut foldout
    Brundage, flat, cardboard 20.00
    Cherubs, 2 pcs 35.00
    Clapsaddle, 1911 . . . . 55.00
Documentary
    Passport, love, 1910 . . . . 45.00
    Wedding certificate, 1914 . . . . 45.00
English Fancy
    5" x 7", lace edged, dressed doll add-on 35.00
    5" x 7", lace edged, litho, pretty girl, verse 35.00
    8" x 10", aquatint, girl and grandmother, c1840 . . . . . 75.00
    8" x 10", aquatint, couple, wedding, c1840 . . . . 125.00
Engraved
    5" x 7", American, verse 35.00
    8" x 10" sheet, English, emb, pg 65.00
    8" x 10" sheet, English, hand colored 45.00
Handmade
    Calligraphy, envelope, 1885 . . . . 135.00
    Cutwork, hearts, 6" x 6", 1855 . . . . 250.00
    Fraktur, cutwork, 1800 . . . . 950.00
    Pen and ink loveknot, 1820 . . . . 275.00
    Puzzle, purse, 14" x 14", 1855 . . . . 450.00
    Theorem, 9" x 14", c1885 . . . . 325.00
    Woven heart, hand, 1840 . . . . 55.00
Honeycomb
    American, kids, tunnel of love 45.00

American, wide-eyed kids, 9" 37.50
German, 1914, white and pink, 11" 75.00
Simple, 1920, Beistle, 8" 17.50
Lace Paper
    American, B & J Cameo Style
        Large 75.00
        Small, 1865 . . . . 45.00
    American, layered, McLoughlin Co., c1880 . . . . 35.00
    Cobweb center, c1855 . . . . 250.00
    English, fancy
        3" x 5", 1865 . . . . 35.00
        5" x 7", 1855 . . . . 75.00
        8" x 10", 1840 . . . . 135.00
    Hand Layered, scraps, 1855 . . . . 65.00
Layered, in orig box
    1875, Howland 75.00
    1910, McLoughlin Co. 45.00
    Orig box, c1890 . . . . 55.00
    Simple, small pc, 1875 . . . . 22.50
    Tiny mirror center, 4" x 6" 75.00
    Whitney, 1875, 5" x 7" 35.00
Pulldown, German
    Airplane, 1914, 8" x 14" 175.00
    Auto, 1910, 8" x 11" x 4" 150.00
    Car and kids, 1920s 35.00
    Dollhouse, large, 1935 . . . . 45.00
    Rowboat, small, honeycomb paper puff 65.00
    Seaplane, 1934, 8" x 9" 75.00
    Tall Ship, 8" x 16" 175.00
Silk Fringed
    Prang, double sided, 3" x 5" 18.50
    Triple layers, orig box 35.00
Standup Novelty
    Cupid, orig box 45.00
    Hands, heart, without orig box 35.00
    Parchment
        Banjo, small, with ribbon 65.00
        Violin, large, boxed 125.00

VALLERYSTHAL GLASS

History: Vallerysthal (Lorraine), France, has been a glass-producing center for centuries. In 1872, two major factories, Vallerysthal glassworks and Portieux glassworks, merged and produced art glass until 1898. Later,

Salt, cobalt blue, ram's head, 3 feet, 2-1/2" d, 1-1/2" h, mkd, $45.

pressed glass animal-covered dishes were introduced. The factory continues to operate today.

Animal Covered Dish
Dog on rug, amber 150.00
Fish, pink 90.00
Frog, green, figural 90.00
Hen on nest, 1-7/8" x 2-3/8", opalescent, sgd 35.00
Robin on nest, blue milk glass 175.00
Box, cov
3-1/2" x 4", blue milk glass 85.00
5" x 3", cameo, dark green, applied and cut dec, sgd
. . . . 950.00
Butter Dish, cov, figural, radish 95.00
Candy Dish, 4-1/8" d, white milk glass, basketweave, rope handles and finial 90.00
Cologne Bottle, 6-3/4" h, cameo, fuchsia flowers and leaves, frosted cranberry ground, gold colored collar and screw stopper, sgd "Cristaherie Le Gantin" 495.00
Dish, cov, amber, ftd, squirrel finial 65.00
Lemon Dish, cov, figural, lemon, opaque yellow 65.00
Plate, 8" d, Thistle pattern, green 70.00
Tumbler, 4" h, cobalt blue 45.00
Vase, 7-3/8" h, tapering cylinder, amber cased over white and clear, acid etched wild grasses and blossoms, enameled pale pink and blue, top and base dec with floral filigree silver mounts, enamel signature, c1900 . . . . 1,400.00

VAN BRIGGLE POTTERY

History: Artus Van Briggle, born in 1869, was a talented Ohio artist. He joined Rookwood in 1887 and studied in Paris under Rookwood's sponsorship from 1893 until 1896. In 1899, he moved to Colorado for his health and established his own pottery in Colorado Springs in 1901.

Van Briggle's work was heavily influenced by the Art Nouveau schools he had seen in France. He produced a great variety of matte-glazed wares in this style. Colors varied.

Artus died in 1904. Anne Van Briggle continued the pottery until 1912.

Marks: The "AA" mark, a date, and "Van Briggle" were incised on all pieces prior to 1907 and on some pieces into the 1920s. After 1920, "Colorado Springs, Colorado" or an abbreviation was added. Dated pieces are the most desirable.

REPRODUCTION ALERT

Van Briggle pottery still is made today. These modern pieces often are mistaken for older examples. Among the glazes used are Moonglo (off white), Turquoise Ming, Russet, and Midnight (black).

References: Susan and Al Bagdade, *Warman's American Pottery and Porcelain*, Wallace-Homestead, 1994; Carol and Jim Carlton, *Colorado Pottery*, Collector Books, 1994; Ralph and Terry Kovel, *Kovels' American Art Pottery*, Crown Publishers, 1993; Richard Sasicki and Josie

Fania, *Collector's Encyclopedia of Van Briggle Art Pottery*, Collector Books, 1993, 1998 value update; David Rago, *American Art Pottery,* Knickerbocker Press, 1997.

Collectors' Club: American Art Pottery Association, 125 E. Rose Ave., St. Louis, MO 63119.

Museum: Pioneer Museum, Colorado Springs, CO.

1901-1920

Candlesticks, pr, 7-1/2" h, handled form, purple and maroon matte glaze, c1913 . . . . 120.00
Chalice, 11 1/2" h, stylized mermaid embracing fish, velvety light green matte glaze, incised logo, name, ate 1902, Roman numeral III, shape No. 1, repaired 14,300.00
Dish, 5 1/2" d, #491, circular, emb stylized black spider, dark green matte ground, incised "AA/Van Briggle/1906/Colorado Springs/491" 450.00
Figure, dragonfly, mulberry, 6 3/4" h, #792, dated 1920 . 200.00
Flower Frog, triple, dated 1914 . . . . 250.00
Jardiniere, 5 1/4" h, emb stylized tulips, mottle blue glaze, incised logo, name, Colorado Springs, shape No. 625
. . . . 715.00
Night Light, 5' h, grape leaf form, light crystalline mulberry glaze
. . . . 150.00
Plaque, 5 1/4" d, spider, green-black matteglaze, incised logo, name, date 1908, shape No. 491 . . . . 770.00
Plate, 8-1/2" d, grapes and leaves, deep burgundy and blue matte glaze, incised marks, c1907-12 . . . . 210.00
Sign, 15" h, cat shape, stylized Art Deco, green, Colorado Springs 225.00
Vase
5" h, molded floral dec, brown, blue, and green matte glaze, incised mark, date under glaze, c1912-19 . . . . 800.00
5" h, 9-1/2" w, molded leaf design to shoulder, maroon and blue matte glaze, post 1920s 300.00
5-1/2" h, 4" d, dark brown clay, vertical ribs, cov in fine pale blue microcrystalline glaze, clay body showing through, incised "AA" 950.00

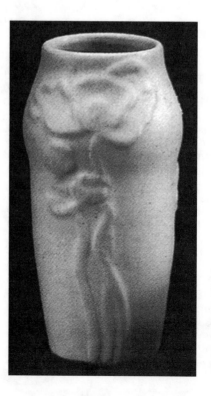

Vase, emb poppies, turquoise matte glaze, incised "AA/1916," 7-1/2" h, 4" d, $850. Photo courtesy of David Rago Auctions, Inc.

5-1/2" h, 6-1/2" d, spherical, emb stylized poppies, dark blue matte glaze, incised "AA/190" under glaze, pre-1910
. . . . 900.00

6-1/2" h, 5-1/4" d, emb row of poppy pods, sinewy stems, dark brown clay, sheer frothy ivory matte glaze, incised "AA VAN BRIGGLE/Colo. Sprg./1907" 3,500.00

7" h, maroon matte glaze, incised marks and date 1914
. . . . 300.00

7" h, 6" d, bulbous, emb stylized feathers under leathery dark green matte glaze, incised "AA," 1907-12 . . . . . . .1,100.00

7-1/4" h, 4-3/4" d, #176, emb trefoils, matte green glaze, incised "AA/VAN BGRIGGLE/1904/176/V," three hairlines
. . . . .1,100.00

7-1/4" h, -1/2" d, bulbous, emb trefoils, black-green matte feathered glaze, incised "AA/Colorado Springs," c1907
. . . . .2,700.00

7-1/2" h, 4" d, emb poppies, turquoise matte glaze, incised "AA/1916" 850.00

8-1/4" h, 5" d, emb dogwood blossoms, sheer dark green glaze, incised "AA/VAN BRIGGLE/COLO.SPRINGS/1906," 1906, minor kiln kiss to side. 2,200.00

9" h, molded flowers on stems, leaves, two-tone green and blue matte glaze, incised marks, c1907-12 . . . . . . 700.00

10" h, molded floral at top, open handles, dark blue and maroon matte glaze, incised mark, c1920 . . . . 475.00

11" h, 4" d, emb peacock feathers, green glaze, blue ground, incised "AA VAN BRIGGLE, 1904/174" 3,500.00

15-1/2" h, 7" d, tapering, stylized yucca leaves, purple glaze, green ground, incised "AA," imp "1915/157," 1915
. . . . .4,750.00

Vessel, 7-1/2" h, 9-1/2" d, squatty, two handles, emb gooseberry leaves and fruit, green glaze, raspberry ground, incised "AA VAN BRIGGLE/1905/82," 1905 . . . . .2,500.00

1921-1968

Bowl

5 1/2" d, Yucca leaves, #747, blue, c1940 . . . . 65.00

8 1/2" d, emb tulip dec, turquoise blue glaze, incised logo, name, Colorado Springs, No. 40, orig flower frog . . . 50.00

Console Set, jet black drip glaze, sgd "Anna Van Briggle, Colorado Springs" 70.00

Figure, Hopi Maiden, blue, c1940 . . . . 150.00

Vase

4-3/4" h, 3-1/2" d, bulbous, emb leaves, amber clay under gunmetal brown glaze, incised "AA," stamped "1939" and "849," c1915. . . . . .1,100.00

9" h, twisted, handle, midnight blue 350.00

VERLYS GLASS

History: Originally made by Verlys France (1931-1960), this Lalique-influenced art glass was produced in America by The Holophane Co. from 1935 to 1951, and select pieces by the A. H. Heisey Co. from 1955 to 1957. Holophane acquired molds and glass formulas from Verlys France and began making the art glass in 1935 at their Newark, Ohio, facility. They later leased molds to the Heisey Co., and in 1966 finally sold all molds and rights to the Fenton Art Glass Co.

The art glass was made in crystal, topaz, amber, rose, opalescent, and Directorie Blue. Heisey added turquoise. Most pieces have etched (frosted) relief designs.

Marks: Verlys France marked the glass with mold impressed "Verlys France" and "A Verlys France." Holo-

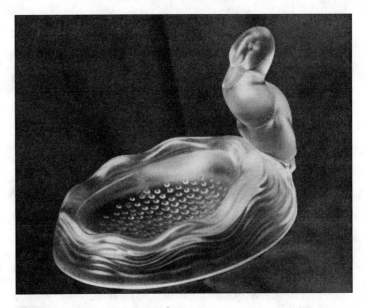

Ashtray, sgd, 6" l oval, $45.

phane (also known as Verlys of America) marked pieces with the mold-impressed "Verlys" and a scratched-script "Verlys" signature. The A. H. Heisey Co. used only a paper label which reads "Verlys by Heisey."

Reference: Carole and Wayne McPeek, *Verlys of America Decorative Glass*, revised ed., published by authors, 1992.

Bowl

Chinois 80.00

Cupid 125.00

Cuspidon 90.00

Orchid. 175.00

Pinecone

Blue 175.00

Opal 175.00

Poppies 200.00

Tassels 150.00

Thistle, topaz 250.00

Tripartite design, frosted

6-1/4" d, pinecones and needles 135.00

8-3/4" d, thistle design 75.00

Water Lily, dusty rose. 500.00

Wild Duck. 175.00

Box, cov, band of flowers 75.00

Candleholders, pr, Eagle. 500.00

Charger, dragonfly 135.00

Dish, cov, 8" d, 1-1/2" lid, three moths and glass knob
. . . . 225.00

Vase, 10" h, mermaids, dolphins, crystal and frosted . . . 750.00

Vase, 8-3/4" h, 9" d, flared colorless oval, press molded Alpine Thistle dec frosted on ext., base inscribed "Verlys"
. . . . 250.00

VILLEROY & BOCH

History: Pierre Joseph Boch established a pottery near Luxembourg, Germany, in 1767. Jean Francis, his son, introduced the first coal-fired kiln in Europe and perfected a water-power-driven

potter's wheel. Pierre's grandson, Eugene Boch, managed a pottery at Mettlach; Nicholas Villeroy also had a pottery nearby.

In 1841, the three potteries merged into the firm of Villeroy & Boch. Early production included a hard-paste earthenware comparable to English ironstone. The factory continues to use this hard-paste formula for its modern tablewares.

References: Susan and Al Bagdade, *Warman's English & Continental Pottery & Porcelain*, 3rd Edition, Krause Publications, 1998; Gary Kirsner, *Mettlach Book*, 3rd ed., Glentiques (P.O. Box 8807, Coral Springs, FL 33075), 1994.

Additional Listings: Mettlach.

Beaker, quarter liter, incised white florals, brown leaves, light green ground, Mettlach #2834 . . . . 90.00
Bowl
    8-1/2" d, spatter, gaudy floral dec, polychrome, mkd "Villeroy & Boch" 45.00
    10-1/2" d, blue floral dec, handles 175.00
Coffeepot, cov, Virginia pattern. 95.00
Cruet, 8-1/2" h, blue and white, orig stopper. 85.00
Demitasse Cup and Saucer, Patermo. 25.00
Mug, 3-1/2" h, tan, leaf and twig dec, twig handle 65.00
Pitcher, 10-5/8"h, six sided, dark gray raised scrolls, leaves, pods, and birds, gray ground, white int., beige crest mark
    . . . . 275.00
Plaque, 12 h, reticulated lilies of the valley dec 225.00
Plate
    9-1/2" d, blue florals, white ground. 35.00
    12-1/2" d, Chintz pattern, marked "Villeroy & Boch," price for 8 pc set 120.00
Stein, 6-1/2" h, half liter, #171, five white figures, blue ground, Mercury mark 225.00
Teapot, 6-1/4" d, blue and white 135.00
Tray, 11" x 16", cavalier, PUG 165.00
Turkey Set, 22-1/2" l platter, ten 10" d plates, blue transfer of turkeys, floral border, few minor flakes. 440.00
Vase, 16-1/4" h, enameled floral and dot dec, blue ground, c1889, Mettlach #1470. . . . . 200.00

WARWICK

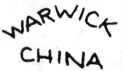

History: Warwick China Manufacturing Co., Wheeling, West Virginia, was incorporated in 1887 and remained in business until 1951. The company was one of the first manufacturers of vitreous glazed wares in the United States. Production was extensive and included tableware, **garden ornaments, and decorative and utilitarian items.**

Pieces were hand painted or decorated with decals. Collectors seek portrait items and fraternal pieces from groups such as the Elks, Eagles, and Knights of Pythias.

Some experimental, eggshell-type porcelain was made before 1887. A few examples are found in the antiques market.

Ale Set, tankard pitcher, seven matching mugs, BPOE emblem and elk dec, shaded brown ground 325.00
Bone Dish, flow blue scenic dec 45.00
Bowl, 4" d, flower and stems dec 72.00
Chocolate Pot, cov, 10-1/2" h, Pansy pattern, flow blue dec, c1893-98 . . . . 300.00
Cider Pitcher, fruit dec, brown glaze 100.00
Cream Soup Bowl, underplate, white, gold trim 20.00
Creamer, speckled blue and white, gold trim, raised leaves around rim, marked "Warwick China". 40.00
Humidor, cov, portrait of woman, brown ground, marked "IOGA"
    . . . . 215.00
Lemonade Pitcher, portrait dec, brown glaze 175.00
Mug
    BPOE emblem and elk dec 35.00
    Monk drinking from mug. 60.00
Portrait Plate, 10" d, Indian, yellow shading to brown ground
    . . . . 75.00
Spittoon, beige ground, red roses 140.00
Tankard, 13" h, portrait of monk and mug of ale. 250.00
Vase
    8" d, ftd, portrait of woman, large hat with peacock feathers, holding rose to her lips, shaded brow to cream ground, marked "IOGA". 125.00
    10" h, amaryllis dec, orange blossoms, brown ground, marked "IOGA". 95.00
    11-1/2" h, ring handles, marked "10 GA Madam LE Brun"
    . . . . 285.00

Charger, village scene, mkd "Villeroy & Boch/Mettlach/Gesehutzt, Remagen Dec 158" imp "1044," 12-3/4 l, $275.

Urn, roses dec, brown ground, two handles, mkd "IOGA," 10" h, $125.

WATCHES, POCKET

History: Pocket watches can be found in many places—from flea markets to the specialized jewelry auctions. Condition of movement is the first priority; design and detailing of the case is second.

Descriptions of pocket watches may include the size (16/0 to 20), number of jewels in the movement, whether the face is open or closed (hunter), and the composition (gold, gold filled, or some other metal). The movement is the critical element since cases often were switched. However, an elaborate case, especially if gold, adds significantly to value.

Pocket watches designed to railroad specifications are desirable. They are between 16 and 18 in size, have a minimum of 17 jewels, adjust to at least five positions, and conform to many other specifications. All are open faced.

Study the field thoroughly before buying. There is a vast amount of literature, including books and newsletters from clubs and collectors.

References: Roy Ehrhardt, *European Pocket Watches*, Book 2, Heart of America Press, 1993; Roy Ehrhardt and Joe Demsey, *Cartier Wrist & Pocket Watches*, Clocks, Heart of America Press, 1992; ——, *Patek Phillipe*, Heart of America Press, 1992; ——, *American Pocket Watch Serial Number Grade Book*, Heart of America Press, 1993; Cooksey Shugart and Richard E. Gilbert, *Complete Price Guide to Watches*, No. 17, Collector Books, 1997.

Periodical: *Watch & Clock Review*, 2403 Champa St., Denver, CO 80205.

Collectors' Clubs: American Watchmakers Institute Chapter 102, 3 Washington Sq, Apt. 3C, Larchmont, NY 10538; Early American Watch Club Chapter 149, P.O. Box 5499, Beverly Hills, CA 90210; National Association of Watch & Clock Collectors, 514 Poplar St., Columbia, PA 17512.

Museums: American Clock & Watch Museum, Bristol, CT; Hoffman Clock Museum, Newark, NY; National Association of Watch and Clock Collectors Museum, Columbia, PA; The Time Museum, Rockford, IL.

Abbreviations:
gf	gold filled
j	jewels
S	size
yg	yellow gold

Dresser

Art Deco, Ermeto, Cartier, coral enamel case, Movado movement, white square dial, silvertone Arabic numeral indicators, silver case with English hallmarks 1,035.00

Fleur-de-lys de Paris, Lenox W. Co., creamtone guillouche enamel dial, gold Arabic numerals, mother-of-pearl bezel and base, engraved gold wash case, in Gothic arch shaped box 145.00

Lapel

Niello, white porcelain dial, black Roman numerals, niello checkerboard pattern, European hallmarks, c1900, some surface scratches 460.00

Patek Philippe & Co., Geneve, 1905-10, 18kt yellow gold, white dial, black and gold Arabic numerals, fancy scroll hands, rose-cut diamond-set bezel, back cover with black enamel rhombic-shaped panels with white painted fleur-de-lis, suspended from shell-form brooch, black and white enamel and rose-cut diamonds, triple signed, Swiss hallmarks, movement needs restoration. 5,750.00

Tiffany & Co., c1900, 18kt yellow gold, white dial, black Arabic numerals, sgd, gold case, back cov set with foil-backed round cabochon sapphire framed in old European-cut diamonds, suspended from open box motif pin with sapphires and old European-cut diamonds in platinum topped gold mount, sgd 3,220.00

Pendant

Mers Mann, Art Deco, hexagonal form, blue guillouche enamel, applied silver and marcasite flower basket surmounted by silver and marcasite top, suspended from silver and tracery enamel bar pin by trace link chains 325.00

Pocket

Bovel & Courvoisier, Neuchatel, 14kt gold, hunter case, matching no. 64795 on movement, dust cover, and case, white porcelain dial, black Roman numerals, subsidiary seconds dial, engraved case, gold-filled 48" l rope chain with seed pearl slide 290.00

Capt., Henry, Geneva, 18kt yellow gold, openface, quarter-hour repeater, fully jeweled nickel movement, #36077, white

Lady's, gold filled case, $190.

enamel dial, Arabic numerals, subsidiary seconds dial, retailed by Hodgson, Kennard & Co., Boston, fitted case, minute hand missing 1,955.00

Goddard, L. D., Worcester, MA, early 19th C, gold, openface, fusee movement, bull's eye crystal, lacking second hand 1,725.00

Guinand, C. L., 14kt gold, open face, no. 31175, creamtone porcelain dial, black Arabic numerals, gold fleur-de-lis hands, subsidiary minutes and seconds dial, triple sgd, engraved gold case 800.00

E. Howard Watch Co., Boston, openface, 14kt yellow gold, 17 jewels, nickel movement, white porcelain dial, black Roman numerals, subsidiary seconds dial, small gold filled watch chain, minor cracks to dial 200.00

Illinois Watch Co., 14kt tricolor gold, white dial, black Roman numerals, subsidiary seconds dial, female portrait on dust cover, case dec with seascape and lighthouse, monogrammed crest, box hinge case 1,495.00

Patek Philippe & Co., Geneve, openface

14kt yellow, gold, numbered on dust cover and movement, highly jeweled movement patent 1891, white porcelain dial, subsidiary dial for seconds, Arabic numerals, monogrammed case, triple sgd, retailed by Shreve, Crump & Low, with 12" l 14kt yellow gold fancy link chain, swivel hook and pocketknife 2,070.00

18kt yellow gold, c1910, 21 jewel nickel movement, eight adjustments, Guillaume balance, size 19 lignes, enamel dial, Arabic numbers, triple sgd with honorable mention at the 1910-11 Geneva Timing Contest, engraved on cov, accompanied by orig Geneva Observatory timing records, orig honorable mention certificate, small crack on dial 4,025.00

18kt yellow gold, 1940s, silvertone dial, goldtone indicators, nickel movement, very thin, 11" 18kt gold watch chain 1,955.00

18kt yellow gold, nickel movement, white enamel dial, Arabic numerals, subsidiary seconds dial, scroll monogram on back, Spaulding & Co. 920.00

18kt yellow gold, 37 jewels, nickel mount made for Bailey & Co., Philadelphia, white porcelain dial, black Roman numerals, subsidiary seconds dial 750.00

S. Silverthau & Sons, 18kt yellow gold, openface, repeater, white dial, black Arabic numerals, subsidiary seconds dial, 14" l fancy link watch chain with swivel hook and T-bar 2,415.00

Smith, Patterson & Co., Boston, 18kt gold, openface, 23 jewels, white porcelain dial, black Arabic numerals, subsidiary seconds dial, blue Arabic minute indicators, monogrammed case, 14kt yellow gold seal set on black grosgrain lapel ribbon, 14kt yellow gold swivel hook 920.00

Vacheron ET Constantin, Geneve, 18kt yellow gold, hunter, 13 jewel, white porcelain dial, black Roman numerals, chased gold case 750.00

Waltham, American, 14kt gold

Hunter case, creamtone dial, black Roman numerals, subsidiary seconds dial, diamond accent on case, 19" l goldtone fancy link chain 1,380.00

White dial, Arabic numerals, subsidiary second dial, 19 jewels, fleur-de-lis design on cover, diamond accents, monogram on back, suspended from bow pin with center diamonds 490.00

Tank

Lady's, vermeil, black dial, silvertone Roman numerals and hands, black "must be Cartier" strap, orig box and documents, minor scratches to crystal 290.00

WATCHES, WRIST

History: The definition of a wristwatch is simply "a small watch that is attached to a bracelet or strap and is worn around the wrist." However, a watch on a bracelet is not necessarily a wristwatch. The key is the ability to read the time. A true wristwatch allows you to read the time at a glance, without making any other motions. Early watches on an arm bracelet had the axis of their dials, from 6 to 12, perpendicular to the band. Reading them required some extensive arm movements.

The first true wristwatch appeared about 1850. However, the key date is 1880 when the stylish, decorative wristwatch appeared and almost universal acceptance occurred. The technology to create the wristwatch existed in the early 19th century with Brequet's shock-absorbing "Parachute System" for automatic watches and Ardien Philipe's winding stem.

The wristwatch was a response to the needs of the entrepreneurial age with its emphasis on punctuality and planned free time. Sometime around 1930 the sales of wristwatches surpassed that of pocket watches. Swiss and German manufacturers were quickly joined by American makers.

The wristwatch has undergone many technical advances during the 20th century including self-winding (automatic), shock-resistance, and electric movements.

References: Hy Brown and Nancy Thomas, *Comic Character Timepieces*, Schiffer Publishing, 1992; Gisbert L. Brunner and Christian Pfeiffer-Belli, *Wristwatches, A Handbook and Price Guide*, Schiffer Publishing, 1997; James M. Dowling and Jeffrey P. Hess, *The Best of Time: Rolex Wristwatches, An Unauthorized History*, Schiffer Publishing, 1996; Roy Ehrhardt and Joe Demsey, *Cartier Wrist & Pocket Watches, Clocks*, Heart of America Press, 1992; ——, *Patek Phillipe*, Heart of America Press, 1992; ——, *Rolex Identification and Price Guide*, Heart of America Press, 1993; Sherry and Roy Ehrhardt and Joe Demesy, *Vintage American & European Wrist Watch Price Guide*, Book 6, Heart of America Press, 1993; Edward Faber and Stewart Unger, *American Wristwatches*, revised ed., Schiffer Publishing, 1996 Anton Kreuzer, *Omega Wristwatches*, Schiffer Publishing, 1996; Heinz Hampel, *Automatic Wristwatches from Switzerland*, Schiffer Publishing, 1997; Fritz von Osterhausen, *Movado History*, Schiffer Publishing, 1996; ——, *Wristwatch Chronometers*, Schiffer Publishing, 1997; Cooksey Shugart and Richard E. Gilbert, *Complete Price Guide to Watches*, No. 17, Collector Books, 1997.

Periodical: *International Wrist Watch*, 242 West Ave., Darien, CT 06820.

Collectors' Clubs: International Wrist Watch Collectors Chapter 146, 5901C Westheimer, Houston, TX 77057; National Association of Watch & Clock Collectors, 514 Poplar St., Columbia, PA 17512; The Swatch Collectors Club, P.O. Box 7400, Melville, NY 11747.

Museums: American Clock & Watch Museum, Bristol, CT; Hoffman Clock Museum, Newark, NY; National Association of Watch and Clock Collectors Museum, Columbia, PA; The Time Museum, Rockford, IL.

Akron, lady's, Retro, 14kt white gold, ruby, and diamond, cov sq coppertone dial, black Roman numerals, red abstract indicators, raised cover set with faceted rubies and diamonds, flanked by ruby and diamond scroll motif, double snake link bracelet. 575.00

Arenbe Watch Co., platinum and diamond, 17 jewels, rect, cream dial, black Arabic numerals, watch and bracelet set with baguette, round and marquise diamonds, platinum mount with millegrain accents 1,610.00

Audemars Piguet, Geneve, man's, 18kt yellow gold, sq silvertone dial, goldtone applied and Arabic numeral indicators, subsidiary seconds dial, brown leather strap, box, crystal chipped. 1,100.00

Bailey, Banks & Biddle Co., lady's, dress, platinum and diamond, C. H. Meylan movement, 18 jewels, silvertone dial, black Roman numerals, diamond bezel flanked by diamond and platinum foliate motif, rose-cut diamond crown, floral engraved back, 14kt white gold bracelet 1,035.00

Brayer, lady's, 14kt yellow gold, textured buckle cover, rope and curb link bracelet, 31.00 dwt. 460.00

Breitling, man's, yellow gold and steel, chronograph, graphite color dial, goldtone subsidiary dials, abstract and Arabic numeral indicators, navy leather strap 920.00

Cartier, man's
18kt yellow gold, rect, convex white dial, black Roman numerals, rounded gold bezel, black leather strap . .1,610.00
18kt yellow gold and steel, Santos, manual wind, white dial, black Roman numerals, date display, second hand sweep, steel band with gold screws. 1,100.00

Concord, lady's, 14kt yellow gold, covered, heavy mesh bracelet, invisible hinged cover, 34.90 dwt 400.00

Cresaux Watch Co., lady's, 14kt gold, 17 jewels, goldtone dial signed "H. W. Beattie and Sons," black abstract indicators, round yellow diamond and diamond-set bezel, yellow gold mesh band 800.00

Elgin, lady's, dress, 18kt gold and diamond, 15 jewels, whitetone dial, blacktone Arabic numerals, engraved bezel, flanked by geometric design, diamond and bead accents, black silk cord band 175.00

Hermes, silver, bracelet-type, Swiss movement, silvertone dial, date aperture and abstract indicators, framed in twisted silver wire freeform design, same style sectioned bracelet, hallmarked 290.00

Gruen Tank, 14K yg, 17 jewel, $65.

Juvenia, Retro, 14kt yellow gold, round dial, slightly curved triangular cover centered by prong set sapphires and diamond, heavy mesh bracelet 575.00

Movado
Lady's, dress, platinum and diamond, silvertone dial, abstract and Arabic numerals, diamond bezel flanked by four round brilliant-cut diamonds in pattern of tapering diagonal squares, 14kt white gold mesh bracelet. 980.00
Lady's, 14kt white gold, cream rect dial, silvertone Arabic numeral and abstract indicators, white gold-filled mesh strap bracelet 90.00

Man's, Kingmatic, 14kt gold, 28 jewels, sq silvertone dial, goldtone indicators, leather strap 345.00

Man's, moonphase triple calendar, Swiss movement, cream dial, applied goldtone abstract and Arabic numeral indicators, month, day, date, subsidiary seconds dial with moon phase, 14kt yellow gold bracelet, scratches to crystal 2,875.00

Patek Philippe, Geneve, man's, 18kt yellow gold
Round silvertone dial, goldtone abstract indicators, black leather strap, boxed 2,185.00
Square silvertone dial, goldtone indicators, subsidiary seconds dial, 18 jewels, black leather strap 2,645.00

Piaget, lady's, Swiss movement, 18kt yellow gold
Goldtone dial, abstract makers, framed with round brilliant-cut diamonds, textured thick 18kt yellow gold band 2,530.00
Silvertone dial, goldtone abstract indicators, diamond frame, gold mesh strap 3,105.00
Rhone Watch Co., Art Deco, 18 jewels, cream dial, black Arabic numerals, framed in diamonds, diamond-set box link bracelet, heavy lead solder 230.00

Rolex
Cellini, man's, 18kt yellow gold, white rect dial, black Roman numeral indicators, brown crocodile strap, Rolex gold buckle 1,610.00
Chronometer, 1950s, 18kt yellow gold, goldtone dial with alternating Roman numerals and abstract indicators, subsidiary seconds dial, leather strap with Rolex gold plated buckle, boxed. 3,335.00
Oyster Perpetual Day-Date, man's, 18kt yellow gold and stainless steel, goldtone dial, abstract indicators, sweeping seconds hand, magnifying glass on date aperture, jubilee bracelet, polished yellow gold central links, minor scratches to crystal 690.00
Oyster Perpetual Dayjust, lady's, 18kt yellow gold, goldtone dial, abstract indicators, date aperture, crenelated bezel, president bracelet, deployment Rolex buckle, orig box with papers, extra links 10,350.00
President Oyster Perpetual Day-Day, man's, 18kt yellow gold, automatic winding, silvertone Florentine dial, magnifier over date aperture, oyster bracelet with deployment clasp. 4,255.00

Vacheron & Constantin, Geneve, man's, 18kt yellow gold, silvered dial, gold baton indicators, Swiss hallmarks, leather strap 1,265.00

WAVE CREST

History: The C. F. Monroe Company of Meriden, Connecticut, produced the opal glassware known as Wave Crest from 1898 until World War I. The company bought the opaque, blown-molded glass blanks from the Pairpoint Manufacturing Co. of New Bedford, Massachusetts, and other glassmakers, including European factories. The Monroe company then decorated the blanks, usually with floral patterns. Trade names used were "Wave Crest Ware," "Kelva," and "Nakara."

References: Wilfred R. Cohen, *Wave Crest*, Collector Books, out-of-print; Elsa H. Grimmer, *Wave Crest Ware*, Wallace-Homestead, out-of-print.

Ash Receiver, 3-1/4" sq, Egg Crate mold, enameled floral dec 180.00

Biscuit Jar, 5-1/4" h, blue and white, Delft dec 550.00

Bon Bon, cov, 8" d, bail handle, rococo mold, sgd 925.00

Box, cov
   3" d, 2-3/4" h, Helmschmid Swirl, soft blue-gray ground, white lily of the valley dec, partial orig lining 150.00
   3" sq, hinged, puffy mold 245.00
   4-1/2" d, 3" h, blown out aster, painted pink, bright yellow center, white enamel, pale blue ground, deeper green hp flowers, black mark. 1,250.00
   5-1/2" d, 3-1/2" h, Helmschmid Swirl, shaded soft beige ground, enameled blue bachelor's buttons and white cosmos, all over gray and green foliage, orig lining and store label 550.00
   5-1/2" d, 3-3/4" h, Helmschmid Swirl, alternating swirls of pale yellow-green with white, hp bright pink floral dec, white enamel, pink banner mark 550.00
   6" d, 3-1/2" h, Kelva, green mottled ground, finely painted pink and white parrot tulips, large green and brown leaves, silver-plated metal mountings, sgd "Kelva" 850.00
   7" d, 4-1/2" h, Helmschmid Swirl, alternating swirls of pale yellow-green with white, hp bright pink floral dec, white enamel, pink banner mark 825.00
   7" d, 4-1/2" h, Helmschmid Swirl, medium beige ground shaded to white, hp all over enameled fern dec, orig lining 750.00
   7" d, 4-1/2" h, Helmschmid Swirl, soft pink/beige ground, all over hp florals, purple, blue and white asters, buds, and leaves, background vines and leaves, orig store label, orig lining 850.00
   7-1/2" d, 6-1/2" h, Swirl pattern, soft pink roses, wild rose and white enamel, metal bottom 850.00

Calling Card Holder, upright rect form, emb frame design, gilt metal rim, cloth lining, hp blue flowers, pink border . . 360.00

Cigar Humidor, 8-3/4" h, blue ground, single petaled pink rose dec, pink "Cigar" signature, pewter collar, bail, and lid fittings, flamed shaped finial, sgd "Kelva" 685.00

Cracker Jar, 10-1/2" h, 6" d, barrel shape, green-blue ground, emb yellow crests, hp yellow and brown wild roses, leaves, and stems, fancy silver-plated hardware 675.00

Creamer and Sugar, 3-1/4" h, blown-out swirls, enameled floral dec 330.00

Cruet, Opalware, dec, orig stopper 200.00

Dresser Box, cov
   5-1/4" d, cut glass, allover cutting, hinged, C. F. Monroe 350.00
   6-3/4" d, 3-3/4" h, opal satin glass, bulbed square box, yellow centered stylized flowers symmetrically arranged, lavender tracery, gilt metal hinged rim 500.00

Fernery
   6-3/4" d, 3-3/4" h, hp white wild roses, leaves, and branches, orig brass swirl rim. 350.00
   7" sq, Egg Crate mold, yellow wild roses, metal twisted rope rim 650.00

Hair Receiver, cov, 5-1/2" d, gold trim, marked "Nakara" 685.00

Humidor, cov, 7-1/2" h, 5-1/2" d, pink emb designs, white satin ground, yellow floral dec, silver plated dome lift-off lid, unmarked 365.00

Jardiniere, 8" h, bulbous body, short cylindrical rim, hp mums and foliate, gold lacy rim trim 550.00

Jewel Tray, 6" l, 2-3/4" h, oval, ftd, Rococo mold, sgd, banner mark, two handles 275.00

Pin Tray, 3-1/4" w, 1-1/2" h, open, Helmschmid Swirl
   Pale blue ground, white lily of the valley dec 75.00
   Pale blue ground, white and blue enameled floral dec 75.00
   Shaded pink ground, blue and purple flowers 75.00

Plate, 7" w, pond lily dec, shaded pale blue ground, reticulated border. 750.00

Salt and Pepper Shakers, pr, 3-1/2" h, 2-1/2" w, shaded yellow to white, pink and green floral transfer dec, old covers 185.00

Spooner, cylindrical paneled rib shape, floral transfer, silver plate rim and loop handles 285.00

Sugar Shaker, 3" h, 3" d, Helmschmied Swirl, caladium leaves, purple centers, white enamel dots, green and brown borders, tiny fuchsia foliated blossom sprays, swirling mottled blue and white ground, orig metal dented lid 685.00

Vase
   5" h, 2-1/2" w, egg shaped body, pale blue ground, hp blue flowers, metal rim and ftd base 475.00
   6-1/2" h, 2-1/2" d, cylindrical, soft pink and beige, white ground, large spray of white and golden asters, white beaded top, metal ftd base 485.00
   6-1/2" h, 2-3/4" d, acorn shaped vase, pale yellow ground, bright yellow flowers, fancy metal base, rim, and handles 475.00
   6-3/4" h, 2-1/2" d, soft pink ground shading to white, blue and pink flowers and leaves, white enameled beads, fancy metal base, rim, and handles. 475.00
   17-3/4" h, ormolu mounts, running nymph and yellow flower, bluish-yellow ground, dark blue accents, two dolphin handles, four dolphin feet, sgd "Trade mark Wave crest," one dolphin handle broken off rim. 1,950.00

Whisk Broom Holder, 10-1/4" l, 7" w, bright solid pink, shield with white, yellow, and purple asters, pale gray ground, ornate metal backing 2,875.00

Ewer, pink and white ground, multicolored floral dec, gilt trim, sgd, metal spout and base, 15-1/2" h, $550.

WEATHER VANES

History: A weather vane indicates wind direction. The earliest known examples were found on late 17th-century structures in the Boston area. The vanes were handcrafted of wood, copper, or tin. By the last half of the 19th century, weather vanes adorned farms and houses throughout the nation. Mass-produced vanes of cast iron, copper, and sheet metal were sold through mail-order catalogs or at country stores.

The champion vane is the rooster—in fact, the name weathercock is synonymous with weather vane—but the styles and patterns are endless. Weathering can affect the same vane differently; for this reason, patina is a critical element in collectible vanes.

Whirligigs are a variation of the weather vane. Constructed of wood and metal, often by the unskilled, whirligigs indicate the direction of the wind and its velocity. Watching their unique movements also provides entertainment.

References: Robert Bishop and Patricia Coblentz, *Gallery of American Weathervanes and Whirligigs*, E. P. Dutton, 1981; Ken Fitzgerald, *Weathervanes and Whirligigs*, Clarkson N. Potter, 1967; A. B. & W. T. Westervelt, *American Antique Weathervanes* (1883 catalog reprint), Dover Publications, 1982.

REPRODUCTION ALERT

Reproductions of early models exist, are being aged, and then sold as originals.

Angel, 35" l, wood, tin trumpet, brown and yellow paint
. . . . .2,500.00
Arrow, 74" l, removed from Orono United Methodist Church, Orono, Maine, steel, cut-out sections, feathered back section with twenty pierced feathers, middle section with scrolls and area of pierced steelwork, shaft with four directionals, large copper housing, north directional broken, center sleeve of arrow where shaft units arrow missing, but present
. . . . .1,900.00

Horse, cast iron, flat, attributed to Massachusetts, c1830, 32" l, $1,500.

Banneret and Sun, 23-1/4" h, 20-3/4" h, sheet copper, attributed to J. Howard, Bridgewater, MA, late 19th C, traces of verdigris, regilt, minor dents and splint. 2,300.00
Bull, 42" l, 30-1/8" h, molded and applied copper, attributed to A. L. Jewell & Co., Waltham, MA, c1875, fine verdigris, bullet holes, minor dents, seam splits 34,500.00
Bull Dog, 30" l, 1920s, tail missing 1,100.00
Cockerel, 31" x 31-1/2", sheet metal, cast iron, and zinc, red tin tail, Rochester Ironwork 1,500.00
Cow, 24" l, copper, solid metal head, horn cracked 600.00
Eagle
    9" h, 17-1/4" w, gilt molded copper, America, 20th C, verdigris surface, contemporary stand 250.00
    18" h, molded copper, America, early 20th C, verdigris surface, dents, seam splits, minor losses 950.00
    19" h, 32-1/2" l, molded copper, America, late 19th/early 20th C, fine verdigris, traces of gilt, old weathered gold paint, minor dents 2,650.00
    21" h, 24-1/2" l, gilt molded copper, America, early 20th C, regilt, minor dents and holes 1,850.00
    21" h, 25-1/2" l, molded copper, A. L. Jewell & Co., Waltham, MA, 1855-67, areas of verdigris, losses to ball, gilt wear, minor dents 3,800.00
    27-1/4" h, 30-3/4" l, gilt molded copper, America, early 20th C, regilt, minor dents 950.00
    104" h overall, eagle 28" h, 36" w, molded copper, on earlier molded copper arrow and architectural wrought iron and copper stand, America, early 20th C 1,725.00
Eagle and Quill, 36-1/2" h, 45" l, molded copper, American, late 19th C, fine verdigris, remnants of old weathered gold paint, minor dents, seam splits, very minor holes 2,650.00
Horse and Sulky, 24-1/2" h, 45-1/4" l, molded copper, St. Julian model, attributed to J. W. Fiske & Co., late 19th C, fine verdigris, areas of gilt. 28,750.00
Horse, jumping, 36-1/2" l, 18" h, gilt molded and applied copper, attributed to A. L. Jewell & Co., Waltham, MA, c1850, old painted surface, repair to tail and base 23,000.00
Horse, running
    15" h, 32" w, trotting, molded copper, Goldsmith's Maid, custom stand, little gold gilt remaining, six bullet holes, some dents 800.00
    15-1/2" h, 26" l, molded copper, painted, minor dents, America, late 19th/early 20th C 500.00
    17" h, 25" d, Blackhawk, gilt molded copper, fine verdigris, America, late 19th C, gilt loss, minor seam splits
    . . . . .3,125.00
    17-1/4" h, 32-1/2" l, trotting, gilt molded copper, old painted surface, America, late 19th C, very minor seam splits, gilt loss. 1,035.00
    19" h, 31" l, gilt molded zinc, scattered dents, America, late 19th C 2,760.00
Rooster
    14" h, wooden, silhouette, crowing, old weathered white repaint, red and black dec, attributed to Amish. 200.00
    20-1/2" h, 20" l, copper body, cast metal feet mounted on board, overall patina 1,300.00
    26-3/4" h, 25" l, gilt cast zinc and sheet copper, J. Howard, Bridgewater, MA, late 19th C, traces of gilt, verdigris surface, imperfections. 3,150.00
Schooner, 59" h, 4" l, gilt dec, two-masted sailing ship in full sail, full bodied hull, rugged sail and mast construction, flying flags, contemporary display stand 4,500.00
Ship, 21" h, 37-3/4" l, carved wood and zinc, attributed to Frank Adams, Martha's Vineyard, MA, c1930, minor cracks
. . . . .1,850.00

Whirligig

Soldier, 17-1/2"h, painted wood, red tunic, late 19th/early 20th C, repairs, repainted. 865.00
Santa and reindeer, 32" l, painted wood, some repair and restoration 175.00
Two men and mule, 21"l, painted wood 110.00
Uncle Sam, 72" h, 48" w, 28" d, carved wood and sheet metal, Uncle Sam sawing log, American flag on flagpole, polychrome dec, Henry Wilson Sargent (Henny Penny), . . Wilmington, MA, dated 1900 .12,650.00

WEBB, THOMAS & SONS

History: Thomas Webb & Sons was established in 1837 in Stourbridge, England. The company probably is best known for its very beautiful English cameo glass. However, many other types of colored art glass were produced, including enameled, iridescent, heavily ornamented, and cased.

References: Charles R. Hajdamach, *British Glass, 1800-1914*, Antique Collectors' Club, 1991.

Additional Listings: Burmese; Cameo; Peachblow.

Bowl
6" w, 6" d, 2" h, Burmese, pink shading to yellow, ruffled corners, turned in sides, sgd on bottom "Thomas Webb & Sons" 250.00
7-1/2" d, 4-7/8" h, glossy peachblow, cream lining, gold prunus and bird dec, three applied reeded feet 850.00
12-1/2" x 5-7/8" x 7" oval, shaded blue, overlay, green and tan enamel leaves, yellow flowers, ruffled 350.00
Bride's Bowl, 12" d, enameled florals, pink shaded to strawberry red ground, sgd 275.00
Cologne Bottle, cameo, carved white florals, amber ground, SS top and mounting 1,450.00
Compote, 5" d, 1-5/8" h, Alexandrite, Optic Honeycomb pattern, pale amber int., 1" w fuchsia band, honey colored wafer base 975.00
Cup and Saucer, handleless, 2-3/4" h, 5" d saucer, cameo, cranberry, carving of prunus blossoms, leaves, branches, and butterfly. 550.00
Goblet, 8-1/2" h, Alexandrite, circular wafer-thing base, twisted stem, four textured leaves applied to base of bow, amber tulip shaped bowl shading to fuchsia 1,850.00
Perfume Bottle, cameo
2-3/4" h, flattened disk, cased turquoise blue, white palm fronts and two flying butterflies, silver rim, swirled screw cap 900.00
3-1/2" h, turquoise, white cameo carved ivy and vine dec, feather border above, hallmarked silver rim, monogrammed screw to ball cover, minor dents 1,350.00
4" h, flattened ovoid, yellow overlaid in Chinese red, cameo carved elaborate trumpet vine and blossoms above leaf-form border edge, hallmarked silver rim, hinged cover, orig glass lined cap 2,760.00
5-1/2" h, 2-3/4' w, sq form, citron yellow, white overlay, carved wild roses, leaves, and buds, orig silver spring hinge cov 1,875.00
Pitcher, MOP satin glass, DQ pattern, dimpled sides, deep rose color, frosted handle. 400.00
Scent Bottle, 2-1/2" d, 3-1/2" h, Burmese, acid finish, gold leaves and berries dec, hallmarked SS screw-on dome cap. 750.00
Toothpick Holder, ball shape, ruffled rim, cream satin, pink int., NTHCS #42 . . . . 165.00

Vase
3" h, 4-1/2" d, yellow satin, heavy gold prunus blossoms, gold butterfly on side, bold band on top and bottom, cream int 325.00
3-1/2" h, 3" d top, Burmese, brightly colored purple prunus blossoms, painted leaves, buds, and stems, deep salmon pink shading to bright yellow 425.00
3-3/4" h, 2-3/4" d top, Burmese, five point petal top, pink and blue prunus blossom dec, sgd "Thomas Webb and Sons Queen's Burmese". 425.00
4" h, 3-3/4' d, squared shape, dimples on each side, shaded blue, gold prunus blossoms and branches, cream lining 245.00
5" h, 6" w, 18" circumference, shaded sky blue to pale white cream, applied crystal edge, enameled gold and yellow flowers, leaves, buds, and butterfly, allover acid-cut basketweave dec. 425.00
5-1/4" h, simulated ivory cameo, brown stain shading to ivory, flowers, leaves, and panel of three birds, scalloped top, sgd 875.00
6" h, gourd shape, gold flowers and insects, shaded brown ground 200.00
7" h, 5" d, basketweave MOP satin, bulbous base shades from deep blue to pale blue, creamy lining 750.00
7-1/2" h, 6-1/2" w, cameo, pillow form, bright blue, white cameo wild rose dec, two large roses, twelve leaves, two rosebuds, large butterfly in flight on reverse, full signature 2,750.00
7-3/4" h, cameo, red ground, white cameo dec, unsigned, chip to rim 300.00
8" h, flared, Wave, electric blue 225.00
8" h, 4" w, satin finish, unlined, pink and white stripes, frilly top, bulbous bottom 425.00
9" h, deep coral red overlay white lining, heavy gold branch and flowers dec 385.00
10-1/2" h, 4" d, bulbous, gold floral dec, prunus blossoms, leaves, branches, pine needles and insect, shaded brown to gold ground, creamy white lining, dec attributed to Jules Barbe 450.00

Vase, cameo, white morning glories, citron ground, mkd, 5-1/8" h, $1,650. Photo courtesy of Garth's Auctions, Inc.

WEDGWOOD

History: In 1754, Josiah Wedgwood and Thomas Whieldon of Fenton Vivian, Staffordshire, England, became partners in a pottery enterprise. Their products included marbled, agate, tortoiseshell, green glaze, and Egyptian black wares. In 1759 Wedgwood opened his own pottery at the Ivy House works, Burslem. In 1764, he moved to the Brick House (Bell Works) at Burslem. The pottery concentrated on utilitarian pieces.

Between 1766 and 1769, Wedgwood built the famous works at Etruria. Among the most-renowned products of this plant were the Empress Catherina of Russia dinner service (1774) and the Portland Vase (1790s). The firm also made caneware, unglazed earthenwares (drabwares), piecrust wares, variegated and marbled wares, black basalt (developed in 1768), Queen's or creamware, and Jasperware (perfected in 1774).

Bone china was produced under the direction of Josiah Wedgwood II between 1812 and 1822 and revived in 1878. Moonlight luster was made from 1805 to 1815. Fairyland luster began in 1920. All luster production ended in 1932.

A museum was established at the Etruria pottery in 1906. When Wedgwood moved to its modern plant at Barlaston, North Staffordshire, the museum was expanded.

References: Susan and Al Bagdade, *Warman's English & Continental Pottery & Porcelain*, 3rd Edition, Krause Publications, 1998; Diana Edwards, *Black Basalt*, Antique Collectors Club, 1994; Robin Reilly, *The New Illustrated Dictionary of Wedgwood*, Antique Collectors' Club Ltd., 1995; ——, *Wedgwood Jasper*, Thomas Hudson, 1994; Peter Williams, *Wedgwood*, Wallace-Homestead, 1992.

Periodical: *ARS Ceramica*, 5 Dogwood Court, Glen Head, NY 11545.

Collectors' Clubs: Wedgwood International Seminar, 22 DeSavry Crescent, Toronto, Ontario M4S 212 Canada; The Wedgwood Society, The Roman Villa, Rockbourne, Fordingbridge, Hants, SP6 3PG, England; The Wedgwood Society of Boston, 28 Birchwood Drive, Hampstead, NH 03841; The Wedgwood Society, of New York, 5 Dogwood Court, Glen Head, NY 11545; Wedgwood Society of Southern California, Inc., P.O. Box 4385, North Hollywood, CA 91617.

Museums: Art Institute of Chicago, Chicago, IL; Birmingham Museum of Art, Birmingham, AL; Brooklyn Museum, Brooklyn, NY; Cincinnati Museum of Art, Cincinnati, OH; City Museum & Art Gallery, Stoke-on-Trent, England; Cleveland Museum of Art, Cleveland, OH; Henry E. Huntington Library and Art Gallery, San Marino, CA; Jones Museum of Glass & Ceramics, East Baldwin, ME; Nassau County Museum System, Long Island, NY; Nelson-Atkins Museum of Art, Kansas City, MO; Potsdam Public Museum, Potsdam, NY; Rose Museum, Brandeis University, Waltham, MA; Victoria & Albert Museum, London, England; Wadsworth Atheneum, Hartford, CT; Wedgwood Museum, Barlaston, Stoke-on-Trent, England.

Basalt

Bowl, 4-1/4" d, black, engine turned body, hand painted floral sprigwork, imp mark, 19th C. 345.00

Cassolette, 9-1/4" h, black, drapery and foliate reliefs, imp Wedgwood & Bentley marks, 18th C, chips to sconce rim, restored foot 1,610.00

Club Jug, 7-1/2" h, black, enamel dec floral sprays, imp marks, c1870, body hairlines 230.00

Figure, black
  12-1/4" h, Apollo, nude standing with cloth draped over arm, imp mark, 19th C, chip to lyre 1,035.00
  16" h, Shakespeare, full figure standing at podium, marked "W.W.," c1850 . . . . .1,200.00

Jar, cov, 4-1/2" h, classical figures, marked "Wedgwood, Made in England" 110.00

Lamp, 8-1/4" h, oval shape, bronzed and gilt black, carved fluting over applied acanthus and bellflower relief, handle formed as female figure seated to one end with book in hand, imp mark, c1875, gilt retouched, finial reglued, socle rim chip 1,320.00

Medallion, Tutankhamun, gold dec chain 175.00

Model, black
  3-1/2" h, cat, c1913 . . . . 550.00
  4-1/4" l, reclining baby, after Della Robbia, imp mark, mid 19th C, foot rim chip. 435.00

Portrait, 3-3/8" x 4-1/4" oval, black, Sir Isaac Newton, self framed, imp mark, 18th C. 230.00

Tea Caddy, cov 5-3/4" h, engine-turned border below classical children in relief, imp marks, late 18th C, rim nicks .1,035.00

Tea Set, engine turned black bodies, 6" h cov teapot with widow finial, 3-3/4" h creamer, 5" d waste bowl, imp marks, 19th C, price for set. 490.00

Basalt, teapot, 8-1/2" h, $120.

Caneware, Sheaf of Wheat, 3-1/2" h, $250.

Vase

10 3/8" h, Encaustic dec, whit and black accented iron red figural design to one side, Greek key gadroons and stiff leaf bands, imp marks, c1840 . . . . .2,300.00

10-1/2" h, cov, putti head modeled handles, body with relief cupid figures supporting wreath, fruiting grapevine border, engine turned to cov, neck and foot, imp circular stamp Wedgwood & Bentley marks, restoration, price for pr
. . . . .6,325.00

Caneware

Game Pie Dish, cov, 9 1 /2" l, oval, molded hare finial, fruiting grapevines, game on body, stained liner, imp mark, mid 19th C. 490.00

Inkwell, 2-1/4" h, black basalt relief, imp mark, c1800, handles restored 375.00

Potpourri, cov, 11-1/2" l, pierced lid, rosso antico fruiting grapevines relief, imp mark, early 19th c, rim chips to married lid, insert missing 410.00

Teapot, cov, 5" h, arabesque molded and spaniel finial, imp mark, c1820, chip to spout and cov collar int. 230.00

Vase, 5-3/4" h, engine-turned borders on either side of rosso antico leafy vinework, imp mark, early 19th C, repair to relief, no cov 115.00

Creamware

Cabaret Tray, 16-1/2" x 12-1/2", Japanned dec 125.00

Dish, 12-1/4" d, polychrome Masonic dec, imp mark, late 18th/19th C. 320.00

Soup Tureen, cov, and Platter, 12-1/4" l tureen, 21-1/2" l platter, iron-red trim, black and green enamel crests, early 19th C, hairline on tureen, wear to platter, price for matching pr
. . . . 415.00

Soup Tureen, cov, stand, 13-1/2" d stand, imp mark, c1800, hairline to cov, foot rim and chip under tureen, price for 3 pc set. 980.00

Teapot, Japanned dec 95.00

Diceware

Cup and Saucer, 5 3/8" d saucer, white running laurel borders, applied yellow quatrefoils, green dip ground, imp mark, late 19th/early 20th C 1,610.00

Tea Set, 5-1/2" h cov teapot, 3-1/4" h creamer, 4" h cov sugar, white running laurel borders, applied yellow quatrefoils, green dip ground, imp mark, late 19th/early 20th C
. . . . .3,335.00

Vase, 8-3/4" h, black jasper ground, central frieze of dancing hours in white relief, lower dice patter band wit yellow quatrefoils, imp mark, mid 19th C, restored base chips, manufactured cov. 1,495.00

Drabware

Teapot, cov, 4-1/2" h, applied blue classical reliefs, imp mark, 19th C. 435.00

Tea Set, 7-1/2"h cov teapot with widow finial, 3 1/8" h creamer, 4" h cov sugar, applied white fruit and floral banding, imp marks, 19th C. 425.00

Jasperware

Bell Pull, 2-1/2" h, white relief of Poor Maria, Lady Templeton design, solid pale blue, late 18th C 345.00

Biscuit Jar, cov, 7-1/2" d, sage green, applied white bust medallions of Washington, Franklin, and Lafayette, acorn finial, minor rim chip. 360.00

Bowl, 10" d, Dancing House, "Wedgwood Made in England" mark

Black and white 600.00

Light blue and white 300.00

Button, 1 3/8" d, white classical relief dec, blue ground, multifaceted cut steel mountings attributed to Matthew Boulton, late 19th C, price for 12 pc set 5,750.00

Cache Pot, blue ground, white grape and leaf garlands, classical theatrical figures, early 20th C 110.00

Candlesticks, pr, 8-1/4" h, light blue and white, dip, mkd "Wedgwood, England" 350.00

Chess Set, 4-1/4" h maximum, 16 pc each side, blue dip and lilac dip base, designed by John Flaxman, Jr., imp marks, late 18th C, minor damage and restoration, price for 32 pc set
. . . . .17,825.00

Clock Garniture, 13" h clock, 9" h pr candlesticks, 12" h pr cov urns, applied black classical medallions between floral swags separated by ram's heads and trophies, yellow dip ground, imp "Etruria" marks, early 20th C, non-operational Bailey, Banks & Biddle, Philadelphia, clock, minor damage and restoration, price for 5 pc set. .2,300.00

Coffee Can and Saucer, 5 3/8" d, 2-1/2" h, white running laurel border, green applied quatrefoils, lilac ground, imp marks, mid 19th C 1,610.00

Cracker Jar, cov

6" h, 5" d, barrel shape, white relief classical figures, dark blue ground, silver plate rim, cov and bail handle, marked "Wedgwood". 200.00

6-1/4" h, bulbous ovoid body, white relief classical figures, dark blue ground, flat silver plate rim, cov, and twisted bail handle, marked "Wedgwood". 220.00

7" h, cylindrical, white relief classical figures, blue ground, flat silver plate cov, lid, bail handle, and base ring, ball feet, marked "Wedgwood, England" 165.00

Creamer and Sugar, cov, blue, marked "Wedgwood, England," price for pr 145.00

Dish, 4-1/2" h, heart shape, white relief classical figures, red ground, marked "Wedgwood, England," c1920 . . . . . 395.00

Jardiniere

4-1/2" h, copper plated, classical relief, imp mark, late 19th C
. . . . 320.00

5-1/4" h, black classical relief, yellow dip, imp mark, 20th C, chip to acanthus relief 375.00

9" h, white classical relief, crimson dip, imp mark, c1920
. . . . .1,265.00

Match Striker/Candleholder, cov, 3-3/4" h, 2 3/8" d, cylindrical body, finial to hold candle, white relief classical figures, blue ground, marked "Wedgwood, England" 225.00

Medallion, oval
  2 5/8 x 3-1/4", white relief of children after Lady Templeton design, dark blue dip, modeled for a buckle, polished edge, imp mark, 18th C 320.00
  3 1/8" l, white classical relief, lilac, green, yellow to dark blue ground, imp mark, early 19th C 1,150.00
Mug
  4-1/4" h, white classical relief, crimson dip, imp mark 1,035.00
  5" h, 3-3/4" d, cylindrical, rope twist handle, silver top rim, white relief classical ladies and cupids on sides, small white medallion at front showing two soldiers, dark blue ground, marked "Wedgwood" 125.00
Pin Tray, 2 3/8" w, 5 7/8" l, white relief classical figures, bleeding green ground, marked "Wedgwood, England" 50.00
Pitcher
  3" h, 2" d, tankard shape, white raised white classical women, grapes and leaves border, lavender ground, marked "Wedgwood England" 85.00
  3-1/2" h, white classical relief, crimson dip, imp mark, c1920 . . . . 750.00
  3-3/4" h, 3-7/8" d, cylindrical, white scrolls and heads of Franklin and Washington, dark green ground, C-scroll handle, marked "Wedgwood, England" 325.00
  6 3/8" h, 3-3/4" d, tankard, cylindrical, white relief classical ladies and cupids, border of relief molded grapes, sage green ground, marked "Wedgwood, England" 155.00
  7-3/4" h, dark blue and white, Portland vase scene, dip, letters 1861 . . . . 500.00
Plaque
  6-1/2" x 23-1/4", rect, white relief Bacchanalian boys after design by Lady Diana Beauclerk, solid light blue, imp mark, 19th C, crazing to relief, plaque restored 1,610.00
  8-3/4" x 18-3/4", rect, white classical relief, pale blue ground, imp mark, late 18th/19th C, giltwood frame 920.00
Portrait Medallion, 45-1/2" l, oval, white relief of Princess of Wales and Prince of Wales, solid blue jasper ground, inscribed titles, imp marks, 19th C, price for pr 520.00
Potpourri Vase, cov, 8" handle to handle, white classical relief, dark blue ground, pierced cov with applied florets, imp mark, mid 19th C, foot rim chips 635.00
Ring Tree, blue and white, "Wedgwood Made in England" mark 125.00
Salt, Imperial, dark blue and white 200.00
Sugar, cov, 4" h, 4 3/8" d, white raised mythological figures, light blue ground, marked "Wedgwood" 120.00
Tea Caddy Spoon, 2 1/8" l, solid blue, shell form bowl, imp mark, early 19th C 435.00
Tea Canister, cov, 5-1/4" h, white classical relief, crimson dip, imp mark, c1920, ball finial missing 920.00
Teapot, cov, 4-1/2" h, black dip, white classical and foliate relief, imp mark, late 19th C 980.00
Urn, cov
  11-1/2" h, light blue and white, #43, "Wedgwood Made in England" mark 350.00
  15" h, two handles, blue and white, classical figures, tapering stem, round shaped foot, reticulated cover, finial reattached 500.00
Vase
  4 7/8" h, Portland, white relief classical figures, dark blue ground, c1840 . . . . 185.00
  5" h
    Green and lilac classical and foliate reliefs, white ground, imp mark, mid 19th C 920.00
    Two handles, white relief classical figures, dark blue ground, marked "Wedgwood, England" 425.00

  5-1/2" h, Portland, white relief classical figures, dark blue ground, c1840 . . . . 250.00
  6-1/2" h, 3" d, angled baluster, handles at shoulder, white relief classical figures, dark blue ground, marked "Wedgwood, England" 225.00
  7-3/4" h, Portland, white relief classical figures, dark blue ground, c1840 . . . . 395.00
Wine Ewer, 16-1/4" h, black dip, white satyr seated on shoulders, ram's head below spout, inscribed under base "J. Sidebotham, July 6, 1882," imp factory mark, c1882, restorations 865.00

Lustres

Bronze, bowl, 6-1/2" d, multicolored fruit ext., MOP lustre int. with fruit, pattern Z5458, printed mark, c1928 . . . . . . 230.00
Dragon, vase, 23-1/4" h, shape #2413, Oriental motif, mottled blue ground, printed mark, c1920, hairline to foot rim, gilt rim wear 750.00
Fairyland
  Punch Bowl, 11-1/4" d, black poplar trees ext., woodland bridge int., pattern Z4968, printed mark, c1925, hairlines, rim chip restored, gilt wear 1,380.00
  Vase
    7-1/4" h, Castle on a Road, daylight coloring, shape #2442, pattern Z4968, printed mark, c1920 . . .3,335.00
    9-1/2" h, Firbolgs, trumpet shape, ruby ground, MOP int., fish border, printed mark, c1920, restored 260.00
    15-3/4" h, Ghostly Wood, cov, shape #2046, pattern Z4968, printed marks, c1920, rim restoration 8,625.00
Fish
  Bowl, K'ang Hsi, 7-1/4" d, mixed blue ext., satin glazed MOP int., pattern Z4920, printed mark, c1920 . . . . 920.00
  Plate, 8-3/4" d, green ground, sponged brown, red and blue, reverse with similar sponging to MOP ground, pattern Z4986, printed mark, c1920 . . . . 345.00
  Hummingbird, vase, 6" h, mottled blue ext., orange int., flying geese border, pattern Z5294, printed mark, c1920, price for pr 750.00
Moonlight
  Caudle Cup and Saucer, 3-3/4" h, imp marks, c1815 . . . . 320.00
  Cup and Saucer, 5-1/2" d, saucer, imp marks, c1810, glaze wear 230.00
  Dish, 11 3/8" h, oval shell shape, imp mark, c1810, price for pr 635.00

Majolica

Compote, 11 1/8" d, multicolored glazes, leaves surrounding central blue medallion, imp mark, c1875 . . . . 345.00
Creamer, cov, 5-1/2" h, cauliflower, molded body, green glazed leaves below cream glazed florets, late 18th C 1,265.00
Game Pie dish, 11" w, 7" d, 6-1/2" h, cover with two bird finial, bottom section with hanging ducks, griffin type handles, manuf Feb. 12, 1868, replaced chip on cover, small hairline 800.00
Plate, seashell shape, pr 250.00
Salt, 1-1/2" d, scrolled tripod base supporting bowl, ram's heads between drapery, imp marks, c1868, int. glaze, nick to one head 345.00
Tile, 8" sq, polychrome dec of bird in flight within water and floral landscape, imp mark, c1877, restored chip 375.00
Vase, 10-1/4" h, glazed brown stoneware, imp mark, c1877 . . . . 230.00

Miscellaneous

Bowl, 10-1/4" h, Liberty Bowl, black transfer dec, sold J E Caldwell & Co. 230.00

Bust, parian

3-1/2" h, Raleigh, inscribed "trial no. 2," imp mark and title, mid 19th C 410.00

14-1/2" h, 8-1/2" d, Milton, by E. W Wyon, marked "Wedgwood" 900.00

Candlestick, 9-3/4" h, blue glaze, molded shell relief surrounding rect base, imp mark and date letters, 1870, chip, glaze flaking, staining, wear 260.00

Cassolette, 9 5/8" h, variegated agate, mounted to stepped basalt plinth, gilding to handles and finial, imp wafer Wedgwood and Bentley wafer mark, gilt wear, rim chips 2,645.00

Chestnut Compote, 8-3/4" d, blue, red, and gilt floral dec, late 19th C, price for pr 230.00

Figure

7" h, Fallow Deer, cream glaze, imp "J. Skeaping," factory mark, c1927 . . . . 200.00

14-1/2" h, Taurus the Bull, modeled and designed by Arnold Machin, black glaze, all over gold printed zodiac symbols, imp mark, c1945 . . . . 415.00

Garden Seat, 17-1/2" h, transfer printed, foliate designed terra cotta colored enamel, cream ground, imp and printed marks, c1891, slight int. glaze line 635.00

Plaque, 4-1/2" x 5 3/8" oval, white terra cotta, depicting Pan and Syrinx in relief, imp Wedgwood and Bentley mark, c1775 . . . . .1,495.00

Plate

7" d, Appledore pattern 22.00

10" d, Ivanhoe series, Black Knight Exchanges with Friar, blue 65.00

Service Plate, 10-5/8" d, bone china, wide powder blue ground, raised gilt scrolled foliate and floral urns, ivory ground center, retailed by T. Goode & Co., Ltd., London, 20th C, set of six 980.00

Serving Dish, 11-3/4" l, oval, three part, armorial crest, blue enamel and gilt trim, colored crests, imp mark, late 18th/early 19th C. 425.00

Teabowl and Saucer, 3-1/2" d saucer, yellow glazed earthenware, green enamel banded bodies, circular black medallions, imp mark, early 19th C 345.00

Teapot, 6" h, 7" w, yellow bamboo, green leaves, imp mark on base with registry mark 350.00

Pearlware

Figure, 7-1/4" h, boy, enamel dec, classical costume, modeled feeding spaniel, imp mark, 19th C, slight foot rim nicks, hand and nose restored, glaze flake 635.00

Pitcher, 7 9/16" h, jug shape, transfer printed black on one side of ship, yellow hull, red, white, and blue American flag and pennant above green sea, black enameled inscription "The Amazon, A. H. Burrows, Commander," reverse with oval scene of ship in distress on stormy sea, red and blue figurehead, under spout dec of eagle beneath 13 stars, banderole inscribed "E Pluribus Unum," worn gilded edge, imp "Wedgwood," c1810, small spout chip 2,300.00

Potpourri Vase, cov, 7-1/2" h, slip dec, central drapery swags within band flanked by engine-turned fluting, imp mark, c1800, vase rim and pierced lid restored 490.00

Weights, 1 to 4", graduated from 1 oz to 7 lb, printed weight and "W. & T Avery Birmingham" on each, imp mark, c1872, minor damage and restoration, price for 8 pc set 1,100.00

Queen's Ware

Centennial Jug, caneware glazed with brown transfers of Independence and Memorial Halls, molded body with star band to rim, ribbed band with thirteen orig states in relief, imp marks, c1874, slight rim line. 200.00

Compote, 6-3/4" h, Japonica pattern, triangular base modeled with three dolphins, gilt and enamel dec, imp mark, c1872 . . . . 345.00

Luncheon Service, brown transfer printed botanical dec, oval serving bowl, four breakfast cups, six butter pats, two coffee cups, two 4-3/4" h compotes, eight 8" d plates, ten 9" d plates, ten 9-7/8" d plates, three oval plates, six sauce dishes, sauce tureen with stand, two 10" l oval serving bowls, oval 9-1/4" d serving dish nine 9" d soup plates, cov oval soup tureen with underdish and ladle, six teacups, oval vegetable bowl with two covers, two circular 9" d cov vegetable bowls, nine 5-1/4" d, saucers, nine 6" d saucers, eight 5" d saucers, c1880, imp marks 980.00

Slop Pail, cov, 11" d, enamel oak leaf border, imp mark, c1886, rim chip repair. 435.00

Vase, cov, 8-1/2" h, engine-turned body, swag drapery bandings, Bacchus head handles, acorn finial, imp mark, mid 19th C. 375.00

Rosso Antico

Club Jug, 4 7/8" h, floral sprays, imp mark, mid 19th C, rim chip and repair. 250.00

Club Pitcher, 4-3/4" h, floral dec, imp mark, mid 19th C 460.00

Creamer, 5" l, basalt creamware trim, hieroglyphics and meander banding, imp mark, early 19th C 575.00

Cup and Saucer, black outlined turquoise enamel and gilt dec, elves scene, cup titled "Get up, silly" and "Hello," 5 3/8" d saucer titled "Look out froggie," imp mark, late 19th C . . 920.00

Figure, 4 5/8" l, boy sleeping, after model of one of the "Five Boys of Fiammingo," imp mark, 19th C 575.00

Plaque, 2-1/4" x 3-1/2" oval, caneware relief, Marriage of Cupid and Psyche, imp mark, early 19th C, mounted in giltwood frame 520.00

Teapot, 5" h, 10" w, black Egyptian motif, alligator finial. 400.00

Vase, 6-1/2" h, basalt classical relief, two handles, mounted atop drum base, imp mark, early 19th C, base nicks, chips, socle restored, no cov 345.00

Stoneware

Mortar and Pestle, 6-1/2" d mortar, 8-1/4" l wood handle pestle imp #3, 19th C 290.00

Sugar, cov, 3" h, three-color glaze, applied green acanthus and lilac bellflowers, imp mark, mid 19th C. 460.00

Vase, 4-1/2" h, white, Portland, painted black ground, classical relief with half-length figure wearing Phyragian cap under base, imp Erturia mark, mid 19th C 635.00

Wine Cask Label, 5-3/4" l, labeled Maderia, Port, Moselle, and Sherry, imp mark, 19th C, price for 4 pc set 500.00

Victoria Ware

Plaque

5 3/8 x 7", white classical relief, deep teal ground, design by Charles Toft, giltwood frame, imp mark, c1880 . . . . 490.00

7-3/4" x 10 7/8" oval, white relief of War & Peace, olive green ground, designed by Charles Toft for 1878 Exhibition, imp mark, c1878, glaze wear and relief repair 690.00

Vase

5" h, portrait, white relief, pale blue ground, iron red ground medallions, black borders, imp mark, c1880 . . . . . . 815.00

7-1/4" h, cov, white dancing hours and foliate relief, deep teal and iron red ground, gilt bacchus-head handles and trim, imp mark, c1875, cov and socle rim restored 865.00

7-1/2" h, cov, white classical and foliate relief, dark blue and burnt red ground, gilt trim, mounted on drum base, imp mark, c1880 . . . . 1,265.00

WELLER POTTERY

History: In 1872, Samuel A. Weller opened a small factory in Fultonham, near Zanesville, Ohio. There he produced utilitarian stoneware, such as milk pans and sewer tile. In 1882, he moved his facilities to Zanesville. Then in 1890, Weller built a new plant in the Putnam section of Zanesville along the tracks of the Cincinnati and Muskingum Railway. Additions followed in 1892 and 1894.

In 1894, Weller entered into an agreement with William A. Long to purchase the Lonhuda Faience Company, which had developed an art pottery line under the guidance of Laura A. Fry, formerly of Rookwood. Long left in 1895, but Weller continued to produce Lonhuda under the new name "Louwelsa." Replacing Long as art director was Charles Babcock Upjohn. He, along with Jacques Sicard, Frederick Hurten Rhead, and Gazo Fudji, developed Weller's art pottery lines.

At the end of World War I, many prestige lines were discontinued and Weller concentrated on commercial wares. Rudolph Lorber joined the staff and designed lines such as Roma, Forest, and Knifewood. In 1920, Weller purchased the plant of the Zanesville Art Pottery and claimed to produce more pottery than anyone else in the country.

Art pottery enjoyed a revival when the Hudson Line was introduced in the early 1920s. The 1930s saw Coppertone and Graystone Garden ware added. However, the Depression forced the closing of the Putnam plant and one on Marietta Street in Zanesville. After World War II inexpensive Japanese imports took over Weller's market. In 1947 Essex Wire Company of Detroit bought the controlling stock, but early in 1948 operations ceased.

References: Susan and Al Bagdade, *Warman's American Pottery and Porcelain*, Wallace-Homestead, 1994; Sharon and Bob Huxford, *Collectors Encyclopedia of Weller Pottery*, Collector Books, 1979, 1998 value update; Ralph and Terry Kovel, *Kovels' American Art Pottery*, Crown Publishers, 1993.

Collectors' Club: American Art Pottery Association, P.O. Box 1226, Westport, MA 02790.

Additional Listings: See *Warman's Americana & Collectibles* for more examples.

Bowl

Burntwood, lions with wings 125.00

Coppertone, green and brown matte glaze cov flower frog on end, 10" l, 5" h, minor bruise 375.00

Glendale, molded design of seagulls, flower frog with molded eggs, sgd, 15" d, 3" h, small flake on frog 700.00

Squirrel, small base chip 115.00

Box, cov, Sicard, crimped and twisted form, irid green, blue, green glaze, gold floral dec, mkd, 6" h, bottom and lid repaired 375.00

Bud Vase, Eocean, 6" 150.00

Candlestick, 14" h, Woodcraft, owl 260.00

Cookie Jar, Mammy 2,495.00

Ewer, Dickensware

Pears on brown branches, green leaves, blue yellow to brow, painted and incised dec, incised mar, incised initials "B.L." 425.00

Two colonialists playing board game, peach to blue, imp mark, 5" h 200.00

Figure

Brighton Woodpecker, 6" h, orig base 375.00

Coppertone, turtle, green and brown matte glaze, 5" l 240.00

Drunken Ducks, yellow, Coppertone base, stamped mark, 15" h, small flake to bottom edge 3,250.00

Hen, six chicks around base, incised mark, 8" h, restored minor flakes 1,600.00

Muskota, fishing boy, 7" h, repaired chip 150.00

Floor Vase, Louwelsa, four sided, blown-out top, scalloped rim, orange and brown poppies, green leaves, unmarked, 23" h, minor flakes at top 1,100.00

Flower Frog, Muskota

Crab, 7" 375.00

Woman on Rock, 7" h, minor flakes 180.00

Garden Ornament, fisher Boy, multicolored, Coppertone base, 20" h, some restoration 500.00

Jardiniere

Flemish, 7" h 200.00

Jap Birdimal, squeeze bag technique landscape, blue trees, yellow moon, imp mark, 8-1/2" h, hairline crack 210.00

Sicard, ftd, brilliant, old irid glaze, red, green, and blue highlights, red int., mkd on side, 8" d, 7" h 650.00

Jardiniere and Pedestal, overall cream floral design, bordered with brown bands, 12-1/2" d, 31" h, minor flakes 425.00

Jug

Dickensware, tan to green, incised and painted fish swimming through waves, imp mark, artist initial, 5-1/2" h 325.00

Dickensware, yellow, green, orange, and brown berry and leaf dec, mkd, initialed "R. G.," 10-1/2" h, mino5 scratches 270.00

Mt. Vernon Bridge, Upjohn 4,150.00

Lamp

Blue Ware, dark blue, girl and yellow garlands, 11" h, 5" w, hairline 200.00

Bronzeware, green and gold metallic glaze, "I" h 400.00

Pitcher, Woodcraft, three fox heads, tree trunk form, 12-1/2" h 500.00

Planter, 10-1/2" w, 6-1/2" h, molded landscape with sheep and flowers, matte green glaze, minor chip repair 375.00

Umbrella Stand, 20" h, 10" d, matte dark green glaze, emb poppies and sunflowers on long stems 1,700.00

Vase

Ardsley, 9" h 90.00

Aurelian, standard glaze, dragon in fire, mkd and sgd "Edward Abel," 12-1/2" h, 5" w 600.00

Blue Ware, 10" h, blue ground, female figure, minor flake 200.00

Blue Ware, 12" h, 6" w. blue ground, several figures 475.00

Bronzeware, metallic red textured glaze, 11" h 800.00

Camelot, 4" h, cream geometric design, yellow matte glaze, mkd 225.00

Chase, 9" h. 375.00
Chengtu, 8" h. 125.00
Claywood, 9" h. 150.00
Coppertone, 7" h, 8-1/2" w, green and rust matte glaze, two
    closed handles, incised signature 600.00
Eocean, 6-1/2" h, green, pink, and cream carp, green to pink
    background, incised signature 1,500.00
Glendale, brown and green, bird nest dec, mkd, 9" h, 8" w
    . . . . 1,000.00
Glenwood, 8-1/4" h, 2 birds with nest. 1,100.00
Greora, 9" h 190.00
Hudson, 7" h, blue, multicolored floral dec, sgd "McLaughlin,"
    orig label, stamp mark 375.00
Hudson, 8-1/4" h 1,800.00
Hudson, 15" h, 7" w, blue ground, white and pink peonies,
    painted and sgd by Pillsbury, mkd 4,500.00
Hudson Pictorial, 11-1/2" h, landscape with snow laden road,
    brown fence running alongside tree line, painted and sgd by
    McLaughlin, incised mark 4,250.00
Jewel, incised fern fronts, swirling blue jewels, dec front and
    back, blue, green, and light pink ground, imp mark, 7-1/2" h
    . . . . 700.00
LaSa, 4" h, bulbous 250.00
Louwelsa, 7-1/2" h, holly berries and leaves, shades of blue,
    imp mark 900.00
Louwelsa, 10-1/2" h, stylized yellow roses, deep emerald
    green ground, sgd "H. Pillsbury," incised mark . . . 2,400.00
Louwelsa, 12" h, matte, deep ruse oak leaves and acorns,
    tan matte ground, sgd "Hester Pillsbury," incised and imp
    marks 1,100.00
Marvo, 7" h 90.00
Perfecto, pink and purple peonies, brown centers, green
    leaves, Dorothy England decorator, 9" h, 9" w 650.00
Scandia, incised black vertical stripes, 9-1/4" h 280.00
Sicard, gold mums with green highlights, purple, blue, and
    red ground, sgd "Weller Sicard," 10-1/2" h 1,700.00
Tutone, Art Deco, 9" 285.00
Warwick, double, 5" 60.00
Woodcraft, 5-1/2" h, #156-2/4 . . . . 100.00
Woodland, Apple Blossom, 10-1/4" x 4-1/4" 250.00
Wall pocket, woman, arms extended, blue matte glaze dress,
    imp mark, 8" l 325.00

Vase, Lasa, 16" h, $2,070. Photo courtesy of Jackson's Auctioneers & Appraisers.

WHALING

History: Whaling items are a specialized part of nautical collecting. Provenance is of prime importance since collectors want assurances that their pieces are from a whaling voyage. Since ship's equipment seldom carries the ship's identification, some individuals have falsely attributed a whaling provenance to general nautical items. Know the dealer, auction house, or collector from whom you buy.

Special tools, e.g., knives, harpoons, lances, and spades, do not overlap the general nautical line. Makers' marks and condition determine value for these items.

References: Nina Hellman and Norman Brouwer, *Mariner's Fancy*, South Street Seaport Museum, Balsam Press, and University of Washington Press, 1992; Martha Lawrence, *Scrimshaw*, Schiffer Publishing, 1993.

Museums: Cold Spring Harbor Whaling Museum, Cold Spring Harbor, NY; Kendall Whaling Museum, Sharon, MA; Mystic Seaport Museum, Mystic, CT; National Maritime Museum Library, San Francisco, CA; New Bedford Whaling Museum, New Bedford, MA; Pacific Whaling Museum, Waimanalo, HI; Sag Harbor Whaling & Historical Museum, Sag Harbor, NY; South Street Seaport Museum, New York, NY.

Additional Listings: Nautical Items; Scrimshaw.

Bag, 19-1/2" l, 11" w, linen, whaleship *Ohio*, holds ship's mail,
    mkd "Ship Ohio/Letter Bag" 800.00
Book
    Etchings of a Whaling Cruise, J Ross Browne, first edition,
        New York, 1846 . . . . 575.00
    Whale Ships and Whaling, George Francis-Dow, Marine Research Society, Salem, MA, 1925 . . . . 125.00
Bookplate, aquatint engraving of whaling scenes, framed,
    French, 19th C, pr 225.00
Box, H & E Howland Whaleship Agents, New Bedford, rosewood, brass bound, lift-out tray, two cut glass ink bottles,
    scrimshaw pen 1,200.00
Busk, whalebone, engraved
    12-11/16" l, dec with various geometric devices, plants,
        three-masted ship under sail, crack, minor chips, minor insect damage 150.00
    14-1/8" l, dec with neoclassical urn with willow, "Love," ship
        under sail, coconut tree, and lighthouse, polychrome highlights, faded, slightly warped, minor crack, 19th C
        . . . . 250.00
Caulking Tool, 4-1/2" l, boat maker's, whale bone 385.00
Crew List, whaleship *Montpelier,* Sept 6, 1853, names, position,
    number of shares in voyages to be received 150.00
Dominoes, bone and ebony, set of 26, few mkd "London"
    . . . . 110.00
Log Book, bark *Pioneer,* Captain James S Hazard, departed
    New Bedford, August 5, 1869, held by US Consol at Mauritins, released and returned by New Bedford on Dec. 1,
    1872, sent home 232 barrels of sperm oil 3,500.00
Print
    "Right Whaling in Behring Straits and Arctic Ocean with its
        Varieties," Benjamin Russell, publisher, John H. Bufford, lithographer, 1871, identified within matrix, chromolithograph
        on paper, framed, sheet size 19-1/8" h, 35-1/4" l, tears and
        losses to margins, staining, not examined out of frame
        . . . . 525.00

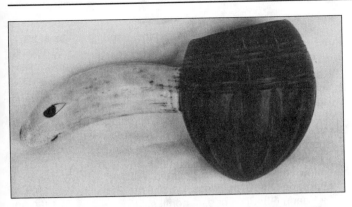

Dipper, sperm whale tooth handle carved as seal, incised dec on coconut shell dipper, 8" w, $395.

"The Whale Fishery, Attacking a 'Right' Whale and 'Cutting In,'" Currier and Ives, John Cameron, lithographer, (Conningham 6623), identified in inscriptions in the matrix, litho with hand coloring on paper, sheet size 21-1/8" h, 28" l, unframed, tears and punctures, staining, toning 1,035.00
Receipt, whale oil purchase, William Rotch & Sons, New Bedford, dated 1811 and 1813, framed, pr 80.00
Sailor's Fid, 11" l, whale bone, old worn surface 200.00
Seam Rubber, whalebone, engraved "T. D. C.," mid 19th C
. . . . .325.00
Ship's Block, 5-1/2" l, double, brass shims, iron hanger, imp metal cross dec on each side 120.00
Sugar Nippers, 12" l, scribe line dec, whalebone handle, wrought iron nippers, mounted on rect wood base, late 18th C, corrosion, cracks to handle 575.00
Try-Square, 11-13/16", whalebone, 19th C. 635.00
Whale's Tooth, engraved, late 19th C, minor crack
  5-1/8" l, dec with elegant lady, seated nude woman, initialed "OM". 950.00
  6-1/4" l, dec with sailor 450.00
  6-1/4" l, dec with spiraling design of various ships under sail, whaling scene, stained. .1,20.00
  7" l, dec with elegant lady. 1,110.00
Whale's Tooth, mounted
  5-1/4" l, plaque reads "This tooth taken from a sperm whale that made 125 barrels of oil. The oil was brought into Nantucket, June 1797," contemporary wood stand 450.00
  19" h, pair of teeth mounted with baleen, naturalistically carved wood base, 19th C, some insect damage to baleen
. . . . .2,990.00

WHIELDON   WHIELDON

History: Thomas Whieldon, a Staffordshire potter, established his shop in 1740. He is best known for his mottled ware, molded in the shapes of vegetables, fruits, and leaves. Josiah Spode and Josiah Wedgwood, in different capacities, had connections with Whieldon.

Whieldon ware is a generic term. His wares were never marked, and other potters made similar items. Whieldon ware is agate-tortoiseshell earthenware, in limited shades of green, brown, blue and yellow. Most pieces are utilitarian items, e.g., dinnerware and plates, but figurines and other decorative pieces also were made.

Cream Jug, 3-1/2" h, baluster, Cauliflower, scrolled foliage handle, silver shape rim, dark green glazed leaves, cream glazed florets, Whieldon/Wedgwood/Greatbatch, c1790 . . .2,250.00

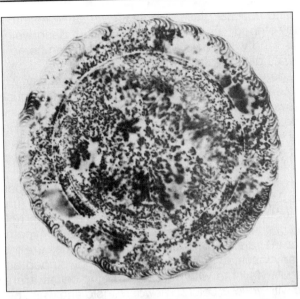

Plate, brown glaze, emb scroll at border, $110.

Dish, 14" l, molded border, scrolls and basketwork, panels, trellis pattern, shaped rim, tortoise shell glaze, hairline, 1760
. . . . .1,650.00
Figure
  2-3/4" h, two nude children resting arm in arm on shrub, applied bird and foliage, translucent brown, green, and gray-blue glazes, c1765, repair to bases, pr 1,035.00
  5" h, cow, standing on freeform base, creamware, translucent brown, yellow, and green glazes, c1780, repairs. .2,300.00
Jar, cov, 2" h, creamware, cylinder shape, mottled gray-green and blue glazes, c1760 . . . . .1,265.00
Plate
  8" d, brown tortoise shell glaze, green and yellow splashes, unmarked. 140.00
  9-3/8" d, trellis diaper molded rim, separated by pairs of feathers, gray splashed glaze with yellow and green splotches, c1760, 9 pc set 3,100.00
  9-1/2" d, black tortoise shell glaze, green, blue, and brown splashes, emb diapered border 390.00
Platter, 17-1/4" l, oval, paneled border, threaded rim, manganese-brown, green, and blue splashes, cream ground
. . . . .290.00
Soup Plate, 9-1/4" d, black tortoise shell glaze, green, blue, brown, and yellow splashes, emb diapered rim 550.00
Sugar, cov, 3-5/8" h, 4-3/8" d, Cauliflower, dark green glazed leaves, cream glazed florets, stains 3,245.00
Tea Canister, 4-1/2" h, Cauliflower, dark green glazed leaves, cream glazed florets, Whieldon/Wedgwood, c1765
. . . . .1,250.00
Teapot, cov
  2-1/2" h, creamware, globular, straight spout, loop handle, mottled brown, blue, and green glazes, c1760 . . .1,265.00
  4" h, Cauliflower, molded lower body and handle, dark green glazed leaves, cream glazed florets, Whieldon/Wedgwood, c1765, base rim chips 1,000.00
  5-3/8" h, molded pineapple form, mold green leaves base, handle, and spout, ochre pineapple body, c1770, restored cracks. 1,035.00

WHIMSIES, GLASS

History: During lunch or after completing their regular work schedule, glassworkers occasionally spent time creating unusual glass objects known as whimsies, e.g. candy-striped canes, darners, hats, paperweights, pipes, and witch balls. Whimsies were taken home and given as gifts to family and friends.

Because of their uniqueness and infinite variety, whimsies can rarely be attributed to a specific glass house or glassworker. Whimsies were created wherever glass was made, from New Jersey to Ohio and westward. Some have suggested that style and color can be used to pinpoint region or factory, but no one has yet developed an identification key that is adequate.

Glass canes are among the most collectible types of whimsies. These range in length from very short (under one foot) to ten feet or more. They come in both hollow and solid form. Hollow canes can have a bulb-type handle or the rarer C- or L-shaped handle. Canes are found in many fascinating colors, with the candy striped being a regular favorite with collectors. Many canes are also filled with various colored powders, gold and white being the most common and silver being harder to find. Sometimes they were even used as candy containers.

References: Gary Baker et al., *Wheeling Glass 1829-1939*, Oglebay Institute, 1994, distributed by Antique Publications; Joyce E. Blake, *Glasshouse Whimsies*, published by author, 1984; Joyce E. Blake and Dale Murschell, *Glasshouse Whimsies: An Enhanced Reference*, published by authors, 1989.

Collectors' Club: Whimsey Club, 522 Woodhall, Newark, NY 14513.

Baton
  59-1/2" l, clear, maroon swirls 330.00
  87" l, hollow, blue and maroon twist 220.00
Bird Fountain, 5-3/4" l, colorless, blown three mold, pontil scar, New England, 1825-40, McKearin GI-12, inner stain
  . . . . 280.00

Witch Ball and Goblet, pink, white, and gold lattice, 7" h goblet, 4" d witch ball, $400.

Cane
  36-3/4" l, clear, square, twisted handle and tip, chips at tip
  . . . . 100.00
  41" l, amber, square, twisted shepherd's crook handle, twisted tip, chips at both ends 140.00
  41" l, opaque white, cased in amber, chips at handle, tip ground 120.00
  45" l, clear, mahogany triple swirl, tip chipped 220.00
Glass, cov, 9" h, aqua, faintly ribbed body, four vertical pinched rigaree bands, four pinched rigaree handles, hollow cover with hen finial, pontil scars on base and cover 400.00
Hat, blown three mold, New England, 1825-40
  McKearin GII-18, colorless, pontil scar, 2" h 110.00
  McKearin GIII-3, colorless, pontil scar 1250.00
  McKearin GIII-23, deep sapphire blue, pontil scar, 2-1/4" h
  . . . . 850.00
Pen Holder, 3" h, 3-1/2" d paperweight base, blown spatter glass, cobalt blue, red, and white solid round sphere, pulled into six coils to hold pen 200.00
Powder Horn, 11" h, Nailsea type blue and white loopings, colorless ground, ftd, tooled ground lip, pontil scar 135.00
Vase, 4" h, blown, witch ball cover, amber, wear, small flake on ball 165.00
Witch Ball and Stand
  9-1/2" h, free blown, deep sapphire blue, pontil scar, attributed to South Jersey, mid 19th C 1,400.00
  9-3/4" h, Nailsea type white loopings, colorless ground, pontil scar, attributed to South Jersey or Pittsburgh area, 1840s
  . . . . 400.00

WILLOW PATTERN CHINA

History: Josiah Spode developed the first "traditional" willow pattern in 1810. The components, all motifs taken from Chinese export china, are a willow tree, "apple" tree, two pagodas, fence, two birds, and three figures crossing a bridge. The legend, in its many versions, is an English invention based on this scenic design.

By 1830, there were more than 200 makers of willow pattern china in England. The pattern has remained in continuous production. Some of the English firms that still produce it are Burleigh, Johnson Bros. (Wedgwood Group), Royal Doulton (continuing production of the Booths' pattern), and Wedgwood.

By the end of the 19th century, production of this pattern spread to France, Germany, Holland, Ireland, Sweden, and the United States. Buffalo Pottery made the first willow pattern in the United States beginning in 1902. Many other companies followed, developing willow variants using rubber-stamp simplified patterns as well as overglaze decals. The largest American manufacturers of the traditional willow pattern were Royal China and Homer Laughlin, usually preferred because it is dated. Shenango pieces are the most desirable among restaurant-quality wares.

Japan began producing large quantities of willow pattern china in the early 20th century. Noritake began about 1902. Most Japanese pieces are porous earthenware with a dark blue pattern using the traditional willow design, usually with no inner border. Noritake did put the pattern on china bodies. Unusual forms include salt and pepper shakers, one-quarter pound butter dishes, and canisters. The most desirable Japanese willow is the fine quality NKT Co. ironstone with a copy of the old Booths pattern. Recent Japanese willow is a paler shade of blue on a porcelain body.

The most common dinnerware color is blue. However, pieces can also be found in black (with clear glaze or mustard-colored glaze by Royal Doulton), brown, green, mulberry, pink (red), and polychrome.

The popularity of the willow design has resulted in a large variety of willow-decorated products: candles, fabric, glass, graniteware, linens, needlepoint, plastic, tinware, stationery, watches, and wall coverings. All this material has collectible value.

Marks: Early pieces of Noritake have a Nippon "Royal Sometuke" mark. "Occupied Japan" may add a small percentage to the value of common table wares. Pieces marked "Maruta" or "Moriyama" are especially valued.

References: Leslie Bockol, *Willow Ware: Ceramics in the Chinese Tradition,* Schiffer Publishing, 1995; Robert Copeland, *Spode's Willow Pattern and Other Designs after the Chinese,* Studio Vista, 1980, 1990 reprint; Mary Frank Gaston, *Blue Willow,* 2nd ed., Collector Books, 1990, 1996 value update.

Periodicals: *American Willow Report,* P.O. Box 900, Oakridge, OR 97463; *The Willow Transfer Quarterly, Willow Word,* P.O. Box 13382, Arlington, TX 76094.

Collectors' Clubs: International Willow Collectors, P.O. Box 13382, Arlington, TX 76094-0382; Willow Society, 39 Medhurst Rd., Toronto Ontario M4B 1B2 Canada.

REPRODUCTION ALERT

The Scio Pottery, Scio, Ohio, currently manufactures a willow pattern set sold in variety stores. The pieces have no marks or backstamps, and the transfer is of poor quality. The plates are flatter in shape than those of other manufacturers.

Note: Although colors other than blue are hard to find, there is less demand; thus, prices may not necessarily be higher priced. Prices below are for blue transfer on white ground, unless otherwise indicated.

Bone Dish, 6-1/4" l, pink, Bailey Walker 20.00
Bowl
    4" d, mkd "Societe Ceramique Willow". 60.00

Berry Bowl, oval, Buffalo China mark, 6-1/2" l, oval, $28.00

5-1/4" d, mkd "Allerton". 10.00
9" d, mkd "Royal" 20.00
Butter Dish, cov, mkd "Societe Ceramique Willow". 90.00
Butter Pat, 3" sq, mkd "Booth's Real Old Willow" 25.00
Cake Plate, pierced sides 65.00
Children's Dishes
    Dinner Service, four plates, cups and saucers, creamer, cov sugar, cov teapot, platter, cov casserole, gravy boat, mkd "Japan". 295.00
    Tea Set, mkd "Occupied Japan," price for 18 pc set 375.00
Creamer, 2-3/8" h, handle, pitcher style, mkd "Shenango" 20.00
Cream Soup, 5" w, red, mkd "Swinnertons," c1930 . . . . . 30.00
Cup and Saucer, mkd "Adams". 25.00
Demitasse Cup and Saucer, mkd "Allerton" 15.00
Egg Cup, 2-1/4" h, border on base, mkd "England" 20.00
Fish Platter, 12" l, 11-1/2" w, dated 1886, mkd "Minton" 650.00
Gravy Boat and Underplate, light blue, mkd "Copeland" 65.00
Hot Water Plate, 11-1/2" w, mkd "Semi-China Warranted," c1830 . . . . 475.00
Jardiniere, 6-1/4" h, 8" d, horizontal ribbing, brown transfer, yellow glaze 400.00
Jug, 6" h, octagonal, blue, serpent handle, Mason's crown mark with "Patent Ironstone China". 360.00
Mug, 4" h, mkd "Doulton" 95.00
Pitcher, 8-1/2" h, mkd "Willow England" 140.00
Plate
    5-3/4" d, mkd "Allerton". 9.50
    6" d, green, mkd "Royal Venton Ware". 15.00
    6-1/4" d, red, mkd "Johnson Brothers" 5.00
    8-1/2" d, ivory ground, scalloped edge, light brown daisy border, blue allover willow pattern, gold bands on edge and base of border 65.00
    9" d, pink, mkd "Allerton" 10.00
    10" d, blue, Two Temples pattern, butterfly border, mkd "W. T. Copeland" 40.00
    10" d, red, mkd "Johnson Brothers" 25.00
Platter
    9-1/2" d, mkd "Allerton". 60.00
    12" l, 9" w, red, mkd "Royal Venton Ware, John Steventon & Sons, Ltd." 50.00
    14" l, English. 175.00
    16" l, 12-1/2" w, mkd "Warranted Staffordshire". 225.00
    18" l, mkd "Allerton" 150.00
    20" l, English. 200.00
Pudding Mold, 5-3/4" d 60.00
Relish Dish, 11" l, divided into three sections, mkd "Booth," c1906 . . . . 275.00
Sauce Boat with Underplate, 14" l. 115.00
Soup Plate, flanged, mkd "Allerton" 25.00
Sugar, cov, 5" h. 55.00
Teapot, cov
    Blue, 5" h, mkd "Sadler, England" 100.00
    Pink, mkd "Royal". 45.00
Tile, 8" sq, mkd "Steele & Wood" 145.00
Toothpick Holder, 1-3/4" h, border at top, English 45.00
Tray, 17-1/4" l, rect, cut corners, blue, gilt rim, mkd "Wedgwood" 315.00
Vegetable Bowl
    8-1/2" d, mkd "Green & Co., England" 40.00
    10" l, dark pink, mkd "Royal Venton, John Steventon & Sons" 35.00

WOODENWARE

History: Many utilitarian household objects and farm implements were made of wood. Although they were subjected to heavy use, these implements were made of the strongest woods and were well cared for by their owners.

References: Arene Burgess, *19th Century Wooden Boxes,* Schiffer Publishing, 1997; George C. Neumann, *Early American Antique Country Furnishing,* L-W Book Sales, 1984, 1993 reprint.

Additional Listings: See *Warman's Americana & Collectibles* for more examples.

Note: This category serves as a catchall for wooden objects, which do not fit into other categories.

Book Press, 55" h, 25" w, 13-3/4" d, wavy birch, threaded shaft and rect press, shaped supports, cockbeaded base with drawer, four sq tapering legs, Federal, New England, c1800 . . . . 1,725.00

Bowl, burl, ash
11" d, 4-3/8" h, old soft finish, good color, int. has wear 880.00
11" d, 5" h, dense burl, refinished, minor age cracks. . 550.00
14-1/4" w, 19" l, 8" h, oval, old refinishing, int. wear, glued "V" shaped repair at rim 1,100.00
15-1/2" d, 6-1/2" h, well figured ash burl, turned detail at top and base, good old finish, minor age crack in rim .9,350.00
16-1/2" d, 6" h, old scrubbed finish, rim handles, minor edge damage and cracks 1,100.00
17-1/4" d, 7-3/4" h, minor crack, rim chips, minute insect damage 1,610.00
17-1/2" d, 4-3/4" h, old soft finish 715.00
19-5/8" d, 6-3/4" h, 19th C, crack, minor rim chips 1,265.00

Bowl, cov, 7" h, 6" d, turned maple, fanciful feather design in reds and greens on ochre ground, attributed to OH, first half 19th C, minor paint loss, old repaired crack 2,645.00

Box
14-1/8" l, burl, dovetailed, molded edge on lid and base, int. till with lid, old brass batwing escutcheons, old soft finish, lock missing 1,825.00
13-1/4" l, curly maple, dovetailed, relief carved designs on scalloped sides, poplar bottom 1,155.00
22-3/4" l, 16-1/2" w, 10" h, pine, molded rect top, staple hinges, dovetailed box, applied molding at base, old natural color, New England, 18th C, missing one cleat 250.00
29" l, 16" w, 23" h, painted and dec, pine, hinged top lifts off, old mustard paint, polychrome painted dec on front (added later), New England, 1830s 885.00

Candle Dryer, 22" h, New England, 19th C, painted, two carved arms, carved drying holes on base and ring-turned post, carved circular base, orig blue-green painted surface, minor paint wear. 575.00

Candle Mold, wood frame
6 pewter tubes, walnut frame 250.00
16 pewter tubes, pine frame. 880.00
18 pewter tube, wick spools and rods, case sgd "H. Tiebe, Nauvoo" 1,815.00
20 tin tubes, one foot missing, one adjusting screw broken 140.00
24 pewter tubes, pine and poplar frame stenciled "W. Humiston/ Maker/ Troy, New York/Warranted/Premium" 1,375.00

Carrier, 7-1/2" w, 6-5/8" d, 9-3/4" h, pine, orig red paint, New England, 19th C 890.00

Carving, 19-1/2" h, 48" l, floral and foliate pierced design, painted blue, repaired, old repaint, 19th C 320.00

Checkerboard, 13" x 23-3/4", primitive, pine, old patina, black stained squares, gallery edge with damage 220.00

Container, cov, 8-1/2" d, 9" h, turned, vinegar grained, America, 19th C. 2,300.00

Dipper, 16-1/4" l, coconut, incised "C. Austin North Kingstown, RI, March 22 1829," dec with crescent moon, sun, heart, pinwheel, fish, ship and human head, geometric border, minor crack. 325.00

Dish, burl
6-3/4" d, 1-7/8" h, old soft finish 385.00
6-3/4" w, 7" l, 2" h, scratch carved ext. "H.A.L. 1841," old worn finish. 360.00

Firkin, 5-1/4" h, 7-1/2" d, cov, bentwood handle fastened with two wood pegs, top with finger lap, orig blue-gray paint 600.00

Flax Wheel, 39" w, 21" d, 38" h, wheel painted black, salmon red and blue trim, inscribed in yellow "Anna Gretta M.D.S. 1859," PA-German, imperfections, incomplete 350.00

Foot Warmer
7" l, 9" w, 7-1/4" h, pine, old red paint, compass star relief carving, drilled holes, some edge damage, sliding door replaced 175.00
7-3/4" l, 8-1/2" w, 6-1/2" h, walnut, dovetailed, orig finish and scorching, pieced circle design with "L. F." and punched date "1814" on sliding lid, wire bale handle 320.00

Game Board
12-1/2" h, 18-3/4" l, carved and painted pine alternating squares of raised panel design, maroon and black paint, America, late 19th/early 20th C 320.00
24" sq, worn old black and brown paint, yellow, red, and blue dec 365.00

Gaming Wheel, 22" d, 32-1/2" h, orig paint, America, late 19th/early 20th C 175.00

Jar, cov, 5-1/4" h, turned tureen, worn dark reddish-brown sponging, hairline in base. 500.00

Lap Desk, 13" l, 10" d, oak and composition, elaborate high relief foliate design, fitted int., Victorian, c1855-60, minor cracking 300.00

Plate Rack, hanging, European
23" h, 30" w, refinished pine, dovetailed frame, shaped ends, some insect damage 250.00
25-1/2" h, 25" w, 8" d, pine, old orange stain, dovetailed, scalloped ends 500.00

Sugar Bucket, mkd "C. S. Hersey," 9-1/2" c, 9" h, $95.

30" h, 42" w, pine with traces of old finish, dovetailed scalloped ends 525.00
34" h, 51" w, pine, very worn brown paint, dovetailed, scalloped ends, worm holes 550.00
Press, 11-3/4" h, 6-1/2" w, cherry, punched detail, single long drawer, old soft finish 625.00
Smoothing Board, chip carved, horse head handle, old dark green, black, and red paint, initialed and dated "1787," insect and edge damage 1,155.00
Spoon Rack
  21" h, 24-1/4" w, 3-1/2" d, double tier, 8 spoon slots at top, center box, shaped sides and back, painted yellow over green 400.00
  24-3/4" h, 11-1/2" w, 5-5/8" d, hanging, pine, cotter pin hinges on lid, dark green paint, attributed to Europe, late 18th C, imperfections 950.00
Sugar Bucket, 11-3/4" h, lid with branded label "E. F. Lane & Co. Marlboro Depot, N.H.," old refinishing, some damage to lid, age crack 175.00
Sugar Firkin, 6-3/4" h, 6-3/4" w, green-blue paint, wire bale handle, fingered bands, one metal base band, slightly tapered sides, wear and slight damage 150.00
Watch Hutch, 10" h, 12" w, 3-3/8" d, painted blue and gray, gilt highlights, carved dec, eagle on ball finial, tall case clock shape, Continental, 19th C 1,265.00

WORLD'S FAIRS and EXPOSITIONS

History: The Great Exhibition of 1851 in London marked the beginning of the World's Fair and Exposition movement. The fairs generally featured exhibitions from nations around the world displaying the best of their industrial and scientific achievements.

Many important technological advances have been introduced at world's fairs, including the airplane, telephone, and electric lights. Ice cream cones, hot dogs, and iced tea were first sold by vendors at fairs. Art movements often were closely connected to fairs, with the Paris Exhibition of 1900 generally considered to have assembled the best of the works of the Art Nouveau artists.

References: *Crystal Palace Exhibition Illustrated Catalogue* (London, 1851), Dover Publications, n.d.; Robert L. Hendershott, *1904 St Louis World's Fair Mementos and Memorabilia*, Kurt R. Krueger Publishing (160 N. Washington, Iola, WI 54945), 1994; Frederick and Mary Megson, *American Exposition Postcards*, The Postcard Lovers, 1992.

Collectors' Clubs: 1904 World's Fair Society, 529 Barcia Dr., St. Louis, MO 63119; World's Fair Collectors' Society, Inc., P.O. Box 20806, Sarasota, FL 34276.

Museums: Buffalo & Erie County Historical Society, Buffalo, NY; California State University, Madden Library, Fresno, CA; 1893 Chicago World's Fair Columbian Exposition Museum, Columbus, WI; Museum of Science & Industry, Chicago, IL; Presidio Army Museum, San Francisco, CA; The Queens Museum, Flushing, NY.

1876, Centennial Exposition, Philadelphia

Paperweight, glass, exposition buildings 90.00
Textile, 19" h, 25-1/2" l, printed in black and red, "Memorial Hall Art Gallery, Centennial 1776-1876," age stains, some purple stains 90.00

(Centennial) Boot, clear glass, metal top, 3-1/2" h, 2" w, $45.

Ticket, United States International Exhibition Package, 3-7/8" x 2-3/8", minor edge discoloration 30.00

1893, Columbian Exposition, Chicago

Advertising Trade Card
  Halveda Milk, evaporated milk and other milk products, fold-out type 50.00
  McLaughlin's Coffee, "Opening of World's Fair," President Cleveland's picture on lower right corner, 7" x 5-1/4" 45.00
Badge, red, white and blue ribbon, eagle and hanging token, one side "World's Columbian Exposition Souvenir, Chicago, IL, 1892-93," other side with illus of Administration Building 85.00
Bank, Administration Building, nickel plated metal, 5" h . . 90.00
Book
  Artistic Guide to Chicago and the World's Columbian Exposition, Charles E. Banks, illus, hard bound 110.00
  In Remembrance of the World's Columbian Exposition, Chicago, Zum Andenken-En Memoire, 1893, 5" x 6", red, hard bound, illus of buildings 45.00
  Official Guide of the World's Columbian Exposition, compiled by J. Flinn, illus, soft bound, dark maroon cov 40.00
  World's Columbian Exposition at Chicago 1492-1892, 1893, hard bound, drawings illus, red, 6-1/4" x 9-1/2" 55.00
  World's Columbian Fair, Chicago, red, hard bound, illus, 7" x 5" 30.00
  World's Columbian Fair, Chicago, 1893, 9" x 5-1/2", tan, black, and gold, pictures of buildings, worn 35.00
Booklet
  "White City by Lake Michigan," Albertype, black and white photos of buildings 35.00
  "World's Fair and Midway Scenes," midway scenes, Government Bldg., German Bldg., Old Vienna, German Exhibit, etc. 6.00
  "World's Fair Souvenir," given out by "Eric Preserving Co., Finest Canned Goods, Buffalo, N. Y., U.S.A.," green cover, pictures of fair, 6-1/4" x 3-1/2" 40.00
Bookmark, woven, 10" l, The Star Spangled Banner, woven on the Exposition Grounds by Phoenix Manufacturing, tassel, mounted on orig paper backing, 6" x 20" walnut frame 200.00
Bottle, pottery, pig shaped, 7-1/4" l, incised "From the World's Fair/ With a little good Old Rye in 1893/ Cut Rates/ To All Points East," Kirkpatrick Bros., Anna, IL 1,760.00

Bowl, 8-1/2" d, porcelain, sq shape, Machinery Bldg and Electric Bldg on inside. 100.00

Dish, quarter-moon shape, lagoon with gondolas, south side of Expo in background 65.00

Glass, 3" h
Etched Art Palace and lake 75.00
Etched flowers and M.B.F., other side "World's Fair 1893"
. . . . 75.00

Match Safe
2-1/2" h, plated metal, "Columbian Fair Souvenir 1492-1892"
. . . . 260.00
3-1/2" l, 1-3/4" w, plated metal, plug tobacco cutter, relief scene of landing of Columbus and wording "Columbian Souvenir 1493, Chicago 1893," patent date 1891, worn
. . . . 45.00

Paperweight, rect, colorful, Machinery Hall, dated 35.00

Pin, 2-1/2" x 1-3/4", Queen's head in foreground, sailing masts in background. 65.00

Pin Box, cov, 1-1/2" x 1/4", Columbian Souvenir 1492-1892, silver finished metal, Columbus landing on cov. 100.00

Plaque, 23" h, 24" w, bronzed three-dimensional plaster relief bust of Shitting Bull, detailed face and head dress, sgd under shoulder, gold lined dec wood frame, attributed to Rupert Schmid 900.00

Pocket Mirror, Model Ranges and Heaters, Providence, RI, World's Best at World's Fair, Chicago, IL, 1893, Sicer Stove Co. 50.00

Token, metal
Columbus on one side, other with three presidents, ring for chain 45.00
Columbus on one side, other with building and "World's Fair, Chicago, 1893," ring for chain 15.00
"Souvenir of World's Columbian Exposition" around edges, info about Chicago in center, other side picture of Landing of Columbus. 18.00
"World's Columbian Exposition," given out at the U.S. Treasury Dept. Exhibit, 1893, dollar size. 25.00

Watch Fob
"Compliments of the Keystone Watch Case Co.," figural
. . . . 35.00
"World's Columbian Exposition Chicago 1893," Columbus landing on one side, other "Chicago 1893," small chain with three small squares with saying on one side, illus on other
. . . . 85.00

1899, Omaha Exposition, toothpick holder, Colorado pattern, etched "Omaha Expo, 1899" 35.00

1901, Pan American Exposition, Buffalo

Bookmark, celluloid, pansy at the top, "Souvenir," fair emblem, "Libby, McNeill & Libby, Chicago," list of food products on back 55.00

Button, 2" w, "Northwestern Consolidated Milling Co.'s Pan-American Souvenir, Cresota Flour, Standard of Excellence" 48.00

Card, 2" x 3-1/2", metal, City Hotel, back with illus of fair, "Pan-American Exposition," Buffalo, 1901, Temple of Music, where President McKinley was show, Sept. 6-died Sept. 14th, 1901 . . . . 50.00

Cup, cov, collapsible, aluminum, lid engraved "Pan American, 1901" 45.00

Match Safe, 2-1/2" h, plated metal, Pan-American Expo, Buffalo 1901, writing on both sides, some wear. 70.00

Paperweight
Rect, Fine Arts Building, black and white. 65.00
Rect, "I was at [buffalo] in 1901," black and white 95.00

Rect, 2-1/2" x 4", glass, photograph of Temple of Music, Electric Tower and Administration Building, small hole in center of photo 80.00

Round, "I was at [buffalo] in 1901," multicolored, made by Empire Art Co. 95.00

Playing Cards, "Official Pan-American Exposition Souvenir Playing Cards," different fair scenes 95.00

Ticket, Buffalo Day, Oct 19, used 25.00

Token, 1-3/4" d, man standing in clouds, one leg bent, resting on another cloud, reaching above his head, wearing hat with sunrays, back with fair emblem, name, and date 25.00

Tray
Oval, metal, flowers and birds border, Electricity Building in center, back "Electricity Building at Buffalo, U.S.A., 1901," tarnished 28.00
Oval, metal, flowers and birds border, U. S. Government Building in center, back "U. S. Government Building at Buffalo, U.S.A. 1901," tarnished 28.00
Round, 3" d, ornate border, center globe and banner "Niagara Falls, Pan-American Exposition 1901," silvered colored metal 48.00
Round, 4" d, flowers and scroll work edges, "1901 Pan American [buffalo] Exposition, Buffalo," brass 65.00

1904, Louisiana Purchase Exposition, St. Louis

Calendar, Coca-Cola, 1909. .8,050.00

Card, signed by Geronimo, pencil annotations of orig owner
. . . . .3,300.00

Creamer, glass, colorless, Star of David pattern, ruby stained top, etched "World's Fair St. Louis, 1904" 130.00

Fan, Keen Kutter Kuttlery advertisement 50.00

Match Safe, 2-3/4" h, plated metal with insert, "Transportation Building," reverse "The Festival Hall and Cascades, St. Louis 1904" 100.00

Pin Tray, aluminum 24.00

Serving Tray, tin, oval, young woman enjoying Coca-Cola
. . . . .3,450.00

Stereo Cards, curved card
Canadian Exhibition Agricultural Building, Replica in Wheat of the Parliament Library at Ottawa, H.C. White Co
. . . . 20.00
Electricity Building, lithographed 10.00
Festival Hall from Cascade Gardens H. C. White 15.00
Grace and Beauty, Italian Section, B.W. Kilburn 15.00

Tip tray, illus of Festival Hall and Cascades, 3-1/4" h, 5" l
. . . . 80.00

Tray, 12" d, Duesseldorfer Beer, baby sucking on bottle of beer, titled "Grand Prize Winners," St. Louis 1904 World's Fair, Chas. W. Shonk Co. litho, rim chips, come overall crazing
. . . . 500.00

1905, Lewis & Clark Centennial, match safe, 2-3/4" h, plated metal with insert, "The Lewis & Clark Centennial, Portland, Oregon, 1905," reverse "Forrestry Building, Lewis and Clark Exposition," minor wear 145.00

1915, Panama Exposition, San Francisco

Bell, metal, bear on Oriental gate, mkd "1915 Panama Exposition" on one side of gate, "1915 San Francisco, Los Angeles, San Diego" on other side, bell mkd "1761, El Camino Real," stamped "Pat. Apld For" 75.00

Tip Tray, Buffalo Brewing Co., children of the world paying homage to Italy, 4-1/4" d 175.00

Tray, Buffalo Brewing Co., titled "San Francisco Exhibition 1915 The Nations Paying Homage to San Francisco," children of

(Chicago) Change purse, white metal top, nautical and patriotic motifs, leather body, 2-3/4" x 1-7/8", $65.

the world paying homage to Italy, Kaufmann & Strauss Co. litho, 12" d, overall soiling, rim chips 225.00

1933, Century of Progress Chicago, 1933

Bank, 4" h, wood, barrel, circular removable tin coin slot, burnt brown lettering 40.00
Bottle, 6" h, 6" d, glass, colorless, GM Building in center, log cabin, teepee 45.00
Compact, 2" d, silvered metal, white enamel accents. . . . 50.00
Plate, china, blue ground, Science Hall scene, Pickard . . 25.00
Thermometer, 5-1/4" x 7-1/4", glass, Golden Temple of Jehol by Night, brass frame, hanging cord 40.00

1939, New York World's Fair, New York

Bank, 3-1/2" h, brass, closed book form, faux smoke-blue leather, raised Trylon and Perisphere, inscription "New York World's Fair 1939" in raised gold letters, Zell Products Co., orig key. 180.00
Decoys, miniature loons, made by George Boyd, Seabrook, NH, documentation of display at fair
    Drake 2,970.00
    Hen. 1,210.00
Hat, official, embroidered front, Trylon and Perisphere, worn by women employees 60.00
Letter Opener, logo handle orig card 20.00
Napkin Ring, bakelite, blue, Trylon and Perisphere 45.00
Pitcher, 4-1/2" h, ceramic, portrait dec, stamped "The American Potter/Joint Exhibit of Capital and Labor/New York World's Fair 1939". 80.00
Poster, 30" x 20", "New York World's Fair," 1939, by Joseph Binder, Art Deco image of yellow and white Trylon and Perisphere, rising over silhouette of New York City, red airplanes, train, and ship. 2,300.00
Scarf, 16-1/2" x 18-1/2", red, white, blue, yellow, and black exhibit buildings, flags and fireworks, turquoise background
. . . . 90.00

1939, Golden Gate International Exposition, San Francisco

Ashtray, white metal 20.00
Glass, 4-3/4" h, colorless, blue Expo symbol under seafood illus, red "Castagnola Bros./Fisherman's Wharf/San Francisco" lettering. 30.00
Plate, 10" d, mkd "Homer Laughlin" 70.00
Scarf, multicolored 40.00

YARD-LONG PRINTS

History: In the early 1900s, many yard-long prints could be had for a few cents postage and a given number of wrappers or box tops. Others were premiums for renewing a subscription to a magazine or newspaper. A large number were advertising items created for a store or company and had calendars on the front or back. Many people believe that the only true yard-long print is 36 inches long and titled "A Yard of Kittens," etc. But lately collectors feel that any long and narrow print, horizontal or vertical, can be included in this category. It is a matter of personal opinion.

Values are listed for full-length prints in near-mint condition, nicely framed, and with original glass.

References: C. G. and J. M. Rhoden and W. D. and M. J. Keagy, *Those Wonderful Yard-Long Prints and More*, Book 1 (1989), Book 2 (1992), Book 3 (1995), published by authors (605 No. Main, Georgetown, IL 61846).

REPRODUCTION ALERT

Some prints are being reproduced. Know your dealer.

Advisors: Charles G. and Joan M. Rhoden, W. D. and M. J. Keagy.

Note: Numbers in parentheses below indicate the Rhoden and Keagy book number and page on which the item is illustrated, e.g. (3-52) refers to Book 3, page 52.

Calendar
    1907, titled "Carrier's Greeting," Peoria Evening Journal, dated 1907 in upper right corner (3-59) 400.00
    1912, Bowles Live Stock Commission Co., "Beauty Among The Roses," split calendar on back, last 3 months, 1912 and first 9 months 1913 (1-10) 400.00
    1913, "Pompeian Beauty," art panel, advertising and calendar on back (2-79) 350.00
    1918, Clay, Robinson & Co. Live Stock Commission, calendar and advertising on front (3-48). 400.00
    1929, Selz Good Shoes, calendar and advertising on front (2-85) 300.00
Print
    Animals
        "In Sunny Africa," #1038, copyright 1904 by Jos. Hoover & Son, print was 4th in series (3-18) 350.00
        Kittens with mother (2-25) 250.00
        Yard of Dogs, copyright 1903 (2-21) 250.00
    Flowers and Fruits
        "American Beauty Roses," by Paul DeLongpre, copyright 1896 by The Art Interchange Co. of New York (2-48)
        . . . . 250.00
        "Assorted Fruit," copyright 1897 by Jos. Hoover & Son, Philadelphia (2-71) 200.00
        Untitled, roses, by Paul DeLongpre, copyright 1895, published by Woolson Spice Co. (3-33) 250.00
    Long Ladies
        Clay, Robinson & Co. Live Stock Commission, c1910, by C.Everett Johnson, artist sgd in lower right (3-43)
        . . . . 350.00
        Diamond Crystal Salt Co., dated 1913, art panel from orig painting by Kaber, lady in light gray dress, white bodice, fox furs on big hat, around shoulders, purple flowers on muff (1-11). 400.00

Hula Girl, sgd "Gene Pressler," girl on surfboard, wearing grass skirt, necklace of shells, bangles on ankles and arms (1-94) 350.00

Hula Girl, sgd "Gene Pressler," girl playing ukulele, wearing grass skirt and hoop earrings (1-95) 350.00

Pabst "American Girl," dark haired beauty in red, band of miniature roses in hair, holding basket of yellow lilies, info on back (1-21) 350.00

Pompeian, by Forbes, 1918, sgd "Sincerely, Mary Pickford," wearing ankle length pink, ruffled dress, holding flowers (1-27) 350.00

Selz Good Shoes, lady in pink dress and black shoes, red flower in hair, holding opera glasses, white plume fan at her side (1-46) 350.00

"Temptation Candy Girl," advertisement on box of chocolates (3-74) 400.00

"The Girl with the Laughing Eyes," copyright 1910 by F. Carlyle, by the Osborne Co., NY (2-92) 250.00

YELLOWWARE

History: Yellowware is a heavy earthenware which varies in color from a rich pumpkin to lighter shades, which are more tan than yellow. The weight and strength varies from piece to piece. Although plates, nappies, and custard cups are found, kitchen bowls and other cooking utensils are most prevalent.

The first American yellowware was produced at Bennington, Vermont. English yellowware has additional ingredients which make its body much harder. Derbyshire and Sharp's were foremost among the English manufacturers.

References: Susan and Al Bagdade, *Warman's American Pottery and Porcelain*, Wallace-Homestead, 1994; William C. Ketchum, Jr., *American Pottery and Porcelain*, Avon Books, 1994; Joan Leibowitz, *Yellow Ware*, Schiffer Publishing, 1985, 1993 value update; Lisa S. McAllister, *Collector's Guide to Yellow Ware*, Collector Books, 1996; Lisa S. McAllister and John L. Michael, *Collecting Yellow Ware*, Collector Books, 1993.

Bowl
5-3/4" d, white band, brown stripes 65.00
8-1/4" d, 3-5/8" h, emb ext., plume-like foliage, green and brown sponging 95.00

9-1/8" d, white stripe with narrow blue center stripe, roughness to top 50.00
Butter Crock, round, emb ribs 95.00
Colander, yellow bands, white int., round 195.00
Crock, 9" h, 6" d, some ext. stains, lid missing 30.00
Figure, 10-3/4" h, seated dog, brown Rockingham glaze, wear on nose, hairlines in front legs, small chips on base . 330.00
Foot Warmer, wedge shape, yellow, cork plug 175.00
Humidor, cov, 9-1/4" h, 6" d, four trophy deer heads, intertwined branches and leaves, base with rabbit and fox, gold highlights, lid with nesting eagle with eggs on rocky area, sgd "K & E 66," some chips to lid, hairline 175.00
Mixing Bowl, 11-5/8" d, 4-3/4" h, pouring spout, emb dec 95.00
Mug, brown and white stripes 195.00
Pitcher
8" h, barrel shape, c1850 . . . . 125.00
8" h, blue stripes 175.00
9" h, emb hunt scene, hanging game and "Miss Miria B Handy, Marion, Mass," brown sponging, blue, green, yellow, and ochre highlights, white slip int. with frog
. . . . 250.00
Rolling Pin, wood handles 175.00
Vase, 9" h, baluster, light sponge dec, emb ribs 40.00
Vegetable Dish, 12-5/8" l, 9-3/4" w, 2" h, eight sided, imp "Bennett & Brothers, Liverpool, Ohio" 475.00
Wash Bowl, 12" d, plain, 1865 . . . . 95.00
Washboard, blue mottled glaze, pine frame, c1880 . . . . 475.00

ZANE POTTERY

History: In 1921, Adam Reed and Harry McClelland bought the Peters and Reed Pottery in Zanesville, Ohio. The firm continued production of garden wares and introduced several new art lines: Sheen, Powder Blue, Crystalline, and Drip. The factory was sold in 1941 to Lawton Gonder.

Reference: Jeffrey, Sherrie, and Barry Hersone, *Peters and Reed and Zane Pottery Experience*, published by authors, 1990.

Additional Listings: Gonder; Peters and Reed.

Bowl, blue band, incised dec, 10-3/4" d, $60.

Bowl, blue band, incised dec, 10-3/4" d, $60.

Bowl, 5" d, brown and blue 50.00
Figure, 10-1/8" h, black cat, green eyes 600.00
Jardiniere, 14-1/2" h, variegated green semi-matte glaze, two
    handles Montene 165.00
Lamp, 11-1/2" h, 5-1/2" w, white ground, green and rust drip
    . . . . 500.00

Vase
    9" h, yellow, green, and black drip over brown. 150.00
    10" h, red clay 275.00
    12" h, black, yellow, green, and brown drip over rust
    . . . . 210.00
    12" h, Persian blue 275.00
    18" h, molded grapes, tan matte 125.00

ZANESVILLE POTTERY

LA MORO

History: Zanesville Art Pottery, one of several potteries located in Zanesville, Ohio, began production in 1900. At first, a line of utilitarian products was made; art pottery was introduced shortly thereafter. The major line was La Moro, which was hand painted and decorated under glaze. The firm was bought by S. A. Weller in 1920 and became known as Weller Plant No. 3.

Marks: The impressed block-print mark "La Moro" appears on the high-glazed and matte-glazed decorated ware.

References: Louise and Evan Purviance and Norris F. Schneider, *Zanesville Art Pottery in Color*, Mid-America Book Company, 1968; Evan and Louise Purviance, *Zanesville Art Tile in Color*, Wallace-Homestead, 1972, out-of-print.

Bowl, 6-1/2" d, mottled blue, fluted edge 42.00
Jardiniere, 9" h, brown and gold glaze 140.00
Paperweight, A. E. Tiling Co., Ltd., 1896, calendar on back
    . . . . 40.00
Tankard, floral dec, artist sgd 320.00

Vase, La Moro, bulbous, cone top and neck, two handles, mkd, 8-3/4" h, $375.

Tile, elk, needlepoint-type technique, "Mosaic" in oval, round cir-
    cle mark, set of sixteen. 300.00
Vase, 8-3/4" h, cone top and neck, bulbous base, two handles,
    La Moro 375.00
Wine Decanter, figural, monk 85.00

ZSOLNAY POTTERY

History: Vilmos Zsolnay (1828-1900) assumed control of his brother's factory in Pécs, Hungary, in the mid-19th century. In 1899, Miklos, Vilmos' son, became manager. The firm still produces ceramic ware.

The early wares are highly ornamental, glazed, and have a cream-colored ground. Eosin glaze, a deep rich play of colors reminiscent of Tiffany's iridescent wares, received a gold medal at the 1900 Paris exhibition. Zsolnay Art Nouveau pieces show great creativity.

Reference: Susan and Al Bagdade, *Warman's English & Continental Pottery & Porcelain, Third Edition*, Krause Publications, 1998; Federico Santi and John Gacher, *Zsolnay Ceramics: Collecting a Culture*, Schiffer Publishing, 1998.

Marks: Originally, no trademark was used; but in 1878,the company began to use a blue mark depicting the five towers of the cathedral at Pécs. The initials "TJM" represent the names of Miklos' three children.

Note: Zsolnay's recent series of iridescent glazed figurines, which initially were inexpensive, now are being sought by collectors and are steadily increasing in value.

Bowl, 7-1/2" h, 5" h, fully reticulated, flower and leaf dec, steel
    blue, rust, yellow, and pink, 4 feet 260.00
Cache Pot
    4-1/2" h, 5" d, form 5897, metallic eosin glaze, high style Se-
    cession design, round raised trademark, minor glaze flakes,
    c1900 . . . . 950.00
    6-3/4" h, multicolored courting couple in landscape scene, in-
    cised "ZW Pecs," hp blue steeple mark, c1880, Armin Klein
    artist 1,650.00
Ewer
    10" h, reticulated, Persian form, crescent finial, minor chips to
    lid 200.00
    12-1/4" h, ftd bulbous form, two scroll handles, applied brown
    speckling and florals, yellow glazed ground. 90.00
Figure
    Caterpillar, 2-3/4" h, Eosine glaze 165.00
    Female, reclining, 10" l, partially clad, green, gold, and pink
    luster glaze, blue and green irid clothing and platform,
    stamp mark 900.00
    Man, sitting on bench, 6" h, 6" w, Eosine glaze 750.00
    Polar bear. 385.00
Inkwell, 4-1/4" h, figural conch shell, crimson and black lustered
    glazes, repair to handle 300.00
Jar, cov, 7" h, blue and cream snowflake design, coral ground,
    painted millennium mark, c1894. . . . . 1,650.00
Pitcher
    5-1/2" h, metallic cream dec, purple-blue metallic ground, mil-
    lennium mark, c1865 . . . . 1,250.00
    18" h, stylized crowing cock, green highly metallic Eosine
    glaze, c1905, round raised mark, minor restoration to beak
    . . . . 4,000.00

Planter, 17-1/2" h, sq, branch form supports, reticulated, irid, molded leaf and vine dec, gold highlights 1,000.00

Plaque, 15-1/4" w, 10-1/4" h, rect, yellow, pink, green, and brown Dutch windmill and horse scene, irid Art Nouveau border, mkd 1,000.00

Plate, 11-1/2" d, 1-3/4" d, pink and yellow carnation flowers, cream ground, 1870s mark 800.00

Stein, half liter, relief design of shield on front, flowers and ribbons on sides, pink glaze, pink glass inlaid lid, crackled finish, Zsolnay Pecs mark. 235.00

Vase

7-3/4" h, Egyptian style, gilted white metal, mottled purple, gold, blue and green Labrador glaze, mount sgd Osiris, c1905. . . . . .2,250.00

8" h, elaborate red, tan, and gold florals, overall irid, wafer mark. 1,100.00

8-1/4" h, 7" w, reticulated ext. resembling Arabic scrollwork 275.00

8-1/2" h, form 6011, landscape dec with trees, highly lustrous eosin leaves, high style dec, Nabis school of design, c1906 . . . . .6,500.00

9" h, shoulder with draped woman, metallic green and blue glaze, stamped mark 600.00

9-1/4" h, double gourd form, highly metallic luster surface, blue, green, and silver Labrador glaze, millennium mark, c1896. . . . . .1,350.00

10-1/2" h, red and putty dec, white glaze, Iznik design, form #3939. . . . . .2,750.00

Vessel, two headed dragon, four legs, green, brown, gold, imp mark, 7-3/4" h, 11-1/2" w, $225.

11-3/4" h, form 7804, metallic gold and blue painted dec, deep burgundy ground, flower and leaf dec, high style Secession design elements, round raised steeple mark, lip repair. 1,750.00

13" h, completely reticulated, double walled 1,500.00

Index

A

ABC Plates, 1
  Glass, 1
  Porcelain or pottery, 1
  Tin, 1
Advertising, 1
Advertising Trade Cards, 9
  Beverages, 9
  Clothing and accessories, 10
  Coffee, 10
  Farm machinery and
    supplies, 10
  Food, 10
  Laundry and soaps, 10
  Medical, 10
  Miscellaneous, 11
  Stoves and ranges, 11
  Thread and sewing, 12
  Tobacco, 12
Agata Glass, 12
Amberina Glass, 12
Amberina Glass, Plated, 14
Amphora, 14
Animal Collectibles, 15
  Barnyard, 16
  Birds, 16
  Cats, 16
  Dogs, 17
  Horses, 17
  Wild Animals, 18
Apothecary, 18
  Apothecary Chest, 19
  Bottle, 19
  Display Case, 20
  Jar, 20
  Mortar and Pestle, 20
  Show Globe, 20
  Show Jar, 21
  Sign, 22
Architectural Elements, 22
Art Deco, 24
Art Nouveau, 26
Art Pottery (General), 28
Arts and Crafts Movement,
  30
Austrian Ware, 32
Autographs, 33
  Colonial America, 34
  Foreign, 34
  General, 34
  Literature, 34
  Military, 35
  Music, 35
  Presidents, 35
  Show Business, 35
  Statesmen 36
Automobiles, 36
Automobilia, 38

B

Baccarat Glass, 39
Banks, Mechanical, 40
Banks, Still, 44
  Cast Iron, 45
  Ceramic/Pottery, 45

  Chalk, 45
  Glass, 46
  Papier-mâché, 46
  Tin, 46
  Wood, 46
Barber Bottles, 46
Barometers, 46
Baskets, 47
Battersea Enamels, 48
Bavarian China, 49
Belleek, 49
  American, 50
  Irish, 50
Bells, 50
Bennington and Bennington-
  Type Pottery, 51
  Bennington Pottery, 52
  Bennington-type, 53
Biscuit Jars, 53
Bisque, 53
Bitters Bottles, 54
Black Memorabilia, 56
Blown Three Mold, 58
Boehm Porcelains, 59
  Birds, 59
  Other, 60
Bohemian Glass, 60
Books, Civil War, 61
Bootjacks, 63
Bottles, General, 63
  Baby and Nursing, 63
  Beverage, 64
  Cosmetic, 64
  Household, 64
  Mineral or spring water, 64
  Utility, 65
Brass, 65
Bread Plates, 66
Bride's Baskets, 66
Bristol Glass, 67
British Royalty
  Commemoratives, 68
Bronze, 70
Buffalo Pottery, 71
  Blue Willow, 71
  Commercial, 72
  Deldare, 72
  Emerald Deldare, 72
  Historical and Commemora-
    tive, 72
  Miscellaneous, 72
Burmese Glass, 72
Busts, 73
Butter Prints, 74
  Mold, 74
  Print, 74

C

Calendar Plates, 75
Calling Card Cases and
  Receivers, 76
  Calling Card Case, 76
  Calling Card Receiver, 76
Cambridge Glass, 76

Cambridge Pottery, 78
Cameo Glass, 79
  American, 79
  English, 79
  Unknown Maker, 80
  Webb, Thomas, & Sons, 80
  French, 80
Cameras, 82
Candlesticks, 83
Candy Containers, 84
Canes, 87
  Cane, 87
  Walking Stick, 87
Canton China, 88
Capo-Di-Monte, 89
Carlsbad China, 90
Carnival Glass, 90
Carousel Figures, 94
Castleford, 95
Castor Sets, 95
Catalogs, 96
Celadon, 98
Celluloid Items, 98
  Advertising and souvenir
    keepsakes, 99
  Decorative albums and box-
    es, 100
  Fashion accessories, 100
  Figural dolls and toys, 101
  Holiday items, 102
  Novelty items, 102
  Toys, 103
  Utilitarian and household
    items, 104
  Vanity items, 104
Chalkware, 105
Character and Personality
  Items, 105
  Character, 106
  Personality, 108
Chelsea, 110
Children's Books, 111
Children's Feeding Dishes,
  113
Children's Nursery Items, 114
Children's Toy Dishes, 115
Chinese Ceramics, 116
  Chinese Export, 116
Chintz China, 117
  Elijah Cotton "Lord Nelson",
    118
  Grimwades Royal Winton,
    118
  James Kent Ltd., 118
  Midwinter Ltd., 118
  A.G. Richardson "Crown Du-
    cal", 118
  Shelley Potteries Ltd., 118
Christmas Items, 119
Cigar Cutters, 120
Cigar Store Figures, 121
Cinnabar, 122
Clewell Pottery, 122
Clarice Cliff, 123
  Wedgwood Reproductions,
    124

Clifton Pottery, 124
Clocks, 125
Cloisonné, 130
Clothing and Clothing
  Accessories, 130
Coalport, 133
Coca-Cola Items, 134
Coffee Mills, 136
  Commercial, 136
  Domestic, 136
Coin-Operated Items, 136
  Arcade, 137
  Gum Machine, 137
  Jukebox, 137
  Slot Machine, 137
  Soda Machine, 137
  Vending Machine, 138
Comic Books, 138
Compacts, 139
Consolidated Glass
  Company, 140
Continental China and
  Porcelain (General), 142
  French, 142
  German, 142
  Italian, 143
Cookie Jars, 143
Copeland and Spode, 145
Copper, 146
Coralene, 147
  China, 147
  Glass, 147
Corkscrews, 148
Cowan Pottery, 148
Cranberry Glass, 149
Crown Milano, 150
Cruets, 151
Cup Plates, 152
  Glass, 152
  Glass, historical, 152
  Porcelain or Pottery, 152
Custard Glass, 153
Cut Glass, American, 155
Cut Velvet, 158
Czechoslovakian Items, 159

D

Dairy Items, 159
Davenport, 161
Decoys, 161
Dedham Pottery, 163
Delftware, 164
Depression Glass, 165
Disneyana, 183
Dollhouses, 185
Dolls, 186
Doorknobs and other
  Builder's Hardware, 191
Doorstops, 192
Dresden/ Meissen, 194
  Dresden, 194
  Meissen, 195
Duncan and Miller, 195
Durand, 196

E

Early American Glass, 197
  Blown, 197
  Lacy, 198
  Pillar Mold, 198
English China and Porcelain
  (General), 198
  Bow, 199
  Bristol, 199
  Caughley, 199
  Derby, 199
  Flight, Barr, & Barr, Worcester, 200
  Ralph Wood, 200
  Worcester, 200
English Soft Paste, 200
  Adams Rose, 200
  Creamware, 200
  Design Spatterware, 200
  Earthenware, 200
  King's Rose, 201
  Pearlware, 201
  Strawberry China, 201
  Yellow Glaze, 201

F

Fairings, Match-strikers, and
  Trinket Boxes, 201
  Fairings, 201
  Match-Strikers, 202
  Trinket Boxes, 202
Fairy Lamps, 202
Famille Rose, 203
  Famille Jaune, 203
  Famille Rose, 203
  Famille Verte, 203
Fenton Glass, 204
Fiesta, 205
Figural Bottles, 207
Findlay Onyx Glass, 208
Fine Arts, 208
Firearm Accessories, 209
Firearms, 210
  Cane Gun, 211
  Derringer, 211
  Musket, 211
  Pepperbox, 212
  Percussion rifle, 212
  Pistol, flintlock, 212
  Pistol, percussion, 212
  Pistol, semi-auto, 212
  Revolver, 212
  Rifle, 213
  Shotgun, 214
Firehouse Collectibles, 214
Fireplace Equipment, 215
Fischer China, 216
Fitzhugh, 217
Flasks, 217
  Ceramic, Bennington-type,
    book shape, glazed,
    chips, 217
  Chestnut, 217
  Historical, 217
  Pictorial, 218
  Pitkin Type, 218
  Pocket, 218
  Portrait, 219
  Scroll, 219
  Sunburst, 219

Flow Blue, 219
Folk Art, 222
Food Bottles, 223
Food Molds, 224
Fostoria Glass, 225
Fraktur, 228
Frankart, 229
Frankoma Pottery, 230
Fraternal Organizations, 231
Fruit Jars, 232
Fry Glass, 233
Fulper Pottery, 233
Furniture, 234
  Beds, 236
  Benches, 237
  Bentwood, 238
  Blanket Chests, 238
  Bookcases, 239
  Boxes, 240
  Cabinets, 241
  Candle Shields, 242
  Candlestands, 242
  Chairs, 243
  Chests of Drawers, 246
  Chests of Drawers, Other,
    248
  Cradles, 250
  Cupboards, 250
  Desks, 252
  Dry Sinks, 253
  Hall Trees and Hat Racks,
    254
  Mirrors, 254
  Rockers, 255
  Secretaries, 256
  Settees, 256
  Sideboards, 257
  Sofas, 258
  Stands, 259
  Steps, 260
  Stools, 260
  Tables, 261

G

Game Plates, 265
  Birds, 265
  Deer, 265
  Fish, 265
  Miscellaneous, 266
Games, 266
Gaudy Dutch, 267
Gaudy Ironstone, 268
Gaudy Welsh, 269
Girandoles and Mantel
  Lustres, 270
  Girandoles, pr, 270
  Mantel Lusters, 270
Goldscheider, 270
Gonder Pottery, 271
Goofus Glass, 271
Gouda Pottery, 272
Graniteware, 273
Greenaway, Kate, 274
Greentown Glass, 274
Grueby Pottery, 276

H

Hair Ornaments, 276

Hall China Company, 277
  Patterns, 277
Hampshire Pottery, 278
Hand-Painted China, 279
Hatpins and Hatpin Holders,
  279
  Hatpin, 280
  Hatpin Holder, 280
Haviland China, 280
Heisey Glass, 281
Holly Amber, 282
Horns, 283
Hull Pottery, 283
  Pre-1950 (matte), 283
  Post 1950, 284
Hummel Items, 284

I

Imari, 285
Imperial Glass, 286
  Art Glass, 286
  Pressed, 287
Indian Artifacts, American,
  287
Indian Tree Pattern, 290
Ink Bottles, 291
Inkwells, 292
Irons, 292
  Charcoal, 293
  Electric, 293
  Flat, 293
  Fulter, 293
  Goffering, 293
  Iron Heater, 293
  Liquid Fuel, 293
  Mangle Board, 293
  Slug, 293
  Small, 293
  Special Purpose, 293
Ironware, 294
Ivory, 295

J

Jade, 296
Japanese Ceramics, 297
Jasperware, 297
Jewel Boxes, 298
Jewelry, 299
Judaica, 306
Jugtown Pottery, 308

K

Kauffmann, Angelica, 309
Kew Blas, 309
Kitchen Collectibles, 310
Kutani, 311

L

Lace and Linens, 312
  Collars, 313
  Collector's Lace, 313
  Doilies, 313
  Handkerchiefs, 314
  Tablecloths, 314
  Veils and shawls, 314

Lalique, 314
Lamp Shades, 315
Lamps and Lighting, 316
  Astral, 317
  Boudoir, 317
  Ceiling, 317
  Chandelier, 317
  Desk, 317
  Early American, 317
  Floor, 317
  Fluid, 318
  Hall, 318
  Student, 318
  Table, 318
Lanterns, 319
Leeds China, 319
Lefton China, 320
Lenox China, 321
Libbey Glass, 322
Limoges, 323
Lithophanes, 323
Liverpool China, 324
Loetz, 325
Luster Ware, 326
  Canary, 326
  Copper, 326
  Pink, 327
  Silver, 327
  Sunderland, 327
Lutz-Type Glass, 327

M

Maastricht Ware, 328
Majolica, 328
Maps, 330
Marblehead Pottery, 331
Mary Gregory Type Glass,
  332
Match Holders, 333
Match Safes, 333
McCoy Pottery, 335
McKee Glass, 336
Medical Items, 337
Medicine Bottles, 339
Mercury Glass, 340
Mettlach, 341
Militaria, 341
  French and Indian War, 342
  Revolutionary War, 342
  Civil War, 343
  Spanish American, 343
  World War I, 344
  World War II, 344
Milk Bottles, 344
Milk Glass, 345
Millefiori, 347
Miniature Lamps, 347
Miniature Paintings, 348
Miniatures, 350
  Child size, 350
  Dollhouse size, 351
Minton China, 351
Mocha, 352
Monart Glass, 353
Mont Joye Glass, 353
Moorcroft, 354
Morgantown Glass Works,
  354

Moser Glass, 357
Mount Washington Glass
    Company, 358
Mulberry China, 360
Musical Instruments, 361
Music Boxes, 362

N

Nailsea-type Glass, 363
Nanking, 364
Napkin Rings, Figural, 365
Nash Glass, 365
Nautical Items, 366
Nazi Items, 367
Netsukes, 368
Newcomb Pottery, 369
Niloak Pottery, Mission Ware,
    370
Nippon China, 1891-1921,
    371
Nodders, 373
Noritake China, 373
North Dakota School of
    Mines, 374
Nutting, Wallace, 375
    Books, 376
    Furniture, 376
    Miscellaneous, 376
    Pictures, 376
    Silhouettes, 377
Wallace Nutting-Like
    Photographers, 377
    David Davidson, 377
    Sawyer, 377
    Fred Thompson, 378
    Minor Wallace Nutting-Like
        Photographers, 378

O

Occupied Japan, 378
OHR Pottery, 379
Old Ivory China, 380
Old Paris China, 381
Old Sleepy Eye, 381
    Mill items, 382
    Pottery and stoneware, 382
Onion Meissen, 382
Opalescent Glass, 383
    Blown, 383
    Novelties, 384
    Pressed, 384
Opaline Glass, 385
Orientalia, 386
Oriental Rugs, 388
Overshot Glass, 390
Owens Pottery, 391

P

Pairpoint, 392
Paper Ephemera, 393
    Billheads and invoices, 393
    Booklets, 394
    Brochures and flyers, 394
    Calendars, 394
    Cigar labels, 395
    Cook booklets, 395

Miscellaneous, 395
    Postcards, 396
Paperweights, 396
    Antique, 397
    Modern, 398
Papier-Mâché, 398
Parian Ware, 399
Pate-De-verre, 399
Pate-Sur-Pate, 400
Pattern Glass, 401
    Actress, 402
    Almond Thumbprint, 402
    Apollo, 403
    Arched Grape, 403
    Argus, 403
    Ashburton, 403
    Atlas, 404
    Austrian, 404
    Banded Portland, 404
    Basketweave, 405
    Beaded Grape, 406
    Bigler, 406
    Bird and Strawberry, 406
    Bleeding Heart, 407
    Block and Fan, 407
    Bow Tie, 407
    Bridal Rosette, 408
    Buckle, 408
    Bull's Eye, 408
    Bull's Eye and Daisy, 409
    Bull's Eye with Diamond
        Point, 409
    Cabbage Rose, 409
    Cable, 409
    Canadian, 410
    Cane, 410
    Comet, 410
    Connecticut, 410
    Crystal Wedding, 411
    Daisy and Button, 411
    Dakota, 412
    Diamond Point, 413
    Egg in Sand, 413
    Excelsior, 413
    Eyewinker, 414
    Finecut, 414
    Flamingo Habitat, 414
    Florida, 414
    Garfield Drape, 415
    Georgia, 415
    Honeycomb, 415
    Horseshoe, 416
    Illinois, 416
    Jacob's Ladder, 417
    Jersey Swirl, 417
    Kansas, 418
    Kentucky, 418
    Loop and Dart, 418
    Louisiana, 418
    Maine, 419
    Maryland, 419
    Mascotte, 419
    Michigan, 420
    Minnesota, 420
    Nevada, 420
    New Jersey, 421
    One Hundred One, 421
    Palmette, 421
    Pennsylvania, 422
    Picket, 422
    Queen Anne, 422
    Red Block, 422
    Skilton, 423
    Spirea Band, 423
    Tennessee, 423
    Texas, 424

Three-Face, 424
    Truncated Cube, 425
    U.S. Coin, 425
    U.S. Sheraton, 425
    Vermont, 426
    Viking, 426
    Waffle and Thumbprint, 426
    Wheat and Barley, 426
    Willow Oak, 427
    Wisconsin, 428
    X-Ray, 428
    Yale, 428
    Zipper, 428
Paul Revere Pottery, 429
Peachblow, 429
    Gunderson, 430
    Mt. Washington, 430
    New England, 430
    Webb, 430
    Wheeling, 430
Peking Glass, 431
Peloton, 431
Perfume, Cologne, and Scent
    Bottles, 432
    Atomizers, 432
    Colognes, 432
    Perfumes, 432
    Perfume Display, 433
    Scents, 433
    Vinaigrettes, 433
Peters and Reed Pottery, 433
Pewter, 434
Phoenix Glass, 435
Phonographs, 436
Photographs, 437
Pickard China, 438
Pickle Castors, 439
Pigeon Blood Glass, 440
Pink Slag, 440
Pipes, 441
Pocket Knives, 442
Poison Bottles, 443
Political Items, 443
Pomona Glass, 446
Portrait Ware, 447
Posters, 447
    Advertising, 448
    Circus, shows, and acts, 448
    Magic, 448
    Movie, 448
    Political and patriotic, 449
    Theater, 449
    Transportation, 449
    Travel, 450
    World War I, 450
    World War II, 450
Pot Lids, 450
Pratt Ware, 451
Prints, 452
Prints, Japanese, 455
Purple Slag (Marble Glass),
    456
Puzzles, 456
    Cardboard, pre-1950, 457
    Cardboard, post-1950, 457
    Children's, 457
    Parker Brothers, Pastime
        Puzzles, plywood, 457
    Straus, Joseph K., plywood,
        457
    Wood and/or handcut,
        pre-1930, 458

Wood and/or handcut,
    1930-40s, 458
Wood and/or handcut, post
    1950, 458

Q

Quezal, 458
Quilts, 459
    Appliqué, 460
    Pieced, 460
Quimper, 461

R

Radios, 463
Railroad Items, 465
Razors, 466
Records, 467
Redware, 468
Red Wing Pottery, 469
Religious Items, 470
Reverse Painting on Glass,
    472
    Portraits, 472
    Scenes, 472
Ridgway, 472
Ring Trees, 473
Rockingham and
    Rockingham
    Brown-Glazed Wares, 473
Rock 'N' Roll, 474
Rockwell, Norman, 476
    Historic 476
    Modern 476
Rogers & Similar Statuary,
    477
    Rogers, 477
    Rogers Type, 477
Rookwood Pottery, 477
Rose Bowls, 479
    Glass, 479
    Porcelain, 480
Rose Canton, Rose
    Mandarin, and Rose
    Medallion, 480
    Rose Canton, 480
    Rose Celadon, 480
    Rose Mandarin, 480
    Rose Medallion, 481
Rosenthal, 481
Roseville Pottery, 482
Royal Bayreuth, 484
    Tapestry, 486
Royal Bonn, 486
Royal Copenhagen, 487
Royal Crown Derby, 488
Royal Doulton, 488
Royal Dux, 490
Royal Flemish, 491
Royal Rudolstadt, 492
Royal Vienna, 492
Royal Worcester, 493
Roycroft, 494
Rubena Glass, 496
Rubena Verde Glass, 496
Russian Items, 496
    Bronze, 497
    Enamel, 497

Icon, 497
Porcelain, 498
Silver, 498
Wood, 498

S

Sabino Glass, 499
Salopian Ware, 499
Salt and Pepper Shakers, 500
  Art Glass (priced individually), 500
  China (priced by set), 500
  Figural and sets (priced by set), 500
  Opalescent (priced individually), 500
  Opaque (priced individually), 500
  Pattern Glass (priced individually), 501
Salt-Glazed Wares, 501
Salts, Open, 501
  Condiment sets with open salts, 502
  Individuals, 502
  Figurals, 502
  Masters, 502
Samplers, 502
Sandwich Glass, 504
Sarreguemines China, 505
Sarsaparilla Bottles, 506
Satin Glass, 506
Satsuma, 507
Scales, 508
Schlegelmilch Porcelains, 508
  E. S. Germany, 509
  R. S. Germany, 509
  R. S. Poland, 510
  R. S. Prussia, 510
  R. S. Suhl, 510
  R. S. Tillowitz, 510
Schneider Glass, 511
Schoenhut Toys, 511
Scientific Instruments, 512
  Microscope, Cary Type, 513
  Microscope, Compound Monocular, 513
  Octant, 514
  Railroad Compass, 514
  Telescope, 514
Scrimshaw, 514
Sevres, 515
Sewing Items, 516
Shaker, 517
Shaving Mugs, 519
  Decorative, 520
  Fraternal, 520
  Occupational, 520
Shawnee Pottery, 520
Silhouettes, 521
  Children, 521
  Groups, 521
  Men, 522
  Pairs, 522
  Women, 522
Silver, 522
  American, 1790-1840, 523
  American, 1840-1920, 524
  Arts & Crafts, 526

Continental, 527
English, 527
English, Sheffield, 530
Silver, Plated, 530
Silver Deposit Glass, 530
Silver Overlay, 531
Smith Bros. Glass, 531
Snuff Bottles, 532
  Bottle, 532
  Box, 534
Soapstone, 534
Souvenir and Commemorative China and Glass, 534
  China, 534
  Glass, 535
Souvenir and Commemorative Spoons, 535
Spangled Glass, 536
Spatter Glass, 536
Spatterware, 537
Spongeware, 538
Sports Cards, 539
  Sports Cards Language, 540
  Baseball, 540
  Football, 541
Sports Collectibles, 541
  Baseball, 542
  Boxing, 542
  Fishing, 543
  Football, 543
  Golf, 543
Staffordshire, Historical, 543
  Adams, 544
  Clews, 544
  Goodwin, Thomas, 1830-40, 545
  Hall, Ralph, Tunstall, 1800-29, 545
  Heath, Joseph & Co., 545
  J. & J. Jackson, 545
  Thomas Mayer, 545
  J. & W. Ridgway and William Ridgway & Co., 545
  Rogers, John & Son, Longport, England, 546
  Stevenson, 546
  Stubbs, 547
  Unknown Maker, 547
  Wood, 548
Staffordshire Items, 549
Staffordshire, Romantic, 550
Stained and/or Leaded Glass Panels, 551
Stangl Pottery Birds, 552
Steiff, 553
Steins, 554
Steuben Glass, 555
  Aurene, 555
  Calcite, 556
  Crystal, 556
  Grotesque, 556
  Ivorene, 556
  Jade, 556
  Miscellaneous, 556
  Pomona Green, 556
  Rosaline, 557
  Verre De Soie, 557
Stevengraphs, 557
  Bookmarks, 557
  Stevengraph, 557

Stevens and Williams, 558
Stickleys, 559
Stiegel-Type Glass, 562
  Enameled, 562
  Etched, 562
  Other, 562
Stoneware, 562
Stoneware, Blue and White, 564
String Holders, 565
Sugar Shakers, 566
  China, 566
  Glass, 566
Surveyors' Instruments, 566
  Reconnaissance Transit, 567
  Surveyors' Compass, 568
  Surveyors' and Engineers' Transit, 568
  Theodolite, 568
  Vernier Compass, 568
  Wye Level, 569
Swords, 569
  US Model 1840, 569
  US Model 1850, 570
  US Model 1860, 570

T

Tea Caddies, 570
Tea Leaf Ironstone China, 571
Teddy Bears, 573
Teplitz China, 574
Textiles, 575
Threaded Glass, 577
Tiffany, 577
  Bronze, 578
  Glass, 579
  Lamp, 579
  Silver and silver plate, 580
Tiffin Glass, 580
Tiles, 582
Tinware, 583
Tinware, Decorated, 584
Tobacco Cutters, 585
Tobacco Jars, 585
Toby Jugs, 585
Tools, 586
Toothpick Holders, 587
Tortoiseshell Items, 588
Toys, 588
Trains, Toy, 597
  American Flyer, 598
  Ives, 598
  Lionel, 598
  Marklin, 599
Tramp Art, 599
Trunks, 600
Tucker China, 601

V

Val St.-Lambert, 602
Valentines, 602
Vallerysthal Glass, 603
Van Briggle Pottery, 604
  1901-1920, 604
  1921-1968, 605
Verlys Glass, 605

Villeroy & Boch, 605

W

Warwick, 606
Watches, Pocket, 607
  Dresser, 607
  Lapel, 607
  Pendant, 607
  Pocket, 607
  Tank, 608
Watches, Wrist, 608
Wave Crest, 609
Weather Vanes, 611
  Whirligig, 612
Webb, Thomas & Sons, 612
Wedgwood, 613
  Basalt, 613
  Caneware, 614
  Creamware, 614
  Diceware, 614
  Drabware, 614
  Jasperware, 614
  Lustres, 615
  Majolica, 615
  Miscellaneous, 616
  Pearlware, 616
  Queen's Ware, 616
  Rosso Antico, 616
  Stoneware, 616
  Victoria Ware, 616
Weller Pottery, 617
Whaling, 618
Whieldon, 619
Whimsies, Glass, 619
Willow Pattern China, 620
Woodenware, 622
World's Fairs and Expositions, 623
  1876, Centennial Exposition, Philadelphia, 623
  1893, Columbian Exposition, Chicago, 623
  1901, Pan American Exposition, Buffalo, 624
  1904, Louisiana Purchase Exposition, St. Louis, 624
  1915, Panama Exposition, San Francisco, 624
  1933, Century of Progress Chicago, 1933, 625
  1939, New York World's Fair, New York, 625
  1939, Golden Gate International Exposition, San Francisco, 625

Y

Yard-Long Prints, 625
Yellowware, 626

Z

Zane Pottery, 626
Zanesville Pottery, 627
Zsolnay Pottery, 627

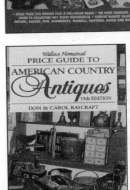

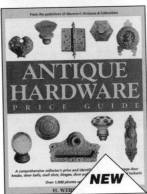

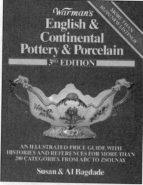

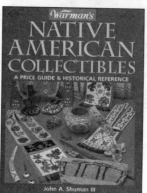